The National GUIDE

TO EDUCATIONAL CREDIT FOR TRAINING PROGRAMS

1989 Edition

Edited by Sylvia W. Galloway and Henry A. Spille

The National Guide is a publication of the Program on Noncollegiate Sponsored Instruction of the American Council on Education's Center for Adult Learning and Educational Credentials. It is a national program, with the following organizations and agencies participating with the Council in the conduct of the Program in their respective states:

The Florida Department of Education
The Illinois Board of Higher Education
The Iowa Coordinating Committee for Continuing Education
The Michigan Board of Education
The New Hampshire Postsecondary Education Commission
The New Jersey Board of Higher Education
The North Carolina Joint Committee on Transfer Students
The Pennsylvania Department of Education
The Tennessee Higher Education Commission
The University of Wisconsin System Consortium
The Vermont Higher Education Council

AMERICAN COUNCIL ON EDUCATION ᴍ MACMILLAN PUBLISHING COMPANY

NEW YORK

Collier Macmillan Publishers
LONDON

Copyright © 1989 by American Council on Education and
Macmillan Publishing Company,
A Division of Macmillan, Inc.

The American Council on Education/Macmillan Series on Higher Education

All rights reserved. No part of this book may be reproduced or
transmitted in any form or by any means, electronic or mechanical,
including photocopying, recording, or by any information storage and
retrieval system, without permission in writing from the Publisher.

Macmillan Publishing Company
866 Third Avenue, New York, NY 10022

Collier Macmillan Canada, Inc.

ISSN 0275-4142

Printed in the United States of America

printing number

1 2 3 4 5 6 7 8 9 10

Program Offices and Cooperating State Agencies

American Council on Education

The American Council on Education is nationally recognized as a major coordinating body for postsecondary education. Within the Council, the Program on Noncollegiate Sponsored Instruction (PONSI®) is administered by The Center for Adult Learning and Educational Credentials. The role of The Center and its policy-making and advisory arm, the Commission on Educational Credit and Credentials, is to give attention to educational credit and credentialing policies for postsecondary education; to foster and operate programs to establish credit equivalencies among educational alternatives; to assist agencies and institutions in providing persons with due recognition for competency, knowledge, and skills, wherever and however obtained; and to provide individuals with an alternative means of demonstrating high school graduating competencies. The Center makes credit recommendations for testing programs such as the College-Level Examination Program (CLEP) and administers the General Educational Development (GED) Testing Service. Other activities of The Center, besides the Program on Noncollegiate Sponsored Instruction (PONSI®) include the evaluation of military formal courses and Army military occupational specialties (MOS's), selected Marine Corps MOS's, and Navy and Coast Guard ratings.

Commission on Educational Credit and Credentials

Jerold Apps, Professor, College of Agriculture & Life Sciences, University of Wisconsin-Madison
Hilton T. Bonniwell, Associate Provost and Dean of Continuing Education, University of Akron
James W. Cleary, President, California State University-Northridge
Richard J. Ernst, President, Northern Virginia Community College
Donald L. Garrity, President, Central Washington University
Sam Gould, Dean, School of Business Administration, University of Dayton
David Reyes-Guerra, Executive Director, Accreditation Board for Engineering and Technology, Inc.
David A. Longanecker, Executive Director, Colorado Commission on Higher Education
Thurston E. Manning, President, Council on Postsecondary Accreditation
Wesley C. McClure, President, Virginia State University
Frank Mouch, President, Saint Leo College
Robert Neilson, Assistant to the President for Higher Education, American Federation of Teachers
Constance Odems, Vice President for Professional Services, American Association of Community and Junior Colleges
Robert Pleasure, Executive Director, George Meany Center for Labor Studies, Inc.
Piedad Robertson, President, Bunker Hill Community College
Oscar Rogers, President, Claflin College
Andrew Sass, Director, American Open University of the New York Institute of Technology
Marilyn Schlack, President, Kalamazoo Valley Community College
Robert Shepack, President, El Paso County Community College
Edwin G. Speir, Jr., President, Georgia College
Bruce T. Shutt, Associate Vice President for Student Affairs and Registrar, University of Georgia
Donald Trotter, Program Manager, AT&T
Franklin B. Walters, Superintendent of Public Instruction, The State of Ohio
C. Wayne Williams, Executive Director, Regents College Degrees and Examination, The University of the State of New York
Larry Williams, Dean of Graduate School and Research, Eastern Illinois University
John A. Yena, Vice President, Johnson and Wales College

Staff

Robert H. Atwell, President, American Council on Education
Henry A. Spille, Vice President, Center for Adult Learning and Educational Credentials
Sylvia W. Galloway, Director, Program on Noncollegiate Sponsored Instruction
Sharron B. Ramos, Assistant to the Director
Dawn K. Simons, Staff Assistant
Joan G. Schwartz, Director of Registries
Jean Gal, Staff Assistant

Florida Department of Education

The State Board of Education is the chief policy-making and coordinating body of public education in Florida. In its work with the Program on Noncollegiate Sponsored Instruction, the Florida Department of Education assists state residents who desire to use the Program's services by acting as a liaison between the noncollegiate and collegiate instructional programs within the state of Florida.

Staff

Betty Castor, Commissioner of Education
W. Cecil Golden, Deputy Commissioner of Education
Jack Tebo, Educational Policy Analyst

Illinois Board of Higher Education

The Illinois Board of Higher Education serves as a coordinating board for postsecondary education. As one of its coordinating efforts, the Board of Higher Education has agreed to serve as the Illinois liaison with the Program on Noncollegiate Sponsored Instruction. By working with this Program, the Board hopes to expand the services being provided to the residents of the state and to bring a closer liaison between those instructional activities that are taking place in noncollegiate organizations and those in higher education.

Staff

Richard D. Wagner, Executive Director
Robert Wallhaus, Deputy Director for Academic and Health Affairs
Kathleen F. Kelly, Associate Director for Academic and Health Affairs (Liaison with the Program on Noncollegiate Sponsored Instruction)
Timothy A. Rock, Assistant Director for Academic and Health Affairs (Liaison with the Program on Noncollegiate Sponsored Instruction)

Iowa Coordinating Committee for Continuing Education

The Iowa Coordinating Committee for Continuing Education (ICCCE), a voluntary statewide organization representing all public and independent postsecondary institutions in Iowa, is recognized by its constituency and by the Iowa Coordinating Council for Post High School Eduation (ICCPHSE). Concerning the Program on Noncollegiate Sponsored Instruction, the ICCCE of the Iowa Board of Regents serves as Iowa's liaison with the American Council on Education.

Staff
Robert Barak, Deputy Executive Director, Iowa Board of Regents (Liaison, Program on Noncollegiate Sponsored Instruction)

Michigan Board of Education

The State Board of Education, established in 1963, serves as the constitutional coordinating agency for postsecondary education and is the single agency for all public agencies, including vocational and adult education. Responsibility for the Program on Noncollegiate Sponsored Instruction is in the Bureau of Educational Services and Adult Extended Learning Services of the State Department of Education, which administers policy as determined by the Board.

Staff

Teressa V. Staten, Associate Superintendent, Bureau of Educational Services
Ronald M. Gillum, State Director, Adult Extended Learning Services, (Liaison with the Program on Noncollegiate Sponsored Instruction)

New Hampshire Postsecondary Education Commission

The New Hampshire Postsecondary Education Commission has legislatively mandated responsibilities for coordination of public and private higher education, including regulation of degree granting authority, receiving and disbursing federal funds for higher education, regulation of private proprietary institutions in the state, and exercises authority over out-of-state institutions of higher education operating in New Hampshire. In addition, the Commission administers various scholarship programs for students attending institutions of higher education. NHTEC (New Hampshire Training and Educational Consultants) has been endorsed by the Commission as the Program on Noncollegiate Sponsored Instruction Coordinator in New Hampshire.

Staff

James Buselle, Executive Director
William G. Andrews, (NHTEC) (Liaison with the Program on Noncollegiate Sponsored Instructions)

New Jersey Board of Higher Education

As the administrative agency of the Board of Higher Education, the New Jersey Department of Higher Education has broad as well as specific responsibilities mandated by law for the coordination and administration of the state system of higher education. The Department is specifically required to "stimulate programs relating to higher education..." and to "encourage co-operative programs by institutions of higher education." Thomas A. Edison State College, New Jersey's college for adults, has assumed responsibility for the Program on Noncollegiate Sponsored Instruction.

Staff

T. Edward Hollander, Chancellor
Michael Meyers, Special Assistant
George A. Pruitt, President, Thomas A. Edison State College
Sonja Eveslage, Director, Corporate Programs, Thomas A. Edison State College
James A. Ratigan, Director, Program on Noncollegiate Sponsored Instruction, Thomas A. Edison State College

North Carolina Joint Committee on College Transfer Students

The North Carolina Joint Committee on College Transfer Students studies problems and recommends policies institutions may use in considering the admission of and the granting of credit to transfer students. The Joint Committee is sponsored by the North Carolina Association of Colleges and Universities in cooperation with The University of North Carolina, the State Board of Community Colleges, and the Association of Independent Colleges and Universities. The Program on Noncollegiate Sponsored Instruction is participated in and supported by the North Carolina Joint Committee on College Transfer Students.

Staff

John F. Corey, Associate Vice President for Planning; The University of North Carolina General Administration (Liaison with the Program on Noncollegiate Sponsored Instruction)

Pennsylvania Department of Education

The Pennsylvania Department of Education provides leadership and service to the consumers and institutions of Basic and Higher Education. The Pennsylvania Department of Education's interest is in providing Pennsylvania's citizens with a wide range of educational and self-improvement alternatives, and because of this the department plays a liaison and endorsement role for the Program on Noncollegiate Sponsored Instruction.

Staff

Thomas K. Gilhool, Secretary of Education
Warren D. Evans, Chief, Division of Postsecondary Education Services

Tennessee Higher Education Commission

The Tennessee Higher Education Commission is the coordinating agency for the public higher education institutions in the state, with responsibilities to approve all proposals for new academic programs or academic administrative units within institutions, to make recommendations to the governor and general assembly for state appropriations, and to develop a master plan for higher education in Tennessee. In addition, the Commission has the responsibility to administer the postsecondary education authorization act and to administer certain federal assistance programs. The Program on Noncollegiate Sponsored Instruction is administered by the section of the Tennessee Higher Education Commission that deals with academic affairs.

Staff

Arliss L. Roaden, Executive Director
Lucius F. Ellsworth, Associate Executive Director for Academic Affairs
George Roberts, Director of Licensure and Veterans Education
Robert R. Appleson, Director of Academic Programs Assessment

University of Wisconsin System

With the consent of its Board of Regents, the University of Wisconsin System plays a liaison and endorsement role for the Program on Noncollegiate Sponsored Instruction. The UW System gives advice and assistance to postsecondary educational institutions in developing policies and practices related to the Program and helps noncollegiate organizations, their employees, and members throughout the state to apply the credit recommendations of the Program.

Staff

Eugene P. Trani, Vice President for Academic Affairs, University of Wisconsin System
Daniel VanEyck, Senior System Academic Planner, University of Wisconsin System

Vermont Higher Education Council

It is the purpose of the Vermont Higher Education Council to foster a community of public and independent institutions of higher education in order to strengthen the quality and value of educational services in Vermont. Vermont institutions of higher education which are certified by the Vermont Board of Education as authorized to grant a postsecondary degree are entitled to membership. The Vermont State Colleges Office of External Programs has assumed responsibility for the Program on Noncollegiate Sponsored Instruction.

Staff

Kenneth G. Kalb, President, Vermont Higher Education Council
Charles I. Bunting, Chancellor, Vermont State Colleges
Brent E. Sargent, Director, Vermont State Colleges Office of External Programs

Foreword

I am pleased to commend to the collegiate and noncollegiate communities the 1989 *National Guide to Educational Credit for Training Programs,* one in a series of ACE guides designed to help institutions give appropriate recognition for learning attained outside their sponsorship.

Since 1945, when the first edition of *A Guide to the Evaluation of Educational Experiences in the Armed Services* was published, the Council has been committed to assisting institutions in their efforts to serve adult learners. Over the last fifteen years, this commitment has been reaffirmed and strengthened with the growth of the Program on Noncollegiate Sponsored Instruction and other evaluation activities of The Center for Adult Learning and Educational Credentials. The ACE Guide Series now includes *A Guide to the Evaluation of Educational Experiences in the Armed Services, The National Guide, Guide to Credit by Examination,* and guides on external degree programs.

The Council urges postsecondary institutions to develop policies that permit the award of credit for learning acquired by students who have successfully completed courses listed in *The National Guide*. For many institutions, long-standing policies on the use of *The Military Guide* will pave the way for the formulation of a policy concerning this companion activity. The policies and procedures used by the Program on Noncollegiate Sponsored Instruction were adapted from those governing the military evaluation program, and the two programs are closely similar.

Institutions without policies on the award of credit for extrainstitutional learning are encouraged by the Council to develop them. The Board of Directors of ACE and the Council on Postsecondary Accreditation, in the statement "Awarding Credit for Extrainstitutional Learning," which appears in this publication, bring this important matter to the attention of the academic community and encourage positive action in developing policies to meet the educational needs of adult students.

The Council is especially pleased to acknowledge the cooperation of the state agencies which have enabled the Program to provide better services to adult students, educational institutions, and noncollegiate organizations in their states. The commitment of these state agencies to provide increased opportunities for adult students and to foster more effective linkages between the collegiate and noncollegiate sectors of postsecondary education attests to a positive direction in American education.

Again, the Council would like to acknowledge its appreciation to the Fund for the Improvement of Postsecondary Education for its support of the Program over the first four years, to the General Motors Foundation for its grants to cover developmental costs, to the W. K. Kellogg Foundation for its commitment to contribute to the Program's support for five years, to Dale Carnegie and Associates, Inc. and the Westinghouse Electric Foundation for their grants to support a special project.

As the Program on Noncollegiate Sponsored Instruction continues to develop, we will look to educational institutions, noncollegiate organizations, and state education agencies for their continued support and advice.

Robert H. Atwell
President
American Council on Education

Statement to Members by the American Association of Collegiate Registrars and Admissions Officers

The American Association of Collegiate Registrars and Admissions Officers welcomes the efforts of The Center for Adult Learning and Educational Credentials in publishing *The National Guide to Educational Credit for Training Programs.*

The National Guide is a valuable tool for extending the concept of awarding credit for learning acquired outside the traditional framework of colleges and universities and is being used more widely than ever before by colleges and universities throughout the country.

Over the years AACRAO has supported and endorsed the Office on Educational Credit and Credentials companion evaluation activity which gives us guidance for credit recommendations for courses sponsored by the armed services. ACE's publication which lists those recommendations, *Guide to the Evaluation of Educational Experiences in the Armed Services,* is an equally valuable resource for AACRAO's members.

The National Guide will continue to gain a wider audience and prove extremely useful to our member institutions. AACRAO commends this series to them as they formulate policies and make decisions on the awarding of credit for course work offered through non-traditional methods.

Robert N. Melott
President
American Association of Collegiate Registrars and Admissions Officers

Statement from the Council on Postsecondary Accreditation

To enable all learners to receive formal recognition for their educational accomplishments however acquired, the Council on Postsecondary Accreditation cooperates with The Center for Adult Learning and Educational Credentials of the American Council on Education in its important work of establishing credit equivalencies for organized learning experiences offered outside of accredited postsecondary institutions and in fostering the use of credit equivalencies by educational institutions. Such extrainstitutional learning includes formal courses sponsored by the military; business; industry; government; voluntary, professional, and religious associations; and labor unions. COPA is the national organization which recognizes and brings together nongovernmental accrediting bodies in the United States. One of COPA's major roles is to assist the accrediting community in identifying and taking positions on common issues and concerns.

COPA commends *The National Guide* to postsecondary institutions as a critically important source of sound and reliable information for use in awarding academic credit for learning acquired in noncollegiate settings.

Thurston E. Manning
President
Council on Postsecondary Accreditation

Contents

Program Offices and Cooperating State Agencies   iii
Foreword   viii
Statement to Members by American Association of Collegiate Registrars and Admissions Officers   ix
Statement from the Council on Postsecondary Accreditation   ix
Introduction   xiii
The Evaluation Process: Procedures and Criteria   xiv
Guidelines for *National Guide* Users in Colleges and Universities   xvii
Questions and Answers for Counselors and Advisers of Adult Students   xvix
How to Use This Guide   xxi
    How to Locate a Course Exhibit   xxi
    How to Read a Course Exhibit   xxi
    Verifying Student Records   xxii
    Awarding Credit Based on the Recommendations   xxiii
    Duplication of Credit   xxiii
    Advisory Service   xxiii
Sample Course Exhibit   xxv
Sample Transcript   xxvi

Course Exhibits

Abu Dhabi National Oil Company Career Development Center/GDC, Inc.   3
American Bankers Association   21
American Center for Technical Arts and Sciences (Formerly Mainline Paralegal Institute)   30
American Conference of Audioprosthology   32
American Educational Institute, Inc.   33
American Institute for Paralegal Studies, Inc.   34
American Institute for Property and Liability Underwriters/Insurance Institute of America   38
American Institute of Banking—Washington, D.C. Chapter   50
American International Group, Inc.   55
American Medical Record Association   56
American Sterilizer Company (AMSCO)   61
Applied Learning, Inc. (Formerly ASI/DELTAK)   64
Applied Power, Inc.—Blackhawk Automotive Division   71
ARA Services, Inc.   72
Armenian National Education Committee (Formerly Woodside Armenian Center)   73
Art Instruction Schools   74
AT&T—Center for Systems Education (Formerly AT&T Company Data Systems Education Group)   76
AT&T—Corporate Education Center, Management Education Training Division   86
AT&T—Marketing Education—Somerset Seminars   89
AT&T—Professional Development Division   102
Automatic Sprinkler Apprenticeship Program, Joint Apprenticeship and Training Committee, Local 669   103
Baroid Corporation Career Development Center (Formerly NL Industries, Inc.)   107
Bell Atlantic Corporation   111
Bell Communications Research, Inc.   136
Bell Communications Research Training and Education Center   137
Bergen County Police Academy   159
Blake Business School   160
Board of Engineers for Rivers and Harbors—U.S. Army Corps of Engineers   167
Brick Computer Science Institute   168
Carolina Power & Light Company   171
The Catholic Home Study Institute   184
The Center for Leadership Development   187
Central Intelligence Agency   189
Certified Employee Benefit Specialist Program   190
Certified Medical Representatives Institute, Inc.   193
The Christopher Academy   200
Chrysler Institute Associate Degree Program   201
Chrysler Motors Advanced Technical Training   209
The Chubb Institute   213
The Cittone Institute   216
College for Financial Planning   220
Computer Learning Center   221
Computer Learning Center of Philadelphia   223
Computer Learning Center of Washington   224
Computer Processing Institute   226
Contel Service Corporation   227
Continental Telecom, Inc.   235
Control Data   236
Crawford Risk Management Services   249
Credit Union National Association—Certified Credit Union Executive Program   252
Dale Carnegie & Associates, Inc.   255
Dana Corporation   257
Data Processing Training, Inc.   259
David C.D. Rogers Associates   260
Defense Mapping Agency—Inter American Geodetic Survey Cartographic School   262
Del Taco Corporation   271
Del Taco, Inc.   272
Department of Defense, Defense Security Institute   273

Digital Equipment Corporation 276
Disabled American Veterans 277
Dow Jones & Company, Inc. 278
Duquesne Light Company 279
Educational Information and Resource Center (EIRC) 283
Electrical Workers, Local Union 26 of the International Brotherhood of Electrical Workers and the Washington, D.C. Chapter of the National Electrical Contractors Association, Joint School 283
Electrical Workers, Local Union 102 of the International Brotherhood of Electrical Workers 284
Electrical Workers, Local Union 164 of the International Brotherhood of Electrical Workers and the Bergen-Hudson County Chapter of the National Electrical Contractors Association Joint Apprenticeship Program 286
English Language Institute of America, Inc. 287
Federal Aviation Administration 288
First Fidelity Bank, N.A., N.J., Management Training Program 324
Florida Bankers' Association 325
Ford National Development and Training Center (Formerly UAW—Ford National Development and Training Center) 326
Fox & Lazo, Inc. 330
Garden State AIB 330
General Electric Company 333
General Motors Corporation 366
General Motors Corporation—Technical Staffs Group and Lansing Automotive Division (Formerly Advanced Engineering Staff [AES]) 369
Georgia Computer Campus (Formerly Georgia Computer Programming Project for Severely Handicapped Persons) 379
Graduate School of Banking at Colorado 380
Graduate School of Banking at the University of Wisconsin–Madison (Central States Conference of Bankers Associates) 381
GTE Service Corporation—GTE Telephone Operations Network Training 383
Health Insurance Association of America 386
Henkels & McCoy, Inc. 387
Illinois Fire Service Institute 388
INACOMP Computer Centers, Inc. 391
Independent School Management 392
Indian Health Service—Tribal Management Support Center 396
Institute for Business and Technology 397
Institute for Citizen Involvement in Education 399
Institute of Certified Professional Managers 399
Institute of Financial Education 401
Institute of Management and Production 408
Insurance Data Management Association 412

Insurance Educational Association 412
International Correspondence Schools 421
International Monetary Fund 441
International PADI, Inc. 442
International Union of Operating Engineers 444
Jamaican Institute of Management 445
Jerrico Corporation 446
Jewish Hospital of St. Louis 448
Joint Apprenticeship Training Committee, International Brotherhood of Electrical Workers Local Union 269, and the National Electrical Contractors Association of Southern New Jersey 449
Katharine Gibbs School 450
Kepner-Tregoe, Inc. 459
Knight-Ridder, Inc. 461
Laubach Literacy Action 465
Massachusetts Bankers Association, Inc. 465
Maynard Management Institute 467
McDonald's Corporation 473
Mercer County Vocational-Technical Schools—Division of Adult Education 477
National Academy for Paralegal Studies, Inc. 478
National Association of Independent Fee Appraisers 481
National Association of REALTORS 482
National Association of Securities Dealers, Inc. 494
National Cryptologic School 494
National Emergency Training Center 515
National Institute of Information Technology 533
National Management Association 534
National Mine Health and Safety Academy 535
National Photographic Interpretation Center 541
National Registry of Radiation Protection Technologists 542
National Sheriffs' Association 543
National Union of Hospital and Health Care Employees, District 1199C 544
National Weather Service Training Center 544
NCR Corporation 552
The Negotiation Institute 572
New England School of Banking 573
New England Telephone Company 574
New Jersey Association of Realtors 578
New Jersey Department of Human Services 579
New Jersey Department of Personnel, Division of Management Training and Employee Services 582
Northern Telecom, Inc., Digital Switching Systems—Technical Training Center 584
O/E Learning, Inc. 586
Offshore Sailing School, Ltd. 587
Ohio Bell Telephone Company 588
Omaha Joint Electrical Apprenticeship and Training Committee 591
Omaha Public Power District 592

Omega Institute 599
Opportunities Academy of Management Training, Inc. 601
Pacific Bell 610
The Palmer School 634
Pitney-Bowes Incorporated 635
PJA School 636
Police Training Institute 638
Ponderosa Inc. 643
Portsmouth Naval Shipyard: Apprenticeship Training 643
Professional Insurance Agents 647
Professional Secretaries International 648
Public Service Electric & Gas 650
Raymond James & Associates, Inc., and Employee Benefits Education and Planning Service, Inc. 651
San Diego Employers Association, Inc. 652
Sandy Corporation—Marketing Educational Services 652
School of Banking of the South 654
Seafarers Harry Lundeberg School of Seamanship 656
Seminary Extension, Southern Baptist Seminaries 667
Southwestern Bell Telephone Company 670
Sun Refining and Marketing Company 680
Syntex Laboratories, Inc. 682
Technical Training Project, Inc. 683
Texas Utilities Electric Corporation (Formerly Texas Utilities Generating Company—TUGCo) 684
Tritone Music 698
Unisys Corporation 699
United States Army Intelligence and Threat Analysis Center 704
United States Army Materiel Command—AMC (formerly United States Army Materiel Development and Readiness Command) 705
United States Department of Agriculture, Graduate School 732
United States Department of Internal Revenue Service, Federal Law Enforcement Training Center 764
United States Department of Justice, Immigration and Naturalization Service, Federal Law Enforcement Training Center 765
United States Department of Justice, U.S. Marshals Service, Federal Law Enforcement Training Center 767
United States Department of Labor, DOL Academy 767
United States Department of the Treasury, Federal Law Enforcement Training Center 771
United States Drug Enforcement Administration 772
United States Food and Drug Administration 773
United States Navy Acquisition Management Training Office 774
United States Office of Personnel Management (OPM) 777
United States Postal Service—Department of Training and Development 781
United States Public Health Service—Indian Health Service 805
U.S. West Learning Systems 807
Western Regional CUNA School for Credit Union Personnel 831
Westinghouse Electric Corporation, Defense and Electronics Center 832
Westinghouse Electric Corporation, Education Center Department 836
Westinghouse Electric Corporation, Integrated Logistic Support Division 840
Westinghouse Electric Corporation, Nuclear Services Division (Formerly Water Reactor Divisions) 840
Whirlpool Corporation 851
Wisconsin Public Service Corporation 854
Wolf Creek Nuclear Operating Corporation (Formerly Kansas Gas & Electric) 859
Xerox Corporation 869
Yankee Atomic Electric Company 879
Young Women's Christian Association of the U.S.A. 881

Appendix: List of Evaluators 887
Index 919

Introduction

The purpose of the Program on Noncollegiate Sponsored Instruction is to help people obtain academic credit for learning acquired outside the sponsorship of colleges and universities by providing educational institutions with reliable information to use in making decisions on credit awards. The Program evaluates and makes credit recommendations for formal educational programs and courses sponsored by noncollegiate organizations who are non-degree granting and who offer courses to their employees, members, or customers. These noncollegiate organizations include business and industry, labor unions, professional and voluntary associations, and government agencies. The credit recommendations are intended to guide colleges and universities as they consider awarding credit to persons who have successfully completed noncollegiate sponsored instruction. In this way, students will be assisted in receiving academic credit for learning gained through such instruction.

The Program is based on the proposition that it is sound educational practice for colleges and universities to grant academic credit for quality educational programs conducted by noncollegiate organizations, provided that the courses are appropriate to an individual's educational program. Moreover, experience has shown that awarding credit for prior learning will in many cases motivate students to enroll in formal postsecondary programs of study.

The Program was begun in July 1974, upon the recommendation of the Carnegie Commission on Nontraditional Study that the American Council on Education's system of evaluating formal courses offered by the armed services be extended to civilian organizations. The criteria and procedures that ACE has used since 1945 in evaluating military courses were adapted for use by the Program on Noncollegiate Sponsored Instruction.

The Program is national in scope, and ACE coordinates the activities of the state Program offices. The eleven states listed on the title page are cooperating with ACE in the conduct of the Program. Thomas A. Edison State College evaluates courses in New Jersey; the Vermont State Colleges Office of External Programs evaluates courses in Vermont; and NHTEC (New Hampshire Training and Education Consultants) evaluates courses in New Hampshire. The ACE Program office evaluates courses elsewhere in the country. The other cooperating states support Program activities and represent the Program in their respective states, but do not conduct course evaluations.

All course evaluations are conducted according to the Program policies and procedures approved by the Commission on Educational Credit and Credentials, the policy-making body for The Center for Adult Learning and Educational Credentials. These policies and procedures appear on pages xiv-xviii. ACE's coordination ensures consistency in the evaluation process. A review committee, with members from each Program office, reviews the results of course evaluations for the Program. The review committee also recommends policy to the Commission on Educational Credit and Credentials.

The American Council on Education encourages other state agencies to participate in the Program and invites them to cooperate with the Council in the conduct of the Program in their respective states.

The National Guide also contains the results of evaluations for apprenticeship programs, which are reported on in this edition. The policies and procedures governing the evaluation of apprenticeship programs closely resemble those used in the evaluation of businesses or corporations and were approved by the Commission on Educational Credit and Credentials in May 1978. A description of the policies and procedures is available upon request.

Additionally, the *Guide* contains credit recommendations for courses offered by home-study schools which are accredited by the National Home Study Council. Here, too, policies and procedures are substantively very close to those used in the evaluation of businesses or corporations and were adopted by the Commission on Educational Credit and Credentials in May 1977. Under these policies, eligibility for review extends only to those accredited home-study courses that include a proctored, comprehensive examination. A description of the policies and procedures is available upon request.

The Evaluation Process: Procedures and Criteria

The credit recommendations in this *Guide* are established through a thorough evaluation process. Noncollegiate organizations participate in the Program on a voluntary basis. Each sponsoring organization selects courses for review with the assistance of Program staff.

Eligibility

1. Organizations eligible to submit educational programs for review are noncollegiate institutions (such as private industry, governmental agencies, labor unions, and associations) which offer courses to their employees, members, or customers. Also eligible are industry-sponsored organizations (e.g., professional, trade, or industrial associations) whose primary or exclusive purpose is to provide occupationally oriented educational programs to members or to the employees of membership or sponsoring organizations.

2. Only educational programs or courses conducted on a formal basis and with official approval of the sponsoring organization are considered. Courses must be under the control of the sponsoring organization. Informal on-the-job training and job experience are not usually reviewed.

Although learning outcomes are the most important basis for making credit recommendations, the following factors must also be considered when selecting courses or programs for review:

    a. The content and rigor of each course must be on the postsecondary level.
    b. The material presented in each course must be on the postsecondary level.
    c. The course must have a prescribed program of instruction.
    d. The instructors should be selected on the basis of their qualifications, including formal education and experience, to teach the subject matter.
    e. The course should serve people who can use the credit recommendations toward a postsecondary credential.
    f. Appropriate procedures (tests, projects, oral quizzes, etc.) must be used in the courses to evaluate student performance. Correspondence and independent study courses must include a proctored examination administered under secure conditions.
    g. Courses conducted over an extended period of time should normally contain at least 30 hours of instruction.
    h. Intensive courses should normally contain at least 35-40 hours of instruction.
    i. Intensive technical courses involving laboratory or workshop exercises should normally contain at least 70-80 hours of instruction.
    j. Individual courses that do not meet the above time requirements may be grouped together for purposes of review if their content is related.
    k. In general, courses offered during the preceding five years are those reviewed.

Documentation

3. Sponsoring organizations submit, in advance of the review, information concerning the administration of their educational programs. This information helps the Program determine whether the organization demonstrates sufficient stability and control to present its courses for review. Information submitted includes a description of the administration of the training program; procedures for selecting and evaluating instructional staff; procedures for course development, evaluation, and revision; and procedures for ensuring consistent quality in programs delivered at multiple locations. This submission becomes part of the Program's permanent record on the sponsoring organization.

4. Each participating organization must maintain permanent and official records of students' participation and performance in any course which is reviewed. The sponsoring organization must demonstrate the capability to store and retrieve student records for the period covered by the credit recommendations.

5. For the evaluation of courses involving classroom instruction, the following information is submitted:
    a. Course syllabus describing the objectives and content.
    b. Instructional materials (textbooks, audiovisual materials, case studies, problems, etc.) used for the course.
    c. Required or suggested qualifications of course participants.
    d. Qualifications of instructional staff.
    e. Techniques (including samples, if available) used to evaluate student performance.
    f. Duration of the course

6. For courses and programs involving other instructional approaches, e.g., videotapes, computers, or independent study courses, some of the foregoing information is not appropriate to the process. However, appropriate and available items must be provided in sufficient detail to allow each course to be judged by the review team.

Selection of Reviewers

7. To conduct initial course reviews, no fewer than three subject matter specialists are used. The names of potential reviewers are solicited from postsecondary institutions, professional and educational associations, accrediting agencies, and noncollegiate organizations.

Among criteria considered in selecting course evaluators are
   a. Area of reviewer competence as evidenced by formal training and experience will closely approximate area of courses being reviewed.
   b. Credibility and reputation among colleagues.
   c. Teaching experience and other aspects of experience in postsecondary settings, including knowledge of curriculum and instruction as evidenced, for example, by having served on a curriculum committee.

The Course Review

8. Review sessions are usually conducted at the location of the organization offering the courses. Organizational staff members familiar with the courses are available to answer questions that may arise during the review of the course materials.

After a thorough review of all the information and materials supplied by the organization, the team members first decide if a course is at the college level. If it is, they then determine the category of credit (described in the section "How To Use This Guide"), the number of credit hours, and the appropriate subject area or areas in which credit can be recommended. Whenever the team establishes a credit recommendation for a course, it has determined that the method of assessment is adequate to judge that students successfully completing the course have mastered the subject matter. The team members also review each course exhibit (the description of the course that will appear in *The National Guide*) to ensure that it adequately describes the course.

If the team recommends that no academic credit be granted, the course will not appear in the *Guide*.

Evaluative Criteria

9. When exercising their professional judgment to determine a credit recommendation, review team members consider the following factors:
   a. The content of a course, its level of difficulty, its applicability to a range of postsecondary programs, and its learning outcomes. These factors are of primary importance.
   b. Distinctive aspects of noncollegiate education, including the background and selection of both instructors and students, the duration of a course, ongoing application of classroom learning in the student's work, and motivational factors.
   c. Duration and concentration of effort in relationship to the generally accepted practice for determining credit in postsecondary institutions. Normally, academic credit is assigned on the basis of one semester credit hour for each 15 classroom contact hours plus 30 hours of outside preparation or equivalent; one semester credit hour for each 30 hours of laboratory work plus necessary outside preparation or equivalent; one semester credit hour for not less than 45 hours of shop instruction (contact hours or equivalent).
   d. For independent study courses and courses delivered by computers, television, and other means, the quality and technical merits of the assessment instruments because of their key role in determining the acquisition of desired learning outcomes.

Credit recommendations made by reviewers are not, however, derived by a simple arithmetic conversion. Intensive courses offered by noncollegiate organizations do not necessarily require as much outside preparation as many regular college courses. Reviewers consider the factors of pre- and postcourse assignments, prior work-related experience, the concentrated nature of the learning experience, and course material reinforcement in the subsequent work setting.

In some cases, the team may cluster a group of two or more related courses which individually are too short to be eligible for review. Courses are combined for review only if they form a coherent sequence and can be viewed as components of a larger course. If appropriate, a single credit recommendation is established for the group of courses and it applies only when a student has completed all courses.

Reasons for failing to recommend credit have included (1) the course is too limited in scope or too narrowly focused to be comparable to that in college programs; (2) the material presented in the course is not comparable to courses offered by colleges and universities; (3) adequate evaluation of student performance is lacking; and (4) the material presented is insufficient for a judgment to be based upon it.

Updating Recommendations

10. Credit recommendations are kept current by the following procedures:
    a. On an annual basis, following the review of a course, a participating organization must submit information on each course for which a credit recommendation has been established. Any indication of a substantive change in a course results in a re-evaluation of the course.
    b. At five-year intervals, each course is reviewed, preferably on site, by a subject-matter specialist to determine if the credit recommendation is still applicable. Ideally, this subject-matter specialist will have been a member of the team that established the initial recommendation. The course materials are compared with those used at the time of the last review. Those courses which are judged to have undergone substantive changes are re-evaluated by a full team.

The course evaluation procedures used by the American Council on Education in the development of credit recommendations for apprenticeship programs and for home study courses are substantially the same as those described above. Descriptions of policies and procedures for the evaluation of apprenticeship programs and home study are available on request from the ACE Program on Noncollegiate Sponsored Instruction office.

Guidelines for National Guide Users in Colleges and Universities

Verification of Course Completion

Educational institutions should require the applicant to verify the fact that he or she has successfully completed such a program or course by having official records submitted. The introduction for each organization listed in *The National Guide* indicates the appropriate source of official student records. Official records may also be supplied by the American Council on Education's Registry of Credit Recommendations. If the student has registered successful course completion in the Registry, he or she can request that a transcript be sent to the institution by the Registry.

Awarding Credit

Credit for those courses evaluated by the Program on Noncollegiate Sponsored Instruction should be considered on the same basis as credit accepted by transcript from another institution. Institutions generally will require the applicant to furnish full information about previous college-level studies and a proposed future program of study before granting credit for such courses.

Applying the Credit to a Student's Program

Credit for a course may be applied to a student's program of study in various ways: (a) applied to the major to replace a required course, (b) applied as an optional course within the major, (c) applied as a general elective, or (d) applied to waive a prerequisite.

Credit for a course taken in a noncollegiate organization should be granted only if the student has not completed a comparable college course. Most often, however, these educational programs do not exactly duplicate college courses but do contain instruction applicable to a general area of collegiate study. In such cases credit can be granted toward required or elective courses in the area, depending on the instructional program at the institution and the specific educational objectives of the individual.

Duplication of Credit

If a student has completed in a noncollegiate organization several courses which are apparently in the same subject area and at the same level, the college official should review the descriptions of these courses for possible duplication of coverage. If it appears that instruction is duplicated among the several courses, officials should apply the credit recommendations so as to avoid granting duplicate credit for the courses. Duplication of course materials is noted only for courses of a single sponsoring organization. Users of *The National Guide* must make their own determinations about duplication of course material in courses offered by different organizations.

Interpreting Grades from Noncollegiate Organizations

Grading systems vary widely among noncollegiate organizations. Most organizations award certificates of successful completion on a pass/fail basis, with no attempt to apply traditional grading practices. A recommendation of academic credit for a course taken in a noncollegiate organization should, therefore, be interpreted as being applicable when the student presents official evidence of having successfully completed or passed the course.

Awarding Credit for Courses Listed in *The National Guide* But Not Covered by the Dates of the Recommendations

Sometimes a student will request credit for a course listed in *The National Guide* but completed by the student prior to the beginning date or after the closing date of the recommendation. The recommendations in *The National Guide* are backdated to the point that the course was first offered in substantially the same form. Sometimes the beginning date indicates the earliest records kept by the organization, even though the course was offered prior to that date. In these cases, institutions can use *The National Guide* as a point of departure when making their own assessments.

When a student requests credit for a course not covered by the recommendations, the institution should, as always, verify the student's completion with the official record. The student should provide additional information on the course, perhaps a course outline or a catalogue from the sponsoring organization, so that the institution can compare that course with the one listed in *The National Guide*. Using the *Guide*, the institution can then make its own assessment.

Interpreting Course Exhibits with Different Versions or Changes in Location, Length, Objectives, Outcomes, Instruction, or Credit Recommendations

Annually, each course exhibit of each organization is reviewed. The review is conducted from information submitted on questionnaires completed by organizational educators and trainers. These persons are requested to make changes in course titles, length, objectives, outcomes, and method of instruction. They are also requested to update the program description preceding their course exhibits. If the PONSI® staff determines that any of these changes may affect the existing credit recommendations, re-evaluations of the courses are conducted. When changes occur to the other items listed above, the course displays are simply changed accordingly. *Guide* users who have questions about any of these kinds of changes are encouraged to call the Progam Advisory Service.

Questions and Answers for Counselors and Advisors of Adult Students

This section is intended for use by persons responsible for helping employees or members make best use of the credit recommendations. Further advice and assistance is available from the Program Advisory Service at the offices listed on pages xxiii and xxiv.

How many credits is each course worth? The recommended number of credits for each course is listed at the end of each course exhibit in *The National Guide*. This recommendation is made by a team of subject matter experts when it has determined that a course is at the college level.

These are recommended credits. A college is not required to grant a student as much credit as recommended by the reviewers, nor is a college limited to granting only that amount of credit. A college may feel that a person's performance in a course deserves additional credit.

How are the credit recommendations used? Primarily to obtain college credit or advanced college placement. It may also be possible to use the credit recommendations for entry into new areas of employment, for job advancement, to obtain salary benefits, and for personal assessment.

Is college credit automatically earned when someone successfully completes a course listed in *The National Guide*? No. Successful completion of such a course results in actual course credit only when the course is accepted toward a degree or certificate at a postsecondary institution. A student who has already taken one of the courses listed in *The National Guide*, or who plans to take one, should contact the admissions office at the college he or she plans to attend to determine the acceptability of the course for academic credit.

Are policies for granting credit the same in all colleges? No. Each college sets its own policies, and these vary from college to college. While one college might not grant credit for successful completion of a course conducted by a noncollegiate organization, others might. It should also be noted that a college may not grant credit but may, instead, waive a prerequisite or a required course.

Each institution and, in many cases, each academic unit and department within each institution, sets its own policies for granting credit. The admissions office in a college should be able to guide students to the appropriate official responsible for making the decision for granting credit.

What should be done if it is found that the organization's official records or the credit recommendations are not being accepted by some colleges? The appropriate Program office should be informed promptly. Often mere lack of familiarity with the Program accounts for a college's refusal to accept records or credit recommendations. A phone call or letter from the appropriate Program office may alleviate that problem. Noncollegiate counselors and advisers should develop for their employees a list of colleges whose policies are favorable toward the employees' educational requirements. Employees will then be spared the time and expense of trial and error.

How much credit may be earned from courses taken in noncollegiate organizations? Institutions have different policies regarding the amount of credit that may be earned off-campus. The student should check with the college he or she plans to attend to determine both the amount of credit which will be granted for such courses and the subject areas in which the college will grant credit for these courses.

When will credit be awarded? In most cases a person should apply for credit when formally applying for admission to a college. A college may grant credit only provisionally at that time and withhold full credit until the student successfully completes at that college either some courses or a specific number of credits.

Can credit be earned for a course completed in the past or taken from a former employer? Yes. The credit recommendation established for each course described in *The National Guide* can be used by anyone who successfully completed the course during the period listed in the *Dates* section of the course exhibit. When "Present" is given as the second date, the course is still being offered by the organization as of the publication date for this edition of *The National Guide*. Each organization listed in *The National Guide* keeps records of its present and former employees who completed the courses during the periods indicated and will supply those records upon request.

When will a college consider granting credit for noncollegiate sponsored instruction? A college will consider granting academic credit to a student for a noncollegiate sponsored course only after receiving an official record from the sponsoring organization or a transcript from the ACE Registry (see below) verifying that the person successfully completed the course.

How are student records for courses listed in *The National Guide* reported to colleges? The sponsoring organization provides the official record at the student's request. If the course completion is registered with the American Council on Education's Registry of Credit Recommendations, the Registry records office will issue an official record at the student's request. Information about the ACE Registry is available from the Program Advisory Service.

The official record or transcript from the Registry will enable a college official to verify the student's successful completion of the course and the date of completion. The source of official student records for each organization is noted in the introduction under each organizational heading.

How are courses listed in *The National Guide* selected for review? With the assistance of the Program staff, each sponsoring organization selects the courses it would like to have reviewed. Individual students may not submit courses for review. Only educational programs conducted on a formal basis and with official approval of the sponsoring organization are listed in *The National Guide*.

Can a person earn credit for courses offered by noncollegiate organizations that are not listed in *The National Guide*? Yes. Some institutions will evaluate students' knowledge individually, either by means of national standardized proficiency examination programs such as the College-Level Examination Program (CLEP) and the College Proficiency Examination Program (CPEP), or by assessment of individual learning experiences through portfolios or institutional examinations. A student should consult with an adviser at the institution where he or she is enrolled or is contemplating enrollment to learn how credit might be awarded for prior learning.

Why do some companies that appeared in previous editions of the *Guide* no longer appear? Organizations that no longer wish to participate in PONSI or adhere to the requirements and procedures of the Program are dropped from the *National Guide*. However, information on the courses formerly evaluated for these companies is available in previous editions of the *National Guide* and from the Program Advisory Service.

How to Use This Guide

The National Guide is intended for use in the academic counseling of students. The credit recommendations and course descriptions provide information for education officials to consider when granting credit to students for learning acquired in noncollegiate organizations.

In order to make the best use of *The National Guide*, careful consideration should be given to this section. It explains the types of courses which may be found in *The National Guide*, how to locate a particular course exhibit, how to interpret course exhibits, how the credit recommendations might be used, and how to receive assistance from the Program offices.

The courses listed in *The National Guide* represent only a small sample of the educational programs conducted by the participating organizations. In addition, many other organizations in the United States conduct a wide range of quality educational programs for their employees or members. These are not included in this edition of *The National Guide* because they have not been submitted for review. Readers are cautioned against making adverse judgments on the educational programs of any noncollegiate organization merely because they are not listed in *The National Guide*. Students who have completed such unlisted courses should be given every consideration in accordance with institutional policies and practices.

It is the policy of the Program to include in *The National Guide* only those courses for which credit recommendations have been made. The Program office will inform college officials, upon request, if a particular course given by one of the participating organizations was reviewed but was not recommended for credit.

How To Locate a Course Exhibit

In the index and in the text of *The National Guide*, each course is listed alphabetically by title under the name of the organization that offers it. Therefore, it is necessary to identify the sponsoring organization before a course can be located. When a group of courses that form an integrated program is reviewed, these courses are listed alphabetically under the title of the program and a paragraph describing the program.

How To Read a Course Exhibit

After each organizational heading there is an introduction that provides general information about the organization, its training and educational activities, the source of official records of student performance in its courses, and the Program office to contact for additional information about the courses. Following the introduction, each course exhibit identifies the course and provides specific information about the course content and the credit recommendation.

Each course exhibit provides the following information (as illustrated on page xxv).

Title. Names of courses parallel course titles used traditionally in colleges and universities. In most cases, the course titles are the official ones used by the sponsoring organizations. However, occasionally the evaluation team assigns an alternate title for more explanation and clarity. When the evaluation team assigns a title, the title used by the sponsoring organization appears in parentheses below the evaluation team's title. Similarly, a course title that a team assigns to a *group* of courses appears first and is followed by a listing of the courses that have been evaluated together to arrive at the credit recommendation. The evaluation team sometimes divides a course into *parts*, in which case the titles assigned by the team are given first, followed by the organization's title in parentheses.

Course number. Official course number, when provided by the organization, in parentheses or brackets following the course title.

Location. The site(s) where the course is offered. Correspondence and independent study courses are identified as such.

Length. Duration of the course in contact hours and, when appropriate, in days or weeks. The length is followed by any additional relevant information describing the course. The term "residential" indicates that the students reside at the location where the course is given for the duration of the course. Correspondence and independent study courses are identified as such.

Dates. The beginning and ending dates of the course, expressed by month and year. The dates cover the period during which the course has been offered with substantially the same content and procedures used at the time of its review; the credit recommendation applies to a person who successfully completed the course during that period. The first date indicates the time from which the recommendation first applies; the second, the time at which the recommendation ceased to apply. When "Present" is given as the second date, the recommendation applies as of the publication date for this edition of *The National Guide*. Program policy is to backdate a credit recommendation no more than 10 years prior to the review date.

Course versions. Generally, if a course has more than one version, a newer version of the course has replaced an earlier one. The reader should be guided by the *Dates* section. When a course has been modified, a closing date will be indicated for the earlier version, with the newer one beginning shortly after the closing date of the first version. Most often, "Present" will be listed as the second date for the newer course, indicating that the course is still offered. When *both* versions have "Present" as the closing date, the two versions are offered concurrently.

The multiple-version format is also used to indicate that a course has undergone modification. The date of modification will be indicated under *Dates*. Wherever the change has occurred, in the length, objective, instruction, or credit recommendation, the reader should be guided by the listing for each version in the *Dates* section.

Objective. The purpose for which the course is offered.

Learning outcome. The abilities or competencies acquired by the student upon successful completion of the course.

Instruction. A description of the major topics covered and teaching methods, materials, and equipment used. Together, the objective and instructional description supplement the credit recommendation by providing essential information about the nature of the course.

Credit recommendation. The category of credit, the number of semester hours recommended, the subject area(s) in which credit might be applied, and the date the course was reviewed.

1. *Categories of Credit:*
   a. *Vocational Certificate.* This category includes course work normally found in year-long certificate programs which are designed to provide students with occupational skills; in many two-year institutions, this type of course work is also found in curricula leading to associate degrees in technical programs. Course content is specialized, and the accompanying shop training emphasizes procedural rather than analytical skills.
   b. *Lower Division Baccalaureate/Associate Degree.* This category includes course work found in programs leading to the Associate in Arts, Associate in Science, and Associate in Applied Science degrees, and introductory-level course work normally found in baccalaureate programs. Emphasis is on learning basic principles that have broad, judgmental application.
   c. *Upper Division Baccalaureate.* This category includes course work usually completed during the last two years of a baccalaureate program. The courses generally involve specialization of a theoretical or analytical nature beyond the introductory level.
   d. *Graduate Degree.* This category includes course work leading to a graduate degree. The courses tend to be oriented toward independent study, original research, critical analysis, and the scholarly and professional application of the specialized knowledge within a discipline.
   NOTE: In some instances, credit is recommended in more than one category. A decision must be made by the college as to which category of credit best applies to a student's educational program.

2. *Semester Hours:* All credit recommendations are made in semester hours. Credit recommendations are not derived by simple arithmetic conversion of contact hours to semester hours; the review teams base their recommendations on both the range and level of complexity of the subject matter covered and the number of contact hours.

3. *Subject Area(s):* In alphabetical order, the recommended subject area(s) in which credit might be applied. The designation of these general areas does not exclude the application of the credit recommendation to other areas not mentioned in the course exhibit.

4. *Date of Review:* The month and year in which the credit recommendation was established is listed in parentheses following the subject area(s).

Verifying Student Records

Students who apply for credit for courses conducted by noncollegiate organizations should be required to submit official records to verify that they successfully completed the courses. Each organization will supply official records at a student's request. The source of official records for each organization is identified in the introduction following each organizational heading.

Registry of Credit Recommendations:

An official transcript record may also be obtained through the American Council on Education's Registry of Credit Recommendations which was established for organizations participating in the Program on Noncollegiate Sponsored Instruction.

The Registry provides a permanent, official record of the courses completed by employees of participating organizations, thus relieving the sponsoring organization of the burden of handling and issuing transcript requests. The employees have continuous access to their records.

The employee can request an official record be sent by the Registry records office to an educational institution, thus facilitating their decisions on awarding credit for noncollegiate sponsored courses.

Awarding Credit Based on the Recommendations

Course information and credit recommendations are provided in *The National Guide* to assist college officials in assessing the applicability of a student's education in a noncollegiate organization to his or her program of collegiate study. Actual credits granted will depend on an institution's degree requirements and general policy on granting credit for college-level learning achieved outside that institution.

Credit for each course may be applied to a student's program of study in various ways: (a) applied to the major to replace a required course, (b) applied as an optional course within the major, (c) applied as a general elective, or (d) applied to waive a prerequisite.

Duplication of Credit

A student may take several courses which are apparently in the same subject area and at the same academic level. Thus, institution officials should carefully review the course objective and instructional description in *The National Guide* for each course the student completed and for which credit is requested. If it appears that major topics of instruction are duplicated among the several courses, officials may wish to adjust the credit recommendations in order to avoid granting duplicate credit. In the *Guide,* duplication of course material is noted only between courses of a single sponsoring organization. Users of *The National Guide* must make their own determination about duplication of course material in courses offered by different organizations.

Advisory Service

A continuing advisory service is provided by each Program office. Publication of *The National Guide* on a regular basis is part of that service. After each edition of *The National Guide* is published, the Program will continue to evaluate courses. The official results of a course review are sent as soon as possible after the review to the sponsoring organization for general distribution to its employees and members. The advisory service will furnish information on courses awaiting publication and will offer assistance in the interpretation of published results. The advisory service will also furnish information on courses for organizations which have been evaluated but which no longer maintain an active status with the program.

Courses awaiting publication will be listed in The Center's newsletter, which is distributed to educational institutions and noncollegiate organizations twice a year.

The appropriate Program office to contact for assistance in regard to a particular course is indicated in the introduction to each group of course exhibits. The offices are:

Program on Noncollegiate Sponsored Instruction
The Center for Adult Learning and Educational
   Credentials
American Council on Education
One Dupont Circle, N.W.
Washington, D.C.   20036
Telephone: (202) 939-9430; or 9431, 9432, or 9433

Program on Noncollegiate Sponsored Instruction
Office of Special Programs
Thomas A. Edison State College
The Kelsey Building
101 West State Street
Trenton, New Jersey   08625
Telephone: (609) 984-1121 or 1168

Program on Noncollegiate Sponsored Instruction
New Hampshire Training and Education
  Consultants
18 Dearborn Street
Milford, NH   03055
Telephone: (603) 673-1524

Program on Noncollegiate Sponsored Instruction
Vermont State Colleges
Office of External Programs
P.O. Box 34
Waterbury, VT   05676-0034
Telephone: (802) 241-3522

Sample Course Exhibit

Course Title: Title (for each course) assigned by sponsoring organization or by program evaluation team.

Location: All locations where course is given.

Length: Duration of the course in contact hours and number of days or weeks over which instruction is delivered.

Dates: Period during which credit recommendation applies. First date denotes beginning point of credit recommendation: second date denotes when the course was eliminated or when credit recommendation ceased to apply. "Present" denotes on-going applicability of the credit recommendations.

Objective: The purpose for which the course was designed. Applies to all versions.

Learning Outcome: Statement(s) explaining the abilities or competencies acquired by the student upon successful completion of the course.

Instruction: Description of instruction, including teaching, methods, facilities, equipment, major subject areas covered. Normally applies to all course versions.

Credit recommendations: Given in four categories: vocational certificate, lower division baccalaureate/associate degree, upper division baccalaureate, and graduate. Expressed in semester hours. Date of evaluation, month and year, in parentheses follows recommendation.

Concepts of Corporate Planning (CCP)

Location: David C.D. Rogers Associates, Wayland, MA.

Length: 43.5 hours (1 week).

Dates: January 1984-Present.

Objectives: To teach the student the evolving concept of strategy and how leading firms make strategic decisions.

Learning Outcome: Upon successful completion of this course, the student will be able to differentiate clearly between strategic and operational decisions, understand how the tools and techniques of strategic planning have evolved since the 1950s, recognize why large corporations are planning innovators, and improve one's skills at strategic planning and the quantification of alternatives.

Instruction: Course covers the concept of strategy, its evolution during the 1950s, 1960s, 1970s and 1980s, the quantification of strategic options and how the premier players practice strategic planning. Extensive use is made of in-depth case studies with 15 videotapes of the actual executives involved. Strategic planning in deregulating industries (financial services and airlines) and strategy implementation is discussed. Methodology includes extensive case discussions, presentations, in-class problems and group preparation sessions.

Credit recommendation: In the upper division baccalaureate or graduate degree category, 3 semester hours in Corporate Planning or as a Business elective (1/88).

NOTE: This edition of *The National Guide* also provides learning outcome statements for courses of selected organizations. Such statements explain the abilities or competencies acquired by the student upon successful completion of the course (Comments from *Guide* users about the addition of learning outcome statements are welcomed.)

Sample Transcript

Registry of Credit Recommendations
American Council on Education
One Dupont Circle • Washington, D.C. 20036
(202) 833-4920

VALIDATION NUMBER: 8700103137
10/03/88

SEND TO:
DR. JAMES   THOMAS
REGISTRAR, SAN FRANCISCO STATE
STATE STREET
SAN FRANCISCO   CA 20079

SEND AT THE REQUEST OF:
JACK   SMITH
1 MAIN ST
FULLERTON   CA 92634

IDENTIFICATION #: 991000000
BIRTH DATE: 9/07/50

COURSE CODE	DATE COMPLETED	COURSE TITLE AND DESCRIPTION
EL10-0001	1/05/86	PRACTICAL ENGLISH & THE COMMAND OF WORDS ENGLISH LANG INST OF AMERICA LD BACC/ASSOC-3 SH: ENGLISH AS AN ELECTIVE AND 1 SH: BUSINESS COMMUNICATION SELF-PACED ADULT ED PROGRAM IN BASIC ENGLISH COMMUNICATION SKILLS. NOTE: CREDIT ONLY IF MONITORED EXAMINATION IS TAKEN.
PB -0010	8/01/85	PLAN WORK(1064);MANAGE PERFORMANCE (1063&1007) PACIFIC BELL LD BACC/ASSOC-2 SH: EMPLOYEE DEVELOPMENT 1 WK (40 HRS).TYPES&CATEGORIES OF CONTROL STRATE- GIES,THEORIES OF PLANNING.SETTING MEASURABLE PERFORM.STANDARDS.TECHNIQUES INCREASE EFFICIENCY.
TACO-0001	6/15/86	MANAGER CANDIDATE COURSE DEL TACO LD BACC/ASSOC-3 SH: COOPERATIVE EDUCATION/INTERN- SHIP IN FOOD SERVICE MANAGEMENT 182 HR. TRAINING IN THE OPERATION OF A RESTAURANT, EMPHASIZING FUNCTIONS OF VARIOUS WORK STATIONS AND INTERPERSONAL RELATIONSHIPS.
		———3 EDUCATIONAL ACTIVITIES ON FILE———

Users are urged to consult the current issue of *The National Guide to Educational Credit for Training Programs*. This publication is available from: Macmillan Publishing Company, Front and Brown Streets, Riverside, N.J. 08370—(800) 257-8247.

The National GUIDE

TO EDUCATIONAL CREDIT FOR TRAINING PROGRAMS

Course Exhibits

Abu Dhabi National Oil Company Career Development Center/GDC, Inc.

GDC, Inc., located in Chicago, Illinois, on the campus of the Illinois Institute of Technology, has worldwide operations in technical and management consulting and manpower training in the energy industry. GDC is strongly committed to the planned development of indigenous energy resources in developing nations. A recent effort in this connection is GDC's work with the Abu Dhabi National Oil Company (ADNOC) in its Career Development Center. This project began as a pilot program for training operators and technicians for a chlor-alkali plant and has expanded into two-year programs in petroleum and chemical-process technology and business training.

The petroleum technology programs include training in mechanical technology, instrument technology, and process plant operations for both petroleum refineries and gas liquefaction plants. Parallel to this program for full-time students is an in-service program for ADNOC employees, who may choose to attend petroleum technology, secretarial, or English language classes on a part-time basis.

In addition to designing curriculum and providing management and training staff, GDC was instrumental in providing architectural services for the refurbishment of the present training facility and the design of a greatly expanded future facility on the same premises.

Source of official student records: ADNOC/GDC, P.O. Box 7181, Abu Dhabi, U.A.E.

Additional information about the courses: Program on Noncollegiate Sponsored Instruction, The Center for Adult Learning and Educational Credentials, American Council on Education, One Dupont Circle, Washington, D.C. 20036.

BUSINESS MANAGEMENT PROGRAM

The Business Management Program includes courses in introductory business and office management skills. The Program enables students to carry out basic responsibilities in an office situation. To be eligible for credit, the student must satisfactorily complete work experience as determined by the Abu Dhabi National Oil Company and entered on the student's record following completion of the Career Development Center Program.

Bookkeeping I
(Accounting I, II, and III)
(Formerly Bookkeeping/Accounting I, II and III)
   Location: Abu Dhabi National Oil Company Career Development Center, Abu Dhabi, United Arab Emirates.
   Length: *Version 1:* 400 hours (40 weeks). *Version 2:* 200 hours (30 weeks).
   Dates: *Version 1:* September 1980-March 1985. *Version 2:* April 1985-Present.
   Objective: To introduce single- and double- entry accounting systems and to apply general accounting procedures to a variety of business situations.
   Learning Outcome: Upon successful completion of this course, the student will be able to record business transactions in journals and ledgers; prepare a balance sheet; and prepare a capital statement.
   Instruction: Topics covered include analysis of business transactions; recording transactions in appropriate journals and ledgers; accounting for payroll, assets, depreciation, accruals, notes, and end-of-period work. A complete accounting cycle for a merchandising corporation is presented. Teaching strategies include lecture/discussion, audio-visual presentations, and problem solving.
   Credit recommendation: In the vocational certificate category, 3 semester hours in Bookkeeping/Accounting (2/81) (1/87). NOTE: This course has been reevaluated and continues to meet requirements for credit recommendations.

Bookkeeping II
(Accounting I, II, and III and Accounting Systems I and II)
   Location: Abu Dhabi National Oil Company Career Development Center, Abu Dhabi, United Arab Emirates.
   Length: 350 hours (50 weeks).
   Dates: April 1985-Present.
   Objective: To provide work experience in various simulated businesses in order to give an overview of how an integrated system functions and how source documents are processed.
   Learning Outcome: Upon successful completion of this course, the student will be able to process the flow of data through the accounting system of simulated businesses; and prepare various reports and schedules, including financial statements.
   Instruction: Topics covered include performance of entire accounting cycle, including original entries, posting, preparation of financial statements and auditing for simulated partnerships, merchandising businesses and corporations. Teaching strategies include lectures, computer laboratory assignments, and case studies.
   Credit recommendation: In the vocational certificate/ Associate in Applied Science degree category, 3 semester hours in Bookkeeping II (1/87).

Business Communications
(Business Correspondence I and II, Oral and Written Communication, Office Correspondence for Commercial Practice)
   Location: Abu Dhabi National Oil Company Career Development Center, Abu Dhabi, United Arab Emirates.
   Length: 200 hours (40 weeks).
   Dates: April 1985-Present.
   Objective: To teach fundamentals of written and oral business communications.

Learning Outcome: Upon successful completion of this course, the student will be able to demonstrate correct use of vocabulary, grammar, punctuation, spelling and composition skills through business letters, reports and forms; use a wordprocessor for written communications, compose business messages, such as letters, memoranda and telex; choose appropriate form of verbal communication in a wide array of business situations; and recognize barriers to, effective techniques for, different modes of, and nonverbal behavior in verbal communication.

Instruction: Topics covered include internal and external business correspondence, oral communication techniques, appropriate use of the wordprocessor, interpretation of managerial directives. Teaching strategies include lecture/demonstration, classroom discussion and written assignments.

Credit recommendation: In the vocational certificate category, 3 semester hours in Business Communications (2/81) (1/87). NOTE: This course has been reevaluated and continues to meet requirements for credit recommendations. Students who receive credit for Business Communications should not receive credit for Business Correspondence.

Business Correspondence
(Business Correspondence I, II and III)

Location: Abu Dhabi National Oil Company Career Development Center, Abu Dhabi, United Arab Emirates.

Length: 300 hours (30 weeks).

Dates: September 1980-December 1986.

Objective: To provide the student with the fundamentals of written business communications so that they may be used effectively as tools for administration and management.

Instruction: Topics in these courses include an overview of business correspondence, the psychology of correspondence, the format of business correspondence, personal business writing, invitation announcements and goodwill messages, sales correspondences, credit and collection correspondence, memoranda, business reports, dictating correspondence, and effective work usage. The instructional methodology consists of lecture, classroom discussion, and written assignments.

Credit recommendation: In the vocational certificate category or in the lower division baccalaureate/associate degree category, 3 semester hours in Business Correspondence (2/81). NOTE: Students who receive credit for Business Correspondence should not receive credit for Business Communications.

Business Mathematics I and II

Location: Abu Dhabi National Oil Company Career Development Center, Abu Dhabi, United Arab Emirates.

Length: 100 hours (20 weeks).

Dates: September 1979-December 1986.

Objective: To provide the student with a knowledge of basic mathematics as applied to the problems of business.

Instruction: Topics covered include general arithmetic, decimals, fractions, applications of percentages, interest calculations, typical payroll and sales computations, and uses of basic calculators for business applications. Computations and terminology related to corporate recordkeeping are also covered. The instructional methodology consists of classroom lecture, discussion, and problem solving.

Credit recommendation: In the vocational certificate category, 2 semester hours in Business Mathematics (2/81). NOTE: Students who receive credit for Business Mathematics I and II should not receive credit for Business Mathematics I, II, and III.

Business Mathematics I, II and III

Location: Abu Dhabi National Oil Company Career Development Center, Abu Dhabi, United Arab Emirates.

Length: 150 hours (30 weeks).

Dates: February 1986-Present.

Objective: To provide students with a knowledge of basic business-related mathematical applications.

Learning Outcome: Upon successful completion of this course, the student will be able to define business mathematical terminology; calculate interest, mark-ups, percentages, net profit, finance charges, cost of goods sold; and identify and analyze business problems, using proper mathematical procedures.

Instruction: Topics covered include basic arithmetic calculations, interest, percentages, mark-ups, profit and loss, inventory, payroll, cash and trade discounts, and graphs. The instructional methodology includes classroom lecture, discussion, and problem solving.

Credit recommendation: In the vocational certificate category or occupational degree category, 3 semester hours in Business Mathematics (1/87). NOTE: Students who receive credit for Business Mathematics I, II, and III should not receive credit for Business Mathematics I, and II.

Computers in Business
(Computers I, II, III and IV)

Location: Abu Dhabi National Oil Company Career Development Center, Abu Dhabi, United Arab Emirates.

Length: 200 hours (40 weeks).

Dates: April 1986-Present.

Objective: To introduce computer terminology and operations via software business applications in word processing spreadsheet and data base programs.

Learning Outcome: Upon successful completion of this course, the student will be able to define computer terms; describe the operation of computer systems; create word processing documents; design, create, and edit database files; design and produce spreadsheets, using a variety of commands; and construct bar charts, pie charts, and XY graphs using the computer.

Instruction: Topics include computer hardware, operating systems, word processing, data base management, computerized accounting systems, graphics and spreadsheets. Methods of instruction include lectures, demonstrations, study assignments, and hands-on experience with the IBM PC and commercial software—WordStar 2000, Lotus 1-2-3, Symphony, d-Base III.

Credit recommendation: In the vocational certificate category and in the lower division baccalaureate/associate degree category, 3 semester hours in Computers in Business (1/87).

Ecomomic Geography I

Location: Abu Dhabi National Oil Company Career Development Center, Abu Dhabi, United Arab Emirates.
Length: 50 hours (10 weeks).
Dates: September 1980-December 1986.
Objective: To familiarize the student with the influence of geographic factors on the development of their natural culture and economy.
Instruction: Covers geographic description of the Middle East, its energy resources and the economy; the availability and use of water resources, agriculture and fishing. Treatment of these subjects is general. Methods of instruction include lecture, model building, and discussion of current events.
Credit recommendation: In the lower division baccalaureate/associate degree category, 1 semester hour in Social Science. (2/81).

Introduction to Economics

Location: Abu Dhabi National Oil Company Career Development Center, Abu Dhabi, United Arab Emirates.
Length: 50 hours (10 weeks).
Dates: November 1984-Present.
Objective: To provide an understanding of the basic concepts of economics and the fundamental mechanisms of an economy.
Learning Outcome: Upon successful completion of this course, the student will be able to define the role of the consumer and producer in the economy; relate the relevant facts, content, and structure of basic economics to current social problems; and describe economic theories that are relevant to the UAE and its role in the world economy.
Instruction: Topics covered include economic systems, production and consumption, supply and demand, national income, international trade and the UAE in world economy. Teaching strategies include lecture/demonstration, audio-visual presentations, and computer simulations.
Credit recommendation: In the vocational certificate category, 1 semester hour in Introduction to Economics (1/87).

Introduction to Supervision
(Principles of Supervision)

Location: Abu Dhabi National Oil Company Career Development Center, Abu Dhabi, United Arab Emirates.
Length: 50 hours (10 weeks).
Dates: February 1985-Present.
Objective: To provide a basic understanding of the techniques of supervision with an overview of the responsibilities of the supervisor.
Learning Outcome: Upon successful completion of this course, the student will be able to state the importance of change within an organization; accept the responsibility for self-improvement; discuss the importance of supervisor to employee communications; and exhibit awareness of conditions necessary for creating a climate for improvement; evaluating ideas and actions; planning; and delegation.
Instruction: Topics covered include developing management-mindedness, self-development, management communication and change, and working with the supervisor. Teaching strategies include classroom lecture, discussion and problem-solving with stated work situations.
Credit recommendation: In the vocational certificate category, 1 semester hour in Introduction to Supervision (1/87).

Management Information Systems
(Management Information Systems I, II)

Location: Abu Dhabi National Oil Company Career Development Center, Abu Dhabi, United Arab Emirates.
Length: 150 hours (20 weeks).
Dates: April 1985-Present.
Objective: To provide an understanding of the role of computers in a management information system and to identify information problems and design and to develop systems to solve these problems.
Learning Outcome: Upon successful completion of this course, the student will be able to define the life-cycle method for managing the four phases of computer information systems; describe the procedures used in a feasibility study; present definitions and information in the following areas: management information systems and distribution data processing; forecast and relate trends in terms of human and information management; and provide an overview of the life-cycle method for managing computer related information systems.
Instruction: Topics covered include the life-cycle method for managing the design and development of information systems; organization and functions of an information service; management information systems and subsystems in the organization; the use of input/output devices in remote entry systems, network systems, and the automated office. Teaching strategies include lectures, computer laboratory assignments, audio/visual presentations, and case study.
Credit recommendation: In the lower division bac-

calaureate/associate degree category, 3 semester hours in Management Information Systems (1/87). NOTE: To be eligible for credit, the student must satisfactorily complete work experience as determined by the Abu Dhabi National Oil Company and entered on the student's record following completion of the Career Development Center Program.

Office Procedures
(Office Organization, Clerical Office Procedures, Records Management)
(Formerly Office Procedures/Clerical Office Procedures I and II, and Office Practices and Office Management)
   Location: Abu Dhabi National Oil Company Career Development Center, Abu Dhabi, United Arab Emirates.
   Length: *Version 1:* 200 hours (20 weeks). *Version 2:* 150 hours (30 weeks).
   Dates: *Version 1:* September 1980-January 1985. *Version 2:* February 1985-Present.
   Objective: To develop skills in and knowledge of basic data processing, as applied to various systems for filing and information retrieval; functions of the business office with an appreciation of various business occupations and administrative services; a variety of practices and techniques involving office operations; and personal and professional office behavior.
   Learning Outcome: Upon successful completion of this course, the student will be able to apply various indexing, transferring, retention and retrieval rules and methods incorporated in current records management procedures; explain the different types of mechanical and electronic data processing machines, describing how data is processed electronically; file information using five different filing systems; identify and describe filing equipment and supplies; operate computational and reproduction equipment; demonstrate appropriate telephone techniques and interpersonal skills; design office environments for business functions and good working conditions; demonstrate correct mail distribution, reception etiquette and verbal skills; describe inventory and stock maintenance; produce and manage typewritten correspondence; and solve simulated office problems.
   Instruction: Topics covered include basic records management procedures, indexing; use of various types of equipment and supplies, processing data with computers and other specialized equipment; office organization; mail; telephone techniques; communication and leadership; management practices; job task analysis; and recordkeeping. Teaching strategies include classroom lecture, discussion and problem solving.
   Credit recommendation: *Version 1:* In the vocational certificate category, 4 semester hours in Office Procedures (2/81). *Version 2:* In the vocational certificate category, 3 semester hours in Office Procedures (1/87). NOTE: This course has been reevaluated and continues to meet requirements for credit recommendations.

Orientation to Business Careers
(Formerly Introduction to Business)
   Location: Abu Dhabi National Oil Company Career Development Center, Abu Dhabi, United Arab Emirates.
   Length: *Version 1:* 100 hours (20 weeks). *Version 2:* 50 hours (10 weeks).
   Dates: *Version 1:* September 1979-December 1986. *Version 2:* January 1987-Present.
   Objective: To provide an understanding of the role of business in the UAE economy, business operations, and the employee's role in the business organization.
   Learning Outcome: Upon successful completion of this course, the student will be able to recognize the various types of business ownership; explain the differences between types of businesses and departments, as divisions within a business; and employ appropriate human relations and work skills in simulated business situations.
   Instruction: Topics covered include types of business ownership; careers within a business organization; money, banking, and transportation systems in the UAE; human relation skills basic to the business environment; and credit. Teaching strategies include lecture/demonstration, classroom discussion and written assignments.
   Credit recommendation: *Version 1:* In the vocational certificate category, 2 semester hours in Introduction to Business (2/81). *Version 2:* In the vocational certificate category, 1 semester hour in Orientation to Business (1/87). NOTE: This course has been reevaluated and continues to meet requirements for credit recommendations.

Principles of Accounting
(Accounting I, II, III, IV, and V and Case Studies—Accounting)
   Location: Abu Dhabi National Oil Company Career Development Center, Abu Dhabi, United Arab Emirates.
   Length: 450 hours (50 weeks).
   Dates: April 1985-Present.
   Objective: To introduce the student to basic accounting principles, including the recording, reporting, and analysis of financial activity.
   Learning Outcome: Upon successful completion of this course, the student will be able to record business transactions; prepare income statement, balance sheets, changes in owners' equity, and statements of change in the financial position; prepare departmental statements; prepare a statement of cost of goods sold; calculate revenues, fixed costs, variable costs and the firm's breakeven point; and analyze financial statements.
   Instruction: Topics covered include the analysis of financial transactions, recording transactions in journals and ledgers, accounting for financial transactions, departmental accounting, financial statement preparation, introduction to cost accounting, and introduction to managerial accounting. Instructional methodology in-

cludes lecture/discussion, audio-visual presentations, problem solving, and case studies.

Credit recommendation: In the lower division baccalaureate/associate degree category, 3 semester hours in Principles of Accounting (1/87).

Principles of Management
(Principles of Management, Management Process I, Management Process II, Case Studies—Management)
  Location: Abu Dhabi National Oil Company Career Development Center, Abu Dhabi, United Arab Emirates.
  Length: 300 hours (30 weeks).
  Dates: April 1985-Present.
  Objective: To provide an introduction to the primary functions of the manager, the primary elements of job specification, departmentalization, span of control, delegation, social concerns and management decisions; and specialization management in areas of marketing and distribution, production, finance, personnel, and public agencies.
  Learning Outcome: Upon successful completion of this course, the student will be able to compare the methods and objectives of recognized managerial philosophies, concepts, and theories; define and describe the major functions of a manager; apply managerial theory to specific problems and scenarios involving organizational relationships, staffing, and supervision; identify the roles and responsibilities of different levels of managers; identify and compare the different organizational areas of managerial specialization; and analyze day-to-day organizational problems and opportunities; and propose management concepts and techniques to resolve the day-to-day problems.
  Instruction: Topics covered include role, responsibilities, functions and environment of management; organizational structure and decision-making; executive-level management assignments, including marketing, production, financial, personnel; and communications; motivation; work groups; and tested theories of supervison. The instructional methodology includes classroom lecture, discussion, problem solving for stated work situations.
  Credit recommendation: In the lower division baccalaureate/associate degree category, 3 semester hours in Principles of Management (1/87).

Principles of Purchasing
(Formerly Purchasing and Storekeeping I)
  Location: Abu Dhabi National Oil Company Career Development Center, Abu Dhabi, United Arab Emirates.
  Length: 50 hours (10 weeks).
  Dates: September 1979-Present.
  Objective: To provide an overview of general purchasing theory with applications pertinent to the purchasing, receiving, and inventory functions in a business.
  Learning Outcome: Upon successful completion of this course, the student will be able to complete purchase requisitions, order forms, and receiving reports; compute quantity, trade and cash discounts; demonstrate skills necessary to the implementation and maintenance of a sound inventory and records system; and identify components of an orderly and secure stockroom.
  Instruction: Topics covered include purchasing and receiving functions, responsibilities, and procedures; inventory records and controls; stockroom procedures, warehousing, and shipping. Teaching strategies include lecture/demonstration, classroom discussion and written assignments.
  Credit recommendation: In the vocational certificate category, 1 semester hour in Principles of Purchasing (2/81) (1/87). NOTE: This course has been reevaluated and continues to meet requirements for credit recommendations.

Recordkeeping
(Formerly Clerical Recordkeeping I and II)
  Location: Abu Dhabi National Oil Company Career Development Center, Abu Dhabi, United Arab Emirates.
  Length: *Version 1:* 200 hours (20 weeks). *Version 2:* 50 hours (10 weeks).
  Dates: *Version 1:* September 1979-December 1986. *Version 2:* January 1987-Present.
  Objective: To familiarize the trainee with procedures and forms necessary for the conduct of routine business activities and the accurate preparation of source documents for those activities.
  Learning Outcome: Upon successful completion of this course, the student will be able to apply entry-level recordkeeping skills; identify and prepare forms commonly utilized in various entry-level clerical occupations; operate the electronic calculator keyboard with the touch system; and state career requirements for a cashier.
  Instruction: Topics covered include basic filing procedures, cashier, daily reports, bank deposits, check writing, reconciliation of bank statements, petty cash, sales, tax, inventory and payroll records, The instructional methodology includes classroom lecture, discussion, and problem solving.
  Credit recommendation: In the vocational certificate category, 1 semester hour in Recordkeeping (2/81)(1/87). NOTE: This course has been reevaluated and continues to meet requirements for credit recommendations.

Typewriting
(Typewriting I and II)
(Formerly Typing I, II, Business Typing I, II)
  Location: Abu Dhabi National Oil Company Career Development Center, Abu Dhabi, United Arab Emirates.
  Length: *Version 1:* 200 hours (40 weeks). *Version 2:* 100 hours (20 weeks).
  Dates: *Version 1:* September 1980-October 1984. *Version 2:* November 1984-Present.
  Objective: To develop a sound technique of touch type-

writing with accuracy and speed, self-confidence, and improved reading and work skills appropriate to the business environment.

Learning Outcome: Upon successful completion of this course, the student will be able to demonstrate work habits that permit accurate and rapid typing; type a minimum of 20 words per minute on a five-minute timed writing test with no more than one error; complete business exercises including business letters, simple manuscripts, business tables and outlines; compose simple correspondence using correct punctuation at the typewriter; and manage the work station in an efficient manner.

Instruction: Topics covered include proper maintenance and care of the typewriter, exercises in the touch system, letter and report writing, tabulation, efficient work habits, and reading improvement techniques. Teaching strategies include instructor demonstration and classroom exercises.

Credit recommendation: *Version 1:* In the vocational certificate category, 4 semester hours in Typewriting (2/81). *Version 2:* In the vocational certificate category, 2 semester hours in Typewriting (1/87). NOTE: This course has been reevaluated and continues to meet requirements for credit recommendations.

ENGLISH AS A SECOND LANGUAGE PROGRAM

Students in the Petroleum and Chemical Technology Program as well as students in the Business Management Program participate in intensive English language classes which provide the requisite skills for speaking, reading, and writing.

English as a Second Language
(Basic English I, II, III, IV; Business English; Technical English)

Location: Abu Dhabi National Oil Company Career Development Center, Abu Dhabi, United Arab Emirates.
Length: 900 hours (60 weeks).
Dates: September 1979-December 1986.
Objective: To provide the trainee with the basic ability to read, write, and speak the English language.
Instruction: Covers English vocabulary, English grammar, oral and aural skills, and the development of writing skills.
Credit recommendation: In the lower division baccalaureate/associate degree category, 3 semester hours in English as a Foreign Language, or English as a Second Language, or Introduction to the English Language (2/81).

PETROLEUM AND CHEMICAL TECHNOLOGY PROGRAM

The Petroleum and Chemical Technology Programs include training in mechanical technology, instrument technology and process plant operations for both petroleum refineries and gas liquefaction plants. The recommendations are primarily applicable to the Associate in Applied Science degree or to certificate programs. To be eligible for credit, students must satisfactorily complete work experience as determined by the Abu Dhabi National Oil Company and entered on the student's record following completion of the Career Development Center.

Analytical Equipment
Location: Abu Dhabi National Oil Company Career Development Center, Abu Dhabi, United Arab Emirates.
Length: 80 hours (20 weeks).
Dates: December 1987-Present.
Objective: To give the student the necessary skills for maintenance, calibration, and use of analytical equipment.
Learning Outcome: Upon successful completion of this course, the student will be able to: (1) use, calibrate, and maintain common analytical equipment such as oxygen analyzers, ultrasonic leak detectors, and other related test equipment; (2) construct, and use calibration curves for equipment; and, (3) use common bridges correctly.
Instruction: Lecture, demonstrations, laboratories, student assignments, tests and evaluation of assigned work are used to teach concepts and skills related to analytical equipment.
Credit recommendation: In the lower division baccalaureate/associate degree category, 4 semester hours in Instrumentation Technology (1/87).

Applied Chemistry I and II
Location: Abu Dhabi National Oil Company Career Development Center, Abu Dhabi, United Arab Emirates.
Length: 100 hours (20 weeks).
Dates: September 1980-Present.
Objective: To provide knowledge of general, basic, and hydrocarbon chemistry in relation to petroleum refineries and petrochemical industry processes.
Learning Outcome: Upon successful completion of this course, the student will be able to perform simple chemical experiments involving preparation of specific solutions; measure PH, demonstrate the safe handling of industrial acids and bases, define the states of matter, explain basic atomic structure and unite; identify common acids and bases and their formulae, identify the differences between inorganic and organic chemistry, define the properties of organic compounds and discuss catalysts; inhibitors, petroleum and natural gas as they relate to the petroleum industry.
Instruction: Lecture, practical laboratory, exercises and on-the-job training in the application of simple chemistry to the petroleum industry.
Credit recommendation: In the vocational certificate category or in the lower division baccalaureate/associate degree category, 3 semester hours in Applied Chemistry

or Chemical Process Technology (2/81) (1/87). NOTE: This course has been reevaluated and continues to meet requirements for credit recommendations.

Applied Physics I and II
Location: Abu Dhabi National Oil Company Career Development Center, Abu Dhabi, United Arab Emirates.
Length: 100 hours (20 weeks).
Dates: September 1980-Present.
Objective: To provide the student with a practical understanding of the basic principles of physics as related to the petroleum industry.
Learning Outcome: Upon successful completion of this course, the student will be able to solve problems related to pressure, force, motion, temperature, liquid level, fluid flow, torque, energy and work, gas lows, lows of conservation modeling, heat, temperature and heat transfer.
Instruction: Lectures, laboratory exercises and experiments in energy, concepts of force, motion, pressure, status of matter, mechanics of fluids, fluids in motion, heat and thermal expansion and contraction.
Credit recommendation: In the vocational certificate category or in the lower division baccalaureate/associate degree category, 3 semester hours in Applied Physics (2/81) (1/87). NOTE: This course has been reevaluated and continues to meet requirements for credit recommendations.

Basic Electricity
Location: Abu Dhabi National Oil Company Career Development Center, Abu Dhabi, United Arab Emirates.
Length: 50 hours (10 weeks).
Dates: *Version 1:* September 1980-December 1986. *Version 2:* January 1987-Present.
Objective: *Version 1:* To provide a practical understanding of basic laws of electricity and applications of those laws by teaching the hazards of electricity and the safety precautions, as well as some basic electrical devices and terminology. *Version 2:* To provide the student with a basic understanding of DC circuits.
Learning Outcome: Upon successful completion of this course, the student will be able to define an electrical circuit; identify electrical components; and make basic circuit calculations and measurements.
Instruction: Lectures and basic experiments in the nature of electricity and electrical energy, concepts of electricity and electrical measurement, Ohm's Law, basic electrical circuits and simple electrical devices, and electrical safety.
Credit recommendation: *Version 1:* In the vocational certificate category, 1 semester hour in Basic Electricity (2/81). *Version 2:* In the lower division baccalaureate/associate degree category, 2 semester hours in Technology (1/87). NOTE: This course has been reevaluated and continues to meet requirements for credit recommendations.

Boiler Control
Location: Abu Dhabi National OIl Company Career Development Center, Abu Dhabi, United Arab Emirates.
Length: 50 hours (10 weeks).
Dates: *Version 1:* September 1980-December 1986. *Version 2:* January 1987-Present.
Objective: This course provides an understanding of process control concepts of steam boiler and furnace operation. The course encompasses combustion control, fuel-water control, fuel control, steam pressure and temperature control, and safety instrumentation. Boiler instrument and control safety practices are stressed as troubleshooting skills are developed through system analysis.
Learning Outcome: Upon successful completion of this course, the student will be able to draw and explain high pressure steam boilers systems, including fuel input control; single, double and three element control systems; combustion air flow and control; the safety systems and safety requirements and be able to analyze and troubleshoot the boiler control systems.
Instruction: *Version 1:* Lectures, discussions and practical experience covering energy production, combustion control, and boiler control. *Version 2:* Lectures, discussions, simulator training and on-the-job training concerning the operation, troubleshooting and control of high pressure steam boilers.
Credit recommendation: *Version 1:* In the lower division baccalaureate/associate degree category, 1 semester hour in Boiler Control Process or Industrial Technology (2/81). *Version 2:* In the lower division baccalaureate/associate degree category, 2 semester hours in Boiler Control Process or Industrial Technology (1/87). NOTE: This course has been reevaluated and continues to meet requirements for credit recommendations.

Boiler Repair and Maintenance
Location: Abu Dhabi National Oil Company Career Development Center, Abu Dhabi, United Arab Emirates.
Length: 50 hours (10 weeks).
Dates: September 1980-Present.
Objective: This course is designed to provide an understanding of boiler inspection, maintenance, and repair practices. Included are causes and effects of fireside and waterside deterioration along with corrective measures, oil and gas burner inspection and maintenance, repairs to safety valves, gauge glasses, burner assemblies, handhole cover plates and other boiler components.
Learning Outcome: Upon successful completion of this course, the student will be able to recognize boiler deterioration problems, recognize boiler defects, explain boiler cleaning practices, repair procedures and safety procedures to be observed while working on boilers.
Instruction: Lecture and discussions on oil and gas fired boilers including boiler inspection, boiler maintenance, and boiler repair.

Credit recommendation: In the vocational certificate category or in the lower division baccalaureate/associate degree category, 2 semester hours in Boiler Repair and Maintenance or Industrial Maintenance (2/81)(1/87). NOTE: This course has been reevaluated and continues to meet requirements for credit recommendations.

Boilers and Water Treatment I and II
 Location: Abu Dhabi National Oil Company Career Development Center, Abu Dhabi, United Arab Emirates.
 Length: 100 hours (20 weeks).
 Dates: *Version 1:* September 1980-December 1986. *Version 2:* January 1987-Present.
 Objective: To provide the student with a basic understanding of boiler types and steam generation.
 Learning Outcome: Upon successful completion of this course, the student will understand and be able to explain and, where appropriate, implement/recognize the following aspects of the boiler: desalination and feedwater treatment practices; high pressure boiler systems and their components; high pressure boiler operating conditions, including safe and efficient operation; high pressure boiler steam, feedwater, and combustion control systems; start-up, operation and shutdown procedures; and boiler malfunction problems.
 Instruction: Lectures, discussions, and practical exercises dealing with the nature of boiling; steam; combustion; boilers, boiler auxiliaries; water treatment; and boiler operation, including start-up and shut-down.
 Credit recommendation: *Version 1:* In the lower division baccalaureate/associate degree category, 3 semester hours in Boiler and Water Treatment or Industrial Technology (2/81). *Version 2:* In the lower division baccalaureate/associate degree category, 4 semester hours in Mechanical Technology (1/87). NOTE: This course has been reevaluated and continues to meet requirements for credit recommendations.

Chemistry for Technologists I and II and Chemical Calculations
 Location: Abu Dhabi National Oil Company Career Development Center, Abu Dhabi, United Arab Emirates.
 Length: 250 hours (60 weeks).
 Dates: September 1985-Present.
 Objective: To give the student a fundamental background in chemistry.
 Learning Outcome: Upon successful completion of this course, the student will be able to define and/or solve problems related to property conversion factors, atomic weights, moles, chemical bonding, periodic properties, oxidation numbers, balancing equations, mole and mass calculations, gas laws, volume and energy calculations, binary compounds, complex compounds, acid-base, oxidation numbers, and organic compounds.
 Instruction: Lecture, laboratory exercises and supervised homework are used to teach basic concepts in Chemistry.
 Credit recommendation: In the lower division baccalaureate/associate degree category, 4 semester hours in General Chemistry (1/87).

Digital and Analog Instruments
 Location: Abu Dhabi National Oil Company Career Development Center, Abu Dhabi, United Arab Emirates.
 Length: 80 hours (20 weeks).
 Dates: February 1986-Present.
 Objective: To acquaint the trainee with digital and analog signal applications, to develop an understanding of microprocessors and their applications to digital and analog instrumentation and to develop the skill needed to maintain analog and digital signal devices.
 Learning Outcome: Upon successful completion of this course, the student will be able to convert between decimal, binary, octal and hexidecimal number systems, identify and read digital code, explain input/output requirements and operation of a 6800 microprocessor, explain computer arithmetic; explain analog-to-digital and digital-to-analog conversions, and how these devices can be used and applied; explain various sensors and transducers used to measure position, motion, flow, force, pressure and level and to utilize these components in an operational microprocessor controlled system in an industrial setting.
 Instruction: Lectures, classroom exercises, laboratory experimentation, supervised homework and on-the-job training in the application of digital and analog devices in a microprocessor controlled system.
 Credit recommendation: In the upper division baccalaureate category, 3 semester hours in Digital and Analog Instrumentation (1/87).

Electrical and Electronic Drawing
 Location: Abu Dhabi National Oil Company Career Development Center, Abu Dhabi, United Arab Emirates.
 Length: 80 hours (20 weeks).
 Dates: August 1985-Present.
 Objective: To provide the student with skills specialized to electrical and electronic circuits.
 Learning Outcome: Upon successful completion of this course, the student will be able to list advantages of cable and harness wiring; recognize and use symbols used in block and logic diagrams; use symbol templates in drawing; and list advantages of pictorial assembly drawings.
 Instruction: Lecture, discussion and laboratory are used to teach concepts and skills related to electrical and electronic circuits.
 Credit recommendation: In the lower division baccalaureate/associate degree category, 3 semester hours in Drafting Technology (1/87).

Electrical Circuits
 Location: Abu Dhabi National Oil Company Career Development Center, Abu Dhabi, United Arab Emirates.

Length: 80 hours (20 weeks).
Dates: September 1985-Present.
Objective: To provide select trainees with additional theoretical exposure to the basic principles for analysis of DC and AC circuits.
Learning Outcome: Upon successful completion of this course, the student will be able to use Kirchhoff's Laws, superposition, Thevenin's Theorem, Norton's Theorem, and other applicable circuit analysis methods to understand electric circuits; determine equivalent resistance, capacitance, inductance, voltages and currents in steady state systems and to verify these by actual measurements in circuits.
Instruction: Lectures, classroom exercises and laboratory experimentation regarding DC and AC steady state circuit operations.
Credit recommendation: In the lower division baccalaureate/associate degree category, 3 semester hours in Basic Electricity or Engineering Technology (1/87).

Electrical Diagrams
Location: Abu Dhabi National Oil Company Career Development Center, Abu Dhabi, United Arab Emirates.
Length: 50 hours (10 weeks).
Dates: November 1986-Present.
Objective: To provide the trainee with an understanding of electrical diagrams and symbols.
Learning Outcome: Upon successful completion of this course, the student will be able to identify and draw various electrical circuit symbols as they pertain to industrial applications, trace through electrical circuit diagrams and to compare these with assembled systems, analyze electrical control diagrams in schematic form, interpret ladder diagrams and their use in explaining industrial electric control circuits.
Instruction: Lectures, discussions and on-the-job training relating to electrical schematic symbols and their use in control system schematics.
Credit recommendation: In the vocational certificate category or in the lower division baccalaureate/associate degree category, 3 semester hours in Motor Control Ladder Diagram Analysis (1/87).

1. Electrical Lab I
2. Electrical Lab II
Location: Abu Dhabi National Oil Company Career Development Center, Abu Dhabi, United Arab Emirates.
Length: 200 hours (20 weeks).
Dates: 1. September 1986-Present. 2. November 1986-Present.
Objective: To introduce the trainee to electrical safety and basic electrical circuit construction techniques.
Learning Outcome: Upon successful completion of this course, the student will be able to develop simple electrical schematics, construct very simple electric circuits, understand resistor color codes, solder connections, crimp and splice wires, install conduit, tape connections, and install lighting circuits in a safe and responsible manner.
Instruction: Laboratory practice in the safe procedures to install electrical wiring.
Credit recommendation: In the vocational certificate category, 4 semester hours in Basic Wiring Practices or in the lower division baccalaureate/associate degree category, 2 semester hours in Basic Wiring Procedures.

Electrical Math I and II
Location: Abu Dhabi National Oil Company Career Development Center, Abu Dhabi, United Arab Emirates.
Length: 100 hours (10 weeks).
Dates: September 1986-Present.
Objective: To enable the trainee to apply theoretical knowledge gained in previous courses to selected mathematical problems pertaining to electrical circuits.
Learning Outcome: Upon successful completion of this course, the student will be able to apply basic arithmetic, algebraic and logic skills to electrical math problems, to systematically solve electrical math problems and to apply their skills to real world equipment and situations.
Instruction: Lectures, practical clasroom exercises and on-the-job training in the application of basic math skills to basic electrical problems.
Credit recommendation: In the vocational certificate category or in the lower division baccalaureate/associate degree category, 2 semester hours in Basic Technical Math or Basic Electricity (1/87).

Electrical Safety
Location: Abu Dhabi National Oil Company Career Development Center, Abu Dhabi, United Arab Emirates.
Length: 80 hours (20 weeks).
Dates: August 1985-Present.
Objective: To create awareness of safe methods/habits when working with electrical circuits and equipment.
Learning Outcome: Upon successful completion of this course, the student will be able to identify potential electrical hazards in a petrochemical plant; be familiar with codes used in the petrochemical industry; know classifications of fires; perform specified safety tests; and list four safeguards to be followed when working on electrical distribution systems.
Instruction: Lecture, demonstrations, audio visuals, laboratory supervised study assignments are used to teach safety measures.
Credit recommendation: In the lower division baccalaureate/associate degree category, 3 semester hours in Industrial Safety (1/87).

Electrical Theory
(Formerly Electrical Mechanical Systems I and II)
Location: Abu Dhabi National Oil Company Career Development Center, Abu Dhabi, United Arab Emirates.
Length: 100 hours (20 weeks).

Dates: September 1980-Present.
Objective: To provide an understanding of the operating characteristics of various electromechanical devices and circuits which are common in the petroleum industry.
Learning Outcome: Upon successful completion of this course, the student will be able to identify various types of electromechanical motors, devices and their symbols, explain how these devices are used in a petrochemical plant, explain simple electromechanical control systems, identify and explain transformers and explain, construct and troubleshoot simple electromechanical control systems.
Instruction: Instructions, practical exercises and on-the-job training in the use of electromechanical systems and devices in the petrochemical plant.
Credit recommendation: In the vocational certificate category or in the lower division baccalaureate/associate degree category, 4 semester hours in Electromechanical Technology or Industrial Electricity (2/81) (1/87). NOTE: This course has been reevaluated and continues to meet requirements for credit recommendations.

1. Electrical Theory I
2. Electrical Theory II
Location: Abu Dhabi National Oil Company Career Development Center, Abu Dhabi, United Arab Emirates.
Length: 200 hours (20 weeks).
Dates: 1. September 1986-Present. 2. November 1986-Present.
Objective: To provide the trainee with an introduction to the basic properties of electric circuits.
Learning Outcome: Upon successful completion of this course, the student will be able to explain current and electron flow; define resistance and the use of Ohm's Law; illustrate the connection and use of an ammeter, a voltmeter and an ohmmeter; define work, power and energy in electric circuits; understand the use of batteries and electromagnetic induction; explain AC generation, frequency, RMS measurement, and AC impedence; understand capacitors, inductors and transformers, their connection, application and maintenance.
Instruction: Lectures, classroom discussions, laboratory exercises and on-the-job training in the application of basic DC and AC electrical theory to industrial situations.
Credit recommendation: In the lower division baccalaureate/associate degree category, 5 semester hours in Basic Electricity (1/87).

1. Electrical Theory III
2. Electrical Lab IV
Location: Abu Dhabi National Oil Company Career Development Center, Abu Dhabi, United Arab Emirates.
Length: 200 hours (10 weeks).
Dates: February 1987-Present.
Objective: To expand the trainee's capabilities in the area of three phase power and its applications to motor starters and motors.
Learning Outcome: Upon successful completion of this course, the student will be able to explain and apply three phase power systems, explain the application of WYE and DELTA systems, utilize three phase power with motor starters and motors, interpret three phase wiring diagrams, to apply these diagrams and to construct these wiring diagrams as they relate to motor systems.
Instruction: Lectures, classroom exercises, laboratory experiments and on-the-job training relevant to three phase electrical power systems and motor control systems.
Credit recommendation: In the vocational certificate category, 6 hours in Motor Control Circuits or in the lower division baccalaureate/associate degree category, 4 semester hours in Motor Control Circuits (1/87).

Electrical Theory and Laboratory Level IV
Location: Abu Dhabi National Oil Company Career Development Center, Abu Dhabi, United Arab Emirataes.
Length: 150 hours (10 weeks).
Dates: April 1987-Present.
Objective: To give the student an understanding of circuit component sizing and troubleshooting of electrical power circuits.
Learning Outcome: Upon successful completion of this course, the student will be able to identify and describe various circuit protection devices, determine motor circuit conductor overload, fuse, disconnect, and conductor size; describe generating stations, transmission substations, distribution substations, transfer switching and fuse coordination; test for short and open circuits; assemble a motor; test a motor circuit, transformer circuit and alarm circuits.
Instruction: Lecture, laboratory exercises and on-the-job training.
Credit recommendation: In the vocational certificate category, 6 semester hours in Electrical Power Circuits or in the lower division baccalaureate/associate degree category, 4 semester hours in Electrical Power Circuits (1/87).

1. Electronic Instrumentation
2. Electronic Devices and Circuits
Location: Abu Dhabi National Oil Company Career Development Center, Abu Dhabi, United Arab Emirates.
Length: 160 hours (40 weeks).
Dates: September 1985-Present.
Objective: To provide the student with knowledge relevant to industrial electronic theory in order to develop and implement electronic maintenance techniques.
Learning Outcome: Upon successful completion of this course, the student will be able to explain the operation of junction diodes, zener diodes, optoelectronic devices, diode limiters, transistors, operational amplifiers, active filters, voltage regulators, oscillators and multi vibrators and to utilize basic electronic devices to construct simple

DC power supplies, voltage doublers, common-emitter amplifiers, and various other simple electronic circuits.

Instruction: Lectures, classroom exercises, laboratory experiments and on-the-job training in the maintenance and application of basic electronic devices to industrial controls.

Credit recommendation: In the lower division baccalaureate/associate degree category, 3 semester hours in Basic Electronics and 2 semester hours in Basic Electronic Laboratory (1/87).

First Aid
Location: Abu Dhabi National Oil Company Career Development Center, Abu Dhabi, United Arab Emirates.
Length: 50 hours (10 weeks).
Dates: September 1980-Present.
Objective: To provide the student with knowledge and skills for emergency first aid care.
Learning Outcome: Upon successful completion of this course, the student will be able to demonstrate first aid techniques for cuts, abrasions, burns, eye injuries, hand injuries, blisters, fractures, sprains, strains, shock, poison and heart attack. Also demonstrate techniques for resuscitation, bandaging and rescue.
Instruction: Lectures, discussion and practical exercises in the purposes and kinds of first aid, wounds, burns, emergency rescue and transfer, respiratory emergency including cardiopulmonary resuscitation, heat reactions, shock, choking, poisoning and treatment of sudden illness.
Credit recommendation: In the lower division baccalaureate/associate degree category, 2 semester hours in First Aid (2/81) (1/87). NOTE: This course has been reevaluated and continues to meet requirements for credit recommendations.

Fuels and Lubricants
Location: Abu Dhabi National Oil Company Career Development Center, Abu Dhabi, United Arab Emirates.
Length: 80 hours (20 weeks).
Dates: April 1987-Present.
Objective: To familiarize the student with fuel lubricant properties along with measurement techniques.
Learning Outcome: Upon successful completion of this course, the student will be able to define the physical properties of liquid and gaseous fuels, lubricating oils and greases; perform calculations on combustion materials and energy balance; and discuss specifications of fuels and lubricants.
Instruction: Lecture, classroom discussions and laboratory are used to teach the student about fuels and lubricants.
Credit recommendation: In the upper division baccalaureate category, 4 semester hours in Petroleum Technology (1/87).

Fundamentals of Fluids
Location: Abu Dhabi National Oil Company Career Development Center, Abu Dhabi, United Arab Emirates.
Length: 80 hours (20 weeks).
Dates: September 1985-Present.
Objective: To enable the student to understand the criteria used for process plant piping.
Learning Outcome: Upon successful completion of this course, the student will be able to explain fluid properties, calculate fluid pressure, use a manometer, define compressible and incompressible fluid, calculate fluid velocity, use the Bernoulli Equation, define laminar flow, turbulent flow and Reynolds Number, calculate pressure loss, flow rates, friction factors and size pipe.
Instruction: Lecture, laboratory exercises, supervised homework and on-the-job training are used to teach the fundamentals of fluids.
Credit recommendation: In the upper division baccalaureate category, 3 semester hours in Fluid Power (1/87).

Hand and Power Tools I
Location: Abu Dhabi National Oil Company Career Development Center, Abu Dhabi, United Arab Emirates.
Length: 50 hours (10 weeks).
Dates: September 1980-Present.
Objective: To provide the student with the skills necessary to safely use basic hand and power tools.
Learning Outcome: Upon successful completion of this course, the student will be able to identify hand and power tools common to the petroleum industry, select and safely use the correct tools for specific operations.
Instruction: Lectures and practical exercises in shop safety, measurement, tool identification, use of general shop and hand tools, power tools, fastening methods, tapping and hand threading. Portable air tools are included.
Credit recommendation: In the vocational certificate category or in the lower division baccalaureate/associate degree category, 1 semester hour in Power Tools or Shop Practices and Procedures (2/81) (1/87). NOTE: This course has been reevaluated and continues to meet requirements for credit recommendations.

Hand and Power Tools II and III
Location: Abu Dhabi National Oil Company Career Development Center, Abu Dhabi, United Arab Emirates.
Length: 100 hours (20 weeks).
Dates: *Version 1:* September 1980-December 1986. *Version 2:* January 1987-Present.
Objective: To provide experienced personnel with the knowledge of how to select and use hand and power tools with emphasis on maintenance procedures, fabrication and safety practices. (These courses are a continuation of Hand and Power Tools I).
Learning Outcome: Upon successful completion of this course, the student will be able to use various rulers,

squares, calipers, dividers, v-blocks, verniers, micrometers, telescoping gauges, screw thread gauges, wire gauges, electric and pneumatic drills and to demonstrate ability to locate, drill and tap a hole accurately and to measure, cut, and thread a pipe accurately.

Instruction: Lectures, demonstrations and practical exercises include review of shop organizations, use of calipers, verniers and micrometers, thread cutting, portable air tools, portable electrical tools, pipefitting and fabrication.

Credit recommendation: *Version 1:* In the vocational certificate or in the lower division baccalaureate/associate degree category, 2 semester hours in Shop Practices and Procedures (2/81). *Version 2:* In the vocational certificate category or in the lower division baccalaureate/associate degree category, 2 semester hours in Shop Practices and Procedures (1/87). NOTE: This course has been reevaluated and continues to meet requirements for credit recommendations.

Heat Transfer Technology
Location: Abu Dhabi National Oil Company Career Development Center, Abu Dhabi, United Arab Emirates.
Length: 80 hours (20 weeks).
Dates: February 1986-Present.
Objective: To enable the student to understand the practical applications of heat transfer in the hydrocarbon processing industry.
Learning Outcome: Upon successful completion of this course, the student will be able to solve steady state heat transfer problems involving conduction through walls, composite walls, and pipe walls; apply the equation for forced convection to fluid flow in pipes; calculate the heat loss by radiation from pipes and storage tanks; use the Fourier Equation for heat exchanger design calculations; calculate the pressure drop in heat exchangers; calculate steam requirements for heating and cooling water requirements to cool or condense process steam; and calculate heat loss from storage tanks and pipes.
Instruction: Lecture, laboratory exercises, supervised homework and on-the-job training are used to teach heat transfer principles.
Credit recommendation: In the upper division baccalaureate category, 3 semester hours in Heat Transfer (1/87).

Hydraulics and Pneumatics I and II
Location: Abu Dhabi National Oil Company Career Development Center, Abu Dhabi, United Arab Emirates.
Length: 100 hours (20 weeks).
Dates: September 1980-Present.
Objective: To provide the student with a basic comprehensive study of hydraulic and pneumatic components and systems related to the petroleum industry.
Learning Outcome: Upon successful completion of this course, the student will be able to demonstrate an understanding of basic hydraulic/pneumatic components and systems, including hydraulic pump, motors and cylinders as well as pneumatic valves, cylinders, motors and compressors by assembling and testing circuits and explaining principles and differences in types of components.
Instruction: Lecture, discussions and practical exercise in basic hydraulic principles, hydraulic systems, hydraulic cylinder operation, hydraulic pumps, hydraulic motors, as well as basic pneumatic principles, air compressors and systems, pressure measurement, pneumatic valves, pneumatic cylinder operation and air motors.
Credit recommendation: In the vocational certificate category or in the lower division baccalaureate/associate degree category, 4 semester hours in Hydraulics and Pneumatics or Instrument Technology (2/81) (1/87). NOTE: This course has been reevaluated and continues to meet requirements for credit recommendations.

Industrial Drawing and Sketching
Location: Abu Dhabi National Oil Company Career Development Center, Abu Dhabi, United Arab Emirates.
Length: 50 hours (10 weeks).
Dates: September 1980-Present.
Objective: To provide the student with the fundamental knowledge and skills necessary to make instrument/electrical diagrams.
Learning Outcome: Upon successful completion of this course, the student will be able to construct isometric/orthographic/multi-view drawings; define and identify types and symbols used in electrical drawings; and demonstrate the purpose of a process flow diagram.
Instruction: Lectures and practical exercises regarding the use and application of drawings in industry and communication generally. Included is the proper use and identification of symbols and freehand sketching.
Credit recommendation: In the vocational certificate category or in the lower division baccalaureate/associate degree category, 3 semester hours in Drafting or Graphics (2/81) (1/87). NOTE: This course is not applicable for Drafting or Mechanical Design majors. This course has been reevaluated and continues to meet requirements for credit recommendations.

Industrial Electronics
(Formerly Industrial Electronics I and II)
Location: Abu Dhabi National Oil Company Career Development Center, Abu Dhabi, United Arab Emirates.
Length: 100 hours (20 weeks).
Dates: *Version 1:* September 1980-December 1986. *Version 2:* January 1987-Present.
Objective: To provide the trainee with an understanding of the function and application of basic electronic components and circuits.
Learning Outcome: Upon successful completion of this course, the student will be able to identify electronic components, their symbols and their use in electronic circuits, be able to use an oscilloscope and multimeter to check and

analyze electronic circuit operation, explain the use and operation of resistors, capacitors, inductors, transformers, transistors, diodes, and other basic electronic circuit components and be able to actually use and apply these electronic components to industrial system control and operation.

Instruction: Lectures, discussions and practical exercises in electronic symbols and abbreviations, electrical energy, series-parallel circuits, use of oscilloscopes, inductance, capacitance, time constants, resonance, discrete solid state components and digital logic.

Credit recommendation: *Version 1:* In the lower division baccalaureate/associate degree category, 4 semester hours in Basic Electronics, Electronics, or Industrial Electronics (2/81). *Version 2:* In the lower division baccalaureate/associate degree category, 4 semester hours in Basic Electronics, Electronics, or Industrial Electronics (1/87). NOTE: This course has been reevaluated and continues to meet requirements for credit recommendations.

Industrial Mathematics I and II
Location: Abu Dhabi National Oil Company Career Development Center, Abu Dhabi, United Arab Emirates.
Length: 100 hours (20 weeks).
Dates: September 1979-Present.
Objective: To provide the student with a basic knowledge of fundamental mathematics relevant to industrial plant operations.
Learning Outcome: Upon successful completion of this course, the student will be able to perform addition, subtraction, multiplication and division of whole numbers, fractions, and decimals; solve percentages, proportions, areas, volume; read graphs, convert units of measurement, weight and temperature; solve specific gravity and pressures; and deal with simple applications of trigonometric quantities.
Instruction: Lectures, practical exercises and on-the-job training in the technical application of mathematics.
Credit recommendation: In the vocational certificate category or in the lower division baccalaureate/associate degree category, 3 semester hours in Industrial Mathematics or Applied Mathematics (2/81) (1/87). NOTE: This course has been reevaluated and continues to meet requirements for credit recommendations.

Industrial Mathematics III
Location: Abu Dhabi National Oil Company Career Development Center, Abu Dhabi, United Arab Emirates.
Length: 80 hours (20 weeks).
Dates: September 1986-Present.
Objective: To provide the trainee with additional advanced mathematical exposure at the algebra level.
Learning Outcome: Upon the successful completion of this course, the student will be able to understand, use, solve, manipulate and interpret algebraic equations; have a basic knowledge of trigonometry; and understand exponentials and logarithms.
Instruction: Lectures, discussions and supervised homework exercises in basic algebra, trigonometry, logarithms, and exponentials.
Credit recommendation: In the lower division baccalaureate/associate degree category, 3 semester hours in College Algebra (1/87).

Industrial Mathematics IV
Location: Abu Dhabi National Oil Company Career Development Center, Abu Dhabi, United Arab Emirates.
Length: 80 hours (20 weeks).
Dates: February 1986-Present.
Objective: To provide students with additional advanced mathematics exposure at the calculus level.
Learning Outcome: Upon successful completion of this course, the student will be able to apply the basic concepts of calculus, including differentiation and integration, the application of calculus to problem solving, and understanding of partial differentiation.
Instruction: Lectures, discussions, classroom exercises and supervised homework dealing with calculus and its application to problem solving.
Credit recommendation: In the lower division baccalaureate/associate degree category, 3 semester hours in Introduction to Calculus (1/87).

Instrumentation
Location: Abu Dhabi National Oil Company Career Development Center, Abu Dhabi, United Arab Emirates.
Length: 50 hours (10 weeks).
Dates: September 1980-Present.
Objective: To give the student an in-depth understanding of timing and troubleshooting of instrument control loops commonly found in petroleum plants.
Learning Outcome: Upon successful completion of this course, the student will be able to interpret and analyze process control loop data, accurately tune and calibrate process control loops, analyze control loop problems and take appropriate corrective action.
Instruction: Lectures, discussions and laboratory exercises regarding the tuning and troubleshooting of various process instrumentation trainers, Moore process control simulator tuning and other process control simulator tuning.
Credit recommendation: In the lower division baccalaureate/associate degree category, 3 semester hours in Industrial Instrumentation or Industrial Technology (2/81) (1/87). NOTE: This course has been reevaluated and continues to meet requirements for credit recommendations.

Instrument Repair and Calibration I and II
Location: Abu Dhabi National Oil Company Career Development Center, Abu Dhabi, United Arab Emirates.
Length: 200 hours (20 weeks).

Dates: September 1980-Present.

Objective: To provide knowledge and skills necessary to repair and calibrate control instruments used in the petrochemical industry.

Learning Outcome: Upon successful completion of this course, the student will be able to calibrate and repair various control valves, positioners, recorders, controllers, alarms, transmitter converters, regulations, dead weight testers, gauges, indicators, minicorder, meters, relays and switches.

Instruction: Lectures and extensive laboratory exercises in fundamentals of control, instrument maintenance, troubleshooting control instrument devices, safety practice in repair and maintenance, control valves, solenoid valves, valve operations, safety valves and relief valves, transmitters, signal conditioner, indicators, controllers and dial indications.

Credit recommendation: In the vocational certificate category or in the lower division baccalaureate/associate degree category, 4 semester hours in Instrument Repair and Calibration or Instrument Technology (2/81) (1/87). NOTE: This course has been reevaluated and continues to meet requirements for credit recommendations.

Instrument Technology

Location: Abu Dhabi National Oil Company Career Development Center, Abu Dhabi, United Arab Emirates.

Length: 50 hours (10 weeks).

Dates: September 1980-Present.

Objective: To introduce techniques and procedures used to install pneumatic instruments using the manufacturers' manuals, data sheets, and loop diagrams.

Learning Outcome: Upon successful completion of this course, the student will be able to identify and explain the purpose of plant drawings, documents, instrument manuals, explosion proof enclosures, and tagging and locking of instruments and list the steps involved in installing pressure transmitters, orifice plates, reading instruments, thermocouples, rotometers and level transmitters.

Instruction: Lecture, discussions and practical exercises in the utilization of documents and procedures, instrument installation practices, transmitter installation, controller, recorder, and indicator installation, control valve and positioner installation and related component installations.

Credit recommendation: In the vocational certificate category, 2 semester hours in Industrial Instrument Installation or Instrument Technology (2/81) (1/87). NOTE: This course has been reevaluated and continues to meet requirements for credit recommendations.

Introduction to Data Processing and Computer Applications

Location: Abu Dhabi National Oil Company Career Development Center, Abu Dhabi, United Arab Emirates.

Length: 80 hours (20 weeks).

Dates: February 1986-Present.

Objective: To teach the student how to operate a computer and to program a computer using BASIC.

Learning Outcome: Upon successful completion of this course, the student will be able to construct flow charts and do program planning; explain computer sub-assemblies and I/O devices; explain storage and file organization; and operate a minicomputer.

Instruction: Lecture and discussion with laboratory are used to introduce the student to the uses of the computer. (Outside work is required).

Credit recommendation: In the lower division baccalaureate/associate degree category, 3 semester hours in Computer Literacy (1/87).

Introduction to Instrumentation
(Formerly Introduction to Instrumentation I and Introduction to Instrumentation II)

Location: Abu Dhabi National Oil Company Career Development Center, Abu Dhabi, United Arab Emirates.

Length: *Version 1:* 50 hours (10 weeks), and 50 hours (10 weeks). *Version 2:* 50 hours (10 weeks).

Dates: *Version 1:* September 1980-December 1986. *Version 2:* January 1987-Present.

Objective: To provide an overview of process instrumentation and control and process measurement through data interpretation.

Learning Outcome: Upon successful completion of this course, the student will be able to explain the function and control of certain process instruments related to a petrochemical plant; explain process variables and the function of instrument control loops; identify various sensory systems and instruments in a petrochemical plant; understand the importance of alarm and safety systems; and inspect and check out the operation of these basic instrument systems.

Instruction: Lectures, demonstrations, practical exercises and on-the-job training in the use of process instrumentation and controls.

Credit recommendation: *Version 1:* In the lower division baccalaureate/associate degree category, 6 semester hours in Introduction to Instrumentation or Instrument Technology (2/81). *Version 2:* In the lower division baccalaureate/associate degree category, 3 semester hours in Introduction to Instrumentation or Instrument Technology (1/87). NOTE: This course has been reevaluated and continues to meet requirements for credit recommendations.

Introduction to Technology I and II

Location: Abu Dhabi National Oil Company Career Development Center, Abu Dhabi, United Arab Emirates.

Length: 100 hours (20 weeks).

Dates: September 1980-Present.

Objective: To reinforce technical vocabulary and terminology related to the petrochemical industry.

Learning Outcome: Upon successful completion of this course, the student will be able to calculate volume; make free hand sketches; work basic mechanical problems; and identify and define operational petrochemical processes.

Instruction: Lectures and practical exercises in drawing and sketching, measurement, energy and force, petroleum production and refining.

Credit recommendation: In the lower division baccalaureate/associate degree category, 2 semester hours in Petroleum Technology (2/81) (1/87). NOTE: This course has been reevaluated and continues to meet requirements for credit recommendations.

Mechanical Blueprint Reading
Location: Abu Dhabi National Oil Company Career Development Center, Abu Dhabi, United Arab Emirates.
Length: 50 hours (10 weeks).
Dates: *Version 1:* September 1980-December 1986. *Version 2:* January 1987-Present.
Objective: To provide the fundamental knowledge and skill required to read and interpret typical mechanical blueprints.
Learning Outcome: Upon successful completion of this course, the student will be able to read and interpret industrial drawings, isometric drawings, blueprints, piping diagrams, maintenance schematics and welding diagrams and to explain sizing, tolerance, and limits of mechanical parts, types of fits, machining processes, exploded views, parts list, and schematics.
Instruction: Lectures and classroom demonstrations in the interpretation of blueprint dimension tolerances, machining details, surface finish sections and auxiliary views, assembly drawings and exploded views, schematics and symbols, piping symbols and diagrams, pipe layout and electrical symbols and diagrams.
Credit recommendation: *Version 1:* In the vocational certificate category or in the lower division baccalaureate/associate degree category, 3 semester hours in Mechanical Blueprint Reading (2/81). *Version 2:* In the vocational certificate category or in the lower division baccalaureate/associate degree category, 2 semester hours in Mechanical Blueprint Reading (1/87). NOTE: This course has been reevaluated and continues to meet requirements for credit recommendations.

Mechanical Elements
Location: Abu Dhabi National Oil Company Career Development Center, Abu Dhabi, United Arab Emirates.
Length: 50 hours (10 weeks).
Dates: September 1980-Present.
Objective: To provide the student with a fundamental working knowledge of mechanics and lubrication.
Learning Outcome: Upon successful completion of this course, the student will be able to compute effort and mechanical advantage for (a) levers, (b) pulleys and block and tackles, and (c) gear boxes; define kinetic and static friction; and recognize and identify different classes of bearings and lubricants.
Instruction: Lectures in simple mechanics, gears, function, bearings, lubrication and sampling methods.
Credit recommendation: In the lower division baccalaureate/associate degree category, 2 semester hours in Industrial or Mechanical Technology (2/81) (1/87). NOTE: This course has been reevaluated and continues to meet requirements for credit recommendations.

Piping and Instrument Diagrams
Location: Abu Dhabi National Oil Company Career Development Center, Abu Dhabi, United Arab Emirates.
Length: 50 hours (10 weeks).
Dates: *Version 1:* September 1980-December 1986. *Version 2:* January 1987-Present.
Objective: To develop the student's understanding and ability to identify, read, and interpret process flow diagrams.
Learning Outcome: Upon successful completion of this course, the student will be able to sketch piping and instrument diagrams; define commonly used petrochemical process plant terminology; and interpret instrument standards and codes.
Instruction: Lectures, and classroom exercises in process equipment, instrument codes and piping and instrumentation diagrams.
Credit recommendation: *Version 1:* In the vocational certificate category or in the lower division baccalaureate/associate degree category, 2 semester hours in Piping and Instrument Diagrams or Instrument Technology (2/81). *Version 1:* In the vocational certificate category, 2 semester hours in Instrument Mechanics (1/87). NOTE: This course has been reevaluated and continues to meet requirements for credit recommendations.

Plant Materials and Equipment
Location: Abu Dhabi National Oil Company Career Development Center, Abu Dhabi, United Arab Emirates.
Length: 50 hours (10 weeks).
Dates: September 1980-Present.
Objective: To provide experience in the procedures and techniques involved in moving and setting up heavy equipment used in the petrochemical industry.
Learning Outcome: Upon successful completion of this course, the student will be able to demonstrate appropriate and/or proper use of a block and tackle, slings, safety precautions, rope size, knots, bends, hitches, wire rope, chains, hand operated hoists, hand signals, coupling devices, scaffolding, ladders, leveling tools and alignment indications; and to explain rope materials and strengths, uses of chains, types of cranes and hoists, lifting fixtures, snatch blocks, scaffolding, safety jacks, skids and leveling tools.
Instruction: Lecture and practical demonstrations regarding rigging, (i.e., ropes, chains, hoists, scaffolds and

fixtures) and the installation and safe application of heavy petrochemical equipment.

Credit recommendation: In the vocational certificate category or in the lower division baccalaureate/associate degree category, 2 semester hours in Plant Material and Practices, Industrial Maintenance, or Industrial Technology (2/81) (1/87). NOTE: This course has been reevaluated and continues to meet requirements for credit recommendations.

Pneumatic Instrumentation
  Location: Abu Dhabi National Oil Company Career Development Center, Abu Dhabi, United Arab Emirates.
  Length: 100 hours (10 weeks).
  Dates: September 1980-Present.
  Objective: To provide an understanding of the concepts and use of pneumatic instrumentation.
  Learning Outcome: Upon successful completion of this course, the student will be able to adjust manual resets and calibrate temperature and pressure transmitters, to draw diagrams and explain force-balance mechanisms, moment-balance mechanisms, relays, pilot valves, feedback circuits, and three-mode controllers.
  Instruction: Lecture, discussion and laboratory exercise in basic computing elements, transmitting devices, pneumatic relays, control valves and positioners and control modes.
  Credit recommendation: In the lower division baccalaureate/associate degree category, 3 semester hours in Pneumatic Instrumentation or Instrument Technology (2/81) (1/87). NOTE: This course has been reevaluated and continues to meet requirements for credit recommendations.

Process Control I and II
  Location: Abu Dhabi National Oil Company Career Development Center, Abu Dhabi, United Arab Emirates.
  Length: 100 hours (20 weeks).
  Dates: September 1980-Present.
  Objective: To provide the student with an understanding of the relationships of the four primary variables in a petrochemical process. (Emphasis placed on refineries. Training is operator oriented).
  Learning Outcome: Upon successful completion of this course, the student will be able to understand control loop components; explain controller operation; and identify problems in loops and report to maintenance.
  Instruction: Lectures, discussions, and practical exercises supplemented by on-the-job training in operating pressure-sensing devices, temperature-sensing devices, level sensors, and flow-measurement devices. Differentiation between a closed and an open loop and the functions of the various elements in a control loop, as well as refinery distillation processes are also studied.
  Credit recommendation: In the lower division baccalaureate/associate degree category, 4 semester hours in Instrument Technology (2/81) (1/87). NOTE: This course has been reevaluated and continues to meet requirements for credit recommendations.

Process Control III
  Location: Abu Dhabi National Oil Company Career Development Center, Abu Dhabi, United Arab Emirates.
  Length: 50 hours (10 weeks).
  Dates: May 1987-Present.
  Objective: To provide the student with an understanding of the relationships of the four primary variables in a petrochemical process. (Emphasis placed on gas plants.) (Training is operator oriented.)
  Learning Outcome: Upon successful completion of this course, the student will be able to identify and work with control loop components; explain controller operation; and identify problems in loop components.
  Instruction: Lecture, discussion and lab demonstration are used to teach the student about the components related to Process Control.
  Credit recommendation: In the lower division baccalaureate/associate degree category, 1 semester hour in Instrument Technology (1/87).

Process Flow Sheets
  Location: Abu Dhabi National Oil Company Career Development Center, Abu Dhabi, United Arab Emirates.
  Length: 50 hours (10 weeks).
  Dates: September 1980-Present.
  Objective: To enable the student to identify, read and interpret diagrams used in the design of petroleum and chemical process plants.
  Learning Outcome: Upon successful completion of this course, the student will be able to interpret process flow sheets (reading of schematics and symbols); and sketch simple process flow diagrams.
  Instruction: Lectures, discussions, and classroom exercises covering technical diagrams of industrial process plants, types of process diagrams, and practice exercises.
  Credit recommendation: In the vocational certificate category, 2 semester hours in Drafting (2/81) (1/87). NOTE: This course has been reevaluated and continues to meet requirements for credit recommendations.

Process Rotating Equipment I
  Location: Abu Dhabi National Oil Company Career Development Center, Abu Dhabi, United Arab Emirates.
  Length: 50 hours (10 weeks).
  Dates: September 1980-Present.
  Objective: To provide the student with an understanding of major rotating equipment used in the petrochemical industry.
  Learning Outcome: Upon successful completion of this course, the student will be able to identify and explain operation of types of pumps, (reciprocating, rotary, centrifugal, propellor, turbine and three control); identify and

explain operation of compressors (reciprocating, rotary); and identify and explain function of couplings and prime movers.

Instruction: Lectures, discussions, and practical exercises in principles and functions of pumps, compressors, and prime movers.

Credit recommendation: In the vocational certificate category or in the lower division baccalaureate/associate degree category, 2 semester hours in Mechanical Technology (2/81) (1/87). NOTE: This course has been reevaluated and continues to meet requirements for credit recommendations.

Process Rotating Equipment II
 Location: Abu Dhabi National Oil Company Career Development Center, Abu Dhabi, United Arab Emirates.
 Length: 50 hours (10 weeks).
 Dates: September 1980-Present.
 Objective: To provide the student with an understanding of centrifugal compressors and gas turbines.
 Learning Outcome: Upon successful completion of this course, the student will be able to trace flow pattern through centrifugal compressors; perform compressor tests for (a) single pump operation and (b) parallel and series operation of compressors; and measure and record pump inlet/outlet pressures, liquid flow, torque, rmp, etc.
 Instruction: Lectures, discussions, and practical exercises in the use of parallel/series pumps, motor current, voltage and speed, pump torque, pressure and liquid flow, radical flow pump/turbine, and 2-state air compressor.
 Credit recommendation: In the lower division baccalaureate/associate degree category, 2 semester hours in Mechanical Technology (2/81) (1/87). NOTE: This course has been reevaluated and continues to meet requirements for credit recommendations.

Process Simulators I and II
 Location: Abu Dhabi National Oil Company Career Development Center, Abu Dhabi, United Arab Emirates.
 Length: 150 hours (20 weeks).
 Dates: September 1980-Present.
 Objective: To provide laboratory exercises emphasizing process operation, analysis of malfunctions, start-up procedures, equipment shutdown, operating procedures for emergency situations, operating safety, safe laboratory procedures.
 Learning Outcome: Upon successful completion of this course, the student will be able to do start-up and shutdown procedures on loops; work with Redox loops (loop tuning); and work with Solver loops (loop tuning).
 Instruction: Lectures, discussions, and practical exercises in operating sensing devices, the use of the Brodhead-Garrett-process simulator, Redox-loop operation, Solvex-loop operation, simultaneous operation of Redox and Solvex loops, bubbles, square-root extractor, the use of the Moore process control simulator, instrument stability.

Credit recommendation: In the lower division baccalaureate/associate degree category, 4 semester hours in Process Control and Instrumentation Technology (2/81) (1/87). NOTE: This course has been reevaluated and continues to meet requirements for credit recommendations.

Process Static Equipment
 Location: Abu Dhabi National Oil Company Career Development Center, Abu Dhabi, United Arab Emirates.
 Length: 50 hours (10 weeks).
 Dates: September 1980-Present.
 Objective: To provide the student with an understanding of the function, construction, and safety limits of static equipment found in the petrochemical industry.
 Learning Outcome: Upon successful completion of this course, the student will be able to cut gaskets, install fittings, identify tubings, identify valve types and oil filters; identify methods of joining a pipe; and know the purpose of expansion joints.
 Instruction: Lectures, discussion and practical exercises on the nature and application of various types of piping and tubing, valves, storage tanks, separations, towers, heat exchangers, fired heaters, ejectors and the effects and prevention of corrosion.
 Credit recommendation: In the lower division baccalaureate/associate degree category, 2 semester hours in Mechanical Technology (2/81) (1/87). NOTE: This course has been reevaluated and continues to meet requirements for credit recommendations.

Process Static Equipment II
 Location: Abu Dhabi National Oil Company Career Development Center, Abu Dhabi, United Arab Emirates.
 Length: 50 hours (10 weeks).
 Dates: September 1980-December 1986.
 Objective: This course is designed to introduce the function and maintenance of static equipment of specific importance to the mechanical technician, and the plant operation in a petrochemical facility. This course covers pipe fittings, filters and strainers, flairs and thermal insulation.
 Instruction: Lecture, discussion and practical exercises in pipe fabrication methods, pipe fittings, valves, distillation towers, heat exchangers, final heaters, filters and strainers, flares and thermal insulation.
 Credit recommendation: In the vocational certificate category or in the lower division baccalaureate/associate degree category, 2 semester hours in Process Static Equipment, Industrial Technology, or Technology (2/81).

Process Systems I and II
(Formerly Process Systems)
 Location: Abu Dhabi National Oil Company Career Development Center, Abu Dhabi, United Arab Emirates.
 Length: 100 hours (20 weeks).
 Dates: *Version 1:* September 1980-December 1986. *Ver-*

sion 2: January 1987-Present.

Objective: To provide the student with an understanding of gas plant operations.

Learning Outcome: Upon successful completion of this course, the student will be able to explain separation, compression, refrigeration, dementhanization, surge drums and boilers.

Instruction: Lecture and group discussion concerning the industrial processing components and relationships of raw materials and products, manufacturing processes, distillation, crystallization solvent extraction, adsorption and absorption, cracking, reforming and other related processes. Student oral presentations are also required.

Credit recommendation: *Version 1:* In the lower division baccalaureate/associate degree category, 3 semester hours in Process Systems, Petrochemical Processes, or Industrial Technology (2/81). *Version 2:* In the lower division baccalaureate/associate degree category, 4 semester hours in Petrochemical Process Systems (1/87). NOTE: This course has been reevaluated and continues to meet requirements for recommendations.

Refrigeration, Cryogenics and Corrosion
Location: Abu Dhabi National Oil Company Career Development Center, Abu Dhabi, United Arab Emirates.
Length: 50 hours (10 weeks).
Dates: September 1980-Present.
Objective: To provide the student with an understanding of L.N.G. operation.
Learning Outcome: Upon successful completion of this course, the student will be able to: (1) identify 3 liquefication cycles; (2) discuss causes and solutions for corrosion problems; (3) cite 6 factors influencing corrosion; and (4) state Joule-Thomson effect and its application.
Instruction: Lecture and discussions in basic refrigeration, fuel preparation, liquefaction cycles, storage of L.N.G., and transportation and revaporization of L.N.G.
Credit recommendation: In the vocational certificate category, 1 semester hour in Petroleum Technology. (2/81) (1/87). NOTE: This course has been reevaluated and continues to meet requirements for credit recommendations.

Repair and Maintenance of Rotating Equipment I and II
Location: Abu Dhabi National Oil Company Career Development Center, Abu Dhabi, United Arab Emirates.
Length: *Version 1:* 200 hours (20 weeks). *Version 2:* 150 hours (20 weeks).
Dates: *Version 1:* September 1980-December 1986. *Version 2:* January 1987-Present.
Objective: To develop the student's ability to repair and maintain skillfully a variety of process rotating equipment, including pumps and compressors, turbines, prime movers, fans, and blowers.
Learning Outcome: Upon successful completion of this course, the student will be able to perform maintenance on an internal combustion engine including replacing rod bearings, lubrication, clean and gap spark plugs, align timing gears, and check ignition wiring; to disassemble and reassemble a centrifugal pump, install pump seals and packing, inspect and align gears, lubricate governors and bearings, install carbon ring and labyrinth seals; to explain the maintenance procedures for I.C. and electric motors, pumps, valves, turbines, bearings, seals and governing systems.
Instruction: Lecture and extensive laboratory exercises in alignment, maintenance, troubleshooting and repair of pumps and compressors, turbines and motor engines, fans and blowers, and maintenance and testing of related equipment.
Credit recommendation: *Version 1:* In the vocational certificate category, 4 semester hours in Industrial Equipment Repair or in the lower division baccalaureate/associate degree category, 3 semester hours in Industrial Technology (2/81). *Version 2:* In the vocational certificate category, 3 semester hours in Industrial Equipment Repair or in the lower division baccalaureate/associate degree category, 2 semester hours in Industrial Technology (1/87). NOTE: This course has been reevaluated and continues to meet requirements for credit recommendations.

Repair and Maintenance of Static Equipment I and II
Location: Abu Dhabi National Oil Company Career Development Center, Abu Dhabi, United Arab Emirates.
Length: 150 hours (20 weeks).
Dates: *Version 1:* September 1980-December 1986. *Version 2:* January 1987-Present.
Objective: To develop fundamental knowledge and skill required for the repair, maintenance, and preventive maintenance of equipment found in the petrochemical processing plant.
Learning Outcome: Upon successful completion of this course, the student will be able to disassemble, inspect, repair, and reassemble a valve; explain the purpose of work orders, ring joints, pipe saddlers, pyrometers, refractory; measure, cut, flange, and solder copper tubing; inspect, test and decoke heating tubes; identify and explain the use of heat exchanger components, valve components and fired heaters; cite hazards and safety procedures associated with maintenance and repair of fired heaters.
Instruction: Lecture and extensive laboratory exercises in job scheduling and planning, maintenance of pipe fittings, maintenance and repair of valves, vessels, heat exchangers and fired heaters.
Credit recommendation: *Version 1:* In the vocational certificate category, 2 semester hours in Industrial Equipment Repair and Maintenance or in the lower division baccalaureate/associate degree category, 1 semester hour in Shop Procedures and Practices or Industrial Technology (2/81). *Version 2:* In the vocational certificate category, 2 semester hours in Industrial Equipment Repair and

Maintenance or in the lower division baccalaureate/associate degree category, 1 semester hour in Shop Procedures and Practices or Industrial Technology (1/87). NOTE: This course has been reevaluated and continues to meet requirements for credit recommendations.

Safety and Fire Prevention
(Formerly Fire Prevention and Plant Safety and Organization)
Location: Abu Dhabi National Oil Company Career Development Center, Abu Dhabi, United Arab Emirates.
Length: *Version 1:* 50 hours (10 weeks) and 50 hours (10 weeks). *Version 2:* 50 hours (10 weeks).
Dates: *Version 1:* September 1980-December 1986. *Version 2:* January 1987-Present.
Objective: To familiarize the student with fire prevention and fire fighting procedures for process plants and with the use of several safety equipment and procedures.
Learning Outcome: Upon successful completion of this course, the student will be able to demonstrate the proper use of personal safety equipment, explosimeters, oxygen meters, gas detectors, ladders, scaffolds, hand trucks and fire fighting equipment and to explain the concepts of safety, accident and fire prevention, methods of fire fighting, safe handling of materials and basic principles of plant organization.
Instruction: Lecture, discussions and classroom exercises in safety and accident prevention, industrial situations and petroleum plant organizations as they relate to safety.
Credit recommendation: In the lower division baccalaureate/associate degree category, 2 semester hours in Safety and Fire Prevention (2/81) (1/87). NOTE: This course has been reevaluated and continues to meet requirements for credit recommendations.

Utility Systems
Location: Abu Dhabi National Oil Company Career Development Center, Abu Dhabi, United Arab Emirates.
Length: 50 hours (10 weeks).
Dates: September 1980-Present.
Objective: To provide the student with a basic understanding of utility systems commonly found in a petrochemical system.
Learning Outcome: Upon successful completion of this course, the student will be able to identify and list problems in plant utility systems; identify subsystem components; and site water treatment methods.
Instruction: Lectures and discussions in operation and control of water systems, air systems, steam systems, condensate systems, fuel-gas systems, purging systems, and drain systems.
Credit recommendation: In the lower division baccalaureate/associate degree category, 1 semester hour in Plant Utility Systems, Industrial Technology, Civil or Mechanical Technology (2/81) (1/87). NOTE: This course has been reevaluated and continues to meet requirements for credit recommendations.

Water Facilities Chemistry
(Water Chemistry)
Location: Abu Dhabi National OIl Company Career Development Center, Abu Dhabi, United Arab Emirates.
Length: 80 hours (20 weeks).
Dates: September 1985-Present.
Objective: To give the student an understanding of the basics of water treatment methods and uses of water in process plants.
Learning Outcome: Upon successful completion of this course, the student will be able to identify the most common dissolved solids and gases formed in raw water and the problems they cause; identify the processes used to treat boiler feedwater, cooling water and drinking water; calculate chemical feed rates to a clarifier; identify methods of introducing chlorine, distillation processes, pretreatment systems for reverse osmosis, ion exchange processing, and calculate consumption rates for an ion exchange process given the design parameters.
Instruction: Lecture, laboratory exercises, supervised homework and on-the-job training are used to teach water chemistry.
Credit recommendation: In the upper division baccalaureate category, 3 semester hours in Water Chemistry (1/87).

Welding
Location: Abu Dhabi National Oil Company Career Development Center, Abu Dhabi, United Arab Emirates.
Length: 50 hours (10 weeks).
Dates: November 1985-Present.
Objective: To provide the student with an understanding of basic welding techniques.
Learning Outcome: Upon successful completion of this course, the student will be able to correctly identify proper cutting and welding tips, set up a gas welding unit, and cut metal with an oxy-acetylene unit; to select proper rods, amperage, prepare metal and join two pieces of metal with an electric welder; and to describe proper safety procedures and techniques used in cutting and welding material.
Instruction: Laboratory exercises and on-the-job training are used to teach welding.
Credit recommendation: In the vocational certificate category or in the lower division baccalaureate/associate degree category, 1 semester hour in Basic Welding or Shop Practices (1/87).

American Bankers Association

The mission of the American Bankers Association (ABA) is to enhance the ability of America's banks and bankers to serve the needs and desires of the American public. ABA serves this mission through activities in government relations, communications, education, and other activities targeted to the specific needs of banks.

The Education Policy and Development Council, made up of senior-level bankers from around the country, guides the work of the Education Policy and Development (EP&D) Group within ABA. The Education Policy and Development Council's missions include banker education, research, evaluation, and program development.

One of the largest adult education programs in the world, the American Institute of Banking (AIB) is also part of EP&D. Over 250,000 students take courses each year through 600 local AIB chapters.

EP&D is in the process of implementing a nationwide system of banker education called the Professional Development Program (PDP). The goals of the PDP are to organize banking education programs into a systematic and logical sequence for bankers and to ensure that these programs are of uniformly high quality across the country. Each AIB chapter operates independently, but is guided by the National Office in Washington. State-sponsored schools, on the other hand, are one- or two-week resident programs established by states, using materials provided by ABA's Professional Development Program.

With the aid of a full-time professional and administrative staff at the National Office within ABA in Washington, D.C., materials are developed, and administrative support is provided to AIB chapters. Long-range planning, research, recordkeeping, and the coordination of conferences, training, workshops, and other programs take place at ABA. This staff also provides chapters with seminar assistance, prepared curricula and texts for over 100 courses and seminars, audio/visual materials, and other forms of educational assistance.

Besides the national headquarters, over 60 chapters located in major metropolitan cities have administrative offices. Most of these chapters also have classroom facilities for courses and seminar offerings housed within their offices.

Along with the above-mentioned facilities, chapters have working relationships with banks, colleges and universities, high schools, and community centers for the use or rental of classroom space. These places are chosen in locations where there is maximum accessibility for bankers.

State-sponsored schools are generally held on college campuses while the college is not in session. Therefore, most schools are held in the summer months. In the event schools must be held at other times during the year, hotel or conference facilities are used.

The selection of teaching staff for state schools is the responsibility of the school's advisory board and the education director. Although each sets its own policies and procedures, they generally include the following: (1) the selection of subject matter specialists with experience in and a commitment to the educational process; (2) a recommendation from senior management or other comparable education program; (3) submission of an application and resume verifying professional history as a banker and/or educator; (4) personal or telephone interview. The American Institute of Banking of the American Bankers Association recommends that its chapters use the specified criteria when selecting their part-time instructors.

ABA's Education Policy and Development Group (EP&D) is responsible for managing the course development and revision process to ensure that a systematic sequence of high-quality, cost-effective educational opportunities is available to bankers.

ABA has recently instituted a comprehensive system to accredit banker education programs. The system is based on the demonstration by a program that it meets or exceeds 15 education standards specified by the EP&D Council. The accreditation process is similar in structure to processes offered in other comparable professions.

It is the intention of ABA, through its accreditation process, to verify that standards are met in the areas of instructor selection, training and review, adequacy of facilities, recordkeeping, governance, course development and evaluation, student evaluation, and instructional materials. Only those state schools and AIB chapters that meet established ABA guidelines and standards will be entitled to use the ACE credit recommendations for their courses.

Source of official student records: Registrar, American Institute of Banking, American Bankers Association, 1120 Connecticut Avenue, N.W., Washington, D.C. 20036.

Additional information about the courses: Program on Noncollegiate Sponsored Instruction, The Center for Adult Learning and Educational Credentials, American Council on Education, One Dupont Circle, Washington, D.C. 20036.

NOTE 1: Courses offered through the American Institute of Banking are frequently offered in affiliation with local community colleges. Some of these community colleges operate on a quarter rather than a semester system, requiring the AIB chapter to structure its courses into a thirty hour format. Although each course is adapted according to its specific characteristics, there are some inherent differences between the forty-five and thirty hour formats.

The forty-five hour format covers all the course objectives of each chapter of the provided text, including those that require deeper levels of applying, analyzing, and synthesizing information. This is accomplished through discussion, exercises, role plays, case studies, and other learning activities designed to improve the conceptual understanding of the content.

The thirty hour format is expected to cover all the chapters in the text with a minimum of related classroom activities.

Credit is also recommended for any courses offered through correspondence study provided that efforts of students using this method are measured by a *proctored* examination at the conclusion of each course.

NOTE 2: The following state bankers association-sponsored schools and American Institute of Banking (AIB) chapters are following guidelines and standards established by the American Bankers Association and are eligible to use the ACE credit recommendations granted to the American Bankers Association:

Akron Chapter, AIB (Ohio)
Atlanta Chapter, AIB (Georgia)
Baltimore Chapter, AIB (Maryland)
Berks County Chapter, AIB (Pennsylvania)
Capital Area Chapter, AIB (Pennsylvania)
Central Atlantic School of Commercial Lending (Pennsylvania Bankers Association)
Cincinnati Chapter, AIB (Ohio)
Columbus Chapter, AIB (Ohio)
Dayton Chapter, AIB (Ohio)
Denver Chapter, AIB (Colorado)
Des Moines Chapter, AIB (Iowa)
East Central Iowa Chapter, AIB (Iowa)
Fox Cities Chapter, AIB (Wisconsin)
Iowa Commercial Lending School (Iowa Bankers Association)
Iowa School of Banking I & II (Iowa Bankers Association)
Iowa Valley Chapter, AIB (Iowa)
Kentucky General Banking School I and II (Kentucky Bankers Association)
Kansas City Chapter, AIB, (Missouri)
Lorain Chapter AIB (Ohio)
Madison Area Chapter, AIB (Ohio)
Marathon Area Chapter, AIB (Wisconsin)
Milwaukee Chapter, AIB (Wisconsin)
Missouri Commercial Lending School (Missouri Bankers Association)
Missouri General Banking School (Missouri Bankers Association)
North Dakota School of Banking (North Dakota Bankers Association)
Northwest Commercial Lending School (Oregon, Washington, and Idaho state bankers associations)
Northwest Intermediate Banking School (Oregon, Washington, and and Idaho state bankers associations)
Oklahoma Commercial Lending School (Oklahoma Bankers Association)
Oklahoma School of Banking (Oklahoma Bankers Association)
Philadelphia Chapter, AIB (Pennsylvania)
Sioux City Iowa Chapter, AIB (Iowa)
Tennessee Commercial Lending School (Tennessee Bankers Assocation)
Tennessee School of General Banking I (Tennesee Bankers Association)
Toledo Chapter, AIB (Ohio)
Valley Forge Chapter, AIB (Pennsylvania)
Waterloo Area Chapter, AIB (Iowa)
Wisconsin Commercial Lending School (Wisconsin Bankers Association)
Wisconsin Consumer Credit School (Wisconsin Bankers Association)
Wisconsin General Banking School (Wisconsin Bankers Association)
York Adams Chapter, AIB (Pennsylvania)

CONSUMER CREDIT/REAL ESTATE FINANCE

Analyzing Financial Statements (6920)

Location: AIB chapters nationwide operating under established ABA guidelines and standards.

Length: *Version 1:* 45 hours (15 weeks - one 3-hour session per week); *Version 2:* 30 hours (10 weeks - one 3-hour session per week).

Dates: November 1985-Present.

Objective: To teach students the basic skills and techniques in analyzing financial statements.

Instruction: The course covers analysis of income statements, analysis of balance sheets, preparation of cash flow statements, and selection and interpretation of ratios. Consideration of future performance is achieved by pre forms analysis, cash budgets, working capital analysis, sensitivity and breakeven analysis, and operating leverage. Lecture and discussion are used.

Credit recommendation: In the upper division baccalaureate category, 3 semester hours in Finance/Accounting (11/85). NOTE: Students who receive credit for this course should not receive credit for Statement Analysis.

Banking and the Plastic Card (6610)
(Formerly Bank Cards)

Location: AIB chapters nationwide operating under established ABA guidelines and standards.

Length: *Version 1:* 45 hours (15 weeks - one 3-hour session per week); *Version 2:* 30 hours (10 weeks - one 3-hour session per week).

Dates: November 1985-Present.

Objective: To provide the student with an understanding of cards used for credit/debt, retail, and travel transactions.

Instruction: Course covers the history and structure of the card system, operational aspects, legal and regulatory issues, and trends. Lecture and discussion are used.

Credit recommendation: *Version 1:* In the vocational certificate or lower division baccalaureate/associate degree category, 2 semester hours in Banking or Consumer Credit. *Version 2:* In the vocational certificate or lower division baccalaureate/associate degree category, 1 semester hour in Banking or Consumer Credit (11/85). NOTE: This course is applicable to an associate degree program.

Consumer Credit 200-Level Curriculum
Location: State-sponsored schools.
Length: 40 hours (1 week).
Dates: August 1985-Present.
Objective: To provide the student with a comprehensive view of the consumer credit function including credit operations, profitability and development of lending skills.
Instruction: Gives a broad view of the consumer credit market, loan types, marketing, analysis, pricing, operations, collections, compliance, and integration in bank asset management. Lecture and discussion are used.
Credit recommendation: In the lower division baccalaureate/associate degree category, 3 semester hours in Consumer Credit Management or Banking (11/85).

Consumer Lending (7008)
Location: AIB chapters nationwide operating under established ABA guidelines and standards.
Length: *Version 1:* 45 hours (15 weeks - one 3-hour meeting per week); *Version 2:* 30 hours (10 weeks - one 3-hour meeting per week).
Dates: November 1985-Present.
Objective: To familiarize students with the techniques, control, generation, and evaluation of consumer loans.
Instruction: Provides overview of consumer credit including loan policy, evaluation and processing of applications, and consumer credit regulation. Lecture and discussion are used.
Credit recommendation: *Version 1:* In the vocational certificate or lower division baccalaureate/associate degree category, 2 semester hours in Banking, Consumer Credit, or Credit Management. *Version 2:* In the vocational certificate or lower division baccalaureate/associate degree category, 1 semester hour in Banking, Consumer Credit, or Credit Management (11/85). NOTE: Course could be integrated with Consumer Credit Analysis to form one 3 semester hour course. Students should not receive credit for this course on the basis of completing Consumer Credit Analysis. This course is applicable to an associate degree program.

Income Property Construction Lending (7801)
(Formerly Construction Lending for Income Properties)
Location: AIB chapters nationwide operating under established ABA guidelines and standards.
Length: Correspondence study. Approximately 4 months.
Dates: November 1985-Present.
Objective: To help the student understand the most important elements of construction lending for income producing commercial real estate.
Instruction: This course offers detailed instruction in the practice of construction lending. Subject matter covered is: (1) theory of commercial construction lending, (2) marketing of financial services, (3) underwriting commercial loans, (4) administration of construction loans.
Credit recommendation: In the lower division baccalaureate/associate degree category, 2 semester hours in Credit Management (11/85).

Income Property Underwriting (7823)
Location: AIB chapters nationwide operating under established ABA guidelines and standards.
Length: Correspondence study or *Version 1:* 45 hours (15 weeks - 3 one-hour sessions per week); *Version 2:* 30 hours (10 weeks - 3 one-hour sessions per week.
Dates: November 1985-Present.
Objective: To give students the basic theory for underwriting income property loans.
Instruction: Course covers the market for permanent loans on income-producing properties and the unique underwriting requirements for different types of properties. Course is delivered using lecture and discussion or by correspondence study.
Credit recommendation: In the vocational certificate or lower division baccalaureate/associate degree category, 2 semester hours in Real Estate Finance (8/85). NOTE: This course is applicable to an associate degree program.

Real Estate Appraisal I (7870)
Real Estate Appraisal II
Location: AIB chapters nationwide operating under established ABA guidelines and standards.
Length: Correspondence study.
Dates: November 1985-Present.
Objective: To introduce students to the theory and practice of real estate appraisal for the purpose of qualifying a practicing real estate appraiser.
Instruction: The course covers the description of real estate and capital markets, land valuation, building valuation, collection and analysis of income and risk data.
Credit recommendation: In the upper division baccalaureate category, 3 semester hours in Real Estate Appraisal (11/85). NOTE: The student must complete both courses to receive credit.

Real Estate Finance (7880)
Location: AIB chapters nationwide operating under established ABA guidelines and standards.
Length: *Version 1:* 45 hours (15 weeks - one 3-hour session per week). *Version 2:* 30 hours (10 weeks - one 3-hour session per week).
Dates: November 1985-Present.
Objective: To give students an understanding of the elements in the real estate credit process, role of real estate loans as a service of commercial banks, real estate lending from the perspectives of buyer, seller, and investor.
Instruction: Covers sources of mortgage credit; federal

assistance in the mortgage market; financing single-family homes, condominiums, and income-producing property; analysis of mortgage credit and real estate investment; construction loan administration; and appraisal of residential and income-producing property. Lecture and discussion are used.

Credit recommendation: *Version 1:* In the lower division baccalaureate/associate degree category, 3 semester hours in Real Estate Finance. *Version 2:* In the lower division baccalaureate/associate degree category, 2 semester hours in Real Estate Finance (11/85).

Residential Mortgage Lending (7802)
(Formerly Construction Lending for Residential Properties)
  Location: AIB chapters nationwide operating under established ABA guidelines and standards.
  Length: Correspondence study. Approximately 4 months.
  Dates: November 1985-Present.
  Objective: The objective of this course is to help the student understand the most important elements of construction lending for residential real estate with the focus on single family homes.
  Instruction: The course covers construction lending for residential real estate, including construction loan processing and administration, underwriting, loan structure, loan documentation.
  Credit recommendation: In the lower division baccalaureate/associate degree category, 2 semester hours in Credit Management (11/85).

COMMERCIAL LENDING

Agriculture Lending: 200-Level Curriculum
  Location: State-sponsored schools.
  Length: 35 hours (1 week).
  Dates: November 1985-Present.
  Objective: To prepare agricultural loan officers and mid-level managers to serve effectively and profitably the needs of American Agriculture.
  Instruction: Content highlights agriculture banking and the economic environment; evaluating borrower management ability; agricultural credit analysis and decision making; structuring agricultural loans; problem loans; loan pricing and customer profitability analysis; loan administration; and financial management issues for rural banks. Lecture and discussion are used.
  Credit recommendation: In the lower division baccalaureate/associate degree category, 2 semester hours in Finance Banking (11/85). Prerequisite of basic course in Finance. NOTE: Students who receive credit for this course should not receive credit for Lending to Agricultural Enterprises. This course is applicable to an associate degree program.

Commercial Lending: 200-Level Curriculum
  Location: State-sponsored schools.
  Length: 37 hours (1 week).
  Dates: November 1985-Present.
  Objective: To train bankers as commercial lenders.
  Instruction: Course covers the economic and business context of commercial lending, analytical and administrative techniques; negotiation, pricing, and structuring the loan. Lecture and discussion are used.
  Credit recommendation: In the upper division baccalaureate category, 3 semester hours in Banking or Finance (11/85).

Commercial Lending (6350)
(Formerly Introduction to Commercial Lending)
  Location: AIB chapters nationwide operating under established ABA guidelines and standards.
  Length: 30 hours (10 weeks).
  Dates: November 1985-Present.
  Objective: To provide prospective loan officers with overview of commercial lending function.
  Instruction: Orients students to the context and structure of commercial loan markets, role of commercial banks, regulation of lending, and methods of managing the lending function.
  Credit recommendation: In the vocational certificate or lower division baccalaureate/associate degree category, 2 semester hours in Banking or Credit Management (11/85). NOTE: Students who receive credit for this course should not receive credit for Corporate Banking: A Practical Approach to Lending. This course is applicable to an associate degree program.

Commercial Loan Officer Development (6360)
(Formerly Loan Officer Development)
  Location: AIB chapters nationwide operating under established ABA guidelines and standards.
  Length: *Version 1:* 45 hours (15 weeks - one 3-hour session per week); *Version 2:* 30 hours (10 weeks - one 3-hour session per week).
  Dates: November 1985-Present.
  Objective: To provide new or prospective commercial loan officers with some of the basic technical and interpersonal skills needed to make successful commercial loans.
  Instruction: Course covers how to conduct an initial loan interview and evaluate the borrower's request; how to gather information necessary to make a sound credit decision and present recommendations to senior loan officers; how to negotiate the terms of the loan with a borrower; how to write credit files and business development call reports; how to recognize and address problem loans; and how to manage both people and task more effectively. Lecture and discussion are used.
  Credit recommendation: *Version 1 and 2:* In the vocational certificate category, 1 semester hour in Banking/Finance (11/85). NOTE: This course is applicable to an

26 American Bankers Association

associate degree program.

International Banking (7710)
Location: AIB chapters nationwide operating under established ABA guidelines and standards.
Length: *Version 1:* 45 hours (15 weeks - one 3-hour session per week); *Version 2:* 30 hours (10 weeks - one 3-hour session per week).
Dates: November 1985-Present.
Objective: To provide the students with a comprehensive overview of the roles-functions banks play in international commerce.
Instruction: The course covers the fundamentals of international banking. It covers inter country funds transfer, international financial institutions, international lending, international currency exchange, and international risk assessment. Lecture and discussion are used.
Credit recommendation: *Version 1:* In the upper division baccalaureate category, 3 semester hours in International Banking. *Version 2:* In the upper division baccalaureate category, 2 semester hours in Banking (11/85).

Letters of Credit (7140)
Location: AIB chapters nationwide operating under established ABA guidelines and standards.
Length: 30 hours (10 weeks).
Dates: November 1985-Present.
Objective: To train bank personnel to examine letters of credit and related documents used in international commerce.
Instruction: This course features a detailed examination of shipping documents and the mechanics of letters of credit, including payment procedures, issuing, advising, and transfer of letters of credit. Lecture and discussion are used.
Credit recommendation: In the upper division baccalaureate category, 1 semester hour in International Finance (11/85).

Statement Analysis (6970)
Location: AIB chapters nationwide operating under established ABA guidelines and standards.
Length: Independent study.
Dates: November 1985-Present.
Objective: To teach the student basic skills of financial statement analysis to new or prospective bank lender or credit analyst.
Instruction: Course teaches basic tools to conduct financial analysis: statement spreading, ratio analysis, trend analysis, funds flow and cash flow analysis, pro forma statement, peak positioning, cash forecasting, and working capital analysis.
Credit recommendation: In the lower division baccalaureate/associate degree category, 3 semester hours in Finance (11/85). NOTE: Credit should not be given for this course and for course Analyzing Financial Statement. This course is applicable to an associate degree program.

OPERATIONS

Accounting Principles I (1000)
(Formerly Accounting Principles and Applications I)
Location: AIB chapters nationwide operating under established ABA guidelines and standards.
Length: *Version 1:* 45 hours (15 weeks - three 1-hour sessions per week); *Version 2:* 30 hours (10 weeks - three 1-hour sessions per week).
Dates: November 1985-Present.
Objective: To provide the student with the basic principles and practices of general accounting procedures.
Instruction: Course emphasizes current practices of accounting procedures and includes coverage of the latest accounting principles as set forth by the Financial Accounting Standards Board. Coverage includes processing accounting information, the accounting cycle, accounting systems and special journals, assets and liabilities. Methods of instruction include lecture, discussion, and classroom exercises.
Credit recommendation: *Version 1:* In the lower division baccalaureate/associate degree category, 3 semester hours in Accounting. *Version 2:* In the lower division baccalaureate/associate degree category, 2 semester hours in Accounting (11/85).

Accounting Principles II (1010)
(Formerly Accounting: Principles and Applications II)
Location: AIB chapters nationwide operating under established ABA guidelines and standards.
Length: *Version 1:* 45 hours (15 weeks - one 3-hour session per week); *Version 2:* 30 hours (10 weeks - one 3-hour session per week).
Dates: November 1985-Present.
Objective: To expand upon the basic principles and practices of general accounting procedures. Introduces broader applications of accounting relative to responsibilities, operations, and control.
Instruction: Course delves into policy analysis and management with emphasis on detailed accounting functions and procedures. Presentation includes corporate accounting, bond and stock investments, analysis and interpretation of financial statements, budgeting, and taxes. Methods of instruction include lecture, discussion, and exercises. Prerequisite: Accounting I.
Credit recommendation: *Version 1:* In the lower division baccalaureate/associate degree category, 3 semester hours in Accounting. *Version 2:* In the lower division baccalaureate/associate degree category, 2 semester hours in Accounting (11/85).

Bank Accounting (7520)
Location: AIB chapters nationwide operating under es-

tablished ABA guidelines and standards.

Length: *Version 1:* 45 hours (15 weeks - one 3-hour session per week); *Version 2:* 30 hours (10 weeks - one 3-hour session per week).

Dates: November 1985-Present.

Objective: To present the principles of accounting as they apply to a financial institution.

Instruction: Contents include basic bank accounting statements of financial position and investments, loans, and depository accounting. Bank performance analysis and governmental reporting are also included in this course. Prerequisite: Accounting I. Methods of instruction include lecture, discussion, and problem solving.

Credit recommendation: *Version 1:* In the lower division baccalaureate/associate degree category, 3 semester hours in Bank Accounting. *Version 2:* In the lower division baccalaureate/associate degree category, 2 semester hours in Bank Accounting (11/85).

Bank Control and Audit (6150)

Location: AIB chapters nationwide operating under established ABA guidelines and standards.

Length: 30 hours (10 weeks - one 3-hour session per week).

Dates: November 1985-Present.

Objective: To present the basic concepts of auditing to the non auditor. Develops a deeper understanding of the role, duties, and responsibilities of the bank auditor.

Instruction: Contents include the nature of bank control and audit, risk exposure, auditing information systems and regulatory compliance. Methods of instruction include lecture, discussion, and classroom exercise.

Credit recommendation: In the lower division baccalaureate/associate degree category, 2 semester hours in Bank Auditing (11/85).

Bank Management (7535)
(Formerly Commercial Bank Management)

Location: AIB chapters nationwide operating under established ABA guidelines and standards.

Length: *Version 1:* 45 hours (15 weeks - one 3-hour session per week); *Version 2:* 30 hours (10 weeks - one 3-hour session per week).

Dates: November 1985-Present.

Objective: To describe and analyze the profitability of various banking functions from the perspective of the simultaneous management of asset, liability, and capital decisions.

Instruction: This course analyzes techniques for managing asset and funding decisions, with special emphasis on the interaction between balance sheet items. Topics covered include lending and investment decisions, deposit functions, liability management, capital decisions, gap management, planning and profitability analysis. Lectures and discussions, supplemented with case materials.

Credit recommendation: *Version 1:* In the upper division baccalaureate category, 4 semester hours in Banking or Finance (11/85). NOTE: Credit hours require completion of 45 hour version of *BOTH* sections of this course. Two credit hours to be granted for completing 30 hours version of *BOTH* courses.

Concepts of Data Processing (2090)
(Formerly Fundamentals of Bank Data Processing)

Location: AIB chapters nationwide operating under established ABA guidelines and standards.

Length: *Version 1:* 45 hours (15 weeks - one 3-hour session per week); *Version 2:* 30 hours (10 weeks - one 3-hour session per week).

Dates: November 1985-Present.

Objective: To introduce bankers to the essential concepts of computers and data processing. To familiarize the student with basic information on data processing, terminology, and current technological trends and developments.

Instruction: Course covers the topic of data processing concepts, principles and uses, the impact of technological change, how to manage change, and the implications and applications for the future. Methods of instruction include lecture, discussion, and some workshop material.

Credit recommendation: *Version 1:* In the lower division baccalaureate/associate degree category, 3 semester hours in Business Administration or Bank Operations. *Version 2:* In the lower division baccalaureate/associate degree category, 2 semester hours in Business Administration or Bank Operations (11/85).

Deposit Operations (6204)

Location: AIB chapters nationwide operating under established ABA guidelines and standards.

Length: *Version 1:* 45 hours (15 weeks - one 3-hour session per week); *Version 2:* 30 hours (10 weeks - one 3-hour session per week).

Dates: November 1985-Present.

Objective: To examine the depository operations of banks within the context of the U.S. payments system.

Instruction: Contents include the deposit operations of banks, the check collection process, and electronic payments mechanism. The course also includes a familiarization of deposit creation and cash management services. Methods of instruction include lecture, discussion, and classroom exercise.

Credit recommendation: *Version 1:* In the vocational certificate or lower division baccalaureate/associate degree category, 2 semester hours in Bank Operations. *Version 2:* In the vocational certificate or lower division baccalaureate/associate degree category, 1 semester hour in Bank Operations (11/85). NOTE: This course is applicable to an associate degree program.

Securities Processing (7240)

Location: AIB chapters nationwide operating under established ABA guidelines and standards.

Length: *Version 1:* 45 hours (15 weeks - one 3-hour session per week); *Version 2:* 30 hours (10 weeks - one 3-hour session per week).

Dates: November 1985-Present.

Objective: To provide a broad knowledge of securities in a banking environment and to develop the skills needed to perform specific securities processing activities.

Instruction: Lecture, discussion of the operational aspects of securities processing. Some workshop material. Highlights types of securities, transactions and markets; processing clearing and settlement operations.

Credit recommendation: *Version 1:* In the vocational certificate or lower division baccalaureate/associate degree category, 2 semester hours in Bank Operations. *Version 2:* In the vocational certificate or lower division baccalaureate/associate degree category, 1 semester hour in Bank Operations (11/85).

MANAGING THE BANK/FINANCIAL COUNSELING/MARKETING

Bank Investments (7200)

Location: AIB chapters nationwide operating under established ABA guidelines and standards.

Length: 30 hours (10 weeks - one 3-hour session per week).

Dates: November 1985-Present.

Objective: To provide students of banking with an introductory overview of the investments function in commercial banking.

Instruction: This course describes various concepts and institutions which are critical to good investment decision-making at commercial banks. Topics covered include investment math, treasury and agency securities, municipal securities, money-market investments, and bond management techniques. Lectures and discussions, with classroom exercises.

Credit recommendation: In the lower division baccalaureate/associate degree category, 2 semester hours in Banking or Finance (11/85).

Management Fundamentals (4140)

Location: AIB chapters nationwide operating under established ABA guidelines and standards.

Length: 45 hours (15 weeks - one 3-hour session per week).

Dates: November 1985-Present.

Objective: To provide a concise, comprehensive overview of the management process. To explain various management theories and approaches.

Instruction: Lecture, discussion, case studies. Focuses on planning, staffing, leading, and controlling.

Credit recommendation: In the lower division baccalaureate/associate degree category, 3 semester hours in Business Administration or Management (11/85).

Marketing for Bankers (7740)

Location: AIB chapters nationwide operating under established ABA guidelines and procedures.

Length: *Version 1:* 45 hours (15 weeks - one 3-hour session per week); *Version 2:* 30 hours (10 weeks - one 3-hour session per week).

Dates: November 1985-Present.

Objective: To provide a thorough grounding in basic marketing principles and theory and their application to banking. To provide an understanding of consumer behavior, marketing research, public relations and communications in marketing, and a marketing plan.

Instruction: Lecture, discussion, workshop—case studies and group discussion. Focuses on the market, the marketing process, and the management of the marketing process.

Credit recommendation: *Version 1:* In the lower division baccalaureate/associate degree category, 3 semester hours in Bank Marketing. *Version 2:* In the lower division baccalaureate/associate degree category, 2 semester hours in Bank Marketing (11/85).

Supervisory Training (4335)

Location: AIB chapters nationwide operating under established ABA guidelines and standards.

Length: 27½ hours (11 weeks).

Dates: November 1985-Present.

Objective: To provide first-line supervisory skills.

Instruction: Lecture, discussion, simulations, and problem solving. Video support is available. Application of managerial skills to the job situation of the new supervisor is emphasized.

Credit recommendation: In the vocational certificate category, 1 semester hour in Management Supervision (11/85).

The Trust Business (8250)

Location: AIB chapters nationwide operating under established ABA guidelines and standards.

Length: *Version 1:* 45 hours (15 weeks - one 3-hour session per week); *Version 2:* 30 hours (10 weeks - one 3-hour session per week).

Dates: November 1985-Present.

Objective: To provide understanding of the trust business, the function of the trust department and how it fits in a bank, its services and their delivery, and the changing role of the trust department.

Instruction: Lecture, discussion, laboratory. Concentrates on the nature, origin, and current status of trusts; trust departments and their customers; and different kinds of trust services, their delivery and marketing.

Credit recommendation: *Version 1:* In the lower division baccalaureate/associate degree category, 3 semester hours in Banking or Finance. *Version 2:* In the lower division baccalaureate/associate degree category, 2 semester hours in Banking or Finance (11/85).

Trust Investments (3540)
(Investment Basics and Beyond)
   Location: AIB chapters nationwide operating under established ABA guidelines and standards.
   Length: *Version 1:* 45 hours (15 weeks - one 3-hour session per week); *Version 2:* 30 hours (10 weeks - one 3-hour session per week).
   Dates: November 1985-Present.
   Objective: To understand investments, portfolio management, and the investment function as they are applied in a bank trust department.
   Instruction: Lecture, discussion, and small group exercises. Highlights securities markets and alternative investment outlets; trust investment operations, techniques and applications, investment policies and portfolio management.
   Credit recommendation: *Version 1:* In the lower division baccalaureate/associate degree category, 3 semester hours in Bank Management or Finance. *Version 2:* In the lower division baccalaureate/associate degree category, 2 semester hours in Bank Management or Finance (11/85).

GENERAL BANKING

Current Issues in Bank Management
(The New World of Commercial Banking)
(Formerly Inside Commercial Banking [1375])
   Location: AIB chapters nationwide operating under established ABA guidelines and standards.
   Length: 45 hours (15 weeks - one 3-hour session per week).
   Dates: November 1985-Present.
   Objective: To explore significant competitive, regulatory, technological, and market related developments currently affecting commercial bank management.
   Instruction: Contents include analysis and discussion of non-bank competition, EFT technology, asset/liability management, interstate banking activities, the Monetary Control Act and global banking. Current issues of effective managerial strategies are also included within the course. Methods of instruction include lecture and discussion.
   Credit recommendation: In the lower division baccalaureate/associate degree category, 3 semester hours in Banking or Finance (11/85).

Law and Banking (3660)
   Location: AIB chapters nationwide operating under established ABA guidelines and standards.
   Length: *Version 1:* 45 hours (15 weeks, one 3-hour session per week); *Version 2:* 30 hours (10 weeks, one-3-hour session per week).
   Dates: November 1985-Present.
   Objective: To present an overview of the legal aspects of banking.
   Instruction: This course examines those aspects of commercial law relevant to banking. Issues covered include: consumer protection, negotiable instruments, secured transactions, documents of title, commercial paper, and alternative legal forms of organization. Lectures and discussions.
   Credit recommendation: In the lower division baccalaureate/associate degree category, 2 semester hours in Banking Law or Commercial Law (11/85).

Law and Banking: Applications (3710)
(Formerly Negotiable Instruments and the Payments Mechanism)
   Location: AIB chapters nationwide operating under established ABA guidelines and standards.
   Length: *Version 1:* 45 hours (15 weeks, one 3-hour session per week); *Version 2:* 30 hours (10 weeks, one 3-hour session per week).
   Dates: November 1985-Present.
   Objective: To provide an introduction to the nature of a negotiable instrument and its role in the payments mechanism.
   Instruction: This course provides a detailed examination of the negotiable instrument; the role of the parties to the instruments, and the means of collecting it through the payments mechanism. Lectures and discussion.
   Credit recommendation: In the lower division baccalaureate/associate degree category, 1 semester hour in Banking Law or Commercial Law (11/85).

Money and Banking (1350)
   Location: AIB chapters nationwide operating under established ABA guidelines and standards.
   Length: *Version 1:* 45 hours (15 weeks - one 3-hour session per week); *Version 2:* 30 hours (10 weeks - one 3-hour session per week).
   Dates: November 1985-Present.
   Objective: To teach the key concepts, theories, processes, and economic and policy interrelationships that link money and banking to the U.S. and world economy.
   Instruction: Lecture, discussion, and laboratory. Covers money, banking, and the payments mechanism; the regulatory environment; the Federal Reserve function and monetary policy; the monetarist fiscalist controversy, the international financial system; and banking issues and trends.
   Credit recommendation: *Version 1:* In the lower division baccalaureate/associate degree category, 3 semester hours in Economics. *Version 2:* In the lower division baccalaureate/associate degree category, 2 semester hours in Economics (11/85).

PDP 200-Level General Banking Curriculum
   Location: University of Georgia, Athens; University of Iowa, Iowa City; Central Michigan University, Mt. Pleasant; St. Olaf College, Northfield, MN; University of North Dakota, Grand Forks; Lewis and Clark College, Portland,

OR; Oklahoma State University, Stillwater, OK; West Virginia University, Morgantown; St. Norbert College, De Pere, WI.
Length: 35-42 hours (5-6 days), Session I; 35-42 hours (5-6 days), Session II.
Dates: May 1984-Present.
Objective: This program seeks to prepare first-level exempt and middle managers to serve effectively and profitably the needs of the banking public.
Instruction: This one-week program (Session I) involves a comprehensive examination of bank management issues such as funding, marketing, lending, investments, trust services, asset-liability control, and changes in the banking environment. Session II covers similar issues at a deeper and more complex level. Lectures, discussion, and problem solving exercises.
Credit recommendation: In the upper division baccalaureate category, 5 semester hours in Banking or Finance for completion of Sessions I and II and Correspondence (11/85). NOTE: Two semester hours for completion of Session I only. Credit is conditional on passing the comprehensive exam in Session I, and on some form of student assessment (to be chosen by each school) in Session II.

Personal Financial Planning
(Financial Planning for Bankers [6535])
Location: AIB chapters nationwide operating under established ABA guidelines and standards.
Length: *Version 1:* 45 hours (15 weeks - one 3-hour session per week); *Version 2:* 30 hours (10 weeks - one 3-hour session per week).
Dates: November 1985-Present.
Objective: To provide bank employees with a basic understanding of the concepts and processes involved in personal financial planning.
Instruction: A discussion of the fundamental concepts of personal financial planning, with emphasis on tax management, insurance, estate planning, and personal cash management.
Credit recommendation: *Version 1:* In the lower division baccalaureate/associate degree category, 2 semester hours in Banking or Business. *Version 2:* In the lower division baccalaureate/associate degree category, 1 semester hour in Banking or Business (11/85).

Principles of Banking (1370)
Location: AIB chapters nationwide operating under established ABA guidelines and standards.
Length: *Version 1:* 45 hours (15 weeks - one 3-hour session per week); *Version 2:* 30 hours (10 weeks - one 3-hour session per week).
Dates: November 1985-Present.
Objective: To provide a comprehensive introduction to the Commercial Banking system.
Instruction: Contents include the history and evolution of American banking, an introduction to the Federal Reserve, the depository, loan and check processing functions, and basic bank accounting. Further explores specialized bank services such as international services, trust functions, and bank regulation. Methods of instruction include lecture, discussion, and classroom exercise.
Credit recommendation: *Version 1:* In the lower division baccalaureate/associate degree category, 3 semester hours in Bank Operations. *Version 2:* In the lower division baccalaureate/associate degree category, 2 semester hours in Bank Operations (11/85).

American Center for Technical Arts and Sciences (Formerly Mainline Paralegal Institute)

The Mainline Paralegal Campus at Wayne, Pennsylvania has been involved in education since 1975. (Its original name, The Mainline Paralegal Institute, was changed in 1986 to reflect its present incorporation.) It is considered one of the pioneers in the field of paralegal education in the United States. A major focus is its evening program which provides continuing education to people already in the fields of law, real estate, banking, and other corresponding endeavors. Recently, a day program was also initiated.

The paralegal program is designed to familiarize the student with the wide range of subjects which form the bulk of the law firm's daily activities. It does not attempt to cover in the same depth those topics which would be taught in a law school curriculum; nor does it attempt to achieve that level of competence expected of a law school student. It does, however, provide a comprehensive review of many aspects of legal practice and prepares individuals to have, at least, entry level competence when they begin employment in a law office.

Source of official student records: American Center for Technical Arts and Sciences, Mainline Paralegal Campus, 100 Lancaster Avenue, Wayne, PA or Registry of Credit Recommendations, The Center for Adult Learning and Educational Credentials, American Council on Education, One Dupont Circle, Washington, D.C. 20036.

Additional information about the courses: Program on Noncollegiate Sponsored Instruction, Thomas A. Edison State College, Kelsey Building, 101 West State Street, Trenton, New Jersey 08625.

Business and Corporate Law I
Location: Wayne, PA.
Length: 45 hours (7 weeks).
Dates: September 1975-Present.
Objective: To familiarize the student with practice and procedure of business and corporate law.
Instruction: This course covers the basic legal principles

applicable to business operations including sole proprietorships, general and limited partnerships, corporations, requirements for formulation, corporate financial structure, meetings, by-law voting powers as well as dividends and other distributions, employment and compensation, agreements regarding share ownership, corporations in foreign jurisdictions, and changes in corporate structure and dissolution.

Credit recommendation: In the lower division baccalaureate/associate degree category, or in the upper baccalaureate category, 3 semester hours in Business Organizations (10/85).

Civil Litigation
Location: Wayne, PA.
Length: 45 hours (7 weeks).
Dates: September 1975-Present.
Objective: To familiarize the student with practice and procedure of civil litigation.
Instruction: Covers civil litigation, introduction to the basic rules that govern the lawsuit, how legal principles are developed by prior court decisions and the remedies at law. The course develops the student's sensitivity to fact gathering processes. Topics include the court system and jurisdiction, review of the law of contracts, laws and evidence, information gathering and investigative strategies, commencement of the lawsuit, settlement of lawsuits and discovery processes, pre-trial, and trial and post-trial activities.
Credit recommendation: In the upper level baccalaureate/associate degree category, 3 semester hours in Civil Litigation (10/85).

Criminal Law
Location: Wayne, PA.
Length: 45 hours (7 weeks).
Dates: September 1975-Present.
Objective: To familiarize the student with practice and procedures of criminal law.
Instruction: This course covers an overview of the criminal justice system, its participants and the various roles they play. Topics include: a review of the sources of criminal law, analysis of criminal procedures from arrest to appeal, classifications of crime, assessment of the constitutional rights of criminal defendants and a knowledge of the defenses. Students will learn to prepare briefs or memoranda of law, rules, orders, motions, and petitions.
Credit recommendation: In the lower division baccalaureate/associate degree category, or in the upper division baccalaureate category, 3 semester hours in Introduction to Criminal Law (10/85).

Debtor/Creditor Relations
Location: Wayne, PA.
Length: 37½ hours (6 weeks).
Dates: September 1975-Present.
Objective: To familiarize the student with practice and procedure of debtor/creditor relations.
Instruction: Covers a specialized overview of the laws applicable to normal debtor/credit relationships. Emphasis on the U.S. Bankruptcy Code and its provisions regarding case administration, disposition of property, protection from creditors, effect of contracts, estate claims, priority of creditors, exemptions, preferences, set-offs and discharge of debts.
Credit recommendation: In the lower division baccalaureate/associate degree category, or in the upper division baccalaureate category, 2 semester hours in Debtor/Creditor Relations (10/85).

Employment Discrimination Law
Location: Wayne, PA.
Length: 30 hours (5 weeks).
Dates: September 1975-Present.
Objective: To familiarize the student with practice and procedure of employment discrimination law.
Instruction: Covers a comprehensive review of the law related to discriminatory practices in the employment sector of our national economy. Topics include: actions, remedies, rights and defenses to discrimination as assessed by case law analysis, statutory review and administrative finding. Also, the EEOC, the Labor Relations Board, the Rehabilitation Act of 1973, and the Civil Rights legislation of the 1960s are considered.
Credit recommendation: In the lower division baccalaureate/associate degree category, or in the upper division baccalaureate category, 2 semester hours in Employment Discrimination Law (10/85).

Employee Retirement Income Security Act (ERISA)
Location: Wayne, PA.
Length: 37½ hours (6 weeks).
Dates: September 1975-Present.
Objective: To familiarize the student with practice and procedure of ERISA.
Instruction: This course examines the Employee Retirement Income Security Act and subsequent tax provisions and their effect in the area of employee benefit plans. Specific attention is given to IRAs, 401K plans, profit sharing strategies, trust agreements, and the procedural filings required for technical deductibility as well as the comprehensive tax implications of these benefit plans.
Credit recommendation: In the lower division baccalaureate/associate degree category, or in the upper baccalaureate category, 2 semester hours in Employee Retirement Income Security Act (10/85).

Estates, Trusts, and Wills
Location: Wayne, PA.
Length: 52½ hours (8 weeks).
Dates: September 1975-Present.
Objective: To familiarize the student with practice and

procedure of estates, trusts, and wills.

Instruction: Covers the filing processes, tax requirements, distribution steps, and accounting strategies in the administration of estates and trusts. The course also covers the theoretical aspects of estates and trusts and provides students with varied strategies and plans in the law of estates, from both the tax and legal perspectives. Students will learn fundamentals of wills and their drafting.

Credit recommendation: In the lower division baccalaureate/associate degree category, or in the upper division baccalaureate category, 3 semester hours in Decedent's Estates (10/85).

Family Law
Location: Wayne, PA.
Length: 22½ hours (4 weeks).
Dates: *Version 1:* September 1976-December 1985. *Version 2:* January 1986-Present.
Objective: To familiarize the student with practice and procedure of family law.
Instruction: *Version 1:* Covers a thorough assessment of the law of domestic relations, particularly the divorce and separation, adoption, custody, alimony, visitation, equitable distribution, and general defenses. Also, emphasis on necessary pleadings and documentations in the visitation, defense, and enforcement of basic family law actions. *Version 2:* Supplements the basic course with additional (outside) work protection from abuse, concerning: rights of women, equitable distribution and other related trends in family law.
Credit recommendation: *Version 1:* In the lower division baccalaureate/associate degree category, or in the upper division baccalaureate category, 1 semester hour in Family Law. *Version 2:* In the lower division baccalaureate/associate degree category or in the upper division baccalaureate category, 2 semester hours in Family Law (10/85).

Law Office Administration
Location: Wayne, PA.
Length: 30 hours (5 weeks).
Dates: *Version 1:* October 1983-December 1985. *Version 2:* January 1986-Present.
Objective: To familiarize the student with practice and procedure of law administration.
Instruction: *Version 1:* Covers the role of management theory and practice in the life of a law office and practice. Emphasis on personnel and staff management accounting and fiscal processes, growth, expansion and control of resources, profit analysis and the computer based application of the above described topics. *Version 2:* Supplements basic course with specific ethical considerations in the daily practice of a legal assistant.
Credit recommendation: *Version 1:* In the lower division baccalaureate/associate degree category or in the upper baccalaureate category, 1 semester hour in Law Office Administration. *Version 2:* In the lower division baccalaureate/associate degree category or in the upper baccalaureate category, 2 semester hours in Law Office Administration (10/85).

Real Estate Law
Location: Wayne, PA.
Length: 45 hours (7 weeks).
Dates: September 1975-Present.
Objective: To familiarize the student with the practice and procedures of real estate.
Instruction: This course covers how to analyze and prepare deeds, mortgages, and other related documents. Students will learn the steps necessary to assist the lawyers in representing the buyer and seller in real estate transactions including the buying and selling of real estate, proper title and conveyancing procedures, securing judgements, liens, residential and commercial leases, dealing with real estate brokers and agents, securing title policies and performing real estate settlements.
Credit recommendation: In the lower division baccalaureate/associate degree category, or in the upper baccalaureate category, 3 semester hours in Real Estate Law (10/85).

Techniques of Legal Research
Location: Wayne, PA.
Length: 45 hours (7 weeks).
Dates: September 1975-Present.
Objective: To familiarize the student with the practices and procedures of legal research.
Instruction: This course familiarizes the student with the principles and strategies of research, types of law books and their scope, citation method, interpreting case and statutory law, legal authority and precedent, annotations, government publications and corresponding kinds of legal writing, organization and format. Emphasis on specific research and writing assignments and maintaining a law library, as well as becoming a competent law library researcher.
Credit recommendation: In the lower level baccalaureate/associate degree category, or in the upper baccalaureate category, 3 semester hours in Introduction to Legal Research or Legal Research and Writing (10/85).

American Conference of Audioprosthology

The original and primary purpose of the American Conference of Audioprosthology is to provide an educational opportunity for those individuals who engage in the dispensing vocation (sales) and assure that they practice professionally, skillfully and ethically. The educational program of A.C.A. contains five courses, structured to conform to a semester hour basis, common to universities. The core faculty is made up of individuals with extensive knowledge and experience in the academic and/or business world. It is the core faculty's responsibility to teach the courses in the A.C.A. program, make suggestions about the use of outside faculty, and periodically review the curriculum. The faculty is also responsible for curriculum revision in light of new knowledge and methodology.

Students must maintain a "C" average in all courses to achieve certification as an Audioprosthologist. Additional reading/study assignments and retesting are given to students who drop below this average, and must repeat the section if they fail.

Source of official student records: Executive Director, American Conference of Audioprosthology, 212 West California, El Paso, Texas 79902.

Additional information about the courses: Program on Noncollegiate Sponsored Instruction, The Center for Adult Learning and Educational Credentials, American Council on Education, One Dupont Circle, Washington, D.C. 20036.

Program in Audioprosthology
  Location: Various locations around the U.S.
  Length: 168 contact hours (14 hours for 12 weekends), plus extensive reading and 90 hours of practicum.
  Dates: January 1978-Present.
  Objective: To provide current and applicable information related to hearing instrument dispensing pertaining to hearing science, audiology, instrumentation and technology, clinical assessment, medical/legal involvement, strategies in selecting and fitting hearing aid devices, and effective counseling.
  Learning Outcome: Upon successful completion of this course, the student will be able to assess the type and magnitude of hearing impairment; analyze and select hearing aids with the appropriate electro-acoustic properties; and manage the professional, technical, and business aspects of being an audioprosthologist.
  Instruction: Course covers hearing science; audiology—techniques and instrumentation; rehabilitation and human communication; small business management; and practicum—hands-on supervised experience. Methodology includes lecture, guest lecture by a specialist, case studies, demonstration and hands-on demonstration of student understanding and ability to analyze clinical data and student practicum.
  Credit recommendation: In the upper division baccalaureate category, 12 semester hours in Audiology and 3 semester hours in related areas such as Small Business Management (8/88).

American Educational Institute, Inc.

The American Educational Institute, Inc., was founded for the purpose of developing job-related law courses for the education of claim department personnel in the casualty insurance business.

AEI maintains a staff of six lawyers, some of whom are admitted in more than one state, and all have experience in the claims area. Some of them have worked fifteen years or more for insurance companies and therefore are fully conversant with the problems in facing the claimsperson daily.

It is they who have developed the essay examination questions which require the student to identify the rule of law or exception that applies to a practical claim situation posed in the questions. The student is required to support his conclusion with sound reasoning. The examining staff then responds directly to each student based on the answer to each part of every question, giving the student the help he or she needs.

A reporting system codes grades received by each active student. This record is forwarded to all companies on a monthly basis. On completion, each student's Final Examination grade is transferred to his company's Management Chart which becomes a permanent record of the training and development for that company.

An Executive Advisory Committee comprised of senior executives from leading insurance companies monitors the course development process which includes an ongoing review of examination questions at monthly meetings.

Source of official student records: AEI, P.O. Box 356, Basking Ridge, New Jersey 07920.

Additional information about the courses: Program on Noncollegiate Sponsored Instruction, Thomas A. Edison State College, 101 West State Street, CN 545, Trenton, New Jersey 08625.

Legal Principles
  Location: Basking Ridge, NJ.
  Length: 116 hours (self-paced).
  Dates: January 1981-Present.
  Objective: To provide the student with an understanding of basic legal principles.
  Instruction: Course covers the development of common law; legal principles involved in contracts, torts, agency, bailments, and damages. Students become acquainted with the significance of subrogation, indemnity, and contribution. Case studies are used throughout to illustrate issues studied. The course is offered by correspondence, designed primarily for self-study with support from small groups or from the professional staff of the Institute.
  Credit recommendation: In the upper division baccalaureate category, 3 semester hours in Legal Environment of Business or Business/Commercial Law (10/84) (3/89). NOTE: To be eligible for credit, student must also

successfully complete the final examination under a proctor approved by the Examination Committee of the American Educational Institute. NOTE: This course has been reevaluated and continues to meet requirements for credit recommendations.

Liability
   Location: Basking Ridge, NJ.
   Length: 194 hours (self-paced).
   Dates: January 1981-Present.
   Objective: To provide the student with an understanding of how selected legal aspects are related to liability insurance.
   Instruction: The first part of the course covers comparative negligence, law of automobile insurance, professional liability, and product liability. The second part of the course covers law of insurance, law of evidence and pleading and practice. Case studies are used throughout to illustrate issues studied. The course is offered by correspondence, designed primarily for self-study with support from small groups or from the professional staff of the Institute.
   Credit recommendation: In the upper division baccalaureate category, 3 semester hours in Advanced Commercial Law or Liability Insurance (10/84) (3/89). NOTE: To be eligible for credit, student must also successfully complete the final examination under a proctor approved by the Examination Committee of the American Educational Institute. NOTE: This course has been reevaluated and continues to meet requirements for credit recommendations.

Property
   Location: Basking Ridge, NJ.
   Length: 163 hours (self-paced).
   Dates: January 1983-Present.
   Objective: To provide the student with an understanding of how selected legal aspects are related to property insurance.
   Instruction: The first part of the course covers the significant issues related to property insurance. Topics include property insurance, standard fire insurance, contract, loss adjustments under fire policy, arson, false swearing, extended coverage endorsement and property insurance forms. The second part of the course includes homeowners; farmowners-ranchowners and mobile homeowners; boat-yacht insurance; commercial property; carriers, warehousemen and other bailors; and agreements of guiding principles and subrogation. Case studies are used throughout to illustrate issues studied. The course is offered by correspondence, designed primarily for self-study with support from small groups or from the professional staff of the Institute.
   Credit recommendation: In the upper division baccalaureate category, 3 semester hours in Advanced Commercial Law or Property Insurance (10/84) (3/89).

NOTE: To be eligible for credit, student must also successfully complete the final examination under a proctor approved by the Examination Committee of the American Educational Institute. NOTE: This course has been reevaluated and continues to meet requirements for credit recommendations.

Worker's Compensation
   Location: Basking Ridge, NJ.
   Length: 123 hours (self-paced).
   Dates: January 1977-Present.
   Objective: To provide the student with understanding of how selected legal aspects are related to workers' compensation.
   Instruction: The course begins with the origin and development of workers' compensation. The course covers federal jurisdiction; workers' compensation and employers' liability policy; social economic and legislative effects; notice, statute of limitations and other procedural matters. Definitions of the essential components involved in workers' compensation (employer, employee, and injury) are provided. Course then reviews benefits, investigation, settlement, hearings, subrogation, contribution, and indemnity and reserves. Case studies are used throughout to illustrate all issues studied. The course is offered by correspondence, designed primarily for self-study with support from small groups or from the professional staff of the Institute.
   Credit recommendation: In the upper division baccalaureate category or in the graduate degree category, 3 semester hours in Worker's Compensation or Social Insurance (10/84) (3/89). NOTE: To be eligible for credit, student must also successfully complete the final examination under a proctor approved by the Examination Committee of the American Educational Institute. NOTE: This course has been reevaluated and continues to meet requirements for credit recommendations.

American Institute for Paralegal Studies, Inc.

The American Institute for Paralegal Studies, Inc., has been offering a comprehensive educational program in the preparation of legal assistants and paralegals since August 1978. The program embarked upon providing a part-time, continuing education opportunity to individuals who desired to enter this novel market.

The Institute's main administrative headquarters is located in Southfield, Michigan. Regional and branch offices are located in Chicago, Illinois; Columbus, Ohio; Jacksonville, Florida; and South Bend, Indiana, with other offices located in Mahwah, New Jersey; Pittsburgh, Pennsylvania; and Oakbrook Terrace, Illinois. The Office of Academic Affairs houses a substantial library of proprietary, scholarly, and academic materials dedicated to the study of legal assistants and paralegals. Textbook preparation and production, as well as course development and revision, are responsibilities of this office. The Institute's curricula underwent a major review in March 1988; however, the curricula is continually reviewed for conceptual efficiency, ensuring that new areas of law and its interpretation are appropriately incorporated. The Curriculum Committee recommends any major changes to a course, which is then submitted to the Office of Academic Affairs to incorporate.

All classroom facilities are located in educational facilities, usually colleges and universities. This type of agreement between the Institute and educational institutions provides accessibility to libraries and resources necessary for students to succeed. The Institute annually searches for faculty by advertising in trade journals, periodicals, local newspapers, and by references of other teaching staff. Instructors are reviewed by the students, who complete evaluation forms during and at the end of a course.

A certificate is awarded to any student who successfully completes a course. Additionally, the Institute has provisions for re-examination, probation, and other academic policies and procedures which insure a just and equitable opportunity to rectify poor performance as well as insure that the Institute adheres to high academic standards. Student grades are recorded by the instructor, who then submits them to either the regional or main office. Once received by the office, grades are recorded in the Institute's database for permanent recordation on a transcript.

Source of official student records: Southfield Regional Office, Dean of Students, Honeywell Center, 17515 West Nine Mile Road, Suite 225, Southfield, Michigan 48075; or Columbus Regional Office, Dean of Students, 2999 East Dublin-Granville Road, Suite 217, Columbus, Ohio 43229; or Chicago Regional Office, Dean of Students, 53 West Jackson, Suite 1140, Chicago, Illinois 60604; or The Registry of Credit Recommendations, The Center for Adult Learning and Educational Credentials, American Council on Education, One Dupont Circle, Suite 1B-20, Washington, D.C. 20036.

Additional information about the courses: Program on Noncollegiate Sponsored Instruction, The Center for Adult Learning and Educational Credentials, American Council on Education, One Dupont Circle, Suite 1B-20, Washington, D.C. 20036.

American Jurisprudence
Location: Various locations throughout the country.
Length: 15 hours (2 days).
Dates: September 1989-Present.
Objective: To familiarize students with the structure and functioning of the American legal system and the role of the paralegal.
Instruction: This course covers the functions and processes of the judicial, administrative, and legislative branches of the government. The role of the legal assistant and the canons of ethics of the American Bar Association are also studied.
Credit recommendation: In the upper division baccalaureate category, 1 semester hour in American Jurisprudence (1/89).

Basic Civil Law
 1. **Tort Law (A-101)**
 2. **Civil Procedure and Evidence (A-102)**
 3. **Family Law (A-105)**
Location: Various locations throughout Connecticut, Illinois, Massachusetts, Michigan, New Jersey, New York, Ohio, Pennsylvania, Rhode Island, and Texas.
Length: 1. 15 hours (2 days); 2. 6 hours (1 day); 3. 15 hours (2 days).
Dates: December 1979-September 1989.
Objective: To master the differing forms of civil actions in law, called torts, including intentional actions, acts of negligence and strict liability torts; to learn the fundamental law of evidence and review the factors which affect the legal admissibility and relevance of all forms of evidence; to review various areas of domestic relations including divorce, annulments, and legal separations.
Instruction: Course includes a thorough examination of all the elements necessary to create a solid cause of action. Consideration is also given to the many defenses available in the civil law including: contributory negligence, comparative negligence and assumption of risk. Course also covers basic concepts in the law of evidence including: burdens of proof, opinion vs. facts, character impeachment and the "Best Evidence" rule, and the problem of "Hearsay." Issues in family law such as custody of children, equitable distribution and support are also analyzed.
Credit recommendation: In the upper division baccalaureate category or in the lower division baccalaureate/associate degree category, 3 semester hours in Basic Civil Law (3/83). NOTE: For credit recommendations, courses 1, 2, and 3 must all be successfully completed.

Business Law
Location: Various locations throughout the country.
Length: 30 hours (5 days).
Dates: September 1989-Present.
Objective: To present the various legal entities including the partnership association and the corporation; to acquaint students with the law of contracts, including an examination of an offer and an acceptance, the capacity to contract, and policies on the enforcement of contracts.
Instruction: The course covers the rights and obligations of a corporation or other business institution. Corporate filing requirements, management, and administration are also covered. Consideration is given to directions, dissolutions, mergers, and liquidations. The student also reviews the general principles of agency law including the master/servant theory. The student examines the major

provisions of the Uniform Commercial Code.

Credit recommendation: In the upper division baccalaureate category or in the lower division baccalaureate/associate degree category, 2 semester hours in Business Law (1/89).

Business Law I
1. **Corporations/Partnerships and Agency (B-202)**
2. **Commercial Law (B-203)**

Location: Various locations throughout Connecticut, Illinois, Massachusetts, Michigan, New Jersey, New York, Ohio, Pennsylvania, Rhode Island, and Texas.
Length: 1. 21 hours (3 days); 2. 15 hours (2 days).
Dates: December 1979-August 1989.
Objective: To present the various legal entities including the partnership association and the corporation; to acquaint students with the law of contracts, including an examination of an offer and an acceptance, the capacity to contract, and policies on the enforcement of contracts.
Instruction: The course covers the rights and obligations of a corporation or other business institution. Corporate filing requirements, management, and administration are also covered. Consideration is given to directions, dissolutions, mergers, and liquidations. The student also reviews the general principles of agency law including the master/servant theory, principal/agent and employer/contractor. The student examines the major provisions of the Uniform Commercial Code.
Credit recommendation: In the upper division baccalaureate category or in the lower division baccalaureate/associate degree category, 2 semester hours in Business Law (3/83). NOTE: For credit recommendations, courses 1 and 2 must both be successfully completed.

Criminal Law and Procedure
Location: Various locations throughout the country.
Length: 15 hours (2 days).
Dates: September 1989-Present.
Objective: To provide students with an overview of criminal law and the procedures and constitutional rights as they apply to criminal cases.
Instruction: This course covers the definition and elements of crimes, including crimes against the person and crimes against property. Procedural and constitutional safeguards and procedures necessary from arrest through trial and sentencing and punishment are reviewed.
Credit recommendation: In the upper division baccalaureate category, 1 semester hour in Criminal Law and Procedure (1/89).

Estates and Trusts (B-204)
Location: Various locations throughout the country.
Length: 24 hours (8 weeks).
Dates: September 1978-Present.
Objective: To give the student a basic understanding of estate planning and administration of decedents' estates.
Instruction: Topics covered include intestacy, wills, probate, federal and state taxes, accounting, and distribution of assets.
Credit recommendation: In the upper division baccalaureate category or in the lower division baccalaureate/associate degree category, 2 semester hours in Estates and Trusts (12/83) (1/89). NOTE: This course has been reevaluated and continues to meet requirements for credit recommendations.

Estates and Trusts II (C-304)
Location: Independent Study
Length: Correspondence program.
Dates: October 1983-Present.
Objective: To give the student a basic understanding of estate planning and administration of decedents' estates.
Instruction: A course in handling of decedents' estates for those who have completed initial introduction to these topics in Estates and Trusts (B-204). Topics covered include: Accumulation of Assets, Filing an Inventory and Payment of Debts; Federal Estate Taxes; Gift Taxes; State Taxes; Formal Accounting; and Distribution of Assets.
Credit recommendation: In the upper division baccalaureate category or in the lower division baccalaureate/associate degree category, 1 semester hour in Estates and Trusts (12/83) (1/89). NOTE: This course has been reevaluated and continues to meet requirements for credit recommendations.

Family Law
Location: Various locations throughout the country.
Length: 15 hours (2 days).
Dates: September 1989-Present.
Objective: To provide students with an overview of family law and procedures for interviewing clients with family law problems.
Instruction: This course covers the wide array of issues that are part of family law, including: marriage, annulments, divorce, property rights and distribution, children visitation, alimony, separation agreements, adoptions, parent and child law. Students learn to interview clients with family law problems and prepare complaints and agreements.
Credit recommendation: In the upper division baccalaureate category, 1 semester hour in Family Law (1/89).

Introduction to Criminal Justice
1. **Legal Investigations (A-104)**
2. **Criminal Law and Procedure (A-106)**
3. **American Jurisprudence (B-201)**

Location: Various locations throughout Connecticut, Illinois, Massachusetts, Michigan, New Jersey, New York, Ohio, Pennsylvania, Rhode Island, and Texas.
Length: 1. 6 hours (1 day); 2. 15 hours (2 days); 3. 9

hours (1 day).

Dates: December 1979-August 1989.

Objective: To provide the student with an overview of techniques employed to engage in successful investigative work including factual analysis and synthesis, gaining access to records and other documentation, and the ability to evaluate leads and sources; a study of the fundamental basis upon which the criminal law exists and to distinguish the major elements of every crime; and review of the basic governmental structure of our society and the impact government has on law-making.

Instruction: Course presents an understanding of how to interview, prepare, and evaluate witnesses for the purposes of present day investigation or any future litigation. Includes a review of the major statutory and common law crimes, their various elements and problems of proof, and specifically covers all major property and personal offenses as well as those offenses which disturb the public order or the public good. Course also covers the numerous procedural issues that arise in the enforcement of criminal codes including all constitutional restrictions on police practice. Course also considers the varied sources of law in American society including the Bill of Rights, and the fundamental aspects of our Court system in the United States including state, federal, and county jurisdictions. Also, the course delves into the numerous ethical problems which arise in the legal system, particularly the lawyer and the Code of Professional Responsibility.

Credit recommendation: In the upper division baccalaureate category or in the lower division baccalaureate/associate degree category, 3 semester hours in Criminal Justice or Paralegal Studies (3/83). NOTE: For credit recommendations, courses 1, 2, and 3 must all be successfully completed.

Introduction to Legal Research and Writing (Legal Analysis and Writing [B-205])

Location: Various locations throughout Connecticut, Illinois, Massachusetts, Michigan, New Jersey, New York, Pennsylvania, Ohio, Rhode Island, and Texas.

Length: 27 hours (9 weeks).

Dates: December 1979-Present.

Objective: To familiarize the student with the essential skills needed to perform legal research and writing, including factual analysis and issue resolution, and Shepardizing.

Instruction: Course covers various sources for research materials, such as digests, reporters, statutory materials, and encyclopedias. Also covered are the proper approach to legal writing, how to prepare memoranda, how to utilize citations, how to evaluate precedents and to formulate logical legal conclusions. Finally, there is extensive library research to solve numerous problems raised in the course; there are also extensive writing projects. The library research and the extensive writing projects are complete outside normal class time, while they are an integral and required part of the course.

Credit recommendation: In the upper division baccalaureate category or in the lower division baccalaureate/associate degree category, 3 semester hours in Legal Research/Legal Writing (3/83) (1/89). NOTE: This course has been reevaluated and continues to meet requirements for credit recommendations.

Legal Research and Writing II (C-301)

Location: Independent Study.

Length: Correspondence Program.

Dates: October 1983-Present.

Objective: To enable the student to review and utilize legal materials available for research purposes.

Instruction: This course is intended for those who have already completed Legal Analysis and Writing (B-205). An independent analysis of and contracted practice in the use of the tools of legal research.

Credit recommendation: In the upper division baccalaureate category or in the lower division baccalaureate/associate degree category, 2 semester hours in Legal Research and Writing II (12/83) (1/89). NOTE: This course has been reevaluated and continues to meet requirements for credit recommendations.

Litigation, Pleadings and Arbitration

Location: Various locations throughout the country.

Length: 42 hours (14 weeks).

Dates: September 1989-Present.

Objective: To introduce students to the major aspects of litigation, pleadings and arbitration as they apply to the work of a paralegal.

Instruction: Course covers client counseling, investigative techniques and processes; the paralegal and civil practice (i.e., commencement of a lawsuit, pleadings, settlement, pre-trial activities), trial procedures, and arbitration and dispute resolution. Methodology includes lecture and discussion.

Credit recommendation: In the upper division baccalaureate category, 3 semester hours in Litigation, Pleadings and Arbitration (1/89).

Personal and Injury Litigation - Torts II (C-303)

Location: Independent Study.

Length: Correspondence program.

Dates: October 1983-Present.

Objective: To enable the student to attain a thorough understanding of personal injury litigations and pleadings that pertain to pre-trial and post-trial activities.

Instruction: For students who have already had a course in basic civil law (e.g., Tort Law [A-101]), this course examines all aspects of personal injury law. Some of the areas reviewed will be the theoretical aspects of negligence, breach, mental and emotional damage, concepts of due care, causation, malpractice, and defenses to causes of action.

Credit recommendation: In the upper division baccalaureate category or in the lower division baccalaureate/associate degree category, 2 semester hours in Torts II (12/83) (1/89). NOTE: This course has been reevaluated and continues to meet requirements for credit recommendations.

Real Estate (C-302)
Location: Independent Study.
Length: Correspondence program.
Dates: October 1983-Present.
Objective: To provide the student with further study of all forms of ownership and a review of basic principles in the sale and exchange of all real estate.
Instruction: This course is recommended for those who have completed Real Estate Transfer and Ownership (A-106). The course will substantially review all forms of ownership in/and from present to future interests, processes of closing and settlement, agreement of sale, modification and adjustment of contracts, recordation, title abstraction, mortgages, and leasing. Course also covers surveys and recording.
Credit recommendation: In the upper division baccalaureate category or in the lower division baccalaureate/associate degree category, 2 semester hours in Real Estate (12/83) (1/89). NOTE: This course has been reevaluated and continues to meet requirements for credit recommendations.

Real Estate Transfer and Ownership (A-106)
Location: Various locations throughout the country.
Length: 21 hours (3 days).
Dates: September 1978-Present.
Objective: To develop the student's understanding of ownership of real property, transfer of such ownership, and the use of legal forms incident thereto.
Instruction: Topics covered in this course are: overview of real property; deeds; liens and other incumbrances on real property; contracts for sale or purchase of real estate; financial instruments; search, examination and title insurance; title closing; landlord and tenant relationships; surveys; and mortgages and financing. As an out-of-class assignment, students are required to prepare all the proper documents used in a "closing" by the buyer and by the seller. Students are also involved in drafting case pleadings and other additional writing assignments outside of the normal class time.
Credit recommendation: In the upper division baccalaureate category or in the lower division baccalaureate/associate degree category, 3 semester hours in Principles and Practice of Real Estate, Real Estate Laws, or Survey of Real Estate (12/83) (1/89). NOTE: This course has been reevaluated and continues to meet requirements for credit recommendations.

Torts and Personal Injury
Location: Various locations throughout the country.
Length: 30 hours (5 days).
Dates: September 1989-Present.
Objective: To provide the student with a thorough overview of traditional and contemporary tort law.
Instruction: This course involves a study of traditional tort law, including intentional torts such as assault and battery, and negligence. Also no-fault laws, products liability, nuisance, misrepresentation, defamation, invasion of privacy, trespass, and workmen's compensation are covered.
Credit recommendation: In the upper division baccalaureate category, 2 semester hours in Tort Law (1/89).

American Institute for Property and Liability Underwriters/Insurance Institute of America

The American Institute for Property and Liability Underwriters and The Insurance Institute of America are companion educational organizations directly supported by the property-liability insurance industry to help meet its personnel development and professional education needs.

The American Institute for Property and Liability Underwriters is responsible for administering the Chartered Property Casualty Underwriter (CPCU) Program. The Insurance Institute offers programs in General Insurance, Insurance Adjusting, Management Studies, Risk Management, and Underwriting. Boards of Trustees made up of representatives of all segments of the property-liability insurance community—mutual and stock companies, agency and brokerage firms, and educators—govern the Institutes.

Courses, offered throughout the United States and abroad, are of three types: (1) formal classes, which may be publicly offered on campuses or privately conducted at insurance companies; (2) informal study groups, which may have a designated leader or shared leadership; and (3) independent study, which primarily benefits those individuals who, because of distance and time factors, choose to study at their own pace. The third type of instruction requires a high degree of self-discipline. The Institutes supply all students, whether they use the formal class, the study group, or the independent study method, with current topical outlines which list the assigned textbooks and their publishers, the weekly readings, illustrative questions applicable to each topic, and suggested effective study methods.

The Institute's national examinations, made up of a series of essay questions, test a candidate's ability to master a body of knowledge and to communicate it clearly to others. Program examinations are three hours in length.

NOTE: The American Institute for Property and Liability Underwriters/Insurance Institute of America sponsors a variety of study programs with a wide range of possible combinations of individual courses from several programs. The credit recommendations which are listed below are based on independent evaluations of the programs. Colleges should carefully consider the possible overlap of courses from different programs before granting students credit for multiple courses.

Source of official student records: Vice President of Examinations, American Institute for Property and Liability Underwriters, Insurance Institute of America, Providence and Sugartown Roads, Malvern, Pennsylvania 19355.

Additional information about the courses: Program on Noncollegiate Sponsored Instruction, The Center for Adult Learning and Educational Credentials, American Council on Education, One Dupont Circle, Washington, D.C. 20036.

ACCREDITED ADVISER IN INSURANCE PROGRAM

(AAI 81) Principles of Insurance Production

Location: Various locations through formal courses, informal study groups, or independent study.

Length: The equivalent of 13 two and one-half hour sessions plus additional preparation.

Dates: December 1981-Present.

Objective: To give the student technical knowledge of insurance products required to meet needs of individuals for personal insurance.

Learning Outcome: Upon successful completion of this course, the student will be able to provide professional level service to individual clients and maintain satisfactory working relationships with insurance.

Instruction: The first eight assignments are concerned with an introduction to insurance, insurance sales, exposure identification, legal liability, and personal lines insurance. The remaining portion of AAI 81 introduces commercial insurance sales, packages, property insurance, and commercial general liability insurance. Specific topics include principles of insurance, insurance law, the sales process, personal insurance coverage, the risk management process with emphasis on exposure identification, and an introduction to commercial insurance.

Credit recommendation: In the upper division baccalaureate category, 2 semester hours in Insurance or General Business (4/87).

(AAI 82) Multiple-Lines Insurance Production

Location: Various locations through formal courses, informal study groups, or independent study.

Length: The equivalent of 13 two and one-half hour sessions plus additional preparation.

Dates: May 1982-Present.

Objective: To give the student technical knowledge of commercial insurance products to meet needs of clients for commercial insurance.

Learning Outcome: Upon successful completion of this course, the student will be able to provide professional level service to commercial clients and maintain satisfactory working relationships with insurance company staff.

Instruction: The entire course is concerned with major commercial lines insurance coverages. Each chapter in the commercial insurance sections of AAI 81 and AAI 82 uses a case approach with four common cases applying to all commercial coverages. Additionally, selling techniques successfully used by agents and brokers around the country illustrate the application of coverage knowledge in the sales process. The final two chapters in AAI 82 discuss account development and use in the case approach to tie together coverages and selling. Specific topics include the major commercial insurance products, package policies, account development, and insurance sales and coverage.

Credit recommendation: In the upper division baccalaureate category, 2 semester hours in Insurance or General Business (4/87).

(AAI 83) Agency Operations and Sales Management

Location: Various locations through formal courses, informal study groups, or independent study.

Length: The equivalent of 13 two and one-half hour sessions plus additional preparation.

Dates: December 1983-Present.

Objective: To provide the student with knowledge of agency operations and sales management in the insurance business.

Learning Outcome: Upon successful completion of this course, the student will be able to provide effective operation of insurance agencies and apply sales management techniques.

Instruction: The content of this course is divided into three major sections. First, agency operations planning, organizing, staffing, directing, and controlling are described. This section also includes material on financial management and other current topics in agency management. The second section, on sales management, examines individual sales plans for producers, risk placement management, competition management, suspecting, and prospecting. The third section of AAI 83 is devoted to ethics and professional liability. Specific topics covered include managerial operations affecting the sale of insurance, personal production planning, automation, ethics, and specific producer topics such as competition, time management, creating a sales proposal, how to sell the underwriter, and the subjects of suspecting, prospecting, and approaching the prospect.

Credit recommendation: In the upper division baccalaureate category, 2 semester hours in Marketing or General Business (4/87).

ASSOCIATE IN INSURANCE ACCOUNTING FINANCE PROGRAM

(AIAF 111) Statutory Accounting for Property and Liability Insurers

Location: Various locations through formal courses, informal study groups, or independent study.

Length: The equivalent of 13 two and one-half hour sessions plus additional preparation.

Dates: January 1985-Present.

Objective: To provide the student with an understanding of state statutory accounting requirements for property liability insurers.

Learning Outcome: Upon successful completion of this course, the student will be able to use knowledge of state statutory accounting for property liability insurance to assemble applicable data needed for required financial statements and reports.

Instruction: Through detailed study of the NAIC Annual Statement for Fire and Casualty Insurance Companies, this course develops the principles of statutory accounting, contrasts them with generally accepted accounting principles, and facilitates the actual preparation of the Annual Statement and other required reports. Specific topics covered include aspects of statutory accounting requirements, including introduction to insurance accounting and finance, annual statement reporting, assets, liabilities and policyholders surplus, estimated liabilities for losses and loss adjustment expenses, earned and unearned premiums (other liabilities, capital, and surplus), insurance company revenues and expenses, written premiums, losses and loss expenses, expenses, investment income; other income, reinsurance accounting, GAAP (other financial reporting requirements).

Credit recommendation: In the upper division baccalaureate category, 2 semester hours in Accounting or Insurance (4/87). NOTE: Students who complete AIAF 111, 112, and 113 should receive 3 semester hours in the graduate category.

(AIAF 112) Insurance Information Systems

Location: Various locations through formal courses, informal study groups, or independent study.

Length: The equivalent of 13 two and one-half hour sessions plus additional preparation.

Dates: January 1986-Present.

Objective: To provide the student with an understanding of fundamental needs, tools, and controls required for development and management of insurance information systems.

Learning Outcome: Upon successful completion of this course, the student will be able to design and effectively manage insurance information systems and coordinate needs of systems users.

Instruction: This course analyzes the recording, processing, and reporting of accounting information for insurance companies. It considers statistical, managerial, and financial reporting requirements and explores the application of computers in insurance. Specific topics covered include aspects of information management systems, computers and insurance, overview of insurance information systems, data flows and data storage, cycles (premium, loss, reserve, reinsurance, treasury investment, payroll, and nonpayroll expenditure), budgeting and planning, management reporting, statistical reporting, data integrity, system controls, auditing.

Credit recommendation: In the upper division baccalaureate category, 2 semester hours in Insurance or Information Systems Management (4/87). NOTE: Students who complete AIAF 111, 112, and 113 should receive 3 semester hours in the graduate category.

(AIAF 113) Insurance Company Finance

Location: Various locations through formal courses, informal study groups, or independent study.

Length: The equivalent of 13 two and one-half hour sessions plus additional preparation.

Dates: September 1986-Present.

Objective: To provide the student with an understanding of basic financial management principles as applied to property and liability insurers as well as understanding of the financial environment in which these companies operate.

Learning Outcome: Upon successful completion of this course, the student will understand application of basic financial management principles in insurance company operations.

Instruction: With an overall emphasis on financial institutions and the larger financial environment, this course presents principles of finance from an insurance company perspective. It includes cash management, capital structure, taxation, financial planning, investment management, and financial markets and instruments. Specific topics covered include elements of finance in insurance, including financial systems, financial management, cash management, capital structure, insurance company income, taxation, financial planning, economic environment, financial markets, money markets, capital markets, investment policy, financial analysis of insurance companies.

Credit recommendation: In the upper division baccalaureate category, 2 semester hours in Economics, Finance, or Insurance (4/87). NOTE: Students who complete AIAF 111, 112, and 113 should receive 3 semester hours in the graduate category.

ASSOCIATE IN CLAIMS PROGRAM

(AIC 31) Principles of Insurance and Property Loss Adjusting
(Formerly ADJ 31)

Location: Various locations through formal courses, in-

formal study groups, or independent study.
Length: 13 lessons.
Dates: May 1967-Present.
Objective: To provide the student with knowledge of selected basic principles of insurance and understanding of property loss adjustment fundamentals.
Learning Outcome: Upon successful completion of this course, the student will be able to apply skillfully insurance principles to solve property loss adjustment procedures.
Instruction: Content covered includes selected principles of insurance, key definitions, insurance contract analysis (including study of the various limitations on amounts of recovery under insurance contracts), fundamental procedures of property loss adjusting, investigation and reports to insurers, and estimation of building losses.
Credit recommendation: In the upper division baccalaureate category, 3 semester hours in Business, Business Law, or Insurance (5/77) (3/82) (4/87). NOTE: This course has been reevaluated and continues to meet requirements for credit recommendations.

(AIC 32) Principles of Insurance and Liability Claims Adjusting
(Formerly ADJ 32)
Location: Various locations through formal courses, informal study groups, or independent study.
Length: 13 lessons.
Dates: May 1967-Present.
Objective: To provide the student with knowledge of basic liability claims adjusting procedures and the human behavioral response, associated with adjusting. Knowledge of functional areas affecting company operations.
Learning Outcome: Upon successful completion of this course, the student will have the ability to initiate and complete the claims investigation process, and understanding of its impact on company operations.
Instruction: Content covered includes functions of claims department, coverage, liability, claims investigation, negotiation, settlement, rehabilitation, organization of insurers, rate making, financial structure, and insurance regulation.
Credit recommendation: In the upper division baccalaureate category, 3 semester hours in Business, Business Law, or Insurance (5/77) (3/82) (4/87). NOTE: This course has been reevaluated and continues to meet requirements for credit recommendations.

(AIC 35) Property Insurance Adjusting
(Formerly ADJ 35)
Location: Various locations through formal courses, informal study groups, or independent study.
Length: 13 lessons.
Dates: May 1967-Present.
Objective: To provide the student with an understanding of concepts relevant to adjustment of property losses.
Learning Outcome: Upon successful completion of this course, the student will be able to apply effectively loss adjustment techniques to complex property insurance losses.
Instruction: Content covered includes apportionment of losses, insurable interest, estimating and adjusting losses (building, personal property, and merchandise), salvage, and business interruption.
Credit recommendation: In the upper division baccalaureate category, 3 semester hours in Business, Business Law, or Insurance (5/77) (3/82) (4/87). NOTE: This course has been reevaluated and continues to meet requirements for credit recommendations.

(AIC 36) Liability Insurance Adjusting
(Formerly ADJ 36)
Location: Various locations through formal courses, informal study groups, or independent study.
Length: 13 lessons.
Dates: May 1967-Present.
Objective: To provide the student with an understanding of legal concepts relevant to adjustment of more complex liability claims.
Learning Outcome: Upon successful completion of this course, the student will have the ability to initiate more complex claims investigation procedures leading to settlement.
Instruction: Content covered includes casualty claims practices, contract law, torts, medical aspects of damages, claims, evaluation, negotiations, settlement, automobile liability, product liability, professional liability, and workers compensation.
Credit recommendation: In the graduate degree category, 3 semester hours in Business, Business Law, or Insurance (5/77) (3/82) (4/87). NOTE: This course has been reevaluated and continues to meet requirements for credit recommendations.

ASSOCIATE IN MANAGEMENT PROGRAM

(AIM 41) The Process of Management
(Formerly MGT 41)
Location: Various locations through formal courses, informal study groups, or independent study.
Length: 12 lessons.
Dates: December 1968-Present.
Objective: To provide the student with knowledge of management concepts and managerial problem solving.
Learning Outcome: Upon successful completion of this course, the student will be able to apply concepts of management in solving insurance management problems.
Instruction: Covers major functions in the management process, organization, motivation, planning and control, and managerial analytical tools.
Credit recommendation: In the upper division baccalaureate category, 3 semester hours in Business Ad-

ministration or Management (5/77) (3/82) (4/87). NOTE: This course has been reevaluated and continues to meet requirements for credit recommendations.

(AIM 42) Management and Human Resources (Formerly MGT 42)
Location: Various locations through formal courses, informal study groups, or independent study.
Length: 12 lessons.
Dates: May 1969-Present.
Objective: To provide the student with knowledge and understanding of human behavior in organizations.
Learning Outcome: Upon successful completion of this course, the student will have the ability to apply principles of human behavior to individuals and groups within an organization.
Instruction: Content covered includes organizational behavior, work groups, individual behavior, two-person work relationship, leadership, group behavior and organizational change.
Credit recommendation: In the upper division baccalaureate category, 3 semester hours in Business Administration or Management (5/77) (3/82) (4/87). NOTE: This course has been reevaluated and continues to meet requirements for credit recommendations.

(AIM 43) Managerial Decision Making (Formerly MGT 43)
Location: Various locations through formal courses, informal study groups, or independent study.
Length: 12 lessons.
Dates: December 1969-Present.
Objective: To provide the student with an understanding of modern decision making tools and techniques.
Learning Outcome: Upon successful completion of this course, the student will have appropriate use of decision making tools and techniques in making management decisions.
Instruction: Content covered includes a systematic framework for evaluation of decisions, sources of inaccuracy and error in decision making, the individual human decision making process, the organizational decision making process, and the role of computers in that process.
Credit recommendation: In the upper division baccalaureate category, 3 semester hours in Business Administration or Management (5/77) (3/82) (4/87). NOTE: This course has been reevaluated and continues to meet requirements for credit recommendations.

(AIM 44) Management in a Changing World (Formerly MGT 44)
Location: Various locations through formal courses, informal study groups, or independent study.
Length: 12 lessons.
Dates: May 1970-Present.
Objective: To provide the student with knowledge of management decision making in a complex and changing world.
Learning Outcome: Upon successful completion of this course, the student will have the ability to apply management theory to business organizations in a changing world with special reference to organization planning and control.
Instruction: Content covered includes organization development, organizational systems strategic planning, systems approach to organizational development, team development, performance appraisals, and stress management.
Credit recommendation: In the upper division baccalaureate category, 3 semester hours in Business Administration or Management (5/77) (3/82) (4/87). NOTE: This course has been reevaluated and continues to meet requirements for credit recommendations.

ASSOCIATE IN LOSS CONTROL MANAGEMENT PROGRAM

(ALCM 71) Hazard Identification and Analysis (Formerly LCM 71)
Location: Various locations through formal courses, informal study groups, or independent study.
Length: 13 lessons.
Dates: January 1979-Present.
Objective: To provide the student with an understanding of the loss control management process, consisting of identifying and analyzing hazards, and developing alternative loss control measures.
Learning Outcome: Upon successful completion of this course, the student will have the ability to use knowledge of hazard identification and analysis to implement loss control programs.
Instruction: Content covered includes in-depth analysis of principles relating to the identification and control of workplace hazards with emphasis on property, accidental, and health hazards.
Credit recommendation: In the upper division baccalaureate category, 3 semester hours in Insurance, Risk Management, or Industrial Safety; or in the graduate degree category, 3 semester hours in Insurance, Risk Management, or Industrial Safety for completion of the two course sequence: ALCM 71 and ALCM 72 (7/79) (3/82) (4/87). NOTE: This course has been reevaluated and continues to meet requirements for credit recommendations.

(ALCM 72) Loss Control Applications and Management
Location: Various locations through formal courses, informal study groups, or independent study.
Length: 12 lessons.
Dates: January 1980-Present.
Objective: To provide the student with an understanding of loss control management processes, including selec-

tion of effective and economical controls to minimize hazards or losses resulting from hazards, implementing these controls and monitoring the results.

Learning Outcome: Upon successful completion of this course, the student will have the ability to apply loss control and management decision techniques to control of losses.

Instruction: Content covered includes application of principles taught in ALCM 71 to designing integrated loss control programs for specific hazards associated with products, workers' compensation, crime, transport and cargo, general liability, and property losses. Special attention is given to problem solving and decision making techniques. Case studies are used.

Credit recommendation: In the upper division baccalaureate category, 3 semester hours in Insurance, Risk Management, or Industrial Safety; or in the graduate degree category, 3 semester hours in Insurance, Risk Management, or Industrial Safety for completion of the two course sequence: ALCM 71 and ALCM 72 (8/82) (4/87). NOTE: This course has been reevaluated and continues to meet requirements for credit recommendations.

ASSOCIATE IN PREMIUM AUDITING PROGRAM

(APA 91) Principles of Premium Auditing

Location: Various locations through formal courses, informal study groups, or independent study.

Length: The equivalent of 13 two and one-half hour sessions plus additional preparation.

Dates: September 1981-Present.

Objective: To provide the student with an understanding of the premium audit function in insurance and of the process that serves as a framework for premium audits.

Learning Outcome: Upon successful completion of this course, the student will have an enhanced competence in premium auditing.

Instruction: The content of this course defines the premium auditing function, establishes its relationship to other insurance company operations, and systematically develops the principles and procedures of insurance premium auditing. The specific topics covered include the nature of premium auditing, insurance company operations, underwriting, insurance law, planning premium audits, review of insured's operations, the insured's employees, evaluation of accounting systems, design of audit programs, auditing EDP accounting systems, verification and analysis, the auditor's report, communication in the premium audit.

Credit recommendation: In the upper division baccalaureate category, 2 semester hours in Accounting or Insurance (4/87).

(APA 92) Premium Auditing Applications

Location: Various locations through formal courses, informal study groups, or independent study.

Length: The equivalent of 13 two and one-half hour sessions plus additional preparation.

Dates: January 1982-Present.

Objective: To provide the student with an understanding of how premium auditing principles are used to determine premiums for specific lines of insurance.

Learning Outcome: Upon successful completion of this course, the student will be able to determine accurately premiums for various lines of insurance using accepted premium auditing principles.

Instruction: The content of this course explores premium determination in a wide variety of property-liability insurance contracts and applies the principles learned in APA 91 to a number of significant and complex premium auditing problems. Specific topics covered include insurance rates and premiums, workers' compensation insurance, workers' compensation premium determination, classification of workers' compensation insurance of maritime workers, general liability: (coverages and premium bases, classification and audit procedures) commercial auto premium determination, truckers premium determination, garage policy premium determination, premium determination of commercial property insurance, other applications and premium auditing careers.

Credit recommendation: In the upper division baccalaureate category, 2 semester hours in Accounting or Insurance (4/87).

ASSOCIATE IN RESEARCH AND PLANNING PROGRAM

(ARP 101) Business Research Methods

Location: Various locations through formal courses, informal study groups, or independent study.

Length: The equivalent of 13 two and one-half hour sessions plus additional preparation.

Dates: September 1983-Present.

Objective: To provide the student with an understanding of methods of effective business research as they relate to property and liability insure.

Learning Outcome: Upon successful completion of this course, the student will be able to apply research skills to property and liability issues and to translate management concerns into research questions.

Instruction: The content of this course discusses the elements of logical analysis and the use of research methods such as measurement, sampling, secondary research, surveys, qualitative techniques, and statistical analysis. This course provides an overview of the research process and the evaluation and reporting of results. The specific topics covered include the nature of business research, scientific thinking, logical arguments, the research process, research design, measurement, sampling, secondary data sources and survey instrument design, scaling and data collection, experimentation, simulation, and qualitative, research techniques, elements of analysis, statistical analysis and research reports.

Credit recommendation: In the upper division baccalaureate category, 2 semester hours in Business Administration, Management, or Insurance (4/87). NOTE: Students who complete ARP 101 and 102 should receive 3 semester hours in the graduate category.

(ARP 102) Strategic Planning for Insurers

Location: Various locations through formal courses, informal study groups, or independent study.

Length: The equivalent of 13 two and one-half hour sessions plus additional preparation.

Dates: January 1984-Present.

Objective: To provide the student with an understanding of the methods of strategic planning as they relate to property and liability insurance.

Learning Outcome: Upon successful completion of this course, the student will be able to apply strategic planning tools and processes to management property and liability companies.

Instruction: The content of this course explores the processes and factors involved in choosing policy directions for insurance firms, including strategic planning, scanning the business, regulatory, and social environments, competitive analysis, forecasting, resource assessment, market strategy, product strategy, systems development, and human resource planning. Specific topics covered include aspects of planning, including corporations and social change, introduction to strategic planning, strategic decision situations, strategic plans, scanning the environment, the business and regulatory environment, forecasting and corporate models, economic forecasting, assessing strengths and weaknesses, competitive positioning and market strategy, product planning and development, systems development, human resource planning.

Credit recommendation: In the upper division baccalaureate category, 2 semester hours in Business Administration, Insurance, or Management (4/87). NOTE: Students who complete ARP 101 and 102 should receive 3 semester hours in the graduate category.

ASSOCIATE IN RISK MANAGEMENT PROGRAM

(ARM 54) Structure of Risk Management Process
(Formerly RM 54)

Location: Various locations through formal courses, informal study groups, or independent study.

Length: 13 lessons.

Dates: May 1967-Present.

Objective: To provide the student with an understanding of exposure identification and evaluation in risk management decision making and of the financial management foundation for choosing risk management alternatives. Knowledge of business organization objectives and general management principles.

Learning Outcome: Upon successful completion of this course, the student will have the ability to identify and analyze various loss and liability exposures and utilize forecasting techniques and cash flow analysis in making risk management decisions.

Instruction: Content covered includes procedures for identifying and analyzing property, income, liability, and personal loss exposures; characteristics of risk control and risk financing techniques; guidelines for selecting appropriate risk management techniques; and, the contribution of proper risk management to an organization's profits and productivity.

Credit recommendation: In the graduate degree category, 3 semester hours in Business Administration, Insurance, or Risk Management (5/77) (3/82) (4/87). NOTE: This course has been reevaluated and continues to meet requirements for credit recommendations.

(ARM 55) Risk Control
(Formerly RM 55)

Location: Various locations through formal courses, informal study groups, or independent study.

Length: 12 lessons.

Dates: May 1967-Present.

Learning Outcome: Upon successful completion of this course, the student will have the ability to use appropriate risk control techniques in dealing with risk management problems.

Instruction: Content covered includes guidelines for selecting risk management techniques, appropriate employment and administration of risk control techniques, and coordination of the total risk management effort.

Credit recommendation: In the graduate degree category, 3 semester hours in Business Administration, Insurance, Management, or Risk Management (5/77) (3/82) (4/87). NOTE: This course has been reevaluated and continues to meet requirements for credit recommendations.

(ARM 56) Risk Financing
(Formerly RM 56)

Location: Various locations through formal courses, informal study groups, or independent study.

Length: 12 lessons.

Dates: December 1973-Present.

Objective: To provide the student with knowledge of risk functioning techniques leading to minimization of financial consequences of losses and claims.

Learning Outcome: Upon successful completion of this course, the student will have the ability to formulate procedures leading to minimization of financial consequences of losses and claims.

Instruction: Content covered includes risk financing techniques; financing property, liability, and personal losses; accounting and tax aspects of accidental losses, risk retention, pricing, selection of insurers, and allocating costs.

Credit recommendation: In the graduate degree category, 3 semester hours in Business Administration, Insurance, Management, or Risk Management (5/77) (3/82) (4/87). NOTE: This course has been reevaluated and continues to meet requirements for credit recommendations.

ASSOCIATE IN UNDERWRITING PROGRAM

(AU 61) Principles of Property Liability and Underwriting
(Formerly UND 61)

Location: Various locations through formal courses, informal study groups, or independent study.
Length: 13 lessons.
Dates: *Version 1:* January 1977-March 1987; *Version 2:* April 1987-Present.
Objective: To enable the student to understand principles, tools, and techniques of property and liability underwriting.
Learning Outcome: Upon successful completion of this course, the student will have the ability to make appropriate property and liability underwriting decisions.
Instruction: Content covered includes underwriting function and decision making process with special attention to coverage analysis, loss control, reinsurance for underwiters, numerical tools, pricing, information/financial analysis, decision making and monitoring, and communications. Case studies are used.
Credit recommendation: *Version 1:* In the upper division baccalaureate category, 3 semester hours in Business Administration or Insurance (5/77) (3/82). *Version 2:* In the upper division baccalaureate category, or in the graduate degree category, 3 semester hours in Business Administration or Insurance for completion of the four course sequence: AU 61, AU 62, AU 63, and AU 64 (4/87). NOTE: This course has been reevaluated and continues to meet requirements for credit recommendations.

(AU 62) Personal Lines Underwriting
(Formerly UND 62)

Location: Various locations through formal courses, informal study groups, or independent study.
Length: 13 lessons.
Dates: *Version 1:* September 1977-March 1987; *Version 2:* April 1987-Present.
Objective: To enable the student to identify, describe, and evaluate factors to consider an underwriting personal lines insurance.
Learning Outcome: Upon successful completion of this course, the student will have the ability to make appropriate personal lines underwriting decisions.
Instruction: Content covered includes nature of personal lines insurance; understanding automobile, residential, farm, ranch, personal inland marine, pleasure boat, and personal liability insurance; electronic data processing and account underwriting. Case studies are used.
Credit recommendation: *Version 1:* In the upper division baccalaureate category, 2 semester hours in Business Administration or Insurance (5/77). *Version 2:* In the upper division baccalaureate category, or in the graduate degree category, 3 semester hours in Business Administration or Insurance for completion of the four course sequence: AU 61, AU 62, AU 63, and AU 64 (9/87). NOTE: This course has been reevaluated and continues to meet requirements for credit recommendations. Students should receive a maximum of 3 hours at the upper division level for any combination of AU 62, AU 63, and AU 64.

(AU 63) Commercial Liability Underwriting
(Formerly UND 63)

Location: Various locations through formal courses, informal study groups, or independent study.
Length: 13 lessons.
Dates: *Version 1:* September 1978-February 1982; *Version 2:* March 1982-Present.
Objective: To enable the student to identify, describe, and evaluate factors to consider in underwriting commercial liability insurance.
Learning Outcome: Upon successful completion of this course, the student will have the ability to make appropriate commercial liability underwriting decisions.
Instruction: Content covered includes legal foundations of liability; underwriting the commercial enterprise (commercial auto liability, general liability, product liability, workers' compensation); medical, professional, and special liability insurance; surety bonds, and account underwriting. Case studies are used.
Credit recommendation: *Version 1:* In the upper division baccalaureate category, 3 semester hours in Insurance (7/79). *Version 2:* In the upper division baccalaureate category, 3 semester hours in Business Administration or Insurance; or in the graduate degree category, 3 semester hours in Business Administration or Insurance for completion of the four course sequence: AU 61, AU 62, AU 63, and AU 64 (3/82)(4/87). NOTE: This course has been reevaluated and continues to meet requirements for credit recommendations.

(AU 64) Commercial Property and Multiple-Lines Underwriting
(Formerly UND 64)

Location: Various locations through formal courses, informal study groups, or independent study.
Length: 13 lessons.
Dates: *Version 1:* January 1979-March 1987; *Version 2:* April 1987-Present.
Objective: To enable the student to understand the basic information and the decision making process involved in making underwriting decisions for commercial property and commercial multiple-line insurance.

Learning Outcome: Upon successful completion of this course, the student will have the ability to effectively use knowledge of commercial property and commercial multiple-lines underwriting to make appropriate underwriting decisions.

Instruction: Content covered includes applications of the underwriting process to commercial property and multiple-lines risks, with emphasis on analyzing frequency and severity of fire and other perils, construction, occupancy hazards and controls, indirect loss exposures, marine risks, crime insurance, and package policies.

Credit recommendation: *Version 1:* In the upper division baccalaureate category, 2 semester hours in Business Administration (7/79) (3/82). *Version 2:* In the upper division baccalaureate category, or in the graduate degree category, 3 semester hours in Business Administration or Insurance for completion of the four course sequence: AU 61, AU 62, AU 63, and AU 64 (4/87). NOTE: Students should receive a maximum of 3 hours at the upper division level for any combination of AU 62, AU 63, and AU 64. This course has been reevaluated and continues to meet requirements for credit recommendations.

CPCU PROGRAM

The goals of the ten CPCU courses listed below are to enable students to (1) describe the broad range of risk management techniques; (2) analyze systematically all types of insurance contracts; (3) describe the coverage provided by approximately 50 property-liability insurance contracts and important types of life and health policy provisions; (4) apply this loss control and loss financing technical knowledge in managing their own loss exposures and those of others; (5) explain the organizational structure and functional roles of the various segments of the insurance industry; (6) describe how insurance fits into and is affected by the economic, legal, financial, and social environment that surrounds it; and (7) understand the nature of professionalism and act within that framework.

Students who satisfactorily complete all ten national examinations and meet ethical and experience requirements are awarded the Chartered Property Casualty Underwriter professional designation.

Prior to 1979, the CPCU program was composed of five 30-lesson courses. In 1979, the academic portion of the program was revised to consist of ten 15-lesson courses. Individuals who have completed courses under the five-course program are given credit for the number of semesters of study they have already completed toward the academic requirements for the CPCU designation, according to a cross-credit schedule.

The ten courses in the current program are described first, followed by a description of the courses in the five-course program. The overall objectives of the two programs are nearly identical. However, the ten-semester program is based on an entirely different set of course materials. The 30-lesson courses culminated in a four-hour essay examination; the 15-lesson courses culminate in a three-hour essay examination.

Accounting and Finance (CPCU 8)
Location: Various locations through formal courses, informal study groups, or independent study.
Length: 15 lessons.
Dates: January 1979-Present.
Objective: To develop an understanding of the basic principles of accounting and finance, and the accounting and finance practices of insurance companies.
Instruction: Covers accounting fundamentals, valuation of balance sheet accounts, income statements, analysis of financial statements, and financial management. Analyzes in detail insurance company accounting and financial management and the relationship between financial analysis and insurance company solvency.
Credit recommendation: In the graduate degree category, 3 semester hours in Accounting, Finance, or Insurance (7/79).

1. Commercial Property Risk Management and Insurance (CPCU 3)
2. Commercial Liability Risk Management and Insurance (CPCU 4)
Location: Various locations through formal courses, informal study groups, or independent study.
Length: 1. 15 lessons; 2. 15 lessons.
Dates: 1. September 1978-Present; 2. January 1979-Present.
Objective: *Course 1:* To provide a detailed understanding of commercial property loss exposures and insurance coverages, along with some noninsurance alternatives. *Course 2:* To provide a detailed understanding of commercial liability loss exposures, along with the insurance and noninsurance techniques available to deal with them.
Instruction: *Course 1:* Includes exhaustive examination of the major property insurance policies and forms available to business, institutions, and other organizations for dealing with fire and allied lines, marine, crime, boiler, and machinery, and some miscellaneous other exposures. Brief consideration is also given to some noninsurance alternatives. *Course 2:* Includes a review of the basic legal concepts which govern the legal liability of business firms for their acts and omissions and an in-depth analysis of these concepts as they apply to specific liability exposures and insurance coverages associated with premises and operations, products and completed operations, contractual and protective agreements, and employee's liability and workers' compensation.
Credit recommendation: *Course 1:* In the upper division baccalaureate category, 3 semester hours in Insurance or Risk Management. *Course 2:* In the upper division baccalaureate category, 3 semester hours in Insurance or Risk Management (7/79). NOTE: A total of 3 semester hours

of graduate credit should be granted when both Course 1 and Course 2 have been completed, but only if Principles of Risk Management and Insurance (CPCU 1) and Personal Risk Management and Insurance (CPCU 2) have also been completed.

Economics (CPCU 9)
  Location: Various locations through formal courses, informal study groups, or independent study.
  Length: 15 lessons.
  Dates: September 1978-Present.
  Objective: To enable students to understand general economic principles at both the micro and macro levels.
  Instruction: Emphasis is placed on the fundamental concepts of micro and macro economics. Subjects covered include product pricing, national income accounting, monetary and fiscal policy, inflation, unemployment, and the international economy.
  Credit recommendation: In the upper division baccalaureate category, 3 semester hours in Economics (7/79).

Insurance Company Operations (CPCU 5)
  Location: Various locations through formal courses, informal study groups, or independent study.
  Length: 15 lessons.
  Dates: September 1978-Present.
  Objective: To familiarize the student with all of the major functional operations of an insurance company and the interrelationships among them.
  Instruction: Examines insurance marketing, underwriting, reinsurance, rate making, claims adjusting, loss control activities, and other functions and activities. With respect to each, current status and development are explored, and the impact of regulation and other social/environmental factors is considered.
  Credit recommendation: In the upper division baccalaureate category, 3 semester hours in Insurance or Risk Management (7/79). NOTE: Students who have also completed Insurance Issues and Professional Ethics (CPCU 10) should be granted 3 semester hours of graduate credit in Insurance or Risk Management.

Insurance Issues and Professional Ethics (CPCU 10)
  Location: Various locations through formal courses, informal study groups, or independent study.
  Length: 15 lessons.
  Dates: January 1979-Present.
  Objective: To identify and analyze major current insurance issues and examine professional ethics in the context of the American Institute Code of Professional Ethics.
  Instruction: Discuss a wide range of current issues relating to property and liability insurance, including price discrimination and regulation, changes in tort law, captive and government insurers, international insurance. Concludes with an examination of professionalism and ethics, including rules, guidelines, and disciplinary procedures.
  Credit recommendation: In the upper division baccalaureate category, 3 semester hours in Insurance or Risk Management (7/79). NOTE: Students who have also completed Insurance Company Operations (CPCU 5) should be granted 3 semester hours of graduate credit in Insurance or Risk Management.

The Legal Environment of Insurance (CPCU 6)
  Location: Various locations through formal courses, informal study groups, or independent study.
  Length: 15 lessons.
  Dates: January 1979-Present.
  Objective: To develop a basic understanding of business and insurance law.
  Instruction: Course is based on general business law, particularly the areas of contract and agency law, and emphasizes the application of business law to insurance situations. Also deals with the rapidly growing areas of administrative and consumer law.
  Credit recommendation: In the upper division baccalaureate category, 3 semester hours in Business Law, Insurance or Risk Management (7/79).

Management (CPCU 7)
  Location: Various locations through formal courses, informal study groups, or independent study.
  Length: 15 lessons.
  Dates: September 1978-Present.
  Objective: To develop in the student an understanding of the principles of management and of organizational behavior and to give the student an introduction to management information systems.
  Instruction: Topics include the historical development of management, basic management functions, behavioral processes, environmental influences, management information systems, and the decision making process.
  Credit recommendation: In the upper division baccalaureate category, 3 semester hours in Business or Management (7/79).

Personal Risk Management and Insurance (CPCU 2)
  Location: Various locations through formal courses, informal study groups, or independent study.
  Length: 15 lessons.
  Dates: January 1979-Present.
  Objective: To apply risk management and insurance concepts to personal loss exposures.
  Instruction: First half of the course describes the nature of the various personal loss exposures and the effect that our changing society has on them. Also covers homeowners insurance contracts, automobile coverages, and life insurance. Second half of the course covers health insurance, retirement planning, investments, and business insurance and estate planning. Course concludes with a

detailed case analysis.

Credit recommendation: In the upper division baccalaureate category, 3 semester hours in Insurance or Risk Management (7/79). NOTE: If students have completed both this course and Principles of Risk Management and Insurance (CPCU 1), they should be granted 3 semester hours of graduate credit in Insurance or Risk Management.

Principles of Risk Management and Insurance (CPCU 1)

Location: Various locations through formal courses, informal study groups, or independent study.

Length: 15 lessons.

Dates: September 1978-Present.

Objective: To introduce the student to the basic concepts of risk management in insurance.

Instruction: Covers risk management concepts; measurement and treatment of loss exposures; insurance and society; related legal concepts such as indemnity, insurable interests, and tort law: fundamentals of insurance contracts.

Credit recommendation: In the upper division baccalaureate category, 3 semester hours in Insurance or Risk Management (7/79). NOTE: If students have completed both this course and Personal Risk Management and Insurance (CPCU 2), they should be granted 3 semester hours of graduate credit in Insurance or Risk Management.

The goals of the five CPCU courses listed below are to enable students to (1) understand major property and liability insurance contracts and the functions insurers perform in providing insurance protection, (2) apply principles of economics, law, finance, and accounting to property-liability insurance as an economic and social institution, and (3) develop the professional attitudes and communication skills needed to channel their knowledge and energy to best serve the insurance public.

Students who satisfactorily complete all five national examinations and meet ethical and experience requirements are awarded the Chartered Property Casualty Underwriter professional designation.

Analysis of Insurance Functions (CPCU II)

Location: Various locations through formal courses, informal study groups, or independent study.

Length: 30 lessons.

Dates: May 1967-Present.

Objective: To develop a thorough understanding of the functional characteristics of insurance company operations, insurance products and services (including loss prevention), and the environment within which the insurance industry operates.

Instruction: Analyzes the formation and organization of insurers, insurance marketing, risk selection, reinsurance, rate making and reserves, loss prevention, the preparation and scope of insurers' financial statements, and claim management. Course also covers human motivation and professional ethics. Students have the option of pursuing an in-depth study of one of three specialty areas of insurance—adjusting, risk management, or underwriting.

Credit recommendation: In the graduate degree category, 3 semester hours in Insurance; or in the upper division baccalaureate category, 6 semester hours in Insurance (5/77).

Economics, Government, and Business (CPCU III)

Location: Various locations through formal courses, informal study groups, or independent study.

Length: 30 lessons.

Dates: May 1967-Present.

Objective: To develop a basic understanding of micro and macro economics and the application of economics to public policy.

Instruction: National income accounting; price determination; income distribution; monetary and fiscal policy; the theory and practice of international trade; public finance; the economics of the firm under competition, oligopoly, and monopoly. Course also treats government regulation of business, particularly of insurance, in an era of growing social responsibility. Antitrust regulation and the control of competition receive special attention, as does the protection of consumers.

Credit recommendation: In the upper division baccalaureate category, 6 semester hours in Business Administration or Economics (5/77).

Insurance and Business Law (CPCU IV)

Location: Various locations through formal courses, informal study groups, or independent study.

Length: 30 lessons.

Dates: May 1967-Present.

Objective: To develop a basic understanding of business and insurance law.

Instruction: The treatment of contract law is followed by several topics on the distinctive features of insurance policies as contracts. The principles of agency and tort law are illustrated extensively with examples and special situations from an insurance setting. This course also covers the law of bailments, commercial paper, corporations, partnerships, real property, and sales.

Credit recommendation: In the graduate degree category, 3 semester hours in Business Law or Insurance; or in the upper division baccalaureate category, 6 semester hours in Business Law or Insurance (5/77).

Insurance Principles and Practices (CPCU I)

Location: Various locations through formal courses, informal study groups, or independent study.

Length: 30 lessons.

Dates: May 1967-Present.

Objective: To provide an in-depth understanding of insurance principles and practices as they are related to contract analysis and application.

Instruction: Covers the nature of risk; risk-handling techniques; provisions of the standard fire insurance contract and many loss exposures, such as business interruption, ocean and inland marine, general liability, workers' compensation, automobile accidents, fidelity, surety, crime, boiler and machinery. Includes an in-depth study of the insurance contracts applicable to the aforementioned risks, and a survey of individual and group life insurance, annuities, and social insurance.

Credit recommendation: In the graduate degree category, 3 semester hours in Insurance; or in the upper division baccalaureate category, 6 semester hours in Insurance (5/77).

Management, Accounting, and Finance (CPCU V)
   Location: Various locations through formal courses, informal study groups, or independent study.
   Length: 30 lessons.
   Dates: May 1967-Present.
   Objective: To develop an understanding of the principles and applications of accounting, corporate finance, and management.
   Instruction: Topics in management are structured around five basic management functions: planning, organizing, directing, leading, and controlling. The accounting topics cover accounting terms and concepts, and their application in managerial decisions and in the interpretation of financial statements. The topics devoted to corporate finance are designed to teach the objectives of financial management and the available methods of obtaining and using financial resources to maximize the profits of a firm.
   Credit recommendation: In the upper division baccalaureate category, 3 semester hours in Management and 4 semester hours in Accounting/Finance; or in the graduate degree category, 3 semester hours in Financial Management (5/77).

PROGRAM IN GENERAL INSURANCE

(INS 21) Property and Liability Insurance Principles
(Formerly General Principles of Insurance)
   Location: Various locations through formal courses, informal study groups, or independent study.
   Length: 12 lessons.
   Dates: *Version 1:* May 1967-February 1982; *Version 2:* March 1982-Present.
   Objective: To provide the student with an understanding of the basic principles of insurance and of the insurance business.
   Learning Outcome: Upon successful completion of this course, the student will be able to apply skillfully basic insurance principles.
   Instruction: Content covered includes the concept of risk, insurance, risk management, insurance contracts, types of insurers, marketing, loss, claim, loss control, underwriting, reinsurance, pricing, and insurance regulations.
   Credit recommendation: In the upper division baccalaureate category, 2 semester hours in Principles of Insurance or General Business (5/77) (3/82) (4/87). NOTE: This course has been reevaluated and continues to meet requirements for credit recommendations.

(INS 22) Personal Insurance
(Formerly Property Insurance)
   Location: Various locations through formal courses, informal study groups, or independent study.
   Length: 12 lessons.
   Dates: *Version 1:* May 1967-February 1982; *Version 2:* March 1982-August 1987.
   Objective: To provide the student with an understanding of the application of property and marine insurance concepts by insurance professionals and other users.
   Learning Outcome: Upon successful completion of this course, the student will be able to apply skillfully principles of property and marine insurance.
   Instruction: Content covered includes property insurance (including fire, indirect losses and business interruption, burglary and theft, boiler and machinery), ocean and inland marine insurance, and personal and business coverages.
   Credit recommendation: *Version 1:* In the upper division baccalaureate category, 1 semester hour in Insurance (5/77) (3/82). *Version 2:* In the upper division baccalaureate category, 2 semester hours in Property Insurance or General Business (4/87). NOTE: This course has been reevaluated and continues to meet requirements for credit recommendations.

(INS 23) Commercial Insurance
(Formerly Casualty Insurance)
   Location: Various locations through formal courses, informal study groups, or independent study.
   Length: 12 lessons.
   Dates: May 1967-August 1987.
   Objective: To provide the student with an understanding of coverages, policy provisions, and concepts in casualty insurance; bonding; and life, health, and social insurance.
   Learning Outcome: Upon successful completion of this course, the student will be able to apply skillfully relevant coverages, provisions, and concepts required of insurance professionals and other users.
   Instruction: Content covered includes casualty insurance (including liability risks, general liability, workers' compensation, automobile and aviation insurance), bonding, and life, health, and social insurance.
   Credit recommendation: In the upper division bac-

calaureate category, 3 semester hours in Casualty Insurance (5/77) (3/82) (4/87). NOTE: This course has been reevaluated and continues to meet requirements for credit recommendations.

American Institute of Banking - Washington, D.C. Chapter

The American Institute of Banking (AIB) is an educational division of the American Bankers Association. Its total membership comprises 18,500 banks and branches.

AIB has over 500 chapters throughout the United States. All activities are initiated by the local chapter, including the choosing of courses and programs, the selection of instructors, and the arrangements for classroom facilities. Although chapters work in cooperation with the national AIB office, each chapter is administratively autonomous. As a result, credit recommendations established for courses offered by a specific chapter apply only to that chapter.

AIB-Washington chapter sponsors a program in contemporary banking subjects for employees of banking institutions in the Washington, D.C., area. Bank officers, attorneys, certified public accountants, and other qualified professionals teach the courses.

Source of official student records: Executive Director, American Institute of Banking, 5010 Wisconsin Avenue, N.W., Suite 105, Washington, D.C. 20016.

Additional information about the courses: Program on Noncollegiate Sponsored Instruction, The Center for Adult Learning and Educational Credentials, American Council on Education, One Dupont Circle, Washington, D.C. 20036.

Accounting I
Location: Various locations in the Washington, D.C. metropolitan area.
Length: 48 hours (16 weeks).
Dates: August 1978-Present.
Objective: To present to the student the basic concepts, theory, and practices of accounting.
Learning Outcome: Upon successful completion of this course, the student will be able to understand basic accounting terms, concepts and principles; understand the accounting cycle; prepare basic financial statements; and analyze, journalize, and post business transactions.
Instruction: Covers accounting terminology; the recording and classifying of financial transactions, including analyzing and posting; the preparation of the trial balance, work sheet, and financial statements; the handling of adjustments, bad debts, inventory, and depreciation.
Credit recommendation: In the lower division baccalaureate/associate degree category, 3 semester hours in Accounting or Business Administration (3/79) (3/84) (3/89). NOTE: This course has been reevaluated and continues to meet requirements for credit recommendations.

Accounting II
Location: Various locations in the Washington, D.C. metropolitan area.
Length: 45 hours (15 weeks).
Dates: September 1978-Present.
Objective: To provide the student with a further understanding of accounting principles and practices, including corporation accounting, taxation, and basic statement analysis.
Learning Outcome: Upon successful completion of this course, the student will be able to apply managerial cost accounting concepts and procedures, including accounting for manufacturing companies and planning, control and decision making; and perform basic financial statement analysis including the statement of cash flows, the balance sheet, and the income statement.
Instruction: Course is a continuation of Accounting I, including partnership accounting, corporation accounting, taxation, responsibility accounting, cost accounting, and basic statement analysis. (Prerequisite: Accounting I.)
Credit recommendation: In the lower division baccalaureate/associate degree category, 3 semester hours in Accounting (3/79) (5/84) (3/89). NOTE: This course has been reevaluated and continues to meet requirements for credit recommendations.

Analyzing Financial Statements
Location: Various locations in the Washington, D.C. metropolitan area.
Length: 45 hours (15 weeks).
Dates: September 1975-Present.
Objective: To provide the student with the basic theory and skills necessary to apply financial analysis to the financial statements, including the statement of cash flows, to evaluate the current and future financial condition of business firms.
Learning Outcome: Upon successful completion of this course, the student will be able to apply financial ratio analysis to the income statement balance sheet to evaluate the business firm's financial condition; analyze the statement of cash flows to determine the firm's capacity to generate internal cash flows and its need for external financing; and prepare pro forma financial statements and cash budgets and use them for financial planning.
Instruction: Course covers financial ratio analysis, statement of cash flows, pro forma financial statements, cash budgets, financial assumptions sensitivity analysis, and break-even analysis. Methodology includes lecture, discussion, and proctored exercises.
Credit recommendation: In the upper division baccalaureate category, 3 semester hours in Accounting or Finance (3/79) (5/84) (3/89). NOTE: This course has been reevaluated and continues to meet requirements for

credit recommendations.

Bank Investments
Location: Various locations in the Washington, D.C. metropolitan area.
Length: 24 hours (3 hours per week for 8 weeks).
Dates: August 1984-Present.
Objective: To teach bankers the fundamentals of investments most often encountered in their work, i.e., treasury securities, government securities, money market investments, and securities markets.
Learning Outcome: Upon successful completion of this course, the student will be able to understand skills needed to coordinate inflows and outflows of bank funds; manage the bank's investment account; and understand key concepts of bank investments and fund management.
Instruction: Course provides an introduction to investment and investment analysis, financial markets, money market investments, federal agency securities, municipal securities, and U.S. Treasury securities. Methodology includes lecture, discussion, and classroom exercises.
Credit recommendation: In the upper division baccalaureate category, 2 semester hours in Banking, Business Administration, or Finance (3/89).

Bank Management
(Commercial Banking)
Location: Various locations in the Washington, D.C. metropolitan area.
Length: 45 hours (15 weeks).
Dates: September 1976-May 1979.
Objective: To provide an understanding of commercial banking and its role in the economy.
Instruction: Commercial bank functions, bank capital and earnings, lending policies and procedures, bank investments, and bank audits.
Credit recommendation: In the lower division baccalaureate/associate degree category, 3 semester hours in Banking (3/79).

Bank Marketing: Theory and Applications
Location: Various locations in the Washington, D.C. metropolitan area.
Length: 45 hours (2½ hours per week for 15 weeks).
Dates: January 1987-Present.
Objective: To provide the student with a basic introduction to marketing and to explore applications of these concepts within a bank setting. Some of the topics presented in this course include marketing management, pricing, market planning, consumer behavior, and marketing research.
Learning Outcome: Upon successful completion of this course, the student will be able to interrelate and coordinate the multi-functions involved in the marketing process; integrate customer behavior factors into plans and strategies; have a better understanding of service offering development processes, pricing decisions, promotional strategies, and delivery alternatives; and be able to specify and use marketing information in marketing decisions.
Instruction: Course covers basic marketing, strategic marketing, understanding the market, marketing mix strategies, and bank marketing topics. Methodology includes lecture and discussion.
Credit recommendation: In the lower division baccalaureate/associate degree category, 3 semester hours in Business Administration, Finance, or Principles of Marketing (3/89).

Business Law
(Banking Law)
Location: Various locations in the Washington, D.C. metropolitan area.
Length: *Version 1:* 20 hours (3 hours for 10 weeks). Students complete 3 hours of outside preparation per week for this course. *Version 2:* 30 hours (3 hours for 10 weeks).
Dates: *Version 1:* October 1981-February 1989. *Version 2:* March 1989-Present.
Objective: To acquaint students with general principles of commercial law emphasizing transactions.
Learning Outcome: Upon successful completion of this course, the student will be able to understand the various aspects of the uniform commercial code; reason through simple legal problems; and understand contract law.
Instruction: Covers principles of commercial law and gives students insight and practice into reasoning through simple legal problems. Lecture and discussion are used to develop the students' appreciation for the legal method of problem analysis and resolution.
Credit recommendation: *Version 1:* In the upper division baccalaureate category, 3 semester hours in Business Law (5/84). *Version 2:* In the upper division baccalaureate category, 2 semester hours in Accounting, Business Administration, Business Law, or Finance (3/89). NOTE: This course has been reevaluated and continues to meet requirements for credit recommendations.

Business Law: Selected Topics
(1. Banking Law/Lending)
(2. Banking Law/Operations)
Location: Various locations in the Washington, D.C. metropolitan area.
Length: *Version 1:* 15 hours (2½ hours for 5 weeks). *Version 2.* 15 hours (3 hours for 5 weeks).
Dates: *Version 1:* May 1984-February 1989. *Version 2:* March 1989-Present.
Objective: *Version 1:* To expand the students' legal knowledge in selected topics in Business Law with special emphasis on bank operations. *Version 2:* To acquaint the student with selected topics in Business Law with special emphasis on bank lending, secured credit, and truth lending.
Learning Outcome: Upon successful completion of this

course, the student will be able to understand the application of business law to bank operations; and relate business law to selected topics including bank lending, secured credit, and truth lending.

Instruction: Concentrates on legal issues which affect the bank employee in a number of areas including check clearance, bank liability, and electronic funds transfers. Methodology includes lecture and discussion.

Credit recommendation: *Version 1:* In the upper division baccalaureate category, 3 semester hours in Business Law (5/84). *Version 2:* In the upper division baccalaureate category, 2 semester hours in Accounting, Business Administration, Business Law, or Finance (3/89). NOTE: Students can receive 1 semester hour for completing either Lending or Operations and 2 semester hours for completing both. NOTE: This course has been reevaluated and continues to meet requirements for credit recommendations.

Cash Management I and II

Location: Various locations in the Washington, D.C. metropolitan area.
Length: 45 hours (2½ hours per week for 15 weeks).
Dates: August 1983-Present.
Objective: This two-part course provides bankers with concise understanding of current and emerging domestic commercial cash management services and systems.
Learning Outcome: Upon successful completion of this course, the student will be able to understand the marketing of cash management services; understand electronic trends related to cash management; and assess cash management needs and problems.
Instruction: Course covers cash collection, short term investment, cash disbursement, information and control, cash management regulation, the corporate services mix, and cash management risk. Methodology includes lecture, discussion, exercises, video, and field visits.
Credit recommendation: In the upper division baccalaureate category, 3 semester hours in Banking, Business Administration, or Finance (3/89).

Commercial Loan Case Simulation

Location: Various locations in the Washington, D.C. metropolitan area.
Length: 10 weeks (3 hour meetings weekly).
Dates: March 1983-April 1986.
Objective: To enable students to analyze and understand actual commercial credit applications and loan pricing in a competitive environment.
Instruction: Commercial Loan Case Simulation is a computer "game" played by teams of three or four lenders competing against each other as they track the decisions made about a group of actual loans over a "four-year" period. The areas of the loan decisions that will be stressed are competitive pricing, business financial statement and management analysis, bank financial performance, goal setting and attainment, and credit investigation, cost/benefit analysis. In addition, to the computer feedback, there will be lectures, individual instructor attention for teams, and small group interaction. Teams of three or four people from the same bank are encouraged to compete against other teams for what is an invaluable learning experience.
Credit recommendation: In the upper division baccalaureate category, 2 semester hours in Finance (5/84).

Consumer Credit (860)

Location: Various locations in the Washington, D.C. metropolitan area.
Length: 45 hours (2½ hours per week for 15 weeks).
Dates: August 1987-Present.
Objective: To provide the student with a basic understanding of credit services available to consumers.
Learning Outcome: Upon successful completion of this course, the student will be familiar with state and federal regulations and laws governing consumer credit; know the various types of consumer loans and the consumer lending process; and understand the planning, organizing, directing, and controlling of the consumer credit function.
Instruction: Course covers consumer credit legislation and regulation, open-end and closed-end consumer credit, credit process, including investigation, decision making, documentation and collection, and credit policies and credit management. Methodology includes lecture, class discussion, and practical exercises.
Credit recommendation: In the lower division baccalaureate/associate degree category, 3 semester hours in Business Administration, Consumer Credit Management, Finance, or Marketing (3/89).

Economics

Location: Various locations in the Washington, D.C. metropolitan area.
Length: 45 hours (15 weeks).
Dates: September 1976-Present.
Objective: To provide the student with knowledge of basic economic principles.
Learning Outcome: Upon successful completion of this course, the student will be able to understand the relationship between micro and macro ecomomic principles and applications; apply the basic concepts of supply, demand, and pricing to banking activities; and apply and understand national income accounting and its contributions to productivity and related topics.
Instruction: Course covers basic economic concepts; measurement of national output and income; national income analysis; monetary and fiscal policy; basic demand, supply, and price concepts.
Credit recommendation: In the lower division baccalaureate/associate degree category, 3 semester hours in Economics (3/79) (5/84) (3/89). NOTE: This course has been reevaluated and continues to meet requirements for credit recommendations.

Fundamentals of Bank Data Processing
  Location: Various locations in the Washington, D.C. metropolitan area.
  Length: 45 hours (15 weeks).
  Dates: September 1978-March 1982.
  Objective: To provide the student with a basic understanding of the fundamentals of data processing and the computer.
  Instruction: Course covers data processing, business applications, punched card systems computer concepts, basic flow-charting, and the programming cycle.
  Credit recommendation: In the lower division baccalaureate/associate degree category, 3 semester hours in Business Administration (3/79).

Installment Credit
  Location: Various locations in the Washington, D.C. metropolitan area.
  Length: 45 hours (15 weeks).
  Dates: September 1976-May 1981.
  Objective: To provide the student with a basic knowledge of installment credit and its administration.
  Instruction: Course covers credit evaluation, techniques of installment lending, leasing of consumer goods, legal aspects of installment credit, collection policies, rate structure.
  Credit recommendation: In the lower division baccalaureate/associate degree category, 3 semester hours in Banking, Business Administration, or Finance (3/79) (5/84). NOTE: This course has been reevaluated and continues to meet requirements for credit recommendations.

International Banking
  Location: Various locations in the Washington, D.C. metropolitan area.
  Length: 30 hours (2 hours per week for 15 weeks).
  Dates: August 1987-Present.
  Objective: To provide the student a broad introductory exposure to the area of international banking and financial transactions. The course covers international operations, credit, and trading exchange policies as they concern the international banking community.
  Learning Outcome: Upon successful completion of this course, the student will be able to evaluate various country risk assessments as they pertain to economic and political factors; understand the international finance transaction; understand the role of correspondent banking as it pertains to international markets; appreciate the trends in international monetary exchange; and translate and evaluate letters of credit both from issuing and utilization standpoint.
  Instruction: Course covers organization and structure of the international monetary markets, how transactions concerning transfer of funds, foreign trade collection, letters of credit, and the basic principles of foreign trade and exchange are examined. Development of policies for exchange by government agencies to facilitate international financial transactions is also covered. Methodology includes lecture, discussion, case preparation and presentation.
  Credit recommendation: In the upper division baccalaureate category, 3 semester hours in Business Administration, Finance, or International Business (3/89).

Introduction to Financial Planning
  Location: Various locations in the Washington, D.C. metropolitan area.
  Length: 45 hours (15 weeks).
  Dates: October 1983-August 1988.
  Objective: To develop the student's awareness of the financial services industry, within both the banking area and other areas as well.
  Instruction: This course provides a broad range of insights into the financial planning industry in which the bankers are becoming more involved as the result of deregulation. Upon completion, students will not be financial planners; they will have an overview of the planning process and what is required to be competitive in the environment of high inflation and taxes. The text is used to provide a source of information upon which case situations are applied. Actual case situations of the instructor are used to reinforce the learning process. Student actual case situations are encouraged.
  Credit recommendation: In the lower division baccalaureate/associate degree category, 3 semester hours in Personal Finance (5/84).

Law and Banking I
  Location: Various locations in the Washington, D.C. metropolitan area.
  Length: 45 hours (15 weeks).
  Dates: September 1975-March 1981.
  Objective: To provide the student with a basic knowledge of business law.
  Instruction: Introduction to business law; the uniform commercial code, including legal rights, contracts, personal property, and bailments; risk and property rights in sales; partnerships, and corporations.
  Credit recommendation: In the upper division baccalaureate category, 3 semester hours in Business Administration (3/79).

Management of Commercial Bank Funds
  Location: Various locations in the Washington, D.C. metropolitan area.
  Length: 45 hours (15 weeks).
  Dates: September 1975-March 1981.
  Objective: To provide the student with an understanding of the principles of funds management in commercial banks.
  Instruction: Course emphasizes the importance of funds management in coordinating policies on loans,

deposits, investments, and capital. (Prerequisite: Accounting I or Economics.)

Credit recommendation: In the upper division baccalaureate category, 3 semester hours in Banking, Business Administration, or Finance (3/79).

Money and Banking
Location: Various locations in the Washington, D.C. metropolitan area.
Length: 45 hours (15 weeks).
Dates: January 1976-Present.
Objective: *Version 1:* To understand the functions of money in the U.S. and how the Federal Reserve and the commercial banking system influence money supply, banking, and availability of credit. *Version 2:* To provide the student with the basic understanding of the history and functions of the American banking system.
Instruction: The development of the U.S. monetary and banking system; Federal Reserve monetary policy and its effect on commercial banking; the quantity theory of money (monetarist approach) and the Keynesian approach; the effectiveness of monetary policy; determination of interest rates; availability of credit. (Prerequisite: Economics.)
Credit recommendation: In the upper division baccalaureate category, 3 semester hours in Economics (3/79) (5/84) (3/89). NOTE: This course has been reevaluated and continues to meet requirements for credit recommendations.

Principles of Banking
(Formerly Principles of Bank Operations)
Location: Various locations in the Washington, D.C. metropolitan area.
Length: 45 hours (15 weeks).
Dates: March 1979-Present.
Objective: To provide the student with an understanding of the fundamentals of bank functions.
Learning Outcome: Upon successful completion of this course, the student will be able to understand and apply the basic principles of banking operations to various types and situations surrounding banking activities; provide a full range of services to customers of a standard or basic banking institution; be able to apply the various banking functions such as check processing, bookkeeping, deposits and others as they pertain to the public; and appreciate the relationship between banks, the community, and various governmental agencies.
Instruction: Course covers negotiable instruments; deposits and payments; loans and investments; basic accounting; marketing, advertising; legal relations with depositors.
Credit recommendation: In the lower division baccalaureate/associate degree category, 3 semester hours in Banking, Business Administration, or Finance (3/79) (5/84) (3/89). NOTE: This course has been reevaluated and continues to meet requirements for credit recommendations.

Principles of Commercial Banking
Location: Various locations in the Washington, D.C. metropolitan area.
Length: 35 hours (10 weeks).
Dates: October 1981-Present.
Objective: To provide the student with an understanding of the fundamentals of bank functions, including the organizational structure and financial management philosophy of banks.
Learning Outcome: Upon successful completion of this course, the student will be able to understand the organizational and financial management philosophy of banks; know the bank functions, including the deposit, lending, and investment functions; analyze bank performance and know bank planning techniques; and be familiar with branch banking, bank holding companies, and international banking.
Instruction: Course covers the role of banking in the economy; banking history; management and internal organization of commercial banks; asset, liability, and capital management; profitability; credit analysis and loan policies; short term and long term loans; real estate and consumer lending; and bank investments.
Credit recommendation: In the upper division baccalaureate category, 3 semester hours in Banking or Finance (5/84) (3/89). NOTE: This course has been reevaluated and continues to meet requirements for credit recommendations.

Real Estate Finance
Location: Various locations in the Washington, D.C. metropolitan area.
Length: 45 hours (2½ hours per week for 15 weeks).
Dates: February 1989-Present.
Objective: To provide the student with a broad understanding of real property finance and its role in meeting the needs of both the borrower and the financial institution.
Learning Outcome: Upon successful completion of this course, the student will be able to understand and appreciate the real estate finance industry; be familiar with underwriting, closing and administration of both residential and income property loans; and apply the fundamental principles of an analysis to real property investment.
Instruction: Course covers real estate law, the lending process, appraisal of both the borrower as well as the properties, various types of properties and peculiarities associated with each. The administrative process and task involved in managing most mortgage departments including constructions loans are also covered. Methodology includes lecture, discussion, cases, and workshops.
Credit recommendation: In the upper division baccalaureate category, 3 semester hours in Business Ad-

ministration, Finance, or Real Estate (3/89).

Trust Banking
Location: Various locations in the Washington, D.C. metropolitan area.
Length: 24 hours (3 hours per week for 8 weeks).
Dates: February 1984-Present.
Objective: To provide the student with a basic knowledge of trust management and operations.
Learning Outcome: Upon successful completion of this course, the student will be able to know the various types of assets managed by trust departments, and the basis of wills and trusts; understand trust investment management; be familiar with corporate trusts, charitable trusts, and consumer trusts; and be familiar with trust operations.
Instruction: Course covers types of assets managed by trust departments, investment management, trusts and wills, fiduciary service to consumers, including estate settlements, corporate and employee benefit trusts, and trust operations. Methodology includes lecture, discussion, and written examinations.
Credit recommendation: In the lower division baccalaureate/associate degree category, 2 semester hours in Business Administration, Finance, or Trust Banking (3/89).

American International Group, Inc.

The education department of the American International Group, Inc. (AIG), headquartered in New York City, conducts training and educational activities in regional offices throughout the United States and Canada. Several professional staff members at the home office engage in both administration and teaching.

AIG courses are developed in response to corporate needs as expressed by senior and/or line management or as uncovered by the education department's on-going needs analyses. Attendance and completion of requirements are criteria for certification of all AIG students.

Source of official student records: The Registrar, Education Department, American International Group, Inc., 70 Pine Street, New York, NY 10005.

Additional information about the courses: Program on Noncollegiate Sponsored Instruction, The Center for Adult Learning and Educational Credentials, American Council on Education, One Dupont Circle, Washington, D.C. 20036.

Administrative Secretary Skills Seminar
Location: New York, NY and regional offices in the U.S. and Canada.
Length: 16 hours (2 days).
Dates: January 1976-September 1985.
Objective: To develop effective communication skills for secretarial personnel.
Instruction: Skills in communication, problem solving, and time management. Lecture, discussion, and case studies are used.
Credit recommendation: In the lower division baccalaureate/associate degree category, 1 semester hour in Office Practices or Secretarial Procedures (3/80).

Basic Typewriting
Location: New York, NY.
Length: 45 hours (over a 2 1/2-month period).
Dates: September 1975-September 1985.
Objective: To refine keyboarding techniques; to produce letters, memoranda, and reports in acceptable business format; and to develop a straight copy typing speed of 40 wpm.
Instruction: Basic typewriting techniques; speed development; and appropriate formats for letters, memos, tabulations, and manuscripts. Lecture, individualized instruction, and laboratory exercises are used.
Credit recommendation: In the lower division baccalaureate/associate degree category, 3 semester hours in Secretarial Science (3/80).

Counselor Selling
Location: New York, NY and regional offices in the U.S. and Canada.
Length: 30 hours (1 week).
Dates: March 1969-September 1985.
Objective: To develop professional counseling and problem-solving techniques in selling, managing, and other working relationships. For sales, managerial, and other professionals.
Instruction: Creativity, motivation, human relations, listening, and other communication skills. Lecture, discussion, role playing, fact finding, presentation, and closing techniques are used.
Credit recommendation: In the lower division baccalaureate/associate degree category, 1 semester hour in General Business or Salesmanship (3/80).

Effective Oral Presentation
Location: New York, NY.
Length: 21 hours (3 days).
Dates: January 1976-September 1985.
Objective: To provide principles and practices of oral communication for professional or managerial personnel.
Instruction: Formal and informal models of oral communication skills, with some emphasis on selection, design, and use of visual aids as a communication technique. Video presentations are taped and critiqued. Lecture, discussion, and classroom exercises are used.
Credit recommendation: In the lower division baccalaureate/associate degree category, 2 semester hours in Oral Communication or Speech (3/80).

Introduction to Gregg Shorthand Theory
   Location: New York, NY.
   Length: 70 hours (over a 3 1/2-month period).
   Dates: February 1978-September 1985.
   Objective: To introduce the theory of Gregg shorthand, to develop an ability to read from plate and personal notes, to take dictation at 60 wpm, and to transcribe dictation in mailable form.
   Instruction: Principles of Gregg shorthand integrating vocabulary, spelling, grammar, and punctuation skills with proper proportion and fluency. Dictation at 60 wpm and transcribing in mailable form.
   Credit recommendation: In the lower division baccalaureate/associate degree category, 3 semester hours in Secretarial Science (3/80).

Principles of Insurance
(New Career Employee Training Program)
   Location: New York, NY.
   Length: 140 hours (4 weeks), plus 60 hours of out-of-class activities.
   Dates: *Version 1:* January 1970-August 1985; *Version 2:* September 1985-Present.
   Objective: *Version 1:* To enable students to understand basic insurance terminology and concepts, and the operation of the insurance industry; to introduce principles and instruments related to coverages and policy provisions for various types of insurance. *Version 2:* To provide students with a basic understanding of the insurance industry.
   Instruction: *Version 1:* Relevant sources of information on and basic language of insurance and the insurance industry. Lectures, field trips, projects, case studies, and demonstrations are used. *Version 2:* Course covers insurance terminology and concepts, the principles, coverages, and policy provisions for specific types of insurance. Lectures by a variety of specialists, field assignments, projects, case studies, and discussion are used.
   Credit recommendation: *Version 1:* In the upper division baccalaureate category, 4 semester hours in Insurance (3/80). *Version 2:* In the upper division baccalaureate or graduate degree category, 3 semester hours in Insurance (9/85). NOTE: This course has been reevaluated and continues to meet requirements for credit recommendations.

Shorthand and Transcription (Gregg/Pitman)
   Location: New York, NY.
   Length: 36 hours (over a 2 1/2-month period).
   Dates: September 1973-September 1985.
   Objective: To review shorthand theory, to introduce transcription techniques, to refine grammar and punctuation skills, and to develop an ability to take dictation at 80 wpm and transcribe in mailable form.
   Instruction: Review Gregg/Pitman theory, phraseology, the writing of shorthand with fluency and proportion, dictation at 80 wpm, and transcribing mailable copy.
   Credit recommendation: In the lower division baccalaureate/associate degree category, 3 semester hours in Secretarial Science (3/80).

Supervisory Management
   Location: New York, NY and regional offices in the U.S.
   Length: 5 hours of lecture plus a wrap-up session; 15 hours of self-study.
   Dates: February 1979-September 1985.
   Objective: To enable the student to understand basic concepts in supervision of employees and the role of supervisors in an organization.
   Instruction: Supervisory skills with preparation of a three-step plan for extension of course content in future supervisory activities. Lectures and self-study materials (audiocassettes and workbooks) with pre- and post-tests used.
   Credit recommendation: In the lower division baccalaureate/associate degree category, 1 semester hour in General Business or Supervision (3/80).

American Medical Record Association

The American Medical Record Association (AMRA) is a nonprofit membership association. Control of the association is by the membership of the association through action of the House of Delegates and of the Board of Directors of the Association. The staff of the Independent Study Division, which is responsible for the administration of the Independent Study Program in Medical Record Technology, includes registered record administrators, administrative personnel, and secretarial-clerical personnel. All Independent Study Division personnel are full time. Instructors, after having been approved through Criteria for Instructors and Instructors Qualification Record for the State of Illinois are required to complete an orientation program prepared by AMRA.

The Essentials of an Accredited Educational program for the Medical Record Technician established by the American Medical Record Association Council on Education in collaboration with the American Medical Association were used to develop the Independent Study Program in Medical Record Technology. The program has been reviewed and approved by the AMRA Council on Education. The Health Record Management in Nursing Homes course, which was discontinued in 1984, was developed as a result of a Health Resources Administration contract from the Department of Health, Education, and Welfare.

External review and assistance in course development are available from the AMRA Council on Education, the professional staff of the AMRA, and instructors.

Source of official student records: Director, American Medical Record Association, Independent Study Division, 875 North Michigan Avenue, Suite 1850, Chicago, IL 60611.

Additional information about the courses: Program on Noncollegiate Sponsored Instruction, The Center for Adult Learning and Educational Credentials, American Council on Education, One Dupont Circle, Washington, D.C. 20036.

Health Record Management in Nursing Homes

Location: Correspondence Program
Length: 12 months (1 year); 14 lessons.
Dates: July 1980-July 1984.
Objective: To provide nursing home personnel with the skills necessary to maintain health care records at the levels required by federal and state governmental regulations.
Instruction: Covers introduction to health care in the United States with emphasis on nursing homes as part of the health care system, basic principles and techniques of communication, introduction to medical terminology, filing and numbering systems, admitting procedures in nursing homes, legal aspects of health records, organizing health record information, analysis of health records, disease classification and coding, statistics, management principles, utilization review procedures, medical care evaluation and PSRO's in nursing homes.
Credit recommendation: Lessons 1-14: In the lower division baccalaureate/associate degree category, 2-4 semester hours in Clinical Practice or Medical Records Technology. Lessons 1-14: In the lower division baccalaureate category or in the graduate degree category, 3 semester hours as an elective in Health Care Administration and other related fields or Social Work. Lessons 12, 13, and 14 only: In the lower division baccalaureate/associate degree category or in the upper division baccalaureate category or in the graduate degree category, 2 semester hours as an elective in Federal Health Regulations (9/80) (7/86). NOTE: These credit recommendations are not additive.

Independent Study Program in Medical Record Technology

Location: Correspondence Program.
Length: 96 lessons over 17 modules (maximum time for completion is 36 months).
Dates: March 1979-Present.
Objective: To improve patient care through increased knowledge of medical record practices and procedures.
Instruction: Covers Orientation to the Health Care Field; Health Record Content and Format; Medical Terminology; Medical Transcription, Numbering and Filing Systems: Indexes, Registers; Legal Aspects of Health Information; Admitting Procedures; Health Statistics; Medical Staff; Basic Pathology of Disease Process; Nomenclature and Classification Systems; Federal Health Programs; Quality Assurance; Trends in Health Care Delivery; Supervisory Principles and Practice; Planning for Health Information Services; Directed Clinical Practice.
Credit recommendation: In the lower division baccalaureate/associate degree category or in the upper division baccalaureate category, 30-33 semester hours in Medical Record Technology (2/80) (7/86). NOTE: This course has been reevaluated and continues to meet requirements for credit recommendations.

1. Orientation to the Health Care Field

Location: Correspondence Program.
Length: *Version 1:* Lessons 1-3 (Module 1 of a 17-module program in medical record technology); *Version 2:* Lessons 1-3 (Module 1 of a 17-module program in medical record technology).
Dates: *Version 1:* March 1979-May 1985; *Version 2:* June 1985-Present.
Objective: *Version 1:* To provide an introduction to the health care field, including the history of medicine and health records, and health care in the United States. *Version 2:* To provide overview of the Health Care Delivery system and the role of the Medical Record Technician.
Instruction: *Version 1:* Overview of the history of medicine and healthy records from ancient times to the present; health care in the United States, including the growth, development, and role of health-related associations, organizations, and local, state, and federal agencies. *Version 2:* Overview of the health care delivery system including health care facilities and services, practitioners, organizations and consumers, content and purposes of the medical record, and a description of American Medical Record Association history and organization.
Credit recommendation: *Version 1:* In the lower division baccalaureate/associate degree category or in the upper division baccalaureate category, 1 semester hour in Community Health, Historical Aspects of Medicine and Health Care, or Introduction to Allied Health Careers (2/80). *Version 2:* In the lower division baccalaureate/associate degree category, 1 semester hour in Introduction to Health Care Delivery Systems, or Introduction to Medical Record Technology (6/85) (7/86). NOTE: This course has been reevaluated and continues to meet requirements for credit recommendations.

2. Health Record Content and Format
(Formerly Module 7)

Location: Correspondence Program.
Length: 7 lessons (Module 2 of a 17-module program in medical record technology).
Dates: March 1979-Present.
Objective: To discuss content and format of the health record in short-term hospitals, skilled nursing and intermediate care facilities, mental health, home health care,

and ambulatory care facilities.

Instruction: Definition and purpose of a health record; arrangement patterns for records; record forms for specific events occurring during stay in hospital; quantitative and qualitative analysis; problem-oriented medical records; minimum information required; major components of history, X-ray, operative reports, and obstetrical health records; source-oriented, integrated, and problem-oriented record formats in skilled nursing, intermediate care, mental health, home health, and ambulatory care facilities.

Credit recommendation: In the lower division baccalaureate/associate degree category or in the upper division baccalaureate category, 3 semester hours in Hospital Administration, Medical Office Assisting, or Medical Record Science (2/80) (7/86). NOTE: This course has been reevaluated and continues to meet requirements for credit recommendations.

3. Medical Terminology
(Formerly Module 2)

Location: Correspondence Program.

Length: 16 lessons (Module 3 of a 17-module program in medical record technology).

Dates: March 1979-Present.

Objective: To help students acquire the specialized vocabulary necessary for reading and understanding the language of medicine and for communicating with other health care professionals.

Instruction: The module consists of 16 lessons. The first introduces word elements used to form medical terms; ten lessons present medical terms pertaining to various body systems; three lessons contain medical terms related to oncology, systemic diseases, and special types of therapies; the last lesson presents terminology relating to anesthesiology, pharmacology, and medicine in general.

Credit recommendation: In the lower division baccalaureate/associate degree category or in the upper division baccalaureate category, 4 semester hours in Medical Terminology or other appropriate health-related programs (2/80) (7/86). NOTE: This course has been reevaluated and continues to meet requirements for credit recommendations.

4. Medical Transcription
(Formerly Module 3)

Location: Correspondence Program.

Length: *Version 1:* 3 lessons (Module 3 of a 17-module program in medical record technology); *Version 2:* 3 lessons (Module 4 of a 17-module program).

Dates: *Version 1:* March 1970-May 1985; *Version 2:* June 1985-Present.

Objective: To provide an introduction to the basic techniques of medical transcription and practical experience in transcribing medical reports.

Instruction: *Version 1:* Covers basic techniques of processing and typing medical reports and provides extensive student practice in typing reports in patient histories and physicals, radiology, operations, pathology, discharge summaries and autopsies. *Version 2:* Self-instructional lessons, practice tapes, and exercises covering dictation and word processing equipment, punctuation and editing, and ethical and legal aspects of medical transcription are used. Extensive practical reinforcement.

Credit recommendation: *Version 1:* In the lower division baccalaureate/associate degree category or in the upper division baccalaureate category, 2 semester hours in Medical Office Transcription, Medical Report Transcription, or Medical Secretarial Transcription (2/80). *Version 2:* in the lower division baccalaureate/associate degree category, 3 semester hours in Medical Record Transcription or in the upper division baccalaureate category, 2 semester hours in Medical Record Transcription (6/85) (7/86). NOTE: This course has been reevaluated and continues to meet requirements for credit recommendations.

5. Numbering and Filing Systems; Indexes; Registers
(Formerly Module 4)

Location: Correspondence Program.

Length: 3 lessons (Module 5 of a 17-module program in medical record technology).

Dates: March 1979-Present.

Objective: To provide an introduction to numbering, filing, and indexing techniques commonly used in health care institutions.

Instruction: Covers acceptable practices in maintaining health records, including types of supplies and equipment used and the common indexes and registers used and the methods used to compile them. In addition, students complete the following practical assignments: organizing a terminal digit file; preparing papers justifying a new and/or existing numbering and filing system for a hospital health information service; practicing alphabetical and phonetical filing, completing an accession register, and thorough Tumor Registry and Cancer Program coverage.

Credit recommendation: In the lower division baccalaureate/associate degree category or in the upper division baccalaureate category, 1 semester hour in Numbering and Filing Systems, Indexes, and Registers Related to Health Information (2/80) (7/86). NOTE: This course has been reevaluated and continues to meet requirements for credit recommendations.

6. Legal Aspects of Health Information

Location: Correspondence Program.

Length: 4 lessons (Module 6 of a 17-module program in medical record technology).

Dates: March 1979-Present.

Objective: To provide knowledge of the legal aspects of health information.

Instruction: Overview of the United States legal system; concepts of confidentiality, patient's rights, consents, and authorization for treatments; the health record as a legal document, release of health information; methods of retention and destruction of health records.

Credit recommendation: In the lower division baccalaureate/associate degree category or in the upper division baccalaureate category, 1 semester hour in Legal Aspects of Health Information in Allied Health Careers or Medical Record Science (2/80) (7/86). NOTE: This course has been reevaluated and continues to meet requirements for credit recommendations.

8. Health Statistics

Location: Correspondence Program.
Length: 6 lessons (Module 8 of a 17-module program in medical record technology).
Dates: March 1979-Present.
Objective: To provide an introduction to and practical application of health statistics, and collection and graphic presentation of statistical data used in the health care field.
Instruction: An introduction to health statistics emphasizing the collection and display of descriptive statistical data such as average length of stay and occupancy, death, autopsy, and infection rates. Students are required to complete the following practical assignments: statistical calculations, census projects, discharge analysis projects, data abstracting, graphic display, and flowcharting.
Credit recommendation: In the lower division baccalaureate/associate degree category or in the upper division baccalaureate category, 1 semester hour in Descriptive Statistical Techniques Applied to the Health Field, Health Information Statistics, or Hospital Statistics (2/80) (7/86). NOTE: This course has been reevaluated and continues to meet requirements for credit recommendations.

9. Medical Staff

Location: Correspondence Program.
Length: 3 lessons (Module 9 of a 17-module program in medical record technology).
Dates: March 1979-Present.
Objective: To discuss the role of the medical staff in various health care settings and outpatient services.
Instruction: Organization of the medical staff in a hospital setting: primary divisions of responsibilities; the bylaws, rules and regulations of the medical staff; responsibilities and functions of the staff for quality medical practice; audits; roles of hospital committees utilization review in the evaluation of health care; role and responsibilities of the medical staff in long-term care facilities and ambulatory care settings.
Credit recommendation: In the lower division baccalaureate/associate degree category or in the upper division baccalaureate category, 1 semester hour in Hospital Administration, Medical Record Science, or Medical and Health-related Career Programs (2/80) (7/86). NOTE: This course has been reevaluated and continues to meet requirements for credit recommendations.

10. Basic Pathology of Disease Process

Location: Correspondence Program.
Length: 24 lessons (Module 10 of a 17-module program in medical record technology).
Dates: March 1979-Present.
Objective: To provide an overview of basic pathology of disease processes.
Instruction: In addition to readings in a basic text on general principles of disease and diseases which affect specific organs of the body, the module is supplemented by 24 lessons, including lessons in vocabulary. Sixteen of the lessons use filmstrips of photomicrographs. Each student receives a portable viewing instrument.
Credit recommendation: In the lower division baccalaureate/associate degree category or in the upper division baccalaureate category, 3 semester hours in introductory courses in Medical Science or Pathophysiology (2/80) (7/86). NOTE: This course has been reevaluated and continues to meet requirements for credit recommendations.

11. Nomenclature and Classification Systems

Location: Correspondence Program.
Length: 3 lessons (Lessons 2, 3, 4). (Module 11 of a 17-module program in medical record technology).
Dates: *Version 1:* March 1979-May 1985; *Version 2:* June 1985-Present.
Objective: *Version 1:* To provide information about the classification systems for health record data. *Version 2:* To provide students with currently accepted knowledge in nomenclature and health record classification systems, and an understanding of their value in the health care setting.
Instruction: *Version 1:* International classification of diseases, diseases for oncology, selected nomenclature and classification systems, and the coding of health information in a variety of settings, including hospitals, skilled nursing facilities, intermediate care facilities, home health programs, and ambulatory care facilities. *Version 2:* Four self-instructional lessons including case history assignments. Covers past and present nomenclature and classification systems including ICD-9-CM and its application to Diagnostic Related Groups. Extensive practice in coding of single diseases and procedures to abstracting complex diagnosis and procedures.
Credit recommendation: *Version 1:* In the lower division baccalaureate/associate degree category or in the upper division baccalaureate category, 2 semester hours in Medical Record Science (2/80). *Version 2:* In the lower division baccalaureate/associate degree category, 4 semester hours in Medical Record Classification Systems or Medical Record Science (6/85) (7/86). NOTE: This course has been reevaluated and continues to meet requirements for credit recommendations.

12. Federal Health Programs

Location: Correspondence Program.

Length: 6 lessons (Module 12 of a 17-module program in medical record technology).

Dates: *Version 1:* March 1979-June 1986; *Version 2:* July 1986-Present.

Objective: To provide an overview of the Department of Health and Human Services, as well as the five major federal health programs: Medicare and Medicaid, Professional Standards Review Organizations, Health Maintenance Organizations, End-State Renal Disease Programs and Health Systems Agencies.

Instruction: *Version 1:* Overview of structure and functions of Department of Health and Human Services; conditions of participation for providers and suppliers of service: requirements and responsibilities of Public Law 92-603 establishing Professional Standards Review Organization (PSRO); responsibilities and structure of Health Maintenance Organization (HMO); structure and function of End-State Renal Disease Program (ESRP); and roles and responsibilities of Health Systems Agencies (HSA). *Version 2:* Overview of the federal government and health care, including a description of the Department of Health and Human Services; financing health care, including information on medicare and medicaid; prospective payment system; Peer Review Organizations (PROs); conditions of participation; and uniform reporting, including information on UHDDS and UB-82.

Credit recommendation: In the lower division baccalaureate/associate degree category or in the upper division baccalaureate category, 2 semester hours in Hospital Administration, Nursing Home Administration, Public Health Administration or in Programs for Physicians' Assistants (2/80) (7/86). NOTE: This course has been reevaluated and continues to meet requirements for credit recommendations.

13. Quality Assurance
(Formerly Medical Care Evaluation)

Location: Correspondence Program.

Length: 4 lessons (Module 13 of a 17-module program in medical record technology).

Dates: March 1979-Present.

Objective: To provide an introduction to the purpose of quality assurance programs in the health care field and the implementation of these programs.

Learning Outcome: Upon successful completion of this course, the student will be able to define quality assurance and describe its importance in health care; discuss the components of a quality assessment program and activities associated with these areas; demonstrate correct handling and utilization of quality assurance data; discuss the relationship between utilization management systems and quality assurance programs; correctly perform admission and continued stay patient reviews, completing all appropriate worksheets; and identify risk factors and determine appropriate risk control activities.

Instruction: Covers basic principles and practices of quality assurance in health care. Students gain practice in characterizing types of quality assurance programs, preparing quality assessment reports, understanding Joint Commission on Accreditation of Hospitals and PRO requirements, preparing patient reviews, preparing Utilization Review Committee reports, understanding the concepts of risk management and utilization of data for implementation of risk control activities.

Credit recommendation: In the lower division baccalaureate/associate degree category or in the upper division baccalaureate category, 2 semester hours in Health Care Quality Assurance Programs and Techniques, Introductory Medical Care Evaluation, or Peer Review in the Health Care Field (2/80) (7/86) (1/88). NOTE: This course had been reevaluated and continues to meet requirements for credit recommendations.

14. Trends in Health Care Delivery

Location: Correspondence Program.

Length: 4 lessons (Module 14 of a 17-module program in medical record technology).

Dates: March 1979-Present.

Objective: To discuss some of the social, legal, and economic questions that are related to the delivery of health care.

Instruction: Covers major issues affecting the health care delivery system; education, certification, and/or licensure, and the probable future of medical record practitioners and other members of the health care team; acute care, ambulatory care, preventive medicine, mental health services, long-term care, and comprehensive health programs; the patient's right to privacy and access to health records; and the effect of federal and state legislation on the health care delivery system.

Credit recommendation: In the lower division baccalaureate/associate degree category or in the upper division baccalaureate category, 1-2 semester hours in Health Care Delivery Systems or Introduction to Hospital Administration (4/80) (7/86). NOTE: This course has been reevaluated and continues to meet requirements for credit recommendations.

15. Supervisory Principles and Practice

Location: Correspondence Program.

Length: 3 lessons (Module 15 of a 17-module program in medical record technology).

Dates: March 1979-Present.

Objective: To become familiar with the principles and techniques essential for effective supervision.

Instruction: Covers fundamental leadership principles and techniques for good management; also provides information on job descriptions, policies and procedures, work schedules, budgets, and employees on-the-job training.

Credit recommendation: In the lower division bac-

calaureate/associate degree category, 1 semester hour in Interpersonal Human Relations, Principles of Supervision and Management or Supervisory Practices in the Health Care Systems (4/80) (7/86). NOTE: This course has been reevaluated and continues to meet requirements for credit recommendations.

16. Planning for Health Information Services
   Location: Correspondence Program.
   Length: 3 lessons (Module 16 of a 17-module program in medical record technology).
   Dates: March 1979-Present.
   Objective: To provide information about some planning techniques and principles that are helpful in planning for health information services in short-term, long-term, or ambulatory care settings.
   Instruction: Covers planning techniques in designing the physical layout and work-flow patterns of a department, including the department's organization, major functions, staffing requirements, recruitment sources, and kinds of intradepartmental communications. Some attention is also given to health care practitioner's role of providing consultation services to other health care facilities.
   Credit recommendation: In the lower division baccalaureate/associate degree category or in the upper division category, 1 semester hour in Health Information Services or Medical Record Services (4/80) (7/86). NOTE: This course has been reevaluated and continues to meet requirements for credit recommendations.

17. Directed Clinical Practice
   Location: Correspondence Program.
   Length: 11 areas (Module 17 of a 17-module program in medical record technology).
   Dates: March 1979-Present.
   Objective: To provide an opportunity to obtain clinical practice in one or more health care facilities under the supervision of a registered record administrator or an accredited record technician.
   Instruction: Covers technical analysis and evaluation of health records; statistical compilation, display, and retrieval of health information; coding and abstracting health information; medicolegal and correspondence procedures; health record storage, retrieval, and control procedures; patient registration; medical transcription procedures; specialized health information registry procedures; utilization review procedures; and patient care evaluation.
   Credit recommendation: In the lower division baccalaureate/associate degree category or in the upper division baccalaureate category, 4-6 semester hours in Clinical Practice in Medical Record Technology (4/80) (7/86). NOTE: This course has been reevaluated and continues to meet requirements for credit recommendations.

American Sterilizer Company (AMSCO)

The American Sterilizer Company (AMSCO) manufactures sterilizers for hospitals, laboratories, and hospital supply distributors. The company employs approximately 2,500 people throughout the North American continent. AMSCO also designs, manufactures, and distributes a broad range of equipment, instruments, and related supplies used primarily in hospitals.

The Education Division conducts resident training programs in management, sales, and service career fields for their employees at the Education Center, which was established in September 1960. Educational seminars in the areas of central service, operating room, materials management, respiratory therapy, and hospital engineering are offered at the Education Center, throughout the country, and abroad to hospital personnel. AMSCO Customer Maintenance Training Programs were incorporated in 1977.

Source of official student records: Manager of Service Training, American Sterilizer Co., 2424 West 23rd Street, Erie, PA 16514.

Additional information about the courses: Program on Noncollegiate Sponsored Instruction, The Center for Adult Learning and Educational Credentials, American Council on Education, One Dupont Circle, Washington, D.C. 20036.

Advanced Management Central Service Seminar
(Alternative Title: Operating Room Service Seminar)
   Location: Erie, PA; locations throughout the United States.
   Length: 32 hours (4 1/2 days); residential.
   Dates: June 1967-August 1983.
   Objective: To present current concepts and practical procedures for improving efficiency and raising standards within a hospital's central service department.
   Instruction: Hospital associated infections; contamination control; chemical disinfectants and concomitant problems; principles and methods of steam sterilization; principles of ethylene oxide gas sterilization; material processing and utilization; instrument processing; packaging requirements; planning concepts; explosion hazards and electrical safety; legal aspects; surgical lighting concepts; surgical draping standards; orthopedic procedures; motivation and communication.
   Credit recommendation: In the upper division baccalaureate category, 1 semester hour in Applied Health Sciences or Management (6/77) (3/82). One credit should be granted for either Operating Room Service Seminar, Central Service Department Seminar, or Combined Central Service and Operating Room and Infection Control Seminar, but not for all three courses.

1. **AMSCAR Service Training or AMSCAR Distribution Systems (CT/AT-7000)**
2. **Engineering Technology Laboratory II (Alternative Title: AMSCOMATIC Washer-Sterilization Training or Material Processing Systems [CT/AT-3000])**

Location: Erie, PA.

Length: 1. 36 hours (4 1/2 days); residential; 2. 34 hours (4 1/2 days); residential.

Dates: 1. January 1977-Present; 2. February 1976-Present.

Objective: To provide the student with hands-on laboratory experience on advanced electromechanical health care equipment.

Instruction: This laboratory deals with exercises on the operation and maintenance of the Amscar and Amscomatic products.

Credit recommendation: In the lower division baccalaureate/associate degree category, 2 semester hours in Engineering Technology Laboratory (2/77) (3/80) (4/88). NOTE: One semester hour for each component, total of 2 semester hours. This course has been reevaluated and continues to meet requirements for credit recommendations.

Basic Biomedical Equipment Maintenance
(Alternative Title: Service II/Surgical Tables and Lights)

Location: Erie, PA.

Length: 29 1/2 hours (4 1/2 days).

Dates: April 1978-Present.

Objective: To provide laboratory experience in electromechanical and hydraulic health care equipment.

Instruction: Electrical mechanical operation and maintenance of operating tables, operating lights, water purification equipment, and glassware washing equipment. Lecture and laboratory experiences are used.

Credit recommendation: In the lower division baccalaureate/associate degree category, 1 semester hour in Basic Biomedical Equipment Maintenance (2/80) (4/88). NOTE: This course has been reevaluated and continues to meet requirements for credit recommendations.

Central Service Department Seminar

Location: Erie, PA; locations throughout the United States.

Length: 32 hours (4 1/2 days); residential.

Dates: June 1967-March 1982.

Objective: To present current concepts and practical procedures for improving efficiency and raising standards within the central service department of a hospital, providing better patient care.

Instruction: Dynamic trends in hospital-associated infections; contamination control; chemical disinfection and concomitant problems; processing and distribution concepts; meeting patient care requirements; principles of steam sterilization; principles of gas sterilization; processing procedures; packaging requirements for hospital operation; electrical safety in hospitals; legal aspects of central service; how the Occupational Safety and Health Act affects hospitals; high purity water and solution processing; budget determination and utilization; motivation and communication.

Credit recommendation: In the upper division baccalaureate category, 1 semester hour in Applied Health Sciences or Management (6/77). NOTE: One credit should be granted for either Central Service Department Seminar, Operating Room Service Seminar, or Combined Central Service and Operating Room Seminar, but not for all 3 courses.

Combined Central Service, Operating Room, and Infection Control Seminar
(Alternative Title: Combined Central Service and Operating Room Seminar)

Location: Erie, PA; locations throughout the United States and abroad.

Length: 38 hours (4 1/2 days); residential.

Dates: February 1976-August 1983.

Objective: To present current concepts and practical procedures for improving efficiency and raising standards in the central service department and in operating room service and infection control.

Instruction: Contamination control; chemical disinfection and concomitant problems; principles of steam and gas sterilization; meeting patient care requirements; planning concepts-surgical suite; explosion and electrical safety; how the Occupational Safety and Health Act affects hospitals; material processing and utilization for the surgical suite; processing and distribution concepts for central service; processing procedures; packaging requirements; high purity water and solution processing; legal aspects relating to hospital personnel; central service budget determination and utilization; surgical lighting concepts; surgical draping standards; establishment of a case cart system; orthopedic procedures; motivation and communication.

Credit recommendation: In the upper division baccalaureate category, 1 semester hour in Applied Health Sciences or Management (6/77). NOTE: One credit should be granted for either Combined Central Service, Operating Room, and Infection Control Seminar; Central Service Seminar; or Advanced Management Central Service Seminar, but not for all 3 courses.

Customer Service V/Eagle 2000 Series Sterilizers

Location: Erie, PA.

Length: 32 hours (4 1/2 days); residential.

Dates: March 1982-August 1983.

Objective: To acquaint students with service and technology of computer-controlled sterilizers.

Instruction: The binary numbers system as it applies to

the computer-controlled sterilizer strategies and techniques for troubleshooting and preventive maintenance of the total sterilizer, laboratory experience on the computer-controlled sterilizer. Lecture, discussion, and laboratory experiences are used.

Credit recommendation: In the lower division baccalaureate/associate degree category, 1 semester hour in Engineering Technology (3/82).

Electromechanical Theories and Practices of Health Care Equipment
(Formerly Electromechanical Principles of Health Care Equipment)
  Location: Erie, PA.
  Length: *Version 1:* 180 hours (5 weeks); *Version 2:* 216 hours (6 weeks); *Version 3:* 288 hours (8 weeks); *Version 4:* 360 hours (9 weeks).
  Dates: *Version 1:* April 1975-February 1982; *Version 2:* March 1982-July 1985; *Version 3:* August 1985-April 1988; *Version 4:* May 1988-Present.
  Objective: To provide students with an introduction to the basic theory, operation, and maintenance of health care equipment and computer control techniques for their operation and maintenance.
  Learning Outcome: Upon successful completion of this course, the student will be able to develop interpersonal skills, analyze-diagnose repair equipment, practice safety; understand and apply basic theories of electronics to actual practice with electromechanical health care equipment; understand and explain the theory of sterilization, sanitation current practices, and prevention; and translate basic theory of physics and mechanics to actual practice on electromechanical equipment.
  Instruction: Major topics covered in the course are basic concepts in electromechanical theory and techniques as they relate to health care equipment, with special emphasis on sterilization, refrigeration, ultrasonic cleaning, surgical tables, and surgical lighting including relevant microcomputer support. Forty percent of the student's time is devoted to extensive laboratory-oriented exercises. Methods of instruction include lecture, discussion, and extensive laboratory exercises are used.
  Credit recommendation: *Version 1:* In the lower division baccalaureate/associate degree category, 6 semester hours in Basic Engineering Technology (2/77). *Version 2:* In the lower division baccalaureate/associate degree category, 8 semester hours in Basic Engineering Technology (3/82). *Versions 3 and 4:* In the lower division baccalaureate/associate degree category, 12 semester hours in Basic Engineering Technology or in the upper division baccalaureate category, 3 semester hours in Advanced Engineering Technology; and in the lower division baccalaureate/associate degree category or in the upper division baccalaureate category, 3 semester hours in Engineering Laboratory (4/88). NOTE: This course has been reevaluated and continues to meet requirements for credit recommendations.

Engineering Service and Technology for Computer-Controlled Sterilizers
(Alternative Title: Eagle Series 2000/Engineering Technology Lab V)
  Location: Erie, PA.
  Length: *Version 1:* 64 hours (2 weeks); *Version 2:* 32 hours (1 week).
  Dates: *Version 1:* February 1979-February 1982; *Version 2:* March 1982-July 1985.
  Objective: To acquaint students with service and technology of computer-controlled sterilizers.
  Instruction: The binary number systems as it applies to the computer-controlled sterilizer; strategies and techniques for troubleshooting and preventive maintenance of the total sterilizer; laboratory experience on the computer-controlled sterilizer. Lecture, discussion, and laboratory experiences are used.
  Credit recommendation: In the lower division baccalaureate/associate degree category, 1 semester hour in Engineering Service and Technology for Computer-Controlled Sterilizers (2/80).

Engineering Technology Laboratory I
(Alternative Title: Specialist Class) (AT/6000)
  Location: Erie, PA.
  Length: 40 hours (5 days); residential.
  Dates: January 1977-July 1985.
  Objective: To provide the student with hands-on laboratory experience on advanced electromechanical health care equipment.
  Instruction: This laboratory deals with exercises on the operation and maintenance of industrial gas console; Lo-Boy; urology table; surgical lighting; Amscope and Chef Center; and other selected products of AMSCO manufacture.
  Credit recommendation: In the lower division baccalaureate/associate degree category, 1 semester hour in Engineering Technology Laboratory (2/77) (3/80). NOTE: This course has undergone a 5-year reevaluation and continues to meet requirements for credit recommendations.

Hospital Engineering Seminar
(Alternative Title: Hospital Directors of Engineering Seminar)
  Location: Erie, PA; locations throughout the United States and Canada.
  Length: 32 hours (4 1/2 days); residential.
  Dates: June 1967-August 1983.
  Objective: To present current concepts and practical applications for improving efficiency and raising the standards in the engineering department of a hospital.
  Instruction: Plant management organization and criteria; medical device legislation and its implications; trends

in hospital associated infections; infection control; cost effectiveness in environmental sanitation; techniques of mechanical washing; explosion hazards and electrical safety; principles of steam and ethylene oxide gas sterilization; legal aspects of the hospital engineering department; water requirement; surgical equipment requirements; how the Occupational Safety and Health Act affects hospitals; communication and motivation.

Credit recommendation: In the upper division baccalaureate category, 1 semester hour in Applied Health Sciences, Biomedical Engineering, or Clinical Engineering (6/77).

Materials Management in Hospitals
  Location: Erie, PA; locations throughout the United States.
  Length: *Version 1:* 38 hours (4 1/2 days); residential. *Version 2:* 32 hours (3 1/2 days); residential.
  Dates: *Version 1:* September 1976-February 1982. *Version 2:* March 1982-August 1983.
  Objective: To present current concepts and practical application of materials management in hospitals.
  Instruction: Administration and scope of responsibilities in materials management; qualifications of a materials manager; materials management organization; purchasing; cost benefits through effective inventory control; materials processing; laundry, pharmacy, dietary departments as elements of materials management; distribution; how the Occupational Safety and Health Act affects materials management; legal aspects; motivation and communication.
  Credit recommendation: In the upper division baccalaureate category, 1 semester hour in Applied Health Sciences or Management (6/77).

1. Training Seminar for Hospital Corporation of America (CT/4000)
2. Engineering Technology Laboratory III (Alternative Title: Customer Service I (CTI/1000)
  Location: Erie, PA.
  Length: 1. 32 hours (4 days); residential; 2. 35 1/2 hours (4 1/2 days); residential.
  Dates: 1. June 1973-Present; 2. January 1977-Present.
  Objective: To provide the participant with hands-on laboratory experience on advanced electromechanical health care equipment.
  Instruction: This laboratory deals with exercises on the operation and maintenance of AMSCO sterilization equipment, ultrasonic cleaning equipment, biological indicators, and instrumentation.
  Credit recommendation: In the lower division baccalaureate/associate degree category, 1 semester hour in Engineering Technology Laboratory (2/77) (3/82) (4/88). NOTE: One semester hour may be granted for work completed in either Training Seminar for Hospital Corporation of America or Customer Service I, but not both.

This course has been reevaluated and continues to meet requirements for credit recommendations.

Applied Learning (Formerly ASI/DELTAK)

Advanced Systems, Incorporated

The Advanced Systems, Incorporated (ASI) in-house instructional system is a grouping of elements designed to supplement and reinforce each other. These elements are designed to achieve quantifiable and measurable changes in behavior, attitudes, and/or skills. ASI materials are structured to maximize effectiveness, and productivity and profitability.

With the ASI system, learning can be in a tutorial or self-study mode so that it is "learner-paced."

By combining full-color video and video graphics, clearly written texts and audio, and problem-driven exercises, ASI provides a powerful medium mix possible for comprehensive skills training. The medium is more than simply the message. ASI's professional media and instructional design specialists select the proper medium to fit the message.

Students taking ASI courses are students from contracted companies who chose between two options: one for college credit and one for a completion certificate. Students taking courses for college credit undergo a proficiency evaluation (final examination) administered at the end of the course(s). This final examination is developed, administered, and graded by Advanced Systems, Incorporated in Elk Grove, Illinois.

It is important to note that all courses, for which credit is recommended, are property of ASI. Any course that is sold to another company no longer is considered ASI property, and therefore, no longer is eligible for a credit recommendation under the Program guidelines.

Source of official student records: Instructional Design Technologist, Advanced Systems, Incorporated, 1801 Tonne Road, Elk Grove Village, Illinois 60007.

Additional information about the courses: Program on Noncollegiate Sponsored Instruction, The Center for Adult Learning and Educational Credentials, American Council on Education, One Dupont Circle, Washington, D.C. 20036.

1414 308X Architecture for the Application Programmer
(Formerly 1412 System/370 Concepts and Facilities)
  Location: Various locations around the country.
  Length: 16-20 hours.
  Dates: *Version 1:* September 1981-November 1986; *Version 2:* December 1986-Present.
  Learning Outcome: Upon successful completion of this

Applied Learning (Formerly ASI/DELTAK) 65

course, the student will be able to: define basic 308X (S/370) terms, e.g., buffer storage, reloadable control registers, rotational position sensing, and decimal, hexadecimal binary conversion; describe and diagram (308X) (S/370) software characteristics including multiprogramming; file organizations, operating system function, and scheduling options. Audiovisual aids, workbooks, and examinations are used.

Instruction: Covers a practical understanding of 308X (System/370) hardware, software, and processing characteristics.

Credit recommendation: *Version 1:* In the lower division baccalaureate/associate degree category, 1 semester hour in System/370 Concepts and Facilities (9/81). *Version 2:* In the lower division baccalaureate/associate degree category, 1 semester hour in 308X Architecture for the Application Programmer (11/86). NOTE: This course has been reevaluated and continues to meet requirements for credit recommendations.

Advanced COBOL Programming
1633 Advanced Structured COBOL (formerly 1626)
1627 Advanced COBOL: Processing Non-Sequential Files
1628 Advanced COBOL: Coding with VSAM Files
1629 Advanced COBOL: Sorting and Advanced Programming Structures
   Location: Various locations around the country.
   Length: 40-45 hours.
   Dates: *Version 1:* June 1981-November 1986; *Version 2:* December 1986-Present.
   Learning Outcome: Upon successful completion of this course, the student will be able to: (1) create and search one and two dimensional tables using linear and binary search methods in ANS COBOL; (2) process non-sequential tables using algorithms, indexing, cylinder concepts, and relevant COBOL techniques; (3) load and access key-sequenced and entry-sequenced files; position VSAM files properly; and describe functions of Invalid Key clause; and (4) use Sort and Merge statements, sections, subprograms, and related ANS COBOL routines with emphasis on structured programming.
   Instruction: Covers the practical use of ANS COBOL instructions in writing table and variable-length records and the practical use of three ANS COBOL organization methods for creating and maintaining non-sequential files. Audiovisual aids, workbooks and examinations are used.
   Credit recommendation: *Version 1:* In the upper division baccalaureate category, 2 semester hours in Advanced COBOL or if taken with 1795 and 1797, 3 semester hours in Advanced COBOL (6/81). *Version 2:* In the lower division baccalaureate/associate degree category, 3 semester hours in Advanced COBOL (11/86). NOTE: This course has been reevaluated and continues to meet requirements for credit recommendations.

Assembler Language Programming
5600 Assembler Language Programming: Basic Techniques
5610 Assembler Language Programming: Binary Instruction Set
4080 MVS/SP JES 2 (Formerly 1795 and 1797)
   Location: Various locations around the country.
   Length: 60-98 hours.
   Dates: *Version 1.* June 1981-November 1986. *Version 2:* December 1986-Present.
   Learning Outcome: Upon successful completion of this course, the student will be able to analyze MFS and JES 2 program dumps; use proper control statements to locate errors; construct IBM Assembler Language programs; and refine techniques acquired in 5600.
   Instruction: Covers the practical use and analysis of MVS/SP dumps for coding and debugging programs of MVS/SP JES 2 dumps and Assembler Language programs. Audiovisual aids, workbooks, and examinations are used.
   Credit recommendation: *Version 1:* In the lower division baccalaureate/associate degree category, 5 semester hours in Assembler Language (6/81). *Version 2:* In the lower division baccalaureate/associate degree category, 3 semester hours in Assembler Language (11/86). NOTE: This course has been reevaluated and continues to meet requirements for credit recommendations.

Computer Operations
4160 Multiple Virtual System (MVS) XA (Formerly 1983 MVS/JES2 System Operator Training)
   Location: Various locations around the country.
   Length: 20-25 hours.
   Dates: September 1981-Present.
   Learning Outcome: Upon successful completion of this course, the student will be able to operate a computer in the MVS/JES2 environment with an understanding of: MVS hardware and terminology; MVS and JES2 commands; and JCL statements.
   Instruction: Covers practical use of techniques and procedures for MVS/JES2 console operation. Audiovisual aids, workbooks, and examinations are used.
   Credit recommendation: In the lower division baccalaureate/associate degree category, 1 semester hour in Computer Operations (9/81) (11/86). NOTE: This course has been reevaluated and continues to meet requirements for credit recommendations.

Data Base Concepts
1. **3801-3807 Data Base: An Introduction**
2. **3808 AITC: How A Data Base Management System (DBMS) Works**
3. **3809 AITC: Data Dictionary**

4. **3810 Data Base Concepts and Fundamentals (consists of 3811-3817)**
   Location: Various locations around the country.
   Length: 26-41 hours.
   Dates: December 1986-Present.
   Learning Outcome: Upon successful completion of these courses, the student will be able to: (1) understand data bases, their organization, advantage of data modeling, the need for security, and value of query languages; (2) be familiar with typical DBMS, the way they manage data, and methods of finding and retrieving items from the data base; (3) have specific knowledge of what a data dictionary is, how it functions, and its value to data base managers in administering and controlling data resources; and (4) define and use proper methods of constructing data bases; describe file organization as related to direct access methods; know the steps needed to create a valid data resource base.
   Instruction: Covers modular exploration of the contemporary data base environment, aimed at providing a generic, primary understanding of the organization, operation, and concepts of data base information systems; introduction to DBMS concepts, their purpose and function in making the data base idea possible; and an introduction to data dictionary/directory system (DD/DS) concepts, and their purpose and function in controlling all items in a data base; Data Base concepts designed to meet the needs of all data processing personnel entering the data base environment for the first time. Audiovisual aids, workbooks, and examinations are used.
   Credit recommendation: In the lower division baccalaureate/associate degree category, 2 semester hours in Data Base Concepts (11/86).

Data Base Design
4505 IMS Concepts
1527 IMS Data Base Design
(Formerly 1525 IMS Concepts and 1527 IMS Data Base Design)
   Location: Various locations around the country.
   Length: 40-52 hours.
   Dates: *Version 1.* September 1981-November 1986. *Version 2:* December 1986-Present.
   Learning Outcome: Upon successful completion of this course, the student will be able to: (1) delineate IMS capabilities in data base recovery and program restart, describe MFS, hierarchial data structure, and define a communications network using logical terminals; and (2) define and describe service analysis tasks, IMS access methods, and create data base descriptions and program specification blocks.
   Instruction: Covers the application for IMS design techniques and procedures and the practical application of data base design techniques. Audiovisual aids, workbooks, and examinations are used.
   Credit recommendation: *Version 1:* In the upper division baccalaureate category, 3 semester hours in IMS Concepts and Data Base Design (9/81). *Version 2:* In the lower division baccalaureate/associate degree category, 3 semester hours in Data Base Design (11/86). NOTE: This course has been reevaluated and continues to meet requirements for credit recommendations.

Data Communications
1. **3501 Fundamentals of Data Communications**
2. **3505 Data Communications Transmission**
3. **4530 IMS/VS Data Communications Programming Overview**
4. **4574 IMS/VS MFS: Concepts and Terminology**
5. **4575 IMS/VS MFS: Control Statement Coding**
   Location: Various locations around the country.
   Length: 28-46 hours.
   Dates: December 1986-Present.
   Learning Outcome: Upon successful completion of these courses, the student will be able to: determine forms and uses of data communications; hardware and software; design and analysis of data communications system; design and analysis of data communications systems to solve business applications; formulate the characteristics and requirements in data transmission which are unique to data communications; be familiar with: bit systems and codes; error detection and control; synchronization; and functional aspects of transmission services; have an overview of IMS-Data Communications parts; describe how data communication transmits, receives, processes, and manipulates messages from and to various terminals; convert a data base program to a data communications environment; and identify IMS input entered thru an unformulated screen; define the importance of an MFS in an IMS system; recognize incorrectly coded assembler macro statements.
   Instruction: Covers a basic understanding of data communications systems; and the characteristics and requirements in data transmission which are unique to data communications systems; the data communications aspect of IMS including the basic concepts of IMS-Data Communications structure, function, and terminology, and the design and construction of application programs; and the coding of basic Message Format Services control statements, and how to tailor MFS to specific installations. Audiovisual aids, workbooks, and examinations are used.
   Credit recommendation: In the lower division baccalaureate/associate degree category, 2 semester hours in Data Communications (11/86).

DL/1 Programming
1. **4511 DL/1 Programming: Transversing the Hierarchy (consists of 4512-4513)**
2. **4515 DL/1 Programming: An overview (consists of 4516-4517)**

3. 4520 DL/1 Programming: Basic Techniques (consists of 4521-4526)
Location: Various locations around the country.
Length: 40-54 hours.
Dates: *Version 1:* September 1981-November 1986. *Version 2:* December 1986-Present.
Learning Outcome: Upon successful completion of these courses, the student will be able to: (1) understand DBMS as it relates to DL/1 Programming and DL/1 hierarchial bases, and apply the rules by which DL/1 uses the data base emphasizing search fields; (2) program in DL/1 to effect a data base using Entry, Linkage, 1/0 area and Segment Search arguments; and (3) code a special DL/1 application program using Sequential, Direct, or Random Access and Insert Function methods; use data base modification with COBOL and PL/I alternatives.
Instruction: Covers the understanding of DL/1 programming describing the basic components of DL/1 hierarchial structure, their relationships, and how DL/1 navigates through the structure; DL/1 programming with emphasis on the personnel involved and system components; and DL/1 programming techniques. After completion of each technique in this course (4520), the student then proceeds to the exercise workbook where all the documentation and specifications can be found to code the required program(s) in either COBOL, Assembler, or PL/I. A total of eleven programs, three of which are optional, can then be compiled and tested against a test data base supplied with the course on a mini magnetic tape reel. The reel and the coordinator guide combine to offer all the information necessary to install a complete test data on any operating system where DL/1 has been previously installed. The COBOL, Assembler, and PL/I solutions for the eleven programs, along with the reports produced by the programs, can be found in a second workbook. Audiovisual aids, workbooks, and examinations are used.
Credit recommendation: *Version 1:* In the upper division baccalaureate degree category, 4 semester hours in DL/1 Programming (9/81). *Version 2:* In the lower division baccalaureate/associate degree category, 3 semester hours in Introduction to DL/1 Programming (11/86). NOTE: This course has been reevaluated and continues to meet requirements for credit recommendations.

Introduction to Computer Fundamentals
5140 ADP Concepts
5141 ADP Fundamentals
Location: Various locations around the country.
Length: 42-58 hours.
Dates: December 1986-Present.
Learning Outcome: Upon successful completion of this course, the student will be able to: (1) understand the significance of computers in one's life with knowledge of hardware, software, data management, and systems development; and (2) understand computer numbering systems, data representation, the control processing unit, peripheral devices, operating systems, program logic, and the need of security in data processing.
Instruction: Covers the basic understanding of computer concepts, the practical understanding of computers and what they are used for. Audiovisual aids, workbooks, and examinations are used.
Credit recommendation: In the lower division baccalaureate/associate degree category, 2 semester hours in Introduction to Computer Fundamentals (11/86).

Introduction to MVS/XA Concepts and Facilities
1. 4010
2. 4020/4310
(Formerly 1790 MVS Concepts and Facilities and 1791 MVS/JES2 System Control Statements)
Location: Various locations in the U.S.
Length: 25-32 hours.
Dates: June 1981-Present.
Learning Outcome: Upon successful completion of these courses, the student will be able to: (1) describe OS, VS, and MVS operating systems; understand functions of Job Control Language; and utilize MVS problem state programs; and (2) understand and use MMVS/JES2 system control statements, cataloged and in-stream procedures.
Instruction: Covers the IBM's MVS operating system and the practical use of MVS/JES2 system control statements for debugging and running programs in an OS/MVS environment. Audiovisual aids, workbooks, and examinations are used.
Credit recommendation: In the lower division baccalaureate/associate degree category, 2 semester hours in MVS Concepts and Facilities (6/81)(11/86). NOTE: This course has been reevaluated and continues to meet requirements for credit recommendations.

Introduction to PL/I Programming (5670-5683)
(Formerly 1672 Mastering PL/I for the Optimizing Compiler)
Location: Various locations around the country.
Length: *Version 1:* 35-40 hours; *Version 2:* 52-65 hours.
Dates: *Version 1:* June 1981-November 1986. *Version 2:* December 1986-Present.
Learning Outcome: Upon successful completion of this course, the student will be able to: (1) know how to manipulate bits, handle data aggregation, and looping techniques; and (2) understand the usage of various PL/I commands; and work with label data, variables, non-consecutive files, and error messages.
Instruction: Covers the practical use of PL/I instructions for writing and debugging programs. Audiovisual aids, workbooks, and examinations are used.
Credit recommendation: In the lower division baccalaureate/associate degree category, 3 semester hours in PL/I (6/81) (11/86). NOTE: This course has been reevaluated and continues to meet requirements for credit

recommendations.

Introduction to Systems Analysis
1. 4701 Developing a Changeable System: Structured Systems Development (consists of 4702-4705)
2. 4711 Structured Systems Analysis & Design: Using Data Flow Diagrams (consists of 4712-4714)
3. 4715 Structured Analysis & Design: Structured Analysis (consists of 4716-4718)

Location: Various locations around the country.
Length: 22-34½ hours.
Dates: September 1981-Present.
Learning Outcome: Upon successful completion of these courses, the student will be able to: (1) describe the elements of structured program design using pertinent symbols for data flow, data storage, and logic process; identify data flow diagrams, decision trees, Structured English; use top-down techniques in building a DP system; (2) construct data flow diagrams using the top-down method and illustrate the various levels of Data Flow diagrams; and (3) redefine the terms of systems analysis to adapt them to Structured Analysis using data dictionary; simplify contents of data stores; specify process logic using decision trees, decision tables, Structured English, and Tight English.
Instruction: Covers the tools of Structured Analysis and techniques of Structured design to develop systems which are easily maintained; the design and use of Data Flow Diagrams as analysis tools for a better interpretation of user requirements; and the basic concepts and tools of structured analysis. Audiovisual aids, workbooks, and examinations are used.
Credit recommendation: In the lower division baccalaureate/associate degree category, 1 semester hour in Structured Systems Analysis (9/81) (11/86). NOTE: This course has been reevaluated and continues to meet requirements for credit recommendations.

Structured COBOL Programming
(Formerly Structured COBOL with Dan McCracken)
Location: Various locations around the country.
Length: 45-90 hours.
Dates: *Version 1:* June 1981-November 1986. *Version 2:* December 1986-Present.
Learning Outcome: Upon successful completion of this course, the student will be able to: (1) know the rules for forming Structured COBOL name fields; (2) write Identification, Environment, Data, and Procedure divisions; (3) define numeric data fields of all types; (4) create COBOL programs using control breaks and developing logic from pseudocode.
Instruction: Covers "Problem-Driven" approach to the essential elements of the ANS COBOL language, including program writing, compiling, debugging, and executing. Audiovisual aids, workbooks, and examinations are used.

Credit recommendation: *Version 1:* In the lower division baccalaureate/associate degree category, 2 semester hours in Structured COBOL, or if taken with 1795 and 1797, 4 semester hours in Structured COBOL (6/81). *Version 2:* In the lower division baccalaureate/associate degree category, 3 semester hours in Structured COBOL (11/86). NOTE: This course has been reevaluated and continues to meet requirements for credit recommendations.

VSAM and Access Methods Services
4040 MVS/SP
4214 VSAM and Basic AMS
(Formerly 1516 VSAM Concepts and 1517 VSAM and Access Methods Services)
Location: Various locations around the country.
Length: 17-28 hours.
Dates: *Version 1:* September 1981-November 1986; *Version 2:* December 1986-Present.
Learning Outcome: Upon successful completion of this course, the student will be able to connect a non-VSAM file to a VSAM file and to create, maintain, and work with VSAM data sets and catalogs.
Instruction: Covers the practical understanding of VSAM and the Access Method Services (AMS) program and the practical application of VSAM and Access Method Services. Audiovisual aids, workbooks, and examinations are used.
Credit recommendation: *Version 1:* In the lower division baccalaureate/associate degree category, 2 semester hours in Disc File Techniques, VSAM Access Methods, or Direct Access Storage Device (9/81). *Version 2:* In the lower division baccalaureate/associate degree category, 1 semester hour in Disc File Techniques, VSAM Access Methods, or Direct Access Storage Device (11/86). NOTE This course has been re-evaluated and continues to meet requirements for credit recommendations.

Introduction to Systems Analysis
1. 2001 Systems: A Phased Approach
2. 2002 Systems: Development Skills
3. 2003 Systems: Preparing the Project Request
4. 2004 Systems: Preparing the System Proposal
5. 2005 Systems: Preparing the Functional Specifications
6. 2006 Analysis and Design Considerations
7. 2007 Systems: Preparing the Design Specifications
8. 2008 Systems: Conducting the Acceptance Test
9. 2009 Systems: Participating in System Evaluation
10. 2012 Documentation Preparation and Distribution

Location: Various locations around the country.
Length: 37-54 hours.
Dates: December 1986-Present.
Learning Outcome: Upon successful completion of these courses, the student will be able to: (1) use a phased approach to systems development and documentation of

the adopted systems; (2) understand the skills of systems analysis with emphasis on the needs of the various types of systems; (3) develop a project request with proper objectives, and documentation; (4) complete the first phase of System Development, defining its purpose, selecting the criteria; and establishing cost/benefit relations; (5) prepare the functional aspects of a system, defining user requirements, management activities, and management control reports; (6) define the purpose of the analysis phase, the activities involved, and the usage of Functional Specifications documents; (7) complete the Design Phase of the system using checkpoints, graphic representation, error parameters, user-specified controls, acceptance testing, and phase-over procedures in installation of a new system; (8) conduct acceptance testing of a system with provisions for proper documentation, user involvement, problem correction, and training of management involved in the system; (9) prepare and analyze an evaluation of a System stating the purpose and role of such evaluation, and delineating the timing, personnel, and alternative actions necessary for its success; and (10) handle complete documentation for a system: using proper standards; producing required documents; and setting up procedures for easy updating of all documents.

Instruction: Covers the understanding of the phased approach to system development; the systems analyst skills of the system development effort; the practical understanding of the Conception phase of System Development and its documentation, the Project Request form; the practical understanding of the Initiation phase of System Development and its documentation, the System proposal; the system requirements contained in the Functional Specifications document; the practical application of analysis, design and documentation techniques for efficient and cost-effective system development; the skills and activities required in the Design Phase of system development; the Construction Phase of the system developed process; the effective preparation and analysis of a System Evaluation Report; and the practical understanding of documentation needs in all phases of system development. Audiovisual aids, workbooks, and examinations are used.

Credit recommendation: No credit. Procedural, but not comparable to a college-level course.

DELTAK, inc.

DELTAK, inc. was formed in 1970 to provide companies with products and services to help them educate their data processing management and line personnel via in-house training programs. Since that time, DELTAK's Delta Vision Library has expanded to include more than 2,300 information and skills training programs for computer professionals and nontechnical computer users, from upper management to staff personnel. All of the courses have been developed to meet exacting standards and provide students with skills designed to increase job proficiency and productivity.

The programs use a combination of text, audio, video, and computer-based instruction to introduce new concepts and build specific job skills. DELTAK's programs are designed for self-instruction; however, they may also be used in a group. They include practice exercises that reinforce learning by simulating actual problems the student encounters on the job, as well as tests to measure student achievement.

Students taking DELTAK courses for college credit are from contracted companies. Upon completion of a course, a proficiency evaluation or final examination developed by DELTAK is administered and graded by the contracting company and forwarded to the American Council on Education's Registry Office for forwarding of the transcript.

All courses taken at contracted companies for which credit is given are the property of DELTAK, inc. All terms and conditions for contracted companies are still in force and binding.

Source of official student records: Director of Human Resources and Training, DELTAK, inc., East/West Technological Center, 1751 West Diehl Road, Naperville, Illinois 60566.

Additional information about the courses: Program on Noncollegiate Sponsored Instruction, The Center for Adult Learning and Educational Credentials, American Council on Education, One Dupont Circle, Washington, D.C. 20036.

ANS COBOL Language (26-3XX)

Location: DELTAK customer locations worldwide.
Length: Variable (60-80 hours).
Dates: June 1979-Present.
Objective: The course is intended to teach the student how to program in ANS COBOL and is especially applicable for persons who will be performing in a structured programming environment. It will also teach a programmer, familiar with other languages, Advanced Techniques in ANS COBOL.

Instruction: In addition to teaching the student to design, code, compile, test and debug ANS COBOL programs, utilizing sequential files, table processing, sort/merge, and report writer, this course teaches the use of nonsequential files (ISAM, VSAM and Direct), modular and advanced programming techniques. The course is essentially self-instructed through the use of text, supplemented by videotape and audio cassette. User organization should provide tutorial assistance, and must provide computer hardware. This series is *also* available in a Computer-Based Training (CBT) format.

Credit recommendation: In the lower division baccalaureate/associate degree category, 4 semester hours in COBOL II (Advanced). It is recommended that a student who completes both 26-2XX and 26-3XX be limited to a total of 7 semester hours for both courses (9/83).

70 *Applied Learning (Formerly ASI/DELTAK)*

Basic and Advanced Troubleshooting in Electronic Systems
   Location: Independent Study.
   Length: 60 hours.
   Dates: January 1984-Present.
   Objective: To give the student an understanding of electronic troubleshooting procedures and test equipment.
   Instruction: Topics include isolating, locating, and verifying problems in electronic systems; preventive maintenance, and repair or replacement of defective components or systems. Instruction involved interactive videodiscs and workbooks.
   Credit recommendation: In the lower division baccalaureate/associate degree category, 1 semester hour in Industrial Technology (7/86).

Basic Electricity and Electronics
   Location: Guided Independent Study.
   Length: 100 hours.
   Dates: October 1985-Present.
   Objective: To provide the student with an understanding of fundamentals of DC and AC circuitry and the application of this knowledge to further study of electronics.
   Instruction: This course requires basic mathematics through an introduction to algebra as determined by diagnostic pretesting. Topics include algebra-based instruction in current/voltage/resistance, direct current, magnetism, DC current, alternating current, capacitance, inductance, transformers, resonance and filters, electronic measurement, electronic diagrams, and safety standards and codes. Instruction involves interactive videodiscs, texts with teacher's guide, lab manuals, and lab kit.
   Credit recommendation: In the lower division baccalaureate/associate degree category, 2 semester hours in Electronics Technology (7/86).

Digital Circuits and Devices
   Location: Guided Independent Study.
   Length: 120 hours.
   Dates: October 1985-Present.
   Objective: To give the student an understanding of basic digital electronics and circuitry.
   Instruction: Topics include digital concepts, numbering systems, digital gates, logic development, logic families, logic simplification, digital integrations, latches/flip-flops/shift registers, counters, digital and analog conversion, memory, and an introduction to computers. Instruction involves interactive videodiscs, texts with teacher's guides, lab manual, and lab kit.
   Credit recommendation: In the lower division baccalaureate/associate degree category, 2 semester hours in Electronics Technology (7/86).

Fundamental Study Skills: Technical Math and Reading
   Location: Independent Study.
   Length: 90 hours.
   Dates: October 1985-Present.
   Objective: To provide the student basic math skills and to improve reading comprehension and study skills.
   Instruction: Topics include basic math skills, number systems through introductory algebra, plus basic reading comprehension and study skills for those being trained in electronics. Instruction utilizes interactive videodiscs and workbooks.
   Credit recommendation: In the vocational certificate category, 2 semester hours in Developmental Studies (7/86).

Course 1 - Introduction to Industrial Control
Course 2 - Introduction to Programmable Control
   Location: Independent Study.
   Length: Course 1 - 30 hours; Course 2 - 36 hours.
   Dates: January 1984-Present.
   Objective: To give the student an understanding of industrial and programmable control systems.
   Instruction: Topics for Course 1 include process control, temperature measurements, relays, switches and sensors, and DC and AC motors. Topics for Course 2 include role of PCs in automated control systems management; control system components, symbols, and documentation; PC system theory, documentation, and troubleshooting. Instruction involves interactive videodiscs and workbooks.
   Credit recommendation: In the lower division baccalaureate/associate degree category, 1 semester hour in Industrial Technology (7/86). NOTE: Students must complete both courses for credit to apply.

Introduction to Microprocessors
   Location: Guided Independent Study.
   Length: 120 hours.
   Dates: October 1985-Present.
   Objective: To give the student an understanding of microprocessor technology.
   Instruction: Topics include an introduction to the Motorola 6802 microprocessor, computer math, support hardware, addressing modes and instruction data sheets, program development, branching/indexing/loops, instructions set, stack and stack pointer, and microprocessor interfacing. Instruction involved interactive videodiscs, texts with teacher's guides, lab manuals, and lab kit.
   Credit recommendation: In the lower division baccalaureate/associate degree category, 2 semester hours in Computer or Electronics Technology (7/86).

Microelectronics: Devices and Applications
   Location: Guided Independent Study.

Length: 100 hours.
Dates: October 1985-Present.
Objective: To give the student exposure to an application of a variety of linear integrated circuit concepts and devices; provides the student a bridge from discrete electronic theory to linear integratged circuitry concepts.
Instruction: Topics include discrete operational amplifiers, IC operational amplifiers, linear operations, comparators, oscillators and function generators, active filters, Norton amplifiers, timers, regulated power supplies, and phase-locked loops. Instruction involves texts with teacher's guide, lab manual, and lab kit.
Credit recommendation: In the lower division baccalaureate/associate degree category, 2 semester hours in Electronics Technology (7/86).

Semiconductors: Circuits and Devices
Location: Guided Independent Study.
Length: 120 hours.
Dates: October 1985-Present.
Objective: To give the student a basic understanding of the fundamentals of semiconductors.
Instruction: Topics include semiconductor theory, PN junction, theory and construction, power supplies, bipolar transistors, semiconductor devices, amplifier operation, oscillator circuits, radio communication fundamentals, and radio frequency test equipment. Instruction involves interactive videodiscs, texts with teacher's guide, lab manuals and lab kit.
Credit recommendation: In the lower division baccalaureate/associate degree category 2 semester hours in Electronics Technology (7/86).

Structured ANS COBOL - Entry Level (26-2XX)
Location: DELTAK customer locations worldwide.
Length: Variable (90-130 hours).
Dates: June 1979-Present.
Objective: The course is intended to teach the student how to program in ANS COBOL and is especially applicable for persons who will be performing in a structured programming environment.
Instruction: The student learns to design, code, compile, test, and debug ANS COBOL programs, utilizing sequential files, table processing, sort/merge, and report writer. Course is essentially self-instructed through use of text, supplemented by videotape and audio cassette. User organization should provide tutorial assistance, and must provide computer hardware. This series is also available in a Computer-Based Training (CBT) format.
Credit recommendation: In the lower division baccalaureate/associate degree category, 4 semester hours in COBOL I (Introductory). The completion of 26-010, 26-020, 26-110, and 26-120 is equal to 1 semester hour at the lower division baccalaureate/associate degree level (9/83).

Understanding Data Processing (7-2XX)
Location: DELTAK customer locations worldwide.
Length: Variable (20-30 hours).
Dates: June 1980-Present.
Objective: To provide the student with a basic introduction to computer science.
Instruction: Course covers information processing, the computer system, information systems, database and distributed systems, data communications and online systems, and the data processing interface. The course is essentially self-instructed through use of text, supplemented by videotape. User organization should provide tutorial assistance.
Credit recommendation: In the lower division baccalaureate/associate degree category, 3 semester hours in Introduction to Computer Science or Data Processing (9/83).

Applied Power, Inc. - Blackhawk Automotive Division

The Automotive Division of Applied Power, Inc. provides equipment and instruction for collision repair through its Blackhawk Training Department. Although headquartered in Milwaukee, Wisconsin, courses of instruction are provided at 10 training facilities located in major population centers throughout the continental United States.

A national director of training is responsible for administration and coordination of the courses of instruction. Locally, at each of the 10 regional facilities, a training manager provides for and supervises instruction. Instructors are required to have 10 years auto body repair experience, instructional skill, communications ability, and adequate references.

Source of official student records: Director and Registrar of Training, Applied Power, Inc., Automotive Division, 11333 West National Avenue, Milwaukee, Wisconsin 53227.

Additional information about the courses: Program on Noncollegiate Sponsored Instruction, The Center for Adult Learning and Educational Credentials, American Council on Education, One Dupont Circle, Washington, D.C. 20036.

New Science of Unibody Repair
Location: 10 branch offices training sites with shop and classroom.
Length: 40 hours (one week when offered at Blackhawk training facilities). The course can be expanded to 80 hours when offered through secondary or postsecondary educational institutions.
Dates: January 1983-Present.
Objective: Provides theory and basic hands-on skills for

proficient unibody collision damage repair. (Unibody auto construction has been rapidly replacing perimeter frame construction in new cars since 1978).

Instruction: Lecture, discussion, demonstration, audiovisual, and hands-on experience are used. Instructional materials include 20 lesson plans, instructor's manual, student workbook, comprehensive slide set, complete taped lecture series, overhead transparencies, quizzes, and tests. The instructional program is designed to provide updating and upgrading for currently employed auto body personnel as well as instructors teaching auto body repair. It is also intended as a component of a secondary school program in auto body repair or as a component of a postsecondary certificate offering or 2 year Associate in Applied Science degree program preparing auto body repair technicians.

Credit recommendation: In the vocational certificate and lower division baccalaureate/associate degree category variable credit from 1-3 semester hours as follows: For the standard 40 hour course offered under industrial or postsecondary auspices, 2 semester hours where a moderate amount of outside study is required and welding instruction (MIG) is provided for (8/83). NOTE: Additional contact hours up to a total of 80 may provide an additional hour of credit.

ARA Services, Inc.

ARA Services, Inc., is an international service management company providing basic services for industry, institutions, and government, including food and refreshment, uniform rental and maintenance, distribution of publications, transportation, health care, and child care. The Air/Leisure Services Sector of ARA Services, Inc., provides fine dining, food and beverage, lodging and recreation services, airport ground-handling services, building maintenance, housekeeping, groundskeeping, and laundry equipment services to its clients.

Source of official student records: ARA Air/Leisure Sector, Personnel Department, Independence Square West, Philadelphia, Pennsylvania 19106.

Additional information about the courses: Program on Noncollegiate Sponsored Instruction, The Center for Adult Learning and Educational Credentials, American Council on Education, One Dupont Circle, Washington, D.C. 20036.

Advanced Management Skills Workshop
Location: Conference centers selected by ARA.
Length: 20 hours (3 days).
Dates: January 1985-Present.
Objective: To give participants an overview of the managerial functions of directing and controlling; to allow participants to review and practice the interpersonal aspects of their jobs and to see how they are perceived by subordinates and how they might improve their effectiveness.

Instruction: Upon completion of this course, participants will display: (1) increased effectiveness in interpersonal skills; (2) enhanced skills in interviewing, coaching, and counseling, delegation and performance appraisal; (3) increased managerial comfort and facility in supervising subordinates in management positions; and (4) improved ability to plan for application of these skills with subordinates. Lecture, discussion, and group exercises are used.

Credit recommendation: In the lower division baccalaureate/associate degree category, 1 semester hour in General Business (3/85).

Management by Objectives
Location: Conference Centers selected by ARA.
Length: 14 hours (2 days).
Dates: January 1985-Present.
Objective: To provide participants with conceptual understanding of managing by objectives, achievement management and business policy and planning; to train participants in the skills of functional job analysis, and drafting and implementing organization mission statements, goals, objectives and action plans.

Instruction: Upon completion of the course, participants will display understanding of effective business planning and will be capable of writing and communicating clear mission statements, organizational goals, objectives and framing action plans.

Credit recommendation: In the lower division baccalaureate/associate degree category, 1 semester hour in General Business (10/85).

Management Expectancy
Location: Conference centers selected by ARA.
Length: 20 hours (3 days).
Dates: January 1985-Present.
Objective: To enable participants to focus on key issues in employee productivity and techniques for performance improvement; to engage in exercises to enhance skills in employee motivation and subordinate development; and to practice techniques for applying the expectancy concept in organizations to establish a setting for successful goal-setting, goal-attainment, and achievement.

Instruction: Upon the completion of this course, participants will display knowledge about their own particular management styles and expectancy, and how these affect employee motivation and productivity. Participants will also be able to understand and practice achievement-leadership behavior, goal-setting, goal-negotiation, and productivity-based performance coaching and feedback. Lecture, discussion, and group exercises are used.

Credit recommendation: In the lower division baccalaureate/associate degree category, 1 semester hour in General Business (3/85).

Service Management Seminar
Location: University of Florida, Management Center, Gainesville, FL.
Length: 40 hours (1 week).
Dates: January 1985-Present.
Objective: To allow participants to discuss and investigate issues of management: assessment, change and conflict, labor relations, business ethics, marketing and strategic planning concepts, organization design and growth, and financial analysis.
Instruction: Upon completion of this course, participants will display: (1) the ability to discuss the organization as a concept and as a reality; (2) knowledge of the integration of strategic planning, marketing, and finance in an achievement leadership framework; and (3) an appreciation for the concept, design, structure, and mission of organizations. Lecture, discussion, and group exercises are used.
Credit recommendation: In the lower division baccalaureate/associate degree category, 3 semester hours in General Business (3/85).

Supervisory Skills Workshop
Location: Conference centers selected by ARA.
Length: 14 hours (2 days).
Dates: January 1985-Present.
Objective: To provide participants with an understanding of the basics of supervision, including effective communication and group dynamics, EEO principles, discipline delegation, selection, and interviewing.
Instruction: Upon completion of this course, participants will be able to: (1) use techniques and job aids to enhance their effectiveness in problem solving, delegating, disciplining, and supervising group activities; (2) display a better understanding of their own leadership styles and needs in order to impact favorably on work-group productivity. Lecture, discussion, and group exercises are used.
Credit recommendation: In the lower division baccalaureate/associate degree category, 1 semester hour in General Business (3/85).

Armenian National Education Committee (Formerly Woodside Armenian Center)

The Siamanto Academy of the Armenian National Education Committee has been headquartered in New York City since September 1983. The educational setting includes a conference room equipped with a complete public address system, podium, chalk/chart/map boards, a piano, projectors (film, slide, overhead) and screens. Additionally, some lecture sessions are conducted at the Armenian National Education Committee's neighboring location in the Prelacy Building of the Armenian Apostolic Church of America. The Prelacy houses a library and offers advantages of a variety of technical and cultural resources.

Source of official student records: Administrator, Siamanto Academy, Armenian National Education Committee, 138 East 39th Street, New York, New York 10016.

Additional information about the courses: Thomas A. Edison State College, Office of Special Programs, 101 West State Street, Trenton, New Jersey 08625; or Program on Noncollegiate Sponsored Instruction, The Center for Adult Learning and Educational Credentials, American Council on Education, One Dupont Circle, Washington, D.C. 20036.

Armenian Ancient and Medieval History
Location: The Woodside Armenian Center, Woodside, NJ and St. Vartanantz Armenian Apostolic Church, Ridgewood, NJ.
Length: 70 hours (60 weeks).
Dates: January 1983-Present.
Objective: To introduce students to ancient and medieval Armenian history covering the period from 1500 B.C. to 1375 A.D.
Instruction: Course covers the relationship between the Armenians and the following empires: Persia, Alexander the Great, Rome, Byzantine, Arab, and early Ottomans; tracing of Armenian religious expression including early duties and Zoroastrian traditions; the analysis of impact of Christianity on the Armenian people including the role of the Armenians during the Crusades.
The material is presented through staff and guest lectures. Homework is assigned regularly, and frequent quizzes and examinations are given in class.
Credit recommendation: In the lower division baccalaureate/associate degree category, 3 semester hours in Ancient/Medieval Armenian History (1/83).

Introduction to Armenian Civilization and Culture
Location: The Woodside Armenian Center, Woodside, NJ and St. Vartanantz Armenian Apostolic Church, Ridgewood, NJ.
Length: 180 hours (90 weeks).
Dates: January 1983-Present.
Objective: To introduce students to Armenian Civilization and Culture through the study of literature, drama, music, and folk dance. A historical perspective is presented and when applicable students participate in the performance of theatre, music, and folk dance.
Instruction: Through the analysis of selected readings the student will correlate and integrate the historical and geographic trends in Armenian literature, music, theatre, and folk dance. The material is presented through staff and guest lectures. Rehearsals and public performances are part of the program. Homework is assigned regularly, and frequent quizzes and examinations are given in class.
Credit recommendation: In the lower division bac-

calaureate/associate degree category, 2-3 semester hours in Introduction to Armenian Civilization and Culture (1/83). NOTE: Two semester hours of credit are recommended for two years (120 hours/60 weeks) of instruction, and three hours of credit are recommended for three years of study (180/90 weeks).

Modern (East and West) Armenian History
   Location: The Woodside Armenian Center, Woodside, NJ and St. Vartanantz Armenian Apostolic Church, Ridgewood, NJ.
   Length: 35 hours (30 weeks).
   Dates: January 1983-Present.
   Objective: To introduce students to modern Armenian history, covering the period from 1375 A.D. to the present.
   Instruction: Course includes: the analysis of Modern West and East Armenian History; identification of related events in Ottoman, late Byzantine, European, Arabian, Russian, Persian, Georgian, and Azeri histories; the analysis of the relationship between the Armenian community and the Ottoman government as reflected in the Millet system; the rise of Armenian nationalism; the course and consequences of the massacres of 1895 and 1915; identification of the events leading to the Armenian Republic of 1918-20; survey of the history of Soviet Armenia, 1920 to present; survey of the selected developments of Turkish history from 1920 to present; survey of the development of the Armenian communities in the Diaspora, 1920 to present.
   The material is presented through staff and guest lectures. Homework is assigned regularly, and frequent quizzes and examinations are given in class.
   Credit recommendation: In the lower division baccalaureate/associate degree category, 3 semester hours in Modern Armenian History (1/83).

Art Instruction Schools

Art Instruction Schools is a wholly owned subsidiary of the Bureau of Engraving, Inc., a privately owned corporation. Located in Minneapolis, Minnesota, the school has offered art courses by correspondence since 1914.

Art Instruction Schools offers Fundamentals of Art and Specialized Art. Fundamentals of Art is a prerequisite for Specialized Art. For each lesson students must submit artwork that demonstrates proficiency in the techniques and concepts presented in the lesson. The assigned artwork evaluates only a portion of the material presented in the lesson, so students may, through independent work and practice, learn more than they are required to demonstrate in the assignments. For this reason, many of the credit recommendations are stated as ranges of credit. Institutions are urged to evaluate portfolios individually to determine the exact amount of credit to be awarded.

Students applying for college credit are required to take proctored, objective art examinations. In Fundamentals of Art, an examination may be taken after Lessons 14 or 22 (at which time a student may apply for credit for the portion completed) or upon completion of the entire Fundamentals of Art program. Similarly, in Specialized Art, students may take an examination after Lesson 17 or upon completion of Specialized Art. They are also required, as part of the examination, to submit a portfolio which is evaluated by a faculty committee and is part of the final grade. Institutions should review the portfolio in determining the credit award.

These examinations were instituted in January 1978, but students who began the programs as early as August 1973 may take the art examination to have the credit recommendations apply to them. Successful completion of the examinations is indicated on the student's record.

Source of official student records: Director of Education, Art Instruction Schools, Inc., 500 South Fourth Street, Minneapolis, Minnesota 55415.

Additional information about the courses: Program on Noncollegiate Sponsored Instruction, The Center for Adult Learning and Educational Credentials, American Council on Education, One Dupont Circle, Washington, D.C. 20036.

Fundamentals of Art
Part 1. Basic Drawing and Design I
Part 2. Basic Drawing and Design II
Part 3. Figure Drawing and Studio Techniques
   Location: Correspondence program.
   Length: 27 lessons (typical student requires two years and over 1,000 hours to complete). *Part 1:* Lessons 1-14; *Part 2:* Lessons 15-22; *Part 3:* Lessons 23-27.
   Dates: *Version 1:* January 1978-June 1988; *Version 2:* July 1988-Present.
   Objective: *Part 1:* To introduce students to drawing, design principles, and color concepts. *Part 2:* To enable students to use a variety of art media and techniques creatively. *Part 3:* To provide students with an understanding of human anatomy that will enable them to draw the nude and draped figure.
   Learning Outcome: Upon successful completion of this course, the student will be familiar with basic drawing, basic color, form, basic design, various media and techniques, studio techniques, cartooning, animal drawing, figure drawing, lettering, and composition.
   Instruction: *Part 1:* Fundamental techniques of drawing to achieve accurate proportions, form, foreshortening, and textures; fundamentals of representational, abstract, and nonobjective designs; application of color principles through planning, mixing, and use. *Part 2:* Drawing and rendering animals; perspective, including one-point to multiple-point, and spacing, shadows, reflections, and plane projections; history and techniques of lettering;

identification of lettering styles; lettering tools; pen and brush lettering and creative lettering; still life art, including positive and negative shapes, sight-size drawing, lighting, backgrounds, enlarging and reducing; pictorial composition. *Part 3:* Figure drawing, including proportions, skeleton, and muscles; action and expressions; foreshortening and distortion; head, hand, and foot studies; drawing the draped figure—with an introduction to fashion illustration; studio techniques, including art studios, care and use of tools and materials, tricks of the trade, the airbrush, mounting photographs and artwork, matting, preparation of keylines (mechanicals or paste-ups), and instructional aids such as the use of a grid.

Credit recommendation: *Version 1:* In the lower division baccalaureate/associate degree category, 4-6 semester hours in Art Education or Studio Art for each part, for a total of 12-18 semester hours (1/78). *Version 2:* In the lower division baccalaureate/associate degree category, 4-8 semester hours in Art Education or Studio Art for each part, for a total of 12-24 semester hours (3/83). *Version 3: In the lower division baccalaureate/associate degree category, 24 semester hours in Art Education or Studio Art (7/88). NOTE: This course has been reevaluated and continues to meet requirements for credit recommendations.*

Specialized Art
Part 1. Design, Composition, and Reproduction
Part 2. Painting Techniques
Part 3. Cartooning
Part 4. Art in Advertising
Part 5. Advanced Drawing and Painting
Part 6. Advanced Illustration

  Location: Correspondence program.
  Length: 27 lessons (typical student requires two years and over 1,400 hours to complete). *Part 1:* Lessons 1-6; *Part 2:* Lessons 7-9; *Part 3:* Lessons 10-12; *Part 4:* Lessons 13-17; *Part 5:* Lessons 18-20; *Part 6:* Lessons 21-27.
  Dates: *Version 1:* January 1978-June 1988; *Version 2:* July 1988-Present.
  Objective: *Part 1:* To provide an understanding of advanced problems in design, reproduction, and composition. *Part 2:* To provide an understanding of various painting techniques and media. *Part 3:* To provide an understanding of cartooning as a creative and expressive art, including the history of cartooning styles and techniques. *Part 4:* To provide an understanding of the functions and responsibilities of an art director and an advertising agency; to provide an awareness of the creative process for an advertisement by analyzing client's needs, researching, and choosing visuals, layout tools and techniques; to develop an understanding of cartoons as part of the advertising message and to experiment with the styles and techniques involved in preparing advertising cartoons. *Part 5:* To enable students to select subjects, compose, use perspective, and apply color theory to drawing from nature and painting portraits. *Part 6:* To familiarize students with the tools and techniques used by professional illustrators; provide students with an understanding of the problems of creating artworks for book, fashion, editorial, and advertising illustrations.
  Learning Outcome: Upon successful completion of this course, the student will be able to design, compose and reproduce; paint; use effective art techniques in cartooning, advertising, drawing and painting; and illustration.
  Instruction: *Part 1:* Commercial printing processes (letterpress and offset lithography), reproduction of art screens, applying tone to line art, color reproduction, silk screening; advanced design problems, processes, techniques, and commercial applications; advanced study of composition, underlying picture patterns, rendering styles, analysis of shapes, values, and color in picture arranging. *Part 2:* Value and color problems in transparent and opaque media; their application to fine art and advertising art. *Part 3:* Study of cartooning using ink, acrylics, Zip-A-Tone shading sheets, colored papers, felt cloth, and other media on illustration boards, texture sheets, acetate, and other surfaces doing dry brush renderings, creating collages, and using other techniques. *Part 4:* Construction of an advertising campaign; service and institutional advertisements; psychology of advertising; functions and responsibilities of the art director; functions of the advertising agency; tools and techniques used in advertising art studios and agencies. *Part 5:* Composition as it relates to landscape space, aerial perspective, drawing and painting portraits, review of head anatomy and form; placement, background considerations, color mixing, and painting methods. *Part 6:* Developing illustrating skills and advanced rendering techniques for book, fashion, editorial, and advertising illustration.
  Credit recommendation: *Version 1: Part 1:* In the upper division baccalaureate category, 4-6 semester hours in Art Education or Studio Art (1/78). *Part 2:* In the upper division baccalaureate category, 2 semester hours in Art Education or Studio Art (1/78). *Part 3:* In the upper division baccalaureate category, 2 semester hours in Art Education or Studio Art (1/78). *Part 4:* In the upper division baccalaureate category, 4-6 semester hours in Art Education or Studio Art (1/78). *Part 5:* In the upper division baccalaureate category, 2 semester hours in Art Education or Studio Art (1/78). *Part 6:* In the upper division baccalaureate category, 6-10 semester hours in Art Education or Studio Art (1/78). Total credit of 20-28 semester hours (1/78) (3/83). *Version 2:* In the upper division baccalaureate category, 28 semester hours in Art Education or Studio Art (7/88). NOTE: This course has been reevaluated and continues to meet requirements for credit recommendations.

ASI/DELTAK

See APPLIED LEARNING

AT&T - Center for Systems Education (Formerly AT&T Company Data Systems Education Group)

The Center for Systems Education is part of the Systems Development and Processing Organization of AT&T. Training and education programs are offered in Piscataway, New Jersey, and other company facilities. The Center provides general systems education and job-related training through instructor-led and self-paced courses, seminars, and hands-on workshops. The organization is driven by user needs, state-of-the-art technology and AT&T methods.

The classrooms and Individualized Learning Center provide a professional learning environment. Instructors, course developers, and training specialists are subject matter experts in their fields, thus assuring the highest quality education and training available.

Source of official student records: CS Ed Registrar, Center for Systems Education, 140 Centennial Avenue, Piscataway, New Jersey 08854.

Additional information about the courses: Program on Noncollegiate Sponsored Instruction, The Center for Adult Learning and Educational Credentials, American Council on Education, One Dupont Circle, Washington, D.C. 20036; or Thomas A. Edison State College, 101 West State Street, CN 545, Trenton, New Jersey 08625.

Advanced Techniques of Instruction (IE8211)
Location: Piscataway, NJ and other AT&T locations.
Length: 37.5 hours (5 days).
Dates: September 1983-Present.
Objective: To help participants identify student/instructor problems and derive solutions for them.
Instruction: This instructor led course utilizes a variety of instructional methods including: lecture, discussions, team exercises, videotaped micro-teaching sessions role play and guided practice. At the conclusion of the course participants will be able to: (1) identify and deal with an assortment of classroom problems; (2) demonstrate knowledge of desirable instructor characteristics and roles; (3) explain and use the principles of small group dynamics and learning theory; (4) identify areas of instructional techniques that require improvement; and (5) discuss advanced concepts of human interaction/teaching methods/human learning.
Credit recommendation: In the upper division baccalaureate category, 2 semester hours in Education or Instructional Technology (7/85).

Analysis and Design Strategies (ADS) (IE3010)
Location: Piscataway, NJ and other AT&T locations; Bell Operating Company locations.
Length: 30 hours (5 days).
Dates: June 1981-Present.
Objective: To provide students with the overall concepts of structured system development.
Instruction: Upon completion of the course, students will be able to: (1) distinguish between logical and physical views of a system; (2) identify the analysis and design tools used to create physical and logical views of a system; (3) identify the products produced by analysis and design; (4) convert the products of analysis into the products of design; (5) identify design tools and how to use them; and (6) convert a properly produced system analysis (standard system specification) into an efficient structured design document.
Credit recommendation: In the upper division baccalaureate degree category, 2 semester hours in Computer Information Systems or Computer Science (7/85).

Assembler Language Coding (IE3135)
(Introduction to Assembler Language Coding)
Location: Piscataway, NJ and other AT&T locations; Bell Operating Company locations.
Length: 30 hours (5 days).
Dates: January 1984-Present.
Objective: To introduce students to the elements of IBM 370 Assembler Language Coding.
Instruction: This course introduces the basic commercial Instruction Set and the use of basic I/O macros. Topics covered include introduction to Assembler, basic instructions, looping and branching, decimal instructions, character handling, QSAM data management. Lecture and labs are used.
Credit recommendation: In the lower division baccalaureate/associate degree category, 2 semester hours in Computer Science or Data Processing (7/85).

Basic FORTRAN (IE3130)
Introduction to FORTRAN
Location: Piscataway, NJ and other AT&T locations; Bell Operating Company locations.
Length: 30 hours (5 days).
Dates: August 1983-Present.
Objective: An introductory level course which will enable programmers to write FORTRAN IV programs which are readable and maintainable.
Instruction: Course includes lecture and laboratory. Topics covered include: Standard FORTRAN statements, data representation and expressions, arithmetic and logical statements, Input/Output statements, and structured programming in FORTRAN.
Credit recommendation: In the lower division baccalaureate/associate degree category, 2 semester hours in Computer Science or Data Processing (7/85).

Basic Training Development Skills Workshop (IE8101)
   Location: Piscataway, NJ and other AT&T locations.
   Length: 35 hours (5 days).
   Dates: *Version 1:* August 1979-May 1983; *Version 2:* May 1983-Present.
   Objective: To introduce the new course developer to a systematic approach to the training development process and to provide "tools" to use in achieving course development goals.
   Instruction: Training requirements analysis, preparation of course objectives, test construction, learning strategies, development of course materials, use of audiovisual media, and course evaluation are covered. Lecture, discussion, and classroom exercises are used.
   Credit recommendation: *Version 1:* In the lower division baccalaureate/associate degree category, 2 semester hours in Education (2/80). *Version 2:* In the upper division baccalaureate category, 2 semester hours in Human Resources Management, Training and Development, or Education (7/85). NOTE: This course has undergone a 5-year reevaluation and continues to meet requirements for credit recommendations.
   ®evised curriculum beginning in May 1983, clearly indicates that this is an "upper level" course offering.

C Initial Designer Training (IE3001)
   Location: Piscataway, NJ; White Plains, NY; Oakton, VA; Atlanta, GA; Cincinnati, OH; Kansas City, KS.
   Length: 375 hours (10 weeks).
   Dates: February 1985-Present.
   Objective: To teach the design skills and C Language programming concepts needed by a programmer/analyst in a UNIX operating system environment.
   Instruction: Course includes lecture, laboratory, and discussion. Topics covered include: the identification and utilization of various steps for systems development; C Language programming, including coding, testing, and debugging under UNIX; and the creation of all necessary documentation.
   Credit recommendation: In the lower division baccalaureate/associate degree category, a total of 6 semester hours consisting of 3 semester hours in C Language and 3 semester hours in Systems Design (7/85).

COBOL Workshop (IE3105)
   Location: Piscataway, NJ and other AT&T locations.
   Length: 75 hours (10 days).
   Dates: November 1983-Present.
   Objective: To present advanced COBOL Coding, Report Writer, COBOL Sorts, and VSAM Access.
   Instruction: Course includes lecture and laboratory. Topics covered include: providing VSAM files in COBOL; processing variable length records in COBOL; data representation and manipulation in COBOL; use of special registers in COBOL maintenance and enhancement of nonstructured COBOL programs; use of COBOL Report Writer features; and testing and debugging of COBOL modules and external and internal sorts.
   Credit recommendation: In the lower division baccalaureate/associate degree category, 4 semester hours in Data Processing or Management Information Systems (7/85).

Computer Communications System Architecture (IE7165)
   Location: Piscataway, NJ and other AT&T locations.
   Length: 24 hours (4 days).
   Dates: January 1976-Present.
   Objective: To introduce the student to the major steps involved in defining communications needs, collecting relevant data, and examining alternative considerations in the selection of appropriate hardware, software, facilities, protocols, and switching methods.
   Instruction: Course includes lecture and discussion. Topics covered include: major areas of computer communications service categories; definition of major components of a computer communications network; differences between bit and character-oriented protocols; identification of traffic-dependent criteria; and the identification of elements in the design of a computer communications network.
   Credit recommendation: In the upper division baccalaureate category, 2 semester hours in Data Processing or Data Communications or Computer Science (7/85).

Concepts of the Integrated Systems Provisioning Process
(Formerly Concepts of Total System Development [IE2000])
   Location: Piscataway, NJ and other AT&T locations.
   Length: 14 hours (2 days).
   Dates: January 1979-Present.
   Objective: To cover the phases and activities required for information systems development projects, and to provide an overview of the total system development methodology.
   Instruction: Upon completion of this course, the student will be able to (1) identify the steps and characteristics of the Total System Development (TSD) process; (2) define a system and list system characteristics; (3) indicate the phase in which the major activities take place in the TSD process; (4) identify subactivities and characteristics that occur during each phase of the TSD process; (5) list the make-up of the system development project team and identify the roles of the team members; (6) identify and list the areas in which documentation is essential in a system development effort; (7) identify and indicate the functions of project management; and (8) identify and list the methods for estimating resources required for a system development effort.
   Credit recommendation: In the lower division baccalaureate/associate degree category, 1 semester hour in

Computer Information Systems, Business Administration, and Information Science (7/85).

Consulting Skills Workshop (IE1500)
Location: Piscataway, NJ and other AT&T locations.
Length: 24 hours (4 days).
Dates: December 1979-Present.
Objective: To enable the manager to understand the dynamics of a client/consultant relationship.
Instruction: At the completion of this workshop, the student consultant, when presented with a simulated client/consultant relationship, will be able to: (1) identify/adopt appropriate roles; (2) determine the suitability of a potential client for subsequent consulting work; (3) identify the four types of consulting technologies and the appropriateness of their use; (4) identify/deal effectively with dilemmas by using appropriate strategies; (5) negotiate contract with the potential client which meets the needs and requirements of both the client and consultant; (6) describe the kind of problems which can arise if there is no formal contract between client and consultant; and (7) understanding the methodology for each phase of a consulting project, which meets the need of client and consultant.
Credit recommendation: In the upper division baccalaureate category, 2 semester hours in Business Management (7/85).

Data Analysis and Logical Data Structuring (IE2530)
Location: Piscataway, NJ and other AT&T locations.
Length: 30 hours (5 days).
Dates: May 1984-Present.
Objective: To provide systems analysts with the basic skills and knowledge needed to perform a feasibility data analysis.
Instruction: The approach to this course involves using a "top-down" approach (entity analysis) to construct and document the "relational" and "usage" views of sample data. Students also learn how to use normalization procedures to clarify and verify a logical data structure. At the conclusion of the course, participants will be able to: (1) explain the purpose of logical data analysis; (2) distinguish difference between a data base and traditional files; (3) construct a complete and accurate relational view of sample data using "top-down" analysis techniques; (4) verify that a data structure is normalized by using "bottom-up" normalization techniques; (5) develop a complete and accurate usage view of sample data; and (6) compare the relational and usage views to verify the accuracy and completeness of the logical data structure.
Credit recommendation: In the upper division baccalaureate degree category, 2 semester hours in Computer Science or Computer Information Systems (7/85). NOTE: Students who already received credit for Logical Data Structuring should receive only 2 semester hours of credit for this course.

Bisync Protocol Analysis (IE7130)
Location: Piscataway, NJ and other AT&T locations.
Length: 24 hours (4 days).
Dates: January 1976-Present.
Objective: To introduce the student to traffic characteristics across the line in a multi-point, leased-line, or polling-mode environment, the establishment and control of the communications link via bisync framing characters, and the various commands, orders, and codes transmitted as message-text for screen formatting in support of transaction processing.
Instruction: Course includes lecture and discussion. Topics covered include: interpretation of a variety of message types flowing across the link; identification of the processes underway between host and the remote station; identification of the external causes and effects of these messages in terms of screen appearance, user actions, and error recovery; identification of error situations and their probable causes; and the creation of control and text messages required to produce particular screens.
Credit recommendation: In the upper division baccalaureate category, 1 semester hour in Data Communications/Operations, Data Processing, or Computer Science (7/85).

Computer Communications System Operations (IE7115)
Location: Piscataway, NJ and other AT&T locations.
Length: 24 hours (4 days).
Dates: January 1976-Present.
Objective: To develop basic skills required to operate in the computer communications environment, which demands knowledge of the network configuration and functions, terminal user functions, and the ability to perform trouble analysis and fault-isolation.
Instruction: This course includes lecture and discussion. Topics covered include: description of various hardware, software, and facilities that make up a computer communications network; the major functions of the Control Center and the responsibilities of its personnel; tools used in performing network monitoring, network control, network analysis, and network diagnostics; identification of discrete steps in a procedure used to resolve network trouble encountered by a terminal user.
Credit recommendation: In the upper division baccalaureate category, 1 semester hour in Data Communications/Operations, Data Processing, or Computer Science (7/85).

Modems and Facilities (IE7120)
Location: Piscataway, NJ and other AT&T locations.
Length: 22-24 hours (4 days).
Dates: June 1982-Present.
Objective: To provide the student with an overview of facilities operation techniques and modulation techniques used by AT&T and approved vendor supplied modems

and DSUs.

Instruction: Course includes lecture and workshops. Topics covered include: description of how data is transmitted over telephone facilities; the functions and characteristics of modems and multiplexors; and troubleshooting data transmission problems on facilities, modems, and multiplexors.

Credit recommendation: In the upper division baccalaureate category, 1 semester hour in Data Communications/Operations, Data Processing, or Computer Science (7/85).

Teleprocessing (T.P.) in the Host (IE7145)

Location: Piscataway, NJ and other AT&T locations.
Length: 24 hours (4 days).
Dates: February 1984-Present.
Objective: To introduce the student to teleprocessing channel programs, control blocks, and the relationships between teleprocessing access method software and hardware components. The emphasis of this course is teleprocessing trouble identification and resolution tools.

Instruction: Course includes lecture, discussion, and laboratory. Course covers the identification of teleprocessing software related trouble indications that may originate from various sources: (a) the network performance monitor; (b) T.P. Access method console; (c) Operating System console; (d) user contact. Also included are: identification of the proper procedure(s) used to isolate/locate the trouble(s); identification of the condition(s) that most likely caused the trouble(s) to occur; and description of the step(s) necessary to resolve/refer the trouble(s).

Credit recommendation: In the upper division baccalaureate category, 1 semester hour in Data Communications/Operations, Data Processing, or Computer Science (7/85).

Terminals and Line Protocol (IE7125)

Location: Piscataway, NJ and other AT&T locations.
Length: 30 hours (5 days).
Dates: September 1983-Present.
Objective: To teach the fundamentals of how terminals operate in a telecommunications environment. Specifically, students will acquire skills on interpreting various forms of asynchronous and synchronous protocols.

Instruction: Course includes lecture, laboratory, and discussion. Topics covered include: asynchronous and synchronous transmissions; the ASCII code set and its control characters; the use of the ANSI X3.64 code; options available on asynchronous terminals, decoding various implementations of BSC protocol; and trouble isolation for asynchronous and synchronous terminals.

Credit recommendation: In the upper division baccalaureate category, 2 semester hours in Data Communications/Operations, Data Processing, or Computer Science (7/85).

Data Gathering for System Development (IE2510)

Location: Piscataway, NJ and other AT&T locations.
Length: 24 hours (4 days).
Dates: October 1983-Present.
Objective: To cover data gathering plans, interviewing techniques, questionnaire design, content analysis, observation, and paperwork flow.

Instruction: In addition to lectures and discussions, students practice data gathering techniques in group exercises and role plays. Upon completion of this course, the student should be able to: (1) plan and organize a data collection project; (2) discuss the advantages and disadvantages of the five major data collection techniques; (3) design, construct, and evaluate a questionnaire; and (4) plan, conduct, and record an interview.

Credit recommendation: In the upper division baccalaureate category, 1 semester hour in Business Administration, Computer Science, or Computer Information Systems (7/85).

Data Processing Concepts for Users (IE2002)

Location: Piscataway, NJ and other AT&T locations.
Length: 18 hours (3 days).
Dates: May 1984-Present.
Objective: To familiarize people lacking backgrounds in data processing with some of the most common concepts and terminology encountered in a mechanized environment.

Instruction: This computer literacy course covers how and why computers are used; how computers work; peripheral equipment; data communications; data base principles; types of software; languages and programming; and current future trends.

Credit recommendation: In the lower division baccalaureate/associate degree category, 1 semester hour in General Education (Computer Literacy) (7/85). NOTE: Not to be used for credit in computer related or other technical degree programs. Students who receive credit for this course should not receive credit for Information Systems Seminar for the Executive.

Data Security and Controls

Location: Data Systems Education Center, Piscataway, NJ and other Bell locations.
Length: 31 hours (1 week).
Dates: April 1979-December 1984.
Objective: To familiarize the student with the need for data security and the basic methods used to provide good security.

Instruction: Need for systems security development, design of countermeasures to meet documented security requirements, continued security maintenance of a data system. Lecture and laboratory are used.

Credit recommendation: In the upper division baccalaureate category, 2 semester hours in Computer Science or Data Processing (2/80).

Human Factors in Computer Systems (IE1002)
Location: Piscataway, NJ and other AT&T locations.
Length: 90 hours (15 days over a 3-month period).
Dates: July 1982-Present.
Objective: To provide the basic education needed to perform human factors activities.
Instruction: Students are exposed to basic human information processing principles via discussions, research, experiments, and testing and then they apply the results to design activities. Upon completion of the course, students should be able to: (1) make and support human factors decisions and recommendations; (2) conduct research in the various subtopics within Human Factors; (3) perform various analysis techniques required to produce human factors products; (4) analyze error rates and costs; (5) design dialog, command language, codes, and error messages; (6) critique the effectiveness of various forms of user documentation for specific use; (7) evaluate screens and forms and make recommendations for improvements; (8) conduct experiments to evaluate problem situations; and (9) apply ergonomic principles to work station design.
Credit recommendation: In the graduate degree category, 3 semester hours in Industrial Engineering, Computer Science, or Computer Information Systems (7/85).

Human Performance Engineering (IE1004)
Location: Piscataway, NJ and other AT&T locations.
Length: 28 hours (4 days).
Dates: September 1982-Present.
Objective: To introduce the participant to the principles and techniques of human factors issues in the design and selection of work procedures, work stations, control panels, and office layout.
Instruction: Upon completion of this course, participants should be able to: (1) discuss the evolution of the human performance engineering field; (2) discuss human factor considerations within each phase of the system development process; (3) identify factors affecting human performance; (4) use anthropometric data charts; and (5) develop a preliminary design for a manual work station and office layout using human factor principles.
Credit recommendation: In the upper division baccalaureate category, 1 semester hour in Business Administration or Industrial Engineering (7/85).

IMS/VS Data Base Implementation
Location: Data Systems Education Center, Piscataway, NJ and other Bell locations.
Length: 60 hours (2 weeks).
Dates: June 1978-December 1984.
Objective: To enable students responsible for implementing IMS/VS data bases(s) to choose and use the most appropriate method.
Instruction: Physical data base descriptions from hierarchical structures; appropriate data base organizations and access methods and related factors. Lecture, discussion, and workshops are used.
Credit recommendation: In the lower division baccalaureate/associate degree category, 2 semester hours in Computer Science or Data Processing (1/80).

IMS/VS Batch Programming (IE3204)
Location: Piscataway, NJ; other AT&T locations; and Bell Operating Company locations.
Length: 30 hours (1 week).
Dates: January 1985-Present.
Objective: To teach the student how to process data stored in an integrated IMS/VS data base in the batch mode.
Instruction: Course includes lecture and laboratory. Topics covered include: IMS/VS data base concepts, Data Language/I calls and segment search arguments, manipulation of data in a batch environment. Additional IMS/VS features such as multiple positioning, variable length segments, segment edit/compression, independent vs. dependent AND, checkpoint/restart.
Credit recommendation: In the upper division baccalaureate category, 2 semester hours in Computer Science or Data Processing (7/85).

IMS/VS Logical Data Base Implementation (IE3308)
Location: Piscataway, NJ; other AT&T locations; and Bell Operating Companies (always taught by headquarters instructors).
Length: 18 hours (3 days).
Dates: January 1985-Present.
Objective: To teach the concepts and implementation techniques of IMS logical relationships. Logical relationships enable the use of network structures in IMS.
Instruction: Course includes lecture and laboratory. Topics covered include: Description of the characteristics and uses of the three types of IMS logical relationships; coding the physical Data Base Description (DBD) parameters necessary to implement logical relationships; drawing the data structures made possible by a given logical relationship; coding logical data base descriptions (logical DBDs); describing the implications of the logical update rules; and describing the procedures necessary to reorganize a data base involved in a logical relationship.
Credit recommendation: In the upper division baccalaureate category, 1 semester hour in Computer Science or Data Processing (7/85).

IMS/VS Physical Data Base Design; Introduction and Techniques (IE3320 and IE3324)
Location: Piscataway, NJ; AT&T Regional Processing Centers; and Bell Operating Companies.
Length: 54 hours (9 days).
Dates: January 1985-Present.
Objective: To provide the transition from logical to physical data base design and also to provide the student with the skills and knowledge necessary to complete IMS/

VS physical data base design. The student will also learn the concepts, structure, and terminology of IMS and the basics of evaluating and tuning a particular physical data base design.

Instruction: Course includes lecture and laboratory. Topics covered include: structural and physical view of data; translating conceptual models into physical design; the use of modeling techniques and tools; and the development of test procedures for a data base to be implemented under a physical design.

Credit recommendation: In the upper division baccalaureate category, 3 semester hours in Computer Science or Data Processing (7/85). NOTE: In order to receive credit, student must complete both courses.

IMS/VS Physical Data Base Implementation (IE3304)
   Location: Piscataway, NJ; other AT&T locations; and Bell Operating Companies.
   Length: 30 hours (5 days).
   Dates: January 1985-Present.
   Objective: To provide the student with an understanding of the physical characteristics of IMS data bases, and the coding of the necessary control blocks to define data bases and programs to IMS.
   Instruction: Course includes lecture and laboratory. Topics covered include: the characteristics of: (a) multiple data set groups; (b) pointer options; (c) segment edit/compression; (d) variable length segments. Also covered are: coding physical Data Base Descriptions (DBDs) for the various data base organizations; coding of Program Specification Blocks (PSBs) required for data base processing; coding of the control statements necessary to pre-build Application Control Blocks; and implementation physical IMS data bases.
   Credit recommendation: In the upper division baccalaureate category, 2 semester hours in Computer Science or Data Processing (7/85).

IMS/VS Programming - Teleprocessing (IE3208)
   Location: Piscataway, NJ; other AT&T locations; and Bell Operating Companies.
   Length: 30 hours (1 week).
   Dates: January 1985-Present.
   Objective: To teach students the difference between the philosophy of teleprocessing and batch processing and to introduce students to MFS and BTS concepts and usages.
   Instruction: Course includes lecture and laboratory. Topics covered include: IMS/VS teleprocessing concepts; coding of message processing and conversational programs; introduction to the use of Message Format Services; and manipulation of Batch Terminal Simulator parameters.
   Credit recommendation: In the upper division baccalaureate category, 2 semester hours in Computer Science or Data Processing (7/85).

IMS/VS Programming (Batch and Teleprocessing)
   Location: Data Systems Education Center, Piscataway, NJ; and other Bell locations.
   Length: 60 hours (2 weeks).
   Dates: June 1976-December 1984.
   Objective: To teach the student how to process data stored in an integrated IMS/VS Data Base in the batch mode.
   Instruction: Data base concepts; data language/I calls; manipulation of data in a batch environment; program debugging in an IMS/VS environment; advanced IMS/VS features such as variable length segments, segment edit/compression, independent versus dependent AND, and system service calls. Lecture, discussion, and workshops are used.
   Credit recommendation: In the lower division baccalaureate/associate degree category, 2 semester hours in Computer Science or Data Processing (2/80).

Information-Mapping, Structured Writing (IE1202)
   Location: Piscataway, NJ and other AT&T locations.
   Length: 24 hours (4 days).
   Dates: June 1980-Present.
   Objective: To teach participants to use this systematic method (Information Mapping) which makes writing simple, clear, more efficient, and more effective.
   Instruction: This instructor-led course emphasizes a modular way of organizing and presenting written materials and a carefully-structured format combining simple graphics and words. Upon completion of this course, the student will be able to: (1) describe Information Mapping Structured Writing; (2) write and edit basic and supplementary types of maps; (3) write and edit a training unit according to the course standards; (4) identify good applications of the structured writing methods; and (5) survey other aspects of this approach, i.e., memos and reports.
   Credit recommendation: In the lower division baccalaureate/associate degree category, 2 semester hours in Business or Managerial Communication (7/85).

Information Systems Analysis Workshop (IE2540)
   Location: Piscataway, NJ and other AT&T locations.
   Length: 90 hours (10 days).
   Dates: June 1984-Present.
   Objective: To apply and integrate the latest techniques and methodologies of system development as part of a process for performing system analysis and logical design.
   Instruction: The students comprise a "development team" simulating a live environment. Starting with a user-proposal report, students will perform the data and function analysis to prepare documentation to be included in the system specifications for the PSS and CSS designers. Upon completion of the course, students will be able to: (1) recognize business objectives and fundamental business needs; (2) create a linkage diagram by identifying

business factors and practices and analyzing data structures; (3) identify logical business events; (4) define business processes, high level functions, and elementary functions; (5) integrate developmental tools and methods; and (6) produce analysis and logical design specifications to support the subsequent physical design.

Credit recommendation: In the graduate level category, 3 semester hours in Business Administration or Computer Information Systems or in the upper level baccalaureate degree category, 5 semester hours in Business Administration or Computer Information Systems (7/85).

Information System Seminar for the Executive (IE2104)
  Location: Central New Jersey "off work" locations.
  Length: 18 hours (3 days).
  Dates: October 1980-Present.
  Objective: To convey the systems development process to students who require a non-technical (user) perspective of information system applications.
  Instruction: The course covers: data processing concepts; the project development life cycle; managing and controlling the project; the project approval process; the role of systems people; systems analysis and design; human factors development; the role of the support organizations; hardware/software/programming languages; data administration; data security and controls; the purpose of EDP audits; data communications; system documentation; and current and future technologies.
  Credit recommendation: In the lower division baccalaureate/associate degree category, 1 semester hour in General Education (Computer Literacy) (7/85). NOTE: This course is not applicable to a computer science degree. Students who receive credit for this course should not receive credit for Data Processing Concepts for Users.

Initial Designer Training 2 (IE3000)
  Location: Piscataway, NJ; White Plains, NY; Oakton, VA; Atlanta, GA; Cincinnati, OH; Kansas City, KS.
  Length: 375 hours (10 weeks).
  Dates: June 1983-Present.
  Objective: To teach the design skills and COBOL programming concepts needed by programmers/analysts regardless of the hardware/software environment in which they will be working.
  Instruction: Course includes lecture, laboratory, and discussion. Topics covered include the identification and utilization of various steps for systems development, structured COBOL programming including coding, testing and debugging, and the creation of all necessary documentation.
  Credit recommendation: In the lower division baccalaureate/associate degree category, a total of 6 semester hours; 3 semester hours in Introduction to COBOL and 3 semester hours in Systems Design (7/85).

Interpersonal Management Skills for Information Systems (IE1800)
  Location: Piscataway, NJ and other AT&T locations.
  Length: 21 hours (3 days).
  Dates: June 1979-Present.
  Objective: To understand the basics of interpersonal skills as they relate to management.
  Instruction: Upon completion of this course, the student should be able to: (1) identify those personal performance situations where performance would be credited, and list the elements of an effective credit; (2) effectively use the skills of "clarifying" and "confirming;" (4) identify the elements and opportunities for the skill of "building;" and (5) select appropriate tactics in "managing differences."
  Credit recommendation: In the upper division baccalaureate category, 1 semester hour in Business Management, Psychology, or Communications (7/85).

Introductory Project Management
1. Introduction to Project Management (IE1602)
2. Project Management Workshops (IE1604)
  Location: Piscataway, NJ and other AT&T locations.
  Length: 1. 18 hours (3 days). 2. 34 hours (5 days).
  Dates: November 1979-Present.
  Objective: To provide the student with detailed conceptual knowledge of the project management process.
  Instruction: Characteristics of a complex systems project; the important aspects of the structure, environment, and vocabulary of project management. Lecture, discussion, and workshops are used.
  Credit recommendation: In the upper division baccalaureate category, 3 semester hours in Business Administration or Management (5/80) (7/85). NOTE: Students must complete both modules to receive credit for the Introductory Project Management. This course has undergone a 5-year reevaluation and continues to meet requirements for credit recommendations.

Logical Data Base Design
  Location: Data Systems Education Center, Piscataway, NJ and other Bell locations.
  Length: 32 hours (1 week).
  Dates: May 1978-August 1984.
  Objective: To provide the student with skills and knowledge necessary to complete logical data base design.
  Instruction: Covers a logical design of a data base, relational and usage requirements of the data base, and the need for controls and security requirements. Lecture and laboratory are used.
  Credit recommendation: In the upper division baccalaureate category, 1 semester hour in Computer Science or Data Processing (2/80).

Logical Data Structuring (IE2532)
  Location: Piscataway, NJ and other AT&T locations.

Length: 18 hours (3 days).
Dates: September 1984-Present.
Objective: To provide programmers with the skills needed to complete logical data base "relational" and "usage" views.
Instruction: In this course students learn how to perform 3-step normalization, how to verify that a data structure is in 3rd Normal Form, and how to document data access and usage requirements. Upon completion of the course students should be able to: (1) explain how a data base differs from traditional file processing; (2) describe how the four phases of data base design are related to each other; (3) construct a relational view of sample; (4) verify that a data structure is normalized; (5) develop a usage view of sample data; and (6) compare relational and usage views to verify the completeness and accuracy of the logical data structure.
Credit recommendation: In the upper division baccalaureate degree category, 1 semester hour in Computer Information Systems or Computer Science (7/85). NOTE: Students who already received credit for Data Analysis and Logical Data Structuring should receive no credit for this course.

Managing the D.P. Professional (IE1802)
Location: Piscataway, NJ and other AT&T locations.
Length: 18 hours (3 days).
Dates: August 1981-Present.
Objective: To improve the understanding of the traits, behaviors, and attitudes that are unique to D.P. professionals and to develop strategies to manage them successfully.
Instruction: Upon completion of the course, participants will be able to: (1) understand today's DP environment - the changing DP industry and its short- and long-term effect of managers; (2) identify and discuss the problems of managing in the new restructured organization; (3) explore more effective leadership styles for managing DP workers; and (4) understanding the team concept and how to build a stronger team.
Credit recommendation: In the upper division baccalaureate category, 1 semester hour in Business Management (7/85).

Managing the Data Systems Manager (IE1804)
Location: Piscataway, NJ and other AT&T locations.
Length: 20 hours (3 days).
Dates: July 1980-Present.
Objective: To examine advanced techniques to maintain manager motivation and to build high-performing teams.
Instruction: Upon completion of the course, the participant will be able to: (1) understand new techniques for managing subordinate managers; (2) coach and develop subordinates; (3) understand advanced techniques to maintain manager motivation; (4) prevent crisis management situations through the use of anticipatory management techniques; and (5) improve the performance evaluation and ranking process.
Credit recommendation: In the upper division baccalaureate category, 1 semester hour in Business Management (7/85).

MVS Workshop (IE4100)
Location: Piscataway, NJ and other AT&T locations.
Length: 90 hours (15 days).
Dates: August 1983-Present.
Objective: To teach MVS batch processing concepts, job control language cataloged procedures and utilities and their use.
Instruction: Course includes lecture and laboratory. Topics covered include: MVS concepts, coding of JCL statements, creating and maintaining cataloged procedures, introduction to storage facilities, and selecting and coding JCL required to execute utilities.
Credit recommendation: In the lower division baccalaureate/associate degree category, 3 semester hours in Computer Science or Data Processing (7/85).

Performance Analysis Workshop (IE1102)
Location: Piscataway, NJ and other AT&T locations.
Length: 18 hours (3 days).
Dates: June 1978-Present.
Objective: To increase the effectiveness and scope of the organization by adapting performance analysis strategies, worth analysis techniques, and the systems approach to training.
Instruction: Upon completion of this course, participants should be able to: (1) apply performance analysis strategies to organizational and individual performance problems; (2) recommend and implement non-training solutions such as feedback systems, incentive systems, and job engineering for appropriate non-training problems; and (3) conduct a worth analysis of training problems (a comparison of the value of solving the problems to the cost of training solutions).
Credit recommendation: In the upper division baccalaureate category, 1 semester hour in Business Administration and Industrial Engineering (7/85).

Personnel Subsystem Testing and Evaluation (IE1400)
Location: Piscataway, NJ and other AT&T locations.
Length: 18 hours (3 days).
Dates: June 1983-Present.
Objective: To present techniques of testing the design of a computer-based system for compatibility with human performance, and for evaluating whether user-related products or documents meet acceptable levels of performance.
Instruction: The course enables the student to be able to design and construct a test plan; to design and construct test items and instructions; to conduct test and analyze

results using representative test subjects; and to evaluate all user-related products for accuracy and quality including procedures, manuals, screens, and training materials.

Credit recommendation: In the lower division baccalaureate/associate degree category, 1 semester hour in Computer Information Systems or Management (7/85). NOTE: Students who have received credit for Structured Test Plans should not receive credit for this course.

Physical Data Base Design (Introduction and Techniques)
Location: Data Systems Education Center, Piscataway, NJ, and other Bell locations.
Length: 60 hours (2 weeks).
Dates: May 1978-December 1984.
Objective: To enable the student to make the transition from logical to physical data base design.
Instruction: Construction of an Information Management System (IMS) that provides a structural view of the data, understanding of the flexibility of the logical data base design, identification of potential back-up and recovery problems. Lecture and laboratory are used.
Credit recommendation: In the upper division baccalaureate category, 2 semester hours in Computer Science or Data Processing (2/80).

PL/1 Workshop (IE3125)
Location: Piscataway, NJ; other AT&T locations; Bell Operating Company locations.
Length: 30 hours (5 days).
Dates: June 1981-Present.
Objective: To teach students the structure, syntax, and instruction set of the PL/1 language.
Instruction: Students are required to code, execute, and debug sample programs in PL/1 using checkout and optimizing compilers. Topics covered include PROCEDURE blocks, sequence of control, stream I/O, built in functions — SUBSTR, INDEX, LENGTH, and VERIFY, storage allocation, record I/O PL/1 subroutines.
Credit recommendation: In the lower division baccalaureate/associate degree category, 2 semester hours in Computer Science or Data Processing (7/85).

Preparing Technical Presentations (IE8320)
Location: Piscataway, NJ and other AT&T locations.
Length: 28 hours (4 days).
Dates: November 1981-Present.
Objective: To prepare managers to be able to plan, prepare, and deliver a presentation.
Instruction: Both informative and persuasive presentations are discussed in detail. Two presentations, one planned and one impromptu, are given by each student during the course. The planned presentation is videotaped and then reviewed in class. Upon completion of this course, the student will be able to: (1) use an efficient and creative approach to prepare a presentation; (2) organize a presentation based on its purpose - persuade, inform, and/or influence attitudes; (3) plan and use visual aids; (4) plan and control audience participation; and (5) plan and deliver a presentation that communicates at the sensory, emotional, and rational levels.
Credit recommendation: In the lower division baccalaureate/associate degree category, 2 semester hours in Public Speaking or Managerial Communications (7/85).

Programmer Basic Training (PBT)
Location: Data Systems Education Center, Piscataway, NJ.
Length: 476 1/4 hours (12.7 weeks).
Dates: January 1975-December 1983.
Objective: To acquaint students with the physical structure and major concepts of a computer, enable students to design and implement a structured COBOL program, test and debug, modify the source statements, understand job control language, and execute various IBM programs.
Instruction: Data processing concepts; data representation; structured programming, design, implementation, and case problems; COBOL; JCL; utilities; cataloged procedures. The COBOL unit of the course emphasizes understanding diagnostic messages, making appropriate corrections to COBOL code, debugging. Students are required to take written tests and execute case studies which adhere to the principles of structured programming, the major emphasis of the course. Lecture, discussion, workshop, and independent study are used.
Credit recommendation: In the lower division baccalaureate/associate degree category or in the upper division baccalaureate category, 6 semester hours in Business, Computer Science, Engineering, Engineering Technology, or Information Science (12/79).

Programmer Productivity Techniques
Location: Data Systems Education Center, Piscataway, NJ.
Length: 30 hours (1 week).
Dates: June 1974-December 1983.
Objective: To enable programmers and managers who develop data processing applications to create error-free programs which are readable, maintainable, and changeable while producing the needed documentation as the program is designed and written.
Instruction: Structured programming; using and creating a HIPO package; translating pseudo-English into a high-level programming language, such as PL/1 or FORTRAN; writing readable COBOL; conducting and participating in walkthrough. Lecture, discussion, and workshops are used.
Credit recommendation: In the lower division baccalaureate/associate degree category, 1 semester hour in Computer Programming (2/80).

Project Management and Leadership
1. Introduction to Project Management
2. Project Leadership Workshop

Location: Data Systems Education Center, Piscataway, NJ.

Length: 1. 20 hours (3 days); 26 hours (4 days). Total 46 hours.

Dates: November 1979-December 1984.

Objective: To provide the student with skills and knowledge required to use methods, tools, and techniques that assure effective performance of project leader responsibilities.

Instruction: Responsibilities and characteristics of a data systems project leader; appropriate organizing and controlling techniques needed to administer a selected project phase subsystem of a test case. Lecture and workshops are used.

Credit recommendation: In the upper division baccalaureate category, 3 semester hours in Business Administration or Management (5/80). NOTE: Students who receive credit for this course should not receive credit for Introductory Project Management.

Project Manager Workshop

Location: Data Systems Education Center, Piscataway, NJ and other Bell locations.

Length: 33 hours (5 days).

Dates: November 1979-September 1984.

Objective: To provide the student with the knowledge and skills needed in using methods, tools, and techniques for effective project management.

Instruction: Responsibilities and characteristics necessary to prepare a complete project development and management plan. Provides practice in project planning, organization, and control of an entire, medium-risk project. Classroom exercises, lecture, workshops, and discussions are used.

Credit recommendation: In the upper division baccalaureate category, 1 semester hour in Business Administration or Management (5/80). NOTE: Students who receive credit for this course by itself should not receive credit for Introductory Project Management.

Structured Test Plans (IE2710)

Location: Piscataway, NJ and other AT&T locations.

Length: 24 hours (4 days).

Dates: January 1978-Present.

Objective: To specify how and when testing activities interact with the Total System Development process; to prepare a test plan and identify various testing methods and test aids.

Instruction: Testing principles and test planning. Includes a presentation of a testing methodology applied to each phase of the Total System Development process. Lecture, discussion, and workshops are used.

Credit recommendation: In the lower division baccalaureate/associate degree category, 1 semester hour in Computer Science or Computer Information Systems (2/80) (7/85). NOTE: Students who have received credit for Personnel Subsystem Testing and Evaluation should not receive credit for this course. This course has undergone a 5-year reevaluation and continues to meet requirements for credit recommendations.

System Design

Location: Data Systems Education Center, Piscataway, NJ.

Length: 60 hours (2 weeks).

Dates: December 1978-December 1984.

Objective: To provide students with the background necessary to enable them to identify and analyze an entity problem and create a logical model of the problem using system analysis methodology.

Instruction: Systems data structure, data flow, function structure, function flow, control, performance criteria, logical subsystems, system implementation and testing. Lecture, discussion, and workshops are used.

Credit recommendation: In the upper division baccalaureate category, 3 semester hours in Information Systems Design (5/80).

Task Analysis (IE1104)

Location: Piscataway, NJ and other AT&T locations.

Length: 15 hours (3 days).

Dates: January 1985-Present.

Objective: To present the fundamental characteristics and applications of task analysis in order to evaluate and improve current systems, modify existing systems, or as a part of total system development in the creation of new systems.

Instruction: Upon completion of this course, the student should be able to: (1) identify the sequence of procedures required to perform task analysis; (2) identify the uses of task analysis in the design of user products and development of systems, modified and new; (3) perform and document task analysis process from planning through the detail analysis phase; and (4) make recommendations for design based upon the task analysis results.

Credit recommendation: In the upper division baccalaureate degree category, 1 semester hour in Computer Information Systems or Management (7/85).

Techniques of Instruction (IE8210)

Location: Piscataway, NJ and other AT&T locations.

Length: 35 hours (5 days).

Dates: March 1978-Present.

Objective: To enable the student to instruct a class efficiently and effectively using balanced instructional techniques and objective performance criteria.

Instruction: Pre-class preparation, ice-breaking, motivation, classroom management, instructional techniques, and end-of-course evaluation. Lecture, discussion, classroom exercises, and micro-teaching are used.

Credit recommendation: In the lower division baccalaureate/associate degree category, 2 semester hours in Education, Human Resources Management, or Training and Development (7/85). NOTE: This course has undergone a 5-year reevaluation and continues to meet requirements for credit recommendations.

Test Design for Course Developers (IE8104)
Location: Piscataway, NJ and other AT&T locations.
Length: 12 hours (2 days).
Dates: August 1983-Present.
Objective: To provide basic information about test design and evaluation for course developers.
Instruction: This instructor-led course is designed for anyone in course development who would like more information about designing tests. Topics addressed include general information about testing, test items and format, and test data evaluation so upon completion of the course the student can: (1) determine which type of test is appropriate for specific applications; (2) design test items that match objectives; (3) create a test document following the recommended format; and (4) evaluate the test data.
Credit recommendation: In the lower division baccalaureate/associate degree category, 1 semester hour in Education (7/85).

User Documentation/Performance Aids Workshop (IE1200)
Location: Piscataway, NJ and other AT&T locations.
Length: 18 hours (3 days).
Dates: June 1980-Present.
Objective: To assist participants develop their skill in the design and construction of performance aids and work procedures for use on the job.
Instruction: This instructor-led workshop addresses products from the Detail and Implementation phases of Total Systems Development, but many of the principles discussed are applicable to other documentation products such as administrative guides, run books, and user guides. Upon completion of this course, the student should be able to: (1) identify the common pitfalls and problems of existing documentation products; (2) reference and apply state-of-the-art documentation principles to the design and presentation of user documents; (3) design documentation products that are clear, legible, easy to scan, and easy to reference; (4) redesign existing products to enhance accessibility, clarity, and organization; and (5) identify strengths, weaknesses, and optimum applications for six documentation formats.
Credit recommendation: In the upper division baccalaureate or lower level baccalaureate/associate degree category, 1 semester hour in Human Resources Management, Training and Development, or Education (7/85).

X.25 Network Architecture (IE7170)
Location: Piscataway, NJ and other AT&T locations.
Length: 24 hours (1 week).
Dates: March 1983-Present.
Objective: To provide a detailed description of X.25 Network Architecture including frame and packet formats with applicable scenarios.
Instruction: Course includes lecture and laboratory. Topics covered include: concepts and basic function of packet switching public data networks; BS.25 protocol characteristics; data transfer and flow control scenarios involving BX.25 packets; major difference between X.25 and BX.25; and a description of packet switching as used by various public networks.
Credit recommendation: In the upper division baccalaureate category, 1 semester hour in Data Processing, Data Communications, or Computer Science (7/85).

AT&T - Corporate Education Center, Management Education Training Division

AT&T's business education curriculum provides fundamental and advanced learning. The curriculum includes principles, theory, and practical application of marketing concepts. These courses are available to management personnel within each of AT&T's lines of business.

University faculty and internal subject matter experts present courses designed with an AT&T perspective. Each faculty member is viewed as a leading authority by business and academia. Primary training facilities are located at the Somerset and Hopewell, New Jersey learning centers. Other AT&T sites are used for remote training needs. Course managers ensure the quality of each course.

Source of official student records: Marketing Curriculum Manager, AT&T Headquarters, 399 Campus Drive, Room C-131315, Somerset, New Jersey 08873.

Additional information about the courses: Program on Noncollegiate Sponsored Instruction, Thomas A. Edison State College, 101 West State Street, CB-545, Trenton, New Jersey 08625.

Applications in Industrial Marketing Research (ME 0957)
Location: Somerset, NJ and other AT&T locations throughout the country.
Length: 40 hours (5 days).
Dates: March 1986-Present.
Objective: To acquaint students with skills to conduct industrial marketing research using conjoint analysis and cluster analysis and multi-dimensional scaling.
Learning Outcome: Upon successful completion of this course, the student will be able to: identify the uses of questionnaires in acquiring market research data; design

questionnaires for use in direct mail, telephone, and personal interviews; list questionnaire difficulties and possible solutions; use MDPREF, MONANOVA and HCLUSTER software for concept testing and product positioning; and interpret and apply the computer generated results to concept and product decisions.

Instruction: This intensive course covers the critical topics of designing questionnaires, and developing and analyzing concept testing methodologies. The course covers the mechanics of questionnaire development for industrial market research. Design issues and execution issues are discussed and resolved with practical recommendations. Concept testing techniques will be discussed and Bell Laboratories developed software for concept testing and product positioning will be utilized. The workshop will demonstrate how conjoint analysis, cluster analysis, and multidimensional scaling may be applied to concept testing and product positioning situations. Prerequisite: ME 0955.

Credit recommendation: In the graduate category, 3 semester hours in Applications in Industrial Marketing Research or Advanced Market Research (11/86).

Business/Consumer Direct Marketing Application (ME 0897)
  Location: Somerset, NJ and other AT&T locations throughout the country.
  Length: 16 hours (2 days).
  Dates: September 1986-Present.
  Objective: To introduce managers to Direct Marketing Applications.
  Learning Outcome: Upon successful completion of this course, the manager will be familiar with: business-to-business megatrends and direct marketing fundamentals; why direct mail is a unique marketing medium; the mathematics used by direct marketers; and business lists and market segmentation.
  Instruction: This course covers direct marketing techniques aimed at the business consumer and international markets. Topics include direct marketing as a cost-effective delivery channel, state of the art techniques and applications.
  Credit recommendation: In the upper division baccalaureate category, 1 semester hour in Business/Consumer Direct Marketing Applications (11/86).

Concepts in Industrial Marketing (ME 0891)
  Location: Somerset, NJ and other AT&T locations throughout the country.
  Length: 40 hours (5 days).
  Dates: January 1986-Present.
  Objective: To acquaint marketing manager with selected key concepts in industrial marketing.
  Learning Outcome: Upon successful completion of this course, the manager will be able to: describe the concept of organizational buying and use this concept as a marketing strategy; define product marketing, including product life cycle, product cannibalism, and economic value to the customer, explain the nature of industrial pricing and perform a pricing analysis; describe how and why industrial markets are segmented and assess various market segmentation alternatives; and apply the appropriate tools and techniques to develop strategies for AT&T.
  Instruction: This course applies marketing principles to industrial, real-world case situations. It emphasizes sales techniques, market segmentation, organization buyer behavior and pricing.
  Credit recommendation: In the upper division baccalaureate category, 3 semester hours in Industrial Marketing Applications (11/86).

Concepts of Promotional Strategy
  Location: Somerset, NJ and other AT&T locations throughout the country.
  Length: 16 hours (2 days).
  Dates: December 1986-Present.
  Objective: To introduce AT&T participants to various promotional concepts and how these concepts can be integrated into an effective promotional strategy.
  Learning Outcome: Upon successful completion of this course, the student will be able to: define the promotional components; advertising, sales promotion, public relations, and personal selling; illustrate the interaction between segmentation, differentiation and positioning; illustrate the campaign; provide an overview of the creative and tactical strategies used in promotion; and demonstrate techniques employed to assess promotional effectiveness.
  Instruction: This course is designed for AT&T employees who interface with customers or design marketing strategies. Various promotional concepts are studied and students are given an opportunity to integrate appropriate concepts into effective promotional strategy. After the two days of class, the students must individually write a complete promotional plan and submit this for review and grading by the instructor. Prerequisites: Successful completion of at least one college or graduate level marketing course. Also, students must read "Guide to Marketing, Media and Production" by Ann Grossman prior to attending course.
  Credit recommendation: In the graduate category, 2 semester hours or in the upper division baccalaureate category, 3 semester hours in Marketing Communications, or Sales Promotion and Advertising Concepts of Effective Promotion or Advertising Principles (11/86).

Consumer Marketing Strategies (ME 0894)
  Location: Somerset, NJ and other AT&T locations throughout the country.
  Length: 24 hours (3 days).
  Dates: July 1986-Present.
  Objective: To introduce managers to selected aspects of

consumer marketing.

Learning Outcome: Upon successful completion of this course, the manager will be able to recognize and be effective in working with: the marketing environment; consumer buyer behavior; advertising and promotion decisions; and product management.

Instruction: This course covers the planning, development and execution of a marketing program directed at consumer markets.

Credit recommendation: In the upper division baccalaureate category, 2 semester hours in Consumer Marketing Management (11/86).

Fundamentals of Marketing Research (ME 0955)

Location: Somerset, NJ and other AT&T locations throughout the country.
Length: 40 hours (5 days).
Dates: January 1986-Present.
Objective: To acquaint students with methodologies of marketing research and measurement.
Learning Outcome: Upon successful completion of this course, the participant will be able to: list the considerations in selecting appropriate research strategies; recognize the various data collection techniques and identify the strengths and weaknesses of each; describe the basic data analysis procedures and their proper application; translate marketing research findings into management recommendations regarding applications to forecasting, market segmentation, and product innovation decision making; and effectively organize and communicate marketing research findings and recommendations.
Instruction: This course provides an introduction to marketing research for individuals conducting research projects, managing the marketing research function, or making decisions based on study results.
Credit recommendation: In the graduate category, 2 semester hours or in the upper division baccalaureate category, 3 semester hours in Fundamentals of Marketing Research (11/86).

Industrial Interviewing and Focus Group Techniques (ME 0958)

Location: Somerset, NJ and other AT&T locations throughout the country.
Length: 32 hours (4 days).
Dates: October 1986-Present.
Objective: To prepare students to conduct focus group depth interviews and other group techniques pertaining to individual market research.
Learning Outcome: Upon successful completion of this course, the participant will be able to: describe the elements of telephone and personal interviewing; identify the proper use of interviewing as a data collection device; conduct personal and telephone interviews to obtain desired market research data; identify the proper uses of focus groups for preliminary market research data collection; list the requirements for designing, conducting, and evaluating industrial focus groups; and use focus group results to guide subsequent market research design development.
Instruction: This intensive workshop presents the critical elements of professional telephone, personal interviewing, and focus group interviewing techniques. Extensive individual exercises are combined with lectures and discussions to demonstrate how essential interviewing is for gathering market research data.
Credit recommendation: In the graduate category, 1 semester hour or in the upper division baccalaureate category, 2 semester hours in Industrial Interviewing and Focus Group Techniques (11/86).

Marketing Decision Making (ME 0954)

Location: Somerset, NJ and other AT&T locations throughout the country.
Length: 32 hours (4 days).
Dates: August 1986-Present.
Objective: To enable managers to make more effective decisions through an understanding of the techniques of marketing decision-making.
Learning Outcome: Upon successful completion of this course, the student will have an understanding of: the decision making process; market analysis; market and sales potential; strategic planning; and developing an integrated marketing plan.
Instruction: The three main areas covered in the course are marketing research, statistical analysis of marketing data, and sales forecasting. The emphasis is on interpretations, not computations. No specific statistical nor quantitative background is required. Students must submit a paper (for grading) after completion of class time.
Credit recommendation: In the graduate category, 2 semester hours in Marketing Decision Making (11/86).

Marketing Entre/Intrapreneurship (ME 0990)

Location: Somerset, NJ and other AT&T locations throughout the country.
Length: 34 hours (3 days).
Dates: August 1986-Present.
Objective: To make executives think like entrepreneurs both within and outside a company environment.
Learning Outcome: Upon successful completion of this course, the manager will be able: to better take appropriate business risks; to evaluate the role of the entreprenuer within the business environment, and to understand the role of the pro-active manager in the business environment.
Instruction: This seminar focuses on a series of topics designed to address and encourage innovation, creativity and entrepreneurship and intrapreneurship within a business enterprise.
Credit recommendation: In the graduate category, 2 semester hours in New Venture Management (11/86).

Product Management Concepts (ME 0896)
   Location: Somerset, NJ and other AT&T locations throughout the country.
   Length: 46 hours (5 days).
   Dates: July 1986-Present.
   Objective: To provide managers with the purposes and techniques of product management.
   Learning Outcome: Upon successful completion of this course, the participant will have an understanding of: the role and responsibilities of the product manager/team; product planning and control; using marketing research for new products; using marketing research for new or established products; forecasting sales for new/established products; product pricing strategies; product channels of distribution strategies; and entre/intrapreneurship in product management.
   Instruction: This course integrates the key concepts pertaining to the planning, development and marketing of existing and new products. The course also presents various techniques, such as marketing forecasting and marketing testing for existing and new products from a strategic point of view.
   Credit recommendation: In the graduate category, 3 semester hours in Product Planning and Management, Applied Marketing Management, Advanced Marketing Management, or Strategic Marketing Management (11/86).

Strategic Physical Distribution Management (ME 0960)
   Location: Somerset, NJ and other AT&T locations throughout the country.
   Length: 24 hours (3 days) on site.
   Dates: July 1986-Present.
   Objective: To provide an understanding of the physical distribution management concept and to encourage interfunctional teamwork necessary for cost-effective provision of products to customers.
   Learning Outcome: Upon successful completion of this course, managers will have an understanding of: integrated physical distribution management concept; physical distribution management in international marketing; order processing to improve profitability; managing customer service to build market share; computer use in physical distribution; and the functions of inventory.
   Instruction: This course examines the linkages and information flows necessary between marketing, manufacturing, finance and data systems to ensure the optimal, cost-effective provision of products to meet customer needs. The course addresses the integration of distribution-related activities including: inventory management, customer service, order processing and production planning. Prior to coming to the class over 18 hours of work (readings and case problems) must be completed and presented to instructor upon arrival. During the class, case study analyses are used and a paper is submitted to the instructor following completion of the class time.
   Credit recommendation: In the graduate category, 2 semester hours in Physical Distribution Management (11/86).

Strategic Pricing for Profitability (ME 0898)
   Location: Somerset, NJ and other AT&T locations throughout the country.
   Length: 16 hours (2 days).
   Dates: July 1986-Present.
   Objective: To acquaint managers with cost and demand oriented approaches to pricing.
   Learning Outcome: Upon successful completion of this course, managers will be able to: recognize various pricing techniques; recognize the difference between cost-based and market-based pricing; and recognize a role of market segmentation for better pricing decisions.
   Instruction: This course illustrates selected pricing procedures. The perceived value concept as an element of pricing strategy is explained through various exercises where managers can apply the principles to specific products and situations. Case study analysis is used throughout the course and a separate term paper must be submitted to the instructor after the class time as part of the course requirements. Prerequisite: Submission of a pricing plan.
   Credit recommendation: In the graduate category, 1 semester hour in Fundamentals of Pricing (11/86).

AT&T - Marketing Education - Somerset Seminars

The Marketing Education - Somerset Seminars group provides basic and advanced education of marketing concepts and techniques of common interest to all headquarters staff personnel. It also provides specific skill training for staff personnel within certain identified organizational groups.

Course delivery is achieved by AT&T subject matter experts and university faculty on AT&T premises. Classroom facilities, audiovisual support, and other student/instructor needs have been designed to ensure an effective learning environment.

Editor's Note: There have been changes in name and organization at AT&T during the six-year period in which some of the following courses have carried credit recommendations. Therefore, in previous editions of the *Guide*, some of these courses were originally listed as being offered by American Telephone and Telegraph Company - Bell System Tariffs and Cost Seminars; American Telephone and Telegraph Company - Marketing Staff and Support Development Group; American Telephone and Telegraph Company - Somerset Seminars; or American Telephone and Telegraph Company - Public Utilities and Education at Somerset Seminars Center.

Source of official student records: Curriculum Manager, AT&T Marketing Education - Somerset Seminars, 100 Davidson Avenue, 3rd Floor, Somerset, New Jersey 08873 or ACE Registry.

Additional information about the courses: Program on Noncollegiate Sponsored Instruction, The Center for Adult Learning and Educational Credentials, American Council on Education, One Dupont Circle, Washington, D.C. 20036; or Thomas A. Edison State College, 101 West State Street, CN 545, Trenton, New Jersey 08625.

A Cost Model for Communications
(Private Line Cost Models and Studies - PLIAC)
(AT&T 108, PUB 303 or SA1060)
 Location: Somerset Seminars Center, Somerset, NJ.
 Length: 40 hours (5 days).
 Dates: January 1984-December 1986.
 Objective: To provide the expertise to effectively prepare and use the Private Line Cost Models and Studies to develop incremental or resource investments and annual costs relevant to Private Line Services. The seminar further provides an understanding of the functions of other models interfacing with Private Line Cost Models and Studies.
 Instruction: This seminar enables participants to define the makeup, structure, and content of the PLIAC Model. It provides an understanding of capabilities and limitations of PLIAC as well as the purpose, content, and interrelationship of supporting files. The participants experience the procedures required to first establish PLIAC data bases, and subsequently to make actual PLIAC runs and analyze the results.
 Credit recommendation: In the graduate degree category, 1 semester hour in Finance or Accounting which would be appropriate in the following degree programs: Operations Research, Finance, Business Administration, Economics, or Accounting (11/85).

Advanced Economic Principles of Network Services Pricing
 Location: Somerset Seminars Center, Somerset, NJ.
 Length: 24 hours (3 days).
 Dates: January 1984-December 1986.
 Objective: This two-day seminar increases the understanding of the application of microeconomic theory in the pricing/costing of intrastate intraLATA services.
 Instruction: This seminar's primary emphasis is on the use of microeconomic principles in analyzing the issues relating to pricing and costing intraLATA services. It includes a brief review of economic analysis; a brief review of market mechanisms and the concept of economic efficiency; a discussion of pricing decisions by the firm and by regulatory bodies. The focus is on intraLATA services pricing issues, emphasizing the local area services.
 Credit recommendation: In the upper division baccalaureate category or in the lower division baccalaureate/associate degree category, 2 semester hours in Economics (11/85).

Advanced Service Management Seminar (BUASM)
 Location: Somerset Seminars Center, Somerset, NJ.
 Length: 40 hours (5 days).
 Dates: January 1984-December 1984.
 Objective: To provide techniques, practices, and systems to successfully select, organize, implement, and evaluate projects. Particular emphasis is placed on management of service operations with project accounting and finance, project organization/control, human resources management, and implementation issues.
 Instruction: Course is divided into three segments: (1) Project Accounting and Financial Management, emphasizes project selection and evaluation and develops criteria for definition of project goals and objectives; (2) Project Organization/Control covers project control, cost control, PERT diagrams, control path management and other techniques for successful management and implementation; (3) Human Resources Management discusses the project team/organization, motivation, implementation factors, and management of change created by the project.
 Credit recommendation: In the graduate degree category, 2 semester hours in Financial Management, Management, or Business Administration (11/85).

Advanced Market Planning (SE1000)
(Formerly Computer Assisted Market Planning [UMMC])
 Location: Somerset Seminars Center, Somerset, NJ.
 Length: 32 hours (4 days).
 Dates: January 1984-Present.
 Objective: To show participants how to implement market strategies through computer simulation.
 Instruction: Course utilizes an interactive computer model that simulates the competitive situation faced by contemporary market planners. Teams of 3-5 persons strive to achieve market share and profit over a several year period. Participants make decisions about cost dynamics, segmentation and positioning, market evolution new product/service development, resource allocation, and the use of market research data. The computer simulation model feeds back the results of team decisions before other decisions can be made. The simulation, plus integrated materials, lectures, and assistance by the seminar faculty leads participants to study a situation in depth, implement a plan, and test decision-making processes. This allows participants to: understand the relationships among the elements of a marketing plan and their impact on company performance, combine tactical with strategic plans and evaluate their effectiveness, develop insight into the dynamics of the marketing process, and learn new ideas for application of marketing resources.
 Credit recommendation: In the upper division baccalaureate degree category, 2 semester hours in Business

Administration, Industrial Marketing, Marketing, or Marketing Management (9/83).

Advanced Quantitative Methods in Marketing (Application of Multivariate Techniques)
   Location: Mt. Laurel, NJ; Atlanta, GA; Denver, CO.
   Length: 34 hours (4 days).
   Dates: January 1980-December 1982.
   Objective: To help students apply advanced statistical techniques to marketing problems.
   Instruction: Covers the fundamentals of multivariate methods and applications to research strategies. Lectures, workshops, practicums, case histories, and criterion testing are used.
   Credit recommendation: In the upper division baccalaureate category, 2 semester hours in Business Analysis, Marketing Research, Quantitative Methods, or Statistics (9/80). (Prerequisite: Statistics course or Quantitative Analysis of Marketing Data within the last three years.)

Analysis of Marketing Data for Management Decision Making (SA4085)
(Formerly Quantitative Analysis of Marketing Data)
   Location: Mt. Laurel, NJ; Atlanta, GA; Denver, CO; Somerset Seminars Center, Somerset, NJ.
   Length: 34 hours (4 days).
   Dates: January 1980-Present.
   Objective: To help managers prepare more meaningful reports, assist them in decision making, and heighten their understanding of statistical analysis.
   Instruction: Emphasizes the application of appropriate statistical techniques. Lectures, individual and group projects, problem solving, and criterion testing are used.
   Credit recommendation: In the upper division baccalaureate category, 2 semester hours in Business Analysis, Marketing, Marketing Research, Quantitative Methods, or Statistics (9/80) (11/85). NOTE: This course has undergone a 5-year reevaluation and continues to meet requirements for credit recommendations.

Capital Cost Methodology (AT&T 312 or PUB 301)
   Location: Somerset Seminars Center, Somerset, NJ.
   Length: 40 hours (1 week).
   Dates: January 1982-September 1984.
   Objective: To provide in-depth knowledge of methodologies and algorithms used in the calculations of the depreciation, post tax income, and taxes associated with cost studies.
   Instruction: This seminar equips managers with the in-depth knowledge required to explain calculations and algorithms of the CAPCOST 2 Model (a cost study tool used to determine capital costs attributable to specific project investments recognizing plant survivor characteristics, accelerated tax depreciation procedures, and investment credit); to understand and make necessary decisions regarding the appropriateness of the variable inputs to the Model (life curves, life tables, service life, etc.); to understand and explain the various elements of the output data.
   Credit recommendation: In the graduate category 2 semester hours or in the upper division baccalaureate category, 3 semester hours in Finance which is appropriate for degree programs in Finance, Public Administration, Management, Economics, or Business Administration (11/85).

Cash Flow Analysis I (AT&T 401A)
   Location: Somerset Seminars Center, Somerset, NJ.
   Length: 32 hours (4 days).
   Dates: January 1984-May 1987.
   Objective: To provide the participants with the skills to perform a valid cash flow analysis without the details of the calculations.
   Instruction: The course provides participants with an understanding of the components of the financial decision environment. Cash flows including representation, reduction to net cash flows; calculation and interpretation of summary measures (net present value) will be presented. This course provides an overview of the Economic Impact and Study System (EISS) and will train participants to enter data, and interpret output results.
   Credit recommendation: In the upper division baccalaureate category, 2 semester hours in Finance or Accounting applicable to Business Administration, Accounting, Finance, Management, or General Business degree programs. NOTE: If this course is followed by and combined with Cash Flow Analysis II (AT&T 401B), then the combined credit recommendation would be 3 semester hours in the above cited level and categories (11/85).

Competitive Marketing Strategies
   Location: Somerset Seminars, Somerset, NJ.
   Length: 19 1/2 hours (3 days).
   Dates: February 1984-December 1986.
   Objective: To acquaint managers with the issues and problems in development of marketing strategies.
   Instruction: The course covers competitive strategy under deregulation as well as segmenting deregulated markets. It contrasts the goals and objectives of regulatory bodies with those of the ultimate consumer, both business and residential. This course includes lectures, discussions, classroom exercises, simulations, problem solving, and case studies.
   Credit recommendation: In the graduate category or in the upper division baccalaureate category, 1 semester hour in Marketing (11/85).

Competitive Pricing Strategy and Tactics (BUCP and SA6010)
(Formerly Competitive Pricing Strategy and Planning [BUCP or SA6010])
   Location: Somerset Seminars Center, Somerset, NJ.

Length: 32 hours (4 days).
Dates: January 1984-Present.
Objective: To provide current approaches and techniques for integrating competitive pricing and marketing strategies, improve pricing decision process skills.
Instruction: Course is designed to prepare participants to develop competitive marketing strategies including definition of a service, selection of the most appropriate strategies to exploit market opportunities, and pricing and distribution strategies. Competitive pricing will be stressed. Competitor analysis for pricing decision making, and evaluation of pricing performance will be included. A computer simulation which integrates these marketing and pricing concepts will be used.
Credit recommendation: In the graduate level category, 2 semester hours in Marketing, Marketing Management, or Business Administration (11/85).

Computer Assisted Market Planning (UNMC)
Location: Somerset Seminars Center, Somerset, NJ.
Length: 40 hours (5 days).
Dates: January 1984-Present.
Objective: To show participants how to implement market strategies through computer simulations.
Instruction: Course utilizes an interactive computer model that simulates the competitive situation faced by contemporary market planners. Teams of 3-5 persons strive to achieve market share and profit over a several year period. Participants make decisions about cost dynamics, segmentation and positioning, market evolution new product/service development, resource allocation, and the use of market research data. The computer simulation model feeds back the results of team decisions before other decisions can be made. The simulation, plus integrated materials, lectures, and assistance by the seminar faculty leads participants to study a situation in depth, implement a plan, and test decision-making processes. This allows participants to: understand the relationships among the elements of a marketing plan and their impact on company performance, combine tactical with strategic plans and evaluate their effectiveness, develop insight into the dynamics of the marketing planning process, and learn new ideas for application of marketing resources.
Credit recommendation: In the upper division baccalaureate degree category, 2 semester hours in Marketing, Industrial Marketing, Marketing Management, or Business Administration (11/85).

Concepts of Capital Costs (CAPCOST)
Location: Somerset Seminars Center, NJ.
Length: 35 hours (1 week).
Dates: January 1981-December 1984.
Objective: To provide the detailed tax and accounting methods utilized in the CAPCOST 2 model, the development of the components of a capital cost (depreciation, post-tax income, and income tax expense) as implemented in the CAPCOST 2 Model and to provide a thorough analysis of the calculations performed by the CAPCOST 2 model.
Instruction: In this seminar such items as the concepts of capital costs, accelerated depreciation, book basis versus tax basis of investment, investment tax credit, and present worth levelized costs are addressed in general terms. The seminar also provides through casework hands-on experience in such areas as procedures for modeling the survivor characteristics of plant investment, ACRS depreciation with salvage and cost of removal, use into the CAPCOST 2 Model. The seminar concludes with an extensive casework utilizing the CAPCOST 2 Model. Lecture, audiovisuals, discussion, casework, time-share computer are used.
Credit recommendation: In the upper division baccalaureate category, 2 semester hours in Business Administration, Public Administration, or Finance and Engineering Economics (12/81).

Concepts of Service and Segment Management (AT&T 504 and SA4040)
Location: Somerset Seminars Center, Somerset, NJ.
Length: 24 hours (3 days).
Dates: January 1984-Present.
Objective: To provide AT&T Marketing personnel with an overview of Service and Segment Management and their interrelationship.
Instruction: This seminar addresses marketing within the AT&T structure, the service development management processes. Participants will be aware of the roles and responsibilities of Service and Segment Management. Sessions on life cycle management, decision and risk analysis, the regulatory process, marketing research, market segmentation, forecasting, and tracking are presented in this seminar.
Credit recommendation: In the upper division baccalaureate degree category, 2 semester hours in Marketing (Marketing Segmentation) for use in degree programs in Marketing or Business Administration (11/85).

Consumer Marketing (SA4100)
(Formerly Applied Consumer Behavior)
Location: Somerset Seminars Center, Somerset, NJ.
Length: 21 hours (3 days).
Dates: January 1985-Present.
Objective: To provide an understanding of the basic concepts of consumer marketing and how they apply to the AT&T residence marketplace. To enumerate ways in which the consumer market can be segmented. To identify the synergies among environmental influences, market research and segmentation, demographics, psychological dimensions, social and cultural factors in understanding the consumer marketplace. To distinguish among the various elements of the marketing mix and how they impact the analysis, development and implementation of marketing

strategies, plans, and programs in the residence market.

Instruction: This course is designed to provide managers with an understanding of consumer marketing and the application of the concepts and practices to AT&T-C Residence Market. It offers participants an introduction to marketing in a competitive environment focusing upon the consumer. Managers are trained in analyzing the residence marketplace and in developing and implementing marketing plans and programs. The course format includes lectures, group participation, and case analysis.

Credit recommendation: In the upper division baccalaureate category, 1 semester hour in Marketing (11/85).

Cost Analysis for Marketing Studies (AT&T 202 and SA2010)
(Formerly Fundamentals of Costing for Pricing Decisions [AT&T 202])
  Location: Somerset Seminars Center, Somerset, NJ.
  Length: 32 hours (4 days).
  Dates: January 1984-Present.
  Objective: To provide an awareness and knowledge of the fundamentals of cost and rate functions.
  Instruction: This seminar is designed to describe and discuss conceptually the Service Management approach. It gives an overview of the role of the Federal Communications and State Commissions in pricing decisions. The seminar describes the questions that an incremental analysis, cash flow analysis, and a fully distributed cost study will answer. The seminar also describes the microeconomics concepts used in service costs work including price demand curve, marginal revenue, marginal costs, elasticity of demand, and cross elastic effects. Participants will identify and compute the components of investment costs, and capital related costs operating expenses. The course describes and defines the purpose of the cost model in regard to translators, unit investments, and annual cost factors.
  Credit recommendation: In the upper division baccalaureate category, 3 semester hours in Economics, Finance, Management, or Business Administration (11/85).

Data Analysis and Regression (AT&T 313)
  Location: Somerset Seminars Center, Somerset, NJ.
  Length: 80 hours (2 weeks).
  Dates: January 1982-December 1983.
  Objective: This seminar provides participants with the skills to apply a variety of data-analytic and regression techniques for modeling and forecasting situations to interpret the statistical and computational output of a variety of regression techniques with particular emphasis on robust and resistant methods; to effectively use computer-generated graphics in both data display, model building, and management presentations; to recognize an appropriate modeling strategy to arrive at practical regression models at reasonable costs; to effectively use statistical computing software for data analysis and regression in an interactive mode; and to prepare, present, and document modeling results for both technical and higher management audiences.
  Instruction: Course is designed to teach student.
  Credit recommendation: In the graduate category, 3 semester hours in Data Analysis and Regression (11/85).

Data Gathering, System Analysis, and Design
  Location: AT&T Training Center, South Plainfield, NJ, and various operating company training centers.
  Length: 26 hours (4 days).
  Dates: October 1980-December 1983.
  Objective: To enable the student to use four major gathering techniques to analyze and design a business system, use data flow diagrams to graphically depict a customer business system, construct decision trees and tables, correctly define data structures and elements, and explain the purpose and function of a data dictionary.
  Instruction: Students are introduced to the top-down approach to systems analysis and design. The key point that students should understand is that systems analysis and design is not a straight-line process. Rather, it requires multiple iterations. Data collection plans and techniques are discussed in detail and students complete exercises requiring the use of interviews, content analysis, and questionnaires to acquire information to be used in system design. Several tools for analysis and design are discussed: flowcharting, DFDs, and HIPO. Data Flow Diagramming is covered in detail and students are asked to complete a high-level DFD for a customer system and a structured walkthrough. Additional symbols and conventions for lower-level DFDs are covered next, and students complete another exercise in charting and presenting a lower-level DFD. Data base concepts addressed are nest-data element, data structures, common files, etc. Process logic is also reviewed, and students are asked to complete exercises in constructing decision trees, decision tables, and writing logic in structured English.
  Credit recommendation: In the lower division baccalaureate/associate degree category, 1 semester hour in Systems Analysis (7/81).

Decision and Risk Analysis (SE9000)
  Location: Somerset Seminars Center, Somerset, NJ.
  Length: 21 hours (3 days).
  Dates: May 1985-Present.
  Objective: To provide students with a set of concepts and techniques that furnish the logic for decision making in the face of uncertainty.
  Instruction: Course examines the role of risk and uncertainty in the managerial decision making process. Lecture, discussion, and demonstrations.
  Credit recommendation: In the graduate category or in the upper division baccalaureate category, 1 semester hour in Decision and Risk Analysis (11/85).

Demand Analysis Techniques (PUB 302)
 Location: Somerset Seminars Center, Somerset, NJ.
 Length: 80 hours (10 days).
 Dates: January 1979-December 1984.
 Objective: To provide a foundation in practical applications of regression analyses and econometric modeling to estimate and forecast demand and revenues for telecommunications products and services.
 Instruction: Course translates microeconomic theory into empirical demand models for telecommunication needs. It teaches participants to define and select appropriate dependent and independent variables when specifying a demand model, course also offers an understanding of major data sources, collection and validity problems with those sources, and identifies potential solutions to these problems.
 Credit recommendation: In the graduate category, 5 semester hours in Business Administration, Economics, Industrial Engineering, Operations Research, Public Administration, Systems Analysis, or Econometrics (11/85).

Demand Analysis Techniques Seminar (DATS)
 Location: Bell System Tariffs and Costs Seminars, Somerset, NJ.
 Length: 85 hours (2 weeks).
 Dates: January 1979-December 1984.
 Objective: To provide the participant with a foundation in the practical applications of regression analysis and econometric modeling to estimate and forecast demand and revenues for telephone products and services. Particular emphasis is given to quantifying the individual factors that impact demand, e.g., elasticity estimation.
 Instruction: This seminar will enable the participant to translate microeconomic theory into empirical demand models for telecommunication needs, and to define and select appropriate dependent and independent variables when specifying a demand model. It will provide an understanding of major data sources, collection and validity problems with those sources, and potential solutions to those problems. In general, the seminar will allow the participant to understand and experience the various aspects of demand analysis, ranging from model specifications to model building, and documentation. Lectures, audiovisuals, individual and group tasks, and guest speakers are used. (Prerequisite: Background in regression analysis, calculus, and economics).
 Credit recommendation: In the graduate category, 5 semester hours in Business Administration, Economics, Industrial Engineering, Operations Research, or Systems Analysis (2/81).

Direct Marketing (SA4110)
 Location: Somerset Seminars Center, Somerset, NJ.
 Length: 17 hours (3 days).
 Dates: June 1985-Present.
 Objective: To provide managers with an overview of the fundamentals of direct marketing.
 Instruction: This course is designed to provide managers with an overview of the field of direct marketing with special emphasis on telemarketing. This course includes lectures, discussion, classroom exercises, simulation, problem solving, and case studies.
 Credit recommendation: In the upper division baccalaureate category, 1 semester hour in Specialty Advertising (11/85).

Economics for Pricing Network Services (PUB 102)
 Location: Somerset Seminars Center, Somerset, NJ.
 Length: 24 hours (3 days).
 Dates: January 1984-December 1984.
 Objective: To provide economic perspectives for understanding the foundation of pricing and costing decisions for intrastate intraLATA services.
 Instruction: This course presents a basic introduction to microeconomics with examples drawn from and related to the telecommunications field. In this course market mechanisms, market analysis, and cost analysis will be discussed. A session on pricing strategies used by the different Regions on specific lines of business will also be presented. Course utilizes a high degree of lecture and instructor/student interaction to achieve its objectives.
 Credit recommendation: In the upper division baccalaureate category or in the lower division baccalaureate/associate degree category, 1 semester hour in Applied Economics, Pricing Strategies, or Business Administration (11/85).

Financial Awareness Seminar (SE9000)
(Introduction to Finance)
 Location: Somerset Seminars Center, Somerset, NJ.
 Length: 14 hours (2 days).
 Dates: November 1984-Present.
 Objective: The course focuses on the financial objectives and structure of AT&T and achieving financial excellence.
 Instruction: The course stresses the use of financial analysis, the management of business and financial risk, cost of capital, and net present value.
 Credit recommendation: In the graduate category or in the upper division baccalaureate category, 1 semester hour in Business Finance, Principles of Finance, Introduction to Finance, or Corporate Finance (11/85).

Financial Awareness Plus Seminar (SA9001)
 Location: Somerset Seminars Center, Somerset, NJ.
 Length: 18 hours (2 1/2 days).
 Dates: November 1984-Present.
 Objective: To improve the level of financial awareness and competency of AT&T managers.
 Instruction: The course content stresses the Wall Street perspective, the use of financial analysis, the management of business and financial analysis, the management of busi-

ness and financial risk, cost of capital, and net present value. Learning points are reinforced through a group exercise, discussion of financially excellent companies, and analysis of a sample case.

Credit recommendation: In the graduate category, 1 semester hour in Business Finance, Principles of Finance, or Corporate Finance (11/85).

Financial Management in Telecommunications
(a) Financial Perspectives on Telecommunications (WSS1)
(b) Financial Management for Services Managers (WSS4)

Location: Somerset Seminars Center, Somerset, NJ.
Length: (a) 8 hours (1 day); (b) 16 hours (2 days).
Dates: January 1984-December 1984.
Objective: (a) To provide participants with a financial analyst's view of telecommunications in a post-divestiture environment. (b) To help participants gain skills to interpret financial strength, expand profits, strengthen cash flow and cash position, locate and determine capital needs, analyze profit margins, measure and improve operating performance.
Instruction: (a) The course provides an understanding of the various forces that affect current telecommunications, e.g., competition, technology, regulation, social changes, judicial and legislative actions and inflation. Participants will gain insights into the new distinct businesses in telecommunications - customer premises, services, local exchange, enhanced services, and manufacturing. (b) This seminar provides participants with an overview for understanding the return-on-investment concept and using it effectively to control and spot developing financial problems. Participants will understand cash flows through a company and how to forecast that flow of cash. It allows participants to analyze changes in volume, price, and cost, elements in the cost of producing a service, what variables affect gross margin, breakeven strategies, cost behavior patterns and the "margin of safety."
Credit recommendation: In the upper division baccalaureate category, 1 semester hour in Financial Management. NOTE: Parts (a) and (b) must both be completed for credit recommendation to apply. No credit recommended for either part alone (11/85).

Financial Management in Telecommunications (SE3000)

Location: Somerset Seminars Center, Somerset, NJ.
Length: 24 hours (3 days).
Dates: January 1985-Present.
Objective: To provide a financial analyst's view of telecommunications in a post divestiture environment.
Instruction: The course provides an introduction to participants with basic financial principles. The course surveys the basic techniques used by money managers to evaluate and improve profit performance by reviewing the financial indicators and ratios used in appraising performance. The course provides an understanding of the various forces that currently affect the telecommunications industry, i.e., competition, technology, regulation, social changes, judicial and legislative factors, and inflation.
Credit recommendation: In the upper division baccalaureate degree category, 1 semester hour in Financial Statement Analysis (11/85).

Financial Planning Control and Decision Making (UMMD and SG1010)
(Formerly Managerial Decision Making Through Financial Planning and Control [UMMD])

Location: Somerset Seminars Center, Somerset, NJ.
Length: 24 hours (3 days).
Dates: January 1984-Present.
Objective: To enable participants to apply financial information to service marketing decisions, perform financial analysis of alternative courses of action, improve profit planning and control processes.
Instruction: Seminar focuses on the financial analysis of ratios and the time value of money. Participants gain the following knowledge for management planning and control: (1) relationship between measurement systems and business strategies, (2) designing the measurement system for specific organizational units, (3) the budgeting process and its behavioral implications, and (4) the relationship between budgeting and the long-range planning systems. Participants learn to identify costs relevant to various decisions, cost-volume-profit relationships, treatment of sunk costs and operating costs, and analyses of complex alternatives.
Credit recommendation: In the upper division baccalaureate category, 1 semester hour in Financial Decision Making, Financial Analysis, Business Administration, or Management (11/85).

Financial Statement Analysis
(a) Understanding Financial Statements (WSS2)
(b) Effective Financial Analysis (WSS3)

Location: Somerset Seminars Center, Somerset, NJ.
Length: (a) 8 hours (1 day); (b) 16 hours (2 days).
Dates: January 1984-December 1984.
Objective: (a) To help participants gain a solid foundation in basic financial principles. (b) To gain a clear understanding of financial statements. Course provides participants with knowledge of how to predict future financial positions, how to measure the degree of risk in marginal accounts, how to use financial ratios, and how to compare financial standings and operating results of similar businesses.
Instruction: (a) Course discusses simplifying financial records, constructing financial statements, providing evaluations to determine progress by examining balance sheet relationships and measuring costs and margins. (b) Course covers financial statements, internal analyses of

the effectiveness of operations and management decisions, capital analyses to determine how management handles money, comparative analyses revealing trends in finances and uncovering problems in marketing and management decisions, and marginal risk analyses in predicting future business prospects.

Credit recommendation: In the upper division baccalaureate category, 1 semester hour in Financial Statement Analysis. NOTE: Parts (a) and (b) must both be completed for credit recommendation to apply. No credit recommended for either part alone (11/85).

Forecasting for Marketing Managers (SA4090) (Formerly Sales Forecasting)
  Location: Somerset Seminars Center, Somerset, NJ.
  Length: 34 hours (4 days).
  Dates: January 1980-Present.
  Objective: To present an intensive treatment of time series analysis, national and regional forecasts, and product and/or service forecasts.
  Instruction: Emphasizes the Delphi technique, sales-force opinions method, executive judgement forecasts, customer surveys, as well as statistical and graphical presentation. Lectures, discussion, and group exercises.
  Credit recommendation: In the upper division baccalaureate category, 2 semester hours in Sales Forecasting (9/80) (11/85).

Fundamentals of Finance and Accounting (UPFF or SE2000)
  Location: Somerset Seminars Center, Somerset, NJ.
  Length: 24 hours (3 days).
  Dates: January 1984-Present.
  Objective: To provide the fundamentals of finance and accounting, furnish an overall understanding of the role of accounting and finance in the success of an enterprise.
  Instruction: Course covers an analysis of financial statements, including the nature of assets, liabilities, and equity. Course includes an examination of financial data, factors that cause fluctuations in the performance of different divisions and service/product lines, and decision rules for top management to improve assessments and predictive ability as well as cash flow and project return on investment.
  Credit recommendation: In the upper division baccalaureate category, 1 semester hour in either finance or accounting (11/85).

Fundamentals of Modern Marketing (AT&T 405A and SA4060)
  Location: Somerset Seminars Center, Somerset, NJ.
  Length: 32 hours (4 days).
  Dates: January 1983-Present.
  Objective: To provide participants with an introductory understanding of the type of marketing decisions made in a large organization.
  Instruction: This seminar provides a general overview of the marketing process as it relates to service marketing. Participants will be offered a basic overview of those marketing principles needed to function effectively in AT&T's new marketing environment. The seminar uses case studies, guest lectures, and relevant current literature.
  Credit recommendation: In the upper division baccalaureate category, 2 semester hours in Introduction to Marketing (9/84).

Integrated Marketing and Financial Strategy (SA4500) (Formerly Financial Applications in Marketing Achieving Customer and Investor Satisfaction)
  Location: Somerset Seminars Center, Somerset, NJ.
  Length: 21 hours (3 days).
  Dates: October 1985-Present.
  Objective: To acquaint students with the role of financial analysis in marketing.
  Instruction: This course presents strategic alternatives in the areas of promotion, price, and distribution as related to the marketing of products and services. The role of financial analysis in the control of marketing mix decisions is also emphasized.
  Credit recommendation: In the graduate category or in the upper division baccalaureate category, 1 semester hour in Marketing (11/83).

International Marketing (AT&T 411 and SA4080)
  Location: Somerset Seminars Center, Somerset, NJ.
  Length: 24 hours (3 days).
  Dates: November 1983-Present.
  Objective: To provide participants with an overview of foreign market opportunities.
  Instruction: This seminar is designed to complement the participant's business experiences. It offers an appreciation of the similarities and differences of doing business in the service sector internationally versus domestically. The seminar uses case studies, guest lectures, and relevant materials from journals and trade magazines.
  Credit recommendation: In the upper division baccalaureate category, 2 semester hours in Introduction to World Resources (9/84).

Introduction to Regulated Utilities (PUB 201)
  Location: Somerset Seminars Center, Somerset, NJ.
  Length: 40 hours (5 days).
  Dates: January 1984-December 1984.
  Objective: To provide an overview of the components of utility pricing and rate case processing.
  Instruction: Course provides an introduction to the elements of a regulated utility. It describes the factors considered in determining the need for rate changes, examines the price structure for key intraLATA service and explains financial and capital components. It also provides an overview of major accounting and reporting systems

used by a utility in operation. Course uses lectures, group discussions, and workshops.

Credit recommendation: In the upper division baccalaureate category, 2 semester hours in Business Administration, Marketing, or Public Administration.

Local Network Services Seminar (LNSS)
(Formerly Exchange Services Seminar [EXS])
  Location: Bell System Tariffs and Costs Seminars, Somerset, NJ.
  Length: 35 1/2 hours (1 week).
  Dates: *Version 1:* May 1980-November 1981. *Version 2:* December 1981-December 1984.
  Objective: *Version 1:* To provide information and knowledge fundamentals to the understanding of key exchange issues and techniques. *Version 2:* To provide a forum for identification and discussion of the pertinent issues impacting the implementation of Local Measured Service and the provision of attendant local area services.
  Instruction: *Version 1:* This seminar addresses exchange service definitions, concepts, pricing and costing methodologies; cost models; economic and market impacts. In addition, the seminar discusses interrelationships between exchange and network services, extended area service optional calling plans, coin operation and service, radio services, and measured service. The seminar provides a group exercise which involves rate structures and levels, the critical need for long-range plans, and awareness of various market impacts. Lectures, audiovisuals, guest speakers, group task performances, and field observations are used. *Version 2:* This seminar utilizes various instructional strategies so that the participants have a high level perception of the application of strategy and development of pricing principles; provides discussion of pertinent issues, primarily from a public acceptance view. Presentation by system subject matter experts and non-Bell consultants will provide current viewpoints on the key local area service issues. Persons completing the seminar should also have a greater understanding of the economic rationale for local area service ratemaking decisions and the need for specific long range planning.
  Credit recommendation: In the upper division baccalaureate category, 1 semester hour in Business Administration, Engineering, or Public Administration (2/81).

Market Segmentation/Buyer Behavior
(Buyer Behavior)
  Location: Somerset Seminars Center, Somerset, NJ.
  Length: 34 hours (4 days).
  Dates: January 1980-Present.
  Objective: To develop the theory of buyer behavior and its impact on market segmentation strategy.
  Instruction: Stresses individual market segmentation in terms of different types of organizations, their sizes, distribution, number, geographical location, and types of purchasing organizations. The customer is studied from a behavioral point of view.
  Credit recommendation: In the upper division baccalaureate category, 2 semester hours in Marketing (9/80) (11/85).

Marketing Communications Workshop (AT&T 502 and SE7000)
(Formerly Media Interaction for Managers [AT&T 502 and SE7000])
  Location: Somerset Seminars Center, Somerset, NJ.
  Length: 24 hours (3 days).
  Dates: January 1984-Present.
  Objective: To provide managers with the communication skills required in an evolving management and marketing culture.
  Instruction: This course concentrates on the following skill training: audience analysis, lecture techniques, effective use of visuals, handling a question/answer sequence, handling adversary questions, panel discussion techniques, effective meeting techniques, television techniques, interview techniques, body language, and proper dress. This course utilizes a high degree of videotaping and individual feedback and critique.
  Credit recommendation: In the graduate degree category, 1 semester hour is appropriate for use in degree programs in Business Communication, Public Administration, Management, or Organizational Behavior (11/85).

Marketing Research (SA4075)
  Location: Somerset Seminars Center, Somerset, NJ.
  Length: 34 hours (4 days).
  Dates: January 1980-Present.
  Objective: To provide students with the basic tools, concepts, and approaches used in data collection in marketing.
  Instruction: Different approaches to data collection, with emphasis on secondary sources, as well as the use of quantitative and qualitative procedures.
  Credit recommendation: In the upper division baccalaureate category, 2 semester hours in Marketing or Marketing Research (9/80) (11/85).

Marketing Strategy (SA4065)
  Location: Somerset Seminars Center, Somerset, NJ.
  Length: 34 hours (4 days).
  Dates: January 1980-Present.
  Objective: To survey marketing operations, market planning, and market research.
  Instruction: Covers subjects related to planning, evaluation, and control in the marketing of services.
  Credit recommendation: In the upper division baccalaureate category, 2 semester hours in Marketing (9/80) (11/85).

Measured Service Issues Seminar

Location: Bell System Tariffs and Cost Seminars, Somerset, NJ.

Length: 44 1/2 hours (1 week).

Dates: October 1979-October 1981.

Objective: To concentrate on all the internal and external issues associated with addressing measured service implementation proposals in both testimony preparation and presentation.

Instruction: This seminar assumes in-depth knowledge of the measured service issue and familiarity with the preparation as discussed in the General Rate and Cost Issue Seminar. MSIS-1 provides participants with the opportunity to discuss the issues with subject matter experts, to monitor lectures by non-Bell consultants, and to receive a high ratio of videotaped role play. This seminar relies on intergroup discussions and task performances to achieve the level of preparedness needed to address effectively the issue before the regulatory bodies. Panel discussions, lectures, individual and group task performances, videotaped role play, evaluation by subject matter experts, and lectures by consultants are used.

Credit recommendation: In the graduate category, 2 semester hours in Business Administration, Law, or Public Administration (2/81).

Microeconomics Seminar (MES)

Location: Bell Systems Tariffs and Cost Seminars, Somerset, NJ.

Length: 23 hours (3 days).

Dates: October 1977-December 1984.

Objective: To increase the awareness and understanding Bell System managers have of the microeconomic theory and the application of that theory in the pricing/costing of telecommunication services.

Instruction: This seminar's primary emphasis is on the use of microeconomics theory in pricing and in regulatory proceedings. The seminar includes introduction to economic analysis; discussion of market mechanisms, e.g., principle components of the market, interplay of supply and demand; analysis of supply and demand, e.g., economic concept, of consumer decision making, price elasticity and cross elasticity, represssion, definition of various costs; discussion of pricing decisions by the firm, pricing decisions by regulatory bodies; discussion of satisfying business objectives and regulatory objectives in a single telephone's pricing policy. The seminar concludes with a discussion of the trends and current issues in the intrastate regulatory arena as seen by a non-Bell consultant. Lecture, discussion, and question/answer sessions are used.

Credit recommendation: In the upper division baccalaureate category or in the lower division baccalaureate/associate degree category, 2 semester hours in Economics (2/81).

Network Cost System and Workshop (AT&T 103 A&B)

Location: Somerset Seminars Center, Somerset, NJ.

Length: 103A. 16 hours (2 days); 103B. 24 hours (2 days).

Dates: January 1984-Present.

Objective: 103A. To provide a perspective on the interstate Network Cost System (NCS) and its application to costs process for the interstate public switched network. 103B. This seminar is sequential to AT&T 103A; it provides the details and specifics of the interstate network service cost system.

Instruction: 103A. The main emphasis on the course will be NCS as a financial analysis tool and will build on principles presented in the Fundamentals of Costing for Pricing Decisions. The course starts with a review and background material on cost concepts and Public Switched Network call and its network components utilized throughout this course, also aggregates the various NCS investment/cost analyses. The NCS Functions module introduces a six-step flowchart of the cost development process. The final two modules are designed to "round out" the NCS course by positioning the NCS in the financial analysis process and presenting an overview of the mechanics of executing NCS.

103B. Section I of the workshop begins by linking with the NCSI courses and these provide a "Systems Approach" diagram, details the various inputs and outputs of NCS. The modules that follow will address each of the input/output items individually and will detail the data selection/specification required to set up NCS. The final module in Section I examines the NCS output and how results are extracted and analyzed based on the study objective. Section II offers the participant the opportunity to apply NCS to three case problems that cover a range of basic NCS studies conducted by the PSN service groups: a marginal analysis, an incremental cost analysis with data extraction for NPCS and cash flow, and a new service analysis for initial rate-setting. The participants will be required to identify the study objective, complete the NCS run request form, and extract/analyze the NCS output.

Credit recommendation: In the upper division baccalaureate category, 2 semester hours in Systems Analysis, Quantitative Methods, or Economics (11/85).

Network Services Issues Seminar (NSIS)
(Formerly General Rate and Cost Issue Seminar [GIS])

Location: Bell System Tariffs and Costs Seminars, Somerset, NJ.

Length: 43 1/2 hours (1 week).

Dates: February 1977-December 1984.

Objective: To provide participants with a clear understanding of the techniques for effective presentation of testimony before regulatory bodies, with experience of the need for consistent approaches in addressing fundamental issues, and with experience of the process for achieving the proper regulatory team (rate, cost, marketing, legal, etc.) interactions.

Instruction: This seminar is considered the foundation of discipline and involves experience in writing testimonies, implementing the methodology for effective presentation of each testimony, opportunity to present the testimony in a simulated role-play performance by subject matter experts. Lectures, guest speakers, videotaped presentations, and individual group tasks are used. The seminar also includes videotaping of role plays and evaluation of participants' performances.

Credit recommendation: In the graduate category, 2 semester hours in Business Administration, Law, or Public Administration (11/85).

Principles of Marketing Management (SE1030) (Marketing Management Program) (UMMP)
   Location: Somerset Seminars Center, Somerset, NJ.
   Length: 24 hours (3 days).
   Dates: January 1984-Present.
   Objective: To provide an understanding of service marketing issues and principles and the roles and tasks of marketers in the strategic planning process. Course also provides a framework for strategic thinking and understanding of the role that marketing research plays in decision making.
   Instruction: Within this program, one module focuses on the fundamentals of marketing, which will cover such topics as marketing planning, buyer behavior, market strategies, product, pricing, distribution, and promotional policies and strategies, and monitoring the marketing plan. Another module provides participants with the understanding of the market research system, the management interface, validity, and approaches to conclusive research. Another module provides product management discussion, market segmentation, trade off analysis, marketing research and forecasting. The final module provides participants with the knowledge of strategic marketing management, the planning concepts and tools.
   Credit recommendation: In the upper division baccalaureate category, 1 semester hour in Business Administration, Marketing, or Marketing Management (9/83).

Public Switched Network Seminar (PSNS)
   Location: Bell System Tariffs and Costs Seminars, Somerset, NJ.
   Length: 35 1/2 hours (1 week).
   Dates: February 1980-December 1984.
   Objective: To provide an in-depth review of the issues associated with the pricing of public switched network services. The material will be of critical importance for understanding the appropriate future pricing policies for PSN services.
   Instruction: This seminar addresses basic components of the public switched network, presents economic theory, and discusses service offering guidelines. It also provides an understanding of various rate design tools, e.g., Message Analysis of Revenue and Customers (MARC); Centralized Message Data Systems (CMDS); WATS Information Systems (WIS); Demand Analysis and cost inputs, such as MIMIC, ODOD, EDA, SCORE; and other appropriate cost supports. Lecture, audiovisuals, group interaction, discussion, and field observations are used.
   Credit recommendation: In the upper division baccalaureate category, 2 semester hours in Business Administration, Communications, Economics, Engineering Economics, Finance, Industrial Engineering, or Public Administration (2/81).

Rate Seminar (RS)
   Location: Bell System Tariffs and Cost Seminars, Somerset, NJ.
   Length: 80 hours (2 weeks).
   Dates: January 1980-December 1984.
   Objective: To provide participants with an overview of the requirements for preparation, design and implementation of basic, nonbasic, network, and special network service rate structures; to expand the knowledge level of those assigned to rate structure work; to provide understanding for those who must relate with rate personnel.
   Instruction: This seminar utilizes subject matter expert (SME) from the various rate and cost disciplines to address the historical and developing principles and concepts used in rate structure design. The seminar presents marketing approaches, changes and challenges to the industry, cost/price theory and application, competition, current proposals in the exchange network, special network services, terminal products, and rate costs preparation. A simulated rate case concludes the seminar with an illustrative experience of rate structure implementation. SME lectures, audiovisuals, individual and group task performance, group discussion, and guest speakers form the seminar process.
   Credit recommendation: In the upper division baccalaureate category, 3 semester hours in Business Administration, Management and/or Marketing, or Public Administration (2/81).

Regulated Pricing and Marketing (AT&T 201)
   Location: Somerset Seminars Center, Somerset, NJ.
   Length: 40 hours (5 days).
   Dates: January 1983-May 1985.
   Objective: To provide an overview of marketing, pricing, and costing in a regulated environment.
   Instruction: The instruction includes marketing and services planning overviews; plus hands-on exercises in marketing of MTS, WATS/800 and Special Network Services. A module addressing basic through advanced Service Management concepts and techniques is included.
   Credit recommendation: In the upper division baccalaureate degree category, 2 semester hours in Marketing

applicable to degree programs in Marketing, Business Administration, or Management (9/83).

Restructure of Private Line Issues (RPLS-1)
   Location: Bell System Tariffs and Cost Seminars, Somerset, NJ.
   Length: 44 3/4 hours (1 week).
   Dates: October 1979-September 1981.
   Objective: To concentrate on all the internal and external issues associated with the reprice restructure of private-line services as they apply to testimony preparation and presentation.
   Instruction: This seminar assumes in-depth knowledge of the private line or special switched network services and familiarity with the preparation and presentation techniques as discussed in the General Rate and Cost Issue Seminar. RPLS-1 provides an overview of pricing/costing principles presented by subject-matter experts; lectures by non-Bell consultants; high ratio of videotaped role play. This seminar relies on intergroup discussions and task performances to achieve the level of preparedness needed to address effectively the issues before the regulatory bodies. Panel discussion, lectures, individual and group task performances, videotaped role play, consultants, and evaluations by subject matter experts are used.
   Credit recommendation: In the graduate category, 1 semester hour in Business Administration, Law, or Public Administration (2/81).

Service Plan Financial Analysis (AT&T 404)
(Analysis for Service Decisions)
   Location: Somerset Seminars Center, Somerset, NJ.
   Length: 32 hours (4 days).
   Dates: January 1984-November 1984.
   Objective: To provide participants with the training to perform and interpret the types of analysis used in the work of the Service Groups, and to adapt to changing or unusual analysis requirements.
   Instruction: This seminar provides participants with the understanding of the analysis tools used in Service Group work, interrelationships, and the use of these tools to perform any of the economic, regulatory, accounting and tracking analyses normally encountered. Analysis systems such as inputs and interpretation of outputs will also be discussed.
   Credit recommendation: In the upper division baccalaureate category, 2 semester hours in Financial Management which could apply to degree programs in Business Administration, Management, or Marketing (11/85).

Special Network Services Seminar (SNSS)
   Location: Bell System Tariffs and Cost Seminars, Somerset, NJ.
   Length: 38 hours (1 week).
   Dates: March 1980-December 1984.
   Objective: To provide personnel in the operating companies' private-line and data-channel organizations with a basic level of job-effectiveness.
   Instruction: This seminar provides participants with an understanding of the basic plant network components used by each of the private-line and data services; provides a description of each service offering, including the market needs and recommended rate structures; analyzes the nature and application of the private-line and general exchange tariffs related to these offerings. Lectures, audiovisuals, casework, discussions, and field observation are used.
   Credit recommendation: In the upper division baccalaureate category, 2 semester hours in Business Administration, Electrical Engineering, Engineering Communications, Industrial Engineering, or Public Administration (2/81).

Stakeholder Analysis (AT&T 503)
(Evaluation of AT&T Interexchange Culture: A Management Technique)
   Location: Somerset Seminars Center, Somerset, NJ.
   Length: 40 hours (1 week).
   Dates: January 1984-Present.
   Objective: To provide participants with an understanding of the evolution occurring in the AT&T culture, to provide the participant with the techniques to cope with the corporate changes, and to provide those techniques needed to address the new stakeholders in the unregulated marketplace.
   Instruction: This seminar addresses the changing environment of business, the stakeholder management philosophy and process, human skills and negotiations. This seminar provides participants with a realistic experience of stakeholder applications by making various external and internal resource people available for each role play required in the specific stakeholder process. This seminar is designed to be easily adaptable to a variety of current issues and concerns. It will constantly by modified to meet identified needs.
   Credit recommendation: In the graduate category, 2 semester hours or in the upper division baccalaureate category, 2 or 3 semester hours in Business Administration, Organizational Behavior, Management, or Public Administration (11/85).

Statistical Analysis in Marketing
(Marketing Statistics)
   Location: Somerset Seminars Center, Somerset, NJ.
   Length: 34 hours (4 days).
   Dates: January 1980-December 1984.
   Objective: To familiarize students with the use and application of statistics in the analysis of marketing data.
   Instruction: The course covers applied sampling techniques, hypothesis testing, analysis of variance, and correlation analysis utilizing marketing data.

Credit recommendation: In the upper division baccalaureate category, 2 semester hours in Business Analysis, Marketing, or Applied Statistics (9/80).

**Strategic Marketing and Process
(Service Planning Seminar [PUB 401])**
  Location: Somerset Seminars Center, Somerset, NJ.
  Length: 24 hours (3 days).
  Dates: January 1983-December 1984.
  Objective: To provide an understanding of strategic marketing concepts and processes as they relate to service management and products.
  Instruction: Course covers marketing fundamentals and the basic of strategic marketing. It addresses the process of strategic marketing decision making, especially decisions involving telecommunications services and product lines.
  Credit recommendation: In the graduate category, 1 semester hour in Marketing, Strategic Marketing, or Business Administration (11/85).

Strategy Analysis for Finance and Marketing (UPSA and SE2010)
  Location: Somerset Seminars Center, Somerset, NJ.
  Length: 24 hours (3 days).
  Dates: January 1984-Present.
  Objective: To focus on the convergence of two functions (finance and marketing) and to address marketing/finance issues at both the level of the managers of individual product-market business/service units and at the level of the overall corporate financial managers.
  Instruction: The program utilizes a decision-making orientation and discusses the elements of a comprehensive marketing strategy with respect to their cost profiles and in developing sustainable competitive roles. Also, measurement of financial performance will be developed and applied to a particular firm in order to determine its success in investing its financial objectives. This course will discuss the impact of competitive marketing decisions on the business's income statement and balance sheet and will consider a systematic approach to analyzing profitability and risk. Procedures for unbundling top-down budget objectives into product-marketing strategy will be discussed and the importance of the consistency of a firm's financial planning will be stressed.
  Credit recommendation: In the upper division baccalaureate category, 1 semester hour as an upper level Business elective (11/85).

Telephone Bypass Opportunities and Local Access (PUB 402)
  Location: Somerset Seminars Center, Somerset, NJ.
  Length: 16 hours (2 days).
  Dates: January 1984-December 1984.
  Objective: To demonstrate the significance of the telephone bypass industry, the innovative application opportunities, and the emerging market structure.
  Instruction: This seminar provides a systematic review of today's telephone network services marketplace, and offers participants an overview of telecommunications, highlighting expected local access marketing strategies for AT&T, other Common Carriers, and large corporate users. These keys for success in the new marketplace are covered: (1) Bypass Technology Economics, (2) Local Access and Charges, and (3) Joint Venture Contracts.
  Credit recommendation: In the graduate category, 1 semester hour in Marketing or Business Administration (11/85).

Terminal Products Issues Seminar (TPIS)
  Location: Bell System Tariffs and Costs Seminars, Somerset, NJ.
  Length: 30 hours (4 days).
  Dates: November 1980-December 1981.
  Objective: To concentrate on all the internal and external issues associated with the implementation of terminal product/service rate proposals before the regulatory bodies.
  Instruction: This seminar assumes in-depth knowledge of the concepts, principles, market considerations associated with the rate design, and levels of terminal products and services; and familiarity with the preparation and presentation techniques as discussed in the General Rate and Cost Issue Seminar. TPIS also provides experience in using tariff-filing support materials in a simulated regulatory implementation process.
  Credit recommendation: In the graduate category, 2 semester hours in Business Administration, Law, or Public Administration (2/81). NOTE: If the student has taken General Rate and Cost Issue Seminar (GIS), then TPIS is recommended for 1 semester hour in the graduate degree category because of duplication.

Theory and Practice of Promotion Management (Advanced Consumer Promotion Management I and II)
  Location: Somerset Seminars Center, Somerset, NJ.
  Length: 35 hours (5 days)
  Dates: July 1985-August 1985.
  Objective: To familiarize the student with the design and implementation of advertising and promotional strategies as part of the overall marketing planning process.
  Instruction: The course covers market segmentation and positioning, scheduling, market selection, message design, media selection, budgeting, and measurement. Particular attention is paid to implementing an advertising/promotion strategy for new products and formulating an annual advertising/promotion calendar for existing products. This course includes lectures, discussions, classroom exercises, simulations, problem solving, and case studies.
  Credit recommendation: In the graduate category, 1

semester hour, or in the upper division baccalaureate category, 2 semester hours in Promotion and Advertsing (11/85). NOTE: Both sections need to be completed to receive credit.

Witness Preparation (AT&T 204, PUB 202, and SA2030)
(Formerly General Witness Preparation [AT&T 204 or PUB 202])
Location: Somerset Seminars Center, Somerset, NJ.
Length: 40 hours (5 days).
Dates: January 1982-Present.
Objective: To provide an understanding of the issues and concerns associated with interstate and intrastate interLATA filings with skill training for presenting testimony by experiencing the rate case process.
Instruction: This seminar provides skill training in writing testimony which addresses interstate and intrastate interLATA issues; implementing the methodology for effective witnessing to each type of testimony; provides the opportunity to present the testimony in a simulated role playing experience of the state and federal regulatory process; describes cross examination tactics, and techniques for dealing with them; identifies the stress associated with formal regulatory presentations and reviews techniques for managing stress levels.
Credit recommendation: In the graduate category, 2 semester hours in Business Communications, Finance, Organizational Behavior, Business Law, or Management (9/83).

Witness Support (AT&T 205, PUB 203, or SA2040)
Location: Somerset Seminars Center, Somerset, NJ.
Length: 40 hours (5 days); no credit recommendations for briefer 2 or 3 day versions.
Dates: January 1983-Present.
Objective: To provide expertise in the process of supporting witnesses; provide skill training or writing testimony, provides participants with the techniques for effective decision making; provides background in persuasive presentation of ideas and concepts.
Instruction: The testimony writing module incorporates successful writing techniques. The seminar concentrates on the management structure and process to ensure that all relevant issues are addressed in a timely manner. It also provides a case management model and the experience of debating deregulation issues. The course concludes with a simulation of a public hearing by a regulatory body.
Credit recommendation: In the graduate category, 3 semester hours in Business Communications, Business Law, Management, Organizational Behavior (11/85). NOTE: Only full 40 hour version of this course carries credit recommendations.

AT&T - Professional Development Division

AT&T - Professional Development Division (PD) is an organization which trains AT&T training professionals. It supports the AT&T business plan in the areas of organizational effectiveness and employee development through the development and delivery of Professional Development courses. These PD courses are designed for training managers, course developers/designers, instructional technologists, and instructor/facilitators. PD also provides development of competency models in both course development and delivery, and in observation and feedback of instructors for their own development. Finally, PD provides consultation with other AT&T organizations concerning their training needs.

Source of official student records: Director, AT&T Professional Development Division, 399 Campus Drive, Somerset, NJ 08873.

Additional information about the courses: Program on Noncollegiate Sponsored Instruction, The Center for Adult Learning and Educational Credentials, American Council on Education, One Dupont Circle, Washington, D.C. 20036.

Basic Instructors Skills (Course QL0101-A)
Location: Somerset, NJ; Cincinnati, OH; and other AT&T locations.
Length: 28 hours (4 days).
Dates: September 1985-Present.
Objective: To enable subject competent employees to teach effectively their own area of competence.
Learning Outcome: At the conclusion of this course, the student will be able to: describe the four learning styles and implication of those styles for instructing; explain the three-step intervention process for handling problem situations in the classrooms; explain the ARCS model of motivation and major strategies for stimulating desire to learn; demonstrate effective techniques for giving and receiving feedback; demonstrate the effective use of questioning skills and presentation skills as major tools for enhancing learning.
Instruction: This course presents various concepts and skills for effective stand-up instruction and participative student center lecture. Course covers the three-step intervention process and uses the ARCS model of motivation. Students prepare and deliver two 20-minute balanced instruction lectures. The course also includes instructor observation, the use of instructor skills inventory and regular quizzes to evaluate student learning.
Credit recommendation: In the upper division baccalaureate category, 2 semester hours in Basic Instructor Skills (1/87).

Instructional Design and Development Workshop (Course QL0303)

Location: Somerset, NJ; Cincinnati, OH; and other AT&T locations.

Length: 40 hours (5 days).

Dates: October 1984-Present.

Objective: To provide the new course developer with the skills and knowledge needed to design courses successfully and effectively.

Learning Outcome: At the conclusion of this course, the student will be able to: describe the techniques to determine performance problems; gather and analyze about job tasks; determine what skills and knowledge should be taught; choose the instructional strategies methods and media for the course; describe the balance instruction technique; describe learning styles and how they relate to the instructional design and development process.

Instruction: This course covers the fundamental principles of instructional designs as presented in a four-step model. Practical application of a model and its underlined principles are emphasis as students design and develop a training package. Students will study task analysis, needs analysis, and job analysis.

Credit recommendation: In the graduate degree category, 3 semester hours in Instructional Design and Development (for those students who already possess a baccalaureate degree or above) or in the upper division baccalaureate category, 3 semester hours for those students who do not already possess a baccalaureate degree (1/87). NOTE: The evaluators determined that if students did not already possess a BA degree or above there was not sufficient indication that they would master a graduate level of the course.

Instructional Writing Workshop (Course QL2001)

Location: Somerset, NJ; Cincinnati, OH; and other AT&T locations.

Length: 35 hours (5 days).

Dates: February 1986-Present.

Objective: To provide instructors the information and hands-on experience needed to design and write a module of instruction for an instructor-led course or a self-paced course. Prerequisite: Successful completion of Instructional Design and Development Workshop (Course QL0303) and a job function which provides experiences in instructional design.

Learning Outcome: Upon completion of this course, students will be able to: conduct a skills, knowledge, or culmination analysis of a topic; determine appropriate test items and design a complete instructional plan for the instructional session; write an instructor guide that includes teaching outlines, course or unit information, and a preface; write a student guide that is intergraded with the instructor guide; conduct a formative evaluation and prepare a formal report of the outcomes.

Instruction: This course provides a hands-on experience in designing and writing a module of instruction for an instructor lead course and a self-paced course. This will include the preparation of an instructor guide, student guide, and other supporting materials. The student will do the various assignments, get immediate feedback on them, and work steadily toward finishing the complete set of materials. Pre- and post-testing, writing projects, and the final written module are all used as an evaluation of the student's performance.

Credit recommendation: In the graduate degree category, 3 semester hours in Instructional Writing (1/87).

Automatic Sprinkler Apprenticeship Program, Joint Apprenticeship and Training Committee, Local 669

All educational/training programs are administered through the educational funds of Local 669 Joint Apprenticeship Training Committee (JATC). The United States Department of Labor approved the apprentice training program and related training in April 1953. The apprentice training program is also recognized by the Federal Bureau of Apprenticeship Training.

This program of courses is offered by correspondence delivery system. Courses are reviewed on a continuous basis. Course development and revisions are based on changes in the codes governing construction, hardware, and procedures and methods relating to the industry. The Department of Independent Learning of The Pennsylvania State University provides instruction and course development, as well as using experts in the trade to provide external review. Tutors/proctors are responsible for assisting apprentices with course-related problems and proctoring examinations. If an apprentice is not in the vicinity of a tutor/proctor, the JATC with the agreement of Penn State has designated the apprentice's supervisor as an acceptable proctor.

To complete a course successfully, the apprentice is required to submit all lessons and examinations associated with a specific course. Students are not permitted to advance to the next course in the program until they have satisfactorily completed (average grade of 60% or better) the previous course. Certificates are only issued upon successful completion of the 19-course program.

Source of official student records: The Transcript Department, 112 Shields Building, The Pennsylvania State University, University Park, Pennsylvania 16802.

Additional information about the courses: Program on Noncollegiate Sponsored Instruction, The Center for Adult Learning and Educational Credentials, American Council on Education, One Dupont Circle, Suite 1B-20, Washington, D.C., 20036.

Courses are listed in numerical order, e.g., ME 5001, ME 5003, etc.

Safety, Rigging, and Scaffolding (ME 5001)
(Formerly ME 990-533)
  Location: Correspondence program.
  Length: 9 independent study lessons.
  Dates: July 1985-Present.
  Objective: To give the student an awareness of safety requirements common to building construction sites.
  Instruction: Course covers safe and proper use of personal protective equipment and tools, handling and storage of materials, fire protection, trenches, welding, first aid, ladders, scaffolding, rigging with cranes, derricks, tackles, winches, and signals. Methodology involves independent study with course guide, optional tutoring, and proctored examination.
  Credit recommendation: In the vocational certificate category, 20 semester hours in Fire Sprinkler System Technology if taken with courses 5001 through 5019 (3/89).

Use and Care of Tools (ME 5003)
(Formerly ME 990-529)
  Location: Correspondence program.
  Length: 12 independent study lessons.
  Dates: February 1987-Present.
  Objective: To provide the student with knowledge of the purpose and the safe and efficient use of tools and materials in the pipe thread industry.
  Instruction: Course covers rules for good practice and safety, OSHA standards, and the use and care of tools used in the pipe trades. Methodology involves independent study with course guide, optional tutoring, supplemental materials, and proctored examination.
  Credit recommendation: In the vocational certificate category, 20 semester hours in Fire Sprinkler System Technology if taken with courses 5001 through 50019 (3/89).

Basic Drawing for the Sprinkler System (ME 5004)
(Formerly ME 990-530)
  Location: Correspondence program.
  Length: 12 independent study lessons.
  Dates: February 1987-Present.
  Objective: To introduce the student to the basic elements of mechanical drawing as it relates to fire sprinkler system.
  Instruction: Course covers blueprint reading, multiview drawings, applications of drawings, size and location dimensioning, rules for dimensioning, scales, thread representation and dimensioning, sections, principles of sketching, the working sketch, isometric drawings, and isometric drawings for piping layouts. Methodology involves independent study with course guide, optional tutoring, supplemental materials, and proctored examination.
  Credit recommendation: In the vocational certificate category, 20 semester hours in Fire Sprinkler System Technology if taken with courses 5001 through 5019, or in the lower division baccalaureate/associate degree category, 12 semester hours in Fire Sprinkler System Technology if taken with courses 5006, 5007, 5009, 5010, 5012, 5013, 5015, 5017, 5018, and 5019 (3/89).

Introduction to Automatic Sprinklers (ME 5005)
(Formerly ME 990-531)
  Location: Correspondence program.
  Length: 12 independent study lessons.
  Dates: August 1986-Present.
  Objective: To provide the student with knowledge of automatic fire sprinkler systems and their installation and inspection.
  Instruction: Course covers fire and its extinguishment, history, value and performance of automatic sprinkler protection, organizations related to the automatic sprinkler industry, factors affecting sprinkler performance, hazard rating and special occupancy conditions, wet-pipe and dry-pipe systems, other types of sprinkler systems, acceptance tests, and flushing sprinkler piping. Methodology involves independent study with course guide, optional tutoring, and proctored examination.
  Credit recommendation: In the vocational certificate category, 20 semester hours in Fire Sprinkler System Technology if taken with courses 5001 through 5019 (3/89).

Reading Automatic Sprinkler Piping Drawings (ME 5006)
(Formerly ME 990-532)
  Location: Correspondence program.
  Length: 12 independent study lessons.
  Dates: October 1984-Present.
  Objective: To provide the student with knowledge of automatic fire sprinkler system drawings.
  Instruction: Course provides an introduction to piping drawings, sprinkling piping, sectional views, underground piping, hydraulically calculated systems, use of materials, deluge system, computer-aided blueprints, and halon system. Methodology involves independent study with course guide, optional tutoring, supplemental materials, and proctored examination.
  Credit recommendation: In the vocational certificate category, 20 semester hours in Fire Sprinkler System Technology if taken with courses 5001 through 5019, or in the lower division baccalaureate/associate degree category, 12 semester hours in Fire Sprinkler System Technology if taken with courses 5004, 5007, 5009, 5010, 5012, 5013, 5015, 5017, 5018, and 5019 (3/89).

Sprinkler Systems Calculations (ME 5007)
(Formerly ME 990-534)
  Location: Correspondence program.

Length: 18 independent study lessons.
Dates: August 1979-Present.
Objective: To provide the student with knowledge of basic mathematics relevant to installation of fire sprinkler systems.
Instruction: Course covers basic arithmetic operations and functions, simple geometry, piping measurement and offsets, pipe bends and piping, piping layouts, piping offsets, and the metric system. Methodology involves independent study with course guide, optional tutoring, and proctored examination.
Credit recommendation: In the vocational certificate category, 20 semester hours in Fire Sprinkler System Technology if taken with courses 5001 through 5019, or in the lower division baccalaureate/associate degree category, 12 semester hours in Fire Sprinkler System Technology if taken with courses 5004, 5006, 5009, 5010, 5012, 5013, 5015, 5017, 5018, and 5019 (3/89).

Installation of Sprinkler Systems (ME 5008)
(Formerly ME 990-535)
Location: Correspondence program.
Length: 15 independent study lessons.
Dates: June 1987-Present.
Objective: To provide the student with knowledge of the rules and regulations governing the design, installation, and testing of fire sprinkler systems.
Instruction: Course covers water supply and system components, spacing, location and position of sprinklers, and hydraulically designed sprinkler systems. Methodology involves independent study with course guide, optional tutoring, supplemental materials, and proctored examination.
Credit recommendation: In the vocational certificate category, 20 semester hours in Fire Sprinkler System Technology if taken with courses 5001 through 5019 (3/89).

Blueprint Reading for the Sprinkler Fitter (ME 5009)
(Formerly ME 990-536)
Location: Correspondence program.
Length: 12 independent study lessons.
Dates: July 1985-Present.
Objective: To provide the student with an understanding and use of isometric and orthographic drawings in fire sprinkler system installation.
Instruction: Course covers isometric drawing in pipe fitting, piping and equipment symbols and nomemclature, progress and instrumentation drawings, orthographic drawings, detailed isometric drawing, spool (shop) drawings, hanger details, and blueprint reading. Methodology involves independent study with course guide, optional tutoring, supplemental materials, and proctored examination.
Credit recommendation: In the vocational certificate category, 20 semester hours in Fire Sprinkler System Technology if taken with courses 5001 through 5019, or in the lower division baccalaureate/associate degree category, 12 semester hours in Fire Sprinkler System Technology if taken with courses 5004, 5006, 5007, 5010, 5012, 5013, 5015, 5017, 5018, and 5019 (3/89).

Architectural Working Drawings for Sprinkler Fitters (ME 5010)
(Formerly AE 990-501)
Location: Correspondence program.
Length: 12 independent study lessons.
Dates: July 1976-Present.
Objective: To provide the student with an understanding of blueprints.
Instruction: Course covers the use of symbols, abbreviations and print types; defining conventions, schedules, and use of scales; drawing interpretation; plan projections, plan scale, and foundation construction types; inspection of floor plans; use of elevations; sectioning, detailing, lumber sizing, and steel framing; mechanical equipment drawings; and plumbing system and sprinkler system types. Methodology involves independent study with course guide, optional tutoring, supplemental materials, and proctored examination.
Credit recommendation: In the vocational certificate category, 20 semester hours in Fire Sprinkler System Technology if taken with courses 5001 through 5019, or in the lower division baccalaureate/associate degree category, 12 semester hours in Fire Sprinkler System Technology if taken with courses 5004, 5006, 5007, 5009, 5012, 5013, 5015, 5017, 5018, and 5019 (3/89).

The Automatic Fire Sprinkler (ME 5011)
(Formerly The Sprinkler Head [990-538])
Location: Correspondence program.
Length: 9 independent study lessons.
Dates: March 1985-Present.
Objective: To provide the student with a basic understanding of operating principles of automatic fire sprinklers.
Instruction: Course covers operating principles and temperature ratings, standard automatic sprinklers, residential sprinklers, special application sprinklers, maintenance of sprinklers, and sprinklers for exposure protection. Methodology involves independent study with course guide, optional tutoring, supplemental materials, and proctored examination.
Credit recommendation: In the vocational certificate category, 20 semester hours in Fire Sprinkler System Technology if taken with courses 5001 through 5019 (3/89).

Sprinkler Systems Water Supply (ME 5012)
(Formerly ME 990-539)
Location: Correspondence program.
Length: 12 independent study lessons.

Dates: August 1985-Present.

Objective: To provide the student with an understanding of the various types of fire sprinkler water supply sources.

Instruction: Course covers the occupancy classification, water supply requirements, supply connections, public water supply systems, fire department connections, backflow prevention, gravity tanks, water level indicators, tank heaters, pressure tanks, embankment tanks, centrifugal fire pumps, horizonatal pumps, vertical shaft turbine-type pumps, controllers, and installation of private fire service mains. Methodology involves independent study with course guide, optional tutoring, and proctored examination.

Credit recommendation: In the vocational certificate category, 20 semester hours in Fire Sprinkler System Technology if taken with courses 5001 through 5019, or in the lower division baccalaureate/associate degree category, 12 semester hours in Fire Sprinkler System Technology if taken with courses 5004, 5006, 5007, 5009, 5010, 5013, 5015, 5017, 5018, and 5019 (3/89).

Types of Fire Protection Systems (ME 5013)
(Formerly ME 990-540)

Location: Correspondence program.
Length: 15 independent study lessons.
Dates: December 1984-Present.

Objective: To provide the student with an understanding of the various types of fire protection systems and their application.

Instruction: Course covers wet-pipe, anti-freeze, dry-pipe, pre-action, and deluge systems; combined dry-pipe and pre-action systems; automatic sprinkler systems with nonfire protection connections; combined sprinkler-standpipe, foam-water, carbon dioxide, and halon systems. Methodology involves independent study with course guide, optional tutoring, and proctored examination.

Credit recommendation: In the vocational certificate category, 20 semester hours in Fire Sprinkler System Technology if taken with courses 5001 through 5019, or in the lower division baccalaureate/associate degree category, 12 semester hours in Fire Sprinkler System Technology if taken with courses 5004, 5006, 5007, 5009, 5010, 5012, 5015, 5017, 5018, and 5019 (3/89).

Special Application Sprinkler Systems (ME 5014)
(Formerly ME 990-541)

Location: Correspondence program.
Length: 12 independent study lessons.
Dates: July 1984-Present.

Objective: To provide the student with an understanding of "rate-of-rise" fire detection technology used in conjunction with sprinkler systems.

Instruction: Course covers the Automatic Sprinkler Corporation's "rate-of-rise" systems, the Grinnel Company's "rate-of-rise" systems, the Viking Corporation's "rate-of-rise" systems, and the Star Electromatic System of Chemetron. Methodology involves independent study with course guide, optional tutoring, and proctored examination.

Credit recommendation: In the vocational certificate category, 20 semester hours in Fire Sprinkler System Technology if taken with courses 5001 through 5019 (3/89).

Hydraulics for the Sprinkler Apprentice (ME 5015)
(Formerly ME 990-542)

Location: Correspondence program.
Length: 6 independent study lessons.
Dates: August 1982-Present.

Objective: To provide the student with knowledge of basic properties of fluids used in operation of fire protection systems and their installation requirements.

Instruction: Course covers specific weight, specific gravity, pressure generation, pressure measurement, sprinkler system design, and pressure losses. Methodology involves independent study with course guide, optional tutoring, and proctored examination.

Credit recommendation: In the vocational certificate category, 20 semester hours in Fire Sprinkler System Technology if taken with courses 5001 through 5019, or in the lower division baccalaureate/associate degree category, 12 semester hours in Fire Sprinkler System Technology if taken with courses 5004, 5006, 5007, 5009, 5010, 5012, 5013, 5017, 5018, and 5019 (3/89).

Sprinkler System Alarms (5016)
(Formerly ME 990-543)

Location: Correspondence program.
Length: 6 independent study lessons.
Dates: November 1979-Present.

Objective: To provide the student with an understanding of fire system alarm systems.

Instruction: Course covers the principles of sprinkler system alarms, wet system water flow alarm methods, water-motor gongs and circuit closers, central station system requirements, and supervisory protection. Methodology involves independent study with course guide, optional tutoring, and proctored examination.

Credit recommendation: In the vocational certificate category, 20 semester hours in Fire Sprinkler System Technology if taken with courses 5001 through 5019 (3/89).

Economics of the Sprinkler Industry (ME 5017)
(Formerly ME 990-544)

Location: Correspondence program.
Length: 9 independent study lessons.
Dates: August 1986-Present.

Objective: To provide the student with an understanding of the economics of the sprinkler industry within the American economic system.

Instruction: Course covers the free enterprise system, needs of people, capital and money, analysis of financial statements, costs, profits, competition, and productivity. Methodology involves independent study with course guide, optional tutoring, and proctored examination.

Credit recommendation: In the vocational certificate category, 20 semester hours in Fire Sprinkler System Technology if taken with courses 5001 through 5019, or in the lower division baccalaureate/associate degree category, 12 semester hours in Fire Sprinkler System Technology if taken with courses 5004, 5006, 5007, 5009, 5010, 5012, 5013, 5015, 5018, and 5019 (3/89).

Human Relations (5018)
(Formerly ME 990-545)
Location: Correspondence program.
Length: 12 independent study lessons.
Dates: February 1987-Present.
Objective: To provide the student with an understanding of the basics of human relations.
Instruction: Course covers the duties and responsibilities of foremen, understanding human nature, planning, the foreman's responsibility for training, giving orders, directions, and suggestions, record keeping and written reports, the foreman and operational costs, other phases of communication, safety, improving work methods and procedures, and getting the job done right. Methodology involves independent study with course guide, optional tutoring, and proctored examination.
Credit recommendation: In the vocational certificate category, 20 semester hours in Fire Sprinkler System Technology if taken with courses 5001 through 5019, or in the lower division baccalaureate/associate degree category, 12 semester hours in Fire Sprinkler System Technology if taken with courses 5004, 5006, 5007, 5009, 5010, 5012, 5013, 5015, 5017, and 5019 (3/89).

Technical Reports (ME 5019)
(Formerly ME 990-546)
Location: Correspondence program.
Length: 6 independent study lessons.
Dates: July 1974-Present.
Objective: To provide the student with the skills necessary to write technical reports relevant to the job.
Instruction: Course covers accident reports, weekly reports (hourly time ticket, weekly progress report), special reports (daily contract change order, day work order), final reports (final "progress" report, contractor's material and test certificate), and adjunct reports (bill of lading, report of inspection). Methodology involves independent study with course guide, optional tutoring, and proctored examination.
Credit recommendation: In the vocational certificate category, 20 semester hours in Fire Sprinkler System Technology if taken with courses 5001 through 5019, or in the lower division baccalaureate/associate degree category, 12 semester hours in Fire Sprinkler System Technology if taken with courses 5004, 5006, 5007, 5009, 5010, 5012, 5013, 5015, 5017, and 5018 (3/89).

Baroid Corporation Career Development Center (Formerly NL Industries, Inc.)

The Baroid Corporation Career Development Center (CDC) is the central training facility of Baroid Corporation, a leading supplier of oilfield products and services. Located in Houston, Texas, the facility is committed to presenting performance-oriented instructional programs to employees and customers of Baroid Corporation.

Secluded on 86 wooded acres, this self-contained complex including housing and dining facilities, has been designed to provide the student with a comfortable environment in which to learn and practice problem-solving skills. Extensive laboratory facilities, heavy equipment bays, training wells, and associated equipment are used by students performing "hands-on" work.

CDC courses are developed to provide the student with both the technical knowledge and skills needed to perform effectively in the ever demanding oil industry. Basic, intermediate, and advanced programs are available and vary in intensity from a few days to several months.

Source of official student records: Student Affairs/Registrar, Baroid Corporation Career Development Center, 3000 North Sam Houston Parkway East, Houston, Texas 77032.

Additional information about the courses: Program on Noncollegiate Sponsored Instruction, The Center for Adult Learning and Educational Credentials, American Council on Education, One Dupont Circle, Washington, D.C. 20036.

Basic Concepts of Open-Hole Logging (135)
Location: Baroid Corporation Career Development Center, Houston, TX.
Length: 112 hours (8 hours per day for 14 days).
Dates: May 1982-December 1985.
Objective: To increase the level of expertise of field engineers in the formal methods of analyzing the information obtained from basic open-hole logs.
Instruction: Basic concepts of open-hole logging including reservoir parameters such as porosity, permeability, oil and water saturation; basic algorithms for interpretation of primary open-hole logs including SP Induction, Micro, Latero and Guard, Density, Neutron, Gamma Ray, and Sonic. Also includes elements of basic petroleum geology and the drilling process. Lecture supplemented with laboratory exercises is used.
Credit recommendation: In the lower division baccalaureate/associate degree category, 4 semester hours in

Well Logging (1/83).

Basic Well Control (149)
  Location: Baroid Corporation Career Development Center, Houston, TX.
  Length: 40 hours (1 week).
  Dates: July 1979-Present.
  Learning Outcome: Upon successful completion of this course, the student will be able to understand well control principles and techniques in the detection, causes, and handling of potential blowout situations.
  Instruction: A group paced course providing both the theoretical and practical understanding of well control principles and techniques in the detection, causes, and handling of potential blowout situations. Classroom lecture/discussion techniques using printed and audiovisual resources. Laboratory exercises utilizing hands-on simulators are emphasized.
  Credit recommendation: In the lower division baccalaureate/associate degree category, 2 semester hours in Petroleum Technology (1/83) (12/88). NOTE: This course has been reevaluated and continues to meet requirements for credit recommendations.

Cased-Hole Log Interpretation (142)
  Location: Baroid Corporation Career Development Center, Houston, TX.
  Length: 48 hours (8 hours per day for 6 days).
  Dates: August 1979-January 1985.
  Objective: To increase the competence level of experienced cased-hole logging engineers in utilizing normal methods of analyzing information obtained from cased-hole logs.
  Instruction: Basic concepts of open-hole log systems including theory of operation, information derived, and practical interpretation; in-depth studies of Gamma Ray, Neutron, Bond Cement, and Casing Inspection logging techniques including advanced interpretation and application of these logs; new developments in cased-hole logging. Lecture and laboratory exercises are used.
  Credit recommendation: In the lower division baccalaureate/associate degree category, 3 semester hours in Well Logging (1/83).

Cased-Hole Wireline Logging (141)
  Location: Baroid Corporation Career Development Center, Houston, TX.
  Length: 140 hours (40 hours per week for 3½ weeks).
  Dates: January 1978-January 1985.
  Objective: To introduce the student to the theory, application, running and interpretation of Gamma Ray, Neutron, Bond Cement, Electronic Casing Caliper, Casing Inspection, and Borehole Compensated Neutron well logs.
  Instruction: Introduction to cased-hole well logging including Gamma Ray, Neutron, Bond Cement, and Casing Inspection/Caliper logging; log theory and interpretation; use of logging instruments to calibrate and record logs; running of logs in a well under field conditions; finishing the log for presentation to the customer. Also includes elements of geology, basic electricity, test equipment, and troubleshooting. Equally divided between classroom study and "hands-on" training.
  Credit recommendation: In the lower division baccalaureate/associate degree category, 4 semester hours in Well Logging (1/83).

Completion/Workover Fluids Technology (154)
  Location: Baroid Corporation Career Development Center, Houston, TX.
  Length: 176 hours (4 weeks and 2 days).
  Dates: April 1982-Present.
  Learning Outcome: Upon successful completion of this course, the student will be able to understand and apply principles related to completion/workover fluids technology.
  Instruction: Self-paced instruction provides training in composition, properties, analysis, and treatment of drilling fluids in addition to the formulation and application of completion fluids. Student manuals guide learning by utilizing extensive printed and audio visual resources and criterion referenced instruction to evaluate progress. Extensive laboratory support is also utilized.
  Credit recommendation: In the upper division baccalaureate category, 4 semester hours in Drilling Fluid Technology (1/83) (12/88). NOTE: This course has been reevaluated and continues to meet requirements for credit recommendations.

Directional Drilling (158)
  Location: Baroid Corporation Career Development Center, Houston, TX.
  Length: 66½-84 hours (2 weeks).
  Dates: May 1984-Present.
  Objective: To provide the student with knowledge and skill for surveying, calculating, and selecting tools to control or deviate borehole trajectories.
  Learning Outcome: Upon successful completion of this course, the student will perform his/her engineering roles related to directional drilling with enhanced competence.
  Instruction: The single-shot instrument; definitions and calculations; orientation and deflection tools; and formation effect, projection and bottom hole assemblies. Students are required to drill (simulation) through wells with employing one of three deflection tools for each well. Laboratory exercises are emphasized.
  Credit recommendation: In the upper division baccalaureate category, 2 semester hours in Geology, Mining, Mineral or Petroleum Engineering (5/87).

Directional Drilling Technology (157)
  Location: Baroid Corporation Career Development

Center, Houston, TX.

Length: 40-50 hours (1 week).

Dates: February 1984-Present.

Objective: To provide the student with an overview of the basic principles of directional drilling.

Learning Outcome: Upon successful completion of this course, the student will understand the principles of directional drilling.

Instruction: Course includes information on directional drilling applications, types of directional wells, directional well planning survey techniques, survey calculations, toolface orientation, kickoff procedures, bottom hole assemblies, and new technology in directional drilling. Lecture, discussion, and laboratory exercises are used.

Credit recommendation: In the lower division baccalaureate/associate degree category, 2 semester hours in Geology, Mining or Mineral Engineering, or Petroleum Engineering (5/87).

Drilling Engineering (165)

Location: Baroid Corporation Career Development Center, Houston, TX.

Length: 130 hours (3 weeks).

Dates: August 1985-Present.

Objective: To provide the student with theory and skills for the development of comprehensive computer programs for drilling engineering.

Learning Outcome: Upon successful completion of this course, the student will be able to design and implement a typical drilling program.

Instruction: Introduction to geological information, origin and occurrence of pore pressure, wireline logs, drilling fluids, solid control equipment, frictional pressure, loss calculations, optimization of hydraulic system, rock bit design, rheology of drilling mud, drilling logs and cost minimization. Lecture, discussion, and workshops are used.

Credit recommendation: In the upper division baccalaureate category, 4 semester hours in Geology, Mining or Mineral Engineering, or Petroleum Engineering (5/87). NOTE: There is considerable overlap between this course and the course entitled Drilling Technology (112).

Drilling Fluids Technology (104)

Location: Baroid Corporation Career Development Center, Houston, TX.

Length: 160-250 hours (4-6 weeks [average]).

Dates: March 1981-Present.

Objective: To provide technical knowledge and skills necessary to formulate, maintain, and treat drilling fluids as required of drilling fluid engineers involved in sales.

Learning Outcome: Upon successful completion of this course, the student will be able to formulate, maintain, and treat drilling fluids systems.

Instruction: A self-paced program covering concepts and application of drilling fluids technology, chemical and physical analysis of fluid properties, diagnosing drilling fluid problems, and drilling fluid treatments. Student manuals (7) guide learning by utilizing extensive printed and audiovisual resources, laboratory exercises, and criterion referenced evaluation to document progress.

Credit recommendation: In the lower division baccalaureate/associate degree category, 6 semester hours in Petroleum Technology (1/83) (12/88). NOTE: This course has been reevaluated and continues to meet requirements for credit recommendations.

Drilling Fluids Technology - Basic

Location: Baroid Corporation Career Development Center, Houston, TX.

Length: 63-82 hours (8-10 days); self-paced.

Dates: February 1983-Present.

Learning Outcome: Upon successful completion of this course, the student will be able to test, formulate, treat, and maintain water-base drilling fluids technology.

Instruction: Covers water-base drilling fluids chemistry, testing procedures, products, and formulation. The theoretical is combined with practical hands-on laboratory exercises in the mixing and testing of the physical and chemical properties of drilling fluids.

Credit recommendation: In the lower division baccalaureate/associate degree category, 3 semester hours in Basic Drilling Fluids Technology (8/83) (12/88). NOTE: This course has been reevaluated and continues to meet requirements for credit recommendations.

Drilling Fluids Technology - Comprehensive

Location: Baroid Corporation Career Development Center, Houston, TX.

Length: 140-174 hours (17½ - 21¾ days); self-paced.

Dates: February 1983-Present.

Learning Outcome: Upon successful completion of this course, the student will be able to formulate, maintain, and treat all classifications of drilling fluids and to understand principles related to mud program design.

Instruction: Covers basic skills of drilling fluids engineering. Major topics include chemical and physical analysis of water and oil-base fluids, clay chemistry, rheology, systems formulation and maintenance, contaminants, products, and introduction to hydraulics and basic mud program design. Problem-solving exercises treat both theoretical and practical areas.

Credit recommendation: In the lower division baccalaureate/associate degree category, 5 semester hours in Advanced Drilling Fluids Technology (8/83) (12/88). NOTE: Students who receive credit for this course should not receive credit for Drilling Fluids Technology - Basic or Intermediate. NOTE: This course has been reevaluated and continues to meet requirements for credit recommendations.

Drilling Fluids Technology - Intermediate
Location: Baroid Corporation Career Development Center, Houston, TX.
Length: 106-127 hours (13-15 days); self-paced.
Dates: February 1983-Present.
Learning Outcome: Upon successful completion of this course, the student will be able to test, formulate, treat, and maintain water-based drilling fluids systems and to understand rheological models and geopressure prediction methods.
Instruction: Covers water-base drilling fluids chemistry, testing procedures, products, systems formulation and pressure calculations. Problem-solving exercises treat both theoretical and practical areas.
Credit recommendation: In the lower division baccalaureate/associate degree category, 4 semester hours in Intermediate Drilling Fluids Technology (8/83) (12/88). NOTE: Students who receive credit for this course should not receive credit for Drilling Fluids Technology - Basic or Comprehensive. NOTE: This course has been reevaluated and continues to meet requirements for credit recommendations.

Drilling Fluids Technology - Refresher
Location: Baroid Corporation Career Development Center, Houston, TX.
Length: 63-80 hours (8-10 days); self-paced.
Dates: February 1983-Present.
Learning Outcome: Upon successful completion of this course, the student will be able to understand and apply the most recent advances in oil-base and water-base drilling fluids technology.
Instruction: Emphasis is placed on the review of chemical and mathematical equations, mud testing and formulation, and contaminant identification. Additional subjects are required in the areas of geopressure detection and balancing, pilot testing, and mud program design for students completing course in less than the prescribed times.
Credit recommendation: In the lower division baccalaureate/associate degree category, 3 semester hours in Basic Drilling Fluids Technology (10/83) (12/88). NOTE: Students who receive credit for this course should not receive credit for Basic, Intermediate, or Comprehensive Drilling Fluids Technology. NOTE: This course has been reevaluated and continues to meet requirements for credit recommendations.

Drilling Technology
(Formerly Applied Drilling Technology 112)
Location: Baroid Corporation Career Development Center, Houston, TX.
Length: 80 hours (2 weeks).
Dates: March 1981-Present.
Learning Outcome: Upon successful completion of this course, the student will be able to understand and apply principles related to drilling technology; and to plan and problem-solve in areas related to drilling operations.
Instruction: Course covers a variety of topics including: well site monitoring, basic geology, pressure problems, fracture gradients, drill string design, rheology, slip velocity, roller cone rotary drilling, minimum cost drilling, diamond bits, and drag bits. Students are also required to master the use of hand-held programmable calculators. Classroom lecture and laboratory are used and supported by reference materials (both printed and audiovisual). Student mastery of criterion referenced tests is required.
Credit recommendation: In the upper division baccalaureate category, 3 semester hours in Petroleum Technology or Petroleum Engineering (1/83) (12/88). NOTE: There is considerable overlap between this course and Drilling Engineering (165). NOTE: This course has been reevaluated and continues to meet requirements for credit recommendations.

Oilwell Pipe Recovery (139)
Location: Baroid Corporation Career Development Center, Houston, TX.
Length: 40 hours (1 week).
Dates: February 1979-January 1985.
Objective: To provide formal instruction on recovery of tubular goods stuck in oil or gas wells; to develop the skills and knowledge required of a pipe recovery engineer.
Instruction: Group-paced instruction covering physical characteristics of oil well tubular goods, downhole well configurations and types of stuck pipe conditions. The course also covers the free-point finder and string shot, procedures and techniques for determining free point and backing-off pipe plus safety procedures and awareness. Lecture/discussion supported by printed and audiovisual references and problem solving techniques are used. (Prerequisite: Basic Wirelines Operations.)
Credit recommendation: In the lower division baccalaureate/associate degree category, 2 semester hours in Petroleum Technology (1/83).

Production Treating Chemicals
Location: Baroid Corporation Career Development Center, Houston, TX.
Length: 112½ classroom/laboratory contact hours (3 weeks [average]).
Dates: August 1981-December 1985.
Objective: To provide students with the knowledge and techniques to sell and service products for the oil and gas production industry through instruction in and application of current industry accepted technology.
Instruction: Group- and/or self-paced instruction covering principles, techniques and equipment required for the effective use of treating chemicals in all phases of oil and gas production, drilling operations, and specialty application. Classroom lecture and laboratory are used supported by printed and audiovisual reference material.

Requires student mastery of criterion referenced tests.
Credit recommendation: In the upper division baccalaureate category, 4 semester hours in Applied Chemistry for the Oil and Gas Industry (1/83).

Programmed Drilling Technology (161)
Location: Baroid Corporation Career Development Center, Houston, TX.
Length: 40 hours (1 week).
Dates: November 1983-Present.
Objective: To train participants to perform "on the spot" calculations which will lead to the solution of a broad spectrum of complex and varied drilling technology problems associated with well pre-planning and drilling operations.
Learning Outcome: Upon successful completion of this course, the student will be able to use hand-held programmable calculators and pre-programmed magnetic cards in drilling activities.
Instruction: Course uses problem solving, using the HP 41CV or TI 59 programmable calculator. Lecture, discussion, and laboratory exercises are used.
Credit recommendation: In the upper division baccalaureate category, 2 semester hours in Geology, Mining, Mineral or Petroleum Engineering (5/87).

Systems Approach to Production Logging (160)
Location: Baroid Corporation Career Development Center, Houston, TX.
Length: 80 hours (2 weeks).
Dates: September 1982-December 1985.
Objective: To provide information and training in order for field personnel to interpret and analyze dynamic well conditions, interpret logs, and take proper course of action.
Instruction: Theory-based course on production logs including Spinner, Fluid identification, Radioactive tracer, and Noise and Temperature surveys. Lecture and discussions are used. Student mastery of criterion based tests is required.
Credit recommendation: In the lower division baccalaureate/associate degree category, 3 semester hours in Petroleum Technology (1/83).

Bell Atlantic Corporation

Since its incorporation in late 1983, Bell Atlantic Corporation has evolved from the parent of a group of regulated telephone utilities serving the mid-Atlantic region of the U.S. into a major source of informative management and communications services and systems, with subsidiary companies operating in regional, national, and international markets.

With revenues exceeding $10 billion and assets of $24 billion, Bell Atlantic, through its core business, is providing state-of-the-art voice and data communications and exchange access services to one of the fastest growing, most densely populated and communications-intensive regions of the United States.

Bell Atlantic's operating telephone companies serve the states of New Jersey, Delaware, Pennsylvania, Maryland, Virginia, West Virginia, and the Distric of Columbia, which have more than 16 million residential, business, and government customers in a geographic area that is home to the U.S. federal government and 85 of the nation's Fortune 500 companies. Its telecommunications network is one of the most technologically advanced in the world and the most cost efficient in the U.S.

Bell Atlantic also provides customers throughout the U.S. and overseas with a range of quality communications services, information products, and related business services.

Source of official student records: PONSI Coordinator, Bell Atlantic Corporation, Network Services, Inc., 13100 Columbia Pike, D16, Silver Spring, Maryland 20904.

Additional information about the courses: Program on Noncollegiate Sponsored Instruction, The Center for Adult Learning and Educational Credit and Credentials, American Council on Education, One Dupont Circle, Washington, D.C. 20036.

ATLAS PROGRAM (AIM TO LEARN AND SUCCEED)

ATLAS offers employees an opportunity, out-of-hours, to enhance their generic skills. The courses range from an extensive Individualized Math and Language program to Test Taking and Thinking Skills. The program is offered throughout the region; however, in Pennsylvania and Delaware it is known as PM Education.

Basic Mathematics
Location: Various locations throughout C&P Telephone Company business area.
Length: 32 weeks; individual sessions ranging from 1-3 hours per week.
Dates: September 1975-Present.
Objective: To train in basic mathematics, from computations with whole numbers through basic algebra.
Instruction: Covers all operations with whole numbers, fractions, decimals, percent, measurements, and algebraic equations. The course is individualized and self-paced, with tutorial assistance and evaluation provided by the instructor.
Credit recommendation: In the lower division baccalaureate/associate degree category, 3 semester hours in Basic Mathematics (5/80) (12/84). NOTE: This course has been reevaluated and continues to meet requirements for credit recommendations.

Effective Writing

Location: Various locations throughout C&P Telephone Company business area.

Length: 30 hours (15 weeks).

Dates: September 1977-Present.

Objective: To improve students' ability to write clear and concise paragraphs, letters, memoranda, and other communications.

Instruction: Presents the qualities of effective writing. Offers opportunity to receive critiques and to revise. The course features lectures and discussions followed by writing laboratory sessions.

Credit recommendation: In the lower division baccalaureate/associate degree category, 1 semester hour in Composition, Written Communication, or Writing Skills (5/80) (12/84). NOTE: This course has been reevaluated and continues to meet requirements for credit recommendations.

English Grammar and Usage

Location: Various locations throughout C&P Telephone Company business area.

Length: 32 weeks; individual sessions ranging from 1-3 hours per week.

Dates: September 1978-Present.

Objective: To teach proper grammatical forms, sentence construction, usage, and punctuation.

Instruction: Covers parts of speech, modifiers, the simple sentence, understanding the sentence unit, building better sentences, using verbs correctly, agreement of subject and verb, case, and using capitals and punctuation correctly. Programmed instruction with tutorial assistance.

Credit recommendation: In the lower division baccalaureate/associate degree category, 1 semester hour in Basic English, Composition, Grammar, or Written Communications (5/80) (12/84). NOTE: This course has been reevaluated and continues to meet requirements for credit recommendations.

Human Relations in Business

Location: Various locations throughout C&P Telephone Company business area.

Length: 30 hours (15 weeks).

Dates: February 1981-Present.

Objective: To develop understanding and practice of human relations skills as they relate to the business setting, emphasizing the development of awareness and personal skills in the areas of interpersonal communication, problem solving, and conflict in organizations.

Instruction: Interpersonal communication, dynamic listening, role playing, problem solving, and case studies through lecture and discussions.

Credit recommendation: In the upper division baccalaureate category, 2 semester hours in Business Administration, Human Relations, Leadership, or Management (2/81) (12/84). NOTE: This course has been reevaluated and continues to meet requirements for credit recommendations.

Oral Communication

Location: Various locations throughout C&P Telephone Company business area.

Length: 24 hours (12 weeks).

Dates: September 1978-Present.

Objective: To foster verbal skills in dialogue and public speaking.

Instruction: Covers basic communication theory and models; listening, perception, and self-awareness; verbal and nonverbal language systems; interpersonal communication; group discussion theory; public communication. Lectures, role playing, and group discussions are used. Prepared talks are presented and evaluated.

Credit recommendation: In the lower division baccalaureate/associate degree category, 2 semester hours in Communications or Speech (5/80) (12/84). NOTE: This course has been reevaluated and continues to meet requirements for credit recommendations.

Skillful Reading

Location: Various locations throughout C&P Telephone Company business area.

Length: 32 weeks; individualized instruction ranging from 103 hours per week.

Dates: September 1975-Present.

Objective: To improve students' reading comprehension.

Instruction: Designed to improve skills in comprehension, vocabulary, observing relationships, discerning details with context, recalling, following directions, interpreting, and understanding figurative language.

Credit recommendation: In the vocational certificate category, 3 semester hours in Reading Comprehension or Basic Skills Development (5/80) (12/84). NOTE: This course has been reevaluated and continues to meet requirements for credit recommendations.

Vocabulary Development

Location: Various locations throughout C&P Telephone Company business area.

Length: 32 weeks; individual sessions ranging from 1-3 hours per week.

Dates: September 1975-Present.

Objective: To improve students' pronunciation and vocabulary at the seventh grade through undergraduate freshman reading levels.

Instruction: Concentrates on vocabulary development. Programmed texts, pretests, posttests, tutorial assistance, and reinforcement exercises are used.

Credit recommendation: In the lower division baccalaureate/associate degree category, 1 semester hour in Written Communications, Composition, Basic English

(5/80) (12/84). NOTE: This course has been reevaluated and continues to meet requirements for credit recommendations.

ENGINEERING TRAINING PROGRAM

The Engineering Training program conducts technical courses for managers in Pennsylvania, Delaware, New Jersey, Maryland, Virginia, West Virginia, and the District of Columbia. For three of their courses (Interoffice Facilities, Current Planning, General Transmission Concepts) students come from all 48 contiguous states.

Source of official student records: Managing Director - Engineering Training Center, Bell Atlantic, 600 Chestnut Street, Room 714, Philadelphia, Pennsylvania 19106.

Additional information about the courses: Program on Noncollegiate Sponsored Instruction, The Center for Adult Learning and Educational Credentials, American Council on Education, One Dupont Circle, Washington, D.C. 20036.

Basic Accounting
(Accounting for Equipment Engineers)
Location: Philadelphia Engineering Training Center.
Length: 33 hours (1 week).
Dates: January 1983-Present.
Objective: Explain basic telephone account concepts including assets, liabilities, retained earnings, operating revenues, and operating expense accounts.
Instruction: Explain various accounting terminology and concepts relating to equipment engineering.
Credit recommendation: In the lower division baccalaureate/associate degree category, 2 semester hours in Principles of Accounting (12/85).

Basic Engineering Economy
Location: Philadelphia Engineering Training Center.
Length: 33 hours (1 week).
Dates: February 1985-Present.
Objective: Identify the various types of cost studies and where they are used as well as identifying common intangible factors and the effect they have on final decisions.
Instruction: Use of time value factors, treatment of inflation, books and tax depreciation.
Credit recommendation: In the lower division baccalaureate/associate degree category, 2 semester hours in Engineering or Engineering Technology (12/85). NOTE: Credit should be granted as an elective.

Capital Utilization Criteria (CUCRIT)
Location: Philadelphia Engineering Training Center.
Length: 33 hours (1 week).
Dates: January 1981-Present.
Objective: To explain and calculate various capital utilization criteria (CUCRIT). To input and run CUCRIT programs. Making reasonable decisions based upon CUCRIT.
Instruction: A "hands-on" course in advanced topics in Engineering Economy. Both problem solving and computer applications are stressed. A case study is included. Extensive use of the computer is incorporated into the instruction.
Credit recommendation: In the lower division baccalaureate/associate degree or in the upper division baccalaureate category, 2 semester hours in Engineering or Engineering Technology (12/85). NOTE: Credit should be granted as an elective.

Concepts in Engineering for Nontechnical Majors
(General Engineering)
Location: Philadelphia, PA.
Length: 66 hours (2 weeks).
Dates: January 1970-Present.
Objective: To expose the nontechnical student to the functions of engineering, including responsibilities, problems, and terminology.
Instruction: Surveys basic switching, traffic engineering, transmission concepts, business information systems, construction programs, development engineering, effective writing, engineering economics, probability, rate engineering, sound, speech and hearing, special networks, special services, switching networks, and time-shared computers. Lecture, discussion, and laboratory are used.
Credit recommendation: In the lower division baccalaureate/associate degree category or in the upper division baccalaureate category, 3 semester hours in a nontechnical curriculum (8/78).

Digital Technology
Location: Philadelphia Engineering Training Center.
Length: 33 hours (1 week).
Dates: January 1982-Present.
Objective: To identify the systems and methods available for management of the digital network. To identify interdisciplinary issues which must be resolved when introducing digital technology.
Instruction: Course includes instruction on basic digital theory and terminology, digital switching machines, and digital interoffice facilities equipment.
Credit recommendation: In the lower division baccalaureate/associate degree category, 2 semester hours in Electrical Technology or Electronic Technology (12/85).

Engineering Economy
Location: Philadelphia, PA.
Length: 66 hours (2 weeks).
Dates: January 1970-December 1988.
Objective: To provide the information necessary to perform a complete engineering economy study.
Instruction: Accounting, mathematics and money, depreciation, division of revenue, inflation, accelerated depreciation, investment tax credit, study techniques.

Lecture, workshop, and laboratory are used.

Credit recommendation: In the lower division baccalaureate/associate degree category or in the upper division baccalaureate category, 3 semester hours in Engineering or Engineering Technology (8/78). NOTE: Credit should be granted as an elective.

FA (Feeder Administration)
  Location: Philadelphia, PA.
  Length: 60 hours (2 weeks).
  Dates: May 1979-December 1988.
  Objective: To provide knowledge and skills in the application of existing economic, electronic, and feeder wire routing programs for the purpose of developing plans for optimum expanded phone usage.
  Instruction: Course covers appropriate economic, electronic, and feeder wire programs; commitment strategies; and monitoring and decision studies. Case studies, lectures, discussion, and laboratories are used.
  Credit recommendation: In the lower division baccalaureate/associate degree category, 2 semester hours in Electrical Technology or Electronic Technology (4/81).

General Transmission Concepts
  Location: Philadelphia Engineering Training Center
  Length: 76 hours (2 weeks).
  Dates: June 1983-Present.
  Objective: To examine the general design requirements for a telephone system using analog and digital carrier, radio or light wave systems.
  Instruction: Topics in this course include: basic telephone equipment operations; design parameters; metallic facilities; introduction to carrier systems; transmission of data.
  Credit recommendation: In the lower division baccalaureate/associate degree category, 4 semester hours in Electrical Technology (12/85).

Interoffice Facilities Current Planning
  Location: Philadelphia Engineering Training Center.
  Length: 40 hours (1 week).
  Dates: February 1983-Present.
  Objective: Development of a current facility and equipment plan. Identify the facility and equipment requirements for a network. To develop a relief and replacement plan for a given network.
  Instruction: Course includes developing and maintaining a planning model; identifying options for relief; and appropriate support documentation.
  Credit recommendation: In the lower division baccalaureate/associate degree category, 2 semester hours in Electrical Technology or Electronic Technology (12/85).

Light Wave Design
  Location: Philadelphia Engineering Training Center
  Length: 34 hours (1 week).
  Dates: November 1984-Present.
  Objective: To provide details required to prepare an engineering job order for digital loop carrier on fiber.
  Instruction: How to prepare fiber cable work prints specifying: (1) remote terminal/fiber hub configurations; (2) hardwired equipment; (3) plug in equipment; and (4) cable details.
  Credit recommendation: In the lower division baccalaureate/associate degree category, 2 semester hours in Electrical Technology or Electronic Technology (12/85).

LROPP (Long-Range Outside Plant Planning)
  Location: Philadelphia, PA.
  Length: 64 hours (2 weeks).
  Dates: September 1979-September 1984.
  Objective: To provide the student with the economic and technical skills and knowledge necessary to develop long-range plans for phone company wire centers.
  Instruction: Course includes tools involved in facilities, forecasting, and planning necessary for phone company wire center development. Lecture, discussion, and classroom exercises are used.
  Credit recommendation: In the lower division baccalaureate/associate degree category, 2 semester hours in Electrical Technology or Electronic Technology as a technical elective (4/81).

Loop Electronics Design
  Location: Philadelphia Engineering Training Center.
  Length: 36 hours (1 week).
  Dates: January 1982-Present.
  Objective: To be able to provide details required to prepare an engineering job order for digital loop carrier systems.
  Instruction: Determining power requirements for remote terminals. Specifying types and locations for terminal plug-ins. Determining splice locations.
  Credit recommendation: In the lower division baccalaureate/associate degree category, 2 semester hours in Electrical Technology or Electronic Technology (12/85).

Loop Electronics Planning
  Location: Philadelphia, PA.
  Length: 37½ hours (5 days).
  Dates: March 1981-December 1981.
  Objective: To provide the student with the tools to make decisions and develop plans for phone company feeder line relief.
  Instruction: Course includes economic analysis for alternate feeder designs; techniques for developing decisions and plans for optimum feeder system. Lecture, discussion, and case studies are used.
  Credit recommendation: In the lower division baccalaureate/associate degree category, 1 semester hour in Electrical Technology or Electronic Technology (4/81).

Methodology (Instructor Training)
　Location: Philadelphia, PA.
　Length: 25 hours (4 days).
　Dates: September 1970-Present.
　Objective: To prepare teachers to use a variety of instructional techniques to enhance the teaching/learning processes.
　Instruction: Course surveys learning theory, instructional methodology, writing learning objectives, and the use of visual aids. Group discussions and simulations are used.
　Credit recommendation: In the upper division baccalaureate category, 1 semester hour in Education (8/78).

MRSE (Mobile Radio Systems Engineering)
　Location: Philadelphia, PA.
　Length: 124 hours (3 weeks).
　Dates: April 1980-December 1988.
　Objective: To develop the necessary skills for the design of two-way mobile radio systems and one-way radio paging systems.
　Instruction: Course includes frequency, site, receiver, antenna, and transmitter power selection procedures; the fundamentals of co-channel and intermodulation interference; and study of signaling systems, remote transmitter control, coupling loss between antennas, and site noise tests. Lectures, discussion, and laboratories are used.
　Credit recommendation: In the lower division baccalaureate/associate degree category, 3 semester hours as a technical elective, or in the upper division baccalaureate degree category, 3 semester hours as a free elective (4/81).

Time Share Cable Sizing Program
ALLOC II, Economic Feeder Admin and Relief, Economic Alternative Selction OSP ÙNE060IIC, NE130IIC, NE080IIC, NE040IIC]
　Location: South Plainfield, NJ; Newark, NJ.
　Length: 56 hours (8 days).
　Dates: January 1981-Present.
　Objective: To enable the student to use TICS program, to create FAS tables and use ALLOC and computer program, to prepare for and conduct an EFAR analysis, and to use the EASOP program to test the economic impact of alternative plans.
　Instruction: Course covers use of TICS program to develop economic cable sizing for feeder cable relief. Next module includes information needed to write the necessary file and run a program using the ALLOC computer program to produce initial run and to analyze the initial output. Following module covers EFAR analysis to determine optimum fill and relief and proper utilization of feeder route in accord with NJB practices. Final module covers gathering necessary information, developing comparable alternatives to be tested, running the EASOP program and evaluating output of the program.
　Credit recommendation: In the lower division baccalaureate/associate degree category, 2 semester hours in Engineering Economics (1/85).

INFORMATION SYSTEMS EDUCATION

Information Systems Education trains employees involved in data systems work and provides education in many disciplines concerned with the development of primarily mainframe computer-based data systems. Courses offered range from basic progrmmer training to operating systems and system analyst training.

Advanced Lotus 1-2-3
　Location: South Plainfield, NJ.
　Length: 21 hours (3 days).
　Dates: June 1985-Present.
　Objective: To present advanced concepts of Lotus 1-2-3- to students who have already mastered fundamentals of Lotus 1-2-3.
　Instruction: Using leader-led tutorials, and laboratory exercises, the course deals with advanced macros, database and statistical analysis, and financial modeling.
　Credit recommendation: In the lower division baccalaureate/associate degree category, 1 semester hour in Business Administration (3/86).

An Introduction to Time Share and Basic Language Programming
1. Time Share Basic
2. Introduction to Honeywell Time Share
　Location: C&P Telephone Company's Information Systems Education Center, Silver Spring, MD, and on-site work location.
　Length: 1. 18 hours (3 days); 2. 23½ hours (4 days).
　Dates: February 1983-Present.
　Objective: This course is intended to introduce students to time sharing commands, operations, editors, and file structures. In the "Basic" programming portion, students design, code, and execute programs.
　Instruction: Video presentation, lecture, labs, and discussion combined with hands-on terminal usage. Course introduces BASIC programming language. At the course's conclusion, students understand functions of current/collector file, system commands, and subsequent operation; use the text editor to create and modify files; and understand the file management supervisor.
　Credit recommendation: In the lower division baccalaureate/associate degree category, 1 semester hour in Data Processing (12/85). NOTE: Students must take both courses to receive credit.

C Programming
　Location: C&P Telephone Company's Information Systems Education Center, Silver Spring, MD.
　Length: 24 hours (4 days).
　Dates: February 1983-Present.

Objective: To enable a student to develop, maintain, or modify C language programs.

Instruction: Course covers C language including basics; time share, basic structures and syntax, program design, arrays, pointers, structured programming concepts, file control, and I/O processing.

Credit recommendation: In the lower division baccalaureate/associate degree category, 1 semester hour in Data Processing (12/85).

Information Management System (IMS)

Location: C&P Telephone Data Systems Training Center.

Length: 62 hours (2 weeks).

Dates: July 1978-Present.

Objective: To introduce students with programming experience to data base concepts and IMS data base management system; to develop skills in access methods of data bases; to process data stored in an IMS data base and to retrieve data from base online systems.

Instruction: Information Management System overview; batch processing and teleprocessing. Overview unit emphasizes the building of data base and various access methods used. Batch unit stresses the use of Data Language One pointers, and command codes. The teleprocessing unit emphasizes message formats, program structure, calls, and conversational processing. Students are required to execute case studies for successful completion of course. Lecture, discussion, workshop, and independent study are used.

Credit recommendation: In the upper division baccalaureate category, 3 semester hours in Data Base Management (12/79) (12/84). NOTE: This course has been reevaluated and continues to meet requirements for credit recommendations.

Introduction to dBase III

Location: South Plainfield, NJ.

Length: 14 hours (2 days).

Dates: June 1985-Present.

Objective: To present students with the fundamentals of Data Base III.

Instruction: Using leader-led tutorials the course deals with the creation of basic files and data entry techniques as well as file manipulation, editing and output.

Credit recommendation: In the lower division baccalaureate/associate degree category, 1 semester hour in Business Administration (3/86).

1. Introduction to IBM PC-XT and DOS
2. Computer Literacy/Do I need a PC?

Location: South Plainfield, NJ.

Length: 1. 7 hours (1 day); 2. 7 hours (1 day).

Dates: June 1985-Present.

Objective: To determine if an employee needs a PC to help perform job in accordance with New Jersey Bell regulations and procedures and to provide an Introduction to I.B.M. PC and disk operating systems.

Instruction: To determine the types of tasks best performed by PC and to provide an introduction to available software to perform these tasks. A general overview of typical hardware/software is presented with a review of N.J. Bell policies regarding computer acquisition and usage. It also provides an introduction to operating procedures of the keyboard and peripherals with detailed PC-DOS commands. The course employs instructor-led tutorials, slide presentations, and hands-on I.B.M. PC lab.

Credit recommendation: In the lower division baccalaureate/associate degree category, 1 semester hour in Business Administration (3/86). NOTE: Students can be admitted directly into the Introduction to IBM PC-XT and DOS course; and if they successfully complete this course, they are eligible for the credit recommendation.

Introduction to Lotus 1-2-3

Location: South Plainfield, NJ.

Length: 14 hours (2 days).

Dates: February 1985-Present.

Objective: To present students with the fundamental concepts of Lotus 1-2-3.

Instruction: Using leader-led tutorials and laboratory exercises, this course will deal with creation, printing, and graphing of spreadsheets.

Credit recommendation: In the lower division baccalaureate/associate degree category, 1 semester hour in Business Administration (3/86).

Programmer Basic Training

Location: Silver Spring, MD.

Length: 472½ hours (13 weeks).

Dates: June 1978-Present.

Objective: To introduce students with no programming experience to the physical structure, major concepts, and application of computers; to develop skills in designing and implementing structured COBOL programs and required documentations; to prepare students to create and modify JCL to execute programs and procedures.

Instruction: Data processing concepts; data representation, structured programming, design, implementation, and case problems; COBOL; JCL; utilities. The COBOL unit of the course emphasizes understanding diagnostic messages, making appropriate corrections to COBOL case, debugging. Students are required to take written tests and execute case studies. Lecture, discussion, workshop, and independent study are used.

Credit recommendation: In the lower division baccalaureate/associate degree category or in the upper division baccalaureate category, 6 semester hours in Business, Computer Science, Engineering, Information Science, or Technology (12/79) (12/84). NOTE: Students may also be awarded credit recommendations in the following manner: (1) in the lower division baccalaureate/associate degree category, 3 semester hours in Introduction to Data Processing; (2) in the upper division baccalaureate category, 3 semester hours in Programming; (3) in the lower division baccalaureate/associate degree category, 3 semester hours in Introduction to Computer Systems.

Programmer Workshop I
  Location: Silver Spring, MD.
  Length: 32½ hours (1 week).
  Dates: February 1979-Present.
  Objective: To introduce systems application.
  Instruction: Covers linkage editor functions; IBM time sharing option; C&P conventions for JCL. Lecture and laboratory activities are used.
  Credit recommendation: In the upper division baccalaureate category, 1 semester hour in Information Systems or Systems Application (5/80) (12/84). NOTE: This course has been reevaluated and continues to meet requirements for credit recommendations.

Programmer Basic Training - COBOL
  Location: Philadelphia, PA.
  Length: 473 hours (13 weeks).
  Dates: February 1977-Present.
  Objective: To introduce students with no programming experience to the physical structure and major concepts of a computer; to develop skills in designing and implementing structured COBOL programs and required documentation; to prepare students to create and modify JCL to execute programs and procedures.
  Instruction: Data processing concepts; data representation; structured programming, design, implementation, and case problems; COBOL; JCL; utilities; cataloged procedures. The COBOL unit of the course emphasizes understanding diagnostic messages, making appropriate corrections to COBOL code, debugging, modularity, the SORT verb, and modular debugging. Students are required to take written tests and execute case studies. Lecture, discussion, workshop, and independent study are used.
  Credit recommendation: In the lower division baccalaureate/associate degree category or in the upper division baccalaureate category, 6 semester hours in Computer Sciences, Engineering, Information Sciences, or Technology (8/78).

MARKETING TRAINING PROGRAM

This regional marketing development and delivery organization has two primary functions: the internal development, or procurement from external sources, of marketing training courses and the delivery of same to the field sales force.

Training is provided to sales personnel in selling and interpersonal skills and in the telecommunications service offerings of the Bell Atlantic Companies (includes New Jersey, Pennsylvania, Delaware, Maryland, Virginia, West Virginia, and Washington, D.C.). The objective is to prepare sales personnel to sell intelligently and aggressively in a highly competitive, sophisticated, and consumer-oriented environment.

Source of official student records: Director, Marketing Training, Bell Atlantic, 3624 Market Street, 5th Floor, Philadelphia, Pennsylvania 19104.

Additional information about the courses: Program on Noncollegiate Sponsored Instruction, The Center for Adult Learning and Educational Credentials, American Council on Education, One Dupont Circle, Suite 1B-20, Washington, D.C., 20036.

Account Executive Selling Skills
  Location: Silver Spring, MD.
  Length: 75 hours (2 weeks).
  Dates: January 1978-December 1984.
  Objective: To instruct personnel in the basic sales skills, including preparatory financial analysis and systems theory.
  Instruction: Financial calculations, sales planning and preparation, conducting a systems study, presentation of results, and cost justification. Lecture, case studies, and role playing are used.
  Credit recommendation: In the upper division baccalaureate category, 3 semester hours in Marketing (12/79).

Advanced Systems Selling for Accounting Executives
  Location: Silver Spring, MD.
  Length: 132 hours (3 weeks).
  Dates: October 1977-December 1984.
  Objective: To instruct personnel in advanced sales skills, including financial analysis, systems analysis, and the various phases of the sales process.
  Instruction: Systems theory, ratio analysis, benefit and investment analysis, economic modeling, behavior modification techniques, the administration and execution of a sales plan through the phases of the systems selling process. Lecture, discussions, case studies, and role playing are used.
  Credit recommendation: In the upper division baccalaureate category, 6 semester hours in Marketing (12/79). NOTE: Students must have successfully completed the course on Account Executive Selling Skills before receiving credit for this course.

Data Processing/Data Communications
  Location: Philadelphia, PA.
  Length: 48½ hours (2 weeks).
  Dates: May 1980-December 1988.
  Objective: To familiarize the student with data processing concepts.
  Instruction: Survey of data processing, including description of hardware, software, flowcharting, program-

ming, systems, and related applications. Lecture, discussion, and laboratory exercises are used.

Credit recommendation: In the lower division baccalaureate/associate degree category, 1 semester hour in Data Processing (4/81) (2/85). NOTE: This course has been reevaluated and continues to meet requirements for credit recommendations.

Information Transmission and Networking (The Network)
Location: New Jersey, Pennsylvania, Delaware, Maryland, Virginia, West Virginia, and Washington, D.C.
Length: 72 hours (9½ days).
Dates: August 1984-Present.
Objective: To provide the student with information in the areas of: transmission and networking fundamentals, telephone system functions, data communications concepts, data transmission digital and analog (Microwave Satellite and Fiber Optic), and existing and proposed network protocols.
Instruction: Course prepares students for a future in data communications with emphasis on services provided by regulated carriers. Students learn through applications, exercises, and mock presentations.
Credit recommendation: In the upper division baccalaureate category, 2 semester hours in Computer Science (12/85).

Personal Selling I
(Account Executive Phase I)
Location: Philadelphia, PA and Silver Spring, MD.
Length: 85 hours (6 weeks).
Dates: January 1984-Present.
Objective: To teach students basic selling skills.
Instruction: This course develops skills for one-to-one promotion based on customer analyses and benefits selling. Lecture, discussion, role playing, and case analyses.
Credit recommendation: In the lower division baccalaureate/associate degree category, 3 semester hours in Personal Selling (12/85).

Personal Selling II
(Account Executive Phase II)
Location: Philadelphia, PA and Silver Spring, MD.
Length: 91½ hours (6 weeks).
Dates: January 1985-Present.
Objective: To teach students advanced selling skills.
Instruction: This course focuses on developing a strategic selling approach and includes competitor analyses, sales plans, presentations, and closing skills. Lecture, discussion, role playing, and case analysis.
Credit recommendation: In the upper division baccalaureate category, 3 semester hours in Personal Selling (12/85).

Selling Skills
(Market Administrator - Voice, Intercity, PBX)
Location: Philadelphia, PA.
Length: *Version 1:* 297 hours (9 weeks); *Version 2:* 468 hours (16 weeks).
Dates: *Version 1:* January 1968-April 1981; *Version 2:* September 1979-December 1982.
Objective: To introduce the student to basic marketing and sales techniques and to develop the student's selling skills.
Instruction: *Versions 1 and 2:* Principles of business, management and economics, pricing tariffs, credit, marketing organization, servicing, selling skills, preparing proposals. Videotape modules, field training, role playing, and program text are used.
Credit recommendation: *Versions 1 and 2:* In the lower division baccalaureate/associate degree category, 4 semester hours in Marketing (Selling Skills) (4/81).

Traffic Theory/Basic Network Design
(Formerly Traffic Theory and Communications Engineering)
Location: Philadelphia, PA.
Length: 30 hours (5 days).
Dates: August 1980-December 1988.
Objective: To teach the student the statistical skills and traffic theories necessary for traffic management.
Instruction: Principles of data collection concepts sampling, probability, and traffic theory. Lecture, discussion, and laboratory exercises are used.
Credit recommendation: In the upper division baccalaureate category, 1 semester hour in Statistics (4/81) (12/85). NOTE: This course has been reevaluated and continues to meet requirements for credit recommendations.

PERFORMANCE IMPROVEMENT RESOURCES

The Performance Improvement Resources program offers clients several activities to improve their organizations' effectiveness. These include performance improvements: organization development, team building, communications, planning, management education courses to enhance managerial skills, and finance and budget courses.

Basic Telephone Accounting
Location: Silver Spring, MD.
Length: 35 hours (1 week).
Dates: December 1975-Present.
Objective: To understand the nature and purpose of accounting.
Instruction: Use of the account to record and accumulate increases and decreases in the items that appear on the financial reports; the processes employed in recording financial data; the eight-step accounting process; application of principles and processes of telephone accounting in

preparing financial reports for a small telephone company. Course uses lecture with visual aids, slide/tape presentations, workbook problems and lesson tests, instructor-led discussions, and case problems involving operations of a small telephone company.

Credit recommendation: In the lower division baccalaureate/associate degree category, 2 semester hours in Principles of Accounting (12/79) (12/84). NOTE: This course has been reevaluated and continues to meet requirements for credit recommendations.

Cost and Accounting Systems
(DOPAC Disk Oriented Property and Cost [2664])
Location: Silver Spring, MD.
Length: 44½ hours (5 days).
Dates: December 1982-December 1988.
Objective: To enable the student to define the overall processing performed on data provided and evaluate when incorrect processing has occurred; identify how transactions are batched, balanced, controlled, generated, corrected, posted, and reported within the system process. Ensure reasonably complete and accurate financial reporting; and evaluate and respond appropriately to feedback received from system users.
Instruction: This course provides a basic overview of the inputs, processes, outputs, and interfaces of a cost accounting system. This is an instructor-led course using lecture/visual aids, instructor-led and group discussions, student materials/reference binders, and case problems/group exercises.
Credit recommendation: In the upper division baccalaureate category, 2 semester hours in Accounting (8/85).

Data Management for Switching Networks
(Data Management No. 5 Crossbar [DM-5])
Location: Silver Spring, MD.
Length: 90 hours (2 weeks).
Dates: November 1978-Present.
Objective: To enable the student to validate and analyze data and suggest proper solutions for all problems.
Instruction: Validation and analysis of the traffic data for switching purposes; the interpretation and application of data directed at each system component, including equipment operation, register scoring sequence, validation of data, and analysis of data. Problem analysis and solutions include dial tone speed, incoming failure to match, overflows, and equipment irregularity. Lecture workshops, flow charts, simulations, classroom and problem-solving exercises are used.
Credit recommendation: In the lower division baccalaureate/associate degree category, 3 semester hours in Electrical Engineering (12/79) (12/84). NOTE: This course has been reevaluated and continues to meet requirements for credit recommendations.

Designing and Conducting Role Play
Location: Various locations throughout C&P Telephone Company business area.
Length: 22½ hours (3 days).
Dates: August 1978-Present.
Objective: To enable participants to understand different role play concepts and techniques; to improve skills in writing, conducting, and critiquing role plays; to apply role-play knowledge and skill to their own specific uses.
Instruction: Developing, designing, and conducting a variety of role plays. Participants develop specific skills in role playing.
Credit recommendation: In the vocational certificate category, 1 semester hour in Communication Skills (12/79) (12/84). NOTE: This course has been reevaluated and continues to meet requirements for credit recommendations.

Developing Additional Managerial Skills
Location: Silver Spring, MD.
Length: 51 hours (1 week).
Dates: June 1971-June 1980.
Objective: To develop and reinforce an understanding of managerial styles and interpersonal skills to promote the growth of management.
Instruction: Application of theories about managerial functions, interpersonal relationships, and human development in organizations. Discussion, lecture, and classroom exercises are used.
Credit recommendation: In the upper division baccalaureate category, 3 semester hours in Business Administration, Educational Administration, or Social Sciences (12/79). NOTE: Students receiving credit for this course should not receive credit for Developing Managers.

Developing Managers
Location: Silver Spring, MD.
Length: 51 hours (1 week).
Dates: June 1971-Present.
Objective: To develop an understanding of managerial styles and interpersonal skills to promote the growth of newly hired or newly promoted management personnel.
Instruction: Introductory application of theories about managerial functions, interpersonal relationships, and human development in organizations. Discussion, lecture, and classroom exercises are used.
Credit recommendation: In the upper division baccalaureate category, 3 semester hours in Business Administration, Educational Administration, or Social Sciences (12/79) (12/84). NOTE: Students receiving credit for this course should not receive credit for Developing Additional Managerial Skills. This course has been reevaluated and continues to meet requirements for credit recommendations.

Developing Managers (G199AIC and G199BIC)
Location: South Plainfield, NJ. and other locations throughout the state.
Length: 35 hours (5 days).
Dates: January 1974-Present.
Objective: To provide managers new to the company or employees newly promoted to management with a knowledge and understanding of their new role.
Learning Outcome: Upon successful completion of this course, the participant will be able to: use the management appraisal process; develop clear, measurable job objectives; focus on the attributes of competent management; and define managerial roles as they relate to corporate objectives.
Instruction: This course is designed to provide a smooth transition into management. Helps new management employees better understand their roles as managers of the business. The program includes guest speakers from various departments. Discussion, role play and trainer observation are used. Conferees are evaluated by this discussion and role play to assure that they meet course objectives.
Credit recommendation: In the lower division baccalaureate/associate degree category, 1 semester hour in Management Development (6/81)(8/86). NOTE: This course has been re-evaluated and continues to meet requirements for credit recommendation.

Dynamics of Management
a. **Developing Managers (G199AIC and G199BIC)**
b. **Managing the Work (G759OIC)**
c. **Problem Solving (G763OIC)**
d. **Situational Leadership (G763OIC)**
e. **Time Management (G190OIC)**
Location: South Plainfield, NJ and other locations throughout the state.
Length: a. 35 hours (5 days); b. 21 hours (3 days); c. 7 hours (1 day); d. 14 hours (2 days); e. 7 hours (1 day).
Dates: a. April 1982-Present; b. January 1981-Present; c. January 1981-Present; d. July 1983-Present; e. April 1976-Present.
Objective: To enable participants to understand their role as manager, to manage work flow, to have a systematic approach for solving problems, to become effective with the Situational Leadership approach, and to learn practical techniques to manage time and gain control of work.
Learning Outcome: Upon successful completion of this series of modules, the participant will be able to: a. *Developing Managers* - develop clear, measureable job objectives; focus on the attributes of competent management; and use skillful communication to enhance managerial style. b. *Managing the Work* - plan and organize work more effectively; and prepare written plans, checkpoint logs and work schedules. c. *Problem Solving* - accurately define a problem and determine if it is worth solving; and select the most efficient solution to the problem. d. *Situational Leadership* - diagnose the readiness of followers to do a specific task or function; and vary leadership styles depending on the situation and the development level of the follower. e. *Time Management* - set long and short term goals; and handle paper work, deal with procrastination, and manage interruptions.
Instruction: This sequence of modules provides an introduction to the role of the manager at New Jersey Bell. In addition to the overview of a corporate manager, the modules focus upon specific areas, managing work, problem solving, situational leadership and time management. The modules clarify the issues involved in each of these types and present a variety of methods of response. The modules are presented only to those in managerial positions and use extensive class exercises. Individual activities, projects or presentations are employed by the instructor to determine that participants are meeting course objectives.
Credit recommendation: In the lower division baccalaureate/associate degree category, 5 semester hours in Dynamics of Management (8/86).

Effective Communicating
a. **Effective Communications Workshop (G761OIC)**
b. **Effective Reading (G212OIC)**
c. **Effective Writing (G197OIC)**
Location: South Plainfield, NJ. and other locations throughout the state.
Length: a. 14 hours (2 days); b. 14 hours (2 days); c. 14 hours (2 days).
Dates: a. April 1982-Present; b. September 1982-Present; c. January 1976-Present.
Objective: To enable participants to communicate in a more effective and businesslike manner whether reading, writing or speaking in public.
Learning Outcome: Upon successful completion of these courses, the participant will be able to: organize a presentation quickly and effectively; give talks confidently and convincingly; determine a purpose and objective for reading; adjust reading rate and technique based on the purpose; organize writing logically; use simple, clear, precise language; and analyze the readibility of letters.
Instruction: In these courses, students present a speech which is videotaped and subsequently critiqued. There is also a pre- and post-testing to measure reading speed and comprehension. Finally, students are required to demonstrate the principles of business writing by applying proper techniques to make sure their writing is clear, concise and understandable.
Credit recommendation: In the lower division baccalaureate/associate degree category, 3 semester hours in Effective Communications (8/86).

First Level Curriculum-Managing Performance
Location: C&P Learning Center, Silver Spring, MD.
Length: 30 hours (4 days).
Dates: July 1982-Present.

Objective: To enable the student to apply and implement the following developmental processes: performance feedback, coaching, career counseling, establishing a motivating atmosphere, and handling formal and informal communication.

Instruction: Course provides new first-level managers with an organized process for conducting work-related discussions with their employees, including ways to plan and follow up on these discussions. Course stresses the use of appropriate communication skills, the provision of a motivating climate, and the removal of roadblocks to effective performance. Lecture and discussion are used.

Credit recommendation: In the lower division baccalaureate/associate degree category, 1 semester hour in Human Relations or Introductory Management (12/84).

Fundamentals of Revenue Accounting
  Location: C&P Learning Center, Silver Spring, MD.
  Length: 32 hours (5 days).
  Dates: December 1984-Present.
  Objective: To provide students with the fundamental principles and concepts of revenue accounting.
  Instruction: Covers general revenue accounting concepts, including accrual accounting, estimates of uncollectability, billing, journalization, source documents, transaction management, and preparation of the associated financial reports. Lecture, discussion, and classroom exercises are used.
  Credit recommendation: In the lower division baccalaureate/associate degree category, 2 semester hours in Principles of Accounting or in the upper division baccalaureate category, 1 semester hour in Intermediate Accounting, or as an elective in the upper division baccalaureate category, 2 semester hours in Accounting (12/84).

Initial Management Training (113)
  Location: Harrisburg, Philadelphia, Pittsburgh, PA.
  Length: 32 hours (1 week).
  Dates: January 1969-January 1984.
  Objective: To identify the functions of management, their applications, and the relationship of managerial behavior to the work situation.
  Instruction: Surveys the initial management principles, behavior, work situation, basic communications and role playing. Group discussion, lectures, and simulations are used.
  Credit recommendation: In the lower division baccalaureate/associate degree category, 1 semester hour in Management (8/78).

Initial Supervisory Training (114)
  Location: Harrisburg, Philadelphia, Pittsburgh, PA.
  Length: 32 hours (1 week).
  Dates: January 1969-January 1984.
  Objective: To identify attitudes and behavior appropriate to a supervisor's position and to enhance the supervisor's relationship with others.
  Instruction: Surveys decision-making processes, motivation, behavior and attitudes, management by objectives and interrelations. Group discussion, lectures, and simulations are used.
  Credit recommendation: In the lower division baccalaureate/associate degree category, 1 semester hour in Management (8/78).

Orientation for New Managers/Supervisors
1. Orientation for New Managers
2. Orientation for New Supervisors
  Location: Philadelphia, Harrisburg, and Pittsburgh, PA.
  Length: 1. 21 hours (3 days); 2. 32 hours (1 week).
  Dates: May 1980-June 1983.
  Objective: To acquaint prospective managers and supervisors with basic management skills.
  Instruction: Basic management objectives, communications skills, personnel problems, leadership styles, motivation. Classroom exercises are used.
  Credit recommendation: In the lower division baccalaureate/associate degree category, 2 semester hours in Management (4/81). NOTE: To be eligible for credit, student must successfully complete both courses.

Instructor Training Workshop
  Location: South Plainfield, NJ.
  Length: 31 hours (5 days).
  Dates: June 1976-Present.
  Objective: To familiarize students with principles, methods, and techniques of instruction to increase their effectiveness as trainers and instructors; to enable students to analyze their own performances through the use of television recording and replay; and to aid students in applying principles of learning.
  Instruction: Covers an examination of the relationship between learners, trainers, and topic; exploration of the effectiveness of the trainer and methods of training; analysis of effective organization of information; and examination of methods to motivate learners. Lectures, case studies, observable behavior, and mastery of tests are used.
  Credit recommendation: In the lower division baccalaureate/associate degree category, 1 semester hour in Workshop Leadership Methods (6/81).

Introduction to Management
(First Level Curriculum - Managing Performance)
  Location: Various locations throughout the C&P Telephone Company network.
  Length: 30 hours (4 days).
  Dates: July 1982-Present.
  Objective: To provide students with an introduction to management techniques with an emphasis on managing performance.

Instruction: Lecture, discussion, and role playing. This course focuses on specific management techniques including employee motivation, performance standards, performance appraisal, and career counseling.

Credit recommendation: In the lower division baccalaureate/associate degree category, 2 semester hours in Basic Management (12/85).

Introduction to Property and Cost Accounting
  Location: C&P Learning Center, Silver Spring, MD.
  Length: *Version 1:* 35 hours (1 week); *Version 2:* 37½ hours (5 days).
  Dates: *Version 1:* December 1972-February 1984; *Version 2:* March 1984-Present.
  Objective: To provide the student with a basic knowledge and understanding of the theory behind each major function of the Property and Cost Office, and a working knowledge of telephone plant accounts and how they affect the financial and productivity reports.
  Instruction: *Version 1:* Covers the accounting process used in classifying, recording, summarizing, and reporting financial transactions involving the addition, retirement, and maintenance of telephone plant accounts. Instructor-led lectures, visual aids, student case problems, discussions, and tests are used. *Version 2:* Covers the review of basic telephone accounting; defines the nature and purpose of property and cost accounting; defines the concept of net plant; provides for the integration of information flow, the allocation of personnel costs, and the use of overhead accounts and preparation of managerial reports. Lecture, discussion, and classroom exercises are used.
  Credit recommendation: In the lower division baccalaureate/associate degree category, 2 semester hours in Cost Accounting, Managerial Accounting, or Principles of Accounting (12/84).

Job Study Workshop
  Location: Silver Spring, MD.
  Length: 32 hours (1 week).
  Dates: May 1978-Present.
  Objective: To enable the student to perform a content analysis of documents used in job performance.
  Instruction: Conduct of a job study interview; recording, referencing, summarizing data; flow chart work activities; and analysis for completeness. Students must demonstrate mastery of subject by providing group outputs that conform to programmed results. Lecture, discussions, classroom exercises, interviews, videotapes, and flow charts are used.
  Credit recommendation: In the upper division baccalaureate category, 1 semester hour in Personnel (12/79) (12/84). NOTE: This course has been reevaluated and continues to meet requirements for credit recommendations.

Management Appraisal Plan Training
  Location: Various locations throughout C&P Telephone Company business area.
  Length: 18 hours (2 days).
  Dates: June 1977-December 1988.
  Objective: To develop the ability to make overall determinations of management potential on the basis of documented behavior and ratings of potential.
  Instruction: A program for new managers who will be doing performance appraisals of subordinates. The course provides a background in appraisals; definition of performance; factors and practical experience in classifying behavior, rating behavior, and giving evaluation feedback. Lecture, discussion, and classroom exercises are used.
  Credit recommendation: In the vocational certificate category, 1 semester hour in Personnel (12/79). NOTE: Not in a position to evaluate until leader's guide is reviewed.

1. Managing the Flow of Work
2. Developing Subordinates
3. Managing the Job
  Location: South Plainfield, NJ.
  Length: 38½ hours (6 days).
  Dates: June 1981-Present.
  Objective: To enable the participant to use a systematic process for planning and monitoring the work flow; develop satisfactory subordinates; and manage his/her job effectively.
  Instruction: Covers managing, supervision, planning, organizing, delegation, problem solving, interviewing and negotiating, time management, and interpersonal skills. Lectures, case studies, observable behavior, and mastery of tests are used.
  Credit recommendation: In the lower division baccalaureate/associate degree category, 2 semester hours in Job Definition and Management (6/81).

1. Managing the Problem-Solving Process
2. Managing to Write
3. Defining the Job
  Location: South Plainfield, NJ.
  Length: 36 hours (6 days).
  Dates: February 1981-Present.
  Objective: To enable the participant to (1) demonstrate a process for solving problems; (2) write memos, letters, and reports, and produce documents which provide maximum impact on the reader; and (3) define thoroughly the job and improve the work group's effectiveness.
  Instruction: Course covers
  1. Describing the problem situation and problem characteristics, determining the problem causes, selecting and evaluating solutions.
  2. Writing memos, letters, reports, and producing documents which provide maximum impact on the readers; defining thoroughly the job in order to improve the work

group's effectiveness.

3. Producing a job definition, reviewing and verifying the job definition, and defining and reviewing the work groups.

Lectures, case studies, observable behavior, and mastery of tests are used.

Credit recommendation: In the lower division baccalaureate/associate degree category, 2 semester hours in Problem Solving (6/81).

Management/Union Relations Workshop
Location: C&P Learning Center, Silver Spring, MD.
Length: 15 hours (2 days).
Dates: February 1982-Present.
Objective: To enable students to examine the basic steps in progressive corrective discipline; demonstrate the recommended procedure for handling refusals to follow instructions; present, through practice, the steps for handling a grievance meeting; prepare a company-initiated change plan according to the recommended procedure; examine communication techniques useful in dealing with labor relations matters; have an opportunity to discuss labor relations questions individual to each participant; and develop personal plans for improving management/union relations.
Instruction: Workshop provides understanding and methods for dealing with selected management/union matters. Skills are developed in corrective progressive discipline, handling grievances, refusals to follow instructions, introducing company-initiated change, and documenting of employee discussions. Practice sessions, written exercises, and group discussions are used.
Credit recommendation: In the vocational certificate category, 1 semester hour in Industrial Relations or Personnel Management (12/84).

1. Methods Development Standards (Module I)
2. Methods Development Standards (Module II)
Location: South Plainfield, NJ.
Length: 30 hours (5 days) - Module I; 60 hours (10 days) - Module II.
Dates: June 1980-Present.
Objective: To enable the participant to develop uniform, high quality methods documents for systems use.
Instruction: Covers the standards by which methods should be developed. The standards comprise nine phases. Each phase embodies a list of activities to perform and disciplines to apply, enabling a project to develop ever increasing levels of detail in a systematic approach toward performance-oriented practices. Lectures, case studies, observable behavior, and mastery of tests are used.
Credit recommendation: *Course 1:* In the lower division baccalaureate/associate degree category, 2 semester hours in Methods Development. *Course 2:* In the lower division baccalaureate/associate degree category, 2 semester hours in Methods Development (6/81).

Methods Developers' Workshop
Location: C&P Learning Center, Silver Spring, MD.
Length: 60 hours (2 weeks).
Dates: February 1982-Present.
Objective: To enable the student to demonstrate a basic understanding of methods development by analyzing case study documents and developing appropriate methods material. Course focuses on analyzing and writing methods, including job aids, throughout the course. Group and individual exercises are used to enable participants to practice developing methods in a systematic way. Participants receive a workbook containing several job aids for use back on the job.
Credit recommendation: In the upper division baccalaureate category, 2 semester hours in Technical Writing or Operations (12/84).

Negotiation Skills Workshop
Location: C&P Learning Center, Silver Spring, MD.
Length: 22½ hours (3 days).
Dates: June 1981-Present.
Objective: To enable the student to understand the basic concepts necessary in effective interpersonal negotiation.
Instruction: Covers a method of resolving differences in a variety of contexts, such as distributing scarce resources, coordinating activities and projects between groups and individuals, and determining the solutions to difficult problems involving conflicts of interest. The win-win model of conflict management is emphasized. Lectures and discussion are used.
Credit recommendation: In the lower division baccalaureate/associate degree category, 1 semester hour in Human Relations or Personnel Relations (12/84).

New Age Thinking (G764OIC)
Location: South Plainfield, NJ and other locations throughout the state.
Length: 24 hours (3 days).
Dates: April 1983-Present.
Objective: To help participants become more productive in their corporate lives through supportive rather than conflicting self image in self or subordinates.
Learning Outcome: Upon successful completion of this course, the participant will be able to: align self image with professional goals; develop new habits and attitudes that support professional goals; correct "mistakes" made by others over whom one has leadership responsibility; and use affirmations and visualizations to attain professional goals.
Instruction: This course is designed to help managers become more productive in their corporate and personal lives. Participants will learn how high performance people enjoy success and fulfillment in all areas on their lives. This course includes standardized lecture and extensive discussion and individual activities. Class size is kept

small and participants are evaluated on this mastery of course objective through individual activities and level of class participation.

Credit recommendation: In the upper division baccalaureate category, 1 semester hour in New Age Thinking or Management Psychology (8/86).

Oral Communication Skills
Location: Various locations throughout C&P Telephone Company business area.
Length: 28½ hours (3 days).
Dates: April 1978-Present.
Objective: To enable participants to prepare and present several oral presentations.
Instruction: Covers the criteria for a good oral presentation and identifies future developmental needs in oral skills for individual students. Discussion, classroom presentations, and films are used.
Credit recommendation: In the vocational certificate category, 1 semester hour in Speech (12/79) (12/84). NOTE: This course has been reevaluated and continues to meet requirements for credit recommendations.

Payroll Accounting (2666)
Location: Silver Spring, MD.
Length: 21 hours (3 days).
Dates: January 1983-Present.
Objective: To enable the student to understand the nature and purpose of payroll accounting; journalize the various employee cash and noncash payments, and understand the related tax treatment; and calculate and journalize the dollar amounts for gross wages, federal income taxes, FICA taxes, allotment withholdings, special payroll transactions, and net pay.
Instruction: Course covers the payroll accounting system. It familiarizes the student with the inputs, outputs, and the related processing functions of payroll accounting. This is an instructor-led course using lecture/visual aids; student workbook problems and tests and instructor-led discussions.
Credit recommendation: In the lower division baccalaureate/associate degree category, 1 semester hour in Accounting (8/85).

Performance Analysis Workshop #204
Location: South Plainfield, NJ.
Length: 19 hours (3 days).
Dates: February 1980-Present.
Objective: To enable the participant to apply performance analysis strategies to organizational performance problems; recommend and implement nontraining solutions - such as feedback systems, incentive systems, and job engineering - for appropriate nontraining problems; conduct a worth analysis of training solutions; and increase the effectiveness of the training organization by adopting performance analysis strategies, worth analysis techniques, and the systems approach to training.
Instruction: Covers identification or isolation of organizational performance problems; determination of the value of correcting the problems; determination of the cause of the problems, by separating problems into those caused by lack of knowledge and those caused by work environment factors, such as lack of feedback, punishment, and poor job design; selection of strategies for solving problems. Lectures, case studies, observable behavior, and mastery of tests are used.
Credit recommendation: In the lower division baccalaureate/associate degree category, 1 semester hour in Performance Analysis (6/81).

Performance Appraisal
a. Communicating for Improved Performance (G770OIC)
b. Evaluation of Potential (G765OIC)
c. Managing Performance (G760OIC)
Location: South Plainfield, NJ and other locations throughout the state.
Length: a. 21 hours (3 days); b. 7 hours (1 day); c. 28 hours (4 days).
Dates: a. December 1985-Present; b. May 1976-Present; c. January 1982-Present.
Objective: To enable managers to deal effectively with people-related performance problems, to determine a subordinate's potential for promotion and, in general, to manage subordinates in a successful manner.
Learning Outcome: Upon successful completion of these courses, the participant will be able to: a. *Communication for Improved Performance* - use a systematic procedure to analyze and respond to performance problems; and conduct problem solving conversations that help solve the problem and maintain or improve relationships. b. *Evaluation of Potential* - observe and classify behaviors relevant to promotion; and document, rate and evaluate behavior related to promotion potential. c. *Managing Performance* - use performance standards as a basis for discussion; reinforce good performance, improve performance, coach, career counsel, and give performance reviews; and create an action plan to remove roadblocks and encourage employees so that they can and desire to do the work.
Instruction: These courses are designed to enable managers to more effectively manage their staff, evaluate individuals for promotion and resolve job performance problems. The participants in the course are evaluated by their specific individual class assignments to demonstrate that they have mastered the course objectives. Videotaped lectures, case studies and role playing are utilized during the courses, as well as a review of pre-class assigned readings.
Credit recommendation: In the upper division baccalaureate category, 3 semester hours in Performance Appraisal or Performance Management (8/86).

Bell Atlantic Corporation 125

Procurement Management Fundamentals
  Location: C&P Learning Center, Silver Spring, MD; New Jersey Bell Training Center, South Plainfield, NJ; Bell of Pennsylvania (various locations).
  Length: Approximately 30 hours (3 days).
  Dates: July 1983-Present.
  Objective: To provide an introductory orientation to the process of procurement of materials and contracting.
  Instruction: Course is an introduction to the procurement field for persons performing procurement functions. The course provides an overview of all the procurement functions, from needs identification to disposition, and defines policies and principles which govern the various functions. Lecture, discussion, and case studies are used.
  Credit recommendation: In the upper division baccalaureate category, 2 semester hours in Procurement and Contracting or Logistics and Materials Management (12/84).

Rate Regulations
(Accounting Witness Support Training [2693])
  Location: Silver Spring, MD.
  Length: 37½ hours (5 days).
  Dates: December 1979-Present.
  Objective: To teach the student the components of the rate base and income statement required to produce an accounting exhibit and the general methodologies and sources of information necessary to develop an accounting exhibit, including: income statement analysis, computation of the cost of capital, and all the other accounting issues.
  Instruction: This course acquaints the students with the major areas and issues in the preparation and presentation of testimony for Rate Case file with state commissions. This is an instructor-led course using lecture/visual aids and instructor-led discussions.
  Credit recommendation: In the upper division baccalaureate category, 2 semester hours in Finance (8/85).

Stress Management (G769OIC)
  Location: South Plainfield, NJ and other locations throughout the state.
  Length: 14 hours (2 days).
  Dates: October 1984-Present.
  Objective: To enable participants to identify their own best range of stress for effective functioning.
  Learning Outcome: Upon successful completion of this course, the participant will be able to: recognize what stress is and what triggers it; examine coping styles and behavior patterns that are developed to deal with stress; manage internal reactions to stress; and apply problem solving skills to stress management.
  Instruction: This course relates stress management to increased productivity, better physical health, more satisfying relationships and a greater sense of well-being. It also relates physical fitness, health and nutrition to stress management.
  Credit recommendation: In the lower division baccalaureate/associate degree category, 1 semester hour in Stress Management (8/86).

1. Supervisory Relationships Training
2. Time Management #190
3. Handling Grievances
4. Social Awareness #196
  Location: South Plainfield, NJ.
  Length: 33¾ hours (5½ days).
  Dates: November 1979-Present.
  Objective: To enable the student to
  1. Teach methods that solve problems supervisors face everyday; sustain open communications between supervisors and subordinates, while maintaining the self-esteem of the employees.
  2. Set long- and short-term goals, set priorities, maintain a daily to-do list, identify time wasters, and take corrective action to eliminate time wasters.
  3. Locate union contract information when necessary, answer questions about provisions of the contract agreement, recognize a grievance situation, and take necessary actions to see a grievance to its conclusion.
  4. Have each participant assess his/her knowledge and beliefs against a set of questions requiring some individual interpretation, and have this individual's knowledge and belief tested in a group situation where different interpretations may exist.
  Instruction: Covers
  1. Encouraging the average employee and increasing the work quantity of subordinates; improving work quality; handling charges of EEO discrimination and reducing employee resistance to a new supervisor; handling problems and discrimination complaints in the absence of written policy, and the steps to take if the initial approach fails; delegating work to subordinates; and applying the course principles to other situations.
  2. The evaluation of resources, examination of principles, time wasters, how to prioritize short- and long-term goals, and the maintenance of a time diary.
  3. How to recognize and handle grievances, and union agreement and arbitration cases.
  4. Problems of managing different individuals and probable causes of these problems.
  Lectures, case studies, observable behavior, and mastery of tests are used.
  Credit recommendation: In the lower division baccalaureate/associate degree category, 1 semester hour in Management of Human Resources (6/81).

Supervisory Relationships - Trainer Workshop
  Location: Various locations throughout C&P Telephone Company business area.
  Length: 40 hours (5 days).
  Dates: December 1972-Present.

Objective: To train second-level managers with the skills necessary to conduct supervisory relationships training courses for first-level managers.

Instruction: Covers guidelines for handling problem situations on the job; supervisory theory; communication techniques; feedback techniques; questioning techniques; techniques for conducting a workshop and handling resistance in the classroom; leadership skills; interpretive skills; skills for working with an adult learner. Lecture, discussion, and classroom exercises are used.

Credit recommendation: In the upper division baccalaureate category, 3 semester hours in Personnel (12/79) (12/84). NOTE: This course has been reevaluated and continues to meet requirements for credit recommendations.

Supervisory Relationships Training

Location: Various locations throughout C&P Telephone Company business area.

Length: 18 hours (one session a week for 5 weeks).

Dates: December 1972-Present.

Objective: To give first-level managers supervisory skills in solving problems, maintaining open communication, and maintaining an employee's self-esteem.

Instruction: Covers guidelines for handling problem situations on the job; supervisory theory; communication techniques; questioning techniques; interpretive skills. Classroom exercises, lecture, and discussion are used.

Credit recommendation: In the lower division baccalaureate/associate degree category, 1 semester hour in Personnel (12/79) (12/84). NOTE: This course has been reevaluated and continues to meet requirements for credit recommendations.

Trainer Workshop

Location: Various locations throughout C&P Telephone Company business area.

Length: 40 hours (5 days).

Dates: August 1978-Present.

Objective: To provide basic learning concepts, training methodologies/techniques, and skill practice for trainers of adult learners.

Instruction: Training methods and learning behavior. Emphasis is placed on the needs of the individual trainer as he/she learns to improve performance of management and nonmanagement employees in industry. Lecture, discussion, group exercises, and individual practice in a simulated training environment are used.

Credit recommendation: In the lower division baccalaureate/associate degree category, 1 semester hour in Educational Methodology or Training Techniques (5/80) (12/84). NOTE: This course has been reevaluated and continues to meet requirements for credit recommendations.

The Total Manager
a. New Age Thinking (G764OIC)
b. Whole Brain Applications (G772OIC)

Location: South Plainfield, NJ and other locations throughout the state.

Length: a. 24 hours (3 days); b. 21 hours (3 days).

Dates: a. April 1983-Present; b. October 1986-Present.

Objective: To enable managers to perform more effectively through identifying a self image that supports professional goals and utilizing creative and analytical skills to accomplish professional goals.

Learning Outcome: Upon successful completion of these modules, the student will be able to: align self image with professional goals; correct "mistakes" made by others over whom one has leadership responsibility; become more effective in activities that require studying and memory; balance academic and creative mental functions to increase learning ability; and remember facts, consolidate information and recall information more effectively.

Instruction: These courses utilize audiovisual information presentations and extensive instructor led discussion and class activities. The courses are designed to make managers much more effective in achieving their professional and organizational goals by a fuller understanding and application of affirmations, visualizations and maximizing use of academic and creative mental functions. Students are evaluated in meeting course objectives by their individual contributions and specific individual activities.

Credit recommendation: In the upper division baccalaureate category, 3 semester hours in The Actualized Manager or Management Psychology (8/86). NOTE: Student must complete both courses for 3 semester hour credit recommendations. Each course alone carries 1 semester hour credit recommendation (see separate listing under individual titles).

Trainer Skills Workshop (G762OIC)

Location: South Plainfield, NJ and other locations throughout the state.

Length: 70 hours (10 days).

Dates: April 1982-Present.

Objective: To provide trainers with the knowledge and skills necessary to instruct in an adult learning environment.

Learning Outcome: Upon successful completion of this course, the participant will be able to: identify various learning styles and adapt teaching methods; instruct effectively in the following formats: lecture, group discussion, demonstration, programmed instruction, role playing and case study; apply the following skills successfully: oral presentation, use of AV, questioning, listening, non-verbal communication, counseling/coaching, managing group dynamics; apply professional and ethical considerations in training; and plan ongoing professional development.

Instruction: This workshop provides trainers with the

knowledge and skills necessary to create an effective learning environment. It describes the key role of the trainer in a climate of rapid change. It assumes that they possess subject matter expertise and course-specific instructional materials, such as a leader's guide and student materials, as required.

Credit recommendation: In the upper division baccalaureate category, 3 semester hours in Training and Development or Manager as Trainer (applicable to a Business or Education curriculum)(8/86).

**Transactional Analysis
(Management Relationships Training [105])**
Location: Harrisburg, Philadelphia, Pittsburgh, PA.
Length: 26 hours (4 days).
Dates: January 1975-Present.
Objective: To recognize major sources of behavior for particular situations and to demonstrate skills in conducting productive communications and promoting mutual understanding.
Instruction: Surveys ego states, diagramming, ulterior transactions, stroking patterns, psychological positions, games, and time structuring. Group discussion, lectures, and simulations are used.
Credit recommendation: In the lower division baccalaureate/associate degree category, 1 semester hour in Management (8/78).

Whole Brain Applications (G7720IC)
Location: South Plainfield, NJ and other locations throughout the state.
Length: 21 hours (3 days).
Dates: October 1986-Present.
Objective: To provide participants with understanding and techniques to increase the mental abilities by using both areas of the brain.
Learning Outcome: Upon successful completion of this course, the participant will be able to: become more effective in activities that require studying and memory; remember facts, consolidate information, and recall information more effectively; and maximize the use of both areas of the brain.
Instruction: This course is offered to management staff in small group settings. The course provides managers with the techniques needed to increase mental abilities, learning potential and organizational skills through proper use of both areas of the brain. Participants are evaluated through the extensive class participation activities and the specific application of techniques as supervised by the instructor.
Credit recommendation: In the upper division baccalaureate category, 1 semester hour in Whole Brain Applications or Management Psychology (8/86).

Written Communication Skills
Location: Various locations throughout C&P Telephone Company business area.
Length: 24 hours (four 6-hour sessions spread over a four-week period).
Dates: May 1977-Present.
Objective: To enable managers to write more effectively.
Instruction: Focuses on skills necessary for organized, clear, accurate, effective business writing. Videotapes, exercises, and discussion are used.
Credit recommendation: In the vocational certificate category, 1 semester hour in English (12/79) (12/84). NOTE: This course has been reevaluated and continues to meet requirements for credit recommendations.

PROJECT TOP GUN

Project Top Gun was designed as a capstone program for Bell Atlantic employees interested in pursuing advanced education and training in information technologies. The Project's curriculum emphasizes the delivery of information technology from the customer's perspective. To develop the curriculum, extensive marketing research was conducted in northern New Jersey, Philadelphia, and in the Washington, D.C. area. Customers' feedback from this research indicated that the focus of the project should be on technological competence and real-life applications of this competence within the telecommunications marketplace.

The five courses (units) within the Project have been designed by consultants with expertise in computer information technology. The courses are routinely reviewed and improved by experts in the field.

Students are nominated for participation in the Project. Successful students must meet the requirements of all five courses (which include written quizzes and tests) and pass a set of comprehensive oral examinations.

Source of official student records: Director, Project Top Gun, Bell Atlantic Corporation, Lafayette Hill, Pennsylvania.

Introduction to Information Technology—Basic Concepts and Market Structure (Top Gun—Unit One)
Location: Eagle Lodge, Lafayette Hill, PA.
Length: 112 hours (14 days).
Dates: January 1987-Present.
Objective: To provide the student with an understanding of information technology and its marketplace.
Learning Outcome: Upon successful completion of this course, the student will be able to define the technological components of the information systems marketplace, including computer and distributed systems, fundamentals of network architecture, and strategic competition in the marketplace.
Instruction: Course covers communications marketplace, information systems, computer systems, communications systems, and communications architecture.

Methodology includes lecture, discussion, and case studies.

Credit recommendation: In the lower division baccalaureate/associate degree category, 6 semester hours in Information Technology (4/89).

Programming Languages, Architecture and Operating Systems, and Communications (Top Gun—Unit Two)
Location: Eagle Lodge, Lafayette Hill, PA.
Length: 112 hours (14 days).
Dates: January 1987-Present.
Objective: To allow the student to examine key elements of information technology.
Learning Outcome: Upon successful completion of this course, the student will be able to understand software management and construction, computer operating systems, and communications.
Instruction: Course consists of three modules: (1) BASIC programming, dBASE III, and a comparison of programming languages; (2) elements of computer architecture and operating systems; (3) communications channels, including components and signal processing and underlying principles of data communications. Prerequisite: Introduction to Information Technology—Basic Concepts and Market Structures (Top Gun—Unit One). Methodology includes lecture, discussion, and laboratory exercises.
Credit recommendation: In the lower division baccalaureate/associate degree category, 6 semester hours in Communications, Computer Systems, and Survey of Programming Languages (4/89).

Computer Network Architecture (Top Gun—Unit Three)
Location: Eagle Lodge, Lafayette Hill, PA.
Length: 112 hours (14 days).
Dates: January 1987-Present.
Objective: To give the student an in-depth understanding of computer networking at the data-link, network, transport, and session layers.
Learning Outcome: Upon successful completion of this course, the student will be able to analyze and evaluate complex computer networks and their protocols.
Instruction: Course covers the major protocols at the data-link, network, transport, and session layers of the ISO OSI (International Standards Organization Open Systems Interconnection) model. Prerequisite: Programming Language, Architecture and Operating Systems, and Communications (Top Gun—Unit Two). College-level mathematics is desirable but not required for this course. Methodology includes lecture, discussion, and laboratory exercises.
Credit recommendation: In the upper division baccalaureate category, 4 semester hours in Computer Networking (4/89).

Information Networks (Top Gun—Unit Four)
Location: Eagle Lodge, Lafayette Hill, PA.
Length: 112 hours (14 days).
Dates: January 1987-Present.
Objective: To give the student an in-depth understanding of Local Area Networks (LANs) and Integrated Services Digital Networks (ISDNs).
Learning Outcome: Upon successful completion of this course, the student will be able to analyze and evaluate Local Area Networks (LANs) and Integrated Services Digital Networks (ISNDs).
Instruction: Course covers topologies, media, and protocols of LANs and the operation and function services of ISDN and voice/data communication. Prerequisite: Computer Network Architecture (Top Gun—Unit Three). College-level mathematics is desirable but not required for this course. Methodology includes lecture, discussion, and case studies.
Credit recommendation: In the upper division baccalaureate category, 4 semester hours in Computer Networking (4/89).

Network Management and Applications (Top Gun—Unit Five)
Location: Eagle Lodge, Lafayette Hill, PA.
Length: 112 hours (14 days).
Dates: January 1987-Present.
Objective: To give the student an understanding of the services provided by the local metropolitan and wide area networks.
Learning Outcome: Upon successful completion of this course, the student will be able to analyze, evaluate, and propose solutions for actual real-world networking problems.
Instruction: Course is composed of two parts. The first part gives a thorough understanding of the services, management, and protocols provided by computer networks. The second part of the course serves as a capstone, integrating material presented in Units 2, 3, and 4 through the use of a series of case studies. Methodology includes lecture, discussion, and case studies. Prerequisite: Information Networks (Top Gun—Unit Four).
Credit recommendation: In the upper division baccalaureate category, 3 semester hours in Computer Science or Information Systems (4/89).

TECHNICAL TRAINING PROGRAM

Technical Services offers training to employees to enable them to perform in both the traditional and latest technologies—from safe pole climbing to digital theory.

Advanced Peripheral Processor Maintenance (1 A ESS Advanced Peripheral Processor Maintenance; No. N691OSC)
Location: South Plainfield, NJ.

Length: Self-paced (approximately 260 hours).
Dates: August 1985-Present.
Objective: To provide the training necessary to perform in-depth trouble shooting on the 1 A ESS system.
Instruction: This course prepares the technician to do in-depth trouble shooting by performing the analyzer's function. Some of the key topics are: 1 A ESS Central Control; 1 A Memory Storage Unit Hardware and Maintenance; 1 A Processor Interface units, Hardware and Maintenance; and 1 A ESS Documentation. (NOTE: the 1 A ESS is a more advanced and more complex version of the 1 ESS switching machine).
Credit recommendation: In the upper division baccalaureate category, 3 semester hours in Electronics Technology (6/86). NOTE: Not applicable as core course in Electrical Engineering or Engineering Technology.

Advanced Peripheral Processor Maintenance (1 ESS Advanced Peripheral Processor Maintenance; No. N691ASC)
Location: South Plainfield, NJ.
Length: Self-paced (approximately 130 hours).
Dates: August 1985-Present.
Objective: To provide the training necessary to perform in-depth trouble shooting on the 1 ESS system.
Instruction: This course prepares the technician to do in-depth trouble shooting by performing the analyst's function. Some of the key topics are: 1 ESS Control Center and Program Fundamentals; 1 ESS Program Store, Call Store, Signal Processor; 1 ESS AMA and TTY Diagnosis; 1 ESS Software and Software Fault Identification; and 1 ESS Processor Trouble Shooting Work Assignments. (NOTE: This course is similar to 1 A ESS Advanced Peripheral Processor Maintenance except that all work is done on the 1 ESS machine).
Credit recommendation: In the upper division baccalaureate category, 2 semester hours in Electronics Technology (6/86). NOTE: Not applicable as course courses in Electrical Engineering or Engineering Technology.

Basic Data Protocol (354)
Location: South Plainfield, NJ.
Length: 32½ hours (Self-paced).
Dates: September 1980-Present.
Objective: Upon completion of the course the student will have the basic protocol knowledge to establish, maintain and repair data circuits that use protocols in interactive data communication equipment.
Instruction: Course includes protocol test equipment and its uses; data speed terminal equipment; protocol trouble isolation; numbering systems/hex, octal, binary, and BCD; formating and coding of standard data characters; protocol error and detection systems.
Credit recommendation: In the lower division baccalaureate/associate degree category, 2 semester hours in Basic Data Protocol (6/82).

1. Basic Drafting (NE1801C)
2. Conduit Drafting (NE1901C)
Location: South Plainfield, NJ; Newark, NJ.
Length: 1. 70 hours (10 days). 2. 49 hours (7 days).
Dates: April 1979-Present.
Objective: 1. To present the basic drafting skills required for performing the duties of an Outside Plant Drafter. 2. To present the basic skills required for the preparation of scaled conduit work prints.
Instruction: 1. This course covers the following two areas: Length and Gauges (route records, symbols, cable capacitors, cross connecting fixtures) and Work Orders (forms, title block, account codes, MCF, terminals involved). 2. This course covers field notes, profile, angles, scaled work prints, drafting techniques, and interpretation of other utility prints.
Credit recommendation: In the lower division baccalaureate/associate degree category, 1 semester hour in Conduit Layout (1/85). NOTE: Credit recommendation is based upon successful completion of Courses 1 and 2.

Basic Electricity and Electronics Course (492)
Location: South Plainfield, NJ.
Length: 78 hours (Self-paced).
Dates: December 1973-Present.
Objective: Upon completion the student will be able to operate test equipment on alternating and direct circuit power supplies, test various electrical and electronic components using the electronic AC-DC volt-meter, function generators, and oscilloscopes.
Instruction: The course covers use of meters, reading circuit diagrams, capacitors, series and parallel circuits, electromagnetism, alternating current, calculating resistance, inductance, RL circuits, effects of capacitance, RC circuits, R.L.C. circuits, transformers, diodes and tubes, transistors, power supplies, amplifiers, and oscillators.
Credit recommendation: In the lower division baccalaureate/associate degree category, 3 semester hours in Basic Electricity and Electronics (6/82).

Computer-Based PBX Systems (Dimension 400 Tier 1 Installation and Repair 208, Dimension 400 Repair-Tier 2 209, CSS 201-2000 Dimension Installation 136, CSS 201-2000 Dimension Tier 2 229)
Location: South Plainfield, NJ.
Length: 169 hours (8½ weeks).
Dates: September 1978-January 1984.
Objective: To train advanced personnel to install and maintain computer-based PBX systems.
Instruction: Instructor-led course uses audiovisual materials and laboratory exercises to cover operation, installation, and maintenance of computer-PBX systems. Includes central processor operation and maintenance, software descriptions, installation testing, and software diagnostic systems.
Credit recommendation: In the lower division bac-

calaureate/associate degree category, 2 semester hours in Computer, Industrial, or Electrical Technology technical electives (6/82).

Custom Telephone Service System (Dimension 400 Tier 1 Installation and Repair 208, Dimension 400 Repair-Tier 2 209, Horizon Computer Communications Systems 237)
Location: South Plainfield, NJ.
Length: 117 hours (3 3/5 weeks).
Dates: September 1978-January 1984.
Objective: Students will be able to operate, install, test, and maintain computer-based PBX systems.
Instruction: Instructor-led course uses lectures and laboratories to cover installation, operation, and maintenance of custom telephone systems related to dimension 40C PBX.
Credit recommendation: In the vocational certificate category, 3 semester hours in Communications Systems Practices (3/87).

Custom Telephone Service System
1. **Dimension 400 Tier 1 Installation and Repair, Course 208**
2. **Dimension 400 Repair - Tier 2, Course 209**
3. **Horizon Communications Systems, Course 237**
Location: South Plainfield, NJ.
Length: 117 hours (3 3/5 weeks).
Dates: September 1975-Present.
Objective: Students will be able to operate, install, test, and maintain microcomputer-based PBX systems.
Instruction: Instructor-led course uses lectures and laboratories to cover installation, operation, and maintenance of custom telephone systems related to dimension 400 PBX.
Credit recommendation: In the vocational certificate degree category, 3 semester hours in Communications System Practices (6/82).

Electronic Switching Systems (431) (Number 1 EES)
Location: South Plainfield, NJ.
Length: 897 hours (138 days).
Dates: December 1973-Present.
Objective: Individuals will be able to characterize data failures, interpret program instructions, apply software diagnostic strategies in troubleshooting, interpret and use program documentation, and use diagnostics in hardware maintenance.
Instruction: The self-paced course orients students to software use and analysis. Course includes topics such as computer concepts, hardware fundamentals, common peripherals, processor and program fundamentals, and memory organization.
Credit recommendation: In the lower division baccalaureate/associate degree category, 3 semester hours in Industrial, Electrical, or Computer Technology technical electives (10/82).

Electronic Switching Systems (458) (Number 1A EES)
Location: South Plainfield, NJ.
Length: 670 hours (103 days).
Dates: April 1977-Present.
Objective: Individuals will be able to characterize data failures, interpret program instructions, apply software diagnostic strategies in troubleshooting, interpret and use program documentation, and use diagnostics in hardware maintenance.
Instruction: This self-paced course orients students to software use and analysis. Course includes topics such as computer concepts, hardware fundamentals, common peripherals, processor and program fundamentals, and memory organization.
Credit recommendation: In the lower division baccalaureate/associate degree category, 3 semester hours in Industrial, Electrical, or Computer Technology technical electives (10/82).

#5 Electronic Switching Systems Method of Operation
Location: South Plainfield, NJ.
Length: 35 hours (1 week).
Dates: December 1984-Present.
Objective: To present a comprehensive data communications course using the #5 ESS system as a vehicle to explain data communications.
Instruction: Using lecture, demonstrations and exercises, the course is a comprehensive overview of the #5 ESS system architecture, hardware options and generic capabilities. Knowledge of terminology and method of operation will be gained by candidates attending this course. Specific items covered are the multimodule configuration, including host and remote operation, 3B-20 Processor, Call Processing, Software Architecture, Traffic Measurement Capability, and the Maintenance Philosophy.
Credit recommendation: In the upper division baccalaureate category, 3 semester hours in Data Communications, Computer Science, or MIS (3/86).

Fundamentals of Data Transmission (Introduction to Data Systems 314, Data Transmission Fundamentals 317, 914 C Data Test Equipment 316)
Location: South Plainfield, NJ.
Length: 66 hours (self-paced).
Dates: February 1975-Present.
Objective: Students will be able to identify forms of data communications; define binary, octal, and hex numbering systems; describe basic computer components; describe modem connections (e.g., RS-232); write simple programs; and perform various tests related to transmission loss.
Instruction: Self-paced course includes text-book in-

struction, media aids, and laboratory experiences.

Credit recommendation: In the lower division baccalaureate/associate degree category, 2 semester hours in Computer, Electrical, or Industrial Technology, Medical Instrumentation Technology, or Humanities electives (10/82).

Fundamentals of Data Transmission: Testing and Service (921A Data Test Set 348, 200 Series Data Sets 349, Dataphone II Service 353)
Location: South Plainfield, NJ.
Length: 91 hours (self-paced).
Dates: September 1980-Present.
Objective: Students will be able to install, test, and service 200 series Data Sets and Dataphone II sets.
Instruction: Self-paced course includes operating specialized test sets used to test synchronous and asynchronous modems; installation, use, testing, and maintenance of various speed modem units.
Credit recommendation: In the lower division baccalaureate/associate degree category, 1 semester hour in Computer, Electrical, or Industrial Technology, Medical Instrumentation Technology, Business, or Humanities electives (10/82). **Prerequisite:** Basic Data Transmission Fundamentals.

Fundamentals of Digital Circuits
(Advanced Electronics Course [493])
Location: South Plainfield, NJ.
Length: 78 hours (Self-paced).
Dates: December 1973-Present.
Objective: Trainees are able to demonstrate computer terminology; solve problems using numbering systems of bases, 2, 8, 10; demonstrate use of Boolean functions; describe operation of core memories, twister memories, ferrods, and fereeds, stored program methods, transistors, pulse nomenclature, clippers, and clampers, wave shaping; use of oscilloscope for digital test measurements.
Instruction: The course covers use of oscilloscope, diodes, transistors, pulse waveshaping, clippers and clampers, numbering systems, basic logic fundamentals, and memory systems. This self-paced course uses tutoring and laboratory work.
Credit recommendation: In the lower division baccalaureate/associate degree category, 3 semester hours in Fundamentals of Digital Circuits (6/82).

Installation and Service of Key Telephone Customer Equipment (COM KEY 2152 Installation 128, Residence Key Telephone System 139, Key Systems Repair 207, 4A Communication System Installation 138)
Location: South Plainfield, NJ.
Length: 27 days (6 weeks).
Dates: March 1979-Present.
Objective: Student will be able to install and service key telephone customer credit.
Instruction: This combined group and self-paced course uses texts, audiovisual aids, and extensive laboratory experience to cover topics such as basic and optional equipment components, planning locations of equipment and cables, installing equipment, installing and troubleshooting Key telephone systems.
Credit recommendation: In the vocational certificate category, 3 semester hours in Key Telephone Customer Equipment Installation Repair (10/82).

Microcomputer Based PBX Systems: Installation and Maintenance
1. Dimension 400-Installation and Maintenance, Course 208
2. Dimension 2000-Installation, Course 136
3. Horizon-Installation, Course 237
Location: South Plainfield, NJ.
Length: 2 4/5 weeks (91 hours).
Dates: September 1975-January 1984.
Objective: To train advanced personnel to install and maintain microcomputer based PBX systems.
Instruction: Instructor led course uses audiovisual materials and laboratory exercises to cover operation, installation, and maintenance of microcomputer based systems. Includes central processor operation and maintenance, software descriptions, installation testing, and software diagnostic systems.
Credit recommendation: In the vocational certificate degree category, 2 semester hours in Computer, Industrial, or Electrical Technology technical electives (6/82).

New Jersey Bell 1 A ESS Overview and Maintenance
1. (System Overview and Software Documentation; No. N 687 OSC)
2. (1/1A SCC ESS Translations; No. 688 OSC)
3. (1 A ESS Peripheral Processor Maintenance; No. N 689 ASC)
Location: South Plainfield, NJ.
Length: 1. Self-paced (approximately 19 hours); 2. Self-paced (approximately 52 hours); 3. Self-paced (approximately 260 hours).
Dates: August 1985-Present.
Objective: 1. To introduce students to the processor and peripheral equipment associated with 1 A ESS. 2. To provide the training necessary to input and verify different types of changes related to SCC Translation Function. 3. To train technicians to perform normal maintenance tasks associated with processor and peripheral equipment in 1 A ESS.
Instruction: 1. Switching technicians assigned to work with the SCC Translations Function of SCC Field Function are introduced to the processor and peripheral equipment associated with 1 A ESS. Students also become familiar with the hardware and software documentation that support the 1 A ESS. 2. This course covers Transla-

tion Introduction; Translation Forms; Translations and Recent Change Verification; Recent Change Procedures; and Translation updates. Simulated work assignments are employed to provide "on the job" conditions. 3. This course covers normal maintenance tasks associated with an SCC Field Assignment. These tasks include peripheral and processor maintenance in 1 A ESS. Topics include: 1/1A Digital Trunk Carrier; 1 A ESS Processor; 3 B Processor; and Attached Processor Interface.

Credit recommendation: In the lower division baccalaureate/associate degree category, 4 semester hours in Microprocessor Based Systems: Maintenance and Troubleshooting (6/86).

New Jersey Bell 1 ESS System Overview and Maintenance
(1. System Overview and Software Documentation; No. N 687 ASC)
(2. 1/1A SCC ESS Translations; No. 688 OSC)
(3. 1 ESS Peripheral Processor Maintenance; No. N 689 ASC)
Location: South Plainfield, NJ.
Length: 1. Self-paced (approximately 19 hours); 2. Self-paced (approximately 52 hours); 3. Self-paced (approximately 182 hours).
Dates: August 1985-Present.
Objective: 1. To introduce students to the processor and peripheral equipment associated with 1 ESS. 2. To provide the training necessary to input and verify different types of changes related to SCC Translation Function. 3. To train technicians to perform normal maintenance tasks associated with processor and peripheral equipment in 1 E ESS.
Instruction: 1. Switching technicians assigned to work with the SCC Translations Function or SCC Field Function are introduced to the processor and peripheral equipment associated with 1 ESS. 2. This course covers Translation Introduction; Translation Forms; Translations and Recent Change Verification; Recent Change Procedures; and Translation updates. Simulated work assignments are employed to provide "on the job" conditions. 3. This course covers normal maintenance tasks associated with an SCC Field Assignment. These tasks include peripheral and processor maintenance in 1 E ESS. Topics include: 1/1A Remreed Frames; 1/1A Digital Carrier Trunk; 1 ESS Processor; and 1 ESS 8K, 32K Callstore Hardware and Maintenance.
Credit recommendation: In the lower division baccalaureate/associate degree category, 3 semester hours in Microprocessor Based Systems: Maintenance and Troubleshooting (6/86). NOTE: Modules 1, 2 & 3 need to be completed for credit recommendation.

New Jersey Bell 507K: Introduction to the 1A Processor
Location: South Plainfield, NJ.
Length: 18 hours (self-paced).
Dates: April 1977-Present.
Objective: To provide the student with the skills needed to progress to more advanced No. 1A-level ESS and to provide the student with practice and skills associated with No. 1A ESS peripheral equipment maintenance.
Instruction: Covers operations, use, fault diagnosis, and repair of No. 1A-level ESS and their related peripheral units, including component identification from schematics, block diagram analysis, program diagnostics and listing, testing procedures for service lines and equipment, logic circuit testing, and central processor hardware operations.
Credit recommendation: In the vocational certificate degree category, 1 semester hour in Switching System Maintenance (6/82).

New Jersey Bell 507AA/AA Sequence
1. 507AA Introduction to Electronic Switching Systems/Second Generation
2. 508A Common Peripheral Units/Second Generation
3. 508AA 1A Technology Common Peripheral Units
Location: South Plainfield, NJ.
Length: 221 hours (self-paced).
Dates: December 1973-Present.
Objective: To provide the student with entry-level skills and knowledge for first- and second-generation electronic switching technology.
Instruction: Covers Electronic Switching Systems overview, numbering systems, diodes and transistors, logic circuits, hardware, oscilloscope usage, basic ESS communication buses, principal components, skills required for locating trouble. Self-paced, practical exercises under supervision of an administrator.
Credit recommendation: In the lower division baccalaureate/associate degree category, 3 semester hours in Introduction to Electronic Switching Systems (6/82).

New Jersey Bell 507B
1. Introduction to No. 1 Electronic Switching Systems (ESS)
2. No. 1 ESS Peripheral Units - On-the-Job Training
Location: South Plainfield, NJ.
Length: 18 hours (self-paced).
Dates: December 1973-Present.
Objective: To provide the student with the skills needed to progress to more advanced No. 1-level ESS and to provide the student with practice and skills associated with No. 1 ESS peripheral equipment maintenance.
Instruction: Covers operations, use, fault diagnostics, and repair of No. 1-level ESS and their related peripheral units, including component identification from schematics, block diagram analysis, program diagnostics and listing, testing procedures for service lines and equipment, logic circuit testing, and central processor hardware operations. Self-paced instruction and practical on-the-job ex-

ercises are used.

Credit recommendation: In the vocational certificate degree category, 1 semester hour in Switching System Maintenance (6/82).

New Jersey Bell 508K Sequence
1. **508KA No. 1/1A Remreed Peripheral Maintenance**
2. **508KB No. 1/1A ESS CMT/MUT Peripheral Unit Maintenance**
3. **508KD No. 1/1A ESS PUC/DCT - Operation and Maintenance**
4. **508KF No. 1 ESS Ferreed Operation and Maintenance**
   Location: South Plainfield, NJ.
   Length: 125½ hours (self-paced).
   Dates: December 1973-Present.
   Objective: To provide the student with the general knowledge and maintenance procedures required to work on first- and second-generation Electronic Switching System (ESS) peripherals.
   Instruction: Covers operation, design, maintenance, and fault diagnosis of first- and second-generation ESS Remreed switching network and its related equipment, including switching path network, trunk switching frames, junction switching, network maintenance, pulse distributing diagnostics, trunk circuit analysis, and digital switching diagnostics. Self-paced instruction and practical exercises are used.
   Credit recommendation: In the vocational certificate degree category, 5 semester hours in Switching System Maintenance (6/82).

New Jersey Bell 509B: No. 1 ESS Central Processor and Program Fundamentals
   Location: South Plainfield, NJ.
   Length: 108 hours (self-paced).
   Dates: December 1973-Present.
   Objective: To provide the student with the skills necessary to characterize data failures in No. 1 Electronic Switching Systems (ESS) Program Store or Call Store memory systems and to identify the specific location of hardware failure.
   Instruction: Covers operation, maintenance, and repair of an advanced-level ESS control unit, including logic circuit analysis, block diagram and timing analysis, address operations, computer system operations, memory addressing (32K and 8K), program instruction codes, core memory operations, program diagnostics, troubleshooting procedures, and repair methods. Self-paced instruction and practical exercises are used.
   Credit recommendation: In the lower division baccalaureate/associate degree category, 3 semester hours in Computer Systems or Logic Circuit Fundamentals (6/82).

New Jersey Bell 534 (A-E) Sequence
1. **534A No. 1 ESS Central Control Language, Hardware, and Maintenance**
2. **534B Program Store Hardware and Maintenance**
3. **534C Call Store Maintenance**
4. **534D No. 1 ESS Central Processor Hardware and Maintenance**
5. **534E Master Control Centers and Associated Frames Diagnostics**
   Location: South Plainfield, NJ.
   Length: 206 hours (self-paced).
   Dates: December 1973-Present.
   Objective: To provide the student with the skills, knowledge, and techniques required to maintain the central processor free of hardware faults.
   Instruction: Course covers central control, program store, call store, signal processor, and master control center. Five modules containing a total of 15 individual units. Tests after each unit. Must obtain 100% on each test prior to continuing. Self-paced, practical exercises under direct supervision of an administrator.
   Credit recommendation: In the vocational certificate degree category, 6 semester hours in Digital Hardware Maintenance (6/82).

New Jersey Bell 534K Sequence
1. **534KA 1A Central Control Organization, Language and Maintenance**
2. **534KB 1A Memory Storage Units Hardware and Maintenance**
3. **534KC 1A Processor Interface Units Hardware and Maintenance**
   Location: South Plainfield, NJ.
   Length: 96 hours (self-paced).
   Dates: April 1977-Present.
   Objective: To provide the student with the skills, knowledge, and techniques required to maintain the central processor free of hardware faults.
   Instruction: Course covers central control, program store, call store, signal processor, and master control center. Three modules containing a total of nine individual units. Tests after each unit. Must obtain 100% on each test prior to continuing. Self-paced, practical exercises under direct supervision of an administrator.
   Credit recommendation: In the vocational certificate degree category, 6 semester hours in Digital Hardware Maintenance (6/82).

New Jersey Bell 539 (A-F) Sequence
1. **539A No. 1 ESS Stored Program Organization**
2. **539B No. 1 ESS Parameters**
3. **539C No. 1 ESS Translations**
4. **539D No. 1 ESS Call Processing**
5. **539E No. 1 ESS Maintenance and Alarm Printouts**
6. **539F No. 1 ESS Maintenance Procedures**
   Location: South Plainfield, NJ.

Length: 212 hours (self-paced).
Dates: December 1973-Present.
Objective: To develop the skills that will enable an individual to perform tasks in the area of software maintenance for No. 1 Electronic Switching Systems (ESS).
Instruction: Covers the use of generic program documentation, locating and clearing parameter and translation problems, applied knowledge of No. 1 ESS Call Processing, resolving audit error printouts, and off-line testing. Self-paced instruction with graded exams serving as the measure of goal accomplishments.
Credit recommendation: In the vocational certificate degree category, 6 semester hours in Switching System Software Diagnostics (6/82).

New Jersey Bell 539K Sequence
1. 539KA 1A ESS Documentation
2. 539KB ESS Translations and Recent Change
3. 539KC 1A Parameters and Call Processing Audits
4. 539KD 1A Memory Administration, Features and Programs
5. 539KE Program Interrupts, Deferred Fault Recovery and Error Analysis
6. 539KF 1A System Recovery
   Location: South Plainfield, NJ.
   Length: 209 hours (self-paced).
   Dates: April 1977-Present.
   Objective: To develop the skills that will enable an individual to perform tasks in the area of software maintenance for No. 1A Electronic Switching System (ESS).
   Instruction: Covers use of generic program documentation, locating and clearing parameter and translation problems, applied knowledge of No. 1A ESS Call Processing, resolving audit error printouts, and off-line testing. Self-paced instruction with graded examinations serving as the measure of goal accomplishments.
   Credit recommendation: In the vocational certificate degree category, 6 semester hours in Switching System Software Diagnostics (6/82).

Office Control
(1/1A ESS SCC Office Control; No. N690OSC)
   Location: South Plainfield, NJ.
   Length: Self-paced (approximately 65 hours).
   Dates: August 1985-Present.
   Objective: To familiarize students with Switching Control Center (SCC) Office Control basic workstation procedures.
   Instruction: This course familiarizes the student with SCC Office Control basic workstation procedures including browsing, making patterns and file manipulation. Simulated work assignments reinforce self-paced course material. Key topics include SCC Operations, Office Control Operations, alarms, audits and emergency action.
   Credit recommendation: In the lower division baccalaureate/associate degree category, 1 semester hour as a Technical Elective (6/86).

Oscilloscopes
   Location: South Plainfield, NJ.
   Length: 13 hours (self-paced).
   Dates: January 1975-Present.
   Objective: To develop proficiency in using oscilloscopes.
   Instruction: Participants learn to set up and calibrate the oscilloscope, measure wave form amplitude polarity and time duration, and use dual trace and delayed sweep features.
   Credit recommendation: In the vocational certificate category, 1 semester hour in Oscilloscopes (10/82).

Outside Plant Engineering Education Program (NE09AIC), (NE09BIC), (NE09CIC)
   Location: South Plainfield, NJ; Newark, NJ.
   Length: 350 hours (10 weeks).
   Dates: February 1976-Present.
   Objective: To provide training in basic skills required by outside plant facility engineers to enable them to effect the design of the outside components of a communication system.
   Instruction: Course covers reading, drawing and interpreting communication line construction work plans. Also addressed are basic electrical communication topics, including sections on electrical protection procedures, estimate preparation, engineering economics, distribution cable design, problem solving, subscriber loop design, etc.
   Credit recommendation: In the lower division baccalaureate/associate degree category, 4 semester hours in Planning and Operations or Industrial Engineering Technology (1/85).

Outside Plant Trunk Facilities Design (NE100ICO)
   Location: South Plainfield, NJ; Newark, NJ.
   Length: 35 hours (5 days).
   Dates: December 1976-Present.
   Objective: To provide basic knowledge of the fundamentals required to design outside plant analog/digital trunk cable facilities.
   Instruction: The course is intended for all engineers involved with the function of providing OSP trunk facilities. In this course, students will demonstrate ability to list all forces included in the company function of providing trunk facilities; describe the job responsibilities of each force; design a loaded and a nonloaded trunk cable facility for wire circuit; and design a trunk cable for T-1 carrier. Students will also demonstrate ability to define the job responsibilities of all forces included in the function of providing trunk facilities.
   Credit recommendation: In the lower division baccalaureate/associate degree category, 2 semester hours as a Communications elective (1/85).

Bell Atlantic Corporation   135

Peripheral Installation and Maintenance
1. Data Speed 40 Dataphone Service, Course 313
2. Synchronous Data Speed 40 (DS40/4) (4540), Course 341
3. COMM-STOR II CSU, Course 355
   Location: South Plainfield, NJ.
   Length: 130 hours (self-paced).
   Dates: February 1974-Present.
   Objective: Students will be able to install, test, and troubleshoot peripheral device controllers, printers, and floppy disks.
   Instruction: This self-paced course includes texts, audiovisual aids, and laboratory experiences. Topics include ASCII/EBCDIC/HEX code synchronous message formats, floppy disks formats and control characteristics, troubleshooting using diagnostic diskettes.
   Credit recommendation: In the lower division baccalaureate/associate degree category, 2 semester hours in Computer, Electrical, or Industrial Technology, Medical Instrumentation Technology, Business, or Humanities electives (6/82).

Peripheral Installation and Maintenance (Data Speed 40 Dataphone Service 313, Synchronous Data Speed 40 [DS40/4] [4540], 34 COMM-STOR II CSU 355)
   Location: South Plainfield, NJ.
   Length: 98 hours (self-paced).
   Dates: October 1976-Present.
   Objective: Students will be able to install, test, and troubleshoot peripheral device controllers, printers, and floppy disks.
   Instruction: This self-paced course includes texts, audiovisual aids, and laboratory experiences. Topics include ASCII/EBCDIC/HEX code synchronous message formats, floppy disk formats and control characteristics, troubleshooting using diagnostic diskettes.
   Credit recommendation: In the lower division baccalaureate/associate degree category, 2 semester hours in Computer, Electrical, or Industrial Technology, Medical Instrumentation Technology, Business, or Humanities electives (10/82).

Radio License - Second Class (326)
   Location: South Plainfield, NJ.
   Length: 200 hours (self-paced).
   Dates: March 1974-Present.
   Objective: The student who successfully completes this course will be able to pass the Federal Communications Commission (FCC) Second Class Radio-Telephone License.
   Instruction: This course covers such topics as DC elements; DC theory; AC theory; inductance - transformers; capacitors; AC circuits; resonance - filters; tubes; basic sold state devices; batteries; motors - generators; AC power supplies; meters, oscilloscopes - decibels, oscillators; AF amplifiers, RF amplifiers; transmitters; AM transmitters; AM receivers; FM receivers, antennas; measuring frequency; microwave; rules-regulations; basic radio law; and basic operation practice.
   Credit recommendation: In the lower division baccalaureate/associate degree category, 2 semester hours in Electronic Communications (6/82).

Repair Transmission (224)
   Location: South Plainfield, NJ.
   Length: 32½ hours (self-paced).
   Dates: December 1973-Present.
   Objective: Trainee will be able to select and apply appropriate test equipment to troubleshoot electrical systems; analyze test results to sectionalize circuit trouble conditions.
   Instruction: Trainee will learn applications of troubleshooting techniques to foreign exchange circuits, tie lines, PBX off-premise circuits, and radio circuits.
   Credit recommendation: In the lower division baccalaureate/associate degree category, 1 semester hour in Electronic Maintenance (6/82).

Subscriber Carrier (NE13OIC)
Lightwave Design (NE31OIC)
   Location: South Plainfield, NJ. Newark, NJ.
   Length: 42 hours (6 days).
   Dates: January 1981-Present.
   Objective: To become familiar with lightwave principles and proper procedures for lightwave cable installation; and to provide information required to design a SLC-96 System.
   Instruction: This detailed design course provides familiarization with Lightwave Theory, Lightguide Cable manufacturing processes, Lightguide Cable characteristics and SLC-96 Lightwave feature. Other topics included in the course are Lightguide digital line design rules, Lightguide Cable grade selection, accounting codes and documentation. Also covered are an understanding of an application of the SLC-96 system.
   Credit recommendation: In the lower division baccalaureate/associate degree category, 2 semester hours in Lightwave Cable Application or Electric Technology (1/85). NOTE: Credit recommendation applies when both modules are successfully complete.

Teletype Fundamentals (328)
   Location: South Plainfield, NJ.
   Length: 45½ hours (self-paced).
   Dates: December 1973-Present.
   Objective: To introduce teletypewriter apparatus and related gear.
   Instruction: Covers teletype signal make-up and selecting codes, transmitting devices, printer mechanisms, tape punches, electrical service units and call controls, motors, data sets, tools and equipment, and troubleshooting.
   Credit recommendation: In the vocational certificate

136 *Bell Atlantic Network Services, Inc.*

degree category, 2 semester hours in Hardware Maintenance (6/82).

Trunk Tester
(1/1A SCC Trunk Tester; No. N686OSC)
   Location: South Plainfield, NJ.
   Length: Self-paced (approximately 65 hours).
   Dates: August 1985–Present.
   Objective: To familiarize students with the SCC Trunk Work Station.
   Instruction: This course is designed to familiarize students with the SCC Trunk Work Station and the SCC Procedures as they apply to Trunk Installation/Maintenance. This course will enable students to perform basic trunk testing, trunk installation and field maintenance.
   Credit recommendation: In the lower division baccalaureate/associate degree category, 1 semester hour in Telephone Switching or as a Technical Elective (6/86).

Underground Conduit Design and Administration (NE14OIC)
   Location: South Plainfield, NJ; Newark, NJ.
   Length: 35 hours (5 days).
   Dates: September 1983–Present.
   Objective: To present major aspects of engineering Outside Plant underground conduit systems.
   Instruction: This course is designed for 1st and 2nd level managers involved in any portion of the O.P. Engineer's job that includes design, cost estimating, contract preparation and control of expenditures for underground conduit jobs. Emphasis will be placed on designing systems within the context of the approved standards. This course provides instruction in the following objectives: Material Selection; Structure Sizing; Manhole Sizing and Construction; Pulling-in-Tension; Design-for-Safety; Route Selection; Research, R/W, Liaison, Environment; Field Survey, Work Prints; Restoration Requirements, and Special Construction.
   Credit recommendation: In the lower division baccalaureate/associate degree category, 2 semester hours in Underground Conduit Design and Administration (1/85).

Bell Atlantic Network Services, Inc.

See BELL ATLANTIC CORPORATION

Bell Communications Research, Inc.

Bell Communications Research, Inc. is a research and development unit. As a research and development house, Bell transforms ideas into products and services. Seven scientists from Bell have won the Nobel Prize. The Bell staff is continually exploring ways to meet the future needs of the business, residence, and network markets.

Bell Communications Research, Inc. is owned by the American Telephone and Telegraph Company (AT&T) and by Western Electric, a manufacturing and supply unit. Bell Communication Research works to bring this nation and the world into the Information Age.
   Source of official student records: Registrar, Bell Communications Research, Inc., 6 Corporate Pl., Piscataway, NJ 08854.
   Additional information about the courses: Thomas A. Edison State College, 101 W. State St., Trenton, NJ 08625.

Basic Programming Sequence (Fundamentals of the UNIX System OS400, UNIX System Files and Commands OS402, Advanced Use of the UNIX Text Editor OS403, Fundamentals of "C" Language Programming PL 730)
   Location: All Bell Communications Research locations.
   Length: 58 1/2 hours (10 days).
   Dates: July 1980–Present.
   Objective: The student will be able to compose correct programs in the "C" programming language; edit, compile, and execute programming effectively; and use operating system features such as text editors and file systems.
   Instruction: Instructor-led or computer-assisted course uses exercises and emphasizes good coding techniques including sequence, selection, repetition, and introductory data structures such as lists and arrays. Students are prepared to design, code, compile, and execute "C" language programs in the UNIX operating system. (UNIX is a trademark of Bell Laboratories.)
   Credit recommendation: In the lower division baccalaureate/associate degree category, 3 semester hours in Computer Science/Business (7/82).

Basic Word Processing Sequence (UNIX System Memorandum Macros WP100, Equation Processing Using the UNIX System WP122, Table Processing Using the UNIX System WP120, UNIX System Phototypesetting WP130)
   Location: All Bell Communications Research locations.
   Length: 18 hours.
   Dates: May 1980–Present.
   Objective: To develop skills in using text processing software for preparing plain texts, tables, and equations. Introduces use of computerized photocomposition techniques.
   Instruction: Lecture and laboratory presentation includes materials on the UNIX system memorandum macros, phototypesetting, and table and equation processing.
   Credit recommendation: In the lower division baccalaureate/associate degree category, 1 semester hour in Computer Science/Word Processing (7/82).

Introduction to "C" Language Programming for Experienced Programmers

   Location: All Bell Communications Research locations.
   Length: 40 hours (1 week).
   Dates: July 1980-Present.
   Objective: Upon completion of this course, the student will be able to (1) write syntactically correct "C" language code; (2) write correct "C" language code in a style that effectively uses structured programming techniques; (3) code "C" language programs using arrays, structures, and pointers; (4) use the standard "C" language library functions; (5) create programs using separately compiled functions; and (6) make effective use of the "C" preprocessor.
   Instruction: The course provides technical personnel experienced in a programming language similar to "C" (e.g., PL/1 or PASCAL) with an understanding of the structure and syntax of "C." The course emphasizes effective coding style and use of structures and pointers. The students are prepared to design, code, compile, and execute "C" programs in the UNIX operating system.
   Credit recommendation: In the lower division baccalaureate/associate degree category, 2 semester hours in Computer Science/Business (7/82).

Bell Communications Research Training and Education Center

Located 30 miles west of Chicago, the Bell Communications Research Training and Education Center (Bellcore TEC) in Lisle, Illinois, offers over 350 courses in a wide variety of telecommunications and other disciplines. Tailored for entry through executive level managers, Bellcore TEC'S job relevant training encompasses UNIX® and C, Telecommunications fundamentals, transmission and data, general technical skills, outside plant, network planning, business and financial management, and more. Bellcore TEC is part of Bell Communications Research which provides technical and administrative services to Bell Regional and Operating Companies.

Established in 1968, Bellcore TEC has kept pace with changes in the technology and structure of the telecommunications industry. Courses are developed and taught by subject matter experts with field experience and up-to-date knowledge in their respective disciplines. Instructors have a personal interest and willingness to share their knowledge with students. Working in tandem with technical experts are training technologists who ensure that course designs meet stringent standards.

Source of official student records: Bellcore TEC Registrar, 6200 Route 53, Lisle, Illinois 60532 (312) 960-6000. Source for additional course information, Bellcore TEC Product Management, 1-800-TEACH-ME.

Additional information about the courses: Program on Noncollegiate Sponsored Instruction, The Center for Adult Learning and Educational Credentials, American Council on Education, One Dupont Circle, Washington, D.C. 20036.

Adult Instructional Methodology: I
(Instructor Skills Workshop)

   Location: Lisle, IL or approved "suitcase" location.
   Length: 40 hours (5 days).
   Dates: July 1986-Present.
   Objective: To provide the student with an understanding of adult learning theory, the instructional process, lecture and discussion techniques, listening, administering self-paced instruction, and group development. Delivery techniques are modeled, then practiced.
   Learning Outcome: Upon completion of this course, the student will be able to complete a self-assessment using an instructor performance model; assess one's own learning style and the importance of knowing the learning styles of students; apply adult learning principles to the classroom environment; practice a four-step instructional process; list and practice the principles for giving and receiving feedback; deliver a lecture; state the principles of self, student, and supervisor evaluation; apply the principles of active listening; manage a classroom discussion; analyze classroom situations and apply proper interventions; specify the major types of out-of-field behavior and practice the means of handling them effectively, and state the elements of one major model of group development.
   Instruction: This course is designed to teach the basic skills and knowledge required to become an effective instructor. Through lectures, videotapes of actual platform performance and group feedback, the novice becomes comfortable in delivering presentations and in administering a variety of instructional techniques. Following lessons on adult learning theory, the four-step instructional process, how to deliver proper lessons, and how to manage discussions, the student delivers a lecture, leads a discussion and experiences some of the roles group members play in a classroom group. This course is primarily designed for newcomers to the training profession with responsibility for delivering adult instruction in a corporate setting. Current instructors, managers of instructors, and course developers would also benefit from attending this course. There are no prerequisites.
   Credit recommendation: In the upper division baccalaureate category, 3 semester hours in Teaching Education in Adult Learning (9/86).

Adult Instructional Methodology II
(Advanced Instructor Skills Workshop)

   Location: Lisle, IL or approved "suitcase" location.
   Length: 40 hours (5 days).
   Dates: July 1986-Present.
   Objective: To provide the student with practice in refining the skills introduced in Instructional Methodology I, particularly in leading discussions, debriefing adult learn-

ing, and in group development.

Learning Outcome: Upon successful completion of this course, the student will be able to demonstrate giving and receiving feedback; handling out-of-field behaviors; platform skills; leading discussions; apply the principles of group development to the classroom; facilitating orientation the first day of class; getting the most out of conflict; confronting undesirable behaviors. State techniques involved in the helping roles as employed by the instructor; state the principles of co-instructing; demonstrate the principles of debriefing/processing a classroom lesson; demonstrate the introduce-manage-debrief model by facilitation: a case study or role play; demonstrate cumulative instructor skills by teaching a back-home lesson; demonstrate a knowledge of the instructor/developer/supervisor training system; discuss applications of instructor ethics, including affirmative action, and review progress made against an instructor performance model.

Instruction: This course refines the delivery and discussion skills established in Methodology I through additional platform practice sessions and group and instructor feedback; however, in this workshop, more attention is directed to advanced teaching techniques and to group development. Three full days are devoted to facilitating case study and role play sessions, with continued group feedback and the use of videotape. The final teaching opportunity is a lesson the student brings from back home. Students are also exposed to techniques that deepen skills in handling most types of classroom situations. Of special benefit is the practice in debriefing or processing learning.

Credit recommendation: In the upper division baccalaureate category, 3 semester hours in Teacher Education Adult Learning (9/86).

Advanced "C" Language Programming
Location: Bellcore TEC, Lisle, IL.
Length: 110 hours (2 weeks).
Dates: June 1987-Present.
Objective: To teach the student how to identify and when to perform system calls and library routines to enable the student to utilize fully the "C" language programming environment and to write "C" programs to accomplish the appropriate system calls and library routines.
Instruction: Covers assorted system calls and subroutines, screen cursor manipulation, process generation and pipes, and UNIX® system V interprocess communication.
Credit recommendation: In the upper division baccalaureate category, 3 semester hours in Computer Science or Data Processing (9/87).

Advanced Strategic Marketing Management
Location: Bellcore TEC, Morristown, NJ.
Length: 37 hours (4½ days).
Dates: December 1985-Present.
Objective: To provide students with a foundation for implementing competitive marketing strategies in today's marketplace through an understanding of key strategic issues such as market segmentation, product positioning and portfolio management, and study of decision-making skills for use in formulating and implementing market strategies.
Instruction: The course uses a computer simulation game called MARKLAND. Markland is designed to improve manager's competitive decision-making skills in the formulation and implementation of marketing strategy. Teams of participants assume the marketing management of "companies" and compete for revenue, share of market and profit over a simulated eight year period. Each team makes decisions in a dynamic and uncertain environment regarding market targets, product positioning, product development, advertising, pricing personal selling, distribution and marketing research.
Credit recommendation: In the graduate category, 1 semester hour in Marketing (9/87).

Applied Communications Fundamentals (ACF)
Location: Bellcore TEC, Lisle, IL.
Length: 240 hours (6 weeks).
Dates: September 1985-May 1988.
Objective: To present the student an overview of telecommunications. To develop an understanding of the planning operations and maintenance of a complete exchange carrier network.
Instruction: Covers a cluster concept approach including the historical development of communications, basic electricity; planning, operations, and maintenance of network systems; state of art fiber optics; and engineering economics with numerous applications; methodology lecture, discussion, and laboratory exercises.
Credit recommendation: In the lower division baccalaureate/associate degree category, 3 semester hours in Telecommunications Management Technology, 3 semester hours in Electronic Communications Technology, and 3 semester hours in Telephone Systems Technology (2/86).

C Language Programming (C-PRB)
Location: Bellcore TEC, Lisle, IL.
Length: 80 hours (2 weeks).
Dates: March 1984-Present.
Objective: To identify the attributes of the C programming language including grammar and syntax, variable, operators, and expressions and the development of Logic flow control.
Learning Outcome: Upon successful completion of this course, the student will be able to write a C Language source program and to accomplish the desired task.
Instruction: Topics covered include: creating, compiling and executing the C program; identifying C Language data types, variables, operators and expressions; using

functions to structure programs in small segments; using pointers to express computation and generate efficient code; use of arrays and other structures, and debugging techniques using C trace and the adb and sdb commands.

Credit recommendation: In the lower division baccalaureate/associate degree category, 3 semester hours in Programming Language (9/86).

Capital Cost Methodology
  Location: Bellcore TEC, Morristown, NJ.
  Length: 35 hours (4½ days).
  Dates: January 1985-Present.
  Objective: To provide the student with an accelerated examination of cost accounting methodologies through the use of a computer-assisted model, CAPCOST.
  Instruction: Study of methodologies and algorithms used in calculating book depreciation, post tax income and income taxes as implemented in the CAPCOST model. Capital costs associated with project investment, plant survivor characteristics and accelerated tax depreciation will be covered using the same model.
  Credit recommendation: In the graduate category, 1 semester hour in Cost Accounting or Financial Management (9/87).

Capital Recovery: Theory
  Location: Bellcore TEC, Lisle, IL; and Morristown, NJ.
  Length: 60 hours (1 week).
  Dates: January 1984-Present.
  Objective: To provide the student with the concepts and principles regarding capital recovery methods and to identify factors in developing capital equipment life estimates. Replacement and substitution techniques are also examined.
  Instruction: Specific topics covered include capital equipment life concepts, depreciation systems and reserves, salvage values, amortization and revenue regulations and requirements. Instruction is provided through lectures, discussion, and self-paced methods.
  Credit recommendation: In the upper division baccalaureate category, 1 semester hour as an Accounting or Finance elective (9/87).

Central Office Grounding (COGRDG)
  Location: Lisle, IL or approved "suitcase" locations.
  Length: 40 hours (1 week).
  Dates: November 1986-Present.
  Objective: To provide the student with the skills necessary to evaluate and specify grounding requirements for a variety of equipment installations.
  Learning Outcome: Upon successful completion of this course, the student will be able to locate a central office principal ground point; conduct a grounding survey, and recommend solutions to problems encountered in the survey.
  Instruction: Major topics covered in the course are types of building grounds, central office ground system, power systems, and AC grounding, and grounding survey. Methods of instruction include lecture, case studies, and laboratory exercises.
  Credit recommendation: In the lower division baccalaureate/associate degree category, 1 semester hour in Industrial Safety or Electrical Networks (4/88).

Competitive Analysis
(Practicing Competitive Analysis)
  Location: Lisle, IL or approved "suitcase" location.
  Length: 36 hours (5 days).
  Dates: January 1984-Present.
  Objective: To provide the student with an understanding of sources and uses of competitive information in a high technology environment. Emphasis is on qualitative and quantitative competitive analysis techniques and methods of projecting the moves of potential competitors.
  Learning Outcome: Upon successful completion of this course, the student will be able to identify critical data needed to perform a competitive analysis; identify sources of legally obtainable data on competitors; use qualitative and quantitative data to develop competitive profiles of real or anticipated competitors; evaluate commercial sources of outside information about industries and specific firms; perform structural analysis of an industry with specific attention to five key variables; describe the increasingly global nature of competitive business forces; perform a competitive analysis using a model introduced in the course; describe the strategic implications of key marketing and financial phenomena, and use objective criteria to assess advantages and disadvantages of proposed new ventures.
  Instruction: This course is led by staff from leading business schools and experienced private consultants. Emphasis is placed on modern competitive strategies. Sources of competitive information and the use of data are developed. Specific examples are used with emphasis on high technology industries. Students practice qualitative and quantitative competitive analysis techniques and lean how to project competitive moves of potential competitors. Course materials consist of cases from business schools including one dealing with a retention/divestiture decision written especially for this course.
  Credit recommendation: In the upper division baccalaureate category, 3 semester hours in Competitive Marketing Analysis. In the graduate degree category, 3 semester hours as a Marketing elective (9/86). NOTE: For students to receive credit, they must have completed Strategic Marketing and Financial Tools.

Competitive Marketing Strategies
  Location: Bellcore TEC Lisle, IL.
  Length: 19½ hours (3 days).
  Dates: February 1984-February 1987.

Objective: To acquaint managers with the issues and problems in development of marketing strategies.

Instruction: The course covers competitive strategy under deregulation as well as segmenting deregulated markets. It contrasts the goals and objectives of regulatory bodies with those of the ultimate consumer, both business and residential. This course includes lectures, discussions, classroom exercises, simulations, problem solving and case studies.

Credit recommendation: In the graduate degree category, 1 semester hour in Marketing (6/86).

Competitive Pricing: Strategy and Tactics

Location: Bellcore TEC, Morristown, NJ.
Length: 32 hours (4 days).
Dates: January 1984-Present.
Objective: To provide current approaches and techniques for integrating competitive pricing and marketing strategies, improve pricing decision process skills.
Instruction: Course is designed to prepare participants to develop competitive marketing strategies including definition of a service, selection of the most appropriate strategies to exploit market opportunities, and pricing and distribution strategies. Competitive pricing will be stressed. Competitor analysis for pricing decision making, and evaluation of pricing performance will be included. A computer simulation which integrates these marketing and pricing concepts will be used.
Credit recommendation: In the graduate degree category, 2 semester hours in Marketing, Marketing Management, or Business Administration (6/86).

Concepts of Corporate Planning

Location: Bellcore TEC, Lisle, IL; Morristown, NJ; and Norwood, MA.
Length: 42 hours (5 days).
Dates: January 1984-Present.
Objective: To teach the student concepts of corporate planning which focuses on the strategic management planning process, including the concepts and skills required to support the process.
Instruction: Students are exposed to the following concepts and techniques: approaches to planning models and processes, environmental analysis, analytical methods, and implication of fixed and variable costs. Instruction is conducted through the use of case studies in a seminar style format.
Credit recommendation: In the graduate category, 3 semester hours in Business Policy/Corporate Strategy (9/87).

Cost Analysis: Service Industry
(Concepts of Service Costs Studies)
Location: Lisle, IL or approved "suitcase" location.
Length: 34 hours (5 days).
Dates: January 1984-Present.

Objective: To provide the student with an understanding of basic concepts, procedures and terminology associated with conducting service cost studies.
Learning Outcome: Upon successful completion of this course, the student will be able to distinguish between investment and expenses; recognize characteristics of a Resource Cost Study; recognize characteristics of capital recurring costs; recognize characteristics of a rate and tariff process; recognize characteristics of microeconomics concepts, and analyze characteristics of Incremental Analysis.
Instruction: This course is designed to provide new and inexperienced Service Costs Analysis with an awareness and knowledge of the concepts of the Service Costs function. It is also intended to provide the prerequisite knowledge required to attend other Service Costs courses.
Credit recommendation: In the upper division baccalaureate category, 3 semester hours in General Business or Economics or Engineering Economics (9/86).

Cost Studies for New Technology

Location: Bellcore TEC, Lisle, IL or approved suitcase locations.
Length: 36 hours (4½ days).
Dates: May 1988-Present.
Objective: To familiarize the student with accounting and economic cost concepts, marginal analysis, and capital budgeting principles and to demonstrate their application to pricing and investment decisions.
Learning Outcome: Upon successful completion of this course, the student will be able to understand accounting and economic treatment of common cost allocation; use marginal cost in pricing decisions; and understand the major methods of capital budgeting.
Instruction: Course covers regulation/cost issues, fixed, variable, marginal cost, and cost of captial and investment ranking methods. Methodology includes intensive reading assignment and lecture followed by a case analysis.
Credit recommendation: In the graduate degree category, 2 semester hours in Business Administration (4/89).

Data Analysis and Regression—Advanced

Location: Bellcore TEC, Lisle, IL.
Length: 35 hours (1 week).
Dates: April 1984-Present.
Objective: To expose students to advanced knowledge in data analysis and regression. Topics such as methods for pooling cross-sectional data, autocorrelation-correction procedures, and robust estimation and regression will be covered.
Instruction: Instruction is conducted in a lecture and problem solving case study format in applying some of the sophisticated data analysis and modeling techniques. Topics covered include a review of multiple regression, autocorrelation correction, pooled regression, techniques for variable selection, robust estimation and regression, sen-

sitivity analysis, multicolineating and simultaneous equation models.

Credit recommendation: In the graduate category, 1 semester hour in Mathematics, Operations Research, or Statistics (9/87).

Data Analysis and Regression—Basic
   Location: Bellcore TEC, Lisle, IL.
   Length: 40 hours (1 week).
   Dates: April 1984-Present.
   Objective: To expose students to analysis techniques such as data analysis and regression methods, including graphical methods of data analysis, modeling strategies, and model validation and correction.
   Instruction: This course provides students with a practical understanding of the statistical and computational aspects of data analysis and regression. Knowledge is acquired through a problem-solving computer-based approach to instruction. Topics include display and analysis, classical linear model, time series analysis, and techniques for presenting model results.
   Credit recommendation: In the graduate category, 1 semester hour in Mathematics, Operations Research, or Statistics (9/87).

Data Communications - Facility at CPE Testing (DC-FACT)
   Location: Lisle, IL.
   Length: 21½ hours (3 days).
   Dates: August 1988-Present.
   Objective: To provide the student with introductory data communications system compatibility concepts and servicing techniques.
   Learning Outcome: Upon successful completion of this course, the student will be able to identify and use test equipment to resolve service problems associated with terminal equipment, modems, service units and telephone company facilities; describe asynchronous and synchronous testing techniques; and segment network facilities and components for testing.
   Instruction: Course covers digital/analog test equipment, modern testing, transmission impairment measurements, terminal equipment testing, and data communications system testing. Methodology includes lecture, discussion, classroom and laboratory exercises.
   Credit recommendation: In the lower division baccalaureate/associate degree category, 1 semester hour in Telecommunications Technology (4/89).

Data Communications - Integrated Services Digital Network (DC-ISDN)
   Location: Lisle, IL.
   Length: 24 hours (3 days).
   Dates: October 1988-Present.
   Objective: To provide the student with an understanding of the major concepts of the Integrated Services Digital Network and its role in the comprehensive network of the future.
   Learning Outcome: Upon successful completion of this course, the student will be able to define ISDN; identify the key attributes of ISDN; and explain the underlying forces of network evolution.
   Instruction: Course covers ISDN attributes, ISDN standard interfaces, ISDN user-to-network interfaces, ISDN call path, ISDN switch architecture, channel protocol, capabilities, ISDN numbering plan, and common channeling signaling system seven (SS7). Methodology includes lecture, discussion, and classroom and laboratory exercises.
   Credit recommendation: In the upper division baccalaureate category, 1 semester hour in Telecommunications Technology (4/89).

Data Communications - Local Area Network (DC-LAN)
   Location: Lisle, IL.
   Length: 40 hours (1 week).
   Dates: July 1988-Present.
   Objective: To provide the student with an in-depth understanding of local area networks (LAN) hardware and software components and the design and capabilities of ETHERNET, STARLAN, and TOKEN RING networks.
   Learning Outcome: Upon successful completion of this course, the student will be able to define LAN parameters; identify various types of LAN configurations; assess LAN service needs and recommended solutions; and implement a LAN.
   Instruction: Course covers introduction and overview of local area networks, LAN topology, cabling plans and media types, network components, LAN applications, interlan connectivity, review of ETHERNET and TOKEN RING design, LAN implementation, and LAN testing. Methodology includes lecture, discussion, and laboratory exercises.
   Credit recommendation: In the lower division baccalaureate/associate degree category, 2 semester hours in Local Area Networks (4/89).

Data Communications - PC Communications (DC-PC COM)
   Location: Lisle, IL.
   Length: 16 hours (2 days).
   Dates: October 1988-Present.
   Objective: To provide the student with an introduction to personal computer interfacing and communication.
   Learning Outcome: Upon successful completion of this course, the student will be able to identify personal computer interfacing techniques; transfer files between personal computers; and describe basic concepts of local area networks.
   Instruction: Course covers introduction to personal

computer communications, personal computer direct link, asychronous modems, and local area networks. Methodology includes lecture, discussion, and classroom and laboratory exercises.

Credit recommendation: In the lower division baccalaureate/associate degree category, 1 semester hour in Computer Science/Business (4/89).

Data Communications - Personal Computer Fundamentals
  Location: Bellcore TEC, Lisle, IL or approved suitcase locations.
  Length: 23 hours (3 days).
  Dates: July 1988-Present.
  Objective: To provide the student with a general understnding of personal computers and their business applications.
  Learning Outcome: Upon successful completion of this course, the student will be able to demonstrate use of fundamental and advanced MS DOS commands; demonstrate use of application packages—WordPerfect, Lotus 1-2-3, dBASE III, Norton Utilities, and Ventura; and interact effectively with business users of personal computers.
  Instruction: Course covers overview of personal computer systems, personal computer terminology, personal computer hardware components, personal computer system software, and personal computer application software. Methodology includes lecture, discussion, case studies, and classroom exercises.
  Credit recommendation: In the lower division baccalaureate/associate degree category, 1 semester hour in Introduction to Personal Computers (4/89).

Data Communications - System Network Architecture (DC-SNA)
  Location: Lisle, IL.
  Length: 35 hours (1 week).
  Dates: January 1989-Present.
  Objective: To provide the student with the structure and composition of SNA and the associated hardware and software.
  Learning Outcome: Upon successful completion of this course, the student will be able to set up synchronous data link control (SDLC) conversion; exhange SNA messages; and view a SNA session.
  Instruction: Course covers SNA overview, SNA layers, data link control, path control, SNA sessions, network management, and new directions in SNA. Methodology includes lecture, discussion, and laboratory exercises.
  Credit recommendation: In the upper division baccalaureate category, 1 semester hour in Advanced Computer Architecture (4/89).

Data Services - Data in the Network (DS-NTWRK)
  Location: Bellcore TEC, Lisle, IL.
  Length: 80 hours (2 weeks).
  Dates: January 1984-Present.
  Objective: To provide the student with the skill and knowledge of data signals including the analysis, implementation, and maintenance of voice band data circuits.
  Instruction: Covers data line signals, cable and carrier facilities, design and impairment limits of data services circuits, and the operation of transmission test sets used for circuit quality analysis. Methodology includes lecture, discussion, and laboratory exercises.
  Credit recommendation: In the upper division baccalaureate category, 3 semester hours in Data Networks (2/86).

Data Services - Digital Data System
  Location: Bellcore TEC, Lisle, IL.
  Length: 92 hours (2½ weeks).
  Dates: January 1984-Present.
  Objective: To gain an understanding of the characteristics of transmitting digital signals; TDM processing; primary functions and service objectives of a digital data system; associated test instruments; design considerations, and diagnostic concepts and applications.
  Instruction: Course content consists of the following subject titles: DDS Overview, Digital Signal Transmission, DDS Equipment Identification, Test Instruments Identification, Circuit Design Guidelines, Basic Network Design, Network Design of Intra-DSA and Long-Haul Facilities, and DDS Coordination. Prerequisites: Basic Circuit and X-mission System Characteristics and DDS Overall Description.
  Credit recommendation: In the upper division baccalaureate category, 2 semester hours in Data Communications or in the lower division baccalaureate/associate degree category, 3 semester hours in Data Communications (9/86).

Data Services - Digital Data System Maintenance
  Location: Bellcore TEC, Lisle, IL.
  Length: 80 hours (2 weeks).
  Dates: April 1984-Present.
  Objective: To provide instruction: in the overall operation of a digital data system; in the use of proper test instruments, job aids and other documentation to perform specific diagnostic checks and DDS equipment tests.
  Instruction: This course provides the student with information sufficient to analyze troubles associated with DDS equipment, facilities, and dataport. In addition, the hands-on approach is used to teach maintenance activities facilitating virtually all the equipment and test facilities in Hub and End offices.
  Credit recommendation: In the lower division baccalaureate/associate degree category, 2 semester hours in

Digital Data Communications (9/86).

Data Services - Network Terminal Equipment
Location: Bellcore TEC, Lisle, IL.
Length: 84 hours (2 weeks).
Dates: January 1984-Present.
Objective: To provide management personnel the skills and knowledge needed to technically support internal data communication systems.
Instruction: Covers advanced concepts necessary to identify problems of timing and compatibility at the digital interface. Emphasis is also given to the study of modems, multiplexers, asynchronous terminals and digital test instruments.
Credit recommendation: In the lower division baccalaureate/associate degree category, 3 semester hours in Digital Data Transmission (9/86).

1. **DC-Introduction to Data Communications (DC-INTRO)**
2. **DC-Basic Protocols (DC-PROT)**
Location: Lisle, IL.
Length: 1. 16 hours (2 days). 2. 24 hours (3 days).
Dates: March 1988-Present.
Objective: 1. To give the student a foundation for all subsequent courses in the Data Communication Training Series. 2. To enable the student to examine the reasons for and advantages of, a layered structure for protocols.
Learning Outcome: Upon successful completion of this course, the student will be able to understand the impact of data speed, transmission impairments, and service degradation on communication systems (DC-INTRO); understand the significance of OSI reference model, packet switching HDLC protocol and X.25 protocol (DC-PROT); and recognize need for protocol conversions to avoid protocol incompatibility in multivendor equipment environments (DC-PROT).
Instruction: Course 1: covers data signals, modulation techniques, transmission media, digital interfocus, multiplexing techniques, and transmission impairments. Course 2: covers standards organizations: ITU, CCITT, ISO, and ANSI, protocol architecture, introduction to protocols, X.25 protocol overview; and network applications. Methods of instruction include lecture, discussion, case studies, and laboratory exercises.
Credit recommendation: In the lower division baccalaureate/associate degree category, 1 semester hour in Data Communications Technology or Telecommunications Technology for the combination of the two courses DC-INTRO and DC-PROT (4/88).

Digital Carrier Maintenance
Location: Lisle, IL.
Length: 74 hours (2 weeks).
Dates: March 1989-Present.
Objective: To provide the student with fundamental concepts of digital encoding, digital transmission, fault locating, and troubleshooting of digital carrier systems.
Learning Outcome: Upon successful completion of this course, the student will be able to describe fundamental concepts of digital carrier systems; identify and troubleshoot digital carrier systems; and trace signal flow on various digital carrier systems.
Instruction: Course covers D4 banks and associated equipment, T1, T1/OS, T1C, and T1D carrier facilities and associated equipment, and trouble analysis. Methodology includes lecture, discussion, and classroom and laboratory exercises.
Credit recommendation: In the upper division baccalaureate category, 3 semester hours in Telecommunications Technology (4/89).

Digital Cross Connect System Fundamentals (DSC-F)
Location: Bellcore TEC, Lisle, IL or approved suitcase locations.
Length: 34 hours (4½ days).
Dates: March 1988-Present.
Objective: To provide the student with an overview of the features, functions, applications, network compatibility and operations systems required for successful integration of DCS frames into emerging digital networks.
Learning Outcome: Upon successful completion of this course, the student will be able to describe the functions, features, and applications of DCS; identify operating systems used to support the maintenance and provisioning of DCS; and identify associated equipment and practices used in conjunction with DCS.
Instruction: Course covers introduction to digital cross-connect systems, DCS data transmission, DCS frame engineering, DCS operating systems, wideband digital cross connect systems, DCS planning considerations, and DCS applications. Methodology includes lecture, discussion, and classroom and laboratory exercises.
Credit recommendation: In the lower division baccalaureate/associate degree category, 2 semester hours in Digital Data Transmission (4/89).

Digital Switch Hardware Maintenance
Location: Bellcore TEC, Lisle, IL.
Length: 72 hours (2 weeks).
Dates: March 1987 - Present.
Objective: To teach students how to identify and resolve hardware problems encountered in the peripheral community of the DMS 100/200 digital switch.
Instruction: Covers documentation/maintenance overview, hardware call flow, peripheral messaging and central message controller, network modules, common peripheral modules, live modules, digital trunk modules, and multiple trouble analysis.
Credit recommendation: In the lower division baccalaureate/associate degree category, 2 semester hours as a Telecommunications elective (9/87).

Digital Switch Programming
Location: Bellcore TEC, Lisle, IL.
Length: 75 hours (2 weeks).
Dates: May 1987-Present.
Objective: To provide the student with the skills to interpret programs employed in the software of a DMS 100/200 switch and the skills to diagnose and resolve equipment failures and call processing problems associated with the software functions performed by the central control complex.
Instruction: Covers DMS 100/200 switch overview, assembly language, protocol language structure/declarations/statements, system commands, software operating system characteristics, call processing, and system restarts/programs/patches.
Credit recommendation: In the lower division baccalaureate/associate degree category, 2 semester hours as a Telecommunications elective (9/87).

DMS-100 Family Capacities
Location: Lisle, IL or approved "suitcase" locations.
Length: 40 hours (1 week).
Dates: March 1987-Present.
Objective: To provide students with the ability to determine realistic main station capacities for the DMS 100/200 switch.
Learning Outcome: Upon successful completion of this course, the student will be able to use the Bellcore TEC "Capacity Cruncher" worksheets to determine hardware capacities; use Northern Telecom's Real Time and Peripheral Real Time Programs (PRTCALC1) to project processor real time capacities; and evaluate the main station capabilities of the DMS 100/200 switch.
Instruction: Major topics covered in the course are introduction to capacities, peripheral modules-lines, peripheral modules-trunks and service circuits, and networks and remotes. Methods of instruction include lecture, case studies, classroom demonstrations and individual student casework on a PC follows each lecture module.
Credit recommendation: In the lower division baccalaureate/associate degree category, 2 semester hours in Telecommunications Technology (4/88).

DMS 100 Family - Hardware Maintenance for Peripherals (DMS-HMP)
(Formerly DMS 100 Family - Traffic Operation Position System [DMS-TOPS])
Location: Lisle, IL.
Length: *Version 1:* 85 hours (2 weeks); *Version 2:* 125 hours (3 weeks).
Dates: *Version 1:* October 1987-March 1989; *Version 2:* April 1989-Present.
Objective: To provide the student with technical skills and knowledge required to maintain TOPS hardware and translations on a routine and trouble report basis.
Learning Outcome: Upon successful completion of this course, the student will be able to maintain TOPS central office and position hardware; detail rating/charging requirements and call processing translations for noncoin, coin, hotel/motel, calling card, and special type calls; and analyze output reports, map functions, and display call for TOPS operating problems.
Instruction: Course covers system description, parameter, hardware, trunking, call processing, rating, charging, coin, mics/accs, OM, output report, OC remote, position, tutor, growth, evolution, force management. Methodology includes lecture, discussion, and classroom and laboratory exercises.
Credit recommendation: In the lower division baccalaureate/associate degree category, 3 semester hours in Telecommunications Equipment Maintenance (4/89).

3B20 Duplex Computer Systems Maintenance (3B-SM)
Location: Bellcore TEC, Lisle, IL.
Length: 123 hours (3 weeks).
Dates: January 1984-Present.
Objective: To teach the fundamentals of the hardware configuration of the 3B20 Duplex Computer and troubleshooting methods, programming techniques used in the 3B processor and the diagnostic language.
Learning Outcome: Upon successful completion of this course, the student will be able to successfully repair troubles in the areas of software, hardware, and database.
Instruction: Course content covers maintenance philosophy of the 3B20 Duplex processor including parity generation and checking, duplication, matching, errors, interrupts, timing audits; documentation, diagnostics, biomation logic analyzer, central control - the core of the 3B20 Duplex processor; microcode, maintenance channels, main store, generic access package (GRASP), direct memory access, and peripheral communications path.
Credit recommendation: In the lower division baccalaureate/associate degree category, 2 semester hours in Introduction to Computer Architecture, and in the upper division baccalaureate category, 2 semester hours in Advanced Computer Architecture (9/86).

3B20 Duplex Computer-System Software (3B-SS)
Location: Bellcore TEC, Lisle, IL.
Length: 144 hours (72 weeks).
Dates: January 1984-Present.
Objective: To teach the system software of the 3B20 Duplex Computer and enable the student to recognize, analyze, and correct software-generated problems.
Learning Outcome: Upon successful completion of this course, the student will know and understand how the system software of the 3B20 Duplex Computer functions; its development in the C Language and UNIX®; to be able to use troubleshooting techniques for software error interrupts and audit failures.
Instruction: The course covers an introduction to the C Language, IS25 Assembly Language and UNIX 2. System

software of the 3B20 Duplex Computer is covered in detail including software documentation and case work, the Generic Access package (GRASP) as a troubleshooting tool; the file system and its debugger, and operating system; the analysis and resolution of software interrupts and audit failures.

Credit recommendation: In the lower division baccalaureate/associate degree category, 2 semester hours and in the upper division baccalaureate category 2 semester hours in Programming Language Systems and Software (9/86).

Economic Evaluation (EE)
Location: Bellcore TEC, Lisle, IL.
Length: 72 hours (1½ weeks).
Dates: January 1984-Present.
Objective: To enable the student to: interpret financial and accounting terminology as it applies to engineering economy studies; identify the relationships between the NPV and NPWE approach to economy studies; explain the relationships between book, tax, and book-tax depreciation; determine the tax effects of accelerated depreciation and investment tax credit in a study; perform a manual after tax cash flow analysis; explain how to properly use (and avoid misuses of) the NPV, NPWE, IROR, DPP, and LTEE evaluators; integrate inflation into a study and determine its impact; identify the capabilities and features of the Capital Utilization Criteria (CUCRIT) program, analyze an economic comparison of two alternatives using Cumulative Discounted Net Cash Flows; test the validity of a study using sensitivity analysis; identify proper and improper techniques for presentation of engineering economy studies; analyze and perform an economic study in group casework, and analyze and describe the income and cash flow effects of an own versus lease study.
Instruction: EE introduces economy concepts beyond the fundamental level. Discounted cash flow methodology provides the framework for discussion of the impacts of accelerated tax depreciation, investment tax credit, expensed capital costs, interest during construction and inflation. The Capital Utilization Criteria (CUCRIT) program is presented and used to perform an economic study. Analysis of the economic evaluators (proper uses and possible misuses) available from the CUCRIT program is covered in detail. Also presented are the basic principles of an own versus lease analysis, sensitivity analysis and economic study presentation techniques. EE is designed for first through third level managers in functions such as economic analysis service costs and construction budget management.
Credit recommendation: In the upper division baccalaureate category, 3 semester hours in Engineering Economics (2/86).

Electrical Protection Fundamentals (EPF)
Location: Bellcore TEC, Lisle, IL.
Length: 35 hours (1 week).
Dates: January 1984-Present.
Objective: To provide the student with the skills necessary to recognize and alleviate problems associated with electrical hazards related to environmental conditions in telecommunications.
Instruction: Covers the methods and devices used to control or mitigate potentials and currents of a magnitude that constitutes a potential hazard to personnel, property, and communications equipment. Voltage and current limitations and protection of optical fiber cables are covered. Methodology includes lecture, discussion, and laboratory exercises.
Credit recommendation: In the lower division baccalaureate/associate degree category, 1 semester hour in Industrial Safety (2/86).

Facilitating Groups and Meetings (FGM)
Location: Lisle, IL and approved "suitcase" locations.
Length: 22.5 hours (3 days).
Dates: February 1984-Present.
Objective: To expose the student to the theory and techniques of managing groups and meetings and provide an appreciation for how and why individuals behave as they do in work groups.
Learning Outcome: Upon successful completion of this course, students will be able to describe how and why people behave as they do in group settings; describe how and why groups behave as they do; identify the ways their behavior as leaders affects their groups' functioning and performance; and identify and develop the skills needed to increase their own effectiveness and the productivity of meetings they conduct.
Instruction: Major topics covered in the course are self-assessment and feedback, forming/norming, interventions, storming, and resources and action planning. Methods of instruction include lecture/discussion, exercises, case analysis/synthesis, and self-assessment profiles.
Credit recommendation: In the upper division baccalaureate category, 1 semester hour in Human Resource Management, Industrial/Organizational Psychology, Organizational Behavior, or Organization Development (4/88).

Fiber Optic Systems - Maintenance (FIBR-MT)
Location: Bellcore TEC, Lisle, IL.
Length: 72 hours (2 weeks).
Dates: January 1986-Present.
Objective: This course is designed to provide instruction in installation, acceptance testing, routine maintenance, and trouble analysis of complete fiber optic telephone systems.
Learning Outcome: Upon successful completion of this course, the student will be able to demonstrate high-level

proficiency in the maintenance of Fiber Optic Systems.

Instruction: This course utilizes a hands-on approach combined with classroom lecture, covering the installation acceptance testing; routine maintenance and trouble analysis of fiber optic transmission; and the operation of various types of test instruments used in Fiber Optic Systems. Prerequisite: DIGCXRMT and FIBR-TEC (both courses).

Credit recommendation: In the lower division baccalaureate/associate degree category, 3 semester hours in Opto-Electronics (9/86).

Fiber Optic Systems - Technical Overview (FIBR-TEC)
Location: Bellcore TEC, Lisle, IL.
Length: 36 hours (1 week).
Dates: January 1985-Present.
Objective: To provide the student an overview of a complete fiber optic system; including operation, trouble shooting procedures, and basic design.
Instruction: Covers the major functions of a complete fiber optic communications system; includes the fundamentals of fiber construction, optical sources, and detectors, waveguides, transmission losses, and safety requirements. Methodology includes lecture, discussion, and laboratory exercises.
Credit recommendation: In the lower division baccalaureate/associate degree category, 2 semester hours on Optoelectronics (2/86).

Field Test Results and Analysis (Field Test Analysis [Trial])
Location: Lisle, IL or approved "suitcase" location.
Length: 16 hours (2 days).
Dates: January 1984-Present.
Objective: To enable the student to analyze data and make recommendations on the appropriate course of action.
Learning Outcome: Upon successful completion of this course, the student will be able to determine the types of data to be collected and the analysis required based upon the field test plan; discriminate between classes of field test data; identify primary problem indicators; identify secondary problem indicators; discriminate the types of data analysis that can be performed: a. during the conduct of each field trial; b. after each field trial is completed; and c. after the field test is completed. Analyze data in terms of the following potential outcomes: a. no revision required; b. revisions/supplement required to training; c. revisions required to field test plan; and d. cancel project.
Instruction: This course covers the principles and practicalities of analyzing data collected during a field test conducted following the Training Development Standards (TDS). The focus is on analyzing data and making recommendations regarding courses of action that are appropriate. However, it also discusses planning aspects of the field test since one must be familiar with the planning in order to carry out the analysis correctly. The principles are developed through lecture and discussion and students develop their skills through individual exercises. This course is intended for course developers who will be conducting a field test of a newly developed course.
Credit recommendation: In the upper division baccalaureate category, 1 semester hour in Education (9/86). NOTE: For a student to receive credit, Introduction to Course Development should be taken as a prerequisite or equivalent.

Finance and Accounting in the Competitive Environment
Location: Bellcore TEC, Lisle, IL or approved suitcase locations.
Length: 43½ hours (1 week).
Dates: January 1984-Present.
Objective: To teach the student the concepts, techniques, and tools of effective and efficient competitive analysis.
Learning Outcome: Upon successful completion of this course, the student will be able to deliniate the five competitive forces on an industry segment, evaluate the strategic position of each firm, calculate the cost structure and financial strength of any competitor, and know how to legally obtain and manipulate information.
Instruction: Course covers the entire breadth of competitive analysis from conceptual framework to how industrial warfare is actually waged, to where to find information and massage it effectively. Considerable emphasis is placed on financial analysis and the use and manipulation of data bases. Competitive battlefield examples are selected to mirror telecommunications strategies. Methodology includes extensive case discussions, presentations, in-class problems, and group preparation sessions.
Credit recommendation: In the upper division baccalaureate category, 3 semester hours in Competitive Marketing Analysis, or in the graduate degree category, 3 semester hours as a Marketing elective (4/89).

Finance and Accounting Issues and Concepts in the Modern Corporation (Formerly Finance and Accounting for the Non-Financial Manager)
Location: Bellcore TEC, Morristown, NJ.
Length: 24 hours (3 days).
Dates: January 1984-Present.
Objective: To provide the fundamentals of finance and accounting, furnish an overall understanding of the role of accounting and finance in the success of an enterprise.
Instruction: Course covers an analysis of financial statements, including the nature of assets, liabilities and equity. Course includes an examination of financial data, factors that cause fluctuations, the performance of different divisions and service/product lines and decision rules for top

management to improve assessments and predictive ability as well as cash flow and project return on investment.

Credit recommendation: In the upper division baccalaureate category, 1 semester hour in either Finance or Accounting (6/86).

Financial Management in Telecommunications
  Location: Bellcore TEC, Morristown, NJ.
  Length: 24 hours (3 days).
  Dates: January 1985-May 1988.
  Objective: To provide a financial analyst's view of telecommunications.
  Instruction: The course provides an introduction to financial principles. The course surveys the basic techniques used by money managers to evaluate and improve profit performance by reviewing the financial indicators and ratios used in appraising performance. The course provides an understanding of the various forces that currently affect the telecommunications industry, i.e., competition, technology, regulation, social changes, judicial and legislative factors and inflation.
  Credit recommendation: In the upper division baccalaureate category, 1 semester hour in Financial Statement Analysis (6/86).

Financial Planning, Control and Decision Making
  Location: Bellcore TEC, Morristown, NJ.
  Length: 24 hours (3 days).
  Dates: January 1984-Present.
  Objective: To enable participants to apply financial information to service marketing decisions, perform financial analysis of alternative courses of action, improve profit planning and control processes.
  Instruction: The course focuses on the financial analysis of ratios and the time value of money. Participants gain the following knowledge for management planning and control: (1) relationship between measurement systems and business strategies; (2) designing the measurement system for specific organizational units; (3) the budgeting process and its behavioral implications, and (4) the relationship between budgeting and the long-range planning systems. Participants learn to identify costs relevant to various decisions, cost-volume-profit relationships, treatment of sunk costs and operating costs, and analyses of complex alternatives.
  Credit recommendation: In the upper division baccalaureate category, 1 semester hour in Financial Decision Making, Financial Analysis, Business Administration, or Management (6/86).

Fundamentals of Instructional Media
(Fundamentals of Media Selection Workshop)
  Location: Lisle, IL or approved "suitcase" location.
  Length: 14 hours (2 days).
  Dates: March 1986-Present.
  Objective: Fundamentals of Media Selection Workshop is a course designed to help students understand how to integrate media into courses they are developing or teaching. Emphasis is placed on matching media to the skills/knowledge to be taught. Media include printed, audiovisual, and hands-on.
  Learning Outcome: Upon successful completion of this course, the student will be able to identify media formats available in a sample training environment; identify the characteristics of the behavior being trained that affect the choice of media format; identify sample resources to assist in determining and selecting media format; identify specific learning characteristics of students that can affect the selection of media format; select the most appropriate media format to communicate specific skill/knowledge objectives, and select and use media based on technical reasons such as adult learning characteristics rather than on personal preference or custom.
  Instruction: This course is intended for individuals who design and develop training. The workshop introduces factors that should be considered when determining whether media are needed; and, when media are needed, Media helps developers identify the most effective medium to use. Students have the opportunity to select media formats using the Job Aid for Selecting Media, observe media production, and learn how to best utilize the media to enable the identified skill/knowledge objectives. There is a precourse assignment that consists of the students selecting several skill/knowledge objectives that they would like to develop with media. This could be for a new course or for a course that is under revision. Students must bring to the workshop both the objectives and the content outlines for the course areas for which the media is to be developed. The precourse assignment also includes a reading assignment that reviews each of the Training Development Standards (TDS) phases of course development, for those not familiar with them. This course is intended for new and experienced course developers and learning or performance technologists.
  Credit recommendation: In the upper division baccalaureate category, 1 semester hour in School of Education (9/86). NOTE: For students to receive credit, Introduction to Course Development must have been completed as a prerequisite or equivalent.

General Transmission Concepts
  Location: Bellcore TEC, Lisle, IL.
  Length: 74 hours (2 weeks).
  Dates: January 1984-Present.
  Objective: To provide General Transmission concepts for managers with responsibilities that are not directly related to transmission.
  Learning Outcome: Upon successful completion of this course, the student will be able to practice effective communications/interaction between transmission and non-transmission personnel in the field of telecommunications.
  Instruction: This course provides instruction in: intro-

duction to electrical signals; telephone switching concepts; customer loop design; network design; network transmission considerations; analog cable carrier; digital carrier theory; and lightwave transmission systems.

Credit recommendation: In the upper division baccalaureate category, 3 semester hours in Introduction to Telecommunications (9/86).

Innovation - Achieving the Future (I-ATF)
Location: Lisle, IL and approved "suitcase" locations.
Length: 22.5 hours (3 days).
Dates: December 1987-Present.
Objective: To provide the student an in-depth understanding of the psychological and business aspects of vision, creativity, and innovation, and to enhance the student's innovative implementation skills.
Learning Outcome: Upon successful completion of this course, the student will be able to apply behavioral and business principles associated with innovation and generate innovative ideas to address problems and opportunities; evaluate individual ideas for merit, fit, and risk; promote and "sell" innovative ideas to others; and implement one's own innovative ideas.
Instruction: Major topics covered in the course are innovative processes, vocabulary, characteristics of innovators, idea generation, solutions and blockage; evaluation and determination of innovation, selling ideas and plans, developing and implementing ideas; surveys, worksheets, and styles. Methods of instruction include lecture, discussion, exercises, videotapes, projects, and case studies.
Credit recommendation: In the upper division baccalaureate category, 1 semester hour in Human Resource Management, Industrial/Organizational Psychology or Organizational Behavior (4/88).

Innovative Marketing Strategies (IMS)
Location: Morristown, NJ and approved "suitcase" locations.
Length: 16 hours (2 days).
Dates: September 1987-Present.
Objective: To provide the student with an understanding that the transition to a deregulated marketplace requires new and innovative strategies in order to compete successfully in a changing environment.
Learning Outcome: Upon successful completion of this course, the student will be able to explain the impact of deregulation on Bell operating companies, identify and develop marketing strategies appropriate for given types of customers with special attention to relevant cost reduction techniques and market segments, and position new services in the marketing strategy portfolio.
Instruction: Major topics covered in the course are history and impact of deregulation, new services, customer service communication, and market segmentation for repositioning Bell operating companies. Methods of instruction include lecture, discussion, and case studies.

Credit recommendation: In the upper division baccalaureate category, 1 semester hour in General Business, Management, Marketing, or Strategic Management (4/88).

Introduction to Telecommunications Concepts
Location: Bellcore TEC, Lisle, IL.
Length: 190 hours (4 weeks).
Dates: October 1986-Present.
Objective: To provide the student with general telecommunications concepts and skills training for telecommunications personnel.
Instruction: Covers history of the Bell System, telecommunications regulatory issues, telecommunications concepts, transmission media, transmission systems, basic switching concepts, PBX systems, data communications, protocols, local area networks, traffic engineering, PBX data/voice generation, advanced networking, network planning and management, office automation, and hands-on laboratory.
Credit recommendation: In the upper division baccalaureate category, 4 semester hours in Telecommunications (9/87).

Introduction to UNIX® Operating System (UNIX INT)
Location: Bellcore TEC, Lisle, IL.
Length: 20 hours (3 days).
Dates: January 1984-Present.
Objective: Use basic UNIX® system terms and concepts, use basic UNIX® system commands, use the UNIX® system user's manual to select and use UNIX® commands, and use the UNIX® system line editor to create and modify files.
Learning Outcome: The student should be able to utilize the basic UNIX® operating system commands on a computer as a user.
Instruction: This course is a dial-up course which will acquaint the student with the basic features of the UNIX® operating system. A product of AT&T BEll Labs, UNIX® is a very powerful and versatile operating system with growing popularity. By working at his/her own pace and reviewing sections as necessary, the student learns how to execute commands, create files, use the editor, and utilize directories to organize files. The student will learn to use the AT&T UNIX® system User Reference Manual, which is provided as part of the precourse package. This manual describes the features of the UNIX® operating system. The student also becomes familiar with some of the system's unique features, which include: making temporary programs by patching existing programs together with pipes, running several programs at the same time by initiating a background process, and reading and sending mail.
Credit recommendation: In the lower division baccalaureate/associate degree category, 1 semester hour in

Computer Science or Telecommunications (9/86).

**Inventory Management
(Inventory Management Fundamentals)**
   Location: Lisle, IL. or approved "suitcase" location.
   Length: 35 hours (4½ days).
   Dates: January 1985-Present.
   Objective: To provide the student with an understanding of the fundamental techniques currently used to improve the productivity of the capital invested in plant and equipment items.
   Learning Outcome: Upon successful completion of this course, the student will be able to state Inventory Management principles to be used to maintain or improve service, improve utilization and optimize capital productivity; develop optimal distribution strategies for various classes of plant; develop stock levels; apply inventory management techniques to planning and introduction of new products, and provide proper input to the Product Management/Line of Business team.
   Instruction: This course is designed to inform managers of fundamental techniques currently being used to improve the productivity of the capital invested in plant and equipment items. During the course, students study the significance of annual carrying charges on reserve inventory; how the inventory loop is used to analyze the interrelationships between the capital and expense budgets; and also the dynamic relationship between service and inventory carrying charges. Students also learn how, and why, inventory management strategies should be modified as a product moves through its life cycle. Two powerful inventory management strategies, aggregation and substitution, are also presented. Throughout the course, students participate in case problems involving inventory management principles. The major case problem requires the students to manage a product over its life cycle.
   Credit recommendation: In the upper division baccalaureate category, 2 semester hours in Inventory Management or Production Operation Management (9/86).

ISDN Switching Fundamentals (ISDN-SWF)
   Location: Lisle, IL.
   Length: 34 hours (1 week).
   Dates: October 1988-Present.
   Objective: To provide the student with a basic overview of loop, switch, and network architecture, types of representative ISDN terminal and applications and maintenance concepts and strategies.
   Learning Outcome: Upon successful completion of this course, the student will be able to describe ISDN; and identify ISDN support protocols, capabilities, and architecture.
   Instruction: Course covers ISDN overview, pocket switching and protocols, major switches 5ESS and DMS 100/200, outside plant, representative terminals, and ISDN maintenance. Methodology includes lecture, discussion, and laboratory exercises.
   Credit recommendation: In the upper division baccalaureate category, 2 semester hours in Telecommunications Software Support (4/89).

1A Maintenance Program - Advanced System Testing
   Location: Bellcore TEC, Lisle, IL.
   Length: 100 hours (2 weeks).
   Dates: January 1984-Present.
   Objective: To teach the student to trouble shoot failures on AT&T's Electronic Switching System of both a hardware and software nature. To implement corrections for failures mentioned above; to prioritize multiple co-existing failures for most efficient recovery, and to be able to direct others in the accomplishment of both 1 and 2 above from a remote location using a telephone.
   Learning Outcome: Upon successful completion of this course, the student will be able to correct most failures of a complex switching processor (AT&T's 1A) both of a hardware or software nature.
   Instruction: This course consists of lectures and case studies conducted in fully equipped labs covering troubleshooting and recovering from hardware and software failures in the complex 1A switching system. Procedures for most efficient recovery are discussed in detail from various standpoints.
   Credit recommendation: In the lower division baccalaureate/associate degree category, 2 semester hours in Software Systems (9/86).

1A Maintenance Program - Attached Processor Systems
   Location: Bellcore TEC, Lisle, IL.
   Length: 110 hours (2 weeks).
   Dates: September 1984-Present.
   Objective: To diagnose and correct mini processor failures, duplex line problems, and mini interface errors. To interpret data, integrate output, and to use documentation and test equipment to diagnose hardware failure.
   Learning Outcome: Upon successful completion of this course, the student will be able to diagnose failure and generally maintain AT&T's 3B mini processor and the accompanying interface device.
   Instruction: This course provides a thorough coverage of AT&T's 3B mini processor as it interacts with a 1A switching mainframe. The 3B is used here primarily to provide additional hard disk capacity. The student is instructed in such areas as, interface hardware, diagnostics, interrupts, file handling, recovery procedures and duplex failures as they relate to the attached 3B processor. This course also covers system recovery techniques for the 1A processor. This is a very technically oriented course of a quite detailed nature.
   Credit recommendation: In the lower division baccalaureate/associate degree category, 3 semester hours in Mini Processor Maintenance (9/86).

1A Maintenance Program - Auxiliary Unit Maintenance

Location: Bellcore TEC, Lisle, IL.
Length: 124-126 hours (2 weeks).
Dates: January 1984-Present.
Objective: In connection with auxiliary units attached to the 1A switching processor, this course will teach the students how these units operate in normal, system reinitialization and processor modes; to locate and correct hardware problems; to diagnose duplex file store failures using tape paged routines; to identify and replace field replaceable components of tape and disk units; to analyze hard copy diagnostic printouts produced by the system in the course of internal audits, and to be able to provide electrical maintenance of these devices through schematic analysis and circuit tracing.
Learning Outcome: Upon successful completion of this course, the student will be competent to maintain auxiliary units (I/O devices) associated with AT&T's 1A switching processor. He should also be able to diagnose faults in these units and take corrective action.
Instruction: The course covers, in great detail, the operation of auxiliary devices to AT&T's 1A switching processor including tape units, tape unit controllers, disk units, data unit selectors, tape transport and buses and their interrelationships. It presents diagnostic techniques through the use of electronic test equipment, hardware documentation, and software aids. It also covers mechanical component failure and repair for the disk and tape units.
Credit recommendation: In the lower division baccalaureate/associate degree category, 3 semester hours in Input/Output Device Maintenance (9/86).

1A Maintenance Program - Control Processor Maintenance

Location: Bellcore TEC, Lisle, IL.
Length: 200 hours (4 weeks).
Dates: January 1984-Present.
Objective: To locate and correct failures in AT&T's 1A central processor using: hardware documentation to follow logic flow of circuits; test equipment for problems beyond diagnostic capabilities of the unit; all 1A software aids; maintenance print outs for repair purposes, and methods available to isolate whether a problem is software or hardware oriented.
Learning Outcome: Upon successful completion of this course, the student will have the capability to diagnose and correct most problems in AT&T's complex 1A central processing unit.
Instruction: This course covers all aspects of maintaining AT&T's 1A central processor. There is liberal hands-on training in the various aspects of the troubleshooting process. A detailed explanation of the operation of the instruments employed is also presented.
Credit recommendation: In the lower division baccalaureate/associate degree category, 5 semester hours in Central Processor Maintenance (9/86).

Management Communications Workshop

Location: Bellcore TEC, Morristown, NJ.
Length: 16 hours (2 days).
Dates: June 1986-Present.
Objective: To provide managers with the communication skills required in an evolving management and marketing culture.
Instruction: The course covers audience analysis, lecture techniques, effective use of visuals, handling a Q&A sequence, adversary questions, panel discussion techniques, and body language. The course uses videotaping and individual feedback.
Credit recommendation: In the graduate degree category, 1 semester hour in Business Communications, Public Administration, Management or Organizational Behavior (6/86).

Managerial Accounting
(Financial Analysis for Business Decisions)

Location: Lisle, IL. or approved "suitcase" location.
Length: 32 hours (4 days).
Dates: January 1984-Present.
Objective: To provide the student with an understanding of concepts of financial and managerial accounting. Emphasis is on managerial accounting concepts, including variable budgets, contribution analysis, break-even analysis and capital investment decisions.
Learning Outcome: Upon successful completion of this course, the student will be able to state eight fundamental accounting conventions; define and perform comparative analysis of each component of an income statement; define and perform comparative analysis of each component of a balance sheet; construct schedules of changes in working capital and a firms' financial position; interpret and project financial statements; discriminate between fixed and variable costs; perform contribution analysis; perform break-even analysis; construct a contribution statement; construct a variable budget, and define and qualify return on investment as a means of evaluating capital investment decisions and operating performance.
Instruction: Covers the concepts of managerial accounting. It focuses on the use of financial accounting documents with specific examples from manufacturing and telecommunications companies. Emphasis is on managerial accounting concepts, including variable budgets, contribution analysis, break-even analysis, and capital investment decisions. This course does not replace the traditional financial accounting course.
Credit recommendation: In the upper division baccalaureate category, 2 semester hours in Managerial Accounting (9/86).

Managing Change in a Changing Environment (MCCE)
Location: Lisle, IL and approved "suitcase" locations.
Length: 22.5 hours (3 days).
Dates: January 1987-Present.
Objective: To develop the student's ability to identify and overcome resistance to change and acquire management skills.
Learning Outcome: Upon successful completion of this course, students will be able to assess their own beliefs and practices associated with change management; anticipate how people and situations will be affected by change and how to identify and overcome resistance to change; and manage change initiation, implementation, and institutionalization; identify organizational change management indicators; and set culture, assess needs and solve problems in ambiguous work environments.
Instruction: Major topics covered in the course are the change chain, understanding an individual's response and reaction to change, and how organization-wide change occurs. Methods of instruction include lecture, discussion, exercises, case analysis/synthesis, and self-assessment profiles.
Credit recommendation: In the upper division baccalaureate category, 1 semester hour in Human Resource Management, Industrial/Organizational Psychology, Organizational Behavior, or Organization Development (4/88).

Managing Costly Group Problems (MCGP)
Location: Lisle, IL and approved "suitcase" locations.
Length: 22.5 hours (3 days).
Dates: January 1986-May 1988.
Objective: To teach students how to prevent and manage interpersonal problems in groups and meetings which cost time, effort, and productivity—and which often occur in the context of a changing corporate environment.
Learning Outcome: Upon successful completion of this course, students will be able to identify and evaluate common costly interpersonal and organizational problems they personally encounter when leading groups and meetings; assess the impact of their own behavior in preventing and/or managing these problems; and anticipate and prevent, before the fact, costly interpersonal and organizational group problems; and implement job-relevant strategies for managing these problems effectively.
Instruction: Major topics covered in the course are facilitating group meetings, models for planning and managing meetings, self-assessment profiles. Methods of instruction include lecture/discussion, exercises, case analysis/synthesis, and self-assessment profiles.
Credit recommendation: In the upper division baccalaureate category, 1 semester hour in Human Resource Management, Industrial/Organizational Psychology, Organizational Behavior, or Organization Development (4/88).

Managing the Boss (MTB)
Location: Lisle, IL and approved "suitcase" locations.
Length: 22.5 hours (3 days).
Dates: October 1986-Present.
Objective: To provide students with an understanding of their individual behavior when dealing with their boss, as well as understanding the boss and the organization for which they both work and develop outcome-oriented strategies for influencing the boss.
Learning Outcome: Upon successful completion of this course, students will be able to support and influence their boss, build upon their boss' strengths, and work effectively with different types of bosses.
Instruction: Major topics covered in the course are "you, your boss, and the environment," coping or quitting and exploring alternatives, and influencing your boss' decisions. Methods of instruction include lecture, discussion, case studies, and self-assessment profile.
Credit recommendation: In the upper division baccalaureate category, 1 semester hour in Human Resource Management, Industrial/Organizational Psychology, Organizational Behavior, or Organization Development (4/88).

Marketing Analysis
(Strategic Marketing and Financial Tools)
Location: Lisle, IL. or approved "suitcase" location.
Length: 35 hours (4 days).
Dates: January 1984-Present.
Objective: To provide the student with an understanding of concepts and procedures for analyzing the economic feasibility of a proposed business plan. It focuses on the strategic process and strategy formulation with emphasis on market forecasting and planning, competitive analysis, pricing, life cycle analysis and evaluating product/service proposals.
Learning Outcome: Upon successful completion of this course, the student will be able to make a preliminary market assessment by performing a situation analysis; develop a preliminary market program for a proposed new product or service; recognize special factors impacting both a product/service and customer markets across product and market life cycles; perform an abbreviated competitive analysis; define the unique selling position for a given product/service; define pricing objectives for a given product/service; recognize key influencing factors leading to a proper pricing decision; recognize the function of distribution channels, define channel objectives, and select a channel appropriate to a specific product/service; establish and justify a proposed price for a given product or service; recognize the costs and revenues associated with alternative product/service proposals; recognize competitive factors associated with cost/revenue analysis impacting product/service decisions, and evaluate the economics of alternative product/service proposals (including break-even and contribution anal-

ysis) as a basis for a "go no/go" decision.

Instruction: This course prepares the student to perform analyses necessary to determine the economic viability of a proposed marketing plan. The course is taught by professors from Lycoming College and Golden Gate University. Basic concepts of strategic planning are discussed and provide a lead-in to the topic of strategy formulation. Market forecasting, market planning, competitive analysis, pricing, life cycle analysis and other topics are introduced. The case study deals with strategy development for bringing to market a telecommunications service offering. The service offering falls under regulation and is characterized by a high incidence of joint costs, most of them of a fixed (not variable) nature. This course deals exclusively with telecommunication product/service offerings in both a regulated and deregulated environment.

Credit recommendation: In the upper division baccalaureate category, 3 semester hours in Strategic Marketing Analysis. In the graduate degree category, 3 semester hours in Marketing as an elective (9/86).

Marketing Strategy
(Advanced Competitive Strategic Analysis)
   Location: Lisle, IL. or approved "suitcase" location.
   Length: 36 hours (5 days).
   Dates: November 1984-Present.
   Objective: To provide the student with an understanding of strategies and procedures for performing a competitive analysis in the telecommunications industry. The course addresses how to utilize tools and techniques for environmental scanning, forecasting and strategic mapping.
   Learning Outcome: Upon successful completion of this course, the student will be able to perform in-depth telecommunication industry analysis; provide insight into changing relationships with suppliers, buyers and competitors; identify the real and anticipated competitors; utilize foremost tools and techniques for environmental scanning, forecasting, and strategic mapping; recognize the implications and components of key financial decisions (e.g., estimating long-term capital needs and alternate sources); describe the implications and components of key financial decisions (e.g., competitive pricing); identify sources of commercial data and collection procedures, and analyze marketing, financial, and operational strategies of competitors.
   Instruction: This course demonstrates how to do competitive analysis and strategic planning in the rapidly evolving telecommunication industry. Exclusive new telecommunication materials have been written specifically for the course by faculty members of Harvard Business School and other leading universities. For example, recently released material includes a detailed discussion of the access charge complexities, the strategy of GTE, ITT's competitive position overseas and domestically, and numerous examples of how to perform strategic mapping of telecommunications competitors. MCI is studied in-depth, including a detailed review of the steps the competitive analyst took to uncover the data legally.
   Credit recommendation: In the upper division baccalaureate category, 3 semester hours in Marketing. In the graduate degree category, 3 semester hours Marketing elective (9/86). NOTE: For students to receive credit they must have completed Strategic Marketing and Financial Tools.

Multivariate Analysis
   Location: Piscataway, NJ or approved "suitcase" location.
   Length: 31 hours (4½ days).
   Dates: June 1985-May 1988.
   Objective: To give the student an understanding of multivariate problem solving, with special attention to computer applications and pre-existing computer packages.
   Learning Outcome: Upon successful completion of this course, the student will be able to problem-solve using matrix algebra, factor analysis, principal component analyses, canonical correlation, computer applications and statistical packages, regression, and linear transformation.
   Instruction: Multivariate Analysis is designed to provide the student with a foundation in the application and development of multivariate analysis techniques. The emphasis in this course is on the practical selection of powerful analysis techniques, and hands-on experience in their use. This course is designed for analysts, statisticians, market researchers, and other technical personnel requiring an understanding of multivariate analysis techniques for applications in survey and market research, demand analysis or other situations where multiple response data must be analyzed.
   Credit recommendation: In the upper division baccalaureate category, 3 semester hours in Multivariate Analysis (9/86).

Planning, Design, and Operation of Telecommunication Systems (PDOTS)
   Location: Bellcore TEC, Lisle, IL.
   Length: 400 hours (9 weeks [previously 10 weeks]).
   Dates: April 1985-Present.
   Objective: To provide students with the theory and concepts underlying the telecommunication network and equipment, its planning and design.
   Instruction: Covers various issues of telecommunication systems including design, operation and planning; introduces basic signal switching theory, networking, marketing, maintenance and various aspects of planning. Methodology includes lecture, discussion, workshop, and laboratory exercises.
   Credit recommendation: In the lower division baccalaureate/associate degree category, 3 semester hours in Communications Technology; in the upper division baccalaureate category, 3 semester hours in Engineering Eco-

nomics; in the upper division baccalaureate category, 3 semester hours in Introduction to Telecommunications; and in the graduate category, 3 semester hours in Telecommunications Switching; in the upper division baccalaureate category, 3 semester hours in Telecommunication Management (2/86).

Principles of Digital Technology (DIG-TECH)
  Location: Bellcore TEC, Lisle, IL.
  Length: 36 hours (1 week).
  Dates: January 1984-Present.
  Objective: To provide an overview of digital transmission and digital switching as related to the telecommunications industry.
  Instruction: Covers pulse code modulation, digital transmission systems, and switch operations as applied to telecommunications. Methodology includes lecture, discussion, and laboratory exercises.
  Credit recommendation: In the lower division baccalaureate/associate degree category, 2 semester hours in Telecommunications Technology (2/86).

Principles of Digtal Transmission (DIGTRAN)
  Location: Lisle, IL and approved "suitcase" locations.
  Length: 68 hours (2 weeks).
  Dates: January 1988-Present.
  Objective: To familiarize students with the techniques of various digital transmission systems, and the advantages and disadvantages of each.
  Learning Outcome: Upon successful completion of this course, the student will be able to design a T1 system and specify the component elements; upgrade to a T1D system; and describe the operation of a lightwave digital transmission system.
  Instruction: Major topics covered in the course are the design of T-Carrier systems, Digital Local Loop systems, and several higher bit-rate systems, including Lightwave Transmission. Methods of instruction include lecture, case studies, and laboratory exercises.
  Credit recommendation: In the upper division baccalaureate category, 3 semester hours in Digital Communications Technology or Electrical Engineering Technology (4/88).

Principles of Noise Measurements and Mitigation (PNMM)
  Location: Bellcore TEC, Lisle, IL.
  Length: 86 hours (2 weeks).
  Dates: January 1984-Present.
  Objective: To provide the student with the basics of noise measurements and the various forms and methods of mitigating the effects of power line induction on telephone facilities.
  Instruction: Covers the methods used to identify noise transients; the means or devices used to suppress these transients and induced harmonic groups; and the effects of unwanted noise on the environment. AC/DC signals and relative spectrum, ISDN spectrum, and the basics of electricity and relative mathematics are covered. Methodology includes lecture, discussion, and laboratory exercises.
  Credit recommendation: In the lower division baccalaureate/associate degree category, 3 semester hours in Noise Rejection Techniques (2/86).

Principles of Telecommunications Environmental Hazards and Protection
  Location: Lisle, IL and other company locations.
  Length: 40 hours (1 week).
  Dates: June 1987-Present.
  Objective: To provide skills needed to maintain and protect power station telecommunications services from the undesired effects of high voltage and environmentally produced hazards.
  Instruction: Course covers an introduction to power stations, power system description, safety, telecommunications service to power stations, power station electromagnetic environment, ground grid testing methods, special protection devices and systems, engineering information, protection engineering of facilities, neutralizing transformer design, installation of protection devices, service to subscribers and administrative considerations.
  Credit recommendation: In the lower division baccalaureate/associate degree category, 1 semester hour in Electronic/Electrical Technology (9/87).

3B Processor - Operations and Data Base Management (3B-ODM)
  Location: Lisle, IL.
  Length: 75 hours (2 weeks).
  Dates: November 1988-Present.
  Objective: To provide the student with the ability to operate the AT&T 3B20 Duplex Processor/Equipment Configuration Data Base and clear basic system faults.
  Learning Outcome: Upon successful completion of this course, the student will be able to operate the 3B20 Duplex Processor, maintain the 3B20 Duplex Processor, and troubleshoot the 3B20 Duplex Processor.
  Instruction: Course covers 3B architecture, Equipment Configuration Data Base, maintenance, file system maintenance, and emergency action/recovery. Methodology includes lecture, discussion, and classroom and laboratory exercises.
  Credit recommendation: In the upper division baccalaureate category, 3 semester hours in Advanced Computer Architecture (4/89).

Product and Market Plans-Design and Implementation (PMP)
  Location: Morristown, NJ and approved "suitcase" locations.
  Length: 24 hours (3 days).
  Dates: October 1987-Present.

Objective: To provide the student with the skills to translate broad corporate strategies into effective action-oriented plans.

Learning Outcome: Upon successful completion of this course, the student will be able to understand the components of a business and marketing plan; understand strategic planning in diversified companies; and assist in the implementation of strategic plans in their operating company.

Instruction: Major topics covered in the course are developing a business and marketing plan, strategy audit, concept of strategy, planning concepts, processes, techniques, and format. Methods of instruction include lecture, discussion, case studies, and a simulated business plan.

Credit recommendation: In the upper division baccalaureate category, 1 semester hour in Marketing or Strategic Management (4/88).

Product Life Cycle Management (PLM)

Location: Morristown, NJ and approved "suitcase" locations.
Length: 24 hours (3 days).
Dates: July 1986-Present.
Objective: To provide the student with the theory and practical applications of developing and marketing a product plan for a service over its product life cycle in the telecommunications industry.

Learning Outcome: Upon successful completion of this course, the student will be able to identify and diagram the product life cycle stages and planning process; describe the types of information needed to successfully complete the annual product life cycle and the role of the product manager; and recognize and demonstrate the application of positioning and the management of strategic variables such as: price, promotion, and life cycle planning for the service offering.

Instruction: Major topics covered in the course are PLC management processes, management and stages, marketing strategies, breakeven analysis, elasticity of demand, and policy and strategy. Methods of instruction include lecture, discussion, projects, and case studies.

Credit recommendation: In the upper division baccalaureate category, 1 semester hour in General Business, Marketing, or Strategic Management (4/88).

Protocol Concepts-1 (PC-1)

Location: Lisle, IL and approved "suitcase" locations.
Length: 40 hours (1 week).
Dates: January 1987-Present.
Objective: To introduce the student to data communications protocols in the global environment of ISDN and Packet Switching networks.

Learning Outcome: Upon successful completion of this course, the student will be able to identify protocol concepts and standards, apply RS-232-C interface techniques using the breakout box; and analyze formats, coding, error control and synchronization procedures.

Instruction: Major topics covered in the course are introduction to protocols, standards organization, DCE/DTE interfaces, X.25 characteristics and operation; and public data network (PDN) to PDN. CCITT Recomendations X.75; environment, link and packet levels; multilink procedures, frame, control field, and flow control; and example call set up are also covered. Methods of instruction include lecture, discussion, and laboratory exercises.

Credit recommendation: In the lower division baccalaureate/associate degree category, 1 semester hour in Data Communications Technology or Telecommunications Technology (4/88).

Protocol Concepts-2 (PC-2)

Location: Lisle, IL and approved "suitcase" locations.
Length: 35 hours (1 week).
Dates: September 1987-Present.
Objective: To provide the student with the fundamental concepts of System Network Architecture (SNA), Local Area Networks (LAN), and Common Channel Signaling (CCS) systems.

Learning Outcome: Upon successful completion of this course, the student will be able to identify hardware and software components associated with SNA, LAN, Packet Switching and SS-7 networks; compare SNA, LAN, Packet Switched and SS-7 structures to the OSI/RM model; and construct packets, frames, and messages for data transmission.

Instruction: Major topics covered in the course are Packet-Network Protocols, System Network Architecture (SNA), Local Area Networks (LAN)/Metropolitan Area Networks (MANS), and Common Channel Signaling System Number 7. Methods of instruction include lecture, discussion, and laboratory exercises.

Credit recommendation: In the lower division baccalaureate/associate degree category, 1 semester hour in Data Communications Technology or Data Networks (4/88).

Quality Assurance for Product Selection, Acquisition and Maintenance (QAPSAM)

Location: Lisle, IL and approved "suitcase" locations.
Length: 32 hours (4 days).
Dates: January 1985-Present.
Objective: To teach the student quality assurance functions utilized for product selection, acquisition, and maintenance.

Learning Outcome: Upon successful completion of this course, the student will be able to identify job relevant quality assurance functions used in product selection, acquisition, and maintenance, and apply these functions to switching, interoffice, and distributing products.

Instruction: Major topics covered in the course are quality assurance, costs, benefits, buyer's responsibility, reliability, product selection, risk, quality control and standards, contract terms and conditions, sampling techniques, reporting and disposition. Methods of instruction include lectures, discussion, videotapes, exercises, case studies, and computer simulations.

Credit recommendation: In the upper division baccalaureate category, 2 semester hours in Operations Management or Production Management (4/88).

Quantitative Forecasting Methods
Location: Bellcore TEC, Lisle, IL.
Length: 88 hours (2 weeks).
Dates: May 1984-Present.
Objective: To give the student an extensive foundation in quantitative model building.
Instruction: Advanced data analysis techniques, both numerical and graphical, are emphasized throughout the course. The first week is devoted to econometric modeling techniques. Simple and multiple regression techniques are covered thoroughly in lecture and extensive computer-based casework. Special indicator variables, sequential modeling, and serial correlation correction methods are applied in casework. Time series analysis and modeling techniques are covered, as well as time series decomposition, seasonal decomposition techniques, time series modeling. Model identification, specification, estimation and evaluation procedures are applied in extensive casework sessions.
Credit recommendation: In the upper division baccalaureate category, 2 semester hours in Accounting or Finance (9/87).

Scientific Sampling I
Location: Bellcore TEC, Wakesha, WI.
Length: 53 hours (4 days).
Dates: August 1985-Present.
Objective: To provide the student with a working knowledge of basic sampling techniques. Selection of appropriate sampling methods will also be evaluated.
Instruction: Topics include simple random sampling techniques, ratio estimates, design and analysis, systematic and replicated sampling and equal probability two-stage sampling. Instructions are presented in a series of lectures, discussion, and class exercises.
Credit recommendation: In the upper division baccalaureate category, 1 semester hour in Statistics (9/87).

Scientific Sampling II
Location: Bellcore TEC, Wakesha, WI.
Length: 48 hours (4 days).
Dates: October 1986-Present.
Objective: To provide the student with a working understanding of more specialized scientific sampling techniques. Students will also become acquainted with values and variances and be able to apply techniques to remedy sampling errors in the sampling process.

Instruction: Course covers salvage techniques, estimation methods, design and analysis procedures, double sampling and misclassification. Also presented is the use of differential methods to formulate expressions for expected values and variances of complex estimation. Instruction is conducted through lecture, class discussion, and class exercises.
Credit recommendation: In the upper division baccalaureate category, 1 semester hour in Statistics (9/87).

Security Personnel Basic Training School (SPBTS)
Location: Bellcore TEC, Lisle, IL or approved suitcase locations.
Length: 72 hours (8 days).
Dates: April 1984-Present.
Objective: To provide the student with the necessary legal background and techniques for conducting an investigation from the beginning to the proper conclusion.
Learning Outcome: Upon successful completion of this course, the student will be able to conduct an investigation from the beginning to its proper conclusion with minimum supervision.
Instruction: Course covers the legal background and methods of conducting an investigation by note taking, interviewing, collection and preservation of evidence, statement taking, report writing, and testifying. Methodology includes lecture, discussion, and judicial moot court participation.
Credit recommendation: In the upper division baccalaureate category, 3 semester hours in Law Enforcement Administration, Pre-law, Security Management, or Sociology (4/89).

Software Fault Analysis
Location: Bellcore TEC, Lisle, IL and other company locations.
Length: 65 hours (1 week).
Dates: June 1987-Present.
Objective: To teach the student the use of the file system debugger, the generic access package, the core dump examiner, the interactive examining tool for address spectrums, and the interactive data base debugger as software troubleshooting tools.
Instruction: Course covers the file system debugger, generic access package, core dump examiner, interactive examining tool, interactive data base debugger. Also includes troubleshooting file systems, system error interrupts, system structures, software system outages, and system audit faults.
Credit recommendation: In the upper division baccalaureate category, 1 semester hour as a Computer Science elective (9/87).

Strategy Analysis for Finance and Marketing
Location: Bellcore TEC, Morristown, NJ.
Length: 24 hours (3 days).

Dates: January 1984-Present.

Objective: To focus on the coverage of finance and marketing and to address marketing/finance issues at both the level of managers of individual produce market business/service units and the overall corporate financial managers.

Instruction: The course covers a comprehensive marketing strategy; develops measurements of financial performance and applies them to a particular firm, discusses the impact of competitive marketing decisions on the income statement and balance sheet and provides a systematic approach to analyzing profitability and risk.

Credit recommendation: In the upper division baccalaureate category, 1 semester hour in an upper division business elective (6/86).

Switch Capacities (5ESS)
Location: Lisle, IL and approved "suitcase" locations.
Length: 32 hours (4½ days [previously 4 days])
Dates: September 1986-Present.
Objective: To provide the student with the ability to analyze selected components and determine 5ESS switch capacities.
Learning Outcome: Upon successful completion of this course, the student will be able to use a PC to enter data for selected components to determine 5ESS switch capacities and analyze and determine items that limit switch capacities.
Instruction: Major topics covered in the course are determination of component capacities, memory administration, and network access line capacities. Methods of instruction include lecture, discussion, and case studies.
Credit recommendation: In the lower division baccalaureate/associate degree category, 2 semester hours in Telecommunications Technology (4/88).

Telecommunications Switch Programming
Location: Bellcore TEC, Lisle, IL.
Length: 180 hours (4 weeks).
Dates: January 1984-Present.
Objective: To enable the student to interpret software documentation, interpret listing in assembler, EPL or DL1 languages, setting up utilities in a 1A system, and determining processor deviation and cause, and appropriate corrective action.
Instruction: Course covers 1A ESS switch documentation, 1A ESS switch language, ESS programming, interrupt analysis, main program structure, input/output processor organization, maintenance control organization, diagnostics and paging, saws audits, software sanity, disk administration, data unit administration, and PR usage.
Credit recommendation: In the lower division baccalaureate/associate degree category, 4 semester hours as a Telecommunications Programming elective (9/87).

Telephone Switch Peripheral Equipment Maintenance I
Location: Bellcore TEC, Lisle, IL.
Length: 136 hours (2 weeks).
Dates: January 1984-Present.
Objective: To enable the student to learn to identify peripheral interconnection schemes, construct diagnostic input messages, and analyze printouts for peripheral fault analysis.
Instruction: Course covers IE/IE ESS peripheral unit overview, parameters, central pulse distributor, signal distributor, scanner, network and controller, fabric, network failures, network analysis tools, trunk and line test panel, F-level interrupts, and ring and tone plant.
Credit recommendation: In the lower division baccalaureate/associate degree category, 3 semester hours in Telecommunications Equipment Maintenance (9/87).

Telephone Switch Peripheral Equipment Maintenance II
Location: Bellcore TEC, Lisle, IL.
Length: 136 hours (2 weeks).
Dates: January 1984-Present.
Objective: To enable the student to learn to use schematics, office drawings, system generated printouts, diagnostics, peripheral address information, appropriate test equipment and total frame outage recovery procedures to restore Remreed, MUT and CMT frames to correct operating parameters.
Instruction: Course covers an overview of the Remreed frame, including the input/output messages, Remreed controller operations, controller diagnostics, network orders, scanner operations, Remreed recovery procedures, MUT and CMT overview, MUT/CMT controller operations, controller diagnostics, and miniature scanner interrogate and readout patterns for MUT and CMT frames.
Credit recommendation: In the lower division baccalaureate/associate degree category, 3 semester hours in Telecommunications Equipment Maintenance (9/87).

Test Development
(Test Development Workshop)
Location: Lisle, IL. or approved "suitcase" location.
Length: 20 hours (2½ days).
Dates: January 1984-Present.
Objective: Test Development Workshop is a basic course in construction and use of classroom tests. The student identifies purpose of testing. Emphasis is placed on constructing various types of tests (i.e., performance, multiple choice, matching, true/false, completion, and short answer). The student learns how to administer, validate test items and develop scoring procedures.
Learning Outcome: This course provides instruction in the following objectives: identify the behavioral and administrative purposes for the various types of tests; identify the performance, conditions and standards of the task being tested; develop test plans that consider constraints

to determine simulation level of test. Construct test items of the following types: performance, multiple choice, matching, true/false, completion, and short answer. Plan for administration of different test types; validate test items, and develop scoring procedures.

Instruction: This course provides instruction in the planning and development of tests to be used in training. The emphasis is on the use and development of performance testing, but traditional modes of testing such as multiple choice and matching are also covered. The actual writing of tests is taught and practiced in a 6-8 hour self-paced module with administrator feedback on tests and practices.

Credit recommendation: In the upper division baccalaureate category, 1 semester hour in Education (9/86). NOTE: For students to receive credit for this course, they must have completed Introduction to Course Development Workshop or equivalent.

TOPS Facilities Management (TOPS-FAM)
  Location: Lisle, IL.
  Length: 130 hours (3 weeks).
  Dates: January 1989-Present.
  Objective: To provide the student with the detailed instruction and hands-on practice needed to maintain and manage DMS TOPS facilities.
  Learning Outcome: Upon successful completion of this course, the student will be able to update TOPS call processing, charging, billing, operational measurements and position translation; analyze system data, service results, and trouble reports to detect and correct TOPS machine and operator-reported problems; and provide technical assistance to Operator Service Center and other department personnel regarding TOPS facilities.
  Instruction: Course covers TOPS network and system architecture, use of table editor and map, TOPS signaling, trunking and hardware, TOPS call processing translations, TOPS operator call processing/queueing, TOPS rating and charging translations, TOPS AMA billing, TOPS operational measurements, and TOPS operator centralization and administration. Methodology includes lecture, discussion, and classroom and laboratory exercises.
  Credit recommendation: In the lower division baccalaureate/associate degree category, 4 semester hours in Telecommunication Equipment Maintenance (4/89).

Training Needs Analysis and Data Collection
(Data Collection and Analysis for Training)
  Location: Lisle, IL or approved "suitcase" location.
  Length: 40 hours (1 week).
  Dates: April 1986-Present.
  Objective: To prepare students to conduct front-end needs analysis, job study and follow-up evaluation phases of course development. Emphasis is placed on applying various analytical techniques, planning data collection and designing data collection instruments.
  Learning Outcome: Upon successful completion of this course, the student will be able to determine causes of performance deficiencies and recommend solutions; prepare a Deficiency Analysis Summary; document performance on a Task Detail and Skill/Knowledge Listing worksheet and flowcharts, using data from a practice interview; plan a data collection effort by describing: a. sample size, b. data sources, and c. data collection techniques. Design data collection instruments, including: a. questionnaire, observation checklist and structured interview.
  Instruction: Following a brief introduction, students immediately begin a case study which integrates skills and knowledge, obtained from the precourse assignment, to analyze deficient performance. Additional skills in applying various analytical techniques, as well as planning data collection and designing data collection instruments, are developed through role play and individual and group exercises. The knowledge and skills obtained through this workshop can be applied by the course developers when conducting front-end needs analysis, job study or follow-up evaluation phases of course development.
  Credit recommendation: In the upper division baccalaureate category, 3 semester hours in Education (9/86). NOTE: For students to receive credit Introduction to Course Development must have been taken as prerequisite or equivalent.

Transmission Theory and Applications (TTAA)
  Location: Bellcore TEC, Lisle, IL.
  Length: 148 hours (4 weeks).
  Dates: January 1984-Present.
  Objective: To provide students with the basic concepts of signals and time sequence relationships, electromagnetic waves and optics including signal transmission systems and communication systems.
  Instruction: Covers general telephony, design principles, metallic facilities, carrier facilities, radio transmission, and data transmission. Methodology includes lectures, discussion, and laboratory demonstrations.
  Credit recommendation: In the lower division baccalaureate/associate degree category, 4 semester hours in Electrical Engineering Principles and in the upper division baccalaureate category, 2 semester hours in Electrical Communications Principles (2/86).

UNIX® Shell Programming (UNIX SHL)
  Location: Bellcore TEC, Lisle, IL.
  Length: 36 hours-(5 days).
  Dates: January 1984-Present.
  Objective: Identify the attributes of the UNIX® shell, describe the result of lock UNIX® shell command line, and given a task, use the UNIX® shell, either as a command language or as an interactive programming language to accomplish the task.
  Learning Outcome: Upon successful completion of this

course, the student will be able to perform necessary commands to the UNIX® operating system.

Instruction: Items that are covered include: basics of the Shell, overview of the UNIX® operating system, parameters (a) positional; (b) keyword; (c) special; and (d) conditional. Pipes, quoting mechanisms, redirections, evaluation, debugging and troubleshooting; loops, signals, nesting, DOT command.

Credit recommendation: In the lower division baccalaureate/associate degree category, 1 semester hour in Operating Systems (9/86).

UNIX® Software For Managers (UNIX MGR)
Location: Bellcore TEC, Lisle, IL.
Length: 34 hours (5 days).
Dates: January 1984-Present.
Objective: Run a shell procedure, use a pipeline, redirect input/output commands, learn advanced UNIX® commands, learn memorandum movers (form commands) to produce reports, and use the VI editor.
Learning Outcome: Upon successful completion of this course, the student will know how to use three major productivity tools: (1) VIC Screen Editor, (2) Memorandum Macros, and (3) Shell Programming Overview.
Instruction: The course provides a deeper understanding of the shell, file system and three major productivity tools. The first tool, VI Screen Editor, gives increased power to easily create and modify most types of files. The second tool, Memorandum Macros enables the student to efficiently produce memos and reports. The third tool, Shell Programming, gives the student the capability to write shell procedures which automate daily tasks and complex command sequences. Throughout the course each individual has access to a terminal for extensive hands-on exercises.
Credit recommendation: In the lower division baccalaureate/associate degree category, 1 semester hour in Office Automation (9/86).

UNIX® System Administration (UNIX ADM)
Location: Bellcore TEC, Lisle, IL.
Length: 74 hours (2 weeks).
Dates: November 1984-Present.
Objective: Check and repair UNIX® file systems, add and remove users, generate a UNIX® system, boot a UNIX® system, make a crash record and perform preliminary analysis, set up a line printer spooling system and a UNIX® communicator network, tune a UNIX® system, and create and use system back-up procedures.
Learning Outcome: Upon successful completion of this course, the student will be able to modify, control and maintain the UNIX® operating system as a system administrate.
Instruction: The course includes: diagnostics and repair of UNIX® file systems; establishing and controlling user access; generating a UNIX® system after installation; booting a UNIX® system; making a crash record and performing preliminary analysis; setting up a line printer spooling system and a communication network between other UNIX® systems; tuning a UNIX® system, and creating and using system back-up procedures.
Credit recommendation: In the upper division baccalaureate category, 3 semester hours in Operating Systems (9/86).

UNIX® System Tools 1
Location: Lisle, IL.
Length: 25 hours (1 week).
Dates: March 1988-Present.
Objective: To provide the application and systems programmers, system analysts, managers and support specialists with an in-depth understanding of and ability to use System V programming commands.
Learning Outcome: Upon successful completion of this course, the student will be able to use the GREP, EGREP, and FGREP commands to locate a specified pattern in a file; use the FIND command to locate files using the appropriate options; use the TR, CUT, and PASTE commands and their appropriate options to edit a file; identify and use the capabilities of the STREAM EDITOR; identify the basic structure of AWK statements; and write own programs.
Instruction: Course covers the UNIX® system commands and utilities including: GREP—locate specific patterns in a file; FIND—locate files; TR, CUT, and PASTE—translate and delete characters, print specific fields or columns of a file, join files horizontally; SED-STREAM EDITOR—edit very large files and files with complicated editing functions; AWK—scan patterns and process text. Methodology includes lecture, discussion, classroom exercises, cse studies, role playing, problem-solving exercises, and homework assignments.
Credit recommendation: In the upper division baccalaureate category, 1 semester hour in UNIX® Operating System Applications (4/89).

UNIX® System Tools 2
Location: Lisle, IL.
Length: 24 hours (3 days).
Dates: March 1988-Present.
Objective: To provide the student with an understanding of and ability to use the UNIX® System V programming tools for managing software development projects.
Learning Outcome: Upon successful completion of this course, the student will be able to use the SCCS commands to administer changes made to files of text; use the MAKE command to maintain, update, and regenerate groups, use the AR command to maintain groups of files organized as a single archive file.
Instruction: Course covers the UNIX® system commands and utilities, including: SCCS-Source Code Control System—important SCCS terms and getting started

with SCCS commands, keywords and generating test files; MAKE-Source Information—important terms, basic operation of MAKE macros; and AR-Archiving Libraries—introduction to libraries, commands, for managing and accessing libraries, compiling and linking libraries, and updating with MAKE. Methodology includes lecture, discussion, and on-line computer exercises.

Credit recommendation: In the upper division baccalaureate category, 1 semester hour in UNIX® Operating System Applications (4/89).

Witness Preparation
Location: Bellcore TEC, Morristown, NJ.
Length: 40 hours (5 days).
Dates: January 1984-Present.
Objective: To provide an understanding of the issues and concerns associated with interstate and intrastate interLATA filings with skill training for presenting testimony by experiencing the rate case process.
Instruction: This seminar provides skills training in writing testimony which addresses interstate and intrastate interLATA issues; implementing the methodology for effective witnessing to each type of testimony; provides the opportunity to present the testimony in a simulated role playing experience of the state and federal regulatory process; describes cross examination tactics, and techniques for dealing with them; identifies the stress associated with formal regulatory presentations and reviews techniques for managing stress levels.
Credit recommendation: In the graduate degree category, 2 semester hours in Business Communications, Finance, Organizational Behavior, Business Law, or Management (6/86).

Witness and Marketing Support
(Formerly Witness Support)
Location: Bellcore TEC, Morristown, NJ.
Length: 32 hours (4 days).
Dates: January 1984-Present.
Objective: The purpose of the seminar is to provide the student with an expertise in the process of supporting witness.
Instruction: The course covers skill training for writing testimony, provides participants with the techniques for effective decision making, including a background in persuasive presentation of ideas and concepts. It concentrates on the management structure and process to ensure that all relevant issues are addressed. It also includes a simulation of a public hearing by a regulatory body.
Credit recommendation: In the graduate degree category, 2 semester hours in Business Communications (6/86).

Bell of Pennsylvania/Diamond State Telephone, A Bell Atlantic Company

See BELL ATLANTIC CORPORATION

Bergen County Police Academy

The Bergen County Police and Fire Academy is a 26-acre facility located in Mahwah, New Jersey. It was established in 1965 and is operated and maintained by the Division of Public Safety Education under the aegis of the Bergen County Executive form of government. A paid staff of 40 and a volunteer instructor staff of over 300 share their expertise through a full range of comprehensive police basic, in-service, specialized and refresher training courses provided to over 11,000 officers in northern New Jersey each year.

Basic Police Training is a 700-hour program conducted twice a year over an eighteen-week period for 200 newly appointed police officers who receive practical lecture, hands-on, and role playing instruction in accordance with the New Jersey Police Training Commission guidelines. The goal of this program is to prepare these officers for the ever-increasing demands placed on the law enforcement professional. Over 200 certified instructors along with audiovisual support and special resources and equipment have been incorporated into the program to facilitate an effective learning experience.

Source of official student records: Director, Division of Public Safety Education, Bergen County Police and Fire Academy, 281 Campgaw Road, Mahwah, NJ 07430.

Additional information about the courses: Thomas A. Edison State College, Program on Noncollegiate Sponsored Instruction, 101 West State Street, Trenton, NJ 08625.

Basic Police Training Course
Location: Mahwah, NJ.
Length: 710 hours (17 weeks).
Dates: October 1985-Present.
Objective: To provide the training (as mandated by New Jersey Police Training Act) to enable the trainee to meet the physical, psychological, legal, and social responsibilities of a police officer within the state of New Jersey.
Learning Outcome: Upon the successful completion of this course, the student will be able to: describe the history and development of enforcement, and the morals and ethics involved in law enforcement; understand the functional components of the criminal justice system and the New Jersey Correctional System; identify factors affecting vehicle operations (maintenance, accidents, etc.); describe and demonstrate the officer's role at an accident and in traffic law enforcement; be familiar with the basics of criminal law, covering topics such as: theft, forgery, disorderly

conduct, use of force, controlled dangerous substances, alcohol use, laws concerning juveniles, etc.; understand and apply the constitutional provisions relating to arrest, search, seizure, and evidence; pursue a criminal investigation, including: preliminary investigation, serious crimes against persons or property, courtroom testimony, etc.; assist with emergency medical care as a first responder or with crash injury management; understand the physical and stress problems that typically affect police officers. Students will also understand the "how, why, and what" of physical education.

Instruction: This course covers the 13 critical learning areas and the 714 specific objectives mandated by the state of New Jersey for the instruction of police officers. All instructors are qualified in their specific area of instruction, complete a methods of instruction course, and are certified to teach by the state, in addition to their normal academic qualifications. The program uses lecture, video, exercises and other methodologies designed to help students learn thoroughly and master all the objectives of the course. This course includes the history, development, and function of the police in a free society. It stresses the relationships among the various components of the criminal justice system. Students also study the philosophy, development, and application of the law of criminal procedure and its constitutional provisions. Included are issues of police authority relative to laws of arrest, search and seizure, and a review of relevant court decisions. Students also analyze the essential elements of investigation as a science of inquiry with an emphasis on the legal significance of evidence. Methods of searching for, collecting, preserving, and evaluating physical evidence are covered. Organizational investigative functions are also reviewed. In emergency medical care, students gain the knowledge and practical skills needed to respond to various situations including: burns, respiratory and cardiac problems, broken bones, etc. Students receive certificates in CPR and First Aid. In physical fitness, students develop and participate in an individualized exercise activity program. They cover a theoretical study of the nature of exercise and its effect on the human body and include topics of: health and fitness, cardiovascular functioning, strength, flexibility, stress, and motor fitness.

Credit recommendation: *Version 1:* In the lower division baccalaureate/associate degree category, 3 semester hours in Introduction to Criminal Justice, 3 semester hours in Criminal Law, 3 semesters hours in Law Enforcement electives, 3 semester hours in Emergency Medical Care, 1 semester hour in Body Conditioning, and 2 semester hours in Foundations of Physical Education, for a total of 15 semester hours (11/87) (4/88). NOTE: After initial site evaluation (11/87), additional data was submitted and a second site visit was arranged. Since all the material belongs to the same program, it has all been incorporated into one final report.

Blake Business School

Blake Business School is devoted entirely to the education and training of students for careers in business. The educational objectives of Blake are to equip its students with the technical skills and motivation to build successful careers and to instill in them a sense of pride and standards of excellence in their endeavors.

Blake Business School is licensed by the New York Education Department and accredited by the Association of Independent Colleges and Schools. Blake is also approved for a variety of financial aid programs, including New York Tuition Assistance Program, Pell Grants, and the Guaranteed Student Loan Program.

Blake's facilities not only provide an effective teaching environment, but enable the school to provide students with a practice intensive program that emphasizes the skills development that is essential to securing employment and high standards of performance. This approach tends to better prepare students for work thus easing their transition from school to the job.

Selection of the teaching staff is the responsibility of the Dean. The Dean reviews resumes and applications that have been submitted, schedules and conducts interviews with those whose educational and professional backgrounds warrant further consideration.

The procedures for revising courses and developing new ones are regulated by the New York State Education Department. As this is normally a two-year process, Blake continuously reviews its program to determine where revisions and new offerings are warranted. This is a coordinated effort by the administration and faculty to assess the strengths and weaknesses of existing courses, review new materials in its field of instruction and discuss the direction courses at Blake should take to remain current with the profession it is training students to enter. The results and recommendations of this process are submitted to the Director of Blake Business School for Final decision.

Source of official student records: Dean, Blake Business School, 145A Fourth Avenue, New York, New York 10003.

Additional information about the courses: Program on Noncollegiate Sponsored Instruction, The Center for Adult Learning and Educational Credentials, One Dupont Circle, Washington, D.C. 20036.

Accounting Essentials (SAE 101)
Location: Blake Business School, New York, NY.
Length: 80 hours (15 weeks).
Dates: July 1986-Present.
Objective: To provide the student with a basic knowledge of accounting systems and methodology.
Learning Outcome: Upon successful completion of this course, the student will (1) be able to use a 10-key calculator in computing accounting data; (2) have knowledge of

the recording procedures and be able to use income statements and balance sheets; and (3) be able to understand accounting methodologies for the preparation of organizational financial statements.

Instruction: Lectures and laboratories covering basic accounting, arithmetic processes; the use and preparation of accounting statements including journals, ledgers, income statement and balance sheets; the process of internal accounts, payrolls, and tax preparation; and specialized accounting books.

Credit recommendation: In the lower division baccalaureate/associate degree category, 3 semester hours in Secretarial Accounting (7/86).

Business Communications I (HBC 101)

Location: Blake Business School, New York, NY.
Length: 80 hours (15 weeks).
Dates: July 1986-Present.
Objective: To give the student a comprehensive review of the basic structure and use of English. Emphasis is placed on basic grammar and rules.
Learning Outcome: Upon successful completion of this course, the student will develop the ability to construct sentences and simple paragraphs for effective communications.
Instruction: Lectures, classroom exercises, and homework cover the essentials of grammar, sentence construction, and continuity of ideas in business writing.
Credit recommendation: In the lower division baccalaureate/associate degree category, 1 semester hour in Fundamentals of Writing (7/86).

Business Communications II (HBC 102)

Location: Blake Business School, New York, NY.
Length: 80 hours (15 weeks).
Dates: July 1986-Present.
Objective: To offer the student a review of basic structures and rules with an emphasis on written communication, correct techniques for composing sentences, paragraphs, and short compositions.
Learning Outcome: Upon successful completion of this course, the student will be able to (1) organize paragraphs in a coherent, sequenced fashion; (2) produce various types of paragraphs; and (3) develop multiparagraph essays.
Instruction: Lectures and exercises cover the planning, organizing, writing, revising, and understanding of sentences, paragraphs, and essays. Review of English grammar and punctuation and spelling improvement.
Credit recommendation: In the lower division baccalaureate/associate degree category, 2 semester hours in English Composition (7/86).

Business Communications III (HBC 103)

Location: Blake Business School, New York, NY.
Length: 80 hours (15 weeks).
Dates: July 1986-Present.
Objective: To provide the student with proficiency in writing business communications.
Learning Outcome: Upon successful completion of this course, the student will be able to (1) identify the components of good business writing; (2) apply good English usage skills to business communications; and (3) compose, organize, and write business letters, reports, and other types of business correspondence.
Instruction: Lectures and exercises cover correct grammatical usage, role of letters in business, communicating in the electronic office, structuring a good business letter, making the letter interesting and easy to read; making letters persuasive. Writing various types of letters (sales, general request, transmittal, information, customer "problem," general response), administrative and personnel communications, letters of application, job acceptance, resignation, writing reports, minutes, memoranda, and resumes.
Credit recommendation: In the lower division baccalaureate/associate degree category, 3 semester hours in Business Communications (7/86).

Business Law (BLW 101)

Location: Blake Business School, New York, NY.
Length: 80 hours (15 weeks).
Dates: July 1986-Present.
Objective: To provide the student with an understanding of the structure of law and its enforcement in the business world.
Learning Outcome: Upon successful completion of this course, the student will be able to define the nature of contracts, the concept of bailment, the major components of commercial paper transactions, and to explain the concepts of employer/employee relationships in different business structures.
Instruction: Lecture and discussion covering legal jurisdictions, court systems, contracts, sales contracts, bailments, commercial paper transactions, agencies, and employment contracts.
Credit recommendation: In the lower division baccalaureate/associate degree category, 3 semester hours in Introduction to Business Law (7/86).

Business Management (BM 101)

Location: Blake Business School, New York, NY.
Length: 80 hours (15 weeks).
Dates: July 1986-Present.
Objective: To provide the student with a broad knowledge of business systems, organization, and functions and their relationship to society.
Learning Outcome: Upon successful completion of this course, the student will be able to describe (1) the functions and purpose of business in the context of the legal and social environments; (2) basic elements in the structure and promotion of enterprise; and (3) the impact of

large corporations on society and the need for regulatory control.

Instruction: Intensive instructor/student interaction in lectures and laboratories covering broad elements of micro and macro comparative economics, private and public enterprise, and the management role of government, the logistics and strategies of firms under conditions of uncertainty, and the role of financial and management information systems in planning and decision making.

Credit recommendation: In the lower division baccalaureate/associate degree category, 3 semester hours in Introduction to Business (7/86).

Business Math I (HBM 101)
   Location: Blake Business School, New York, NY.
   Length: 80 hours (15 weeks).
   Dates: July 1986-Present.
   Objective: To provide the student with the fundamentals of business mathematics.
   Learning Outcome: Upon successful completion of this course, the student will understand whole numbers, fractions, and decimals and the calculus of business transactions, purchasing, payroll, and interest determination.
   Instruction: Lectures and problem solving covering whole numbers, fractions, decimals, percents, mathematics of buying and selling, payrolls, and simple interest calculations.
   Credit recommendation: In the lower division baccalaureate/associate degree category, 2 semester hours in Business Math (7/86).

Business Math II (HBM 102)
   Location: Blake Business School, New York, NY.
   Length: 80 hours (15 weeks).
   Dates: July 1986-Present.
   Objective: To provide the student with the ability to apply mathematical principles in business transactions.
   Learning Outcome: Upon successful completion of this course, the student will be able to calculate discounts and compound interest, mortgage points, and taxes, personal insurance rates and premiums; construct depreciation schedules under a variety of accepted methods and develop financial analysis statements.
   Instruction: Lecture and problem solving exercises covering bank discounts, compound interest, stocks and bonds, loans, real estate, insurance, and depreciation calculations.
   Credit recommendation: In the lower division baccalaureate/associate degree category, 3 semester hours in Business Math (7/86).

Computer Programming (BCP 101)
   Location: Blake Business School, New York, NY.
   Length: 80 hours (15 weeks).
   Dates: July 1986-Present.
   Objective: To provide the student with the ability to develop and code programs in BASIC that will solve business problems.
   Learning Outcome: Upon successful completion of this course, the student will be able to code and run business programs in BASIC.
   Instruction: Utilizing lectures and laboratory experience, the student learns the BASIC programming language including subtotals, looping, branching, Go-sub and return, Do-loops, tables, sort, random and sequential processing.
   Credit recommendation: In the lower division baccalaureate/associate degree category, 2 semester hours in BASIC Computer Programming (7/86).

Computer Theory (BCT 101)
   Location: Blake Business School, New York, NY.
   Length: 80 hours (15 weeks).
   Dates: July 1986-Present.
   Objective: To provide the student with an understanding of how computers function and of basic hardware and software used in business applications integrated and systems fashion.
   Learning Outcome: Upon successful completion of this course, the student will be able to describe the major components and functions of a computer. The student will have an understanding of operating systems and will be able to identify major languages and explain how programs work. The student will be able to describe systems implementation which includes hardware, software, personnel, planning, evaluation and implementations. The student will also understand the concepts of networking and computer communications.
   Instruction: Primarily through lecture the students learn the history of computers and how they work (e.g, basic concepts, the uses for, and capabilities of computers are covered, including computer communication and networking).
   Credit recommendation: In the lower division baccalaureate/associate degree category, 2 semester hours in Introduction to Data Processing (7/86). NOTE: Credit for this course is excluded if credit is awarded for Introduction to Data Processing (BDP 101).

Data Entry Applications (BDE 101)
   Location: Blake Business School, New York, NY.
   Length: 80 hours (15 weeks).
   Dates: July 1986-Present.
   Objective: To develop the ability to perform machine operations and use computer business application packages.
   Learning Outcome: Upon successful completion of this course, the student will be familiar with computer applications in general and will utilize specific application packages including DBase II; Lotus 1, 2, 3; Multiplan; and Visicalc.
   Instruction: Utilizing lecture and laboratory experi-

ence, the student learns to operate microcomputers and runs business programs for inventory, sales, accounts receivable and payable, bank reconciliation, payroll and general ledgers. Also included is a review of COBOL and BASIC languages.

Credit recommendation: In the lower division baccalaureate/associate degree category, 3 semester hours in Microcomputer Operations (7/86).

Economics (BEC 101)
Location: Blake Business School, New York, NY.
Length: 80 hours (15 weeks).
Dates: July 1986-Present.
Objective: To provide the student with a survey of micro- and macroeconomics.
Learning Outcome: Upon successful completion of this course, the student will have a broad knowledge of the operation of the U.S. economic system to include: (1) pricing and its relation to demand and supply; (2) the role of money; (3) production and employment; (4) methods of economic analysis; (5) bases for the development of economic policies; and (6) relationship to international economics.
Instruction: Lectures covering micro- and macroeconomics, economic analysis scarcity, competition, pricing, antitrust loans, the characteristics of money, price indexing, inflation, tax, and trade policies.
Credit recommendation: In the lower division baccalaureate/associate degree category, 3 semester hours in Introduction to Economics (7/86).

Electronic Office Procedures (102)
Location: Blake Business School, New York, NY.
Length: 80 hours (15 weeks).
Dates: April 1988-Present.
Objective: To provide the student with a comprehensive understanding of how to manage a modern-day office.
Learning Outcome: Upon successful completion of this course, the student will be able to function in a contemporary office setting using electronic equipment and processing information requisite for the successful completion of responsibilities associated with such activities as mail distribution, meeting planning, and payroll management.
Instruction: Course covers career planning and goal setting, output and reprographics, manual and electronic distribution and communication methods, telephone technology and techniques, time management and work organization, meeting planning, basic principles of mathematics and general accounting, payroll management, basic supervisory skills and techniques, and the management of automated office systems. Methodology includes lecture, discussion, and practical exercises.
Credit recommendation: In the lower division baccalaureate/associate degree category, 3 semester hours in Automated Office Management or Secretarial Science (4/89).

Human Relations (HHR 101)
Location: Blake Business School, New York, NY.
Length: 80 hours (15 weeks).
Dates: July 1986-Present.
Objective: To introduce the student to broad factors involving organizational behavior and personal development.
Learning Outcome: Upon successful completion of this course, the student will have a broad understanding of organizational operations as influenced by different management styles. The student will have a knowledge of factors associated with personal development.
Instruction: Intensive instructor/student interaction to provide for a broad survey of human relations in organizations, strategies for improving employee relations, motivational instrument, personal development requirements, and effective supervision.
Credit recommendation: In the lower division baccalaureate/associate degree category, 3 semester hours in Survey of Human Resource Management (7/86).

Introduction to Data Processing (BDP 101)
Location: Blake Business School, New York, NY.
Length: 80 hours (15 weeks).
Dates: July 1986-Present.
Objective: To provide the student with a fundamental understanding of data processing and problem-solving. The student will become familiar with COBOL and BASIC programming languages.
Learning Outcome: Upon successful completion of this course, the student will be able to flowchart a problem and identify the data processing functions required.
Instruction: Through lectures, the student learns the history and components of data processing, automated data processing and various systems and programs. The student is also given information on COBOL programming and flowcharts, and is required to write a BASIC program.
Credit recommendation: In the lower division baccalaureate/associate degree category, 2 semester hours in Introduction to Business Data Processing (7/86). NOTE: Credit for this course is excluded if student has credit for Computer Theory (BCT 101).

Microcomputer Operation: Word Processing Applications
Location: Blake Business School, New York, NY.
Length: 80 hours (15 weeks).
Dates: April 1988-Present.
Objective: To introduce the student to word processing on microcomputers.
Learning Outcome: Upon successful completion of this course, the student will be able to understand basic principles of word and information processing; and input, format, revise, and output documents.
Instruction: Course introduces the student to correct

terminology and machine operations associated with the general use of microcomputers for word processing. Methodology includes lecture, discussion, and hands-on exercises.

Credit recommendation: In the lower division baccalaureate/associate degree category, 3 semester hours in Introduction to Word Processing (4/89).

Office Procedures (SOP 101)
   Location: Blake Business School, New York, NY.
   Length: 80 hours (15 weeks).
   Dates: July 1986-Present.
   Objective: To prepare the student to perform the procedures necessary to function effectively and efficiently in today's office.
   Learning Outcome: Upon successful completion of this course, the student will develop an understanding of acceptable skills, attitudes, and personal traits required in the business environment. The student will be able to describe, understand, and perform the basic duties and responsibilities of a secretary. Student will demonstrate skill in processing information and in handling oral and written communications and filing systems. Student will develop successful job-seeking techniques.
   Instruction: Personal and professional characteristics of the professional secretary, organization of the office, handling oral and written communications, planning work and setting priorities, using different types of filing systems, keeping financial records, making travel arrangements, assisting with meetings, understanding the role of the supervisor, development of job-seeking techniques (resume, application, interview, job sources, professional growth); discussion, lecture, and simulation are used.
   Credit recommendation: In the lower division baccalaureate/associate degree category, 3 semester hours in Secretarial Science (7/86).

Records Management (BRM 101)
   Location: Blake Business School, New York, NY.
   Length: 80 hours (15 weeks).
   Dates: July 1986-December 1988.
   Objective: To provide the student with an understanding of the origins of information, the document cycle, and various methods of storage from manual to advanced electronic data files.
   Learning Outcome: Upon successful completion of this course, the student will understand the nature of records management and major filing methods for storage and retrieval of information.
   Instruction: Instruction and laboratory work covering alphabetical, subject, and geographic methods of record storage, storing cycles, retrieval cycles, and the organization and operation of a records management system.
   Credit recommendation: In the lower division baccalaureate/associate degree category, 3 semester hours in Records Management (7/86).

Shorthand I (SSH 101)
   Location: Blake Business School, New York, NY.
   Length: 80 hours (15 weeks).
   Dates: July 1986-Present.
   Objective: To provide the student with an understanding of the principles of Alpha Hand notetaking, and the development of reading and writing skills using this system.
   Learning Outcome: Upon successful completion of this course, the student will be able to identify and write basic Alpha letters, combinations, endings, prefixes, and suffixes; master Alpha Bit Speed Builders; identify and write typical letter combinations; write phrases, sentences, and paragraphs with good structure; read notes back fluently; develop dictation speeds from 50 to 70 words per minute; and transcribe letters and memos with 95 percent accuracy.
   Instruction: Introduction to Alpha Hand theory; English usage and rules of punctuation; practice in commonly used words and phrases; city and state abbreviations; increased vocabulary and sentence structure; building of reading and writing skills, and different letter styles and letter placement.
   Credit recommendation: In the lower division baccalaureate/associate degree category, 3 semester hours in Secretarial Science (7/86).

Shorthand II (SSH 102)
   Location: Blake Business School, New York, NY.
   Length: 80 hours (15 weeks).
   Dates: July 1986-Present.
   Objective: To provide the student with a review of Alpha Hand theory; to enable the student to take dictation at progressively higher rates of speed and transcribe accurately from notes.
   Learning Outcome: Upon successful completion of this course, the student will have dictation speeds from 60 to 80 words per minute with 95 percent accuracy in transcriptions.
   Instruction: Introduction to transcription techniques; vocabulary building and sentence structure; proofreading exercises; sustained dictation at varying rates of speed; grammar, punctuation, paragraphing, and spelling review; instruction and practice in skills and knowledge essential to sustained shorthand writing; review of Alpha Hand principles.
   Credit recommendation: In the lower division baccalaureate/associate degree category, 2 semester hours in Secretarial Science (7/86).

Shorthand III (SSH 103)
   Location: Blake Business School, New York, NY.
   Length: 80 hours (15 weeks).
   Dates: July 1986-Present.
   Objective: To enable the student to combine Alpha Hand, English, and typewriting abilities to produce maila-

ble transcripts.

Learning Outcome: Upon successful completion of this course, the student will have dictation speeds from 70 to 90 words per minute and transcription of business letters with 95 percent accuracy. Development of effective transcription techniques.

Instruction: Reading and writing familiar material; new vocabulary and theory review; mastery of reference books and manuals; sustained dictation at progressively higher rates of speed; office-style dictation; grammar, punctuation, sentence structure; use of carbons and envelopes; transcription techniques, including correction and proofreading.

Credit recommendation: In the lower division baccalaureate/associate degree category, 2 semester hours in Secretarial Science (7/86).

Shorthand IV (SSH 104)

Location: Blake Business School, New York, NY.
Length: 80 hours (15 weeks).
Dates: October 1986-Present.
Objective: To enable the student to improve and develop additional skills in sustained dictation and transcription, using the Alpha Hand system, and to master techniques of machine transcription.

Learning Outcome: Upon successful completion of this course, the student will have dictation speeds from 90 to 110 words per minute and transcription of business correspondence with 95 percent accuracy. Development of good listening skills; proficiency in transcribing numbers; establishment of good working habits and development of the ability to use transcribing equipment effectively.

Instruction: Emphasis on dictation and transcription from notes and machine transcribers at progressively faster rates of speed. English usage and rules of punctuation, expanded business vocabulary, effective use of reference books and office manuals, practice in commonly used words and phrases, expansion of transcription skills to include written communication forms such as memorandum reports, manuscripts, articles, itineraries, and two-page letters. Use of shortcut dictation and proofreading techniques; office-style dictation.

Credit recommendation: In the lower division baccalaureate/associate degree category, 2 semester hours in Secretarial Science (7/86).

Typing I (ST 101)

Location: Blake Business School, New York, NY.
Length: 80 hours (15 weeks).
Dates: July 1986-Present.
Objective: To enable the student to develop basic typewriting techniques and mastery of the keyboard.

Learning Outcome: Upon successful completion of this course, the student will know the keyboard by touch; be able to enter data attractively on a page; arrange and type letters, envelopes, tables, and simple reports; and type a minimum of 25 words per minute on a three-minute timing with a five-error limit. (Previous requirement was 30 words per minute.)

Instruction: Proper techniques for operation and care of typewriter, touch control of the keyboard, speed and accuracy drills, learning of letter and number reaches, centering vertically and horizontally, rough drafts and proofreader's symbols, correct preparation of personal and business letters, tables, reports, interoffice memos, and envelopes.

Credit recommendation: In the lower division baccalaureate/associate category, 2 semester hours in Typewriting (7/86).

Typing II (ST 102)

Location: Blake Business School, New York, NY.
Length: 80 hours (15 weeks).
Dates: July 1986-Present.
Objective: To enable the student to refine basic typewriting techniques and to develop higher speed and greater proficiency in typing business documents.

Learning Outcome: Upon successful completion of this course, the student will be able to type a minimum of 40 words per minute on a five-minute timing with less than three errors and to arrange and type business correspondence in correct formats. (Previous minimum was 35 words per minute.)

Instruction: Review of proper techniques for operation of typewriter, speed and accuracy building, formatting and typing of letters, manuscripts, tabulations, memos, rough drafts, and statistical material. Proofreading and correction techniques.

Credit recommendation: In the lower division baccalaureate/associate degree category, 2 semester hours in Typewriting (7/86).

Typing III (ST 103)

Location: Blake Business School, New York, NY.
Length: 80 hours (15 weeks).
Dates: July 1986-Present.
Objective: To enable the student to perfect basic typewriting techniques, and to build speed, accuracy and endurance. To enable the student to type a wide variety of business communications effectively and correctly.

Learning Outcome: Upon successful completion of this course, the student will be able to do straight copy speed at a minimum of 40 words per minute on a five-minute timing with less than three errors, and compose, edit, and correct copy at the typewriter.

Instruction: Proper techniques for error analysis and correction, speed and accuracy building, practice and instruction in typing tables, statistical copy, vertical and horizontal rulings, rough drafts, different styles of letters, business forms, and manuscripts. Practice in typing employment communications and composing follow-up letters.

Credit recommendation: In the lower division baccalaureate/associate degree category, 2 semester hours in Typewriting (7/86).

Typing IV (ST 104)
Location: Blake Business School, New York, NY.
Length: 80 hours (15 weeks).
Dates: July 1986-Present.
Objective: To enable the student to effectively and efficiently apply typewriting skills to a variety of projects typical in an office environment.
Learning Outcome: Upon successful completion of this course, the student will be able to do straight copy speed at a minimum of 55 words per minute on a five-minute timing with less than three errors, read and follow directions accurately and efficiently, and prepare and evaluate typed production problems.
Instruction: Practice in analyzing and correcting errors, remediation practice, speed and accuracy building, correct use of reference manuals, timed production problems in mailable formats, typing business documents in administrative, financial, executive, sales, purchasing, and government offices, rough drafts and memos, use of reprographic materials, and review of language arts skills.
Credit recommendation: In the lower division baccalaureate/associate degree category, 2 semester hours in Typewriting (7/86).

Word Processing I (SWP 101)
Location: Blake Business School, New York, NY.
Length: 80 hours (15 weeks).
Dates: July 1986-Present.
Objective: To introduce the student to the concepts of the traditional office and the effect of office automation; the concept of information processing, the components of the electronic office, and the application of technology to business.
Learning Outcome: Upon successful completion of this course, the student will understand the need for information processing and identify the components of the electronic office and acquire an understanding of the total operating system in a changing office environment of word/information processing.
Instruction: Sixty hours of lecture and demonstration, twenty hours of laboratory practice, with intensive instructor/student interaction covering the effect of automation, impact of voice processing, machine dictation and transcription, components of documenting and storage, electronic communication, components of word/information processing workstation, methods of storing and retrieving information, types of peripheral devices for printing information.
Credit recommendation: In the lower division/baccalaureate/associate degree category, 3 semester hours in Introduction to Word/Information Processing (7/86).

Word Processing II Basic Function (SWP 102)
Location: Blake Business School, New York, NY.
Length: 80 hours (15 weeks).
Dates: July 1986-Present.
Objective: To introduce the student to applications for the word processor stressing keyboard techniques and basic machine operations.
Learning Outcome: Upon successful completion of this course, the student will be able to input, format, revise, and print a document.
Instruction: Twenty hours of lecture and demonstration and sixty hours of hands-on applications, with intensive instructor/student interaction covering non-display word processor, basic operations, special functions, document inputting, letters, tables, and reports.
Credit recommendation: In the lower division baccalaureate/associate degree category, 2 semester hours in Word Processing Applications (7/86).

Word Processing III Application (SWP 103)
Location: Blake Business School, New York, NY.
Length: 80 hours (15 weeks).
Dates: July 1986-Present.
Objective: To provide the student with a review of the basic functions and a knowledge of advanced functions in word processing.
Learning Outcome: Upon successful completion of this course, the student will be able to input multipage documents, and revise manually and automatically; demonstrate pagination; merge, copy files and disks; and demonstrate print changes.
Instruction: Twenty hours of lecture and demonstration and sixty hours of hands-on application with intensive instructor/student interaction covering basic and advanced functions including pagination, merging, copy and print functions, and preparation of special documents.
Credit recommendation: In the lower division baccalaureate/associate degree category, 2 semester hours in Word Processing Applications (7/86).

Word Processing IV (SWP 104)
Location: Blake Business School, New York, NY.
Length: 80 hours (15 weeks).
Dates: July 1986-Present.
Objective: To provide the student with the ability to use transcription equipment with the word processor.
Learning Outcome: Upon successful completion of this course, the student will understand the proper use of dictation/transcription equipment and procedures and the techniques for production of mailable copy documents on the word processors.
Instruction: Twenty hours of lecture and demonstration and sixty hours of applications using Wang systems, covering document typing, letters, manuscripts, merge operations, reports, and statistics.
Credit recommendation: In the lower division bac-

calaureate/associate degree category, 2 semester hours in Word Processing Transcription and Applications (7/86).

Word Processing Applications: Wang
  Location: Blake Business School, New York, NY.
  Length: 80 hours (15 weeks).
  Dates: April 1988-Present.
  Objective: To give the student an understanding of the use and application of the Wang word processing system.
  Learning Outcome: Upon successful completion of this course, the student will be able to use basic and advanced functions of the Wang word processing system.
  Instruction: Course covers commands, functions, and techniques required to apply the Wang word processing system in an office setting. Methodology includes hands-on or practical exercises and discussion.
  Credit recommendation: In the lower division baccalaureate/associate degree category, 2 semester hours in Word Processing Applications (4/89).

Word Processing Applications: Wordstar, Display Write 4, WordPerfect, Multimate
  Location: Blake Business School, New York, NY.
  Length: 80 hours (15 weeks).
  Dates: April 1988-Present.
  Objective: To provide the student with the ability to use a variety of word processing software packages.
  Learning Outcome: Upon successful completion of this course, the student will be able to load a program, enter and edit text, paginate and print documents using Wordstar, Display Write 4, WordPerfect, and Multimate.
  Instruction: Course covers the commands, functions, and techniques required to apply Wordstar, Display Write 4, WordPerfect, and Multimate in an office setting. Methodology includes hands-on or practical exercises and discussion.
  Credit recommendation: In the lower division baccalaureate/associate degree category, 2 semester hours in Word Processing Applications (4/89).

Board of Engineers for Rivers and Harbors - U.S. Army Corps of Engineers

The Water Resources Planning Associates Program has been designed as an eleven-month internship to provide additional training for selected employees of the U.S. Army Corps of Engineers. It is conducted annually by the Board of Engineers for Rivers and Harbors at Fort Belvoir, Virginia.

The emphasis of the Program is on applied water resources policy and planning techniques, methods, and decision making.

The Planning Associate receives on-the-job and specialized training in the laws, policies, criteria, and procedures that apply to the U.S. Army Corps of Engineers' Civil Works planning, and participates in seminars on specialized aspects of planning. Numerous opportunities are provided for in-depth discussions with leaders in the water resources field from governmental agencies, private organizations, and educational institutions.

Senior planners from the Board staff and the Headquarters, U.S. Army Corps of Engineers provide most of the classroom instruction. The curriculum is supplemented with intensive short-term courses and field investigations. Experts from outside the organization are chosen by background, personal knowledge of qualifications, and recommendations of the professional staff.

The student-selection process each year is aimed at assembling students with various backgrounds in scientific training. The backgrounds of the students, who work in teams, facilitate working with interdisciplinary problems. Criteria for admission include a bachelor's degree, four years of experience with the U.S. Army Corps of Engineers, two of which are in water resources planning, and recommendation from supervisors.

Source of official student records: Chief, Education Policy Division, Board of Engineers for Rivers and Harbors, Kingman Building, Fort Belvoir, Virginia 22060.

Additional information about the courses: Program on Noncollegiate Sponsored Instruction, The Center for Adult Learning and Educational Credentials, American Council on Education, One Dupont Circle, Washington, D.C. 20036.

Water Resources Planning Associates Program
  Location: Fort Belvoir, VA.
  Length: *Version 1:* 10½ months; *Version 2:* 11 months (including approximately 45 days of field trips and 2 weeks teaching).
  Dates: *Version 1:* January 1983-May 1987; *Version 2:* June 1987-Present.
  Objective: The objective of the program is to develop generalist planners who will manage complex planning studies and who will be capable of integrating future needs and available resources into viable plans which are technically, socially, and politically acceptable.
  Learning Outcome: Upon successful completion of this course, the student will be able to manage a complex water resources planning study including environmental, engineering, and economic aspects, in coordination with local municipalities, other governmental agents, and outside interests; and to become knowledgeable in legislative processes.
  Instruction: Lectures, discussions, field trips, case studies, and practice teaching on the fundamentals of hydrology, economics, environmental science, decision-making, problem-solving, management by objectives, and policy and planning procedures as they relate to current water

resources planning problems. Instruction methods are geared to developing attitudes and skills necessary for the generalist-water resources planner operating in a team leader mode.

Credit recommendation: *Version 1:* In the upper division baccalaureate category, 3 semester hours in Engineering Economics and in the upper division baccalaureate or graduate category, 8 semester hours in Applied Environmental Sciences, or in the upper division baccalaureate category, 3 semester hours in Engineering Economics and in the upper division baccalaureate or graduate category, 9 semester hours in Water Resources Planning (2/83). NOTE: Graduate credit given should be applicable only at the Master's degree level. *Version 2:* In the graduate category, 3 semester hours in Engineering Economics and in the graduate category, 9 semester hours in Water Resources Planning, and in the graduate category, 3 semester hours in Advanced Management Skills (11/88). NOTE: This course has been reevaluated and continues to meet requirements for credit recommendations.

Brick Computer Science Institute

Brick Computer Science Institute (BSCI) was founded in 1970 for the purpose of providing quality education in the principles of computer hardware, software, and high technology areas. The goal of BCSI is to provide the best instruction in the latest state of the art, preparing students for the complexities of the data processing industry. BCSI utilizes a distributed data processing network of remote and local computer systems to provide students with exposure to multiple programming environment.

BCSI is accredited by the National Association of Trade and Technical Schools and is a member of the Private Career Schools Association of New Jersey and is licensed by the Department of Education, Division of Vocational and Technical Careers.

Source of official student records: Dean of Faculty, Brick Computer Science Institute, 525 Route 70, Brick, New Jersey 08723.

Additional information about the courses: Program on Noncollegiate Sponsored Instruction, Thomas A. Edison State College, 101 West State Street, CN 545, Trenton, New Jersey 08625.

Active Circuits and Lab (953)
  Location: Brick, NJ.
  Length: 135 hours (27 days).
  Dates: January 1976-Present.
  Objective: To familiarize students with semiconductor devices and their applications.
  Instruction: This course introduces the student to a variety of semiconductor devices and their applications. Some devices are diodes (including zeners, etc.), transistors (BJT, FET and phototransistors), thyristors, and operational amplifiers. Theory and lab also cover regulated and nonregulated power supplies. Basic circuit analysis, troubleshooting techniques and applications to realistic situations are stressed.
  Credit recommendation: In the lower division baccalaureate/associate degree category, 4 semester hours in Introduction to Solid State Devices (5/84).

Advanced ANSI COBOL (301.2)
  Location: Brick, NJ.
  Length: 70 hours (14 days).
  Dates: January 1980-Present.
  Objective: To teach students advanced methods and techniques of COBOL programming.
  Instruction: This course builds upon the concepts in Introduction to ANSI COBOL (301.1). There is continued work on application programming, testing and debugging, file handling, documentation, and screen formatting. The course also includes table handling, editing, sequential and ISAM file updating and sort/merge techniques.
  Credit recommendation: In the lower division baccalaureate/associate degree category, 4 semester hours in COBOL II (5/84).

Advanced RPG II (205.2)
  Location: Brick, NJ.
  Length: 70 hours (14 days).
  Dates: January 1980-Present.
  Objective: To instruct students in the advanced concepts and techniques of the RPG II programming language.
  Instruction: Project and program requirements will progress with additional concepts such as multiple record tapes, array processing, table processing, matching record and sequential access methods. Project portfolios will be developed which demonstrate complete program documentation techniques.
  Credit recommendation: In the lower division baccalaureate/associate degree category, 3 semester hours in Advanced RPG II (5/84).

Assembler Programming (308)
  Location: Brick, NJ.
  Length: 75 hours (15 days).
  Dates: July 1982-Present.
  Objective: To present students with the basic techniques to write Assembler Programs in Series 1 Assembler.
  Instruction: Course covers an introduction to IBM Series 1 Assembler concepts; register management, loops, and subroutines. Actual programs will be written to access a file, perform mathematical calculations, and generate reports.
  Credit recommendation: In the lower division bac-

calaureate/associate degree category, 4 semester hours in Assembler Language (5/84).

Basic Electronics I (952.1)
Location: Brick, NJ.
Length: 80 hours (17 days).
Dates: January 1976-Present.
Objective: To familiarize the student with the fundamentals of electricity and electronics, related to the nature of electricity and D.C. circuit analysis.
Instruction: This course covers the fundamentals of electricity and electronics. Topics included are nature of electricity, D.C. circuits, Kirchoff's Laws, networks, and meters.
Credit recommendation: In the lower division baccalaureate/associate degree category, 3 semester hours in Electronics I (D.C. Circuits) (5/84).

Basic Electronics II (952.2)
Location: Brick, NJ.
Length: 85 hours (17 days).
Dates: January 1976-Present.
Objective: To familiarize students with fundamentals of electricity related to A.C. circuit analysis.
Instruction: Course covers A.C. signal generation. Topics in the course include reactance, complex circuit analysis, time constants, filters, resonance, and an introduction to test equipment care and use.
Credit recommendation: In the lower division baccalaureate/associate degree category, 3 semester hours in Electronics II (A.C. Circuits) (5/84).

Basic Mathematics for Electronics (951)
Location: Brick, NJ.
Length: 60 hours (12 days).
Dates: January 1979-Present.
Objective: To train students in basic math, algebra and trigonometry skills.
Instruction: The arithmetic processes are reviewed with positive and negative decimal numbers and fractions. The lessons progress through the basic aspects of algebra, trigonometry, and logarithmic operations.
Credit recommendation: In the lower division baccalaureate/associate degree category, 3 semester hours in Basic Mathematics (5/84).

Basic Programming (945)
Location: Brick, NJ.
Length: 45 hours (9 days).
Dates: January 1976-Present.
Objective: To give students a clear understanding of the fundamentals of programming in the BASIC language.
Instruction: This course presents the fundamentals of programming in the BASIC language. Topics in the course are flowcharting, coding, and interactive programming. Specific items covered are BASIC control statements, loops and arrays, library function, DEF statements, input printing, and string data.
Credit recommendation: In the lower division baccalaureate/associate degree category, 2 semester hours in BASIC Programming (5/84).

CICS/VS (307)
Location: Brick, NJ.
Length: 60 hours (12 days).
Dates: January 1981-Present.
Objective: To teach students to code, debug, and execute CICS/VS applications and to write macro level programs for screen formatting.
Instruction: The course provides an application programmer with a COBOL background the necessary knowledge to code, debug, and execute a command level CICS/VS application. In the course, a student writes macro level programs to format a screen which will be used to interactively update a VSAM file. Student will also be using an IBM Series/1 as a remote job entry terminal online to an IBM 4331 mainframe.
Credit recommendation: In the upper division baccalaureate or lower division baccalaureate/associate degree category, 2 semester hours in CICS/VS (5/84).

EDP Applications and Systems (305)
Location: Brick, NJ.
Length: 60 hours (12 days).
Dates: January 1980-Present.
Objective: To instruct students in Business Systems concepts such as system concepts, components of a business computer system, file design, payroll, accounts payable, invoicing, accounts receivable, inventory, etc.
Instruction: This course covers business applications and systems, the techniques of systems analysis, computer programming, and systems documentation. Emphasis is placed on basic accounting principles.
Credit recommendation: In the lower division baccalaureate/associate degree category, 3 semester hours in Introduction to Business Systems (5/84).

IBM Series/1 Disk and Magnetic Tape System with Telecommunications (214)
Location: Brick, NJ.
Length: 175 hours (14 weeks).
Dates: January 1982-Present.
Objective: To familiarize students with the control and operations of the IBM Series/1 minicomputer.
Instruction: Course provides complete coverage of the control, operations, and "operators maintenance" aspects of a functioning Series/1 minicomputer. Features and functions applicable to all Series/1 environments and the use of JCL in these environments are also covered.
Credit recommendation: In the vocational certificate category, 4 semester hours or in the lower division baccalaureate/associate degree category, 2 semester hours in

IBM Series/1 (5/84).

Introduction to ANSI COBOL (301.1)
Location: Brick, NJ.
Length: 90 hours (18 days).
Dates: January 1980-Present.
Objective: To instruct students in basic methods and techniques of COBOL programming.
Instruction: This course provides the basic concepts of COBOL programming so that the student can solve a wide variety of business programming problems using structured techniques. Mathematical functions, computing statements, headings, final totals, comparing, testing and debugging application programs, documentation, and control breaks are covered in this course.
Credit recommendation: In the lower division baccalaureate/associate degree category, 4 semester hours in COBOL I (5/85).

Introduction to Data Processing (941)
Location: Brick, NJ.
Length: 30 hours (6 days).
Dates: January 1980-Present.
Objective: To familiarize students with common fundamental concepts which are found in all data processing systems.
Instruction: Course covers all data processing systems that have certain common fundamental concepts and operational principles. The modules cover storage devices, central processing unit, input/output devices, teleprocessing, stored program concepts, programming language techniques, operating system, data security and integrity.
Credit recommendation: In the lower division baccalaureate/associate degree category, 2 semester hours in Introduction to Data Processing (5/84).

Micro Computer Hardware and Software with Lab (956)
Location: Brick, NJ.
Length: 125 hours (25 days).
Dates: January 1980-Present.
Objective: To familiarize students with the operational aspects of a microcomputer and the application of software concepts.
Instruction: Through the actual construction of a Z-80 Microprocessor, the student will become familiar with the microprocessor, Z-80 firmware and hardware, such as random access memory, read only memory, counter time circuit, serial input-output circuits, address buss, data buss, and Z-80 interrupts. Also presented is digital asynchronous communications and debugging of a Z-80 system.
Credit recommendation: In the lower division baccalaureate/associate degree category, 3 semester hours in Microcomputer Hardware and 3 semester hours in Microcomputer Software (5/84).

Micro Electronics with Lab (954)
Location: Brick, NJ.
Length: 140 hours (28 days).
Dates: January 1980-Present.
Objective: To familiarize students with digital logic circuiting and various data codes.
Instruction: This course teaches number systems, Boolean algebra, codes, basic computer circuiting, and the use of test equipment. The three numbering systems taught are binary, octal, and hexadecimal. Boolean algebra contains AND, OR, NOT and postulates. ASCII, BCD, and EBCDIC are codes taught to describe the exchange of data between computer circuits. Basic computer circuiting studies include Boolean functions, flip flops, registers, counters, decoders, timing circuits, Arithmetic and Logic Unit and random access memory.
Credit recommendation: In the lower division baccalaureate/associate degree category, 4 semester hours in Digital Circuits (5/84).

OS/JCL with VSAM Concepts (946)
Location: Brick, NJ.
Length: 75 hours (15 days).
Dates: January 1980-Present.
Objective: To provide students with an introduction to the concepts and application of OS/JCL and the relationship between application programs and an operating system.
Instruction: This course builds a working knowledge of OS/JCL through the use of JCL (Job Control Language) by stressing the following: (1) Job execute, DD, advanced DD statement; (2) compile, link and go job streams; (3) linkage editor and loader; (4) OS libraries and utilities; (5) ISAM files; (6) VSAM files. Students will code and actually run their OS/JCL job streams through a scan program.
Credit recommendation: In the lower division baccalaureate/associate degree category, 3 semester hours in OS/JCL (5/84).

RPG II Programming (205.1)
Location: Brick, NJ.
Length: 65 hours (13 days).
Dates: January 1980-Present.
Objective: To instruct students in the basic concepts and techniques of the RPG II programming language.
Instruction: RPG II is an application oriented language used to generate business reports. The student will learn how to access a file and produce a report. Basic mathematical functions will be covered along with report headings, total lines, compare operations, and control break processing. Students will construct, code, and run programs for business applications.
Credit recommendation: In the lower division baccalaureate/associate degree category, 2 semester hours in RPG II (5/84).

Carolina Power & Light Company

The Nuclear Training Section (NTS) of Carolina Power & Light Company is responsible for providing technical education and training to Reactor Operators (RO) and Senior Reactor Operators (SRO) at the Company's three nuclear plants. This is accomplished through a combination of classroom, simulator, and on-the-job training conducted at each nuclear plant and the Shearon Harris Energy & Environmental Center. The Reactor Operator training programs at all three CP&L nuclear plants also include a course on the PULSTAR research reactor at North Carolina State University.

The NTS is part of the Operations Training and Technical Services Department of the Operations Support Group. It is comprised of eight functional units. Five units are located at the central training facility, the Shearon Harris Energy & Environmental Center (SHE&EC), in New Hill, North Carolina. In addition, a training unit is assigned to each of the three nuclear plants. Each plant training unit is managed by a Manager-Training who reports off site to the Manager-Nuclear Training.

Carolina Power & Light Company's training programs are developed utilizing a job task analysis. Training programs derived from a job task analysis utilize criterion-referenced technology in lesson plans and other training materials. The training programs are conducted by individuals who are highly qualified in both technical and teaching skills.

Each training program is designed to facilitate the evaluation and appraisal of each student's comprehension and degree of mastery of the subject by both written and oral examinations. Training programs embody both the academic and practical aspects of the subject. Training programs are modified as necessary to reflect new regulatory requirements, operating experiences of CP&L and the nuclear industry, INPO evaluations, CP&L audits, and plant modifications.

Source of official student records: (A) Training Manager, Carolina Power & Light Company, H.B. Robinson Steam Electric Plant, P.O. Box 790, Hartsville, SC 29550; (B) Training Manager, Carolina Power & Light Company, Shearon Harris Nuclear Power Plant, Box 165, New Hill, NC 27562; (C) Training Manager, Carolina Power & Light Company, Brunswick Steam Electric Plant, P.O. Box 10429, Southport, NC 28461; (D) Nuclear & Simulator Training Director, Carolina Power and Light Company, Harris Energy & Environmental Center, Route 1, Box 327, New Hill, NC 27562; (E) Director, Nuclear Reactor Program Department of Nuclear Engineering, Box 7909, North Carolina State University, Raleigh, NC 27695-7909.

Additional information about the courses: Program on Noncollegiate Sponsored Instruction, The Center for Adult Learning and Educational Credentials, American Council on Education, One Dupont Circle, Washington, D.C. 20036.

BRUNSWICK STEAM ELECTRIC PLANT: REACTOR OPERATOR TRAINING

Reactor Operator: Simulator
(ROAO1B-RO Simul)

Location: Brunswick Steam Electric Plant, Southport, NC.

Length: 368 hours (20 weeks); 28 hours classroom instruction, 340 hours simulator.

Dates: January 1984-Present.

Objective: To provide the student with instruction and practical operating experience to conduct normal, abnormal, and emergency power plant operation as it applies to a BWR nuclear power plant reactor operator.

Learning Outcome: Upon successful completion of this course, the student will be able to perform plant startups and shutdowns under normal and abnormal operating conditions; diagnose and mitigate malfunctions; institute appropriate emergency operating procedures in nuclear power plants.

Instruction: Course covers subjects related to BWR power plant operations including plant startups, shutdowns, normal operation, abnormal operation, and emergency conditions.

Credit recommendation: In the upper division baccalaureate category, 3 semester hours in Nuclear Engineering Technology (12/87).

Reactor Operator Systems: Nuclear Steam Supply Systems and Design Considerations
(ROAO1B-Prim. Syst.)

Location: Brunswick Steam Electric Plant, Southport, NC.

Length: 420 hours (13 weeks); 100 hours classroom instruction and 320 hours on-the-job training.

Dates: January 1984-Present.

Objective: To provide the student with instruction on nuclear steam supply systems and design considerations (primary systems) as they apply to a nuclear power plant reactor operator.

Learning Outcome: Upon successful completion of this course, the student will be able to describe the design and operation of the following general systems: reactor coolant systems; fuel handling system; instrumentation and control systems; containment and support systems; reactor protection systems; and engineering safety systems.

Instruction: Course covers classroom and on-the-job training (OJT) related to nuclear steam supply system and design considerations including the design and operation of a boiling water reactor, its support system, emergency safeguards, and the licensing and technical specifications under which the operating license is issued.

Credit recommendation: In the lower division bac-

Reactor Operator Systems: Power Plant Engineering Systems
(ROAO1B-Sec. and Elec. Systems)
Location: Brunswick Steam Electric Plant, Southport, NC.
Length: 300 hours (10 weeks); 100 hours classroom instruction and 200 hours on-the-job training.
Dates: January 1984-Present.
Objective: To provide the student with instruction on power plant engineering systems (secondary and electrical) as they apply to a nuclear power plant reactor operator.
Learning Outcome: Upon successful completion of this course, the student will be able to describe the design and operation of the following general systems: main and auxiliary steam systems; condensate and feedwater systems; main turbine and associated support systems; and electrical systems associated with the secondary plant.
Instruction: Course covers classroom and on-the-job training (OJT) related to power plant engineering systems including steam distribution systems, electrical distribution and operation, condensate and feedwater, main turbine and generator, and auxiliary systems including emergency power.
Credit recommendation: In the lower division baccalaureate/associate degree category, 3 semester hours in Nuclear Engineering Technology (12/87).

Reactor Operator Theory: Chemistry
(ROAO1B-CH)
Location: Brunswick Steam Electric Plant, Southport, NC.
Length: 16 hours (2 days).
Dates: January 1984-Present.
Objective: To provide instruction on chemistry as it applies to a nuclear power plant reactor operator.
Learning Outcome: Upon successful completion of this course, the student will have an understanding of the importance associated with maintaining chemistry controls.
Instruction: Course covers subjects related to chemistry, including structure of matter; atomic structure; chemical activity (valence bonding and covalent bonding); solutions; ionization; acid, bases, and salts; conductivity; BWR chemistry (corrosion and water quality control); BWR radiochemistry; and removal of activation products.
Credit recommendation: In the lower division baccalaureate/associate degree category, 1 semester hour in Chemistry (12/87).

Reactor Operator Theory: Heat Transfer, Fluid Flow, and Thermodynamics
(ROAO1B-HT, FF, TH) (A and B)
Location: Brunswick Steam Electric Plant, Southport, NC.
Length: *Version A:* 40 hours (1 week). *Version B:* 80 hours (2 weeks).
Dates: *Version A:* January 1984-October 1987. *Version B:* October 1987-Present.
Objective: To provide the student with sufficient instruction on heat transfer, fluid flow, and thermodynamics as it applies to nuclear power plant operation.
Learning Outcome: Upon successful completion of this course, the student will be able to understand the essential heat transfer, fluid mechanics, and thermodynamic principles relative to nuclear power plant operation; perform calculations to estimate temperatures, pressures, and thermodynamic properties associated with essential plant systems.
Instruction: Course covers subjects related to heat transfer, fluid flow, and thermodynamics including laws and methods of heat transfer; boiling heat transfer (critical heat flux, two-phase flow, and flow patterns in heated vertical tube); thermal stresses; fluid statics; fluid flow; pumps, valves, and turbine theory; and nozzles.
Credit recommendation: In the upper division baccalaureate category, 3 semester hours in Nuclear Engineering Technology (12/87). NOTE: Credit cannot be give for the Version A course and the Control Operator Candidate course.

Reactor Operator Theory: Reactor Core Analysis and Mitigating Core Damage
(ROAO1B-RCA & MCD)
Location: Brunswick Steam Electric Plant, Southport, NC.
Length: 24 hours (1 week).
Dates: January 1984-Present.
Objective: To provide the student instruction on reactor core analysis and mitigating core damage as they apply to a nuclear power plant reactor operator.
Learning Outcome: Upon successful completion of this course, the student will be able to state expected responses to various events; explain instrument responses to various events; define various terms; state radiological consequences both on-site and off-site; and become familiar with process computer.
Instruction: Course covers reactor core analysis and mitigating core damage including transient analysis, accident analysis, mitigating core damage, thermal limits, core power response, and process computer.
Credit recommendation: In the lower division baccalaureate/associate degree category, 1 semester hour in Nuclear Engineering Technology (12/87). NOTE: Credit should not be awarded for both Senior Reactor Operator: Reactor Core Analysis and Mitigating Core Damage (ROAO2B-RCA & MCD) and this course.

Reactor Operator Theory: Reactor Theory
(ROAO1B-RT) (A and B)

Location: Brunswick Steam Electric Plant, Southport, NC.

Length: *Version A:* 80 hours (2 weeks). *Version B:* 120 hours (3 weeks).

Dates: *Version A:* June 1983-October 1987. *Version B:* October 1987-Present.

Objective: To provide instruction on reactor theory as it applies to a nuclear power plant reactor operator.

Learning Outcome: Upon successful completion of this course, the student will be able to define some physics terms; describe the structure of the atom; make radioactive decay calculations; make static and dynamic reactor calculations using the six factor equation and the reactor equation; describe and calculate various coefficients; and describe and calculate reactivity effects.

Instruction: Course covers subjects related to reactor theory, including properties of matter and energy, nuclear physics and reactions, reactor physics, reactivity effects and variations, reactor kinetics, subcritical theory, various coefficients, poisoning, power distribution, and reactivity control during operation.

Credit recommendation: *Version A:* In the lower division baccalaureate/associate degree category, 2 semester hours in Nuclear Engineering Technology. *Version B:* In the lower division baccalaureate/associate degree category, 3 semester hours in Nuclear Engineering Technology (12/87).

BRUNSWICK STEAM ELECTRIC PLANT: SENIOR REACTOR OPERATOR TRAINING

Senior Reactor Operator: Operational Administration
(ROAO2B-OPADMIN)

Location: Brunswick Steam Electric Plant, Southport, NC.

Length: 88 hours (4 weeks).

Dates: January 1984-Present.

Objective: To provide instruction on operational administration as it applies to a nuclear power plant senior reactor operator.

Learning Outcome: Upon successful completion of this course, the student will be able to describe and explain the implications, definitions, limitations, compliance, and bases for technical specifications and the various parts of the code of federal regulations; describe the interrelationships between on-site and off-site emergency organizations; and perform administrative aspects for various maintenance tasks.

Instruction: Course covers subjects including administrative procedures, administrative instructions, operating instructions, appropriate parts of the code of federal regulations, regulatory compliance instructions, maintenance procedures, technical specifications and their bases, and plant emergency plan.

Credit recommendation: In the upper division baccalaureate category, 3 semester hours in Nuclear Plant Management (12/87).

Senior Reactor Operator: Plant Systems Review and Upgrade
(ROAO2B-Review)

Location: Brunswick Steam Electric Plant, Southport, NC.

Length: 240 hours (6 weeks).

Dates: January 1984-Present.

Objective: To provide the student with a review of reactor operator theory and systems courses as it applies to a nuclear power plant senior reactor operator. It should provide the student with an in-depth and integrated understanding of essential plant systems and their interrelationships.

Learning Outcome: Upon successful completion of this course, the student will be able to demonstrate a thorough and integrated understanding of plant systems relative to operating procedures, technical specifications and design limitations. This level of understanding should also be evident with respect to operational procedures and limits imposed by reactor physics, heat transfer, fluid flow, thermodynamics, and general laws of physics and chemistry.

Instruction: Course covers subjects related to a review of reactor operator theory and systems course including reactor theory; heat transfer, fluid flow, and thermodynamics; chemistry; radiological control; instrumentation; and plant systems.

Credit recommendation: In the upper division baccalaureate category, 5 semester hours in Nuclear Engineering Technology (12/87).

Senior Reactor Operator: Reactor Core Analysis and Mitigating Core Damage
(ROAO2B-RCA & MCD)

Location: Brunswick Steam Electric Plant, Southport, NC.

Length: 20 hours (1/2 week).

Dates: January 1984-Present.

Objective: To provide instruction on reactor core analysis and mitigating core damage as they apply to a nuclear power plant senior reactor operator.

Learning Outcome: Upon successful completion of this course, the student will be able to state expected responses to various events; explain instrument responses to various events; define various terms; state radiological consequences both on-site and off-site; and become familiar with process computer.

Instruction: Course covers reactor core analysis and mitigating core damage including transient analysis, accident analysis, mitigating core damage, thermal limits, core power response, and process computer.

Credit recommendation: In the lower division baccalaureate/associate degree category, 1 semester hour in

Nuclear Engineering Technology (12/87). NOTE: Credit should not be awarded for both Reactor Operator: Reactor Core Analysis and Mitigating Core Damage (ROAO1B-RCA & MCD) and this course.

Senior Reactor Operator: Simulator (ROAO2B-SRO Simul)

Location: Brunswick Steam Electric Plant, Southport, NC.

Length: 200 hours (10 weeks); 60 hours classroom instruction and 140 hours simulator.

Dates: January 1984-Present.

Objective: To provide the student with instruction and practical operating experience to supervise normal, abnormal, and emergency power plant operation as it applies to a BWR nuclear power plant senior reactor operator.

Learning Outcome: Upon successful completion of this course, the student will be able to supervise normal and abnormal plant startups and shutdowns; perform transient and accident analyses; direct emergency operations; evaluate plant operations relative to technical specifications.

Instruction: Course covers subjects related to the supervision of power plant operation including diagnosing problems and applying technical specifications to plant start-ups, shutdowns, normal operation, abnormal operation, and emergency conditions.

Credit recommendation: In the upper division baccalaureate category, 2 semester hours in Nuclear Engineering Technology (12/87).

H.B. ROBINSON STEAM ELECTRIC PLANT: REACTOR OPERATOR TRAINING

Reactor Operator: Emergency Operating Procedures (Including Dedicated Shutdown Procedures) ROAO1R-EOP, ARP)

Location: H.B. Robinson Steam Electric Plant, Hartsville, SC.

Length: 56 hours (1.4 weeks); 42 hours lecture/discussion and 14 hours self-study.

Dates: January 1983-Present.

Objective: To provide instruction on emergency operating procedures and dedicated shutdown procedures as they apply to a nuclear power plant reactor operator.

Learning Outcome: Upon successful completion of this course, the student will be able to state, list, discuss and/or describe conditions which require the initiation of the various procedures; be familiar with and understand the steps, actions, and equipment necessary to effect the various procedures.

Instruction: Course covers subjects related to emergency operating procedures, dedicated shutdown procedures including plant emergency operating procedures, dedicated shutdown procedures, and fire protection.

Credit recommendation: In the lower division baccalaureate/associate degree category, 1 semester hour in Nuclear Engineering Technology (12/87). NOTE: Credit should not be awarded for both Senior Reactor Operator: Emergency Operating Procedures (Including Dedicated Shutdown Procedures) (ROAO2R-EOP, ARP) and this course.

Reactor Operator: Simulator (ROAO1R-RO Simul)

Location: Shearon Harris Energy & Environmental Center, New Hill, NC and H.B. Robinson Steam Electric Plant, Hartsville, SC.

Length: 240 hours (6 weeks).

Dates: January 1983-Present.

Objective: To provide the student with instruction and practical operating experience to conduct normal, abnormal, and emergency plant operation as it applies to a PWR nuclear plant reactor operator.

Learning Outcome: Upon successful completion of this course, the student will be able to perform plant startups and shutdowns under normal and abnormal operating conditions; diagnose and mitigate malfunctions; institute appropriate emergency operating procedures in nuclear power plants.

Instruction: Course covers subjects related to PWR power plant operations including startups, shutdowns, normal operations, abnormal operations, and emergency conditions.

Credit recommendation: In the upper division baccalaureate category, 2 semester hours in Nuclear Engineering Technology (12/87).

Reactor Operator Systems: Nuclear Steam Supply Systems and Design Considerations (ROAO1R-Prim. Syst.)

Location: H.B. Robinson Steam Electric Plant, Hartsville, SC.

Length: 495 hours (12.4 weeks); 135 hours classroom instruction and 360 hours on-the-job training.

Dates: January 1983-Present.

Objective: To provide the student with instruction on nuclear steam supply systems and design considerations (primary systems) as they apply to a nuclear power plant reactor operator.

Learning Outcome: Upon successful completion of this course, the student will be able to describe the design and operation of the following general systems: reactor coolant systems; fuel handling system; instrumentation and control systems; chemical and volume control system; containment and support system; reactor protection systems; and radioactive waste handling and processing systems.

Instruction: Course covers classroom and on-the-job training (OJT) related to nuclear steam supply systems and design considerations including reactor coolant systems; nuclear fuel, incore instrumentation, NIS, CVCS, fuel handling, RHR, primary sampling, CCW, spent fuel pit, containment and support, HVAC, engineered safety features, rod control, rod position indication, snubbers, reactor protection, radiation monitoring, solid radwaste, liquid radwaste, and gaseous radwaste.

Credit recommendation: In the lower division baccalaureate/associate degree category, 5 semester hours in Nuclear Engineering Technology (12/87).

Reactor Operator Systems: Plant Systems Review and Upgrade (Prelicense Review)
(ROAO1R-PLR)

Location: H.B. Robinson Steam Electric Plant, Hartsville, SC.

Length: 100 hours (2.5 weeks).

Dates: January 1983-Present.

Objective: To provide the student with instruction on plant systems review and upgrade (prelicense review) as it applies to a nuclear power plant reactor operator. The student should obtain an integrated knowledge of essential plant systems and their interrelationships.

Learning Outcome: Upon successful completion of this course, the student will be able to demonstrate an improved and integrated knowledge of plant systems relative to plant operating procedures, technical specifications, and design limitations.

Instruction: Course covers subjects related to plant systems review and update.

Credit recommendation: In the upper division baccalaureate category, 2 semester hours in Nuclear Engineering Technology (12/87).

Reactor Operator Systems: Power Plant Engineering Systems
(ROAO1R-Sec. and Elec. Systems)

Location: H.B. Robinson Steam Electric Plant, Hartsville, SC.

Length: 265 hours (6.6 weeks); 105 hours classroom instruction and 160 hours on-the-job training.

Dates: January 1983-Present.

Objective: To provide the student with instruction on power plant engineering systems (secondary and electrical) as they apply to a nuclear power plant reactor operator.

Learning Outcome: Upon successful completion of this course, the student will be able to describe the design and operation of the following general systems: main and auxiliary steam systems; condensate and feedwater systems; main turbine and associated support systems; steam generator and associated support systems; and electrical systems associated with the secondary plant.

Instruction: Course covers classroom and on-the-job training (OJT) related to power plant engineering systems (secondary and electrical systems) including secondary sampling system, service water, main and auxiliary steam, steam generator, steam generator water level control, main turbine and reheaters, turbine auxiliary system, oil analysis, turbine control, condensate, feedwater system, extraction steam, feedwater heater, vents and drains, fire protection system, main generator, generator auxiliaries, AC electrical systems, diesel generators, DC electrical systems, plant computer, circulating water, plant air, plant compressed gas.

Credit recommendation: In the lower division baccalaureate/associate degree category, 3 semester hours in Nuclear Engineering Technology (12/87).

Reactor Operator Theory: Chemistry
(ROAO1R-CH)

Location: H.B. Robinson Steam Electric Plant, Hartsville, SC.

Length: 20 hours (2.5 days); 15 hours lecture/discussion and 5 hours self-study.

Dates: January 1983-Present.

Objective: To provide the student with instruction on chemistry as it applies to a nuclear plant reactor operator.

Learning Outcome: Upon successful completion of this course, the student will have an understanding of fundamental chemistry concepts and the important role chemistry plays in the performance and safety of a nuclear power plant.

Instruction: Course covers subjects related to chemistry including chemistry fundamentals review, corrosion and corrosion control, radiation chemistry, secondary chemistry, hazardous chemicals, sampling techniques, and water treatment.

Credit recommendation: In the lower division baccalaureate/associate degree category, 1 semester hour in Chemistry (12/87).

Reactor Operator Theory: Heat Transfer, Fluid Flow, and Thermodynamics
(ROAO1R-HT, FF, TH)

Location: H.B. Robinson Steam Electric Plant, Hartsville, SC.

Length: 80 hours (2 weeks); 60 hours lecture/discussion and 20 hours self-study.

Dates: January 1983-Present.

Objective: To provide the student with sufficient instruction on heat transfer, fluid flow, and thermodynamics as it applies to nuclear power plant operation.

Learning Outcome: Upon successful completion of this course, the student will be able to understand the essential heat transfer, fluid mechanics, and thermodynamic principles relative to nuclear power plant operation; perform calculations to estimate temperatures, pressures, and thermodynamic properties associated with essential plant systems.

Instruction: Course covers subjects related to heat transfer, fluid flow, and thermodynamics including properties of working fluids, phases of matter, laws of thermodynamics, steam tables, limits, Bernoulli's equation, pump laws, heat balance, and Rankine cycle.

Credit recommendation: In the upper division baccalaureate category, 3 semester hours in Nuclear Engineering Technology (12/87).

Reactor Operator Theory: Material Science (ROAO1R-Mt Sc)

Location: H.B. Robinson Steam Electric Plant, Hartsville, SC.

Length: 20 hours (2.5 days); 15 hours lecture/discussion and 5 hours self-study.

Dates: January 1983-Present.

Objective: To provide instruction on material science as it applies to a nuclear power plant reactor operator.

Learning Outcome: Upon successful completion of this course, the student will be able to describe, state, list, define and/or explain the concepts and phenomena covered in the course description.

Instruction: Course covers subjects related to material science including atomic interactions and order in microstructures, classification of crystalline materials, imperfection in materials, stress and strain, mechanical properties of materials, mechanisms of deformation and fracture, toughness testing, effects of radiation on materials, alloys, nuclear fuel and cladding, brittle fracture in reactor vessels, heat-up and cool-down considerations.

Credit recommendation: In the lower division baccalaureate/associate degree category, 1 semester hour in Material Science (12/87).

Reactor Operator Theory: Mathematics (ROAO1R-MATH)

Location: H.B. Robinson Steam Electric Plant, Hartsville, SC.

Length: 28 hours (3.5 days); 21 hours lecture/discussion and 7 hours self-study.

Dates: January 1983-Present.

Objective: To provide the student with sufficient instruction to perform essential calculations for operating a nuclear power plant.

Learning Outcome: Upon successful completion of this course, the student will be able to perform calculations required to operate a nuclear power plant.

Instruction: Course covers fundamentals of algebra, graphs and functions, exponential and logarithmic functions, and trigonometry.

Credit recommendation: In the lower division baccalaureate/associate degree category, 1 semester hour in Mathematics (12/87).

Reactor Operator Theory: Mitigating Core Damage (ROAO1R-MCD)

Location: H.B. Robinson Steam Electric Plant, Hartsville, SC.

Length: 60 hours (1.5 weeks); 45 hours lecture/discussion and 15 hours self-study.

Dates: January 1983-Present.

Objective: To provide instruction on mitigating core damage as it applies to a nuclear power plant reactor operator.

Learning Outcome: Upon successful completion of this course, the student will be able to list, describe, and explain the parameters, symptoms, alarms, causes, and indications which could result in core damage; state, explain, and list the actions, procedures, and conditions which would mitigate core damage.

Instruction: Course covers subjects related to mitigating core damage including fuel rod temperature profiles, core thermal limits, natural circulation, fission product containment, post accident radiation monitoring, TM 1-2 event, reactivity and power distribution anomalies, heat removal by secondary system, expected transients, and integrated system responses.

Credit recommendation: In the lower division baccalaureate/associate degree category, 2 semester hours in Nuclear Engineering Technology (12/87).

Reactor Operator Theory: Radiological Control (Health Physics) (ROAO1R-HP)

Location: H.B. Robinson Steam Electric Plant, Hartsville, SC.

Length: 28 hours (3.5 days); 21 hours lecture/discussion and 7 hours self-study.

Dates: January 1983-Present.

Objective: To provide the student with instruction on radiological control as it applies to a nuclear power plant reactor operator.

Learning Outcome: Upon successful completion of this course, the student will have an understanding of radioactivity, contamination, health effects, and emergency responses.

Instruction: Course covers subjects related to radiological control (health physics) including terminology and decay equations, properties and interactions of radiation, units of exposure and dose, biological effects of radiation, dose rate and shielding, detector principles, emergency response plan, and initial dose projections.

Credit recommendation: In the lower division baccalaureate/associate degree category, 1 semester hour in Nuclear Engineering Technology (12/87).

Reactor Operator Theory: Reactor Theory (ROAO1R-RT)

Location: H.B. Robinson Steam Electric Plant, Hartsville, SC.

Length: 80 hours (2 weeks); 60 hours lecture/discussion and 20 hours self-study.

Dates: January 1983-Present.

Objective: To provide instruction on reactor theory as it applies to a nuclear power plant reactor operator.

Learning Outcome: Upon successful completion of this course, the student will be able to define some physics terms; describe the structure of the atom; make radioactive decay calculations; make static and dynamic reactor calculations using the six factor equation and the reactor equation; describe and calculate various coefficients; and describe and calculate reactivity effects.

Instruction: Course covers subjects related to reactor theory, including properties of matter and energy, nuclear physics and reactions, reactor physics, reactivity effects and variations, reactor kinetics, subcritical theory, various coefficients, poisoning, power distribution, and reactivity control during operation.

Credit recommendation: In the lower division baccalaureate/associate degree category, 2 semester hours in Nuclear Engineering Technology (12/87).

H.B. ROBINSON STEAM ELECTRIC PLANT: SENIOR REACTOR OPERATOR TRAINING

Senior Reactor Operator: Administration, Procedures, and Bases
(ROAO2R-PROC, AOP)

Location: H.B. Robinson Steam Electric Plant, Hartsville, SC.

Length: 628 hours (15.5 weeks); 100 hours classroom instruction and 528 hours on-the-job training.

Dates: January 1983-Present.

Objective: To provide instruction on administration, procedures, and bases as they apply to a nuclear power plant senior reactor operator.

Learning Outcome: Upon successful completion of this course, the student will be able to describe and explain the implications, definitions, limitations, compliance, and bases for technical specifications and the various parts of the code of federal regulations; describe the interrelationships between on-site and off-site emergency organizations; perform administrative aspects for various plant maintenance tasks; and list responsibilities of personnel from general plant manager to radiation control technician under certain circumstances.

Instruction: Course covers topics related to administration, procedures, and bases including health physics administrative guidelines, procedures, contamination control policies and procedures, off-site release of gaseous and liquid radioactive effluents, health administrative radiation work permits, emergency response plans, technical specifications, and fuel follow procedures.

Credit recommendation: In the upper division baccalaureate category, 3 semester hours in Nuclear Plant Management (12/87).

Senior Reactor Operator: Advanced Transient and Accident Analysis
(ROAO2R-ATAA)

Location: H.B. Robinson Steam Electric Plant, Hartsville, SC.

Length: 48 hours (1.2 weeks); 36 hours lecture/discussion and 12 hours self-study.

Dates: January 1983-Present.

Objective: To provide instruction on advanced transient and accident analysis as it applies to a nuclear power plant senior reactor operator.

Learning Outcome: Upon successful completion of this course, the student will be able to list, state, explain and/or describe indications or situations that could be potentially damaging to the reactor system; and describe action that should be taken by the operator to prevent such damage.

Instruction: Course covers subjects related to advanced transient and accident analysis including fuel rod temperature profiles, reactor heat generation, core thermal limits, natural circulation, fission product containment, postaccident radiation monitoring, incore thermocouple system, large and small break LOCA, steam generator tube rupture, and brittle fracture and the reactor vessel.

Credit recommendation: In the upper division baccalaureate category, 2 semester hours in Nuclear Engineering Technology (12/87).

Senior Reactor Operator: Emergency Operating Procedures (Including Dedicated Shutdown Procedures)
(ROAO2R-EOP, ARP)

Location: H.B. Robinson Steam Electric Plant, Hartsville, SC.

Length: 56 hours (1.4 weeks); 42 hours lecture/discussion and 14 hours self-study.

Dates: January 1983-Present.

Objective: To provide instruction on emergency operating procedures and dedicated shutdown procedures as they apply to a nuclear power plant senior reactor operator.

Learning Outcome: Upon successful completion of this course, the student will be able to state, list, discuss and/or describe conditions which require the initiation of the various procedures; and be familiar with and understand the steps, actions, and equipment necessary to effect the various procedures.

Instruction: Course covers subjects related to emergency operating procedures, dedicated shutdown procedures, including plant emergency operating procedures, dedicated shutdown procedures, and fire protection.

Credit recommendation: In the lower division baccalaureate/associate degree category, 1 semester hour in Nuclear Engineering Technology (12/87). NOTE: Credit should not be awarded for both Reactor Operator: Emergency Operating Procedures (Including Dedicated Shutdown Procedures) (ROAO1R-EOP, ARP) and this course.

Senior Reactor Operator: Plant Systems Review and Upgrade
(ROAO2R-PLR)

Location: H.B. Robinson Steam Electric Plant, Harts-

ville, SC.
Length: 100 hours (2.5 weeks); 75 hours lecture/discussion and 25 hours self-study.
Dates: January 1983-Present.
Objective: To provide the student with a review of reactor operator theory and systems courses as it applies to a nuclear power plant senior reactor operator. It should provide the student with an in-depth and integrated understanding of essential plant systems and their interrelationships.
Learning Outcome: Upon successful completion of this course, the student will be able to demonstrate a thorough and integrated understanding of plant systems relative to operating procedures, technical specifications and design limitations. This level of understanding should also be evident with respect to operational procedures and limits imposed by reactor physics, heat transfer, fluid flow, thermodynamics, and general laws of physics and chemistry.
Instruction: Course covers subjects related to plant systems review and upgrade (prelicense review) including reactor theory; heat transfer, fluid flow, and thermodynamics; chemistry; health physics; systems; routine and emergency reporting requirements; and Westinghouse major design base accidents.
Credit recommendation: In the upper division baccalaureate category, 3 semester hours in Nuclear Engineering Technology (12/87).

**Senior Reactor Operator: Simulator
(ROAO2R-SRO Simul)**
Location: Shearon Harris Energy & Environmental Center, New Hill, NC and H.B. Robinson Steam Electric Plant, Hartsville, SC.
Length: 120 hours (3 weeks).
Dates: January 1983-Present.
Objective: To provide the student with instruction and practical operating experience to supervise normal, abnormal, and emergency power plant operation as it applies to a PWR nuclear power plant senior reactor operator.
Learning Outcome: Upon successful completion of this course, the student will be able to supervise normal and abnormal plant start-ups and shutdowns; perform transient and accident analyses: direct emergency operations; and evaluate plant operations relative to technical specifications.
Instruction: Course covers subjects related to supervising and directing operators during plant start-ups, shutdown, normal operations, abnormal operations, and emergency conditions.
Credit recommendation: In the upper division baccalaureate category, 1 semester hour in Nuclear Engineering Technology (12/87).

**Senior Reactor Operator Theory: Electrical Science
(ROAO2R-ELEC)**
Location: H.B. Robinson Steam Electric Plant, Hartsville, SC.
Length: 60 hours (1.5 weeks); 45 hours lecture/discussion and 15 hours self-study.
Dates: January 1983-Present.
Objective: To provide the student with instruction on electrical science as it applies to a nuclear power plant senior reactor operator.
Learning Outcome: Upon successful completion of this course, the student will be able to describe, define, and/or calculate the basic properties of electrical circuits, components, and devices.
Instruction: Course covers subjects related to electrical science including fundamental concepts, AC circuit fundamentals, three-phase generation, transformer theory, power system control and protection, station AC, emergency diesel generators, electrical components and systems, DC electrical system, transistors, and thermocouples.
Credit recommendation: In the upper division baccalaureate category, 2 semester hours in Electrical Engineering Technology (12/87).

SHEARON HARRIS NUCLEAR POWER PLANT: REACTOR OPERATOR TRAINING

**Reactor Operator: Simulator (SHNPP)
(RO6CO2H-RO Simul)**
Location: Shearon Harris Energy and Environmental Center, New Hill, NC.
Length: 360 hours (9 weeks).
Dates: January 1983-Present.
Objective: To provide the student with instruction and practical operating experience on normal, abnormal, and emergency power plant operation as it applies to a PWR nuclear power plant reactor operator.
Learning Outcome: Upon successful completion of this course, the student will be able to perform plant startups and shutdowns under normal and abnormal operating conditions; diagnose and mitigate malfunctions; institute appropriate emergency operating procedures in nuclear power plants.
Instruction: Course covers subjects related to PWR power plant operation including plant startups, shutdowns, normal operation, abnormal operation, and emergency conditions.
Credit recommendation: In the upper division baccalaureate category, 3 semester hours in Nuclear Engineering Technology (12/87).

**Reactor Operator Systems: Nuclear Steam Supply Systems and Design Considerations
(RO6CO2H-Prim. Syst.)**
Location: Shearon Harris Energy and Environmental

Center, New Hill, NC.

Length: 240 hours (6 weeks); 80 hours classroom instruction and 160 hours on-the-job training.

Dates: March 1983-Present.

Objective: To provide the student with instruction on nuclear steam supply systems and design considerations (primary systems) as they apply to a nuclear power plant reactor operator.

Learning Outcome: Upon successful completion of this course, the student will be able to describe the design and operation of the following general systems: reactor coolant systems; safety systems; containment systems; safety-related auxiliary systems; radioactive waste processing systems; and instrumentation and control systems.

Instruction: Course covers classroom and on-the-job training (OJT) related to nuclear steam supply systems and design considerations including reactor coolant systems, safety systems, containment systems, safety-related auxiliary systems, radioactive waste processing systems, and instrumentation and control systems.

Credit recommendation: In the lower division baccalaureate/associate degree category, 3 semester hours in Nuclear Engineering Technology (12/87).

Reactor Operator Systems: Plant Systems Review and Upgrade (Prelicense Review)
(RO6CO2H-PLR)

Location: Shearon Harris Energy and Environmental Center, New Hill, NC.

Length: 150 hours (4 weeks)

Dates: October 1982-Present.

Objective: To provide the student with instruction on plant systems review and upgrade (prelicense review) as it applies to a nuclear plant reactor operator. The student should obtain an integrated knowledge of essential plant systems and their interrelationships.

Learning Outcome: Upon successful completion of this course, the student will be able to demonstrate an improved and integrated knowledge of plant systems relative to plant operating procedures, technical specifications and design limitations.

Instruction: Course covers subjects related to plant systems review and upgrade.

Credit recommendation: In the upper division baccalaureate category, 2 semester hours in Nuclear Engineering Technology (12/87).

Reactor Operator Systems: Power Plant Engineering Systems
(RO6CO2H-Sec. and Elec. Systems)

Location: Shearon Harris Energy and Environmental Center, New Hill, NC.

Length: 560 hours (14 weeks); 200 hours classroom instruction and 360 hours on-the-job training.

Dates: March 1983-Present.

Objective: To provide the student with instruction on power plant engineering systems (secondary and electrical) as they apply to a nuclear power plant reactor operator.

Learning Outcome: Upon successful completion of this course, the student will be able to describe the design and operation of the following general systems: main and auxiliary steam systems, condensate and feedwater systems, main turbine and associated support systems; steam generator and associated support systems; and electrical systems associated with the secondary plant.

Instruction: Course covers classroom and on-the-job training related to power plant engineering systems including secondary PWR systems and electrical systems.

Credit recommendation: In the lower division baccalaureate/associate degree category, 6 semester hours in Nuclear Engineering Technology (12/87).

Reactor Operator Theory: Electrical Sciences
(RO6CO2H-ELEC)

Location: Shearon Harris Energy and Environmental Center, New Hill, NC.

Length: 30 hours (1 week); 22 hours lecture/discussion and 8 hours self-study.

Dates: October 1982-Present.

Objective: To provide the student with instruction on electrical sciences as it applies to a nuclear power plant reactor operator.

Learning Outcome: Upon successful completion of this course, the student will have a basic knowledge of voltage, current, and resistance in DC and AC electrical circuits; circuit laws and nomenclature, as well as the operation of electrical instruments.

Instruction: Course covers subjects related to electrical sciences including AC circuit fundamentals, DC theory and circuits, DC measurement, AC generation, motors, load sharing, and voltage regulation.

Credit recommendation: In the lower division baccalaureate/associate degree category, 1 semester hour in Electrical Engineering Technology (12/87).

Reactor Operator Theory: Heat Transfer, Fluid Flow, and Thermodynamics
(RO6CO2H-HT, FF, TH)

Location: Shearon Harris Energy and Environmental Center, New Hill, NC.

Length: 80 hours (2 weeks); 60 hours lecture/discussion and 20 hours self-study.

Dates: October 1982-Present.

Objective: To provide the student with sufficient instruction on heat transfer, fluid flow, and thermodynamics as it applies to nuclear power plant operation.

Learning Outcome: Upon successful completion of this course, the student will be able to understand the essential heat transfer, fluid mechanics, and thermodynamic principles relative to nuclear power plant operation; perform calculations to estimate temperatures, pressures, and thermodynamic properties associated with essential plant systems.

Instruction: Course covers subjects related to heat transfer, fluid flow, and thermodynamics including reactor heat transfer, heat exchangers, design and operational limits: Rx core thermal parameters, fluid statics, fluid flow dynamics, fluid mechanics in pumps and piping, fluid mechanics in the turbine, natural circulation, instrumentation, the properties of water, reactor and pressurizer thermo, steam generator thermo, turbine thermo and the Rankine cycle, condenser/tertiary system thermo.

Credit recommendation: In the upper division baccalaureate category, 3 semester hours in Nuclear Engineering Technology (12/87).

Reactor Operator Theory: Material Sciences (RO6CO2H-Mt Sc, PTS)

Location: Shearon Harris Energy and Environmental Center, New Hill, NC.

Length: 30 hours (4 days); 22 hours lecture/discussion and 8 hours self-study.

Dates: October 1982-Present.

Objective: To provide instruction on material sciences and pressurized thermal shock as it applies to a nuclear power plant reactor operator.

Learning Outcome: Upon successful completion of this course, the student will be able to describe, state, list, define and/or explain the concepts and phenomena covered in the course description.

Instruction: Course covers subjects related to material science including mechanical metallurgy, material properties, nuclear core design, plant materials, reactor vessel stress and embrittlement, and pressurized thermal shock.

Credit recommendation: In the lower division baccalaureate/associate degree category, 1 semester hour in Material Science (12/87).

Reactor Operator Theory: Mathematics (RO6CO2H-MATH)

Location: Shearon Harris Energy and Environmental Center, New Hill, NC.

Length: 36 hours (1 week); 26 hours lecture/discussion and 10 hours self-study.

Dates: October 1982-Present.

Objective: To provide the student with sufficient instruction to perform essential calculations for operating a nuclear power plant.

Learning Outcome: Upon successful completion of this course, the student will be able to perform all essential calculations required to operate a nuclear power plant.

Instruction: Course covers fundamentals of algebra, graphs and functions, exponential and logarithmic functions, trigonometry and calculus.

Credit recommendation: In the lower division baccalaureate/associate degree category, 1 semester hour in Mathematics.

Reactor Operator Theory: Operation and Administration (RO6CO2H-OPADMIN)

Location: Shearon Harris Energy and Environmental Center, New Hill, NC.

Length: 175 hours (4.4 weeks); 153 hours lecture/discussion and 22 hours self-study.

Dates: October 1987-Present.

Objective: To provide instruction on plant operation procedures and administration as they apply to a nuclear power plant reactor operator.

Learning Outcome: Upon successful completion of this course, the student will be able to state, list, and/or define terms, safety limits, and certain requirements for technical specifications as they related to nuclear power plant reactor operations.

Instruction: Course covers subjects related to plant operation procedures and administration including technical specifications, general procedures, emergency procedures, plant procedures, and abnormal operating procedures.

Credit recommendation: In the lower division baccalaureate/associate degree category, 3 semester hours in Nuclear Engineering Technology (12/87).

Reactor Operator Theory: Radiation Protections and Chemistry (RO6CO2H-RP, CH)

Location: Shearon Harris Energy and Environmental Center, New Hill, NC.

Length: 40 hours (1 week).

Dates: October 1982-Present.

Objective: To provide the student with instruction on radiation protection and chemistry as it applies to a nuclear power plant reactor operator.

Learning Outcome: Upon successful completion of this course, the student will have an understanding of radioisotopes, the interaction and health effects of ionizing radiation as well as nuclear power plant chemistry.

Instruction: Course covers subjects related to radiation protection and chemistry including radioactivity concepts, radiation interaction with matter, health effects, radiation detection, chemistry fundamentals, corrosion, primary and secondary chemistry, and hazardous chemicals.

Credit recommendation: In the lower division baccalaureate/associate degree category, 2 semester hours in Nuclear Engineering Technology (12/87).

Reactor Operator Theory: Reactor Theory (RO6CO2H-RT)

Location: Shearon Harris Energy and Environmental Center, New Hill, NC.

Length: 80 hours (2 weeks); 70 hours lecture/discussion and 10 hours self-study.

Dates: October 1982-Present.

Objective: To provide instruction on reactor theory as

it applies to a nuclear power plant reactor operator.

Learning Outcome: Upon successful completion of this course, the student will be able to define some physics terms; describe the structure of the atom; make radioactive decay calculations; make static and dynamic reactor calculations using the six factor equation and the reactor equation; describe and calculate various coefficients; and describe and calculate reactivity effects.

Instruction: Course covers subjects related to reactor theory, including properties of matter and energy, nuclear physics and reactions, reactor physics, reactivity effects and variations, reactor kinetics, subcritical theory, various coefficients, poisoning, power distribution, and reactivity control during operation.

Credit recommendation: In the lower division baccalaureate/associate degree category, 2 semester hours in Nuclear Engineering Technology (12/87).

SHEARON HARRIS NUCLEAR POWER PLANT: SENIOR REACTOR OPERATOR TRAINING

Senior Reactor Operator: Plant Systems Review and Upgrade
(SO6COOH-PLR)

Location: Shearon Harris Energy and Environmental Center, New Hill, NC.

Length: 130 hours (4 weeks).

Dates: October 1982-Present.

Objective: To provide the student with a review of reactor operator theory and systems courses as it applies to a nuclear power plant senior reactor operator. It should provide the student with an in-depth and integrated understanding of essential plant systems and their interrelationships.

Learning Outcome: Upon successful completion of this course, the student will be able to demonstrate a thorough and integrated understanding of plant systems relative to operating procedures, technical specification and design limitations. This level of understanding should also be evident with respect to operational procedures and limits imposed by reactor physics, heat transfer, fluid flow, thermodynamics, and general laws of physics and chemistry.

Instruction: Course covers subjects related to plant systems review and upgrade (prelicense review) including reactor theory; heat transfer, fluid flow, and thermodynamics; chemistry; radiation protection; general procedures, emergency operating procedures and plant procedures.

Credit recommendation: In the upper division baccalaureate category, 3 semester hours in Nuclear Engineering Technology (12/87).

Senior Reactor Operator: Simulator (SHNPP)
(SO6COOH-SRO Simul)

Location: Shearon Harris Energy and Environmental Center, New Hill, NC.

Length: 160 hours (4 weeks).

Dates: January 1983-Present.

Objective: To provide the student with instruction and practical operating experience to supervise normal, abnormal, and emergency power plant operation as it applies to a PWR nuclear power plant senior reactor operator.

Learning Outcome: Upon successful completion of this course, the student will be able to supervise normal and abnormal plant startups and shutdowns; perform transient and accident analyses: direct emergency operations; and evaluate operations relative to technical specifications.

Instruction: Course covers subjects related to the supervision of power plant operation including transient and accident analysis, diagnosing problems and applying technical specificaitons to plant startups, shutdowns, normal operation, abnormal operation, and emergency conditions.

Credit recommendation: In the upper division baccalaureate category, 2 semester hours in Nuclear Engineering Technology (12/87).

Senior Reactor Operator Theory: Electrical Science
(SO6COOH-ELEC)

Location: Shearon Harris Energy and Environmental Center, New Hill, NC.

Length: 40 hours (1 week); 26 hours lecture/discussion and 14 hours self-study.

Dates: October 1982-Present.

Objective: To provide the student with instruction on electrical science as it applies to a nuclear power plant senior reactor operator.

Learning Outcome: Upon successful completion of this course, the student will be able to describe, define and/or calculate the basic properties of electrical circuits, components, and devices.

Instruction: Course covers subjects related to electrical sciences including AC circuit fundamentals; three-phase power generation; fundamental electrical concepts; generator paralleling and load sharing; generator voltage regulation and stability operations; generator operational limitations; brushless excitation system; transformer theory and construction; voltage control and protective relaying; switchgear theory; lead acid batteries; DC motors; three-phase AC motors; motor starter control; restart criteria for major motors; semiconductor, diodes, and transistors.

Credit recommendation: In the upper division baccalaureate category, 2 semester hours in Electrical Engineering Technology (12/87).

Senior Reactor Operator Theory: Mitigating Core Damage
(SO6COOH-MCD)

Location: Shearon Harris Energy and Environmental Center, New Hill, NC.

Length: 25 hours (4 days); 23 hours lecture/discussion and 2 hours self-study.

Dates: October 1984-Present.

Objective: To provide instruction on mitigating core damage as it applies to a nuclear power plant senior reactor operator.

Learning Outcome: Upon successful completion of this course, the student will be able to state expected plant response to various events; list methods of recovery from various events; explain instrument responses to various events; list operator actions; and state radiological consequences both on-site and off-site for various events.

Instruction: Course covers mitigating core damage including post accident cooling, small break LOCA with no high head safety injection, loss of feedwater induced loss of coolant accidents, vital process instrumentation, accident response of incore and excore instrumentation, post-accident primary radiochemistry, radiological aspects of core damage, and loss of all AC power.

Credit recommendation: In the lower division baccalaureate/associate degree category, 1 semester hour in Nuclear Engineering Technology (12/87).

Senior Reactor Operator Theory: Operation and Administration
(SO6COOH-OPADMIN)

Location: Shearon Harris Energy and Environmental Center, New Hill, NC.

Length: 70 hours (2 weeks); 61 hours lecture/discussion and 9 hours self-study.

Dates: October 1987-Present.

Objective: To provide instruction on plant operation procedures and administration as it applies to a nuclear power plant senior reactor operator.

Learning Outcome: Upon successful completion of this course, the student will be able to describe and explain the implications, definitions, limitations, compliance, and bases for technical specifications; describe interrelationships between on-site and off-site emergency organizations; perform administrative aspects for various plant tasks; and list responsibilities of personnel from general plant manager to radiation control technicians under certain circumstances.

Instruction: Course covers plant operation procedures and administration including technical specifications, emergency plan plant procedures, and advanced operating practices.

Credit recommendation: In the upper division baccalaureate category, 2 semester hours in Nuclear Plant Management (12/87).

Senior Reactor Operator Theory: Transient and Accident Analysis
(SO6COOH-T&AA)

Location: Shearon Harris Energy and Environmental Center, New Hill, NC.

Length: 50 hours (1.5 weeks); 47 hours lecture/discussion and 3 hours self-study.

Dates: October 1984-Present.

Objective: To provide instruction on transient and accident analysis as it applies to a nuclear power plant senior reactor operator.

Learning Outcome: Upon successful completion of this course, the student will be able to analyze indications from instruments relative to possible abnormal events and be capable of specifying appropriate corrective actions.

Instruction: Course covers subjects related to transient and accident analysis including instrument failure analysis, introduction to accident analysis, primary induced reactivity addition accidents, increased secondary heat removal, decreased secondary heat removal, loss of coolant accident, steam generator tube rupture, loss of flow accident, anticipated transients without trip, heat source and hot channel factors, hydrogen generation and control, fission product containment, normal and abnormal transient analysis, TMI-2 and other operational experience reports, brittle fracture and the reactor vessel.

Credit recommendation: In the upper division baccalaureate category, 2 semester hours in Nuclear Engineering Technology (12/87).

SHEARON HARRIS ENERGY & ENVIRONMENTAL CENTER: CONTROL OPERATOR CANDIDATE TRAINING

COC: Chemistry and Material Science
(COBOIN-CH, MS)

Location: Shearon Harris Energy and Environmental Center, New Hill, NC.

Length: 33 hours (10 weeks).

Dates: January 1983-December 1986.

Objective: To provide the student with instruction on chemistry and material science as they apply to a nuclear power plant reactor operator.

Learning Outcome: Upon successful completion of this course, the student will be able to define and explain basic chemical terms and reactions, understand corrosion, radiation chemistry and hazardous chemicals, and understand properties associated with nuclear power plant materials.

Instruction: Course covers subjects related to chemistry and material science including chemistry fundamentals, corrosion, radiation chemistry, feed and condensate chemistry, hazardous chemicals, water treatment, and the fundamentals of material science from stress and strain through the use of testing to determine the properties of metals.

Credit recommendation: In the lower division baccalaureate/associate degree category, 1 semester hour in Chemistry (12/87).

COC: Electrical Science, Instrumentation and Control (COBOIN-EL, IC)
  Location: Shearon Harris Energy and Environmental Center, New Hill, NC.
  Length: 35 hours (10 weeks).
  Dates: January 1983-December 1986.
  Objective: To provide instruction on the science of electricity generation and instrumentation and control as they apply to a nuclear power plant reactor operator.
  Learning Outcome: Upon successful completion of this course, the student will be able to describe, define and/or calculate the basic properties of electrical circuits and devices.
  Instruction: Course covers subjects related to electrical science and instrumentation and control including AC circuits through three-phase generators, AC and DC motors, power system control and protection, and semiconductor theory.
  Credit recommendation: In the upper division baccalaureate category, 2 semester hours in Electrical Engineering Technology (12/87).

COC: Health Physics (COBOIN-HP)
  Location: Shearon Harris Energy and Environmental Center, New Hill, NC.
  Length: 25 hours (10 weeks).
  Dates: January 1983-December 1986.
  Objective: To provide instruction on health physics as it applies to a nuclear power plant reactor operator.
  Learning Outcome: Upon successful completion of this course, the student will have an understanding of radioactive decay, biological effect, radiation dose, radiation monitoring, dose levels, and emergency plans.
  Instruction: Course covers subjects related to health physics including how to control exposure to radioactive isotopes, measurement of radiation fields, identification and exposure limits for radioactive isotopes, the use of protective clothing and respirators, and the calculation of possible effects of a release of radioactive isotopes.
  Credit recommendation: In the lower division baccalaureate/associate degree category, 1 semester hour in Nuclear Science (Health Physics) (12/87).

COC: Heat Transfer, Fluid Flow, and Thermodynamics (COBOIN-TH, HT, and FF)
  Location: Shearon Harris Energy and Environmental Center, New Hill, NC.
  Length: 68 hours (10 weeks).
  Dates: January 1983-December 1986.
  Objective: To provide instruction on thermodynamics, heat transfer, and fluid flow as they apply to a nuclear power plant reactor operator.
  Learning Outcome: Upon successful completion of this course, the student will be able to understand heat transfer, fluid mechanics, and thermodynamic principles; perform calculations to estimate temperatures, pressures, and thermodynamic properties associated with essential plant systems.
  Instruction: Course covers subjects related to thermodynamics, heat transfer, and fluid flow including the first and second laws of thermodynamics through energy, enthalpy, entropy, and the general energy equation; the properties of water in all phases, steam tables, Mollier diagram; conductive, convective, and radioactive heat transfer; pump head and head loss calculations.
  Credit recommendation: In the upper division baccalaureate category, 3 semester hours in Nuclear Engineering Technology (12/87).

COC: Mathematics and Physics (COBOIN-MA, PHY)
  Location: Shearon Harris Energy and Environmental Center, New Hill, NC.
  Length: 33 hours (10 weeks).
  Dates: January 1983-December 1986.
  Objective: To provide the student with instruction on mathematics and physics as they apply to a nuclear power plant reactor operator.
  Learning Outcome: Upon successful completion of this course, the student will be able to define, explain and/or solve various arithmetic operations, algebraic terms, systems of linear equations, trigonometric functions, and physics problems for nuclear power plants.
  Instruction: Course covers subjects related to mathematics and physics including arithmetic operations, algebra, logarithms, geometry, trigonometry, unit conversion, differential and integral calculus, basic physics from Newton's laws through the concepts of work and energy.
  Credit recommendation: In the lower division baccalaureate/associate degree category, 1 semester hour in Science (12/87).

COC: Reactor Theory (COBOIN-RT)
  Location: Shearon Harris Energy and Environmental Center, New Hill, NC.
  Length: 69 hours (10 weeks).
  Dates: January 1983-December 1986.
  Objective: To provide instruction on reactor theory as it applies to a nuclear power plant reactor operator.
  Learning Outcome: Upon successful completion of this course, the student will have knowledge of concepts related to atomic and nuclear physics as well as basic nuclear reactor theory.
  Instruction: Course covers subjects related to reactor theory including the details of atomic structure and radioactive decay of elements, the behavior and control of the neutron flux in a power reactor, and those factors necessary to achieve and maintain a critical reactor.
  Credit recommendation: In the lower division baccalaureate/associate degree category, 2 semester hours in

Nuclear Engineering Technology (12/87).

NORTH CAROLINA STATE UNIVERSITY, BURLINGTON LABORATORY: REACTOR OPERATOR TRAINING

Radiation Control and Measurement Laboratory (ROT-201)

Location: Burlington Laboratory, NCSU Campus, Raleigh, NC.
Length: 28 hours (1 week); 10.5 hours lecture and 17.5 hours laboratory.
Dates: January 1978-January 1981.
Objective: To introduce techniques relating to health physics measurements at nuclear power plants.
Learning Outcome: Upon successful completion of this course, the student will have knowledge of survey instrument operation, monitoring techniques, water chemistry procedures, and the use of anti-contamination clothing.
Instruction: Course covers the basic principles used in radiation detection and process instrumentation in commercial nuclear power plants. Topics include the various techniques of radiation monitoring, personnel monitoring, reactor nuclear instrumentation, contamination control, process measurement, and water chemistry analysis as applicable to commercial power reactor plants.
Credit recommendation: In the lower division baccalaureate/associate degree category, 1 semester hour in Nuclear Science (Health Physics) (12/87). NOTE: Credit should not be awarded for both Nuclear Engineering Fundamentals Laboratory (ROT-301) and this course.

Nuclear Engineering Fundamentals Laboratory (ROT-301)

Location: Burlington Laboratory, NCSU Campus, Raleigh, NC.
Length: 31.5 hours (1 week); 11.5 hours lecture and 20 hours laboratory.
Dates: February 1985-Present.
Objective: To provide knowledge and experience relating to radiation control and thermal hydraulic processes applicable to nuclear reactors.
Learning Outcome: Upon successful completion of this course, the student will have been introduced to radiation monitoring concepts, fluid systems, and heat transfer.
Instruction: Course covers radiation measurement, radiation shielding, heat transfer and fluid flow in reactors, and power plant thermodynamics.
Credit recommendation: In the lower division baccalaureate/associate degree category, 1 semester hour in Nuclear Engineering Technology (12/87).

Nuclear Reactor Operations Laboratory (ROT-401)

Location: Burlington Laboratory, NCSU Campus, Raleigh, NC.
Length: 38 hours (1 week); 11.5 hours lecture and 26.5 hours laboratory.
Dates: January 1978-Present.
Objective: To provide the student with experience relating to the operation of a light water reactor.
Learning Outcome: Upon successful completion of this course, the student will have an increased understanding of practical concepts related to the operation of a nuclear reactor.
Instruction: Course covers topics pertinent to the design and operation of commercial power reactors which are presented and demonstrated through laboratory experiments. Topics include subcritical behavior, reactor statics, reactor kinetics, transient analysis, and reactor safety considerations.
Credit recommendation: In the lower division baccalaureate/associate degree category, 1 semester hour in Nuclear Engineering Technology (12/87).

The Catholic Home Study Institute

The Catholic Home Study Institute (CHSI) was established in 1983 by the Roman Catholic Church as a correspondence institute for training adults in the tenents, principles, history and practices of the Roman Catholic Church. The Institute, which is accredited by the Accrediting Commission of the NHSC, is a non-profit corporation in the State of Virginia governed by a seven member board made up of both Catholic clergy and laity with wide experience in the field of education.

In November 1983, CHSI was designated a Pontifical Institute by the Vatican office for religious education. This approval entitles CHSI students to earn a Pontifical Diploma (teaching certificate) for successfully completing fifteen correspondence courses in designated subjects.

CHSI maintains a computerized data base on each student. It is updated weekly and printed monthly for the purpose of maintaining a system of motivation letters. It also indicates course completion dates, grades, college credits earned, personal data and payment period.

Because of the unique nature of correspondence education, the teaching staff for each course includes the following three persons: (1) the course author who writes the course manual, (2) the staff instructor who is a trained religious educator. (He or she evaluates the written assignments and examinations, maintains personal contact through motivation letters and telephone calls, and is responsible for calculating the final grade, and (3) the staff theologian who handles specific theological questions and is available to students for consultation by letter or telephone.

The performance of the teaching staff is monitored on a regular basis by the Executive Director who reviews all incoming mail daily. Performance is measured by student course evaluation, student correspondence, re-enrollment rates and a complaint file, all of which are reviewed weekly by the Executive Director.

CHSI seeks course authors who (1) have a Ph.D. or its equivalent, unless other credentials are equally suitable, (2) have at least three years teaching experience at the college level in the subject area of interest and, (3) have publishing experience and/or a published textbook that could be used as the text for the course. Many CHSI course authors are renowned in their fields.

Source of official student records: Department of Student Services, CHSI, 9 Loudoun Street, S.E., Leesburg, Virginia 22075.

Additional information about the courses: Program on Noncollegiate Sponsored Instruction, The Center for Adult Learning and Educational Credentials, American Council on Education, One Dupont Circle, Suite 1B-20, Washington, D.C. 20036.

Catechesis of the High School Student (101-0901)
  Location: Home Study.
  Length: 9 lessons (Approximately 6 months required for course completion).
  Dates: March 1987-Present.
  Objective: To present the methods and psychology of teaching religion to the high school age student. Includes official Church documents and terminology on how to present theological concepts and methods of lesson planning.
  Instruction: Identifies the characteristics of youth, the "whole person" approach to catechetics; defines "real assent" and lists principle teaching tools, emphasizes lesson planning, the place of imagination, memory, intellect and will along with effective and proven teaching techniques. Explains appropriate and established means of motivation.
  Credit recommendation: In the upper division baccalaureate category, 3 semester hours in Psychology or Religious Education (4/87).

Christian Spirituality in the Catholic Tradition (101-0701)
  Location: Home Study.
  Length: 10 lessons (Approximately 6 months required for course completion).
  Dates: May 1987-Present.
  Objective: To examine the historical development and theological elements of Catholic spiritual traditions from the early Church Fathers to the nineteenth century.
  Instruction: Introduction to the origin and development of Christian asceticism, identifying the early and subsequent spiritual schools and their leaders. Following chapters trace the emergence of western monasticism with emphasis on Augustine and Benedict. Continues the development of spirituality through the subsequent centuries up until modern times.

  Credit recommendation: In the upper division baccalaureate category, 3 semester hours in Religious Studies or Theology (1/87).

The Church and Human Destiny (101-0103)
  Location: Home Study.
  Length: 17 lessons (Approximately 6 months required for course completion).
  Dates: May 1986-Present.
  Objective: To introduce the student to doctrinal theology that examines the fundamental teachings of the Catholic Church as contained in the Third Article of the Apostles Creed — the Church and Eschatology.
  Instruction: The final articles of the Creed: the foundation of the Church, its four marks, ecumenism, church-state relations, religious freedom, eschatology: the four last things (heaven, hell, death, and judgement).
  Credit recommendation: In the lower division baccalaureate/associate degree category, 3 semester hours in Religious Studies or Theology (1/87).

God, Man, and the Universe (101-0101)
  Location: Home Study.
  Length: 13 lessons (Approximately 6 months required for course completion).
  Dates: May 1986-Present.
  Objective: To introduce the student to doctrinal theology that examines the fundamental teachings of the Catholic Church as contained in the First Article of the Apostles Creed — God the Creator, original sin and the fall of man.
  Instruction: Introductory study of Revelation, the relationship between Sacred Scripture and Sacred Tradition; the first articles of the Creed: God the Creator, the Trinity, Providence, the Angels, Satan, Original Sin — the fall of man, evolution.
  Credit recommendation: In the lower division baccalaureate/associate degree category, 3 semester hours in Religious Studies or Theology (1/87).

Introduction to Sacred Scripture (101-0401)
  Location: Home Study.
  Length: 14 lessons (Approximately 6 months required for course completion).
  Dates: March 1987-Present.
  Objective: To familiarize the student with terminology of the study of Sacred Scripture; provides the tools for examining specific books of the Old and New Testaments in future courses; examines the Vatican II document *Dei Verbum* which deals with study of Sacred Scripture.
  Instruction: Introduces basic scriptural concepts: inspiration, inerrancy, and canonicity. Traces the origin of the Bible, the transmission of the text; explains the different versions of the biblical texts, the major pertinent documents of the Church dealing with Scripture. Discusses the scope of hermeneutics, the presuppositions affecting inter-

pretation, textural criticism, the contribution of archaeology and geography. Explains and critiques methods of redaction and exegesis.

Credit recommendation: In the lower division baccalaureate/associate degree category, 3 semester hours in Religious Studies or Theology (4/87).

Jesus Christ, Mary, and the Grace of God (101-0102)
Location: Home Study.
Length: 16 lessons (Approximately 6 months required for course completion).
Dates: May 1986-Present.
Objective: To introduce the student to doctrinal theology that examines the fundamental teachings of the Catholic Church as contained in the Second Article of the Apostles Creed—Jesus Christ, Mary, and divine grace.
Instruction: The second article of the Creed: Jesus Christ in Sacred Scripture, the Church's teaching on the Person and work of Jesus Christ, the Hypostalic Union, heresies, the role of Mary, the doctrine of grace, the virtues and gifts of the Holy Spirit.
Credit recommendation: In the lower division baccalaureate/associate degree category, 3 semester hours in Religious Studies or Theology (1/87).

Nature of Christian Spirituality (101-0702)
Location: Home Study.
Length: 13 lessons (Approximately 6 months required for course completion).
Dates: March 1987-Present.
Objective: This course aims to define the nature and source of Christian Spirituality and demonstrates, at the same time, how it differs from all other religious, i.e., its peculiarities and uniqueness.
Instruction: Introduces a study of Christian holiness, examines the relevant instruments employed by the Holy Spirit in inviting and leading the Christian to a more intimate union with God: grace, revelation, the meaning and relationship of old and new covenants, the significance of the cross of redemption. Develops understanding of agape and the Church. Reviews the theology of St. Thomas concerning God's love and sanctifying grace. Explores the roles of Son and Spirit in the spiritual life of the human person. Integrates the charismatic and the hierarchical aspects of ecclesial life. Concludes with an exposition of the place of the Sacraments in the growth of holy community with emphasis on the primacy and centrality of the Eucharist.
Credit recommendation: In the upper division baccalaureate category, 3 semester hours in Religious Studies or Theology (4/87).

The Philosophy of Communism (101-0802)
Location: Home Study.
Length: 9 lessons (Approximately 6 months required for course completion).
Dates: March 1987-Present.
Objective: To present the philosophical and historical setting for the emergence of communism, its founders, proponents, its philosophy and how it impacts on Catholicism in various parts of the world. Communism is viewed in contrast to the Roman Catholic Faith.
Instruction: Traces the evolution of society that preceded the emergence of radical socialism; shows Marx as its logical leader; explains "dialectical materialism" and covers the range of Marxist concepts and principles dealing with materialism, the human person, the state, private ownership, religion; gives Marxist prophecy concerning present world; discusses the proletarian revolution, the communist future; and explains the effect of communism on the Church.
Credit recommendation: In the upper division baccalaureate category, 3 semester hours in Philosophy, Political Science or Religious Studies (4/87).

The Ten Commandments Today, Part A (101-0301)
Location: Home Study.
Length: 10 lessons (Approximately 6 months required for course completion).
Dates: May 1986-Present.
Objective: To introduce the student to moral theology, its terms and concepts and to provide detailed application of concepts to first five commandments of the Decalogue seen from the point of view of Scripture and Church teaching.
Instruction: Introduction to moral theology: moral responsibility, conscience, objective moral principles, the first five commandments according to Scripture and Church teaching.
Credit recommendation: In the lower division baccalaureate/associate degree category, 3 semester hours in Religious Studies or Theology (1/87).

The Ten Commandments Today, Part B (101-0302)
Location: Home Study.
Length: 13 lessons (Approximately 6 months required for course completion).
Dates: May 1986-Present.
Objective: To continue the study of basic moral theological principles, the last five commandments of the Decalogue in Scripture and Church teaching.
Instruction: A continuation of 101-0301: the basic principles of moral theology, the last five commandments.
Credit recommendation: In the lower division baccalaureate/associate degree category, 3 semester hours in Religious Studies or Theology (1/87).

Theology of the Sacraments, Part One (101-0201)
Location: Home Study.
Length: 9 lessons (Approximately 6 months required for course completion).
Dates: April 1986-Present.

Objective: To introduce the student to sacramental theology, to liturgy, and to the theological/historical development of Eucharist and Penance.

Instruction: An introduction to liturgy and the Sacraments of Eucharist and Penance, their history and theology.

Credit recommendation: In the lower division baccalaureate/associate degree category, 3 semester hours in Religious Studies or Theology (1/87).

Theology of the Sacraments, Part Two (101-0202)
Location: Home Study.
Length: 12 lessons (Approximately 6 months required for course completion).
Dates: April 1987-Present.
Objective: A continuation of the study of sacramental theology dealing with the historical and theological development of the Sacraments of Baptism, Confirmation, Marriage, Holy Orders and Anointing of the Sick. A brief study is made of related subjects such as sacramentals, Liturgy of the Hours and indulgences.

Instruction: Continues the study of the Sacraments not treated in Part One: Baptism, Confirmation, Holy Orders, Marriage, and the Anointing of the Sick. Explains "Sacramental character," the ministers of the Sacraments, the requirements for valid reception, the appropriate grace of each Sacrament and discusses sacramentals.

Credit recommendation: In the lower division baccalaureate/associate degree category, 3 semester hours in Religious Studies or Theology (1/87).

The Center for Leadership Development

The Center for Leadership Development (which administers the Institutes for Organization Management and the Academy Program) was formerly a department of the U.S. Chamber of Commerce, but in 1986 became a part of the National Chamber Foundation, an independent nonprofit, public policy research and educational organization affiliated with the U.S. Chamber. The educational direction of the National Chamber Foundation lies largely in the area of public policy. The Foundation conducts seminars and public conferences in areas of public policy, and considers the publication of these proceedings as well as other publications part of its educational mandate. The Institutes are conducted seven times a year, at seven different university sites. The Academy is conducted once a year at the University of Notre Dame.

The Center for Leadership Development provides the business community with a variety of educational programs, currently in five key areas: educational programs for local chamber of commerce and trade/professional association executives; public policy seminars for business leaders; training programs for new Center speakers and faculty; scholarships for qualifying business, association and chamber executives; publishing program to develop and publish educational materials. The Center currently administers and/or manages three programs: Institutes for Organization Management and Corporate Executive Development.

The Institutes for Organization Management and Academy are programs founded on a strong management development philosophy. The elements of this philosophy include the following tenets: the opportunity to develop management abilities which should be available to all voluntary organization executives; management is a highly valuable organization resource; individual effort is the essence of development; the opportunity for decision-making experience must be present; development must center on future as well as present positions; management development is a continuing process; standards are needed for appraising management performance; the management development program should be periodically evaluated; and general management concepts should be stressed for chief paid executives as well as managers of special departments. Six years are required to complete the Institutes for Organization Management Program and three years are required to complete the Academy Program.

Course development is accomplished by the Center's Board of Trustees, a Curriculum Review Committee, and Faculty Chairs who are responsible for the actual course content. Students participating in the six-year Institutes must achieve eighty percent mastery of the material to receive credit recommendations. Students participating in the Academy Program are required to complete a research paper at the conclusion of the three-year program to be eligible for credit recommendations.

Source of official student records: Enrollment Secretary, Center for Leadership Development, National Chamber Foundation, 1615 H Street, N.W., Washington, D.C. 20062.

Additional information about the courses: Program on Noncollegiate Sponsored Instruction, The Center for Adult Learning and Educational Credentials, American Council on Education, One Dupont Circle, Washington, D.C. 20036.

Applied Management
1. **Development and Management of Members and Volunteers**
2. **Chambers/Associates: An Overview**
3. **Membership Operations**
4. **Public Relations**
5. **Sources of Non-Dues Income**
6. **Community Analysis and Development**

Location: Various locations throughout the United States.

Length: 6 seminars, each three hours in length, over a six-year period with pre-test and extensive outside reading.

Dates: June 1988-Present.

Objective: To provide the student with an overview of the role of the chambers and associations with focus on the structure, membership operations, public relations, dues income, and community analysis and development.

Learning Outcome: Upon successful completion of this course, the student will be able to understand the functions and roles of a chamber manager; learn how to create a sound chamber policy; identify resources available to professions to help them deal with situations; understand the importance of membership to the overall chamber effectiveness; gain a better understanding of the differences between services and sources of income; understand the public relations role in the management process; establish and maintain a positive relationship between the chamber and the media; identify the most important target markets for public relations; develop methods to find out *why* a particular community is unique; identify low-cost, time-saving resources to aid in economic and community development; know the differences between dues income and non-dues income; identify possible new sources of income for participating organizations; and understand the pros and cons of other sources of income for organizations.

Instruction: During the first year, the course "Development and Management of Members and Volunteers" allows active participation while reinforcing the most important aspects of volunteer recruitment and motivation. An overview of the chamber covers basic organizational steps in creating and managing a chamber of commerce effectively. Basic membership operations is also covered during the first year when a review of various types of membership sales, increase and retention programs are reviewed such as those being used successfully around the United States. The "Public Relations" course is offered during the third year and helps the student to gain a clearer understanding of the public relations process and the tools and skills necessary to implement an on-going plan. The fifth course, "Commmunity Analysis and Development," introduces the student to the analytical tools needed to assess change, identify community leadership, and strengths and weaknesses within the local community. The sixth course, "Sources of Non-Dues Income," helps students to understand ways to generate income and develop funds for his/her organization. Methodology includes lecture, experiential learning/exercises, simulations, role plays, and case studies.

Credit recommendation: In the lower division baccalaureate/associate degree category, 2 semester hours in Applied Management (1/89).

Business and Society
1. **Ethics for the Executive and the Organization**
2. **Technology and Human Values**
3. **Rights, Interests, Law**
4. **Government Relations**
5. **Anti-Trust**
6. **Chambers Association Law**

Location: Various locations throughout the United States.

Length: 6 seminars, each three hours in length, over a six-year period with pre-test and extensive outside readings.

Dates: June 1988-Present.

Objective: To introduce the student to technology ethics, the law, and government as they influence the role of business in society.

Learning Outcome: Upon successful completion of this course, the student will be able to think critically about new developments in technology; relate conceptions of human rights to competing philosophies of business and society; and think critically about the ethical responsibilities of executives.

Instruction: Course covers ethics for the executive and the human rights organization, individual and group behavior and the law, technology, human values, and government behavior. Methodology includes lecture, discussion, classroom exercises, and films.

Credit recommendation: In the lower division baccalaureate/associate degree category, 2 semester hours in Business and Society (1/89).

Economics
1. **Finance/Budgeting**
2. **Microeconomy**
3. **Macroeconomy**

Location: Various locations throughout the United States.

Length: 3 seminars, each three hours in length, over a six-year period with pre-test and extensive outside readings.

Dates: June 1988-Present.

Objective: To provide the student with an examination of operation, nature, and structure of the economy as well as the effects of macroeconomic policies and the control of cash flow and investments.

Learning Outcome: Upon successful completion of this course, the student will be able to understand the structure of the American economy and the roles of consumers, business, labor, and government; be familiar with alternative fiscal and monetary policies and their impact on achieving economic goals; know how to plan and control cash flows and be familiar with corresponding investment vehicles.

Instruction: Course covers the structure of the American economy, economic roles of consumers, labor, business firms, and government, macroeconomic goals and their attainment, monetary and fiscal policies, and planning and controlling cash flow. Methodology includes lecture, discussion, classroom exercises, and an open-book pre-test.

Credit recommendation: In the lower division bac-

calaureate/associate degree category, 1 semester hour in Principles of Economics (1/89).

Organizational Behavior
1. Group Analysis
2. Group Motivation
3. Leadership
4. Conflict Management
5. Interpersonal Communication
6. Organizational Communications
7. Communication Skills
8. Applied Decision-Making
9. The Art of Negotiation
10. Interpersonal Power Relations
11. Power and Influence in Groups
12. The Changing Organization
13. Organizing Power Structures

Location: Various locations throughout the United States.
Length: 13 seminars, each three hours in length, over a six-year period with pre-test and extensive outside readings.
Dates: June 1988-Present.
Objective: To introduce the student to the study of the behavior of individuals and groups in organizations.
Learning Outcome: Upon successful completion of this course, the student will be able to gain an increased understanding of human behavior; improve his/her communication skills; recognize range of human needs; work more effectively with groups within organizations; and grasp the roles of power and leadership in organizational effectiveness.
Instruction: Course covers group analysis, group motivation, leadership, conflict management, interpersonal communication, organizational communications, communication skills, applied decision-making, the art of negotiation, interpersonal power relations, power and influence in groups, the changing organization, and organizing power structures. Methodology includes lecture, discussion, and classroom exercises.
Credit recommendation: In the upper division baccalaureate category, 4 semester hours in Organizational Behavior (1/89).

Principles of Management
1. Management Information Systems
2. Managerial Planning
3. The Art of Successful Management
4. Strategic Planning
5. Information Collecting for Decision Making
6. Contemporary Management for Voluntary Organizations
7. Staff Development and Administration
8. The Executive Role and Position

Location: Various locations throughout the United States.
Length: 8 seminars, each three hours in length, over a six-year period.
Dates: June 1988-Present.
Objective: To provide the student with an examination of the issues and interrelationships of planning and controlling within a group context, and management of the flow of information.
Learning Outcome: Upon successful completion of this course, the student will be able to know how managerial planning contributes to achieving the objectives of the organization; understand the role of the executive and staff in planning and setting priorities; understand the importance and methods of staff development and administration; and know how to plan an information system using staff and volunteers.
Instruction: Course covers strategic planning, management by objectives, roles of the executives and staff in planning, staff development and administration, management information systems, and the art of successful management. Methodology includes lecture, discussion, classroom exercises, and an open-book pre-test.
Credit recommendation: In the lower division baccalaureate/associate degree category, 3 semester hours in Principles of Management (1/89).

Central Intelligence Agency

This is the capstone course for the Central Intelligence Agency's Acquisition Management Program. It is designed for engineers and other employees responsible for managing engineering systems acquisitions.

Source of official student records: Career Development Officer, Directorate of Science and Technology, Washington, D.C. 20505.

Additional information about the courses: Program on Noncollegiate Sponsored Instruction, The Center for Adult Learning and Educational Credentials, American Council on Education, One Dupont Circle, Washington, D.C. 20036.

Issues in Program Management in Government Procurement
(The John J. Crowley Memorial Engineering Management Seminar)
Location: CIA headquarters, Washington, D.C.
Length: 46 hours (includes 10 hours of pre-course reading, 28 hours of classroom work, and 8 hours of discussion which involves a guest lecturer and individual case preparation).
Dates: January 1980-Present.
Objective: To enable the student to develop skills and knowledge to manage procurement contracts in research, development, and engineering.
Learning Outcome: Upon successful completion of this

course, the student will understand the management of government contracting officers, representatives and program managers in the solicitation, evaluation, selection, and monitoring of government contracts.

Instruction: This course explores common pitfalls of government contract officers technical representatives in contract monitoring through an analysis of applicable case studies. The course leads to an improved understanding of roles, functions, and relationships of the contracting officer, the contracting officer's technical representatives, and program manager in effective management of an engineering systems development procurement. Lecture, discussion, and case studies are used. Prerequisite: Students who receive credit for this course must have had previous course experience in contract management, three-to-five years of relevant work experience, and permission of the instructor.

Credit recommendation: In the upper division baccalaureate category, 3 semester hours in Program Management in Schools of Business Administration, or in the graduate degree category, 2 semester hours in Program Management in Schools of Business Administration or in Engineering Administration for students with a degree in engineering (4/87).

Certified Employee Benefit Specialist Program

The International Foundation of Employee Benefit Plans and the Wharton School of the University of Pennsylvania cosponsor the Certified Employee Benefit Specialist (CEBS) Program. The International Foundation is responsible for the overall administration of the program, while the Wharton School is responsible for the academic content and educational standards.

The International Foundation is the largest educational organization in the employee benefits field and is dedicated to enhancing the skills and knowledge of those who have responsibility for employee benefit plans. The Foundation annually sponsors educational meetings; administers the CEBS Program; publishes news and information periodicals, research reports, and books; and makes available the services of its Library/Information Center.

The Wharton School's joint sponsorship of the CEBS Program with the International Foundation is an extension of its long interest in adult education.

This ten-course, professional designation program has a threefold purpose:

(1) to enhance individual capabilities for fulfilling responsibilities in the employee benefit sector at a high performance level;

(2) to bestow a measure of professional recognition on those persons who achieve significant competence in the field, as evidenced by passing a series of national examinations; and

(3) to assist the public in evaluating the academic qualifications and competence of persons having responsibilities for employee benefit plans.

To provide participants maximum flexibility for taking courses and preparing for examinations, three different study methods are available: (1) formal classes which are offered at over 70 colleges and universities throughout the United States, (2) study groups, and (3) independent study.

Study materials for the courses can be ordered directly from the International Foundation or can be obtained from some university bookstores offering the CEBS Program. Examination centers are located throughout the country.

Successful completion of a CEBS course is based on passing the national examination. In order to qualify for the CEBS designation, candidates must pass all ten examinations, meet Precertification Standards, and abide by the Principles of Conduct.

Source of official student records: CEBS Department, International Foundation for Employee Benefit Plans, P.O. Box 69, 18700 West Bluemound Road, Brookfield, Wisconsin 53008-0069.

Additional information about the courses: Program on Noncollegiate Sponsored Instruction, The Center for Adult Learning and Educational Credentials, American Council on Education, One Dupont Circle, Washington, D.C. 20036.

CEBS Course I
Life, Health, and Other Group Benefit Programs

Location: Various locations throughout the U.S.

Length: 75 hours (self-study) and 94 hours (formal class sessions).

Dates: January 1979-Present.

Objective: To provide the student with knowledge of the various methods used to protect against the financial consequences resulting from illness, disability, unemployment and premature death using both public and private sector institutional arrangements.

Instruction: Covers the functional approaches to employee benefit planning, social insurance, the group insurance mechanism, life insurance benefits, medical expense benefits, disability income, dental and vision care, prepaid legal services, property and liability insurance benefits, and other benefit plans. Self-study, group study, or formal class sessions are used.

Credit recommendation: In the upper division baccalaureate category, 4 semester hours, or in the graduate degree category, 3 semester hours in Life and Health Insurance, Group Life and Health Insurance, or Employee Benefit Programs (3/81) (4/86). NOTE: This course has been reevaluated and continues to meet requirements for credit recommendations.

CEBS Course II
Pension Plans
  Location: Various locations throughout the U.S.
  Length: 75 hours (self-study) and 94 hours (formal class sessions).
  Dates: January 1978-Present.
  Objective: To teach the student contemporary fundamentals of pension plans, as well as the federal tax considerations and the reporting, disclosure, and other regulations in the management of pension plans.
  Instruction: The course covers the history and development of pension plans, plan design, funding aspects, disclosure requirements, taxation, and plan termination insurance. Self-study, group study, or formal class sessions are used.
  Credit recommendation: In the upper division baccalaureate category, 4 semester hours, or in the graduate degree category, 3 semester hours in Advanced Life Insurance and Pension Plans, or Pension Plans. (3/81) (4/86). NOTE: This course has been reevaluated and continues to meet requirements for credit recommendations.

CEBS Course III
Social Security, Savings Plans, and Other Retirement Arrangements
  Location: Various locations throughout the U.S.
  Length: 75 hours (self-study) and 94 hours (formal class sessions).
  Dates: June 1978-Present.
  Objective: To provide the student with knowledge and understanding of various privately sponsored retirement income vehicles as well as the Social Security system and its provisions.
  Instruction: Topics include profit-sharing plans, thrift and savings plans, employee stock ownership and stock bonus plans, plans for the self-employed, individual retirement accounts, tax deferred annuities, and special executive retirement arrangements. The course also covers old age, survivors, disability and health insurance unemployment compensation, and worker's compensation. Self-study, group study, or formal class sessions are used.
  Credit recommendation: In the upper division baccalaureate category, 4 semester hours, or in the graduate degree category, 3 semester hours in Social Insurance; Social Security; or Social Security, Savings Plans, and Other Retirement Arrangements (3/81) (4/86). NOTE: This course has been reevaluated and continues to meet requirements for credit recommendations.

CEBS Course IV
Management Principles
  Location: Various locations throughout the U.S.
  Length: 75 hours (self-study) and 94 hours (formal class sessions).
  Dates: June 1978-Present.
  Objective: To provide the student with knowledge of the universal concept of management as a process with special emphasis being placed on the environment, structure, and methodology of employee benefits management. The principles, theories, and concepts covered will be used by an individual to staff and administer employee benefit plan operations effectively.
  Instruction: The course includes management organization, human factors in organizing, decision making, planning, controlling, and activation. The principles, concepts, and terminology are applicable to any type of management setting, such as employee benefit systems, manufacturing enterprises, hospitals, sales organizations, and educational institutions. Self-study, group study, or formal class sessions are used.
  Credit recommendation: In the upper division baccalaureate category, 3 semester hours in Management or Organizational Behavior (3/81) (4/86). NOTE: This course has been reevaluated and continues to meet requirements for credit recommendations.

CEBS Course V
Contemporary Legal Environment of Employee Benefit Plans
  Location: Various locations throughout the U.S.
  Length: 75 hours (self-study) and 94 hours (formal class sessions).
  Dates: June 1977-Present.
  Objective: To provide a general knowledge of the legal system and basic understanding of concepts and principles of the legal environment in which employee benefit plans exist and function.
  Instruction: The course covers legal procedure, agency contracts, personal and real property, mortgages, wills, estates, commercial paper, partnerships, corporations, and trusts. Self-study, group study, or formal class sessions are used.
  Credit recommendation: In the upper division baccalaureate category, 3 semester hours in Business/Commercial Law, or Legal Environment of Business (3/81) (4/86). NOTE: This course has been reevaluated and continues to meet requirements for credit recommendations.

CEBS Course VI
Accounting and Information Systems
  Location: Various locations throughout the U.S.
  Length: 75 hours (self-study) and 94 hours (formal class sessions).
  Dates: June 1979-Present.
  Objective: To provide the student with a general knowledge of accounting concepts and information systems.
  Instruction: Covers financial and managerial concepts, noncurrent assets, stockholders equity and long term liabilities, analysis of financial statements, income measurement, control through standard costs, budgeting, cost volume-profit analysis, employee benefit accounting and management information systems. The limitations of ac-

counting and information systems as applied to employee benefit plans are analyzed. Self-study, group study, or formal class sessions are used.

Credit recommendation: In the upper division baccalaureate category, 3 semester hours in Accounting (3/81) (4/86). NOTE: This course has been reevaluated and continues to meet requirements for credit recommendations.

CEBS Course VII
Asset Management
Location: Various locations throughout the U.S.
Length: 75 hours (self-study) and 94 hours (formal class sessions).
Dates: June 1979-Present.
Objective: To provide the student with an understanding of the investment process related to employee benefit plans. Both theory and practice are covered with emphasis on the practical application of important investment concepts.
Instruction: Covers investment objectives, security markets, investment timing, portfolio theory, capital asset pricing theory, portfolio management, technical analysis, and evaluation of financial performance. Self-study, group study, or formal class sessions are used.
Credit recommendation: In the upper division baccalaureate category, 3 semester hours in Asset Management, Investments, Investment Analysis, or Investment Management (3/81) (4/86). NOTE: This course has been reevaluated and continues to meet requirements for credit recommendations.

CEBS Course VIII
Personnel and Labor Relations
Location: Various locations throughout the U.S.
Length: 75 hours (self-study) and 94 hours (formal class sessions).
Dates: January 1980-Present.
Objective: To provide the student with a basic understanding of the labor relations movement in the United States and general knowledge of the union-management process.
Instruction: Covers employer-employee relations with a special focus on collective bargaining. Topics include personnel relations, manpower planning, recruitment and selection, personnel evaluation, wage and salary administration, and employee benefit plans. Self-study, group study, or formal class sessions are used.
Credit recommendation: In the upper division baccalaureate category, 3 semester hours, or in the graduate degree category, 2 semester hours in Human Resources Management, Labor Relations/Industrial Relations, or Personnel Administration (3/81) (4/86). NOTE: This course has been reevaluated and continues to meet requirements for credit recommendations.

CEBS Course IX
Employee Benefit Plans and the Economy
Location: Various locations throughout the U.S.
Length: 75 hours (self-study) and 94 hours (formal class sessions).
Dates: January 1980-Present.
Objective: To provide the student with a general knowledge of microeconomic principles and how they impact on employee benefit plans.
Instruction: Covers the economic principle underlying inflation, national income, business cycles, employment levels, money and banking, monetary and fiscal policy, and international economics. Other topics include analysis of the impact of such economic principles on employee benefits; the economic impact of pension plans; and the ways in which unemployment and inflation affect Social Security, pension plans, and health and welfare plans. Self-study, group study, or formal class sessions are used.
Credit recommendation: In the upper division baccalaureate category, 3 semester hours in Economic Principles, General Economics, or Macroeconomics (3/81) (4/86). NOTE: This course has been reevaluated and continues to meet requirements for credit recommendations.

CEBS X
Contemporary Benefit Issues and Administration
Location: Various locations throughout the U.S.
Length: 75 hours (self-study) and 94 hours (formal class sessions).
Dates: June 1980-Present.
Objective: To provide the student with knowledge of contemporary issues affecting employee benefit plans and of the principles of employee benefit plan administration.
Instruction: Covers issues involving fiduciary responsibility concepts for employee benefit plans, actuarial issues, management of pension plan assets, accounting for pension costs, taxation and administration of employee benefit plans, qualified retirement plans for small business, managing employee health benefits and international employee benefit plans. Methodology includes case analyses to supplement prepared readings. Self-study, group study, or formal class sessions are used. It is recommended that this course be taken last or concurrently with the last CEBS course(s) taken.
Credit recommendation: In the upper division baccalaureate category, 4 semester hours, or in the graduate degree category, 3 semester hours in Advanced Personnel Administration, Contemporary Benefit Issues and Administration, or Employee Benefits (3/81) (4/86). NOTE: This course has been reevaluated and continues to meet requirements for credit recommendations.

Certified Medical Representatives Institute, Inc.

The Certified Medical Representatives Program was established to provide and administer a complete educational and professional development program designed primarily for the needs of medical representatives employed in the United States and Canada.

The curriculum has been designed in a broad manner in order to enforce and complement the sales-training programs offered by pharmaceutical companies. Courses and examinations have been developed under the supervision of educators in various universities throughout the United States.

Upon successful completion of required scientific subjects and other elective courses which are closely related to his or her professional responsibilities, the medical representative is awarded the C.M.R. designation by the Institute. The C.M.R. award certifies the professional competency of the representative in pertinent areas of knowledge and signifies a certified career representative.

Source of official student records: Certified Medical Representatives Institute, Inc., 4316 Brambleton Avenue, S.W., Roanoke, Virginia 24018.

Additional information about the courses: Program on Noncollegiate Sponsored Instruction, The Center for Adult Learning and Educational Credentials, American Council on Education, One Dupont Circle, Washington, D.C. 20036.

Anatomy (1-A)
Location: CMR Institute Centers located regionally throughout the U.S.
Length: Self-study.
Dates: December 1968-February 1989.
Objective: To provide the student without an educational background in human anatomy with a basic understanding of the structure of the human body.
Instruction: Covers the cell, tissues, and the skeletal, muscular, cardiovascular, nervous, digestive, respiratory, urinary, reproductive, endocrine, and integumentary systems. While the course includes the study of both gross and microscopic structures and their relationships to systems, detailed anatomical relationships are not considered. Methodology includes self-study and examination.
Credit recommendation: In the lower division baccalaureate/associate degree category, 2 semester hours in Nursing, Occupational Therapy Assistants, or Physical Therapy (4/80).

Behavioral Pathology and Treatment (7-A)
Location: CMR Institute Centers located regionally throughout the U.S.
Length: Self-study.
Dates: January 1989-Present.
Objective: To provide the student with an overview of the major categories of behavioral disorders and to describe the methods of psychotherapy and pharmacotherapy used in their treatments.
Learning Outcome: Upon successful completion of this course, the student will be able to process basic knowledge in psychotherapy; and become familiar with the pharmacology related to behavioral disorders.
Instruction: Course provides introduction to psychotherapy, psychonalytic theory and modern psychotherapy, an overview of behavioral disorders which includes pharmacology and neurotransmitter activity. The course also covers a list of behavioral disorders which includes some of the following: anxiety disorders, affective (mood) disorders, psychotic disorders, organic mental disorders, and impulse control disorders. Methodology includes self-study with text, audiotape, and pre- and post-tests, progress checks, and final examination.
Credit recommendation: In the lower division baccalaureate/associate degree category, 3 semester hours in Abnormal Psychology (1/89).

Biochemistry (2-A, 2-B)
Location: CMR Institute Centers located regionally throughout the U.S.
Length: Self-study.
Dates: December 1975-December 1988.
Objective: To provide the student with a basic knowledge and understanding of biochemical principles and mechanisms.
Instruction: Topics include carbohydrates, lipids, proteins, digestion and absorption, nutrition, nucleic acids, energy metabolism, and biochemical regulation. Intermediary metabolism and the role of enzymes are discussed in some detail. Emphasis is placed on human biochemical processes and controls.
Credit recommendation: In the lower division baccalaureate/associate degree category, 3 semester hours in Survey of Biochemistry (4/80).

Cardiovascular System (6-C)
Location: CMR Institute Centers located regionally throughout the U.S.
Length: Self-study.
Dates: January 1988-Present.
Objective: To provide the student with a broad understanding of the mechanisms of the cardiovascular system, pharmacological applications and disorders of the system.
Learning Outcome: Upon successful completion of this course, the student will be able to describe the anatomy, physiology and functions of the cardiovascular system; describe common disorders of the cardiovascular system-etiology and symptoms; and describe therapeutic classes of drugs appropriate for cardiovascular disorders.
Instruction: Course covers functions and components of the cardiovascular system, circulation, lymphatic sys-

tem, cardiovascular system disorders, and related pharmacology. Methodology includes self-study with text, audiotape, pre- and post-tests, progress checks, and final examination.

Credit recommendation: In the lower division baccalaureate/associate degree category, 2 semester hours in Allied Health, Health Sciences, Human Biology, or Nursing (2/89). NOTE: Students who complete this course in combination with Digestive, Endocrine, Integumentary, Musculoskeletal, Nervous, Reproductive, Respiratory, Sensory Organs, and Urinary Systems should receive 8 semester hours in Anatomy, 8 semester hours in Physiology, and 4 semester hours in Applied Pharmacology.

Clinical Drug Interactions (2-J)
Location: CMR Institute Centers located regionally throughout the U.S.
Length: Self-study.
Dates: December 1976-December 1988.
Objective: To provide the student with basic information about the interactions of commonly prescribed drugs.
Instruction: Covers drug interactions related to absorption, chemical reactions, excretion, and metabolism of routine drugs. The roles of the pharmacist, hospital personnel, and patients in preventing adverse interactions are also included. Self-instructional course including workbook and audiotape presentation.
Credit recommendation: In the lower division baccalaureate/associate degree category, 2 semester hours in Introduction to Drug Interactions or an Allied Health or Nursing elective (4/80).

Digestive System (6-H)
Location: CMR Institute Centers located regionally throughout the U.S.
Length: Self-study.
Dates: September 1987-Present.
Objective: To provide the student with an understanding of the digestive system and its role in digestion and absorption of food substances to provide the body's need for energy and nutrients.
Learning Outcome: Upon successful completion of this course, the student will be able to describe the anatomy and physiology of the digestive system and its role in conversion of foods to energy and absorbed nutrients; describe disorders of the digestive system and the pharmacology of drug classes relevant to these disorders.
Instruction: Course covers the structure and function of the digestive system, the physiology of digestion and absorption, disorders of the system and the pharmacology of drugs related to digestive system disorders. Methodology includes self-study with text, audiotape, pre- and post-test, progress checks, and final examination.
Credit recommendation: In the lower division baccalaureate/associate degree category, 2 semester hours in Allied Health, Health Sciences, Human Biology, or Nursing (2/89). NOTE: Students who complete this course in combination with Cardiovascular, Endocrine, Integumentary, Musculoskeletal, Nervous, Reproductive, Respiratory, Sensory Organs, and Urinary Systems should receive 8 semester hours in Anatomy, 8 semester hours in Physiology, and 4 semester hours in Applied Pharmacology.

Endocrine System (6-F)
Location: CMR Institute Centers located regionally throughout the U.S.
Length: Self-study.
Dates: May 1988-Present.
Objective: To provide the student with a broad understanding of how the endocrine system influences growth and development, reproduction, homeostasis, and energy production, utilization and storage, and the pharmacology related to the system.
Learning Outcome: Upon successful completion of this course, the student will be able to describe the endocrine system (structure and function) and its component parts; describe the hormones of the endocrine system and their roles; and describe common disorders of the system, their diagnosis and related pharmacology.
Instruction: Course covers the anatomy and physiology of the endocrine system and its components; disorders of the system; and pharmacology related to the endocrine system. Methodology includes self-study with text, audiotape, pre- and post-tests, progress checks, and final examination.
Credit recommendation: In the lower division baccalaureate/associate degree category, 2 semester hours in Allied Health, Health Sciences, Human Biology, or Nursing (2/89). NOTE: Students who complete this course in combination with Cardiovascular, Digestive, Integumentary, Musculoskeletal, Nervous, Reproductive, Respiratory, Sensory Organs, and Urinary Systems should receive 8 semester hours in Anatomy, 8 semester hours in Physiology, and 4 semester hours in Applied Pharmacology.

Ethics (2-E)
Location: CMR Institute Centers located regionally throughout the U.S.
Length: Self-study.
Dates: December 1969-December 1988.
Objective: To present considerations of the medical (pharmaceutical) representative's legal and moral responsibilities and obligations in his/her unique role.
Instruction: The course considers doctrinal or theoretical and practical applications. The first section of the text reviews the history of technical thought and the principles which have engaged minds from the earliest days. The remaining discussion is devoted to the meaning of the theoretical in terms of issues facing persons who work in the medical sciences. Self-study and examination are used.
Credit recommendation: In the lower division baccalaureate/associate degree category or in the upper divi-

sion baccalaureate degree category, 2 semester hours in Medical Ethics for Allied Health Fields, Nursing, or in prehealth professional programs such as Dentistry, Medicine, or Pharmacy (4/80).

Governmental Regulations (1-F)
Location: CMR Institute Centers located regionally throughout the U.S.
Length: Self-study.
Dates: December 1975-December 1988.
Objective: To familiarize the student with a broad coverage and interpretation of major and significant regulations which influence or control the development and distribution of pharmaceutical products; effects of these regulations on the medical representative's job and his/her relationships with employers and clients.
Instruction: Provides a better understanding of the medical representative's obligations and responsibilities as well as general exposure to the broad scope of regulations governing the manufacturing and distribution of drugs. The course also covers general considerations in business law and outlines essentials of the federal insurance program for the aged (Medicare). Self-study and examination are used.
Credit recommendation: In the lower division baccalaureate/associate degree category, 2 semester hours in pre-pharmacy or pharmacy assisting programs (4/80).

Healthcare Community (7-D)
Location: CMR Institute Centers located regionally throughout the U.S.
Length: Self-study.
Dates: January 1989-Present.
Objective: To provide the student with an overview of healthcare providers, funding, and delivery.
Learning Outcome: Upon successful completion of this course, the student will be able to become knowledgeable about the professionals of the healthcare community, their roles, educational backgrounds, and perspectives; become knowledgeable of healthcare funding from the private and public (government) sectors; and become knowledgeable of the healthcare inpatient and outpatient delivery systems.
Instruction: Course covers current issues that affect the relationships between professional groups; the education and development of physicians; types of physicians; a description of the roles of nurses, physician assistants, pharmacists, dentists, and other healthcare professionals. Also covered is the role of professional associates in the healthcare community; an overview of healthcare funding and private health insurances; a discussion of government programs such as Medicare and Medicaid recent developments in healthcare delivery; demographics and attitudes of patients and a description of hospitals and long-term care facilities. Methodology includes self-study with text, audiotape, pre- and post-tests, progress checks and final examination.
Credit recommendation: In the lower division baccalaureate/associate degree category, 3 semester hours in Allied Health or Health Care Administration (2/89).

History of the Pharmaceutical Industry (2-F)
Location: CMR Institute Centers located regionally throughout the U.S.
Length: Self-study.
Dates: December 1977-December 1988.
Objective: To provide the student with information about the background and development of the pharmaceutical industry from its beginning to the present.
Instruction: The text consists of three essays, each designed to give a historic overview of the significant phases in the development of the pharmaceutical industry. The text is designed to relate the industry to important events in the history of healing. Self-study and examination are used.
Credit recommendation: In the lower division baccalaureate/associate degree category or in the upper division baccalaureate category, 1 semester hour in Pharmaceutical History for pharmacy or pharmacy assistant majors or any other student interested in medicine/pharmacy history as an elective (4/80).

Human Body, Pathology and Treatment (5-A)
Location: CMR Institute Centers located regionally throughout the U.S.
Length: Self-study.
Dates: May 1987-Present.
Objective: To provide the student with a basic knowledge and understanding of the body systems and their functions.
Learning Outcome: Upon successful completion of this course, the student will be able to describe basic anatomy and physiology of the human body including body systems and funcitons; describe in general terms approaches to disease prevention and treatment; correctly use basic medical terminology in discussions of body systems and pathology.
Instruction: Course covers objectives and concerns of the health profession, basic body chemistry, body cells, tissues and defenses, body systems, and treatment approaches. Methodology includes self-study with text, audiotape, pre- and post-tests, progress checks, and final examination.
Credit recommendation: In the lower division baccalaureate/associate degree category, 3 semester hours in Introductory Human Biology (2/89).

Immune System (6-D)
Location: CMR Institute Centers located regionally throughout the U.S.
Length: Self-study.
Dates: May 1988-Present.

Objective: To provide the student with general knowledge of the components and functions of the immune system.

Learning Outcome: Upon successful completion of this course, the student will be able to discuss the immune response with respect to cellular interactions in both humoral and cell mediated responses; discuss disorders related to the immune system including the disease process and methods of treatment; relate the pharmacology of drugs relevant to immune system disorders to the total concept of the immune system physiology.

Instruction: Course covers production and function of the cells of the immune system, structure and function of antibodies, humoral and cell medicated immunity, immune response, hypersensitivity, autoimmunity, immunodeficiency disorders including acquired immune deficiency syndrome, pharmacology of drugs relevant to immune system disorders and the production of immunity and transplant immunology. Methodology includes self-study with text, audiotape, pre- and post-tests, progress checks, and final examination.

Credit recommendation: In the lower division baccalaureate/associate degree category, 3 semester hours in Basic Immunology (2/89).

Integumentary System (6-B)

Location: CMR Institute Centers located regionally throughout the U.S.

Length: Self-study.

Dates: September 1987-Present.

Objective: To provide the student with a broad understanding of the anatomy and physiology of the integumentary system and pharmacology as it relates to the skin.

Learning Outcome: Upon successful completion of this course, the student will be able to describe the anatomy and physiology of the integumentary system; describe common disorders of the system, causes, symptoms, and treatments.

Instruction: Course covers the anatomy and physiology of the integumentary system, pharmacology of drugs related to skin disorders, disorders of the integumentary system including etiology, symptoms, and treatments. Methodology includes self-study with text, audiotape, pre- and post-tests, progress checks, and final examination.

Credit recommendation: In the lower division baccalaureate/associate degree category, 2 semester hours in Allied Health, Health Sciences, Human Biology, or Nursing (2/89). NOTE: Students who complete this course in combination with Cardiovascular, Digestive, Endocrine, Musculoskeletal, Nervous, Reproductive, Respiratory, Sensory Organs, and Urinary Systems should receive 8 semester hours in Anatomy, 8 semester hours in Physiology, and 4 semester hours in Applied Pharmacology.

Introduction to Disease States (2-I)

Location: CMR Institute Centers located regionally throughout the U.S.

Length: Self-study.

Dates: December 1976-December 1988.

Objective: To provide the student with a general understanding of basic human pathology.

Instruction: Course covers pathological conditions associated with the major body systems, genetic disorders, methods of injury, and the human body's defense mechanisms. Self-instruction.

Credit recommendation: In the lower division baccalaureate/associate degree category or in the upper division baccalaureate category, 3 semester hours in Introduction to Human Pathology for Allied Health, Principles of Human Disease, Nursing, or undergraduate programs in the health field (4/80).

Introduction to Pharmacology (5-B)

Location: CMR Institute Centers located regionally throughout the U.S.

Length: Self-study.

Dates: May 1987-Present.

Objective: To provide the student with a broad understanding of basic pharmacology.

Learning Outcome: Upon successful completion of this course, the student will be able to describe basic principles of drug actions and interactions including adverse reactions and factors modifying response; describe actions of drugs by therapeutic classes; discuss the techniques by which drugs are administered to treat diseases.

Instruction: Course covers basic principles of drug actions and interactions; therapeutic classes of drugs-antiinflammatory drugs, cardiovascular drugs, antihistamines, hormones, gastrointestinal drugs, and antineoplastic drugs and drug administration. Methodology includes self-study with text, audiotape, pre- and post-tests, progress checks, and final examination.

Credit recommendation: In the lower division baccalaureate/associate degree category, 3 semester hours in Introduction to Pharmacology (2/89).

Medical Terminology (1-E)

Location: CMR Institute Centers located regionally throughout the U.S.

Length: Self-study.

Dates: December 1972-December 1988.

Objective: To provide the student with a working knowledge of medical terminology that will enable him/her to write and converse in the medical community.

Instruction: Covers the derivation and definition of medical terms, their spelling and pronunciation. Recognition of Greek and Latin roots and affixes are stressed. Cassette tapes are included to demonstrate correct pronunciation. Self-instruction.

Credit recommendation: In the lower division baccalaureate/associate degree category, 3 semester hours in Medical Terminology (4/80).

Microbiology (2-C)
Location: CMR Institute Centers located regionally throughout the U.S.
Length: Self-study.
Dates: December 1975-December 1988.
Objective: To provide the student with a basic knowledge of terminology and mechanisms associated with the microbiology.
Instruction: Presents an overview of microbial morphology, growth characteristics, and environmental interactions. Major pathogens are discussed individually with relation to the above topics. Basic laboratory procedures are described. Self-instruction.
Credit recommendation: In the lower division baccalaureate/associate degree category, 2 semester hours in Introduction to Microbiology, Microbiology for Nonscience Majors, or Survey of Microbiology (4/80).

Musculoskeletal System (6-A)
Location: CMR Institute Centers located regionally throughout the U.S.
Length: Self-study.
Dates: September 1987-Present.
Objective: To provide the student with a broad understanding of the anatomy and physiology of the musculoskeletal system and pharmacology as it relates to the system.
Learning Outcome: Upon successful completion of this course, the student will be able to describe the anatomy and physiology of the skeletal system, common disorders of the system, and pharmacology of drugs related to the system, as well as describe the anatomy and physiology of the skeletal system, common disorders of the system, and pharmacology of drugs related to the system.
Instruction: Course covers the anatomy and physiology of the musculoskeletal system, disorders of the system and pharmacology related to the system. Methodology includes self-study with text, audiotape, pre- and post-tests, progress checks, and final examination.
Credit recommendation: In the lower division baccalaureate/associate degree category, 2 semester hours in Allied Health, Health Sciences, Human Biology, or Nursing (2/89). NOTE: Students who complete this course in combination with Cardiovascular, Digestive, Endocrine, Integumentary, Nervous, Reproductive, Respiratory, Sensory Organs, and Urinary Systems should receive 8 semester hours in Anatomy, 8 semester hours in Physiology, and 4 semester hours in Applied Pharmacology.

Nervous System (6-E)
Location: CMR Institute Centers located regionally throughout the U.S.
Length: Self-study.
Dates: September 1988-Present.
Objective: To provide the student with an understanding of the fundamentals of neuroanatomy and neurophysiology.
Learning Outcome: Upon successful completion of this course, the student will be able to describe the anatomy and physiology of the nervous system (central, peripheral, and autonomic); describe neurologic disorders, their etiology and pharmacology related to nervous system disorders.
Instruction: Course covers the anatomy and physiology of the nervous system and its component parts, common disorders of the nervous system, and related pharmacology. Methodology includes self-study with text, audiotape, pre- and post-tests, progress checks, and final examination.
Credit recommendation: In the lower division baccalaureate/associate degree category, 2 semester hours in Allied Health, Health Sciences, Human Biology, or Nursing (2/89). NOTE: Students who complete this course in combination with Cardiovascular, Digestive, Endocrine, Integumentary, Musculoskeletal, Reproductive, Respiratory, Sensory Organs, and Urinary Systems should receive 8 semester hours in Anatomy, 8 semester hours in Physiology, and 4 semester hours in Applied Pharmacology.

Pharmaceutical and Medical Research (7-B)
Location: CMR Institute Centers located regionally throughout the U.S.
Length: Self-study.
Dates: January 1989-Present.
Objective: To provide the student with a general knowledge of the pharmaceutical and medical research process.
Learning Outcome: Upon successful completion of this course, the student will be able to identify types of research, institutions, and personnel; discuss the various governmental regulations affecting research with respect to clinical trials, ethics, and cost constraints; describe the basics of scientific methodology and the statistics of sampling, hypothesis testing, and data analysis.
Instruction: Course covers types of research and research institutions, governmental regulation, clinical trials, research design, methodology and analysis including scientific methodology, data collection and statistical analysis, cost analysis and ethical constraints. Methodology includes self-study with text, audiotape, pre- and post-tests, progress checks, and final examination.
Credit recommendation: In the lower division baccalaureate/associate degree category, 3 semester hours in Introduction to Research Methodology or Survey of Research Methods (2/89).

Pharmaceutical Industry (7-C)
Location: CMR Institute Centers located regionally throughout the U.S.
Length: Self-study.
Dates: January 1989-Present.
Objective: To provide the student with information about the background and development of the phar-

maceutical industry from its beginning to the present.

Learning Outcome: Upon successful completion of this course, the student will be able to understand the evolution of the pharmaceutical industry; gain knowledge in the development and distribution of pharmaceutical products; become familiar with the American pharmaceutical industry and advancements in manufacturing, science, and technology that helped it develop.

Instruction: The text consists of three chapters, an audiotape, glossary, chart of important professional organizations for pharmacists and pharmaceutical companies. Progress checks are interspersed throughout the course. Course covers contributions of early drug wholesalers to the pharmaceutical industry in America; factors that contributed to the increasing costs of drug research and development, as well as the high cost of drug research and development in affecting the pharmaceutical industry. Methodology includes self-study with text, audiotape, pre- and post-tests, progress checks, and final examination.

Credit recommendation: In the lower division baccalaureate/associate degree category, 3 semester hours in Pharmaceutical History for pharmacy or pharmacy assistant majors or any other students interested in Medicine or Health Sciences (2/89).

Pharmaceutical Marketing (2-H)
  Location: CMR Institute Centers located regionally throughout the U.S.
  Length: Self-Study.
  Dates: December 1975-December 1988.
  Objective: To provide the student with knowledge about fundamental principles of the marketing structure in the pharmaceutical industry.
  Instruction: Discussion of the specific factors involved in manufacturing and marketing of products of the pharmaceutical industry; discussion of the unique position of the medical representative in the marketing structure; and a broad discussion of the interaction of external forces as they relate to the marketing of pharmaceutical products. Self-study, programmed instruction, and examination are used.
  Credit recommendation: In the lower division baccalaureate/associate degree category or in the upper division baccalaureate category, 2 semester hours in Principles of Pharmaceutical Marketing for pharmacy or pharmacy assistant majors (4/80).

Pharmacology I (1-B)
  Location: CMR Institute Centers located regionally throughout the U.S.
  Length: Self-study.
  Dates: December 1976-December 1988.
  Objective: To provide the student with an overview of the modes of action of the most commonly prescribed pharmaceuticals.
  Instruction: Covers fundamental principles of drug action with emphasis on locally acting drugs and central nervous system drugs. Course may be followed by Pharmacology II. Self-instruction.
  Credit recommendation: In the lower division baccalaureate/associate degree category or in the upper division baccalaureate category, 2 semester hours in Introduction to Pharmacology or Nursing Pharmacology (4/80).

Pharmacology II (1-C)
  Location: CMR Institute Centers located regionally throughout the U.S.
  Length: Self-study.
  Dates: December 1976-December 1988.
  Objective: To provide the student with a basic knowledge and understanding of pharmacology. This course is taken in conjunction with, or following completion of, Pharmacology I.
  Instruction: Topics include antihistamine drugs, cardiovascular drugs, agents affecting the kidney and electrolyte balance, antineoplastic drugs, anti-infective drugs, endocrine products, and vitamins. Emphasis is placed on the nature, effects, and mechanisms of the action of drugs.
  Credit recommendation: In the lower division baccalaureate/associate degree category or in the upper division baccalaureate category, 2 semester hours in Introduction to Pharmacology or Nursing Pharmacology (4/80).

Physiology (1-D)
  Location: CMR Institute Centers located regionally throughout the U.S.
  Length: Self-study.
  Dates: December 1969-December 1988.
  Objective: To provide the student with a basic knowledge and understanding of physiological processes and controls in humans.
  Instruction: Topics include cell physiology, nerve-muscle physiology, the cardiovascular system, respiration, renal physiology, digestion, and endocrinology. Each topic is treated in considerable detail.
  Credit recommendation: In the lower division baccalaureate/associate degree category, 3 semester hours in Human Physiology (4/80).

Psychology (2-D)
  Location: CMR Institute Centers located regionally throughout the U.S.
  Length: Self-study.
  Dates: December 1979-December 1988.
  Objective: To provide the student with a basic knowledge of psychology, guidance in self-development, and an understanding of the needs and motivations of others.
  Instruction: A survey of psychology, including behavior modification, psychological development, emotions, perception, motivation, behavior disorders, memory, intelli-

gence and heredity, biofeedback, psychopharmacology, and the dynamics of personal interactions. Self-instruction.

Credit recommendation: In the lower division baccalaureate/associate degree category, 3 semester hours in Introduction to Psychology or Social Psychology (4/80).

Reproductive Systems (6-K)
  Location: CMR Institute Centers located regionally throughout the U.S.
  Length: Self-study.
  Dates: January 1988-Present.
  Objective: To provide the student with a general knowledge of the structure and function of the male and female reproductive systems.
  Learning Outcome: Upon successful completion of this course, the student will be able to name and give the function of the organs in the male and female reproductive systems; briefly describe the major disorders of the male and female reproductive systems; relate reproductive disorders to the recommended drug treatments and discuss the mechanism of the drug action.
  Instruction: Course covers the anatomy and physiology of the male and female reproductive systems, disorders of the reproductive systems, and methods of diagnosis and pharmacology relevant to the reproductive systems. Methodology includes self-study with text, audiotape, pre- and post-tests, progress checks, and final examination.
  Credit recommendation: In the lower division baccalaureate/associate degree category, 2 semester hours in Allied Health, Health Sciences, Human Biology, or Nursing (2/89). NOTE: Students who complete this course in combination with Cardiovascular, Digestive, Endocrine, Integumentary, Musculoskeletal, Nervous, Respiratory, Sensory Organs, and Urinary Systems should receive 8 semester hours in Anatomy, 8 semester hours in Physiology, and 4 semester hours in Applied Pharmacology.

Research Methods (2-G)
  Location: CMR Institute Centers location regionally throughout the U.S.
  Length: Self-study.
  Dates: December 1977-December 1988.
  Objective: To provide the medical representative with training in reading, comprehending, and evaluating articles in the literature which report on drug research.
  Instruction: Topics include the scientific method, observation, classification, data collection and analysis, descriptive statistical methods, and inferential statistics.
  Credit recommendation: In the lower division baccalaureate/associate degree category, 2 semester hours in Survey of Research Methods (4/80).

Respiratory System (6-I)
  Location: CMR Institute Centers located regionally throughout the U.S.
  Length: Self-study.
  Dates: September 1987-Present.
  Objective: To provide the student with an understanding of the structure of the respiratory system and its role in oxygen and carbon dioxide exchange.
  Learning Outcome: Upon successful completion of this course, the student will be able to describe structure and functions of the respiratory system and describe common disorders of the system and classes of drugs relevant to treatment of these disorders.
  Instruction: Course covers structure and functions of the respiratory system, mechanics of breathing, gas exchange, disorders of the system and the pharmacology relating to anti-inflammatory agents, central nervous system drugs, autonomic system drugs, expectorants and bronchodilators in relation to these disorders. Methodology includes self-study with text, audiotape, pre- and post-tests, progress checks, and final examination.
  Credit recommendation: In the lower division baccalaureate/associate degree category, 2 semester hours in Allied Health, Health Sciences, Human Biology, or Nursing (2/89). NOTE: Students who complete this course in combination with Cardiovascular, Digestive, Endocrine, Integumentary, Musculoskeletal, Nervous, Reproductive, Sensory Organs, and Urinary Systems should receive 8 semester hours in Anatomy, 8 semester hours in Physiology, and 4 semester hours in Applied Pharmacology.

Sensory Organs (6-G)
  Location: CMR Institute Centers located regionally throughout the U.S.
  Length: Self-study.
  Dates: September 1988-Present.
  Objective: To provide the student with an understanding of the structure and functions of the sensory organs.
  Learning Outcome: Upon successful completion of this course, the student will be able to describe the anatomy and physiology of the sensory organs and describe common disorders of the sensory organs-etiology, diagnosis, and pharmacology related to disorders.
  Instruction: Course covers the receptor functions, vision, hearing and equilibrium, taste, smell; disorders and pharmacology related to disorders of the sensory organs. Methodology includes self-study with text, audiotape, pre- and post-tests, progress checks, and final examination.
  Credit recommendation: In the lower division baccalaureate/associate degree category, 2 semester hours in Allied Health, Health Sciences, Human Biology, or Nursing (2/89). NOTE: Students who complete this course in combination with Cardiovascular, Digestive, Endocrine, Integumentary, Musculoskeletal, Nervous, Reproductive, Respiratory, and Urinary Systems should receive 8 semester hours in Anatomy, 8 semester hours in Physiology, and 4 semester hours in Applied Pharmacology.

Trends and Issues in Healthcare (7-E)
  Location: CMR Institute Centers located regionally throughout the U.S.
  Length: Self-study.
  Dates: September 1988-Present.
  Objective: To enhance the students' awareness of a variety of current trends and issues in healthcare.
  Learning Outcome: Upon successful completion of this course, the student will be able to understand the effects of cost containment on the health care industry; have some understanding of technological developments in the medical industry; become familiar with the changing healthcare delivery system and the medical malpractice crisis.
  Instruction: Course covers description of how public support for the medical establishment influenced its growth during the 1960s and 1970s. Trends in healthcare are analyzed. A discussion/overview of the changing healthcare delivery system; the medical malpractice crisis; society's response to epidemic and catastrophic diseases; healthcare on the uninsured and underinsured; transplants and allocations of organs; foregoing or terminating life-sustaining treatments; abortions; Medicare and Medicaid programs and the percentage of each healthcare dollar that goes toward physician fees and hospital costs. Methodology includes self-study with text, audiotape, pre- and post-tests, progress checks, and final examination.
  Credit recommendation: In the lower division baccalaureate/associate degree category, 2 semester hours in Allied Health or Health Care Administration (2/89).

Urinary System (6-J)
  Location: CMR Institute Centers located regionally throughout the U.S.
  Length: Self-study.
  Dates: September 1987-Present.
  Objective: To provide the student with general knowledge of the anatomy and physiology of the urinary system.
  Learning Outcome: Upon successful completion of this course, the student will be able to identify the organs of the urinary system, including the parts of the kidney and nephron; describe the physiology of urine formation including regulation of urine composition; briefly describe major disorders of the urinary system including methods of diagnosis and treatment.
  Instruction: Course covers urinary system anatomy, with strong emphasis on the kidney, physiology or urine formation, disorders of the urinary system, diagnostic procedures, and pharmacology relevant to urinary system disorders. Methodology includes self-study with text, audiotape, pre- and post-tests, progress checks, and final examination.
  Credit recommendation: In the lower division baccalaureate/associate degree category, 2 semester hours in Allied Health, Health Sciences, Human Biology, or Nursing (2/89). NOTE: Students who complete this course in combination with Cardiovascular, Digestive, Endocrine, Integumentary, Musculoskeletal, Nervous, Reproductive, Respiratory, and Sensory Organs Systems should receive 8 semester hours in Anatomy, 8 semester hours in Physiology, and 4 semester hours in Applied Pharmacology.

Chesapeake and Potomac Telephone Company (C&P), A Bell Atlantic Company

See BELL ATLANTIC CORPORATION

The Christopher Academy

The Christopher Academy, in conjunction with the Saint Nicholas Montessori College, England and/or Ireland provides training in the Montessori Method. This training consists of the philosophy and theories of Dr. Montessori, as well as how to present the Montessori curriculum and materials to children from 2½ to 5 years of age.

The courses are delivered by experts in the Montessori Method of education. The initial phase of this training is accomplished through a 9- to 24-month correspondence program involving reading materials, assignments and examinations. The workshop section is presented in an actual Montessori classroom so the student teachers can see the full advantage of the Montessori curriculum.

  Source of official student records: American Council on Education, Registry of Credit Recommendations, One Dupont Circle, Washington, DC 20063.
  Additional information about the courses: Program on Noncollegiate Sponsored Instruction, The Center for Adult Learning and Educational Credentials, American Council on Education, One Dupont Circle, Washington, DC 20036 or Thomas A. Edison State College, 101 West State Street, CN 545, Trenton, NJ 08625.

(a) St. Nicholas Montessori Training Course I
(b) Workshop
  Location: (a) Independent Study; (b) Westfield, NJ.
  Length: (a) 9 to 24 months; (b) 60 hours (10 days)
  Dates: July 1986-Present.
  Objective: To acquaint teachers with the Montessori philosophy and method of education and to prepare them to become qualified as Montessori teachers.
  Learning Outcome: Upon completion of this program, the teacher will be able to discuss the Montessori philosophy of education, and the growth and development of a child from birth to 5 years of age; to develop a Montessori curriculum, with appropriate stress on all physical, emotional and educational needs for a child from 2½ to 5 years old; to demonstrate skills in the use of Montessori

apparatus and activities.

Instruction: This course provides its student teachers with the qualifications to teach in a Montessori school or classroom. It emphasizes the Montessori theory and philosophy as well as instruction in the use of Montessori apparatus.

Credit recommendation: In the upper division baccalaureate category, 6 semester hours in Early Childhood Education (9/88).

Chrysler Institute Associate Degree Program

The Associate Degree Program is the equivalent of a two-year college program. It was designed to furnish full-time employees with knowledge and practical skills that would contribute to improved performance on present and future jobs and help in preparation for increased or new responsibilities. The curriculum includes subjects in mathematics, communication, interpersonal skills, management, business, manufacturing technology, as well as surveys of organizational areas such as finance, industrial engineering, manufacturing engineering, personnel, production, production control, and quality control.

The facilities used for classes are selected because of their proximity to the employees' workplace or residence. Classes are held in the metropolitan Detroit area and in Belvedere, Illinois; VanWert, Ohio; Indianapolis, Indiana; and St. Louis/Fenton, Missouri.

Courses are jointly developed through cooperation of the Chrysler Institute Course Development Specialist, experienced instructors, and resource personnel in the academic area of study for each course. Course Development Specialists approve the completed course outlines, syllabi, weekly lesson plans, text materials, and examinations. Instructors are interviewed and selected by the Manager of the Associate Degree Program, after analysis of the instructor's work experience, education, interests, and special accomplishments. Instructors are college graduates, with training or experience in the subject area being taught. The instructor's performance is reviewed by program staff by end-of-course evaluation submitted by all students; verbal feedback from students; and classroom monitoring by the Program Manager, Administrator, and Course Development Specialist.

Certification of completion of a course is based upon the student's satisfactory completion of a specific number of course assignments and written examinations. Instructors submit a class grade report to the office, showing names of students, test scores, overall score and course letter grade, plus the formula used to determine the grades awarded. All pertinent information is entered in the computer system for permanent record retention.

Source of official student records: Registrar, Central Michigan University, Mt. Pleasant, Michigan 48859.

Additional information about the courses: Program on Noncollegiate Sponsored Instruction, The Center for Adult Learning and Educational Credentials, American Council on Education, One Dupont Circle, Washington, D.C. 20036.

Applied Behavioral Science (PSY203)
Location: Chrysler facilities located in Michigan, Missouri, Indiana, Ohio, and Illinois.
Length: 36 hours (12 weeks).
Dates: April 1974-Present.
Objective: To provide students with a deeper insight into their own behavior and that of the people who work for and with them.
Learning Outcome: Upon successful completion of this course, the student will be able to understand how individuals affect the behavior of people in groups and how groups affect the behavior of an individual; relate theories of organizational behavior to more effective resolutions of conflicts in the workplace; and understand the causes of self, peer, and employee behavior.
Instruction: Course covers psychosocial phenomena in the workplace, theories of motivation, need-achievement theory, behavioral modification; group dynamics, and personality theories. Methodology includes lecture, discussion, classroom exercises with psychological instruments and film.
Credit recommendation: In the lower division baccalaureate/associate degree category, 3 semester hours in Psychology (4/88).

Basic Economics (ECON101)
Location: Chrysler facilities located in Michigan, Missouri, Indiana, Ohio, and Illinois.
Length: 36 hours (12 weeks).
Dates: March 1984-Present.
Objective: To provide the student with a basic overview of the economy as a sub-system of the social order.
Learning Outcome: Upon successful completion of this course, the student will be able to understand the mutual cause-and-effect relationship between a democratic society and their free enterprise economy; critique reliability of economic data, speculation, and theorizing; and understand the nature and role of American fiscal policy.
Instruction: Course covers economic measurements and business fluctuations, gross national product, role of money in the economy, tools of economic analysis, role of government in the economy, and the federal reserve system. Methodology includes lecture, discussion, and classroom exercises.
Credit recommendation: In the lower division baccalaureate/associate degree category, 3 semester hours in Basic Economics (4/88).

Business Law (201)
Location: Chrysler facilities located in Michigan, Missouri, Indiana, Ohio, and Illinois.
Length: 36 hours (12 weeks).
Dates: August 1983-Present.
Objective: To provide the student with an understanding of the legal system and its relationship to companies, covering contracts, insurance and property, including court structure overview.
Learning Outcome: Upon successful completion of this course, the student will be able to demonstrate a basic knowledge of legal aspects of partnerships, contracts and corporations; demonstrate a basic understanding of personal property, sales, wills, insurance and bankruptcy; and demonstrate a working knowledge of how business law affects their daily lives at work and at home.
Instruction: Course covers business law courts and court procedure, contracts, personal property sales, commercial paper, partnerships, an overview of corporation, insurance, and wills, inheritance, and bankruptcy. Methodology includes primarily lecture, some case study, problem-solving involvement by students.
Credit recommendation: In the lower division baccalaureate/associate degree category, 2 semester hours in Business Law (4/88).

Computer Usage in Manufacturing Operations (MT106)
Location: Chrysler facilities located in Michigan, Missouri, Indiana, Ohio, and Illinois.
Length: 36 hours (12 weeks).
Dates: September 1979-Present.
Objective: To provide the student with a general orientation to computers and their uses—data processing, equipment, and programming.
Learning Outcome: Upon successful completion of this course, the student will be able to understand historical development and computer use in business; S functions, how computers operate; hands-on demonstration; define a typical data processing organization; understand present use and future role of computers in business and plant operations; and explain systems analysis and programming languages.
Instruction: Course covers history of calculating, overview of data characteristics, data storage/information processing/data entry, introduction to microcomputers, field trips to major data processing center, overview of systems analysis and programming, and telecommunications and terminal usage. Methodology includes lecture, films, hands-on experience and term paper.
Credit recommendation: In the lower division baccalaureate/associate degree category, 3 semester hours in Introduction to Computers/Computer Information Science (4/88).

Creative Thinking in the Industrial Environment (CT101)
Location: Chrysler facilities located in Michigan, Missouri, Indiana, Ohio, and Illinois.
Length: 36 hours (12 weeks).
Dates: March 1984-Present.
Objective: To provide the student with an introduction to techniques and approaches to creative thinking, problem solving, critiquing, criticism, and persuasion.
Learning Outcome: Upon successful completion of this course, the student will be able to understand principles and techniques of creative thinking; know how to critique own ideas and express them logically; demonstrate problem-solving techniques; and demonstrate knowledge of the art of persuasion for more effective communication.
Instruction: Course covers developing creative thinking processes, the art of curiosity, the creative process, problem solving—identification, investigation, possible solutions, refine one solution, build a persuasive case, and fundamentals of logic. Methodology includes lecture, discussion, and student reports.
Credit recommendation: In the lower division baccalaureate/associate degree category, 2 semester hours in Logic (4/88).

The Environment of Business (BUS101)
Location: Chrysler (facilities located at McNichols Training Center, Mott Training Center, Center Line Training Center, New Training Center, and Chrysler).
Length: 36 hours (12 weeks).
Dates: April 1978-Present.
Objective: To introduce the student to the significance of the private enterprise system and the means by which management operates within the bounds of ethics, social decency, and the law.
Learning Outcome: Upon successful completion of this course, the student will be able to identify the various types of business organizations and the advantages/disadvantages of each; understand the ethical considerations of business situations; and understand the interrelationships between government, business, and industry.
Instruction: Course covers overview of management practices and procedures (productivity, staffing, pricing, produce distribution, law and ethics in business, and labor-management relations). Methodology includes lecture/discussion.
Credit recommendation: In the lower division baccalaureate/associate degree category, 2 semester hours in General Management (4/88).

Fundamental Electronics I (ITE101)
Location: Chrysler facilities located in Michigan, Missouri, Indiana, Ohio, and Illinois.
Length: 36 hours (12 weeks).
Dates: January 1983-Present.
Objective: To introduce the student to various electron-

ic components as well as the relationships between electricity and magnetism, current, voltage, resistance, and power.

Learning Outcome: Upon successful completion of this course, the student will be able to solve basic problems involving current, voltage, resistance, and power; use a multimeter to measure current, voltage, and resistance; and draw a schematic diagram of a simple electronic circuit.

Instruction: Course covers current, voltage, resistance, magnetism, electrical measurements, and inductance and capacitance. Methodology includes lecture, discussion, homework, and laboratory work.

Credit recommendation: In the lower division baccalaureate/associate degree category, 2 semester hours in Introduction to DC Electronics as an elective in a division of Engineering other than Electronics (4/88).

Fundamental Electronics II (ITE102)
  Location: Chrysler facilities located in Michigan, Missouri, Indiana, Ohio, and Illinois.
  Length: 36 hours (12 weeks).
  Dates: January 1986-Present.
  Objective: To introduce the student to AC theory, its generation and measurement, applications of capacitive circuits, inductive circuits, and transformers.
  Learning Outcome: Upon successful completion of this course, the student will be able to read an oscilloscope and interpret an AC sine wave's amplitude and frequency; calculate the voltage, current, and impedance of RC, RL, LC, and RCL series and parallel circuits; and describe the operation and use of AC motors as related to current, voltage, and power.
  Instruction: Course covers AC motors, capacitance and capacitors, power in AC circuits, inductance and inductors, transformers, tuned circuits, and resonance. Methodology includes lecture, discussion, demonstration, and transparencies.
  Credit recommendation: In the lower division baccalaureate/associate degree category, 2 semester hours in Basic AC Electronics (4/88).

Industrial Hydraulics (ITH101)
  Location: Chrysler facilities located in Michigan, Missouri, Indiana, Ohio, and Illinois.
  Length: 36 hours (12 weeks).
  Dates: January 1983-Present.
  Objective: To introduce the student to the basic physical concepts and fundamentals of pressure and flow. The course also includes hydraulic components and their use in hydraulic systems.
  Learning Outcome: Upon successful completion of this course, the student will be able to develop an understanding of how work is accomplished through hydraulics; develop an understanding of how hydraulic controls determine system performance; and identify various components within a hydraulic system.
  Instruction: Course covers force and pressure, hydraulic actuators, hydraulic pumps, pressure controls, directional controls, and flow controls. Methodology includes lecture, transparencies, videotape, and class instruction.
  Credit recommendation: In the lower division baccalaureate/associate degree category, 2 semester hours in Basic Hydraulics (4/88).

Industrial Mathematics (MATH101)
  Location: Chrysler facilities located in Michigan, Indiana, Ohio, and Illinois.
  Length: 36 hours (12 weeks).
  Dates: October 1971-Present.
  Objective: To provide the student with basic mathematical skills in the areas of addition, subtraction, multiplication, and division of whole numbers, fractions, exponents, and decimals.
  Learning Outcome: Upon successful completion of this course, the student will be able to solve problems (for the correct answer) involving ratios and proportions; solve problems of multiplication, addition, and subtraction of fractions; and solve for the unknown in equations.
  Instruction: Course covers whole numbers, common fractions, decimal fractions, measurement, percentages, algebra, equations, ratios and proportions, exponents, and radicals. Methodology includes lecture and classroom exercises.
  Credit recommendation: In the lower division baccalaureate/associate degree category, 2 semester hours in Basic Mathematics (4/88).

Industrial Mathematics-Algebra (MATH102)
  Location: Chrysler facilities located in Michigan, Indiana, Ohio, and Illinois.
  Length: 36 hours (12 weeks).
  Dates: October 1971-Present.
  Objective: To provide the student with skills in solving algebraic problems involving addition, subtraction, multiplication, and division of integers and real numbers, powers and roots, exponents and radicals, factoring, and algebraic equations.
  Learning Outcome: Upon successful completion of this course, the student will be able to solve for the unknown in an equation; change a given number to a radical of exponent form; and write an equation of a line passing through a given point with a given slope.
  Instruction: Course covers simple equations, multiplication, division and factoring, fractions, equations with more than one unknown, quadratic equations, and graphical methods. Methodology includes lecture and classroom exercises.
  Credit recommendation: In the lower division baccalaureate/associate degree category, 2 semester hours in Basic Algebra (4/88).

Industrial Supervisory Practices (SUPV101)
Location: Chrysler facilities located in Michigan, Missouri, Indiana, Ohio, and Illinois.
Length: 36 hours (12 weeks).
Dates: December 1983-Present.
Objective: To provide the student with a better understanding of the problems and practices of industrial supervision.
Learning Outcome: Upon successful completion of this course, the student will be able to accept the presence of conflict in organizations, minimize it, and build an atmosphere that encourages cooperation; recognize the values in different styles of leadership; and appraise employee performance.
Instruction: Course covers supervisor's role in an organization, equal employment opportunities, employee safety and health, handling complaints, avoiding grievances, group dynamics, and conflict versus cooperation. Methodology includes lecture, discussion, and classroom exercises.
Credit recommendation: In the lower division baccalaureate/associate degree category, 3 semester hours in Personnel (4/88).

Interpersonal Communications (COM106)
Location: Chrysler facilities located in Michigan, Missouri, Indiana, Ohio, and Illinois.
Length: 36 hours (12 weeks).
Dates: March 1982-Present.
Objective: To provide the student with the ability to promote and sustain better communication with others.
Learning Outcome: Upon successful completion of this course, the student will be able to interact with others more effectively both at work and personally; identify the differences between constructive and destructive criticism; and effectively challenge and evaluate ideas and concepts of others.
Instruction: Course covers techniques of constructive criticism; active listening skills; conflict resolution techniques; self-awareness skills for constructive interactions; small group interaction techniques; and interviewing techniques. Methodology includes lecture and discussion.
Credit recommendation: In the lower division baccalaureate/associate degree category, 3 semester hours in Interpersonal Communications (4/88).

Introduction to Industrial Engineering (IE101)
Location: Chrysler facilities located in Michigan, Missouri, Indiana, Ohio, and Illinois.
Length: 36 hours (12 weeks).
Dates: September 1972-Present.
Objective: To provide the student with an understanding of the industrial engineering function and its relationship to the other functions in an organization. The course includes direct labor control (including work standards), indirect manufacturing expense, methods improvements, and cost reduction.
Learning Outcome: Upon successful completion of this course, the student will be able to develop a better understanding of the importance of cost control within the manufacturing expense budget system; develop an understanding of various incentive plans or systems; and develop an understanding of the uses, purposes, and advantages of electronic work sampling.
Instruction: Course covers method improvement, cost control, work standards and man assignment, work simplification, work measurement, developing indirect labor standards and manpower controls, work sampling procedure, electronic work sampling, and incentive systems. Methodology includes lectures, role playing, and time studies cases.
Credit recommendation: In the lower division baccalaureate/associate degree category, 3 semester hours in Motion and Time Study (4/88).

Introduction to Psychology (PSY101)
Location: Chrysler facilities located in Michigan, Missouri, Indiana, Ohio, and Illinois.
Length: 36 hours (12 weeks).
Dates: August 1983-Present.
Objective: To provide the student with an understanding of and familiarity with the basic concepts, theories, and principles of psychology and how they relate to the work environment.
Learning Outcome: Upon successful completion of this course, the student will be able to understand the process of learning and apply the learning principles in behavior modification and training programs; understand the theories and knowledge regarding human differences and behavior; and understand the concept and application of motivation.
Instruction: Course covers basic concepts, theories, and principles of psychology; cognitive processes (learning, remembering, thinking, intelligence); concept of motivation; and individual and social processes (personality, social influences, group dynamics). Methodology includes lecture, discussion, and films.
Credit recommendation: In the lower division baccalaureate/associate degree category, 3 semester hours in General Psychology (4/88).

Introduction to Statistics (STAT201)
Location: Chrysler facilities located in Michigan, Missouri, Indiana, Ohio, and Illinois.
Length: 36 hours (12 weeks).
Dates: January 1982-Present.
Objective: To provide the student with an introduction to the vocabulary and capabilities of probability and statistics as tools for analysis and decision making.
Learning Outcome: Upon successful completion of this course, the student will be able to better use probability and statistics for the sake of analyzing problems and mak-

ing decisions; interpret the results of statistical analyses; and compute sample statistics and population parameters.

Instruction: Course covers basic probability theory, sampling and sampling distributions, estimation, hypothesis testing, and forecasting. Methodology includes lecture, discussion, and classroom exercises.

Credit recommendation: In the lower division baccalaureate/associate degree category, 3 semester hours in Statistics (4/88).

Introduction to Writing (COM102)

Location: Chrysler facilities located in Michigan, Missouri, Indiana, Ohio, and Illinois.
Length: 36 hours (12 weeks).
Dates: October 1971-Present.
Objective: To provide the student with an overview of basic English language skills including structure and grammar.
Learning Outcome: Upon successful completion of this course, the student will be able to demonstrate improved spelling; accurately use parts of speech; and demonstrate a knowledge of punctuation.
Instruction: Course covers spelling, parts of speech, punctuation, and phrases and clauses. Methodology includes lecture, drills, and exercises.
Credit recommendation: In the lower division baccalaureate/associate degree category, 2 semester hours in Basic English (4/88).

Labor Relations (PERS201)

Location: Chrysler facilities located in Michigan, Missouri, Indiana, Ohio, and Illinois.
Length: 36 hours (12 weeks).
Dates: March 1982-Present.
Objective: To provide the student with an understanding of organized labor and the management community.
Learning Outcome: Upon successful completion of this course, the student will be able to understand the labor contract negotiation process and the administration of the agreement; understand the wage, institutional, and administrative issues under collective bargaining; and cope with union behavior, structure, governing practices, and operation.
Instruction: Course covers historical background of labor, legal, framework of labor, union behavior, bargaining process, grievance procedures, arbitration, wage issues, and collective bargaining. Methodology includes lecture, discussion, and classroom exercises.
Credit recommendation: In the lower division baccalaureate/associate degree category, 3 semester hours in Industrial Relations (4/88).

Manufacturing Engineering Survey (ME101)

Location: Chrysler facilities located in Michigan, Missouri, Indiana, Ohio, and Illinois.
Length: 36 hours (12 weeks).
Dates: April 1972-Present.
Objective: To familiarize the student with the history and development of manufacturing engineering and its role in the manufacturing environment.
Learning Outcome: Upon successful completion of this course, the student will be able to develop an understanding of process planning, tooling, and material handling; develop an understanding of manufacturing research, development and manufacturing; and develop an understanding of process engineering, work planning, and plant maintenance.
Instruction: Course covers the manufacturing engineering function, cost estimating, preproduction planning, work measurement and standards, capital equipment and facilities, plant engineering, material handling engineering, special processes, tooling, work planning, process engineering, and mechanization and automatic assembly. Methodology includes lecture, discussion, and plant tours.
Credit recommendation: In the lower division baccalaureate/associate degree category, 3 semester hours in Introduction to Manufacturing Engineering (4/88).

Personnel Practices Survey (PERS101)

Location: Chrysler facilities located in Michigan, Missouri, Indiana, Ohio, and Illinois.
Length: 36 hours (12 weeks).
Dates: October 1971-Present.
Objective: To provide the student with a basic understanding of personnel practices as they relate to industrial and business management.
Learning Outcome: Upon successful completion of this course, the student will be able to understand the importance of personnel selection in the building of a productive and stable work force; effectively utilize human resources; and understand employee compensation programs, financial incentive plans, and employee benefits.
Instruction: Course covers collective bargaining, union organization and behavior, conflict resolution, organizational structures, career development, supervision, and performance evaluation. Methodology includes lecture, discussion, and classroom exercises.
Credit recommendation: In the lower division baccalaureate/associate degree category, 3 semester hours in Personnel Management (4/88).

Plant Finance Overview (FIN101)

Location: Chrysler facilities located in Michigan, Indiana, Ohio, and Illinois.
Length: 36 hours (12 weeks).
Dates: September 1973-Present.
Objective: To familiarize the student with the basic functions of accounting and its role in the business environment. The course includes accounting, bookkeeping, cost determination, voucher systems, pay practices, and auditing techniques.
Learning Outcome: Upon successful completion of this

course, the student will be able to identify basic accounting practices, enter all business transactions in account in either debit or credit columns correctly, and develop books of entry and ledgers.

Instruction: Course covers accounting—the language, measuring business, completing the accounting cycle, purchases of sales merchandising, corporations, inventories, income taxes, and forms of business organization. Methodology includes lecture and classroom exercises.

Credit recommendation: In the lower division baccalaureate/associate degree category, 3 semester hours in Basic Accounting (4/88).

Principles and Structuring of Organizations Management (MGT203)
Location: Chrysler facilities located in Michigan, Missouri, Indiana, Ohio, and Illinois.
Length: 36 hours (12 weeks).
Dates: April 1974-Present.
Objective: To provide the student with an understanding of the nature of business and industrial organizations and how work is coordinated within them, to familiarize the student with structuring of organizations, its parameters, environments, power systems, flow systems, functions, and interrelationships.
Learning Outcome: Upon successful completion of this course, the student will be able to demonstrate knowledge of five basic parts of an organization; describe unit groups and unit size influence on an organization; understand comparison of Japanese and American styles of organization and management; describe vertical and horizontal centralization and decentralization; and understand key factors of organizational structuring.
Instruction: Course covers five basic parts of an organization; techniques used to coordinate employees efforts; organizational superstructure and influence of unit group and unit size; Japanese organization and management style as compared to American style; vertical and horizontal centralization and decentralization; and organizational structuring. Methodology includes lecture and individual student presentations.
Credit recommendation: In the lower division baccalaureate/associate degree category, 3 semester hours in Management (4/88).

Principles of Industrial Psychology (PSY110)
Location: Chrysler facilities located in Michigan, Missouri, Indiana, Ohio, and Illinois.
Length: 36 hours (12 weeks).
Dates: October 1971-Present.
Objective: To provide the student with an awareness of psychological issues relevant to the operation of industrial organizations.
Learning Outcome: Upon successful completion of this course, the student will be able to better understand human beings and the factors which influence them and their performance as employees; use motivational patterns to increase employee participation and job satisfaction; and understand the impact of conformity on organizational behavior.
Instruction: Course covers concepts and models of organizational behavior; theories of motivated behavior; appraising and rewarding performance; psychology of attitudes; leadership styles; communication within an organization; and psychological factors that lead to resistance and change. Methodology includes lecture, discussion, and classroom exercises.
Credit recommendation: In the lower division baccalaureate/associate degree category, 3 semester hours in Industrial Psychology (4/88).

Principles of Management (MGT101)
Location: Chrysler facilities located in Michigan, Missouri, Indiana, Ohio, and Illinois.
Length: 36 hours (12 weeks).
Dates: October 1971-Present.
Objective: To introduce the student to the functions of management: planning, organizing, directing, controlling, and staffing.
Learning Outcome: Upon successful completion of this course, the student will be able to utilize effective planning as a management tool for reaching goals; use improved problem-solving and decision-making skills; and understand the supervisory role in management.
Instruction: Course covers management styles, techniques of delegation, decision making, staffing, employee appraisal, and planning/goal-setting. Methodology includes lecture, discussion, classroom exercises, and films.
Credit recommendation: In the lower division baccalaureate/associate degree category, 2 semester hours in Introduction to Management (4/88).

Print Reading (ME102)
Location: Chrysler facilities located in Michigan, Indiana, Ohio, and Illinois.
Length: 36 hours (12 weeks).
Dates: January 1972-Present.
Objective: To provide the student with skills in interpreting basic mechanical drawings of parts and tools used in the manufacturing environment.
Learning Outcome: Upon successful completion of this course, the student will be able to draw and/or interpret three views of a part, dimension parts, and cut sections simple part drawings.
Instruction: Course covers orthographic projection, dimensioning, tolerances, threads, sections, sketching, and metrics. Methodology includes lectures and classroom exercises in mechanical parts drawing and interpretation of drawing.
Credit recommendation: In the lower division baccalaureate/associate degree category, 2 semester hours in Blueprint Reading (4/88).

Problem Solving and Productivity (SUPV102)
  Location: Chrysler facilities located in Michigan, Missouri, Indiana, Ohio, and Illinois.
  Length: 36 hours (12 weeks).
  Dates: January 1985-Present.
  Objective: To provide the student with basic skills that can be applied to solving day-to-day problems that affect work group productivity.
  Learning Outcome: Upon successful completion of this course, the student will be able to identify factors affecting the productivity of an operation; understand the relationship between productivity, cost effectiveness, and utilization of resources; and present project proposals in a convincing manner.
  Instruction: Course covers cause analysis, decision making, presentation skills, problem evaluation and solving, and plan analysis. Methodology includes lecture, discussion, and classroom exercises.
  Credit recommendation: In the lower division baccalaureate/associate degree category, 2 semester hours in General Management (4/88).

Procurement and Production Control (PC101)
  Location: Chrysler facilities located in Michigan, Missouri, Indiana, Ohio, and Illinois.
  Length: 36 hours (12 weeks).
  Dates: October 1971-Present.
  Objective: To familiarize the student with the responsibility of the procurement and production control organization. Topics covered include product engineering data, schedule analysis and float establishment, and material release and follow-up.
  Learning Outcome: Upon successful completion of this course, the student will be able to develop an understanding of the relationship of the purchasing activity to production control; develop an understanding of inventory control; and develop an understanding of just-in-time material flow and computer systems applications.
  Instruction: Course covers quality, specifications of standardization; purchasing; sourcing; forecasting; inventory control; production control; transportation; and material control. Methodology includes lecture and discussion.
  Credit recommendation: In the lower division baccalaureate/associate degree category, 3 semester hours in Production Control (4/88).

Production Processes Survey (MT101)
  Location: Chrysler facilities located in Michigan, Missouri, Indiana, Ohio, and Illinois.
  Length: 36 hours (12 weeks).
  Dates: April 1973-Present.
  Objective: To provide the student with an overview of production methods and equipment in manufacturing.
  Learning Outcome: Upon successful completion of this course, the student will be able to understand production processes used in manufacturing industries; know origin and processing of materials used in auto industry production; understand machine and cutting tools and quality control in production; explain thought processes used by a process engineer in manufacturing; and have a knowledge of adaptation processes through plant tours and visits.
  Instruction: Course covers characteristics, classifications, and sources of materials; plant tours and then discussion of them; hot and cold working of metals/welding; plastics processing; metal cutting; boring and drilling machines; milling machine; grinding wheel technology; gear terminology; and quality assurance. Methodology includes lectures, films, tours, and student presentations.
  Credit recommendation: In the lower division baccalaureate/associate degree category, 3 semester hours in Manufacturing Technology (4/88).

Quality Control Survey (QC101)
  Location: Chrysler facilities located in Michigan, Missouri, Indiana, Ohio, and Illinois.
  Length: 36 hours (12 weeks).
  Dates: September 1972-Present.
  Objective: To provide the student with knowledge that defines quality control responsibilities at various organizational levels, quality control concepts, principles, and services to other manufacturing functions.
  Learning Outcome: Upon successful completion of this course, the student will be able to develop an understanding of the interactions of a quality system with productivity and cost; develop an understanding of frequency distributions, histograms, and normal distribution curves; and develop an understanding of statistical process control.
  Instruction: Course covers basic programs for quality control, controls and procedures, cost/profit, and statistical methods of quality control Methodology includes lecture and discussion.
  Credit recommendation: In the lower division baccalaureate/associate degree category, 3 semester hours in Introduction to Quality Control (4/88).

Reading and Study Skills (COM101)
  Location: Chrysler facilities located in Michigan, Missouri, Indiana, Ohio, and Illinois.
  Length: 36 hours (12 weeks).
  Dates: October 1971-Present.
  Objective: To provide the student with the skills necessary to improve basic reading and study skills with special emphasis on vocabulary comprehension and development.
  Learning Outcome: Upon successful completion of this course, the student will be able to demonstrate basic ability to use dictionary, take notes, control own time, use memory, use library, and use textbooks; demonstrate techniques for improving reading comprehension; and have basic knowledge of how to outline, summarize, and skim

read.

Instruction: Course covers motivational skills, word skills, dictionary use; study skills, notetaking, book marking; reading comprehension skills; textbook notetaking; memory techniques; objective and essay test taking; and use of headings, signal words. Methodology includes lecture and practice of skills.

Credit recommendation: In the lower division baccalaureate/associate degree category, 2 semester hours in Study Skills (4/88).

Sociology (SOC101)
Location: Chrysler facilities located in Michigan, Missouri, Indiana, Ohio, and Illinois.
Length: 36 hours (12 weeks).
Dates: December 1982-Present.
Objective: To provide the student with a broad overview of sociological perspectives and the impact of social structure on individual attitudes and behaviors.
Learning Outcome: Upon successful completion of this course, the student will be able to explain the elements of culture and social organization; have knowledge of social roles, human groupings, and social millieu; understand social norms, deviance and expectations; explain stratification, classes, social mobility and power; have knowledge of changing American family structure; understand how education transmits cultural knowledge, values, skills and rituals; understand interrelationships of population, health, urban life and environment; and understand collective behavior and social change.
Instruction: Course covers impact of social structure upon individual attitudes and behaviors; socialization, social roles of men and women (time, class, culture); human groupings, social milieu; deviance, social norms, expectations; stratification, classes, inequalities, social mobility; power, political, economic; minorities, group status; changing American family structure; education, transmitting skills, knowledge, values, and rituals; Durheimian perspective of religion; population, health, urban life and environment; social movements and social change; and relationships between theory and sociological research. Methodology includes lecture and discussion.
Credit recommendation: In the lower division baccalaureate/associate degree category, 3 semester hours in Sociology (4/88).

Speech Skills (COM204)
Location: Chrysler facilities located in Michigan, Missouri, Indiana, Ohio, and Illinois.
Length: 36 hours (12 weeks).
Dates: April 1973-Present.
Objective: To foster verbal skills in dialogue and public speaking.
Learning Outcome: Upon successful completion of this course, the student will be able to organize and express ideas more clearly; understand the relationships among beliefs, motivation, credibility, and persuasion; find or develop supporting materials to effectively prepare speeches; and utilize skills in presenting and delivering a variety of speeches.
Instruction: Course covers speech writing, use of visual aids, persuasion, listening as a communication skill, and critiquing speeches of others. Methodology includes lecture, discussion, and speeches presented in class.
Credit recommendation: In the lower division baccalaureate/associate degree category, 3 semester hours in Speech (4/88).

Stamping Technology (MT202)
Location: Chrysler facilities located in Michigan, Missouri, Indiana, Ohio, and Illinois.
Length: 36 hours (12 weeks).
Dates: October 1971-Present.
Objective: To provide the student with an understanding of the principles involved with pressworking metals and an introduction to stamping presses, material and equipment usage.
Learning Outcome: Upon successful completion of this course, the student will be able to develop an understanding of the various types of presses used in stamping operations; develop an understanding of the various types of dies used; and develop an understanding of the physical factors in forming steel.
Instruction: Course covers types of presses, types of steel and metal blanking operations, metal drawing operations, forming operations, piercing and trimming operations, and progressive dies. Methodology includes lectures, discussions, and classroom exercises.
Credit recommendation: In the lower division baccalaureate/associate degree category, 3 semester hours in Stamping Technology (4/88).

Writing Skills (COM103)
Location: Chrysler facilities located in Michigan, Missouri, Indiana, Ohio, and Illinois.
Length: 36 hours (12 weeks).
Dates: January 1972-Present.
Objective: To improve the student's writing skills through emphasis on composition, outlining, and paragraph structure.
Learning Outcome: Upon successful completion of this course, the student will be able to write simple, uncomplicated sentences using familiar words; write conversationally with the reader in mind; use correct "person" in writing; demonstrate writing clarity; demonstrate effective word usage; demonstrate effective paragraph structure; demonstrate effective outlining techniques; demonstrate effective report and business letter writing.
Instruction: Course covers clarity and simplicity in writing, writing in conversational manner, word selection, outlining, paragraph structuring, and report writing and business letters. Methodology includes some lecture and

videotape presentations, extensive written assignments and exercises for in-class discussion and critique.

Credit recommendation: In the lower division baccalaureate/associate degree category, 3 semester hours in Composition (4/88).

Chrysler Motors Advanced Technical Training

Chrysler Motors Advanced Technical Training (A.T.T.) is a department of Chrysler Motors' Human Resources Office. The primary responsibility of A.T.T. is to provide technical training programs that improve the skills and productivity of Chrysler employees, specifically those in production, skilled trades, supervisory and engineering positions.

A.T.T. classes are conducted at the Featherstone Road Engineering Center, Auburn Hills, Michigan; Chrysler Engineering Center, Highland Park, Michigan; and over 30 plant locations in the Chrysler organization. Classrooms are equipped with fully operational trainer units to support each course. Standard industrial equipment and tools are used to increase the value of the laboratory learning experience.

Courses are designed and developed by department task groups, working in conjunction with plant and industry representatives to address the technical training needs of the company. Successful completion of courses is based on a passing test score, completion of all assigned laboratory exercises, and meeting minimum attendance requirements.

Source of official student records: Advanced Technical Training Records Office, Chrysler Motors, Featherstone Road Engineering Center, 2301 Featherstone Road, Auburn Hills, Michigan 48057.

Additional information about the courses: Program on Noncollegiate Sponsored Instruction, The Center for Adult Learning and Educational Credentials, American Council on Education, One Dupont Circle, Washington, D.C., 20036.

Advanced Cincinnati Milacron T*3786 (CIM 201)
Location: Chrysler locations worldwide.
Length: 40 hours (1 week).
Dates: May 1987-Present.
Objective: To develop the student's skills to program, operate, and troubleshoot the T*3786 Cincinnati Milacron Robot.
Learning Outcome: Upon successful completion of this course, the student will be able to program the robot using the teach pendant; match commands with descriptions of functions; and identify wiring schemes for I/O modules.
Instruction: Course covers system operation, programming procedures and commands, installation procedures, and maintenance. Methodology includes lecture and laboratory exercises.
Credit recommendation: In the lower division baccalaureate/associate degree category, 2 semester hours in Robotics (9/88). NOTE: To receive credit for this course, students must have successfully completed Industrial Robotics (ROB 101).

Air Logic (ALG 101)
Location: Chrysler locations worldwide.
Length: 40 hours (1 week).
Dates: April 1985-Present.
Objective: To enable the student to set up and troubleshoot air logic systems.
Learning Outcome: Upon successful completion of this course, the student will be able to match circuit functions of air logic components to their symbols; fabricate, operate, and analyze various air logic circuits; and identify basic air logic circuits and the sequence of operation of the system.
Instruction: Course covers fundamentals of compressed air; power valve symbology; comparison of electrical relays versus pneumatic air logic components and functions; ladder diagrams; and troubleshooting procedures and techniques. Methodology includes lecture and laboratory.
Credit recommendation: In the lower division baccalaureate/associate degree category, 2 semester hours in Pneumatic Logic Controls (9/88).

ASEA IRB/90 (ASA 201)
Location: Featherstone Road Engineering Center and various Chrysler Corporation locations.
Length: 80 hours (2 weeks).
Dates: June 1988-Present.
Objective: To enable the student to program, operate, troubleshoot, and maintain ASEA IRB 90/2 industrial robots.
Instruction: Course covers robot specifications, system components/operations, safety, programming procedures, command, maintenance, and troubleshooting. Methodology includes lecture, demonstration, and laboratory exercises.
Credit recommendation: In the lower division baccalaureate/associate degree category, 3 semester hours in Robotics Technology (4/89). NOTE: Credit should not be awarded for both this course and KUKA IR662/100 (KUK 201).

Electronic Fuel Injection Systems (PO5 EFI)
Location: Chrysler Engineering Center and various Chrysler Corporation locations.
Length: 40 hours (1 or 2 weeks).
Dates: June 1988-Present.
Objective: To provide the student with the basic knowledge to diagnose an improperly functioning vehicle using

the latest electronic test equipment.

Instruction: Course covers the starting system, computers, power/ground systems, ignition systems, throttle body assembly, sensors, EGR system, and charging systems. Methodology includes lecture and laboratory exercises.

Credit recommendation: In the lower division baccalaureate/associate degree category, 2 semester hours in Automotive Technology (4/89).

Hydraulic Systems Analysis (HSA 201)
Location: Featherstone Road Engineering Center and various Chrysler Corporation locations.
Length: 40 hours (1 week).
Dates: June 1988-Present.
Objective: To familiarize the student with the various components in a hydraulic system and how they are integrated for system operation.
Instruction: Course covers hydraulic systems (input and output devices), control valves, fluids and fluid conditioning, fluid conductors and connectors, and fluid power analysis. Methodology includes lecture and demonstration.
Credit recommendation: In the lower division baccalaureate/associate degree category, 2 semester hours in Fluid Power Technology (4/89).

Industrial Electrical Controls (IEC 101)
Location: Chrysler locations worldwide.
Length: 80 hours (2 weeks).
Dates: January 1983-Present.
Objective: To enable the student to repair, maintain, and troubleshoot relay-based machine controls used in manufacturing.
Learning Outcome: Upon successful completion of this course, the student will be able to understand and repair basic components used in relay-based machines including motors and motor control systems; troubleshoot manufacturing systems using relay-based logic controls; and maintain relay-based machines to operate safely under manufacturing conditions.
Instruction: Course covers electrical safety, electrical testing, surge protection switches, relays, solenoids, contactors, AC motors, magnetic motor starters, jogging circuits, circuit breakers, ladder diagrams, preventive maintenance, and troubleshooting control circuits. Methodology includes lecture and laboratory.
Credit recommendation: In the lower division baccalaureate/associate degree category, 4 semester hours in Electrical Control Systems or Electrical Power Technology (9/88).

Industrial Electronics (IET 200)
Location: Liberty Development Center, Auburn Hills, MI.
Length: 200 hours (1 day per week for 25 weeks).
Dates: January 1983-Present.
Objective: To give the student a survey of the basic electronic theory and application of electronics circuits and systems used in industrial electronics controls and processing systems.
Learning Outcome: Upon successful completion of this course, the student will be able to demonstrate the basic knowledge required to effectively troubleshoot and maintain industrial electronic control systems; develop an understanding of basic circuits used in industrial control and logic systems; and develop the proper use of test equipment for proper troubleshooting techniques used in industrial control systems.
Instruction: Course covers review of DC and AC circuit fundamentals, solid state fundamentals and circuit applications, use of IC's and digital electronics in microprocessors and applications in resistance welding, motor controls, position control systems, and robotics. Methodology include lecture and laboratory.
Credit recommendation: In the lower division baccalaureate/associate degree category, 8 semester hour in Fundamentals of Industrial Electronics (9/88).

Industrial Hydraulic Technology (HYD 101)
Location: Chrysler locations worldwide.
Length: 80 hours (2 weeks).
Dates: January 1983-Present.
Objective: To provide the student with the necessary experience to develop those skills enabling him/her to set up, troubleshoot, and maintain hydraulic systems.
Learning Outcome: Upon successful completion of this course, the student will be able to identify various hydraulic components by their ANSI symbols and function within the hydraulic system; calculate pressures and flows required for simple hydraulic systems; and read hydraulic prints and understand function of system operation.
Instruction: Course covers hydraulic transmission of energy; controls of hydraulic energy: pressure, flow, direction; and hydraulic energy input and output devices: pumps, motors, and cylinders. Methodology includes lecture and laboratory.
Credit recommendation: In the lower division baccalaureate/associate degree category, 3 semester hours in Basic Hydraulics (9/88).

Industrial Pneumatic Technology (PNU 101)
Location: Chrysler locations worldwide.
Length: 40 hours (1 week).
Dates: February 1985-Present.
Objective: To provide the student with the experiences necessary to develop those skills enabling him/her to set up, troubleshoot, and maintain pneumatic systems.
Learning Outcome: Upon successful completion of this course, the student will be able to identify various pneumatic components by their ANSI symbols and functions within the pneumatic system; identify characteristics of

directional valves given their ANSI symbols; and identify pneumatic components from prints.

Instruction: Course covers energy transmission using pneumatic systems, control of pneumatic energy, and air preparation. Methodology includes lecture and laboratory.

Credit recommendation: In the lower division baccalaureate/associate degree category, 2 semester hours in Basic Pneumatics (9/88).

Industrial Robotics (ROB 101)

Location: Chrysler locations worldwide.
Length: 40 hours (1 week).
Dates: January 1983-Present.
Objective: To introduce the student to robotic technology, hardware devices and concepts related to industrial devices.
Learning Outcome: Upon successful completion of this course, the student will be able to identify terminology used in robotic applications; identify advantages and disadvantages of various safety devices used in conjunction with robots; and operate a robot using the teach pendant.
Instruction: Course covers robotic classification and operating systems; safety; mechanics of robotics and drive systems; control panels; and programming. Methodology includes lecture, demonstration and laboratory.
Credit recommendation: In the lower division baccalaureate/associate degree category, 2 semester hours in Manufacturing Engineering or Robotics (9/88).

KUKA IR662/100 (KUK 201)

Location: Featherstone Road Engineering Center and various Chrysler Corporation locations.
Length: 80 hours (2 weeks).
Dates: February 1989-Present.
Objective: To enable the student to program, operate, maintain, and troubleshoot KUKA IR662/100 industrial robots.
Instruction: Course covers robot specifications, system components/operations, safety, programming procedures, commands, maintenance, and troubleshooting. Methodology includes lecture, demonstration, and laboratory exercises.
Credit recommendation: In the lower division baccalaureate/associate degree category, 3 semester hours in Robotics Technology (4/89). NOTE: Credit should not be awarded for both this course and ASEA IRB/90 (ASA 201).

Microprocessors 6800/6502 (MPU 101)

Location: Chrysler locations worldwide.
Length: 80 hours (2 weeks).
Dates: June 1985-Present.
Objective: To give the student a general understanding of microprocessors including programming and troubleshooting the Motorola 6800/6502.
Learning Outcome: Upon successful completion of this course, the student will be able to understand block diagrams and logic systems used in microprocessors; understand the application of digital logic and programming used in microprocessors; and identify basic troubleshooting techniques used in microprocessors.
Instruction: Course covers number systems used in microprocessors, digital logic, mathematical operation and microprocessor concepts, introduction to programming, memory storage, decoding, and troubleshooting microprocessor. Methodology includes lecture and laboratory.
Credit recommendation: In the lower division baccalaureate/associate degree category, 4 semester hours in Industrial Controls or Industrial Electronics (9/88).

PRAB F600 Control (PRB 206)

Location: Featherstone Road Engineering Center and various Chrysler Corporation locations.
Length: 80 hours (2 weeks).
Dates: November 1986-Present.
Objective: To prepare the student to operate, program, and edit programs for the PRAB F600 robot.
Instruction: Course covers general safety, robot movement control, major component description and location, system theory of operation, control operation, basic programming, and maintenance. Methodology includes lecture, demonstration, and laboratory exercises.
Credit recommendation: In the lower division baccalaureate/associate degree category, 3 semester hours in Robotic Technology (4/89). NOTE: Credit should not be awarded for both this course and PRAB F700 Control (PRB 207).

PRAB F700 Control (PRB 207)

Location: Featherstone Road Engineering Center and various Chrysler Corporation locations.
Length: 80 hours (2 weeks).
Dates: November 1987-Present.
Objective: To prepare the student to operate, program, and edit programs for the PRAB F700 robot.
Instruction: Course covers general safety, robot movement control, major component description and location, system theory of operation, control operation, basic programming, and maintenance. Methodology includes lecture, demonstration, and laboratory exercises.
Credit recommendation: In the lower division baccalaureate/associate degree category, 3 semester hours in Robotic Technology (4/89). NOTE: Credit should not be awarded for both this course and PRAB F600 Control (PRB 206).

Programmable Controllers—Modicon 484 (MOD 104)

Location: Chrysler locations worldwide.
Length: 40 hours (1 week).
Dates: November 1983-Present.

Objective: To provide the student with experiences designed to help him/her install, repair, and operate the Modicon 484 programmable controller.

Learning Outcome: Upon successful completion of this course, the student will be able to identify specific hardware and their functions on the Modicon 484 controller; operate the 484 using Modicon software programs; and identify problems indicated by the controllers diagnostic program.

Instruction: Course covers power supplies, processor, system software, I/O hardware, programming and power distribution. Methodology includes lecture and laboratory.

Credit recommendation: In the vocational category, 2 semester hours in Industrial Electrical Controls (9/88).

Programmable Controllers—Modicon 584 (MOD 105)
Location: Chrysler locations worldwide.
Length: 80 hours (2 weeks).
Dates: September 1985-Present.
Objective: To develop the student's skills in the operation of the Modicon 584 controller with a P190 terminal using user programs.

Learning Outcome: Upon successful completion of this course, the student will be able to properly install all appropriate cables to the 584; properly set all switches and pins; and convert a relay logic diagram into a 584 program.

Instruction: Course covers block diagrams and main-frame hardware and configurations: I/O section hardware, conversion from relay logic to P.C. logic, Modicon 584 element references, timer instructions, and configuring Modicon 584 system I/O. Methodology includes lecture and laboratory.

Credit recommendation: In the vocational certificate category, 4 semester hours in Industrial Electrical Controls (9/88).

Programmable Controllers PLC-2 Family (BAB 102)
Location: Chrysler locations worldwide.
Length: 40 hours (1 week).
Dates: November 1983-Present.
Objective: To give the student an understanding of the parameters required for installing, operating, and basic troubleshooting the PLC-2 controller, including program editing.

Learning Outcome: Upon successful completion of this course, the student will be able to understand the operations and interfacing parameters of the PLC-2 controller; demonstrate the use and application of the PLC-2 controller in an industrial application; and identify the diagnostic troubleshooting indicators of the PLC-2 controller.

Instruction: Course covers 2/30 processor, cable installations, control functions for PLC-2 controller, logic diagrams, and hardware troubleshooting of PLC-2 controller. Methodology includes lecture and laboratory.

Credit recommendation: In the vocational certificate category, 2 semester hours in Industrial Electrical Controls (9/88).

Programmable Controllers PLC-2 Family Advanced Program (AAB 202)
Location: Chrysler locations worldwide.
Length: 40 hours (1 week).
Dates: November 1983-Present.
Objective: To give the student an understanding of the operation and programming of controller (PLC-2).

Learning Outcome: Upon successful completion of this course, the student will be able to input information and data into PLC-2 controller and analyze program operation; program PLC-2 controller to perform and control operation; and edit and troubleshoot program problems regarding the PLC-2.

Instruction: Course covers arithmetic instructions, program control, data transfer and comparison, subroutine and file concepts, sequencing and block transfer instructions. Methodology includes lecture and laboratory.

Credit recommendation: In the vocational certificate category, 2 semester hours in Industrial Electrical Controls (9/88).

Programmable Controllers PLC-3 and PLC-3/10 (BAB 103)
Location: Chrysler locations worldwide.
Length: 80 hours (2 weeks).
Dates: November 1983-Present.
Objective: To enable the student to understand the parameters required for installation, operation, and basic troubleshooting of the PLC-3 and PLC-3/10 controllers.

Learning Outcome: Upon successful completion of this course, the student will be able to understand the operations and interfacing parameters of the PLC-3 and PLC-3/10 controllers, demonstrate the use and application of the PLC-3 and PLC-3/10 controllers in an industrial application; and identify the diagnostic troubleshooting operations of the PLC-3 and PLC-3/10 controllers.

Instruction: Course covers PLC-3 processor, cable installation, relay ladder diagram conversion, processor mode selection and operation, diagnostic logic for PLC-3 processor, and hardware troubleshooting of PLC-3 and PLC-3/10 systems. Methodology includes lecture and laboratory.

Credit recommendation: In the vocational certificate category, 4 semester hours in Industrial Electrical Controls (9/88).

Programmable Controllers PLC-3 and PLC 3/10 Advanced Program (AAB 203)
Location: Chrysler locations worldwide.
Length: 40 hours (1 week).
Dates: September 1985-Present.
Objective: To introduce the student to the advanced

operation and programming of PLC-3 and PLC-3/10 controllers and the utilization of the advanced instruction set to support machine diagnostics.

Learning Outcome: Upon successful completion of this course, the student will be able to input information and data into the PLC-3 and PLC-3/10 controllers and analyze program operation; program PLC-3 and PLC-3/10 controllers to perform and control operations; and edit and troubleshoot programming problems regarding the PLC-3 and PLC-3/10 controllers.

Instruction: Course covers PLC-3 controller, memory organization, forces, functions and instructions for PLC-3, file concepts and instructions, FIFO, block transfer instructions, analog input and output usage. Methodology includes lecture and laboratory.

Credit recommendation: In the vocational certificate category, 2 semester hours in Industrial Electrical Controls (9/88).

Programmable Controllers PLC-5 Family (BAB 105)
Location: Chrysler locations worldwide.
Length: 40 hours (1 week).
Dates: April 1988-Present.

Objective: To develop the student's skills in the operation of the Allen Bradley PLC-5/15 family controllers with a 1784-T50 terminal.

Learning Outcome: Upon successful completion of this course, the student will be able to convert a relay logic diagram into a PLC-5/15 program; identify various faults in operation of controller; and properly set all switches and jumpers.

Instruction: Course covers power supplies, processor boards, chassis component identification, introduction to T50 terminal, programming, and introduction to MS DOS. Methodology includes lecture and laboratory.

Credit recommendation: In the vocational certificate category, 2 semester hours in Industrial Electrical Controls (9/88).

Resistance Welding Technology (RWT 101)
Location: Chrysler locations worldwide.
Length: 40 hours (1 week).
Dates: January 1983-Present.

Objective: To provide the student with a basic knowledge for the analysis of problems in the weld zone.

Learning Outcome: Upon successful completion of this course, the student will be able to demonstrate the ability to safely set up a welding situation; demonstrate the ability to compensate for factors that affect the welding process; and distinguish the quality of a given weld.

Instruction: Course covers safety, resistance welding, weld quality, weld hardware, weld machines, and troubleshooting. Methodology includes lecture and laboratory.

Credit recommendation: In the lower division baccalaureate/associate degree category, 2 semester hours in Welding Technology (9/88).

Vehicle Electrical/Electronic Systems (PO1 VEE)
Location: Chrysler Engineering Center and various Chrysler Corporation locations.
Length: 40 hours (1 or 2 weeks).
Dates: June 1988-Present.

Objective: To provide the student with the basic understanding of automotive electrical systems and related electronic components.

Instruction: Course covers the fundamentals of electricity, electronic symbols and wiring diagrams, use of test equipment, diagnostic techniques and introduction to multiplexing. Methodology includes lecture and laboratory exercises.

Credit recommendation: In the lower division baccalaureate/associate degree category, 2 semester hours in Automotive Technology (4/89).

Weld Controllers (RWC 101)
Location: Chrysler locations worldwide.
Length: 40 hours (1 week).
Dates: March 1984-Present.

Objective: To provide the student with a basic understanding of the installation, programming, and editing of a "Pertron" or a "Medar" Basic Weld controller.

Learning Outcome: Upon successful completion of this course, the student will be able to identify component parts and their functions; identify steps to be taken when given the status of diagnostic indicators; and diagnose and isolate a defective part within the weld controller.

Instruction: Course covers safety, functions, hardware and programming of the "Pertron" and "Medar" WC-2 controllers. Methodology includes lecture and laboratory.

Credit recommendation: In the lower division baccalaureate/associate degree category, 2 semester hours in Welding Technology (9/88). NOTE: To receive credit for this course, the student must have received credit for Resistance Welding Technology (RWT 101).

The Chubb Institute

Founded in 1970 by Chubb & Son Inc., the insurance group, The Chubb Institute is an independent business that provides classroom training in business-oriented computer subjects to the public and industry. The career division provides entry-level business programming training both to self-sponsored individuals and to company-sponsored students; the corporate division provides company customers with advanced programming courses for their experienced programmers and introductory computer courses for their non-data processing personnel. The Institute has a traditional approach to training, featuring experienced instructors who also have work experience in the field, a classroom environment to stimulate student/instructor interaction, and a skills oriented curriculum supported by practical workshop exercises.

The Chubb Institute is located in Parsippany, NJ and uses its parent company's computer center, one of the largest and most advanced in the state. The Institute is linked to this computer center via a telecommunications network by computer terminals and remote job entry equipment.

The Chubb Institute's entry-level programming curriculum is approved by the New Jersey Department of Education, approved for veterans' training, and the Institute is accredited by the Accrediting Commission of the National Association of Trade and Technical Schools.

Introductory Note:

Students take Introduction to Computer Systems (ICS), Programming Fundamentals (PRF), and Basic Program Design (BPD) in combination, not as stand-alone courses. Therefore, no credit is recommended if any one of these is taken alone.

When all three are completed, i.e., ICS, PRF, and BPD, a cumulative total of 7 semester hours is recommended, 3 in Introduction to Data Processing (lower division baccalaureate/associate), 1 in Machine Organization (upper division baccalaureate), and 3 in Assembler Language I (upper division baccalaureate or lower division baccalaureate/associate).

If ICS and PRF are completed, but not BPD, a total of 4 semester hours are recommended, 3 in Introduction to Data Processing (lower division baccalaureate/associate) and 1 in Machine Organization (upper division baccalaureate).

If PRF and BPD are completed, but not ICS, 3 semester hours in Assembler Language I (upper division baccalaureate or lower division baccalaureate/associate) are recommended.

Source of official student records: Education Services, Chubb Institute, Box 342, 8 Sylvan Way, Parsippany, NJ 07054-0342.

Additional information about the courses: Program on Noncollegiate Sponsored Instruction, Thomas A. Edison State College, Kelsey Building, 101 West State Street, Trenton, NJ 08625.

Applications Laboratory (LABS)
Location: Parsippany, NJ.
Length: 125 hours (5 weeks).
Dates: January 1974-Present.
Objective: To provide a student with Advanced COBOL and Assembler techniques including Structured programming techniques, Program linkage, documentation, file structure, data base concepts and VSAM file processing.
Instruction: This course consists of lecture and work sessions. Students design, code, test and debug four programs of varying complexity. Topics covered in the course are: Structured Programming Techniques, data base systems, minicomputers, Advanced COBOL techniques and Advanced Assembler techniques. Also covered are program linkage, VSAM file processing, program documentation and computer output to microfilm. In all their projects students are required to write the JCL needed to run the projects. All projects consist of multiple steps and include source library maintenance.

Credit recommendation: In the upper division baccalaureate category, 3 semester hours in COBOL II and 3 semester hours in Assembler Language II (11/83). NOTE: When taken after COBOL and Assembler Language this course provides rich application skills comparable to a second semester in both of these topics.

Assembler Language (ASM)
Location: Parsippany, NJ.
Length: 75 hours (3 weeks).
Dates: January 1974-Present.
Objective: To introduce students to fixed-point, decimal, and logical instructions, QSAM I/O macros, and Assembler program structure.
Instruction: Topics covered in this course are: Fixed-point, decimal and logical instructions; Data definition statements; Base registers, entry and return linkage; I/O Macros; EDIT, and TRT instructions. Course also covers: Multiple base registers; Multiple CSECTs; ADCONS, VCONS, LTORG, DSECT; BHX, BXLE; Linkage Editor and Loader functions; Basic dump debugging; Mainline and subroutine structures (BAL, CALL); Functions of the Assembler Translator program; Workshops are included in this unit with emphasis on coding readable and maintainable assembler programs. Students design, code, test and debug one program.

Credit recommendation: In the upper division baccalaureate or lower division baccalaureate/associate degree category, 3 semester hours in Computer Systems or Computer Organization (11/83).

Basic Program Design (BPD)
Location: Parsippany, NJ.
Length: 75 hours (3 weeks).
Dates: January 1974-Present.
Objective: To present the most common data processing problems encountered in an applications environment, and to teach students how to analyze these problems, design solutions, select appropriate test data, validate the problem solutions, and finally to apply these techniques to the development of a (computer based) systems.
Instruction: This course is mainly through lecture with about 15 hours of lab time. Students are required to design and flowchart two major problems. The course covers Methods for problem analysis and program design, Flowcharting techniques, and Mainline and subroutine logic. Students learn the logic involved in: data validation (single and multiple error analysis), sequence checks (ascending and descending keys), loop structure, master file updates; match programs, control breaks and summary reports,

and table handling.

Credit recommendation: In the upper division baccalaureate or lower division baccalaureate/associate degree category, 3 semester hours in Assembler Language I (when student also completes Programming Fundamentals) (11/83). NOTE: When a student has completed Introduction to Computer Systems, Programming Fundamentals and Basic Program Design, there is a cumulative total of 7 semester hours of credit recommended. 3 semester hours (lower division baccalaureate) in Introduction to Data Processing, 1 semester hour (upper division baccalaureate) in Machine Organization and 3 semester hours (upper division) in Assembler Language I.

COBOL Language (COB)
Location: Parsippany, NJ.
Length: 75 hours (3 weeks).
Dates: January 1974-Present.
Objective: To introduce students to ANS COBOL coding rules, COBOL program structure, data definition and manipulation, input and output operations.
Instruction: This course covers: Divisions of a COBOL program; Arithmetic verbs; I/O verbs; Data definitions (77, 88, 01-49); MOVE, IF, PERFORM; and Table handling. It also covers Indexing, subscripting; SEARCH; SORT (USING, GIVING, INPUT PROCEDURE, OUTPUT PROCEDURE); Program linkage; COBOL LISTING MAPS; Sequential and VSAM file processing. Emphasis is placed on coding techniques that produce readable and maintainable COBOL programs. Students design, code, test and debug a COBOL program that edits the transaction file that is input to the Inventory project. The program produces an edited transaction disk file and a formatted error report.
Credit recommendation: In the upper division baccalaureate category, or lower division baccalaureate/associate degree category, 3 semester hours in COBOL I (11/83).

Introduction to Computer Systems (ICS)
Location: Parsippany, NJ.
Length: 23 hours (5 days).
Dates: January 1974-Present.
Objective: To provide a thorough introduction to computer systems, computer concepts, programming, and data processing terminology. A basic introduction to binary and hexadecimal systems is also covered.
Instruction: The course introduces students to the components of a computer system including: Descriptions of data storage hardware, including disks, drums, tapes, card readers, printers (impact and laser), and MSS; Main storage; Arithmetic/Logic Unit; and Control Unit. Also covered are: Storage addressing (absolute addresses, relative addresses), Binary and hexadecimal number systems (binary and hexadecimal arithmetic), and the steps involved in problem solving. Finally this course treats the differences between logical and physical records, file organizations, record formats, and basic operating system concepts.
Credit recommendation: In the lower division baccalaureate/associate degree category, if Programming Fundamentals (PRF) is also successfully completed, 3 semester hours in Introduction to Data Processing and in the upper division baccalaureate level category, 1 semester hour in Machine Organization (11/83). NOTE: No credit recommended if Introduction to Computer Systems taken alone.

Operating Systems (OS/VS)
Location: Parsippany, NJ.
Length: 75 hours (3 weeks).
Dates: January 1974-Present.
Objective: To introduce students to Operating Systems Fundamentals, MVS, JCL, MVS Data Management Utilities, and MVS Debugging using System Dumps.
Instruction: In the Operating Systems Fundamentals section the functional components of the Operating System are covered with emphasis on the development of conceptual understanding of the job, task, and data management facilities. In the MVS JCL section emphasis is placed on both JCL syntax and coding techniques. The JOB, EXEC, and DD statements and related parameters are covered in-depth as is the use and manipulation of Cataloged Procedures. The Data Management Utilities section presents the IBM Data Management Utilities most often used by applications programmers. Finally in the MVS Debugging section debugging MVS dumps are covered through the use of the Operating System control blocks. Lectures cover task and data management processing and the use of dump information in identifying logic errors.
Credit recommendation: In the upper division baccalaureate category, 3 semester hours in Operating Systems Fundamentals (11/83).

Programming Fundamentals (PRF)
Location: Parsippany, NJ.
Length: 75 hours (3 weeks).
Dates: January 1974-Present.
Objective: To provide an in-depth coverage of the principles of program execution, input/output operations, and IBM S/360 - S/370 machine code instructions, and an introduction to IBM machine language instruction set.
Instruction: This course covers machine code programming using fixed point, logical, and decimal instructions, and data formats (fixed-point, zoned, packed, logical). The IBM S/360 - S/370 interrupt handling system in relation to multiprogramming, Task Dispatcher, TCB, and Task status are covered, as well as the relationship between CPU, channels, control units, and devices. Physical I/O and Logical I/O, (CCW, CAW, CSW, I/O Supervisor), characteristics of Sequential, Indexed, Direct and Parti-

tioned Data Sets and tape and disk concepts complete this course. Lecture is used throughout this course with a dozen hours of laboratory work.

Credit recommendation: When taken with Introduction to Computer Systems in the lower division baccalaureate/associate degree category, 3 semester hours in Introduction to Data Processing and in the upper division baccalaureate category, 1 semester hour in Machine Organization. When taken with Basic Program Design (BPD) in the upper division baccalaureate or lower division baccalaureate/associate level, 3 semester hours in Assembly Language I (11/83). NOTE: It is not anticipated that any student would take only Programming Fundamentals, and there was no appropriate credit recommendation for this course if taken alone.

The Cittone Institute

The Cittone Institute started its Computer Repair/Robotics school in March 1984 for industry. In September 1984 the program was reorganized giving the students the technical training necessary for the Analog and Digital Electronics for Computers and Robotics. This training gives the student a minimum of forty percent hands-on laboratory work and sixty percent of classroom theory in a lecture, conference, and discussion method to involve the student in the program with highly qualified instructors. The students must select their own projects and design and build their projects in two semesters.

The Computer Repair/Robotics school provides the training for the self sponsored individual, veteran sponsored individuals and company sponsored students.

The program is 1800 hours long and consists of Module 110 Direct Current Theory, Module 120 Alternating Current Theory, Module 130 Semiconductor and Industrial Circuits, Module 210 Digital Electronics, Module 220 Microprocessor technology, and Module 230 Computer Systems, Computer Systems, Computer Peripherals, Robotics, and Data Communications. There are four major examinations used as a tool for measuring satisfactory completion of each module.

The Cittone Institute curriculum is approved by the New Jersey State Department of Education, approved for veterans' training, and New Jersey State Department for Vocational Rehabilitation. The Institute is also accredited by ASICS.

Source of official student records: Education Services, Cittone Institute, 1697 Oaktree Road, Edison, New Jersey 08820.

Additional information about the courses: Thomas A. Edison State College, Program on Noncollegiate Sponsored Instruction, 101 West State Street, Trenton, New Jersey 08625 or American Council on Education, Registry of Credit Recommendations, One Dupont Circle, Washington, DC 20063.

COMPUTER REPAIR AND ROBOTICS

The Computer Repair/Robotic school provides the training for the self-sponsored individual, veteran sponsored individuals, and company sponsored students. The program is 1800 hours in length and consists of Module 110 Direct Current Theory, Module 120 alternating Current Theory, Module 130 Semiconductor and Industrial Circuits, Module 210 Digital Electronics, Module 220 Microprocessor technology, and Module 230 Computer Systems, Computer Systems, Computer Peripherals, Robotics, and Data Communications. There are four major examinations used as a tool for measuring satisfactory completion of each module.

Alternating Current Module (D120 or E120)
  Location: Edison, NJ.
  Length: 300 hours (12 weeks).
  Dates: April 1984-Present.
  Objective: To provide the student with the level of knowledge to support and understand the theory, application, and specification of alternating current.
  Learning Outcome: Upon completion of this module which will provide the level of knowledge to support and understand the theory, application, and specification of alternating current, the student will be able to: (1) describe the concepts of magnetism and electro magnetism; (2) illustrate the characteristics of inductor and the generation of AC using varying magnetic field; (3) describe and analyze capacitance and capacitive reactance and their applications for sinusoidal voltages; (4) describe and analyze the characteristics of inductors and capacitors for DC and AC sources; (5) perform experiments that will validate the effects of impedance and current effects in series and parallel resonance circuits.
  Instruction: This course provides an introduction to the basics of alternating current, in-depth studies of alternating voltage and alternating current, inductive circuits, capacitive circuits, resistive circuits, and combination of resistive, inductive, and capacitive circuits. Also covered are networks analysis and complex numbering for AC circuits; resonance and filters; AC meters, power supplies and oscilloscopes, and basic vacuum tubes. Mathematics skills are covered as needed to complete the work with AC circuits. Mathematics skills are expanded to include working complex numbers and right oblique triangle solutions. Algebra is expanded to include simultaneous equations. The students are introduced to exponential and logarithmic equations as well as rectangular notations and polar coordinates. Students conduct laboratory experiments to verify and reinforce classroom lectures. Students assemble components to complete various circuits in order to verify the reactance of components with alternating current and receive practice in use of AC meters and oscilloscopes and

an introduction to troubleshooting technique.

Credit recommendation: In the lower division baccalaureate/associate degree category, 4 semester hours in Alternating Current (8/88).

Computer System, Peripherals and Robotics (D230 or E230)
  Location: Edison, NJ.
  Length: 300 hours (12 weeks).
  Dates: April 1984-Present.
  Objective: To provide the student with the level of knowledge to support and understand the theory, application, and specification of microprocessor technology.
  Learning Outcome: Upon completion of this module, the student will be able to: (1) perform experiments utilizing the operation system (load, start, and keep account of several running tasks in a multiuser environment); (2) perform experiments analyzing the operation of various types of input/output ports; and troubleshoot the system and repair to component level; (3) perform experiments to determine the internal functions of a printer; troubleshoot and repair to component level; (4) identify the various parts of robotic systems; program to control the robot; (5) analyze the operation of a robotic system software; analyze and troubleshoot a hydraulic system; (6) analyze and troubleshoot the control circuitry of the robot (DC, AC and Stepping motors); (7) perform experiments by writing a program in basic and machine code to control various types of robots for the purpose of analyzation and troubleshooting; (8) design digital circuitry to achieve external control of motors; analyze the operation of motors; analyze the operation of the simulator control circuitry; (9) analyze the software and its interaction with various mechanical components of manipulators to recognizing problems when they occur.
  Instruction: The student will be introduced to mainframe, minicomputer and microcomputer systems and robotics. This module will encompass computer memory units, CPU interfacing and controllers, peripheral devices, magnetic tapes, visual display units (VDU), disk drives (floppy disk, hard disk, removable, and permanent), and printers. Serve control system of a robot, actuators, and sensors are included. Students will study these techniques with various test equipment. Troubleshooting techniques are reinforced and refined with "hands-on" experiments. This will include using various computer systems and their associated peripheral devices as well as robotic control systems.
  Credit recommendation: In the lower division baccalaureate/associate degree category, 1 semester hour in Introduction to Robotics, 2 semester hours in Computer Peripherals, and 1 semester hour in Computer Systems (8/88).

Digital Electronics (D210 or E210)
  Location: Edison, NJ.
  Length: 300 hours (12 weeks).
  Dates: April 1984-Present.
  Objective: This course covers digital electronics which is the foundation for all computerized equipment. Emphasis is placed on the numbering systems. All types of logic families, logic gates, flip-flops, counters, registers, memory techniques, D/A and A/D conversions, universal asynchronous receivers transmitters (UARTs) and conversions of digital code to American Standard Code for Information Interchange (ASCII) are studied.
  Learning Outcome: Upon successful completion of this course, the student will be able to (1) describe and perform experiments to support the theory and verification of logic outputs, logic gates, and evaluate their truth tables; (2) analyze, test, and troubleshoot prototypes; design and evaluate logic outputs; (3) analyze and design circuits containing counters, decoders, and flip-flops; (4) perform and analyze current and voltage specification of logic circuits with asynchronous and asynchronous circuits; (5) perform experiments using different type converters to consolidate the theory learned.
  Instruction: Students will assemble components in a configuration to produce operational circuits and to verify their skills by using appropriate test equipment.
  Credit recommendation: In the lower division baccalaureate/associate degree category, 4 semester hours in Digital Electronics (8/88).

Direct Current (D110 or E110)
  Location: Edison, NJ.
  Length: 300 hours (12 to 25 weeks).
  Dates: April 1984-Present.
  Objective: To provide the student with the level of knowledge to support and understand the theory, application, and specification of direct current.
  Learning Outcome: Upon successful completion of this module, the student will be able to: (1) describe the nature of electricity and perform experiments verifying elements of electricity using formulas and basic test equipment; (2) describe series, parallel, and series-parallel circuits (voltage, resistance, short current, etc.) and perform experiments verifying voltage, current resistance, open and short circuits in series-parallel circuit using basic test equipment; (3) perform experiments verifying resistor power rating, use of rheostats and potentiometers and their proper use; (4) perform experiments verifying design techniques and the operation of DC meters; (5) perform experiments verifying the practical application of the network theorems, characteristics of batteries, and the phenomenon of magnetism.
  Instruction: This module introduces the student to basic principles of electricity and electronics. Ohm's law, Kirchoff laws, network theorems, series and parallel resistance in DC networks, voltage and current dividers, conductors and insulators, magnetism and batteries are studied and analyzed in detail together with basic measur-

ing equipment and component identification. Fundamental mathematics skills necessary for the understanding of basic electronics are studied and practiced. Students will conduct laboratory experiments (about 40 percent of total course time) to verify and reinforce classroom lectures from direct current theory. This includes assembling components to form series, parallel and combination series-parallel circuits; and applying basic mathematics skills to analyze the circuit and verify results by using basic test-measuring equipment. Laboratory safety practices are emphasized.

Credit recommendation: In the lower division associate/baccalaureate degree category, 4 semester hours in Direct Current (8/88).

Microprocessor Technology (D220 or E220)
Location: Edison, NJ.
Length: 300 hours (12 weeks).
Dates: April 1984-Present.
Objective: To provide the student with the level of knowledge to support and understand the theory, application, and specification of microprocessor technology.

Learning Outcome: Upon successful completion of this course, the student will be able to: (1) describe the characteristic of and perform experiments on the Hickok K6800 Microcomputer related to starting up and running the microcomputer uisng the MC6800, Zilog Z80, and Intel 8086 microprocessors; (2) perform experiments using the microcomputer to control the complete system, to include start-up DMA control and program execution; (3) perform experiments that execute programs and diagnostic routines; troubleshoot and debug each program and verify the correct operation; (4) write software programs for the purpose of troubleshooting and debugging; (5) perform troubleshooting experiments, identify the symptoms, isolate the fault(s) and present written reports, specifying the corrective action necessary.

Instruction: Microprocessors and their applications are covered in the class. Microcomputer timing diagrams and analysis are covered; MPU-to-Random access memory interface is studied. Machine language and systems operations will be taught as well as addressing modes available to microprocessors. MPU architecture and its features (differences and similarities in existing architecture) as well as applications of stacks, subroutines, and interrupts are analyzed. Student will gain a thorough understanding of the microprocessor hardware and schematics. Advanced status/dynamics troubleshooting for both catastrophic and intermittent failures will be emphasized. Maintenance via structures and their understanding will be studied. Hands-on troubleshooting with various types of test equipment will enhance their ability to perform on microprocessor-type equipment.

Credit recommendation: In the lower division baccalaureate/associate degree category, 2 semester hours in Assembly Language and 2 semester hours in Computer Circuits (8/88).

Semiconductor Principles Module (D130 or E130)
Location: Edison, NJ.
Length: 300 hours (12 weeks).
Dates: April 1984-Present.
Objective: To provide the student with the level of knowledge to support and understand the theory, application, and specification of semiconductor theory.

Learning Outcome: Upon successful completion of this course, the student will be able to: (1) describe and analyze semiconductor physics, differences between semiconductors, conductors and insulators; (2) perform experiments to demonstrate forward and reverse biasing of the PN junction diode, and different characteristics of different types of diodes; (3) perform experiments to demonstrate bipolar transistor characteristics; (4) perform experiments to demonstrate common emitter, common collector, and common base configurations and their applications; (5) perform experiments to demonstrate different classes of amplifiers and their applications; (6) perform experiments to demonstrate the characteristics of JFET and MOSFET transistors and their applications.

Instruction: In this course, principles of semiconductors will be studied in depth by applying knowledge gained from DC and AC theories. The studies of semiconductors will be the analysis of the PN junction diode, special diodes, bipolar transistors, unipolar transistors thyristro family, and operational amplifiers. Biasing and various configurations for each of the semiconductor components to include coupling networks will be studied. Students construct operational circuits with diodes, transistors, and operational circuits with diodes, and operational amplifiers and then analyze each circuit using power supplies, multimeters, frequency counters, signal generators, and oscilloscopes.

Credit recommendation: In the lower division baccalaureate/associate degree category, 5 semester hours in Semiconductor Principles (8/88).

COMPUTER PROGRAMMING

BASIC Programming with Flowcharting (CP902)
Location: Edison, NJ.
Length: 125 hours (5 weeks).
Dates: January 1986-Present.
Objective: To introduce students to programming languages and the use of algorithms and flowcharting techniques. BASIC programming problems are coded and executed on the IBM-PC.

Learning Outcome: Upon successful completion of this course, the student will be able to: (1) define and analyze the problem; (2) determine the logic necessary to solve the problem; (3) write the appropriate code to solve the problem; (4) use structure and discipline in a step-by-step methodology in dealing with sequential and direct files with sequential or random processing.

Instruction: This course introduces students to the discipline of computer programming, using the BASIC language. Emphasis will be on structured program design and program writing. The overall intention of this course is to teach the student the use of the PC, the function of the disk operating system, and the BASIC language in business applications.

Credit recommendation: In the lower division baccalaureate/associate degree category, 3 semester hours in BASIC Programming (10/88).

COBOL (CP904)

Location: Edison, NJ.
Length: 250 hours.
Dates: September 1981-Present.

Objective: To provide students with an understanding of the fundamental principles of computer programming. ANSI COBOL is used as the programming language.

Learning Outcome: Upon successful completion of this course, the student will: (1) be able to write structured ANS COBOL programs; (2) process the knowledge of programming and information processing concepts necessary to write both elementary and advanced programs; (3) be oriented toward effective, efficient standardized code.

Instruction: Students will become proficient in American National Standard (ANS) COBOL. Beginning with the four divisions of COBOL program, the student will progress to control, arithmetic, and input-output verbs. Advanced techniques of internal sorting, indexing, subscripting, and linkage sections are covered. Structured programming is taught and enforced. Students are required to code and test programs using each of the above-mentioned techniques including indexed files. Various debugging tools will be explained; students will learn correct syntax, as well as logic errors. VSAM concepts will be discussed; random and dynamic processing will be used where applicable.

Credit recommendation: In the lower division baccalaureate/associate degree category, 3 semester hours in COBOL I (10/88).

Data Base III (CP903)

Location: Edison, NJ.
Length: 50 hours (2 weeks).
Dates: May 1987-Present.

Objective: To give the student a solid introduction to Data Base programming.

Learning Outcome: Upon successful completion of this course, the student will: (1) understand the basic concepts of data bases; (2) be familiar with the Data Base commands necessary to program in this language; and (3) understand the concept of interactive programming.

Instruction: This course covers fields and data base files and their formations. The course also includes how to create files, enter data, use and list commands, and adding data with Append. The student will be responsible for creation of a Customer Information File as well as an Inventory Information File.

Credit recommendation: In the lower division baccalaureate/associate degree category, 1 semester hour in Data Base III (10/88).

Introduction to Computers (CP901)

Location: Edison, NJ.
Length: 25 hours (1 week).
Dates: September 1981-Present.

Objective: To introduce the student to terms and concepts necessary to become an efficient data processing professional.

Learning Outcome: Upon successful completion of this course, students will: (1) have a clear understanding of computer terminology and concepts; (2) be able to explain the differences between the three categories of computers (hardware) as well as the differences between high level programming languages (software); and (3) will understand the operations of the computer system, as well as possess the ability to code and implement a small BASIC program.

Instruction: This course presents background information to help clarify the students' perspective on computers. Topics discussed include: trends, fundamental concepts of a computer system, categories of computer usage, and an overview of computer applications. Also included are data organization storage concepts and a general overview of systems. The course expands on MIS concepts and applications of the computer by examining how computers are used in business and government.

Credit recommendation: In the lower division baccalaureate/associate degree category, 1 semester hour in Introduction to Computers (10/88).

RPG II and RPG III (CP906)

Location: Edison, NJ.
Length: 150 hours (6 weeks).
Dates: January 1984-Present.

Objective: To explain to the student the current state-of-the-art applications of RPG II.

Learning Outcome: Upon successful completion of this course, the student will: (1) have a working knowledge of RPG II; (2) be familiar with the concepts of RPG III; (3) be able to analyze code and debug business applications problems in RPG II; (4) be able to determine when it is best to program in RPG and when other languages might prove more useful. The student will also learn how to create data files through Interactive Programming and Screen Design.

Instruction: The student is required to complete a series of entries on pre-defined specifications forms that basically define the file description input, calculation, and output processed. The student will learn RPG II programming in relation to business situations using current state-of-the-art applications. In addition, proper programming form that focuses on overall logical design and procedures for file maintenance, report generation and record inquiry, using on-line real-time applications will be covered. An overview of RPG III concepts emphasizing data base technology will also be introduced.

Credit recommendation: In the lower division baccalaureate/associate degree category, 3 semester hours in RPG II (10/88).

College for Financial Planning®

The College for Financial Planning®, a nonprofit education institution, offers a curriculum to prepare individuals for testing by the International Board of Standards and Practices for Certified Financial Planners, Inc. (IBCFP). The Certified Financial Planner*TM (CFP*TM) Professional Education Program consists of six separate parts, each of which is followed by a corresponding national IBCFP test. It is designed for self-study, utilizing unique study materials that include textbooks and study guides specially prepared by the academic staff of the College. Classroom instruction also is available through the College's adjunct faculty and affiliate colleges and universities, as well as through select corporations. Individuals who complete the CFP Program learn to recognize existing and potential client problems and to recommend solutions over a broad range of financial circumstances.

To qualify for certification by the IBCFP, an individual must fulfill certain requirements, including submission of a transcript indicating completion of a financial planning education program that has been registered with the IBCFP and successful completion of the six-part national IBCFP certification examination series.

In 1984, the College developed the Financial Paraplanner Program to provide administrative and support personnel in financial services with the opportunity to gain knowledge of basic financial planning concepts and skills.

The College for Financial Planning®, located in Denver, Colorado, was established in 1972.

Source of official student records: College for Financial Planning®, 9725 East Hampden Avenue, Denver, Colorado 80231.

Additional information about the courses: Program on Noncollegiate Sponsored Instruction, The Center for Adult Learning and Educational Credentials, American Council on Education, One Dupont Circle, Washington, D.C. 20036.

Financial Paraplanner Program

Location: Available at various locations nationally and internationally.
Length: Approximately 150 to 225 hours of self-study.
Dates: February 1985-Present.
Objective: To introduce the financial planning assistant to financial planning, concepts, and terminology.
Instruction: Course covers topical areas included in the objectives with periodic examination at various collegiate institutions.
Credit recommendation: In the lower division baccalaureate/associate degree category, 3 semester hours in Business Administration (2/85).

The following courses are arranged in numerical sequence, i.e., CFP I, CFB II, etc.

Introduction to Financial Planning (CFP I)

Location: Available nationally and internationally at various locations.
Length: Approximately 180 hours of self-study.
Dates: November 1975-Present.
Objective: To present the six-stage financial planning process and an introduction to regulations affecting financial planners. To present the concepts of communication skills, the economic environment, and the time value of money. To provide an introduction and overview of the content of the Program Parts II through VI.
Instruction: Course includes an introduction to personal financial planning, regulation, communication techniques, time value of money, the economic environment, risk management, investments, retirement plans, personal income tax planning and estate planning. Proctored examinations are required at a variety of collegiate institutions.
Credit recommendation: In the upper division baccalaureate category, 3 semester hours in Business Administration or Financial Planning (12/81) (2/85). NOTE: This course has been reevaluated and continues to meet requirements for credit recommendations.

Risk Management (CFP II)

Location: Available at various locations nationally and internationally.
Length: Approximately 180 to 210 hours of self-study.
Dates: November 1975-Present.
Objective: To give students an understanding of risk management and risk analysis including interpreting the insurance contract; coverages provided by property and liability insurance; the areas of life and health insurance; group and social insurance; the organization and internal functions of private insurers; and to enable the student to demonstrate an understanding of processes associated with the determination of insurance needs and purchase of insurance products.
Instruction: Course covers all topical areas included in the objectives with periodic proctored examinations at various collegiate institutions.
Credit recommendation: In the upper division baccalaureate category, 3 semester hours in Business Administration or Insurance (12/81) (2/85). NOTE: This

course has been reevaluated and continues to meet requirements for credit recommendations.

Investments (CFP III)
Location: Available at various locations both nationally and internationally.
Length: Approximately 150 to 225 hours of self-study.
Dates: November 1975-Present.
Objective: To provide the student with an understanding of the economic and business environment; to provide the fundamentals of investments, including tools and mechanics of investing, security markets, tax considerations, sources of investment risk, and the analysis of corporate financial statements; to provide a knowledge of valuation techniques, portfolio construction and management process, and asset categories.
Instruction: Course covers topical areas included in the objectives with periodic proctored examinations at various collegiate institutions.
Credit recommendation: In the upper division baccalaureate category, 3 semester hours in Business Administration or Finance (12/81) (2/85). NOTE: This course has been reevaluated and continues to meet requirements for credit recommendations.

Tax Planning and Management (CFP IV)
Location: Available at various locations nationally and internationally.
Length: Approximately 210 hours of self-study.
Dates: November 1975-Present.
Objective: To provide the student with an understanding of the fundamentals of individual income tax; considerations in selecting a business form; tax planning for the acquisition and disposition of property; tax advantaged investments; tax planning alternatives; tax traps; and personal tax management processes.
Instruction: Course covers topical areas included in the objectives with periodic proctored examinations at various collegiate institutions.
Credit recommendation: In the upper division baccalaureate category, 3 semester hours in Business Administration or Tax Accounting (12/81) (2/85). NOTE: This course has been reevaluated and continues to meet requirements for credit recommendations.

Retirement Planning and Employee Benefits (CFP V)
Location: Available at various locations nationally and internationally.
Length: Approximately 150 hours if independent study.
Dates: November 1975-Present.
Objective: To provide the student with an understanding of personal retirement planning, qualified retirement plans; government-sponsored retirement plans, and employee benefits involving group life and medical insurance and related programs, and nonqualified deferred compensation.
Instruction: Course covers topical areas included in the objectives with periodic proctored examinations at various collegiate institutions.
Credit recommendation: In the upper division baccalaureate category, 3 semester hours in Business Administration or Financial Planning (12/81) (2/85). NOTE: This course has been reevaluated and continues to meet requirements for credit recommendations.

Estate Planning (CFP VI)
Location: Available at various locations nationally and internationally.
Length: Approximately 210 hours of self-study.
Dates: February 1985-Present.
Objective: To introduce the student to the fundamentals of an estate plan, including federal estate and gift taxation as well as specific exclusion and valuation techniques that reduce the size of the gross estate; to enable the student to provide specific estate planning recommendations.
Instruction: Course covers topical areas included in the objectives with periodic proctored examinations at various collegiate institutions.
Credit recommendation: In the upper division baccalaureate category, 3 semester hours in Business Administration or Insurance (2/85).

Computer Learning Center

The Computer Learning Center is owned and operated by the Airco Educational Services Division of the BOC Group, Inc., in Montvale, New Jersey. Airco entered the career training field in 1968 as a commitment to provide marketable skills to underemployed and unemployed persons.

In 1976, Airco acquired the Computer Learning Center operations. The Computer Learning Center is designed to provide quality training responsive to the needs in the data processing community. Computer Learning Center facilities have expanded nationally and are now located in many large metropolitan areas.

All computer Learning Center schools are accredited by the Accrediting Commission of either the Association of Independent Colleges and Schools (AICS) or the National Association of Trade and Technical Schools (NATTS). Several Computer Learning Center schools hold dual accreditation.

The administration of the school is comprised of six (6) departments: Admissions, Financial Aid, Business, Student Services, Education, and Placement.

Source of official student records: Director of Student Services, Computer Learning Center, 160 East Route 4, Paramus, New Jersey 07652.

Additional information about the courses: Program on Noncollegiate Sponsored Instruction, Thomas A. Edison State College, 101 West State Street, CB-545, Trenton, New Jersey 08625.

Assembler Language Coding (CP-301)
  Location: Paramus, NJ.
  Length: 200 hours (40 days).
  Dates: April 1983-Present.
  Objective: To enable students to understand and utilize OS JCL and utilities and to code and debug assembler programs using VSAM and non-VSAM methods.
  Instruction: This course covers concepts of symbolic language, assembler processing, data representation, standard instruction set, machine format, decimal instructions, defined storage, defined constants, base register, decimal alignment, explicit addressing, table processing, program structure, loop control, closed subroutines, and debugging techniques.
  Students learn how to code and run a program by (1) incorporating disk-to-print moves, compares and headings; (2) using control break, logic, packed decimal instructions, editing techniques and print overflow concept; (3) utilizing OS sort features; (4) executing a sequential update, using two input files, minor totals, line counters, and output-to-disk concepts; (5) creating an indexed sequential file, using the required MACROs; (6) using explicit addressing techniques and loops; and (7) using three input files, one of which is to be updated based on specifications from a flowchart (maintenance).
  Credit recommendation: In the lower division baccalaureate/associate degree category, 5 semester hours in Assembler Language and in the lower division baccalaureate/associate degree category, 1 semester hour in OS Job Control Language and Utilities (2/85).

DOS/Operations (CO-401)
  Location: Paramus, NJ.
  Length: 200 hours (40 days).
  Dates: April 1983-Present.
  Objective: To enable students to operate a large mainframe computer system with a full complement of peripheral devices.
  Instruction: Covered are the concepts of DOS Operating Systems, multiprogramming, multiprocessing, data management, task management, queue management, foreground partitions, background partitions, DOS operator commands, DOS utility programs, DOS Job Control Language, spooling, Power II, Power II Operator Commands, Power Job Entry Control Language, and DOS IPL.
  Students will further learn to respond to DOS console messages with appropriate DOS operator response, to work with DOS job control language, diagnose job control errors, and respond with appropriate corrections.
  Credit recommendation: In the lower division baccalaureate/associate degree category, 6 semester hours in DOS/Operations (2/85).

Introduction to Data Processing (DP-100)
  Location: Paramus, NJ.
  Length: 100 hours (20 days).
  Dates: February 1983-Present.
  Objective: To provide students with an introduction to data processing and to lay the foundation for subsequent computer courses.
  Instruction: This course presents an overview of the data processing industry—its history and growth, its application to contemporary society, its terminology and its possible impact on the future growth of our society. Also covered are concepts of components of the computer, internal processing, data formats, access methods, and logic and flowcharting.
  Credit recommendation: In the lower division baccalaureate/associate degree category, 3 semester hours in Introduction to Data Processing, and in the lower division baccalaureate/associate degree category, 1 semester hour in Job Control Language (2/85).

OS/Operations (CO-400)
  Location: Paramus, NJ.
  Length: 200 hours (40 days).
  Dates: June 1983-Present.
  Objective: To enable students to comprehend and execute the IPL process for an IBM OS System.
  Instruction: Covered in this course are the concepts of operating systems, interleaving, multiprogramming, multiprocessing, interrupts, control programs, management routines, reader/interpreter, initiator/terminator, output writers, main storage, virtual storage, partitions, regions, operating commands, spooling, OS Job Control Language, and utility programs.
  Students will also learn to execute and comprehend the IPL process for an IBM OS System; respond to OS Console messages with appropriate responses, display techniques used to order and execute work on system and diagnose error messages relative to the Operating System and Job Control Language and take appropriate action to rectify said errors. Students will further understand the internal working of the Operating System and the internal logic involved in job processing; the use and function of Job Control Language in job processing; the function of a spooling system. Students will code and execute IBM utility programs.
  Credit recommendation: In the lower division baccalaureate/associate degree category, 3 semester hours in OS/Operations and in the lower division baccalaureate/associate degree category, 3 semester hours in OS/Job Control Language and Utilities (2/85).

RPG II Programming (DP-200)
  Location: Paramus, NJ.
  Length: 100 hours (20 days).

Dates: March 1983-Present.
Objective: To enable students to understand concepts of RPG II, generate RPG II programs, and execute programs.
Instruction: This course is designed to enable the student to (1) understand the concepts of RPG logic flow, indicator usage, arithmetic operations, control levels, compare operations, indexed sequential files, disk storage and retrieval, sort/merge, subroutines, tables, and arrays; (2) transfer information from one file to another using IBM utility programs for listing input and output files; (3) complete a card to print RPG II program using arithmetic operations and report headings; (4) generate sorted input data and complete RPG programs using level breaks for major and minor totals; and (5) complete an RPG II program using indexed sequential input and table look-up.
Credit recommendation: In the lower division baccalaureate/associate degree category, 3 semester hours in RPG II (2/85).

Structured Programming in COBOL (CP-300)
Location: Paramus, NJ.
Length: 200 hours (40 days).
Dates: April 1983-Present.
Objective: To enable students to comprehend COBOL language in terms of structural and top down coding techniques.
Instruction: Upon course completion, the student will (1) understand the concepts of compilers, linkage editors, load module, COBOL coding standards, file processing, indexed sequential file coding standards, control break processing, sort features, table handling, editing input and output, debugging, documentation, IBM 4341 JCL; (2) understand the flow of an inventory system which has been prepared to comprehensively present the ANSI COBOL instruction set; (3) use ANSI COBOL concepts in flowcharting, coding, testing, debugging, and documenting these problems with emphasis on structured design; (4) code and run a card-to-print program with output headings and page counters; code and run programs which edit both input and output data; code and run programs which manipulate tables by means of interactive loops, as well as serial and binary searches; code and run a program which sorts an input file and executes control break processing of the output; and (5) master Job Control Language, its syntax and its manipulative concepts relative to job execution; and a general understanding of operating system concepts.
Credit recommendation: In the lower division baccalaureate/associate degree category, 5 semester hours in COBOL (2/85).

Computer Learning Center of Philadelphia

The Computer Learning Center provides an educational career program that prepares students desiring jobs as entry level data processing professionals. The educational program at Computer Learning Center is directed toward preparing students to develop technical skills, to understand the application of such skills, and to develop professional attitudes and behaviors related to study, work habits, interpersonal communications, self-discipline, and confidence.

A faculty of mature and competent data processing professionals teaching in a professional and demanding atmosphere enables the students to make rapid progress in skills that will gain them recognition from employers in the data processing field.

Source of official student records: Director, Computer Learning Center, 30th & Market Streets, Philadelphia, Pennsylvania 19104.

Additional information about the courses: Program on Noncollegiate Sponsored Instruction, The Center for Adult Learning and Educational Credentials, American Council on Education, One Dupont Circle, Washington, D.C. 20036.

Assembler Language (CP-301)
Location: Computer Learning Center, Philadelphia, PA.
Length: 204 hours (34 days).
Dates: April 1979-Present.
Objective: To provide the student with an elementary, business oriented, introduction to Assembler Language.
Instruction: Upon completion of the course, the student will understand the following concepts: general registers, defined storage, defined constants, base and displacement addressing, symbolic addressing, instruction sets, internal data format, decimal arithmetic. Also discussed are closed and open subroutines, loops, table look-up techniques, masking, tape and disk operations, Job Control Language, and core dump debugging.
Credit recommendation: In the lower division baccalaureate/associate degree category, 2 semester hours in Computer Science or Data Processing or in the vocational certificate category, 4 semester hours in Data Processing (3/85).

DOS Operations (CO-401)
Location: Computer Learning Center, Philadelphia, PA.
Length: 204 hours (34 days).
Dates: April 1979-Present.
Objective: To provide the student with skills related to the manipulation of equipment executing under the Disk Operating System.

Instruction: Upon completion of this course, the student will understand the following concepts: components of a data processing system, program execution, foreground and background partitions, task management, job management, spooling, IPL programs, batch mode operations, error messages, and diagnostics. In addition, the student will be familiar with the operation and maintenance of card reader/punch, printer, tape units, and disk units. The student will also be able to use the vendor-supplied utilities for the system.

Credit recommendation: In the vocational certificate category, 9 semester hours in Data Processing (3/85).

Introduction to Data Processing (DP-100)

Location: Computer Learning Center, Philadelphia, PA.

Length: 102 hours (17 days).

Dates: February 1979-Present.

Objective: To provide the student with an introduction to data processing including physical components of computers, internal processing concepts, and data representation.

Instruction: Upon completion of the course, the student will be able to identify computer components, manipulate binary and hexadecimal numbers, identify and convert EBCDIC code, develop introductory flowcharts, and acquire an overview of the history of computers.

Credit recommendation: In the lower division baccalaureate/associate degree category, 2 semester hours in Data Processing or General Studies, or in the vocational certificate category, 4 semester hours in Data Processing (3/85).

OS Job Control Language (DP-200)

Location: Computer Learning Center, Philadelphia, PA.

Length: 102 hours (17 days).

Dates: July 1982-Present.

Objective: To provide the student with an introduction to the coding and understanding of Job Control language for IBM computers.

Instruction: Upon completion of the course, the student will have a knowledge of Job Control language format and syntax, catalogued procedures, data retention, generation of data sets, space allocation, data control block characteristics, system and data set maintenance through the use of IBM supplied utility programs, rerunning of systems that have abnormally terminated, and condition codes to bypass the processing of certain job sets.

Credit recommendation: In the lower division baccalaureate/associate degree category, 3 semester hours in Computer Science or Data Processing or in the vocational certificate category, 6 semester hours in Data Processing (3/85).

OS Operations (CO-400)

Location: Computer Learning Center, Philadelphia, PA.

Length: 204 hours (34 days).

Dates: April 1979-Present.

Objective: To provide the student with technical understanding and practical experience related to the internal and external control of a mainframe computer by an OS Operating System.

Instruction: Upon completion of this course, the student will understand the following concepts: console messages, multiprogramming, multiprocessing, interrupts, management routines, main storage, virtual storage, partitions, regions, spooling and control programs. The students will receive training in various types of OS Operating Systems.

Credit recommendation: In the vocational certificate category, 9 semester hours in Data Processing (3/85).

Structured Programming in COBOL (CP-300)

Location: Computer Learning Center, Philadelphia, PA.

Length: 204 hours (34 days).

Dates: April 1979-Present.

Objective: To provide the student with the knowledge and skills required to master both fundamental and some advanced concepts of programming in structured COBOL.

Instruction: The student will learn the following programming concepts: table handling, subscripting, indexing, sort, search, search-all, sequential access, indexed sequential access, multilevel control breaks, editing, report-writing feature, debugging techniques, and documentation.

Credit recommendation: In the lower division baccalaureate/associate degree category, 6 semester hours in Computer Science or Data Processing or in the vocational certificate category, 12 semester hours in Data Processing (3/85).

Computer Learning Center of Washington

The Computer Learning Center of Washington is certified by the Association of Independent Colleges and Schools and the National Association of Trade and Technical Schools. The Center has an education division which is divided into day and evening schools. Each school has its own director. The Director of Education is responsible for the overall administration of both day and evening schools. All instructors must have two years of field experience or a baccalaureate. Instructors are reviewed formally on an annual basis by the Director of the Day or Evening School.

Source of official student records: Director of Education, Computer Learning Center of Washington, 6666 Commerce Street, Springfield, Virginia 22150.

Additional information about the courses: Program on Noncollegiate Sponsored Instruction, The Center for Adult Learning and Educational Credentials, American Council on Education, One Dupont Circle, Washington, D.C. 20036.

1. Assembler Language Programming (Introduction)
2. Assembler Language Programming (Advanced)
   Location: Computer Learning Center of Washington, Springfield, VA.
   Length: 1. 77 hours (5.7 weeks). 2. 77 hours (5.7 weeks).
   Dates: January 1981-Present.
   Objective: To enable the student to understand the concepts and facilities of assembler language coding and to apply this knowledge in programming complex problems and analyzing the function and process of other programming languages.
   Instruction: This course provides the basic machine language functions and the fundamentals of ALC. Concepts and exercises include instruction sets, internal data formats, coding form, and formation of symbolic names, instruction formats, move instructions and propagation methods, general registers, base and displacement addressing, symbolic addressing, assembler vs. executable instructions, calculations, editing, fixed-point arithmetic, loop concepts, table look-up techniques, processing variable length records, tape and disk operations, core dump investigation and analysis, and OS/JCL. Projects include a minimum of four functioning and documented programs. Teaching methodologies include lecture, group discussion, laboratory activity, and regular outside assignments.
   Credit recommendation: In the lower division baccalaureate/associate degree category, 6 semester hours in Computer Science or Data Processing (1/84).

1. COBOL Programming (Introduction)
2. COBOL Programming (Advanced)
   Location: Computer Learning Center of Washington, Springfield, VA.
   Length: 1. 104 hours (4 weeks). 2. 99 hours (3.60 weeks).
   Dates: January 1981-Present.
   Objective: To provide the student with the knowledge and skills to understand the concepts and facilities of ANSI COBOL, including word formation and punctuation and the basic structure of a COBOL program and apply this knowledge to solve business problems.
   Instruction: Course includes word formation and punctuation and the basic structure of a COBOL program. OS systems concepts and JCL are utilized. Techniques and concepts covered include table handling, subscripting and indexing, sort, search, sequential access (tape, card, disk), multi-level control breaks, editing raw data, ISAM files (creation and update), debugging (trace, exhibit, procedure division maps and core dumps), and OS/JCL. Projects include a minimum of four functioning programs, fully documented. Teaching methodologies include lecture, group discussion, laboratory activity, and regular outside activities.
   Credit recommendation: In the lower division baccalaureate/associate degree category, 6 semester hours in Computer Science or Data Processing (1/84).

FORTRAN Programming
   Location: Computer Learning Center of Washington, Springfield, VA.
   Length: 104 hours (4 weeks).
   Dates: August 1980-Present.
   Objective: To enable the student to develop the knowledge and skills to write and debug FORTRAN programs using I/O, format statements, DO loops, arrays and subroutines.
   Instruction: This course provides basic and expanded programming skills in FORTRAN IV. Basic skills include arithmetic, move, compare, and branching instructions, DO-Loops, file processing, FORMAT statements, explicit and implicit type statements, manipulation of alphanumeric data, array handling and initialized fields. Expanded skills include linkage, COMMON statements, sorts, multi-dimensional array handling, computer graphics, debugging techniques and use of sub-routines. A minimum of two scientific and/or business application programs are required, fully documented. Teaching methodologies include lecture, group discussion, laboratory activity, and regular outside activities.
   Credit recommendation: In the lower division baccalaureate/associate degree category, 3 semester hours in Computer Science or Data Processing (1/84).

Introduction to Data Processing for Programmers (Introduction to Data Processing)
   Location: Computer Learning Center of Washington, Springfield, VA.
   Length: 104 hours (3.78 weeks).
   Dates: August 1980-Present.
   Objective: To introduce the student to DP history, understand computer hardware and terminology, develop programming techniques and logic charts, use JCL and utility programs, and understand the relationship between decimal, hexadecimal, and binary number systems.
   Instruction: Course is designed as a prerequisite for Programming majors. An overview of the data processing industry which includes its history, growth, applications in modern society, career path choices, and terminology is presented. Basic computer systems concepts are presented. These include hardware and software components, system configuration, number systems, and programming logic with an emphasis on appropriate JCL problem solv-

ing techniques, such as flowcharting, pseudo code, and documentation. Projects include a multi-step file-to-file utility job, requiring OS job control statements, keypunch of the job control stream, and input/output design. Teaching methodologies include lecture, group discussion, some laboratory activity, and regular outside assignments.

Credit recommendation: In the lower division baccalaureate/associate degree category, 6 semester hours in Computer Science or Data Processing (1/84).

Systems Analysis and Design
  Location: Computer Learning Center of Washington, Springfield, VA.
  Length: 55 hours (2 weeks).
  Dates: January 1981-Present.
  Objective: To provide the student with the basic knowledge and skills to use the techniques and concepts of Systems Analysis and Design.
  Instruction: This course examines and utilizes the techniques and concepts of Systems Analysis and Design. Topics include data gathering, problem identification/analysis/solution, analysis approach, design methods, documentation techniques, systems designs, file design, form design, hardware and software considerations, procedural methods, presentation techniques, and system flowcharting techniques. Projects of limited scope are assigned to illustrate concepts. Teaching methodologies include lecture, group discussion, laboratory activity, and regular outside activities.
  Credit recommendation: In the lower division baccalaureate/associate degree category, 3 semester hours in Computer Science or Data Processing (1/84).

Computer Processing Institute

  Source of official student records: Computer Processing Institute, 81 East Route 4, Paramus, New Jersey 07652.
  Additional information about the courses: Thomas A. Edison State College, Office of Special Programs, Director of Special Programs, 101 West State Street, Trenton, New Jersey 08625; or Program on Noncollegiate Sponsored Instruction, The Center for Adult Learning and Educational Credentials, American Council on Education, One Dupont Circle, Washington, D.C. 20036.

Alternating Current Theory (ET 603)
Alternating Current Theory Laboratory (ET 604)
  Location: East Hartford, CT; Bridgeport, CT; Paramus, NJ; Woburn, MA.
  Length: 120 hours (4 weeks).
  Dates: January 1982-Present.
  Objective: To introduce students to the basic theory and practical applications of alternating current circuits.
  Instruction: The effect of AC in capacitive and inductive circuits is studied. Topics include oscilloscope operation, energy storage, electromagnetic fields, resonance and bandwidth, filters, and transformers. Lab topics include analysis of AC circuits using audio generators, oscilloscopes, isolation transformers, measuring voltage and phase relationships in capacitive and inductive circuits, and frequency response.
  Credit recommendation: In the lower division baccalaureate/associate degree category, 3 semester hours in Alternating Current (8/85). NOTE: This is not an engineering curriculum course but could apply to an electronics technology curriculum or to other degree programs, as appropriate.

Basic Electricity and DC Circuits (ET 601)
Basic Electricity and DC Circuits Laboratory (ET 602)
  Location: East Hartford, CT; Bridgeport, CT; Paramus, NJ; Woburn, MA.
  Length: 120 hours (4 weeks).
  Dates: September 1984-Present.
  Objective: To introduce students to basic electricity and DC circuits.
  Instruction: Basic electrical phenomena and electron theory and how these relate to static and dynamic electrical forces, concepts of resistance, voltage, current, and power. Ohm's law is introduced as a tool to applications in analysis of DC circuits. Resistor networks, voltage dividers, and meter movements are discussed. Lab topics cover basic technical mathematics and mechanical concepts, soldering techniques, construction of DC circuits, measuring resistance, voltage and current using VOM, DMM, and power supplies, and construction and analysis of DC meters using meter movements.
  Credit recommendation: In the lower division baccalaureate/associate degree category, 3 semester hours in Basic Electricity and DC circuits (8/85). NOTE: This is not an engineering curriculum course but could apply to an electronics technology curriculum or to other degree programs, as appropriate.

Electronics Circuits I & II (ET 605, ET 607)
Electronics Circuits I & II Laboratory (ET 606, ET 608)
  Location: East Hartford, CT; Bridgeport, CT; Paramus, NJ; Woburn, MA.
  Length: 200-240 hours.
  Dates: January 1982-Present.
  Objective: To introduce students in the fundamentals of electronic semiconductor devices.
  Instruction: The course focuses on the description and operation of circuits using diodes and bipolar transistors. Topics include semiconductor rectifiers, filters, regulators, characteristic curves, feedback, biasing, coupling techniques, class of operation, and the gain and impedance characteristics of transistor configurations. Lab topics include construction and analysis of circuits, and diagnosis

of circuit malfunctions using test equipment. The second half of the course studies Field Effect Transistors (FETs), operational amplifiers, and thyristors and analyzes applications of circuits using active devices. Topics include frequency response, feedback, bandwidth, slew rate, characteristic curves, and coupling. Lab topics include construction and analysis of circuits, and diagnosis of circuit malfunctions using test equipment.

Credit recommendation: In the lower division baccalaureate/associate degree category, 5 semester hours in Electronic Circuits or Semiconductor Devices (8/85). NOTE: This is not an engineering curriculum course but could apply to an electronics technology curriculum or to other degree programs, as appropriate.

Digital Techniques and Circuits (ET 609)
Digital Techniques and Circuits Laboratory (ET 610)
   Location: East Hartford, CT; Bridgeport, CT; Paramus, NJ; Woburn, MA.
   Length: 150 hours (5 weeks).
   Dates: January 1982-Present.
   Objective: To introduce students to the fundamentals of digital electronic theory and equipment.
   Instruction: Number systems, gate, Boolean algebra, combinational and sequential digital networks. Topics include adders, comparators, encoders and decoders, multiplexers and demultiplexers, flip-flops, and counters and registers. Various integrated circuit technologies and their electrical characteristics are compared. Lab topics include construction and analysis of circuit operation to check operation against concepts learned in theory sessions.
   Credit recommendation: In the lower division baccalaureate/associate degree category, 4 semester hours in Digital Electronics (8/85). This is not an engineering curriculum course but could apply to an electronics technology curriculum or to other degree programs, as appropriate.

Microprocessor Electronics (ET 611)
(Also titled: Microprocessor Fundamentals (ME 614)
Microprocessor Electronics Laboratory (ET 612)
(Also titled: Microprocessor Fundamentals Laboratory (ME 615)
   Location: East Hartford, CT; Bridgeport, CT; Paramus, NJ; Woburn, MA.
   Length: 300 hours (10 weeks).
   Dates: January 1982-Present.
   Objective: To provide students with an understanding of microprocessor theory and operations.
   Instruction: Microprocessor theory and system hardware based on the 6502. Topics include: system architecture, instruction set, addressing modes, flowcharting techniques, generation of signals, data transfer, timing requirements, and "handshaking." Lab topics include analysis, composition, documentation, and debugging of instruction lists in machine code, troubleshooting techniques and tools, analysis of waveforms generated in a running program, and interrupts.
   Credit recommendation: In the lower division baccalaureate/associate degree category, 4 semester hours in Microprocessor Electronics or Microcomputers (8/85). NOTE: This is not an engineering curriculum course but could apply to an electronics technology curriculum or to other degree programs, as appropriate.

Contel Service Corporation

Contel Service Corporation (formerly Continental Telephone Company) was founded in 1960, and began operations in 1961 with the acquisition of a single Central Illinois company that served 2,100 telephones. Within five years, Continental was providing communication services to more than a half million telephones in 34 states. Ten years later, Contel had acquired 500 companies and integrated them into one of America's largest independent telecommunications networks. Most of the company's customers reside in small towns and suburban areas, but Contel provides telephone service to schools, hospitals, industry and various institutions. In addition to providing regulated telephone services, Contel is also engaged in business communications systems, information services, international consulting and contracting, and network services domestically and overseas. Its Telephone Operations Sector is divided into 3 Regions and 12 Operating Divisions that collectively provide service to more than three million telephones across the United States.

The Information Services (IS) Training and Development Department provides training in the areas of computer literacy, personal computers, programming languages, Digital VAX/VMS, and Honeywell DPS8/SP86 technologies. IS recognizes that a properly trained technical staff and a well informed user community are the most important components in any information system. During the past seven years, the training program of professionally developed and delivered data processing courses has reached over 8,000 Contel and external and client customers.

The functions of the IS Training and Development Department include the development, evaluation, and revision of the information services training curriculum, classroom instruction, coordination and distribution of multimedia training, and evaluation of student progress.

Education facilities at Contel include training rooms, computer terminals, personal computers, audiovisual aids, screen projection devices, overhead projector, slide projector, writing boards, flip charts, network connections, and other learning materials necessary for instruction.

Course development and revisions are based on the information services training requirements of Contel's staff in accordance with the overall business plan of the corporation.

Instructional staff are hired explicitly for the purpose of developing and teaching IS training courses. Appointment of teaching staff members is based upon their previous experiences as instructor/trainers, their educational backgrounds, ability to communicate effectively, and familiarity with the information services field.

Students who successfully complete the courses are awarded the Certificate of Achievement from Contel IS Training and Development.

Source of official student records: Manager, IS Training and Development Department, Contel Service Corporation, 245 Perimeter Center Parkway, Atlanta, Georgia 30346.

Additional information about the courses: Program on Noncollegiate Sponsored Instruction, The Center for Adult Learning and Educational Credentials, American Council on Education, One Dupont Circle, Washington, D.C. 20036.

ADE Training (09038)
(Formerly [VAX04])

Location: Various Contel sites around the country.
Length: 16 hours (2 days).
Dates: August 1985-Present.
Objective: To provide a comprehensive study of Digital's ADE (Application Design Environment) software package which includes ability to create tables of information, maintain that information, and select from those tables information that meets various criteria.
Learning Outcome: Upon successful completion of this course, the student will be able to determine types of applications where the use of ADE is appropriate; create, modify, and delete tables of information; extract information from a table; use the report writer; and produce graphs.
Instruction: Course provides a comprehensive study of Digital's ADE (Application Design Environment) software. Topics include understanding and using ADE terminology, making worksheets, developing and using tables, sorting data, performing compound searches, producing graphs, creating, using and updating reports, and recognition of ADE efficiency considerations and its limitations. Methodology includes lecture, classroom exercises, and laboratory.
Credit recommendation: In the lower division baccalaureate/associate degree category, 1 semester hour in Computer Science or Data Processing (4/87).

Advanced DATATRIEVE with FMS (D9032)
(Formerly [VAX06])

Location: Various Contel sites around the country.
Length: 24 hours (3 days).
Dates: October 1984-Present.
Objective: To provide the student already familiar with DATATRIEVE the ability to set protections, prepare sophisticated reports, create procedures, and use the advanced features of DATATRIEVE.
Learning Outcome: Upon successful completion of this course, the student will be able to write and execute comprehensive, formatted reports; create Screen Forms for either viewing or storing data; interpret and alter DATATRIEVE protections; use Cross, Views and Tables to facilitate data retrieval; restructure existing data files; and create procedures to be used to store reports and other data retrieval techniques.
Instruction: Course covers DATATRIEVE report writing, creating and executing DATATRIEVE procedures, using DATATRIEVE tables, creating forms with FMS and using them with DATATRIEVE, access control lists and DATATREIVE protections, DATATRIEVE intrinsic functions, use the CROSS clause to combine two domains, restructuring with DATATRIEVE, and DATATRIEVE optimization techniques. Methodology includes lecture, classroom exercises, and laboratory.
Credit recommendation: In the lower division baccalaureate/associate degree category, 1 semester hour in Computer Science or Data Processing (4/87).

ALL-IN-1 Version 2 (D9039)
(Formerly [VAX23])

Location: Various Contel sites around the country.
Length: 16 hours (2 days).
Dates: September 1985-Present.
Objective: To provide the student with a working knowledge of the Version 2 "ALL-IN-1" professional workstation management system used on the VAX minicomputer.
Learning Outcome: Upon successful completion of this course, the student will be able to access ALL-IN-1 and traverse its many layers of menus; create, edit, and print documents using ALL-IN-1 Version 2; create, send, and receive electronic messages to and from other ALL-IN-1 users; manage appointments and meetings by using ALL-IN-1's time management application; and maintain and manage documents and message folders in order to optimize the use of storage space and to expedite the retrieval of these items.
Instruction: Course covers introduction to ALL-IN-1 Version 2 and comparison to Version 1, WPS-PLUS word processing, list processing, electronic messaging, time management, distribution lists, interrupt menus, editor menus, scratch pad, and user profile. Methodology includes lecture, classroom exercises, and laboratory.
Credit recommendation: In the lower division baccalaureate/associate degree category, 1 semester hour in Office Systems Technology (4/87).

Azrex Training (D9026)
(Formerly [AZ7])

Location: Various Contel sites around the country.

Length: 16 hours (2 days).
Dates: July 1984-Present.
Objective: To introduce the student to the facilities and features of the AZ7 data management system.
Learning Outcome: Upon successful completion of this course, the student will be able to examine and alter files using AZ7 techniques; interpret and create an AZ7 dictionary; write queries that generated comprehensive reports; store and edit created queries; and run queries either on-line or batch.
Instruction: Covers concepts of AZ7 dictionaries, creation of dictionaries, on-line inquiry and report writing, password protection for files and fields, use of summary statistics, and multiple reports from one query. Methodology includes lecture and laboratory.
Credit recommendation: In the lower division baccalaureate/associate degree category, 1 semester hour in Computer Science or Data Processing (4/87).

BASIC Micro Programming (D9036)
(Formerly [BAS01])
Location: Various Contel sites around the country.
Length: 40 hours (1 week).
Dates: April 1985-Present.
Objective: To introduce programming concepts and techniques using Microsoft BASIC.
Learning Outcome: Upon successful completion of this course, the student will be able to draw flowcharts to illustrate program logic; write BASIC programs to utilize one and two dimensional arrays; build and use data files; write a BASIC sort routine; write a BASIC program using branching and looping; and implement formatting procedures for program output to screen and printer.
Instruction: Covers coding, testing, and developing programs using the Microsoft BASIC language in a minicomputer. Topics include BASIC arithmetic statements, input/output statements, branching and looping, manipulating algebraic and string data, building and using data files, using one and two dimensional arrays, special functions, and implementation of formatting procedures for output.
Credit recommendation: In the lower division baccalaureate/associate degree category, 2 semester hours in Computer Science or Data Processing (4/87).

BASIC Programming (BAS01)
Location: Contel, Wentzville, MO; Dulles, VA; and Bakersfield, CA.
Length: *Version 1:* 24 hours (two 3-hour sessions per week over 4 weeks). *Version 2:* 36 hours (two 3-hour sessions per week over 6 weeks).
Dates: September 1980-December 1984.
Objective: To introduce programming concepts and techniques using BASIC language.
Learning Outcome: Upon successful completion of this course, the student will be able to draw flowcharts to illustrate program logic, write BASIC programs to utilize one and two dimensional arrays, build and use data files, write a BASIC sort routine, write a BASIC program using branching and looping, and implement formatting procedures for program output.
Instruction: Course gives introduction to the BASIC language, with emphasis on programming techniques. Topics covered include algebraic and string manipulation, logic flow, program structure, formatted output, lists and tables, and file manipulations (Prerequisite: Introduction to TSS [TSS01]).
Credit recommendation: In the lower division baccalaureate/associate degree category, 1 semester hour in Computer Science or Data Processing (9/81) (4/87).

COBOL-74 Specifics (D9008)
(Formerly [CBL74])
Location: Various Contel sites around the country.
Length: 40 hours (1 week).
Dates: February 1983-Present.
Objective: To provide the student with a thorough knowledge of the structure of a Honeywell COBOL-74 program, emphasizing the differences between the 1968 and 1974 releases.
Learning Outcome: Upon successful completion of this course, the student will be able to draw flowcharts; write COBOL-74 programs which include the following: branching, and looping techniques, internal sorts, tables, subscripts and indexes; and interpret internal data structure formats.
Instruction: Covers new Procedure Division verbs in COBOL-74 Sort/Merge package, indexed file I/O and efficiency techniques, and COBOL-74 Debug facility components. Methodology includes lecture, classroom exercises, and laboratory.
Credit recommendation: In the lower division baccalaureate/associate degree category, 2 semester hours in Computer Science or Data Processing (4/87).

Computer Fundamentals for Engineering Applications (D9048)
(Formerly [CFENG])
Location: Various Contel sites around the country.
Length: 36 hours (1 week).
Dates: August 1986-Present.
Objective: To provide an overview of the hardware and software options available in Contel's nationwide network.
Learning Outcome: Upon successful completion of this course, the student will be able to describe major computer components along with basic data processing concepts and terminology; design a relatively simple computer program using the correct flowcharting symbols; create and modify files using TSS commands and the text editor available on the Honeywell DPS8; create, code, and execute BASIC programs of various complexity on a mi-

crocomputer; describe the system configuration of the DPS6 and VAX computer and the Contel software products available on them; define the basic components and terminology of the personal computer and the most widely used PC software products; and determine the most appropriate combinations of hardware and software for accomplishing various engineering tasks.

Instruction: Course covers an overview of mainframe systems, manipulation of data through the time share TSS editor, accessing the subsystem, libraries, miscellaneous utilities, programming concepts and flowcharting, BASIC programming, and overviews minicomputer and microcomputer systems. Methodology includes lecture and laboratory.

Credit recommendation: In the lower division baccalaureate/associate degree category, 2 semester hours in Computer Science or Data Processing (4/87).

DATATRIEVE Training (D9031)
(Formerly [VAX05])

Location: Various Contel sites around the country.
Length: 16 hours (2 days).
Dates: January 1984-Present.
Objective: To provide the student with a working knowledge of DATATRIEVE for data management applications.

Learning Outcome: Upon successful completion of this course, the student will be able to create DATATRIEVE domains, record definitions and data files; store data in data files; retrieve data and print out a simple report; modify the data in the data file; and erase the data in the data file.

Instruction: Course covers information storage and retrieval, DATATRIEVE domains and files, accessing a domain and DTR permissions, forming record streams, using record selection expression (RSE), boolean expressions in DATATRIEVE, sorting records in a record stream, forming and naming collections, directing reports to disk files and printers, sorting new records in a DATARETRIEVE domain, updating information through DATARETRIEVE, erasing records with DATATRIEVE, and sequential vs. indexed file considerations.

Credit recommendation: In the lower division baccalaureate/associate degree category, 1 semester hour in Computer Science or Data Processing (4/87).

DECMATE Word Processing (D9060)
(Formerly [DEC01])

Location: Various Contel sites around the country.
Length: 24 hours (3 days).
Dates: October 1986-Present.
Objective: To provide the student with a comprehensive understanding of the DECMATE work processing system.

Learning Outcome: Upon successful completion of this course, the student will be able to create, modify, and print documents using the DECMATE system; develop customized form letters using DECMATE's list and sort processing capabilities; proofread documents with DECSPELL; and receive electronic mail messages.

Instruction: Course covers word processing skills including initialization, handling, backup and recovery of document diskettes, use of menus and special function keys, maintaining a document index, creating and editing documents, controlling print settings and printing documents, controlling the screen and page environment, search methods, list processing and sort processing, abbreviation and library documents and special consideration using hard disk systems. Methodology includes lecture, classroom exercises and laboratory.

Credit recommendation: In the lower division baccalaureate/associate degree category, 1 semester hour in Word Processing (4/87).

Distributed Customer Record Information System (D9042)
(Formerly [DCR10])

Location: Various Contel sites around the country.
Length: 96 hours (3 weeks).
Dates: September 1985-Present.
Objective: To provide the DCRIS computer operator the conceptual framework and the practical application necessary to operate the Honeywell DPS6 computer running the DCRIS application.

Learning Outcome: Upon successful completion of this course, the student will be able to recognize and define various terms associated with a DCRIS service Office; name and properly use the hardware components of a typical DCRIS System; sign on and bring up the operating system, the TDS system, and the DCRIS system; perform routine commands using MOD600 and the Editor; explain EC data flows in relation to data base activity; recognize the roles various components play in building actual ECs; explain a console listing in relation to operator generated input and system generated responses or messages; perform morning and evening batch work for file transfer and data base update; execute (if necessary) various programs related and associated with conversion process; and execute the proper restart/recovery procedures ensuring data base integrity and file protection.

Instruction: Covers Honeywell DPS/6 hardware configuration for the DCRIS, the GCOS6 MOD600 operating system commands, the MOD600 Editor functions and the transaction driven system. Topics include data processing concepts, DCRIS service office interview, DCRIS hardware configuration, GCOS6 MOD600 operating system, GSOS6 MOD600 Editor, TDS, overview of conversion procedures, DCRIS operator procedures, and system restart/recovery procedures. Methodology includes lecture, classroom exercises and laboratory.

Credit recommendation: In the lower division bac-

calaureate/associate degree category, 3 semester hours in Computer Operations (4/87).

DPS MOD600 Utilization (D9027)
(Formerly [DPS6])
Location: Various Contel sites around the country.
Length: 24 hours (3 days).
Dates: November 1985-Present.
Objective: To provide the student with the capability of issuing commands, running utilities, and writing command files within the Honeywell DPS6 MOD600 operating system.
Learning Outcome: Upon successful completion of this course, the student will be able to perform routine file maintenance on his/her interactive account; use the line editor; perform program development using the COBOLA compiler; use the MOD600 linker to create a bound unit; use the operating system utilities for sorting files; and create command files called ECs.
Instruction: Course covers introduction to MOD600 operating environment; file and directory components; file maintenance; editor usage; program development, language processors and linking; utilities; and Execution Control Language (ECL).
Credit recommendation: In the lower division baccalaureate/associate degree category, 1 semester hour in Computer Science or Data Processing (4/87).

FORTRAN (D9004)
(Formerly [FOR01])
Location: Various Contel sites around the country.
Length: 40 hours (1 week).
Dates: *Version 1:* June 1980-April 1987. *Version 2:* May 1987-Present.
Objective: To provide a working knowledge of the FORTRAN programming language.
Learning Outcome: Upon successful completion of this course, the student will be able to access sequential and random files through FORTRAN I/O statement; call user-written and FORTRAN supplied functions and subroutines; manipulate data in one line, two and three dimensional arrays; and compile, link and execute FORTRAN programs in the batch and interactive modes.
Instruction: Covers coding, testing, and debugging FORTRAN programs in the timesharing and batch environment. Topics include the basic elements of the FORTRAN language, input/output statements, branching and looping techniques, advanced input/output statements, sequential file input/output techniques, arrays and subscripted variables, FORTRAN supplied functions and subroutines, random file input/output techniques, batch timesharing FORTRAN comparisons, and libraries and run time options. Methodology includes lecture, classroom exercises and laboratory.
Credit recommendation: *Version 1:* In the lower division baccalaureate/associate degree category, 3 semester hours in Computer Science or Data Processing; or in the upper division baccalaureate category, 2 semester hours in Engineering or Business Administration (9/81). *Version 2:* In the lower division baccalaureate/associate degree category, 2 semester hours in FORTRAN (4/87). NOTE: This course has been reevaluated and continues to meet requirements for credit recommendations. NOTE: The reduction in credit hours recommended is not a result of a curriculum change at Contel. The reduction is a result of the re-positioning of FORTRAN in traditional college curricula.

Freelance Plus Graphics (D9080)
Location: Various Contel sites around the country.
Length: 16 hours (2 days).
Dates: June 1988-Present.
Objective: To provide the student with an understanding of the concepts, features, and uses of the Freelance Plus Graphics package.
Learning Outcome: Upon successful completion of this course, the student will be able to construct and edit charts, graphs, and diagrams; plot single and multiple drawings; and impart Lotus 1-2-3 files for graphical display.
Instruction: Course covers the commands for creation, selection, editing, and manipulating graphics objects, and interfacing Lotus 1-2-3 files and automating production of multiple plots. Methodology includes lecture and laboratory.
Credit recommendation: In the lower division baccalaureate/associate degree category, 1 semester hour in Office Systems Technology (4/89). NOTE: Credit should be granted only if the student has taken an introduciton to personal computers course.

Honeywell Job Control Language (D9007)
(Formerly [JCL77])
Location: Various Contel sites around the country.
Length: 24 hours (3 days).
Dates: May 1982-Present.
Objective: To provide an overview of the operating system (GCOS), job flow, and supporting hardware and software.
Learning Outcome: Upon successful completion of this course, the student will be able to define the primary elements of the job control language and the function performed by specific control records; write the basic JCL records necessary to run a job in the Honeywell batch environment; construct files and catalogs for user applications; write the JCL records necessary to convert data from one media device to another using Bulk Media Conversion, Utility and UTL2 software; and define system files and job flow.
Instruction: Course covers JCL statement format, understanding Job Activity Relationships, File Management Supervisor (FMS), JCL to compile and execute programs,

system files and job flow, bulk media conversion, and utility. Methodology includes lecture, classroom exercises, and laboratory.

Credit recommendation: In the upper division baccalaureate category, 1 semester hour in Computer Science or Data Processing (4/87).

Intermediate Timeshare (D9001)
(Formerly [TSS02])
Location: Various Contel sites around the country.
Length: 16 hours (2 days).
Dates: August 1980-Present.
Objective: To develop the capability of using advanced text editor techniques.
Learning Outcome: Upon successful completion of this course, the student will be able to reformat and print a text file using RUNOFF subsystem commands; execute the commands of the CONVERT subsystem; utilize the JOUT functions and related commands; set up jobs for deferred processing; and create and execute a command file.
Instruction: Course covers deferred file processing, command file processing and the RUNOFF, CONVERT, and JOUT subsystems. Topics include short review of the major subsystems, application of advanced text editor techniques, reformatting text files utilizing the RUNOFF subsystem, and using the five commands of the CONVERT subsystem. Methodology includes lecture and laboratory. Prerequisite: Introduction to Timesharing (TSS01) or proficiency with the Honeywell TSS.
Credit recommendation: In the lower division baccalaureate/associate degree category, 1 semester hour in Computer Science or Data Processing (4/87).

Introduction to Data Processing and Data Communications (D9037)
(Formerly [DPCOM])
Location: Various Contel sites around the country.
Length: 24 hours (3 days).
Dates: October 1984-Present.
Objective: To provide an introduction to data communications, data processing, and a basic understanding of the microcomputer software products LOTUS 1-2-3 and dBASE II Plus.
Learning Outcome: Upon successful completion of this course, the student will be able to define the components of a data communication system and the differences between digital and analog signals; identify the various designs of network architecture; name the differences between micro, mini, and mainframe computers; and create spreadsheets and databases.
Instruction: Course covers discussion of the basic data communication concepts; data processing terminology; the hardware, software, operating systems currently on the market today; demonstrations of the electronic spreadsheet; and the use of a database management system. Methodologies include lecture, classroom exercises, and laboratory.
Credit recommendation: In the lower division baccalaureate/associate degree category, 1 semester hour in Computer Science or Data Processing (4/87).

Introduction to dBASE III Plus (D9056)
(Formerly [DB310])
Advanced dBASE III Plus (D9058)
(Formerly [DB320])
Location: Various Contel sites around the country.
Length: 16 hours (2 days).
Dates: October 1986-Present.
Objective: To provide the skills needed to maintain, manipulate and report the information held in a database, and to learn structured programming techniques using dBASE III Plus.
Learning Outcome: Upon successful completion of this course, the student will be able to create and maintain a database, create reports and customized data entry forms, design a dBASE III Plus application system, identify and use structured programming techniques, write application procedures and generate complex reports, and document the system application.
Instruction: Course covers storage and retrieval of database information with the use of dBASE III Plus, fundamental programming concepts, data entry techniques and controls, report generation using dBASE III Plus procedures, and menu driven and interactive systems. Methodology includes lecture, classroom exercises and laboratory.
Credit recommendation: In the lower division baccalaureate/associate degree category, 1 semester hour in Computer Science or Data Processing (4/87). NOTE: Both courses must be completed to receive credit.

Introduction to Designing Oracle/SQL*Forms (D9106)
Location: Various Contel sites around the country.
Length: 24 hours (3 days).
Dates: February 1989-Present.
Objective: To provide the student with skills necessary to use SQL*Forms in the development of forms applications.
Learning Outcome: Upon successful completion of this course, the student will be able to plan the physical layout and form characteristics of a SQL*Form; develop an SQL*Form utilizing defaults and simple triggers; and develop a complete application utilizing menus and SQL*Forms.
Instruction: Course covers operating SQL*Forms application, using the Runform program, developing and planning a form, modifying a SQL*Form, and developing a complete application using menus and SQL*Forms. Methodology includes lecture and laboratory.
Credit recommendation: In the lower division baccalaureate/associate degree category, 1 semester hour in

Data Processing (4/89).

Introduction to Oracle/SQL*Plus (D9102)
Location: Various Contel sites around the country.
Length: 24 hours (3 days).
Dates: January 1988-Present.
Objective: To provide the student with an understanding of relational database concepts of Oracle, and of Contel's shared data environment strategy.
Learning Outcome: Upon successful completion of this course, the student will be able to initialize Oracle using SQL*Plus; write, execture, save, and reuse SQL queries; save and format query results; and explain Conel's shared data environment strategy.
Instruction: Course covers relational data base benefits and concepts, Oracle initializing log-in/log-out procedures, writing SQL*Plus queries, executing, formatting, and saving queries, overview of SQL*Calc, SQL*Forms, and Easy*SQL, and Contel's shared data environment strategy. Methodology includes lecture, classroom exercises, video, and laboratory.
Credit recommendation: In the lower division baccalaureate/associate degree category, 1 semester hour in Data Processing (4/89).

Introduction to Oracle/SQL*Calc (D9108)
Location: Various Contel sites around the country.
Length: 16 hours (2 days).
Dates: February 1989-Present.
Objective: To provide the student with an understanding of spreadsheet concepts and Oracle implementation of the concepts.
Learning Outcome: Upon successful completion of this course, the student will be able to utilize basic SQL*Calc commands; utilize SQL statements to bring data base information into a spreadsheet; perform what-if analysis; and create a data base table from spreadsheet information.
Instruction: Course covers generic spreadsheet terms, SQL*Calc commands, executing Oracle commands, manipulating Oracle data from a spreadsheet, and building Oracle tables from spreadsheet data. Methodology includes lecture, classroom exercises, and laboratory.
Credit recommendation: In the lower division baccalaureate/associate degree category, 1 semester hour in Data Processing (4/89). NOTE: Credit should be granted only if the student has successfully completed Introduction to Oracle/SQL*Plus (D9102).

Introduction to Systems Analysis and Design (D9174)
Location: Various Contel sites around the country.
Length: 24 hours (3 days).
Dates: January 1989-Present.
Objective: To provide the student with knowledge of general concepts and standard techniques used in design, analysis, and construction of computer software systems.
Learning Outcome: Upon successful completion of this course, the student will be able to identify phases involved in the software development process; and apply techniques and tools of the software development process.
Instruction: Course covers the components of system development lifecycle, standard tools and techniques for problem definition, functional analysis, and logical and physical design phases, and prototyping, testing, security, and control issues. Methodology includes lecture, classroom exercises, and video presentation.
Credit recommendation: In the upper division baccalaureate degree category, 2 semester hours in Computer Science or Data Processing (4/89).

Introduction to Time Sharing (D9000)
(Formerly [TSS01])
Location: Various Contel sites around the country.
Length: 24 hours (3 days).
Dates: April 1980-Present.
Objective: To provide the learner with a working knowledge of the Honeywell TSS and its major subsystems.
Learning Outcome: Upon successful completion of this course, the student will be able to execute the commands of the Honeywell timeshare system command language; create file space, file content and subcatalogs, modify file content, file and subcatalog attributes; assign passwords and permissions to files and subcatalogs; change the User-ID password; and use the page-print and sort utilities of the timeshare system.
Instruction: Topics include data processing concepts, the Honeywell Time Share Executive, the command language, the ABACUS subsystem, the Text Editor subsystem, the page print system and the ACCESS subsystem. This course is intended for the user with little or no data processing experience, or someone who is new to the Honeywell System.
Credit recommendation: In the lower division baccalaureate/associate degree category, 1 semester hour in Computer Science or Data Processing (9/81) (4/87). NOTE: This course has been reevaluated and continues to meet requirements for credit recommendations.

Lotus 1-2-3 (D9021)
Advanced Lotus 1-2-3 (D9034)
(Formerly [LOT02])
Location: Various Contel sites around the country.
Length: 16 hours (One 8-hour session per course).
Dates: February 1985-Present.
Objective: To provide an introduction to Lotus 1-2-3, and Advanced Lotus 1-2-3- functions.
Learning Outcome: Upon successful completion of this course, the student will be able to use Lotus 1-2-3 software to sort, query and analyze information; create and use macros; use cross tabulation analyses; and transfer non-Lotus files into a Lotus spreadsheet.
Instruction: Course covers personal computer opera-

tions and Lotus 1-2-3 software. Topics include entering data, using labels and formulas, sorting data, graphing data, querying a database to locate list of delete records, cross tabulating, analyzing of data, using macros, and file imports. Methodology includes lecture, classroom exercises, and laboratory.

Credit recommendation: In the lower division baccalaureate/associate degree category, 1 semester hour in Computer Science or Data Processing (4/87). NOTE: Both courses must be completed to receive credit.

Lotus 1-2-3 Macros (D9150)
 Location: Various Contel sites around the country.
 Length: 16 hours (2 days).
 Dates: February 1989-Present.
 Objective: To provide the student with an understanding of Lotus 1-2-3 Macros as an aid to complex spreadsheet manipulations.
 Learning Outcome: Upon successful completion of this course, the student will be able to create macros to perform a variety of operations; edit and debug macros; and demonstrate familiarity with advanced macro techniques.
 Instruction: Course provides an overview of macros, creation of macros for formatting, displaying, and printing, and macro command language, subroutines, conditionals, and automatic execution. Methodology includes lecture, classroom exercises, and laboratory.
 Credit recommendation: In the lower division baccalaureate/associate degree category, 1 semester hour in Office Systems Technology (4/89). NOTE: Credit should be granted only if the student has completed an introduction and an advanced Lotus course.

Personal Computer (DOS Operating System) (D9020/9122)
 Location: Various Contel sites around the country.
 Length: 16 hours (2 days with intervening application time of 2 weeks).
 Dates: January 1988-Present.
 Objective: To provide the student with a knowledge of personal computers and the DOS operating system.
 Learning Outcome: Upon successful completion of this course, the student will be able to identify and define hardware and software components of personal computers; and create, modify, access, and use DOS files and directory.
 Instruction: Course covers the physical layout of personal computers, files, and DOS commands. Methodology includes lecture, classroom exercises, and laboratory.
 Credit recommendation: In the lower division baccalaureate/associate degree category, 1 semester hour in Data Processing or Office Systems Technology (4/89).

20/20 (D9033)
(Formerly [52020])
 Location: Various Contel sites around the country.
 Length: 16 hours (2 days).
 Dates: March 1985-Present.
 Objective: To provide a working knowledge of an integrated electronics spreadsheet using 20/20/ software package designed for VAX minicomputer system.
 Learning Outcome: Upon successful completion of this course, the student will be able to create and maintain relatively complex spreadsheets; combine, sort and query spreadsheet data; create formulas; and format selected cells for appearance and practical purposes.
 Instruction: Course covers the basic skills needed to use a spreadsheet approach to data management. Topics include spreadsheet concepts; creation and maintenance of a spreadsheet; cell addresses and ranges; copy, cut and paste procedures; and sorting and querying data. Methodologies include lecture, classroom exercises and laboratory.
 Credit recommendation: In the lower division baccalaureate/associate degree category, 1 semester hour in Computer Science or Data Processing (4/87).

VAX/VMS Commands and Utilities I (D9024)
(Formerly [VAX10])
 Location: Various Contel sites around the country.
 Length: 24 hours (3 days).
 Dates: February 1983-Present.
 Objective: To provide the student with the information needed to perform non-privileged user tasks under the VAX/VMS operating system.
 Learning Outcome: Upon successful completion of this course, the student will be able to perform routine file maintenance on a VMS system; create and use directories and subdirectories; establish file and directory protections; use the line editor (EDT); use the sort/merge utilities; and write simple command procedures to be processed interactively.
 Instruction: Covers VAX/VMS concepts and terminology, VAX/VMS user software overview, DCL command structure, directory and subdirectory concepts, the EDT editor, sort/merge techniques, program development, and command procedure fundamentals.
 Credit recommendation: In the lower division baccalaureate/associate degree category, 1 semester hour in Computer Science or Data Processsing (4/87).

VAX/VMS Commands and Utilities II (D9025)
(Formerly [VAX20])
 Location: Various Contel sites around the country.
 Length: 16 hours (2 days).
 Dates: March 1984-Present.
 Objective: To provide the experienced VAX/VMS programmer with advanced tools to make the individual a more effective user of the VAX/VMS operating system.
 Learning Outcome: Upon successful completion of this course, the student will be able to use the features of the full screen editor (EDT); appreciate the use of logical

names and symbols; write command procedures for terminal interaction; create user libraries; create and run batch procedures; and manage procedures in the batch and print queries.

Instruction: Covers the full screen editor (EDT), logical names and symbols, command procedure concepts, user libraries, using the Linker effectively, volume initialization and backup utilities, batch processing, and queue management. Methodology includes lecture, classroom exercises, and laboratory. Prerequisite: VAX/VMS Commands and Utilities I.

Credit recommendation: In the lower division baccalaureate/associate degree category, 1 semester hour in Computer Science or Data Processing (4/87).

VAX/VMS Minicomputer Concepts (D9017)
(Formerly [VAX01])
Location: Contel, Wentzville, MO.
Length: 24 hours (3 days).
Dates: January 1983-Present.
Objective: To introduce the student to VAX-11 concepts, terminology, and hardware and software components.

Learning Outcome: Upon successful completion of this course, the student will be able to identify the hardware and software components of a VAX-11 minicomputer; understand the VAX-11 architecture and characteristics of the VAX/VMS operating system; interpret internal data representation; work hexadecimal arithmetic and conversions; and differentiate between exceptions and interrupts.

Instruction: Covers an overview of VAX-11 architecture and peripherals, characteristics and functions of the VAX/VMS operating system, internal data representation, and memory management in the VAX-11. Methodology includes lecture and classroom exercises.

Credit recommendation: In the lower division baccalaureate/associate degree category, 1 semester hour in Computer Science or Data Processing (4/87).

WordPerfect 5.0: Module 1 (D9176)
WordPerfect 5.0: Module 2 (D9178)
Location: Various Contel sites around the country.
Length: *Module 1:* 16 hours (2 days); *Module 2:* 16 hours (2 days).
Dates: February 1989-Present.
Objective: To provide the student with an understanding of basic and advanced features of WordPerfect.

Learning Outcome: Upon successful completion of this course, the student will be able to enter, edit, modify, format, and print a text file; manipulate and maintain multiple files; and use various fonts and graphics.

Instruction: Course covers commands for entering, editing, modifying, formatting, and printing a text file, function keys and their uses, and editing, formatting, and sorting features. Methodology includes lecture, classroom exercises, and laboratory.

Credit recommendation: In the lower division baccalaureate/associate degree category, 1 semester hour in Office Systems Technology (4/89). NOTE: Credit should be granted only upon successful completion of both Module 1 and Module 2.

Continental Telecom, Inc.

Continental Telecom, Inc., (CONTEL) is the nation's third largest independent telephone company. Employing approximately 22,000 people, Continental provides telephone service to principally suburban and rural communities in 38 states and the Caribbean.

The Department of Management and Organizational Development, located in the Corporate headquarters in Atlanta, Georgia, writes and revises all of the class material. Courses stress basic fundamentals of management. Although directed more toward the introductory levels (supervisors and superintendents), the courses also serve as review and brush-up sessions for higher levels of management.

The corporate staff is responsible for qualifying instructors, as well as for quality control of the program.

Source of official student records: Eastern Region: Personnel Development Manager, CONTEL Service Corporation, P.O. Box 401, Merrifield, Virginia 22116. Central Region: Personnel Development Manager, CONTEL Service Corporation, 600 Mason Ridge Center Drive, St. Louis, Missouri 60141. Western Region: Personal Development Manager, CONTEL Service Corporation, 1350 Norris Road, Bakersfield, California 93308.

Additional information about the courses: Program on Noncollegiate Sponsored Instruction, The Center for Adult Learning and Educational Credentials, American Council on Education, One Dupont Circle, Washington, D.C. 20036.

Better Business Writing
Location: *Version 1:* Bakersfield, CA; Victorville, CA; Dallas, TX; Phoenix, AZ; Bellevue, WA; St. Charles, MO; Leesburg, VA. *Version 2:* Bakersfield, CA; Washington, DC; St. Louis, MO.
Length: *Version 1:* 36 hours (1 week); *Version 2:* 40 hours (1 week).
Dates: *Version 1:* August 1978-December 1982; *Version 2:* January 1983-Present.
Objective: To develop the students' written communications skills.
Instruction: Principles and application of effective written communications, with emphasis on clarity, precision, and easy-to-read letters, memos, and reports. Methodology includes lectures, writing, and critiques of written assignments by instructor and class participants.

Credit recommendation: *Version 1:* In the lower division baccalaureate/associate degree category, 2 semester hours in Business Administration or Business Communication (8/78). *Version 2:* In the lower division baccalaureate/associate degree category, 3 semester hours in Business Administration or Business Communication (1/83). NOTE: This course has undergone a 5-year reevaluation and continues to meet requirements for credit recommendations.

Management Studies Workshop
   Location: Bakersfield, CA; Washington, DC; St. Louis, MO.
   Length: 40 hours (1 week).
   Dates: July 1982-Present.
   Objective: To acquaint middle management employees with both the human relations and technical skills necessary for improving performance within an organization.
   Instruction: Evaluating performance, managing stress, leadership, problem solving and decision making, delegation, labor relations, and communication skills. Includes lectures, case studies, role playing and oral presentations.
   Credit recommendation: In the lower division baccalaureate/associate degree category, 3 semester hours in Business Administration or Management (1/83).

Orientation to Management
(Basic Supervisory Management Program - CORE)
(Formerly Initial Management Training)
   Location: *Version 1:* Bakersfield, CA; Victorville, CA; Dallas, TX; Phoenix, AZ; Bellevue, WA; St. Charles, MO; Leesburg, VA. *Version 2:* Bakersfield, CA; Washington, DC; St. Louis, MO.
   Length: *Version 1:* 36 hours (1 week); *Version 2:* 40 hours (1 week).
   Dates: *Version 1:* August 1978-December 1982; *Version 2:* Version 2: January 1983-Present.
   Objective: To provide the student with a concise preview of and preparation for a managerial/supervisory job with emphasis on communication.
   Instruction: Communications skills and application of selected management principles to the solution of job-related problems. Role of the manager; conducting meetings; decision making; responsibility and authority; induction of new employees; affirmative action; listening techniques; dealing with paper, promotion, and attitude surveys. Methodology includes lecture, subgroup exercises, role plays, case studies, discussion, and audiovisual aids.
   Credit recommendation: *Version 1:* In the lower division baccalaureate/associate degree category, 2 semester hours in Business Administration, Management, or Public Administration (8/78). *Version 2:* In the lower division baccalaureate/associate degree category, 3 semester hours in Business Administration, Management, or Public Administration, or as a business elective in programs such as Nursing, Technology, Education, etc. (1/83). NOTE: This course has undergone a 5-year reevaluation and continues to meet requirements for credit recommendations.

Control Data

Control Data, a multinational corporation with headquarters in Minneapolis, Minnesota, provides products and services based on computer technologies.

The application of computer-based education technology is an integral part of Control Data's educational offerings. These offerings include: computer-based education (PLATO) products and services, an entry-level vocational school system (Control Data Institutes), a seminar division, customer training, and a curriculum development department that customizes courses. All computer-assisted and computer-managed instruction is supplemented by texts and/or workbooks and multimedia presentations.

Control Data's Education Center Network offers independent-study, computer-based education courses. These centers are located in most major metropolitan areas and serve Control Data employees and employees of other corporations.

Procedures followed by army education service centers should be designed in accordance with guidelines established by Control Data Corporation. Moreover, any army education service center which delivers ACE-credit recommended courses developed by CDC must maintain a formal liaison with CDC and must deliver CDC courses, grades (if such is the case), and certificates of completion in accordance with CDC administrative requirements which are based on CDC's adherence to the policies and procedures of ACE/PONSI.

Source of official student records: The American Council on Education Registry of Credit Recommendations or the Education Center Registrar, Education and Training, Control Data, 8100 34th Avenue South, Mailing Address Box 0, Minneapolis, Minnesota 55440.

Additional information about the courses: Program on Noncollegiate Sponsored Instruction, The Center for Adult Learning and Educational Credentials, American Council on Education, One Dupont Circle, Washington, D.C. 20036.

BUSINESS/MANAGEMENT CURRICULUM

Accounts Receivable Collection Techniques
   Location: Various Control Data sites around the country.
   Length: Approximately 16 hours (computer-based instruction).
   Dates: October 1979-Present.
   Objective: To recognize the importance of accounts receivable collections and to apply various collections

skills (letters, telephone, customer visits) to job situations.

Learning Outcome: Upon successful completion of this course, the student will be able to handle collection more efficiently.

Instruction: Incorporates the basic accounts receivable files and reports with the three primary collection techniques: written, telephone, and personal visits. Simulation exercises, multimedia presentations, and drill and practice are used.

Credit recommendation: In the lower division baccalaureate/associate degree category, 1 semester hour in Accounts Receivable Collection Techniques (11/81) (6/86). NOTE: This course has been reevaluated and continues to meet requirements for credit recommendations.

Affirmative Action Management Sequence

Location: Various Control Data sites around the country.

Length: Approximately 25 hours (computer-based instruction).

Dates: October 1979-Present.

Objective: To develop a knowledge of relevant laws, executive orders, and their application in actual and hypothetical situations; to develop an awareness of the past and present climate of racial and sex discrimination; to identify and to develop positive approaches for counteracting discriminatory processes and behavior.

Learning Outcome: Upon successful completion of this course, the student will be aware of the legal, interpersonal and managerial ramifications of racism and sexism.

Instruction: Equal employment opportunity and affirmative action laws and executive orders, consequences of noncompliance, understanding racial and sex discrimination, identifying and counteracting discriminatory behavior. Simulation exercises, multimedia presentations, and drill and practice are used.

Credit recommendation: In the upper division baccalaureate category, 1 semester hour in Affirmative Action Programs and Human Relations (8/79) (6/86). NOTE: This course has been reevaluated and continues to meet requirements for credit recommendations.

Analytic Accounting

Location: Various Control Data sites around the country.

Length: Approximately 16 hours (computer-based instruction).

Dates: October 1979-January 1983.

Objective: To attain applied knowledge of financial accounting concepts.

Instruction: Provides practice in applying financial accounting concepts in the following areas: balance sheets; income statements; measuring income for both merchandising and manufacturing companies; justifying the acquisition and amortization of fixed assets, long term debt, and equity; and analyzing the flow of business funds. Simulation exercises, multimedia presentations, and drill and practice are used.

Credit recommendation: In the lower division baccalaureate/associate degree category, 1 semester hour in Principles of Accounting (11/81).

Basic Management (Resource Management, Supervisory Success, Time Management, Effective Supervision)
(Formerly Resource Management, Supervisory Success, Time Management)

Location: Various Control Data sites around the country.

Length: *Version 1:* Approximately 28 hours (computer-based instruction). *Version 2:* Approximately 36 hours (computer-based instruction).

Dates: May 1980-Present.

Objective: To enable the participant to understand lower-level management concepts that deal with effective supervision, communication, planning, motivation, resource and time management.

Learning Outcome: Upon successful completion of this course, the student will understand management and personnel dynamics at the first level of supervision.

Instruction: Covers lower-level management concepts. Simulation exercises, multimedia presentations, and drill and practice are used.

Credit recommendation: In the lower division baccalaureate/associate degree category, 1 semester hour in Basic Management (11/81) (6/86). NOTE: This course has been reevaluated and continues to meet requirements for credit recommendations.

Better Business Letters

Location: Various Control Data sites around the country.

Length: Approximately 13 hours (computer-based instruction).

Dates: October 1979-Present.

Objective: To increase efficiency and effectiveness by producing low-cost business letters that communicate persuasively, enthusiastically, and effectively.

Learning Outcome: Upon successful completion of this course, the student will have enhanced written communication skills.

Instruction: Covers techniques for producing business letters and memoranda that communicate in an effective manner. Simulation exercises, multimedia presentations, and drill and practice are used.

Credit recommendation: In the vocational certificate category, 1 semester hour in Business Communication about subject area of program (11/81) (6/86). NOTE: This course has been reevaluated and continues to meet requirements for credit recommendations.

Building Your Own Business and Obtaining Financing *(Version 2)*
(Formerly Building Your Own Business) *(Version 1)*
Location: Various Control Data sites around the country.
Length: Version 1: Approximately 39 hours (computer-based instruction). *Version 2:* Approximately 43 hours (computer-based instruction).
Dates: Version 1: October 1979-May 1986. *Version 2:* June 1986-Present.
Objective: To enable the participant to understand and readily identify the primary considerations that must be addressed in founding or expanding a small business.
Learning Outcome: Upon successful completion of this course, the student will be able to integrate the various activities necessary to found or expand a small business.
Instruction: A survey course in starting, improving, and/or expanding a business. Simulation exercises, multimedia presentations, and drill and practice are used.
Credit recommendation: Version 1: In the lower division baccalaureate/associate degree category, 1 semester hour in Introduction to Small Business Management (11/81). *Version 2:* In the lower division baccalaureate/associate degree category, 2 semester hours in Introduction to Small Business Management (6/86). NOTE: This course has been reevaluated and continues to meet requirements for credit recommendations.

Business Systems Analyst Sequence
Location: Various Control Data sites around the country.
Length: Approximately 117 hours (computer-based instruction).
Dates: October 1979-Present.
Objective: To help prepare the student to become a business systems analyst in terms of computer concepts and the business environment.
Learning Outcome: Upon successful completion of this course, the student will understand the basic tasks involved in successfully designing, developing, implementing and evaluating a business information system and be able to apply that understanding to case studies.
Instruction: The student is provided with basic tools of the systems analyst and then with the procedures needed to design, develop, and implement a business information system. Covers computer system hardware, basic elements of COBOL programming, introduction to computer systems, and data base management systems. Simulation exercises, multimedia presentations, and drill and practice are used.
Credit recommendation: In the lower division baccalaureate/associate degree category, 3 semester hours in Business Systems Analysis (11/81) (6/86). NOTE: This course has been reevaluated and continues to meet requirements for credit recommendations.

Communications and Consulting Skills Sequence
(Communication Skills, Consulting Skills, The Helping Relationship)
Location: Various Control Data sites around the country.
Length: Approximately 27 hours (computer-based instruction).
Dates: May 1983-Present.
Objective: To provide the student with the basic skills pertaining to communication, consulting, cooperation, and listening.
Learning Outcome: Upon successful completion of this course, the student will have more effective interpersonal relations.
Instruction: Identification and improvement of communication styles; improvement of listening; and establishing cooperative relationships in personal and professional settings.
Credit recommendation: In the lower division baccalaureate/associate degree category, 1 semester hour in Communications (6/86).

Computer Hardware
(Introduction to Computer Hardware Sequence, Disc Drive Fundamentals, the Disc Pack)
Location: Various Control Data sites around the country.
Length: Approximately 57 hours (computer-based instruction).
Dates: October 1979-November 1983.
Objective: To familiarize the student with computer numbering systems, equipment, flow charting, and programming.
Instruction: Covers computer math, introduction to data processing, and machine language programming. Simulation exercises, multimedia presentations, and drill and practice are used.
Credit recommendation: In the lower division baccalaureate/associate degree category, 3 semester hours in Survey of Computer Hardware and Principles (11/81).

Consumer Finance
(Credit and the Consumer, Insurance and the Consumer, Investing and the Consumer, Money Management and the Consumer)
Location: Various Control Data sites around the country.
Length: Approximately 36 hours (computer-based instruction).
Dates: October 1979-August 1983.
Objective: To enable the participant to understand the general principles of consumer finance.
Instruction: From the viewpoint of the consumer, the course covers money management, the wise use of credit, insurance, and investment. Simulation exercises, multimedia presentations, and drill and practice are used.

Credit recommendation: In the lower division baccalaureate/associate degree category, 1 semester hour in Consumer Finance (for Non-Business Students) (11/81).

CREATE Curriculum
Location: Various Control Data sites around the country.
Length: Approximately 250 hours (computer-based instruction).
Dates: October 1979-Present.
Objective: To provide training in the design, development, and implementation of CAI and CMI courseware.
Learning Outcome: Upon successful completion of this course, the student will understand the fundamentals of curriculum design and its implementation through CAI and CMI.
Instruction: Provides training in the skills required for designing, developing, and managing the development of individualized instruction. Covers CREATE fundamentals, design, development, PLATO Author Language, CAI, CMI, and management. Simulation exercises, multimedia presentations, and drill and practice are used. Prerequisite: Introduction to Computer-Based Education.
Credit recommendation: In the graduate degree category, 8 semester hours in Development and Design of CAI and CMI using CREATE (PLATO) (11/81) (6/86). NOTE: This course has been reevaluated and continues to meet requirements for credit recommendations.

Economics
Location: Various Control Data sites around the country.
Length: Approximately 30 hours (computer-based instruction).
Dates: October 1979-January 1983.
Objective: To enable the participant to understand selected economic principles.
Instruction: Covers the basic aspects of macro- and microeconomics. Topics covered include price discrimination, demand and supply, imperfect competition, antitrust policy, and international trade. Simulation exercises, multimedia presentations, and drill and practice are used.
Credit recommendation: In the lower division baccalaureate/associate degree category, 2 semester hours in Economics (11/81).

Foundations of Corporate Financial Management
(Capital Budgeting, Financing for Long-Term Growth, Short-Term Financial Planning Sequences)
Location: Various Control Data sites around the country.
Length: Approximately 82 hours (computer-based instruction).
Dates: September 1979-Present.
Objective: To provide a thorough understanding of the principles of corporate financial management.
Learning Outcome: Upon successful completion of this course, the student will understand the basic processes for financial management of a corporation.
Instruction: Topics include an introduction to capital budgeting, the effect of taxes and the uncertain economy on budgeting, capital structure and financial leverage, cost of capital, dividend policy and retention of earnings, issuance of capital stock, intermediate and long-term financing, leasing, merges and acquisitions, and inventory control. Simulation exercises, multimedia presentations, and drill and practice are used.
Credit recommendation: In the upper division baccalaureate category, 3 semester hours in Foundations of Corporate Financial Management (8/79) (6/86). NOTE: This course has been reevaluated and continues to meet requirements for credit recommendations.

Fundamentals of Finance and Accounting for Non-Financial Managers
Location: Various Control Data sites around the country.
Length: Approximately 20 hours (computer-based instruction).
Dates: October 1979-Present.
Objective: To enable participants to understand how finance relates to their own management specialty and the financial implications of daily managerial decision-making.
Learning Outcome: Upon successful completion of this course, the student will better understand budgeting and financial statements, and the vocabulary of accounting and finance.
Instruction: Covers financial functions: introduction to managerial accounting, cost behavior, financial planning and budget, return on investment and financial statement analysis. Simulation exercises, multimedia presentations, and drill and practice are used.
Credit recommendation: In the lower division baccalaureate/associate degree category, 1 semester hour in Basic Finance (for Non-Financial Managers) (11/81) (6/86). NOTE: This course has been reevaluated and continues to meet requirements for credit recommendations.

Introduction to Data Processing and Data Base Management
(Data Base Management System Environment, Introduction to Data Processing for Managers)
Location: Various Control Data sites around the country.
Length: Approximately 14 hours (computer-based instruction).
Dates: October 1979-Present.
Objective: To present an overview of the state of the art in computerized data processing and an awareness of the difference between traditional data processing and data base management.

Learning Outcome: Upon successful completion of this course, the student will understand the difference between traditional data processing and data base management, and be aware of the use of data base management as a tool for managers.

Instruction: Covers computer hardware and software, automated business systems, and data base management. Simulation exercises, multimedia presentations, and drill and practice are used.

Credit recommendation: In the lower division baccalaureate/associate degree category, 1 semester hour in Introduction to Data Processing and Data Base Management (11/81) (6/86). NOTE: This course has been reevaluated and continues to meet requirements for credit recommendations.

Introduction to Programming in BASIC
(Introduction to Programming in BASIC, BASIC Programming Techniques)

Location: Various Control Data sites around the country.

Length: Approximately 45 hours (computer-based instruction).

Dates: August 1980-Present.

Objective: To provide a practical introduction to programming techniques through the use of the BASIC language.

Learning Outcome: Upon successful completion of this course, the student will have an elementary knowledge of the function of computers and the vocabulary and syntax of the BASIC programming language.

Instruction: Introduces advanced programming techniques through use of the BASIC language. Covers structured programming fundamentals, iterative and logical loop programming, array handling techniques, function and subroutine use, and file processing methods. Simulation exercises, multimedia presentations, and drill and practice are used.

Credit recommendation: In the lower division baccalaureate/associate degree category, 1 semester hour in Introduction to Programming in BASIC (11/81) (6/86). If taken with Introduction to Computers, then 2 semester hours are recommended in the same category. (No credit is recommended for Introduction to Computers if taken separately.) NOTE: This course has been reevaluated and continues to meet requirements for credit recommendations.

Managerial Accounting
(Financial Management Sequence, Understanding Financial Statements Sequence)

Location: Various Control Data sites around the country.

Length: Approximately 72 hours (computer-based instruction).

Dates: June 1979-Present.

Objective: To provide background in managerial accounting techniques and practices.

Learning Outcome: Upon successful completion of this course, the student will understand the basic techniques and vocabulary of accounting, especially cost accounting.

Instruction: Review of accounting fundamentals; basics of income statements and balance sheets; cost systems, cost reporting, classification of costs, burden costs, cost standards and variances, determination of profits, valuation of inventories, long-range planning, budgeting, budget control; basics of financial statement analysis and the basics of constructing pro-forma financial statements.

Credit recommendation: In the lower division baccalaureate/associate degree category or in the upper division baccalaureate category, 3 semester hours in Managerial Accounting (8/79) (6/86). NOTE: This course has been reevaluated and continues to meet requirements for recommendations.

Managerial Planning, Organizing, and Controlling Curriculum

Location: Various Control Data sites around the country.

Length: Approximately 35 hours (computer-based instruction).

Dates: October 1979-April 1984.

Objective: To enable the participant to improve managerial skills in planning and budgeting, organizing, and controlling work flow.

Instruction: Covers management issues and tasks relevant to the interrelated responsibilities of planning and budgeting. Topics include the use of principles of organizing structures, interrelated communication systems, management-by-objectives, and the achievement of departmental plans. Simulation exercises, multimedia presentations, and drill and practice are used.

Credit recommendation: In the upper division baccalaureate category, 2 semester hours in Management (11/81).

Managerial Success Curriculum

Location: Various Control Data sites around the country.

Length: Approximately 26 hours (computer-based instruction).

Dates: May 1980-Present.

Objective: To enable the participants to improve managerial effectiveness and their personal roles as a change agent.

Learning Outcome: Upon successful completion of this course, the student will better understand the role of the effective middle manager.

Instruction: Focuses on middle management. Covers the expansion of managerial perspective, motivation, communication, the setting of objectives, and performance appraisal. Simulation exercises, multimedia presentations, and drill and practice are used.

Credit recommendation: In the lower division baccalaureate/associate degree category, 1 semester hour in Management and Supervision (11/81) (6/86). NOTE: This course has been reevaluated and continues to meet requirements for credit recommendations.

Mathematics of Life Insurance

Location: Various Control Data sites around the country.

Length: Approximately 15 hours (computer-based instruction).

Dates: November 1981-January 1983.

Objective: To provide a basic understanding of life insurance mathematics.

Instruction: Covers the fundamentals of mathematics as they apply to probability, mortality, gross premiums, net premiums, policy reserve, nonforfeiture value, surplus, dividends, and asset share. Simulation exercises, multimedia presentations, and drill and practice are used.

Credit recommendation: In the lower division baccalaureate/associate degree category, 1 semester hour in Mathematics of Life Insurance (11/81).

Office Communication and Behavior (Excel)

Location: Various Control Data sites around the country.

Length: Approximately 21 hours (computer-based instruction).

Dates: June 1979-Present.

Objective: To improve proficiency in handling office problems and in supporting the activities of managers.

Learning Outcome: Upon successful completion of this course, the student will understand the political and social forces present in the work environment.

Instruction: Topics include the manager's job, managerial styles, coping with change, successful communications, developing a professional approach, criticism and job responsibilities, setting performance standards, effective use of time, and career goal considerations.

Credit recommendation: In the vocational certificate category, 1 semester hour in Secretarial Science (8/79) (6/86). NOTE: This course has been reevaluated and continues to meet requirements for credit recommendations.

Principles of Real Estate Appraisal

Location: Various Control Data sites around the country.

Length: Approximately 20 hours (computer-based instruction).

Dates: November 1981-Present.

Objective: To enable students to perform real property appraisals using the field's basic concepts and standards.

Learning Outcome: Upon successful completion of this course, the student will understand the variables affecting a real estate appraisal.

Instruction: Covers the cost, income, and market data approaches to appraising real estate. Simulation exercises, multimedia presentations, and drill and practice are used.

Credit recommendation: In the vocational certificate category, 1 semester hour in Real Estate Appraisal (11/81) (6/86). NOTE: This course has been reevaluated and continues to meet requirements for credit recommendations.

Problem Analysis and Decision Making

Location: Various Control Data sites around the country.

Length: Approximately 24 hours (computer-based instruction).

Dates: October 1979-Present.

Objective: To enable the participant to develop an understanding of a systematic approach to problem analysis and decision making and be able to apply effective decision making skills.

Instruction: The decision making process as a whole is studied, including its relationship to problem analysis with emphasis on the Alpha-Omega method. Included are the factors involved in making a choice and follow-up on that choice. Simulation exercises, multimedia presentations, and drill and practice are used.

Credit recommendation: In the upper division baccalaureate category, 1 semester hour in Problem Analysis and Decision Making (11/81).

Selling: The Psychological Sequence
(Effective Sales Calls, Selling: The Psychological Approach, Telephone as a Sales Tool, Value Selling)
(Version 2)
(Formerly Effective Sales Calls, Selling: The Psychological Approach, Telephone as a Sales Tool)
(Version 1)

Location: Various Control Data sites around the country.

Length: *Version 1:* Approximately 25½ hours (computer-based instruction). *Version 2:* Approximately 42½ hours (computer-based instruction).

Dates: *Version 1:* October 1979-May 1986. *Version 2:* June 1986-Present.

Objective: To enable the participant to develop a psychological approach to selling.

Learning Outcome: Upon successful completion of this course, the student will become a better salesperson and be able to prepare a value selling presentation.

Instruction: A basic psychological approach to selling. Topics include the development of the psychological approach to selling, using the telephone as a sales tool, effective sales calls, and organizing a sales strategy. Simulation exercises, multimedia presentations, and drill and practice are used.

Credit recommendation: *Version 1:* In the lower division baccalaureate/associate degree category, 1 semester hour in Basic Selling or Introduction to Sales (11/81). *Version 2:* In the lower division baccalaureate/associate degree category, 2 semester hours in Basic Selling or Introduction to Sales (6/86). NOTE: The student should not receive credit for both Selling or Sales Techniques: The Psychological Sequence and Selling: The Strategic Approach Sequence. NOTE: This course has been reevaluated and continues to meet requirements for credit recommendations.

Selling: The Strategic Approach Sequence
(The Strategic Process; Time and Territory
Management; Account Control, Executive Selling; The
Telephone as a Sales Tool; Value Selling)
   Location: Various Control Data sites around the country.
   Length: Approximately 39½ hours (Computer-instruction).
   Dates: November 1983-Present.
   Objective: To provide a framework for selling.
   Learning Outcome: Upon successful completion of this course, the student will be able to organize a sales presentation incorporating a value selling analysis.
   Instruction: Developing a strategic process, effective time and territory management, maintaining control of accounts, and executive and value selling.
   Credit recommendation: In the lower division baccalaureate/associate degree category, 2 semester hours in Basic Selling or Introduction to Sales (6/86). NOTE: The student should not receive credit for both Selling: The Strategic Approach Sequence and Selling: The Psychological Sequence.

WILDWAYS: Understanding Wildlife Conservation
   Location: Various Control Data sites around the country.
   Length: Approximately 20 hours (computer-assisted instruction).
   Dates: June 1985-Present.
   Objective: To provide basic understanding of wildlife and its role in the Western Hemisphere's ecology and society, the fundamentals of how living systems work and interrelate, and the need for urgency in supporting wildlife conservation.
   Instruction: The eight sections of the course are: Beginnings: Earth and Life, Basic Necessities of Life, Importance of Wildlife, Population Ecology, Community Ecology, Extinction, Wildlife Management, and Citizen Action. The course, combining perspectives from the biological and sociological disciplines, helps people learn more about animal life and emphasizes support of wildlife conservation. Instruction is individualized, computer-based supplemented by a text, and provided at learning centers staffed for technical assistance.
   Credit recommendation: In the lower division baccalaureate/associate degree category, 1 semester hour in Environmental Science, Environmental Technology, Environmental Education (7/85).

COMPUTER SCIENCE/MATHEMATICS CURRICULUM

Ada Programming Fundamentals
(Ada Overview, Ada Programming: Fundamentals)
   Location: Various Control Data Sites around the country.
   Length: Approximately 40 hours (computer-based instruction).
   Dates: August 1985-Present.
   Objective: To understand the Ada programming environment and to learn the basics of Ada and introduce effective design and development methods.
   Learning Outcome: Upon successful completion of this course, the student will be able to understand the rationale of the design and development of the Ada programming language, the effective use of Ada to improve cost efficiency and productivity throughout the software life cycle; to write and compile Ada programs encompassing basic features such as objects, subprograms and packages; and to use Ada program structure concepts.
   Instruction: The development of the understanding of productivity, reliability, and the economics of problem solving associated with the development and maintenance of computer software, the effective use of Ada concepts and terminology, the impact of Ada on software design and development, the basic Ada program units and structure concepts, syntax and types, and central structure. Prerequisite: The ability to program in a higher level language (e.g., PASCAL, FORTRAN, COBOL, JOVIAL).
   Credit recommendation: In the lower division baccalaureate/associate degree category, 1 semester hour in Computer Science (6/86).

Advanced Ada and Software Engineering
(Ada Programming: Advanced Features; Ada
Programming: Software Engineering)
   Location: Various Control Data sites around the country.
   Length: Approximately 60 hours (computer-based instruction).
   Dates: November 1985-Present.
   Objective: To identify attributes of numeric and private types, the syntax and use of unconstrained arrays, and the concept and use of exception processing capabilities; and to use these concepts in software engineering.
   Learning Outcome: Upon successful completion of this course, the student will be able to write and compile Ada programs making use of numeric and private types, the syntax for unconstrained arrays, the exception processing capabilities, the syntax of composite types, the characteristics of access types, the use of explicit type conversions,

the use of discriminated records and variant records and generics, the use of the Ada programming environment for the design and development of major software.

Instruction: The development of Ada programs using numeric and private types, data structures, type conversion and unconstrained arrays, discriminated records and generics, library issues and exceptions, concurrency. The issues of portability, machine dependency and library routines, design and program structure. Prerequisite: Ada Programming Fundamentals.

Credit recommendation: In the upper division baccalaureate category, 2 semester hours in Computer Science (6/86). NOTE: If the course is supplemented with programming assignments, the credit recommendation is 3 semester hours Computer Science in the upper division baccalaureate category.

Algebra

Location: Various Control Data sites around the country.

Length: Approximately 75 hours (computer-based instruction).

Dates: April 1983-Present.

Objective: Provides practice, workbook exercises, tutorials, and testing on topics normally found in a one-year (elementary or beginning) Algebra course.

Learning Outcome: Upon successful completion of this course, the student will be able to solve algebraic problems (nonverbal and verbal) that require the knowledge of integers, rationals, and real numbers, sets and set notation, exponents (integer and rational), absolute value, variables, polynomials, factoring, rational expressions, equalities and inequalities, graphing (one and two dimensional), and introductory probability.

Instruction: The course covers sets and numbers, exponents (integer and rational), polynomials, factoring, solutions of: first and second (quadratic) degree equations, first degree inequalities, systems of two linear equations, and first and second degree verbal problems; rational expressions, graphs (one and two dimensional); and a brief introduction to elementary probability. Prerequisites: Mastery of basic mathematics (i.e., addition, subtraction, multiplication, division, fractions, decimals, ratio/proportion/percent).

Credit recommendation: In the lower division baccalaureate/associate degree category, 2 semester hours in Algebra (6/86).

Calculus 1

Location: Various Control Data sites around the country.

Length: Approximately 125 hours (computer-based instruction).

Dates: June 1984-Present.

Objective: To introduce students to the fundamentals of differential and integral calculus, equivalent to the first semester of college calculus, and to prepare them for study in the physical sciences, engineering, or for further study in calculus.

Learning Outcome: Upon successful completion of this course, the student will understand the basic concepts and theories of calculus and will be able to apply this knowledge to the analysis and accurate solution of graphical, geometrical, and physical problems utilizing differentiation and integration.

Instruction: Calculus 1 is a first semester of college calculus. Topics include limits and limit theories, continuity, definition and applications of the derivative including related rates, maxima-minima theory, and graphical analysis, the chain rule, techniques of differentiation, the indefinite and definite integral, fundamental theorem of calculus, applications of the definite integral to geometric and physical problems. Individualized instruction consisting of textbook reading and practice problems and computer-assisted lessons with problem solving and self-testing, delivered by the PLATO computer-based educational system. Prerequisite: Precalculus or equivalent.

Credit recommendation: In the lower division baccalaureate/associate degree category, 4 semester hours in Calculus (6/86).

Calculus 2

Location: Various Control Data sites around the country.

Length: Approximately 90 hours (computer-based instruction).

Dates: August 1985-Present.

Objective: To provide instruction equivalent to second semester calculus with emphasis on transcendental functions, techniques and applications of the integral, and sequences and series.

Learning Outcome: Upon successful completion of this course, the student will be able to diagnose and solve calculus problems involving inverse functions, integration techniques and applications, and be able to apply the appropriate theories to test for convergence of infinite series.

Instruction: Calculus 2 is a second semester college calculus course. Topics include properties of inverse functions, differentiation and integration of transcendental functions, L'Hopital's Rule, and indeterminate forms, applications of the integral, numerical integration, improper integrals, test for convergence of sequences and series. Individualized instruction consisting of textbook reading and practice problems and computer-assisted lessons with problem solving and self-testing delivered by the PLATO computer-based educational system. Prerequisite: Calculus 1 or equivalent.

Credit recommendation: In the lower division baccalaureate/associate degree category, 4 semester hours in Calculus (6/86).

Chemistry 1

Location: Various Control Data sites around the country.

Length: Approximately 90 hours (computer-based instruction).

Dates: July 1983-Present.

Objective: To give the student a basic introduction to chemistry, exclusive of laboratory, and to prepare them for further study in chemistry.

Instruction: Course covers measurement and calculations; classification of matter; atoms, molecules, and ions; chemical formulas and equations; thermochemistry; physical behavior of gases; electronic structure of atoms; chemical bonding; liquids and solids; intermolecular forces; properties of solutions. Individualized instruction consisting of assigned reading and computer-assisted lessons involving drill, practice and testing delivered by the PLATO computer-based education system. Prerequisite: 2 years of high school algebra and 1 year high school chemistry.

Credit recommendation: In the lower division baccalaureate/associate degree category, 3 semester hours in Chemistry (7/83).

Chemistry 2

Location: Various Control Data sites around the country.

Length: Approximately 95 hours (computer-based instruction).

Dates: January 1986-Present.

Objective: To provide instruction equivalent to second semester of college chemistry, exclusive of laboratory. Emphasis is on kinetics, thermodynamics, and gaseous and aqueous equilibria.

Learning Outcome: Upon successful completion of this course, the student will be able to apply their understanding of chemical concepts to solve problems involving reaction kinetics, gas phase equilibria, acid-base chemistry, solution equilibria, electrochemistry, thermodynamics, and coordination chemistry.

Instruction: Chemistry 2 is a non-laboratory course in second semester college chemistry. Topics include reaction rates and mechanisms, gas phase equilibira, equilibrium calculations, acid-base definitions, acid-base and solubility equilibria, applications of thermodynamics, electrochemistry, chemistry of the representative elements, coordination chemistry. Individualized instruction consisting of textbook reading and practice problems with computer-assisted lessons and self-tests delivered by the PLATO computer-based education. Prerequisite: Chemistry 1 or equivalent.

Credit recommendation: In the lower division baccalaureate/associate degree category, 3 semester hours in Chemistry (6/86). NOTE: This is a non-laboratory course.

Computer Literacy

Location: Various Control Data sites around the country.

Length: Approximately 50 hours (computer-based instruction).

Dates: August 1985-Present.

Objective: To overcome "computer anxiety," understand computer life skills, become informed on public policy concerning computers and computer-related products. Achieve computer skills in word processing, spread sheets, and simple data analysis.

Learning Outcome: Upon successful completion of this course, the student will understand how to use the computer to improve study and work skills, how computers affect their lives directly or indirectly, and how to be effective consumers of computer products and services.

Instruction: Topics covered include computer careers, computers in the classroom, history of computers, computer crime, robotics, computers and government, electronic funds transfer, human factors, privacy, social values, artificial intelligence, supercalc, data file fundamentals, word processing fundamentals, spread sheet, and computers and the future. No prerequisites required.

Credit recommendation: In the lower division baccalaureate/associate degree category, 2 semester hours in Computer Science (6/86). NOTE: If the course material is supplemented by laboratory exercises using word processing, supercalc, spreadsheets, then the credit recommendation is 3 semester hours in Computer Science in the lower division baccalaureate/associate degree category.

Data Communications

Location: Various Control Data sites around the country.

Length: Approximately 16 hours (computer-based instruction).

Dates: March 1982-Present.

Objective: To study how computer systems interconnect through common carrier communications networks.

Learning Outcome: Upon successful completion of this course, the student will be able to understand terminology commonly used in describing data communication systems, recognize the types of data communication services available, identify data communication hardware and their operational characteristics, recognize types of data transmission techniques, and recognize typical problems and failures.

Instruction: The topics covered include introduction to communication, basic communication systems, communication facilities and common carriers, data communication hardware, communication problems and systems maintenance. Prerequisite: basic electronics and computer fundamentals.

Credit recommendation: In the lower division baccalaureate/associate degree category, 1 semester hour in Computer Science (6/86). NOTE: If the course material is supplemented by a laboratory, the credit recommendation is 2 semester hours in Computer Science in the lower division baccalaureate/associate degree category.

Data Representation
   Location: Various Control Data sites around the country.
   Length: Approximately 11 hours (computer-based instruction).
   Dates: March 1982-Present.
   Objective: To introduce students to representation of numerical data within the computer.
   Learning Outcome: Upon successful completion of this course, the student will be able to convert numbers from one number base to another; perform binary, octal, and hexadecimal arithmetic operations; and recognize characteristics of computer data representation codes.
   Instruction: Topics include number base conversions, computer arithmetic, and data representation codes. Individualized instruction consisting of reading and computer-assisted lessons delivered by the PLATO computer-based educational system. No prerequisites.
   Credit recommendation: In the vocational certificate category, 1 semester hour in Computer Technology (6/86).

Introduction to Microprocessors
(Microprocessors: A Short Course)
   Location: Various Control Data sites around the country.
   Length: Approximately 75 hours (computer-based instruction).
   Dates: July 1980-Present.
   Objective: To give the student a working knowledge of the concepts, terminology, and analysis of basic microprocessor circuits.
   Learning Outcome: Upon successful completion of this course, the student will be able to understand the basics of microprocessors, operate and program microprocessors (machine language); and understand microprocessor components, circuitry for external interfaces, and simple machine language programming.
   Instruction: The course covers introduction to fundamental information on computer systems, logic fundamentals, microprocessor introduction, microprocessor fundamentals, machine language, instruction flow, memory and microprocessor interfacing, D/A and A/D, serial and parallel, troubleshooting, and introduction to high level languages. Prerequisites: Basic electronics or equivalent.
   Credit recommendation: In the lower division baccalaureate/associate degree category, 3 semester hours in Computer Science and Computer Engineering (6/86). NOTE: Recommendation requires lab activities.

Introduction to RPG II Programming
   Location: Various Control Data sites around the country.
   Length: Approximately 48 hours (computer-based instruction).
   Dates: March 1982-Present.
   Objective: To train students in Introductory RPG II Programming.
   Instruction: Course covers both the theory and practical applications of the RPG II language. A total of five major RPG II programs are written. The programs are specifically designed to provide experience in printing elementary reports, calculations and comparisons, multiple records, move operations, and control level indicators. Instruction utilizes a series of simulation exercises, multimedia presentations, and drill and practice.
   Credit recommendation: In the lower division baccalaureate/associate degree category, 1 semester hour in RPG II Programming (7/83).

Job Control Language (IBM OS/VS JCL)
   Location: Various Control Data sites around the country.
   Length: Approximately 50 hours (computer-based instruction).
   Dates: March 1982-Present.
   Objective: To present introductory concepts of IBM OS/VS JCL for the IBM/370 and 303X environments. To introduce the process of creating and accessing files, writing procedures, using procedure libraries, and JCL programmer utilities and error diagnostics.
   Learning Outcome: Upon successful completion of this course, the student will be able to explain JCL statements, create and access files and identify multistep jobs in relation to files, create procedures for modification functions, identify and explain specific utilities, write procedures for tape and disk media, and debug JCL errors.
   Instruction: The topics covered include Introduction to JCL, statements, file procedures, modification functions, utilities, performance requirements. Programming assignments are not included in the course. Prerequisite: Introductory course in higher level language (e.g., COBOL, FORTRAN, PASCAL).
   Credit recommendation: In the lower division baccalaureate/associate degree category, 2 semester hours in Computer Science (6/86). NOTE: If the course material is supplemented with programming assignments, then the credit recommendation is 3 semester hours in Computer Science in the lower division baccalaureate/associate degree category.

PASCAL
   Location: Various Control Data sites around the country.
   Length: Approximately 90 hours (computer-based instruction).

Dates: June 1984-Present.

Objective: To teach students to use a modular approach and basic control structure in the design and writing of programs in the PASCAL language.

Learning Outcome: Upon successful completion of this course, the student will understand the modular top-down approach and basic control structure in the design and writing of programs in the PASCAL language.

Instruction: The course discusses computer concepts, PASCAL structures, problem solving, control structure, attributes of data, modularity, and introduction to data structure. Emphasis is on algorithm development. Programming assignments are not included in the course. No prerequisites.

Credit recommendation: In the lower division baccalaureate/associate degree category, 2 semester hours in Computer Science (6/86). NOTE: If the course material is supplemented with programming assignments, then the credit recommendation is 3 semester hours in Computer Science in the lower division baccalaureate/associate degree category.

Physics I

Location: Various Control Data sites around the country.

Length: Approximately 90 hours (computer-based instruction).

Dates: July 1983-Present.

Objective: To enable the student to understand and explain the fundamental concepts, definitions, and relations of elementary Newtonian mechanics and apply them to solve problems in mechanics.

Instruction: Covers subject areas basic to the understanding of mechanics including kinematics in one and two dimensions, force, particle statics and dynamics, work and energy, impulse and momentum, rotational motion and angular momentum rigid body motion, conservation of energy and momentum, and simple harmonic motion. The course is taught by personalized self instruction (PSI) using PLATO computer-based education. Prerequisite: mathematics through differential calculus and co-registration in integral calculus.

Credit recommendation: In the lower division baccalaureate/associate degree category, 4 semester hours in Physics (7/83). NOTE: This is a calculus-based physics course not including laboratory.

Precalculus

Location: Various Control Data sites around the country.

Length: Approximately 120 hours (computer-based instruction).

Dates: September 1984-Present.

Objective: To provide the student with the understanding and skills in college algebra and trigonometry functional analysis, and analytic geometry necessary for the study of calculus.

Learning Outcome: Upon successful completion of this course, the student will be able to formulate and solve problems in elementary functional analysis; trigonometric, logarithmic, and exponential functions; and in analytic geometry of second degree curves.

Instruction: Precalculus is a course in elementary functions designed to prepare students for successful study of calculus. Topics include properties of real numbers, algebraic operations, equations and inequalities, graphical representation of algebraic relations. Analysis of second degree curves, logarithmic, exponential, and trigonometric functions and their graphs, trigonometric identities and equations, applications of trigonometry. Individualized instruction consisting of textbook reading and practice problems and computer-assisted lessons with self-tests delivered by the PLATO computer-based educational system. Prerequisite: 3 years of high school mathematics or equivalent.

Credit recommendation: In the lower division baccalaureate/associate degree category, 4 semester hours in Precalculus Mathematics (6/86).

Structured COBOL Programming

Location: Various Control Data sites around the country.

Length: Approximately 295 hours (computer-based instruction).

Dates: March 1982-Present.

Objective: To train students in elementary and advanced structured COBOL programming.

Instruction: This course covers the structure of the COBOL language and its use in a variety of practical problems. Topics include structured documentation, COBOL reports and tables, structured analysis and design; and validating, sorting, and updating sequential files. Instruction utilizes a series of simulation exercises, multimedia presentations, and drill and practice.

Credit recommendation: In the lower division baccalaureate/associate degree category, 3 semester hours in COBOL Programming and 2 semester hours in Advanced COBOL Programming (7/83).

Structured FORTRAN Programming

Location: Various Control Data sites around the country.

Length: Approximately 75 hours (computer-based instruction).

Dates: July 1983-Present.

Objective: To train students in FORTRAN Programming.

Instruction: The course covers both the theory and practical applications of the FORTRAN Language. Topics include FORTRAN concepts, I/O capabilities, array processing, and subprogram and cases. Instruction utilizes a series of simulation exercises, multimedia presentations, and classroom exercises.

Credit recommendation: In the lower division baccalaureate/associate degree category, 2 semester hours in FORTRAN Programming (7/83).

Structured Programming with FORTRAN 77
  Location: Various PLATO sites around the country.
  Length: Approximately 90 hours (computer-based instruction).
  Dates: July 1983-Present.
  Objective: To provide the student with the skills and knowledge necessary to solve problems using structured programs and modular techniques using the FORTRAN 77 programming language.
  Instruction: The course is designed to teach students to develop computer programs using the "top-down" design and structured programming of the FORTRAN language. Topics include: programming and computers, basic sequential programs, modular design, control structures, repetition and arrays, character data, subprograms, and formulated input and output. Instruction utilizes exercises, simulation, and computer-based modules.
  Credit recommendation: In the lower division baccalaureate/associate degree category, 3 semester hours in Programming (7/83).

MECHANICAL ENGINEERING CURRICULUM

Advanced ICEM Design/Drafting
a. ICEM Design/Drafting II (Advanced Topics)
b. ICEM Design/Drafting 3-D (Techniques)
  Location: Various Control Data sites around the country.
  Length: a. 3 days (half lecture/half laboratory). b. 2 days (half lecture/half laboratory).
  Dates: January 1986-Present.
  Objective: a. To understand and apply advanced features of ICEM Design/Drafting. b. To instruct experienced ICEM users in special techniques for working in 3-dimensions.
  Learning Outcome: Upon completion of this course, the student will be able to: a. use the full range of capabilities of ICEM Design/Drafting; b. develop fundamental procedures for working in a flexible work plane to create 3-dimensional drawings.
  Instruction: Course covers user defined symbols, patterns-templates, part merge, tablet programming, analysis, view layout, attribute management, trace and plot files, user technology file, canon; and fundamentals of 3-dimensional approach, modals that identify display parameters, exploring advantages of flexible work plane, setting depth, using transform coordinates, and view layout construction to format drawings.
  Credit recommendation: In the upper division baccalaureate category, 2 semester hours in Design and Drafting (6/86). NOTE: Students may receive 1 semester hour for completion of course "a" and 1 semester hour for completion of course "b."

Basic ICEM Design/Drafting
a. ICEM Design/Drafting Introduction (PLATO)
b. ICEM Design/Drafting I (Basic)
  Location: Various Control Data sites around the country.
  Length: a. 22 hours (computer-based instruction). b. 5 days (half lecture/half laboratory).
  Dates: January 1986-Present.
  Objective: To enable the user to construct, manipulate, dimension, display, file, and retrieve parts and production drawing on their graphics terminals.
  Learning Outcome: Upon successful completion of this course, the student will be able to perform basic drafting tasks at the computer graphics terminal. Drawings can be filed and recalled from computer storage.
  Instruction: Course "a" covers explanation of points, lines, arcs, and circles, storage and retrieval of parts; trim and delete functions; drafting modals and dimensions; offset curves, fillets, chamfers, and centerlines, zoom and view control. Course "b" covers all of "a" above plus string, projected entity, and Z clip functions; selective view blanking, hidden line removal, detail magnification; creation and retrieval of patterns; and grid and stretch functions.
  Credit recommendation: In the lower division baccalaureate/associate degree category, 3 semester hours in Design and Drafting (6/86). NOTE: Student may receive 1 semester hour for completion of course "a" and 2 semester hours for completion of course "b."

Fluid Power Systems
a. Hydraulic Power Fundamentals
b. Pneumatic Power Fundamentals
  Location: Various Control Data sites around the country.
  Length: a. 65 hours. b. 47 hours (computer-based instruction).
  Dates: September 1983-Present.
  Objective: To learn the importance and functioning of Fluid Power and Control Systems. To learn to interpret fluid circuit diagrams.
  Learning Outcome: Upon successful completion of this course, the student will understand fluid power transfer and have the ability to select components and assemble into fluid power systems.
  Instruction: Course "a" covers basic hydraulic relations, hydraulic components and circuits, and hydraulic system maintenance and troubleshooting. Course "b" covers preparation and distribution of air in pneumatic systems, use of compressed air in pneumatic systems, safety in pneumatic systems, pneumatic system maintenance and troubleshooting.
  Credit recommendation: In the vocational certificate

category, 3 semester hours as a technical elective for engineering students (6/86). NOTE: Students may receive 1 semester hour for course "a" and 2 semester hours for course "b."

ICEM Engineering Data Library
a. ICEM Engineering Data Library Usage
b. ICEM Engineering Data Library Data Base Administration
c. ICEM Engineering Data Library Implementation Workshop

Location: Various Control Data sites around the country.
Length: a. 2 days (lecture/laboratory). b. 2 days (lecture/laboratory). c. 3 days (assigned to team).
Dates: January 1986-Present.
Objective: EDL performs both application management and engineering data management functions. a. Enable users to understand the capabilities and use the menus to accomplish data management tasks. b. Allows the DBA administrator to initiate new users, delete users, modify menus, add vendors, and modify application procedures. c. Implementation and customizaton of EDL for specific installations. Case studies are used.
Learning Outcome: Upon successful completion of this course, the student will be able to a. log in/out of EDL, access and manage files, transfer drawings between applications, access multiple applications, and release drawing to text file; b. understand how to adapt and operate EDL to meet needs of their organization, and c. the Engineering Data Manager will understand how to implement and customize EDL for specific installations and know the tools available to accomplish the customization.
Instruction: Course covers EDL advantages and terminology, adding, deleting, and retrieving modals and parts, file security, releasing drawings, interfacing with ICEM applications, relating drawings to engineering documentation files, modifying EDL menu and error messages, initiating new users, selected query update commands, updating vendor information, generating EDL reports, loading and unloading data from data-bases, establishing security, integrating applications, real world implementation, challenges, analyzing implementation process in laboratories, and solving problems as team members.
Credit recommendation: In the upper division baccalaureate category, 2 semester hours in Engineering Data Base Library Usage and Administration (6/86).

ICEM Numerical Control (N/C)
Location: Various Control Data sites around the country.
Length: 5 days (half lecture/half laboratory).
Dates: January 1986-Present.
Objective: This course teaches experienced numerical control personnel how to use ICEM Numerical Control to create and machine parts.
Learning Outcome: Upon successful completion of this course, the student will have set up and machined a part requiring at least four tool paths.
Instruction: Course covers planning a part, modal settings, point-to-point tool path generation, mill tooth path generation, composite tool paths, display and edit, post processors, and machine tape transfer.
Credit recommendation: In the upper division baccalaureate category, 1 semester hour in Numerical Control (6/86).

ICEM Solid Modeling
Location: Various Control Data sites around the country.
Length: 5 days (half lecture/half laboratory).
Dates: January 1986-Present.
Objective: To use the ICEM Solid Modeling System to create 3-dimensional solid models of mechanical parts including color-shaded models, and to analyze mass properties.
Learning Outcome: Upon successful completion of this course, users will construct and manipulate solid models, produce and modify color-shaded pictures of models, calculate mass properties, and be able to link to and from ICEM Design/Drafting.
Instruction: Course covers solid modeling concepts, user interface, construction using primitives, animation commands, shaded pictures, mass properties, links to/from ICEM Design/Drafting, edge files, parameterized objects, potential applications areas, and relationship to overall ICEM system.
Credit recommendation: In the upper division baccalaureate category, 1 semester hour in Design and Drafting (6/86).

Industrial Electronics
Location: Various Control Data sites around the country.
Length: 345 hours (computer-based instruction).
Dates: November 1982-Present.
Objective: To understand and apply number systems such as binary, octal, decimal, and hexadecimal. To understand and apply principles of semiconductors, circuit analysis, and essential measuring instruments.
Learning Outcome: Upon successful completion of this course, the student will have a working knowledge of electronic circuits and components and the logic of computer operation, understand basic computer components and logic circuits, and be capable of troubleshooting practices.
Instruction: Course covers basic electronics, semiconductor electronics, and digital electronics.
Credit recommendation: In the vocational certificate category, 5 semester hours as a technical elective (6/86).

Mechanisms
  Location: Various Control Data sites around the country.
  Length: 91 hours (computer-based instruction).
  Dates: June 1981-Present.
  Objective: To identify and study proper installation, operation, and maintenance of common mechanisms including gears, belt drives, bearings, and shafts.
  Learning Outcome: Upon successful completion of this course, the student will have the ability to successfully install the mechanisms studied.
  Instruction: Course covers machine elements, gear drive systems, gear maintenance, belt drive systems, chain drive systems, bearing types, shaft drives, bearing maintenance, troubleshooting, and preventive maintenance.
  Credit recommendation: In the lower division baccalaureate/associate degree category, 1 semester hour in Engineering for Non-Engineering and Non-Science majors (6/86).

Power System Stability and Control
(Automatic Generation Control, Power System Stability, Power Oscillation Due to Xenon Poisoning of Nuclear Reaction, Three Bus Power System Load Flow, Voltage Ampier Reactor
  Location: Various Control Data sites around the country.
  Length: Approximately 53 hours (computer-based instruction).
  Dates: August 1984-Present.
  Objective: To learn benefits and principles of operation of typical automatic controls of electric power generating systems; learn how various operational factors affect electric power generator system stability; understand influence of xenon poisoning on reactor power oscillation; understand load and voltage control in three bus power system; understand relationship of real and reactive power, VAR sources, and flow of power in control of electric power systems.
  Learning Outcome: Upon successful completion of this course, the student will have an improved understanding and performance in the operation of complex electric power generation systems.
  Instruction: Course covers preliminary ideas and definitions, governing speed change, reactions to change in load, frequency control, economic control, steady state, perturbations to steady state, torque variations, large disturbances, maximum excursion (deviation), transient stability, xenon production, xenon dynamics, relation between power and voltage in three bus system, and elementary theory of reactive power in VAR flow systems.
  Credit recommendation: In the vocational certificate category, 2 semester hours as a technical elective (6/86). NOTE: Students must complete all modules to receive credit.

Robotics Sequence
(Introduction to Robotics, Robotics Literacy, Robotics Safety, Working with Robots, Robot Drive Systems, Teach Mode Programming, Troubleshooting)
  Location: Various Control Data sites around the country.
  Length: Approximately 25 1/4 hours (computer-based instruction).
  Dates: August 1983-Present.
  Objective: Describe robots and robotic functions; define commonly used robot terminology and functions; delineate equipment, procedures, and legal requirements for safe robot operation; identify kinds of robots with applications and information resources; functioning and maintenance of typical pneumatic, hydraulic, and electric drive and positioning systems; learn techniques for programming and checking by teach mode process; diagnose and solve robot problems using maintenance manuals.
  Learning Outcome: Upon successful completion of this course, the student will have limited skills in selection, safe installation, operation, and routine maintenance of robotic systems.
  Instruction: Course covers industrial robots, robot components, robotic terminology, positioning and control limitations, end of arm tooling-grippers, drive systems, servo and non-servo control, robot communications, safety-hazard elimination, manipulator specification and operation, teach mode programming, and troubleshooting and maintenance.
  Credit recommendation: In the vocational certificate or lower division baccalaureate/associate degree category, 1 semester hour as a technical elective (6/86). NOTE: Students must complete all modules to receive credit.

Crawford Risk Management Services

The education and training component of Crawford Risk Management Services is the Corporate Training Department, a part of the Human Resources Division. The Department has three primary segments: Claims Administration Training, which has a Director and four instructors; Rehabilitation and Management Training, which has a Director, two instructors, and two support staff; and Training Services which has a Manager and five support staff members.

Instructors are Crawford Risk Management Services employees who are experts in the areas in which they instruct. The instructors are periodically reviewed by trained staff members to ascertain that training methods are met and procedures remain current and realistic. Experts from the Home Office as well as from the seven Regional Offices monitor several classes per year and submit written reports to the Director of Corporate Training. Classes are held in four classrooms, each equipped with video projectors and other audiovisual aids/devices.

Course are developed and revised by consultation with in-house experts in the Home Office and Regional Offices, in their respective fields of expertise. All courses and supporting material are submitted to that particular expert in the Home Office for review and approval before being implemented.

Certification of completion of a course is based upon evidence that the student has mastered the course content. This involves grading examination papers, and averaging grades. All daily quizzes and final examinations require a minimum grade of 70 for acceptable course completion. Student successful completion records are maintained and filed on Crawford's computer system.

Source of official student records: Director of Corporate Training, Crawford Risk Management Services, P.O. Box 5047, Atlanta, Georgia 30302.

Additional information about the courses: Program on Noncollegiate Sponsored Instruction, The Center for Adult Learning and Educational Credentials, American Council on Education, One Dupont Circle, Washington, D.C. 20036.

Advanced Branch Office Management (0001)
 Location: Atlanta, GA.
 Length: 50 hours (1 week).
 Dates: October 1982-Present.
 Objective: To give the student orientation and skill training in branch office management.
 Learning Outcome: Upon successful completion of this course, the student will be able to perform all of the duties associated with the proper management of a branch office. This will include the analysis and proper utilization of all financial documents in branch operations; supervision of subordinates and leadership styles; organizing, planning, delegating and communicating; office procedures; sales techniques and business planning. The student will report directly to a regional manager.
 Instruction: Participants receive training/information in the areas of supervision-leadership styles; organization, delegating, communicating; statistical management; office procedures; personnel files/interview techniques; sales and business planning.
 Credit recommendation: In the graduate category, 1 semester hour in Management (8/87).

Advanced Casualty Claims Adjusting (0002)
 Location: Atlanta, GA.
 Length: 50 hours (1 week).
 Dates: January 1984-Present.
 Objective: To provide the student with knowledge to adjust advanced workers' compensation, environmental pollution, products and professional liability cases; and to use effectively rehabilitation and structured settlements in claim settlements. Attention is given to litigation supervision.
 Learning Outcome: Upon successful completion of this course, the student will be able to handle casualty claim files of a serious nature involving claims to be analyzed, investigated and concluded in the areas of environmental pollution liability, products liability, serious workers' compensation and professional liability. The student will be able to utilize structured settlements in the course of handling these files and be able to properly assist defense attorneys in those files which are litigated. The student will work under the supervision of a branch manager or supervisor.
 Instruction: Subjects covered include settlement of advanced workers' compensation losses, environmental pollution, products and professional liability losses, and the use of rehabilitation and structured settlements in claims settlement. Application of the subject matter covered is practiced in case situations.
 Credit recommendation: In the upper division baccalaureate category, 1 semester hour in Business Law, General Business, Insurance, or Risk Management (8/87).

Advanced Property Loss Adjusting (0003)
 Location: Atlanta, GA.
 Length: 115 hours (2 weeks).
 Dates: August 1978-Present.
 Objective: To enable students who are experienced property loss adjusters to handle commercial losses with emphasis on retail stock and business interruption cases.
 Learning Outcome: Upon successful completion of this course, the student will be able to perform the duties of a property general adjuster in the handling of commercial claim files dealing with reporting forms, business interruption losses, analysis of income statements, stock values, etc. The student will work under the supervision of the branch manager.
 Instruction: This course involves business interruption coverages and adjusting procedures, guiding principles, reporting forms, stock losses and related book inventories and computations, arson investigation and reporting, and the use of technical experts.
 Credit recommendation: In the upper division baccalaureate category, 3 semester hours in General Business, Insurance, or Risk Management (8/87).

Branch Office Management (0004)
 Location: Atlanta, GA.
 Length: 63 hours (1 week).
 Dates: July 1983-Present.
 Objective: To enhance a supervisor's ability to communicate effectively, develop employee sales skills, and increase employee motivation.
 Learning Outcome: Upon successful completion of this course, the student will be able to perform all duties associated with the management of a branch office, including utilization of all financial documents, supervision,

organizational communications and motivational techniques. The student will work under the direction of a branch manager.

Instruction: A variety of techniques, including lecture/discussion, case study, demonstration, video role playing, individual/group activities and guest speakers, are used to enhance student skills in supervision-leadership styles, organizing, delegating, communicating statistical management, personnel file/interview and sales techniques.

Credit recommendation: In the upper division baccalaureate or graduate category, 2 semester hours in Management (8/87).

Casualty Claim Adjusting (0005)
   Location: Atlanta, GA.
   Length: 200 hours (4 weeks).
   Dates: January 1975-Present.
   Objective: To provide the student with the basic knowledge skills needed to begin a career as a Casualty Claims Adjuster.
   Learning Outcome: Upon successful completion of this course, the student will be able to perform the duties of a Casualty Claims Adjuster in the handling of claim files, including the analysis of coverage and investigation of the facts, evaluation of damages and liability, settlement or conclusion of the claim, and reports. The student conducts these activities under the supervision of the Branch Manager or Supervisor.
   Instruction: This course includes principles of insurance, adjuster law, automobile coverages, introduction to material damage appraising and workers' compensation, homeowners coverages, general liability coverages, liability claims investigation techniques, claim forms and reports, claim evaluation, litigation procedures and human relations. Skills are learned through a variety of cases that are assigned to each student to be investigated and handled from the opening to the closing of the claim file.
   Credit recommendation: In the upper division baccalaureate category, 4 semester hours in General Business, Insurance, or Risk Management (8/87).

Heavy Equipment Material Damage Appraisal (0006)
   Location: Atlanta, GA.
   Length: 95 hours (2 weeks).
   Dates: November 1983-Present.
   Objective: To teach the student to prepare appraisals on tractor-trailer vehicles, refrigerated vans, tank trucks, furniture vans, and off-the-road heavy equipment.
   Learning Outcome: Upon successful completion of this course, the student will be able to perform duties required of a heavy equipment appraiser including the inspection, analysis, and evaluation of various types of damage to tractors, trailers, refrigerated vans, tank trucks, furniture vans, and off-the-road heavy equipment, and preparation of written appraisals on the cost of repairing heavy equipment or determination of the actual cash value and salvage value in the event of a total loss. The student will work under the supervision of the Branch Manager or Supervisor.
   Instruction: Course includes instruction in the use of various publications and accepted repair techniques on heavy equipment units, nomenclature of various types of heavy equipment, inspecting and analyzing damages, detecting and eliminating problems relating to overlap, included operations, and conjunctive straightening. The course includes visits to repair facilities and manufacturers of heavy equipment.
   Credit recommendation: In the vocational certificate category, 2 semester hours in General Electives (8/87).

Material Damage Appraisal (0007)
   Location: Atlanta, GA.
   Length: 192 hours (3 weeks).
   Dates: December 1974-Present.
   Objective: To teach the student to prepare properly a material damage appraisal on passenger cars and motorcycles.
   Learning Outcome: Upon successful completion of this course, the student will be able to perform all duties associated with the job of a material damage appraiser and will be able to inspect, analyze, and determine damage to all types of passenger cars and motorcycles and to prepare written appraisals on the cost of repairs or actual cash value in the event of a total loss. The student will work under the supervision of a branch manager or supervisor.
   Instruction: Course includes introduction to the use of flat rate manuals, detecting and eliminating problems related to overlap, included operations and conjunctive straightening, and appraisal writing. The course involves making field appraisals on damaged automobiles and motorcycles.
   Credit recommendation: In the vocational certificate category, 3 semester hours in General Electives (8/87).

Property Loss Adjusting (0008)
   Location: Atlanta, GA.
   Length: 230 hours (4 weeks).
   Dates: August 1978-Present.
   Objective: To provide the student with the basic knowledge and skills needed to begin a career as a property claims adjuster.
   Learning Outcome: Upon successful completion of this course, the student will be able to handle personal and commercial property loss files. This will include the ability to analyze coverage, investigate facts, determine damage to residential dwellings, conclude the loss, and report findings accurately. The student will work under the supervision of the branch manager or supervisor.
   Instruction: The course includes an analysis of residential, commercial and condominium coverages, replacement cost and actual cash value, business interruption coverages, the Unfair Claims Settlement Practices Act

and extra contractual liability, construction terminology, areas and materials quantities computations, property loss files, salvage and subrogation reporting guidelines, automated value appraisals, risk surveys, and the use of experts.

Credit recommendation: In the upper division baccalaureate category, 4 semester hours in General Business, Insurance, or Risk Management (8/87).

Specialized Rehabilitation Counseling (0009)
Location: Atlanta, GA.
Length: 80 hours (2 weeks).
Dates: September 1983-Present.
Objective: To upgrade the student's skills and increase the knowledge of the vocational and medical aspects of rehabilitation.
Learning Outcome: Upon successful completion of this course, the student will be able to handle files and perform all duties associated and required of a medical or vocational rehabilitation consultant in a branch office. This will include the ability to analyze injuries, classifications of work that could be performed by the disabled person, report findings and conclude the claim. The students will work under the supervision of the branch manager or a supervisor.
Instruction: Students' rehabilitation skills are enhanced in the areas of private rehabilitation and the rehabilitation process, medical disabilities, insurance law, time management, report writing, and analysis of skills, other medical services, job development/job analysis, and testimony. Instruction includes lecture/discussion, demonstration, case study, video, role playing, individual/group activities, and guest speakers.
Credit recommendation: In the graduate category, 2 semester hours as an elective in General Business, Health Sciences, Human Resources, Insurance, Nursing, Rehabilitation Counseling, or Risk Management (8/87).

Workers' Compensation Claims Adjusting (0010)
Location: Atlanta, GA.
Length: 95 hours (2 weeks).
Dates: March 1986-Present.
Objective: To enable the student to analyze, investigate, control, and conclude workers' compensation claims.
Learning Outcome: Upon successful completion of this course, the student will be able to perform all of the duties required of a workers' compensation claims adjuster. This will include the analysis of the coverage, determination of proper jurisdiction, investigation of facts, evaluation of injuries, establishment of the proper weekly wage and compensation rate, completion of all forms required of the various state jurisdictions, reporting and concluding the claim properly. The student will be able to handle workers' compensation claims files upon completion of the class working under the supervision of a branch manager or supervisor.

Instruction: Students develop knowledge of the principles of insurance, workers' compensation laws, the Workers' Compensation and Employers Liability Policy, determination of average weekly wage, compensation rate, waiting period, healing period, type of disabilities, investigative techniques of death claims, independent contractor relationships, extraterritorial jurisdictions, dual- or multi-employment situations and medical aspects of injuries.

Credit recommendation: In the upper division baccalaureate category, 2 semester hours in General Business, Insurance, or Risk Management (8/87).

Credit Union National Association - Certified Credit Union Executive Program

The Certified Credit Union Executive (CCUE) Program is sponsored by the Credit Union National Association (CUNA). CUNA is the national trade association for 22,000 credit unions in the United States. The CCUE program is primarily an independent study program developed by an advisory committee of credit union executives and educators. However, in some localities CCUE courses are also offered by colleges in a conventional classroom format. The CCUE program was initiated in 1975 and is a professional development program for credit union personnel.

To participate in the CCUE program, a candidate must be actively engaged in the credit union industry and must complete a curriculum of ten independent study courses designed to broaden knowledge and enhance management skills. Successful completion of all ten courses qualifies a candidate for CCUE designation.

Course completion is validated by national examinations prepared by college and university professors, and administered under strict control in colleges and universities in the candidates' home areas. The program is primarily designed for self-study, and participants desiring professional assistance may contact the CCUE Coordinator at CUNA.

Textbooks are selected by college and university faculty members, and study guides to accompany the textbooks are prepared by faculty members. Review guides are available for examination preparation.

Source of official student records: Coordinator, Certified Credit Union Executive Program, CUNA, P.O. Box 431, Madison, Wisconsin 53701.

Additional information about the courses: Program on Noncollegiate Sponsored Instruction, The Center for Adult Learning and Educational Credentials, American Council on Education, One Dupont Circle, Washington, D.C. 20036.

Accounting I #400
  Location: Independent study program.
  Length: 15 self-paced lessons. (Formerly 10 self-paced lessons.)
  Dates: January 1975-Present.
  Objective: To provide knowledge of basic accounting principles and applications.
  Learning Outcome: Upon successful completion of this course, the student will understand accounting principles so that they may be applied to credit union needs.
  Instruction: Course emphasis is on those areas of financial accounting relevant to external reporting by credit unions. Topical areas include: accounting principles, basic accounting cycle and financial statements, analysis of revenue and expense; analysis of asset, liability and equity accounts, preparation of financial statements, and present value concepts. This course is a prerequisite for Accounting II.
  Credit recommendation: In the lower division baccalaureate/associate degree category, 3 semester hours in Accounting (6/81) (7/86). NOTE: This course has been reevaluated and continues to meet requirements for credit recommendations.

Accounting II #410
  Location: Independent study program.
  Length: 10 self-paced lessons.
  Dates: January 1975-May 1987.
  Objective: To provide the knowledge of managerial accounting and how it applies to the decision making process.
  Learning Outcome: Upon successful completion of this course, the student will understand the relationship of accounting data to management decisions.
  Instruction: Course emphasis is on the preparation and use of reports for management decision making. Topical areas include: management accounting, cost behavior, cost flows and capital budgeting, financial statement analysis, measuring performance, planning and control, budgeting, standard costing, internal control, audits, and cost allocations. Accounting I is a prerequisite for this course.
  Credit recommendation: In the upper division baccalaureate category, 3 semester hours in Managerial Accounting (6/81) (7/86). NOTE: This course has been reevaluated and continues to meet requirements for credit recommendations.

Business Law #1000
(Formerly Business Law #10)
  Location: Independent study program.
  Length: 15 self-paced lessons. (Formerly 10 self-paced lessons.)
  Dates: *Version 1:* January 1975-June 1986; *Version 2:* July 1986-Present.
  Objective: To provide an understanding of business law concepts and terms and to acquaint personnel with the application of these concepts and terms to the operation of credit unions.
  Learning Outcome: Upon successful completion of this course, the student will understand basic business law concepts and terms.
  Instruction: Course provides a well-rounded study of business law and a working knowledge of legal terminology. Topics include social forces and legal rights; contracts, including nature, offer and acceptance, capacity, mutuality and consideration, legality, form and interpretation, transfer of rights, and discharge; agency; commercial paper, including nature, negotiability and transfer, rights of parties, notes and drafts, bankruptcy, and management of corporation. Methodology involves self-study utilizing a study guide, a text, and a review guide for examination preparation.
  Credit recommendation: *Version 1:* In the upper division baccalaureate category, 2 semester hours in Business Law I (Contracts and Negotiable Instruments) (6/81). *Version 2:* In the lower division baccalaureate/associate degree and in the upper division category, 3 semester hours in Business Law (7/86). NOTE: This course has been reevaluated and continues to meet requirements for credit recommendations.

Credit and Collections #900
(Formerly Credit and Collections #9)
  Location: Independent study program.
  Length: 11 self-paced lessons.
  Dates: January 1975-Present.
  Objective: To develop knowledge of credit granting and collection techniques with application to credit unions.
  Learning Outcome: Upon successful completion of this course, the student will understand the basic elements and principles of granting credit and collection techniques.
  Instruction: Course covers various aspects of credit. Topics include nature and role of credit; types of consumer credit, and their management and investigation; basis of credit decision; decision and salesmanship in consumer credit; numerical scoring systems, collection policies, practices, and systems; and business and government credit functions, and control of credit operations. Methodology involves self-study utilizing a study guide, a text, and a review guide for examination preparation.
  Credit recommendation: In the lower division baccalaureate/associate degree category, 2 semester hours in Credit and Collections (6/81) (7/86). NOTE: This course has been reevaluated and continues to meet requirements for credit recommendations.

Economics #600
(Formerly Economics, Government, and Business #6)
  Location: Independent study program.
  Length: 13 self-paced lessons.
  Dates: *Version 1:* January 1975-June 1986; *Version 2:* July 1986-Present.

Objective: To provide knowledge of general economic principles with special reference to their effect on credit unions.

Learning Outcome: Upon successful completion of this course, the student will have an understanding of national economic policies, such as monetary and fiscal policy, and their effect on credit unions and their customers.

Instruction: This course comprises a systematic study and searching analysis of economic activity. Topics include basic economic concepts and national income; pricing, supply, and demand; incomes and living standards; business organization; labor and industrial relations and the economic role of government; national income, savings, investment, and consumption; income determination, business cycles, and forecasting; prices and money, the banking system, and monetary policy; fiscal policy and price determination; pricing and the productive factors, wages, interest, and profits; international trade and finance; and economic problems and alternate economic systems. Methodology involves self-study utilizing a study guide, a textbook, and a review guide for examination preparation.

Credit recommendation: *Version 1:* In the lower division baccalaureate/associate degree category, 2 semester hours in General Economics (6/81). *Version 2:* In the lower division baccalaureate/associate degree category, 3 semester hours in Economics (7/86). NOTE: This course has been reevaluated and continues to meet requirements for credit recommendations.

Financial Counseling #800
(Formerly Financial Counseling #8)

Location: Independent study program.

Length: 15 self-paced lessons. (Formerly 13 self-paced lessons.)

Dates: January 1975-Present.

Objective: To provide understanding of the basic elements of personal financial planning; and to apply elements of personal financial planning through the use of a counseling model.

Instruction: Course provides instruction and material that enable the counselor to meet the demands of the credit union members. Topics include family resource management and consumer decision making; consumer credit; family budget components; social security, life insurance, and annuities; savings and investments; estate planning, wills, and trusts; consumer education; types and techniques of counseling; and evaluation and ethics. Methodology involves self-study utilizing study guide, a self-directed practicum, texts, and a review guide for examination preparation.

Credit recommendation: In the lower division baccalaureate/associate degree category, 3 semester hours in Personal Finance (6/81) (7/86). NOTE: This course has been reevaluated and continues to meet requirements for credit recommendations.

Introduction to Credit Unions #100
(Formerly Foundation and Structure of Credit Unions #1)

Location: Independent study program.

Length: 14 self-paced lessons. (Formerly 15 self-paced lessons.)

Dates: January 1975-Present.

Objective: To provide knowledge of the historical origin of credit unions, to broaden understanding of credit union philosophy, and to review credit union organization and working relationships.

Instruction: The course covers credit union origins and introduction into North America; depression and credit union development; new leadership, World War II, postwar expansion; credit union as a legal entity; development and functioning of board of directors; motive power for a credit union; ethics in the credit union; and credit union relationships and professionalism. Methodology involves self-study utilizing a study guide, recommended texts, and a review guide for examination preparation.

Credit recommendation: In the lower division baccalaureate/associate degree category, 2 semester hours in History and Organization of Credit Unions (6/81) (7/86). NOTE: This course has been reevaluated and continues to meet requirements for credit recommendations.

Management #200
(Formerly Management #2)

Location: Independent study program.

Length: 13 self-paced lessons.

Dates: *Version 1:* January 1975-June 1986; *Version 2:* July 1986-Present.

Objective: To provide knowledge of the fundamentals of management and organizational behavior and the application of this knowledge to the management and operation of credit unions.

Learning Outcome: Upon successful completion of this course, the student will be able to apply the techniques of management and styles of supervision of credit union employees.

Instruction: This course presents the principles of sound management. Topics include motivation, organizing, human factors in organizing, decision making, planning, leadership and directing, controlling, and management and development. Methodology involves self-study utilizing a study guide, selected texts, and a review guide for examination preparation.

Credit recommendation: *Version 1:* In the lower division baccalaureate/associate degree category, 2 semester hours in Principles of Management (6/81). *Version 2:* In the lower division baccalaureate/associate degree category, 3 semester hours in Principles of Management (7/86). NOTE: This course has been reevaluated and continues to meet requirements for credit recommendations.

Marketing #700
(Formerly Marketing #7)
  Location: Independent study program.
  Length: 10 self-paced lessons.
  Dates: January 1975-Present.
  Objective: To further students' knowledge and understanding of how goods and services are marketed with specific attention to marketing techniques related to credit union products and services.
  Learning Outcome: Upon successful completion of this course, the student will have an understanding of marketing strategy and its effect on credit union managerial decisions.
  Instruction: Course covers the facts and principles of marketing. Topics include the marketing concept and structure; market information and buyer behavior; consumer and intermediate customers' buying behavior; product, packaging, and branding decisions; consumer and industrial goods; product planning and time-place utility; channels of distribution; promotion; pricing; strategy and integrating the market program; and controlling marketing programs and the cost-value to society. Methodology involves self-study utilizing a study guide, test-book, supplemental readings, and a review guide for examination preparation.
  Credit recommendation: In the lower division baccalaureate/associate degree category, 2 semester hours in Principles of Marketing (6/81) (7/86). NOTE: This course has been reevaluated and continues to meet requirements for credit recommendations.

Personnel Administration #300
(Formerly Office and Personnel Administration #3)
  Location: Independent study program.
  Length: 12 self-paced lessons.
  Dates: January 1975-Present.
  Objective: To provide knowledge of office administration principles and practices with specific application to credit unions.
  Learning Outcome: Upon successful completion of this course, the student will have an understanding of office and personnel administration emphasizing management's authority and responsibility in supervisory situations.
  Instruction: Course topics include systems and procedures, office layout, records management, information media, supervisory skills, staff development, salary administration, job evaluation, labor relations, performance appraisal and training methods, benefit programs, and management's responsibility and dealing with people. Methodology involves self-study utilizing a study guide, selected texts, and a review guide for examination preparation.
  Credit recommendation: In the lower division baccalaureate/associate degree category, 2 semester hours in Office and Administrative Management (6/81) (7/86). NOTE: This course has been reevaluated and continues to meet requirements for credit recommendations.

Risk Management and Insurance #500
(Formerly Risk Management and Insurance #5)
  Location: Independent study program.
  Length: 12 self-paced lessons. (Formerly 10 self-paced lessons.)
  Dates: *Version 1:* January 1975-June 1986; *Version 2:* July 1986-Present.
  Objective: To provide knowledge of concepts and principles of business insurance and risk management, and to provide experience in applying these concepts to credit unions.
  Learning Outcome: Upon successful completion of this course, the student will be able to understand the basic ideas, problems and principles found in various types of modern insurance and other methods of managing risks.
  Instruction: Course covers concepts and principles needed to produce and operate a program of risk measurement and control. Topics include the concept of risk; the risk management function; identification, measurement, and control of risk; important concepts of insurance; property and liability risk exposures and insurance; personal risk exposure and the uses of life and health insurance; the institution and selection of insurance organizations; risk management in credit unions; selection and application of noninsurance tools; and selection and application of various types of insurance. Methodology involves self-study utilizing a study guide, text, supplemental readings, a self-directed practicum, and a review guide for examination preparation.
  Credit recommendation: *Version 1:* In the upper division baccalaureate category, 2 semester hours in Business Insurance and Risk Management (6/81). *Version 2:* In the lower division baccalaureate/associate degree or in the upper division category, 2 semester hours in Business Insurance and Risk Management (7/86). NOTE: This course has been reevaluated and continues to meet requirements for credit recommendations.

Dale Carnegie & Associates, Inc.

Dale Carnegie Training® includes the development of effective communication and improved human relations, motivational selling skills, goal-oriented management, personnel development and improved customer relations. Courses are conducted by licensed sponsors and Institutes located throughout the United States and several foreign countries.

Instructors are selected mainly from the executive and managerial ranks. All instructors must complete a formal Instructor Training Conference conducted by a field Instructor Trainer of the Department of Instruction. Upon completion of the Training Conference, potential instructors work with an experienced instructor for one or two cycles of the course. All instructors are evaluated annually by the Department of Instruction.

Records of Dale Carnegie & Associates, Inc. are on file for the period 1959 to date. Local licenses and Institutes offering Dale Carnegie Courses® maintain their own records. Regular visits by staff members of Dale Carnegie & Associates, Inc., assure that facilities and record-keeping systems are adequate.

Source of official student records: Vice President, Department of Instruction, Dale Carnegie & Associates, Inc., 1475 Franklin Avenue, Garden City, New York 11530.

Additional information about the courses: Program on Noncollegiate Sponsored Instruction, The Center for Adult Learning and Educational Credentials, American Council on Education, One Dupont Circle, Washington, D.C. 20036.

Dale Carnegie Course

Location: Dale Carnegie & Associates, Inc., Garden City, NY and all other Dale Carnegie® locations worldwide.

Length: 14 weeks (3½ hours per week, 49 credit hours and 21 to 56 hours of outside preparation and activities required).

Dates: January 1980-Present.

Objective: To enhance the student's communications and interpersonal relations skills and to build student's self-confidence.

Learning Outcome: Upon successful completion of this course, the student will be able to function even more comfortably and effectively in a conference setting, work environment, or social arena where good interpersonal relations are essential; organize and express thoughts more clearly; and, understand the reasons behind the principles of effective public speaking and human relations skills.

Instruction: Major topics covered in the course are organization and presentation of ideas, goal setting, how to develop self-confidence. Personal involvement and participation are encouraged and reinforced through discussions, workshops, classroom exercises, simulations, and problem solving. Emphasis is on individual progress and is measured by the instructor's and student's regular evaluation of that progress.

Credit recommendation: In the lower division baccalaureate/associate degree category, 3 semester hours in Oral Communications or Public Speaking (4/83) (5/88). NOTE: This course has been reevaluated and continues to meet requirements for credit recommendations.

Dale Carnegie Management Seminar

Location: Dale Carnegie & Associates, Inc., Garden City, NY and all other Dale Carnegie® locations worldwide.

Length: 6 weeks, (3 hours per week for 18 contact hours and 9 hours of outside preparation required).

Dates: January 1981-Present.

Objective: To provide the student with a basic understanding of principles and skills of management.

Learning Outcome: Upon successful completion of this course, the student will be able to perform more effectively as a manager by being able to plan, organize, direct, coordinate, control management functions, and motivate and influence colleagues and subordinates more positively.

Instruction: Major topics covered in the course are planning, organizing for effective performance, directing coordinated activities; and controlling various parts of the organization. Lectures, discussions, workshops, and laboratories are designed to provide personal application throughout seminar sessions. The seminars are constructed to provide participants with a clear picture of an effective manager in action.

Credit recommendation: In the upper division baccalaureate category, 2 semester hours in Principles and Practice of Management (4/83) (5/88). NOTE: This course has been reevaluated and continues to meet requirements for credit recommendations.

Dale Carnegie Sales Course

Location: Dale Carnegie & Associates, Inc., Garden City, NY and all other Dale Carnegie® locations worldwide.

Length: 12 weeks (3½ hours per week, 42 contact hours and 18 hours of outside preparation and activities required).

Dates: January 1983-Present.

Objective: To strengthen students in generic principles and techniques of sales with emphasis on human relations in the selling process.

Learning Outcome: Upon successful completion of this course, the student will be able to plan a sales presentation; communicate more effectively with prospective buyers; and stimulate interest in prospective buyers.

Instruction: Major topics covered in the course are how to organize a sales presentation, influence prospective buyers, close the sale, and prospect for new purchasers. Discussions, workshops, and laboratory experience designed to emphasize participation in the classroom as well as the working environments. Written and oral reports required at each following session to provide student/instructor interaction and progress evaluation.

Credit recommendation: In the lower division baccalaureate/associate degree category, 3 semester hours in the Principles and Practice of Selling (4/83) (5/88). NOTE: This course has been reevaluated and continues to meet requirements for credit recommendations.

Dana Corporation

Dana Corporation, a multinational company with approximately 24,000 U.S. employees in sixty-four plants, manufactures and markets proprietary components and systems for the transmission and control of power in the vehicular and industrial markets.

To facilitate a promote-from-within policy, each division of the company sponsors local training, sends people to association or university sponsored workshops and seminars, and encourages the use of a tuition refund plan for undergraduate and postgraduate college courses. Personal growth also takes place through active job-rotation programs.

At the corporate level Dana University exists for management development education. Through nearly 100 one-week course offerings annually, Dana University reaches almost half of the company's 4,000 managers each year. Programs are conducted by a full-time central staff and are presented in Toledo, in Dana plant cities, and overseas.

Source of official student records: President, Dana University, Dana Corporation, P.O. Box 1000, Toledo, OH 43697.

Additional information about the courses: Program on Noncollegiate Sponsored Instruction, The Center for Adult Learning and Educational Credentials, American Council on Education, One Dupont Circle, Washington, D.C. 20036.

Asset Management
Location: Toledo, OH; various field locations.
Length: 48 hours (1 week).
Dates: April 1977-Present.
Objective: To provide students with an understanding of money management and the effect of decisions on the profit center in a manufacturing organization.
Instruction: Teams of students study the effects of routine factory cost decisions on the financial management of the organization. Discussion and team activities lead to the development of long-range objectives, which in turn contribute to an understanding of asset management in the manufacturing organization. Prerequisite: Cost Control for Profit Planning.
Credit recommendation: In the lower division baccalaureate/associate degree category, 3 semester hours in Management (4/77) (7/82). NOTE: This course has undergone a 5-year reevaluation and continues to meet requirements for credit recommendations.

Business Practices
Location: Toledo, OH; various field locations.
Length: 33 hours (1 week).
Dates: April 1977-June 1982.
Objective: To improve students' skills in written and oral communications and to provide them with an understanding of management relationships and practices.
Instruction: Case studies, written exercises, and films are used extensively along with some lectures in which theory is presented. Specific techniques are discussed for improving skills in preparing written communications, in listening, and in conducting meetings. These are brought together in group discussions, group dynamics exercises, and individual work on a "manager's in-basket" case.
Credit recommendation: In the lower division baccalaureate/associate degree category, 2 semester hours in Business Communications (4/77) (7/82). NOTE: This course has undergone a 5-year reevaluation and continues to meet requirements for credit recommendations.

Effective Speaking
(Alternative Title: Speech Workshop)
Location: Toledo, OH; various field locations.
Length: 40 hours (1 week).
Dates: April 1977-Present.
Objective: To develop skills in organizing and delivering oral presentations.
Instruction: Preparation, analysis, and presentation of impromptu, persuasive, and informative speeches. Methodology includes the use of video tape to critique performance and improve individual effectiveness.
Credit recommendation: In the lower division baccalaureate/associate degree category, 3 semester hours in Speech (4/77) (7/82). NOTE: This course has undergone a 5-year reevaluation and continues to meet requirements for credit recommendations.

Fundamentals of Supervision III
Location: Toledo, OH; various field locations.
Length: 36 hours (1 week).
Dates: April 1977-July 1981.
Objective: To provide first-line supervisors with an understanding of (1) the effects of costs on the financial performance of a manufacturing organization and (2) labor-management relations and grievance procedures.
Instruction: Cost decision making theory is examined in the context of burden studies, machine utilization, schedules, inventory costing, and investment concerns. Labor relations theory is reviewed with role playing of labor-management negotiations as they relate to grievance procedures and the arbitration process.
Credit recommendation: In the lower division baccalaureate/associate degree category, 1 semester hour in Management and 1 semester hour in Labor-Management Relations (4/77) (7/82). NOTE: This course has undergone a 5-year reevaluation and continues to meet requirements for credit recommendations.

Intermediate Management
Location: Toledo, OH; various field locations.
Length: 50 hours (1 week).

Dates: April 1977–July 1983.

Objective: To develop the student's skills in the use of management by objectives.

Instruction: Application of management by objectives in a supervisor-subordinate situation, including specific applications, skill building, and critique. The methodology involves a case study analysis, using a team approach and applying management by objectives to a plant situation. An in-basket exercise is used in which participants are given the opportunity to establish and implement a system of management by objectives.

Credit recommendation: In the lower division baccalaureate/associate degree category, 3 semester hours in Management (4/77) (7/82). NOTE: This course has undergone a 5-year reevaluation and continues to meet requirements for credit recommendations.

Managerial Styles Seminar

Location: Toledo, OH; various field locations.

Length: *Version 1:* 50 hours (1 week); 30 hours of preparatory independent study; *Version 2:* 60 hours (1*/2 weeks); 30 hours of preparatory independent study.

Dates: April 1977–Present.

Objective: To develop students' skills in identifying and assessing managerial behavior so that they might gain insight into their own managerial styles and the effects of different styles on team action.

Instruction: Working in teams, the students engage in exercises designed to identify managerial styles and to determine their impact on others. A laboratory approach is used and includes discussion periods, case studies, and a feature-length movie.

Credit recommendation: In the lower division baccalaureate/associate degree category, 3 semester hours in Management (4/77) (7/82). This course has undergone a 5-year reevaluation and continues to meet requirements for credit recommendation.

Manufacturing Costs and Controls
(Alternative Title: Cost Control for Profit Planning)

Location: Toledo, OH; various field locations.

Length: 48 hours (1 week).

Dates: April 1977–Present.

Objective: To develop the students' skills in analyzing cost factors, including manpower, materials, and machines.

Instruction: Covers a standard cost system, direct and indirect material and labor costs, fixed and variable expense, and burden absorption. Methodology includes participant involvement in a series of management simulation exercises related to the cost and profit consequences of such factors as volume change, purchased material cost change, and product mix change.

Credit recommendation: In the lower division baccalaureate/associate degree category, 3 semester hours in Management (4/77) (7/82). NOTE: This course has undergone a 5-year reevaluation and continues to meet requirements for credit recommendation.

Principles of Organizational Behavior
(Alternative Title: Fundamentals of Supervision II)

Location: Toledo, OH; various field locations.

Length: 35 hours (1 week).

Dates: April 1977–Present.

Objective: To improve the first-line supervisor's understanding of the principles of organizational behavior.

Instruction: Motivational theories of Maslow and McGregor and the managerial grid as they apply to manufacturing organizations; the effect of different decision making and managerial styles on human relations. Methods include case studies, lectures, discussion, and role playing.

Credit recommendation: In the lower division baccalaureate/associate degree category, 2 semester hours in Management (4/77) (7/82). NOTE: This course has undergone a 5-year reevaluation and continues to meet requirements for credit recommendations.

Problem Solving and Decision Making

Location: Toledo, OH; various field locations.

Length: 44 hours (1 week).

Dates: April 1977–Present.

Objective: To develop the students' skills in applying appropriate management principles to problem analysis and decision making.

Instruction: Working in simulated management teams, students participate in case studies and exercises in the area of situation analysis, problem analysis, and decision making. Applications are made to writing performance standards, selecting new hires, preparing development plans, evaluating communication, and improving meeting effectiveness.

Credit recommendation: In the lower division baccalaureate/associate degree category, 3 semester hours in Management (4/77) (7/82). NOTE: This course has undergone a 5-year reevaluation and continues to meet requirements for credit recommendations.

Sales Development

Location: Toledo, OH; various field locations.

Length: 40 hours (1 week).

Dates: April 1977–Present.

Objective: To provide students with knowledge of the sales organization and the sales functions of the organization, and to develop the sales skills of individual student participants.

Instruction: Lectures and discussion cover the salesman's responsibilities and the marketing function of the organization as they relate to the individual salesman. Market forecasting, product liability, and persuasive sales techniques are included. Role playing and video tape techniques are also used.

Credit recommendation: In the lower division baccalaureate/associate degree category, 3 semester hours in Sales Management (4/77) (7/82). NOTE: This course has undergone a 5-year reevaluation and continues to meet requirements for credit recommendations.

Supervisory Management
(Alternative Title: Fundamentals of Supervision I)
   Location: Toledo, OH; various field locations.
   Length: 34½ hours (1 week).
   Dates: April 1977-Present.
   Objective: To improve the supervisory skill and knowledge of new and experienced first-time supervisors.
   Instruction: The theory and practical application of management and human relations principles to labor relations, grievance, and arbitration procedures. lecture, case studies, and discussion are used.
   Credit recommendation: In the lower division baccalaureate/associate degree category, 2 semester hours in Management (4/77) (7/82). NOTE: This course has undergone a 5-year reevaluation and continues to meet requirements for credit recommendations.

Data Processing Training, Inc.

Data Processing Training, Inc., located in Indiana, is a provider of industrial and corporate computer training. Instructors possess a bachelor's degree or higher, and/or extensive experience in the computer field, prior experience in training adults or professionals in the application of computers, prior training in data processing technology. Instructors are evaluated by means of unannounced reviews, by review of student evaluation forms, and when applicable, by review of director or contact personnel evaluation forms.

Courses, materials, and visual aids are constantly reviewed. Instructors, lab assistants, and students may also submit ideas and/or comments concerning the classroom and materials. Students have the opportunity to enhance skills and make up sessions during "open lab." Students master course content by performing hands-on tasks and exercises on individual computer workstations. Certification of completion of a course is based upon demonstratable evidence that the student has mastered the course content. Students who have not successfully mastered course content are tutored until the course content has been mastered. Student records are recorded via computer database, which tracks and records the attendance of each student. These records are printed and filed at the end of the course session.

   Source of official student records: Data Processing Training, Inc., R.R. #4, Box 314, Peru, Indiana 46970, ATTN: Transcripts.

   Additional information about the courses: Program on Noncollegiate Sponsored Instruction, The Center for Adult Learning and Educational Credentials, American Council on Education, One Dupont Circle, Washington, D.C. 20036.

Computer Literacy (DP 101)
(Data Processing Awareness)
   Location: Kokomo, IN.
   Length: 30 hours (5 weeks).
   Dates: August 1988-Present.
   Objective: To introduce the student to the capabilities and limitations of microcomputer hardware and software and to familiarize the student with computer technology.
   Learning Outcome: Upon successful completion of this course, the student will be able to operate microcomputer hardware and write introductory applications using spreadsheet, database, and word processing software.
   Instruction: Course covers the history of computers, word processing, database management, spreadsheet and graphing, and operating system and programming languages. Methodology includes lecture, hands-on training, and laboratory work.
   Credit recommendation: In the lower division baccalaureate/associate degree category, 2 semester hours in Computer Applications or Microcomputer Applications (3/89).

Introduction to Microcomputer Applications (DP 102)
(Advanced Data Processing Awareness)
   Location: Kokomo, IN.
   Length: 30 hours (5 weeks).
   Dates: August 1988-Present.
   Objective: To provide the student with proficiency in the use of microcomputer operating systems, software packages, and their integration.
   Learning Outcome: Upon successful completion of this course, the student will be able to use operating system commands and its file system; write integrated applications using spreadsheet, database, and word processing software; and recognize programming language statements.
   Instruction: Course covers microcomputer operating system commands and file system, word processing, database management, and spreadsheets and graphing. Methodology includes lecture, hands-on training, and laboratory (independent) work.
   Credit recommendation: In the lower division baccalaureate/associate degree category, 2 semester hours in Microcomputer Applications (3/89).

Introduction to Spreadsheet Applications (DP 201)
(Spreadsheet Data Processing Course)
   Location: Kokomo, IN.
   Length: 30 hours (5 weeks).
   Dates: August 1988-Present.

Objective: To provide the student with the skills to efficiently develop spreadsheet applications.

Learning Outcome: Upon successful completion of this course, the student will be able to develop spreadsheet applications; and develop applications which integrate spreadsheet, graphing, database, and automated keystroke features.

Instruction: Course covers the Lotus 1-2-3 environment, worksheet design, graphing, database operation, and keystroke automation. Methodology includes lecture, hands-on training, and laboratory (individual) work.

Credit recommendation: In the lower division baccalaureate/associate degree category, 2 semester hours in Computer Applications, Data Processing, or Microcomputer Applications (3/89).

David C.D. Rogers Associates

Rogers Associates prides itself on having top quality presentations with up-to-date materials. Founded by Dr. David C.D. Rogers, the company develops courses for particular industries (automobile, telecommunications, financial services) for very specific client needs. Case material is selected from that publicly available; cases are chosen to mirror situations and problems faced by the client. When outside cases and technical notes are not available, experienced case writers are hired to write them.

The training components of Rogers Associates consists of five full-time people, three of whom participate in the managing and teaching of the programs. In addition, there are four to six subcontractors who are professors at Harvard, Stanford, and Wharton. Outside technical specialists (from the venture capital industry) deliver a one-hour lecture in one course. Instructors are selected on a "word of mouth" reputation basis, after careful checking with many references (other professors, deans, corporate training directors, Rogers Associates alumni, etc.). Dr. Rogers monitors the first two trial, day-long sessions of each new instructor to ensure the presentation is dynamic and intellectually challenging. Subsequent sessions are monitored periodically without prior notice by a staff member. In addition, students are asked for verbal and written feedback on each instructor, and the staff holds frequent meetings to discuss course content, changes, and ensure program continuity. Course content is continually compared with that offered by other institutions and updated to keep pace with the rapidly changing telecommunications industry.

Student records are maintained on computer disks, with each student's name, address, and course completion date. The records are updated weekly. Interactive case classes have many advantages, significantly the fact that the depth of participant understanding and knowledge is very visible. It is clear to the instructor and other students who is understanding the subject matter and who is lost. Each program has several group presentations, much individual case discussion, and sufficient in-class problems to ensure that only those who have mastered the course will receive certification. Students who do not master the course are encouraged to repeat the program.

Source of official student records: Administrative Assistant, David D.C. Rogers Associates, 260 Boston Post Road, Suite 1, P.O. Box 438, Wayland, Massachusetts 01778.

Additional information about the courses: Program on Nocollegiate Sponsored Instruction, The Center for Adult Learning and Educational Credentials, American Council on Education, One Dupont Circle, Washington, D.C. 20036.

Advanced Competitive Strategic Analysis (ACSA)

Location: David C.D. Rogers Associates, Wayland, MA.

Length: 43½ hours (1 week).

Dates: January 1988-Present.

Objective: To teach the student the parameters of the information systems industry, the role of telecommunications, the strategic position of the key players and how to do competitive analysis and strategic planning in the rapidly evolving hi-tech environment.

Learning Outcome: Upon successful completion of this course, the student will be able to diagnose the strategies and the competitive advantage of a wide range of firms (from emerging entrants to market leaders); interpret the financial implications of alternate capital formation; utilize scenario planning (in lieu of single-point forecasts), and understand the key technologies in telecommunications.

Instruction: Course covers competitive analysis and strategic planning in the rapidly evolving telecommunications industry. The entire information systems industry will be mapped and the strategies of key players and new entrants dissected. Cases and videotapes of the executives involved permit in-depth analysis of strategy, technology, and competitive position. In addition, the techniques of scenario planning, capital formation, and strategy implementation will be detailed. Methodology includes extensive case studies, presentations, in-class problems, and group preparation sessions.

Credit recommendation: In the upper division baccalaureate category, 3 semester hours in Marketing, or in the graduate degree category, 3 semester hours as a Marketing elective (1/88).

Advanced Marketing Strategies (AMS)

Location: David C.D. Rogers Associates, Wayland, MA.

Length: 43½ hours (1 week).

Dates: January 1988-Present.

Objective: To teach the student those areas of marketing most elusive to telecommunications managers: positioning products in deregulated global markets, managing third party distribution channels, and implementing marketing strategy in hostile environments.

Learning Outcome: Upon successful completion of this course, the student will be able to analyze complex global marketing situations; evaluate objectively the positioning of products/services and choice of channels; and determine how to attract and retain key customers in the face of competitors with seeming competitive advantage.

Instruction: Course covers building on an understanding of basic marketing tools and strategies, focusing on four key areas telecommunications managers find most challenging: product positioning and market segmentation with global competition; strategic realignments against newly deregulated competitors; the selection, nurturing, and protection of third party distribution channels; and implementing marketing strategy, particularly through a direct salesforce. New interactive cases, lecture-discussions, and videotapes of the managers involved show how a major consumer marketer positions itself in global markets and "goes to war," and then how another major company's large salesforce attacks industrial consumers; details of the deregulation of the cable T.V. industry show how regional firms can combine sophisticated market intelligence with a salesforce to capture potential BOC markets; distribution channels management in the information systems industry with filmed examples; sophisticated market research techniques, forecasting and computer modeling; and an in-depth look at consortium marketing with EDS and the difference between marketing products and services are discussed. Methodology includes extensive case discussions, presentations, in-class problems, and group preparation sessions.

Credit recommendation: In the graduate degree category, 3 semester hours in Marketing Strategies or as a Marketing elective (1/88).

Competition in Telecommunications (CIT)

Location: David C.D. Rogers Associates, Wayland, MA.
Length: 20½ hours (2½ days).
Dates: January 1988-Present.
Objective: To teach the student the parameters of the information systems industry, the role of telecommunications, the strategic position of key players and the concepts of competitive analysis.
Learning Outcome: Upon successful completion of this course, the student will be able to diagnose the competitive advantage of a wide range of firms, analyze their strategies, and quantify the impact of alternate strategic decisions.
Instruction: Course introduces the concepts of competitive analysis in the rapidly evolving telecommunications industry, which will be mapped and the key players dissected. The complex issues of access charges will be analyzed in depth as will the evolution of a key competitor. Methodology includes extensive case discussions, presentations, in-class problems, and group preparation sessions.

Credit recommendation: In the upper division baccalaureate category, 1 semester hour in Economics or as a Business elective, or in the graduate degree category, 1 semester hour in a specialized curriculum such as Telecommunications (1/88).

Concepts of Corporate Planning (CCP)

Location: David C.D. Rogers Associates, Wayland, MA.
Length: 43½ hours (1 week).
Dates: January 1988-Present.
Objective: To teach the student the evolving concept of strategy and how leading firms make strategic decisions.
Learning Outcome: Upon successful completion of this course, the student will be able to differentiate clearly between strategic and operational decisions, understand how the tools and techniques of strategic planning have evolved since the 1950s, recognize why large corporations are planning innovators, and improve one's skills at strategic planning and the quantification of alternatives.
Instruction: Course covers the concept of strategy, its evolution during the 1950s, 1960s, 1970s, and 1980s, the quantification of strategic options and how the premier players practice strategic planning. Extensive use is made of in-depth case studies with 15 videotapes of the actual executives involved. Strategic planning in deregulating industries (financial services and airlines) and strategy implementation is discussed. Methodology includes extensive case discussions, presentations, in-class problems, and group preparation sessions.

Credit recommendation: In the upper division baccalaureate or graduate degree category, 3 semester hours in Corporate Planning or as a Business elective (1/88).

Finance and Accounting for Managers (FAM)

Location: David C.D. Rogers Associates, Wayland, MA.
Length: 30 hours (3 days).
Dates: January 1988-Present.
Objective: To teach nonfinancial managers what they need to know about both external and internal financial statements and sufficient background to discover useful information from competitors' public statements.
Learning Outcome: Upon successful completion of this course, the student will be able to dissect external statements and analyze the future differential revenues and costs of any decision.
Instruction: Course covers in depth the concepts and tools financial people use to construct and analyze balance sheets, income statements, and statements of changes in financial position (funds flow or cash flow) in addition to a working knowledge of what the "Notes to Financial

Statements" usually contain and what to deduce from them. Also covered are methods of relevant cost analysis (product versus period cost, variable versus fixed, incremental versus full, and opportunity versus historical); the uses of contribution analysis; the breakeven chart; variable budgeting and variance analysis; return on investment both for capital projects and performance evaluation; and the strategic implications of high fixed cost versus high variable cost structures. Methodology includes extensive case discussions, presentations, in-class problems, and group preparation sessions.

Credit recommendation: In the upper division baccalaureate category, 1 semester hour in Accounting, Finance, or General Business Administration (1/88).

Finance and Accounting in the Competitive Environment
(Formerly Practicing Competitive Analysis)

Location: David C.D. Rogers Associates, Wayland, MA.
Length: 43½ hours (1 week).
Dates: January 1984-Present.
Objective: To teach the student the concepts, techniques, and tools of effective and efficient *quantified* competitive analysis.
Learning Outcome: Upon successful completion of this course, the student will be able to delineate the five competitive forces on an industry segment, evaluate the strategic position of each firm, calculate the cost structure and financial strength of any competitor, and know how to legally obtain and manipulate information.
Instruction: Course covers the entire breadth of competitive analysis from conceptual framework to how industrial warfare is actually waged, to where to find information and massage it effectively. Assuming most participants will be unfamiliar or uncomfortable with accounting, most class sessions are devoted to (a) financial analysis (analyzing and projecting balance sheets, income statements and cash flows) and (b) relevant costs (product vs. period, variable vs. fixed, incremental vs. full and opportunity vs. historical) for understanding and anticipating competitors' discussions. How to use numbers derived from external—and usually public—sources is stressed. Methodology includes extensive case discussions, presentations, in-class problems, and group preparation sessions.
Credit recommendation: In the upper division baccalaureate category, 3 semester hours in Competitive Marketing Analysis, or in the graduate degree category, 3 semester hours as a Marketing elective (1/88).

Marketing Tools and Strategies (MKTS)

Location: David C.D. Rogers Associates, Wayland, MA.
Length: 43½ hours (1 week).
Dates: January 1988-Present.
Objective: To teach the student the latest marketing tools and techniques emphasizing product positioning, competitive pricing, and the role of the product-market manager.
Learning Outcome: Upon successful completion of this course, the student will be able to diagnose marketing situations, analyze customer needs, quantify the value of product/services to market segments, understand the role of product/market managers and apply marketing tools, concepts, and models.
Instruction: Course covers the latest tools and techniques for effective and efficient marketing. Interactive cases and lectures demonstrate how top market/product/LOB managers in matrix organizations ply their trade so successfully and how the leading marketers use price to introduce products, promote high tech services, milk so-called "cash cows" properly, and reposition products and services into target market segments. New materials will show the day-to-day short- and long-term pressures on product managers, in-depth detail of how pricing decisions should be made, spell out the methodology of quantifying advertising and promotion decisions, and explore the relationships between marketing and sales force management. Technical areas such as computer modeling, marketing research and numbers for marketing decision making will be covered as well as a detailed explanation of what should be in an effective marketing or LOB plan.
Credit recommendation: In the upper division baccalaureate category, 3 semester hours in Strategic Market Analysis, or in the graduate degree category, 3 semester hours as a Marketing elective (1/88).

Defense Mapping Agency - Inter American Geodetic Survey Cartographic School

The Defense Mapping Agency-Inter American Geodetic Survey Cartographic School was established in 1952 in order to transfer technology to Latin America by offering training in specialized skills required in the fields of geodesy, photogrammetry, and cartography. This training (in the Spanish language generally and in English with simultaneous interpretation when required) serves to assist national cartographic agencies to develop personnel, conform to standard norms of accuracy and precision, and become self-sustaining and interacting in the exchange of data and ideas between Latin American agencies and DMA-IAGS. The training is provided primarily at the DMA-IAGS Cartographic School in Fort Clayton, Panama; however, special courses/training is also presented in the host country upon special request. Over 5,500 students have received training through the school since 1952.

Source of official student records: Director, Defense Mapping Agency-Inter American Geodetic Survey Cartographic School, Drawer 936, APO, Miami 34004.

Additional information about the courses: Program on Noncollegiate Sponsored Instruction, The Center for Adult Learning and Educational Credentials, American Council on Education, One Dupont Circle, Washington, D.C. 20036.

Aeronautical Cartography (C-205)

Location: DMA-IAGS Cartographic School, Fort Clayton, Panama.

Length: 160 contact hours (4 weeks; 8 hours per day; 40 hours per week).

Dates: May 1982-Present.

Objective: To train aeronautical charting specialists in the methods needed to produce ICAO and PAIGH-approved specification charts as applied to in the production of Latin American aeronautical charts. Skills in data research handling and manipulation relating to chart specifications are emphasized.

Instruction: Covers the science of producing an aeronautical chart using conventional cartography technology; basic projections, specialized math computations of arc distance and maximum elevation, source map reduction or enlargement, detail selection concepts, and an intensive study of specifications and chart format. Exercises include using projector and photographic techniques of data scaling. Students are also required to perform rigorous detail selection and elimination decisions. Finally, students are closely monitored and exercises in the selection of maximum elevation computations which can constitute the greatest hazard to flying. Upon successful completion of the course, the student should be able to satisfy all national aeronautical charting agency requirements and operations while working under initial general supervision.

Credit recommendation: In the lower division baccalaureate/associate degree category, 2 semester hours in Map Reading and Interpretation, Introduction to Cartography, or Map Drafting (4/84).

Advanced Photogrammetry
Modern Photogrammetry (P-401)

Location: DMA-IAGS Cartographic School, Fort Clayton, Panama.

Length: 6 weeks (240 hours).

Dates: April 1984-Present.

Objective: To provide students with training in the latest advances in photogrammetry; to illustrate the latest procedures used with modern photogrammetric techniques.

Instruction: Covers photogrammetric mathematics; imaging systems and aerial cameras; photogrammetric project planning; rectification and space resection; analytical aerotriangulation; automated systems and products; special applications; satellite photogrammetry; and photo interpretation. Prerequisite: wide knowledge and experience in photogrammetry as a technical manager. 12 hours lecture, 6 hours discussion, and 22 hours of laboratory per week.

Credit recommendation: In the upper division baccalaureate or graduate degree category, 4 semester hours in Photogrammetry and Surveying (4/84).

Automated Cartography (C-302)

Location: DMA-IAGS Cartographic School, Fort Clayton, Panama.

Length: 400 contact hours (10 weeks; 8 hours per day; 5 days per week).

Dates: March 1983-Present.

Objective: To provide the training necessary for the student to perform a wide variety of computer mapping assignments including the application of theoretical principles necessary to replicate standard analog maps and charts in digital format, using necessary hands-on training.

Instruction: This course examines glossaries of terms used in digital cartography with emphasis on those terms pertaining to the PDP-11 series computers which is the interactive graphics system used at the Cartographic School. There is some discussion of types of equipment that make up each of the subsystems in a basic computer cartographic system with some description of the function and specification of each device. A basic understanding of the software specifications needed for various mapping requirements is provided, including the speed and frequency of data access, coordinate transformations, editing, symbolization, and line encoding. An examination is made of the type of equipment best suited to individual program mapping needs. Methods of data organization and line storage are analyzed. Each student receives hands-on training with the interactive graphics system. This includes gathering source materials and preparing them for CAGS digitizing, data entry, display commands, edit commands, and plot commands. Training with various CAGS utility programs is provided. There is instruction in cartographic basic plotting software. A simple plot programming exercise is completed by each student.

Credit recommendation: In the upper division baccalaureate category, 5 semester hours in Automated or Advanced Cartography, Computer Science, Photogrammetry, Geography, and Civil Engineering (4/84).

Automated Cartography-Digitizing System Operator (C-103)
(Formerly Map Digitizing Technology)
(Map Digitizer Operator [C-103])

Location: DMA-IAGS Cartographic School, Fort Clayton, Panama.

Length: 160 hours (4 weeks); 15 hours per week of lecture, 25 hours per week of practice, laboratory, problems, examinations.

Dates: April 1983-Present.

Objective: To train cartographic technicians to operate

an interactive graphic system work station to digitize standard large-scale topographic map products.

Instruction: Map digitizing with an interactive graphics system. Replication of standard topographic maps by means of the digital process. Line digitizing, stream digitizing, names placement, automated grid generation, data storage and retrieval. Practice in all aspects of map digitizing.

Credit recommendation: In the lower division baccalaureate/associate degree category, 2 semester hours in Surveying Technology, Cartographic Technology, or Engineering Technology or Computer Science (4/84).

Basic Photographic Sciences (C-111)
Location: DMA-IAGS Cartographic School, Fort Clayton, Panama.
Length: 400 hours (10 weeks); 10 hours preparation per week.
Dates: April 1984-Present.
Objective: To familiarize students with basic photographic sciences as a technique applied in laboratory practice; photo processes including factors which affect photo image, quality, contrast, distortion, and background information on types of film, their densities and qualities; and tone printing and use of photomechanical process camera and other photo work for use in photomosaicking and mapping products.
Instruction: Photographic process; factors affecting photo images (basic optics applied to photograph); photo lab equipment and materials orientation; types of films and their photographic qualities; photo processing techniques and procedures (basic photochemistry); photomechanical graphic arts products (line and halftone products); quality control techniques and procedures (basic densitometry); equipment maintenance and lab housekeeping.
Credit recommendation: In the lower division baccalaureate/associate degree category, 5 semester hours in Cartography, Photogrammetry, or Photographic Sciences (4/84).

Cartographic Data Base Concepts (C-305)
Location: DMA-IAGS Cartographic School, Fort Clayton, Panama.
Length: 120 contact hours (3 weeks; 8 hours per day; 40 hours per week).
Dates: November 1984-Present.
Objective: The major goal is to provide advanced training with different data base concepts with the specific goal of fostering standardized cartographic data bases for Latin American countries. The express purpose is to stimulate and enhance exchange programs and standardize map symbology, type styles, and formats.
Instruction: The course assumes considerable background and training in cartography among persons who might be working in a Latin American country at national mapping agency. The course provides the data base manager and systems personnel with background and understanding for the implementation of cartographic data base schemas. There is a focus on planning, implementation, and production requirements essential to the design and installation of a functional cartographic data base.
Credit recommendation: In the lower division baccalaureate/associate degree category, 2 semester hours in Map Reading and Interpretation, Management, or Systems Analysis (4/84).

Cartographic Management
Cartographic Production Supervisor (C-303)
Location: DMA-IAGS Cartographic School, Fort Clayton, Panama.
Length: 120 contact hours (3 weeks; 8 hours per day at 40 hours per week).
Dates: November 1979-Present.
Objective: To provide training to supervisors and potential supervisors at the production level in cartography and geodesy institutions in the modern concepts of supervision.
Instruction: The goal of this course is to provide training in the supervision and management aspects of production cartography, geodesy, or field surveys. There is a concern on planning for work flow and cost estimates, especially as these might relate to the interface with photogrammetry, photographic laboratories and editing requirements. Emphasis is on proper scheduling, planning and the appropriate utilization of human resources and production equipment. Methods of time estimation, record keeping, work assignment, equipment and material requisitioning, priority establishment and other general office practices are covered in the course. There is an effort made at dealing with the improvement of the working environment and from this developing an increased productivity. The final goal is to allow the course participants to improve existing responsibilities or assume new supervisory responsibilities within a product unit.
Credit recommendation: In the lower division baccalaureate/associate degree category, 2 semester hours in Business Administration, Management, Public Administration, or Personnel Supervision (4/84). NOTE: Students who receive credit for this course should not receive credit for F-306 or P-303. Credit can be changed in subject area after field experience (for all three).

Cartographic Techniques for Space Imagery (C-307)
Location: DMA-IAGS Cartographic School, Fort Clayton, Panama.
Length: 320 contact hours (8 weeks; 8 hours per day; 40 hours per week).
Dates: April 1984-Present.
Objective: To familiarize students with the special cartographic applications of space imagery.
Instruction: Covers the general principles of remote

sensing and its physical base. Detailed studies are made on the cartographic applications of Landsat, and the large format camera on-board the space shuttle. Students are taught about map projections and grid formats commonly used for sensor data adjustments. The students prepare semicontrolled photomosaics by conventional techniques including color photomosaicking. This practical experience includes map and chart production including data compilation, color separation, and printing using modern color proof systems. The final goal is to provide training that enables the student to use space imagery to prepare a map.

Credit recommendation: In the lower division baccalaureate/associate degree category, 2 semester hours in Map Reading and Interpretation, Introduction to Cartography, or Introduction to Remote Sensing; and in the upper division baccalaureate category, 2 semester hours in Cartography, Photography, or Photo-Laboratory Color Processing. (4/84).

Cartographic Techniques for Thematic Mapping (C-304)

Location: DMA-IAGS Cartographic School, Fort Clayton, Panama.

Length: 320 contact hours (8 weeks; 8 hours per day; 40 hours per week).

Dates: March 1981-Present.

Objective: To train students, with some background in cartography, in the design, compilation, and reproduction of thematic map products.

Instruction: The student is given training in how to handle thematic (statistical) data in order to convert it to graphical formats. Discussion focuses on nominal, ordinal, and interval-ratio concepts of data handling as reduced to point, line, and area symbology in graphical displays, especially in map formats. The student develops a practical working knowledge in the design, construction, and reproduction of thematic maps. More than one quarter of the course is concerned with photolithographic processes, process color printing, and color proofing. There is some application of satellite imagery for natural resource mapping as well as quality control and editing techniques.

Credit recommendation: In the upper division baccalaureate category, 4 semester hours in Map Reading and Interpretation, Cartography, Color Printing, or Photographic Sciences (4/84).

Cartography (201)
(Formerly Map Reading Interpretation and Introductory Cartography)

Location: DMA-IAGS Cartographic School, Fort Clayton, Panama.

Length: 400 hours (10 weeks).

Dates: September 1979-Present.

Objective: To present general theory of projections and grid systems, principles of map sheet format and design, and cartographic compilation techniques and procedures for medium- and small-scale maps.

Instruction: Emphasizes topographic mapping with some attention given to thematic mapping; photolab processing for cartography and map sheet design; color separation; working with various types of cartographic equipment. Training helps students develop cartographic skills and techniques; for example, design and color separation of large-scale city maps, large-, medium-, and small-scale topographic maps, and color-enhanced photo maps. A student who completes this course should be able to design, execute, and reproduce a professional looking map under general supervision.

Credit recommendation: In the lower division baccalaureate/associate degree category, 3 semester hours in Map Reading and Interpretation; and in the upper division baccalaureate category, 3 semester hours in Introductory Cartography, for a total of 6 hours (4/80).

Color Separation Technician (C-101)

Location: DMA-IAGS Cartographic School, Fort Clayton, Panama.

Length: 320 hours (8 weeks); 6 hours per week of lecture, 31½ hours per week of laboratory, and 2½ hours per week for contingencies.

Dates: April 1984-Present.

Objective: (1) To train students to the level of performance as cartographic technicians in the color separation of standard large scale products. (2) To familiarize students with standard operating procedures, specifications, and work methods for a complete range of the color separation process.

Instruction: The course is designed for the entrance level technician in the Latin American national mapping agencies. The training is given in techniques and procedures of color separation by means of plastic scribing. The student is required to prepare a color separation map, type overlays, and process color proofs. Training includes type placement, use of cuts, selection and application of screens and patterns. Use and care of equipment is emphasized. Upon successful completion of the course the student should be capable of filling the position of cartographic technician in national mapping agency, performing color separation scribing under general supervision. The skills learned are applicable to the production of map products which meet National Cartographic Standards.

Credit recommendation: In the lower division baccalaureate/associate degree category, 3 semester hours in Surveying Technology, Cartographic Technology, or Engineering Technology (4/84).

Control Surveys
Field Surveys (F-201)

Location: DMA-IAGS Cartographic School, Fort Clayton, Panama.

Length: 400 hours (10 weeks).

Dates: April 1980-Present.

Objective: To prepare students who already possess basic surveying skills for more advanced and specialized aspects of surveying such as photogrammetric control surveys and geodetic operations, including preliminary computations.

Instruction: Introduction to basic principles of surveying theory, aerial photography, and maps; strength of figure; spherical excess, triangulation; preliminary quadrilateral adjustment and side checks; geographic and Universal Transverse Mercator computations; electronic traversing, differential leveling, picture point surveys.

Credit recommendation: In the upper division baccalaureate category, 6 semester hours in Cartography, Civil Engineering, Civil Engineering Technology, Geodetic Science, Photogrammetry, Surveying, or Surveying Technology (4/80).

Digital Methods of Terrain Modeling
(Digital Terrain Modeling [P-307])

Location: DMA-IAGS Cartographic School, Fort Clayton, Panama.

Length: 120 hours (3 weeks).

Dates: April 1984-Present

Objective: To provide students with a knowledge of the techniques and procedures in generation, storage, editing, and retrieval of digital terrain models (DTM) and their application in various mapping, charting, and geodetic problems.

Instruction: Covers types of data used and criteria for data selection; the collection process and file generation; model linkage, and the editing process. Analytic plotters, orthophoto systems and other stereodigitizing systems are studied. Overall instruction provides the photogrammetrist with the skills of DTM generation and applications. Prerequisite: Student needs knowledge of algebra and trigonometry, experience in stereocompilation and a course in or experience in FORTRAN programming; Course P-201 or equivalent experience.

Credit recommendation: In the upper division baccalaureate category, 2 semester hours in Cartography, Earth Sciences, Photogrammetry, Surveying, or Computer Science (4/84).

Fundamentals of Remote Sensing
(Independent study program - comparable to P-311 - Introduction to Remote Sensing)

Location: DMA-IAGS Cartographic School, Fort Clayton, Panama, or anywhere the equipment is available to project the visual tapes and audio explanations.

Length: *Variable,* depending on the individual student. The tapes can be reviewed a number of times until the material they contain is fully understood. (At least 19 hours to review all the tapes.) 19 lessons.

Dates: March 1981-Present.

Objective: The objectives of this self-paced course are similar to the classroom type course P-311 listed in this section of the *National Guide.* The modules selected present a systematic overview of the field of remote sensing in logical step-by-step manner that, to some extent, build on the previous lessons. The goal is to give the student a fundamental overview of remote sensing.

Instruction: Introduces students to remote sensing, discusses the electromagnetic spectrum, photographic and electronic processes of acquiring remote sensing data. Multispectral data manipulation is considered. There are units on radar, thermal infrared, reflected infrared, and the use of the computer to deal with digital data. Attention is given to the temporal aspects of remote sensing data and how it changes with time. This independent study, or self-paced, course is designed around the Purdue University series of modules on remote sensing. The modules have been modified and supplemented in some cases where appropriate.

Credit recommendation: In the lower division baccalaureate/associate degree category, 2 semester hours in Remote Sensing of the Environment (4/84). NOTE 1: This course might be offered in Geography, Geological Sciences, Forestry, Agriculture, or Engineering Sciences. To some extent it would depend on the individual university and where, or in what discipline, a course in remote sensing is offered. NOTE 2: Because this is a self-paced course with no interaction with an instructor or other students, and no practical field experience with remote sensing imagery, it cannot be given the same upper division credit as DMA-IAGS course P-311, Introduction to Remote Sensing.

Geodesy (Geodmetric, Physical, Satellite) (F-401)

Location: DMA-IAGS Cartographic School, Fort Clayton, Panama.

Length: 340 hours (6 weeks); 20 hours per week lecture; 20 hours per week computer laboratories, problems, examinations.

Dates: January 1981-Present.

Objective: To update professional geodesists and the managers of technical projects with the latest technology available in theoretical and applied geodesy. The graduate will be aware of the new geodetic positioning systems and their applicability to this job.

Instruction: Covers mathematical properties of the ellipsoid, geodesics, and the solution of spherical and ellipsoidal triangles; geodetic datums; elements of least squares theory; direct and inverse problems in geodesy; Laplace Azimuths, deflection of the vertical, and datum transformations; introduction to theory of the potential of gravitation; normal gravity, gravity measurements, and gravity anomalies; the geoid and height systems; astro-geodetic and astro-gravimetric procedures; space geodesy, including orbital mechanics and perturbation theory; visual, photographic, and electronic observations of satellites; and ionospheric and tropospheric refraction.

Credit recommendation: In the upper division baccalaureate or graduate degree category, 4 semester hours in Geodetic Science, Surveying, or Surveying Science (4/84).

Geodetic Computations (F-203)

Location: DMA-IAGS Cartographic School, Fort Clayton, Panama.

Length: *Version 1:* 240 hours (6 weeks). *Version 2:* 280 hours (7 weeks).

Dates: July 1980-Present.

Objective: To prepare students for checking preliminary geodetic computations and performing final computations and adjustment of local geodetic networks, such as leveling, traversing, and triangulation.

Instruction: Plane coordinate system; Transverse Mercator, Lambert Conformal, and other project systems; transformation of Universal Transverse Mercator to geographic coordinates and vice versa; familiarization with electronic calculators; adjustment of triangulation, traversing, and level nets, including introduction to least squares; geographic position determinations.

Credit recommendation: In the upper division baccalaureate category, 4 semester hours in Civil Engineering, Civil Engineering Technology, Geodetic Science, Surveying, or Surveying Technology (4/80).

Geodetic Computations and Adjustments
(Automated Geodetic Computations and Adjustments [F-304])

Location: DMA-IAGS Cartographic School, Fort Clayton, Panama.

Length: *Version 1:* 240 hours (6 weeks); 15 hours per week lecture, 1 hour per week discussion, 24 hours per week laboratories, problems, examinations. *Version 2:* 280 hours (8 weeks).

Dates: January 1982-Present.

Objective: To prepare students in advanced geodetic computations and adjustments, including error analyses and identification or areas for reobservation.

Instruction: Covers advanced adjustment of observations and analyses of error propagation; matrix methods; practice in adjustment of level nets, trilaterations, triangulation, and traverses; two dimensional conformal coordinate transformation; error ellipses; curve fitting; and use of the VAX computer.

Credit recommendation: In the upper division baccalaureate or graduate degree category, 4 semester hours in Civil Engineering, Civil Engineering Technology, Geodetic Science, Surveying, or Surveying Technology (4/84).

Geodetic Management
(Field Surveys Supervisor [F-303])

Location: DMA-IAGS Cartographic School, Fort Clayton, Panama.

Length: 120 hours (3 weeks); 10 hours per week lecture, 30 hours per week problems, examinations, etc.

Dates: November 1979-Present.

Objective: To instruct students in the supervision and management of geodetic, photogrammetric and cartographic production operations.

Instruction: Concepts of planning, scheduling, and optimum utilization of equipment and human resources are presented. General office practices including time estimates, record keeping, requisitions, and establishment of priorities are studied. Preparation of operating instructions and written communications are included.

Credit recommendation: In the lower division baccalaureate/associate degree category, 2 semester hours in Business Administration, Management, Public Administration, or Personnel Administration (4/84). NOTE: Students who receive credit for this course should not receive credit for C-303 or P-303.

Gravity Surveys
(Land Gravity Surveys [F-207])

Location: DMA-IAGS Cartographic School, Fort Clayton, Panama.

Length: 280 hours (7 weeks); 9 hours per week lecture, 8 1/3 hours per week discussion, 22 2/3 hours per week laboratory, examinations, etc.

Dates: January 1982-April 1985.

Objective: To produce personnel who are capable of performing land gravity surveys in accordance to established specifications and standards and who can recognize and apply the requirements for geodetic and regional land gravity surveys and conduct the field operations.

Instruction: Covers gravity survey accuracy standards and techniques for geodetic and/or geophysical surveys; gravity anomalies; field gravity recording, description forms, and computations; and practice in collecting gravity data and computations.

Credit recommendation: In the upper division baccalaureate category, 3 semester hours in Civil Engineering, Civil Engineering Technology, Geodetic Sciences, Geophysics, Surveying, or Surveying Technology (4/84).

Hydrographic Surveying (F-204)

Location: DMA-IAGS Cartographic School, Fort Clayton, Panama, and Hydrographic Survey Assistance Program, U.S. Naval Oceanographic Office (HYSAP).

Length: 320 hours (8 weeks); 8 hours per week lecture, 2 hours per week discussion, 30 hours per week workshop and laboratory.

Dates: January 1977-Present.

Objective: To familiarize the student with the general principles used in hydrographic surveying. Emphasis is placed on the application of hydrographic instrumentation including electronic positioning systems.

Instruction: This course is designed for the student who expects to be engaged in the planning, field operations, and processing of hydrographic surveys. In addition, the student will be exposed to geodetic survey instrumentation, field techniques, and computations necessary to establish horizontal control necessary for hydrography. The course will consist of both classroom lectures and field operations where students will receive hands-on experience in operation of instrumentation and data collection.

Credit recommendation: In the upper division baccalaureate or graduate degree category, 4 semester hours in Civil Engineering Technology, Geodetic Science, Hydrographic Science, Surveying, or Surveying Technology (4/84).

Introduction to Automated Cartography (Automated Cartography [C-302])

Location: DMA-IAGS Cartographic School, Fort Clayton, Panama.
Length: 320 hours (8 weeks).
Dates: May 1980-Present.
Objective: To introduce the basic principles of automated cartography.
Instruction: The course covers techniques by which information can be transferred from an air photo, remote-sensing imagery, map, or other graphic medium to a computer system to produce a final cartographic product. The course allows students to make decisions on the applicability and need for automated systems in mapping projects. This course does not train expert technicians to manipulate or operate an automated cartographic system; students are trained to plan and produce mapping products using an automated system. Instruction includes work with stereo and linear digitalization systems. The relationship among hardware, software, and graphics is discussed. Applications in storage, generation, and updating of mapping data are also considered as are topographic and thematic mapping. The course is divided equally between lecture (theory) and hands-on training with computer hardware.
Credit recommendation: In the upper division baccalaureate category, 4 semester hours in Introduction to Automated Cartography (4/80).

Introduction to Computer Programming Using FORTRAN, Independent Study

Location: DMA-IAGS Cartographic School, Fort Clayton, Panama.
Length: 4 weeks (10 lessons).
Dates: January 1981-Present.
Objective: This self-paced course will give students a proficiency in the FORTRAN language.
Instruction: Covers arithmetic and logical principles; batch and interactive forms for reading and writing information; loops; predefined and user-defined programs; one- and two-dimensional arrays; attacking and debugging problems. It provides a working knowledge of FORTRAN and an introduction to the power of computer operating systems. Includes a step-by-step approach to computer programming using the FORTRAN language. No mathematics beyond the high school level is required.
Credit recommendation: In the lower division baccalaureate/associate degree category, 1 semester hour in Cartography, Earth Sciences, Photogrammetry and Surveying, or Computer Sciences (4/84)

Introduction to Digital Image Analysis (A201)

Location: DMA-IAGS Cartographic School, Fort Clayton, Panama.
Length: 320 hours (8 weeks).
Dates: April 1984-Present.
Objective: To instruct students in the use of computer assisted systems to analyze and process digital imagery.
Instruction: Covers review of fundamental remote sensing; principles of digital image processing; image enhancement; image rectification; image classification; Landsat 4; study of the program package ERDAS. Students produce classified or thematic maps and evaluate mapping accuracy using statistical methods combined with ground measurements. Course covers the concepts and use of Landsat computer compatible tapes (CCT) for automated image processing and data analysis. An image analysis system interfaced to a PDP 11/70 computer is used. Software enables student to manipulate multispectral digital data for automatic feature classification and generation of thematic map data. 2 hours lecture, 8 hours discussion, and 20 hours laboratory per week. Prerequisite: P-311, Introduction to Remote Sensing or equivalent.
Credit recommendation: In the upper division baccalaureate category, 2 semester hours in Earth Sciences, Cartography, Photogrammetry, or Computer Sciences (4/84).

Introduction to Minicomputers, Independent Study

Location: DMA-IAGS Cartographic School, Fort Clayton, Panama.
Length: 16 lessons.
Dates: April 1984-Present.
Objective: This is a self-paced course that introduces students to computer system concepts, peripherals, and memory principles, and prepares them for programming in assembly and high-level language.
Instruction: Gives a system overview, terms and conventions; problem solving; number systems; computer arithmetic; logic and hardware basics; instruction sets; main memory; central processor; peripheral devices; bus structure; general software, file organization; programming language; I/O techniques; operating systems. Emphasis is placed on the fundamentals necessary in the minicomputer field, teaching arithmetic computations and conversions in numbering systems. Prerequisite: high school education, course in computer science (e.g., Introduction to Computer Programming).
Credit recommendation: In the lower division baccalaureate/associate degree category, 2 semester hours in

Cartography, Earth Sciences, Photogrammetry and Surveying, or Computer Sciences (4/84).

Introduction to Remote Sensing (I-302)

Location: DMA-IAGS Cartographic School, Fort Clayton, Panama.
Length: 200 hours (5 weeks).
Dates: April 1980-February 1985.
Objective: To give the student an overview of remote sensing from the visible portion of the electromagnetic spectrum to the microwave region.
Instruction: The students do laboratory and field problems using imagery from each of the major regions in the electromagnetic spectrum. The objective is to introduce the students to the various kinds of environmental data which can be interpreted from remote sensing imagery. The course consists of a combination of lecture, discussion, laboratory, and field work. After an introduction to the theory of electromagnetic energy and the energy environment, attention is focused on theory and practical (hands-on) experiences with various forms of remote sensing imagery, including air photographs, color infrared photographs, thermal infrared imagery, passive and active microwave, and the multispectral imagery, especially landsat products. The students do both laboratory and field mapping projects, individually and in group assignments.
Credit recommendation: In the upper division baccalaureate category or in the graduate degree category, 3 semester hours in Introduction to Remote Sensing (4/80).

Introduction to Remote Sensing/Image Analysis (A-101)

Location: DMA-IAGS Cartographic School, Fort Clayton, Panama.
Length: 160 contact hours (4 weeks); 40 hours per week, 8 hours per day.
Dates: April 1974-Present.
Objective: To introduce students to the field of remote sensing; to provide insight on the capabilities and limitations of remote sensing systems and techniques, especially as these relate to potential mapping and charting applications.
Instruction: There is a review of remote sensing systems and techniques; this includes color photography, image analysis, active and passive microwave, and infrared data, as acquired from the ground, aircraft, and satellites. There is field experience with remote sensing imagery. There is concern for quantitative techniques especially using computers for data manipulation. Concepts of data processing, pattern recognition, and numerical analysis are covered. The course focuses on numerical analysis of multispectral satellite data like that produced by LANDSAT.
Credit recommendation: In the upper division baccalaureate category, 2 semester hours in Remote Sensing of the Environment (4/84). NOTE: This course might be offered in Geography, Geological Sciences, Forestry, Agriculture, or Engineering Sciences. To some extent it would depend on the individual university and where, or in what discipline, a course in remote sensing is offered.

Map Maintenance (I-201)

Location: DMA-IAGS Cartographic School, Fort Clayton, Panama.
Length: 160 hours (4 weeks).
Dates: April 1980-Present.
Objective: To provide the necessary background to deal with problems of evaluating the need for and updating of maps. The course emphasizes the need for and updating of maps. The course emphasizes the methods, procedures, and equipment necessary in analyzing and updating maps in a systematic, timely, and economic manner.
Instruction: This course assumes a considerable amount of training and background on the part of the individual participants. It will be concerned with the managerial decisions and judgments in map revision. These decisions must be based on professional training broadly oriented in air photo interpretation, photogrammetry, cartography, remote sensing, and management. Recognizing that not all participants will have this background, some equipment and technology familiarization will be provided, but this is essentially a theoretical background course designed for midlevel managers who have considerable previous technological background.
Credit recommendation: In the upper division baccalaureate category or in the graduate degree category, 3 semester hours in Cartography, Map Interpretation, and Photogrammetry (4/80). NOTE: Students in the last year of a 4-year collegiate program and especially students at the master's level would benefit from this course.

Modern Cartography (C-401)

Location: DMA-IAGS Cartographic School, Fort Clayton, Panama.
Length: 240 contact hours (6 weeks; 40 hours per week; 8 hours per day).
Dates: July 1973-Present.
Objective: To update professional cartographers and the managers of technical projects or agencies with the current "state-of-the-art" and leading edge of research in cartography.
Instruction: This course is normally taught by leading experts from U.S. universities. Included are insights into the theory of geometric map design, symbology and type styles, graphic, color and texture schemes used in cartography. Both demonstration and "hands-on" training with computer graphics systems are provided using examples of topographic, thematic, and statistical cartography and computer graphics are discussed. There are two phases to the course: (1) modern concepts of conventional cartography, and (2) modern concepts of digital cartography. The emphasis is on the interface between both these phases of

cartography with special concern for those students who have not been involved in computer-assisted cartographic operations.

Credit recommendation: In the upper division baccalaureate or graduate degree category, 4 semester hours in Advanced Cartography, Computer Sciences, or Computer Graphics (4/84).

Nautical Cartography (204)
(Formerly Nautical Chart Construction)
   Location: DMA-IAGS Cartographic School, Fort Clayton, Panama.
   Length: 320 hours (8 weeks).
   Dates: December 1969-Present.
   Objective: To provide a foundation for planning, supervising, and executing the construction and updating of nautical charts.
   Instruction: Oceanography, navigation, nautical cartographic theory, projections, chart planning and design, marginal chart data, topography, bathymetry, hydrography, navigational data, traffic limits, magnetism, and chart revision.
   Credit recommendation: In the upper division baccalaureate category, 4 semester hours in Cartography, Navigation, Oceanography, or Surveying (4/80).

Orthophotography (P-302)
   Location: DMA-IAGS Cartographic School, Fort Clayton, Panama.
   Length: 320 hours (8 weeks).
   Dates: November 1983-Present.
   Objective: To provide the student with the theoretical background and practical aspects of various systems used in orthophotography.
   Instruction: In-depth development of geometry of tilted photography and its relationship to orthophotos; types and characteristics of various orthophoto systems; use of orthophoto products; instrumental training (Kern OP-2, Wild OR-1); laboratory work on an orthophotography project, including photo lab processing. Prerequisite: Students need a working knowledge of algebra and trigonometry and experience in stereocompilation and lab processing. Also Photogrammetry P-201.
   Credit recommendation: In the upper division baccalaureate category, 4 semester hours in Cartography, Earth Sciences, or Photogrammetry (4/84).

Photogrammetric Aerotriangulation
(Semianalytical and Analytical Triangulation [P-304])
   Location: DMA-IAGS Cartographic School, Fort Clayton, Panama.
   Length: 640 hours (16 weeks).
   Dates: January 1980-Present.
   Objective: To present the fundamentals of control extension by semianalytical (independent model) and analytical aerotriangulation, the necessary measurements and error analysis, and the necessary data processing so that students can plan, supervise, and execute a variety of control extension projects and evaluate errors in the system.
   Instruction: Mathematics of analytical triangulation, independent model triangulation, data acquisition for IMT, computer programs for IMT, analytical aerotriangulation, data acquisition for analytical triangulation, computer programs for analytical triangulation, statistical analysis of triangulation results.
   Credit recommendation: In the graduate degree category, 8 semester hours in Applied Mathematics or Photogrammetry (4/80). NOTE: If the student has completed the first 8 weeks covering independent model triangulation, he or she should receive 4 graduate credits. If the student continues through the next 8 weeks, he or she should receive 8 graduate credits.

Photogrammetric Applications Program (P-301)
   Location: DMA-IAGS Cartographic School, Fort Clayton, Panama.
   Length: 400 hours (10 weeks).
   Dates: November 1983-Present.
   Objective: To provide the student with knowledge about all aspects of software for photogrammetric and remote sensing applications.
   Instruction: Review of basic mathematics in photogrammetry and remote sensing. Analytical photogrammetry and generalized solution; mathematical modeling for photogrammetric problems; existing programs. Modifications of existing programs; programming for photogrammetric applications; debugging new programs; fictitious data generation; testing and execution. Prerequisite: F-304.
   Credit recommendation: In the upper division baccalaureate or graduate degree category, 5 semester hours in Applied Mathematics, Photogrammetry, and Computer Science (4/84).

Photogrammetric Production Supervisor (P-303)
(Formerly Photogrammetric Management)
   Location: DMA-IAGS Cartographic School, Fort Clayton, Panama.
   Length: 120 hours (3 weeks); 10 hours of lecture, 30 hours of laboratory per week.
   Dates: November 1979-Present.
   Objective: To provide training to supervisors at the production level in photogrammetry.
   Instruction: Covers supervisory skills related to photogrammetric production. Emphases are on management techniques, methods, and procedures, including planning, project programming, and scheduling.
   Credit recommendation: In the lower division baccalaureate/associate degree category, 2 semester hours in Business Administration, Management, Public Administration, or Personnel Administration (4/84). NOTE: Stu-

dents who receive credit for this course should not receive credit for F-306 or C-303.

Photogrammetry (P-201)
Location: DMA-IAGS Cartographic School, Fort Clayton, Panama.
Length: 400 hours (10 weeks).
Dates: September 1979-Present.
Objective: To teach the fundamentals of aerial and terrestrial photogrammetry and the ground control requirements for scale determination and map compilation; to introduce the orientation of a stereoscopic model in a first- and second-order plotter; and to introduce advanced techniques of control extension by the method of independent models.
Instruction: Calculation of grid coordinates; coordinate transformation; basic geometry of aerial photographs; cartographic cameras; ground control; orientation and compilation of a stereoscopic model in optical train stereo-plotter; map symbols; scribing; flight planning; introduction to aerial triangulation.
Credit recommendation: In the upper division baccalaureate category, 5 semester hours in Cartography, Earth Sciences, Geodetic Sciences, Photogrammetry, or Surveying (4/80).

**Preparation of Landsat Mosaics
(Independent Study Program)**
(This course is somewhat similar in organization and content to DMA-IAGS course C-307, Cartographic Techniques for Space Imagery, listed in this section of the *National Guide*).
Location: DMA-IAGS Cartographic School, Fort Clayton, Panama, or anywhere the equipment is available to project the visual tapes and audio explanations.
Length: *Variable,* depending on the individual student. The tapes can be reviewed a number of times until the material they contain is fully covered. (About 80 contact hours are required to work through the entire set of tapes and examinations.)
Dates: April 1983-Present.
Objective: To provide the student a background on the NASA-Landsat series of satellites, with special emphasis on the multispectral scanning systems (MSS) and the methods and techniques whereby the imagery produced by this system can be formatted together into an image mosaic covering a larger area of the earth than does a single Landsat scene.
Instruction: Covers the Landsat data collection systems, especially the multispectral scanning system (MSS). After reviewing this system and the data (imagery) it produces, the student will then be shown techniques on how this data can be used to join independent Landsat scenes into a mosaic covering a large area. The student will be shown how to do this mosaicking but will not be expected to produce an actual mosaic and have it reviewed.

Credit recommendation: In the lower division baccalaureate/associate degree category, 2 semester hours in Map Reading and Interpretation, Introduction to Cartography, Introduction to Photography, Photo-Laboratory Color Processing (4/84). NOTE: Because this is a self-paced course with no interaction with an instructor or other students and no practical experience in producing a Landsat mosaic, it cannot be given the same upper division credit as DMA-IAGS C-307 listed in the *National Guide.* Prerequisite: Students should have an introductory course in remote sensing such as Fundamentals of Remote Sensing.

Satellite Doppler Positioning (F-303)
Location: DMA-IAGS Cartographic School, Fort Clayton, Panama.
Length: 240 hours (6 weeks).
Dates: October 1979-May 1986.
Objective: To teach competent field surveyors to acquire valid horizontal and vertical position information from doppler satellites, as well as to test and maintain doppler receiving equipment in the field.
Instruction: Basic concepts of geodetic satellite systems; doppler satellite positioning concepts; doppler observation techniques; ground survey ties and photoidentification; satellite, ground support, and user subsytems; satellite messages and geodetic uses; various doppler receiver procedures; orbital information; practical exercises in observing, operating, and maintaining equipment; preliminary evaluation of collected horizontal and vertical position data.
Credit recommendation: In the upper division baccalaureate category or in the graduate degree category, 4 semester hours in Aerospace Engineering, Civil Engineering, Civil Engineering Technology, Geodetic Science, Photogrammetry, Surveying, or Surveying Technology (4/80).

Del Taco Corporation

The Del Taco Corporation, part of the food service industry, is a national corporation with primary emphasis on Mexican food. Del Taco units also offer hamburgers, french fries, and milk shakes.

The Del Taco training functions are administered by the Corporate Managers of Training and Operations Development at the National Office in College Park, Georgia. District offices are located in Atlanta, Dallas, and Houston. Managers of training and development direct the training programs in these districts. The Corporate Manager of Training and Operations Development is responsible for curriculum and instructional changes.

Course instructors are selected on the basis of their successful completion of the Del Taco Development Program. Instructors are also given "train-the-trainers workshops" before they teach courses.

Source of official student records: Del Taco Corporation, Manager of Training and Development, 4854 Old National Highway, College Park, Georgia 30337; or 16720 Hedgecroft, Houston, Texas 77060; or 506 Fountain Parkway, Grand Prairie, Texas 75050.

Additional information about the courses: Program on Noncollegiate Sponsored Instruction, The Center for Adult Learning and Educational Credentials, American Council on Education, One Dupont Circle, Washington, D.C. 20036.

Manager Candidate Course
   Location: Atlanta, GA; Dallas, TX; Houston, TX.
   Length: 182 hours (1 month).
   Dates: September 1978-Present.
   Objective: To provide students with knowledge of the operation of a restaurant, emphasizing the functions of the various work stations and including the importance of interpersonal relationships within those work stations.
   Instruction: Gives basic information on restaurant management, uses controlled work experience with complementary classroom experiences and review. Student progress is monitored by trainers who supervise the learning as well as use of written exams.
   Credit recommendation: In the lower division baccalaureate/associate degree category, 3 semester hours in Cooperative Education/Internship in Food Service Management (11/80).

Manager Training Program, Phases I, II, and III
   Location: Atlanta, GA; Dallas, TX; Houston, TX.
   Length: 785 hours (6 months).
   Dates: September 1978-Present.
   Objective: To provide students with a management perspective and the techniques necessary for the successful operation and control of a food service operation.
   Instruction: Covers personnel practices and applications, along with food service management skills in the work setting. Classroom lectures, controlled work experience, and written examinations are used to ensure the successful accomplishment of the stated objectives.
   Credit recommendation: In the lower division baccalaureate/associate degree category, 3 semester hours in Food Service Management or Cooperative Education/Internship in Food Service Management; or in the upper division baccalaureate category, 3 semester hours in Personnel Management (11/80).

Del Taco, Inc.

Del Taco, Inc., is a major fast food restaurant chain with outlets in the California and Arizona market place. The product line is primarily Mexican food but also offers the traditional hamburger line.

All management training is administered through the corporate office in Costa Mesa, California, under the direction of a corporate training manager. All personnel entering into the Del Taco Training Program receive a thorough indoctrination into the principles and practices of restaurant operations and sound business management. The training program provides a combination of classroom training with qualified instructors, and individual, one-on-one, on-the-job training with field trainers. In order to obtain proficiency and recognition as a store manager, the matriculation process requires approximately eight to twelve months of training.

Source of official student records: Del Taco, Inc., Director of Personnel, 345 Baker St., Costa Mesa, CA 92626.

Additional information about the courses: Program on Noncollegiate Sponsored Instruction, The Center for Adult Learning and Educational Credentials, American Council on Education, One Dupont Circle, Washington, D.C. 20036.

Manager Candidate Course
   Location: Costa Mesa, CA, and various locations in California and Arizona.
   Length: 182 hours (1 month).
   Dates: September 1978-Present.
   Objective: To provide a working knowledge of the operation of a restaurant, emphasizing the functions of the various work stations and including interpersonal relationships.
   Instruction: This course utilizes controlled work experience with complementary classroom experiences and review. Student progress is monitored by trainers who supervise the learning as well as use of written exams.
   Credit recommendation: In the lower division baccalaureate/associate degree category, 3 semester hours in Cooperative Education/Internship in Food Service Management (1/82).

Manager Training Program, Phases I, II, and III
   Location: Costa Mesa, CA, and various locations in California and Arizona.
   Length: 6 months plus an 8-hour graduation class after Phase I.
   Dates: September 1978-Present.
   Objective: To provide a step-by-step familiarization with management perspective and techniques necessary to the successful operation and control of a food service operation.
   Instruction: Demonstrated knowledge of personnel

practices and applications, along with food service management skills is emphasized in the work setting. Classroom lectures, controlled work experience, and written examinations are used to ensure the successful accomplishment of the stated objectives.

Credit recommendation: In the lower division baccalaureate/associate degree, 3 semester hours in Food Service Management; upper division baccalaureate category, 3 semester hours in Personnel Management; lower division baccalaureate/associate degree category, 3 semester hours in Cooperative Education/Internship in Food Service Management (1/82). Students may receive a total of 9 semester hours for this program.

Department of Defense, Defense Security Institute

The U.S. Department of Defense Security Institute (DoDSI) is an activity established by the Secretary of Defense. The Institute is under the management oversight, policy direction, and technical guidance of the Deputy Under Secretary of Defense (Policy).

The Institute serves as the Department of Defense focal point for promoting activities supporting DoD security programs in education and training, research and development, and career development. The Institute presents courses of instruction, including resident, field extension, and correspondence, relating to the Department of Defense Security Programs. These courses are designed for U.S. Government personnel, plus selected employees and representatives of U.S. industry.

Four operating departments manage and provide the education, training, and special publications and products for DoDSI. The Educational Programs Department primarily produces or coordinates production of the DoDSI recurring and special publications and products and produces or supports development of correspondence courses. These publications include a topical bulletin on security and a periodical of news clippings of security interest. The Industrial Security Department primarily produces and conducts courses and special training in the DoD Industrial Security program, the Key Assets Protection Program, and in automated information systems security. The Personnel Security Investigations Department produces and conducts courses and special training in the DoD personnel security investigations. Finally, the Security Management Department produces and conducts courses and special training in the DoD information security program, personnel security program, and in general security requirements and management.

Selection procedures for faculty members must conform to requirements by the Federal Government's Office of Personnel Management (OPM). Applicants must submit a personal qualification statement which is reviewed by panel members selected for their expertise in the subject area. Knowledge, skills, abilities, education, work experience, and other pertinent qualifying information is used to determine the rating of an applicant. The instructors are evaluated twice yearly by their supervisors who observe them teaching a course, and then provide feedback and critique on their performances. Department chairpersons also evaluate the instructors by other means.

In order to receive a course diploma, students must demonstrate mastery of course content through formal examination, formally evaluated criterion exercises, the completion of graded written exercises, faculty observation and evaluation, and graded homework assignments or some combination thereof. For most courses, students who do no meet minimum academic or performance standards are given a certificate or letter of attendance in lieu of a course diploma. In all courses, the faculty identify the marginal student early on in the course. All students are assigned to faculty advisors, and when students develop academic or performance problems, their advisors work with them in free time to improve their mastery of the required knowledge or skills.

Source of official student records: Registrar, Department of Defense Security Institute, c/o Defense General Supply Center, Richmond, Virginia 23297-5091.

Additional information about the courses: Program on Noncollegiate Sponsored Instruction, The Center for Adult Learning and Educational Credentials, American Council on Education, One Dupont Circle, Washington, D.C. 20036.

Defense Industrial Security Programs I and II
Essentials of Industrial Security Management
Automated Data Processing Concepts and Terms
Physical Security
  Location: Correspondence course.
  Length: Self-study (approximately 72 hours).
  Dates: January 1986-Present.
  Objective: To provide the student with an overview of the Defense Industrial Security Program and Defense Investigative Service.
  Learning Outcome: Upon successful completion of this course, the student will be able to demonstrate an understanding of organization, missions, functions, and history of Defense Investigative Service and Defense Industrial Security Program; demonstrate an understanding of industrial personnel security clearance program and process; demonstrate a basic understanding of Defense Industrial Security Program structure and function; demonstrate a basic understanding of protective barriers, lighting, locks, and security process in physical security administration; and identify functions and characteristics of computer systems.
  Instruction: Course covers Defense Investigative Service structure and functions, Defense Industrial Security Program structure and functions, processing of govern-

ment clearances, facility security administration, principles and criteria of physical security, and basic concepts of automated data processing.

Credit recommendation: In the vocational certificate category, 3 semester hours in Principles of Industrial Security (10/88).

Introduction to Security Administration
(DoD Security Specialist Course [5220.9])

Location: Richmond, VA.
Length: 102 hours (3 weeks).
Dates: September 1986-Present.
Objective: To provide the student with an introduction to security programs, policies, and procedures as they apply to the security specialist field.

Learning Outcome: Upon successful completion of this course, the student will be able to identify major security programs for safeguarding classified and sensitive government information; demonstrate a basic knowledge of policies and principles inherent in each program; and apply the basic principles of security to development, implementation, and evaluation of programs within home agencies.

Instruction: This course is designed to examine the information, physical, industrial, personnel, computer, communications, and operations security programs through an intensive curriculum of lectures, discussion, study, exams, and exercises. These programs are integrated through discussion, study, and exercises in security management, inspections and oversight, and education and training.

Credit recommendation: In the lower division baccalaureate/associate degree category, 3 semester hours in Introduction to Security Administration (10/88).

Personnel Security Adjudications (Correspondence Course)
(DoD Basic Personnel Security Adjudications Correspondence Course)

Location: Correspondence course.
Length: Self-study (approximately 50 hours).
Dates: July 1988-Present.
Objective: To prepare DoD personnel security adjudicators for attendance in the DoD Basic Personnel Security Adjudications Course (resident phase) by introducing students to the DoD Personnel Security Program and the process of making personnel security determinations.

Learning Outcome: Upon successful completion of this course, the student will be able to identify appropriate national security threats; demonstrate an understanding of methods, policies and procedures employed by Defense Investigative Service, Office of Personnel Management, and other investigative agencies in the conduct of security investigations; and demonstrate an ability to analyze, weigh, decide, and act on given personnel security information.

Instruction: Course covers introduction to the personnel security program; employing activities' initial responsibilities; personnel security investigations; central adjudication; adjudicative issues; and continuous evaluation. Lessons deal with the history, foundation, and scope of the personnel security program; the responsibilities and methods of the various agencies involved in the personnel security program; the investigations used in the personnel security program, with explanation of their uses, elements and idiosyncrasies; the adjudicator's responsibilities; and the adjudication policy guidelines. This course is a prerequisite for DoD Basic Personnel Security Adjudications.

Credit recommendation: In the vocational certificate category, 2 semester hours in Personnel Security Adjudications (10/88).

Personnel Security Adjudications
(DoD Basic Personnel Security Adjudications Course [5220.11])

Location: Richmond, VA.
Length: 88 hours (2½ weeks).
Dates: October 1988-Present.
Objective: To provide the student with a structured approach to security adjudication and evaluation of investigation results. Emphasis is on the practical application involving student decision-making and "how to do" exercises.

Learning Outcome: Upon successful completion of this course, the student will be able to process personnel security information (i.e., analyze, weigh, and decide on personnel security investigation); evaluate the results of investigations and reports of derogatory information against the current adjudicative criteria to determine necessary actions warranted and the adequacy of the investigation on information; and differentiate between position sensitivity and security determination requirements and involved agencies, rules, and procedures.

Instruction: This course is designed to teach the basic skills and knowledge required of an adjudicator working in a DoD Central Adjudication Facility. Through lectures, discussions, and extensive classroom exercises, the student learns how to review personnel security investigations and other sources of information for completeness, validity, and required action. Major emphasis is on applying the DoD adjudication policy when reviewing investigations to make personnel security determinations. Case studies are used throughout to illustrate issues discussed. Exercises include using the Defense Central Index of Investigations, scoping and summarizing investigations, identifying adjudicative issues, and applying each of the adjudication guidelines. The DoD Basic Personnel Security Adjudications Correspondence Course is a prerequisite.

Credit recommendation: In the lower division baccalaureate/associate degree category, 3 semester hours in Personnel Security Adjudications (10/88).

Personnel Security Investigations Course (5220.8)
Location: Richmond, VA.
Length: 131 hours (4 weeks).
Dates: January 1984-Present.
Objective: To provide newly assigned special agents with introductory training in agency policies and procedures.
Learning Outcome: Upon successful completion of this course, the student will be able to demonstrate an understanding of Defense Investigative Service (DIS) jurisdiction, investigative procedure legislation; demonstrate practical knowledge of interviewing techniques, including non-verbal communication and techniques of effective listening as applied to DIS duties; and demonstrate an understanding of DIS policy and procedures as applied in background investigation/periodic reinvestigation procedures.
Instruction: This course is designed to teach the basic skills and knowledge necessary for competent performance by individuals new to the personnel security investigative field. The course is an intense, performance-oriented experience covering all aspects of personnel security investigations from origin of the investigation with an authorized requestor, through case handling, investigative methods and techniques, administrative requirements of proper, accurate, and complete report writing to processing and return of the comprehensive investigation to the requestor. Through lectures, demonstrations, group activities, and extensive practical application the student becomes comfortable and successful at performing the various investigative duties. Through observation and videotaping, student performance is evaluated and feedback provided to enable the individual to attain a satisfactory performance level directly related to the job.
Credit recommendation: In the lower division baccalaureate/associate degree category, 3 semester hours in Principles of Personnel Security, or in the lower division baccalaureate/associate degree category, 2 semester hours in Principles of Personnel Security; or in the lower division baccalaureate/associate degree category, 1 semester hour in Personnel Security Investigations (10/88).

Principles of Industrial Security
(Industrial Security Specialist Course—Basic and Advanced [5220.2])
Location: Richmond, VA.
Length: 227½ hours (6½ weeks).
Dates: July 1986-Present.
Objective: To provide comprehensive and formal classroom education and training for DoD industrial security representatives assigned to positions in the Defense Industrial Security Program, including the conduct of surveys, inspections, education and training functions, and administrative inquiries.
Learning Outcome: Upon successful completion of this course, the student will be able to perform the functions of a DoD Industrial Security Representative; accomplish facility inspections; assess and provide guidance on internal security controls and security violations; and evaluate and certify computer systems for processing classified information.
Instruction: This course is designed to teach the necessary skills and program knowledge required to evaluate effectively the implementation of the Defense Industrial Security Program in industry. The underlying focus of discussions and practical exercises is to direct the students' attention to the main purpose of the Defense Industrial Security Program, i.e., protection of classified information. This discourages the Industrial Security Representative from having a narrow view to the "requirements" set forth in the *Industrial Security Manual,* and permits effective program implementation in varying environments. The course is intended for persons serving as Department of Defense Industrial Security Representatives. Program policies and requirements are presented in lecture format. Discussions and practical exercises are used to demonstrate the application of policies and requirements. The Defense Industrial Security Programs I and II; Essentials of Industrial Security Management, and Automated Data Processing Concepts and Terms correspondence course is a prerequisite.
Credit recommendation: In the lower division baccalaureate/associate degree category, 3 semester hours in Principles of Industrial Security or Industrial Security Administration, and in the lower division baccalaureate/associate degree category, 1 semester hour in Practicum in Industrial Security (10/88).

Principles of Information Security
(Information Security Management [5220.7])
Location: Richmond, VA.
Length: 67 hours (2 weeks).
Dates: October 1987-Present.
Objective: To provide the student with a comprehensive understanding of the Defense Information Security Program, including proper classification, downgrading and declassification of information, and safeguarding of classified information.
Learning Outcome: Upon successful completion of this course, the student will be able to demonstrate a basic understanding of the principles of information security management and have the ability to apply them within their employing activities; demonstrate an awareness of organizations involved in the DoD Information Security Program; and identify and utilize the official literature in the field of information security program.
Instruction: This course is designed to teach the basic skills and knowledge required to effectively implement the Department of Defense Information Security Program in an organization. Students are encouraged to focus on the purpose and goals underlying requirements—rather than

viewing them simply as "rules"—to permit effective program implementation in widely varying environments. Key policy developers from the Information Security Oversight Office and Office of the Secretary of Defense lecture on current program developments and discuss issues of concern with students. The course is primarily intended for persons serving as Security Managers within the meaning of the Department of Defense Information Security Regulation. People in similar positions in other Executive Branch organizations and persons working in related disciplines would also benefit from the course. The first week of the course (which focuses on classification management) is open to employees of contractors participating in the Defense Industrial Security Program. Program policies and requirements are presented in lectures and quizzes. Classroom discussions and practical exercises are used to demonstrate application of policies and requirements in a variety of specific situations.

Credit recommendation: In the lower division baccalaureate/associate degree category, 2 semester hours in Principles of Information Security (10/88).

Digital Equipment Corporation

Digital Equipment Corporation is dedicated to the design, manufacturing, and marketing of networked computer systems worldwide. Digital's South Burlington manufacturing plant makes available to its employees many sources of training in the areas of business and engineering. Their certification as a "Class A" manufacturing plant is partly based upon the excellence in employee training to ensure continual improvement in employee skills. The Production/Inventory Control Training Program encompasses five distinct courses of study in the field of Materials Management: Materials Requirement Planning, Inventory Management, Capacity Requirements Planning, Production Activity Control, and Master Planning. The associated Purchasing Training Program is a single course in Industrial Purchasing.

The intent of these programs is to hone student skills and prepare them for professional certification examinations: the American Production and Inventory Control Society's (APICS) Certified Production and Inventory Control Manager award and the National Association of Purchasing Management's (NAPM) Certified Purchasing Manager award.

Source of official student records: College Program Director, Digital Equipment Corporation, 115 Kimball Avenue, South Burlington, Vermont 05401.

Additional information about the courses: Vermont State Colleges, Office of External Programs, P.O. Box 34, Waterbury, Vermont 05676.

PRODUCTION/INVENTORY CONTROL AND PURCHASING PROGRAMS

Capacity Requirements Planning
  Location: South Burlington, VT.
  Length: 30 hours (10 weeks).
  Dates: September 1986-Present.
  Objective: To provide students with a solid background in calculating capacity, obtaining and interpreting inputs for capacity requirements planning (CRP), completing the CRP process, analyzing results, resolving potential problems, and monitoring capacity.
  Instruction: Topics include calculating capacity, obtaining and interpreting inputs for capacity requirements planning (CRP), completing the CRP process, analyzing results, resolving potential problems, and monitoring capacity.
  Credit recommendation: In the lower division baccalaureate/associate degree category, 2 semester hours in Capacity Requirements Planning (9/86).

Inventory Management
  Location: South Burlington, VT.
  Length: 30 hours (10 weeks).
  Dates: September 1986-Present.
  Objective: To provide students with the principles, concepts, and techniques for planning and controlling inventory at all stages of the manufacturing/distribution cycle.
  Instruction: Topics include how to establish an inventory management plan, control that plan, and monitor performance.
  Credit recommendation: In the lower division baccalaureate/associate degree category, 2 semester hours in Inventory Management (9/86).

Master Planning
  Location: South Burlington, VT.
  Length: 30 hours (10 weeks).
  Dates: September 1986-Present.
  Objective: To explain how a company's objectives and operating philosophy are established and how a business plan is executed.
  Instruction: Students learn to develop inputs for a production plan, to include forecasting policies and procedures, and to establish and review master production schedule (MPS) policies and procedures. Students also learn how to consolidate demand into factory requirements, produce an MPS, and measure the performance of an MPS.
  Credit recommendation: In the lower division baccalaureate/associate degree category, 2 semester hours in Master Planning (9/86).

Material Requirements Planning
  Location: South Burlington, VT.
  Length: 30 hours (10 weeks).

Dates: September 1986-Present.

Objective: To familiarize individuals with the MRP system and teach them how to develop and use a bill of material.

Instruction: Material Requirements Planning (MRP) is a set of production and inventory control techniques in which all future demands for work are generated by a master schedule. The Materials Requirements Planning course is designed to teach individuals how to develop and use a bill of material, one of the four sources of the MRP system data inputs. Topic areas include sources of MRP input; developing a materials requirement plan; policies, capabilities, and methods; order quantity methods; and execution of the material requirements plan.

Credit recommendation: In the lower division baccalaureate/associate degree category, 2 semester hours in Material Requirements Planning (9/86).

Production Activity Control
Location: South Burlington, VT.
Length: 30 hours (10 weeks).
Dates: September 1986-Present.

Objective: To teach individuals how to control production in both the push and pull production environments.

Instruction: This course focuses on production activity control in the job shop, repetitive, and process manufacturing environments. Students learn to plan production releases, authorize and begin production, control the flow of work after release, and measure production data. For the pull environment, students learn to prepare work cells for production, how to control production as it moves through the process, and how card signaling systems work. Students also learn how to capture production data and prepare for changes in products.

Credit recommendation: In the lower division baccalaureate/associate degree category, 2 semester hours in Production Activity Control (9/86).

Purchasing
Location: South Burlington, VT.
Length: 45 hours (15 weeks).
Dates: September 1986-Present.

Objective: To familiarize individuals with the functional disciplines of industrial purchasing, including negotiations, legal aspects, contracts, cost/price analysis, vendor analysis, quality, and materials management.

Instruction: Attention is focused on purchasing's responsibilities for and contributions to more profitable manufacturing operations and managing the supplier base.

Credit recommendation: In the lower division baccalaureate/associate degree category, 3 semester hours in Purchasing (9/86).

Disabled American Veterans

The Disabled American Veteran's (DAV) Structured and Continuing Training Program is designed for use by rehabilitated National Service Officers (NSOs) who have completed a sixteen month on-the-job training program. The program covers four important areas: anatomy, pathology, physiology, and Veterans Administration laws. It is a comprehensive course developed for the purpose of enhancing job-related skills such as paralegal and paramedical principles needed to represent veterans before the Department of Veterans Affairs.

To address those needs, seven key elements were developed for the training program: the DAV Supplement to Veterans Administration (VA) Schedule for Rating Disabilities (SRS), the Supervisor's Training Manual (STM), the National Service Officers' Workbook, videotapes, audio cassettes, interactive computer programs, and medical charts. Students are taught by tenured National Service Officers with expertise in the subject matter. Training class instructors are monitored by staff members of the National Organization.

Students are required to successfully complete each section of the training program. Student progress is monitored at the National Service and Legislative Headquarters. Monitored computer tests are administered after completion of each training module with a final examination upon completion of the course. The Director is issued a weekly computer generated report of the progress of all students. Students who do not master the subject matter, as determined through testing, are rescheduled for additional sessions.

Source of official student records: National Service Director, National Service and Legislative Headquarters, 807 Maine Avenue, S.W., Washington, D.C. 20024.

Additional information about the courses: Program on Noncollegiate Sponsored Instruction, The Center for Adult Learning and Educational Credentials, American Council on Education, One Dupont Circle, Washington, D.C. 20036.

Disabled American Veterans (DAV) Continuing Training Program for National Service Officers (NSOs)
Location: Cincinnati, OH; Dallas, TX; and various locations.
Length: 17 self-paced units of instruction.
Dates: July 1987-Present.

Objective: To provide the student with an overview of human anatomy and various pathophysiological processes and conditions for use in relation to disability compensation.

Instruction: Course covers the endocrine system, mental disorders, dental and oral conditions, the hemic and lymphatic system, the skin, the musculoskeletal system, the gynecological system, the genitourinary system, systemic diseases, the digestive system, the respiratory system, the ears, the eyes, the cardiovascular system, organic diseases of the central nervous system, and the application of pathophysiological conditions to specific Veterans Administration compensation and rating systems. Methodology includes self-study workbooks, group discussions and presentations, videotapes, and audio cassettes. Also includes computerized evaluations.

Credit recommendation: In the lower division baccalaureate/associate degree category, 3 semester hours in Human Anatomy, in the lower division baccalaureate/associate degree category, 2 semester hours in Basic Pathophysiology or Medical Terminology, and in the lower division baccalaureate/associate degree category, 1 semester hour in Administrative Law for Legal Assisting/Paralegal program for a total of 6 semester hours.

Dow Jones & Company, Inc.

The Plant Communications Technical Training Department provides technical education programs for engineering and other technical personnel at Dow Jones.

Programs are taught by a training staff skilled in advanced systems and technology and pre-trained on the equipment or systems for which they must prepare student documentation and course outlines (or scripts, depending upon the availability of developmental documentation).

Classroom facilities are available at a number of locations at the South Brunswick, New Jersey campus. Some courses, however, are conducted at sites in New York, Florida, Texas, California, Illinois, Massachusetts, and other locations.

Audiovisual support and other student/instructor communication aids have been incorporated in the training programs to ensure student success.

Source of official student records: Training Manager, Plant Communications Department, Dow Jones and Company, Inc., Box 300, Princeton, NJ 08543-0300 or Registry of Credit Recommendations, The Center for Adult Learning and Educational Credentials, American Council on Education, One Dupont Circle, Washington, D.C. 20036.

Additional information about the courses: Program on Noncollegiate Sponsored Instruction, Thomas A. Edison State College, 101 West State Street, Trenton, New Jersey 08625.

AVANTI

Location: South Brunswick, NJ.
Length: 27 hours (5 days).
Objective: To train students on the operation and operational troubleshooting procedures on the AVANTI System.
Instruction: This course introduces students to the high-speed multiplexer with full DS-1 frame formatting capability for telecommunications purposes. Network functions and operation; hardware, framing, and menu; RS 232 Networking; system diagnostics and maintenance are included.
Credit recommendation: In the upper division baccalaureate category, 1 semester hour in Computer Technology. If student has also completed DataBak, then a total of 2 semester hours in Digital Communications or Telecommunications (10/87).

DataBak

Location: South Brunswick, NJ.
Length: 30 hours (5 days).
Dates: June 1987-Present.
Objective: To teach students to program and to maintain electronically the DataBak System which is a tie-in system to pagination and satellite operations.
Instruction: This course covers DataBak operation and coding. It includes an overview of the VM02 and VM21; and removable and fixed-disk storage.
Credit recommendation: In the upper division baccalaureate category, 1 semester hour in Computer Technology. If student has also completed AVANTI, then a total of 2 semester hours in Digital Communications or Telecommunications (10/87).

CDC 9710/9715 Disk Drives

Location: South Brunswick, NJ.
Length: 30 hours (5 days).
Dates: March 1986-Present.
Objective: To teach technicians how to calibrate, maintain, and troubleshoot CDC 9710/9715 disk drives.
Instruction: This course covers the function, purpose, and physical description of the disk drives. Control card and I/O board; and theory of operation are also included. Finally general maintenance information is covered.
Credit recommendation: In the upper division baccalaureate category, 1 semester hour in Computer Disk Drive or Computer Technology Elective (10/87). NOTE: This recommendation duplicates the credit for Disk Drive 9766.

CDC 9766 Disk Drive

Location: South Brunswick, NJ.
Length: 24 hours (4 days).
Dates: January 1986-Present.
Objective: To teach technicians how to calibrate and maintain 9766 disk drives.
Instruction: This course covers the description, physical and functional, of the disk drive; control and indicators and theory of operation. Power supply and power system functions and troubleshooting procedures and logic charts are also included.

Credit recommendation: In the upper division baccalaureate category, 1 semester hour in Computer Disk Drives or Computer Technology Elective (10/87). NOTE: This recommendation duplicates the credit for Disk Drive 9710/9715.

Pagination
  Location: South Brunswick, NJ.
  Length: 207 hours (7 weeks).
  Dates: May 1985-Present.
  Objective: To enable students to understand, maintain, and troubleshoot the Triple I-Dow Jones Pagination System.
  Instruction: This course covers the hardware and software of the file managers, graphic arts generators, video display terminals, various disk drives, and complex electronics, both hard-wired and modular. At the conclusion of the course students must understand and be able to maintain the system. The pagination training program is divided into three sessions with a one- to three-week interval between each session.
  Credit recommendation: In the upper division baccalaureate category, 4 semester hours in Machine Language Programming or Computer Technology or Introduction to Specialized Pagination System (10/87). NOTE: As a special prerequisite to this course, students must successfully complete proctored examinations in the (120-160 hour) home study course III-15 Programming. This course provides Dow Jones engineers and technicians the necessary software background to troubleshoot III computers and/or master the pagination system.

Duquesne Light Company

Duquesne Light Company is committed to both fossil and nuclear power generation for meeting the energy needs of its customers. The Company recognizes the importance of producing power in a safe and reliable manner and is therefore dedicated to excellence of operation of its facilities. The Duquesne Light Company considers a realistic but effective nuclear training program is the basic foundation to achieve excellence of operation at its nuclear facilities.

It is the intent of the Duquesne Light Company's nuclear training center to train individuals for responsible positions in the operation of its nuclear facilities. It is also the intention of Duquesne Light Company to provide training programs that are properly balanced to meet the training needs of operations and the needs of its customers for safe, reliable and economical electrical energy.

The nuclear training staff is organized to provide a large part of the training service required for Nuclear Division personnel and Company support personnel. To ensure that nuclear training is uniform within the Company, a Corporate Training Committee has been established. This Committee has developed procedures and guidelines for all Company Service Departments and Divisions that support the operation of the Company's nuclear facilities. Job duties are analyzed to ensure that Company supervisory personnel engaged in safety-related activities at Duquesne Light Company's nuclear facilities are given required and job specific training.

In addition, the Company is a member of the Institute of Nuclear Power Operations (INPO) and supports its goals and objectives to achieve excellence of operation and training.

Source of official student records: Duquesne Light Company, Nuclear Division, P.O. Box 4, Shippingport, Pennsylvania 15077-0004.

Additional information about the courses: Program on Noncollegiate Sponsored Instruction, The Center for Adult Learning and Educational Credentials, American Council on Education, One Dupont Circle, Washington, D.C. 20036.

NUCLEAR TRAINING

Basic Nuclear Physics
  Location: Shippingport, PA.
  Length: 104 hours (13 days).
  Dates: June 1983-Present.
  Objective: To provide students with the knowledge required to describe the production of energy from the fission process and to apply knowledge of the structure of matter and nuclear processes to other training topics.
  Instruction: Lecture/discussion format. Atomic structure, nuclear physics, mass defect and binding energy, radioactive decay, decay chain and activity, atomic and nuclear interactions, fission and doppler effect, fission rate and power, neutron production, neutron generation and criticality.
  Credit recommendation: In the lower division baccalaureate/associate degree category, 3 semester hours in Nuclear Engineering/Nuclear Engineering Technology (10/86).

Chemistry Fundamentals
  Location: Beaver Valley Power Station, Shippingport, PA.
  Length: 30 hours (1 week).
  Dates: November 1981-Present.
  Objective: To introduce the student to the fundamentals of inorganic chemistry.
  Learning Outcome: Upon successful completion of this course, the student will be able to: describe the three phases of matter and their properties. Understand the Bohr model of the atom and the structure of the periodic table; understand the concepts of atomic and molecular weight and perform calculations relating to the above; understand the ideas of chemical valence of compounds;

understand types of molecular bonds. Balance chemical formulas, calculate amounts of products, give the amounts of reactants and basic chemical rate of change problems; understand solutions to chemistry and perform calculations on the molarity of solutions boiling point elevation and freezing point depression properties of solutions; and understand basic concepts of electrochemistry.

Instruction: Bohr model of atom, periodic table qualitative properties of the phases of matter, atomic and molecular weights, chemical valence, different types of chemical bonds, chemical equations, chemical rate of change, heat of formation, basic solution chemistry, boiling point elevation, freezing point depression, electrochemical calculations, basic nuclear chemistry. Lecture and discussion are used.

Credit recommendation: In the lower division baccalaureate/associate degree category, 2 semester hours in General Chemistry (1/88).

Electrical Circuits and Applications
a. Electrical Fundamentals
b. Electrical Practical

Location: Shippingport, PA.
Length: a. 36 hours (14 days). b. 51.6 hours (8 days).
Dates: September 1982-Present.
Objective: *Fundamentals:* to provide the student with a knowledge of basic electrical concepts, DC circuits, basic AC concepts and circuits, operation of AC generators, motors and transformers, basic semiconductor theory and applications. *Practical:* To provide a student with knowledge of power plant circuit breaker operation; electrical schematics, 345 KV and 138 KV switchyards, main generator operation, metering and protective relaying.
Instruction: *Fundamentals:* Lecture/discussion format. Voltage, current, resistance, Kirchoff's laws, bridge circuits, electromagnetism, basic AC concepts, AC circuit analysis, AC generators, 3-phase circuits, instrument transformers, motors; semiconductors. *Practical:* Symbol review, circuit breakers; 480V/4KV/OCB's and SF6, reading schematics, 345 and 138 KV switchyards, main generator; construction/voltage regulator/parallel operation, metering, protective relaying.
Credit recommendation: In the lower division baccalaureate/associate degree category, 3 semester hours in Survey of Electric Circuits (10/86).

Instructor Development
Location: Beaver Valley Power Station, Shippingport, PA.
Length: 66 hours (7 days).
Dates: December 1984-Present.
Objective: To provide the student with a knowledge of the Systematic Approach to Training (S.A.T.) including: the basics of learning, the adult learning process, course design and development, effective course instruction and implementation, effective evaluation, counseling and tutoring, and supervisory skills. To provide the student with appropriate practice instructional workshops, provide instructions and practice in job task analysis, objective writing, and exam writing and preparation.
Learning Outcome: Upon successful completion of this course, the student will be able to: describe factors of learning including systematic approach to training; the adult learning process, and motivation; construct a training course, including terminal objectives, enabling objectives, and lesson plan format; develop and implement a training program; develop and conduct training program evaluations, counsel, and tutor students; describe effects of attitudes, change, conditioning, motivation and personnel development; methods of overcoming motivation problems; communication and listening problems; how to develop proper assertive behavior and methods of dealing with stress; requirements of goal setting; and provide a practice teaching lesson.
Instruction: Course covers basics of learning, creating learning objectives and lesson plans, implementing a training plan, conduct training planning, methods of counseling, tutoring and student/teacher interaction. Practicum includes student's preparation and presentation of a one hour sample lecture. Examinations used to evaluate performance.
Credit recommendation: In the upper division baccalaureate category, 3 semester hours in Methodology of Teaching Technical Courses (1/88).

Instrumentation and Control Fundamentals
Location: Beaver Valley Power Station, Shippingport, PA.
Length: 120 hours (3 weeks).
Dates: March 1985-Present.
Objective: To provide the student with the knowledge of basic sensor concepts, neutron detection methods, and analog and digital process control concepts.
Learning Outcome: Upon successful completion of this course, the student will be able to explain the following: operation of pressure, level, flow, neutron flux; dynamic compensation, signal control modes; relationship of proportional, rate and reset controllers, basic pneumatic and electronic controllers; basic operational amplifier circuits including summers, multipliers and comparators; in addition the student will be able to draw basic logic symbols and application circuits and analyze applications of control circuits.
Instruction: Course covers basic sensors and transducers for measurement of temperature, pressure, fluid level, flow, position, and neutrons. Also, sensor and transducer reliability and failure analysis. Also, basic process control and control circuits. Lecture and discussion are used.
Credit recommendation: In the lower division baccalaureate/associate degree category, 3 semester hours in Process Instrumentation and Control Fundamentals (1/88).

Materials for Power Plants
(Materials for Licensed Operations)
   Location: Shippingport, PA.
   Length: 44 hours (6 days).
   Dates: February 1982-Present.
   Objective: To provide students with the knowledge needed to relate material selection to plant system limitations; describe the effects of radiation on plant materials and fully explain the basis for Beaver Valley Power Station Technical Specifications which are founded upon maintaining system/component integrity under physical stress.
   Instruction: Lecture/discussion format. Properties of metals including physical properties and load dependent properties; selection of plant materials; testing of materials; fracture and failure modes; linear elastic fracture mechanics; radiation effects on materials; pressurized thermal shock; heatup curve and cooldown curve development; Beaver Valley Power Station Technical Specifications related to materials including generators; and Code of Federal Regulations 10CFR50 (Appendix G&H).
   Credit recommendation: In the lower division baccalaureate/associate degree category, 1 semester hour in Theory of Nuclear Plant Materials (10/86).

Mitigating Core Damage/Accident Transient Analysis
   Location: Shippingport, PA.
   Length: 152 hours (19 days).
   Dates: January 1984-Present.
   Objective: To provide the student with the knowledge needed to describe the nuclear power plant response to various transients, the nuclear power plant response to various accidents, and to explain how to mitigate the consequences of various plant transients and accidents.
   Instruction: Fundamentals review, power distribution, transient analysis - normal/abnormal, accident analysis - reactivity addition accident/LOCA's miscellaneous, mitigating core damage - post accident cooling/potentially damaging operating conditions/small break loss of coolant with no high head safety injection/loss of feedwater induced loss of coolant accident/main stream break review/steam generator overfill/loss of all AC, EOP-7/pressurized thermal shock/incore thermocouple maps/vital process instrumentation/instrument qualification and accident response of excore instrumentation/accident response of incore instrumentation/post accident primary radiochemistry. Lecture discussion format.
   Credit recommendation: In the upper division baccalaureate category, 4 semester hours in Nuclear Engineering (10/86).

Radiation, Radiation Protection, and Radiation Survey
(Operator Radiation Safety Training/Radiation Survey Meter Qualifications)
   Location: Shippingport, PA.
   Length: 120 hours (15 days).
   Dates: November 1982-Present.
   Objective: To provide students with instruction in fundamental radiation protection techniques, regulations, and guidelines governing radiation exposure and radiation survey techniques and including the proper use of radiation survey instruments.
   Instruction: Lecture/discussion/demonstration format. Review of basic nuclear concepts, radiation quantities and units, biological effects of radiation, limits, guides and areas, radiation protection techniques, radioactive contamination control, radioactive material control, environmental considerations and emergency planning. The radiation detection and measurement section covers radiation detection, radiological surveys and portable instrumentation, radiation monitoring system, radiation accident monitors.
   Credit recommendation: In the lower division baccalaureate/associate degree category, 3 semester hours in Nuclear Engineering Technology/Health Physics and Radiation Safety Technology (10/86).

Radiation Technician Training Program
   Location: Beaver Valley Power Station, Shippingport, PA.
   Length: 80 hours (2 weeks).
   Dates: June 1981-Present.
   Objective: To introduce the student to the basic results of Nuclear Theory.
   Learning Outcome: Upon successful completion of this course, the student will be able to: perform half-life calculations; understand the ideas of cross-section and ionization, and relate these to the range of penetration of radiation in matter; cover the theory of photoelectric, Compton effect, and pair production; develop working knowledge of units of radiation measurement, linear attenuation, and buildup in the case of thick absorbers; perform calculations on neutron penetration and activation; become knowledgeable about the biological hazards of different sources of radiation; discuss nuclear stability comparing coulombic and nuclear force. Mass defect theory, and nuclear binding energy; quantitative discussion of nuclear decay rates. Discussion of units of radiation measurement and comparison of Co-60 to beta emitter units of activity comparison; students learn how to perform exposure and dose calculations; discussion of biological effectiveness and quality factor; understand definitions of Roentgen, rad, rem, and perform conversion calculations.
   Instruction: Course covers review of atomic structure, ionization, nuclear cross-section, range and attenuation, biological hazards of radiation sources. The electromagnetic processes associated with ionizing radiation, Compton effect, photoelectric effect, and pair production. Neutron attenuation and activation in matter. Unit conversions, biological effectiveness calculations, exposure and dose calculations. Quantitative calculations of nuclear decay rates.
   Credit recommendation: In the lower division bac-

calaureate/associate degree category, 2 semester hours in Basic Nuclear Theory (1/88).

Reactor Plant Systems
Location: Beaver Valley Power Station, Shippingport, PA.
Length: 960 hours (29 weeks).
Dates: November 1982-Present.
Objective: To provide the student with a knowledge of the various reactor plant systems as they apply to a nuclear power plant reactor operator.
Learning Outcome: Upon successful completion of this course, the student will be able to write a description of the function of systems and components, system flow paths, instrumentation and control of each component and the response of the system to an accident condition; and interpret all available indications from systems to determine the plant status and compliance with technical specifications.
Instruction: Course covers lecture, simulation, and on-the-job training. The student covers reactor systems, engineered safeguards, instrumentation, waste disposal, primary cooling, ventilation, primary support, and process computers.
Credit recommendation: In the lower division baccalaureate/associate degree category, 20 semester hours (15 academic semester hours and 5 on-the-job training semester hours) in Nuclear Engineering Technology (1/88).

Reactor Theory
(Reactor Theory for Licensed Operators)
Location: Shippingport, PA.
Length: 160 hours (22 days).
Dates: May 1983-Present.
Objective: To provide the student with the knowledge required to describe the neutron life cycle and to predict and explain reactor response.
Instruction: Lecture/discussion format. Neutron diffusion, neutron leakage, neutron multiplication, reactivity, period/startup rate, subcritical multiplication, coefficients and reactor control, fission product poisoning, delayed neutrons, transient reactor behavior, reactor startup and shutdown, power distribution and peaking factors.
Credit recommendation: In the lower division baccalaureate/associate degree category, 4 semester hours in Nuclear Engineering Technology (10/86).

Simulator Training (For Licensed Nuclear Reactor Operators)
Location: Beaver Valley Power Station, Shippingport, PA.
Length: 171 hours (3½ weeks).
Dates: February 1985-Present.
Objective: To provide simulator instruction for the student as it applies to a nuclear power plant reactor operator.
Learning Outcome: Upon successful completion of this course, the student will be able to utilize the appropriate controls, indications and instrumentation to operate each of the systems; utilize the appropriate indications and instrumentation to assess the plant status, and predict and explain the response of plant parameters during the various evolutions.
Instruction: Course covers lecture and simulator evolutions. The student participates in all phases of simulated reactor operations from shutdown to full power operations including unusual and accident situations.
Credit recommendation: In the upper division baccalaureate category, 2 semester hours in Nuclear Engineering (1/88).

Thermodynamics for Licensed Operators (2404)
Location: Shippingport, PA.
Length: 183 hours (5 weeks).
Dates: May 1982-Present.
Objective: To provide students with an understanding of basic thermodynamic concepts and a survey of heat transfer and fluid flow processes, heat and energy cycles with applications to nuclear power plant operations.
Instruction: Non-calculus discussions of laws of thermodynamics; the general energy equation, properties of water; methods of heat transfer; fluid statics; fluid mechanics - Bernoulli's principle. Conceptual discussions of compressible and incompressible flow, fluid measurements, pumps, valves, systems; ideal and real gases; Cycles - Carnot, Rankine, Rankine Regenerative Reheat, Refrigeration; Reactor Thermal and Hydraulic Limits. Lecture and discussion are used.
Credit recommendation: In the upper division baccalaureate degree category, 3 semester hours in Nuclear Technology (1/84).

Turbine Plant Systems
Location: Beaver Valley Power Station, Shippingport, PA.
Length: 920 hours (28 weeks).
Dates: June 1982-Present.
Objective: To provide the student with a knowledge of the various turbine plant systems as they apply to a nuclear power plant reactor operator.
Learning Outcome: Upon successful completion of this course, the student will be able to write the function of the various systems; draw the basic system flow path; describe in detail the operation, control, and location of the major components of the various systems; and explain system procedures.
Instruction: Course covers lecture, simulation, and on-the-job training. The student covers electrical distribution, steam cycle, turbine-generator, cooling, secondary support, personnel safety, and administrative procedures.
Credit recommendation: In the lower division bac-

calaureate/associate degree category, 18 semester hours (13 academic semester hours and 5 on-the-job training semester hours) in Nuclear Engineering Technology (1/88).

Educational Information and Resource Center (EIRC)

For nearly twenty years, the Educational Information and Resource Center (EIRC) has developed programs to meet a variety of educational and social needs for the state of New Jersey. Its success in meeting those needs resulted in an expansion of its original mission as an educational support organization to a multi-faceted resource center for many public agencies, professional groups, and the public at large.

EIRC has the core capability to provide training and technical assistance in all areas of professional development. It provides assistance through workshops and seminars which have given thousands of educators, administrators, and human service personnel the knowledge necessary to keep current on issues affecting their professions and their careers.

Source of official student records: Associate Director of Educational Services, RD #4, Box 209, Sewell, NJ 08080.

Additional information about the courses: Program on Noncollegiate Sponsored Instruction, Thomas A. Edison State College, Kelsey Building, 101 West State Street, Trenton, NJ 08625.

Early Childhood Curriculum
Location: Various locations throughout New Jersey.
Length: 45 hours (9 days).
Dates: September 1985-Present.
Objective: To provide an introduction to selected topics to Early Childhood Curriculum.
Instruction: This course consists of a series of modules. Lectures, discussion, and classroom exercises are utilized. The topics covered are: Concepts and Values in Early Childhood, Observing and Rewarding Behavior, Teaching Techniques, Art, Science, Social Studies, Children with Special Needs.
Credit recommendation: In the lower division baccalaureate/associate degree category, 3 semester hours in Selected Topics in Early Childhood Curriculum (9/85).

Relationship Within the Preschool Setting
Location: Various locations throughout New Jersey.
Length: 50 hours (10 days).
Dates: September 1985-Present.
Objective: To offer students an understanding of relationships that exist within preschool environment between children, staff and parents, and to extend this knowledge toward appropriate strategies for classroom management.
Instruction: This course consists of a series of modules. Lectures, discussion, and classroom exercises are utilized. The topics covered are: Child Development, Human Sexuality and Abuse, Classroom Management, Staff Self Concept, Advanced Discipline, and Communicating with Parents.
Credit recommendation: In the lower division baccalaureate/associate degree category, 3 semester hours in Relationships within the Preschool Setting (9/85).

Electrical Workers, Local Union 26 of the International Brotherhood of Electrical Workers and the Washington, D.C. Chapter of the National Electrical Contractors Association, Joint School

Electrical Workers Local 26 represents 1,900 workers performing electrical work in the Washington, D.C. metropolitan area. They are classified as inside wiremen and are responsible for the final delivery of current at consumers' outlets. Their four years of apprenticeship training, which includes 180 hours of classroom instruction and 2000 hours of on-the-job training each year, is administered jointly by Local 26 and the Washington, D.C. Chapter of the National Electrical Contractors Association. The training enables each worker to read blueprints; to work safely with high voltages; and to install, repair, and service complicated electrical equipment and controls.

To receive journeyman status, all four years of the program must be completed. Each year approximately 100 members of Local 26 graduate from the Electrician Apprentice program.

Source of official student records: Director, Electrical Workers Joint Apprenticeship Committee, Local 26, I.B.E.W., 6200 Kansas Avenue, N.E., Washington, D.C. 2011.

Additional information about the courses: Program on Noncollegiate Sponsored Instruction, The Center for Adult Learning and Educational Credentials, American Council on Education, One Dupont Circle, Washington, D.C. 20036.

Electrician Apprentice (Inside)
Location: International Brotherhood of Electrical Workers Local 26 and the National Electrical Contractors Association Joint School, Washington, D.C. Job sites in the Washington, D.C. area.
Length: Four years.
Dates: January 1971-Present.
Objective: To prepare apprentices for journeyman status in the electrical construction (inside) industry.
Instruction: *First year:* Principles of direct current, al-

ternating current, and electromagnetism; knowledge and application of National Electrical Code requirements pertaining to cable, conduit, and grounding; operation of electric motors; Ohm's law, series circuits, parallel circuits, magnetism, and motors; safety procedures and first aid resuscitation; reading and sketching of elevation views and plot plans, including symbols and scales used; materials used in the electrical construction industry, such as wires, cables, conduit, conductors, insulation, joints, fasteners, and fuses; under supervision, installation of electrical apparatus such as cables, conduit, tubing, outlet boxes, outlets, fixtures, and securing and holding devices at various job sites; orientation to the apprenticeship form of education and training, the electrical industry, the history of the electrical industry, the International Brotherhood of Electrical Workers, local union by-laws, and the history of the operation and contribution of the National Electrical Contractors Association.

Second year: Use and installation of electric meters; National Electrical Code requirements relating to grounding conductors, branch circuits, and transformers; use of algebra and trigonometry in making mathematical calculations; types, construction, winding ratios, functions, and classifications of transformers; operating principles and functions of incandescent lamps, alarms, and refrigeration and air conditioning components; capacitance, inductance, reactance, and RLC circuits; electric motor mechanical drive and load connections; use of architect's blueprint and layouts; use and care of tools of the industry; circuit testing; first aid procedures, including those for electric shock victims; safety rules and practices for the electrical construction industry. Apprentices perform more complex work tasks through a series of six-month job rotations.

Third year: National Electrical Code requirements for capacitors, electric motors, hazardous locations, and Class I, II, and III installations; use of blueprints pertaining to structural details, floor plan specifications, floor ducts, service entrances, circuits, and riser circuits; electrical wiring and distribution systems; electrical theory pertaining to alternating currents, alternating current motors and transformers, power factor and correction, and primary and secondary connections; analysis of malfunctions and repair of remote controls, protection devices, and alternating current motor controls. Apprentices apply knowledge by assuming increasingly complex responsibilities and performing increasingly complex tasks in work settings that are rotated each six months.

Fourth year: Knowledge and application of National Electrical Code requirements pertaining to wire closets, junction boxes, and stairway and emergency lighting; metric system conversions; application of rules to radiation exposure, protection, reaction, and other features of nuclear safety; transistor principles circuits and vacuum tube fundamentals; ;use of electronic testing equipment; basic rectifier circuits, amplifier circuits, special circuit applications, and transistor use; static control fundamentals, including concepts, circuits, analyses, and applications; alternating current applications in industrial electricity; fundamentals of temperature, pressure, and flow; instrumentation systems; installation and testing of electrical construction materials; use of electrical construction equipment

Credit recommendation: *First year:* In the lower division baccalaureate/associate degree category, 2 semester hours in Basic Electricity, 1 in National Electrical Code, 1 in Blueprint Reading and Sketching, 1 in Orientation to Electrical Construction, 1 in Electrical Construction Materials and Methods, and 1 in field experience in Electrical Construction, for a total of 7 semester hours (9/77).

Second year: In the lower division baccalaureate/associate degree category, 4 semester hours in Basic Electricity, 3 in Electrical Construction Materials and Methods, 2 in field experience in Electrical Construction, 2 in National Electrical Code, 2 in Technical Mathematics, 2 in Bluepirnt Reading and Sketching, 1 in Orientation to Electrical Construction, 1 in Safety and First Aid, and 1 in Shop Practices, for a total of 18 semester hours (9/77).

Third year: In the lower division baccalaureate/associate degree category, 4 semester hours in Basic Electricity, 4 in Electrical Construction Materials and Methods, 3 in National Electrical Code, 3 in Blueprint Reading and Sketching, 3 in field experience in Electrical Construction, 2 in Technical Mathematics, 2 in Industrial Electricity, 1 in Motor Controls, 1 in Orientation to Electrical Construction, 1 in Safety and First Aid, and 1 in Shop Practices, for a total of 25 semester hours (9/77).

Fourth year: In the lower division baccalaureate/associate degree category, 5 semester hours in Electrical Construction Materials and Methods, 4 in Basic Electricity, 4 in National Electrical Code, 4 in Blueprint Reading and Sketching, 4 in field experience in Electrical Construction, 3 in Industrial Electricity, 2 in Safety and First Aid, 2 in Motor Controls, 2 in Technical Mathematics, 2 in Shop Practices, 2 in Electronics, 1 in Instrumentation, and 1 in Orientation to Electrical Construction, for a total of 36 semester hours (9/77).

NOTE: The credit recommendations are cumulative; readers should use the recommendation that corresponds to the number of years completed by the student.

Electrical Workers, Local Union 102 of the International Brotherhood of Electrical Workers

The Electrical Workers, IBEW Local 102, represents some 500 construction workers performing electrical work in the Passaic County and parts of Bergen County, New Jersey area. The members represented by Local 102 are classified as inside and outside wireman and are responsible for the final delivery of current at consumers' outlets. Their four years of apprenticeship training includes a minimum of 144 hours of classroom instruction and 1,750 hours of on-the-job training each year and is administered jointly by Local 102 and the Passaic County division of the Northern New Jersey chapter of the National Electrical Contractors Association. The training enables each to read blueprints; to work safely with high voltages; and to install, repair, and service complicated electrical equipment and controls on residential, commercial, and industrial projects.

The location of Local 102's training facilities is the Passaic County Vocational Technical School, 45 Rhinehart Road in Wayne, New Jersey. Local 102 has several classrooms in this modern facility which include lecture, lab, demonstration, and workshop rooms. They have a full complement of the latest electrical training equipment on which experiments and troubleshooting problems are performed in a lab setting. A variety of workshops are also in use including electrical installation, wire, and welding shops. There is a library of the latest print materials, as well as a variety of media materials including films and overhead transparencies. These facilities together provide an excellent setting for the furtherance of the objectives of the program.

As this is a national standardized training program, the course materials are periodically reviewed, updated (annually) and revised by the National Joint Apprenticeship and Training Committee. The prerequisite for journeyperson training courses are included in the apprenticeship training program. As this is a very competitive and dangerous occupation, it is essential that all of the members working in the field are fully trained in all phases of the job. To achieve journeyperson status, all four years must be successfully completed.

Source of official student records: Training Director, IBEW Local 102, 234 McLean Boulevard, Paterson, New Jersey 07504.

Additional information about the courses: Thomas A. Edison State College, Program on Noncollegiate Sponsored Instruction, 101 West State Street, CN545, Trenton, New Jersey 08625.

Electrician Apprentice (Inside)
  Location: Paterson, NJ.
  Length: 4 years.
  Dates: June 1978-Present.
  Objective: To prepare apprentices for journeyman status in the electrical construction (inside) industry.
  Instruction: *First year:* Principles of direct current, alternating current and electromagnetism; knowledge and application of National Electrical Code requirements pertaining to cable, conduit, and grounding; operation of electric motors; Ohm's law, series circuits, parallel circuits, magnetism, and motors, safety procedures and first aid resuscitation; reading and sketching of evaluation views and plot plans, including symbols and scales used; materials used in the electrical construction industry, such as wires, cables, conduit, conductors, insulation, joints, fasteners, and fuses; under supervision, installation of electrical apparatus such as cables, conduit, tubing, outlet boxes, outlets, fixtures, and securing and holding devices at various job sites; orientation to the apprenticeship form of education and training, the electrical industry, the history of the electrical industry, the International Brotherhood of Electrical Workers, local union by-laws, and the history of the operation and contribution of the National Electrical Contractors Association.

Second year: Use and installation of electric meters; National Electrical Code requirements relating to grounding conductors, branch circuits, and transformers; use of algebra and trigonometry in making mathematical calculations; types, construction, winding ratios, functions, and classifications of transformers; operating principles and functions of incandescent lamps, alarms, and refrigeration and air conditioning components; capacitance, inductance; reactance, and RLC circuits; electric motor mechanical drive and load connections; use of architect's blueprint and layouts; use and care of tools of the industry; circuit testing; first aid procedures, including those for electric shock victims; safety rules and practices for the electrical construction industry. Apprentices perform more complex work tasks through a series of six-month job rotations.

Third year: National Electrical Code requirement for capacitors, electric motors, hazardous locations, and Class I, II, and III installations; use of blueprints pertaining to structural details, floor plan specifications, floor ducts, service entrances, circuits, and riser circuits; electrical wiring and distribution systems; electrical theory pertaining to alternating currents, alternating current motors and transformers, power factor and correction, and primary and secondary connections; analysis of malfunctions and repair of remote controls, protection devices, and alternating current motor controls. Apprentices apply knowledge by assuming increasingly complex responsibilities and performing increasingly complex tasks in work settings that are rotated each six months.

Fourth year: Knowledge and application of National Electrical Code requirements pertaining to wire closets, junction boxes, and stairway and emergency lighting; metric system conversions; application of rules to radiation exposure, protection, reaction, and other features of nuclear safety; transistor principles and circuits, use of electronic testing equipment; basic rectifier circuits, amplifier circuits, special circuit applications, and transistor use; static control fundamentals, including concepts, circuits, analysis, and applications; alternating current applications in industrial electricity; fundamentals of temperature, pressure, and flow; instrumentation systems; installation and testing of electrical construction materials; use of electrical construction equipment.

Credit recommendation: *First year:* In the lower division baccalaureate/associate degree category, 2 semester hours in Basic Electricity, 1 in National Electrical Code, 2 in Blueprint Reading and Sketching, and 2 in field experience in Electrical Construction, 1 in Technical Mathematics, for a total of 8 semester hours.

Second year: In the lower division baccalaureate/associate degree category, 1 semester hour in Basic Electricity, 2 in field experience in Electrical Construction, 1 in National Electrical Code, 1 in Technical Mathematics, 1 in Blueprint Reading and Sketching, for a total of 6 semester hours.

Third year: In the lower division baccalaureate/associate degree category, 2 semester hours in Basic Electricity, 1 in National Electrical Code, 1 in Blueprint Reading and Sketching, 2 in field experience in Electrical Construction, 3 in Motor Controls, 2 in Electrical Machinery for a total of 11 semester hours.

Fourth year: In the lower division baccalaureate/associate degree category, 1 in National Electrical Code, 3 in field experience in Electrical Construction, 1 in Motor Controls, 4 in Electronics, 1 in Electrical Machinery for a total of 10 semester hours.

NOTE: Total number of credits for successful completion of all four (4) years: 5 semester hours in Basic Electricity, 4 in Blueprint Reading and Sketching, 4 in Electronics, 3 in Electrical Machinery, 9 in Field Experience in Electrical Construction, 4 in Motor Controls, 4 in National Electrical Code, 2 in Technical Mathematics, for a total of 35 semester hours (6/88).

Electrical Workers, Local Union 164 of the International Brotherhood of Electrical Workers, AFL-CIO, Bergen and Hudson Counties, New Jersey, and the Bergen-Hudson County Chapter of the National Electrical Contractors Association Joint Apprenticeship Training Program

Electrical Workers, Local 164 represents some 800 journeypersons in the Bergen-Hudson County, New Jersey area. The members represented by Local 164 are classified as inside and outside wirepersons and are responsible for the final delivery of current at consumers' outlets. Their four years of apprenticeship training which includes 161 hours of classroom instruction and 1,650 hours of on-the-job training each year, is administered jointly by Local 164 and the Bergen-Hudson Division of the Northern New Jersey Chapter of the National Electrical Contractors Association. The training enables each to read blueprints; to work safely with high voltages; and to install, repair, and service complicated electrical equipment and controls on residential, commercial and industrial projects.

The permanent location of Local 164's training facilities is 61 Kansas Avenue, Hackensack, New Jersey. Local 164 has a large classroom in this modern facility which also includes a lab with a full complement of the latest electrical training equipment on which experiments and troubleshooting problems are performed. There is a library of the latest printed materials, as well as a variety of mediated materials including films and overhead transparencies, and video cassettes. These facilities together provide an excellent setting for the furtherance of the objectives of the program. Apprentices in Local 164 attend class during the day of a full-time, paid basis and the instruction is provided by a full-time professional instructor.

As this is a national standardized training program, the course materials are periodically reviewed, updated (annually) and revised by the National Joint Apprenticeship and Training Committee. The prerequisites for journeyperson training courses are included in the apprenticeship training program. As this is a very competitive and dangerous occupation, it is essential that all of the members working in the field are fully trained in all phases of the job.

To achieve journeyperson status, all four years must be successfully completed, as well as successful performance on the rigorous final apprenticeship exam (this final exam required of all local 164 apprentices is beyond standard, national IBEW requirements).

Source of official student records: Director, Electrical Workers Joint Apprenticeship Training Committee, Local 164, IBEW, AFL-CIO, 61 Kansas Street, Hackensack, New Jersey 07601. Students should request records directly from ACE Registry of Credit Recommendations.

Additional information about the courses: Director of Program on Noncollegiate Sponsored Instruction, Thomas A. Edison State College, 101 West State Street, CN545, Trenton, New Jersey 08625.

Electrician Apprentice (Inside)
Location: Hackensack, NJ.
Length: 4 years.
Dates: September 1972-Present.
Objective: To prepare apprentices for journeyperson status in the electrical construction (inside) industry.
Instruction: *First year:* Principles of direct current, alternating current, and electromagnetism; knowledge and application of National Electrical Code requirements pertaining to cable, conduit, and grounding; operation of electric motors; Ohm's law, series circuits, parallel circuits, magnetism, and motors; safety procedures and first aid resuscitation; reading and sketching of elevation views and plot plans, including symbols and scales used; materials used in the electrical construction industry, such as wires, cables, conduit, conductors, insulation, joints, fasteners, and fuses; under supervision, installation of electri-

cal apparatus such as cables, conduit, tubing, outlet boxes, outlets, fixtures, and securing and holding devices at various job sites; orientation to the apprenticeship form of education and training, the electrical industry, the history of the electrical industry, the International Brotherhood of Electrical Workers, local union by-laws, and the history of the operation and contribution of the National Electrical Contractors Association.

Second year: Use and installation of electric meters; National Electrical Code requirements relating to grounding conductors, branch circuits, and transformers; use of algebra and trigonometry in making mathematical calculations; types, construction, winding ratios, functions, and classifications of transformers; operating principles and functions of incandescent lamps, alarms, and refrigeration and air conditioning components; capacitance, inductance, reactance, and RLC circuits; electric motor mechanical drive and load connections; use of architect's blueprint and layouts; use and care of tools of the industry; circuit testing; first aid procedures, including those for electric shock victims; safety rules and practices for electrical construction industry. Apprentices perform more complex work tasks through a series of one-year job rotations.

Third year: National Electrical Code requirements for capacitors, electric motors, hazardous locations, and Class I, II, and III installations; use of blueprints pertaining to structural details, floor plan specifications, floor ducts, service entrances, circuits, and riser circuits; electrical wiring and distribution systems; electrical theory pertaining to alternating currents, alternating current motors and transformers, power factor and correction, and primary and secondary connections; analysis of malfunctions and repair of remote controls, protection devices, and alternating current motor controls. Apprentices apply knowledge by assuming increasingly complex responsibilities and performing increasingly complex tasks in work settings that are rotated each one year.

Fourth year: Knowledge and application of National Electrical Code requirements pertaining to wire closets, junction boxes, and stairway and emergency lighting; metric system conversions; application of rules to radiation exposure, protection, reaction and other features of nuclear safety; transistor principles, circuits, and use of electronic testing equipment; basic rectifier circuits, amplifier circuits, special circuit applications, and transistor use; static control fundamentals, including concepts, circuits, analyses, and applications; alternating current applications in industrial electricity; fundamentals of temperature, pressure, and flow; instrumentation systems; installation and testing of electrical construction materials; use of electrical construction equipment. Each apprentice in this local must complete the required Red Cross First Aid course and earn the CPR Certificate; this requirement exceeds national IBEW standards.

Credit recommendation: *First year:* In the lower division baccalaureate/associate degree category, 2 semester hours in Basic Electricity, 1 in National Electrical Code, 1 in Blueprint Reading and Sketching, and 2 in field experience in Electrical Construction, 2 in Technical Mathematics, for a total of 8 semester hours.

Second year: In the lower division baccalaureate/associate degree category, 2 semester hours in Basic Electricity, 2 in field experience in Electrical Construction, 1 in National Electrical Code, 1 in Technical Mathematics, 1 in Blueprint Reading and Sketching, for a total of 7 semester hours.

Third year: In the lower division baccalaureate/associate degree category, 1 semester hour in Basic Electricity, 1 in National Electrical Code, 1 in Blueprint Reading and Sketching, 2 in field experience in Electrical Construction, 2 in Motor Controls, for a total of 7 semester hours.

Fourth year: In the lower division baccalaureate/associate degree category, 1 in National Electrical Code, 1 in Blueprint Reading and Sketching, 2 in field experience in Electrical Construction, 2 in Motor Controls, 3 in Electronics, 1 in Safety and First Aid, and 4 in Electrical Construction, Materials and Methods, for a total of 14 semester hours.

NOTE: Total number of credits for successful completion of all four (4) years: 5 semester hours in Basic Electricity, 4 in Blueprint Reading and Sketching, 3 in Electronics, 1 in Safety and First Aid, 8 in Field Experience in Electrical Construction, 4 in Electrical Construction, Materials and Methods, 4 in Motor Controls, 4 in National Electrical Code, 3 in Technical Mathematics, for a total of 36 semester hours (5/83) (7/88). NOTE: These courses have been reevaluated and continue to meet requirements for credit recommendations.

English Language Institute of America, Inc.

The English Language Institute offers one course, *Practical English and the Command of Words.* The Institute, in offering the course, recognizes that effective communication is a demand of contemporary business life, and the prerequisite of effective communication is mastery of its basic tool: language.

The Institute has offered this course since 1955. Course Developers skilled in communication skills have been used periodically to revise the course. Students who take the Institute ACE credit-recommended course usually are employees of business and government agencies that approve the course for employee participation. However, individuals can and do take the course independently.

A final exam is developed by the Institute, administered (and monitored) by a sponsoring business or government agency and scored by the Institute or can be administered and monitored directly by the Institute.

Source of official student records: Director, English Language Institute of America, 332 S. Michigan Avenue, Chicago, Illinois 60604.

Additional information about the courses: Program on Noncollegiate Sponsored Instruction, The Center for Adult Learning and Educational Credentials, American Council on Education, One Dupont Circle, Washington, D.C. 20036.

Practical English and the Command of Words
Location: Employees of businesses and governmental agencies located throughout the United States and individual independent study at location of choice.
Length: Self-paced.
Dates: July 1979-Present.
Objective: To provide a self-study educational program for adults in basic English communication skills.
Instruction: Practical English skills are covered through 52 four-page units on vocabulary development, pronunciation, grammar and usage, spelling, speech, word meaning, punctuation, sentence structure, paragraph organization, and telephone courtesy. The user has an opportunity to plan his/her course of study and to determine areas that need review by using self-administered, self-scored pre-tests and quarterly post-tests.
Credit recommendation: In the lower division baccalaureate/associate degree category, 3 semester hours in English as an elective in Grammar and Usage, and in the lower division baccalaureate/associate degree category, 1 semester hour in Business Communication (1/84). NOTE: In order to receive credit, students must take and successfully pass a final examination developed by the English Language Institute. The final examination can be administered (and monitored) by a company training officer and scored by the Institute *or* it can be administered, monitored, and scored directly by the Institute.

Federal Aviation Administration

The Federal Aviation Administration (FAA), a component of the United States Department of Transportation, serves primarily to ensure aviation safety, promote air commerce, and support national security through management of the National Airspace System. Training programs are offered to employees in each of the 11 FAA regions in the United States.

FEDERAL AVIATION ADMINISTRATION ACADEMY

The FAA Academy was established in the summer of 1959 to administer the Agency's technical training programs. FAA personnel must be familiar with current aviation concepts, knowledge, and skills, and must also acquire advanced knowledge and skills in order to operate and maintain new equipment as it is developed. Training is provided for air traffic control specialists, engineers, technicians, and pilots. In addition, a wide range of instructor development courses is offered to ensure the efficiency and effectiveness of Academy technical instructors.

The courses listed below are part of the training program of the Instructor Resources Section, a division of the Training Methods and Operations Branch, FAA Academy. Courses are taught at the FAA Academy in Oklahoma City and at various FAA regional locations. Professional education specialists administer instructor development programs for Academy instructors and supervisors, regional staffs, Department of Transportation (DOT) personnel, and international personnel. In addition, they provide a wide range of educational consulting services which include follow-up instructor evaluations of the Academy's technical instructor staff.

Source of official student records: Registrar Unit, AAC-911A, Federal Aviation Administration Academy, Aeronautical Center, P.O. Box 25082, 5400 S. MacArthur, Oklahoma City, Oklahoma 73125.

Additional information about the courses: Program on Noncollegiate Sponsored Instruction, The Center for Adult Learning and Educational Credentials, American Council on Education, One Dupont Circle, Washington, D.C. 20036.

Academy Instructor Training (Basic) (10520)
Location: FAA Academy, Oklahoma City, OK.
Length: 120 hours (3 weeks).
Dates: April 1983-Present.
Objective: To provide the student with an understanding of classroom instruction.
Learning Outcome: Upon successful completion of this course, the student will have a knowledge of factors affecting learning, leadership, counseling, equal employment opportunity; and develop skills in use of training aids, materials, classroom management, human relations practices, and teaching techniques.
Instruction: Course covers oral communication, training aids and materials, classroom management, methods and techniques of instruction, and interpersonal relations. Methodology includes lecture, discussion, and role playing.
Credit recommendation: In the upper division baccalaureate category, 3 semester hours in Behavioral Science or Educational Methods (9/88).

Advanced Instructor Training (10511)
(Formerly Academy Instructor Training - Advanced)
Location: FAA Academy, Oklahoma City, OK.
Length: 40 hours (1 week).
Dates: February 1974-Present.
Objective: To improve the experienced instructor's competency in teaching, classroom management, and in-

terpersonal relationships.

Learning Outcome: Upon successful completion of this course, the student will be able to demonstrate methods of instruction; and demonstrate skill managing the learning process.

Instruction: Course covers group dynamics, methods of instruction, and assessing teaching effectiveness. Methodology includes lecture, discussion, team activity, case studies, and role playing.

Credit recommendation: In the upper division baccalaureate category, 2 semester hours in Human Relations or Psychology (8/78) (9/88). NOTE: This course has been reevaluated and continues to meet requirements for credit recommendations.

Air Carrier Operations Indoctrination (20700)
Location: FAA Academy, Oklahoma City, OK.
Length: 160 hours (4 weeks).
Dates: October 1982-Present.
Objective: To provide the student with an introduciton for air carrier operations inspector's job functions.
Learning Outcome: Upon successful completion of this course, the student will be able to demonstrate an understanding of flight standards and air carrier mission; and demonstrate skills in performing inspector job functions.
Instruction: Course covers accident prevention, instrument flying rating, aircraft familiarization (Cessna 340-A; 172), test standards, evaluation techniques, qualifications pilot examiners, V.F.R. maneuvers, cross country flight planning, conduct of tests, air transport pilot certification, commercial pilot certification, airmen certification-written tests, surveillance/air worthiness, flight instructor certificaiton, aircraft ratings, crew member qualification, pilot certification, and student certification. Methodology includes lectures and discussion.
Credit recommendation: In the upper division baccalaureate category, 4 semester hours in Aviation Technology (9/88).

Air Traffic Control Beacon Integrator 5 (40383)
Location: FAA Academy, Oklahoma City, OK.
Length: 80 hours (2 weeks).
Dates: January 1982-Present.
Objective: To train the student to evaluate, modify, maintain, and certify the ATCBI-5 system.
Learning Outcome: Upon successful completion of this course, the student will be able to operate and evaluate the ATCBI-5 system using video and RF test sets; and be able to troubleshoot and correct malfunctions.
Instruction: Course covers system concepts, pulse mode generator, transmitter, receiver, stagger/de-stagger, control circuits and test sets. Methodology includes lecture and discussion, with laboratory activities.
Credit recommendation: In the lower division baccalaureate/associate degree category, 2 semester hours in Electronics Technology (9/88).

Curriculum Development (10512)
Location: FAA Academy, Oklahoma City, OK.
Length: 80 hours (2 weeks).
Dates: November 1972-Present.
Objective: To improve the instructor's competency in curriculum development.
Learning Outcome: Upon successful completion of this course, the student will be able to understand rationale in curriculum develpment; demonstrate instructional methods; and demonstrate knowledge of curriculum design.
Instruction: Course covers curriculum rationale, course design, validation, and methods of instruction. Methodology includes lecture, discussion, and laboratory assignments.
Credit recommendation: In the upper division baccalaureate category, 3 semester hours in Curriculum (8/78) (9/88). NOTE: This course has been reevaluated and continues to meet requirements for credit recommendations.

Designing Programmed Instruction (10525)
(Formerly Instructional Materials Development [10515])
Location: FAA Academy, Oklahoma City, OK.
Length: 120 hours (3 weeks).
Dates: March 1973-Present.
Objective: To improve the experienced instructor's competency in the development of course materials.
Learning Outcome: Upon successful completion of this course, the student will be able to demonstrate skill in development of self-instructional materials; and to prepare new materials and tests for selected subject areas.
Instruction: Course covers the design of self-instructional materials, learning objectives, teaching activities, testing techniques, and behavioral objectives. Methodology includes self-instructional activities with monitoring and evaluation by educational specialist.
Credit recommendation: In the upper division baccalaureate category, 3 semester hours in Curriculum or in Programmed Instruction (8/78) (9/88). NOTE: This course has been reevaluated and continues to meet requirements for credit recommendations.

Facility Instructor Training (10501)
Location: FAA Academy, Oklahoma City, OK.
Length: 100 hours (2 weeks, 3 days).
Dates: *Version 1:* June 1977-January 1988; *Version 2:* February 1988-Present.
Objective: To develop the new instructor's understanding of and competency in learning theory, training methods, and classroom management.
Learning Outcome: Upon successful completion of this course, the student will be able to demonstrate an understanding of learning theory, training methods, and classroom management.
Instruction: Course covers planning and conducting

training, methods of training, use and preparation of audiovisual aids, classroom management, and lesson plan development. Methodology includes lecture, discussion, student participation, and presentations.

Credit recommendation: In the lower division baccalaureate/associate degree category, 3 semester hours in Behavioral Sciences or Educational Methods (8/78) (9/88). NOTE: Credit should not be granted both for this course and for Basic Instructor Training (10510). NOTE: This course has been reevaluated and continues to meet requirements for credit recommendations.

Flight Control System (22462)
  Location: FAA Academy, Oklahoma City, OK.
  Length: 240 hours (6 weeks).
  Dates: October 1982-Present.
  Objective: To provide the avionics maintenance technician with the knowledge and ability to perform testing, troubleshooting, repair, and modification of the FCS-105 Flight Control System and the MC-103 Compass System.
  Learning Outcome: Upon successful completion of this course, the student will be able to demonstrate skill in repairing, troubleshooting, and modification of the FCS-105 Flight Control System and MC-103 Magnetic Compass System.
  Instruction: Course covers logic circuits, circuit analysis, maintenance, and calibration. Methodology includes lecture, discussion, and laboratory activity.
  Credit recommendation: In the upper division baccalaureate category, 6 semester hours in Avionics (9/88).

Fundamentals of Microprocessors (22470)
  Location: Will Rogers Field, Oklahoma City, OK.
  Length: 120 hours (3 weeks).
  Dates: June 1981-Present.
  Objective: To provide the student with knowledge of the hardware and software operation of the Intel 8085 microprocessor.
  Learning Outcome: Upon successful completion of this course, the student will be able to convert from one number base to another; interpret simple programs written in assembly or machine language; write and debug microprocessor programs; and troubleshoot and repair microprocessor controlled circuits.
  Instruction: Course covers microprocessor fundamentals, introduction to programming, microprocessor system hardware, microprocessor software, and troubleshooting microprocessor systems. Methodology includes lecture, laboratory exercises, and written and performance examinations.
  Credit recommendation: In the lower division baccalaureate/associate degree category, 3 semester hours in Microprocessor Technology (9/88).

Instructional Testing (10513)
  Location: FAA Academy, Oklahoma City, OK.
  Length: 80 hours (2 weeks); residential.
  Dates: November 1976-Present.
  Objective: To improve the experienced instructor's competency in test construction and administration, particularly criterion-referenced assessment.
  Learning Outcome: Upon successful completion of this course, the student will be able to demonstrate skill in test construction and administration; and demonstrate an understanding of testing rationale.
  Instruction: Course covers criterion-referenced evaluation, verbal and motor performance, item analysis, and administrative procedures. Methodology includes lecture, discussion, and laboratory activities.
  Credit recommendation: In the upper division baccalaureate category, 3 semester hours in Evaluation and Measurement (8/78) (9/88). NOTE: This course has been reevaluated and continues to meet requirements for credit recommendations.

AIR TRAFFIC TRAINING

(Courses are listed in numerical order)

Air Traffic Control Specialist and/or Facility Instructor Training (10510)
(Terminal, En Route - Instruction)
(This is a job classification, not a course title)
  Location: FAA Academy, Oklahoma City, OK.
  Length: 3,540 hours (2 years).
  Dates: May 1969-Present.
  Objective: To provide Federal Aviation Administration staff with an extensive, supervised experience in classroom instruction, supervision, and curriculum development.
  Instruction: *1. Instructor:* The typical instructor at the Federal Aviation Administration Academy is a journeyman specialist selected for assignment to the Academy on the basis of superior competency in his/her field. After undergoing training in basic instructional methods, the person is given responsibility for presenting both lecture/discussion and laboratory sessions. Normally instructors are also required to complete an advanced course in instructor training within a year of assignment to the Academy. The person teaches for a minimum of two years at the Academy, during which time his/her performance is regularly and carefully critiqued in terms of rigorous instructor performance standards. *2. Lead Instructor:* For Instructors Assigned Positions as Lead Instructors responsibility includes supervision of classroom lecture/discussions and laboratory sessions. They function as first level supervisors to students acting as liaisons between Federal Aviation Administration management instructors, and the students. Lead Instructors administer all tests, schedule classroom and laboratory activities, counsel students on academic and personal problems, and insure adherence to Academy policies and procedures. It is the Lead Instructor's responsibility to assure that a class

is managed according to Academy guidelines and the Federal Aviation Administration's National Training Plan, and that course or curriculum objectives are met. *3. Development/Revision:* If the instructor is assigned to the Academy's Development/Revision Unit after one year of teaching, the person is responsible for the development of curriculum, and instructional and testing material, including audio/visual aids, lesson plans, course outlines, reference materials, lab guides, and individualized instruction materials. The person's performance in this unit is regularly and carefully evaluated, and additional training is provided by a supervisor or through additional classroom study, as needed.

Credit recommendation: *1. Instructor:* In the upper division baccalaureate category, 3 semester hours equivalent to a college-supervised student teaching field experience in Secondary of Postsecondary Education. *2. Lead Instructor:* Instructors who served in this capacity for one or more years; in the upper division baccalaureate category, 3 semester hours equivalent to a college-supervised student teaching field experience and in the upper division baccalaureate category, 3 semester hours of Educational Program Management. *3. Development/Revision:* Instructors who are assigned to Development/Revision unit for one or more years, in the upper division baccalaureate category, 3 semester hours equivalent to a college-supervised student teaching field experience, and in the upper division baccalaureate category, 3 semester hours of Curriculum Development and Instruction (10/82). NOTE: To validate individual's performance, students must submit Standard Form 172. NOTE 1: For credit to be awarded in student teaching, Basic Instruction Training (10510) and Facilities Instruction Training (10501) must have been satisfactorily completed. NOTE 2. For credit to be awarded in Program Management, Instruction Testing (10513) and Training for Advanced Instructors (10511) must have been completed satisfactorily. NOTE 3: For credit to be awarded as Curriculum Development, Curriculum Development (10512) and Instruction Materials Development (10515) must have been satisfactorily completed.

Jovial Programming (12002)
Location: FAA Academy, Oklahoma City, OK.
Length: 160 hours.
Dates: May 1982-Present.
Objective: To introduce students to programming concepts and techniques.
Instruction: Covers elementary concepts of computer programming; Jovial as a language (IBM 9020); use of library routines to do mathematical calculations, data-movements, comparison, conversions, and input/output operations; keypunch operation. Lecture and discussion on programming using the IBM 9020 computer with practical exercises in lab using a punch card environment are used.

Credit recommendation: In the lower division baccalaureate/associate degree category, 3 semester hours in Computer Science or Data Processing (10/82).

IBM 360 Operating System (12003)
Location: FAA Academy, Oklahoma City, OK.
Length: 160 hours.
Dates: November 1981-Present.
Objective: To provide students with an understanding of applications of software using the job control language for IBM 360 operating system; to enable students to develop, code, and execute routines using JCL procedures to sort, merge and run utility programs.
Instruction: Lecture, discussion and application of software, JCL control language using the IBM 360 system. Hands-on lab is provided.
Credit recommendation: In the lower division baccalaureate/associate degree category, 3 semester hours in Computer Science or Data Processing (10/82).

Obstruction Evaluation and Airport/Airspace Analysis (12050)
Location: FAA Academy, Oklahoma City, OK.
Length: 200 hours.
Dates: January 1978-Present.
Objective: To enable students to understand responsibilities of the Federal Aviation Administration in integrating commercial construction peripheral to any airport.
Instruction: Covers analysis and completion of administrative efforts in obstruction/hazard evaluation; skills interpreting and applying Federal Aviation Administration regulations, specifications and associated Federal, State, and municipal laws, regulations and ordinances focusing on safe aircraft operation. Lecture and discussion activities in a classroom environment are the primary instructional vehicles. Case problems in an individual effort environment with a low student-teacher ration, i.e., 4:1, is the manner of skill achievement evaluation.
Credit recommendation: In the lower division baccalaureate/associate degree category, 3 semester hours in Management (10/82). NOTE: Students who receive credit for this course should *not* receive credit for 12051 or 12052.

Basic Obstruction Evaluation and Airport/Airspace Analysis (12051)
Location: FAA Academy, Oklahoma City, OK.
Length: 96 hours.
Dates: October 1978-Present.
Objective: To enable students to understand the basic in Federal Aviation Administration responsibilities for local community commercial, non-federal projects which may have an impact on Federal Aviation Administration jurisdiction on airports and in airspace.
Instruction: Covers analysis of projected construction

for obstruction and hazard criteria; interpretation of appropriate regulations for analyzing and judging obstruction standards adherence. Lecture and discussion are used. Case studies in the form of actual problems taken from Federal Aviation Administration files form the basis of skill application exercises.

Credit recommendation: In the lower division baccalaureate/associate degree category, 1 semester hour in Management (10/82). NOTE: Students who receive credit for this course should *not* receive credit for 12050 or 12052.

Advanced Air Traffic Control for International Participants (50003)
   Location: FAA Academy, Oklahoma City, OK.
   Length: 320 hours.
   Dates: January 1972-Present.
   Objective: To enable students to apply separation standards.
   Instruction: Covers identification of vector and separate aircraft; advisories coordination of air traffic; emergency assistance. Lecture, discussion, and practical exercises are used.
   Credit recommendation: In the lower division baccalaureate/associate degree category, 3 semester hours in Aviation Management (10/82).

Facility Management and Administration for International Participants (50004 and 14002)
   Location: FAA Academy, Oklahoma City, OK.
   Length: 160 hours (4 weeks).
   Dates: January 1972-Present.
   Objective: To enable students to understand and to apply basics of management to realistic (case study) problems under staff supervision and critique.
   Instruction: Covers management fundamentals; application of skills evidenced in test question and case study analyses. Lecture and discussion are the primary learning mechanisms. Application of materials learned (principles, theories, guidelines) is accomplished, individually or in small group environments.
   Credit recommendation: In the upper division baccalaureate category, 3 semester hours in Engineering Management or MBA Curricula (10/82).

Airspace Management (50010)
   Location: FAA Academy, Oklahoma City, OK.
   Length: 56 hours.
   Dates: January 1975-Present.
   Objective: To enable students to develop, review, coordinate, and recommend proposals for the assignment and use of navigable airspace.
   Instruction: Covers location of information, determination and application of procedures, recognition of criteria, designation of special use airspace and establishment of routes. Lecture, discussion, and classroom exercises are used.
   Credit recommendation: In the lower division baccalaureate/associate degree category, 3 semester hours in Aviation Management (10/82).

Fundamentals of Air Traffic Control (50022)
   Location: FAA Academy, Oklahoma City, OK.
   Length: 120 hours.
   Dates: January 1976-Present.
   Objective: To train personnel to understand factors affecting the operation of aircraft within the National Airspace and to relate these factors to the wide variety of aircraft now flying.
   Instruction: Topics include: Principles of Flight, Aircraft identification and performance, aviation weather, navigation, federal regulations, communication, ATC services, radar, flight assistance service. Lecture and discussion are used.
   Credit recommendation: In the lower division baccalaureate/associate degree category, 2 semester hours in Aviation Management (10/82).

Terminal Phase III - Control Tower Operation (50023)
   Location: FAA Academy, Oklahoma City, OK.
   Length: 120 hours (3 weeks).
   Dates: *Version 1:* January 1976-December 1979. *Version 2:* January 1980-Present.
   Objective: To train students in the operation of tower operation related to Terminal Phase III-Control.
   Instruction: Covers administrative and procedural skills associated with the operation of the Flight Data/Clearance Delivery, Ground Control, and Local Control positions in the Tower. Lecture, discussion, and laboratory exercises are used.
   Credit recommendation: In the vocational certificate category, 3 semester hours in Aviation Technology or Control Tower Operations (10/82).

Terminal Phase IV, Non-Radar Air Traffic Control (50024)
   Location: FAA Academy, Oklahoma City, OK.
   Length: 200 hours.
   Dates: *Version 1:* January 1976-August 1982. *Version 2:* September 1982-Present.
   Objective: To enable the student to understand and develop skills in non-radar air traffic control.
   Instruction: Emphasis is placed on flight operations direction of traffic without a radar. Lecture/discussion prepares the student for the laboratory effort. Laboratory assignments require approximately 50 percent of the course.
   Credit recommendation: In the vocational certificate category, 3 semester hours in Tower/Airport Operation (10/82).

Federal Aviation Administration 293

Radar Air Traffic Control Phase 10-A (50026)
  Location: FAA Academy, Oklahoma City, OK.
  Length: 136 hours.
  Dates: *Version 1:* April 1980-July 1982. *Version 2:* August 1982-Present.
  Objective: To develop the student's knowledge and skill for radar controlling of in-flight aircraft traffic.
  Instruction: Gives understanding of radar equipment benefits as extension of controller's capability and the limits of the technology/equipment in aiding visual and instrument oriented traffic. Laboratory exercise is the major means to instruction in this course. Two thirds or more of the student's time is spent completing assignments made in class lectures. Phase tests and a controller test are the measures of course skill achievement.
  Credit recommendation: In the vocational certificate category, 3 semester hours in Airport Management, Aircraft Control, or Tower Operator (10/82).

Flow Management Weather Coordinator (50112/55138)
  Location: *50112:* Training at Federal Aviation Administration, Oklahoma City, OK. *55138:* Training at field offices by academy trained instructors using FAA Academy Lesson Plans.
  Length: 64 hours (2 weeks).
  Dates: *Version 1:* September 1978-June 1982. *Version 2:* July 1982-Present.
  Objective: To train flow controllers and supervisors in current and forecast aviation weather, to teach the use of weather information to promote safe air traffic control.
  Instruction: Covers current and forecast aviation weather. Lecture and discussion with supervised laboratory exercises are used.
  Credit recommendation: In the upper division baccalaureate category, 3 semester hours in Meteorology, Aeronautical Sciences (10/82).

Fundamentals of Air Traffic Control (50122)
  Location: FAA Academy, Oklahoma City, OK.
  Length: 120 hours.
  Dates: January 1976-Present.
  Objective: To train personnel to understand factors affecting the operation of aircraft within the national airspace and to related these factors to the wide variety of aircraft now flying.
  Instruction: Topics include: Principles of flight, aircraft identification and performance, aviation weather, navigation, federal regulations, communication, ATC services, radar flight assistance service. Lecture and discussion are used.
  Credit recommendation: In the lower division baccalaureate/associate degree category, 2 semester hours in Aviation Management (10/82).

Non-Radar Air Traffic Control (50123)
  Location: FAA Academy, Oklahoma City, OK.
  Length: 312 hours (8 weeks).
  Dates: January 1976-Present.
  Objective: To train students in the rules and procedures governing the control of air traffic along with the governing theory and principles.
  Instruction: Through a number of practical exercises involving real time problem solving, developing and processing flight plans, computation and application of separation standards, performance of correct departure and arrival procedures, and establishment and maintenance of smooth flow control procedures are covered.
  Credit recommendation: In the lower division baccalaureate/associate degree category, 6 semester hours in Aeronautical Studies, Aviation Management, or Aviation Technology (10/82).

Enroute Radar Initial Qualification Training, Phase 10A (50125 [formerly 50124])
  Location: FAA Academy, Oklahoma City, OK.
  Length: *Version 1:* 250 hours. *Version 2:* 136 hours.
  Dates: *Version 1:* April 1980-August 1982. *Version 2:* September 1982-Present.
  Objective: To teach students the fundamentals, procedures and techniques of Enroute Radar air traffic control.
  Instruction: Lecture/discussion for about one third of the course and supervised laboratory (practice) for the other two thirds of the course are used to cover principles, basic concepts, and techniques associated with radar air traffic control.
  Credit recommendation: In the lower division baccalaureate/associate degree category, 3 semester hours in Aviation Technology (10/82).

Basic Aviation and Air Traffic (50312)
  Location: FAA Academy, Oklahoma City, OK.
  Length: 680 hours.
  Dates: *Version 1:* January 1972-December 1977. *Version 2:* January 1978-Present.
  Objective: To provide minority and female students with special aviation and air traffic programs in order to increase their opportunities for employment in air traffic control.
  Instruction: Gives orientation to aviation, history of civil aviation, principles of aerodynamics, weather, navigation, and air traffic control. Lecture and laboratory exercises are used.
  Credit recommendation: In the lower division baccalaureate/associate degree category, 3 semester hours in Aviation and 3 semester hours in General Education as an elective (10/82).

ARTS III for Data Systems Specialist (53003)
  Location: FAA Academy, Oklahoma City, OK.
  Length: *Versions 1 and 2:* 440 hours. *Version 3:* 240 hours (6 weeks).
  Dates: *Version 1:* March 1972-May 1982. *Version 2:*

June 1982-April 1987. *Version 3:* May 1987-Present.

Objective: To train software automation specialists in the use of the machine and assembly language used by the Univac Ultra 30 Computer.

Learning Outcome: Upon successful completion of this course, the students will be able to flowchart, code, debug, and document Ultra 30 Computer programs.

Instruction: This course includes instruction in numbering systems, machine code, assembly code, flowcharting, debugging, hardware architecture, subroutines, I/O and system interrupts.

Credit recommendation: *Versions 1 and 2:* In the lower division baccalaureate/associate degree category, 7 semester hours in Computer Science and Data Processing (10/82). *Version 3:* In the lower division baccalaureate/associate degree category, 4 semester hours in Computer Technology (5/87). NOTE: This course has been reevaluated and continues to meet requirements for credit recommendations.

ARTS III: A Programmer (53010)
(Air Traffic Control Automated Radar Terminal System)

Location: FAA Academy, Oklahoma City, OK.
Length: 272 hours.
Dates: *Version 1:* August 1978-May 1982. *Version 2:* June 1982-Present.

Objective: To prepare students to serve as data system specialists for field support of National Air Traffic Control Automated Radar Terminal systems.

Instruction: Lecture and discussion with hands-on laboratory exercises are used to teach multiprocessing and other principles related to air traffic control automated radar terminal systems.

Credit recommendation: In the lower division baccalaureate/associate degree category, 3 semester hours in Computer Programming or Data Processing (10/82).

ARTS III Operating and Programming the Disc System (53012)

Location: FAA Academy, Oklahoma City, OK.
Length: 80 hours (2 weeks).
Dates: *Version 1:* February 1978-August 1980. *Version 2:* September 1980-Present.

Objective: To enable students to operate and program a disc system.

Instruction: Covers (1) software management utilizing magnetic disk storage, (2) care and maintenance of disc packs; and (3) programming and operation of printers and data recorders. Lecture, discussion, and laboratory are used.

Credit recommendation: In the vocational certificate category, 3 semester hours in Computer Peripheral Operations and/or in the lower division baccalaureate/associate degree category, 1 semester hour in Computer Science or Data Processing (10/82).

ARTS II For Data Systems Specialist (53020)

Location: FAA Academy, Oklahoma City, OK.
Length: 296 hours.
Dates: *Version 1:* March 1978-September 1981. *Version 2:* October 1981-Present.

Objective: Prepare data systems specialist. To prepare students to become data systems specialists.

Instruction: Instruction uses lecture and laboratory exercises involving computer organization, assembly language programming fundamentals of number systems flow charts, LSI-2 mini-computer, and software maintenance using the Burroughs Computer.

Credit recommendation: In the lower division baccalaureate/associate degree category, 4 semester hours in Computer Science or Data Processing (10/82).

Adaptation and Operations (53122)

Location: FAA Academy, Oklahoma City, OK.
Length: 256 hours.
Dates: *Version 1:* March 1974-July 1979. *Version 2:* August 1979-Present.

Objective: To familiarize students with records contained in a Federal Aviation Administration specialized data base.

Instruction: Covers basic computer operations so students can adapt and update the data base, computer messages, and peripheral programs useful to the Air Route Center's operations. Lecture and discussion about Airway and Airspace structure with hands-on lab are provided. The course emphasized procedural skills.

Credit recommendation: In the vocational certificate category, 2 semester hours in Computer Operations or Data Entry or in the lower division baccalaureate/associate degree category, 2 semester hours in Computer Science (10/82). NOTE: This course is a Data Base Management course for a large computer system (IBM 9020).

NAS Data Processing Functions (53129)

Location: FAA Academy, Oklahoma City, OK.
Length: 134 hours.
Dates: *Version 1:* October 1978-December 1981. *Version 2:* January 1982-Present.

Objective: To provide students with an understanding of the application of systems analysis to Enroute Operational Computer Program, using already learned computer skills to assemble, execute and analyze failures of the Program. Graduates will have a comprehensive knowledge of the Enroute Operational Computer Program at the completion of this course.

Instruction: Lecture instruction supplemented by laboratory efforts on the IBM 360 system. Classroom lectures take up over 85 percent of the course, the material is then applied in intensive laboratory sessions. Weekly tests monitor the learning progress.

Credit recommendation: In the vocational certificate category, 2 semester hours in Data Entry or Computer

Operations (10/82).

Hardware Familiarization and Programming EARTS Software (53133)
   Location: FAA Academy, Oklahoma City, OK.
   Length: 40 hours.
   Dates: *Version 1:* August 1978-July 1980. *Version 2:* August 1980-Present.
   Objective: To provide students with an understanding of the EARTS program and equipment.
   Instruction: Lecture/discussion technique is used for two thirds of the class with approximately one third devoted to laboratory exercises in order to cover topics associated with EARTS computer hardware and software.
   Credit recommendation: In the lower division baccalaureate/associate degree category, 1 semester hour in Application of Programming (10/82).

Basic Assembler Language (53135)
   Location: FAA Academy, Oklahoma City, OK.
   Length: 256 hours.
   Dates: July 1982-Present.
   Objective: To introduce students to concepts of basic assembler language.
   Instruction: Covers fixed point instruction set, decimal instruction set, and a logic set; use of linking program modules and debugging of systems software; experience in writing off-line facility programs and other systems programs. Lecture and discussion are used. Hands-on programming is provided during supervised laboratory sessions.
   Credit recommendation: In the lower division baccalaureate/associate degree category, 3 semester hours in Computer Science or Data Processing (10/82).

Fundamentals of Digital Logic (54004)
   Location: FAA Academy, Oklahoma City, OK.
   Length: 120 hours.
   Dates: July 1982-Present.
   Objective: To provide students with an understanding of basic digital logic.
   Instruction: Covers basic principles of operation of the microprocessor (6800); basic concepts of programming a microprocessor; execution of a program, addressing modes, and experiments. This is a self-paced course that uses the Heathkit study materials, plus hands-on experience with the Heathkit trainer. The final exam is proctored.
   Credit recommendation: In the lower division baccalaureate/associate degree category, 3 semester hours in Microprocessor or Microcomputer (10/82).

Flight Data (55026)
   Location: Field facilities throughout the United States.
   Length: 160 hours.
   Dates: *Version 1:* January 1976-December 1979. *Version 2:* January 1980-Present.
   Objective: To familiarize the student with scope of airport services and their relation to the Federal Aviation Administration air traffic control.
   Instruction: Includes tower equipment, flight data requirements and forms completion procedures, airport specialized circumstances affecting flight procedures and applicable emergency procedures for accidents, special flight operation and other incidents. Programmed self-study.
   Credit recommendation: In the vocational certificate category, 2 semester hours in Airport Management (10/82).

Phase VII Clearance Delivery (55027)
   Location: Field facilities throughout the United States.
   Length: 20 hours.
   Dates: *Version 1:* January 1976-December 1979. *Version 2:* January 1980-Present.
   Objective: To provide students with basics related to clearance delivery.
   Instruction: Covers introductory Federal Aviation Administration air traffic procedures. Correspondence course.
   Credit recommendation: In the vocational certificate category, 1 semester hour in Air Traffic Control (10/82).

Ground Control (55028)
   Location: Field facilities throughout the United States.
   Length: 80 hours.
   Dates: *Version 1:* January 1976-December 1979. *Version 2:* January 1980-Present.
   Objective: To teach the student procedures pertinent to ground control.
   Instruction: Covers basic airport operations pertaining to aircrafts and their characteristics as they impact on airport systems. Programmed self-instruction.
   Credit recommendation: In the vocational certificate category, 2 semester hours in Airport Management (10/82).

Local Control (55029)
   Location: Field facilities throughout the United States.
   Length: 80 hours.
   Dates: *Version 1:* January 1978-December 1979. *Version 2:* January 1980-Present.
   Objective: To familiarize the student with airport operating procedures.
   Instruction: Covers night time operations and the impact of night/low visibility operations on various types of aircrafts. Programmed self-instruction is used.
   Credit recommendation: In the vocational certificate category, 2 semester hours in Airport Management (10/82).

Non-Radar Terminal Control (55030)
   Location: Field facilities throughout the United States.
   Length: 120 hours.
   Dates: January 1978-Present.
   Objective: To enable the student to apply Federal Aviation Administration established standards to moderately dense aircraft flying traffic.
   Instruction: Covers maintenance of aircraft clearances in space dimensions, maintenance of accepted discipline levels of proper pre and post flight data submitted from aircraft crews and Federal Aviation Administration facilities. Programmed self-study.
   Credit recommendation: In the vocational certificate category, 2 semester hours in Airport Management (10/82).

Radar Position Certification (55031)
   Location: Field facilities throughout the United States.
   Length: 200 hours (80 hours of classroom instruction, 120 hours of on-the-job training).
   Dates: August 1982-Present.
   Objective: To enable students to retain the skill level reached in Federal Aviation Administration resident course 50026, Terminal Radar Initial Qualification Training.
   Instruction: On-the-job training and lecture/discussion. Through on-the-job training primarily, this course covers those skills needed to qualify for Radar Position Certification.
   Credit recommendation: In the vocational certificate category, 2 semester hours in Aviation Management or Tower Operation (10/82).

On-the-Job Training in NAS (55103)
   Location: Field training for the Federal Aviation Administration Academy, Oklahoma City, OK.
   Length: 720 hours.
   Dates: *Version 1:* August 1972-September 1975. *Version 2:* October 1975-Present.
   Objective: To provide students with guidelines for on-the-job training at the ARTCC.
   Instruction: On-the-job training covering NAS adaptation and operations.
   Credit recommendation: In the vocational certificate category, 4 semester hours in Aviation Technology or in the lower division baccalaureate/associate degree category, 2 semester hours in Computer Science or Data Processing (10/82).

On-the-Job Training, Final Functional Area Checkout (55104)
   Location: Field training from the Federal Aviation Administration Academy, Oklahoma City, OK.
   Length: 960 hours.
   Dates: *Version 1:* August 1972-September 1975. *Version 2:* October 1975-Present.
   Objective: To enable students to apply knowledge obtained in programming courses.
   Instruction: On-the-job training which outlines training related to computer programming.
   Credit recommendation: In the vocational certificate category, 5 semester hours in Aviation Technology or Computer Operations (10/82).

Assistant Controller Position Qualification and Certification (55126)
   Location: Field facilities throughout the United States.
   Length: 80 hours (2 weeks).
   Dates: *Version 1:* January 1976-May 1986. *Version 2:* June 1986-Present.
   Objective: To qualify the student to perform the full range of assistant controller duties and to obtain certification on all assistant controller positions of operation in an assigned area of specialization.
   Learning Outcome: Upon successful completion of this course, the student will be able to demonstrate the ability to receive, process and deliver flight plan information; effectively communicate and/or coordinate; enter flight data into the computer directly; coordinate flight processing errors with the FDCS, DSC, or the appropriate controller, as required; service the flight strip printer; and process flight plans manually.
   Instruction: On-the-job training. The full range of assistant controller duties.
   Credit recommendation: In the vocational certificate category, 2 semester hours in Aviation Technology (10/82) (5/87). NOTE: This course has been reevaluated and continues to meet requirements for credit recommendations.

Preliminary Radar-Associated/Non-Radar Control Training and Assistant Controller Duties (55127)
   Location: Field facilities throughout the United States.
   Length: 320 hours (8 weeks).
   Dates: *Version 1:* January 1976-October 1980. *Version 2:* November 1980-Present.
   Objective: To provide the student with background knowledge on Special Military Operations, Letters of Agreement, Phraseology and Strip Marking in preparation for entry into radar-associated/nonradar training.
   Learning Outcome: Upon successful completion of this course, the student will be able to have a general understanding of En Route Air Traffic Control; know the procedures for Special Military Operations; know the requirements, limitations and procedures as stated in Letters of Agreement/facility orders pertinent to the assigned area of specialization; complete a number of phraseology/strip marking exercises; and prepare a detailed map of the assigned area of specialization.
   Instruction: Covers Special Military Operations, Letters of Agreement, phraseology and strip marking, a general review of En Route Air Traffic Control and the

specific assigned area of specialization. Programmed learning capsules and exercises developed by the Academy and facility are used.

Credit recommendation: In the vocational certificate category, 2 semester hours in Aviation Technology (10/82) (5/87). NOTE: This course has been reevaluated and continues to meet requirements for credit recommendations.

Radar Associated/Non-Radar Controller Training (55128)
  Location: Field facilities throughout the U.S. - Air Route Traffic Control Center (ARTCCs).
  Length: 240 hours (6 weeks).
  Dates: January 1976-Present.
  Objective: To enable the student to perform as a radar associated/non-radar controller.
  Instruction: Covers all appropriate regulations and procedures and their application to the safe and efficient movement of air traffic. Topics include but are not limited to: Area Navigation, Radar Identification, Separation, Communications, Route and Altitude Assignment, Clearances, Departure, Arrival, Approaches, Holding and Emergency Procedures.
  Credit recommendation: In the lower division baccalaureate/associate degree category, 3 semester hours in Aviation Technology (10/82).

Initial Radar Position Qualification Certification Phase (55129)
  Location: Field facilities throughout the United States.
  Length: *Version 1:* 60 hours. *Version 2:* 120 hours (maximum of 14 weeks).
  Dates: *Version 1:* January 1976-May 1986. *Version 2:* June 1986-Present.
  Objective: To qualify the student to perform the full range of duties and to attain certification on two radar-associated/nonradar control positions of operation in an area of specialization.
  Learning Outcome: Upon successful completion of this course, the student will be able to correctly demonstrate the ability to initiate and accept radar handoffs and point-outs; perform appropriate changeover procedures to Transition to and from the primary back-up system; maintain separation using prescribed standards; issue departure clearances; provide beacon code assignments to IFR aircraft; provide assistance to aircraft experiencing inflight emergencies; provide control to aircraft experiencing radio communication failure; employ holding procedures; recognize sector saturation and employ procedures to prevent or alleviate this control problem; provide weather advisories; maintain board management; enter flight data into the computer; effectively communicate over interphone or radio; and apply hijacked aircraft control procedures.
  Instruction: On-the-job training leading to qualification for radar-associated/nonradar controller duties on two sectors within an area of specialization. These sectors are selected for OJT and evaluation is based on their potential to provide the student with a realistic but fair standard in demonstrating an ability to handle all control situations anticipated in the assigned area of specialization.
  Credit recommendation: In the vocational certificate category, 3 semester hours in Aviation Technology (10/82) (5/87). NOTE: This course has been reevaluated and continues to meet requirements for credit recommendations.

Final Radar-Associated/Non-Radar Control Position Qualification and Certification (55130)
  Location: Field facilities throughout the United States.
  Length: 80 hours (18 weeks).
  Dates: *Version 1:* January 1976-May 1986. *Version 2:* June 1986-Present.
  Objective: To qualify the student to perform the full range of duties and attain certification on all the radar-associated/nonradar positions of operation in the area of specialization.
  Learning Outcome: Upon successful completion of this course, the student will be able to perform, independently and under general supervision, all duties of a radar-associated/nonradar controller on all the sectors in his/her assigned area of specialization.
  Instruction: This phase of training shall be administered in an operational environment, with on-the-job training, as assigned, and supervised by the first level supervisor.
  Credit recommendation: *Version 1:* In the vocational certificate category, 3 semester hours in Aviation Technology or Practical Arts (10/82). *Version 2:* In the vocational certificate category, 2 semester hours in Aviation Technology (5/87). NOTE: This course has been reevaluated and continues to meet requirements for credit recommendations.

Initial Radar Control Position Qualification and Certification - Phase XII (55132)
  Location: FAA Academy, Oklahoma City, OK.
  Length: 240 hours.
  Dates: October 1982-Present.
  Objective: To qualify persons to perform certification on radar positions in an area of specialization.
  Instruction: On-the-job training covering techniques related to initial radar control position.
  Credit recommendation: In the vocational certificate category, 3 semester hours in Aviation Technology or Practical Arts (10/82).

Final Radar Control Position - Phase XIII (55133) (Formerly 55130)
  Location: Field facilities throughout the United States.
  Length: *Version 1:* 60 hours. *Version 2:* 80 clock hours

per position.

Dates: *Version 1:* October 1982-August 1985. *Version 2:* September 1985-Present.

Objective: To train personnel to qualify and be certified at the final radar control position full performance level.

Learning Outcome: Upon successful completion of this course, the students will perform the same skills outlined in Phase XII: initial and continued aircraft identification, separation of aircraft in radar and non-radar environments, holding procedures, beacon code assignments, use of correct communication procedures, sequencing of aircraft, handoffs to and from adjacent controller/facilities, recognize and alleviate sector saturation, provide advisory and assistance as needed, detect and report equipment malfunctions, changeover to backup systems, and perform position relief briefing.

Instruction: Lab course with full-time instruction on radar procedures for each position to include: initial and continued aircraft identification; separation in radar and non-radar environments, use of proper communication procedures, sequencing of and handoffs to and from adjacent controller/facilities, provide advisories and emergency assistance as needed, report system malfunctions and changeover backup systems, and perform position relief briefing.

Credit recommendation: *Version 1:* In the vocational certificate category, 3 semester hours in Aviation Technology or Practical Arts (10/82). *Version 2:* In the vocational certificate category, 2 semester hours in Aviation Technology (5/87). NOTE: Credit should not be granted for both this course and for Phase XII Initial Radar Control Position Qualification and Certification (55132). This course has been reevaluated and continues to meet requirements for credit recommendations.

Predevelopmental, Phase III Field Environmental Training (55313)

Location: Field facilities throughout the United States.
Length: 324 hours.
Dates: *Version 1:* December 1978-December 1979. *Version 2:* January 1980-Present.
Objective: To orient students to actual job tasks and skills. Job exposure.
Instruction: Gives on-the-job training and uses criterion tests as study aids.
Credit recommendation: In the vocational certificate category, 1 semester hour in Aviation Technology or Practical Arts (10/82).

Predevelopmental, Phase IV - Option Determination (55314)

Location: Field facilities throughout the United States.
Length: 130 hours.
Dates: June 1979-Present.
Objective: To familiarize students with equipment used in daily operations.

Instruction: On-the-job training covering the basic operational tasks of any of the major positions within an assigned option.
Credit recommendation: In the vocational certificate category, 1 semester hour in Aviation Technology or Practical Arts (10/82).

AIRPORT TRAINING

(Courses are listed in numerical order)

Airport Paving (06005)

Location: FAA Academy, Oklahoma City, OK.
Length: 80 hours (2 weeks).
Dates: June 1971-Present.
Objective: To provide students with the knowledge necessary to survey, design, and construction of airport paving projects. The construction phase is theoretical only. The course treats soil investigation, pavement design (flexible and rigid), surfacing and overlays, pavements for light and heavy aircraft, and pavement evaluation. This course also will be applicable to other paving projects constructed with concrete and/or asphalt.
Instruction: Lecture and laboratory and visits from experts from various industrial and educational facilities, including: (a) Troyler Laboratories, (use of technology in nuclear testing-moisture density gauges; (b) Asphalt Institute (motivation over field inspection); (c) CMI (construction equipment); (d) University of Maryland (construction technology), and (e) Portland Cement (construction characteristics), knowledge of civil or general engineering required because of the level of mathematical calculations and graph interpretations. Knowledge of computer operation would be helpful if not essential.
Credit recommendation: In the upper division baccalaureate category, 3 semester hours in Civil Engineering and General Engineering (10/82).

Airport Engineering (06012)

Location: FAA Academy, Oklahoma City, OK.
Length: 36 hours (1 week).
Dates: March 1976-Present.
Objective: The course is primarily for airport consultants and airport engineers who need to build expertise in Federal Aviation Administration regulations affecting airport design, construction standards and inspection techniques. Course materials in *Pavement Design* and *Airport Lighting* and *NAVAIDS* will be helpful (if not essential) as a prerequisite for this survey course.
Instruction: The course is primarily lecture using transparencies to support the material in the following areas: subgrade and soil testing; flexible airport paving; rigid airport paving; gradients and drainage; skid resistant surfacing; airport lighting; runway and edge markings, power requirements, AC and DC and radio controls.
Credit recommendation: In the upper division bac-

calaureate category, 2 semester hours in Civil Engineering/General Engineering (10/82).

Airport Planning for Non-Federal Aviation Administration Personnel (06013)
  Location: FAA Academy, Oklahoma City, OK.
  Length: 36 hours (1 week).
  Dates: January 1977-Present.
  Objective: To assist non-Federal Aviation Administration personnel in the development of airport master plans which are consistent with Federal Aviation Administration standards of quality and completeness.
  Instruction: Presents major aspects of airport master plan development including site selection, land and plans, aircraft factors in runway length and capacity, airport layout, noise control, airspace requirements, environmental assessments and reports, aeronautical activity forecasts, and airport systems plans.
  Credit recommendation: In the lower division baccalaureate/associate degree category, 2 semester hours in Airport Management (elective) (10/82).

Project Engineering (06018)
  Location: FAA Academy, Oklahoma City, OK.
  Length: 80 hours (2 weeks).
  Dates: December 1977-Present.
  Objective: This course is designed for airport engineers who wish to upgrade their knowledge in airport standards; paving, legating, grading, drainage, and general design. In addition, techniques are developed in the area of inspecting and testing.
  Instruction: Instruction includes a two-week sequence in the following areas: land acquisition, airport landscaping, soils and testing, airport paving theory (flexible and rigid), joints, overlaps, and evaluation, federal assistance grants. The last day is an airport paving workshop where students may simulate airport planning and work problems related to airport paving. Final exam is provided.
  Credit recommendation: In the upper division baccalaureate category, 2 semester hours in Civil Engineering/Airport Engineering (10/82).

Airport NAVAIDS and Lighting (06019)
  Location: FAA Academy, Oklahoma City, OK.
  Length: 36 hours (1 week).
  Dates: October 1980-Present.
  Objective: This course is designed primarily for airport engineers seeking expertise in Federal Aviation Administration airport regulations and design procedures. The students will develop expertise in airport site engineering including airport lighting systems designs and NAVAIDS.
  Instruction: The course is primarily lecture with practical problems to support: airport marking, practical lighting procedures, visual approach guidance systems, inspection of lighting systems, taxiway signs and radio controls, navigation aids and AC and DC power systems. A workshop on the last day is designed to provide students with practical problem-solving in airport lighting and NAVAIDS.
  Credit recommendation: In the upper division baccalaureate category, 2 semester hours in Civil Engineering/General Engineering (10/82).

Recurrent Engineering (06021)
  Location: FAA Academy, Oklahoma City, OK.
  Length: 36 hours (1 week).
  Dates: January 1977-Present.
  Objective: The objective of this course is to give practicing engineers an opportunity to update in Federal Aviation Administration design and construction methods and techniques. A prerequisite to this course is *Airport Paving* (or equivalent experience). Subject matter may vary depending upon current regulations and techniques.
  Instruction: The same materials are used for this course as used in *Airport Paving*. The last two days of this course is presented by guest instructors; e.g., a representative from the Bureau of Standards and a representative from the Airport engineers area.
  Credit recommendation: In the upper division baccalaureate category, 1 semester hour in Civil Engineering/General Engineering (10/82).

Airport Master Planning (06022)
  Location: FAA Academy, Oklahoma City, OK.
  Length: 36 hours (1 week).
  Dates: January 1978-Present.
  Objective: To prepare airport planners for developing and gaining approval of a master plan for airports from basic utility size to major carrier facilities.
  Instruction: Presents major aspects of airport master plan development including site selection, land use plans, aircraft factors in runway length and capacity, airport layout, noise controls, airspace requirements, environmental assessments and reports, aeronautical activity forecasts, and airport systems plans.
  Credit recommendation: In the lower division baccalaureate/associate degree category, 2 semester hours in Airport Management (Elective) (10/82).

Relocation Assistance (06027)
  Location: FAA Academy, Oklahoma City, OK.
  Length: 36 hours (1 week).
  Dates: *Version 1:* January 1976-December 1976. *Version 2:* January 1977-Present.
  Objective: This course is designed for Airport personnel who have the responsibility in reviewing and approving the relocation assistance and payments program from an ADAP project. It will cover the implementations of the provisions of Title II of the Uniform Relocation Assistance and Real Properties Acquisition Policies Act of 1970 and OST Regulations, Part-5. This training is intend-

ed for personnel assigned to positions requiring this knowledge.

Instruction: The student will be given the basic philosophy, policies, and criteria of the Uniform Relocation Assistance and Real Property Acquisition Policies Act of 1970. The student will be able to apply the provisions of the Act in simulated problems, assessing the claims, determining the payments, finding replacement housing, and determining the advisory services to displaced persons in accordance with the Act, consists of 14 hours of lecture and 22 hours of supervised laboratory. This course is based on a case study.

Credit recommendation: In the upper division baccalaureate category, 1 semester hour in Urban Planning, City Planning, General Business, or Public Administration (10/82).

Land Appraisal and Title Opinion (06028)
 Location: FAA Academy, Oklahoma City, OK.
 Length: 40 hours (1 week).
 Dates: January 1976-Present.
 Objective: To improve students understanding of procedures in land acquisition procedures; reviews sponsor's land appraisal to assure conformance with prescribed procedure; and examines eligibility, allowability, and reasonableness of land costs for land acquisition.
 Instruction: Reviews philosophy, policy and criteria of Title III of the Uniform Relocation Assistance and Real Estate Property Acquisition Policies Act of 1970; examines various appraisal methods; and examines the validity of title opinion.
 Credit recommendation: In the upper division category, 2 semester hours in Real Estate (10/82).

Airport Management for Internationals (06032)
 Location: FAA Academy, Oklahoma City, OK.
 Length: 300 hours (8 weeks).
 Dates: June 1982-Present.
 Objective: To provide students with an understanding of air secting, terminal and landside operation of an airport including financial, management, and operation responsibilities.
 Instruction: Topics include airport management principles; airport financing; master planning; airport systems; airport sites. Airport forecasting; National Airport system plan; runways; airport capacity; airport revenues; fixed based operators; international regulations; airline and ramp operations. Airport landing and handling fees; airline, airport regulations; air cargo; transportation pricing. The course utilizes a series of authorities in airport management as guest lectures; and on-site airport visits. A written examination is required.
 Credit recommendation: In the lower division baccalaureate/associate degree category, 3 semester hours in Airport Management (Elective) (10/82).

Environmental Assessment (12000)
 Location: FAA Academy, Oklahoma City, OK.
 Length: 72 hours (2 weeks).
 Dates: May 1976-Present.
 Objective: To provide students with a fundamental knowledge of environmental assessment; requirements and procedures relative to Airport/Aircraft development and operation.
 Instruction: The major topics include legislative mandates, identification of impacts, effects, causes of aircraft noise, air pollution, impact of vegetation and wildlife; documentation outlines; processing information, consultation process; public involvement, legal implications.
 Credit recommendation: In the lower division baccalaureate/associate degree category, 2 semester hours in Airport Management or Environmental Science as an elective (10/82).

AIRWAY FACILITIES

(Courses are listed in numerical order)

Back-Up Emergency Communications (BUEC) System (40008 - 40009)
 Location: FAA Academy, Oklahoma City, OK.
 Length: 158 hours (4 weeks).
 Dates: November 1975-Present.
 Objective: To provide students with an understanding of the installation, evaluation, modification, maintenance, or certification of the remote site back-up Emergency Communication System.
 Instruction: Utilizing lecture and lab, study the operation of transmitters, receivers, power supply, synthesizer and control circuits. Equipment alignment procedures. Test equipment and transceiver troubleshooting techniques.
 Credit recommendation: In the lower division baccalaureate/associate degree category, 3 semester hours in Electronics Technology (11/82). NOTE: Credit should not be granted both for these courses and for the combined courses (40027 and 40028).

High Capacity Voice Recorder Runway Visual Range Equipment Type (40016)
 Location: FAA Academy, Oklahoma City, OK.
 Length: 120 hours (3 weeks).
 Dates: November 1982-Present.
 Objective: To teach technicians to install, maintain, and evaluate the high capacity voice recorder system.
 Learning Outcome: Upon successful completion of this course, the student learns the basics of magnetic recording and the operation of the 8966 HCVR system. The student learns recording, tape transport, reproduction and repair of the system.
 Instruction: The course teaches the principles of magnetic recording, the operation of a high capacity voice

recording system. The course is half class and half laboratory. The lab stresses troubleshooting and system operation of the 8966 HCVR.

Credit recommendation: In the lower division baccalaureate/associate degree category, 2 semester hours in Electronics Technology (5/87).

Data Terminal Equipment, Display and Keyboard (40019)

Location: FAA Academy, Oklahoma City, OK.
Length: 156 hours (4 weeks).
Dates: September 1982-Present.
Objective: To prepare Airway Facilities personnel for the maintenance, evaluation, or certification of Data Terminal Equipment.
Instruction: The course consists of classroom lectures and lab sessions concerning display and keyboard, terminal controller, and journal.
Credit recommendation: In the lower division baccalaureate/associate degree category, 3 semester hours in Electronics Technology (11/82).

Back-up Emergency Communications (BUEC) System (40027 - 40028)

Location: FAA Academy, Oklahoma City, OK.
Length: 158 hours (4 weeks).
Dates: December 1981-Present.
Objective: To provide students with an understanding of installation, evaluation, and maintenance, of Back-Up Emergency Communications Systems at remote and ARTCC locations.
Instruction: Subjects include operation of transmitters, receivers, power supply, synthesizer and control circuits. Equipment alignment procedures test equipment and transceiver troubleshooting techniques.
Credit recommendation: In the lower division baccalaureate/associate degree category, 3 semester hours in Electronics Technology (11/82). NOTE: Credit should not be granted for both these courses and for the combined courses (40008 and 40009).

Communications Equipment (40029)

Location: FAA Academy, Oklahoma City, OK.
Length: Approximately 103 hours, but variable due to computerized instruction.
Dates: October 1982-Present.
Objective: To prepare personnel for the installation, maintenance, and evaluation of VHF and UHF communication equipment.
Instruction: Utilizing computer based and directed instruction, areas covered include: mathematics review, theory and operation of solid state VHF and UHF transmitters and receivers, audio control lines, and antennas and transmission lines.
Credit recommendation: In the vocational certificate or lower division baccalaureate/associate degree category, 2 semester hours in Electronics Technology (11/82).

Cable Fault Analysis Engine Control Panels (40121)

Location: FAA Academy, Oklahoma City, OK.
Length: 80 hours (2 weeks).
Dates: April 1985-Present.
Objective: To provide instruction and practice in cable fault location and repair of the fault.
Learning Outcome: Upon successful completion of this course, the students learn the construction of power cables, including the materials used for the conductor, insulation, and shielding. The students learn the installation, maintenance, and repair of power cables, how to test the insulation, and locate faults.
Instruction: The course teaches the installation, maintenance and evaluation of buried power and control cables. Includes hands-on practice in cable splicing techniques, cable analysis and cable fault location. Types of cables, insulation and shielding are covered in a course that is about half class and half application.
Credit recommendation: In the vocational certificate category, 2 semester hours in Electrical Power (5/87).

Power Conditioning System for Radar Microwave Link (40122)

Location: FAA Academy, Oklahoma City, OK.
Length: 80 hours (2 weeks).
Dates: June 1977-Present.
Objective: To train Airways Facilities technicians and engineers for installation, operation, evaluation, and repair of PCS/RML systems.
Instruction: A 50 percent lecture, 50 percent lab course studying system concepts, circuit analysis, operation, evaluation, maintenance procedures, troubleshooting, and fault correction down to component level.
Credit recommendation: In the lower division baccalaureate/associate degree category, 2 semester hours in Electronics Technology (11/82).

Engine Control Panels (40127)

Location: FAA Academy, Oklahoma City, OK.
Length: *Version 1:* 192 hours (4½ weeks); *Version 2:* 200 hours (5 weeks).
Dates: November 1984-Present.
Objective: To provide the student with the knowldege of the operation of a gasoline-diesel electrical power generating system, including the control panel.
Learning Outcome: Upon successful completion of this course, the student will be able to test the system to determine if it is operating properly; determine the faulty component if the system does not operate properly; and replace the faulty component and make the system operational.
Instruction: Course covers the internal combustion engine, the generator and the control panel for three electrical power generation systems. Methodology includes

laboratory exercises and lecture.

Credit recommendation: In the vocational certificate category, 4 semester hours in Automotive, Diesel, or Electrical Technology (5/87) (9/88). NOTE: This course has been reevaluated and continues to meet requirements for credit recommendations.

Heating, Ventilating, Air Conditioner (40132)
Location: FAA Academy, Oklahoma City, OK.
Length: 160 hours (4 weeks).
Dates: January 1979-Present.
Objective: To teach responsible personnel the installation, maintenance, and evaluation of boilers and heavy duty air conditioning systems.
Learning Outcome: Upon successful completion of this course, the students learn the basic operation of boiler and air conditioning units. Students learn the principle of centrifugal refrigeration units and chillers. The operation and repair of the control panel, fuel system, water distribution, water testing, and air distribution system.
Instruction: The course covers the operation, evaluation, and maintenance of boilers and heavy duty air conditioning systems. The course includes the construction and operation of boilers/air conditioners, troubleshooting, water analysis and treatment, safety, centrifugal chillers, motors, control panel, water distribution system, air handling equipment and auxiliary equipment. The course is half lecture, half lab.
Credit recommendation: In the vocational certificate or lower baccalaureate/associate degree category, 3 semester hours in Environmental Science/HVAC (5/87).

Environmental System Control (40133)
Location: FAA Academy, Oklahoma City, OK.
Length: 160 hours (4 weeks).
Dates: May 1984-Present.
Objective: To teach service technicians to evaluate, calibrate and maintain pneumatic control systems used in heating, ventilating, and air conditioning systems.
Learning Outcome: Upon successful completion of this course, the students learn the basics of air psychrometries and environmental conditioning processes, and pneumatic control fundamentals. The students learn the operation of thermostats, humidistats, and methods of transmission of data. System balancing is learned.
Instruction: The course teaches the maintenance, calibration, and operation of pneumatic controls and devices. The Johnson, Honeywell, Robertshaw, Barbara-Coleman, and Powers systems are covered. The properties of psychrometries and environmental air conditioning are covered along with troubleshooting, calibration and balancing of systems. The course is half lecture and half lab.
Credit recommendation: In the vocational certificate or lower division baccalaureate/associate degree category, 3 semester hours in Environmental Science/HVAC (5/87).

Electrical Principles (47600)
(Formerly 40135)
Location: FAA Academy, Oklahoma City, OK.
Length: 240 hours average (6 weeks). Course length is somewhat variable due to individualized, computerized instruction.
Dates: *Version 1:* October 1981-January 1983; *Version 2:* February 1983-Present.
Objective: *Version 1:* To provide students with the basic electrical principles and solid state technology introduction required for future study. *Version 2:* To teach the student the basics of electricity and the solid state devices related to control of electric generators.
Learning Outcome: Upon successful completion of this course, the student will be able to solve DC circuit problems on paper and in the laboratory; solve AC circuit problems with an algebraic approach and in the laboratory; and describe the operation of basic solid state devices.
Instruction: *Version 1:* This course is a computer-based and monitored program. The subject areas include the following: mathematics, transformers, 3-phase power, AC and DC electricity, and power supplies. *Version 2:* The course covers basic DC and AC circuits, and the fundamentals of solid state devices. Methodology includes self-paced, computer-aided instruction, including laboratory exercises, with written and practical proctored exams.
Credit recommendation: *Version 1:* In the vocational certificate or lower division baccalaureate/associate degree category, 4 semester hours in Electronics Technology (11/82). *Version 2:* In the vocational certificate category, 4 semester hours in Electrical/Electronics Technology (9/88). NOTE: This course has been reevaluated and continues to meet requirements for credit recommendations.

Exide Uninterruptible Power Supply (40145)
(Formerly 40149)
Location: FAA Academy, Oklahoma City, OK.
Length: 80 hours (2 weeks).
Dates: *Version 1:* July 1986-August 1988; *Version 2:* September 1988-Present.
Objective: To teach the student the testing and maintenance of the Exide Uninterruptible Power Supply (UPS).
Learning Outcome: Upon successful completion of this course, the student will be able to test the Exide power supply to determine if it is operating properly; and repair the Exide power supply if it is faulty.
Instruction: Course covers overall operation and maintenance of the Exide UPS, including the proper care of the storage batteries. Methodology includes laboratory exercises and lecture.
Credit recommendation: *Version 1:* In the vocational certificate category, 1 semester hour in Electronics Technology (5/87). *Version 2:* In the vocational certificate category, 2 semester hours in Electrical/Electronics Technology (9/88). NOTE: This course has been reevaluated and continues to meet requirements for credit

recommendations.

VHF/UHF Direction Finder Equipment (40225)
(Formerly 40225 and 40227)
   Location: FAA Academy, Oklahoma City, OK.
   Length: 160 hours (4 weeks).
   Dates: December 1973-Present.
   Objective: To provide students with understanding of the installation, evaluation, and maintenance of the FA 5530 Doppler DF system.
   Learning Outcome: Upon successful completion of this course, the students learn the Doppler DF theory and develop skills in system alignment, preventative and corrective maintenance, and system troubleshooting.
   Instruction: Topics include antenna systems, receiver system, control line frequence slight operation, control system and data system. Approximately half classroom participation and half laboratory.
   Credit recommendation: In the lower division baccalaureate/associate degree category, 1 semester hour in Electronics Technology (11/82) (5/87). NOTE: This course has been reevaluated and continues to meet requirements for credit recommendations.

Solid State VOR Transmitter Assembly (40230)
   Location: FAA Academy, Oklahoma City, OK.
   Length: 80 hours (2 weeks).
   Dates: June 1980-Present.
   Objective: To provide students with an understanding of the installation, maintenance, and evaluation of VOR facilities.
   Instruction: A lecture/lab course involving transmitter circuitry and goniometer circuitry.
   Credit recommendation: In the lower division baccalaureate/associate degree category, 1 semester hour in Electronics Technology (11/82).

AN/GRN-27 (40232)
   Location: FAA Academy, Oklahoma City, OK.
   Length: 120 hours (3 weeks).
   Dates: October 1982-Present.
   Objective: To train technicians to install, maintain, evaluate, and modify the AN/GRN-27 instrument landing system.
   Learning Outcome: Upon successful completion of this course, the students learn the operation and maintenance of AC and DC power systems, localizer/glide slope monitor, control unit, remote control and monitor pad, marker beacon system, antenna system, and localizer transmitter.
   Instruction: This is a lecture/laboratory course on the AN/GRN-27 instrument landing system. Course covers the operation down to the component level. Transistor and logic circuit operation is taught with heavy emphasis on troubleshooting. Transistors, receivers, antennas, and power supply are included.
   Credit recommendation: In the lower division baccalaureate/associate degree category, 3 semester hours in Electronic/Communications (5/87).

ILS Concepts (40233)
   Location: FAA Academy, Oklahoma City, OK.
   Length: 80 hours (2 weeks).
   Dates: March 1986-Present.
   Objective: To teach the basic concepts used in instrument landing systems and to prepare systems for equipment courses.
   Learning Outcome: Upon successful completion of this course, the students learn the basic operation of instrument landing systems and fundamentals of antenna systems, amplitude, modulation, glide slope RP and DDM, v-ring RP, ILS waveforms, test equipment and radiation patterns. The difference in depth of modulation, proximity effects and monitor networks are learned.
   Instruction: The course covers the basics of installation, evaluation, modification and maintenance of instrument landing systems in general as well as any one of several instrument landing systems by teaching the basics of modulation, antennas, proximity effects, monitor networks, localizer radiation patterns and glide slope patterns. The course is half classroom and half lab.
   Credit recommendation: In the lower division baccalaureate/associate degree category, 2 semester hours Electronic Communication (5/87).

ILS Wilcox Mark 1-A (40235)
   Location: FAA Academy, Oklahoma City, OK.
   Length: 120 hours (3 weeks).
   Dates: July 1975-Present.
   Objective: To teach technicians to install, do preventive maintenance and repair of the Instrument Landing Systems Equipment (Wilcox Mark 1-A).
   Instruction: The course covers the operation of the overall system from a block diagram and functional theory of operation basis; transmitters; oscillator/keyer; modulator; antennas; and monitor. Students receive practice in operation and troubleshooting in lab. One-half of time on instruction and one-half in lab.
   Credit recommendation: In the lower division baccalaureate/associate degree category, 2 semester hours in Communications Electronics (5/87).

ILS Capture Effect Glide Slope (40240)
   Location: FAA Academy, Oklahoma City, OK.
   Length: 40 hours (1 week).
   Dates: February 1975-Present.
   Objective: To teach the student the operation and maintenance of the Capture Effect Glide Slope system.
   Learning Outcome: Upon successful completion of this course, the student will be able to operate the Capture Effect Glide Slope; perform maintenance techniques; calibrate the equipment; and diagnose faults within the Capture Effect Glide Slope system.

Instruction: Course covers the principles of transmitters and receivers, and the operation and maintenance of the Capture Effect Glide Slope system. Methodology includes lecture and laboratory exercises.

Credit recommendation: In the lower division baccalaureate/associate degree category, 1 semester hour in Electronics Technology (5/87) (9/88). NOTE: This course has been reevaluated and continues to meet requirements for credit recommendations.

Runway Visual Range Equipment Tasker 500 Series (40252)

Location: FAA Academy, Oklahoma City, OK.
Length: 120 hours (3 weeks).
Dates: *Version 1:* March 1976-January 1984. *Version 2:* February 1984-Present.
Objective: To provide students with an understanding of the installation, evaluation, maintenance, and certification of the Tasker 500 system.
Learning Outcome: Upon successful completion of this course, the student will understand system integration, signal data converter, integrated circuit devices, graphic recorder, functions and sequence of operation, and remote programmer, decoding and remote display operation.
Instruction: A lecture/lab course concerning system integration, integrated circuit devices, graphic recorders, signal data converter modules and display operations.
Credit recommendation: In the lower division baccalaureate/associate degree category, 2 semester hours in Electronics Technology (11/82) (5/87). NOTE: This course has been reevaluated and continues to meet requirements for credit recommendations.

Solid State Direction Finder Equipment (40257)

Location: FAA Academy, Oklahoma City, OK.
Length: 80 hours (2 weeks).
Dates: October 1981-Present.
Objective: To provide students with an understanding of the proper routing performance checks; to perform troubleshooting, and repair and modifications on the VHF/DF Type FA 9964 Equipment.
Instruction: Utilizing lecture and lab techniques, study the operational performance checks, bearing display, control assembly, antenna systems, and remote maintenance monitoring systems.
Credit recommendation: In the lower division baccalaureate/associate degree category, 2 semester hours in Electronics Technology (11/82). NOTE: Credit should not be granted both for this course and for (40225 and 40227).

Distance Measuring Equipment Cardion DME-9639 (40258)

Location: FAA Academy, Oklahoma City, OK.
Length: 80 hours (2 weeks).
Dates: January 1979-Present.

Objective: To provide students with training in installation, maintenance, or evaluation of the Cardion Models FA-8974 or FA-9639.
Instruction: A lecture/lab course involving the following transmitter, receiver, monitor, and transponder data flow and circuits.
Credit recommendation: In the lower division baccalaureate/associate degree category, 2 semester hours in Electronics Technology (11/82).

Surveillance Radar Unit (40307)
(Formerly Radar Systems ARSR-1D, 1E, 1F)

Location: FAA Academy, Oklahoma City, OK.
Length: *Version 1:* 176 hours (4¼ weeks); *Version 2:* 120 hours (3 weeks).
Dates: *Version 1:* October 1981-August 1988; *Version 2:* September 1988-Present.
Objective: To teach the student the installation, evaluation, and maintenance of the Long Range Radar System ARSR 1/2.
Learning Outcome: Upon successful completion of this course, the students will be able to operate, install, evaluate performance, and maintain the ARSE 1/2 Surveillance Radar.
Instruction: Course covers main power control, RF monitor, STC generator, transmitter-magnetron, transmitter-amplitron, transmitter H.V. interlocsk, DMTI processor, video distribution and troubleshooting. Methodology includes lecture, laboratory, and equipment testing.
Credit recommendation: In the lower division baccalaureate/associate degree category, 3 semester hours in Electronics Technology (5/87) (9/88). NOTE: This course has been reevaluated and continues to meet requirements for credit recommendations.

Radar Microwave Link/Repeater (RML) (40320)

Location: FAA Academy, Oklahoma City, OK.
Length: 88 hours (11 days).
Dates: November 1972-Present.
Objective: To develop the students' ability to analyze the RML system for correct performance and to diagnose and repair any fault in the system.
Instruction: Two thirds lecture, one third laboratory. Course addressing the theory of operation, signal flow, detailed circuit analysis, fault diagnosis, system/subsystem alignment, theory and application of special test equipment.
Credit recommendation: In the lower division baccalaureate/associate degree category, 2 semester hours in Electronics Technology (11/82).

Bright 2/4 Radar Indicator (40327)

Location: FAA Academy, Oklahoma City, OK.
Length: 120 hours.
Dates: October 1977-Present.

Objective: To enable the electronic technician to perform maintenance, testing, and adjustment of Bright Radar Indicator Tower Equipment.

Learning Outcome: Upon successful completion of this course, the student will be able to troubleshoot video systems; use block diagrams to describe system functions; and know theory of operation and maintenance of television systems, including video camera.

Instruction: The course contains the theory of operation, maintenance, and troubleshooting of a closed circuit television system. The system is known as the Brite 2/4 system. Does not include television.

Credit recommendation: In the lower division baccalaureate/associate degree category, 2 semester hours in Electronic/Communications Technology (5/87).

Solid State Video Mappers (40328)
  Location: FAA Academy, Oklahoma City, OK.
  Length: 40 hours (1 week).
  Dates: December 1980-Present.
  Objective: To enable Federal Aviation Administration technicians and engineers to certify, maintain, and modify solid state video mappers.
  Instruction: 50 percent lecture, 50 percent laboratory on video mapping principles, timing, sweep generation, video circuits, monitors and digital to analog azimuth conversion. Maintenance and troubleshooting.
  Credit recommendation: In the lower division baccalaureate/associate degree category, 1 semester hour in Electronics Technology (11/82).

Air Route Surveillance Radar-3 (40331)
  Location: FAA Academy, Oklahoma City, OK.
  Length: *Version 1:* 600 hours (15 weeks); *Version 2:* 560 hours (14 weeks).
  Dates: *Version 1:* January 1982-August 1988; *Version 2:* September 1988-Present.
  Objective: To prepare the student to maintain, install, modify, and certify the ARSR-3 Surveillance Radar System.
  Learning Outcome: Upon successful completion of this course, the student will be able to initialize and configure the ARSR-3 system; perform periodic maintenance on the ARSR-3; and locate, isolate, and correct malfunctions.
  Instruction: Course covers a functional analysis of the ARSR-3 Surveillance Radar System, including data flow, operational analysis of the transmitter, receiver, RF distribution system, the ARSR antenna system, and the Remote Maintenance Monitor. Methodology includes lecture, laboratory sessions, and examinations.
  Credit recommendation: *Version 1:* In the lower division baccalaureate/associate degree category, 12 semester hours in Electronics Technology (11/82). *Version 2:* In the upper division baccalaureate category, 6 semester hours in Electronics Technology (9/88). NOTE: This course has been reevaluated and continues to meet requirements for credit recommendations.

Airport Surveillance Radar System ASR-8 (40333)
  Location: FAA Academy, Oklahoma City, OK.
  Length: 240 hours (6 weeks).
  Dates: March 1981-Present.
  Objective: To train personnel to evaluate radar system operation, isolate defective circuits, take proper corrective measures, use test equipment, and be able to adapt to Airport Surveillance Radar.
  Learning Outcome: Upon successful completion of this course, the students will understand principles of operation; detailed circuit analysis; system maintenance; and troubleshooting.
  Instruction: Course covers system concepts, timing, klystron transmitter, normal receivers, video processor, MTI (Moving Target Indicator), STC (Sensitivity Time Controls), remote site equipment, control systems, heavy emphasis on troubleshooting. 60% lecture, 40% lab. Prerequisite: Radar Principles A (40329) and B (40330).
  Credit recommendation: In the lower division baccalaureate/associate degree category, 4 semester hours in Radar Technology (5/87).

Air Traffic Control Beacon Interrogator (40335)
  Location: FAA Academy, Oklahoma City, OK.
  Length: 96 hours (2½ weeks).
  Dates: November 1982-Present.
  Objective: To enable technicians and engineers to maintain, certify, and modify the Air Traffic Beacon Interrogator.
  Instruction: Classroom subjects include: systems concepts, pulse mode generator, transmitter receiver, monitors, control circuits, and beacon test set. Lab sessions develop skills in systems alignment, systems performance analysis, fault diagnosis, and use of test equipment.
  Credit recommendation: In the lower division baccalaureate/associate degree category, 2 semester hours in Electronics Technology (11/82).

Radar Beacon Interrogator ATCBI-5 (40339)
  Location: FAA Academy, Oklahoma City, OK.
  Length: 80 hours (2 weeks).
  Dates: January 1986-Present.
  Objective: To train personnel for evaluation modification, maintenance or certification of the ATCBI-5 system.
  Learning Outcome: Upon successful completion of this course, the students learn principles of operation, system evaluation, test set characteristics, troubleshooting, and certification requirements.
  Instruction: A course of study in system concepts, pulse mode generator, transmitter, receiver, stagger/de-stagger, SLS/ISIS monitors, control circuits, and Beacon test sets.
  Credit recommendation: In the lower division baccalaureate/associate degree category, 2 semester hours in Electronics Technology (5/87).

Airport Surveillance Radar (ASR) (40342)
Location: FAA Academy, Oklahoma City, OK.
Length: 120 hours (3 weeks).
Dates: May 1981-Present.
Objective: To enable students to analyze the ASR-4/5/6 system for correct performance. To diagnose and repair any fault in the system.
Instruction: Lecture/laboratory course on: circulating trigger loop, modulate, transmitter, receives, video cancellation, radar control system, power supplies, and video monitoring equipment.
Credit recommendation: In the lower division baccalaureate/associate degree category, 2 semester hours in Electronics Technology (11/82).

Radar Microwave Link System (40344/76)
Location: FAA Academy, Oklahoma City, OK.
Length: 160 hours (4 weeks).
Dates: May 1981-Present.
Objective: To prepare a technician or engineer to properly analyze the entire radar microwave link repeater system for correct performance, and be able to diagnose and repair any fault which may occur in the system, including major assemblies, modules, and components.
Instruction: Subject areas covered include: RF microwave generation, transmission and reception, frequency modulation concepts, receivers, system alignment and certification.
Credit recommendation: In the lower division baccalaureate/associate degree category, 3 semester hours in Electronics Technology (11/82).

Bright Radar Indicator Tower Equipment (40345)
Location: FAA Academy, Oklahoma City, OK.
Length: 120 hours (3 weeks).
Dates: July 1981-Present.
Objective: To provide training for technicians responsible for the alignment and maintenance of Bright Radar Indicator Tower Equipment video display systems.
Learning Outcome: Upon successful completion of this course, the student will be able to perform alignment procedures on the Plan Position Indicator (PPI) and on the Vidicon video camera; use resolution pattern test equipment for realistic optimum alignment; and recognize system problems and perform fault analysis.
Instruction: Classroom instruction, laboratory exercises, and written examinations are used to teach the analysis of circuitry and system functions by major blocks consisting of PPI type deflection and related video circuitry; digital timing generations; television displays; and interrelated control functions.
Credit recommendation: In the lower division baccalaureate/associate degree category, 2 semester hours in Electron Video Technology (5/87).

Radar Beacon Performance Remote System Monitor (40378)
Location: FAA Academy, Oklahoma City, OK.
Length: 48 hours (1 week, 1 day).
Dates: *Version 1:* August 1981-August 1988; *Version 2:* September 1988-Present.
Objective: To teach the student the operation, maintenance, and certification of the Radar Beacon Remote System Monitor.
Learning Outcome: Upon successful completion of this course, the student will be able to describe the operation of the system; test the system and determine any fault; and repair the system for proper operation.
Instruction: Course covers the block diagram of the entire system, the receiver circuits, decoder/encoder circuits, transmitter, and monitor. Troubleshooting the system is also covered. Methodology includes lecture and on-the-job training.
Credit recommendation: *Version 1:* In the vocational certificate or lower division baccalaureate/associate degree category, 1 semester hour in Electronics Technology (11/82). *Version 2:* In the lower division baccalaureate/associate degree category, 1 semester hour in Electronics Technology (9/88). NOTE: This course has been reevaluated and continues to meet requirements for credit recommendations.

Air Traffic Control Beacon Integrator 5 (ATCBI) (40383)
Location: FAA Academy, Oklahoma City, OK.
Length: 80 hours (2 weeks).
Dates: January 1982-Present.
Objective: To train personnel for installation, evaluation, modification, maintenance, or certification of the ATCBI-5 system.
Instruction: A course of study in: system concepts, pulse mode generator, transmitter, receiver, stagger/destagger, SLS/ISLS, monitors, control circuits, and Beacon test sets.
Credit recommendation: In the lower division baccalaureate/associate degree or upper division baccalaureate category, 2 semester hours in Electronics Technology (11/82).

Electronics Technician Qualification Course Phase I (40509)
Location: FAA Academy, Oklahoma City, OK.
Length: 300 hours (7½ weeks).
Dates: January 1972-Present.
Objective: To train electronic technicians in the fundamentals of basic electronics.
Instruction: Computer based instruction including: AC/DC math, electron theory, Ohm's Law, electromagnetism, capacitance, reactance, series-parallel bridge circuits, network theorems, transient analysis, resonance, filters, and test equipment.

Credit recommendation: In the vocational certificate or lower division baccalaureate/associate degree category, 4 semester hours in Electronics Technology (11/82).

Ultra Programming (42008)
  Location: FAA Academy, Oklahoma City, OK.
  Length: 120 hours (3 weeks).
  Dates: January 1975-Present.
  Objective: To prepare technicians and engineers to analyze the operational program, select, and interpret any special software features necessary for analyzing on-line system performance.
  Instruction: A study of: symbolic coding format, assembler basics, form directives, expressions, DO directives, MACROS, and correlation of operational program instruction listings to program data by sub-program analysis.
  Credit recommendation: In the lower division baccalaureate/associate degree category, 3 semester hours in Computer Science (11/82).

Automated Radar Terminal System Common Course (42009)
  Location: FAA Academy, Oklahoma City, OK.
  Length: 240 hours (6 weeks).
  Dates: March 1978-Present.
  Objective: To prepare a technician or engineer to analyze the equipment common between the ARTS III and ARTS III-A system for normal operation, and be able to trouble-shoot the entire system.
  Instruction: Utilizing two thirds lecture and one third lab subject areas include: peripheral adapter module (PAM), which includes interfacility data sets, magnetic tape control unit, communications teletype adapter, and related material.
  Credit recommendation: In the lower division baccalaureate/associate degree category, 5 semester hours in Electronics Technology (11/82).

Automated Radar Tracking System III-A (42011)
  Location: FAA Academy, Oklahoma City, OK.
  Length: 200 hours (5 weeks).
  Dates: January 1976-Present.
  Objective: Provide technicians and engineers with training to analyze for normal operation equipment associated with the ARTS III-A system and will be able to diagnose and correct any fault which occurs in the ARTS III-A system, subsystem or individual modules or the associated interface circuitry.
  Instruction: Units of study include: IOPB Diagnostic Program, Reconfiguration and Fault Detection (RFDU) unit, RFDU Diagnostic program, Multiplexer Display Buffer Memory (MDBM), Data Entry and Display Subsystem (DEDS)/MDBM Diagnostic Program and Operational program (ARTS III-A) layout.
  Credit recommendation: In the lower division baccalaureate/associate degree category, 4 semester hours in Electronics Technology (11/82). NOTE: Credit should not be granted for both this course and for 24014.

Automated Radar Terminal System (ARTS III-A) Update (42014)
  Location: FAA Academy, Oklahoma City, OK.
  Length: 240 hours (6 weeks).
  Dates: March 1978-Present.
  Objective: To enable students to analyze equipment associated with the ARTS III-A system and diagnose and correct any fault in the system, subsystem, individual modules and associated interface circuitry.
  Instruction: Two-thirds lecture, one-third laboratory. Includes: IOP/IOPB differences, IOPB diagnostic program, reconfiguration and fault detection unit (RFDU), RFDU diagnostic program, multiplex display buffer memory (MDBM), data entry and display subsystem (DEDS)/MDBM diagnostic program and ARTS III-A operational program layout.
  Credit recommendation: In the lower division baccalaureate/associate degree category, 4 semester hours in Electronics Technology (11/82). NOTE: Credit should not be granted for both this course and 42011.

Input/Output Processor (IOP) (42017)
  Location: FAA Academy, Oklahoma City, OK.
  Length: 320 hours (8 weeks).
  Dates: January 1976-Present.
  Objective: To provide technicians and engineers with training to analyze the operation of the input output processor for normal performance and be able to analyze, diagnose, and correct any fault which may occur in the equipment or its associated interface.
  Instruction: Using a 3/4 lecture and 1/4 laboratory course breakdown, the topic areas are: system introduction, processor instruction set, input/output instruction set, principles of programming, processor hardware, I/O hardware, and memory and utility software.
  Credit recommendation: In the lower division baccalaureate/associate degree category, 6 semester hours in Electronics Technology (11/82).

Enroute Automated Radar Tracking System (42021)
  Location: FAA Academy, Oklahoma City, OK.
  Length: 160 hours (4 weeks).
  Dates: March 1982-Present.
  Objective: To provide technicians and engineers training to analyze for normal operation of equipment associated with the EARTS system and diagnose and correct faults within the system, subsystem, or individual modules associated with the interface circuitry.
  Instruction: A study of: ULTRA symbolic instruction, EARTS operational program, fault analysis, system level troubleshooting.
  Credit recommendation: In the lower division bac-

calaureate/associate degree category, 3 semester hours in Electronics Technology (11/82).

Interface Buffer Adapter and Generator (42024)
Location: FAA Academy, Oklahoma City, OK.
Length: 120 hours (3 weeks).
Dates: March 1982-Present.
Objective: To enable the technician or engineer to analyze the operation of the Interface Buffer Adapter and Generator for correct performance and be able to diagnose and correct any fault which may occur in the subsystem or its associated interface circuitry.
Instruction: A 3/4 lecture and 1/4 laboratory course. The topics covered include: display console interface, microexecutions program, diagnostic programs, logic diagrams, maintenance procedures, fault diagnostics, performance analysis, associated operational software, system and subsystem concepts and troubleshooting.
Credit recommendation: In the lower division baccalaureate/associate degree category, 3 semester hours in Electronics Technology or Computer Science (11/82).

Continuous Data Recording System (42025)
Location: FAA Academy, Oklahoma City, OK.
Length: 160 hours (4 weeks).
Dates: March 1981-Present.
Objective: To enable students to analyze the CDR system for correct performance; to diagnose and correct any fault which may occur in the CDR system and its interface circuitry.
Instruction: This 3/4 lecture and 1/4 laboratory course includes; disc drive units, disc control units, printer control units, printer logic and printer mechanical unit.
Credit recommendation: In the lower division baccalaureate/associate degree category, 4 semester hours in Electronics Technology (11/82).

Data Processing Subsystem (42027)
Location: FAA Academy, Oklahoma City, OK.
Length: 480 hours (12 weeks).
Dates: March 1982-Present.
Objective: To enable the technician or engineer to analyze the data processing subsystem for normal operation and will be able to analyze, diagnose, and correct fault which may occur in the subsystem or its associated interface circuitry.
Instruction: This lecture/lab course involves the following subjects: Input/output processor modification, centralized memory access unit, reconfiguration and fault detection unit, memory, and associated diagnostics and operational software.
Credit recommendation: In the lower division baccalaureate/associate degree category, 10 semester hours in Computer Science (11/82).

Enroute Automated Radar Tracking System Data Acquisition Subsystem (42028)
Location: FAA Academy, Oklahoma City, OK.
Length: 240 hours (6 weeks).
Dates: January 1982-Present.
Objective: To provide training for engineers and technicians to analyze the EARTS Data Acquisition Subsystem for correct performance and be able to diagnose and correct any fault which may occur in the subsystem of interface circuitry.
Instruction: A study of the theory of operation on the communication multiplexer controller (CMC), console data terminal, CARD reader and controller, real time clock unit, WWV receiver unit, Magnetic Tape Transport (MTT), formatter, Magnetic Tape Controller (MTC), diagnostic programs and operational software.
Credit recommendation: In the lower division baccalaureate/associate degree category, 4 semester hours in Electronics Technology (11/82).

Automated Radar Terminal System (ARTS II) for Supervisors (42029)
Location: FAA Academy, Oklahoma City, OK.
Length: 48 hours (1 week, 1 day).
Dates: December 1981-Present.
Objective: To provide students with an overview of the ARTS II for supervisory personnel.
Instruction: A 3/4 lecture and 1/4 laboratory course including: system overview, diagnostic and utility programs, certification and preventive maintenance.
Credit recommendation: In the upper division baccalaureate/associate degree category, 1 semester hour in Electronics Technology (11/82).

Automated Radar Terminal System II (42031)
Location: FAA Academy, Oklahoma City, OK.
Length: 480 hours (12 weeks).
Dates: January 1982-Present.
Objective: To provide technicians with maintenance and operational expertise in process, I/O controller, modern, display, and bus hardware and assembler, operating system, and diagnostic software.
Instruction: A 3/4 CBI/lecture, 1/4 laboratory course. Topics: basic computer logic, number systems/conversions, hardware interface, processor operations, I/O operations; assembly language programming, programming techniques, diagnostics, and system configuration.
Credit recommendation: In the lower division baccalaureate/associate degree category, 8 semester hours in Electronics Technology (11/82).

Computer Update Equipment (43416)
Location: FAA Academy, Oklahoma City, OK.
Length: 200 hours (5 weeks).
Dates: August 1980-Present.
Objective: To train personnel responsible for the

maintenance, evaluation, modification, or certification of the Computer Update Equipment.

Learning Outcome: Upon successful completion of this course, the student will learn to make checks, adjustments, and diagnose malfunctions in the CUE system.

Instruction: The course includes study of NRKM, Console Equipment, Interface, AC Power monitor, and Core Memory.

Credit recommendation: In the lower division baccalaureate/associate degree category, 3 semester hours in Computer Systems Technology (5/87).

Data Receiver Group/IFDS (43417)

Location: FAA Academy, Oklahoma City, OK.
Length: 144 hours (3½ weeks)
Dates: June 1983-Present.
Objective: To train technicians the operation and maintenance of the Data Receiving and the Inter-Facility Data Set.

Learning Outcome: Upon successful completion of this course, the students learn the basic operation of each piece of equipment in the Data Receiver Group and the Inter-Facility Data Set; and the operation of the overall systems. Students learn to do operational checks, make voltage measurements and troubleshooting to locate faulty parts.

Instruction: The course teaches the equipment operation and repair of the Data Receiving Group and the Inter-Facility Data Set. The course is 50 percent lab where the operation and troubleshooting is covered in a hands-on style of instruction. Equipment includes digital logic, counters, registers, number base converters, coders, decoders, and processor, used in data reception and transmission. The CRT, modem, and printer are taught.

Credit recommendation: In the lower division baccalaureate/associate degree category, 3 semester hours in Electronics/Data Communications (5/87).

Test Equipment Console Test (43419)

Location: FAA Academy, Oklahoma City, OK.
Length: 240 hours (6 weeks).
Dates: 1977-Present.
Objective: To provide the student with the skills necessary to operate, maintain, and test the Test Equipment Console (TEC).

Learning Outcome: Upon successful completion of this course, the student will understand the conversion of numbers from one base to another, such as hexidecimal to binary; write a simple machine language program; understand the use of flowcharts and diagnostic tests; understand the tracing of electronic circuits and logic diagrams; and understand the interfacing of peripherals to DATA BUS (TTY, TTL, and RS 232).

Instruction: The course consists of machine language programming of a 16 bit computer, data storage using core and static MOS memory, TTL to RS 232 interfacing, direct and indexed addressing, use of diagnostic software, and peripheral controllers.

Credit recommendation: In the lower division baccalaureate/associate degree category, 4 semester hours in Electronic/Computer Technology (5/87).

Computer Display Channel Processor (43423)

Location: FAA Academy, Oklahoma City, OK.
Length: 956 hours (24 weeks).
Dates: November 1975-Present.
Objective: To prepare students to assume the responsibility for the maintenance of the Computer Display Channel Processor subsystem.

Instruction: The course is presented in a lab/lecture structure. Subject areas include: Programming, data strings, central processor, test cart, operational programs, input/output control, high speed filters, and configuration and control monitor.

Credit recommendation: In the lower division baccalaureate/associate degree or upper division baccalaureate category, 14 semester hours in Computer Science or Electronics Technology (11/82).

Computer Display Channel for Technicians (43426)

Location: FAA Academy, Oklahoma City, OK.
Length: 400 hours (10 weeks).
Dates: January 1975-Present.
Objective: To train technicians to install, do preventative maintenance and repair to the computer display channel Equipment and Radar Display systems.

Learning Outcome: Upon successful completion of this course, the student will be able to do detailed maintenance and repair for a computer displayed radar system.

Instruction: The course teaches the system down to the component level. There is a great deal of digital logic, transistor theory, registers, counters, displays, A to D, D to A, CRT circuitry (video amplifiers, etc.), operational amplifiers, keyboard operation and multiplexing. There are classes and labs on equipment operation and fault isolation.

Credit recommendation: In the lower division baccalaureate/associate degree category, 15 semester hours in Computer Electronics, Digital Controls, or Digital Electronics (5/87).

Computer Display Channel for Software (43451)

Location: FAA Academy, Oklahoma City, OK.
Length: 320 hours (8 weeks).
Dates: March 1984-Present.
Objective: To provide theoretical and practical training necessary to maintain the software used to control the Computer Display Channel Systems.

Learning Outcome: Upon successful completion of this course, the students will have skills in the following areas: verifying new and revised CDC operational programs; analyzing program discrepancies; coding emergency patches; and maintaining CDC hardware/software integrity.

Instruction: Subject areas include study of on-line operational programs, test and maintenance programs, and off-line maintenance programs. The course is approximately 50 percent lecture, 50 percent laboratory.
Prerequisite: CDC Programming and Data Structure.
Credit recommendation: In the upper division baccalaureate category, 4 semester hours in Computer Science Technology (5/87).

IBM 029 Card Punch and IBM 129 Card Punch - Print-Verifier (43456)
Location: FAA Academy, Oklahoma City, OK.
Length: 156 hours (4 weeks).
Dates: January 1980-Present.
Objective: To prepare students to repair and maintain the 029 card punch and 129 card punch - print-verifier machine.
Instruction: The course consists of classroom lectures, laboratory sessions, and examinations. Classroom subjects are theory of operation, electrical and electronic circuits, adjustment procedures, and corrective maintenance procedures.
Credit recommendation: In the vocational certificate category, 3 semester hours in Computer Equipment Repair (11/82).

IBM 9020-A Processing (43461)
Location: FAA Academy, Oklahoma City, OK.
Length: 636 hours (16 weeks).
Dates: December 1978-December 1987.
Objective: To provide technicians and engineers training in the operation, maintenance, and troubleshooting of the IBM Model 9020-A.
Instruction: This course covers the operation and maintenance of the processing portion of the 9020-A computers, and includes the CE (Model 1), SE (Model 8), and the IOCE.
Credit recommendation: In the lower division baccalaureate/associate degree or upper division baccalaureate category, 12 semester hours in Electronics Technology or Computer Science (11/82).

Enroute Automated Radar Tracking System Display (EARTS) (43467)
Location: FAA Academy, Oklahoma City, OK.
Length: 120 hours (3 weeks).
Dates: October 1981-Present.
Objective: To train personnel to install, evaluate, modify, and maintain EARTS display.
Instruction: In this lecture/laboratory course, plan view display operation is taught. Laboratory sessions develop skills in equipment routine checks, alignment, test procedures, use of test equipment, and fault diagnosis.
Credit recommendation: In the lower division baccalaureate/associate degree category, 2 semester hours in Electronics Technology (11/82).

IBM System 360 Operating System (43468)
Location: FAA Academy, Oklahoma City, OK.
Length: 152 hours (3 weeks and 4 days).
Dates: July 1981-December 1987.
Objective: To prepare students to program the 2314 DASF, operate the DS-360, apply utility programs and run problem programs on the DS-360.
Instruction: The course is two-thirds lecture, one-third laboratory. Presentation of operating systems, structure and function, lab control language, utility programs, and IBM BAL programming under DS-360.
Credit recommendation: In the lower division baccalaureate/associate degree or upper division baccalaureate category, 2 semester hours in Computer Science (11/82).

Flight Data Processing and Monitor for Jovial Programming System (43469)
Location: FAA Academy, Oklahoma City, OK.
Length: 236 hours (6 weeks).
Dates: March 1979-Present.
Objective: To provide students with training in the NAS monitor, flight data processing, program alerts, and support processors for system performance officers and specialists.
Instruction: 30 hours lecture, 10 hours lab per week. Topics covered include: Systems Introduction, NAS monitor, and FDP. Support Processors and Program Alerts are also covered.
Credit recommendation: In the lower division baccalaureate/associate degree or upper division baccalaureate category, 6 semester hours in Computer Science (11/82).

NAS Enroute Operational Program for Engineers (43470)
Location: FAA Academy, Oklahoma City, OK.
Length: 236 hours (6 weeks).
Dates: November 1981-Present.
Objective: To prepare engineers in the operation of the National Airspace Operational program in the areas of the operational monitor, Flight Data Processing, and Radar Data Processing.
Instruction: Utilizing a 4 to 1 lecture/lab ratio, this course addresses the following areas at the engineering level: element error analysis and configuration program, flight data processing, off-line processing programs, system messages, and radar data processing. All areas involve the use and analysis of Basic Assembler Language and Jovial Programming Language.
Credit recommendation: In the upper division baccalaureate or graduate category, 8 semester hours in Computer Science (11/82).

NAS System Interfaces for Systems Performance Specialists (43471)
Location: FAA Academy, Oklahoma City, OK.
Length: 196 hours (4 weeks - 4½ days).
Dates: March 1981-December 1987.
Objective: To develop the students' expertise in the software interface of all input/output devices to the 9020 Central Computer Complex.
Instruction: To include introduction to NAS interface and interface with: maintenance diagnostic monitor, channel interface, input/output typewriter, flight data entry and printout, teletype, flight strip printer control module, direct access storage facility, common digitizer; coded time source, non-radar keyboard multiplexer, and computer display channel.
Credit recommendation: In the upper division baccalaureate/associate degree category, 5 semester hours in Computer Science (11/82).

Central Control and Monitoring System (CCMS) Maintenance (43472)
Location: FAA Academy, Oklahoma City, OK.
Length: 320 hours (8 weeks).
Dates: May 1986-Present.
Objective: To train personnel responsible for the operation, maintenance, and evaluation of central control and monitoring systems.
Learning Outcome: Upon successful completion of this course, the students will be able to perform routine checks and adjustments; and equipment evaluation and fault diagnosis.
Instruction: The course includes computer programming, debugging, data storage and read-out; computer I/O devices; interfacing and computer organization. The course is approximately half lecture, half lab.
Credit recommendation: In the lower division baccalaureate/associate degree category, 6 semester hours in Computer Technology (5/87).

Direct Access Radar Channel System for Technicians (43473)
Location: FAA Academy, Oklahoma City, OK.
Length: *Version 1:* 276 hours (7 weeks). *Version 2:* 360 hours (9 weeks).
Dates: July 1978-Present.
Objective: To prepare students for the responsibility of maintenance of the Direct Access Radar Channel System.
Instruction: The course consists of classroom lectures, examinations, and laboratory sessions. Subject areas include: national airspace system/prime comparison, system operation, system reconfiguration capability, and display generator unit interface equipment.
Credit recommendation: In the lower division baccalaureate/associate degree category, 4 semester hours in Electronics Technology (11/82).

Central Control and Monitoring System (CCMS) Remote Operator (43474)
Location: FAA Academy, Oklahoma City, OK.
Length: 80 hours (2 weeks).
Dates: January 1979-Present.
Objective: To develop the students' skills in operating central control and monitoring systems and maintenance of remote sensors and Data Gathering Panel (DGP).
Learning Outcome: Upon successful completion of this course, the students learn how to operate and maintain remote sensors and Data Gathering Panels.
Instruction: Utilizing a 50 percent lecture and 50 percent lab course breakdown, the material covered includes: (1) digital logic; (2) general theory of Central Control and Monitoring System; and (3) the operation involved in that system.
Credit recommendation: In the vocational certificate category, 1 semester hour in Vocational Electronics (5/87).

Common Digitizer Height Only (43477)
Location: FAA Academy, Oklahoma City, OK.
Length: 120 hours (3 weeks).
Dates: November 1982-Present.
Objective: To provide electronics technicians and engineers the theory of operation and troubleshooting procedures for the height and military functions of the common digitizer AN/FYO-47.
Instruction: This lecture/lab course addresses request message format and processing, timing circuits, coordinate data converter, mode control height circuits, output message generating and transfer, aims, and normal detection.
Credit recommendation: In the lower division baccalaureate/associate degree category, 3 semester hours in Computer Science or Electronics Technology (11/82).

Direct Access Radar Channel System for Engineers (43479)
Location: FAA Academy, Oklahoma City, OK.
Length: 40 hours (1 week).
Dates: August 1982-Present.
Objective: To prepare engineers and software specialists for the installation, maintenance, and evaluation of the Direct Access Radar Channel equipment.
Instruction: The course consists of classroom lectures, examinations, and laboratory sessions. Subject areas include: basic programming data flow, system theory, and error analysis.
Credit recommendation: In the upper division baccalaureate/associate degree category, 1 semester hour in Computer Science or Electronics Technology (11/82).

Radar Data Processing for Systems Performance Specialist (43483)
Location: FAA Academy, Oklahoma City, OK.

Length: *Version 1:* 156 hours (3 weeks, 4½ days). *Version 2:* 200 hours (5 weeks).
Dates: *Version 1:* August 1982-December 1983. *Version 2:* January 1984-Present.
Objective: To prepare systems performance specialists for field responsibility of diagnosing problems in the NAS enroute operational programs and its related hardware subsystems.
Learning Outcome: Upon successful completion of this course, the student will be able to identify major tasks performed by MRDP; recognize data types passed to various subsystems; define search areas; list tasks, function and printouts of RTOC; and understand parameters associated with dynamic simulator processing and identify subprograms.
Instruction: The course provides detailed training in radar data processing and radar offline support procedures.
Credit recommendation: *Version 1:* In the lower division baccalaureate/associate degree category, 4 semester hours in Computer Science (11/82). *Version 2:* In the lower division baccalaureate/associate degree category, 2 semester hours in Radar Systems (5/87). NOTE: This course has been reevaluated and continues to meet requirements for credit recommendations.

IBM 9020-A System Hardware for Engineers (43489)
Location: FAA Academy, Oklahoma City, OK.
Length: 88 hours (2 weeks, 1 day).
Dates: August 1980-December 1987.
Objective: To provide students with an overview of the theory of operation and system integration of the IBM 9020-A central computer complex.
Instruction: A lecture/lab course involving theory or operation and system concepts associated with the IBM Model 7201-01 Computer Element; Model 7251-08 Storage Elements, Model 7231-02, Input/Output Control Element, Check Report Analysis, Diagnostic Instruction, Maintenance Aids, and Diagnostic Aids.
Credit recommendation: In the lower division baccalaureate/associate degree category, 2 semester hours in Electronics Technology or Computer Science (11/82). NOTE: Credit should not be granted both for this course and for course 43490.

IBM 9020-D System Hardware for Engineers (43490)
Location: FAA Academy, Oklahoma City, OK.
Length: 88 hours (2 weeks and 1 day).
Dates: August 1980-December 1987.
Objective: To provide students with an overview on the theory of operations and systems integration of the IBM 9020-A central computer complex.
Instruction: This course is composed of 3/4 lecture and 1/4 lab. Content includes: Theory and operation of the IBM 7201-02 computer element and IBM 7251-09 storage element; check report analysis; diagnose instruction, and general system operation.
Credit recommendation: In the lower division baccalaureate/associate degree category, 2 semester hours in Electronics Technology or Computer Science (11/82). NOTE: Credit should not be granted both for this course and for course 43489.

IBM 9020-A/D System Common Hardware for Engineers (43491)
Location: FAA Academy, Oklahoma City, OK.
Length: 180 hours (4½ weeks).
Dates: August 1980-December 1987.
Objective: To provide students with an overview of operational theory and system integration of common elements to the IBM 9020 models A and D.
Instruction: 3/4 lecture, 1/4 laboratory theory, operation, and systems integration of the input/output control elements and all peripheral devices including disc storage
Credit recommendation: In the lower division baccalaureate/associate degree category, 4 semester hours in Electronics Technology and Computer Science (11/82).

Direct Access Radar Channel System Software (43520) (Formerly 43480)
Location: FAA Academy, Oklahoma City, OK.
Length: *Version 1:* 476 hours (12 weeks). *Version 2:* 640 hours (16 weeks).
Dates: November 1982-Present.
Objective: To provide direct access radar channel system performance specialists with theoretical and practical training on the Direct Access Radar Channel operational program and support programs.
Instruction: The course consists of classroom instruction, examinations, and laboratory sessions. Subject areas include: operational programs, test and maintenance programs, and diagnostic software.
Credit recommendation: In the lower division baccalaureate/associate degree or in the upper division baccalaureate category, 6 semester hours in Electronics Technology or Computer Science (11/82).

Basic Multi Channel Recorder Theory (44006)
Location: Correspondence course from the FAA Academy, Oklahoma City, OK.
Length: 40 hours (1 week).
Dates: August 1981-Present.
Objective: To teach magnetic recording theory, magnetic head operation, digital recording techniques, tape drive systems, and transport systems.
Learning Outcome: Upon successful completion of this course, the students learn the principles of magnetism, magnetic bias, and equalization as applied to magnetic recording heads. They learn digital recording techniques and tape drive systems (servomechanisms). Students learn about tape transport systems and power supplies.
Instruction: The course covers the basic theory of mag-

netic recording. It includes the principles of magnetism, magnetic bias, gaps, azimuth, and skew for tape heads. The theory of tape transport systems and speed control are taught along with digital recording techniques.

Credit recommendation: In the lower division baccalaureate/associate degree category, 1 semester hour in Electromechanical Technology (5/87).

Diesel Engine Generators (44102)

Location: Correspondence course from the FAA Academy, Oklahoma City, OK.
Length: 45 hours.
Dates: August 1985-Present.
Objective: To teach basic principles, concepts, terminology and definitions of diesel engine generators and associated control panels.
Learning Outcome: Upon successful completion of this course, the student will be able to describe basic diesel engine operation; understand Bosch, Caterpillar, GMC, Rooso Master, and Cummins PT fuel systems; understand techniques related to a variety of speed governors; trace control signals through the control panel schematics; and understand brushless exciters and voltage regulation.
Instruction: Topics include basic diesel engine operation, fuel systems, governors, and control panels.
Credit recommendation: In the vocational certificate category, 2 semester hours in Diesel Mechanics (5/87).

Air Conditioning (44106)

Location: FAA Academy, Oklahoma City, OK.
Length: 30 hours.
Dates: May 1969-Present.
Objective: To teach students introductory principles of air conditioning.
Learning Outcome: Upon successful completion of this course, the student will be able to define basic refrigeration and air conditioning terms; explain the function of major system components using simple diagrams; and use refrigerant tables and charts.
Instruction: A correspondence study course to teach the student principles of refrigeration, properties of air, and the basic air conditioning system.
Credit recommendation: In the vocational certificate category, 2 semester hours in Air Conditioning or Practical Arts (5/87).

Semi-Conductor Devices (44417)

Location: Correspondence Course for the FAA Academy, Oklahoma City, OK.
Length: 120 hours (3 weeks).
Dates: November 1979-Present.
Objective: To provide training in the areas of semiconductor fundamentals, diodes, zenus, bi-polar transistors, FETs, thyristors, ICs, and optoelectronics.
Learning Outcome: Upon successful completion of this coruse, the students will be able to describe the electrical characteristics of semiconductors; explain how most important semiconductor devices operate; properly handle semiconductor components; and test various semiconductor devices.
Instruction: This course covers the operation and characteristics of the most widely used semiconductor devices. A training manual, cassette tapes, and 27 electronics components are furnished. Eleven experiments are conducted by the student. A supervised final exam is administered.
Credit recommendation: In the lower division baccalaureate/associate degree category, 1 semester hour in Semiconductor Devices (5/87).

ILS (Wilcox Mark I-D/E/F) (47702)

Location: FAA Academy, Oklahoma City, OK.
Length: 156 hours.
Dates: July 1984-Present.
Objective: To provide technicians with the skills and knowledge to install, maintain, and modify the Wilcox Mark 1-D/E/F Localizer System.
Learning Outcome: Upon successful completion of this course, the student will be able to measure RF power, percent of modulation, and distortion of carrier and sideband; use logic truth tables, block diagrams and schematic diagrams to troubleshoot the system; perform routine maintenance of Localizer; and have knowledge and skill to perform a complete system alignment and/or adjustment.
Instruction: One hundred and four clock hours of computer-based instruction describing the theory of operations, system principles, calibration, and fault analysis of the ILS Localizer. Fifty-two clock hours of practical laboratory experience involving operation, alignment, and maintenance.
Credit recommendation: In the lower division baccalaureate/associate degree category, 3 semester hours in Communication Electronics (5/87).

Mark 1F-Instrument Handling System (47703)

Location: FAA Academy, Oklahoma City, OK.
Length: 156 hours (4 weeks).
Dates: July 1984-Present.
Objective: To teach the student the theory of operation and maintenance of the Mark 1D/E/F ILS Glide Slope system.
Learning Outcome: Upon successful completion of this course, the student will be able to explain the block diagram of the system; test and troubleshoot the system; and repair the system to operate correctly.
Instruction: Course covers the power supply, transmitter, antenna, monitor, and localizer systems of the Mark 1D/E/F. System analysis, inspection, and troubleshooting are covered. Methodology includes lecture and on-the-job training.
Credit recommendation: In the lower division baccalaureate/associate degree category, 2 semester hours in

Electronics Technology (5/87) (9/88). NOTE: This course has been reevaluated and continues to meet requirements for credit recommendations.

FLIGHT STANDARDS

(Courses are listed in numerical order)

Federal Aviation Administration Douglas DC-9 Air Carrier Training Unit (20006)
  Location: FAA Academy, Oklahoma City, OK.
  Length: 168 hours (4 weeks, 1 day).
  Dates: October 1982-Present.
  Objective: This course is designed to train Air Carrier Operations Inspectors for initial qualification and standardization in DC-9 aircraft.
  Instruction: Instruction is given through lectures, pre- and post-flight briefings, and simulator and flight experiences. Subject areas include aircraft systems and equipment, limitations, performance, maneuvers, and emergency procedures.
  Credit recommendation: In the upper division baccalaureate category, 6 semester hours in Flight Technology (10/82). NOTE: Credit for this course precludes credit for 20007.

Boeing 727 Inspector Pilot and Flight Engineer Initial Qualification Course (20007)
  Location: FAA Academy, Oklahoma City, OK.
  Length: 200 hours (5 weeks).
  Dates: October 1982-Present.
  Objective: This course is designed to train Air Carrier Operations Inspectors for initial qualification and standardization in Boeing 727 aircraft.
  Instruction: Instruction is given through lectures, pre- and post-flight briefings, and simulator and flight experience. Subject areas include aircraft systems and equipment, limitations, performance, maneuvers, and emergency procedures.
  Credit recommendation: In the upper division baccalaureate category, 7 semester hours in Flight Technology (10/82). NOTE: Credit for this course precludes credit for 20006.

Air Carrier Operations Indoctrination (21607)
  Location: FAA Academy, Oklahoma City, OK.
  Length: 160 hours (4 weeks).
  Dates: October 1982-Present.
  Objective: To provide indoctrination for Air Carrier Operations Inspectors in the job functions required of this specialty.
  Instruction: Course consists of lectures and discussions on inspector job functions, improving personal relations and effectiveness and aeromedical training. The subject areas are related to the overall subjects of flight standards and air carrier mission.
  Credit recommendation: In the upper division baccalaureate category, 4 semester hours in Aviation Technology (10/82).

B-737 Aircraft Systems (21806)
  Location: FAA Academy, Oklahoma City, OK.
  Length: 80 hours (2 weeks).
  Dates: October 1982-Present.
  Objective: This course is designed to provide the maintenance or electrical/electronics inspector a working knowledge of Boeing 737 aircraft systems for the safety regulatory function.
  Instruction: Course includes study of the following systems: electrical power, fuel, anti- and de-icing systems, air conditioning and pressurization, hydraulic, landing gear and brake, flight controls, oxygen and emergency equipment, flight instruments and auto pilot. Instruction includes formal classroom lectures, class discussion and seminars, supervised laboratory and workshop experiences and homework assignments.
  Credit recommendation: In the upper division baccalaureate category, 3 semester hours in Aviation Technology (10/82). NOTE: Credit for this course excludes credit for 21800, 21807, and 21808.

DC-9 Aircraft Systems (21807)
  Location: FAA Academy, Oklahoma City, OK.
  Length: 80 hours (2 weeks).
  Dates: October 1982-Present.
  Objective: This course is designed to provide the maintenance or electrical/electronics inspector a working knowledge of Douglas DC-9 aircraft systems for the safety/regulatory function.
  Instruction: Course includes study of the following systems: electrical power, fuel, anti- and de-icing system, air conditioning and pressurization, hydraulic, landing gear and brake, flight controls, oxygen and emergency equipment, flight instruments and autopilot. Instruction includes formal classroom lectures, class discussions and seminars, supervised laboratory and workshop experiences and homework assignments.
  Credit recommendation: In the upper division baccalaureate category, 3 semester hours in Aviation Technology (10/82). NOTE: Credit for this course excludes credit for 21800, 21806, and 21808.

B-727 Aircraft Systems (21808)
  Location: FAA Academy, Oklahoma City, OK.
  Length: 80 hours (2 weeks).
  Dates: October 1982-Present.
  Objective: This course is designed to provide the maintenance on electrical/electronics inspectors a working knowledge of B-727 aircraft systems for the safety/regulatory function.
  Instruction: Course includes study of the following systems: electrical power, fuel, anti- and de-icing systems, air

conditioning and pressurization, hydraulic, landing gear and brake, flight controls, oxygen and emergency equipment, flight instruments and auto pilot. Instruction includes: formal classroom lectures, class discussion seminars, supervised lab and workshop experiences.

Credit recommendation: In the upper division baccalaureate category, 2 semester hours in Aviation Technology (10/82). NOTE: Credit for this course excludes credit for 21800, 21806, and 21807.

General Aviation Aircraft Alteration (21811)
Location: FAA Academy, Oklahoma City, OK.
Length: 76 hours (2 weeks).
Dates: October 1982-Present.
Objective: To prepare Airworthiness Inspectors for the task of approving aircraft alterations and installations.
Instruction: This course covers those areas which may be subject to alteration on general aviation aircraft such as electrical, avionics, propulsion, honeycomb products, fuel and oil, fiberglass and plastics, vacuum, and oxygen system. Learning takes place through lectures and laboratory experiences.
Credit recommendation: In the lower division baccalaureate category, 1 semester hour in Aviation Technology (10/82).

General Purpose Helicopter (21812)
Location: FAA Academy, Oklahoma City, OK.
Length: 80 hours (2 weeks).
Dates: October 1982-Present.
Objective: To provide basic knowledge of helicopters for Airworthiness Inspectors and Manufacturing Inspectors.
Instruction: Course consists of lectures and discussions on the design, construction, and maintenance of the leading type-certificated helicopters. A 2½ day field trip to an industry site is included.
Credit recommendation: In the lower division baccalaureate category, 2 semester hours in Aviation Technology (10/82).

Aircraft Maintenance Reliability Programs (21813)
Location: FAA Academy, Oklahoma City, OK.
Length: 80 hours (2 weeks).
Dates: October 1982-Present.
Objective: To train Airworthiness Inspectors to perform evaluation and surveillance of aircraft maintenance reliability or condition-monitoring maintenance programs.
Instruction: This course consists of lectures, workshops and homework assignments pertaining to calculations, organizing data, control charts, analysis techniques, electronic data processing, reliability and condition-monitoring maintenance methods. A review of FAR's, handbooks, circulars, etc., pertaining to reliability and condition-monitoring maintenance programs.

Credit recommendation: In the upper division baccalaureate category, 3 semester hours in Aviation Maintenance Technology (10/82).

General Aviation Jet Powerplants (21814)
Location: FAA Academy, Oklahoma City, OK.
Length: 76 hours (2 weeks).
Dates: October 1982-Present.
Objective: This course provides a general knowledge of general aviation jet powerplants for General Airworthiness Inspectors.
Instruction: Subject areas include: turbine powerplant analysis, turbine powerplant regulations, general aviation turbine powerplant familiarization, jet powerplant fuel and oils, powerplant accessories and associated equipment, and maintenance and inspection of turbine powerplants. Learning is acquired through lecture and laboratory experiences.
Credit recommendation: In the lower division baccalaureate category, 3 semester hours in Aviation Maintenance Technology (10/82).

Introduction to Executive Jet-Powered Aircraft (21816)
Location: FAA Academy, Oklahoma City, OK.
Length: 80 hours (2 weeks).
Dates: October 1982-Present.
Objective: To familiarize General Aviation Inspectors with the basic concepts of the systems and capabilities of small, executive jet aircraft.
Instruction: Subjects presented in lectures, and workshops include: executive turbine aircraft design features, high speed airfoil sections, vortex generators, mach trim, and other aerodynamic components of executive jet aircraft. Familiarization with functioning and operation of representative systems and power plants is included.
Credit recommendation: In the lower division baccalaureate category, 2 semester hours in Aviation Maintenance Technology (10/82). NOTE: Credit for this course excludes credit received for 21817.

Lear Jet and Sabreliner Aircraft Systems (21817)
Location: FAA Academy, Oklahoma City, OK.
Length: 80 hours (2 weeks).
Dates: October 1982-Present.
Objective: To familiarize General Aviation Airworthiness Inspectors with the systems and components of Lear Jet and Sabreliner aircraft.
Instruction: Lectures and laboratory workshop classes covering: aircraft design features, hydraulic systems, environmental control systems, fuel systems, instruments, navigation equipment, weight and balance, and operation limitation.
Credit recommendation: In the lower division baccalaureate category, 2 semester hours in Aviation Maintenance Technology (10/82). NOTE: Credit for this course excludes credit for 21816.

Allison Convair 580 Maintenance and Inspection (21831)
Location: FAA Academy, Oklahoma City, OK.
Length: 80 hours (2 weeks).
Dates: October 1982-Present.
Objective: To familiarize line mechanics and inspectors responsible for maintaining Allison Convair 580 aircraft with required maintenance procedures.
Instruction: This course consists of classroom lecture and study on the following subject areas pertaining to Allison Convair 580 aircraft; electrical systems, aircraft bleed system, hydraulic power system, landing gear, brakes, flaps, door and stairs, A/C and pressurization, fuel system, and locating components on the aircraft.
Credit recommendation: In the lower division baccalaureate category, 2 semester hours in Aviation Maintenance Technology (10/82). NOTE: Credit for this course excludes credit received from 21838 and 21840.

B-727 Aircraft and JT8D Engine Maintenance and Inspection (21838)
Location: FAA Academy, Oklahoma City, OK.
Length: 120 hours (3 weeks).
Dates: October 1982-Present.
Objective: To provide mechanics and/or inspection/quality control personnel who need a working knowledge on Boeing 727 aircraft systems and the JT8D engine to maintain the airworthiness of the Boeing 727 aircraft.
Instruction: Instruction in the form of lectures and laboratory assignments includes: design features and construction, hydraulic systems, landing gear, brakes and AFT airstairs, flight controls, electrical systems, oxygen and emergency equipment, pneumatic system, air conditioning and pressurization, ice and rain protection, fire detection and control, Pratt and Whitney JT8D power plant, fuel system, and APU.
Credit recommendation: In the lower division baccalaureate category, 3 semester hours in Aviation Maintenance Technology (10/82). NOTE: Credit for this course excludes credit received for 21840 and 21831.

DC-9 Airframe and Powerplant Maintenance and Inspection (21840)
Location: FAA Academy, Oklahoma City, OK.
Length: 120 hours (3 weeks).
Dates: October 1982-Present.
Objective: To provide mechanics and/or inspection personnel with a working knowledge of DC-9 aircraft systems.
Instruction: This course consists of classroom lecture and study on hydraulic power system, landing gear and brake systems, power plants, pneumatic system, air conditioning and pressurization systems, fuel systems, APU, systems operation in the DC-9 cockpit procedure trainer.
Credit recommendation: In the lower division baccalaureate category, 3 semester hours in Aviation Maintenance Technology (10/82). NOTE: Credit for this course excludes credit received for 21838 and 21831.

Emergency Evacuation and Survival Equipment (Airworthiness) (21843)
Location: FAA Academy, Oklahoma City, OK.
Length: 36 hours (1 week).
Dates: October 1982-Present.
Objective: To provide the Airworthiness Inspector with an update in the state-of-the art changes involving emergency equipment on newer aircraft, especially large and wide-bodied jets.
Instruction: Course involves classroom lectures, laboratory experiences and field training and includes the following topics: exits, lighting, evacuation slides, flotation equipment, supplemental oxygen, maintenance manual requirements, miscellaneous equipment, and FARs.
Credit recommendation: In the lower division baccalaureate category, 1 semester hour in Aircraft Maintenance Technology (10/82).

Omega/Area Navigation Systems (21845)
Location: FAA Academy, Oklahoma City, OK.
Length: *Version 1:* 80 hours (2 weeks). *Version 2:* 76 hours (2 weeks).
Dates: October 1982-Present.
Objective: This course is designed for Federal Aviation Administration Aviation Safety Inspectors (Avionics) involved in certification, surveillance and approval of VLF/Omega/RNAU Navigation Systems.
Instruction: Students receive instruction on the characteristics, limitations, and error sources of VLF/Omega/RNAU systems, Federal Aviation Regulations, approval procedures, maintenance requirements, and practice problems in conformity inspections. Course includes training on Loran "C" and microwave landing systems.
Credit recommendation: In the upper division baccalaureate category, 1 semester hour in Avionics or Electronics (10/82).

Flight Control Systems (22462)
Location: FAA Academy, Oklahoma City, OK.
Length: 240 hours (6 weeks).
Dates: October 1982-Present.
Objective: To provide the Avionics Maintenance Technician with the knowledge and ability to perform testing, troubleshooting, repair, and modification of the FCS-105 Flight Control System and the MC-103 Compass System.
Instruction: Students obtain knowledge and skills in the areas of theory of flight, logic circuits review, circuit analysis, maintenance and calibration of the FCS-105 Flight Control System and MC-103 Magnetic Compass System.
Credit recommendation: In the upper division baccalaureate category, 6 semester hours in Avionics (10/82).

Non-Destructive Testing (22502)
  Location: FAA Academy, Oklahoma City, OK.
  Length: 80 hours (2 weeks).
  Dates: October 1982-Present.
  Objective: To familiarize Federal Aviation Administration inspectors and quality control specialists with types/principles/and procedures for Non-Destructive Testing of aircraft components.
  Instruction: Subject areas covered in lectures and laboratory sessions include evaluation of non-destructive testing methods, application, limitations and surveillance of methods. Students will detect metal defects, cracks, changes in material properties, manufacturing voids, mechanical defects and thickness measurements.
  Credit recommendation: In the upper division baccalaureate category, 2 semester hours in Aeronautical Engineering (10/82).

Introduction to Aircraft Flutter (22504)
  Location: FAA Academy, Oklahoma City, OK.
  Length: 80 hours (2 weeks).
  Dates: October 1982-Present.
  Objective: To acquaint aerospace engineers with the behavior of aircraft under certain aerodynamic conditions, i.e., aircraft flutter, tubular analysis, flutter prevention and flight testing.
  Instruction: This course serves as an introduction to aircraft flutter analysis and includes the following subjects: aircraft vibration, introduction to flutter, vibration testing, review of mathematics, two and three dimensional flutter analysis, tubular analysis, flutter prevention criteria, and flutter flight testing. Learning methods include classroom lectures, discussion and seminars and problem solving activities covering analyses of flutter reports.
  Credit recommendation: In the upper division baccalaureate category, 3 semester hours in Aeronautical Engineering (10/82).

Introduction to Aircraft Vibration (22505)
  Location: FAA Academy, Oklahoma City, OK.
  Length: 80 hours (2 weeks)
  Dates: October 1982-Present.
  Objective: To provide engineers with an understanding of the theory and application of vibration testing and analysis.
  Instruction: Subject areas include a review of mathematics and mechanics, free and forced-damped systems, unbalance and balancing equipment, absorbers and dampers, vibration equipment and its use, engine and propeller vibration, helicopter vibration and a complete ground vibration survey on an actual airframe.
  Credit recommendation: In the upper division baccalaureate category, 3 semester hours in Aeronautical Engineering (10/82).

Certification and Surveillance of NDT Repair Stations and Facilities (22520)
  Location: FAA Academy, Oklahoma City, OK.
  Length: 80 hours (2 weeks).
  Dates: October 1982-Present.
  Objective: To familiarize Federal Aviation Administration inspection and engineering personnel with in-depth training in radiographic and eddy current non-destructive testing.
  Instruction: Lecture subjects include theory and practical application of radiography and eddy current NDT methods, certification and surveillance of NDT repair stations with emphasis on certification of repair stations to conduct NDT inspections of the Beech 18. Laboratory exercises will consist of "hands-on" set up and operation of equipment and interpretation of results.
  Credit recommendation: In the upper division baccalaureate category, 2 semester hours in Aeronautical Engineering (10/82).

Loads Analysis for Small Airplanes (22521)
  Location: FAA Academy, Oklahoma City, OK.
  Length: 80 hours (2 weeks).
  Dates: October 1982-Present.
  Objective: To acquaint engineers with the knowledge and procedures involved in the evaluation of loads reports for FAR Part 23 airplanes (small airplanes).
  Instruction: Instruction includes both lecture and laboratory experiences and covers the following subjects: methods of loads analysis, aerodynamics, design data, critical loading conditions, airfoil characteristics, airplane balancing, wing load and landing loads.
  Credit recommendation: In the lower division baccalaureate category, 3 semester hours in Aeronautical Engineering (10/82).

Evaluation of Aviation Management Systems (22600)
  Location: FAA Academy, Oklahoma City, OK.
  Length: 78 hours (2 weeks).
  Dates: October 1982-Present.
  Objective: To provide basic management auditing and analysis techniques to qualified journeyman aviation safety inspectors.
  Instruction: Material covered includes: types of organizations, problem decisions, organizational principles, management concepts and principles, organization evaluation and planning; and essentials of management information systems design. Instruction includes: lecture/discussion, workshops, and problem-solving projects.
  Credit recommendation: In the lower division baccalaureate category, 3 semester hours in Aviation Management or Business Management (10/82).

LOGISTICS

(Courses are listed in numerical order)

Fundamentals of Procurement (07001)
Location: FAA Academy, Oklahoma City, OK.
Length: 120 hours (3 weeks); residential.
Dates: July 1969-Present.
Objective: To train entry level procurement personnel in essential legal and regulatory framework for the government acquisition process and the interrelationship of the procurement function with other logistics functions.
Instruction: General policies relative to procurement responsibility and authority, ethics and standard of conduct, specifications, formal advertising, negotiations and administration. Lectures, discussion, and case studies. (No prerequisites).
Credit recommendation: In the lower division baccalaureate/associate degree category, 3 semester hours in General Business (10/82).

Procurement for Technical Personnel (07004)
Location: FAA Academy, Washington and Regional Headquarters, and U.S. Coast Guard Headquarters.
Length: 40 hours (1 week).
Dates: December 1970-Present.
Objective: To provide technical and professional personnel with an understanding of the procurement process as related to contracting with contractors, and coordination with procurement personnel.
Instruction: Process of procurement management; involving the preparation and release of procurement requests, solicitation of contract awards, and procurement management after contract award. Other topics include: specifications, source selection, contractor responsibility, contract types, nature and scope of contract administration, modification and termination.
Credit recommendation: In the lower division baccalaureate/associate degree category, 2 semester hours in Management, Business Administration, or Logistics (10/82).

Real Estate for Federal Aviation Administration Contracting Officers (07005)
Location: FAA Academy, Oklahoma City, OK.
Length: 72 hours (2 weeks).
Dates: *Version 1:* April 1971-December 1980. *Version 2:* January 1981-Present.
Objective: To provide training for Realty Contracting Officers involved in purchase and leasing of real estate property for Federal use.
Instruction: Lectures, workshops, discussion, problem solving and examination on major issues of real estate including appraisal; negotiation, acquisitions and condemnation; title evidence; land measurement; leasing; and real estate property record systems. Particular reference to Federal laws on land acquisition for Federal use.
Credit recommendation: In the upper division category, 3 semester hours in Real Estate Principles (10/82).

Advanced Procurement and Contracting (07007)
Location: FAA Academy, Oklahoma City, OK.
Length: 80 hours (2 weeks, 5 days/week).
Dates: *Version 1:* January 1972-December 1977. *Version 2:* January 1978-Present.
Objective: When completing the course, the student will be able to (a) plan procurement at top levels; (b) plan procurement for multi-years; (c) calculate life cycle costing; (d) demonstrate competency in pricing and cost analysis; (e) identify and manipulate various contracts, and (f) demonstrate expertise in handling disputes. Using the procedures and materials in the lecture and laboratory and to achieve at least a minimum level of competency.
Instruction: The instruction consists of approximately 68 hours of lecture (34 per week) and approximately 12 hours of laboratory (6 hours per week). The students will necessarily be working presently either in procurement and management status in procurement; forty-five students are generally enrolled.
Credit recommendation: In the elective area in the lower division baccalaureate/associate degree category, 2 semester hours in Business Administration/Materials Management (10/82).

Federal Procurement Law (07010)
Location: FAA Academy, Oklahoma City, OK.
Length: 104 hours (3 weeks); residential.
Dates: July 1971-Present.
Objective: To provide comprehensive training for Federal Aviation Administration employees whose positions require a basic understanding of contract law and its application.
Instruction: Power to contract, authority of individual agents, contract formation principles, interpretation, modification and equitable adjustments, delays, default, inspection, acceptance and warranties. Case studies and group reports are used in this seminar.
Credit recommendation: In the upper division baccalaureate category, 3 semester hours in Management (10/82).

Construction Contracting (07013)
Location: FAA Academy, Oklahoma City, OK.
Length: 76 hours (2 weeks).
Dates: January 1975-Present.
Objective: To provide training for entry level and operating specialists engaged in the procurement of construction for Federal Aviation Administration.
Instruction: Procurement requests, labor standards, liquidated, formal advertising, alternate bids, contractor responsibility, protests, changes, delays, defaults, inspections, and acceptance.
Credit recommendation: In the lower division baccalaureate/associate degree category, 2 semester hours in Business Management (10/82).

Operations and Supply Support (07014)
Location: FAA Academy, Oklahoma City, OK.
Length: 64 hours (2 weeks).
Dates: August 1976-Present.
Objective: To assist Federal Aviation Administration logistics clerks and administrative personnel in the development of an understanding of the basic principles in operations and supply support.
Instruction: Major topics covered in this course are introduction to inventory input, pipeline of supply. The Federal Aviation Administration support system procedure, Economic Order Quantity (EOQ): the use catalog and receiving procedure, shipping government bills of lading (GBL), local purchase, depot operations (tour of depot) and materials requirements, system evaluation, the role of the contracting officer representative, and responsibilities for operating material.
Credit recommendation: In the lower division baccalaureate/associate degree category, 2 semester hours in Business Management/Logistics (10/82).

Material Management (07015)
Location: FAA Academy, Oklahoma City, OK.
Length: 64 hours (2 weeks).
Dates: February 1979-Present.
Objective: To develop a basic understanding of material management and day to day operation of management of the Federal Aviation Administration Material system for logistics clerical and administrative personnel in the Federal Aviation Administration Academy.
Instruction: Instruction includes topics of supply cycle, project material, provisioning process, failure under warranty, cataloging, capitalization, express materials and motor vehicle management.
Credit recommendation: In the lower baccalaureate/associate degree category, 2 semester hours in Management/Logistics: Elective (10/82).

CENTER FOR MANAGEMENT DEVELOPMENT

(Courses are listed in numerical order.)
Source of official student records: FAA Center for Management Development, 4500 Palm Coast, Parkway East, Palm Coast, FL 32037.
Additional information about the courses: Program on Noncollegiate Sponsored Instruction, The Center for Adult Learning and Educational Credentials, American Council on Education, One Dupont Circle, Washington, D.C. 20036.

Performance Improvement and Employee Appraisal (01201)
Location: FAA Center for Management Development, Palm Coast, FL.
Length: 35 hours (1 week); residential.
Dates: August 1972-November 1979.
Objective: To improve the supervisor's understanding and application of FAA approaches to employee performance improvement and appraisal.
Instruction: Performance standards, human relations and communications, employee development programs, the performance appraisal process, counseling. Lectures, discussions, and classroom exercises are used. Prerequisite: Supervisory Initial Course (01200) or Managerial Initial Course (01300).
Credit recommendation: In the upper division baccalaureate category, 2 semester hours in Management or Public Administration (5/76).

Labor Relations for Management (01202)
Location: FAA Center for Management Development, Palm Coast, FL.
Length: 35 hours (1 week); residential.
Dates: November 1973-December 1979.
Objective: To provide line managers with an in-depth understanding of labor contract administration consistent with Executive Order 11491 and interpretations, and with FAA labor policy and philosophy.
Instruction: Public sector labor-management-union relations, Federal Code of Fair Labor Practices, unfair labor practices, contract negotiations, grievance systems, arbitration. Lecture, discussion, and classroom exercises are used. Prerequisite: Supervisory Initial Course (01200) or Managerial Initial Course (01300).
Credit recommendation: In the upper division baccalaureate category, 2 semester hours in Labor Relations (5/76).

Constructive Discipline (01203)
Location: FAA Center for Management Development, Palm Coast, FL.
Length: 35 hours (1 week); residential.
Dates: October 1975-Present.
Objective: To strengthen the ability of managers to maintain organizational discipline in a positive manner.
Instruction: Role and forms of discipline, means of achieving constructive discipline, appropriate use of corrective and disciplinary actions, the FAA disciplinary systems. Lecture, discussion, case studies, and role playing are used. Prerequisite: Supervisory Initial Course (01200) or Managerial Initial Course (01300).
Credit recommendation: In the upper division baccalaureate category, 2 semester hours in Management or Public Administration (5/76).

Supervisor's Course - Phase I (01260)
Location: FAA Center for Management Development, Palm Coast, FL.
Length: 99 hours (3 weeks).
Dates: July 1982-Present.
Objective: To develop supervisory skills for a new or relatively inexperienced supervisor.

Instruction: The instruction provides a wide spectrum of critical and primary skills, such as interactive skills, counseling, interpersonal skills, performance appraisal, and development; conduct and discipline.

Credit recommendation: In the lower division baccalaureate category, 5 semester hours in Supervision Management (10/82).

Supervisor's Course - Phase II (01226)
(Interpersonal Behavior In Problem Solving)
Location: FAA Center for Management Development, Palm Coast, FL.
Length: 59 hours (2 weeks).
Dates: September 1977-Present.
Objective: To develop interpersonal skills in managerial problem solving.
Instruction: To develop an understanding of the interpersonal roles of the supervisor and managerial situations; skills in interpersonal behavior, problem solving, and counseling.
Credit recommendation: In the upper division baccalaureate category, 3 semester hours in Supervision Management (10/82).

Managerial Initial Course (01300)
Location: FAA Center Management Development, Palm Coast, FL.
Length: 75 hours (2 weeks); residential; includes 42 hours of lecture/discussion and 33 hours of classroom exercises.
Dates: July 1975-Present.
Objective: To provide managers with the concepts and applications of a systems approach to results-based management.
Instruction: Systems, organization theory, communications, group behavior, management by objectives, evaluation and control, decision making, integrating the individual and the organization. Emphasis is on the functions of planning and organizing. Methodology includes lecture, discussion, case studies, and role playing.
Prerequisite: Supervisory Initial Course (01200).
Credit recommendation: In the upper division baccalaureate category, 4 semester hours in Management or Public Administration (5/76). NOTE: The content of this course overlaps to a large extent with that of Management for Program Managers (01509). Credit should not be granted for both courses.

Managerial Effectiveness (01302)
Location: FAA Center for Management Development, Palm Coast, FL.
Length: 35 hours (1 week); residential.
Dates: December 1972-November 1976.
Objective: To improve the manager's capabilities in a goals-oriented approach to planning and interpersonal relationships.
Instruction: Management philosophy, organizational theory, communications, group processes, leadership styles. Methodology includes lecture, discussion, role playing, and multimedia instruction. **Prerequisite:** Managerial Initial Course (01300).
Credit recommendation: In the upper division baccalaureate category, 2 semester hours in Management or Public Administration (5/76).

Resource Management (01303)
Location: FAA Center for Management Development, Palm Coast, FL.
Length: 59 hours (7½ days); residential.
Dates: March 1976-Present.
Objective: To provide the manager with the financial knowledge and skills to manage human, physical, and technical resources effectively.
Instruction: The federal budgeting process, public laws and policies, development of objectives, financial forecasting, setting of standards, cost estimating, scheduling and controlling. Lectures, discussion, and simulations are used. **Prerequisite:** Supervisory Initial Course (01200) or Managerial Initial Course (01300).
Credit recommendation: In the upper division baccalaureate category, 3 semester hours in Public Administration (5/76).

Managing Change (01306)
Location: FAA Center for Management Development, Palm Coast, FL.
Length: 27 hours (3½ days).
Dates: October 1986-Present.
Objective: To help the student to get a better understanding of himself/herself related to attitudes toward change and to be more skillful in acquiring change in subordinates.
Learning Outcome: Upon successful completion of this course, students will have a knowledge of one's own attitude toward change, the necessity for and scope of change in society today, motivations theories such as Maslow's Needs Hierarchy, Hygiene/Motivation, directive/supportive behavior, leadership styles, decision making, problem analysis, etc. The manager's role in making changes, overcoming resistances.
Instruction: The course content includes motivational theories, the manager's role in acquiring change, how to overcome resistance and strategies to effectively accomplish change. The course uses lectures, written handouts, group interaction, and films to present the course material.
Credit recommendation: In the upper division baccalaureate category, 2 semester hours in Business Administration or Management (5/87).

Computer Based Support for Managerial Decision Making (01307)
Location: FAA Center for Management Development,

Palm Coast, FL.
Length: 60 hours (7½ days).
Dates: December 1986-Present.
Objective: To teach the knowledge and skills necessary to utilize microcomputers with a view towards optimizing alternatives to meet the criteria for an acceptable solution and support of managerial decision making.
Learning Outcome: Upon successful completion of this course, the student learns to use the personal computer and utilize the computer software in making management decisions.
Instruction: The course utilizes the IBM PC and the latest software packages such as: Decision Aid, Howard Project Manager, Smart Data Manager, and Symphony. The course utilizes lecture (35 percent), hands-on training (55 percent), and case studies.
Credit recommendation: In the lower division baccalaureate/associate degree category or in the upper division baccalaureate category, 3 semester hours in Computer Science, Data Processing, or Management (5/87).

Equal Employment Opportunity Counselor Effectiveness Training (01505)
Location: FAA Center for Management Development, Palm Coast, FL.
Length: 35 hours (1 week); residential.
Dates: February 1974-Present.
Objective: To improve the effectiveness of the Equal Employment Opportunity counselor's implementation of Executive Order 12478.
Instruction: Equal Employment Opportunity programs and their relationship to FAA organization and programs, human behavior in counseling, effective interpersonal communication to influence behavior, handling of discrimination complaint procedures. Lecture, discussion, role playing, and case studies are used.
Credit recommendation: In the upper division baccalaureate category, 2 semester hours in Public Administration (5/76).

Management for Program Managers (01509)
Location: FAA Center for Management Development, Palm Coast, FL.
Length: 75 hours (2 weeks); residential.
Dates: August 1974-Present.
Objective: To improve the managerial capabilities of staff personnel who manage programs rather than organizations.
Instruction: Systems and organization theory, management methods for program management, establishing objectives, human factors, problem analysis, decision making. Lectures, discussion, case studies, and role playing are used.
Credit recommendation: In the upper division baccalaureate category, 4 semester hours in Management or Public Administration (5/76). NOTE: The content of this course overlaps to a large extent with that of the Managerial Initial Course (01300). Credit should not be granted for both courses.

Facilitator's Training Course (01523)
Location: Field facilities throughout the United States.
Length: 68 hours (8½ days).
Dates: February 1985-Present.
Objective: To prepare the student to function as a facilitator by more directly involving employees in agency goals, resolution of organizational problems, and improvement of work situations.
Learning Outcome: Upon successful completion of this course, the student will be able to identify and explain the major components of QWL and how the program should be initiated and maintained; describe and apply the role of the facilitator in a QWL effort; identify various aspects of human behavior and how it influences organizational effectiveness; determine the need for design and implementation of an organizational evaluation plan; select and apply appropriate group problem-solving techniques; select appropriate data-gathering models and apply appropriate techniques as a facilitator, group leader, or member; and plan, organize and deliver a recommendation presentation to management.
Instruction: This course is designed to train individuals to facilitate group problem-solving processes. While there is some lecture/theory, this course is primarily workshop/experimental learning.
Credit recommendation: In the upper division baccalaureate category, 3 semester hours in Business Administration or Management (5/87).

Discrimination Complaints Investigation Course (01525)
Location: FAA Center for Management Development, Palm Coast, FL.
Length: 51 hours (6½ days).
Dates: March 1986-Present.
Objective: To teach the student how to plan and conduct a systematic search for fact and evidence when conducting a fact finding investigation of a discrimination complaint.
Learning Outcome: Upon successful completion of this course, the student will be able to explain the discrimination complaint procedure; determine the basis for filing an EEO discrimination complaint; and prepare an investigation report file.
Instruction: Course covers the history and policy of Equal Employment Opportunity (EEO), discrimination complaint procedure, EEO theories of discrimination, planning the investigation, and conducting the investigation. Methods include interviewing techniques, sworn statements or affidavits, and writing the investigative reports. Role plays, critiques, and workshops are used.

Credit recommendation: In the lower division baccalaureate/associate degree category or in the upper division baccalaureate category, 2 semester hours in Business Administration or Management (5/87).

Work Group Facilitator's Course (01528)
Location: Field facilities throughout the United States.
Length: 38 hours (5 days).
Dates: June 1983-Present.
Objective: To prepare the student to function as a work group facilitator by more directly involving employees in agency goals, resolution of organizational problems, and improvement of work situations.
Learning Outcome: Upon successful completion of this course, the student will be able to identify the role of human relations in the organization, areas of caution, who is responsible for it; and relate the roles and values of individuals and groups, what their similarities and differences are.
Instruction: This course is designed for individuals who have been selected to become Work Group Facilitators, the course consists of classroom and workshop activity with emphasis on learning in the areas of group dynamics, group roles and values, group data gathering/problem analyzing/decision-making procedures, and the ability to make an effective presentation to management.
Credit recommendation: In the upper division baccalaureate category, 2 semester hours in Business Administration or Management (5/87).

Developing Human Relations Skills
Location: FAA Center for Management Development, Palm Coast, FL.
Length: 67 hours (2 weeks); residential.
Dates: December 1976-Present.
Objective: To provide employees with an understanding of and an opportunity to practice the skills needed for effective conduct of human relations in the organization.
Instruction: Covers a broad spectrum of knowledge and skills required for effective human relations. Topics include human understanding, self-analysis, listening, stress, group relations, and interpersonal relations. Methods used stress individual and group exercises, practice presentation, and role playing.
Credit recommendation: In the lower division baccalaureate/associate degree category or in the upper division baccalaureate category, 4 semester hours in General Management or Social Sciences (9/77).

Staff Specialist
Location: FAA Center for Management Development, Palm Coast, FL.
Length: 35 hours (1 week); residential.
Dates: June 1974-Present.
Objective: To improve the performance of staff personnel in accomplishing studies and preparing reports.
Instruction: Staff functions in problem analysis and decision making; human relations and communications in conducting, preparing, and presenting staff studies. Lecture, discussion, case problems, and class exercises are used.
Credit recommendation: In the upper division baccalaureate category, 2 semester hours in Management or Public Administration (5/76).

CENTER FOR MANAGEMENT DEVELOPMENT/CORRESPONDENCE COURSES

(Courses are listed in numerical order)
Source of official student records: FAA Center for Management Development, 4500 Palm Coast Parkway East, Palm Coast, FL 32037.
Additional information about the courses: Program on Noncollegiate Sponsored Instruction, The Center for Adult Learning and Educational Credentials, American Council on Education, One Dupont Circle, Washington, D.C. 20036.

1. **A Positive Approach to Discipline (14001)**
2. **Effective Organization of Work (14006)**
3. **Human Relations in Supervision (14003)**
   Location: Field facilities throughout the United States.
   Length: Self-paced must be completed in 15 weeks.
   Dates: August 1980-Present.
   Objective: To develop skills and abilities of the supervisor.
   Instruction: Course 1 covers organizing and planning of work to be accomplished, determining employee qualifications, training needs for new employees, and effective group communications; Course 2 covers employee discipline, dissatisfaction, complaints, and grievances; Course 3 covers effective leadership, individual behavior and attitudes of workers, different management styles, and employee counseling. Directed study and related workshop (12 hours of group activity). Tests, self-evaluation, and peer evaluation are used as assessment task to determine course grade.
   Credit recommendation: In the lower division baccalaureate/associate degree category, 1 semester hour in Front-line Supervision (10/82). NOTE: (1) 14002, Fundamentals of Supervision must have been completed satisfactorily for this award to be made. (2) The 1 hour of credit is for successful completion *of all three courses.*

Fundamentals of Supervision (14002)
Location: Field facilities throughout the United States.
Length: 12-18 months.
Dates: January 1981-Present.
Objective: To improve the Federal Aviation Administration employee's knowledge of principles of management.
Instruction: Covers supervisor's responsibilities, leader-

ship, selecting and assigning employees, morale, and job performance. Self-paced correspondence course.

Credit recommendation: In the lower division baccalaureate/associate degree category, 2 semester hours in Front-line Supervision (10/82).

Introduction to Foreign Service (14007)
  Location: Field facilities throughout the United States.
  Length: Approximately 20 hours.
  Dates: December 1980-Present.
  Objective: To teach some of the knowledge needed to plan for and begin a foreign assignment.
  Instruction: Covers general information necessary for preparing for foreign assignments. Self-paced correspondence course.
  Credit recommendation: In the lower division baccalaureate/associate degree category, 1 semester hour in Foreign Service (10/82).

1. Briefing and Presentation Techniques (14010)
2. Conference Techniques in Every-Day Management (14000)
  Location: Field facilities throughout the United States.
  Length: 1. 15 weeks; 2. 15 weeks.
  Dates: October 1980-Present.
  Objective: To develop students' oral and communication skills.
  Instruction: *Course 1:* Gives an overview of the system of activities required to provide managerial personnel with information and successful presentations. Understand the need for audience analysis, proper visual aids, proper vocabulary selection and post presentation analysis. Home study by correspondence.
  Credit recommendation: In the lower division baccalaureate/associate degree category, 2 semester hours in Business Administration or Management (10/82). NOTE: Student must complete both courses for *any* credits.

1. Writing Improvement (14014)
2. Report Analysis and Consolidation (14027)
  Location: FAA Academy, Oklahoma City, OK.
  Length: 15 weeks.
  Dates: *Version 1:* June 1980-Present. *Version 2:* March 1981-Present.
  Objective: To improve the students' writing ability.
  Instruction: *Course 1:* covers aspects of grammar necessary to achieve good writing; *Course 2:* covers technical report writing, organization and presentation. Self-paced correspondence course.
  Credit recommendation: In the lower division baccalaureate/associate degree category, 2 semester hours in Technical Report Writing (10/82). NOTE: For the 2 semester hours credit to be awarded both courses must have been completed satisfactorily.

1. Basic Clerical/Secretarial Techniques (14015)
2. Advanced Secretarial Course (14016)
  Location: Field facilities throughout the United States.
  Length: 1. 15 weeks; 2. 15 weeks.
  Dates: October 1980-Present.
  Objective: To provide students with an understanding of the secretarial function.
  Instruction: *Course 1:* covers responsibilities within the organization of the secretarial position; the needs of the organization personnel lateral to, above and below the secretary's job; *Course 2:* covers the executive/upper management needed for secretarial expertise in the management functions. Correspondence course.
  Credit recommendation: In the lower division baccalaureate/associate degree category, 1 semester hour in Administration, Management, or Office Management (10/82). NOTE: Both courses must be completed before any credit is granted.

Staff Specialist (14019 Books I & II)
  Location: Field facilities throughout the United States.
  Length: 15 weeks.
  Dates: *Version 1:* June 1974-March 1982. *Version 2:* April 1982-Present.
  Objective: To develop staff skills in studying, analyzing and recommending alternative solutions to problems for management.
  Instruction: Covers staff personnel responsibilities and staff-report-formats necessary to large organizations. Correspondence by home study.
  Credit recommendation: In the lower division baccalaureate/associate degree category, 2 semester hours in Management (10/82).

1. Principles of Instruction (14022)
2. On-the-Job Training Techniques (14018)
  Location: Field facilities throughout the United States.
  Length: 1. 4 months (2 lessons); 2. 4 months (Phase I-6 lessons; Phase II-20 hours for a 6 member group - 10 sessions of 2 hours each).
  Dates: August 1980-Present.
  Objective: To provide students with a basic understanding of what is required to be an effective Federal Aviation Administration instructor.
  Instruction: Covers leadership and management skills to prepare and conduct on-the-job training; provides skill building assignments.
  Credit recommendation: In the lower division baccalaureate/associate degree category, 2 semester hours in Education (10/82). NOTE: Credit should be awarded upon satisfactory completion of *both* courses. No credit should be awarded for each individual course.

Budgeting and Resource Management (14024)
  Location: Field facilities throughout the United States.
  Length: 15 weeks.

Dates: June 1980-Present.
Objective: To introduce students to the Federal Budget process, in general and as it applies to the Federal Aviation Administration.
Instruction: Covers planning programming and budgeting system (PPBS) applied to Federal Aviation Administration resource management. Correspondence course.
Credit recommendation: In the lower division baccalaureate/associate degree category, 1 semester hour in Management (10/82).

Program Analysis and Review (14026)
  Location: Field facilities throughout the United States.
  Length: 15 weeks.
  Dates: September 1981-Present.
  Objective: To give students an understanding of the Federal Aviation Administration program manager in a multi-discipline project.
  Instruction: Covers integration and management of resources across several distinct skills. Correspondence course.
  Credit recommendation: In the lower division baccalaureate/associate degree category, 2 semester hours in Business or Management (10/82).

1. **Use and Conservation of Personnel, Money, and Materials (14005)**
2. **Basic Employment Practices (14029)**
3. **Position Management and Classification (14030)**
  Location: FAA Academy, Oklahoma City, OK.
  Length: 15 weeks.
  Dates: August 1980-Present.
  Objective: To develop the skills and abilities of the supervisor.
  Instruction: *Course 1:* covers effective employee utilization, effective use of people, increasing productivity, conserving money and material, and evaluating program effectiveness; *Course 2:* covers recruitment, staffing and organizing, compensation, employee development, group and individual problems, and health services for the employee; *Course 3:* covers work position - position description, classification, evaluation of the position, establishment of a position, and determining appropriate standards for comparison of positions. Directed study and related workshop.
  Credit recommendation: In the lower division baccalaureate/associate degree category, 1 semester hour in Fundamentals of Supervision (10/82). NOTE: (1) 14002, Fundamentals of Supervision must have been completed satisfactorily for this award to be made. (2) The 1 hour of credit is for successful completion of *all three courses.*

1. **Management by Objectives (14004)**
2. **Supervisory Guide (14021)**
3. **Labor Relations (14028)**
  Location: Field facilities throughout the United States.
  Length: 1. 15 weeks; 2. 15 weeks; 3. 15 weeks.
  Dates: December 1981-Present.
  Objective: To provide students with a knowledge of management principles.
  Instruction: *Course 1:* covers the planning and implementing use of the technique Management by Objectives; *Course 2:* covers the Blake/Mouton Management Grid to assist the individual in selecting personal management style and its alternatives; *Course 3:* covers the evolution of and Federal response to organized labor unions as a force in the Federal Aviation Administration; grievance procedures including arbitration and mediation of labor disputes. Correspondence courses.
  Credit recommendation: In the lower division baccalaureate/associate degree category, 1 semester hour in Management (10/82). NOTE: (1) These three courses serve to fulfill a one semester credit course. (2) Students must have also completed either 14019 or 14026 to receive this credit.

First Fidelity Bank, N.A., N.J., Management Training Program

The First Fidelity Bank Management Training Program is one of the methods used to identify and train future management talent. The program is specially designed to recruit and develop candidates who aspire to leadership position.

The Management Training Program is a seven month classroom-based program. Participants complete 4 months of challenging graduate-level coursework which includes: Managerial Accounting, Corporate Finance, Money and Banking, and Commercial Credit and Lending. During this phase of the program, trainees also participate in seminars and training sessions in assigned banking department functions: Time Management, Communications, Presentation Skills, and Business Writing.

The second phase of the program offers a series of rotations through a variety of major banking departments.

Assignment into a Career Path is made 6 to 8 months after beginning the program.

Source of official student records: Assistant Vice President, Career Planning and Development, First Fidelity Bank, N.A., New Jersey, 500 Broad Street, Newark, New Jersey 07192.

Additional information about the courses: Program on Noncollegiate Sponsored Instruction, The Center for Adult Learning and Educational Credentials, American Council on Education, One Dupont Circle, Washington, D.C. 20036 or Thomas A. Edison State College, 101 West State Street, CN545, Trenton, New Jersey 08625.

Corporate Finance (515)
  Location: Newark, NJ.

Length: 54 hours (4 weeks).
Dates: July 1985-Present.
Objective: To familiarize students with the basic concepts and principles of finance, and to introduce students to the techniques of financial decisions using financial concepts and principles.
Instruction: The course covers an introduction to financial analysis using ratios and concepts of return and risk. Investment decisions: capital budgeting, working capital, management of current assets; and financing decisions: financial planning, leverage, cost of capital, valuation and dividend policy are studied. An introduction to capital markets is also provided.
Credit recommendation: In the graduate degree category or in the upper division category, 3 semester hours in Corporate Finance (5/86).

Managerial Accounting (505)
Location: Newark, NJ.
Length: 75 hours (5 weeks).
Dates: July 1985-Present.
Objective: To develop the logic of accounting, including identification and measurement of financial events and accounts, recording procedures and preparation of financial statements, and to examine measurement and interpretation of specific accounts appearing on financial statements.
Instruction: This accounting course is presented in two parts: the first develops an understanding of the basic logic of accounting, including identification and measurement of accounting events, recording procedures, and preparation of financial statements. The second part focuses on measurement and interpretation of specific events and accounts, including accounting for inventory, long-lived assets, stockholders equity, taxes, long-term liabilities, leases, intercorporate investments, pensions, and cash flow statements.
Credit recommendation: In the graduate degree category, 3 semester hours in Managerial Accounting or in the upper division baccalaureate category, 4 semester hours in Managerial Accounting (5/86).

Money and Banking (495)
Location: Newark, NJ.
Length: 45 hours (3 weeks).
Dates: July 1985-Present.
Objective: To enable the trainees to understand the structure and operations of the domestic and international financial systems, with special emphasis on banking.
Instruction: Economic fundamentals included in this course are the operations of the banking system, the business cycle and economic indications, interest rate determination, term structure of interest rates, and factors effecting exchange rates. Banking topics include the structure of the U.S. banking system, money and capital markets, banks' balance sheets, Eurodollars and other international topics. A banks simulation game concludes the course.
Credit recommendation: In the upper division baccalaureate category, 3 semester hours in Money and Banking (5/86).

Florida Bankers' Association

Sponsored by the Florida Bankers' Association, the Florida School of Banking enables bank personnel at the supervisory and junior officer level to increase their knowledge about the banking industry and the economy. It is intended as preparation for the advanced schools of banking.

To graduate, students must attend three 1-week summer sessions at the University of Florida and complete final examinations and extension problems. For evaluation purposes, courses that are offered throughout the three years of the program are grouped together. Therefore, students requesting credit must have completed the entire program.

Source of official student records: Registrar, Florida School of Banking, Florida Bankers' Association, P.O. Box 6847, Orlando, Florida 32853.

Additional information about the courses: Program on Noncollegiate Sponsored Instruction, The Center for Adult Learning and Educational Credentials, American Council on Education, One Dupont Circle, Washington, D.C. 20036.

Accounting
1. Accounting I
2. Accounting II
3. Bank Accounting and Auditing (deleted as of 8/80)
4. Bank Management Simulation Game
   Location: University of Florida, Gainesville, FL.
   Length: 1. 9½ hours; 2. 9½ hours; 3. 4½ hours (deleted as of 8/80); 4. 9½ hours. Total 33 hours (28½ hours as of 8/80) and 80-130 hours of independent study.
   Dates: August 1970-Present.
   Objective: To provide the student with an understanding of and the ability to apply accounting principles.
   Instruction: Accounting objectives; measurement of income and preparation of financial statements; the accounting cycle; adjusting entries; preparation of financial statements and discussion of their interrelationships; statement interpretation, analysis, and application; application of accounting systems and the auditing function. In the Bank Simulation Game, students work in groups to make decisions and determine policy in the operation of a commercial bank. Accounting reports and their interpretations are used to make decisions and formulate strategies. Lecture, discussion, and home study problems are used.

Credit recommendation: In the lower division baccalaureate/associate degree category, 3 semester hours in Accounting (8/78).

Commercial Bank Management
1. Fiduciary Services
2. Bank Credit
3. Uniform Commercial Code
4. Marketing
5. Communications
6. Personnel Management
7. Introduction to Data Processing %1142 8. Bank Management Simulation Game
   Location: University of Florida, Gainesville, FL.
   Length: 1. 1½ hours; 2. 17 hours; 3. 4½ hours; 4. 3½ hours; 5. 1½ hours; 6. 3 hours; 7. 3 hours; 8. 9½ hours. Total 25½ hours and 50-65 hours of independent study.
   Dates: August 1970-Present.
   Objective: To provide an analysis of the operations and management of commercial banks.
   Instruction: The development of a credit policy; organization for credit administration; principles of credit analysis; types of loans; the trust and fiduciary function; commercial bank business development and marketing; community relations; the communications process; motivation and supervision of personnel; the application of the Uniform Commercial Code to commercial bank operations; computer applications and system selection. Bank Simulation Games enables students to formulate and test bank decisions and strategies.
   Credit recommendation: In the upper division baccalaureate category, 2 semester hours in Bank Management (8/78).

Macroeconomics and Introduction to Money and Banking
1. Money and Banking
2. Sources and Uses of Economic Data
3. Regulation
4. Federal Reserve System
5. Risk Management
6. Investments
7. Money and Capital Markets
   Location: University of Florida, Gainesville, FL.
   Length: 1. 10½ hours; 2. 3 hours; 3. 3½ hours; 4. 4½ hours; 5. 4½ hours; 6. 4½ hours; 7. 6 hours. Total 36 hours and 53-85 hours of independent study.
   Dates: August 1970-Present.
   Objective: To provide an understanding of the American economy, business cycles, and the influence of the federal reserve system on the financial markets.
   Instruction: The concept of money and the money creation process; the economic role of commercial banks; review of the Federal Reserve System; monetary policy instruments; regulation of financial institutions; determinants of the term structure of interest rates; flow of funds analysis; availability of investment funds; theories of bank asset and liability management; liquidity analysis; the use of economic data, its measurement and reliability; basic statistical analysis; impact of bank regulation.
   Credit recommendation: In the lower division baccalaureate/associate degree category, 3 semester hours in Economics (8/78).

Ford National Development and Training Center (Formerly UAW—Ford National Development and Training Center)

The United Auto Workers and the Ford Motor Company established the Employe Development and Training Program in the 1982 Collective Bargaining Agreement. The Agreement charters the Program to be responsive to the personal, educational, and training needs of UAW-represented hourly employes of Ford Motor Company.

The Program is administered by the UAW—Ford National Development and Training Center located in Dearborn, Michigan, under the direction of a Joint Governing Body comprised of Company and UAW representatives.

Ford Motor Company manufactures, assembles, and markets its cars, trucks, tractors, and related automotive products through independent dealerships in the United States and Canada.

The Company has almost 112,000 hourly, UAW-represented employes working in 20 states. In all, there are 96 plants, parts distribution centers, and research and engineering facilities.

The International Union, United Automotive, Aerospace, and Agricultural Implement Workers of America (UAW) serves more than 1,500,000 active and retired workers throughout the United States and the Dominion of Canada. Through its Education Department and staff, it reaches out annually to its members with a variety of educational programs on a continuing basis. The Education Department, under the guidance and administration of the International Union President and headed by a department director, is comprised of a national staff with an additional national department staff member assigned to each of the eighteen regions of the UAW in the United States and Canada. In addition to the national staff located at the Union headquarters in Detroit, Michigan, and the eighteen regions of the UAW, nine additional staff members throughout the union are assigned, on a half-time basis, to the dual roles of education and citizenship activities.

In addition to the many and varied educational programs carried on by the Education Department staff, many other national departments assume similar educational roles in the process of performing their duties and responsibilities to the membership of the International

Union, UAW.

Programs and workshops are prepared and presented to the leadership of the UAW in such diverse areas as consumer affairs; citizenship and legislative activities; veterans' benefits; time study and engineering; arbitration services; concerns of the elderly and retired workers; community services (including a large and comprehensive listing of programs affecting the good and welfare of union members, both at the workplace and in their communities); women's programs (activities and educational services affecting women workers and families); public relations and publicity (including communication skills and media media skills, e.g., shop papers, radio, video, training); conservation; recreation and leisure-time activities; civil rights; occupational safety and health educational programs and training; and training programs for local union officers and negotiators throughout the various bargaining units of the International Union. Courses are continually being developed and presented to the elected local union leaders and to rank-and-file members by staff personnel.

Workshops are held at the International Union headquarters, at the eighteen regional offices, at local union halls of the 1,650 local unions of the International Union, at the three UAW Family Education Centers (in Onaway, Michigan; Port Elgin, Ontario; and at Ottawa, Illinois) and at several university campuses throughout the country.

Company-sponsored education and training courses are offered through its Human Resources Development Center, Robotics and Automation Applications Consulting Center, and Service Training Center in Dearborn, Michigan, and on-site at plant locations throughout the country.

Courses are currently listed under two major areas: Employe Development and Technology.

Source of official student records: UAW—Ford National Development and Training Center, P.O. Box 6002, Dearborn, Michigan 48121.

Additional information about the courses: Program on Noncollegiate Sponsored Instruction, The Center for Adult Learning and Educational Credentials, American Council on Education, One Dupont Circle, Washington, D.C. 20036-1193.

EMPLOYE DEVELOPMENT

Employe Involvement Process
   Location: UAW—Ford National Development and Training Center and the Botsford Inn.
   Length: 28 hours (3½ days).
   Dates: *Version 1:* January 1981-January 1985; *Version 2:* February 1985-Present.
   Objective: To enable participants to become familiar with the employe involvement process and its implementation within organizations.
   Instruction: Course covers management/union commitment for employe involvement, management styles, organizational diagnosis, communications, pilot area selection factors, and group dynamics. Topics are presented through group exercises, lecture, and discussion.
   Credit recommendation: *Version 1:* In the lower division baccalaureate/associate degree category, 1 semester hour in Human Services Related Programs, Labor Studies, or Management. *Version 2:* In the lower division baccalaureate/associate degree category, 2 semester hours in Human Services Related programs, Labor Studies, or Management (2/85).

Group Problem Solving
   Location: Ford Human Resource Development Center.
   Length: 32 hours (1 week).
   Dates: September 1984-Present.
   Objective: To provide participants training and experience in group problem-solving processes, procedures, and analysis.
   Instruction: This train the trainer workshop provides participants with knowledge of various problem solving methods and skills essential to leading problem solving groups within the organization. The program focuses on the development of communication skills, techniques for group decision making, and problem and decision analysis skills through various presentations and individual/group activities. Lecture and discussion are used.
   Credit recommendation: In the lower division baccalaureate category, 2 semester hours in Human Services, Behavioral Sciences, Management Sciences, Social Work, or Sociology (9/84).

Instructional Skills Workshop
   Location: Ford Human Resource Development Center.
   Length: 24 hours (1 week).
   Dates: January 1983-Present.
   Objective: To prepare personnel to conduct workshop and training programs.
   Instruction: The purpose of the course is to enable analysis of instructional style and its impact on learner expectations, learn and apply group process instructional techniques and learn to communicate in results-oriented, learner based behavioral terms. Lecture and discussion are used.
   Credit recommendation: In the lower division baccalaureate/associate degree category, 1 semester hour in General Education or General Studies (9/84).

Successful Retirement Planning: Instructor Training
   Location: UAW—Ford National Development and Training Center.
   Length: 44 hours (6 days).
   Dates: August 1984-Present.
   Objective: To train participants to deliver retirement planning programs.
   Instruction: The purpose of the course is to provide a

review of the instructional skills necessary and the information base required to deliver a program on retirement planning that include the following units: Planning Health, Medication and Drugs, Social Security, Benefits, Money, Legal, and Leisure.

Credit recommendation: In the lower division baccalaureate/associate degree or upper division baccalaureate category, 3 semester hours in Human Services Related Programs or Labor Studies (2/85).

Time Management and Effective Listening
Location: Ford Human Resource Development Center.
Length: 16 hours (2 days).
Dates: February 1984-Present.
Objective: To teach the student principles of effective listening and time management in personal and professional activities.
Instruction: The effective listening module is designed to teach participants the principles of analyzing listening skills, the motivational value of effective listening, components of communication and communication break down, the characteristics of effective listening and personal strategies for active listening. The time management module emphasizes principles of time management, cost analysis of participation time problem areas in time management and principles and practices of effective time management, planning and scheduling. Workshops are used.
Credit recommendation: In the lower division baccalaureate/associate degree category, 1 semester hour in General Education or General Studies (9/84).

TECHNOLOGY

Basic Electronics
(Solid State Electronics)
Location: UAW—Ford National Development and Training Center.
Length: Self-paced (approximately 60 hours).
Dates: January 1984-Present.
Objective: To acquaint personnel with some of the basic elements of electric circuits and electronic circuit.
Instruction: Self-paced practical exercises in the basic components and equations used in electronic circuit troubleshooting, including Ohm's Law, resistance, capacitance, inductance, phase angles, series and parallel operation of these components, diodes, zener diodes, SCRs, triads, transistors, operational amplifiers, transformers, voltage regulation, multivibrators, and the basic testing and troubleshooting of circuitry containing these elements.
Credit recommendation: In the lower division baccalaureate/associate degree category, 3 semester hours in Basic Electronic Laboratory (9/84).

Basic Electronic Measuring Equipment
1. Use of the Volt-Ohm-Millian Meter (Simpson 260)
2. Using the Oscilloscope
Location: Ford Human Resource Development Center.
Length: 1. 8 hours (1 day); 2. 40 hours (5 days).
Dates: September 1982-Present.
Objective: To train personnel in the correct use of a Simpson 260 multimeter and a particular oscilloscope.
Instruction: Self-paced practical exercises in the use, operation, and application of a Simpson 260 multimeter and a particular oscilloscope the employe has brought with him/her to class, including reading different meter scales, measurement of resistances, voltages and currents, the characteristics of various wave forms, types of probes and probe coupling, dual trace and storage scope operation and multiple time bases and delay operation.
Credit recommendation: In the vocational certificate degree category, 2 semester hours in Basic Electronic Laboratory (9/84).

Basic Hydraulics
Location: UAW—Ford National Development and Training Center.
Length: Self-paced (approximately 100 hours).
Dates: January 1974-Present.
Objective: To enable participants to develop skills in identifying typical hydraulic components, their symbology and their interrelationship within hydraulic systems.
Instruction: This covers the basic principles of the physics of fluids, hydraulic presssure, directional and flow control valves. The various types of hydraulic pumps and motors and their operation. The use of hydraulic trainer devices provides hands-on experiences in circuit fabrication with quick-disconnect components.
Credit recommendation: In the lower division baccalaureate/associate degree category, 2 semester hours in Basic Hydraulics (9/84).

Electro-Mechanical Logic Controls for Industrial Machines
1. Relay Logic Program
2. Advanced Relay Logic Program
Location: Ford Human Resource Development Center.
Length: 1. 40 hours (1 week); 2. 40 hours (1 week).
Dates: 1. August 1980-June 1982; 2. July 1982-Present.
Objective: To enable the participant to identify actual control components and their symbology, interpret ladder logic prints, and troubleshoot relay logic systems.
Instruction: Audio, video, and computer assisted practice exercises are used to provide knowledge of and symbology for electro-mechanical devices, such as transformers, timers, temperature and pressure switches and other standard industrial controls. Ladder control circuit diagrams and sequence of operation charts are implemented to provide experience in troubleshooting relay logic systems.

Credit recommendation: In the lower division baccalaureate/associate degree category, 2 semester hours in Industrial Electro-Mechanical Programs for Course 1, and in the lower division baccalaureate/associate degree category, 2 semester hours in Industrial Electro-Mechanical Programs for Course 2 (9/84).

Introduction to Automated Systems
1. **Robotics Overview (Module I)**
2. **Robotics/Automation Evaluation and Application Methodology (Module II)**
3. **Brand Oriented Robot Workshop (Module IV)**

Location: Robotics and Automation Applications Consulting Center and selected plant sites.
Length: 1. 7 hours (1 day); 2. 14 hours (2 days); 3. 35 hours (5 days).
Dates: April 1983-Present.
Objective: To provide personnel with an introduction to a variety of robots and with an approach to selecting and implementing a flexible automated system.
Instruction: Lectures and practical exercises in the capabilities of robots, the basic application of robots, the programming of robots, safety issues relating to robots, basic adjustments and troubleshooting of robot systems, types of robots (point to point, nonservo, and continuous path servo types) and the selection and implementation of automation systems.
Credit recommendation: In the lower division baccalaureate/associate degree category, 3 semester hours in Introduction to Automated Systems (9/84).

Introduction to Design for Automation
1. **Robotics Overview (Module I)**
2. **Automation Friendly Design (Module V)**

Location: Robotics and Automation Applications Consulting Center and selected plant sites.
Length: 1. 7 hours (1 day); 2. 14 hours (2 days).
Dates: December 1984-Present.
Objective: To provide personnel with an introduction to robots and an awareness of the contribution of product design in automating production systems.
Instruction: Lectures and practical exercises in the capabilities of robots, the basic application of robots, the basic safety issues relating to robots, the planning criteria for automation, the guidelines for the shaping, joining, and fitting of parts for automation, and the implementation of automated systems.
Credit recommendation: In the lower division baccalaureate/associate degree category, 1 semester hour in Introduction to Design for Automation (9/84). NOTE: Credit recommendation is contingent upon one class completing the course.

Introduction to Robotics
1. **Robotics Overview (Module I)**
2. **Specific Application Instruction (Module III)**
3. **Specific Manufacture Robot Training (Module VI)**

Location: Robotics and Automation Applications Consulting Center and selected plant sites.
Length: 1. 7 hours (1 day); 2. 21 hours (3 days); 3. 21 hours (3 days).
Dates: April 1983-Present.
Objective: To train personnel in the basic aspects of robots.
Instruction: Lectures and practical experience in the application of typical robots, safety considerations surrounding robots, performance parameters, basic operation, pendant programming, operational adjustments, troubleshooting techniques, and practical applications including start up procedures, error codes, operation and adjustment of some peripherals, the mechanical drive systems (axis drives, harmonic drives, ball screws, wrist linkage, and hard stops), electrical diagrams and electronic systems and the adjustments of typical resolves, limits, synchronizing switches and regulators.
Credit recommendation: In the lower division baccalaureate/associate degree category, 2 semester hours in Introduction to Robotics (9/84). NOTE: Since Modules III and VI are virtually duplicates, students may receive the 2 semester hours credit recommendation for completing the following combinations of modules: Modules I, III, and VI; or Modules I and II; or Modules I and VI.

Programmable Logic Controller Maintenance
(Allen-Bradley Programmable Controller Maintenance Program)

Location: Ford Human Resource Development Center.
Length: 80 hours (2 weeks).
Dates: August 1980-Present.
Objective: To train participants to service programmable controllers by developing knowledge of the controllers' functions, their relationship to external machine elements, and the basic sections within the controller (input decision, output, and their functions).
Instruction: This course examines the programmable controller, its function, and the relationship to the overall manufacturing system. Components associated with local and remote systems are identified as major replaceable components. Means of recording, loading, and verifying ladder logic are practiced. CRT programming panels are used for troubleshooting and modifying ladder logic.
Credit recommendation: In the lower division baccalaureate/associate degree category, 3 semester hours in Basic Electronics (9/84). NOTE: Students who receive credit for this course should not receive credit for Modicon Programmable Controller Maintenance Training Program. The materials covered in both courses are similar in content.

Programmable Logic Controller Maintenance Training Program
(Modicon Programmable Controller Maintenance Training Program)
  Location: Ford Human Resource Development Center.
  Length: 80 hours (2 weeks).
  Dates: August 1981-Present.
  Objective: To train participants to service programmable controllers by developing a knowledge of the controllers' functions, their relationship to external machine elements, and the basic sections within the controller (input decision, output) and their functions.
  Instruction: This course examines the programmable controller, its function, and the relationship to the overall manufacturing machine system. Components associated with local and remote systems are identified as are major replaceable components. Means of recording, loading, and verifying ladder logic are practiced. CRT programming panels are used for troubleshooting and modifying ladder logic.
  Credit recommendation: In the lower division baccalaureate/associate degree category, 3 semester hours in Basic Electronics (9/84). NOTE: Students who receive credit for this course should not receive credit for Allen-Bradley Programmable Controller Maintenance Training Program. The materials covered in both courses are similar in content.

Troubleshooting Strategy
  Location: Ford Human Resource Development Center.
  Length: 16-24 hours (2-3 days).
  Dates: August 1980-Present.
  Objective: To provide maintenance personnel with a systematic procedure for troubleshooting a faulty system.
  Instruction: Computer assisted instruction relating to the basic concepts of troubleshooting procedures, system flow diagrams, localization of fixed and directable flow sequences, fault isolation, feedback systems, and practical exercises pertaining to these troubleshooting procedures.
  Credit recommendation: In the vocational certificate degree category, 1 semester hour in Basic Troubleshooting Practices (9/84).

Fox & Lazo, Inc.

Fox & Lazo, Inc. Realtors is the largest independently owned real estate agency in the Delaware Valley/Greater Philadelphia area. Its educational division was developed over ten years ago with the goal of providing quality instruction and education for Fox & Lazo's sales associates.

All new sales people are required to attend the Professional Real Estate Orientation (PRO) program.

The objective of the course is to give a thorough indoctrination to the business of real estate, the selling process, and services offered by Fox & Lazo. As a result of this course, clients/customers receive the best professional and ethical services available within the industry when they deal with Fox & Lazo agents.

Source of official student records: Director of Student Records, Fox & Lazo, 30 Washington Avenue, Haddonfield, New Jersey 08033.

Additional information about the courses: Program on Noncollegiate Sponsored Instruction, Thomas A. Edison State College, 101 West State Street, Trenton, New Jersey 08625.

Professional Real Estate Orientation (PRO) CII
  Location: Haddonfield, NJ.
  Length: 80 hours (4 weeks).
  Dates: January 1982-Present.
  Objective: To develop an understanding of the real estate profession and to develop the skills necessary in the sales profession.
  Instruction: This course is designed to teach the techniques of successful selling, especially as related to real estate. Specific topics covered in this course are: prospecting, the approach, sales presentation, answering objections, and closing the sale.
  Credit recommendation: In the lower division baccalaureate/associate degree category, 3 semester hours in Salesmanship or Real Estate Practices (4/85).

Garden State AIB

The American Institute of Banking (AIB) is an educational division of the American Bankers Association, the national organization of the banking industry. Its total membership includes some 18,500 banks and branches, about 97 percent of the nation's commercial banks. AIB is part of the Education Group, one of the six working groups of the Association.

AIB has more than 500 chapters throughout the United States. An organized chapter assures that the Institute's work can be carried on from year to year.

All activities are initiated by the local chapter, including the choosing of courses and programs, the selection of instructors, and the arrangements for classroom facilities. While chapters work in cooperation with the national AIB office, each chapter is administratively autonomous. As a result, credit recommendations established for courses offered by a specific chapter apply only to that chapter.

The Garden State AIB sponsors a program in contemporary banking subjects for employees of banking institutions in the following New Jersey counties: Essex, Hudson, Mercer, Morris, Passaic, Sussex, and Warren.

Source of official student records: Garden State AIB, 400 Broadacres, Suite 30, Bloomfield, NJ 07003 or Program on Noncollegiate Sponsored Instruction, The Center for Adult Learning and Educational Credentials, American Council on Education, One Dupont Circle, Washington, D.C. 20036.

Additional information about the courses: Thomas A. Edison State College, 101 W. State Street, Trenton, NJ 08625.

Accounting I
Location: Various locations in New Jersey.
Length: 45 hours (15 weeks).
Dates: January 1977-Present.
Objective: To enable the student to understand the basic concepts, theories, and practices of business accounting.
Instruction: Covers analysis of business transactions, the accounting cycle, special journal and ledgers, end-of-cycle procedures, payrolls and control systems, payables and receivables, valuation of other assets, taxes, and the accrual basis. Lectures, discussion, classroom exercises, problem solving.
Credit recommendation: In the lower division baccalaureate/associate degree category, 3 semester hours in Accounting I (1/82) (4/87). NOTE: This course has been reevaluated and continues to meet requirements for credit recommendations.

Accounting II
Location: Various locations in New Jersey.
Length: 45 hours (15 weeks).
Dates: January 1977-Present.
Objective: To build on the basic principles in the Accounting I offering.
Instruction: Covers advanced concepts and techniques of departmentalized accounting, the partnership accounting cycle, branch and home office accounting, corporation accounting, responsibility and cost accounting, budgeting, reporting, statement analysis, and an overview of data processing. Lectures, discussion, classroom exercises, problem solving.
Credit recommendation: In the lower division baccalaureate/associate degree category, 3 semester hours in Accounting II (1/82) (4/87). NOTE: This course has been reevaluated and continues to meet requirements for credit recommendations.

Analyzing Financial Statements
Location: Various locations in New Jersey.
Length: *Version 1:* 45 hours (15 weeks); *Version 2:* 30 hours (10 weeks).
Dates: *Version 1:* January 1977-December 1986. *Version 2:* January 1987-Present.
Objective: To enable the student to understand financial statement analysis through evaluation of past and current financial conditions, diagnosis of and suggested remedies for any existing financial problems, and forecasting of future trends.
Instruction: The course is organized into 4 main sections: cash inflows and outflows; an analysis on selected financial statements; tools of financial statement analysis; and techniques of financial statement analysis. Lectures, discussion, classroom exercises, problem solving.
Credit recommendation: In the upper division baccalaureate category, 3 semester hours in Analyzing Financial Statements. *Version 1:* 3 semester hours; *Version 2:* 2 semester hours (1/82) (4/87). NOTE: This course has been reevaluated and continues to meet requirements for credit recommendations.

Bank Management
Location: Various locations in New Jersey.
Length: 45 hours (15 weeks).
Dates: January 1977-Present.
Objective: To enable the student to apply management principles to banking operations.
Instruction: Covers the nature and objectives of banking, setting of objectives, organizational planning, staffing, management controls, and relationship between management principles and selected banking functions. Lectures, discussion, classroom exercises, problem solving. Prerequisite: Introduction to Banking or Banking Principles course. NOTE: This course duplicates Bank Management Seminar*.
Credit recommendation: Upper division baccalaureate category, 3 semester hours in Bank Management Seminar (1/82) (4/87). NOTE: This course has been reevaluated and continues to meet requirements for credit recommendations.

Bank Management Seminar*
Location: Various locations in New Jersey.
Length: 45 hours (15 weeks).
Dates: January 1978-December 1985.
Objective: To enable the student to apply management principles to banking operations.
Instruction: Covers the nature and objectives of banking, setting of objectives, organizational planning, staffing, management controls, and relationship between management principles and selected banking functions. Lectures, discussion, classroom exercises, problem solving. Prerequisite: Introduction to Banking or Banking Principles course. NOTE: This course duplicates Bank Management.
Credit recommendation: In the upper division baccalaureate category, 3 semester hours in Bank Management Seminar (1/82).

Business and Banking Law 1
(Formerly Law and Banking)
Location: Various locations in New Jersey.
Length: 45 hours (15 weeks).
Dates: January 1977-Present.
Objective: To enable the student to understand general legal principles and selected legal issues of importance to

bankers.

Instruction: Covers the court system, civil procedure, contracts, personal property, real property, torts, crime trusts, agency and partnership, corporations, sales, commercial paper, secured transactions, and consumer regulations. Lectures, discussion, classroom exercises, problem solving.

Credit recommendation: In the upper division baccalaureate category, 3 semester hours in Introduction to Law and Banking (1/82) (4/87). NOTE: The course has been reevaluated and continues to meet requirements for credit recommendations.

Economics
    Location: Various locations in New Jersey.
    Length: 45 hours (15 weeks).
    Dates: *Version 1:* January 1977-December 1986; *Version 2:* January 1987-Present.
    Objective: To enable the student to understand the basic principles of economics.
    Instruction: *Version 1:* Covers basic economics concepts, macro and micro principles. Topics include supply and demand, income determination, business cycles and forecasting, prices and money, the banking system deposit creation, and monetary policy. Lectures, discussion, classroom exercises, problem solving. *Version 2:* This course sets forth the current principles explaining how our economic system operates. It takes up the determination of relative value in markets with different types of competition, and applies the underlying principles of incomes and commodities. The course also offers a basic introduction to the arenas of international economics and finance.
    Credit recommendation: *Version 1:* In the lower division baccalaureate/associate degree category, 2 semester hours in Economics (1/82) (4/87). *Version 2:* In the lower division baccalaureate/associate degree category, 3 semester hours in Economics (1/82) (4/87). NOTE: This course has been reevaluated and continues to meet requirements for credit recommendations.

Financial Marketing
(Formerly Bank Marketing and Marketing for Business)
    Location: Various locations in New Jersey.
    Length: 45 hours (15 weeks).
    Dates: January 1977-Present.
    Objective: To enable the student to understand the basic principles of marketing as applied to banking.
    Instruction: Covers the concepts and philosophies of marketing including market research; consumer behavior; motivation; strategies related to product, price, promotion, and place; public relations; advertising and selling; and planning. Lectures, discussion, classroom exercises, problem solving.
    Credit recommendation: In the upper division baccalaureate category, 3 semester hours in Bank Marketing or Business elective (1/82) (4/87). NOTE: This course has been reevaluated and continues to meet requirements for credit recommendations.

Fundamentals of Supervision
(Formerly Supervision and Personnel Administration)
    Location: Various locations in New Jersey.
    Length: 45 hours (15 weeks).
    Dates: *Version 1:* January 1977-December 1986; *Version 2:* January 1987-Present.
    Objective: To provide an understanding of management philosophies and techniques for first-line supervisors. This course is designed to aid first-line supervisors in making a smooth transition from expert in a particular task to the role of a supervisor who must produce results through the efforts of other people.
    Instruction: *Version 1:* Covers developing management-mindedness, self-development, communication, management of change, superior-subordinate relationships, understanding, motivation, training; grievances handling, planning, delegating, decision making, and performance review. Lectures, discussion, classroom exercises, problem solving. *Version 2:* This course focuses on the managerial process: planning, organizing, staffing, directing, and controlling. Practical case studies are used to apply these concepts to realistic situations. The course also treats basic management considerations and the area of labor relations.
    Credit recommendation: *Version 1:* In the lower division baccalaureate/associate degree category, 2 semester hours in Supervisor Management or Business Elective (1/82). *Version 2:* In the lower division baccalaureate/associate degree category, 3 semester hours in Supervisor Management or Business Elective (4/87). NOTE: This course has been reevaluated and continues to meet requirements for credit recommendations.

Loan and Discount
    Location: Various locations in New Jersey.
    Length: 45 hours (15 weeks).
    Dates: January 1977-Present.
    Objective: To enable the student to understand the loan and discount function in a commercial bank.
    Instruction: Covers notes, guarantees, collateral agreements, and secured transactions. Lectures, discussion, classroom exercises, problem solving.
    Credit recommendation: In the upper division baccalaureate category, 3 semester hours in Loan and Discount (1/82) (4/87). NOTE: This course has been reevaluated and continues to meet requirements for credit recommendations.

Money and Banking
    Location: Various locations in New Jersey.
    Length: 45 hours (15 weeks).
    Dates: *Version 1:* January 1977-December 1986; *Ver-

sion 2: January 1987-Present.

Objective: To enable the banking student to learn the practical aspects of money and banking and basic monetary theory.

Instruction: *Version 1:* Covers economic stabilization, types of spending, the role of gold, limitations of central bank control, government fiscal policy, the balance of payments, and foreign exchange. Lectures, discussion, classroom exercises, problem solving. *Version 2:* This course applies basic economic principles to the field of banking. It covers the economy, how it works; the Federal Reserve System; the business of banking; monetary policy, its impact on financial markets and banks; alternate theories of money's role in the economy; fiscal policy, and trends in banking.

Credit recommendation: *Version 1:* In the upper division baccalaureate category, 2 semester hours in Money and Banking (1/82). *Version 2:* In the upper division baccalaureate category, 3 semester hours in Money and Banking (4/87). NOTE: This course has been reevaluated and continues to meet requirements for credit recommendations.

Principles of Banking

Location: Various locations in New Jersey.
Length: 45 hours (15 weeks).
Dates: *Version 1:* January 1977-December 1986; *Version 2:* January 1987-Present.

Objective: To provide the student with a basic understanding of commercial banking.

Instruction: *Version 1:* The course surveys internal operations of commercial banks including documents and language of banking, deposit functions, relationships with depositors, specialized banking services, regulations, and examination. Lectures, discussion, classroom exercises, problem solving. *Version 2:* This course offers a comprehensive introduction to the diversified services offered by the banking industry today. It covers banking, history and economic and community environment; documents and language of banking; bank services; deposit and check processing; bank loans and investments; trust departments; specialized services; and bank regulations.

Credit recommendation: *Version 1:* In the lower division baccalaureate/associate degree category, 2 semester hours in Introduction to Banking (1/82). *Version 2:* In the lower division baccalaureate/associate degree category, 3 semester hours in Introduction to Banking (4/87). NOTE: This course has been reevaluated and continues to meet requirements for credit recommendations.

Real Estate and Mortgage Principles
(Formerly Real Estate Finance)

Location: Various locations in New Jersey.
Length: 45 hours (15 weeks).
Dates: January 1977-Present.

Objective: To enable the student to understand real estate from the viewpoint of the mortgage loan officer.

Instruction: Covers the mortgage market acquisition of mortgage portfolio, mortgage plans and procedures, mortgage loan processing and servicing, and portfolio management. Lectures, discussion, classroom exercises, problem solving.

Credit recommendation: In the upper division baccalaureate degree category, 3 semester hours in Real Estate Finance (1/82) (4/87). NOTE: This course has been reevaluated and continues to meet requirements for credit recommendations.

Trust Business
(Formerly Trust Functions and Services)

Location: Various locations in New Jersey.
Length: 45 hours (15 weeks).
Dates: January 1977-Present.

Objective: To enable the student to understand the function and services offered by institutions engaged in the trust business.

Instruction: Covers trusts, wills, estate administration, personal agencies, corporate agencies, property rights, trust funds, and employee benefit accounts. Lectures, discussion, classroom exercises, problem solving.

Credit recommendation: In the upper division baccalaureate category, 3 semester hours in Trust Functions and Services or Business elective (1/82) (4/87). NOTE: This course has been reevaluated and continues to meet requirements for credit recommendations.

Trust Operations

Location: Various locations in New Jersey.
Length: 45 hours (15 weeks).
Dates: January 1977-Present.

Objective: To enable the student to understand the fundamental functions of trust operations.

Instruction: Covers orientation and history of trust operations, central depositories and security movement and control, retirement trusts and common fund accounting, corporate trust, fiduciary tax, fiduciary accounting, statutes and regulatory requirements, trust auditors, and trust profitability. Lectures, discussion, classroom exercises, problem solving.

Credit recommendation: In the upper division baccalaureate category, 3 semester hours in Trust Operations or Business electives (1/82) (4/87). NOTE: This course has been reevaluated and continues to meet requirements for credit recommendations.

General Electric Company

The General Electric Company (GE) is engaged primarily in developing, manufacturing, and marketing a wide variety of products used in the generation, transmission, distribution, control, and utilization of electricity. As a result of corporate research and development, GE has also developed businesses in such areas as communications, plastics, medical systems, aircraft engines, and ship propulsion systems. In 1980, GE employed approximately 402,000 persons in 142 business operations worldwide.

GE offers many courses to its employees to help accelerate their professional and managerial career development. Whether the courses are single offerings or are part of an integrated program of study, they are all designed to help individual employees perform more effectively on current jobs, prepare for new jobs, or gain greater personal satisfaction from their work.

Courses are grouped alphabetically under the title of the program of which they are a part. A brief description of the purpose and general content of each program precedes the group of courses the program comprises.

AIRCRAFT ENGINE BUSINESS GROUP (OHIO)

Aircraft Engines is a component of General Electric, headquarterd in Cincinnati, with 19,000 employees in its Evendale plant. Courses are offered as on-company-time workshops, university or vocational school-based programs, and After Hours courses. The following courses are offered as After Hours courses of the Evendale program. These courses are administered for GE by Raymond Walters College of the University of Cincinnati, under a contract signed in 1984.

Registration is handled through advertisement in a catalog, the *Guide to Growth*, and the plant newspaper with participants submitting applications directly to the instructors, and overall registration coordinated by a UC administrator. Students are measured against identified goals and objectives. Some courses require written tests, other courses have identified measurements. The successful completion of a course is recorded by the instructor on a course attendance record and certificates are given to students. An "Objective Status Card" is used when a student has not passed a course and they have the option of attempting to pass the course a second time.

New courses are developed according to business needs. Some courses are designed at corporate GE training and instructors are certified to teach this material. The course writer/designer identifies goals, objectives, and lesson plans, and at times prepares the method of evaluating student learning. A team of consultants from UC provide training in course development/instruction for the instructors and are available for assistance. More than one-half of the After Hours courses are taught in classrooms at Raymond Walters College. They are equipped with audiovisual equipment, and textbooks purchased under contract at UC. Other classes are taught either in the Computer Training Lab provided to GE by Scarlet Oaks Vocational School, or in one of five HRD in-plant classrooms in the Evendale plant.

Most of the After Hours course instructors are GE personnel. Applicants submit a resume with applicable credentials prior to an interview and evaluation of subject and content knowledge. The selected individual is then trained to teach a given course. The designer of the course, normally an in-house expert, is also the instructor. Instructors are evaluated by a proctored evaluation at the end of each course. The evaluation is reviewed and a summary of results is reported, a compilation of which is sent to each instructor.

Source of official student records: After Hours Program Administrator, GE Aircraft Engines, Mail Drop G9, 1 Neumann Way, Cincinnati, OH 45215.

Additional information about the courses: Program on Noncollegiate Sponsored Instruction, The Center for Adult Learning and Educational Credentials, American Council on Education, One Dupont Circle, Washington, D.C. 20036.

Aerodynamics (E-307)
Location: Raymond Walters College, Cincinnati, OH. (Previously General Electric, Evendale, OH.)
Length: 60 hours (30 weeks; 2 hours per week).
Dates: September 1971-Present.
Objective: To give the student a broad but reasonable thorough understanding of the basic principles of fluid mechanics especially as they relate to aircraft flight and turbo-machinery, and to develop the skills necessary to compute solutions to various flowfields.
Learning Outcome: Upon successful completion of this course, the student will be able to identify and describe distinguishing features of subsonic, transonic, and supersonic flowfields; describe the fundamental equations of fluid mechanics and the types of analytical procedures available; select the appropriate type of analysis to be used to solve a specified flowfield; compute the aerodynamic and thermodynamic properties of a flowfield including shock waves, expansion fans, and the effects of viscosity; and apply aerodynamic theory to the design of inlets, fans, compressors, turbines, and exhaust nozzles.
Instruction: Course covers subsonic and supersonic aerodynamics. It is particularly useful for those individuals who have a technical background and interact with aerodesigners but have no formal aero training.
Credit recommendation: In the upper division baccalaureate category or in the graduate degree category, 3 semester hours in Aerospace or Mechanical Engineering (11/87).

Career Planning Workshop (P215)
Location: General Electric, Evendale, OH.
Length: 28 hours (7 weeks; 4 hours per week).
Dates: July 1988-Present.
Objective: To make students aware of their career-related skills, including their strengths and weaknesses, establish realistic career goals, and explore alternative ca-

reer paths.

Learning Outcome: Upon successful completion of this course, the student will be able to acknowledge their talents, skills and values; list and review key elements in logical career planning; and assess their potential and plan for their next career change.

Instruction: Course covers self-assessment, value systems, techniques of interviews and career mapping; power, politics, and burnout are also discussed as related to career planning. Methodology includes lecture, discussion, class presentation, book review, and homework assignments.

Credit recommendation: In the lower division baccalaureate/associate degree category, 2 semester hours in Human Resource Development or Personnel Development (10/88).

C Programming (C-146)
   Location: General Electric, Evendale, OH. (Raymond Walters College, Cincinnati, OH.)
   Length: 24 hours (12 weeks, 2 hours per week).
   Dates: June 1987-Present.
   Objective: To develop the student's understanding of effective use of the C programming language.
   Learning Outcome: Upon successful completion of this course, the student will be able to write, compile, and execute structured C programs; understand fundamental C language data types; create complex data structures in C; use accepted style conventions and create their own coding conventions; make effective use of the preprocessor in producing modulerized readable code; and understand portability considerations for C language programs designed to run in the Evendale data processing environment.
   Instruction: Course covers data types, operators, control structures, functions, elementary arrays, advanced arrays, pointers and structures, the preprocessor, advanced topics. Class sessions include lectures, discussions, assignments, quizzes and exams. Student must earn 75 points out of 100 possible points to receive a certificate.
   Credit recommendation: In the lower division baccalaureate/associate degree category, 2 semester hours in Computer Science or Data Processing (11/87).

Descriptive Geometry I (M020)
   Location: General Electric, Evendale, OH.
   Length: 35 hours (14 weeks; 2½ hours per week).
   Dates: April 1987-Present.
   Objective: To develop the student's skills to reinforce perception of related orthographic projection principles and stimulate the development of the student's depth perception and visualization abilities essential for creative design.
   Learning Outcome: Upon successful completion of this course, the student will be able to apply principles of orthographic projection and descriptive geometry for the solution of space problems and true graphic presentations with efficient use of time and effort; use of problem-solving techniques to find true length of lines, true position of points, planes and solids; accurately and clearly define intersections of lines, points, planes, solids, and development problems.
   Instruction: Course covers orthographic projection including definition of lines and planes; piercing points involving intersecting and parallel planes; plane tangencies, including development and intersections and perspective projection. Methodology includes lectures, quizzes, tests, and homework problems.
   Credit recommendation: In the lower division baccalaureate/associate degree category, 2 semester hours in Industrial Technology (10/88).

Descriptive Geometry II (M021)
   Location: General Electric, Evendale, OH.
   Length: 35 hours (14 weeks; 2½ hours per week).
   Dates: September 1987-Present.
   Objective: To enhance the student's skills in the area of orthographic projection, depth perception, and visualization as related to graphic resolution of geometric problems.
   Learning Outcome: Upon successful completion of this course, the student will be able to apply graphic problem-solving techniques in various combinations to determine geometric shapes and their relative positions in space; apply principles of descriptive geometry; and interpret the graphic problem resolution process.
   Instruction: Course covers orthographic projection, piercing points, and plane tangencies with applications to practical problems; development is also covered with emphasis on transitional shapes. Methodology includes lectures, quizzes, tests, and homework problems.
   Credit recommendation: In the lower division baccalaureate/associate degree category, 2 semester hours in Industrial Technology (10/88).

Effective Creativity (P223)
   Location: General Electric, Evendale, OH.
   Length: 30 hours (12 weeks; 2½ hours per week).
   Dates: October 1988-Present.
   Objective: To provide the student with a set of techniques for applying creativity, abilities present in individuals, and to improve the student's problem solving abilities.
   Learning Outcome: Upon successful completion of this course, the student will be able to apply techniques of deliberate creativeness, such as brainstorming, association, and storyboarding; choose and apply appropriate techniques for problem solving; design a new system of behaviors based on resistance to change.
   Instruction: Course covers definition, rules, and principles of creativity; association techniques, brainstorming, attribute listing technique, symetics techniques, storyboarding techniques, and managing and selling creative ideas. Methodology includes lecture, discussion, home-

work assignments, and book review.

Credit recommendation: In the upper division baccalaureate category, 2 semester hours in Business Administration (Effective) (10/88). NOTE: This course has application in Personnel Development, Human Relations, Group Dynamics, and Interpersonal Communications.

Effective Listening (P224)

Location: General Electric, Evendale, OH.
Length: 25 hours (10 weeks; 2½ hours per week).
Dates: October 1988-Present.
Objective: To develop the student's four essential abilities to effective listening—overcoming distractions, maintaining emotional control, detecting the central ideas in a message, and evaluating the message.
Learning Outcome: Upon successful completion of this course, the student will be able to use greater logic in listening; effectively evaluate what is heard by detecting the central idea; solve interpersonal problems caused by miscommunications.
Instruction: Course covers communication model and process, ten major barriers to effective listening, strategies to overcome distractions, methods to maintain emotional control in stressful listening situations, and the function and dimension of nonverbal communication. Methodology includes lecture, discussion, guest speakers, tests, homework assignments, and class interaction in small groups.
Credit recommendation: In the lower division baccalaureate/associate degree category, 2 semester hours in Communications or Speech (10/88).

Effective Presentation (P-225)

Location: Raymond Walters College, Cincinnati, OH.
Length: 37-1/2 hours (15 weeks; 2-1/2 hours per week).
Dates: September 1982-Present.
Objective: To develop and enhance the student's oral and written skills in a professional manner, and to allow the student to demonstrate presentation skills in a concise and organized presentation.
Learning Outcome: Upon successful completion of this course, the student will be able to organize ideas and speech outlines; properly generate charts and viewgraphs that support the presentation; achieve the ability to present subject matter with greater confidence; improve the skill to be concise in both written and oral communication; deal in an effective manner with external as well as internal customers; express themselves more clearly and creatively, not only in the job, but also in community relations; read a speech or prepared text properly; achieve the ability to constructively critique through class participation; and conduct meetings and conferences.
Instruction: Course covers effective presentation as a necessity in today's business world. This course will provide students with the tools to improve themselves by providing a more professional approach to representing our business. Each student is required to give a 3-minute speech each week. Speeches will require proper usage of objects, flip charts, and viewgraphs. The student will advance through demonstrated ability which will be enhanced through the use of proper critiquing, along with observance of fellow students. Storyboarding techniques will be introduced. Methodology includes student presentations, video-taping, lectures, and discussion.
Credit recommendation: In the lower division baccalaureate/associate degree category, 2 semester hours as a General Elective (11/87).

Feedback Control Theory and Design of Digital Control Systems (E-315) (E-316)

Location: Raymond Walters College, Cincinnati, OH.
Length: 60 hours (30 weeks, 2 hours per week).
Dates: September 1982-Present.
Objective: To allow the student to formulate the methods required to understand feedback control specifications and design; to apply both analytical and graphical techniques to the specification and design of a turbofan engine control system; and to formulate the methods needed to generate and interpret digital feedback control specifications and designs.
Learning Outcome: Upon successful completion of this course, the student will be able to formulate the open and closed loop response characteristics of feedback control systems; understand control system specifications and then develop a feedback system which will satisfy them; apply graphical and analytical complex frequency techniques to the analysis and design of closed loop feedback control systems; apply the real time methods of modern control theory to the analysis and design of control systems; analyze control system test data to determine if the feedback control meets specifications; understand the techniques needed to generate and interpret digital feedback control system specifications and designs; design proportional-integral-derivative (PID), phase-lead, and phase-lag digital controllers using frequency techniques; design digital control systems using pole placement and linear quadratic optimal criteria, with implementation using state estimators (observers) and Kalman filters; implement digital control systems using microcomputer techniques; understand the problems of implementing digital controllers on microcomputers; and review the microcomputer hardware used in digital control systems in order to accurately implement all control law algorithms.
Instruction: Course covers the techniques which are required to analyze, specify, and design feedback control systems. It will include both the analytical and graphical methods for both the frequency and real time approach. This course is directed toward the engineer who is interested in working in the feedback controls field or is required to interface with control system personnel. Methodology includes lectures and homework problems.
Credit recommendation: In the upper division bac-

calaureate category or in the graduate degree category, 3 semester hours in Electrical or Mechanical Engineering (11/87).

Gas Turbine Fundamentals (E-333)
  Location: Raymond Walters College, Cincinnati, OH and General Electric, Evendale, OH.
  Length: 60 hours (30 weeks, 2 hours per week).
  Dates: September 1972-Present.
  Objective: To develop the student's understanding of basic aero-thermodynamic concepts related to the principal gas path components and to develop the student's communication capability with the various aero-component design groups.
  Learning Outcome: Upon successful completion of this course, the student will be able to conduct basic aerodynamic and thermodynamic calculations related to gas turbines; develop thermodynamic cycle studies to select appropriate engine configurations; layout preliminary flowpath design of turbojet engines; and establish vector diagrams to satisfy component requirements.
  Instruction: Course covers aero-thermodynamic design of the gas turbine engine including the principal gas path components. It is useful for those employees who have a desire to gain a broader understanding of gas turbines as propulsion devices. Methodology includes lectures, design reviews, homework problems, and exams.
  Credit recommendation: In the upper division baccalaureate category or in the graduate degree category, 3 semester hours in Aerospace or Mechanical Engineering (11/87).

Mechanical Design and Mechanical Vibration Theory (E-353) (E-354)
  Location: Raymond Walters College, Cincinnati, OH.
  Length: 40 hours (20 weeks, 2 hours per week).
  Dates: September 1982-Present.
  Objective: To broaden the engineer's knowledge of the fundamentals of mechanical design theory, emphasizing the basics and limitations of the theories. In addition, to give the design engineer the necessary background to understand and solve practical vibration problems in the jet engine.
  Learning Outcome: Upon successful completion of this course, the student will be able to apply currently available solutions and methods to the design process with a knowledge of the theory limitations; select and apply energy methods for the approximate and rapid solution to complex problems; apply the various theories of failure, with a knowledge of their mechanisms and limitations; formulate solutions to simple problems involving creep effects; solve vibration problems for idealized systems; predict the vibration behavior of real engine systems by use of idealized equivalents; apply numerical methods to determine the vibration characteristics in real engine systems; and identify and understand the general characteristics and behavior of the vibrating systems.
  Instruction: Course covers the theories underlying stress analysis and mechanics of materials as applied to design and also to identify the limitations and assumptions which affect results. Emphasis is on fundamentals rather than on specific design techniques. In addition, this course is designed to provide engineers with a basic understanding of vibration theory, and to relate the results for simple systems to complex structural behavior. Methodology includes lectures, homework problems, and exams.
  Credit recommendation: In the upper division baccalaureate category or in the graduate degree category, 2 semester hours in Mechanical Engineering (11/87).

Principles of Production and Inventory Management (M-062)
  Location: General Electric, Evendale, OH.
  Length: 60 hours (20 weeks, one 3-hour meeting per week).
  Dates: September 1984-Present.
  Objective: To provide the student with an understanding of the basic principles of production and inventory control and basic understanding of Materials Requirements Planning (MRP).
  Learning Outcome: Upon successful completion of this course, the student will be able to distinguish between formal/informal systems; apply specific forecasting principles and techniques; measure and analyze forecasting errors; define and be able to evaluate where, and where not to use a recorder point system; define what a Material Requirements Planning system is and where it applies; effectively calculate order quantities; define basic scheduling and loading techniques; apply techniques to control manufacturing cycle times; use dispatch techniques to control manufacturing cycle times; distinguish "symptoms" from "diseases" in production inventory control systems; distinguish how various techniques relate to one another in a P&IC system; and use every opportunity to effect cost reductions and systems improvements.
  Instruction: This is an American Production and Inventory Control Society (APICS) course covering the basics and techniques of Production and Inventory Control. It is intended for employees interested in working in production or inventory control and prepares students with the APICS certification examination. Coverage includes forecasting systems, production planning, inventory control practices and techniques, material requirements planning, need scheduling, capacity planning and control.
  Credit recommendation: In the lower division baccalaureate/associate degree category, 4 semester hours in Operations Management (11/87).

Value Engineering (E305)
  Location: General Electric, Evendale, OH.
  Length: 40 hours (10 weeks; 4 hours per week).
  Dates: September 1987-Present.

Objective: To provide the student with an understanding of value engineering methodology as an effective strategy to improve design, manufacturing processes, procedures, and systems.

Learning Outcome: Upon successful completion of this course, the student will be able to associate costs with the functions achieved; determine function worth; use function analysis to become more creative; realize the value of teamwork; sell ideas more effectively. This course is certified by the Society of American Value Engineers and completion satisfies the education requirement for Certified Value Specialist.

Instruction: Course teaches the Value Engineering five-step plan: Information; Creativity; Evaluation; Planning; Reporting and Implementing. Covered are: function analysis and evaluation; value concepts; history of value engineering; concept of worth. Methodology includes lecture, discussion, and team reports on projects.

Credit recommendation: In the lower division baccalaureate/associate degree category, 2 semester hours in Value Engineering (10/88).

AIRCRAFT ENGINE BUSINESS GROUP - MANUFACTURING MATERIALS AND PROCESSES PROGRAM (MASSACHUSETTS)

General Electric has developed programs that prepare key personnel in manufacturing to deal with the processes, materials, equipment, and technology of aircraft engine production. Included are the several segments of Level II (numbered 2.-). Instructors are GE technical personnel involved in development and application of manufacturing processes.

Source of official student records: Learning Resource Center, General Electric, Mail Drop 153TL, 1000 Western Avenue, Lynn, Massachusetts 01910.

Additional information about the courses: Program on Noncollegiate Sponsored Instruction, The Center for Adult Learning and Educational Credentials, American Council on Education, One Dupont Circle, Washington, D.C. 20036.

Computer-Aided Manufacturing (M2.4)
(Formerly M2.11)

Location: Lynn, MA.

Length: 36 hours (9 weeks).

Dates: *Version 1:* September 1982-January 1989; *Version 2:* February 1989-Present.

Objective: To develop the student's knowledge of the capabilities, applications, investments, and human considerations necessary to initiate and maintain a computer-aided manufacturing system.

Learning Outcome: Upon successful completion of this course, the student will be able to demonstrate knowledge of capabilities of computer-aided manufacturing; demonstrate knowledge of the application of computer-aided manufacturing; and understand investments and human factors necessary to initiate and maintain a computer-aided manufacturing system.

Instruction: Course covers study of small, medium, and large scale computers; interactive graphics; automatically programmed tools; computer-aided design; closed loop machining; quality control-advanced systems; factory management systems; group technology; computer-aided process planning; and future trends. Methodology includes lecture, demonstration, discussion, and examinations.

Credit recommendation: *Version 1:* In the upper division baccalaureate category, 3 semester hours in Engineering Technology or Management (12/83). *Version 2:* In the upper division baccalaureate category, 3 semester hours in Manufacturing Engineering Technology or as an elective in Industrial Management (2/89). NOTE: This course has been reevaluated and continues to meet requirements for credit recommendations.

Conventional Metal Removal (M2.1)
(Formerly Conventional Metal Remover [M2.1])

Location: Lynn, MA.

Length: 40 hours (10 weeks).

Dates: *Version 1:* September 1978-January 1989; *Version 2:* February 1989-Present.

Objective: To introduce the basic conventional metal removal processes to supervisory and nontechnical professionals.

Learning Outcome: Upon successful completion of this course, the student will be able to explain the significance of machining operations in the manufacturing process; and understand the machining process including the effects of feed rates, speed, machine rigidity, and tool vibration on part integrity.

Instruction: Course covers the study of machinability theory, chip formation, cutting tool forces, and the machine tool application. Discussion of machine speeds and feeds as applied to surface finish, tool life, power requirements, and parts integrity. Methodology includes lecture, demonstration, audiovisual aids, and examinations.

Credit recommendation: *Version 1:* In the lower division baccalaureate/associate degree category, 3 semester hours in Manufacturing Engineering Technology; or in the lower division baccalaureate/associate degree category or in the upper division baccalaureate category, 3 semester hours in Industrial Management (12/78) (12/83). *Version 2:* In the lower division baccalaureate/associate degree category, 3 semester hours in Manufacturing Engineering Technology; or in the lower division baccalaureate/associate degree category or in the upper division baccalaureate category, 3 semester hours as an elective in Industrial Management (2/89). NOTE: This course has been reevaluated and continues to meet requirements for credit recommendations.

Fabricated Parts Seminar (M2.10F)
Location: Lynn, MA.
Length: *Version 1:* 24 hours (6 weeks); *Version 2:* 20 hours (5 weeks).
Dates: *Version 1:* April 1979-March 1986; *Version 2:* April 1986-Present.
Objective: To introduce supervisory and nontechnical professionals to problem areas and the integration of processes unique to the fabrication of aircraft engine sheet metal parts.
Learning Outcome: Upon successful completion of this course, the student will be able to define a fabricated part; understand the key elements necessary to establish a manufacturing plan for the production of fabricated parts; and understand the techniques and be familiar with available resources for solving technical manufacturing problems associated with fabricated parts.
Instruction: Course covers every step of the planning, production, and troubleshooting of fabricated parts. A team project to develop a sample manufacturing plan is required. Methodology includes lecture, discussion, demonstration, audiovisual aids, and examinations. (Prerequisites: Sheet Metal, Joining, and Quality Control.)
Credit recommendation: *Version1:* In the lower division baccalaureate/associate degree category, 2 semester hours in Manufacturing Engineering Technology; or in the upper division baccalaureate category, 2 semester hours in Management (4/80) (12/83). *Version 2:* In the lower division baccalaureate/associate degree category, 2 semester hours in Manufacturing Engineering Technology; or in the upper division baccalaureate category, 2 semester hours as an elective in Industrial Management (2/89). NOTE: This course has been reevaluated and continues to meet requirements for credit recommendations.

Joining (M2.5)
Location: Lynn, MA.
Length: 40 hours (10 weeks).
Dates: *Version 1:* September 1978-January 1989; *Version 2:* February 1989-Present.
Objective: To introduce supervisory and nontechnical professionals to joining techniques used in jet aircraft engines.
Learning Outcome: Upon successful completion of this course, the student will be able to demonstrate knowledge of metal joining techniques; identify and describe the capabilities and benefits of various joining techniques; describe fixtures, fit and tolerance, requirements, inspection, and operating problems associated with various welding techniques.
Instruction: Course covers fixtures; fit and tolerances; operator requirements; equipment certification; inspection; typical operating problems associated with resistance welding; gas tungsten arc welding; brazing; electron beam welding as applied to aluminum, cobalt, nickel, titanium base alloys, and selected stainless steels. Methodology includes lecture, demonstration, audiovisual aids, and examinations.
Credit recommendation: *Version 1:* In the lower division baccalaureate/associate degree category, 3 semester hours in Manufacturing Engineering Technology; or in the lower division baccalaureate/associate degree category or in the upper division baccalaureate category, 3 semester hours in Industrial Management (12/78) (12/83). *Version 2:* In the lower division baccalaureate/associate degree category, 3 semester hours in Manufacturing Engineering Technology; or in the lower division baccalaureate/associate degree category or in the upper division baccalaureate category, 3 semester hours as an elective in Industrial Management (2/89). NOTE: This course has been reevaluated and continues to meet requirements for credit recommendations.

Manufacturing Methods and Processes (M10)
Location: Lynn, MA.
Length: 76 hours (19 weeks).
Dates: *Version 1:* September 1982-September 1985; *Version 2:* October 1985-Present.
Objective: To teach the student the basic knowledge of manufacturing methods in preparing a detailed plan for manufacturing components.
Learning Outcome: Upon successful completion of this course, the student will be able to evaluate manufacturing methods for producing a machine component; understand the common procedures used in manufacturing machine components; evaluate drawings, time standards, and quality cost/manufacturing losses associated with manufacturing processes.
Instruction: Course covers the study of value engineering, design engineering, design and application of castings, forgings, weld fixtures, machining fixtures, press and die work procedures, application of heat treating and cutting tools. Also includes methods paperwork, process drawing, process analysis, time standards, quality cost/manufacturing losses and customer complaint handling. Methodology includes lecture, discussion, audiovisual aids, projects, and examinations.
Credit recommendation: *Version 1:* In the upper division baccalaureate category, 4 semester hours in Engineering Technology or Management (12/83). *Version 2:* In the upper division baccalaureate category, 4 semester hours in Manufacturing Engineering Technology or as an elective in Industrial Management (2/89). NOTE: This course has been reevaluated and continues to meet requirements for credit recommendations.

Miscellaneous Processes (M2.6)
Location: Lynn, MA.
Length: 30 hours (7½ weeks).
Dates: *Version 1:* September 1978-January 1989; *Version 2:* February 1989-Present.

Objective: To introduce supervisors and nontechnical professionals to several industrial processes.

Learning Outcome: Upon successful completion of this course, the student will be able to describe the purpose, process, and effect of heat treating on materials; describe the purpose, materials, and procedures in chemical cleaning processes; describe the purpose, materials, and procedures of thermal spray processes; describe the purpose, materials, and procedures of shot peening processes.

Instruction: Course covers heat treating, cleaning, shot peening, and thermal spraying of specialized materials used in turbines and jet aircraft engines. Methodology includes lecture, demonstration, audiovisual aids, and examinations.

Credit recommendation: *Version 1:* In the lower division baccalaureate/associate degree category, 3 semester hours in Manufacturing Engineering Technology; or in the lower division baccalaureate/associate degree category or in the upper division baccalaureate category, 3 semester hours in Industrial Management (12/78) (12/83). *Version 2:* In the lower division baccalaureate/associate degree category, 3 semester hours in Manufacturing Engineering Technology; or in the lower division baccalaureate/associate degree category, or in the upper division baccalaureate category, 3 semester hours as an elective in Industrial Management (2/89). NOTE: This course has been reevaluated and continues to meet requirements for credit recommendations.

Non-Conventional Metal Removal
(Formerly Electrical Discharge Machining [M2.3])
   Location: Lynn, MA.
   Length: *Version 1:* 20 hours (10 weeks); *Version 2:* 24 hours (12 weeks).
   Dates: *Version 1:* January 1979-March 1984; *Version 2:* April 1984-Present.
   Objective: To introduce the electrical discharge machining process to supervisory and nontechnical professionals.
   Learning Outcome: Upon successful completion of this course, the student will be able to determine when to use electrical discharge machining processes and how to evaluate as well as optimize the cost of electrical discharge machining operations; effectively manage electrical discharge machining processes; acquire a knowledge of the operation and use of laser systems for metal removal.
   Instruction: Course covers electrical discharge machining principles as they relate to equipment operation, effects of process parameters on machined dimensions and surface characteristics, effects on metal removal rate and tool wear, selection of parameters for machining operations, and process capability. Non-conventional metal removal techniques using laser systems are also covered in the course. Examples of machining operations, estimation of machining time, equipment, and safety are covered in lecture and discussion. Methodology includes lecture, demonstration, audiovisual aids, discussion, and examinations.
   Credit recommendation: *Version 1:* In the lower division baccalaureate/associate degree category, 2 semester hours in Manufacturing Engineering Technology; or in the upper division baccalaureate category, 2 semester hours in Management (4/80) (12/83). *Version 2:* In the lower division baccalaureate/associate degree category, 2 semester hours in Manufacturing Engineering Technology; or in the upper division baccalaureate category, 2 semester hours as an elective in Industrial Management (2/89). NOTE: This course has been reevaluated and continues to meet requirements for credit recommendations.

Numerical Control (M2.2)
   Location: Lynn, MA.
   Length: *Version 1:* 32 hours (8 weeks); *Version 2:* 42 hours (11 weeks).
   Dates: *Version 1:* September 1978-December 1980; *Version 2:* January 1981-Present.
   Objective: To introduce supervisory and nontechnical professionals to numerical control as applied to machine tool processes.
   Learning Outcome: Upon successful completion of this course, the student will be able to understand components, advantages, and applications of numerical control machines; understand the use of computers and robotics in the manufacturing process.
   Instruction: Course covers the history of numerical control; programming; lathe specifications and tooling; tape coding; interactive graphics; computerized coordinate measuring machines. Methodology includes lecture, demonstration, audiovisual aids, and examinations.
   Credit recommendation: *Version 1:* In the lower division baccalaureate/associate degree category, 3 semester hours in Manufacturing Engineering Technology; or in the lower division baccalaureate/associate degree category or in the upper division baccalaureate category, 3 semester hours in Industrial Management (12/78) (12/83). *Version 2:* In the lower division baccalaureate/associate degree category, 3 semester hours in Manufacturing Engineering Technology; or in the lower division baccalaureate/associate degree category or in the upper division baccalaureate category, 3 semester hours as an elective in Industrial Management (2/89). NOTE: This course has been reevaluated and continues to meet requirements for credit recommendations.

Quality Control (M2.7RF)
   Location: Lynn, MA.
   Length: *Version 1:* 24 hours (6 weeks); *Version 2:* 40 hours (10 weeks).
   Dates: *Version 1:* March 1979-April 1985; *Version 2:* May 1985-Present.
   Objective: To acquaint supervisors and nontechnical personnel with quality control system, instrumentation,

and procedures.

Learning Outcome: Upon successful completion of this course, the student will be able to understand quality control systems and the organization required to implement quality control; explain principles and applications of relevant instruments and testing techniques; apply quality control measures to manufacturing processes.

Instruction: *Version 1:* Course provides in-depth coverage of nondestructive testing as well as information on penetrant die techniques, ultrasonics, X-ray, gauging, and measurement. Also covers quality control functions as they relate to the total manufacturing process. *Version 2:* Course covers quality control systems, quality control organization, and testing and evaluation techniques. Methodology includes lecture, demonstration, case studies, audiovisual aids, and examinations.

Credit recommendation: *Version 1:* In the lower division baccalaureate/associate degree category, 2 semester hours in Industrial Management or Manufacturing Engineering Technology (4/80) (12/83). *Version 2:* In the lower division baccalaureate/associate degree category, 2 semester hours in Manufacturing Engineering Technology, or as an elective in Industrial Management; or 3 semester hours in Manufacturing Engineering Technology or as an elective in Industrial Management (2/89). NOTE: This course has been reevaluated and continues to meet requirements for credit recommendations.

Rotating Parts Seminar (M2.9R)
   Location: Lynn, MA.
   Length: 30 hours (7½ weeks).
   Dates: *Version 1:* April 1979-January 1989; *Version 2:* February 1989-Present.
   Objective: To introduce supervisory and nontechnical professionals to the processes and problem areas inherent in the manufacturing of rotating aircraft engine parts.
   Learning Outcome: Upon successful completion of this course, the student will be able to define characteristics, design, and functions of rotating parts used in aircraft engines; explain the purpose and characteristics of engineering drawings and their impact on the manufacturing process for rotating parts; understand and present the development and uses of a manufacturing plan for typical rotating parts.
   Instruction: *Version 1:* Presents every step of the planning, production, and troubleshooting of typical jet engine rotating parts. A team project to develop a sample manufacturing plan is required. (Prerequisites: Conventional Metal Removal, Non-Conventional Metal Removal, Numerical Control, and Quality Control.) *Version 2:* Course covers rotating parts of aircraft engines, engineering and process drawings, and manufacturing plans. Methodology includes lecture, discussion, demonstration, audiovisual aids, team project, and examination.
   Credit recommendation: *Version 1:* In the lower division baccalaureate/associate degree category, 2 semester hours in Manufacturing Engineering Technology; or in the upper division baccalaureate category, 2 semester hours in Management (4/80) (12/83). *Version 2:* In the lower division baccalaureate/associate degree category, 2 semester hours in Manufacturing Engineering Technology; or in the upper division baccalaureate category, 2 semester hours as an elective in Industrial Management (2/89). NOTE: This course has been reevaluated and continues to meet requirements for credit recommendations.

Sheet Metal (M2.4)
   Location: Lynn, MA.
   Length: *Version 1:* 38 hours (9½ weeks); *Version 2:* 30 hours (8 weeks).
   Dates: *Version 1:* September 1978-June 1986; *Version 2:* July 1986-Present.
   Objective: To introduce supervisory personnel and nontechnical professionals to sheet metal manufacturing processes.
   Learning Outcome: Upon successful completion of this course, the student will be able to understand the properties of sheet metals; understand the relationship between the properties of sheet metals and various forms of sheet metal processing.
   Instruction: Course covers specifications, physical properties, testing, equipment, tools and dies, materials phenomena, sheet metal manufacturing processes. Methodology includes lecture, demonstration, audiovisual aids, and examinations.
   Credit recommendation: *Version 1:* In the lower division baccalaureate/associate degree category, 2 semester hours in Manufacturing Engineering Technology; or in the lower division baccalaureate/associate degree category or in the upper division baccalaureate degree category, 3 semester hours in Industrial Management (12/78) (12/83). *Version 2:* In the lower division baccalaureate/associate degree category, 2 semester hours in Manufacturing Engineering Technology; or in the lower division baccalaureate/associate degree category, or in upper division baccalaureate degree category, 2 semester hours as an elective in Industrial Management (2/89). NOTE: This course has been reevaluated and continues to meet requirements for credit recommendations.

AIRCRAFT ENGINE BUSINESS GROUP - AFTER-HOURS COURSES

The course listed below is one of many opportunities available to aircraft engine business group employees of Lynn. It is offered at the close of the working day.

Source of official student records: Personnel Development Office, General Electric, Mail Drop 14508, 1000 Western Avenue, Lynn, Massachusetts 01910.

Additional information about the courses: Program on Noncollegiate Sponsored Instruction, The Center for Adult Learning and Educational Credentials, American

General Electric Company

Council on Education, One Dupont Circle, Washington, D.C. 20036.

High Temperature Metallurgy (E80)
(Formerly M9)
   Location: Lynn, MA.
   Length: 40 hours (20 weeks); one 2-hour meeting per week.
   Dates: December 1968-Present.
   Objective: To give engineers and supervisory personnel with engineering backgrounds an understanding of high temperature alloys and their application.
   Instruction: Crystal structure of metals; equilibrium diagrams; strengthening mechanisms; properties of metals at elevated temperatures; creep rupture; fatigue; oxidation; corrosion; surface treatments; protective coatings, with a special emphasis on superalloys. Methodology includes lecture, projects, and presentations.
   Credit recommendation: In the upper division baccalaureate category, 3 semester hours in Engineering or Metallurgy (12/78) (12/83). NOTE: This course has been reevaluated and continues to meet requirements for credit recommendations.

APPRENTICESHIP TRAINING PROGRAM - LYNN RIVER WORKS

The courses that follow are conducted by the Apprenticeship Office of the Lynn Relations Operation. Three years of classroom training, in conjunction with three years of hands-on shop training, produce qualified machinists for the two GE businesses at the Lynn River Works: the Power Generation Group and the Aircraft Engine Business Group. Apprentice trainees are usually hired for this program, but selected employees may also be admitted.

Source of official student records: Manager-Apprentice Training, General Electric Company, Mail Drop 37717, 1100 Western Avenue, Lynn, Massachusetts 01910.

Additional information about the courses: Program on Noncollegiate Sponsored Instruction, The Center for Adult Learning and Educational Credentials, American Council on Education, One Dupont Circle, Washington, D.C. 20036.

Applied Engineering Mechanics
   Location: Lynn, MA.
   Length: 54 hours (18 weeks).
   Dates: December 1968-April 1989.
   Objective: To provide a basic knowledge of statics and some dynamics as a foundation for more advanced courses in mechanics and strength of materials.
   Instruction: Principles of statics, coplaner force systems, parallel force systems, friction, principles of dynamics, kinematics of rectilinear motion, variable acceleration, kinetics of rectilinear motion, systems of bodies in motion, hydraulics.
   Credit recommendation: In the lower division baccalaureate/associate degree category, 3 semester hours in Manufacturing Engineering Technology (12/78) (12/83). NOTE: This course has been reevaluated and continues to meet requirements for credit recommendations.

APT Programming
(Automatically Programmed Tools Programming)
   Location: Lynn, MA.
   Length: 54 hours (18 weeks).
   Dates: October 1983-April 1989.
   Objective: To prepare the student to understand, interpret, and utilize a numerical control machining language.
   Instruction: Machine language, flowcharting, production part programming, verification and post processing. Methodology includes lecture, demonstration, field trip, and practical exercises.
   Credit recommendation: In the lower division baccalaureate/associate degree category, 3 semester hours in Engineering Technology (12/83).

College Algebra
   Location: Lynn, MA.
   Length: 54 hours (18 weeks).
   Dates: December 1968-April 1989.
   Objective: To provide a working ability in algebra at college level.
   Instruction: Set theory, exponents in multiplications, products involving multinomials, division (exponents with multinomials), binomial products, factoring, complex fractions, laws of exponents, roots, radicals, liner equations, quadratic equations, complex numbers, functions, graphs of linear functions, elimination of a variable, determinants, ratio and proportion, variation, permutations, combinations.
   Credit recommendation: In the lower division baccalaureate/associate degree category, 3 semester hours in College Algebra (12/78) (12/83). NOTE: This course has been reevaluated and continues to meet requirements for credit recommendations.

Computer Science
   Location: Lynn, MA.
   Length: 54 hours (18 weeks).
   Dates: December 1968-April 1989.
   Objective: To provide an introduction to the operations of computers and programming in BASIC.
   Instruction: History of computers, flow charting statements and sequences, input/output, arithmetic operations, alphanumerics, functions and subroutines, program writing in BASIC, Methodology includes lecture and demonstration.
   Credit recommendation: In the lower division baccalaureate/associate degree category, 3 semester hours in Computer Technology and Programming (12/78) (12/

Engineering Graphics I
(Formerly Blueprint I)
  Location: Lynn, MA.
  Length: 54 hours (18 weeks).
  Dates: December 1968-April 1989.
  Objective: To introduce basic blueprint interpretation.
  Instruction: Interpretation of industrial drawings, orthographic projection, line values, decimal dimensions, tolerances, rotated sections, sectioning, partial views, and baseline dimensioning. Methodology includes lecture and practical exercises.
  Credit recommendation: In the lower division baccalaureate/associate degree category, 1 semester hour in Manufacturing Engineering Technology (12/78) (12/83). NOTE: This course has been reevaluated and continues to meet requirements for credit recommendations.

Engineering Graphics II
(Formerly Blueprint II)
  Location: Lynn, MA.
  Length: 54 hours (18 weeks).
  Dates: December 1968-April 1989.
  Objective: To provide a knowledge of advanced blueprint interpretation.
  Instruction: Point-to-point dimensioning; representation of screw threads; classification of fits; thread symbols; auxiliary views; phantom outlines; structural steel shapes; finishes; sketching of objects by oblique, perspective, isometric methods; special sections; special methods of showing combined sections; auxiliary views; assembly drawings; combined assembly and detail drawings; pictorial assembly drawings; multiscale drawings; and drawings with complex parts.
  Credit recommendation: In the lower division baccalaureate/associate degree category, 2 semester hours in Manufacturing Engineering Technology (12/78) (12/83). NOTE: This course has been reevaluated and continues to meet requirements for credit recommendations.

Fundamentals of Numerical Control
  Location: Lynn, MA.
  Length: 54 hours (18 weeks)
  Dates: December 1968-April 1989.
  Objective: To provide an introduction to the operation of numerically controlled machine tool programming and tape punching.
  Instruction: Value of numerical control to manufacturing; engineering and management; numerical control cost; needs and accuracy; definitions; types of signals; types of input media and coding; methods of measuring and comparing input and feedback signals; numerical control history; types; similarity and reliability; pros and cons of numerical control quality and tooling cost; basis for numerical control dimensioning; introduction to punched tape; word identification; auxiliary functions; incremental dimensioning; computer programming; input and output of APT programming; timesharing. Methodology includes lecture and demonstration.
  Credit recommendation: In the lower division baccalaureate/associate degree category, 2 semester hours in Manufacturing Engineering Technology (12/78) (12/83). NOTE: This course has been reevaluated and continues to meet requirements for credit recommendations.

Interactive Graphics
  Location: Lynn, MA.
  Length: 54 hours (18 weeks).
  Dates: October 1983-April 1989.
  Objective: To provide a broad understanding and appreciation for computer graphics hardware and software.
  Instruction: Explanation of various hardware peripherals used in the computer graphics facility. Methodology includes hands-on instruction using appropriate training manuals and the creation of engineering drawings using IAG equipment. Systems commands, pen strokes and macro creation are applied to an engineering drawing chosen by the student.
  Credit recommendation: In the lower division baccalaureate/associate degree category, 1 semester hour in Engineering Technology (12/83).

Machine Shop Theory
  Location: Lynn, MA.
  Length: 54 hours (18 weeks).
  Dates: December 1968-April 1989.
  Objective: To provide the basics in machine shop technology.
  Instruction: Safety; drilling; use of hand tools, lathes, millers, grinders; gear cutting; special machines; surface measurement and supportive skills, such as precision measuring, lay out, heat treating, and metal testing. Methodology includes lecture, demonstration, and extensive practical exercises.
  Credit recommendation: In the lower division baccalaureate/associate degree category, 3 semester hours in Manufacturing Engineering Technology (12/78) (12/83). NOTE: This course has been reevaluated and continues to meet requirements for credit recommendations.

Manufacturing Engineering
  Location: Lynn, MA.
  Length: 54 hours (18 weeks).
  Dates: December 1968-April 1989.
  Objective: To provide an overview of manufacturing engineering and its role in industry.
  Instruction: Work measurement, product planning, facilities planning, OSHA, sampling, economic analysis. Methodology includes lecture, discussion, and team projects.

Credit recommendation: In the lower division baccalaureate/associate degree category, 2 semester hours in Manufacturing Engineering Technology (12/78) (12/83). NOTE: This course has been reevaluated and continues to meet requirements for credit recommendations.

Measurements
Location: Lynn, MA.
Length: 27 hours (9 weeks).
Dates: December 1968-December 1983.
Objective: To develop skill and understanding of precision measurement and its history in related manufacturing.
Instruction: Study of a wide range of measuring instruments, including micrometers, verniers, depth and height gauges, indicators, sine bars, and surface plate set-ups. Methodology includes lecture, audiovisual aids, demonstration, and extensive practical exercises.
Credit recommendation: In the lower division baccalaureate/associate degree category, 1 semester hour in Manufacturing Engineering Technology (12/78).

Metallurgy/Materials
(Formerly Metallurgy)
Location: Lynn, MA.
Length: 54 hours (18 weeks).
Dates: December 1968-April 1989.
Objective: To provide a broad introduction to metallurgy as a basis for more advanced materials engineering courses.
Instruction: Atomic arrangements, solidification, phase diagrams, precipitation hardening, ferrous heat treating operations, hot and cold working, corrosion studies. Methodology includes lecture, demonstration, and laboratory.
Credit recommendation: In the lower division baccalaureate/associate degree category, 3 semester hours in Manufacturing Engineering Technology (12/78) (12/83). NOTE: This course has been reevaluated and continues to meet requirements for credit recommendations.

Quality Control
Location: Lynn, MA.
Length: 27 hours (9 weeks).
Dates: December 1968-April 1989.
Objective: To provide an overview of quality control and its application to industrial processes.
Instruction: Total quality control, quality policies, reproduction quality evaluation, cost of quality, conformance and product auditing, quality planning, statistical method of control, nondestructive testing. Methodology includes lecture and case studies.
Credit recommendation: In the lower division baccalaureate/associate degree category, 2 semester hours in Manufacturing Engineering Technology (12/78) (12/83). NOTE: This course has been reevaluated and continues to meet requirements for credit recommendations.

Mechanics of Materials
(Formerly Strength of Materials)
Location: Lynn, MA.
Length: 54 hours (18 weeks).
Dates: December 1968-April 1989.
Objective: To teach students how to make basic stress calculations for structure.
Instruction: Study of stresses and deformations involved in tension, compression, bending, torsion, and some combined stresses. Methodology includes lecture, demonstration, audiovisual aids, and practical training.
Credit recommendation: In the lower division baccalaureate/associate degree category, 2 semester hours in Manufacturing Engineering Technology (12/78) (12/83). NOTE: This course has been reevaluated and continues to meet requirements for credit recommendations.

Technical Communications
Location: Lynn, MA.
Length: 54 hours (18 weeks).
Dates: December 1968-April 1989.
Objective: To develop the ability to communicate technical information effectively.
Instruction: Sentence structure and word usage emphasizing clarity and conciseness. A written report, oral presentations, and a term paper are required.
Credit recommendation: In the lower division baccalaureate/associate degree category, 1 semester hour in Technical Writing (12/78) (12/83). NOTE: This course has been reevaluated and continues to meet requirements for credit recommendations.

Tool Design
Location: Lynn, MA.
Length: 54 hours (18 weeks).
Dates: December 1968-April 1989.
Objective: To provide a working knowledge of basic tool design.
Instruction: Cutting tools, locating fixtures, clamping methods, gauge design, single stage blanking and piercing dies, bending dies, plastic tools, design requirements of numerically controlled tooling. Methodology includes lecture, audiovisual aids, demonstration, and practical exercises.
Credit recommendation: In the lower division baccalaureate/associate degree category, 3 semester hours in Manufacturing Engineering Technology (12/78) (12/83). NOTE: This course has been reevaluated and continues to meet requirements for credit recommendations.

Trigonometry
Location: Lynn, MA.
Length: 54 hours (18 weeks).
Dates: December 1968-April 1989.

Objective: To provide the ability to perform calculations involving trigonometric functions and logarithms.

Instruction: Trigonometric functions, tables of trigonometric functions and solutions of right triangles, trigonometric identities, graphical presentation of the trigonometric functions, trigonometric equations and inverse functions, logarithms, oblique triangles, vectors and applications, complex numbers.

Credit recommendation: In the lower division baccalaureate/associate degree category, 3 semester hours in Trigonometry (12/78) (12/83). NOTE: This course has been reevaluated and continues to meet requirements for credit recommendations.

MACHINIST/TOOLMAKER APPRENTICE PROGRAM

The General Electric Apprentice Training Program, established at the beginning of the century, is among the oldest continuing industrial apprentice programs in the United States. The Machinist/Toolmaker Apprentice Program, as it is called in Rutland, Vermont, includes 6,000 hours of on-the-job learning and 750 hours if instruction in twenty separate course areas. The program teaches the operation of a full range of state-of-the-art shop machinery, gives students experience in the machinist and toolmaker trades, and provides a sound theoretical background in the required mathematics, physics, manufacturing, and materials and processes areas.

The credit recommendations apply only to individuals who have successfully completed the entire three years of the program for the period January 1977 to the present.

Source of official student records: Apprentice Program Director, General Electric Company, 210 Columbian Avenue, Rutland, Vermont 05701.

Additional information about the courses: Vermont State Colleges, Office of External Programs, P.O. Box 34, Waterbury, Vermont 05676.

Computer Science
(Formerly Introduction to Computers)

Location: Rutland, VT.

Length: *Version 1:* 26 hours (10 weeks); *Version 2:* 39 hours (11 weeks).

Dates: *Version 1:* January 1977-January 1987. *Version 2:* February 1987-Present.

Objective: To present the fundamentals of computer programming using the BASIC language.

Instruction: Using a lecture and laboratory format, this course provides instruction in branching, looping, one- and two-dimensional arrays, and library functions.

Credit recommendation: *Version 1:* In the lower division baccalaureate/associate degree category, 1 semester hour in Introduction to Computers (6/83). *Version 2:* In the lower division baccalaureate/associate degree category, 2 semester hours in Programming in BASIC (9/86). NOTE: This course has been reevaluated and continues to meet requirements for credit recommendations.

Effective Presentation and Career Management Skills
(Formerly Effective Presentation)

Location: Rutland, VT.

Length: *Version 1:* 32 hours (16 weeks); *Version 2:* 32 hours (16 weeks).

Dates: *Version 1:* January 1977-January 1987. *Version 2:* February 1987-Present.

Objective: To enable students to develop clarity and confidence in interpersonal communications.

Instruction: This course introduces students to preparing and delivering various types of presentations in class and in the work place. Emphasis is placed on organization of material and adaptation of content to a wide range of audiences.

Credit recommendation: *Version 1:* In the lower division baccalaureate/associate degree category, 3 semester hours in Effective Oral Communication (6/83). *Version 2:* In the lower division baccalaureate/associate degree category, 3 semester hours in Effective Oral Communication (9/86). NOTE: This course has been reevaluated and continues to meet requirements for credit recommendations.

Electricity I & II

Location: Rutland, VT.

Length: *Version 1:* 94 hours (36 weeks); *Version 2:* 102 hours (36 weeks).

Dates: *Version 1:* January 1977-January 1987. *Version 2:* February 1987-Present.

Objective: To present students the basic elements of electricity and electronics.

Instruction: Study of the basic elements of electricity and electronics. Electricity topics include direct current, resistive networks, Ohm's and Kirchoff's laws, alternating current circuits under steady state and transient conditions. Basic electronics topics include solid state components and circuits, logic and integrated circuits. Practical applications are included.

Credit recommendation: *Version 1:* In the lower division baccalaureate/associate degree category, 4 semester hours in Survey of Electricity and Electronics (6/83). *Version 2:* In the lower division baccalaureate/associate degree category, 4 semester hours in Survey of Electricity and Electronics (9/86). NOTE: This course has been reevaluated and continues to meet requirements for credit recommendations.

Fundamentals of Numerical Control and Numerical Control Programming
(Formerly Numerical Control Programming)

Location: Rutland, VT.

Length: *Version 1:* 23 hours (9 weeks). *Version 2:* 54 hours (18 weeks).

Dates: *Version 1:* January 1977-January 1987. *Version*

2: February 1987-Present.

Objective: To enable students to become proficient in the programming and use of numerically controlled machines.

Instruction: Topics include: coordinate systems, incremental and absolute systems, tape coding, linear and circular interpolation. APT language is presented and used in the program development and machining of several parts.

Credit recommendation: *Version 1:* In the lower division baccalaureate/associate degree category, 2 semester hours in Introduction to Numerical Control Part Programming (6/83). *Version 2:* In the lower division baccalaureate/associate degree category, 4 semester hours in Numerical Control Programming and Applications (9/86). NOTE: This course has been reevaluated and continues to meet requirements for credit recommendations.

Industrial Hydraulics

Location: Rutland, VT.

Length: *Version 1:* 47 hours (18 weeks). *Version 2:* 51 hours (18 weeks).

Dates: *Version 1:* January 1977-January 1987. *Version 2:* February 1987-Present.

Objective: To provide students with an introduction to the operation and uses of hydraulic components used in an industrial setting.

Instruction: Operation and uses of hydraulic components such as pumps, motors, actuators, and 2-, 3-, 4-, and 5-way control valves are studied. A design project utilizing these components is required. Fundamentals of fluid pressure and flow are also presented.

Credit recommendation: *Version 1:* In the lower division baccalaureate/associate degree category, 1 semester hour in Survey of Industrial Hydraulics (6/83). *Version 2:* In the lower division baccalaureate/associate degree category, 1 semester hour in Survey of Industrial Hydraulics (9/86). NOTE: This course has been reevaluated and continues to meet requirements for credit recommendations.

Industrial Physics
(Formerly Physics)

Location: Rutland, VT.

Length: *Version 1:* 67 hours (26 weeks). *Version 2:* 85 hours (26 weeks).

Dates: *Version 1:* January 1977-January 1987. *Version 2:* February 1987-Present.

Objective: To provide students with an algebra-based introduction to the general principles of classical mechanics.

Instruction: An algebra-based introduction to classical mechanics. Topics include kinematics, solid and fluid statics, and dynamics. Laboratory component included.

Credit recommendation: *Version 1:* In the lower division baccalaureate/associate degree category, 3 semester hours in Topics in Physics (6/83). *Version 2:* In the lower division baccalaureate/associate degree category, 4 semester hours in Physics I (9/86). NOTE: This course has been reevaluated and continues to meet requirements for credit recommendations.

Mechanical Drawing I & II
(Formerly Blue Print Reading I & II)

Location: Rutland, VT.

Length: *Version 1:*, 93 hours (36 weeks). *Version 2:* 100 hours (36 weeks).

Dates: *Version 1:* January 1977-January 1987. *Version 2:* February 1987-Present.

Objective: To provide the student with basic knowledge to interpret symbols and understand drafting conventions as they appear on engineering drawings.

Instruction: This course develops skills in understanding drafting conventions and preparing simple drawings. Topics include orthographic projection, axial and sectional views, dimensioning, true position and geometric tolerancing in accordance with ANSI standards.

Credit recommendation: *Version 1:* In the lower division baccalaureate/associate degree category, 3 semester hours in Engineering Drawing Interpretation (6/83). *Version 2:* In the lower division baccalaureate/associate degree category, 3 semester hours in Technical Drawing Interpretation (9/86). NOTE: This course has been reevaluated and continues to meet requirements for credit recommendations.

Mechanisms

Location: Rutland, VT.

Length: 51 hours (18 weeks).

Dates: February 1987-Present.

Objective: To provide students with an introduction to the study of mechanisms.

Instruction: This course presents a graphically-based study of displacement, velocity, and acceleration of 4-bar linkages, utilizing graphic techniques of analysis.

Credit recommendation: In the lower division baccalaureate/associate degree category, 3 semester hours in Mechanisms (9/86).

Metallurgy

Location: Rutland, VT.

Length: *Version 1:* 47 hours (18 weeks). *Version 2:* 54 hours (18 weeks).

Dates: *Version 1:* January 1977-January 1987. *Version 2:* February 1987-Present.

Objective: To present the physical and mechanical properties of metals and alloys.

Instruction: This course covers crystalline structure, binary equilibrium diagrams, microstructure, and hardenability aspects of metallurgy.

Credit recommendation: *Version 1:* In the lower division baccalaureate/associate degree category, 3 semester hours in Metallurgy (6/83). *Version 2:* In the lower division baccalaureate/associate degree category, 3 semester hours in Metallurgy (9/86). NOTE: This course has been reevaluated and continues to meet requirements for credit recommendations.

Shop Theory/Materials and Processes
  Location: Rutland, VT.
  Length: *Version 1:* 49 hours (21 weeks). *Version 2:* 66 hours (20 weeks).
  Dates: *Version 1:* January 1977-January 1987. *Version 2:* February 1987-Present.
  Objective: To provide students with an in-depth exposure to processes and materials involved in manufacturing.
  Instruction: This course explores various processes of manufacturing such as casting, forging, and welding, including gas, arc, and resistance. Operations performed by lathes, mills, drills, and grinders are studied, and projects using those machines are completed. Material selection and planning for manufacturing operations are also included.
  Credit recommendation: *Version 1:* In the lower division baccalaureate/associate degree category, 4 semester hours in Manufacturing Processes (6/83). *Version 2:* In the lower division baccalaureate/associate degree category, 4 semester hours in Manufacturing Processes (9/86). NOTE: This course has been reevaluated and continues to meet requirements or credit recommendations.

Statics
(Formerly Applied Mechanics/Applied Strength of Materials)
  Location: Rutland, VT.
  Length: *Version 1:* 94 hours (36 weeks). *Version 2:* 51 hours (18 weeks).
  Dates: *Version 1:* January 1977-January 1987. *Version 2:* February 1987-Present.
  Objective: *Version 1:* To offer students an introduction to composition and resolution of forces as applied to trusses and machine parts. *Version 2:* To provide students a noncalculus-based presentation of planar and nonplanar force systems.
  Instruction: *Version 1:* Composition and resolution of forces, torsion, shear, and moment diagrams, stresses and deflections of beams are taught. *Version 2:* This course is a a noncalculus-based presentation of coplanar and noncoplanar force systems, including parallel, concurrent, and nonconcurrent. Friction is also introduced.
  Credit recommendation: *Version 1:* In the lower division baccalaureate/associate degree category, 3 semester hours in Introduction to Statics and Strength of Materials (6/83). *Version 2:* In the lower division baccalaureate/associate degree category, 3 semester hours in Statics (9/86). NOTE: This course has been reevaluated and continues to meet requirements for credit recommendations.

Statistics/Inspection Techniques
(Formerly Industrial Problem Solving/Statistics/Inspection Techniques)
  Location: Rutland, VT.
  Length: *Version 1:* 55 hours (29 weeks). *Version 2:* 57 hours (19 weeks).
  Dates: *Version 1:* January 1977-January 1987. *Version 2:* February 1987-Present.
  Objective: To provide an introduction to measurement and statistical sampling techniques.
  Instruction: This course provides an introduction to measurement techniques, including use of such instruments as graduated scales, gauge blocks, dial indicators, and verniers. Basic statistical sampling techniques, data analysis, and probability evaluation based on normal curve distribution are discussed.
  Credit recommendation: *Version 1:* In the lower division baccalaureate/associate degree category, 3 semester hours in Industrial Problem Solving. *Version 2:* In the lower division baccalaureate/associate degree category, 2 semester hours in Introduction to Quality Control (9/86). NOTE: This course has been reevaluated and continues to meet requirements for credit recommendations.

Strength of Materials
(Formerly offered as part of Statics/Applied Strength of Materials, outline above)
  Location: Rutland, VT.
  Length: *Version 1:* Not offered as separate course in Version 1. *Version 2:* 51 hours (18 weeks).
  Dates: *Version 1:* January 1977-January 1987. *Version 2:* February 1987-Present.
  Objective: To provide students with an algebra-based presentation of strength of materials.
  Instruction: An algebra-based presentation of strength of materials, including basic stress and strain, temperature stresses, torsion, centroids, moments of inertia, stresses and deflections of beams, statically indeterminate problems, combined stresses, and columns.
  Credit recommendation: *Version 1:* N/A (6/83). *Version 2:* In the lower division baccalaureate/associate degree category, 3 semester hours in Strength of Materials (9/86). NOTE: This course has been reevaluated and continues to meet requirements for credit recommendations.

Technical Mathematics
(Formerly Algebra/Trigonometry)
  Location: Rutland, VT.
  Length: *Version 1:* 93 hours (36 weeks). *Version 2:* 67 hours (25 weeks).
  Dates: *Version 1:* January 1977-January 1987. *Version 2:* February 1987-Present.
  Objective: To provide students with an understanding of the relation of mathematics to engineering applications and to help students develop an appreciation of the importance of precision in mathematical thought.

Instruction: This course includes the use of the pocket calculator, solution of linear and quadratic equations, exponents and radicals, logarithms, exponential functions, sine and cosine laws, binomial expansion and progressions, vectors, operations with imaginary and complex numbers, polar and rectangular coordinates, trigonometric identities and equations, and graphs of trigonometric functions.

Credit recommendation: *Version 1:* In the lower division baccalaureate/associate degree category, 5 semester hours in College Algebra and Trigonometry (6/83). *Version 2:* In the lower division baccalaureate/associate degree category, 5 semester hours in Technical Mathematics (9/86). NOTE: This course has been reevaluated and continues to meet requirements for credit recommendations.

Tool Design

Location: Rutland, VT.
Length: *Version 1:* 47 hours (18 weeks). *Version 2:* 51 hours (18 weeks).
Dates: *Version 1:* January 1977-January 1987. *Version 2:* February 1987-Present.
Objective: To help the student develop skills in design procedures, techniques, and practices related to tool making.
Instruction: Design procedure, techniques, and practices of tool making, cutting tools, drill jigs, and fixtures are studied. Locating and clamping, materials selection techniques, fixtures for numerically controlled machining are also presented. Design projects are completed in conjunction with the tool room.
Credit recommendation: *Version 1:* In the lower division baccalaureate/associate degree category, 3 semester hours in Tool Making (6/83). *Version 2:* In the lower division baccalaureate/associate degree category, 3 semester hours in Tool Making (9/86). NOTE: This course has been reevaluated and continues to meet requirements for credit recommendations.

MEDICAL EDUCATION PROGRAMS, MEDICAL SYSTEMS DIVISION

The Medical Systems Division, General Electric Company, manufactures and distributes equipment and provides services in the fields of radiology, computer tomography, nuclear medicine, ultrasound, monitoring, and dental radiography. The division headquarters, in Milwaukee, Wisconsin, is the center of educational activities.

Medical education programs are independent of the product line and are not involved with promotional activities or employee service training activities. The goal of the programs is to impart a large volume of information in a limited period of time. Students come from all areas of the medical field and have diverse backgrounds. Information that participants gain can be immediately applied in the clinical situation.

Source of official student records: Registry of Credit Recommendations, Office on Educational Credit and Credentials, American Council on Education, One Dupont Circle, Washington, D.C. 20036.

Additional information about the courses: Program on Noncollegiate Sponsored Instruction, The Center for Adult Learning and Educational Credentials, American Council on Education, One Dupont Circle, Washington, D.C. 20036.

Advanced Concepts in Nuclear Medicine

Location: Oconomowoc, WI; Las Vegas, NV.
Length: 41 hours (5 days).
Dates: August 1978-March 1982.
Objective: To present new and advanced technologies in nuclear medicine.
Instruction: Explains the dynamic vascular techniques used in organ evaluation.
Credit recommendation: In the upper division baccalaureate category, 2 semester hours in Advanced Nuclear Medicine Techniques and 1 semester hour in Techniques Seminar (8/79).

Basics of Nuclear Medicine

Location: Oconomowoc, WI; Las Vegas, NV.
Length: 91 hours (over 2 weeks).
Dates: February 1976-March 1982.
Objective: To impart the fundamental principles of nuclear medicine.
Instruction: A comprehensive program covering clinical hospital rotations, detector systems, equipment and health physics, history, mathematics, nuclear and atomic physics, quality control, radiation biology, radiation detectors, radiation units, radionuclide production, radiopharmaceuticals, regulatory control, and statistics of nuclear medicine. An introduction to computers, computerized tomography, nuclear dynamics, thermography, and radioimmunoassay ultrasound is included.
Credit recommendation: In the lower division baccalaureate/associate degree category or in the upper division baccalaureate category, 3 semester hours in Introduction to Nuclear Medicine (8/79).

Basics of Ultrasound

Location: Oconomowoc, WI; Las Vegas, NV.
Length: 37 hours (5 days).
Dates: January 1979-March 1982.
Objective: To impart basic principles of ultrasound including wave theory, generation frequency, transduction, and measurement; selected clinical applications of ultrasound equipment.
Instruction: Basic principles of ultrasound. Students are instructed in clinical procedures indications, contraindications, and techniques.
Credit recommendation: In the lower division bac-

calaureate/associate degree category or in the upper division baccalaureate category, 1 semester hour in Applied Physics (Sound), Biomedical Engineering, Electromechanical Laboratory, or Principles of Ultrasound Equipment (8/79).

Comprehensive Nuclear Medicine
  Location: Jacksonville, FL; Las Vegas, NV; various other locations in the U.S.
  Length: 30 hours (3 days).
  Dates: November 1979-March 1982.
  Objective: To cover the basic and advanced concepts of nuclear medicine.
  Instruction: A didactic overview of nuclear medicine principles, including health physics, instrumentation and procedures, mathematics, radiation biology, radiation physics, radioactive transmutation, units, radio pharmaceuticals.
  Credit recommendation: In the lower division baccalaureate/associate degree category, 1 semester hour in Introduction to Nuclear Medicine (8/79).

Computed Tomography Series
  Part 1: Principles of Computed Tomography
  Part 2: Quality Assurance in Computed Tomography
  Part 3: Quality Control in Computed Tomography
  Location: Oconomowoc, WI.
  Length: 1. 40 hours (5 days); 2. 24 hours (3 days); 3. 16 hours (2 days).
  Dates: June 1979-March 1982.
  Objective: To provide a fundamental understanding of principles of and quality control in computed tomography.
  Instruction: Basic radiography and computers, emphasizing computed tomography equipment, quality control, and quality assurance. Methodology includes audiovisual aids and limited laboratory observations.
  Credit recommendation: In the lower division baccalaureate/associate degree category or in the upper division baccalaureate category, 2 semester hours in Introduction to Radiography or electives in Advanced Radiographic Equipment. Part 1, when taken separately, 1 semester hour in Introduction to Radiography (8/79).

Dynamics in Nuclear Medicine
  Location: Oconomowoc, WI; Las Vegas, NV.
  Length: 30 hours (3 days).
  Dates: September 1979-March 1982.
  Objective: To teach specific advanced techniques of dynamics and the use of equipment involved in applying these techniques.
  Instruction: Advanced techniques in nuclear medicine, including angiography, cerebral dynamics, cardiac imaging and function studies, perfusion studies. Instruction about principles of the equipment and computers involved in these procedures is included.
  Credit recommendation: In the upper division baccalaureate category, 1 semester hour in Nuclear Medicine Seminar or Project and 1 semester hour in Advanced Nuclear Medicine Techniques (8/79).

Management Processes
  Location: Oconomowoc, WI; Las Vegas, NV.
  Length: 48 hours (5 days).
  Dates: October 1979-March 1982.
  Objective: To teach participants to use management techniques that can be applied to the work environment in decision analysis and problem analysis.
  Instruction: Focus on decision analysis, methods of handling complex situations, problem analysis, and supervisor and personnel problems. A combined lecture/discussion learning experience using the Kepner-Tregoe approach to problem solving.
  Credit recommendation: In the upper division baccalaureate category, 1 semester hour in Administration, Business, Health Administration, Hospital/Clinic Administration, Management, or Personnel Administration (8/79).

Nuclear Cardiology
  Location: Oconomowoc, WI; Las Vegas, NV.
  Length: 30 hours (3 days).
  Dates: November 1979-March 1982.
  Objective: To present principles and techniques of nuclear cardiology.
  Instruction: Injection techniques; dynamic flow studies; cardiac ejection fractions and their use in evaluation of function; output; wall motion; other aspects of the cardiovascular system.
  Credit recommendation: In the lower division baccalaureate/associate degree category or in the upper division baccalaureate category, 1 semester hour in Cardiovascular Anatomy or Cardiovascular Physiology, or a practicum in Nuclear Cardiology or Nuclear Medicine (8/79).

Nuclear Medicine Registration and Certification
  Location: Oconomowoc, WI; Las Vegas, NV; and various other locations in the U.S.
  Length: 45 hours (1 week).
  Dates: August 1978-March 1982.
  Objective: To cover the principles of nuclear medicine deemed essential for certified nuclear medicine technologists.
  Instruction: An overview of the major principles in nuclear medicine emphasizing mathematical computations and their application to the field of nuclear medicine.
  Credit recommendation: In the lower division baccalaureate/associate degree category, 1 semester hour in Medicine Mathematics or Seminar in Nuclear Medicine (8/79).

Principles of Cardiovascular Monitoring
  Location: Oconomowoc, WI; Las Vegas, NV.
  Length: 38 hours (5 days).
  Dates: October 1979-March 1982.
  Objective: To provide an understanding of the basic physiology of the heart, particularly in relation to basic and advanced life support and cardiovascular monitoring.
  Instruction: Principles of the cardiovascular system, including the common abnormal functions as indicated by cardiovascular monitoring systems; the origin and sequence of the electrocardiogram. Vascular pressures are discussed. Principles of cardiovascular monitoring devices are developed and explored from the viewpoint of the monitoring specialist. Includes instruction in basic electronic terminology, grounds, isolated circuits, leakage current, and basic mechanisms of monitoring. Lecture and discussion are used.
  Credit recommendation: In the lower division baccalaureate/associate degree category and in the upper division baccalaureate category, 1 semester hour in Clinical Medicine, Emergency Medicine, First Aid, or Health Education (8/79).

Quality Control and Compliance in Nuclear Medicine
  Location: Oconomowoc, WI; Las Vegas, NV.
  Length: 30 hours (3 days).
  Dates: October 1979-March 1982.
  Objective: To explain the procedures necessary for compliance with professional and government agencies.
  Instruction: Quality control as applied to radiopharmaceuticals, nuclear instrumentation, and nuclear procedures. Compliance techniques to meet and exceed the requirements of the Nuclear Regulatory Commission, Food and Drug Administration, Occupational Safety and Health Administration, and Joint Commission on Hospital Accreditation. Classroom lectures are used.
  Credit recommendation: In the lower division baccalaureate/associate degree category and in the upper division baccalaureate category, 1 semester hour in Nuclear Medicine Quality Control and Compliance or 1 semester hour in Radiation Safety (8/79).

Quality Control and Compliance in Ultrasound
  Location: Oconomowoc, WI; Las Vegas, NV.
  Length: 30 hours (3 days).
  Dates: October 1979-March 1982.
  Objective: To introduce basic quality control techniques consistent with requirements of the Bureau of Medical Devices, Bureau of Radiologic Health, Joint Commission on Hospital Accreditation, and National Electrical Manufacturers Association. Participants should be able to accurately analyze a quality control program.
  Instruction: An overview of basic principles of ultrasound followed by detailed presentations on quality control and compliance. Designed for health professionals who have previous knowledge about optimum image quality. Program is a three-day lecture course.
  Credit recommendation: In the lower division baccalaureate/associate degree category, 1 semester hour in Principles of Ultrasound Equipment (8/79).

Radioisotope Handlers
  Location: Oconomowoc, WI; Las Vegas, NV.
  Length: 30 hours (3 days).
  Dates: April 1979-March 1982.
  Objective: To provide the theoretical and practical knowledge necessary to respond to a variety of routine emergency radioisotope materials management situations in such a way as to comply with local and federal requirements.
  Instruction: A comprehensive three-day program designed for individuals who work with or around radioisotope sources, as well as those who supervise operations in which radioisotopes are involved. Basic principles of mathematics, physics, radiation biology, radioisotope chemistry instrumentation, radiation protection, and emergency procedures. Radiation protection includes the practical aspects of regulations, protection standards, surveys for exposure and contamination, and the handling of sealed and unsealed sources. Participants must complete mock manipulation, wipe testing, and exposure surveys. Leak testing wipes or smears as well as techniques for measurement will be completed by each member of the class.
  Credit recommendation: In the lower division baccalaureate/associate degree category or in the upper division baccalaureate category, 1 semester hour in Physics, Radiation Biology, Radiation Chemistry, Radiation Physics, or Radiation Safety (8/79).

Radiological Series
1. Introduction to Radiologic Techniques
2. Quality Assurance in Radiology
3. Radiology Registration and Certification
4. Standardization of Radiologic Techniques
5. Understanding X-Ray Generation
  Location: Oconomowoc, WI.
  Length: 1. 40 hours (5 days); 2. 40 hours (5 days); 3. 40 hours (5 days); 4. 24 hours (3 days); 5. 24 hours (3 days).
  Dates: October 1979-March 1982.
  Objective: To teach in coherent sequence the principles and procedures associated with the radiologic science area.
  Instruction: *Course 1:* A basic introductory program of classroom instruction designed for a rapid coverage of the basic scientific principles of radiology. Electronics, health physics, physics, radiation biology, X-ray emissions and techniques; introduction to special physiological and social problems associated with this field. Students will complete courses in chemistry, human anatomy, mathematics, and physiology. *Course 2:* A classroom and laboratory program designed to teach the theory and practice of

quality assurance in radiology. Covers Department of Health and Human Services requirements and the techniques for compliance with quality assurance criteria. Participants will learn how to use their equipment to make meaningful measurements of filtration, KVP, MA, time, and tube alignments. Collimator specifications and compliance will be developed. *Course 3:* Classroom presentation designed for rapid instruction in basic principles of radiological sciences. Darkroom chemistry, instrumentation, health physics, mathematics, physics, radiation biology, radiation physics, techniques, and exposure factors will be covered. Instruction will help participant prepare for examinations in radiology; each participant must complete multiple choice examination questions covering each area of study. Computed tomography, nuclear medicine, radiation therapy, and ultrasound will be reviewed in this program. *Course 4:* A classroom presentation developing the procedure for departmental standardization of techniques. Covers the basic concepts affecting the machine's output. Participants develop procedures that will allow an analysis of technique factors and how they change. With these data, participants develop a uniform program for standardization as suggested by the Joint Commission on Hospital Accreditation and the American College of Radiology. *Course 5:* A classroom didactic presentation designed for a comprehensive, up-to-date presentation of the principles of X-ray generation and their application. The generator, X-ray tube, controlling devices, and associated equipment will be covered, along with beam quality and quantity factors, pulse shape, three phases, types of targets, and output-heat unit curves.

Credit recommendation: *Course 1:* In the lower division baccalaureate/associate degree category, 2 semester hours in Radiology Sciences. *Course 2:* In the lower division baccalaureate/associate degree category, 2 semester hours in Radiology Sciences. *Course 3:* In the lower division baccalaureate/associate degree category, no credit is given. *Course 4:* In the lower division baccalaureate/associate degree category, 1 semester hour in Radiology Sciences. *Course 5:* In the lower division baccalaureate/associate degree category, 1 semester hour in Radiology Sciences.

Radiological Techniques in Dentistry

Location: Oconomowoc, WI; Omaha, NE; Las Vegas, NV.

Length: 30 hours (3 days).

Dates: September 1979-March 1982.

Objective: To cover the functional aspects of dental radiography.

Instruction: The principles of film processing and exposure techniques, health physics, radiation biology, and X-ray production will be covered, with an emphasis on the use of dental radiographic systems. The participants will be instructed on the use of collimation, filtration, and technique factors of KV, MA, and time as they relate to problems associated with dental radiography. Contrast, distortion, exposure factors, latitude, magnification, minification, quality assurance, quality control, and resolution will also be covered. Equipment selection and film processing techniques for dental radiography, operation, registration, and shielding are analyzed.

Credit recommendation: In the lower division baccalaureate/associate degree category and in the upper division baccalaureate category, 1 semester hour in Dental Assisting and Dental Hygiene (8/79).

RESEARCH AND ENGINEERING PROFESSIONAL DEVELOPMENT PROGRAM

The courses listed below are part of the Research and Engineering Professional Development Program conducted by General Electric's Re-Entry and Environmental Systems Division (RESD) at its offices in Philadelphia and neighboring locations. The courses are offered to employees of the division and are supervised and taught by qualified staff of RESD. Included below are courses of the centrally administered General Electric Financial Management Program (FMP). These courses are highly intensive and selective in admissions.

Source of official student records: Technical Director, Professional Development and Education Program, General Electric Company, Re-Entry and Environmental Systems Division, 3198 Chestnut Street, Philadelphia, Pennsylvania 19101. NOTE: Courses whose titles are followed by an asterisk are offered through Financial Management Program Administration, Corporate Financial Manpower Operation, General Electric Company, 3135 Easton Turnpike, Mail Drop W2A, Fairfield, Connecticut 06431.

Additional information about the courses: Program on Noncollegiate Sponsored Instruction, The Center for Adult Learning and Educational Credentials, American Council on Education, One Dupont Circle, Washington, D.C. 20036.

Advanced Computer Techniques
(Advanced Programming Techniques [C-235])

Location: Philadelphia and Valley Forge, PA.

Length: 30 hours (15 weeks).

Dates: February 1977-December 1985.

Objective: To provide advanced instruction on the efficient use of hardware and software to students familiar with basic programming.

Instruction: Text editing; time sharing; media conversion; magnetic tape contrasted with disc files; plotting; computer costs. Lecture and computer problem solving are used.

Credit recommendation: In the lower division baccalaureate/associate degree category, 2 semester hours in Computer Sciences (1/77).

Advanced Financial Accounting*
(Financial Accounting [FMP-102])
  Location: Philadelphia, PA.
  Length: 24 hours (12 weeks).
  Dates: January 1971-December 1985.
  Objective: To train students to apply basic accounting theories and techniques to balance-sheet accounts, studies, and special accounting problems.
  Instruction: All balance-sheet accounts; consolidated financial statements; foreign exchange accounting; fund flow/cash flow; federal, state, and local taxes. Involves lecture, discussion, and homework projects.
  Credit recommendation: In the upper division baccalaureate category, 3 semester hours in Accounting (1/77).

Auditing (FMP-301)*
  Location: Philadelphia, PA.
  Length: 26 hours (13 weeks).
  Dates: January 1969-December 1985.
  Objective: To enable participants to audit and evaluate accounting and management systems.
  Instruction: Principles and practices of auditing as applied to cash, receivables, inventory, plant and equipment, liabilities, net worth, and operations. Includes review of internal control systems. Involves lecture, discussion, and homework projects.
  Credit recommendation: In the upper division baccalaureate category, 3 semester hours in Accounting (1/77).

Basic Electronics (EE-115)
  Location: Philadelphia, PA.
  Length: 24 hours (12 weeks).
  Dates: September 1977-December 1985.
  Objective: To provide students with a basic understanding of the laws of electricity and magnetism, and to prepare the students for a more detailed course in the fundamentals of circuit design.
  Instruction: Physics associated with electrical technology; electrostatics and DC circuitry; electromagnetic effects; the theory of AC circuitry; application of electrical laws and principles. Includes detailed treatment of the functions and performance characteristics of common state-of-the-art electronic devices. More advanced topics, such as noise, transient effects, and instrumentation, are introduced and explained. Methodology includes lecture and laboratory.
  Credit recommendation: In the lower division baccalaureate/associate degree category, 2 semester hours in Electronics (1/77). NOTE: Recommendation does not apply to science and engineering majors.

Calculus I (AM-175)
  Location: Philadelphia, PA.
  Length: 30 hours (15 weeks).
  Dates: September 1976-December 1985.
  Objective: To provide a standard first-semester calculus course that would be useful to technicians pursuing undergraduate degrees.
  Instruction: Algebra, functions, limits, derivations, differentiation, application of the derivative, the definite integral, infinite limits and limits of sequences, exponential functions, logarithmic functions, trigonometric functions. Employs lecture and problem solving as homework and classwork.
  Credit recommendation: In the lower division baccalaureate/associate degree category, 3 semester hours in Mathematics (1/77). NOTE: Recommendation does not apply to science and engineering majors.

Calculus II (AM-275)
  Location: Philadelphia, PA.
  Length: 30 hours (15 weeks).
  Dates: September 1976-December 1985.
  Objective: To provide a standard second-semester calculus course that would be useful to technicians pursuing undergraduate degrees.
  Instruction: Inverse functions, finding antiderivatives, the definite integral, paths, infinite sequences and series, power series and polynomial approximation, vectors in the plane, functions of two variables. Employs lecture and problem solving as homework and classwork.
  Credit recommendation: In the lower division baccalaureate/associate degree category, 3 semester hours in Mathematics (1/77). NOTE: Recommendation does not apply to science and engineering majors.

College Math I (AM-172)
College Math II (AM-272)
  Location: Philadelphia, PA.
  Length: *Version 1:* 30 hours (15 weeks). *Version 2:* 45 hours (15 weeks).
  Dates: *Version 1:* September 1975-April 1978. *Version 2:* May 1978-December 1985.
  Objective: To provide a basic college freshman mathematics course that would be useful to technicians and others pursuing undergraduate degrees.
  Instruction: *Version 1:* Set theory, logic, number theory, algebra, geometry, trigonometry (2 hours only), matrices, probability and statistics, introduction to calculus and statistics. Method includes lecture and classroom and homework problem solving. *Version 2:* Set theory, logic, number systems, algebra, probability, statistics, matrices, game theory, computer applications, trigonometry, polynomials, factoring, quadratic equations, irrational equations, logarithms, calculus. Methodology includes lecture and classroom and homework problem solving.
  Credit recommendation: *Version 1:* In the lower division baccalaureate/associate degree category, 3 semester hours in Mathematics (1/77). NOTE: Recommendation does not apply to science and engineering majors. *Version*

2: In the lower division baccalaureate/associate degree category, 6 semester hours in Mathematics (5/78). NOTE: Recommendation does not apply to science and engineering majors.

Computer-aided Circuit Design and Analysis (EE-117)
 Location: Philadelphia and Valley Forge, PA.
 Length: 36 hours (12 weeks).
 Dates: September 1975-December 1985.
 Objective: To provide students with a working knowledge and understanding of the techniques of computer-aided circuit analysis.
 Instruction: The responses of semiconductors, integrated circuits, and discrete circuits to various frequency and time-varying stimuli are evaluated. Methods for describing the behavior of active nonlinear elements to the computer are explained and compared. Comparison between expected theoretical analysis and computed results is made. Limited studies of optimization and sensitivity analysis are covered. Methodology includes lecture, discussion, and laboratory.
 Credit recommendation: In the upper division baccalaureate category, 3 semester hours in Electrical Engineering as a professional elective (1/77).

Designing with Microprocessors (EE-213)
 Location: Philadelphia, PA.
 Length: 64 hours (16 weeks).
 Dates: September 1974-December 1985.
 Objective: To teach participants the fundamental theory of microcomputer architecture, to acquaint them with the state-of-the art of microprocessor hardware, and to give them experience in programming for microprocessor usage so that they can design actual subsystems.
 Instruction: Covers the theory and application of microprocessors in design. Data on currently available hardware are provided, and hands-on experience is obtained.
 Credit recommendation: In the lower division baccalaureate/associate degree category, 3 semester hours in Engineering (1/77).

Effective Management Planning (MT-105)
 Location: Philadelphia, PA.
 Length: 26 hours (13 weeks).
 Dates: February 1976-December 1985.
 Objective: To provide planning within organizations in order to broaden participants' understanding of the planning function.
 Instruction: Strategic, product, operational, program, engineering, and financial planning. Method includes lecture and case study. A history of the evolution of corporate planning and techniques for selling the plan are also included.
 Credit recommendation: In the upper division baccalaureate category, 2 semester hours in Management (1/77).

Information Systems (FMP-302)*
 Location: Philadelphia, PA.
 Length: 24 hours (12 weeks).
 Dates: January 1969-December 1985.
 Objective: To introduce planning and implementation of information systems from the management and business viewpoint.
 Instruction: Designing, programming, developing, and managing computer-based data systems for business and financial operations. Method includes lecture, discussion, and case study.
 Credit recommendation: In the lower division baccalaureate/associate degree category or in the upper division baccalaureate category, 2 semester hours in Computer and Information Science (1/77).

Introduction to Chemistry I (AC-181)
 Location: Philadelphia and King of Prussia, PA.
 Length: 60 hours (30 weeks).
 Dates: September 1975-December 1985.
 Objective: To provide students with an understanding of the basic concepts of chemistry and how these concepts relate to the materials and processes used in the aerospace industry.
 Instruction: Atomic theory and structure of compounds; oxygen, oxidation, and combustion; gas laws-hydrogen; molecules and molecular weights; general classification of compounds; classification of the elements; structure of the atom and the theory of valence; water; carbon; solutions and colloids; halogens; alkali metals; ionization; chemical equilibrium; nitrogen and ammonia. Method includes lecture and discussion.
 Credit recommendation: In the lower division baccalaureate/associate degree category, 2 semester hours in Chemistry (1/77). NOTE: Recommendation does not apply to science and engineering majors.

Introduction to Chemistry II (AC-281)
 Location: Philadelphia and King of Prussia, PA.
 Length: 60 hours (30 weeks).
 Dates: September 1975-December 1985.
 Objective: To provide students with an understanding of the basic concepts of chemistry and how these concepts relate to the materials and processes used in the aerospace industry.
 Instruction: The sulfur family, electrochemistry, organic chemistry, aliphatic hydrocarbons, olefins, free radicals, aromatic hydrocarbons, alcohols, phenols, ethers, halides, amines and derivatives, aldehydes, ketones, acids, polyfunctional compounds, organic polymers, carbohydrates, amino acids, peptides and proteins, biochemical reactions, biosynthesis, general biological reactions. Method includes lecture and discussion.
 Credit recommendation: In the lower division baccalaureate/associate degree category, 2 semester hours in Chemistry (1/77). NOTE: Recommendation does not ap-

ply to science and engineering majors.

Management Cost Accounting*
(Management Accounting [FMP-202])
   Location: Philadelphia, PA.
   Length: 34 hours (17 weeks).
   Dates: January 1971-December 1985.
   Objective: To provide students with an understanding of cost accounting as a quantitative device used by managers to select and research objectives.
   Instruction: General cost accounting concepts, job order costs, standard costs, process costs, direct costing, and government contract costing. Involves lecture, discussion, and homework projects.
   Credit recommendation: In the upper division baccalaureate category, 3 semester hours in Accounting (1/77).

Materials Engineering I (ME-121)
   Location: Valley Forge Space Center, Valley Forge, PA.
   Length: 60 hours (30 weeks).
   Dates: September 1974-December 1985.
   Objective: To provide students with an introduction to materials science.
   Instruction: Principles underlying structure, properties, and behavior of engineering materials, including metals, ceramics, and polymers. Bonding; crystal structure; defect structure; alloying; mechanical, electronic, and magnetic properties in relation to structure; phase equilibrium; phase transformation. Instruction is chiefly lecture.
   Credit recommendation: In the lower division baccalaureate/associate degree category, 3 semester hours in Engineering (1/77).

Probability Theory
(Probability Theory for Engineering Applications [AM-174])
   Location: Philadelphia, PA.
   Length: 32 hours (16 weeks).
   Dates: September 1977-December 1985.
   Objective: To establish a foundation in mathematical probability theory.
   Instruction: Basic mathematical probability theory with calculus; set theory as a basis for probability; probability axioms; the concept of a random variable; distributions, density functions, moments, and characteristic functions; conditional marginal and joint distributions; and functions of random variables. Lecture, discussion, and homework problems are used.
   Credit recommendation: In the upper division baccalaureate category, 3 semester hours in Mathematics (1/77).

Supervisory Development and Organization Renewal Workshop (MT-2020)
   Location: Philadelphia, PA.
   Length: 45-50 hours (16 sessions).
   Dates: September 1977-December 1985.
   Objective: To broaden the experienced supervisor's understanding of human behavior and of his or her impact on others; to improve supervisory skills and ability to influence the organizational environment through planned problem-solving strategies; to give the supervisor a greater sense of participation in the management process.
   Instruction: The course is divided into three major phases: theory, practices, and implementation and follow-up. Topics include motivation, transactional analysis, leadership styles, group dynamics, and problem solving. Students attend management training sessions and then apply their knowledge in identifying and solving problems in their work situations. Method emphasizes discussion and workshop.
   Credit recommendation: In the upper division baccalaureate category, 3 semester hours in Organizational Behavior/Management (1/77).

Survey of Accounting and Financial Techniques
(An Introduction to Finance [MT-202])
   Location: Philadelphia, PA.
   Length: 26 hours (13 weeks).
   Dates: February 1977-December 1985.
   Objective: To familiarize employees with the basic tools of accounting and financial management.
   Instruction: Basic accounting theory, cost accounting concepts, cost control, federal and state taxation, cash flow, budgeting government contracts, information systems. Method includes lecture, classroom discussion, and exercises.
   Credit recommendation: In the lower division baccalaureate/associate degree category, 2 semester hours in Business Administration (1/77). NOTE: This recommendation applies to nonbusiness curricula.

Survey of Topics in Structural Analysis
(Modern Structural Analysis I [ME-122])
   Location: Philadelphia and Valley Forge, PA.
   Length: 60 hours (30 weeks).
   Dates: September 1977-December 1985.
   Objective: To provide design engineers with a survey of selected topics in structural analysis.
   Instruction: Covers elastic analysis of indeterminate structures, using the finite element method. Provides an introduction to fracture mechanics and the analysis and design of composite materials. Lecture, discussion, and problem solving are employed.
   Credit recommendation: In the upper division baccalaureate category, 2 semester hours in Structural Engineering (1/77).

Value Engineering
(Value Analysis [MT-104 or MT-204])
  Location: Philadelphia and Valley Forge, PA.
  Length: 40 hours (13 weeks).
  Dates: February 1975-December 1985.
  Objective: To familiarize managers with the analysis and solution of engineering and organizational problems through the systematic implementation of value engineering principles.
  Instruction: History of value engineering/value analysis, job plan application, types of value, information phase, functional analysis, systems technique. Method includes lecture, discussion, and workshop.
  Credit recommendation: In the upper division baccalaureate category, 3 semester hours in Operations Management (1/77).

NOTE:

The General Electric courses in the programs that follow have been evaluated and recommended for credit by the New York Regents Program on Noncollegiate Sponsored Instruction. For additional information about these courses, contact the New York Regents Program on Noncollegiate Sponsored Instruction, Cultural Education Center, Empire State Plaza, Albany, New York 12230.

ADVANCED COURSE IN ENGINEERING

The Advanced Course in Engineering was originally established in 1923 to supply the General Electric Company with engineers who possessed sufficient breadth and depth of technical understanding to make basic contributions in the development of new or improved products. The objectives of the course are to provide the recent technical college graduate with
  the ability to identify and solve real engineering problems;
  competence in writing engineering reports;
  an understanding of the use and misuse of mathematical analysis and other ways of solving engineering problems;
  an understanding that the engineer's primary purpose is not mathematical virtuosity, but the improvement of methods and products.
  The Advanced Course is a three-year program consisting of the company-taught A-, B-, and C-courses, and periods of formal academic study on campus. The course material is continually reviewed, revised, and updated. It includes pertinent basics, state-of-the art analytical techniques, and topical emphasis relative to changing business needs and products. Graduates of the program earn the company's advanced course certificate.
  The A-course is taught with basic uniformity at the General Electric locations at which it is conducted, and the credit recommendation for that course applies to all those locations. The B- and C-courses treat subject areas that have special applications to each plant, and the credit recommendations established for those two courses apply only to the locations indicated.
  Source of official student records: Manager, Advanced Courses, General Electric Company, 29ESE, Bridgeport, Connecticut 06602.
  Additional information about the courses: New York Regents Program on Noncollegiate Sponsored Instruction, Cultural Education Center, Empire State Plaza, Albany, New York 12230.

A-Course
  Location: Various company locations throughout the U.S. and Canada.
  Length: 136 hours (34 weeks); approximately 680 hours are devoted to problem solving outside of class.
  Dates: January 1965-Present.
  Objective: To develop the ability to solve engineering development and design problems.
  Instruction: Engineering analysis (application of mathematical techniques to many technical areas). Vibrational analysis, E&M fields, control theory, probability and random variables, heat transfer, structure analysis. Assigned problems support the classwork, are completed outside the class, and are submitted to the instructor for review.
  Credit recommendation: In the graduate degree category, 12 semester hours in Engineering Analysis or Engineering Science (or 4 semester hours in Applied Mathematics) (6/75). NOTE: The course is broadly interdisciplinary in nature and may not be sufficiently specialized for full credit in highly specialized degree programs.

B-Course
  Location: Aerospace Control Systems Department, Binghamton, NY (1/70-12/74 only); Aerospace Electronics Systems Department, Utica, NY; Military Electronic Systems Operations, Syracuse, NY.
  Length: *Version 1:* 64 hours (16 weeks); approximately 320 hours are devoted to problem solving outside of class. *Version 2:* 112 hours (28 weeks); approximately 480 hours are devoted to problem solving outside of class. *Version 3:* 124 hours (31 weeks); approximately 465 hours are devoted to problem solving outside of class. *Version 4:* 92 hours (23 weeks); approximately 345 hours are devoted to problem solving outside of class.
  Dates: *Version 1:* January 1970-December 1975. *Version 2:* January 1976-December 1979. *Version 3:* January 1980-December 1980. *Version 4:* January 1981-Present.
  Objective: To teach classical communications theory with emphasis on selected current engineering problems.
  Instruction: *Versions 1, 2, 3, and 4:* Amplitude, frequency, and digital modulation schemes; information theory; hypothesis testing; parametric estimation. Kalman filtering and radar design. Assigned problems support the classwork, are completed outside of class, and are submitted to the instructor for review. *Version 2, 3, and 4:* Also

include probability theory and stochastic processes, Hilbert transforms and complex envelope, extended information theory concepts, electro-optics, statistical detection theory, sonar techniques, electronic countermeasures.

Credit recommendation: *Version 1:* In the graduate degree category, 6 semester hours in Communications Theory and Systems (6/75). *Versions 2 and 3:* In the graduate category, 12 semester hours in Communications Theory and Systems (8/76). *Version 4:* In the graduate degree category, 9 semester hours in Communications Theory and Systems (9/81).

C-Course
Location: Aerospace Control Systems Department, Binghamton, NY (1/70-12/74 only); Aerospace Electronic Systems Products Department, Utica, NY; Military Electronic Systems Operations, Syracuse, NY.
Length: *Version 1:* 128 hours (32 weeks); approximately 480 hours are devoted to problem solving outside of class. *Version 2:* 92 hours (23 weeks); approximately 345 hours are devoted to problem solving outside of class.
Dates: *Version 1:* January 1970-December 1979. *Version 2:* January 1980-Present.
Objective: To teach classical control theory, digital controls, optimal control, and computer applications and systems.
Instruction: Classical controls, optimal control, digital signal processing, linear programming, dynamic programming, numerical methods, calculus of variations, integral equations, Markov processes, queuing theory, digital design, microprocessors, computer systems. Assigned problems support the classwork, are completed outside of class, and are submitted to the instructor for review.
Credit recommendation: *Version 1:* In the graduate degree category, 12 semester hours in Electrical Engineering (or 10 semester hours in Computer Science) (6/75). *Version 2:* In the graduate degree category, 9 semester hours in Electrical Engineering (or 7 semester hours in Computer Science) (9/81).

CONTINUING EDUCATION PROGRAM

The courses listed below are part of the Continuing Education Program which is conducted at many General Electric plants, including the following locations in New York State: Auburn, Binghamton, Brockport, Hudson Falls, Schenectady, Syracuse, and Utica.

The courses are offered to General Electric employees wishing to add to or reinforce their knowledge of the field of manufacturing. The courses cover such topics as mathematics, manufacturing management, and computers.

Please note that the credit recommendations apply to *all* locations where the program is conducted.

Source of official student records: Manufacturing Education Representative in the plant where the courses were completed; or Corporate Engineering and Manufacturing, Technical Education Operation, General Electric Company, 9285 Boston Avenue, (29EE), Bridgeport, Connecticut 06601.

Cases in Manufacturing Management (AMS 303)
Location: General Electric plants: Auburn, Hudson Falls, Schenectady, Syracuse, and Utica, NY; locations throughout the U.S. and overseas.
Length: 20 hours (10 weeks).
Dates: January 1965-Present.
Objective: To introduce the student to the various problems resulting from the interaction of manufacturing management with the other functional areas of the firm.
Instruction: A case-study approach is used to deal with manufacturing and business management problems. Discussion of each case to identify the real problem or problems and the important considerations involved. Each case is an actual situation in which a manufacturing problem is interrelated with one or more of the other key business functions (marketing, engineering, finance, relations). Involves applications of concepts covered in Basic Manufacturing Studies courses.
Credit recommendation: In the upper division baccalaureate category, 1 semester hour in Manufacturing Management (2/75).

GESIMTEL (Simulation with Teleprocessing) (AMS 311)
Location: General Electric plants: Auburn, Hudson Falls, Schenectady, Syracuse, and Utica, NY; locations throughout the U.S. and overseas.
Length: 24 hours (8 weeks).
Dates: January 1973-Present.
Objective: To provide the student with a background in general purpose system simulation and its application.
Instruction: A study of computer simulation techniques. The GESIMTEL system; modeling methods; control language; I/O format; debugging; applications to algebraic and probabilistic problems.
Credit recommendation: In the lower division baccalaureate/associate degree category or in the upper division baccalaureate category, 2 semester hours in Business Administration or Computer Science (2/75).

Mathematical Methods and Models
1. Advanced Methods and Models (AMS 152)
2. Basic Mathematics (AMS 151)
Location: General Electric plants: Auburn, Hudson Falls, Schenectady, Syracuse, and Utica, NY; locations throughout the U.S. and overseas.
Length: 1. 18 hours (9 weeks); 2. 16 hours (8 weeks).
Dates: January 1965-Present.
Objective: To provide the student with basic mathematical background and skills needed in creating mathematical models and in simulating systems.
Instruction: Introduction to descriptive statistics; re-

view of high school algebra; introduction to calculus and partial derivatives; elements of matrices; language of set theory; compound interest; simulation; linear programming; multiple regression.

Credit recommendation: In the lower division baccalaureate/associate degree category or in the upper division baccalaureate category, 2 semester hours in Business Administration or Economics (2/75).

Probabilistic Models (AMS 154)
  Location: General Electric plants: Auburn, Hudson Falls, Schenectady, Syracuse, and Utica, NY; locations throughout the U.S. and overseas.
  Length: 16 hours (8 weeks).
  Dates: January 1965-Present.
  Objective: To introduce the student to statistical and probabilistic ideas through Markov and stochastic processes with application to queuing theory.
  Instruction: Basic ideas of probability; binomial and geometric distribution; Markov processes, uniform and normal distribution; Monte Carlo method, queuing theory, decision models and metamathematics; statistics (means, variances, and correlation coefficients).
  Credit recommendation: In the upper division baccalaureate category, 1 semester hour in Business Administration or Economics (2/75).

Regression Analysis (AMS 320)
  Location: General Electric plants: Bethesda, MD; Schenectady, NY; Wilmington, NC.
  Length: 24 hours (12 weeks).
  Dates: January 1969-May 1980.
  Objective: To provide the student with applied knowledge of basic regression models.
  Instruction: Simple linear regression model, multiple regression models, least-squares method of estimating the parameters of the models, interpretation of computer output.
  Credit recommendation: In the upper division baccalaureate category, 1 semester hour in Business Administration or Economics (2/75).

Statistical Inference (AMS 153)
  Location: General Electric plants: Auburn, Hudson Falls, Schenectady, Syracuse, and Utica, NY; locations throughout the U.S. and overseas.
  Length: 16 hours (8 weeks).
  Dates: January 1965-Present.
  Objective: To provide the student with a background in statistical inference for computer applications.
  Instruction: Background in statistical inference involving numerical data. Statistical populations, principles of sampling, statistical estimation, quantitative conclusions, statistical decisions.
  Credit recommendation: In the upper division baccalaureate category, 1 semester hour in Business Administration or Mathematics (2/75).

FIELD ENGINEERING PROGRAM

The courses listed below are part of the Field Engineering Program (Mechanical). The Program was established in 1966 by the Installation and Service Engineering Division. Its purpose is to prepare individuals who have a sound academic and practical background for the position of Field Engineer or Field Representative. Persons holding these positions provide field engineering services on power generation equipment: gas and steam turbines, turbogenerators, and marine propulsion machinery. Services include technical direction of installation, start-up, emergency repairs, and maintenance; and project planning and management for all aspects of the work. Courses are conducted at the Field Engineering Development Center in Schenectady, New York.

Source of official student records: Manager, Internal Technical Training (Mechanical), Field Engineering Development Center, General Electric Company, 2690 Balltown Road, Schenectady, New York 12309.

Applied Electrical Principles
  Location: Field Engineering Development Center, Schenectady, NY.
  Length: 60 hours (4 weeks).
  Dates: January 1979-Present.
  Objective: To provide an understanding of the practical application of electrical engineering principles to rotating machinery, related equipment, and systems, with particular emphasis on applications to gas turbines and steam turbines.
  Instruction: Review of basic electrical theory; electrical meters and measurement; electrical diagrams; motor controls, installation, and maintenance; electrical construction practices; electrical control equipment; electrical safety; large generator construction and operation. Laboratory sessions focus on AC and DC circuits, measuring instruments, and motor controls.
  Credit recommendation: In the upper division baccalaureate category, 3 semester hours in Electrical Measurements Laboratory (2/79). NOTE: A student should complete either Gas Turbine Technology or Steam Turbine Technology to receive credit for this course.

Applied Mechanical Principles
  Location: Field Engineering Development Center, Schenectady, NY.
  Length: 80 hours (4 weeks).
  Dates: January 1979-Present.
  Objective: To provide an understanding of the practical application of mechanical engineering principles as they apply to rotating machinery, related equipment, and systems, with particular emphasis on applications to gas turbines and steam turbines.

Instruction: Interpretation of engineering drawings, techniques in project planning, use of precision measuring instruments, alignment techniques, threaded fasteners, piping, gears, welding procedures and techniques, nondestructive testing, techniques in lifting and rigging, hydraulic controls.

Credit recommendation: In the lower division baccalaureate/associate degree category, 4 semester hours in Mechanical Engineering Laboratory (2/79). NOTE: A student should complete either Gas Turbine Technology or Steam Turbine Technology to receive credit for this course.

Gas Turbine Technology
Location: Field Engineering Development Center, Schenectady, NY.
Length: 200 hours (5 weeks); additional one-week field trip.
Dates: January 1979-Present.
Objective: To develop an understanding of the fundamental principles of gas turbine design, construction, operation, and maintenance.
Instruction: Gas turbine theory and component functions; gas turbine auxiliary systems; gas turbine installation; gas turbine controls, start-up, and operation; gas turbine maintenance. Lectures are supplemented by laboratory sessions and field trips. Prerequisites: Applied Electrical Principles and Applied Mechanical Principles.
Credit recommendation: In the upper division baccalaureate category, 5 semester hours in Gas Turbine Technology (3 lecture, 2 laboratory) (2/79). NOTE: In addition to submitting an official student record, the Field Engineering Training Center should submit a copy of the student's Field Engineering Program Performance Evaluation before a college grants credit for this course.

Steam Turbine Technology
Location: Field Engineering Development Center, Schenectady, NY.
Length: 240 hours (6 weeks); additional one-week field trip.
Dates: January 1979-Present.
Objective: To develop an understanding of the fundamental principles of steam turbine design, construction, operation, and maintenance.
Instruction: Steam turbine theory and component functions; steam turbine auxiliary systems; steam turbine installations; steam turbine controls, start-up, and operation; steam turbine maintenance. Lectures are supplemented by laboratory sessions and field trips. Prerequisites: Applied Electrical Principles and Applied Mechanical Principles.
Credit recommendation: In the upper division baccalaureate category, 6 semester hours in Steam Turbine Technology (4 lecture, 2 laboratory) (2/79). NOTE: In addition to submitting an official student record, the Field Engineering Development Center should submit a copy of the student's Field Engineering Program Performance Evaluation before a college grants credit for this course.

OTHER ENGINEERING COURSES

Abnormal Event Analysis (8470)
Location: General Electric Training Facility, San Jose, CA; customer sites.
Length: 40 hours (1 week).
Dates: April 1981-Present.
Objective: To enable the participant to identify, classify, and assess abnormal events and accidents in a boiling water reactor plant, with emphasis on mitigation and recovery.
Instruction: Level instrumentation; nuclear system pressure increase events; moderator temperature decrease events; positive reactivity insertion events; loss of feedwater events; core flow decrease events; core flow increase events; loss of coolant accidents; anticipated transient without scram; containment response; emergency procedure guidelines.
Credit recommendation: In the upper division baccalaureate category, 1 semester hour in Engineering or Engineering Technology (5/82).

Boiling Water Reactor Chemistry (8510)
Location: General Electric Vallecitos Nuclear Center, Pleasanton, CA.
Length: 480 hours (12 weeks).
Dates: May 1972-Present.
Objective: To provide the participant with the knowledge necessary to understand, analyze, and exercise control over the chemistry and radiochemistry of a boiling water reactor.
Instruction: Calibration and use of counting instrumentation, including liquid scintillation systems, high resolution gamma spectrometry, and alpha-beta proportional counters; process radiation monitors; radiochemical separation procedures and techniques; atomic absorption spectroscopy; spectrophotometry; activity balances; gaseous waste analysis; liquid waste release; cleanup systems. Integrated laboratory exercises.
Credit recommendation: In the upper division baccalaureate category, 6 semester hours (4 lecture, 2 laboratory) in Chemistry, Engineering, or Engineering Technology; or in the graduate degree category, 3 semester hours in Chemistry or Engineering (5/82).

Boiling Water Reactor Chemistry for Shift Technical Advisors (8535)
Location: General Electric Vallecitos Nuclear Center, Pleasanton, CA; customer sites.
Length: 40 hours (1 week).
Dates: April 1980-Present.
Objective: To provide the participant with an introduc-

tion to the chemistry of boiling water reactors, basic cause and effect chemical relationships, and laboratory counting and process monitoring systems.

Instruction: Plant chemistry; process radiation monitors; sampling; data logging; ion exchange; cleanup systems; gaseous waste analysis. No laboratory work is included.

Credit recommendation: In the lower division baccalaureate/associate degree category, 1 semester hour in Engineering Technology (5/82).

Boiling Water Reactor Chemistry for Technicians (8520)
   Location: General Electric Vallecitos Nuclear Center, Pleasanton, CA; customer sites.
   Length: 240 hours (6 weeks).
   Dates: January 1979-Present.
   Objective: To develop the participant's proficiency in techniques for radiochemical and chemical analyses of liquids and gases associated with the operation of a boiling water reactor.
   Instruction: Sample collection and preparation; atomic absorption and spectrophotometric analyses; radiochemical separations; radiation detection and measurement.
   Credit recommendation: In the lower division baccalaureate/associate degree category, 2 semester hours in Chemistry, Engineering, or Engineering Technology (5/82).

Core Management Engineering (8450)
   Location: General Electric Training Facility, San Jose, CA; customer sites.
   Length: 120 hours (3 weeks).
   Dates: November 1979-Present.
   Objective: To provide the participant with an understanding of the concepts and techniques of boiling water reactor core management.
   Instruction: Core thermal limits; fuel and exposure accounting; core component lifetime; core design; control rod pattern and sequence development; fuel cycle analysis; fuel performance; operating strategies; cycle extensions.
   Credit recommendation: In the upper division baccalaureate category, 2 semester hours in Engineering or Engineering Technology (5/82). NOTE: Credit award for this course should be reduced to 1 semester hour if credit has already been awarded for Station Nuclear Engineering (8410).

1. Corrosion in Boiling Water Reactors (8455)
2. Nuclear Materials (8445)
   Location: General Electric Training Facility, San Jose, CA; customer sites.
   Length: 1. 20 hours (2 1/2 days); 2. 20 hours (2 1/2 days).
   Dates: April 1981-Present.
   Objective: *Course 1:* To provide the participant with the principles of corrosion as they apply to the design and operation of a boiling water reactor. *Course 2:* To provide the participant with the principles of metal properties and failure mechanisms.
   Instruction: *Course 1:* Economics of corrosion; corrosion fundamentals; corrosion in boiling water reactors; metallurgical factors; testing for, and mitigation of, stress corrosion. *Course 2:* Uniaxial stress and strain; plastic flow and fracture; mechanisms of flow and fracture in metals; time-dependent deformation processes; fracture toughness; radiation effects.
   Credit recommendation: In the upper division baccalaureate category or in the graduate degree category, 1 semester hour in Engineering (5/82). NOTE: Courses 1 and 2 must *both* be completed to receive credit.

Degraded Core Training, Part I (8480)
   Location: General Electric Training Facility, San Jose, CA; customer sites.
   Length: 20 hours (2 1/2 days).
   Dates: May 1981-Present.
   Objective: To enable the participant to recognize conditions associated with inadequate core cooling and core degradation in boiling water reactors.
   Instruction: Heat sources; gas generation; core cooling mechanisms; fuel and core damage threshold; recognition of inadequate core cooling conditions.
   Credit recommendation: In the lower division baccalaureate/associate degree category, 1 semester hour in Engineering or Engineering Technology (5/82).

Engineering Fundamentals (8435)
   Location: General Electric Training Facility, San Jose, CA; customer sites.
   Length: 40 hours (1 week).
   Dates: March 1981-Present.
   Objective: To introduce the participant to the fundamentals of thermodynamics, heat transfer, and fluid flow.
   Instruction: Elementary thermodynamics; elementary heat transfer; fluid statics; fluid dynamics.
   Credit recommendation: In the lower division baccalaureate/associate degree category, 1 semester hour in Engineering or Engineering Technology (5/82).

Fundamentals of Nuclear Engineering (8460)
   Location: General Electric Training Facility, San Jose, CA; customer sites.
   Length: 120 hours (3 weeks).
   Dates: September 1980-Present.
   Objective: To provide the participant with a basic understanding of reactor physics and thermal-hydraulics related to core power response.
   Instruction: Reactor functions; thermal-hydraulics; core reactivity; nuclear instrumentation; process computer; fuel management.
   Credit recommendation: In the upper division bac-

calaureate category, 3 semester hours in Engineering or Engineering Technology; or in the graduate degree category, 2 semester hours in Engineering (5/82). NOTE: Credit should *not* be awarded for this course if it has already been awarded for Nuclear Engineering for Operators, Station Nuclear Engineering (8410), or Station Nuclear Engineering Refresher (8420).

Health Physics and Radiological Emergencies (8560)
 Location: General Electric Vallecitos Nuclear Center, Pleasanton, CA; customer sites.
 Length: 40 hours (1 week).
 Dates: August 1981-Present.
 Objective: To provide the participant with a working knowledge of health physics and radiation protection, with emphasis on emergency situations.
 Instruction: Radiation fundamentals; sources of radioactivity in a boiling water reactor; biological effects of radiation; radiation protection regulations; radiation detection instruments; operational health physics; radiological emergencies.
 Credit recommendation: In the upper division baccalaureate category, 1 semester hour in Engineering, Engineering Technology, Health Physics, or related sciences (5/82).

Health Physics Technology (8555)
 Location: General Electric Vallecitos Nuclear Center, Pleasanton, CA; customer sites.
 Length: 120 or 160 hours (3 or 4 weeks).
 Dates: January 1976-Present.
 Objective: To provide the participant with an understanding of the basic principles of radiation and radioactive decay; to provide the participant with a working knowledge of radiation protection principles, techniques, and procedures.
 Instruction: Radioactivity and radiation; radiation interaction with matter; biological effects of radiation; radiation detection principles and instruments; Federal regulations and guides; contamination control.
 Credit recommendation: In the upper division baccalaureate category, 3 semester hours in Engineering, Engineering Technology, Health Physics, or related sciences (5/82).

Nuclear Engineering for Operators
 Location: General Electric Training Facility, San Jose, CA; customer sites.
 Length: 40 hours (1 week).
 Dates: January 1982-Present.
 Objective: To familiarize the participant with the basic engineering aspects of reactor physics and thermal-hydraulics related to core power response.
 Instruction: Thermal-hydraulics; core power response; thermal limits; core reactivity and control; process computer applications.
 Credit recommendation: In the lower division baccalaureate/associate degree category, 1 semester hour in Engineering or Engineering Technology (5/82). NOTE: Credit should *not* be awarded for this course if it has already been awarded for Fundamentals of Nuclear Engineering (8460), Station Nuclear Engineering (8410), or Station Nuclear Engineering Refresher (8420).

Nuclear Materials (8445)
 SEE Corrosion in Boiling Water Reactors (8455).

Radiological Engineering (8550)
 Location: General Electric Vallecitos Nuclear Center, Pleasanton, CA.
 Length: 320 hours (8 weeks).
 Dates: March 1978-Present.
 Objective: To provide the participant with a detailed understanding of nuclear science and radiation measurement methods; to provide the participant with practical experience in radiation protection programs for nuclear power reactors.
 Instruction: Radiation fundamentals; external gamma and beta dosimetry; biological effects of radiation; internal contamination and dosimetry; health physics instrumentation; Federal regulations and guides; contamination control; radiation monitoring; radiation exposure control; boiling water reactor health physics operation; environmental monitoring; meteorology; boiling water reactor accident analysis. Integrated laboratory and practical exercises.
 Credit recommendation: In the upper division baccalaureate category, 6 semester hours (3 lecture, 3 laboratory) in Engineering, Engineering Technology, Health Physics, or related sciences; or in the graduate degree category, 3 semester hours in Engineering, Health Physics, or related sciences (5/82).

Station Nuclear Engineering (8410)
 Location: General Electric Training Facility, San Jose, CA; customer sites.
 Length: 160 or 200 hours (4 or 5 weeks).
 Dates: January 1976-Present.
 Objective: To provide the participant with a basic understanding of reactor physics, chemistry, and thermal-hydraulics related to core power response, with emphasis on assessment and optimization of core performance.
 Instruction: Reactor physics; thermal-hydraulics; core reactivity; nuclear instrumentation; boiling water reactor chemistry; process computer; fuel management; plant operating strategy.
 Credit recommendation: In the upper division baccalaureate category, 4 semester hours in Engineering or Engineering Technology; or in the graduate degree category, 3 semester hours in Engineering (5/82).

Station Nuclear Engineering Refresher (8420)
 Location: General Electric Training Facility, San Jose,

CA; customer sites.
  Length: 80 hours (2 weeks).
  Dates: September 1980-Present.
  Objective: To review the basic principles of reactor physics, chemistry, and thermal-hydraulics related to core power response, with emphasis on assessment and optimization of core performance.
  Instruction: Selected topics in reactor physics, thermal-hydraulics, core reactivity, nuclear instrumentation, boiling water reactor chemistry, process computer, fuel management, and plant operating strategy.
  Credit recommendation: In the upper division baccalaureate category, 2 semester hours in Engineering or Engineering Technology (5/82). NOTE: Credit should *not* be awarded for this course if it has already been awarded for Fundamentals of Nuclear Engineering (8460), Nuclear Engineering for Operators, or Station Nuclear Engineering (8410).

INSTRUMENTATION AND CONTROL COURSES

Feedwater Control
  Location: General Electric Training Facility, San Jose, CA; customer sites.
  Length: 40 hours (1 week).
  Dates: August 1981-Present.
  Objective: To familiarize the participant with the theory and operation of feedwater control in boiling water reactors.
  Instruction: Feedback amplifier concepts; principle of automatic control; level theory; feedwater control system theory; instrumentation functions.
  Credit recommendation: In the lower division baccalaureate/associate degree category, 1 semester hour in Engineering or Engineering Technology (5/82). NOTE: No more than 3 credits in Engineering should be awarded for any combination of this course and GE MAC 5000 Instrumentation (8650), Process Instrumentation and Control (8630), and Recirculation Flow Control (8635).

GE MAC 5000 Instrumentation (8650)
  Location: General Electric Training Facility, San Jose, CA; customer sites.
  Length: 40 hours (1 week).
  Dates: August 1979-Present.
  Objective: To provide the participant with a review of the principles of automatic control systems; to familiarize the participant with maintenance requirements and system drawings of the GE MAC 5000 process instrumentation system.
  Instruction: Control system principles; GE MAC 5000 instrumentation, including control units, transmitters, power supplies, alarm units, function generators, recorders, and converters.
  Credit recommendation: In the lower division baccalaureate/associate degree category, 1 semester hour in Engineering or Engineering Technology (5/82). NOTE: No more than 3 credits in Engineering should be awarded for any combination of this course and Feedwater Control, Process Instrumentation and Control (8630), and Recirculation Flow Control (8635).

Nuclear Instrumentation (8610)
  Location: General Electric Training Facility, San Jose, CA.
  Length: 200 hours (5 weeks).
  Dates: January 1978-Present.
  Objective: To enable the participant to demonstrate an understanding of generic and specific power plant nuclear instrumentation systems; to enable the participant to demonstrate the ability to test, calibrate, and troubleshoot representative instruments.
  Instruction: Principles of nuclear radiation detector operation; start-up range monitoring system; traversing in-core probe system; process radiation monitoring systems.
  Credit recommendation: In the upper division baccalaureate category, 3 semester hours in Engineering; or in the upper division baccalaureate category, 4 semester hours in Engineering Technology (5/82).

Process Instrumentation and Control (8630)
  Location: General Electric Training Facility, San Jose, CA.
  Length: 160 hours (4 weeks).
  Dates: June 1977-Present.
  Objective: To familiarize the participant with specific nuclear power plant instrumentation and control systems and their maintenance requirements.
  Instruction: Fundamentals of automatic process control; Bailey signal conditioners; temperature, pressure, flow, and level control theory.
  Credit recommendation: In the lower division baccalaureate/associate degree category, 3 semester hours in Engineering or Engineering Technology (5/82). NOTE: No more than 3 credits in Engineering should be awarded for any combination of this course and Feedwater Control, GE MAC 5000 Instrumentation (8650), and Recirculation Flow Control (8635).

Recirculation Flow Control (8635)
  Location: General Electric Training Facility, San Jose, CA.
  Length: 120 hours (3 weeks).
  Dates: August 1979-Present.
  Objective: To familiarize the participant with the theory and operation of recirculation flow control systems in boiling water reactors, and to enable the participant to inspect and calibrate related equipment.
  Instruction: Operational amplifier theory; Foxboro operational amplifier calibration; recirculation system description and control; Modicon programmable controller operation and control.

Credit recommendation: In the lower division baccalaureate/associate degree category, 2 semester hours in Engineering or Engineering Technology (5/82). NOTE: No more than 3 credits in Engineering should be awarded for any combination of this course and Feedwater Control, GE MAC 5000 Instrumentation (8650), and Process Instrumentation and Control (8630).

Rod Control and Information System (8625)
Location: General Electric Training Facility, San Jose, CA.
Length: 320 hours (8 weeks).
Dates: January 1979-Present.
Objective: To familiarize the participant with a specific nuclear power plant instrumentation and control system based on digital logic; to enable the participant to perform circuit analysis, tests, and troubleshooting on the BWR/6 rod control and information system.
Instruction: Presentation of detailed information on BWR/6 rod drive control system digital logic, transponder functions, circuit analysis of specific circuit cards, and testing of transponders and circuit cards.
Credit recommendation: In the upper division baccalaureate category, 3 semester hours in Engineering; or in the upper division baccalaureate category, 5 semester hours in Engineering Technology (5/82). NOTE: Credit should *not* be awarded for this course if it has already been awarded for Rod Drive Control System (8620).

Rod Drive Control System (8620)
Location: General Electric Training Facility, San Jose, CA.
Length: 200 hours (5 weeks).
Dates: January 1981-Present.
Objective: To familiarize the participant with BWR/5 nuclear power plant rod drive control systems and their maintenance requirements.
Instruction: Description of the rod drive control system, rod sequence control system, rod position information system, and the rod worth minimizer for BWR/5 plants.
Credit recommendation: In the upper division baccalaureate category, 3 semester hours in Engineering; or in the upper division baccalaureate category, 4 semester hours in Engineering Technology (5/82). NOTE: Credit should *not* be awarded for this course if it has already been awarded for Rod Control and Information System (8625).

MANAGEMENT PROBLEMS ANALYSIS PROGRAM

The courses listed below constitute the Management Problems Analysis (MPA) Program. It is an 11-month program designed to teach modern quantitative techniques and to effectively apply those methods to the analysis of business problems and to the subsequent decision-making process.

Each student completes all eight modules which make up the program during the course of the 11 months. Each program participant is required to attend classroom instruction, and to write seven reports which describe his or her application of newly learned techniques to specific on-the-job problems. At the end of the program, the student is required to submit a major project, which usually involves another 60 hours of independent study.

Since its inception in 1962, MPA has been offered at 21 GE locations, and since 1973 has been offered at the following ten locations: Chicago, Illinois; Evendale, Ohio; Fort Wayne, Indiana; Louisville, Kentucky; Lynn, Massachusetts; Milwaukee, Wisconsin; Philadelphia, Pennsylvania; Pittsfield, Massachusetts; Schenectady, New York; and Valley Forge, Pennsylvania. The credit recommendations listed below apply to all locations where the program has been offered since 1973.

Source of official student records: Manufacturing Education Representative in the plant where the courses were completed; or Corporate Engineering and Manufacturing, Technical Education Operation, General Electric Company, 1285 Boston Avenue (29EE), Bridgeport, CT 06601.

Economic Analysis of Alternatives
Location: Various General Electric locations.
Length: 24 hours.
Dates: January 1973-Present.
Objective: To provide the student with an appreciation of the time value of money and its effect on the decision-making process.
Instruction: The effects of time on the economic analysis of alternatives. Concepts of compound interest, present value analysis and internal rate of return, the effect of taxes and depreciation on cash flows.
Credit recommendation: In the graduate degree category, 1 semester hour in Business Administration or Engineering Management (2/75).

GESIMTEL (Simulation with Teleprocessing)
Location: Various General Electric locations.
Length: 24 hours.
Dates: January 1973-Present.
Objective: To provide the student with practical background in using General Purpose System Simulator (GPSS) and its application in graphical data analysis and statistical inference.
Instruction: Background in GESIMTEL and its applications. The GESIMTEL system, modeling techniques, computer I/O formats, histograms, probability plots, crossplots, applications to manufacturing information systems (marketing, engineering, and finance).
Credit recommendation: In the graduate degree category, 2 semester hours in Business Administration or Engineering Management (2/75).

Introduction to Probability Theory and Descriptive Statistics
  Location: Various General Electric locations.
  Length: 18 hours.
  Dates: January 1973-Present.
  Objective: To provide the student with basic probabilistic concepts and skills in combinatorial computations and an understanding of and skill in using frequency distribution.
  Instruction: Basic probability theory (sets, sample space, events, symbolic probabilities, probability computations, probability trees, combinatorial computations); frequency distribution; grouping of individual data; histograms and frequency polygons; calculation of mean, variance, and standard deviation; uniform and normal distribution.
  Credit recommendation: In the graduate degree category, 1 semester hour in Business Administration, Economics, or Engineering Management (2/75).

Modeling
  Location: Various General Electric locations.
  Length: 36 hours.
  Dates: January 1973-Present.
  Objective: To provide the student with a first simulation experience and to provide the student with some basic discrete and continuous probability distributions.
  Instruction: Introduction to modeling and use of random numbers; Bernoulli processes; Poisson processes; Bayesian inference. In particular, the binomial, geometric, Pascal, Poisson, exponential, and gamma distributions. Applications to queuing theory, inventory, and man/machine mixture problems.
  Credit recommendation: In the graduate degree category, 2 semester hours in Business Administration, Economics, or Engineering Management (2/75).

Operations Research and Applications Training
  Location: Various General Electric locations.
  Length: 45 hours.
  Dates: January 1973-Present.
  Objective: To familiarize the student with quantitative models useful for decision making and the steps involved in incorporating these into a business strategy.
  Instruction: A series of mathematical models and techniques useful in decision making. Linear programming models, PERT/CPM, forecasting techniques, the learning curve, reliability concepts. Discussion involving the development of skills in planning decision making strategies and presenting conclusions and recommendations is included.
  Credit recommendation: In the graduate degree category, 3 semester hours in Business Administration or Engineering Management (2/75).

Regression Analysis
  Location: Various General Electric locations.
  Length: 39 hours.
  Dates: January 1973-Present.
  Objective: To provide the student with applied knowledge of linear statistical models.
  Instruction: Applied linear statistical models dealing with simple and multiple regression models and analysis of variance models. Least squares method, simple and multiple Rho-square polynomial regression models, stepwise procedures, multicolinearity, computer application, ANOVA with one- and two-variable models, cross and nested models, various designs of experiment. No calculus background is assumed.
  Credit recommendation: In the graduate degree category, 3 semester hours in Business Administration, Economics, or Industrial Engineering (2/75).

Statistical Inference
  Location: Various General Electric locations.
  Length: 30 hours.
  Dates: January 1973-Present.
  Objective: To provide the student with applied knowledge of various statistical inference methods.
  Instruction: Statistical inference methods dealing with estimation of mean, difference between two means, variance, ratio of variances (hypothesis testing and confidence interval methods); Goodness of Fit test; graphical data analysis.
  Credit recommendation: In the graduate degree category, 2 semester hours in Business Administration, Economics, or Engineering Management (2/75).

Time-Sharing System and Applications
  Location: Various General Electric locations.
  Length: 18 hours.
  Dates: January 1973-Present.
  Objective: To provide the student with background in BASIC programming techniques and their applications to management problem analysis programs.
  Instruction: Background in time-sharing systems and applications. Flowcharting, BASIC language coding, editing, debugging, file organization subroutine, GE Mark III time-sharing system principles and operations, statistical analysis program packages. Hands-on applications, problem solving, and project design are emphasized.
  Credit recommendation: In the graduate degree category, 1 semester hour in Business Administration, Computer Science, or Engineering Management (2/75).

MANUFACTURING STUDIES PROGRAM

The courses listed below are part of a two-year integrated curriculum called the Manufacturing Studies Program. Each course meets for two hours per week after working hours. Two courses are taken concurrently from September to June. The Program is conducted at many GE plants including the following locations in New York State: Auburn, Binghamton, Brockport, Hudson Falls, Schenectady, Syracuse, and Utica.

The general objective of the program is to provide an opportunity for individuals capable of college-level work to further develop knowledge and technical abilities applicable in such fields as manufacturing supervision, materials management, manufacturing engineering, quality control, information systems, and employee relations. The program is designed for engineers, specialists, supervisors, and managers.

Because of the modular structure of the curriculum, the courses have been grouped together in order to establish appropriate credit recommendations. While credit recommendations have been made for each separate group of courses, when awarding credit particular consideration should be given to those who have completed the total program.

Please note that the credit recommendations listed below apply to all GE locations where the program is offered.

Source of official student records: Manufacturing Education Representative in the plant where the courses were completed; or Corporate Engineering and Manufacturing, Technical Education Operation, General Electric Company, 1285 Boston Avenue (29EE), Bridgeport, CT 06601.

Computer Programming and Data Analysis (Unit I)
1. **Data Analysis and Probability Evaluation (MFG 220)**
2. **Introduction to Computers (MFG 111 or 111B)**
3. **Manufacturing Information Systems (MFG 211)**

   Location: General Electric plants: Auburn, Hudson Falls, Schenectady, Syracuse, and Utica, NY; locations throughout the U.S. and overseas.
   Length: 1. 24 hours (12 weeks); 2. 20 hours (10 weeks); 3. 20 hours (10 weeks).
   Dates: September 1965-Present.
   Objective: To provide an introduction to basic concepts in computer programming and statistical analysis.
   Instruction: Characteristics and limitations of computers; use of FORTRAN and BASIC programming language in solving problems; introductory statistical concepts (measures of central tendency and variability, statistical inference, discrete sampling distributions, and correlations analysis).
   Credit recommendation: In the upper division baccalaureate category, 3 semester hours in Computer Programming and Data Analysis (2/74).

Industrial Engineering (Unit II)
1. **Manufacturing Materials and Processes (MFG 108)**
2. **Product Engineering (MFG 250)**

   Location: General Electric plants: Auburn, Hudson Falls, Schenectady, Syracuse, and Utica, NY; locations throughout the U.S. and overseas.
   Length: 1. 24 hours (12 weeks); 2. 10 hours (5 weeks).
   Dates: September 1965-Present.
   Objective: To provide the student with knowledge of manufacturing processes and the product engineering function.
   Instruction: Study of manufacturing processes and the product engineering function. Introduction to productivity and total design, casting processes, basic machinery and metal forming processes, metal joining processes; use of excellent problems treating these topics. Brief treatment of the type of work involved in designing a product and the impact of the design phase on the manufacturing function, engineering data base, and product documentation.
   Credit recommendation: In the upper division baccalaureate category, 3 semester hours in Industrial Engineering (2/74).

Managerial Accounting and Cost Analysis (Unit III)
1. **Economic Analysis of Alternatives (MFG 130)**
2. **Introduction to Accounting Principles (MFG 25)**
3. **Operating Costs, Budgets, and Measurements (MFG 125)**

   Location: General Electric plants: Auburn, Hudson Falls, Schenectady, Syracuse, and Utica, NY; locations throughout the U.S. and overseas.
   Length: 1. 24 hours (12 weeks); 2. 6 hours (3 weeks); 3. 20 hours (10 weeks).
   Dates: September 1965-Present.
   Objective: To provide an introduction to basic accounting concepts and principles.
   Instruction: Basic introduction to accounting concepts and principles with strong emphasis on managerial use of accounting information. Introduction to accounting statements and principles; brief treatment of statement preparation, T-accounts, ledger and journal entries; introduction to cost concepts and analysis, incremental and sunk costs, and budgeting: capital budgeting (discounted cash flows, tax considerations, and alternative equipment replacement policies).
   Credit recommendation: In the upper division baccalaureate category, 3 semester hours in Managerial Accounting and Cost Analysis (2/74).

Manufacturing Management (Unit IV)
1. **Manufacturing Engineering (MFG 204)**
2. **Materials Management (MFG 215)**
3. **Quality Control (MFG 217)**

   Location: General Electric plants: Auburn, Hudson Falls, Schenectady, Syracuse, and Utica, NY; locations throughout the U.S. and overseas.
   Length: 1. 24 hours (12 weeks); 2. 24 hours (12 weeks); 3. 24 hours (12 weeks).
   Dates: September 1965-Present.
   Objective: To provide an introduction to manufacturing management.

Instruction: Introduction to management problems in designing and controlling production systems; methods for designing a production process (preparation of plant layouts, job designs, production standards, and assembly line balances); study of the problems of planning and controlling production (forecasting demand, inventory control, production scheduling, and purchasing and traffic management); procedures for organizing the quality control function in manufacturing and the statistical control of product quality variables.

Credit recommendation: In the upper division baccalaureate category, 3 semester hours in Manufacturing Management (2/74).

Personnel Administration (Unit V)
1. **Employee Relations in Manufacturing (MFG 105)**
2. **Individual and Group Relations on the Job (MFG 102)**
3. **Manufacturing Organization and Supervision (MFG 101)**

Location: General Electric plants: Auburn, Hudson Falls, Schenectady, Syracuse, and Utica, NY; locations throughout the U.S. and overseas.

Length: 1. 16 hours (8 weeks); 2. 24 hours (12 weeks); 3. 16 hours (8 weeks).

Dates: September 1965-Present.

Objective: To provide knowledge of the organization and management of a firm.

Instruction: General approach to the organization and management of a firm; special emphasis on the engineering-type organizations and the interpersonal relationships which exist and operate in such an institution; specific aspects of the personnel function; general areas of motivation, organization behavior, and manpower planning.

Credit recommendation: In the upper division baccalaureate category, 3 semester hours in Personnel Administration (2/74).

OPERATOR TRAINING COURSES

BWR Hot License Qualification (8140)
Location: General Electric BWR Operator Training Center, Morris, IL.
Length: 96 hours (2 weeks).
Dates: January 1982-Present.
Objective: To provide the participant with a working knowledge of boiling water reactor control room operations and procedures.
Instruction: Practical simulator exercises in normal operation and routine testing; anticipated abnormal conditions; postulated emergency sequences.
Credit recommendation: In the upper division baccalaureate category, 2 semester hours in Engineering Technology (6/82). NOTE: Credit should *not* be awarded for this course if it has already been awarded for BWR Operator Training (8120) or BWR/6 Operator Training (8220).

BWR Observation Training (8335)
Location: Various utility sites.
Length: 160 hours (4 weeks).
Dates: May 1980-Present.
Objective: To provide the participant with a working knowledge of boiling water reactor systems integration and procedures through plant observation, lectures, and discussions.
Instruction: Lectures on, and observation of, plant systems and layout, routines and procedures during normal and abnormal operation and surveillance, and organizational responsibilities and activities.
Credit recommendation: In the upper division baccalaureate category or in the graduate degree category, 1 semester hour in Engineering; or in the upper division baccalaureate category, 2 semester hours in Engineering Technology (6/82). NOTE: Credit should *not* be awarded for this course if it has already been awarded for BWR Operator Training (8120).

BWR Operator Training (8120)
Location: General Electric BWR Operator Training Center, Morris, IL.
Length: 368 hours (9 weeks).
Dates: January 1976-Present.
Objective: To provide the participant with a working knowledge of boiling water reactor systems integration and procedures through simulator exercises, plant observation, lectures, and discussions.
Instruction: Practical simulator exercises in normal operation and routine testing; anticipated abnormal conditions; postulated emergency sequences; plant observation of operational and safety systems, including layout.
Credit recommendation: In the upper division baccalaureate category or in the graduate degree category, 3 semester hours in Engineering; or in the upper division baccalaureate category, 5 semester hours in Engineering Technology (6/82). NOTE: Credit should *not* be awarded for this course if it has already been awarded for BWR Hot License Qualification (8140), BWR Observation Training (8335), or BWR/6 Operator Training (8220).

BWR/6 Operator Training (8220)
Location: General Electric BWR Operator Training Center, Tulsa, OK.
Length: 320 hours (9 weeks).
Dates: May 1980-Present.
Objective: To provide the participant with a working knowledge of boiling water reactor (BWR/6) control room operations and procedures.
Instruction: Practical simulator exercises in normal operation and routine testing; anticipated abnormal conditions; postulated emergency sequences.
Credit recommendation: In the upper division bac-

calaureate category or in the graduate degree category, 2 semester hours in Engineering; or in the upper division baccalaureate category, 4 semester hours in Engineering Technology (6/82). NOTE: Credit should *not* be awarded for this course if it has already been awarded for BWR Hot License Qualification (8140) or BWR Operator Training (8120).

1. BWR Technology (8330)
2. BWR Technology (8331)
 Location: *Course 1:* General Electric BWR Operator Training Center, Morris, IL; General Electric BWR Operator Training Center, Tulsa, OK; customer sites. *Course 2:* General Electric BWR Operator Training Center, Morris, IL.
 Length: 1. 200 hours (5 weeks); 2. 120 hours (3 weeks).
 Dates: August 1975-Present.
 Objective: To provide the participant with a working knowledge of the design objectives and physical operation of boiling water reactor systems.
 Instruction: *Course 1:* Reactor vessel and internals; fuel; coolant, control, safety, and balance-of-plant systems; plant operating principles. *Course 2:* Reactor vessel and internals; fuel; coolant, control, safety, and balance-of-plant systems; system operating principles.
 Credit recommendation: *Course 1:* In the upper division baccalaureate category or in the graduate degree category, 3 semester hours in Engineering; or in the upper division baccalaureate category, 5 semester hours in Engineering Technology (6/82). *Course 2:* In the upper division baccalaureate category or in the graduate degree category, 2 semester hours in Engineering; or in the upper division baccalaureate category, 3 semester hours in Engineering Technology (6/82).

General Motors Corporation

General Motors (GM) manufactures and markets automotive products through a network of independently owned dealerships that covers the United States and Canada.

General Motors offers management, technical, and special courses on a corporation-wide basis and for individual units of the corporation and their dealerships. In 1976, the training function was administratively reorganized. The former Education and Training Department is now divided into three separate units: Continuing Engineering Education, Education and Training, and Marketing Educational Services.

The headquarters for the three units is in Flint, Michigan, and uses the facilities of the General Motors Institute, a 4-year accredited institution which is a wholly owned subsidiary of the GM Corporation.

CONTINUING ENGINEERING EDUCATION

This unit conducts engineering/technical courses for plant and division personnel. The courses listed below are conducted in Flint, Michigan, and at plant locations throughout the corporation. Instructional staff are drawn primarily from the faculty of the General Motors Institute.

Source of official student records: Director, Continuing Engineering Education, General Motors Institute, 1700 West Third Avenue, Flint, MI 48502.

Additional information about the courses: Program on Noncollegiate Sponsored Instruction, The Center for Adult Learning and Educational Credentials, American Council on Education, One Dupont Circle, Washington, D.C. 20036.

Design of Computerized Real-Time Data Acquisitions, and Process Control Systems (0221)
(Formerly Computer Process Control [0221])
 Location: General Motors, Flint, MI.
 Length: 48 hours (5 days); residential.
 Dates: May 1971-April 1980.
 Objective: To provide knowledge and experience in the application of minicomputers to machine and industrial processes.
 Instruction: Considers process computer concepts, including data acquisition, control computations, and output actuation for real-time systems. Input/output devices, software program implementation, detailed considerations for the computerized control of small manufacturing processes. Emphasis on practical, hands-on experience.
 Credit recommendation: In the upper division baccalaureate category, 2 semester hours in Engineering or Engineering Technology (7/75).

Engineering Economy Analysis of Plant Projects
(Formerly Engineering Economy [0293])
 Location: General Motors, Flint, MI, and plant locations.
 Length: 80 hours (10 days); residential.
 Dates: February 1966-September 1977.
 Objective: To present methods and develop expertise for evaluating the economic aspects of engineering decisions.
 Instruction: The development of evaluation and decision criteria for an engineering approach to economic evaluation. Depreciation practices, alternative comparisons, economic life studies, tax implications, retirement and replacement studies, structuring for economic improvement. Case study examples are used.
 Credit recommendation: In the upper division baccalaureate category, 2 semester hours in Engineering or Engineering Technology (7/75).

**Introduction to Data Sampling and Analysis
(Quality Control and Industrial Statistics I [0201])**
　　Location: General Motors, Flint, MI, and plant locations.
　　Length: 80 hours (2 weeks); residential.
　　Dates: January 1974-April 1980.
　　Objective: To introduce students to methods of sampling in the manufacturing environment so they can gather, reduce, and evaluate data for quality control purposes.
　　Instruction: Introduction to probability and probability density functions; histogram construction; mean and variance estimation; use of control and defect charts; performing process capability studies; use of AOQ and AOQL sampling methods. Lectures and problem sessions are used.
　　Credit recommendation: In the lower division baccalaureate/associate degree category, 3 semester hours in Engineering or Engineering Technology (7/75).

**Introduction to Human Performance
(Human Performance [0272])**
　　Location: General Motors, Flint, MI.
　　Length: *Version 1:* 80 hours (10 days); residential; *Version 2:* 40 hours (1 week); residential.
　　Dates: *Version 1:* February 1966-September 1977. *Version 2:* May 1979-April 1980.
　　Objective: To relate the psychological and physical attributes of people to system design and performance evaluation.
　　Instruction: Introduction to various human attributes as they relate to the industrial setting. Human information processing and coding, vision and light, hearing and noise, motivational aspects of work, anthropometry, fatigue, job enrichment, accident characteristics. Lectures and discussions are used.
　　Credit recommendation: In the lower division baccalaureate/associate degree category, 2 semester hours in Engineering or Management (7/75).

**Introduction to Industrial Statistics
(Quality Control and Industrial Statistics II [0202])**
　　Location: General Motors, Flint, MI, and plant locations.
　　Length: 80 hours (10 days); residential.
　　Dates: May 1972-April 1980.
　　Objective: To introduce the student to basic statistical concepts necessary for analysis of quality and/or engineering problems.
　　Instruction: Empirical distributions, hypothesis testing, point and interval estimating, analysis of variance, simple and multiple regression models, design of experiments, optimal sampling techniques. Lectures and problem sets are used extensively.
　　Credit recommendation: In the upper division baccalaureate category, 3 semester hours in Engineering or Engineering Technology (7/75).

Introduction to Minicomputer Programming (0223)
　　Location: General Motors, Flint, MI.
　　Length: 48 hours (5 days); residential.
　　Dates: May 1971-April 1980.
　　Objective: To provide an introduction to minicomputer hardware and software with the major emphasis on programming.
　　Instruction: Machine organization, specifications, and operating characteristics from the user point of view. Assembly-level programming; debugging; flow charting; software aids. Emphasis is on laboratory hands-on experience.
　　Credit recommendation: In the lower division baccalaureate/associate degree category or in the upper division baccalaureate category, 2 semester hours in Engineering, Engineering Technology, or Machine Technology (7/75).

Methods Analysis and Basic Time Study (0273)
　　Location: General Motors, Flint, MI, and plant locations.
　　Length: 76 hours (10 days); residential.
　　Dates: September 1968-April 1980.
　　Objective: To provide people working in methods and time study departments with a working knowledge of techniques and methodologies necessary to evaluate and improve industrial operations.
　　Instruction: Review of the classic procedures necessary to perform both methods analysis and time studies. Evaluation of worker motion patterns; activity breakdowns; work flow and process analysis; statistics of time studies; human relations; time study methods; delay allowances; human performance factors; engineering economy in man-machine systems. Lectures and laboratory sessions are used along with a manual.
　　Credit recommendation: In the upper division baccalaureate category, 3 semester hours in Engineering or Engineering Technology (7/75).

Noise Control (0213)
　　Location: General Motors, Flint, MI.
　　Length: 40 hours (5 days); residential.
　　Dates: November 1964-April 1980.
　　Objective: To provide engineers with contemporary knowledge of concepts, techniques of measurement, and interpretation of data related to noise.
　　Instruction: Introduction to noise and acoustical physics; OSHA and GM noise regulation procedures; hearing physiology and audiometric testing; machine and equipment noise abatement specifications; architectural physics; noise measurement and control concepts and methods; vibration analysis. Lectures, seminars, and laboratory exercises are used.
　　Credit recommendation: In the upper division baccalaureate category, 2 semester hours in Engineering (7/75).

Nondestructive Evaluation (0252)
Location: General Motors, Flint, MI, and plant locations.
Length: 40 hours (5 days) residential; *or* 40 hours (10 weeks) with weekly sessions.
Dates: January 1970-April 1980.
Objective: To provide process and design engineers, vendor source inspectors, and reliability and quality control personnel with an understanding of the fundamentals of nondestructive evaluation methods.
Instruction: Study of the nondestructive evaluation methods with emphasis on radiography, ultrasonics, eddy currents, acoustical emission, holography, and stress analysis techniques. Principles of each test method are identified and the advantages and limitations indicated. Laboratory exercises illustrate the fundamental concepts discussed in the classroom and provide an opportunity to work on practical inspection problems.
Credit recommendation: In the lower division baccalaureate/associate degree category or in the upper division baccalaureate category, 2 semester hours in Engineering Technology or Manufacturing Engineering (7/75).

Plant Layout and Materials Handling (0274)
Location: General Motors, Flint, MI.
Length: 80 hours (2 weeks); residential.
Dates: December 1964-April 1980.
Objective: To develop a working knowledge of the fundamentals of plant layout and material handling and provide an ability to recognize and solve related problems involving planning, design, operation, and control of space and equipment.
Instruction: Introduction to the basic concepts involved in the analysis and solution of plant layout and material handling problems. Graphical layout techniques, travel charting, block area diagramming, computer simulations. Workshop projects provide an opportunity to relate the theories to the solution of practical problems. Plant visitations allow observation of the principles in practice.
Credit recommendation: In the upper division baccalaureate category, 3 semester hours in Architectural Science or Engineering (7/75).

Project Management Using Network Planning Techniques (0292)
(Formerly Critical Path Planning [0292])
Location: General Motors, Flint, MI, and plant locations.
Length: 40 hours (5 days); residential.
Dates: October 1968-April 1980.
Objective: To acquaint students with the use of critical path planning methods in the analysis of typical industrial situations.
Instruction: The course introduces and demonstrates the use of CPM in several industrial problems. Network diagramming, time compression methods, Gantt charting, use of computer algorithms, PERT. Methodology includes lectures and problem sessions.
Credit recommendation: In the upper division baccalaureate category, 2 semester hours in Engineering, Engineering Technology, or Management (7/75).

Reliability Engineering (0205)
Location: General Motors, Flint, MI, and plant locations.
Length: *Version 1:* 40 hours (5 days); residential. *Version 2:* 24 hours (3 days); residential.
Dates: *Version 1:* April 1972-May 1979. *Version 2:* May 1979-April 1980.
Objective: To explore the concepts of reliability, focusing on the prediction and analysis of product failures and using the methods of probability.
Instruction: Survey of reliability analysis includes a review of probability, distribution functions, and the three areas of reliability. Techniques are developed for life test design, evaluation, and reliability prediction using the Weibull and other distributions. Includes applications and examples.
Credit recommendation: In the upper division baccalaureate category, 1 semester hour in Engineering or Engineering Technology (7/75).

Resistance Welding (0237)
(Formerly Spot and Projection Welding)
Location: General Motors, Flint, MI, and plant locations.
Length: 40 hours (5 days); residential; *or* 40 hours (10 weeks) with weekly sessions.
Dates: October 1969-April 1980.
Objective: To provide welding supervisors, welder repairmen, process engineers, and quality control personnel with an understanding of the fundamentals of resistance welding processes.
Instruction: Study of resistance welding processes with considerable emphasis on spot and projection applications. Treatment of material properties; weld quality considerations; welding fixtures; production schedules; safety requirements. Laboratory exercises augment classroom discussions and provide an opportunity to solve practical manufacturing problems.
Credit recommendation: In the lower division baccalaureate/associate degree category or in the upper division baccalaureate category, 2 semester hours in Engineering Technology or Manufacturing Engineering (7/75).

EDUCATION AND TRAINING

The management courses listed below are offered to plant and division management in Flint, MI, and four field centers: Buffalo, NY; Indianapolis, IN; Dayton, OH; and

Detroit, MI.

Source of official student records: Director, Education and Training, General Motors Corporation, 1700 West Third Avenue, Flint, MI 48502.

Additional information about the courses: Program on Noncollegiate Sponsored Instruction, The Center for Adult Learning and Educational Credentials, American Council on Education, One Dupont Circle, Washington, D.C. 20036.

Basic Management for First-Line Supervisors - Engineering/Technical (0004)

  Location: General Motors, Flint, MI; field centers.

  Length: 40 hours (5 days); 6 hours of preparatory independent study.

  Dates: September 1974-April 1980.

  Objective: To examine and develop fundamental skills in technical staff supervision.

  Instruction: Basic financial management (return on investment); human behavior as it relates to small-group performance; communication in conflict resolution; the supervision of technical staff. Methodology includes participant involvement in a series of management simulation exercises related to the work environment.

  Credit recommendation: In the lower division baccalaureate/associate degree category, 3 semester hours in Management (4/75).

Basic Management for First-Line Supervisors in Manufacturing (0003)

  Location: General Motors, Flint, MI; field centers.

  Length: 40 hours (5 days); 6 hours of preparatory independent study.

  Dates: September 1974-April 1980.

  Objective: To examine and develop the fundamental skills of plant supervision.

  Instruction: Basic financial management (manufacturing costs), human behavior as it relates to job performance, communication in conflict resolution, application of performance analysis concepts. Methodology includes participant involvement in a series of management simulation exercises related to the work environment.

  Credit recommendation: In the lower division baccalaureate/associate degree category, 3 semester hours in Management (4/75).

Basic Management for First-Line Supervisors of Salaried Employees (0005)

  Location: General Motors, Flint, MI; field centers.

  Length: 40 hours (5 days); 6 hours of preparatory independent study.

  Dates: November 1974-April 1980.

  Objective: To examine and develop the fundamental skills of office supervision.

  Instruction: Basic financial management (return on investment), human behavior as it relates to job performance, communication in conflict resolution, employee performance management (including management by objectives). Methodology includes participant involvement in a series of management simulation exercises.

  Credit recommendation: In the lower division baccalaureate/associate degree category, 3 semester hours in Management (4/75).

Intermediate Management for General Supervisors in Manufacturing (0010)

  Location: General Motors, Flint, MI; field centers.

  Length: 42 hours (5 days); 6 hours of preparatory independent study.

  Dates: December 1974-April 1980.

  Objective: To provide second-level supervisors with the knowledge and skills necessary to manage foremen in plant operations.

  Instruction: Analysis and improvement of human performance, the relationship of managerial behavior to employee performance, utilization of the problem-solving process. Methodology includes case studies, role play, personal assessment using video replay, and analysis.

  Credit recommendation: In the upper division baccalaureate category, 3 semester hours in Management or Organizational Behavior (4/75).

Intermediate Management for General Supervisors of Salaried Employees (0011)

  Location: General Motors, Flint, MI; field centers.

  Length: 42 hours (5 days); 6 hours of preparatory independent study.

  Dates: December 1974-April 1980.

  Objective: To provide the second-level supervisor with the knowledge and skills necessary to manage salaried supervisors in nonmanufacturing operations.

  Instruction: Analysis and improvement of human performance, the relationship of managerial behavior to employee performance, utilization of the problem-solving process. Methodology includes case studies, role play, personal assessment using video replay, and analysis.

  Credit recommendation: In the upper division baccalaureate category, 3 semester hours in Management or Organizational Behavior (4/75).

General Motors Corporation - Technical Staffs Group and Lansing Automotive Division (Formerly Advanced Engineering Staff [AES])

The Education Program is tailored to promote the GM mission by maintaining a learning culture which promotes creativity, fosters investigation and encourages open-minded and creative ideas.

Courses are offered to all levels of the staff by a wide range of educational sources with an emphasis on graduate-level engineering curricula that may be taken for degree credit.

The Education Program includes a Certificate in Advanced Engineering coupled with a Purdue University master's degree, a Certificate of Doctoral Studies in Engineering coupled with a University of Michigan (Ann Arbor) Ph.D. in Mechanical Engineering or Electricl Engineering and Computer Science, and a Certificate in Advanced Technology coupled with a Wayne State University bachelor's degree.

Courses listed below are offered at the GM Technical Center in Warren, Michigan; the Milford Proving Ground in Milford, Michigan, and the Lansing Engineering Center in Lansing and Troy, Michigan.

Source of official student records: Education Program Administrator, General Motors Technical Center, Warren, Michigan 48090-9040.

Additional information about the courses: Program on Noncollegiate Sponsored Instruction, The Center for Adult Learning and Educational Credentials, American Council on Education, One Dupont Circle, Washington, D.C. 20036.

Advanced Artificial Intelligence
Location: General Motors Technical Center, Warren, MI.
Length: 36 hours (12 weeks, 3 hours per week).
Dates: January 1986-Present.
Objective: To provide an understanding of advanced topics in Artificial Intelligence and Expert Systems.
Instruction: Topics include natural language processing, word expert theory, computer vision, and learning systems.
Credit recommendation: In the graduate degree category, 2 semester hours in Electrical, Mechanical, or Manufacturing Engineering, or Computer Science (6/86).

Advanced Computer Graphics and Computer Aided Design
Location: General Motors Technical Center, Warren, MI.
Length: 45 hours (15 weeks, 3 hours per week).
Dates: September 1986-Present.
Objective: To provide intense coverage of advanced topics in Computer Graphics and Computer Aided Design.
Instruction: Course covers review of CAD software packages. Emphasis on raster graphics. Design of applications programs.
Credit recommendation: In the graduate degree category, 3 semester hours in Electrical, Mechanical, or Manufacturing Engineering (6/86).

Advanced Finite Element Methods
Location: General Motors Technical Center, Warren, MI.
Length: 45 hours (15 weeks, 3 hours per week).
Dates: January 1986-Present.
Objective: To provide engineers with tools to analyze the more common types of vibratory and nonlinear problems with MSC/NASTRAN.
Instruction: The course covers special matrices, nonlinear equation solvers, optimal dynamic design and transient heat conduction.
Credit recommendation: In the graduate degree category, 3 semester hours in Mechanical Engineering (6/86).

Advanced Robotic Systems
Location: General Motors Technical Center, Warren, MI.
Length: 45 hours (15 weeks, 3 hours per week).
Dates: September 1986-Present.
Objective: To provide advanced developments in robotics from a system standpoint.
Instruction: Course covers robot geometries and dynamics; vision, robot selection, and implementation of industrial robots, as well as robot work cell design.
Credit recommendation: In the graduate degree category, 3 semester hours in Industrial, Mechanical, or Manufacturing Engineering (6/86). NOTE: Course is not to be taken for credit by one who has already had Analytical Methods in Robotics.

Analytical Methods in Robotics
Location: General Motors Technical Center, Warren, MI.
Length: 45 hours (15 weeks, 3 hours per week).
Dates: September 1986-Present.
Objective: To provide an understanding of the concepts in the design and operation of robotic systems.
Instruction: Course covers feedback control systems; arm control; applications of microcomputer distributed systems to robotics control; and discussion of command languages.
Credit recommendation: In the graduate degree category, 3 semester hours in Industrial, Mechanical, Electrical, or Manufacturing Engineering (6/86). NOTE: Course is not to be taken for credit by one who has had Advanced Robotic Systems.

Artificial Intelligence
Location: General Motors Technical Center, Warren, MI.
Length: 45 hours (15 weeks); one 3-hour meeting per week.
Dates: September 1985-Present.
Objective: To provide engineers with a general introduction to the methods and applications of artificial intelligence.

Instruction: Topics covered include: philosophical foundations and problems, application areas, problem representation, computer game-playing, problem solving paradigm, problem reduction, state space search, application of heuristics, control metaphors, hierarchy and heterarchy, object-oriented control, demons, production systems, computer vision and human vision, logic and theorem-proving, and natural language understanding.

Credit recommendation: In the graduate degree category, 3 semester hours in Artificial Intelligence (7/85).

Automated Manufacturing

Location: General Motors Technical Center, Warren, MI.

Length: 45 hours (15 weeks); one 3-hour meeting per week.

Dates: September 1985-Present.

Objective: To provide engineers with practical application skills in the design and layout of automated manufacturing systems.

Instruction: Topics covered include: CAD/CAM, computer graphics (hardware and software), analysis of automated flowlines, simulations and modeling of manufacturing systems, introduction to SIMAN (simulation software), group technology, production management systems, data base management, and flexible manufacturing systems.

Credit recommendation: In the graduate degree category, 3 semester hours in Manufacturing (7/85).

Automotive Electronics

Location: General Motors Technical Center, Warren, MI.

Length: 45 hours (15 weeks, 3 hours per week).

Dates: September 1986-Present.

Objective: To provide the service technician with more specific current technology background in automotive control systems, maintenance, removal and replacement (R&R).

Instruction: Course covers computer command control fundamentals, electronic spark control, advanced computer command control, and electronic fuel injections. Methods are lecture, video, and hands-on demonstrations covering operation and servicing of sensors, fuel injection systems, etc.

Credit recommendation: In the vocational certificate category, 2 semester hours in Automotive Electronics Service (6/86).

Automotive Fundamentals

Location: General Motors Technical Center, Warren, MI.

Length: 45 hours (15 weeks, 3 hours per week).

Dates: January 1986-Present.

Objective: To provide the student with an overview of the subsystems of the automobile.

Instruction: A description of the engine, drive line, and chassis with emphasis on performance, ride, and economy.

Credit recommendation: In the lower division baccalaureate/associate degree category, 3 semester hours as a general elective for the non-automotive major (6/86).

Basic Circuits and Electronics

Location: General Motors Technical Center, Warren, MI.

Length: 45 hours (15 weeks, 3 hours per week).

Dates: September 1986-Present.

Objective: To provide a refresher for electrical engineers and familiarization for non-electrical engineers.

Instruction: Topics covered include Kirchoffs laws, network theorems and DC and AC circuit analysis, electronic devices and applications (e.g., amplifiers, power supplies), op-amps, and some switching circuits. Lecture and discussion, and some lab demonstrations are used.

Credit recommendation: In the lower division baccalaureate/associate degree category, 3 semester hours for Electrical Engineers in Electrical Engineering Technology. In the upper division baccalaureate category, 3 semester hours for Non-electrical Engineers in Electrical Engineering Technology (6/86).

Basic Electrical Circuits and Instrumentation

Location: General Motors Technical Center, Warren, MI.

Length: 45 hours (15 weeks, 3 hours per week).

Dates: April 1984-Present.

Objective: To develop introductory circuits and instrumentation background for engineering technician level.

Instruction: Course introduces basic theories of electricity. Emphasis is placed on safety, tools and materials of the trade. Types of circuits, nomenclature, units of measurement. The correct use of basic measuring units is emphasized.

Credit recommendation: In the lower division baccalaureate/associate degree category, 3 semester hours in Electrical/Electronic Engineering Technology (6/86).

Chassis Design and Vehicle Dynamics

Location: General Motors Technical Center, Warren, MI.

Length: 45 hours (15 weeks); one 3-hour meeting per week.

Dates: September 1985-Present.

Objective: To provide a background in chassis design and vehicle dynamics for engineers.

Instruction: Topics covered include: steering and suspension parameters and their effects upon vehicle ride and handling characteristics, computer simulation studies and a systems approach to the analysis and synthesis of the dynamic behavior of vehicle vibrating systems, including

structural and acoustical considerations.
Credit recommendation: In the graduate degree category, 3 semester hours in Automotive Performance (7/85).

Combustion Engine Emissions and Control
Location: General Motors Technical Center, Warren, MI.
Length: 45 hours (15 weeks, 3 hours per week).
Dates: September 1986-Present.
Objective: To provide an understanding of the formation and control of emissions from combustion engines.
Instruction: Course covers emission formation in diesel and gasoline engines, methods of controlling emissions and their effectiveness, and the effect of emission control on fuel economy.
Credit recommendation: In the graduate degree category, 3 semester hours in Mechanical Engineering (6/86).

Compiler Design
Location: General Motors Technical Center, Warren, MI.
Length: 45 hours (15 weeks, 3 hours per week).
Dates: September 1985-Present.
Objective: To provide an in-depth exposure to the design and construction of compilers and programming systems.
Instruction: Course covers formal language theory, design of programming languages, parsing techniques, code generation, systems integration, and documentation.
Credit recommendation: In the graduate degree category, 3 semester hours in Computer Science or Electrical Engineering (6/86).

Computer-Aided Electrical Engineering
Location: General Motors Technical Center, Warren, MI.
Length: 45 hours (15 weeks); one 3-hour meeting per week.
Dates: September 1985-Present.
Objective: To provide engineers and technicians with tools and skills to use the computer in electrical engineering.
Instruction: Topics covered include: modern techniques for solving electrical engineering problems on the digital computer, solution of linear and non-linear algebraic equations, integration, solution of ordinary and partial differential equations and random number generation with applications to power systems, control systems, communication systems, and circuit design.
Credit recommendation: In the upper division baccalaureate category, 3 semester hours in Computer Aided Analysis of Electronic Circuits (7/85).

Computer Architecture
Location: General Motors Technical Center, Warren, MI.
Length: 45 hours (15 weeks); one 3-hour meeting per week.
Dates: September 1985-Present.
Objective: To provide engineers with an understanding of computer organization and architecture.
Instruction: Topics include: stored program computers, organization of arithmetic-logic unit, control processing unit, main and auxiliary memory, input/output unit, microprogramming control and distributed processing computer networks, architecture of mainframe computers, and microprocessors and parallel and pipeline processing.
Credit recommendation: In the graduate degree category, 3 semester hours in Computer Architecture (7/85).

Computer Graphics
Location: General Motors Technical Center, Warren, MI.
Length: 45 hours (15 weeks); one 3-hour meeting per week.
Dates: September 1985-Present.
Objective: To provide manufacturing systems and product design engineers with an introductory background and first-hand experience in computer graphics system design in order to strengthen their understanding of current state-of-the-art systems.
Instruction: Topics covered include: overview of modern raster based computer graphics systems, solid modeling, area scan, color theory and applications, hidden surface removal, shading, animation, hardware. Programming examples using the IBM PC XT to illustrate algorithms for points, lines, and arcs; transformations, and scaling. Overview of more complex techniques as hidden line removal, shading, solid modeling, interactive techniques and input-output devices.
Credit recommendation: In the graduate degree category, 3 semester hours in Computer Graphics (7/85).

Computer Information Processing and Control
Location: General Motors Technical Center, Warren, MI.
Length: 45 hours (15 weeks); one 3-hour meeting per week.
Dates: September 1985-Present.
Objective: To provide manufacturing system engineers with knowledge of computer systems used to acquire and process data, perform logical decisions based upon the data, and use the results to control systems and processes.
Instruction: Topics covered include: overview of the techniques used to monitor and control physical processes using digital computers, elements of information processing systems, real time operating systems, real time programming using high-level languages, control strategies, data base design, multiprogramming and multitasking systems, design techniques used to control repetitive manufacturing processes, relay solid state logic and programmable controller implementation.

Credit recommendation: In the graduate degree category, 3 semester hours in Real Time Processing and Control (7/85).

Computer Integrated Design and Manufacturing

Location: General Motors Technical Center, Warren, MI.

Length: 45 hours (15 weeks); one 3-hour meeting per week.

Dates: September 1985-Present.

Objective: To provide engineers with a background in computer programming and manufacturing with practical skills in computer integrated product design and manufacturing.

Instruction: Topics covered include: product design and information, marketing and financial data for manufacturing planning, static and dynamic aspects of manufacturing planning for the operating strategy of the physical plant, monitoring and control systems studied as a part of the dynamic operating system, nodes and path concepts and cell models as tools for system design, computer graphics, graphics exchange standards, information analysis of wire frame and solid modeling systems. Variant and generative planning systems, automated time standards, numerical control systems, interfaces to manufacturing resource planning systems, factory management and plant monitoring and control.

Credit recommendation: In the graduate degree category, 3 semester hours in Computer Aided Design and Manufacturing (7/85).

Computer Programming in BASIC

Location: General Motors Technical Center, Warren, MI.

Length: 45 hours (15 weeks, 3 hours per week).

Dates: September 1985-Present.

Objective: To teach fundamental concepts of the BASIC programming language and to teach operation of the IBM PC/XT Personal Computer.

Instruction: An introduction to BASIC and the IBM PC/XT. Topics include: introduction to computer components, disk drives, a disk operating system (DOS), files, and software use. Also, BASIC operation commands such as RUN, LIST, LOAD; BASIC program statements including INPUT, READ, PRINT; program branching using GO TO; conditional statements using IF-THEN; file control statements using open, print #, INPUT #, loop control using FOR-NEXT statements, array handling using single and double subscripted arrays. Several student created programs using the PC are required.

Credit recommendation: In the lower division baccalaureate/associate degree category, 3 semester hours in Introduction to Programming using BASIC (6/86).

Corrosion

Location: General Motors Technical Center, Warren, MI.

Length: 36 hours (12 weeks, 3 hours per week).

Dates: September 1986-Present.

Objective: To provide an understanding of the determination of the causes of corrosion and methods of prevention.

Instruction: Course covers forms of corrosion, design for the avoidance of corrosion, degradation of nonmetallic materials.

Credit recommendation: In the upper division baccalaureate category, 2 semester hours in Manufacturing, Chemical, or Mechanical Engineering (6/86).

Database Systems

Location: General Motors Technical Center, Warren, MI.

Length: 45 hours (15 weeks, 3 hours per week).

Dates: January 1986-Present.

Objective: To provide an understanding of the design and implementation of database systems.

Instruction: Course covers design and manipulation of a database, the review of database management systems, and the implementation of a given database on a commercial database management system.

Credit recommendation: In the upper division baccalaureate category, 3 semester hours in Computer Science, or Electrical Engineering (6/86).

Design and Analysis of Experiments

Location: General Motors Technical Center, Warren, MI.

Length: 45 hours (15 weeks, 3 hours per week).

Dates: January 1986-Present.

Objective: To provide an understanding of the development of design of experiments.

Instruction: Course covers: multifactor experiments, investigation of fixed, random, and mixed models and the development of factorial experiments.

Credit recommendation: In the upper division baccalaureate category, 3 semester hours in Mechanical or Electrical Engineering (6/86).

Design for Manufacturability

Location: General Motors Technical Center, Warren, MI.

Length: 45 hours (15 weeks); one 3-hour meeting per week.

Dates: September 1985-Present.

Objective: To provide design and manufacturing systems engineers with knowledge of the interrelationships between product design and manufacturing methods.

Instruction: Topics covered include: functional analysis, value analysis, assembly considerations, service considerations, material-process cost trade-offs, process capabilities and optimization.

Credit recommendation: In the graduate degree category, 3 semester hours in Manufacturing (7/85).

Design Sensitivities and Optimization
Location: General Motors Technical Center, Warren, MI.
Length: 15 hours (15 weeks, 1 hour per week).
Dates: May 1986-Present.
Objective: To provide an understanding of the process of investigation of optimization techniques in design.
Instruction: Course covers overview and examples of design sensitivity and optimal design procedures and examples.
Credit recommendation: In the graduate degree category, 1 semester hour in Mechanical Engineering (6/86).

Digital Signal Processing
Location: General Motors Technical Center, Warren, MI.
Length: 45 hours (15 weeks, 3 hours per week).
Dates: September 1986-Present.
Objective: To provide the understanding of the application of signal analysis techniques to practical problems.
Instruction: Course covers development of a general signal space based on multidimensional linear spaces as well as methods for characterizing signals by properties such as energy, power, instantaneous frequency, signal dimensionibility and time width band product as well as the application to practical problems.
Credit recommendation: In the graduate degree category, 3 semester hours in Electrical Engineering (6/86).

Engine Design
Location: General Motors Technical Center, Warren, MI.
Length: 45 hours (15 weeks); one 3-hour meeting per week.
Dates: September 1985-Present.
Objective: To provide a background in modern vehicle power plant design and analysis for engineers.
Instruction: Topics covered include: Thermodynamic cycles, typical engine configurations for reciprocating, rotary, and turbine engines, balancing, bearing loads, fuel systems, combustion processes and emissions, and performance characteristics.
Credit recommendation: In the upper division baccalaureate category, 3 semester hours in Engines (7/85).

Feedback Control Systems
Location: General Motors Technical Center, Warren, MI.
Length: 45 hours (15 weeks); one 3-hour meeting per week.
Dates: September 1985-Present.
Objective: To provide engineers with practical tools and applications for feedback control in manufacturing systems.
Instruction: Topics covered include: transfer functions, performance of feedback control systems, root-locus method, frequency domain analysis and stability, mathematical modeling, including inductance, resistance and capacity for fluid, thermal and mechanical systems, reactive processes and controllers case studies of actual industrial systems in providing competence in design, selection, and maintenance of electromechanical, pneumatic, thermal, and hyrdraulic systems.
Credit recommendation: In the upper division baccalaureate category, 3 semester hours in Feedback Control (7/85).

Finite Element Methods
Location: General Motors Technical Center, Warren, MI.
Length: 45 hours (15 weeks); one 3-hour meeting per week.
Dates: September 1985-Present.
Objective: To provide engineers with an in-depth presentation to finite element analysis with an emphasis on linear static analysis in mechanical and structural design.
Instruction: Topics covered include: the line element, interpolation, coordinate systems, rigid body motion, bending elements, virtual work, plate and shell elements, modeling strategy, bandwidth, convergence, solid elements, thermal stresses, Gaussian quadrature, parametric elements, optimal design and steady-state conduction.
Credit recommendation: In the graduate degree category, 3 semester hours in Finite Element Analysis (7/85).

Fracture and Fatigue Considerations in Design
Location: General Motors Technical Center, Warren, MI.
Length: 45 hours (15 weeks, 3 hours per week).
Dates: January 1986-Present.
Objective: To provide a comprehensive review of fracture and fatigue processes in materials with emphasis on mechanics.
Instruction: Course covers mechanics of brittle fracture, elastic-plastic fracture, fracture toughness, high and low cycle fatigue, fatigue-crack growth, fail-safe designs and fracture control.
Credit recommendation: In the upper division baccalaureate category, 3 semester hours in Engineering Mechanics or Mechanical Engineering (6/86).

Geometrical and Physical Optics
Location: General Motors Technical Center, Warren, MI.
Length: 45 hours (15 weeks, 3 hours per week).
Dates: October 1985-Present.
Objective: To learn the principles of classical optics and optical systems.
Instruction: Lectures in optics including first and third order geometrical optics, paraxial theory; ray tracing,

stops and apertures; aberration reduction; optical design using matrix methods; transverse wave motion; simple harmonic motion; interferometry; diffraction; and fourier optical methods. Prerequisites: knowledge of harmonic motion; wave equity; Taylor and MacClarin's Series, Laplace transforms.

Credit recommendation: In the upper division baccalaureate category, 3 semester hours in Electrical and Mechanical Engineering (6/86).

Geometric Tolerancing
Location: General Motors Technical Center, Warren, MI.
Length: 20 hours (10 weeks, 2 hours per week).
Dates: January 1986-Present.
Objective: To develop technical knowledge and skills needed to prepare and interpret engineering drawings using the geometric dimensioning and tolerancing system.
Instruction: This course covers geometric dimensioning and tolerancing per the American National Standards Institute (ANSI) Y14.5m-1982 Standard through the use of video tapes.
Credit recommendation: In the lower division baccalaureate/associate degree category, 1 semester hour in Engineering Graphics (6/86).

Heat and Mass Transfer
Location: General Motors Technical Center, Warren, MI.
Length: 45 hours (15 weeks, 3 hours per week).
Dates: January 1986-Present.
Objective: To provide and develop an understanding of basic heat and mass transfer.
Instruction: Course covers heat and mass transfer by diffusion in one-dimensional, two-dimensional, transient, periodic, and phase change systems, convective heat transfer for external and internal flows, similarity and integral solution methods. Turbulence, buoyancy driven flows, convection with phase change, radiation exchange between surfaces and radiation transfer in absorbing-emitting media.
Credit recommendation: In the upper division baccalaureate category, 3 semester hours in Mechanical or Manufacturing Engineering (6/86).

Hydraulics and Pneumatics
Location: General Motors Technical Center, Warren, MI.
Length: 45 hours (15 weeks, 3 hours per week).
Dates: January 1986-Present.
Objective: To provide the student with experiences designed to: recognize hydraulic and pneumatic components both physically and symbolically; read hydraulic and pneumatic circuit diagrams; design and draw simple hydraulic and pneumatic circuits; and size and specify components.
Instruction: This course is designed for the individual who has had no formal training in industrial hydraulics. Representative industrial circuits are analyzed for function, efficiency, and component sizing. Design rules and practices are within the component/system approach.
Credit recommendation: In the upper division baccalaureate degree category, 3 semester hours in Engineering Technology (6/86).

Information Structures
Location: General Motors Technical Center, Warren, MI.
Length: 45 hours (15 weeks, 3 hours per week).
Dates: September 1985-Present.
Objective: To develop an understanding of efficient algorithms for data manipulation, searching, and sorting.
Instruction: Course covers development of sequential, linked, and circular lists, binary through representation, and sorting.
Credit recommendation: In the upper division baccalaureate category, 3 semester hours in Computer Science or Manufacturing Engineering (6/86).

Image Processing
Location: General Motors Technical Center, Warren, MI.
Length: 45 hours (15 weeks); one 3-hour meeting per week.
Dates: September 1985-Present.
Objective: To provide manufacturing systems engineers with knowledge of human and electromechanical image processing with applications for robotics and machine vision.
Instruction: Topics covered include: Elements of human vision and image modeling, image sampling, quantization, enhancement, two-dimensional filtering, transforms, extraction, edges, texture, shape, image segmentation, relaxation and other iterative methods in image analysis, image registration, matching, and geometrical transforms.
Credit recommendation: In the graduate category, 3 semester hours in Image Processing (7/85).

Integrated Optics
Location: General Motors Technical Center, Warren, MI.
Length: 45 hours (15 weeks); one 3-hour meeting per week.
Dates: September 1985-Present.
Objective: To provide engineers having a sound background in electromagnetic fields and semiconductor devices with a working knowledge of integrated optics.
Instruction: Topics covered include: optical waveguide theory, waveguide fabrication techniques, scattering and absorption losses, radiation losses, couplers, and modulators, light emission in semiconductors, lasers, integrated

detectors, industrial applications of integrated optics, and current developments in integrated optics.

Credit recommendation: In the graduate degree category, 3 semester hours in Optics (7/85).

Introduction to Microcomputers
  Location: General Motors Technical Center, Warren, MI.
  Length: 45 hours (15 weeks, 3 hours per week).
  Dates: September 1986-Present.
  Objective: To introduce students interested in application of digital logic to commercially available microprocessors such as Intel 8080.
  Instruction: Lecture and lab covering binary, hexadecimal number systems, addition 80/85 instruction. 80/85 architecture, logic gates, flags and jumps, routines and terms, priority encoder, debounce and terms. 8 bit/7 segment display, LED binary count. Flowchart/debug techniques and terms. Binary arithmetic, BCD and rounding, negative numbers. Subroutines, calls and stack management. Nine lab meetings, 3 programs, 2 exams, and 1 project assignment. Labs include use of SDK-85 trainer.
  Credit recommendation: In the lower division baccalaureate/associate degree category, 2 semester hours in Electrical/Electronic Technology (6/86).

Machine Elements
  Location: General Motors Technical Center, Warren, MI.
  Length: 45 hours (15 weeks, 3 hours per week).
  Dates: September 1986-Present.
  Objective: To develop entry level abilities in the analysis, design, and selection of basic machine elements.
  Instruction: Course includes analysis of power screws, mechanical fasteners, springs and friction devices (bearings, clutches, bands and breaks), through lectures, demonstrations and some laboratory.
  Credit recommendation: In the upper division baccalaureate category, 3 semester hours in Mechanical Engineering (6/86).

Machine Tool Design
  Location: General Motors Technical Center, Warren, MI.
  Length: 45 hours (15 weeks, 3 hours per week).
  Dates: May 1986-Present.
  Objective: To introduce the student to the concepts of machine tool design with a view of kinematics and production accuracy.
  Instruction: This course provides a systematic approach to machine tool design. Topics include: basis for selection of machine tool feeds and speeds; gear box design; bearing, spindle, slideway design; differential design; and mechanical, electrical, and hydraulic machine tool drives.
  Credit recommendation: In the upper division baccalaureate degree category, 3 semester hours in Mechanical Engineering (6/86).

Manufacturing Processes
  Location: General Motors Technical Center, Warren, MI.
  Length: 45 hours (15 weeks, 3 hours per week).
  Dates: September 1986-Present.
  Objective: To provide students with the fundamentals of manufacturing processes.
  Instruction: Course covers the manufacturing processes of plastic molding, power metallurgy, molding and welding processes, adhesive bondings, protective surface treatments. Also included are metal removal and metal forming processes. Course materials are presented by video tape, lectures, and demonstrations.
  Credit recommendation: In the lower division baccalaureate/associate degree category, 3 semester hours in Manufacturing Engineering (6/86).

Manufacturing Quality Assurance
  Location: General Motors Technical Center, Warren, MI.
  Length: 45 hours (15 weeks); one 3-hour meeting per week.
  Dates: January 1976-Present.
  Objective: To provide engineers with a background in statistical methods with practical knowledge in quality assurance.
  Instruction: Topics covered include: techniques for assuring product quality by controlling production processes, principles and techniques of process validation and local optimization, concepts related to producing accuracy testing, tolerance charting, and Run Sum procedures used in validating operations, tolerance analysis, process capability, process control, acceptance sampling, quality costs, and quality circles.
  Credit recommendation: In the graduate degree category, 3 semester hours in Quality Assurance (7/85).

Mechanical Power Transmissions
  Location: General Motors Technical Center, Warren, MI.
  Length: 45 hours (15 weeks, 3 hours per week).
  Dates: September 1986-Present.
  Objective: To provide students in mechanical engineering with entry level abilities in the analysis, design, and selection of basic mechanical power transmission components and systems.
  Instruction: Course covers analysis and design of gears, chains, bolts, shafts, and power screws through the use of lecture, demonstrations, and some laboratory.
  Credit recommendation: In the upper division baccalaureate category, 3 semester hours in Mechanical Engineering (6/86).

Modern Control Theory
Location: General Motors Technical Center, Warren, MI.
Length: 45 hours (15 weeks, 3 hours per week).
Dates: September 1986-Present.
Objective: To provide an understanding of optimization methods for systems and control.
Instruction: Course covers introduction to methods of obtaining the extremum of a nondynamic or dynamic system and their use in control system design, linear programming, search methods, nonlinear and dynamic programming for discrete time as well as continuous time systems and applications.
Credit recommendation: In the upper division baccalaureate category, 3 semester hours in Mechanical or Electrical Engineering (6/86).

Modern Engineering Materials
Location: General Motors Technical Center, Warren, MI.
Length: 45 hours (15 weeks); one 3-hour meeting per week.
Dates: September 1985-Present.
Objective: To provide product design and manufacturing systems engineers with a background in modern engineering materials.
Instruction: Topics covered include: relationships among properties, composition, structure and processing of ceramics, polymers and metals, behavior of various materials resulting from different fabrication and service conditions, material data used in development of product and process design information, and materials selection, testing, behavior, and design.
Credit recommendation: In the graduate degree category, 3 semester hours in Materials (7/85).

Noise Control
Location: General Motors Technical Center, Warren, MI.
Length: 45 hours (15 weeks, 3 hours per week).
Dates: September 1986-Present.
Objective: To learn basic physics, physiological effects, and control of noise and related legislation.
Instruction: Lectures and video tapes include behavior of sound waves, physiology of the ear, decibels, sound levels, sound and vibration instruments; noise legislation including OSHA and EPA criteria; control of noise including absorption, transmission loss, filters, mufflers, vibration, and hearing protection. Homework problems and projects illustrate theoretical principles.
Credit recommendation: In the upper division baccalaureate category, 3 semester hours in Industrial Engineering (6/86).

Nondestructive Testing and Evaluation
Location: General Motors Technical Center, Warren, MI.
Length: 45 hours (15 weeks, 3 hours per week).
Dates: September 1986-Present.
Objective: To learn the theory of nondestructive testing of metallic components without altering properties, using Magnetic Particle testing; Liquid Penetrant testing, and Eddy Current testing.
Instruction: Lectures and video tapes describing the theories and applications of nondestructive metallic metal testing including Magnetic Particle, Liquid Penetrant, and Eddy Current. Also included is equipment set-up, calibration, and application. Course is designed to meet American Society of Nondestructive Testing No. SNG-TC-IA Level II requirements.
Credit recommendation: In the upper division baccalaureate category, 3 semester hours in Metallurgical Engineering or Nuclear Engineering Technology (6/86).

Pattern Recognition
Location: General Motors Technical Center, Warren, MI.
Length: 45 hours (15 weeks, 3 hours per week).
Dates: September 1986-Present.
Objective: To provide an understanding of the basic concepts of pattern recognition and artificial intelligence.
Instruction: Course covers theory of neural nets, basic pattern recognition techniques, and training methods, visual and speech recognition mechanics, and heuristic programming.
Credit recommendation: In the graduate degree category, 3 semester hours in Computer Science or Electrical Engineering (6/86).

Polymer Engineering
Location: General Motors Technical Center, Warren, MI.
Length: 45 hours (15 weeks, 3 hours per week).
Dates: January 1986-Present.
Objective: To develop an understanding of polymer processing, flow in tubes, calendaring, and extrusion.
Instruction: Course covers introduction to polymers with emphasis on basic properties, adhesion, solubility, and rheology. Injection molding and screw extruder design.
Credit recommendation: In the upper division baccalaureate category, 3 semester hours in Mechanical, Chemical, or Manufacturing Engineering (6/86).

Polymer Processes
Location: General Motors Technical Center, Warren, MI.
Length: 36 hours (12 weeks, 3 hours per week).
Dates: January 1986-Present.
Objective: To provide students with the ability to develop injection molded products.
Instruction: Course covers polymer definitions, ma-

chine description and setup, mold design, and product design.

Credit recommendation: In the upper division baccalaureate category, 2 semester hours in Manufacturing or Mechanical Engineering (6/86).

Random Variables and Signals

Location: General Motors Technical Center, Warren, MI.

Length: 45 hours (15 weeks, 3 hours per week).

Dates: May 1986-Present.

Objective: To educate the student on applications of probability theory to engineering problems.

Instruction: Course covers engineering application of probability theory; dependence, correlation and regression; multivariate Gaussian distribution; stochastic processes, spectual densities, random inputs to linear systems; Gaussian processes.

Credit recommendation: In the graduate degree category, 3 semester hours in Electrical, Mechanical, or Manufacturing Engineering (6/86).

Resistance Welding Processes

Location: General Motors Technical Center, Warren, MI.

Length: 45 hours (15 weeks, 3 hours per week).

Dates: September 1986-Present.

Objective: To teach the student principles of resistance welding processes including process parameters, joint design, tooling design, controls and instrumentation.

Instruction: Course includes lectures describing resistance welding theories including spot, resistance, projection, seam, flash, butt and electro-brazing. Also, welding of low and high carbon steel, stainless, coated and plated materials. Also, welding of aluminum, magnesium, copper, nickel alloys and dissimilar materials. Resistance welding machines, controls, and power distribution.

Credit recommendation: In the lower division baccalaureate/associate degree category, 3 semester hours in Manufacturing Engineering Technology (6/86).

Robotic Systems

Location: General Motors Technical Center, Warren, MI.

Length: 45 hours (15 weeks); one 3-hour meeting per week.

Dates: September 1985-Present.

Objective: To provide manufacturing systems engineers with an applications overview of robotics.

Instruction: Topics covered include: Recursive Newton-Euler and Lagrangian dynamics formulations, improved trajectory generation algorithms, comparative control methods for robot manipulations and compliance modeling, applications overview and work cell integration and design.

Credit recommendation: In the graduate degree category, 3 semester hours in Robotic Dynamics and Control (7/85).

Statistics for Technicians

Location: General Motors Technical Center, Warren, MI.

Length: 45 hours (15 weeks, 3 hours per week).

Dates: September 1986-Present.

Objective: To learn basic statistical concepts and to apply these concepts in the solution of problems using algebraic techniques.

Instruction: Lectures with video tape supplement include description of sample data, statistical nomenclature, probability, frequency distributions, sampling, estimation, testing hypothesis, correlation, and regression. Practice problems included to illustrate theoretical concepts.

Credit recommendation: In the lower division baccalaureate/associate degree category, 3 semester hours in Elementary Statistics (6/86).

Strength of Materials

Location: General Motors Technical Center, Warren, MI.

Length: 45 hours (15 weeks, 3 hours per week).

Dates: September 1986-Present.

Objective: To provide the student the opportunity to solve simple problems of stress analysis by developing an understanding of and an ability to apply the principles of mechanics of deformable solids.

Instruction: Topics in this course include: stress, strain, Hooke's Law, thermal stresses, beams, principal stresses and strains, and columns. Lectures and demonstrations are used.

Credit recommendation: In the upper division baccalaureate category, 3 semester hours in Mechanical Engineering (6/86).

Technical Drawing

Location: General Motors Technical Center, Warren, MI.

Length: 45 hours (15 weeks, 3 hours per week).

Dates: September 1986-Present.

Objective: To introduce the student to the fundamentals of drafting procedures and the tools required to complete industrial drawings.

Instruction: This course deals with the fundamentals, analysis, and procedures of projection. Such topics as scales, isometric drawings, definitions, applications of terms, true size of planes, parallelism, auxiliary views, classification of lines and planes are covered.

Credit recommendation: In the lower division baccalaureate/associate degree category, 2 semester hours in Engineering Drawing (Graphics) (6/86).

Turbomachinery

Location: General Motors Technical Center, Warren,

MI.
Length: 45 hours (15 weeks, 3 hours per week).
Dates: September 1986-Present.
Objective: To study advanced topics in turbomachinery.
Instruction: Course covers design and aerodynamic analysis of axial and radial flow gas compressors and turbine, blade element performance, secondary flow, centrifugal compression modeling, rotating stall and surge.
Credit recommendation: In the graduate degree category, 3 semester hours in Mechanical Engineering (6/86).

Vehicle Performance and Transmission Design
Location: General Motors Technical Center, Warren, MI.
Length: 45 hours (15 weeks); one 3-hour meeting per week.
Dates: September 1985-Present.
Objective: To provide a background in vehicle performance and current transmission design practices for engineers.
Instruction: Topics covered include: effects of such variables as N/V ratio, drag coefficient, weight, rolling resistance, and grade on acceleration and fuel consumption rates, transmission design practices such as manual transmission gear trains and synchronizers, bearing loads, ratio selection, torque converters, planetary gear trains, friction elements, control systems; current CVT designs and requirements for nontraditional power plants.
Credit recommendation: In the upper division baccalaureate category, 3 semester hours in Automotive Performance (7/85).

VLSI Design
Location: General Motors Technical Center, Warren, MI.
Length: 45 hours (15 weeks); one 3-hour meeting per week.
Dates: September 1985-Present.
Objective: To provide engineers with a general introduction to very large-scale integrated circuits.
Instruction: Topics covered include: MOS transistor, MOSFET and the inverter, MOSFET inverter and simple gates, pass transistor networks for gating, MOS memory, logic arrays, finite state machines, structured design examples, integrated circuit fabrication, MOS processing, cell generation and lithography, mask patterns and their constraints, mask layout, circuit performance, resistance and capacitance, device models and scaling.
Credit recommendation: In the graduate degree category, 3 semester hours in VLSI Design (7/85).

Georgia Computer Campus (Formerly Georgia Computer Programming Project for Severely Handicapped Persons)

Georgia Computer Campus, (formerly Georgia Computer Programming Project of Goodwill Industries of Atlanta, Inc.) was founded in November, 1979, and offers a nine month, 35 hour per week data processing training program to 17 qualified disabled students. The goal of this project is to train and place between 10 and 17 students annually as entry-level computer programmers.

The project operates with a manager, one full-time instructor, a part-time instructor, an admissions coordinator, a secretary, and a Business Advisory Council.

Facilities include specialized adaptive devices, a classroom, conference area, and a terminal room. All eleven terminals are linked with the CDC Cyber at the Georgia Institute of Technology.

The course was developed by the project's Curriculum Committee and the instructor to conform to academic standards and to specific needs in private industry. The committee reviews and updates the curriculum on a regular basis. All instructional staff have had extensive on-the-job experience.

Source of official student records: Project Director, Georgia Computer Campus, 430 10th Street, ATDC-South Building, Suite 201, Atlanta, Georgia 30318.

Additional information about the courses: Program on Noncollegiate Sponsored Instruction, The Center for Adult Learning and Educational Credentials, American Council on Education, One Dupont Circle, Washington, D.C. 20036.

Advanced Programming: PASCAL and COBOL
Location: O'Keefe Building, Georgia Institute of Technology, Atlanta, GA.
Length: 385 hours (11 weeks).
Dates: March 1980-Present.
Objective: To introduce the student to a second language (PASCAL). Students also implement a large system project.
Instruction: Teaches applications of logic and design skills in a second language (PASCAL) through lecture, discussion and laboratory work. More than half of the course work is devoted to the implementation of a large system project using COBOL.
Credit recommendation: In the lower division baccalaureate/associate degree or upper division baccalaureate category, 3 semester hours in Data Processing (12/82).

Business Communication Skills
Location: O'Keefe Building, Georgia Institute of Technology, Atlanta, GA.
Length: 45 hours (29 weeks).

Dates: October 1982-Present.
Objective: To develop the written and oral communications skills of computer programmer students to enhance the job seeking process and to promote effective communications required in the team environment of the data processing field.
Instruction: Written and oral business communication skills are developed through lectures, workshops, assignments, and role-laying exercises. Several field trips to data processing departments are made during the 29-week course.
Credit recommendation: In the lower division baccalaureate/associate degree category, 1 semester hour per term for a total maximum of 3 hours in Business Communication (12/82).

COBOL II
Location: O'Keefe Building, Georgia Institute of Technology, Atlanta, GA.
Length: 397 hours (11 weeks).
Dates: March 1980-Present.
Objective: To develop COBOL programming proficiency, incorporating advanced programming techniques.
Instruction: Covers table handling, sequential and direct access file techniques. Students utilize team projects to design and code application programs. Methodology includes lecture, discussion and extensive laboratory activity.
Credit recommendation: In the lower division baccalaureate/associate degree or upper division baccalaureate category, 3 semester hours in Data Processing (12/82).

Introduction to Data Processing - COBOL I
Location: O'Keefe Building, Georgia Institute of Technology, Atlanta, GA.
Length: 397 hours (11 weeks).
Dates: March 1980-Present.
Objective: To teach students to write, debug, and document computer programs in COBOL programming language.
Instruction: Students are introduced to basic data processing theory. Utilizes flowcharts and pseudocode to express problem definition and solution method. Solutions are converted to COBOL language. Lecture and discussion are used, with heavy laboratory emphasis.
Credit recommendation: In the lower division baccalaureate/associate degree or upper division baccalaureate category, 3 semester hours in Data Processing (12/82).

Graduate School of Banking at Colorado

The Graduate School of Banking at Colorado, established in 1950, provides a program of continuing education and research for practitioners in banking and finance. The student body is composed of bank officers, savings and loan officers, and officials of banking regulatory agencies.

The curriculum emphasizes policy and management problems; it focuses on the tools of bank management and the analytical framework within which general management problems can be recognized and solved. Course offerings are designed and coordinated by the director who works closely with faculty of practicing bankers, academicians, and other professionals. The curriculum is reviewed mainly by the Board of Trustees.

Attendance at three 2-week summer sessions conducted on the campus of the University of Colorado, participation in evening seminar programs, and completion of extension work are required for graduation. For evaluation purposes, courses offered throughout the three years of the program have been grouped together. Thus, students requesting credit must have completed the entire program.

All participants must pass an examination at the end of each annual session. Successful completion of the examination and extension work is indicated on the student's record.

The recommendations listed below apply only to those who complete the total program and not to individual courses or sections.

Source of official student records: Registrar, Graduate School of Banking at Colorado, University of Colorado, Campus Box 411, Boulder, Colorado 80309.

Additional information about the courses: Program on Noncollegiate Sponsored Instruction, The Center for Adult Learning and Educational Credentials, American Council on Education, One Dupont Circle, Suite 1B-20, Washington, D.C., 20036.

Bank Lending
  1. **Financial Analysis**
  2. **Commercial Lending**
  3. **Banking for the Small Business**
  4. **Consumer Lending or Loan Workouts**

Location: Graduate School of Banking at Colorado, University of Colorado, Boulder, CO.
Length: 38 hours (5 days) for students with previous lending experience; 46 hours (1 week) for students with no previous lending experience.
Dates: August 1988-Present.
Objective: To provide the student with an understanding of the basic concepts and the practical application of current analytical techniques related to the lending function of a financial institution.

Instruction: Course covers financial statement preparation, techniques of credit analysis, loan pricing decisions, short-term versus long-term debt structure, and commercial loan portfolio management. In addition, the student will elect further concentration in either Consumer Lending or Loan Workouts, specifically involving bankruptcy recoveries. If the student has no experience in lending, then the course Workshop on Agricultural Lending is recommended. Methodology includes lecture, discussion, cases, group processes, and computer simulation.

Credit recommendation: In the lower division baccalaureate/associate degree category, 2 semester hours in Bank Lending, Finance, or as a Business elective (4/89). NOTE: If the student has had no prior experience in lending, then Basic Credit for Non Lenders is required to earn this credit recommendation.

Management of Financial Institutions
1. Business Law in Banking
2. Economics of Banking
3. Banking Strategies for the 1990s
4. Asset/Liability Management I
5. Asset/Liability Management II
6. Investments and the Money Market
7. Financial Planning
8. Managing Bank Performance
9. BankSim

Location: Graduate School of Banking at Colorado, University of Colorado, Boulder, CO.
Length: 112 hours (2½ weeks).
Dates: August 1988-Present.
Objective: To allow the student to explore the management of financial institutions in the context of basic and advanced problems encountered in the banking industry.
Instruction: Course covers legal aspects of banking, bank regulation, monetary policy, macroeconomics, interest rate behavior, strategic planning, bank investments, asset/liability management, and financial planning. Students are recommended to take the course Electronic Banking. Methodology includes lecture, discussion, cases, group processes, and computer simulation.
Credit recommendation: In the upper division baccalaureate category, 4 semester hours in Bank Management, Finance, or as a Business elective (4/89).

Marketing Management
1. Marketing Bank Services
2. Planning Case
3. Banking Services Case
4. New Business Development
5. Formulating Bank Strategy
6. Contemporary Bank Issues
7. Managing Human Resources
8. Case in Non-Bank Competition

Location: Graduate School of Banking at Colorado, University of Colorado, Boulder, CO.
Length: 44½ hours (5 days).
Dates: August 1988-Present.
Objective: To provide the student with an understanding of basic concepts and approaches to marketing management of financial institutions.
Instruction: Course covers marketing bank service, planning as related to marketing bank services, developing new business, the environment within which marketing occurs, managing human resources, non-bank competitors in financial markets, and issues related to the quality of service. Students are recommended to take the course Quality of Service. Methodology involves lecture, discussion, cases, group processes, and computer simulation.
Credit recommendation: In the upper division baccalaureate category, 2 semester hours in Marketing, Marketing Management, or as a Business elective (4/89).

Graduate School of Banking at the University of Wisconsin-Madison (Central States Conference of Bankers Associates)

The Graduate School of Banking, established in 1945, provides a program of continuing education and research for practitioners in banking and finance. The student body is composed of bank officers and officials of banking regulatory agencies.

The curriculum emphasizes policy and management problems; it focuses on the tools of bank management and the analytical framework within which general management problems can be recognized and solved. Course offerings are designed and coordinated by an academic dean who works closely with faculty of practicing bankers, academicians, and other professionals.

Attendance at three 2-week summer sessions conducted on the campus of the University of Wisconsin-Madison, participation in evening seminar programs, and completion of extension work are required for graduation. For evaluation purposes, courses offered throughout the three years of the program have been grouped together. Thus, students requesting credit must have completed the entire program.

All participants must pass an examination at the end of each annual session. Successful completion of the examination and extension work is indicated on the student's record.

The recommendations listed below apply only to those who complete the total program and not to individual courses or sections.

Source of official student records: Registrar, Graduate School of Banking, 122 West Washington Avenue, Madison, WI 53703.

Additional information about the courses: Program on Noncollegiate Sponsored Instruction, The Center for

Adult Learning and Educational Credentials, American Council on Education, One Dupont Circle, Washington, D.C. 20036.

Commercial Lending
(Formerly 1. Commercial Loan Administration, 2. Commercial Loan Analysis, 3. Specialized Lending, 4. Lending to Agribusiness, 5. Loan Administration, 6. Income Property Mortgage Lending)
 1. Commercial Loan Analysis
 2. Commercial Loan Management
 3. Commercial Loan Sensitivity Analysis
 4. Financing Closely-Held Business
 5. Legal Aspects of Lending
 6. Credit and Asset/Liability Policy
 7. Agricultural Lending
 8. Income Property Mortgage Lending

Location: University of Wisconsin-Madison.
Length: *Version 1:* 32½ hours; *Version 2:* 36 to 44 hours covering modules of a three-year program; *Version 3:* 36 to 42½ hours covering modules of a three-year program.
Dates: *Version 1:* August 1977-April 1986; *Version 2:* May 1986-June 1988; *Version 3:* July 1988-Present.
Objective: To provide students with an understanding of basic concepts and analytical techniques related to commercial loan administration and practice.
Instruction: Lecture, discussion, and extension problems are used to cover topics related to loan structure and administration; loan analysis; consumer and agricultural lending.
Credit recommendation: *Version 1:* In the upper division baccalaureate category or in the graduate degree category, 2 semester hours in Finance (12/76) (6/81). *Version 2:* In the upper division baccalaureate category or in the graduate degree category, 2 semester hours in Finance (5/86). NOTE: This course has been reevaluated and continues to meet requirements for credit recommendations.

Investments
(Formerly 1. Investments, 2. Portfolio in Asset/Liability Management, 3. Cash Management, 4. Cash for Community Banks)
 1. Investments
 2. Cash Management for Community Banks
 3. Commodity Options
 4. Cash Management for Corporate Customers
 5. New Investment Products

Location: University of Wisconsin-Madison.
Length: *Version 1:* 34½ hours; *Version 2:* 19 to 22 hours covering modules of a three-year program; *Version 3:* 16 to 31 hours covering modules of a three-year program.
Dates: *Version 1:* August 1977-April 1986; *Version 2:* May 1986-June 1988; *Version 3:* July 1988-Present.
Objective: To provide students with an understanding of investment principles and the formulation and analysis of cash and portfolio management strategies.
Instruction: Lecture, discussion, and extension problems are used to cover topics such as principles of investment, asset/liability portfolio management, and money management.
Credit recommendation: *Version 1:* In the upper division baccalaureate category or in the graduate degree category, 2 semester hours in Finance (12/76) (6/81). *Version 2:* In the upper division baccalaureate category or in the graduate degree category, 2 semester hours in Investments or Finance (5/86). NOTE: This course has been reevaluated and continues to meet requirements for credit recommendations.

Management of Financial Institutions
(Formerly 1. Bank Marketing, 2. Bank Performance Analysis, 3. Economic and Monetary Policy, 4. Asset/Liability Management, 5. Law and Regulation in Banking, 6. Retail Banking, 7. Topics in Bank Management, 8. Evaluation of Country Risk for Banks, 9. Changing Consumer Market for Financial Services, 10. Bank Management)
 1. Bank Marketing
 2. Bank Performance Analysis
 3. Economic and Monetary Policy
 4. Asset/Liability Management
 5. Law and Regulation in Banking
 6. Retail Banking
 7. Emerging Issues in Bank Management
 8. Commercial Business Development
 9. Value Pricing
 10. Bank Management Simulation
 11. Credit and Asset/Liability Policy
 12. Evaluating the Trust Department
 13. Managing the Trust Department
 14. New Product Strategies
 15. Marketing Issues
 16. The Financial Planning in the Community Bank
 17. Financial Planning
 18. Personal Financial Planning
 19. Plan for a Winning Strategy

Location: University of Wisconsin-Madison.
Length: *Version 1:* 59½ hours; *Version 2:* 127 to 142 hours covering modules of a three-year program; *Version 3:* 107½ to 122½ hours.
Dates: *Version 1:* August 1977-April 1986; *Version 2:* May 1986-June 1988; *Version 3:* July 1988-Present.
Objective: To explore the management of financial institutions in the context of basic and advanced problems.
Instruction: Lecture, discussion, extension problems, and evening seminar programs are used to cover topics such as economics and monetary policy; asset and liability management; regulatory issues; and strategies for effective bank management.
Credit recommendation: *Version 1:* In the upper division baccalaureate category or in the graduate degree category, 4 semester hours in Finance (12/76) (6/81). *Version*

2: In the upper division baccalaureate category, 4 semester hours in Bank Management or Finance and in the graduate degree category, 4 semester hours in Advanced Bank Management or Finance (5/86). NOTE: This course has been reevaluated and continues to meet requirements for credit recommendations.

Principles of Management
(Formerly 1. Managerial Practice, 2. Human Resources Management, 3. Leadership Through Effective Staff Management, 4. Improving Problem Solving)
 1. Managerial Practice
 2. Human Resource Management
 3. Leadership Through Effective Staff Management
 4. Improving Problem Solving
 5. Ethics in Banking
 6. Managing Employees in the 1990s
Location: University of Wisconsin-Madison.
Length: *Version 1:* 22 to 26 hours covering modules of a three-year program; *Version 2:* 21½ to 30½ hours covering modules of a three-year program.
Dates: *Version 1:* May 1986-June 1988; *Version 2:* July 1988-Present.
Objective: To enable students to understand their roles as bank managers and to examine a variety of techniques and problems applicable to management of human resources.
Instruction: Lecture, discussion, case studies, extension problems, and exercises are used to cover topics such as leadership, problem-solving and decision-making, and personal and group development.
Credit recommendation: In the upper division baccalaureate category, 2 semester hours in Principles of Management (5/86).

GTE Service Corporation - GTE Telephone Operations Network Training

GTE Telephone Operations Network Training provides conceptual and skill training to the salaried engineering, construction, and planning staffs of the GTE Telephone Operating Companies. The courses taught generally have a high technology telecommunications focus. They are developed using a systematic criterion referenced instruction method.

Students attending the courses increasingly possess one or more academic degrees and must demonstrate competency in the courses before receiving credit. A variety of learning strategies including lecture, discussion, laboratory activities, and examinations are utilized.

The training facility is located in DFW Airport, Texas, but a great deal of the instruction is done at various locations throughout the United States. The instructors chosen to present the courses are selected for their specific expertise in engineering, planning, or construction work functions.

Source of official student records: Director, Training Administration, GTE Service Corporation, GTE Place, P.O. Box 619060, West Airfield Drive, DFW Airport, Texas 75261-9060.

Additional information about the courses: Program on Noncollegiate Sponsored Instruction, The Center for Adult Learning and Educational Credentials, American Council on Education, One Dupont Circle, Washington, D.C. 20036.

Advanced Data Communications Analysis (8121)
Location: GTE Service Corporation, DFW Airport, TX.
Length: 160 hours (4 weeks), (80 hours lecture, 80 hours laboratory).
Dates: April 1983-January 1986.
Objective: To enable the student to analyze terminal equipment, data facilities, data communications equipment, data link control protocols and identify and isolate problems related to defective data communication.
Instruction: Covers data transmission, data communications equipment, data link control, data terminal equipment, channel impairments, RS-232C interface and data set operations testing. Methodology includes lecture, discussion, laboratory exercises, and examinations.
Credit recommendation: In the upper division baccalaureate category, 4 semester hours in Data Communications (9/84).

Basic Data Transmission Engineering (8122)
Location: GTE Service Corporation, DFW Airport, TX, and at telephone company sites.
Length: 64 hours (2 weeks).
Dates: June 1983-Present.
Objective: To provide the student with a general knowledge of terminal equipment, telegraph carriers, limited distance modems, wideband applications, digital data service, and Dataphone II requirements. Also to develop the skills required to design voice-bank private line and switched data services.
Instruction: Covers facility identification, determining of routing, transmission requirements, and device selection for the design of both private line and DDD data circuits. Also includes identification of data equipment such as terminals, telegraph carrier, digital multiplexer and network diagnosis control system. Methodology includes lecture and laboratory activities.
Credit recommendation: In the upper division baccalaureate, or graduate degree category, 3 semester hours in Transmission Engineering (9/84).

Basic Engineering—Outside Plant (8090)

Location: GTE Service Corporation, DFW Airport, TX, and at telephone company sites.
Length: 78 hours (2 weeks).
Dates: July 1984-Present.
Objective: To provide competencies so that students can construct structurally sound, safe, and reliable outside plant facilities that meet the legal, economic, and service demands of today's technology.
Instruction: Covers plant record systems, communications cables, structural engineering including aerial facilities and manholes, permits, rights of way, cable facilities, protection and noise, work order production and construction drawings. Methodology includes lecture, discussion, workshop, and laboratory activities.
Credit recommendation: in the lower division baccalaureate/associate degree category, 2 semester hours in Construction Technology (9/84).

Basic Transmission Engineering (8015)

Location: GTE Service Corporation, DFW Airport, TX, and at telephone company sites.
Length: 80 hours (2 weeks).
Dates: June 1982-Present.
Objective: To develop competencies so that students can become familiar with and identify virtually all types of components and engineering areas in communications transmission, select components for specific applications, prepare reports on noise and switching problems. List uses of fiber optics, radio and microwave and explain data modulation.
Instruction: Covers sound, telephone instruments, transmission units and measurements, analog transmission, digital transmission, loop design, toll switching, noises, fiber optics communication, protection, radio and microwave and data modulation. Methodology includes lecture, discussion, workshop, and laboratory activities.
Credit recommendation: In the lower division baccalaureate/associate degree category, 3 semester hours in Communications Engineering Technology (9/84).

Customer Loop Design (8141)

Location: GTE Service Corporation, DFW Airport, TX, and at telephone company sites.
Length: 80 hours (2 weeks).
Dates: April 1983-Present.
Objective: To provide the student with competencies to design advanced circuits for loop transmissions systems, quality cost effective systems, document transmission loops to match amplifier or loop extenders, provide adjustments prior to barrier use. Develop system plan to include installation, work order drawings, detailing distribution and equipment purchasing information.
Instruction: Covers modern techniques and components, design of efficient and economical loop using multi-channel analog carrier, planning for future expansion and remote pair gain devices. Methodology includes lecture, discussion, workshop, and laboratory activities.
Credit recommendation: In the upper division baccalaureate category, 3 semester hours in Communication Systems (9/84).

Data Communications Concepts (8023)

Location: GTE Service Corporation, DFW Airport, TX, and at telephone company sites.
Length: 40 hours (1 week).
Dates: July 1983-Present.
Objective: To provide the student with an in-depth description of concepts and technologies related to data communications.
Instruction: Covers concepts and technologies of data communications, computer input-output requirements, data communications equipment, data link protocols, and network related topics. Methodology includes lecture, class discussion, in-class projects and examinations.
Credit recommendation: In the lower division baccalaureate/associate degree category, 2 semester hours in Introduction to Computers and Data Communications (9/84).

Digital Network Concepts (8060)

Location: GTE Service Corporation, DFW Airport, TX, and at telephone company sites.
Length: 80 hours (2 weeks).
Dates: April 1983-Present.
Objective: To provide the student with a knowledge of digital technology sufficient to understand the digital telephony techniques of transmission, multiplexing, and switching.
Instruction: Covers basic digital concepts, A/D and D/A conversion, digital transmission and multiplexing, digital switching, time division switching, packet switching, local digital networks and other digital telephony techniques. Methodology includes lecture, discussion, and practical exercises.
Credit recommendation: In the upper division baccalaureate category, 3 semester hours in Communications Network Subsystem (9/84).

Engineering Economics (8070)

Location: GTE Service Corporation, DFW Airport, TX, and at telephone company sites.
Length: 80 hours (2 weeks).
Dates: March 1983-Present.
Objective: To provide the student with the knowledge to identify major line items indicated on financial statements and develop the necessary skills to make financial decisions.
Instruction: Covers basic accounting concepts, introduction to financing, mathematics of money, nature of costs, capital repayment and depreciation, inflation and the cost of money, economy study techniques, and owning

versus leasing. Methodology includes lecture, discussion, and practical exercises.

Credit recommendation: In the lower division baccalaureate/associate degree, or in the upper division baccalaureate category, 3 semester hours in Engineering Economics (9/84).

Fiber Optic Communications Engineering (8133)
   Location: GTE Service Corporation, DFW Airport, TX, and at telephone company sites.
   Length: 38 hours (1 week).
   Dates: April 1983-Present.
   Objective: To provide the student with a knowledge of the principles of optic fiber communications necessary to engineer optical fiber communication systems.
   Instruction: Covers and introduction to fiber optic technology, lightwave theory, fiber manufacturing, optical test equipment and span testing techniques, fiber splicing, light sources, photodetectors, fiber optic cable installation and testing methods, system planning and other related system engineering topics. Methodology includes lecture, practical exercises, and examinations.
   Credit recommendation: In the upper division baccalaureate, or graduate degree category, 2 semester hours in Communications Engineering (9/84).

Introduction to Packet Switching Networks (8134)
   Location: GTE Service Corporation, DFW Airport, TX, and at telephone company sites.
   Length: 40 hours (1 week).
   Dates: April 1984-Present.
   Objective: To enable the student to identify the structure, equipment, interfaces, and management practices of packet switching networks. Also identified are the various functions and interactions required of packet switching software.
   Instruction: Covers technical descriptions and management practices of packet switching technology, interface-protocols and CCITT standards; physical frame and packet levels of X.25, S.3/ITI, X.28, and X.29 interfaces and IBM 3270 support. Methodology includes lecture, class presentations, class projects, and examinations.
   Credit recommendation: In the upper division baccalaureate, or graduate degree category, 2 semester hours in Network Theory (9/84).

Metallic Trunk Carrier Transmission Engineering (8129)
   Location: GTE Service Corporation, DFW Airport, TX, and at telephone company sites.
   Length: 40 hours (1 week).
   Dates: February 1984-Present.
   Objective: To provide competencies so that students can identify types of transmission cables, select proper cables for specific routings, discriminate between analog and digital carrier systems, design a carrier span according to GTE standards, and select proper test equipment and testing procedures.
   Instruction: Covers types and uses of various communication cables, analog and digital concepts, carrier spans and GTE standards and troubleshooting procedures. Methodology includes lecture, discussion, and laboratory activities.
   Credit recommendation: In the lower division baccalaureate/associate degree category, 2 semester hours in Basic Electrical Circuits (9/84).

Microprocessor Fundamentals (8137)
   Location: GTE Service Corporation, DFW Airport, TX, and at telephone company sites.
   Length: 64 hours (2 weeks).
   Dates: January 1984-Present.
   Objective: To provide the student with the knowledge to operate and program a microprocessor controlled system. This course is designed around the Heathkit Microprocessor Trainer, ET-3400 including the Motorola 6800 Microprocessor.
   Instruction: Covers microprocessor architecture, numbering systems, flowcharting, machine language programming, and the mechanics of the Heathkit Microprocessor Trainer, ET-3400 including the Motorola 6800 Microprocessor. Methodology includes lecture, discussion, and extensive "hands-on" laboratory exercises.
   Credit recommendation: In the upper division baccalaureate category, 2 semester hours in Microprocessor Programming (9/84).

Microwave Radio Engineering (8138)
   Location: GTE Service Corporation, DFW Airport, TX, and at telephone company sites.
   Length: 72 hours (2 weeks).
   Dates: June 1980-Present.
   Objective: To enable students to apply the basic theory and concepts of microwave radio propagation, antenna, wave guide transmission lines and transmission objectives to the design of microwave transmission systems.
   Instruction: Covers microwave radio theory and concepts and the design fundamentals for microwave radio systems including FCC regulations, route designs and site selection, trouble investigation and plant performance. Methodology includes lecture, class presentations, design projects, and examinations.
   Credit recommendation: In the upper division baccalaureate, or graduate degree category, 3 semester hours in Microwave Engineering Design (9/84).

Protection and Noise (8119)
   Location: GTE Service Corporation, DFW Airport, TX, and at telephone company sites.
   Length: 80 hours (2 weeks).
   Dates: June 1982-Present.
   Objective: To develop competencies so that students

can design grounding circuits, specify protection components to protect employees, consumers, and equipment from hazardous voltages, utilize proper procedures to correct corrosion problems, troubleshoot and repair noise problems.

Instruction: Covers designing and testing ground circuits, lighting protection circuits, troubleshooting for industrial standards, performing accident investigations, writing reports, evaluating and correcting corrosion problems, and analyzing noise to mitigate the problem. Methodology includes lecture, discussion, workshops, and laboratory activities.

Credit recommendation: In the lower division baccalaureate/associate degree, or in the upper division baccalaureate category, 3 semester hours in Electronic Engineering Technology (9/84).

Special Circuits Design Engineering (8123)
Location: GTE Service Corporation, DFW Airport, TX, and at telephone company sites.
Length: 80 hours (2 weeks).
Dates: June 1982-Present.
Objective: To provide the student with competencies to interpret a universal service order, identify equipment and design circuits necessary to interface switched circuits with private line special service voice circuits.
Instruction: Covers the functions of the intercompany service coordination plan, requirements for industry standards, facilities necessary and troubleshooting of malfunctioning circuits. Methodology includes lecture, discussion, and laboratory activities.
Credit recommendation: In the upper division baccalaureate category, 3 semester hours in Communications Circuit Design (9/84).

Traffic Concepts (8118)
Location: GTE Service Corporation, DFW Airport, TX, and at telephone company sites.
Length: 80 hours (2 weeks).
Dates: June 1982-Present.
Objective: To provide the student with a knowledge of telephone traffic concepts sufficient to understand telephone traffic engineering.
Instruction: Covers probability theory as applied to telephone traffic, sampling theory as applied to traffic studies, telephone traffic blocking and delays, data validation and analysis, trunk management, load balancing, and other switching system concepts related to telephone traffic engineering.
Credit recommendation: In the upper division baccalaureate category, 3 semester hours in Network Systems Analysis (9/84).

Health Insurance Association of America

The Health Insurance Association of America (HIAA), located in Washington, D.C., is a voluntary trade association whose membership consists of approximately 340 insurance companies which are responsible for about 85 percent of the United States and 90 percent of the Canadian health insurance business written by insurance companies. The general purpose of the Association is to promote the development of voluntary health insurance for the provision of sound protection against loss of income and financial burden resulting from sickness or injury.

The Association has sponsored a formal educational program since 1958 that currently consists of a two-part individual health insurance course and a three-part life/health insurance course. These courses are designed to give the student comprehensive knowledge and understanding of the technical as well as the socioeconomic aspects of the group life/health and individual health insurance business.

Achievement in these course is assessed through a comprehensive examination for each course part. Students' principal method of preparation for final examinations is through independent study, with on-the-job experience and, in some instances, classroom instruction supplementing this study. HIAA provides self-study materials that candidates can use to prepare for examinations. Guides for Course Leaders are available for Group Life/Health Parts A and B. Course content and examinations are constantly reviewed and updated by persons knowledgeable and active in the various specialties of the health insurance business.

Source of official student records: Insurance Education Program, Health Insurance Association of America, 1025 Connecticut Avenue, N.W., Washington, D.C. 20036.

Additional information about the courses: Program on Noncollegiate Sponsored Instruction, The Center for Adult Learning and Educational Credentials, American Council on Education, One Dupont Circle, Washington, D.C. 20036.

1. Group Life/Health Insurance: Parts A and B
2. Group Life/Health Insurance: Part C
Location: Various locations throughout the United States.
Length: Self-study (approximately 150 hours, including test preparation and testing time). (Parts A and B: approximately 100 hours; Part C: approximately 50 hours).
Dates: *Version 1:* September 1979-April 1988; *Version 2:* May 1988-Present.
Objective: To furnish students with a comprehensive knowledge of the technical and socioeconomic aspects (Parts A and B) as well as the advanced and specialty areas (Part C) of the group life and health insurance busi-

ness.

Learning Outcome: Upon successful completion of this course, the student will be able to understand the need for life and health insurance and the historical development, structure, and regulation of group life and health insurance business; understand and skillfully and professionally use the fundamentals of group life and health insurance; and understand and explain the role and contribution of the group life and health insurance business in the financing and administration of health care systems and premature death.

Instruction: Part A: Covers development of group health insurance, analysis of coverages, marketing, underwriting, pricing and rate making. Part B: The contract, issue and administration, claims, financial analysis of group operations, regulations, and taxation, industry organizations. Part C: Design and funding of group life and health insurance for traditional insurance coverages, retired employee, flexible benefits, rehabilitation, automobile, homeowners and legal programs; health care cost containment approaches, thorough introduction to data processing and its function in group insurance. Instructor-directed or self-instructional with supervised examinations.

Credit recommendation: *Version 1:* Parts A and B: In the upper division baccalaureate category, 3 semester hours in Business Administration, or in the upper division baccalaureate or graduate category, 2 semester hours in Health Care Administration. Part C: In the upper division baccalaureate or graduate category, 2 semester hours in Business Administration or Insurance; and in the lower division baccalaureate/associate degree category, 1 semester hour in Data Processing (5/83). *Version 2:* Parts A and B: In the upper division baccalaureate category, 3 semester hours in Business Administration, or in the graduate category, 2 semester hours in Business Administration or Health Care Administration. Part C: In the upper division baccalaureate category or graduate category, 2 semester hours in Business Administration or Health Care Administration (5/88). NOTE: This course has been reevaluated and continues to meet requirements for credit recommendations.

Individual Health Insurance: Parts A and B

Location: Various locations throughout the United States.

Length: Self-study (approximately 100 hours, including test preparation and testing time).

Dates: May 1968-Present.

Objective: To enable students to have an in-depth understanding of individual health insurance and of the social and economic responsibilities of the industry.

Learning Outcome: Upon successful completion of this course, the student will be able to understand the need for medical expense and disability insurance and the historical development, structure, and regulation of the individual health insurance business; understand and skillfully and professionally use the fundamentals of individual health insurance; and understand and explain the role and contribution of the individual health insurance business in the financing and administration of health care systems.

Instruction: Part A: History and development of health insurance; types of coverage; contracts; marketing; and understanding. Part B: Claims; premiums and rates; regulation and taxation; government program (U.S. and foreign); cost, delivery, and financing of health care. Instructor-directed or self-instructional with supervised examinations.

Credit recommendation: In the upper division baccalaureate category, 3 semester hours in Business Administration, Insurance, or Marketing (6/77) (5/83) (5/88). NOTE: This course has been reevaluated and continues to meet requirements for credit recommendations.

Henkels & McCoy, Inc.

Henkels & McCoy, Inc., founded in 1923, is a highly diversified multinational engineering, management, construction, and maintenance company. Its 5,300 employees represent all of the engineering disciplines and craft orientations needed to complete projects in engineering, communications, pipelining, electric transmission and distribution systems, and industrial construction services.

Job training is an important element in the company's philosophy. Instruction is based on a practical combination of classroom sessions and hands-on experience in real or simulated field conditions. Henkels & McCoy is involved in job development and placement programs for private industry as well as for government agencies. From these programs emerge an ongoing flow of properly trained technicians to serve in an increasingly complex technological world.

Source of official student records: National Manager, Training Services, Henkels & McCoy, Inc., Jolly Road, Blue Bell, Pennsylvania 19422.

Additional information about the courses: Compact Lifelong Educational Opportunities (CLEO), 37 South 16th Street, Philadelphia, Pennsylvania 19102 or Program on Noncollegiate Sponsored Instruction, The Center for Adult Learning and Educational Credentials, American Council on Education, One Dupont Circle, Washington, D.C. 20036.

Cable Television Technician Course

Location: Locations throughout the country including remote job sites.

Length: 350 hours (10 weeks, 35 hours weekly); 152 hours lecture and 198 hours laboratory.

Dates: October 1982-Present.

Objective: To provide a basic knowledge of broad band

coaxial transmission and aerial/underground construction for application in a working environment.

Instruction: Covers *Electrical Circuits:* Ohm's Law, decibel theory, logarithms, series/parallel circuits, CATV electronics, broadcast transmission, reception, system layout and operation, signal processing equipment, broad band amplifiers, channel allocations, signal evaluations, test equipment, plant operation/maintenance. *Construction:* Codes, blueprint reading, physical plant, safety, materials and equipment, cable installation techniques, supervision, record keeping, regulations, customer relations. Includes lecture, laboratory, practical exercises.

Credit recommendation: In the lower division baccalaureate/associate degree category, 4 semester hours in Communication Systems (4/84).

Key System Installer
Location: Locations throughout the country including remote job sites.
Length: 350 hours (10 weeks, 35 hours weekly); 105 hours lecture and 245 hours laboratory.
Dates: February 1983-Present.
Objective: To provide a basic knowledge of telephony, key system installation, writing layout and testing to be used in a working environment.
Instruction: Covers cable color codes and pair counts; blueprints, wiring diagrams and schematic reading; cable termination; key service units; test equipment; Main Distributing Frame layout and installation; K.S.U. troubleshooting methods and techniques; electromechanical and electronic intercoms; phones and enhanced feature units; binary and hexadecimal counting for programming electronic key systems. Includes lecture, laboratory, and practical exercises.
Credit recommendation: In the lower division baccalaureate/associate degree category, 4 semester hours or in the vocational certificate category, 12 semester hours in Communications Systems (4/84).

Illinois Fire Service Institute

The Illinois Fire Service Institute is the mandated State Fire Training Academy for Illinois. Implemented in the fiscal year 1974-75, it is responsible for developing and implementing training programs that address the needs of the fire service. To achieve the success of the educational program, classrooms, drill grounds, and specialized training areas are used to train and educate the students.

Courses are revised and developed according to recognized needs. Certain courses undergo constant review because of the nature of the material, while others receive periodic evaluation by instructors and national standards. The courses are under constant scrutiny to insure that the information is current and useful to the student. Not all courses are certified, however, certification for courses is dependent upon two factors—practical exercises and examinations. The student has the option to participate in the certification process and can retest for certain skill areas that are evaluated during the course. All courses, certified or not, require demonstrated skills.

All student records are filed in the computer system (according to an ID number) which helps to determine the student's progress. Each course that is successfully completed is noted on the student's individual record.

Source of official student records: The Illinois Fire Service Institute, 1208 West Peabody Drive, 202 Old Agricultural Engineering Building, Urbana, Illinois 61801.

Additional information about the courses: Program on Noncollegiate Sponsored Instruction, The Center for Adult Learning and Educational Credentials, American Council on Education, One Dupont Circle, Washington, D.C. 20036.

Arson Investigation I
(A. Fire Arson Investigation Module I)
(B. Fire Arson Investigation Module II)
Location: University of Illinois or selected off-campus sites.
Length: A. 40 hours (1 week). B. 40 hours (1 week) for a total of 80 hours (2 weeks).
Dates: October 1982-Present.
Objective: To train fire and police personnel in theory and behavior of fire, sources of fire ignition, building construction as it affects fire spread, fire cause and point of origin, indicators of arson, vehicle fires, and other related material.
Learning Outcome: Upon successful completion of this course, the student will be able to understand fire/arson investigation, including the chemistry of fire; understand the types of building construction, types of loading and building elements that may increase or decrease fire growth, and understand how to conduct a fire investigation.
Instruction: Course covers fire behavior, building construction; automatic fire detection and supervision system, determining cause and point of origin; accidental fire hazards and causes, incendiary fire causes and indicators, vehicle fires, sketching; appropriate field demonstrations, field interviews, gathering information and evidence, recording facts and observations, recognizing motivations of arsonists, identifying fires set by explosion, and working within legal guidelines. Lecture, discussion, and practical exercises are used.
Credit recommendation: In the upper division baccalaureate category, 3 semester hours in Criminal Justice, Fire Science, Insurance, or Law Enforcement (10/87). NOTE: To receive credit, students must complete both courses.

Arson Investigation II
(Fire Arson Investigation Module III)
   Location: University of Illinois or selected off-campus sites.
   Length: 40 hours (1 week).
   Dates: October 1982-Present.
   Objective: To provide the student with the knowledge and skills required to detect arson patterns and motives in a variety of settings.
   Learning Outcome: Upon successful completion of this course, the student will be able to understand intelligence systems, crime laboratory, interview and communications techniques, fatal fires, photography, and arson for profit.
   Instruction: Course covers administrative units, intelligence systems, crime laboratory, photography, interviews and communication techniques, fatal fires, arson for profit, and arson prevention programs. Lecture, discussion, and practical exercises are used. **Prerequisite:** Arson Investigation I.
   Credit recommendation: In the upper division baccalaureate category, 1 semester hour in Criminal Justice, Fire Science, Fire Technology, Insurance, or Law Enforcement (10/87).

Curriculum and Course Design I
(Fire Service Instructor I)
   Location: University of Illinois or selected off-campus sites.
   Length: 40 hours (1 week).
   Dates: January 1977-Present.
   Objective: To provide the student with an understanding of the methods of learning.
   Learning Outcome: Upon successful completion of this course, the student will be able to understand techniques related to teaching.
   Instruction: Course covers communication, concepts of learning, human relations in the teaching-learning environment, methods of teaching, organizing the learning environment, performance evaluation, records and reports, testing and evaluation, the instructor's role and responsibilities, the lesson plan, the teaching technique and the use of instructional materials. Lecture, discussion, role playing, audiovisual aids, and practical exercises are used.
   Credit recommendation: In the lower division baccalaureate/associate degree category, 3 semester hours in Education Methods of Teaching, Fire Science, or Fire Technology (10/87).

Curriculum and Course Design II
(Fire Service Instructor II)
   Location: University of Illinois or selected off-campus sites.
   Length: 40 hours (1 week).
   Dates: January 1977-Present.
   Objective: To instruct fire service personnel in the following areas: developing performance objective, lesson plan, instructional aids, evaluation systems, references and records, and reports.
   Learning Outcome: Upon successful completion of this course, the student will be able to develop performance objectives, lesson plans, instructional aids, evaluation systems, references and records, and reports.
   Instruction: Course covers preparation of instructional materials, techniques of testing and evaluation, writing behavioral objectives or performance objectives, lesson plan development, teaching/learning process, methods of instruction, records and reports, and references. Lecture, discussion, role playing, audiovisual aids, and practical exercises are used. **Prerequisite:** Instructor I or Curriculum and Course Design I.
   Credit recommendation: In the upper division baccalaureate category, 3 semester hours in Education, Fire Science, Fire Technology, or Methods of Teaching (10/87).

Curriculum and Course Design III
(Instructor III-Advanced Teaching Methods or Fire Service Instructor III-Methods of Instruction)
   Location: University of Illinois or selected off-campus sites.
   Length: 80 hours (2 weeks).
   Dates: January 1985-Present.
   Objective: To instruct the student in advanced methods of curriculum and course design.
   Learning Outcome: Upon successful completion of this course, the student will be able to analyze fire service occupations, prepare instructional materials, understand principles of technical writing, and techniques of administering tests and evaluation; the student will also know how to write behavioral objectives.
   Instruction: Course covers approaches to training, systems design, developing terminal objectives, instructional techniques, technical writing, course design and sequencing, analysis of evaluation systems (including entire tests, test items, and statistical), course materials development, design and development of instructional aids, the equal opportunity law, and impact of the instructional program and records and reports. Lecture, discussion, role playing, audiovisual aids, and practical exercises are used. **Prerequisite:** Curriculum and Course Design II.
   Credit recommendation: In the upper division baccalaureate category, 3 semester hours in Education, Fire Science Technology, or Methods of Teaching (10/87).

Fire Department Management I
   Location: University of Illinois or selected off-campus sites.
   Length: 40 hours (5-8 hour meetings per week or weekends).
   Dates: September 1984-Present.
   Objective: To introduce the student to the basic princi-

ples of management.

Learning Outcome: Upon successful completion of this course, the student will be able to understand the role and function of the Fire Officer I; basic management principles and concepts; leadership; motivation; organizational culture; concepts of change; giving orders; the disciplinary process; performance appraisal; and public relations and public education.

Instruction: Course covers role and function of a Fire Officer I, goals and objectives of the fire service, leadership styles and patterns, supervisor and subordinate relations, sources of fire officer power, the fire officer's role as a manager, basic organizational concepts and principles, motivation and discipline, basic performance appraisal interviewing, and public relations. Lecture and discussion are used.

Credit recommendation: In the lower division baccalaureate/associate degree category or in the upper division baccalaureate category, 3 semester hours in Business Administration, Fire Science, Management, or Public Management (10/87).

Fire Department Management II

Location: University of Illinois or selected off-campus sites.

Length: 40 hours (5- to 8-hour meetings per week or weekends).

Dates: September 1984-Present.

Objective: To provide the student with the skills related to successful management.

Learning Outcome: Upon successful completion of this course, the student will be able to understand basic communication skills; written communications; group dynamics; conflict resolution; and stress management.

Instruction: Course covers writing records and reports, nature and structure of a work group, types and functions of small groups, factors affecting group job performance, leadership within a work group, building group cohesion and morale, formal and informal communication channels, communication and self-disclosure patterns in a fire company, and interpersonal and intergroup conflicts. Lecture and discussion are used.

Credit recommendation: In the lower division baccalaureate/associate degree category or in the upper division baccalaureate category, 3 semester hours in Business Administration, Fire Science, Management, or Public Management (10/87).

Fire Department Management III

Location: University of Illinois or selected off-campus sites.

Length: 40 hours (5-8 hour meetings per week or weekends).

Dates: January 1985-Present.

Objective: To provide the student with an understanding of key management techniques.

Learning Outcome: Upon successful completion of this course, the student will be able to understand the role and function of the Fire Officer II; the functions of management; coaching and counseling; time management; decision making; management by objectives; program analysis; and budgeting techniques.

Instruction: Course covers role and function of a Fire Officer II, managing programs and supervisors, the Fire Officer II and the management cycle, time management, delegation, decision-making, management by objectives, motivation, counseling subordinates, management versus leadership, and basic budgeting techniques.

Credit recommendation: In the upper division baccalaureate category, 3 semester hours in Business Administration, Fire Science, Management, or Public Management (10/87).

Fire Department Management IV

Location: University of Illinois or selected off-campus sites.

Length: 40 hours (5-8 hour meetings per week or weekends).

Dates: January 1985-Present.

Objective: To provide the student with negotiation and human relation skills related to successful management.

Learning Outcome: Upon successful completion of this course, the student will be able to understand leadership development; fire officer liability; dealing with the news media; image development; labor relations; hiring and promotional systems; personnel management; and special topics.

Instruction: Course covers public relations and public education; dealing with the media; personnel management; labor relations in the public sector; collective bargaining problems; criminal, civil and administrative liability; hiring and promotion interviews; job appraisal interview systems, disciplinary hearings; avoiding lawsuits and suspensions; training for leadership; and communication within organizational structures. Lecture and discussion are used.

Credit recommendation: In the upper division baccalaureate category, 3 semester hours in Business Administration, Fire Science, Management, or Personnel Management (10/87).

Fire Prevention Officer I

Location: University of Illinois or selected off-campus sites.

Length: 240 hours (6 weeks).

Dates: September 1982-Present.

Objective: To lead the student to certification at three levels: Fire Investigator I, Fire Prevention Education Officer I, and Fire Inspector I.

Learning Outcome: Upon successful completion of this course, the student will be able to understand the methods and applications of inspection techniques, interpretation and application of fire codes, fire hazards and causes, elements of building construction, and fire protection devices.

Instruction: Course covers inspection techniques, interpretation and application of fire codes, fire hazards and causes, elements of building construction, and fire protection devices. Students must successfully complete this course in order to satisfy requirements for certification as Fire Investigator I, Fire Prevention Education Officer I, and Fire Inspector I. This course is very specialized and covers topics in an in-depth manner. Lecture and discussion are used.

Credit recommendation: In the lower division baccalaureate/associate degree category, 6 semester hours in Fire Science or Fire Technology (10/87).

Hazardous Materials: Chemistry
  Location: University of Illinois or selected off-campus sites.
  Length: 80 hours (2 weeks).
  Dates: April 1986-Present.
  Objective: To provide the student with a basic understanding of principles related to organic and inorganic chemistry.
  Learning Outcome: Upon successful completion of this course, the student will be able to understand aspects of inorganic and organic chemistry necessary to prepare the hazardous materials first responder or response team member to evaluate a hazardous materials incident scene and initiate appropriate corrective action in accordance with proper safety procedures.
  Instruction: Topics include a survey lecture on physical chemistry, chemical formula writing, types of reactions, math review, atomic theory, chemical equations, molecular theory, chemical changes, common organic compounds, incident analysis and mitigation, identification of unknowns, hydrocarbons, and toxicology.
  Credit recommendation: In the lower division baccalaureate/associate degree category, 3 semester hours in Emergency Medical Services, Fire Science, Fire Technology, or Law Enforcement (10/87).

Tactics and Strategy II
  Location: University of Illinois or selected off-campus sites.
  Length: 40 hours (1 week).
  Dates: October 1982-Present.
  Objective: To provide the student with the appropriate strategies and tactics for managing or directing fire fighting operations.
  Learning Outcome: Upon successful completion of this course, the student will be able to direct multi-company or department fire fighting operations.
  Instruction: Course covers fire ground management, strategic concepts in fire fighting, manpower utilization, hazardous materials, disaster management, and simulated fire problems. Lecture and practical exercises are used.
  Credit recommendation: In the lower division baccalaureate/associate degree category, 3 semester hours in Fire Science or Fire Technology (10/87).

INACOMP Computer Centers, Inc.

INACOMP Educational Services (IES) which has been in existence since 1982 is a division of Inacomp Computer Centers, Inc. Inacomp Computer Centers, Inc. has been in existence since 1976 and provides computer training, hardware, software, and support services. Corporate headquarters are located in Troy, Michigan.

IES training programs include courses in computer literacy, software applications in the areas of word processing, spreadsheets, database, and technical computer-related courses such as Computer Aided Design (CAD).

The programs are nationally coordinated and monitored in order to help maintain consistency across multiple locations. Supervisors of the program are located at the Troy, Michigan location and all course policies, procedures and guidelines originate and are handled through that office.

IES provides instructors and all necessary instructional and reference materials to teach the course objectives. IES classrooms are equipped with computer workstations for hands-on training.

Where instruction takes place on-site at a particular business or industry rather than at an Inacomp location, IES provides the instruction, all of the course materials and the course equipment (hardware and software) at the designated site.

Teaching staff is selected through the resume and interview process. Selection is based upon the following criteria: knowledge of Disk Operating System (DOS), knowledge of course subject matter, professionalism, interpersonal communications skills, and experience. Course development and revision takes place when the need has been identified by either course evaluation form responses or market analysis information. When the need has been identified, the national instructional coordinator works with the curriculum specialist and "master" instructors who have developed the appropriate area of expertise.

Source of official student records: INACOMP Educational Services, Office of the Registrar, 1800 West Maple Road, Troy, Michigan 48084.

Additional information about the courses: Program on Noncollegiate Sponsored Instruction, The Center for Adult Learning and Educational Credentials, One Dupont Circle, Washington D.C. 20036.

Advanced Computer Literacy
  Location: At various locations in thirteen states with

regional bases in Michigan, California, Illinois, Florida and Georgia.

Length: 30 hours (12 weeks; can be scheduled differently).

Dates: January 1987-Present.

Objective: To introduce the student to advanced features of: Microcomputer Operating Systems for Hard Disk, Word Processing, Spreadsheet, and Data Base Application Software.

Learning Outcome: Upon successful completion of this course, the student will understand basic computer architecture and be able to use microcomputer word processing, spreadsheets, data base software, and operating systems commands.

Instruction: Concepts covered include: hard disk operating system commands, elementary basic language commands, spreadsheets, word processing, data base, and introduction to the use of microcomputers in data communication. Includes opportunity for hands-on experience.

Credit recommendation: In the lower division baccalaureate/associate degree category, 2 semester hours in Microcomputer Applications (3/87).

Basic Computer Literacy

Location: At various locations in thirteen states with regional bases in Michigan, California, Illinois, Florida, and Georgia.

Length: 30 hours (12 weeks; can be scheduled differently).

Dates: January 1987-Present.

Objective: To introduce the student to computer hardware and some commonly used microcomputer software packages.

Learning Outcome: Upon successful completion of this course, the student will understand basic microcomputer terminology and hardware components and gain elementary skills in using spreadsheets, word processing, database, and the disk operating system.

Instruction: Elementary concepts (including DOS) and terminology of microcomputers and introduction to software packages, including: word processing, spreadsheet, database, and operating systems. Includes opportunity for hands-on experience.

Credit recommendation: In the lower division baccalaureate/associate degree category, 1 semester hour in Microcomputer Applications (3/87).

Computer Aided Design (CAD)

Location: At various locations in thirteen states with regional bases in Michigan, California, Illinois, Florida and Georgia.

Length: 30 hours (10 weeks; can be scheduled differently).

Dates: January 1987-Present.

Objective: To introduce the student to the essential components of Microcomputer Based CAD Systems and Application.

Learning Outcome: Upon successful completion of this course, the student will understand the use and role of microcomputers in CAD applications. Application software will be used to introduce basic CAD commands, and design drawings.

Instruction: Microcomputer hardware components required for CAD; CAD software commands; and elementary drawing design using CAD software are covered. Included opportunity for hands-on experience.

Credit recommendation: In the upper division baccalaureate category, 2 semester hours in Computer Aided Design (3/87).

Independent School Management

Independent School Management (ISM) is a consulting and service firm committed to the development of cost effective, efficient management of private-independent schools. Research, on-site consulting, problem analysis, and theory development are all part of its ongoing activities, the results of which are shared in publications, seminars, and workshops.

The Management Institutes are offered in response to the needs of the independent school community. To complement graduate education programs that primarily relate to administrators in the public sector, the ISM workshops are targeted to key administrators of private independent schools. The workshops provide practical information. Techniques, concepts, designs, and theories have been developed and tested by ISM through on-site consultation at hundreds of different types of private-independent schools. Each workshop and seminar takes place under the guidance of men and women with experience in several private-independent schools.

Most of the workshops are operated during the Summer Institute that is held at Washington College in Chestertown, Maryland. Other fall and winter workshops are held in Wilmington, Delaware, using hotel facilities.

Source of official student records: Director of Management Institutes, Independent School Management, 1316 North Union Street, Wilmington, Delaware 19806-2594.

Additional information about the courses: Program on Noncollegiate Sponsored Instruction, The Center for Adult Learning and Educational Credentials, American Council on Education, One Dupont Circle, Washington, D.C. 20036.

Administering the Small Private-Independent School

Location: Chestertown, MD.

Length: 42 hours (6 days).

Dates: July 1984-Present.

Objective: To provide practical information and techniques for administering a small private-independent school with a limited budget and support staff.

Instruction: Covers general elements of private-independent school administration (role of the head, staffing, working with trustees, business management, curriculum and scheduling, external relations, stress and conflict management, effecting change) from the perspective of a small school headmaster. Methodology includes lecture, discussion, and handouts.

Credit recommendation: In the upper division baccalaureate or graduate category, 1 semester hour in School Administration (8/85).

Advanced Business Management for Private-Independent Schools

Location: Chestertown, MD.
Length: 42 Hours (6 days).
Dates: July 1985-Present.
Objective: To provide independent school managers with advanced training in the areas of financial management, administrative accounting, risk analysis, insurance, property management, budgeting, legal aspects of various decisions, and establishing administrative policies.
Instruction: Methodology includes lecture, discussions, handouts, financial and budgeting problems, cases, and readings. Special attention is given to the financial and legal impacts of school decisions on the budgeting process.
Credit recommendation: In the graduate category, 1 semester hour in School Business Management (8/85).

Catholic School Governance: Managing Change

Location: Chestertown, MD.
Length: 21 Hours (3 days).
Dates: July 1985-July 1986.
Objective: To provide the emerging lay leadership (trustees and heads) of Catholic schools with understanding and skills for effective governance in times of change.
Instruction: Analyzes the shift from religious to lay leadership and the resulting emergence of advisory and lay governing boards. Addresses questions of philosophy, trust, ownership, super-boards, board responsibility, appointment of heads, finances, and marketing. Methodology includes lecture, discussion, handouts, and use of visuals.
Credit recommendation: In the upper division baccalaureate or graduate category, 1 semester hour in Educational Administration (8/85).

Fund Raising for Private-Independent Schools

Location: Chestertown, MD.
Length: 21 hours (3 days).
Dates: July 1980-Present.
Objective: To provide private-independent school Heads and trustees with an understanding of basic fund raising methods, operations, and staffing and an appreciation of their appropriate role in overseeing the development program.
Instruction: An introduction to development, components of the development program, and basic fund raising techniques for administrators and board members who will oversee development functions in private-independent schools. Methodology includes lecture, discussion, display of materials and handouts.
Credit recommendation: In the upper division baccalaureate category, 1 semester hour in Educational Administration (8/85).

Extending Student Counselor's Role in Private-Independent Schools

Location: Chestertown, MD.
Length: 21 hours (3 days).
Dates: July 1985-Present.
Objective: To provide counselors in an independent school with additional tools and techniques by which to extend and improve its student assistance programs. The course emphasizes contemporary student distresses and needs which usually can be favorably impacted by early recognition and counselor involvement.
Instruction: Methodology includes extensive readings of handouts, lecture on theory and practice of counseling, discussion, shared case evaluations, and early identification of student life problems associated with emotional distress, peer pressures, social isolation, drug use, delinquency, causes of various disorders (and student suicide). Emphasis is upon early problem recognition, evaluation, and counseling.
Credit recommendation: In the upper division baccalaureate or graduate category, 1 semester hour in Counselor Education (8/85).

In-Service Workshop for Private-Independent School Headmasters

Location: Chestertown, MD.
Length: *Versions 1 and 2:* 60 hours (11 days).
Dates: July 1982-Present.
Objective: To provide experienced private-independent school Headmasters with information and techniques for analyzing and managing their schools.
Instruction: Applies models of private-independent school operation and governance to the varied responsibilities of Headmasters, including constituent relations, curriculum development, non-academic programs, personnel management, internal policy, trustee relations, physical plant operations, financial management, and institutional advancement. Methodology includes lecture, discussion, and handouts.
Credit recommendation: In the upper division baccalaureate or graduate category, 2 semester hours in Educational Administration (8/85).

Managing the Private-Independent Elementary School
Location: Chestertown, MD.
Length: 21 hours (3 days).
Dates: July 1980-Present.
Objective: To provide information and techniques for operating the elementary division of a private-independent school.
Instruction: Applies concepts of problem solving, communications, testing, leadership, school organization, staffing, and supervision to the management of a private-independent elementary school. Methodology includes lecture, discussion, case studies, and handouts.
Credit recommendation: In the upper division baccalaureate category, 1 semester hour in Elementary Education Administration (8/85).

Managing the Private-Independent Middle School
Location: Chestertown, MD.
Length: *Version 1:* 21 hours (3 days); *Version 2:* 42 hours (6 days).
Dates: July 1981-Present.
Objective: To apply selected management techniques to the administration of a middle school division of a private-independent school.
Instruction: Analyzes the needs of early adolescents and the appropriate educational environment for these middle-school students. Attention is given to parent relations, goal setting and planning, staffing, and management techniques. Methodology includes lecture, discussion, and handouts.
Credit recommendation: In the upper division baccalaureate category, 1 semester hour in Junior High School Administration (8/85).

Marketing the Private-Independent School: Student Recruitment and Retention
Location: Chestertown, MD.
Length: 42 hours (6 days).
Dates: July 1982-Present.
Objective: To provide independent school administrators with the concepts and applications of successful marketing by way of market planning strategy development, promotion, and selling. Well designed marketing programs lead to successful student recruitment and retention results.
Instruction: Methodology includes a review of marketing literature and applications in non-profit organizations, and relevance to school management; lecture and discussions; individualized development of market plans and strategies, case problems and discussions, and implementation of recruiting and retention programs.
Credit recommendation: In the upper division baccalaureate or graduate category, 1 semester hour in School Administration (8/85).

Operating a Private-Independent School Business Office
Location: Chestertown, MD.
Length: 42 hours (6 days).
Dates: July 1977-Present.
Objective: To provide an overview of the duties, organization and management aspects of operating a business office in an independent school; and explore representative topics and problems of finance, budgeting, investment practices, physical plant, taxation, and managerial role of the business officer.
Instruction: Methodology includes lecture, discussion, regular handouts, short problems, design of forms, interpreting rules and school policies, and review of representative problems and issues that face the business officer of an independent school.
Credit recommendation: In the upper division baccalaureate or graduate category, 1 semester hour in School Administration (8/85).

Operating the Private-Independent School Development Program - 3dd
Location: Chestertown, MD.
Length: 42 hours (6 days).
Dates: July 1979-Present.
Objective: To provide understanding of and techniques for management of a development (fund raising) program.
Instruction: Covers principal functions of a school development office: long-range planning, annual fund, capital campaign, foundation/corporate solicitation, planned giving, solicitation techniques, and use of computers in development. Methodology includes lecture, discussion, handouts, and in-class projects.
Credit recommendation: In the graduate category, 2 semester hours in Financial Resource Development (8/85).

Overview of Business and Financial Management in Private-Independent Schools
Location: Chestertown, MD.
Length: 21 hours (3 days).
Dates: July 1977-Present.
Objective: To introduce principles and applications of basic accounting, business and financial management for independent schools; and to orient school Heads to the operator of a business office.
Instruction: Lecture and discussion of problems.
Credit recommendation: In the upper division baccalaureate or graduate category, 1 semester hour in School Administration or Leadership (8/85).

Presiding Over the Private-Independent School Board of Trustees
Location: Chestertown, MD.
Length: 21 hours (3 days).
Dates: July 1979-Present.

Objective: To review the legal and political setting in which school boards operate, to explore representative board problems and issues, and to provide trustees and board chairpersons with skills for successful board management.

Instruction: Covers origin and responsibilities of governing boards for private-independent schools, board composition and organization, responsibilities of board presidents and other officers, and behavior of board members. Methodology includes seminar, lecture, group discussions, and extensive readings, case problems, simulated board exercises.

Credit recommendation: In the graduate category, 1 semester hour in Educational Administration or Leadership (8/85).

The Private-Independent School Admissions Office

Location: Chestertown, MD.
Length: 21 hours (3 days).
Dates: July 1985-Present.
Objective: To provide information on the operation of an independent school admissions office; and to relate admissions procedures and techniques to marketing and recruiting concepts.

Instruction: Covers operations of a private-independent school admissions office, how to interest prospective students, internal procedures for data collection and evaluation, fee structure and financial aids, retention techniques, parent relations and working with the school Head. Methodology includes lecture, discussion, and handouts.

Credit recommendation: In the upper division baccalaureate category, 1 semester hour in Student Personnel Administration (8/85).

Private-Independent School Curriculum Analysis and Coordination

Location: Chestertown, MD.
Length: 21 hours (3 days).
Dates: July 1984-Present.
Objective: To provide a framework for analyzing elements of the school environment that impact the curriculum, and to provide techniques for scheduling and implementing the school curriculum.

Instruction: Covers analysis of the community, parents, students, faculty, and school resources and their implications for the school curriculum. Special attention is given to scheduling and implementation of the school curriculum. Methodology includes lecture, discussion, and handouts.

Credit recommendation: In the upper division baccalaureate category, 1 semester hour in School Curriculum (8/85). This credit recommendation will apply if the course goes beyond the personal experience of the instructor by examining insights about curriculum development and evaluation found in the literature of the curriculum field.

Private-Independent School Scheduling: Designs, Process, Techniques

Location: Chestertown, MD.
Length: 42 hours (6 days).
Dates: July 1975-Present.
Objective: To provide administrators with the principles and diverse applications of scheduling models to independent school decisions, particularly pre-registration and registration, and curricula planning. A variety of scheduling models and designs are introduced along with computer-supported scheduling routines.

Instruction: Methodology includes lecture, discussion, handouts, cases, readings, and solving a variety of independent school scheduling problems.

Credit recommendation: In the upper division baccalaureate or graduate category, 1 semester hour in School Administration (8/85).

The Compleat Private-Independent School Secretary

Location: Chestertown, MD.
Length: 21 hours (3 days).
Dates: July 1980-Present.
Objective: To improve communication skills of the Head's secretary, review office leadership styles, and provide an overview of office management topics and administrative techniques which improve productivity.

Instruction: Methodology includes lecture, discussion, current problems, review of office administration principles and practices, and recent developments in word processing and other information handling procedures.

Credit recommendation: In the vocational certificate category, 1 semester hour in Office Administration or Secretarial Studies (8/85).

Women as School Administrators in Private-Independent Schools

Location: Chestertown, MD.
Length: 21 hours (3 days).
Dates: July 1985-Present.
Objective: To examine the role and leadership styles of women administrators in independent schools, to improve managerial skills of participants, and to explore professional development options of women executives.

Instruction: Covers female psychological development, management styles and techniques, conflict resolution, decision making, and collaboration all within the context of leadership of female administrators. Methodology includes seminar, surveys and self-evaluation, critiques from literature, current problems and conflict resolution.

Credit recommendation: In the graduate category, 1 semester hour in Administration or Leadership (8/85).

Indian Health Service - Tribal Management Support Center

The Tribal Management Support Center (TMSC) functions within the director's office of the Office of Research and Development, an Indian Health Service (IHS) Headquarters component geographically located in Tucson, Arizona.

TMSC was established to provide a broad spectrum of services nationwide to all recognized Indian and Alaskan Native Tribes, tribal organizations, and the Indian Health Service through technical consultation and assistance, systems development, and training in the management and administration of health programs and institutions.

The Training Services component of TMSC provides a professional staff to develop courses, instruct, and manage all formal educational training by the Center; and coordinates all training efforts promoted by the Center but carried on by outside agencies or institutions. TMSC courses are specifically designed to meet the explicit goals and objectives of the various Indian and Alaska Native tribes, their organizations, and the Indian Health Service nationwide.

TMSC maintains a Curriculum Review Committee to monitor TMSC courses for quality of course content and instruction as well as cultural/audience appropriateness.

Source of official student records: Registrar and Chief of Training, Tribal Management Support Center, Training Services, P.O. Box 11340, Tucson, Arizona 85734.

Additional information about the courses: Program on Noncollegiate Sponsored Instruction, The Center for Adult Learning and Educational Credentials, American Council on Education, One Dupont Circle, Washington, D.C. 20036.

Health Service Personnel Administration (Federal) (HSPF 400, A,B,C)

Location: Tribal Management Support Center, Tucson, AZ. Field locations by special arrangement.
Length: 105 hours (3 weeks).
Dates: April 1980-Present.
Objective: To develop a basic understanding and working knowledge of personnel management and administration in the federal system.
Instruction: Covers the history and role of the federal personnel system; position classification and pay management; standards of performance and appraisal; adverse actions and grievance procedures; labor-management relations; recruitment and staffing; personnel records and reports; employee benefits; employee development; commissioned corps; and special conditions and restrictions. Lecture, discussion, supervised programmed learning, and written exercises are used.
Credit recommendation: In the lower division baccalaureate/associate degree category, 3 semester hours in Business Administration, Personnel Administration, or Public Administration (9/80).

Health Service Personnel Administration (Tribal) (HSPT 400)

Location: Tribal Management Support Center, Tucson, AZ. Field locations by special arrangement.
Length: 35 hours (1 week).
Dates: January 1981-Present.
Objective: To provide a working knowledge of personnel management and administration.
Instruction: Covers position classification and pay management, standards of performance and appraisal, adverse actions and grievance procedures, recruitment and staff, personnel records, employee benefits, employee development, and special conditions and restrictions. Lecture, discussion, supervised programmed learning, and written exercises are used.
Credit recommendation: In the lower division baccalaureate/associate degree category, 2 semester hours in Business Administration, Personnel Administration, or Public Administration (9/80).

Office Management and Administration (OMA 400)

Location: Tribal Management Support Center, Tucson, AZ. Field locations by special arrangement.
Length: 35 hours (1 week).
Dates: April 1980-Present.
Objective: To provide basic instruction in ten functional areas of office support services and to broaden students' knowledge in those areas. Emphasis is given to developing skills and introducing basic principles and functions.
Instruction: Provides comprehensive survey of office management support services and procedures and in-depth discussion of routine office services tasks, such as records management, communications, mail processing, reports, and equipment management. Develops specialized skills in forms design, office space planning, and travel arrangements. Uses reference materials published by the federal government. Lecture, discussion, and workshops are used.
Credit recommendation: In the vocational certificate category or in the lower division baccalaureate/associate degree category, 2 semester hours in Office Management or Secretarial Science (9/80).

Principles of Management and Leadership (MAN 200 A & B)

Location: Tribal Management Support Center, Tucson, AZ. Field locations by special arrangement.
Length: 42 hours (3 days per week for 2 weeks).
Dates: November 1979-Present.
Objective: To present basic management and leadership principles and their application to actual management situations.

Instruction: Covers principles of basic management and supervisory responsibilities, including planning, organizing, controlling, communicating, motivating, and decision making. Leadership instruction is provided, with units in employee individuality, personality and behavior, three-way communications, discipline, complaints and grievances, employee development, and job satisfaction and morale. Discussion, lecture, and workshop/simulation exercises are used.

Credit recommendation: In the lower division baccalaureate/associate degree category, 2 semester hours in Business Administration or Public Administration (9/80).

Training the Trainer (TT 100)
Location: Tribal Management Support Center, Tucson, AZ. Field locations by special arrangement.
Length: 35 hours (1 week).
Dates: July 1980-Present.
Objective: To provide trainers with a practical overview of training methods to improve the quality of their training.
Instruction: Covers techniques of assessing training needs, writing performance objectives, developing course content, selection and use of training aids, development of materials, and presentation skills. Lecture, discussion, workshops, and videotapes are used.
Credit recommendation: In the vocational certificate category or in the lower division baccalaureate/associate degree category, 2 semester hours in Communication or Community Services (9/80).

Using the Computer as a Management Tool (MAN 400)
Location: Tribal Management Support Center, Tucson, AZ. Field locations by special arrangement.
Length: 22 hours (3 days).
Dates: May 1980-Present.
Objective: To help managers increase their understanding of the practical procedures for using the computer and to improve communications between operating managers and data processing professionals.
Instruction: Covers basic vocabulary and concepts of data processing, including system and computer language, how to identify information needs, how to communicate those needs to the people responsible for data processing, and how computer systems can improve management. Discussion, lecture, and workshop/simulation exercises are used.
Credit recommendation: In the lower division baccalaureate/associate degree category, 1 semester hour in Management or Public Administration (9/80).

Wang Word Processing (WP 100 A & B)
Location: Tribal Management Support Center, Tucson, AZ.
Length: 35 hours (1 week).
Dates: June 1980-Present.
Objective: To train clerical operators in word processing, and give them the ability to proficiently operate the Wang word processor.
Instruction: Covers the concepts of word processing and operation of the Wang word processor. Students will learn to use these machines proficiently, enter and retrieve documents, and edit in the easiest possible manner. Lecture, discussion, and workshops are used.
Credit recommendation: In the vocational certificate category or in the lower division baccalaureate/associate degree category, 2 semester hours in Office Management or Secretarial Science (9/80).

Institute for Business and Technology

The Institute for Business and Technology (IBT) offers training programs in: Word Processing, Computer Operations, Computer Programming, General Secretary, Executive, Legal and Medical Secretary. IBT has locations in Newark and Jersey City, New Jersey; Atlanta, Georgia; Philadelphia, Pennsylvania; and Richmond, Virginia. The main campus manages all the schools from its headquarters in Newark, New Jersey. The curriculum and academic standards are uniform.

Programs of study are offered during the day (full-time) or evening (part-time). Full-time students attend classes 25 hours per week, Monday through Friday and part-time students attend 16 hours per week, Monday through Thursday.

Students progress through the curriculum following a sequential order of general business courses, which provide the foundation needed for the students to succeed in their chosen areas of specialization. Students are required to complete all courses satisfactorily and to develop skill proficiency in typewriting and word processing courses to be eligible for a diploma or certificate.

IBT is accredited by the Accrediting Commission of the Association of Independent Colleges and Schools.

Source of official student records: Dean, Academic Programs, Institute of Business and Technology, 3 William Street, Newark, NJ 07102.

Additional information about the courses: Program on Noncollegiate Sponsored Information, Thomas A. Edison State College, 101 West State Street, Trenton, NJ 08625.

Business Law (Bus 103)
Location: Newark, NJ and Jersey City, NJ.
Length: 50 hours (10 weeks).
Dates: January 1985-Present.
Objective: To introduce students to fundamental concepts of law and how the law impacts upon their business and personal life.
Instruction: This course covers an introduction to fun-

damentals of law including contracts, wills, estates, and other legal corporate documents. In a simulated manner students prepare the filing of papers of incorporation. Students, also, learn how legal rules and procedures impact on daily life. A midterm, a final examination, and student project are required.

Credit recommendation: In the lower division baccalaureate/associate degree category, 3 semester hours in Personal Law (7/86).

Business Mathematics (Bus 107)
   Location: Newark, NJ and Jersey City, NJ.
   Length: 50 hours (10 weeks).
   Dates: January 1985-Present.
   Objective: To teach students the applications of basic mathematical functions to business-related activities.
   Instruction: This course covers the developing of mathematical competencies necessary to perform day-to-day business transactions such as banking and credit, trade and cash discounts, record keeping, payroll, taxes, inventory, and depreciation.
   Credit recommendation: In the lower division baccalaureate/associate degree category, 3 semester hours in Business Mathematics (7/86).

Introduction to Word Processing
   a. Computer and Word Processing Concepts (Bus 104)
   b. Introduction to Word Processing (WP 107)
   c. Word Processing and Lab (WP 108)
   Location: Newark, NJ and Jersey City, NJ.
   Length: a. 50 hours (10 weeks); b. 50 hours (10 weeks); c. 150 hours (10 weeks).
   Dates: January 1985-Present.
   Objective: a. To teach students the fundamentals of using microcomputers effectively. b. To provide necessary skills for students to maximize their efficiency in Word Processing. c. To enable students to operate state-of-the-art Word Processing CRT equipment.
   Instruction: a. The course provides an historical overview of the development of the computer and Word Processing equipment. Students also learn detailed vocabulary for use with Word Processing. b. This course provides the word processing concepts and materials from input to distribution. Students gain step-by-step theoretical knowledge necessary for creating, revising, formulating, and producing office documents. Proofreading and editing skills are also covered. A midterm and final examination are required. c. This is a hands-on course in which all the information learned in WP 107 is applied. Students create and edit documents, store, and retrieve documents, file maintenance and special functions are also covered. A midterm and final examination are required.
   Credit recommendation: In the lower division baccalaureate/associate degree category, 4 semester hours in Introduction to Word Processing (7/86).

Keyboarding (Typ 101)
   Location: Newark, NJ and Jersey City, NJ.
   Length: 50 hours (10 weeks).
   Dates: January 1985-Present.
   Objective: To teach computer operators and programming students the alphabetic and numeric keyboarding.
   Instruction: In this course students use the touch typing method to learn the alphabetic and numeric keyboard. Students are required to achieve a gross typing speed of 20 words per minute as determined by a services of speed tests.
   Credit recommendation: In the lower division baccalaureate/associate degree category, 1 semester hour in Keyboarding (7/86).

Office Technology
   a. Office Simulation (Bus 106)
   b. Professional Preparation (Bus 105)
   c. Records Management (Bus 102)
   d. Speech and Communication (Eng 103)
   Location: Newark, NJ and Jersey City, NJ.
   Length: a. 50 hours (10 weeks); b. 25 hours (5 weeks); c. 25 hours (5 weeks); d. 50 hours (10 weeks).
   Dates: April 1985-Present.
   Objective: a. To acquaint students with actual procedures in a simulated office environment. b. To prepare students for successful career planning. c. To develop students' efficiency in filing procedures and maintaining office records. d. To assist students develop effective written and oral communication skills.
   Instruction: a. In this course the teacher acts as office supervisor and assigns students specific tasks. These include greeting visitors, handling the phone, typing, filing, etc. Students are given performance evaluation. b. This course covers the essential steps in a successful search and securement of employment. c. This course teaches students the functions and procedures of records management in the business office. Emphasis is placed upon soft and hard copy filing and cross reference techniques between paper and electronic storage. A final exam is required. d. This course teachers students basic oral and written communication correspondences necessary in a business office. A formal speech and a final examination are required.
   Credit recommendation: In the lower division baccalaureate/associate degree category, 1 semester hour in Office Technology (7/86).

Typing
   a. Beginning Typing (Typ 102)
   b. Intermediate Typing (Typ 103)
   c. Production Typing (Typ 104)
   Location: Newark, NJ and Jersey City, NJ.
   Length: a. 100 hours (10 weeks); b. 100 hours (10 weeks); c. 100 hours (10 weeks).
   Dates: January 1985-Present.

Objective: a. To teach students functions of the typewriter and the keyboard by using the touch method. b. To teach in-depth application of skills acquired in beginning. c. To improve typing skills of students and to increase their efficiency in office situations.

Instruction: a. In this course students learn typewriting skills and are tested for speed and accuracy throughout the course. b. In this course business letters, memorandums, and manuscript typing are covered; students also learn random business forms, statistical tabulation, and formal reports. Students must achieve a minimum of 37 words per minute as well as pass a final examination. c. Students in this course learn two-page letters, multipage reports, letters with tabulations in the body, and manuscripts with footnotes. A minimum speed of 58 words per minute and final examination are required.

Credit recommendation: In the lower division baccalaureate/associate degree category, 5 semester hours in Typing (7/86).

Institute for Citizen Involvement in Education

The Institute for Citizen Involvement in Education, formerly Schoolwatch, Inc., is a nonprofit coalition of business, civic, and religious organizations that monitors implementation of New Jersey's state education laws. In particular, the Institute monitors the implementation of the Public School Education Act of 1975. Known as the T&E law (thorough and efficient), this legislation defines "thorough" and "efficient" and calls for fiscal reform in the state.

The Institute is governed by an eight-member volunteer board chaired by Robert Woodford, Chair of the New Jersey Business and Industry Council. Other members represent the state Chamber of Commerce, New Jersey Taxpayers Association, New Jersey Bell, The Ecumenical Ministry, the Puerto Rican Congress, and The Educational Law Center.

A major concern of the Institute is to improve the involvement and effectiveness of parents in the public schools. The course described here addresses that concern. Parent volunteers are the course participants.

Source of official student records: Institute for Citizen Involvement in Education, Passaic County Community College, College Boulevard, Patterson, New Jersey 07509.

Additional information about the courses: Thomas A. Edison State College, Program on Noncollegiate Sponsored Instruction, Office of Special Programs, 101 W. State St., Trenton, New Jersey 08625.

Public Policy and Public Schools

Location: Various New Jersey School Districts.
Length: *Version 1:* 120 hours (30 weeks); *Version 2:* 80 hours (24 weeks).
Dates: *Version 1:* September 1982-June 1984; *Version 2:* September 1984-Present.
Objective: To increase the degree of involvement and to enhance the effectiveness of parents in the public schools.
Instruction: Parent volunteers are the course participants. The instructor-led course uses simulations, presentations, reading and writing assignments to cover federal, state, and local legislative and fiscal policies including school budgets; school district organization; discipline; curriculum; testing; effective schools research; parent roles and family roles; and communication in schools. The learning outcomes of the course are: to enable students to describe, analyze, and evaluate issues surrounding or involved in distribution of power and decision making, equity, resource provision, control, and innovation, and to enable students to collect and evaluate information; to enable students to describe, analyze, and evaluate issues surrounding or involved in testing, discipline, parenting skills, and curriculum development; to enhance the ability of students to work effectively in groups and make written and public presentations; to increase student capabilities to apply knowledge and participate effectively in public policy making in education.

Credit recommendation: *Version 1:* In the lower division baccalaureate/associate degree category, 3 semester hours in Political Science/Public Policy, 3 semester hours in Educational Psychology or Tests and Measurements, and 3 semester hours in Communications or Introductory Speech. *Version 2:* In the lower division baccalaureate/associate degree category, 3 semester hours in Political Science or Public Policy and 3 semester hours in Introductory Speech or Communications (5/85). NOTE: This course is taught in a very integrated manner over a full term of 24 weeks. If a student completes only one half of the course (12 weeks), 3 semester hours in either Political Science/Public Policy or Introductory Speech/Communications. In the first half of the course there is an extensive communications component but the content is primarily Public Policy. A total of 3 semester hours should be awarded, but it could properly be given in either discipline.

Institute of Certified Professional Managers

The Institute of Certified Professional Managers, established in 1974, provides an opportunity for managers to attain the designation of CM (Certified Manager) by achieving passing scores on three examinations. In addition to this independent certification procedure, the Institute seeks to instill a commitment to lifelong learning in the management field through a formal recertification process.

Examinations cover Administrative Skills, Interpersonal Skills, and Personal Skills of managers and are given twice yearly (on the first Saturdays of May and November) at various locations in the U.S. and abroad. These examinations require demonstration of knowledge of management principles and practices in the areas of leadership, achievement of organizational objectives, motivation of subordinates, and general managerial behavior. Each examination contains 120 multiple-choice questions and takes two hours. All three need not be taken at one time and each may be taken again, if failed.

Since October 1982, preparatory course appropriate to each of the three examinations have been available through the Institute.

Maintenance of the CM designation requires that proof of continued study in the field of management be presented at five-year intervals.

Source of official student records: Institute of Certified Professional Managers, James Madison University, Harrisonburg, Virginia 22807.

Additional information about the courses: Program on Noncollegiate Sponsored Instruction, The Center for Adult Learning and Educational Credentials, American Council on Education, One Dupont Circle, Washington, D.C. 20036.

Administrative Skills for the Manager

Location: Various; materials suitable for self-study, use by study groups, or in a formal course.

Length: Varies with mode of delivery; 20 hours (10 weeks) if a course.

Dates: October 1982-Present.

Objective: To prepare the student for Part II of a standardized examination on administrative skills of effective managers.

Learning Outcome: Upon successful completion of this course, the student will be able to understand planning and control processes; know guidelines and tools of compensation management, including forecasting, flow charts, and budgeting; know uses of business mathematics in statistical decision making; understand the role and application of computers in MIS; and understand relationships among business, government, and labor.

Instruction: Course covers legal, economic, and business influences on management; planning; building organizational staff and structure; controlling; and management and analysis of information. Methodology includes study manual, lecture, discussion, and study questions, depending on mode of delivery. A *Leader's Guide,* which includes examples and illustrations, is available to assist individual learners, study group leaders, or instructors of more formal courses.

Credit recommendation: In the upper division baccalaureate category, 1 semester hour in Principles of Management (Administrative Skills of Managers) (8/83) (4/88). NOTE 1: This course has been reevaluated and continues to meet requirements for credit recommendations. NOTE 2: Credit should be given only if the student passes the corresponding part of the Professional Managers Certification examination.

Interpersonal Skills for the Manager

Location: Various; materials suitable for self-study, use by study groups, or in a formal course.

Length: Varies with mode of delivery; 20 hours (10 weeks) if a course.

Dates: October 1982-Present.

Objective: To prepare the student for Part III of a standardized examination on interpersonal skills of effective managers.

Learning Outcome: Upon successful completion of this course, the student will be able to demonstrate knowledge of individual psychology and group dynamics; understand approaches to leadership that insure loyalty and cooperation; understand ways to motivate people to maximum potential; understand the complex roles of unions in today's society; and develop a framework for human resource planning and management.

Instruction: Course covers management of human resources; understanding individual behavior, group dynamics, motivational theories, leadership, unions, management and communication, conflict causes and resolution, and effective utilization of human resources. Methodology includes study manual, lecture, discussion, and study questions depending on mode of delivery. A *Leader's Guide,* which includes examples and illustrations, is available to assist individual learners, study group leaders, or instructors of more formal courses.

Credit recommendation: In the upper division baccalaureate category, 1 semester hour in Principles of Management (Interpersonal Skills of Effective Managers) (8/83) (4/88). NOTE 1: This course has been reevaluated and continues to meet requirements for credit recommendations. NOTE 2: Credit should be given only if the student passes the corresponding part of the Professional Managers Certification examination.

Personal Skills for the Manager

Location: Various; materials suitable for self-study, use by study groups, or in a formal course.

Length: Varies with mode of delivery; 20 hours (10 weeks) if a course.

Dates: October 1982-Present.

Objective: To prepare the student for Part I of a standardized examination on personal skills of effective managers.

Learning Outcome: Upon successful completion of this course, the student will be able to understand their own personal work situation; understand basic responsibilities of managers in organizations; understand the manager's role in supervision and achievement of organizational goals; and use key skills of managers in time management, communication, and delegation of authority.

Instruction: Course covers the manager as a person, a leader, a communicator, and a professional; creativity and change; the manager and time; decision making; delegation; and self-development. Methodology includes study manual, lecture, discussion, and study questions, depending on mode of delivery. A *Leader's Guide,* which includes examples and illustrations, is available to assist individual learners, study group leaders, or instructors of more formal courses.

Credit recommendation: In the upper division baccalaureate category, 1 semester hour in Principles of Management (Personal Skills of Managers) (8/83) (4/88). NOTE 1: This course has been reevaluated and continues to meet requirements for credit recommendations. NOTE 2: Credit should be given only if the student passes the corresponding part of the Professional Managers Certification examination.

Institute of Financial Education

The Institute of Financial Education is the educational affiliate of the United States League of Savings Associations. The league is the national trade association serving the savings association business.

The Institute provides multilevel professional education and training programs for savings association personnel involved in both operations and management functions. Programs are delivered through correspondence instruction, in-house training, resident schools, and a network of 220 local chapters. These programs are designed to help savings association personnel obtain the knowledge skills, and attitudes needed for efficient functioning in the various departments of a savings association.

The courses listed below constitute those required for the Institute's three diploma programs: the Certificate of Achievement, the Diploma of Merit, and the Degree of Distinction. The three programs represent a building process which begins with introductory technical business courses (Certificate), proceeds to specific technical business courses (Diploma), and ends with those broader conceptual courses (Degree) which enable students to become effective managers. Human relations and communication courses are required on the first two levels to ensure effective performance in a service-oriented, high customer-contact business. On the third level, personnel management is required to familiarize the student with the basic concepts of supervision and management.

The credit recommendations for the courses listed below apply to all chapters. Consistency is ensured through the central development of course materials and examinations. The Institute also provides chapters with guidelines for the selection and evaluation of instructors.

The credit recommendations also apply to the correspondence versions of the courses listed below. An optional proctored final examination was instituted in May 1978 for students taking the correspondence course and wishing to apply for academic credit. Students completing the courses prior to that data may also take the proctored final examination to be eligible for credit. Successful completion of the proctored examination is indicated on the student's record. This examination should not be confused with the open-book final examination which is completed at home by all students taking the correspondence courses.

Source of official student records: Manager of Scholastic and Membership Records, The Institute of Financial Education, 111 East Wacker Drive, Chicago, Illinois 60601.

Additional information about the courses: Program on Noncollegiate Sponsored Instruction, The Center for Adult Learning and Educational Credentials, American Council on Education, One Dupont Circle, Washington, D.C. 20036.

1. Accounting Principles for Savings Institutions (004)
2. Accounting Practices for Savings Institutions (005)
(Formerly 1. Savings and Loan Accounting I)
(Formerly 2. Savings and Loan Accounting II)
  Location: Chapters throughout the United States.
  Length: 48 hours (24 weeks).
  Dates: July 1979-Present.
  Objective: To introduce the accounting process in general terms for all employees of savings institutions.
  Instruction: This course covers the basic aspects of the accounting process as applied to savings institutions including (1) the functions of bookkeeping, accounting, and auditing and their interrelationships, (2) the definitions of cash accounting and accrual accounting systems, (3) preparation and analysis of balance sheets, income statements, etc., (4) the internal relationships among the departments of a savings institution as they affect information about transactions and the development of institutional statements, (5) the concept of time value of money, (6) the specific accounting procedure related to the savings and lending functions. The course also covers the techniques necessary to perform many accounting procedures such as those for savings accounts, mortgage loans, payroll, etc. The teaching methodology is lecture, discussion, and classroom exercises.
  Credit recommendation: In the lower division baccalaureate/associate degree category, 3 semester hours in Accounting for Financial Institutions (7/85). NOTE: To be eligible for credit, students must take both courses.

Basic Business English (017)
  Location: Correspondence study.
  Length: Approximately 24 hours.
  Dates: July 1982-Present.

Objective: To introduce basic English grammar, spelling, and punctuation as applied to business writing.

Instruction: This course covers the components of basic English including sentence structure, spelling, and punctuation. Emphasis is on proper use of tense, subject-verb agreement as well as analysis of the parts of speech. The common errors of punctuation and spelling are reviewed. Since this is a correspondence course, considerable opportunity for practice and self-testing are provided.

Credit recommendation: In the lower division/associate degree category, 1 semester hour in Basic Skills or Basic English (7/85).

Business Math Review (064)

Location: Chapters throughout the United States.
Length: 24 hours (12 weeks).
Dates: June 1983-Present.
Objective: Provides the student with a review of basic arithmetic operations and their application in business situations. Topics include checking accounts reconciliation, payroll and interest calculations, depreciation, and stock and bond pricing.

Instruction: Presents mathematical operations using business applications. Emphasizes topics such as checking account reconciliation, credit card transactions, payroll records, simple and compound interest, and present value tables. Additional consideration is given to APR interest calculations, depreciation methods, and mortgage loan amortization. Methodology includes lecture, discussion, and problem solving.

Credit recommendation: In the lower division baccalaureate/associate degree category, 2 semester hours in Business Mathematics (7/85).

Commercial Banking (081)

Location: Chapters throughout the United States.
Length: 24 hours (12 weeks).
Dates: December 1984-Present.
Objective: Provides the student with an examination of the organization, structure, and management of the commercial banking system within a deregulated environment.

Instruction: Covers the elements of federal and state banking regulation. Explores bank mergers, branch banking, and interstate banking. Describes the components of assets and liability managements and their effect on bank profitability. Presents policies and practices relating to lending, investments, trust services, and international banking. Methodology includes lecture and discussion.

Credit recommendation: In the lower division baccalaureate/associate degree category, 1 semester hour in Banking or Finance (7/85).

1. **Commercial Law I (043)**
2. **Commercial Law II (044)**

Location: Chapters throughout the United States.
Length: 48 hours (24 weeks).
Dates: July 1980-Present.
Objective: To acquaint the student with general concepts and principles of business law and to enable students to apply legal principles to business problems.

Instruction: Commercial Law I covers contract law and the law of personal and real property, insurance law, bankruptcy, mortgages, and landlord-tenant relationships. Commercial Law II covers commercial paper, partnerships, corporations, security and secured transactions.

Credit recommendation: In the lower division baccalaureate/associate degree category, 3 semester hours in General Business or Commercial Law (7/85). NOTE: To be eligible for credit, student must complete both courses.

Commercial Lending for Savings Institutions (079)

Location: Chapters throughout the United States.
Length: 24 hours (12 weeks).
Dates: January 1983-Present.
Objective: To provide students with an introduction to Commercial Lending. The course provides a basic overview of terms, concepts, and techniques related to business lending.

Instruction: Presents the economic and competitive factors that influence commercial lending. Describes the components of major financial statements, presents an introduction to financial statement analysis, and credit analysis of the potential borrower. Further discusses loan administration including bankruptcy proceedings. Methodology includes lecture, discussion, and case analysis.

Credit recommendation: In the lower division baccalaureate/associate degree category, 1 semester hour in Commercial Lending or Banking (7/85).

Communication Skills for Business: Talking and Listening (066)

Location: Chapters, nationally.
Length: 24 hours (12 weeks).
Dates: August 1975-Present.
Objective: To provide an understanding of the basic elements of communication and to introduce the skills necessary to interact in a business setting.

Instruction: Covers the elements of interpersonal communications and discussion skills, with emphasis on speech communication and society, messages and meanings, feedback, nonverbal communication, attention and listening, decision making, barriers and breakdowns, persuasion, conflict, troubled talk, and skill building. Methodology includes lecture, discussion, small-group interaction, and role playing.

Credit recommendation: In the lower division baccalaureate/associate degree category, 1 semester hour in Communications (4/77) (7/85). NOTE: This course has been reevaluated and continues to meet requirements for credit recommendations.

Consumer Lending (077)
Location: Chapters throughout the United States.
Length: 24 hours (12 weeks).
Dates: September 1981-Present.
Objective: Provides the student with an introduction to consumer credits and consumer lending activities. The course provides an introduction to the various types of credit sources, laws and regulations, loan mathematics, and organization of consumer credit activities.
Instruction: Covers the types and sources of consumer credit. Identifies the state and federal statutes and regulations relating to consumer credit operations. Introduces credit mathematics such as monthly payment calculation, APR, add-on and discount interest. Describes the perfection of security interest and the loan evaluation process. Methodology includes lecture, discussion, and case studies.
Credit recommendation: In the lower division baccalaureate/associate degree category, 1 semester hour in Banking or Consumer Lending (7/85).

Economics I (024)
Economics II (025)
Location: Chapters throughout the United States.
Length: 48 hours (24 weeks).
Dates: September 1973-July 1985.
Objective: To provide students with an understanding of the basic terminology of economics and to familiarize them with the theories of choice, economic motivation, market structure, inflation, and unemployment.
Instruction: Introduction to supply and demand, scarcity and utilization of economic resources, the price system, and income and expenditure flow. Also covered are goals of full employment and price stability, investment and consumption, money and banking, monetary and fiscal policy, and theories of economic growth. Methodology includes lecture, discussion, and classroom exercises.
Credit recommendation: In the lower division baccalaureate/associate degree category, 3 semester hours in Economics (7/85). NOTE: To be eligible for credit, student must complete both courses.

Economics (082)
Location: Chapters throughout the United States.
Length: 24 hours (12 weeks).
Dates: February 1985-Present.
Objective: To introduce major economic terminology, concepts and relationships, and to survey the tools available to evaluate fundamental economic behavior.
Instruction: The course covers the basic concepts from both micro and macro-economics including supply and demand, competition, monopoly, oligopoly, scarcity and production, production costs, taxation, inflation and unemployment. Emphasis is also placed on current economic issues such as international trade and monetary policy. The teaching methodology is lecture and discussion.
Credit recommendation: In the lower division baccalaureate/associate degree category, 1 semester hour in Economics (7/85).

Effective Business Writing (018)
Location: Chapters throughout the United States.
Length: 24 hours (12 weeks).
Dates: September 1974-Present.
Objective: To provide an understanding of the concepts, form, and style used in writing effective business correspondence and reports.
Instruction: Covers principles of writing, punctuation, and sentence structure. The following types of letters are examined: friendly, bad news, persuasive requests, collection, and goodwill. Additionally, effective reports and direct requests are reviewed. Methodology includes lecture, discussion, writing practice, and analysis.
Credit recommendation: In the lower division baccalaureate/associate degree category, 1 semester hour in Written Communications (4/77) (7/85). NOTE: This course has been reevaluated and continues to meet requirements for credit recommendations.

Effective Speaking (019)
Location: Chapters throughout the United States.
Length: 24 hours (12 weeks).
Dates: September 1984-Present.
Objective: To introduce fundamental speaking skills and to provide the student with practice to become an effective and confident speaker.
Instruction: Barriers to communication with an audience, controlling stage fright, speech delivery, composing speeches, types of speeches, group discussion. Students organize, present, and evaluate informative and persuasive speeches and speeches for special occasions.
Credit recommendation: In the lower division baccalaureate/associate degree category, 2 semester hours in Communications (4/77) (7/85). NOTE: This course has been reevaluated and continues to meet requirements for credit recommendations.

1. **Financial Institutions I (030)**
2. **Financial Institutions II (031)**
Location: Chapters throughout the United States.
Length: 48 hours (24 weeks).
Dates: September 1972-July 1985.
Objective: To provide an understanding of financial agencies and institutions and the process involved in money and credit flow.
Instruction: Covers financial and monetary institutions and their interrelationships with and influence on money and capital markets; examines corporate financial policies and practices as well as business and consumer finance. Methodology includes lecture and discussion. Course is also available through correspondence study.

Credit recommendation: In the upper division baccalaureate category, 3 semester hours in Financial Institutions (4/77).

Financial Statement Analysis (073)
Location: Chapters throughout the United States.
Length: 24 hours (12 weeks).
Dates: September 1983-Present.
Objective: To introduce the concepts and techniques necessary to analyze financial statements of prospective borrowers.
Instruction: This course covers the concepts of risk, profitability, solvency, liquidity, and leverage. The analytical techniques for examining income statements and for evaluating liability are studied. Flow-statements, financial ratios, pro-forma statements, and cash budgets are explained in relation to financial analysis of business managed by prospective borrowers. The lecture-discussion approach is used along with case analyses and other classroom exercises.
Credit recommendation: In the lower division baccalaureate/associate degree category, 1 semester hour in Finance (7/85).

Housing Construction (Principles and Practices) (033)
Location: Chapters throughout the United States.
Length: 24 hours (12 weeks).
Dates: November 1983-December 1988.
Objective: To provide an understanding of basic construction terminology and concepts and the construction techniques used in the production of housing.
Instruction: Covers materials and construction techniques in all components of the housing structure, including floor, wall, and roof systems, interior and exterior finishes, heat control and insulation, passive heating and cooling, wiring, and plumbing. Lecture and discussion are used.
Credit recommendation: In the lower division baccalaureate/associate degree category, 1 semester hour in Real Estate or Construction Principles (7/85).

Human Relations in Business (061)
Location: Chapters throughout the United States.
Length: 24 hours (12 weeks).
Dates: September 1975-Present.
Objective: To provide the student with an introduction to Business Psychology and personal adjustment.
Instruction: The psychology of work; motivation theory; social interaction; personality development; conflict, frustration, and stress; self-awareness, behavior modification, and group dynamics. Methodology includes lecture, discussion, case problems, and group interaction.
Credit recommendation: In the lower division baccalaureate/associate degree category, 2 semester hours in General Psychology (4/77) (7/85). NOTE: This course has been reevaluated and continues to meet requirements for credit recommendations.

Human Resources Management (067)
Location: Chapters throughout the United States.
Length: 24 hours (12 weeks).
Dates: August 1984-December 1988.
Objective: To introduce the various aspects of personnel management including selection, training, and compensation. Emphasis is on the management of human resources in a changing society. The functions of human resources management are treated within the context of the savings institution.
Instruction: The course covers the basic principles of personnel management in a changing society. The selection process is examined as are such functions as training and compensation. The various aspects of the selection decision making process are studied in light of needs and savings institutions.
Credit recommendation: In the upper division baccalaureate category, 1 semester hour in Management or Personnel Management (7/85).

Income Property Lending (080)
Location: Chapters throughout the United States.
Length: 24 hours (12 weeks).
Dates: June 1983-Present.
Objective: To explain the considerations of the mortgage loan officer in negotiating, closing, and administering both construction and permanent loans on income properties.
Instruction: Covers the forms and documentation required for income property lending, project evaluation, borrower analysis, and the processes of loan negotiation, structuring, servicing, problem loan resolution, and loan workouts. Apartment buildings, office buildings and shopping centers are considered emphasizing market studies, appraisals, and financial ratios used with borrower and project evaluations. Methodology includes lecture and discussion.
Credit recommendation: In the upper division baccalaureate category, 1 semester hour in Real Estate or Banking (7/85).

1. Individual Retirement Accounts/Keogh Plans (076)
2. NOW Accounts (816)
Location: Chapters throughout the United States.
Length: 24 hours (12 weeks).
Dates: June 1984-December 1988.
Objective: 1. Provides the student with background knowledge of IRA, SEPPs, and Keogh accounts. The course reflects eligibility requirements and contribution limits of the Tax Equity and Fiscal Responsibility Act of 1982. 2. Provides the student with an examination of the history and development of NOW accounts and their legal requirements. Describes the check clearing system, endorsements, and methods of interest calculation.

Instruction: 1. Covers the major legislation authorizing IRAs and Keogh accounts. Describes the legal relationships created under pension plans and their documentation. Presents tax benefits and penalties, customer eligibility, fiduciary responsibilities and reporting requirements for retirement accounts. Methodology includes lecture and discussion. 2. Presents the elements of NOW accounts and their legal requirements. Describes the role of the Federal Reserve, correspondent banks, and the Federal Home Loan Bank in the clearing of NOW drafts. Further explores check processing and the role of NOW account department personnel. Methodology includes lecture, discussion, and case studies.

Credit recommendation: In the vocational certificate category, 1 semester hour in Banking (7/85). NOTE: To be eligible for credit, students must complete both courses.

Introduction to Electronic Data Processing (053)
Location: Chapters throughout the United States.
Length: 24 hours (12 weeks).
Dates: June 1984-Present.
Objective: To introduce the field of electronic data processing through a nontechnical survey of the capabilities of computers as applied to the needs of savings institutions, and to familiarize the student with the breadth and depth of computer hardware and software appropriate to data processing needs in the savings field.
Instruction: Covers such topics as: (1) the components, capabilities, and limitations of computer systems, (2) the types of processing systems, (3) major developments in computer technology, (4) considerations in developing computer programs, (5) the concept of systems and program flowcharts, (6) the characteristics of storage devices, (7) computer security, and (8) direct applications of computer technology for the savings institution. The teaching methodology used is lecture, discussion, and classroom demonstration.
Credit recommendation: In the lower division baccalaureate/associate degree category, 1 semester hour in Data Processing or Computer Science (7/85).

Introduction to the Savings Institution Business (060)
Location: Chapters throughout the United States.
Length: 24 hours (12 weeks).
Dates: September 1973-Present.
Objective: To provide an introductory understanding of the business world with an emphasis on the role of savings associations in that environment.
Instruction: Forms of business organization, the modern business enterprise, the Federal Reserve and Federal Home Loan Bank systems, introduction to computer technology, securities markets, financial intermediaries, the savings and investment processes. Emphasized throughout are the history and expansion of savings associations, and the role of savings associations in the business community and society. Methodology includes lecture and discussion. Course is also available through correspondence study.

Credit recommendation: In the lower division baccalaureate/associate degree category, 1 semester hour in Introduction to Business (4/77) (7/85).

1. Managing Deposit Accounts and Services (009)
2. Deposit Accounts and Services (008)
(Formerly Savings Accounts Administration and Savings Accounts)
Location: Chapters, nationally.
Length: 48 hours (24 weeks).
Dates: September 1974-Present.
Objective: To provide an understanding of the solicitation, maintenance, and administration of savings funds from a legal perspective.
Instruction: Provides an analysis of the contractual and legal nature of savings accounts. Types of ownership and types of savings accounts, insurance of proxy procedures, loans secured by savings accounts, dormant or inactive accounts, accounts of decedents, savings account terminology, additional services to savers. Emphasis is placed on analysis of savings department services. Methodology includes lecture and discussion.
Credit recommendation: In the upper division baccalaureate category, 3 semester hours in General Business (4/77) (7/85). NOTE: To be eligible for credit, student must complete both courses. These courses have been reevaluated and continue to meet requirements for credit recommendations.

Marketing for Financial Institutions (063)
Location: Chapters throughout the United States.
Length: 24 hours (12 weeks).
Dates: January 1983-Present.
Objective: Provides the student with a basic introduction to marketing and explores applications of these concepts within a financial institution setting. Some of the topics presented in this course include marketing management, pricing, market planning, and marketing research.
Instruction: Explores the external marketing environment and presents consumer behavior analysis. Identifies primary and secondary sources of market research information. Analyzes pricing decisions and the cost effectiveness of services. Describes the function and use of advertising, public relations, and personal selling within the financial services industry. Methodology includes lecture, discussion, case studies, and role playing.
Credit recommendation: In the lower division baccalaureate/associate degree category, 1 semester hour in Financial Institutions Marketing or Banking (7/85).

Money and Banking (030)
(Formerly Financial Institutions)
Location: Chapters throughout the United States.
Length: 24 hours (12 weeks).

Dates: July 1985-Present.

Objective: To provide an understanding of financial agencies and institutions and the processes involved in money and credit flow.

Instruction: Covers financial and monetary institutions and their interrelationships with an influence on money and capital markets; examines corporate financial policies and practices as well as business and consumer finance. Methodology includes lecture and discussion.

Credit recommendation: In the upper division baccalaureate category, 1 semester hour in Banking Financial Institutions (7/85).

Mortgage Loan Servicing (029)
Location: Chapters throughout the United States.
Length: 24 hours (12 weeks).
Dates: June 1983-Present.

Objective: To cover the loan servicing function from the time of closing until final payment, focusing on the procedures used in the daily loan servicing operations.

Instruction: Covers the organization of the loan servicing department, the handling of escrow accounts, processing contract changes, the legal and economic effects of delinquency on the lender, and the handling of delinquencies, foreclosures, and real estate owned. Alternative mortgage programs, FHA and VA loans, and secondary mortgage market activity are examined as they pertain to the mortgage servicing function. Lecture and discussion are used.

Credit recommendation: In the lower division baccalaureate/associate degree or vocational certificate categories, 1 semester hour in Banking (7/85).

Personal Investments (027)
Location: Chapters throughout the United States.
Length: 24 hours (12 weeks).
Dates: July 1985-Present.

Objective: Provides the student with basic techniques, vehicles, and strategies for implementing investment goals in a portfolio context. Explores the basic information needed to aid individual investors so that they can make sound investment decisions.

Instruction: Presents the economic, market, and price function of different types of investment markets. Evaluates and contrasts the investment characteristics of debt securities, common and preferred stock, mutual funds, real estate, stock options, and commodities. Further applies fundamental and technical analysis to identify the proper timing of an investment decision. Methodology includes lecture, discussion, and case studies.

Credit recommendation: In the upper division baccalaureate category, 1 semester hour in Investments (7/85).

Personal Money Management (032)
Location: Chapters throughout the United States.
Length: 24 hours (12 weeks).
Dates: July 1983-Present.

Objective: Provides the student with a basic introduction to Personal Money Management with emphasis on credit management, insurance coverage, investment decisions, and estate planning.

Instruction: Interrelates money management with personal assets, budgeting, and financial resources and goals. Explains the methods of insuring assets. Analyzes the need for property insurance, liability coverage, auto, health, and life insurance. Discusses the basic concepts of investments, tax and estate planning. Emphasis is on designing and implementing overall effective money management strategies. Methodology includes lecture and discussion.

Credit recommendation: In the lower division baccalaureate/associate degree category, 1 semester hour in Personal Finance (7/85).

Principles of Management
Location: Chapters throughout the United States.
Length: 24 hours (12 weeks).
Dates: July 1984-Present.

Objective: To introduce the concept of management including planning, leading, organizing and controlling an enterprise. Emphasis is on the relation of theory to practice as applied to savings institutions. Skills are practiced during applications to real situations.

Instruction: The course covers the fundamental principles of management. Topics covered are planning, and decision making theory; the relationship among authority, responsibility and power; the constructive use of conflict; and the benefits of improving productivity. The methodology includes discussion and classroom exercises such as role playing, simulations, and case study analysis.

Credit recommendation: In the upper division baccalaureate category, 1 semester hour in Business Administration or Management (7/85).

1. Real Estate Law I (006)
2. Real Estate Law II (007)
Location: Chapters throughout the United States.
Length: 48 hours (24 weeks).
Dates: July 1983-Present.

Objective: To provide an understanding of the legal principles governing real estate transactions, mortgage contracts, land use controls, rehabilitation, racial discrimination, and taxes. Condominiums, cooperatives, planned unit developments, and mobile homes are discussed.

Instruction: 1. Covers the legal concept of land, estates in real property, land descriptions, the law of agency, contracts for the sale of land, deeds, closing the transaction, escrows, evidence of title, insurance, and co-ownership. 2. Covers real estate financing instruments (use of existing mortgages, purchase money mortgages, wraparounds, and junior mortgages), the due-on-sale clause, installment contracts, ground leases, foreclosure and redemption, land use controls, condominiums, cooperatives, planned unit developments, rehabilitation, landlord-tenant, racial discrimination, and taxes. Lecture and discussion are used.

Credit recommendation: In the upper division baccalaureate category, 3 semester hours in Banking or Real Estate (7/85). NOTE: To be eligible for credit, student must complete both courses.

1. Real Estate Principles I (015)
2. Real Estate Principles II (016)
  Location: Chapters throughout the United States.
  Length: 48 hours (24 weeks).
  Dates: September 1976-Present.
  Objective: To provide the student with a foundation in the legal, economic, and governmental aspects of real estate.
  Instruction: An examination of principles and practices of real estate relative to the savings association business. Includes a study of real estate administration, the process of making and implementing real estate decisions, evaluation principles, analysis of locations, and land use. Also included are subdivision and land development, property management, instruments of financing, mortgage lending, and urban and rural development. Lecture, discussion, and classroom exercises are used.
  Credit recommendation: In the upper division baccalaureate category, 3 semester hours in Real Estate Principles (4/77) (7/85). NOTE: To be eligible for credit, student must complete both courses. This course has been reevaluated and continues to meet requirements for credit examination.

Residential Appraising (013)
  Location: Chapters throughout the United States.
  Length: 24 hours (12 weeks).
  Dates: July 1979-Present.
  Objective: To provide an understanding of the basic concepts and techniques pertaining to the appraisal of residential housing.
  Instruction: Covers the appraisal principles and the appraisal process, local economic analysis, housing markets and neighborhood analysis, site analysis, and valuation, highest and best use, improvement analysis, the market comparison, cost and gross rent multiplier approaches to value estimation and preparation of a short-form appraisal. Emphasis is placed in basic residential appraisal techniques in order to understand the role of the appraiser in the mortgage lending process. Lecture and discussion are used.
  Credit recommendation: In the lower division baccalaureate/associate degree category, 1 semester hour in Real Estate (7/85).

Residential Mortgage Lending
  Location: Chapters throughout the United States.
  Length: 24 hours (12 weeks).
  Dates: July 1981-Present.
  Objective: To explain the procedures in originating, processing, and servicing residential mortgage loans and to acquaint the student with the types of residential mortgage loans which federally chartered savings institutions can make.
  Instruction: Covers the regulations and laws governing residential mortgage lending by savings associations, the functions of the mortgage loan department, analysis of risk and appraisals in residential mortgage lending, the origination, closing, servicing, foreclosure, and workouts of residential mortgage loans, types of loans, and the secondary mortgage market. Lecture and discussion are used.
  Credit recommendation: In the lower division baccalaureate/associate degree category, 1 semester hour in Banking or Real Estate (7/85).

Savings Institution Operations
(Formerly Savings Association Operations [062])
  Location: Chapters throughout the United States.
  Length: 24 hours (12 weeks).
  Dates: June 1977-Present.
  Objective: To introduce the role of savings association in the modern business world with emphasis on theory and practice of internal operations.
  Instruction: The savings function; operations of the savings department; the lending function; operations of the loan department; additional association services; accounting operations; internal auditing, electronic data processing, and other support services; personnel functions and processes; marketing elements and concepts; management principles in action. Lecture and discussion are used.
  Credit recommendation: In the lower division baccalaureate/associate degree category, 2 semester hours in General Business (4/77) (7/85). NOTE: This course has been reevaluated and continues to meet requirements for credit recommendations. Course is also available through correspondence study.

1. Supervisory Personnel Management I (047)
2. Supervisory Personnel Management II (048)
  Location: Chapters throughout the United States.
  Length: 48 hours (24 weeks).
  Dates: September 1976-Present.
  Objective: To provide students with an understanding of organization and behavior theory and practice necessary to enable them to become effective supervisors.
  Instruction: Content is developed within the framework of the five managerial functions of planning, organizing, staffing, directing, and controlling. Role of the supervisor, effective decision making, employee need satisfaction, responsibility and delegation, time management skills, hiring practices and employee appraisal, motivation and

control techniques for managerial personnel.

Credit recommendation: In the lower division baccalaureate/associate degree category, 3 semester hours in Management (4/77) (7/85). NOTE: to be eligible for credit, student must complete both courses. This course has been reevaluated and continues to meet requirements for credit recommendations.

Techniques for Customer Counseling
Location: Chapters throughout the United States.
Length: 24 hours (12 weeks).
Dates: July 1980-Present.
Objective: Provides the students with effective interviewing techniques and methods of formulating their own strategies for discovering and meeting customer needs. The course provides the opportunity to learn and practice skills necessary to effectively communicate with customers.
Instruction: Explores counseling and advising techniques. Describes how values, beliefs, and attitudes affect the purchase decision. Explains the importance of verbal and nonverbal communication, and demonstrates effective listening skills. Further discusses cross selling techniques useful to a savings counselor. Methodology includes lecture, discussion, and role playing.
Credit recommendation: In the lower division baccalaureate/associate degree category, 1 semester hour in Sales (7/85).

Institute of Management and Production

The Institute of Management and Production (IMP) is a Human Resource Development Institution which provides a wide range of Management Services and Training Programs to companies and other organizations in both the private and public sectors of the economy.

IMP has, as its primary objective, the improvement of organizational capability with emphasis on the improvement of proficiency, productive performance and personal growth of people.

IMP works closely with companies to help them to analyze the factors contributing to performance levels and assist them in finding solutions to the problems of low productivity.

Following a formal as well as informal needs assessment of its primary target group - companies in the business community - professional staff of the Institute initiate and develop particular programs for which they identify appropriate instructors. On occasion a particular course may be developed by adjunct faculty and found suitable for implementation in the Institute's program.

The Institute of Management and Production operates its programs and services with full time professional and administrative staff members. The staff, with the assistance of an adjunct faculty provide professional training and consultancy services to clients.

Source of official student records: The Program Officer, Institute of Management and Production, 17 Worthington Avenue, Kingston 5, Jamaica, West Indies.

Additional information about the courses: Program on Noncollegiate Sponsored Instruction, The Center for Adult Learning and Educational Credentials, American Council on Education, One Dupont Circle, Washington, D.C. 20036.

Basic Accounting
Location: Institute of Management and Production, Kingston, Jamaica.
Length: Approximately 82 hours (one 3-hour class per week for 27 weeks).
Dates: September 1988-Present.
Objective: To provide the student with an appreciation of the role of accounting within the organization and an understanding of the techniques of collecting and processing accounting data.
Instruction: Lecture, discussion, and classroom exercises are used to introduce the role of accounting information for managers, owners, and creditors. The student learns to gather and record data in the accounting system and to use internal controls to reduce errors. Students will then learn to use this data to produce simple financial statements.
Credit recommendation: In the lower division baccalaureate/associate degree category, 3 semester hours in Basic Accounting (4/89).

Basics of Accounting and Financial Control (B2)
Location: Institute of Management and Production, Kingston, Jamaica.
Length: 24 hours (one 3-hour session for 8 weeks).
Dates: January 1980-Present.
Objective: To acquaint non-financial staff with the elements of accounting systems and give an understanding of financial statements.
Instruction: Course introduces the concept of a double entry bookkeeping system and explains the role of the accounting department in the firm. It is designed to enhance the non-financial employee's understanding of financial statements. Methodology includes a combination of lecture, discussion, and practical exercises.
Credit recommendation: In the vocational certificate category, 1 semester hour in Basics of Accounting (4/89).

Business Administration
Location: Institute of Management and Production, Kingston, Jamaica.
Length: Approximately 82 hours (one 3-hour class per week for 27 weeks).
Dates: September 1988-Present.

Objective: To give the student a basic understanding of the administration of an organization and an appreciation of basic administrative procedures.

Instruction: Course covers organization structures, administrative systems, information technology, performance reviews, and the physical work environment. Methodology includes lecture and discussion.

Credit recommendation: In the lower division baccalaureate/associate degree category, 2 semester hours in Introduction to Business (4/89).

Business Administration (Company Administration) (Formerly Management Program)

Location: Institute of Management and Production, Kingston, Jamaica.

Length: 138 hours (26 weeks; two three-hour sessions per week, plus field work for six weeks).

Dates: May 1984-Present.

Objective: To provide students with the basic tools for monitoring and managing the acquisition and allocation of funds, and the production and marketing process within the business enterprise; to give students information on the legal requirements of company operation and the legal framework within which companies are formed and operated in Jamaica; and to give students basic skills in problem recognition, data collection, and quantitative situation analysis.

Instruction: Lecture, discussion, classroom exercises and a special project are used in the teaching of company finance, company law, production and marketing, data interpretation for decision making, and management. A six-week field work component completes the program.

Credit recommendation: In the lower division baccalaureate/associate degree category, 4 semester hours in Introduction to Business or 1 semester hour in each of the following four areas: Finance, Law, Management, and Marketing (2/86).

COBOL Programming (D5)

Location: Institute of Management and Production, Kingston, Jamaica.

Length: 36 hours with a 20-hour minimum microcomputer laboratory.

Dates: January 1979-Present.

Objective: To provide the student with the tools necessary to code and test programs using COBOL.

Instruction: Language procedure, basic structure analysis, top down review coding and testing. Prerequisite: Student must have successfully completed D1 and D2.

Credit recommendation: In the lower division baccalaureate/associate degree category, 2 semester hours in Business Administration, Computer Science or Data Processing (2/86).

Communication

Location: Institute of Management and Production, Kingston, Jamaica.

Length: Approximately 82 hours (one 3-hour class per week for 27 weeks).

Dates: September 1988-Present.

Objective: To improve the student's ability to communicate information in written and oral forms.

Instruction: Course covers information-selecting and using appropriate methods and formats of communication; persuading, identifying false arguments, formulating and defending rational arguments—engaging in constructive discussion; and operating, structure, and use of communication systems within an organization, selection and use of appropriate communications, matching messages to needs, information storage, retrieval, report writing; cooperating-group working, different types of individuals within the group, analysis of attitudes, feelings, and objectives of self, motivation to work, source of conflict, and nature of negotiations. Methodology includes lecture, discussion, simulation, video-taping, audio cassettes, group assignments, role playing, games, use of films, and individual project assignments.

Credit recommendation: In the lower division baccalaureate/associate degree category, 3 semester hours in Business Communications (4/89).

Computer Concepts in Business

Location: Institute of Management and Production, Kingston, Jamaica.

Length: 84 hours (one 3-hour class per week for 28 weeks).

Dates: September 1988-Present.

Objective: To provide the student with an understanding of computer concepts used in the business environment.

Instruction: Course covers computer literacy: history, keyboarding, introduction to personal computers, data processing terminology, hardware and software, and a visit to local data processing installations; system analysis and design: introduction to system analysis, management information system, organization of a data processing department; role of system analyst; system programmer; and the electronic office. Methodology includes lectures, films, videotapes, a visit to data processing installations, and microcomputer exposures.

Credit recommendation: In the lower division baccalaureate/associate degree category, 2 semester hours in Computer Information Systems or Data Processing (4/89).

Data Processing Program
Basic Language for Microcomputer Users (D10)

Location: Institute of Management and Production, Kingston, Jamaica.

Length: 42 hours with a 20-hour minimum microcomputer laboratory (14 three-hour sessions).

Dates: January 1979-Present.

Objective: To provide the student with tools necessary to code and test programs using the BASIC Language; and to introduce the student to the ways in which BASIC and computers can be applied to the solution of realistic problems.

Instruction: Course gives students an introduction to the computer and to the concepts of flowcharting; assignment statements and functions, input/output statements, control structures; file processing statements. Lecture, discussion, and case studies are used. Prerequisite: Student must have successfully completed D1 and D2.

Credit recommendation: In the lower division baccalaureate/associate degree category, 2 semester hours in Business Administration, Computer Science or Data Processing (2/86).

Human Resource Development

Location: Institute of Management and Production, Kingston, Jamaica.

Length: 60 hours (20 weeks; one three-hour session per week).

Dates: October 1982-Present.

Objective: To give students an understanding of the training function; to instruct them in the design and evaluation of training programs.

Instruction: This course is delivered in lecture, discussion and case formats. The course begins with an analysis of management functions, organizational dynamics, and the role of the training function. It examines concepts, principles, methods, and techniques for developing human resources.

Credit recommendation: In the upper division baccalaureate category, 2 semester hours in Personnel Management (2/86).

Introduction to Data Processing
Course 1: Introduction to the Computer for Beginners - D1
Course 2: Fundamentals of Programming - D2

Location: Institute of Management and Production, Kingston, Jamaica.

Length: 48 hours (8 three-hour sessions for both course 1 and 2).

Dates: January 1979-Present.

Objective: To provide students with a fundamental knowledge of date processing systems and functions related to computer programming.

Instruction: This course examines the elements of a data processing system and equips participants to be more effective in their day to day dealing with a computer center. Specific areas covered will include: History of Information Processing, The Computer Hardware and Software, Data Collection, Programming, Organization and Methods, Systems Analysis and Design, Environmental Considerations, Future Developments. Lecture and discussion are used.

Credit recommendation: In the lower division baccalaureate/associate degree category, 3 semester hours in Business Administration, Computer Science, or Data Processing (2/86).

Labor Relations in Jamaica
1. Collective Bargaining (G3)
2. Industrial Relations, Issues, and Review (G4)
3. Labor Laws in Jamaica (G6)

Location: Institute of Management and Production, Kingston, Jamaica.

Length: 54 hours (3 courses with one 3-hour session for 6 weeks respectively).

Dates: January 1980-Present.

Objective: To give the student an understanding of labor relations in Jamaica.

Instruction: Course covers the history of the union movement in Jamaica, the collective bargaining process, and legislation affecting industrial relations in Jamaica. Methodology includes lecture, discussion, and case studies.

Credit recommendation: In the lower division baccalaureate/associate degree category, 3 semester hours in Labor Relations in Jamaica (4/89). NOTE: Students must successfully complete all three courses to receive credit.

Management of Data Processing Installations (D8)

Location: Institute of Management and Production, Kingston, Jamaica.

Length: 24 hours (8 sessions at 3 hours each).

Dates: January 1979-Present.

Objective: To provide the student with information on the principles of management that allow for the full utilization of data processing capabilities in support of organizational objectives.

Instruction: Course covers pre-installation planning, installation, organizing the data processing department, the management of a distributed data processing unit, and maintaining data processing efficiency in a changing environment. Lecture and discussion are used. Prerequisite: Students must complete D1 and D2 and D5 or D6.

Credit recommendation: In the lower division baccalaureate/associate degree category, 1 semester hour in Data Processing or Management (2/86).

Marketing

Location: Institute of Management and Production, Kingston, Jamaica.

Length: 22 hours (1½ hours per week for 14 weeks).

Dates: September 1988-Present.

Objective: To provide the student with an overview of marketing elements and concepts, with emphasis on formulating a simple marketing plan.

Instruction: Course covers the nature of marketing; analysis of marketing: definition of markets, target market selection, sales forecasting, buying behavior; market research; product and price decisions; pricing methods, pricing structure, pricing policy, and competition; distribution; promotion, advertising and sales; and organizing and managing marketing strategies. Methodology includes lecture, case studies, and development of a marketing plan.

Credit recommendation: In the lower division baccalaureate/associate degree category, 1 semester hour in Marketing as an elective (4/89).

Personnel Management
1. **Introduction to Personnel management (G1)**
2. **Personnel Management: Skills and Techniques (G2)**

   Location: Institute of Management and Production, Kingston, Jamaica.
   Length: 42 hours (1. eight 3-hour sessions; 2. six 3-hour sessions).
   Dates: January 1980-Present.
   Objective: To give the student a basic understanding of the principles of industrial psychology, personnel development, and organization management as they relate to the management of personnel.
   Instruction: Course covers the principles of employee recruitment and selection, performance appraisal and training, wage and salary administration, leadership and supervision, employee motivation, communication, and career development. Methodology includes lecture and discussion.
   Credit recommendation: In the lower division baccalaureate/associate degree category, 2 semester hours in Personnel Management (4/89). NOTE: Students must successfully complete both courses to receive credit.

Principles of Public Relations
   Location: Institute of Management and Production, Kingston, Jamaica.
   Length: 22 hours (1½ hours per week for 14 weeks).
   Dates: September 1989-Present.
   Objective: To give the student an appreciation for the principles of public relations and provide exposure to specific public relations activities.
   Instruction: Course explains the main principles of public relations as a management function, explores a variety of public relations activities, and allows students to experience some aspects of media operations. Methodology includes lecture, discussion, and field trips to media houses.
   Credit recommendation: In the lower division baccalaureate/associate degree category, 1 semester hour in Public Relations (4/89).

Principles of Supervision
1. **Fundamentals of Supervisory Practice**
2. **Supervisory Management—Part I**
3. **Supervisory Management—Part II**

   Location: Institute of Management and Production, Kingston, Jamaica.
   Length: *Course 1:* 24 hours (nine 2-hour, 45 minute sessions); *Course 2:* 24 hours (eight 3-hour sessions); *Course 3:* 24 hours (eight 3-hour sessions).
   Dates: September 1988-Present.
   Objective: *Course 1:* To provide the student with an overview of the principles involved in the supervision of people. The course explores the scientific yet sensitive approach to the supervision of Jamaican employees. *Course 2:* To provide the student with basic management principles with applications to work situations. *Course 3:* To provide the student with advanced supervisory management principles with emphasis on individual differences, personality and behavior, discipline, communication improvement, job satisfaction and self-actualization by guiding and developing the employee.
   Learning Outcome: *Course 1:* Upon successful completion of this course, the student will be able to describe the basic requirements of supervision and apply these supervision principles to his/her own on-the-job circumstances. *Course 2:* Upon successful completion of this course, the student will be able to describe basic management principles and how they apply to local business and industries; apply these principles to his/her own work environment. *Course 3:* Upon successful completion of this course, the student will be able to identify and adapt the qualities of leadership; understand what makes people different, and what causes frustration of employees; identify barriers to communication, handle grievances, and counsel and motivate employees.
   Instruction: *Course 1:* Course covers leadership, management, human relations, and case studies involving understanding people, individual differences, improving job relations, bringing out the best in people, the decision-making process, and delegating work. Methodology includes lecture, discussion, role playing, and case studies. *Course 2:* Course covers the nature of management, planning, organizing, controlling, standard/appraisal, communications, motivation, and decision making. Methodology includes lecture, discussion, film-case studies, and practice exercises. *Course 3:* Course covers leadership, qualities and attributes of effective supervision, four elements of effective leadership in business, and differences between leadership and management. Methodology includes lecture, discussion, and case study analysis.
   Credit recommendation: In the lower division baccalaureate/associate degree category, 3 semester hours in Supervision (4/89). NOTE: Students must successfully complete all three courses to receive credit.

Report Program Generator II (D6)
   Location: Institute of Management and Production, Kingston, Jamaica.
   Length: 36 hours with a 20-hour minimum microcomputer laboratory (12 three-hour sessions).
   Dates: January 1979-Present.
   Objective: To introduce the student to program writing

and testing.

Instruction: Course gives an introduction to programming and program definitions, operation codes, and information on debugging techniques. Lecture and discussion are used. Prerequisite: Student must have successfully completed D1 and D2.

Credit recommendation: In the lower division baccalaureate/associate degree category, 2 semester hours in Computer Science or Data Processing (2/86).

Systems Analysis and Design
1. Fundamentals of Systems Analysis (D3)
2. Systems Analysis (D4)

Location: Institute of Management and Production, Kingston, Jamaica.
Length: 48 hours (8 three-hour sessions for both course 1 and 2).
Dates: January 1979-Present.
Objective: To provide the student with the fundamental knowledge and skills to use the techniques and concepts of Systems Analysis and Design.
Instruction: Course one gives an introduction to the role of systems analysis including information gathering, information analysis, data capture, input-output design, system specification, implementation, feasibility study, appraisal of hardware with regard to systems needs, and presentation of findings. Course two covers the process of systems development, systems design process, file concepts and structures, timing, systems testing, data control, systems security and recovery, documentation, transaction processsing. Lecture and discussion are used.
Credit recommendation: In the lower division baccalaureate/associate degree category, 3 semester hours in Business Administration, Computer Science or Data Processing (2/86).

Insurance Data Management Association

Insurance Data Management Association (IDMA) is a nonprofit professional association dedicated to increasing the level of professionalism among insurance data managers. Fifty-three insurance organizations are represented by nearly five hundred individual members nationwide. In addition to a seven-course curriculum, successful completion of which leads to certification as a Certified Data Manager (CDM), the Association sponsors technical seminars, conducts meetings and forums for pertinent topics, and produces a tort reform analysis package.

The IDMA curriculum incorporates three courses from the Insurance Institutes of America as well as four IDMA-designed courses. Curriculum activities are coordinated by the Education Committee, advised by an Academic Advisory Committee. Courses are designed to facilitate self-study and performance is tested in examinations administered twice yearly.

Source of official student records: Administrator, Insurance Data Management Association, 85 John Street, New York, New York 10038.

Additional information about the courses: Program on Noncollegiate Sponsored Instruction, Center for Adult Learning and Educational Credentials, American Council on Education, One Dupont Circle, Washington, D.C. 20036-1193.

Data Administration
Location: Correspondence Program.
Length: 150 hours (15 weeks).
Dates: August 1987-Present.
Objective: To provide students with a solid perspective on data management to enhance their effectiveness as data managers.
Learning Outcome: Upon successful completion of this course, the student will be able to understand and appreciate the importance and necessity of management of information to the successful functioning of a company; appreciate and understand that data is an important resource of every company and should be handled with careful consideration as would other company resources: e.g., funds, personnel, natural resources; understand the importance of database management and the need to develop and create models for new systems should the need arise.
Instruction: Definition and benefits of data administration; standards, policies and procedures for data use; data organization; data administration, management and quality considerations; principles and use of data dictionary; data dictionary and directory systems-design, meta-entities, input and output; implementation (developer's and user's viewpoint); and distributed database environment and auditing.
Credit recommendation: In the graduate degree or upper division baccalaureate category, 3 semester hours in Management of Information Systems (4/88). NOTE: This course is particularly applicable to computer systems or business degree programs.

Insurance Educational Association

The Insurance Educational Association (IEA) is a voluntary, nonprofit corporation, organized for the purpose of meeting the needs of people for education in the fields of risk and insurance.

The IEA provides students with the preparation necessary for professional certification for careers in insurance, risk management and employee benefits. In addition, it provides continuing education for persons employed within these industries.

Courses offered may lead to preparation for national examinations offered by The American Institute for Property and Liability Underwriters/Insurance Institute of America, and the International Foundation of Employee Benefit Plans in its Certified Employee Benefit Specialist program. Students successfully completing national examinations in these programs may apply to these organizations which are listed elsewhere in this *National Guide,* to receive appropriate academic credit recommendations. To be eligible for credit, students should have received at least a grade of "C."

Other specialized, technical classes are offered and may apply toward the IEA's certificate programs. These include (1) Commercial Multiple Line Insurance and (2) Workers' Compensation Claims.

IEA is approved by the California State Superintendent of Public Instruction, and all instructors are licensed through the office of the superintendent. The association provides seminars, workshops, self-instructional courses, and special programs in all aspects of insurance, from basic indoctrinary courses to advanced technical and managerial studies.

Source of official student records: Northern California - Insurance Educational Association, 300 Montgomery Street, San Francisco, California 94104. Southern California - Insurance Educational Association, 901 Dove Street, Newport Beach, California 92660.

Additional information about the courses: Program on Noncollegiate Sponsored Instruction, The Center for Adult Learning and Educational Credentials, American Council on Education, One Dupont Circle, Washington, D.C. 20036.

NOTE: To be eligible for credit, students should receive at least a grade of "C." Courses marked with an asterisk are based on materials developed by the American Institute for Property and Underwriters/Insurance Institute of America. In order to avoid duplication of credit, close attention should be paid to course titles and descriptions when granting credit for the courses below and those offered by the American Institute.

Accounting and Finance (CPCU VIII)*
   Location: Various locations throughout CA.
   Length: 40 hours (17 weeks).
   Dates: March 1979-March 1984.
   Objective: To develop an understanding of the principles and applications of accounting and finance and how they relate to insurance.
   Instruction: Emphasizes the principles of basic accounting and finance. The accounting topics cover accounting terms, concepts, and a review of financial statements. The finance portions are designed to cover the principles of corporate financial management. The final topics relate specifically to property and liability insurance company accounting and finance. Lecture and discussion are used.
   Credit recommendation: In the upper division baccalaureate category, 3 semester hours in Finance or Insurance (6/79). NOTE: Because this course is sometimes found in community college curricula, it is also appropriate for the granting of 3 units of lower division credit at a community college.

Automobile Insurance (CA3)
   Location: Various locations throughout CA.
   Length: 30 hours (13 weeks).
   Dates: September 1968-June 1984.
   Objective: To provide a survey of the basic automobile coverages.
   Instruction: Analysis of the family auto policy, the basic auto policy, the personal auto policy, and the garage liability policy. Lecture and class discussion are used.
   Credit recommendation: In the lower division baccalaureate/associate degree category or in the upper division baccalaureate category, 1 semester hour in Insurance (6/78) (3/84). NOTE: This course has undergone a 5-year reevaluation and continues to meet requirements for credit recommendations.

Casualty Insurance (INS23)*
   Location: Various locations throughout CA.
   Length: 30 hours (13 weeks).
   Dates: September 1970-March 1984.
   Objective: To provide concepts peculiar to the common casualty, surety, and multiple-line contracts. Primary emphasis is placed on understanding coverages and policy provisions.
   Instruction: Contracts studied include the Family Automobile Policy; Workers' Compensation and Employers' Liability Policy; Owners', Landlords', and Tenants' Liability Policy; Comprehensive General Liability Policy; comprehensive personal liability coverage, life and health insurance coverages; the liability insurance aspects of modern multiple-line contracts.
   Credit recommendation: In the lower division baccalaureate/associate degree category or in the upper division baccalaureate category, 2 semester hours in Insurance (5/78) (3/84). NOTE: This course has undergone a 5-year reevaluation and continues to meet requirements for credit recommendations.

Commercial Automobile Insurance Coverages (CA5)
(Formerly Liability Insurance [Advanced] [CA5])
   Location: Various locations throughout CA.
   Length: 30 hours (12 weeks).
   Dates: September 1972-December 1988.
   Objective: To provide an advanced survey of casualty insurance coverage, forms, and underwriting.
   Instruction: Coverage, forms, and underwriting of Comprehensive General Liability, including Products and Completed Operations, Broad Form Property Damage, Contractual, Personal Injury, and the implications of recent contract changes.

Credit recommendation: In the upper division baccalaureate category, 1 semester hour in Insurance (5/78) (3/84). NOTE: This course has undergone a 5-year reevaluation and continues to meet requirements for credit recommendations.

Commercial Inland Marine (PR21)
  Location: Various locations throughout CA.
  Length: 30 hours (12 weeks).
  Dates: January 1968-December 1988.
  Objective: To provide an understanding of commercial inland marine forms and coverages, including underwriting and rating.
  Instruction: Definitions of Marine Insurance, Basic Inland Marine Coverages, Transportation Insurance, Transit Insurance Coverage, Motor Truck Cargo Insurance, Air Cargo, Instrumentalities of Transportation, Time Element Coverages, Dealers Insurance, Bailees and Bailees Customers Coverage, and Contractors Equipment.
  Credit recommendation: In the upper division baccalaureate category, 2 semester hours in Insurance (6/78) (3/84). NOTE: This course has undergone a 5-year reevaluation and continues to meet requirements for credit recommendations.

Commercial Liability Insurance Coverages (CA4) (Formerly Insurance Coverages [CA4])
  Location: Various locations throughout CA.
  Length: 30 hours (12 weeks).
  Dates: September 1977-Present.
  Objective: To provide a basic survey of casualty insurance coverages and forms.
  Instruction: Casualty rules, manuals, classifications, and rating. Coverages include Owners, Landlords, and Tenants, Manufactures and Contractors, Contractual, Protective, Products, Completed Operations, Blanket Contractual, Broad Form Property Damage, Fire Legal Liability, Crime, and Fidelity.
  Credit recommendation: In the lower division baccalaureate/associate degree category, 1 semester hour in Insurance (5/78) 3/84. NOTE: This course has undergone a 5-year reevaluation and continues to meet requirements for credit recommendations.

Commercial Liability Risk Management and Insurance (CPCU IV)*
  Location: Various locations throughout CA.
  Length: 40 hours (17 weeks).
  Dates: March 1979-March 1984.
  Objective: To apply the risk management process to commercial liability loss exposures and analyze contracts in this area.
  Instruction: Emphasizes the analysis of commercial liability loss exposures and then examines the insurance coverages designed to meet those exposures. Premise and operations, products and completed operations, contractual and protective liability, employer's liability and workers' compensation, motor vehicles, and professional liability will be discussed along with surety bonds. Lecture and discussion are used.
  Credit recommendation: In the upper division baccalaureate category, 3 semester hours in Insurance (6/79). NOTE: Because this course is sometimes found in community college curricula, it is also appropriate for the granting of 3 units of lower division credit at a community college.

Commercial Liability Underwriting (UND 63)*
  Location: Various locations throughout CA.
  Length: 30 hours (13 weeks).
  Dates: March 1979-March 1984.
  Objective: To apply the underwriting decision-making process to commercial property exposures.
  Instruction: Emphasizes the major types of commercial liability insurance and includes the use of reinsurance and surplus lines and the handling of special accounts and large exposures. Lecture and discussion are used.
  Credit recommendation: In the upper division baccalaureate category, 3 semester hours in Insurance (6/79). NOTE: Because this course is sometimes found in community college curricula, it is also appropriate for the granting of 3 units of lower division credit at a community college.

Commercial Multi-Peril Package Policies (MU31)
  Location: Various locations throughout CA.
  Length: 30 hours (12 weeks).
  Dates: February 1971-December 1985.
  Objective: To provide an in-depth analysis of commercial multi-peril package policy forms and underwriting.
  Instruction: Actual cash value versus replacement cost, demolition coverage, SMP programs and eligibility, time element coverages, liability underwriting, crime, boiler and machinery, property underwriting.
  Credit recommendation: In the upper division baccalaureate category, 2 semester hours in Insurance (5/78) (3/84). NOTE: This course has undergone a 5-year reevaluation and continues to meet requirements for credit recommendations.

Commercial Property and Multiple-Line Underwriting (UND 64)*
  Location: Various locations throughout CA.
  Length: 30 hours (13 weeks).
  Dates: March 1979-March 1984.
  Objective: To apply the underwriting decision-making process to commercial liability exposures.
  Instruction: Emphasizes the analysis of the loss potential of fire and allied perils, the evaluation of property hazards and methods of underwriting and pricing major property lines and package policies. Lecture and discussion are used.

Credit recommendation: In the upper division baccalaureate category, 3 semester hours in Insurance (6/79). NOTE: Because this course is sometimes found in community college curricula, it is also appropriate for the granting of 3 units of lower division credit at a community college.

Commercial Property Insurance Coverages (PR20) (Formerly Property Insurance Coverages [PR20])
  Location: Various locations throughout CA.
  Length: 30 hours (12 weeks).
  Dates: September 1977-Present.
  Objective: To provide an understanding of commercial property forms and coverages, including direct and consequential loss.
  Instruction: Standard fire policy, extended coverage forms, sprinkler leakage, earthquake, flood contingent loss from operation of building laws, and business interruption.
  Credit recommendation: In the lower division baccalaureate/associate degree category, 1 semester hour in Insurance (5/78) (3/84). NOTE: This course has undergone a 5-year reevaluation and continues to meet requirements for credit recommendations.

Commercial Property Risk Management and Insurance (CPCU III)*
  Location: Various locations throughout CA.
  Length: 40 hours (17 weeks).
  Dates: September 1978-March 1984.
  Objective: To apply the risk management process to commercial property loss exposures and analyze contracts in this area.
  Instruction: Emphasizes the analysis of commercial property exposures and forms - fires and allied lines, business interruption, ocean and inland marine, crime, and combination policies. Noninsurance techniques, such as loss control and transfer, are also discussed. Lecture and discussion are used.
  Credit recommendation: In the upper division baccalaureate category, 3 semester hours in Insurance (6/79). NOTE: Because this course is sometimes found in community college curricula, it is also appropriate for the granting of 3 units of lower division credit at a community college.

Economics (CPCU IX)*
  Location: Various locations throughout CA.
  Length: 40 hours (17 weeks).
  Dates: September 1978-March 1984.
  Objective: To provide an understanding of basic micro- and macroeconomic principles.
  Instruction: Emphasizes product pricing; distribution of income; savings, investment, and consumption; monetary and fiscal policy; and the economics of social issues. Lecture and discussion are used.

Credit recommendation: In the lower division baccalaureate/associate degree category, 3 semester hours in Economics (6/79). NOTE: Because this course is sometimes found in community college curricula, it is also appropriate for the granting of 3 units of lower division credit at a community college.

Fire Protection Engineering (PR30)
  Location: Various locations throughout CA.
  Length: 30 hours (12 weeks).
  Dates: February 1976-May 1986.
  Objective: To provide a basic understanding of fire protection engineering.
  Instruction: Automatic sprinkler systems; portable fire extinguishing equipment; special extinguishing systems, such as Halon 1301; carbon dioxide and hi-ex foam; water supply systems and hydraulic analysis; fire pumps; signal systems; building construction and facilities; special hazards evaluation and control.
  Credit recommendation: In the upper division baccalaureate category, 2 semester hours in Fire Protection or Insurance (5/78) (3/84). NOTE: This course has undergone a 5-year reevaluation and continues to meet requirements for credit recommendations.

Fire Protection Engineering (Phase II) (PR30A)
  Location: Various locations throughout CA.
  Length: 30 hours (12 weeks).
  Dates: February 1977-May 1986.
  Objective: To provide an advanced understanding of fire protection engineering.
  Instruction: An advanced course covering high-rise protection, arson, radiation hazards, heat and smoke detectors, transportation fire hazards, fire hazards during earthquake and flood. Analysis of the chemistry and physics of fire protection engineering.
  Credit recommendation: In the upper division baccalaureate category, 2 semester hours in Insurance or Fire Protection (5/78) (3/84). NOTE: This course has undergone a 5-year reevalaution and continues to meet requirements for credit recommendations.

Hazard Identification and Analysis (LCM 71)*
  Location: Various locations throughout CA.
  Length: 30 hours (13 weeks).
  Dates: March 1979-March 1984.
  Objective: To examine the fundamental principles relating to identification and control of the hazards of the workplace.
  Instruction: Emphasis on health hazards, accidental hazards, and property hazards, stressing identification of the conditions which lead to accidents and techniques for abating these hazards.
  Credit recommendation: In the upper division baccalaureate category, 3 semester hours in Engineering, Health and Safety, or Insurance (6/79). NOTE: Because

this course is sometimes found in community college curricula, it is also appropriate for the granting of 3 units of lower division credit at a community college.

Insurance Company Operations (CPCU V)*
Location: Various locations throughout CA.
Length: 40 hours (17 weeks).
Dates: September 1978-March 1984.
Objective: To develop a thorough understanding of the functional characteristics of insurance company operations.
Instruction: Emphasizes the analysis of the following areas of company operations: marketing, underwriting, reinsurance, rate making, claims adjusting, loss control activities, and other insurance functions and activities. Lecture and discussion are used.
Credit recommendation: In the upper division baccalaureate category, 3 semester hours in Insurance (6/79). NOTE: Because this course is sometimes found in community college curricula, it is also appropriate for the granting of 3 units of lower division credit at a community college.

Insurance Issues and Professional Ethics (CPCU X)*
Location: Various locations throughout CA.
Length: 40 hours (17 weeks).
Dates: March 1979-March 1984.
Objective: To analyze selected major problems in the insurance industry and to analyze the American Institute Code of Professional Ethics.
Instruction: Covers major problems and issues in the insurance industry such as discrimination, primacy, trends in tort law, open rating, government insurers, inflation, professional liability for health care providers, captives, wrap-up insurance, international insurance, insurance theory, and insurance professionalism. Lecture and discussion are used.
Credit recommendation: In the upper division baccalaureate category, 3 semester hours in Insurance (6/79). NOTE: Because this course is sometimes found in community college curricula, it is also appropriate for the granting of 3 units of lower division credit at a community college.

Law of Torts (LA1)
Location: Various locations throughout CA.
Length: 30 hours (12 weeks).
Dates: September 1969-Present.
Objective: To provide an understanding of the basic principles of tort law.
Instruction: Intentional torts, proof of negligence, breach of duty, causation, proximate cause, damages, defenses, imputed negligence, survival and wrongful death, joint tortfeasors, owners and occupiers of land, strict liability, products liability. Lecture and discussion are used.
Credit recommendation: In the lower division baccalaureate/associate degree category, 2 semester hours in Business Law or Insurance (6/78) (3/84). NOTE: This course has undergone a 5-year reevaluation and continues to meet requirements for credit recommendations.

Legal Environment of Insurance (CPCU VI)*
Location: Various locations throughout CA.
Length: 40 hours (17 weeks).
Dates: March 1979-March 1984.
Objective: To develop a basic understanding of business and insurance law.
Instruction: Covers the areas of general business law, particularly the areas of contract and agency law, and emphasizes the application of business law to insurance situations.
Credit recommendation: In the upper division baccalaureate category, 3 semester hours in Business Law or Insurance (6/79). NOTE: Because this course is sometimes found in community college curricula, it is also appropriate for the granting of 3 units of lower division credit at a community college.

Liability Insurance Adjusting (ADJ36)*
Location: Various locations throughout CA.
Length: 30 hours (13 weeks).
Dates: September 1969-March 1984.
Objective: To provide an understanding of the concepts of legal duty, breach of legal duty, doctrine of proximate cause, and the evaluation of damages; to explore the basis of legal liability; to study the investigation and disposition of liability claims.
Instruction: Introductory material on medical knowledge needed by adjusters, study of adjuster-lawyer and adjuster-physician relationships, special problems regarding the settlement of workers' compensation claims. Investigation and evaluation problems are examined at a level more advanced than in previous courses in the program. Lecture and discussion are used.
Credit recommendation: In the upper division baccalaureate category, 3 semester hours in Business, Business Law, or Insurance (6/78).

Management (CPCU VII)*
Location: Various locations throughout CA.
Length: 40 hours (17 weeks).
Dates: September 1978-March 1984.
Objective: To develop an understanding of the principles of management.
Instruction: Emphasizes the management process, organizational design, planning, control, motivation, leadership, group behavior, communications, management information systems, entrepreneurship, and career development. Lecture and discussion are used.
Credit recommendation: In the upper division baccalaureate category, 3 semester hours in Management (6/79). NOTE: Because this course is sometimes found in

community college curricula, it is also appropriate for the granting of 3 units of lower division credit at a community college.

Management and Human Resources (MGT42)*
  Location: Various locations throughout CA.
  Length: 30 hours (13 weeks).
  Dates: September 1968-March 1984.
  Objective: To provide an understanding of human behavior within an organization.
  Instruction: Utilizes the behavioral sciences to provide analytical tools for the study of behavior in organizational settings. A series of cases assists in the development of skills in diagnosing "people problems" and determining effective ways of responding to them as a manager. Emphasizes the development of practical solutions to problems affected by human considerations. Lecture and discussion are used.
  Credit recommendation: In the upper division baccalaureate category, 3 semester hours in Business Administration or Management (6/78).

Management in a Changing World (MGT44)*
  Location: Various locations throughout CA.
  Length: 30 hours (13 weeks).
  Dates: September 1968-March 1984.
  Objective: To examine management decision making within the context of broad social and political considerations.
  Instruction: The political and social environment and the constraints which it places on management; trends in management practices and emerging concepts about the management of human and technological change. Lecture and discussion are used.
  Credit recommendation: In the upper division baccalaureate category, 3 semester hours in Business Administration or Management (6/78).

Managerial Decision Making (MGT43)*
  Location: Various locations throughout CA.
  Length: 30 hours (13 weeks).
  Dates: September 1968-March 1984.
  Objective: To acquaint students with modern decision-making tools and techniques.
  Instruction: Develops a systematic framework for the evaluation of decisions. Particular attention is given to the sources of error in decision making. Study of the individual and organizational decision-making process, and the role of the computer in an organization. Lecture and discussion are used.
  Credit recommendation: In the upper division baccalaureate category, 3 semester hours in Business Administration or Management (6/78).

Personal Lines Insurance (MU32)
  Location: Various locations throughout CA.
  Length: 30 hours (12 weeks).
  Dates: March 1975-December 1988.
  Objective: To provide the student with a survey of personal lines forms, coverages, and underwriting.
  Instruction: Emphasizes contractual coverages as related to all personal lines including family automobile, dwelling fire, homeowners, personal inland marine, personal umbrella and personal watercraft. Rating procedures and underwriting considerations as related to each line of insurance are reviewed.
  Credit recommendation: In the lower division baccalaureate/associate degree category, 2 semester hours in Insurance (5/78) (3/84). NOTE: This course has undergone a 5-year reevaluation and continues to meet requirements for credit recommendations.

Personal Lines Underwriting (UND62)*
  Location: Various locations throughout CA.
  Length: 30 hours (13 weeks).
  Dates: September 1978-March 1984.
  Objective: To provide an understanding of the underwriting of personal lines of property liability insurance.
  Instruction: Underwriting personal auto, homeowners, comprehensive personal liability, personal umbrella, personal articles floaters, and other personal lines. The application of the underwriting principles developed in the preceding course, Underwriting UND61. Lectures and discussions are used.
  Credit recommendation: In the upper division baccalaureate category, 3 semester hours in Insurance (5/78).

Personal Risk Management and Insurance (CPCU II)*
  Location: Various locations throughout CA.
  Length: 40 hours (17 weeks).
  Dates: March 1979-March 1984.
  Objective: To apply the risk management process to personal loss exposures and analyze personal lines contracts.
  Instruction: Emphasizes the analysis of personal insurance policies such as automobile, homeowners, life and health contracts; and includes social insurance, employee benefit plan, and estate planning. Lecture and discussion are used.
  Credit recommendation: In the upper division baccalaureate category, 3 semester hours in Insurance (6/79). NOTE: Because this course is sometimes found in community college curricula, it is also appropriate for the granting of 3 units of lower division credit at a community college.

Principles of Insurance (INS21)*
  Location: Various locations throughout CA.
  Length: 30 hours (13 weeks).
  Dates: September 1970-March 1984.
  Objective: To provide an understanding of the basic principles of insurance as well as the nature and operation

of the insurance business.

Instruction: Analyzes the use of probability distributions; indemnity; insurable interest; coinsurance; subrogation; proximate cause; requisites of insurable risk; use of deductibles; valued policies. Insurance company operations such as rate making, underwriting, marketing, and adjusting. Government regulations, reinsurance, functions of insurance agents and brokers, historical development of the insurance mechanism, organization of insurance entities.

Credit recommendation: In the lower division baccalaureate/associate degree category or in the upper division baccalaureate category, 2 semester hours in Insurance (5/78).

Principles of Insurance and Liability Claim Adjusting (ADJ32)*

Location: Various locations throughout CA.
Length: 30 hours (13 weeks).
Dates: May 1970-March 1984.
Objective: To introduce basic liability claim adjusting and the human behavioral response.
Instruction: The functional areas of rating and underwriting, as well as the subjects of regulation, reinsurance, and company organization are explored. Includes legal liability hazards and the investigation, evaluation, negotiation, and settlement of bodily injury and property damage claims. Emphasizes adjustment of automobile liability and physical damage claims and losses. Introduces fundamental concepts of the no-fault approach to automobile insurance reform. Special attention is devoted to the subject of understanding human behavior of claimants. Lecture and discussion are used.
Credit recommendation: In the lower division baccalaureate/associate degree category, 3 semester hours in Business, Business Law, or Insurance (6/78).

Principles of Insurance and Property Loss Adjusting (ADJ31)*

Location: Various locations throughout CA.
Length: 30 hours (13 weeks).
Dates: January 1970-March 1984.
Objective: To examine the basic principles of insurance and the fundamental areas of property loss adjusting with emphasis on the adjustment of personal property losses.
Instruction: Emphasizes property loss adjustment procedure, including investigation, negotiation, and settlement. Determination of coverage, value, and loss is included. Attention is given to estimating building losses and construction costs along with reporting procedures. Lecture and discussion are used.
Credit recommendation: In the lower division baccalaureate/associate degree category, 3 semester hours in Business, Business Law, or Insurance (6/78).

Principles of Property and Liability Underwriting (UND61)*

Location: Various locations throughout CA.
Length: 30 hours (13 weeks).
Dates: February 1977-March 1984.
Objective: To introduce students to underwriting decision making on two levels: individual risk underwriting and the underwriting management of a company's entire operation.
Instruction: A discussion of the underwriting function, its nature, purpose, and organization, is followed by an analysis of the underwriting decision-making process. Underwriting and fundamentals, including coverage analysis, loss control, reinsurance, necessary numerical tools. Financial analysis and pricing are also examined.
Credit recommendation: In the upper division baccalaureate category, 3 semester hours in Insurance (5/78).

Principles of Risk Management and Insurance (CPCU I)*

Location: Various locations throughout CA.
Length: 40 hours (17 weeks).
Dates: September 1978-March 1984.
Objective: To provide an understanding of the risk management process and develop a framework for the analysis of insurance contracts.
Instruction: Emphasizes techniques for managing pure loss exposures, the insurance environment, basic legal concepts, and fundamentals of insurance contracts. Lecture and discussion are used.
Credit recommendation: In the upper division baccalaureate category, 3 semester hours in Insurance (6/79). NOTE: Because this course is sometimes found in community college curricula, it is also appropriate for the granting of 3 units of lower division credit at a community college.

Process of Management (MGT41)*

Location: Various locations throughout CA.
Length: 30 hours (13 weeks).
Dates: September 1968-March 1984.
Objective: To introduce the student to the study of management and managerial problem solving.
Instruction: Major functions in the management process: organization, motivation, planning, and control; analytical tools used by managers. Cases based on actual organizational experience are used to apply concepts in solving management problems. Lecture and discussion are used.
Credit recommendation: In the upper division baccalaureate category, 3 semester hours in Business Administration or Management (6/78).

Property Insurance (INS22)*

Location: Various locations throughout CA.
Length: 30 hours (13 weeks).

Dates: September 1970-March 1984.

Objective: To provide an understanding of coverages, policy provisions, and concepts common to property insurance.

Instruction: Study of contracts and forms, including the standard fire policy, extended coverage endorsements, dwelling and contents form, building and contents form, bailees' customers policy, and property coverage provided by multiple-line contracts.

Credit recommendation: In the lower division baccalaureate/associate degree category or in the upper division baccalaureate category, 2 semester hours in Insurance (5/78).

Property Insurance Adjusting - Advanced (ADJ35)*

Location: Various locations throughout CA.
Length: 30 hours (13 weeks).
Dates: January 1970-March 1984.

Objective: To provide in-depth information on the subject of apportionment, insurable interest, loss estimation, and limitations on the amount of insurer's liability (including replacement cost and contribution).

Instruction: Adjustment of building losses (including valuation), merchandise and fixture losses, reporting form losses, business interruption insurance losses. Lecture and discussion are used.

Credit recommendation: In the upper division baccalaureate category, 3 semester hours in Business, Business Law, or Insurance (6/78).

Risk Control (RM55)*

Location: Various locations throughout CA.
Length: 30 hours (13 weeks).
Dates: February 1972-June 1984.

Objective: To provide information on best use of risk management techniques which minimize the financial consequences of a casualty loss: risk avoidance, loss prevention or reduction, and risk transfer to noninsurance organizations.

Instruction: Describes when and to what extent each risk-control technique should be employed, how each should be administered, and how each should be monitored for the control and coordination of the total risk-management effort. Students use guidelines for selecting risk-management techniques.

Credit recommendation: In the upper division baccalaureate category or in the graduate degree category, 3 semester hours in Insurance (5/78). NOTE: To be eligible for credit at the graduate level, the student should receive at least a grade of "B."

Risk Financing (RM56)*

Location: Various locations throughout CA.
Length: 30 hours (13 weeks).
Dates: September 1973-March 1984.

Objective: To complete the risk-management decision-making process with respect to risk-financing techniques, concentrating on the selection, implementation, and monitoring of the methods by which an organization can obtain funds to minimize the financial consequences of a casualty loss.

Instruction: Course emphasizes risk retention and commercial insurance. The financial guidelines from Risk Management 54 are applied to such topics as setting the amounts of self-insured retention, negotiating with admitted and nonadmitted insurers, and coordinating self-insurance with commercial insurance.

Credit recommendation: In the upper division baccalaureate category or in the graduate degree category, 3 semester hours in Insurance (5/78). NOTE: To be eligible for credit at the graduate level, the student should receive at least a grade of "B."

Structure of the Risk-Management Process (RM 54)*

Location: Various locations throughout CA.
Length: 30 hours (13 weeks).
Dates: February 1972-March 1984.

Objective: To introduce exposure identification and evaluation into the risk-management decision-making process and to lay the financial-management foundation for choosing the best risk-management alternative. Students should be familiar with the objectives of a business organization and the principles of general management.

Instruction: Procedures for identifying and analyzing property, income, liability, and personnel loss exposures; general characteristics of the various risk control and risk financing techniques; guidelines for selecting the most appropriate risk management techniques for each exposure. These guidelines demonstrate how proper risk management helps to achieve the organization's overall profits and productivity.

Credit recommendation: In the upper division baccalaureate category or in the graduate degree category, 3 semester hours in Insurance (5/78). NOTE: To be eligible for credit at the graduate level, the student should receive at least a grade of "B."

Surety Bonding (BO 1)

Location: Various locations throughout CA.
Length: 30 hours (12 weeks).
Dates: September 1973-Present.

Objective: To introduce the basic principles and nomenclature of suretyship.

Instruction: Basic principles of suretyship: judicial, license and permit, contract, and miscellaneous surety. Basic financial statement analysis, underwriting approaches and fundamentals are studied from the standpoint of the underwriter and producer. Lecture and discussion are used.

Credit recommendation: In the lower division baccalaureate/associate degree category, 2 semester hours in Insurance (6/78) (3/84). NOTE: This course has under-

Workers' Compensation (Advanced) (CA9A)
Location: Various locations throughout CA.
Length: 30 hours (13 weeks).
Dates: September 1974-Present.
Objective: To develop decision-making abilities in dealing with workers' compensation insurance plans.
Instruction: General rules, classification procedures, premium calculations, experience rating plans, administration of workers' compensation boards and bureaus, state funds, assigned risk plans. This course is built on the basic concepts presented in CA9. Lecture and discussion are used.
Credit recommendation: In the upper division baccalaureate category, 1 semester hour in Insurance (6/78) (3/84). NOTE: This course has undergone a 5-year reevaluation and continues to meet the requirements for credit recommendations.

Workers' Compensation (Basic) (CA9)
Location: Various locations throughout CA.
Length: 30 hours (12 weeks).
Dates: September 1972-Present.
Objective: To introduce the basic concepts of Workers' Compensation Insurance.
Instruction: Fundamentals of Workers' Compensation; analysis of the policy forms, LS and HW, Jones Act, Rules, Rates, and Classification. Lecture and discussion are used.
Credit recommendation: In the lower division baccalaureate/associate degree category, 1 semester hour in Insurance (5/78) (3/84). NOTE: This course has undergone a 5-year reevaluation and continues to meet requirements for credit recommendations.

Workers' Compensation Claims (Advanced) (CA11)
Location: Various locations throughout CA.
Length: 30 hours (12 weeks).
Dates: February 1975-Present.
Objective: To provide coverage at an advanced level of current case law involved with employment, injury, and permanent disability.
Instruction: Functioning of the Workers' Compensation Appeals Board, analysis of current case law concerning compensable injuries, degree of disability, rehabilitation. Lecture and discussion are used.
Credit recommendation: In the upper division baccalaureate category, 2 semester hours in Insurance (5/78) (3/84). NOTE: This course has undergone a 5-year reevaluation and continues to meet requirements for credit recommendations.

Workers' Compensation Claims (Basic) (CA10)
Location: Various locations throughout CA.
Length: 30 hours (12 weeks).
Dates: September 1974-Present.
Objective: To provide a basic understanding of the workers' compensation claims process.
Instruction: Workers' compensation insurance claims adjusting, investigation required to determine application of the law and its interpretation, payment of benefits, subrogation. Lecture and discussion are used.
Credit recommendation: In the upper division baccalaureate category, 2 semester hours in Insurance (5/78) (3/84). NOTE: This course has undergone a 5-year reevaluation and continues to meet the requirements for credit recommendations.

Workers' Compensation Claims - Medical Terms and Applications
(Formerly Medical Management of Workers' Compensation Claims [CA12])
Location: Various locations throughout CA.
Length: 30 hours (12 weeks).
Dates: September 1974-Present.
Objective: To provide students with the ability to recognize and define medical word roots, prefixes, suffixes, and related disease and surgical terms.
Instruction: An introduction to medical language, anatomy, and physiology. This course prepares the student to understand and process workers' compensation medical claims. Series of lectures by medical injury specialists and discussion are used.
Credit recommendation: In the upper division baccalaureate category, 1 semester hour in Insurance or Medical Technology (5/78) (3/84). NOTE: This course has undergone a 5-year reevaluation and continues to meet requirements for credit recommendations.

Workers' Compensation: Permanent Disability Rating (CA13)
Location: Various locations throughout CA.
Length: 30 hours (12 weeks).
Dates: September 1974-Present.
Objective: To rate permanent disability cases both objective and subjective based on medical reports.
Instruction: Covers the mechanics of rating and the interpretation of medical reports including multiple disabilities, bilateral and ambidextrous disabilities and subsequent injuries fund.
Credit recommendation: In the upper division baccalaureate category, 1 semester hour in Insurance (3/84).

Workers' Compensation Rehabilitation (CA14)
Location: Various locations throughout CA.
Length: 30 hours (12 weeks).
Dates: September 1977-Present.
Objective: To provide an understanding of the administration of the Workers' Compensation Rehabilitation program as outlined in the Rules and Regulations.

Instruction: History and concept, organization and authority, due process, qualifying the injured worker, role of the rehabilitation representative, evaluation, testing and plan maintenance. Lecture and discussion are used.

Credit recommendation: In the upper division baccalaureate category, 1 semester hour in Health Care Administration or Insurance (6/78) (3/84). NOTE: This course has undergone a 5-year reevaluation and continues to meet requirements for credit recommendations.

International Correspondence Schools

The International Correspondence Schools (ICS) Education Service Center is located in Scranton, Pennsylvania. It is this location which is charged by The National Education Corporation (NEC) with the delivery of the course in computer literacy.

ICS is itself a world leader in the field of independent learning. Since its founding in 1891, ICS has pioneered in the development of self-paced independent study materials. Its entire business is devoted to the development, marketing, and servicing of vocational and avocational instructional materials. ICS has developed such innovative educational aids as Dial-A-Question, a toll-free educational assistance system, and Tel-Test, a sophisticated interactive testing device which utilizes telephone communication between the student and the institution.

ICS has a permanent faculty of over 20 people plus additional support personnel. Aided by contemporary data processing equipment, the institution has enrolled close to 8 million students. In 1983, enrollments in courses offered by ICS and its companion institution NACS (North American Correspondence Schools) topped 50,000.

A charter member of the National Home Study Council, ICS is accredited by the Council and is also licensed by the Pennsylvania Department of Education. National Education Corporation is also a member of the National Home Study Council.

National Education Corporation (NEC) is a world leader in the field of human resource development. It has worldwide operations in vocational and industrial training, educational publishing, and home health care services. It is the sponsoring organization for the Computer Literacy Course which was originally developed by the International Correspondence Schools (ICS) Independent Study Division.

Source of official student records: Director, Center for Degree Studies, International Correspondence Schools, Scranton, Pennsylvania 18515.

Additional information about the courses: Program on Noncollegiate Sponsored Instruction, The Center for Adult Learning and Educational Credentials, American Council on Education, One Dupont Circle, Washington, D.C. 20036. Program on Noncollegiate Sponsored Instruction, Thomas A. Edison State College, 101 West State Street, CN 545, Trenton, New Jersey 08625.

A-C and D-C Motors and Controls
Location: Self study.
Length: Correspondence Program.
Dates: January 1980-Present.
Objective: To provide the student with an understanding of direct-current generators and motors, alternating-current motors, and the methods of controlling such equipment.

Learning Outcome: Upon successful completion of this course, the student will be able to understand the construction, operation, rating and maintenance of different types of A-C and D-C motors and generators; manual and circuit protective devices.

Instruction: Principles of generator and motor operation; ratings and efficiency; principles of induction motors and synchronous motors; performance and speed control; single-phase motors; principles of motor control system; motor-circuit protective devices; solid-state drive systems; SCRs as A-C to D-C converters; installation and maintenance of drive systems.

Credit recommendation: In the lower division baccalaureate/associate degree category, 2 semester hours in Electrical/Electronic Technology, or A-C and D-C Motors (11/84) (4/89). NOTE: This course has been reevaluated and continues to meet requirements for credit recommendations.

Accounting I
Location: Self study.
Length: Correspondence Program.
Dates: January 1981-Present.
Objective: To provide the student with basic understanding of principles of accounting including the balance sheet and income statement; to provide practice in making journal entries. Student will be able to read and interpret financial reports; record financial transactions; establish a trial balance; make appropriate journal entries and post to the general ledger; and make adjustments.

Learning Outcome: Upon successful completion of this course, the student will be able to prepare all required procedures in the accounting cycle and payroll calculations.

Instruction: A review of the nature of accounting; financial reports, including the balance sheet and income statement. Recording transactions, the trial balance, journal entries, and posting. Adjustments, and cash versus accrual method of accounting. The work sheet, the accounting cycle. Accounts and procedures for a merchandising business, special journals, payroll accounting.

Credit recommendation: in the lower division baccalaureate/associate degree category, 3 semester hours in Accounting (4/86).

Accounting II
  Location: Self study.
  Length: Correspondence Program.
  Dates: January 1981-Present.
  Objective: To expand the student's knowledge developed in first part of Accounting and to explain more detailed uses of accounting techniques. Student will be able to identify and distinguish several types of fixed assets; to establish accounting procedures for current and long term liabilities; and to complete an entire accounting cycle for a corporation.
  Learning Outcome: Upon successful completion of this course, the student will be able to prepare and analyze financial statements and present the concepts of assets and liabilities as they apply to business organizations.
  Instruction: An explanation of cash, accounts receivable, notes receivables, investments, and inventory. Also, the nature of fixed assets, accounting for current and long-term liabilities. Particular emphasis is placed on partnership accounting and corporate ownership and management. A comprehensive case study dealing with the entire accounting cycle for a merchandising firm operating as a corporation is included.
  Credit recommendation: In the lower baccalaureate/associate degree category, 3 semester hours in Accounting (4/86).

Advertising Principles
  Location: Self study.
  Length: Correspondence Program.
  Dates: March 1984-Present.
  Objective: To give the student a general introduction to advertising, its function and role. Student will be able to place advertising among the other appropriate marketing functions; to describe the steps necessary to build an advertising organization; to identify outside specialists; and to construct an advertising plan.
  Learning Outcome: Upon successful completion of this course, the student will understand the techniques of advertising, the function of advertising, and the role of advertising.
  Instruction: The purpose of this course is to describe, at a very basic level, the techniques of advertising, the function of advertising, in the marketing area, and the role of advertising in the marketplace.
  Credit recommendation: In the vocational certificate category, 1 semester hour in Marketing (4/86).

American Literature
  Location: Self study.
  Length: Correspondence Program.
  Dates: June 1978-December 1986.
  Objective: To provide the student with understanding and appreciation of major authors and forms of writing as found in American Literature - An Introductory Overview.
  Instruction: America's literature evolving into art form from its Puritan beginnings to the twentieth century.
  Credit recommendation: In the lower division baccalaureate/associate degree category, 3 semester hours in American Literature (11/84).

Analytic Geometry and Calculus
  Location: Self study.
  Length: Correspondence Program.
  Dates: October 1975-Present.
  Objective: To provide the student with a basic foundation in analytic geometry and a broad coverage of topics in differential and integral calculus.
  Learning Outcome: Upon successful completion of this course, the student will be able to apply principles of analytic geometry and differential and integral calculus.
  Instruction: Rectangular coordinates; graphs of linear equations; conic sections; exponential, logarithmic, and trigonometric functions; continuity; limits; derivatives and their applications, including derivatives of implicit functions, parametric equations, and trigonometric, exponential, hyperbolic, and logarithmic functions; integrals and their applications; methods of integration; polar coordinates.
  Credit recommendation: In the lower division baccalaureate/associate degree category, 4 semester hours in Analytic Geometry and Calculus (11/84) (4/89). NOTE: This course has been reevaluated and continues to meet requirements for credit recommendations.

Applications of Industrial Electronics
  Location: Self study.
  Length: Correspondence Program.
  Dates: January 1982-Present.
  Objective: To provide the student with a qualitative understanding of the color TV system, electronic systems applications and industrial systems troubleshooting techniques.
  Learning Outcome: Upon successful completion of this course, the student will be able to qualitatively understand the color TV system, electronic systems applications, and industrial systems troubleshooting techniques.
  Instruction: Color TV system; basic industrial electronic systems application; voltage and frequency controllers; nondestructive test equipment; resistance welding equipment; dielectic and induction heating; cranes, scales, and materials handling. Advanced troubleshooting; analysis of systems; test equipment applications; safe troubleshooting practices; troubleshooting industrial systems.
  Credit recommendation: In the lower division baccalaureate/associate degree category, 3 semester hours in Electrical/Electronic Technology or Application of Industrial Electronics (11/84) (4/89). NOTE: This course has been reevaluated and continues to meet requirements for credit recommendations.

Applied Math
Location: Self study.
Length: Correspondence Program.
Dates: January 1980-Present.
Objective: To provide the student with a foundation in the use of metrics, and a working knowledge of the application of certain topics in calculus which are needed in the electronics field of technology.
Learning Outcome: Upon successful completion of this course, the student will be able to use metrics and basic calculus in solving problems encountered in electronics.
Instruction: Use of metrics; use of calculus in electrical and electronic circuits; graphic differentiation; applications of derivatives and differentials; Kirchhoff's Laws; differentiating circuits; higher order derivatives; maxima and minima; partial occurrences of maxima and minima; integration; electrical applications of integration; integrating circuits; graphic approach to integration; integrating instruments; polar coordinates; derivatives of trigonometric functions and their applications to electronics; logarithmic and exponential functions; natural logarithms; electrical transients in RC and RL circuits; hyperbolic functions; introduction to partial derivatives of transistor and electron-tube parameters; maxima and minima with partial derivatives; gradients; integration techniques; application of double integrals to electrical circuits.
Credit recommendation: In the lower division baccalaureate/associate degree category, 3 semester hours in Applied Math (11/84) (4/89). NOTE: This course has been reevaluated and continues to meet requirements for credit recommendations.

Basic Surveying I
Location: Self study.
Length: Correspondence Program.
Dates: January 1978-Present.
Objective: To introduce students to the fundamentals of plane surveying; including distant measurement, leveling, and transit work.
Learning Outcome: Upon successful completion of this course, the student will be able to work proficiently with various surveying tools and equipment.
Instruction: Covers principles of taps and accessories; electronic measurements; leveling; use of transit and theodolite; adjustment of instruments; angle measurements; triangulation; trigonometric leveling; balancing traverse; error of sure; computation of area by latitudes and departures. NOTE: Does not include field exercises with surveying instruments.
Credit recommendation: In the lower division baccalaureate/associate degree category, or in the upper division baccalaureate category, 2 semester hours in Basic Surveying I or 1 semester hour in Basic Surveying I when applied to Engineering major (11/84) (4/89). NOTE: Before credit is awarded student should have completed a basic surveying lab course or have equivalent field experience. NOTE: This course has been reevaluated and continues to meet requirements for credit recommendations.

Basic Surveying II
Location: Self study.
Length: Correspondence Program.
Dates: January 1980-Present.
Objective: To introduce the student to the principles of highway curve geometry.
Learning Outcome: Upon successful completion of this course, the student will be able to conduct basic surveys that involve a variety of curves: horizontal, vertical, compound, spiral, etc.
Instruction: Tangents and horizontal curves; grades and vertical curves; compound and reverse curves; transition curves; superelevation; field layout of simple, compound, and spiral curves; vertical parabolic curves; elevations on vertical curves. NOTE: Course does not include field exercise with surveying instruments.
Credit recommendation: In the lower division baccalaureate/associate degree or in the upper division baccalaureate category, 2 semester hours in Basic Surveying II or 1 semester hour in Basic Surveying II when applied to Engineering major (11/84) (4/89). NOTE: This course has been reevaluated and continues to meet requirements for credit recommendations.

Business Communication
(Communications/Modern Language Expression)
Location: Self study.
Length: Correspondence Program.
Dates: January 1981-Present.
Objective: To introduce the student to elements of communication necessary for success in business. Student will be able to apply principles of grammar to writing samples; to develop an effective speaking technique; to list steps in constructing business letters; and to list steps necessary for preparation of a report.
Learning Outcome: Upon successful completion of this course, the student will understand how to prepare a speech and the mechanics of letter styles and advanced writing techniques.
Instruction: Study of parts of speech, proper usage, punctuation and capitalization, vocabulary building, and sentence structure. How to prepare a speech, conversational speech, conferences, public speaking, and parliamentary procedure. Mechanics of letter style and advanced writing techniques. Scope of report writing, examples of body, paragraph system. A project is included.
Credit recommendation: In the lower division baccalaureate/associate degree category, 2 semester hours in Business Communications (4/86).

Business Law I
Location: Self study.

Length: Correspondence Program.
Dates: January 1981-Present.
Objective: To introduce the student to the study of law and how it applies to contemporary business. Student will be able to describe and distinguish types of international law; to identify and explain which Constitutional Amendments affect everyday life; to identify and explain differences in types of contracts; to explain the roles of parties in a contract; and to interpret contractual capacities of minors and insane persons.
Learning Outcome: Upon successful completion of this course, the student will understand the nature and administration of law, the law of bankruptcy, and commercial paper.
Instruction: An introduction to the study of law, its nature and administration. The law contracts, bankruptcy and commercial paper.
Credit recommendation: In the lower division baccalaureate/associate degree category, 2 semester hours in Business Law (4/86).

Business Law II
Location: Self study.
Length: Correspondence Program.
Dates: January 1981-Present.
Objective: To provide the student with an expansion upon subjects covered in Business Law I and to provide more concrete examples of role of law in business. Student will be able to explain nature of Agency relationship and how one can be created; to explain a partnership and major characteristics of a corporation; to explain differences in types of stock and the advantages and disadvantages of each; and to identify significant pieces of legislation affecting laws of trade.
Learning Outcome: Upon successful completion of this course, the student will have a good understanding of agency, partnership, real property, corporation, and trade regulations.
Instruction: A study of agency, partnerships, real property, and corporations, and concluding with an introduction to trade regulations.
Credit recommendation: In the lower division baccalaureate/associate degree category, 2 semester hours in Business Law (4/86).

Business Statistics
Location: Self study.
Length: Correspondence Program.
Dates: January 1981-Present.
Objective: Student will be introduced to modern business statistical techniques and solve many sample problems. Students will be able to construct a graph, chart a table to display analysis results. Student will be able to list properties of arithmetic mean. Student will be able, given both grouped and ungrouped data, to perform several types of analysis. Student will be able to measure deviation or variation of data about a control valve. Student will be able to use devices such as time series correlation to forecast future.
Learning Outcome: Upon successful completion of this course, the student will understand the presentation of data, frequency distributions, averages, correlation, forecasting, and the theory of probability and statistical inference.
Instruction: Course content includes presentation of data, frequency distributions, averages, dispersion and skewness, index numbers, time series analysis, correlation and forecasting, introduction to the theory of probability and statistical inference.
Credit recommendation: In the lower division baccalaureate/associate degree category, 2 semester hours in Business Math (4/86).

Circuits and Components Testing
Location: Self study.
Length: Correspondence Program.
Dates: January 1982-Present.
Objective: To provide the student with an understanding of reactive circuits and to perform electrical and electronics measurements experiments by using a measurements trainer.
Learning Outcome: Upon successful completion of this course, the student will be able to understand reactive circuits and to perform basic electrical and electronics measurements.
Instruction: Reactive circuits; resistance, capacitance and inductance; reactance and impedance; resonant circuits; applications of resonant circuits. D-C principles experiments; A-C principles and components experiments; electrical measurements and instruments experiments; electronic measurements and instruments experiments; reactive circuits experiments; electronic components experiments; basic electronic circuits experiments.
Credit recommendation: In the lower division baccalaureate/associate degree category, 3 semester hours in Electrical/Electronic Technology or Circuits Testing (11/84) (4/89). NOTE: This course has been reevaluated and continues to meet requirements for credit recommendations.

Communications
Location: Self study.
Length: Correspondence Program.
Dates: October 1975-Present.
Objective: To develop student's capability in using correct English and in preparing various types of reports.
Learning Outcome: Upon successful completion of this course, the student will be able to communicate effectively and accurately through a report format.
Instruction: The course covers relationship of words, phrases, and clauses; rule for capitalization, abbreviations, and punctuation; effective speech; principles of good letter

writing; scope of report writing; component parts of reports; gathering and arranging facts and data; rough draft; rewriting; examples of introduction and body; headings; summarizing conclusion; checklist; synopsis, typing details.

Credit recommendation: In the lower division baccalaureate/associate degree category, 2 semester hours in Communications (11/84) (4/89). NOTE: This course has been reevaluated and continues to meet requirements for credit recommendations.

Composition and Rhetoric
  Location: Self study.
  Length: Correspondence Program.
  Dates: *Version 1:* September 1984-March 1989; *Version 2:* April 1989-Present.
  Objective: To provide the student with both theoretical and practical experience in writing.
  Learning Outcome: Upon successful completion of this course, the student will be able to write and speak coherently.
  Instruction: Course provides practice in expository writing and the application of rhetorical principles. Wide variety of reading to stimulate good writing and skill in composition. Also students will be able to understand and apply rhetorical principles through written assignments.
  Credit recommendation: *Version 1:* In the lower division baccalaureate/associate degree category, 2 semester hours in Composition and Rhetoric (11/84). *Version 2:*
  In the lower division baccalaureate/associate degree category, 3 semester hours in Composition and Rhetoric (4/89). NOTE: This course has been reevaluated and continues to meet requirements for credit recommendations.

Computer Literacy and Programming in BASIC
  Location: Independent study course, offered to students at their own residences or within their companies.
  Length: Approximately 225 hours of independent study.
  Dates: March 1983-Present.
  Objective: To provide the student with fundamental computer concepts; flow charting and BASIC programming including graphics, arrays, functions and file handling techniques.
  Learning Outcome: Upon successful completion of this course, the student will be able to understand fundamental computer concepts, flowcharting and programming using BASIC language.
  Instruction: This is an independent study course consisting of 11 institutional units complete with a microcomputer and a user's manual. Major topics include: computer parts and components; BASIC language and personal computers; peripherals and systems; software and program writing; the microprocessor unit; input and output devices; formats and displays; auxiliary storage and data organization; developing a program; using the flowchart and worksheet; arithmetic functions and applications; comparing and branching; tables and arrays; sorting and merging; running; editing, and debugging a program.

Credit recommendation: In the lower division baccalaureate/associate degree category, 3 semester hours in BASIC Programming and in the lower division baccalaureate/associate degree category, 2 semester hours in Computer Literacy (5/84) (4/89). NOTE: This course may be used to satisfy graduate requirements for teacher in-service training in Introduction to Computers. NOTE: This course has been reevaluated and continues to meet requirements for credit recommendations.

1. **Computer Science I (Computer Applications and Operations)**
2. **Computer Science II (BASIC Programming Fundamentals)**
  Location: Self study.
  Length: Correspondence Program.
  Dates: *Version 1:* February 1984-December 1987; *Version 2:* January 1988-Present.
  Objective: To provide the student with fundamental computer concepts; flowcharting and BASIC programming including graphics, arrays, functions, and file handling techniques.
  Learning Outcome: Upon successful completion of this course, the student will be able to understand the fundamentals of programming, flowcharting, and data representation.
  Instruction: *Version 1:* Course 1. Elementary programming and hardware concepts and terminology, data representation, flowcharting and elementary BASIC programming concepts. Lecture materials emphasize microcomputers. Course 2. Comparing and branching; selecting alternative paths; translating two-directional flowcharts into linear programs, using multiple comparisons; subtotaling; internal subroutines; multiple control breaks; defining a table; loading and printing numeric arrays; searching a table; maintaining a data file; alphabetic and numeric sequencing; coding sorts; merging files; formatting lines; columns and references; producing graphics; reverses and output; using pexels; creating graphs. (Prerequisite: Computer Science I.) *Version 2:* Course 1. Elementary programming and hardware concepts and terminology, data representation, flowcharting and elementary BASIC programming concepts. Lecture materials emphasize microcomputers. Course 2. Comparing and branching; selecting alternative paths; translating two-directional flowcharts into linear programs, using multiple comparisons; subtotaling; internal subroutines; multiple control breaks; defining a table; loading and printing numeric arrays; searching a table; maintaining a data file; alphabetic and numeric sequencing; coding sorts; merging files; formatting lines; columns and references; producing graphics; reverses and output; using pixels. (Prerequisite: Computer Science I.)

Credit recommendation: *Version 1:* In the lower division baccalaureate/associate degree category, 3 semester hours in BASIC Programming and in the lower division baccalaureate/associate degree category, 2 semester hours in Computer Literacy (11/84). NOTE: Both Computer Science I and II must be successfully completed for credit recommendations to apply. *Version 2:* In the lower division baccalaureate/associate degree category, 6 semester hours in BASIC Programming and Computer Literacy (4/89). NOTE: This course has been reevaluated and continues to meet requirements for credit recommendations.

Computer Science III—Computer and FORTRAN Fundamentals
  Location: Self study.
  Length: Correspondence Program.
  Dates: *Version 1:* January 1982-March 1989; *Version 2:* April 1989-Present.
  Objective: To provide the student with a fundamental understanding of the FORTRAN IV programming language. Also, to offer an overview of computer application in industry and electronics is provided.
  Learning Outcome: Upon successful completion of this course, the student will be able to understand concepts of FORTRAN; write simple FORTRAN programs; and understand how computers are used in industry and electronics.
  Instruction: Course covers basic industrial computer systems; computer fundamentals; digital and analog systems; software and programming; computer-aided control systems; interfacing principles. FORTRAN IV programming; fundamental FORTRAN IV concepts; writing simple FORTRAN program; statement functions; use of magnetic tapes and disks; review of function and subroutine subprograms. (Prerequisite: Technical Mathematics I and II.)
  Credit recommendation: *Version 1:* In the lower division baccalaureate/associate degree category, 2 semester hours in FORTRAN (11/84). *Version 2:* In the lower division baccalaureate/associate degree category, 3 semester hours in FORTRAN (4/89). NOTE: This course has been reevaluated and continues to meet requirements for credit recommendations.

Concrete
  Location: Self study.
  Length: Correspondence Program.
  Dates: January 1982-Present.
  Objective: To provide the student with an understanding of how concrete is produced, tested, and used in the field.
  Learning Outcome: Upon successful completion of this course, the student will be able to test and analyze the quality of concrete in the field.
  Instruction: Production of concrete; proportioning of concrete mixes; tests for concrete; field methods in concrete construction.
  Credit recommendation: In the lower division baccalaureate/associate degree category, or in the upper division baccalaureate category, 1 semester hour in Concrete (11/84) (4/89). NOTE: This course has been reevaluated and continues to meet requirements for credit recommendations.

Cost Accounting
  Location: Self study.
  Length: Correspondence Program.
  Dates: January 1981-Present.
  Objective: To provide the student with understanding of cost accounting concepts and the ability to develop timekeeping and payroll reports. Student will be able to explain necessity for cost information; to record entries dealing with raw materials acquisition, labor costs, overhead costs, warehousing and sales; how to interpret a job cost system after it is installed; and to account for work in process in proper terms.
  Learning Outcome: Upon successful completion of this course, the student will be able to use cost data in budgeting and capital planning for various types of manufacturing operations.
  Instruction: Cost accounting concepts and the interpretation of reports. Development of timekeeping and payroll procedures. The setting of overhead rates. Accounting for scrap, spoiled, and defective goods. Accounting for by-products, development of cost analyses, process cost accounting, job-order cost accounting, standard costs.
  Credit recommendation: In the upper division baccalaureate category, 3 semester hours in Accounting (4/86).

Earthwork
  Location: Self study.
  Length: Correspondence Program.
  Dates: January 1980-Present.
  Objective: To perform earthwork volume computations.
  Learning Outcome: Upon successful completion of this course, the student will be able to conduct field and office work in the area of cut-fill calculations, embankment analysis and grade establishment.
  Instruction: Course covers surveys for determining grade; cross-sectioning; earthwork computations; formation of embankments; shrinkage and swell; moving cut to fill; mass diagrams.
  Credit recommendation: In the lower division baccalaureate/associate degree category, 1 semester hour in Earthwork (11/84) (4/89). NOTE: Can also apply to Engineering majors. NOTE: This course has been reevaluated and continues to meet requirements for credit recommendations.

Economics I
Location: Self study.
Length: Correspondence Program.
Dates: January 1981-Present.
Objective: To provide the student with a general survey course which is designed to introduce student to basic concepts of economics. Student will be able to describe a business cycle; to explain importance concept of Gross National Product; to list four assumptions concerning consumer behavior; to explain differences between foreign and domestic trade; and to define and give examples of non competitive market structures.
Learning Outcome: Upon successful completion of this course, the student will understand macro and micro economic concepts, the economizing problem, and its future implications.
Instruction: This course defines the economizing problem, develops it, and explores its future implications. The course emphasizes economic growth. Macro and micro economic concepts are examined in terms of a discussion of three fundamental economic questions: (1) What is to be produced? (2) Where is it to be produced? and (3) How is it to be produced?
Credit recommendation: In the lower division baccalaureate/associate degree category, 3 semester hours in Economics (4/86).

Economics II
Location: Self study.
Length: Correspondence Program.
Dates: April 1986-Present.
Objective: To provide the student with an understanding of general concepts of economics and emphasizes concepts like inequality and poverty. Also includes a discussion of Managerial Economics. Student will be able to list and explain some of the reasons for differences in money income received by individual; to differentiate between the economics growth problems facing more versus less developed countries; to identify and explain major differences between different economic systems; and to identify different kinds of markets.
Learning Outcome: Upon successful completion of this course, the student will have an expanded understanding of macro and micro economic concepts and will have a knowledge of the economics of inequality and poverty.
Instruction: This course continues the study of macro and micro economic concepts. Emphasis is placed upon the economics of inequality and poverty. The material is organized to answer two fundamental questions: (1) To whom shall resources be distributed? (2) When will the "poverty amidst plenty" problem be resolved?
Credit recommendation: In the lower division baccalaureate/associate degree category, 3 semester hours in Economics (4/86).

Electrical/Electronic Measurements and Instruments
Location: Self study.
Length: Correspondence Program.
Dates: January 1982-Present.
Objective: To familiarize the student with transformers and the various electrical and electronic meters/testing devices that are used in troubleshooting/monitoring circuits.
Learning Outcome: Upon successful completion of this course, the student will be able to understand how various test instruments work and how they are used. The course also provides an introduction to transformers.
Instruction: Transformer fundamentals; electrical measurements and instruments; checking simple circuits; troubleshooting with basic meters; how a voltmeter works; how an ammeter works; A-C measuring instruments; miscellaneous electrical measuring instruments. Electrical measurements and instruments; electronic quantities and testing principles; multipurpose test instruments; bridge-type instruments; oscilloscopes; component testers; digital test equipment.
Credit recommendation: In the lower division baccalaureate/associate degree category, 1 semester hour in Electrical/Electronic Technology or Electrical/Electronic Measurements (11/84) (4/89). NOTE: This course has been reevaluated and continues to meet requirements for credit recommendations.

Electrical Installation Practices
Location: Self study.
Length: Correspondence Program.
Dates: January 1980-Present.
Objective: To provide the student with a foundation in basic wiring, plus an understanding of the National Electrical Code.
Learning Outcome: Upon successful completion of this course, the student will be able to have a very good understanding of wiring new as well as old work; rules covered in National Electrical Code Book.
Instruction: Review of sizing conduit, conductors, and boxes; review of circuits; testing circuits; running cable; cutting openings; mounting and grounding boxes; preparing cable and installing cable in boxes; wiring commonly used devices; plugs and receptacles; line and extension cords; split-wired and switched receptacles; switch circuits; dimmers; wiring and mounting lampholders and lighting fixtures; use of nipples and hickeys; wiring appliance circuits; wiring doorbell circuits and electric space heaters; conduit bending; raceways; busways; industrial power distribution systems; definitions and explanation of code.
Credit recommendation: In the lower division baccalaureate/associate degree category, 2 semester hours in Electrical/Electronic Technology or Electronic Installation Practices (11/84) (4/89). NOTE: This course has been reevaluated and continues to meet requirements for

credit recommendations.

Electrical Machines
Location: Self study.
Length: Correspondence Program.
Dates: January 1980-Present.
Objective: To provide the student with the knowledge needed to apply, in industrial settings, fractional-horsepower motors, direct-current machines, alternators, alternating-current motors and the knowledge to perform efficiency tests on them.
Learning Outcome: Upon successful completion of this course, the student will be able to define and compute the efficiency of fractional-horse powered motors, direct-current machines, transformers, synchronous alternating-current machines and induction machines.
Instruction: Principles and characteristics of D-C and A-C machines; electrical connections; rating; performance and speed control; thermal overload protection; types of drive systems; efficiency of D-C and A-C machines and transformers.
Credit recommendation: in the lower division baccalaureate/associate degree category, 3 semester hours in Electrical/Electronic Technology or Electrical Machines (11/84) (4/89). NOTE: This course has been reevaluated and continues to meet requirements for credit recommendations.

Electronic Circuits
Location: Self study.
Length: Correspondence Program.
Dates: January 1982-Present.
Objective: To widen the student's knowledge of electronic circuits and their applications including an introduction to electronic systems using block diagram techniques. Also provides an introduction to troubleshooting methods and philosophy.
Learning Outcome: Upon successful completion of this course, the student will be able to understand basic troubleshooting methods and philosophy, understand a wider range of circuits, and understand block diagrams of electronic systems.
Instruction: Electronic systems; electronic devices and amplification; audio and R-F circuits; oscillators, feedback and waveform generators; electronic power supply systems; industrial receivers, transmitters, and video systems; servo and control systems; pulse and logic circuits; programmable controllers and microprocessor. Troubleshooting electronic equipment and systems; logical troubleshooting methods; instrument selection; measuring techniques; interpreting data and results; use of manufacturers' instructions; test instruments maintenance.
Credit recommendation: In the lower division baccalaureate/associate degree category, 1 semester hour in Electrical/Electronic Technology or Electronic Circuits (11/84) (4/89). NOTE: This course has been reevaluated and continues to meet requirements for credit recommendations.

Electronic Instrumentation and Control
Location: Self study.
Length: Correspondence Program.
Dates: January 1982-Present.
Objective: To provide the student with an understanding of the function and use of circuit testing devices, instruments and their control, and electronic circuit applications found within industry.
Learning Outcome: Upon successful completion of this course, the student will be able to understand the function and use of circuit testing devices, control circuits, and electronic circuit applications found within industry.
Instruction: Automatic testing of electronic devices; electronic instrumentation and control: physical properties and their measurement Part 1; physical properties and their measurement Part 2; measuring instruments and signal processing; transducers; introduction to control systems; controllers; control system methods; data logging, transmission, and display; control applications, maintenance and troubleshooting. Industrial electronic circuit applications: interfacing process variables; motor control and servo systems; numeric control systems; programmable controllers; industrial robots.
Credit recommendation: In the lower division baccalaureate/associate degree category, 3 semester hours in Electrical/Electronic Technology or Electronic Instrumentation (11/84) (4/89). NOTE: This course has been reevaluated and continues to meet requirements for credit recommendations.

Engineering Economy
Location: Self study.
Length: Correspondence Program.
Dates: October 1978-Present.
Objective: To provide a basis for making economic decision in equipment selection or replacement.
Learning Outcome: Upon successful completion of this course, the student will be able to understand the information necessary to make an equipment selection or replacement decision based on economics and various procedures used to make the decsion.
Instruction: Cash flow; time value of money; investment methods; use of interest tables; engineering valuation; canons of ethics for engineers. (Prerequisite: Technical Mathematics I.)
Credit recommendation: In the lower division baccalaureate/associate degree category, 1 semester hour in Introduction to Engineering Economy (11/84) (4/89). NOTE: This course has been reevaluated and continues to meet requirements for credit recommendations.

Engineering Materials
Location: Self study.

International Correspondence Schools 429

Length: Correspondence Program.
Dates: January 1982-Present.
Objective: To introduce the student to nature and properties of metallic and nonmetallic materials.
Learning Outcome: Upon successful completion of this course, the student will be able to understand the composition and properties of metallic and nonmetallic materials.
Instruction: Course covers composition and properties of metals, ceramics, concrete, glass, graphite, plastics, and wood. (Prerequisite: Technical Science.)
Credit recommendation: In the lower division baccalaureate/associate degree category, 2 semester hours in Engineering Materials, Engineering Technology (11/84) (4/89). NOTE: This course has been reevaluated and continues to meet requirements for credit recommendations.

Engineering Mechanics
Location: Self study.
Length: Correspondence Program.
Dates: January 1977-Present.
Objective: To introduce the student to the study of the effect of forces on stationary and moving bodies.
Learning Outcome: Upon successful completion of this course, the student will be able to understand the basic relation between force and energy and stationary or moving bodies.
Instruction: Scope of engineering mechanics; collinear and concurrent forces; center of gravity of bodies; free-body diagrams; characteristics of friction; bodies on level and inclined surfaces; kinematics; translation and rotation; kinetics; force-mass-acceleration method; collision of two bodies. (Prerequisite: Technical Mathematics I and II.)
Credit recommendation: In the lower division baccalaureate/associate degree category, 3 semester hours in Elements of Statics and Dynamics or Engineering Technology (11/84) (4/89). NOTE: This course has been reevaluated and continues to meet requirements for credit recommendations.

Federal Taxation
Location: Self study.
Length: Correspondence Program.
Dates: January 1981-Present.
Objective: To provide the student with understanding of principles of tax laws plus simple instructions on tax preparation and savings. Concentrates on individual tax return. Student will be able to identify and apply many of the principles required for completion of a tax return; to identify legitimate deductions and place them in proper positions; to calculate gains and losses for both business and non-business transactions; and to calculate and claim depreciation.
Learning Outcome: Upon successful completion of this course, the student will be able to present tax-planning concepts for personal and business decision making and preparation of federal income tax returns.
Instruction: This course provides a practical study of government income tax regulations, including a history of federal income tax and tax-saving principles, and instruction on completing individual returns. It also covers briefly income tax regulations as applied to partnerships and corporations.
Credit recommendation: In the upper division baccalaureate category, 3 semester hours in Accounting (4/86).

Fluid Mechanics
Location: Self study.
Length: Correspondence Program.
Dates: January 1980-Present.
Objective: To introduce students to the study of fluid flow in open and closed channels.
Learning Outcome: Upon successful completion of this course, the student will be able to assist in the design and analysis of various types of fluid flow in open and closed channels.
Instruction: Properties of materials; intensity of pressure; flow of liquids through pipes; Bernoulli's theorem; resultant forces due to liquid pressure; center of pressure; Chezy-Darcy formula; Hazen-Williams formula; Reynolds number; flow of water in open channels; rate of discharge through wires. (Prerequisite: Engineering Mechanics.)
Credit recommendation: In the lower division baccalaureate/associate degree category, 3 semester hours in Fluid Mechanics, or Engineering Technology (11/84) (4/89). NOTE: This course has been reevaluated and continues to meet requirements for credit recommendations.

Fundamentals of Electricity
Location: Self study.
Length: Correspondence Program.
Dates: January 1982-Present.
Objective: To provide the student with a qualitative approach to basic concepts in A-C and D-C electricity.
Learning Outcome: Upon successful completion of this course, the student will be able to understand Ohm's law; basic circuit arrangements; the student will be familiar with alternators, generators, and transformers.
Instruction: D-C principles: nature of electricity; preventive maintenance; electric cells and batteries; electrical components and Ohm's Law; basic circuit arrangements; electrical language and hardware; magnetism and electromagnetism; D-C generators. A-C principles and components: alternators; transformers; inductance and capacitance; A-C circuits; rectification and electronic devices; electric energy distribution; types of electric circuits.
Credit recommendation: In the lower division baccalaureate/associate degree category, 1 semester hour in Fundamentals of Electricity for majors in Electrical/Electronics Technology; 3 semester hours for non Electrical/

Electronics majors (11/84) (4/89). NOTE: This course has been reevaluated and continues to meet requirements for credit recommendations.

Fundamentals of Electronics
  Location: Self study.
  Length: Correspondence Program.
  Dates: January 1982-Present
  Objective: To provide the student with a qualitative understanding of various electronic components and how they are used in the various types of electronic circuits.
  Learning Outcome: Upon successful completion of this course, the student will be able to recognize typical components and circuits as they appear on a schematic, plus have a qualitative understanding of their operation.
  Instruction: Electrical components; resistive, capacitive, and inductive components; basic semiconductor components; semiconductor switching devices; special semiconductor devices; rectifiers and electron tubes; switching and connection devices; basic electronic circuits; logic circuits; gating and counting circuits; pulse digital circuits.
  Credit recommendation: In the lower division baccalaureate/associate degree category, 3 semester hours in Electrical/Electronics Technology, or Fundamentals of Electronics (11/84) (4/89). NOTE: This course has been reevaluated and continues to meet requirements for credit recommendations.

General Psychology
  Location: Self study.
  Length: Correspondence Program.
  Dates: February 1977-December 1986.
  Objective: To provide the student with an understanding and familiarity with the basic concepts, theories, and principles of psychology. To familiarize students with psychological methodologies.
  Instruction: An introductory course, including historical development of scientific psychology, methods of obtaining behavioral data, human development, cognitive processes, awareness, motivation, emotion, personality, normal and abnormal behavior, and interpersonal relations.
  Credit recommendation: In the lower division baccalaureate/associate degree category, 2 semester hours in General Psychology (11/84).

Geodetic Surveying
  Location: Self study.
  Length: Correspondence Program.
  Dates: January 1980-Present.
  Objective: To introduce the student to advanced topics in Land Surveying.
  Learning Outcome: Upon successful completion of this course, the student will be able to conduct city surveys.
  Instruction: Course covers horizontal and vertical control surveys; monuments and markers; triangulation surveys; state plane coordinate systems; methods of projection; construction and maintenance surveys; subdivision of city blocks into lots.
  Credit recommendation: In the lower division baccalaureate/associate degree category, or in the upper division baccalaureate category, 2 semester hours in Land Surveying II or 1 semester hour in Land Surveying III when applied to an Engineering major (11/84) (4/89). NOTE: This course has been reevaluated and continues to meet requirements for credit recommendations.

Highway Construction and Design I
  Location: Self study.
  Length: Correspondence Program.
  Dates: January 1980-Present.
  Objective: To introduce students to the principles of design and analysis of embankments and subgrades, drainage, highway location and traffic control facets of highway/road work.
  Learning Outcome: Upon successful completion of this course, the student will be able to compute cuts and fills, estimate the effects of route design on drainage, and select the best possible route for a proposed road.
  Instruction: This course covers soil studies; subgrades and drainage; location surveys; selection of route; establishing grade lines; traffic studies; signs; volume and speed studies; safety appurtenances.
  Credit recommendation: In the lower division baccalaureate/associate degree category, 2 semester hours in Highway Construction and Design I (11/84) (4/89). NOTE: Course should not be applied to an Engineering major. NOTE: This course has been reevaluated and continues to meet requirements for credit recommendations.

Highway Construction and Design II
  Location: Self study.
  Length: Correspondence Program.
  Dates: January 1980-Present.
  Objective: To continue the student's exposure to the factors involved in highway work in which the student learns about low cost road surfaces, hard pavements, and the structural design of pipe culverts.
  Learning Outcome: Upon successful completion of this course, the student will be able to ascertain the characteristics of various subgrade soils, prepare each soil for service as a roadbed and design roads paved with concrete or asphalt.
  Instruction: The course covers maintenance of untreated surfaces; stabilized soil-bound surfaces; rigid concrete pavements; flexible bituminous pavements; design of pipe culverts.
  Credit recommendation: In the lower division baccalaureate/associate degree category, 2 semester hours in Highway Construction and Design II (11/84) (4/89). NOTE: Course should not be applied to an Engineering

major. NOTE: This course has been reevaluated and continues to meet requirements for credit recommendations.

Industrial Psychology
Location: Self study.
Length: Correspondence Program.
Dates: *Version 1:* October 1975-March 1989; *Version 2:* April 1989-Present.
Objective: To provide the student with an awareness of psychological issues relevant to the operation of industrial organizations.
Learning Outcome: Upon successful completion of this course, the student will be able to understand organizational dynamics involving interrelationships of people, processes, and procedures.
Instruction: Course covers the application of psychology to industrial organizations; psychology of attitudes; morale and group processes; supervisory leadership; measuring proficiency; selection and placement; psychological tests; design of jobs and man-machine systems; training in organizations; motivation at work; fatigue; accidents and their prevention; psychological factors in labor turnover; counseling, interviewing, and job contacts; organizational psychology.
Credit recommendation: *Version 1:* In the lower division baccalaureate/associate degree category, 2 semester hours in Management or Psychology (11/84). *Version 2:* In the lower division baccalaureate/associate degree category, 3 semester hours in Industrial Psychology (4/89). NOTE: This course has been reevaluated and continues to meet requirements for credit recommendations.

Industrial Systems
Location: Self study.
Length: Correspondence Program.
Dates: January 1980-Present.
Objective: To provide the student with a qualitative understanding of industrial systems involving the use of storage batteries, lighting controls, motor controls, and telemetering devices.
Learning Outcome: Upon successful completion of this course, the student will be able to understand the different methods of switching in residential and commercial buildings; principle of motor control and symbols; definition and classification of telemetering; be familiar with many types of storage batteries.
Instruction: Characteristics and applications of storage batteries; lighting control systems; principles of motor control systems; control components; protective devices; solid-state motor drive systems; definition and classification of telemetering systems; transmission data signals; computations in telemetering; telemetering for automatic control; electric power systems control.
Credit recommendation: In the lower division baccalaureate/associate degree category, 3 semester hours in Electrical/Electronics Technology or Industrial Systems (11/84) (4/89). NOTE: This course has been reevaluated and continues to meet requirements for credit recommendations.

Intermediate Accounting I
Location: Self study.
Length: Correspondence Program.
Dates: April 1986-Present.
Objective: To expand upon general principles studied in previous courses while providing more detailed knowledge of complex subjects. Students will be able to explain the objectives of a financial statement; describe the basic assumptions of all accounting; prepare solutions to practice problems; display compound interest, present value and annuities in proper fashion; how to account for cash and short term investments; and how to use several methods of accounting for inventory.
Learning Outcome: Upon successful completion of this course, the student will be able to apply accounting theory, concepts and procedures to financial problems pertaining to stock, investments, and intangibles.
Instruction: A comprehensive study of contemporary accounting theory, concepts, and procedures and their application to financial reporting. Intermediate problems pertaining to cash, receivables, inventories, plant and equipment, and investments in securities.
Credit recommendation: In the upper division baccalaureate category, 3 semester hours in Accounting or Intermediate Accounting I (4/86).

Intermediate Accounting II
Location: Self study.
Length: Correspondence Program.
Dates: January 1981-Present.
Objective: To provide the student with an expansion on materials presented in Intermediate Accounting I and to provide deeper understanding of accounting principles. Student will be able to understand and account for current liabilities and bonds payable and retainer earnings and dividends; to explain and calculate concepts of book value, earnings per share; to account for long term leases and pensions; income taxes; to make accounting changes and correct errors; and to create a statement of changes in financial positions.
Learning Outcome: Upon successful completion of this course, the student will be able to prepare reports disclosing changes in financial position, income tax allocation, and future and present value concepts and application.
Instruction: A continuation of Intermediate Accounting I. Intermediate problems pertaining to current and long-term liabilities, stockholders' equity, pensions, and income taxes; financial statement analysis, price-level accounting, and fund and cash flow reporting.
Credit recommendation: In the upper division baccalaureate category, 3 semester hours in Accounting (4/86).

Introduction to Business
Location: Self study.
Length: Correspondence Program.
Dates: January 1981-Present.
Objective: To provide the student with a general understanding of major functions of contemporary business. Student will be able to describe business enterprise cycle and describe roles we play. Students will be able to name functional divisions of a business enterprise.
Learning Outcome: Upon successful completion of this course, the student will have a basic understanding of business—finance, production, marketing, and administration.
Instruction: A study of business and its functions, including finance, production, marketing, and administration. This functional study is developed around a framework involving goal setting, organizational design, and decision making.
Credit recommendation: In the lower division baccalaureate/associate degree category, 2 semester hours in Business Administration or Management (4/86).

Introduction to Computer Concepts (Business Data Processing)
Location: Self study.
Length: Correspondence Program.
Dates: January 1981-Present.
Objective: To provide the student with an introduction to business data processing. Student will learn how to define scope and purpose of investigation. Student will be able to explain differences in numbering systems and how to convert to and from decimal systems; to identify and draw flow charting symbols; to construct an elementary flow chart; to convert symbolic to object programs; and to discuss methods of converting a system.
Learning Outcome: Upon successful completion of this course, the student will understand the techniques of electronic data processing. Goal setting, organizational design, and decision making are included.
Instruction: A nontechnical course in modern business data processing—what it is and what it can do. An introduction to the field for those who want the techniques of electronic data processing. This course includes consideration of the systems investigation, defining scope and purpose.
Credit recommendation: In the lower division baccalaureate/associate degree category, 3 semester hours in Business Management, Computer Information Systems, or Data Processing (4/86).

Introduction to Microprocessors
Location: Self study.
Length: Correspondence Program.
Dates: January 1983-Present.
Objective: To introduce the student to the fundamentals and uses of computers in business and industry. This is followed by coverage of the basics of microprocessors, what they are comprised of, how they operate, and how useful they are in industry.
Learning Outcome: Upon successful completion of this course, the student will be able to understand the operation, organization, and typical uses for microprocessors.
Instruction: Introduction to computers; introduction to microprocessor applications; microprocessor basics.
Credit recommendation: In the lower division baccalaureate/associate degree category, 1 semester hour in Electrical/Electronics Technology or Introduction to Microprocessors (11/84) (4/89). NOTE: This course has been reevaluated and continues to meet requirements for credit recommendations.

Introduction to Sociology
Location: Self study.
Length: Correspondence Program.
Dates: July 1977-December 1986.
Objective: To enable the student to interpret sociological theory and to apply the methods used in sociology. The student will also be able to identify and assess basic structures in social life and the process of socialization, social change, deviant behavior and social control.
Instruction: An introduction to the fundamental concepts of human society; to the social dimensions of culture, institutions, personality, ecology, and their basic interaction processes; and to social order and social change.
Credit recommendation: In the lower division baccalaureate/associate degree category, 2 semester hours in Introduction to Sociology (11/84).

Kinematics
Location: Self study.
Length: Correspondence Program.
Dates: January 1980-Present.
Objective: To introduce students to the study of linkages, cams, and gears.
Learning Outcome: Upon successful completion of this course, the student will be able to understand the basic principles of linkages, gears, and cams.
Instruction: Linkages; quick-return mechanisms; kinematics of link mechanisms; spur gearing, worm, and worm gears; gear cutting; use of gear trains; compound gearing; ratchet mechanisms; types and uses of cams; fundamentals of cam motion; cam profiles. (Prerequisite: Engineering Mechanics.)
Credit recommendation: In the lower division baccalaureate/associate degree category, 3 semester hours in Kinematics or Engineering Technology (11/84) (4/89). NOTE: This course has been reevaluated and continues to meet requirements for credit recommendations.

Land Surveying
Location: Self study.

Length: Correspondence Program.
Dates: January 1980-Present.
Objective: To introduce the student to boundary surveying computations and legal aspects of land surveying.
Learning Outcome: Upon successful completion of this course, the student will be able to perform field and office operations in property surveys and resurveys and be knowledgeable in the legal area of surveying.
Instruction: Course covers determination of true meridian; latitudes and longitudes; rectangular system of dividing land; subdivision of townships and sections; identifying and restoring corners; correction of defects in original surveys; legal descriptions. Methodology involves hands-on proficiency of procedures such as the calculation of EDMs and total stations in the resident laboratory at a major university location.
Credit recommendation: In the lower division baccalaureate/associate degree category, or in the upper division baccalaureate category, 2 semester hours in Land Surveying I when applied to an Engineering major (11/84) (4/89). NOTE: This course has been reevaluated and continues to meet requirements for credit recommendations.

Linear and Digital Integrated Circuits
Location: Self study.
Length: Correspondence Program.
Dates: January 1982-Present.
Objective: To provide the student with an understanding of the functions and uses of linear and digital integrated circuits. Also included with this course is a Digital Trainer. The student performs assigned experiments involving logic circuits, pulse circuits, and linear/digital IC circuits.
Learning Outcome: Upon successful completion of this course, the student will be able to understand the functions and uses of linear and digital integrated circuits. Completing the experiments will provide experience in handling, using, and testing ICs.
Instruction: Linear and digital integrated circuits; linear and digital circuit principles; integrated circuit techniques; linear integrated circuits; digital integrated circuits; integrated circuit logic systems; troubleshooting linear and digital IC systems; pulse circuits experiments; logic circuits experiments; linear and digital integrated circuits experiments.
Credit recommendation: In the lower division baccalaureate/associate degree category, 3 semester hours in Electrical/Electronics Technology or Linear and Digital Integrated Circuits (11/84) (4/89). NOTE: This course has been reevaluated and continues to meet requirements for credit recommendations.

Managerial Accounting
(Advanced Accounting)
Location: Self study.
Length: Correspondence Program.
Dates: January 1981-Present.
Objective: To provide the student with an understanding of more complex aspects of accounting theory plus significant opportunity for practice. Student will be able to provide for the organization, liquidation or uncorporation of a partnership in accounting system; to understand and explain the nature and principles of fund accounting; to handle consignment sales and establish proper accounting methods for consignee and consignor; and to begin to establish a consolidated financial statement.
Learning Outcome: Upon successful completion of this course, the student will be able to apply theory and practice issues in income and value measurement and report for multicorporate enterprises and business combinations.
Instruction: A study of advanced accounting concepts, including partnerships, installment sales, consignments, home office and branch, business combinations and fund accounting.
Credit recommendation: In the upper division baccalaureate category, 3 semester hours in Accounting (4/86).

Manufacturing Processes
Location: Self study.
Length: Correspondence Program.
Dates: January 1980-Present.
Objective: To introduce the student to common industrial and manufacturing processes.
Learning Outcome: Upon successful completion of this course, the student will be able to understand the basic concepts and practaices of common industrial and manufacturing practices.
Instruction: Course covers cutting tools; machine tools; powder metallurgy; hot and cold working of materials; stamping, drawing and forming; heat treatment; welding techniques; special forming techniques; electrical and chemical machining; tension, compression, torsion, impact and hardness testing of materials; nondestructive testing techniques; use of vernier calipers, micrometers, gages, gage blocks, and sine bars; basic numerical control; numerical control programming. Methodology involves hands-on proficiency of machining through the use of lathes, drill presses, milling machines, and grinders in the resident laboratory at a major university location. (Prerequisite: Techncial Mathematics I.)
Credit recommendation: In the lower division baccalaureate/associate degree category, 4 semester hours in Manufacturing Processes or Engineering Technology (11/84) (4/89). NOTE: This course has been reevaluated and continues to meet requirements for credit recommendations.

Marketing Research
Location: Self study.
Length: Correspondence Program.
Dates: January 1981-Present.

Objective: To give the student an introduction to techniques of marketing research plus practice in using devices for measuring decision making. Student will be able to identify which market factors can or cannot be controlled; to list factors which limit success of market research; to describe key aspects of methods used in market research; to perform calculations to determine square root, normal and standard deviation; to identify and explain advantages and limitations on uses of secondary research; and to apply techniques for editing and tabulation.

Learning Outcome: Upon successful completion of this course, the student will understand marketing research procedures, sampling, primary and secondary data sources, data analysis, and summary statistics.

Instruction: The nature and scope of marketing research, including marketing research procedures, are described. Also covered in detail are the topics of sampling and sampling methods, primary and secondary data sources, questionnaire scales, data analysis and development of summary statistics.

Credit recommendation: In the upper division baccalaureate category, 2 semester hours in Marketing Research (4/86).

Math for Business and Finance

Location: Self study.
Length: Correspondence Program.
Dates: January 1981-Present.
Objective: To provide the student with mathematical skills required in entry level contemporary business positions. Student will be able to employ problem solving skills; to calculate percents, discounts and interest; to calculate gross profit and loss, net profit and loss and depreciation; to identify positive and negative numbers; and to add, subtract, multiply and divide algebraic expressions.

Learning Outcome: Upon successful completion of this course, the student will understand interest, installment buying, pricing, depreciation, investments, and insurance. Symbols and their application, equations and formulas, and the importance of statistics are included.

Instruction: A review of percentages, discounts, interest, present worth, sinking funds, and installment buying. Includes pricing, depreciation, investments, and insurance. The use of symbols and their application, equations and formulas, importance of statistics—table and chart construction.

Credit recommendation: In the lower division baccalaureate/associate degree category, 2 semester hours in Business Math (4/86).

Mechanical Design I

Location: Self study.
Length: Correspondence Program.
Dates: *Version 1:* January 1980-December 1985. *Version 2:* January 1986-Present.
Objective: *Version 1:* To introduce the student to study of material failure theories, and analysis of shafts, beams, column, gears, gear trains, belts, clutches, and brakes. *Version 2:* To familiarize the student with the design of basic machine components.

Learning Outcome: Upon successful completion of this course, the student will be able to understand the information necessary for the successful design of basic machine components and to calculate basic ball and roller bearing loads.

Instruction: *Version 1:* Course covers stress analysis; Mohr's circle; stress-strain relations; torsion; curved beams; deflection analysis; strain energy; column design; statistics in mechanical design; normal distribution; toughness; hardness; strength of machine members; stress concentration; theories of failure; reliability; notch sensitivity. (Prerequisites: Mechanics of Materials; Manufacturing Processes; Analytic Geometry; and Calculus.) *Version 2:* Course reviews mechanics and strength of materials; friction and lubrication; bearings; shaft design and seals; fasterners; couplings; keys; retaining rings; welding and weld design; belting; chain drives; hoists and conveyors; and ropes. Methodology involves hands-on proficiency of welding in the resident laboratory at a major university location. (Prerequisites: Mechanics of Materials and Manufacturing Processes.)

Credit recommendation: In the lower division baccalaureate/associate degree category, 3 semester hours in Mechanical Design I or Engineering Technology (11/84) (4/89). NOTE: This course has been reevaluated and continues to meet requirements for credit recommendations.

Mechanical Design II

Location: Self study.
Length: Correspondence Program.
Dates: *Version 1:* January 1980-December 1985; *Version 2:* January 1986-Present.
Objective: *Version 1:* To provide the student with continued studies in the design of machine elements based upon the principles of material failure theory. *Version 2:* To provide the student with continued studies in the design of machine components based upon the principles of force analysis as well as areas of good practice and judgment.

Learning Outcome: Upon successful completion of this course, the student will be able to understand the design of basic machine components as a continued study from Mechanical Design I.

Instruction: *Version 1:* Course covers thread standards; threaded fasteners; bolted and riveted joints; strength of welded joints; design of springs; ball and roller bearings; bearing friction; bearing life; thrust bearings; lubrication of bearings; design of journal bearings; design of spur, helical, worm, and bevel gears; design of power transmission shafts; design of clutches, brakes, couplings, belts, and roller chains. (Prerequisite: Mechanical Design I.)

Version 2: Course covers brakes; clutches; power screws; gears; cams; spring design; flywheels; miscellaneous machine elements; and power units. Methodology involves hands-on proficiency of welding in the resident laboratory at a major university location.

Credit recommendation: In the lower division baccalaureate/associate degree category, 3 semester hours in Mechanical Design II or Engineering Technology (11/84) (4/89). NOTE: This course has been reevaluated and continues to meet requirements for credit recommendations.

Mechanical Drawing
Location: Self study.
Length: Correspondence Program.
Dates: January 1985-Present.
Objective: To introduce students to the basics of mechanical drawing.
Learning Outcome: Upon successful completion of this course, the student will be able to prepare geometrical, projection, and introductory mechanical drawings.
Instruction: Drawing equipment; lettering; eight drawing plates; 721, 722, and 723, geometrical drawing problems; 724, projections of simple solids; 725, foreshortened views in projection; 726, common conventions; 727, lifting and test cover; 728, hanger assembly.
Credit recommendation: In the vocational certificate category, 1 semester hour in Mechanical Drawing (11/84) (4/89). NOTE: This course has been reevaluated and continues to meet requirements for credit recommendations.

Mechanics of Materials
Location: Self study.
Length: Correspondence Program.
Dates: January 1985-Present.
Objective: To enable the student to calculate reactions, stresses, shear and bending moment, deformation and deflection; moment of inertia, section modules, and radius of gyration.
Learning Outcome: Upon successful completion of this course, the student will be able to calculate siimple stresses, reactions at beam support, as well as other technical data needed for basic column design.
Instruction: The course includes simple stresses; fixed and moving loads on beams; reactions at beam support; continuous beams; points on inflection; shear and bending moment diagrams; moment of inertia and section modulus; theory of column design; radius of gyration.
Credit recommendation: In the lower division baccalaureate/associate degree category, 2 semester hours in Mechanics of Materials or Engineering Technology (11/84) (4/89). NOTE: Credit recommendation is not appropriate for Engineering majors. NOTE: This course has been reevaluated and continues to meet requirements for credit recommendations.

Microprocessor Application
Location: Self study.
Length: Correspondence Program.
Dates: January 1982-Present.
Objective: To provide the student with an understanding of the functional application of a microprocessor; simple machine language programming and an introduction to microprocessor interfacing. Student learning is reinforced through the use of a microprocessor trainer.
Learning Outcome: Upon successful completion of this course, the student will be able to understand the functional application of a microprocessor; simple machine language programming and basic microprocessor interfacing principles.
Instruction: Working with an uncomplicated microprocessor, the MC 6802, Part 1; microprocessor programming principles, Part 1; working with an uncomplicated microprocessor, the MC 6802, Part 2; microprocessor programming principles, Part 2; interfacing through serial and parallel ports; troubleshooting microprocessor equipment, Part 2; other families of microprocessors; microprocessor experiments.
Credit recommendation: In the lower division baccalaureate/associate degree category, 3 semester hours in Electrical/Electronics Technology or Microprocessor Applications (11/84) (4/89). NOTE: This course has been reevaluated and continues to meet requirements for credit recommendations.

Personal Financial Management
Location: Self study.
Length: Correspondence Program.
Dates: March 1984-Present.
Objective: To give the student an introduction to concepts of personal financial management which provides student with general understanding of principles of management and financing of assets. Student will be able to list and explain concepts of personal financial management; to list key factors considered in acquisition of assets; and to explain how to use borrowed funds to finance the purchase of assets.
Learning Outcome: Upon successful completion of this course, the student will be able to apply decision-making procedures to realistic problems such as budgets, insurance, real estate, and security buying.
Instruction: A study of the fundamental concepts and importance of personal financial management. The course involves the management and financing of fundamental assets including how to protect against events that might make good asset and liability management useless.
Credit recommendation: In the lower division baccalaureate/associate degree category, 2 semester hours in Personal Finance (4/86).

Personnel Management
Location: Self study.

Length: Correspondence Program.
Dates: April 1986-Present.
Objective: To provide the student with an overview of major concepts in personnel management, including an understanding of the role of the personnel department, the work environment, employee's compensation, policy formulation, recruitment and selection, labor relations, human resource development, and other selected areas.
Learning Outcome: Upon successful completion of this course, the student will understand the role of the personnel department in the selection, orientation, and training of employees. Personnel policies, employee evaluation, and wage and salary administration are covered.
Instruction: A study of the role of the personnel department in the selection, orientation, and training of employees. Among the topics covered are the procedure used in the formulation of personnel policies, employee evaluation programs, and wage and salary administration. The effect of unionism on personnel management is also reviewed.
Credit recommendation: In the lower division baccalaureate/associate degree category, 2 semester hours in Personnel Management/Human Resource Management (4/86).

Physical Science
Location: Self study.
Length: Correspondence Program.
Dates: January 1983-Present.
Objective: To provide the student with a foundation in science by surveying basic aspects of chemistry, mechanics, heat, sound, light, electricity, earth science, and space science.
Learning Outcome: Upon successful completion of this course, the student will be able to apply fundamental principles of chemistry, mechanics, heat, sound, light, electricity, earth science, and space science.
Instruction: Basic concepts of physical science with particular emphasis on mechanics, heat, sound, light, chemistry, electricity, earth science, and space science.
Credit recommendation: In the lower division baccalaureate/associate degree category, 3 semester hours in Physical Science (11/84) (4/89). NOTE: This is a nonlaboratory science course. NOTE: This course has been reevaluated and continues to meet requirements for credit recommendations.

Physics
Location: Self study.
Length: Correspondence Program.
Dates: January 1981-Present.
Objective: To develop the student's technical understanding of heat, electricity, light, and sound.
Learning Outcome: Upon successful completion of this course, the student will be able to understand basic principles of heat, electricity, light, and sound.
Instruction: Heat: nature of heat; transfer of heat; relationship between pressure, volume, temperature; weight of gases and the gas constant; expansion of gases; compression of gases; closed cycles; carnots cycle. Electricity: voltage, current, conductance, and resistance; conductors, insulators, and semiconductors; electric cells and batteries; resistors; switches; parallel, series, and series-parallel circuits; Ohm's Law; electric power; electric energy; analysis of D-C circuits; generator and motor action; theory of alternating currents; A-C circuits; principle of transformers; A-C machines. Light: nature of light; reflection of light; optical mirrors; optical instruments; lasers. Sound: relation of sound to wave motion; nature, properties, and sources of sound; functions of the ear; infrasonics and ultrasonics; doppler effect; focusing of sound; absorption of sound; loudness; decibels; transducers.
Credit recommendation: In the lower division baccalaureate/associate degree category, 3 semester hours in Physics (11/84) (4/89). NOTE: This course has been reevaluated and continues to meet requirements for credit recommendations.

Planning and Control
Location: Self study.
Length: Correspondence Program.
Dates: January 1980-Present.
Objective: To introduce students to planning and scheduling of production activities with a focus on volume and quality of production.
Learning Outcome: Upon successful completion of this course, the student will be able to understand the nature of production including materials handling, acquisitions and forecasting, as well as quality costs and control.
Instruction: Nature of production control; demand forecasting. Economic order quantity; critical-path method; quality costs and their control inspection function; vendor relation; manufacturing planning for quality; quality improvement; fundamentals of materials control; acquisition of materials; storage of materials; control of materials during manufacture; paper-work control; systems approach to materials control. (Prerequisite: Technical Mathematics I).
Credit recommendation: In the lower division baccalaureate/associate degree category, 3 semester hours in Production Planning and Control or Engineering Technology (11/84) (4/89). NOTE: This course has been reevaluated and continues to meet requirements for credit recommendations.

Plant Facilities
Location: Self study.
Length: Correspondence Program.
Dates: January 1984-Present.
Objective: To introduce the student to elements of plant layout and materials handling.
Learning Outcome: Upon successful completion of this

course, the student will be able to understand what information is necessary for the development of a plant layout and the procedures and tools used for development and presentation of layouts.

Instruction: Plant layout; definition; scope, importance, advantages, and nature of layout projects; effect of storage, services, and materials handling on plant layout; collection and analysis of data necessary for the development and presentation of layouts; industrial layout; growth planning; manufacturing plant layouts; industrial layout; warehouse design; types of warehouses; use of computer; design factors; alternatives and implementation; materials handling; introduction; sealing equipment; trucks; conveyors; pneumatic systems; bulk handling systems and components; grab attachments; long distance transportation; auxiliary equipment; specialized components. (Prerequisite: Technical Mathematics I.)

Credit recommendation: In the lower division baccalaureate/associate degree category, 2 semester hours in Production Facilities Planning or Engineering Technology (11/84) (4/89). NOTE: This course has been reevaluated and continues to meet requirements for credit recommendations.

Principles of Finance
Location: Self study.
Length: Correspondence Program.
Dates: January 1981-Present.
Objective: To introduce the student to the history of money and the role of finance in business organizations. Student will be able to identify and list qualities and functions of money; to list and explain differences in types of credit; to explain and use financial ratios and also the methods used to evaluate capital funding; to explain sources for funding a long term debt; and to list courses of business failure.
Learning Outcome: Upon successful completion of this course, the student will understand the role of finance in various business organizations, capital budgets, sources of funds, marketing securities, capital structure, foreign expansion, and reorganization.
Instruction: Includes a review of the history of money, monetary systems, and credit. also covered are the role of finance in various forms of busines organizations, capital budgeting, sources of funds, marketing securities, capital structure, foreign expansion, and reorganization of a business firm.
Credit recommendation: In the lower division baccalaureate/associate degree category, 2 semester hours in Principles of Finance (4/86).

Principles of Management
Location: Self study.
Length: Correspondence Program.
Dates: January 1981-Present.
Objective: To introduce the student to basic concepts of management and to impress upon the student the importance of these concepts. Students will be able to identify and explain differences between management functions and responsibilities; to identify and distinguish basic leadership styles; to list procedures for reorganization; to provide examples of functions of management; and to list and describe factors important to controlling cost and simplifying work.
Learning Outcome: Upon successful completion of this course, the student will understand the basic management concepts, employee behavior, morale, complaints and grievances, training, and communication.
Instruction: This course emphasizes the importance of management in the business enterprise. Concepts such as leadership, functions of management, employee behavior morale, complaints, and grievances training and communications are covered.
Credit recommendation: In the upper division baccalaureate category, 3 semester hours in Principles of Management or Supervision (4/86).

Principles of Marketing
Location: Self study.
Length: Correspondence Program.
Dates: January 1981-Present.
Objective: To provide the student with a general understanding of the principles of marketing and product management. Student will be able to discriminate between industrial and consumer marketing activities; to develop an integrated marketing plan; to list and distinguish between internal and external factors involved in introducing new products; to list and prioritize the aspects of physical distribution; and to list factors in site location.
Learning Outcome: Upon successful completion of this course, the student will understand the importance of marketing and product management, behavioral science approach, and managing the marketing function.
Instruction: This course introduces the meaning of marketing and product management. Emphasis is place on the behavioral science approach to marketing, the tools of marketing, and managing the marketing function.
Credit recommendation: In the lower division baccalaureate/associate degree category, 2 semester hours in Marketing or Sales (4/86).

Production Management
Location: Self study.
Length: Correspondence Program.
Dates: January 1981-Present.
Objective: To introduce the student to the production function with emphasis on plant layout, production planning and safety. Student will be able to define plant layout and discuss factors which influence plant layout decision; to describe several types of forecasts and apply statistical methods for forecast control; to calculate quality costs and controls; and to discuss advantages and disadvantages of

differing types of plant layouts.

Learning Outcome: Upon successful completion of this course, the student will understand the production function. This includes plant layout, production planning, material control, production techniques, material inspection, and occupational safety.

Instruction: An introduction to the production function, including factors affecting plant layout, nature and purpose of production planning, factors in material control, purchasing techinques, materials inspection, analysis of customers' complaints, and occupational safety.

Credit recommendation: In the lower division baccalaureate/associate degree category, 2 semester hours in Production Management (4/86).

Public Relations
Location: Self study.
Length: Correspondence Program.
Dates: April 1986-Present.
Objective: To provide the student with a general understanding of the role of public relations in contemporary business. Student will be able to list differences between corporate reporting and agency reporting relationships; to list and define special techniques used in dealing with the press; to identify all publics with which all Public Relations Departments deal; and to list and apply techniques for good writing for public relations.

Learning Outcome: Upon successful completion of this course, the student will understand the responsibility of the public relations department, and dealings with the press, community, employees, and customers.

Instruction: This course deals with the evolution of public relations, including the organization and responsibility of a public relations department and the importance of communications research. Special emphasis is placed on dealing with the press, government, community, employees, and customers. The course concludes with the techniques of good public relations writing.

Credit recommendation: In the lower division baccalaureate/associate degree category, 2 semester hours in Public Affairs, Public Communication, Public Information, or Public Relations (4/86).

Pulse and Logic Circuits
Location: Self study.
Length: Correspondence Program.
Dates: January 1982-Present.
Objective: To provide the student with a qualitative knowledge of pulse circuits and logic circuits. The course includes purpose configuration, applications, and troubleshooting of such circuits.

Learning Outcome: Upon successful completion of this course, the student will be able to qualitatively understand pulse and logic circuits, typical troubleshooting procedures, and applications.

Instruction: Pulse circuits: pulse techniques; pulse generators; waveshaping circuits; timing and synchronization; pulse circuit applications; troubleshooting pulse circuits. Logic circuits: logic circuit fundamentals; introduction to number systems; logic devices and diagrams; logic families; applications of logic circuits; troubleshooting logic circuits.

Credit recommendation: In the lower division baccalaureate/associate degree category, 1 semester hour in Electrical/Electronics Technology or Pulse and Logic Circuits (11/84) (4/89). NOTE: This course has been reevaluated and continues to meet requirements for credit recommendations.

Reinforced Concrete Design
Location: Self study.
Length: Correspondence Program.
Dates: January 1985-Present.
Objective: To enable the student to acquire design ability involving reinforced concrete beams and columns.

Learning Outcome: Upon successful completion of this course, the student will be able to design and detail a variety of reinforced concrete member shapes, one-way slabs, long and short columns and prestressed beams.

Instruction: The course covers design and analysis of rectangular beams, T-beams, double-reinforced beams.

Credit recommendation: In the lower division baccalaureate/associate degree category, 2 semester hours in Reinforced Concrete Design or Engineering Technology (11/84) (4/89). NOTE: This course has been reevaluated and continues to meet requirements for credit recommendations.

Retailing
Location: Self study.
Length: Correspondence Program.
Dates: January 1983-Present.
Objective: To introduce the student to general principles regarding organization of retail stores and sound merchandising. Student will be able to list steps in retail management decision making process; to list and explain key items in retailing; and to list key elements in structure of a retail business including pricing policy.

Learning Outcome: Upon successful completion of this course, the student will understand the organization of retail stores, merchandising principles, and the management of a successful retail business.

Instruction: The purpose of this course is to present, at an introductory level, an analysis on the basics of retailing, management of a successful retail business, and merchandising principles.

Credit recommendation: In the vocational certificate category, 1 semester hour in Marketing (4/86).

Sales Management
Location: Self study.
Length: Correspondence Program.

Dates: January 1981-Present.

Objective: To give the student general introduction to the sales function with emphasis on management of sales force. Also student learns of relationship between sales, marketing and product development. Student will be able to identify steps necessary for the establishment of a sales organization; to list advantages of sales contests; to list essential elements in recruiting sales personnel; and to list key elements in the role of sales manager.

Learning Outcome: Upon successful completion of this course, the student will understand the relation of sales management to other departments, the organization of the sales force, and information on the product and the marketplace.

Instruction: The field of sales management is analyzed including organization of the sales force and the relations of the sales organization to other internal departments and the external community. Also covered in this course are the product and the marketplace.

Credit recommendation: In the upper division baccalaureate category, 2 semester hours in Sales Management (4/86).

Securities and Investments
Location: Self study.
Length: Correspondence Program.
Dates: January 1981-Present.

Objective: To provide the student with introduction to general principles of investment decision making. Student will be able to evaluate securities issued in stock and bond markets; to identify and discuss unique characteristics of various securities; and to identify steps in investment decision process.

Learning Outcome: Upon successful completion of this course, the student will be able to make investment decisions, evaluate corporate security, dividend policies and analyze organization and operation of stock and bond markets.

Instruction: This course discusses the basic principles underlying investment decisions. It includes a comprehensive study of securities and markets, fundamental and technical analysis, and portfolio selection.

Credit recommendation: In the lower division baccalaureate/associate degree category, 3 semester hours in Finance (4/86).

Structural Steel Design
Location: Self study.
Length: Correspondence Program.
Dates: January 1985-Present.

Objective: To develop the students capability in the design of steel beams, columns, and connections.

Learning Outcome: Upon successful completion of this course, the student will be able to design and detail rolled steel shapes used in building frames, connections, steel beams and columns, and composite steel/concrete items.

Instruction: The course covers selection of rolled steel shapes for beams and column; allowable unit stresses; design of connections; eccentric loading; design of column base plates.

Credit recommendation: In the lower division baccalaureate/associate degree category, 2 semester hours in Structural Steel Design (11/84) (4/89). NOTE: Course should not be applied to Engineering major. NOTE: This course has been reevaluated and continues to meet requirements for credit recommendations.

Technical Mathematics I
Location: Self study.
Length: Correspondence Program.
Dates: *Version 1:* January 1983-December 1986; *Version 2:* January 1987-Present.

Objective: *Version 1:* To introduce the student to the history of engineering, and to provide basic algebra skills necessary to solve technical problems. *Version 2:* To provide the student with basic algebra skills necessary to solve technical problems.

Learning Outcome: Upon successful completion of this course, the student will be able to solve technical problems involving the use of basic algebra skills.

Instruction: *Version 1:* Overview of the history of engineering; formulas; operations on signed numbers, polynomials, and rational expressions; factoring; solution of linear systems, including the methods of determinants; graphs and graphical solutions of linear and quadratic equations; exponents; radicals; logarithms; imaginary numbers; technical applications are included. *Version 2:* Formulas; operations of signed numbers, polynomials, and rational expressions; factoring; solution of linear systems including the methods of determinants; graphs and graphical solutions of linear quadratic equations; exponents; radicals; logarithms; imaginary numbers; technical applications are included.

Credit recommendation: In the lower division baccalaureate/associate degree category, 2 semester hours in Technical Mathematics or Algebra (11/84) (4/89). NOTE: Course should not be applied to Science or Engineering majors. NOTE: This course has been reevaluated and continues to meet requirements for credit recommendations.

Technical Mathematics II
Location: Self study.
Length: Correspondence Program.
Dates: January 1983-Present.

Objective: To provide the student with a basic knowledge of plane geometry and plane trigonometry.

Learning Outcome: Upon successful completion of this course, the student will be able to understand the basic principles of plane geometry and plane trigonometry.

Instruction: Practical geometry: points, lines, surfaces and angles; perpendicular and parallel lines; triangles;

quadrilaterals; other polygons; the circle, arcs and areas of figures bounded by them; areas and volumes of solids; plane trigonometry: solving a triangle; deriving trigonometric functions; trigonometric and geometric identities; values for the trigonometric functions; using the table of natural trigonometric functions; interpolations; solving the right triangle; solving the right triangle by using logarithms; angles and their measurement; degrees and radians; rectangular coordinates; the trigonometric formulas; finding the values of the functions of angles; reduction formulas; solving the oblique triangle; law of tangents; using half-angle formulas; area of a triangle; radius of an inscribed circle; radius of a circumscribed circle.

Credit recommendation: In the lower division baccalaureate/associate degree category, 2 semester hours in Technical Mathematics or Trigonometry for non-Engineering majors (11/84) (4/89). NOTE: Course should not be applied to Science or Engineering majors. NOTE: This course has been reevaluated and continues to meet requirements for credit recommendations.

Technical Materials
 Location: Self study.
 Length: Correspondence Program.
 Dates: January 1980-Present.
 Objective: To introduce the student to nature and properties of metallic and nonmetallic elements.
 Learning Outcome: Upon successful completion of this course, the student will be able to understand the basic nature and properties of metallic and nonmetallic elements.
 Instruction: Use of metrics; fundamental laws of chemistry; metallic and nonmetallic elements; organic chemistry; unit operations; composition and properties of materials. (Prerequisite: Technical Mathematics I.)
 Credit recommendation: In the lower division baccalaureate/associate degree category, 3 semester hours in Engineering Materials (including Chemistry) or Engineering Technology (11/84) (4/89). NOTE: This course includes the contents and recommendation of 2 semester hours for Engineering Materials course. NOTE: This course has been reevaluated and continues to meet requirements for credit recommendations.

Technical Science
 Location: Self study.
 Length: Correspondence Program.
 Dates: January 1982-Present.
 Objective: To provide the student with a foundation for the application and use of metrics; and to have the student develop an understanding of technical and mathematical aspects of heat, elements of chemistry, and engineering chemistry.
 Learning Outcome: Upon successful completion of this course, the student will be able to understand the basic application and use of metrics along with the technical and mathematical aspects of heat, elements of chemistry, and engineering chemistry.
 Instruction: Use of metrics; nature of heat; expansion of gases; carnot's cycle, fundamental laws of chemistry; metallic and nonmetallic elements; organic chemistry, unit operations. Mathematical modeling and problem solving is used extensively.
 Credit recommendation: In the lower division baccalaureate/associate degree category, 2 semester hours in Technical Science (11/84) (4/89). NOTE: This course has been reevaluated and continues to meet requirements for credit recommendations.

1. **Tool Design I**
2. **Tool Design II**
 Location: Self study.
 Length: Correspondence Program.
 Dates: *Version 1:* January 1980-December 1986; *Version 2:* January 1987-Present.
 Objective: To provide the student with an understanding of the principles of tool planning.
 Learning Outcome: Upon successful completion of this course, the student will be able to understand and perform processes associated with tool planning.
 Instruction: *Version 1:* Course 1. Single-point, multiple-point, and rotary tools; control of tool wear and failure; types of work-holding devices; power presses; shearing and die-cutting; design of piercing, blanking, and compound dies. (Prerequisite: Manufacturing Processes or Production Processes.) Course 2:. Principles of gaging; types and applications of inspection gages; tools for soldering, brazing, and mechanical joining processes; general considerations in tool design; safety; tool materials; heat-treating; fits and tolerances. (Prerequisite: Tool Design I.) *Version 2:* Course 1. Single-point, multiple-point, and rotary tools; control of tool wear and failure; types of work-holding devices; jig and fixture design; power presses; shearing and die-cutting; design of piercing, blanking, and compound dies. Course 2. Principles of gaging; types and applications of gages; tools for soldering, brazing, and mechanical joining processes; general considerations in tool design; gage materials; fits and tolerances; fundamentals of numerical control; and overview of CAD in tool design. Methodology for both courses involves hands-on proficiency in material testing procedures and a brief overview of CAD/CAM in the resident laboratory at a major university location.
 Credit recommendation: *Version 1:* In the lower division baccalaureate/associate degree category, 3 semester hours in Introduction to Tool Design or Engineering Technology (11/84). *Version 2:* In the lower division baccalaureate/associate degree category, 6 semester hours in Tool Design or Engineering Technology (4/89). NOTE: This course has been reevaluated and continues to meet requirements for credit recommendations.

Topographic Drawing and Surveying
  Location: Self study.
  Length: Correspondence Program.
  Dates: *Version 1:* January 1980-March 1989; *Version 2:* April 1989-Present.
  Objective: To develop the student's ability in technical drawing by preparing five geometrical drawing plates plus four mapping plates. The study of topographic surveying is also covered.
  Learning Outcome: Upon successful completion of this course, the student will be able to prepare drawing and mapping plates; and understand principles of topographic surveying.
  Instruction: The course includes use of drafting instruments; azimuths and bearings of lines; topographic symbols and contours; plotting cross sections and profiles; city and village maps; determination of distance by stadia; stadia surveys for locating topography; plane-table surveying; topographic maps; methods of control. Methodology involves hands-on proficiency of drafting in the resident laboratory at a major university location.
  Credit recommendation: *Version 1:* In the lower division baccalaureate/associate degree category or in the upper division baccalaureate category, 2 semester hours in Topographic Drawing and Surveying or 1 semester hour when applied to an Engineering major (11/84). *Version 2:* In the lower division baccalaureate/associate degree category, 3 semester hours in Topographic Drawing and Surveying (4/89). NOTE: This course has been reevaluated and continues to meet requirements for credit recommendations.

International Monetary Fund

The Training and Development Unit (TDU) of the International Monetary Fund is the educational arm of the Staff Development Division which is part of the Administration Department. The TDU delivers training through a combination of in-house and external programs. The in-house programs include in-service training courses, seminar programs, language training, and the Learning Center.

The TDU is equipped with one general purpose classroom that provides the proper learning space for communications, economic/professional, and management and organizational development courses. The facility also houses the two technology training classrooms. The microcomputer training room enables instruction on PC software and Fund-specific software (JOLIS), and the NBI Word Processing training classroom enables instruction on the full range of word processing features available to NBI implemented departments.

Participants are nominated and selected by the Training Contacts of their Departments to attend courses. The class roster is entered into a computer database and at the end of each completed in-service course, the instructor reports those students who have successfully completed the course and those who have not. The students who elect to receive credit will have the appropriate credits entered in the computer and attached to their transcript.

Source of official student records: Training and Development Unit, Room 6-309, International Monetary Fund, 700 19th Street, N.W., Washington, D.C. 20431.

Additional information about the courses: Program on Noncollegiate Sponsored Instruction, The Center for Adult Learning and Educational Credentials, American Council on Education, One Dupont Circle, Washington, D.C. 20036.

1. **CMC 100 Overview of Personal Computers**
2. **CMC 101 Microcomputer Fixed Disk Management**
3. **CMC 200 Lotus 1-2-3**
4. **CMC 201 Advanced Lotus 1-2-3**
  Location: Washington, D.C.
  Length: 1. 8 hours (1 day). 2. 3 hours (½ day). 3. 16 hours (2½ days). 4. 12 hours (2 days).
  Dates: May 1987-Present.
  Objective: To provide students with a knowledge of the use of microcomputers in an IBM environment, skill in basic operations required in managing disks and files, and an understanding of advanced concepts required for use of Lotus 1-2-3 software.
  Learning Outcome: Upon successful completion of this course, students will have the ability to demonstrate basic microcomputer functions and capabilities; manage data on a fixed disk system; use Lotus to prepare spreadsheets, graphs and charts, and to print, save, and retrieve files.
  Instruction: Content includes uses and operations of IBM microcomputers and an introduction to IBM PC hardware and software, disk operating system, and DOS commands; creating and working with subdirectories and techniques for managing data on a fixed disk; Lotus basics; spreadsheet design, saving and retrieving files, and use of Lotus built-in functions. Instruction involves lecture, demonstration, and hands-on experience.
  Credit recommendation: In the lower division baccalaureate/associate degree category, 1 semester hour in Data Processing (6/87). NOTE: Students must take all four courses to receive credit.

MGT 3 Management Development Course
  Location: Washington, D.C.
  Length: 40 hours of instruction plus 4 hours of outside preparation (1 week).
  Dates: March 1986-Present.
  Objective: To provide students with the skill to select, direct, support, reinforce, and develop human resources.
  Learning Outcome: Upon successful completion of this course, students will have the ability to communicate effectively, provide feedback, delegate, appraise perfor-

mance, plan, and interview when managing personnel.

Instruction: Content includes fundamentals of human resource planning, decision making, staff interviewing and selection, communication skills, performance appraisal, coaching, feedback techniques, reinforcement, leadership, and motivation. Instruction involves lecture, discussion, and case studies.

Credit recommendation: In the upper division baccalaureate or graduate category, 1 semester hour in Human Resource Development or Management (6/87).

International PADI, Inc.

International PADI, Inc. is a professional organization whose activities center around the training of scuba divers and scuba diving instructors. PADI's goal is to promote the training and education of the general public in the proper techniques of participating in recreational underwater activities and the advancement of those activities.

As a professional association, PADI has three types of members: (1) supervisory, (2) instructional, and (3) retail. PADI members in a supervisory category include PADI Divemasters and Assistant Instructors. These members have completed courses allowing them to perform limited teaching activities and primarily act as supervisory personnel during diving instructional activities conducted by fully qualified PADI Instructors. PADI members belonging to the instructional category include PADI Underwater Instructors, Open Water Scuba Instructors, Master Instructors and Course Directors (instructor trainers). These members have completed specific qualification programs allowing them to teach the general public how to scuba dive and in the case of the Course Directors, train instructors. Professional retail dive stores whose business it is to sell scuba equipment and provide instruction, equipment rentals, equipment repair and other related services may also become members.

PADI is international in scope. Branch and service offices are located in Australia, Canada, Switzerland, Japan, New Zealand, Norway and Sweden. PADI Headquarters is located in the United States. Translations of many PADI training materials are available in Dutch, English, French, German, Italian, Japanese, Norwegian, Spanish and Swedish.

The PADI method of diving instruction is based on progressive training in the classroom, pool, and open water.

Instructor ethics, teaching methods and course equipment are monitored by PADI Headquarters to uphold PADI training standards, Records are required to be maintained on all courses conducted under the sanction of PADI.

PADI does not "select" its teaching staff *per se*. Rather, qualified individuals must complete training programs specific to the type of PADI courses they wish to teach. Experienced scuba divers that wish to become PADI Instructors must successfully complete a series of instructor preparation and evaluation courses.

All PADI courses are developed in terms of demonstrable student performance. PADI course materials employ the concepts of mastery learning based on student-centered objectives and the curriculum is performance-based, rather than time-based.

Students are not certified as PADI divers until all cognitive and motor-skills performance objectives are mastered. Students who have not demonstrated an acceptable level of performance typically matriculate to another course or begin remedial training with the instructor until all cognitive or motor-skill performance objectives are met.

Student records are kept at two levels: (1) PADI members are required to maintain records of the students in their courses, and (2) PADI Headquarters maintains records of students receiving course completion documents.

Source of official student records: PADI, Office of Academic Transcripts, 1243 East Warner Avenue, Santa Ana, California 92705.

Additional information about the courses: Program on Noncollegiate Sponsored Instruction, The Center for Adult Learning and Educational Credentials, American Council on Education, One Dupont Circle, Washington, D.C. 20036.

Open Water Diver
Location: Various locations throughout the U.S. and internationally, including PADI Affiliated Dive Stores, Santa Ana, CA.
Length: 30 hours (flexible modular schedule).
Dates: January 1978-Present.
Objective: To provide students the necessary entry-level knowledge and skills to scuba dive.
Learning Outcome: Upon successful completion of this course, the student will be able to engage in beginning recreational scuba diving activities in local aquatic environments without direct or indirect supervision by a certified diving instructor.
Instruction: Unit lectures with A/V materials, demonstrations and discussions. Evaluation through written unit quizzes and final exam. Topics include: adapting to the underwater world, underwater communications, dive planning, diving equipment, boat diving, health for diving, dive tables, marine life identification and the underwater environment. Course also includes skill development in a confined water (e.g., pool) situation and practical application of acquired skills in an open water environment (e.g., ocean, lake, spring, quarry).
Credit recommendation: In the lower division baccalaureate/associate degree category, 1 semester hour in Recreation or Physical Education (3/87).

Advanced Open Water Diver

Location: Various locations throughout the U.S. and internationally, including **PADI** Affiliated Dive Stores, Santa Ana, CA.

Length: 23 hours (flexible modular schedule).

Dates: January 1980-Present.

Objective: To provide advanced training that will expand the student's openwater diving capabilities.

Learning Outcome: Upon successful completion of this course, the student will be able to demonstrate ability to navigate underwater; demonstrate skills for limited visibility and night diving and demonstrate proper deep diving procedures.

Instruction: Unit lectures and demonstrations. Evaluation through written and performance testing. Topics include underwater phenomena, your body and diving, diving procedures, the diving environment and deep diving.

Credit recommendation: In the lower division baccalaureate/associate degree category, 1 semester hour in Recreation or Physical Education (3/87).

Rescue Diver

Location: Various locations throughout the U.S. and internationally, including **PADI** Affiliated Dive Stores and PADI International College, Santa Ana, CA.

Length: 25 hours (flexible modular schedule).

Dates: January 1984-Present.

Objective: To become knowledgeable in recognizing signs and symptoms of aquatic stress/potential rescue situations as related to scuba diving. To become competent in scuba diving rescue and emergency procedures.

Learning Outcome: Upon successful completion of this course, the student will be able to demonstrate knowledge of the physiology and psychology of scuba-related rescue situations; demonstrate the skills of effecting a scuba-related rescue; and demonstrate the application of emergency procedures.

Instruction: Unit lectures and demonstrations. Evaluation through written and performance testing. Topic areas include first aid for diving maladies, first aid for marine injuries, emergency procedures, rescue equipment, panic syndrome, distress recognition, self-rescue, rescue entries and approaches, use of extensions and floats, assists, transporting, submerged diver rescue, missing diver procedures, in-water artificial respiration, equipment considerations, rescue exits and accident recording and reporting.

Credit recommendation: In the lower division baccalaureate/associate degree category, 1 semester hour in Recreation or Physical Education (3/87).

Divemaster

Location: Various locations throughout the U.S. and internationally, including **PADI** Affiliated Dive Stores and PADI International College, Santa Ana, CA.

Length: 50 hours (flexible modular schedule).

Dates: January 1985-Present.

Objective: To provide certified rescue divers with the knowledge and skills to organize, conduct and supervise recreational diving activities.

Learning Outcome: Upon successful completion of this course, the student will be able to plan safe and successful dives, including boat dives; supervise students in training; supervise deep and specialized diving; and demonstrate first aid and CPR procedures.

Instruction: Unit lectures and demonstrations. Evaluation through written and performance testing. Topics include the role of the divemaster, dive planning, dive management and control, how to supervise students in training, boat diving supervision and control, deep diving supervision and supervision of specialized diving activities.

Credit recommendation: In the lower division baccalaureate/associate degree category, 2 semester hours in Recreation or Physical Education (3/87).

Instructor Development

Location: Various locations throughout the U.S. and internationally, including **PADI** Affiliated Dive Stores and PADI International College, Santa Ana, CA.

Length: 57½ hours (flexible modular schedule).

Dates: August 1984-Present.

Objective: To provide certified PADI Divemasters and Assistant Instructors the knowledge and skills necessary to teach recreational scuba diving.

Learning Outcome: Upon successful completion of this course, the student will be able to demonstrate competence in teaching methodology; and familiarity with the entire PADI Instructional System.

Instruction: Lecture/discussion/demonstration. Unit lectures with A/V materials. Classroom exercises. Pool sessions to allow students to demonstrate teaching proficiency. Open water to allow students to demonstrate teaching proficiency. Topics include diving industry overview, overview and analysis of all PADI courses, lesson planning and delivery, teaching and using the PADI Dive Tables, techniques for teaching in a pool environment, open water problem solving, opportunities for the professional diving instructor, noninstructional duties, PADI standards and procedures, the PADI continuing education system, and marketing and promotion for the professional instructor.

Credit recommendation: In the upper division baccalaureate category, 2 semester hours in Physical Education, Recreation or Education (3/87).

Professional Scuba Equipment Repair

Location: PADI International College, Santa Ana, CA.

Length: 38½ hours (1 week).

Dates: January 1982-Present.

Objective: To provide students with the knowledge and

develop the skills necessary to maintain and/or repair scuba-related equipment properly.

Learning Outcome: Upon successful completion of this course, the student will be able to demonstrate knowledge of the mechanics of operation of scuba-related equipment and demonstrate proper care, maintenance, and repair of scuba-related equipment.

Instruction: Lecture/discussion with use of audiovisual materials. Laboratory/shop hands-on training. Evaluation through written examinations and proficiency testing. The course teaches the procedures for maintenance and repair of scuba equipment.

Credit recommendation: In the lower division baccalaureate/associate degree category, 1 semester hour in Recreation or Physical Education (3/87).

Retail Store Sales and Operations
Location: PADI International College, Santa Ana, CA.
Length: 66 hours (2 weeks).
Dates: January 1984-Present.
Objective: To train students in the essentials of retail management and operations as these relate to a professional dive store.

Learning Outcome: Upon successful completion of this course, the student will be able to understand the essentials required to set up and operate a professional dive store utilizing marketing, advertising, inventory control, merchandising and financial management skills; demonstrate the ability to design and develop diving newsletters that coordinate store activities with local and distant diving opportunities; conduct diver travel programs; and sell equipment.

Instruction: Unit lectures with audiovisual, demonstrations and role playing. Evaluation is through written examinations and demonstrations by students.

Credit recommendation: In the lower division baccalaureate/associate degree category, 4 semester hours in Business Management or Physical Education (3/87).

Underwater Photography Instructor
Location: PADI International College, Santa Ana, CA.
Length: 48 hours (1 week).
Dates: February 1986-Present.
Objective: To train instructors to take underwater photos and teach others the basics.

Learning Outcome: Upon successful completion of this course, the student will be able to discuss camera and film functions; discuss and demonstrate equipment care and maintenance; and discuss and demonstrate underwater picture composition, use of strobes, and macro-photography.

Instruction: Lecture/discussion with use of audiovisual materials and classroom assignments. Evaluation through written examinations and demonstrations both in the pool and open water assignments. Topics include camera function, how film works and film types, camera care and maintenance, strobe photography, available light photography, using a light meter, composition and modeling techniques, macro-photography, slide presentation techniques, use of underwater photography for diver marketing, orientation to teaching PADI Underwater Photography courses.

Credit recommendation: In the lower division baccalaureate/associate degree category, 2 semester hours in Recreation, Physical Education, Visual Arts, or Education (3/87).

International Union of Operating Engineers

The International Union of Operating Engineers is a 360,000-member AFL-CIO affiliated craft union with jurisdiction over heavy equipment operators and mechanics, surveyors, stationary engineers, and petrochemical refinery workers.

The Department of Education and Training works with other administrative departments at the International Headquarters in Washington, D.C. to offer courses in trade union education in the following areas: training fund administration, pension fund administration, shop steward and grievance skills, organizing, and safety and health.

Source of official student records: General Secretary-Treasurer, International Union of Operating Engineers, 1125 17th Street, N.W., Washington, D.C. 20036.

Additional information about the courses: Program on Noncollegiate Sponsored Instruction, The Center for Adult Learning and Educational Credentials, American Council on Education, One Dupont Circle, Washington, D.C. 20036.

Hazardous Waste Materials Training
Location: U.S. Mine Safety and Health Academy, Beckley, WV.
Length: 80 hours (2 weeks).
Dates: January 1988-Present.
Objective: To train instructors for locals to give courses in proper procedures and personnel protection with emphasis on hazardous waste disposal sites.

Learning Outcome: Upon successful completion of this course, the student will be able to understand the legal and biological limits on exposure to hazardous materials; instruct others on the potential dangers and proper amelioration procedures when working at hazardous waste disposal sites and to train workers in the use of personnel protective equipment.

Instruction: Course covers basic concepts in industrial hygiene, toxicology, hazard identification, the use of material safety data sheets, monitoring equipment, respirators and self-contained breathing apparatus, other personnel protective equipment and clothing, techniques of site remediation, decontamination, and emergency response procedures.

Credit recommendation: In the lower division baccalaureate/associate degree category, 3 semester hours in Environmental Engineering or Waste Management (8/88).

Jamaican Institute of Management

The Jamaican Institute of Management (JIM) is an independent non-profit, non-political membership organization, established in 1967 by a group of businessmen to promote professional management and raise the standard of management in Jamaica.

The Institute is dedicated to the purpose of promoting the better management of enterprises in both private and public sectors in Jamaica. It is an Institute for persons and organizations concerned with and interested in Management, and is the oldest management development institution in the country.

The Institute maintains classroom facilities at its Head Office and in rented quarters, in near proximity in the capital city of Kingston. In addition the same courses are now being offered in regional capitals in Mandeville and Montego Bay approximately 70-150 miles away respectively.

The courses are of uniform quality in all respects at all locations, including course duration, content and selection of faculty staff.

Courses are usually initiated by the Faculties based on perceived need of the business community (or special needs survey) then examined by the Board of Studies, reviewed by the Programmes Advisory Committee for appropriateness and recommended to the Executive committee for approval.

An Instructor's performance is progressively assessed by a faculty of professionals and academic staff (with a Faculty Head) reporting to a Board of Studies established to assist the Executive Director in the formulation of policies affecting management training and in the maintenance of good standards in all aspects of course and student performance.

Source of official student records: Assistant Director, Program Research and Development, Jamaican Institute of Management, 15 Hillcrest Avenue, Kingston 6, Jamaica, West Indies.

Additional information about the courses: Program on Noncollegiate Sponsored Instruction, The Center for Adult Learning and Educational Credentials, American Council on Education, One Dupont Circle, Washington, D.C. 20036.

Financial Management and Advanced Financial Management
(Diploma in Financial Management and Accounting)
  Location: Financial and Accounting College of Training, Kingston, Jamaica.
  Length: 210 hours (35 weeks; 2 three-hour meetings per week).
  Dates: January 1984-Present.
  Objective: To provide students with an understanding of the concepts and principles of financial planning and control and to develop the student's analytical and managerial skills particularly related to the Jamaican environment.
  Credit recommendation: In the upper division baccalaureate category, 3 semester hours in Principles of Financial Management and in the upper division baccalaureate category, 3 semester hours in Advanced Financial Management (2/86).

Introduction to Business and Principles of Management
(Diploma in Management Studies)
  Location: Financial and Accounting College of Training, Kingston, Jamaica.
  Length: 210 hours (35 weeks; 2 three-hour meetings per week).
  Dates: January 1984-Present.
  Objective: To provide students with formal training in the theoretical and practical aspects of management.
  Instruction: Lecture and discussion, case studies, film presentations, management games, simulation exercises and a special project are used in the teaching of principles of management and elements of economics; quantitative aspects of management including business statistics and operations research; fundamentals of data processing; financial management and accounting; industrial psychology; and the legal environment of business.
  Credit recommendation: In the lower division baccalaureate/associate degree category, 3 semester hours in Introduction to Business and in the upper division baccalaureate category, 3 semester hours in Principles of Management (2/86).

Personnel Management and Industrial Relations
(Diploma in Personnel Management)
  Location: Jamaican Institute of Management, Kingston, Jamaica.
  Length: 210 hours (35 weeks; 2 three-hour meetings per week).
  Dates: January 1985-Present.
  Objective: To provide students with a sound knowledge of personnel management processes, approaches, and techniques; to give students a theoretical base in personnel management as well as knowledge and skills in various aspects of personnel administration as they apply to the local environment.

Instruction: Lecture and discussion, case studies, film presentations, management games, simulation exercises, and special job-related projects are used in teaching of topics covering management of the personnel function, psychological aspects of personnel administration, industrial relations, training and staff development, and interview techniques.

Credit recommendation: In the upper division baccalaureate category, 4 semester hours in Personnel Management and in the upper division baccalaureate category, 2 semester hours in Industrial Relations in the West Indies (2/86).

Principles of Marketing and Marketing Management
(Diploma in Marketing)

Location: Financial and Accounting College of Training, Kingston, Jamaica.

Length: 210 hours (35 weeks; 2 three-hour meetings per week).

Dates: January 1984-Present.

Objective: To provide students with a sound knowledge and understanding of key principles and applications of marketing mix strategies.

Instruction: Lecture and discussion, case studies, film presentations, and project assignments are used in the teaching of topics covering principles and practices of marketing; quantitative aspects of marketing; marketing behavior, principles of export marketing, planning the marketing effort, and organization behavior.

Credit recommendation: In the upper division baccalaureate category, 3 semester hours in Principles of Marketing and in the upper division baccalaureate category, 3 semester hours in Marketing Management (2/86).

Principles of Management
(Certificate in Management Studies)

Location: Financial and Accounting College of Training, Kingston, Jamaica.

Length: 150 hours (25 weeks; 2 three-hour meetings per week).

Dates: January 1984-Present.

Objective: To introduce students to the nature, scope and functions of management, and to relate that knowledge to certain specialized, job-related skills.

Instruction: Lecture and discussion, programmed instruction, film presentations, case studies, games, and simulation exercises are used in the teaching of topics covering management principles; basics of accounting and internal control; statistics for business managers; introductory personnel management; and leadership skills.

Credit recommendation: In the vocational certificate category, 4 semester hours in Principles of Management (2/86).

Principles of Supervision
(Certificate in Supervision)

Location: Jamaican Management Institute, Kingston, Jamaica.

Length: 150 hours (25 weeks; 2 three-hour meetings per week).

Dates: January 1984-Present.

Objective: To introduce students to basic supervisory skills.

Instruction: Lecture and discussion.

Credit recommendation: In the vocational certificate degree category, 4 semester hours in Principles of Supervision (2/86).

Jerrico Corporation

Jerrico Corporation and its subsidiaries operate, franchise, and service Long John Silver's Seafood Shoppes and Jerry's Restaurants, and sell food, supplies, and restaurant equipment.

The Jerrico CENTER for Training and Development serves the educational and training needs of Long John Silver's and Jerry's Restaurant operations and support functions. It is a residential facility located on the campus of Transylvania University in Lexington, Kentucky.

The CENTER's staff is responsible for the design of courses for delivery at the CENTER and in the field. Field training occurs in Phases I and II of the Basic Management Program (see below) under the direction of training managers who have successfully completed the "Train the Trainer" course. The delivery of field training is under the control of the CENTER.

Source of official student records: Vice President of Training, Jerrico CENTER, P.O. Box 11988, Lexington, Kentucky 40579.

Additional information about the courses: Program on Noncollegiate Sponsored Instruction, The Center for Adult Learning and Educational Credentials, American Council on Education, One Dupont Circle, Washington, D.C. 20036.

BASIC MANAGEMENT TRAINING PROGRAM

The Basic Management Training Course is a three-phase program for management trainees in Long John Silver's restaurants. The Phase I program takes place in an approved training restaurant under the supervision of a restaurant manager who has been trained as a field instructor. The Phase II program is also conducted at a Long John Silver's restaurant, and is devoted to the mastery of a designated number of management tasks. The third phase is a two week residential phase conducted at the Jerrico CENTER. Phase III is attended by trainees who have successfully completed Phases I and II. Trainees who have not attended Phase I and II attend the basic management training course, which includes topics covered in the first two phases of the program.

The program is oriented toward competency-based learning and students are assessed on the basis of performance in specific areas.

Basic Management Training Program
  Phase I
  Phase II
  Phase III
  Location: Long John Silver Training restaurants.
  Length: 1. 120 hours (3 weeks). 2. Self-paced over 3 weeks. 3. 72 hours (2 weeks); residential.
  Dates: *Version 1:* Courses 1 and 2: July 1976-May 1985; Course 3: September 1977-May 1985. *Version 2:* Courses 1, 2, and 3: June 1985-Present.
  Objective: To provide managerial candidates with basic operational and managerial skills to direct a single-unit food service operation.
  Instruction: The food service production component provides the skills necessary to operate efficiently a limited-menu facility. Covers methods of food preparation, portion and cost control, and equipment maintenance. The management component provides an introduction to productivity, communications, leadership, motivation, scheduling, and problem solving.
  Credit recommendation: *Version 1:* In the lower division baccalaureate/associate degree category, 1 semester hour in Quantity/Food Production and in the lower division baccalaureate/associate degree category or in the upper division baccalaureate category, 3 semester hours in Management (10/77). *Version 2:* In the lower division baccalaureate/associate degree category, 1 semester hour in Cooperative Education/Coordinated Internship of a Food Service Program, and in the lower division baccalaureate/associate degree category, or in the upper division baccalaureate category, 3 semester hours in Management (6/85). NOTE: To be eligible for credit, student must complete all three courses. This course has been reevaluated and continues to meet requirements for credit recommendations.

Basic Management Training Program Course
(Formerly Basic Management Training Program, Phase III)
  Location: Jerrico CENTER, Lexington, KY.
  Length: 72 hours (2 weeks); residential.
  Dates: March 1977-Present.
  Objective: To provide managerial candidates who have not attended Phases I and II with basic operational and managerial skills for a single-unit food service facility.
  Instruction: Productivity, communications, leadership, motivation, scheduling, problem solving. Emphasis is on human relations.
  Credit recommendation: In the lower division baccalaureate/associate degree category or in the upper division baccalaureate category, 3 semester hours in Management (10/77) (6/85). NOTE: This course has been reevaluated and continues to meet requirements for credit recommendations.

Executive Career Development Workshop
  Location: Jerrico CENTER, Lexington, KY.
  Length: 40 hours (1 week); residential.
  Dates: May 1982-Present.
  Objective: To provide district director level managers with the corporate philosophy, structure and job responsibilities of corporate management.
  Instruction: Selected topics in the areas of restaurant management, personnel, law, marketing, accounting, real estate, and purchasing are covered. Methodology includes presentations by guest lecturers and small group discussion.
  Credit recommendation: In the upper division baccalaureate degree category, 1 semester hour in Management (6/85).

Supervisory Development Course
  Location: Jerrico CENTER, Lexington KY.
  Length: 40 hours (1 week); residential; approximately 10 hours in evening sessions.
  Dates: September 1977-Present.
  Objective: To provide managers who have responsibility for several food service operations with the skills to develop, implement, and control performance standards.
  Instruction: Using an action plan, participants establish and evaluate performance standards. Topics covered include organizing, planning, leading, directing, and controlling. Methodology includes role playing, discussion, and small-group exercises.
  Credit recommendation: In the upper division baccalaureate category, 3 semester hours in Management (10/77) (6/85). NOTE: This course has been reevaluated and continues to meet requirements for credit recommendations.

Train the Trainer
  Location: Jerrico CENTER, Lexington, KY.
  Length: 40 hours (1 week); residential; approximately 10 hours in evening sessions.
  Dates: February 1976-Present.
  Objective: To provide the manager with an understanding of his/her role and responsibility as a trainer of personnel.
  Instruction: Development of training skills through role playing, discussion, lesson plan writing, and small-group work. Emphasis on analyzing subject matter and applying education principles.
  Credit recommendation: In the upper division baccalaureate category, 3 semester hours in Education, Management, or Personnel (10/77) (6/85). NOTE: This

course has been reevaluated and continues to meet requirements for credit recommendations.

Jewish Hospital of St. Louis

The Jewish Hospital of St. Louis was founded in 1900 as a nonprofit, nonsectarian voluntary general hospital and is a major teaching affiliate of the Washington University School of Medicine. It is dedicated to a broad range of acute, chronic, and specialized medical care, to health professional education, to various forms of community service, and to investigational research. The Hospital seeks to provide such resources as necessary to guarantee excellence in the training of health professionals, in the promotion of health, and the delivery of health care to the sick.

The Jewish Hospital offers a wide array of medical services to the patient population including anesthesiology, dentistry, home care, medicine, neurology, obstetrics/gynecology, ophthalmology, otolaryngology, pathology and laboratory medicine, pediatrics, psychiatry, radiology, rehabilitation medicine, and surgery.

Source of official student records: Director of the Department of Education, The Jewish Hospital of St. Louis, 216 So. Kingshighway, St. Louis, MO 63110.

Additional information about the courses: Program on Noncollegiate Sponsored Instruction, The Center for Adult Learning and Educational Credentials, American Council on Education, One Dupont Circle, Washington, D.C. 20036.

The American Council on Education would like to acknowledge the support of Webster College, St. Louis, Missouri, in coordinating the course evaluation for the Jewish Hospital of St. Louis.

Assertiveness Training
  Location: St. Louis, MO.
  Length: 16 hours (2 hours per week for 8 weeks or 8 hours for 2 days).
  Dates: September 1981-July 1987.
  Objective: Upon completion of the course the student will be able to describe basic theories of assertive behavior; identify personal rights and the rights of others in various situations; discriminate between nonassertive, assertive, and aggressive responses to specific situations; and evaluate his or her personal "assertive presentation of self," including verbal and nonverbal mannerism.
  Instruction: Course prepares the student to evaluate human interaction from the perspective of an active, nonthreatening, rational person. It provides the theoretical framework to help the student become more sensitive to others and to modify behavior patterns when appropriate. Methods include group activity and video taping.
  Credit recommendation: In the lower division baccalaureate/associate degree category, 1 semester hour in Counseling, Psychology, and Sociology (8/82).

Basic Critical Care Nursing Course
  Location: St. Louis, MO.
  Length: *Version 1:* 68 hours (2 weeks, 6.8 hours/day); *Version 2:* 73½ hours (2 weeks and one day).
  Dates: October 1976-Present.
  Objective: To prepare registered nurses to perform on a safe beginning practitioner level in the critical care area. The learner will be able to demonstrate a theoretical knowledge of critical care nursing and safely apply it to a variety of critically ill patients.
  Instruction: Pathophysiology of the cardiac and respiratory systems and related phamacology are studied in depth. Interpretation of electrocardiography is introduced and practiced along with maintenance of artificial life support systems. Methodology includes lectures, discussions, audiovisual materials, handouts, examinations, case study, and hands-on experience with relevant equipment. The course is designed for experienced registered nurses.
  Credit recommendation: In the lower division baccalaureate/associate degree category or in the upper division baccalaureate category, 3 semester hours in Medical/Surgical Nursing (6/82).

1. **Management I**
2. **Management II**
  Location: St. Louis, MO.
  Length: 33 hours (1½ hours per week for 22 weeks); *Version 1:* Management I - 12 weeks; *Version 2:* Management I - 14 weeks; *Version 1:* Management II - 12 weeks; *Version 2:* Management II - 13 weeks.
  Dates: January 1979-July 1987.
  Objective: To provide students with basic management principles as they relate to effective supervision, personnel management, and human relations.
  Instruction: Basic management theory is covered including fundamental concepts of planning, organizing, and control processes; motivation; incentives; leadership, communications and interpersonal relations. Instructional methods include classroom discussion, lectures, group activities, audiovisual materials, and project assignments.
  Credit recommendation: In the lower division baccalaureate/associate degree category, 2 semester hours in Business Administration, Management, or Personnel Administration (6/82). Students must complete both courses in order for the credit recommendations to apply.

1. **Motivational Dynamics I**
2. **Motivational Dynamics II**
  Location: St. Louis, MO.
  Length: 32 hours (2 hours per week); M.D. I: 2 hours per week for 12 weeks; M.D. II: 2 hours per week for 4 weeks.
  Dates: February 1980-July 1987.

Objective: To provide managers with an in-depth study of the modern psychological theories of management-worker relationships and the approaches to mastering managerial motivational skills.

Instruction: Instruction in motivation theories, productivity and morale, communication, group behavior, time management, decision making, management by objectives, and total performance management. Methods of instruction include lecture, class participation, audiovisuals, student workbooks, selected readings, and problem solving.

Credit recommendation: In the lower division baccalaureate/associate degree category or upper division baccalaureate category, 2 semester hours in Business Management elective, Human Resource Development or Psychology elective, and Personnel Administration (6/82). Students must complete both courses in order for the credit recommendations to apply.

Nursing Management
  Location: St. Louis, MO.
  Length: *Version 1:* 22 hours (2 hours per week for 11 weeks). *Version 2:* (28 hours per week for 14 weeks).
  Dates: *Version 1:* September 1976-August 1982. *Version 2:* September 1982-July 1987.
  Objective: To enable the student to define tasks and responsibilities of nurse managers and to develop a working knowledge of those factors which contribute to collateral relations in first-line management.
  Instruction: *Version 1:* Covers basic management theory including the fundamental concepts of planning, organizing, directing, evaluating, labor relations, and organization finance. Focus is on intraorganizational behavior at the level of the first-line supervisor. Course is designed for registered nurses who have had a minimum of one year's work experience and who are potential nurse managers. Techniques include lecture, classroom activities, reading assignments, role playing, and student projects. *Version 2:* Same as Version 1 with the addition of a segment covering general management theory.
  Credit recommendation: *Version 1:* In the upper division baccalaureate category, 1 semester hour in Health Facilities Management or Nursing Management. *Version 2:* In the upper division baccalaureate category, 2 semester hours in Health Facilities Management or Nursing Management (6/82).

Stress Management
  Location: St. Louis, MO.
  Length: 16 hours (2 hours per week for 8 weeks).
  Dates: September 1982-July 1987.
  Objective: Upon completion of the course, the student will be able to describe stress reactions, the dynamics of perception as it relates to stress, mental techniques that reduce stress, to identify personal sources of stress, and to demonstrate various relaxation techniques.

Instruction: Focus is on the sources of stress, the identification of stressful situations, and the many coping mechanisms productively used to ameliorate stress. Emphasis throughout course is on self-analysis and improvement.

Credit recommendation: In the lower division baccalaureate/associate degree category, 1 semester hour in Counseling and Psychology (6/82).

Joint Apprenticeship Training Committee, International Brotherhood of Electrical Workers Local Union 269, and the National Electrical Contractors Association of Southern New Jersey

I.B.E.W. Local Union 269 represents some 350 construction workers performing various electrical work in the Mercer, Burlington, and Bucks Country areas. A four-year apprenticeship training program includes 210 hours of classroom instruction and 2,000 hours of on-the-job training each year and is administered by Local 269 and the Southern Chapter of the National Electrical Contractors Association. The training enables each apprentice to read blueprints, to work safely with high voltages and to install, repair, and service electrical equipment and controls on residential, commercial, and industrial projects.

Local 269 has its own training facilities adjacent to the Union Offices. The facilities have several classrooms, labs, and demonstration and workshop rooms with a variety of workshops including electrical installation, wire and welding shops. The facilities also have a library with printed materials, overhead transparencies and films. The library is available to apprentices and journeypersons for their personal research. To receive journeyman status, all four years of the program must be completed.

Source of official student records: Training Director, I.B.E.W. Local 269 J.A.T.C., 676 Whitehead Road, Trenton, New Jersey 08648.

Additional information about the courses: Thomas A. Edison State College, Program on Noncollegiate Sponsored Instruction, 101 West State Street, CN545, Trenton, New Jersey 08625.

Electrician Apprentice (Inside)
  Location: Trenton, NJ.
  Length: Four years.
  Dates: September 1978-Present.
  Objective: To prepare apprentices for journeymen status in the electrical construction (inside) industry.
  Instruction: *First year:* Principles of direct current, alternating current and electromagnetism; knowledge and application of National Electrical Code requirements per-

taining to cable, conduit, and grounding; operation of electric motors; Ohm's law, series circuits, parallel circuits, magnetism, and motors, safety procedures and first aid resuscitation; reading and sketching of evaluation views and plot plans, including symbols and scales used; materials used in the electrical construction industry, such as wires, cables, conduit, conductors, insulation, joints, fasteners, and fuses; under supervision, installation of electrical apparatus such as cables, conduit, tubing, outlet boxes, outlets, fixtures, and securing and holding devices at various job sites; orientation to the apprenticeship form of education and training, the electrical industry, the history of electrical industry, the International Brotherhood of Electrical Workers, local union by-laws, and the history of the operation and contribution of the National Electrical Contractors Association.

Second year: Use and installation of electric meters; National Electrical Code requirements relating to grounding conductors, branch circuits, and transformers; use of algebra and trigonometry in making mathematical calculations; types, construction, winding ratios, functions, and classifications of transformers; operating principles and functions of incandescent lamps, alarms, and refrigeration and air conditioning components; capacitance, inductance; reactance, and RLC circuits; electric motor mechanical drive and load connections; use of architect's blueprints and layouts; use and care of tools of the industry; circuit testing; first aid procedures, including those for electric shock victims; safety rules and practices for the electrical construction industry. Apprentices perform more complex work tasks through a series of six-month job rotations.

Third year: National Electrical Code requirement for capacitors, electric motors, hazardous locations, and Class I, II, and III installations; use of blueprints pertaining to structural details, floor plan specifications, floor ducts, service entrances, circuits, and rise circuits; electrical wiring and distribution systems; electrical theory pertaining to alternating currents, alternating current motors and transformers, power factor and correction, and primary and secondary connections; analysis of malfunctions and repair of remote controls, protection of devices, and alternating current motor controls. Apprentices apply knowledge by assuming increasingly complex responsibilities and performing increasingly complex tasks in work settings that are rotated each six months.

Fourth year: Knowledge and application of National Electrical Code requirements pertaining to wire closets, junction boxes, and stairway and emergency lighting; metric system conversions; application of rules to radiation exposure, protection, reaction, and other features of nuclear safety; transistor principles and circuits, use of electronic testing equipment; basic rectifier circuits, amplifier circuits, special circuit applications, and transistor use; static control fundamentals, including concepts, circuits, analysis, and applications; alternating current applications in industrial electricity; fundamentals of temperature, pressure, and flow; instrumentation systems; installation and testing of electrical construction materials; use of electrical construction equipment.

Credit recommendation: *First year:* In the lower division baccalaureate/associate degree category, 4 semester hours in Basic Electricity, 1 in National Electrical Code, 1 in Blueprint Reading and Sketching, and 2 in field experience in Electrical Construction, 1 in Technical Mathematics, for a total of 9 semester hours.

Second year: In the lower division baccalaureate/associate degree category, 4 semester hours in Basic Electricity, 5 in field experience in Electrical Construction, 2 in National Electrical Code, 1 in Technical Mathematics, 2 in Blueprint Reading and Sketching, 4 in Electrical Machinery, and 1 in Safety and First Aid for a total of 19 semester hours.

Third year: In the lower division baccalaureate/associate degree category, 4 semester hours in Basic Electricity, 3 in National Electrical Code, 3 in Blueprint Reading and Sketching, 7 in field experience in Electrical Construction, 1 in Technical Mathematics, 2 in A.C. Machinery, 1 in Safety and First Aid for a total of 27 semester hours.

Fourth year: In the lower division baccalaureate/associate degree category, 4 semester hours in Basic Electricity, 1 semester hour in Technical Mathematics, 4 in National Electrical Code, 4 in Blueprint Reading and Sketching, 9 in field experience in Electrical Construction, 2 in Safety and First Aid, 3 in Motor Controls, 3 in Electronics, 4 in Electrical Machinery, 2 in A.C. Machinery for a total of 36 semester hours (1/84). NOTE: The credit recommendation is cumulative; readers should use the recommendation that corresponds to the number of years completed by the student.

Katharine Gibbs School

Since its founding in 1911 by Katharine Gibbs, the school has grown from a two-room unit in Providence, R.I., to an eight-school organization that prepares over 4,000 graduates a year for positions as executive secretaries.

The educational objective of the Katharine Gibbs School are supported by a selective admissions policy, a carefully structured curriculum offering courses both in business subjects and in the liberal arts, and a credentialed teaching staff that includes a full-time faculty as well as adjunct professors from near-by colleges and universities.

Katharine Gibbs School prepares its students for entry-level executive secretarial positions via the following full-time programs: The One-Year Executive Secretarial Program, The One-Year Advanced Executive Secretarial Program, The One-Year Word Processing Program, The Special Program for College Women, and The Two-Year

Liberal Arts-Secretarial Program. College graduates may also obtain entry-level secretarial skills in an eleven-week training program called ENTREE. In addition, the school offers day and evening adult training programs, and specialized evening courses and seminars.

The essence of the Gibbs education, however, is more than its curriculum. Today, as always, Gibbs places a high priority on each person's growth as a total professional who will be involved in a creative interaction of business relationships that demand a unique blend of strengths. Gibbs seeks to instill in students a high degree of confidence and determination, a respect for their own attitudes and standards, and an ambition to pursue even greater responsibilities and achievements.

It is the commitment to the total professional that is at the heart of the Gibbs educational philosophy.

Credit recommendations are intended for use by students who take the one-year program.

Source of official student records: General Administrative Offices of Katharine Gibbs Schools are located at 200 Park Avenue, New York, NY 10166. Transcripts for individual students are available from the specific Gibbs School they attended.

Additional information about the courses: Thomas A. Edison State College, Program on Noncollegiate Sponsored Instruction, 101 West State Street, CN545, Trenton, NJ 08625.

Accounting I #403
(Also offered as Basic Accounting)
Location: Montclair, NJ; Boston, MA; Norwalk, CT; Huntington, NY; New York, NY.
Length: 51 hours (17 weeks).
Dates: September 1973-Present.
Objective: To introduce accounting fundamentals and cover generally accepted accounting principles and financial reporting standards.
Instruction: Basic accounting principles are explained through textbook and workbook exercises. Students learn the accounting cycle, develop mastery in skills such as recording daily transactions, and preparation of trial balances and financial statements. Attention is also given to payroll deductions and employer's taxes.
Credit recommendation: In the lower division baccalaureate/associate degree category, 3 semester hours in Principles of Accounting (5/83).

Accounting I #409
Location: All Katharine Gibbs Schools.
Length: 51 hours (17 weeks).
Dates: September 1973-Present.
Objective: To give word processing program students the fundamental principles and practical applications of accounting.
Instruction: Accounting principles and the accounting cycle are presented in this class. Also, students learn to record daily business transactions and prepare financial statements. In addition to lectures in the above topics, the course includes exercises to develop proficiency in basic computational skills.
Credit recommendation: In the lower division baccalaureate/associate degree category, 3 semester hours in Principles of Accounting (5/83).

Accounting II #403.2
(Also offered as under Gibbs titles of Intermediate Accounting)
Location: Montclair, NJ; Boston, MA; Norwalk, CT; Huntington, NY.
Length: 51 hours (17 weeks).
Dates: September 1973-Present.
Objective: To build upon basic accounting theory including partnership and corporate accounting.
Instruction: This course builds upon basic theory and includes partnership and corporate accounting, introduction to cost accounting, budgeting and managerial concepts, statement analysis, and statement of changes in financial position. (Prerequisite: Accounting I #403.)
Credit recommendation: In the lower division baccalaureate/associate degree category, 3 semester hours in Principles of Accounting II (5/83).

Accounting Essentials #401
Also listed as Managerial Accounting #402.
Location: All Katharine Gibbs Schools.
Length: 19 hours (19 weeks).
Dates: September 1973-January 1985.
Objective: To present an introduction to principles and practical applications of accounting essentials.
Instruction: The fundamental principles and practical applications of accounting are presented through weekly lectures. Topics include: accounting cycle, methods of recording basic transactions in a combined cash journal, posting to the ledger, and preparing a monthly trial balance.
Credit recommendation: In the lower division baccalaureate/associate degree category, 1 semester hour in Accounting Essentials (5/83).

Administrative Assistant I
(Administrative Assistant: Supervisory Skills)
Location: Montclair, NJ.
Length: 23 hours (11 weeks).
Dates: January 1983-September 1985.
Objective: To increase personal effectiveness in supervisory capacity.
Instruction: Course explores management skills through reading lectures and case studies. Management by objectives, human resource development, communication and problem solving techniques are also introduced.
Credit recommendation: In the lower division baccalaureate/associate degree category, 1 semester hour in

Office Administration (5/83).

Administrative Assistant II
(Administrative and Office Management)
   Location: Montclair, NJ.
   Length: 23 hours (11 weeks).
   Dates: January 1983-September 1985.
   Objective: To help students learn the role and duties of the administrative assistant.
   Instruction: Course covers: role of an administrative assistant in the corporate structure, organization of office systems and time utilization. Oral presentation and time management skills are also covered in the lectures of the course.
   Credit recommendation: In the lower division baccalaureate/associate degree category, 1 semester hour in Administrative Assistant (5/83).

Advanced Typewriting
   Location: Montclair, NJ.
   Length: 32 hours (8 weeks).
   Dates: January 1983-Present.
   Objective: To develop speed and accuracy through the use of proper typing techniques and to gain skill in the typing of office production tasks.
   Instruction: In this course the student works on the development of speed and accuracy and begins to work on business production problems. Course also covers: review of basic skills and techniques, centering, letters, tables, and reports.
   Credit recommendation: In the lower division baccalaureate/associate degree category, 1 semester hour in Typing (5/83).

Beginning Typewriting
   Location: Montclair, NJ.
   Length: 32 hours (8 weeks).
   Dates: June 1983-Present.
   Objective: To learn touch typewriting through mastery of the keyboard and to begin to develop speed and accuracy.
   Instruction: Course covers introduction to keyboard, correct typewriting techniques and some introductory production exercises. Student learns to correctly type simple business letters and reports.
   Credit recommendation: In the lower division baccalaureate/associate degree category, 1 semester hour in Typing (5/83).

Business English
   Location: All Katharine Gibbs Schools.
   Length: 34 hours (34 weeks).
   Dates: September 1980-Present.
   Objective: To strengthen business vocabulary and to communicate effectively in business.
   Instruction: Course consists of a review of basic English fundamentals including grammar, spelling and punctuation. There is an emphasis on strengthening the business vocabulary.
   Credit recommendation: In the lower division baccalaureate/associate degree category, 1 semester hour in Business Program or Business Elective (5/83).

Business Law #603
   Location: Montclair, NJ; Boston, MA, Huntington, NY; Norwalk, CT; New York, NY.
   Length: 51 hours (17 weeks).
   Dates: September 1973-Present.
   Objective: To introduce legal principles, obligations and rights.
   Instruction: Through lectures, the following topics are covered: contracts, negotiable instruments, family law, ownership of real estate and personal property. The rights that ensure an individual's legal protection are also included.
   Credit recommendation: In the lower division baccalaureate/associate degree category, 3 semester hours in Business Law (5/83).

Business Writing
(English IV, Business Writing Seminar #303)
   Location: Montclair, NJ; Boston, MA; Norwalk, CT; Huntington, NY; New York, NY.
   Length: 51 hours (17 weeks).
   Dates: September 1973-June 1985.
   Objective: To provide opportunity for students to examine, implement, and reinforce techniques for the development of effective communication skills in business situations.
   Instruction: Course covers business research techniques and procedures and provides experience in preparing a variety of business reports. Emphasis is placed on the development of a clear, concise writing style. Topics covered include: Introduction to Business Writing; Letters and Memos; Customer Relations; Administrative Communication; and Management and Employment Communications.
   Credit recommendation: In the upper division baccalaureate category or lower division baccalaureate/associate degree category, 3 semester hours in English or in Business Communications (5/83).

Effective Writing
(Effective Business Writing Part of Continuing Education Program)
   Location: Montclair, NJ.
   Length: 30 hours (10 weeks).
   Dates: January 1983-Present.
   Objective: To develop skill in using the English language clearly, concisely, and correctly. Course provides opportunity for practical and effective application of basic English concepts to specific business writing situations.

Instruction: Course is based upon a review of English fundamentals, and their practical application to business correspondence. Intensive practice in writing accurately, clearly, concisely, and effectively is offered.

Credit recommendation: In the lower division baccalaureate/associate degree category, 2 semester hours in English Composition (5/83).

Economic History #703
Location: Norwalk, CT.
Length: 51 hours (17 weeks).
Dates: September 1978-Present.
Objective: To study the economic forces that have shaped past and recent history.
Instruction: This course emphasizes the economic forces rather than the political events that have shaped the past and present. The evolution of economic societies from the traditional to the market and command economics are reviewed. The course stresses society's impact on the economy and the concept of evolutionary economic history throughout the lectures and discussions.
Credit recommendation: In the lower division baccalaureate/associate degree category, 3 semester hours in Social Science Elective (5/83).

Economics I - #506 or #806
Location: Montclair, NJ; Huntington, NY; Boston, MA; Norwalk, CT; New York, NY.
Length: 51 hours (17 weeks).
Dates: September 1973-Present.
Objective: To introduce students to the concepts and theories of macroeconomics.
Instruction: An examination of the central problems of the economy with a focus on the determination of natural income and employment. Other topics in the course include: price systems, monetary and fiscal policies, business cycles, and to role of international trade in the economy.
Credit recommendation: In the lower division baccalaureate/associate degree category, 3 semester hours in Principles of Macroeconomics (5/83).

Economics II - #809, #542, or #506.2
Location: Boston, MA; Montclair, NJ; Huntington, NY; Norwalk, CT; New York, NY.
Length: 51 hours (17 weeks).
Dates: September 1973-Present.
Objective: To introduce students to concepts and theories of microeconomics.
Instruction: In this course the laws of supply and demand and pricing, as they relate to the business firm, are explored. Topics covered in the course include: the stock market, introduction to labor economics, and women's role in the labor force. Some individual topic research by students supplement the lecture approach of the course.
Credit recommendation: In the lower division baccalaureate/associate degree category, 3 semester hours in Principles of Microeconomics (5/83).

Fundamentals of Writing
1. **English I (301-304 or 309)**
2. **English II (301.2, 304.2, 309.2, or 302)**
3. **English III (301.2)**
   Location: All Katharine Gibbs Schools.
   Length: 1. 68 hours (17 weeks); 2. 68 hours (17 weeks); 3. 51 hours (17 weeks).
   Dates: September 1973-Present.
   Objective: To refresh students on basic mechanisms of grammar and punctuation; to review basic principles of writing and apply that knowledge to business writing.
   Instruction: Through lecture and extensive drill in punctuation, dictionary use, proofreading, vocabulary building, sentence structure and grammar, students develop mastery of basic mechanics of written English. This course also provides means for each student to develop a clear and accurate writing style. The skills of reading, writing, and rewriting are emphasized in the opportunities provided for students to compose various kinds of modern business correspondence.
   Credit recommendation: If student completes 1 and 2, in the lower division baccalaureate/associate degree category, 1 semester hour in Review Mechanics of English. If student completes 1, 2, and 3, in the lower division baccalaureate/associate degree category, 3 semester hours in Freshman Composition (5/83).

History of Modern World I
(Introduction to Modern Civilization #701 or #813.)
Location: Boston, MA; Norwalk, CT; Montclair, NJ; Huntington, NY; New York, NY.
Length: 51 hours (17 weeks).
Dates: September 1973-Present.
Objective: To give students an understanding of major movements and trends in the world with an emphasis on European development in the period from 1789 to 1870.
Instruction: Through study of the historical and political events that have shaped the modern world from the French Revolution to the unification of Germany, the student gains an appreciation of past causes and present effects. Topics emphasized include: the impact of revolution in modern history, the rise of national states, the development of modern democracy, and the evolution of modern capitalism and its critics. Lecture, discussion, and debate are utilized.
Credit recommendation: In the lower division baccalaureate/associate degree category, 3 semester hours in History (5/83).

History of Modern World II
(Modern World: A World in Flux #701.2 or #814)
Location: Boston, MA; Norwalk, CT; Montclair, NJ; Huntington, NY; New York, NY.
Length: 51 hours (17 weeks).

Dates: September 1973-Present.

Objective: To give students an understanding of major movements and trends in the world during the period from 1870 to the present.

Instruction: The emphasis in this course is on international developments since the unification of Germany. Particular focus is place on the effects of imperialism on the modern world, changing political alliances, the problems of emerging nations, and the social and political ramifications of such events. Lecture, discussion, and debate are utilized.

Credit recommendation: In the lower division baccalaureate/associate degree category, 3 semester hours in History (5/83).

Humanities I (702)
(Introduction to the Humanities)

Location: Montclair, NJ; Boston, MA; Norwalk, CT; Huntington, NY; New York, NY.

Length: 51 hours (17 weeks).

Dates: September 1973-Present.

Objective: To acquaint students with the sources of classical and contemporary thought and to familiarize them with the development of cultural trends as reflected by leading writers.

Instruction: Through selected readings in philosophy and literature, the student develops an appreciation for the major intellectual and aesthetic values that have contributed to Western cultural heritage. Selected readings include: *The Conscience Reader,* Shrodes et al.; *Man's Search for Meaning,* Frankl; *Siddhartha,* Hesse; *Long Day's Journey Into Night,* O'Neill; and *Othello,* Shakespeare. Lecture and discussion methods are used.

Credit recommendation: In the lower division baccalaureate/associate degree category, 3 semester hours in Humanities or Liberal Arts electives (5/83).

Humanities II (714 or 702.2)
(Humanities: The American Experience)

Location: Montclair, NJ; Norwalk, CT; Huntington, NY; Boston, MA.

Length: 51 hours (17 weeks).

Dates: September 1973-Present.

Objective: To develop an understanding of the American character through an examination of selected themes as reflected by representative writers.

Instruction: In this course selected topics may include: the Puritan experiment, frontier influence, legacy of abundance, reform impulse, and the impacts of immigration, industrialization and urbanization. Selected writers may include: John Cawelti, Nathaniel Hawthorne, Toni Morrison, Upton Sinclair, and F. Scott Fitzgerald. Class utilizes lecture, discussion and workshop presentations.

Credit recommendation: In the lower division baccalaureate/associate degree category, 3 hours in Humanities or Liberal Arts electives (5/83).

Industrial and Organizational Psychology (538, 806, or 810)
(Also offered as Psychology of the Work Place)

Location: Boston, MA; Huntington, NY; Montclair, NJ.

Length: 51 hours (17 weeks).

Dates: September 1981-Present.

Objective: To be able to apply the methods, facts and principles of psychology to people at work.

Instruction: This course focuses on the application of psychological principles to business situations. Problem employee attitudes, working conditions, and work job selection techniques and tactics are reviewed. Lecture and case discussion, quizzes, mid-term and final exams are utilized.

Credit recommendation: In the lower division baccalaureate/associate degree category, 3 semester hours in Industrial and Organizational Psychology (5/83).

Intermediate Gregg Shorthand and Transcription

Location: Montclair, NJ.

Length: 56 hours (14 weeks).

Dates: January 1983-Present.

Objective: To develop ability to take sustained dictation at minimum of 80-100 w.p.m.

Instruction: Course includes a review of Gregg Theory, typing drills and dictation exercises. Students also do transcriptions of varied business correspondence. Students must take dictation at a minimum of 80 w.p.m. with standard error limit by the end of the course.

Credit recommendation: In the lower division baccalaureate/associate degree category, 2 semester hours in Gregg Shorthand (5/83).

Intermediate Typewriting

Location: Montclair, NJ.

Length: 32 hours (8 weeks).

Dates: January 1983-Present.

Objective: To increase accuracy, speed, and master typing for integrated office projects.

Instruction: Students develop speed through straight copy typing which includes letters, tables, and reports. Simulated office projects and assignments are also provided. At conclusion of course, students type at least 40 w.p.m. with a maximum of 2 errors on standard tests.

Credit recommendation: In the lower division baccalaureate/associate degree category, 1 semester hour in Typing (5/83).

Introduction to Business
(Offered as: Basic Business Organization #503; or Introduction to Business Management #504 and #504.2; or Principles of Business Management #505)

Location: All Katharine Gibbs Schools.

Length: 51 hours (17 weeks).

Dates: September 1973-Present.

Katharine Gibbs School

Objective: To explore the nature and overall structure of business as they relate to the functions of management: planning, directing, organizing and controlling.

Instruction: Course explores various types of business enterprises. Communications within an organization, the staffing of organizations, and the development of a managerial style are also covered. Topics include: product marketing, short and long term financial methods, physical distribution and risk management.

Credit recommendation: In the lower division baccalaureate/associate degree category, 3 semester hours in Introduction to Business (5/83).

Introduction to Data Processing (539) (Information Processing)
  Location: Montclair, NJ.
  Length: 51 hours (17 weeks).
  Dates: September 1982-Present.
  Objective: To introduce students to the field of Data Processing and to develop an awareness of computer systems utilized in the office environment.
  Instruction: Course covers basic concepts of data processing, its evolution, its impact on the business office and its operations. Computer hardware and software are studied from a conceptual (not a "hands-on") approach through lecture and discussion.
  Credit recommendation: In the upper division baccalaureate category or lower division baccalaureate/associate degree category, 2 semester hours in Data Processing (5/83).

Introduction to Gregg Shorthand
  Location: Montclair, NJ.
  Length: 56 hours (14 weeks).
  Dates: January 1983-Present.
  Objective: To learn the Gregg Shorthand system in order to take timed dictation at 60 w.p.m.
  Instruction: Course covers theory and principles of Gregg Shorthand, business vocabulary and an introduction to dictation and English review. Student learns to take time dictation at 60 w.p.m.
  Credit recommendation: In the lower division baccalaureate/associate degree category, 2 semester hours in Shorthand (5/83).

Introduction to Psychology #805
  Location: Montclair, NJ; Boston, MA; Huntington, NY; Norwalk, CT.
  Length: 51 hours (17 weeks).
  Dates: Montclair, NJ: September 1973-Present; Boston, MA: September 1973-Present; Huntington, NY: September 1976-Present; Norwalk, CT: September 1976-Present.
  Objective: To be able to understand and discuss the breadth of fundamental psychological concepts.
  Instruction: Such topics as research methods, human development, individual differences, intelligence testing, human learning procedure and processes, memory, emotions, motivation, abnormal behavior, personality, psychotherapy, and social behavior are examined by lecture, discussions, and collateral readings.
  Credit recommendation: In the lower division baccalaureate/associate degree category, 3 semester hours in Introduction to Psychology (5/83).

Introduction to Sociology #815, 806, or 819
  Location: Montclair, NJ; Norwalk, CT.
  Length: 51 hours (17 weeks).
  Dates: September 1981-Present.
  Objective: To familiarize students with the sociological perspective and to acquaint students with the body of research methods used in studying human social behavior.
  Instruction: Introduction to basic concepts in sociology, analyzing the works of leading sociologists and major trends in the development of sociological thought. Lectures, discussions, and collateral readings including such topics as sociological imagination, social stratification, sex roles in society, the family, urbanization, and race relations.
  Credit recommendation: In the lower division baccalaureate/associate degree category, 3 semester hours in Introduction to Sociology (5/83).

Introduction to Theatre (705-712 or 723)
  Location: Montclair, NJ; Boston, MA; Norwalk, CT.
  Length: 51 hours (17 weeks).
  Dates: September 1980-June 1985.
  Objective: To provide students with a framework for the history of the theatre and a basic analysis of dramatic literature.
  Instruction: This course encourages students to understand and appreciate theatre production through a selective study of plays and criticisms. Lectures, discussions and collateral readings emphasize the development of the theatre from Greek drama to the present. The course presents a history of theatre rather than an overview of how Theatre works. Field trips, films, and recordings supplement the course.
  Credit recommendation: In the lower division baccalaureate/associate degree category, 2 semester hours in Theatre or Drama (5/83).

Legal Office Practice (103)
  Location: All Katharine Gibbs Schools.
  Length: 30 hours (15 weeks).
  Dates: September 1973-Present.
  Objective: To familiarize students with legal terminology and legal office procedures.
  Instruction: Legal terminology, with accompanying Gregg Shorthand outlines, is presented to students. Dictation in specialized areas of law (e.g. real estate, litigation) is given. Course also covers procedures practiced in the law office and the use of legal forms.

Credit recommendation: In the lower division baccalaureate/associate degree category, 1 semester hour in Legal Office Practice (5/83).

Legal Secretary (540)
  Location: Montclair, NJ.
  Length: 51 hours (17 weeks).
  Dates: September 1980-Present.
  Objective: To familiarize students with legal terminology and the operational procedures of a legal office.
  Instruction: Students explore the functions of the secretary in the legal office. After learning general legal secretarial procedures, students develop a knowledge of specialized areas such as: real estate, litigation, appeals, and wills and estates.
  Credit recommendation: In the lower division baccalaureate/associate degree category, 2 semester hours in Office Procedures for Legal Secretary (5/83).

Machine Transcription (901)
(Machine Transcription/Word Processing Typewriting)
  Location: All Katherine Gibbs Schools.
  Length: 68 hours (17 weeks).
  Dates: September 1973-Present.
  Objective: To develop machine transcription skills which will enable students to transcribe dictated material in mailable form from machine dictation.
  Instruction: This course will develop machine transcription skills enabling students to transcribe material in mailable form at marketable production speeds. Students also apply English skills learned in Business Communication Courses.
  Credit recommendation: In the lower division baccalaureate/associate degree category, 2 semester hours in Transcription in Secretarial Science Program (5/83).

Mathematics for Business (533)
  Location: Boston, MA.
  Length: 51 hours (17 weeks).
  Dates: September 1982-Present.
  Objective: To teach students the application of mathematics in business and in their personal use.
  Instruction: Basics of business mathematics are covered through such topics as checking accounts, interest, inventory and depreciation. Students learn how to find practical solutions to mathematics problems that arise daily in business.
  Credit recommendation: In the lower division baccalaureate/associate degree category, 2 semester hours in Business Math (5/83).

Medical Office Practice (103)
  Location: All Katharine Gibbs Schools.
  Length: 30 hours (15 weeks).
  Dates: September 1973-Present.
  Objective: To familiarize students with the duties of the medical secretary and medical terminology.
  Instruction: Students receive practice in taking medical dictation: histories, medical reports, etc. They also learn the business procedures of medical offices and how to type medical forms.
  Credit recommendation: In the lower division baccalaureate/associate degree category, 1 semester hour in Medical Office Practice (5/83).

Modern American Literature 704, 706, or 722.
  Location: Montclair, NJ; Huntington, NY; Norwalk, CT.
  Length: 51 hours (17 weeks).
  Dates: September 1980-Present.
  Objective: To broaden the student's cultural perspective and to develop an awareness of literature as a reflection of American society.
  Instruction: Course includes selected readings in literature and provides students with an appreciation of major literary figures and their works, novels, and short stories, and poetry from the mid-nineteenth century to the present. Lecture and independent research encourage the development of critical judgement in evaluating the contribution of the writer to society.
  Credit recommendation: In the lower division baccalaureate/associate degree category, 3 semester hours in Literature (5/83).

Office Procedures (532)
  Location: All Katharine Gibbs Schools.
  Length: 51 hours (17 weeks).
  Dates: September 1981-Present.
  Objective: To help students develop skill in business procedures.
  Instruction: Course emphasizes office systems and procedures. Student also develops skills in basic secretarial tasks such as travel arrangements, planning itineraries, maintaining financial records, filing and records management. Class activities include simulated office workshop.
  Credit recommendation: In the lower division baccalaureate/associate degree category, 2 semester hours in Office Procedures (5/83). NOTE: This course overlaps materials in courses 501, 508, and 509 so a maximum of 2 semester hours should be given for any combination of these courses.

Oral Communication (310 or 308)
  Location: All Katharine Gibbs Schools.
  Length: 34 hours (17 weeks).
  Dates: September 1973-June 1985.
  Objective: To develop skill in preparing and delivering a well-organized speech.
  Instruction: Course covers main speech forms, elements of a communication model and audience analysis. Conflict between verbal and nonverbal communication is considered, together with listening and feedback techniques.

Class drills and exercises are given to help students prepare and deliver effective speeches.

Credit recommendation: In the lower division baccalaureate/associate degree category, 2 semester hours in Speech (5/83).

Principles of Marketing #543
Location: Norwalk, CT.
Length: 51 hours (17 weeks).
Dates: September 1981-Present.
Objective: To understand the consumer market and the art of the advertising.
Instruction: Course covers the fundamentals of marketing, including the consumer's role, pricing, advertising and promotion and distribution. Attention is paid to the special vocabulary used in marketing and advertising.
Credit recommendation: In the lower division baccalaureate/associate degree category, 3 semester hours in Principles of Marketing (5/83).

Secretarial Procedures (507 and 507.2)
(Administrative Secretary I and II)
Location: Boston, MA; New York, NY.
Length: 30 hours (30 weeks).
Dates: September 1973-June 1985.
Objective: To introduce the student to the secretarial and administrative work required in an office.
Instruction: Course focuses on simulated office situations demanding judgement and initiative, decision making, organizing and planning work, and meeting deadlines. Procedures for modern filing systems are stressed.
Credit recommendation: In the lower division baccalaureate/associate degree category, 1 semester hour in Secretarial Procedures (5/83).

Secretarial Procedures (501)
Location: All Katharine Gibbs Schools.
Length: 30 hours (15 weeks).
Dates: September 1973-June 1985.
Objective: To introduce student to a high level of secretarial and administrative work.
Instruction: Competencies necessary for carrying out administrative office duties are taught through individual and group projects and simulated office situations. Basic topics such as filing and telephone techniques are also covered.
Credit recommendation: In the lower division baccalaureate/associate degree category, 1 semester hour in Secretarial Procedures (5/83). NOTE: Course overlaps materials from courses 508-532 and 509, so a maximum of 2 semester hours should be given for any combination of these courses.

Secretarial Procedures (508 and 508.2)
(Advanced Secretarial Procedures I and II)
Location: All Katharine Gibbs Schools.
Length: 30 hours (30 weeks).
Dates: September 1973-June 1985.
Objective: To introduce student to a high level of secretarial and administrative work.
Instruction: Introduces students to changing role of secretary. Students learn a variety of business procedures including: filing, telephone technique, listing priorities, assembling facts, etc. so that they can correlate secretarial skills and administrative ability.
Credit recommendation: In the lower division baccalaureate/associate degree category, 1 semester hour in Secretarial Procedures (5/83). NOTE: This course overlaps materials covered in courses 501-509 and 532, therefore, a maximum of 2 semester hours should be awarded for any combination of these courses.

Secretarial Procedures (509)
(Administrative Procedures)
Location: Montclair, NJ; Boston, MA; New York, NY; Norwalk, CT.
Length: 51 hours (17 weeks).
Dates: September 1973-Present.
Objective: To introduce students to secretarial and administrative work required in an office.
Instruction: Course consists of administrative secretarial projects in a simulated office environment. Student learns basic office administrative skills to research and assemble data, set priorities, and organize tasks.
Credit recommendation: In the lower division baccalaureate/associate degree category, 2 semester hours in Secretarial Procedures (5/83). NOTE: This course greatly overlaps courses 501, 508, and 532, therefore a student should be granted a maximum of 2 semester hours for this subject.

Shorthand I (104)
Location: Montclair, NJ; Boston, MA; Norwalk, CT; Huntington, NY.
Length: 85 hours (17 weeks).
Dates: September 1973-Present.
Objective: To introduce student to theory and principles of shorthand and to develop basic skills in this area.
Instruction: Introduction to thorough knowledge of Gregg Shorthand with an emphasis on shorthand theory so that foundation is laid for taking dictation at advanced speeds in subsequent courses. Speed level in this course is 50 w.p.m. with standard 10% error.
Credit recommendation: In the upper division baccalaureate category or lower division baccalaureate/associate degree category, 3 semester hours in Shorthand (5/83).

Shorthand I and II (101, 102, 109, 110)
Location: All Katharine Gibbs Schools
Length: 290 hours (34 weeks).
Dates: September 1973-Present.
Objective: To develop to mastery level theory and performance of Gregg Shorthand.
Instruction: Course is designed to enable students to learn principles of Gregg Shorthand. Early emphasis is placed on sustained dictation speeds to facilitate accurate transcription. Student also learns to transcribe from dictation machines. Dictation discs are provided for out-of-class practice. Wireless dictation equipment is used for speed building. When sufficient speed and accuracy are developed, student concentrates on building good transcription techniques. Students must attain 100 w.p.m. with 10% standard error.
Credit recommendation: In the upper division baccalaureate category or lower division baccalaureate/associate degree category, 8 semester hours in Gregg Shorthand (5/83). NOTE: Shorthand I and II must both be completed for credit recommendation.

Shorthand II (105)
Location: Montclair, NJ; Boston, MA; Norwalk, CT; Huntington, NY.
Length: 85 hours (17 weeks).
Dates: September 1973-Present.
Objective: To master shorthand theory and to gain skill in constructing new outlines and to develop a constantly increasing shorthand vocabulary with accuracy and fluency.
Instruction: After a thorough review of the basic principles of Gregg Shorthand, course focuses upon building sustained dictation speed and increasing shorthand vocabulary. Students must attain at least 70 w.p.m. with standard 10% error.
Credit recommendation: In the upper division baccalaureate category or lower division baccalaureate/associate degree category, 3 semester hours in Shorthand (5/83). NOTE: Part of this course is listed separately on the Gibbs transcript as Introduction to Transcript (107) although it is taught as a single integrated course. Therefore, the student's record must also show completion of Introduction to Transcription for credit recommendation to apply.

Shorthand III (106)
Location: Montclair, NJ; Boston, MA; Norwalk, CT; Huntington, NY.
Length: 85 hours (17 weeks).
Dates: September 1973-Present.
Objective: To build upon previous theory and skill and to meet qualifying standard of at least 80 w.p.m.
Instruction: Dictation skills that meet demanding business requirements are further developed. Most of the course time is devoted to laboratory dictation exercises with supplemented lecture sessions. This is the third course in the Shorthand sequence and students must meet minimum speed of 80 w.p.m. with standard error.
Credit recommendation: In the upper division baccalaureate category or lower division baccalaureate/associate degree category, 2 semester hours in Shorthand (5/83). NOTE: Part of this course is listed separately on the Gibbs transcript as Advanced Transcription (107.2) although it is taught as a single integrated course. Therefore, the student's record must also show completion of Advanced Transcription for credit recommendation to apply.

Shorthand III and IV (103 and 104)
Location: All Katherine Gibbs Schools.
Length: 250 hours (34 weeks).
Dates: September 1973-Present.
Objective: To develop ability to take sustained dictation, using Gregg Shorthand, to reach a speed of 100 w.p.m.
Instruction: Speed development with accuracy is the emphasis of this course which begins with a thorough review of Gregg Shorthand. Transcription techniques are introduced and combined with correct English usage to prepare students to produce correspondence that will meet demanding business requirements. Students must attain dictation speed of 100 w.p.m. with standard error factor.
Credit recommendation: In the lower division baccalaureate/associate degree category, or in the upper division baccalaureate category, 8 semester hours in Shorthand (5/83). NOTE: Shorthand III and IV must both be completed for credit recommendation.

Stenoscript
Location: All Katharine Gibbs Schools.
Length: 85 hours (34 weeks).
Dates: September 1980-Present.
Objective: To develop knowledge of an alphabetic shorthand system.
Instruction: Students are taught stenoscript and build speed and skill through drill and exercise. In the course students learn to produce mailable business correspondence at a rate of 60 w.p.m. with 10% error on standard tests.
Credit recommendation: In the lower division baccalaureate/associate degree category, 2 semester hours in Stenoscript (5/83).

Typewriting
Location: All Katharine Gibbs Schools.
Length: 87 hours (34 weeks).
Dates: September 1980-Present.
Objective: To learn touch typewriting techniques and gain mastery of the typewriter keyboard.
Instruction: Course introduces students to basic type-

writing techniques and through intensive classroom drills develops speed and accuracy to achieve a level of 40 w.p.m. with 2% error on standardized tests.

Credit recommendation: In the lower division baccalaureate/associate degree category, 2 semester hours in Typing (5/83).

Typing I or III
(Courses 201, 203, 205, 207, 209, or 211)
Location: All Katharine Gibbs Schools.
Length: 153 hours (17 weeks).
Dates: September 1973-Present.
Objective: To learn correct typewriting techniques and mastery of keyboard in order to produce typewritten material with accuracy and speed.
Instruction: Course stresses proper typing techniques; mastery of keyboard, typing of business letters, tables, forms and reports. Student must pass five minute timing with minimum speed of 27 net words per minute (after error deduction).
Credit recommendation: In the lower division baccalaureate/associate degree category, 3 semester hours in College Typing (5/83). NOTE: Typing I and III are essentially the same course and are offered under a variety of course numbers as cited above.

Typing II or IV
(Courses 202, 204, 206, 208, 210, or 212)
Location: All Katharine Gibbs Schools.
Length: 153 hours (17 weeks).
Dates: September 1973-Present.
Objective: To develop typing speed and accuracy at the advanced level.
Instruction: In addition to typing business letters, forms, and reports, students receive training for a variety of business environments. Students must pass five minute timed writing with minimum speed of 50 net words per minute (after error reduction).
Credit recommendation: In the lower division baccalaureate/associate degree category, 3 semester hours in Typing (5/83). NOTE: Typing II and IV are essentially the same course and are offered under a variety of course numbers as listed above.

Word Processing Concepts (900)
Location: All Katharine Gibbs Schools.
Length: 68 hours (17 weeks).
Dates: September 1981-Present.
Objective: To acquaint students with the history of word processing and its evolution in the business office.
Instruction: Course presents the theory and evolution of word processing in the business world. The various computer capabilities and management systems for word processing are explored as well as the human aspects of utilization. This lecture course addresses the people, equipment, and systems involved in word processing in some detail.
Credit recommendation: In the upper division baccalaureate category or lower division baccalaureate/associate degree category, 3 semester hours in Word Processing Concepts (5/83).

Kepner-Tregoe, Inc.

Kepner-Tregoe, Inc. is a firm engaged in organization development and research. It was founded in 1958 by Dr. Charles H. Kepner and Dr. Benjamin Tregoe.

Kepner-Tregoe specializes in management and organization development with emphasis on problem analysis, decision analysis, performance analysis, situational leadership and strategy formulation. Kepner-Tregoe programs have been translated into 13 languages and have been used in 44 countries.

Students taking Kepner-Tregoe courses are from contracted companies. These participants choose between two options: obtaining college credit or receiving a completion certificate. Students taking courses for college credit undergo a proficiency evaluation (final examination) administered at the end of the courses(s). This final examination is developed, administered and graded by Kepner-Tregoe in Princeton, New Jersey.

Source of official student records: Program Coordinator, Kepner-Tregoe, Inc., P.O. Box 704, Research Road, Princeton, New Jersey 08540.

Additional information about the courses: Thomas A. Edison State College, Program on Noncollegiate Sponsored Instruction, Director of Special Programs, 101 West State Street, CN 545, Trenton, New Jersey 08625.

Apex
Location: Various locations around the country and select locations worldwide.
Length: 52-60 hours (1 week).
Dates: July 1981-December 1982.
Objective: To improve the managerial skills of persons in manufacturing or the service industry (banks, etc.).
Instruction: Covers situations appraisal, problem analysis, decision analysis, and potential problem analysis. Prework, lectures, and in-class participation are used. Course also includes a constant testing for understanding and further honing of management skills, application of management skills, and planning for their future use.
Credit recommendation: In the upper division baccalaureate or graduate degree category, 3 semester hours in Business Administration, Management, and/or Public Administration (7/81).

Fulcrum
Location: Various locations around the country and select locations worldwide.

Length: 26 hours (3 days).
Dates: July 1981-Present.
Objective: To enable participants (office workers and middle management) to improve their managerial skills.
Instruction: Covers situation appraisal problem analysis, decision analysis, and potential problem analysis. Prework, lectures, and in-class participation are used. Course also includes a constant testing for understanding and further honing of management skills, application of management skills, and planning for their future use.
Credit recommendation: In the lower division baccalaureate/associate degree category, 2 semester hours in Business Administration or Management (7/81) (4/87). NOTE: This course has been reevaluated and continues to meet requirements for credit recommendations.

Genco
Location: Various locations around the country and select locations worldwide.
Length: 52-60 hours (1 week).
Dates: July 1981-Present.
Objective: To improve the managerial skills of persons at the middle-management level in manufacturing.
Instruction: Covers situation appraisal, problem analysis, decision analysis, and potential problem analysis. Prework, lectures, and in-class participation are used. Course also includes a constant testing for understanding and further honing of management skills, application of management skills, and planning for their future use.
Credit recommendation: In the upper division baccalaureate degree category, 3 semester hours in Business Administration or Management (7/81) (4/87). NOTE: This course has been reevaluated and continues to meet requirements for credit recommendations.

Government Management Seminar (GMS)
Location: Various locations around the country and select locations worldwide.
Length: 52-60 hours (week).
Dates: July 1981-December 1985.
Objective: To improve managerial skills of government workers.
Instruction: Covers situation appraisal, problem analysis, decision analysis, and potential problem analysis. Prework, lectures, and in-class participation are used. Course also includes a constant testing for understanding and further honing of management skills, application of management skills, and planning for their future use.
Credit recommendation: In the upper division baccalaureate degree category, 3 semester hours in Management or Public Administration (7/81).

Problem Solving and Decision Making (PSDM)
Location: Various locations around the country and select locations worldwide.
Length: 1. 36 hours (3 days); 2. 52 hours (5 days: 3 days of PSDM and 2 days of application).
Dates: July 1981-Present.
Objective: To enable participants to improve their managerial skills.
Instruction: Covers situation appraisal, problem analysis, decision analysis, and potential problem analysis. Prework, lecture, and in-class participation are used. Course also includes a constant testing for understanding and further honing of management skills, application of management skills, and planning for their future use.
Credit recommendation: In the upper division baccalaureate category, 2 semester hours in Business Administration or Management (7/81) (4/87). NOTE: This course has been reevaluated and continues to meet requirements for credit recommendations.

Project Management
Location: Various locations around the country and select locations worldwide.
Length: 21 hours (3 days).
Dates: August 1986-Present.
Objective: To develop an understanding and application of principles of Project Management.
Instruction: This course discussed in depth the three phases of project management—project definition, project planning, and project implementation. It teaches techniques for setting project objectives, developing a work breakdown structure, allocating resources, and developing a project plan. The program covers technical tools such as network diagramming and human management techniques. Participants practice these techniques and case situations and then apply them to their own projects during the program.
Credit recommendation: In the upper division baccalaureate degree category, 1 semester hour in Project Management, Business Administration, or Management (4/87).

Managing Involvement (Formerly Telos)
Location: Various locations around the country and select locations worldwide.
Length: 22 hours (2½ days).
Dates: July 1981-Present.
Objective: To enable participants (top and middle management) to improve their managerial skills by using common sense approach to decide when and how to involve others in resolving a concern.
Instruction: Covers situational appraisal and managerial leadership behavior. Prework, lecture, and in-class participation are used. Course also includes a constant testing for understanding and further honing of management skills, application of managerial skills, and planning for their use.
Credit recommendation: In the upper division baccalaureate category, 1 semester hour in Business Administration or Management (7/8) (4/87). NOTE: This course

has been reevaluated and continues to meet requirements for credit recommendations.

Vertex
  Location: Various locations around the country and select locations worldwide.
  Length: 52-60 hours (4½ days).
  Dates: July 1981-December 1984.
  Objective: To improve managerial skills of persons in sales and marketing.
  Instruction: Covers situation appraisal, problem analysis. Prework, lectures, and in-class participation are used. Course also includes a constant testing for understanding and further honing of management skills, application of management skills, and planning for their future use.
  Credit recommendation: In the upper division baccalaureate category, 3 semester hours in Business Administration or Management (7/81).

Knight-Ridder, Inc.

Knight-Ridder, Inc. is a nationwide information and communications company engaged in newspaper publishing, business news and information services, electronic retrieval services, news graphics, and photo services, cable television, and newsprint manufacturing.

With 29 daily newspapers, it is the second largest newspaper company in the United States in terms of newspaper circulation (4.85 million, Sunday; 3.96 million, daily) and total revenues ($2.1 billion). Knight-Ridder's various information services reach more than 100 million people daily in 89 countries.

From 1984 to 1988, Knight-Ridder newspapers were honored to receive 25 Pulitzer Prizes, journalism's highest award—the greatest number received by any newspaper organization.

Knight-Ridder, Inc. offers many personal professional management development courses to its employees to help them accelerate their professional and managerial career development. Many of these courses are offered under the auspices of the Knight-Ridder Institute of Training, located in Miami, Florida. Though primarily for employees of Knight-Ridder, the courses are open to limited attendance by persons outside the company.

Source of official student records: Personnel Division, Knight-Ridder, Inc., 1 Herald Plaza, Miami, Florida 33101.

Additional information about the courses: Program on Noncollegiate Sponsored Instruction, The Center for Adult Learning and Educational Credentials, American Council on Education, One Dupont Circle, Washington, D.C. 20036.

Advertising Sales Management
  Location: Miami, FL.
  Length: 40 hours (1 week); residential; 8 hours pre-course work.
  Dates: November 1979-Present.
  Objective: To assist new sales managers in the development of managerial objectives, attitudes, and skills.
  Instruction: Emphasis is placed on learning managerial responsibilities in relation to selection and evaluation of new employees, acquisition of leadership skills, techniques for training and evaluating staff, development of selling by objectives programs, and how to utilize market research to determine consumer behavior. Participants also learn to correlate media strategy and decisions and the role of planning in advertising management. Methodology includes lecture, discussion, case studies, and practical exercises.
  Credit recommendation: In the lower division baccalaureate/associate degree category or in the upper division baccalaureate category, 3 semester hours in Marketing Management (8/82) (12/88). NOTE: This course has been reevaluated and continues to meet requirements for credit recommendations.

Application of Modern Computer Technology to Newspaper Operations
  Location: Miami, FL.
  Length: 40 hours (1 week); residential.
  Dates: October 1972-January 1989.
  Objective: To give newspaper managers a practical understanding of how computers and related electronic systems work and how they are used in business operations, circulation information systems, mailroom operations, and the newsroom.
  Instruction: A survey of topics in computer sciences including binary numbers, computer logic, hardware, software, and basic programs. Introduces business and newspaper applications. Methodology includes lecture, discussion, and laboratory workshops.
  Credit recommendation: In the lower division baccalaureate/associate degree category, 3 semester hours in Computer Science (2/78) (8/82) (12/88). NOTE: This course has been reevaluated and continues to meet requirements for credit recommendations.

Career Planning and Counseling
  Location: Miami, FL.
  Length: 40 hours (1 week); residential; 4 hours pre-course work.
  Dates: March 1982-January 1988.
  Objective: To identify skills and clarify values and objectives of managers, editors, and supervisors with the formulation of individual plans of action for professional growth. Participants are assisted in managing nonpromotable employees through counseling, motivation, and techniques in redirecting subordinates.
  Instruction: Emphasis is placed on the elements of an effective career plan, an approach to planning a career,

and overcoming career development problems. Participants develop an understanding of nonpromotability and techniques to revitalize static careers. Methodology includes lectures, discussion, skills inventories, exercises in value clarification, texts, and films.

Credit recommendation: In the lower division baccalaureate/associate degree category, 2 semester hours in Career Planning and 1 semester hour in Personnel Administration (8/82).

Circulation Management
Location: Miami, FL.
Length: 40 hours (1 week); residential; 4 hours of precourse work.
Dates: June 1973-Present.
Objective: To assist circulation managers and managers from other departments in developing key marketing-management skills.
Instruction: The management cycle; problem solving; consumer information systems; marketing and promotion problems are addressed. In-basket exercises and case studies are used to develop skills in applying appropriate management techniques to the solution of problems and improvement of operations of the circulation department.
Credit recommendation: In the lower division baccalaureate/associate degree category, 3 semester hours in Marketing Management (9/77) (8/82) (12/88). NOTE: This course been reevaluated and continues to meet requirements for credit recommendations.

Effective Human Relations
Location: Miami, FL.
Length: 40 hours (1 week); residential; 4 hours of precourse work.
Dates: June 1971-January 1988.
Objective: To provide managers with understanding, information, and skills in human relations within the organization.
Instruction: Varieties of managerial styles and behavior; motivation theories; means to develop effective relations with subordinates, peers, and supervisors in an organization. Methodology includes individual and team exercises, videotaped role play, case studies, and audiovisuals.
Credit recommendation: In the lower division baccalaureate/associate degree category or in the upper division baccalaureate category, 3 semester hours in Supervision (9/77) (8/82). NOTE: This course has been reevaluated and continues to meet requirements for credit recommendations.

Effective Management Skills
Location: Miami, FL.
Length: 40 hours (1 week); residential; 6 hours of precourse work.
Dates: October 1978-Present.
Objective: To develop effective management skills for new managers and editors.
Learning Outcome: Upon successful completion of this course, the student will be able to define the "process" school of management; understand and apply the management functions, including planning, organizing, directing, and controlling; and apply motivation and teamwork skills to the organizational environment.
Instruction: Course covers the management process; management functions, including planning, organizing, directing, and controlling; leadership versus management; management by objectives; the communication process; visionary leadership; motivation and group behavior; and the control process. Methodology includes lectures, case studies, self-assessment inventories, role playing, business games, team exercises, and audiovisuals.
Credit recommendation: In the lower division baccalaureate/associate degree category or in the upper division/baccalaureate category, 3 semester hours in Principles of Management (8/82) (12/88). NOTE: This course has been reevaluated and continues to meet requirements for credit recommendations.

Effective Newspaper Design and Graphics Editing
Location: Miami, FL.
Length: 40 hours (1 week); residential; 2 to 4 hours of precourse work.
Dates: October 1978-January 1989.
Objective: To develop the creative and technical skills of newspaper layout editors, picture editors, and design editors.
Instruction: Emphasizes hands-on experience in the organization, packaging, and layout of a newspaper. Course includes news hole efficiency, instant-art capabilities, type selection, tools of the trade, graphic capabilities of computer editing systems, redesign and prototype development, news-art department coordination, and photo, art, and graphics editing. Methodology includes lectures, discussions, hands-on kits for individual and team exercises, slides, and other visual aids.
Credit recommendation: In the lower division baccalaureate/associate degree category, 3 semester hours in Newspaper Design and Graphics Editing (8/82) (12/88). NOTE: This course has been reevaluated and continues to meet requirements for credit recommendations.

Financial Management for Non-Financial Executives
Location: Miami, FL.
Length: 40 hours (1 week); residential.
Dates: September 1972-Present.
Objective: To familiarize participants with the vocabulary and concepts of finance and accounting; to provide ability to interpret and analyze financial reports as a basis for decision making.
Instruction: Basic financial vocabulary; analysis of transactions; recording and summarizing of accounting

information; generally accepted accounting principles; financial reports; ratio analysis; cost and profit relationships; capital budgeting; ROI and the auditing and treasurer functions are covered. Methodology includes lecture, discussion, case studies, and practical exercises.

Credit recommendation: In the lower division baccalaureate/associate degree category or in the upper division baccalaureate category, 3 semester hours in Financial Management (2/78) (8/82) (12/88). NOTE: This course has been reevaluated and continues to meet requirements for credit recommendations.

Improving Personnel Selection
  Location: Miami, FL.
  Length: 40 hours (1 week); residential.
  Dates: March 1975-Present.
  Objective: To provide line supervisors with interviewing, testing, and selection techniques.
  Instruction: Preparation for and conduct of the interview; reference checks; test administration; making the selection decision; equal employment considerations are covered. Methodology includes lecture and emphasizes role playing, which is videotaped and critiqued.
  Credit recommendation: In the upper division baccalaureate category, 3 semester hours in Business Administration, General Management, or Personnel Administration (9/77) (8/82) (12/88). NOTE: This course has been reevaluated and continues to meet requirements for credit recommendations.

Interpersonal and Organizational Communications
  Location: Miami, FL.
  Length: 40 hours (1 week); residential; 4 hours of pre-course work.
  Dates: February 1972-January 1988.
  Objective: To provide line managers with information and experiences to increase their understanding and effectiveness in verbal and nonverbal communications.
  Instruction: Major emphasis is placed on one-on-one communications between a manager and individuals with whom he or she works. Specific interview situations relate to employment (hiring and exit), counseling, disciplining, and appraisal. Methodology includes case studies, team exercises, role playing and critique, and audiovisual aids.
  Credit recommendation: In the lower division baccalaureate/associate degree category, 2 semester hours in Communications or General Management (9/77) (8/82). NOTE: This course has been reevaluated and continues to meet requirements for credit recommendations.

Knight-Ridder Supervisory Training
  Location: Miami, FL.
  Length: 40 hours (1 week); residential; 8 hours of pre-course work.
  Dates: September 1977-January 1988.
  Objective: To develop the skills of experienced personnel directors, trainers, and department heads in education and training methodology.
  Instruction: Covers techniques of instruction, such as lecture, audiovisual, role playing, and case study. Selected current management topics are examined. Methodology emphasizes practical exercises.
  Credit recommendation: In the upper division baccalaureate category, 3 semester hours in Educational Methodology or Personnel Administration (9/77) (8/82). NOTE: This course has been reevaluated and continues to meet requirements for credit recommendations.

Making Effective Presentations
  Location: Miami, FL.
  Length: 40 hours (1 week); residential.
  Dates: August 1976-Present.
  Objective: To provide principles and practices of oral communication to top level supervisors.
  Instruction: Covers the communication process, preparing informal and formal presentations; presenting technical information, and the use of visual aids and effective presentation techniques. Managers acquire understanding of principles through self-instruction materials and case studies. Skills are developed by making presentations which are videotaped and critiqued.
  Credit recommendation: In the lower division baccalaureate/associate degree category or in the upper division baccalaureate category, 3 semester hours in Communications or Speech (9/77) (8/82) (12/88). NOTE: This course has been reevaluated and continues to meet requirements for credit recommendations.

Marketing (Classified—The Action Approach)
  Location: Miami, FL.
  Length: 40 hours (1 week); residential; 6 hours of pre-course work.
  Dates: March 1975-January 1989.
  Objective: To provide sales, advertising, and management training to managers and supervisors of classified advertising departments.
  Instruction: Covers the role of the classified manager, selecting and training sales people, measuring and evaluating their performance, the "positive selling" approach, creative copywriting, and sales incentives programs. Instructional methods include lectures, in-basket exercises, role playing, and workshops.
  Credit recommendation: In the lower division baccalaureate/associate degree category or in the upper division baccalaureate category, 3 semester hours in Marketing (9/77) (8/82) (12/88). NOTE: This course has been reevaluated and continues to meet requirements for credit recommendations.

Newspaper Production Techniques (Formerly Modern Newspaper Programs)
  Location: Miami, FL.

Length: 40 hours (1 week); residential.
Dates: April 1971-Present.
Objective: To provide an understanding of the integrated systems employed in newspaper production including direct experience with techniques, tools, and equipment.
Instruction: Covers ad service and editorial composition, engraving, stereotype, pressroom, and mailroom. Methodology includes some lecture but emphasis is on hands-on experience and tutoring by staff in each department.
Credit recommendation: In the lower division baccalaureate/associate degree category, 2 semester hours in General Business Administration, or in the upper division baccalaureate category, 2 semester hours in Graphics, Industrial Arts, or Journalism (2/78) (8/82) (12/88). NOTE: This course has been reevaluated and continues to meet requirements for credit recommendations.

Newsroom Management
Location: Miami, FL.
Length: 40 hours (1 week); residential; 2 or 3 hours precourse work.
Dates: October 1979-Present.
Objective: To meet the managerial needs of the newly promoted editor as well as reporters about to make the transition into management.
Instruction: Shows how to apply successful managerial techniques and managerial skills to the newsroom environment of the 1990s. Defines the role of the editor, styles of leadership, methods of evaluating employees and potential employees; examines how to analyze and resolve interpersonal problems, and budget planning. Methodology includes lectures, discussion, individual and team exercises, and audiovisuals.
Credit recommendation: In the lower division baccalaureate/associate degree category, or in the upper division baccalaureate category, 3 semester hours in Newsroom Management (8/82) (12/88). NOTE: This course has been reevaluated and continues to meet requirements for credit recommendations.

Organization and Team Development
Location: Miami, FL.
Length: 40 hours (1 week); residential; 3 hours of precourse work.
Dates: March 1977-Present.
Objective: To provide editors, general managers, and division directors with an understanding of individual and group behavior.
Learning Outcome: Upon successful completion of this course, the student will be able to understand how different management styles influence behavior; identify factors that influence individual and team behavior; develop organizational consensus; and identify aspects of effective management and leadership.
Instruction: Examines the forces influencing individual and team behavior, communication techniques, theories of leadership and motivation, self-analysis and evaluation, and planning strategies for change. Methodology includes lectures, individual and team exercises, case studies, films, and other visual aids.
Credit recommendation: In the lower division baccalaureate/associate degree category, or in the upper division baccalaureate category, 3 semester hours in General Management or Organizational Behavior (8/82) (12/88). NOTE: This course has been reevaluated and continues to meet requirements for credit recommendations.

Problem Solving and Decision Making
Location: Miami, FL.
Length: 40 hours (1 week); residential; 3 hours of precourse work and a a minimum of 8 hours of outside preparation during the course.
Dates: March 1971-Present.
Objective: To provide the manager with skills used in rational problem analysis, problem solving, and decision making.
Learning Outcome: Upon successful completion of this course, the student will be able to determine the appropriate method to analyze and verify the cause of a specific organizational problem; establish a criteria for decision making; and develop specific planning skills for decision making.
Instruction: Course covers a systematic and logical approach to information gathering and analysis, problem solving, cause analysis, decision making, plan analysis, and situation review. Methodology includes small group discussion and case studies. A film series is also used.
Credit recommendation: In the lower division baccalaureate/associate degree category or in the upper division baccalaureate category, 3 semester hours in General Management (9/77) (8/82) (12/88). NOTE: This course has been reevaluated and continues to meet requirements for credit recommendations.

Training, Developing, and Evaluating Your Employees
Location: Miami, FL.
Length: 40 hours (1 week); residential; 4 hours of precourse work.
Dates: December 1972-January 1989.
Objective: To develop in managers the skills needed to evaluate employee performance and to provide needed training and development.
Instruction: Programmed instruction, films, case studies, and role playing are utilized to teach supervisory techniques for observing and evaluating performance, determining development needs, conducting development interviews, and on-the-job training.
Credit recommendation: In the lower division baccalaureate/associate degree category, 2 semester hours in General Management (9/77) (8/82) (12/88). NOTE: This course has been reevaluated and continues to meet re-

quirements for credit recommendations.

Laubach Literacy Action

The Laubach Literacy Action (LLA) is the U.S. program of Laubach Literacy International. Started in 1968, LLA provides a channel for coordinating and exchanging volunteer literacy expertise and experience.

LLA has built its program upon the 40 years of Laubach Literacy activity with trained volunteers in the United States. Laubach Literacy International, founded in 1955, functions worldwide to teach adult non-readers to read and write.

LLA's tutor-training programs are delivered to over 700 affiliate literacy groups by 1,200 qualified trainers. Teaching materials, curricula, and certification standards for tutors and their trainers are coordinated by LLA.

Source of official student records: Laubach Literacy Action, Box 131, Syracuse, New York 13210.

Additional information about the courses: Program on Noncollegiate Sponsored Instruction, The Center for Adult Learning and Educational Credentials, American Council on Education, One Dupont Circle, Washington, D.C. 20036.

Teaching English to Speakers of Other Languages
Location: Local affiliates throughout the U.S.
Length: 40 hours (13 weeks); 15 hours classroom instruction (2 weeks), 21 hours practicum, and 4 hours supervision (11 weeks).
Dates: January 1976-Present.
Objective: To train volunteers to teach speakers of other languages oral and written skills in English.
Instruction: Covers techniques for teaching English as a Second Language. Presents the Laubach Way to English Series, principles of understanding cultural differences among learners, the speech sounds of English, and the practice of specific techniques for teaching oral and written English skills. Introduces tutors to use of additional methods and materials supplementary to the core curriculum useful in meeting the needs of individual learners.
Credit recommendation: In the lower division baccalaureate/associate degree category or in the upper division baccalaureate category, 2 semester hours in Education or Linguistics (1/76) (10/87). NOTE: This course has been reevaluated and continues to meet requirements for credit recommendations.

Teaching of Basic Reading and Writing Skills to Adult Nonreaders
(Formerly Teaching of Basic Reading and Writing Skills to Older Nonreaders)
Location: Local affiliates throughout the U.S.
Length: 40 hours (14 weeks); 12 hours classroom instruction (2 weeks), 24 hours practicum, and 4 hours supervision (12 weeks).
Dates: January 1976-Present.
Objective: To train volunteers to teach English-speaking adult nonreaders to read and write.
Instruction: Covers techniques for teaching reading and writing to the older nonreaders. Introduces tutors to writing simple stories for beginning adult readers, using a controlled vocabulary. Students learn to conduct tutorial teaching sequences using the Laubach Way to Reading Series. Students learn how to supplement core curriculum with a variety of teaching techniques and additional reading materials. Instruction includes lecture, discussion, role playing, a supervised practicum, and an examination.
Credit recommendation: In the lower division baccalaureate/associate degree category or in the upper division baccalaureate category, 2 semester hours in Adult Basic Education or Reading Education (1/76) (10/87). Course could also be used to meet requirements for graduate credit recommendations. NOTE: This course has been reevaluated and continues to meet requirements for credit recommendations.

Writing for New Readers
Location: Local affiliates throughout the U.S.
Length: 20 hours (3-4 days).
Dates: January 1976-October 1988.
Objective: To train volunteer tutors to write reading materials for beginning adult readers using the Laubach method.
Instruction: Develops skills in writing high-interest low-level materials that can be reproduced for basic literacy instruction. Students complete three major writing assignments and in class evaluate them for appropriateness of content and quality of writing. Assignments are preceded by discussion of the needs of the target audience, principles and methods of writing for that audience, use of appropriate word lists. Overview of production, copywriting, and distribution of materials. Prerequisite: Teaching of Basic Reading and Writing Skills to Adult Nonreaders or Teaching English to Speakers of Other Languages.
Credit recommendation: In the upper division baccalaureate category, 1 semester hour in Communications, Education, or English (1/76).

Massachusetts Bankers Association, Inc.

The Massachusetts Bankers Association (MBA) is a trade association which represents 270 mutual savings banks, stock savings banks, and commercial banks in Massachusetts, with assets totaling $125 billion. The MBA staff is organized in seven departments: Education and Management Development, Finance and Administration,

Legislative and Regulatory Affairs, Public Affairs and Marketing, Research and Planning, Member Services, and Trust. The Massachusetts School of Financial Studies (MSFS) was founded in 1961 as the School of Savings Banking. The name was changed in 1984 to reflect the program's increased emphasis on financial and management studies.

The Massachusetts School of Financial Studies is located at the Center for Executive Education, Babson College, Wellesley, Massachusetts. The Center's facilities include lecture theaters which feature audiovisual equipment and small break-out rooms which surround the lecture theaters. Students can be divided into small groups for discussion, problem solving, and case study activities.

The director of Education and Management Development is advised by an Education and Management Development Committee composed of senior bank executives. The Committee meets four times annually to discuss additions to the curriculum, program quality, and admissions and standards. Programs are changed and revised in response to industry trends and changes as well as proposed introduction of a subject of importance to the industry. During this process, consultants are used as resources in revision and development.

The MSFS selects faculty from leading academic, government, business, and financial organizations. An advanced degree or significant experience (over five years) in a specialty is required. The prospective faculty member is interviewed by the director of Education and Management Development, qualifications are weighed carefully, and recommendations from peers and students are considered for a faculty position. MSFS instructors are evaluated frequently and systematically. A faculty member is present during all class presentations, and students complete an evaluation for each segment of the program. The information is evaluated by the director, who then counsels the instructor.

Source of official student records: Vice President and Director of Education and Management Development, Massachusetts Bankers Association, Prudential Tower, Suite 550, Boston, Massachusetts 02199.

Additional information about the courses: Program on Noncollegiate Sponsored Instruction, The Center for Adult Learning and Educational Credentials, American Council on Education, One Dupont Circle, Suite 1B-20, Washington, D.C. 20036.

MSFS-Business Policy

Location: Babson College Center for Executive Education, Wellesley, MA.

Length: Length of the program is 294 hours. Due to the integrated nature of the material, credit should be awarded only upon completion of the full two years.

Dates: April 1982-Present.

Objective: To develop in the student an understanding of financial management problems in banks, and to expose them to a wide range of operating decisions.

Learning Outcome: Upon successful completion of this course, the student will be able to understand vocabulary and basic concepts of strategic planning; use a simulation model for strategic planning; and understand the relationship between corporate culture and successful creation and implementation of a plan.

Instruction: Course covers operational and strategic long range planning; definition of objectives, goals, and strategies; use of simulation modeling and cases to develop decision-making skills; and alternative perspectives of strategic planning. Methodology includes lecture, discussion, cases, simulation modeling, and small-group processes.

Credit recommendation: In the upper division baccalaureate category, 3 semester hours in Business Policy, Economics, or General Business (2/89). NOTE: Credit awarded only on completion of the full two-year program.

MSFS-Human Resource Management

Location: Babson College Center for Executive Education, Wellesley, MA.

Length: Length of the program is 294 hours. Due to the integrated nature of the material, credit should be awarded only upon completion of the full two years.

Dates: April 1982-Present.

Objective: To instruct students in the concepts and techniques necessary to understand and manage employees in an organization.

Learning Outcome: Upon successful completion of this course, the student will be able to demonstrate communication and career planning skills; analyze the dynamics of human behavior and conflict resolution in the workplace; and describe and explain management styles and the role of human resources management in an organization.

Instruction: Course covers business communication, recruitment, staffing and training, human relations and motivation, and salary and benefits administration. Methodology includes lecture, discussion, cases, simulation modeling, and small-group processes.

Credit recommendation: In the upper division baccalaureate category, 3 semester hours in General Business or Human Resource Management (2/89). NOTE: Credit awarded only on completion of the full two-year program.

MSFS-Investments

Location: Babson College Center for Executive Education, Wellesley, MA.

Length: Length of the program is 294 hours. Due to the integrated nature of the material, credit should be awarded only upon completion of the full two years.

Dates: April 1982-Present.

Objective: To provide students with a basic understanding of the principles of investments with special emphasis on money and capital markets, investment instruments, interest rate forecasting, and portfolio policy, with specific attention to bank investments.

Learning Outcome: Upon successful completion of this course, the student will be able to identify and explain investment characteristics, objectives, and risks; describe, calculate, and compare yields on various investments; and explain the function and importance of investment banking.

Instruction: Course is an introduction to risk and return, investment mathematics including yield calculations and present value analysis, money and capital market securities, and bank asset liability-asset management. Methodology includes lecture, discussion, cases, simulation modeling, and small-group processes.

Credit recommendation: In the upper division baccalaureate category, 3 semester hours in Business, Economics, or Finance (2/89). NOTE: Credit awarded only on completion of the full two-year program.

MSFS-Lending Fundamentals

Location: Babson College Center for Executive Education, Wellesley, MA.

Length: Length of the program is 294 hours. Due to the integrated nature of the material, credit should be awarded only upon completion of the full two years.

Dates: April 1982-Present.

Objective: To provide students with an understanding of the fundamentals of residential real estate and commercial lending.

Learning Outcome: Upon successful completion of this course, the student will be able to identify and describe the properties of residential mortgages; conduct preliminary financial analysis of residential and commercial borrowers; and describe and explain the workings of the secondary market for residential mortgages.

Instruction: Course covers for residential real estate lending: profitability of the mortgage product; first mortgage products; second mortgages and secured equity lines of credit; secondary mortgage market including underwriting, types of sales, servicing, and profit analysis. Course covers for the commercial lending market: analysis of credit risk; secured and unsecured loans; lines of credit; term loans; revolving credit agreements, and letters of credit. Methodology includes lecture, discussion, cases, simulation modeling, and small-group processes.

Credit recommendation: In the upper division baccalaureate category, 3 semester hours in Business, Economics, or Finance (2/89). NOTE: Credit awarded only on completion of the full two-year program.

MSFS-Marketing of Financial Services

Location: Babson College Center for Executive Education, Wellesley, MA.

Length: Length of the program is 294 hours. Due to the integrated nature of the material, credit should be awarded only upon completion of the full two years.

Dates: April 1982-Present.

Objective: To provide students with an understanding of the marketing function of a financial institution and the steps necessary to develop and implement marketing strategy.

Learning Outcome: Upon successful completion of this course, the student will be able to identify and describe market research and its uses; explain product development, pricing, and management; and describe the role of marketing in advertising and public relations.

Instruction: Course covers marketing promotion, pricing, product and market research, marketing strategy, product profitability analysis, and new product entry strategies. Methodology includes lecture, discussion, cases, simulation modeling, and small-group processes.

Credit recommendation: In the upper division baccalaureate category, 3 semester hours in Marketing or as a Business Elective (2/89). NOTE: Credit awarded only on completion of the full two-year program.

MSFS-Principles of Management

Location: Babson College Center for Executive Education, Wellesley, MA.

Length: Length of the program is 294 hours. Due to the integrated nature of the material, credit should be awarded only upon completion of the full two years.

Dates: April 1982-Present.

Objective: To instruct students in the concepts, techniques, and current issues in managing an organization.

Learning Outcome: Upon successful completion of this course, the student will be able to prepare long- and short-term plans for an organization; analyze the major functions of planning, organizing, leading, and controlling; and respond to pressures both inside and from outside the organization.

Instruction: Course covers strategic planning, decision making, delegating, stockholder relations, and ethics. Methodology includes lecture, discussion, cases, simulation modeling, and small-group processes.

Credit recommendation: In the upper division baccalaureate category, 3 semester hours in General Business or Management (2/89). NOTE: Credit awarded only on completion of the full two-year program.

Maynard Management Institute

The Maynard Management Institute provides training in industrial engineering techniques. The Institute teaches courses related to the engineering strategies developed by the late Dr. H.B. Maynard, the author of many books, including the *Industrial Engineering Handbook* and *Methods-Time Measurement*. The Methods Time Management (MTM) system and other systems using predetermined times for measuring work productivity (e.g., MOST—Maynard Operation Sequence Technique) serve as the basis for Institute courses. Courses also include other production control and cost reduction techniques as well as supervisory training. The objectives of each of the courses is to train people who will in turn help reduce production costs.

Source of official student records: Maynard Management Institute, 201 S. College Street, Charlotte, NC 28244.

Additional information about the courses: Program on Noncollegiate Sponsored Instruction, Thomas A. Edison College, 101 W. State Street, CN545, Trenton, New Jersey 08625.

Clerical MOST (M007/L008)
Location: Charlotte, NC; Pittsburgh, PA; Los Angeles, CA; and various client locations throughout the United States.
Length: 40 hours (Self-paced).
Dates: January 1983-Present.
Objective: To prepare students to use Clerical MOST for improving methods, developing accurate and consistent standards, establishing work loads, and improving workplace layouts in clerical areas.
Instruction: This course covers an introduction to work measurement and clerical MOST. It includes Sequence Models Definitions and Usage: general MOVE, controlled MOVE, equipment use, and tool use. There are specific applicator practice, systematic development of standards using clerical MOST, and an overview of MOST systems family.
Credit recommendation: In the upper division baccalaureate category, 2 semester hours in Industrial Engineering technical elective (6/88).

Fundamentals of Cost Reduction (M301)
Location: Charlotte, NC; Pittsburgh, PA; Los Angeles, CA; and various client locations throughout the United States.
Length: 40 hours (Self-paced).
Dates: January 1972-Present.
Objective: To provide students with a working knowledge of basic methods engineering concepts by emphasizing methods improvement and labor cost reduction.
Instruction: This multimedia course uses programmed instruction, filmed demonstrations, laboratory exercises, textbook readings, and discussion with instructor. The course introduces principles of scientific management and work measurement, plant layout, operations analysis, methods improvement, process charting, work sampling, and wage incentive systems.
Credit recommendation: In the upper division baccalaureate degree category, 2 semester hours in Industrial Engineering technical electives (3/82) (6/88). NOTE: This course has been reevaluated and continues to meet the requirements for credit recommendations.

Fundamentals of Methods Engineering and Time Study (M303)
Location: Charlotte, NC; Pittsburgh, PA; Los Angeles, CA; and various client locations throughout the United States.
Length: 80 hours (Self-paced).
Dates: March 1972-Present.
Objective: To provide training in methods analysis, fundamentals of stop-watch time studies, process charting, and cost reduction techniques.
Instruction: The multimedia course includes slide-tapes, filmed demonstration, programmed instruction, laboratory exercises, textbook reading, and discussion with instructor. The course outlines principles and applications of scientific management and work measurement including work measurement techniques, management methods, plant layout, operations analysis, methods improvement, process charting, time study procedures, and performance rating.
Credit recommendation: In the upper division baccalaureate degree category, 3 semester hours in Industrial Engineering technical electives (3/82) (6/88). NOTE: This course has been reevaluated and continues to meet the requirements for credit recommendations.

Fundamental Principles of Supervision (M401)
Location: Charlotte, NC; Pittsburgh, PA; Los Angeles, CA; and various client locations throughout the United States.
Length: 40 hours (Self-paced).
Dates: April 1979-Present.
Objective: To increase new supervisors' or managers' effectiveness by developing skills in using four basic resources: people, capital, materials, and machinery.
Instruction: This course develops understanding of the supervisors' role in the organization as well as the required job skills (e.g., delegating, planning, leading, producing) and develops skills in human and labor relations, budgeting and cost reduction.
Credit recommendation: In the lower division baccalaureate/associate degree category, 2 semester hours in Supervisory Management or Industrial Engineering free electives (3/82) (6/88). NOTE: This course has been reevaluated and continues to meet the requirements for credit recommendations.

Fundamentals of Time Study (M201)
Location: Charlotte, NC; Pittsburgh, PA; Los Angeles, CA; and various client locations throughout the United States.
Length: 40 hours (Self-paced).
Dates: June 1972-Present.
Objective: To enable students to understand the concepts of time study and performance rating and to become competent in setting standards using stop-watch methods.
Instruction: The multimedia course includes slide-tape,

filmed demonstrations, programmed instruction, laboratory exercises, textbook readings, and discussion with instructor. The course introduces principles and practices of scientific management and work measurement, time study procedures, performance rating, operations analysis, motion economy and work place layout; develops skills in time study, performance rating, and allowance applications.

Credit recommendation: In the upper division baccalaureate degree category, 2 semester hours in Industrial Engineering technical electives (3/82) (6/88). NOTE: This course has been reevaluated and continues to meet the requirements for credit recommendations.

Industrial Engineering Basics (M405)
Location: Charlotte, NC; Pittsburgh, PA; Los Angeles, CA; and various client locations throughout the United States.
Length: 40 hours (Self-paced).
Dates: June 1976-Present.
Objective: To provide managers with an understanding of basic industrial engineering concepts and techniques. Emphasis is on methods engineering concepts and work study techniques including understanding of MOST and Methods-Time Measurement using Predetermined Times and Time Study.
Instruction: The course introduces basic concepts of time study and predetermined times to the non-industrial engineer. Concepts include performance rating, methods improvement, process charting, operations analysis, work simplification, plant layout, and motion economy.
Credit recommendation: In the lower division baccalaureate/associate degree category, 2 semester hours in Introduction to Industrial Engineering or Business Management electives (3/82) (6/88). NOTE: This course has been reevaluated and continues to meet the requirements for credit recommendations.

Industrial Engineering for the Supervisor (M402, 403, 404)
Location: Charlotte, NC; Pittsburgh, PA; Los Angeles, CA; and various client locations throughout the United States.
Length: 40 hours (Self-paced).
Dates: January 1972-Present.
Objective: To enable supervisors to understand and participate in a progressive cost reduction program using industrial engineering techniques and approaches to work study.
Instruction: The course includes methods improvement, first-line manager's view of cost control, motion economy and work place layout, introduction to plant layout, operations analysis, performance rating, work sampling, operator training and understanding of work measurement principles and practice.
Credit recommendation: In the upper division baccalaureate category, 2 semester hours in Industrial Engineering or Business Management. (3/82) (6/88). NOTE: This course has been reevaluated and continues to meet the requirements for credit recommendations. NOTE: This course is not recommended for Industrial Engineering majors.

Maintenance Planner and Scheduler (M511)
Location: Charlotte, NC; Pittsburgh, PA; Los Angeles, CA; and various client locations throughout the United States.
Length: 16 hours (Self-paced).
Dates: February 1987-Present.
Objective: To provide participants with a knowledge of the proper way to plan and schedule maintenance work.
Instruction: This course covers an overview of maintenance management, work order system, job planning, scheduling, slotting and estimating exercises, and flow of work orders.
Credit recommendation: In the lower division baccalaureate/associate degree category, 1 semester hour in Industrial Engineering Basics or General Management elective (6/88).

Maxi MOST (L015)
Location: Charlotte, NC; Pittsburgh, PA; Los Angeles, CA; and various client locations throughout the United States.
Length: 32 hours (Self-paced).
Dates: January 1983-Present.
Objective: To prepare students to use Maxi MOST to develop accurate standards, improve methods, establish work loads, improve workplace layouts.
Instruction: This course covers a review of equipment handling sequences. Topics covered are: introduction of Maxi MOST sequence models, part handling, tool use, machine handling, exercises, extensive applicator practice, systematic development of standards using Maxi MOST, and the certification exam.
Credit recommendation: In the upper division baccalaureate category, 2 semester hours in Industrial Engineering technical elective (6/88).

Maxi MOST Computer Supplementary Module (L059)
Location: Charlotte, NC; Pittsburgh, PA; Los Angeles, CA; and various client locations throughout the United States.
Length: 24 hours (Self-paced).
Dates: June 1986-Present.
Objective: To prepare participants to use the MOST Computer systems Maxi MOST module.
Instruction: This course includes preparation for the certified computer MOST applicator to use the MOST Computer Systems Maxi MOST Module. Specific topics covered are: Work area layout, method description, keywords, part handling format, tool use format, machine

manipulation; movement of items within the work area, controlled MOVE sentence format, and Maxi MOST application.

Credit recommendation: In the upper division baccalaureate category, 1 semester hour in Industrial Engineering technical electives (6/88).

Methods Engineering (M302)

Location: Charlotte, NC; Pittsburgh, PA; Los Angeles, CA; and various client locations throughout the United States.

Length: 80 hours (Self-paced).

Dates: March 1972-Present.

Objective: To provide training in methods analysis, fundamentals of stop-watch time studies, process charting and cost reduction techniques.

Instruction: The multimedia course includes slide-tapes, filmed demonstration, programmed instruction, laboratory exercises, textbook reading, and discussion with instructor. The course outlines principles and applications of scientific management and work measurement, including methods time management (MTM), time study procedures, management methods, plant layout, motion economy, work place layout, process charting, job evaluation, and break-even analysis.

Credit recommendation: In the upper division baccalaureate degree category, 3 semester hours in Industrial Engineering technical electives (3/82) (6/88). NOTE: This course has been reevaluated and continues to meet requirements for credit recommendations.

Mini MOST Computer Supplementary Module (L057)

Location: Charlotte, NC; Pittsburgh, PA; Los Angeles, CA; and various client locations throughout the United States.

Length: 24 hours (Self-paced).

Dates: June 1986-Present.

Objective: To prepare participants for the certified MOST computer systems Mini MOST module.

Instruction: This course focuses on preparing entry data for generating Mini MOST analysis on the system and filing into the sub-operation data base. Determining the differences between basic and mini MOST. It includes work area, layout method description, keywords, general MOVE Sentence Format, and Mini MOST application.

Credit recommendation: In the upper division baccalaureate category, 1 semester hour in Industrial Engineering technical elective (6/88).

MOST Computer (L052)

Location: Charlotte, NC; Pittsburgh, PA; Los Angeles, CA; and various client locations throughout the United States.

Length: 40 hours (Self-paced).

Dates: January 1984-Present.

Objective: To prepare participants to use computer MOST, developing accurate and consistent standards, improve methods, and improving workplace layout establishing work loads.

Instruction: This course covers an introduction to work measurement and MOST. Specific topics covered are: General MOVE, controlled MOVE, tool use, equipment handling, and exercises. It also includes key words for all sequence models, work area, and work area layout; editing routines; mass update and utilities, certification exam.

Credit recommendation: In the upper division baccalaureate category, 2 semester hours in Industrial Engineering technical elective (6/88).

MOST Computer Systems (L051)

Location: Charlotte, NC; Pittsburgh, PA; Los Angeles, CA; and various client locations throughout the United States.

Length: 80 hours (Self-paced).

Dates: March 1984-Present.

Objective: To prepare participants to use MOST Computer systems to develop accurate and consistent standards.

Instruction: This course covers an introduction to work measurement and MOST. It includes General MOVE, controlled MOVE, tool use, equipment handling, exercises, keywords for all sequence models, work area, and work area layout, editing routines, standards data base, mass update, utilities and certification exam.

Credit recommendation: In the upper division baccalaureate category, 3 semester hours in Industrial Engineering technical elective (6/88). NOTE: This course includes material covered in Basic MOST (M001) course. If the student has already completed M001, only 2 semester hours of credit should be awarded for L051.

Predetermined Time Systems—MTM-1 (M101)

Location: Charlotte, NC; Pittsburgh, PA; Los Angeles, CA; and various client locations throughout the United States.

Length: 80 hours (Self-paced).

Dates: March 1972-Present.

Objective: To enable the student to use Methods-Time Measurement I (MTM-1), a system for analyzing activities completed in 30 seconds or less. The system is used to improve methods, develop accurate and consistent standards, establish work loads, and design workplace layouts. Successful completion of the course leads to certification as an MTM-1 applicator.

Instruction: The multimedia course includes videotapes, filmed demonstrations, programmed instruction, laboratory exercises, textbook reading, and discussion with instructor. The course introduces scientific management, work measurement, and motion economy principles; explains basic MTM motion; develops skills in simultaneous and combined motion application and methods improvement by using laboratory analysis and exercises, certifies students as MTM-1 applicators.

Credit recommendation: In the upper division baccalaureate degree category, 3 semester hours in Industrial Engineering technical electives (3/82) (6/88). NOTE: This course has been reevaluated and continues to meet the requirements for credit recommendations.

Predetermined Time Systems—MTM-2 (M105)
Location: Charlotte, NC; Pittsburgh, PA; Los Angeles, CA; and various client locations throughout the United States.
Length: 32 hours (Self-paced).
Dates: June 1972-June 1986.
Objective: To enable the student to understand the theory and practice of Methods Time Measurement II, a system for analyzing activities completed in 31 to 60 seconds. The system is used to improve methods, develop accurate and consistent standards, establish workloads, and design workplace layouts. Successful completion leads to certification as an MTM-2 applicator.
Instruction: The multimedia course uses programmed instruction, filmed demonstrations, laboratory exercises, textbook readings, and discussion with instructor. The course defines MTM-2 motion categories, introduces principles of application, develops skills through laboratory exercises, and certifies students as MTM-2 applicators.
Credit recommendation: In the upper division baccalaureate category, 2 semester hours in Industrial Engineering technical elective (3/82) (6/88). NOTE: This course has been reevaluated and continues to meet the requirements for credit recommendations.

Predetermined Time Systems—MTM2B (M106)
Location: Charlotte, NC; Pittsburgh, PA; Los Angeles, CA; and various client locations throughout the United States.
Length: 80 hours (Self-paced).
Dates: June 1972-June 1986.
Objective: To enable the student to understand the theory and practice of Methods Time Measurement I (MTM-1), a system for analyzing activities completed in 30 seconds or less, and to apply MTM-2 for analyzing activities completed in 31 to 60 seconds. The system is used to improve methods, develop accurate and consistent standards, establish work loads, and design workplace layouts. Successful completion leads to certification as an MTM-2 applicator.
Instruction: The multimedia course includes slid-tapes, filmed demonstrations, programmed instruction, laboratory exercises, textbook readings, and discussion with instructor. The course introduces scientific management, work measurement, and motion economy principles, develops skills in simultaneous and combined motion application and methods improvement through laboratory analysis and exercises, and certifies individuals as MTM-1 applicators.

Credit recommendation: In the upper division baccalaureate category, 3 semester hours in Industrial Engineering technical elective (3/82) (6/88). NOTE: This course has been reevaluated and continues to meet the requirements for credit recommendations.

Predetermined Time Systems—MTM3 (M107)
Location: Charlotte, NC; Pittsburgh, PA; Los Angeles, CA; and various client locations throughout the United States.
Length: 32 hours (Self-paced).
Dates: June 1972-June 1986.
Objective: To enable the student to use Methods Time Management III (MTM-3) independently or in conjunction with MTM-1 or MTM-2. MTM-3 is used on the non-repetitive operations of one minute or longer. The system is used to establish standards, develop standard data, improve methods, and determine work loads. Successful completion leads to certification as an MTM-3 applicator.
Instruction: The multimedia course includes slide-tapes, filmed demonstrations, programmed instruction laboratory exercises, textbook reading, and discussion with instructor. The course defines MTM-3 motions and application principles, develops application skills, and certifies completers as MTM-3 applicators.
Credit recommendation: In the upper division baccalaureate category, 2 semester hours in Industrial Engineering technical elective (3/82) (6/88). NOTE: This course has been reevaluated and continues to meet the requirements for credit recommendations.

Predetermined Time System—Basic MOST (L002 or M001)
Location: Charlotte, NC; Pittsburgh, PA; Los Angeles, CA; and various client locations throughout the United States.
Length: 40 hours (Self-paced).
Dates: June 1974-Present.
Objective: To provide students with the ability to apply Basic MOST, a method of work measurement using predetermined times. Using MOST, the student will be able to analyze work cycles of 30 seconds or more in order to improve methods, develop accurate and consistent standards, establish work loads, and design workplace layouts. The final examination leads to certification as a Basic MOST applicator.
Instruction: L002 uses a lecture/discussion format. M001 uses lecture, discussion, multimedia, and laboratory exercises.
Credit recommendation: In the upper division baccalaureate category, 2 semester hours in Industrial Engineering technical electives (3/82) (6/88). NOTE: This course has been reevaluated and continues to meet the requirements for credit recommendations.

Predetermined Time Systems—Mini MOST (L004)

Location: Charlotte, NC; Pittsburgh, PA; Los Angeles, CA; and various client locations throughout the United States.

Length: 32 hours (Self-paced).

Dates: June 1974-Present.

Objective: To prepare industrial employees to use Mini MOST, a predetermined time system for measuring work performances.

Instruction: Lecture/discussion format. Students can use the system to measure performance in work cycles of 31 seconds to 1 minute in order to improve methods, develop accurate and consistent standards, establish work loads, and design workplace layouts. The final examination leads to certification as a Mini MOST applicator.

Credit recommendation: In the upper division baccalaureate category, 2 semester hours in Industrial Engineering technical electives (3/82) (6/88). NOTE: This course has been reevaluated and continues to meet the requirements for credit recommendations.

Standard Data Development (L701)

Location: Charlotte, NC; Pittsburgh, PA; Los Angeles, CA; and various client locations throughout the United States.

Length: 24 hours (Self-paced).

Dates: June 1983-Present.

Objective: To prepare participant to develop standard data.

Instruction: This course covers an introduction to standard data concepts and understanding of benefits, values, and limitations of standard data. Promotes an understanding of the basic principles of standard data development. Provides specific training in the critical skills of recognizing and documenting essential input requirements for the effective development of standard data. It includes introduction to standard data concepts, data development, development of worksheets, work management manual, and occurrency frequency and group procedures.

Credit recommendation: In the upper division baccalaureate category, 1 semester hour in Industrial Engineering technical electives (6/88).

Supervisor's Cost Reduction (M304)

Location: Charlotte, NC; Pittsburgh, PA; Los Angeles, CA; and various client locations throughout the United States.

Length: 24 hours (Self-paced).

Dates: March 1972-Present.

Objective: To give supervisors an awareness of cost reduction by exploring techniques of profit improvement. Key emphasis is on methods improvement and labor cost reduction.

Instruction: The multimedia course includes slide-tapes, filmed demonstration, programmed instruction, laboratory exercises, textbook reading, and discussion with instructor. The course introduces theories and practices of labor cost reduction including cost reduction principles, motion economy and workplace layout, operations analysis, process charting, work sampling, operator training, and attitudes required for successful implementation.

Credit recommendation: In the lower division baccalaureate/associate degree category, 1 semester hour in Industrial Engineering technical electives. The course is recommended for nonmajors (3/82) (6/88). NOTE: This course has been reevaluated and continues to meet the requirements for credit recommendations.

Time Study Engineering (M202)

Location: Charlotte, NC; Pittsburgh, PA; Los Angeles, CA; and various client locations throughout the United States.

Length: 80 hours (Self-paced).

Dates: March 1972-Present.

Objective: To enable the student to apply standard industrial engineering methods analysis concepts by practicing time study methods using stop-watch techniques and applying work sampling techniques.

Instruction: The multimedia course includes programmed instruction, filmed demonstrations, laboratory exercises, textbook readings, and instructor discussion. The course introduces principles of scientific management and work measurement including time study procedures and practice, performance rating, operations analysis, motion economy and workplace layouts, work sampling and simplification, and process charting.

Credit recommendation: In the upper division baccalaureate category, 3 semester hours in Industrial Engineering technical electives (3/82) (6/88). NOTE: This course has been reevaluated and continues to meet the requirements for credit recommendations.

Universal Maintenance Standards (M501)

Location: Charlotte, NC; Pittsburgh, PA; Los Angeles, CA; and various client locations throughout the United States.

Length: 32 hours (Self-paced).

Dates: June 1966-Present.

Objective: To provide maintenance planners/analysts or other management personnel concerned with measurement and control of maintenance labor with the skills to apply Universal Maintenance Standards (UMS) techniques.

Instruction: The course provides appropriate work measurement training then introduces maintenance managers to and builds skills in developing universal data, establishing benchmark standards, using spread sheets in determining standard times for work orders, and comparing work content.

Credit recommendation: In the upper division baccalaureate category, 1 semester hour in Industrial Engineering technical electives (3/82) (6/88). NOTE: This course has been reevaluated and continues to meet the requirements for credit recommendations.

McDonald's Corporation

The McDonald's Corporation provides training for its management personnel at Hamburger University and Regional Training Departments. The courses offered are designed to improve the skills and knowledge of management personnel in the McDonald's Corporation. This includes specific on-the-job training as well as comprehensive skills and knowledge involved in restaurant management and food service equipment for various levels of management personnel.

Course delivery is carried out by McDonald's Corporation instructional and corporate staff within Hamburger University and at Regional Training Departments.

All McDonald's training courses are systematically designed and offered at either Hamburger University or at Regional Training Departments.

Classrooms, audiovisual support, and other student/instructor facilities have been designed to ensure an effective learning environment.

In addition to the training offered to management personnel, specialized training for home office staff is provided at the corporate headquarters in Oak Brook.

Source of official student records: Dean, Hamburger University, Ronald Lane, Oak Brook, IL 60521.

Additional information about the courses: Program on Noncollegiate Sponsored Instruction, The Center for Adult Learning and Educational Credentials, American Council on Education, One Dupont Circle, Washington, D.C. 20036.

Advanced Operations
Location: Hamburger University, Oak Brook, IL.
Length: 70 hours (2 weeks).
Dates: *Version 1:* January 1974-December 1983; *Version 2:* January 1984-Present.
Objective: To provide managers with a knowledge of restaurant management and food service equipment.
Instruction: Covers personnel management, skill development and equipment operation, maintenance, and troubleshooting. Individual lessons prepared around specific objectives augmented by audiovisual presentations, lecture-discussion workshops, and testing are used. (Prerequisites: Basic Operations, Intermediate Operations, Applied Equipment, and Management Development I, II, III.)
Credit recommendation: *Version 1:* In the lower division baccalaureate/associate degree category, 2 semester hours in Food Service Equipment; and in the upper division baccalaureate category, 2 semester hours in Personnel Management (10/80). *Version 1:* In the lower division baccalaureate/associate degree category, 1 semester hour in Food Service Equipment and in the upper division baccalaureate category, 3 semester hours in Restaurant Management (7/85). NOTE: This is the fourth course in a four-course sequence in food management training. This course has been reevaluated and continues to meet requirements for credit recommendation.

Advanced Restaurant Management
Location: Hamburger University, Oak Brook, IL.
Length: 35 hours (1 week).
Dates: *Version 1:* December 1977-December 1983; *Version 2:* January 1984-December 1988.
Objective: To strengthen students' decision-making ability in a variety of complex operational situations in restaurants.
Instruction: A senior level seminar that includes advanced management techniques, operational procedures, profits, cost and pricing, local store marketing and personnel administration. Lecture and discussion are used.
Credit recommendation: *Version 1:* In the upper division baccalaureate category, 2 semester hours in Seminar in Restaurant Management and Finance (10/80). *Version 2:* In the upper division baccalaureate category, 2 semester hours in General Management (7/85). NOTE: This course has been reevaluated and continues to meet requirements for credit recommendations.

Applied Equipment
Location: Hamburger University, Oak Brook, IL; McDonald's Regional Training Centers.
Length: 62½ hours (32½ hours of classwork in one week; and 30 hours of laboratory work in 90 days).
Dates: August 1980-Present.
Objective: To provide knowledge and skill in working with all components of food-service equipment, including equipment parts identification, basic operations, calibration, preventive maintenance, and troubleshooting.
Instruction: Presents key information on the operation and repair of equipment with emphasis on theory of systems as well as practical applications. After the classroom experience, students must complete a workbook which is designed to enrich and personalize their experience in their restaurant. A combination of classroom lecture and laboratory (in-store) hands-on instruction is used. (Prerequisites: Basic and Intermediate Operations plus Management Development I, II, and 3 months of III.)
Credit recommendation: In the lower division baccalaureate/associate degree category, 3 semester hours in Food Service Equipment Engineering (10/80) (7/85). NOTE: This is the third course in a four-course sequence in Food Management Training. This course has been reevaluated and continues to meet requirements for credit recommendations.

Area Supervisor's Development Program (Volume I)
  Location: McDonald's Regional Training Centers.
  Length: 120 hours (3 months).
  Dates: January 1980-Present.
  Objective: To prepare the newly promoted area supervisor to assume mid-management responsibilities and make a smooth transition from restaurant operations.
  Instruction: Covers personal development, transition from store to region, orientation, supervision, profit and loss, field operations, and human resources. Course is self-paced.
  Credit recommendation: In the lower division baccalaureate/associate degree category, 2 semester hours in Cooperative Education (10/80) (7/85). NOTE: This course has been reevaluated and continues to meet requirements for credit recommendations.

Basic Operations
  Location: Hamburger University, Oak Brook, IL; McDonald's Regional Training Centers.
  Length: 38 1/4 hours (1 week).
  Dates: January 1979-Present.
  Objective: To augment and complete management trainees' individualized instruction in basic operational functions of restaurant management.
  Instruction: *Version 1:* Course is divided into seven product areas, covering raw product, equipment operations, finished quality, and other areas covering production, personnel, maintenance, and general operation. Individual lessons prepared around specific objectives, lecture-discussion workshops, and testing. *Version 2:* Course is divided into topical areas covering raw products, production and quality control, communications, time management, training, service, security, personnel and maintenance. Lecture, discussions, and demonstrations are employed. (Prerequisite: Management Development Program I.)
  Credit recommendation: In the lower division baccalaureate/associate degree category, 2 semester hours in Food Service Management (10/80) (7/85). NOTE: This course is the first course in a four-course sequence in food management training. This course has been reevaluated and continues to meet requirements for credit recommendations.

Field Consultants
  Location: Hamburger University, Oak Brook, IL.
  Length: 30 hours (1 week).
  Dates: December 1975-Present.
  Objective: To analyze the operational level of the restaurant and to provide professional advice, methods, and direction to owners and operators in the areas of sales, financial, and reinvestment matters.
  Instruction: Covers owner/operator expectations, strategies of effective consultation and financial concepts. Lecture and discussion are used. (Prerequisite: Advanced Operations within the past 3 years.)
  Credit recommendation: In the upper division baccalaureate category, 2 semester hours in Food Service Management (10/80) (7/85). NOTE: This course has been reevaluated and continues to meet requirements for credit recommendations.

Field Consultant Development Program
  Location: McDonald's Regional Offices
  Length: 120 hours (3 months).
  Dates: February 1981-Present.
  Objective: To prepare the newly promoted field consultant to assume the responsibilities of a business management consultant representing the mutual interests of the independent operators and the parent company.
  Instruction: Under the direction of the field service managers, the field consultant is introduced to the various functions, and supporting personnel relative to the conduct of the position. Covers licensing, consultations with owner operators, financial reviews, specialized departmental orientations, and operator evaluation.
  Credit recommendation: In the lower division baccalaureate/associate degree category, 2 semester hours in Cooperative Education in Restaurant Management (7/85).

Intermediate Operations
  Location: Hamburger University, Oak Brook, IL; McDonald's Regional Training Centers.
  Length: *Version 1:* 25 hours (3 days); *Version 2:* 35 hours (5 days).
  Dates: *Version 1:* August 1978-August 1982; *Versions 2:* September 1982-Present.
  Objective: To analyze and reinforce the second assistant's instruction in the successful operation of a restaurant.
  Instruction: Covers personnel skills in orientation and training, knowledge of equipment function and maintenance, scheduling, and record keeping. Consists of individual lessons prepared around specific objectives and augmented by audiovisual presentations, lecture-discussions workshops, and testing. Prerequisite: Basic Operations plus three months' experience in management training and completion of the McDonald's Management Development II.
  Credit recommendation: *Version 1:* In the lower division baccalaureate/associate degree category, 1 semester hour in Food Service Management (10/80). *Version 2:* In the lower division baccalaureate/associate degree category, 2 semester hours in Food Service Management (7/85). NOTE: This is the second course in a four-course sequence in food management training. This course has been reevaluated and continues to meet requirements for credit recommendations.

Management Development Program I, II, III, & IV (Formerly 1. Management Development Program I, II, III, & IV; 2. Registered Applicants Program I & II).
   Location: Hamburger University, Oak Brook, IL; McDonald's Regional Training Centers.
   Length: *Version 1:* Approximately 6 months to 2 years; *Version 2:* 1 to 2 years.
   Dates: *Version 1:* September 1977-February 1985; *Version 2:* March 1985-Present.
   Objective: To prepare students to assume the responsibilities of food-service management by providing experience carrying out the functions of the trainee, second assistant, first assistant, and store manager/owner-operator.
   Instruction: Covers basic food service operations, basic management functions and applications, and advanced-management control. The trainee's performance is evaluated by supervisory personnel according to established performance objectives. On-the-job training is used.
   Credit recommendation: In the lower division baccalaureate/associate degree category, 6 semester hours in Cooperative Education/Coordinated Internship of a food service program (10/80) (7/85). NOTE: Students may receive the credit for either the Management Development Program or the Registered Applicant Program but not both. This course has been reevaluated and continues to meet requirements for credit recommendation.

Management Skills
   Location: McDonald's Corporation, Oak Brook, IL (McDonald's Headquarters).
   Length: 24 hours (one 3-hour session per week for 8 weeks).
   Dates: December 1978-January 1983.
   Instruction: Covers the nature of management, planning, organization, control, standards and appraisal, communication, motivation, and decision making. Classroom presentations, reading assignments, workshops, and general class discussions are used.
   Credit recommendation: In the lower division baccalaureate/associate degree category, 2 semester hours in Principles of Management (10/80).

Management Skills Development
   Location: Hamburger University, Elk Grove, IL.
   Length: 15 hours (2 days).
   Dates: September 1978-January 1983.
   Objective: To enable supervisors to develop skills in personnel practices, time management, setting objectives, and individual management.
   Instruction: Covers personal time planning, writing and evaluating work-related objectives, interpersonal communication skills, and analysis of managerial styles. Lecture, discussion, and practical exercises are used.
   Credit recommendation: In the lower division baccalaureate/associate degree category, 1 semester hour in Personnel Management (10/80).

Managing the McDonald's Team
   Location: McDonald's Regional Training Centers.
   Length: 43 hours (1 week).
   Dates: December 1979-May 1983.
   Objective: To provide store managers and area supervisors with information about and skills in the team approach to management.
   Instruction: Covers communication, delegation, motivation, managerial climate, leadership styles, development of individuals, training and performance appraisal, and goal setting.
   Credit recommendation: In the upper division baccalaureate category, 3 semester hours in Senior Seminar in Business Administration/Management (10/80).

Operations Department Head's Class
   Location: Hamburger University, Oak Brook, IL.
   Length: 34 hours (1 week).
   Dates: April 1980-Present.
   Objective: To provide midlevel managers with advanced training in the areas of food service leadership and operational decision making.
   Instruction: Covers personnel and performance appraisal, leadership, problem analysis, decision making, marketing analysis, owner/operator relations, and building construction. Lecture and case studies are used.
   Credit recommendation: In the upper division baccalaureate category, 2 semester hours in Advanced Food Service Management (10/80) (7/85). NOTE: This course has been reevaluated and continues to meet requirements for credit recommendations.

Personnel Orientation Program (PDP)
   Location: McDonald's Regional Offices.
   Length: 5 months covering 200 hours of independent work supervised by regional personnel managers.
   Dates: September 1983-Present.
   Objective: To introduce the student to human resource management practices in the field of restaurant management.
   Instruction: A combination of supervised and independent study covering a survey of human resource management practices in the restaurant industry.
   Credit recommendation: In the lower division baccalaureate/associate degree category, 2 semester hours in A Survey of Human Resource Management (7/85).

Personnel Recruiter Program (Volume I PDP)
   Location: McDonald's Regional Offices.
   Length: 9 months covering 192 hours of independent work supervised by regional personnel managers.
   Dates: September 1983-Present.
   Objective: To provide the student with a knowledge of organizational objectives and personnel hiring practices

with emphasis on salary administration, philosophy, salary ranges, and management opportunities.

Instruction: A combination of supervised and independent study covering the recruiting philosophy and practices of the restaurant industry.

Credit recommendation: In the upper division baccalaureate category, 2 semester hours in Human Resource Selection Management (7/85).

Personnel Assistant Program (Volume II PDP)

Location: McDonald's Regional Offices.
Length: 11 months covering 235 hours of independent work supervised by Regional Personnel Manager.
Dates: September 1983-Present.
Objective: To provide the student with a knowledge of human resources practices in the restaurant industry.
Instruction: A combination of supervised and independent study covering the general areas of human resources management towards the assumption of duties as a personnel manager.
Credit recommendation: In the upper division baccalaureate category, 2 semester hours in Human Resource Policies and Practices (7/85).

Personnel Supervisor Program (Volume III PDP)

Location: McDonald's Regional Offices.
Length: 11 months covering 235 hours of independent work supervised by regional personnel managers.
Dates: September 1984-Present.
Objective: To provide the student with the ability to perform effectively as a human resource manager.
Instruction: A combination of supervised and independent study covering recruiting, labor relations, wages, and salary administration, affirmative action, EEOC, career development planning and counseling, and benefits administration.
Credit recommendation: In the upper division baccalaureate category, 2 semester hours in Human Resource Supervision (7/85).

Personnel Manager Program (Volume IV PDP)

Location: McDonald's Corporation (Headquarters), Oak Brook, IL; McDonald's Regional Offices.
Length: 15 months covering 325 hours of independent work supervised by national personnel consultants.
Dates: July 1985-Present.
Objective: To provide the student with the knowledge and understanding of, and the ability to manage human resources in the restaurant industry.
Instruction: A combination of supervised and independent study covering all of human resource management facets at an advanced level in the restaurant industry.
Credit recommendation: In the upper division baccalaureate category, 3 semester hours in Advanced Human Resource Management (7/85).

Presentation Skills I & II

Location: Hamburger University, Oak Brook, IL.
Length: 15 hours (2 days).
Dates: January 1978-Present.
Objective: To identify techniques necessary for successful oral communication.
Instruction: Emphasizes use of eye contact, gestures, voice and emotion; managing distractor and distractions; responding to questions; and the major tasks of a facilitator. Student practice sessions feature videotape feedback and instructor critiques. Lectures and workshops are used.
Credit recommendation: In the lower division baccalaureate/associate degree category, 1 semester hour in Oral Communications or Public Speaking (10/80) (7/85). NOTE: This course has been reevaluated and continues to meet requirements for credit recommendations.

Supervisory Management Skills (Area Supervisor's Class)

Location: Hamburger University, Oak Brook, IL.
Length: 40 hours (1 week).
Dates: *Version 1:* September 1975-February 1982; *Version 2:* March 1982-Present.
Objective: To prepare students to successfully manage multiunit food service operations.
Instruction: *Version 1:* Covers personnel and food service management. Lecture and discussion are used. *Version 2:* Covers responsibilities of an area supervisor, labor relations, personnel management, leadership, accounting, security, operational procedures and time management. Lecture and discussion are used.
Credit recommendation: *Version 1:* In the lower division baccalaureate/associate degree category, 1 semester hour in Food Service Management and 1 semester hour in Personnel Management (10/80). *Version 2:* In the upper division baccalaureate category, 2 semester hours in Supervisory Management (7/85). NOTE: This course has been reevaluated and continues to meet requirements for credit recommendations.

1. Training Consultant's Development
2. Training Consultants

Location: Hamburger University, Oak Brook, IL; McDonald's Regional Training Centers.
Length: 1. Self-paced, approximately 20-25 hours; 2. Classroom, 31 hours (1 week).
Dates: April 1977-Present.
Objective: To instruct training consultants in presentation skills and to develop an understanding of the conceptual framework in which training activities take place.
Instruction: Provide practice in individual presentation skills and a general exposure to the areas of verifying training needs, appropriate training methods, effective use of visual aids, lesson plan preparation, and testing. Course 1 is self-paced; lecture, discussion, and practice teaching

exercises are used in Course 2.

Credit recommendation: In the upper division baccalaureate category, 3 semester hours in Educational Methodology (10/80) (7/85). NOTE: This course has been reevaluated and continues to meet requirements for credit recommendations.

Mercer County Vocational-Technical Schools - Division of Adult Education

The Mercer County Vocational-Technical Schools is a public county school system offering secondary and adult/postsecondary programs to area residents. The adult education division offers related instruction in technical education, apprenticeship training, trade and industrial education, health/medical related education and avocational program disciplines. Most adult programs are delivered on a part-time, two-night per week basis. Program offerings range from four months to four years in duration.

Students enrolled within the adult electrical program may be admitted as either formal apprentices or related trade and industrial students.

Source of official student records: Supervisor, Adult/Post Secondary Education, Mercer County Vocational Adult Evening School, 1085 Old Trenton Road, Trenton, New Jersey 08690.

Additional information about the courses: Program on Noncollegiate Sponsored Instruction, Thomas A. Edison State College, 101 West State Street, Trenton, New Jersey 08625.

AC Circuits
(a. Fundamentals of AC Theory)
(b. AC Circuit Characteristics)
Location: Trenton, N.J.
Length: a. 36 hours (12 weeks); b. 36 hours (12 weeks).
Dates: September 1980-Present.
Objective: a. To present the theory of AC circuits and electromagnetism. b. To present the related theory and related math to RL, RC, and RLC circuits.
Instruction: a. This course covers AC waveforms and generations, transformers theory and types and losses, inductance and capacitance, capacitive AC circuits and AC power transmission. b. This module includes RC and RL circuits, impedance, RLC circuits, resonance, resonant and filter circuits.
Credit recommendation: In the lower division baccalaureate/associate degree category, 3 semester hours in AC Circuits (6/86). NOTE: If student has only classroom instruction and no outside related work, only 2 semester hours.

DC Circuits
(a. Electromagnetic Fundamentals)
(b. Circuits Concepts)
Location: Trenton, NJ.
Length: a. 36 hours (12 weeks). b. 36 hours (12 weeks).
Dates: September 1980-Present.
Objective: a. To enable students to explain concepts of current and voltage; electricity and magnetism. b. To enable students to understand fundamental circuit concepts.
Instruction: a. This course covers a basic introduction to: atom and matter electron theory, current and voltage, magnetism/electricity, and basic related math. b. This course includes the following topics: resistance, Ohm's Law, series and parallel circuits, Kirchoff Laws, DC circuits.
Credit recommendation: In the lower division baccalaureate/associate degree category, 3 semester hours in DC Circuits (6/86). NOTE: If student has only classroom instruction and no outside related work, only 2 semester hours.

Electrical Machinery
(a. DC Machinery and Control)
(b. AC Motors)
(c. AC Machinery and Controls)
(d. Three-Phase Alternators)
Location: Trenton, N.J.
Length: a. 36 hours (12 weeks); b. 36 hours (12 weeks); c. 36 hours (12 weeks); d. 36 hours (12 weeks).
Dates: September 1980-Present.
Objective: a. To enable students to explain the operating principles of different types of generators and motors and to understand how to control them. b. To enable students to be able to select the proper type of motor. c. To enable the student to analyze problems in motor and control circuits. d. To enable students to explain the electrical operating principles of three phase alternators.
Instruction: a. Topics in this course are generator and motor operation, DC shunt and and series motors, DC compound wound motors, industrial control and DC rectifiers, and principles of automatic motor control. b. In this course the topics include single phase capacitor, repulsion, repulsion-induction, universal motor disassembly, squirrel cage and synchronous motors. c. In this course the topics include wound rotor motor control, circuit logic, reversing rotation and speed control, starting current and power factors, starting and running protection, testing A/C motors and troubleshooting. d. Topics in this course are principles of operation, types of alternators, frequency variation, DC field excitations, alternator output, two-watt meter and polyphase-watt meter method of power measurement, and transmission devices.
Credit recommendation: In the lower division baccalaureate/associate degree category, 4 semester hours in Electrical Machinery (6/86). NOTE: If student has only classroom instruction and no outside related work, only 3 semester hours.

Industrial Electricity
  (a. Transformers)
  (b. Polyphase Circuits)
Location: Trenton, N.J.
Length: a. 36 hours (12 weeks); b. 36 hours (12 weeks).
Dates: September 1980-Present.
Objective: a. To present the operating principles of transformers. b. To present the uses and advantages of each polyphase system.
Instruction: a. This course covers induced current, single-phase, delta-connected transformers, wye-connected tranformers, wye-delta-connected transformers, instrument and autotransformers.
b. Included in this course are two, three and six phase connections; calculation and correction of power failure; high voltage services, terminations and testing. Also safety considerations are covered.
Credit recommendation: In the lower division baccalaureate/associate degree category, 3 semester hours in Industrial Electricity (6/86). NOTE: If student has only classroom instruction and no outside work, only 2 semester hours.

National Electrical Code
  (a. Residential Wiring)
  (b. Commercial Wiring)
  (c. Industrial Wiring)
  (d. Lighting Systems)
Location: Trenton, N.J.
Length: a. 36 hours (12 weeks); b. 36 hours (12 weeks); c. 36 hours (12 weeks); d. 36 hours (12 weeks).
Dates: September 1980-Present.
Objective: a. To enable students to be familiar with the code requirements for installation of residential services and wiring systems. b. To enable students to be familiar with the code requirements for installation of commercial services and wiring systems. c. To enable students to be familiar with the code requirements for installation of industrial services and wiring systems. d. To enable students to design the installation of residential, commercial and industrial lighting systems reflecting code requirements if given a skeletal blueprint.
Instruction: a. This course covers calculations and installation for single dwelling and apartment services, utility company requirements, special circuits, electric heating and wiring of residential dwellings. b. This course covers calculations and installation of commercial services, panel board selection, short circuit protection, branch and appliance circuit installation and special circuits. c. Topics covered in this course include: plans and sitework, light industrial service installations, unit substations, feeder bus systems, panel boards, branch circuits, HVAC facilities and system protection. d. This course covers incandescent and electric discharge lighting, residential and commercial requirements and installations, low voltage and emergency lighting systems, security and sign lighting.

Credit recommendation: In the lower division baccalaureate/associate degree category, 4 semester hours in National Electrical Code (6/86). NOTE: If student has only classroom instruction and no outside related work, only 3 semester hours.

Survey of Basic Electronics
  (a. Solid State Digital Electronics I)
  (b. Solid State Digital Electronics II)
Location: Trenton, N.J.
Length: a. 36 hours (12 weeks); b. 36 hours (12 weeks).
Dates: September 1980-Present.
Objective: a. To enable students to identify and troubleshoot solid state and I C switching circuits. b. To enable students to identify and perform basic troubleshooting procedures on MOS type circuits and the microprocessor.
Instruction: a. Topics in this course include comparisons of discrete components and integrated circuits, combinational logic circuits and their implementation. Also covered are coding and decoding systems, pulse circuits, counters and shift registers. b. In the course CMOS devices and CMOS logic gates are covered. Sequential circuits, microcomputer systems and the central processor are studied. Memories, programming and operating cycles are also introduced.
Credit recommendation: In the lower division baccalaureate/associate degree category, 3 semester hours in Survey of Basic Electronics (6/86). NOTE: If student has only classroom instruction and no outside related work, only 2 semester hours.

National Academy for Paralegal Studies, Inc.

The National Academy for Paralegal Studies, Inc., is an educational institution offering paralegal training courses throughout the United States primarily on campuses of colleges and universities. The program is geared to the adult working student and is taught over a period of nine months. A student can enroll for the program throughout the year. The program is licensed or approved by the Department of Education in each state in which it is offered. The program is taught two or three evenings a week, three hours per session. All courses are taught by attorneys and legal professionals.

Source of official student records: Educational Coordinator, National Academy for Paralegal Studies, Inc., P.O. Box 835, 1 Lethbridge Plaza, Suite 23, Mahwah, New Jersey 07430.

Additional information about the courses: Program on Noncollegiate Sponsored Instruction, The Center for Adult Learning and Educational Credentials, American Council on Education, One Dupont Circle, Suite 1B-20, Washington, D.C., 20036 or Program on Noncollegiate

Sponsored Instruction, Thomas A. Edison State College, 101 West State Street, CN 545, Trenton, New Jersey 08625.

Basic Civil Law
  1. **Tort Law (A-101)**
  2. **Civil Procedure and Evidence (A-102)**
  3. **Family Law (A-105)**

Location: Various locations throughout the United States.

Length: 1. 15 hours; 2. 6 hours; 3. 15 hours.

Dates: 1979-Present.

Objective: 1. To master the differing forms of civil actions in law, called torts, including intentional actions, acts of negligence, and strict liability torts. 2. To learn the fundamental law of evidence and review the factors which affect the legal admissibility and relevance of all forms of evidence. 3. To review various areas of domestic relations including divorce, annulments and legal separations.

Instruction: 1. Course includes a thorough examination of all the elements necessary to create a solid cause of action. Consideration is also given to the many defenses available in the civil law including: contributory negligence, comparative negligence and assumption of risk. 2. Course covers basic concepts in the law of evidence including: burdens of proof, opinion vs. facts, character impeachment and the "Best Evidence" rule, and the problem of "Hearsay." 3. The course will also analyze other important issues in family law such as custody of children, equitable distribution and support.

Credit recommendation: In the upper division baccalaureate category or the lower division baccalaureate/associate degree category, 3 semester hours in Basic Civil Law. For credit recommendation, numbers 1, 2, and 3 must all be successfully completed (3/83) (4/89). NOTE: This course has been reevaluated and continues to meet requirements for credit recommendations.

Business Law 1
  1. **Corporations/Partnerships and Agency (B-202)**
  2. **Commercial Law (B-203)**

Location: Various locations throughout the United States.

Length: 1. 21 hours; 2. 15 hours.

Dates: 1979-Present.

Objective: 1. To present the various legal entities including the partnership, association, and the corporation. 2. To make the student acquainted with a basic understanding of the law of contracts, including an examination of an offer and an acceptance, the capacity to contract, and policies on the enforcement of contracts.

Instruction: 1. The course covers the rights and obligations of a corporation or other business institution. Corporate filing requirements, management and administration are also covered. Consideration is given to directions, dissolutions, mergers, and liquidations. The student also reviews the general principles of agency law including the master/servant theory, principal/agent and employer/contractor. 2. The student examines the major provision of the Uniform Commercial Code.

Credit recommendation: In the upper division baccalaureate category or the lower division baccalaureate/associate degree category, 2 semester hours in Business Law. For credit recommendation, numbers 1 and 2 must both be successfully completed (3/83) (4/89). NOTE: This course has been reevaluated and continues to meet requirements for credit recommendations.

Estates and Trusts (B-204)

Location: Various locations throughout the United States.

Length: 24 hours (8 weeks).

Dates: September 1978-Present.

Objective: To develop a basic understanding of estate planning and administration of decedents estates.

Instruction: Topics covered in this course are: intestacy, wills, probate, federal and state taxes, accounting and distribution of assets.

Credit recommendation: In the upper division baccalaureate category or the lower division baccalaureate/associate degree category, 2 semester hours in Estates and Trusts (12/83) (4/89). NOTE: This course has been reevaluated and continues to meet requirements for credit recommendations.

Estates and Trusts II (C-304)

Location: Correspondence Program.

Length: Independent Study.

Dates: October 1983-Present.

Objective: To further develop the basic understandings of estate planning and administration of decedents estates (begun in Estates and Trusts [B-204]).

Instruction: A further course in handling of decedents estates for those who have completed initial introduction to these topics in Estates and Trusts (B-204). Topics covered include: accumulation of assets, filing an inventory and payment of debts, federal estate taxes, gift taxes, state taxes, formal accounting, and distribution of assets.

Credit recommendation: In the upper division baccalaureate category or the lower division baccalaureate/associate degree category, 1 semester hour in Estates and Trusts (12/83) (4/89). NOTE: This course has been reevaluated and continues to meet requirements for credit recommendations.

Introduction to Criminal Justice
  1. **Legal Investigations (A-104)**
  2. **Criminal Law and Procedure (A-106)**
  3. **American Jurisprudence (B-201)**

Location: Various locations throughout the United States.

Length: 1. 6 hours; 2. 15 hours; 3. 9 hours.

Dates: 1979-Present.

Objective: 1. Overview of techniques employed to engage in successful investigative work including factual analysis and synthesis, gaining access to records and other documentation, and the ability to evaluate leads and sources. 2. A study of the fundamental basis upon which the criminal law exists and to distinguish the major elements of every crime. 3. A review of the basic governmental structure of our society and the impact government has on law-making.

Instruction: 1. Course presents an understanding of how to interview, prepare and evaluate witnesses for the purposes of present-day investigation or any future litigation. 2. Course includes a review of the major statutory and common law crimes—their various elements and problems of proof, and specifically covers all major property and personal offenses as well as those offenses which disturb the public order or the public good. Course also covers the numerous procedural issues that arise in the enforcement of criminal codes including all constitutional restrictions on police practice. 3. The course considers the varied sources of law in American society including the Bill of Rights, and the fundamental aspects of our court system in the United States including state, federal, and county jurisdictions. Also, the course delves into the numerous ethical problems which arise in the legal system, particularly the lawyer and the Code of Professional Responsibility.

Credit recommendation: In the upper division baccalaureate category or the lower division baccalaureate/associate degree category, 3 semester hours in Criminal Justice or Paralegal Studies. For credit recommendation, numbers 1, 2, and 3 must all be completed successfully (3/83) (3/88).

**Introduction to Legal Research and Writing
(Legal Analysis and Writing [B-205])**
  Location: Various locations throughout the United States.
  Length: 27 hours (9 weeks).
  Dates: 1979-Present.
  Objective: To familiarize the student with the essential skills needed to perform legal research and writing, including factual analysis and issue resolution, and Shepardizing.
  Instruction: Course covers various sources for research materials, such as digests, reporters, statutory materials and encyclopedias. Also covered are the proper approach to legal writing, how to prepare memoranda, how to utilize citations, how to evaluate precedent and to formulate logical legal conclusions. Finally there is extensive library research to solve numerous problems raised in the course. There are also extensive writing projects.
  Credit recommendation: In the upper division baccalaureate category or the lower division baccalaureate/associate degree category, 3 semester hours in Legal Research-Legal Writing (3/83) (3/88).

Legal Research and Writing II (C0301)
  Location: Correspondence Program.
  Length: Independent Study.
  Dates: October 1983-Present.
  Objective: To review and utilize legal materials available for research purposes.
  Instruction: This course is intended for those who have already completed Legal Analysis and Writing (B-205). An independent analysis of and concentrated practice in the use of the tools of legal research.
  Credit recommendation: In the upper division baccalaureate category or the lower division baccalaureate/associate degree category, 2 semester hours in Legal Research and Writing II (12/83) (4/89). This course has been reevaluated and continues to meet requirements for credit recommendations.

Personal and Injury Litigation - Torts II (C-303)
  Location: Correspondence Program.
  Length: Independent Study.
  Dates: October 1983-Present.
  Objective: To attain a thorough understanding of personal injury litigations and pleadings that pertain to pretrial and post-trial activities.
  Instruction: For students who have already had a course in basic civil law (e.g., Tort Law [A-101]), this course examines all aspects of personal injury law. Some of the areas reviewed will be the theoretical aspects of negligence, breach, mental and emotional damage, concepts of due care, causation, malpractice, and defenses to causes of action.
  Credit recommendation: In the upper division baccalaureate category or the lower division baccalaureate/associate degree category, 2 semester hours in Torts II (12/83) (4/89). NOTE: This course has been reevaluated and continues to meet requirements for credit recommendations.

Real Estate (C-302)
  Location: Correspondence Program.
  Length: Independent Study.
  Dates: October 1983-Present.
  Objective: To further study all forms of ownership and to review basic principles in the sale and exchange of all real estate.
  Instruction: This course is recommended for those who have completed Real Estate Transfer and Ownership (A-106). The course will substantially review all forms of ownership in and from present to future interests, processes of closing and settlement, agreement of sale, modification and adjustment of contracts, recordation, title abstraction, mortgages, and leasing. Course also covers surveys and recording.
  Credit recommendation: In the upper division bac-

calaureate category or the lower division baccalaureate/associate degree category, 2 semester hours in Real Estate. (12/83) (4/89). NOTE: This course has been reevaluated and continues to meet requirements for credit recommendations.

Real Estate Transfer and Ownership (A-106)
  Location: Various locations throughout the United States.
  Length: 21 hours.
  Dates: September 1978-Present.
  Objective: To develop an understanding of ownership of real property, transfer of such ownership, and ability to use legal forms, incident thereto.
  Instruction: Topics covered in this course are: overview of real property; deeds; liens and other incumbrances on real property; contracts for sale or purchase of real estate; financial instruments; search, examination, and title insurance; title closing; landlord and tenant relationships; surveys; mortgages and financing.
  Credit recommendation: In the upper division baccalaureate category or the lower division baccalaureate/associate degree category, 3 semester hours in Survey of Real Estate or Real Estate Laws or Principles of Real Estate (12/83) (4/89). NOTE: This course has been reevaluated and continues to meet requirements for credit recommendations.

National Association of Independent Fee Appraisers

The National Association of Independent Fee Appraisers was founded in 1961 as a nonprofit, professional society of real estate appraisers and is incorporated under the laws of the state of Arizona.

Today the association has chapters throughout the United States and Canada, and continues to grow not only in number, but also in stature.

The Association's objective is to raise the standards of the profession, gain recognition for "its members as qualified appraisers and promote fellowship among the appraisers." This further affords reasonable assurance to the public of the professional skill, integrity and responsibility of the membership.

Members of the association are comprised of full time professional real estate appraisers and others in related fields such as real estate, banking, building construction, governmental agencies and savings and loan associations.

Source of official student records: National Association of Independent Fee Appraisers, 7501 Murdoch Avenue, St. Louis, Missouri.

Additional information about the courses: Program on Noncollegiate Sponsored Instruction, The Center for Adult Learning and Educational Credentials, American Council on Education, One Dupont Circle, Washington, D.C. 20036.

Farm, Ranch, and Rural Appraisal
  Location: Various locations throughout the United States.
  Length: 21 hours (3 days).
  Dates: February 1980-Present.
  Objective: To train individuals in the principles and procedures of farm, ranch, and rural appraisal.
  Instruction: This course is designed to make participant aware of the reason for conclusions of value and to present a method of writing an acceptable farm appraisal. Students learn to effectively use data sources, inspection of the farm, three approaches to value; case studies and report writing.
  Credit recommendation: In the upper division baccalaureate or in the lower division baccalaureate/associate degree category, 1 semester hour in Farm, Ranch and Rural Appraisal (3/85).

Income Property Appraising
  Location: Various locations throughout the United States.
  Length: 24 hours (3 days classroom, plus extended independent studies).
  Dates: April 1976-Present.
  Objective: To train individuals in the principles and procedures of income property appraising.
  Instruction: This course is designed to give participants an understanding of the forces that create and affect value and to provide the techniques and methods to process income into value. Topics covered in this course include: three approaches to value and when to apply them, processing and analyzing income, capitalization, rate development, compound interest, techniques of capitalization and case studies. In addition to the classroom hours, there is an extended independent study culminating in a detailed narrative income property appraisal report.
  Credit recommendation: In the upper division baccalaureate or in the lower division baccalaureate/associate degree category, 3 semester hours in Income Property Appraisal (3/85). NOTE: To be eligible for the credit recommendation students must submit a narrative appraisal report on an income producing property and attain the Senior Member IFAS, designation.

Principles of Residential Real Estate Appraising
  Location: Various locations throughout the United States.
  Length: 24 hours (3 days classroom, plus independent study).
  Dates: October 1975-Present.
  Objective: To train individuals in the principles and procedures of residential real estate appraising.
  Instruction: This course covers the elements involved in

residential appraising. Topics include value, definition and kinds, forces and factors that influence value, principles and construction. The appraisal process is divided into identifying the problem, gathering data, approach to value, and correlation and final value. In addition to the classroom hours there is an extended independent study culminating in a detailed narrative residential appraisal report.

Credit recommendation: In the upper division baccalaureate or in the lower division baccalaureate/associate degree category, 3 semester hours in the Principle of Real Estate Appraising (3/85). NOTE: To be eligible for the credit recommendation students must submit a narrative residential appraisal report and attain the member, IFA designation.

National Association of REALTORS®

The National Association of REALTORS®, with offices in Chicago and Washington, D.C., provides a facility for education, research, and exchange of information for those engaged in the recognized branches of the real estate business.

The National Association of REALTORS®, through State Associations, Local Boards and Societies, Institutes and Councils (e.g., American Institute of Real Estate Appraisers, REALTORS® Land Institute, Institute of Real Estate Management, Society of Industrial and Office REALTORS®, and REALTORS® National Marketing Institute) offers programs of education on a nationwide basis to assist members to achieve higher levels of professional development and excellence in their field of specialized activity. These various programs lead to designations that are recognized throughout the real estate and related industries as indicators of superior achievement and knowledge.

REALTORS® is a registered collective membership mark which may used only by real estate professionals who are members of the National Association of REALTORS® and to subscribe to its strict Code of Ethics.

Source of official student records: Individual Affiliate, Council, State Association, or Society. Addresses are available from the National Association of REALTORS, 777 14th Street, N.W., Washington, D.C. 20005.

Additional information about the courses: Program on Noncollegiate Sponsored Instruction, The Center for Adult Learning and Educational Credentials, American Council on Education, One Dupont Circle, Washington, D.C. 20036.

AMERICAN INSTITUTE OF REAL ESTATE APPRAISERS

Basic Real Estate Valuation (EX 1A-2)
(Basic Valuation Procedures)
   Location: At various locations throughout the U.S. and Canada.
   Length: 30 hours (1 week).
   Dates: October 1973-June 1988.
   Objective: To enable students to explore the valuation techniques and procedures required for the appraisal of real estate.
   Instruction: Lectures, discussions, case studies, and laboratory exercises are employed to cover the valuation process, site valuation, cost estimating, depreciation, and cooperative and summary market data.
   Credit recommendation: In the lower division baccalaureate/associate degree category, 2 semester hours in Basic Real Estate Valuation (10/83).

Capitalization Theory and Techniques - Part A (EX 1B-1)
   Location: At various locations throughout the U.S. and Canada.
   Length: 30 hours (1 week).
   Dates: October 1973-June 1988.
   Objective: To familiarize students with the methods and techniques used in Real Estate Valuation with emphasis on income capitalization.
   Instruction: A lecture and drill problem course including case study on income/expense analysis treating real estate capitalization processes.
   Credit recommendation: In the upper division baccalaureate category, 2 semester hours in Capitalization Theory and Techniques (10/83).

Capitalization Theory and Techniques - Part B (EX 1B-2)
   Location: At various locations throughout the U.S. and Canada.
   Length: 30 hours (1 week).
   Dates: October 1973-June 1988.
   Objective: To familiarize students with the methods and techniques used in real estate valuation with emphasis on mathematics of yield capitalization.
   Instruction: Lecture and drill problem course including review and correction of homework problems covering annuity yields, AIREA financial tables, income analysis and projection, yield rates, and appraisal of lease interests.
   Credit recommendation: In the upper division baccalaureate category, 2 semester hours in Capitalization Theory and Techniques (10/83).

Capitalization Theory and Techniques - Part C (EX 1B-3)
   Location: At various locations throughout the U.S. and Canada.
   Length: 30 hours (1 week).
   Dates: October 1973-July 1987.

Objective: To familiarize students with the methods and techniques used in real estate valuation with emphasis on mathematical measurements and investment concept analysis.

Instruction: Lecture and drill problem course covering mathematical measurements and concepts of investment analysis using payback periods, net present value, internal rate of return, etc.

Credit recommendation: In the upper division baccalaureate category, 2 semester hours in Capitalization Theory and Techniques (10/83).

Case Studies in Real Estate Valuation (EX 2-1)

Location: At various locations throughout the U.S. and Canada.
Length: 30 hours (1 week).
Dates: October 1973-June 1988.
Objective: To enable the student to apply principles, theories, and techniques of capitalization approach to real estate valuation.
Instruction: Lecture and case study methods to analyze and solve the cases pertaining to evaluation of various and different property types.
Credit recommendation: In the upper division baccalaureate category, 2 semester hours in Case Studies in Real Estate Valuations (10/83).

Industrial Valuation (EX 7)

Location: At various locations throughout the U.S. and Canada.
Length: 30 hours (1 week).
Dates: October 1973-June 1988.
Objective: To provide participants with skills in the valuation of industrial properties with emphasis on market value of general purpose structures and user value of general purpose structures for limited purpose properties.
Instruction: Lecture, discussion, and problem solving exercises are used to demonstrate principles and techniques of analysis of industrial property valuation.
Credit recommendation: In the upper division baccalaureate category, 2 semester hours in Industrial Valuation (10/83).

Introduction to Real Estate Investment Analysis (EX 6)
(Real Estate Investment Analysis)

Location: At various locations throughout the U.S. and Canada.
Length: 30 hours (1 week).
Dates: October 1973-June 1988.
Objective: To provide the student with an overview of the field of investment analysis towards more advanced study in the field.
Instruction: Lecture, discussion, and laboratory covering investment criteria, economic risk, and cash flow forecasting.

Credit recommendation: In the upper division baccalaureate category, 2 semester hours in Introduction to Real Estate Analysis (10/83).

Litigation Valuation (EX 4)

Location: At various locations throughout the U.S. and Canada.
Length: 30 hours (1 week).
Dates: October 1973-June 1988.
Objective: To familiarize the appraiser with the techniques of preparation and testimony in the litigation process.
Instruction: Lecture, discussion, report writing, and case study in relation to Eminent Domain, highest and best use, damages and benefits, and easement acquisition in litigation proceedings.
Credit recommendation: In the upper division baccalaureate category, 2 semester hours in Litigation Values (10/83).

Principles of Real Estate Appraisal (EX 1A-1/8-1)
(Real Estate Appraisal Principles)

Location: At various locations throughout the U.S. and Canada.
Length: 30 hours (1 week).
Dates: October 1973-June 1988.
Objective: To provide students with an overview of the real estate appraisal process.
Instruction: Lecture, discussion, and interactive sessions covering fundamental appraisal principles and practical methods necessary to gather, interpret, and analyze relevant market data toward the valuation process.
Credit recommendation: In the lower division baccalaureate/associate degree category, 2 semester hours in Principles of Real Estate Appraisal (10/83).

Professional Appraisal Standards (EX 2-3/8-3)
(Standards of Professional Practice)

Location: At various locations throughout the U.S. and Canada.
Length: 20 hours (3½ days).
Dates: October 1973-June 1988.
Objective: To provide institute members and candidates an understanding of ethical conduct and standards, including the bylaws and regulations of the Appraisal Institute.
Instruction: Lecture, discussion, and case studies of professionalism, discipline, and regulation of the Institute.
Credit recommendation: In the upper division baccalaureate category, 1 semester hour in Professional Appraisal Standards (10/83).

Quantitative Methods (EX 11)

Location: At various locations throughout the U.S. and Canada.
Length: 30 hours (1 week).

Dates: October 1973–November 1986.
Objective: To provide the participant with the knowledge of the tools and applications of quantitative methods as applicable to real estate valuation.
Instruction: Lecture, workshops, classroom exercises, and drill problems designed to acquaint the students with quantitative techniques and applications.
Credit recommendation: In the upper division baccalaureate category, 2 semester hours in Quantitative Methods (10/83).

Real Estate Market Analysis (EX 10)
Location: At various locations throughout the U.S. and Canada.
Length: 30 hours (1 week).
Dates: October 1973–June 1988.
Objective: To provide the participants with understanding of the role of market analysis in feasibility studies, along with the ability to analyze, interpret, and present the data relating to market studies.
Instruction: Lectures, discussions, and workshops on the design and preparation of real estate market studies.
Credit recommendation: In the upper division baccalaureate category, 2 semester hours in Real Estate Marketing Analysis (10/83).

Residential Valuation (EX 8-2)
Location: At various locations throughout the U.S. and Canada.
Length: 30 hours (1 week).
Dates: October 1973–June 1988.
Objective: To enable students to explore the valuation techniques and procedures for the appraisal of residential real estate.
Instruction: Lecture, discussion, and case study are used to provide practical knowledge in the cost, income, and market value methods of appraisal techniques.
Credit recommendation: In the lower division baccalaureate/associate degree category, 2 semester hours in Residential Valuation (10/83).

Rural Valuation (EX 3)
Location: At various locations throughout the U.S. and Canada.
Length: 30 hours (1 week).
Dates: October 1973–June 1988.
Objective: To provide participants with analytical procedures and methods for interpreting appraisal data with special attention to farms, permanent plantings, livestock operations, and transitional lands.
Instruction: Lecture, discussions, case studies, and classroom exercises are used to analyze a variety of non-urban properties.
Credit recommendation: In the upper division baccalaureate category, 2 semester hours in Rural Valuation (10/83).

Valuation Analysis and Report Writing (EX 2-2)
Location: At various locations throughout the U.S. and Canada.
Length: 30 hours (1 week).
Dates: October 1973–June 1988.
Objective: To provide participants with skills in analyzing valuation situations and preparing appraisal reports.
Instruction: Lecture, discussion workshops, and in-class presentations are used to develop skills in individual appraisal report writing.
Credit recommendation: In the upper division baccalaureate category, 2 semester hours in Valuation Analysis and Report Writing (10/83).

REALTORS® NATIONAL MARKETING INSTITUTE

A. COMMERCIAL INVESTMENT REAL ESTATE COUNCIL

Advanced Real Estate Taxation and Investments (CI-103)
(Advanced Real Estate Taxation and Marketing Tools for Investment Real Estate)
Location: At various locations in the U.S.
Length: 40 hours (1 week).
Dates: *Version 1:* October 1973–May 1988; *Version 2:* June 1988–Present.
Objective: To provide the participant with the capability to recognize and advise on the tax implications of purchase and disposition of investment properties.
Learning Outcome: Upon successful completion of this course, the student will be able to describe the impact of taxation and investments; evaluate the tax entities and ownership forms involving real estate; and describe the tax implications of various financing methods.
Instruction: *Version 1:* Classroom exercises, simulations, and problem solving are used to provide an overview of federal tax, tax adjustment, and operations, dispositions, partnerships, corporations, and exchanges. *Version 2:* Course covers tax calculations relating to individuals and various ownership forms; taxes other than income taxes; tax accounting—terms and methods; basis and adjustments for property acquisition; and real estate operations and dispositions. Methodology includes lecture, discussion and problem solving utilizing various tax forms.
Credit recommendation: *Version 1:* In the upper division baccalaureate category, 3 semester hours in Advanced Real Estate Investment and Taxation (10/83). *Version 2:* In the upper division baccalaureate category, 2 semester hours in Taxation (6/88). NOTE: This course has been reevaluated and continues to meet requirements for credit recommendations.

Behavioral Aspects of Investment (CI-104)
(The Impact of Human Behavior on Commercial Investment Decision Making)

Location: At various locations throughout the U.S.
Length: 40 hours (1 week).
Dates: *Version 1:* October 1973-May 1988; *Version 2:* June 1988-Present.
Objective: To help students develop skills in technical and human relations aspects of commercial investments.
Learning Outcome: Upon successful completion of this course, the student will be able to have sufficient understanding of his/her role as a salesperson, humanist, and professional investment counselor; have sufficient self-awareness, as well as understanding of others for personal management and successful sales; and use basic communication skills.
Instruction: *Version 1:* Role playing and case studies are used to facilitate broker-client relationships and provide deeper understanding of investor motivations and communication skills. *Version 2:* Course covers the CCIM as a salesperson, humanist, and investment counselor; understanding ourselves; the process of understanding others; developing communicaiton skills; and effective management of yourself and the sales process. Role playing and case studies are used to facilitate broker-client relationships, and provide deeper understanding of investor motivation and communication.
Credit recommendation: *Version 1:* In the upper division baccalaureate category, 3 semester hours in Real Estate Investment (10/83). *Version 2:*
In the lower division baccalaureate/associate degree category, or in the upper division baccalaureate category, 2 semester hours in Real Estate Investment (6/88). NOTE: This course has been reevaluated and continues to meet requirements for credit recommendations.

Case Studies in Commercial Investment Real Estate Brokerage (CI-105)

Location: At various locations throughout the U.S. and Canada.
Length: 40 hours (1 week).
Dates: *Version 1:* October 1973-May 1988; *Version 2:* June 1988-Present.
Objective: To provide participants with computer skills required for analyzing commercial-investment real estate transactions and an understanding of commercial-investment brokerage.
Learning Outcome: Upon successful completion of this course, the student will be able to make decisions involving cash flow analysis, rates of return, and tax considerations in the formation of investment plans, and to utilize computer-based systems to analyze related problems and to develop plans.
Instruction: *Version 1:* Case studies, role playing, and microcomputers are used to develop decision-making skills involving properties based on cash flow analysis, rates of return, and tax consideration in the formation of investment plans. *Version 2:* Course covers investment choices, cash flow, capitalization and equity return rates, investor qualification, presentation skills, taxation and investment base determination. Methodology includes lecture, discussion, and many case studies.
Credit recommendation: *Version 1:* In the upper division baccalaureate category, 3 semester hours in Case Studies in Commercial Investment (10/83). *Version 2:* In the upper division baccalaureate category, 2 semester hours in Real Estate Management (6/88). NOTE: This course has been reevaluated and continues to meet requirements for credit recommendations.

Fundamentals of Real Estate Investment and Taxation (CI-101)

Location: At various locations in the U.S.
Length: 40 hours (1 week).
Dates: *Version 1:* October 1973-May 1988; *Version 2:* June 1988-Present.
Objective: To provide the student with the knowledge of investment goals and opportunities, and the skills with which to achieve these goals.
Learning Outcome: Upon successful completion of this course, the student will be able calculate amortization, determine appreciation and depreciation; balance financial variables, model cash flows; and manage an investment portfolio.
Instruction: *Version 1:* Lecture, discussion and laboratory sessions. Covers basic tools and techniques necessary to analyze and evaluate real estate, including cash flow analysis, net operating income estimation and valuation models. *Version 2:* Course covers value assessment, cash flow, capital recovery, depreciation, financial variables, capital gains, market analysis, liquidity, and taxation. Methodology includes lecture and discussion.
Credit recommendation: *Version 1:* In the upper division baccalaureate category, 3 semester hours in Fundamentals of Real Estate (10/83). *Version 2:* In the upper division baccalaureate category, 2 semester hours in Taxation (6/88). NOTE: This course has been reevaluated and continues to meet requirements for credit recommendations.

Real Estate Investment Analysis (CI-102)
(Fundamentals of Location and Market Analysis)
(Formerly Real Estate Investment Decisions [CI-102])

Location: At various locations throughout the U.S.
Length: 40 hours (1 week).
Dates: *Version 1:* October 1973-May 1988; *Version 2:* June 1988-Present.
Objective: To provide students with the ability to develop feasibility studies for real estate investment decisions.
Learning Outcome: Upon successful completion of this course, the student will be able to describe the economic models for eal estate, investment analysis; review urban

growth trends and relate these to real estate investment decisions; and analyze the impact of alternative methods of financing.

Instruction: *Version 1:* Case studies supplemented by lectures, discussions, and laboratory exercises are used to develop analytic skills relevant to students in defining markets, financial application, loans, leasing and special requirements of industrial and office space, and shopping centers, etc. *Version 2:* Course covers market analysis, location and demand analysis, forecasting and feasibility analysis, leasing alternatives, and financing methods. Methodology includes lecture, discussion, and case studies.

Credit recommendation: *Version 1:* In the upper division baccalaureate category, 3 semester hours in Real Estate Investment Decisions (10/83). *Version 2:* In the upper division baccalaureate category, 2 semester hours in Real Estate Investments (6/88). NOTE: This course has been reevaluated and continues to meet requirements for credit recommendations.

B. RESIDENTIAL SALES COUNCIL

Listing Strategies for the Residential Specialist (RS-201)
(Formerly Real Estate Sales [RS-101])
   Location: At various locations throughout the U.S. and Canada.
   Length: 14-21 hours (2-3 days).
   Dates: October 1973-June 1988.
   Objective: To provide the participant with an understanding of the communication process between seller and buyer in the promotion and exchange of real estate transactions.
   Instruction: Lectures, discussions, workshops, and training aids committed to the process involved in listing marketing and servicing of real estate transactions.
   Credit recommendation: In the lower division baccalaureate/associate degree category, 1 semester hour in Real Estate Sales (10/83).

Making Money Selling and Investing in Single Family Residences (RS-204)
(Formerly Homes and Condominiums as Investment Vehicles [RS-104])
   Location: At various locations throughout the U.S. and Canada.
   Length: 16-23 hours (2-3 days).
   Dates: October 1973-June 1988.
   Objective: To provide the residential sales associates with knowledge of the single-family home/condominium as an investment in today's economy.
   Instruction: Lecture, discussion, workshops, and laboratories provide the residential salesperson with the basic knowledge and skills necessary to analyze the investment potential of homes, condominiums, and townhouses.
   Credit recommendation: In the lower division baccalaureate/associate degree category, 1 semester hour in Homes and Condominiums as Investment Vehicles (10/83). NOTE: No credit should be given for this course if CI-102 credit is received.

Personal and Career Management for the Residential Specialist (RS-203)
(Formerly Time and Stress Management [RS-103])
   Location: At various locations throughout the U.S. and Canada.
   Length: 13-20 hours (2-3 days).
   Dates: October 1973-June 1988.
   Objective: To provide the participant with an understanding of organization and stress and time management.
   Instruction: Lectures, discussion, and films presentations concentrated toward the creation and implementation of management and communication skills.
   Credit recommendation: In the lower division baccalaureate/associate degree category, 1 semester hour in Time and Stress Management (10/83).

C. REAL ESTATE BROKERAGE COUNCIL

How to Improve Image and Increase Market Share (CRB-303)
(Formerly How to Plan and Implement Marketing Strategies for a Real Estate Business: Improving Image and Market Share [MM-303])
   Location: At various locations throughout the U.S. and Canada.
   Length: 20 hours (3 days).
   Dates: *Version 1:* October 1973-December 1985; *Version 2:* January 1985-June 1988.
   Objective: To provide participants with knowledge of activities and principles involved in basic tasks of marketing management with attention to developing, executing and evaluating effective, integrated programs towards meeting customer needs.
   Instruction: Lecture, discussion, and workshops are used to develop marketing management skills including marketing opportunity analysis, research and information systems, product/service and communications.
   Credit recommendation: In the lower division baccalaureate/associate degree category, 1 semester hour in Principles of Real Estate Marketing Management (10/83).

How to Manage the Finances: Risks of a Real Estate Brokerage (CRB-302)
(Formerly How to Manage the Financial Resources and Risks of a Real Estate Business: Evaluating Aspects of Management Decisions Before Implementation [MM-302])
   Location: At various locations throughout the U.S. and Canada.
   Length: *Version 1:* 20 hours (3 days); *Version 2:* 30

hours (4 days).

Dates: *Version 1:* October 1973-December 1985; *Version 2:* November 1984-June 1988.

Objective: To provide participants with the ability to achieve greater productivity from employees through human relations techniques.

Instruction: Lectures, workshops, and classroom exercises covering organizational strategies, motivational theories, communication leadership and transactional analysis involved in achieving increased effectiveness of human resources.

Credit recommendation: In the lower division baccalaureate/associate degree category, 1 semester hour in Personnel Administration (10/83).

How to Plan for Profit and Growth (CRB-301)
(Formerly How to Manage a Real Estate Office Profitably: Managing for Profit and Growth [MM-301])

Location: At various locations throughout the U.S. and Canada.

Dates: *Version 1:* October 1973-December 1985; *Version 2:* November 1984-June 1988.

Objective: To enable the student to develop the foundations for effectively managing a real estate brokerage office with special attention to planning, organizing, staffing, training, budgeting, and decision making.

Instruction: Lectures, workshops, and classroom exercises provide the student with an understanding of the basic functions of owning or operating a real estate office.

Credit recommendation: In the lower division baccalaureate/associate degree category, 1 semester hour in Office Management (10/83).

How to Recruit, Train, and Retain Real Estate Sales Associates and Increase Productivity (CRB-304)
(Formerly How to Recruit, Train, and Retain Real Estate Sales Associates: Leading, Communicating, Motivating the Team to Greater Productivity [MM-304])

Location: At various locations throughout the U.S. and Canada.

Length: *Version 1:* 20 hours (3 days) for MM-202 and 20 hours (3 days) for MM-204; *Version 2:* 40 hours (6 days) for MM-304; *Version 3:* 30 hours (4 days).

Dates: *Version 1:* October 1973-December 1985; *Version 2:* January 1985-June 1988.

Objective: To provide participants with the ability to achieve greater productivity from employees through human relations techniques geared toward motivating sales associates.

Instruction: Lectures, workshops, and classroom exercises covering recruitment, selection, organizational strategies, motivational theories, communication leadership and transactional analysis involved in achieving increased effectiveness of human resources.

Credit recommendation: *Version 1:* In the lower division baccalaureate/associate degree category, 1 semester hour in Personnel Administration for MM-202 and MM-204, respectively (10/83). *Version 2:* In the lower division baccalaureate/associate degree category, 2 semester hours in Personnel Administration (5/85).

Real Estate Business Decision-Making Computer Simulated Management Game (CRB-305)
(Formerly Computer Supported Marketing Techniques [MM-205])

Location: At various locations throughout the U.S. and Canada.

Length: 28 hours (4 days).

Dates: *Version 1:* October 1973-December 1985; *Version 2:* January 1985-June 1988.

Objective: To offer students a computer-based team analysis of the management decisions necessary to provide a profit objective in the residential real estate office.

Instruction: Computer-based team case study as affects the profit and loss function of the residential real estate office.

Credit recommendation: In the upper division baccalaureate category, 1 semester hour in Computer Supported Marketing Techniques (10/83).

Sales Strategies for the Residential Specialist (RS202)
(Formerly Real Estate Marketing [RS-102])

Location: At various locations throughout the U.S. and Canada.

Length: 14-21 hours (2-3 days).

Dates: October 1973-June 1988.

Objective: To provide the participant with an understanding of real estate transactional analysis, prospecting and servicing requirements.

Instruction: Lectures, discussion, workshops, and training aids covering the characteristics and requirements of the professional sales representative.

Credit recommendation: In the lower division baccalaureate/associate degree category, 1 semester hour in Real Estate Marketing (10/83).

SOCIETY OF INDUSTRIAL AND OFFICE REALTORS®

Industrial Real Estate (SIR-I)

Location: At various locations throughout the U.S. and Canada.

Length: 33 hours (1 week).

Dates: October 1973-June 1988.

Objective: To provide the participant with a knowledge of appraisal theory and assignment towards the marketing process in Industrial Real Estate transactions. Leases, lease forms, and negotiating processes are included.

Instruction: A one-week intensive lecture, discussion, workshop experience is included to provide the student an understanding of appraisal theory. The marketing and industrial process, leasing and negotiation in real estate transactions is included.

Credit recommendation: In the lower division baccalaureate/associate degree category, 2 semester hours in Industrial Real Estate I (10/83).

Industrial Real Estate (SIR-II)

Location: At various locations throughout the U.S. and Canada.

Length: 50 hours (1 week).

Dates: October 1973-June 1988.

Objective: To provide the student with a knowledge of marketing and financial processes involved in industrial real estate transactions to include a review of market trends, buy/lease considerations and fundamentals of investment analysis.

Instruction: An intensive one-week period of lectures, discussions, and case studies designed to provide an understanding of selected markets and financial processes involved in industrial real estate transactions.

Credit recommendation: In the upper division baccalaureate category, 3 semester hours in Industrial Real Estate II (10/83).

Office Leasing Administration (SIR-III)

Location: At various locations throughout the U.S. and Canada.

Length: 45 hours (1 week).

Dates: October 1973-June 1988.

Objective: To provide the participant with an understanding of office leasing, its market, inventory systems, identifying and qualifying prospects and the negotiation process.

Instruction: A one-week intensive period of lectures, discussions, and workshops designed to provide for the understanding of office leasing processes and administration.

Credit recommendation: In the upper division baccalaureate category, 3 semester hours in Office Leasing Administration (10/83).

REALTORS® LAND INSTITUTE

Agricultural Land Brokerage (FLI-220)

Location: At various locations throughout the U.S. and Canada.

Length: 24 hours (4 days).

Dates: October 1973-June 1988.

Objective: To provide the participant with an understanding of crop and product classification, financing, farm management, and future trends.

Instruction: Lecture, discussion and problem solving techniques are used to analyze the current agricultural market with special attention to infrastructure, timing, and future trends.

Credit recommendation: In the lower division baccalaureate/associate degree category, 1 semester hour in Agricultural Land Brokerage (10/83).

Agricultural Land Valuation (FLI-161)
(Establishing Market Value of Agricultural Land)

Location: At various locations throughout the U.S. and Canada.

Length: 12 hours (1½ days).

Dates: October 1973-June 1988.

Objective: To provide the participant with a knowledge of the agricultural land market and the methods needed to analyze it.

Instruction: Lecture and discussion techniques are utilized towards an understanding of the practical aspects of rural property.

Credit recommendation: In the lower division baccalaureate/associate degree category, 1 semester hour in Agricultural Land Valuation (10/83).

Alternative Real Estate Marketing Techniques (FLI-163)
(Exchanging and Creative Marketing Techniques)

Location: At various locations throughout the U.S. and Canada.

Length: 18 hours (3 days).

Dates: October 1973-April 1986.

Objective: To provide the participant with the ability to develop nontraditional techniques of marketing; with special attention to property exchange and pyramiding.

Instruction: Lecture and discussion are used to acquaint the student with non-monetary property marketing techniques.

Credit recommendation: In the lower division baccalaureate/associate degree category, 1 semester hour in Real Estate Marketing (10/83).

Brokering Transitional Properties (FLI-230)

Location: At various locations throughout the U.S. and Canada.

Length: 18 hours (3 days).

Dates: October 1973-June 1988.

Objective: To acquaint the participant with the knowledge of marketing analysis, feasibility studies, methods of acquisition, financing, construction and the final marketing of the real estate property.

Instruction: Lecture and case study approach covering marketing analysis, feasibility studies, methods of acquisition, financing, construction, and final marketing of a real estate project. The use of computers for analysis and land inventory is included.

Credit recommendation: In the lower division baccalaureate/associate degree category, 1 semester hour in Property Brokering (10/83).

Estate Planning (FLI-160)
(Personal Estate Planning)
Location: At various locations throughout the U.S. and Canada.
Length: 12 hours (2 days).
Dates: October 1973-April 1985.
Objective: To provide the participant with an understanding of tax and legal aspects of accumulation, conservation, and disposition of real property and other personal assets.
Instruction: Lectures and discussions designed to provide the student with the ability to recognize and deal with client needs in the areas of ownership, estate and trust.
Credit recommendation: In the lower division baccalaureate/associate degree category, 1 semester hour in Estate Planning (10/83).

Introduction to Federal Taxes and Real Estate (FLI-166)
Location: At various locations throughout the U.S. and Canada.
Length: 18 hours (3 days).
Dates: October 1973-June 1988.
Objective: To provide the participants with the tax knowledge that is vital to the success of the REALTOR.
Instruction: Lectures and discussion to alert the REALTOR to new possibilities of using the tax laws and regulations to benefit participants involved in real estate transactions.
Credit recommendation: In the lower division baccalaureate/associate degree category, 1 semester hour in Federal Taxation and Real Estate (10/83).

Land Return Analysis (FLI-164)
Location: At various locations throughout the U.S. and Canada.
Length: 18 hours (3 days).
Dates: October 1973-June 1988.
Objective: To introduce the student to discounted cash flow analysis involving present and future values of investments.
Instruction: Lecture and case study approach pertaining to discounted cash flow analysis to establish criterion for comparison of alternative investments.
Credit recommendation: In the lower division baccalaureate/associate degree category, 1 semester hour in Land Return Analysis (10/83).

EDUCATION DIVISION

Real Estate Securities Licensing Course (22L)
Location: At various locations throughout the U.S. and Canada.
Length: 22 hours (3½ days).
Dates: October 1973-February 1986.
Objective: To prepare the student for the NASD Series 22 exam, as well as providing background information on tax-advantaged investments.
Instruction: Primarily a lecture course designed to assist students in preparing for the NASD Series 22 exam.
Credit recommendation: In the lower division baccalaureate/associate degree category, 1 semester hour in Real Estate Securities Licensing (10/83). NOTE: Credit for this course excludes credit for Self Study Program, provided the NASD Series 22L examination is passed.

Tax Advantaged Investments - Self Study Program
Location: Self Study.
Length: 40 hours.
Dates: October 1973-January 1987.
Objective: To provide students with a working knowledge of tax-advantaged investments and direct participation programs and to assist students in preparing for the NASD Series 22L examination.
Instruction: A home study course designed to cover various forms of ownership, products, tax implications, and regulations.
Credit recommendation: In the lower division baccalaureate/associate degree category, 1 semester hour in Tax Advantaged Investments - Self Study (10/83). NOTE: Credit for this course is based on the student's passing the NASD 22L examination.

INSTITUTE OF REAL ESTATE MANAGEMENT

Asset Management (703)
Location: At various locations throughout the U.S. and Canada.
Length: 31 hours (1 week).
Dates: October 1973-December 1983.
Objective: The course is designed to introduce the student to current techniques and trends involved in the evaluation of institutional portfolios.
Instruction: Lecture and discussion pertaining to real estate, financing, taxation, and ownership in the context of world economic influences.
Credit recommendation: In the upper division baccalaureate category, 2 semester hours in Real Estate Asset Management (10/83).

Management Practices and Techniques (702)
(Advanced Management Practices and Techniques)
Location: At various locations throughout the U.S. and Canada.
Length: *Version 1:* 31 hours (1 week); *Version 2:* 40 hours (5 days).
Dates: *Version 1:* October 1973-May 1988; *Version 2:* June 1988-Present.
Objective: *Version 1:* The course is designed to upgrade the management skills of CPM1 executives through lecture, group discussion and group exercises. *Version 2:* To expand the management skills of CPM1 executives.

Learning Outcome: Upon successful completion of this course, the student will be able to utilize work groups in formulating decisions; engage in strategic planning, and effectively manage people and time; and delegate authority.

Instruction: *Version 1:* Primarily a lecture and discussion course for executives including workshop on setting strategy and building organizational structure in participants' companies. *Version 2:* Course covers strategic planning, exploring corporate cultural, work groups, employee motivation, conflict management, organizational performance and complex decision management. Methodology includes lecture, discussion, and case studies.

Credit recommendation: *Version 1:* In the upper division baccalaureate category, 2 semester hours in General Management (10/83). *Version 2:* In the lower division baccalaureate/associate degree category or in the upper division baccalaureate category, 2 semester hours in Management (6/88). NOTE: This course has been reevaluated and continues to meet requirements for credit recommendations.

Property Management (RM-304)
(Condominiums and Cooperative Associations)
(Principles of Condominimum and Cooperative Association Management)

Location: At various locations throughout the U.S. and Canada.

Length: 33 hours (1 week).

Dates: October 1973-December 1984.

Objective: To provide the student with operational skills required to manage condominiums and cooperative associations.

Instruction: Lecture, classroom exercises, simulation, and problem solving involving management agreements, rental analysis, leases, financial management, and maintenance of condominiums and cooperative associations.

Credit recommendation: In the upper division baccalaureate category, 2 semester hours in Property Management (Condominiums and Cooperative Associations) (10/83). NOTE: Credit for this course excludes credit for Property Management (Residential) RM-301, Property Management (Office Buildings) RM-302, and Property Management (Commercial Buildings and Shopping Centers) RM-303.

Property Management I
(Successful On-Site Management 101)
(Formerly A Survey of Property Management [RM-101])

Location: At various locations throughout the U.S. and Canada.

Length: *Version 1:* 45 hours (variable time formats); *Version 2:* 45 hours (6 days).

Dates: *Version 1:* October 1973-May 1988; *Version 2:* June 1988-Present.

Objective: To provide an introduction to management theories, marketing procedures, and employee-tenant relationships as they relate to the property manager.

Learning Outcome: Upon successful completion of this course, the student will be able to understand the roles and functions of management, and to prepare and implement effective marketing procedures; comply with affirmative marketing and other equal opportunity requirements of federal, state, and local laws; and select and manage service contractors, hire and supervise employees, work with resident organizations, and conduct scheduled inspections.

Instruction: *Version 1:* Lecture, discussion workshop, laboratory, films, and field study; and problem-solving supplemented with appropriate training aids. *Version 2:* Course covers management process, public relations, product preparation and marketing, risk management, and legal aspects. Methodology includes lecture, discussion, workshop, films, and field study.

Credit recommendation: *Version 1:* In the lower division baccalaureate/associate degree category, 3 semester hours in A Survey of Property Management (10/83). *Version 2:* In the lower division baccalaureate/associate degree category, 2 semester hours in Property Management (6/88). NOTE: This course has been reevaluated and continues to meet requirements for credit recommendations.

Property Management II
(Marketing and Management of Residential Property #301)
(Formerly Property Management [RM-301])

Location: At various locations throughout the U.S. and Canada.

Length: *Version 1:* 33 hours (1 week); *Version 2:* 42 hours (6 days).

Dates: *Version 1:* October 1973-May 1988; *Version 2:* June 1988-Present.

Objective: To provide the student with the ability to manage a residential complex.

Learning Outcome: Upon successful completion of this course, the student will be able to prepare a management operating manual, management agreements, and leases; prepare required budgets and financial reports; and recommend property management improvements.

Instruction: *Version 1:* Lecture, classroom exercise, simulations, and problem solving involving management agreements, rental analysis, leases, financial management, and maintenance of residential property. *Version 2:* Course covers property inspection, operating manuals, management agreements, leases, fiscal reports, rental analysis and property improvements. Methodology includes lecture, discussion, simulations, and problem solving.

Credit recommendation: *Version 1:* In the upper division baccalaureate category, 2 semester hours in Property Management (Residential) (10/83). NOTE: Credit for this course excludes credit for Property Management

(Office Building) RM-302, Property Management (Condominiums and Cooperative Associations) RM-304, and Property Management (Residential) RM-301. *Version 2:* In the lower division baccalaureate/associate degree category, or in the upper division baccalaureate category, 2 semester hours in Property Management (6/88). NOTE: This course has been reevaluated and continues to meet requirements for credit recommendations. NOTE: Students may receive credit for only one course of Property Management 301, Property Management 302, Property Management 303, or Property Management 304.

Property Management III
(Leasing and Management of Office Buildings 302)
(Formerly Property Management [RM-302])

Location: At various locations throughout the U.S. and Canada.

Length: *Version 1:* 33 hours (1 week); *Version 2:* 35 hours (6 days).

Dates: *Version 1:* October 1973-May 1988; *Version 2:* June 1988-Present.

Objective: To provide the student with operational skills needed to operate an office building.

Learning Outcome: Upon successful completion of this course, the student will be able to manage tenant suite development, budgeting, and building maintenance; and set up management operations for a new building.

Instruction: *Version 1:* Lecture, classroom exercises, simulations, and problem solving involving management agreements, rental analysis, leases, financial management, and maintenance of office buildings. *Version 2:* Course covers property inspection, management agreements, space measurement, rental analysis, budgeting, lease negotiation, and maintenance. Methodology includes lecture, discussion, workshops, and problem solving.

Credit recommendation: *Version 1:* In the upper division baccalaureate category, 2 semester hours in Property Management (Office Buildings) (10/83). NOTE: Credit for this course excludes credit for Property Management (Residential) RM-301, Property Management (Commercial Buildings and Shopping Centers) RM-303, and Property Management (Condominiums and Cooperative Associations) RM-304. *Version 2:* In the lower division baccalaureate/associate degree category, or in the upper division baccalaureate degree category, 2 semester hours in Property Management (6/88). NOTE: This course has been reevaluated and continues to meet requirements for credit recommendations. NOTE: Students may receive credit for only one course of Property Management 301, Property Management 302, Property Management 303, or Property Management 304.

Property Management IV
(Commercial Buildings and Shopping Centers 303)
(Formerly Property Management [RM-303])

Location: At various locations throughout the U.S. and Canada.

Length: *Version 1:* 33 hours (1 week); *Version 2:* 35 hours (6 days).

Dates: *Version 1:* October 1973-May 1988; *Version 2:* June 1988-Present.

Objective: To provide the student with operational skills required to manage commercial buildings and shopping centers.

Learning Outcome: Upon successful completion of this course, the student will be able to manage store tenant development, budgeting and commercial area management; and prepare market analyses.

Instruction: *Version 1:* Lecture, classroom exercises, simulations, and problem solving involving management agreements, rental analysis, leases, financial management, and maintenance of commercial buildings and shopping centers. *Version 2:* Course covers property inspection, management and tenant agreements, rental analysis, financial management, and property maintenance. Methodology includes lecture, discussion, workshops, and problem solving.

Credit recommendation: *Version 1:* In the upper division baccalaureate category, 2 semester hours in Property Management (Commercial Buildings and Shopping Centers) (10/83). NOTE: Credit for this course excludes credit for Property Management (Residential) RM-301, Property Management (Office Buildings) RM-302, and Property Management (Condominiums and Cooperative Associations) RM-304. *Version 2:* In the lower division baccalaureate/associate degree category, or in the upper division baccalaureate category, 2 semester hours in Property Management (6/88). NOTE: This course has been reevaluated and continues to meet requirements for credit recommendations. NOTE: Students may receive credit for only one course of Property Management 301, Property Management 302, Property Management 303, or Property Management 304.

Property Management V
(Problem Solving and Decision Making for Property Management 500)

Location: At various locations throughout the U.S. and Canada.

Length: 30 hours (5 days).

Dates: February 1988-Present.

Objective: To provide students with the skills necessary to identify property management related problems, research information sources, propose solutions, make decisions, and communicate the decisions to appropriate recipients.

Learning Outcome: Upon successful completion of this course, the student will be able to write a formal letter of authorization with management plan proposals and how to set related fees; be able to describe a property's physical and financial condition; and conduct a market study.

Instruction: Course covers problem identificaiton, analysis, solving and testing, and maintenance plan overview. Methodology includes lecture and workshop.

Credit recommendation: In the upper division baccalaureate category, 2 semester hours in Property Management (6/88).

Real Estate Investment Management
(Managing Real Estate and Investment)
(Formerly Management of Real Estate Investment [(RM-400])

Location: At various locations throughout the U.S. and Canada.

Length: *Version 1:* 31 hours (1 week); *Version 2:* 35 hours (6 days).

Dates: *Version 1:* October 1973-May 1988; *Version 2:* June 1988-Present.

Objective: To provide an understanding of real estate investment management, including ownership, budgeting and finance, and long-range planning in the context of general economic conditions.

Learning Outcome: Upon sucessful completion of this course, the student will be able to prepare financial analyses utilizing present value and rates of return; utilize valuation and budgeting techniques; and analyze cost recovery and its impact on real property.

Instruction: *Version 1:* Lecture, classroom exercises, simulations, and problem solving including valuation, leasing, cost recovery, cash flow analysis, and long-range budget and long-range management plan. *Version 2:* Course covers forms of ownership, financial calculations, lease and valuation analysis, time value of money, income tax considerations, cash flow and tax analysis. Methodology includes lecture, discussion, and workshops.

Credit recommendation: *Version 1:* In the upper division baccalaureate category, 2 semester hours in Property Management (10/83). *Version 2:* In the lower division baccalaureate/associate degree category, or in the upper division baccalaureate category, 2 semester hours in Property Management (6/88). NOTE: This course has been reevaluated and continues to meet requirements for credit recommendations.

Real Estate Office Management
(Managing the Real Estate Office)
(Formerly Real Estate Information and Management System 701)

Location: At various locations throughout the U.S. and Canada.

Length: 28 hours (3 days).

Dates: *Version 1:* October 1973-May 1988; *Version 2:* June 1988-Present.

Objective: To provde the CPM1 with methods to improve the performance standards in office management procedures, introduce new accounting and management information systems and learn techniques on how to acquire new business.

Learning Outcome: Upon successful completion of this course, the student will be able to select and manage people, get new business, and establish fees; utilize accounting and management information systems; and conduct client relations and discern future opportunities.

Instruction: *Version 1:* Primarily a lecture and discussion course including group reports covering real estate information and management. *Version 2:* Course covers human resources, accounting and information systems, office management techniques, new business acquisition, contracts and insurance.

Credit recommendation: *Version 1:* In the upper division baccalaureate category, 1 semester hour in Real Estate Management Information Systems (10/83). *Version 2:* In the lower division baccalaureate/associate degree category, or in the upper division baccalaureate category, 1 semester hour in Real Estate Office Management (6/88). NOTE: This course has been reevaluated and continues to meet requirements for credit recommendations.

Real Estate Planning (501) (Residential)
(Long Range Management Plan for Residential Properties)

Location: At various locations throughout the U.S. and Canada.

Length: 30 hours (3 days).

Dates: October 1973-June 1988.

Objective: To provide participants with the ability to develop a management plan for the operation of residential real estate in the context of existing economic conditions.

Instruction: Case study, lecture, on site inspection, including plan preparation are used to teach students techniques of real estate planning for residential areas.

Credit recommendation: In the upper division baccalaureate category, 1 semester hour in Real Estate Planning (10/83). NOTE: Credit in this course excludes credit in course 503, Real Estate Planning (Commercial Stores and Shopping Centers).

Real Estate Planning (502) (Office Buildings)
(Long Range Management Plan for Office Buildings)

Location: At various locations throughout the U.S. and Canada.

Length: 30 hours (1 week).

Dates: October 1973-June 1988.

Objective: To provide participants with the ability to develop a management plan for the operation of office buildings in the context of existing economic conditions.

Instruction: Case study, lecture, on-site inspection including plan preparation are used to teach students the techniques of real estate planning for office buildings.

Credit recommendation: In the upper division baccalaureate category, 1 semester hour in Real Estate Planning (Commercial Stores and Shopping Centers) (10/83). NOTE: Credit in this course excludes credit in Course

501, Real Estate Planning (Residential) and Course 503, Real Estate Planning (Commercial Stores and Shopping Centers).

Real Estate Planning (503) (Commercial Stores and Shopping Centers)
(Long Range Plan for Commercial Stores and Shopping Centers)

Location: At various locations throughout the U.S. and Canada.
Length: 30 hours (1 week).
Dates: October 1973-June 1988.
Objective: To provide participants with the ability to develop a management plan for the operation of commercial stores and shopping centers in the context of existing economic conditions.
Instruction: Case study, lecture, on-site inspection including plan preparations are used to teach students the techniques of real estate planning for commercial stores and shopping centers.
Credit recommendation: In the upper division baccalaureate category, 1 semester hour in Real Estate Planning (Office Buildings) (10/83). NOTE: Credit in this course excludes credit in Course 501, Real Estate Planning (Residential) and Course 502, Real Estate Planning (Office Buildings).

Public Housing Management
(Professional Management of Government-Assisted Housing 305)

Location: At various locations throughout the U.S. and Canada.
Length: 40 hours (5 days).
Dates: February 1986-Present.
Objective: To provide the student with the basic elements necessary to manage government-assisted housing.
Learning Outcome: Upon successful completion of this course, the student will be able to write management policies and procedures, and management agreements and to set fees; inspect property and plan maintenance; and identify components of the lease and lease clauses.
Instruction: Course covers rental analysis, leases, maintenance, fiscal reporting, budgeting and financial controls, management agreements and fees, property inspection, and human relations. Methodology includes lecture, discussion, and workshop.
Credit recommendation: In the upper division baccalaureate category, 2 semester hours in Management (6/88).

REALTOR® INSTITUTE PROGRAM

The Education Division of the National Association of REALTORS®, with offices in Chicago, Illinois and Washington, D.C., administers and regulates an extensive program of instruction in real estate in cooperation with affiliated state organizations in all 50 states, plus three territories. The Education Division has established, with much consultation and consensus from practitioners in the field, twelve required topics which comprise approximately half of the Realtor Institute Program. State Associations provide instruction and evaluation for the required topics as well as for an equal amount of optional topics selected to meet different state needs and interests. The Education Division ensures reasonable comparability and quality among the programs by providing instructional outlines, reference books, criteria for instructor selection and evaluation, and recommendations for examinations. In addition, each GRI Program must submit materials for recertification every 3 years and be prepared for site visitation from members of the Education Division staff.

Source of official student records: Affiliated State Associations in the 23 states reviewed by the American Council on Education. Specific names and addresses are available from the National Association of REALTORS, Education Division, 777 14th Street, N.W., Washington, D.C. 20005.

Additional information about the courses: Program on Noncollegiate Sponsored Instruction, Office on Educational Credit and Credentials, American Council on Education, One Dupont Circle, Washington, D.C. 20036.

Graduate Realtors Institute (GRI) Courses I, II, III.
Location: Affiliated State Associations in the following 23 states: Arkansas, California, Connecticut, Delaware, Florida, Georgia, Hawaii, Idaho, Illinois, Indiana, Maine, Maryland, Massachusetts, Missouri, Nevada, New Hampshire, Oregon, Pennsylvania, South Carolina, Tennessee, Vermont, Virginia, Wisconsin. The New Jersey Association of Realtors was reviewed by Thomas A. Edison State College under the auspices of the American Council on Education. It is presented in a separate exhibit.
Length: 30-45 hours (1 week per course; 90-135 hours for the GRI Program).
Dates: October 1974-Present.
Objective: To offer a program of continuing education for the professional real estate licensee which provides a foundation for building the skills needed for career success and for better service to the public. The program aims to educate and train in all areas of the real estate business. The GRI Program provides a broad base for more advanced and specialized education offered through institutions of higher education or through the state associations affiliated with NAR.
Instruction: This 3-course sequence provides lecture and discussion in various areas of real estate. Required topics in approximately half of the program are listing property, marketing and servicing listed property, residential construction and energy, pricing properties for sale, completing the transaction, real estate law, time management, common-ownership forms, government effects on

real estate, financing the sale, other business and education opportunities in real estate, and code of ethics. The remaining half of the program consists of real estate topics selected by the state associations to meet particular needs and interests of the individual states.

Credit recommendation: In the lower division baccalaureate/associate degree category, 6 semester hours in Business/Real Estate (10/84). NOTE: Credit is recommended only for the entire program of 3 courses. No credit is given for individual courses.

National Association of Securities Dealers, Inc.

The National Association of Securities Dealers, Inc. (NASD), is the primary organization of the securities industry and is responsible for the regulation of the over-the-counter securities market. The NASD was established by the 1938 Maloney Act amendments to the Securities Exchange Act of 1934. The principle behind the legislation is that of cooperative regulation by which voluntary associations of broker-dealers regulate themselves under the oversight of the Securities and Exchange Commission. The NASD is the only securities association to have been established under the legislation. Today, its membership comprises approximately 90% of the nation's broker-dealers. The NASD, in addition to enforcing federal securities laws as well as the broader ethical requirements of its own rules which obligate members to observe high standards of commercial honor, also operates a nationwide electronic "stockmarket" for OTC securities called "NASDAQ."

To ensure that its staff has the necessary knowledge, the NASD developed its own training/education program for its regulatory personnel. Two 3-week training sessions, conducted in a formal classroom environment, are required for each professional staff member as part of his or her overall training. Each class stresses subjects dealing with the various types and forms of securities products, financial and operational analysis, and securities laws and the rules and regulations thereunder.

The NASD's training program has two objectives. The first is to enable a participant to master the major aspects of federal securities laws and disciplines relating to the investment banking and securities business and to demonstrate that knowledge by on-site inspections of the business of investment bankers and securities broker-dealers. The second objective is to enable a participant to learn how to analyze the financial and operational systems of the investment community and to demonstrate that knowledge by capital analyses and operational audits.

Source of official student records: National Association of Security Dealers, Inc., 9513 Key West Avenue, Rockville, Maryland 20850.

Additional information about the courses: Program on Noncollegiate Sponsored Instruction, The Center for Adult Learning and Educational Credentials, American Council on Education, One Dupont Circle, Washington, D.C. 20036.

1. Investments and/or Brokerage Accounting
2. Securities, Regulation, Law, and Self-Regulation
   Location: Washington, DC.
   Length: 210 hours (6 weeks); plus a pre-phase component.
   Dates: July 1975-Present.
   Objective: To enable a participant to master the major aspects of federal securities laws and disciplines relating to the investment banking and securities business and to demonstrate that knowledge by examining the business of investment bankers or securities broker-dealers.
   Instruction: Course covers comparisons of the auction and negotiated markets and the exchange specialist and over-the-counter market making systems; investment banking and the capital formation process; operations of a securities firm. Course also covers the Securities Act of 1933, Securities Exchange Act of 1934, and the elements of discovering and proving a market manipulation. A detailed explanation of securities products and the federal regulations governing them is provided on such instruments as options municipal securities, government-guaranteed mortgaged-backed securities, direct participation programs (e.g., real estate syndications, oil and gas programs, cattle-feeding programs), commodity futures, investment banking, and secondary market making. Emphasis is placed upon broker-dealer operations and their specialized accounting systems, Federal Reserve System credit regulations and margin rules, coupled with the exhaustive analysis of financial and capital data, and operational audits. Lecture, discussions, and classroom exercises are used.
   Credit recommendation: In the upper division baccalaureate category or in the graduate degree category, 3 semester hours in Investments and/or Brokerage Accounting and Operation. In the upper division baccalaureate category or in the graduate degree category, 3 semester hours in Securities, Regulation, and Law, for a total of 6 hours (7/81). NOTE 1: Participants must complete both Phases I and II in order to receive credit (7/87). NOTE 2: This course has been reevaluated and continues to meet requirements for credit recommendations.

National Cryptologic School

The National Cryptologic School operates under the Government Employees Training Act and applicable Department of Defense directives. It provides training in Cryptology and related activities to military and civilian personnel of the U.S. Government. The School is organized into four departments: Language Department, Intelligence and Analysis Department, Science and Technology Department, and Cryptologic Management Department.

Source of official student records: Registrar, National Cryptologic School, Fort George G. Meade, Maryland 20755, ATTN: E1.

Additional information about the courses: Program on Noncollegiate Sponsored Instruction, The Center for Adult Learning and Educational Credentials, American Council on Education, One Dupont Circle, Washington, D.C. 20036.

COMPUTER SOFTWARE AND OPERATIONS DIVISION

The Computer Software and Operations Division is one of several departments in the Science and Technology Department. It provides training for computer operators and programmers as well as systems analysts, engineers, and mathematicians.

ALGOL Programming (MP-243)
Location: National Cryptologic School, Ft. Meade, MD.
Length: 45 hours (5 weeks).
Dates: August 1969-Present.
Objective: To provide an understanding of the ALGOL programming language, and to teach the student to program in ALGOL.
Instruction: Origins of the ALGOL language, writing and debugging of at least four ALGOL programs, presentation of various programming techniques useful in the solution of selected problems. Instruction by lecture, discussion, and computer usage. **Prerequisite:** Mechanics of Algebra (MA-012) or college-level algebra and demonstrated competency in another programming language.
Credit recommendation: In the upper division baccalaureate category, 2 semester hours in Computer Science (11/75) (12/80). NOTE: This course has undergone a 5-year reevaluation and continues to meet the requirements for credit recommendations.

APL Programming (MP-188)
Location: National Cryptologic School, Ft. Meade, MD.
Length: 40 hours (5 weeks).
Dates: November 1973-December 1988.
Objective: To teach the student the APL programming language.
Instruction: Develops the ability to use APL as an effective tool for the solution of operational problems. Covers syntax and semantics of APL commands and operators used in selected quantitative problems. Instruction by lectures, discussion, and the use of interactive computer terminals. **Prerequisite:** Mechanics of Algebra (MA-012) or college-level algebra.
Credit recommendation: In the upper division baccalaureate category, 2 semester hours in Computational or Quantitative Research Methods (11/75) (12/80). NOTE: This course has undergone a 5-year reevaluation and continues to meet the requirements for credit recommendations.

Burroughs B6700/7000 Advanced Technical Skills (MP-1H6)
(Formerly Burroughs B6700 Advanced Technical Skills [MP-1H6])
Location: National Cryptologic School, Ft. Meade, MD.
Length: 70 hours (2 weeks).
Dates: July 1974-Present.
Objective: To provide the experienced operator with an in-depth understanding from an operational viewpoint of the internal functions of the Burroughs B6700 MCP Operating System software.
Instruction: In-depth study of the concepts and facilities of the Burroughs B6700 MCP Operating System and the use of its job control statements; emphasis on data management and system utilities. **Prerequisite:** Burroughs B6700 Systems Software (MP-1H5) and FORTRAN for Operators (MP-166).
Credit recommendation: In the lower division baccalaureate/associate degree category, 2 semester hours in Data Processing (9/77) (11/82). NOTE: This course has undergone a 5-year reevaluation and continues to meet requirements for credit recommendations.

Burroughs B6700/7000 Systems Software (MP-1H5)
(Formerly Burroughs B6700 Systems Software [MP-1H5])
Location: National Cryptologic School, Ft. Meade, MD.
Length: 35 hours (1 week).
Dates: July 1973-Present.
Objective: To enhance the apprentice operator's ability to interact with the Burroughs B6700 Operating System software.
Instruction: System reconfiguration, initialization memory control, work flow language and management, input/output subsystem, operator MCP communications and data communication. **Prerequisite:** Introduction to Computer Systems Operations (MP-154).
Credit recommendation: In the lower division baccalaureate/associate degree category, 1 semester hour in Data Processing (9/77) (11/82). NOTE: This course has undergone a 5-year reevaluation and continues to meet the requirements for credit recommendations.

CDC 6600 Series Advanced Technical Skills (MP-1P6) (Formerly [MP-1B6])

Location: National Cryptologic School, Ft. Meade, MD.

Length: 35 hours (1 week).

Dates: July 1971-Present.

Objective: To provide the experienced operator with an in-depth understanding from an operational viewpoint of the internal functions of the CDC 6600 SCOPE Operating System software.

Instruction: In-depth study of the concepts and facilities of the CDC 6600 SCOPE Operating System and the use of job control statements. **Prerequisite:** FORTRAN for Operators (MP-166) and CDC 6600 Series System Software (MP-1B5).

Credit recommendation: In the lower division baccalaureate/associate degree category, 1 semester hour in Data Processing (9/77) (11/82). NOTE: This course has undergone a 5-year reevaluation and continues to meet the requirements for credit recommendations.

CDC 6600 Series System Software (MP-1P5) (Formerly [MP-1B5])

Location: National Cryptologic School, Ft. Meade, MD.

Length: 35 hours (1 week).

Dates: July 1970-Present.

Objective: To enhance the apprentice operator's ability to interact with the CDC 6600 SCOPE Operating Series software.

Instruction: Overview of the concepts and facilities of the CDC 6600 SCOPE Operating System and the use of its job control statements. **Prerequisite:** Introduction to Computer Systems Operations (MP-154).

Credit recommendation: In the lower division baccalaureate/associate degree category, 1 semester hour in Data Processing (9/77) (11/82). NOTE: This course has undergone a 5-year reevaluation and continues to meet the requirements for credit recommendations.

COBOL Programming (MP-230)

Location: National Cryptologic School, Ft. Meade, MD.

Length: 72 hours (8 weeks).

Dates: August 1969-Present.

Objective: To teach students to write, debug, and document computer programs in COBOL compiler language.

Instruction: Includes mechanics of COBOL, use and syntactic aspects of the COBOL language, punctuation and coding sheet rules, data structure, types of data items, file and record description entries, use of I/O, arithmetic, data manipulation, switching and linkage verbs, arithmetic and conditional expressions, defining tables with emphasis on retrieval methods, and writing and debugging of at least three COBOL programs. Self-paced program instruction approach used with access to instructor when needed. **Prerequisite:** Introduction to Computer Science (MP-160) or equivalent.

Credit recommendation: In the lower division baccalaureate/associate degree category, 3 semester hours in Data Processing (11/75) (12/80). NOTE: This course has undergone a 5-year reevaluation and continues to meet the requirements for credit recommendations.

Programming for Operators (MP-166) (Formerly FORTRAN for Operators [MP-166])

Location: National Cryptologic School, Ft. Meade, MD.

Length: 40 hours (1 week).

Dates: January 1971-Present.

Objective: To familiarize computer operators with the FORTRAN language.

Instruction: Introduces basic features of FORTRAN and the programming environment. Covers concepts of FORTRAN commands, including input/output instructions, data manipulation, and data structure. Instruction by lecture, laboratory, and computer usage. **Prerequisite:** Familiarity at the operator's level with a specific computer system's operation.

Credit recommendation: In the vocational certificate category, 2 semester hours in Data Processing; or in the lower division baccalaureate/associate degree category, 1 semester hour in Data Processing (11/75) (12/80). NOTE: This course has undergone a 5-year reevaluation and continues to meet the requirements for credit recommendations.

FORTRAN Programming (MP-227)

Location: National Cryptologic School, Ft. Meade, MD.

Length: 45 hours (5 weeks).

Dates: December 1974-Present.

Objective: To enable the student to write programs in structured FORTRAN.

Instruction: General history and philosophy of compiler languages with detailed background of the FORTRAN language; detailed examination of the FORTRAN language; detailed examination of the structured programming constructs, and, more specifically, their implementation in FORTRAN; writing and debugging of at least four FORTRAN programs; presentation of various programming techniques useful in the efficient solution of frequently encountered problems. Instruction by lecture, discussion, and computer usage. **Prerequisite:** Introduction to Computing or equivalent.

Credit recommendation: In the lower division baccalaureate/associate degree category, 2 semester hours in Computer Science (11/75) (12/80). NOTE: This course has undergone a 5-year reevaluation and continues to meet the requirements for credit recommendations.

General Programming Techniques (MP-430)

Location: National Cryptologic School, Ft. Meade, MD.
Length: 40 hours (10 weeks).
Dates: June 1974-Present.
Objective: To provide a background in the use of advanced general techniques in programming.
Instruction: Course covers top-down design, structured programming, sorting, table look-up techniques, dynamic programming, data structures, dynamic storage allocation, character strings, data compression, and profiling. The student demonstrates knowledge of the above through completion of a group project using these techniques. Instruction by lecture, discussion, laboratory, and computer usage. **Prerequisites:** Introduction to Computing or equivalent; FORTRAN Programming (MP-227) or equivalent; and Introduction to Computer Science Mathematics (MA-400) or equivalent.
Credit recommendation: In the upper division baccalaureate category, 3 semester hours in Computer Science (11/75) (12/80). NOTE: This course has undergone a 5-year reevaluation and continues to meet the requirements for credit recommendations.

Version 1. IBM 360 Job Control Language (MP-268)
Version 2. IBM 370 Job Control Language (MP-368)

Location: National Cryptologic School, Ft. Meade, MD.
Length: 32 hours (2 weeks).
Dates: *Version 1:* November 1969-December 1975; *Version 2:* January 1976-Present.
Objective: *Version 1:* To teach the preparation of control statements for the S360/OS. *Version 2:* To teach the preparation of control statements for the S370/VS.
Instruction: *Version 1:* Discussion of syntax of job control language required to perform the elementary functions of job, task, and data management. Instruction by lecture, discussion, laboratory, and computer usage. *Version 2:* This version deals with the IBM-370 computer, which replaced the IBM-360 computer. The course remains substantially the same, with minor adjustments for the new computer.
Credit recommendation: *Versions 1 and 2:* In the vocational certificate category, 2 semester hours in Data Processing; or in the lower division baccalaureate/associate degree category, 1 semester hour in Data Processing (11/75) (12/80). NOTE: This course has undergone a 5-year reevaluation and continues to meet the requirements for credit recommendations.

IBM 360 System Software (OS) (MP-1D5)

Location: National Cryptologic School, Ft. Meade, MD.
Length: 40 hours (5 days).
Dates: July 1971-November 1976.
Objective: To introduce the student to technical concepts of OS/360.
Instruction: Reviews 360 hardware features relevant to OS operations; explains the operating system components and their interrelationships, including interrupt systems, principles of multiprogramming and Job Control Language (JCL), critical OS utilities and Recovery Management Support functions. Instruction by lecture and discussion. **Prerequisite:** IBM 360 (MP-1A4) or equivalent.
Credit recommendation: In the vocational certificate category, 2 semester hours in Data Processing; or in the lower division baccalaureate/associate degree category, 1 semester hour in Data Processing (11/75) (12/80). NOTE: This course has undergone a 5-year reevaluation and continues to meet the requirements for credit recommendations.

370 MVS Advanced Technical Skills (MP-156)
(Formerly IBM 370 MVS Advanced Technical Skills [MP-156])

Location: National Cryptologic School, Ft. Meade, MD.
Length: 70 hours (2 weeks).
Dates: July 1976-Present.
Objective: To provide the experienced operator with an in-depth understanding from an operational viewpoint of the internal functions of the 370 MVS Operating System software.
Instruction: In-depth study of the concepts and facilities of the 370 MVS Operating System and the use of its job control statements; emphasis on data management operations (including VSAM); system utilities; 3850 Mass Storage System. **Prerequisite:** FORTRAN for Operators (MP-166) and Introduction to the 370 MVS Operating System (MP-1S5).
Credit recommendation: In the lower division baccalaureate/associate degree category, 2 semester hours in Data Processing (9/77) (11/82). NOTE: This course has undergone a 5-year reevaluation and continues to meet the requirements for credit recommendations.

Introduction to the 370 MVS Operating System (MP-155)
(Formerly IBM 370 MVS Operating System [MP-155])

Location: National Cryptologic School, Ft. Meade, MD.
Length: 35 hours (1 week).
Dates: July 1976-Present.
Objective: To enhance the apprentice operator's ability to interact with the 370 Operating System software.
Instruction: Overview of the concepts and facilities of the 370 MVS Operating System and the use of its job control statements; introduction to data management (including VSAM). **Prerequisite:** Introduction to Computer Systems Operations (MP-154).

Credit recommendation: In the lower division baccalaureate/associate degree category, 2 semester hours in Data Processing (9/77) (11/82). NOTE: This course has undergone a 5-year reevaluation and continues to meet the requirements for credit recommendations.

IBM Assembly Language Programming (MP-335)
(Formerly IBM 370 Programming [MP-335])
Location: National Cryptologic School, Ft. Meade, MD.
Length: 100 hours (5 weeks).
Dates: July 1974-Present.
Objective: To teach the student programming in the IBM 370 assembler language.
Instruction: The standard instruction set is covered in detail. Students learn to write instructions in both the symbolic and explicit forms, to use macros involving QSAM access, to make use of debugging aids which include the dump macros and an interpretation of an OS hexadecimal dump, to write a structured program using IBM macros and the subroutine linkages between assembly language and FORTRAN programs. Instruction includes lecture, discussion, laboratory, and computer usage. **Prerequisite:** FORTRAN Programming (MP-227) or equivalent.
Credit recommendation: In the lower division baccalaureate/associate degree category, 3 semester hours in Data Processing (11/75) (12/80). NOTE: This course has undergone a 5-year reevaluation and continues to meet requirements for credit recommendations.

Modern Computer Architecture (MP-410)
(Formerly Introduction to Computer Hardware [MP-410])
Location: National Cryptologic School, Ft. Meade, MD.
Length: 40 hours (5 weeks).
Dates: September 1973-Present.
Objective: To provide and introduction to the principles of digital computer design.
Instruction: Covers Boolean algebra, hardware circuitry, elementary digital computer design, subcomponent design, high-speed arithmetic techniques, implementation of arithmetic operations, control operations, input/output operation, and storage techniques. Lecture, discussion, and laboratory are used. (Prerequisite: Successful completion of an assembly language programming course.)
Credit recommendation: In the upper division baccalaureate category, 3 semester hours in Computer Science (11/75) (12/80). NOTE: This course has undergone a 5-year reevaluation and continues to meet the requirements for credit recommendations.

Introduction to Computer Systems Operations (MP-154)
Location: National Cryptologic School, Ft. Meade, MD.
Length: 70 hours (2 weeks).
Dates: July 1974-Present.
Objective: To provide an introduction to data processing terminology and methodology.
Instruction: Computer history, numbering systems, components of digital computers, characteristics of assemblers and compilers, characteristics of I/O devices, operating systems. Programming, specific types of business applications, and punch card processing are not emphasized.
Credit recommendation: In the lower division baccalaureate/associate degree category, 2 semester hours in Data Processing (9/77) (11/82). NOTE: This course has undergone a 5-year reevaluation and continues to meet the requirements for credit recommendations.

Introduction to Computing
(Introduction to Computer Science [MP-160])
Location: National Cryptologic School, Ft. Meade, MD.
Length: 60 hours (3 weeks).
Dates: April 1970-Present.
Objective: To introduce underlying concepts in computing and to provide a base for programming language courses.
Instruction: General consideration of computer history, number systems, conversion from a number in any base and its equivalent in any other base, binary arithmetic, the coding of numerical and character data, explanation of the five components of a digital computer (input, output, control, arithmetic/logic, memory), the six steps of computer programming development (problem analysis, flowcharting, coding, debugging, production run, documentation). Emphasis will be placed on flowcharting and coding. Within coding, the concept of assembly and high-level languages are covered and a simple FORTRAN program is coded. Instruction by lecture and discussion. **Prerequisite:** Mechanics of Algebra (MA-012) or college-level algebra.
Credit recommendation: In the lower division baccalaureate/associate degree category, 2 semester hours in Computer Science (11/75) (12/80). NOTE: This course has undergone a 5-year reevaluation and continues to meet the requirements for credit recommendations.

Model 204 Information Retrieval Language (MP-185)
Location: National Cryptologic School, Ft. Meade, MD.
Length: 36 hours (4 weeks).
Dates: June 1973-Present.
Objective: To explain and demonstrate instructions for utilizing retrieval capabilities of the CCA Model 204 System.
Instruction: General use of the Model 204 remote terminal; system control commands, including sign-on

procedures, opening and closing files; retrieving stored information; outputting retrieved information in the format desired; performing arithmetic or conditional operations with stored information; updating or deleting old information; storing new information; use of the editor; functions. Instruction by lecture, discussion, laboratory, and computer usage.

Credit recommendation: In the vocational certificate category, 2 semester hours in Data Processing; or in the lower division baccalaureate/associate degree category, 1 semester hour in Data Processing (11/75) (12/80). NOTE: This course has undergone a 5-year reevaluation and continues to meet the requirements for credit recommendations.

Version 1. PDP-11 Programming (MP-375)
Version 2. PDP-11 Programming (MP-377)

Location: National Cryptologic School, Ft. Meade, MD.

Length: *Version 1:* 120 hours (3 weeks); *Version 2:* 200 hours (5 weeks).

Dates: *Version 1:* November 1973-April 1976; *Version 2:* May 1977-December 1988.

Objective: To teach students to write and execute assembly language programs using the PDP-11 instruction set.

Instruction: *Versions 1 and 2:* Covers communications with the DOS operating system using monitor commands and programmed request (I/O), editing of source language programs, debugging and modifying programs using ODT subsystem, and managing and manipulating files using PDP. Instruction by lecture, discussion, laboratory, and computer usage. **Prerequisites:** Competence in an assembly language. *Version 2:* Additional instruction on the operation of the computer, using a specific operating system to support requirements for PDP-11 operations.

Credit recommendation: *Versions 1 and 2:* In the vocational certificate category, 6 semester hours in Data Processing; or in the lower division baccalaureate/associate degree category, 3 semester hours in Data Processing (11/75) (12/80). NOTE: This course has undergone a 5-year reevaluation and continues to meet the requirements for credit recommendations.

Phase V CDC 7600 System (IDA) Software Concepts (MP-1K5)

Location: National Cryptologic School, Ft. Meade, MD.

Length: 35 hours (1 week).

Dates: July 1971-Present.

Objective: To enhance the apprentice operator's ability to interact with the CDC 7600 IDA Operating System software.

Instruction: Overview of the concepts and facilities of the CDC 7600 IDA Operating System and the use of its job control statements. **Prerequisite:** Introduction to Computer Systems Operations (MP-154).

Credit recommendation: In the lower division baccalaureate/associate degree category, 1 semester hour in Data Processing (9/77) (11/82). NOTE: This course has undergone a 5-year reevaluation and continues to meet the requirements for credit recommendations.

Phase VI CDC 7600 System (IDA) Advanced Technical Skills (MP-1K6)

Location: National Cryptologic School, Ft. Meade, MD.

Length: 35 hours (1 week).

Dates: July 1972-Present.

Objective: To provide the experienced operator with an in-depth understanding from an operational viewpoint of the internal functions of the CDC 7600 IDA Operating System software.

Instruction: In-depth study of the concepts and facilities of the CDC 7600 IDA operating system and the use of its job control statements. (Prerequisite: FORTRAN for Operators [MP-166] and Phase V CDC 7600 System [IDA] Software Concepts [MP-1K5].)

Credit recommendation: In the lower division baccalaureate/associate degree category, 1 semester hour in Data Processing (9/77) (11/82). NOTE: This course has undergone a 5-year reevaluation and continues to meet the requirements for credit recommendations.

PL/1 Programming (MP-242)

Location: National Cryptologic School, Ft. Meade, MD.

Length: 72 hours (8 weeks).

Dates: October 1969-Present.

Objective: To teach the student to write, debug, and document programs in the PL/1 compiler language.

Instruction: Examination of PL/1, writing and debugging at least four PL/1 programs, class discussion of various sample programs, presentation of various programming techniques useful in the efficient solution of frequently encountered problems. Instruction by lecture, discussion, and computer usage. (Prerequisite: College-level algebra course or Mechanics of Algebra [MA-012] and demonstrated competency in another programming language.)

Credit recommendation: In the lower division baccalaureate/associate degree category, 3 semester hours in Data Processing (11/75) (12/80). NOTE: This course has undergone a 5-year reevaluation and continues to meet the requirements for credit recommendations.

Systems Software
(Introduction to Computer Software [MP-420])

Location: National Cryptologic School, Ft. Meade, MD.

Length: 48 hours (5 weeks).

Dates: September 1973-Present.

Objective: To provide an introduction to the field of general systems programming and an understanding of how operating systems and compilers are constructed and implemented.

Instruction: Detailed discussion and investigation of the nature and characteristics of systems programs; systems design; structural programming; optimization; language utility, microprogramming, compilers, and operating systems. Lecture and discussion are used. **Prerequisites:** FORTRAN Programming (MP-227) and successful completion of an assembly language programming course.

Credit recommendation: In the upper division baccalaureate category, or in the graduate degree category, 3 semester hours in Computer Science or Data Processing (11/75) (12/80). NOTE: This course has undergone a 5-year reevaluation and continues to meet the requirements for credit recommendations.

Univac 494 Advanced Technical Skills (MP-1C6)

Location: National Cryptologic School, Ft. Meade, MD.
Length: 35 hours (1 week).
Dates: July 1972-Present.
Objective: To provide the experienced operator with an in-depth understanding from an operational viewpoint of the internal functions of the Univac 494 Operating System software.

Instruction: In-depth study of the concepts and facilities of the Univac 494 Operating System and the use of its job control statements; programming techniques; machine language instructions; input and output conventions; program segmentation; FORTRAN programming; file control; debugging aids; file standards; communications. **Prerequisite:** FORTRAN for Operators (MP-166) and Univac 494 System Software (MP-1C5).

Credit recommendation: In the lower division baccalaureate/associate degree category, 1 semester hour in Data Processing (9/77) (11/82). NOTE: This course has undergone a 5-year reevaluation and continues to meet the requirements for credit recommendations.

Univac 494 HOLDER System Software (MP-1G5)

Location: National Cryptologic School, Ft. Meade, MD.
Length: 35 hours (1 week).
Dates: July 1975-Present.
Objective: To enhance the apprentice operator's ability to interact with the Univac 494 Real Time Interrupt Processing executive software.

Instruction: Overview of the concepts and facilities of the Univac 494 Real Time Interrupt Processing Executive Operating System and the use of its job control statements. **Prerequisite:** Introduction to Computer Systems Operations (MP-154).

Credit recommendation: In the lower division baccalaureate/associate degree category, 1 semester hour in Data Processing (9/77) (11/82). NOTE: This course has undergone a 5-year reevaluation and continues to meet the requirements for credit recommendations.

Univac 494RYE System Software (MP-1C5)

Location: National Cryptologic School, Ft. Meade, MD.
Length: 35 hours (1 week).
Dates: July 1971-March 1979.
Objective: To enhance the apprentice operator's ability to interact with the Univac 494 Operating System software.

Instruction: Overview of the concepts and facilities of the Univac 494 Operating System and the use of its job control statements to schedule, prioritize, log, and monitor system operation. **Prerequisite:** Introduction to Computer Systems Operations (MP-154).

Credit recommendation: In the lower division baccalaureate/associate degree category, 1 semester hour in Data Processing (9/77) (11/82). NOTE: This course has undergone a 5-year reevaluation and continues to meet the requirements for credit recommendations.

Univac 1100 Advanced Training Skills (MP-1E6)
(Formerly Univac 1108 Advanced Technical Skills [MP-1E6])

Location: National Cryptologic School, Ft. Meade, MD.
Length: 35 hours (1 week).
Dates: July 1973-Present.
Objective: To provide the experienced operator with an in-depth understanding from an operational viewpoint of the internal functions of the Univac 1108 EXEC 8 Operating System software.

Instruction: In-depth study of the concepts and facilities of the Univac 1108 EXEC 8 Operating System and the use of its job control language. **Prerequisite:** FORTRAN for Operators (MP-166) and Univac 1108 Systems Software (MP-1E5).

Credit recommendation: In the lower division baccalaureate/associate degree category, 1 semester hour in Data Processing (9/77) (11/82). NOTE: This course has undergone a 5-year reevaluation and continues to meet the requirements for credit recommendations.

Univac 1100 Systems Software (MP-1E5)
(Formerly Univac 1108 Systems Software [MP-1E5])

Location: National Cryptologic School, Ft. Meade, MD.
Length: 35 hours (1 week).
Dates: July 1972-Present.
Objective: To enhance the apprentice operator's ability to interact with the Univac 1108 EXEC 8 Operating System software.

Instruction: Overview of the concepts and facilities of the Univac 1108 EXEC 8 Operating System and the use of its job control statements. **Prerequisite:** Introduction to Computer Systems Operations (MP-154).

Credit recommendation: In the lower division baccalaureate/associate degree category, 1 semester hour in Data Processing (9/77) (11/82). NOTE: This course has undergone a 5-year reevaluation and continues to meet the requirements for credit recommendations.

LANGUAGE DEPARTMENT

The Language Department is one of several departments in the Language and Analysis Faculty. It provides training in different languages to those in language-associated jobs. The first course listed below (Introduction to Linguistic Theory) is followed by courses arranged alphabetically by title under language (Arabic, Chinese, Hebrew, etc.).

Introduction to Linguistic Theory (LG-130)
  Location: National Cryptologic School, Ft. Meade, MD.
  Length: 60 hours (6 weeks).
  Dates: July 1972-Present.
  Objective: To introduce the basic principles of phonetics, phonemics, morphology, and syntax.
  Instruction: Study of the principles of phonetics, phonemics, morphology, and syntax. Analysis of the principles underlying different writing systems. Exercises in various forms of linguistic analysis, including establishment of phonemic status, determining distribution and conditioning of allophones, segmentation of utterances into morphemes, determining distribution and conditioning of allomorphs and morphophonemic changes, IC analysis, and descriptions of syntactic features. Emphasis is both synchronic and diachronic. Lecture, discussion, and laboratory exercises are used.
  Credit recommendation: In the lower division baccalaureate/associate degree category, 3 semester hours in Linguistics (3/80) (10/85). NOTE: This course has been reevaluated and continues to meet requirements for credit recommendations.

ARABIC

Arabic Syria Course (AA-111)
(Levantine Arabic Course)
  Location: National Cryptologic School, Ft. Meade, MD.
  Length: 480 hours (12 weeks, 40 hours per week).
  Dates: April 1985-Present.
  Objective: To enable the student to listen, read, understand, and answer questions about everyday topics in Syrian/Levantine Arabic.
  Learning Outcome: Upon successful completion of this course, the student will be able to live in Syria having little difficulty in communicating in the dialect dealing with everyday topics in terms of reading, writing, and speaking.
  Instruction: Grammatically, from the prerequisites, the student would have covered the main sentence structure and derivation system in addition to reading and writing. In this course, the student is more exposed to the Levantine Arabic spoken dialect at length and would be getting familiar with everyday topics.
  Credit recommendation: In the upper division baccalaureate category, 6 semester hours in Arabic (6/87). NOTE: Students must have completed the L2 Level or the intermediate level in the grammar of Standard Arabic to receive this credit.

Basic Modern Standard Arabic (AA-10A)
  Course 1: Basic Modern Standard Arabic
  Course 2: Intermediate Modern Standard Arabic
  Location: National Cryptologic School, Ft. Meade, MD.
  Length: *Version 1:* 1520 hours (38 weeks); classroom and self-study included. *Course 1:* 1010 hours (25 weeks); *Course 2:* 510 hours (13 weeks). *Version 2:* 1880 hours total.
  Dates: *Version 1:* July 1974-April 1984; *Version 2:* May 1984-Present.
  Objective: To provide a thorough knowledge of the basic grammatical features of modern standard Arabic and to provide a moderately broad familiarity with newspaper vocabulary and skills in listening comprehension, transcription, and translation into English.
  Instruction: This course is the equivalent of three years intensive study (five hours weekly) with strong emphasis on military and political vocabulary. Special emphasis is placed on grammatical structures, and listening and reading for understanding.
  Credit recommendation: *Course 1:* In the lower division baccalaureate/associate degree category, 20 semester hours in Basic Modern Standard Arabic; *Course 2:* In the upper division baccalaureate category, 10 semester hours in Intermediate Modern Standard Arabic (3/80) (10/85). NOTE: This course has been reevaluated and continues to meet requirements for credit recommendations.

Basic Modern Standard Arabic (AA-15A)
  Location: National Cryptologic School, Ft. Meade, MD.
  Length: 1880 hours (47 weeks).
  Dates: November 1983-Present.
  Objective: To provide a thorough knowledge of the basic grammatical features of modern standard Arabic and to provide a moderately broad familiarity with newspaper vocabulary and skills in listening comprehension, transcription, and translation into English.
  Learning Outcome: Upon successful completion of this course, the student will be able to write a summary in English of an Arabic text at the L2 Level; translate a text into good English; write a summary of a voice recording

in Modern Standard Arabic at L2 Level (news segment); transcribe a news segment in Arabic script; and conjugate verbs in all forms.

Instruction: This course is the equivalent of three years intensive study (five hours weekly) with strong emphasis on military and political vocabulary. Special emphasis is placed on grammatical structures, and listening and reading for understanding. The final six weeks of the curriculum consists of transcription and translation of Arabic operational material.

Credit recommendation: In the lower division baccalaureate/associate degree category, or in the upper division baccalaureate category, 32 semester hours in Modern Standard Arabic (6/87).

Intermediate Arabic Structure (AA-201)
(Arabic Morphology)
 Location: National Cryptologic School, Ft. Meade, MD.
 Length: 160 hours (4 weeks, 8 hours per day).
 Dates: January 1985-Present.
 Objective: To provide a comprehensive, detailed study of Arabic grammar at the intermediate level, utilizing Arabic grammar terms; and to give students the ability to recognize and "read through" errors in an Arabic text and to use sophisticated lexical aids.
 Learning Outcome: Upon successful completion of this course, the student will be able to provide diacritical marks for an unvoweled Arabic text (L3 Level); correct grammatical errors; conjugate verbs in the past, present, and imperative tenses; and poise sentences (L3 Level).
 Instruction: This course is designed for students who have already acquired a basic foundation in Arabic vocabulary and grammar, i.e., they have taken the "Basic Modern Standard Arabic" courses (AA-10A or AA-15A), or the equivalent; it is designed to provide the mechanics needed to deal with more sophisticated written and recorded materials.
 Credit recommendation: In the upper division baccalaureate category, 4 semester hours in Modern Standard Arabic (6/87).

CHINESE

Chinese Refresher II (CI-152)
(Formerly Basic Chinese Structure II [CI-102])
(Formerly Basic Structure of Written Chinese [CI-102])
 Location: National Cryptologic School, Ft. Meade, MD.
 Length: 480 hours (12 weeks).
 Dates: December 1970-Present.
 Objective: To master 500 selected key compounds for use in intermediate-level reading and translation from written standard Chinese into English, as well as for aural comprehension.
 Instruction: Vocabulary introduced through the medium of example sentences and passages for reading, and aural comprehension through the use of tapes. Written tests and aural tests on tape for testing of skills in comprehension, translation, and transcription.
 Credit recommendation: In the upper division baccalaureate category, 10 semester hours in Chinese (Mandarin) (3/80) (10/85). NOTE: This course has been reevaluated and continues to meet requirements for credit recommendations.

Intermediate Readings in Chinese (CI-244)
(Formerly Newspaper/Broadcast Chinese II [C-141])
(Formerly Advanced Newspaper Chinese [CI-104])
 Location: National Cryptologic School, Ft. Meade, MD.
 Length: 480 hours (12 weeks).
 Dates: December 1970-Present.
 Objective: To develop ability to translate a wide range of advanced level material from Chinese newspapers, to comprehend, transcribe, and translate long narratives and dialogues from Chinese news broadcasts and radio interviews.
 Instruction: Reading advanced level articles from current Chinese newspapers; developing ability to read Chinese newspapers freely; training in listening to current news broadcasts and radio interviews on tape, leading to development of ability to comprehend, transcribe, and translate Mandarin Chinese radio broadcasts freely.
 Credit recommendation: In the upper division baccalaureate category, 10 semester hours in Chinese (Mandarin) (3/80) (10/85). NOTE: This course has been reevaluated and continues to meet requirements for credit recommendations.

Newspaper/Broadcast Chinese I (CI-243)
(Formerly CI-103)
(Formerly Newspaper Chinese [CI-103])
 Location: National Cryptologic School, Ft. Meade, MD.
 Length: 480 hours (12 weeks).
 Dates: December 1970-Present.
 Objective: To translate material from Taiwanese, Hong Kong, and People's Republic of China newspaper articles into English, through the use of selected current articles; and to comprehend, transcribe, and translate Chinese news broadcasts, using current Voice of America material on tape in Mandarin.
 Instruction: Reading of selected articles from Chinese, Taiwanese, and People's Republic of China newspaper textbooks; developing reading ability using current newspaper articles with prepared vocabulary notes; training in aural comprehension of taped, current Voice of America news broadcasts in Mandarin Chinese.
 Credit recommendation: In the upper division baccalaureate category, 10 semester hours in Chinese (Man-

darin) (3/80) (10/85). NOTE: This course has been reevaluated and continues to meet requirements for credit recommendations.

FRENCH

Intermediate French Translation (FE-270)
   Location: National Cryptologic School, Ft. Meade, MD.
   Length: 128 hours (8 weeks, two 8-hour sessions per week).
   Dates: February 1985-Present.
   Objective: To enable students to progress from Level II to Intermediate Level III in French to English translation skills.
   Learning Outcome: Upon successful completion of this course, the student will be able to translate into English relatively complex authentic texts from French newspapers and magazines dealing with all aspects of world culture, society, and technology.
   Instruction: This course is divided into 5 segments, with each segment containing 44 relatively complex texts on political, economic, legal, technological, military and/or scientific topics taken from authentic sources written in French. Comprehension and final translation are achieved through vocabulary enrichment and sentence analysis.
   Credit recommendation: In the upper division baccalaureate category, 3 semester hours in Intermediate French Translation (6/87).

GERMAN

Introduction to German (GR-010)
   Location: National Cryptologic School, Ft. Meade, MD.
   Length: 100 hours (4 weeks, three 8-hour sessions per week).
   Dates: March 1986-Present.
   Objective: Students should be able to find items belonging to specific classes, to determine the principal participants in the exchange, and to relate the general substance in the form of a summary, and are expected to operate at an 80% level of accuracy.
   Learning Outcome: Upon successful completion of this course, the students, using given texts, will be able to answer questions derived from the text with an 80% accuracy and write summary statements.
   Instruction: This course covers sound systems and basic grammar in the German language. Phonology, orthography, morphology, and syntax are covered using practical exercises.
   Credit recommendation: In the lower division baccalaureate/associate degree category, 6 to 8 semester hours in Introductory German (6/87).

German for Reading Knowledge (GR-145)
(Basic German Reading)
   Location: National Cryptologic School, Ft. Meade, MD.
   Length: 144 hours (4 weeks).
   Dates: June 1986-Present.
   Objective: This course enables students who have had formal academic German training to refresh their skills in reading the language for understanding.
   Learning Outcome: Upon successful completion of this course, the students will have developed their reading and comprehension skills through exposure to periodical articles with different styles and different purposes in the German language.
   Instruction: The course covers synthesizing and writing summary statements without the use of a dictionary. The topics for discussion are taken from international, local, and general news items in German newspapers and magazines. The students' studies involve the reading of German for understanding.
   Credit recommendation: In the upper division baccalaureate category, 6 semester hours in German for Reading Knowledge (6/87).

Intermediate German Review (GR-153)
(German Refresher Maintenance Course)
   Location: National Cryptologic School, Ft. Meade, MD.
   Length: *Version 1:* 220 hours (6 weeks); *Version 2:* 240 hours.
   Dates: August 1985-Present.
   Objective: To enable students to raise their language to a Level 2 capacity. This course is for students who have lost their previous language proficiency through a long period of non-language use.
   Learning Outcome: Upon successful completion of this course, the students who have had formal academic German training should be able to read, translate, transcribe, listen, and understand beyond the Level 2 training in this language.
   Instruction: The course covers grammar, translation, and transcription components and allows students to work at their own pace in a formal environment.
   Credit recommendation: In the upper division baccalaureate category, 12 semester hours in Intermediate German Review (6/87).

HEBREW

Intermediate Hebrew Reading Comprehension (HB-240)
(Formerly Basic Hebrew Reading Comprehension [HB-240])
   Location: National Cryptologic School, Ft. Meade, MD.
   Length: 320 hours (40 hours per week for 8 weeks).

Dates: January 1984-Present.

Objective: To enable the student to comprehend written Hebrew on topics of current political and military interest of intermediate difficulty.

Instruction: This course emphasizes the reading and translating of Hebrew texts which are primarily drawn from newspaper articles. Course materials are of an intermediate level of difficulty.

Credit recommendation: In the lower division baccalaureate/associate degree category, 6 semester hours in Intermediate Hebrew (10/85).

Basic Hebrew Refresher (HB-150)

Location: National Cryptologic School, Ft. Meade, MD.

Length: 320 hours (40 hours per week for 8 weeks).

Dates: January 1977-January 1986.

Objective: To give the student competency in understanding spoken and written Hebrew on an elementary-intermediate level.

Instruction: A review of basic grammar and vocabulary, with particular emphasis on reading, translation, and transcription. Course content emphasis is on military and political affairs.

Credit recommendation: In the lower division baccalaureate/associate degree category, 6 semester hours in Hebrew (10/85).

Basic Modern Standard Hebrew (IU-10A)

Course 1: Basic Modern Standard Hebrew
Course 2. Intermediate Modern Standard Hebrew

Location: National Cryptologic School, Ft. Meade, MD.

Length: 1880 hours (47 weeks); classroom and self-study included. *Course 1:* 1200 hours (30 weeks); *Course 2:* 600 hours (15 weeks).

Dates: October 1974-January 1985.

Objective: To provide a thorough knowledge of Hebrew grammar and the ability to read newspaper articles of moderate difficulty.

Instruction: This course corresponds to completion of an advanced intermediate college program. Emphasis is placed on broad knowledge of political and military vocabulary and the acquisition of listening, speaking, transcription, and translation skills.

Credit recommendation: *Course 1:* In the lower division baccalaureate/associate degree category, 20 semester hours in Basic Modern Standard Hebrew; *Course 2:* In the upper division baccalaureate category, 10 semester hours in Intermediate Modern Standard Hebrew (3/80) (10/85). NOTE: This course has been reevaluated and continues to meet requirements for credit recommendations.

Intermediate Hebrew Structure (HB-200)

Location: National Cryptologic School, Fort Meade, MD.

Length: 480 hours (40 hours per week for 12 weeks).

Dates: January 1977-Present.

Objective: To enable the student to comprehend spoken and written modern Hebrew, specifically news broadcasts, newspapers, military communications, and similar technical material of an advanced level.

Instruction: The analysis of advanced Hebrew texts drawn primarily from Israeli journals, magazines, newspapers, and news broadcasts.

Credit recommendation: In the upper division baccalaureate category, 9 semester hours in Advanced Hebrew (10/85).

Intermediate Hebrew Structure (Intermediate Hebrew [IU-250])

Location: National Cryptologic School, Ft. Meade, MD.

Length: 1200 hours (30 weeks); classroom and self-study included.

Dates: November 1975-October 1985.

Objective: To provide students who have one year of prior experience in intensive Hebrew with further study of the language.

Instruction: This course corresponds to an intensive advanced intermediate-level college course emphasizing military and political vocabulary. The first 480 hours (12 weeks) is an intensive review of materials covered in Basic Modern Standard Hebrew and strengthens the basic skills of speaking, understanding, reading, and writing.

Credit recommendation: In the upper division baccalaureate category, 16 semester hours in Intermediate Hebrew (10/85).

IRAQI

Basic Colloquial Iraqi (AA-112)

Location: National Cryptologic School, Ft. Meade, MD.

Length: 480 hours (12 weeks, 40 hours per week).

Dates: March 1986-Present.

Objective: To enable the student to read, write, transcribe, and translate colloquial Iraqi Arabic at ILR Proficiency Skill Level 1.

Learning Outcome: Upon successful completion this course, the student achieves listening, reading, and writing proficiency at the ILR Level 1 Limited speaking competence.

Instruction: This course presupposes completion of AA-10A (Basic Modern Standard Arabic) or its equivalent. It provides extensive drill practice in the phonology, morphology, and syntax of the Iraqi Arabic dialect. There is primary concentration on reading, writing, and translating a wide range of situational dialogues, texts, and proverbial expressions.

Credit recommendation: In the upper division baccalaureate category, 8 semester hours in Colloquial Iraqi

Arabic (10/87).

ITALIAN

Basic Italian (IA-10A)
Location: National Cryptologic School, International Tower, Baltimore, MD.
Length: 720 hours (18 weeks), classroom and self-study included.
Dates: January 1985-Present.
Objective: To enable the student with little or no knowledge of the language to perform with proficiency in the basic skills of listening, speaking, reading, and writing.
Instruction: Comprehensive presentation of grammar, vocabulary, writing system, and phonology. Extensive use of texts, supplementary native materials, and accompanying tapes. Intensive aural-oral drilling used throughout.
Credit recommendation: In the lower division baccalaureate/associate degree category, 10-12 semester hours in Italian (10/85). NOTE: Transcriptions and native text readings go beyond first year Italian level of difficulty.

Intermediate Italian Translation (IA-270)
Location: National Cryptologic School, Ft. Meade, MD.
Length: 128 hours (8 weeks, classroom, and self-study included).
Dates: March 1986-Present.
Objective: To enable Level 2 Italian students to improve Italian to English translation skills to a Level 3 proficiency.
Learning Outcome: Upon successful completion of this course, the student will be able to translate Level 3 materials dealing with military, political, economic, technological, and scientific subjects.
Instruction: Primary emphasis is on improving translation skills, using contemporary native materials. Teacher contact supplemented by computer exercises. In-depth grammar review as warranted.
Credit recommendation: In the lower division baccalaureate/associate degree category, 3 semester hours in Italian (6/87). NOTE: Level to be determined by placement examination.

Rapid Survey of Italian Structure (IA-020)
Location: National Cryptologic School, Ft. Meade, MD.
Length: 128 hours (8 weeks, classroom and self-study included).
Dates: July 1984-Present.
Objective: To enable a student with translation proficiency in a foreign language to acquire Level 2 translating skills in Italian.
Learning Outcome: Upon successful completion of this course, the student will be able to translate Level 2 materials from Italian to English.
Instruction: Primary emphasis is on developing reading/translation skills, using native materials dealing with contemporary issues. Comprehensive presentation of Italian grammar, receptive rather than active.
Credit recommendation: In the lower division baccalaureate/associate degree category, 3 semester hours in Italian (6/87). NOTE: Level to be determined by placement examination.

JAPANESE

Basic Japanese Level I (JP-101)
(Formerly Basic Japanese Structure [JP-101])
Location: National Cryptologic School, Ft. Meade, MD.
Length: 480 hours (12 weeks).
Dates: April 1975-Present.
Objective: To develop basic skills in listening, speaking, reading, and writing, with structural points introduced inductively.
Instruction: Development of basic Japanese language skills, using intensive training in listening, speaking, reading, and writing. Extensive use of text, supplementary materials, and accompanying tapes.
Credit recommendation: In the lower division baccalaureate/associate degree or in the upper division baccalaureate category, 10 semester hours in Japanese (3/80) (10/85). NOTE: This course has been reevaluated and continues to meet requirements for credit recommendations.

Basic Japanese Level II (JP-102)
(Formerly Basic Japanese Structure [JP-102])
Location: National Cryptologic School, Ft. Meade, MD.
Length: 480 hours (12 weeks).
Dates: April 1975-Present.
Objective: Starting at 101 level, to continue developing skills in listening, speaking, reading, and writing, with structural points learned inductively.
Instruction: Development of Japanese language skills beyond the 101 level, using intensive training in listening, speaking, reading, and writing. Extensive use of text, supplementary materials, and accompanying tapes.
Credit recommendation: In the lower division baccalaureate/associate degree category or in the upper division baccalaureate category, 10 semester hours in Japanese (3/80) (10/85). NOTE: This course has been reevaluated and continues to meet requirements for credit recommendations.

Basic Japanese Level III (JP-103)
(Formerly Basic Japanese Structure [JP-103])
Location: National Cryptologic School, Ft. Meade, MD.

Length: 480 hours (12 weeks).
Dates: April 1975-Present.
Objective: Starting at 102 level, to continue developing skills in listening, speaking, reading, and writing, with structural points learned inductively; and to develop proficiency in major sentence patterns.
Instruction: Development of Japanese language skills beyond the 102 level, using intensive training in listening, speaking, reading, and writing. Extensive use of text, supplementary materials, and accompanying tapes. Translation skills are emphasized.
Credit recommendation: In the lower division baccalaureate/associate degree category or in the upper division baccalaureate category, 10 semester hours in Japanese (3/80) (10/85). NOTE: This course has been reevaluated and continues to meet requirements for credit recommendations.

Basic Japanese Level IV (JP-104)
(Formerly Basic Japanese Structure [JP-104])
Location: National Cryptologic School, Ft. Meade, MD.
Length: 480 hours (12 weeks).
Dates: April 1975-Present.
Objective: Starting at 103 level, to continue developing translation and comprehension skills, achieving proficiency in all major sentence patterns.
Instruction: Development of Japanese language skills beyond the 103 level, using intensive training in listening, speaking, reading, and writing. Extensive use of text, supplementary materials, and accompanying tapes. Translation skills for newspaper and journal articles emphasized.
Credit recommendation: In the lower division baccalaureate/associate degree category or in the upper division baccalaureate category, 10 semester hours in Japanese (3/80) (10/85). NOTE: This course has been reevaluated and continues to meet requirements for credit recommendations.

KOREAN

Basic Korean Refresher Course (KR-150)
Location: National Cryptologic School, Ft. Meade, MD.
Length: 360 hours (15 weeks).
Dates: June 1985-Present.
Objective: To enable students who have had one year prior Korean language learning experience, but who have lost broad-base language competency, to regain that competency so that they are able to translate and transcribe Level 2 materials.
Learning Outcome: Upon successful completion of this course, the student will be able to translate and transcribe Level 2 selections.
Instruction: This course is the equivalent of a one-year intensive Korean language course, enhancing functional Korean competence by reviewing basic grammar and vocabulary with particular emphasis on translation, transcription, and reading.
Credit recommendation: In the upper division baccalaureate category, 7 semester hours in Basic Korean Refresher Course (6/87).

Basic Korean Structure I (KR-101)
(Formerly Basic Korean Structure [KR-101])
Location: National Cryptologic School, Ft. Meade, MD.
Length: 480 hours (12 weeks); classroom instruction and self-study included.
Dates: October 1979-Present.
Objective: To provide students who have no language background in Korean with a knowledge of basic vocabulary, structure, and simple Chinese characters of the language in order to conduct a simple conversation on a familiar topic and to read.
Instruction: Introduction to the phonology, morphology, syntax, and writing systems of Korean orthography "Hangu'l" and to simple Chinese characters. Development of basic skills in speaking and reading. Audiolingual approach is used.
Credit recommendation: In the lower division baccalaureate/associate degree category or in the upper division baccalaureate category, 10 semester hours in Korean (3/80) (10/85). NOTE: This course has been reevaluated and continues to meet requirements for credit recommendations.

Basic Korean Structure II (KR-102)
(Formerly Basic Korean Structure [KR-102])
Location: National Cryptologic School, Ft. Meade, MD.
Length: 480 hours (12 weeks), classroom instruction and self-study.
Dates: January 1979-Present.
Objective: To provide students possessing a basic understanding of Korean (101 level), additional training in listening, speaking, reading. Translation skills emphasized. Additional Chinese characters are introduced.
Instruction: Development of Korean language skills using the intensive model with emphasis on translation skills. Audiolingual mode with accompanying text.
Credit recommendation: In the lower division baccalaureate/associate degree or in the upper division baccalaureate category, 10 semester hours in Korean (10/85).

Basic Korean Structure III (KR-103)
(Formerly Basic Korean Structure [KR-103])
Location: National Cryptologic School, Fort Meade, MD.
Length: 480 hours (8 hours/day, 5 days per week for 12 weeks), classroom instruction and self-study included.
Dates: January 1979-Present.

Objective: To provide the student with continued skill development in the Korean language beyond the 102 level. Translation skills emphasized. Additional Chinese characters are introduced.

Instruction: Development of Korean language skills beyond 102 level utilizing intensive training in listening and translating. Intermediate level Chinese characters are presented.

Credit recommendation: In the lower division baccalaureate/associate degree category or in the upper division baccalaureate category, 10 semester hours in Korean (10/85).

Basic Korean Structure IV (KR-104)
(Formerly Basic Korean Structure [KR-104])

Location: National Cryptologic School, Fort Meade, MD.

Length: 480 hours (8 hours per day, 5 days per week for 12 weeks), classroom instruction and self-study included.

Dates: January 1979-Present.

Objective: To provide the student with continued development of language ability starting at 103 level; to develop skill in reading, translating and transcribing colloquial Korean. Additional Chinese characters are introduced.

Instruction: Development of Korean language skills beyond 103 level using intensive training in primarily reading, translating, and transcribing of colloquial Korean. Study of grammatical topics, including post positions, verbalizers, and style levels. Extensive use of texts and supplemental materials. Advanced level Chinese characters are covered.

Credit recommendation: In the lower division baccalaureate/associate degree category or in the upper division baccalaureate category, 10 semester hours in Korean (10/85).

PORTUGUESE

Basic Portuguese (PT-10A)

Location: National Cryptologic School, Fort Meade, MD.

Length: *Version 1:* 880 hours (22 weeks). *Version 2:* 800 hours (20 weeks).

Dates: January 1985-Present.

Objective: To provide the student with the ability to understand the Portuguese language through development of his/her listening and reading skills; ultimately the student will be able to speak and write the language.

Instruction: Oral exercises covering the structure of the language as used in Brazil, assignments such as interpretation of newscasts and texts are well presented in order to enable the student to build up self-confidence in speaking and writing the language.

Credit recommendation: In the lower division baccalaureate/associate degree, 14 semester hours in Portuguese (10/85).

Basic Portuguese Transcription (PT-120)

Location: National Cryptologic School, Ft. Meade, MD.

Length: 96 hours (12 days, 8 hours per day).

Dates: July 1986-Present.

Objective: To enable the student to develop competency in transcribing and identifying the nature of subject spoken in one or more dialects of the Portuguese language (Brazilian, Continental, or African).

Learning Outcome: Upon successful completion of this course, the student will be able to transcribe, after a general comprehension of text heard, 85% of it, composed of 200-300 words. If full comprehension is not attained, the student will still be able to understand the subject of selected spoken texts. The classroom exercises along with the tapes and the video will enable the student to become an effective language analyst. The texts are geared towards a practical understanding of the Portuguese language.

Instruction: The course covers tapes and videos in the three modes of Portuguese: Brazilian, Continental, and African. Students are required to listen to selected texts, transcribe, gist, skim and scan relevant information contained in the texts. Usually, the texts are well pronounced and clear radio broadcast or television news.

Credit recommendation: In the lower division baccalaureate/associate degree category, 3 semester hours in Portuguese (6/87).

Portuguese for Spanish Linguistics (PT-021)

Location: National Cryptologic School, Ft. Meade, MD.

Length: 144 hours (9 weeks, two 8-hour meetings per week).

Dates: July 1984-Present.

Objective: To use effectively the student's knowledge of Spanish, emphasizing the similarities of the two languages, as well as the contrasts between them.

Learning Outcome: Upon successful completion of this course, the student will be able to read and fully understand Level 2 texts from Brazilian magazines, such as *Veja* and *Visao,* and newspapers such as *O Globo,* considered the best written texts in the current Brazilian press. The student will learn grammar in a practical way: by reading the selected texts after a brief introduction on the main characteristics of a given grammatical situation. The Spanish formation mastered by the student serves as a foundation for the contrasts, comparisons, and similarities between the two languages.

Instruction: The course covers the reading and understanding of Brazilian news and advertising, in a global comprehension of the language. The grammar is reviewed with the presentation of the texts. Designed for students who already know Spanish.

Credit recommendation: In the lower division baccalaureate/associate degree category, 4 semester hours in Portuguese (6/87). NOTE: Credit should not be granted for both this course and Rapid Survey of Portuguese (PT-020).

Rapid Survey of Portuguese (PT-020)
   Location: National Cryptologic School, Ft. Meade, MD.
   Length: 192 hours (12 weeks, two 8-hour meetings per week).
   Dates: July 1984-Present.
   Objective: To use effectively the student's knolwedge of Spanish, emphasizing the similarities of the two languages, as well as the contrasts between them.
   Learning Outcome: Upon successful completion of this course, the student will be able to read and fully understand Level 2 texts from Brazilian magazines, such as *Veja* and *Visao*, and newspapers such as *O Globo*, considered the best written texts in the current Brazilian press. The student will learn grammar in a practical way: by reading the selected texts after a brief introduction on the main characteristics of a given grammatical situation. The Spanish formation mastered by the student serves as a foundation for the contrasts, comparisons, and similarities between the two languages.
   Instruction: The course covers the reading and understanding of Brazilian news and advertising, in a global comprehension of the language. The grammar is reviewed along the presentation of texts.
   Credit recommendation: In the lower division baccalaureate/associate degree category, 6 semester hours in Portuguese (6/87). NOTE: Credit should not be granted for both this course and Portuguese for Spanish Linguistics (PT-021).

RUSSIAN

Accelerated Intermediate Intensive Russian (Russian Refresher [RU-250])
(Formerly Basic Russian Refresher [RS 151])
   Location: National Cryptologic School, Ft. Meade, MD.
   Length: 224 hours (14 weeks); two full-day sessions per week; classroom instruction and self-study included.
   Dates: April 1975-December 1985.
   Objective: To provide students who have one year of prior experience in Russian with further study of the language.
   Instruction: This course is the equivalent of a one-year intensive intermediate Russian course in an accelerated form. Perfects the four basic skills of speaking, understanding, reading, and writing. Audiolingual approach is used.
   Credit recommendation: In the lower division baccalaureate/associate degree category, 10 semester hours in Russian (5/76) (11/82). NOTE: If this course is completed after Russian 105 and/or Russian 110, credit should be reduced. This course has undergone a 5-year reevaluation and continues to meet the requirements for credit recommendations.

Advanced Russian Conversation and Composition I (RU-310)
(Formerly Intermediate Russian Seminar [RS 260])
   Location: National Cryptologic School, Ft. Meade, MD.
   Length: 160 hours (10 weeks); two full-day sessions per week; classroom instruction and self-study included.
   Dates: December 1972-Present.
   Objective: To enable students to perfect speaking skills, aural comprehension, and understanding of selected grammar problems; and to express themselves in writing.
   Instruction: This course corresponds to a fourth-year Russian conversation and composition course. Emphasis is on stylistics and idiomatic usage.
   Credit recommendation: In the upper division baccalaureate category, 3 semester hours in Russian (5/76) (11/82). NOTE: This course has undergone a 5-year reevaluation and continues to meet requirements for credit recommendations.

Advanced Russian Conversation and Composition II (RU-311)
(Formerly Advanced Russian Seminar [RS 360])
   Location: National Cryptologic School, Ft. Meade, MD.
   Length: 160 hours (10 weeks); two full-day sessions per week; classroom instruction and self-study included.
   Dates: September 1971-December 1988.
   Objective: To enable students to perfect speaking skills, aural comprehension, understanding of selected grammar problems; and to express themselves in writing.
   Instruction: This course is a continuation of RU-310, at the fourth-year level. Emphasis is on stylistics and idiomatic usage.
   Credit recommendation: In the upper division baccalaureate category, 3 semester hours in Russian (5/76) (11/82). NOTE: This course has undergone a 5-year reevaluation and continues to meet the requirements for credit recommendations.

Advanced Russian Reading (Intermediate Russian Reading [RU-240])
(Formerly Basic Russian Reading [RS 140]
   Location: National Cryptologic School, Ft. Meade, MD.
   Length: 112 hours (7 weeks); two full-day sessions per week; classroom instruction and self-study included.
   Dates: September 1974-December 1985.
   Objective: To enable students who have an intermediate knowledge of Russian to acquire further skills in reading Russian periodicals.
   Instruction: Corresponds to one semester of a third-year nonintensive Russian course with emphasis on read-

ing and abstracting technical texts and primary Soviet sources. (Prerequisite: Intermediate Russian or equivalent.)

Credit recommendation: In the upper division baccalaureate category, 3 semester hours in Russian (5/76) (11/82). NOTE: This course has undergone a 5-year reevaluation and continues to meet the requirements for credit recommendations.

Advanced Russian Translation (RU-270)
(Russian Translation Techniques [RU-270])
(Formerly Intermediate Russian Translation [RS 200])
   Location: National Cryptologic School, Ft. Meade, MD.
   Length: *Version 1:* 192 hours (12 weeks); two full-day sessions per week; classroom instruction and self-study included. *Version 2:* 128 hours (8 weeks); two full-day sessions per week. *Version 3:* 160 hours (10 weeks); two full-day sessions per week.
   Dates: *Version 1:* January 1976-December 1976. *Version 2:* January 1977-Present.
   Objective: To enable students with advanced knowledge of Russian to develop and perfect written translation skills.
   Instruction: *Versions 1 and 2:* Corresponds to one semester of a fourth-year nonintensive Russian course in written translation. Uses contemporary Russian texts. *Version 2:* Students are required to demonstrate greater proficiency to enter the course. The time devoted to technical translation has been reduced.
   Credit recommendation: *Versions 1, 2, and 3:* In the upper division baccalaureate category, 3 semester hours in Russian (5/76) (11/82). NOTE: This course has undergone a 5-year reevaluation and continues to meet the requirements for credit recommendations.

Intensive Basic and Intermediate Russian
(Comprehensive Russian [RU-15A]))
(Formerly [15A])
   Location: National Cryptologic School, Ft. Meade, MD.
   Length: *Version 1:* 2240 hours (58 weeks); *Version 2:* Approximately 2080 hours (52 weeks); classroom instruction and self-study included.
   Dates: January 1973-Present.
   Objective: To bring the student, in the shortest possible time, to the level of fluency generally acquired in two years of language study.
   Instruction: This course is the equivalent of a two-year basic and intermediate intensive Russian program. Develops the four basic skills: speaking, understanding, reading, and writing. Audiolingual approach is used.
   Credit recommendation: In the lower division baccalaureate/associate degree category, 22 semester hours in Russian (5/76) (11/82). NOTE: This course has undergone a 5-year reevaluation and continues to meet the requirements for credit recommendations.

Intermediate Intensive Russian
(Intermediate Russian Structure I [RU-201])
(Formerly Basic Russian Refresher [RS 150])
   Location: National Cryptologic School, Ft. Meade, MD.
   Length: *Version 1:* 480 hours (12 weeks); classroom instruction and self-study included. *Version 2:* 400 hours (10 weeks).
   Dates: January 1971-Present.
   Objective: To provide students who have one year of prior experience in Russian with further study of the language.
   Instruction: This course is the equivalent of a one-year intensive intermediate Russian course. Perfects the four basic skills of speaking, understanding, reading, and writing. Audiolingual approach is used.
   Credit recommendation: In the lower division baccalaureate/associate degree category, 10 semester hours in Russian (5/76) (11/82). NOTE: If this course is completed after Intermediate Russian and/or Intermediate Spoken Russian I, credit should be reduced. This course has undergone a 5-year reevaluation and continues to meet the requirements for credit recommendations.

Intermediate Russian
(Russian Structure II [RU-102])
(Formerly Basic Russian Structure [RS 105]
   Location: National Cryptologic School, Ft. Meade, MD.
   Length: *Version 1:* 240 hours (16 weeks); classroom instruction and self-study included; *Version 2:* 240 hours (12 weeks); classroom instruction and self-study included.
   Dates: September 1975-Present.
   Objective: To provide students who have a basic knowledge of Russian with further language development emphasizing reading.
   Instruction: This course is the equivalent of a second-year, nonintensive Russian course with emphasis on reading. Uses a grammar/translation approach. (Prerequisite: Russian Structure I or one year of college-level Russian.)
   Credit recommendation: In the lower division baccalaureate/associate degree category, 6 semester hours in Russian (5/76) (11/82). NOTE: This course has undergone a 5-year reevaluation and continues to meet the requirements for credit recommendations.

Intermediate Spoken Russian I
(Basic Conversation and Composition [RU-110])
(Formerly Basic Colloquial Russian [RS 110])
   Location: National Cryptologic School, Ft. Meade, MD.
   Length: 160 hours (10 weeks); two full-day sessions per week; classroom instruction and self-study included.
   Dates: March 1974-December 1975.

Objective: To enable students who have a basic knowledge of Russian to acquire further skills in spoken Russian.

Instruction: This course corresponds to the first semester of a second-year, nonintensive Russian course. Emphasizes aural comprehension and oral production. Audiolingual approach is used. (Prerequisite: Russian Structure I or one year of college-level Russian.)

Credit recommendation: In the lower division baccalaureate/associate degree category, 3 semester hours in Russian (5/76) (11/82). NOTE: This course has undergone a 5-year reevaluation and continues to meet the requirements for credit recommendations.

Russian Linguistics (RU-230)
(Formerly Introduction to Russian Linguistics [RS 130])
  Location: National Cryptologic School, Ft. Meade, MD.
  Length: *Version 1:* 128 hours (8 weeks); *Version 2:* 96 hours (8 weeks); 3 half-days.
  Dates: *Version 1:* April 1976-January 1987. *Version 2:* February 1987-Present.
  Objective: To familiarize the student with the basic principles of the phonological and morphological structure of contemporary standard Russian.
  Instruction: The topics covered in this course include: orthography, articulatory phonetics, phonemics, stressed and unstressed vowels, phonological analysis of colloquial speech, morphology, and morphophonemics. Instruction includes practical application of principles to recorded speech in a language laboratory.
  Credit recommendation: In the upper division baccalaureate category, 3 semester hours in Russian Linguistics (5/76) (11/82). NOTE: This course has undergone a 5-year reevaluation and continues to meet the requirements for credit recommendations.

Russian Structure I (RU-101)
(Formerly Introductory Russian [RS 010])
  Location: National Cryptologic School, Ft. Meade, MD.
  Length: 225 hours (15 weeks); classroom instruction and self-study included.
  Dates: January 1973-Present.
  Objective: To provide students who have no background in Russian with a knowledge of the basic vocabulary and structure of the language.
  Instruction: This course is the equivalent of a nonintensive, first-year Russian course. Develops the four basic skills: speaking, understanding, reading, and writing. Audiolingual approach is used.
  Credit recommendation: In the lower division baccalaureate/associate degree category, 6 semester hours in Russian (5/76) (11/82). NOTE: This course has undergone a 5-year reevaluation and continues to meet the requirements for credit recommendations.

Russian Textual Analysis I (RU-202)
  Location: National Cryptologic School, Ft. Meade, MD.
  Length: 240 hours (8 hours/day, 3 days/week, 10 weeks).
  Dates: January 1980-Present.
  Objective: To develop reading skills and text processing strategies. To enable students to comprehend straightforward, non-technical writing which appears in Soviet and Russian emigre periodicals; to increase aural comprehension and speaking skills.
  Instruction: Focus of this course is on developing reading skills through the application of techniques of textual analysis. Listening, speaking, and writing skills are also improved. Corresponds to a third year reading and conversation course.
  Credit recommendation: In the upper division baccalaureate category, 6 semester hours in Russian (11/82).

Russian Textual Analysis II (RU-203)
(Formerly Intermediate Russian Structure)
  Location: National Cryptologic School, Ft. Meade, MD.
  Length: *Version 1:* 128 hours (8 weeks), two full day sessions/week; *Version 2:* 160 hours (8 hours/day, 2 days/week, 10 weeks).
  Dates: *Version 1:* October 1974-September 1981; *Version 2:* October 1981-Present.
  Objective: To enable students to read standard Russian texts on several stylistic levels. To prepare students for advanced courses in translation.
  Instruction: Focus is on dealing with problems of syntax and gaining practice in restructuring Russian texts to produce smooth English translations. Corresponds to one semester of a fourth year translation course.
  Credit recommendation: *Version 1:* In the upper division baccalaureate category, 1 semester hour in Russian (5/76). *Version 2:* In the upper division baccalaureate category, 4 semester hours in Russian (11/82).

Workshop in Russian Stylistics (RU-280)
(Formerly Intermediate Colloquial Russian [RS 210])
  Location: National Cryptologic School, Ft. Meade, MD.
  Length: 160 hours (10 weeks); two full-day sessions per week; classroom instruction and self-study included.
  Dates: March 1974-Present.
  Objective: To enable students to appreciate fine points of Russian usage.
  Instruction: A tool-of-research course for the purpose of developing a deeper understanding of the more intricate patterns of Russian usage.
  Credit recommendation: In the upper division baccalaureate category, 1 semester hour in Russian (5/76)

(11/82). NOTE: This course has undergone a 5-year reevaluation and continues to meet the requirements for credit recommendations.

SPANISH

Basic Spanish Structure (SN-100)
(Formerly Basic to Intermediate Spanish Language Course I & II [SN-100])
  Location: National Cryptologic School, Fort Meade, MD.
  Length: 240 hours (6 weeks, 5 days per week).
  Dates: April 1983-Present.
  Objective: To develop the student's reading comprehension and listening skills based on grammatical sequences. Emphasis on vocabulary, translations, and transcription.
  Instruction: General basic level intensive Spanish course. Emphasis on developing reading comprehension and listening skills, vocabulary, and military and radio terminology, translation, and transcription. Graded presentation of grammar and individualized instruction. Extensive use of text, periodicals, and tapes. Frequent quizzes and diagnostic tests.
  Credit recommendation: In the lower division baccalaureate/associate degree category, 12-16 hours in Spanish (10/85). NOTE: This course covers basic to intermediate college level Spanish (12 to 16 semester hours or four college semesters).

Intermediate Spanish Translation (SN-270)
  Location: National Cryptologic School, Ft. Meade, MD.
  Length: 128 hours (8 weeks, 16 hours per week).
  Dates: February 1985-Present.
  Objective: This course is designed to assist Spanish translators in improving their ability translating Spanish to English from Level 2 to Level 3.
  Learning Outcome: Upon successful completion of this course, the student will be able to do analysis and translation of relatively complex texts on political, economical, military and/or scientific topics from authentic sources written in Spanish.
  Instruction: The course covers a text of semi-technical subject matter in Spanish. The student will write a translation into English using general and technical reference sources.
  Credit recommendation: In the upper division baccalaureate category, 4 semester hours in Spanish (6/87).

Spanish Refresher Course (SN-154)
(Basic Spanish Refresher)
  Location: National Cryptologic School, Ft. Meade, MD.
  Length: *Version 1:* 80 hours (2 weeks, 8 hours a day); *Version 2:* 240 hours (6 weeks).
  Dates: February 1986-Present.
  Objective: To provide students with basic knowledge of the Spanish language with the opportunity to further develop basic skills in listening, speaking, reading, and writing to an intermediate level.
  Learning Outcome: Upon successful completion of this course, the student will be able to comprehend the written Level 2 language of newspapers or magazine articles on personal, government, military, or commercial documents; write basic information items; and understand basic oral communication.
  Instruction: The course covers a review of basic grammar and vocabulary, with special emphasis on reading, translation, and transcription. Extensive listening practice and grammatical quizzes. Use of periodicals and video materials.
  Credit recommendation: In the lower division baccalaureate/associate degree category, 6 semester hours in Spanish (6/87).

Spanish Refresher Course - Reading (SN-151)
(Basic Spanish Refresher - Reading)
  Location: National Cryptologic School, Ft. Meade, MD.
  Length: 80 hours (2 weeks, 8 hours a day).
  Dates: August 1982-Present.
  Objective: This course enables students who have had formal academic training to refresh their skills in reading the Spanish language for understanding to Level 2 and 3.
  Learning Outcome: Upon successful completion of this course, the student will be able to read a text from a current Latin American or Spanish newspaper or magazine and understand military, political, or technical articles, and write a summary or gist.
  Instruction: The course covers reading of current newspaper and magazine articles on government, military, and political subjects. Materials are graded on the intermediate level. Students work at their own pace.
  Credit recommendation: In the lower division baccalaureate/associate degree category, 2 semester hours in Spanish (6/87).

Spanish Refresher Course - Translation (SN-152)
(Basic Spanish Refresher - Translation)
  Location: National Cryptologic School, Ft. Meade, MD.
  Length: 80 hours (2 weeks, 8 hours a day).
  Dates: June 1987-Present.
  Objective: This course enables students who have had formal academic training in the Spanish language to refresh their skills in translating intermediate level Spanish texts from Spanish to English to Level 2 or 3.
  Learning Outcome: Upon successful completion of this course, the student will be able to read a text from a current Latin American or Spanish newspaper or magazine and write a translation from Spanish to English.

Instruction: The course covers translation of current newspaper and magazine articles on government, military, and political subjects. Materials are graded on the intermediate level. Students work at their own pace.

Credit recommendation: In the lower division baccalaureate/associate degree category, 2 semester hours in Spanish (6/87).

Spanish Refresher Course - Transcription (SN-153)
(Basic Spanish Refresher - Transcription)
Location: National Cryptologic School, Ft. Meade, MD.
Length: 80 hours (2 weeks, 8 hours a day).
Dates: August 1982-Present.
Objective: This course enables students who have had formal academic training in Spanish to refresh their ability to transcribe intermediate Spanish Level 2 text material.
Learning Outcome: Upon successful completion of this course, the student will be able to produce a verbatim transcription in Spanish from a text of aural Spanish information.
Instruction: The course covers transcription of currently taped radio and audio materials on government, military, and political issues. Students work at their own pace.
Credit recommendation: In the lower division baccalaureate/associate degree category, 2 semester hours in Spanish (6/87).

TURKISH

Basic Modern Turkish (TR-10A)
Location: National Cryptologic School, Ft. Meade, MD.
Length: *Version 1:* 1200 hours (30 weeks), *Version 2:* 1880 hours; classroom and self-study included.
Dates: *Version 1:* December 1975-April 1984, *Version 2:* May 1984-Present.
Objective: To provide a strong knowledge of and fluency in using the grammatical structures of Turkish. A general vocabulary is developed with some introduction to newspaper Turkish.
Instruction: This course is the equivalent of a two-year basic and intermediate intensive Turkish program. It develops the four basic skills: speaking, understanding, reading, and writing. Modified audiolingual approach is used; in addition to spoken exercises, grammar explanations, translation, and reading are emphasized.
Credit recommendation: In the lower division baccalaureate/associate degree category, or in the upper division baccalaureate category, 20 semester hours in Turkish (3/80) (10/85). NOTE: This course has been reevaluated and continues to meet requirements for credit recommendations.

MANAGEMENT EDUCATION DEPARTMENT

Management Education Department is a department of the Cryptologic Management Faculty. It provides supervisory, managerial, executive management education to all levels of management at the National Cryptologic School. It is also responsible for providing functional management training to meet agency needs.

Behavioral Sciences Concepts and Applications in Management
(Cryptologic Management for Supervisors [MC-120])
Location: National Cryptologic School, Ft. Meade, MD.
Length: 70 hours (2 weeks).
Dates: September 1969-Present.
Objective: To enable students to increase their effectiveness as first-line supervisors through knowledge of behavioral sciences and their applications to management.
Instruction: Interpersonal communications and conflict resolution, performance appraisal and counseling, leadership styles and group behavior, management of personnel, motivational theories and applications. Lecture, discussion, case studies, and group exercises are used.
Credit recommendation: In the upper division baccalaureate category, 2 semester hours in Business Administration or Management (9/76) (11/82). NOTE: A substantial portion of the material covered in this course is covered in MC-210. Therefore, credit should not be granted for MC-210 if it is granted for Behavioral Sciences Concepts and Applications in Management. This course has undergone a 5-year reevaluation and continues to meet the requirements for credit recommendations.

1. Clerical Orientation (OS-052)
2. (Formerly Clerical Introduction [OS-051] or [OS-050])
Location: National Cryptologic School, Ft. Meade, MD.
Length: 1. 24 hours (3 days); 2. 32 hours (4 days).
Dates: June 1971-Present.
Objective: To enable the employee to upgrade clerical skills.
Instruction: Introduction to clerical procedures, including filing, drafts, proofreading, and use of office machines; mail management; managing paperwork flow. Lecture discussion, and practical exercises are used.
Credit recommendation: In the lower division baccalaureate/associate degree category, 1 semester hour in Secretarial Science (9/76) (11/82). NOTE: This course has undergone a 5-year reevaluation and continues to meet the requirements for credit recommendations.

Cryptologic Management for Managers (MC-210)
Location: National Cryptologic School, Ft. Meade, MD.

Length: 70 hours (2 weeks).
Dates: September 1973-June 1985.
Objective: To enable midlevel managers to broaden their knowledge of modern management concepts, philosophy, and techniques as well as of behavioral science.
Instruction: Components of the management process, organization theory, motivation, job enrichment, management by objectives, network theory and analysis, transactional analysis, organization development. Lecture, discussion, case studies, and practical exercises are used.
Credit recommendation: In the upper division baccalaureate category or in the graduate degree category, 3 semester hours in Business Administration or Management (9/76) (11/82). NOTE: A substantial portion of the material presented in this course is covered in Behavioral Sciences Concepts and Applications in Management. Therefore, credit should not be granted for Behavioral Sciences Concepts and Applications in Management if it is granted for MC-210. This course has undergone a 5-year reevaluation and continues to meet the requirements for credit recommendations.

Introduction to Management
(Cryptologic Management for Interns [MC-107])
Location: National Cryptologic School, Ft. Meade, MD.
Length: 35 hours (1 week).
Dates: March 1975-August 1979.
Objective: To enable new supervisors to develop interpersonal administrative skills to improve job performance.
Instruction: The functions of supervision, styles of leadership, personnel practices, interpersonal communications, motivation, performance appraisal and counseling, decision making and problem solving. Lecture, discussion, case studies, and group exercises are used. **Prerequisites:** Assigned to a supervisory position; completion of Cryptologic Management for Managers (MC-210) and Cryptologic Management for Supervisors (MC-120); voluntary participation.
Credit recommendation: In the lower division baccalaureate/associate degree category, 2 semester hours in Business Administration or Management (9/76) (11/82). NOTE: Credit should be granted for this course or for MC-105, but not for both. This course has undergone a 5-year reevaluation and continues to meet the requirements for credit recommendations.

Introduction to Supervision [MC-105]
Location: National Cryptologic School, Ft. Meade, MD.
Length: 35 hours (1 week).
Dates: September 1970-Present.
Objective: To enable new supervisors to develop interpersonal and administrative skills to improve their job performance.
Instruction: The functions of supervision, styles of leadership, personnel practices, interpersonal communications, motivation, performance appraisal and counseling, decision making and problem solving. Lecture, discussion, case studies, and group exercises are used.
Credit recommendation: In the lower division baccalaureate/associate degree category, 2 semester hours in Business Administration or Management (9/76) (11/82). NOTE: Credit should be granted for this course or for Introduction to Management (MC-107) but not for both. Additionally, a substantial portion of the material in this course is covered in MC-120. This course has undergone a 5-year reevaluation and continues to meet the requirements for credit recommendations.

Managerial Grid Seminar (MG-240)
Location: National Cryptologic School, Ft. Meade, MD.
Length: 50 hours (5½ days); residential; 30 hours preparatory independent study.
Dates: January 1967-December 1988.
Objective: To enable managers to understand and apply the management grid concept.
Instruction: Introduction to the managerial grid; clarification of the grid concept, with special emphasis on application of grid techniques. Extensive use is made of practical exercises.
Credit recommendation: In the upper division baccalaureate category, 2 semester hours, or in the graduate degree category, 1 semester hour, in Business Administration or Management (9/76).

Organizational Problem Solving for Executives (MC-320)
(Formerly Executive-Level Problem Analysis and Decision Making Seminar [MG-320])
Location: National Cryptologic School, Ft. Meade, MD.
Length: 50 hours (5½ days); residential; 30 hours preparatory independent study.
Dates: July 1969-September 1982.
Objective: To enable executive-level managers to improve their ability to integrate the concepts of problem solving and decision making with those of the communication process.
Instruction: Communication, planning, and problem solving; concept integration; quantitative decision making; problem diagnosis and means-ends analyses; group process and individual approaches. Extensive use is made of case studies and practical exercises.
Credit recommendation: In the upper division baccalaureate category or in the graduate degree category, 3 semester hours in Management (9/76) (11/82). NOTE: Credit should be granted for this course or for MG-230, but not for both. This course has undergone a 5-year reevaluation and continues to meet the requirements for

credit recommendations.

Organizational Problem Solving for Managers (MC-230)
(Formerly Manager-Level Decision Making Seminar [MG-320])
  Location: National Cryptologic School, Ft. Meade, MD; San Angelo, TX.
  Length: 50 hours (5½ days); residential; 30 hours preparatory independent study.
  Dates: December 1970-December 1988.
  Objective: To enable midlevel managers to improve their ability to integrate the concepts of problem solving and decision making with those of the communication process.
  Instruction: Communication, planning, and problem solving; concept integration; total systems integration; problem diagnosis and means-ends analyses; group process and individual approaches. Extensive use is made of case studies and practical exercises.
  Credit recommendation: In the upper division baccalaureate category or in the graduate degree category, 3 semester hours in Management (9/76) (11/82). NOTE: Credit should be granted for this course or for MG-320, but not for both. This course has undergone a 5-year reevaluation and continues to meet the requirements for credit recommendations.

Procurement
(Procurement Management for Technical Personnel [MT-420])
  Location: National Cryptologic School, Ft. Meade, MD.
  Length: *Version 1:* 30 hours (5 weeks); two 3-hour meetings per week. *Version 2:* 30 hours (5 days); two 3-hour meetings per day. *Version 3:* 35 hours (5 days).
  Dates: December 1966-Present.
  Objective: To provide personnel whose assignment is related to procurement with an understanding of the regulatory, procedural, and statutory requirements that form the basis of the contract function in Defense Procurement.
  Instruction: Procurement planning, national policy and source selection, types of contracts. Lecture and discussion are used.
  Credit recommendation: In the upper division baccalaureate category, 1 semester hour in Business Administration or Marketing (9/76) (11/82). NOTE: This course has undergone a 5-year reevaluation and continues to meet requirements for credit recommendations.

Transactional Analysis (MG-255)
  Location: National Cryptologic School, Ft. Meade, MD.
  Length: 28 hours (2 weeks); two full-day sessions per week; 8 hours preparatory independent study.
  Dates: October 1975-April 1976.
  Objective: To enable managers to improve management skills through interpersonal communications.
  Instruction: Definition of ego states, application of ego states in interpersonal communications, role of transactional analysis. Lecture and discussion are used, with special emphasis on practical exercises.
  Credit recommendation: In the upper division baccalaureate category, 1 semester hour in Behavioral Science (9/76) (11/82). NOTE: This course has undergone a 5-year reevaluation and continues to meet requirements for credit recommendations.

MATHEMATICS DEPARTMENT

Combinatorial Mathematics (MA-414)
  Location: National Cryptologic School, Fort Meade, MD.
  Length: 48 hours (6 hours per week for 8 weeks).
  Dates: January 1975-Present.
  Objective: To introduce students to the advanced principles of combinatorial theory and illustrate a wide range of current and potential applications.
  Instruction: Lecture, exercises, and advanced problems on techniques of enumeration, generating functions and recursions, Mobus inversion in partially order set, fast transformations, systems of distinct representatives, lating squares, finite geometries, Hadamard matrices, block design and difference sets, code design.
  Credit recommendation: In the graduate category, 3 semester hours in Advanced Operations Research (I.E., or E.E.), Artificial Intelligence, or Mathematics (special topics) (10/85).

Fourier Analysis for Cryptanalysis
(Fourier Analysis; or Advanced Topics in Fourier Analysis [MA 302])
  Location: National Cryptologic School, Fort Meade, MD.
  Dates: January 1975-Present.
  Objective: To provide students with an extensive coverage of Fourier Analysis, and advanced coverage of select Fourier Analysis applications in engineering and physics.
  Instruction: Lecture, discussion, exercises, (unsolved) problems, overview of the many applications of the Fourier Transformation and its many forms, continuous, discrete, multidimensional, optical transformations. Review of complex variable theory, Residue Theorem, Cauchy-Schwartz, Rumann-Lebesgue Lemma. Research on present, real-world applications and problem solving.
  Credit recommendation: In the graduate category, 3 semester hours in Applied Mathematics, Electrical Engineering Applications of Fourier Analysis, or Physics (10/85).

Introduction to Astrodynamics (MA 500)
  Location: National Cryptologic School, Fort Meade, MD.
  Length: 48 hours (6 hours per week for 8 weeks).
  Dates: January 1975-Present.
  Objective: To introduce students to the concepts and applications of astrodynamics.
  Instruction: Lecture, discussion, exercises, and problems dealing with such concepts as coordinate systems and time scales and references; two-body problem; perturbations, special and general; powered flight; orbit determination and tracking.
  Credit recommendation: In the graduate category, 3 semester hours in Astronomy, Geophysics, Mathematical Modeling, or Operations Research (10/85).

Introduction to Computer Science Math (MA 400)
  Location: National Cryptologic School, Fort Meade, MD.
  Length: 60 hours (6 hours per week for 10 weeks).
  Dates: July 1976-Present.
  Objective: To provide students with mathematical knowledge and skills, beyond college and intermediate algebra, with which to proceed into math-related computer coursework and applications, and statistics.
  Instruction: Lecture, exercises, and problems in the topical areas of linear functions, arrays and matrices, polynomial functions, exponential and logarithmic functions, logic tables, and Boolean algebra.
  Credit recommendation: In the lower division baccalaureate/associate degree category, 3 semester hours in Finite Mathematics or Pre-Calculus Math (10/85).

Mathematical Statistics (MA 146)
  Location: National Cryptologic School, Fort Meade, MD.
  Length: 60 hours (6 hours per week for 10 weeks).
  Dates: January 1975-Present.
  Objective: To provide students with an advanced coverage of statistics utilizing calculus-based mathematics (integral calculus required).
  Instruction: Nature of statistical methods; elementary sampling theory for one variable; correlation, regression, and theoretical frequency distributions for studying these; general principles for hypothesis testing and estimation; testing goodness of fit; small sample distributions; cryptologic examples and exercises. Course stresses both theory and cryptologic applications.
  Credit recommendation: In the upper division baccalaureate or graduate degree category, 2 semester hours in Economics, Math Statistics, or M.B.A. Stat/Quantitative Applications (10/85).

Probability and Statistics (MA 144)
(Social Sciences Statistics)

(Economics/Business Administration Statistics)
  Location: National Cryptologic School, Fort Meade, MD.
  Length: 72 hours (3 hours per day, 2 days per week for 12 weeks).
  Dates: July 1976-Present.
  Objective: To provide students with an introduction and overview of the theory and applications of probability, descriptive statistics, and statistical testing.
  Instruction: Lecture, exercises, problems, and examinations over permutations, combinations, probability rules, Bayes rule; descriptive statistics; binomial, hypergeometric and normal distributions; point and interval estimation; sampling; hypothesis testing; student's t-distribution, chi-square, regression and correlation analysis, non-metric statistics.
  Credit recommendation: In the lower division baccalaureate/associate degree category, 3 semester hours in Business Administration or Economics (10/85).

Probability Theory (MA 145)
  Location: National Cryptologic School, Fort Meade, MD.
  Length: 60 hours (6 hours per week for 10 weeks).
  Dates: January 1975-Present.
  Objective: To provide students with an advanced coverage of probability theory utilizing calculus-based mathematics (integral calculus required).
  Instruction: Probability theory as a study of mathematical models of random phenomena; basic probability theory; random variables; independence and dependence; Markov chains; numerical-valued random phenomena; mean and variance of a probability law; normal, Poisson, and related probability laws; cryptologic examples and exercises.
  Credit recommendation: In the upper division baccalaureate or graduate category, 2 semester hours in Economics, M.B.A. Stat/Quantitative Applications, or Math Statistics (10/85).

National Emergency Training Center

The National Emergency Training Center (NETC) is a training facility where training opportunites are offered in fire prevention and control and emergency management through the National Fire Academy and the Emergency Management Institute. Situated on a 107-acre campus near historic Gettysburg, the two institutions maintain 19 fully equipped classrooms and can accommodate up to 1,000 students with housing for over 540.

The training institutions are the development and delivery elements of the Office of Training which integrates a diversity of training efforts sponsored by the various program offices in the Federal Emergency Management

Agency (FEMA). NETC provides cost-effective, safe, facilities that maximize student comfort and educational resources.

Source of official student records: Office of Admissions and Registration, National Emergency Training Center, 18625 South Seton Avenue, Emmitsburg, MD 21727.

Additional information about the courses: Program on Noncollegiate Sponsored Instruction, The Center for Adult Learning and Educational Credentials, American Council on Education, One Dupont Circle, Washington, D.C. 20036.

NATIONAL FIRE ACADEMY

The National Fire Academy works to enhance the ability of the fire service and applied professions to deal most effectively with the fire problem. The Academy is authorized by the Federal Fire Prevention and Control Act of 1974 to provide training and education through programs delivered on-campus at the Emmitsburg training site and through courses delivered off-campus in every state. Off-campus training is handled in cooperation with state and local fire training officials.

On the Emmitsburg campus, the Academy offers specialized training courses and advanced management programs of national impact. These courses and programs are offered in a concentrated, residential setting most conducive for such intensive learning. On-campus resident programs are targeted to middle and top-level fire officers, fire service instructors, selected technical professionals, and representatives from the allied professions.

Advanced Fire Safety (R341)
(Formerly Management or Administration of Public Fire Education)
  Location: Emmitsburg, MD.
  Length: 80 hours (2 weeks).
  Dates: October 1984-Present.
  Objective: To provide the student with the necessary knowledge and skill to formulate and administer a public education program in fire prevention.
  Learning Outcome: Upon successful completion of this course, the student will be able to create an education package which includes a planning process for fire safety; demonstrate selecting appropriate instructional strategies related to task analysis; and create a criterion-referenced test with three types of questions.
  Instruction: Course covers sharing with other participants one program, program element, audiovisual element, or other public education from home-based public education program; and apply accepted principle statistical analysis and a cost benefit analysis.
  Credit recommendation: In the lower division baccalaureate/associate degree category, 2 semester hours in Educational Administration, Fire Administration, or Introductory Management (3/83) (12/88). NOTE: This course has been reevaluated and continues to meet requirements for credit recommendations.

Advanced Incident Command
(Formerly Incident Command II)
  Location: Emmitsburg, MD.
  Length: 57 hours (2 weeks).
  Dates: July 1980-August 1985.
  Objective: To provide students with an understanding of complex firesite operations. Focus is on multiple company response and efficient utilization of available and prospective resources in managing major incidents.
  Instruction: Course provides students with an understanding of complex firesite tactics and fire operations. Emphasis is given to the study of multiple company resources on combating multiple company fires. The study of multiple unit response, staff and command operations, and organization and utilization of staff and nonfire support is undertaken as an integral part of the course. It also provides an opportunity to improve ground organization with multiple unit response. Lecture, discussion, and media techniques are used.
  Credit recommendation: In the upper division baccalaureate category, 3 semester hours in Fire Science (6/81).

Arson Detection
  Location: Emittsburg, MD.
  Length: 36½ hours (1 week).
  Dates: July 1978-March 1985.
  Objective: To provide students with a basic understanding of arson motivation to enable them to relate types of fires to certain individuals and groups. To provide overviews of evidence-collection procedures and of legal requirements governing fire-scene searches. To suggest the proper demeanor for courtroom testimony.
  Instruction: Covers method of determining the point of origin of a fire, what indicators to search for at the fire scene, and how to evaluate fire-scene conditions to determine the fire's probable cause. Students are taught to interpret the visual indicators which make possible a preliminary determination of cause of death when fatalities are associated with fires, and learn the procedures to follow in such cases. Discriminating between accidental and incendiary fire causes, handling operations at the fire scene, collecting and preserving evidence, and recording information for support of later arson investigations are also covered. This course is not designed to fill the more advanced needs of the fire investigator. Lecture, discussion, and media techniques are used.
  Credit recommendation: In the lower division baccalaureate/associate degree category, 2 semester hours in Criminal Justice, Fire Science, Insurance, or Investigation (6/81).

Building Construction: Non-Combustible and Fire Resistive (F150)
  Location: Host sites throughout the United States.
  Length: 16 hours (2 days).
  Dates: July 1983-Present.
  Objective: To enable the student to cite key features of non-combustible or fire-resistive buildings that affect emergency operations. Fire and life safety concerns that exist in non-combustible and fire-resistive structures are studied.
  Instruction: This course links the key features of non-combustible and fire-resistive structures that affect emergency operations. The fire behaviors of steel and concrete are presented so that the effect of their presence in non-combustible or fire-resistive structures may be better anticipated. Basic principles that apply to the spread of fire, products of combustion in structures and special problems with interior finishes and building elements are discussed. Testing methods for materials are covered. The unique problems of conducting emergency operations in buildings under construction are studied. Lecture, discussion and simulation exercises are used.
  Credit recommendation: In the lower division baccalaureate/associate degree category, 1 semester hour in Construction Technology or Fire Science (8/86).

Building Construction: Principles—Wood and Ordinary Construction (F100)
  Location: Host sites throughout the United States.
  Length: 16 hours (2 days).
  Dates: July 1982-Present.
  Objective: To enable the student to recognize construction types, design, alternation consequences, materials used, and their influence on the building's reaction to fire. In a tactical situation construction features and resultant potential hazards to firefighters are studied.
  Instruction: This course provides students with the information of how the construction type, alterations, design and materials influence a building's reaction to fire. The principle of "fireground" reading of a building and the value of relevant advance information about buildings are explained. Major areas of study include building stability and resistance to fire, special hazards to firefighters and construction elements, and the determination of likely paths of fire extension. Lecture, discussion and simulation exercises are used.
  Credit recommendation: In the lower division baccalaureate/associate degree category, 1 semester hour in Construction Technology or Fire Science (8/86).

Chemistry of Hazardous Materials (R-234)
(Formerly Hazardous Materials I)
  Location: Emittsburg, MD.
  Length: *Versions 1 & 2:* 84 hours (2 weeks); *Version 3:* 95 hours (2 weeks).
  Dates: *Version 1:* January 1981-February 1983; *Version 2:* March 1983-November 1988; *Version 3:* December 1988-Present.
  Objective: To provide students a sound understanding of the basic chemistry of hazardous materials, key properties of important hazardous materials products, and significant storage and handling requirements for hazardous materials in their normal environment.
  Instruction: *Versions 1 and 2:* Course provides the basic knowledge required to evaluate potential hazards and behaviors of materials considered dangerous. Emphasis is on the underlying reasons for recommended handling of hazardous materials, with the hope this knowledge will lead to improve decision making and safer operations and handling. For fire officers who may be involved in hazardous-material incidents or in the inspection of occupancies, vehicles, watercraft, or aircraft containing hazardous materials. Lecture, discussion, laboratory, and workshops are used. *Version 3:* Increased emphasis is placed on the chemistry of hazardous materials.
  Credit recommendation: *Version 1:* In the lower division baccalaureate/associate degree category, 2 semester hours in Engineering, Fire Science Chemistry, General Science, or Physical Science (6/81). *Version 2:* In the lower division baccalaureate/associate degree category, 3 semester hours in Engineering, Fire Science Chemistry, General Science, or Physical Science (3/83). *Version 3:* In the upper division baccalaureate category, 4 semester hours in Engineering, Fire Science Chemistry, General Science, or Physical Science (12/88). NOTE: This course has been reevaluated and continues to meet requirements for credit recommendations.

Code Management: A Systems Approach (R101)
  Location: Emmitsburg, MD.
  Length: 68 hours (15 weeks; 2 one-hour meetings per week).
  Dates: August 1988-Present.
  Objective: To develop the student's awareness of code management functions as an integrated system and to enhance management skills in areas of system analysis, knowledge of codes, code development and adoption, code management, and evaluation of code functions.
  Learning Outcome: Upon successful completion of this course, the student will have knowledge of analyzing specific codes systems; be able to apply and evaluate knowledge of code systems; and role play a comprehensive code adoption hearing.
  Instruction: Course covers system analysis, data collection, risk analysis, codes, codes in the United States, fire in America, general scope of codes, scope of building codes, fire codes, model consensus codes, code groups, standards, appeals process, application of codes, code development research, new technology, data analysis, and adopting effective laws.
  Credit recommendation: In the upper division baccalaureate or graduate category, 3 semester hours in Ad-

ministrative Law, Decision Making, Legal Environment of Management as Business, Management, Policy Development, or Policy Formation (12/88).

Command and Control of Fire Department Operations (R304)
  Location: Emmitsburg, MD.
  Length: 63 hours (2 weeks).
  Dates: February 1986-Present.
  Objective: To enable the student to take initial command and control emergencies of greater alarm level using a planned management system. To provide the student with techniques and skills necessary for firefighter safety and survival.
  Instruction: This course links two subjects of importance to fireground managers: operations and safety. The course is devoted to command and control for chief officers in charge of several companies or who initially command greater alarm incidents. Major areas of study include pre-incident preparation, size-up, an incident command system, and incident management. Principles of safety and survival and causes of fatalities among firefighters are stressed throughout the course. Physical fitness and stress management are also emphasized. Lecture, discussion, student activities, and various media are used.
  Credit recommendation: In the upper division baccalaureate category, 3 semester hours in Fire Science (8/86).

Command and Control of Fire Department Operations at Catastrophic Disasters (R308)
(Formerly Command and Control of Fire Department Operations at Earthquake and Other Catastrophic Disasters [R308])
  Location: Emmitsburg, MD.
  Length: 65 hours (2 weeks).
  Dates: April 1986-Present.
  Objective: To provide fire commanders and emergency control officers with the necessary knowledge, skills, and attitudes for commanding fire department field operations during a large scale natural disaster such as: an earthquake, hurricane, tornado, or flood.
  Instruction: The course covers the extensive aspects of damage, problems, and issues involved with catastrophic disasters. Special consideration is given to the effect of these conditions on fire units' functions. In addition, the course views carefully the command and control of Fire Service Operations within an incident Command System Structure. The positive effect of the Integrated Emergency Management System (IEMS) is also covered. Lecture, media, simulations and student projects are used.
  Credit recommendation: In the upper division baccalaureate category, 3 semester hours in Emergency Management, Environmental Science, or Fire Science (8/86).

Community Fire Defenses: Challenges and Solutions
  Location: Emmitsburg, MD.
  Length: 16 hours (2 days).
  Dates: November 1983-Present.
  Objective: To enable students to use a workable problem solving process for analyzing risk and addressing community fire protection.
  Instruction: Course provides training in analyzing data, identifying problems, formulating objectives, analyzing casual factors, developing selection criteria, identifying alternative solutions, developing implementation strategies and designing an evaluation plan. Lecture, discussion, media and application activities are used.
  Credit recommendation: In the lower division baccalaureate/associate degree category, 1 semester hour in Fire Science (8/85).

Community Fire Protection: Planning (R802)
  Location: Emmitsburg, MD.
  Length: 40 hours (1 week).
  Dates: July 1988-Present.
  Objective: To develop and provide students with the planning skills necessary from a technical and political standpoint to effectively plan a local fire program.
  Learning Outcome: Upon successful completion of this course, the student will be able to evaluate the community needs associated with risk of fire; select and evaluate the most efficient system in developing community fire protection programs; and define and design a fire and life safety system for a community.
  Instruction: Course covers planning strategy, analysis of current systems including risk, developing solutions and action plans to be implemented and evaluate the various problems associated with community fire planning.
  Credit recommendation: In the upper division baccalaureate category, 2 semester hours in Administration, Fire Science, Management, or Public Administration (12/88).

Emergency Medical Service and Administration: An Overview
  Location: Emmitsburg, MD and host sites throughout the United States.
  Length: 16 hours (2 days).
  Dates: April 1981-Present.
  Objective: To provide students with an overview of the skills needed to design and manage an emergency medical services organization unit.
  Instruction: The EMS Administration course will provide the fire and rescue service manager with an overview of the issues associated with the development of an EMS Program. Specific topics include resources and constraints to system development impact of EMS on capital and operation costs of the fire department mechanisms for medical control and quality assurance, sources of support, implementation, and administration of EMS service, and

legal implications of EMS. Individual and group activities provide opportunities for interaction among participants. Lecture, discussion and media techniques are used.

Credit recommendation: In the lower division baccalaureate/associate degree category, 1 semester hour in Emergency Management, Fire Science, Health Safety or Public Administration (8/85).

Fire Arson Investigation
(Formerly Arson Investigation)
Location: Emmitsburg, MD.
Length: *Version 1:* 90 hours (3 weeks); *Version 2:* 80 hours (2 weeks).
Dates: *Version 1:* January 1978-August 1985; *Version 2:* September 1985-Present.
Objective: *Version 1:* To enable students to conduct legal investigations of fires which occur in their jurisdictions. *Version 2:* To enable students to properly identify the origin and cause of a fire, conduct a technically and legally proper scene and follow-up investigation, and properly pursue the case throughout the judicial system.
Instruction: *Version 1:* Course provides training for personnel primarily responsible for the investigation of fire-related incidents. It is an in-depth course dealing with methods and techniques of conducting a legal investigation into all aspects of fire. The course deals with fire investigation and prosecution of arson. Students will be able to determine the origin and cause of a fire and prepare the necessary forms, sketches, and reports an investigation requires. The identity of common motives encountered in fire investigations, and collection and preservation of evidence which may be used to prove some fact or occurence is covered. The course includes both classroom and application, where knowledge and experience are acquired from observation of actual building-burning, scene examinations, and case development. Lecture, discussion, and media techniques are used. *Version 2:* Course provides training in fire investigation. The course is a rigorous treatment in which objectives are accomplished through concentrated effort in the classroom and laboratory. It identifies recommended methods for conducting legal fire investigations which culminate when appropriate, in prosecution for arson. Emphasis is given to determining origin and cause of the fire as well as motivation of the firesetter. Details of investigation, insurance, fire protection systems, types of fires, incendiary devices, legal aspects, interviews, evidence collection and information management are provided. Lecture, discussion, media, laboratory work and application activities are used.
Credit recommendation: *Version 1:* In the lower division baccalaureate/associate degree category, 4 semester hours in Criminal Justice, Fire Science, Insurance, or Investigation (6/81). *Version 2:* In the upper division baccalaureate or graduate degree category, 3 semester hours in Arson Investigation, Criminal Justice, Fire Science, or Insurance (7/86). NOTE: This course has been reevaluated and continues to meet requirements for credit recommendations.

Fire Command Operations (R801)
Location: Emmitsburg, MD.
Length: 35 hours (1 week).
Dates: July 1988-Present.
Objective: To develop the student's skills, technique, and knowledge for managing and directing operations at emergency sites.
Learning Outcome: Upon successful completion of this course, the student will be able to apply the "Incident Command System" in organizing emergency procedures at various kinds of sites and under varying types of conditions and situations; coordinate the activities of multiple skill units; and provide a concentrated effort at effecting solutions in emergency situations.
Instruction: Course covers identifying problems, planning, pre-planning, intra-agency corrdination, incident identification, management, and strategic planning.
Credit recommendation: In the upper division baccalaureate category, 2 semester hours in Fire Science, Human Resource Management, Occupational Health and Safety, or Public Management (12/88). NOTE: Credit for Incident Command Systems should not be awarded if credit is awarded for this course.

Fire Executive Development III
(Formerly Senior Executive Development)
Location: Emmitsburg, MD.
Length: 76½ hours (2 weeks).
Dates: January 1980-Present.
Objective: To enable students to identify the role and responsibilities of the fire executive and current and future challenges affecting that role; and to provide students with a knowledge of the effective use of management concepts and techniques as well as current issues in management.
Instruction: Course provides an opportunity for senior-level fire executives to expand their managerial approaches and improve the effectiveness of their organizations by applying current theories of management. Subject areas include the emerging role and responsibilities of executives, future trends in American communities, policy formulation and planning, legal dimensions of the fire service, management of human and physical resources, personnel management, and fire department effectiveness and productivity. Students are generally senior-level fire officers, state fire marshals, and assistant state fire marshals. Lecture and discussion are used.
Credit recommendation: In the graduate degree category, 3 semester hours or in the upper division baccalaureate category, 4 semester hours in Business Administration, Fire Science Management or Public Administration (6/81) (7/86). NOTE: This course has been reevaluated and continues to meet requirements for credit recommendations.

Firefighter Health and Safety: Program Implementation and Management

Location: Emmitsburg, MD and host sites throughout the United States.

Length: 16 hours (2 eight-hour days).

Dates: May 1986-Present.

Objective: To provide the student with an understanding of general health and safety guidelines and practices needed by firefighters.

Learning Outcome: Upon successful completion of this course, the student will be able to identify and analyze firefighter health and safety concerns; determine the components of an effective department health and safety program; and understand the steps and process necessary to design and implement such a program.

Instruction: Course covers safety as an attitude, developing a health and safety program, laws, standards and regulations, health maintenance and physical fitness, stress, emergency scene safety, and safety investigation.

Credit recommendation: In the lower division baccalaureate/associate degree category, or in the upper division baccalaureate category, 2 semester hours in Engineering (Industrial), Fire Science, Health Promotion, Health Safety, or Occupational Safety (12/88).

Firefighter Safety and Survival: Company Officer's Responsibility

Location: Emmitsburg, MD and host sites throughout the United States.

Length: 16 hours (2 eight-hour days).

Dates: June 1985-Present.

Objective: To provide the student with an appreciation of the seriousness of the firefighter injury and death problems and to provide an awareness of techniques for reducing injuries and deaths.

Learning Outcome: Upon successful completion of this course, the student will be able to understand the causes of injury and death; understand the behavior problems and attitudes that are addressed; identify health and fitness programs related to injury and death; identify hazardous situations found in training; identify and correct five station hazards; identify and resolve hazards responding to and returning from a fire; identify and enforce procedures to improve incident scene safety; and identify safety and survival tips.

Instruction: Course provides an explanation of firefighter injuries and deaths; firefighter health and fitness, safety in training, station and response preparation safety, incident safety, post-incident safety, and survival tips.

Credit recommendation: In the lower division baccalaureate/associate degree category, 1 semester hour in Fire Administration, Fire Management, or Fire Science (12/88).

Fire Prevention Specialist I
(Formerly Fundamentals of Fire Prevention I)

Location: Emmitsburg, MD.

Length: 57 hours (2 weeks).

Dates: July 1980-Present.

Objective: To teach beginning fire inspectors how to apply a code or recognized standard during the process of an inspection.

Instruction: Areas of study include property classification: storage, handling, and transportation of flammable and combustible liquids, and of compressed and liquefied gases. Special hazards; review and maintenance of fire protection equipment and systems; and installation, maintenance, and use of heating and cooling equipment are included. The course is designed to meet the professional development needs of the fire prevention specialist or fire inspector by providing the skills and abilities necessary to conduct technical fire inspections. Students learn working definitions of codes and ordinances and the intents and scopes of their own codes. Through practice, they become conversant with a variety of codes. Finally, the course attempts to strengthen the skills of recognition, observation, and listening, which are needed to enforce the codes properly and correct violations. The applicant should have at least two years of fire-suppression experience or equivalent fire-related training. The student should be a prospective or newly appointed inspector and have less than one year actual inspection experience. Lecture, discussion and media techniques are used.

Credit recommendation: In the lower division baccalaureate/associate degree category, 3 semester hours in Fire Science (6/81) (7/86). NOTE: This course has been reevaluated and continues to meet requirements for credit recommendations.

Fire Prevention Specialist II
(Formerly Fundamentals of Fire Prevention II)

Location: Emmitsburg, MD.

Length: 57 hours (2 weeks).

Dates: July 1981-Present.

Objective: To improve and enhance students' technical and conceptual problem-solving abilities in the area of fire prevention.

Instruction: This advanced course is designed and intended to meet the development needs of the fire inspector. Course covers advanced problem-solving, decision-making, and specific areas of concern, such as plan review, inspection, tests of fire-protection systems, effective communications, and code interpretation. Topics include fire-protection systems, code enforcement, emergency evacuation planning, the issuance of permits and certificates of occupancy, records and record-keeping systems, fire safety evacuation plans, and a broad overview of the scope of the inspector's responsibilities and concerns. Lecture, discussion and media techniques are used. (Prerequisite: Fire Prevention Specialist I; or demonstration, by virtue of prior education and experience in an organized fire prevention bureau, of knowledge and skills which constitute the Fire Inspector Professional Qualifications).

Credit recommendation: In the lower division baccalaureate/associate degree category, 2 semester hours in Fire Science (6/81) (7/86). NOTE: This course has been reevaluated and continues to meet requirements for credit recommendations.

Fire Risk Analysis (A Systems Approach)
  Location: Emmitsburg, MD and host sites throughout the United States.
  Length: 16 hours (2 days).
  Dates: July 1984-December 1988.
  Objective: To enable fire service managers to identify the needs and capabilities of community fire defense systems through the application of systematic risk analysis techniques.
  Instruction: This course examines community fire defenses as a system and provides fire service managers with a system concept to identify and measure risk level and the level of protection provided by existing resources. Topics in the course include problem identification, community fire protection systems models, risk analysis, effectiveness and efficiency considerations. Lecture, discussion, and media techniques are used.
  Credit recommendation: In the lower division baccalaureate/associate degree category, 1 semester hour in Administration, Fire Science, or Management (8/85).

Fire Science Course Development
(Formerly Fire Science Course Development)
  Location: Emmitsburg, MD.
  Length: *Version 1:* 68 hours (2 weeks); *Version 2:* 71 hours (2 weeks).
  Dates: May 1980-Present.
  Objective: To teach trainers how to design courses which are tailored to meet specific objectives.
  Instruction: Course prepares fire-service personnel to design and develop curricula. It identifies the components of a typical training program and provides trainers with the necessary planning, research, writing, and evaluation skills to design and successfully implement a training program. A systematic process is used; learning principles and design criteria are considered. Functioning as members of project groups, students design and develop a course and lesson plans. Students are not expected to deliver a similar course in their jurisdictions. Lecture, discussion, and laboratories are used. (Prerequisite: Fire Service Instructional Methodology.)
  Credit recommendation: In the upper division baccalaureate category, 3 semester hours in Education or Fire Science (6/81) (7/86). NOTE: This course has been reevaluated and continues to meet requirements for credit recommendations.

Fire Service Financial Management
  Location: Emmitsburg, MD.
  Length: *Version 1:* 74 hours (2 weeks); *Version 2:* 81 hours (2 weeks).
  Dates: *Version 1:* January 1986-April 1988; *Version 2:* May 1988-Present.
  Objective: *Version 1:* To provide fire service managers with the necessary techniques to effectively identify, prepare, justify, and manage the components of an operating budget. Steps of typical budget preparation cycles are identified, the inter-relationships of each step in the cycle and the result of each step are analyzed. *Version 2:* To develop the capability of the student to manage a fire department financial program, to include the planning for and design of the financial system as well as budget preparation, justification, and administration.
  Learning Outcome: Upon successful completion of this course, the student will be able to design and develop the fire department financial system; design, develop, present, and justify the budget; and administer the fire department financial system.
  Instruction: *Version 1:* This course will assist fire service managers in planning and managing their fire department's fiscal program. The course will lead the participants through a cyclical process of effectively identifying, preparing, and justifying the components of a budget, including assessing budgetary needs, developing long-range financial revenues, understanding the technical and political aspects of preparing a budget, administering a budget, managing revenues and evaluating the efficiency and effectiveness of funded programs. Lecture, discussion and simulation exercises are used. *Version 2:* Course covers the financial management cycle to include system design, budget preparation, budget justification, and budget administration.
  Credit recommendation: In the upper division baccalaureate category, 3 semester hours in Business Administration, Fire Science, or Public Administration (8/86) (12/88). NOTE: This course has been reevaluated and continues to meet requirements for credit recommendations.

Fire Service Information Management
  Location: Emmitsburg, MD.
  Length: 57 hours (2 weeks).
  Dates: October 1984-Present.
  Objective: To provide students with the appropriate theory, information and technical requirement to enable them to effectively design, acquire and implement a multi-user information system suitable for a local fire service agency.
  Instruction: The course is intended to provide fire service personnel with background and necessary information required to develop, plan and acquire an operating information system. A variety of teaching methods, such as lectures, discussion, case study and simulation are used.

The course is planning oriented with emphasis on the decision making process required to rent or purchase a information system. Group and individual projects are discussed and graded.

Credit recommendation: In the upper division baccalaureate category, 2 semester hours in Business or Engineering Administration, Fire Science, or Management (8/85).

Fire Service Instructional Methodology
(Formerly Educational Methodology)
   Location: Emmitsburg, MD.
   Length: 64 hours (2 weeks).
   Dates: January 1980-Present.
   Objective: To teach fire service instructors and trainers how to organize and teach a lesson or course effectively.
   Instruction: Covers educational concepts necessary to train prospective trainers. The first stage of the course delivers specific information about student-trainers' objectives, teaching strategies, instructional aids and media, lesson planning, and testing. Students engage in applied performance activities to demonstrate understanding of concepts. The second stage requires students to design instructional approaches, create instructional materials, and demonstrate training deliveries for peer and instructor evaluation. In addition, students are provided with opportunities to refine the techniques they will apply as trainers. Lecture, discussion, and media techniques are used.
   Credit recommendation: In the upper division baccalaureate category, 3 semester hours in Education or Fire Science (6/81) (7/86). NOTE: This course has been reevaluated and continues to meet requirements for credit recommendations.

Fire Service Leadership/Communications
(Formerly Executive Development II/Leadership and Communications)
   Location: Emmitsburg, MD.
   Length: 93½ hours (3 weeks).
   Dates: November 1981-September 1988.
   Objective: To develop mid-level fire service managers' understanding of leadership styles and situations when each is most effective; to increase managers' skills and knowledge in the areas of supervisory skills, personal counseling, motivation, and communication skills, both oral and written.
   Instruction: This course is designed to analyze leadership styles and develop an individual's effectiveness in oral and written communication. It focuses on three managerial techniques which include leader match training, the behavioral modeling approach and goal setting techniques. It also incorporates both effective written and oral communication skills within the framework of leadership skills and their importance to effectiveness management. Lecture and discussion are used.
   Credit recommendation: In the upper division baccalaureate category, 3 semester hours in Business Administration, Fire Science, Management, or Public Administration (1/81) (7/86). NOTE: This course has been reevaluated and continues to meet requirements for credit recommendations.

Fire Service Organizational Theory
(Executive Development II: Middle Management I)
(Formerly Executive Development for Middle Management I)
   Location: Emmitsburg, MD.
   Length: 75½ hours (2 weeks).
   Dates: July 1981-September 1985.
   Objective: To enable students to develop and improve skills of mid-level responsibilities.
   Instruction: Course covers strategic and operational planning, financing, and budgeting, resource allocation, fire-loss analysis, risk-level clarification, and public relations. It is designed to provide present or future mid-level fire-service managers with an understanding of current management functions and their practical application in daily problem-solving. Workshop exercises, case studies, force-field analysis, lecture, and discussion are used.
   Credit recommendation: In the upper division baccalaureate category, 3 semester hours in Business Administration, Fire Science, Management, or Public Administration (6/81).

Hazardous Materials Tactical Considerations
(Formerly Hazardous Materials II)
   Location: Emmitsburg, MD.
   Length: *Version 1:* 60 hours (2 weeks); *Version 2:* 79 hours (2 weeks). Lecture/discussion, laboratory, workshops, and evening classes.
   Dates: January 1981-Present.
   Objective: To provide students with knowledge and skills to evaluate and manage properly incidents involving hazardous materials.
   Instruction: Prepares fire officers and other emergency personnel to command an incident involving hazardous materials. Physical handling of the materials rather than the chemical properties of the materials is emphasized. The discussion of chemical properties will be adequate for understanding the reasons for specific handling of the materials under various conditions and circumstances. Evaluative capabilities will be enhanced by the study of carrier and labeling requirements and other available information. Lecture, discussion, laboratory, and workshop are used.
   Credit recommendation: *Version 1:* In the lower division baccalaureate/associate degree category, 2 semester hours in Engineering, Fire Science Chemistry, General Science, or Physical Science (6/81). *Version 2:* In the lower division baccalaureate/associate degree category, 3 semester hours in Engineering, Fire Science Chemistry, General Science, or Physical Science (7/86). NOTE: This

course has been re-evaluated and continues to meet requirements for credit recommendations.

Hazardous Substance Specialist
(Formerly Hazardous Materials Substance Specialist)
  Location: Emittsburg, MD.
  Length: 120 hours (3 weeks).
  Dates: March 1985-September 1987.
  Objective: To give students an understanding of the basic chemistry of hazardous materials, key properties of hazardous material products, and the proper measures for the safe control of hazardous materials. Students will also learn about specific codes, standards, and regulations of fire protection safety.
  Instruction: Hazardous Substance Specialist is designed to meet the needs of those fire service individuals who will be responsible for code compliance and fire prevention, specifically in the area of hazardous materials. The first 2 weeks of the course is heavily oriented to chemistry of hazardous materials to provide the student with a basic knowledge of the compatibility of products considered to be hazardous. The third week involves the student with the study of the appropriate National Fire Protection Agency (NFPA) codes and right-to-know laws dealing with the storage and handling of hazardous materials. Lecture, discussion, and media techniques are used.
  Credit recommendation: In the lower division baccalaureate/associate degree category, 3 semester hours in Engineering, Fire Science Chemistry, General Science or Physical Science (8/85).

Incident Command System
  Location: Emmitsburg, MD and host sites throughout the United States.
  Length: 16 hours (2 eight-hour days).
  Dates: May 1988-Present.
  Objective: To allow the student to demonstrate the need for an organized approach to managing emergency incidents, to identify the laws and standards requiring this approach, to identify the elements of an emergency response system, and to assess department capabilities for implementing such a system.
  Learning Outcome: Upon successful completion of this course, the student will be able to demonstrate the need for an organized approach to emergency incidents; identify the laws and standards requiring this approach; identify the elements of an effective system; and evaluate his/her department capabilities.
  Instruction: Course covers the need for organized incident management; the laws and standards requiring same; the components of such a system; relationship between business management and incident management; the NFA model of such a system; and other examples of incident management systems.
  Credit recommendation: In the lower division baccalaureate/associate degree category, 1 semester hour in Administration, Fire Science, or Management (12/88). NOTE: Credit for Fire Command Operations should not be awarded if credit is awarded for this course.

Instructors Program Level I—Chemistry of Hazardous Materials
  Location: Emmitsburg, MD and host sites throughout the United States.
  Length: 80 hours (2 weeks).
  Dates: February 1988-Present.
  Objective: To enable the student to instruct in the area of hazardous materials. Particular attention is directed toward the chemistry of the various types of materials such as acids, salts, plastics, and petroleum products of various kinds. The course has two primary objectives: methodology of instruction in hazardous materials and the chemical and physical problems associated with hazardous materials.
  Learning Outcome: Upon successful completion of this course, the student will be able to teach courses associated with hazardous materials from the standpoint of teaching methodology as well as present the material of a technical nature associated with hazardous chemicals and products.
  Instruction: Course covers basic chemistry, elements, the use of the periodic table, as well as an understanding of the combination of elements into complex compounds. Various kinds of salts are discussed. Organic compounds and their properites are explained and investigated. Fuels and the handling of incidents involving fuels are used as examples. Liquids and gases are also covered. Cryogenics, lecture, workshop, and videotapes are used as teaching methodologies.
  Credit recommendation: In the upper division baccalaureate category, 3 semester hours in Chemistry, Educational Methodology, Fire Prevention Chemistry, Physical Science, Science, or Teaching Methods (12/88).

Interpersonal Dynamics in Fire Service Organizations
(Formerly Executive Development for Middle Management II)
  Location: Emittsburg, MD.
  Length: 73½ hours (2 weeks).
  Dates: October 1981-Present.
  Objective: To enable students to enhance development of personal, interpersonal, and group behavior skills; and to enable students to identify, describe, and explain the concepts and techniques involved in effective human resource development and utilization especially as they pertain to managerial productivity.
  Instruction: Course is designed to provide present or future mid-level fire-service managers with the basic knowledge and skills required to become effective human resource managers. Topics include leadership styles, conflict resolution, counseling, team building, delegation, personnel management, stress management, and interpersonal relationships. Workshop exercises, case

studies, force-field analysis, lecture, and discussion are used.

Credit recommendation: In the upper division baccalaureate category, 3 semester hours in Business Administration, Fire Science, Management, or Public Administration (6/81) (7/86). NOTE: This course has been reevaluated and continues to meet requirements for credit recommendations.

Introduction to Fire Safety Education (R115)
Location: Emmitsburg, MD.
Length: 89 hours (2 weeks).
Dates: October 1985-Present.
Objective: To enable the student to identify fire/burn problems, design and implement information and education programs and evaluate their effects.
Instruction: The course is designed as an introduction to the concepts and techniques of fire safety information and education. Students learn the five-step planning process for public fire safety education programs. Appropriate media channel selection for the message and effective delivery is facilitated through student presentations and experience in a media workshop. Data acquisition, strategic information and education planning, product development, delivery, and evaluation are used to improve communication skills and foster effective fire service education. The course involves extensive student participation in learning activities and presentations, followed by videotape feedback.
Credit recommendation: In the upper division baccalaureate category, 3 semester hours in Fire Science (8/86).

Leadership and Incident Command/Communications Course
(Formerly Incident Command I)
Location: Emmitsburg, MD.
Length: 56 hours (2 weeks).
Dates: July 1981-September 1984.
Objective: To provide students with an understanding of the principles of fire-site management and basic familiarization with tactics and strategies associated with fire-control methods and accepted fire fighting practices.
Instruction: Course covers basic fire fighting considerations of initial fire-site operations and fire fighting methods for typical occupancies. It is geared to a three-company response with two pumping units and ladder operations. Role play, simulation, and case studies are used.
Credit recommendation: In the upper division baccalaureate category, 2 semester hours in Fire Science (6/81).

Management of a Fire Preventive Program (R225)
Location: Emmitsburg, MD.
Length: 72 hours (2 weeks).
Dates: August 1985-Present.
Objective: To enable fire prevention managers to plan and execute effective fire prevention functions in their communities.
Instruction: The course examines contemporary issues in the management of fire prevention functions. Top level fire managers address present day and potential challenges in fire prevention. Topics include effective management principles, leadership styles, structure of the fire prevention bureau, technical skills of the fire prevention manager, promoting fire prevention, and the law in fire prevention. Modern management literature is integrated with fire prevention concepts. Lecture, discussion, and student activities are used.
Credit recommendation: In the upper division baccalaureate category, 3 semester hours in Fire Science, Public Administration or Principles of Management (8/86).

Management of Emergency Medical Services
(Management of Emergency Medical Services for the Fire Service)
Location: Emmitsburg, MD.
Length: 61 hours (2 weeks).
Dates: January 1981-Present.
Objective: To help upgrade the fire-service manager's skills and knowledge in planning, implementing, and evaluating an emergency medical service program within the fire department. The course emphasizes the manager's role with the fire department, although the system management functions are also considered.
Instruction: Covers systematic approaches for the management of emergency medical services system. Resources for and constraints on system development, impact on capital and operating cost of the fire department, mechanisms for medical control and quality assurance, sources of support, implementation and administration of emergency medical services are included. The course provides a high degree of student involvement in both individual and group activities. A unique learning opportunity in the course is the student's development of a simulated system called "Metropolis." For fire-service managers who are beginning emergency medical services or are considering upgrading an existing service. Lecture and discussion are used.
Credit recommendation: In the upper division baccalaureate category, 3 semester hours in Engineering Administration, Fire Science, or Health Care Administration (6/81) (7/86). NOTE: This course has been reevaluated and continues to meet requirements for credit recommendations.

Managing the Code Process
(Formerly Codes and Ordinances)
Location: Emmitsburg, MD.
Length: 69 hours (2 weeks).
Dates: July 1981-June 1985.

Objective: To enable students to develop, apply, and enforce codes properly upon return to their local jurisdictions. To help students understand the principles, history, function, development, and application of codes and ordinances, as well as understand administrative procedures, working relationships, with various segments of the community, and legal implications related to codes and ordinances.

Instruction: The course is designed to meet the professional needs of code administrators and enforcers who must be familiar with the development, application, and enforcement of the codes. Topics for study include introduction to fire building codes; development, adoption, and implementation of fire building codes; and the code-revision process. Code-development background and the general need for codes and ordinances are also explored. Lecture, discussion, and classroom exercises are used.

Credit recommendation: In the lower division baccalaureate/associate degree category, 3 semester hours in Business Law or Fire Science (6/81).

Personal Effectiveness
(Fire Service Supervisor: Personal)

Location: Emmitsburg, MD and state fire-training academies.

Length: 16 hours (2 days).

Dates: August 1983-Present.

Objective: To provide fire service managers and supervisors with basic supervisory skills and techniques that will improve their personal effectiveness as key leaders.

Instruction: The course reviews basic skills and techniques that will assist the individual in improving his/her personal effectiveness. Among the topics considered in the course are: management culture, leadership managerial style and personal performance; time management; stress management; and personal professional development planning.

Credit recommendation: In the upper division baccalaureate category, 1 semester hour in Business Management, Behavioral Science, Fire Science, Principles of Management, or Supervision (8/86).

Planning for a Hazardous Materials Incident
(Formerly Hazardous Materials III)

Location: Emmitsburg, MD.

Length: 55½ hours (2 weeks). Approximately three-fourths lecture, and one-fourth laboratory, discussion, and workshops.

Dates: May 1980-April 1984.

Objective: To prepare students to plan for and manage a hazardous materials incident. Major subject areas include the community's potential for disaster, government and private sector capability and assistance, interagency relations, command organization, emergency response teams, and preparation of operational guidelines for the management of hazardous-materials programs.

Instruction: Major subject areas include the community's potential for disaster, government and private sector capability and assistance, interagency relations, command organization, emergency response teams, and preparation of a hazardous-materials-incident management manual. For senior-level fire and rescue officers who may have planning and operational responsibility. Other participants may be selected from allied professions with similar command and/or planning responsibilities. Lecture, discussion, laboratory, and workshop are used.

Credit recommendation: In the lower division baccalaureate/associate degree category, 3 semester hours in Engineering, Fire Science Chemistry, General Science, or Physical Science (6/81).

Plans Review for Inspectors (R102)
(Formerly Overview of Plans Review for Inspectors)

Location: Emmitsburg, MD.

Length: *Version 1:* 66 hours (2 weeks); 30 hours lecture, 10 hours discussion, 26 hours lab. *Version 2:* 74 hours (2 weeks); 30 hours lecture, 10 hours discussion, 8 hours classroom, 26 hours lab.

Dates: *Version 1:* October 1982-November 1988; *Version 2:* December 1988-Present.

Objective: *Version 1:* To introduce the student to plan review systems confirming compliance with applicable codes and standards and to develop a report identifying at least five positive and five negative elements of the student's local plan review system along with recommended changes. *Version 2:* To develop the student's understanding of plan review systems confirming compliance with applicable codes and standards and provide an understanding of architect/designer submitted drawings.

Learning Outcome: Upon successful completion of this course, the student will be able to evaluate a set of construction documents for compliance with applicable codes and standards; and develop the skills and attitude required to make his/her unit effective in the plans review process.

Instruction: *Version 1:* Course gives an overview of a systematic checklist approach to verifying that a complete set of construction documents complies with applicable codes. Also introduces applicable standards for the design of sprinkler, standpipe, fire alarm and detection systems, and fire pump installation. Lecture, discussion, and laboratory exercises are used. *Version 2:* Topics are centered around providing knowledge and developing attitudes helpful in establishing a competent review organization. The course also deals with the "how-to's" of reviewing construction documents.

Credit recommendation: *Version 1:* In the upper division baccalaureate category, 2 semester hours in Environmental Science, Fire Administration, or Management, or in the lower division baccalaureate/associate degree category, 2 semester hours in Fire Engineering, Fire Science, or Fire Technology (3/83). *Version 2:* In the upper division baccalaureate category, 3 semester hours in Environmental Science or Fire Administration, or in the lower division baccalaureate/associate degree category, 3 semester hours in Fire Engineering, Fire Science, or Fire Technology (12/88). NOTE: This course has been reevaluated and continues to meet requirements for credit recommendations.

Public Fire Education Specialist
(Formerly Public Information)
   Location: Emmitsburg, MD.
   Length: 33 1/3 hours (1 week).
   Dates: February 1980-April 1985.
   Objective: To assist students in the design, development, and presentation of fire safety education programs. Students learn communication skills needed to construct public relations programs, speeches, public service announcements, and news releases; and the instructional skills needed to construct behavioral objectives and educational programs and activities.
   Instruction: Covers the design, development, and delivery of public fire safety education and public relations programs in the community. Students increase their communication skills in speaking, writing, and use of media; apply behavioral objectives; utilize evaluation techniques; and match instructional methodology to the learner. Topics include high-risk attitudes, behavior, and environments; and related public education programs. Lecture, discussion, and media techniques are used.
   Credit recommendation: In the lower division baccalaureate/associate degree category, 2 semester hours in Communications, Fire Science, or Public Information (6/81).

Strategic Analysis of Executive Leadership (R125)
   Location: Emmitsburg, MD.
   Length: 72 hours (2 weeks).
   Dates: July 1987-Present.
   Learning Outcome: Upon successful completion of this course, the executive fire officer will be able to conceptualize and employ the key processes used by executive-level managers.
   Instruction: An examination of contemporary public sector and fire service issues using a case study approach to enhance the ability to perform at the executive level. Social and behavioral frameworks are provided for application to administration of fire programs.
   Credit recommendation: In the graduate degree category, 3 semester hours in Business Management, Human Resource Management, Organizational Behavior, Public Management, or Supervision (7/87).

Strategic Analysis of Fire Department Operations
(Strategy in Operations of Fire Departments)
   Location: Emmitsburg, MD.
   Length: 67 hours (2 weeks).
   Dates: November 1984-Present.
   Objective: To provide the students with strategic management principles to address special command problems posed by major incidents involving major life and property loss.
   Instruction: Course prepares the student with managerial principles through course studies and supportive material and instruction which enable the (learner) student to understand, analyze, manage, control, and evaluate incidents involving major life and property loss. Lecture, discussion, media techniques, and student activities are used.
   Credit recommendation: In the upper division baccalaureate category, 3 semester hours in Business Administration, Fire Science, Management, or Public Administration (8/85).

Strategic Analysis of Fire Prevention Programs (R309)
   Location: Emmitsburg, MD.
   Length: 83 hours (2 weeks).
   Dates: *Version 1:* March 1987-November 1988; *Version 2:* December 1988-Present.
   Objective: *Version 1:* To develop the students' awareness of fire prevention as a key method of achieving the department mission; to provide the skills needed to design and implement a fire prevention program; and to develop a strategy for fire prevention in the local community. *Version 2:* To enable students to provide leadership in fire prevention attitude, awareness, and implementation efforts in their home communities.
   Learning Outcome: *Version 1:* Upon successful completion of this course, the participant will have an awareness of and positive attitude towards fire prevention as a major method of accomplishing the fire department mission; be able to analyze, implement, and evaluate an effective fire prevention program; and be successful in providing leadership and direction for fire prevention efforts in their home communities. *Version 2:* Upon successful completion of this course, the student will have developed an awareness of and positive attitude towards fire prevention as a major method of accomplishing the fire department mission; be able to analyze, implement, and evaluate an effective fire prevention program; and provide leadership and direction for fire prevention efforts in one's home communities.
   Instruction: This course examines community fire protection and fire service issues using a case study approach to enhance the officer's ability to perform at the executive level. Emphasis is on transfer of skills to local organizations. An independent research project is included as a major component of the course.
   Credit recommendation: *Version 1:* In the upper division baccalaureate category, 3 semester hours in Community Development, Fire Prevention Engineering, Labor Planning, or Occupational Health and Safety (7/87). *Version 2:* In the upper division baccalaureate or graduate degree category, 3 semester hours in Community Devel-

opment, Fire Prevention Engineering, Labor Planning, or Occupational Health and Safety (12/88).

Tactical Operations for Company Officers I (TOCO I)
Location: Emmitsburg, MD.
Length: 16 hours (2 eight-hour days).
Dates: April 1988-Present.
Objective: To provide the student with basic knowledge of tactics and incident command techniques necessary to effectively manage and direct company-level tactical operations.
Learning Outcome: Upon successful completion of this course, the student will be able to know the multiple roles of the company officer; know the techniques for gathering and developing incident information; know the methods for utilizing strategic information; and know the organization and management of incident resources and the appreciation of the incident command system at the company level.
Instruction: Course covers multiple roles of the company officer, techniques for gathering and developing incident information, the organization and management of incident resources; application of the incident command system at the company level; and using strategic information.
Credit recommendation: In the lower division baccalaureate/associate degree category, or in the upper division baccalaureate category, 2 semester hours in Fire Science or Strategic Planning (12/88).

Tactical Operations for Company Officers II (TOCO II)
Location: Emmitsburg, MD.
Length: 16 hours (2 eight-hour days).
Dates: April 1988-Present.
Objective: To provide the student with the basic knowledge and tactics and incident command techniques necessary to effectively manage and direct company-level tactical operations.
Learning Outcome: Upon successful completion of this course, the student will be able to learn the responsibilities of the company officer to provide for safety of firefighters; know the five basic categories of apparatus placement; demonstrate and explain proper apparatus placement to accomplish the specific tactical objectives; know use of entry techniques as essential to facilitate all other tactical operations; and review the common obstructions encountered in entry operations and the methods used to gain entry.
Instruction: Course covers introduction, apparatus placement, entry, water supply, hose lines, salvage, utility control and overhaul, laddering, ventilation, search and rescue, tactical operations (basic incidents), and tactical operations (complex incidents).
Credit recommendation: In the lower division baccalaureate/associate degree category, 2 semester hours in Emergency Management, Fire Science, or Strategic Management, or in the upper division baccalaureate category, 1 1 semester hour in Emergency Management, Fire Science, or Strategic Management (12/88).

Team Effectiveness
(Fire Service Supervisor: Team)
Location: Emmitsburg, MD and state fire training academies.
Length: 16 hours (2 days).
Dates: November 1983-Present.
Objective: To introduce fire service managers and supervisors to basic skills and techniques that will improve their ability to relate to others in the work environment. Service managers will be expected to incorporate the principles of team building in their daily jobs.
Instruction: This course is geared toward the team leader's needs of fire service supervisors and program managers. While primarily focused on the manager's interpersonal skills, other topics covered include: motivation, interpersonal communications, counseling, group dynamics, and conflict resolution. Lecture, discussion, media and student activities are used.
Credit recommendation: In the upper division baccalaureate category, 1 semester hour in Behavioral Science, Business Management, Fire Science, Principles of Management or Supervision (8/86).

Use Of Microcomputers For Fire Service Management
Location: Emmitsburg, MD.
Length: 86 hours (2 weeks).
Dates: October 1982-Present.
Objective: To familiarize the student with the application of low-cost microcomputer technology to the management of fire service and EMS organizations.
Instruction: The course uses lecture, demonstrations and group projects to introduce the student to microcomputer applications in fire service and EMS organizations. Subjects include: Decision Support Systems, Data Collection, Analysis and Reporting and Organizational Implications. "Hands-on" experience with microcomputer hardware and commercial software is available in a microcomputer laboratory.
Credit recommendation: In the lower division baccalaureate/associate degree category, 2 semester hours in Emergency Medicine, Fire Administration, Fire Management, or Fire Science (3/83).

Wildland/Urban Interface Fire Protection: A National Problem with Local Solutions
Location: Self-study course.
Length: Self-paced (approximately 32 hours).
Dates: November 1988-Present.
Objective: To increase the student's level of understanding of the wildland/urban interface problem and to provide effective and defensible strategies and solutions in

protecting the interfaces of people and their environment. The interface between rural/urban and developed/undeveloped areas are of particular concern.

Learning Outcome: Upon successful completion of this course, the student will be able to assess the interface problem associated with fire and develop solutions; establish the relationship between fire and regulation; and develop programs on enforcement, public education, and maintaining community support.

Instruction: This is a self-study, self-paced instructional course designed to motivate students to undertake a comprehensive fire prevention and protection program for the urban interface.

Credit recommendation: In the vocational certificate, or lower division baccalaureate/associate degree category, 1 semester hour in Civil Engineering, Environmental Management, Range Management, Urban and Regional Planning, or Urban Policy (12/88).

EMERGENCY MANAGEMENT INSTITUTE

The Emergency Management Institute (EMI) serves as a national focal point for development and delivery of civil defense/emergency management training to enhance emergency management capabilities of federal, state, and local governments, and the private sector. It administers both resident and nonresident training programs. Nearly 4,000 students participate annually in resident training activities. Another 200,000 students participate in nonresident training activities sponsored by the Institute and conducted by State emergency management agencies.

Training activities, which consist of courses, workshops, seminars, conferences, teleconferences, and exercises are conducted throughout the United States. EMI's curriculum addresses all phases of emergency management, mitigation, preparedness, response and recovery, and applies emergency management concepts and experiential information to hazards ranging from earthquakes to hazardous materials to nuclear attack.

1. Basic Skills For Emergency Program Managers
   Module I: Leadership and Influence
   Module II: Decision Making and Problem Solving
   Module III: Effective Communications
2. Module IV: Creative Financing

Location: State Offices of Emergency Management nationwide.

Length: 1. *Module I:* 20 hours (3 days of classroom instruction); *Module II:* 8 hours (1 day of classroom instruction); *Module III:* 15 hours (2 days of classroom instruction). 2. *Module IV:* 16 hours (2 days of classroom instruction).

Dates: 1. November 1982-Present; 2. November 1982-Present.

Objective: 1. *Module I:* To provide students with concepts of leadership, influence, power relationships and conflict mediation in the community setting. *Module II:* To provide students with concepts of various decison-making and problem-solving processes and the ability to apply these in the emergency management setting. *Module III:* To provide students with concepts of communication and presentation skills in the community setting. 2. *Module IV:* To provide students with skills in effective budget planning, budget presentation to community budget authorities, and determination of alternative funding sources and mechanisms.

Learning Outcome: 1. *Module I:* Upon successful completion of this course, the student will be able to determine personal values, influence style, leadership style, and power bases as they apply to interpersonal relations and group dynamics. *Module II:* Upon successful completion of this course, the student will be able to draw conclusions regarding individual and the group decision-making process. *Module III:* Upon successful completion of this course, the student will be able to identify and utilize both verbal and nonverbal communications techniques in developing a structured presentation. 2. *Module IV:* Upon successful completion of this course, the student will be able to list and describe basic emergency management creative financing concepts; describe standard elements of proposals and utilize them in a team development process; and evaluate creative financing activities and apply them in development of a community plan.

Instruction: 1. *Module I:* Lectures, discussions, exercises in organizational behavior, conflict management, interpersonal relations and group dynamics in an emergency setting. *Module II: Covers decision-making process and theory as applied in emergency situations. Lectures, discussions, case study. Module III*: Covers communication issues for emergency managers, the communication cycle, nonverbal communication, and public speaking. 2. *Module IV:* Covers public budgeting, grantsmanship, and financial planning for emergency managers. Lectures and exercises.

Credit recommendation: 1. In the lower division baccalaureate/associate degree category, 3 semester hours in Emergency Management or Public Administration. 2. In the lower division baccalaureate/associate degree category, 1 semester hour in Public Administration (fund-raising or grantsmanship) or Emergency Management (3/84) (6/88). NOTE: This course has been reevaluated and continues to meet requirements for credit recommendations.

Civil Defense Systems, Programs and Policies (E-371)
Location: State Offices of Emergency Management nationwide.
Length: 32 hours (4 days).
Dates: August 1988-Present.
Objective: To provide the participant with a history, mission, and status of civil defense system in the United States. It demonstrates how the nuclear attack preparedness also enhances and supports natural and technological

hazard preparedness.

Learning Outcome: Upon successful completion of this course, the student will be able to demonstrate the merit of civil defense; explain assumptions of designation of specific potential targets; describe the effects of the air and ground bursts on population; identify references, program guidance and other resources; and prepare a presentation for promoting sound and effective civil defense programs.

Instruction: Course covers introduction to civil defense, national security threats—nuclear attacks, effects of nuclear war, civil defense system, program and policies, and communicating with varied publics. Methodology includes lecture and discussion.

Credit recommendation: In the lower division baccalaureate/associate degree category, or in the upper division baccalaureate category, 1 semester hour in Emergency Management, Public Administration, Public Works, Urban Services Delivery, or Planning (6/88).

Emergency Planning Course

Location: State Offices of Emergency Management nationwide.

Length: 27 hours (4½ days of classroom instruction and post-class practicum).

Dates: October 1982-Present.

Objective: To provide students with advanced competency in planning skills for emergency situations.

Learning Outcome: Upon successful completion of this course, the student will be able to establish a planning framework for emergency management; develop an emergency planning strategy and integrate principles of group processes, team building, and decision making; and evaluate the adequacy of existing plans.

Instruction: Covers needs assessment (hazard/vulnerability analysis) techniques, comprehensive planning, action planning and organization development in the emergency planning process. Lectures, discussions, individual and group activities including pre- and post-class projects.

Credit recommendation: In the upper division baccalaureate category, 2 semester hours in Public Administration (planning) or Emergency Management (3/84) (6/88). NOTE: This course has been reevaluated and continues to meet requirements for credit recommendations.

Executive Development for Emergency Program Managers (E-215)

Location: State Offices of Emergency Management nationwide.

Length: 78 hours (2 weeks).

Dates: January 1985-Present.

Objective: To provide the participant with in-depth knowledge about executive management and leadership skills for helping the manager plan and implement a good emergency response.

Learning Outcome: Upon successful completion of this course, the student will be able to be aware of legal issues in the local emergency management system; develop a strategic management plan for their jurisdiction; assess the current status of their emergency management system, formulate techniques for long-range planning and strategies; and develop alternative marketing approaches for involving the community in planning and carrying out emergency management goals.

Instruction: Course covers legal issues, strategic management, executive skills, community involvement, and stress management. Methodology includes lecture and discussion.

Credit recommendation: In the upper division baccalaureate category, 3 semester hours in Administrative Principles of Management (6/88).

Exercise Design

Location: All States and U.S. Trust Territories.

Length: 22½ hours (3 days).

Dates: March 1984-Present.

Objective: To teach emergency managers how to design, conduct and evaluate the effectiveness of disaster exercises.

Instruction: Course prepares emergency management personnel to identify, design, and conduct simulation exercises to evaluate the preparedness posture of local jurisdiction. It identifies the four types of exercise, emphasizes the team approach to exercising, and allows students to develop and conduct exercises.

Credit recommendation: In the lower division baccalaureate/associate degree category, 1 semester hour in Emergency Management or Public Administration (8/86). NOTE: Students who receive credit for this course should not receive credit for Exercise Design—Train-the-Trainer.

Exercise Design—Train-the-Trainer

Location: Emergency Management Institute, Emmitsburg, MD.

Length: 32 hours (4 days).

Dates: March 1984-Present.

Objective: To train instructors in the techniques and methodology for presenting Exercise Design course materials to emergency program managers at state and local government level.

Instruction: Course provides techniques and methodology to prepare emergency program managers to identify, design, and conduct simulation exercises to evaluate the preparedness posture of the local jurisdiction. Course identifies four types of exercises, emphasizes team approach to exercise development, execution, and critique.

Credit recommendation: In the upper division baccalaureate category, 2 semester hours in Emergency Management or Public Administration (8/86). NOTE: Students who receive credit for this course should not receive credit for Exercise Design.

Fallout Shelter Analysis

Location: Emergency Management Institute, Emmitsburg, MD, and various NATO Air Force Bases in Europe.

Length: 55½ hours (2 weeks).

Dates: August 1976-Present.

Objective: To train architects and engineers in the methods of fallout shelter analysis and design.

Instruction: The course covers basic nuclear physics; nuclear weapons; radiation shielding; FEMA fallout shelter analysis; estimating and analyzing shelter yield; and fallout shelter analysis by programmable pocket calculators and by computer. Lecture, discussion, classroom exercises, problem-solving, and written examinations are used.

Credit recommendation: In the graduate degree category, 4 semester hours in Architecture, Civil Engineering, Emergency Planning, or Public Administration (8/86).

Fundamentals: For Radiological Monitor and Radiological Response Teams
(Based upon two NETC courses: [1] Fundamentals Course for Radiological Monitors; [2] Fundamentals Course for Radiological Response Teams)

Location: Emergency Management Institute field locations.

Length: 1. 12 hours (2 days). 2. 31 hours (1 week).

Dates: November 1984-Present.

Objective: To provide participants with appropriate knowledge and skills related to monitoring radiation and performing as a member of a radiological response team.

Instruction: Lecture, discussion and exercises covering an overview of radiological emergencies, radiation fundamentals, biological effects and risks, radiological monitoring instruments, exposure and contamination control techniques, on-scene assessment, and special nuclear attack considerations.

Credit recommendation: In the lower division baccalaureate/associate degree category, 3 semester hours in Radiological Science (8/85). NOTE: In order to receive credit, students must complete both courses.

Fundamentals for Radiological Officers

Location: Emergency Management Institute for field locations.

Length: 30 hours (1 week).

Dates: November 1984-Present.

Objective: To provide state and local radiological officers with the knowledge and skills necessary to implement initial protective actions in a radiological emergency, and to apply planning and management principles to the design and administration of a radiological protection system.

Instruction: Lecture, discussion and exercises in radiological response planning, managing a protection system, state and local system issues, and advanced concepts in radiological sciences and nuclear attack considerations.

Credit recommendation: In the upper division baccalaureate category, 2 semester hours in Radiation Emergency Management and Radiological Sciences (8/85).

Hazardous Materials Contingency Planning

Location: FEMA Emergency Management Institute, EPA Edison, New Jersey Training, and State Emergency Management Offices.

Length: 29 hours (5 days).

Dates: January 1986-Present.

Objective: To provide students with advanced competency, knowledge and skills in hazardous materials planning and response techniques.

Instruction: Course covers Haz Mar Hazard Vulnerability; assessment of resources; development of Haz Mar Contingency Plan; development of fixed site Haz Mar Contingent Plan. Basic chemistry is strongly recommended as a prerequisite for this course. Lectures, discussion, exercises, individual and group activities.

Credit recommendation: In the graduate degree category, 2 semester hours in Emergency Management or Public Administration (8/86).

Introduction to Emergency Management

Location: State Offices of Emergency Management nationwide.

Length: 27 hours (4½ days—23 hours lecture and discussion, 4 hours workshop)

Dates: April 1983-Present.

Objective: To describe elements of an integrated emergency management system, necessity for emergency management teamwork and the identification of hazards and hazard sources all of which lead to a personal emergency management strategy.

Learning Outcome: Upon successful completion of this course, the student will be able to identify hazards and draw conclusions regarding scope, importance, and implications to the community; describe operational elements of a comprehensive emergency management system; and identify fundamental organizational characteristics and the relationship between individual and group behavior.

Instruction: Covers community needs assessment for emergency management, systems approach to emergency management, community organization development, and management planning for community emergencies. Lecture and discussion are used.

Credit recommendation: In the lower division baccalaureate/associate degree category, 2 semester hours in Emergency Management or Public Administration (3/84) (6/88). NOTE: This course has been reevaluated and continues to meet requirements for credit recommendations.

Methods and Techniques of Adult Learning (E-204)
  Location: Emergency Management Institute, Emmitsburg, MD, and State Offices of Emergency Management nationwide.
  Length: 32½ hours (4 days).
  Dates: August 1987-Present.
  Objective: To familiarize experienced emergency management trainers with adult learing theory with reference to adult learning techniques, media usage, presentation topics, and training techniques.
  Learning Outcome: Upon successful completion of this course, the student will be able to provide students with a series of alternative techniques to present information in the most efficient and effective method; know something about classroom environment for learning; carry out appropriate communications principles and techniques; and plan and perform a team teaching activity that incorporates one or more instructional techniques.
  Instruction: Course covers introduction and overview, presentation, media usage, practical applications, and evaluation. Methodology includes lecture and discussion.
  Credit recommendation: In the upper division baccalaureate category, 2 semester hours in Education, Educational Methods, Extension Education, Psychology of Learning, or Training Methods (6/88).

Microcomputer Applications in Emergency Management
  Location: Emergency Management Institute, Emmitsburg, MD.
  Length: 37 classroom hours and 15 hours evening lab work (5 days).
  Dates: June 1985-Present.
  Objective: To introduce emergency managers who use, or plan to use, microcomputers in a systems development process for designing and implementing a computerized information system.
  Instruction: Covers introduction to microcomputer laboratory; management overview; application to emergency management; identifies resources, word processing software application; evaluates alternative hardware and software systems; addresses communications, data base management and spreadsheet software application. Course includes lectures, demonstrations, discussions and practical application in microcomputer operations.
  Credit recommendation: In the upper division baccalaureate category, 3 semester hours in Emergency Management or Public Administration (8/86).

Natural Hazards Mitigations (Inland) (E-306)
  Location: National Emergency Training Center, Emmitsburg, MD.
  Length: 30 hours (4½ days).
  Dates: March 1989-Present.
  Objective: To introduce concepts and skills of mitigation planning for application in general community planning processes.
  Learning Outcome: Upon successful completion of this course, the student will be able to apply knowledge and skills to the local context of mitigation planning processes, legal and liability issues, hazards assessment, and implementation strategies.
  Instruction: Course covers local context of mitigation planning, hazards assessment, legal issues in mitigation, implementation strategies, and action steps. Methodology includes lecture, exercises, and case study.
  Credit recommendation: In the upper division baccalaureate category, 1 semester hour in Emergency Management (6/88).

Natural Hazards Recovery (Coastal) (E-313)
  Location: National Emergency Training Center, Emmitsburg, MD.
  Length: 30 hours (4½ days).
  Dates: March 1989-Present.
  Objective: To provide information on disaster recovery, planning techniques, political and community context of disaster recovery, post-disaster mitigation planning, community planning, and implementation assessment techniques.
  Learning Outcome: Upon successful completion of this course, the student will be able to apply a working knowledge of effective approaches, tools and techniques to initiate pre-disaster recovery planning in their communities; and relate disaster recovery planning to mitigation and general community planning.
  Instruction: Course covers disaster recovery planning, recovery organizing priorities, community infrastructure recovery, state and federal assistance, land use planning, and building codes in post-disaster mitigation. Methodology includes lecture and exercises.
  Credit recommendation: In the upper division baccalaureate category, 1 semester hour in Emergency Management (6/88).

Radiological Accident Assessment
  Location: Emergency Management Institute, Emmitsburg, MD.
  Length: 30 hours (1 week).
  Dates: June 1985-Present.
  Objective: This course is designed for individuals who have, or will have, responsibilities for helping to assess the radiological consequences to the public following an accidental release of radioactivity from a nuclear facility. It will provide knowledge and skills required to make recommendations to public officials to minimize the hazards to people, animals, and the food chain.
  Instruction: Lectures, discussion, and exercises in accident classifications and protective action decision making, projection methods, off-site monitoring, and meteorology.
  Credit recommendation: In the upper division baccalaureate or graduate category, 2 semester hours in Ra-

diological Sciences (8/85).

Radiological Emergency Preparedness Planning
Location: Emergency Management Institute, Emmitsburg, MD.
Length: 34 hours (1 week).
Dates: January 1985-Present.
Objective: To provide federal, state, local, and private industry radiological planners with federal guidance for planning around nuclear power generating stations.
Instruction: Lectures, discussions and workshops in hazard analysis, reactor safety, accident classification, protective actions, off-site monitoring and instrumentation, integrated emergency management information systems, media relations, and disaster related needs of the handicapped, disabled, and elderly.
Credit recommendation: In the upper division baccalaureate category, 2 semester hours in Public Administration (8/85).

Radiological Emergency Response
Location: Nevada Test Site in Las Vegas
Length: 56 hours (2 weeks).
Dates: August 1985-Present.
Objective: To provide persons assigned to state and local radiological emergency response teams with "hands-on" experience in simulated radiation accidents.
Instruction: Lectures, discussions and exercises in basic principles and procedures of nuclear physics, map reading, environmental sampling, radiological area control, respiratory protection, field instrument techniques, personnel and equipment anti-contamination, and hot-line procedures and personnel monitoring.
Credit recommendation: In the lower division baccalaureate/associate degree category, 3 semester hours in Radiological Sciences (8/85).

Radiological Monitors Instructor (Part l)
Location: Emergency Management Institute field locations.
Length: 24 hours (3 days).
Dates: August 1985-Present.
Objective: To provide qualified instructors with knowledge and skills necessary to teach the "Fundamentals Course for Radiological Monitors."
Instruction: Lectures, discussions, and exercises in student recruitment and scheduling, instructional techniques and methodology, expedient radiological training, source handling techniques, and student teaching.
Credit recommendation: In the lower division baccalaureate/associate degree category, 2 semester hours in Radiological Science Education (8/85).

State Radiological Officer Management
Location: Emergency Management Institute, Emmitsburg, MD.
Length: 35 hours (1 week).
Dates: February 1985-Present.
Objective: To provide state-level radiological protection officers with knowledge and skills required to develop and manage an integrated state radiological protective system.
Instruction: Lectures, discussions and workshops in integrated state radiological protection systems, management principles and practices, planning and evaluation, and radiological intelligence gathering, processing, and reporting.
Credit recommendation: In the upper division baccalaureate category, 2 semester hours in Public Administration (8/85).

Train the Trainer for Radiological Instructors III
Location: Emergency Management Institute, Emmitsburg, MD.
Length: 35 hours (1 week).
Dates: May 1984-Present.
Objective: To qualify trainers as Radiological Instructor III to teach the Fundamentals Course for Radiological Response Teams, the "Fundamentals Course for Radiological Officers," and the "Radiological Monitor Instructor Course."
Instruction: Lectures, discussions, and workshops on the content and presentation of course materials in the "Fundamentals Course for Radiological Response Teams," "Fundamentals Course for Radiological Officers," and the "Radiological Monitor Instructor Course."
Credit recommendation: In the upper division baccalaureate category, 2 semester hours in Radiological Science Education (8/85).

Shelter Systems Officer
Location: Emergency Management Institute, Emmitsburg, MD.
Length: 32 hours (1 week).
Dates: June 1981-Present.
Objective: To provide students with an understanding of the responsibilities of a Shelter Systems Officer, i.e., planning the system, managing the system, and training Shelter Managers.
Instruction: Course covers the basic elements of the Integrated Emergency Management System; definitions, terms, and concerns related to shelter management; development, operation and management of a shelter system; basic communications skills and governmental responsibilities for shelter operations. Lectures, discussions and applied exercises are employed in the conduct of this course.
Credit recommendation: In the lower division baccalaureate/associate degree category, 2 semester hours in Emergency Management or Public Administration (8/86).

Shelter Systems Officer Train-the Trainer

Location: Emergency Management Institute, Emmitsburg, MD.

Length: 33½ hours (1 week).

Dates: July 1981-Present.

Objective: To train instructor personnel in techniques and methodology for instructing emergency management personnel around the three basic responsibilities of the Shelter Systems Officer, i.e., planning the system, managing the system, and training Shelter Managers.

Instruction: Course covers basic elements of the Integrated Emergency Management System; definitions, concerns and terms related to shelter management; development, operation and management of a shelter system; basic communications skills and governmental responsibility for shelter operations. Lectures, discussions, and applied exercises are employed in the conduct of this course. Students must demonstrate knowledge of educational methodologies and techniques.

Credit recommendation: In the upper division baccalaureate category, 2 semester hours in Emergency Management or Public Administration (8/86). NOTE: Students who receive credit for this course should not receive credit for Shelter Systems Officer.

National Institute of Information Technology

The National Institute of Information Technology (NIIT) was established in 1981 to fulfill the crucial need for skilled manpower in the area of computers. NIIT has a variety of courses in computer education and training designed to meet the needs of various regions throughout India. NIIT's computer education and training centers are operated in over 30 locations which include Bombay, Delhi, Madras, Bangalore, Calcutta, Hyderabad, and Pune.

Formal courses, seminars, workshops, and other educational and training activities at NIIT fall into four areas: Education (EDN), Network Center Education (NCE), Corporate Training (CTP), and Professional Development Workshops (PDW).

The Education (EDN) computer courses at NIIT are conducted in-house and are organized into four categories which include a literacy or introductory series, a career series, a career upgrade series, and an end user skill series.

Courses are developed on the basis of the need to keep students current in the computer science field. The need for a course usually originates from requests by the various NIIT regional staff. Such requests are reviewed by the Head, Education Planning Group in Delhi. After a detailed analysis which involves further research into the suitability of proposed new courses and discussions with faculty and other NIIT administrators, pilot courses are developed. Prior to the final release of any new course, the pilot-phase is extensively reviewed and revised if required by research and validation teams. On-going courses are regularly revised, based on faculty feedback, poor student performance over two continuous courses, changing market requirements, and poor student feedback on the effectiveness of course material.

Faculty members at NIIT have education and training in computer science and/or management information systems. They are selected from leading management or academic institutions within India. Because of the ever evolving nature of the computer science field, one month out of every year is devoted to faculty training. In addition to this mandatory faculty training program, the performances of faculty are reviewed on a regular basis.

Student performance is evaluated by a series of quizzes, module tests, and comprehensive final examinations which are in place for each of the courses within EDN.

Source of official student records: Head, Education Planning Group, National Institute of Information Technology, B4/144 Safdarjung Enclave, New Delhi 110026, India.

Additional information about the courses: Program on Noncollegiate Sponsored Instruction, The Center for Adult Learning and Educational Credentials, American Council on Education, One Dupont Circle, Washington, D.C. 20036.

COBOL Programming and Application
(Certificate in COBOL Programming [CCP])

Location: Various locations offered by NIIT in India.

Length: 140 hours (22 weeks); 3 two-hour meetings per week, plus an eight-hour project.

Dates: April 1986-Present.

Objective: To train students to become proficient COBOL programmers.

Learning Outcome: Upon successful completion of this course, the student will be able to understand the workings of a computer system; break a problem down into its composite parts and then structure the problem into flowchart form; and write COBOL programs for varied case studies.

Instruction: Course covers a basic overview of computers which includes a brief history, coverage of typical items in computer systems (i.e., keyboards, video display units, printers, etc.), types of computer systems (centralized, decentralized, and distributed), a review of programming logic techniques relating to problem solving, programming constructs and flowcharting which includes structuring of programs and flowcharts relating to commercial programming with hands-on operation and programming to develop abilities in report generation, control break, and file merge problems. COBOL exposure relates to ANSI COBOL and its use in commercial data processing and includes exposure to table handling, accessing, indexed files, subprograms, and other related COBOL program structures. Methodology includes lectures, practical exercises, self-paced learning, student/instructor consultation sessions, reading assignments in NIIT prepared text, booklets, and extensive program development, compiling and execution on in-house computers.

Credit recommendation: In the lower division baccalaureate/associate degree category, 1 semester hour in Introduction to Computers and in the upper division baccalaureate and graduate category, 4 semester hours in COBOL Programming and Applications (3/89).

Computer-Based Business Systems
(Diploma in Systems Management [DSM])
  Location: Various locations offered by NIIT in India.
  Length: 264 hours (52 weeks); 3 two-hour meetings per week, plus a forty-eight hour project.
  Dates: April 1986-Present.
  Objective: To provide the student with the skills and experience to support computer-based problem solving.
  Learning Outcome: Upon successful completion of this course, the student will be able to understand the workings of a computer system; break a problem down into its composite parts and then structure the problem into a flowchart form; write COBOL programs for varied case studies; use micro database and spreadsheet programs; and use basic concepts to analyze and interpret problems into a logical format useful for structuring computer programs.
  Instruction: Course covers a basic overview of computers which includes a brief history, coverage of typical items in computer systems (i.e., keyboards, video display units, printers, etc.), types of computer systems (centralized, decentralized, and distributed), a review of programming logic techniques relating to problem solving, programming constructs and flowcharting, which includes structuring of programs and flowcharts relating to commercial programming with hands-on operation and programming to develop abilities in report generation, control break and file merge problems. COBOL exposure relates to ANSI COBOL and its use in commercial data processing and includes exposure to table handling, accessing, indexed files, subprograms and other related COBOL program structures, exposure to advanced computer languages applicable to spreadsheet analysis and database management (dBase III), additional exposure to structuring of problems into flowcharts, data dictionaries, inventory control, payroll and product planning and control, software development procedures including all stages from initial development through testing and finally handing over to external users, and procedures to select and appraise the quality and usage of small computer systems. Methodology includes lectures, practical exercises, self-paced learning, student/instructor consultation sessions, reading assignments in NIIT prepared text, booklets, and extensive program development, compiling and execution on in-house computers, as well as a major project which will allow the student to demonstrate his/her mastery of all the course components.
  Credit recommendation: In the lower division baccalaureate/associate degree category, 3 semester hours in Introduction to Computers, in the upper division baccalaureate or graduate category, 4 semester hours in COBOL Programming, in the lower division baccalaureate/associate degree category, 3 semester hours in Computer Programming, and in the upper division baccalaureate category, 3 semester hours in Advanced Computer Programming Applications (3/89). NOTE: Students who receive total credit for this course should not receive credit for Certificate in COBOL Programming.

National Management Association

The National Management Association is one of the oldest and largest organizations espousing management as a profession and the personal and professional development of the manager. Founded in the early nineteen hundreds at the Dayton Engineering Laboratories Company by the famous inventor, Charles Kettering, it became the National Association of Foremen in 1925. In 1957 the name was changed to the National Management Association.

The NMA has affiliated chapters throughout the U.S.A. and in some overseas locations. The organization is committed to bringing its members the latest state of the art thinking in management training through its professional development course materials. To enhance managerial interactions, all course materials are prepared with a complete discussion leader guide to be used in a group discussion learning format.

Source of official student records: National Management Association, Professional Development Division, 2210 Arbor Boulevard, Dayton, OH 45439.

Additional information about the courses: Program on Noncollegiate Sponsored Instruction, The Center for Adult Learning and Educational Credentials, American Council on Education, One Dupont Circle, Washington, D.C. 20036.

Supervisory and Management Skills Program
(Formerly First Line Supervisor Program)
  Course 1: Introduction to Supervision
  Course 2: Management Principles
  Course 8: Leadership Development
  Location: Nationwide.
  Length: 42 hours (21 weeks); 2 hours of pre-course work.
  Dates: September 1980-Present.
  Objective: To develop an understanding of the supervisor's role within the organization or environment; to deve-

lop an understanding of the basic principles of management, and to develop an understanding of supervisory leadership.

Instruction: The introductory course covers the supervisory setting, and the role of the supervisor as leader, problem-solver, and person. The principles course treats the organization as a system within which the classic management functions of planning, organizing, directing, and controlling are examined. The leadership course considers the environment of the supervisor and his interpersonal and organizational role. Instruction and methods used in all of the above include videotapes, lectures, role playing, quizzes, situational problems, and reading assignments.

Credit recommendation: In the lower division baccalaureate/associate degree category, 3 semester hours in Management and Supervision (8/83).

Supervisory and Management Skills Program
(Formerly First Line Supervisor Program)
   Course 3: Communication Skills
   Course 4: Interpersonal Relations
   Location: Nationwide.
   Length: 28 hours (14 weeks); 2 hours of pre-course work.
   Dates: July 1981-Present.
   Objective: To provide the supervisor with knowledge and skills in order to increase his understanding and effectiveness in communicating both verbally and nonverbally.
   Instruction: Major emphasis in this course is focused on the basics of communication in working with people. Specific information includes: oral and written communication; handling meetings and conferences, dealing with communication in the organization. Methodology includes: reading assignments, case studies; team exercises, role playing and critiques, audiovisual aids, and tests.
   Credit recommendation: In the lower division baccalaureate/associate degree category, 2 semester hours in Business Communications, Communications, Human Behavior or Interpersonal Dynamics (8/83).

Supervisory and Management Skills Program
(Formerly First Line Supervisor Program)
   Course 5: Developing Employee Performance
   Course 6: Challenge of a New Employee
   Course 7: Counseling
   Location: Nationwide.
   Length: 42 hours (2 hours per week for 21 weeks); 3 hours pre-course work.
   Dates: July 1982-Present.
   Objective: To provide participants with an introduction to contemporary principles and practices of hiring, developing and maintaining productive employees.
   Instruction: Emphasis will be placed upon hiring, orientation and training of new employees; the development and implementation of personnel management systems; and the role of the counseling as a corrective strategy.

Methods of instruction includes videotape cases, classroom discussion, individual/team exercises, readings and tests.
   Credit recommendation: In the lower division baccalaureate/associate degree category, 2 semester hours in Personnel Management (8/83).

Supervisory and Management Skills Program
(Formerly First Line Supervisor Program)
   Course 9: Business Concepts
   Course 10: Law for the Layman
   Location: Nationwide.
   Length: 28 hours (14 weeks); 2 hours of pre-course work.
   Dates: January 1983-Present.
   Objective: To provide supervisors with an understanding and working knowledge of business, legal concepts and practices.
   Instruction: Emphasis is placed on economic systems, management information systems, financial management systems; quality and productivity, the changing business world, employee and employment law, and government regulations. Methodology includes lecture and discussion, videotapes, and case studies.
   Credit recommendation: In the lower division baccalaureate/associate degree category, 2 semester hours in Contemporary Business Issues (8/83).

National Mine Health and Safety Academy

The mission of the National Mine Health and Safety Academy of the U.S. Department of Labor is to provide education and training services in support of the Mine Safety and Health Administration's effort to reduce accidents and improve health conditions in the Nation's mines and mineral industries.

The Academy provides a wide range of education and training for Coal and Metal/Nonmetal mine inspectors and other technical specialists required to enforce the provisions of the Federal Mine Safety and Health Act of 1977. Training is also offered, on safety and health and management subjects, to selected mine employees, and qualified mining students to enhance their knowledge of and compliance with the 1977 Act.

Source of official student records: Student Services Coordinator, National Mine Health and Safety Academy, P.O. Box 1166, Beckley, West Virginia 25802-1166.

Additional information about the courses: Program on Noncollegiate Sponsored Instruction, The Center for Adult Learning and Educational Credentials, American Council on Education, One Dupont Circle, N.W., Washington, D.C. 20036

Accident Analysis and Problem Identification
Location: National Mine Health and Safety Academy, Beckley, WV.
Length: 28 hours (1 week).
Dates: October 1985-Present.
Objective: To survey new accident prevention techniques and their solutions by group problem solving exercises and conceptual overview of the results.
Instruction: Covers logic of technique, customizing solutions, physical barrier analysis, human barrier analysis, planned inquiry, on-site concerns, optimizing resources used in analyzing accidents and gathering field data. Methodology includes lecture, discussion, classroom exercises, case studies, and problem solving.
Credit recommendation: In the lower division baccalaureate/associate degree category, 2 semester hours in Accident Prevention and Safety (4/86).

Accident Prevention in the Mining Industry
Location: National Mine Health and Safety Academy, Beckley, WV.
Length: 35 hours (5 days).
Dates: September 1980-Present.
Objective: To teach accident prevention with emphasis on mine safety.
Instruction: Covers accident investigation and analysis, job safety analysis, behavioral aspects of accident prevention, and related methodology. Includes lecture, discussion and classroom exercises.
Credit recommendation: In the lower division baccalaureate/associate degree category, 2 semester hours in Accident Prevention and Safety (4/86).

Accident Prevention Techniques
Location: National Mine Health and Safety Academy, Beckley, WV and at various coal and metal/nonmetal mine sites throughout the United States.
Length: 21 hours (3 days).
Dates: May 1980-Present.
Objective: To teach general accident prevention with emphasis on mine safety.
Instruction: Covers accident/incident analysis, analyzing performance problems, communications and effective safety, safety awareness, motivation, managing stress, job safety analysis, job observation, accident investigation and mine safety program rating procedures. Methodology includes lecture, discussion, and classroom exercises.
Credit recommendation: In the lower division baccalaureate/associate degree category, 1 semester hour in Accident Prevention and Safety (4/86).

Applied Communication Techniques
Location: National Mine Health and Safety Academy, Beckley, WV.
Length: 56 hours (2 weeks).
Dates: December 1983-Present.
Objective: To provide the participant training in listening skills, interviewing, conducting pre-inspection conferences, case-study problem-solving, and the presentation of evidence in court in situations involving mine safety violations.
Instruction: Covers the communication skills needed by an inspector in order to conduct inspection conferences and make courtroom appearances. Methodology includes lecture, discussion, case-studies, problem-solving, videotapes, and extensive role playing.
Credit recommendation: In the upper division baccalaureate category, 3 semester hours in Interviewing or Interviewing and Interrogation Procedures (4/86).

Coal Mine Dust Control
Location: National Mine Health and Safety Academy, Beckley, WV.
Length: 28 hours (4 days).
Dates: September 1985-Present.
Objective: To present the various techniques useful for dust control emphasizing the current technology.
Instruction: Covers problems associated with coal mine dust control; suppression techniques, social-medical problems associated with coal mine dust control, and problems arising from specific mining techniques as applied to coal mine dust management. Methodology includes lecture, discussion, laboratory exercises and workshops.
Credit recommendation: In the upper division baccalaureate category, 2 semester hours in Mine Atmosphere and Detection Instruments (4/86).

Coal Mine Explosion Prevention
Location: National Mine Health and Safety Academy, Beckley, WV.
Length: 28 hours (4 days).
Dates: February 1983-Present.
Objective: To learn to recognize, evaluate and control explosion hazards in coal mines.
Instruction: Covers historical background; study of methane, coal dust and ignition sources; sealing and ventilation, explosives use and characteristics; inspection and preventive measures.
Credit recommendation: In the upper division baccalaureate category, 2 semester hours in Mine Safety (4/86).

Coal Preparation
Location: National Mine Health and Safety Academy, Beckley, WV.
Length: 56 hours (8 days).
Dates: June 1986-Present.
Objective: To enable employees and industry personnel to recognize and understand the function of the individual processes of coal preparation and the hazards associated with each.
Instruction: Covers chemical properties of coal, electri-

cal properties of coal, physical properties of coal, mechanical sampling, laboratory determination, uses of coal, mine property data collection, screening, dense medium process and hydraulic separation, fine coal benefication, dry concretation, mechanical dewatering, thermal drying, dust control, coal storage, unit train loading, barge and ship loading, waste disposal, noise control, fire protection. Methodology includes lecture, discussion, computer assisted instruction, video tape and field trips.

Credit recommendation: In the upper division baccalaureate category, 3 semester hours in Coal Preparation (4/86).

Communication Skills I or Communication, Interpersonal, Small Group

Location: National Mine Health and Safety Academy, Beckley, WV and other mine sites.

Length: 28 hours (4 days).

Dates: April 1981-Present.

Objective: To provide participants an opportunity to learn and practice the effective use of interpersonal, intrapersonal, and small group communication skills.

Instruction: Covers barriers to communication, listening skills, group problem-solving, verbal and non-verbal communication; small group communications, values conflict resolution, and a review of the effects of stress. Methodology includes discussion, mini-lectures, experiential activities, practice teaching, role-playing, and problem-solving.

Credit recommendation: In the lower division baccalaureate/associate degree category, 2 semester hours in Communication, Helping Skills, or Interpersonal Relations (4/86).

Courtroom Procedures

Location: National Mine Health and Safety Academy, Beckley, WV.

Length: 28 hours (4 days).

Dates: July 1986-Present.

Objective: To prepare the journey man coal mine inspector for appearances in court.

Instruction: Course covers listening skills, interviewing, role of the inspector, importance of note making, the role of the commission and courts, elements in a citation, evidence in hearings, and understanding the procedures in preparing to testifying in court. Methodology includes lecture, discussion, case-studies, problem-solving, and extensive role-playing.

Credit recommendation: In the lower division baccalaureate/associate degree category, 2 semester hours in Court Room Procedures or Trial Practices. NOTE: Credit should not be awarded for both this course and the Applied Communication Techniques course (4/86).

Effective Writing

Location: National Mine Health and Safety Academy, Beckley, WV.

Length: 28 hours (4 days).

Dates: November 1978-Present.

Objective: To understand the techniques for effective, simple and logical writing.

Instruction: Covers elements of grammar, mechanics of writing, report writing, effective sentences, effective paragraphs, and the various aspects of effective writing. Methodology includes lecture, discussion, films, and writing exercises.

Credit recommendation: In the lower division baccalaureate/associate degree category, 1 semester hour in Business Communication (4/86).

Electrical Permissibility

Location: National Mine Health and Safety Academy, Beckley, WV.

Length: 16 hours (3 days).

Dates: June 1976-Present.

Objective: To provide an understanding of permissibility locations where permissible equipment is required.

Instruction: Covers concepts and application of permissibility, component requirements, tables and specifications, inspection activities, explosion proof electrical compartments, audible warning devices, and citation description. Methodology includes lectures, classroom discussions, and laboratory exercises.

Credit recommendation: In the lower division baccalaureate/associate degree category, 1 semester hour in Electrical Permissibility (4/86).

Electricity and Permissibility for the Non-Electrical Inspector

Location: National Mine Health and Safety Academy, Beckley, WV.

Length: 28 hours (4 days).

Dates: March 1983-Present.

Objective: To review the basic principles of electricity; to show how the principles are applied in coal mining.

Instruction: Covers voltage, current and resistance and how to calculate these in electrical circuits, single and thru-phase circuits, grounding, overload protection, checking methane, monitors and permissibility of electrical face equipment, electrical shock and physiological consequences. Methodology includes lecture, discussion, and laboratory experiences.

Credit recommendation: In the lower division baccalaureate/associate degree category, 2 semester hours in Mine Electricity and Permissibility (4/86).

First Responder

Location: National Mine Health and Safety Academy, Beckley, WV.

Length: 40 hours (1 week).

Dates: March 1983-Present.

Objective: To provide training in emergency care services rendered to victims of accidents and illness from those who are apt to be the first responding to an accident.

Instruction: Covers the roles and responsibilities of the first responder, the human body, patient examination, CPR, injuries to organs and extremities, heart attack, emergency childbirth, skull and chest injuries, poisons and drugs, triage, and burns. Methodology includes lecture, discussion, and laboratory instruction.

Credit recommendation: In the lower division baccalaureate/associate degree category, 2 semester hours in Health Education or CPR (4/86).

General Math or Introduction to Algebra

Location: National Mine Health and Safety Academy, Beckley, WV.
Length: 35 hours (1 week).
Dates: September 1985-Present.
Objective: To review math skills to qualify students to take advanced math courses.
Instruction: Covers a review of basic mathematics, experiences in practical applications, new vocabulary that applies to the material, problem-solving, operations with real numbers, exponents, radicals, polynomials, algebraic fractions, functions and graphing with exponential and logarithmic functions. Methodology includes lecture and classroom exercises.
Credit recommendation: In the lower division baccalaureate/associate degree category, 2 semester hours in General Mathematics (4/86).

Hazardous Materials

Location: National Mine Health and Safety Academy, Beckley, WV.
Length: 40 hours (1 week).
Dates: March 1982-Present.
Objective: To introduce the student to the problems of hazardous materials and hazardous waste disposal.
Instruction: Covers hazard recognition and evaluation; physical controls and identification during manufacture, storage, and handling; and personal protective equipment. Methodology includes lecture, discussion and laboratory exercises.
Credit recommendation: In the upper division baccalaureate category, 3 semester hours in Hazardous Materials (4/86).

Health Hazards in Mining

Location: National Mine Health and Safety Academy, Beckley, WV.
Length: 35 hours (1 week).
Dates: October 1983-Present.
Objective: To understand the basic principles of industrial hygiene and the diverse fields that this specialty encompasses.
Instruction: Covers fundamental concepts of industrial hygiene, health hazards associated with the respiratory system, occupational skin disorders, particulates exposure, hearing impairment, industrial dermatoses, documentation of exposure, industrial noise, ventilation and protective equipment. Methodology includes lecture, discussion, and laboratory exercises.
Credit recommendation: In the upper division baccalaureate category, 3 semester hours in Health Hazards in Mining (4/86).

Hoisting (Mine Elevators)

Location: National Mine Health and Safety Academy, Beckley, WV.
Length: 21 hours (3 days).
Dates: April 1980-Present.
Objective: To acquaint the student with the requirements of the ANSI A17.1 1984 and A17.2 1985 codes relative to elevator installation, inspection and maintenance.
Instruction: Covers drum, brakes, cage attachments, surry area; field trip to inspect gear driven and gearless hoists; study of American National Standards Institute code requirements on installation, maintenance, testing and inspection. Methodology includes lecture, discussion and field trips.
Credit recommendation: In the upper division baccalaureate degree category, 1 semester hour in Mine Hoist Operations (4/86).

Human Factors Engineering

Location: National Mine Health and Safety Academy, Beckley, WV.
Length: 28 hours (4 days).
Dates: December 1981-Present.
Objective: To be acquainted with concepts that enable the student to recognize, evaluate and control human factors engineering problems in the mining industry.
Instruction: Covers perceived mining needs in the human factors engineering field, primary goals of human factors and accidents, population stereotypes, design and operation of mining machines, decreasing the mine machine human factors problems, mine machine control, human factors in mine machine designs, training miners on the mine machine system, human lag time, and use of signals. Methodology includes lecture, discussion, and laboratory exercises.
Credit recommendation: In the upper division baccalaureate category, 2 semester hours in Human Factors Engineering (4/86).

Instructor Training

Location: National Mine Health and Safety Academy, Beckley, WV.
Length: 21 hours (3 days).
Dates: March 1983-Present.
Objective: To provide instructors with the fundamentals of curriculum design, evaluation techniques, and in-

structional strategies.

Instruction: Covers the development of behavioral objectives, development of criterion tests, planning of instructional activities, development of lesson plans, and development and use of audiovisuals. Methodology includes lecture, discussion, and videotaped presentations.

Credit recommendation: In the lower division baccalaureate/associate degree category, 1 semester hour in Teaching Methods (4/86).

Introduction to Mining

Location: National Mine Health and Safety Academy, Beckley, WV.

Length: 21 hours (3 days).

Dates: March 1981-Present.

Objective: Provides the participant with a general understanding of mining history, development, systems terminology, procedures, methods, and health and safety activities.

Instruction: Covers introduction to mining, history-geology-exploration in mining, environmental factors, survey and mapping, mining methods, hoisting-haulage, coal preparation, mineral processing, health and safety activities. Methodology includes lecture, discussion, laboratory exercises, and field trips.

Credit recommendation: In the lower division baccalaureate/associate degree category, 1 semester hour in Introduction to Mining (4/86).

Man, Machine and the Environment

Location: National Mine Health and Safety Academy, Beckley, WV.

Length: 35 hours (1 week).

Dates: July 1981-Present.

Objective: To acquaint the student with the basic principles used by human factor engineering in the design of mining systems.

Instruction: Covers industry "population stereotypes," early studies of human factors engineering, survey of human factors in underground bituminous coal mining, improving the safety and quality of consumer products, effects of sound and noise, work stations for operators, restrictions of detents on component controls, and residual energy. Methodology includes lecture, discussion, and laboratory exercises.

Credit recommendation: In the upper division baccalaureate category, 2 semester hours in Man, Machines and the Environment in the Mining Industry (4/86).

Mine Disaster Procedures

Location: National Mine Health and Safety Academy, Beckley, WV.

Length: 28 hours (1 week).

Dates: March 1981-Present.

Objective: To identify the types of rescue equipment, procedures for their use, and methods for mine rescue.

Instruction: Covers principles of mine rescue, mine emergency operations, history of disaster prevention activities, mine gasses, detection instruments, respiratory protection, rescue team activities, tactical procedures, map exercises and mine emergency operations system.

Credit recommendation: In the lower division baccalaureate/associate degree category, 2 semester hours in Mine Disaster Procedures (4/86).

Mine Electricity (Metal/Nonmetal Mines)

Location: National Mine Health and Safety Academy, Beckley, WV.

Length: 56 hours (8 days).

Dates: February 1982-Present.

Objective: To provide inspectors with an understanding of electricity and the electrical standards in 30 CFR for use in their inspection activities.

Instruction: Covers basic electrical terms and circuits; transformers and connections; systems grounding; electrical substations and related equipment; circuit breakers; substation perimeter fencing requirements; permissibility and permissibility standards; and inspection procedures to ascertain compliance with standards. Methodology includes lecture, discussion, and laboratory exercises.

Credit recommendation: In the lower division baccalaureate/associate degree category, 3 semester hours in Mine Electricity (4/86).

Mine Haulage and Transportation

Location: National Mine Health and Safety Academy, Beckley, WV.

Length: 35 hours (1 week).

Dates: March 1982-Present.

Objective: To introduce the student to the various systems used for haulage and transportation of product, supplies and personnel in surface and underground mining.

Instruction: Covers the recognition and the evaluation of hazardous conditions relating to surface and underground haulage, knowledge of hoisting systems, wire rope technology, static load safety factors, inspection techniques, inspection procedures for conveyor belt-roller type slippage switch. Methodology includes lecture, discussion, and laboratory exercises.

Credit recommendation: In the upper division baccalaureate category, 2 semester hours in Mine Haulage and Transportation (4/86).

Mine Safety and Health Legislation

Location: National Mine Health and Safety Academy, Beckley, WV.

Length: 35 hours (1 week).

Dates: November 1982-Present.

Objective: To acquaint the student in the history of Mine Safety and Health Legislation in the United States.

Instruction: Covers the functions of the Bureau of Mines and its functions and limitations, mine safety and health 1910 to present, Mine Safety and Health Act of 1977 and reasons for its establishment, problems of miner's pneumonconoisis, and extent of mine disasters. Methodology includes lecture, discussion, classroom exercises and library research.

Credit recommendation: In the upper division baccalaureate category, 2 semester hours in Mine Safety and Health Legislation (4/86).

Philosophical Concepts of Mine Safety and Health
Location: National Mine Health and Safety Academy, Beckley, WV.
Length: 35 hours (1 week).
Dates: December 1981-Present.
Objective: To provide the student with the opportunity to explore and discuss various factors which have had impact upon the philosophy of health and safety in the industrial environment.
Instruction: Covers social factors which influence one's philosophy, the effects of organized labor upon the philosophy of health and safety in the workplace, Federal laws pertaining to health and safety, and comparison of foreign countries' philosophies on health and safety. Methodology includes lecture and discussion.
Credit recommendation: In the upper division baccalaureate category, 3 semester hours in Philosophical Concepts of Mine Safety and Health (4/86).

Public Speaking and Briefing Techniques
Location: National Mine Health and Safety Academy, Beckley, WV and selected MSHA field locations.
Length: 28 hours (4 days).
Dates: June 1984-Present.
Objective: To provide public speaking and briefing skills techniques, knowledge, and workshop practice to increase job effectiveness.
Instruction: Covers public speaking fears, public communication objectives, speaking effectively, preparing a speech, planning a speech, speaking aids, conducting question and answer sessions, and communications by voice and action. Methodology includes lecture, discussion, classroom exercises, role-playing, films, and video-tapes.
Credit recommendation: In the lower division baccalaureate/associate degree category, 2 semester hours in Speech, or Public Speaking (4/86).

Research Applications in Occupational Education
Location: National Mine Health and Safety Academy, Beckley, WV.
Length: 40 hours (1 week).
Dates: September 1983-Present.
Objective: A study of methodology, application, analysis, and synthesis of research in occupational education.
Instruction: Covers a review of current occupational studies, clustered by areas, with attention to statistical techniques, data collecting, data handling and the audience and impact of particular projects and research organizations. Methodology includes lecture, discussion, and library exercises.
Credit recommendation: In the upper division baccalaureate category, 2 semester hours in Research Application in Occupational Education (4/86).

Resident IV Industrial Hygiene II
Location: National Mine Health and Safety Academy, Beckley, WV.
Length: 56 hours (2 weeks).
Dates: March 1984-Present.
Objective: To understand instrumentation and documentation principles of industrial hygiene.
Instruction: Covers industrial noise, ionizing radiation, non-ionizing radiation, temperature extremes, ergonomics, biological hazards, industrial toxicology and levels of exposure to determine compliance with applicable regulations. Methodology includes lecture, discussion, and classroom exercises.
Credit recommendation: In the upper division baccalaureate category, 3 semester hours in Industrial Hygiene (4/86).

Roof Control for the Specialist
Location: National Mine Health and Safety Academy, Beckley, WV.
Length: 28 hours (4 days).
Dates: June 1977-Present.
Objective: To train inspectors to recognize and minimize the hazards created by roof and rib conditions.
Instruction: Covers basic geology as it relates to coal bearing and nearby strata, effects of water and temperature on rock, rock stresses, poisson effect; roof control methods and procedures, roof bolting systems and trusses; laboratory and test procedures to evaluate anchorage; and inspection procedures. Methodology includes lecture, discussion, films, and laboratory exercises.
Credit recommendation: In the lower division baccalaureate/associate degree category, 2 semester hours in Roof and Rib Control (4/86).

Stress - Its Implications in Health and Safety
Location: National Mine Health and Safety Academy, Beckley, WV.
Length: 40 hours (1 week).
Dates: November 1984-Present.
Objective: To introduce the student to the problems of stress in the work environment.
Instruction: Covers the sources of stress, physiological effects of stress, psychological effects of stress, relaxation techniques, stress management, and the financial implications of stress in industry. Methodology includes lecture, discussion, and laboratory exercises.
Credit recommendation: In the upper division baccalaureate category, 3 semester hours in Stress and Its

Impact on Safety and Health in Mining (4/86).

Substance Abuse or (Alcohol and Drug Abuse)
  Location: National Mine Health and Safety Academy, Beckley, WV and in the field.
  Length: 28 hours (4 days).
  Dates: February 1983-Present.
  Objective: To explore the history of the rise of the chemical dependency problem in society and its impact on the individual and industry.
  Instruction: Covers the history of drug culture development, identification of licit and illicit substances in the workplace, the physiological effects of drugs on the human body and mind, signs and symptoms of a chemical substance abuser, legality of pre-employment drug screening, search and seizure, the financial impact on the industrial setting, and the role of and employee assistance program. Methodology includes lecture, discussion, case studies, and labor.
  Credit recommendation: In the lower division baccalaureate/associate degree category, 2 semester hours in Alcohol and Drug Abuse, Substance Abuse, Alcohol and Health, or Drug Abuse (4/86).

System Safety Engineering
  Location: National Mine Health and Safety Academy, Beckley, WV.
  Length: 28 hours (4 days).
  Dates: August 1978-Present.
  Objective: To acquaint the student with established system safety engineering concepts and techniques and the ability to apply those techniques in the analysis of safety hazards.
  Instruction: Covers the basic components of a "system," system characteristics that constitute a measure of "system effectiveness," methods that may be used to gain understanding of system operations, five phases in the system life cycle model, qualitative and quantitative evaluation of system safety engineering, Job Safety Analysis, and Fault Free Analysis. Methodology includes lecture, discussion, and case studies.
  Credit recommendation: In the upper division baccalaureate category, 2 semester hours in System Safety Engineering in the Mining Industry (4/86).

Ventilation
  Location: National Mine Health and Safety Academy, Beckley, WV.
  Length: 28 hours (4 days).
  Dates: February 1983-Present.
  Objective: To review the principles of coal mine ventilationa and applicable ventilation regulations.
  Instruction: Covers mine gases, abandoned areas, sealed areas, air velocity measurements, face ventilation, longwalls, rock dusting, job areas, ventilation plans, calculation of face liberation, and leakage. Methodology includes lecture, discussion, and laboratory exercises.
  Credit recommendation: In the lower division baccalaureate/associate degree category, 2 semester hours in Coal Mine Ventilation (4/86).

National Photographic Interpretation Center

The advanced Remote Image Sensor Training Program is a 66-hour, 11-day, performance-based, criterion-referenced learning experience and is designed to provide the necessary background knowledge relating to remote sensing system-specific imaging principles required to exploit imagery collected by a remote sensor collection system. The major goal of the Course is to help the experienced Imagery Analyst learn to use remote sensing system-specific imagery for the prompt and confident exploitation and interpretation of imagery. The Course also provides opportunities to apply previously learned remote sensing system-specific principles, knowledge and procedures as the students compare images of familiar types of Military Order of Battle subjects.

The Course covers only topics which will aid the experienced Imagery Analyst in extraction of the pertinent information from the actual images and to evaluate their interpretability. The Course deliberately avoids covering generic remote sensing theory, the detailed design and/or the mathematical derivations of the sensor system performances. The principles learned in this Course provide the knowledge of remote sensing system-specific principles utilized in interpreting imagery generated from the sensor system and to describe the sensor collection system and its modes of operation, viewing angle limitations, the collection access areas, mode considerations and concepts, operational film titling and formatting, collection trade-off considerations and stereo imagery.

  Source of official student records: Chief, Training Division, National Photographic Interpretation Center, CIA, Washington, D.C. 20505.

  Additional information about the courses: Program on Noncollegiate Sponsored Instruction, The Center for Adult Learning and Educational Credentials, American Council on Education, One Dupont Circle, Washington, D.C. 20036.

Active Remote Sensor Image Analysis Training Program
(Advanced Remote Sensor Image Analysis Training Program) (ARSIA-TP)
  Location: National Photographic Interpretation Center.
  Length: 66 hours (11 days).
  Dates: June 1984-Present.
  Objective: To provide students with the necessary back-

ground knowledge of active remote sensing systems necessary for analysis and interpretation of images obtained from such systems.

Instruction: The course assumes previous knowledge and experience in analysis and interpretation of imagery from sensors operating in the visible region. The course includes both classroom lectures and laboratory exercises. Topics include principles and signature analysis, data processing techniques, fundamentals of the sensor collection system, analysis and interpretation of imagery for orders of battle.

Credit recommendation: In the upper division baccalaureate or graduate degree category, 2 semester hours in Remote Sensing Interpretation (11/85).

National Imagery Analysis Course

Location: National Photographic Interpretation Center, Washington, D.C.

Length: *Version 1:* 269 hours (10 weeks); *Version 2:* 360 hours (12 weeks).

Dates: *Version 1:* January 1986-December 1988; *Version 2:* January 1989-Present.

Objective: To provide skills and acquire fundamental knowledge needed to effectively interpret, analyze, and report on imaged objects, facilities, and phenomena.

Learning Outcome: Upon successful completion of this course, the student will possess the capability to interpret remote sensing imagery, be knowledgeable of recognition features of foreign military industrial equipment, and site configuration and understand the use of reference material such as maps and guides to perform imagery analysis.

Instruction: The course provides knowledge and experience in interpretation and analysis of imagery from a variety of remote sensing systems. The course includes lectures, instructional media presentations, and a heavy reliance on laboratory exercises. Topics include fundamentals of imaging sensors systems, military organization and structure, recognition of military and cultural objects, facilities and phenomena, and auxiliary topics.

Credit recommendation: In the upper division baccalaureate or graduate degree category, 6 semester hours in Imagery Analysis, Remote Sensing Techniques, or Imagery Interpretation (4/87).

National Registry of Radiation Protection Technologists

The National Registry of Radiation Protection Technologists evolved out of the nuclear industry need for responsible and competent protection technologists, as a standard measure to promote improved training programs and curricula, and to recognize the motivation and achievement of individual professionals. The objective of the Registry is to encourage and promote the education and training of Radiation Protection Technologists and, by so doing, promote and advance the science of Health Physics.

Source of official student records: Executive Secretary, National Registry of Radiation Protection Technologists, P.O. Box 6974, Kennewick, WA 99336.

Additional information about the courses: Program on Noncollegiate Sponsored Instruction, The Center for Adult Learning and Educational Credentials, American Council on Education, One Dupont Circle, Suite 1B-20, Washington, D.C., 20036 or Program on Noncollegiate Sponsored Instruction, Thomas A. Edison State College, 101 West State Street, CN 545, Trenton, New Jersey 08625.

National Registry of Radiation Protection Technologists

Location: Various locations throughout the U.S.

Length: Independent study.

Dates: November 1978-present.

Objective: To promote technical competence in the radiation protection field at the operational level by establishing a standard of excellence for the radiation protection technologist.

Instruction: Prior to sitting for the Registry, applicants must be high school graduates, have at least 5 years qualified experience in the field of radiation protection and be currently working in the field. Students prepare for the Registry through independent study. They must have supervisor and professional recommendations as conditions for qualifying for the Registry.

Topics covered in the Registry include: Introduction to atomic and nuclear physics; natural and artificial radioactivity; decay schemes; nuclear reactions including fission and fusion; interaction of radiation with matter; radiation quantities and units; shielding; biological effects of radiation; radiation protection standards and regulations; principles of radiation detection and detection devices; counting systems and assay of alpha, beta, and gamma emitters; survey and monitoring equipment; external radiation exposure and protection techniques; radiation safety and control; accelerator and reactor health physics; medical radiation physics.

Registry also covers an introduction to radiation protection, including radiation sources, radiation dose and dose measurement, radiation exposure, radiation protection techniques, monitoring methods and instruments, contamination control and waste storage, facility design, hazards analysis, and applied health physics techniques for the safe handling and control of radioactive material. Laboratory experience provides students practical knowledge of equipment and practices of current use in the radiation protection field, and gives some of the practical aspects of radiation safety and control.

Each applicant also has applied work experience as a health physics technician at a government laboratory or a radiation facility of some industry, hospital, or education and research institution.

Credit recommendation: In the lower division baccalaureate/associate degree category, 6 semester hours in Introduction to Radiological Science; in the upper division baccalaureate category, 8 semester hours in Radiation Detection and Measurement; in the upper division baccalaureate category, 8 semester hours in Radiation Protection and Control; and in the upper division baccalaureate category, 8 semester hours in Applied Health Physics Internship (11/88). NOTE: For those students who already possess a baccalaureate degree, these upper level baccalaureate credit recommendations can be considered graduate level recommendations. The academic content is comparable to graduate school courses in these same subject areas.

National Sheriffs' Association

The National Sheriffs' Association is a nonprofit professional service organization dedicated to enhancing the professional capabilities of criminal justice agencies and personnel in the United States and to promoting effective law enforcement and correctional services at the county and local level.

Although the NSA's primary area of responsibility is in meeting the needs of America's 3,100 sheriffs and their departments, the Association's professional responsibility also encompasses more than 41,000 members who are employed by federal, state, county, and municipal criminal justice agencies nationwide.

Since 1940, the National Sheriffs' Association has provided a broad range of professional services to sheriff departments and the law enforcement practitioners who are members of the Association. One of the organizational objectives enumerated in the charter requires the Association to "promote the Law Enforcement profession by providing appropriate educational courses of higher learning."

To facilitate this mission the Association makes a concerted effort to provide meaningful training programs on an ongoing basis. Hundreds of training projects to improve the professional knowledge and skills of criminal justice personnel at all levels have used instructional materials prepared by the Association.

The Training/Professional Development Section is a branch of the Professional Services Division and has the responsibility for facilitating all training programs offered by the Association.

The Jail Officers' Training Program is designed to fulfill basic training needs of jail officers through a course of independent study by correspondence. It has also been designed to serve as an in-class basic training program.

Source of official student records: National Sheriffs' Association, 1450 Duke Street, Alexandria, Virginia 22314-3490.

Additional information about the courses: Program on Noncollegiate Sponsored Instruction, The Center for Adult Learning and Educational Credentials, American Council on Education, One Dupont Circle, Washington, D.C. 20036.

Fundamentals of Adult Detention
(Jail Officers' Training Program)

Location: Various sites certified by the National Association of State Directors of Law Enforcement Training.

Length: 80 hours (2 weeks) as a classroom course or approximately 6 months as a correspondence course.

Dates: July 1982-Present.

Objective: At the conclusion of this course, the student will be able to understand the historical perspectives of the detention center environment; understand the importance of the legal ramifications of their assigned responsibilities; identify their role in the communication process of the total institution; understand the rules, regulations, and procedures regarding the security of the inmates, staff, and facility; identify and address the special medical, social, and psychological needs encountered in the detention environment; and understand the decision making and problem solving responsibilities involved in working with the confined.

Instruction: This course examines the elements impacting upon the adult detention environment. Included are the historical perspectives, legal ramifications, and the role and responsibilities of the detention personnel. Special sections of the course cover the following topics: basic issues—the American jail, legal rights and responsibilities within the corrections environment, litigation procedure, written communications, role concepts, attitudes, and interpersonal communication, dealing with stress; security —basic jail security principles, books and admissions, classification of inmates, disciplinary procedures contraband control, key and tool control, patrol procedures in the jail, escort of inmates, hostage incidents in the jail, release procedures; special procedures—sick call, recreation and visiting, diabetic and epileptic inmates, medical problems confronting women inmates, drug withdrawal in the jail, alcohol abuse emergencies in the jail, psychological disorders (psychopathic and neurotic personalities), homosexual behavior in the jail, suicide prevention; and supervision—supervising inmates (principles and skills), personal supervision situations in housing and general areas, special supervision problems in the jail, supervision of inmates in dining areas, and the supervision of minimum security inmates. This course is delivered by classroom instruction or correspondence study.

Credit recommendation: In the vocational certificate or lower division baccalaureate/associate degree category, 3 semester hours in Administration of Justice, Criminal Justice, or Social Science (12/84). NOTE: This course may be substituted for a course in Introduction to Corrections.

National Union of Hospital and Health Care Employees, District 1199C

The National Union of Hospital and Health Care Employees, District 1199C, represents the workers of approximately 50 hospitals and health care facilities in the Philadelphia area. The Training and Upgrading Fund is an educational program established as a result of collective bargaining agreements with many of the health care institutions and is a cooperative union-management operation.

The Training and Upgrading Fund was established in Philadelphia in 1974 and provides educational services on several levels. In addition to a tuition reimbursement program and a full-time scholarship program, there is a Continuing Education Program. This program offers college-level courses, high school equivalency courses, and technical in-service training.

Since June 1978, the Continuing Education Program has been offering college-level courses. The courses are taught at the union headquarters after working hours and are open to all union members. Basic collegiate courses in mathematics, English, and social sciences are offered.

Source of official student records: Training and Upgrading Office, National Union of Hospital and Health Care Employees, District 1199C, 1317 Race Street, Philadelphia, Pennsylvania 19107.

Additional information about the courses: Program on Noncollegiate Sponsored Instruction, The Center for Adult Learning and Educational Credentials, American Council on Education, One Dupont Circle, Washington, D.C. 20036.

Algebra and Calculus
(Calculus I)
Location: Philadelphia, PA.
Length: 45 hours (9 weeks).
Dates: June 1978-Present.
Objective: To provide students with a basic college-level calculus course.
Instruction: Graphs, functions, derivatives, differentiation, second derivatives, antiderivatives, the fundamental theorem of calculus, applications of calculus in the biological sciences or in business. Lecture, problems, mid-term and comprehensive final examination are used.
Credit recommendation: In the lower division baccalaureate/associate degree category, 3 semester hours in Mathematics (7/78).

Elementary Statistics
Location: Philadelphia, PA.
Length: 45 hours (9 weeks).
Dates: September 1978-Present.
Objective: To provide students with a basic understanding of descriptive statistics, including an introduction to inferential statistics.
Instruction: Frequency distributions, measures of central tendency, permutation, binomial distributions, normal distributions, sampling techniques, and statistical inferences. Lecture, discussion, and homework are used.
Credit recommendation: In the lower division baccalaureate/associate degree category, 3 semester hours in Statistics (7/78).

National Weather Service Training Center

The National Weather Service, an agency within the National Oceanic and Atmospheric Administration (NOAA) and the U.S. Department of Commerce, established the Training Center to provide residence courses in meteorology, electronics, management, and supervision for employees. Limited space is made available to personnel of other U.S. government agencies and to foreign countries which have cooperative weather program agreements with the United States. The Center also administers a correspondence program for National Weather Service employees.

Source of official student records: Coordinator of Student Affairs, National Weather Service Training Center, 617 Hardesty, Kansas City, Missouri 64124.

Additional information about the courses: Program on Noncollegiate Sponsored Instruction, The Center for Adult Learning and Educational Credentials, American Council on Education, One Dupont Circle, Washington, D.C. 20036.

Air Pollution Meteorology (APMO1)
Location: National Weather Service Training Center, Kansas City, MO.
Length: 64 hours (2 weeks).
Dates: May 1975-November 1979.
Objective: To enable professional meteorologists to serve as air pollution specialists.
Instruction: Forecasting the atmosphere's ability to transport and dilute emitted pollutants, recognition of pending atmospheric stagnation, sources and hazards of various pollutants, Briggs plume rise equations, atmospheric dispersion equations.
Credit recommendation: In the upper division baccalaureate category or in the graduate degree category, 2 semester hours in Meteorology (10/77).

AMOS (Automatic Meteorological Observing System) III-70/73 S-02-02
Location: National Weather Service Training Center,

Kansas City, MO.

Length: 64 hours (8 working days).

Dates: January 1972-Present.

Objective: To provide technicians who are familiar with digital techniques with the knowledge and skills necessary to install, calibrate, and maintain the NWS-AMOS III systems.

Instruction: Provides detailed coverage of circuits and mechanical components, automatic programming, sensors, pulse coding, and manual programming. Laboratory exercises, calibration, and troubleshooting of complete operational systems are used.

Credit recommendation: In the lower division baccalaureate/associate degree category, 2 semester hours in Digital Equipment Diagnostics and Repair (8/80) (11/85). NOTE: This course has been reevaluated and continues to meet requirements for credit recommendations.

ART (Automatic Radio Theodolite) Rawin System J-12-03

Location: National Weather Service Training Center, Kansas City, MO.

Length: 96 hours (12 days).

Dates: May 1984-Present.

Objective: To provide electronics technicians with the knowledge and skills required to align, calibrate, and maintain the ART system and associated ground equipment.

Instruction: Upper air sounding systems; principles of tracking active targets by conical scanning; system operation and diagnostic evaluation to subsystem and LRU levels, including the upper air minicomputer; alignment, calibration, troubleshooting, and repair of ART systems. Lecture and extensive laboratory exercises.

Credit recommendation: In the lower division baccalaureate/associate degree category, 2 semester hours in Electronic Systems (11/85). NOTE: This course is essentially identical to GMD RAWIN System J-10-03 and WBRT-RAWIN System J-11-03; credit should be awarded for no more than one of these courses.

Automation of Field Operations and Services (AFOS I) M-04-04

Location: National Weather Service Training Center, Kansas City, MO.

Length: *Version 1:* 144 hours (18 working days). *Version 2:* 184 hours (23 working days).

Dates: *Version 1:* May 1978-October 1985. *Version 2:* November 1985-Present.

Objective: To prepare experienced electronics technicians to activate newly installed AFOS systems and to run quality assurance tests on the equipment. To enable technicians to diagnose trouble to board level 50 percent of the time and 80 percent of the time with phone advice from a systems specialist.

Instruction: Presents an overview of the national computer distributed system with protocol for information transfer within the system. Also covers the real-time disk operating system used in AFOS; computer architecture with emphasis on diagnostic and troubleshooting procedures; subsystems, including the disk controller and drive; synchronous and asynchronous modems; graphics display module; printer/plotter; alphanumeric display module; and systems interface modules. Lecture, laboratory work, extensive use of audiovisual materials, and testing are used. (Prerequisites: Solid State and Digital Logic Y-02-03, or its equivalent, and Computer Technology Y-03-01).

Credit recommendation: In the lower division baccalaureate/associate degree category, 4 semester hours in Computer System Maintenance and Repair (8/80) (11/85). NOTE: This course has been reevaluated and continues to meet requirements for credit recommendations.

Automation of Field Operations and Services (AFOS II A & B) M-05-07, M-08-04

Location: National Weather Service Training Center, Kansas City, MO.

Length: *Version 1:* 264 hours (33 working days). *Version 2:* 280 hours (35 working days).

Dates: *Version 1:* May 1978-October 1985. *Version 2:* November 1985-Present.

Objective: To supplement knowledge gained from the AFOS I course, M-04-04, with a more in-depth study of each subsystem in the nationally distributed computer communications system. Emphasis is given to diagnostic and troubleshooting procedures. Graduates should be able to repair independently 80 percent of malfunctions and give phone advice to less experienced electronics technicians.

Instruction: Covers each subsystem of the AFOS system down to chip level. Detailed subsystem schematics, as well as system software, are studied. Advanced diagnostic and troubleshooting procedures are covered and practiced in a coordinate laboratory. (Prerequisite: Automation of Field Operations and Services AFOS I M-04-04).

Credit recommendation: In the upper division baccalaureate category, 4 semester hours in Advanced Digital and Computer Circuitry; in the lower division baccalaureate/associate degree category, 4 semester hours in Digital Equipment and Computer Equipment Diagnostics and Repair (8/80) (11/85). NOTE: This course has been reevaluated and continues to meet requirements for credit recommendations. Students who complete the course should be extremely well versed in digital electronics, computer circuitry, and computer system diagnostics and troubleshooting.

Computer Technology Y-03-01

Location: National Weather Service Training Center, Kansas City, MO.

Length: *Version 1:* 40 hours (5 working days). *Version 2:* 32 hours (4 working days).

Dates: *Version 1:* May 1978-October 1985. *Version 2:* November 1985-Present.

Objective: To introduce minicomputer systems architecture. To develop skills in interpreting and running short programs using the NOVA computer instruction set. To demonstrate how to boot-up the system's operating system software from disk.

Instruction: Covers minicomputer systems architecture and programming using the NOVA computer instruction set. Students should become familiar with short programs that use peripheral devices. Students are also introduced to the use of canned diagnostic programs. The course includes lecture/discussion and laboratory work.

Credit recommendation: In the lower division baccalaureate/associate degree category, 1 semester hour in Computers (8/80) (11/85). NOTE: Course is too specialized to be substituted for the usual computer programming course found in lower division technical programs. This course has been reevaluated and continues to meet requirements for credit recommendations.

Device for Automatic Remote Data Collection (DARDC) B-07-02

Location: National Weather Service Training Center, Kansas City, MO.

Length: 64 hours (8 working days).

Dates: July 1972-Present.

Objective: To enable students to install, operate, and localize trouble to block or card level using visual and/or audio outputs from the DARDC to a TTY or DARDC test set. (A DARDC is a device that measures wind speed, direction, temperature, dew point, and precipitation at a remote site and forwards the data over telephone lines or by radio transmission to a central point.)

Instruction: Starts with a system overview, including the actual DARDC unit, telephone coupler, solar panel, battery charger, DARDC simulator, and test set; reviews basic digital COS/MOS circuitry, including gates, flip-flops, shift registers, four-bit adders, A/D converters, phase-locked loop, parity generator/checker, voltage comparator, voltage-to-frequency converters, and the ASCII code; treats in detail the proper installation and operation of each major component of the system; emphasizes diagnostic and troubleshooting procedures to board level. Lecture, laboratory work, and out-of-class problem solving are used. (Prerequisite: Solid State Electronics and Digital Logic course Y-02-03.)

Credit recommendation: In the lower division baccalaureate/associate degree category, 2 semester hours in Digital Equipment Diagnostics and Repair (8/80) (11/85). NOTE: This course has been reevaluated and continues to meet requirements for credit recommendations.

Digital Video Integrator Processor (Logicon DVIP) R-13-02

Location: National Weather Service Training Center, Kansas City, MO.

Length: 64 hours (8 working days).

Dates: May 1978-October 1979.

Objective: To teach qualified electronics technicians the methods of improving accuracy of radar displays through digital quantitizing of data, and the circuit theory needed to accomplish this work.

Instruction: Logic diagrams; linear and digital modules; and various digital operations, such as integration, division, and addition, are studied. Although applied to specific equipment, the concepts covered have many other applications.

Credit recommendation: In the upper division baccalaureate category, 2 semester hours in Digital Systems (8/80) (11/85). NOTE: Credit should not be given if it has been awarded for WSR (Weather Service Radar)-57/DVIP Radar System R-08-06 or WSR (Weather Service Radar) 74C Radar System R-12-04. This course has been reevaluated and continues to meet requirements for credit recommendations.

Flash Flood Forecasting (FFF01)

Location: National Weather Service Training Center, Kansas City, MO.

Length: 64 hours (2 weeks).

Dates: July 1978-Present.

Objective: To develop the abilities of the professional meteorologist to deal effectively with the flash flood phenomenon through the use of specialized techniques and forecasting tools; and to enable the professional hydrologist to recognize flash flood threats and furnish the meteorologist with the appropriate hydrologic guidance.

Instruction: Flash flood hydrology and hydrologic guidance materials; flash flood meteorology and climatology; uses of radar and satellite data; flash flood planning and preparedness. Instruction involves lectures, demonstrations, and case studies.

Credit recommendation: In the upper division baccalaureate category or in the graduate degree category, 2 semester hours in Hydrology or Meteorology (7/79).

Fundamentals of Meteorology (Formerly Basic Meteorology)

Location: Honolulu, HI.

Length: 184 hours (5 weeks).

Dates: February 1973-February 1976.

Objective: To qualify meteorological technicians to deliver weather briefings to pilots.

Instruction: Lectures and practical exercises in basic meteorology, reading forecasts, and communication techniques in providing weather briefings to pilots. Also includes instruction in elementary aeronautics.

Credit recommendation: In the lower division baccalaureate/associate degree category, 3 semester hours in Meteorology (10/77) (8/82). NOTE: This course has undergone a 5-year reevaluation and continues to meet the requirements for credit recommendations.

GMD (Ground Meteorological Device) RAWIN System J-10-03
  Location: National Weather Service Training Center, Kansas City, MO.
  Length: 104 hours (13 working days).
  Dates: January 1960-Present.
  Objective: To provide electronics technicians with the skills required to install, align, calibrate, and maintain the GMD-1 RAWIN system and associated ground equipment.
  Instruction: Covers upper air sounding systems, radiosonde operation, principles of tracking active targets by conical scanning, frequency-to-voltage conversion, null-balance recording systems, and alignment, calibration, troubleshooting, and repair of GMD-1 systems. Lecture and laboratory exercises are used.
  Credit recommendation: In the lower division baccalaureate/associate degree category, 2 semester hours in Electronic Systems (8/80) (11/85). NOTE: This course is essentially identical to WBRT (Weather Bureau Radio Theodolite) RAWIN System J-11-03; therefore, credit should not be awarded for both this course and WBRT. This course has been reevaluated and continues to meet requirements for credit recommendations.

Instructor Training (ITT01)
  Location: National Weather Service Training Center, Kansas City, MO.
  Length: 72 hours (9 days).
  Dates: January 1974-Present.
  Objective: To prepare effective instructors for training programs.
  Learning Outcome: Upon successful completion of this course, the student will be able to analyze student learning processes, teaching methods, and course material; prepare effective courses and course materials; conduct instruction using appropriate methods.
  Instruction: Course covers psychology of learning, motivation; instuctional stages, methods, and techniques; instructor personality and characteristics; training aids; communication, speech techniques, and voice development; and test construction. Methodology includes lecture, discussion, group critique of student instructional presentations, out-of-class assignments, and evaluation of student's teaching ability, and examinations.
  Credit recommendation: In the lower division baccalaureate/associate degree category, or in the upper division baccalaureate category, 1 semester hour in Education or Human Resource Development (2/77) (4/82) (7/88). NOTE: This course has been reevaluated and continues to meet requirements for credit recommendations.

Integrated Circuits and Application Concepts Y-02-03 (Formerly Solid State and Digital Logic Y-02-03)
  Location: National Weather Service Training Center, Kansas City, MO.
  Length: 104 hours (13 working days).
  Dates: June 1975-Present.
  Objective: To provide electronics technicians with a basic understanding of integrated circuits and computer logic.
  Instruction: The digital portion of the course covers number systems, Boolean algebra, logic elements, logic trees, and various kinds of flip-flops in counting and register circuits. The linear portion covers the basics of integrated operational amplifiers and some of their applications. Half of the course is devoted to lecture/discussion and half to laboratory work. This course has been offered as a self-paced personal computer course since August 1983.
  Credit recommendation: In the lower division baccalaureate/associate degree category, 3 semester hours in Linear and Digital Electronics (8/80) (11/85). NOTE: This course has been reevaluated and continues to meet requirements for credit recommendations.

Introduction to Meteorology (Basic Meteorological Technician [BMT01])
  Location: National Weather Service Training Center, Kansas City, MO.
  Length: 304 hours (8 weeks).
  Dates: April 1974-January 1978.
  Objective: To qualify the student to enter the meteorological technician/observer job series.
  Instruction: Lecture, hands-on training, and practical sessions in basic meteorology, weather code interpretation, instrument operation and observation, communication equipment operation, and weather station operation. Also includes instruction in basic English (oral and written skills), basic mathematics, and geography. Course does not require knowledge of calculus.
  Credit recommendation: In the lower division baccalaureate/associate degree category, 4 semester hours in Meteorology (3 semester hours in lecture and 1 semester hour in laboratory) (10/77).

Meteorology (RAD06) (Formerly RAD01, RAD02, LWR01, RAD03, RAD05)
  Location: National Weather Service Training Center, Kansas City, MO.
  Length: 104 hours (3 weeks, plus approximately 1 week of prior self-study and examination on course modules sent in advance).
  Dates: October 1987-Present.
  Objective: To apply radar theory and principles to the practical use of National Weather Service radar data.
  Learning Outcome: Upon successful completion of this course, the student will be able to: apply radar theory and

principles to the operation and interpretation of NWS field radars, air traffic radars, and the proposed NEXRAD doppler radar system; identify proper operating and checking procedures for the appropriate radar system and encode radar system information; apply contemporary severe thunderstorm, flash flood, and tropical cyclone models to collection and interpretation of radar data.

Instruction: Course covers applied physics of radar operation, descriptive and comparative study of weather radars, observation and coding techniques, interpretation of radar displays, including doppler in terms of atmospherical processes, and warning and forecasting operations. Methodology includes lectures, discussion, demonstration, case studies, use of field radar equipment and radar simulator systems, out-of-class assignments, and examinations.

Credit recommendation: In the upper division baccalaureate category, 3 semester hours in Radar Meteorology (7/88). NOTE: This course contains primarily the same content and has the same credit recommendation of all former versions of the course listed here.

Microprocessor: Fundamental Concepts and Applications Y-04-02

Location: National Weather Service Training Center, Kansas City, MO.
Length: 56 hours (7 working days).
Dates: July 1979-Present.
Objective: To introduce experienced electronics technicians to this "state-of-the-art" technology to enable them to use both software and hardware in a variety of ways. Graduates should be able to apply this knowledge in operating microprocessor-based equipment in the National Weather Service.

Instruction: The course is developed around the Z80A microprocessor. Computer architecture, the Z80A instruction set, CP/M operating system, basic 80 language and program development and debugging, arithmetic routines, timing loops, I/O programming and interfacing, and using the microcomputer for real-time applications. There is introduction to CP/M assembly languages, register change and *call* instruction sets, and the generation of short assembly language programs. Block diagrams are used with microcomputers for laboratory practice. (Prerequisite: A digital electronics background.)

Credit recommendation: In the upper division baccalaureate category, 3 semester hours in Introduction to Microcomputers (8/80) (11/85). NOTE: This course has been reevaluated and continues to meet requirements for credit recommendations.

Radar Meteorology - A Short Course (RAD03) (Formerly [RSC01])

Location: National Weather Service Training Center, Kansas City, MO.
Length: 104 hours (3 weeks).
Dates: November 1977-March 1984.
Objective: To enable the student to apply radar principles and theory to the practical operation of weather radars, and to interpret and disseminate accurate radar data.

Instruction: Radar principles; interpretation of radar scope depictions; measurement techniques; integration and analysis; the dissemination of radar information. (Prerequisite: Mathematics through trigonometry and one year of college physics).

Credit recommendation: In the upper division baccalaureate category, 3 semester hours in Meteorology (10/77) (4/82). NOTE: This course has been reevaluated and continues to meet the requirements for credit recommendations.

Radar Meteorology - WSR-57 (RAD01)

Location: National Weather Service Training Center, Kansas City, MO.
Length: 144 hours (4 weeks).
Dates: January 1972-September 1983.
Objective: To enable the student to apply radar principles and theory to the practical operation of the WSR-57, to operate the WSR-57 at an acceptable level of competence, and to interpret and disseminate accurate radar data.

Instruction: Theory and operation of the primary weather surveillance radar used by the National Weather Service, basic mathematical and physical principles in radar, radar principles, radio wave propagation, interpretation of radar scope depictions, measurement techniques, integration and analysis, the dissemination or radar information.

Credit recommendation: In the upper division baccalaureate category, 3 semester hours in Meteorology (10/77).

Radar Meteorology - WSR-74 (RAD02) (Formerly [LWR01])

Location: National Weather Service Training Center, Kansas City, MO.
Length: 144 hours (4 weeks).
Dates: December 1974-September 1983.
Objective: To enable the student to apply radar principles and theory to the practical operation of the WSR-74, to operate the WSR-74 at an acceptable level of competence, and to interpret and disseminate accurate radar data.

Instruction: Theory and operation of the local warning surveillance radar used by the National Weather Service, mathematical and physical principles in radar, radar principles, radio wave propagation, interpretation of radar scope depictions, measurement techniques, integration and analysis, dissemination of radar information.

Credit recommendation: In the upper division baccalaureate category, 3 semester hours in Meteorology (10/77).

Radar Meteorology (RAD05)
(Formerly RAD01, RAD02, LWR01)
Location: National Weather Service Training Center, Kansas City, MO.
Length: 144 hours (4 weeks).
Dates: October 1983-Present.
Objective: To enable the student to apply radar principles and theory to the practical operation of National Weather Service meteorological radars, to operate these radars at an acceptable level of competence and to interpret and disseminate accurate radar data.
Instruction: Theory and operation of weather surveillance radars used by the National Weather Service, mathematical and physical principles in radar, radar physics, radio wave propagation, interpretation of radar scope depictions, measurement techniques, integration and analysis, dissemination of radar information.
Credit recommendation: In the upper division baccalaureate category, 3 semester hours in Meteorology (6/83).

Radar Users' Course (RAD04)
Location: National Weather Service Training Center, Kansas City, MO.
Length: *Version 1:* 64 hours (2 weeks). *Version 2:* 104 hours (3 weeks).
Dates: December 1980-Present.
Objective: To train meteorologists and meteorological technicians to apply radar principles and theory, use radar products, and employ radar interpretation techniques for weather forecasting and warning.
Instruction: Instruction and practical exercise in the application of radar data to weather forecasting and warning. Specifically includes discussion of radar physics, propagation, and principles; radar data interpretation and weather station operation and responsibilities. Lecture, discussion, and classroom exercise are used along with the WRT 78 radar simulator and an operational WSR 74C.
Credit recommendation: In the upper division baccalaureate category, 2 semester hours in Radar Meteorology (8/82).

Radar Users' Course (RAD07)
(Formerly Radar Users' Course [RAD04])
Location: National Weather Service Training Center, Kansas City, MO.
Length: 64 hours (2 weeks plus approximately 1 week prior self-study and examination on course modules sent in advance).
Dates: October 1987-Present.
Objective: To apply radar principles and theory, use radar products, and employ radar interpretation techniques for weather forecasting and warning.
Learning Outcome: Upon successful completion of this course, the student will be able to: interpret coded data from NWS field radars, air traffic radars, and the proposed NEXRAD doppler radar system; distinguish among various radar systems in terms of weather depiction; use contemporary severe thunderstorm, flash flood, and tropical cyclone models to collect and interpret the radar data.
Instruction: Course covers applied physics of radar operation, descriptive and comparative study of weather radars, decoding of radar reports, interpretation of radar displays including doppler in terms of atmospheric processes. Methodology includes lecture, discussion, classroom demonstrations, case studies, use of field radar and radar simulator systems, out-of-class assignments, and examinations.
Credit recommendation: In the upper division baccalaureate category, 2 semester hours in Radar Meteorology (7/88). NOTE: This course contains primarily the same content as RAD04.

RAMOS (Remote Automated Meteorological Observation System) S-03-02
Location: National Weather Service Training Center, Kansas City, MO.
Length: 64 hours (8 working days).
Dates: August 1977-Present.
Objective: To provide electronics technicians experienced in digital logic the knowledge and skills necessary to install, calibrate, and maintain the RAMOS system.
Instruction: Covers in detail all mechanical components, module block diagrams, and maintenance procedures. Also examines the circuitry on each data card. Test procedures are reviewed. Lecture and laboratory sessions are used.
Credit recommendation: In the lower division baccalaureate/associate degree category, 2 semester hours in Solid State Electronics (8/80) (11/85). NOTE: This course has been reevaluated and continues to meet requirements for credit recommendations.

Station Management and Supervision (MGT01)
Location: National Weather Service Training Center, Kansas City, MO.
Length: 104 hours (3 weeks).
Dates: January 1978-Present.
Objective: To develop leadership and administrative skills of managers and supervisors.
Learning Outcome: Upon successful completion of this course, the student will be able to supervise the work of subordinate employees; perform personnel actions; demonstrate leadership abilities; and perform various administrative functions associated with management of a weather station.
Instruction: Course covers supervisory skills, leadership and management theory, functions of a manager, communicating with individuals and groups, discipline and morale, performance appraisals and training, weather station management, labor-management relations, equal

employment opportunity practices, administrative guidance materials, organization and mission of the National Weather Service. Methodology includes lecture, discussion, case studies, classroom exercises, out-of-class assignments, and examinations.

Credit recommendation: In the upper division baccalaureate degree category, 4 semester hours in Personnel Administration, Public Administration, or Public Management, or in the graduate degree category, 3 semester hours in Personnel Administration, Public Administration, or Public Management (8/82) (7/88). NOTE: This course has been reevaluated and continues to meet requirements for credit recommendations.

Surface Instruments Maintenance Training (SIMT) X-02-04

Location: National Weather Service Training Center, Kansas City, MO.

Length: 160 hours (20 working days).

Dates: December 1972-Present.

Objective: To provide experienced electronics technicians with the skills necessary to install, calibrate, and maintain the surface measurement equipment used by the National Weather Service.

Instruction: Covers basic principles of servo positioning systems, digital logic for common data recorders, digital decoding, temperature, wind speed, and direction, dew point, precipitation recorders, cloud height indicators, and radiation recorders. Lecture, discussion, and laboratories are used.

Credit recommendation: In the upper division baccalaureate category, 3 semester hours in Meteorological Instrumentation (8/80) (11/85). NOTE: This course has been reevaluated and continues to meet requirements for credit recommendations.

Upper Air Minicomputer M-03-06

Location: National Weather Service Training Center, Kansas City, MO.

Length: 240 hours (30 working days).

Dates: February 1978-February 1985.

Objective: To discuss in detail the subsystems of the Model 3610 upper air minicomputer system, including NOVA minicomputer, paper-tape reader, paper-tape punch, keyboard, printer, link mag tape transport, and T.I. Silent-700 data terminal. To enable students to use diagnostic programming, static testing, schematics, and oscilloscope to trace malfunctions to chip level.

Instruction: Presents overview of the upper air minicomputer; review of Boolean algebra; basic digital building blocks, including BCD counters, shift registers, binary-to-octal decoders; NOVA architecture and instruction set; use of diagnostic routines; use of oscilloscope in isolating computer troubles to chip level; peripherals and peripheral control cards. Half of the course features lecture/discussion and half laboratory work.

Credit recommendation: In the lower division baccalaureate/associate degree category, 5 semester hours in Computer and Digital Equipment Diagnostics and Repair (8/80) (11/85). NOTE: This course has been reevaluated and continues to meet requirements for credit recommendations.

Upper Air Observations (UAO01)

Location: National Weather Service Training Center, Kansas City, MO.

Length: 224 hours (6 weeks).

Dates: December 1974-April 1984.

Objective: To enable meteorological technicians to take, record, and disseminate rawinsonde observations.

Instruction: A practical course providing instruction in flight equipment preparation, balloon release, instrument tracking, and data reduction by computer methods. Also includes interpolation and extrapolation techniques, encoding and decoding data, selecting mandatory and significant levels, and operation of communications equipment. Course does not require knowledge of calculus.

Credit recommendation: In the lower division baccalaureate/associate degree category, 2 semester hours in Meteorological Instrumentation Laboratory (10/77) (4/82). NOTE: This course has undergone a 5-year reevaluation and continues to meet the requirements for credit recommendations.

NOAA Weather Radio (NWR) (B422/B222) B-16-03 (Formerly VHF Weather Warning System [B422/B220D] B-16-03)

Location: National Weather Service Training Center, Kansas City, MO.

Length: 104 hours (13 working days).

Dates: September 1977-Present.

Objective: To teach well-qualified electronics technicians to install, maintain, and monitor the technical operations of the VHF weather warning systems.

Instruction: Covers basics and applied studies of magnetic-tape recording systems, control logic, and the theory and use of VHF transmitters - their control circuitry and diagnostic methods. Lecture, discussion, and laboratory exercises are used.

Credit recommendation: In the lower division baccalaureate/associate degree category, 3 semester hours in Radio Systems (8/80) (11/85). NOTE: This course has been reevaluated and continues to meet requirements for credit recommendations.

Weather Bureau Radar Remote 1 and 2 R-05-03

Location: National Weather Service Training Center, Kansas City, MO.

Length: 136 hours (17 working days).

Dates: May 1969-November 1983.

Objective: To provide electronics technicians with the

knowledge and skills required to install, activate, align, and maintain the Weather Bureau Radar Remoting (WBRR) systems.

Instruction: Covers slow-scan-video remoting techniques; vidicon and iatron operation; FM data transmission by telephone lines; and the theory and mechanics of operation, alignment, troubleshooting, and repair of the WBRR radar remoting units. Lecture and laboratory exercises are used.

Credit recommendation: In the lower division baccalaureate/associate degree category, 3 semester hours in Electronics Systems (8/80).

WBRT (Weather Bureau Radio Theodolite) RAWIN System J-11-03

Location: National Weather Service Training Center, Kansas City, MO.
Length: 104 hours (13 working days).
Dates: January 1960-November 1985.
Objective: To provide electronics technicians with the knowledge and skills required to install, align, calibrate, and maintain the WBRT RAWIN system.

Instruction: Covers upper air sounding systems; radiosonde operations; principles of tracking active targets by conical scanning; frequency-to-voltage conversion; null-balance recording systems; and alignment, calibration, troubleshooting, and repair of WBRT systems. Lecture and laboratory exercises are used.

Credit recommendation: In the lower division baccalaureate/associate degree category, 2 semester hours in Electronics Systems (8/80). NOTE: This course is essentially identical to GMD (Ground Meteorological Device) RAWIN System J-10-03; therefore, credit should not be awarded for both this course and GMD RAWIN System J-10-03.

Weather Bureau Radar Remote Recorder (WBRR-4 and RRM Models) R-06-02

Location: National Weather Service Training Center, Kansas City, MO.
Length: 80 hours (10 working days).
Dates: May 1969-November 1983.
Objective: To provide electronics technicians with the knowledge and skills required to install, activate, align, and maintain the WBRR-4 fascimile recorder.

Instruction: Covers AM and FM demodulation circuitry; facsimile transmission; recording principles; servo systems; logic circuits; and alignment, troubleshooting, and repair of the WBRR-4 and RRM recorders. Lecture and laboratory exercises are used.

Credit recommendation: In the lower division baccalaureate/associate degree category, 2 semester hours in Electronics Systems (8/80).

Weather Service Operations (WSO01)

Location: National Weather Service Training Center, Kansas City, MO.
Length: 144 hours (4 weeks).
Dates: May 1970-Present.
Objective: To increase the Weather Service Specialist's ability to use all National Weather Service products and programs and to improve his/her ability to communicate weather information.

Instruction: Lectures and practical exercises in three major subject areas: oral and written communications, preparation of adapted local forecasts from National Meteorological Center Guidance products, and special topics. The communications area covers preparation of weather reports and pilot briefings through videotaped student presentations. Special topics include flash flood warnings, hydrology, aviation weather, hurricanes, winter storms, and severe local storms. This course is equivalent to a first course in synoptic meteorology.

Credit recommendation: In the lower division baccalaureate/associate degree category, 1 semester hour in Communications, and in the upper division baccalaureate category, 3 semester hours in Meteorology (10/77) (4/82). NOTE: This course has undergone a 5-year reevaluation and continues to meet the requirements for credit recommendations.

Weather Service Operations (WSO02)
(Formerly Weather Service Operations [WSO01])

Location: National Weather Service Training Center, Kansas City, MO.
Length: 104 hours (13 days).
Dates: October 1988-Present.
Objective: Application of National Weather Service guidance programs and products in making weather forecasts.

Learning Outcome: Upon successful completion of this course, the student will be able to determine relative strengths and limitations of various guidance products and other forecast tools, apply large scale numerical guidance products to local forecast problems; and use meteorological dynamics to forecast various weather phenomena.

Instruction: Course covers AFOS operations, guidance products, use of satellite and radar imagery, meteorological analysis techniques, severe weather, and hydrology. Methodology includes lecture, discussion, case studies, field trips, forecast presentations, out-of-class assignments, and examinations.

Credit recommendation: In the upper division baccalaureate category, 3 semester hours in Synoptic Meteorology (7/88). NOTE: This course has primarily the same course content as WSO01.

WSR (Weather Service Radar) - 57/DVIP Radar System R-08-06

Location: National Weather Service Training Center, Kansas City, MO.

Length: 240 hours (30 working days).
Dates: September 1959-Present.
Objective: To enable well-qualified electronics technicians to install, calibrate, maintain, and monitor the operation of the complete WSR-57 weather radar, including the digital video integrator processor system.
Instruction: Covers radar systems in general, with emphasis on the WSR-57. Detailed study is made of the electronic circuitry, electromechanical components, microwave techniques, power measurements, integrated circuits, and the digital video integrator processor.
Credit recommendation: In the upper division baccalaureate category, 4 semester hours in Radar Systems, *and* 2 semester hours in Digital Systems (8/80) (11/85). NOTE: Students who take WSR-57 Radar Systems, but who do not take DVIP Radar Systems should only receive 4 semester hours in Radar Systems at the upper division level. This course has been reevaluated and continues to meet requirements for credit recommendations.

WSR (Weather Service Radar) 74C Radar System R-12-04
Location: National Weather Service Training Center, Kansas City, MO.
Length: 160 hours (20 working days).
Dates: December 1976-Present.
Objective: To provide electronics technicians with the knowledge and skills needed to activate, calibrate, and maintain the WSR-74C meteorological radar system and the associated Digital Video Integrator and Processor (DVIP).
Instruction: Covers radar system principles, WSR-74C characteristics, subsystem details and theory of operation; alignment, calibration, troubleshooting, and repair techniques; integrated circuits, functioning, and maintenance of the DVIP. Lecture and laboratory sessions are used.
Credit recommendation: In the upper division baccalaureate category, 2 semester hours in Radar Systems *and* 2 semester hours in Digital Systems (8/80) (11/85). NOTE: This course has been reevaluated and continues to meet requirements for credit recommendations.

NCR Corporation

NCR Corporation develops, manufactures, markets, installs, and services total business information processing systems.

NCR is a multinational corporation and its staff consists of approximately 67,000 employees. On a worldwide basis, the Corporation conducts a wide range of training and education in technical and nontechnical, management, and nonmanagement subjects for employees and customers.

NCR MANAGEMENT COLLEGE

The NCR Management College is responsible for the Company's worldwide management education programs and activities. Through the line organizations that conduct them, the Management College is responsible for assuring that these programs and activities maintain a high level of quality, are cost effective, and are coordinated with the objectives and strategies of the Corporation. Each course taught under the auspices of the Management College is individually tailored to an important segment of NCR's management group and then further customized to meet the special requirements of the organized unit involved.

Source of official student records: Assistant Vice President, NCR Management College and Career Development Center, NCR Corporation, Dayton, Ohio 45479.

Additional information about the courses: Program on Noncollegiate Sponsored Instruction, The Center for Adult Learning and Educational Credentials, American Council on Education, One Dupont Circle, Washington, D.C. 20036.

Administrative Management (820500)
Location: Dayton, OH.
Length: 40 hours (1 week).
Dates: May 1980-July 1985.
Objective: To improve the knowledge and skills that are necessary for the performance of basic administrative management functions and tasks.
Instruction: Course focuses on administrative practices, management philosophy, information systems, and financial and personnel management. Lectures, discussions, case studies, and laboratory exercises are used. (Prerequisite: Basic Management [022503].)
Credit recommendation: In the lower division baccalaureate/associate degree category, 2 semester hours in Administrative Management (3/81). NOTE: Credit should not be granted for both this course and Corporate Management (822505), Data Center Sales Management (824505), District Sales Management (024505), or Field Engineering Management (813500).

Advanced Management Skills (M25402)
Location: Dayton, OH and selected national and international sites.
Length: 64 hours (16 weeks).
Dates: September 1987-Present.
Objective: To give the student the opportunity to integrate the functional areas of finance, operations, marketing, and strategy using an increasingly complex simulation.
Learning Outcome: Upon successful completion of this course, the student will be able to understand comprehensive theory and applications in the areas of marketing, finance, operations, and strategy with demonstrated abili-

ty to apply concepts to simulated business situations.

Instruction: Covers the functional areas of finance, marketing, operations, and strategy moving through four levels of increasing complexity. Integration is achieved through the use of computer simulations at each level. Methodology includes lecture, discussion, computer simulations, and classroom exercises.

Credit recommendation: In the upper division baccalaureate category, 3 semester hours in Business Policy and Strategic Management (9/87).

Behavior Modeling (811501)
   Location: Dayton, OH and selected national sites.
   Length: 32 hours (eight 4-hour sessions: 2 sessions per week for 4 weeks).
   Dates: November 1980-January 1981.
   Objective: To improve the student's interpersonal skills and present theories and practices for management of human resources.
   Instruction: The course covers supervision, motivation, performance measurement and appraisal. Lectures, discussions, role-play exercises, cassettes, and audiovisual presentations are used.
   Credit recommendation: In the lower division baccalaureate/associate degree category, 2 semester hours in Management of Human Resources or Personnel Management (3/81).

Coaching and Counseling (850505)
   Location: Dayton, OH and selected national and international sites.
   Length: 40 hours (5 days).
   Dates: October 1983-Present.
   Objective: To give the student the opportunity to achieve better performance through greater fulfillment by being able to coach and counsel employees.
   Learning Outcome: Upon successful completion of this course, the student will be able to recognize managerial situations requiring coaching and counseling skills and implement the skills correctly and effectively.
   Instruction: Covers performance management, employee development, performance appraisal, and personal effectiveness. Methodology includes lecture, discussion, and role playing.
   Credit recommendation: In the upper division baccalaureate category, 2 semester hours in Management (9/87).

Corporate Management (822505)
   Location: Dayton, OH.
   Length: 40 hours (1 week).
   Dates: November 1980-November 1984.
   Objective: To improve the knowledge and skills that are essential for the performance of basic corporate management functions and tasks.
   Instruction: The course focuses on management philosophy, management styles and practices, organizational concepts, problem solving, and financial and personnel management. Lectures, discussions, case studies, and laboratory exercises are used. (Prerequisite: Basic Management [022503].)
   Credit recommendation: In the upper division baccalaureate category, 2 semester hours in Management Practices (3/81). NOTE: Credit should not be granted for both this course and Administrative Management (820500), Data Center Sales Management (824505), District Sales Management (024505), or Field Engineering Management (813500).

Course Development Workshop (020005)
   Location: Self-instruction offered at NCR Education Center, Dayton, OH; Technical Education Center, Dayton, OH; and NCR international sites: Sheldon, England; Sydney, Australia; and Tokyo, Japan.
   Length: *Version 1:* 60 hours (2 weeks); *Version 2:* 80 hours (2 weeks).
   Dates: December 1977-Present.
   Objective: To enable participants to acquire and demonstrate competence in skills needed to develop and implement courses in a criterion-referenced format.
   Instruction: Course is an example of criterion-referenced instruction - a way of organizing and managing instruction according to the mastery or competency concept. Each participant is expected to perform to a prescribed criterion on each module of instruction before being certified to advance to the next module. Students study only those modules that are concerned with skills they need but do not have. Participants demonstrate their proficiency (by way of criterion tests) whenever they feel ready to do so. Each course participant will spend as much or as little time as may be required to achieve mastery of essential skills.
   Credit recommendation: In the upper division baccalaureate or graduate degree category, 3 semester hours in Education (12/83) (9/87). NOTE: This course has been reevaluated and continues to meet requirements for credit recommendations.

Data Center Sales Management (824505)
   Location: Dayton, OH.
   Length: 40 hours (1 week).
   Dates: October 1980-June 1984.
   Objective: To improve the knowledge and skills that are necessary for performance of basic sales management functions and tasks.
   Instruction: The course explores the basic managerial functions related to a data center sales organization. Topics include managing the manager's activities, managing company resources, sales analysis, and managing the sales force. Lectures, discussions, cases, and problem-solving exercises are used. (Prerequisite: Basic Management [022503].)

Credit recommendation: In the lower division baccalaureate/associate degree category, 2 semester hours in Marketing Management (3/81). NOTE: Credit should not be granted for both this course and Administrative Management (820500), Corporate Management (822505), District Sales Management (024505), or Field Engineering Management (813500).

Data Pathing Systems Engineering Management (825505)
  Location: Dayton, OH.
  Length: 40 hours (1 week).
  Dates: October 1980-December 1985.
  Objective: To improve the knowledge and skills that are necessary for performance of the basic data pathing systems engineering management functions and tasks.
  Instruction: Topics include managing yourself, business planning and forecasting, postsale support planning, asset management, reporting system, and management of equipment and human resources. Lectures, discussions, and projects are used. (Prerequisite: Basic Management [022503].)
  Credit recommendation: In the lower division baccalaureate/associate degree category, 2 semester hours in Principles of Industrial Management (3/81). NOTE: Credit should not be granted for both this course and Systems Engineering Management (812500).

Development and Production Management (814500) (Formerly Engineering Management [814500])
  Location: Dayton, OH and selected national and international sites.
  Length: 40 hours (1 week).
  Dates: February 1980-December 1985.
  Objective: To improve the knowledge and skills that are essential for performance of the basic engineering management functions and tasks.
  Instruction: The course focuses on the broad topics of managerial responsibilities, organizational objectives and policies, financial management, personnel management, and managerial styles. Lectures, discussions, and exercises are used. (Prerequisite: Basic Management [022503].)
  Credit recommendation: In the upper division baccalaureate category, 2 semester hours in Personnel Management (3/81).

District Sales Management (024505)
  Location: Dayton, OH and selected national and international sites.
  Length: 40 hours (1 week).
  Dates: January 1979-July 1985.
  Objective: To improve the knowledge and skills that are necessary for performance of the basic managerial functions related to sales organization.
  Instruction: Topics include managing the sales force and the firm's assets within the territory. Methodology includes lectures, discussions, cases, simulations, and videocassette presentations. (Prerequisite: Basic Management [022503].)
  Credit recommendation: In the lower division baccalaureate/associate degree category, 2 semester hours in Marketing Management (3/81). NOTE: Credit should not be granted for both this course and Administrative Management (820500), Corporate Management (822505), Data Center Sales Management (824505), or Field Engineering Management (813500).

Effective Teaching (015005)
  Location: Dayton, OH and selected national and international sites.
  Length: 40 hours (1 week).
  Dates: October 1975-Present.
  Objective: To improve the student's instructional skills and knowledge of the teaching and learning process.
  Instruction: Provides an overview of the psychology of teaching and of learning the stages in the course development process. Alternative delivery methods are discussed. At the end of the week students prepare and present sample lessons which are videotaped for immediate feedback and student evaluation. Lectures, discussions, audiovisuals, training aids, and workshops are used.
  Credit recommendation: In the lower division baccalaureate/associate degree category, 3 semester hours in Education (3/81) (9/87). NOTE: This course has been reevaluated and continues to meet requirements for credit recommendations.

Effective Technical Writing (028505)
  Location: Dayton, OH and selected national and international sites.
  Length: 32 hours (4 days).
  Dates: December 1974-May 1982.
  Objective: To develop the student's skills in technical report writing.
  Instruction: The course covers principles and applications of effective technical report writing, with emphasis on preparation, research, organization, writing, and revision. The student submits the outline of a final report and the report itself, and takes a final examination at the end of the course. Lectures, discussions, and in-class writing exercises are used.
  Credit recommendation: In the lower division baccalaureate/associate degree category, 2 semester hours in Technical Report Writing (3/81).

1. Executive Development Program - Law (823504)
2. Executive Development Program - International Economy (840504)
(Formerly Executive Development Program [823504]
  Location: Dayton, OH.
  Length: 24 hours (8 days).
  Dates: 1. January 1981-May 1982; 2. June 1982-Febru-

ary 1984.

Objective: To provide high level corporate executives with a deeper understanding of the legal, political, technological, social and cultural environment of a multinational firm.

Instruction: One seminar is offered each year, with each seminar covering a different topic. The initial seminar focused on "Law and Society." Topics for subsequent seminars will be selected from a wide range, such as the impact of new technologies, the importance of history and philosophy to better understand the present and future, and the international economy. A combination of lectures by and discussions with university faculty are utilized.

Credit recommendation: In the graduate degree category, 2 semester hours in Business Administration or Management (3/81).

Field Engineering Management (813500)
Location: Dayton, OH and selected national and international sites.
Length: 40 hours (1 week).
Dates: December 1979-July 1985.
Objective: To improve the knowledge and skills that are necessary for performance of the basic field engineering management functions and tasks.
Instruction: The course focuses on the management of field engineering resources, financial resources, and personnel. Lectures, discussions, and outside study activities are used. **Prerequisite:** Basic Management (022503).
Credit recommendation: In the lower division baccalaureate/associate degree category, 2 semester hours in Operations Management (3/81). NOTE: Credit should not be granted for both this course and Administrative Management (820500), Corporate Management (822505), Data Center Sales Management (824505), or District Sales Management (024505).

Financial Management (021505)
Location: Dayton, OH and selected national and international sites.
Length: 32 hours (4 days), plus 10 hours of preparation required before the course begins.
Dates: February 1976-Present.
Objective: To improve the student's knowledge of and skills in managing the assets of the corporation.
Instruction: The course covers managerial accounting, cost behavior, R.O.I., financial reports analysis, and profit planning and control. Lectures and discussions are supplemented by extensive use of case studies and simulations. Prerequisite: Basic Management (022503) and Accounting Essentials.
Credit recommendation: In the lower division baccalaureate/associate degree category, 2 semester hours in Corporation Finance, Financial Management, or Managerial Accounting (3/81) (9/87). NOTE: This course has been reevaluated and continues to meet requirements for credit recommendations.

Financial Management for D&PG Managers (815500)
Location: Dayton, OH.
Length: 40 hours (1 week).
Dates: January 1980-December 1985.
Objective: To understand the uniform concepts, policies, and practices of financial management within the Development and Production Group and to improve the student's knowledge of and skills in managing the assets of the corporation.
Instruction: The course covers basic concepts in cost accounting (cost/volume/profit/price analysis, variances, job costing, and product cost), research and development (planning and reporting, external reporting), product management, performance appraisal, and motivation. Lectures, discussions, and case analyses are used. Prerequisite: Accounting Essentials.
Credit recommendation: In the upper division baccalaureate category, 2 semester hours in Managerial Accounting (3/81).

Influence Management (M29505)
Location: Dayton, OH and selected national and international sites.
Length: 16 hours (2 days).
Dates: September 1987-Present.
Objective: To enhance the student's knowledge and skills in three areas critical to successful influence including communication, building and maintaining relationships and establishing and using influence.
Learning Outcome: Upon successful completion of this course, the student will be able to demonstrate improved interpersonal communications, human relations skills, and strategic use of influence.
Instruction: Covers the concept of influence; how it differs from power, authority and leadership; and how it is developed through a structured approach to the use of interpersonal skills. Methodology includes discussion, role playing, analysis of video presentations and readings.
Credit recommendation: In the upper division baccalaureate category, 1 semester hour in Management (9/87).

Introduction to Management
(Principles of Management [859503])
Location: Self-instruction.
Length: Approximately 40-45 hours over 12-15 weeks.
Dates: December 1982-Present.
Objective: To enable students to become familiar with the management functions, management concepts, and skills that lead to success as a manager.
Instruction: Course introduces major management functions and many specific skills used by successful managers. Course is structured around four management functions: planning, organizing, controlling, and coor-

dinating. An overview of management and recent developments in managerial practice, decision making, and behavioral science are provided.

Credit recommendation: In the lower division baccalaureate/associate degree category, 2 semester hours in Introduction to Management (12/83) (9/87). NOTE: This course has been reevaluated and continues to meet requirements for credit recommendations.

Introduction to Time Management, Public Speaking, and Stress Management
(Time Management, Interpersonal Communication, Stress Management [849505])
   Location: NCR Education Center, Dayton, OH.
   Length: 36 hours (1 week).
   Dates: January 1983-December 1985.
   Objective: To enable students to increase managerial efficiency and effectiveness by improving time management, public speaking, and stress management.
   Instruction: Course introduces concepts that will improve job efficiency. Students learn (1) basic principles and techniques of time management using topics such as goal-setting, delegation, and conducting effective meetings; (2) how to improve presentation skills for large groups and one-to-one communication; (3) how to reduce and handle negative stress factors. Lecture and discussion are used.
   Credit recommendation: In the lower division baccalaureate/associate degree category, 1 semester hour as an elective in the area of Interpersonal Communications (12/83).

Introduction to Quality Circles
(Action Team Leader Training [841505])
   Location: NCR Education Center, Dayton, OH.
   Length: *Version 1:* 28 hours (3½ days). *Version 2:* 32 hours (4 days).
   Dates: May 1980-June 1984.
   Objective: To introduce students to the concept of quality circles.
   Instruction: The course content includes: the history and development of quality circles; concepts of productivity; principles of participative management; the origin of quality circle activities in NCR; brainstorming techniques; problem identifications; gathering and using data; group dynamics in problem solving; cause and effect analysis in problem solving; management presentation; structure of quality circles/action teams in NCR; and content and sequence of member training. Lecture and discussion are used.
   Credit recommendation: In the upper division baccalaureate category, 1 semester hour in Production/Operations Management (12/83).

Introduction to Quality Improvement
(Juran on Quality Improvement [842501])
   Location: NCR Development and Production facilities and NCR Education Center, Dayton, OH.
   Length: 32 hours (2 hours per week for 16 weeks).
   Dates: May 1982-Present.
   Objective: To enable students to apply decision making methods to solve specific plant problems in product defect or difficulty and to improve product quality.
   Instruction: This course focuses on basic problem solving techniques related to improving product quality. The course emphasizes collecting and analyzing data to find the cause of a quality problem and applying decision making tools to solve actual quality problems. Quality teams generally have about eight members from various organizations within the Development and Production facilities, e.g., Engineering, Quality Assurance, Personnel Resources, etc. Students learn quality improvement concepts and apply them to a specific quality problem in their location. The cross-fertilization of perspectives and increased communication are major outcomes for most quality teams. Lecture, discussion, and videotapes are used.
   Credit recommendation: In the lower division baccalaureate/associate degree category, 2 semester hours in Business Administration or Engineering Technology (12/83) (9/87). NOTE: This course has been reevaluated and continues to meet requirements for credit recommendations.

Presentation Skills (94005)
   Location: Dayton, OH and selected national and international sites.
   Length: 16 hours (2 days).
   Dates: February 1986-Present.
   Objective: To prepare the student for oral presentations to groups through instruction in the preparation and presentation of various topics.
   Learning Outcome: Upon successful completion of this course, the student will be able to make effective and assured presentations.
   Instruction: The course covers methods for organizing information and presenting it effectively to an audience. Participants make a ten minute presentation at the beginning and at the conclusion of the course. Methodology includes discussion, role playing, and video tapes.
   Credit recommendation: In the lower division baccalaureate/associate degree category, 1 semester hour in Speech Communication (9/87).

Principles of Management (859503)
(Formerly Basic Management [022503])
   Location: Worldwide.
   Length: 40 hours of self-instruction (15 weeks).
   Dates: September 1976-June 1985.
   Objective: To develop knowledge of management functions, concepts, and skills. For those individuals who currently hold or have been identified to move into management positions.
   Instruction: A controlled, self-directed course.

Through the combined use of audiocassettes and written text, the course covers the major management functions: planning, organizing, controlling, and leading, along with an explanation of specific management skills used by successful managers. Five cases are completed by the student and evaluated by a qualified instructor. A final examination is administered at completion of the course.

Credit recommendation: In the lower division baccalaureate/associate degree category, 2 semester hours in Principles of Management (3/81).

Project Planning and Management for Software Development
(Project Planning and Management [831505])
   Location: NCR Development and Production facilities and NCR Education Center, Dayton, OH.
   Length: 47 hours (1 week; 10-12 hours per day).
   Dates: May 1981-September 1985.
   Objective: To provide students with a framework for planning, organizing, and managing a software development project.
   Instruction: Course familiarizes participants with the Standard Development Process (SDP), planning for a development project within the SDP framework, and management tools and techniques to facilitate the planning and controlling of the plan. Course includes necessary steps and considerations for project planning and management and emphasizes the life of the project from design to completion. Included are the tools and techniques of planning and design and the role of the project manager in executing and controlling the project. Lecture and discussion are used.
   Credit recommendation: In the upper division baccalaureate category, 2 semester hours as an elective in Industrial Engineering or Production/Operations Management (12/83).

Purchasing Education - Phase I (053001)
   Location: NCR Education Center, Dayton, OH.
   Length: 36 hours (1 week).
   Dates: January 1975-Present.
   Objective: To provide students with purchasing principles and types of negotiation strategies.
   Instruction: Course covers purchasing principles, negotiation skills in purchasing and materials handling, and interface with vendors, engineers, and company departments. It also includes a discussion of the legal implications of purchasing and a brief introduction to the value analysis process. Lecture and discussion are used.
   Credit recommendation: In the upper division baccalaureate category, 1 semester hour in Purchasing Management (12/83) (9/87). NOTE: This course has been reevaluated and continues to meet requirements for credit recommendations.

Purchasing Education - Phase II (054001)
   Location: NCR Education Center, Dayton, OH.
   Length: 36 hours (1 week).
   Dates: January 1975-Present.
   Objective: To provide students with senior-level purchasing techniques and an introduction to management practices.
   Instruction: Concepts emphasized are the vendors selection process, development of purchasing plans, extended procurement, legal aspects of purchasing (particularly Uniform Commercial Code-U.C.C.), and negotiation skills. Students are also given Phase II of basic electronics and an orientation to material requirements planning at a major corporation. Lecture and discussion are used.
   Credit recommendation: In the upper division baccalaureate category, 1 semester hour in Purchasing Management (12/83) (9/87). NOTE: This course has been reevaluated and continues to meet requirements for credit recommendations.

Systemedia District Management (816500)
   Location: Dayton, OH and selected national and international sites.
   Length: 1. 45 hours (1 week) plus 20 hours of required preparation before the course begins; 2. 51 hours (6 days) plus 10 hours of required preparation before the course begins; 3. 40 hours (5 days).
   Dates: 1. July 1979-May 1982; 2. June 1982-December 1985; 3. January 1986-December 1986.
   Objective: To improve the student's knowledge of and skills in the management functions of planning, organizing, and controlling operations.
   Instruction: The course covers such topics as management by objectives, district analysis, sales forecasts, developing the territory, recruiting, and supervision. Lectures, discussions, and classroom exercises are used. Prerequisite: Basic Management (022503).
   Credit recommendation: In the upper division baccalaureate category, 3 semester hours in Sales Management (3/81).

Systems Engineering Management (812500)
   Location: Dayton, OH and selected national and international sites.
   Length: 40 hours (1 week).
   Dates: November 1979-October 1985.
   Objective: To improve the knowledge and skills that are necessary for performance of the basic systems engineering management functions and tasks.
   Instruction: Topics include managing yourself, business planning and forecasting, Pert charting, CPM, and managing human and corporate resources. (Prerequisite: Basic Management [022503].)
   Credit recommendation: In the lower division baccalaureate/associate degree category, 2 semester hours in Principles of Industrial Management (3/81). NOTE:

Credit should not be granted for both this course and Data Pathing Systems Engineering Management (825505).

Targeted Performance Management (M01505)
   Location: Dayton, OH and selected national and international sites.
   Length: 24 hours (3 days).
   Dates: November 1985-Present.
   Objective: To develop a manager's ability to identify typical employee problem situations and act in an effective manner to plan, manage, and appraise employee performance.
   Learning Outcome: Upon successful completion of this course, the student will be able to identify performance problems and plan, coach, and appraise performance in a standardized and effective manner that results in a positive impact on employee motivation and performance.
   Instruction: Course covers performance planning, performance tracking, effective conduct of performance appraisal and employee development. Methodology includes lecture, discussion, case studies, role playing, and audiovisual presentations.
   Credit recommendation: In the upper division baccalaureate category, 1 semester hour in Management (9/87).

Technical and Report Writing (835005)
(Formerly Effective Business Writing [027505])
   Location: Dayton, OH and selected national and international sites.
   Length: 40 hours (1 week).
   Dates: April 1979-December 1985.
   Objective: To prepare managers, accountants, and other nontechnical professional employees to write effective business letters, memoranda, reports, procedures, policies, etc.
   Instruction: Emphasis is placed on preparation, research, organization, writing, and revision. Both reports and letter writing are covered in detail. Lectures, discussions, classroom exercises, and other writing activities are used.
   Credit recommendation: In the lower division baccalaureate/associate degree category, 2 semester hours in Business Communications and Report Writing (3/81).

NCR CUSTOMER AND SUPPORT EDUCATION

NCR's Customer and Support Education organization is responsible for the education of the Corporation's software support personnel, as well as education of customers who are using NCR systems. In the United States, this education takes place at centers in Atlanta, Chicago, Dallas, Dayton, Denver, Los Angeles, New York, and San Diego.

Customer and Support Education courses are developed to exacting standards and are taught by a professional staff of instructors. In addition to the classroom courses, Customer and Support Education offers a wide range of self-instruction courses.

Source of official student records: Director, Customer and Support Education, NCR Education Center, 101 W. Schantz Avenue, Dayton, Ohio 45479.

Additional information about the courses: Program on Noncollegiate Sponsored Instruction, The Center for Adult Learning and Educational Credentials, American Council on Education, One Dupont Circle, Washington, D.C. 20036.

Advanced 2950 Programming (N05105)
   Location: NCR Education Centers at Dayton, OH and Tampa, FL.
   Length: 40 hours (5 days).
   Dates: January 1981-December 1985.
   Objective: To provide the knowledge required to create or modify application programs of the NCR-2950 general purpose terminal using the BASIC language.
   Instruction: Covers the use of numerous I/O devices and includes the use of several file handling methods. Also studies system statements, utilities and diagnostics. Methodology includes lectures and programming workshops.
   Credit recommendation: In the lower division baccalaureate/associate degree category, 1 semester hour in BASIC Programming (11/82).

Advanced NCR VRX COBOL (N08105)
(Formerly Accelerated NCR VRX COBOL [31505])
   Location: Selected NCR Education Centers in the U.S.
   Length: 45 hours (1 week).
   Dates: July 1982-Present.
   Objective: To furnish an experienced COBOL programmer with the unique features and programming techniques associated with the NCR Virtual Resource Executive (VRX) COBOL.
   Instruction: The course concentrates on common advanced programming techniques for NCR VRX COBOL in combination with operating system concepts. Workshop exercises permit the student to code, compile, and test COBOL programs using NCR VRX COBOL. Online Program Development (OLPD) is available for the students to use in creating programs and test jobs.
   Credit recommendation: In the upper division baccalaureate category, 1 semester hour in COBOL Programming (11/82) (9/87). This course has been reevaluated and continues to meet requirements for credit recommendations.

Automatic Teller Machine/Automated System Generator (ATM/ASG) H05835
   Location: NCR Education Center, Dayton, OH and Chicago, IL Education Center.
   Length: 38 hours (4 days).
   Dates: October 1980-December 1985.

Objective: To prepare the student in generating an Automatic Teller Machine (ATM) load tape using the Automated System Generator (ASG) process.

Instruction: Emphasis is placed on card formats, hardware configuration, encryption, ASG program options, loading, balancing, replenishing of the ATM, reading the listing, and applying patches. Methodology includes lecture, discussion, and workshops.

Credit recommendation: In the lower division baccalaureate/associate degree category, 1 semester hour in Data Processing (11/82).

BASIC for the 2157 (N30145)

Location: NCR Education Centers in the U.S.
Length: 80 hours (2 weeks).
Dates: March 1987-Present.

Objective: To enable the student to create and maintain BASIC programs under the MRX operating system for the Midline General Purpose Terminal using the minimal standard BASIC programming language with NCR extensions.

Learning Outcome: Upon successful completion of this course, the student will be able to use operating system and BASIC statements to code, debug, and execute interactive programs; perform hardware diagnostics; and explain system utilities and file types.

Instruction: Course covers BASIC programming for the Midline 2157 Distributed Transaction Processing Terminal, including system commands and program statements, file types available through VAST and on cassette, the use of flex disk and mass memory, and functions of Midline system utilities. Methodology includes lecture, discussion, and laboratory exercises.

Credit recommendation: In the lower division baccalaureate/associate degree category, 2 semester hours in BASIC Programming (9/87). NOTE: Students who receive credit for this course cannot receive credit for BASIC Programming (N02105).

BASIC Programming (N02105)

Location: Various NCR Customer and Support Education Centers in the U.S.
Length: 40 hours (1 week).
Dates: October 1980-Present.

Objective: To enable the student to code, enter, debug, save, and execute a BASIC program.

Instruction: Course covers fundamental concepts of BASIC programming through a problem-oriented approach. Sequential files, screen and printer formats, and data precision handling are studied in sample business applications. Workshop exercises enable the student to write, test, and debug programs following classroom examples. Lecture is also used.

Credit recommendation: In the lower division baccalaureate/associate degree category, 1 semester hour in BASIC Programming (10/81) (9/87). NOTE: This course has been reevaluated and continues to meet requirements for credit recommendations.

Basic Systems Analysis Skills (490000)

Location: Various NCR Customer and Support Education Centers in the U.S.
Length: 70 hours (2 weeks).
Dates: November 1975-Present.

Objective: To give the student a basic framework for performing analysis of a new EDP (Electronic Data Processing) system by presenting a standard software development cycle, emphasizing those portions where the analyst is heavily involved.

Instruction: Course covers beginning systems analysis, offering a basic framework for analyzing existing information processing systems and designing new EDP systems. It follows a standard system development cycle. A realistic case study is used to reinforce the concepts that are presented in the course. Lecture, video, audio, and workshop sessions are used.

Credit recommendation: In the upper division baccalaureate category, 2 semester hours in Systems Analysis (10/81) (9/87). NOTE: This course has been reevaluated and continues to meet requirements for credit recommendations.

"C" Programming for Entry Level Programmers (N32105)

Location: Selected NCR Education Centers in the U.S.
Length: 80 hours (2 weeks).
Dates: January 1986-Present.

Objective: To enable the student to develop, maintain, and modify "C" programs at an entry level.

Learning Outcome: Upon successful completion of this course, the student will be able to code, compile, and develop "C" programs using preprocessor directives, data types, control flow statements, pointers, arrays, and multiple functions using "C" libraries.

Instruction: Covers the "C" language's strengths and versatility, the ability of "C" to be machine-independent, and the language's accommodation to structured programming. Methodology includes lecture, discussion, laboratory exercises, projects, and examinations.

Credit recommendation: In the lower division baccalaureate/associate degree category, 2 semester hours in "C" Programming (9/87).

"C" Programming (N16105)

Location: Selected NCR Education Centers in the U.S.
Length: 40 hours (1 week).
Dates: August 1983-Present.

Objective: To enable students to develop, maintain, or modify "C" programs.

Instruction: Course covers "C" language including basics; types, operators, and expressions; control flow statements; functions; pointers; structures; input/output;

low-level input/output; and compiling and executing. Lecture and workshops are used.

Credit recommendation: In the lower division baccalaureate/associate degree category, 1 semester hour in "C" Programming (7/84) (9/87). NOTE: This course has been reevaluated and continues to meet requirements for credit recommendations.

"C" Programming Advanced (N19105)
Location: Selected NCR Education Centers in the U.S.
Length: 40 hours (1 week).
Dates: July 1985-Present.
Objective: To enable the student to develop, maintain, and modify "C" programs at an advanced level.
Learning Outcome: Upon successful completion of this course, the student will be able to code, compile, and debug "C" programs in an advanced mode using I/O headers, and linking source and object modules. Students will also learn to create a library, use the MAKE command, debug programs using ADB/SDB, and create and modify files.
Instruction: Course covers advanced techniques in "C" programming including standardization and efficiency of programs; file handling; "C" functions and complete programs; fundamental and derived types; definitions and declarations; and creation of system commands. Methodology includes lectures, laboratory exercises, projects, and examinations.
Credit recommendation: In the lower division baccalaureate/associate degree category, 1 semester hour in Advanced "C" Programming (9/87).

COBOL 74 (484100)
Location: Various NCR Customer and Support Education Centers in the U.S.
Length: 80 hours (2 weeks).
Dates: *Version 1:* November 1978-August 1987; *Version 2:* Sept. 1987-Present.
Objective: To enable the student to code, compile, test, and debug programs written in an NCR COBOL programming language based on American National Standard COBOL 74.
Learning Outcome: Upon successful completion of this course, the student will be able to code magnetic file programs using the NCR COBOL language, and write, test, and debug programs using sequential, random, and dynamic access files.
Instruction: Course covers source level programming techniques associated with an NCR COBOL language based on American National Standard COBOL 1974. Through a problem-oriented approach, the student writes magnetic file programs using an NCR COBOL programming language. Sequential, random, and dynamic access of files are studied. Workshop exercises permit students to extend their knowledge via program writing, testing, and debugging. Lecture is also used.

Credit recommendation: *Version 1:* In the upper division baccalaureate category, 2 semester hours in COBOL Programming (10/81). *Version 2:* In the lower division baccalaureate/associate degree category, 2 semester hours in COBOL Programming (9/87). NOTE 1: Students who receive credit for this course should not receive credit for COBOL 74 - Self-Instruction (484102). NOTE 2: This course has been reevaluated and continues to meet requirements for credit recommendations.

1. COBOL 74 (484100)
2. Structured COBOL (379105)
Location: Various NCR Customer and Support Education Centers in the U.S.
Length: 1. 80 hours (2 weeks); 2. 20 hours (1 week).
Dates: *Version 1:* August 1977-August 1987; *Version 2:* September 1987-Present.
Objective: To enable the student to code, compile, test, and debug programs written in an NCR COBOL programming language based on American National Standard COBOL 74. The student will also participate in structured walkthroughs and use structured programming techniques, as well as testing and implementation techniques, to help achieve the goal of structured programming.
Learning Outcome: Upon successful completion of this course, the student will be able to use structured programming techniques and apply them to program design and coding; understand the history, theory, and relationships between structured systems design and programming using sequential, random, and dynamic access files.
Instruction: Courses cover source level programming techniques; specific structured programming techniques are applied to program design and coding. Reviews history and theories of structured systems development methodology, relationship between structured programming and structured systems design. Sequential, random, and dynamic access of files are also covered. Lecture, discussion, and workshop exercises are used.
Credit recommendation: *Version 1:* In the upper division baccalaureate category, 3 semester hours in COBOL Programming (10/81). *Version 2:* In the lower division baccalaureate/associate degree category, 3 semester hours in COBOL Programming (9/87). NOTE 1: Students who receive credit for this course should not receive credit for COBOL 74 - Self-Instruction (484102). NOTE 2: This course has been reevaluated and continues to meet requirements for credit recommendations.

COBOL 74 - Self-Instruction (484102)
Location: Self-instruction course available from NCR Corporation.
Length: Self-paced (average completion time is 40 hours).
Dates: August 1977-Present.
Objective: To enable the student to code, compile, test,

and debug programs written in an NCR COBOL programming language based on American National Standard COBOL 1974.

Learning Outcome: Upon successful completion of this course, the students will be able to code, test, and debug programs at an entry level, at their own pace. The students will be prepared to extend their knowledge through experience.

Instruction: Course covers NCR COBOL source language, which is based on American National Standard COBOL 1974. Course prepares students to use all the basic elements of the COBOL language, and enables them to grow in ability as they acquire programming experience. Each lesson contains explanations and descriptions of the COBOL language, exercises to be completed at various points, and sample solutions to exercises. This is a self-instruction course.

Credit recommendation: *Version 1:* In the upper division baccalaureate category, 1 semester hour in COBOL Programming (10/81). *Version 2:* In the lower division baccalaureate/associate degree category, 1 semester hour in COBOL Programming (9/87). NOTE 1: Students who receive credit for this course should not receive credit for COBOL 74 (484100). NOTE 2: this course has been reevaluated and continues to meet requirements for credit recommendations.

1. COBOL 74 - Self-Instruction (484102)
2. Structured COBOL (379105)

Location: Various NCR Customer and Support Education Centers in the U.S.

Length: *Version 1:* Self-paced (average 40 hours); *Version 2:* 20 hours (1 week).

Dates: August 1977-Present.

Objective: To enable the student to code, compile, test, and debug programs written in an NCR COBOL programming language based on American National Standard COBOL 74. The student will also use structured program techniques, testing, and implementation techniques to help achieve the goal of structured programming.

Learning Outcome: Upon successful completion of this course, the student will be able to use structured programming techniques and apply them to program design and coding; understand the history, theory, and relationships between structured systems design and programming using sequential, random, and dynamic access files.

Instruction: Courses cover source language based on American National Standard COBOL 1974 and basic elements of the COBOL language. Also covered are specific structured programming techniques applied to program design and coding, history and theories of structured systems development methodology. The relationship between structured programming and structured systems design is also covered. Self-instruction, lecture, and workshop exercises are used.

Credit recommendation: *Version 1:* In the upper division baccalaureate category, 2 semester hours in COBOL Programming (10/81). *Version 2:* In the lower division baccalaureate/associate degree category, 2 semester hours in COBOL Programming (9/87). NOTE 1: Students who receive credit for this course receive additional credit for COBOL 74 (484100). NOTE 2: This course has been reevaluated and continues to meet requirements for credit recommendations.

COBOL 74 VRX/E (N34105)

Location: NCR Education Centers in the U.S.

Length: 80 hours (2 weeks).

Dates: June 1987-Present.

Objective: To enable the student to code, compile, test, and debug programs written in NCR COBOL based on the American National Standard COBOL 1974 with the NCR VRX/E (Virtual Resource Executive) extensions.

Learning Outcome: Upon successful completion of this course, the student will be able to understand, create, and access sequential, relative, and indexed files using the sequential, random, and dynamic access methods; use table processing techniques; and code, compile, execute, and debug COBOL programs using the VRX/E operating system.

Instruction: Course covers source-level programming techniques associated with an NCR COBOL language based on American National Standard COBOL 1974 with NCR VRX/E extensions. Course concentrates on the new features in the implementation of the NCR VRX/E COBOL language. Methodology includes lecture, discussion, and laboratory exercises.

Credit recommendation: In the lower division baccalaureate/associate degree category, 2 semester hours in COBOL Programming (9/87).

1. COBOL Programming (Accelerated NCR VRX COBOL)
(Formerly COBOL Programming [315105])
2. Advanced NCR VRX COBOL (NO8105)

Location: Various NCR Customer and Support Education Centers in the U.S.

Length: 40 hours (1 week).

Dates: *Version 1:* August 1978-May 1982; *Version 2:* June 1982-Present.

Objective: To enable the student to code programs using NCR VRX (Virtual Resource Executive) COBOL.

Instruction: Course furnishes an experienced COBOL programmer with the unique programming techniques associated with the NCR VRX COBOL. Course concentrates on the new features in the implementation on the NCR VRX COBOL language. Online Program Development is available for the students to use in creating programs and jobs. Lecture and workshop exercises are used.

Credit recommendation: *Version 1:* In the upper division baccalaureate category, 1 semester hour in COBOL

Programming (10/81). *Version 2:* In the lower division baccalaureate/associate degree category, 1 semester hour in COBOL Programming (9/87). NOTE: This course has been reevaluated and continues to meet requirements for credit recommendations.

Computer Assisted Instruction Development Techniques (089005)
 Location: NCR Education Center (Sugar Camp), Dayton, OH.
 Length: 40 hours (1 week).
 Dates: April 1984-December 1986.
 Objective: To enable the student to use traditional as well as new techniques to develop courseware to present interactive self-instruction education to a learner through the medium of a microcomputer.
 Instruction: Course reviews the preliminary activities of course development, introduces the attributes of self-instruction, and provides students with the skills to develop a lesson using computer assisted instruction. Lecture and workshop are used.
 Credit recommendation: In the upper division baccalaureate category, 1 semester hour in Curriculum Development (7/84).

Data Base Design (D06005)
 Location: Selected NCR Education Centers in the U.S.
 Length: 41-44 hours (1 week).
 Dates: November 1981-Present.
 Objective: To provide the student with concepts basic to data base and a recognized logical design methodology, independent of any given data base management system.
 Learning Outcome: Upon successful completion of this course, the student will be able to describe a file management system in terms of the relationship between the data files and the application programs; describe a data base management system in terms of the relationship between the data files and the application program; and list three advantages the data base approach has over a file management system.
 Instruction: The student will be taught to identify basic data objects of interest to an enterprise, identify, and classify all relationships among these data objects, identify all attributes and identifiers of these data objects and these relationships, generate an overall, conceptual model of the data resources and construct and validate a logical framework (SCHEMA) for the data base.
 Credit recommendation: In the upper division baccalaureate category, 1 semester hour in Data Base Management (11/82) (9/87). NOTE: This course has been reevaluated and continues to meet requirements for credit recommendations.

EDP Concepts (402002)
 Location: Self-instruction course available from NCR Corporation.
 Length: Self-paced (average completion time is 50 hours).
 Dates: January 1976-Present.
 Objective: To provide the student with a knowledge of fundamentals of electronic data processing. Emphasis is on EDP terminology, concepts, and problem solving using flowcharts.
 Instruction: Course covers data processing terminology, batch and data communications logic presented by flowcharts, hardware and software definitions and elements, file devices and concepts, and EDP audit and system controls. This is a self-instruction course.
 Credit recommendation: In the lower division baccalaureate/associate degree category, 1 semester hour in Introduction to Data Processing or Data Processing Principles (10/81) (9/87). NOTE 1: This course and NEAT/3 Programming (404102) are equivalent to Elementary Systems and Software-NEAT/3 (435100). NOTE 2: This course has been reevaluated and continues to meet requirements for credit recommendations.

Elementary Systems and Software - NEAT/3 (435100)
 Location: Various NCR Customer and Support Education Centers in the U.S.
 Length: 96 hours (3 weeks).
 Dates: October 1971-Present.
 Objective: To provide the student with basic programming capability in the NCR NEAT/3 language within a father-son processing environment.
 Instruction: Course covers all phases of programming, operations, and software while teaching the NEAT/3 language. Within a father-son processing environment, the students learn fundamental system design considerations and program flowcharting techniques; and NEAT/3 coding, testing, and symbolic debugging. Essential operating software routines and console operations are covered by extensive hands-on experience with the NCR computer hardware. All course topics are interwoven for practical application through a tutorial payroll system. Lecture, discussion, and workshop exercises are used.
 Credit recommendation: In the lower division baccalaureate/associate degree category, 2 semester hours in NEAT/3 Programming and in the lower division baccalaureate/associate degree category, 1 semester hour in Introduction to Data Processing (10/81) (9/87). NOTE 1: This course is equivalent to NEAT/3 Programming (404102) and EDP Concepts (402002). NOTE 2: This course has been reevaluated and continues to meet requirements for credit recommendations.

2160 Food Service System Installation - UO2445
 Location: NCR Education Center, Dayton, OH.
 Length: 78 hours (2 weeks).
 Dates: September 1980-Present.
 Objective: To teach a student how to install the 2160 point-of-sale terminal. Provides training in implementa-

tion, maintenance and modification of the data base by the 2160 system.

Instruction: The course covers data base development and maintenance, report generation, software installation and in-service diagnostics. The course includes lectures and the development of a case study.

Credit recommendation: In the lower division baccalaureate/associate degree category, 2 semester hours in Data Processing (11/82) (9/87). NOTE 1: If this course is used in conjunction with GO3845 (2140 Programming and Systems Installation), a total of 3 semester hours is recommended. NOTE 2: This course has been reevaluated and continues to meet requirements for credit recommendations.

Fundamentals of Computers and Programming Logic (680005)
Location: NCR Education Centers in the U.S.
Length: 32 hours (4 days).
Dates: April 1985-November 1988.
Objective: To provide the student with a knowledge of the fundamentals of computer concepts and programming, including computer systems and logic flowcharting.
Learning Outcome: Upon successful completion of this course, the student will be able to identify and define the components of a computer system; and design flowcharts of solutions to data processing problems.
Instruction: Course covers the computer systems terminology, including software concepts, file types, and processing considerations. Programming logic is introduced through flowcharts. Methodology includes lecture, discussion, and classroom exercises.
Credit recommendation: In the lower division baccalaureate/associate degree category, 1 semester hour in Introduction to Data Processing or Data Processing Principles (9/87).

IMOS TRAN-PRO Concepts (R13805)
Location: NCR Education Center, Atlanta, GA.
Length: 16 hours (2 days).
Dates: January 1982-December 1985.
Objective: To introduce the concepts, terminology and the hardware/software requirements related to the IMOS Transaction Processing System.
Instruction: Teaches transaction processing overview, hardware, TRAN-PRO features and functions, functional components, communication control, system files and tablets, and utilities. Methodology includes projects, presentations and examinations.
Credit recommendation: In the upper division baccalaureate category, 1 semester hour in Information Systems (11/82). NOTE: Students must also complete IMOS TRAN-PRO Installation and Support (R15805).

IMOS TRAN-PRO Installation and Support (R15805)
Location: NCR Education Center, Atlanta, GA.
Length: 22 hours (3 days).
Dates: January 1981-December 1985.
Objective: To introduce the procedures and techniques necessary to generate and maintain IMOS TRAN-PRO software.
Instruction: The course describes recommended design considerations, presents procedures and utilities to define a TRAN-PRO system, covers the actual operation of the TRAN-PRO system, and provides diagnostic tools.
Credit recommendation: In the upper division baccalaureate category, 1 semester hour in Information Systems (11/82). NOTE: Students must also complete IMOS TRAN-PRO Concepts (R18305).

IMOS TRAN-PRO Programming (R14105)
Location: NCR Education Center, Atlanta, GA.
Length: 40 hours (1 week).
Dates: January 1982-December 1985.
Objective: To introduce the special techniques necessary to define IMOS TRAN-PRO terminal transactions and the associated COBOL 74 application programs.
Instruction: The course trains a student to design and debug key and screen formats as well as COBOL application programs to interact with them. Selected utilities involving TRAN-PRO are also discussed. Methodology includes lecture, discussions, and workshops.
Credit recommendation: In the upper division baccalaureate category, 1 semester hour in Advanced Programming (11/82).

IMOS V Operating System (K08105)
Location: Selected NCR Education Centers in the U.S.
Length: 38 hours (1 week).
Dates: January 1981-Present.
Objective: To prepare the student to generate, operate, and maintain an Interactive Multiprogramming Operating System (IMOS) V Operating system.
Instruction: The course covers configuring and generating the IMOS V software, constructing system command files, and using the utility features of the operating system, which include editing, compilation and execution of COBOL programs. Methodology includes lectures and team environment workshops.
Credit recommendation: In the upper division baccalaureate category, 1 semester hour in Operating Systems (11/82) (9/87). NOTE: This course has been reevaluated and continues to meet requirements for credit recommendations.

Industrial Data Systems (D11625)
Location: NCR Education Centers at Dayton, OH and Sunnyvale, CA or on-site (if requested).
Length: 44 hours (1 week).
Dates: June 1981-December 1985.

Objective: To present the objectives, requirements, and operations of industrial manufacturing; explains modern techniques of factory management, with study of the manufacturing process and the information flow necessary to support it.

Instruction: Includes an introduction to industrial management and organization. Industrial departments are discussed. Other topics considered are planning and forecasting, inventory management, bill of material processing, priority and capacity planning and manufacturing control.

Credit recommendation: In the lower division baccalaureate/associate degree category, 1 semester hour in Industrial Management (11/82).

Interactive Manufacturing Control Systems (IMCS) II (W18425)

Location: NCR C.A.S.E. Education Centers and on-site at NCR District Offices or Customer's location.
Length: 50 hours (1 week).
Dates: September 1981-Present.
Objective: To introduce the student to the fundamental data files, programs, daily processing procedures, and conversion techniques for the Bill of Material, Inventory Management, Routing and the Material Requirements Planning modules of the NCR IMCS II software application.

Instruction: Teaches the student system overview, concepts and design, maintenance, cost control, material movement, inquiry, report and installation techniques for the application areas listed in objectives. Methodology includes lecture, discussion, workshops and audiovisuals.

Credit recommendation: In the lower division baccalaureate/associate degree category, 1 semester hour in Data Processing (11/82) (9/87). NOTE: This course has been reevaluated and continues to meet requirements for credit recommendations.

Introduction to Interactive COBOL Programming (364105)

Location: Various NCR Customer and Support Education Centers in the U.S.
Length: 120 hours (3 weeks).
Dates: *Version 1:* October 1971-August 1987; *Version 2:* September 1987-December 1988.
Objective: To enable the student to analyze a problem, design a solution for an interactive environment, code an application program in a structured manner using an NCR COBOL language, and successfully debug the coded application programs.

Learning Outcome: Upon successful completion of this course, the student will be able to code, test, and debug programs that involve sequential, random, dynamic, and relative files being accessed in an interactive environment.

Instruction: Course introduces COBOL as it is used in an interactive programming environment. Provides the student with concepts useful in diagnosing a problem, designing a programmable solution, and writing application programs in a structured manner. Furnishes the student with source level programming techniques associated with an NCR COBOL programming language based on American National Standard COBOL 1974. Lecture, classroom exercises, simulations, and problem-solving exercises are used.

Credit recommendation: *Version 1:* In the upper division baccalaureate category, 3 semester hours in COBOL Programming (10/81). *Version 2:* In the lower division baccalaureate/associate degree category, 3 semester hours in COBOL Programming (9/87). NOTE: This course has been reevaluated and continues to meet requirements for credit recommendations.

Introduction to VRX Operating System (331105) (Formerly VRX Operating System Utilization [331105])

Location: Various NCR Customer and Support Education Centers in the U.S.
Length: 40 hours (1 week).
Dates: October 1977-Present.
Objective: To enable the student to prepare and execute jobs using 8000-series computer and the VRX Operating System.

Instruction: Course covers preparation and execution of jobs under Virtual Resource Executive (VRX). Course includes guidelines for optimizing program and system applications in a virtual storage environment based on available statistics and tools. Lecture, discussion, and workshop exercises are used.

Credit recommendation: In the lower division baccalaureate/associate degree category, 1 semester hour in Computer Operations (10/81) (9/87). NOTE: This course has been reevaluated and continues to meet requirements for credit recommendations.

IRX Operating System (369105)

Location: All NCR Customer and Support Education Centers.
Length: 48-52 hours (1 week).
Dates: December 1978-December 1987.
Objective: To train the student to modify an existing operating system, construct system command files, perform daily start procedures and use all utility features of the operating system including editing, compiling, and executing of programs.

Instruction: Course includes discussion of systems configurations and software generation, system and disk utility routines, system commands and messages, program compilation and execution, error procedures and reporting, and submitted batch processes.

Credit recommendation: In the upper division baccalaureate category, 1 semester hour in Operating Systems (11/82) (9/87). NOTE: This course has been reevaluated and continues to meet requirements for credit recommendations.

ITEM (W37425)
Location: Any C.A.S.E. education center or on-site if hardware is appropriate.
Length: 42 hours (1 week).
Dates: June 1982-Present.
Objective: To teach the student how to install and generate the Interactive Technique for Effective Management (ITEM) and to use the system in inventory management.
Instruction: Introduces the student to the fundamental data files, daily processing operations, and conversion of the Interactive Technique for Effective Management (ITEM) software package. Methodology includes lecture, discussion, and workshops.
Credit recommendation: In the lower division baccalaureate/associate degree category, 1 semester hour in Data Processing (11/82) (9/87). NOTE: This course has been reevaluated and continues to meet requirements for credit recommendations.

ITX Operating System (K21805)
Location: Selected NCR Education Centers in the U.S.
Length: 40 hours (1 week).
Dates: May 1983-Present.
Objective: To enable the student to use and support others who use the Interactive Transaction Executive (ITX) operating system.
Learning Outcome: Upon successful completion of this course, the student will be able to use ITX functions to process tasks; use the ITX system commands; control printer operations; execute utility programs; interact with the Audit Trail Utility; create and use control strings; and understand initial installation procedures.
Instruction: Course covers preparation and execution of jobs using the ITX operating system, including the system command language, system and terminal operations, process control, file management, streaming tape utility, printer operations, file editing, control strings, batch processing, system utilities, programmer functions, and installation. Methodology includes lecture, discussion, and laboratory exercises.
Credit recommendation: In the upper division baccalaureate category, 1 semester hour in Operating Systems (9/87).

ITX Operating System Advanced (K32805)
Location: Selected NCR Education Centers in the U.S.
Length: 40 hours (1 week).
Dates: October 1983-Present.
Objective: To enable the student to employ advanced skills in designing, implementing, and maintaining the Interactive Transaction Executive (ITX) Operating System.
Learning Outcome: Upon successful completion of this course, the student will be able to design and generate the ITX Operating System; create command files; use the integrated features; maintain files; determine memory requirements; program efficient operations; analyze status messages and resolve error conditions.
Instruction: Course covers advanced techniques in enhancing the performance of the ITX Operating System using system and programming tools, programming languages, system monitoring, system performance, debugging, data capture, error checking, job analysis, SCL, integration, virtual memory, and diagnostics. Methodology includes lecture, discussion, and laboratory exercises.
Credit recommendation: In the upper division baccalaureate category, 2 semester hours in Advanced Operating Systems (9/87).

Modular Lodging System (MLS) Installation (U10445)
Location: NCR Sugar Camp Education Center, Dayton, OH.
Length: 45 hours (1 week).
Dates: February 1982-December 1985.
Objective: To teach the student to install, modify, and maintain a Modular Lodging System (MLS).
Instruction: Course prepares the student for software installation, screen modifications, and maintenance of an installed system. The course is presented by lecture, in-class exercises, and hands-on workshops.
Credit recommendation: In the lower division baccalaureate/associate degree category, 1 semester hour in Data Processing (11/82).

NCR Century to VRX Migration (319105)
Location: Atlanta, GA and Los Angeles, CA Education Centers.
Length: 126-132 hours (3 weeks).
Dates: June 1978-December 1985.
Objective: To teach the student to initialize, create and execute jobs under, interpret system reports from, and recover aborted jobs using the Virtual Resource Executive (VRX).
Instruction: Course includes discussion of 8000 V-series hardware, virtual storage concepts, Job Control Language, compilers, Link Editor, Online Program Development, VRX files including Criterion Access Method, telecommunications, multitasking, Dynamic Storage Area and system and job recovery. Methodology includes lecture, discussion, and workshops.
Credit recommendation: In the upper division baccalaureate category, 3 semester hours in Operating Systems (11/82).

NCR 605/608 Hardware and Programming (463205)
Location: Sugar Camp Education Center, Dayton, OH.
Length: 78-84 hours (8 days).
Dates: March 1977-December 1985.
Objective: To teach the student to write an assembler

program for an NCR 605, 606 607, or 608 processor.

Instruction: Course covers machine instructions, pseudo instructions, error trapping concepts, systems design, programming methods and techniques, and use of utility programs. Methodology includes lecture and hands-on programming.

Credit recommendation: In the lower division baccalaureate/associate degree category, 2 semester hours in Assembly Language Programming (11/82).

NCR 7750 DDPS and RPS Systems and Programming (243835)

Location: NCR Corporate Education Center, Dayton, OH.

Length: 120 hours (3 weeks).

Dates: July 1978-July 1988.

Objective: To enable the student to configure basic 7750 systems, begin the planning of the system installation, and complete systems and tables construction programming. In addition, the student will have extensive knowledge of uses, applications, and operations of the system.

Instruction: Course covers in-depth details of the NCR 7750 Distributive Document Processing System (DDPS) and Remittance Processing System (RPS) and its hardware, and the detailed programming of the application sets that are used by the RECAPS application software. Course is for those persons who are ready to begin the planning and programming for a specific installation. Lecture, discussion, and workshop exercises are used.

Credit recommendation: In the lower division baccalaureate/associate degree category, 3 semester hours in Programming (10/81) (9/87). NOTE: This course has been reevaluated and continues to meet requirements for credit recommendations.

NCR TOTAL (372105)

Location: Various NCR Customer and Support Education Centers in the U.S.

Length: 36 hours (1 week).

Dates: October 1978-Present.

Objective: To enable the student to define, program, and maintain a TOTAL data base system.

Instruction: Course covers programming, implementing, maintaining, and supporting a TOTAL data base system. Course includes general background information on data base systems, considerations and requirements for designing and building a TOTAL data base, information on the utility routines available, and writing of programs utilizing the TOTAL data base management system. Lecture, discussion, and workshop exercises are used.

Credit recommendation: In the upper division baccalaureate category, 1 semester hour in Data Base Concepts (10/81) (9/87). NOTE: This course has been reevaluated and continues to meet requirements for credit recommendations.

NCS Operations (367905)

Location: Various NCR Customer and Support Education Centers in the U.S.

Length: 31½ hours (4½ days).

Dates: December 1978-December 1986.

Objective: To enable the student to perform the required daily tasks of operating an NCR N-Mode computer system. Daily start procedures, handling errors and other problems, and following system run books to run production jobs are all stressed in this course.

Instruction: Course covers daily operations of a computer system operating under N-Mode software in a production environment. Both NCR Century and Criterion systems are discussed. Lecture, discussion, and workshop exercises are used.

Credit recommendation: In the lower division baccalaureate/associate degree category, 1 semester hour in Computer Operations (10/81).

NEAT/3 Programming (404102)

Location: Self-instruction course available from NCR Corporation.

Length: Self-paced (average completion time is 60 hours).

Dates: January 1975-Present.

Objective: To provide the student with the skills and knowledge required of an entry-level NEAT/3 programmer.

Instruction: Course covers NEAT/3 programming. An introduction to NCR Century hardware and software is followed by lessons on data structure and definition, data management instructions, I/O commands, table manipulations, and printing. This is a self-instruction course.

Credit recommendation: In the lower division baccalaureate/associate degree category, 2 semester hours in NEAT/3 Programming (10/81) (9/87). NOTE 1: This course and EDP Concepts (402002) are equivalent to Elementary Systems and Software-NEAT/3 (435100). NOTE 2: This course has been reevaluated and continues to meet requirements for credit recommendations.

Online Systems Design (318005)

Location: *Version 1:* NCR Education Centers in Los Angeles, CA and Dayton, OH; *Version 2:* Selected NCR Education Centers.

Length: *Version 1:* 60 hours (1½ weeks); *Version 2:* 40 hours (1 week).

Dates: *Version 1:* February 1980-September 1987. *Version 2:* October 1987-Present.

Objective: To enable the student to describe online system development methods and procedures and the concepts and considerations related to the design of online systems; to explain the use of the mathematical simulation approach utilizing queuing theory.

Learning Outcome: Upon successful completion of this course, the student will be able to solve performance problems related to design, implementation, operation, and optimization for real-time transaction processing systems.

Instruction: Course covers many facets of the design of online systems and provides a basis for making decisions related to these considerations. The first phase of the course includes a review of basic concepts and a discussion of system development methods and procedures. The second phase considers, in more detail, each design factor and focuses on programming structure and technique. An appropriate program design workshop is part of this phase. The third phase of the course deals with performance estimating. A mathematical simulation utilizing queuing theory is taught. Phase three involves a computerized work simulation. Lecture and discussion are also used.

Credit recommendation: *Version 1:* In the upper division baccalaureate category, 2 semester hours in Online Systems Design (10/81). *Version 2:* In the upper division baccalaureate category, 1 semester hour in Online Systems Design (9/87). NOTE: This course has been reevaluated and continues to meet requirements for credit recommendations.

PASCAL Programming (N25105)

Location: Selected NCR Education Centers in the U.S.
Length: 40 hours (1 week).
Dates: June 1984-December 1988.
Objective: To enable students to design, code, compile, and debug PASCAL programs.
Instruction: Course provides a programmer with an introduction to the PASCAL programming language. It combines a series of lectures and workshop exercises which enable students to code, compile, debug, and execute PASCAL programs. Covers programming calculations; procedures; case and for structures; procedures with parameters; if structure; while and repeat structures; functions; ordinal types; introduction of structured types; records; arrays; files, and sets.
Credit recommendation: In the lower division baccalaureate/associate degree category, 1 semester hour in PASCAL Programming (7/84) (9/87). NOTE: This course has been reevaluated and continues to meet requirements for credit recommendations.

Problem Determination for SNA (677005)

Location: NCR Education Centers in Atlanta, GA and Dayton, OH.
Length: 80 hours (10 days).
Dates: August 1984-Present.
Objective: To enable the student to interpret SNA formats and protocols using appropriate tools to isolate problem SNA devices.
Learning Outcome: Upon successful completion of this course, the student, if given a trace of an SNA session, will be able to: identify and describe typical SNA messages; list and describe a sequence of events for SNA processes; interpret the information in the Transmission Header and the Request/Response Headers; and interpret the information provided by the NCCF, NPDA, and NLDM that will assist in identifying SNA problems.
Instruction: Course covers SNA overview, Problem Determination Methodology, hardware tools, Transmission Header and Request/Response Header, network initialization, network communications control facility, VTAM and NCP tools, LU-LU session establishment, the BIND command, presentation services formats, function management headers, network deactivation, NPDA (Network Problem Determination Application), and NLDM (Network Logical Data Manager). Methodology includes lecture, discussion, and laboratory exercises.
Credit recommendation: In the upper division baccalaureate category, 2 semester hours in Computer Systems Networking (9/87).

2140 Programming and System Installation (G03845)

Location: NCR Sugar Camp Education Center, Dayton, OH.
Length: 92 hours (2 weeks).
Dates: September 1981-December 1985.
Objective: Teaches 2140 (point of sale terminal) features and options, and describes the general purpose application programs available. It also describes terminal configuration options and teaches the student how to program the optional peripheral interfaces for in-house communications, common carrier communications, data capture, and optical character reader (OCR).
Instruction: Covers hardware and applications, program selection, marketing support plan, program load procedure and operations, program modifications, data capture programming and tape analysis, optical character recognition programming, and in-house and common carrier communication. Methodology includes lectures, projects, workshops, presentations, and examinations.
Credit recommendation: In the lower division baccalaureate/associate degree category, 2 semester hours in Data Processing (11/82). NOTE: If this course is used in conjunction with U02445 (2160 Food Service System), a total of 3 semester hours is recommended.

PROGRESS Programming Fundamentals (R47105)

Location: Selected NCR Education Centers in the U.S.
Length: 36 hours (1 week).
Dates: October 1986-Present.
Objective: To enable the student to design and program a database system using a relational DB language.
Learning Outcome: Upon successful completion of this course, the student will be able to develop procedures to maintain a database (DB) using PROGRESS; use a Data Dictionary to define the DB; format screens and reports; redirect I/O; create menus; and ensure data integrity in a multiuser environment.
Instruction: Course covers database programming for students familiar with DOS and UNIX® operating sys-

tems using a relational DBMS called PROGRESS. Methodology includes lecture, discussion, and laboratory exercises.

Credit recommendation: In the upper division baccalaureate category, 1 semester hour in Advanced Database Management (9/87).

RM/COS Operating System (K42805)
Location: Selected NCR Education Centers in the U.S.
Length: 28 hours (4 days).
Dates: January 1984-Present.
Objective: To enable the student to use procedures required to install, configure, and run the operating system.
Instruction: Course covers the installation and use of the RM/COS operating system. Most aspects of the operating system will be covered, with emphasis on normal operating procedures. Lecture and workshop are used.
Credit recommendation: In the upper division baccalaureate category, 1 semester hour in Computer Science (7/84) (9/87). NOTE: This course has been reevaluated and continues to meet requirements for credit recommendations.

STORES Systems and Operations (U06845)
Location: NCR Sugar Camp Education Center, Dayton, OH.
Length: 88 hours (8 days).
Dates: February 1981-Present.
Objective: To provide the knowledge, skill, and practice required to operate and maintain STORES system applications for a retail point-of-sale system.
Instruction: Course includes hardware components, basic online operations, after-hours operations, system applications, system maintenance, problem isolation and reporting, operator documentation/training and communication and considerations. Methodology includes lectures and workshops.
Credit recommendation: In the upper division baccalaureate category, 2 semester hours in Systems Implementation (11/82) (9/87). NOTE: This course has been reevaluated and continues to meet requirements for credit recommendations.

STORES System Generation and Installation U07445
Location: Sugar Camp Education Center, Dayton, OH.
Length: *Version 1:* 77-84 hours (7 days); *Version 2:* 56 hours (7 days).
Dates: *Version 1:* February 1981-August 1987; *Version 2:* September 1987-December 1988.
Objective: To provide the student with the knowledge, skills and practice required to generate and install STORES processors as part of an online retail point of sale system.
Instruction: Course includes system configuration, installation planning, file considerations, application parameterization, STORES generator, system-building utilities, system documentation, and a tutorial workshop covering generation, design, building, testing, and debugging. Methodology includes lecture, discussion, and workshops.
Credit recommendation: In the lower division baccalaureate/associate degree category, 1 semester hour in Systems Implementation (11/82) (9/87). NOTE: This course has been reevaluated and continues to meet requirements for credit recommendations.

Structured Design (378105)
Location: *Version 1:* NCR Education Centers in Dallas, TX and Dayton, OH; *Version 2:* NCR Education Center in Dayton, OH.
Length: 30 hours (1 week).
Dates: November 1978-December 1988.
Objective: To enable students to design programs and systems using structured design techniques.
Learning Outcome: Upon successful completion of this course, the student will be able to develop a working knowledge of the tools and techniques used for system and program design, including methods for functional decomposition and parsing, methods of evaluation and review; and design the structure of medium or large-sized programs.
Instruction: Course covers tools and techniques used for system and program design. These techniques include methods for functional decomposition and parsing, and also methods of evaluation and review. Lecture and workshop exercises are used.
Credit recommendation: In the upper division baccalaureate category, 1 semester hour in Structured Design (10/81) (9/87). NOTE: This course has been reevaluated and continues to meet requirements for credit recommendations.

Telecommunications
Location: NCR Technical Education Center, Miamisburg, OH.
Length: 104 hours (13 days).
Dates: August 1978-Present.
Objective: To provide the student with a knowledge of telecommunication fundamentals, telephone system functions, data communication concepts, signal rate/modulation, definition of line signals; signal correction, EIA interface, modern principles/features; DAA, Dial/Answer; line fault isolation; data scope, ascynchronous/binary synchronous protocols; communication equipment/cable installation; data communication tester; and data link control protocol.
Learning Outcome: Upon successful completion of this course, the student will be able to provide assistance in the installation and maintenance of communication systems.
Instruction: Course prepares the student for a future in Data Communications. Aspects of Data Communication Systems are considered with theory being supported by hands-on experience using an extensive array of communi-

cations equipment. Students learn to assist in communication-related installations and problems without the specific product training. Use of the spectron 601 data scope and the Tektronix 832 data communications tester are covered. Lecture, discussion, and workshop are used.

Credit recommendation: In the upper division baccalaureate category, 4 semester hours in Computer Engineering or Computer Science (7/84) (9/87). NOTE: This course has been reevaluated and continues to meet requirements for credit recommendations.

UNIX® Operating System
1. UNIX® Operating System (K22805)
2. UNIX® System Administration (K28905)

Location: Selected NCR Education Centers in the U.S.
Length: 1. 40 hours (1 week). 2. *Version 1:* 30 hours (4 days); *Version 2:* 40 hours (5 days).
Dates: 1. January 1983-Present. 2. *Version 1:* October 1983-Present; *Version 2:* January 1989-Present.
Objective: Course 1: To enable students to use the UNIX® Operating System in daily computing activities. Course 2: To enable students to install, configure, maintain, and manage the UNIX® System; to monitor and record system use; and to create and maintain files.
Instruction: Course 1: Details the use of the command programming language of the UNIX® Operating System. Use of UNIX® commands and the Bourne Shell for daily operations and software development are presented. Emphasis is placed on the areas of system operations, the command programming language, and various utilities and software tools. Course 2: Covers the role of the UNIX® System Administrator including his/her responsibility for installation, maintenance, and management of the system. Course is designed to teach students the tools available within UNIX® that help the system administrator perform his/her job. Lecture, discussion, and workshop are used.
Credit recommendation: In the lower division baccalaureate/associate degree category, 3 semester hours in Computer Science (7/84) (9/87). NOTE 1: Students who only take Course 1 (K22805) may receive credit in the lower division baccalaureate/associate degree category, 1 semester hour in Computer Science. NOTE 2: This course has been reevaluated and continues to meet requirements for credit recommendations.

UNIX® Shell Programming (N29105)
Location: NCR Education Centers in Atlanta, GA; Chicago, IL; Dayton, OH; and Los Angeles, CA.
Length: *Version 1:* 32 hours (4 days); *Version 2:* 40 hours (1 week).
Dates: *Version 1:* July 1985-December 1988; *Version 2:* January 1989-Present.
Objective: To be able to write and execute shell programs utilizing any of the shell facilities, utilize selected UNIX® commands in a shell program, utilize the NCR menu commands and optimize a shell program for maximum efficiency.
Learning Outcome: Upon successful completion of this course, the student will be able to write and execute efficient shell programs and design a menu program utilizing shell commands; and utilize the NCR menu to create additional menus that can process shell commands.
Instruction: Course covers user defined variables, positional parameters, shell special variables, I/O redirection, conditional executions, iterative execution, conditional substitution, restricted shells, selected case execution, background processing, pipes and filters, option processing, argument lists, and sequential handling. Methodology includes lecture, discussion, and laboratory exercises.
Credit recommendation: In the upper division baccalaureate category, 1 semester hour in UNIX® Shell Programming (9/87).

UNIX® System Tuning (K51805)
Location: NCR Education Centers in Atlanta, GA; Chicago, IL; Dayton, OH; and New York, NY.
Length: *Version 1:* 37 hours (1 week); *Version 2:* 40 hours (1 week).
Dates: *Version 1:* March 1986-December 1988; *Version 2:* January 1989-Present.
Objective: To provide skills needed to improve system performance by altering kernel parameters.
Learning Outcome: Upon successful completion of this course, the student will be able to describe the major functions of the UNIX® system; describe a process; explain the purpose, use, and alterability of the system tables; detail the CU allocation algorithms; describe swapping and how system tuning affects it; explain demand paging; describe I/O management with regard to systems parameters; demonstrate and describe methods of interprocess communications; and improve system performance through tuning the kernel.
Instruction: Course covers UNIX® operating system overview; internal file mechanics; process management, kernel functions; I/O systems; /etc/crash; interprocess communications; and system design and fine tuning. Methodology includes lecture, discussion, and laboratory exercises.
Credit recommendation: In the upper division baccalaureate category, 1 semester hour in UNIX® Operating System (9/87).

Variable Item Processing System (V14435)
Location: NCR Education Center at Chicago, IL.
Length: 38 hours (4 days).
Dates: May 1981-December 1986.
Objective: To teach the student how to install the modules of the Variable Item Processing System (VIPS).
Instruction: Course teaches the student how to select compile options, set monitor flags and bit weights, and build sort tables to customize the Variable Item Process-

ing System (VIPS) modules.

Credit recommendation: In the lower division baccalaureate/associate degree category, 1 semester hour in Data Processing (11/82).

VRX Operations (330905)

Location: Various NCR Customer and Support Education Centers in the U.S.
Length: 40 hours (1 week).
Dates: August 1980-Present.
Objective: To enable the student to operate an NCR computer system using the VRX Operating System.
Instruction: Course presents operating procedures used on an NCR 8000-Series Processor using the Virtual Resource Executive (VRX) Operating System. System initialization, job flow, displays, responses, and unsolicited input are discussed. Hands-on workshop allows each student to enter jobs, request displays, and respond to system messages. Utility routines, restart, and run-book procedures are discussed and practiced in workshop. Lecture is also used.
Credit recommendation: In the lower division baccalaureate/associate degree category, 1 semester hour in Computer Operations (10/81) (9/87). NOTE: This course has been reevaluated and continues to meet requirements for credit recommendations.

VRX Problem-Solving Techniques (K07105)

Location: Various NCR Customer and Support Education Centers in the U.S.
Length: 37 hours (1 week).
Dates: September 1980-Present.
Objective: To enable the student to detect and isolate problems in programs that operate under the VRX Operating System.
Instruction: Course covers detection and isolation of problems in user programs. Course includes a discussion of the VRX (Virtual Resource Executive) Operating System and its relationship to the user job. Memory dumps are used to reinforce the discussions, and debugging exercises are used when applicable.
Credit recommendation: In the upper division baccalaureate category, 1 semester hour in Operating Systems (10/81) (9/87). NOTE: This course has been reevaluated and continues to meet requirements for credit recommendations.

VRX Telecommunications (MCS only) (389105)

Location: NCR Regional Education Centers in the U.S.
Length: 40 hours (1 week).
Dates: May 1979-Present.
Objective: To teach the student to program the Virtual Resource Executive (VRX) telecommunication systems using Network Description Language (NDL) and Message Control System (MCS).
Instruction: Course covers introduction to VRX telecommunications, VRX Network Description Language (NDL) and Message Control System (MCS), MCS multiple task programming interface, and system and job recovery. Methodology includes lecture and workshops.
Credit recommendation: In the upper division baccalaureate category, 1 semester hour in Telecommunications (11/82) (9/87). NOTE: This course has been reevaluated and continues to meet requirements for credit recommendations.

NCR NEW INSTRUCTIONAL TECHNOLOGIES

New Instructional Technologies (NIT) develops training materials such as video tapes, slides, and computer-assisted instruction to support classroom training; but their largest mission is to develop self-instruction courses using the newest form of educational delivery-interactive videodisc.

Interactive videodisc courses are available at most of the NCR district offices, manufacturing plants, and regional training centers. An NCR InteracTV-2 videodisc system, a modified PC which can control and display video segments from a Pioneer or Hitachi videodisc player, is located at each of those sites.

Pre-tests help the student determine what content to study, and post-tests evaluate the student's progress. Each videodisc course is designed to be delivered without the aid of an instructor or subject matter expert.

Source of official student records: Director, NCR Technical Education, NCR Technical Education Center, 9391 Washington Church Road, Miamisburg, OH 45342.

Additional information about the courses: Program on Noncollegiate Sponsored Instruction, The Center for Adult Learning and Educational Credentials, American Council on Education, One Dupont Circle, Washington, DC 20036.

Data Communications: Concepts

Location: NCR Education Centers in the U.S.
Length: 24 hours (self-paced instruction).
Dates: January 1987-Present.
Objective: To provide the student with the vocabulary and concepts necessary to communicate and work effectively in a data communications environment.
Learning Outcome: Upon successful completion of this course, the student will be able to identify elements and functions of a communications system; identify the basic types of telephone company services; identify the advantages and disadvantages of dial-up versus dedicated lines; distinguish between simplex, half duplex, and full duplex transmission; and identify the considerations relative to line turnaround on a 2-wire versus 4-wire circuit.
Instruction: Course covers communications systems, telephone systems, communications circuits, transmission methods, modulation techniques, and special purpose devices and services. Methodology includes individualized,

self-paced learning on interactive videodisc. Students are expected to extend their learning through additional reading and exercises. Student progress is monitored through a computerized tracking system.

Credit recommendation: In the lower division baccalaureate/associate degree category, 2 semester hours in Computer Engineering or Computer Science (9/87).

Data Communications: Fault Analysis (000106)

Location: NCR Education Centers in the U.S.
Length: 28 hours (self-paced instruction).
Dates: January 1987-Present.
Objective: To provide the student with the knowledge required to isolate data communication hardware failures.
Learning Outcome: Upon successful completion of this course, the student, given a faulty communication link, will be able to isolate a hardware failure to an adapter, modem, DAA, or telephone company line.
Instruction: Course covers telephone company line signal considerations, modem operational principles, line fault analysis, modem features and options, adapter/modem interface, DAAs and auto dialers, and fault analysis. Methodology includes individualized, self-paced learning on interactive videodisc. Students are expected to extend their learning through additional reading and exercises. Student progress is monitored through a computerized tracking system.
Credit recommendation: In the upper division baccalaureate category, 2 semester hours in Computer Engineering or Computer Science (9/87).

Data Processing: Concepts and Systems (000115)

Location: Selected NCR Education Centers and District Offices in the U.S.
Length: 8 hours (self-paced instruction equivalent to 16 hours traditional instruction).
Dates: June 1987-Present.
Objective: To enable the student to understand data processing concepts including hardware, software, data, and procedures.
Learning Outcome: Upon successful completion of this course, the student will be able to describe data, information, MIS, operations; identify and differentiate hardware, software, firmware, peripherals, and programs; describe computer languages, applications, systems, utilities, data hierarchy, and security.
Instruction: Covers data processing concepts and systems including procedures, hardware, software, firmware, data, I/O devices, CPU, storage, types of computers, types of processing and security. Methodology includes individualized, self-paced learning on interactive videodisc. Students are expected to extend their learning through additional reading and exercises. Student progress is monitored through a computerized tracking system.
Credit recommendation: In the lower division baccalaureate/associate degree category, 1 semester hour in Introduction to Data Processing (9/87).

Personal Computers: Concepts (000112)

Location: Selected NCR Education Centers and District Offices in the U.S.
Length: 8 hours (self-paced instruction equivalent to 16 hours traditional instruction).
Dates: January 1987-Present.
Objective: To enable the student to understand personal computer (PC) concepts and terminology, including hardware, software, and peripherals.
Learning Outcome: Upon successful completion of this course, the student will be able to identify types of PCs; the PC elements and their function; explain I/O and I/O devices; understand RAM, ROM, and MS/PC-DOS; name some of the common PC programming languages, software packages, and compatibility features.
Instruction: Course covers PC hardware and software including PC systems, basic elements and dataflow, devices, ROM, RAM, operating systems, programming languages, application programs, and compatibility. Methodology includes individualized, self-paced learning on interactive videodisc. Students are expected to extend their learning through additional reading and exercises. Student progress is monitored through a computerized tracking system.
Credit recommendation: In the lower division baccalaureate/associate degree category, 1 semester hour in Introduction to Personal Computers (9/87).

Personal Computers: DOS (000115)

Location: Selected NCR Education Centers and District Offices in the U.S.
Length: 8 hours (self-paced instruction equivalent to 16 hours traditional instruction).
Dates: January 1987-Present.
Objective: To enable the student to understand the personal computer (PC) disk operating system (DOS) including PC-related concepts.
Learning Outcome: Upon successful completion of this course, the student will be able to identify DOS commands, disk drives, valid file names, and specifications; know control keys and functions; use the text editor; and identify disk management, file management, and system management systems.
Instruction: Course covers PC environment and commands including PC-related definitions, drives, diskettes, files, control keys, editor, command types and formats, disk management, directory and system management, and I/O. Methodology includes individualized, self-paced learning on interactive videodisc. Students are expected to extend their learning through additional reading and exercises. Student progress is monitored through a computerized tracking system.
Credit recommendation: In the lower division baccalaureate/associate degree category, 1 semester hour in

Introduction to Personal Computers (9/87).

Retail Environments: Concepts (000128)
  Location: NCR Education Centers.
  Length: 8 hours (self-paced instruction).
  Dates: March 1987-Present.
  Objective: To provide the student with the basic terminology and concepts necessary to communicate with customers in the retail environment.
  Learning Outcome: Upon successful completion of this course, the student will be able to identify the primary functions of retailing; define merchandising terminology; identify four major retail industry classifications; list the three levels of retail communication structure; distinguish between independent and chain retailing; specify the steps in automated back office flow; and given various accounting terms, specify their meaning within the retail environment.
  Instruction: Course covers retail industry overview, inventory and merchandise cycle, merchandise flow, posterminals, accounting and back office information flow, and financial and management reports. Methodology includes individualized, self-paced learning on interactive videodisc. Students are expected to extend their learning through additional reading and exercises. Student progress is monitored through a computerized tracking system.
  Credit recommendation: In the lower division baccalaureate/associate degree category, 1 semester hour in Retailing (9/87).

Video Displays: Concepts (000111)
  Location: Selected NCR Education Centers and District Offices in the U.S.
  Length: 8 hours (self-paced instruction equivalent to 16 hours traditional instruction).
  Dates: January 1987-Present.
  Objective: To enable the student to understand concepts related to video display terminal (VDT) product specifications.
  Learning Outcome: Upon successful completion of this course, the student will be able to identify VDT block diagrams, monitors, CRT elements, raster scanning, character displays, waveforms, circuitry, signals, control logic, monochrome and color displays, and various graphic generation techniques.
  Instruction: Course covers display techniques, video circuitry and color CRTs including elements of the CRT and VDT, raster scanning, character display, deflection waveforms, video monitor circuitry and control logic, color monitors and graphics. Methodology includes individualized, self-paced learning on interactive videodisc. Students are expected to extend their learning through additional reading and exercises. Student progress is monitored through a computerized tracking system.
  Credit recommendation: In the lower division baccalaureate/associate degree category, 1 semester hour in Computer Engineering or Computer Science (9/87).

Video Display: Fault Analysis (000131)
  Location: Selected NCR Education Centers and District Offices in the U.S.
  Length: 8 hours (self-paced instruction equivalent to 16 hours traditional instruction).
  Dates: June 1987-Present.
  Objective: To enable the student to install and maintain video display terminals (VDT) and monitors with minimum product specific training.
  Learning Outcome: Upon successful completion of this course, the student will be able to identify site and cabling needs for VDTs, VDT configuration and functions, communication parameters, safety factors, adjustment procedures, replaceable modules, diagnostics, fault symptoms, communication ports, white-balance, purity, and convergence adjustments.
  Instruction: Course covers installation, adjustments, fault isolation and repair including configuration parameters, installation procedures, monochrome adjustments, modular VDT construction, hardware fault isolation, part replacement procedures, troubleshooting simulations and color servicing considerations. Methodology includes individualized, self-paced learning on interactive videodisc. Students are expected to extend their learning through additional reading and exercises. Student progress is monitored through a computerized tracking system.
  Credit recommendation: In the lower division baccalaureate/associate degree category, 1 semester hour in Computer Engineering or Computer Science (9/87).

The Negotiation Institute

The Negotiation Institute is dedicated to advancing the skills and corresponding arts in the processes of negotiations. Founded in 1968, the Negotiation Institute has conducted seminars in over 1,000 American locations, as well as 20 overseas locations. Graduate schools of business, law schools, and graduate and accounting schools have regularly offered the Institute's negotiation seminars.

The seminar technique, running either 2 to 3 days, is the primary mode of educational delivery. Students are required to engage in extensive reading, problem solving, discussion, and case interaction.

The Negotiation Institute's administrative offices are located in New York City. Classroom facilities for the seminars are usually in business conference centers, continuing education centers, college classrooms, or seminar facilities. Instructional staff are proficient negotiators typically with extensive legal, corporate, and negotiating experience.

Source of official student records: The Secretary, The Negotiation Institute, 230 Park Avenue, New York, New York 10169.

Additional information about the courses: Program on Noncollegiate Sponsored Instruction, The Center for Adult Learning and Educational Credentials, American Council on Education, One Dupont Circle, Washington, D.C. 20036.

The Art of Negotiation
Location: 220 Park Avenue, New York, NY and various locations throughout the United States.
Length: 16-24 hours (2 or 3 days depending on the inclusion of a one-day computer-supported negotiation exercise [3rd day only]).
Dates: September 1985-Present.
Objective: To provide the student with the knowledge of the principles of negotiations and the ability to apply negotiating skills to a variety of negotiation and/or arbitration situations.
Instruction: Required reading prior to in-residence program. Lectures, discussions, and computer-assisted instruction are employed towards the understanding of communications and behavioral patterns to identify hidden problems in the negotiation process; to understand, and identify motivational factors; to recognize failure factors in negotiations; to develop strategies for the solution of difficult negotiation problems; to understand non-verbal communications; to administer agreements following the completion of negotiations; and to recognize the diverse characteristics of negotiating environments.
Credit recommendation: In the upper division baccalaureate category, 2 semester hours in Introduction to the Art of Negotiation (9/85). NOTE: Without computer-supported segment, the credit recommendation is in the upper division baccalaureate category, 1 semester hour in Introduction to the Art of Negotiating.

New England School of Banking

The New England School of Banking offers a program in banking education for junior and middle management bankers. The Commercial Banking Major was established in 1957. The Trust Major was added in 1967. The school is sponsored by the six New England state bankers' associations.

Each major is a two-year summer program (one-week resident session each year). The majors are designed to increase students' knowledge of the technical and managerial aspects of their own specialists and to introduce them to other commercial and trust banking subjects. The school faculty is drawn from both the academic and banking communities. Lectures, case studies, role playing, workshops, and computer simulations are used.

The goal of the school is to provide bankers with the knowledge needed to assume greater responsibility, an understanding of the complexity of the industry, and an awareness of banking's role in today's society.

Source of official student records: Executive Director, New England School of Banking, P.O. Box 431, North Kingstown, RI 02852.

Additional information about the courses: Program on Noncollegiate Sponsored Instruction, The Center for Adult Learning and Educational Credentials, American Council on Education, One Dupont Circle, Washington, D.C. 20036.

Commercial Banking Major
Location: Williams College, Williamstown, MA.
Length: 73 hours (2 weeks) and 110 hours of independent study.
Dates: June 1980-Present.
Objective: To expand students' knowledge of the technical and managerial aspects of their own specialties and to introduce them to other commercial banking subjects in a rapidly changing banking environment.
Instruction: Covers the history of banking, American financial system, management of bank assets and liabilities analysis of financial statements, bank investments, lending and loan administration, sales management and marketing, financial instruments and markets, and related bank management topics such as communications and personnel. In the bank simulation game, students work in groups to make decisions and determine policy in the operation of a commercial bank. In addition to on-campus instruction, students are assigned case problems to be completed between the 2 resident sessions for evaluation by an instructor.
Credit recommendation: In the upper division baccalaureate category, 3 semester hours in Bank Management; in the upper division baccalaureate category, 2 semester hours in Business Policy; and in the upper division baccalaureate category, 1 semester hour in Capital Markets (6/82). These credit recommendations are cumulative.

Trust Banking Major
Location: Williams College, Williamstown, MA.
Length: 73 hours (2 weeks) and 110 hours of independent study.
Dates: June 1980-Present.
Objective: To increase students' knowledge of the technical and managerial aspects of their own specialties and to introduce them to other trust banking subjects in a rapidly changing banking environment.
Instruction: Covers trust investments, fiduciary tax, fiduciary law, and trust department operations. The methods of instruction include workshops, seminars, and group discussions. In addition to on-campus study, students are assigned case problems to be completed between the 2

resident sessions for evaluation by an instructor.

Credit recommendation: In the upper division baccalaureate category, 3 semester hours in Wills, Trusts, and Estates; in the upper division baccalaureate category, 2 semester hours in Estate Taxation; and in the upper division baccalaureate category, 1 semester hour in Bank Management (6/82). These credit recommendations are cumulative.

New England Telephone Company

The New England Telephone Company is part of NYNEX. It provides telecommunications services to all New England states except Connecticut. The Training, Development, and Consulting Division of New England Telephone allows for a centralized point of contact for all employee educational developmental and consulting needs plus the support services required to provide them. It is responsible for the delivery, development, and revision of educational material required by New England Telephone.

Training and education programs are offered at the Marlboro Learning Center, Marlboro, Massachusetts, at other company facilities, and various locations throughout the five state area.

Instructors are selected through their prior work experience and subject matter expertise, in addition to their formal educational background. Their performance is reviewed periodically through classroom observations conducted by their immediate supervisor and through student evaluations of the courses, their content and delivery.

Course development and revision is based on the Trainer's Library. External review and assistance are not used in course development.

Source of official student records: Marlboro Learning Center, Administrative Services-Budgets, 280 Lock Drive, Marlboro, Massachusetts 01752.

Additional information about the courses: Program on Noncollegiate Sponsored Instruction, The Center for Adult Learning and Educational Credentials, American Council on Education, One Dupont Circle, Washington, D.C. 20036.

BUSINESS/MANAGEMENT COURSES

Asbestos Recognition and Abatement (EB23000)
   Location: Marlboro Learning Center, Marlboro, MA; Boston, MA.
   Length: 20 - 24 hours (2½ days - 3 days)
   Dates: January 1987-Present.
   Objective: To provide the student with an overview of origin, use, current environmental and medical concerns of asbestos and the current Environmental Protection Agency and the Occupational Safety and Health Administration standards. The course also covers current industry standards for removal of asbestos.
   Learning Outcome: Upon successful completion of this course, the student will be able to describe the background of asbestos, including the current glossary of asbestos related terms, and the current use of asbestos in the industry; name the current legislative and regulatory requirements associated with asbestos use and removal, including those mandated by the EPA and OSHA; name the health effects associated with asbestos; describe the asbestos removal methods currently being used in the industry; name and describe the engineering controls employed to confine and minimize airborne fibers within an asbestos removal area; name and describe the asbestos sampling and analysis techniques used to determine the existence or concentration of asbestos fibers; describe current asbestos waste disposal requirements; and name and describe the items to be considered by the owner/building manager when faced with an asbestos removal project.
   Instruction: Course covers definition of asbestos and the use of asbestos in the industry, understanding current regulations concerning the use and removal of asbestos, health effects associated with asbestos, and current disposal requirements. Methodology includes lecture and discussion.
   Credit recommendation: In the lower division baccalaureate/associate degree category, 1 semester hour in Architectural Engineering, Environmental Control, Hazardous Materials, or Public Administration (1/89).

Business Meeting Skills (PB11500)
   Location: Marlboro Learning Center, Marlboro, MA.
   Length: 17½ hours (2½ days).
   Dates: April 1987 - Present.
   Objective: To provide the student with an understanding and appreciation of the importance of a conference, the understanding of leader/group relationships, and an understanding of how to design and plan a conference.
   Learning Outcome: Upon successful completion of this course, the student will be able to use the meeting as a successful management tool within a realistic time frame; plan an effective meeting—members, agenda, facilities, objectives, etc.; establish a climate for communication and utilize audiovisual materials; sharpen problem-solving and decision-making skills; manage hostility, argument, disinterest, and uneven participation; and recognize hidden agendas, inappropriate audiovisual support, autocratic leadership, and incorrect formats.
   Instruction: Course covers dyadic interviews with feedback, conference planning, conference tools and techniques, role playing, and decision making. Methodology includes lecture, classroom discussion, exercises, and videotapes.
   Credit recommendation: In the lower division baccalaureate/associate degree category, 1 semester hour in Business Communications (1/89).

Communications Workshop (PB11300)
Location: Marlboro Learning Center, Marlboro, MA.
Length: 34 hours (5 days).
Dates: January 1983-Present.
Objective: To provide the student with a wide range of communication skills and competencies (verbal and nonverbal) and outlines guidelines for improved communication.
Learning Outcome: Upon successful completion of this course, the student will be able to identify and remove barriers to communication and emphasize the power of listening; learn to give, receive and use feedback; gauge the effects of assumptions, inferences, individual needs and stereotypes, and create a climate of trust; develop specific personal guidelines for communicating.
Instruction: Course covers communication skills, communication competencies, group dynamics and processing, importance of feedback, and function (group). Methodology includes lecture, discussion, classroom exercises, and case studies.
Credit recommendation: In the lower division baccalaureate/associate degree category, 2 semester hours in Business Communications or Communications (1/89).

Investment in Excellence (PB16200)
Location: Marlboro Learning Center, Marlboro, MA and various locations throughout New England.
Length: 21½ hours (3 days).
Dates: October 1983-Present.
Objective: To provide the student with the personal and developmental skills necessary and to raise awareness and competence in the areas of stress management, leadership, autonomy, and risk taking which will enhance job productivity.
Learning Outcome: Upon successful completion of this course, the student will be able to tap his/her unlimited potential for development; regard change as a challenge, not as a threat; unlock his/her creativity to reach a higher level of accomplishment; become a powerful, significant, positive force to his/herself and others; visualize his/herself in stimulating new areas of living; utilize self-talk, imagination, and emotion to set and achieve goals; and take risks, gain from new experiences, and take giant steps towards a more rewarding professional and personal life.
Instruction: Instruction covers positive thinking, self-image, habits and attitudes, motivation, self-esteem, goal setting, and feedback techniques. Methodology includes lecture, discussion, and use of videotapes.
Credit recommendation: In the lower division baccalaureate/associate degree category, 1 semester hour in Communications, Human Relations, or Psychology (1/89).

Labor Relations (PB05000)
Location: Marlboro Learning Center, Marlboro, MA.
Length: 17 hours (2 days).
Dates: April 1984-Present.
Objective: To provide the student with an understanding of labor relations principles, the grievance process, and highlight the importance of understanding an administration of the contract.
Learning Outcome: Upon successful completion of this course, the student will be able to interpret various statements and locate the aid of the contract appropriate article references to substantiate responses; define "due process of discipline" according to established procedures; document statements and participatory discussions according to prescribed guidelines; demonstrate managerial technique in simulated discipline and grievance discussions; state an understanding of the grievance procedure as written in contract; define arbitration and expedited arbitration as described in the contract, and describe the effects of decisions resulting from arbitration and expedited arbitration.
Instruction: Course covers labor relations principles, discipline and grievance, contract administration, and documentation. Methodology includes role playing, videotapes, and class discussion.
Credit recommendation: In the lower division baccalaureate/associate degree category, 1 semester hour in Labor Relations or Labor Studies (1/89).

Principles of Supervision: Managerial Task Cycle (PB16900)
Location: Various locations throughout New England.
Length: 26½ hours (4 days).
Dates: November 1985-Present.
Objective: To teach the student a system of management that focuses on results-oriented, specific skills that are applicable across a wide variety of functional tasks accomplished through support and cooperation of manager's reporting people and peers. The Wilson Survey is used to show management styles.
Learning Outcome: Upon successful completion of this course, the student will be able to apply the "management task cycle" in their own setting; use survey feedback results to put skills into perspective and start managing more effectively; use on-on-one communication as a powerful tool; improve problem-solving and objective-setting skills; write effective goal statements; develop a personal management action plan; deal successfully with people problems; develop and motivate employees; give effective feedback; develop and use coaching guides; handle conflict.
Instruction: Course covers clarifying goals, planning, and problem solving; facilitating the work of others, obtaining and providing feedback, exercising control, and reinforcing performance and interpersonal relations. Methodology includes lecture, discussion, and the use of audiotapes.
Credit recommendation: In the upper division baccalaureate category, 2 semester hours as an elective in

Management or Supervision (1/89).

Situational Leadership II (PB16100)
Location: Marlboro Learning Center, Marlboro, MA and various locations throughout New England.
Length: 18 hours (3 days).
Dates: August 1983-Present.
Objective: To provide the student with the skills necessary for effective leadership, performance problem solving, delegation of responsibility, and provide the knowledge necessary to adapt a management style suited to both people and the organization.
Learning Outcome: Upon successful completion of this course, the student will be able to recognize that there is no "one best" leadership style; discover the three secrets of the one-minute manager: goal setting, praising, and reprimand (feedback); determine the leadership style appropriate for a given situation; practice and apply situational leadership in various situations; determine his/her own leadership style in a problem-solving work group; diagnose the development level of subordinates for key tasks; understand various strategies for changing personal leadership style to meet the needs of those with whom one works; behavioral flexibility, self objectivity, group dynamics, performance appraisal, decision making, and awareness of social environment.
Instruction: Course covers notetaking, personal power, levels of change, pyramidal organizations, behavioral theories X and Y, and supervision. Methodology includes lecture, discussion, and the use of videotapes.
Credit recommendation: In the lower division baccalaureate/associate degree category, 1 semester hour in Management or Supervision (1/89).

Stress Management: A Positive Strategy (PB03000)
Location: Marlboro Learning Center, Marlboro, MA.
Length: 13½ hours (2 days).
Dates: January 1986-Present.
Objective: To provide the student with effective ways of dealing with professional and personal stress and define the manager's role and responsibility for stress management.
Learning Outcome: Upon successful completion of this course, the student will be able to understand the concept of stress and what triggers it in one's life; know how stress affects performance, interpersonal relationships, and health; identify the signs of chronic, damaging stress; understand one's role as a manager in dealing with stress in the workplace; learn how to use effective stress management techniques.
Instruction: Course covers awareness, self-assessment, rational emotional thinking, and problem solving. Methodology includes lecture, discussion, and use of videotapes.
Credit recommendation: In the upper division baccalaureate category, 1 semester hour in Management, Psychology, or Supervision (1/89).

Telemarketing (CA60600)
(Residence Representative Initial Training)
Location: Boston, MA.
Length: 277 hours (7½ weeks).
Dates: February 1981-Present.
Objective: To provide the student with training for non-management personnel so he/she can perform the functions of a residence service representative using a variety of mechanized systems via a computer terminal.
Learning Outcome: Upon successful completion of this course, the student will be able to handle customer complaints; resolve inquiries; collect overdue bills; acquire selling skills; process requests involving service by using a computer terminal; develop positive customer relations.
Instruction: Course covers all aspects of the very broad issues of customer/service relationships. Methodology includes laboratory exercises, lecture, discussion, case study, problem solving, and hands-on computer terminal practice.
Credit recommendation: In the lower division baccalaureate/associate degree category, 3 semester hours in Customer Relations or Telemarketing (1/89).

Trainer Skills Workshop (PB13300)
Location: Marlboro Learning Center, Marlboro, MA and various locations throughout New England.
Length: 65 hours (2 weeks).
Dates: January 1983-Present.
Objective: To provide the student with skills such as oral presentation, use of visual aids, questioning, listening, group management, interventions, discussion simulation, and coaching which will help the participant be an effective trainer.
Learning Outcome: Upon successful completion of this course, the student will be able to describe the role of the trainer in a climate of rapid change; conduct an assessment of personal abilities; identify various learning styles; instruct effectively in the following formats—lecture, group discussion, demonstration, programmed instruction, role play, and case study; apply oral presentation skills, use of audiovisual aids, questioning skills, listening skills, nonverbal communication skills, and group management skills; employ professional and ethical points in training; create an effective learning climate.
Instruction: Course covers expectations, learning agreement and groups, presentation skills, listening, questioning, discussion and obtaining feedback from students, self-assessment, and group development with the use of role playing and case studies. A development of techniques to be used by trainer in the classroom. Methodology includes lecture, discussion, role playing, and case studies.
Credit recommendation: In the upper division baccalaureate category, 3 semester hours in Instruction De-

sign or Training and Development (1/89).

Writer's Workshop (PB11600)
  Location: Marlboro Learning Center, Marlboro, MA and various locations throughout New England.
  Length: 19½ hours (3 days).
  Dates: July 1982-Present.
  Objective: To provide the student with instruction and practice in editing and developing clear, concise communication skills in written correspondence.
  Learning Outcome: Upon successful completion of this course, the student will be able to organize writing logically, using clear, precise language; determine correct paragraph construction; sequence paragraphs effectively; edit for results; use correct syntax; use reference material; and organize ideas to be persuasive.
  Instruction: Course covers grammar reviews, sentence and paragraph structure, and writing skills and styles. Methodology includes class discussion, student presentations, and case exercises.
  Credit recommendation: In the lower division baccalaureate/associate degree category, 1 semester hour in Business Communications or Development Education (1/89).

COMPUTER SCIENCE COURSES

Concepts of Total System Development
  Location: Marlboro Learning Center, Marlboro, MA.
  Length: 22½ hours (3 days).
  Dates: August 1981-Present.
  Objective: To develop the role of systems development, the characteristics and functions of systems management within a framework that is useful in the design of machine and personnel subsystems.
  Learning Outcome: Upon successful completion of this course, the student will be able to explain the general environment and information needs brought about by modern computers; explain what makes "total system development" different from other system development approaches.
  Instruction: Course describes the major activities of design, implementation, conversion, performance review and support of the total system process. Methodology includes lectures, discussion, and limited laboratory work.
  Credit recommendation: In the upper division baccalaureate category, 1 semester hour in Business Administration, Management, or Engineering Administration (4/83) (1/89). NOTE: Credit should not be awarded if credit has already been received for Introduction to Project Management. NOTE: This course has been reevaluated and continues to meet requirements for credit recommendations.

Introduction to Project Management
  Location: Marlboro Learning Center, Marlboro, MA.
  Length: 22½ hours (3 days).
  Dates: February 1982-Present.
  Objective: To provide the student with a conceptual knowledge of the project management process and enable the student to develop the use of various strategies in managing a project within the confines and boundaries of major service suppliers.
  Learning Outcome: Upon successful completion of this course, the student will be able to define a project and list the important characteristics of a project; describe the primary function of project management in general; identify significant aspects of the development history of the project management system; describe the relationship between project management and new products, methods and procedures, new services, and the methodology required to deliver the end product of the projects.
  Instruction: Course details the basic tenets of project management within a systems framework. Explains the role of various operating personnel in project management. Methodology includes lecture, discussion, and classroom exercises are used.
  Credit recommendation: In the upper division baccalaureate category, 1 semester hour in Business Administration, Engineering Administration, or Management (4/83) (1/89). NOTE: Credit should not be awarded if credit has already been received for Concepts of Total System Development course. NOTE: This course has been reevaluated and continues to meet requirements for credit recommendations.

Programmer Basic Training
  Location: New England Telephone, Boston, MA.
  Length: 37½ hours (15½ weeks).
  Dates: *Version 1:* February 1978-December 1988; *Version 2:* January 1989-Present.
  Objective: To acquaint students with the physical structure and major concepts of a computer, enable students to design and implement a structured COBOL program, test and debug, modify the source statements, understand job control language, and execute various IBM programs.
  Learning Outcome: Upon successful completion of this course, the student will be able to design, implement, test, and debug COBOL on PL/1 programs; create and modify JCL to execute programs and procedures; describe the physical structure and major concepts of a computer.
  Instruction: Course covers data processing concepts; data representation; structured programming, design, implementation, and case problems; COBOL; JCL; utilities; cataloged procedures. The COBOL unit of the course emphasizes understanding diagnostic messages, making appropriate corrections to COBOL code, debugging. Students are required to take written tests and execute case studies which adhere to the principles of structured programming, the major emphasis of the course. A combination of lecture and machine-based, self-paced programmed instruction are used.

Credit recommendation: *Version 1:* In the upper division baccalaureate category, 1 semester hour in Introduction to Data Processing or Computer Science; in the upper division baccalaureate category, 6 semester hours in Programming; in the upper division baccalaureate category, 3 semester hours in Business Administration, Computer Science, Information Science, Engineering, Management, or System Management (4/83). NOTE: Students are able to receive a maximum of 10 semester hours for this course. *Version 2:* In the lower division baccalaureate/associate degree category, 6 semester hours in Programming; in the lower division baccalaureate/associate degree category, 3 semester hours in Business Administration, Computer Science, Engineering, Information Science, Management, or System Management (1/89). NOTE: Students are able to receive a maximum of 10 semester hours for this course. NOTE: This course has been reevaluated and continues to meet requirements for credit recommendations.

New Jersey Association of Realtors

The following courses are sponsored by the New Jersey Association of Realtors, Edison, New Jersey.

Source of official student records: New Jersey Association of Realtors, 295 Pierson Avenue, P.O. Box 2098, Edison, New Jersey 08837.

Additional information about the courses: Thomas A. Edison State College, Office of Special Programs, Director of Special Programs, 101 West State Street, Trenton, New Jersey 08625.

Graduate Realtors Institute (GRI) Course I
Location: Various locations throughout New Jersey.
Length: 30 hours (10 3-hour sessions).
Dates: September 1974-Present.
Objective: To train persons to function effectively in the residential real estate brokerage business.
Instruction: Covers organized real estate industries, urban development, legal environment of real estate, industries, construction, prospecting for listings, real estate contracts, market analysis for listings price, financing, qualifying the buyer, showing the property, obtaining and presenting the offer, and career management.
Credit recommendation: In the lower division baccalaureate/associate degree category, 4 semester hours in Principles and Practices of Real Estate, when GRI Course II and III are also completed (12/83). NOTE: Credit recommendation (total of 4 semester hours) only applies if GRI I, II, and III are all completed; no recommendation for any single course.

Graduate Realtors Institute (GRI) Course II
Location: Various locations throughout New Jersey.
Length: 30 hours (10 3-hour sessions).
Dates: September 1974-Present.
Objective: To train persons to function effectively in the residential real estate brokerage business.
Instruction: Covers communication, real estate market analysis, creative financing, advertising, real property and capital gains taxation, residential subdivisions, condominium residential trade-in and guaranteed sales, and real estate counseling.
Credit recommendation: In the lower division baccalaureate/associate degree category, 4 semester hours in Principles and Practices of Real Estate, when GRI I and III are also completed (12/83). NOTE: Credit recommendation (total of 4 semester hours) only applies if GRI I, II, and III are all completed; no recommendation for any single course.

Graduate Realtors Institute (GRI) Course III
Location: Various locations throughout New Jersey.
Length: 30 hours (10 3-hour sessions).
Dates: September 1974-Present.
Objective: To train persons to function effectively in the residential real estate brokerage business.
Instruction: Covers investment real estate, estimating cash flow, pricing investment property, taxation and real estate investment, financing investment real estate, applications of cost estimating, industrial real estate, commercial real estate, managing investment property, real estate exchanges, managing broker operations.
Credit recommendation: In the lower division baccalaureate/associate degree category, 4 semester hours in Principles and Practices of Real Estate, when GRI I and II are also completed (12/83). NOTE: Credit recommendation (total of 4 semester hours) only applies if GRI I, II, and III are all completed; no recommendation for any single course.

Graduate Realtors Institute (GRI) Course IV
Location: Various locations throughout New Jersey.
Length: 30 hours (10 3-hour sessions).
Dates: August 1971-Present.
Objective: To prepare realtors to qualify for New Jersey Brokers license examination.
Instruction: Covers laws-rules-regulations, interest in realty, how title is held, real estate contracts, liens, leases, mortgages-financing, deeds and legal descriptions, voluntary and involuntary alienation, settlement procedures and settlement sheets, mathematics-broker level, discrimination-investment, and real estate commission rules and regulations.
Credit recommendation: In the lower division baccalaureate/associate degree category, 2 semester hours in Principles and Practices of Real Estate, for those who have already completed GRI I, II, and III (12/83). NOTE: Therefore, completion of GRI I, II, III, and IV yields a cumulative total of 6 semester hours.

New Jersey Bell, A Bell Atlantic Company

See BELL ATLANTIC CORPORATION

New Jersey Department of Human Services

The Office of Manpower Planning, Development, and Training is the central training division for the New Jersey Department of Human Services, which employs approximately 23,000 people. This Office is responsible for the coordinating, monitoring, and evaluating of all departmental training efforts, the development and promulgation of training policies and procedures, the systematic development of all departmental managers and supervisors, and the delivery of training programs which cross divisional and institutional lines.

All facilities chosen for the training programs must facilitate group process, provide the opportunity for small-group work when necessary, be aesthetically pleasing, be well lighted and ventilated, be accessible for trainees, and have appropriate audiovisual aids and materials.

Source of official student records: Director, Office of Human Resource Development, New Jersey Department of Human Services, 3131 Princeton Pike, Lawrenceville, NJ 08648.

Additional information about the courses: Thomas A. Edison State College, Program on Noncollegiate Sponsored Instruction, 101 West State Street, Trenton, New Jersey 08625.

Executive Development Seminar (Basic)
Location: Various locations in New Jersey.
Length: 45 hours (5 days, 3 evenings).
Dates: October 1981-December 1983.
Objective: To enable students to evaluate their own leadership styles and make modifications in their own operating units; and to utilize concepts which will be results-oriented within their own operating units.
Instruction: Covers management techniques, cohesion, managerial practice, human response development, planning, organizing, directing, communication, motivation, and organizational change. Lecturettes, audiovisual aids, hand-out materials, experiential group activities/discussions, role-play simulations, case studies/participant presentations with feedback, individual inventories, and dialogue with instructor are used.
Credit recommendation: In the graduate degree category, 3 semester hours in Management Development, Organizational Behavior, Organization Development and Change, or Team Building (10/81).

Executive Development Seminar (Follow-Up)
Location: Various locations in New Jersey.
Length: 23 hours (3 days).
Dates: October 1981-December 1983.
Objective: To enable students to apply the most recent managerial concepts and theories, as well as plan, organize, and control operating units and make better use of available human resources.
Instruction: Covers dynamics of organizational trust, team building, leadership effectiveness, and stress. Lecturettes, audiovisual aids, hand-out materials, experiential group activities/discussions, role-play simulations, case studies/participant presentations with feedback, individual inventories, and dialogue with instructor are used.
Credit recommendation: In the graduate degree category, 1 semester hour in Management Development Seminar (10/81).

Gerontology Training Series
Location: Various Department of Human Services locations in New Jersey.
Length: 36 hours (in class) and supervised application in practical settings.
Dates: September 1983-Present.
Objective: To prepare staff members (ranging from direct care workers to physicians to CEOs) to address the holistic needs of the elderly and the problems they encounter when providing services to the elderly.
Learning Outcome: Upon successful completion of this course, students will be able to: (1) identify and describe principles of gerontology and techniques of care for the institutionalized elderly; (2) express positive attitudes about the institutionalized elderly; (3) apply knowledge and skills learned in training to on-the-job situations; and (4) better understand relationship between institution and community and focus upon ways to utilize outside resources.
Instruction: This course is made up of 12 modules covering a wide range of areas in the field of aging. It includes ways the staff can address the needs of the elderly, stressing quality of life and prevention strategies. Topics include: normal aging process, common problems of aging and the effects of institutionalization. Knowledge of gerontology is coupled with approaches to promote individuality, independence, and respect.
Credit recommendation: In the upper division baccalaureate category, 3 semester hours in Gerontological Studies or Human Services. If participant already possesses a baccalaureate degree and successfully completes a "research paper" read by a qualified independent assessor, then on the graduate level, 3 semester hours in Gerontological Studies or Human Services (8/87).

Special Management Topics
1. Management "B" - Management by Objectives/Standards of Performance

2. Management "C" - Interviewing and Counseling
3. Management "D" - Motivation/Communication
4. Management "E" - Performance Appraisal/Standards
5. Management "F" - Problem Solving/Decision Making
6. Management "G" - Transactional Analysis
7. Management "H" - Employee Relations and Grievance Handling
8. Management "I" - Equal Employment Opportunity
9. Management "J" - Assertiveness Training
10. Management "K" - Stress Management
11. Management "L" - Team Building/Group Dynamics
12. Women in Management

Location: Various locations in New Jersey.
Length: 12 hours (2 days) for each Management course "B" through "L;" 18 hours (3 days) for Women In Management.
Dates: October 1981-Present.
Objective: To enable students to:

1. Identify organizational and individual objectives and determine the procedures necessary to achieve them, and to write and use objectives in formulating decisions and policies for the organization.

2. Extract pertinent information for interviewing situations, and deal effectively with a variety of job-related situations which necessitate good rapport and communication skills.

3. Develop and sustain an organizational environment which will motivate employees and to apply a variety of motivational techniques to improve the organizational climate of the work unit.

4. Improve the work unit's performance by increasing knowledge of, approaches to, and techniques for performance appraisal, and to write standards in the context of MBO theories and the Performance Assessment Review (PAR).

5. Identify and analyze the causes of problems, and to develop appropriate options for resolving problems.

6. Improve the organizational climate and the flow of communications through a greater understanding of interpersonal relations, and to analyze interpersonal problems and examine relationships among members of the work unit.

7. Recognize the role and responsibilities of the supervisor in the equitable disposition of grievances, and handle situations before they become grievable issues.

8. Site EEO legislation, identify discrimination on the job, and interview and counsel employees in compliance with EEO Regulations.

9. Define and distinguish assertive, passive, and aggressive behavior and identify verbal and nonverbal components of these behaviors.

10. Recognize clues that trigger counterproductive stress and learn to use stress creatively and to change negative perceptions.

11. Effectively use techniques to deal with change and resistance through team building, and develop sharply defined objectives as a team leader.

12. To enable participants to understand the nature and scope of some internal, interpersonal, and structural barriers to advancement that women face; and to develop strategies utilizing personal strengths and abilities to overcome barriers to advancement.

Instruction: Covers:

1. Goal and objective clarification, setting standards, utilizing time-management techniques, and relating standards to organizational goals.

2. Communication theory, counseling employees, listening skills, and role-play exercises.

3. Motivation concepts, change, verbal and nonverbal modalities, and listening and feedback.

4. Instructional techniques to enhance skills and improve organizational effectiveness.

5. Problem analysis and decision making.

6. Transactional analysis as a management tool, and analyzing transactions and improving interpersonal communications.

7. Handling of grievances, unionism, role playing.

8. EEO legislation, regulation, and guidelines; discrimination complaint process; and interviewing and counseling skills.

9. Basic human rights, assertion, and communication skills.

10. Defining stress, sources of stress, self-motivation, and tension levels.

11. Team building, group dynamics.

12. Covers the nature and scope of traditional socialization, communication and self-assessment, time-management skills, managing change, problem solving and decision making, leadership, assertion techniques, conflict resolution, and career pathing and planning. Lecturettes, audiovisual aids, hand-out materials, experiential group activities/discussions, role-play simulations, case studies/participant presentations with feedback, individual inventories, and dialogue with instructor are used.

Credit recommendation: In the upper division baccalaureate category, 2 semester hours in Management Development (10/81) (3/87). This credit recommendation applies for successful completion of any three of these courses. Four credits should be awarded for completion of any six of the courses. NOTE: This course has been reevaluated and continues to meet requirements for credit recommendations.

Management II Basic (Mid-level Management)
Location: Various locations in New Jersey.
Length: 30 hours (1 week).
Dates: October 1981-Present.

Objective: To enable the student to develop a sound management system and solve management problems.

Instruction: Covers the application of the management functions of planning, organizing, directing, and controlling, and their relations to decision making. Lecturettes, audiovisual aids, hand-out materials, experiential group activities/discussions, role-play simulations, case studies/participant presentations with feedback, individual inventories, and dialogue with instructor are used.

Credit recommendation: In the upper division baccalaureate category, 2 semester hours in basic Principles of Supervision (10/81) (3/87). This course material is no longer included by most colleges as part of their business major, but is still applicable, as appropriate, to any other degree program, or as business electives. NOTE: This course has been reevaluated and continues to meet requirements for credit recommendation.

Management III Basic (Supervisory Level)

Location: Various locations in New Jersey.
Length: 30 hours (1 week).
Dates: October 1981-Present.
Objective: To enable the student to perform the tasks of a supervisor (i.e., planning, control, organization, problem solving, and decision making).

Instruction: Covers the role of the supervisor, leadership style and application, planning, problem solving and decision making, group dynamics, time management, communication styles, and assertive supervision. Lecturettes, audiovisual aids, hand-out materials, experiential group activities/discussions, role-play simulations, case studies/participant presentations with feedback, individual inventories, dialogue with instructor are used.

Credit recommendation: In the upper division baccalaureate category, 2 semester hours in Basic Principles of Supervision (10/81) (3/87). This course material is no longer included by most colleges as part of their business major, but is still applicable, as appropriate, to any other degree program, or as a business elective. NOTE: This course has been reevaluated and continues to meet requirements for credit recommendation.

Prediction and Prevention of Aggressive Behavior in the System (CRPI)

Location: Various Department of Human Services locations in New Jersey.
Length: *Version 1:* 40 hours (5 days); *Version 2:* 32 hours (4 days).
Dates: *Version 1:* June 1980-May 1985; *Version 2:* June 1985-Present.
Objective: To develop skills in predicting and preventing "acting out" client behavior. This course is designed for all staff who provide services to clients in a residential setting.

Instruction: This course teaches specific skills in nonphysical client control and also emphasizes verbal communication skills. Methods of instruction include interactive lectures; self-instruction multimedia learning modes such as work books, videotapes, and slide-tapes; role playing and field observation.

Credit recommendation: In the upper division baccalaureate degree category, 2 semester hours in Counseling, Special Education, Rehabilitation, or Human Services (6/82) (8/87). NOTE: This course has undergone a 5-year reevaluation and continues to meet the requirements for credit recommendations.

Psychiatric Rehabilitation Practitioner Training (M882)

Location: Greystone Park, NJ.
Length: *Version 1:* 148 hours (21 days); *Version 2:* 84 hours (12 days).
Dates: *Version 1:* April 1984-April 1986; *Version 2:* April 1986-Present.
Objective: To provide necessary skills in Psychiatric Rehabilitation to enable staff to work more effectively with resident clients.

Learning Outcome: At the conclusion of this course, the trainee should be able to conduct the functional and resource assessment; determine skill intervention and set time frames; direct skills teaching; utilize interviewing techniques; and make skill-language translations.

Instruction: This course covers an overview of Psychiatric Rehabilitation methods, including the goals of Psychiatric Rehab, the three phases of Psychiatric Rehab, and a comparison between physical and psychiatric rehabilitation. Each of the three phases (diagnostic, planning, and intervention) is then studied in more detail.

Credit recommendation: In the lower division baccalaureate/associate category, 3 semester hours in Psychiatric Rehabilitation Training Development or Human Service elective (not a core course) (12/87).

Psychiatric Rehabilitation Trainer Development (M-883)

Location: Greystone Park, NJ.
Length: 70 hours (3 month supervised internship).
Dates: September 1983-Present.
Objective: To enable trainees to present Psychiatric Rehabilitations Practitioner Training Course to other staff members.

Learning Outcome: At the completion of this course, trainees should be able to: deliver complete Psychiatric Rehabilitation program to practitioners; modify programs to suit learners' needs; and facilitate implementation of Psychiatric Rehabilitation into clinical areas of hospital.

Instruction: This course involves a two-week classroom component followed by a three-month supervised internship. Topics included in the classroom section are platform skills, methods of presentation, use of media, lesson planning and intervention strategies for the difficult learner. In the internship, students actually present training course under supervision of senior trainer.

Credit recommendation: In the lower division baccalaureate/associate degree category, 2 semester hours in Applied Training Procedures (12/87).

Training for Trainers - Crisis Recognition, Prevention, and Intervention
(Formerly Delivering Crisis Management Prevention Program, or Train the Trainers)
Location: Various Department of Human Services locations in New Jersey.
Length: Version 1: 120 hours (15 days); *Version 2:* 96 hours (12 days).
Dates: Version 1: May 1980-May 1985; *Version 2:* June 1985-Present.
Objective: To develop trainer's competence in delivering training in verbal, nonintrusive, nonphysical control to predict and prevent "acting out" client behavior.
Instruction: Introduce students to training strategies including behavioral rehearsal, communications skills, and methods of presentations. Teaches specific skills in non-physical client control.
Credit recommendation: In the upper division baccalaureate category, 5 semester hours in Special Education, Rehabilitation, or Human Services (6/82) (8/87). NOTE: This course has undergone a 5-year reevaluation and continues to meet the requirements for credit recommendations.

New Jersey Department of Personnel, Division of Management Training and Employee Services

The Division of Management Training and Employee Services within the Department of Personnel provides training and education to all levels of government employees. The Division provides practical instruction to meet the ever-increasing demands of governmental organizations.

Since 1960, these training opportunities have been available to address everyday technical, management, maintenance, and clerical concerns of managers and executives.

Course offerings include clerical skills training, communications, health and safety, management and labor relations. In addition to these courses, tailor-made programs are available. These programs are available throughout the state.

Source of official student records: Registrar, New Jersey Department of Personnel, Central Training Center, Front and Stockton Street, CN318, Trenton, New Jersey 08625.

Additional information about the courses: Thomas A. Edison State College, Office of Special Programs, Director of Special Programs, 101 West State Street, Trenton, New Jersey 08625.

Leading and Directing
(Level 1 of CPM Program)
Location: Trenton, NJ and other locations throughout the state.
Length: 30 hours (6 hour sessions over 5 weeks).
Dates: February 1983-Present.
Objective: To present managers (supervisors) with theory and techniques of successful management.
Learning Outcome: Upon successful completion of this course, the manager will have a more effective understanding of: the six managerial functions; the role of the supervisor; motivation, its theory and reinforcement; leadership, its theory and styles; and discipline, traditional approval, and preventive techniques.
Instruction: This course focuses on the individual manager's role, strengths and weaknesses as they relate to various managerial functions and the one-on-one relationship of leading and directing others. To complete the course, students must pass a written examination and present an in-class practicum relating a theory from class to their practicum situation.
Credit recommendation: In the upper division baccalaureate category, with completion of Levels 2 and 3, a total recommendation of 3 semester hours in Organizational Behavior and 3 semester hours in Human Resources Management or Management in the Public Sector (11/86).

Organizing
(Level 2 of CPM Program)
Location: Trenton, NJ and other locations throughout the state.
Length: 30 hours (6 hour sessions over 5 weeks).
Dates: February 1983-Present.
Objective: To explore and develop the manager's role in developing high performance work groups.
Learning Outcome: Upon successful completion of this course, the manager will have a more effective understanding of: relationship of power and authority; delegation; group dynamics and team building; managing conflict; and EEO and Affirmative Action.
Instruction: This course amplifies the topics introduced in Level 1 by further examining their relevance to the managerial function of organizing. The overall focus of this level is on the manager's role in developing high performance work groups. To complete the course students must pass a written examination and present an in-class practicum relating a theory from class to their practicum situation. Prerequisite: successful completion of Level 1 of CPM Program.
Credit recommendation: In the upper division baccalaureate category, with successful completion of Levels 1 and 3, a total recommendation of 3 semester hours in Organizational Behavior and 3 semester hours in Human

Resources Management or Management in the Public Sector (11/86).

Planning
(Level 3 of CPM Program)
Location: Trenton, NJ and other locations throughout the state.
Length: 30 hours (6 hour sessions over 5 weeks).
Dates: February 1983-Present.
Objective: To enable managers to study and utilize the skills necessary to manage the planning function.
Learning Outcome: Upon successful completion of this course, the manager will have a more effective understanding of: problem solving; decision making; management by objectives; and performance appraisal.
Instruction: This course provides participants with an opportunity to learn about and experiment with the skills and strategies necessary to manage the planning function. It is the experience for participants who will be eligible for the Certificate in Supervisory Management. Students work with a problem solving model, a decision making model, determining and writing statements, performance planning and the appraisal interview. To complete the course, students must pass a written examination and present an in-class practicum relating a theory from class to their practicum situation.
Credit recommendation: In the upper division baccalaureate category, with successful completion of Levels 1 and 2, a total recommendation of 3 semester hours in Organizational Behavior and 3 semester hours in Human Resources Management or Management in the Public Sector (11/86).

Management Functions in State Government
(Level 4 of CPM Program)
Location: Trenton, NJ and other locations throughout the state.
Length: 39 hours (6 hour sessions over 6½ weeks).
Dates: October 1983-Present.
Objective: To extend the manager's concern from the individual employee and the employee group to the overall organization.
Learning Outcome: Upon successful completion of this course, the manager will have a more effective understanding of: the role of management in government; organizational systems and structures; public personnel and motivation; decision making theory, structure and styles; management budget process; budget development and planning; and the context of public management in a political (interest group) environment.
Instruction: This course is designed to introduce students to relevant theories and models of administrative theory and organization, as well as major issues facing local, state and federal governments. Key modules focus upon developing skills of the public manager as an effective problem solver. In addition to written examinations, students must also submit a research paper to successfully complete the course. Prerequisite: successful completion of Levels 1, 2 and 3 of the CPM Program.
Credit recommendation: In the graduate degree or upper division baccalaureate category, 3 semester hours in Public Administration (11/86).

Managerial Tools for Today's Executive
(Level 5 of CPM Program)
Location: Trenton, NJ and other locations throughout the state.
Length: 72 hours (6 hour sessions over 12 weeks).
Dates: January 1984-Present.
Objective: To prepare managers to make sound fiscal and policy decisions in an ever-changing environment.
Learning Outcome: Upon successful completion of this course, the manager will have a more effective understanding of: administrative law; analytical skills; capital budgeting; the New Jersey Budget Process; and an executive's use of computing and microcomputing.
Instruction: This course concentrates on the tools needed by managers to make decisions which have an organizational impact. Public finance and administrative law topics are covered intently. Also about half the class time is devoted to the use of computers by managers, providing an integrated overview of the computer as a managerial tool. This course includes written examinations and a separate written project for successful completion. Prerequisite: successful completion of Level 4 of CPM Program.
Credit recommendation: In the graduate degree or upper division baccalaureate category, 3 semester hours in Introduction to Microcomputers for Managers or Management Information Systems in the Public Sector (11/86). NOTE: Not a computer science course: 2 semester hours in Public Finances and 1 semester hour in Administrative Law.

Organizational and Human Resources Development
(Level 6 of CPM Program)
Location: Trenton, NJ and other locations throughout the state.
Length: 39 hours (6 hour sessions over 6½ weeks).
Dates: May 1984-Present.
Objective: To prepare managers to provide and guide effective change within their organization.
Learning Outcome: Upon successful completion of this course, the manager will have a more effective understanding of: techniques of organizational development; productivity and employee participation; participatory techniques for organization units; and strategies for placement change.
Instruction: This course focuses primarily on the manager's role in managing change within the organization. An in-depth look at organizational development and team building is undertaken as part of this course. This

course includes written examinations and an out-of-class project for successful completion. Prerequisite: successful completion of Level 5 of CPM Program.

Credit recommendation: In the graduate degree or upper division baccalaureate category, 3 semester hours in Organizational Development or Organizational Change and Development (11/86).

NL Industries, Inc.

See BAROID CORPORATION

Northern Telecom, Inc., Digital Switching Systems - Technical Training Center

Northern Telecom has two Technical Training Centers, one located in Raleigh, North Carolina and the other in Sacramento, California. Each of these centers is equipped and staffed to provide customer training to personnel from those companies that purchase switching systems from the Digital Switching Systems division.

Northern Telecom, Inc. supplies telecommunications and electronic office systems to the telecommunications industry, business, institutions, and government. The company employs over 15,000 people in its 16 manufacturing plants, research and development facilities, and marketing, sales, and service offices across the country. It is a wholly-owned subsidiary of Northern Telecom Limited, Canada.

The Customer Product Training departments provide engineering, administration, and maintenance training programs in support of various Digital Multiplex System (DMS) sales. This group also provides various programs in basic telecommunications and telephony.

Colocated with the Customer Training group is the Management Development group which provides courses for personal growth in supervisory/management skills, customer relations, time management, interviewing, assertiveness, performance appraisal, sales, and sales management skills.

The Technical Development group is headed by a director responsible for the administration, development, presentation, and evaluation functions. Reporting to the director are five managers, each responsible for one of the following: Administration, DMS-10 and DMS-100 Instruction, Course Development, and Operator training. A full-time instructor/developer staff, selected for their subject matter expertise and teaching/development abilities, design, develop, and present these programs in a modern facility utilizing state-of-the-art educational techniques and operational Northern Telecom switching systems.

Source of official student records: Manager, Training Administration, Northern Telecom Technical Training Center, P.O. Box 10185, 1000 Wade Avenue, Raleigh, North Carolina 27605.

Additional information about the courses: Program on Noncollegiate Sponsored Instruction, The Center for Adult Learning and Educational Credentials, American Council on Education, One Dupont Circle, Washington, D.C. 20036.

Digital Multiplex System-1 (DMS-1) System Maintenance (100)

Location: NTI Technical Training Center, Raleigh, NC.

Length: 40 hours (1 week); 16 hours lecture and 24 hours fault-find and troubleshooting.

Dates: March 1978-December 1985.

Objective: To provide personnel with hands-on instruction which will enable them to perform maintenance functions, e.g., diagnostic testing, analysis, and locating and clearing system malfunctions.

Instruction: A treatment of Digital concepts including analog-to-Digital conversion, Digital multiplex theory, and pulse code modulation. These concepts will be applied to the principles of operation and maintenance of the DMS-1 system. (Prerequisite: Basic telephony course or equivalent experience.)

Credit recommendation: In the lower division baccalaureate/associate degree category, 1 semester hour in Engineering Technology (7/81).

Digital Multiplex System-10 (DMS-10) Method of Operation/Traffic Provisioning (210)

Location: NTI Technical Training Centers, Raleigh, NC and Sacramento, CA.

Length: 40 hours (1 week).

Dates: September 1977-Present.

Objective: To acquire a basic understanding of Digital terminology and concepts as they relate to transmission and switching systems. Student will be able to apply knowledge of the structure of DMS-10 hardware and software to system traffic problems.

Instruction: Digital concepts and specifics of the DMS-10 system operation, including hardware and software. Provisioning worksheets are completed to determine equipment configurations based on traffic measurements. Lecture and case studies/discussion formats are used. (Prerequisite: Basic telephony course or equivalent experience.)

Credit recommendation: In the lower division baccalaureate/associate degree category, 1 semester hour in Engineering Technology (7/81).

DMS-10 System Translations (211)

Location: NTI Technical Training Centers, Raleigh, NC and Sacramento, CA.

Length: 40 hours (1 week).
Dates: September 1977-Present.
Objective: To understand the architecture of the minicomputer-driven switching system model and acquire in-depth knowledge of the methods and procedures for developing the data base for the model.
Instruction: An overview of the system architecture, emphasizing relationships of software to hardware, is presented early in the course. Subsequent instruction includes the reason for a data base, procedures for developing the base information, and a comprehensive problem requiring the student to construct a workable data base for the model system at the training center.
Credit recommendation: In the lower division baccalaureate/associate degree category, 1 semester hour in Computer Engineering and 2 semester hours in Introduction to Data Processing (7/81).

DMS-10 System Maintenance (220)
Location: NTI Technical Training Centers, Raleigh, NC and Sacramento, CA.
Length: *Version 1:* 200 hours (5 weeks); *Version 2:* 160 hours (4 weeks).
Dates: September 1977-Present.
Objective: To acquire an in-depth understanding of the DMS-10 switching system, including hardware, flow diagrams, microprogramming, and data conversion.
Instruction: Digital concepts, including analog-to-Digital conversion, are covered to introduce the student to digital technology. The DMS-10 system is introduced with the system hardware configuration, leading into concepts on the digital switching network, computer bus timing, network bus timing, the computer's MOS memory configuration, and its operation in a coherent digital switching system. I/O programming, diagnostic and data flow charts, troubleshooting techniques and fault recovery procedures are discussed in detail and applied through interactive laboratory work exercises. All of these concepts are then applied to the principles of operational hardware maintenance and the administration of the system's software structure.
Credit recommendation: In the lower division baccalaureate/associate degree category, 3 semester hours in Computer Hardware, 3 semester hours in Microprocessor Fundamentals, and 2 semester hours in Introduction to Data Processing (7/81).

Digital Multiplex System-100/200 (DMS-100/200) System Method of Operation/Traffic Provisioning (310)
Location: NTI Technical Training Centers, Raleigh, NC and Sacramento, CA.
Length: *Version 1:* 80 hours (2 weeks); *Version 2:* 64 hours (8 days).
Dates: November 1979-Present.
Objective: To provide an overview of the DMS-100 family method of operation and related planning activities to include digital overview, hardware description, and software capabilities.
Instruction: This course focuses on equipment and provides a general description of system components and software structure. Hardware/software relationships are applied to the area of traffic provisioning. Lectures, class discussion, and laboratories are used. (Prerequisite: Basic telephony course or equivalent experience.)
Credit recommendation: In the lower division baccalaureate/associate degree category, 1 semester hour in Engineering Technology (7/81).

DMS-100/200 System Translations (311)
Location: NTI Technical Training Centers, Raleigh, NC and Sacramento, CA.
Length: 80 hours (2 weeks).
Dates: September 1977-Present.
Objective: To understand the architecture of the minicomputer-driven switching system model and acquire an in-depth knowledge of the methods and procedures for developing the data base for the model.
Instruction: An overview of the system architecture, emphasizing relationships of software to hardware, is presented early in the course. Subsequent instruction includes the reason for a data base, procedures for developing the base information, and a comprehensive problem requiring the student to construct a workable data base for the model system at the training center.
Credit recommendation: In the lower division baccalaureate/associate degree category, 3 semester hours in Introduction to Data Processing (7/81).

DMS-100/200 System Maintenance (320)
Location: NTI Technical Training Centers, Raleigh, NC and Sacramento, CA.
Length: *Version 1:* 200 hours (5 weeks); *Version 2:* 160 hours (4 weeks).
Dates: November 1979-Present.
Objective: To acquire in-depth understanding of the DMS-100/200 digital switching system. System hardware/software, A/D data conversion, flowcharts, microprogramming, troubleshooting, and preventive maintenance procedures are included.
Instruction: Digital concepts, including analog-to-Digital conversion and various numbering systems, are covered to introduce the student to digital technology. The DMS-100/200 system is introduced with the system hardware configuration, leading into concepts on digital switching networks, computer bus timing, network bus timing, CPU/MOS memory operation, data programming, diagnostic and troubleshooting flow charts, and fault-recovery procedures. Basic analog and digital transmission systems and how they interface with the switching system are discussed. These concepts will be applied to operational, system administrative, and maintenance

procedures.

Credit recommendation: In the lower division baccalaureate/associate degree category, 3 semester hours in Computer Hardware, 3 semester hours in Microprocessor Fundamentals, and 2 semester hours in Introduction to Data Processing (7/81).

O/E Learning, Inc.

Comprehensive computer-based training is the trademark of O/E Learning, Inc. based in Troy, Michigan. Training is provided for all segments of business from the factory floor to the executive offices. There are also fully equipped computer training facilities which accommodate both large and small groups. For on-site training, O/E can install and operate a training facility in an office or plant. The curricula is tailored to specific needs and optimizes the use of valuable employee time. O/E also works in the vocational and job training areas and can help design vocational re-education plans.

Source of official student records: O/E Learning, Inc., 3290 West Big Beaver, Suite 116, Troy, Michigan 48084.

Additional information about the courses: Program on Noncollegiate Sponsored Instruction, The Center for Adult Learning and Educational Credentials, American Council on Education, One Dupont Circle, Washington, D.C. 20036.

Computer Awareness Training Phase I
  Location: O/E Learning, Inc., Troy, MI. and other locations in the U.S.
  Length: 30 hours (12 weeks - 2½ hours per week).
  Dates: January 1986-Present.
  Objective: To provide the student with a basic knowledge of Computer terminology; capabilities and limitations of computers; and the fundamentals of hardware and software in a variety of environmental uses.
  Instruction: Lectures, presentations and laboratories with intensive emphasis on hands-on experiences by each student using a variety of software programs for the microcomputer.
  Credit recommendation: In the lower division baccalaureate/associate degree category, 2 semester hours in Introduction to Microcomputers (1/86).

Computer Awareness Training Phase II
  Location: O/E Learning, Inc., Troy MI. and other locations in the U.S.
  Length: 30 hours (12 weeks - 2½ hours per week).
  Dates: January 1986-Present.
  Objective: To familiarize the student with advanced capabilities of commonly used microcomputer software. Application software instruction focuses on word processing, spreadsheets, and data base management.
  Instruction: Lecture, presentations and laboratories with intensive emphasis on hands-on experiences by each student using a variety of software programs for the microcomputer.
  Credit recommendation: In the lower division baccalaureate/associate degree category, 2 semester hours in Introduction to Microcomputer Applications (1/86).

Lotus
  Location: O/E Learning, Inc., Troy, MI and other sites nationwide.
  Length: 30 hours (12 weeks).
  Dates: January 1986-Present.
  Objective: To teach Lotus 1-2-3 software.
  Learning Outcome: Upon successful completion of this course, the student will be familiar with Lotus 1-2-3 software package commands and facilities.
  Instruction: Lotus spreadsheet commands, graphics commands, file management commands, and introduction to Lotus macro instructions. This course covers every aspect of Lotus 1-2-3 and how to apply it to a business environment. Advanced Awareness Training II is a prerequisite to Lotus 1-2-3. Lotus 1-2-3 is not the spreadsheet used in Advance Awareness Training II. Multiplan and Visicalc are used as spreadsheet packages in this advanced course.
  Credit recommendation: In the lower division baccalaureate/associate degree category, 2 semester hours in Data Processing (10/86).

Personal Finances
  Location: O/E Learning, Inc., Troy MI and other sites nationwide.
  Length: 20 hours (8 weeks).
  Dates: January 1987-Present.
  Objective: To introduce personal finance concepts regarding investments, wills, property ownership, real estate, insurance, fringe benefits and consumerism.
  Learning Outcome: Upon successful completion of this course, the student will be able to create a financial plan to be used in each individual's personal planning.
  Instruction: Discussion and use of comprehensive practice set workbook which includes actual preparation of a wide variety of applicable data forms for personal financial planning.
  Credit recommendation: In the lower division baccalaureate/associate degree category, 2 semester hours in Business Administration (10/86). NOTE: This course is most applicable for elective credit.

Robotics Awareness Training Phase III
  Location: O/E Learning, Inc., Troy, MI and other locations in the U.S.
  Length: 30 hours (12 weeks - 2½ hours per week).
  Dates: January 1986-Present.
  Objective: To provide the student with basic knowledge

of the various classes and levels of robots; to introduce the student to the programming requirements of robots and microbots with the computer; and to create an understanding of control commands and robot safety factors.

Instruction: Lectures, presentations and laboratories with intensive emphasis on hands-on experience by each student on computer supported robotic operations. Instruction is supplemented by manuals in microbots and a handbook on working robots.

Credit recommendation: In the vocational certificate and/or lower division baccalaureate/associate degree category, 2 semester hours in Introduction to Robotics (10/86).

Offshore Sailing School, Ltd.

The Offshore Sailing School is headquartered in Ft. Myers, Florida. Four resort locations are managed from the headquarters. The School provides instruction in sailing for those people visiting the resort locations. Boats used by the School are 27 feet Olympic class sailboats called Solings, modern cruising boats such as Hunter 40s, a Mooring 50, a Pearson, modern racing boats, and the Laser 28s.

All instructors are active racing sailors. The instructional staff undergoes periodic review which includes a student evaluation and performance review by the operations manager. Prospective instructors are required to pass a written examination before they are included as Offshore Sailing instructors.

Course development is handled by the office in Ft. Myers. In general, courses are developed by the management with input from the Training Committee of the United States Yacht Racing Union, the governing body of sailing.

Source of official student records: Operations Manager, Offshore Sailing School, 16731 McGregor Boulevard, Suite 110, Ft. Myers, Florida 33903.

Additional information about the courses: Program on Noncollegiate Sponsored Instruction, The Center for Adult Learning and Educational Credentials, American Council on Education, One Dupont Circle, Washington, D.C. 20036.

Bareboat Cruising Preparation

Location: City Island, NY; Captiva Island, FL; Tortola, British Virgin Islands.
Length: 26 hours (1 week).
Dates: January 1975-Present.
Objective: To give the student the ability to operate larger chartered cruising sailboats without assistance of a professional captain and/or crew.
Instruction: Topics include a more in-depth consideration of skills for sailboat and equipment operation and maintenance beyond those introduced in previous courses (Learn to Sail, and Advanced Sailing). Emphasis is on cruising in larger sailboats for extended periods of time without expert assistance, and on coping with the greater natural forces involved when sailing larger boats. Methods of instruction include lecture, audiovisual presentations, and practical applications aboard cruising sailboats. (Prerequisite: Learn to Sail or equivalent experience.)
Credit recommendation: In the lower division baccalaureate/associate degree category, 1 semester hour in Sailing (9/85).

Learn to Sail

Location: City Island, NY; Captiva Island, FL; Tortola, British Virgin Islands; and Cape Cod, MA.
Length: 26 hours (1 week).
Dates: January 1975-Present.
Objective: To provide the student with knowledge of basic sailing terms, theory, and equipment; ability to prepare and equip a boat for sailing; and ability to sail a boat in a safe and seamanlike manner.
Instruction: Topics include sailing and sailboat nomenclature; sailing theory; basic seamanship, technical sailing skills; wind (apparent versus true) and weather conditions; marine safety; mooring, anchoring, and docking techniques; rules of the road; man overboard rescue techniques; basic navigation; and grounding recovery techniques. Methods of instruction include lecture, audiovisual presentations, and practical applications afloat.
Credit recommendation: In the lower division baccalaureate/associate degree category, 1 semester hour in Sailing (9/85).

Advanced Sailing
(Formerly Sailing and Cruising)

Location: City Island, NY; Captiva Island, FL.
Length: 26 hours (1 week).
Dates: January 1982-Present.
Objective: To provide the student with an understanding of advanced sailing theory and techniques; an ability to cope with emergency situations; skill in applying advanced sailing and cruising techniques; and an ability to sail solo in a small cruising sailboat.
Instruction: Topics include sail characteristics, shape, and control; advanced sailboat handling; spinnaker handling; mechanical maintenance; emergency procedures; piloting; and radio-telephone operation. Methods of instruction include lecture, audiovisual presentations and practical application afloat aboard cruising sailboats. (Prerequisite: Learn to Sail or equivalent experience.)
Credit recommendation: In the lower division baccalaureate/associate degree category, 1 semester hour in Sailing (9/85).

Sailboat Racing

Location: Captiva Island, FL.
Length: 26 hours (1 week).

Dates: January 1975-Present.

Objective: To reinforce the student's understanding of basic seamanship and preparation for racing; to give the student knowledge of advanced seamanship; and to teach him/her to apply seamanship knowledge and skills under actual racing conditions and appreciate sailboat racing as a participatory sport.

Instruction: Topics include racing rules and tactics, sail trim, helmsmanship, advanced sail handling, and sailboat racing psychology. Methods include lecture, audiovisual presentations, and practical application aboard racing sailboats. (Prerequisite: Learn to Sail or equivalent experience.)

Credit recommendation: In the lower division baccalaureate/associate degree category, 1 semester hour in Sailing (9/85).

Ohio Bell Telephone Company

The Ohio Bell Telephone Company is part of Ameritech, Inc. and provides telecommunications services within the state of Ohio. The Ohio Bell Employee Development Department develops and maintains the educational resources that support Ohio Bell's Corporate and Personnel Departmental objectives.

Training and education programs are offered at the Technical Training Center and other company facilities throughout the state. Course offerings range from job-specific to more generic and are added to the curriculum on an as needed basis. Both vendor courses and Ohio Bell (Ameritech)-developed courses are included in the curriculum. All courses are required to meet the Ohio Bell training development standards as those standards pertain to subject matter, job relevancy, instructional efficiency, and evaluation appropriateness.

The developmental process involves using both subject matter experts and training development technologies. Each new and existing course is extensively "pre-trialed" with representative student populations prior to acceptance.

Instructors are selected based on their qualifications—performance demonstration and personal interviews. Methods used to evaluate student mastery of the course content include written tests, in-class demonstrations, oral tests, and in-class case problems (both individual and group). Unsuccessful students may repeat the entire course or selected portions. Successful completions are entered into a computer database and completion notices are sent to each student's supervisor for review with the student. The notice is then entered into the student's personal file. A hard copy is also kept in the training center's file.

Source of official student records: Employee Development Department, Ohio Bell Telephone Company, Room 740, 45 Erieview Plaza, Cleveland, Ohio 44114.

Additional information about the courses: Program on Noncollegiate Sponsored Instruction, The Center for Adult Learning and Educational Credentials, American Council on Education, One Dupont Circle, Washington, D.C. 20036.

Communications Skills Workshop (6110)
Location: Ohio Bell Technical Training Center, Boston Heights, OH.
Length: 24 hours (3 days).
Dates: June 1987-Present (previously December 1987-Present).
Objective: To develop the student's ability to promote and sustain better communications in the workplace.
Learning Outcome: Upon successful completion of this course, the student will be able to communicate more effectively; determine what is important to the speaker and the listener; and encourage others to solve work related problems and to improve performance.
Instruction: This instructor-led course teaches basic interpersonal skills that have application in the day-to-day management of performance and leadership of others. Correct application of these skills can enhance individual and group performance. Methodology includes group discussion, skill practice, role playing, videotape and programmed instruction.
Credit recommendation: In the lower division baccalaureate/associate degree category, 1 semester hour in Management or a related field (3/88).

Data Communications Concepts (5605)
Location: Cleveland, OH and other on-site locations.
Length: 20 hours (3 days).
Dates: January 1981-Present.
Objective: To provide the student with an introduction to data communications concepts and methods.
Learning Outcome: Upon successful completion of this course, the student will be able to understand the components and characteristics of transmission; understand the characteristics of a sine wave, modulation methods; understand the difference between parallel and serial transmission, asynchronous and synchronous transmission and three circuit types; understand station controller functions, transmission terminal types and functions; understand the meaning of network configuration terms and communication processing functions; understand multiplexing methods; and understand the difference between private network, network architecture, value added networks, and packet switching.
Instruction: The course covers components and characteristics of data communications; modulation methods and characteristics; types of transmission circuits and protocols; network types and functions; transmission equipment and functions; and network architecture.
Credit recommendation: In the lower division bac-

calaureate/associate degree category, 1 semester hour in Data Communications Concepts (3/88).

Data Processing Concepts (5604)
  Location: Cleveland and Columbus, OH.
  Length: 20 hours (3 days).
  Dates: January 1987-Present.
  Objective: To provide the student with an introduction to computers and data processing for non-technical personnel so that the student is able to understand the basic operations of computers and their use in many aspects of business, social, and physical sciences.
  Learning Outcome: Upon successful completion of this course, the student will be able to distinguish between data processing and data communications, and between data and information; identify central processing unit components and functions, primary and secondary storage devices, and the characteristics of input/output devices; identify different levels of programming languages, major categories of software and identify examples of application software; identify the function of operating systems software utilities software; identify the characteristics of number systems; and describe the major file organization methods.
  Instruction: Course covers data processing and data communications and their differences, computer systems components, storage systems, systems and applications software, programming languages, and coding and numbering schemes.
  Credit recommendation: In the lower division baccalaureate/associate degree category, 1 semester hour in Computer and Information Science (3/88).

Financial Operations (6013)
  Location: Ohio Bell Technical Training Center, Boston Heights, OH.
  Length: 16 hours (2 days).
  Dates: January 1987-Present.
  Objective: To provide the student with knowledge of the structure and components of a financial statement.
  Learning Outcome: Upon successful completion of this course, the student will be able to understand accounting processes; changes in income statements and balance sheets; the relationship of functional accounting to the uniform system of accounts; cash flow management; book depreciation as an expense as well as accelerated depreciation methods resulting in tax deferrals; and understand the development and control of a construction budget.
  Instruction: Course covers the introduction to accounting and financial statements, cash management, and depreciation and taxes through lecture and discussion, classroom exercises, and videotape.
  Credit recommendation: In the lower division baccalaureate/associate degree category, 1 semester hour in Principles of Financial Management or a related field (3/88).

Innovative Problem Solving (6113)
  Location: Ohio Bell Technical Training Center, Boston Heights, OH.
  Length: 32 hours (4 days).
  Dates: May 1987-Present.
  Objective: To provide students with the skills they need to solve problems, respond to opportunities, develop improvements, and establish plans. The course provides the structure to minimize uncertainty and allows the manager to be flexible and opportunity-driven in today's environment.
  Learning Outcome: Upon successful completion of this course, the student will be able to assess and clarify complex situations and determine how to prioritize and handle individual concerns; identify efficiently the cause or causes of problems and also capitalize on opportunities to improve and enhance performance; and make well-balanced choices from among an array of alternatives considering both how alternatives meet organizational criteria and how to manage potential problems. In addition, participants learn how to create alternatives using a variety of creative thinking processes.
  Instruction: Course is designed both to ensure optimum learning and to provide maximum opportunity for on-job application. The program uses a specific, predictable learning model to accomplish these objectives: after the introduction of a skill, the facilitator uses a model situation to demonstrate how to use the skill in its entirety. The model helps participants understand how the skill works before they actually learn how to use it. Lecture, discussion, and classroom exercises are used.
  Credit recommendation: In the upper division baccalaureate category, 2 semester hours in Management or a related field (3/88).

Leadership Strategies Workshop (6111)
  Location: Ohio Bell Technical Training Center, Boston Heights, OH.
  Length: 32 hours (4 days).
  Dates: October 1987-Present.
  Objective: To enable the student to examine contemporary management techniques for optimum leadership in the work environment.
  Learning Outcome: Upon successful completion of this course, the student will be able to create a climate of performance with fulfillment and learning with trust; improve performance and contribute to their learning and growth; create goals that are responsive to the needs of co-workers; and be more effective as a manager.
  Instruction: Course covers contemporary leadership styles and their applications to management. Topics include communication techniques, decision making, and supervisory theory. Lecture, discussion, and classroom exercises are used.
  Credit recommendation: In the lower division baccalaureate/associate degree category, 2 semester hours in

Organizational Behavior (3/88).

Listening Skills (6016)
  Location: Ohio Bell Technical Training Center, Boston Heights, OH.
  Length: 16 hours (2 days).
  Dates: January 1979-Present.
  Objective: To enable the student to examine strategies for improving listening skills as a managerial tool.
  Learning Outcome: Upon successful completion of this course, the student will be able to identify barriers to listening; become active listeners; listen effectively for content and feeling; and develop better interpersonal communication skills.
  Instruction: Course covers listening as a communication skill, and establishing effective interpersonal relationships. The course analyzes the importance of effective listening skills as a necessary managerial tool. Lecture, discussion, and classroom exercises are used.
  Credit recommendation: In the lower division baccalaureate/associate degree category, 1 semester hour in Interpersonal Communication (3/88).

New Age Thinking for Achieving Your Potential (6018)
  Location: Ohio Bell Technical Training Center, Boston Heights, OH.
  Length: 32 hours (4 days).
  Dates: January 1981-Present.
  Objective: To provide students with an understanding of their own talents, resources, and abilities to succeed.
  Learning Outcome: Upon successful completion of this course, the student will be able to gain awareness of his/her potential; learn to use techniques of affirmation, visualization, and imagery to tap existing resources; and eliminate self-imposed barriers.
  Instruction: Course covers goal setting, interpersonal communication, problem solving, self-esteem, motivation, and acceptance of and planning for change. The course increases the students' awareness of the potential for self-development. Lecture, discussion, video and classroom exercises are used.
  Credit recommendation: In the lower division baccalaureate/associate degree category, 2 semester hours in Personnel Development (3/88).

Risk Management Workshop (6019)
  Location: Ohio Bell Technical Training Center, Boston Heights, OH.
  Length: 16 hours (2 days).
  Dates: January 1981-Present.
  Objective: To provide students with an understanding of risk-taking and its impact on behavior and performance and the ability to analyze the risk-taking climate in an organization and the opportunities for risk in specific situations.
  Learning Outcome: Upon successful completion of this course, the students will be able to assess their risk-taking styles and assume responsibility for risk-taking challenges in their organizations; practice risk-taking behaviors and learn alternatives to their current approach to risk-taking; and develop a plan for applying their newly acquired skills back on the job.
  Instruction: Lecture, discussion, and exercises are used to provide coverage of risk-taking behavior. The course defines risk-taking looks at the impact of this type of behavior on performance and helps to identify opportunities for risk-taking in the work setting. Students will learn about the following aspects of risk-taking: the definition; the benefits and consequences; risk-taking styles; the challenge of risk-taking; and the challenge of risk-taking versus stagnation on the job.
  Credit recommendation: In the lower division baccalaureate/associate degree category, 1 semester hour in Management or a related field (3/88).

Trainer Workshop (6004)
  Location: Ohio Bell Technical Training Center, Boston Heights, OH.
  Length: 40 hours (5 days).
  Dates: January 1981-Present.
  Objective: To provide the student with the teaching skills essential for effective industrial training.
  Learning Outcome: Upon successful completion of this course, the student will be able to establish an appropriate classroom environment for adult learners; present the four-step instructional process linking trainer behavior with expected results; and display a variety of teaching methods and evaluation techniques.
  Instruction: Course covers the philosophy of adult education, including learning characteristics, learning styles, learning environments, and the ethical considerations in training. Methodology includes lecture, discussions, student presentations, instructor role modeling using a variety of techniques.
  Credit recommendation: In the upper division baccalaureate category, 3 semester hours in Industrial Education or a related field (3/88). NOTE: It should be assumed that the persons taking this course have a functional knowledge of human development.

Transmission Principles (5901)
  Location: Cleveland and Columbus, OH.
  Length: 36 hours (4 days).
  Dates: January 1981-Present.
  Objective: To provide the student with an overview of telecommunications networks including the characteristics of voice and data information carrier systems, of how information is reproduced and converted for transmission, to identify the characteristics of information carrier systems.
  Learning Outcome: Upon successful completion of this course, the student will be able to identify the difference

between analog and digital signals; the difference between the characteristics of sine waves and rectangular waves on time and frequency domain drawings; various digital signal formats; terms and concepts associated with signal propagation; various methods of error detection and correction; random noise and its cause and effects; features of common channel interoffice signalling systems; characteristics of space, frequency and time division switches; modulation terminology and schemes and their use with modems; the terminology and requirements for telecommunications lines; and the impairments encountered on private lines, data and DATAPHONE Digital Services circuits.

Instruction: Course covers switching and the advantages and disadvantages of a network using switching hierarchy; analog and digital transmission methods; impairments of data transmission lines; and limits on data rates and current transmission lines.

Credit recommendation: In the upper division baccalaureate category, 2 semester hours in Data Transmission (3/88).

Omaha Joint Electrical Apprenticeship and Training Committee

The primary responsibility of the Omaha Joint Electrical Apprenticeship and Training Committee is the training of men and women to step into the industry as qualified journeymen electricians. The second responsibility lies in providing upgrade courses for those who are already journeymen. The Committee is jointly sponsored and financed by agreement between the local office of the National Electrical Contractors Association, and the local unit of the International Brotherhood of Electrical Workers. The training enables students to accept the responsibilities of a skilled craftsman. The journeyman can increase his/her knowledge of new materials and techniques and, the customer benefits through being able to rely on an efficient workman for wiring installations and electrical services.

The Joint Apprenticeship and Training Committee is composed of persons who are appointed for a three year term of service and are selected because of their interest in training. All members work at maintaining a high standard of excellence in those selected for apprenticeship, and then in their performance while in training. The committee meets once a month with the director of training to review progress and solve any problems. The Committee also reviews the quality of instruction and approves the materials and training aids used and seeks to prevent an apprentice from failing, by dealing directly with the apprentice that may be having problems. Because all members of the Committee are directly involved in the electrical construction field either as a contractor or his representative, or are journeymen electricians, they are keenly aware of what is needed in the way of training to produce new input into the labor pool.

The Omaha program maintains its own Training Center. It is an electrical showplace wired with various automatic control systems which give the apprentices an exposure to the advantages of adequate wiring. The Center is equipped not only with the hand tools of the electrical trade, but also many of the power tools used by electricians. The Center also has many training aids for hands-on training in setting up control circuits, electronics, refrigeration and air conditioning, as well as the tools needed to help in developing manipulative skills. A library of audiovisual materials and an electrical resource library for both the instructors and apprentices are also available.

Source of official student records: Omaha Joint Electrical Apprenticeship Committee, 8946 "L" Street, Omaha, NE 68127.

Additional information about the courses: Program on Noncollegiate Sponsored Instruction, The Center for Adult Learning and Educational Credentials, American Council on Education, One Dupont Circle, Washington, D.C. 20036.

Electrical Apprenticeship Training
  Location: Omaha Joint Electrical Apprenticeship and Training Committee, Omaha, NE.
  Length: Four years.
  Dates: July 1973–Present.
  Objective: To prepare apprentices for journeyman status in the electrical construction (inside) industry.
  Instruction: *First year:* Principles of direct current, alternating current, and electromagnetism; knowledge and application of National Electrical Code requirements pertaining to cable, conduit, and grounding; operation of electric motors; Ohm's Law, series circuits, parallel circuits, magnetism, and motors; safety procedures and first aid resuscitation; reading and sketching of elevation views and plot plans, including symbols and scales used; materials used in the electrical construction industry, such as wires, cables, conduit, conductors, insulation, joints, fasteners, and fuses; under supervision, installation of electrical apparatus such as cables, conduit, tubing, outlet boxes, outlets, fixtures, and securing and holding devices at various job sites; orientation to the apprenticeship form of education and training, the electrical industry, the history of the electrical industry, the International Brotherhood of Electrical Workers, local union by-laws, and the history of the operation and contribution of the National Electrical Contractors Association.

Second year: Use and installation of electric meters; National Electrical Code requirements relating to grounding conductors, branch circuits, and transformers; use of algebra and trigonometry in making mathematical calculations; types of construction, winding ratios, functions, and classifications of transformers; operating principles and functions of incandescent lamps, alarms, and refrigeration and air conditioning components; capacitance, inductance, reactance, and RLC circuits; electric motor mechanical drive and load connections; use of architect's blueprint and layouts; use and care of tools of the industry; circuit testing; first aid procedures, including those for electric shock victims; safety rules and practices for the electrical construction industry. Apprentices perform more complex work tasks through a series of six-month job rotations.

Third year: National Electrical Code requirements for capacitors, electric motors, hazardous locations, and Class I, II and III installations; use of blueprints pertaining to structural details, floor plan specifications, floor ducts, service entrances, circuits, and riser circuits; electrical wiring and distribution systems; electrical theory pertaining to alternating currents, alternating current motors and transformers, power factor and correction, and primary and secondary connections; analysis of malfunctions and repair of remote controls, protection devices, and alternating current motor controls. Apprentices apply knowledge by assuming increasingly complex responsibilities and performing increasingly complex tasks in work settings that are rotated each six months.

Fourth year: Knowledge and application of National Electrical Code requirements pertaining to wire closets, junction boxes, and stairway and emergency lighting; metric system conversions; application of rules to radiation exposure, protection, reaction, and other features of nuclear safety; transistor principles and circuits and vacuum tube fundamentals; use of electronic testing equipment; basic rectifier circuits, amplifier circuits, special circuit applications, and transistor use; static control fundamentals, including concepts, circuits, analyses, and applications; alternating current applications in industrial electricity; fundamentals of temperature, pressure, and flow; instrumentation systems; installation and testing of electrical construction materials; use of electrical construction equipment.

Credit recommendation: *First year:* In the lower division baccalaureate/associate degree category, 2 semester hours in Basic Electricity, 1 in National Electrical Code, 1 in Blueprint Reading and Sketching, 1 in Orientation to Electrical Construction, 1 in Electrical Construction Materials and Methods, and 1 in field experience in Electrical Construction, for a total of 7 semester hours (7/83).

Second year: In the lower division baccalaureate/associate degree category, 4 semester hours in Basic Electricity, 3 in Electrical Construction Materials and Methods, 2 in field experience in Electrical Construction, 2 in National Electrical Code, 2 in Technical Mathematics, 2 in Blueprint Reading and Sketching, 1 in Orientation to Electrical Construction, 1 in Safety and First Aid, and 1 in Shop Practices, for a total of 18 semester hours (7/83).

Third year: In the lower division baccalaureate/associate degree category, 4 semester hours in Basic Electricity, 4 in Electrical Construction Materials and Methods, 3 in National Electrical Code, 3 in Blueprint Reading and Sketching, 3 in field experience in Electrical Construction, 2 in Technical Mathematics, 2 in Industrial Electricity, 1 in Motor Controls, 1 in Orientation to Electrical Construction, 1 in Safety and First Aid, and 1 in Shop Practices, for a total of 25 semester hours (7/83).

Fourth year: In the lower division baccalaureate/associate degree category, 5 semester hours in Electrical Construction Materials and Methods, 4 in Basic Electricity, 4 in National Electrical Code, 4 in Blueprint Reading and Sketching, 4 in field experience in Electrical Construction, 3 in Industrial Electricity, 2 in Safety and First Aid, 2 in Motor Controls, 2 in Technical Mathematics, 2 in Shop Practices, 2 in Electronics, 1 in Instrumentation, and 1 in Orientation to Electrical Construction, for a total of 36 semester hours (7/83).

NOTE: The credit recommendations are cumulative; readers should use the recommendation that corresponds to the number of years completed by the student.

Omaha Public Power District

Omaha Public Power District (OPPD) was created in August 1945 under the authority of the Enabling Act as a public corporation and political subdivision of the State of Nebraska. OPPD provides electric service in the City of Omaha, Nebraska, and adjacent territory. The service area is approximately 5,000 square miles, with an estimated population of 555,000. Omaha, with an estimated population of 335,000 within the corporate limits, is the largest city in the State of Nebraska and is the only community among the 49 cities and villages served by the District with a population of more than 35,000.

The Training Organization of the Nuclear Operations Division develops and delivers performance based training to all personnel assigned to the Fort Calhoun Nuclear Power Station located in Washington County, Nebraska. In April 1988, the training programs were accredited and OPPD was installed as a full member of the National Academy for Nuclear Training.

Source of official student records: Supervisor, Training Support, c/o Omaha Public Power District, Fort Calhoun Nuclear Power Station, 1623 Harney, Omaha, Nebraska 68102.

Additional information about the courses: Program on Noncollegiate Sponsored Instruction, The Center for Adult Learning and Educational Credentials, American Council on Education, One Dupont Circle, Washington, D.C. 20036.

Process Measurement Fundamentals (ACE I&C 88-01)
  Location: Omaha Public Power District, Ft. Calhoun Nuclear Station.
  Length: 72 hours (9 weeks).
  Dates: July 1987-Present.
  Objective: To review the instruments and measurement techniques used to determine temperature, pressure, and liquid level.
  Learning Outcome: Upon successful completion of this course, the student will be able to use level, fluid flow, temperature and pressure instruments; and troubleshoot simple instrumentation systems.
  Instruction: Course covers unit conversion, constructing and plotting of graphs, pressure measurements, liquid level measurements, fluid-flow measurements, temperature measurements, and instrumentation troubleshooting. Methodology includes lecture, videos, demonstration, and problem sessions.
  Credit recommendation: In the vocational certificate category, 2 semester hours in Basic Process Measurements/Industrial Processes (7/88).

Basic Electronics (ACE I&C 88-02)
  Location: Omaha Public Power District, Ft. Calhoun Nuclear Station.
  Length: 64 hours (8 weeks).
  Dates: January 1988-Present.
  Objective: To provide the student with an understanding of electronic circuits and operation.
  Learning Outcome: Upon successful completion of this course, the student will be able to apply Kirchoff's voltage and current laws; understand basic operational amplifier circuits; and understand transistor biasing and small-signal analysis.
  Instruction: Course covers electrical circuits and theory, Kirchoff's voltage and current laws, semiconductor principles, semiconductor diode applications and circuits, transistor amplifiers and oscillators, specialized electronic devices (tunnels, UTTs, SCRs, etc.), and operational amplifiers and circuits. Methodology includes lecture, classroom exercises, and video.
  Credit recommendation: In the lower division baccalaureate/associate degree category, 2 semester hours in Basic Electronics/Electrical Engineering (7/88). NOTE: If this course and Electrical Circuits, Machinery and Instruments (ACEOPS 88-04) are taken, then a total of 4 semester hours is awarded in Electrical Technology/Engineering.

Fundamentals of Digital Electronics (ACE I&C 88-03)
  Location: Omaha Public Power District, Ft. Calhoun Nuclear Station.
  Length: 96 hours (12 weeks).
  Dates: January 1988-Present.
  Objective: To provide the student with a fundamental understanding of digital electronics and displays.
  Learning Outcome: Upon successful completion of this course, the student will be able to understand the basic structure of various number systems (binary, octal, hexidecimal, etc.); identify and describe the function of AND, NOT, NAND, OR, NOR, etc.; and identify and describe the operation of various digital circuits (two-line to four-line decoders, multiplexers, etc.).
  Instruction: Course covers number system and digital codes, digital logic and technology, digital circuits (ANDs, ORs, NORs, decoders, etc.), digital displays, digital bus concepts, and power supplies. Methodology includes lecture, classroom exercises, video, and laboratory.
  Credit recommendation: In the lower division baccalaureate/associate degree category, 3 semester hours in Basic Electronics/Electrical Engineering (7/88).

Basic Mathematics (ACEEM 88-01) or (ACEHP 88-07)
  Location: Omaha Public Power District, Ft. Calhoun Nuclear Station.
  Length: 30 hours (5 six-hour meetings).
  Dates: January 1988-Present.
  Objective: To provide the student with a review of basic algebra and trigonometry commonly used in electrical circuits and applications.
  Learning Outcome: Upon successful completion of this course, the student will be able to solve linear and non-linear equations; graph linear and non-linear equations; use basic geometry formulas; and use trig-functions in solving right triangles.
  Instruction: Course covers the Pythagorean theorem, law of sines and cosines, quadratic equations, linear interpolation, function graphs and straight lines, and point-slope formula of a straight line. Methodology includes lecture and classroom exercises.
  Credit recommendation: In the vocational certificate category, 2 semester hours in Basic Algebra and Right Triangle Trigonometry (7/88).

Electrical Circuits Lab (ACEEM 88-02)
  Location: Omaha Public Power District, Ft. Calhoun Nuclear Station.
  Length: 106 hours (7 weeks).
  Dates: January 1988-Present.
  Objective: To provide the student with the ability to demonstrate analytical and practical applications of basic electrical circuits.
  Learning Outcome: Upon successful completion of this course, the student will be able to use an oscilloscope effectively; use a digital multimeter; and connect, test, evaluate, and troubleshoot basic electrical circuits.
  Instruction: Course covers electrical symbols and abbreviations, electronic power supplies, Ohm's law, Kirchoff's law, Thevenin and Norton's theorems, maximum power transfer, reading electrical diagrams, three-phase

circuits, vectors and phasors, electronic and transistor fundamentals, and amplifiers. Methodology includes lecture, videos, laboratory and classroom exercises.

Credit recommendation: In the lower division baccalaureate/associate degree category, 3 semester hours in Basic Electrical Circuits/Electrical Engineering (7/88).

Motors, Generators and Transformers (ACEEM 88-03)
  Location: Omaha Public Power District, Ft. Calhoun Nuclear Station.
  Length: 71 hours (4 weeks).
  Dates: January 1988-Present.
  Objective: To provide a fundamental knowledge of motor, generator and transformer theory and application.
  Learning Outcome: Upon successful completion of this course, the student will be able to perform transformer, generator and motor maintenance; and connect transformers, generators and motors in various configurations.
  Instruction: Course covers single-phase motor principles, three-phase AC induction motor principles, DC motors/generators, electromagnetic induction, transformer principles and operations, and instrument transformers. Methodology includes lecture, laboratory, and classroom exercises.
  Credit recommendation: In the vocational certificate category, 3 semester hours in Electrical Power Technology (7/88).

Electronics Lab (ACEEM 88-04)
  Location: Omaha Public Power District, Ft. Calhoun Nuclear Station.
  Length: 125 hours (8 weeks).
  Dates: January 1988-Present.
  Objective: To establish a broad knowledge base in both power and digital electronics.
  Learning Outcome: Upon successful completion of this course, the student will be able to construct and test digital electronic circuits; and construct and test power and advanced analog circuits.
  Instruction: Course covers power electronics, industrial electronics, instrumentation, and digital electronics. Methodology includes lecture, classroom exercises, video, and laboratory.
  Credit recommendation: In the lower division baccalaureate/associate degree category, 3 semester hours in Basic Electronics/Electrical Engineering (7/88).

Reactor Theory and Core Physics (ACEOPS 88-01)
  Location: Omaha Public Power District, Ft. Calhoun Nuclear Station.
  Length: 136 hours (24 four-hour and 5 eight-hour meetings).
  Dates: January 1987-Present.
  Objective: To provide the student with information on the properties of neutrons, the static and dynamic behavior of the reactor, the flux characteristics and coefficients of the reactor, and an operational and experimentation setting at a research reactor to demonstrate many of the concepts studied in the classroom.
  Learning Outcome: Upon successful completion of this course, the student will be able to describe, define, list and/or calculate: various neutron processes (i.e., slowing down, diffusion); radial and axial flux and power distribution; reactivity effects of various coefficients on reactivity; six factor formula; static and dynamic behavior of reactor; power ranges and the behavior of the reactor in different power ranges as reactivity changes; and a variety of "classical" reactor experiments.
  Instruction: Course covers neutron slowing down, thermal diffusion of neutrons, flux profiles; neutron life-cycle and the six-factor formula, criticality determination, various reactor parameter variation effects on criticality, reactivity changes; power ranges, sources of reactor neutrons, delayed neutrons reactor dynamics, start-up rate, reactor response to reactivity change, power decrease effects, shutdown effects; fast and thermal flux spatial variation effects upon power distribution, research reactor experiments. Methodology includes illustrated lecture, discussion, problem solving, and experimentation with a research reactor.
  Credit recommendation: In the lower division baccalaureate/associate degree category, 6 semester hours in Nuclear Engineering/Nuclear Technology (7/88).

Applied Thermodynamics (ACEOPS 88-02)
  Location: Omaha Public Power District, Ft. Calhoun Nuclear Station.
  Length: 60 hours (1½ weeks).
  Dates: January 1987-Present.
  Objective: To provide the student with a quantitative and qualitative understanding of the thermodynamics, heat transfer, and fluid-flow phenomena.
  Learning Outcome: Upon successful completion of this course, the student will be able to apply and understand the basic laws of thermodynamics; apply fluid statics, hydraulics, and pressure measurements; and understand basic heat transfer phenomena.
  Instruction: Course covers the first and second laws of thermodynamics, basis heat transfer principles, and reactor core heat generation and removal. Methodology includes lecture and classroom exercises.
  Credit recommendation: In the lower division baccalaureate/associate degree category, 2 semester hours in Applied Sciences/Mechanical Engineering (7/88).

Introduction to Thermodynamics (ACEOPS 88-03)
  Location: Omaha Public Power District, Ft. Calhoun Nuclear Station.
  Length: 81 hours (2 weeks).
  Dates: January 1985-Present.
  Objective: To provide the student (at an introductory level) with a basic understanding of the thermodynamics,

heat transfer, and fluid-flow phenomena.

Learning Outcome: Upon successful completion of this course, the student will be able to understand international units associated with fluid mechanics and thermodynamics; understand the first and second laws of thermodynamics; and understand the principles behind turbine generator design and operation.

Instruction: Course covers the steam power cycle, heat at work, steam and turbine generation, pumps and fluid flow, reactor fuel and core design, and valve principles. Methodology includes lecture, video, and classroom exercises.

Credit recommendation: In the vocational certificate category, 3 semester hours in Fluid Mechanics/Thermodynamics (7/88).

Electrical Circuits, Machinery and Instruments (ACEOPS 88-04)

Location: Omaha Public Power District, Ft. Calhoun Nuclear Station.

Length: 80 hours (2 weeks).

Dates: July 1985-Present.

Objective: To provide the student with a knowledge of basic electrical concepts, AC and DC circuits, AC generators, motors, transformers, and control instrumentation.

Learning Outcome: Upon successful completion of this course, the student will be able to describe, define and/or calculate the basic properties of electrical circuits, devices, and control instruments.

Instruction: Course covers current and voltage laws, AC and DC circuit analysis, power factor, AC and DC motors and generators, rectifiers; phase relationships in resistive, inductive and capacitive circuits, RLC series and parallel circuit analysis, circuit time constants; applications and control systems and control instrumentation. Methodology includes illustrated lecture, discussion, problem solving, and plant tour.

Credit recommendation: In the lower division baccalaureate/associate degree category, 3 semester hours in Electrical Technology/Electrical Engineering (7/88). NOTE: If both this course and Basic Electronics (ACE I&C 88-02) are taken, then a total of 4 semester hours is awarded in Electrical Technology/Engineering.

Applied Calculus (ACEOPS 88-05)

Location: Omaha Public Power District, Ft. Calhoun Nuclear Station.

Length: 40 hours (1 week).

Dates: January 1987-Present.

Objective: To provide the student with a knowledge of the basic concepts in and ability to solve problems using differential and integral calculus as it applies to a nuclear power plant reactor operator.

Learning Outcome: Upon successful completion of this course, the student will be able to calculate the limit of a function, list the properties of limits and apply them to the solution of problems involving limits; determine if a function is continuous at a point; define and evaluate the derivative of a function; define and evaluate the integral of a function; and use the concept of rate of change to solve rate problems that involve multiple additive rates.

Instruction: Course covers limits, continuity, differentiation, integration; applications to radioactive decay problems, equilibrium equation for fission products, and the first and second kinetics equations. Methodology includes lecture, discussion, and problem solving.

Credit recommendation: In the lower division baccalaureate/associate degree category, 2 semester hours in Mathematics (7/88).

Trigonometry (ACEOPS 88-06)

Location: Omaha Public Power District, Ft. Calhoun Nuclear Station.

Length: 40 hours (1 week).

Dates: January 1986-Present.

Objective: To provide the student with an understanding of the trigonometric functions, graphing of the functions and trigonometric identities, with an emphasis on right triangle trigonometry and vector analysis.

Learning Outcome: Upon successful completion of this course, the student will be able to use trigonometric relationships and concepts to graph the functions and solve for unknowns; use trigonometric tables; use trigonometric identities to solve for unknown values; convert from radians to degrees and vice versa; and use vector analysis to determine resultant vectors with the proper magnitude and direction.

Instruction: Course covers the wrapping function, properties of the trigonometric functions, graphs of the trigonometric functions, fundamental identities, trigonometric formulas, inverse trigonometric functions, right triangle trigonometry, law of sines and law of cosines, vectors and trigonometry, vector addition, and scalar product. Methodology includes lecture and problem solving.

Credit recommendation: In the lower division baccalaureate/associate degree category, 2 semester hours in Mathematics (7/88).

Algebra (ACEOPS 88-07)

Location: Omaha Public Power District, Ft. Calhoun Nuclear Station.

Length: 40 hours (1 week).

Dates: July 1985-Present.

Objective: To provide the student with the ability to solve algebraic equations and to understand exponents, logarithms, and graphs.

Learning Outcome: Upon successful completion of this course, the student will be able to describe the construction of a cartesian coordinate system; graph relationships with respect to a cartesian coordinate system; solve for unknowns of a second degree equation; solve algebraic word problems; work with exponents, powers, radicals, logarithms, and scientific notation; and plot functions on semi-log and log-log scales.

Instruction: Course covers fractions, exponentials, powers, radicals, scientific notation, common and natural logarithms, algebraic operations, algebraic equations, systems of equations, matrices, algebraic word problems, and functions and graphs. Methodology includes lecture and problem solving.

Credit recommendation: In the lower division baccalaureate/associate degree category, 2 semester hours in Mathematics (7/88).

Introduction to Personnel Management (ACEOPS 88-08)

Location: Omaha Public Power District, Ft. Calhoun Nuclear Station.

Length: 16 hours (3 days).

Dates: January 1987-Present.

Objective: To provide the student with the skills needed to communicate effectively, plan projects, delegate authority, and manage.

Learning Outcome: Upon successful completion of this course, the student will be able to organize and prepare effective oral and written business communications; identify/set goals and delegate responsibilities; and determine what, when, and how to coach/counsel others.

Instruction: Course covers how to manage your boss, rate yourself, setting priorities, guidelines for effective delegation, the ABCs of management, improving below average performance, and self-assessment profiles and motivation. Methodology includes lecture and classroom exercises.

Credit recommendation: In the lower division baccalaureate/associate degree category, 1 semester hour in Personnel Management (7/88). NOTE: Credit should not be awarded for both this course and Introduction to Management Skills (ACEOPS 88-09).

Introduction to Management Skills (ACEOPS 88-09)

Location: Omaha Public Power District, Ft. Calhoun Nuclear Station.

Length: 30 hours (4 days).

Dates: January 1987-Present.

Objective: To provide the student with the skills needed to communicate effectively, plan projects, delegate authority, and manage.

Learning Outcome: Upon successful completion of this course, the student will be able to organize and prepare effective oral and written business communications; identify/set goals and delegate responsibilities; and determine what, when, and how to coach/counsel others.

Instruction: Course covers how to manage your boss, rate yourself, setting priorities, guidelines for effective delegation, the ABCs of management, improving below average performance, and self-assessment profiles and motivation. Methodology includes lecture and classroom exercises.

Credit recommendation: In the lower division baccalaureate/associate degree category, 1 semester hour in Personnel Management (7/88). NOTE: Credit should not be awarded for both this course and Introduction to Personnel Management (ACEOPS 88-08).

Radiological Protection (ACEOPS 88-10)

Location: Omaha Public Power District, Ft. Calhoun Nuclear Station.

Length: 44 hours (6 days).

Dates: January 1987-Present.

Objective: To provide instruction in radiological protection.

Learning Outcome: Upon successful completion of this course, the student will be able to discuss basic principles of nuclear physics; learn biological effects and risks; explain federal and OPPD limits and guidelines for radiation exposures; and explain basic radiological protection techniques.

Instruction: Course covers radioactive decay, radiation interaction with matter, units of measurement, biological effects, radiation protection manual, shielding, contamination, and respiratory protection. Methodology involves lecture.

Credit recommendation: In the lower division baccalaureate/associate degree category, 1 semester hour in Nuclear Engineering Technology (7/88).

Radiation Protection and Detection (ACEOPS 88-11)

Location: Omaha Public Power District, Ft. Calhoun Nuclear Station.

Length: 36 hours (5 days).

Dates: January 1986-January 1987.

Objective: To provide instruction in the fundamentals of radiation protection and detection for a nuclear power plant operator.

Learning Outcome: Upon successful completion of this course, the student will be able to explain the construction and operation of various types of radiation detectors; discuss radiation spectroscopy; discuss principles of nuclear physics; explain federal and OPPD limits and guidelines for radiation exposures; and explain radiation protection techniques for external and internal exposure.

Instruction: Course covers gas-filled detectors, scintillation, semiconductor self-powered, portable radiation monitors, area monitors, radioactive decay, radiation interaction with matter, units of measurements, biological effects, exposure guidelines, and techniques for radiation protection. Methodology involves lecture.

Credit recommendation: In the lower division baccalaureate/associate degree category, 1 semester hour in Nuclear Engineering Technology (7/88).

Basic Concepts of Water Chemistry (ACEOPS 88-13)

Location: Omaha Public Power District, Ft. Calhoun Nuclear Station.

Length: 70 hours (2 weeks).

Dates: January 1987-Present.

Objective: To provide the student with instruction in fundamental water chemistry as it applies to a nuclear power plant.

Learning Outcome: Upon successful completion of this course, the student will be able to define and/or discuss concepts and principles, and perform basic analyses in fundamental chemistry with emphasis on applications in water chemistry and water treatment for the performance and safety of a nuclear power reactor.

Instruction: Course covers chemistry fundamentals, corrosion and corrosion control, water treatment quality and purity, physical and chemical methods for removal of water impurities, and general chemistry techniques used in water chemistry analysis. Methodology includes lecture, discussion, and laboratory.

Credit recommendation: In the lower division baccalaureate/associate degree category, 3 semester hours in Chemistry (7/88).

Basic Concepts of Mechanics, Heat, Electricity and Atomic Physics (ACEOPS 88-14)

Location: Omaha Public Power District, Ft. Calhoun Nuclear Station.

Length: 42 hours (1 week).

Dates: January 1986-Present.

Objective: To provide a survey of various topics in mechanics, heat, electricity, and atomic physics.

Learning Outcome: Upon successful completion of this course, the student will be able to define terms and list units; state laws and explain concepts; and perform calculations and solve problems for a variety of topics related to mechanics, heat, electricity, and atomic physics.

Instruction: Course covers systems of units: English-metric; mass; force; work; energy; power; Newton's laws; electric charge; Coulomb's law; electric fields; temperature; heat; heat transfer; specific heat; enthalpy; entropy; electrostatic potential; atomic structure; nuclear structure; isotopes; mass energy conversion; mass defect; binding energy; fuels: fissile, fissionable, fertile; nuclear interactions and reactions; radioactive decay and types of radiation; and the chart of nuclides. Methodology includes illustrated lecture, discussion, and problem solving.

Credit recommendation: In the lower division baccalaureate/associate degree category, 2 semester hours in Physics (7/88).

Introduction to Nuclear Physics and Power Reactors (ACEHP 88-01)

Location: Omaha Public Power District, Ft. Calhoun Nuclear Station.

Length: 36 hours (1 week).

Dates: January 1988-Present.

Objective: To provide instruction in basic nuclear physics concepts and an overview of power reactors.

Learning Outcome: Upon successful completion of this course, the student will be able to explain the way in which an atom is constructed; discuss sources of radioactivity; explain radiation interaction with matter; discuss the origin of radionuclides; and discuss the design of different power reactors.

Instruction: Course covers the basic atomic nature of matter, binding energy, mass defect, mass energy equivalence, man-made and natural radioactivity, types of radiation, major reactor primary components and control systems utilized in a pressurized water reactor. Methodology involves lecture.

Credit recommendation: In the lower division baccalaureate/associate degree category, 1 semester hour in Radiation Protection Technology (7/88).

Health Physics Fundamentals (ACEHP 88-02)

Location: Omaha Public Power District, Ft. Calhoun Nuclear Station.

Length: 40 hours (5 days).

Dates: January 1988-Present.

Objective: To provide an introduction of health physics fundamentals for radiation protection.

Learning Outcome: Upon successful completion of this course, the student will be able to define basic terms used in radiation protection programs; describe radiation sources and doses; apply basic principles of radioactive decay; and describe the neutron activation process.

Instruction: Course covers basic nuclear terminology, data references, radiation sources, radioactive decay, introduction to radiation, and radiation interactions with matter. Methodology involves lecture.

Credit recommendation: In the lower division baccalaureate/associate degree category, 1 semester hour in Radiation Protection Technology (7/88).

Radiation Measurements, Calculations and Material Handling (ACEHP 88-03)

Location: Omaha Public Power District, Ft. Calhoun Nuclear Station.

Length: 27 hours (4 days).

Dates: January 1988-Present.

Objective: To provide instruction on radiation measurements, basic methods of calculation and radioactive material handling.

Learning Outcome: Upon successful completion of this course, the student will be able to explain the basic principles of radiation detection and measurement; calculate various sample activity concentrations; identify the characteristics and pre-operational testing methods for survey instruments; and describe regulations associated with receipt and shipment of radioactive material.

Instruction: Course covers methods for measuring different types of radiation; calculating parameters that affect sample activity and volume; design characteristics for specific survey instruments; and proper classification, packaging, and shipping of radioactive materials. Methodology involves lecture.

Credit recommendation: In the lower division baccalaureate/associate degree category, 1 semester hour in Radiation Protection Technology (7/88).

Radiation Biology and Exposure Control (ACEHP 88-04)

Location: Omaha Public Power District, Ft. Calhoun Nuclear Station.
Length: 34 hours (4½ days).
Dates: January 1988-Present.
Objective: To provide instruction on radiation biology and radiation exposure as it applies to a radiation protection technician.
Learning Outcome: Upon successful completion of this course, the student will be able to describe the biological effects of ionizing radiation; and perform basic calculations associated with radiation exposure reduction.
Instruction: Course covers cell structure, cell radiosensitivity, scope of regulatory guides 8.13 and 8.29, linear energy transfer, quality factor, exposure rates from radiation sources, ALARA considerations and radiation shielding.
Credit recommendation: In the lower division baccalaureate/associate degree category, 1 semester hour in Radiation Protection Technology (7/88).

Environmental Radioactivity and Accident Evaluation (ACEHP 88-05)

Location: Omaha Public Power District, Ft. Calhoun Nuclear Station.
Length: 21 hours (2 ¾ days).
Dates: January 1988-Present.
Objective: To provide instruction on environmental radioactivity and accident analysis as it applies to a radiation protection technician.
Learning Outcome: Upon successful completion of this course, the student will be able to describe environmental considerations associated with the operation of a nuclear power plant; discuss radiological incident responses; and apply basic principles of incident and accident evaluation.
Instruction: Course covers site selection, land and water food cycles, environmental monitoring, health physics, incident responses, and classes of accidents considered in FSARs. Methodology involves lecture.
Credit recommendation: In the lower division baccalaureate/associate degree category, 1 semester hour in Radiation Protection Technology (7/88).

Airborne Radioactivity Monitoring and Control (ACEHP 88-06)

Location: Omaha Public Power District, Ft. Calhoun Nuclear Station.
Length: 42 hours (5¼ days).
Dates: January 1988-Present.
Objective: To provide instruction on airborne radioactivity monitoring and control as it applies to a radiation protection technician.
Learning Outcome: Upon successful completion of this course, the student will be able to describe the typical sources, causes, sample collection and analysis of airborne radioactivity; apply basic principles to respiratory protection; and explain regulations.
Instruction: Course covers collection and analysis of airborne contaminants, sources and causes of airborne radioactivity, understand the use of different types of respiratory equipment, and learn regulations associated with respiratory programs. Methodology involves lecture.
Credit recommendation: In the lower division baccalaureate/associate degree category, 2 semester hours in Radiation Protection Technology (7/88).

Dosimetry and Contamination Control (ACEHP 88-08)

Location: Omaha Public Power District, Ft. Calhoun Nuclear Station.
Length: 49 hours (7 days).
Dates: January 1988-Present.
Objective: To provide instruction on internal and external radiation dosimetry including contamination control.
Learning Outcome: Upon successful completion of this course, the student will be able to specify the principles of operation of dosimetry instruments; apply basic concepts of internal dosimetry; and explain the principles of contamination control.
Instruction: Course covers instruction on self-reading, thermoluminescent, alarming and remote readout dosimeters, fundamental internal dosimetry, general decontamination techniques, and typical contamination control devices. Methodology involves lecture.
Credit recommendation: In the lower division baccalaureate/associate degree category, 2 semester hours in Radiation Protection Technology (7/88).

Chemistry Lecture (ACECH 88-01)

Location: Omaha Public Power District, Ft. Calhoun Nuclear Station.
Length: 98 hours (13 days).
Dates: January 1988-Present.
Objective: To provide a foundation of chemistry principles.
Learning Outcome: Upon successful completion of this course, the student will be able to discuss atomic structure; compound formation and chemical reactions; discuss the fundamental concepts of gases, acids, bases and salts; and electrical properties of solutions.
Instruction: Course covers pH, atomic structure, properties of gases, compounds, chemical reactions, acids and bases, solutions and specific power plant chemistry. Me-

thodology involves lecture.

Credit recommendation: In the lower division baccalaureate/associate degree category, 3 semester hours in Chemistry Lecture (7/88).

Radiochemistry I (ACECH 88-02)
Location: Omaha Public Power District, Ft. Calhoun Nuclear Station.
Length: 51 hours (1½ weeks).
Dates: January 1988-Present.
Objective: To provide instruction on radiochemistry fundamentals.
Learning Outcome: Upon successful completion of this course, the student will be able to discuss the fundamentals of radiochemistry and radioactive decay; discuss the fundamental concepts associated with reactor plant chemistry.
Instruction: Course covers rate of radioactive decay, interaction of radiation with matter, sources of reactor coolant radiation, effects of power level and time at power on radioactivity production, counting instrumentation, and liquid scintillation counting techniques. Methodology involves lecture.
Credit recommendation: In the upper division baccalaureate category, 2 semester hours in Chemistry (7/88).

Radiochemistry II (ACECH 88-03)
Location: Omaha Public Power District, Ft. Calhoun Nuclear Station.
Length: 66 hours (1½ weeks).
Dates: January 1988-Present.
Objective: To provide instruction on advanced radiochemistry.
Learning Outcome: Upon successful completion of this course, the student will be able to discuss the basic techniques associated with MCA calibration; discuss the basic concepts associated with counting instrumentation; discuss the fission product releases; and describe the parameters used to evaluate primary and secondary leakage.
Instruction: Course covers gamma ray spectrometer, defective fuel and core damage, primary to secondary leakage and steam generator tube rupture, borated water problems, and toxic gas monitors. Methodology includes lecture and laboratory.
Credit recommendation: In the upper division baccalaureate category, 3 semester hours in Chemistry (7/88).

Omega Institute

Since 1980, Omega Institute has been actively involved in providing comprehensive paralegal training for the greater Philadelphia and southern New Jersey community.

Although Omega has facilities both in Cherry Hill and Cinnaminson, New Jersey, all of the paralegal classes are held at the Cinnaminson location.

The program of study consists of four hundred and fifty hours of classroom instruction and a one hundred and fifty hour internship where the student is placed on the job in an actual legal environment to utilize and refine his/her skills. The classroom portion of the course is further divided into a series of daily "labs" which are designed to provide the student with assignments that a working paralegal would actually encounter. The entire program strongly emphasizes the development of practical job-related skills.

Daytime classes are held Monday through Friday (9:00 A.M. to 3:00 P.M. and evening classes are held Monday, Wednesday, and Thursday 6:00 P.M. to 10:00 P.M.

Omega Institute is accredited by the Association of Independent Colleges and Schools (AICS) and is involved with a host of local, state, and national paralegal associations.

Source of official student records: Omega Institute, Route 130, South Cinnaminson, New Jersey 08077, or The Registry of Credit Recommendations, American Council on Education, One Dupont Circle, Washington, D.C. 20036.

Additional information about the courses: Program on Noncollegiate Sponsored Instruction, The Center for Adult Learning and Educational Credentials, American Council on Education, One Dupont Circle, Washington, D.C., 20036 or the Program on Noncollegiate Sponsored Instruction, Thomas A. Edison State College, 101 West State Street, CN 545, Trenton, New Jersey 08625.

Constitutional Law and Governmental Agencies
  a. Administrative Law (#202)
  b. Public Rights and Remedies (#206)
Location: Cinnaminson, NJ.
Length: *a.* 25 hours (4 days); *b.* 24 hours (4 days).
Dates: January 1984-Present.
Objective: *a.* To introduce students to the purpose and function of various governmental administrative agencies; *b.* To introduce students to the area of basic constitutional rights.
Instruction: *a.* This course includes an overview of various federal and state administrative agencies, working of these agencies and the forms used within them, utilization of paralegals within the government agencies. Stress is on the nature of administrative agencies, their proceedings, hearings, findings, and function of the paralegal as advocate within Public Law in contrast and relation to Private Law.
b. This course covers a study of the basic constitutional rights, focusing on such contemporary issues as Civil Rights, Welfare Rights, Tenant and Housing Rights, Fair/Equal Employment Rights and Consumer Rights. In addition to regular written exercises, the students must

pass a midterm and a final examination in both *a.* and *b.*

Credit recommendation: In the lower division baccalaureate/associate degree category, 3 semester hours in Constitutional Law and Governmental Agencies (6/86) (11/88).

Corporate Law (#203)
Location: Cinnaminson, NJ.
Length: 40 hours (7 days).
Dates: January 1984-Present.
Objective: To provide an overview to corporate law and to enable students to assist with legal documents in this field.
Instruction: This course is a survey of the basic principles of the various forms of business, including the sole proprietorship, the partnership, and the corporation. Students are instructed in the formation, operation, and dissolution of these forms of business. Students are taught how to prepare the basic legal documents connected with this field of law including, but not limited to, documents necessary for incorporation, amendments to a corporate charter, by-laws, and director's meetings and minutes, stock certificates, corporate resolutions, corporate minutes, fictitious name applications and partnership agreements. In addition to regular written exercises, the students must pass a midterm and a final examination.
Credit recommendation: In the lower division baccalaureate/associate degree category, 2 semester hours in Corporate Law (6/86) (11/88).

Civil Litigation Practice
a. Judgments, Executions & Remedies (#204)
b. Civil Litigation (#207)
Location: Cinnaminson, NJ.
Length: *a.* 35 hours (6 days); *b.* 48 hours (8 days).
Dates: January 1984-Present.
Objective: *a.* To present a summary of debtor/creditor law; *b.* To introduce students to civil court procedures.
Instruction: *a.* The first portion of this course summarizes the areas of debtor/creditor law and examines creditor's rights in attachment, garnishment, replevin, receivership, and execution sales, followed by an overview of secured transactions covering creditors with special rights. The second portion of this course is devoted to bankruptcy practice and covers in detail the law and procedures for processing a Chapter 7, Chapter 11, or Chapter 13 bankruptcy petition together with creditor's and bankrupt's rights and defenses. In the final portion of this course, students are exposed to a review of the basic systems and procedures used in legal systems and offices with special emphasis on alternative forms of filing systems, organization of work schedules, and management of office personnel.
b. This course examines the functions and processes of our judicial system and the role of a legal assistant in the law with emphasis on the canons of ethics of the American Bar Association and the National Association of Legal Assistants. This area analyzes civil court procedure rules and filing requirements.

In addition to regular written exercises, the students must pass a midterm and a final examination in both *a.* and *b.*

Credit recommendation: In the lower division baccalaureate/associate degree category, 4 semester hours in Civil Litigation Practice (6/86) (11/88).

Contract Law (#205)
Location: Cinnaminson, NJ.
Length: 36 hours (6 days).
Dates: January 1984-Present.
Objective: To provide students with an overview of Commercial Law.
Instruction: This course provides students with an overview of the field of commercial law with emphasis on the formation of contracts, consideration, statute of frauds, the capacity to contract, third-party beneficiaries, parole evidence, breach of contract, and remedies. Instructions in these areas will center on the Uniform Commercial Code and students will gain experience in basic contract drafting techniques. In addition to regular written exercises, the students must pass a midterm and a final examination.
Credit recommendation: In the lower division baccalaureate/associate degree category, 2 semester hours in Contract Law (6/86) 11/88).

Legal Research and Writing (#208)
Location: Cinnaminson, NJ.
Length: 36 hours (6 days).
Dates: January 1984-Present.
Objective: To present an introduction to the area of Legal Research and Writing.
Instruction: This course provides an introduction to the federal and state systems of legal research with utilization of primary sources, secondary materials, and related finding tools. Examination and instruction on the use of the legal library, legal terminology, the structure and citation of court opinions, the writing of legal memoranda and briefs; and the development of other appropriate legal writing techniques are also included. In additions to regular written exercises, the students must have two graded memoranda.
Credit recommendation: In the lower division baccalaureate/associate degree category, 2 semester hours in Legal Research and Writing (6/86) (11/88).

Estates and Trusts (#209)
Location: Cinnaminson, NJ.
Length: 36 hours (6 days).
Dates: January 1984-Present.
Objective: To present an introduction to the Probate Court System and activities related to it.
Instruction: This course includes a study of the New

Jersey Probate Court system, including probate procedures and administration of estates, methods for settlement of estates, inheritance and estate taxes. Estate planning and review of the techniques and principles applicable thereto; preparation of will and trust documents. In addition to regular written exercises, the students must pass a midterm and a final examination.

Credit recommendation: In the lower division baccalaureate/associate degree category, 2 semester hours in Estates and Trusts (6/86) (11/88).

Domestic Relations (#210)
Location: Cinnaminson, NJ.
Length: 36 hours (6 days).
Dates: January 1984-Present.
Objective: To present an overview of the legal issues involved in Domestic Relations.
Instruction: This course covers the law of domestic relations, including marriage annulment, dissolution and judicial separation, alimony, legitimacy of children, custody and adoption. It also points out means to obtain basic divorce information while working under the supervision of a lawyer, and using the data to pursue successful completion of divorce. In addition to regular written exercises, the students must pass a midterm and a final examination.
Credit recommendation: In the lower division baccalaureate/associate degree category, 2 semester hours in Domestic Relations (6/86) (11/88).

Real and Personal Property (#211)
Location: Cinnaminson, NJ.
Length: 42 hours (7 days)
Dates: January 1984-Present.
Objective: To present an overview of the Real and Personal Property.
Instruction: This course surveys the types and ways of owning real and personal property with an emphasis on estates in land, future interest, concurrent and marital estates, easements and covenants. Students gain experience in these various interests in property and how they are created, including liens, mortgages, and the methods for transferring title to land. In addition to regular written exercises, the students must pass a midterm and a final examination.
Credit recommendation: In the lower division baccalaureate/associate degree category, 2 semester hours in Real and Personal Property (6/86) (11/88).

Torts (#213)
Location: Cinnaminson, NJ.
Length: 42 hours (7 days).
Dates: January 1984-Present.
Objective: To familiarize students with the provisions of the Law of Torts.
Instruction: This course gives students an overview of traditional tort law, including intentional torts such as battery, assault, false imprisonment, conversion and emotional distress and negligent torts, along with their defenses. Students are also instructed in the areas of strict liability, nuisance, misrepresentation, defamation, invasion of privacy and trespass, and finally in New Jersey no-fault law. In addition to regular written exercises, the students must pass a midterm and a final examination.
Credit recommendation: In the lower division baccalaureate/associate degree category, 2 semester hours in Torts (6/86) (11/88).

Opportunities Academy of Management Training, Inc.

The Opportunities Academy of Management Training, Inc. was founded in September 1974 with the goal of providing community-based management, operational, and economic development training, as well as other services, for a broad range of clients. The objectives of the Academy are (1) to provide training programs for the Opportunities Industrialization Center's (OIC) national and international network; and (2) to provide the nonprofit sector with a resource of management skills training courses for professionals and paraprofessional who help minorities and disadvantaged populations improve their performance and potential.

The Academy offers a broad range of courses which deal with identifying management and operational needs, promoting economic development, providing career development, and facilitating financial management.

Source of official student records: Director's Office, Opportunities Academy of Management Training, Inc., 1415 North Broad Street, Philadelphia, Pennsylvania 19122.

Additional information about the courses: Program on Noncollegiate Sponsored Instruction, The Center for Adult Learning and Educational Credentials, American Council on Education, One Dupont Circle, Washington, D.C. 20036.

Adult Basic Education
Location: Regional Centers throughout the U.S.
Length: 30 hours (1 week).
Dates: May 1979-Present.
Objective: To provide the student with an analysis of problems associated with adult basic education and techniques for solving those problems.
Learning Outcome: Upon successful completion of this course, the student will be able to understand the basic characteristics of adult education students; and develop a curriculum for adult basic education students.
Instruction: Course emphasizes the characteristics of adult basic education students, development of curriculum, and counseling/instructional strategies. Workshop, laboratory, discussion, and lecture are used.

Credit recommendation: In the lower division baccalaureate/associate degree category, 2 semester hours in Education or Communications (12/79) (2/88). NOTE: This course has been reevaluated and continues to meet requirements for credit recommendations.

Advanced Adult Basic Education
  Location: Regional Centers throughout the U.S.
  Length: 30 hours (1 week).
  Dates: February 1983-Present.
  Objective: To enable the student to expand on the knowledge learned in Adult Basic Education and identifying the unique characteristics of adult learners as well as analyze appropriate teaching styles.
  Learning Outcome: Upon successful completion of this course, the student will be able to discuss the unique characteristics of adult learners; and practice teaching styles and different techniques.
  Instruction: Course content includes an analysis of the characteristics of adult learners, teaching styles and techniques, and curriculum development, with strong emphasis on affective learning, motivation, communication, and personal growth. Use of lectures, small-group exercises, and self-assessment. **Prerequisite:** Adult Basic Education.
  Credit recommendation: In the upper division or graduate degree category, 2 semester hours in Education (for example Counseling Education, Urban Education, Education Psychology, Adult Education) (3/83) (3/88). NOTE 1: Students who receive credit for this course should not receive credit for Affective Education and Advanced Affective Education. NOTE 2: This course has been reevaluated and continues to meet requirements for credit recommendations.

Advanced Affective Educational Techniques
  Location: Regional Centers throughout the U.S.
  Length: 30 hours (1 week).
  Dates: February 1983-Present.
  Objective: To allow the student to explore the use of advanced affective education as an instructional method in order to involve individuals in the learning process through dedicated and experiential learning.
  Learning Outcome: Upon successful completion of this course, the student will be able to process affective education techniques into existing curriculum; and integrate effective and cognitive dimensions of learning and teaching in the classroom.
  Instruction: Major emphasis is on learning advanced affective educational techniques and the process of integrating them into existing curriculum or programs through small group activities, structured exercises, outside assignments, self-assessment instruments and lectures. Emphasis is on the importance of integrating the effective and cognitive dimensions of learning and teaching in the classroom.
  Credit recommendation: In the upper division baccalaureate category, or in the graduate degree category, 2 semester hours in Administration (e.g., Personnel), Education (e.g., Counselor Education, Education Psychology, Humanistic Education, Urban Education), or Psychology (3/83) (3/88). NOTE 1: Students who receive credit for this course should not receive credit for Affective Education or Advanced Adult Basic Education Techniques. NOTE 2: This course has been reevaluated and continues to meet requirements for credit recommendations.

Advanced Counseling
  Location: Regional Centers throughout the U.S.
  Length: 30 hours (1 week).
  Dates: February 1983-Present.
  Objective: To teach the student advanced approaches and methods used in individuals, group and career counseling.
  Learning Outcome: Upon successful completion of this course, the student will be able to conduct personal growth groups; facilitate group sessions and assessments of clients; and increase communication skills through self-awareness and self-reliance.
  Instruction: The course is designed to review the dynamics of human behavior in order to increase communication effectiveness, self-awareness and self reliance. An overview of advanced communication, structuring and conducting personal growth groups, facilitating group sessions and assessments of clients, counselors and programs will be covered through lecturable group experience, individual assessments, homework, team building exercises. Student who wish to receive credit in Career Counseling must have taken Counseling for the Disadvantaged.
  Prerequisite: For Career Counseling credit, Counseling for the Disadvantaged must be taken.
  Credit recommendation: In the upper division baccalaureate category, or in the graduate degree category, 2 semester hours in Education (e.g., Adult Education, Counseling Education, Urban Education, Vocational Education), Social Work, or Social Welfare (3/83) (3/88). NOTE: This course has been reevaluated and continues to meet requirements for credit recommendations.

Advanced Job Development
  Location: Regional Centers throughout the U.S.
  Length: 30 hours (1 week).
  Dates: April 1981-Present.
  Objective: To allow the student explore with participants up-to-date methods and techniques of job development.
  Learning Outcome: Upon successful completion of this course, the student will be able to obtain and hold a job; implement EEO policy and legal aspects of development; and document employer contacts and conduct follow-up studies on job placements.
  Instruction: Course covers the techniques for getting and holding the right job, EEO policy and the legal aspects

of development, labor market analysis, documentation of employer contacts and follow-up, and utilization of the Dictionary of Occupational Titles.

Credit recommendation: In the upper division baccalaureate category, 2 semester hours in Distributive Education, Career or Occupational Counseling, Urban Education, or Social Welfare (3/83) (3/88). NOTE 1: Students who receive credit for this course should not receive credit for Employment Analysis: Development and Placement for the Disadvantaged. NOTE 2: This course has been reevaluated and continues to meet requirements for credit recommendations.

Advanced Management Skill Training

Location: Regional Centers throughout the U.S.
Length: 30 hours (1 week).
Dates: August 1981-Present.
Objective: To increase the effectiveness of experienced managers and administrators, through a survey of management theories and their application to participants' own organizations.
Learning Outcome: Upon successful completion of this course, the student will be able to implement theories of management and organizational development; conduct performance appraisal, financial monitoring, problem analysis, and conflict management; and design a strategic plan for his/her own organization.
Instruction: Provides an extensive review of major contemporary theories of management and organizational development, along with specific information on management techniques, such as performance appraisal, financial monitoring, problem analysis, and conflict management. Culminates in a planning exercise in which each participant designs a strategic plan for his/her own organization. Specific content and format may vary, depending on the particular location and participants served.
Credit recommendation: In the graduate degree category, 2 semester hours in Administration or Management (3/83) (3/88). NOTE: This course has been reevaluated and continues to meet requirements for credit recommendations.

Advanced Motivation

Location: Regional Centers throughout the U.S.
Length: 30 hours (1 week).
Dates: March 1981-Present.
Objective: To provide the student with knowledge and experimental exercises for those directly involved in the process of motivating others.
Learning Outcome: Upon successful completion of this course, the student will be able to utilize techniques of motivation, interpersonal communication, group dynamics, and life planning; and reassess and redefine personal needs and motivation.
Instruction: Course covers review of the major theories and techniques of motivation, interpersonal communication both verbal and nonverbal, group dynamics, and life planning. The course is structured to provide opportunities for participants to reassess and redefine personal needs and motivation.
Credit recommendation: In the upper division baccalaureate or graduate degree category, 2 semester hours in Counseling Psychology, Counseling, Adult Education, or Social Work (3/83) (3/88). NOTE: This course has been reevaluated and continues to meet requirements for credit recommendations.

Affective Education

Location: Philadelphia, PA and other regional locations.
Length: 30 hours (1 week).
Dates: March 1978-May 1984.
Objective: To explore the use of affective education as an instructional method in order to involve individuals in the learning process.
Instruction: Course covers the study of people, their perceptions, and experiential learning; identification of dysfunctional behavioral patterns and their effect on interpersonal relations and the accomplishment of group tasks. Role playing, gaming, simulation, lecture, and laboratory are used.
Credit recommendation: In the upper division baccalaureate category or in the graduate degree category, 2 semester hours in Administration (e.g., Personnel), Education (e.g., Counselor Education, Educational Psychology, Humanistic Education, Urban Education), or Psychology (3/78) (3/83). NOTE 1: Students who receive credit for this course should not receive credit for Advanced Adult Basic Educational Techniques or Advanced Affective Educational Techniques. NOTE 2: This course has been reevaluated and continues to meet requirements for credit recommendations.

Community Corporate Planning Process

Location: Regional Centers throughout the U.S.
Length: 30 hours (1 week).
Dates: January 1980-Present.
Objective: To allow the student to examine the community economic development and corporate planning processes.
Learning Outcome: Upon successful completion of this course, the student will be able to understand and analyze long- and short-term economic planning; and understand various components essential to effective corporate planning.
Instruction: Course covers detailed analysis of long- and short-term economic planning, investment methodologies, and the various components essential to effective corporation planning. Methodology includes lecture, discussion, case studies, small- and large-group interaction.
Credit recommendation: In the lower division bac-

calaureate/associate degree category, 3 semester hours in Urban Studies (12/79) (3/88). NOTE: This course has been reevaluated and continues to meet requirements for credit recommendations.

Community Economic Development Policy and Analysis
   Location: Regional Centers throughout the U.S.
   Length: 30 hours (1 week).
   Dates: January 1980-Present.
   Objective: To provide the student with a general foundation in the theory, technology, process, and art of local economic development.
   Learning Outcome: Upon successful completion of this course, the student will be able to understand the theory and history of community economic development; and analyze the current federal and state policies affecting community development programs.
   Instruction: Course covers presentation of community economic development theory and history, terms and concepts used in the community economic development field, survey of organizational models, analysis of current federal and state policies affecting community-development programs. Lecture, discussion, and laboratory are used.
   Credit recommendation: In the upper division baccalaureate category, 3 semester hours in Economics, Sociology, or Urban Studies (12/79) (3/88). NOTE: This course has been reevaluated and continues to meet requirements for credit recommendations.

Community Involvement
   Location: Regional Centers throughout the U.S.
   Length: 30 hours (1 week).
   Dates: February 1976-Present.
   Objective: To enable students to work effectively within the community.
   Learning Outcome: Upon successful completion of this course, the student will be able to utilize community resources in the initiation and operation of community-based organizations; and refer to proper community group.
   Instruction: Course describes ways in which the community can become involved in the initiation and operation of community-based organizations modeled after Opportunities Industrialization Centers. The community includes poor people, clients, service vendors, labor unions, and industry. Methodology includes laboratory, discussion, and workshop.
   Credit recommendation: In the lower division baccalaureate/associate degree category, 2 semester hours in Social Work or Urban Studies (12/79) (3/88). NOTE: This course has been reevaluated and continues to meet requirements for credit recommendations.

Community Participation in Local Economic Development
   Location: Regional Centers throughout the U.S.
   Length: 30 hours (1 week).
   Dates: January 1980-Present.
   Objective: To acquaint the student with processes, problems, and issues involved in dealing with community economics.
   Learning Outcome: Upon successful completion of this course, the student will be able to assess community needs and translate the needs into strategies; and organize the community for effective participation in the Community Economic Development process.
   Instruction: Course covers the role of the community in the local economic decision-making process, including assessing community needs, translating needs into strategies, and organizing the community for effective participation in the Community Economic Development process.
   Credit recommendation: In the upper division baccalaureate category, 3 semester hours in Social Work or Urban Studies (12/79) (3/88). NOTE: This course has been reevaluated and continues to meet requirements for credit recommendations.

Comprehensive Employment and Training Act
   Location: Philadelphia, PA and other regional locations.
   Length: 30 hours (1 week).
   Dates: September 1975-March 1983.
   Objective: To present a history of manpower programs, emphasizing recent CETA legislation in order to create effective manpower systems.
   Instruction: Course covers techniques for implementing the legislation review models for effective program design. Reviews recent PSE amendments and explores their impact on the economy. Covers manpower policy, CETA, PSE Title VI Project, Youth Legislation (Job Corps, Youth Adult Conservation Corps, Youth Entitlement, Comprehensive Youth Program). Lecture, workshop, and laboratory are used.
   Credit recommendation: In the graduate degree category, 2 semester hours in Human Resources, Labor Policy, Public Administration, or Urban Education (3/78) (3/83). NOTE: This course has been reevaluated and continues to meet requirements for credit recommendations.

Corporate Training for Nonprofit Organizations
   Location: Philadelphia, PA and other regional locations.
   Length: 32 hours (1 week).
   Dates: March 1978-Present.
   Objective: To enable supervisors and managers to develop and use a comprehensive corporate plan based on management and behavioral theories.
   Learning Outcome: Upon successful completion of this

course, the student will be able to implement corporate planning and action steps; develop operational goals and unit objectives; and conduct budgeting and performance assessments.

Instruction: Course covers corporate planning, operational goals, unit objectives, budgeting, action steps, performance assessment. Lecture, discussion, and laboratory are used.

Credit recommendation: In the graduate degree category, 2 semester hours in Administration or Management (3/78) (3/83) (3/88). NOTE: This course has been reevaluated and continues to meet requirements for credit recommendations.

Counseling for the Disadvantaged
  Location: Philadelphia, PA and other regional locations.
  Length: 30 hours (1 week).
  Dates: October 1975-Present.
  Objective: To teach the student the approaches and methods used in career counseling for the economically disadvantaged.
  Instruction: Course covers counseling techniques, the uses and limitations of counseling in manpower programs, vocational assessment, and role definition of counselors. Case study, lecture, and laboratory are used.
  Credit recommendation: In the upper division baccalaureate category or in the graduate degree category, 2 semester hours in Education (e.g., Adult Education, Counseling Education, Urban Education, Vocational Education) or Social Welfare (3/78) (3/83) (3/88). NOTE: This course has been reevaluated and continues to meet requirements for credit recommendations.

Employment Analysis: Development and Placement for the Disadvantaged
(Job Development for the Disadvantaged)
  Location: Philadelphia, PA and other regional locations.
  Length: 30 hours (1 week).
  Dates: October 1975-March 1984.
  Objective: To introduce methods and techniques for developing employment opportunities for the disadvantaged.
  Instruction: Course presents a method for creating and using an employment information and placement system. Affirmative action, in-service training models, follow-up techniques in field visitation, development of employer advisory committees. Lecture and laboratory are used.
  Credit recommendation: In the upper division baccalaureate category, 2 semester hours in Education (e.g., Distributive Education, Urban Education) or Social Welfare (3/78) (3/83). NOTE 1: Students who receive credit for this course should not receive credit for Advanced Job Techniques. NOTE 2: This course has been reevaluated and continues to meet requirements for credit recommendations.

Employment and Training Services to Ex-Offenders
  Location: Regional Centers throughout the U.S.
  Length: 30 hours (1 week).
  Dates: March 1977-Present.
  Objective: To familiarize students with the goals and structure of manpower programs for ex-offenders.
  Learning Outcome: Upon successful completion of this course, the student will be able to utilize laws regarding ex-offenders' right to work; and develop techniques for teaching and counseling ex-offenders.
  Instruction: Course covers profile of the ex-offender, laws regarding ex-offenders' right to work, techniques for teaching and counseling ex-offenders. Lectures, group and individual exercises, films, and visits to a detention center are used.
  Credit recommendation: In the lower division baccalaureate/associate degree category, 2 semester hours in Education, Criminal Justice, Social Work, or Social Welfare (12/79) (3/88). NOTE: This course has been reevaluated and continues to meet requirements for credit recommendations.

Employment and Training Services to Former Drug Abusers
(Employment and Training Services to Ex-Substance Abusers)
  Location: Regional Centers throughout the U.S.
  Length: 30 hours (1 week).
  Dates: September 1979-Present.
  Objective: To provide the student with practical information and develop vocational counseling skills for counselors, instructors, and job developers serving former drug abusers.
  Learning Outcome: Upon successful completion of this course, the student will be able to implement communication and counseling techniques in serving former drug abusers; survey community resources including rehabilitation programs; and teach effectively with former drug abusers.
  Instruction: Course covers discussion of motivation, communication, counseling techniques; survey of community resources, including rehabilitation programs, testing services, film libraries, etc., in the local area. Lectures, group discussion, and group exercises are used.
  Credit recommendation: In the vocational certificate category, 2 semester hours in Criminal Justice, Social Work, or Social Welfare (12/79) (3/88). NOTE: This course has been reevaluated and continues to meet requirements for credit recommendations.

Employment and Training Services to Limited English-Speaking Populations
  Location: Regional Centers throughout the U.S.
  Length: 30 hours (1 week).

Dates: August 1979-Present.
Objective: To allow the student to identify the special needs and problems of persons with limited English-speaking ability.
Learning Outcome: Upon successful completion of this course, the student will be able to understand acculturation process; implement equal educational opportunity; and utilize diverse media for teaching English as a Second Language.
Instruction: Topics covered include acculturation processes, unemployment, equal educational opportunity, diverse media for teaching English as a second language, available community resources, practical expressions, and dialogues. Methodology includes case studies, discussions, laboratory learning experiences, and lecture.
Credit recommendation: In the lower division baccalaureate/associate degree category, 2 semester hours in Education, English as a Second Language, Social Work, or Urban Studies (12/79) (3/88). NOTE: This course has been reevaluated and continues to meet requirements for credit recommendations.

Employment and Training Services to Older Workers
Location: Regional Centers throughout the U.S.
Length: 30 hours (1 week).
Dates: September 1979-Present.
Objective: To sensitize participants to cultural attitudes toward older persons and to examine the social service needs of America's aging population.
Learning Outcome: Upon successful completion of this course, the student will be able to understand the legal rights of older persons and some of their needs; and develop social service needs for older person.
Instruction: Course covers profile of the aging population; brief overview of the legal rights of older persons, their needs in the areas of counseling, education and job training, health, recreation, and consumer awareness; survey of community resources for older persons. Methodology includes lecture, discussion, and group and individual exercises.
Credit recommendation: In the lower division baccalaureate/associate degree category, 2 semester hours in Social Welfare, Sociology, or Urban Studies (12/79) (3/88). NOTE: This course has been reevaluated and continues to meet requirements for credit recommendations.

Functions of a Manager
Location: Philadelphia, PA and other regional locations.
Length: 32 hours (1 week).
Dates: December 1973-March 1984.
Objective: To increase the effectiveness of supervisors and managers by providing knowledge of modern management concepts and techniques as they relate to planning, leadership, organization, and control.
Instruction: Course covers time management priority setting, decision making, staff selection and development, analysis of performance discrepancies, and communication. Lecture, discussion, and case studies are used.
Credit recommendation: In the graduate degree category, 2 semester hours in Business Administration or Management (3/78) (3/83). NOTE: This course has been reevaluated and continues to meet requirements for credit recommendations.

Fundamentals of the Local Economic Development Process
Location: Regional Centers throughout the U.S.
Length: 30 hours (1 week).
Dates: January 1980-Present.
Objective: To enable the student to identify techniques for assessing community needs for economic development.
Learning Outcome: Upon successful completion of this course, the student will be able to assess community needs for economic devleopment; gain knowledge about public and private resources available to promote development; and present organizational strategies for commercial development.
Instruction: Course covers analysis of local economic forces, introduction to information sources and techniques for analyzing local economic problems and formulating development strategies, and examination of case studies of local development organizations. Lecture, discussions, and group and individual exercises are used.
Credit recommendation: In the upper division baccalaureate category, 2 semester hours in Economics, Economic Geography, or Urban Studies (12/79) (3/88). NOTE: This course has been reevaluated and continues to meet requirements for credit recommendations.

Improving Management Skills
Location: Philadelphia, PA and other regional locations.
Length: 32 hours (1 week).
Dates: January 1975-March 1984.
Objective: To enable supervisors and managers to improve their ability to use the concepts of problem solving and decision making in the communication process.
Instruction: Course covers styles of managing conflict, conducting meetings, conference and group interaction, planning and proposal analysis, transactional analysis, business writing. Lecture, discussion, and case studies are used.
Credit recommendation: In the graduate degree category, 2 semester hours in Administration or Management (3/78) (3/83). NOTE: This course has been reevaluated and continues to meet requirements for credit recommendations.

Introduction of Accounting and Internal Control
Location: Philadelphia, PA and other regional loca-

tions.
Length: 30 hours (1 week).
Dates: December 1977-Present.
Objective: To provide the student with a basic understanding of the accounting cycle.
Learning Outcome: Upon successful completion of this course, the student will be able to understand the accounting cycle; and record, classify, summarize, and report on financial information.
Instruction: Course covers the accounting cycle, including recording, classifying, summarizing, reporting; accounting equation, including assets and liabilities, fund balancing, including general cash disbursements, receipts and payroll journals; trial balancing, including balance sheets, statement of revenue and expenses, statement of functional expenses; internal control, including accounting controls and management controls. Lecture and laboratory are used.
Credit recommendation: In the lower division baccalaureate/associate degree category, 2 semester hours in Accounting (3/78) (3/83) (3/88). NOTE: This course has been reevaluated and continues to meet requirements for credit recommendations.

Management and Ownership Training
Location: Philadelphia, PA and other regional locations.
Length: *Version 1:* 390 hours (13 weeks); day. *Version 2:* 182 hours (14 weeks); night.
Dates: January 1968-March 1984.
Objective: To provide persons who are entering business, who own businesses, or who are interested in managing businesses owned by other persons with training on how to own and operate successful businesses.
Instruction: *Versions 1 and 2:* Course covers ownership, management, business mathematics, finance, business communication, business law, accounting and taxation, business and politics, marketing, federal taxation, economic concepts, and stock and bonds. *Version 1:* An internship model for individuals with no business experience. *Version 2:* A work-study model for persons with business experience who work in a business setting. Course uses internship, lecture, seminar, and laboratory.
Credit recommendation: *Versions 1 and 2:* In the upper division baccalaureate category, 30 semester hours, or in the graduate degree category, 30 semester hours, or in the graduate degree category, 15 semester hours in Administration, Business, or Management (3/78) (3/83). NOTE: This course has been reevaluated and continues to meet requirements for credit recommendations.

Management Control in Nonprofit Organizations
Location: Philadelphia, PA and other regional locations.
Length: 30 hours (1 week).
Dates: November 1976-March 1984.
Objective: To provide the student with knowledge and skills in structuring financial and statistical data for management planning, control, and evaluation.
Instruction: Course covers fundamentals of management control in nonprofit organizations, e.g., output measures, program accounting, responsibility accounting, other control concepts, relationship of program and responsibility structure, and management cycle. Lecture and laboratory are used.
Credit recommendation: In the upper division baccalaureate category or in the graduate degree category, 2 semester hours in Administration or Management (3/78) (3/83). NOTE: This course has been reevaluated and continues to meet requirements for credit recommendations.

Management Skills for Economic Development
Location: Regional Centers throughout the U.S.
Length: 30 hours (1 week).
Dates: January 1980-Present.
Objective: To enable the student to analyze the role of management in economic development.
Learning Outcome: Upon successful completion of this course, the student will be able to understand the theories and concepts of management.
Instruction: Course covers theories and concepts of management, along with specific economic development models. Methodology includes lecture, guided discussions, role playing, and laboratory learning experiences.
Credit recommendation: In the lower division baccalaureate/associate degree category, 2 semester hours in Management or Urban Studies (12/79) (3/88). NOTE: This course has been reevaluated and continues to meet requirements for credit recommendations.

Managerial Accounting
Location: Regional Centers throughout the U.S.
Length: 30 hours (1 week).
Dates: January 1980-Present.
Objective: To provide the student with basic information about accounting in profit and nonprofit organizations.
Learning Outcome: Upon successful completion of this course, the student will be able to compute balance sheets, income statements and cash flow; and understand financial statement analysis and financial forecasting.
Instruction: Course covers balance sheets, income statements, cash flow, financial statement analysis, and financial forecasting. Lectures and exercises are used.
Credit recommendation: In the lower division baccalaureate/associate degree category, 2 semester hours in Accounting (12/79) (3/88). NOTE: This course has been reevaluated and continues to meet requirements for credit recommendations.

Manpower Services to Disadvantaged Youth
Location: Philadelphia, PA and other regional loca-

tions.
Length: 30 hours (1 week).
Dates: March 1978-Present.
Objective: To help the student understand, work with, and provide manpower services for youth.
Learning Outcome: Upon successful completion of this course, the student will be able to develop strategies to work with disadvantaged youth; and develop techniques for recruiting and placing disadvantaged youth.
Instruction: Course identifies manpower needs of youth, presents strategies which serve the economically disadvantaged. Identification and recruitment; basic education; vocational training; counseling and placement; potential occupational development to obtain regular competitive employment; job and labor market information; community resources and referral agencies; the criminal justice system relative to youth and models of youth programs, e.g., Neighborhood Youth Corps (NYC), Urban Conservations Corps (UCC), Job Corps, and Urban Career Education Center (UCEC). Lecture, discussion, and laboratory are used.
Credit recommendation: In the upper division baccalaureate category or in the graduate degree category, 2 semester hours in Education (e.g., Counselor Education, Urban Education), Human Services, Juvenile Justice, Public and Urban Policy, or Social Work (3/78) (3/83) (3/88). NOTE: This course has been reevaluated and continues to meet requirements for credit recommendations.

Methods in Prevocational Training
(Prevocational Training)
Location: Philadelphia, PA and other regional locations.
Length: 30 hours (1 week).
Dates: November 1975-Present.
Objective: To teach instructors methodology for providing basic education to adults.
Learning Outcome: Upon successful completion of this course, the student will be able to develop and select materials necessary for the design and implementation of adult basic education programs.
Instruction: Course covers methods of motivation and individualized instruction, and development and selection of materials necessary for the design and implementation of adult basic education programs. Lecture, laboratory, and workshops are used.
Credit recommendation: In the upper division baccalaureate category, 2 semester hours in Education (3/78) (3/83) (3/88). NOTE: This course has been reevaluated and continues to meet requirements for credit recommendations.

Motivating the Disadvantaged
Location: Philadelphia, PA and other regional locations.
Length: 30 hours (1 week).
Dates: October 1975-March 1984.
Objective: To provide the student with knowledge about attitudes and expectations of the disadvantaged and unemployed.
Instruction: Course covers philosophies and models of human motivation (Maslow, McGregor); counseling and testing; methods, techniques, and strategies for motivating; and staff development and communications techniques. Lecture, discussion, and laboratory are used.
Credit recommendation: In the upper division baccalaureate category or in the graduate degree category, 2 semester hours in Education (e.g., Counselor Education, Psychology of Education, Urban Education) and Psychology (3/78) (3/83). NOTE: This course has been reevaluated and continues to meet requirements for credit recommendations.

Open-Entry/Open-Exit Skill Training
Location: Philadelphia, PA and other regional locations.
Length: 30 hours (1 week).
Dates: September 1976-March 1984.
Objective: To provide the student instructional methods for use in training groups with people of varied backgrounds and skill levels.
Instruction: Course covers techniques for planning and implementation of a particular skill training system, including organization and management of open-entry/open-exit skill training; role of the counselor and job developer; techniques for developing curriculum; in-service training for instructors and staff; role of employer in developing curriculum; placement from open-entry/open-exit skill training. Lecture, workshops, and laboratory are used.
Credit recommendation: In the upper division baccalaureate category, 2 semester hours in Education (e.g., Adult Education, Counselor Education, Urban Education, or Vocational Education) (3/78) (3/83). NOTE: This course has been reevaluated and continues to meet requirements for credit recommendations.

Personnel Management
Location: Philadelphia, PA and other regional locations.
Length: 32 hours (1 week).
Dates: December 1977-March 1984.
Objective: To increase managers' effectiveness in personnel relations.
Instruction: Course covers selection and development of subordinates, appraisal by objectives, grievance handling, the manager and the law, and analysis of performance discrepancies. Lecture, discussion, and case studies are used.
Credit recommendation: In the graduate degree category, 2 semester hours in Administration or Management (3/78) (3/83). NOTE: This course has been reevaluated

Program Assessment and Evaluation
Location: Philadelphia, PA and other regional locations.
Length: 30 hours (1 week).
Dates: August 1976-Present.
Objective: To introduce the student to methods used to determine how effectively a program achieves its objectives.
Learning Outcome: Upon successful completion of this course, the student will be able to discuss the use of manual and computerized information systems; and develop tools for assessing and evaluating programs.
Instruction: Course covers various levels of review; direct service component operation, prime sponsorships, state and federal levels; effect of formative and summative evaluation on operation; manual and computerized information systems. Lecture and case studies are used.
Credit recommendation: In the graduate degree category, 2 semester hours in Administration, Educational Psychology, Management, Public and Urban Policy, or Urban Education (3/78) (3/83) (3/88). NOTE: This course has been reevaluated and continues to meet requirements for credit recommendations.

Program Planning Design and Implementation
Location: Philadelphia, PA and other regional locations.
Length: 30 hours (1 week).
Dates: October 1977-Present.
Objective: To provide the student with strategies and techniques for integrated planning and implementing of program operations.
Learning Outcome: Upon successful completion of this course, the student will be able to provide program implementation skills; establish objectives for performance; and integrate planning process between supervisors and line staff.
Instruction: Course covers fundamentals of manpower planning, leadership styles and their effects on planning, planning curriculum, program implementation skills, establishing objectives and performance standards, and integration of planning process between supervisors and line staff. Lecture and case studies are used.
Credit recommendation: In the upper division baccalaureate category or in the graduate degree category, 2 semester hours in Administration or Management (3/78) (3/83) (3/88). NOTE: This course has been reevaluated and continues to meet requirements for credit recommendations.

Proposal Writing and Fund Development
(Employment and Training, Planning Proposal Writing and Fund Development)
Location: Regional Centers throughout the U.S.
Length: 30 hours (1 week).
Dates: March 1982-Present.
Objective: To assist the student in developing effective skills in proposal writing for the purpose of fund raising and public relations.
Learning Outcome: Upon successful completion of this course, the student will be able to effectively write proposals; participate in fund raising activities; and create and present the needs of an organization to the private and public sector for development of fund raising purpose.
Instruction: The content of this course is designed to developmentally teach the skills needed in proposal writing, fund raising and public relations. Participants will learn through step by step exercises how to create and present the needs of an organization to the private and public sector for development of fund raising purpose.
Credit recommendation: In the graduate degree category, 2 semester hours in Administration/Management, Adult Education, Urban Studies, or Organization Development (3/83) (3/88). NOTE: This course has been reevaluated and continues to meet requirements for credit recommendations.

Seminar on the Job Training Partnership Act
Location: Regional Centers throughout the U.S.
Length: 30 hours (1 week).
Dates: January 1983-Present.
Objective: To assist individuals in organizations to understand the Job Training Partnership Act.
Learning Outcome: Upon successful completion of this course, the student will be able to understand the purpose and scope of the Job Training Partnership Act; and understand how the JTPA can effectively serve the unemployed through training.
Instruction: This seminar will examine the purpose and scope of the Job Training Partnership Act. The content of the course will include the Job Training Partnership Act, the Regulations and many other items, pamphlets and books of information that will be of interest and value to the participants. This process of the seminar will be a flexible one which will focus on involving the group members in discussion, strategies, actions, and other pertinent activities viewed as meaningful and profitable for the individual and the organization.
Credit recommendation: In the graduate degree category, 2 semester hours in Management, Public Administration, or Urban Studies (3/83) (3/88). NOTE: This course has been reevaluated and continues to meet requirements for credit recommendations.

Team Building
(Formerly Management Through Teamwork)
   Location: Philadelphia, PA and other regional locations.
   Length: 32 hours (1 week).
   Dates: April 1974-Present.
   Objective: To enable supervisors and managers to increase their effectiveness through study of behavioral science and its application to management.
   Learning Outcome: Upon successful completion of this course, the student will be able to understand interpersonal communications and conflict resolutions; understand the different leadership styles; and understand the importance of team building.
   Instruction: Course covers interpersonal communications and conflict resolution, leadership styles and group behavior, motivational themes and applications, management of personnel. Lecture, discussion, and case studies are used.
   Credit recommendation: In the graduate degree category, 2 semester hours in Administration or Management (3/78) (3/83) (3/88). NOTE: This course has been reevaluated and continues to meet requirements for credit recommendations.

Tool for Better Management
   Location: Philadelphia, PA and other regional locations.
   Length: 32 hours (1 week).
   Dates: May 1976-March 1984.
   Objective: To provide supervisors and managers with techniques for problem solving and analysis.
   Instruction: Course covers management by objectives, transactional analysis, PERT (Program Evaluation Review Techniques). Lecture, discussion, simulation, and case studies are used.
   Credit recommendation: In the graduate degree category, 2 semester hours in Administration or Management (3/78) (3/83). NOTE: This course has been reevaluated and continues to meet requirements for credit recommendations.

Vocational Education Instruction
   Location: Philadelphia, PA and other regional locations.
   Length: 30 hours (1 week).
   Dates: January 1978-Present.
   Objective: To provide the student with methods for systematic development of vocational instruction.
   Learning Outcome: Upon successful completion of this course, the student will be able to develop strategies for instructional development and implementation; and develop materials and activities for target populations.
   Instruction: Course covers strategies for instructional development and implementation, developing materials and activities for the target population, use of on-the-job training site work experience and work simulation, improving course effectiveness, and performance measurement. Lecture, discussion, workshop, and laboratory are used.
   Credit recommendation: In the upper division baccalaureate category, 3 semester hours in Education (e.g., Industrial Arts, Vocational Education) (3/78) (3/83) (3/88). NOTE: This course has been reevaluated and continues to meet requirements for credit recommendations.

Pacific Bell

Pacific Bell is a public utility located in California with 64,000 employees. The training department is composed of two districts responsible to an assistant vice president of employee placement and training, a unit of the company's human resources department. The company offers employee referral and educational assistance through the Tuition Aid Office.

Courses are systematically designed in accordance with the Pacific Bell Training Development Guidelines. Instructors are full-time Pacific Bell employees selected for their subject matter expertise and teaching skills. Classroom facilities, audiovisual support, and other needs have been designed to ensure an effective learning environment.

Source of official student records: Pacific Bell Training Department, Tuition Aid Office, 2600 Camino Ramon, Room 2N400-L, San Ramon, California 94583 or ACE Registry of Credit Recommendation, The Center for Adult Learning and Educational Credentials, American Council on Education, One Dupont Circle, Washington, D.C. 20036.

Additional information about the courses: Program on Noncollegiate Sponsored Instruction, The Center for Adult Learning and Educational Credentials, American Council on Education, One Dupont Circle, Washington, D.C. 20036.

Account Executive Selling Skills (45500)
(Formerly [02009])
   Location: Oakland and Los Angeles, CA.
   Length: 70 hours (2 weeks).
   Dates: August 1982-Present.
   Objective: To instruct personnel in basic sales skills, including preparatory financial analysis and systems theory.
   Instruction: Financial calculations, sales planning and preparation, conducting a systems study, presentation and results, and cost justification. Lecture, case studies, and role playing are used.
   Credit recommendation: In the upper division baccalaureate category, 3 semester hours in Marketing (11/84).

Account Inquiry Initial Training (02549)
  Location: Various locations throughout California.
  Length: 296 hours (7 weeks).
  Dates: May 1986-Present.
  Objective: To train service representatives in customer relations functions.
  Learning Outcome: Upon successful completion of this course, the student will be able to: (1) handle customer billing inquiries; (2) market company products and services effectively; (3) demonstrate positive customer contact skills; (4) collect overdue accounts; (5) handle claims and process adjustments; (6) process returned checks; and (7) handle annoyance calls.
  Instruction: Covers development of employee skills enabling them to interact effectively with customers over the phone. Utilizes lectures, case studies, group exercises, role playing, and interaction with computer ordering and billing systems.
  Credit recommendation: In the lower division baccalaureate/associate degree category, 3 semester hours in Basic Customer Relations (11/86). NOTE: Credit for this course is excluded if prior credit for courses RASC (02321A), Basic RTOC (02321B), Inside Selling Skills (02148), or Basic Selling Skills (02130) has been granted.

Advanced PC Users Series: Operating Systems (1407), Project Management (1426), Local Networks (1423)
  Location: Various locations throughout California.
  Length: 21 hours (3 days).
  Dates: August 1984-Present.
  Objective: To acquaint students with the more advanced microcomputer applications, including DOS commands, project management with Time Line, and networking with PC Connection.
  Learning Outcome: Upon successful completion of this course, the student will be able to configure a PC to print graphic, format output to the display and customize the keyboard; create batch files to eliminate repetition key strokes; use Time Line as a planning and tracking tool for project management and control; and use PC Connection to create network servers and work stations.
  Instruction: In the Advanced DOS course, editing keys, special commands, DOS filters, modes of operations, system prompt, system configuration, debugging programs and directory manipulation are covered. The Time Line basics include: creating schedules, managing projects and resources; and generating reports. The PC Networks course covers net/one and the network administrator, creating the system, managing the network; and using the network.
  Credit recommendation: In the lower division baccalaureate/associate degree category, 1 semester hour in Computer Information Systems, Data Processing, or Management Information Systems (8/87).

1 AESS Attached Processor System Maintenance (05602)
  Location: Various training locations throughout California and Nevada.
  Length: 21 hours (3 days).
  Dates: August 1983-Present.
  Objective: To provide students with the fundamental knowledge and skills necessary to troubleshoot and maintain the attached processor system.
  Instruction: Covers API frame description and theory, API diagnostics and translations, system update and recovery, system communications and system maintenance. Methodology includes four units of self-paced instruction. Students must demonstrate mastery learning before proceeding to the next lesson.
  Credit recommendation: In the vocational certificate category, 1 semester hour in Digital Hardware Maintenance (8/85).

1 AESS Common Peripheral Units (05606)
  Location: Various training locations throughout California and Nevada.
  Length: 140 hours (4 weeks).
  Dates: June 1981-Present.
  Objective: To provide the student with the fundamental knowledge and skills to locate and resolve basic controller troubles in second generation technology and peripheral units.
  Instruction: Covers circuitry, troubleshooting and maintenance of central pulse distributor, Remreed line switch circuitry, Triac signal distributor, and miniature scanner circuitry. Methodology includes four units of self-paced instruction and hands-on work assignments using training modules which contain circuitry similar to that actually found in ESS offices. Unit tests consist of written questions and laboratory applications.
  Credit recommendation: In the vocational certificate category, 4 semester hours in Digital Hardware Maintenance (8/85).

1 AESS Peripheral Units (05642)
  Location: Various training locations in California.
  Length: 172 hours (5 weeks).
  Dates: January 1982-Present.
  Objective: To present general knowledge and maintenance procedures required for maintaining peripheral equipment.
  Instruction: Covers introduction to Remreed Switching Network, associated switching frames, network maintenance. Course requires student to use Bell Documentation and interact with a computer which simulates ESS. Methodology includes modules which are divided into lessons, each of which is followed by a test.
  Credit recommendation: In the vocational certificate category, 5 semester hours in Switching Systems Maintenance (8/85).

1 AESS Processor Hardware Language (05643)
Location: Various training locations in California.
Length: 105 hours (3 weeks).
Dates: August 1982-Present.
Objective: To provide the student with skills, knowledge and techniques required to maintain the central processor free of hardware faults.
Instruction: Covers the organization of central control, the basic program language, diagnostic analysis procedures, memory storage units and processor interface units. Methodology includes self-paced instruction and practical exercises.
Credit recommendation: In the vocational certificate category, 4 semester hours in Digital Hardware Maintenance (8/85).

1 AESS Processor Introduction (05641)
Location: Various training locations in California.
Length: 21 hours (3 days).
Dates: May 1982-Present.
Objective: To provide students with general knowledge of the IA processor, to resolve a simple power and diagnostic failures.
Instruction: Covers identification of IA Processor units and subunits and their functions. Trouble conditions involving simple failures, along with remedial actions, are covered. Automatic Message Accounting System is presented. Methodology includes self-paced instruction.
Credit recommendation: In the vocational certificate category, 1 semester hour in Switching System Maintenance (8/85).

1 AESS System Operation (05645)
Location: Various training locations in California.
Length: 190 hours (5½ weeks).
Dates: August 1982-Present.
Objective: To develop the skills that will enable students to perform tasks in area of software maintenance for No. 1 Electronic Switching Systems (ESS).
Instruction: Covers use of documentation, locating and clearing parameter and translation problems, emergency procedures, analysis of problems. Methodology includes self-paced instruction.
Credit recommendation: In the vocational certificate category, 6 semester hours in Switching Systems Software Diagnostics (8/85).

Affirmative Action (01005)
Location: Various locations throughout California.
Length: 16 hours (2 days).
Dates: January 1985-Present.
Objective: To enable students to understand EEO and Affirmative Action, explore their own issues and concerns relative to the topic, and to clarify their role in EEO/Affirmative Action programs.
Learning Outcome: Upon successful completion of this course, the student will be able to: (1) understand the legal and historical background of EEO/Affirmative Action; (2) define what discrimination/reverse discrimination is and is not; (3) demonstrate how Affirmative Action benefits all employees; (4) understand the organization's commitment to EEO/AA; and (5) understand their role in Affirmative Action and how it related to their own career development.
Instruction: Course covers legal aspects of EEO/AA, developing Affirmative Action plans and objectives, perceptions of discrimination, reverse discrimination, the older employee, the additionally challenged, selection decisions, defining sexual harassment, problem resolution, and the future of affirmative action. Teaching methodology includes lecture, discussion, and videotapes.
Credit recommendation: In the upper division baccalaureate category, 1 semester hour in Affirmative Action (11/86).

Air Dryer Maintenance (06238)
Location: Anaheim, CA.
Length: 28 hours (4 days).
Dates: January 1982-Present.
Objective: To train students in the functioning of air dryers and how to analyze and diagnose air dryer malfunction.
Instruction: Course covers fundamental principles of air drying and the major characteristics of various types of air dryers. Methodology includes lectures and practical exercises in each module.
Credit recommendation: In the vocational certificate category, 1 semester hour in Pneumatics (8/85).

Arbitration Advocacy
Location: Arrowhead, Redwood City, and other educational facilities.
Length: 40 hours (4½ days).
Dates: January 1983-Present.
Objective: To prepare the student to effectively function as an advocate for the company in mediation/arbitration and arbitration proceedings.
Learning Outcome: Upon successful completion of this course, the student will be able to understand the history, theory, and mechanics of arbitration (with specific emphasis on Pacific Bell); prepare a case file, formulate issues, prepare and deliver opening statements and closing arguments; and select and prepare witnesses, testimony, exhibit, and prepare post-hearing briefs.
Instruction: Course covers laws affecting and giving authority to arbitration and a union's duty of fair representation; arbitration case preparation techniques; formulation of issues; preparation and delivery of opening statements and closing arguments; witness selection and preparation; preparation of testimony and exhibits; conducting witness examination; and preparation of post-hearing briefs. Methodology includes cases, lecture, group

discussion, videotapes, writing exercises, and oral presentation.

Credit recommendation: In the upper division baccalaureate category, 3 semester hours, or in the graduate category, 2 semester hours in Business, Economics, Government, Labor Relations, or Labor Studies (9/88).

Assistant Manager Initial Training Business (AMIT) (02773/77/79/82/83/89/93/94)

Location: Various training locations throughout California and Nevada.

Length: 28-32 hours (4 days).

Dates: August 1984-Present.

Objective: To present the student with concepts and principles for effective people and time management.

Instruction: Covers conducting a group meeting management of the services representatives floor, interviewing and counseling employees; time management, job motivation and enrichment principles, and positive communication techniques. Methodology includes lecture, discussion, video tapes, and student role playing.

Credit recommendation: In the lower division baccalaureate/associate degree category, 2 semester hours in Principles of Supervision (11/84).

Basic Electricity (04005)

Location: Various locations throughout California.

Length: 40 hours (1 week).

Dates: February 1981-Present.

Objective: To provide personnel with the training required to solve fundamental electrical problems and to apply proper safety precautions as they relate to electrical equipment.

Instruction: Covers the basic topics of electrical current voltage and resistance. Fundamentals of troubleshooting series and parallel circuits are included. Specific topics include: Electromagnetism, Inductive and Capacitive Reactance, Semiconductor Rectifiers and Impedance. This is a self-paced program designed by the Westinghouse Learning Corporation for the Bureau of Naval Personnel. The Pacific Bell Company has modified it to meet specific on-the-job needs which results in heavy emphasis on direct current circuits.

Credit recommendation: In the vocational certification category, 3 semester hours in Basic Electricity (11/84).

Basic Engineering Economy (25052)

Location: Various training locations throughout California and Nevada.

Length: 40 hours (1 week).

Dates: July 1977-December 1988.

Objective: To enable the student to define the terms and symbols used in the mathematics of money.

Instruction: Covers methods used to compare alternating course of action in financial decision making, including the different types of cost studies used in investment analysis. Methodology includes lecture, discussion, and classroom exercises and problem solving.

Credit recommendation: In the upper division baccalaureate category, 1 semester hour in Engineering Economics (11/84).

Basic Network Design (02257)

Location: Sacramento, Los Angeles, San Diego, and Oakland, CA.

Length: 24 hours (3 days).

Dates: March 1987-Present.

Objective: To provide the student with a thorough understanding of data collection, design terminology and criteria, and computer-based design tools.

Learning Outcome: Upon successful completion of this course, the student will have a thorough understanding of data collection (how to, and interpretation); have a thorough understanding of design terminology and criteria; effectively use data and design criteria with computer-based design tools, i.e., SWAT, RDF/FEX optimizer; understand effect on design output if certain design criteria are changed; and be able to incorporate design output into proposal form for customers.

Instruction: Course covers theory, general terminology used in network design including definition, conversions, and traffic characteristics. Course is delivered by computer-based training and instructor. This course includes CBT and Leader-led.

Credit recommendation: In the lower division baccalaureate/associate degree category, 1 semester hour in Computer Information Systems, Data Processing, or Telecommunications (8/87).

Basic Selling Skills (02130)

Location: Oakland and Los Angeles, CA.

Length: 40 hours (1 week).

Dates: April 1984-Present.

Objective: To provide students with specific sales information to determine customer needs and to satisfy these needs with company products and services.

Instruction: Covers the basic selling techniques of data gathering, customer approach, buying motives, handling objectives, and closing the sale. Methodology includes instructor led discussion, student exercises, and simulation.

Credit recommendation: In the lower division baccalaureate/associate degree category, 2 semester hours in Principles of Salesmanship (8/85).

Beginning Lotus 1-2-3 (01414)
Intermediate Lotus 1-2-3 (01402)
Advanced Lotus 1-2-3

Location: Los Angeles, Pasadena, Tustin, San Ramon, Oakland, San Diego, Sacramento, San Jose, and San Francisco, CA.

Length: 21 hours for 1402, 1411, 1414 series. Series must be taken on non-consecutive days.

Dates: August 1984-Present.

Objective: To introduce user participants to the basic concepts of the spreadsheet program Lotus 1-2-3. To provide beginning, intermediate, and advanced instruction and practice in the use and application of the Lotus 1-2-3 software package.

Learning Outcome: Upon successful completion of this course, the student will be able to: issue commands, correct mistakes, and convert a ledger account into an electronic spreadsheet using a microcomputer and the Lotus 1-2-3 spreadsheet program; write and test complex formulas, to protect data from erasure, to maneuver large blocks of numerical data, to create and manipulate multiple graphs, and to design special and attractive printing techniques; and, control the operation and appearance of a spreadsheet, to use management commands and functions, to analyze data with Data-branch commands, and to construct 1-2-3 macros.

Instruction: The course provides a comprehensive introduction to the concepts and utilization of the Lotus 1-2-3 spreadsheet program. Covers command sequences, creation and manipulation of spreadsheets, graphing, special printing techniques, use of formulas, management commands and functions, analyzing information with Data-branch commands, and construction of 1-2-3 macros.

Credit recommendation: In the vocational certificate or lower division baccalaureate/associate degree category, 1 semester hour in Data Processing or Management Information Systems (11/86).

Beginning WordPerfect (1427A); Intermediate Word Perfect (1427B); Advanced WordPerfect (1427C)

Location: Various locations throughout California.
Length: 21 hours (3 days).
Dates: August 1984-Present.

Objective: To provide the student with a solid introduction to the word processing program WordPerfect, by emphasizing those skills and concepts most used in the business world.

Learning Outcome: Upon successful completion of this course, the student will be able to use a personal computer to create, edit, and print documents.

Instruction: A comprehensive three-part series of classes consisting of beginning, intermediate, and advanced topics in the word processing program, Word Perfect. Covers editing, printing, and merge techniques, as well as formatting features. Teaching methodology includes lecture and laboratory experience.

Credit recommendation: In the lower division baccalaureate/associate degree category, 1 semester hour in Business Administration, Data Processing, or Management Information Systems (8/87).

Building Industry Consultant (05726) (Formerly Building Energy Consultant [25606])

Location: Various training locations throughout California and Nevada.
Length: 100 hours (2 weeks).
Dates: January 1979-Present.

Objective: To enable the student to design a building communications system from the point of building entry through the building distribution to the individual outlets.

Instruction: Covers the plans design for components in the physical distribution of telephone systems throughout a facility. Methodology includes lecture, role playing, and problem solving.

Credit recommendation: In the lower division baccalaureate/associate degree category, 6 semester hours in Construction Technology (11/84).

Cable Fault Locating (06215)

Location: Emeryville and Orange, CA.
Length: 40 hours (5 days).
Dates: September 1984-Present.

Objective: To provide the student with the skills and knowledge to perform fault isolation on communications cables.

Learning Outcome: Upon successful completion of this course, the student will be able to perform various measurements using test sets; write and interpret the results of tests conducted; and measure and isolate faults in aerial, underground, and buried communications cables.

Instruction: Course covers fault isolation techniques, test set understanding and operation, and decision making based on field results.

Credit recommendation: In the lower division baccalaureate/associate degree category, 2 semester hours in Electronics Technology or Telecommunications (9/88).

Cable Pressurization Engineering (03400)

Location: Various locations in California.
Length: 32 hours (1 week).
Dates: February 1984-Present.

Objective: To train students in applying proper guidelines when placing exchange feeder cable in an existing standardized cable pressure system.

Instruction: Covers an overview of the cable pressure system and air pipe routes, manifold assemblies, pressure transducers, meter panels; methods of updating a Cable Pressure Key map; recalculating Optimum Air Usage for manifolds, air pipe routes, and meter panels. Methodology includes lecture, discussion, and final examination.

Credit recommendation: In the lower division baccalaureate/associate degree category, 1 semester hour in Pneumatics (8/85).

Cable Repair - Fault Locating (06215)

Location: Various training locations throughout California and Nevada.

Length: 40 hours (1 week).
Dates: January 1981-Present.
Objective: To train the student to understand the application of various test sets to the cable fault locating process and be able to locate any fault within the capability of the selected test set.
Instruction: Covers electrical measurement to fault, tracing of the tone to fault, application of high voltage, sectionalizing; uses of volt-ohmeter, open fault locator, open-split locator, and various fault locators. Methodology includes nine independent units supported by printed materials and audio cassette tapes with significant hands-on application of 15 cable fault location test sets.
Credit recommendation: In the vocational certificate category, 1 semester hour in Electronics Technology (8/85).

CBT Design and Development (01500)
Location: Various training locations throughout California.
Length: 14 hours (2 days).
Dates: February 1985-Present.
Objective: To provide course developers and managers with the ability to design, develop, and evaluate computer-based training courseware.
Instruction: Covers the fundamental principles for the design and development of computer-based training courseware through instructional techniques, reference materials, cost considerations, courseware evaluations and customizing courses to meet special needs of the target audience. Methodology includes lecture, group discussion, and projects which can be implemented in the students actual work environment.
Credit recommendation: In the upper division baccalaureate category, 1 semester hour in Education (8/85).

Computer Systems Concepts (02262)
Location: Los Angeles and Oakland, CA.
Length: 40 hours (5 days).
Dates: November 1986-Present.
Objective: To provide the student with an understanding of computer hardware, operating systems, and systems software.
Learning Outcome: Upon successful completion of this course, students will have an understanding of hardware processing, transactions, and characteristics of operating systems. Students will be able to estimate sizing requirements, develop and cost detailed computer configurations, and evaluate the effectiveness of current computer systems at the mainframe and minicomputer level.
Instruction: Course covers the detailed operation of computer hardware, operating systems, and systems software. Hardware at the mainframe, minicomputer, and microcomputer levels are discussed. Specific operating systems covered include: MVS, VM, VMS, and DOS. Systems analysis includes hardware and system sizing as well as system evaluation. Performance monitoring, tuning, and capacity planning are discussed in the context of current computer operations. Homework assignments in addition to reading include hardware comparison, operating system evaluation, minicomputer sizing and configuration analysis, and mainframe performance analysis. Course prerequisite includes coursework in data processing, telecommunications, and computer programming.
Credit recommendation: In the upper division baccalaureate category, 3 semester hours in Computer Science or Computer Information Systems, or in the graduate degree category, 2 semester hours in Management (11/86). NOTE: Text is suitable for upper division baccalaureate or introductory graduate student if theoretical concepts are treated. Instructor's manual and student guides do not appear to deal with the theoretical concepts in an in-depth manner. Prerequisites of the students do not suggest graduate treatment.

Contemporary Collective Bargaining
Location: Arrowhead and Redwood City, CA.
Length: 40 hours (4½ days).
Dates: January 1986-Present.
Objective: To provide the student with a fundamental understanding of the contemporary collective bargaining process and prepare him/her to contribute to the company's negotiation effort in either a minor or major role.
Learning Outcome: Upon successful completion of this course, the student will be able to conduct research necessary to support a company's bargaining prepartion effort; analyze provision of external collective bargaining agreements; prepare bargaining proposals and supporting rationale; prepare responses to union demands with supporting rationale; write clear, unambiguous contract language; record collective bargaining minutes; and properly funciton as a member of the bargaining team.
Instruction: Course covers laws defining the duty to bargain; mandatory, permissive and illegal issues; unfair labor practices; election petitions; functions and powers of the NLRB; picketing; union tactics before, during, and after bargaining; bargaining preparation; conduct of negotiations; rules of contract language construction; and preparation of proposals, and responding to demands. Methodology includes cases, lecture, oral presentation, group discussion, and writing exercises.
Credit recommendation: In the upper division baccalaureate category, 3 semester hours, or in the graduate category, 2 semester hours in Business, Economics, Government, Labor Relations, or Labor Studies (9/88).

Data Processing/Data Communications (45503) (Formerly [02024])
Location: Oakland and Los Angeles, CA.
Length: 36 hours (1 week).
Dates: July 1981-Present.
Objective: To enable students to develop knowledge

needed to identify and solve customer DP/DC System problems.

Instruction: Covers technological applications in a manual environment; data processing and data communications. Course progresses from a simple batch system to a complex distributed application information system. Case exercises and multiple applications are used to reinforce concepts. Home assignments before and during the course are very strongly emphasized.

Credit recommendation: In the upper division baccalaureate category, 3 semester hours in Business Administration, Computer Science, or Data Processing (11/84).

dBASE III Users Series: Introduction to dBASE III (1405A); Using dBASE III (1405B); Applying dBASE III (1405C)

Location: Los Angeles, Pasadena, Tustin, San Ramon, Oakland, San Diego, Sacramento, San Jose, and San Francisco, CA.

Length: 21 hours (3 days, 7 hours per day).

Dates: August 1984-Present.

Objective: To provide students with a comprehensive learning experience on the relational database program called dBASE III plus.

Learning Outcome: Upon successful completion of this course, the student will be able to design, create, and modify a database.

Instruction: Course covers basic definitions and terminology involved with databases and progresses to programming specific applications with dBASE, including design, creation, and modification of a database; creation of database screens; retrieval of information from multiple databases; creating reports; and writing dBASE III Plus programs.

Credit recommendation: In the lower division baccalaureate/associate degree category, 1 semester hour in Computer Information Systems, or Data Processing (8/87).

DOS Concepts and Beginning RBASE 5000 for Hard Disk PC Systems
(Alternate Title: Beginning RBASE 5000 [01424], DOS for the Hard Disk [01403] and Advanced RBASE 5000 [01431]).

Location: Los Angeles, Pasadena, Tustin, San Ramon, Oakland, San Diego, Sacramento, San Jose, and San Francisco, CA.

Length: 21 hours (3 days).

Dates: August 1984-Present.

Objective: To acquaint students with disk operating system concepts for a hard disk-based PC system and to introduce them to data base concepts through the use of RBASE 5000.

Learning Outcome: Upon successful completion of this course, the student will learn the general makeup of a PC system and its operating system software; concepts of a relational database and how to create, update, and utilize one through the study of RBASE 5000.

Instruction: The course includes two basic sections: (1) The first segment provides an explanation of the components of a typical computer system, tips on the safe and efficient operation of a computer and hands-on experience in a variety of basic computing techniques. (2) The second segment is a detailed introduction to the basics of the RBASE 5000 database software package. Through extensive hands-on exercises, the student learns many of the advanced features of the package, including relational commands, data-entry rules and passwords, and the use of the Forms and Reports mode.

Credit recommendation: In the vocational certificate or lower division baccalaureate/associate degree category, 1 semester hour in Business Administration, Data Processing, or Management Information Systems (11/86).

DOS Concepts, Wordstar, and Lotus 1-2-3 for the Hard Disk PC System
(Alternate Title: DOS for the Hard Disk [01403], Beginning Lotus 1-2-3 [01414], Beginning Wordstar [01415])

Location: Los Angeles, Pasadena, Tustin, San Ramon, Oakland, San Diego, Sacramento, San Jose, and San Francisco, CA.

Length: 21 hours (3 days).

Dates: August 1984-Present.

Objective: To provide the student with a solid introduction to the operations and appreciations of microcomputers through the use of Wordstar and Lotus 1-2-3.

Learning Outcome: Upon successful completion of this course, the student will be able to use a personal computer to create, edit, and print test documents and will also be able to create a spreadsheet, convert it into an effective graph, then print it.

Instruction: The course is a connected series made up of three principal elements. The first element is for introduction to the operating system for a hard disk PC system. Emphasis is placed on the study of files, organization of the hard disk, formatting, copying and locking up files, and use of directories. The second element is devoted to a treatment of Wordstar. All functions needed to begin using this word processing package are covered, the last element included is a study of Lotus 1-2-3. Lotus basics, window commands, worksheet structure, graphing capabilities, and an introduction to hard copy features are included.

Credit recommendation: In the vocational certificate or lower division baccalaureate/associate degree category, 1 semester hour in Data Processing, Business Administration, or Management Information Systems (11/86).

Ease Authoring (01501)
Location: Various training locations throughout Cali-

fornia.
Length: 24 hours (3 days).
Dates: February 1985-Present.
Objective: To provide an experienced CBT author, who has successfully completed the CBT Design and Development course with a basic framework of the Phoenix Ease authoring system to create efficient, cost effective courses.
Instruction: Covers the structure of the Phoenix Ease authoring system and creating a mini course which can be customized to place emphasis on the author's particular needs. Methodology includes lecture, discussion, and laboratory activities geared to an author's needs.
Credit recommendation: In the upper division baccalaureate category, 1 semester hour in Education (8/85).

EDP Concepts for Business (02267)
Location: Various locations throughout California.
Length: 19 hours (2 days).
Dates: July 1987-Present.
Objective: To provide the student with an understanding of the basic elements of data processing.
Learning Outcome: Upon successful completion of this course, the student will recognize the definition of data processing; identify the primary purpose of CPU; identify hardware elements of a data processing system; and identify the functions of the CPU components.
Instruction: Course covers computer components, computer terminology, and definitions, programs, purpose and definition, major types of programs, program components, and system development basics.
Credit recommendation: In the lower division baccalaureate/associate degree category, 1 semester hour in Business Administration or Data Processing (8/87).

Effective Communicating Seminar (21008)
Location: Various locations throughout California.
Length: 16 hours (2 days).
Dates: April 1987-July 1988.
Objective: To increase the student's confidence in verbal communication through skill building that focuses on organizing information, presentation style, and listening involvement techniques.
Learning Outcome: Upon successful completion of this course, the student will have enhanced his/her ability to: communicate in pressure situations; deal with impromptu presentations; involve listerners; and evaluate presentations of self and others.
Instruction: Course covers planning/organizing a presentation, communications skills and techniques, developing visual aides, handling of questions and answers, and listener involvement techniques. Teaching methodology includes lecture, discussion, and video taping.
Credit recommendation: In the lower division baccalaureate/associate degree category, 1 semester hour in Communications (8/87).

1. Effective Presentations (1040)
2. Leading Discussion Meetings (1030)
Location: Various training locations throughout California.
Length: 40 hours (1 week).
Dates: January 1974-Present.
Objective: *Course 1:* To enable the student to plan, develop, and deliver an effective presentation. *Course 2:* To enable the student to prepare and lead discussion meetings.
Instruction: *Course 1* covers the knowledge and skills required for preparations, including the selection of visual aids. Students will prepare and deliver two final presentations. *Course 2* covers knowledge and skills required for planning and leading discussion meetings. Students demonstrate acquired skills by leading two discussion meetings. Methodology includes lecture, discussion, workshop, and other audiovisual aids.
Credit recommendation: In the lower division baccalaureate/associate degree category, 2 semester hours in Management Communication (11/84).

Electronic Spreadsheets: Enhancing Lotus 1-2-3 with Freelance, HAL, and Manuscript (1439, 1440, 1441) (Lotus Products User Series: Lotus Freelance, Lotus HAL, Lotus Manuscript)
Location: Various California locations.
Length: 24 hours (3 days).
Dates: August 1985-Present.
Objective: To provide the student who has mastered Lotus 1-2-3 with additional software power to enhance their applications on IBM-PC and compatible computers.
Learning Outcome: Upon successful completion of this course, the student will be able to create and display graphics with Freelance-Plus; enhance Lotus spreadsheet with HAL; and enhance word processing capabilities with Manuscript.
Instruction: Course covers detailed procedures to use Freelance, HAL, and Manuscript. Specific topics include creating a pie chart, creating a text chart, design and editing everyday graphics, importing worksheet data, maps, working with HAL tables, using Macros, linking data in different worksheets, using the document outliner, creating a structured document, columns and tables, and printing. Methodology includes lectures and hands-on activities.
Credit recommendation: In the lower division baccalaureate/associate degree category, 1 semester hour in Computer Information Systems or Data Processing (9/88). NOTE: It is recommended that a student be granted credit in only one word processing course (i.e., Multimate, Displaywrite, Wordstar, etc.).

Electronic Spreadsheets: EXCEL on MacIntosh (1433, 1434, 1442)
(MacIntosh and EXCEL Users Series: Meet the Mac, Beginning, Intermediate and Advanced)
   Location: Various California locations.
   Length: 24 hours (3 days).
   Dates: August 1985-Present.
   Objective: To provide the student with an understanding and knowledge in using EXCEL on a McIntosh computer.
   Learning Outcome: Upon successful completion of this course, the student will be able to manage a disk on a MacIntosh computer; create a spreadsheet, graph with EXCEL on the MacIntosh computer; and use a database including how to sort, search, and retrieve with EXCEL.
   Instruction: Course includes two segments. The first segment provides an explanation of the components of a MacIntosh computer and how it works. The second segment provides the student with detailed procedures in using the drawing package, hypercard, worksheet, printing, database structures, creating and printing charts. Methodology includes lectures and hands-on activities.
   Credit recommendation: In the lower division baccalaureate/associate degree category, 1 semester hour in Computer Information Systems or Data Processing (9/88). NOTE: It is recommended that a student be granted credit in only one word processing course (i.e., Multimate, Displaywrite, or Wordstar, etc.).

Engineering Economy - Advanced (25053)
   Location: Various training locations throughout California and Nevada.
   Length: 72 hours (1½ weeks).
   Dates: September 1984-December 1988.
   Objective: To enable the student to interpret financial and accounting terminology as it applies to engineering economy studies. To identify the relationships of various financial analysis approaches, and to identify the proper techniques for presentation of engineering economy studies.
   Instruction: Covers how to integrate complex financial considerations into the decision making process and analysis. Methodology includes lecture, discussion, classroom exercises, simulation, and problem solving.
   Credit recommendation: In the upper division baccalaureate category, 3 semester hours in Engineering Economics (11/84).

1 ESS Central Processor and Programming Fundamentals (5620)
   Location: Various training locations throughout California.
   Length: 123 hours (3 weeks).
   Dates: June 1984-Present.
   Objective: To provide the student with the skills necessary to characterize data failures in No. 1 Electronic Switching Systems Program Store or Call Store memory systems and to interpret program instructions and apply software diagnostic tactics in locating system hardware failures.
   Instruction: Covers operation, maintenance, and repair of an advanced-level ESS control unit, including logic circuit analysis, block diagram and timing analysis, address operations, computer system operations, memory addressing (32K and 8K), program instruction codes, core memory operations, program diagnostics, troubleshooting procedures, and repair methods. Methodology includes self-paced instruction and practical exercises.
   Credit recommendation: In the lower division baccalaureate/associate degree category, 3 semester hours in Computer Systems or Logic Circuit Fundamentals (8/85).

1 ESS Central Processor Hardware Maintenance (05625)
   Location: Various training locations throughout California and Nevada.
   Length: 140 hours (4 weeks).
   Dates: June 1984-Present.
   Objective: To provide standard training for operating company personnel assigned to maintain the No. 1E-ESS system.
   Instruction: Course covers central control, program store, call store, signal processor language, master control center, and No. 1 ESS processor units trouble analysis. Six modules containing a total of 17 individualized units. Test after each unit. Student must obtain 100 percent on each test to move to next lesson. Methodology includes self-paced, practical exercises under the direct supervision of the faculty.
   Credit recommendation: In the vocational certificate category, 4 semester hours in Digital Hardware Maintenance (8/85).

1 ESS Common Peripheral Units (05605)
   Location: Various training centers throughout California and Nevada.
   Length: 63 hours (2 weeks).
   Dates: August 1981-Present.
   Objective: To provide training which enables the student to use standard references and test equipment to locate hardware trouble in ESS peripheral units.
   Instruction: Covers schematic drawings, identification of troubles associated with the scanner interrogate and readout circuitry, the network controller logic, buffer registers, group check and path selection circuitry of the switching network; an ESS source circuit (touch-tone detector); the signal distributor circuitry and matrix selection. Methodology includes four units of self-paced, programmed instruction and hands-on work assignments using ESS peripheral units. Unit tests consist of written questions and laboratory exercises.
   Credit recommendation: In the vocational certificate

category, 2 semester hours in Digital Hardware Maintenance (8/85).

ESS Introduction (05600)
Location: Various training locations throughout California and Nevada.
Length: 85 hours (2 weeks).
Dates: January 1984-Present.
Objective: To provide the fundamental knowledge and skills prerequisite to stored program switching systems using minicomputer fundamentals.
Instruction: Covers basic and intermediate computer concepts, call processing, numbering systems, diodes and transistors, electrostatic discharge, hardware familiarization, schematics, Belpac, BSPs, and ESS communication buses. Methodology includes the instructional workbench delivery system utilizing the UNIX operating system. Unit tests accompany each of the 15 modules.
Credit recommendation: In the lower division baccalaureate/associate degree category, 2 semester hours in Electronics Technology (8/85).

1 ESS Method of Operation (05115)
1 ESS Translations Basic (05120)
Location: Various training locations throughout California and Nevada.
Length: 70 hours (2 weeks).
Dates: August 1980-Present.
Objective: To provide skills and knowledge to enable entry level students to perform tasks in area hardware and software maintenance of No. 1 Electronic Switching Systems (ESS).
Instruction: Covers a basic understanding of how a No. 1 ESS system works and its methods of operation; details how to match software items with their definitions; and traces the basic translations used in call processing. Methodology includes lecture, discussion, and classroom exercises.
Credit recommendation: In the vocational certificate category, 2 semester hours in Switching System Maintenance (8/85).

2 ESS Method of Operation (05145)
Location: Various training locations throughout California and Nevada.
Length: 35 hours (1 week).
Dates: August 1980-Present.
Objective: To provide the student with a fundamental understanding of the No. 2 ESS systems features, terminology, and the skills necessary to maintain equipment.
Instruction: Covers operations, use, fault diagnosis, and repair of No. 2 level ESS, including component identification from schematics, block diagram analysis, program diagnostics and testing, testing procedures for service lines and equipment, logic circuit testing and control hardware operations. Methodology includes lecture, discussion, and classroom exercises.
Credit recommendation: In the vocational certificate category, 1 semester hour in Switching System Maintenance (8/85).

1 ESS System Operations (05630)
Location: Various locations in California and Nevada.
Length: 140 hours (4 weeks).
Dates: June 1984-Present.
Objective: To enable the student to be knowledgeable in the operation and maintenance of a No. 2 ESS system.
Instruction: Covers the No. 1 ESS operational environment and provides the knowledge and skills necessary to analyze and clear systems troubles. Methodology includes individualized self-instructional workbooks, office assignments and laboratory for hands-on experience and job relevant testing.
Credit recommendation: In the vocational certificate category, 4 semester hours in Switching Systems Software Diagnostics (8/85).

Fiber Optics: Sales (02165) or Technical (02166)
Location: Various locations throughout California.
Length: 16 hours (2 days).
Dates: July 1987-Present.
Objective: To provide the student with an understanding of fiber optics systems and light transmission theory.
Learning Outcome: Upon successful completion of this course, the student will be able to identify and understand fundamentals of fiber optics technology.
Instruction: Course covers fundamentals of fiber optics technology; performance characteristics such as speed, error rates; fiber optics systems including transmitters, multiplexers and comparison with other types of transmission systems; applications; Pacific Bell fiber systems; and fiber optics capabilities and performance. Course is delivered by computer-based training.
Credit recommendation: In the lower division baccalaureate/associate degree category, 1 semester hour in Data Processing or Telecommunications (8/87). NOTE: Students may receive credit for Fiber Optics (Sales) or Fiber Optics (Technology), but not both.

Fundamentals of Computer Operations (50001)
(Introduction to Computer Organization)
Location: Various locations throughout California.
Length: 20 hours (5 days).
Dates: August 1986-Present.
Objective: To provide students with an understanding of the major components of a typical computer system.
Learning Outcome: Upon successful completion of this course, the student will be able to identify a minimum of eighteen data processing terms and will be able to label a block diagram of a computer system.
Instruction: Course covers the data processing cycle; computer hardware, software, and peripheral equipment;

data representation; instruction formats; and external storage. Course is delivered by computer-based training.

Credit recommendation: In the lower division baccalaureate/associate degree category, 1 semester hour in Data Processing (8/87).

1. Goal Setting Skills (1006)
2. Managing Performance (1063)
   Location: Various training locations throughout California.
   Length: 40 hours (1 week).
   Dates: January 1981-December 1988.
   Objective: *Course 1:* To train the student in the process of goal setting and practice the interpersonal communication skills necessary to negotiate and finalize mutual goals. *Course 2:* To teach the student a process that will help plan, conduct, and follow up discussions with employees.
   Instruction: *Course 1* covers setting performance standards and writing goals in relation to various leadership styles. *Course 2* covers setting specific and measurable performance standards, a work-related discussion process, communication skills, and a process for coaching and counseling employees' performance. Methodology includes lecture, discussion, workshop, lab, and audiovisual aids.
   Credit recommendation: In the lower division baccalaureate/associate degree category, 1 semester hour in Career Development (11/84).

Improving Performance (01009)
   Location: Various locations throughout California.
   Length: 16 hours (2 days).
   Dates: April 1986-Present.
   Objective: To provide students with an understanding of the performance appraisal process, and to develop the skills necessary to set performance standards and conduct performance reviews.
   Learning Outcome: Upon successful completion of this course, the student will be able to: (1) determine measurable job standards; (2) prepare for and plan strategies for conducting appraisal interviews; (3) guide an appraisal discussion using the skills of listening, questioning, handling conflict, negotiating and reaching resolution; and (4) set performance objectives that relate to employee needs.
   Instruction: Presents performance appraisal as an integral part of managing and improving productivity. Covers performance appraisal skills, performance standards, identifying job parts, setting objectives, formal performance appraisals, coaching, developing action plans, solving problems and documenting past performance.
   Credit recommendation: In the upper division baccalaureate category, 1 semester hour in Performance Appraisal (11/86).

Information Mapping (01267)
   Location: Various locations throughout California.
   Length: 40 hours (1 week).
   Dates: June 1976-Present.
   Objective: To improve student's ability to write business documents utilizing the Information Mapping method.
   Instruction: Covers Information Mapping as a technique for gaining a practical skill in using a structured format to write business documents; a means to organize material and present information clearly; how to organize large or complex information into manageable units that are easy to read and understand. Methodology includes self-paced written materials with some instructor-led discussion.
   Credit recommendation: In the upper division baccalaureate category, 2 semester hours in Principles of Information Mapping (8/85).

Influence Management (01015)
   Location: Various locations throughout California.
   Length: 24 hours (3 days).
   Dates: September 1984-Present
   Objective: To improve the manager's ability to work with and through others.
   Learning Outcome: Upon successful completion of this course, the student will have: (1) an awareness of the influence process; (2) a plan for improvement in performing high priority influence practices; (3) improved influence practices and tactics to allow them to implement their plan; (4) a system for tracking the progress of their plan; and (5) plans for involving others in their improvement efforts.
   Instruction: Covers identification of the manager's influence environment, conflict anticipation and management in working relationships, methods of enhancing rapport in the work group, and the effective use of influence to make high-quality decisions. Methodology includes a pre-course computerized feedback on the participant's influence skills as compared to the top managers in the Fortune 500 companies. Utilizes lectures, audiovisual materials, group exercises, and role playing.
   Credit recommendation: In the upper division baccalaureate category, 1 semester hour in Organizational Behavior (11/86).

Information Transport Technologies (02207)
   Location: Oakland and Los Angeles, CA.
   Length: 32 hours (4 days).
   Dates: December 1985-Present.
   Objective: To provide participants with an understanding of telecommunications networks.
   Learning Outcome: Upon successful completion of this course, the student will be able to: (1) describe the types and characteristics of voice and data information carrying systems, their benefits and limitations; (2) define basic principles of signal propagation, modulation, analog/digital modulations and transmission performance; and (3)

describe the switching hierarchy and switching principles.

Instruction: Course provides an overview of switching technology, transmission media and carrier systems, transmission impairments, data transmission and digital transmission media, digital networks and ISDN.

Credit recommendation: In the vocational certificate or lower division baccalaureate/associate degree or upper division baccalaureate category, 2 semester hours in Telecommunications Technology (11/86).

Inside Selling Skills (02148)
   Location: Oakland and Los Angeles, CA.
   Length: 40 hours (1 week).
   Dates: January 1984-Present.
   Objective: To provide students with the appropriate sales techniques to determine customer needs and to satisfy these with specific products and services.
   Instruction: Covers the basic selling techniques of time management, buying motives, needs analysis, handling objectives, and closing the sale. Methodology includes lectures, discussions, classroom exercises, simulations, and problem solving techniques.
   Credit recommendation: In the lower division baccalaureate/associate degree category, 2 semester hours in Principles of Salesmanship (8/85).

Instructor Competencies (01226)
(Formerly Trainer Skills Workshop [01245])
   Location: Various training locations throughout California.
   Length: 76 hours (2 weeks).
   Dates: May 1982-Present.
   Objective: To provide the student with teaching skills essential for effective industrial training.
   Instruction: Covers the philosophy of adult education including learning characteristics, learning styles, instructional methods, creation of effective learning climates, and the ethical considerations in training. Methodology includes lecture, discussion, and laboratory exercises involving class presentations utilizing various instructional methods.
   Credit recommendation: In the upper division baccalaureate category, 3 semester hours in Instructional Design (11/84).

Integrated Application Software: Beginning DOS and Total Engineering Support System (TESS) (1403, 1437)
   Location: Various California locations.
   Length: 24 hours (3 days).
   Dates: August 1985-Present.
   Objective: To provide the student with a comprehensive undertanding of IBM-PC microcomputer, PC-DOS, and the Total Engineering Support System (TESS) software.
   Learning Outcome: Upon successful completion of this course, the student will be able to perform basic DOS operations, including managing a hard disk; use TESSOM communications program; and log on the PACTIME 1, upload and download files.
   Instruction: Course includes two segments. The first segment provides an explanation of the components of an IBM-PC system and how it works along with DOS. The second segment provides the student with an understanding of Total Engineering Support System (TESS) and developing operation skills with modules of *Functions, Abeyance, Editor, Phones,* and *TESSMAIL;* and familiarity with the *TESSCOM* communications system. Methodology includes lectures and hands-on activities.
   Credit recommendation: In the lower division baccalaureate/associate degree category, 1 semester hour in Computer Information Systems or Data Processing (9/88).

Integrated Application Software: Total Engineering Support System (TESS) and PC-DOS (1436)
   Location: Various California locations.
   Length: 24 hours (3 days).
   Dates: August 1985-Present.
   Objective: To provide the student with a comprehensive understanding of the Total Engineering Support System (TESS) software.
   Learning Outcome: Upon successful completion of this course, the student will be able to use TESSOM communications program; log on the PACTIME 1, upload and download files; and use DOS commands.
   Instruction: Course includes two segments. The first segment provides detailed procedures in using TESSOM communications software with an understanding of Total Engineering Support System (TESS) and developing operation procedures with modules of *Functions, Abeyance, Editor, Phones,* and *TESSMAIL.* The second segment covers the overview of an IBM-PC XT computer system, including DOS commands. Methodology includes lectures and hands-on activities.
   Credit recommendation: In the lower division baccalaureate/associate degree category, 1 semester hour in Computer Information Systems or Data Processing (9/88). NOTE: It is recommended that a student be granted credit in only one word processing course (i.e., Multimate, Displaywrite, Wordstar, etc.).

1. **Interpersonal Skills (1000)**
2. **Influence Management (01029) (Formerly 1015)**
   Location: Various training locations throughout California.
   Length: 35 hours (1 week).
   Dates: August 1982-Present.
   Objective: *Course 1:* To enable the student to develop an awareness of personal leadership styles and assess their effect on employee behavior. *Course 2:* To enable the student to improve substantially the students' personal performance in building, using, and sustaining influence.

Instruction: *Course 1* offers a choice of learning tools which impact awareness and perception leading to behavior change on the job, e.g., Firo B. *Course 2* covers an awareness of the influence process, how it works on the job and the application of selected practices and tactics to improve performance. Methodology includes lecture, discussion, laboratory, and audiovisual aids.

Credit recommendation: In the upper division baccalaureate category, 2 semester hours in Organizational Behavior (11/84).

Introduction to Basic Accounting (02264)
Location: San Francisco, CA.
Length: 21 hours (3 days).
Dates: September 1986-Present.
Objective: To give the student a general background in basic accounting that assists the student in understanding and using financial statements.
Learning Outcome: Upon successful completion of this course, the student will understand the basic language and concepts of financial accounting; be able to prepare basic financial statements; and use basic analytical tools to interpret financial statements.
Instruction: Introduces basic accounting principles and definitions. Covers journal entries, the general ledger, income statements, and balance sheets.
Credit recommendation: In the lower division baccalaureate/associate degree category, 1 semester hour in Introduction to Accounting (8/87).

Introduction to CBT: Design and Development (01502 and 01504)
Location: Oakland, CA.
Length: 40 hours (5 days).
Dates: February 1988-Present.
Objective: To provide the student with the ability to identify the benefits of CBT, determine its applicability to a given project, and to design, develop, and document a CBT course.
Learning Outcome: Upon successful completion of this course, the student will be able to identify the benefits of CBT; identify the differences and similarities between CBT and other training methods; determining if CBT is the appropriate media for a given project based on design complexity and testing, audience, cost, and content considerations; indentify activities relating to CBT development in each phase of the development process; document CBT constraints, special teaching strategies and lesson sequences; select CBT instrucitonal strategies to incorporate into course design documentaiton; write a CBT lesson; and incorporate CBT system, delivery, and maintenance requirements into printed student and administrator materials.
Instruction: Course covers concepts of CBT, CBT selection considerations, CBT development time and costs, the CBT development process, course design requirements, and CBT instruction strategies. Methodology includes lecture, discussion, and laboratory exercises.
Credit recommendation: In the upper division baccalaureate category, 3 semester hours in Educational Methodology (9/88).

Introduction to "C" Programming (59787)
Location: Oakland, CA.
Length: 40 hours (5 days).
Dates: May 1984-Present.
Objective: To provide the student with the ability to use the basic structure and syntax of "C" language to design, code test, and execute programs.
Learning Outcome: Upon successful completion of this course, the student will be able to describe how an application program interfaces with the UNIX System; discuss the basic structure and syntax of the "C" programming language; design programs using arrays, pointers, and structured programming concepts; handle file control via storage management and I/O processing; design and code "C" programs in a UNIX environment; and compile and execute "C" programs.
Instruction: Course covers structure of the language; declaration of variables; arithmetic processing; logical constructs; loop exit instructions; array processing; pointer processing; functions other than main; structure variable processing; storage management; I/O processing; executing commands from programs; and compilation and executing.
Credit recommendation: In the lower division baccalaureate/associate degree category, 2 semester hours in Computer Science or Data Processing (8/87).

Introduction to Data Base Management Systems (52311)
Location: Concord, San Ramon, Anaheim, and Irvine, CA.
Length: 24 hours (self-paced).
Dates: October 1987-Present.
Objective: To teach the student fundamental concepts of data base management systems (DBMS) and to prepare students for more intensive study of a selected DBMS.
Learning Outcome: Upon successful completion of this course, the student will be able to distinguish between file and data base structures; define schemes and subschemes; define logical and physical structure; explain how data dictionaries are used; compare hierarchical, network, and relational DBM structures; and demonstrate familiarity with issues of data integrity and internal and external threats to it.
Instruction: Course covers definition of a data base, logical and physical structures, data languages, tree structures, various file organization methods, and data integrity, privacy, and security. Methodology involves computer-based training.
Credit recommendation: In the lower division bac-

calaureate/associate degree category, 2 semester hours in Computer Science, Data Processing, or Management Information Systems (9/88). NOTE: Students who receive credit for this course should not receive credit for Unisys Data Base Concepts and Unisys 1100 Series System Concepts.

Introduction to DBASE II/III (01405)
Communications with Microcomputers (01406)
Advanced DOS (01407)

Location: Los Angeles, Pasadena, Tustin, San Ramon, Oakland, San Diego, Sacramento, San Jose, and San Francisco, CA.

Length: 21 hours (3 days).

Dates: August 1984-Present.

Objective: To provide students with an understanding of database management systems through the use of DBASE II and III and the study of advanced DOS concepts.

Learning Outcome: Upon successful completion of this course, the student will be able to: understand the concept of database, create a database, search for data, edit database files, generate reports, and manage multiple files.

Instruction: Database organization and management. File creation and file management including addition, deletion, editing, search and modification. A review/introduction to P/C data communications. Hands-on experience and instruction of the Hazar 1200 and setting up communications between computers. Instruction in advanced functions available in DOS.

Credit recommendation: In the vocational certificate or lower division baccalaureate/associate degree category, 1 semester hour in Information Systems, Business Administration, or Data Processing (11/86).

Introduction to JCL (52142)
(JCL 1)

Location: Various locations throughout California.

Length: 24 hours (3 days).

Dates: April 1985-Present.

Objective: To provide students with the necessary skills to write the job control statements required to process a basic one-step job.

Learning Outcome: Upon successful completion of this course, the student will know the purpose of JCL and be able to explain how it is used in the computer operations environment.

Instruction: Course is divided into fourteen units. Included in these units are: need for JCL in an IBM environment; relationships between hardware and software; syntax for formatting JCL statements; and a criterion test for the course. Course uses computer-based training.

Credit recommendation: In the lower division baccalaureate/associate degree category, 2 semester hours in Computer Science, Data Processing, or Management Information Systems (8/87).

Introduction to Management and Supervision (45900-A)
(Residence Manager Initial Training)

Location: Sacramento, Oakland, Pasadena, Los Angeles, Tustin, and San Diego, CA.

Length: 64 hours (8 eight-hour days).

Dates: January 1988-Present.

Objective: To prepare the manager for his/her role by studying the principles of effective job management and practicing the related skills.

Learning Outcome: Upon successful completion of this course, the student will be able to provide quality customer service; coach and develop subordinates towards effective performance; and utilize the skills necessary for effective supervision.

Instruction: Course covers coaching and development; learning and demonstrating the different feedback techniques; conducting a monitoring session; demonstrating a coaching session; professionalism; effective communication; group meetings; goal setting; establishing daily priorities; and payroll. Methodology includes lecture, group discussion, role playing and quizzes.

Credit recommendation: In the lower division baccalaureate/associate degree category, or vocational certificate category, 3 semester hours in Principles of Supervision or Management and Supervision (9/88).

Introduction to Management Skills (1060A)

Location: Various training locations throughout California.

Length: 40 hours (1 week).

Dates: January 1981-December 1988.

Objective: To help prepare first level managers for supervisory and managerial roles by teaching the principles and practices of administrative responsibilities.

Instruction: Covers company goals, structure, supervisorial policies, policies and principles of management, with an emphasis on the supervisory functions toward career guidance and counseling, managing employee attendance, and nonmanagement employee evaluations. Methodology includes lecture, discussion, group and individual role playing, in-class written exercises, and some self-paced individual study.

Credit recommendation: In the lower division baccalaureate/associate degree category, 1 semester hour in General Management (11/84).

Introduction to Management Skills (1060B)

Location: Various training locations throughout California.

Length: 40 hours (1 week).

Dates: January 1981-December 1988.

Objective: To teach management skills to first-level managers who are in a non-supervisory role.

Instruction: Covers the four management tasks of planning, organizing, directing, and controlling; time management techniques, company goals and the effects of competition; use of administrative references; the manager's responsibilities in the management evaluation process; communication skills with emphasis on active learning. Methodology includes lecture, discussion, workshop, classroom exercises, and role playing.

Credit recommendation: In the lower division baccalaureate/associate degree category, 2 semester hours in General Management (11/84).

Introduction to Personal Computing (42011 or 42011P) (Personal Computing)
Location: Various Business Marketing locations throughout California.
Length: 5-15 hours (Interactive Video).
Dates: June 1987-Present.
Objective: To provide students with an understanding of the types of computers and their components, computer assembly, and basic operation.
Learning Outcome: Upon successful completion of this course, the student will gain a basic understanding of microcomputers and their use. It should make the student more confident and comfortable in operating a microcomputer.
Instruction: Course covers computer types, computer components, computer assembly, data entry, editing, and computer selection. Course is delivered by interactive video and workbook assignment.
Credit recommendation: In the lower division baccalaureate/associate degree category, 1 semester hour in Business Administration or Data Processing (8/87).

1. Job Aid Analysis and Design (1265)
2. Development of Instructional Materials (1207)
Location: Various training locations throughout California.
Length: 84 hours (2 weeks plus one day).
Dates: December 1982-Present.
Objective: To prepare a trainer to determine which behavior should be job aided, design and construct job aids, and apply appropriate training course design to produce both lecture and self-instructing training courses.
Instruction: Covers job study and training design, formation, and sequencing of prime units, development of a module plan and predicting and matching learning problems with selected teaching strategies. Methodology includes lecture, discussion, workshop, and laboratory activities.
Credit recommendation: In the upper division baccalaureate category, 3 semester hours in Curriculum Design (11/84).

Labor Laws and Labor History
Location: Arrowhead, Redwood City, CA and other educational sites.
Length: 40 hours (4½ days).
Dates: January 1983-Present.
Objective: To provide the student with a fundamental knowledge of the history of labor in America and the various laws impacting on the employer-employee relationship.
Learning Outcome: Upon successful completion of this course, the student will be able to provide competent advice and counsel on the handling of strike/picketing situations; effectively coordinate with the NLRB in the conduct of representation elecitons; conduct research of applicable case law as necessary to provide effective advice and counsel; and investigate unfair labor practice charges and State Labor Commission complaints and prepare appropriate responses in light of the case facts and applicable law.
Instruction: Course covers important events in American labor history; beginnings of English labor law; the evolution of U.S.labor law and the provisions of various Acts affecting the employer-employee-union relationship; an in-depth examination of the provisions of the National Labor Relations Act (NLRA), California State Labor Code and Industrial Welfare Commission Rules and Labor Code and Industrial Welfare Commission rules and regulations. Methodology includes lecture, group discussions, and case studies.
Credit recommendation: In the upper division baccalaureate category, 3 semester hours in Business, Economics, Government, Labor Relations, or Labor Studies (9/88).

Loop Lightwave Engineering (03301)
Location: Various training locations throughout California and Nevada.
Length: 40 hours (5 days).
Dates: December 1984-Present.
Objective: To train distribution service engineers in the methods and procedures required to plan and design a lightwave system in the subscriber loop.
Instruction: Covers an overview of theory of lightwaves, equipment used to operate a lightwave system; step-by-step procedures to develop a lightwave plan including a subscriber loop; step-by-step procedures to design a lightwave job and an overview of installation and maintenance activities. Methodology includes lecture, discussion, classroom exercises and simulated problem solving.
Credit recommendation: In the lower division baccalaureate/associate degree category, 2 semester hours in Electronic Communication Systems (8/85).

Managing Professional Growth (01012)
Location: Various locations throughout California.
Length: 16 hours (2 days).
Dates: April 1986-Present.
Objective: To guide the participant toward an understanding of personal values and individual strengths and

weaknesses as they relate to career development.

Learning Outcome: Upon successful completion of this course, the student will be able to: (1) identify personal values; (2) assess their own strengths and weaknesses; (3) identify skills required to perform a job; and (4) prepare a framework for career development.

Instruction: Covers value clarification, development of a personal definition of job satisfaction, identification of special talents, description of development needs, and individualized development strategy. Methodology includes a pre-workshop assignment completed by both the participant and manager as well as lecture, classroom exercises, and discussion.

Credit recommendation: In the upper division baccalaureate category, 1 semester hour in Performance Appraisal (11/86).

Management Skill Development Series (42327 or 42327P)

Location: Various Business Marketing locations throughout California.
Length: 20-40 hours (Interactive Video).
Dates: July 1987-Present.
Objective: To develop and/or improve the management skills of managers in the ten skill areas listed in the instruction section. To develop/enhance the student's managerials skills.
Learning Outcome: Upon successful completion of this course, the student will be able to use basic management skills required for an effective supervisor.
Instruction: Course uses computer software to assist students in development of their management skills and provides them a tool for assessing their skill level in the ten areas. The course consists of ten modules that deal with: Organization and Planning; Control and Follow-up; Decisiveness; Decision Making; Perception; Interpersonal Relations; Leadership; Flexibility; Oral Communication; and Written Communication. The student uses video and workbook assignments to learn these skills. Length of the course does not include time for outside preparation with workbook assignments. Students are expected to complete the course within a 4-6 week timeframe.
Credit recommendation: In the lower division baccalaureate/associate degree category, 2 semester hours in Principles of Management (8/87).

Marketing Residence Service Representative Basic-RASC (02321-A)
(Billing Group - Residence)
Location: Various locations throughout California.
Length: 240 hours (6 weeks).
Dates: September 1984-Present.
Objective: To provide training to nonmanagement personnel in performing service representative functions.
Instruction: Covers training in handling customer questions and complaints, collection and adjustments of overdue bills in a professional manner. Methodology includes self-paced learning under an instructor's guidance and student application practice sessions.
Credit recommendation: In the lower division baccalaureate/associate degree category, 3 semester hours in Customer Relations (8/85).

Marketing Residence Service Representative Basic-RTOC (02321-B)
(Order Group-Residence)
Location: Various locations throughout California.
Length: 240 hours (6 weeks).
Dates: September 1984-Present.
Objective: To prepare service representatives for customer contact and to recommend various company products.
Instruction: Covers selling skills, customer relations, repair calls, and contact memos. Methodology includes self-paced learning under instructor guidance.
Credit recommendation: In the lower division baccalaureate/associate degree category, 3 semester hours in Customer Relations (8/85).

Marketing Service Representative Basic Training (05899)
Location: Various locations throughout California.
Length: 270 hours (36 days).
Dates: March 1985-Present.
Objective: To train service representatives.
Learning Outcome: Upon successful completion of this course, the student will be able to demonstrate verbal skills related to effective interaction with customers; describe phone network services; negotiate and process orders using current computer networks, includes orders for new installatons, disconnects, and additions to existing services.
Instruction: Course covers development of employee skills enabling them to interact effectively with customers over the phone. Utilizes lectures, class discussion, and laboratory exercises.
Credit recommendation: In the lower division baccalaureate/associate degree category, 3 semester hours in Basic Market Service Representation (8/87). NOTE: Credit for this course is excluded if prior credit for courses RASC (02321A), Basic RTOC (02321B), Account Inquiry Initial Training (02549), Inside Selling Skills (02148), or Basic Selling Skills (02130) has been granted.

Methods Development Workshop (1204)
Location: Various training locations throughout California.
Length: 76 hours (2 weeks).
Dates: March 1983-Present.
Objective: To train the student in the techniques and philosophy of methods development.
Instruction: Covers all necessary activities involved in

the method development process and produce a method (given a case) with all required components. Methodology includes lecture, discussion workshop, and laboratory.

Credit recommendation: In the lower division baccalaureate/associate degree category, 1 semester hour in Business Administration (11/84).

Microcomputer Fundamentals (1400)
  Location: Oakland and Los Angeles, CA.
  Length: 21 hours (3 days).
  Dates: August 1984-Present.
  Objective: To enable the student to identify, connect, and use microcomputers including peripheral equipment. To learn to use various software programs including word processing, spreadsheet, and communications.
  Instruction: Covers the use of components, and software and various application examples. Methodology includes lecture, video, and class discussion with extensive computer use.
  Credit recommendation: In the lower division baccalaureate/associate degree category, 1 semester hour in Introduction to Microcomputer Concepts (11/84).

Multimate Mod. I (01416-A)
Multimate Mod. II (01416-B)
DOS for the Hard Disk (01403)
  Location: Los Angeles, Pasadena, Tustin, San Ramon, Oakland, San Diego, Sacramento, San Jose, and San Francisco, CA.
  Length: 21 hours (3 days).
  Dates: August 1984-Present.
  Objective: To introduce user participants to the basic concepts of the Multimate word processing software.
  Learning Outcome: Upon successful completion of this course, user participants will be able to: (1) understand the makeup of a computer system and the nature and use of DOS; (2) use Multimate to create, edit, and print documents, letters and reports; and (3) use formatting features and text enhancements associated with Multimate.
  Instruction: A familiarization course for first time computer users. Includes an explanation of the use and care of computer system components and an introduction to the basic concepts and capabilities of the Multimate word processing software. Covers basic editing, formatting, print commands, use of tabs, copying, speller and thesaurus usage.
  Credit recommendation: In the vocational certificate or lower division baccalaureate/associate degree category, 1 semester hour in Business Administration, Data Processing, or Management Information Systems (11/86). NOTE: Keyboarding skills might need to be treated; could be part of prerequisite package.

MVS Concepts (52314)
  Location: Concord, San Ramon, San Diego, and San Francisco, CA.
  Length: 24 hours (3 days).
  Dates: June 1987-Present.
  Objective: To teach the student computer operations personnel basic MVS concepts.
  Learning Outcome: Upon successful completion of this course, the student will be able to explain the concept of vertical storage; demonstrate a clear understanding of MVS; and understand the components of operating system software.
  Instruction: Course covers hardware components, data retrieval and organization, operating system software, and JCL basics, programs, and procedures.
  Credit recommendation: In the lower division baccalaureate/associate degree category, 1 semester hour in Data Procesing ((/88).

Network Fundamentals (05710)
  Location: Los Angeles, San Diego, Sacramento, San Mateo, Tustin, and various suitcase locations.
  Length: 80 hours (2 weeks).
  Dates: December 1984-Present.
  Objective: To acquaint the student with network design concepts, network components, analog and digital transmission, radio and other network transmission media.
  Learning Outcome: Upon successful completion of this course, the student will understand terminology and network design concepts; and be familiar with multiplexing, switching, transmission systems, analog and digital transmission characteristics and network applications.
  Instruction: Course explains network design and switching system concepts; network duplications; transmission systems including radio and fiber; analog and digital transmissions characteristics; and modulation and multiplexing techniques.
  Credit recommendation: In the lower division baccalaureate/associate degree category, 5 semester hours in Telecommunications Management or Telecommunications Technology (11/86).

Network Traffic Concepts (23719)
  Location: Various training locations throughout California and Nevada.
  Length: 36 hours (1 week).
  Dates: December 1981-Present.
  Objective: To enable the student to recognize the theories and principals of network administration and network switching engineering, and to recognize the interrelationship and appropriate application of these theories and principles.
  Instruction: Covers the underlying concepts governing the design and administration of the telephone switching system. Methodology includes lecture, workshop, discussion, and classroom exercises.
  Credit recommendation: In the upper division baccalaureate category, 3 semester hours in Information Systems or Telecommunications (11/84).

New Age Thinking for Achieving Your Potential (01093)

Location: Various locations throughout California.
Length: 20 hours (3 days).
Dates: January 1981-Present.
Objective: To guide the salaried participant toward an understanding and acceptance of his or her own talents and resources, instill belief in personal ability to succeed, and expand vision of available opportunities.
Instruction: Covers applied techniques for developing potential, both personally and professionally based on the implementation of modern concepts of self-image psychology. Methodology includes videotaped lectures, classroom discussion and laboratory work.
Credit recommendation: In the lower division baccalaureate/associate degree category, 1 semester hour in Personal Growth and Development Seminar (8/85).

New Age Thinking for Achieving Your Potential (1093-A)

Location: Various locations throughout California.
Length: 13 hours (2 days).
Dates: January 1984-Present.
Objective: To guide the non-salaried participant toward an understanding and acceptance of his or her own talents and resources, instill belief in personal ability to succeed, and expand vision of available opportunities.
Instruction: Covers applied techniques for developing potential, both personally and professionally based on the implementation of modern concepts of self-image psychology. Methodology includes videotaped lectures, classroom discussion, and laboratory work.
Credit recommendation: In the lower division baccalaureate/associate degree category, 1 semester hour in Personal Growth and Development Seminar (8/85).

Paradox Users Series: Introduction to Paradox (1425); Using Paradox (1425A); Applying Paradox (1425B)

Location: Various locations throughout California.
Length: 21 hours (3 days).
Dates: August 1984-Present.
Objective: To familiarize students with the relational database program called Paradox. This course takes the beginning database user from introductory through advanced levels of Paradox.
Learning Outcome: Upon successful completion of this course, the student will be able to understand the concepts of relational databases; enter, update, edit, and delete database information; query and sort the database; format and print reports and tables; customize forms; and design a summary report.
Instruction: Introduces the student to database concepts, definitions and terminology used by Paradox. Covers the creation, addition, editing, and deletion of files. It also covers data manipulation funcitons, how to create tables, Paradox querying abilities, customized forms and data summary. The teaching methodology utilizes classroom lectures and personal computer usage.
Credit recommendation: In the lower division baccalaureate/associate degree category, 1 semester hour in Business Administration, Data Processing, or Management Information Systems (8/87).

PC and Symphony Users Series: Hard Disk and DOS (1403); Beginning Symphony (1417); Advanced Symphony (1422)

Location: Various locations throughout California.
Length: 21 hours (3 days).
Dates: August 1984-Present.
Objective: To familiarize the student with the fundamental aspects of using a personal computer and DOS. Students will gain an understanding of what Symphony is, and how to use it at an advanced level to build spreadsheets and graphs.
Learning Outcome: Upon successful completion of this course, the student will understand what DOS is and how to use it; be able to construct Symphony spreadsheets; be able to construct Symphony graphs; be able to perform advanced spreadsheet calculations; and be able to use Symphony macro commands.
Instruction: Introduces the student to floppy and hard disk computer systems and usage of the more important DOS utilities. It then covers basic and advanced elements of Symphony spreadsheets and graphics including the design and use of spreadsheets and graphics, macro commands, and customized menus. The teaching methodology utilizes classroom lectures and personal computer usage.
Credit recommendation: In the lower division baccalaureate/associate degree category, 1 semester hour in Business Administration, Data Processing, or Management Information Systems (8/87).

PC and Wordstar Users Series: Beginning WI Hard Disk and DOS (1403); Beginning Wordstar (1415); Advanced Wordstar (1432)

Location: Various locations throughout California.
Length: 21 hours (3 days).
Dates: August 1984-Present.
Objective: To provide the student with an introduction to the operation of microcomputers through the use of Wordstar.
Learning Outcome: Upon successful completion of this course, the student will be able to use a personal computer to create, edit, and print documents.
Instruction: A comprehensive three-part series of classes concentrating on familiarizing a new user with the PC, its operating system, and its word processing applications. Emphasis is placed on the study of file, organization of the hard disk, formatting, copying and backing up files, and use of directories. The second element is devoted to the beginning use of the word processing software and

covers editing and printing techniques as well as formatting. The third element covers more advanced formatting editing techniques as well as creating more complex documents and merge procedures.

Credit recommendation: In the lower division baccalaureate/associate degree category, 1 semester hour in Business Administration, Data Processing, or Management Information Systems (8/87).

Performance Data Collection and Analysis (01206A) (Techniques of Data Collection and Analysis)
Location: Oakland and Tustin, CA.
Length: 22½ hours (3 days, 7½ hours per day).
Dates: March 1987-Present.
Objective: To provide students with an understanding of data collection methods and analysis of job performance.
Learning Outcome: Upon successful completion of this course, the student will be able to determine causes of performance deficiencies and solutions by using a series of data analysis techniques such as content analysis, input/output analysis, decision analysis, contingency analysis, and analysis of work products. The student will be able to collect data using a variety of techniques such as personal interviews, focus group interviews, observations, and questionnaires.
Instruction: Course is designed to provide instruction in specific performance data collection techniques, includes sample sizes and data sources. Worksheets and flow charts are utilized. A deficiency analysis summary is used to conclude reports.
Credit recommendation: In the lower division baccalaureate/associate degree category, 2 semester hours in Management Information Systems (8/87).

1. Planning Controlling the Work (1064)
2. Managing Performance (1063)
3. Taking Charge of Time (1007)
Location: Various training locations throughout California.
Length: 40 hours (1 week).
Dates: January 1981-December 1988.
Objective: *Course 1:* To introduce the student to strategies of control and their impact on motivation and to enable the student to plan and monitor work more effectively. *Course 2:* To teach the student a process that will help him/her plan, conduct, and follow-up discussions with employees. *Course 3:* To enable the student to evaluate the students use of time and apply scientific time management techniques to job activities.
Instruction: *Course 1* identifies the types and categories of control strategies, theories of planning, and an 8-step process of planning and monitoring and its application to specific case studies. *Course 2* covers setting specific and measurable performance standards, a work related discussion process, communication skills and a process for coaching and counseling employee performance. *Course 3:* covers the evaluation and processing of time management techniques and includes choosing five techniques which will increase personal effectiveness and efficiency. Methodology includes lecture, discussion, workshop, lab, and audiovisual aids.
Credit recommendation: In the lower division baccalaureate/associate degree category, 2 semester hours in Employee Development (11/84).

Principles of Digital Technology (05703) (Formerly 25050)
Location: Various training locations throughout California and Nevada.
Length: 36 hours (1 week).
Dates: April 1981-Present.
Objective: To enable the student to interpret, identify, and describe the digital technology currently in use, the evolution of the technology, and the methods for management of the technology.
Instruction: Covers the digital technology utilized in the communications network and develops an understanding of basic digital theory and terminology. Methodology includes lecture, discussion, workshop, and classroom exercises.
Credit recommendation: In the upper division baccalaureate category, 2 semester hours in Information Science or Telecommunications (11/84).

Principles of Engineering Economy and Economic Alternative Selection for Outside Plant (EASOP) (03361 - 03374)
Location: Various training locations throughout California.
Length: 40 hours (1 week).
Dates: March 1981-December 1988.
Objective: To provide the student with the basic skills and knowledge to complete an economic study using manual, engineering, and computer-based analysis techniques.
Instruction: Covers basic concepts of accounting and financing up to and including the cash flows associated with various projects. Methodology includes laboratory exercises and self-paced instruction.
Credit recommendation: In the upper division baccalaureate category, 1 semester hour in Engineering Economics (11/84).

Project Management: Sales Version (42605) or Staff Version (42607)
Location: Los Angeles and Oakland, CA.
Length: 24 hours (3 days).
Dates: March 1987-Present.
Objective: To teach the student the concepts and methodologies of project management and to provide techniques which increase the ability to manage products.

Learning Outcome: Upon successful completion of this course, the student will understand and be able to apply concepts of project management to projects of various sizes and types; be able to apply work breakdown structures to specific projects; understand how and why projects can fail; and be able to use project management tools and automated aids.

Instruction: Course covers methodologies and specific techniques for managing projects of various sizes and types. Provides both behavioral science and quantitative analysis views of project management which emphasize the importance of a systematic approach to project planning and execution. Methodology includes lecture, discussion, laboratory, and class presentation.

Credit recommendation: In the upper division baccalaureate category, 2 semester hours in Project Management (8/87). NOTE: Students may receive credit for Project Management (Sales Version) or Project Management (Staff Version), but not both.

Protocol-Asynchronous and Bisynchronous (51538)
(Data Communications Protocols—Asynchronous and Bisynchronous)
  Location: San Ramon and San Diego, CA.
  Length: 24 hours (3 days).
  Dates: August 1986-Present.
  Objective: To provide the student with a basic understanding of data base utility, messages, and device status.
  Learning Outcome: Upon successful completion of this course, the student will be able to understand the function of protocols; be able to define and understand the basic functions of network software, CSUs, BETA Sets, CIUs and terminals; and understand the differences and functions of asynchronous and bisynchronous protocols.
  Instruction: Course covers an introduction to protocols and network hardware functions. Methodology includes lecture and laboratory assignments.
  Credit recommendation: In the upper division baccalaureate category, 1 semester hour in Data Communications or Telecommunications (9/88).

Public Packet Switching Service (02128)
  Location: Los Angeles and Oakland, CA.
  Length: 16 hours (2 days).
  Dates: January 1985-Present.
  Objective: To train managers in the new product of Public Packet Switching.
  Instruction: Covers training in and marketing of the new product, Public Packet Switching, Standard and Optional Features, Applications, Basic Operation of PPS Network, and other Packet Switching Networks. Methodology is primarily lecture with laboratory.
  Credit recommendation: In the lower division baccalaureate/associate degree category, 1 semester hour in Marketing (8/85).

Right of Way (ROW) (05716)
(Formerly 25600)
  Location: Various training locations throughout California and Nevada.
  Length: *Version 1:* 41 hours (1 week); *Version 2:* 80 hours (2 weeks).
  Dates: *Version 1:* October 1980-August 1988; *Version 2:* September 1988-Present.
  Objective: To train the student in the various procedures required to secure easement acquisitions.
  Instruction: Covers the proper acquisition of easements across private property, Real Estate Law, Title Search, Legal Description Writing Interpreting, Appraising Real Estate for easement compensation, and negotiating skills. Methodology includes lecture, discussion, workshop, and lab experiences.
  Credit recommendation: *Version 1:* In the lower division baccalaureate/associate degree category, 3 semester hours in Civil Engineering Technology (11/84). *Version 2:* In the lower division baccalaureate/associate degree, or vocational certificate category, 3 semester hours in Civil Engineering Technology, Real Estate, or as a Business elective (9/88).

Right of Way Appraisal (05732)
(Right of Way Essentials)
  Location: San Mateo, CA or other client locations.
  Length: 40 hours (5 days).
  Dates: January 1985-Present.
  Objective: To prepare the student in the acquisition, writing, and/or interpreting of easement descriptions.
  Learning Outcome: Upon successful completion of this course, the student will be able to write accurate grants of easement; determine the current ownership of a particular piece of land; appraise the value of an easement; run a chain of title; examine and interpret surveys, deeds, and easements; and negotiate a signed easement from the property owner.
  Instruction: Course covers application of real property law concepts, determining grantors, title search, appraising real property, and writing accurate grants and easements. Methodology includes lecture, group discussions, cases, and videotape.
  Credit recommendation: In the lower division baccalaureate/associate degree, or vocational certificate category, 3 semester hours in Civil Engineering Technology, Real Estate, or as a Business elective (9/88).

Sales Skills (05846-D)
  Location: Various locations throughout California.
  Length: 37½ hours (1 week, 7½ hours per day).
  Dates: March 1985-Present.
  Objective: To introduce students to basic selling skills so they can recognize and assess customer needs, recommend appropriate services and products, overcome customer objections, and close the sale.

Learning Outcome: Upon successful completion of this course, the student will be able to improve sales performance in the field.

Instruction: A six-step sales model is employed which covers sales planning, approaching the customer, data gathering, solutions development, closing the sale, and post-sales follow-up. The teaching methodology includes lectures, class discussion, exercises, and case studies.

Credit recommendation: In the lower division baccalaureate/associate degree category, 2 semester hours in Principles of Salesmanship (8/87).

SCC Trunk Tester (05617)
Location: Various training locations in California and Nevada.
Length: 56 hours (8 days).
Dates: January 1985-Present.
Objective: To enable students upon completion of the course to acquire the skills and knowledge necessary to perform the following tasks in the switching control center: trunking and facilities, interoffice signaling, transmission, trunk orders, trunk testing, administration, and full maintenance.
Instruction: Covers and familiarizes the student with the switching control center (SCC) and trunk work station as well as SCC procedures as they apply to the trunk installation/maintenance function. This course will enable the student to perform basic trunk testing, trunk installation, and trunk field maintenance. Methodology includes self-paced instruction.
Credit recommendation: In the lower division baccalaureate/associate degree category, 2 semester hours in Electronics Technology (8/85).

Spreadsheets, Graphics, Word Processing and Database Using Symphony
(Alternate Title: Symphony Spreadsheets and Graphics [01417], Symphony Word Processing [01420], Symphony Database [01421])
Location: Los Angeles, Pasadena, Tustin, San Ramon, Oakland, San Diego, Sacramento, San Jose, and San Francisco, CA.
Length: 21 hours (3 days).
Dates: August 1984-Present.
Objective: Students completing this course will understand what the software package Symphony is, what it includes, and how to use its features to build spreadsheets, do word processing, and to create a database.
Learning Outcome: Upon completion of this course, the student can build and print a simple spreadsheet, create and print a graph from information in a spreadsheet, create and edit text documents, and can create and manage a database.
Instruction: The course covers the fine separate environments included in the Symphony software package.
Credit recommendation: In the vocational certificate or lower division baccalaureate/associate degree category, 1 semester hour in Data Processing, Business Administration, or Management Information Systems (MIS) (11/86). NOTE: Essentially a lab course.

Strategic Management Writing (01019)
Location: Oakland, San Ramon, Los Angeles, Tustin, San Diego, and Pasadena, CA.
Length: 16 hours (2 eight-hour days).
Dates: September 1987-Present.
Objective: To increase the students' capability in using the processes needed for effective written communication.
Learning Outcome: Upon successful completion of this course, the student will be able to apply problem-solving techniques in the planning stage; do a variety of outlining procedures—clustering, tree branching—for organizing large numbers of ideas; produce drafts rapidly; make specific changes in sentences and paragraphs to increase readability; and fine-tune the professional image he/she projects in his/her writing.
Instruction: Course covers how to get started, without pain; how to overcome communications barriers; how to communicate outside your department; how to polish your style; how to develop persuasive strategies; and how to develop strategic writing techniques to improve letters, memos and reports. Methodology includes lecture, discussion, demonstration, writing exercises, problem solving, quizzes, and presentations.
Credit recommendation: In the lower division baccalaureate/associate degree, or vocational certificate category, 1 semester hour in Business Administration, Business Communication, or Management and Supervision (9/88).

Structured COBOL (58524)
(Introduction to Structured COBOL Programming)
Location: Oakland, CA.
Length: 80 hours (2 weeks).
Dates: January 1986-Present.
Objective: To introduce the student to the essential elements of the ANS COBOL language. Major topics include program writing, compiling, debugging, and executing.
Learning Outcome: Upon successful completion of this course, the student will be able to list syntax rules; write an identification division, a configuration section, an environment division, a data division, and a procedure division using the ANS COBOL language.
Instruction: Course covers various naming conventions and rules for writing all major divisions of a COBOL program. It also covers data representation, file/merge procedures, and formatting of output reports. Course is self-paced using video and tutor/student instruciton.
Credit recommendation: In the lower division baccalaureate/associate degree category, 3 semester hours in Computer Information Systems, Computer Science, or

Data Processing (8/87).

Systems Analysis and Design (02256)
  Location: Los Angeles and Oakland, CA.
  Length: 40 hours (5 days).
  Dates: October 1986-Present.
  Objective: To provide the student with an understanding of life cycle as a methodology and analysis and design skill.
  Learning Outcome: Upon successful completion of this course, the student will be able to collect data, interview, define problems, prepare and support proposals, and oversee installations and operations.
  Instruction: Course presents method of data collection, problem definition, analysis, systems planning, and design in support of proposal preparation, and follow-up, installation and operations. The post-implementation review is also covered. Examples and case studies are used in the course. Techniques are presented for tracking progress in analysis and design as well as for evaluating situations.
  Credit recommendation: In the upper division baccalaureate category, 3 semester hours in Computer Information Systems (11/86). NOTE: No graduate credit; students do not have prerequisites to suggest graduate. Text material is at undergraduate level.

System Design Consultant Communication Skills (02138)
  Location: Various training locations throughout California and Nevada.
  Length: 24 hours (3 days).
  Dates: October 1982-December 1988.
  Objective: To teach the student effective communication skills in a technical environment, with the client and other members of the marketing team through consideration of basic communication models and techniques and the design and development of technical reports, sales proposals, and presentations.
  Instruction: Covers communications concepts and techniques, proposal strategies, understanding one's audience, presentation style and techniques, effective use of language and English skills, managing and rehearsing presentations.
  Credit recommendation: In the upper division baccalaureate category, 2 semester hours in Business Communications (11/84).

Telemarketing Concepts and Sales Process (02145-A)
  Location: Oakland and Los Angeles, CA.
  Length: 24 hours (3 days).
  Dates: January 1985-Present.
  Objective: To provide students with skills required to understand telecommunications marketing which can assist potential customers of the company's product and services.
  Instruction: Covers telecommunications technology as a marketing tool in a well organized marketing program. Marketing strategies, the sales process and information gathering are included. Methodology includes lectures and customer led discussions as well as classroom exercises and problem solving.
  Credit recommendation: In the lower division baccalaureate/associate degree category, 1 semester hour in Marketing Seminar (8/85).

Telemarketing Design and Implementation Workshop (02145-D)
  Location: Oakland and Los Angeles, CA.
  Length: 24 hours (3 days).
  Dates: February 1985-Present.
  Objective: To provide students with basic information to assist customers in designing a general telecommunication marketing system.
  Instruction: Covers telemarketing systems design through casework analysis and documentation. Methodology includes lectures and instructor led discussions with student analysis of case problems.
  Credit recommendation: In the lower division baccalaureate/associate degree category, 1 semester hour in Marketing Seminar (8/85).

Television Fundamentals and Signal Analysis (Basic) (04457)
  Location: Various training locations throughout California and Nevada.
  Length: 40 hours (1 week).
  Dates: May 1984-Present.
  Objective: To provide the student with the necessary basic and common background information required by persons working in the television field.
  Instruction: Covers four parts: Black and White Television, Color Television, Television Testing, and Television Transmission Systems. Basic concepts and principles are stressed with hands-on participation in the demonstration sessions. Methodology includes lecture, reading, and classroom demonstration involving the use of TV monitors and test signal generators. It is not a TV repair course. (Possession of an FCC radio license is prerequisite for the course.)
  Credit recommendation: In the lower division baccalaureate/associate degree category, 3 semester hours in Basic Television Theory (11/84).

Transmission Fundamentals (02139)
  Location: Oakland and Los Angeles, CA.
  Length: 32-34 hours (1 week).
  Dates: February 1979-December 1988.
  Objective: To introduce the student to concepts of data transmission.
  Instruction: Covers basic skills necessary to establish and maintain data transmission facilities and to perform required transmission tests, analyze results to determine if

requirements are met and take corrective action when necessary. Individualized, self-instructional workbooks with audiotape and laboratory for hands-on experience and job-relevant testing.

Credit recommendation: In the lower division baccalaureate/associate degree category, 2 semester hours in Data Transmission Fundamentals (11/84). NOTE: This course should only be used for elective credit.

UNISYS Database Concepts and UNISYS 1100 Series System Concepts (52698 and 52691)
   Location: Hayward, San Ramon, and San Diego, CA.
   Length: 20 hours (2½ days).
   Dates: January 1986-Present.
   Objective: To teach the student fundamental concepts of data and hierarchical and relational data base management systems (DBMS) operating system concepts for the UNISYS 1100.
   Learning Outcome: Upon successful completion of this course, the student will be able to define a database and understand basic database terminology; understand hierarchical and relational databases; be familiar with the three types of hierarchical databases and the terminology used in describing relational databases; define and understand the main functions of the UNISYS 1100 operating system; and have a basic understanding of runstream processing on the 1100.
   Instruction: Course covers basic database terminology, hierarchical database concepts, relational database concepts, the fine main components of the UNISYS operating system, and runstream processing on the UNISYS 1100 mainframe. Methodology includes discussion and computer-based training.
   Credit recommendation: In the lower division baccalaureate/associate degree category, 2 semester hours in Computer Science, Data Processing, or Management Information Systems (9/88). NOTE: Students who receive credit for this course should not receive credit for Introduction to Data Base Management Systems.

UNISYS Peripheral Subsystems (52660)
   Location: Hayward, San Ramon, and San Diego, CA.
   Length: 20 hours (2½ days).
   Dates: April 1987-Present.
   Objective: To teach the student operator procedures for certain UNISYS computer peripheral devices.
   Learning Outcome: Upon successful completion of this course, the student will be able to do keyins on the UTS 20 and UTS 60 consoles; boot the UTS 60; change the paper in the pagewriter; understand the functions of the tape controllers and tape drives; mount tapes and clean the tape drives; reload the 0770 printer with paper; understand the disk subsystem and the pathways to the central complex; understand the operator control panels on the disk drives; know where to look for the error codes on both types of disk drives, the 8480 and the 8481; know how to IML the disk controller; understand the concept of caching and the cache terms; and know the cache operator keyins.
   Instruction: Course covers consoles and pagewriters, tape controllers and drives, the model 0770 printer, and cache memory. Methodology includes lecture and laboratory.
   Credit recommendation: In the vocational certificate category, 1 semester hour in Data Processing (9/88).

Utilities (Survey of IBM Utilities Progress) (52139)
   Location: Concord, Hayward, San Ramon, and San Diego, CA.
   Length: 20 hours (2½ days).
   Dates: June 1984-Present.
   Objective: To teach computer systems operators the purpose and use of utilities progress and the utilities manual.
   Learning Outcome: Upon successful completion of this course, the student will be able to describe the purpose of utility programs; identify the type of utility program; and use a utilities manual.
   Instruction: Course covers the IBM utility manual, the more commonly used utilities, and techniques for copying from one storage medium to another.
   Credit recommendation: In the lower division baccalaureate/associate degree category, 1 semester hour in Computer Science, Data Processing, or Management Information Systems (9/88).

The Versatile Organization (42000 or 42000P) (Social Styles/Interpersonal Skills)
   Location: Various Business/Consumer Marketing locations throughout California.
   Length: 8-13 hours (Interactive Video).
   Dates: November 1986-Present.
   Objective: To enable students to observe behavioral characteristics of Customers/Managers/Subordinates in a non-judgemental way and from those observations be able to be versatile in meeting the expectations of people different or same as themselves.
   Learning Outcome: Upon successful completion of this course, the student will be able to discriminate degrees of assertiveness and responsiveness in people based on their behavior, so as to classify them in one of four social types; identify the need and expectations of each social style; and design and implement appropriate strategies for interacting with each style.
   Instruction: Course presents the idea that behavior reflects preferred styles for interacting with others. Covers how to observe behavioral characteristics in a non-judgemental way and to develop appropriate interpersonal skills for (versatility) dealing with the different styles. The course is self-paced and utilizes interactive video.
   Credit recommendation: In the lower divsion baccalaureate/associate degree category, 1 semester hour in

Interpersonal Skills (8/87).

Voice Network Design (45510)
(Formerly 02132)
Location: Oakland and Los Angeles, CA.
Length: 32 hours (1 week).
Dates: November 1982-Present.
Objective: To teach the student the statistical skills and traffic theories necessary for traffic management.
Instruction: Principles of data collection concepts sampling, probability, and traffic theory. Lecture, discussion, and laboratory exercises are used.
Credit recommendation: In the upper division baccalaureate category, 1 semester hour in Statistics (11/84).

Wang Word Processing Training (00029)
Location: Various training locations throughout California.
Length: 20 hours (3 days).
Dates: January 1980-Present.
Objective: To provide students with training on how to use a WANG word processing system to create, edit, print, and store documents at the introductory level.
Instruction: Covers introductory word processing concepts and basic machine operation to create, edit, print, and store documents. Methodology includes self-paced instruction using CRT work stations, video monitors, and practical applications in a variety of business documents.
Credit recommendation: In the lower division baccalaureate/associate degree category, 1 semester hour in Beginning Word Processing Application (8/85).

1. Winning (1003)
2. Interpersonal Skills (1000)
3. Problem Solving (1064)
Location: Various training locations throughout California.
Length: 40 hours (1 week).
Dates: January 1981-December 1988.
Objective: *Courses 1 and 2:* To enable the student to develop an awareness of the impact of individual leadership styles on motivation and to assess behavior patterns as they enhance or impede effective communication in the workplace. *Course 3:* To enable the student to use a practical and sequential method in analyzing and solving problems.
Instruction: *Courses 1 and 2* cover a choice of learning tools which impact awareness and perception leading to behavior change on the job, e.g., Firo B., Situational Leadership, Johari Window, etc. *Course 3* covers a step-by-step process model for solving problems. Methodology includes discussion, role play exercises, and audiovisual media.
Credit recommendation: In the lower division baccalaureate/associate degree category, 2 semester hours in Human Relations and in Supervision (11/84).

Word Processing Concepts and the Use of Displaywrite (1444A, 1444B, 1444C)
(Displaywrite4 Users Series: Beginning, Intermediate, and Advanced)
Location: Los Angeles, Pasadena, San Jose, San Ramon, Tustin, Oakland, San Diego, Sacramento, and San Francisco, CA.
Length: 24 hours (3 days).
Dates: August 1985-Present.
Objective: To teach the student beginning, intermediate, and advanced concepts of the Displaywrite word processing software package.
Learning Outcome: Upon successful completion of this course, the student will be able to create, edit, and print documents, letters, and reports; save and load documents; create and use Stop codes; create, edit, and execute keystroke programs; create, use, and print a paragraph library; and work with ASCII files.
Instruction: Course covers review of microcomputer fundamentals and the hardware required to run Displaywrite, beginning Displaywrite concepts, including creating, editing, formatting, printing, and saving a document, intermediate Displaywrite concepts, including merging documents, creating and making labels, pagination, table construction, and keystroke programming, and advanced Displaywrite concepts, including retrieving ASCII files and advanced math, marking tables for revision, and drawing with the cursor.
Credit recommendation: In the lower division baccalaureate/associate degree category, 1 semester hour in Business Administration, Data Processing, or Management Information Systems (9/88). NOTE: It is recommended that a student be granted credit in only one word processing concepts course (i.e., Multimate, Displaywrite, Wordstar, etc.).

Word Processing Concepts and the Use of Multimate (1416A, 1416B, 1416C)
(Multimate Users Series: Beginning, Intermediate, and Advanced)
Location: Los Angeles, Pasadena, San Jose, San Ramon, Tustin, Oakland, San Diego, Sacramento, and San Francisco, CA.
Length: 24 hours (3 days).
Dates: August 1985-Present.
Objective: To teach the student beginning, intermediate, and advanced concepts of the Multimate word processing software package.
Learning Outcome: Upon successful completion of this course, the student will be able to create, edit, and print documents, letters, and reports; format documents, letters, and reports; edit previously created documents; and create and edit key procedures and the customer dictionary.
Instruction: Course covers review of microcomputer fundamentals and the hardware required to run Multi-

mate; beginning Multimate concepts; intermediate Multimate concepts, including key procedures, merges, pagination, libraries, and the thesaurus; advanced features of Multimate, such as line and box drawing, updating records, creating and manipulating columns, editing the custom dictionary and file conversion. Methodology involves lecture.

Credit recommendation: In the lower division baccalaureate/associate degree category, 1 semester hour in Business Administration, Data Processing, or Management Information Systems (9/88). NOTE: It is recommended that a student be granted credit in only one word processing course (i.e., Multimate, Displaywrite, Wordstar, etc.).

Word Processing Concepts: MS-Word on MacIntosh (1433, 1435, 1443)
(MacIntosh and Microsoft Word Users Series: Meet the Mac, Beginning, Intermediate, and Advanced)
  Location: Various California locations.
  Length: 24 hours (3 days).
  Dates: August 1985-Present.
  Objective: To provide the student with an understanding and skills in using MS-Word on a MacIntosh computer.
  Learning Outcome: Upon successful completion of this course, the student will be able to create, edit, and print documents with Word; use software options to scroll, select, and to work with ruler line; create, edit, and manipulate columns; and use graphics in documents.
  Instruction: Course includes two segments. The first segment provides an explanation of the components of a MacIntosh computer system and how it works. The second segment provides the student with detailed operation procedures of MS-Word software. Specific topics include Word fundamentals, scrolling, selecting, editing, working with the ruler, tables and columns, graphics, and printing. Methodology includes lectures and hands-on activities.
  Credit recommendation: In the lower division baccalaureate/associate degree category, 1 semester hour in Computer Information Systems or Data Processing (9/88). NOTE: It is recommended that a student be granted credit in only one word processing course (i.e., Multimate, Displaywrite, Wordstar, etc.).

Writing Management Reports (01266)
  Location: Various training locations throughout California.
  Length: 24 hours (3 days).
  Dates: November 1984-Present.
  Objective: To enable managers to write reports more effectively, applying the basic principles of Information Mapping.
  Instruction: Covers basic principles of Information Mapping writing methods; includes the writing of memos and reports that involves how the mind processes information. Methodology includes lecture, discussion, and student exercises.
  Credit recommendation: In the upper division baccalaureate category, 1 semester hour in Management Report Writing (8/85).

The Palmer School

The Palmer School was founded in 1885 as a shorthand school by Orson R. Palmer. Throughout the years, the curriculum expanded to include the business courses that today prepare students for a career in the business community. Students wishing to become enrolled must pass entrance tests in mathematics, reading comprehension, and language skills. They must also display a positive attitude toward business training, responsibility, and personal achievement. A teaching staff provides education in business training.

In October 1983, Educom, Inc.—a publicly held corporation—purchased The Palmer School. Through this purchase, Educom, Inc. has combined 100 years of business education with today's technological era.

Source of official student records: Registrar, Palmer School, 1118 Market Street, Philadelphia, Pennsylvania 19107.

Additional information about the courses: Compact for Lifelong Educational Opportunities (CLEO), 37 South 16th Street, Philadelphia, Pennsylvania 19102 or Program on Noncollegiate Sponsored Instruction, The Center for Adult Learning and Educational Credentials, American Council on Education, One Dupont Circle, Washington, D.C. 20036.

Accounting
1. Accounting I
2. Accounting II
3. Accounting III
  Location: Palmer School, Philadelphia, PA.
  Length: 60 hours (1½ weeks).
  Dates: September 1977-Present.
  Objective: *Course 1:* To introduce students to basic accounting concepts as they apply to service and merchandising business. *Course 2:* To expand the students' knowledge of merchandising business organized as proprietorships and partnerships and to introduce manufacturing accounting concepts and corporate accounting. *Course 3:* To enable students to study in greater detail transactions unique to corporations and managerial decision making.
  Instruction: *Course 1:* Introduces the basic accounting cycle of a service and merchandising business. Includes such topics as journalizing, posting, trial balance, special journals, work sheet, adjusting entries, closing entries, balance sheet, financial statements, accounting for returns,

allowances, discounts, and bank reconciliations. *Course 2:* Broadens the students' knowledge of basic accounting concepts and includes such topics as receivables and payables, merchandise inventory, plant assets and depreciation, accruals and deferrals, and principles of good internal control, including voucher, payroll, and data processing systems. Introduces partnership and corporate accounting, dividends, problems of measurement and reporting, and long-term financing and investment. Prerequisite: Accounting I. *Course 3:* An analysis of corporate financial and managerial accounting which includes financial statement analysis, changes in financial position, cost accounting for a manufacturing enterprise, and decision making aids such as capital budgeting, rate of return, and break-even analyses. (Prerequisite: Accounting II.) Lecture and teacher-supervised discussion and laboratory are used.

Credit recommendation: In the lower division baccalaureate/associate degree category, 6 semester hours in Business Administration; or 9 semester hours in the vocational certificate degree category (6/84).

Business Law I
Location: Palmer School, Philadelphia, PA.
Length: 60 hours (1½ week).
Dates: September 1977-Present.
Objective: To provide the business student with a basic understanding of the legal environment in which business is conducted, an awareness of legal rights and remedies and the ability to recognize contract law situations requiring legal counsel.
Instruction: An overview of the nature and operation of the legal system in the United States. Course content includes contracts, bailments, sales, warranties, and product liabilities. Lecture and teacher-supervised discussion and laboratory are used.
Credit recommendation: In the lower division baccalaureate/associate degree category, or in the upper division baccalaureate category, 3 semester hours in Business Administration (6/84).

Business Law II
Location: Palmer School, Philadelphia, PA.
Length: 60 hours (1½ weeks).
Dates: September 1977-Present.
Objective: To provide students with an awareness of the legal environment in which business transactions are completed; an understanding that business decisions must be considered in light of their legal consequences; a comprehension of the legal rights and responsibilities of business owners, consumers and workers; and a knowledge of the legal remedies available to injured parties.
Instruction: A continuation of Business Law I including commercial and administrative law with emphasis on commercial paper, agency, employment business organization, real property and inheritance, insurance and secured transactions. Lecture and teacher-supervised discussion and laboratory are used.
Credit recommendation: In the lower division baccalaureate/associate degree category or in the upper division baccalaureate category, 3 semester hours in Business Administration (6/84).

Introduction to Business
Location: Palmer School, Philadelphia, PA.
Length: 60 hours (1½ weeks).
Dates: September 1977-Present.
Objective: To give the students a review of all functional areas of business; to provide students with a practical approach to the operations of American business; and to motivate and prepare students for the business world.
Instruction: A study of business organizations in the United States, and a detailed examination of the functional aspects of management. Lecture and teacher-supervised discussion and laboratory are used.
Credit recommendation: In the lower division baccalaureate/associate degree category, or in the vocational certificate degree category, 3 semester hours in Business Administration (6/84).

Pitney-Bowes Incorporated

At Pitney-Bowes Inc., the Sales Training Department is charged with providing both newly hired sales representatives and the field sales force with the necessary tools to perform effectively. As an integral part of marketing services, the Department provides both formal and field training.

Formal training is offered at the Pitney-Bowes National Sales Training Center, a spacious and comfortably facility that creates an excellent atmosphere for learning.

A carefully trained team of 11 instructors constitutes the teaching force. Instructors have been selected on the basis of achieving their objectives in field sales and sales management positions as well as on their college degrees.

Source of official student records: Pitney-Bowes Inc., Sales Training Center, 201 Aberdeen Parkway, Peachtree, Georgia 30269-1422.

Additional information about the courses: Thomas A. Edison State College, Program on Noncollegiate Sponsored Instruction, Office of Special Programs, 101 W. State St., Trenton, NJ 08625.

Introduction to Selling
Location: Pitney-Bowes National Training Center, Cherry Hill, NJ.
Length: 50 hours (7 days).
Dates: January 1981-Present.
Objective: To develop new employees' understanding of the sales process and improve their sales skills.

Instruction: Covers current concepts and practices pertaining to the sales process, including produce analysis, the approach, effective interviewing, effective presentation, handling objections, and closing the sale. Also emphasizes verbal communications skills. Methods of instruction include interactive lectures; self-instructional multimedia learning modes such as work books, videotapes, and slide-tapes; role-playing, and field observation.

Credit recommendation: In the lower division baccalaureate/associate degree category, 3 semester hours in Marketing (5/82).

PJA School

The PJA School provides a Paralegal Training Program designed to educate students for employment as entry level paralegals. The 300 hour Program consists of the eight areas of study presented in the course displays below. Classroom activities are supplemented by trips taken within the parameters of class times. The School also offers an optional Internship opportunity to those students desiring to avail themselves of it at the completion of their paralegal classroom work. The PJA School's educational objective is to give students the skills which will allow them to work as entry level legal assistants. This entails imparting legal theory, presenting practical skills and giving background enrichment. The program has been licensed by the Pennsylvania Department of Education (Board of Private Business Schools) and accredited by the National Association of Trade and Technical Schools. The PJA School employs a small faculty of practicing attorneys. The faculty is evaluated by students at the end of each class. The PJA School conducts extensive evaluations of its students. These evaluations consist both of periodic examinations and written assignments. The examinations, which contain both objective sections and essay questions, are designed to check the student's retention of theory and terminology, while the written assignments are designed to monitor the student's practical drafting skills.

Source of official student records: Director of Admissions, The PJA School, 7900 West Chester Pike, Upper Darby, Pennsylvania 19082.

Additional information about the courses: Program on Noncollegiate Sponsored Instruction, The Center for Adult Learning and Educational Credentials, American Council on Education, One Dupont Circle, Washington, D.C. 20036.

Business Entities

Location: Upper Darby, PA.
Length: Day: 36 hours (6 weeks); five 1.2 hour meetings per week. Night: 36 hours (12 weeks); one 3 hour meeting per week. Saturday: 36 hours (9 weeks); one 4 hour meeting per week.
Dates: January 1982-Present.
Objective: To give students both basic knowledge of business organizations and skills to assist in their operation.
Learning Outcome: Given the task of reading and interpreting a Partnership Agreement, the student successfully completing this course will be able to accomplish the job with a minimum of assistance. Faced with the assignment of drafting a Pennsylvania Articles of Incorporation and Registry Statement, the student will be able to complete the task without assistance. The successful student will also, when necessary, be able to identify the nature of a business by examining its structure, financing, and extent of government control. When asked to describe corporate management and financing, the successful student will be able to give a comprehensive overview. When necessary, the student will also be able to identify different methods for corporate takeover, different mechanisms for the combining of corporations, the major functions of the Securities Exchange Commission, the classic common law and SEC Fiduciary Duties, and the dynamics of corporate dissolution and liquidation.
Instruction: The student learns the various types of Pennsylvania business entities and formats from sole proprietorships through partnerships to corporations. Extensive time is spent on the corporate form. Appropriate documents are drafted. Lecture and discussion are used.
Credit recommendation: In the lower division baccalaureate/associate degree category or in the upper division baccalaureate category, 3 semester hours in Business Corporations or Business Entities (5/86).

Civil Litigation

Location: Upper Darby, PA.
Length: Day: 42 hours (6 weeks); five 1.4 meetings per week. Night: 42 hours (12 weeks); one 3.5 hour meeting per week. Saturday: 42 hours (11 weeks); one 4 hour meeting per week.
Dates: January 1982-Present.
Objective: To give the student comprehensive instruction on the theories and practical application of Pennsylvania and federal procedural law with a view toward the student obtaining skills to provide independent litigation support.
Learning Outcome: Given the name of Pennsylvania, New Jersey, or Federal Court, the student successfully completing this course will be able to identify the court system to which it belongs and the level of the court. Given a hypothetical dispute, the student will be able to identify it as a contract or tort situation and be able to analyze the relative merits of both sides' cases. When asked to draft a Pennsylvania or Federal Court Civil Complaint, the successful student will be able to do so. Given the task of answering the Civil Complaint, once again the successful student will be able to do so. When asked to prepare or answer a Request for Production of Documents

or Interrogatories, the student will be able to do so with minimal supervision by an attorney. Faced with the task of preparing a Notice of Deposition or Subpoena, the student will be able to complete the assignment without error. Asked to digest a deposition, the student will be able to do so in the style demonstrated in his text materials. Given the assignment of preparing a Pre-Trial Memorandum, the successful student will be able to do so with minimal attorney supervision. When asked to prepare settlement papers, the student will be able to comply without mistake, while, when requested to maintain files and a reminder or "tickler" system, the student will again be able to do so without error. The successful student will also be able to prepare without assistance a Pennsylvania Motion or Answer to Motion when asked to do so and to identify the purpose and sequence of civil trial states when requested.

Instruction: This course deals with the essentials of handling a lawsuit. Students learn the Pennsylvania, New Jersey, and Federal Court systems, and a background of substantive law. They learn how to handle a lawsuit from beginning to end, including filing pleadings and handling discovery. Lecture and discussion are used.

Credit recommendation: In the lower division baccalaureate/associate degree category, 3 semester hours in Paralegal Studies or in the upper division baccalaureate category, 3 semester hours as an elective in Legal Studies (5/86).

Criminal Law

Location: Upper Darby, PA.

Length: Day: 42 hours (6 weeks); five 1.4 hour meetings per week. Night: 42 hours (12 weeks); one 3.5 hour meeting per week. Saturday: 42 hours (11 weeks); one 4 hour meeting per week.

Dates: January 1982-Present.

Objective: To acquaint students with the definitions of various crimes, the nature of the criminal process and the area of Constitutional Criminal Law.

Learning Outcome: Upon successful completion of this course, the student will, when faced with the description of a criminal act, be able to identify the crimes committed. When dealing with a client, the successful student will be able to describe the criminal process and its various stages. When given the description of a certain activity by the police or the judiciary, the successful student will be able to identify areas of Constitutional misconduct. Moreover, when asked to, the successful student will be able to draft an Entry of Appearance, Petition for a Change of Venue, or Petition to Suppress Evidence.

Instruction: Students learn the essentials of the criminal system—both substantive criminal law and criminal procedure. Attention is given to Constitutional considerations and the drafting of papers. Lecture and discussion are used.

Credit recommendation: In the lower division baccalaureate/associate degree category, 3 semester hours in Criminal Procedures (5/86).

Domestic Relations

Location: Upper Darby, PA.

Length: Day: 36 hours (6 weeks); five 1.2 hour meetings per week. Night: 36 hours (12 weeks); one 3.0 hour meeting per week. Saturday: 36 hours (9 weeks); one 4 hour meeting per week.

Dates: January 1982-Present.

Objective: To acquaint the student with major areas of family law and to give the student the skills to deal with these areas.

Learning Outcome: Upon successful completion of this course, the student will, given the task of dealing with a client contemplating marriage, be able to indicate the statutory requirements for marriage and the requirements for a valid prenuptial agreement. When dealing with a divorced spouse, the successful student will be able to identify and describe the various mechanisms for the enforcement of support. When working with prospective adoptive parents, the student will be able to describe the adoption procedure and draft an Adoption Petition. Given the task of discussing parental rights and duties with clients, the successful student will be able to describe these rights and duties in a comprehensive manner. When working with divorcing clients, the successful student will be able to describe divorce procedure to the clients and to draft divorce complaints, answers, motions and related documents.

Instruction: This course covers family law—the judicial resolution of disputes and questions involving the family. Divorce, separation, support, custody and adoption in Pennsylvania court systems are covered. Students learn to handle a divorce case from beginning to end. Lecture and Discussion are used.

Credit recommendation: In the upper division baccalaureate or graduate category, 3 semester hours as an elective in Legal Studies (5/86).

Legal Research

Location: Upper Darby, PA.

Length: Day: 60 hours (6 weeks); five 2 hour meetings per week. Night: 60 hours (12 weeks); one 5 hour meeting per week. Saturday: 60 hours (15 weeks); one 4 hour meeting per week.

Dates: January 1982-Present.

Objective: To give students basic research skills in how to read cases and statutes, how to write memoranda of law, how to find the law, and how to update the law.

Learning Outcome: Upon successful completion of this course, the student will, when asked, be able to read a case opinion, construct an outline of the opinion, and convert the outline into a written memorandum of law. When given a research assignment, the successful student will be able to find a case on a certain legal topic in a Law Encyclopedia or Digest, to find a certain statute in a Statute Book, to find a certain rule of court in a Rule Book, and to find a certain legal form in a Form Book. When asked, the successful student will also be able to Shepardize a case.

Instruction: The student learns the valuable skills of finding law and analyzing it. Students learn to use the law library and the books in it. Substantial attention is given to reading cases. Shepardization is covered. Lecture and discussion are used.

Credit recommendation: In the lower division baccalaureate/associate degree category, 2 semester hours as an elective in Legal Studies (5/86).

Real Property
  Location: Upper Darby, PA.
  Length: Day: 36 hours (6 weeks); five 1.2 hour meetings per week. Night: 36 hours (12 weeks); one 3 hour meeting per week. Saturday: 36 hours (9 weeks); one 4 hour meeting per week.
  Dates: January 1982-Present.
  Objective: To give students both knowledge and skills in real estate law.
  Learning Outcome: Upon successful completion of this course, the student will, when speaking with a client, be able to identify and describe such different types of land ownership as Free Simple, Life Estate, Cooperative and Condominium, Joint Tenancy, Tenancy in Common, and Tenancy by the Entireties. When asked to assist in the preparation of preliminary real estate transaction papers, the successful student will be able to draft an Exclusive Sales Brokerage Agreement, a Buyer's Financial Information Form, a Buyer's Estimated Settlement Costs Form, and a Seller's Estimated Proceeds Form. When assisting in the transaction, the successful student will be able to draft an Agreement of Sale, a Mortgage, A Mortgage Note, a Deed and a Settlement Sheet. When assisting in a Landlord-Tenant situation, the successful student will be able to draft a Landlord-Tenant Complaint and a form lease. In counseling clients, the successful student will also be able to describe such land use control mechanisms as zoning, easements, restrictive convenants and reciprocal negative easements.
  Instruction: Students learn real estate law. The basic roots of English and American property law are covered in the first half of the course. Deeds, mortgages, leases and contracts in Pennsylvania legal practice constitute the second portion of the semester. Lecture and discussions are used.
  Credit recommendation: In the lower division baccalaureate/associate degree category, 3 semester hours in Fundamentals of Real Estate (5/86).

Wills and Estates
  Location: Upper Darby, PA.
  Length: Day: 36 hours (6 weeks); five 1.2 hour meetings per week. Night: 36 hours (12 weeks); one 3 hour meeting per week. Saturday: 36 hours (9 weeks); one 4 hour meeting per week.
  Dates: January 1982-Present.
  Objective: To give students both knowledge of probate issues and the skills to deal with probate problems.
  Learning Outcome: Upon successful completion of this course, the student will, in dealing with a client, be able to list the steps in the probate of both Testate and Intestate estates. When asked to, the student will be able to assist the attorney in the handling of these steps. In addition, when necessary the successful student will be able to draft a Simple Will, Self-Proved Will Affidavits and Codicils without assistance. Given the task of distinguishing among different types of insurance policies, trusts and estates arising from status, the successful student will be able to accomplish the task without assistance. Moreover, when asked to assist in the preparation of the Federal Estate Tax return, the student will be able render assistance in filling in the simple General Information, Asset and Liability schedules.
  Instruction: This course equips a student to handle an estate from the filing of initial papers to the final distribution of assets. Attention is given to drafting documents, including estate tax forms. Students learn how to interview executors and administrators. Lecture and discussion are used.
  Credit recommendation: In the upper division baccalaureate category, 3 semester hours as an elective in Legal Studies (5/86).

Police Training Institute

The Police Training Institute maintains its central administrative offices in Champaign/Urbana and, with its full-time staff and the assistance of many adjunct staff throughout the state of Illinois, provides training for approximately 5,000 Illinois police officers each year. Since the creation of the Institute in 1955, over 70,000 Illinois police officers have been trained there in various programs and activities.

Source of official student records: Director, Police Training Institute, University of Illinois, 409 East Chalmers, Room 209, Champaign, Illinois 61820.

Additional information about the courses: Program on Noncollegiate Sponsored Instruction, The Center for Adult Learning and Educational Credentials, American Council on Education, One Dupont Circle, Washington, D.C. 20036.

Advanced Law for Youth Officers
  Location: Champaign, or other locations in Illinois.
  Length: 36 hours (1 week).
  Dates: September 1976-Present.

Objective: To prepare students to handle youthful offender cases from detection to adjudication.

Instruction: Covers case law, including its historical and legal roots, in the judicial processing of children and youth; legal philosophy and rationale for precedent-setting decisions by the U.S. Supreme Court; Illinois-revised statutes as they pertain to and affect youth; recent Illinois apellate court decisions and national trends in youth law; educational trends in law-focused education in the schools; and information necessary to write an operating procedure defining criteria to follow when mechanical devices are used in the juvenile investigative process. Lecture is used.

Credit recommendation: In the lower division baccalaureate/associate degree category, 2 semester hours in Counseling, Criminal Justice, Criminology, Juvenile Delinquency, Juvenile Justice, or Sociology (3/80) (4/86). NOTE: This course has been reevaluated and continues to meet requirements for credit recommendations.

Basic Correctional Officers

Location: Champaign, or other locations in Illinois.
Length: 200 hours (5 weeks).
Dates: November 1985-Present.

Objective: To prepare basic correctional officer students to assume the duties and responsibilities which are relevant to a recruit correctional officer.

Instruction: Course includes at the introductory level, instruction in law, operations, investigations, correctional officer proficiency and human behavior. Methods used include lecture/discussion, case studies, computer-based instruction, computer managed instruction and practical exercises.

Credit recommendation: In the lower division baccalaureate/associate degree category, 3 semester hours in Criminal Justice or Corrections (4/86).

Basic Law Enforcement I

Location: Champaign, or other locations in Illinois.
Length: 160 hours (4 weeks).
Dates: May 1966-November 1969.

Objective: To provide a basic knowledge of procedures and practices involved in basic law enforcement.

Instruction: Covers issues related to the police and the public; legal concerns such as civil rights, court organization and procedures in Illinois, laws of arrest, and rules of evidence; traffic; criminal investigations; records and reports; patrol procedures; and specialized subjects including emergency aid to persons, juvenile matters, firearms training, and testifying in court. Lecture, discussion, and problem solving are used.

Credit recommendation: In the lower division baccalaureate/associate degree category, 5 semester hours in Basic Law Enforcement (8/80) (4/86). NOTE: Students who receive credit for this course should not receive credit for Basic Law Enforcement II, III, or IV. This course has been reevaluated and continues to meet requirements for credit recommendations.

Basic Law Enforcement II

Location: Champaign, or other locations in Illinois.
Length: 560 hours (14 weeks).
Dates: March 1974-June 1974.

Objective: To provide the necessary knowledge and performance skills to assume the responsibilities and duties of a recruit peace officer.

Instruction: Covers foundations of law enforcement and enforcement skills through a process of sequential learning that enables the student to demonstrate learning in law, behavior, physical skills, practices, and procedures. Lecture, discussion, and practical application with field experience are used.

Credit recommendation: In the lower division baccalaureate/associate degree category, 12 semester hours in Basic Law Enforcement (8/80) (4/86). NOTE: Students who receive credit for this course should not receive credit for Basic Law Enforcement I, III, or IV. This course has been reevaluated and continues to meet requirements for credit recommendations.

Basic Law Enforcement III

Location: Champaign, or other locations in Illinois.
Length: 244 hours (6 weeks).
Dates: December 1969-July 1982.

Objective: To prepare students to assume the obligations, tasks, and responsibilities necessary for efficient and judicious exercise of their authority and duties within the criminal justice system.

Instruction: Covers basic knowledge of the law enforcement function. Includes instruction on Illinois criminal and vehicle codes, judicial due process and related legal subjects, patrol practices and procedure, traffic law enforcement, human behavior, juvenile matters, criminal investigation. Also develops basic skills in making arrests, using firearms, stopping vehicles, handling crimes in progress, dealing with family disturbances, writing reports, and testifying in court. Lecture, classroom, and problem solving exercises are used.

Credit recommendation: In the lower division baccalaureate/associate degree category, 3 semester hours in Criminal Law, 3 semester hours in Patrol, and 2 semester hours in Traffic (8/80) (4/86). NOTE: Students who receive credit for this course should not receive credit for Law for Police or for Basic Law Enforcement I, II, or IV. This course has been reevaluated and continues to meet requirements for credit recommendations.

Basic Law Enforcement IV

Location: Champaign, or other locations in Illinois.
Length: 400 hours (10 weeks).
Dates: July 1982-Present.

Objective: To prepare students to assume the obligations attendant to the proper function of a recruit peace officer; to develop attitudinal and performance skills necessary for efficient and judicious exercise of authority and duties within the criminal justice system; to provide the foundation for a common quality of police protection and service by law enforcement personnel throughout the state of Illinois.

Instruction: Covers basic knowledge of the law enforcement function. Includes instruction on Illinois criminal and vehicle codes, judicial due process and related legal subjects, patrol practices and procedure, traffic law enforcement, human behavior, juvenile matters, criminal investigation. Also develops basic skills in making arrests, using firearms, stopping vehicles, handling crimes in progress, dealing with family disturbances, writing reports, and testifying in court. Lecture, classroom and problem solving exercises are used.

Credit recommendation: In the lower division baccalaureate/associate degree category, 4 semester hours in Criminal Law; in the lower division baccalaureate/associate degree category, 4 semester hours in Police Function and Human Behavior; in the lower division baccalaureate/associate degree category, 2 semester hours in Patrol Techniques (6/83) (4/86). NOTE: Students who receive credit for this course should not receive credit for Law for Police or Basic Law Enforcement I, II, or III. This course has been reevaluated and continues to meet requirements for credit recommendations.

Child Sex Exploitation
  Location: Champaign, or other locations in Illinois.
  Length: 32 hours (1 week).
  Dates: September 1985-Present.
  Objective: To assist criminal justice practitioners and allied child welfare personnel to understand, appreciate, and recognize the dynamics of child sex exploitation, including the nature of the pederphiles.
  Instruction: Covers psychosexual deviancy, laws pertaining to sex offenses against children, the nature and extent of child sex exploitation, the development of proactive investigative processes, interviewing sex offenders and sex-crime victims, and the establishment of a "preventive" network for combating sex exploitation. Methods include lecture, discussion, computer assisted instruction, case studies, role playing, and multimedia.
  Credit recommendation: In the lower division baccalaureate/associate degree category, 2 semester hours in Criminal Justice or in Social Work/Child Welfare, or 1 semester hour in Sociology or Psychology (Deviancy) (4/86).

Crime Prevention Officers
  Location: Champaign, Western Springs, or other locations in Illinois.
  Length: 80 hours (2 weeks).
  Dates: December 1973-December 1988.
  Objective: To prepare students for the specialized areas of crime prevention.
  Instruction: Covers requirements of an effective crime prevention program within the local police department; conducting and reporting of security surveys of building; procedures for submitting recommendations for improved security; techniques to reduce criminal opportunity; effective use of security hardware, such as alarms, lighting, and locks; role of construction engineering and design in preventing crime; and organizing effective crime prevention programs within the community.
  Credit recommendation: In the vocational certificate category, 1 semester hour in Crime Prevention Activity (3/80) (4/86). NOTE: This course has been reevaluated and continues to meet requirements for credit recommendations.

Crime Scene Technician
(Formerly Physical Evidence Technician)
  Location: Champaign, or other locations in Illinois.
  Length: 80 hours (2 weeks).
  Dates: *Version 1:* December 1973-December 1980; *Version 2:* January 1981-Present.
  Objective: *Version 1:* To provide the skills required to process effectively a crime scene for physical evidence. *Version 2:* To develop student-technician proficiency in knowledge and skills relative to the appropriate evidentiary processing of a crime scene.
  Instruction: *Version 1:* Legal considerations in search and seizure that relate to physical evidence and its admissibility in court; evidence potential; laboratory assistance and capability; crime scene requirements; and evidence processing. Specific skills developed in the course are crime scene and evidence photography; casting and molding; latent print restoration on a variety of surfaces; field comparison of fingerprints; crime scene sketching (field and court purposes); notetaking, including description of evidence and special report requirements; and packing, custody, and transmittal of various items of physical evidence. Lecture and laboratory are used. *Version 2:* Covers the application of meticulous methods to recognize, identify, collect, process, and preserve from contamination all macroscopic and microscopic materials relative to the criminal activity. Topics of instruction are role of the evidence technician, laws of evidence, an overview of physical evidence, role of the coroner/medical examiner, forensic pathology, forensic odontology, forensic toxicology, forensic etymology, questionable death investigation, pediatric evidence, sex crime evidence, gunshot evidence, blood splatters, forensic anthropology, mass disasters, forensic laboratory assistance, firearms identification, questioned documents, security of physical evidence, scene sketching, evidence technician testimony and courtroom exhibits, arson evidence, technician reports and records, vehicular physical evidence, scene search kits/equipment, impression evidence, crime science management, suicide/

homicide scenes, sudden infant death, explosive bomb scenes. Lecture, discussion, case histories, and practical exercises are used.

Credit recommendation: *Versions 1 and 2:* In the lower division baccalaureate/associate degree category, 4 semester hours in Forensic Science or Police Science (3/80) (4/86). NOTE: This course has been reevaluated and continues to meet requirements for credit recommendations.

Criminal Investigation
  Location: Champaign, or other locations in Illinois.
  Length: 80 hours (2 weeks).
  Dates: August 1968-Present.
  Objective: To acquaint the student with the investigation process and to present examples of the applications of the process to the investigation of various types of crimes.
  Instruction: Processing crime scene evidence, development of investigative leads at the crime scene, follow-up resources, identification of suspects, questioning of witnesses and suspects, investigative reporting, case preparation, and court testimony. Lecture and classroom exercises are used.
  Credit recommendation: In the lower division baccalaureate/associate degree category, 2 semester hours in Criminal Investigation (3/80) (4/86). NOTE: This course has been reevaluated and continues to meet requirements for credit recommendations.

Field Training Officer
  Location: *Version 1:* Champaign, Western Springs, or other locations in Illinois; *Version 2:* Champaign or other locations in Illinois.
  Length: *Version 1:* 80 hours (2 weeks); *Version 2:* 82 hours (2 weeks).
  Dates: *Version 1:* April 1973-June 1983; *Version 2:* July 1983-Present.
  Objective: To develop skills necessary for effective and meaningful field training to recruit officers; to provide methods of assessing recruit officer proficiency and ability to perform in the law enforcement profession.
  Instruction: *Version 1:* Covers teaching in a coach-pupil relationship, critiquing and evaluating performance, planning for progressive learning experiences, effective use of field training records, techniques for directing motivation and problem solving, and utilizing available resources for field training. *Version 2:* Similar to version one but with added emphasis on methods of instruction, principles of learning, and coach-pupil interactions.
  Credit recommendation: *Version 1:* In the vocational certificate category, 1 semester hour in Teaching Techniques (3/80). *Version 2:* In the lower division baccalaureate/associate degree category, 1 semester hour in Teaching Techniques (6/83) (4/86). NOTE: This course has been reevaluated and continues to meet requirements for credit recommendations.

First Line Supervision or Police Supervision
  Location: Champaign, or other locations in Illinois.
  Length: 79 hours (2 weeks).
  Dates: December 1967-Present.
  Objective: To acquaint students with basic principles of supervision applied to contemporary law enforcement issues from a practical rather than theoretical point of view.
  Instruction: Covers basic principles of supervision from a practical rather than theoretical point of view. Includes principles of supervision, leadership development, human relations and training, personnel evaluation and rating procedures, communication, and semantics. Lecture, discussion, and case studies are used.
  Credit recommendation: In the lower division baccalaureate/associate degree category, 3 semester hours in Office Management, Personnel Administration, Police Science, or Principles of Supervision (3/80) (4/86). NOTE: This course has been reevaluated and continues to meet requirements for credit recommendations.

Fundamentals of Burglary Investigation
  Location: Champaign, or other locations in Illinois.
  Length: 40 hours (1 week).
  Dates: September 1974-December 1988.
  Objective: To aid students in improving skills necessary for the preliminary investigation of burglary incidents.
  Instruction: Covers burglary prevention programs, review of legal matters affecting burglary incidents, types and techniques of burglary, stages and approaches to investigation, crime scene requirements for security and protection evidence, questioning witnesses and suspects. Lecture and classroom exercises are used.
  Credit recommendation: In the lower division baccalaureate/associate degree category, 1 semester hour in Criminal Investigation (3/80) (4/86). NOTE: Students must have completed Criminal Investigation before receiving credit for this course. Students cannot receive credit for this course and Homicide/Sex Investigation. This course has been reevaluated and continues to meet requirements for credit recommendations.

Homicide/Sex Investigation
  Location: Champaign, Western Springs, or other locations in Illinois.
  Length: 40 hours (1 week).
  Dates: September 1976-Present.
  Objective: To prepare investigative personnel to handle and process homicide or sexual misconduct incidents.
  Instruction: Covers legal review, including recent court decisions affecting murder, manslaughter, rape and other sex offense incidents; crime scene and evidence photography; evidence collection and laboratory processing; interviewing techniques, including special requirements for females, juveniles, and the handicapped; peculiar investigative techniques in questionable death cases; rape offender profiles; assistance for rape victims; special inves-

tigative techniques for sex offense incidents; and major case coordination. Lecture and classroom exercises are used.

Credit recommendation: In the lower division baccalaureate/associate degree category, 1 semester hour in Criminal Investigation (3/80) (4/86). NOTE: Students must have completed Criminal Investigation before receiving credit for this course. Students cannot receive credit for this course and Fundamentals of Burglary Investigation. This course has been reevaluated and continues to meet requirements for credit recommendations.

Introduction to Teaching Techniques
1. Police Instructors
2. Police In-Service Trainers

Location: Champaign, or other locations in Illinois.
Length: 72 hours (2 weeks).
Dates: 1. September 1978-Present; 2. June 1976-December 1988.
Objective: To enable students to develop instructional materials and procedures effective in achieving stated educational goals.
Instruction: Covers planning of effective classes for practitioners within the criminal justice system, utilizing effective instructional techniques to motivate students, measuring learning outcomes, and evaluating student performance. Lecture, discussion, and some microteaching are used.
Credit recommendation: In the lower division baccalaureate/associate degree category, 3 semester hours in Teaching Techniques (3/80) (4/86). NOTE: This course has been reevaluated and continues to meet requirements for credit recommendations.

Law for Police II
(Formerly Law for Police I)
Location: Champaign, or other locations in Illinois.
Length: *Version 1:* 40 hours (1 week); *Version 2:* 32 hours (1 week).
Dates: *Version 1:* March 1968-September 1984; *Version 2:* September 1984-Present.
Objective: To provide students with an updated and practical understanding of legal matters affecting the law enforcement function.
Instruction: *Version 1:* Covers constitutional law; Illinois criminal code; juvenile court act; civil rights and civil liability; police discretionary powers; rules of evidence, statements, admissions, and confessions; legal questions and answers; and current court decisions. Lecture is used. *Version 2:* Covers jurisdiction, law of admission, rights of the accused, criminal offenses in Illinois, use of force, civil rights and civil liability, laws of arrest, search and seizure, Illinois criminal code, legal aspects of drinking, driver enforcement, rules of evidence and identification procedures. Methods include lecture, discussion, and computer-based (Plato) instruction.

Credit recommendation: In the graduate or upper division baccalaureate category, 3 semester hours in Substantive and Procedural Criminal Law (4/86). NOTE: Students who receive credit for this course should not receive credit for Basic law Enforcement I, II, III, IV, or Law for Police I.

Management Techniques
(Formerly Law Enforcement Executive Management or Police Executive Development)
Location: Champaign, or other locations in Illinois.
Length: *Version 1:* 80 hours (2 weeks); *Version 2:* 36 hours (1 week).
Dates: *Version 1:* March 1968-March 1985; *Version 2:* April 1985-December 1988.
Objective: *Version 1:* To provide in-depth knowledge of contemporary management techniques and tools that will enhance the student's ability to function as a line or staff manager in a law enforcement agency. *Version 2:* To develop further the student's knowledge of management techniques and tools that will enable the student to function more effectively as a law enforcement administrator/manager.
Instruction: *Version 1:* Covers decision making, management by objectives, behavioral sciences, leadership, personnel management, planning, fiscal management, police productivity, managerial concepts, public speaking, and selected contemporary management resources and problems. Lecture, discussions, and classroom exercises are used. *Version 2:* Covers principles of management and organizational communications, establishment of organizational goals and objectives, managerial liability, management of the police operation, personnel management, organizational planning, and dynamics of decision making. Methods include lecture, discussion, case studies, and film.
Credit recommendation: *Version 1:* In the lower division baccalaureate/associate degree category, 3 semester hours in Police Administration or Principles of Management (3/80). *Version 2:* In the lower division baccalaureate/associate degree category, 2 semester hours in Police Administration/Management (4/86). NOTE: This course has been reevaluated and continues to meet requirements for credit recommendations.

Police Community Relations
Location: Champaign, or other locations in Illinois.
Length: 40 hours (1 week).
Dates: December 1968-December 1988.
Objective: To provide information on how to improve the police image and relations in the community.
Instruction: Covers improvement of the police image in the community; historical development of police-community relations; citizens' rights; crowd, mob, and riot behavior; rumor control; surveying citizens' attitudes; understanding violence in America; techniques for reducing

conflict behavior; using community resources; work skills for police-community relations officers; developing programs through crime prevention; and police-community relations and team policing. Lecture is used.

Credit recommendation: In the lower division baccalaureate/associate degree category, 3 semester hours in Criminal Justice, Police Science, Sociology, or Urban Affairs (3/80) (4/86). NOTE: Only students who have completed the basic course in law enforcement should receive credit for this course. This course has been reevaluated and continues to meet requirements for credit recommendations.

Youth Officers
  Location: Champaign, or other locations in Illinois.
  Length: 80 hours (2 weeks).
  Dates: December 1967-Present.
  Objective: To prepare students for the specialized function of handling cases involving youth and the legal processes attendant to juvenile offenders.
  Instruction: Covers theories of delinquency causation, understanding adolescent behavior, delinquency in Illinois, research on delinquency, special juvenile problem areas, Illinois Juvenile Court Act, laws and court decisions affecting juveniles, roles of state's attorney and public defender, police juvenile enforcement, policy and procedures in processing juveniles, investigative techniques, interpersonal communications, questioning juveniles, police-school relations, state and local community resources, crisis intervention techniques, the rehabilitative process, child abuse and neglect, youth alcohol and drugs, counseling techniques for youth officers, juvenile record systems, delinquency prevention strategies, and problems facing the youth officer. Lecture and classroom exercises are used.
  Credit recommendation: In the lower division baccalaureate/associate degree category, 4 semester hours in Counseling, Criminal Justice, Criminology, Juvenile Delinquency, Juvenile Justice, or Sociology (3/80) (4/86). NOTE: This course has been reevaluated and continues to meet requirements for credit recommendations.

Ponderosa Inc.

Ponderosa Inc. operates and licenses budget-priced Ponderosa Steakhouse restaurants. The system consists of approximately 460 company-operated and 235 licensee-operated steakhouses covering twenty-nine states and nine Canadian provinces.

The Ponderosa Development Institute (PDI), located at corporate headquarters in Dayton, Ohio provides training and development opportunities for management and employees of Ponderosa Inc. In addition to PDI, Ponderosa maintains twelve district training facilities in its various operation areas.

The training function in Ponderosa consists of three components: Operations Training, Classroom Instruction and Design, and Communication and Training Design. These components are responsible for the design and instruction of training and development programs offered at PDI and field locations.

Steakhouse Training and Education Program (STEP) is a specific training program for all entry level steakhouse managers. STEP is designed to produce qualified, well-trained general business managers to operate Ponderosa Steakhouses. Participants are evaluated on their performance as measured against well-defined objectives.

Source of official student records: Supervisor of Classroom Instruction and Design, Ponderosa Inc., P.O. 578, Dayton, Ohio 45401.

Additional information about the courses: Program on Noncollegiate Sponsored Instruction, The Center for Adult Learning and Educational Credentials, American Council on Education, One Dupont Circle, Washington, D.C. 20036.

Steakhouse Training and Education Program (STEP)
  Location: Dayton, OH; Saugus, MA; Middlebury Heights, OH.
  Length: 172 hours (3 weeks at District Training Facilitiy and 1 week at Ponderosa Development Institute).
  Dates: January 1980-Present.
  Objective: To provide managerial candidates with the managerial and technical skills necessary to operate a single unit food service operation.
  Instruction: The content of STEP is organized under 3 major areas: maximizing sales, cost containment, and human resource management. Topic areas include advertising, marketing, inventory control, labor scheduling, maintenance, hiring, training, leadership, communication, motivation, coaching, team building, performance appraisal, unionization, quality assurance, food preparation, and safety and security.
  Credit recommendation: In the lower division baccalaureate/associate degree category, 3 semester hours in Personnel Supervision, 3 semester hours in Cost and Quality Control in Food Operations, and 2 semester hours in Food Production (2/82).

Portsmouth Naval Shipyard: Apprenticeship Training

The Portsmouth Naval Shipyard repairs and retrofits naval vessels, with special expertise in nuclear missile-carrying submarines. The shipyard employs skilled workers in a number of apprenticeship-type occupations such as carpentry, electrical work, painting, pipefitting, welding, shipfitting, mechanics, and rigging. The program extends over a period of four years and combines classroom trade instruction, academic instruction, and on-the-job training. The academic instruction covers four areas: science, math, communications, and mechanical drawing. The instructional staff consists of certified teachers plus adjunct, part-time instructors. Course outlines and daily lesson plans are developed and implemented under the supervision of the Apprenticeship Program Administrator.

Source of official student records: Commander, Apprenticeship Program, Portsmouth Naval Yard, Code 180-2, Building 99, Portsmouth, New Hampshire 03801.

Additional information about the courses: Program on Noncollegiate Sponsored Instruction, The Center for Adult Learning and Educational Credentials, American Council on Education, One Dupont Circle, Washington, D.C. 20036.

Architectural Drawing
 Location: Portsmouth Naval Shipyard, Portsmouth, NH.
 Length: 32 hours (3 weeks).
 Dates: May 1982-Present.
 Objective: To enable the student to: understand building materials and general construction principles; understand the basics of architectural structure and the critical role foundations play in building design; become competent in elementary architectural draftsmanship particularly capable in room by room planning and site planning; and design and draft a basic home plan which includes appropriate dimensions, plot plans, floor plans, exterior elevations and specifications.
 Instruction: This course enables students to learn general theory and practice in building and architectural design. Concentrated analysis is given to foundations, joints, rafters, roofing, and stair and sill layout. Other issues to be considered include floor plans, architectural design and general space utilization as well as elevation techniques in home design.
 Credit recommendation: In the lower division baccalaureate/associate degree category, 2 semester hours in Architectural Drawing (5/85).

1. Basic Mathematics and Algebra
2. Geometry, Trigonometry, and Statistics
 Location: Portsmouth Naval Shipyard, Portsmouth, NH.
 Length: 1. 112 hours (2 weeks). 2. 96 hours (2 weeks).
 Dates: May 1982-Present.
 Objective: *Course 1:* To enable the student to calculate fractions, decimals, powers, percentages and square roots; become adept at solving ratios, proportions; become competent in the measurement of the English and metric systems of measurement; determine, calculate and simplify algebraic expressions including the quadratic and linear equation, word problems, and variable analysis; and understand and determine logarithms, antilogarithms, exponents and radicals. *Course 2:* To enable the student to discern fundamental geometric concepts and differentiate and calculate problems involving common solid figures; express numerical and literal trigonometric functions of angles and the relationships between linear and directional distances; determine trigonometric values; and understand the fundamental theory and practical applications of descriptive statistics, otherwise known as charting.
 Instruction: *Course 1* is a comprehensive overview of the application, investigation, and theoretical analysis of fundamental mathematics and algebraic problem solving, and provides students with a firm foundation in mathematical theory which is immediately utilized in practical applications. Topical coverage includes fractions, ratios, weights and measures, linear equations, exponents and radicals, and quadratic equations. *Course 2* highlights geometric function problem solving and conceptualizations. This course also delves into trigonometric reasoning including function, tables, oblique problems, and other practical applications. Finally, course provides a rudimentary analysis of statistical process, specifically charting techniques and method.
 Credit recommendation: *Course 1:* In the lower division baccalaureate/associate degree category, 3 semester hours in Basic Mathematics. *Course 2:* In the lower division baccalaureate/associate degree category, 3 semester hours in General Mathematics/Statistics (5/85).

Blueprint Reading and Shop Sketching
 Location: Portsmouth Naval Shipyard, Portsmouth, NH.
 Length: 48 hours (4 weeks).
 Dates: May 1982-Present.
 Objective: To enable the student to: become aware of the basic processes in the creation and design of blueprints; gain insight and knowledge into the skills of interpreting blueprints, and their overall reading; identify tolerance and allowance limits in blueprint and engineering drawings; recognize and discern blueprint information which consists of threading and welding symbols; highlight dimensions and tolerance variables in the blueprint; identify the differing types of drawings and newly emerging types of reproduction; become familiar with geometric principles relevant to the interpretation of shop sketches; and become skilled in sketching tasks at the shop level.
 Instruction: This is a basic course in blueprint and shop sketch interpretation and analysis. Blueprints, sketches, and technical drawings will be thoroughly evaluated as to angle projection, view perception, alignment and other auxiliary views, line conventions, tolerances, allowances, and mechanical nomenclature. The course provides ample opportunity to interpret the contents of a blueprint and to become familiar with emerging techniques of reproduction such as check prints, microfilm, and cronaflex.
 Credit recommendation: In the vocational certificate

category, 3 semester hours in Blueprint Reading and Shop Sketching (5/85).

Engineering Drawings - The Application of Mechanical Design
Location: Portsmouth Naval Shipyard, Portsmouth, NH.
Length: 48 hours (4 weeks).
Dates: May 1982-Present.
Objective: To enable the student to: understand the terms, definitions and formulas relevant to the design and drawing of gears, cams, and other engineering systems; become skilled in the design and drawing of cam displacement diagrams as well as spur and bevel gear pictorials; become competent in the construction of working drawings which represent the proper working relationship of parts to the whole machine; and supply illustrations which might be used for catalog and other illustrative purposes.
Instruction: This is a course emphasizing the skills of drawing and design in an engineering context. The main thrust of the course is its emphasis on practical review and application of common engineering subject matter including spur and bevel gears, cams, typologies in motion and the resulting working drawings. Lecture and demonstration are used.
Credit recommendation: In the lower division baccalaureate/associate degree category, 2 semester hours in Engineering Drawings (5/85). NOTE: This course is a useful supplement to the course entitled Mechanical Design (Machine Design).

Engineering Graphics
(Mechanical Drawing)
Location: Portsmouth Naval Shipyard, Portsmouth, NH.
Length: 90 hours (10 weeks).
Dates: May 1982-Present.
Objective: To enable the student to: become familiar with the required equipment for successful mechanical drawings; understand the importance of pre-planning in mechanical drawing with a review of dimensioning, lettering, and space allotment; master the necessary geometric principles essential in mechanical drawing including angles, quadrants, ground line and surface to projection planes; become competent in orthographic processes in mechanical drawing including varied view analysis, visualization and sketch dimensions; become proficient in the drawing of pictorial forms, isometrics, projections, oblique figures; and become capable of drawing threaded forms and representations, keys, and assembly and detail representations.
Instruction: The course permits students a practical education in the rudiments and intricacies of mechanical drawing and draftsmanship. Students will regularly draw to appropriate dimension and scope a variety of isometric and pictorial forms, threaded materials and assembly and detail drawings. Equally essential to the courses' design is its emphasis on the theoretical foundations of mechanical drawing with consideration being given to dimensioning, lettering, visualization, and space allotment.
Credit recommendation: In the lower division baccalaureate/associate degree category, 3 semester hours in Engineering Graphics (5/85).

Human Behavior and Leadership
Location: Portsmouth Naval Shipyard, Portsmouth, NH.
Length: 32 hours (3 weeks).
Dates: May 1982-Present.
Objective: To enable the student to: understand the principal factors shaping human behavior including self actualization, perception and needs assessment; become familiar with the external factors such as work and supervising conditions which influence human behavior; gain understanding into the role of pre-conception and its effect on individuality, and resulting performance; evaluate and analyze methods of human conflict and typical responses to personal frustration and aggression; become aware of the impact stress plays on the mental state of the person; analyze the communication process and acquire the means to be a successful communicator; focus on the transactional management style of human behavior and conditioning; understand various aspects of group dynamics and membership including status, identification, social structure and goal orientation; and become familiar with successful strategies in problem solving and decision making.
Instruction: This course assesses principal motivational and behavioral factors in the molding and shaping of human behavior. Emphasis is given to the transactional schools of thought. Attention will be given to the dynamics of human interaction as it affects persons in the workplace. Topics such as stress, judgement, perception are crucial to human evaluation and are covered in depth. Practical guidelines and insights are also provided in the areas of human communication, problem solving, and effective group interaction.
Credit recommendation: In the lower division baccalaureate/associate degree category, 2 semester hours in Interpersonal Communications (5/85).

Mechanical Design
(Machine Design)
Location: Portsmouth Naval Shipyard, Portsmouth, NH.
Length: 48 hours (4 weeks).
Dates: May 1982-Present.
Objective: To enable the student to: become familiar with the forces which cause acceleration and are often determinative in the feasibility of a machine design; understand physical laws concerning work, energy, power, mass and torque, and examine the interlocking relationship that

exists between them; design formulas for the construction of shafts to resist torsion; comprehend the factors of stress, fatigue, torsion, bending, and deflection in the design of machines, as well as the influence of elasticity and deformation; understand the various keys, belt pulleys and gears that can be used to diffuse or transmit power; become aware of the essential parts in the design of a spur gear; assess the critical role couplings play in an overall efficient machine design; understand that friction is an effective means of transmitting power and learn the operations of clutches, bearings, and springs.

Instruction: This course covers the necessary theories of science in the design and construction of machinery. In sum, the course is an explanatory review of the parts and pieces which are necessary for the eventual design of an operating machine. Transmissions, shafts, keys, pulleys, couplings, clutches, bearings, and springs are all reviewed. In addition, the student has the opportunity to evaluate theoretical problems in machine design, such as force, motion, elasticity, and principles of horsepower and torque.

Credit recommendation: In the lower division baccalaureate/associate degree category, 3 semester hours in Mechanical Design (5/85).

Metallurgy
Location: Portsmouth Naval Shipyard, Portsmouth, NH.
Length: 48 hours (4 weeks).
Dates: May 1982-Present.
Objective: To enable the student to: define all properties associated with metals; become familiar with the various tests and scientific processes utilized in the production and analysis of metals; understand the refinement techniques utilized in steel processing, particularly cold and hot working methods; become able to identify the inherent structural characteristics of metals and be adept at identifying alloy materials; discern the various modes of heat treating of materials, as well as other surface hardening techniques; comprehend alloys and their characteristics; analyze the structure and properties of case irons, aluminum, magnesium, titanium, and other relevant light metals; and assess the nature of all bearing metals such as bronze, copper, and tin.

Instruction: This course reviews the usage and make-up of metals in a modern industrial society. Specific topics for analysis include the production of iron and steel, refinement technologies, physical and mechanical properties of metals, theoretical applications relevant to alloys, bearing metals and non-ferrous materials, as well as a coverage of various surface and coating treatment methods of metals.

Credit recommendation: In the lower division baccalaureate/associate degree category, 3 semester hours in Metallurgy (5/85).

Oral Communications
Location: Portsmouth Naval Shipyard, Portsmouth, NH.
Length: 48 hours (9 weeks).
Dates: May 1982-Present.
Objective: To enable the student to: become comfortable and assured when speaking in front of a group or large audience; understand steps that are crucial to proper explanation, oral communication and demonstration; see the value in criticizing in a constructive way; increase his or her skill at fielding questions from an audience; and improve his or her self-image as an orator and translate that assurance to the workplace.

Instruction: This is a practical course designed to markedly improve a student's speaking and oratory skills. In more focused terms, the course allows a student the opportunity to participate in speaking assignments from an extemporaneous talk to a short presentation on a current event. Student assignments are geared to a self-improvement and self-enhancement in the workplace with the eventual hope that students will be able to relate their ideas more cogently and persuasively.

Credit recommendation: In the lower division baccalaureate/associate degree category, 3 semester hours in Oral Communications (5/85).

Physics
Location: Portsmouth Naval Shipyard, Portsmouth, NH.
Length: 64 hours (6 weeks).
Dates: May 1982-Present.
Objective: To enable the student to: understand the relationships that exist between acceleration, velocity distance, time, form and to discern the differences in motion; master fundamental laws of motion, including Newton's rules, principles of work and energy and the transformation thereof; acquire a fundamental knowledge of basic machines and their capacity as well as parts essential to machinery such as pulleys, belts, chains, and gears; comprehend the laws relevant to friction, inclined planes, and general motion; analyze basic atomic structure and models and more precisely conceptualize nuclear processes such as radioactivity, reactors, and fusion; understand the properties essential to solid materials like density, elasticity, malleability and ductibility; analyze the principles of stress, strain, and mass acceleration; understand various properties of liquids; discern the relationship between pressure and depth and its influence on solid materials; understand Boyle's law on pressure and gas properties; become skilled in the measurement and evaluation of temperature, heat, and energy on solids and liquids, gases, specifically as these processes cause expansion and contraction; and analyze heat, its transfer, conduction, and convection issues.

Instruction: This course provides students with a foundation in the science of physics the study of both matter energy, and of the factors which make industry and advanced technology possible. Topics for analysis and application include a study of motion, energy, friction, atomic structure, density, pressure, hydraulics, heat, conduction, and the measurement and assessment of physical properties.

Credit recommendation: In the lower division baccalaureate/associate degree category, 3 semester hours in General Physics (5/85).

**Sheet Metal Fabrication and Design
(Pattern Drafting)**
  Location: Portsmouth Naval Shipyard, Portsmouth, NH.
  Length: 48 hours (4 weeks).
  Dates: May 1982-Present.
  Objective: To enable the student to: become aware of the various equipment needed to successfully draft pattern work; attain proficiencies in parallel, and radial line problems and developments in pattern drafting; understand the techniques of triangulation in pattern drafting; develop fundamental math skills; and use special remedies and suggestions in pattern drafting which assist in the design and interpretation of these materials.
  Instruction: This course presents general theory and practice in the art of draftsmanship in pattern work, such as sheet metal mechanics, heating, ventilations, cornice work, and heavy plate work. Problems are provided to the student for continuous practice and reinforcement. Topics covered include pattern drafting by parallel line, radial line, and triangulation methodologies.
  Credit recommendation: In the vocational certificate category, 3 semester hours in Sheet Metal Fabrication and Design (5/85).

Strength of Materials
  Location: Portsmouth Naval Shipyard, Portsmouth, NH.
  Length: 48 hours (4 weeks).
  Dates: May 1982-Present.
  Objective: To enable the student to: assess the influence of stress and strain by force, shearing or compression has on the strength of materials including temperature, riveted connections, structural joints and welds; define and discuss loads on beams and solve beam reaction problems; identify and discuss vertical shear valves, shear diagrams and bending moments, and corresponding stress; become adept at identifying the deflection level in beams, as well as their slope and curvature; and understand how to evaluate the relative strength of wood, steel, and aluminum columns and the influence of corresponding stress and shear.
  Instruction: This course introduces the student to the strength, inherent or acquired, in materials used for construction. Beam deflections, curvature, bending, and slope of materials are thoroughly reviewed. More specific attention is given to the strength of steel, wood, and aluminum columns, and the influence of stress and strain on the materials. Other materials in the course include rivetng influences on condition of materials, joints by weld, and various forms of stress.
  Credit recommendation: In the lower division baccalaureate/associate degree category, 3 semester hours in Strength of Materials (5/85).

Professional Insurance Agents

The Professional Insurance Agents (P.I.A.) is a membership association representing more than 40,000 independent insurance agencies in the United States.

P.I.A. disseminates information on education, legislation, and public relations and represents its members in all of these areas.

P.I.A.'s Education Department conducts numerous training seminars and schools at locations throughout the country. Its major educational effort is a three-week, live-in program, conducted on a college campus. This program is taught by professional educators and experienced independent insurance agents.

Source of official student records: Director of Education, Education Department, National Association of Professional Insurance Agents, 400 North Washington Street, Alexandria, Virginia 22314.

Additional information about the courses: Program on Noncollegiate Sponsored Instruction, The Center for Adult Learning and Educational Credentials, American Council on Education, One Dupont Circle, Washington, D.C. 20036.

**PIA Insurance School at Drake University
(Formerly Basic Insurance School)**
  Location: Drake University, Des Moines, IA.
  Length: 121 hours (3 weeks) residential, plus approximately 40 hours of preparatory independent study.
  Dates: January 1976-Present.
  Objective: To familiarize the student with the fundamentals of business and personal risk, and with the basic principles of insurance contracts with emphasis on casualty and liability insurance.
  Learning Outcome: Upon successful completion of this course, the student will be able to analyze business and personal risks inherent in commercial and personal activities; select appropriate insurance contracts to cover effectively property and liability risks; recommend legal and financial clauses in insurance contracts for specialized coverages in a wide variety of industries.
  Instruction: Course covers lectures, discussions, and case studies analyzing basic principles of insurance, reviewing the structure of the insurance industry, introducing legal concepts. Provides extensive contract and form

analysis for fire and allied insurance lines including ocean and inland marine, automobile, home owners, liability, workers compensation, crime, bonding, ranch and farm owners insurance combination policies. Introduces life and health insurance. Emphasis is shared between commercial and personal applications.

Credit recommendation: In the lower division baccalaureate/associate degree category or in the upper division baccalaureate category, 3 semester hours in Principles of Insurance and 3 semester hours in Property and Liability Contract Analysis (7/78) (7/83) (2/88). NOTE: This course has been reevaluated and continues to meet requirements for credit recommendations.

Professional Secretaries International

Professional Secretaries International (formerly National Secretaries Association) is a nonprofit association founded in 1942, with chapters throughout the 50 states, Canada, and Puerto Rico, and affiliate chapters around the world. The association's aim is to elevate secretarial standards and offer opportunities for professional and personal growth and development to achieve that goal.

THE INSTITUTE FOR CERTIFYING SECRETARIES

The Institute for Certifying Secretaries is a department of Professional Secretaries International. The Institute was established by PSI in 1949 and is staffed by representatives from management, business education, and PSI. The institute's program was established to develop and administer the Certified Professional Secretary (CPS) Examination, which is the recognized standard of proficiency in the secretarial profession. In order to qualify to take the CPS Examination, candidates must meet specific educational and work experience requirements established by the Institute.

The CPS Examination is a two-day, six-part examination. All parts of the examination consist of multiple-choice questions, which include problem solving, knowledge of facts, and application of theory.

Formal courses are not required before taking the examination; however, many candidates find it necessary to take formal or review courses, or to do extensive independent study in each of the areas in which they will be examined. The Institute does not sponsor courses to help candidates prepare for the examination, but it does publish a study outline and a bibliography of books and periodicals dealing with each part of the examination.

Source of official student records: Executive Director, Professional Secretaries International, 301 East Armour Boulevard, Kansas City, Missouri 64111-1299.

Additional information about the courses: Program on Noncollegiate Sponsored Instruction, The Center for Adult Learning and Educational Credentials, American Council on Education, One Dupont Circle, Washington, D.C. 20036.

Part I: Behavioral Science in Business
(Formerly Environmental Relationships in Business)

Location: Examination centers in the U.S., Canada, Puerto Rico, Jamaica, and Malaysia.

Length: *Version 1:* 105 minutes (150 questions); *Version 2:* 105 minutes (100 questions); *Version 3:* 105 minutes (120 questions).

Dates: *Versions 1 and 2:* May 1971-May 1986; *Version 3:* June 1986-Present.

Objective: To test the candidate's understanding of the principles of human relations and organizational dynamics in the workplace.

Instruction: Focuses on the needs, motivation, nature of conflict, problem-solving techniques, essentials of supervision and communication, leadership styles, and understanding of the informal organization.

Credit recommendation: *Versions 1 and 2:* In the lower division baccalaureate/associate degree category, 3 semester hours in Human Relations or Psychology (1/76) (11/81). *Version 3:* In the lower division baccalaureate/associate degree category, 3 semester hours in Psychology, Secretarial Skills, Administration and Organization, or Human Relations in Business; and in the lower division baccalaureate/associate degree category, 1 semester hour in Principles of Human Resources Management and 1 semester hour in Management of Organizational Behavior (6/86). NOTE: This course has been reevaluated and continues to meet requirements for credit recommendations.

Part II: Business Law
(Formerly Business and Public Policy)

Location: Examination centers in the U.S., Canada, Puerto Rico, Jamaica, and Malaysia.

Length: *Versions 1 and 2:* 105 minutes (100 questions); *Version 3:* 105 minutes (100 questions).

Dates: *Versions 1 and 2:* May 1971-May 1986; *Version 3:* June 1986-Present.

Objective: To test the candidate's knowledge of the major elements of business law involved in the secretary's daily work.

Instruction: Contracts and bailments, law of agency and sales, insurance, negotiable instruments, real property and public policy in the form of governmental regulatory legislation are covered.

Credit recommendation: *Versions 1, 2, and 3:* In the lower division baccalaureate/associate degree category or in the upper division baccalaureate category, 3 semester hours in Business Law (1/76) (11/81) (6/86). NOTE: This course has been reevaluated and continues to meet requirements for credit recommendations.

Part III: Economics and Management

Location: Examination Centers in the U.S., Canada, Puerto Rico, Jamaica, and Malaysia.

Length: *Versions 1 and 2:* 105 minutes (100 questions); *Version 3:* 105 minutes (120 questions).

Dates: *Version 1:* May 1971-October 1981; *Version 2:* November 1981-May 1986; *Version 3:* June 1986-Present.

Objective: To test the candidate's understanding of the basic concepts of business operation.

Instruction: *Version 1:* The economics portion covers basic concepts of economics (private property, supply and demand, markets), national income and its determinants, the labor force, the financial system, federal income taxes for business, business involvement in social programs and related legislation, and international trade. The management portion covers principles of management and elements of business operation, including personnel, financial, production, and marketing management. *Version 2:* The economics portion covers basic concepts of economics (private property, supply and demand, markets), national income and its determinants, the financial system, business involvement in social programs and related legislation, and international trade. The management portion covers the basic management functions (planning, organizing, directing, and controlling); management trends; and various fields of management, including production, marketing, and personnel. *Version 3:* The economics portion covers basic concepts of economics (private property, supply and demand, and markets), national income and its determinants, the financial system, business involvement in current social and economic programs, and international trade. The management portion covers the basic management functions (planning, organizing, leading, controlling, and communicating), fields of management (human resources, production, marketing, and public relations), forms of business organization, and decision-making processes.

Credit recommendation: *Version 1:* In the lower division baccalaureate/associate degree category, 6 semester hours in Economics or Management (1/76). *Version 2:* In the lower division baccalaureate/associate degree category, 2 semester hours in Economics and 3 semester hours in Management (11/81). *Version 3:* In the lower division baccalaureate/associate degree category, 3 semester hours in Economics, 3 semester hours in Principles of Management, 1 semester hour in Marketing, and 1 semester hour in Human Resources Management (6/86) (11/86). NOTE: This course has been reevaluated and continues to meet the requirements for credit recommendations.

Part IV: Accounting
(Formerly Financial Analysis and the Mathematics of Business)

Location: Examination centers in the U.S., Canada, Puerto Rico, Jamaica, and Malaysia.

Length: 120 minutes (100 questions).

Dates: May 1971-Present.

Objective: To test the candidate's knowledge of basic accounting procedures.

Instruction: Focuses on the theory and classification of accounts, the accounting cycle, financial statements, interest and discounts, cost analysis, budgets, forecasting, and the analysis and interpretation of financial statements, insurance, and budgets and forecasting.

Credit recommendation: In the lower division baccalaureate/associate degree category, 4 semester hours in Accounting (1/76) (11/81) (6/86) (11/86). NOTE: This course has been reevaluated and continues to meet requirements for credit recommendations.

Part V: Communication Applications (effective with 1983 exam)
Part V: Office Administration and Communication (effective with 1984 exam)
(Formerly Secretarial Skills and Decision Making)

Location: Examination centers in the U.S., Canada, Puerto Rico, Jamaica, and Malaysia.

Length: 120 minutes (120 questions).

Dates: *Version 1:* May 1971-October 1981; *Version 2:* November 1981-May 1986; *Version 3:* June 1986-Present.

Objective: To measure the secretary's proficiency in office administration and communication.

Instruction: Office administration aspect covers executive travel, office management, records management, and reprographics. Communications aspect covers written business communication, editing, abstracting, and preparing communications in final format.

Credit recommendation: *Version 1:* In the lower division baccalaureate/associate degree category, 9 semester hours in Shorthand, Transcription, and/or Typewriting (1/76). *Version 2:* In the lower division baccalaureate/associate degree category, 6 semester hours in Typewriting, 6 semester hours in Shorthand, and 3 semester hours in Office Procedures (11/81). *Version 3:* In the lower division baccalaureate/associate degree category, 3 semester hours in Office Procedures or Administration Management and 3 semester hours in Business Communications (6/86) (11/86). NOTE: Additional credit in shorthand, transcription or typewriting may be granted based on institutional policies in these skill areas. This course has been reevaluated and continues to meet requirements for credit recommendations.

Part VI: Office Administration and Technology (effective with 1983 exam)
Part VI: Office Technology (effective with 1984 exam)
(Formerly Office Procedures and Administration)

Location: Examination centers in the U.S., Canada, Puerto Rico, Jamaica, and Malaysia.

Length: *Versions 1 and 2:* 75 minutes (100 questions); *Version 3:* 105 minutes (120 questions).

Dates: *Version 1:* May 1971-October 1981; *Version 2:*

November 1981-May 1986; *Version 3:* June 1986-Present.

Objective: To test the candidate's knowledge of office technology.

Instruction: *Version 1:* Electronic data processing; communications media; records management; office systems, layout and design. *Version 2:* Focuses on word processing; electronic data processing; communication techniques; executive travel; secretarial planning; work simplification, including office system design; and reprographics. *Version 3:* Covers the secretary's responsibilities created by word and data processing, communications media, advances in office management, technological applications, records management technology, and reprographics technology.

Credit recommendation: *Version 1:* In the lower division baccalaureate/associate degree category or in the upper division baccalaureate category, 6 semester hours in Office Management or Office Procedures (1/76). *Version 2:* In the lower division baccalaureate/associate degree category, 3 semester hours in Office Administration or Office Management (11/81). *Version 3:* In the lower division baccalaureate/associate degree category, 6 semester hours in Office Technology or in the lower division baccalaureate/associate degree category, 3 semester hours in Automated Office Administration and 3 semester hours in Communications Technology (6/86) (11/86). NOTE: This course has been reevaluated and continues to meet requirements for credit recommendations.

Public Service Electric & Gas

The Personnel Development Department of Human Resources is devoted to improving the skills of PSE&G employees, increasing individual and team performance on the job and facilitating the personnel growth and development of PSE&G employees.

The Personnel Development Department will accomplish this mission through the following strategies: provide appropriate training opportunities at all employees' level; act as the corporate resource for increasing productivity through improved performance appraisal systems; disseminate information about training and development opportunities and related services throughout the Company; encourage ongoing relationships with academic and professional institutions to keep abreast of current trends in the field of Training and Development.

Training at PSE&G is viewed as a continuing process to assure high quality performance on the part of the entire work force at all levels of the organization.

Prior to participation in any program, it is important that participants and their supervisors clarify together the specific objectives for attendance at any given workshop. This process allows the individuals to approach their training experience with a clear set of learning goals.

Source of official student records: American Council on Education, Registry of Credit Recommendations, One Dupont Circle, Washington, D.C. 20063.

Additional information about the courses: Program on Noncollegiate Sponsored Instruction, The Center for Adult Learning and Educational Credentials, American Council on Education, One Dupont Circle, Washington, D.C. 20036 or Thomas A. Edison State College, 101 West State Street, CN 545, Trenton, New Jersey 08625.

Oral Presentation Skills

Location: Various PSE&G locations throughout New Jersey.

Length: 16 hours (2 days).

Dates: August 1983-Present.

Objective: To improve the verbal and nonverbal skills necessary for formal presentations and group discussions.

Learning Outcome: At the end of the workshop, participants will be able to control nervousness and turn it from a negative destructive force into a positive constructive force; recognize and eliminate restraining inhibitions; use five forms of evidence for maximum persuasion; prepare effective visual aids and use them to achieve action and understanding; control a question and answer session with group; design, plan, and present a written script.

Instruction: This program presents specific techniques for improving oral presentation skills. Areas such as audience analysis, preparation, delivery, relaxation, and confidence building will be covered. Participants will be required to make several oral presentations to demonstrate acquired skills to satisfaction of class instructor. Videotape will be used to define individual strengths and weaknesses.

Credit recommendation: In the lower division baccalaureate/associate degree category, 1 semester hour in Speech Workshop (8/88).

Systematic Analysis of Ideas

Location: Various PSE&G locations throughout New Jersey.

Length: 30 hours (5 days).

Dates: August 1978-Present.

Objective: To teach participants how to prepare and present persuasive recommendations.

Learning Outcome: At the end of the workshop, participants will be able to determine the other person's real, but often hidden objectives and goals and relate their idea, plan, or recommendation to those objectives; generate interest for their idea or recommendation when dealing with complacent, self-satisfied people; organize and present ideas and recommendations concisely and to answer questions and objections in advance; calm emotion and more effectively handle confrontation; handle and express themselves in strenuous and difficult situations; handle objections, such as "We've always done it that way."

Instruction: The course analyzes the required behavior

that must exist between two people if successful communication is to take place. The course also prepares a speaker to analyze, organize and think from a listener's point of view, so that this behavior can be maintained when the listener is being persuaded to make a change. There is a sequence of communication which must be used if a person is willing to change behavior. If the sequence is not used, the person may resist change. The course examines both logical and emotional elements of communication, and discusses when to use each one most effectively.

Credit recommendation: In the lower division baccalaureate/associate degree category, 2 semester hours in Persuasive Communications (8/88).

Supervisory Training Program (Part 1 and 2)
    Location: Salem and Newark, NJ.
    Length: *Part 1.* 30 hours (5 days) separated by 3 months; *Part 2.* 12 hours (2 days).
    Dates: March 1983-Present.
    Objective: To provide first-line supervisors with the skills necessary to manage work, people, and self.
    Learning Outcome: At the end of the workshop, participants will be able to: (1) manage themselves and others and do the supervisor's job more effectively; implement decisions; (2) manage time better; (3) gain consensus, support, and communicate effectively; (4) listen effectively and solve problems, including sensitive personnel situations (e.g., performance appraisal, alcoholism, and drugs); (5) implement a behavioral performance model of supervision; delegate and schedule work fairly and realistically.
    Instruction: This workshop explores basic management skills and clarifies the major roles and responsibilities of a supervisor. Through various activities, participants will learn the methods that help motivate employees to achieve and maintain high performance levels. In addition, the workshop clarifies the many regulations and procedures that impact a supervisor's job.
    Credit recommendation: In the lower division baccalaureate/associate degree category, 3 semester hours in Principles and Practices of Supervision (8/88).

Raymond James & Associates, Inc. and Employee Benefits Education and Planning Service, Inc.

The educational program is offered by Raymond James Financial Planning Division, a Registered Investment Advisor/SEC, and the Employee Benefits Education and Planning Service (EBEPS).

The curriculum design, course text, and courses were developed by professional educators who hold advanced degrees. These educators have more than two decades of teaching experience in public schools, colleges, and adult education programs. They supervise changes in both the text and curriculum, and play an active role in the delivery of courses to students. All course review and assistance is provided by an internal professional staff which includes investment advisors, legal counsel, authors, trainers, CPAs, and CFPs.

Instructors are required to have a bachelor's or advanced degree, and must have completed the employee benefit training program, combined with financial planning experience or the successful completion of the CFP and/or CPA program. Additionally, prior seminar or formal educational teaching ability must be demonstrated along with having successfully taught the full curriculum under supervision. Instructors are reviewed by in-class supervisory and student written evaluations. They are submitted and approved by the curriculum committee before the instructor is assigned to teach a subsequent course.

Sessions are taught at the employment location which allows a high level of employee attendance, flexible scheduling, and a familiar setting. All educational equipment is provided by the organization. Registration sheets containing personal data entries and attendance sheets are required for each class meeting. This information is used to create a computerized data base containing all pertinent student information. Completion of class projects requiring demonstration of skills in constructing personal financial planning and investment strategies are required. Students may, at the organization's discretion, repeat the course.

Source of official student records: Registrar, Registry of Credit Recommendations (ROCR), The Center for Adult Learning and Educational Credentials; American Council on Education, One Dupont Circle, Washington, D.C. 20036.

Additional information about the courses: Program on Noncollegiate Sponsored Instruction, The Center for Adult Learning and Educational Credentials, American Council on Education, One Dupont Circle, Washington, D.C., 20036.

1. Personal Investment Planning
(Investment Planning)
2. Personal Financial Planning
(Financial Planning with Employee Benefits)
    Location: Various locations nationally.
    Length: 18 hours (2 days).
    Dates: April 1989-Present.
    Objective: 1. To develop the students' ability to identify clear investment objectives and match those objectives with appropriate investment alternatives. 2. To introduce employees to financial planning concepts that have been tailored to their organization's specific benefits program.
    Instruction: Course covers investor attitudes, risk levels, banking services, credit unions, insurance services, stocks, mutual funds, real estate, limited partnerships, tangible investments, tax strategies, life cycle financial

planning, optimum utilization of employee benefits, asset accumulation, cash management, estate planning, and retirement income maintenance. Students also complete a generic case study in financial planning. Methodology includes lecture, discussion, case study work, and problem solving.

Credit recommendation: In the lower division baccalaureate/associate degree category, 1 semester hour in Finance (4/89). NOTE: Students must successfully complete both courses to receive the credit recommendation.

San Diego Employers Association, Inc.

The San Diego Employers Association is a nonprofit voluntary association of business managers. It was incorporated in 1939 and provides professional industrial relations and labor relations services to over 1,200 member companies.

One aspect of its services is its ongoing program of education to strengthen and improve supervisors' ability to manage employees effectively. Emphasis is placed on broadening the supervisor's capabilities under rapidly changing business conditions.

Source of official student records: Director, Management Development, San Diego Employers Association, Inc., Suite 225, 9245 Sky Park Ct., San Diego, California 92123.

Additional information about the courses: Program on Noncollegiate Sponsored Instruction, The Center for Adult Learning and Educational Credentials, American Council on Education, One Dupont Circle, Washington, D.C. 20036.

Graduate Seminar for Supervisors
(Advanced Workshop for Supervisors)
   Location: San Diego, CA.
   Length: 24 hours (8 weeks).
   Dates: January 1973-Present.
   Objective: To improve the supervisory skills and knowledge of supervisors.
   Instruction: A continuation of the basic workshop for supervisors with emphasis on experiential application and role-playing exercises. Lecture, discussion, and case studies are used.
   Credit recommendation: In the lower division baccalaureate/associate degree category, 1 semester hour in Management (6/78). NOTE: Successful completion of Workshop for Supervisors and Graduate Seminar for Supervisors is equivalent to a three-unit course in Supervision.

Workshop for Supervisors
   Location: San Diego, CA.
   Length: 30 hours (10 weeks).
   Dates: September 1968-Present.
   Objective: To improve the managerial skills and knowledge of supervisors.
   Instruction: A basic course in supervision, including communications, leadership, labor law, employment law, human relations, grievances, training, and performance evaluation. Lectures, audiovisual aids, role playing, and problem solving are used.
   Credit recommendation: In the lower division baccalaureate/associate degree category, 2 semester hours in Management (5/78).

Sandy Corporation - Marketing Educational Services

The Sandy Corporation - Marketing Educational Services offers courses to General Motors sales personnel and dealership management personnel. The courses listed below are offered in Flint, MI and in 5 campus centers in Atlanta, GA; Fort Worth, TX; Philadelphia, PA; San Francisco and Pomona, CA. Courses are also conducted at campus locations in Canada.

Source of official student records: President, Marketing Educational Services, Sandy Corporation, 1500 West Big Beaver Road, Troy, Michigan 48084.

Additional information about the courses: Program on Noncollegiate Sponsored Instruction, The Center for Adult Learning and Educational Credentials, American Council on Education, One Dupont Circle, Washington, D.C. 20036.

Dealership Management Development (0147)
   Location: Phoenix, AZ; Atlanta, GA; Flint, MI; Troy, MI.
   Length: 160 hours (4 weeks).
   Dates: August 1973-Present.
   Objective: To provide prospective dealers with knowledge of dealership organization and functions, and to enable them to develop the management skills required to successfully operate an automotive dealership.
   Instruction: Personnel, financial, and physical plant requirements of automotive dealerships and their relationship to finance companies, customers, employees, and the community. Methodology includes team teaching, case studies, and a computerized dealership simulation.
   Credit recommendation: In the upper division baccalaureate category, 6 semester hours in Management (4/75) (10/80). NOTE: This course has undergone a 5-year reevaluation and continues to meet the requirements for credit recommendations.

1. Fundamentals of Management for Parts Managers (X121)
2. Personnel Management for Parts Managers (X122)

3. Financial Management for Parts Managers (X123)
4. Operations Management for Parts Managers (X124)

Location: Flint, MI; Newark, DE; Atlanta, GA; Chicago, IL; Ft. Worth, TX; Los Angeles, CA; San Francisco, CA; Vancouver, British Columbia; London and Ottawa, Ontario; and other locations as necessary.

Length: 1. 34 hours (1 week); 6 hours of preparatory independent study; 2. 34 hours (1 week); 8 hours of preparatory independent study; 3. 36 hours (1 week); 8 hours of preparatory independent study; 4. 34 hours (1 week); 16 hours of preparatory independent study.

Dates: 1. October 1975-Present; 2. March 1976-Present; 3. August 1976-Present; 4. February 1977-Present.

Objective: To provide parts managers with the knowledge and skills required to perform essential managerial functions in automotive dealership settings.

Instruction: *Course 1:* Teaches fundamentals of management and the application of management processes to promotional strategies, customer relations, merchandising, etc., within the dealership environment. *Course 2:* Covers staffing, performance evaluation, employee relations, motivation, and communications. *Course 3:* Covers statement analysis, parts department analysis, expense management, and forecasting using a computerized dealership simulation to develop financial management skills. *Course 4:* Covers analysis of gross profit, profit-expense relationships, inventory management, merchandising, and the development of plans to improve operations. Lectures, discussions, case studies, and simulation exercises are used in all courses.

Credit recommendation: In the lower division baccalaureate/associate degree category, 6 semester hours in Automotive Technology or Management (8/76) (10/80). NOTE: To be eligible for credit, student must successfully complete Courses 1, 2, 3, and 4. All these courses have undergone a 5-year reevaluation and continue to meet the requirements for credit recommendations.

1. Fundamentals of Management for Sales Managers (X101)
2. Personnel Management for Sales Managers (X102)
3. Financial Management for Sales Managers (X103)
4. Operations Management for Sales Managers (X104)

Location: Flint, MI; Newark, DE; Atlanta, GA; Chicago, IL; Ft. Worth, TX; Los Angeles, CA; San Francisco, CA; Vancouver, British Columbia; London and Ottawa, Ontario; and other locations as necessary.

Length: 1. 36 hours (1 week); 8 hours preparatory independent study; 2. 36 hours (1 week); 8 hours preparatory independent study; 3. 36 hours (1 week); 12 hours preparatory independent study; 4. 36 hours (1 week); 16 hours preparatory independent study.

Dates: 1. February 1974-Present; 2. February 1974-Present; 3. February 1974-Present; 4. October 1975-Present.

Objective: To provide sales managers with the knowledge and skill required to perform essential managerial functions in automotive dealership settings.

Instruction: *Course 1:* Teaches fundamentals of management and the application of management processes to promotional strategies, customer relations, merchandising, etc., within the dealership environment. *Course 2:* Covers staffing, performance evaluation, quality of work life, motivation, and communications. *Course 3:* Covers variable and fixed expenses, profit determination, methods of analysis, expense management, and forecasting using a computerized dealership simulation to develop sales management skills. *Course 4:* Covers analysis of profit objectives, developing a sales force, communicating with customers and salespersons, selling intangibles, and strengthening relationships between customers and the dealership. Lectures, discussions, case studies, and simulation exercises are used in all courses.

Credit recommendation: In the lower division baccalaureate/associate degree category, 6 semester hours in Automotive Technology or Management (8/76) (10/80). NOTE: To be eligible for credit, student must successfully complete Courses 1,2,3,4. All these courses have undergone 5-year reevaluation and continue to meet the requirements for credit recommendations.

1. Fundamentals of Management for Service Managers (X111)
2. Personnel Management for Service Managers (X112)
3. Financial Management for Service Managers (X113)
4. Operations Management for Service Managers (X114)

Location: Flint, MI; Newark, DE; Atlanta, GA; Chicago, IL; Ft. Worth, TX; Los Angeles, CA; San Francisco, CA; Vancouver, British Columbia; London and Ottawa, Ontario; and other locations as necessary.

Length: 1. 36 hours (1 week); 10 hours preparatory independent study; 2. 36 hours (1 week); 10 hours preparatory independent study; 3. 36 hours (1 week); 12 hours preparatory independent study; 4. 34 hours (1 week); 14 hours preparatory independent study.

Dates: 1. February 1974-Present; 2. February 1974-Present; 3. February 1974-Present; 4. May 1975-Present.

Objective: To provide service managers with the knowledge and skills required to perform essential managerial functions in automotive dealership settings.

Instruction: *Course 1:* Teaches fundamentals of management and the application of management processes to promotional strategies, customer relations, merchandising, etc., within the dealership environment. *Course 2:* Covers staffing, performance evaluation, employee relations, motivation, and communications. *Course 3:* Covers forecasting, service department analysis, and expense management using a computerized dealership simulation to develop financial management skills. *Course 4:* Covers analysis of service department functions, gross profit potential, resource utilization, decision implementation, and the development of plans to improve operations. Lectures, discussions, case studies, and simulation exercises are used in all courses.

Credit recommendation: In the lower division baccalaureate/associate degree category, 6 semester hours in Automotive Technology or Management (8/76) (10/80). NOTE: To be eligible for credit, student must successfully complete Courses 1, 2, 3, and 4. All these courses have undergone 5-year reevaluation and continue to meet the requirements for credit recommendations.

General Motors Field Management Development Program (0161)
Location: General Motors Institute, Flint, MI; and selected General Motors divisions and dealerships.
Length: *Version 1:* 1,040 hours (26 weeks); 11 weeks of classroom instruction and a 15-week internship. *Version 2:* 840 hours (21 weeks); 11 weeks of classroom instruction and a 10-week internship.
Dates: *Version 1:* January 1972-December 1976. *Version 2:* January 1977-August 1987.
Objective: To provide participants with a comprehensive understanding of the marketing and sales functions of franchise retail organizations that have single-source suppliers.
Instruction: The general management section includes financial management, service and sales agreements, a computerized dealership simulation, and maintaining a positive manufacturer-dealer relationship. The retail merchandising segment teaches product information, distribution, marketing, advertising, merchandising, and customer service. Automotive technology covers automotive basics, electronics, air-conditioning, and parts and accessories. Internships include an orientation to home and allied factories. Interns participate in a classroom orientation, in a retail dealership, and also a wholesale field office.
Credit recommendation: *Versions 1 and 2:* In the upper division baccalaureate category, 6 semester hours in General Management, 5 semester hours in Retail Merchandising, and 5 semester hours in Automotive Technology; for district managers, 3 additional semester hours in internship in Retail Merchandising; for parts and service managers, 3 additional semester hours of internship in Automotive Technology (4/75) (10/80). NOTE: this course has undergone a 5-year reevaluation and continues to meet the requirements for credit recommendations.

School of Banking of the South

The School of Banking of the South, established in 1950, provides an advanced course of study in banking for bank officers and other bank professionals. The three-year program covers bank management and operations topics, including monetary economics and regulatory theory and practice.

The School involves students in the learning process, stimulating them to acquire a better understanding of their banks and the bank's role in a changing environment. Students consider a variety of solutions to problems of their banks and weigh the effects of each.

Attendance at the three two-week summer sessions conducted on the campus of Louisiana State University, Baton Rouge, and completion of extension work are required for graduation. For evaluation purposes, courses that are offered throughout the three years of the program were grouped together. Thus, students requesting credit must have completed the entire program.

Source of official student records: Registrar, School of Banking of the South, P.O. Box 17680-A, Louisiana State University, Baton Rouge, Louisiana 70893.

Additional information about the courses: Program on Noncollegiate Sponsored Instruction, The Center for Adult Learning and Educational Credentials, American Council on Education, One Dupont Circle, Washington, D.C. 20036.

Business Policy
1. First-year Cases
2. Simulation I
3. Second-year Cases
4. Bank Simulation II

Location: Louisiana State University, Baton Rouge, LA.
Length: 1. 7½ hours (1 week); 2. 15 hours (1 week); 3. 17 hours (1 week); 4. 23 hours (2 weeks); 20 additional hours of group work in the evening are also required.
Students also complete one extension problem requiring approximately 40 hours of independent study.
Dates: Completion in 1973-Present.
Objective: Through the use of case studies and management interactive games, to enable students to formulate, analyze, and enact strategies for managing a financial institution.
Instruction: This course involves continued participation throughout the three-year program by requiring the student to formulate and implement policy in the areas of lending, investing, planning, deposit management, reporting, capital, cost control, and liquidity management. The Stanford Bank Management simulator is used in the first year. Cases throughout the program cover special credit areas, specific phases of bank management, and business finance. Third-year students apply policy decisions through the FDIC computer simulation management game.
Credit recommendation: In the upper division baccalaureate category or in the graduate degree category, 4 semester hours in Management (5/78).

Commercial Lending and Credit Analysis
1. Commercial Bank Credit IA

2. **Commercial Bank Credit IB**
3. **Consumer Credit**
4. **Real Estate Finance**

Location: Louisiana State University, Baton Rouge, LA.

Length: 1. 8½ hours (1 week); 2. 9 hours (1 week); 3. 8½ hours (1 week); 4. 8½ hours (1 week).

Students also complete four extension problems requiring approximately 160 hours of independent study.

Dates: Completion in 1973-Present.

Objective: To teach the fundamentals of commercial lending and analytical techniques used in loan and credit decisions.

Instruction: Covers basic accounting and financial techniques used to analyze income statements, balance sheets, and other financial data. Deals with credit criteria, analysis of loan applications, lending policies, and loan reviews. Covers accounts receivable financing, term loans, seasonal loans, problem loans, loan workouts, and loan profitability. Contains considerable coverage of real estate financing, including mortgage lending, principles of real estate valuation, and problem real estate loans. Also deals with consumer credit, including auto lending, bank charge cards, second mortgage loans, collections, and consumer credit regulation.

Credit recommendation: In the upper division baccalaureate category or in the graduate degree category, 3 semester hours in Banking or Finance (5/78).

Economics
1. **Monetary Economics**
2. **Interpreting Economic Change**
3. **Economics II** *or*
4. **Agribusiness (dropped effective January 1982)**

Location: Louisiana State University, Baton Rouge, LA.

Length: 1. 8½ hours (1 week); 2. 8½ hours (1 week); 3. 8½ hours (1 week).

Students also complete three extension problems requiring approximately 120 hours of independent study.

Dates: Completion in 1973-Present.

Objective: To provide an understanding of the role of the banking system in the economy and of the nature, causes, measurement, and interpretaiton of business fluctuations.

Instruction: *Courses 1 and 2:* A review of the market system, economic stabilization and the banking system, interpretation of monetary policy, development of the present banking system, nature of business fluctuations, causes and measurement of business cycles, review of information sources, indicators of economic activity, analysis of price indexes, leading theoretical models of inflation, judging turning point in business fluctuations. *Course 3:* A review of the commercial bank as a business form with emphasis on financial management for banks; term structure of interest rates; theories of the determination of the yield curve; methods of forecasting, including time series decomposition and a description of economic models. *Course 4:* Agricultural economics with specific reference to farm credit problems; the nature of agricultural production, including number and size of farms, cost structure in farming, capital investment in farming, and trends in farm income; governmental programs and policies affecting the agriculture industry; the operation of commodity markets.

Credit recommendation: In the upper division baccalaureate category, 3 semester hours in Economics (5/78). NOTE: All student complete courses 1 and 2 and either 3 *or* 4, for a total of three courses.

Legal Environment of Business
1. **Banking Law I**
2. **Banking Law II**
(Formerly Regulatory Problems)
3. **Labor Relations**

Location: Louisiana State University, Baton Rouge, LA.

Length: 1. 9 hours (1 week); 2. 8½ hours (1 week); 3. 8½ hours (1 week).

Students also complete an extension problem requiring approximately 40 hours of independent study.

Dates: Completion in 1973-Present.

Objective: To provide a study of the regulatory environment of banking.

Instruction: A review of regulations involved in a consumer law compliance examination, such as Truth-in-Lending Equal Credit Opportunity Act, Holder-in-Due-Course rule, Fair Credit Billing Act, Fair Credit Reporting Act, usury legislation, and loans to executive officers; a review of various legal aspects of bills and notes; the regulations involved in employee relations such as the Fair Labor Standards Act, sex and age discrimination regulations, OSHA, workers' compensation, EEOC problems, and affirmative action plans; a review of banking and the laws relating to privacy, the financial institutions regulatory act, the community reinvestments act, and prospects for future developments in bank regulation.

Credit recommendation: In the upper division baccalaureate category, 2 semester hours in Business Administration (5/78).

Management of Financial Institutions
1. **Investments**
2. **Bank Management**
(Formerly Special Banking Problems)
3. **Bank Marketing**
4. **Staff Management**
5. **Trusts Procedures** or
6. **International Finance (dropped effective January 1982)**
7. **Bank Pricing** or
(Formerly Retail Banking)

**8. Profit Planning
(Formerly Information Systems)
9. Innovative Management**
   Location: Louisiana State University, Baton Rouge, LA.
   Length: 1. 8½ hours (1 week); 2. 8½ hours (1 week); 3. 8½ hours (1 week); 4. 8½ hours (1 week); 5 or 6. 6 hours (1 week); 7 or 8. 7½ hours (1 week); 9. 7½ hours (1 week).
   Students also complete four extension problems requiring approximately 160 hours of independent study.
   Dates: Completion in 1973-Present.
   Objective: To examine a variety of managerial techniques and problems applicable to financial institutions.
   Instruction: The analysis and management of municipal bonds, U.S. government and agency bonds, bills, and notes; bank marketing, including sales, promotion, and marketing management; staff management issues, including personnel planning, human relations, leadership, motivation, and communication. Also deals with special topical problems in bank management such as capital planning, risk management, and accounting. *Course 5:* The organization and management of bank trust departments, supervision of trust investments, tax matters, estate planning, other trust-related matters. *Course 6:* Basics of foreign trade and foreign banking operations, collections and discounts, exchange controls, letters of credit, banking practices. *Course 7:* The major forces of change in the current banking environment - particularly as these factors relate to development of technology based delivery systems for retail services. *Course 8:* The use of financial information for setting objectives and establishing responsibilities for performance. Specific subjects include financial information and management, profit planning and responsibility reporting, cost accounting, pricing of bank services, funds transfer systems, and budgeting. *Course 9:* The dynamics of management in the context of increasing information about behavior data processing and economics; interpersonal communication, motivation, and management.
   Credit recommendation: In the upper division baccalaureate category or in the graduate degree category, 3 semester hours in Banking or Finance (5/78). NOTE: All students complete Course 1-4 *and* Course 5 or 6 *and* Course 7 or 8, for a total of six courses.

Seafarers Harry Lundeberg School of Seamanship

The Seafarers Harry Lundeberg School of Seamanship, founded in 1967, provides academic and career programs for boatmen and unlicensed seafarers. The purpose of the school is to train, guide, and encourage young people to pursue careers on the seas or on America's network of inland and coastal waterways, as well as to upgrade seafarers and boatmen to higher ratings. The school is administered by a joint board of trustees representing private American shipowners and the Seafarers International Union.

The school conducts both academic and vocational programs. The academic program consists of an adult basic education program, a high school equivalency program, and a two-year college program. Vocational programs are developed and expanded as changes in industry or in Coast Guard regulations occur.

The courses listed below are part of the training or upgrading programs. Many of the courses include hands-on experience aboard vessels as well as in the school's laboratories.

Source of official student records: Director of Vocational Education, Seafarers Harry Lundeberg School of Seamanship, Piney Point, Maryland 20674.

Additional information about the courses: Program on Noncollegiate Sponsored Instruction, The Center for Adult Learning and Educational Credentials, American Council on Education, One Dupont Circle, Washington, D.C. 20036.

**Able Seaman
(Formerly Lifeboat and Able Seaman)
   Part 1: Basic Seamanship
   Part 2: Navigation
   Part 3: First Aid and Safety**
   Location: Seafarers Harry Lundeberg School of Seamanship, Piney Point, MD.
   Length: *Version 1:* Approximately 240 hours (5 weeks, 5 days); residential. *Part 1:* 144 hours; *Part 2:* 36 hours; *Part 3:* 22 hours.
   Version 2: Approximately 320 hours (8 weeks).
   Version 3: 110 hours (4 weeks).
   Dates: *Version 1:* October 1975-December 1984. *Version 2:* January 1982-October 1986. *Version 3:* January 1985-Present.
   Objective: To provide the student with a sufficient understanding of life saving and seamanship skills to prepare for endorsement by the Coast Guard as an Able Seaman.
   Learning Outcome: Upon successful completion of this course, the student will be able to acquire working knowledge of the following subjects to enable the student to perform duties as qualified Able Seaman Unlimited, Able Seaman Limited, or Able Seaman Special: rules of the road; use of the magnetic and gyro compasses; use of booms; running rigging; winches; CPR; first aid; firefighting; manila and wire splicing; rigging and using stages; hitches and boatswains chairs; lifesaving equipment; aids to navigation; helmsmanship and lookout duties; and splices used aboard ship.
   Instruction: *Versions 1 and 2: Part 1:* Lifeboat handling; deck seamanship; marlinspike seamanship; helmsmanship; cargo handling; rigging; *Part 2:* Rules of the road;

bearings; aids to navigation; magnetic compass; radio use; *Part 3:* Treatment of wounds, shock, fractures, and burns; artificial respiration; toxic substances; survival measures; prevention and treatment of diseases; introduction to use of shipboard safety equipment; proper storage and handling of hazardous materials; fire prevention and shipboard fire fighting. *Version 3:* Course covers duties of Able Seaman aboard ship; ship construction and terminology; characteristics of SIU contracted ships; ship's organization; ship's control; bridge equipment and instruments; helmsmanship; basic fix plotting; compass (magnetic and gyro); aids to navigation (bouyage); rules of the nautical road; firefighting; and ship's sanitation.

Credit recommendation: *Versions 1 and 2: Part 1:* In the lower division baccalaureate/associate degree category, 6 semester hours in Seamanship. *Part 2:* In the lower division baccalaureate/associate degree category, 2 semester hours in Coastwise Navigation and Piloting. *Part 3:* In the lower division baccalaureate/associate degree category, 1 semester hour in First Aid and Safety (11/77) (6/82). NOTE 1: Further credit may be granted for Part 3 upon institutional evaluation. *Version 3:* In the lower division baccalaureate/associate degree category, 3 semester hours in Seamanship, 2 semester hours in Coastwise Navigation and Piloting, and 1 semester hour in First Aid and Safety (2/88). NOTE 2: This course has been reevaluated and continues to meet requirements for credit recommendations.

Advanced Deck - Inland and Oceans

Location: Seafarers Harry Lundeberg School of Seamanship, Piney Point, MD.

Length: *Version 1:* 80 hours (2 weeks); *Version 2:* 70 hours (2 weeks).

Dates: *Version 1:* May 1975-January 1988; *Version 2:* February 1988-Present.

Objective: To provide students with the skills required to perform the entry rating jobs in the deck and engine department on board merchant ships and towing vessels.

Instruction: *Version 1:* Topics covered are deck and engine skills and their practical application, work habits on board ship, and actual shipboard work. Lecture, discussion, and lab, with an emphasis on on-the-job training, are used. *Version 2:* Topics covered are deck department watches, pneumatic tools, electrical tools, priming and painting, maintain lines, heaving line, lock and lines, and safety aboard ships, and electrical safety.

Credit recommendation: In the lower division baccalaureate/associate degree category, 2 semester hours in Seamanship (6/82) (2/88). NOTE: This course has been reevaluated and continues to meet requirements for credit recommendations.

Assistant Cook Utility
(Formerly Assistant Cook)

Location: Seafarers Harry Lundeberg School of Seamanship, Piney Point, MD.

Length: *Version 1:* 208 hours (6 weeks); residential; 42 hours lecture and discussion, 30 hours laboratory, and 136 hours workshop; *Version 2:* 280 hours (7 weeks).

Dates: *Version 1:* September 1976-December 1985; *Version 2:* January 1986-Present.

Objective: *Version 1:* To develop the skills of food service workers and enable them to perform the duties of assistant cook. *Version 2:* To develop the skills of food service workers and enable them to perform the duties of assistant cook with special emphasis on food production.

Learning Outcome: Upon successful completion of this course, the student will be able to maintain the ship galley in a sanitary condition; prepare salads in a ship galley; prepare pasta and rice in a ship galley; prepare vegetables in a ship galley; prepare breakfast in a ship galley; and, prepare a night luncheon in a ship galley.

Instruction: Course covers preparation, cooking, and serving of vegetables (fresh, canned, and frozen), cooked salads, sandwiches, and breakfast foods. The basics of food preparation, including sanitation, dietary values, work organization, and the use of recipes, are emphasized.

Credit recommendation: *Version 1:* In the lower division baccalaureate/associate degree category, 3 semester hours in Quantity Food Production and 3 semester hours in Food Preparation (9/78). *Version 2:* In the lower division baccalaureate/associate degree category, 3 semester hours in Quantity Food Production, 4 semester hours in Food Preparation, and 1 semester hour in Kitchen Supervision (2/88). NOTE: This course has been reevaluated and continues to meet requirements for credit recommendations.

Basic Deck

Location: Seafarers Harry Lundeberg School of Seamanship, Piney Point, MD.

Length: 36 hours (2 weeks).

Dates: June 1972-Present.

Objective: To provide students with the skills required to perform the entry rating jobs aboard merchant ship and towing vessels.

Learning Outcome: Upon successful completion of this course, the student will be able to tie knots, use shipboard terminology, and stand shipboard watches.

Instruction: Course covers nautical time, standing watch, knot tying, and shipboard functions. Lecture, discussion, and lab are used.

Credit recommendation: In the lower division baccalaureate/associate degree category, 2 semester hours in Seamanship (6/82) (2/88). NOTE: This course has been reevaluated and continues to meet requirements for credit recommendations.

Basic Engine

Location: Seafarers Harry Lundeberg School of Seamanship, Piney Point, MD.

Length: *Version 1:* 46 hours (2 weeks); *Version 2:* 40 hours (2 weeks).

Dates: *Version 1:* May 1975-January 1988; *Version 2:* February 1988-Present.

Objective: To familiarize the student with steam and diesel engine plants, their operation, systems and associated parts. Students also learn the care and use of hand and power tools through actual machine shop practice.

Learning Outcome: Upon successful completion of this course, the student will be able to utilize basic hand tools and be familiar with basic ships engine systems (steam and diesel).

Instruction: Course covers the theory of operation, construction, and routine maintenance of diesel and steam power plants. Boilers and their operation, steam turbines and auxiliary equipment, and basic operation of the steam and water cycle are also covered. Lecture, discussion, and lab are used.

Credit recommendation: *Version 1:* In the lower division baccalaureate/associate degree category, 3 semester hours in Marine Engineering (6/82). *Version 2:* In the lower division baccalaureate/associate degree category, 2 semester hours in Marine Engineering (2/88). NOTE: This course has been reevaluated and continues to meet requirements for credit recommendations.

Basic Steward

Location: Seafarers Harry Lundeberg School of Seamanship, Piney Point, MD.

Length: *Version 1:* 70 hours (2 weeks); residential; 10 hours lecture and laboratory and 25 hours workshop per week; *Version 2:* 140 hours (4 weeks).

Dates: *Version 1:* May 1975-January 1988; *Version 2:* February 1988-Present.

Objective: *Version 1:* To develop the skills required to perform entry-level jobs in maritime food service departments. *Version 2:* To develop skills required to perform entry-level jobs in maritime food service departments with emphasis on food preparation and production.

Learning Outcome: Upon successful completion of this course, the student will be able to perform entry-level jobs in merchant vessel steward departments; prepare basic salads, vegetables, and breakfast cooking; understand the units of measure, identify galley equipment, and correctly use knives.

Instruction: *Version 1:* Covers food service operations, kitchen responsibilities and safety, use of kitchen utensils and tools, use of measurements and recipes, and quantity food preparation. *Version 2:* Covers food service operations, kitchen responsibilities and safety, use of kitchen utensils and tools, use of measurements and recipes, and quantity food preparation and production.

Credit recommendation: *Version 1:* In the lower division baccalaureate/associate degree category, 2 semester hours in Introductory Food Service Operations (9/78). *Version 2:* In the lower division baccalaureate/associate degree category, 4 semester hours in Introductory Food Service Operations (2/88). NOTE: This course has been reevaluated and continues to meet requirements for credit recommendations.

Celestial Navigation

Location: Seafarers Harry Lundeberg School of Seamanship, Piney Point, MD.

Length: *Version 1:* 186 hours (4-6 weeks); *Version 2:* 157 hours (5 weeks).

Dates: *Version 1:* September 1979-January 1988; *Version 2:* February 1988-Present.

Objective: *Version 1:* To provide the student with a knowledge of all aspects of celestial navigation that are required for licensing as Towboat Operation-Oceans, Master/Mate of Uninspected Vessels not over 300 gross tons, Master/Mate of Freight and Towing Vessels, and Third Mate candidate. *Version 2:* To enable the student to understand all aspects of celestial navigation that are required for licensing as Towboat Operator-Oceans, Master/Mate of Uninspected Vessels not over 300 gross tons, Master/Mate of Freight and Towing Vessels, Third Mate Unlimited, and Second Mate Unlimited.

Learning Outcome: Upon successful completion of this course, the student will be able to have basic knowledge of theory of nautical astronomy and time; determine sunrise/sunset/moonrise/moonset/civil twilight; determine latitude by polaris; determine time of LAN; determine latitude by meridian altitude; determine compass error using amplitudes and azimuths of celestial bodies; have basic knowledge of marine sextant, sextant errors and practical use; and determine position using LOP's of sun, moon, planets, and stars and plotting same.

Instruction: *Version 1:* Course covers computing time of sunrise, sunset, twilight, moonrise and moonset, determining compass error by amplitude and azimuth, latitude by polaris, determining time of meridian passage of the sun, latitude by meridian altitude of the sun, position by sun line, use and adjustments of the sextant, underway practical experience in celestial navigation, review of the international and inland rules of the road. Lecture, discussion, and lab are used. *Version 2:* The celestial course includes the following major topics: nautical astronomy; time; sunrise/sunset/moonrise/moonset; Greenwich Hour angle and declination; latitude by polaris observation; time of local apparent noon; sextant corrections; latitude by observation at local apparent noon; and sunlines.

Credit recommendation: In the lower division baccalaureate/associate degree category, 8 semester hours in Celestial Navigation, 1 semester hour in First Aid and Safety, and 1 semester hour in Rules of the Road (6/82) (2/88). NOTE: This course has been reevaluated and continues to meet requirements for credit recommendations.

Chief/Assistant Engineer - Uninspected Motor Vessels (Formerly License Diesel Engineer - Uninspected)

Location: Seafarers Harry Lundeberg School of Seamanship, Piney Point, MD.

Length: *Version 1:* 235 hours (8 weeks); *Version 2:* 320 hours (10 weeks).

Dates: *Version 1:* January 1978-January 1988; *Version 2:* February 1988-Present.

Objective: To provide the student with sufficient knowledge to pass the U.S. Coast Guard Chief Engineer or Assistant Engineer Diesel License of specified horsepower on uninspected vessels.

Learning Outcome: Upon successful completion of this course, the student will be able to sit for United States Coast Guard Chief or Assistant Engineer Uninspected Motor Vessels.

Instruction: To include training in pumps, compressors, heat exchanges, propellors, shafting, steering systems, valves, instruments, lubrication, inspections, ship construction, damage control, reduction gears, diesel construction, diesel principles, fuel injection, starting systems, governors, boilers, direct current components, alternating current components, batteries, refrigeration, fire fighting, emergency equipment, Coast Guard regulations, pollution laws, sanitary systems, and First Aid. The practical engine training includes extensive operation of maintenance on the school's tugs and in the engine shop. In addition, an applicant must hold a First Aid and CPR certificate which is offered at the school. Lecture, discussion, and lab are used.

Credit recommendation: *Version 1:* In the lower division baccalaureate/associate degree category, 9 semester hours in Diesel Engine Technology (6/82). *Version 2:* In the lower division baccalaureate/associate degree category, 9 semester hours in Diesel Engine Technology, 1 semester hour in Electricity, 1 semester hour in First Aid/CPR, and 1 semester hour in Industrial Safety (2/88). NOTE: This course has been reevaluated and continues to meet requirements for credit recommendations.

Chief Cook

Location: Seafarers Harry Lundeberg School of Seamanship, Piney Point, MD.

Length: *Version 1:* Approximately 242 hours (8 weeks); residential; 50 hours lecture and discussion, 54 hours laboratory, and 138 hours workshop; *Version 2:* 333 hours (9 weeks).

Dates: *Version 1:* September 1976-January 1988; *Version 2:* February 1988-Present.

Objective: *Version 1:* To teach a cook and baker (second cook) to serve as chief cook. *Version 2:* To upgrade qualified members of the Steward's department to Chief Cook.

Learning Outcome: Upon successful completion of this course, the student will be able to operate galley equipment; satisfy general and specific sanitation and safety requirements; operate most cutting equipment and identify cuts of meat; maintain inventory control records; prepare meats, seafood, poultry, soups, sauces, and gravies; supervise galley personnel; and produce menus and meals aboard ship.

Instruction: *Version 1:* Topics include principles of preparation of meats, poultry, seafood, soups, sauces, and gravies; quantity preparation of these foods; identification of meat cuts by the use of charts; work organization; sanitation; the use of recipes. *Version 2:* Topics include principles of preparation of meats, poultry, seafood, soups, sauces, and gravies; quantity preparation of these foods; identification of meat cuts by the use of charts; work organization; sanitation; the use of recipes, work supervision, and maintaining inventory control are also covered in this course.

Credit recommendation: *Version 1:* In the lower division baccalaureate/associate degree category, 3 semester hours in Food Preparation and 3 semester hours in Quantity Food Production (9/78). *Version 2:* In the lower division baccalaureate/associate degree category, 4 semester hours in Food Preparation, 3 semester hours in Quantity Food Production, and 3 semester hours in Kitchen Supervision (2/88). NOTE: This course has been reevaluated and continues to meet requirements for credit recommendations.

Chief Steward

Location: Seafarers Harry Lundeberg School of Seamanship, Piney Point, MD.

Length: *Version 1:* Approximately 232½ hours (8 weeks); residential; 72 hours lecture and discussion, 86 hours laboratory, and 74½ hours workshop; *Version 2:* 324 hours (9 weeks).

Dates: *Version 1:* September 1975-January 1988; *Version 2:* February 1988-Present.

Objective: *Version 1:* To teach chief cooks the duties of mess steward. *Version 2:* To provide the management and operational skills necessary for successful operation of the stewards department aboard ship.

Learning Outcome: Upon successful completion of this course, the student will be able to plan menus; supervise subordinates; organize and operate the steward department; cook; type; and conduct an inventory control system.

Instruction: *Version 1:* A comprehensive course covering organization, work supervision, menu planning, inventory control, requisitioning procedures, and sanitation. Includes all aspects of food production and nutrition. Also includes typing, first aid, CPR, and safety. *Version 2:* A comprehensive course covering organization, work supervision, menu planning, inventory control, requisitioning procedures, sanitation, all aspects of food production, nutrition, typing, and safety.

Credit recommendation: *Version 1:* In the lower division baccalaureate/associate degree category, 2 semester hours in First Aid and Cardiopulmonary Resuscitation, 4 semester hours in Food Service Organization and Supervision, and 2 semester hours in Quantity Food Production (9/78). NOTE: Credit for typing on the basis of institutional assessment. *Version 2:* In the lower division baccalaureate/associate degree category, 2 semester hours in Nutrition, 6 semester hours in Food Management, and 2 semester hours in Quantity Food Production (2/88). NOTE 1: This course has been reevaluated and continues to meet requirements for credit recommendations. NOTE 2: Credit for typing on the basis of institutional assessment.

Coastwise Navigation and Piloting (Quartermaster)
Location: Seafarers Harry Lundeberg School of Seamanship, Piney Point, MD.
Length: *Version 1:* 64 hours (2 weeks); residential; *Version 2:* 132 hours (3 weeks); residential; *Version 3:* 168 hours (8 weeks).
Dates: *Version 1:* October 1972-March 1977; *Version 2:* April 1977-October 1985; *Version 3:* June 1982-December 1985.
Objective: To provide the student with a working knowledge of marine navigation.
Instruction: *Version 1:* Same as Version 2 (below) but coverage is less complete. Tides and currents, electronic aids to navigation, and sounding are not covered. *Version 2:* Use of magnetic and gyro compass; rules of the road; international codes and signals; bridge publications and instruments; aids to navigation; use of radar; loran, fathometers, and RDF; tides and currents. **Prerequisite:** Lifeboatman and Able Seaman course or Coast Guard endorsement as Able Seaman Unlimited Any Waters. *Version 3:* Same as Version 2, but includes more practical training.
Credit recommendation: *Version 1:* In the lower division baccalaureate/associate degree category, 3 semester hours in Navigation (11/77). *Version 2:* In the lower division baccalaureate/associate degree category, 6 semester hour in Navigation (11/77). *Version 3:* In the lower division baccalaureate/associate degree category, 7 semester hours in Navigation (6/82). NOTE: This course has been reevaluated and continues to meet requirements for credit recommendations.

Conveyorman
Location: Seafarers Harry Lundeberg School of Seamanship, Piney Point, MD.
Length: *Version 1:* 34 hours (indicates number of hours devoted to instruction in Welding); *Version 2:* Approximately 100 hours (4 weeks).
Dates: *Version 1:* February 1980-January 1988; *Version 2:* February 1988-Present.
Objective: To teach the student the use, maintenance, and repair of marine conveyor systems.

Learning Outcome: Upon successful completion of this course, the student will be able to operate cargo handling equipment aboard bulk carriers; and perform basic gas and air welding functions.
Instruction: Consists of introduction to types and developments of self-unloaders, conveyorman belt construction and types, belt adjustments, belt splicing procedures and practical application, related electrical AC and DC systems, practical electrical troubleshooting, electrical test equipment, power failure testing, hydraulic ram theory, practical hydraulic troubleshooting, pipe fitting and threading, gate construction, maintenance and operation, as well as oxyacetylene cutting and electric and welding shop practical training. Lecture, discussion, and lab are used.
Credit recommendation: *Version 1:* In the lower division baccalaureate/associate degree category, 2 semester hours in Welding (6/82). NOTE: While this course is at the postsecondary level, it does not equate directly to standard collegiate course offerings. Institutional evaluation of the applicability of this course and of appropriate credit is recommended. *Version 2:* In the vocational certificate category, 3 semester hours in Conveyor Operation and Maintenance (2/88). NOTE: This course has been reevaluated and continues to meet requirements for credit recommendations.

Cook and Baker
Location: Seafarers Harry Lundeberg School of Seamanship, Piney Point, MD.
Length: *Version 1:* 208 hours (6 weeks); residential; 40 hours lecture and discussion, 22 hours laboratory, and 146 hours workshop; *Version 2:* 302 hours (9 weeks).
Dates: *Version 1:* September 1976-January 1988; *Version 2:* February 1988-Present.
Objective: *Version 1:* To teach assistant cooks to bake. *Version 2:* To provide the skills required to perform shipboard baking and breakfast preparation.
Learning Outcome: Upon successful completion of this course, the student will be able to operate the equipment found in the bake shop; understand the different methods of measuring in a bake shop; prepare pastry, pies, gelatins, puddings, custards, cookies, icings, bread and rolls; be familiar with safety and sanitation procedures in the bake shop, and be able to name and explain functions of different ingredients used in baking.
Instruction: *Version 1:* Topics include baking breads, rolls, pies, cakes, cookies, and breakfast pastries. Students concentrate on dessert and breakfast preparations, sanitation, and work organization. Careful attention to recipe requirements is highlighted. *Version 2:* Topics include baking breads, rolls, pies, cakes, cookies, and breakfast pastries. Students concentrate on dessert and breakfast preparations, sanitation, and work organization. Careful attention to recipe requirements is highlighted. Emphasis is placed on baking theory and on the job preparation and

production of bread and rolls, pastries, cakes, pie doughs and fillings, cookies and icings.

Credit recommendation: *Version 1:* In the lower division baccalaureate/associate degree category, 3 semester hours in Baking and 3 semester hours in Quantity Food Production (9/78). *Version 2:* In the lower division baccalaureate/associate degree category, 6 semester hours in Baking and 3 semester hours in Quantity Food Production (2/88). NOTE: This course has been reevaluated and continues to meet requirements for credit recommendations.

Diesel Engines (MET 209)

Location: Seafarers Harry Lundeberg School of Seamanship, Piney Point, MD.

Length: *Version 1:* 128 hours (3 weeks, 4 days); residential; 34 hours lecture/discussion and 6 hours laboratory/workshop per week; *Version 2:* 180 hours (6 weeks); including approximately 50 hours laboratory/workshop.

Dates: *Version 1:* January 1975-January 1988; *Version 2:* February 1988-Present.

Objective: To provide the student with the knowledge to operate small diesel engines.

Learning Outcome: Upon successful completion of this course, the student will be able to disassemble, diagnose, repair, reassemble, and tune-up a high speed diesel engine; perform maintenance on diesel engine air intake systems; and troubleshoot low, medium, and high speed performing diesel engines.

Instruction: *Version 1:* Types, design, construction, and characteristics of various diesel engines; diesel nomenclature and principles of operation; introduction to the fuel, air, lubrication, and exhaust systems; the use of various gauges, meters, and instruments used on diesel engines; the care, operation, maintenance, and recording of diesel engine performance signals used between bridge and engine room; basic fire fighting; first aid and safety. *Version 2:* More in-depth coverage of air intake system; fuel injectors, lubrication systems, governors, and plant automation.

Credit recommendation: *Version 1:* In the lower division baccalaureate/associate degree category, 6 semester hours in Diesel Engines (11/77) (6/82). *Version 2:* In the lower division baccalaureate/associate degree category, 9 semester hours in Diesel Engine Technology (2/88). NOTE: This course has been reevaluated and continues to meet requirements for credit recommendations.

Electro-Hydraulic System Maintenance
(Hagglund Crane Maintenance)

Location: Seafarers Harry Lundeberg School of Seamanship, Piney Point, MD.

Length: 180 hours (6 weeks).

Dates: February 1988-Present.

Objective: To provide the Electro-Hydraulic Technician with the theoretical knowledge and practical skills to maintain, troubleshoot, and repair complex electrically controlled, hydraulic systems.

Learning Outcome: Upon successful completion of this course, the student will be able to read and interpret manufacturer's instructions, diagrams, operations and maintenance manuals; perform routine tests and inspections; and train operator in routine maintenance and inspection procedures.

Instruction: Course covers basic hydraulics, electrical control of hydraulic systems, deck cranes (specifically Hagglunds type TAP 1626, TG3632, TG2432).

Credit recommendation: In the vocational certificate category, 6 semester hours in Electro-Hydraulic Control Systems (2/88).

Fireman, Oiler, and Watertender
(Formerly Fireman, Watertender, and Oiler)

Location: Seafarers Harry Lundeberg School of Seamanship, Piney Point, MD.

Length: *Version 1:* 56 hours (2 weeks); *Version 2:* 84 hours (3 weeks); *Version 3:* Approximately 144 hours (4-6 weeks); residential; includes 14 hours supervised independent study; *Version 4:* 180 hours (8 weeks).

Dates: *Version 1:* June 1972-August 1975; *Version 2:* September 1975-September 1976; *Version 3:* October 1976-January 1988; *Version 4:* February 1988-Present.

Objective: *Versions 1 and 2:* To review the theoretical and practical knowledge required to perform the job of fireman/watertender or oiler aboard ship. *Versions 3 and 4:* To provide students with the theoretical and practical knowledge required to perform the job of fireman/watertender or oiler aboard ship.

Learning Outcome: Upon successful completion of this course, the student will be able to sit for the United States Coast Guard Unlicensed rating as Fireman, Oiler, Watertender (FOWT)

Instruction: *Versions 1 and 2:* Same as Version 3 except coverage is less in-depth. *Version 3:* Parts of a boiler and their functions; the steam and water cycle; fuel oil and lube oil systems; fire-fighting and emergency procedures. Use of a simulator in putting boilers on the line; changing burners; operating auxiliary equipment; and starting and securing main engines. *Version 4:* Parts of a boiler and their functions; the steam and water cycle; fuel oil and lube oil systems; fire-fighting and emergency procedures. Use of a simulator in putting boilers on the line; changing burners; operating auxiliary equipment; starting and securing main engines; diesels, refrigeration, and auxiliary systems.

Credit recommendation: *Versions 1 and 2:* In the lower division baccalaureate/associate degree category, 2 semester hours in Marine Engineering (11/77). *Version 3:* In the lower division baccalaureate/associate degree category, 6 semester hours in Marine Engineering (6/82). *Version 4:* In the lower division baccalaureate/associate degree category, 6 semester hours in Basic Marine Engineering, 1 semester hour in Diesel Technology, and 1 semester hour in Refrigeration Technology (2/88). NOTE: This course has been reevaluated and continues to meet requirements for credit recommendations.

First Class Pilot
  Location: Seafarers Harry Lundeberg School of Seamanship, Piney Point, MD.
  Length: 197 hours (7 weeks).
  Dates: June 1973-Present.
  Objective: To prepare the student to successfully complete the U.S. Coast Guard First Class Pilot Examination.
  Learning Outcome: Upon successful completion of this course, the student will be able to adequately perform all functions of a First Class Pilot.
  Instruction: *Version 1:* Course covers first aid and life saving, piloting and coastwise navigation, rules of the road, electronic aids to navigation, marine meteorology, advanced seamanship, and marine investigation regulations. Lecture, discussion, and lab are used. *Version 2:* Course covers rules of the road, local area knowledge, chart sketching, instruments and accessories, piloting, tides and currents, ship handling, and weather. First aid, CPR, and firefighting offered if necessary.
  Credit recommendation: In the lower division baccalaureate/associate degree category, 1 semester hour in First Aid and Life Saving, 5 semester hours in Piloting and Coastwise Navigation, 2 semester hours in Rules of the Road; 1 semester hour in Electronic Aids to Navigation; 1 semester hour in Marine Meteorology; 1 semester hour in Advanced Seamanship; and 1 semester hour in Marine Investigation/Regulations (6/82) (2/88). NOTE: This course has been reevaluated and continues to meet requirements for credit recommendations.

Hydraulics
  Location: Seafarers Harry Lundeberg School of Seamanship, Piney Point, MD.
  Length: 82 hours (4 weeks).
  Dates: September 1987-Present.
  Objective: To provide a basic understanding and troubleshooting knowledge of hydraulic systems.
  Learning Outcome: Upon successful completion of this course, the student will be able to read a hydraulic system design; understand how a hydraulic system works; and troubleshoot and repair hydraulic systems, particularly as they relate to the shipping industry.
  Instruction: Course covers a general introduction to the principles and applications of fluid dynamics relating to cargo handling systems. Hydraulic troubleshooting and repair procedures are also covered.
  Credit recommendation: In the lower division baccalaureate/associate degree category, 4 semester hours in Introduction to Hydraulics (2/88).

Lifeboat (NST 102)
  Location: Seafarers Harry Lundeberg School of Seamanship, Piney Point, MD.
  Length: *Version 1:* 60 hours (2 weeks); *Version 2:* 70 hours (2 weeks).
  Dates: *Version 1:* June 1972-January 1988; *Version 2:* February 1988-Present.
  Objective: *Version 1:* To give the student a knowledge of the nomenclature of lifeboats and liferafts, survival and abandon ship procedures; students are also given 30 hours of actual rowing experience. *Version 2:* To provide the student with a sufficient understanding of lifesaving techniques, equipment, and practical boat handling procedures.
  Learning Outcome: Upon successful completion of this course, the student will be able to pass United States Coast Guard examination and receive an endorsement as Lifeboatman.
  Instruction: *Version 1:* Topics include emergency duties, lifeboat construction, lifeboat launching and recovery, basic compass in navigation, liferaft construction, liferaft launching and maintenance, and use of all lifeboat and liferaft equipment. Survival methods such as abandon ship procedures, hypothermia prevention, eating and drinking to survive, helicopter rescue procedures, and use of the emergency radio and signals to attract attention are also covered. Laboratory experience (i.e., indoor and on the water) is stressed. *Version 2:* Topics include emergency duties, lifeboat construction, lifeboat launching and recovery, basic compass in navigation, liferaft construction, liferaft launching and maintenance, and use of all lifeboat and liferaft equipment. Survival methods such as abandon ship procedures, hypothermia prevention, eating and drinking to survive, helicopter rescue procedures, and use of the emergency radio and signals to attract attention are also covered. Laboratory experience (i.e., indoor and on the water) is stressed including 30 hours of actual rowing experience.
  Credit recommendation: In the lower division baccalaureate/associate degree category, 2 semester hours in Seamanship (6/82) (2/88). NOTE: This course has been reevaluated and continues to meet requirements for credit recommendations.

Liquid Cargo Operations
(Pump Room Operations and Maintenance)
  Location: Seafarers Harry Lundeberg School of Seamanship, Piney Point, MD.
  Length: *Version 1:* Approximately 222 hours (6 weeks); *Version 2:* 180 hours (6 weeks).
  Dates: *Version 1:* April 1979-January 1988; *Version 2:* February 1988-Present.
  Objective: To train the student in pumpman operation and maintenance and liquid cargo operations.
  Learning Outcome: Upon successful completion of this course, the student will be able to perform the duties of pumpman; perform valve and pump repair; and operate loading and discharging procedures.

Instruction: Consists of fire fighting and safety, first aid, cargo properties and emergency procedures, tanker development and construction, operation and maintenance of valves and pumps, loading procedures, cargo pump operation, cargo measurement, discharging procedures, ballasting procedures, tank cleaning, inert gas systems, pollution control, cargo control system, and hydraulics and machine shop. Lecture and lab are used.

Credit recommendation: *Version 1:* In the lower division baccalaureate/associate degree category, 3 semester hours in Machine Shop Practices and 4 semester hours in Liquid Cargo Operations (6/82). *Version 2:* In the lower division baccalaureate/associate degree category, 3 semester hours in Machine Shop Practices, and 3 semester hours in Liquid Cargo Operations (2/88). NOTE: This course has been reevaluated and continues to meet requirements for credit recommendations.

Marine Electrical Maintenance

Location: Seafarers Harry Lundeberg School of Seamanship, Piney Point, MD.

Length: *Version 1:* 198 hours (5 weeks, 2 days); residential; *Version 2:* 240 hours (8 weeks).

Dates: *Version 1:* October 1975-May 1982; *Version 2:* June 1982-Present.

Objective: To provide the student with the theoretical and practical knowledge required to act as a troubleshooter and to repair motors, generators, controllers, and signal appliances.

Learning Outcome: Upon successful completion of this course, the student will be able to perform routine maintenance and repair and troubleshoot; rotating electrical machinery; lighting systems; galley equipment; cargo handling equipment; and ships interior communications.

Instruction: *Version 1:* Electrical theory and power systems; electrical measuring instruments; classroom and practical training in the control, operation, maintenance, troubleshooting, and repair of AC and DC motors and generators; controllers and sold-state motor control. **Prerequisite:** Qualified Marine Engine Department, endorsement, or endorsement as Electrician. *Version 2:* Same as Version 1, but includes more practical training.

Credit recommendation: *Version 1:* In the lower division baccalaureate/associate degree category, 8 semester hours in Electricity (11/77). NOTE: If student has completed QMED course, a maximum of 8 semester hours in Electricity should be granted. *Version 2:* In the lower division baccalaureate/associate degree category, 9 semester hours in Electricity (6/82) (2/88). NOTE: This course has been reevaluated and continues to meet requirements for credit recommendations.

Master/Mate Freight and Towing

Location: Seafarers Harry Lundeberg School of Seamanship, Piney Point, MD.

Length: 35 hours (10 weeks).

Dates: February 1988-Present.

Objective: To offer classroom instruction leading to United States Coast Guard certification as Master/Mate of Freight and Towing vessels of not more than 1,600 gross tons.

Learning Outcome: Upon successful completion of this course, the student will be able to have basic knowledge of tugboat use and operation; tows, types of barges, terminal operations, safety, firefighting capability and off-shore supply; marine meteorology; rules of the road; electronic aids to navigation; advanced seamanship; first aid and lifesaving; piloting and coastwise navigation; and marine resuscitation (CPR).

Instruction: Course covers rules of the road, ship construction, cargo gear, ship handling, tides and currents, instruments and accessories, weather, rules and regulations, stability, ships business, charts and piloting. First aid, CPR, and firefighting are also offered.

Credit recommendation: In the lower division baccalaureate/associate degree category, 1 semester hour in First Aid and Lifesaving (CPR), 5 semester hours in Piloting and Coastwise Navigation, 2 semester hours in Rules of the Road, 1 semester hour in Electronic Aids to Navigation, 1 semester hour in Marine Meteorology, 1 semester hour in Advanced Seamanship, and 1 semester hour in Rules and Regulations (2/88).

Original Third Assistant Engineer, Steam and/or Motor - Inspected
(Formerly Third Assistant Engineer Steam and/or Motor - Inspected)

Location: Seafarers Harry Lundeberg School of Seamanship, Piney Point, MD.

Length: *Version 1:* 248 hours (10 weeks); *Version 2:* 278 hours (11 weeks).

Dates: *Version 1:* January 1981-January 1988; *Version 2:* February 1988-Present.

Objective: To provide the student with sufficient knowledge to pass the U.S. Coast Guard Third Assistant Engineer Unlimited License Examination.

Learning Outcome: Upon successful completion of this course, the student will be able to sit for Original Third Assistant Engineer's License.

Instruction: Course covers engine room watching aboard deep sea ships and operation and maintenance of all machinery located in the engine spaces. This course includes advanced electricity, electronics, propulsion and steering systems, boilers, turbines, diesels, safety, hydraulics, air conductors, and refrigeration and distilling units. Lecture and discussion are used.

Credit recommendation: *Version 1:* In the lower division baccalaureate/associate degree category, 3 semester hours in Electricity, 2 semester hours in Industrial Safety, 2 semester hours in Diesel Power, 1 semester hour in First Aid and CPR, and 4 semester hours in Ship Systems and Auxiliary Equipment (6/82). *Version 2:* In the lower division baccalaureate/associate degree category, 3 semester hours in Electricity, 2 semester hours in Industrial Safety, 2 semester hours in Diesel Engine Technology, 1 semester hour in First Aid and CPR, and 4 semester hours in Ship Systems and Auxiliary Equipment or Power Plant Technology (2/88). NOTE: This course has been reevaluated and continues to meet requirements for credit recommendations.

Process Control Instrumentation (Automation)
Location: Seafarers Harry Lundeberg School of Seamanship, Piney Point, MD.
Length: *Version 1:* 106 hours (3 weeks and 4 days); *Version 2:* Approximately 120 hours (4 weeks).
Dates: *Version 1:* November 1979-January 1988; *Version 2:* February 1988-Present.
Objective: To teach the student about process control instrumentation for automated vessels.
Learning Outcome: Upon successful completion of this course, the student will be able to operate and maintain marine type combustion control equipment; operate and maintain marine type feedwater regulation equipment; and operate and maintain drilling plant control equipment.
Instruction: Covers process control instrumentation including automated boiler equipment, pneumatics, systems analysis and the operation of remote controls for all components in the steam and water cycle. The course also covers level, temperature, flow, force, weight and motion measurement, final control elements, safety calibration, and testing procedures. Lecture and lab (classroom and practical training) are used.
Credit recommendation: In the lower division baccalaureate/associate degree category, 7 semester hours in Process Control Instrumentation (6/82) (2/88). NOTE: This course has been reevaluated and continues to meet requirements for credit recommendations.

Qualified Members of the Engine Department (QMED), Four-Week Version
   Part 1: Principles of Electricity
   Part 2. Principles of Refrigeration
   Location: Seafarers Harry Lundeberg School of Seamanship, Piney Point, MD.
   Length: 98 hours (4 weeks); residential. *Part 1:* 48 hours; *Part 2:* 46 hours.
   Dates: October 1972-June 1982.
   Objective: To provide the student with the knowledge required for certification for Qualified Marine Engine Department (QMED) and to operate and repair refrigeration and electrical equipment.
   Instruction: *Parts 1 and 2:* Same as six-week version.
   Credit recommendation: *Part 1:* In the lower division baccalaureate/associate degree category, 2 semester hours in Electricity. *Part 2:* In the lower division baccalaureate/associate degree category, 2 semester hours in Refrigeration (11/77).

Qualified Members of the Engine Department (QMED), Six-Week Version
   Part 1: Principles of Electricity
   Part 2: Principles of Refrigeration
   Part 3: Principles of Steam Generation Systems
   Location: Seafarers Harry Lundeberg School of Seamanship, Piney Point, MD.
   Length: 124 hours (6 weeks); residential. *Part 1:* 48 hours; *Part 2:* 46 hours; *Part 3:* 30 hours.
   Dates: November 1972-October 1973.
   Objective: To provide the student with the knowledge required for certification for Qualified Marine Engine Department (QMED) and to operate and repair refrigeration and electrical equipment and to introduce the student to the operation of industrial steam generation systems.
   Instruction: *Part 1:* Same as eight-week version except less time is devoted to AC and DC electricity. *Part 2:* Same as eight-week version except less time is devoted to review. *Part 3:* Covers boiler theory.
   Credit recommendation: *Part 1:* In the lower division baccalaureate/associate degree category, 2 semester hours in Electricity. *Part 2:* In the lower division baccalaureate/associate degree category, 2 semester hours in Refrigeration. *Part 3:* In the lower division baccalaureate/associate degree category, 1 semester hour in Steam Generation Systems (11/77) (6/82). NOTE: This course has been reevaluated and continues to meet requirements for credit recommendations.

Qualified Members of the Engine Department (QMED), Eight-Week Version
   Part 1: Principles of Electricity
   Part 2: Principles of Refrigeration
   Part 3: Principles of Steam Generation Systems
   Location: Seafarers Harry Lundeberg School of Seamanship, Piney Point, MD.
   Length: 242 hours (8 weeks); residential. *Part 1:* 66 hours; *Part 2:* 64 hours; *Part 3:* 112 hours.
   Dates: October 1973-May 1977.
   Objective: To provide the student with the knowledge required for certification for QMED and to operate industrial steam generation systems.
   Instruction: *Part 1:* Same as 12-week version, with less time devoted to placed electrical measuring instruments, soldering, brazing, and welding. *Part 2:* Same as 12-week version, with less time devoted to troubleshooting procedures. *Part 3:* Same as 12-week version, with less time devoted to fuels.
   Credit recommendation: *Part 1:* In the lower division baccalaureate/associate degree category, 3 semester hours in Electricity (11/77). *Part 2:* In the lower division baccalaureate/associate degree category, 3 semester hours in Refrigeration (11/77). *Part 3:* In the lower division baccalaureate/associate degree category, 6 semester hours in

Steam Generation Systems (11/77).

Qualified Members of the Engine Department (QMED), Twelve-Week Version
  Part 1: Principles of Electricity
  Part 2: Principles of Refrigeration
  Part 3: Principles of Steam Generation Systems
  Part 4: First Aid and Safety
  Location: Seafarers Harry Lundeberg School of Seamanship, Piney Point, MD.
  Length: 336 hours (12 weeks); residential. *Part 1:* 76 hours; *Part 2:* 74 hours; *Part 3:* 162 hours; *Part 4:* 24 hours.
  Dates: June 1977-Present.
  Objective: To provide the student with the knowledge required for certification for Qualified Marine Engine Department (QMED) and to provide a thorough understanding of industrial steam generation systems.
  Learning Outcome: Upon successful completion of this course, the student will be able to obtain United States Coast Guard QMED endorsement which includes ratings for pumpman, refrigeration engineer, machinist, electrician, deck engineer, junior engineer, and deck engine mechanic (DEMAC).
  Instruction: *Part 1:* Fundamental concepts of electricity; batteries; electrical circuits; magnetism and electromagnetic circuits; transformers; AC motors and generators; use and care of electrical instruments; troubleshooting of electrical equipment; starting, securing, and paralleling turbo generators; placed electrical measuring instruments; soldering, brazing, and welding; fire-fighting and emergency procedures. *Part 2:* Principles of refrigeration; compressors; receivers; dehydrators; valves (solenoids, therm-expansion, packless); evaporators; testing for and repairing leaks. Emphasizes troubleshooting and refrigeration problems. *Part 3:* Operation, use, and repair of pumps; boiler theory and boiler water treatment; piping, tubing, and valves; automation principles; evaporators; fuels. *Part 4:* Preparation for emergency at sea; work safety; emergency first aid and procedures; controlling and extinguishing shipboard fires.
  Credit recommendation: *Part 1:* In the lower division baccalaureate/associate degree category, 4 semester hours in Electricity. *Part 2:* In the lower division baccalaureate/associate degree category, 4 semester hours in Refrigeration. *Part 3:* In the lower division baccalaureate/associate degree category, 9 semester hours in Steam Generation Systems. *Part 4:* In the lower division baccalaureate/associate degree category, 1 semester hour in First Aid and Safety (11/77) (6/82). *Version 2: Part 1:* In the lower division baccalaureate/associate degree category, 4 semester hours in Electricity. *Part 2:* In the lower division baccalaureate/associate degree category, 4 semester hours in Refrigeration. *Part 3:* In the lower division baccalaureate/associate degree category, 9 semester hours in Power Plant Technology or Steam Generation Systems. *Part 4:* 1 semester hour in First Aid and Safety (2/88). NOTE: This course has been reevaluated and continues to meet requirements for credit recommendations.

Refrigerated Containers/Advanced Maintenance
  Location: Seafarers Harry Lundeberg School of Seamanship, Piney Point, MD.
  Length: 210 hours (6 weeks).
  Dates: February 1988-Present.
  Objective: To provide theoretical background and practical experience in the construction, operation, maintenance, and repair of refrigerated container systems, including engine, refrigeration, and electrical systems.
  Learning Outcome: Upon successful completion of this course, the student will be able to perform standard refrigeration service techniques and system diagnosis; perform electrical troubleshooting on refrigerated container units; conduct a compressor overhaul; and assume the duties of a maintenance electrician aboard container ships relative to refrigerated containers.
  Instruction: Course covers review of refrigeration systems; capacity control, refrigerants, etc., applied electricity; wiring diagrams, motors, etc.; diesel engines; systems operation, maintenance and troubleshooting. Laboratory work on actual units of various manufacture and design.
  Credit recommendation: In the lower division baccalaureate/associate degree category, 2 semester hours in Refrigeration Technology, 2 semester hours in Diesel Technology, and 1 semester hour in Electrical Maintenance (2/88).

Refrigeration Systems Maintenance and Operation (Formerly Maintenance of Shipboard Refrigeration Systems)
  Location: Seafarers Harry Lundeberg School of Seamanship, Piney Point, MD.
  Length: 218 hours (5 weeks, 4 days); residential.
  Dates: December 1975-Present.
  Objective: To provide the student with the theoretical and practical knowledge required to repair a refrigeration system.
  Learning Outcome: Upon successful completion of this course, the student will be able to perform routine maintenance on ship stores, refrigeration and air conditioning plants; and troubleshoot shipboard refrigeration equipment.
  Instruction: Basic refrigeration, refrigeration components; maintenance of refrigeration systems; parts of replacement and overhaul; electrical circuitry; electrical wiring and troubleshooting. **Prerequisite:** Qualified Marine Engine Department, Any Rating Endorsement, or endorsement as Refrigeration Engineer and Electrician.
  Credit recommendation: *Version 1:* In the lower division baccalaureate/associate degree category, 10 semester hours in Refrigeration (11/77) (6/82). NOTE: If student has completed QMED course, a maximum of 10 semester

hours in Refrigeration should be granted. *Version 2:* In the lower division baccalaureate/associate degree category, 10 semester hours in Refrigeration/Air Conditioning Technology (2/88). NOTE: This course has been reevaluated and continues to meet requirements for credit recommendations.

Third Mate - Inspected Vessels
   Location: Seafarers Harry Lundeberg School of Seamanship, Piney Point, MD.
   Length: 311 hours (10 weeks).
   Dates: January 1981-Present.
   Objective: To provide the student with sufficient knowledge to pass the U.S. Coast Guard Third Mate Unlimited License Examination.
   Instruction: *Version 1:* Course covers celestial navigation, coastwise navigation, rules of the road, marine meteorology, seamanship, and cargo handling. Lecture, discussion, and lab are used. *Version 2:* Course covers rules of the road, ship construction, cargo gear, ship handling, tides and currents, instruments and accessories, weather, rules and regulations (CFR), stability, ships business, and charts and piloting. First aid, CPR, and firefighting are also offered.
   Credit recommendation: In the lower division baccalaureate/associate degree category, 3 semester hours in Celestial Navigation, 4 semester hours in Coastwise Navigation, 3 semester hours in Rules of the Road, 1 semester hour in Marine Meteorology, 2 semester hours in Seamanship, and 2 semester hours in Cargo Handling (6/82) (2/88). NOTE: This course has been reevaluated and continues to meet requirements for credit recommendations.

Towboat Cook
   Location: Seafarers Harry Lundeberg School of Seamanship, Piney Point, MD.
   Length: *Version 1:* 277 hours (6 weeks); residential; 29 hours lecture and discussion, 24 hours laboratory, and 224 hours workshop; *Version 2:* 240 hours (6 weeks).
   Dates: *Version 1:* September 1976-December 1979; *Version 2:* January 1980-Present.
   Objective: To develop the skills required to independently operate a food service kitchen serving up to twelve people.
   Learning Outcome: Upon successful completion of this course, the student will be able to perform as cook onboard tugs and towboats.
   Instruction: A comprehensive course in food principles and preparation of the following: baked goods, breakfast, vegetables, sandwiches, salads, meats, fish, beverages, soups, and sauces. Other topics include work scheduling and organization, menu planning, purchasing and storage of supplies, and sanitation.
   Credit recommendation: In the lower division baccalaureate/associate degree category, 7 semester hours in Food Preparation (9/78) (2/88). NOTE: This course has been reevaluated and continues to meet requirements for credit recommendations.

Towboat Operator (Inland and Oceans, 200 Miles)
   Location: Seafarers Harry Lundeberg School of Seamanship, Piney Point, MD.
   Length: *Version 1:* 210 hours (5 weeks, 4 days); residential; includes 20 hours supervised independent study and 24 hours license preparation review; *Version 2:* 244 hours (7 weeks); *Version 3:* 238 hours (7 weeks).
   Dates: *Version 1:* April 1973-May 1982; *Version 2:* June 1982-January 1988; *Version 3:* February 1988-Present.
   Objective: To provide the student with a sufficient understanding of the principles of towboat operation, U.S. Coast Guard rules and regulations, and rules of the road (inland and international) to obtain a license as a towboat operator.
   Instruction: *Version 1:* Rules of the Road; use of magnetic compass; operation and use of navigational instruments and accessories; tides and currents; emergency signals; use of charts in navigation; aids to navigation; lifesaving and simple first aid; fire-fighting; regulations and laws applicable to the operation of a towing vessel; pollution prevention and control. Course leads to licensing as 1st or 2nd class operator of uninspected towing vessels on inland waters or on oceans (not more than 200 miles off-shore). *Version 2:* Same as Version 1, but includes more practical training. *Version 3:* Course covers earth coordinates and charts; instruments and accessories; compasses, dead reckoning and piloting; aids to navigation (buoys and lights); navigation publications; electronic navigation; tides and currents; weather; rules of the road; seamanship and safety; and rules and regulations.
   Credit recommendation: *Version 1:* In the lower division baccalaureate/associate degree category, 8 semester hours in Navigation (11/77). *Version 2:* In the lower division baccalaureate/associate degree category, 9 semester hours in Navigation (6/82). *Version 3:* In the lower division baccalaureate/associate degree category, 9 semester hours in Towboat Operations (2/88). NOTE: This course has been reevaluated and continues to meet requirements for credit recommendations.

Towboat Operator (Western Rivers)
   Location: Seafarers Harry Lundeberg School of Seamanship, Piney Point, MD.
   Length: 108 hours (2 weeks, 4 days); residential; includes 10 hours supervised independent study and 16 hours license preparation review; 33 hours lecture/discussion and 7 hours laboratory/workshop per week.
   Dates: May 1973-July 1983.
   Objective: To provide the student with a sufficient understanding of towboat operation, U.S. Coast Guard rules and regulations, and rules of the road for western rivers to obtain a license as a towboat operator.
   Instruction: Rules of the road; operation and use of

river piloting instruments and accessories; emergency signals; use of river charts; aids to piloting; boatmanship for western rivers; regulations and laws applicable to the operation of a towing vessel; pollution prevention and control. Course leads to licensing as 1st or 2nd class operator of uninspected vessels on western rivers. Lecture and discussion receive more emphasis than hands-on exercises.

Credit recommendation: In the lower division baccalaureate/associate degree category, 5 semester hours in River Piloting (11/77) (6/82). NOTE: This course has been reevaluated and continues to meet requirements for credit recommendations.

Union Education
Location: Seafarers Harry Lundeberg School of Seamanship, Piney Point, MD.
Length: 40 hours (5 one-hour meetings for 8 weeks).
Dates: May 1975-February 1988.
Objective: To provide the student with a foundation on which to establish his ideas about unions, and to help the student gain an understanding of the history of the labor movement in America.
Instruction: Covers growth of the labor movement from 1894 to the present, changes that have taken place in unions, relationships with management and government, vacation, pension and welfare plans, politics, and law. Lecture and discussion are used.
Credit recommendation: In the lower division baccalaureate/associate degree category, 1 semester hour in Labor Education (11/82).

Union Leadership
(Alternative Title: Union History)
Location: Seafarers Harry Lundeberg School of Seamanship, Piney Point, MD.
Length: 160 hours (4 weeks).
Dates: April 1978-February 1988.
Objective: To provide students with a working knowledge of union matters so that they can act as union representatives, officials, or shop stewards aboard ship.
Instruction: Covers the historical, economic, and social development of the Seafarers' Union. Also includes history of the labor movement from 1884 to present. The formation, organization, constitution, and contract functions are examined in relation to the members' responsibilities. The backgrounds of international and local maritime unions and their associations are also covered. Lecture, discussion, and field trips are used.
Credit recommendation: In the lower division baccalaureate/associate degree category, 2 semester hours in Labor Studies or Labor Relations (11/82).

Variable Speed DC Drives
(Marine Electronics)
Location: Seafarers Harry Lundeberg School of Seamanship, Piney Point, MD.
Length: 180 hours (6 weeks).
Dates: February 1988-Present.
Objective: To provide the electrical maintenance technician with the theory of DC drive systems and the construction, operation, maintenance, and repair of electronic DC motor drive systems.
Learning Outcome: Upon successful completion of this course, the student will be able to perform routine tests and inspections and conduct routine maintenance of electronic DC motor drive systems; and read and interpret manufacturers' operations and maintenance instructions and diagrams.
Instruction: Course covers DC motors and generators; operation and maintenance; power electronics; diodes SCR's; power modules; crane electrical distribution; relay logic and operation; LASH I and II systems; and electronic component alignment.
Credit recommendation: In the lower division baccalaureate/associate degree category, 2 semester hours in Industrial Electronics Laboratory (2/88).

Welding (MET 120)
Location: Seafarers Harry Lundeberg School of Seamanship, Piney Point, MD.
Length: 120 hours (4 weeks).
Dates: September 1973-Present.
Objective: To provide the student with the skills required to perform basic welding and cutting jobs aboard ship.
Learning Outcome: Upon successful completion of this course, the student will be able to perform basic welding and cutting including flat, horizontal, vertical, and pipe welds; and be able to do flat brazing and oxyacetylene cutting.
Instruction: Course offers practical training in electric welding and oxyacetylene cutting and brazing. Lecture and discussion with an emphasis on lab experiences are used.
Credit recommendation: In the lower division baccalaureate/associate degree category, 4 semester hours in Welding (6/82) (2/88). NOTE: This course has been reevaluated and continues to meet requirements for credit recommendations.

Seminary Extension, Southern Baptist Seminaries

Seminary Extension is an external theological education program of the six theological seminaries of the Southern Baptist Convention: Southern Baptist Theological Seminary, Southwestern Baptist Theological Seminary, Golden Gate Baptist Theological Seminary, New Orleans Baptist Theological Seminary, Southeastern Baptist Theological Seminary, and Midwestern Baptist Theological

Seminary. Each of these institutions is accredited by its regional accrediting agency and by the Association of Theological Schools.

The program of Seminary Extension includes two delivery systems: The Home Study Institute, which offers correspondence courses and other forms of home study, and a network of more than 300 extension centers.

To meet the needs of students with a wide range of educational backgrounds, Seminary Extension offers courses on three levels of difficulty. Basic Curriculum courses (in English and Spanish) are designed for pastors who have had only limited formal education. Courses in the College-Level curriculum are for pastors and lay persons who are qualified to perform satisfactorily on a college level. The Personal-Career Development Series contains noncredit learning resources primarily for seminary alumni. The courses listed below are in the College-Level Curriculum.

Source of official student records: Seminary Extension Department, 460 James Robertson Parkway, Nashville, Tennessee 37219.

Additional information about the courses: Program on Noncollegiate Sponsored Instruction, The Center for Adult Learning and Educational Credentials, American Council on Education, One Dupont Circle, Washington, D.C. 20036.

Advanced Exposition
(Alternative Title: Principles of Preaching) (PM 0253)
(Formerly PR 113)
  Length: 16 lessons.
  Dates: January 1978-Present.
  Objective: To prepare the student to develop, deliver, and evaluate sermons.
  Instruction: Understanding and appreciating the work of preaching; extensive written work in conception, outlining, and drafting of oral presentations; using resources for ideas, texts, and topics guidance in various appropriate methods of oral presentations; instruction in long-range preaching plans.
  Credit recommendation: In the upper division baccalaureate category, 1-3 semester hours in Communications or Homiletics (2/77) (9/82). NOTE: This course has undergone a 5-year reevaluation and continues to meet requirements for credit recommendations.

Biblical Backgrounds (BB 0101)
(Formerly BB 101)
  Length: 16 lessons.
  Dates: January 1978-Present.
  Objective: To survey systematically the historical geography and archaeology of Bible lands and peoples as a prerequisite to interpreting the Bible's meaning for today.
  Instruction: Events from the time of the patriarchs to the time of apostolic church; the world of the Bible in its historical context; political, cultural, economic, and religious factors influencing biblical figures.
  Credit recommendation: In the lower division baccalaureate/associate degree category, 1-3 semester hours in Archaeology, History, or Religion (11/77) (9/82). NOTE: This course has undergone a 5-year reevaluation and continues to meet requirements for credit recommendations.

Dynamics of Teaching (RE 0264)
(Formerly RE 115)
  Length: 16 lessons.
  Dates: January 1978-Present.
  Objective: To introduce students to some basic principles of the teaching-learning process and to develop students' teaching skills.
  Instruction: A survey of the nature of the relation of the teacher to the teaching task; the steps in lesson-plan development; the use of teaching aids.
  Credit recommendation: In the lower division baccalaureate/associate degree category, 3 semester hours in Education (11/77) (9/82). NOTE: This course has undergone a 5-year reevaluation and continues to meet requirements for credit recommendations.

History of Christian Thought (CH 0212)
(Formerly HCT 174)
  Length: 16 lessons.
  Dates: January 1978-Present.
  Objective: Using primary documents, to present the widely influential components of Christian thought from the Apostolic Age to the English Reformation.
  Instruction: An examination and interpretation of numerous historical sources, using a broad chronological framework. In the study of the English Reformation, particular emphasis is given to Baptist thought.
  Credit recommendation: In the graduate degree category, 1-3 semester hours in History of Religion, Religion, or Theology (11/77) (9/82). NOTE: This course has undergone a 5-year reevaluation and continues to meet requirements for credit recommendations.

History of Christianity (CH 0211)
(Formerly CH 154)
  Length: 16 lessons.
  Dates: January 1978-Present.
  Objective: To introduce the major historical periods and movements of Christianity.
  Instruction: Factors that influenced Christianity and were influenced by it. Instruction includes perspectives on the great movements and heresies in Christian history.
  Credit recommendation: In the upper division baccalaureate category, 1-3 semester hours in History of Religion (11/77) (9/82). NOTE: This course has undergone a 5-year reevaluation and continues to meet requirements for credit recommendations.

How to Understand the Bible (BB 0100)
(Formerly BB 100)
  Length: 16 lessons.
  Dates: January 1978-Present.
  Objective: To introduce the student to the nature, purpose, and interpretation of the Bible.
  Instruction: Begins with a basic survey of the Bible and progresses through the Bible as literature, principles of biblical interpretation, canonical development, form criticism, placement in the world of sacred scriptures.
  Credit recommendation: In the lower division baccalaureate/associate degree category or in the upper division baccalaureate category, 1-3 semester hours in History, Humanities, or Religion (11/77) (9/82). NOTE: This course has undergone a 5-year reevaluation and continues to meet requirements for credit recommendations.

Introduction to Christian Ethics (CE 0230)
(Formerly Christian Ethics)
  Length: 16 lessons.
  Dates: January 1978-Present.
  Objective: To introduce the ethical teaching of the Bible as a foundation for the responsibilities of marriage and family living, race relations, economic and political life.
  Instruction: A comprehensive exploration of the Old and New Testament ethics and an examination of contemporary social, economic, and political issues as they relate to personal ethics.
  Credit recommendation: In the upper division baccalaureate category, 1-3 semester hours in Ethics, Philosophy, Religion, or Sociology (11/77) (9/82). NOTE: This course has undergone a 5-year reevaluation and continues to meet requirements for credit recommendations.

New Testament Survey, Part III (NT 0167)
(Formerly Introduction to the New Testament, Part II, NT 122)
  Length: 16 lessons.
  Dates: January 1978-Present.
  Objective: To introduce the student to an historical survey of the New Testament documents, stressing why these books were chosen for the canon and how the authors selected their contents.
  Instruction: Covers the New Testament, book by book, from the Acts of the Apostles through the Revelation of John.
  Credit recommendation: In the lower division baccalaureate/associate degree category, 1-3 semester hours in Humanities or Religion (11/77) (9/82). NOTE: This course has undergone a 5-year reevaluation and continues to meet requirements for credit recommendations.

New Testament Theology (TH 0201)
(Formerly TH 436)
  Length: 16 lessons.
  Dates: January 1978-Present.
  Objective: To present thematically the teaching of the New Testament based upon exegesis.
  Instruction: Teachings of the New Testament, including the Bible, God, humanity, sin, salvation, the church, the ordinances, the ministry, the Christian life, the kingdom, and the ultimate goal of humanity, and of history.
  Credit recommendation: In the graduate degree category, 1-3 semester hours in History of Religion, Religion, or Theology (11/77) (9/82). NOTE: This course has undergone a 5-year reevaluation and continues to meet requirements for credit recommendations.

The Pastor as Counselor
(Pastoral Care PM 0251)
(Formerly PM 153)
  Length: 16 lessons.
  Dates: January 1978-Present.
  Objective: To provide an understanding of the processes of caring for and counseling church members and others.
  Instruction: The pastor's role as counselor; personal problems and self-definition; dealing with issues such as grief, marriage conflict, vocational choice, and child-parent relationships.
  Credit recommendation: In the graduate degree category, 1-3 semester hours in Pastoral Counseling (11/77) (9/82). NOTE: This course has undergone a 5-year reevaluation and continues to meet requirements for credit recommendations.

The Pastor as a Person (PM 0250)
(Formerly PM 163)
  Length: 16 lessons.
  Dates: January 1978-Present.
  Objective: To introduce the student to the nature of the pastor's life and ministry in today's world.
  Instruction: An exploration of the essential factors of the pastor's personal function, with attention to role fulfillment, personal investment, value systems, and growth potential.
  Credit recommendation: In the graduate degree category, 1-3 semester hours in Pastoral Ministries (11/77) (9/82). NOTE: This course has undergone a 5-year reevaluation and continues to meet requirements for credit recommendations.

Pastoral Ministries (PM 0252)
(Formerly PM 133)
  Length: 16 lessons.
  Dates: January 1978-Present.
  Objective: To provide an understanding of the life and work of the pastor in relation to the church's total mission, with attention to the minister's various roles and functions.
  Instruction: A guide to the main functions of the parish pastor, such as leading in worship, visiting, counseling,

conducting weddings and funerals, and financial management. Attention is also given to the minister's own growth.

Credit recommendation: In the graduate degree category, 3 semester hours in Pastoral Ministries (11/77) (9/82). NOTE: This course has undergone a 5-year reevaluation and continues to meet requirements for credit recommendations.

Public Worship (PM 0254)
(Formerly PW 173)
   Length: 16 lessons.
   Dates: January 1978-Present.
   Objective: To consider the nature, history, and purpose of corporate worship.
   Instruction: An examination of worship from the perspectives of personal experience, theology, psychology, Bible, Christian history, music, and various elements in public worship. Special attention is given to developing skill in planning and conducting public worship.
   Credit recommendation: In the upper division baccalaureate category, 1-3 semester hours in Religion (11/77) (9/82). NOTE: This course has undergone a 5-year reevaluation and continues to meet requirements for credit recommendations.

Systematic Theology (TH 0200)
(Formerly ST 136)
   Length: 16 lessons.
   Dates: *Version 1:* January 1978-August 1982; *Version 2:* September 1982-Present.
   Objective: To provide a comprehensive presentation of the methodical interpretation and organization of the teachings of Christianity.
   Instruction: Using accepted tools of logic, course explores in depth Christian doctrines, with emphasis on revelation. God, creation of humanity, the person and work of Jesus Christ, the church, the Christian life, and the Christian hope.
   Credit recommendation: *Version 1:* In the graduate degree category, 6 semester hours in History of Religion, Religion, or Theology (11/77). *Version 2:* In the graduate degree category, 1-6 semester hours in the same subject areas as noted above (9/82). NOTE: This course has undergone a 5-year reevaluation and continues to meet requirements for credit recommendations.

Southwestern Bell Telephone Company

Southwestern Bell Telephone Company is a public utility with corporate headquarters in St. Louis, Missouri. The education division is composed of five districts with main offices located in Irving (Dallas), Texas. The company provides curricula that include: marketing, sales, customer contact, information services, engineering, supervision, administration, technical skills and safety.

Courses are designed in accordance with Southwestern Bell Telephone Training Development Guidelines. Instructors and developers are full-time Southwestern Bell Telephone employees.

Source of official student records: Southwestern Bell Telephone Company, 4250 Duncan, St. Louis, Missouri 63310.

Additional information about the courses: Program on Noncollegiate Sponsored Instruction, The Center for Adult Learning and Educational Credentials, American Council on Education, One Dupont Circle, Washington, D.C. 20036.

MANAGEMENT

Account Inquiry Center
   Location: Arkansas, Kansas, Missouri, Oklahoma, and Texas.
   Length: 40 hours (1 week).
   Dates: January 1979-Present.
   Objective: To provide the student with initial training as service representatives.
   Learning Outcome: Upon successful completion of this course, the student will be able to use effective interpersonal skills and knowledge to represent the company to the customer; handle credit, billing, and collection procedures; and suggest services to meet customer needs.
   Instruction: Course covers communication skills, credit procedures, billing and collection procedures, customer accounts, and customer relations. Methodology includes lecture, multiple experiential methods, and on-the-job training.
   Credit recommendation: In the lower division baccalaureate/associate degree category, 2 semester hours in Customer Relations, or in the vocational certificate category, 3 semester hours in a vocational/technical curriculum (7/88).

Assistant Manager Job Design
   Location: Dallas, TX.
   Length: 40 hours (1 week).
   Dates: January 1980-Present.
   Objective: To train the student how to function as first level managers of customer services with specific job activities and procedures.
   Learning Outcome: Upon successful completion of this course, the student will be able to practice the procedures inherent in the job of supervisor of customer services; and integrate policies, procedures, and regulations to achieve departmental objectives.
   Instruction: Course covers location of reference material, training employees, safety, meetings, employee privacy, reports and logs, procedures, customer screening, employee absence control, credit management, scheduling, discipline, performance appraisal, and management/un-

ion relations. Methodology includes lecture and multiple experiential methods.

Credit recommendation: In the lower division baccalaureate/associate degree category, 2 semester hours in Introduction to Supervision (7/88).

Fundamentals of Selling (615001)
  Location: St. Louis, MO and Dallas, TX.
  Length: 40 hours (1 week).
  Dates: September 1985-Present.
  Objective: To instruct the student in basic sales skills in communications services.
  Learning Outcome: Upon successful completion of this course, the student will be able to prepare sales approach to a customer; deliver a sales presentation; and effectively close a sale.
  Instruction: Course covers qualifying customers, designing sales approaches, outlining sales presentations, and delivering and practicing techniques for presentations. Methodology includes lecture and multiple experiential exercises.
  Credit recommendation: In the lower division baccalaureate/associate degree category, 2 semester hours in Personal Selling/Salesmanship (7/88).

Leadership Skills Workshop
  Location: Management Development Training Centers in Arkansas, Kansas, Missouri, Oklahoma, and 3 centers in Texas.
  Length: 24 hours (3 days).
  Dates: October 1972-Present.
  Objective: To introduce the student to functions and responsibilities of first level managers and to introduce the student to various leadership decision styles and explore their impact on work group dynamics.
  Learning Outcome: Upon successful completion of this course, the student will be able to identify, choose, and develop a flexible personal leadership style; and create an effective and productive small work group.
  Instruction: Course covers time management, planning and implementation, problem solving, decision making, communication feedback, small group dynamics, decision styles, conducting meetings, formal presentations, and moving operations from one location to another. Methodology includes lecture and multiple experiential methods.
  Credit recommendation: In the upper division baccalaureate category, 1 semester hour in Introduction to Supervision or Leadership (7/88).

Supervisory Skills Workshop
  Location: All Management Training Centers in Arkansas, Kansas, Missouri, Oklahoma, and 3 locations in Texas.
  Length: 16 hours (2 days).
  Dates: April 1987-Present.
  Objective: To provide the student with supervisory knowledge and skills in dealing with employees and procedures in the work environment.
  Learning Outcome: Upon successful completion of this course, the student will be able to organize on-the-job training; evaluate a nonmanagement employee using a standardized performance appraisal procedure; and solve supervisory problems and recommend decisions concerning employees.
  Instruction: Course covers interpersonal skills including training and evaluating employees, conflict resolution, union-management relations, and decision making. Methodology includes lecture and multiple experiential methods.
  Credit recommendation: In the upper division baccalaureate category, 1 semester hour in Introduction to Supervision (7/88).

Trainer Skills Workshop
  Location: St. Louis, MO and Dallas, TX.
  Length: 64 hours (8 days).
  Dates: January 1981-Present.
  Objective: To orient the student to the training function and uses of instructional methodologies for the purpose of developing and practicing instructional skills.
  Learning Outcome: Upon successful completion of this course, the student will be able to develop a training course using multiple instructional methodologies; conduct a training course; and evaluate the effectiveness of training skills and of a training course.
  Instruction: Course covers purpose and functions of the trainer, learning processes and characteristics of adults, instructional methods, and presentation skills. Methodology includes lecture and multiple experiential exercises.
  Credit recommendation: In the graduate category, 3 semester hours in Instructional Methods (7/88).

MARKETING

Communispond Effective Presentation Skills (CEPS)
  Location: St. Louis, MO; Irving, TX; Houston, TX; San Antonio, TX.
  Length: 16 hours (2 days).
  Dates: December 1984-Present.
  Objective: To help the student improve presentation skills, avoid nervousness, organize subject matter, develop visualization and visual aids, fielding questions, and controlling dialog.
  Learning Outcome: Upon successful completion of this course, the student will be able to make oral presentations with relative ease; organize materials and physical arrangements; and control a discussion.
  Instruction: Course covers physical skills in presentation; organization and visualization of content material; delivery of oral presentations with visual aids; and stimu-

lating questions and discussion. Methodology includes oral presentations, exercises, and group discussions.

Credit recommendation: In the vocational certificate category, 1 semester hour in Oral Presentations or Speech (1/89).

Effective Sales Management (ESM)
   Location: Irving, TX; St. Louis, MO.
   Length: 28 hours (3½ days).
   Dates: December 1987-Present.
   Objective: To provide the student with a definition of the sales manager's role, development of attitudes, leadership, performance criteria, and evaluation standards for a sales group.
   Learning Outcome: Upon successful completion of this course, the student will be able to understand the function of the sales manager; utilize a variety of motivational tools in directing subordinates; and supervise, correct, and evaluate the subordinate's selling techniques.
   Instruction: Course covers the role of the sales manager; attitudes, motivation, and leadership principles; and setting standards, forecasting and performance management. Methodology includes lecture, case study, role play, and practical exercises.
   Credit recommendation: In the upper division baccalaureate category, 2 semester hours in Sales Management (1/89).

Financial Selling Skills
   Location: Irving, TX.
   Length: 32 hours (4 days).
   Dates: September 1988-Present.
   Objective: To provide the student with a foundation in fundamental concepts of finance in order to apply financial concepts to the process of selling.
   Learning Outcome: Upon successful completion of this course, the student will be able to understand the major financial concepts, terms and techniques; apply financial principles to a client's problem and situation; and use financial motivation to close a sale.
   Instruction: Course covers a glossary of accounting and finance terminology; problems in various financial analyses and techniques; and introduction of financial criteria into a sales presentation and close.
   Credit recommendation: In the upper division baccalaureate category, 3 semester hours in Marketing, or in the lower division baccalaureate/associate degree category, 3 semester hours in Finance (1/89).

Fundamentals of Selling (615001)
   Location: St. Louis, MO; Dallas, TX.
   Length: 40 hours (1 week).
   Dates: September 1985-Present.
   Objective: To instruct the student in basic sales skills in communication services.
   Learning Outcome: Upon successful completion of this course, the student will be able to prepare sales approach to a customer; deliver a sales presentation; and effectively close a sale.
   Instruction: Course covers qualifying customers, designing sales approaches, outlining sales presentations, and delivering and practicing techniques for presentations. Methodology includes lecture and multiple experiential exercises.
   Credit recommendation: In the lower division baccalaureate/associate degree category, 2 semester hours in Personal Selling/Salesmanship (7/88).

Introduction to Sales Training Supervision (Supervisory Consultant Selling Skills [615002])
   Location: St. Louis, MO; Irving, TX.
   Length: 24 hours (3 days).
   Dates: January 1988-Present.
   Objective: To provide the student with a basis for evaluating and advising sales people in making an initial sales contact, and the development and use of effective selling skills.
   Learning Outcome: Upon successful completion of this course, the student will be able to identify and use the steps in making an initial contact with a client; determine whether the sales person's activity and sales technique are effective or not; and identify ways of developing improved selling skills.
   Instruction: Course provides a review of selling fundamentals, coaching and development of selling skills, and practice and evaluation of sales technique. Methodology includes lecture, group discussion, group exercises, written exercises, role playing, and videotape/slides.
   Credit recommendation: In the upper division baccalaureate category, 1 semester hour in Sales Supervision (1/89).

Introduction to UNIXR Operating Systems and Shell Programming
(1. UNIX Orientation [8500], 2. The Shell and Editing [8510], 3. Tools [8540], 4. Shell Programming [8580])
   Location: St. Louis, MO; and training centers in Kansas, Arkansas, Oklahoma, and Texas.
   Length: 1. 7½ hours (1 day); 2. 22½ hours (3 days); 3. 7½ hours (1 day); 4. 24 hours (3 days).
   Dates: January 1986-Present.
   Objective: To give the student a general awareness of data processing, basic concepts, and some elementary hands-on experience with hardware and software systems.
   Learning Outcome: Upon successful completion of this course, the student will be able to access the UNIX system and use system communications; build a personal file system that includes directions; use basic shell commands and central structures; use shell quoting mechanisms to escape the meaning of special characters; use redirection of input and output in conjunction with shell programs; use special shell variables and parameters and user-defined

variables within a shell program; and use interactive execution of a shell program as well as commands and facilities.

Instruction: Course covers orientation to the UNIX system, basic shell commands, use of the UNIX system for progam development, documentation, and data processing, and programming language capabilities of the UNIX shell. Methodology includes lecture, discussion, and classroom exercises.

Credit recommendation: In the lower division baccalaureate/associate degree category, 3 semester hours in Computer Information Systems, Computer Science, or Data Processing (1/89). NOTE: Students must complete all four courses to receive the credit.

Negotiating Successfully (NS)
Location: Irving, TX; St. Louis, MO.
Length: 24 hours (3 days).
Dates: February 1987-Present.
Objective: To provide the student with a basis for planning and participating in a negotiation session by defining interests and issues, confronting differences and achieving agreement or consensus.
Learning Outcome: Upon successful completion of this course, the student will be able to plan and participate in a negotiation; analyze the positions and disagreements; and be able to assist in resolution of conflicts.
Instruction: Course covers analysis and planning of a negotiation; listening skills, body language; analysis of differences and conflict; and methods of achieving agreement or consensus. Methodology includes class book, flip charts, videotape, practice in role playing, and discussion.
Credit recommendation: In the lower division baccalaureate/associate degree category, 1 semester hour in Interpersonal Skills or Sales (1/89).

1. Sales Presentation Skills
2. Communispond Effective Presentation Skills
3. Versatile Sales Person
Location: Irving, TX.
Length: 1. 20 hours (2½ days); 2. 16 hours (2 days); 3. 16 hours (2 days).
Dates: March 1987-Present.
Objective: To provide the student with the ability to identify and practice the selling skills which minimize interference and noise in sales presentation delivery; create a physical environment and an appropriate format and delivery of a sales presentation with different media.
Learning Outcome: Upon successful completion of this course, the student will be able to develop confidence in the development and delivery of a sales presentation; use visual aids effectively in making sales; and use techniques of various audio and visual media.
Instruction: Course covers audience analysis, planning of physical arrangements, choice and use of visual aids, and effective delivery and dialog.
Credit recommendation: In the lower division baccalaureate/associate degree category, 2 semester hours in Sales (1/89). NOTE: Students must complete all three courses to receive the credit.

Sales Strategies and Tactics—Account Executive (SS&T-AE)
Location: St. Louis, MO; Irving, TX; Kansas City, MO.
Length: 40 hours (5 days).
Dates: October 1987-Present.
Objective: To develop the skills of the student, sales account executive or other manager, in reaching sales objectives, teaching and supervisory sales planning, developing effective relationship to the sales territory, and leadership of a sales group.
Learning Outcome: Upon successful completion of this course, the student will be able to lead a sales team, teach and reinforce sales planning; become a role model for the sales force; and help sales people develop self confidence and competence in selling.
Instruction: Course covers strategic sales planning, territory management, opportunity management, and sales call development and delivery. Methodology includes lecture, exercises, and role playing.
Credit recommendation: In the upper division baccalaureate category, 3 semester hours in Sales Management (1/89).

Versatile Sales Person
Location: St. Louis, MO; Irving, TX.
Length: 16 hours (2 days).
Dates: June 1981-Present.
Objective: To provide the student with a basis for evaluating human behavior and interaction. Social style analysis is used to differentiate clients and define differentiated responses and tactics to sell heterogenous clienteles.
Learning Outcome: Upon successful completion of this course, the student will be able to classify customers according to assertiveness and responsiveness; analyze mannerisms, speech, work areas and social styles; and use social style in the design of sales strategy.
Instruction: Course covers social style awareness, analysis and application, analyze mannerisms, speech and work areas, and practice in application of social style theory in setting. Methodology includes class discussions, exercises, role playing, examinations, projects, and presentations.
Credit recommendation: In the lower division baccalaureate/associate degree category, 1 semester hour in Human Behavior in Organizations or Salesmanship (1/89).

TECHNICAL

Attached Processor Maintenance (515.4)
(3B20 Processor Operation and Maintenance, and 1A-APS Maintenance)
Location: Advanced Education Center, Irving, TX.
Length: 71 hours (2 weeks).
Dates: January 1983-Present.

Learning Outcome: Upon successful completion of this course, the student will be able to understand the circuiting of a large attached computer processor; correct malfunctions in a large attached computer processor; and analyze diagnostic information from an attached computer processor to determine problem areas.

Instruction: Course covers troubleshooting on an attached computer processor supplementing a telephone switching CPU. Methodology involves self-paced instruction.

Credit recommendation: In the lower division baccalaureate/associate degree category, 2 semester hours in Electronics (3/89). NOTE: This course, combined with 1/1A ESS Peripheral Maintenance (515.1) and 1/A ESS Processor Maintenance (515.2) comprise course 1/1A ESS Peripheral/Processor Maintenance (515.0) for 5 semester hours. Credit should be awarded for either this sequence of courses, or for course 515.0, but not both.

Cable Repair - Fault Locating (D-401)
Location: Houston, TX; Oklahoma City, OK; and St. Louis, MO.
Length: 32 hours (4 days).
Dates: February 1985-Present.

Objective: To teach students how to locate a fault on an underground or aerial cable.

Learning Outcome: Upon successful completion of this course, the student will be able to determine the starting point, test set choice and data analysis method necessary to clear a cable fault; operate various fault locating test sets; and locate faults in cables and locate and stake the path of a buried cable.

Instruction: The course teaches how to locate faults on underground and aerial cables using standard test equipment. Methodology includes self-paced, individualized programmed instruction.

Credit recommendation: In the vocational certificate category, 1 semester hour in Telecommunications (7/88).

Computer CPU and Peripheral Maintenance (515.0)
(1/1A ESS Peripheral/Processor Maintenance)
Location: Advanced Education Center, Irving, TX.
Length: 215 hours (5½ weeks).
Dates: January 1983-Present.

Objective: To teach the student to maintain computer hardware, including a large CPU and specialized telephone peripheral equipment.

Learning Outcome: Upon successful completion of this course, the student will be able to diagnose, analyze, and correct malfunctions on specialized switching computer peripherals, telephone switching CPUs, and attached processors to telephone switching computers.

Instruction: Course provides hands-on training in troubleshooting phone trunk lines, peripheral control units, digital carriers, analog CPU hardware (1 and 1A switching computer), and attached processor. Methodology involves self-paced instruction.

Credit recommendation: In the lower division baccalaureate/associate degree category, 5 semester hours in Electronics (3/89). NOTE: This course, combined with courses 1/1A ESS Peripheral Maintenance (515.1), 1/A ESS Processor Maintenance (515.2), and 3B20 Processor Operation and Maintenance and 1A-APS Maintenance (515.4) comprise a course sequence for 5 semester hours. Credit should be awarded for either this sequence or this course, but not both.

Computer CPU Maintenance (515.2)
(1A ESS Processor Maintenance)
Location: Advanced Education Center, Irving, TX.
Length: 32 hours (4 days).
Dates: January 1983-Present.

Objective: To teach students to maintain a large telephone switching CPU.

Learning Outcome: Upon successful completion of this course, the student will be able to interpret and react to CPU interrupts, retrieve and analyze self diagnostic information from the CPU, and recover the system from a malfunction.

Instruction: Course covers troubleshooting a large switching CPU, including CPU interrupts, deferral fault recognition, and system recovery. Methodology involves self-paced instruction.

Credit recommendation: In the lower division baccalaureate/associate degree category, 1 semester hour in Electronics (3/89). NOTE: This course, combined with Specialized Computer Peripheral Maintenance (515.1) and 1A-APS Maintenance (515.4) comprise course Computer CPU and Peripheral Maintenance (515.0) for 5 semester hours. Credit should be awarded for either this sequence of courses, or for course 515.0, but not both.

Data Communications Technology (1025)
Location: Advanced Education Center, Irving, TX.
Length: 80 hours (2 weeks).
Dates: November 1988-Present.

Objective: To provide students with a comprehensive understanding of data communication fundamentals.

Learning Outcome: Upon successful completion of this course, the student will be able to install and maintain various types of modems and data service units; convert from one numbering system to another; use a data line monitor to observe and analyze data; understand modulation and mulitplexing schemes; and understand various data communications protocols.

Instruction: Course covers analog and digital transmission requirements, numbering systems, data codes and error checking schemes, elements of digital logic, modulation and multiplexing, and transmission protocols. Methodology includes lecture, discussion, and laboratory exercises.

Credit recommendation: In the lower division baccalaureate/associate degree category, 3 semester hours in Computer Science, Electronics Technology, or Telecommunications (3/89).

Design Center Engineering (D-651)
Location: Advanced Education Center, Irving, TX.
Length: 52 hours (7 days).
Dates: June 1981-Present.

Objective: To give the student a fundamental overview of telephone in communications network/facility planning and design.

Learning Outcome: Upon successful completion of this course, the student will be able to define telephone engineering terminology; use telephone planning documents; and describe the telephone network planning organization and process.

Instruction: Course covers the organization of telephone engineering function, definition of engineering terms, engineering documents, and distribution planning tasks. Methodology includes lecture, discussion, and computer-assisted classroom projects/exercises.

Credit recommendation: In the upper division baccalaureate category, 1 semester hour in Telecommunications (3/89).

Digital Circuit Technology (262)
Location: Advanced Education Center, Irving, TX.
Length: 56 hours (1½ weeks).
Dates: September 1987-Present.

Objective: To provide the student with the technical knowledge to install and maintain digital data circuits.

Learning Outcome: Upon successful completion of this course, the student will be able to demonstrate an understanding of basic digital terminology; identify the levels of digital hierarchy; perform the turn-up of both dataport networks and digital data banks; and locate and clear DDB circuit trouble.

Instruction: Course covers the theory of data communications, multiplexing, timing and synchronization issues, digital and circuit operation, and testing procedures. Methodology includes lecture, discussion, and laboratory exercises.

Credit recommendation: In the lower division baccalaureate/associate degree category, 2 semester hours in Electronics Technology or Telecommunications (3/89).

Economic Study Module (ESM) (D-686)
Location: Southwestern Bell Education Centers.
Length: 18 hours (1½ days).
Dates: February 1984-Present.

Objective: To give the student an understanding of the theory and application of engineering economics related to provide telecommunications transmission capacity.

Learning Outcome: Upon successful completion of this course, the student will be able to prepare input mask on the cathode ray terminal for the problem file and the user cost data file; analyze and return ESM programs for smoothed results; and evaluate the alternatives selected.

Instruction: Course covers economics concepts, time value of money, discounting net cash flow, present worth, and the application of economic study module software. Methodology includes lecture, discussion, and computer-assisted instruction.

Credit recommendation: In the upper division baccalaureate category, 1 semester hour in Engineering Economics or Telecommunications (3/89). NOTE: Credit is awarded only if Loop Engineering Assignment Data (D-685) is successfully completed.

Fiber Optics (112)
Location: Advanced Education Center, Irving, TX.
Length: 40 hours (1 week).
Dates: January 1989-Present.

Objective: To provide the student with knowledge of fiber optic theory, typical system application, use of WORD document, and hands-on technical experience in the installation and maintenance of high and low-speed fiber optic systems.

Learning Outcome: Upon successful completion of this course, the student will have a working knowledge in the installation and maintenance of fiber optic systems using WORD documents, test equipment, and technical documentation.

Instruction: Course covers the basic principles of digital transmissions, fiber optic technology, digital performance testing, and low and high-speed light-guide systems. Methodology includes lecture, discussion, and laboratory exercises.

Credit recommendation: In the upper division baccalaureate category, 1 semester hour in Computer Science, Electronics Technology, or Telecommunications (3/89).

Fundamental Electrical Circuits/Telehone Transmission (311)
(Fundamentals of Analog Transmission)
Location: Advanced Education Center, Irving, TX.
Length: 40 hours (1 week).
Dates: February 1983-Present.

Objective: To train students to apply general principles of electrical circuits to telephone voice transmission.

Learning Outcome: Upon successful completion of this course, the student will be able to apply standard electrical testing techniques to telephone voice circuits; understand signalling loops; and adjust line quality to telephone standards.

Instruction: Course covers the use of volt/Ohm meters and other specialized instruments, basic signalling techniques, including E₁M, DX and SF, and line quality monitoring and adjustment. Methodology includes lectures and laboratory exercises.

Credit recommendation: In the lower division baccalaureate/associate degree category, 1 semester hour in Electrical Circuits (3/89).

Fundamentals of Electricity in Telephony (D-314)

Location: St. Louis, MO; Houston, TX; and Oklahoma, OK.
Length: 16 hours (2 days).
Dates: February 1988-Present.
Objective: To provide the student with an understanding of elementary electrical and transmission terminology concepts.
Learning Outcome: Upon successful completion of this course, the student will be able to define basic electrical terms, symbols, and units of measure; calculate value of an unknown electrical property using Ohm's Law; and recognize various factors that affect loss or gain in electrical signals.
Instruction: Course covers electric circuits, circuit impairments, and telephone circuits. Methodology involves computer-assisted instruction.
Credit recommendation: In the lower division baccalaureate/associate degree category, 1 semester hour in Electric Technology or Physics (3/89).

I/IA ESS Overview and Software (513)

Location: Dallas, TX.
Length: 32 hours (4 days).
Dates: May 1986-Present.
Objective: To provide the student with an understanding of the Number One ESS Processor and Software documentation.
Learning Outcome: Upon successful completion of this course, the student will be able to describe the Number One ESS Processor and the peripheral equipment; identify and interpret input and output messages, and locate suspected faulty circuit packs; and identify software documentation.
Instruction: Course covers the identification of the I/IA processor, the peripheral equipment and the hardware/software documentation, and the identification of input and output messages, and alarms in order to locate faulty circuit packs. Methodology includes programmed, self-paced instruction.
Credit recommendation: In the vocational certificate category, 1 semester hour in Electromechanical Troubleshooting (7/88).

IMS Basic Data Communications Programming and Message Format Service (5035)

Location: St. Louis, MO.
Length: 40 hours (1 week).
Dates: February 1988-Present.
Objective: To teach the student how to program in an IMS Data Base/Data Communications environment.
Learning Outcome: Upon successful completion of this course, the student will be able to use an IMS online system for application development and implementation; use SWBT IMS guidelines and standards in the development of online IMS programs; and use BTS and the test IMS online systems to debug application programs.
Instruction: Course covers programming concepts of the IMS Data Base/Data Communications system including basic DC concepts and terminology associated with the IMS online system. Methodology includes lecture, in-class exercises, and workshop problems.
Credit recommendation: In the upper division baccalaureate category, 2 semester hours in Data Processing (7/88).

IMS/VS: DL/I Programming (ICS/TE 5022)

Location: St. Louis, MO.
Length: 64 hours (8 days).
Dates: March 1983-Present.
Objective: To teach the student to program in an IMS batch environment using DL/I coding.
Learning Outcome: Upon successful completion of this course, the student will be able to describe DL/I terminology and its relationship within the database; code and test programs to access a DL/I database to skip, insert segments, delete segments, and execute path calls; and use the IMS program to retrieve and insert segments in a database.
Instruction: Course teaches how to use programming code to alter and control the IMS databases. Methodology includes lecture and programming laboratory.
Credit recommendation: In the upper division baccalaureate category, 2 semester hours in Computer Science or Data Processing (7/88).

Introduction to C Programming

Location: St. Louis, MO; and training centers in Kansas, Arkansas, Oklahoma, and Texas.
Length: 40 hours (5 days).
Dates: January 1986-Present.
Objective: To provide the experienced programmer with knowledge of the basic structure and syntax of the C programming language.
Learning Outcome: Upon successful completion of this course, the student will be able to create, compile, and execute basic C programs in the UNIX environment; describe how a C program interfaces with the UNIX system; and describe the use of arithmetic, logical, and relational operators in the C language.

Instruction: Course covers fundamental data types, operators and data conversion, control structures and statements, decimal data types and functions, storage classifications, pointers, and libraries. Methodology includes lecture, discussion, classroom exercises, and problem solving.

Credit recommendation: In the lower division baccalaureate/associate degree category, 2 semester hours in Computer Information Systems, Computer Science, or Data Processing (1/89).

Introduction to ESS and Minicomputer Fundamentals (511)

Location: Dallas, TX.
Length: 80 hours (10 days).
Dates: December 1983-Present.
Objective: To provide the student with general knowledge in computer fundamentals as used in the stored program switching system.

Learning Outcome: Upon successful completion of this course, the student will be able to understand the binary, octal, and hexidecimal numbering systems; describe the operation of diodes and transistors and applications in logic and computer fundamentals; and describe the use of the oscilloscope in analyzing the equipment and communication busses.

Instruction: Course consists of basic electronic component operation in the digital logic application area. Number bases are covered with application to computers. The oscilloscope is taught and its application to troubleshooting the computer and the communication busses. Methodology includes self-paced, programmed instruction.

Credit recommendation: In the lower division baccalaureate/associate degree category, 2 semester hours in Electronics Technology (7/88).

Light Guide Design (D-680)

Location: Advanced Education Center, Irving, TX.
Length: 40 hours (1 week).
Dates: January 1983-Present.
Objective: To teach the student to design fiber optic transmission systems, and study the latest technology in design criteria.

Learning Outcome: Upon successful completion of this course, the student will be able to describe properties of lightwave and fiber optic transmission systems; design fiber optic transmission loops; and specify test criteria and procedures for fiber optic transmission systems.

Instruction: Course covers principles of lightwave transmission, fiber optic technology, digital data transmission, and multiplexing/demultiplexing. Methodology includes lecture, discussion, classroom exercises, and computer-assisted instruction.

Credit recommendation: In the upper division baccalaureate category, 1 semester hour in Telecommunications (3/89).

Loop Electronics Design (D-663)

Location: Irving, TX; St. Louis, MO; and Oklahoma City, OK.
Length: 40 hours (1 week).
Dates: January 1984-Present.
Objective: To teach the student to produce detailed technical design of digital carrier systems.

Learning Outcome: Upon successful completion of this course, the student will be able to design communications loop remote terminal and repeater locations; produce detailed network testing and conditioning specifications; and describe digital communication loop design requirements.

Instruction: Course covers basic analog and digital switching, basic signal impairment, and digital loop design. Methodology includes lecture, discussion, and computer-assisted design projects.

Credit recommendation: In the upper division baccalaureate category, 1 semester hour in Telecommunications (3/89).

Loop Engineering Assignment Data (D-685)

Location: Southwestern Bell Education Centers.
Length: 24 hours (3 days).
Dates: April 1982-Present.
Objective: To teach the student the development, structure, and application of Loop Engineering Information Systems (LEIS).

Learning Outcome: Upon successful completion of this course, the student will be able to state the purpose and describe the operation of an automated data collection analysis program; use automated planning reports to complete loop technology planning activities; and use the UNIX operating system to create, edit, and print automated planning documents and reports.

Instruction: Course covers the fundamentals of Loop Engineering Information System (LEIS), UNIX operating system, use of the UNIX editor (vi), use of database reports, and generation and use of Loop Engineering Reports. Methodology includes lecture, discussion, computer-assisted instruction, and laboratory projects.

Credit recommendation: In the upper division baccalaureate degree category, 1 semester hour in Telecommunications (3/89). NOTE: Students may receive credit only if Economic Study Workshop (D-686) has been successfully completed.

Loop Technology Planning Fundamentals (D-694)

Location: Advanced Education Center, Irving, TX.
Length: 40 hours (1 week).
Dates: August 1988-Present.
Objective: To teach the student fundamental communications loop technology planning skills.

Learning Outcome: Upon successful completion of this course, the student will be able to establish network planning areas; gather necessary design and planning data; and analyze existing loop technology plans.

Instruction: Course covers loop technology planning fundamentals, long-range planning consideration, planning software tools, and loop technology planning tasks. Methodology includes lecture, discussion, case studies, and computer/video-assisted instruction.

Credit recommendation: In the upper division baccalaureate category, 1 semester hour in Telecommunications (3/89).

Noise Reduction (D-313)

Location: St. Louis, MO; Houston, TX; and Oklahoma City, OK.
Length: 12 hours (1½ days).
Dates: January 1987-Present.
Objective: To provide the student with knowledge of the basic electrical circuit characteristics and techniques for noise reduction on such a circuit.
Learning Outcome: Upon successful completion of this course, the student will be able to trace current flow through a DC circuit; define circuit loss and its effect on transmission; and determine the source of noise in a circuit.
Instruction: Course covers basic DC circuits, basic AC circuits, and noise reduction. Methodology involves computer-assisted instruction.
Credit recommendation: In the lower division baccalaureate/associate degree category, 1 semester hour in Electric Technology or Physics (3/89).

Phone Trunk Testing (512)
(SCC Trunk Tester)

Location: Advanced Education Center, Irving, TX.
Length: 65 hours (1½ weeks).
Dates: January 1983-Present.
Objective: To familiarize the student with the Switching Control Center (SCC) and phone trunk work station as well as SCC procedures as they apply to phone trunk installation and maintenance functions.
Learning Outcome: Upon successful completion of this course, the student will be able to perform basic phone trunk testing; phone trunk installation; and phone trunk field maintenance.
Instruction: Course covers the switching control center activities of trunking and facilities, interoffice signalling, transmission, trunk orders, trunk testing, administration, and full maintenance. Methodology involves self-instruction.
Credit recommendation: In the lower division baccalaureate/associate degree category, 2 semester hours in Data Communications, Teleprocessing, or as a technical elective (3/89).

Report Writing Using the Fourth Generation Language (4GL) FOCUS

1. FOCUS Report Writing (5305)

2. FOCUS Advanced Reporting Techniques (5330)
Location: St. Louis, MO; Dallas, TX; and various locations in the five-state Southwestern Bell area.
Length: 21 hours (4 days).
Dates: April 1987-Present.
Objective: To instruct the student in the techniques of creating reports from existing databases using the 4GL FOCUS.
Learning Outcome: Upon successful completion of this course, the student will be able to generate and format reports that select certain database fields, sort these fields as needed, and summarize the selected fields; join FOCUS files; use multiple verbs, sort phrases, and "if tests" in multiple reports; and merge subsets of two or more databases into a new hold file.
Instruction: Course covers FOCUS overview, report requests, data selection, summarization, and computation, report formatting, join command, table command option, and setting the environment. Methodology includes lecture, discussion, and laboratory exercises.
Credit recommendation: In the lower division baccalaureate/associate degree category, 1 semester hour in Computer Information Systems (CIS), Computer Science, or Data Processing (3/89). NOTE: In order for the student to receive credit, both courses must be successfully completed. Credit should be awarded for either this course sequence (5305, 5330) or course sequence (5310, 5320, and 5330), but not for both.

Specialized Computer Peripheral Maintenance (515.1)
(1/1A ESS Peripheral Maintenance)

Location: Advanced Education Center, Irving, TX.
Length: 90 hours (2½ weeks).
Dates: January 1983-Present.
Objective: To teach the student to diagnose problems and make fixes to specialized telephone peripheral equipment.
Learning Outcome: Upon successful completion of this course, the student will be able to diagnose malfunctions in computer switching peripheral units; analyze the cause of a computer switching peripheral malfunction; and correct a computer peripheral malfunction.
Instruction: Course covers peripheral maintenance in 1/1A common remreed frames, combined miscellaneous and miniaturized universal trunk frames, 1/1A peripheral unit controller, and 1/1 digital carrier trunk. Methodology involves self-paced instruction.
Credit recommendation: In the lower division baccalaureate/associate degree category, 2 semester hours in Electronics (3/89). NOTE: This course, combined with Computer CPU Maintenance (515.2) and Attached Processor Maintenance (515.4) comprise the course Computer CPU and Peripheral Maintenance (515.0) for 5 semester hours. Credit should be awarded for either this sequence of courses, or for course 515.0, but not both.

Specialized Telephone Software Applications (514)
(1/1A ESS SCC Translations)
Location: Advanced Education Center, Irving, TX.
Length: 72½ hours (1¾ weeks).
Dates: January 1983-Present.
Objective: To teach the student to use specialized telephone software that analyzes incoming phone requests digit by digit.
Learning Outcome: Upon successful completion of this course, the student will be able to understand specialized telephone translation software, implement changes to the system through specialized telephone translation software and recover from malfunctions of specialized telephone translation software.
Instruction: Course covers simulator training in specialized telephone translation software, including updating a translation database and debugging software malfunctions. Methodology involves computer-assisted self-instruction.
Credit recommendation: In the lower division baccalaureate/associate degree category, 2 semester hours in Computer Software (3/89).

Subscriber Loop Carrier 96 (D-407)
Location: Dallas, TX; Houston, TX; Oklahoma City, OK; and St. Louis, MO.
Length: 40 hours (1 week).
Dates: April 1987-Present.
Objective: To introduce the student to subscriber loop systems, such as the SLC-96, including the input and output signals.
Learning Outcome: Upon successful completion of this course, the student will be able to maintain a SLC-96 system; set up and test a central office and a remote terminal; and be able to use the task oriented practice (TOP) flow chart system.
Instruction: Course teaches the installation, start up, and troubleshooting of the Subscriber Loop Carrier 97 (SLC 96) system. The course includes both the central office terminal and the remote terminal. Methodology includes programmed instruction, discussion, lecture, and video. Half the course is hands-on laboratory experiences.
Credit recommendation: In the vocational certificate category, 1 semester hour in Telecommunications (7/88).

UNIX® Systems Programming
(1. C UNIX Interface [8555]; 2. Advanced Shell Programming [8585])
Location: St. Louis, MO.
Length: 1. 40 hours (5 days); 2. 24 hours (3 days).
Dates: August 1988-Present.
Objective: To enable the experienced C programmer to perform routine systems programming tasks using C language system calls as well as being able to perform some of these tasks using the UNIX operating systems shell language.
Learning Outcome: Upon successful completion of this course, the student will be able to use the C libraries to develop C interfaces to the UNIX operating system; and understand and use the systems programming capabilities of the shell language.
Instruction: Course covers advanced aspects of the C programming language, fiber and I/O, process creation and management, creating and customizing a shell environment, monitoring and control of processes through the shell language. Methodology includes lecture and discussion. Prerequisite: The student is assumed to be an experienced C language programmer and has a working knowledge of the internals of the UNIX operating system.
Credit recommendation: In the upper division baccalaureate category, 3 semester hours in Computer Information Systems, Computer Science, or Data Processing (1/89). NOTE: Students must complete both courses to receive the credit.

Use of Fourth Generation Language (4GL) FOCUS
  1. **FOCUS Report Preparation, File Design, and Maintenance (5310)**
  2. **FOCUS Application Development Techniques (5320)**
  3. **FOCUS Advanced Reporting Techniques (5330)**
Location: St. Louis, MO.
Length: 52 hours (8 days).
Dates: August 1986-Present.
Objective: To introduce the student to the basic techniques of creating reports and techniques for defining, creating, and updating databases using FOCUS.
Learning Outcome: Upon successful completion of this course, the student will be able to generate reports from selected fields in a database, and sort and summarize report fields; create master file descriptions, and new files or update existing ones; and understand the differences in the summary functions of Subtotal, Summarize, and Recompute.
Instruction: Course provides an introduction to FOCUS, basic report formats, arithmetic and grouping functions, file design and maintenance, joining files, modifying databases, prompt transactions, table command review, define command, match command and alternate file views. Methodology includes lecture, discussion, and laboratory exercises.
Credit recommendation: In the lower division baccalaureate/associate degree category, 2 semester hours in Computer Information Systems (CIS), Computer Science, or Data Processing (3/89). NOTE: Credit should be awarded for this course sequence (5310, 5320, 5330) or course sequence (5305 and 5330), but not for both.

Wiring Specialized Telephone Circuits (A) (901)
(Installation and Maintenance of Special Circuits)
Location: Advanced Education Center, Irving, TX.
Length: 160 hours (4 weeks).

Dates: January 1980-Present.

Objective: To provide the student with in-depth instruction in the use and maintenance of specially designed telephone circuits.

Learning Outcome: Upon successful completion of this course, the student will be able to install new specially designed telephone circuits; and isolate and repair trouble in specially designed telephone circuits.

Instruction: Course covers the installation and repair of specially designed telephone circuits for use in WATS lines, ATM lines and others. Methodology includes lecture, discussion, and laboratory exercises.

Credit recommendation: In the lower division baccalaureate/associate degree category, 4 semester hours in Electrical Circuits (3/89). NOTE: This course is the same as course 20002 in content; however, it is twice as long and contains many more practice exercises.

Sun Refining and Marketing Company

The education/training component of the Sun Refining and Marketing Company falls into three categories: Management/Supervisory, providing in-house developed programs for managers and supervisors, focusing on leadership skill development; Technical, providing craft, mechanical and operators with both the classroom and on-the-job training needed to technically perform their jobs; and External/Professional Development, emphasizing special needs (managerial or technical), employees are sent to external programs such as the University of Michigan (i.e., Labor Relations program), AMA (i.e., Interpersonal Skills Workshop), NTL (i.e., Human Interaction), or programs on special equipment or processes.

Certification is part of an on-going, three-year process. Students must pass each of the 36 tests offered. When all 36 tests are successfully completed along with their on-the-job requirements, they are certified by the State as an Apprentice. In addition, students need to qualify for four jobs in their work units in the same three-year period. To do this, they must be able to demonstrate to their supervisors (through the actual operation of the plant and equipment) the ability to transfer the knowledge learned to their job. Students who do not meet the acceptable level of learning are given extra tutoring and attention by a full-time trainer. If a student continues to fail tests or does not demonstrate the transfer of knowledge, he/she is terminated from the program.

The Manager, Human Resources Development, provides consulting and training expertise to the Refinery's personnel; develops and implements various training programs for all levels of personnel; works with the Operations Department Training Committee to develop training system and programs and annually reviews the progress of the program. When needed changes are identified, the Committee works with the American Petroleum Institute for updates. Training experts are utilized from the American Petroleum Institute and consultants to (or in) other oil companies.

Learning facilities include the Education/Conference Center, located within a few miles from the Refinery. This Center has five classrooms and an auditorium; an on-site building dedicated to technical training which has three classrooms, complete with audiovisual equipment; each operating unit, where the students train on-the-job, has a training room. All facilities provide the quality environment needed to be conducive to learning. For programs which require easy access to the facility, students learn some theory and can immediately transfer that knowledge in the plant. Off-site locations are utilized for programs where participants need to be removed from the work site and "experience" new learnings.

Source of official student records: Manager, Human Resources Development, Sun Refining and Marketing Company, P.O. Box 426, Marcus Hook, Pennsylvania 19061.

Additional information about the courses: Program on Noncollegiate Sponsored Instruction, The Center for Adult Learning and Educational Credentials, American Council on Education, One Dupont Circle, Washington, D.C. 20036.

Basic Operator Training
(Basic Training)

Location: Marcus Hook Refinery, Marcus Hook, PA.

Length: 70 hours (2 weeks).

Dates: May 1983-Present.

Objective: To provide students with an overview of refinery unit operations.

Learning Outcome: Upon successful completion of this course, the student will be able to describe function of process equipment and terms such as oil flow; valves; cooling towers; pumps and pump operation; steam turbines; distillation processes; process instrumentation; head transfer and heat exchangers; compressors; gauges; drains and vents; heaters; electrical switchgear, and operator responsibilities.

Instruction: Course covers communications, refinery operator duties, refinery process sampling, handling hydrocarbons, pump operation and maintenance, basic physical and chemical terminology, valves and valve operations, heat transfer, heaters, electrical switches, motor starters, compressors, air handling systems, steam and steam generation, steam traps, and water treatment. Methodology includes lecture, videotape, and field trip.

Credit recommendation: In the lower division baccalaureate/associate degree category, 2 semester hours in Survey of Chemical Unit Operations (4/88).

Introduction to Teaching Techniques
(Train the Trainer)
  Location: Marcus Hook Refinery, Marcus Hook, PA.
  Length: 21 hours (3 days).
  Dates: January 1985-Present.
  Objective: To provide technically skilled personnel with the fundamentals of the technical/learning process needed to become a technical instructor.
  Learning Outcome: Upon successful completion of this course, the student will be able to apply principles of effective classroom teaching; write objectives for his/her training program; apply procedures of group dynamics to obtain appropriate student participation; and demonstrate techniques in actual teaching situations.
  Instruction: Course covers classroom teaching basics including effective presentations, use of visuals, communication techniques and use of split feedback; developing a training program including determining content, participant's needs, how to format materials, how to create pre/post test instruments, objective preparation, and lesson plan development; what a training model is, how people learn, how to check for learning, and how to make learning interesting; group dynamics, including stages of group participation, how to get participation, how to deal with problem situations; and learning logistics, including classroom set-up, teacher preparation, environment, field versus class instruction, and three practice teaching sessions. Methodology includes lecture, videotape, and student practice teaching session.
  Credit recommendation: In the upper division baccalaureate category, 1 semester hour in Fundamentals of Teaching Methods (4/88).

Refinery Operator Program
(Apprenticeship Related Studies Program)
  Location: Marcus Hook Refinery, Marcus Hook, PA.
  Length: 36 months (includes 3 hours self-study per week).
  Dates: July 1978-Present.
  Objective: To provide operators with knowledge to learn the safe operation of the refinery process.
  Learning Outcome: *First Year, Modules 1-12:* Upon successful completion of this course, the apprentice operator will attain a knowledge of accident control, fire fighting, and mechanics of fluids and pumps; know the various aspects of operating a refinery safely and how to respond to emergencies such as fire; be able to demonstrate a knowledge of how his/her work unit interacts and affects other parts of the refinery process through semiannual written and oral quizzes.
  Second Year, Modules 13-24: Upon successful completion of this course, the apprentice operator will describe behavior of compressible and non-compressible fluids; explain differences in temperature scales, fahrenheit, and rankine; describe fundamental gas laws; describe theory of operation of: centrifugal compressors and positive displacement compressors; fundamental magnetic properties; electric current generation; theory of operation of three-phase and single-phase motors including: induction, wound rotor, and synchronous; explain principles of steam turbines, condensing and non-condensing turbines, turbine governors; explain principles and construction of combustible gas turbines; explain use of couplings, gear trains and V-belt drives; explain principles of steam engines and steam reciprocating pumps; explain basic principles of heat transfer; explain construction and use of heat exchangers; and have completed one year of field work related to course topics.
  Third Year, Modules 25-36: Upon successful completion of this course, the apprentice operator will know the various types of refinery furnaces, the operations of furnace components, furnace heat transfer and explain the relationship between fuel, air, source of ignition and control for efficient operation; explain cooling tower construction and heat transfer and the significance of water conditioning for efficient operation; explain the refinery distillation process including fractionating equipment, factors for control and problem solving skills to correct abnormal operation and to maximize distillation efficiency; avoid waste of utilities and fuel to reduce costs in refinery operations; explain the role of various instruments for efficient refinery operation including control of operating variables such as temperature, pressure, liquid level and flow rates, use specialized analytical instruments, alarms; explain the nature of the process control loop, control needs, and how to identify controller problems.
  Instruction: *First Year, Modules 1-12:* Course covers accident control techniques, including safe and unsafe acts; fire fighting, fuels and combustion, water, extinguishers and foams, tactics and strategy; mechanics of fluids, chemical and physical nature of fluids, behavior of gases, statics of fluids and fluids in motion; pumps, centrifugal, positive displacement, reciprocating, pump valves, and operating maintenance of pumps.
  Second Year, Modules 13-24: Course covers centrifugal and positive displacement compressors, A-C motors, steam turbines, steam reciprocating pumps, valves, basic heat theory and heat transfer.
  Third Year, Modules 25-36: Course covers operation, control and safety of refinery furnaces, distillation units, cooling towers, instrumentation, process control tests, and cost reduction.
  Credit recommendation: *First Year:* In the lower division baccalaureate/associate degree category, 3 semester hours in Safety-Firefighting and Accident Control, 3 semester hours in Mechanics of Fluids, and 3 semester hours in Mechanical Elements-Pumps, for a total of 9 semester hours.
  Second Year: In the upper division baccalaureate category, 6 semester hours in Fluid Mechanics Technology and 3 semester hours in Fluids Mechanics Technology Laboratory, for a total of 9 semester hours.

Third Year: In the upper division baccalaureate category, 3 semester hours in Chemical Unit Operations Technology, 2 semester hours in Chemical Unit Operations Laboratory, 3 semester hours in Refinery Process Instrumentation and Control, and 1 semester hour in Refinery Process Instrumentation and Control Laboratory, for a total of 9 semester hours (4/88). NOTE: The credit recommendations are cumulative; readers should use the recommendation that corresponds to the number of years completed by the student.

Syntex Laboratories, Inc.

Syntex Laboratories is a pharmaceutical company headquartered in Palo Alto, California. The Continuing Education Department has developed the Syntex Professional Development Program (SPDP) to provide advancement opportunities, increased recognition, and added training for its sales representatives. The SPDP offers five progressive levels for the Syntex representative to achieve career advancement.

An employee's movement from one level to the next requires the completion of a prescribed self-study curriculum designed to sharpen and increase the representative's professional skills. The curriculum includes the study of advanced education modules in the areas of Dermatology, Arthritis, Obstetrics, and Gynecology. Each module consists of more than 1,000 pages of text book material. Successful completion of these modules requires mastery of an exam which is administered biannually through the Control Data Corporation Plato Terminal Network System located throughout the country.

Source of official student records: Office of Continuing Education Manager, Training and Education Department of Syntex Laboratories, 3401 Hillview Avenue, Palo Alto, CA 94304.

Additional information about the courses: Program on Noncollegiate Sponsored Instruction, The Center for Adult Learning and Educational Credentials, American Council on Education, One Dupont Circle, Washington, D.C. 20036.

Advanced Medical Education: Arthritis I, II, III

Location: Course developed and offered by Syntex Laboratories, Inc., Palo Alto, CA. Examinations offered in regional Control Data Learning Center using Plato Learning Management System.
Length: Self-study.
Dates: June 1981-Present.
Objective: To provide the Certified Medical Representative (CMR) with a comprehensive overview and understanding of arthritis conditions, their causes, and consequences, their diagnosis, and their therapies. Specifically, the course provides the CMR with the knowledge to discuss with physicians their concerns in the area of arthritis.
Instruction: Topics include basic anatomy and physiology related to rheumatic diseases; pharmacology of antirheumatic drugs; etiology, pathogenesis, laboratory findings and therapies in rheumatoid arthritis and other rheumatoid diseases; disorder of joints and related structures; metabolic bone and joint diseases. The student utilizes the same textbooks currently adopted in medical schools along with a study guide developed by Syntex Laboratories, Inc. The course is conducted in 3 modules with an examination following each module. Successful completion of 1 module is essential before advancing to the next in sequence.
Credit recommendation: In the upper division baccalaureate category, 6 semester hours in Medical and Health-Related Career Programs (1/82).

Advanced Medical Education Course: Dermatology I, II, III

Location: Course developed and offered by Syntex Laboratories, Inc., Palo Alto, CA. Examinations offered in regional Control Data Learning Centers using Plato Learning Management System.
Length: Self-study.
Dates: June 1981-Present.
Objective: To provide the Certified Medical Representative (CMR) with a comprehensive overview of dermatologic conditions including etiology, pathology, diagnosis, and treatment. Specifically the course provides the CMR with the knowledge and background necessary to be able to discuss these conditions with physicians.
Instruction: Includes the following: structure and functions of the skin, physiologic and histopathologic reaction, principles of clinical diagnosis, and specific dermatologic conditions with therapeutic approaches for each. Textbooks currently used include those used in medical schools and include approaches and alternatives in diagnosis and therapy. The course is conducted in 3 modules with an examination following each module. Successful completion of the previous module is essential for advancement to the next module.
Credit recommendation: In the upper division baccalaureate category, 8 semester hours in Medical and Health-Related Career Programs (1/82).

Advanced Medical Education: Obstetrics and Gynecology I, II, III

Location: Course developed and offered by Syntex Laboratories, Inc., Palo Alto, CA. Examinations offered in regional Control Data Learning Center using Plato Learning Management System.
Length: Self-study.
Dates: June 1981-Present.
Objective: To provide the Certified Medical Representative (CMR) with a comprehensive overview of obstetri-

cal and gynecological anatomy and physiology along with associated conditions of their management. The course is focused on the ability of the CMR to relate with health professionals in the obstetrics-gynecology (OB-GYN) health specialty.

Instruction: Provides a modular learning approach on content related to the reproductive system. Included in this content are the history and physical examination of the reproductive system, common normal variations, and pathological disease status. Course materials center on the medical/pharmaceutical management of these conditions.

The course consists of 3 self-programmed modules. Evaluation occurs at the end of each module, and successful completion of the previous module is prerequisite for advancement to the next module.

Credit recommendation: In the upper division baccalaureate category, 6 semester hours in Medical and Health-Related Career Programs (1/82).

Technical Training Project, Inc.

Technical Training Project, Inc. (TTP) was created by a consortium of eleven pharmaceutical companies in the New Jersey-New York area as a private nonprofit organization.

The project's purpose was to combat the problems of unemployment and underemployment among minority groups and other disadvantaged people. To do this, TTP created its own curriculum and training schedule, so that within a sixteen-week work-study period, the trainee would acquire technical competence, discipline, motivation, and skills to qualify for an entry-level laboratory technician position.

TTP moved from a smaller and crowded facility at 162 Broad Street, Newark, New Jersey to Essex County College, Newark, New Jersey, where it leases space as of August 1, 1987.

The trainee goes through an intensive academic course of study taught by the staff of TTP. In addition, scientists from various companies provide lectures to supplement the training process.

TTP uses the laboratories of the sponsoring companies for the On-Job-Training phase of the program. Here a trainee works in the laboratory under the supervision of a skilled professional and is exposed to state-of-the-art equipment.

Through the years TTP has continuously reviewed its curriculum to ensure it is keeping pace with the needs of industry. This is accomplished through a Technical Advisory Committee, comprised of scientists from the companies meeting with the staff. Areas of academic and laboratory concentrations are discussed as are choice of textbooks.

Source of official student records: Technical Training Project, Inc. at Essex County College, 303 University Avenue, Newark, New Jersey 07102.

Additional information about the courses: Program on Noncollegiate Sponsored Instruction, The Center for Adult Learning and Educational Credentials, American Council on Education, One Dupont Circle, Washington, D.C. 20036 or Program on Noncollegiate Sponsored Instruction, Thomas A. Edison State College, 101 West State Street, CN545, Trenton, New Jersey 08625.

Laboratory Technician Program
 Location: Newark, NJ.
 Length: 800 hours (20 weeks).
 Dates: July 1978-Present.
 Objective: To train individuals for entry-level positions as laboratory technicians in an industrial laboratory so that individuals with little or no background in the sciences can pursue a career in science or allied health.
 Learning Outcome: Upon completion of the training program, individuals will be able to: (a) understand biology, bacteriology, physiology, microbiology, and pharmacology as related to laboratory work, i.e., bacterial culture, soil sampling, human anatomy, cell biology; (b) use chemicals, materials, and lab equipment; (c) handle mathematical calculations and general concepts of normality, dilution, weighing samples, and use of lab equipment; (d) maintain lab reports on all experiments; (e) perform various techniques of wet and dry analysis; and (f) apply theory to work experience in the laboratories of sponsoring companies.
 Instruction: This intensive program mixes classroom and on-the-job training in technical and laboratory skills. The curriculum provides 32 hours of classroom and 8 hours of laboratory work each week with an emphasis on basic organic and inorganic chemistry and mathematics, and an introduction to biochemistry, biology, anatomy, physiology, and microbiology.

Topics included in the curriculum are: an introduction to chemistry including atomic structure, periodic law, states of matter, acid-base equilibrium, solutions and oxidation-reduction; laboratory techniques, gravimetric volumetric, spectrometric methods of chemical analysis are emphasized along with preparations, extractions, types of chromatography and distillation; also an introduction to organic chemistry and industrial processes; the position and function of the chemical industry and specific topics of contemporary interest are highlighted.

Methods of showing data and performing chemical calculations using logarithms, algebra, graphic methods and electronic calculations are studied using typical industrial problems. Modern analytical techniques are also studied including spectral methods, polarimetry, and refractometry.

There is also a modern approach to the study of the biological sciences emphasizing the ultrastructure and function of the macromolecular constituents of the cell, and those fundamental chemical principles necessary for the understanding of cellular metabolism. Principles of biochemical activities and protoplasmic organization inherent in living cells are studied. To meet specific needs of the chemical technologist, topics are selected from arithmetic, algebra, some geometry, logarithms, and graphic analyses. Finally, there is a six-week on-the-job internship where the students work under professional supervision in the laboratory of one of the sponsoring pharmaceutical or chemical companies.

Credit recommendation: In the lower division baccalaureate/associate degree category, 4 semester hours in College Chemistry I, 4 in College Chemistry II, 3 in Chemistry Seminar, 3 in Chemical Calculations, 5 in Instrumental Methods, 4 in Introduction to Fundamentals of Cell Chemistry, 3 in Technical Mathematics, and 3 in Chemical Technology Internship; for a grand total of 29 semester hours (7/88).

Texas Utilities Electric Corporation (Formerly Texas Utilities Generating Company - TUGCo)

The Athens Training Center (ATC) was established in 1975 to serve the TU Electric and Texas Utilities Mining Company in the craft areas of power plant operations, electrical maintenance, electronics, mechanical maintenance, warehouse, chemical lab, instruments and controls, and strip mining operations. These crafts are directly related to a steam electric generating (lignite, gas, and oil-fired boiler) system and strip mining operations that provide the lignite which is used as a fuel. These steam electric stations contribute to the overall electric generation for the Texas Utilities system.

The primary function of the ATC is to provide "state of the art" training in the various technical areas of operations and maintenance that is specific to this type of business. There are approximately 12,000 employees working at one of the 24 different plant and 10 different mine sites who may require some level of training by the ATC. The ATC provides about two-thirds of its training at Athens and the remainder at the various plant and mine sites and company offices. Each site has at least one classroom available on-site for use by the ATC training personnel. Classroom facilities have been designed specifically for the purpose of industrial training. All classrooms have complete audiovisual support equipment, writing and drawing boards, and special lighting. The ATC is designed to ensure an effective learning environment.

The ATC's training specialists are full-time instructors selected for their expertise, communication skills, and adaptability to teach. Most were selected after being employed by the TU Electric System for a long period of time, working into a supervisory position, and proving their expertise in the areas they would be required to teach. Each department has a coordinator, working with the Supervisor of Curriculum Planning and Scheduling to occasionally visit the classroom and evaluate the instructor and the material being taught. The instructor is required to formally meet with the Training Manager, Supervisor of Curriculum Planning and Scheduling, and the Department Coordinator twice each year for review and evaluation.

Course development is a joint project with the instructor, the Supervisor of Curriculum Planning and Scheduling, the Audio-Visual Department, and possibly an on-site engineer to accumulate the best material available and assemble it for classroom use. All training material is periodically reviewed by the instructor and Supervisor of Curriculum Planning and Scheduling to ensure its currency.

Each student is pretested at the beginning and posttested at the end of each course. Both grades are handwritten on a contact hour card by the instructor and turned in to the office staff. The staff then inputs the grades into a computer whose mainframe is housed in Dallas. A printout of any and all grades, date taken, and grades received for any student can be received upon written request. Each student must make a grade of 70 to pass and move on to the next course. In some cases, the student must demonstrate, using hands-on, to prove that he/she can actually perform the task. If the student has not demonstrated an acceptable level of learning, he/she may require additional tutoring, or be recycled through the course.

Source of official student records: Training Manager, Athens Training Center, Route 2, Box 2234, Athens, Texas 75751.

Additional information about the courses: Program on Noncollegiate Sponsored Instruction, The Center for Adult Learning and Educational Credentials, American Council on Education, One Dupont Circle, Washington, D.C. 20036.

AC Circuits (E-7)
Location: Athens, TX.
Length: 36 hours (1 week).
Dates: September 1976-Present.
Objective: To provide the student with the basic knowledge of electrical and electronic fundamentals.
Learning Outcome: Upon successful completion of this course, the student will be able to apply basic rules of theory to AC circuits containing both resistive and reactive components, use test equipment (including oscilloscope) to verify calculations and as an effective means of troubleshooting AC (Basic) circuits, apply Phythagorean's Theorem and basic trigonometry to problems of AC theory, and to understand and apply the concepts

of power factor connection using charts and tables.

Instruction: Course covers the fundamentals of electricity and magnetism, the relationships between voltage, resistance, and currents, and fundamental direct current circuit analysis. Instruction is provided in the basics of vacuum tube and semiconductor operation. Also studied are alternating current fundamentals as applied to the power industry.

Credit recommendation: In the lower division baccalaureate/associate degree category, 2 semester hours in Fundamentals of Electricity (9/82) (11/87). NOTE: This course has been reevaluated and continues to meet requirements for credit recommendations.

ARC Welding (QR-10)
   Location: Athens, TX.
   Length: 36 hours (1 week).
   Dates: *Version 1:* September 1976-November 1987; *Version 2:* December 1987-Present.
   Objective: To provide general orientation and application to gas tungsten and shielded metal-arc welding processes at the introductory to certification competency level.
   Learning Outcome: Upon successful completion of this course, the student will be able to produce a full penetration quality weld using welding procedures that meet or exceed ASME code requirements, select type and size welding electrodes for general field welds, and to select a proper welding machine to be used and make all necessary connections and adjustments to produce a quality weld.
   Instruction: The student is introduced to arc welding processes and applies theory and procedures in a laboratory setting. Study also includes safety and health, equipment start-up, adjustments, shutdown, and appropriate positions for various types of welding. Follow-up field experience required for full credit.
   Credit recommendation: *Version 1:* In the lower division baccalaureate/associate degree category, 3 semester hours in Vocational/Technical Education (9/82). *Version 2:* In the lower division baccalaureate/associate degree category, 2 semester hours in Vocational/Technical Education (11/87). NOTE: This course has been reevaluated and continues to meet requirements for credit recommendations.

Basic Hydraulics and Troubleshooting (M-11)
   Location: Athens, TX.
   Length: 36 hours (1 week).
   Dates: February 1979-March 1987.
   Objective: To develop a working knowledge of hydraulic systems at the level necessary to maintain properly and repair hydraulic systems.
   Instruction: Course covers basic operating principles of hydraulic systems including fluid flow, power determination, hydraulic transfer, and pressure/movement characteristics. Also, study and application includes strainers and filters, reservoirs, pumps, piping, valves, cylinders, and motors. Students apply theory in laboratory settings. Eight hours of outside study assignments.
   Credit recommendation: In the lower division baccalaureate/associate degree category, 2 semester hours in Vocational/Technical Education (9/82).

Basic Metallurgy (M-6)
(Formerly Industrial Materials - Metals and Non-Metals [M-6])
   Location: Athens, TX.
   Length: 36 hours (1 week).
   Dates: January 1979-February 1987.
   Objective: To obtain information that is particularly beneficial to maintenance personnel in the application and use of metals and non-metals.
   Instruction: Designed to provide a basic knowledge of the properties and behavior of various metals and non-metals used by industrial plants for both production and maintenance. Non-metal materials include plastic, rubber, wood, and chemical compounds. Metals denote both metals and alloys. The course is taught in 25 hours of lecture/discussion, 11 hours of laboratory work, with 8 hours of outside study assignments.
   Credit recommendation: In the lower division baccalaureate/associate degree category, 2 semester hours in Vocational/Technical Education (9/82).

Basic Pneumatics and Troubleshooting (M-12)
   Location: Athens, TX.
   Length: 36 hours (1 week).
   Dates: July 1979-May 1987.
   Objective: To develop an understanding of pneumatic system principles necessary to initiate corrective action and reduce equipment failure and/or breakdown.
   Instruction: Study is made of the operating principles that determine the action and operation of pneumatic systems. Topics include air compressors, air treatment, piping-hoses-fittings, valves, cylinders, and motors. Also, the common types of industrial pneumatic equipment are studied. Eight hours of outside study assignments are required.
   Credit recommendation: In the lower division baccalaureate/associate degree category, 2 semester hours in Vocational/Technical Education (9/82).

Basic Shop Mathematics (B-1 & B-2)
(Formerly B-3)
   Location: Athens, TX.
   Length: *Version 1:* 36 hours (1 week); *Version 2:* 72 hours (2 weeks).
   Dates: January 1977-November 1987.
   Objective: To explain the nature and meaning of numbers and how to use them, and the fundamental application of mathematics in solving work-related problems.
   Instruction: Basic introduction to fractions, decimals,

algebraic formulas, ratio percentages, powers and roots, geometry, area and volume, and trigonometry and minicomputer for application to workshop situations. Lectures are augmented by 15 hours of outside study assignments.

Credit recommendation: In the lower division baccalaureate/associate degree category, 3 semester hours in Introductory Mathematics (9/82).

Basic Vibration Training and Simple Balancing (QR-524)
  Location: Plant sites and mine sites.
  Length: 24 hours (3 days).
  Dates: January 1986-Present.
  Objective: To teach students to develop skills necessary for proper use of vibration measuring equipment.
  Learning Outcome: Upon successful completion of this course, the students will be able to operate vibration measurement equipment at their locations and record readings which are accurate and legible, determine if unbalance of rotating parts is the problem and determine if one of the four methods of balancing can be used, and to balance rotating parts to within manufacturer's specifications using one of four methods for balancing covered in class.
  Instruction: Course covers causes and characteristics of vibration, vibration measurement equipment and positions for measuring vibration. Vibration equipment is used to provide practical experience necessary for balancing rotating equipment using the single plane vector method, single plane vector method without phase, one run method, overhung rotor method, and four step method.
  Credit recommendation: In the lower division baccalaureate/associate degree category, 1 semester hour in Vocational/Technical Education electives (11/87).

Batteries and DC Circuits (E-6)
  Location: Athens, TX.
  Length: 36 hours (1 week).
  Dates: September 1976-Present.
  Objective: To provide a thorough knowledge of the maintenance techniques required by the use of battery operated equipment and a fundamental review of series and parallel DC circuits.
  Learning Outcome: Upon successful completion of this course, the student will be able to use terminology as may be encountered in vendor's publications/technical manuals; understand voltage, current, resistance and power in DC series and parallel circuits, use a volt-Ohm-Milliameter in a circuit verify calculations, and apply principles of safety and application in the maintenance/use of lead-acid batteries.
  Instruction: Course covers the theory of operation and use of the various types of batteries, their characteristics, limitations, maintenance requirements, and types of DC circuits that normally use battery power. A review of series and parallel DC circuits is provided.
  Credit recommendation: In the lower division baccalaureate/associate degree category, 2 semester hours in Electrical Technology (9/82) (11/87). NOTE: This course has been reevaluated and continues to meet requirements for credit recommendations.

Better Plant Operation Through Chemistry (O-9)
  Location: Athens, TX.
  Length: 36 hours (1 week).
  Dates: May 1986-Present.
  Objective: To introduce the student to the advantages of adequate chemical usages in a power plant.
  Learning Outcome: Upon successful completion of this course, the student will be able to understand basic water chemistry and its importance within the water/steam cycle of the power plant process, identify the differences between water treatment for drum and supercritical once through boilers, and recognize the water cleaning process for improved boiler performance.
  Instruction: Course covers the study of water and its impurities, clarification and filtration, sodium zeolite softening, demineralization, deareation, steam generation, internal treatment, phosphate treatment, and steam purity.
  Credit recommendation: In the lower division baccalaureate/associate degree category, 2 semester hours in Vocational/Technical Education (11/87).

Blueprint Reading (B-5)
(Formerly Introduction to Blueprints [B-4])
  Location: Athens, TX.
  Length: 36 hours (1 week).
  Dates: September 1975-Present.
  Objective: To introduce blueprint interpretation.
  Learning Outcome: Upon successful completion of this course, the student will be able to know vocabulary of ten line meanings; draw estimated angles, irregular curves, arcs and circles, ellipses and sold objects showing three dimensions; identify and draw front, top, side auxiliary; draw isometric, oblique, and perspective projections; determine the general tolerances according to number of decimal places; recognize scale and how to use it; and to define and recognize bevel, rack, spur, spliac, etc.
  Instruction: Course covers role of blueprints in industry. How to read blueprints, focusing on machine, hydraulic and pneumatic, building, electrical, pipe system and sheet metal drawing. Sketching is also required. Methodology includes lecture and laboratory, with 20 hours of outside study.
  Credit recommendation: In the lower division baccalaureate/associate degree category, 2 semester hours in Technical Programs (9/82) (11/87). NOTE: This course has been reevaluated and continues to meet requirements for credit recommendations.

Boiler Fundamentals and Operation (O-11)
(Formerly Boiler Operations [O-8])
  Location: Athens, TX.

Length: 36 hours (1 week).
Dates: September 1975-Present.
Objective: To provide information needed for the student to utilize basic procedures for the operation of controlled and combined circulation units.
Learning Outcome: Upon successful completion of this course, the student will be able to describe the water flow cycle in natural circulation boiler, the water flow cycle in a forced circulation boiler, describe the principles of operation for steam drum internals, economizer inlet, furnace riser inlets, and steam quality control.
Instruction: Course covers general boiler operation procedures, including precautions to be observed during the operation of steam generating facilities. Topics include pre-operation and start-up procedures, operations, shutdown, restart, emergency procedures, and furnace explosions.
Credit recommendation: In the lower division baccalaureate/associate degree category, 2 semester hours in Vocational/Technical Education (9/82) (11/87). NOTE: This course has been reevaluated and continues to meet requirements for credit recommendations.

Control Circuits (E-14)
(Formerly Alternating Current Control Equipment [E-14])
Location: Athens, TX.
Length: 36 hours (1 week).
Dates: *Version 1:* August 1978-November 1987; *Version 2:* December 1987-Present.
Objective: To provide the student with an understanding of the characteristics, specifications, and operating requirements of control devices.
Learning Outcome: Upon successful completion of this course, the student will be able to explain the difference between manual, automatic and magnetic controls, explain logic for control circuits, describe the operation of thermal and magnetic overloads, and explain the operation and uses of devices such as push buttons, selector switch, joy stick, limit switch, and pressure switch.
Instruction: Course covers control devices such as timing and operating sequencing controls. Operation of motors and other devices under hazardous conditions is also studied. Twenty hours of outside study assignments.
Credit recommendation: *Version 1:* In the lower division baccalaureate/associate degree category, 3 semester hours in Electrical Technology (9/82). *Version 2:* In the lower division baccalaureate/associate degree category, 2 semester hours in Electrical Technology (11/87). NOTE: This course has been reevaluated and continues to meet requirements for credit recommendations.

Control Wiring Diagrams and Electrical Troubleshooting (QR-17)
Location: Athens, TX.
Length: 36 hours (1 week).
Dates: May 1976-Present.
Objective: To provide elementary training in DC current circuits.
Instruction: To provide coverage in the basics of electrical schematic diagrams, the use of Ohm's Law, circuit calculations, and basic faultfinding techniques.
Credit recommendation: In the lower division baccalaureate/associate degree category, 2 semester hours in Electrical Technology (9/82) (11/87). NOTE: This course has been reevaluated and continues to meet requirements for credit recommendations.

Coupling and Shaft Alignment Level I (M-14)
(Formerly Introductory Coupling and Shaft Alignment - Level I [M-14])
Location: Athens, TX.
Length: 36 hours (1 week).
Dates: *Version 1:* September 1981-November 1987; *Version 2:* December 1987-Present.
Objective: To develop an ability to maintain equipment in a closely aligned condition to the degree necessary for minimum vibration, maximum bearing and coupling life, and high power efficiency.
Learning Outcome: Upon successful completion of this course, the student will be able to perform all tasks necessary for the preparation of alignment of shafts for maintaining equipment in a closely aligned condition; set up dial indicators to obtain accurate measurements of misalignment; and to correct for any soft foot condition that may exist.
Instruction: Course applies the geometry of alignment to any laboratory experience for proper adjustments or high speed equipment relative to load and temperature. Manufacturing tolerances, equipment wear, distortions, repair procedures, and inspection techniques are studied.
Credit recommendation: *Version 1:* In the lower division baccalaureate/associate degree category, 3 semester hours in Vocational/Technical Education (9/82). *Version 2:* In the lower division baccalaureate/associate degree category, 2 semester hours in Vocational/Technical Education (11/87). NOTE: This course has been reevaluated and continues to meet requirements for credit recommendations.

Coupling and Shaft Alignment Level II (M-15)
(Formerly Advanced Coupling and Shaft Alignment-Level II [M-15])
Location: Athens, TX; Trinidad S.E.S.
Length: 36 hours (1 week).
Dates: *Version 1:* September 1981-November 1987; *Version 2:* December 1987-Present.
Objective: To develop an ability to maintain equipment in a closely aligned condition to the degree necessary for minimum vibration, maximum bearing and coupling life, and high power efficiency.
Learning Outcome: Upon successful completion of this

course, the student will be able to align shafts to a degree required for minimum vibration, maximum bearing and rotating element lift, and high power efficiency.

Instruction: Course applies the geometry of alignment to any laboratory experience for proper adjustments or high speed equipment relative to load and temperature. Manufacturing tolerances, equipment wear, distortions, repair procedures, and inspector techniques are studied.

Credit recommendation: *Version 1:* In the lower division baccalaureate/associate degree category, 3 semester hours in Vocational/Technical Education (9/82). *Version 2:* In the lower division baccalaureate/associate degree category, 2 semester hours in Vocational/Technical Education (11/87). NOTE: This course has been reevaluated and continues to meet requirements for credit recommendations.

DC Motors and Generators (E-11)
(Formerly Direct Current Equipment and Controls [E-11])
  Location: Athens, TX.
  Length: 36 hours (1 week).
  Dates: January 1978-Present.
  Objective: To provide the student with the ability to understand the characteristics, specifications, and proper use of DC generators, motors, and power supplies.
  Learning Outcome: Upon successful completion of this course, the student will be able to explain the operational characteristics of series, shunt, and compound DC motors and generators, know the differences between starting rheostats and speed controllers, demonstrate in hands-on exercises the differences between a separately excited and self-excited generator, and to explain how voltage build-up occurs in a self-excited DC generator.
  Instruction: Course covers the principles of DC power generation, DC motors, relay devices, semiconductor control systems, and maintenance practices necessary for reliable operation. Twenty hours of outside study assignments.
  Credit recommendation: In the lower division baccalaureate/associate degree category, 2 semester hours in Industrial Electrical Technology (9/82) (11/87). NOTE: This course has been reevaluated and continues to meet requirements for credit recommendations.

Drive Components (M-10)
  Location: Athens, TX.
  Length: 36 hours (1 week).
  Dates: September 1975-Present.
  Objective: To develop an understanding of how drive components work, how they are constructed, and their designed functions.
  Learning Outcome: Upon successful completion of this course, the student will be able to install and maintain drive components such as belts, chains and gears; determine ratios related to pulleys, sprockets, and gears; and to determine torque, horsepower, and efficiency of rotating equipment.
  Instruction: Course covers construction and application of many of the common and special couplings, clutches, v-belt drives, chain drives, speed reducers, gears, brakes, and motors used in industry. Emphasis is also placed on special materials and maintenance requirements.
  Credit recommendation: In the lower division baccalaureate/associate degree category, 2 semester hours in Vocational/Technical Education (9/82) (11/87). NOTE: This course has been reevaluated and continues to meet requirements for credit recommendations.

Electrical Distribution (O-10)
  Location: Athens, TX.
  Length: 36 hours (1 week).
  Dates: June 1986-Present.
  Objective: To learn the operation and characteristics of high voltage switchyards, breakers, transformers, metering devices, and protective relaying.
  Learning Outcome: Upon successful completion of this course, the student will be able to define a polyphase system; calculate power and power factor within a polyphase system; to calculate voltage, amps, and resistance; and the applications for transformers.
  Instruction: Course covers an introduction to electrical diagrams and the functions of a power plant's basic electrical systems. Areas of study include polyphase circuits, three phase wye connections, three phase delta connections, basic principles of transformers, switchyard breaker operations, and different zones of protection in switchyards.
  Credit recommendation: In the lower division baccalaureate/associate degree category, 2 semester hours in Vocational/Technical Education (11/87).

Electrical Protective Devices (E-10)
(Formerly Electrical Protective Devices [E-9])
  Location: Athens, TX.
  Length: 36 hours (1 week).
  Dates: May 1977-Present.
  Objective: To provide the student with the expertise necessary to understand, specify, and properly use electrical protective devices such as overload protectors.
  Learning Outcome: Upon successful completion of this course, the student will be able to describe operation of fuses, molded case circuit breakers, ground fault circuit interrupters, ground fault protection, ground fault indication and overload protection; understand and apply device ratings IAW and NCED for safe, coordinated, and maximum protection of equipment, circuits and personnel; and perform short circuit calculations using the point-to-point method and charts/tables method.
  Instruction: Course covers the various protective devices and circuit interrupters, their characteristics, economic value, principles of operation, and related safety

procedures to be followed.

Credit recommendation: In the lower division baccalaureate/associate degree category, 2 semester hours in Electrical Technology (9/82) (11/87). NOTE: This course has been reevaluated and continues to meet requirements for credit recommendations.

Electrical Troubleshooting (E-15)
Location: Athens, TX.
Length: 36 hours (1 week).
Dates: *Version 1:* November 1978-November 1987; *Version 2:* December 1987-Present.
Objective: To provide an understanding of a systematic approach to locating faults in electrical control and power circuits.
Learning Outcome: Upon successful completion of this course, the student will be able to review the vital portions of the preceding Electrical Long Range courses that will be helpful in successful troubleshooting, use ladder diagrams and Control Wiring Diagrams (CWD) to identify current paths and voltage distribution to various components, identify and locate (with test equipment), opens and short circuits in control circuits, and to use simulators and CWDs to fabricate and troubleshoot realistic motor control circuits.
Instruction: Course covers detailed use of schematic diagrams and organized approaches to locating malfunctions in control circuits, DC motors, AC motors, lighting distribution circuits as well as electronic power control equipment. Twenty hours of outside study assignments.
Credit recommendation: *Version 1:* In the lower division baccalaureate/associate degree category, 3 semester hours in Industrial Electrical Technology (9/82). *Version 2:* In the lower division baccalaureate/associate degree category, 2 semester hours in Industrial Electrical Technology (11/87). NOTE: This course has been reevaluated and continues to meet requirements for credit recommendations.

Electrical Wiring and National Electric Code (E-8)
(Formerly Electrical Measuring Instruments [E-8])
Location: Athens, TX.
Length: 36 hours (1 week).
Dates: February 1977-July 1987.
Objective: To provide an overall review of the types and principles of operation of common electrical instruments used in normal maintenance procedures in the electrical power field.
Instruction: Instruction covers the general principles of operation, use and limitations of DC and AC electrical measuring instruments in common use by maintenance personnel. Instruction is also provided in the use of power-factor, multimeter, recording and electronic instruments. Approximately 8 hours outside study is required.
Credit recommendation: In the lower division baccalaureate/associate degree category, 3 semester hours in Electrical Instrumentation (9/82).

Electronics I (QR-412)
(Formerly Electronics I [QR-12])
Location: Athens, TX.
Length: 36 hours (1 week).
Dates: March 1977-Present.
Objective: To provide training in basic electronics.
Learning Outcome: Upon successful completion of this course, the student will be able to solve basic electronic problems using current voltage and resistance; explain the relationship between current, voltage and resistance, between electricity and magnetism; and to construct DC circuits using resistors, switches, lamps and batteries; read a schematic diagram of a basic DC circuit; use a multimeter to read voltage, current and resistance; and use capacitors and inductors in DC circuits.
Instruction: Course covers electrical current flow, voltage rise and drop, Ohm's Law, magnetism, basics of electrical instruments, and the concept of inductance and capacitance. Ten hours of outside study required.
Credit recommendation: In the lower division baccalaureate/associate degree category, 2 semester hours in Electronics (9/82) (11/87). NOTE: This course has been reevaluated and continues to meet requirements for credit recommendations.

Electronics II (QR-413)
(Formerly Electronics II [QR-13])
Location: Athens, TX.
Length: 36 hours (1 week).
Dates: March 1977-Present.
Objective: To provide basic instruction in principles of alternating currents.
Learning Outcome: Upon successful completion of this course, the student will be able to know the difference between AC and DC and list the advantages of AC over DC; describe the operation of a basic AC generator; determine the RMS, peak, peak to peak, period and frequency of an AC wave form; measure AC values using an oscilloscope and an AC voltmeter; and to analyze AC circuits that contain resistors, inductors and capacitors and solve for capacitive reactance, inductive reactance, current, voltage, true power, reactive power, impedance, phase angle, and power factor.
Instruction: Course covers AC fundamentals, measuring instruments, properties of capacitors and inductances, and elementary AC circuit analysis. Ten hours of outside study assignments.
Credit recommendation: In the lower division baccalaureate/associate degree category, 2 semester hours in Electronics (9/82) (11/87). NOTE: This course has been reevaluated and continues to meet requirements for credit recommendations.

Electronics III (QR-414)
(Formerly Electronics III [QR-14])
  Location: Athens, TX.
  Length: 36 hours (1 week).
  Dates: *Version 1:* March 1977-November 1987; *Version 2:* December 1987-Present.
  Objective: To provide basic knowledge of semiconductor devices.
  Learning Outcome: Upon successful completion of this course, the student will be able to describe the electrical characteristics of semiconductor material, name the advantages that semiconductors have over vacuum tubes, explain how semiconductor devices operate and how to properly bias them, recognize the schematic symbols for the various semiconductor devices, and to test semiconductor devices to see if they are functioning properly.
  Instruction: Course covers semiconductor fundamentals, diodes, zener diodes, bipolar transistor operation and characteristics, field effect transistors, and integrated circuit fundamentals. Ten hours of outside study assignments.
  Credit recommendation: *Version 1:* In the lower division baccalaureate/associate degree category, 3 semester hours in Electronics (9/82). *Version 2:* In the lower division baccalaureate/associate degree category, 2 semester hours in Electronics (11/87). NOTE: This course has been reevaluated and continues to meet requirements for credit recommendations.

Electronics IV (QR-415)
(Formerly Electronics IV [QR-15])
  Location: Athens, TX.
  Length: 36 hours (1 week).
  Dates: *Version 1:* March 1977-November 1987; *Version 2:* December 1987-Present.
  Objective: To provide instruction in the basics of operational amplifiers and control circuitry.
  Learning Outcome: Upon successful completion of this course, the student will be able to identify the three basic transistor amplifier circuit configurations and describe their operation, define direct current amplifiers, audio amplifiers, video amplifiers, IF and RF amplifiers, define the applications of differential amplifiers, comparators, summing amplifiers and difference amplifiers using operational amplifiers, and to identify and explain the operation of power supply filters, rectifiers, and regulators.
  Instruction: Course covers analog semiconductor amplifiers, DC and high frequency amplifiers, operational amplifiers, analog servo controls, and power supplies. Ten hours of outside study required.
  Credit recommendation: *Version 1:* In the lower division baccalaureate/associate degree category, 3 semester hours in Electronics (9/82). *Version 2:* In the lower division baccalaurate/associate degree category, 2 semester hours in Electronics (11/87). NOTE: This course has been reevaluated and continues to meet requirements for credit recommendations.

Electronics V (QR-416)
(Formerly Electronics V [QR-16])
  Location: Athens, TX.
  Length: 36 hours (1 week).
  Dates: *Version 1:* March 1977-November 1987; *Version 2:* December 1987-Present.
  Objective: To provide introduction to and study of digital techniques.
  Learning Outcome: Upon successful completion of this course, the student will be able to convert decimal numbers to binary and hexadecimal; convert binary and hexadecimal numbers to decimal; determine the binary ASCII code for any letter or number; list the logic levels and operating characteristics for TTL, N-MOS, CMOS, IIL, and ECL logic families; recognize and use Boolean expressions to identify digital signal names; and to recognize the symbols and truth tables for common logic gates and flip-flops.
  Instruction: Course covers digital techniques, digital devices, logic circuits, digital integrated circuits, Boolean algebra, registers, logic clocks, combination logic, digital design, and applications. Ten hours of outside study assignments.
  Credit recommendation: *Version 1:* In the lower division baccalaureate/associate degree category, 3 semester hours in Electronics (9/82). *Version 2:* In the lower division baccalaureate/associate degree category, 2 semester hours in Electronics (11/87). NOTE: This course has been reevaluated and continues to meet requirements for credit recommendations.

Electronics VI (QR-605)
  Location: Athens, TX.
  Length: 36 hours (1 week).
  Dates: June 1986-Present.
  Objective: To learn digital circuit components and their operations and practical methods of implementing circuit design.
  Learning Outcome: Upon successful completion of this course, the student will be able to determine the binary sequence and operation of synchronous counters, asynchronous counters, modulo-n counters, shift registers, and ring counters from a schematic diagram, list applications for these sequential logic circuits, determine the output states and operation of decoders, ecoders, multiplexers, demultiplexers, binary comparators and adders, and diode matrix Read Only Memories, list applications for these combinational logic circuits, and to apply the knowledge gained to analyzing digital equipment schematics.
  Instruction: Course is a continuation of digital circuit components, their functions and methods of implementing circuit design.
  Credit recommendation: In the lower division baccalaureate/associate degree category, 2 semester hours in

Electronics (11/87).

Elements of Mechanics (M-7)
  Location: Athens, TX.
  Length: 36 hours (1 week).
  Dates: September 1975-Present.
  Objective: To provide important facts required to understand the many facets of mechanics necessary to maintenance work.
  Learning Outcome: Upon successful completion of this course, the student will be able to identify and apply the basic principle of forces, motion, work and energy, area and volume to mechanic systems; use the principles of force, motion, work and energy, area and volume to determine if problems exist in a mechanical system; apply the principles of the six simple machines to help in completing jobs such as rigging, and material handling with maximum efficiency and safety; and select the proper threaded fastener for jobs being performed and install the fastener with the proper lubrication and torque.
  Instruction: Course covers such fundamental concepts as force, motion, friction, and work and energy. The application of these concepts to simple machinery, fasteners, and the use of tools is emphasized.
  Credit recommendation: In the lower division baccalaureate/associate degree category, 2 semester hours in Vocational/Technical Education (9/82) (11/87). NOTE: This course has been reevaluated and continues to meet requirements for credit recommendations.

Fluid Power Systems (M-11)
  Location: Athens, TX.
  Length: 36 hours (1 week).
  Dates: January 1988-Present.
  Objective: To learn to identify and schematically draw at least five components of a basic hydraulic and pneumatic system.
  Learning Outcome: Upon successful completion of this course, the student will be able to identify components of a fluid power system from the components themselves and from schematic drawings or blueprints; and to maintain, troubleshoot, and repair components of a fluid power system.
  Instruction: Course covers basic principles of hydraulic and pneumatic systems as they relate to industrial application. Topics include compressors/pumps, head exchangers, high pressure filtration, central valves, pressure relief valves, cylinders, motors, symbols and schematics, and basic systems designs.
  Credit recommendation: In the lower division baccalaureate/associate degree category, 2 semester hours in Vocational/Technical Education (11/87).

Generator Fundamentals and Operation (O-13)
(Formerly Generator Fundamentals and Operations [O-10])
  Location: Athens, TX.
  Length: 36 hours (1 week).
  Dates: September 1975-Present.
  Objective: To develop and advance student knowledge of turbine and generator operations.
  Learning Outcome: Upon successful completion of this course, the student will be able to have a thorough understanding of magnetic fields and magnetic lines of force, identify the components of a large AC generator, identify the components of different excitation systems, a cooling system, generator leads cooling system, the seal oil system, identify and explain the generation devices, and to demonstrate on the simulator, the proper operation of the generator.
  Instruction: Course covers an advanced understanding of turbines, generators, and auxiliary systems to ensure safe, efficient operations.
  Credit recommendation: In the lower division baccalaureate/associate degree category, 2 semester hours in Vocational/Technical Education (9/82) (11/87). NOTE: This course has been reevaluated and continues to meet requirements for credit recommendations.

Heat Rate Improvement (O-14)
  Location: Athens, TX.
  Length: 36 hours (1 week).
  Dates: October 1986-Present.
  Objective: To acquaint the student with the relationship between efficiency and heat rate and its impact upon the operator.
  Learning Outcome: Upon successful completion of this course, the student will be able to identify cost of fuel, kilowatts and new plants; understand efficiency versus heat rate; identify the basic and most complex plant cycles within the power generation process; identify boiler, turbine and generator efficiency and how to figure for each or together, and to recognize miscellaneous losses within power plant cycle and the entire power generation process.
  Instruction: Course covers the relationship between operator efficiency and heat rate. Topics include the relationship between heat rate and efficiency; heat rate and plant cycles, boiler operations, turbine operations, back pressure and feedwater heaters, fundamentals of a generator, and dispatching.
  Credit recommendation: In the lower division baccalaureate/associate degree category, 2 semester hours in Vocational/Technical Education (11/87).

Lubrication and Bearings (M-8)
  Location: Athens, TX.
  Length: 36 hours (1 week).
  Dates: June 1987-Present.
  Objective: To provide a knowledge of lubrication prin-

ciples and procedures as they relate to industrial maintenance; and to develop an understanding of the general principles of bearing operations.

Learning Outcome: Upon successful completion of this course, the student will be able to properly administer lubricants to a bearing, determine how to choose a lubricant for a certain piece of equipment, describe various bearings and where they are used in various pieces of equipment, apply lubricants using various lubricating methods and determine which method is best for a situation, and to troubleshoot and repair a Lincoln lubricating system.

Instruction: Course covers the principles, characteristics, and applications of lubricants. Bearing lubrication methods are covered with emphasis on basic bearings, sliding surface bearing failure, rolling contact bearing replacements, and bearing housings.

Credit recommendation: In the lower division baccalaureate/associate degree category, 2 semester hours in Vocational/Technical Education (11/87).

Materials (M-6)

Location: Athens, TX.
Length: 36 hours (1 week).
Dates: January 1986-Present.
Objective: To provide students with knowledge of common material found at utility electrical work stations.
Learning Outcome: Upon successful completion of this course, the student will be able to identify materials such as metals, plastics, liquids, and gases by their physical and chemical properties, and to identify the effect that environmental changes such as heat and pressure have on different materials.
Instruction: Course covers a basic knowledge of the properties and behavior of various materials used by industrial plants for both production and maintenance. Materials covered include metallics, polymerics, ceramics and others, with destructive and nondestructive testing emphasized.
Credit recommendation: In the lower division baccalaureate/associate degree category, 2 semester hours in Vocational/Technical Education (11/87).

Measurements (B-3)

Location: Athens, TX.
Length: 36 hours (1 week).
Dates: *Version 1:* March 1977-November 1987; *Version 2:* December 1987-Present.
Objective: To develop skill and understanding of precision measurement and its applications in industry.
Learning Outcome: Upon successful completion of this course, the student will be able to identify and determine the values of quantities which describe objects, processes and systems which may be encountered in steam electric stations and lignite mines, define and understand units of measurement used throughout the U.S. and Europe, and to be able to calculate said quantities if needed.
Instruction: Course covers study of the units of measurement, including metric, linear, motion, force, bulk, comparison and surface, temperature, fluid and electrical, and the related instruments. Methodology includes lectures, discussion, and textbooks, with 10 hours of outside study required.
Credit recommendation: *Version 1:* In the lower division baccalaureate/associate degree category, 3 semester hours in Manufacturing Engineering Technology (9/82). *Version 2:* In the lower division baccalaureate/associate degree category, 2 semester hours in Manufacturing Engineering Technology (11/87). NOTE: This course has been reevaluated and continues to meet requirements for credit recommendations.

Microprocessor I (QR-482)

Location: Athens, TX.
Length: 36 hours (1 week).
Dates: January 1986-Present.
Objective: To provide an introduction to microcomputer basics.
Learning Outcome: Upon successful completion of this course, the student will be able to perform conversions between binary, octal, decimal, and hexadecimal including fractional, integer, signal, and unsigned numbers; determine the ASCII and Baudot codes for any letter or number; perform binary addition, subtraction, multiplication, and division; describe the detailed sequential execution of the fetch and execute cycles for simple instructions, and write simple straight line programs.
Instruction: Course covers the number systems used with microprocessors and computers, microprocessor hardware, microprocessor basics, computer arithmetic, and an introduction to programming.
Credit recommendation: In the lower division baccalaureate/associate degree category, 1 semester hour in Computer Science (11/87).

Microprocessor II (QR-483)

Location: Athens, TX.
Length: 36 hours (1 week).
Dates: January 1986-Present.
Objective: To provide a study of the 6800 microprocessor and the application of microprocessors in computers.
Learning Outcome: Upon successful completion of this course, the student will be able to describe the hardware architecture of the Motorola 6800 microprocessor, define the inherent, immediate, direct, extended, relative, and indexed addressing modes used by the 6800 microprocessor, use the stack and interrupt instructions to write real time subroutines, describe the algorithms used for many of the common "device driver" programs, and write functional machine language programs for the 6800 microprocessor.
Instruction: Course covers a continuation of Micro-

processor I, using the 6800 Microprocessor unit, students study address modes available, stack operations, subroutines, input/output, and interrupts.

Credit recommendation: In the lower division baccalaureate/associate degree category, 1 semester hour in Computer Science (11/87).

Microprocessor III (QR-573)
  Location: Athens, TX.
  Length: 36 hours (1 week).
  Dates: January 1986-Present.
  Objective: To provide the student with the ability to understand the fundamentals of interfacing.
  Learning Outcome: Upon successful completion of this course, the student will be able to describe the connection and operation of digital buses and 3-state logic drivers; describe the timing diagrams and waveforms generated by the 6800 microprocessor system while executing instructions; define the function and purpose of each connecting pin on the 6800 chip; determine from schematic diagrams the proper connection and hardware address of memory chips, displays, keyboards, and other common peripherals, and interconnect and write programs to operate the Peripheral Interface Adaptor IC in experiments which generate music and operate A/D and D/A converters.
  Instruction: Course covers the fundamentals of interfacing, random access memory, interfacing with display, switches, and the operation of peripheral interface adapter.
  Credit recommendation: In the lower division baccalaureate/associate degree category, 1 semester hour in Computer Science (11/87).

Oxyacetylene Welding (QR-520)
  Location: Athens, TX.
  Length: 36 hours (1 week).
  Dates: January 1986-Present.
  Objective: To provide a general orientation to the oxyacetylene welding process.
  Learning Outcome: Upon successful completion of this course, the student will be able to set up oxyacetylene welding equipment to be used in heating, cutting, braze welding, and fusion welding, to weld materials to be repaired using oxyacetylene process, and to select proper welding tip, gas pressures, and welding rod.
  Instruction: The student is introduced to oxyacetylene welding process and applies theory and procedures in a laboratory setting. Study also includes safety, equipment start-up, adjustments, shutdown, and appropriate positions for various types of welding.
  Credit recommendation: In the lower division baccalaureate/associate degree category, 2 semester hours in Vocational/Technical Education (11/87).

Piping Systems and Pumps (M-12)
(Formerly Piping Systems and Pumps [M-13])
  Location: Athens, TX.
  Length: 36 hours (1 week).
  Dates: May 1982-Present.
  Objective: To gain practical knowledge about piping systems and pumps that are a vital part of plant operations.
  Instruction: Concerned with various piping systems and pumps. Topics include forms of piping, fittings, valves, strainers, filters, traps, pump applications, pump selection, types of pumps, packing and seals, and pump maintenance. The course is taught in 12 hours of lecture/discussion, 24 hours of laboratory work, and 4 hours of outside review.
  Credit recommendation: In the lower division baccalaureate/associate degree category, 2 semester hours in Vocational/Technical Education (9/82) (11/87). NOTE: This course has been reevaluated and continues to meet requirements for credit recommendations.

Plant Protective Devices (O-15)
  Location: Athens, TX.
  Length: 36 hours (1 week).
  Dates: October 1986-Present.
  Objective: To provide the student with the expertise necessary to understand, specify, and use plant protective devices.
  Learning Outcome: Upon successful completion of this course, the student will be able to learn the nature of plant protection, causes of equipment failure, the function and scope of electrical protective systems, generator protective devices, motor protective devices, and to describe the various supervisory devices on the turbine.
  Instruction: Course covers the fundamentals of plant protective devices and their protective schemes. Topics include protective devices, electrical protective devices, boiler and turbine protection, logic diagrams, and integral plant protection.
  Credit recommendation: In the lower division baccalaureate/associate degree category, 2 semester hours in Vocational/Technical Education (11/87).

Power Plant Auxiliary Equipment (O-7)
  Location: Athens, TX.
  Length: 36 hours (1 week).
  Dates: September 1975-Present.
  Objective: To develop a basic understanding of boiler fundamentals through study and application relative to steam generator production.
  Learning Outcome: Upon successful completion of this course, the student will be able to explain the principle of condenser operation, identify different condenser designs, two types of feedwater heaters, define the application of unit heat balance, identify major classifications of pumps, and describe principle operation of major pumps.

Instruction: Material includes steam generator components, combined circulation heat transfer, theory of combustion, fluid flow circuits, air flow circuits, fuel systems, pulverizers, feeders, sulzer valves, safety valves, and air heaters as applied to steam generator production. Simulators are used to provide practical "hands-on" experience. Outside preparation of 12 hours is required.

Credit recommendation: In the lower division baccalaureate/associate degree category, 2 semester hours in Vocational/Technical Education (9/82) (11/87). NOTE: This course has been reevaluated and continues to meet requirements for credit recommendations.

Power Plant Fundamentals (O-6)
(Formerly Power Fundamentals [O-6])
Location: Athens, TX.
Length: 36 hours (1 week).
Dates: September 1975-Present.
Objective: To prepare the student to become skilled as a power plant operator by introducing basic power plant fundamentals as a prerequisite.

Learning Outcome: Upon successful completion of this course, the student will be able to describe properties of matter, identify forms of energy including thermal, mechanical, and internal; describe basic chemical concepts with regard to atomic structure and the law of combining weights; measure heat energy in BTU and identify the elements of fuel content; and to describe the three types of heat transfer within the power generation process.

Instruction: Introduces the student to basic concepts of physics, chemistry, and thermodynamics as they relate to power plant mechanisms and production of electrical power. Outside study assignments of 20 hours are required.

Credit recommendation: In the lower division baccalaureate/associate degree category, 2 semester hours in Vocational/Technical Education (9/82) (11/87). NOTE: This course has been reevaluated and continues to meet requirements for credit recommendations.

Power Plant Simulator Training (QR-645)
Location: Athens, TX.
Length: 36 hours (1 week).
Dates: August 1986-Present.
Objective: To learn operation of the power plant simulator, using safe, proper operating procedures and to demonstrate proper responses to malfunctions.

Learning Outcome: Upon successful completion of this course, the student will be able to train plant operators to be proficient in their jobs by knowing power plant systems, being able to differentiate between normal and abnormal conditions, knowing what actions to take in the event abnormal conditions arise, and preventing unit trips caused by human error.

Instruction: Course covers basic concepts of operating a power plant through simulator training. Topics include simulator familiarization, unit operation, valve operation, start-up procedures, feedwater heaters, generator, turbine operations, and responses to minor and major malfunctions.

Credit recommendation: In the lower division baccalaureate/associate degree category, 2 semester hours in Vocational/Technical Education (11/87).

Principles and Applications of Lubrication (M-8)
Location: Athens, TX.
Length: 36 hours (1 week).
Dates: September 1975-July 1986.
Objective: To provide a knowledge of lubrication principles and procedures as they relate to industrial maintenance.

Instruction: Explains the principles and procedures of lubrication including how oils and grease reduce friction, prevent corrosion, dampen shock, and cool equipment. The course is taught in 25 hours of lecture/discussion, 10 hours of laboratory work, with 8 hours of outside study assignments.

Credit recommendation: In the lower division baccalaureate/associate degree category, 2 semester hours in Vocational/Technical Education (9/82).

Principles of Bearings Operation (M-9)
Location: Athens, TX.
Length: 36 hours (1 week).
Dates: September 1975-October 1986.
Objective: To develop an understanding of the general principles of bearings operations.

Instruction: Covers the correct design, selection, and installation of bearings and shafts to assure proper performance of equipment. The course is taught in 25 hours of lecture/discussion, 11 hours of laboratory work, with 8 hours of outside study assignments.

Credit recommendation: In the lower division baccalaureate/associate degree category, 2 semester hours in Vocational/Technical Education (9/82).

Pumps (O-8)
Location: Athens, TX.
Length: 36 hours (1 week).
Dates: March 1986-Present.
Objective: To increase the knowledge and skill level of the student in the area of pumps, with primary emphasis on dynamic pumps.

Learning Outcome: Upon successful completion of this course, the student will be able to describe the top three groups of pump classifications, be able to assemble or disassemble a very simple pump, identify the relationship between static head and static pressure, and the specific gravity of a fluid and its effect on fluid itself, identify different types of heads within a pumping system, and to describe five methods for measuring flow within a system.

Instruction: Course covers pump classification, static

head and static pressure measurement, types of heads and their measurement, various heads such as suction, lift and discharge heads, flow measurements, performance identification of pumps, and centrifugal pump construction.

Credit recommendation: In the lower division baccalaureate/associate degree category, 2 semester hours in Vocational/Technical Education (11/87).

Pumps and Piping (M1-12)
   Location: Athens Training Center, Athens, TX.
   Length: 36 hours (1 week).
   Dates: April 1988-Present.
   Objective: To teach practical knowledge about piping systems and pumps that are a vital part of plant operations.
   Learning Outcome: Upon successful completion of this course, the student will be able to identify pump design features and their functions and determine why a pump is not performing at its rated capacity, how to disassemble and inspect pumps for worn or damaged parts, and to reassemble and reinstall pumps for maximum efficiency and reliability.
   Instruction: Course covers forms of piping, fittings, valves, strainers, filters, traps, pump applications, pump selection, types of pumps, packing and seats, and pump maintenance.
   Credit recommendation: In the lower division baccalaureate/associate degree category, 2 semester hours in Vocational/Technical Education (11/87).

Rigging, Hydraulic Crane, Forklift (M-13)
   Location: Athens Training Center, Athens, TX.
   Length: 36 hours (1 week).
   Dates: May 1988-Present.
   Objective: To provide technical and practical training in the areas of safe rigging, hydraulic crane and forklift operation.
   Learning Outcome: Upon successful completion of this course, the student will be able to operate forklifts in work areas and in various conditions, rig hydraulic cranes and determine how much weight the crane can lift at various boom angles and positions, and safely operate a hydraulic crane.
   Instruction: Course covers technical information and operations related to rigging, hydaulic cranes and forklifts. Topics include wire, rope, fiber rope, chain, rigging hardware, reeving, slings, safety, load charts, weight estimates, capacity charts, and load signals.
   Credit recommendation: In the lower division baccalaureate/associate degree category, 2 semester hours in the Vocational/Technical Education elective (11/87).

Safety and Relief Valves (QR-637)
   Location: Plant sites.
   Length: 24 hours (3 days).
   Dates: January 1986-Present.
   Objective: To provide information on the necessary steps in dismantling, inspecting, lapping, micro finishing, reassembling and resetting safety and relief valves.
   Learning Outcome: Upon successful completion of this course, the student will be able to disassemble, inspect, repair, reassemble, and properly set popping pressure and blowdown on safety and relief valves following Texas Boiler Law and code. After successful completion of this course, student may be commissioned by the Texas Boiler Division to set and seal valves.
   Instruction: Explains functions of safety and relief valves; valve maintenance; valve disassembly, valve repair, valve reassembly, and valve setting.
   Credit recommendation: In the lower division baccalaureate/associate degree category, 1 semester hour in Vocational/Technical Education electives (11/87).

Schematics and Symbols (B-4)
(Formerly Reading Schematics and Symbols [B-5])
   Location: Athens, TX.
   Length: 36 hours (1 week).
   Dates: *Version 1:* November 1976-November 1987; *Version 2:* December 1987-Present.
   Objective: To develop the ability to read schematics of electrical, piping, and fluid power systems.
   Learning Outcome: Upon successful completion of this course, the student will have been introduced with understanding to fundamentals of electricity and sufficient knowledge of electrical symbols to enable personnel to trace current through an electrical schematic, and be able to use electrical schematics and wiring diagrams to solve problems easier than before.
   Instruction: Course covers introduction to schematics and symbols through the study of guidelines for reading electrical and fluid power schematics, electrical diagrams, and electrical piping, and fluid power, and welding symbols. Methodology includes lecture and laboratory with 10 hours of outside study.
   Credit recommendation: *Version 1:* In the lower division baccalaureate/associate degree category, 3 semester hours in Technical Programs (9/82). *Version 2:* In the lower division baccalaureate/associate degree category, 2 semester hours in Technical Programs (11/87). NOTE: This course has been reevaluated and continues to meet requirements for credit recommendations.

Solid State Devices (E-8)
   Location: Athens, TX.
   Length: 36 hours (1 week).
   Dates: January 1985-Present.
   Objective: To identify the different solid state devices on a schematic diagram and explain their operation.
   Learning Outcome: Upon successful completion of this course, the student will be able to apply a basic understanding of semiconductor materials, troubleshoot diodes/rectifiers (both half and full wave) filters and simple

regulators as commonly encountered in solid state systems; be familiar with and use applicable terminology as may be found in technical manuals, i.e., characteristic curves, ratings, derating, voltage multiplier, LCD, LED, SCR, and other "alphabet soup" components; test, troubleshoot, and maintain circuits that include transistor switches, transducers, SCRs, DIAC/TRIACs, UJTs, FETs, and ICs (novice level), and to use the oscilloscope to examine circuit function.

Instruction: This course provides instruction in the functions and electrical characteristics of semiconductors, diodes, how temperature affects voltage regulation, and the relationship between the base, emitter, and collection of a bipolar transistor. How to read and describe the operation of various solid state devices from a given control schematic is included.

Credit recommendation: In the lower division baccalaureate/associate degree category, 2 semester hours in Electrical Technology (11/87).

Supervisor-Employee Relations (S-202)
(Formerly Supervisor-Employee Relations [S-2])
  Location: *Version 1:* Athens, TX; *Version 2:* Dallas Training Center, Dallas, TX.
  Length: 36 hours (1 week).
  Dates: *Version 1:* September 1981-November 1987; *Version 2:* December 1987-Present.
  Objective: To increase the supervisory skills and understanding of human behavior through problem solving strategies.
  Learning Outcome: Upon successful completion of this course, the student will be able to compare the stereotyped image of the boss of the old days with the reality of today's supervisor; how to organize and conduct a meeting to make it the valuable two-way communication medium it should be; deal with complaints so that workers feel they get a fair hearing; and how the supervisor can help create the feeling of unity.
  Instruction: Includes representing management, understanding people, assigning tasks, teaching employee planning, conducting meetings, handling complaints, administering discipline, and building good relationships. Methodology emphasizes lecture/discussion centered on audiovisuals based upon supervisory problems; 10 hours of outside study assignments required.
  Credit recommendation: *Version 1:* In the lower division baccalaureate/associate degree or upper division baccalaureate category, 3 semester hours in Management or Education (9/82). *Version 2:* In the lower division baccalaureate/associate degree category, 2 semester hours in Management of Education (11/87). NOTE: This course has been reevaluated and continues to meet requirements for credit recommendations.

Supervisory Development (S-1)
  Location: Athens, TX.
  Length: 40 hours (1 week).
  Dates: June 1977-November 1987.
  Objective: To improve the supervisory skills and knowledge of new and experienced supervisors.
  Instruction: Covers leadership qualities and basic styles, leader-follower relationships, shaping of attitudes, methods of on-the-job training, application of leadership concepts, and solving performance problems. Methodology emphasizes lecture discussion with use of case studies; 10 hours outside study required.
  Credit recommendation: In the upper division baccalaureate or lower division baccalaureate/associate degree category, 3 semester hours in Management (9/82).

Three-Phase Motors (E-13)
(Formerly Solid State Devices [E-13])
  Location: Athens, TX.
  Length: 36 hours (1 week).
  Dates: *Version 1:* May 1978-November 1987; *Version 2:* December 1987-Present.
  Objective: To provide the student with an understanding of the characteristics, specifications, starting and operating requirements of three-phase motors.
  Learning Outcome: Upon successful completion of this course, the student will be able to explain the operating characteristics for AC motors and alternators, draw a schematic for an across-the-line magnetic starter and connect diagram in laboratory, explain the operation of a wound-rotor motor and the purpose of secondary resistors, and use basic schematics for operation of reduced voltage starter and auto transformer compensator.
  Instruction: Course covers the principles of three-phase motors and alternators, their operating characteristics and proper maintenance procedures. Twenty hours of outside study assignments.
  Credit recommendation: *Version 1:* In the lower division baccalaureate/associate degree category, 3 semester hours in Electrical Technology (9/82). *Version 2:* In the lower division baccalaureate/associate degree category, 2 semester hours in Electrical Technology (11/87). NOTE: This course has been reevaluated and continues to meet requirements for credit recommendations.

Transformers (E-11)
(Formerly Transformers and Alternating Current Circuits [E-9])
  Location: Athens, TX.
  Length: 36 hours (1 week).
  Dates: May 1977-July 1987.
  Objective: To provide study of the principles of AC currents of circuits containing inductance, capacitance, and resistive loads that are supplied by transformers.
  Instruction: Instruction in single and three-phase AC circuits, concept of electrical impedance, AC power and power-factor determination, principles of transformer operation, connections, and maintenance. Eight hours of

outside study assignments.

Credit recommendation: In the lower division baccalaureate/associate degree category, 3 semester hours in Electrical Troubleshooting (9/82).

Transformers and Circuit Breakers (E-12)
(Formerly Single-Phase Motors [E-12])
Location: Athens, TX.
Length: 36 hours (1 week).
Dates: *Version 1:* March 1978-November 1987; *Version 2:* December 1987-Present.
Objective: To teach the student to understand the characteristics, specifications, proper use, and maintenance of the various types of fractional horsepower, single-phase motors.
Learning Outcome: Upon successful completion of this course, the student will be able to explain what is meant by a polyphase system; draw a schematic for wye and delta connected transformers and connect them in hands-on exercises; calculate voltage and current for various transformer connections, explain differences between two wire and three wire secondary systems, and to adjust the contacts for air and oil circuit breakers using maintenance manuals and schematics.
Instruction: Course covers the principles of single-phase fractional horsepower motors, starting and operating characteristics, and proper maintenance procedures. Included in the course is instruction in synchronous repeaters and servomechanism devices.
Credit recommendation: *Version 1:* In the lower division baccalaureate/associate degree category, 3 semester hours in Industrial Electrical Technology (9/82). *Version 2:* In the lower division baccalaureate/associate degree category, 2 semester hours in Industrial Electrical Technology (11/87). NOTE: This course has been reevaluated and continues to meet requirements for credit recommendations.

Turbine Fundamentals and Operation (O-12)
(Formerly Turbine Fundamentals and Operation [O-9])
Location: Athens, TX.
Length: 36 hours (1 week).
Dates: September 1975-Present.
Objective: To develop basic knowledge of electrical theory, meters, and distribution systems needed to understand electrical systems, turbines, and generators within a power plant.
Learning Outcome: Upon successful completion of this course, the student will be able to learn about various types of basic turbine designs, identify nomenclature for turbine parts, understand protection of turbine speed through control mechanisms and design types, identify supervisory instrumentation need and reasonable limits.
Instruction: Course covers various types of steam turbines and generators in conjunction with basic electricity, three-phase AC generators, transformer principles, voltage and frequency conditions, transmission and distribution, protective equipment, instrumentation and transformers. Proper maintenance practices are also taught.
Credit recommendation: In the lower division baccalaureate/associate degree category, 2 semester hours in Vocational/Technical Education (9/82) (11/87). NOTE: This course has been reevaluated and continues to meet requirements for credit recommendations.

Valves (M-9)
Location: Athens, TX.
Length: 36 hours (1 week).
Dates: August 1987-Present.
Objective: To learn to disassemble, inspect, check seating, packing, and reassemble valves.
Learning Outcome: Upon successful completion of this course, the student will be able to disassemble, inspect, and repair various valves by lapping the seat and checking with Prussian Blue, and to properly reassemble and install valves.
Instruction: Course covers six different valves and their uses. These include safety, gate, globe, diaphragm, butterfly, solenoid, and control valves. Valve packing and types of controllers are also studied.
Credit recommendation: In the lower division baccalaureate/associate degree category, 2 semester hours in Vocational/Technical Education elective (11/87).

Wiring and the National Electrical Code (E-9)
Location: Athens, TX.
Length: 36 hours (1 week).
Dates: January 1983-Present.
Objective: To provide an understanding and interpretation of National Electrical Codes.
Learning Outcome: Upon successful completion of this course, the student will be able to locate specific information (on request) in the current edition of the NEC; practice principles relating to conduit bending; locate and accumulate information (on demand) from architectural and electrical prints for a commercial/industrial installation; apply NEC rules for selection of materials and installation of services, feeders/meins, and branch circuits; and for a given installation, select wire size, insulation type and properly rated devices (I.A.W. the NEC) along with switches, receptacles, low voltage equipment/wiring, and luminaires/lamps.
Instruction: Course covers how to make an electrical installation, selecting wire size, insulation, devices, conduit type and size in accordance with NEC requirements. How to interpret and utilize construction related documents for safe and effective installation of electrical systems is taught. Emphasis is placed on blueprint reading with instruction in motor, air conditioning and lighting installations.
Credit recommendation: In the lower division baccalaureate/associate degree category, 2 semester hours in

Electrical Technology (11/87).

Tritone Music

Tritone Music, founded in 1977 by Michael Freeman, is incorporated as a limited company under the statutes of the Province of Ontario, Canada. In 1987, Tritone Music officially registered as a business in Niagara Falls, New York, under the name of The American Institute of Music. In 1988, Tritone Music was accepted for membership in the Private Career Educational Council of Canada, and was accredited by the National Home Study Council

Tritone Music was founded to prepare students for the music theory examinations of the Canadian Conservatory system. Students take these courses to prepare for entry into college music programs; seek advanced standing or supplementary instruction in their college music programs; aim to write the Advanced Placement Music examinations of the College Board; and to prepare music teachers and students for the Teacher Certification examinations.

The Structured Learning Programs courses are designed according to the examination curriculum requirements of the Canadian Conservatory system. The course content match exactly the Conservatory syllabi and are revised as necessary. Students are provided with all course materials, textbooks, and supplementary materials necessary to complete the courses. Students are gently prodded to complete and return all homework assignments which include short-answer responses, exercises, and essays. Students also take the semiannual national testing of the Canadian Conservatories. Students who do poorly on the examinations are given another opportunity to retake the examination after Tritone Music staff have evaluated a copy of it and have determined where the problem lies. Student records are kept (in both hard copy and soft copy form) concerning all personal information, grades, course completion, examination results, and correspondence.

Source of official student records: In Canada, write to: Tritone Music, 5803 Yonge Street, Suite 106, Willowdale, Ontario, Canada M2M 3V5; in the United States, write to: Tritone Music, P.O. Box 2000, Niagara Falls, New York 14109-2000.

Additional information about the courses: Program on Noncollegiate Sponsored Instruction, The Center for Adult Learning and Educational Credentials, American Council on Education, One Dupont Circle, Washington, D.C. 20036.

Diatonic Harmony
(Grade III Harmony)
Location: Correspondence course.
Length: Self-paced.
Dates: January 1984-Present.
Objective: To provide the student with an understanding of the basic concepts of diatonic harmony.
Learning Outcome: Upon successful completion of this course, the student will be able to write diatonic utilizing four-part figured bass harmony; write short diatonic melodies; and identify simple structural forms.
Instruction: Course covers diatonic triads in major and minor keys; four-part figured bass writing; study of melody, simple formal structures and harmonic analysis.
Credit recommendation: In the lower division baccalaureate/associate degree category, 3 semester hours in Harmony (7/88).

Chromatic Harmony
(Grade IV Harmony)
Location: Correspondence course.
Length: Self-paced.
Dates: January 1984-Present.
Objective: To provide the student with an understanding of the basic concepts of chromatic harmony.
Learning Outcome: Upon successful completion of this course, the student will be able to write chromatic using four-part figured bass harmony; write twelve to sixteen measure melodies; and identify sonata allegro form and fugue.
Instruction: Course covers modulation; most chromatic chords; four-part figured bass writing, including non-harmonic tones; harmonic analysis; study of sonata allegro form and fugue.
Credit recommendation: In the lower division baccalaureate/associate degree category, 3 semester hours in Harmony (7/88).

18th-Century Counterpoint
(Grade IV Counterpoint)
Location: Correspondence course.
Length: Self-paced.
Dates: January 1984-Present.
Objective: To provide the student with a knowledge of two-part 18th-century contrapuntal techniques.
Learning Outcome: Upon successful completion of this course, the student will be able to write two-part counterpoint.
Instruction: Course covers two-part contrapuntal writing including modulation, motivic unity, imitation and invertible counterpoint.
Credit recommendation: In the upper division baccalaureate category, 2 semester hours in Counterpoint (7/88).

Music Appreciation: Music of the 19th Century
(Grade III History)
Location: Correspondence course.
Length: Self-paced.
Dates: January 1986-Present.
Objective: To provide the student with a survey of his-

tory in the 19th century.

Learning Outcome: Upon successful completion of this course, the student will be able to understand 19th-century musical characteristics and genres.

Instruction: Course covers the art song, program music, concerto, nationalism, symphony, opera, and choral music.

Credit recommendation: In the lower division baccalaureate/associate degree category, 2 semester hours in Music Appreciation (7/88). NOTE: This course is for non-music majors.

Music Appreciation: Music from the Middle Ages Through the Classical Period
(Grade IV History)
Location: Correspondence course.
Length: Self-paced.
Dates: January 1986-Present.
Objective: To provide the student with a survey of music from 800 to 1800.
Learning Outcome: Upon successful completion of this course, the student will be able to understand musical characteristics and genres from the Middle Ages through the Classical Period.
Instruction: Topics in this course cover music from the Middle Ages, Renaissance, Baroque, Rococo, and Classical Periods.
Credit recommendation: In the lower division baccalaureate/associate degree category, 2 semester hours in Music Appreciation (7/88). NOTE: This course is for non-music majors.

Music Appreciation: Music of the 20th Century and Music of Canada
(Grade V History)
Location: Correspondence course.
Length: Self-paced.
Dates: January 1986-Present.
Objective: To provide the student with a survey of 20th-century music as well as the music of Canada.
Learning Outcome: Upon successful completion of this course, the student will be able to understand musical characteristics and genres of 20th-century and Canadian music.
Instruction: Course covers impressionism, polytonality, atonality, electronic music, aleatoric music, jazz, and the music of Canada.
Credit recommendation: In the lower division baccalaureate/associate degree category, 2 semester hours in Music Appreciation (7/88). NOTE: This course is for non-music majors.

UAW—Chrysler National Training Center

See CHRYSLER INSTITUTE ASSOCIATE DEGREE PROGRAM

UAW—Ford National Development and Training Center

See FORD NATIONAL DEVELOPMENT AND TRAINING CENTER

Unisys Corporation

Unisys is a world leader in the electronics-based information systems industry. The Corporation and its subsidiaries serve customers operating in key industry sectors, including financial manufacturing, government, education, health care, hospitality, distribution, and services.

Principal Unisys products include computers and computer-based systems, office automation systems, media products, special purpose products and services, peripheral devices, business forms and office supplies, and a range of applications software products and professional services.

Nearly 64,000 people are employed by Unisys and its subsidiaries, some 6,500 of them scientist and engineers. Marketing operations are conducted in nearly 100 countries through 1,200 marketing and support offices. Engineering and manufacturing operations include 64 major facilities located in 13 countries.

Source of official student records: Corporate Education Service, Unisys Corporation, One Unisys Place, Suite 3-C-83, Detroit, Michigan 48232. Source of official student records for Field Engineering Courses: Manager, Field Engineering Education, Unisys Corporation, 707 West Milwaukee Avenue, Room 1M26, Detroit, Michigan 48202.

Additional information about the courses: Program on Noncollegiate Sponsored Instruction, The Center for Adult Learning and Educational Credentials, American Council on Education, One Dupont Circle, Washington, D.C. 20036.

S3000 Document Processor (382861)
Location: Unisys Corporation Training Center, Lisle, IL.
Length: 192 hours (24 days, 8 hours per day).
Dates: January 1983-Present.
Objective: This course is designed to provide the student with a working knowledge of the S3000 document processing system. The student should be able to complete

most tasks associated with the operation, maintenance, and repair of the S3000 system. The course is laboratory-based with these objectives in mind.

Instruction: The course is designed in a lab/lecture format. The topics of processor-to-data communications associated with the S3000 MTR are discussed in lab then review and/or related experiments are performed.

Credit recommendation: In the upper division baccalaureate category, 4 semester hours in Computer Science or Electrical Engineering (11/85).

Fundamentals of Data Communications (385050)

Location: Unisys Corporation Training Centers, Lisle, IL; Malvern, PA; and El Monte, CA.

Length: 40 hours (1 week).

Dates: August 1982-Present.

Objective: To provide students with the skills and knowledge required for the maintenance of a Data Communications Network, and the isolation of systems failure to a major component.

Instruction: Basic data communication format, RS-232C interface signals and sequence of operations, troubleshooting RS-232C interface problems, the basic principles of multipoint line discipline, and modems and lease lines are covered. Lectures and lab exercises emphasize troubleshooting a Data Communications Network, using specialized digital test equipment.

Credit recommendation: In the lower division baccalaureate/associate degree category, 2 semester hours in Data Communications (10/84).

B7900 Hardware and Maintenance (337909)

Location: Unisys Corporation Training Center, Lisle, IL.

Length: 232 hours (5 weeks and 4 days).

Dates: January 1985-Present.

Objective: To teach students the basic skills to perform preventive maintenance, execute online test routines, verify proper operation and repair the hardware for the B7900.

Instruction: Lectures and laboratories are geared to present the IDA functions and procedures. Students should be able to perform fault isolation procedure on the auxiliary processor (AP), host data unit (HDU), input-output data communications (IODU), and input-output system module (IOSM). With the basic skills developed in this course, students will be able to perform preventive maintenance, verify proper operation, and repair the hardware for the B7900.

Credit recommendation: In the upper division baccalaureate category, 5 semester hours in Computer Science or Hardware Maintenance (11/85).

Introduction to COBOL Processor Operation and Maintenance (332900)

Location: Unisys Corporation Training Centers, El Monte, CA; and Malvern, PA.

Length: 184 hours (23 days).

Dates: June 1982-Present.

Objective: To teach students the skills and knowledge needed to install, maintain, and troubleshoot a super minicomputer designed for data processing applications.

Instruction: Topics studied include system architecture, processor unit, memory unit power subsystem, console operation, I/O operation, system maintenance, use of diagnostic programs, and the skills needed to troubleshoot to the component level in the processor and memory. Lecture/laboratory and simulated exercises. Heavy emphasis on laboratory experience. The laboratory exercises are performed on a system with a 32-bit work length that can perform only byte processing, and the system is designed to optimize the execution of COBOL programs in a time sharing environment.

Credit recommendation: In the lower division baccalaureate/associate degree category, 4 semester hours in Computer Technology or Electronic Technology or the upper division baccalaureate category, 3 semester hours in Computer Technology or Electronic Technology (10/84). NOTE: Credit applies to BSET non-ABET approved program.

Introduction to Computer Mainframe Operation and Maintenance (335900)

Location: Unisys Corporation Training Center, Lisle, IL.

Length: 120 hours (15 days).

Dates: March 1982-Present.

Objective: To provide students with the basic skills and knowledge required to install, maintain, and troubleshoot a typical computer mainframe.

Instruction: Lectures and laboratories are based on a single processor machine using a 56-bit work, stack operation, virtual memory extension, and a single-bus architecture designed for single task, multi-user operation. Topics include an overview of systems architecture, use of systems software, operator console operation, processor operation, memory operation, I/O operations, maintenance procedures, power subsystems, maintenance logs, diagnostic programs, and system troubleshooting.

Credit recommendation: In the upper division baccalaureate category, 4 semester hours in Computer Mainframe Operations and Maintenance (10/84). NOTE: Credit applies in a BSET non-ABET approved program.

Introduction to Computer Systems Operation (388100)

Location: Unisys Corporation Training Center, Lisle, IL.

Length: 80 hours (2 weeks).

Dates: July 1981-Present.

Objective: To introduce students to basic computer systems concepts.

Instruction: Systems software and its installation, systems storage structure, file orientation and intrinsic systems utilities are covered. Lectures and laboratories designed to facilitate student use of operating systems commands and tasks of a computer operator.

Credit recommendation: In the lower division baccalaureate/associate degree category, 2 semester hours in Computer Operations or Data Processing (10/84).

Introduction to Disk Pack Drive Operation and Maintenance (333400)

Location: Unisys Corporation Training Centers, Lisle, IL; El Monte, CA.

Length: 56 hours (7 days).

Dates: May 1984-Present.

Objective: To teach students the skills and knowledge required for the installation, maintenance, and troubleshooting of a disk pack drive.

Instruction: Topics include drive characteristics, media format, installation procedures, use of disk drive exerciser, use of diagnostic maintenance logs, head alignment, preventive maintenance, and troubleshooting control logic, servo subsystem, read/write subsystem, and power supply. Lectures and laboratories emphasizing the operation, installation, preventive maintenance, and adjustment of disk pack drives.

Credit recommendation: In the lower division baccalaureate/associate degree category, 2 semester hours in Disk Pack Drive Maintenance and Operations (10/84). NOTE: Credit applies in a non-ABET approved program. Only 1 semester hour recommended if student has credit for Unisys Course 320532 or 320536.

Introduction to Dual-Processor Mini-Computer Operation and Maintenance (321965)

Location: Unisys Corporation Training Center, Lisle, IL.

Length: 80 hours (10 days).

Dates: September 1983-Present.

Objective: To teach students the skills and knowledge needed to install, maintain, and troubleshoot a dual-processor minicomputer system designed to provide multi-user and/or multi-processing operation.

Instruction: Topics include basic operational concepts, use of the operator terminal, use of operating system software, I/O operations, disk subsystem controller operation, maintenance procedures, use of diagnostic programs, memory subsystem operation, remote diagnostic features, use of system documentation, and system troubleshooting to the module level. Lectures and laboratories with emphasis on systems diagnostics and test routines.

Credit recommendation: In the upper division baccalaureate category, 2 semester hours in Dual-Process Minicomputer Operation and Maintenance (10/84). NOTE: Credit for 321966 excludes credit for this course.

Introduction to Dual-Processor Mini-Computer Operation and Maintenance (321966)

Location: Unisys Corporation Training Center, Lisle, IL.

Length: 40 hours (5 days).

Dates: September 1983-Present.

Objective: To teach students the skills and knowledge needed to install, maintain and troubleshoot a dual-processor mini-computer system designed to provide multi-user and/or multi-processing operation.

Instruction: Topics include basic operational concepts, use of the operator terminal, use of operating system software, I/O operations, disk subsystem controller operation, maintenance procedures, use of diagnostic programs, memory subsystem operation, remote diagnostic features, use of system documentation, and system troubleshooting to the module level. Lectures and laboratories with emphasis on systems diagnostics and test routines.

Credit recommendation: In the upper division baccalaureate category, 2 semester hours in Dual-Process Mini-Computer Operation and Maintenance (10/84). NOTE: Credit for 321965 excludes credit for this course.

Introduction to Fixed Disk Drive Operation and Maintenance of Medium and Small Systems (320536)

Location: Unisys Corporation Training Centers, Lisle, IL; El Monte, CA; and Malvern, PA.

Length: 40 hours (5 days).

Dates: January 1981-Present.

Objective: To develop the students' skills and knowledge required for the installation and maintenance of fixed drive magnetic disk drive.

Instruction: Topics include drive characteristics, power sequencing operation, servo logic operation, servo timing, read/write logic, maintenance procedures, mechanical adjustments, and troubleshooting. Lectures and laboratory exercises stressing installation, maintenance and repair procedures.

Credit recommendation: In the lower division baccalaureate/associate degree category, 1 semester hour in Disk Operation and Maintenance (10/84). NOTE: Credit applies in BSET non-ABET approved program. Credit for this course excludes credit for 320532.

Introduction to Fixed Disk Drive Operation and Maintenance of Small Systems (320532)

Location: Unisys Corporation Training Centers, Lisle, IL; El Monte, CA; and Malvern, PA.

Length: 40 hours (5 days).

Dates: January 1981-Present.

Objective: To develop the students' skills and knowledge required for the installation and maintenance of fixed drive magnetic disk drive.

Instruction: Topics include drive characteristics, power sequencing operation, servo logic operation, servo timing, read/write logic, maintenance procedures, mechanical adjustments, and troubleshooting. Lectures and laboratory exercises stressing installation, maintenance and repair procedures.

Credit recommendation: In the lower division baccalaureate/associate degree category, 1 semester hour in Disk Operation and Maintenance (10/84). NOTE: Credit applies in BSET non-ABET approved program. Credit for this course excludes credit for 320536.

Introduction to Large Computer Mainframes Operation and Maintenance (337800)

Location: Unisys Corporation Training Center, Malvern, PA.

Length: 192 hours (24 days).

Dates: November 1980-Present.

Objective: To teach students the skills and knowledge needed to install, maintain, and troubleshoot a large computer and mainframe.

Instruction: The course covers a system using three central processors, three I/O data channels and a bus matrix. Topics include overall system operation, operating procedures, maintenance procedures, diagnostic programs, online peripheral testing, and system level troubleshooting. This course is taught by lecture and lab exercises. Approximately 25 percent of the class time is devoted to lecture.

Credit recommendation: In the upper division baccalaureate or lower division baccalaureate/associate degree category, 4 semester hours in Electronic Technology or Computer Maintenance or Computer Science (10/84). NOTE: BSET non-ABET approved.

Introduction to Multi-Processor System Maintenance (320901)

Location: Unisys Corporation Training Center, Lisle, IL.

Length: 160 hours (4 weeks).

Dates: August 1982-Present.

Objective: To familiarize students with installation and maintenance of a multi-user, multi-tasking computer system.

Instruction: Elements of system software are covered and utilized in conjunction with isolating hardware failures related to various subsystems and/or component parts. This course is conducted using a traditional lecture/laboratory structure with the document component instruction assigned to laboratory work in diagnostic programs for maintenance, processor subsystem operation, ROM memory features, and I/O interface operation and troubleshooting. The laboratory exercises are conducted on a system using 8-bit words and four to eight processors. One processor is allocated to executing the operating system. The processors provide concurrent operation. (Prerequisite to 387610).

Credit recommendation: In the upper division baccalaureate category, 5 semester hours in a non-ABET approved Engineering Technology Program with a computer specialty option (10/84).

Introduction to Non-Impact Printers (339193)

Location: Unisys Corporation Training Center, Lisle, IL.

Length: 80 hours (10 days).

Dates: May 1983-Present.

Objective: To teach students the skills and knowledge needed to install, maintain, and troubleshoot a non-impact ink printer.

Instruction: Topics studied include operating procedures, ink subsystem operation, heater components, logic circuits, preventive maintenance, and troubleshooting procedures. Lecture/laboratory and simulation exercises with actual equipment. (Prerequisite B9134/37/38, 331309).

Credit recommendation: In the lower division baccalaureate/associate degree category, 1 semester hour in Electromechanical Technology (10/84).

Introduction to Software Concepts (388006)

Location: Unisys Corporation Training Center, Lisle, IL.

Length: 120 hours (15 days).

Dates: January 1979-Present.

Objective: To introduce students to software concepts for computer maintenance technicians. Students study the message processing language used as part of the computer management system, operation system, a block structured language derivative of PASCAL and ALGOL.

Instruction: Topics studied include file organization and access, file types, arrays and indexing, compiler operation, simple programming exercises, program dump analysis, and the use of operating system features as a diagnostic aid. Lecture/laboratories.

Credit recommendation: In the lower division baccalaureate/associate degree and upper division baccalaureate category, 4 semester hours in Electronics, Computer Maintenance, or Computer Science (10/84). NOTE: BSET non-ABET approved.

Introduction to Tape Subsystems (333312)

Location: Unisys Corporation Training Center, Lisle, IL.

Length: 112 hours (14 days).

Dates: April 1984-Present.

Objective: To introduce students to the principles, operation, and maintenance of a tape controller unit and associated drive.

Instruction: Key topics include RAM loaders, tape control unit power sequencing, self-diagnostic testing procedures, reel and capstan control systems including servo operation and pneumatic system operation. Lecture/laboratory with approximately 38 hours of lecture and 57 hours of laboratory.

Credit recommendation: In the lower division baccalaureate/associate degree category, 3 semester hours in Computer Peripherals (10/84).

Introduction to Teaching Methods (399100)

Location: Unisys Corporation Training Centers nationwide.

Length: 80 hours (2 weeks).

Dates: March 1982-Present.

Objective: To introduce students to principles and practice of modern teaching methodology.

Instruction: The science of learning is reviewed, and behavioral objectives are studied relative to preparation and presentation of lecture/laboratory sessions. Emphasis is on the preparation of instructional objectives. The method of instruction includes traditional lecture/discussion format. In addition, students are supervised in the preparation and presentation of lecture/laboratory simulated exercises.

Credit recommendation: In the upper division baccalaureate category, 3 semester hours in Instructional Methods (10/84).

Large Mainframe Central Processing Operation and Maintenance (337803)

Location: Unisys Corporation Training Center, Malvern, PA.

Length: 232 hours (29 days).

Dates: August 1981-Present.

Objective: To provide students with the skills and knowledge needed to install, maintain, and troubleshoot the central processor modules of large computer mainframes.

Instruction: The laboratory exercises are conducted on a system with a 52-bit word length, three processors, three I/O data channels, and a bus matrix designed to operate in a multi-processing, time sharing environment. Topics studied include stack operations, off-line processor testing with a maintenance panel, program control unit, data reference unit, instruction execution, store queue, memory access, bus control, installation, use of diagnostic programs, installation, use of the logic, and other instruments needed to troubleshoot to the component level. Lecture/laboratory and simulation exercises.

Credit recommendation: In the upper division baccalaureate category, 5 semester hours in Mainframe Processor Operations and Maintenance - BSET (10/84).

CP3680/CP3685 Maintenance (387523)

Location: Unisys Corporation Training Center, Lisle, IL.

Length: 112 hours (3 weeks).

Dates: June 1984-Present.

Objective: To teach students a working knowledge of the CP3680/CP3685 and its related systems such as disk, tape, and terminals.

Instruction: Lectures and laboratories are geared to provide students with the basic skills in operating the CP3680/CP3685. Topics include the installation of hardware, the configuration of the operational system, and system maintenance.

Credit recommendation: In the upper division baccalaureate category, 3 semester hours in Computer Science or Electrical Engineering (11/85).

Maintenance and Operation (333401)

Location: Unisys Corporation Training Center, Lisle, IL.

Length: 40 hours (1 week).

Dates: November 1983-Present.

Objective: To develop the students' knowledge and skills necessary to install and operate a B9494-5/10 fixed drive in the B2000-7000 system configuration and perform the required preventive maintenance; to develop the students' skills required to isolate failures in the drive and replace components; to enable students to perform head disk assembly replacement.

Instruction: Lecture/lab format is used to cover the procedures necessary to repair any B9494-5/10 fixed disk drive in subsystem with B9387-51/52 for medium and large systems. The course covers such topics as drive overview, maintenance procedures, power-up sequences, CM/DMS servo-logic and timing, and read/write logic.

Credit recommendation: In the upper division baccalaureate category, 1 semester hour in Computer Science or Electrical Engineering (11/85).

Maintenance and Operation of Character Recognition System (339196)

Location: Unisys Corporation Training Center, Lisle, IL.

Length: 120 hours (15 days).

Dates: June 1983-Present.

Objective: To teach students the skills and knowledge needed to install, maintain, and troubleshoot an electromechanical character recognition system used to process and sort encoded documents or 51 column cards.

Instruction: Topics include basic system overview, motor controls, character recognition processing, document feeder and separator operation, impact endorser operation, system timing, preventive maintenance, installation procedures, and troubleshooting. The course is taught by lecture and laboratory exercises. Approximately 60 percent of the class activity is laboratory exercises.

Credit recommendation: In lower division baccalaureate/associate degree category, 3 semester hours in Electronics or Electromechanical Technology (10/84).

Microcomputer System Maintenance (387610)

Location: Unisys Corporation Training Center, Lisle, IL.

Length: 160 hours (4 weeks).

Dates: March 1982-July 1985.

Objective: To teach students the skills and knowledge needed to install, troubleshoot, and maintain a typical microcomputer system.

Instruction: Topics include software system operation, use of diagnostic programs for maintenance, basic system troubleshooting, peripheral troubleshooting, preventive maintenance, system installation procedures, and use of maintenance documentation. This course is taught by lecture and laboratory exercises. Approximately 65 percent of the class time is devoted to laboratory activity. The laboratory exercises are based on an 8-bit machine implemented with four LSI integrated circuits including a memory extension unit to provide an address space of one megabyte.

Credit recommendation: In the upper division baccalaureate category, 3 semester hours in Computer System Architecture and 2 semester hours in Peripheral Device Theory and Operation (10/84).

Microfilm Module Installation and Maintenance (382860)

Location: Unisys Corporation Training Center, Lisle, IL.

Length: 56 hours (7 days).

Dates: December 1978-Present.

Objective: To provide students with the ability to isolate and repair any malfunction in the microfilm module of a computer supported document provision system.

Instruction: Lecture and extensive laboratories to provide the student with the requisite skills for microfilm repair including the photography and processing of document images on film. Topics include microfilm interface operation, controller operation, use of microfilm subsystem exerciser, film processing techniques, lens focusing adjustments, handling and care of optics, subsystem maintenance, and troubleshooting procedures.

Credit recommendation: In the lower division baccalaureate/associate degree category, 1 semester hour in Electromechanical Technology or Photography (10/84). NOTE: Credit is applicable to a non-ABET approved program.

Operations and Software (337908)

Location: Unisys Corporation Training Center, Lisle, IL.

Length: 232 hours (6 weeks).

Dates: October 1984-Present.

Objective: To provide students with the necessary basic skills to program, compile, and execute work flow language for the system; to perform any operator task to operate and maintain the 7900 system equipment; and to update, install, troubleshoot and otherwise maintain the equipment and software.

Instruction: Students should be able to write programs for work flow, update and install software. Skills will be developed to enable students to develop performance and availability reports. Troubleshooting for general system failures as well as repair for bringing the system back online are an integral part of the instruction.

Credit recommendation: In the upper division baccalaureate category, 5 semester hours in Computer Science (11/85).

Principles and Practice of Course Development (399202)

Location: Unisys Corporation Training Centers nationwide.

Length: 64 hours (8 days).

Dates: March 1982-Present.

Objective: To provide students with the ability to formulate course and instructional objectives based on a formalized needs analysis study.

Instruction: Topics include developing an audience description, task analysis preparation, design specification, conducting design reviews, preparing practice and evaluation plans, developing student and instructor guides, and the preparation of computer-aided instruction. The method of instruction includes lectures, supervised workshops, and student presentations emphasizing the design, construction, review, and evaluation processes.

Credit recommendation: In the upper division baccalaureate category, 3 semester hours in Principles of Course Development (10/84).

United States Army Intelligence and Threat Analysis Center

The U.S. Army Intelligence and Threat Analysis Center (ITAC) provides to the Department of the Army and, as required, to the Department of Defense (DOD) comprehensive general intelligence and counterintelligence analysis and production reflecting the capabilities, vulnerabilities, and threats to the Army from foreign military and security forces—current and projected. This mission remains the same in war and peace. Although the Center's studies are produced mainly for Army and DOD decision makers, the national intelligence community also relies on them. The studies—geared to enable better development of plans, policies, and capabilities for controlling potential conflicts—range from analyses of foreign military capabilities, hostile intelligence, and terrorist threats to potential battlefield environments.

The Introduction to Strategic Intelligence Production course was developed with assistance from ITAC's reserve detachment commanders, the National Defense University, the Naval War College, the Defense Intelligence Agency, the Defense Intelligence College, the National Cryptologic School/National Security Agency, and the U.S. Army Intelligence Center and School. Hand-outs, bibliographies, references, referrals, and lesson plans are provided for the students. Selected blocks of instruction are presented by guest instructors from the Office of the Joint Chiefs of Staff, the Defense Intelligence Agency, the National Photographic Interpretation Center, the National Security Agency, the Office of the Deputy Chief of Staff for Intelligence, and the U.S. Army Foreign Service and Technology Center.

Instructors are nominated based on their educational background and/or experience in the subject area. Instructors are evaluated by pre-briefing the course manager or their branch and division chiefs and also by student evaluations. Students have three chances to complete satisfactorily weekly objective exams, two writing assignments, and two briefings. Students who have not demonstrated an acceptable level of learning have the opportunity to attend the course again.

Source of official student records: CDR, USAITAC, ATTN: AIAIT-AA (MAJ Heverly), Building 203, Stop 314, Washington Navy Yard, Washington, D.C. 20374-2136.

Additional information about the courses: Program on Noncollegiate Sponsored Instruction, The Center for Adult Learning and Educational Credentials, American Council on Education, One Dupont Circle, Washington, D.C. 20036.

Introduction to Strategic Intelligence Production (Formerly Introduction to Strategic Intelligence Analysis)
   Location: Washington, D.C.
   Length: *Version 1:* 105 hours (3 weeks); *Version 2:* 70 hours (2 weeks).
   Dates: October 1988-Present.
   Objective: To provide the student with an understanding of the fundamentals of strategic intelligence production.
   Learning Outcome: Upon successful completion of this course, the student will be able to conduct research using online information data bases; access the intelligence collection system; utilize imagery, signals, and human intelligence; validate data; develop strategic intelligence forecasts; relate managerial processes to strategic intelligence production; present effective findings and recommendations.
   Instruction: Course covers national foreign intelligence community; elements of strategic intelligence analysis; intelligence collection management; research support resources; imagery, signals, and human intelligence; military capabilities and scientific and technical intelligence; financial management; long-range forecasting; modeling; ground forces organization, equipment, and operations; and effective briefing and writing. Methodology includes lecture, discussion, group project, readings, research and writing exercises, simulated briefings, and examinations.

Credit recommendation: *Version 1:* In the upper division baccalaureate category, 3 semester hours in Military Science, National Security Affairs, Political Science, or Public Policy (2/89). *Version 2:* In the upper division baccalaureate category, 2 semester hours in Military Science, National Security Affairs, Political Science, or Public Policy (2/89).

United States Army Materiel Command - AMC (Formerly DARCOM - United States Army Materiel Development and Readiness Command)

The U.S. Army Materiel Command (AMC) has the School of Engineering and Logistics at the Red River Army Depot; the School serves as an on-site education facility for interns. The present missions of the School are to provide training in the six career fields: Supply Management, Maintenance Management, Maintainability, Safety, Product/Production, and Quality/Reliability. Additionally, the School teaches the Pre-Engineering Physical Science Program; provides special course, research, and consulting services; and participates in writing AMC publications. All the programs prepare the AMC interns for journeyman level performance in the various career fields at AMC.

Source of official student records: Chief, Department of Engineering or Chief, Department of Materiel Readiness, AMC School of Engineering and Logistics, Red River Army Depot, Texarkana, Texas 75507.

Additional information about the courses: Program on Noncollegiate Sponsored Education, The Center for Adult Learning and Educational Credentials, American Council on Education, One Dupont Circle, Washington, D.C. 20036.

SUPPLY MANAGEMENT PROGRAM

The Supply Management Program consists of three phases. Phase I has 1,520 hours (38 weeks) of formal academic instruction at the School of Engineering and Logistics in Texarkana, Texas. This training is standard training for all career interns. It is supplemented by appropriate on-the-job training at the local depot activity and temporary duty travel to selected activities. Phase II consists of basic skill development, rotational, on-the-job training in the Supply Management and related career fields at the intern's permanent duty location. The length of training provided during Phase II varies from 14 to 40 weeks. Phase III consists of intensified specialized training in the functional area to which the career intern is assigned upon completion of the total training program. The graduate is prepared for positions in General Supply, Inventory Management, Distribution Facilities and Storage Management, and Preservation and Packaging.

Acquisition and Contracting
  Location: School of Engineering and Logistics, Red River Army Depot.
  Length: 20 hours (1 week).
  Dates: January 1975-Present.
  Objective: To enable the student to comprehend the acquisition process for Military equipment. Procurement Law and relationships to all Logistics areas.
  Instruction: Lecture and discussion. Evaluation by examination. Course provides an introduction to the acquisition of materiel including the legislative framework, formal advertising, negotiations, types of contracts, and contracting officers' responsibilities.
  Credit recommendation: In the graduate degree category, 1 semester hour in Business Management (6/84).

Administrative Systems and Design
  Location: School of Engineering and Logistics, Red River Army Depot.
  Length: 50 hours (2½ weeks).
  Dates: June 1980-Present.
  Objective: To teach the student the planning procedures for office communications and paperwork flow in an organization.
  Instruction: Lecture and student project. Project presentation is critiqued. Course covers functions of management and the role of administrative systems. The student uses management analysis techniques, including forms of analysis and layout planning.
  Credit recommendation: In the graduate degree category, 2 semester hours in Management (6/84).

Cataloging
  Location: School of Engineering and Logistics, Red River Army Depot.
  Length: 20 hours (1 week).
  Dates: January 1975-Present.
  Objective: To enable the student to comprehend the Federal and Army cataloging procedures.
  Instruction: Lecture, discussion, and laboratory exercises. Evaluation by examination. Course covers application of Federal and Army cataloging procedures to management-cataloging related problems.
  Credit recommendation: In the lower division baccalaureate/associate degree category, 1 semester hour in Management (6/84).

Defense Inventory Simulation (DIMSIM)
  Location: School of Engineering and Logistics, Red River Army Depot.
  Length: 50 hours (2 weeks).
  Dates: January 1975-Present.
  Objective: A computer simulation which requires students to analyze complex logistical data and to make decision on various logistics functions. With emphasis on Inventory Management.
  Instruction: Lecture and simulation exercises. Evaluation by simulation performance. Course includes practical application of management tools and techniques such as inventory policies, variables safety levels, moving average, exponential smoothing, and planned overhaul program.
  Credit recommendation: In the graduate degree category, 2 semester hours in Management (6/84).

Department of Army Publication
  Location: School of Engineering and Logistics, Red River Army Depot.
  Length: 40 hours (2 weeks).
  Dates: January 1975-Present.
  Objective: To teach the student the policies, responsibility and procedures governing official publications and blank forms used by the Army.
  Instruction: Lecture, laboratory, and workshops are all used. Evaluation is through exercises and examinations. Military and Federal specifications and stock standards are covered.
  Credit recommendation: In the upper division baccalaureate category, 2 semester hours in Management (6/84).

Direct Support/General Support Supply Procedures
  Location: School of Engineering and Logistics, Red River Army Depot.
  Length: 30 hours (2 weeks).
  Dates: January 1975-Present.
  Objective: To teach the student what the Direct Support/General Support Supply Procedures system is and to calculate supply performance of a Direct Supply Unit in terms of supply satisfaction and accommodation.
  Instruction: Lecture. Evaluation by examination. Course covers concepts of demand supported stockage and economic order quantity; requisitioning objectives, reorder points, safety levels, order ship times and operating levels at the Direct Support Unit level; retention policy; stock record keeping policy and procedures; replenishment, issue and receiving; air lines of communication; location survey/inventory procedures; alternate methods of supply; methods of measuring supply support and performance; and class of supply structure.
  Credit recommendation: In the upper division baccalaureate category, 1 semester hour in Management (6/84).

Financial Management
  Location: School of Engineering and Logistics, Red River Army Depot.
  Length: 15 hours (5 3-hour meetings).
  Dates: January 1975-Present.
  Objective: To provide the student with a knowledge of

the overall DOD and Army financial management structure.

Instruction: Lecture and classroom exercises. Evaluation by examination. Course concentrates on those aspects of financial management, such as the stock funds, that are most affected by the actions of graduate interns.

Credit recommendation: In the graduate degree category, 1 semester hour in Financial Management (6/84).

Integrated Logistics Support

Location: School of Engineering and Logistics, Red River Army Depot.
Length: 60 hours (3 weeks).
Dates: January 1975-Present.
Objective: To teach the student the phases and possible problem areas in the life cycle of an end item.
Instruction: Lecture and discussion. Evaluation by examination. Course includes the interfaces that occur internally within AMC, and externally with other elements in the DA and DOD.
Credit recommendation: In the graduate degree category, 3 semester hours in Management (6/84).

Introduction to CCSS
(Commodity Command Standard System)

Location: School of Engineering and Logistics, Red River Army Depot.
Length: 20 hours (1 week).
Dates: January 1975-Present.
Objective: To provide the student with a knowledge of the Commodity Command Standard System for Inventory Management.
Instruction: Lecture, discussion, and laboratory exercises. Evaluation by examination. Course describes how provisioning, cataloging, supply control, maintenance, and international logistics are performed within the Commodity Command Standard System.
Credit recommendation: In the upper division baccalaureate category, 1 semester hour in Management (6/84).

Issues

Location: School of Engineering and Logistics, Red River Army Depot.
Length: 20 hours (1 week).
Dates: January 1975-Present.
Objective: To provide the student with a comprehensive study of the standard depot system stock control procedures used in processing materiel release orders and related supply documents and issuing materiel within the AMC distribution system.
Instruction: Lecture, discussion, laboratory exercises, and research. Evaluation by examination. Course covers terms, policies, responsibilities, and procedures used for materiel release order processing of general supplies, shipment planning, stock selection, issues and warehouse details consolidation, packing and marking, outloading operations, special processing, related documentation, performance reporting. Depot Direct Support System (DSS) procedures, containerization, and preparation of materiel for Consolidation Containerization Points (CCP).

Credit recommendation: In the upper division baccalaureate category, 1 semester hour in Industrial Management (6/84).

Logistic Support Exercise

Location: School of Engineering and Logistics, Red River Army Depot.
Length: 40 hours (1 week).
Dates: January 1975-Present.
Objective: To allow the student to test management skills in the initial and follow-up support of a weapon system.
Instruction: Lecture and extensive use of practical exercises. Evaluation by analyzing exercise results. A management decision making exercise in which the student plays a particular role in support of an end item. The roles the student must play are maintenance manager, item manager, comptroller, and battalion supply manager. Costs are affixed to all decisions made by the student.
Credit recommendation: In the graduate degree category, 3 semester hours in Management (6/84).

Maintenance Management

Location: School of Engineering and Logistics, Red River Army Depot.
Length: 23 hours (1 week).
Dates: January 1975-Present.
Objective: To provide the student with a knowledge of the entire Army maintenance system.
Instruction: Lecture, discussion and laboratory. Evaluation by examination. Course covers the varied aspects of equipment maintenance from the types of maintenance accomplished, the organizations involved and reponsibilities at each level, the proper initiation of a maintenance program, through the financial and procedural means of controlling maintenance costs and production. Army Maintenance systems and coding procedures are discussed.
Credit recommendation: In the upper division baccalaureate category, 1 semester hour in Management (6/84).

Management Analysis

Location: School of Engineering and Logistics, Red River Army Depot.
Length: 64 hours (2 weeks).
Dates: January 1975-Present.
Objective: To provide the student with the theory and application of qualitative and quantitative methods which can be used in conducting a decision risk analysis.
Instruction: Lecture and laboratory. Case studies are

emphasized. Evaluation through examination. Course includes analytical techniques, decision analysis, subjective estimating network techniques, and simulation.

Credit recommendation: In the upper division baccalaureate category, 2 semester hours in Management and in the graduate degree category, 1 semester hour in Management (6/84).

Management Information Systems

Location: School of Engineering and Logistics, Red River Army Depot.
Length: 80 hours (4 weeks).
Dates: January 1975-Present.
Objective: To provide the student with a knowledge of Advanced Data Processing (ADP) systems so that students will be able to program a computer, understand computer terminology, and develop automated systems.
Instruction: Lecture and laboratory. Evaluation by weekly examinations. Course covers FORTRAN statements: input/output statements, control statements, subscripted variables, DO loops; basic FORTRAN program operation; disk input/output. An overview of computer technology is also given.
Credit recommendation: In the graduate degree category, 3 semester hours in Data Processing (6/84).

Management of Major Items

Location: School of Engineering and Logistics, Red River Army Depot.
Length: 40 hours (1 week).
Dates: June 1980-Present.
Objective: To introduce the student to methods used in managing major items.
Instruction: Lecture and laboratory. Evaluation by examination. Funding, computing requirements and the Army Materiel Plan are included.
Credit recommendation: In the upper division baccalaureate category, 2 semester hours in Management (6/84).

Management of Secondary Items

Location: School of Engineering and Logistics, Red River Army Depot.
Length: 120 hours (6 weeks).
Dates: January 1975-Present.
Objective: To introduce the student to the techniques of Inventory Management of secondary items at the wholesale level.
Instruction: Lecture and laboratory exercises. Evaluation through weekly examinations. Course includes management of secondary items; organization for inventory management; selective item management; data integration and standardization; commodity command standard system structures; return disposal, output products, and file structure.
Credit recommendation: In the graduate degree category, 3 semester hours in Management (6/84).

Military Standard Data Systems (MSDS)

Location: School of Engineering and Logistics, Red River Army Depot.
Length: 60 hours (3 weeks).
Dates: January 1975-Present.
Objective: To teach the student the various military standard systems, such as MILSTRIP, MILSTRAP, MILSTAMP, UMMIPS, MILSCAP, and MILSTEP.
Instruction: Lecture and laboratory. Evaluation through examinations, presentations, and projects. The development, scope, relationship, and use of each of these systems is covered. Forms, formats, and codes applicable to each of these systems are also covered.
Credit recommendation: In the upper division baccalaureate category, 1 semester hour in Military Science (6/84).

Oral Communications

Location: School of Engineering and Logistics, Red River Army Depot.
Length: 60 hours (3 weeks).
Dates: January 1975-Present.
Objective: To provide students with an awareness of the importance of effective communications within any organization and to provide practice in making prepared presentations, and briefings.
Instruction: Lecture and student presentations. Evaluation of student presentations and weekly examinations.
Credit recommendation: In the lower division baccalaureate/associate degree category, 3 semester hours in Speech (6/84).

Physical Inventory

Location: School of Engineering and Logistics, Red River Army Depot.
Length: 20 hours (1 week).
Dates: January 1975-Present.
Objective: To provide the student with a knowledge of the physical inventory system, with interface between the depots and accountable supply distribution activities.
Instruction: Lecture, discussion, laboratory exercises, and research. Evaluation by examination. Course covers terms and definitions applicable to the physical inventory at all supply levels for general supplies and ammunition. Location survey procedures, types of inventories, location record audit/match procedures, adjustments of records, performance reporting, registration of small arms, Materiel Release Details and Physical Inventory Quality Control are explained.
Credit recommendation: In the upper division baccalaureate category, 1 semester hour in Industrial Management (6/84).

Preservation and Packaging
Location: School of Engineering and Logistics, Red River Army Depot.
Length: 20 hours (1 week).
Dates: January 1975-Present.
Objective: To provide the student with the capability for working as a preservation and packaging specialist in the GS-2032 career field and related areas.
Instruction: Lecture and laboratory exercises. Evaluation by examination. Methods of cleaning preservation and packaging in accordance with military and civilian specifications studied in depth.
Credit recommendation: In the upper division baccalaureate category, 1 semester hour in Industrial Management (6/84).

Production Planning and Control
Location: School of Engineering and Logistics, Red River Army Depot.
Length: 40 hours (2 weeks).
Dates: January 1975-Present.
Objective: To instruct the student in missions and functions of an Army Production Planning and Control organization.
Instruction: Lecture, laboratory, and research. Evaluation by examination. Course covers the purpose and functions of a depot supply product planning and control organization and its relationship with Materiel Readiness Command and the Depot System Command. Students work with a product planning and control related group project.
Credit recommendation: In the graduate degree category, 1 semester hour in Industrial Management (6/84).

Quality Assurance
Location: School of Engineering and Logistics, Red River Army Depot.
Length: 20 hours (1 week).
Dates: January 1975-Present.
Objective: To provide the student with a knowledge of quality control assurance and how it relates to other logistics and management activities.
Instruction: Lecture, research, and practical exercises. Evaluation by examination. Course covers basic methods used in cleaning, drying, preserving, wrapping, packaging, and marking.
Credit recommendation: In the upper division baccalaureate category, 1 semester hour in Business Management (6/84).

Receiving
Location: School of Engineering and Logistics, Red River Army Depot.
Length: 20 hours (1 week).
Dates: January 1975-Present.
Objective: To show the student functions of National Inventory Control Points within the Materiel Readiness Commands.
Instruction: Lecture, video cassettes, and a field trip. Evaluation through examination. Course stresses the function of depots. The receiving function is used as a central point of receipt in the supply system.
Credit recommendation: In the upper division baccalaureate category, 1 semester hour in Industrial Management (6/84).

Research Project
Location: School of Engineering and Logistics, Red River Army Depot.
Length: 40 hours (2 weeks).
Dates: January 1975-Present.
Objective: To allow students to develop a research paper on a topic related to logistics or management.
Instruction: Lecture and student reports, both oral and written. Both written and oral reports are evaluated; both must be passed.
Credit recommendation: In the graduate degree category, 2 semester hours in Directed Research in Management (6/84).

Security Assistance Management
Location: School of Engineering and Logistics, Red River Army Depot.
Length: 32 hours (2 weeks).
Dates: January 1975-Present.
Objective: To enable the student to comprehend the history, role, and operation of the U.S. Security Assistance Management Program.
Instruction: Lecture and discussion. Evaluation by examination. Topics include military assistance through grant aid and international military education and training; foreign military sales; the role of organization in the Department of Defense; financial requirements; quality assurance terms; North Atlantic Treaty and Multi-National programs; and the role of major subordinate command organizations and responsibilities.
Credit recommendation: In the graduate degree category, 1 semester hour in Management (6/84).

Standard Army Intermediate Level Supply Subsystem (SAILS)
Location: School of Engineering and Logistics, Red River Army Depot.
Length: 24 hours (8 days).
Dates: January 1975-Present.
Objective: To show the student how Standard Army Intermediate Level Supply Subsystem (SAILS) operates and its importance to the operation of the retail system/wholesale system of Inventory Management.
Instruction: Lecture and laboratory. Evaluation through multiple choice examinations. Course covers the basic computer files and selected input documents and

output products of the SAILS system.

Credit recommendation: In the upper division baccalaureate category, 1 semester hour in Management (6/84).

Statistical Analysis

Location: School of Engineering and Logistics, Red River Army Depot.
Length: 60 hours (3 weeks).
Dates: January 1975-Present.
Objective: To give the student a general knowledge of the use of statistics by managers and to enable the student to apply certain techniques to management problems.
Instruction: Lecture and problem solving. Evaluation through examinations. Introduction to probability, probability distributions, and statistical inference. Testing of hypothesis using f and t tests. Use of methods of tests for independence, single regression, and analysis of variance.
Credit recommendation: In the graduate degree category, 3 semester hours in Business Statistics (6/84).

Stratification

Location: School of Engineering and Logistics, Red River Army Depot.
Length: 20 hours (1 week).
Dates: June 1984-Present.
Objective: To show the student the concept of "time-phased simulation of buy."
Instruction: Lecture and discussion. Evaluation by examination. Principles of demand supported stockage and their relationship to secondary items budget process are also covered.
Credit recommendation: In the upper division baccalaureate category, 1 semester hour in Management (6/84).

Supply Simulation (SUPSIM)

Location: School of Engineering and Logistics, Red River Army Depot.
Length: 20 hours (1 week).
Dates: January 1975-Present.
Objective: To provide the students with a knowledge in system requirements of DS/DS and SAILS, using a computer simulation of Stock Control and Inventory Management.
Instruction: A computer-assisted exercise that allows the participant to use knowledge gained in Unit and Organization Supply, Direct and General Support Supply, and Standard Army Intermediate Supply Subsystem in making supply management decisions typical of those required at this level of supply.
Credit recommendation: In the graduate degree category, 1 semester hour in Management (6/84).

Techniques of Management

Location: School of Engineering and Logistics, Red River Army Depot.
Length: 40 hours (1 week).
Dates: January 1975-Present.
Objective: To provide the student with an understanding of widely used principles, philosophies, tools, and applications of management.
Instruction: Lecture, discussion, in-basket exercises, and research. Evaluation by examination.
Credit recommendation: In the upper division baccalaureate category, 3 semester hours in Management (6/84).

Transportation Management

Location: School of Engineering and Logistics, Red River Army Depot.
Length: 15 hours (1 week).
Dates: January 1975-Present.
Objective: To provide the student with a basic knowledge of transportation management and its relationship to other areas of management, and logistics.
Instruction: Lecture. Evaluation by examination. Course gives an introduction to transportation and traffic management agencies; freight services; classifications; rates and tariffs; routing and documentation of freight; loss and damage in shipment; household goods and personal baggage, containerizations and trends in transportation.
Credit recommendation: In the upper division baccalaureate category, 1 semester hour in Management (6/84).

Unit and Organization Supply Procedures

Location: School of Engineering and Logistics, Red River Army Depot.
Length: 26 hours (2 weeks).
Dates: January 1975-Present.
Objective: To teach the student policies and procedures used at the unit and organizational level of supply in the United States Army.
Instruction: Lecture and laboratory. Evaluation by oral and written examinations. Topics include the organization for supply at the user/Direct Supply level; the Army Authorizations Documents System and its impact on supply; preparation and maintenance of property books; preparation of a request for issue, follow-up, and cancellation, maintenance of the Document Register; sources of supply available to the unit; use of repair parts technical manuals, prescribed load list procedures; applicable supply terminology.
Credit recommendation: In the upper division baccalaureate category, 1 semester hour in Military Science (6/84).

Warehousing and Materiels Handling

Location: School of Engineering and Logistics, Red River Army Depot.

Length: 20 hours (1 week).
Dates: January 1975-Present.
Objective: To teach the student types of materiel stored, types of storage facilities, safety, policies, and storage management systems used in warehousing.
Instruction: Lecture and laboratory. Evaluation by examination. Course covers planning storage; space requirement factors; effective use of storage space; stock location system; storage procedures; commingled storage; storage for other services; types and application of Materiels Handling Equipment; planning materiels handling operations; selection of Materiels Handling Equipment (MHE); computing MHE requirements; innovations in materiels handling and its interface with the Depot Modernization Program.
Credit recommendation: In the upper division baccalaureate category, 1 semester hour in Industrial Management (6/84).

Written Communications
Location: School of Engineering and Logistics, Red River Army Depot.
Length: 40 hours (2 weeks).
Dates: January 1975-Present.
Objective: To study communication models, analysis of group communication with emphasis on organizational communications.
Instruction: Lecture and problem solving. Evaluation through weekly examinations. Course covers effective writing and research techniques.
Credit recommendation: In the upper division baccalaureate category, 3 semester hours in Communications or Technical Writing (6/84).

MAINTENANCE MANAGEMENT PROGRAM

The Maintenance Management Program consists of 35 weeks (1,400 hours) of formal academic instruction. This formal academic instruction is supplemented by appropriate on-the-job training at the local activity and temporary duty travel visits to selected installations. At the conclusion of this program, the graduate is prepared for positions in maintenance management and production and control.

Acquisition and Contracting
Location: School of Engineering and Logistics, Red River Army Depot.
Length: 20 hours (3 weeks).
Dates: January 1975-Present.
Objective: To comprehend the acquisition process for military equipment, procurement law, and relationships to all logistics areas.
Instruction: Lecture and discussion. Evaluation by examination. Course provides an introduction to the acquisition negotiations, types of contracts, and contracting of officers' responsibilities.
Credit recommendation: In the graduate degree category, 1 semester hour in Introduction to Business Management (6/84).

Administrative Systems
Location: School of Engineering and Logistics, Red River Army Depot.
Length: 50 hours (2½ weeks).
Dates: June 1980-Present.
Objective: To teach the student the planning procedures for office communication and paperwork flow in an organization.
Instruction: Lecture and student project. Project presentation is critiqued. Course covers management analysis techniques such as forms analysis and layout planning.
Credit recommendation: In the graduate degree category, 2 semester hours in Management (6/84).

Aircraft
Location: School of Engineering and Logistics, Red River Army Depot.
Length: 26 hours (2 weeks).
Dates: January 1975-Present.
Objective: To give the student a knowledge of the principles of flight, aircraft parts and functions, and Army aircraft uses, normally required of a maintenance manager.
Instruction: Lecture. Evaluation through weekly examinations. Course covers characteristics of both fixed wing and rotary wing aircraft. Includes a discussion of aircraft engines, hydraulics, transmissions, and a description of Army aircraft.
Credit recommendation: In the lower division baccalaureate/associate degree category, 1 semester hour in Military Science (6/84).

Automotive Principles
Location: School of Engineering and Logistics, Red River Army Depot.
Length: 60 hours (4 weeks).
Dates: February 1982-Present.
Objective: To provide the student with a basic understanding of how all systems on an automotive vehicle operate.
Instruction: Lecture. Evaluation through weekly examinations. Course covers engines, fuel systems, cooling systems, lubrication, brakes, power train, steering, and electrical systems.
Credit recommendation: In the vocational certificate degree category, 2 semester hours in Automotive or Mechanical Engineering (6/84).

Blueprint Reading
Location: School of Engineering and Logistics, Red River Army Depot.
Length: 40 hours (2 weeks).

Dates: February 1982-Present.
Objective: To provide the student with a knowledge of drafting principles so that students will be able to read prints.
Instruction: Lecture and laboratory. Evaluation through weekly tests. Students learn to complete drawings, extract data from prints, and sketch various geometrical shapes.
Credit recommendation: In the lower division baccalaureate/associate degree category, 2 semester hours in Drafting (6/84).

Defense Inventory Management Simulation (DIMSIM)
Location: School of Engineering and Logistics, Red River Army Depot.
Length: 50 hours (2 weeks).
Dates: January 1975-Present.
Objective: A computer simulation which requires students to analyze complex logistical data and to make decisions on various logistics functions.
Instruction: Lecture and simulation exercises. Evaluation by simulation performance. Emphasis is on inventory management.
Credit recommendation: In the graduate degree category, 2 semester hours in Management (6/84).

Department of Army Publication
Location: School of Engineering and Logistics, Red River Army Depot.
Length: 40 hours (2 weeks).
Dates: January 1975-Present.
Objective: To teach the student the policies, responsibility, and procedures governing official publications and blank forms used by the Army.
Instruction: Lecture, laboratory, and workshops are all used. Evaluation is through exercises and examinations. Military and Federal specifications and stock standards are covered.
Credit recommendation: In the upper division baccalaureate category, 2 semester hours in Management (6/84).

Electronics
Location: School of Engineering and Logistics, Red River Army Depot.
Length: 40 hours (3 weeks).
Dates: February 1982-Present.
Objective: To teach the student how to recognize various electrical/electronic components, know what their function is in a circuit, and analyze circuits using test equipment to identify faculty components.
Instruction: Lecture and laboratory. Five projects are worked through in lab. Evaluation is through examination. Course covers basic principles of electricity and its use in Army equipment.
Credit recommendation: In the lower division baccalaureate/associate degree category, 1 semester hour in Electrical/Electronics Technology or Industrial Arts (6/84).

Financial Management
Location: School of Engineering and Logistics, Red River Army Depot.
Length: 20 hours (1 week).
Dates: January 1975-Present.
Objective: To provide the student with a knowledge of the overall DOD and Army financial management structure.
Instruction: Lecture and classroom exercises. Evaluation by examination. Course concentrates on those aspects of financial management, such as the stock funds, that are most affected by the actions of graduate interns.
Credit recommendation: In the graduate degree category, 1 semester hour in Financial Management (6/84).

Integrated Logistics Support
Location: School of Engineering and Logistics, Red River Army Depot.
Length: 60 hours (3 weeks).
Dates: January 1975-Present.
Objective: To learn the phases and possible problem areas in the life cycle of an end item, including the interfaces that occur internally within DARCOM, and externally with other elements in the Department of the Army and the Department of Defense.
Instruction: Lecture and discussion. Evaluation by examination. Course covers the development of the maintenance concept of the materiel need and progresses through the feasibility, design, development, testing, evaluation, procurement and production phases.
Credit recommendation: In the graduate degree category, 3 semester hours in Management (6/84).

Introduction to the Army in the Field
Location: School of Engineering and Logistics, Red River Army Depot.
Length: 24 hours (1 week).
Dates: January 1975-Present.
Objective: To teach the student how the Army and supporting government agencies are organized, and relate to each other.
Instruction: Lecture. Evaluation through examination. Instruction illustrates the operational and technical chains of command.
Credit recommendation: In the upper division baccalaureate category, 1 semester hour in Military Science (6/84).

Logistic Support Exercise
Location: School of Engineering and Logistics, Red River Army Depot.
Length: 40 hours (1 week).

Dates: January 1975-Present.

Objective: To allow the student to test management skills in the initial and follow-up support of a weapon system.

Instruction: Lecture and extensive use of practical exercises. Evaluation by analyzing exercise results. Exercise includes the development of a prototype weapon system, its initial fielding and provisioning, and its logistics support for 36 months. Costs are affixed to all decisions made by the student.

Credit recommendation: In the graduate degree category, 3 semester hours in Management (6/84).

Maintenance Management Program: Research Project

Location: School of Engineering and Logistics, Red River Army Depot.

Length: 40 hours (2 weeks).

Dates: January 1975-Present.

Objective: To allow the student to develop a research paper on a topic related to logistics.

Instruction: Lecture and student reports, both oral and written. Both written and oral reports are evaluated, both must be passed. Subjects must relate to logistics or management.

Credit recommendation: In the graduate degree category, 2 semester hours in Directed Research Management (6/84).

Management Information Systems

Location: School of Engineering and Logistics, Red River Army Depot.

Length: 80 hours (4 weeks).

Dates: January 1975-Present.

Objective: To provide the student with a knowledge of advanced data processing systems so that students will be able to program a computer, understand computer terminology, and develop automated systems.

Instruction: Lecture and laboratory. Evaluation by weekly examinations. Course covers FORTRAN statements, FORTRAN program, disk input/output, and general information on computer technology.

Credit recommendation: In the graduate degree category, 3 semester hours in Data Processing (6/84).

Missiles and Rockets

Location: School of Engineering and Logistics, Red River Army Depot.

Length: 25 hours (1 week).

Dates: February 1982-Present.

Objective: To familiarize the student with basic principles of missiles and rockets.

Instruction: Lecture. Evaluation through examination. Maintenance problems are emphasized.

Credit recommendation: In the lower division baccalaureate/associate degree category, 1 semester hour in Military Science (6/84).

Oral Communications

Location: School of Engineering and Logistics, Red River Army Depot.

Length: 60 hours (3 weeks).

Dates: January 1975-Present.

Objective: To provide students with an awareness of the importance of effective communications within any organization and to provide practice in making prepared presentations and briefings.

Instruction: Lecture and student presentations. Evaluation of student presentations and weekly examinations. Course includes key points on proper presentations such as vocal, physical, emotional, and intellectual behavior on the platform.

Credit recommendation: In the lower division baccalaureate/associate degree category, 3 semester hours in Speech (6/84).

Program Planning and Control

Location: School of Engineering and Logistics, Red River Army Depot.

Length: 78 hours (7 weeks).

Dates: January 1975-Present.

Objective: To teach the student how to plot a production schedule that will meet a production deadline when placed in a production control situation.

Instruction: Lecture and discussion are used. Evaluation is through examination. Course covers principles and fundamentals of program planning and control as applied to various types of activities.

Credit recommendation: In the graduate degree category, 4 semester hours in Industrial Management (6/84).

Quality Assurance

Location: School of Engineering and Logistics, Red River Army Depot.

Length: 20 hours (1 week).

Dates: January 1975-Present.

Objective: To provide the student with a knowledge of quality control/assurance and how it relates to other logistics and management activities.

Instruction: Lecture, research, and practical exercises. Evaluation by examination.

Credit recommendation: In the upper division baccalaureate category, 1 semester hour in Introduction to Business Management (6/84).

Reliability, Availability, and Maintainability

Location: School of Engineering and Logistics, Red River Army Depot.

Length: 20 hours (1 week).

Dates: January 1975-Present.

Objective: To teach the student the basic elements, theory, and practical application of reliability engineering.

Instruction: Lecture only. Evaluation through examination. Course covers the theories and techniques pertinent to the evaluation of engineering problems in system reliability, maintainability, and other measures of system effectiveness.

Credit recommendation: In the graduate degree category, 1 semester hour in Industrial Engineering (6/84).

Statistical Analysis
   Location: School of Engineering and Logistics, Red River Army Depot.
   Length: 60 hours (3 weeks).
   Dates: January 1975-Present.
   Objective: To provide the student with a general knowledge of the use of statistics by managers and the application of certain techniques to management problems.
   Instruction: Lecture and problem solving. Evaluation through examinations. Introduction to probability, probability distributions, and statistical inference. Testing of hypotheses using f and t tests. Use of methods of tests for independence, single regression, and analysis of variance.
   Credit recommendation: In the graduate degree category, 3 semester hours in Business Statistics (6/84).

Supply, Storage, and Transportation Procedures
   Location: School of Engineering and Logistics, Red River Army Depot.
   Length: 80 hours (4 weeks).
   Dates: January 1975-Present.
   Objective: To introduce the student to inventory management and the Army Supply system.
   Instruction: Lecture and laboratory. The course is laboratory oriented. Topics covered include Commodity Command Standard System structure, capabilities, and functions.
   Credit recommendation: In the upper division baccalaureate category, 1 semester hour in Military Science (6/84).

Techniques of Management
   Location: School of Engineering and Logistics, Red River Army Depot.
   Length: 20 hours (3 weeks).
   Dates: January 1975-Present.
   Objective: To provide the student with an understanding of widely used principles, philosophies, tools, and applications of management.
   Instruction: Lecture, discussion, in-basket exercises, and research. Evaluation by examination. Course covers topics in organizational behavior and group dynamics.
   Credit recommendation: In the upper division baccalaureate category, 2 semester hours in Management (6/84).

Written Communications
   Location: School of Engineering and Logistics, Red River Army Depot.
   Length: 40 hours (2 weeks).
   Dates: January 1975-Present.
   Objective: To give the student an understanding of communication models, analysis of group communication with emphasis on organizational communications.
   Instruction: Lecture and problem solving. Evaluation through weekly examinations. Course covers effective writing and research techniques.
   Credit recommendation: In the upper division baccalaureate category, 3 semester hours in Communications or Technical Writing (6/84).

QUALITY AND RELIABILITY ENGINEERING PROGRAM

The Quality and Reliability Engineering Program has been designed to provide the training required to assure that new Army systems are developed and fielded with the highest levels of quality and reliability characteristics. This is a structured two-year training program that consists of classroom instruction, self-development activities, and specialized on-the-job training.

Army Manufacturing and Testing Technology (88532)
   Location: School of Engineering and Logistics, Red River Army Depot.
   Length: 50 hours (5 weeks).
   Dates: July 1980-Present.
   Objective: To provide the student with information on the Army's Manufacturing Methods and Technology Program.
   Instruction: Lecture and outside work. Evaluation through examination. Course covers concepts and methods with emphasis on procedures and techniques associated with AMC Manufacturing Methods and Technology program and Materiels Testing Program. Covers nondestructive testing and special acceptance inspection equipment.
   Credit recommendation: In the lower division baccalaureate/associate degree category, 3 semester hours in Engineering Technology (6/84).

Computer Simulation Techniques (88559)
   Location: School of Engineering and Logistics, Red River Army Depot.
   Length: 70 hours (10 weeks).
   Dates: February 1981-Present.
   Objective: To give the student a knowledge of modeling, simulation techniques, and computer-aided technology.
   Instruction: Lectures, laboratory, and research. Evaluation through examinations and written reports. Course covers generation of random numbers, Monte Carlo simulations, GASP IV simulation language, and numerical control and computer-aided design in manufacturing.
   Credit recommendation: In the graduate degree category, 4 semester hours in Industrial Engineering (6/84).

U.S. Army Materiel Command - AMC

Design by Reliability (88587)
Location: School of Engineering and Logistics, Red River Army Depot.
Length: 60 hours (10 weeks).
Dates: May 1981-Present.
Objective: To provide the student with methods applicable to design optimization.
Instruction: Lecture and laboratory exercises. Evaluation by examination. Course covers stress/strength analysis, failure modes and effects analysis, fault tree analysis, probabilistic design, and optimization techniques.
Credit recommendation: In the graduate degree category, 3 semester hours in Industrial Engineering (6/84).

End of Course Projects (88586)
Location: School of Engineering and Logistics, Red River Army Depot.
Length: 40 hours (1 week).
Dates: January 1981-Present.
Objective: To allow the student to apply what he has learned during each session and obtain a working knowledge of the Army developmental process.
Instruction: Lecture and practical exercises. Evaluation by written examination and reports. Projects will be performed to allow students to apply knowledge and techniques learned throughout the Quality and Reliability Engineering Training Program.
Credit recommendation: In the upper division baccalaureate category, 1 semester hour in Management (6/84).

Engineering Applications for Computers (88558)
Location: School of Engineering and Logistics, Red River Army Depot.
Length: 70 hours (10 weeks).
Dates: January 1980-Present.
Objective: To teach the student scientific computer programming theory.
Instruction: Lecture and laboratory with outside assignments. Evaluation through examination and research papers. Course covers FORTRAN statements, FORTRAN programming, and disk input/output.
Credit recommendation: In the upper division baccalaureate category, 4 semester hours in Computer Science (6/84).

Maintainability Analysis and Design (88517)
Location: School of Engineering and Logistics, Red River Army Depot.
Length: 60 hours (10 weeks).
Dates: May 1981-Present.
Objective: To provide the student with techniques in maintainability which are used in product quality assurance.
Instruction: Lecture and laboratory exercises. Evaluation by examination. Course covers quantitative and qualitative terms, system requirements and characteristics, demonstration techniques, allocation and prediction, and design factors.
Credit recommendation: In the graduate degree category, 3 semester hours in Industrial Management (6/84).

Mathematical Statistics for Product Assurance (88511)
Location: School of Engineering and Logistics, Red River Army Depot.
Length: 60 hours (10 weeks).
Dates: January 1980-Present.
Objective: To teach the student probability theory, random variables probability distribution, expected values, and related statistical techniques.
Instruction: Lecture, practical exercises, and research. Evaluation through examinations and research paper. Course covers statistical concepts required for product assurance.
Credit recommendation: In the graduate degree category, 3 semester hours in Statistics (6/84).

Problems in Quality and Reliability Engineering II (88585)
Location: School of Engineering and Logistics, Red River Army Depot.
Length: 120 hours (20 weeks).
Dates: May 1981-Present.
Objective: To provide the student with advanced study and research in the field of Quality and Reliability Engineering.
Instruction: Lecture and research. Evaluation by research project. Course requires original research (analysis, writing, reporting, and publication) in an Army problem area.
Credit recommendation: In the graduate degree category, 6 hours in Graduate Research (6/84).

Procurement Policies and Procedures for Engineers (88506)
Location: School of Engineering and Logistics, Red River Army Depot.
Length: 50 hours (5 weeks).
Dates: July 1980-Present.
Objective: To give the student a working knowledge of the defense procurement system for technical personnel.
Instruction: Lecture and practical assignments. Evaluation through written examinations and reports. Course covers legal aspects, policies, and procedures.
Credit recommendation: In the upper division baccalaureate category, 3 semester hours in Business Administration (6/84).

Product Assurance Management and Engineering I (88503)
Location: School of Engineering and Logistics, Red River Army Depot.

Length: 60 hours (10 weeks).
Dates: January 1980-Present.
Objective: To give the student a survey of the various product assurance management and technical tools, techniques, and technical guidance (including Army regulations, standards, pamphlets, directives, and other published material).
Instruction: Lecture and laboratory. Evaluation through examinations and written reports. Emphasis is placed on the Army equipment life cycle and its relationship to product assurance and tests.
Credit recommendation: In the lower division baccalaureate/associate degree category, 3 semester hours in Military Science (6/84).

Product Assurance Management and Engineering II
Location: School of Engineering and Logistics, Red River Army Depot.
Length: 50 hours (5 weeks).
Dates: January 1980-Present.
Objective: To provide the student with a knowledge of product assurance and engineering with increasing emphasis on the management of product assurance and its interface with other functional areas.
Instruction: Lecture and outside work. Evaluation is through examinations and written reports. Course covers maintenance, logistics, laboratories, and design items. Includes a discussion of how quality impacts design practices and reviews quality design techniques available to the engineer.
Credit recommendation: In the lower division baccalaureate/associate degree category, 3 semester hours in Industrial Management (6/84).

Reliability Analysis and Design (88526)
Location: School of Engineering and Logistics, Red River Army Depot.
Length: 60 hours (10 weeks).
Dates: February 1981-Present.
Objective: To teach the student quantitative reliability analysis techniques used in engineering design.
Instruction: Lecture and laboratory. Evaluation through written tests. Course includes system effectiveness parameters, reliability growth, reliability prediction and allocation, and reliability modeling techniques for systems.
Credit recommendation: In the graduate degree category, 3 semester hours in Industrial Engineering (6/84).

Software Quality
Location: School of Engineering and Logistics, Red River Army Depot.
Length: 50 hours (10 weeks).
Dates: July 1983-Present.
Objective: To give the student a set of design measures, strategies, management and technical tools, techniques and technical guidance.
Instruction: Lecture and outside study. Evaluation through examination. Course includes regulations, standards, pamphlets, and directives.
Credit recommendation: In the upper division baccalaureate category, 3 semester hours in Industrial Management (6/84).

Statistical Methods in Reliability (88525)
Location: School of Engineering and Logistics, Red River Army Depot.
Length: 60 hours (10 weeks).
Dates: November 1980-Present.
Objective: To provide the student with the theories and techniques pertinent to the solution of engineering problems in system reliability, maintainability, and other measures of effectiveness.
Instruction: Lecture and laboratory. Evaluation through written examinations and reports. Course covers reliability, reliability measurements, static reliability models, probabilistic design, and dynamic probability models.
Credit recommendation: In the graduate degree category, 3 semester hours in Industrial Engineering (6/84).

Statistical Quality Control (88514)
Location: School of Engineering and Logistics, Red River Army Depot.
Length: 60 hours (10 weeks).
Dates: January 1975-Present.
Objective: To provide the student with statistical methods used in industrial quality control.
Instruction: Lecture and laboratory. Evaluation through written examinations and reports. Course includes aspects of the physical application of the process control theory and techniques, sampling plans, and military standards for inspection.
Credit recommendation: In the graduate degree category, 3 semester hours in Industrial Engineering (6/84).

System Assessment Techniques
Location: School of Engineering and Logistics, Red River Army Depot.
Length: 60 hours (10 weeks).
Dates: November 1980-Present.
Objective: To provide the student with a detailed discussion of system assessment techniques and the Army's Assessment Program.
Instruction: Lecture and practical exercises. Evaluation by examination. Course includes studies of Army discipline reviews, the Standard Army Maintenance System, sample data collection, and industries assessment programs.
Credit recommendation: In the graduate degree category, 3 semester hours in Statistics (6/84).

Technical Data Package Development (88504)
  Location: School of Engineering and Logistics, Red River Army Depot.
  Length: 40 hours (1 week).
  Dates: May 1981-Present.
  Objective: To introduce the student to the policies, procedures, and responsibilities for the acquisition, preparation, review, proofing, maintenance, improvement, control, and transmission of the Technical Data Package for procurement and production purposes.
  Instruction: Lecture, with evaluation by examination. Course covers history and controls, technical data package, management and control systems; information storage retrieval, specifications and standardization, product assurance, and technical documentation.
  Credit recommendation: In the upper division baccalaureate category, 2 semester hours in Military Science (6/84).

Techniques in Operations Research (88520)
  Location: School of Engineering and Logistics, Red River Army Depot.
  Length: 60 hours (10 weeks).
  Dates: January 1980-Present.
  Objective: To teach the student the operations research field and operations research techniques.
  Instruction: Lecture and laboratory exercises. Evaluation through examinations and written reports. Course covers production and inventory control, linear programming, game theory, and dynamic programming.
  Credit recommendation: In the graduate degree category, 3 semester hours in Industrial Engineering (6/84).

Test and Evaluation Management (88530)
  Location: School of Engineering and Logistics, Red River Army Depot.
  Length: 60 hours (10 weeks).
  Dates: January 1980-Present.
  Objective: To give the student an understanding of the testing procedures occurring during the development of new materiel systems, and the evaluation that are performed to determine the technical and military worth of the materiel under test.
  Instruction: Lectures and laboratory. Evaluation through examinations and written reports. Emphasis is placed on the interrelationship of development and operational tests and their evaluations. The coordinated test program, test schedule, review committees, and the development of the test and evaluation master plan are discussed.
  Credit recommendation: In the upper division baccalaureate category, 3 semester hours in Industrial Engineering (6/84).

Test Engineering and Analysis (88531)
  Location: School of Engineering and Logistics, Red River Army Depot.
  Length: 60 hours (10 weeks).
  Dates: February 1981-Present.
  Objective: To provide the student with the statistical model-building technology.
  Instruction: Lecture and laboratory. Evaluation through examinations and written reports. Course covers the design and evaluation of tests, methods of collecting test data and test evaluation techniques used within the Army.
  Credit recommendation: In the graduate degree category, 3 semester hours in Statistics (6/84).

PRE-ENGINEERING FOR PHYSICAL SCIENTIST PROGRAM

The Pre-Engineering Program has been designed to train highly qualified mathematics and physical science majors for entry into one of the four engineering programs. The program requires an undergraduate background in math, physics, or chemistry with a minimum of 60 hours in one or a combination of these fields.

Electrical Fields and Circuits (87504)
  Location: School of Engineering and Logistics, Red River Army Depot.
  Length: 91 hours (6½ weeks)
  Dates: January 1975-Present.
  Objective: To enable the student to analyze and design electrical systems.
  Instruction: Lecture, practical exercises, and research. Evaluation through examination. Course covers basic concepts of electrical fields and circuits.
  Credit recommendation: In the upper division baccalaureate category, 4 semester hours in Electrical Engineering (6/84).

Engineering Materiels (87503)
  Location: School of Engineering and Logistics, Red River Army Depot.
  Length: 74 hours (6 weeks).
  Dates: January 1975-Present.
  Objective: To enable the student to select appropriate materiels for engineering applications after considering service life, corrosion, and environmental effects.
  Instruction: Lecture, practical exercises, and research. Evaluation through examination. Course covers metals, polymers, and ceramics.
  Credit recommendation: In the upper division baccalaureate category, 3 semester hours in Mechanical Engineering (6/84).

Statics and Dynamics (87501)
  Location: School of Engineering and Logistics, Red River Army Depot.
  Length: 93 hours (13 weeks).

Dates: January 1975-Present.
Objective: To give the student an understanding of the relationships of basic force, mass, and acceleration; to apply these relationships in solving engineering problems, and to use vector methods to analyze the kinematic and dynamic behavior of solid bodies.
Instruction: Lecture, practical exercises, and research. Evaluation by examination. Course covers the fundamental concepts and principal units, methods of problem solution, and the importance of numerical accuracy.
Credit recommendation: In the lower division baccalaureate/associate degree category, 4 semester hours in Mechanical Engineering (6/84).

Strength of Materiels (87502)
Location: School of Engineering and Logistics, Red River Army Depot.
Length: 73 hours (5 two-hour meetings and 1 individual problem session per week for 6½ weeks).
Dates: January 1975-Present.
Objective: To enable the student to analyze forces on materiels to ascertain required strengths and design parameters.
Instruction: Lecture, practical exercises, and research. Evaluation through examination. Course covers stress and strain, torsion on circular shafts, torsion shear flow, deflection of beams, statically indeterminate beams, buckling, and combination stress.
Credit recommendation: In the upper division baccalaureate category, 3 semester hours in Mechanical Engineering (6/84).

Thermodynamics (87505)
Location: School of Engineering and Logistics, Red River Army Depot.
Length: 76 hours (5 two-hour meetings and 2 one-hour individual problem sessions per week for 6½ weeks).
Dates: January 1975-Present.
Objective: To enable the student to apply thermodynamics principles in solving practical problems.
Instruction: Lecture, practical exercises, and research. Evaluation by examination. Course covers the principles of work and heat transfer, and the laws of thermodynamics.
Credit recommendation: In the upper division baccalaureate category, 3 semester hours in Mechanical Engineering (6/84).

MAINTAINABILITY ENGINEERING PROGRAM

The Maintainability Engineering Program is designed to provide the engineering skills that are necessary to affect systems design and support with the goal of reducing the cost of operating and maintaining Army equipment in today's environment. The training objective is thirty engineering graduates per year.

Advanced Topics in Reliability and Maintainability Engineering (82545)
Location: School of Engineering and Logistics, Red River Army Depot.
Length: 60 hours (10 weeks); 6 one-hour meetings per week.
Dates: February 1981-Present.
Objective: To give students a detailed treatment of advanced topics in reliability and maintainability, as a follow-up to the methods in reliability and maintainability, and the maintainability analysis course.
Instruction: Five hours lecture per week plus one hour laboratory per week. Evaluation covers reliability estimation, reliability growth, software reliability, and reliability centered maintenance.
Credit recommendation: In the graduate degree category, 3 semester hours in Industrial Engineering (12/84).

Army Systems Management and Engineering (82506)
Location: School of Engineering and Logistics, Red River Army Depot.
Length: 60 hours (10 weeks); 6 one-hour meetings per week.
Dates: September 1976-Present.
Objective: To provide the student with a comprehensive study of the organization, management tools, and procedures used to develop army equipment.
Instruction: Five hours lecture per week plus one hour laboratory per week. Evaluation through written examinations. Course covers defense management organizations, level of army maintenance, materiel acquisition management, Army planning and budgeting for system development, and acquisition of Army systems.
Credit recommendation: In the upper division baccalaureate category, 3 semester hours in Military Science (12/84).

Computer Simulation for System Design (82559)
Location: School of Engineering and Logistics, Red River Army Depot.
Length: 70 hours (10 weeks); 7 one-hour meetings per week.
Dates: February 1977-Present.
Objective: To provide students with an understanding of the theory of generating random numbers.
Instruction: Five hours lecture per week plus two hours laboratory per week. Evaluation through written examination. Detailed studies of simulation languages and practical experience with simulator languages are included.
Credit recommendation: In the graduate degree category, 3 semester hours in Computer Science (12/84).

Computer Science (82558)
Location: School of Engineering and Logistics, Red River Army Depot.
Length: 70 hours (10 weeks); 7 one-hour meetings per

week.

Dates: September 1976-Present.

Objective: To provide students with an understanding of scientific computer programming theory and application. Introduce FORTRAN, and discuss scientific and engineering applications.

Instruction: Five hours lecture per week plus two hours laboratory per week. Evaluation through written examination. Course covers an introduction to FORTRAN and discussion of scientific and engineering applications.

Credit recommendation: In the lower division baccalaureate/associate degree category, 3 semester hours in Computer Science (12/84).

Design of Engineering Experiments (82519)

Location: School of Engineering and Logistics, Red River Army Depot.

Length: 60 hours (10 weeks); 6 one-hour meetings per week.

Dates: February 1977-Present.

Objective: To provide students with an understanding of statistical model building technology so that students can use data collection and analysis skills; planning is emphasized to optimize information and cost of experiments.

Instruction: Five hours lecture per week plus one hour laboratory per week. Evaluation through written examinations. Course covers linear regression, multiple regression, nonlinear regression, one-way analysis of variance, and blocked designs.

Credit recommendation: In the graduate degree category, 3 semester hours in Industrial Engineering (12/84).

Human Operations in Complex Systems (82560)

Location: School of Engineering and Logistics, Red River Army Depot.

Length: 60 hours (10 weeks); 6 one-hour meetings per week.

Dates: September 1976-Present.

Objective: To provide students with an understanding of how human physiological and environmental factors affect system performance.

Instruction: Five hours lecture per week plus one hour laboratory per week. Evaluation through written examinations. Human engineering tools for systematic analysis identification, and evaluation of man-machine systems are provided along with the development of human factors and system procedures for operation and maintenance of complex equipment.

Credit recommendation: In the graduate degree category, 3 semester hours in Industrial Engineering (12/84).

Logistics Support Analysis (82518)

Location: School of Engineering and Logistics, Red River Army Depot.

Length: 70 hours (10 weeks); 7 one-hour meetings per week.

Dates: February 1981-Present.

Objective: To orient students to the Army Logistics Support System.

Instruction: Five hours lecture per week plus one hour discussion per week and one hour laboratory per week. Evaluation through written examination. Emphasis is placed on the methods and techniques for analyzing and assessing the effectiveness of the support system and on ILS in ensuring the compatibility of equipment and its support system.

Credit recommendation: In the upper division baccalaureate category, 3 semester hours in Industrial Engineering (12/84).

Maintainability Analysis (82517)

Location: School of Engineering and Logistics, Red River Army Depot.

Length: 60 hours (10 weeks); 6 one-hour meetings per week.

Dates: February 1977-Present.

Objective: To provide students with techniques which can be used for system analysis relative to maintainability areas.

Instruction: Five hours lecture per week plus one hour laboratory per week. Evaluation through written examinations. Course covers maintainability quantitative and qualitative terms, maintainability as a system characteristic, maintainability demonstration techniques, maintainability allocation and prediction, and maintainability design factors.

Credit recommendation: In the graduate degree category, 3 semester hours in Industrial Engineering (12/84).

Maintainability Case Studies (82516)

Location: School of Engineering and Logistics, Red River Army Depot.

Length: 60 hours (10 weeks); 6 one-hour meetings per week.

Dates: February 1981-Present.

Objective: To provide students with examples of specific applications of reliability and maintenance principles in acquisition of army equipment by following selected items through the development cycle to monitor maintainability inputs and accomplishments.

Instruction: Five hours lecture per week plus one hour laboratory per week. Evaluation through written examinations. Course covers U.S. Army equipment's research and development cycle, selected current systems, and state-of-the-art developments in reliability and maintainability.

Credit recommendation: In the upper division baccalaureate category, 3 semester hours in Military Science (12/84).

Mathematical Statistics I (82511)
Location: School of Engineering and Logistics, Red River Army Depot.
Length: 60 hours (10 weeks); 6 one-hour meetings per week.
Dates: September 1976-Present.
Objective: To provide the student with an understanding of various statistical methods.
Instruction: Five hours lecture per week plus one hour laboratory per week. Evaluation through written examinations. Course covers basic probability theory, random variables, sums of random variables, and expected values.
Credit recommendation: In the graduate degree category, 3 semester hours in Statistics (12/84).

Management Techniques—Parts I and II (82508) (82509)
Location: School of Engineering and Logistics, Red River Army Depot.
Length: 70 hours (10 weeks); 7 one-hour meetings per week.
Dates: September 1980-Present.
Objective: To make the student proficient in those management techniques that will be required in their civil service center.
Instruction: Five hours lecture per week plus one hour discussion per week, plus one hour laboratory per week. Evaluation through written examination. Course covers managerial processes, management information systems, and personnel processes.
Credit recommendation: In the upper division baccalaureate category, 3 semester hours in Management (12/84).

Mathematical Statistics II (82512)
Location: School of Engineering and Logistics, Red River Army Depot.
Length: 60 hours (10 weeks); 6 one-hour meetings per week.
Dates: November 1976-Present.
Objective: To provide students with an understanding of sampling distribution, parameter estimation, hypothesis testing, and statistical experimental design.
Instruction: Five hours lecture per week plus one hour laboratory per week. Evaluation through written examination. Course covers sampling statistics and distributions, estimation of parameters, and application of hypotheses.
Credit recommendation: In the graduate degree category, 3 semester hours in Statistics (12/84).

Problem Solving Techniques (82570)
Location: School of Engineering and Logistics, Red River Army Depot.
Length: 60 hours (10 weeks); 6 one-hour meetings per week.
Dates: February 1974-Present.
Objective: To provide students with scientific and engineering approaches to problem solving and decision making.
Instruction: Five hours lecture per week plus one hour laboratory per week. Evaluation by examination. Course includes presentations of optimization problems, Markov decision processes, decision risk analysis, and dynamic programming.
Credit recommendation: In the graduate degree category, 3 semester hours in Operations Research (12/84).

Problems in Maintainability Engineering I
Location: School of Engineering and Logistics, Red River Army Depot.
Length: 60 hours (10 weeks); 6 one-hour meetings per week.
Dates: February 1977-Present.
Objective: To give students advanced study and research in the field of maintainability engineering.
Instruction: Two hours lecture per week plus four hours research per week. Evaluation through research reports. Course covers research sources, research techniques, and topic selection.
Credit recommendation: In the graduate degree category, 3 semester hours in Industrial Engineering (12/84).

Problems in Maintainability Engineering II (82585)
Location: School of Engineering and Logistics, Red River Army Depot.
Length: 60 hours (10 weeks); 6 one-hour meetings per week.
Dates: May 1977-Present.
Objective: To demonstrate to students advanced engineering capability through resolution of one or two problems by professional problem-solving and documentation techniques.
Instruction: One hour lecture per week plus five hours research per week. Evaluation of research reports. Each student does original research on an Army problem area.
Credit recommendation: In the graduate degree category, 3 semester hours in Industrial Engineering (12/84).

Statistical Methods in Reliability and Maintainability (82525)
Location: School of Engineering and Logistics, Red River Army Depot.
Length: 60 hours (10 weeks); 6 one-hour meetings per week.
Dates: February 1977-Present.
Objective: To provide students with an understanding of statistical methods used in industrial quality control.
Instruction: Five hours lecture per week plus one hour laboratory per week. Evaluation through written examinations. Course includes aspects of the physical application of the process control theory and techniques,

significant tests, sampling plans, and military standards for inspection.

Credit recommendation: In the graduate degree category, 3 semester hours in Industrial Engineering (12/84).

Techniques in Cost Estimation (82566)
Location: School of Engineering and Logistics, Red River Army Depot.
Length: 60 hours (10 weeks); 6 one-hour meetings per week.
Dates: November 1976-Present.
Objective: To provide students with an understanding of the theories and techniques pertinent to the solution of engineering problems in system reliability, maintainability, and other measures of effectiveness.
Instruction: Five hours lecture per week plus one hour laboratory per week. Evaluation through written examinations. Course covers interest and economic equivalence; evaluating replacement alternative and public activities; and risk, uncertainty, and economic modeling.
Credit recommendation: In the graduate degree category, 3 semester hours in Economic Analysis (12/84).

Techniques in Operations Research (82520)
Location: School of Engineering and Logistics, Red River Army Depot.
Length: 60 hours (10 weeks); 6 one-hour meetings per week.
Dates: September 1976-Present.
Objective: To provide students with specific capabilities in operations research.
Instruction: Five hours lecture per week plus one hour laboratory per week. Evaluation through written examinations. Course covers operations research techniques such as production and inventory control; linear programming; queuing theory, game theory; and dynamic programming.
Credit recommendation: In the graduate degree category, 3 semester hours in Operations Research (12/84).

SAFETY ENGINEERING PROGRAM

The objective of the Safety Engineering Program is the design and operation of systems and facilities that are free from injury-producing conditions. The recruiting goal is twenty engineers per year. During their second year, the interns attend specialized safety short courses at the Field Safety Activity.

Chemical Safety in the Industrial Environment (84569)
Location: School of Engineering and Logistics, Red River Army Depot.
Length: 60 hours (10 weeks).
Dates: March 1979-Present.
Objective: To introduce students to the chemical compounds and solutions used in the Army-Industrial Complex; review their properties, use, and limitations.
Instruction: Five hours lecture per week plus one hour laboratory per week. Evaluation through written examinations, projects, and presentation. Students study the effect of chemical compounds on the human body and methods of protection against them. Specific techniques for use in recognition and control of chemical hazards are presented. Safety engineering techniques, methods, and criteria are discussed for selecting, testing, and using special protective equipment in situations where hazards cannot be eliminated.
Credit recommendation: In the graduate degree category, 3 semester hours in Industrial Safety or Engineering (12/84).

Computer Science (84558)
Location: School of Engineering and Logistics, Red River Army Depot.
Length: 70 hours (10 weeks).
Dates: January 1974-Present.
Objective: To provide students with an understanding of scientific computer programming theory and application.
Instruction: Five hours per week lecture plus two hours per week laboratory. Evaluation through written examinations. Course covers an introduction to FORTRAN, COBOL, and other programming languages, and discussion of scientific and engineering applications.
Credit recommendation: In the lower division baccalaureate/associate degree category, 3 semester hours in Computer Science (12/84).

Engineering Statistics (84511)
Location: School of Engineering and Logistics, Red River Army Depot.
Length: 60 hours (10 weeks).
Dates: January 1974-Present.
Objective: To provide students with an understanding of basic probability theory, random variables, sums of random variables, and expected values.
Instruction: Five hours lecture per week plus one hour laboratory per week. Evaluation through written examinations. Course covers probability theory, random variables and probability distributions, algebra of expectation, sums of random variables.
Credit recommendation: In the graduate degree category, 3 semester hours in Statistics (12/84).

Experimental Design (84519)
Location: School of Engineering and Logistics, Red River Army Depot.
Length: 60 hours (10 weeks).
Dates: January 1977-Present.
Objective: To provide students with information on model building technology and engineering experimentation methods.

Instruction: Five hours lecture per week plus one hour laboratory per week. Evaluation through written examinations. Course includes data collection and analysis, empirical development of parameters, and time dependent models. The applications of experimental design to safety research are stressed.

Credit recommendation: In the graduate degree category, 3 semester hours in Industrial Engineering (12/84).

Human Factors Engineering in Systems Design (84568)

Location: School of Engineering and Logistics, Red River Army Depot.

Length: 50 hours (10 weeks).

Dates: June 1982-Present.

Objective: To provide students with an understanding of an industrially oriented human engineering tool for systematic analysis.

Instruction: Lecture only. Evaluation through written examinations. Course provides an identification and evaluation of man-machine systems leading to the development of human factors data design and hardware, personnel subsystems, and system procedures for operations and maintenance.

Credit recommendation: In the graduate degree category, 3 semester hours in Industrial Engineering (12/84).

Principles of Management (84508)

Location: School of Engineering and Logistics, Red River Army Depot.

Length: 50 hours (5 weeks).

Dates: September 1976-Present.

Objective: To make the student proficient in those management techniques necessary for managers during career progression.

Instruction: Nine hours lecture per week plus one hour laboratory per week. Evaluation through written examinations, reports, and presentations. Course includes studying top level decision making structures; identifying and assessing the economic and social forces affecting defense decisions; analyzing various management systems, philosophies and theories and their applications, limitations, and values to the Army: and by presenting oral and written solutions of specified management problems. The structure of staff studies and engineering reports are given special emphasis.

Credit recommendation: In the upper division baccalaureate category, 3 semester hours in Management (12/84).

Principles of Radiological Safety Engineering (84549)

Location: School of Engineering and Logistics, Red River Army Depot.

Length: 60 hours (10 weeks).

Dates: January 1978-Present.

Objective: To provide students with an understanding of the basic theory of nuclear reactions, radioactivity, and sources of radiation and their interaction with matter.

Instruction: Five hours lecture per week plus one hour laboratory. Evaluation through written examinations and project presentations. Course covers atomic structure and radiation, radiation effects and dosimetry, radioactive materiel transportation, radioactive commodity system safety, internal and external permissible exposure limits, and protection against external radiation.

Credit recommendation: In the graduate degree category, 3 semester hours in Safety Engineering (12/84).

Principles of Safety (84540)

Location: School of Engineering and Logistics, Red River Army Depot.

Length: 50 hours (5 weeks).

Dates: December 1984-Present.

Objective: To provide students with a foundation in the field of safety and the discipline of safety engineering.

Instruction: Ten hours lecture per week. Evaluation through written examinations, projects, and presentations. Course covers evolution of safety and safety engineering, theories of accident causation, safety standards, and codes, and the Occupational Safety and Health Act.

Credit recommendation: In the upper division baccalaureate category, 3 semester hours in Safety Engineering (12/84).

Problems in Safety Engineering (84585)

Location: School of Engineering and Logistics, Red River Army Depot.

Length: 60 hours (10 weeks).

Dates: June 1985-Present.

Objective: To test the students' understanding of important concerns in safety engineering.

Instruction: Lecture and laboratory. Evaluation through research paper in safety engineering.

Credit recommendation: In the graduate degree category, 3 semester hours in Safety Engineering (12/84).

Product Reliability and Safety (84566)

Location: School of Engineering and Logistics, Red River Army Depot.

Length: 60 hours (10 weeks).

Dates: September 1977-Present.

Objective: To provide students with an understanding of the specialized emphasis required to develop the ability to function in the product design process as a specialist in safety engineering.

Instruction: Five hours lecture per week plus one hour laboratory per week. Evaluation through written examinations, projects, and presentations. Accident prevention and human factor principles are brought to focus upon specific problems of accident elimination as related to product liability and safety.

Credit recommendation: In the graduate degree category, 3 semester hours in Industrial Management (12/84).

Radiological Safety and Hazards Evaluation (84550)
Location: School of Engineering and Logistics, Red River Army Depot.
Length: 60 hours (10 weeks).
Dates: April 1978-Present.
Objective: To present students with pertinent information concerning the evaluation and control of various ionizing and nonionizing radiations. Safety control techniques are of primary importance.
Instruction: Five hours per week lecture plus one hour per week laboratory. Evaluation through written examinations. Course covers X-ray safety, protection against internal radiation, nuclear reactor safety, handling and disposal of radioactive materiel, radiation detection and measurement, and radiation control and licensing requirements.
Credit recommendation: In the graduate degree category, 3 semester hours in Safety Engineering (12/84).

Reliability Engineering (84525)
Location: School of Engineering and Logistics, Red River Army Depot.
Length: 60 hours (10 weeks).
Dates: April 1981-Present.
Objective: To provide students with an understanding of the theories and techniques pertinent to the solution of engineering problems in system reliability.
Instruction: Five hours lecture per week plus one hour laboratory. Evaluation through written examinations. Statistical techniques for predicting and assessing reliability, reliability measures, and probabilistic design are covered.
Credit recommendation: In the graduate degree category, 3 semester hours in Industrial Engineering (12/84).

Safety Aspects of Facilities Design (84562)
Location: School of Engineering and Logistics, Red River Army Depot.
Length: 60 hours (10 weeks).
Dates: September 1977-Present.
Objective: To provide students with an understanding of specialized training in the design of buildings and similar facilities from the standpoint of accident elimination.
Instruction: Five hours lecture per week plus one hour laboratory per week. Evaluation through written examinations, projects, and presentations. The generalized safety and human factors principles included in the prerequisite courses are used in specific problems of safety related to facilities designed for use by human beings. Emphasis is placed on environmental effects and control, flow of traffic (human and materiel) and access to facilities.
Credit recommendation: In the upper division baccalaureate category, 3 semester hours in Safety Engineering (12/84).

Safety Considerations in Electrical/Electronic Systems Design (84531)
Location: School of Engineering and Logistics, Red River Army Depot.
Length: 60 hours (10 weeks).
Dates: April 1983-Present.
Objective: To provide students with the knowledge and understanding of electrical energy hazards and appropriate control measures to minimize personnel injury and equipment damage.
Instruction: Five hours lecture per week plus one hour laboratory per week. Evaluation through written examinations, project, and presentation. Course covers a review of electrical circuits, hazards, created by electrical and electromagnetic energy, effect of current flow on personnel, and abnormal circuit conditions.
Credit recommendation: In the lower division baccalaureate/associate degree category, 3 semester hours in Technology (12/84).

Safety Engineering Tools and Techniques
Location: School of Engineering and Logistics, Red River Army Depot.
Length: 60 hours (10 weeks).
Dates: April 1984-Present.
Objective: To provide students with an understanding of the basic tools and techniques developed to use in applying management information systems programs to safety management and engineering functions.
Instruction: Lecture, laboratory, exercises, simulations, and problem solving. Evaluation through examinations. Course covers development of a safety data file program and a safety management control technique program. Students also develop and run a computer simulation of a safety engineering problem.
Credit recommendation: In the upper division baccalaureate category, 3 semester hours in Industrial Management (12/84).

Safety in the Occupational Environment I (84564)
Location: School of Engineering and Logistics, Red River Army Depot.
Length: 60 hours (10 weeks).
Dates: September 1981-Present.
Objective: To provide students with the knowledge and understanding of materiels and techniques essential to the detection, evaluation, and control of certain known physical occupational hazards with emphasis on hazards most common in industrial environments.
Instruction: Five hours lecture per week plus one hour laboratory per week. Evaluation through written examinations, projects, and presentations. Course covers ventilation, heat stress, noise control and hearing conversion, vibration, and illumination.
Credit recommendation: In the upper division baccalaureate category, 3 semester hours in Safety Engineer-

ing (12/84).

Safety in the Occupational Environment II (84572)
Location: School of Engineering and Logistics, Red River Army Depot.
Length: 60 hours (10 weeks).
Dates: November 1981-Present.
Objective: To enable students to apply OSHA and AMC safety standards to practices and methods used in industrial operations.
Instruction: Five hours lecture per week plus one hour laboratory per week. Evaluation through written examinations. Course covers industrial manufacturing and maintenance process, principles of machine guarding, safety in welding operations, materiel handling safety. OSHA standards and safety surveys, and industrial hygiene.
Credit recommendation: In the upper division baccalaureate category, 3 semester hours in Safety Engineering (12/84).

Statistical Quality Control (84514)
Location: School of Engineering and Logistics, Red River Army Depot.
Length: 60 hours (10 weeks).
Dates: May 1974-Present.
Objective: To provide students with an understanding of statistical methods use in industrial quality control.
Instruction: Five hours lecture per week plus one hour laboratory per week. Evaluation by examinations, projects, and presentations. Course covers aspects of physical application of the process control theory and technique, significance tests, sampling plans, and military standards for inspection.
Credit recommendation: In the graduate degree category, 3 semester hours in Quality Control (12/84).

Systems Safety Engineering (84567)
Location: School of Engineering and Logistics, Red River Army Depot.
Length: 60 hours (10 weeks).
Dates: April 1977-Present.
Objective: To provide students with information on the tools and techniques required to provide safety engineering output in various stages during system design.
Instruction: Five hours per week lecture plus one hour laboratory per week. Evaluation through examinations, projects, and presentations. Course covers the relationship of safety with the reliability and maintainability disciplines; and the management of an effective system safety program.
Credit recommendation: In the graduate degree category, 3 semester hours in Safety Engineering (12/84).

Systems Safety Management (84571)
Location: School of Engineering and Logistics, Red River Army Depot.
Length: 60 hours (10 weeks).
Dates: January 1980-Present.
Objective: To give students a comprehensive study of the role of the Army System Safety Program in overall systems management.
Instruction: Five hours per week plus one hour laboratory per week. Evaluation through written examinations, projects, and presentations. Emphasis is placed on the integration of the Army System Safety effort in the overall system management model and establishment of a system safety organization that allows flexibility and procedures. The student must complete a project for developing system safety input and present the results to the class.
Credit recommendation: In the upper division baccalaureate category, 3 semester hours in Military Science (12/84).

PRODUCT/PRODUCTION ENGINEERING PROGRAM

The goal of the Product/Production Engineering Program is to ensure that Army Materiel is designed and produced in the most economical, cost-effective manner possible, and to ensure that Army Technology represents the current state-of-the-art in manufacturing technology. The training objective is thirty engineering graduates each year.

Army Manufacturing Technology (83506)
Location: School of Engineering and Logistics, Red River Army Depot.
Length: 60 hours (10 weeks).
Dates: January 1976-Present.
Objective: To give students an introduction to Army producibility engineering programs.
Instruction: Six hours lecture per week. Evaluation through written examination. Course covers producibility, producibility engineering and planning, military adaptation of commercial items, manufacturing methods and technology, value engineering, and productivity.
Credit recommendation: In the upper division baccalaureate category, 3 semester hours in Military Science (12/84).

Computer Science (83558)
Location: School of Engineering and Logistics, Red River Army Depot.
Length: 70 hours (10 weeks).
Dates: January 1980-Present.
Objective: To provide the student with an understanding of scientific computer programming theory, FORTRAN programming language, and scientific and engineering applications.
Instruction: Course covers computer fundamentals, basic FORTRAN, advanced FORTRAN, and brief ses-

sions on other programming languages.

Credit recommendation: In the upper division baccalaureate category, 4 semester hours in Computer Science (12/84).

Computers in Manufacturing (83554)

Location: School of Engineering and Logistics, Red River Army Depot.

Length: 90 hours (20 weeks).

Dates: December 1984-Present.

Objective: To advance students knowledge of the uses of computers in manufacturing and manufacturing support.

Instruction: Six one-hour meetings per week for the first ten weeks, then three one-hour meetings per week for second ten weeks. Lecture and laboratory. Evaluation through written examinations. Course covers simulations, random number generation, numerical control, computer-aided manufacture, and integrated manufacturing.

Credit recommendation: In the graduate degree category, 4 semester hours in Industrial Engineering (12/84).

Cost Estimating for Engineering

Location: School of Engineering and Logistics, Red River Army Depot.

Length: 40 hours (1 week).

Dates: January 1976-Present.

Objective: To aid students involved in weapon systems cost estimating at research and development activities.

Instruction: A seminar approach is used. Twenty-two and one-half hours of lecture per week plus seventeen and one-half hours of workshop per week. Topics stressed are design to cost estimating, statistics, economic analysis, and trace. Case studies are used.

Credit recommendation: In the upper division baccalaureate category, 2 semester hours and 1 semester hour in the graduate degree category in Military Science (12/84).

Economic Analysis (83507)

Location: School of Engineering and Logistics, Red River Army Depot.

Length: 60 hours (6 weeks).

Dates: January 1976-Present.

Objective: To give students concepts concerning economic considerations and problems that will improve their decision making skills and abilities. Analytic techniques used in cost estimating are stressed.

Instruction: Seven hours lecture per week plus three hours laboratory per week. Evaluation through written examinations, in-class exercises, and homework. Course covers interest and economic equivalence, evaluating replacement alternatives and public activities, and risk, uncertainty, and economic modeling.

Credit recommendation: In the graduate degree category, 3 semester hours in Economic Analysis (12/84).

Engineering Management

Location: School of Engineering and Logistics, Red River Army Depot.

Length: 50 hours (10 weeks).

Dates: September 1976-Present.

Objective: To provide students with management techniques.

Instruction: Five hours lecture per week. Evaluation through written examinations and reports. Course includes the study of top level decision making structures, analysis of economic and social forces affecting defense decisions, and study of various management system philosophies and theories. Study of staff studies and engineering reports is stressed.

Credit recommendation: In the upper division baccalaureate category, 3 semester hours in Management (12/84).

Mathematical Statistics for Product Assurance (83513)

Location: School of Engineering and Logistics, Red River Army Depot.

Length: 60 hours (10 weeks).

Dates: January 1980-Present.

Objective: To provide students with an understanding in probability theory, random variables probability distribution, expected values, and related statistical techniques.

Instruction: Lecture, practical exercises, and research. Evaluation through examinations and research paper. Course covers probability theory, random variables and probability distributions, sums of random variables, sampling distributions, estimation of parameters, application of hypotheses, and experimental design.

Credit recommendation: In the graduate degree category, 3 semester hours in Statistics (12/84).

Materiel Acquisition Management (83509)

Location: School of Engineering and Logistics, Red River Army Depot.

Length: 60 hours (10 weeks).

Dates: January 1976-Present.

Objective: To give students an understanding of materiel acquisition management and its application to Army Materiel.

Instruction: Five hours lecture per week plus one hour laboratory per week. Evaluation through written examinations. Course covers life-cycle model, configuration management, force modernization process, weapon system and equipment support analysis, and financial management.

Credit recommendation: In the lower division baccalaureate/associate degree category, 3 semester hours in Military Science (12/84).

Microprocessor Controls (83510)

Location: School of Engineering and Logistics, Red River Army Depot.

Length: 60 hours (10 weeks).
Dates: January 1983-Present.
Objective: To provide students with a working knowledge of the use of microprocessor systems for monitoring and controlling physical processes.
Instruction: Three hours lecture per week plus three hours laboratory. Evaluation through written examinations. Course covers microprocessor fundamentals, microprocessor operations, memory technology, peripheral support, and industrial microprocessors application.
Credit recommendation: In the upper division baccalaureate category, 3 semester hours in Engineering (12/84).

Operational Analysis for Production Systems (83520)
Location: School of Engineering and Logistics, Red River Army Depot.
Length: 60 hours (10 weeks).
Dates: September 1976-Present.
Objective: To provide a survey of uses of operations research techniques.
Instruction: Five hours lecture per week plus one hour laboratory per week. Evaluation through written examination.
Credit recommendation: In the graduate degree category, 3 semester hours in Industrial Management (12/84).

Problems in Product/Production Engineering I & II (83585)
Location: School of Engineering and Logistics, Red River Army Depot.
Length: 120 hours for both I & II (20 weeks).
Dates: January 1976-Present.
Objective: To allow students to research and study assigned problems. Techniques concerning documentation and professional problem solving are stressed.
Instruction: Section I: Deals with familiarization of library, research proposals, and topic selection. Two 2½-hour meetings per week plus one hour laboratory per week. Section II: Deals with writing and presenting the research results. Two 2½-hour meetings per week plus one hour laboratory per week.
Credit recommendation: In the graduate degree category, 6 semester hours in Graduate Research (12/84). NOTE: Students must complete both I and II to receive any credit.

Procurement Policies and Procedures for Engineers (83503)
Location: School of Engineering and Logistics, Red River Army Depot.
Length: 50 hours (5 weeks).
Dates: January 1976-Present.
Objective: To give students a working knowledge of the defense procurement system.
Instruction: Lecture and practical assignments. Evaluation through written examination and reports. Legal aspects, procedures, and policies concerning contracts are studied.
Credit recommendation: In the upper division baccalaureate category, 3 semester hours in Management (12/84).

Product/Production Engineering I (83502)
Location: School of Engineering and Logistics, Red River Army Depot.
Length: 80 hours (13 weeks).
Dates: January 1976-Present.
Objective: To provide students with an understanding of the scope of AMC product/production engineering. Activities concerning interrelationships among materials, production, and selection for uses in design.
Instruction: Lecture and laboratory. Evaluation through written examination. Course gives product/production engineering overview; covers research, development and acquisition policies and procedures, materiel characteristics, and uses production processes.
Credit recommendation: In the upper division baccalaureate category, 3 semester hours in Mechanical Engineering (12/84).

Product/Production Engineering II (83505)
Location: School of Engineering and Logistics, Red River Army Depot.
Length: 100 hours (11 weeks).
Dates: January 1976-Present.
Objective: To further students' understanding of principles learned in Product/Production Engineering I.
Instruction: Lecture and laboratory. Evaluation through written examination. Course covers inspection, machining process, and production equipment; joining processes; and finishing and surface treatments. Also includes plant visits in Dallas.
Credit recommendation: In the graduate degree category, 3 semester hours in Mechanical Engineering (12/84).

Product/Production Engineering III (83600)
Location: School of Engineering and Logistics, Red River Army Depot.
Length: 60 hours (10 weeks).
Dates: January 1983-Present.
Objective: To give students an in-depth exposure to manufacturing and testing of electronic devices and nonmetals such as various plastics.
Instruction: Five hours lecture per week plus one hour laboratory. Evaluation through written examinations. Course covers material characteristics, nonmetal production processes, and electronic production processes.
Credit recommendation: In the graduate degree category, 3 semester hours in Mechanical Engineering (12/84).

Product/Production Planning and Control (83508)
   Location: School of Engineering and Logistics, Red River Army Depot.
   Length: 60 hours (10 weeks).
   Dates: January 1976-Present.
   Objective: To familiarize students with management role, concept, and techniques used in the Department of Defense and related commercial facilities.
   Instruction: Five hours lecture per week plus one hour laboratory per week. Evaluation through written examinations. Course covers cost/schedule control system, network-based management techniques, line of balance, plant operations management, project management, and production management.
   Credit recommendation: In the upper division baccalaureate category, 3 semester hours in Management (12/84).

Production Modeling Techniques (83576)
   Location: School of Engineering and Logistics, Red River Army Depot.
   Length: 60 hours (10 weeks).
   Dates: January 1983-Present.
   Objective: To provide students with an understanding of scientific and engineering approaches to the modeling of production systems.
   Instruction: Five hours lecture per week plus one hour laboratory per week. Evaluation through written examinations. Course covers Markov processes, forecasting techniques, and munitions production systems.
   Credit recommendation: In the graduate degree category, 3 semester hours in Industrial Engineering (12/84).

Production Quality Control (83514)
   Location: School of Engineering and Logistics, Red River Army Depot.
   Length: 60 hours (10 weeks).
   Dates: January 1975-Present.
   Objective: To teach students statistical methods as used in industrial quality control.
   Instruction: Five hours lecture per week plus one hour laboratory per week. Evaluation through written examinations and reports. Process control theory, sampling plans, and military standards for inspection are used.
   Credit recommendation: In the graduate degree category, 3 semester hours in Quality Control (12/84).

Production Systems Design
   Location: School of Engineering and Logistics, Red River Army Depot.
   Length: 60 hours (10 weeks).
   Dates: January 1976-Present.
   Objective: To teach students the techniques and considerations involved in planning, designing, and modernizing production systems.
   Instruction: Five hours per week plus one hour laboratory per week. Evaluation through written examinations. Course covers introduction to plant layout, system engineering of production lines and equipment, production lead-time estimating, and production planning and control.
   Credit recommendation: In the upper division baccalaureate category, 3 semester hours in Industrial Engineering (12/84).

Statistical Methods and Systems Reliability (83525)
   Location: School of Engineering and Logistics, Red River Army Depot.
   Length: 60 hours (10 weeks); 6 one-hour meetings per week.
   Dates: February 1977-Present.
   Objective: To provide students with an understanding of statistical methods used in industrial quality control.
   Instruction: Five hours lecture per week plus one hour laboratory per week. Evaluation through written examinations. Course includes aspects of the physical application of the process control theory and techniques, significant tests, sampling plans, and military standards for inspection.
   Credit recommendation: In the graduate degree category, 3 semester hours in Industrial Engineering (12/84).

Technical Data Package Development/Preparation (83504)
   Location: School of Engineering and Logistics, Red River Army Depot.
   Length: 40 hours (1 week).
   Dates: January 1976-Present.
   Objective: To introduce students to policies, procedures, and the responsibility of acquisition, preparation, review, and proofing of technical data packages.
   Instruction: Five 8-hour lecture sessions per week. Evaluation through written examination. Course covers technical data package and its background and history; management and control systems; information storage retrieval; specifications and standardization; product assurance; and technical documentation.
   Credit recommendation: In the upper division baccalaureate category, 3 semester hours in Military Science (12/84).

SOFTWARE ENGINEERING PROGRAM

Advanced Microprocessors (81541)
   Location: School of Engineering and Logistics, Red River Army Depot.
   Length: 50 hours (10 weeks: two 1-hour lectures/week; one 3-hour lab/week).
   Dates: August 1986-Present.
   Objective: To provide the student with hands-on experience using an INTEL 80286 uP. Programming and interfacing are emphasized.

Learning Outcome: Upon successful completion of this course, the student will be able to program using assembler language; measure and convert signals, and know bus communication protocols.

Instruction: An in-depth study of programming techniques and details for currently utilized processors. In addition, applications of microprocessors for robotics, process control, and process inspection are discussed. Major topics include: process automation, measurement, signal generation and conversion, interfacing, programming techniques, and application.

Credit recommendation: In the graduate category, 2 semester hours in Electrical Engineering or Software Engineering (9/87).

Computer Simulation and Communication Techniques (81559)

Location: School of Engineering and Logistics, Red River Army Depot.

Length: 80 hours (10 weeks: five 1-hour lectures/week; one 3-hour lab/week).

Dates: August 1986-Present.

Objective: To teach the student analysis and design methods used in simulation and communication networks.

Learning Outcome: Upon successful completion of this course, the student will be able to work with simulation methods (Monte Carlo method) and program with GASP IV; understand and use hardware and interface standards and protocols; and understand distributed computing systems.

Instruction: An introduction to digital simulation techniques and methods, data communications, techniques and computer networking methods. Emphasis is placed on utilization of presented materials as tools in development and testing of real-time distributed software systems. Major topics are digital simulation techniques, data communications techniques, and distributed computing systems. Student evaluation is achieved by exams (65%), homework (15%), and labs (20%).

Credit recommendation: In the graduate category, 3 semester hours in Computer Engineering or Computer Science (9/87).

Computer Techniques for Engineers (81558)

Location: School of Engineering and Logistics, Red River Army Depot.

Length: 70 hours (10 weeks: five 1-hour lectures/week; two 1-hour labs/week).

Dates: August 1986-Present.

Objective: To teach the student some important elements concerning systems architecture and selected programming languages (high level).

Learning Outcome: Upon successful completion of this course, the student will be able to read and understand operation of programs written in FORTRAN, COBOL, PASCAL, and C languages; understand language design characteristics such as structures, data types, run-time considerations, interpretative languages, lexical analysis and passing.

Instruction: A survey of computer systems architecture, programming languages, and operating systems used within the Army for engineering applications, business applications, and for real-time applications. A brief introduction to FORTRAN syntax and programming concepts emphasizing engineering applications is provided. Major topics are computer system architecture, programming languages/operating systems, and FORTRAN programming. Student evaluation is achieved through hourly exams and lab exercises.

Credit recommendation: In the graduate category, 3 semester hours in Computer Engineering or Computer Science (9/87).

Current Topics in Software Engineering (81590)

Location: School of Engineering and Logistics, Red River Army Depot.

Length: 90 hours (10 weeks: one 1-hour lecture/week; 80 hours of conference attendance).

Dates: August 1986-Present.

Objective: To provide the student with an understanding of current concerns/development in software engineering.

Learning Outcome: Upon successful completion of this course, the student will have an understanding of the current happenings and developments in software engineering.

Instruction: The course provides an understanding of current happenings and developments in software engineering. It includes guest lecturers from within the Army, software engineering comments, and attendance at nationally recognized software symposia.

Credit recommendation: In the graduate category, 3 semester hours in Computer Engineering, Computer Science, or Software Engineering (9/87).

Economic Analysis and Software Life-Cycle Costs (81566)

Location: School of Engineering and Logistics, Red River Army Depot.

Length: 60 hours (6 weeks: five 1-hour lectures/week; five 1-hour labs/week).

Dates: August 1986-Present.

Objective: To provide the student with an understanding of economic considerations, concepts, and problems designed to improve decision making, analytical abilities, and methods of evaluation.

Learning Outcome: Upon successful completion of this course, the student will be able to demonstrate an understanding of interest and economic equivalence, replacement alternatives and public activities, risks, uncertainty, economic modeling, and software life-cycle cost evaluation.

Instruction: Major topics include interest and economic equivalence; evaluating replacement alternatives and public activities; risk, uncertainty, and economic modeling; and software life-cycle cost evaluation.

Credit recommendation: In the graduate category, 3 semester hours in Economics, Computer Engineering, Computer Software, or Software Engineering (9/87).

Embedded Computer Algorithms (81550)

Location: School of Engineering and Logistics, Red River Army Depot.

Length: 60 hours (10 weeks: four 1-hour lectures/week; one 2-hour lab/week).

Dates: August 1986-Present.

Objective: To teach the student theory and application of information structures and algorithms to design, implementation, and maintenance of real-time systems.

Learning Outcome: Upon successful completion of this course, the student will be able to apply theory of structures and algorithms to real-time applications such as data acquisition, process control, and interfacing.

Instruction: Course provides an introduction to the theory of information structures and algorithms and their application to design implementation of real-time systems. Major topics are linear, tree, and graph structures; memory management; algorithm design and analysis; and real-time applications. Student evaluation is achieved by three examinations (90%) and selected programs (10%).

Credit recommendation: In the graduate category, 3 semester hours in Computer Science or Software Engineering (9/87).

Mathematical Statistics (81511)

Location: School of Engineering and Logistics, Red River Army Depot.

Length: 66 hours (11 weeks: six 1-hour lectures/week).

Dates: August 1986-Present.

Objective: To provide the student with an in-depth study of statistical techniques used to assess system performance based on sample data.

Learning Outcome: Upon successful completion of this course, the student will be able to solve basic engineering problems of a statistical nature; read advanced texts and journals in research fields; and communicate statistical techniques with other engineers and managers.

Instruction: Major topics are probability theory; probability distributions; goodness of assessment values, and sample data collection.

Credit recommendation: In the upper division baccalaureate category, 3 semester hours in Mathematical Statistics (9/87).

Microprocessor Controls (81540)

Location: School of Engineering and Logistics, Red River Army Depot.

Length: 140 hours (10 weeks: three 4-hour lectures/week; one 2-hour lab/week).

Dates: August 1986-Present.

Objective: To give the student an understanding of microprocessor architecture, numbers, computer codes and arithmetic, and assembly language programming.

Learning Outcome: Upon successful completion of this course, the student will be able to recall components and functions making up a microprocessor; and do limited programming in assembly language.

Instruction: Instruction covers microcomputer operations and architecture, memory technology, peripheral support, and microcomputer applications in control. Instruction is through lecture and laboratory. Evaluation through examination.

Credit recommendation: In the upper division baccalaureate category, 3 semester hours in Computer Engineering (9/87).

Problems in Software Engineering I and II (81585)

Location: School of Engineering and Logistics, Red River Army Depot.

Length: 60 hours (10 weeks: six 1-hour lectures/week; 1-2 hours of lecture, 4-5 hours of study time).

Dates: August 1986-Present.

Objective: To provide the student with advanced study and research in the field of software engineering. Emphasis is placed on the role of communication skills such as organizing ideas, writing, structure and content of proposals, technical reports, manuals, and other software project documentation.

Learning Outcome: Upon successful completion of this course, the student will be familiar with research sources and will be able to demonstrate research techniques, select a research topic, do research, develop a research proposal, prepare a formal research report, and present and defend a completed report.

Instruction: Major topics include familiarization with research sources, research techniques and topic selection, research problem selection and proposal development, performance of research, preparation of formal research report, and report presentation and defense.

Credit recommendation: In the graduate category, 6 semester hours in General Studies or Interdisciplinary Studies (9/87). NOTE: Three (3) semester hours should be applied to Introduction to Graduate Studies and three (3) semester hours should be applied to Thesis Writing.

Project Management (81508)

Location: School of Engineering and Logistics, Red River Army Depot.

Length: 60 hours (10 weeks: six 1-hour lectures/week).

Dates: August 1986-Present.

Objective: To give the student an introduction to the concept of project/system management organizations, the general operating procedures and funding criteria for project management, and the roles and responsibilities of project managers.

Learning Outcome: Upon successful completion of this course, the student will be able to trace the history of the development of modern management thought; exhibit a working knowledge of personnel administration in a federal service; describe the work of modern management theorists including (but not limited to) Maslow, McGregor, Herzberg, and McClellan. Discuss in detail the functions of management: planning, organizing, controlling, and conducting; and apply the techniques of PERT and CPM.

Instruction: Course covers a history of management thought, personnel administration in the federal service, the works of modern management theorists, the functions of management, and the techniques of PERT and CPM.

Credit recommendation: In the upper division baccalaureate category, 3 semester hours in Business Administration or Management (9/87).

Software Configuration Management (51576)
Location: School of Engineering and Logistics, Red River Army Depot.
Length: 50 hours (10 weeks: five 1-hour lectures/week).
Dates: August 1986-Present.
Objective: To present the student with the concepts, policies, and administrative requirements of configuration management.
Learning Outcome: Upon successful completion of this course, the student will be able to explain hardware configuration management practices; explain software configuration management practices; and apply configuration management principles of: configuration identification, configuration control, configuration status accounting, and configuration auditing to a software development project.
Instruction: Major topics are management aspects, specifications and engineering drawing, and configuration control.
Credit recommendation: In the graduate category, 3 semester hours in Computer Science or Software Engineering (9/87).

Software Engineering Concepts I (81530)
Location: School of Engineering and Logistics, Red River Army Depot.
Length: 66 hours (11 weeks: six 1-hour lectures/week).
Dates: August 1986-Present.
Objective: To provide the student with a set of design measures, strategies, technical tools and techniques for software development.
Learning Outcome: Upon successful completion of this course, the student will be able to use the tools, techniques, and methodologies appropriate for use during analysis, design, and coding activities; implement management controls that will lend traceability and visibility to software development and maintenance activities.

Instruction: Major topics are software systems analysis, system design methodology, and programming methodology.
Credit recommendation: In the upper division baccalaureate category, 3 semester hours in Computer Science or Software Engineering (9/87).

Software Engineering Concepts II (81531)
Location: School of Engineering and Logistics, Red River Army Depot.
Length: 66 hours (11 weeks: six 1-hour lectures/week).
Dates: August 1986-Present.
Objective: To present the student with principles of design, implementation, debugging, testing, documentation, and maintenance of *team* oriented software projects.
Learning Outcome: Upon successful completion of this course, the student will be able to identify problems associated with team oriented software projects; use software testing and debugging techniques; and employ methods of measuring software quality.
Instruction: Course covers software quality assurance and software testing. Evaluation through examination; course taught through lectures.
Credit recommendation: In the graduate category, 3 semester hours in Computer Engineering, Computer Science, or Software Engineering (9/87).

Software Engineering Using ADA I (81520)
Location: School of Engineering and Logistics, Red River Army Depot.
Length: 99 hours (11 weeks: five 1-hour lectures/week; two 2-hour labs/week.
Dates: August 1986-Present.
Objective: To provide the student with an introduction to the ADA programming language. Topics include data abstraction and types, packages, generic program units, and input/output.
Learning Outcome: Upon successful completion of this course, the student will be able to describe the situations that led to the development and use of ADA; describe how the use of ADA enforces the use of software engineering principles such as abstraction, information hiding and modularity; and write programs in ADA using statements and constructs; such as, array slices and attributes, unconstrained arrays, text/character/string IO, and aggregates.
Instruction: Major topics are software engineering overview; ADA programming language and coding; and ADA programming support environment.
Credit recommendation: In the upper division baccalaureate category, 3 semester hours in Computer Science (9/87).

Software Engineering Using ADA II (81521)
Location: School of Engineering and Logistics, Red River Army Depot.
Length: 99 hours (11 weeks: five 1-hour lectures/week;

two 2-hour labs/week.

Dates: August 1986-Present.

Objective: To provide the student with an understanding of how ADA programming deals with exception handling and concurrent programming, as related to real-time processing problems.

Learning Outcome: Upon successful completion of this course, the student will be able to demonstrate exception handling programming; and demonstrate concurrent programming of real-time processing problems.

Instruction: Course presents advanced features of ADA programming language. Topics covered include tasks, exception handling and concurrent programming, as relating to real-time processing problems. Presentation through lecture and labs. Evaluation through exams and performance testing in lab. Grade of 70% considered passing.

Credit recommendation: In the graduate category, 3 semester hours in Computer Engineering, Computer Science, or Software Engineering (9/87).

Software Engineering Workshop (81586)

Location: School of Engineering and Logistics, Red River Army Depot.

Length: 60 hours (10 weeks: six 1-hour lectures/week).

Dates: August 1986-Present.

Objective: To give the student the opportunity to participate as a team member in a complete software development project. The size and scope of the project is such that the software development tools and techniques presented in the previous course will be used.

Learning Outcome: Upon successful completion of this course, the student will be able to design and develop a software system.

Instruction: In the course, students are assigned to project teams which design and develop a software system.

Credit recommendation: In the graduate category, 3 semester hours in Computer Engineering, Computer Science, or Software Engineering (9/87).

Software Technical Data Package Development (81504)

Location: School of Engineering and Logistics, Red River Army Depot.

Length: 50 hours (10 weeks: five 1-hour lectures/week).

Dates: August 1986-Present.

Objective: To familiarize the student with policies, procedures, and responsibilities for the acquisition, review, preparation, proofing, maintenance, control, and transmission of a technical data package.

Learning Outcome: Upon successful completion of this course, the student will be able to use the methodology required by the Army Materials Command for developing a technical data package; introduce this methodology for development of software technical data packages; and demonstrate technical data package development through individual and group projects.

Instruction: Course covers the components of a technical data package and the steps used to develop a technical data package. Student evaluation is achieved through homework and quizzes (10%), group project(s) (30%), and written exams (60%).

Credit recommendation: In the upper division baccalaureate category, 3 semester hours in Military Science (9/87). NOTE: While similar material is covered in public education—this material appears to be too closely tied to DOD STD-2167 to be generally applicable.

Systems Engineering (81515)

Location: School of Engineering and Logistics, Red River Army Depot.

Length: 50 hours (10 weeks: five 1-hour lectures/week).

Dates: August 1986-Present.

Objective: To give the student an introduction to the processes and patterns of systems engineering: planning, organization, and management of programs for developing large, highly complex systems with special emphasis on problems of embedded computers and relationships between hardware and software.

Learning Outcome: Upon successful completion of this course, the student will be able to identify and practice methods of overcoming conceptual blocks to problem solving; define the basic concepts of general systems thinking as applied to complex system development; define and use systems engineering tools and techniques as aids in the development of large, complex systems; and relate systems engineering techniques to the development of systems with embedded computer resources.

Instruction: Major topics are systems concepts, systems engineering methods, and embedded computer systems principles.

Credit recommendation: In the graduate category, 3 semester hours in Business Administration, Computer Engineering, Computer Science, or Software Engineering (9/87).

Systems Reliability (81525)

Location: School of Engineering and Logistics, Red River Army Depot.

Length: 60 hours (five 1-hour lectures/week; one 1-hour lab/week).

Dates: August 1986-Present.

Objective: To enable the student to make reliability calculations, reliability tests, and to apply reliability management techniques.

Learning Outcome: Upon successful completion of this course, the student will be able to identify reliability parameters; make system reliability calculations; and use reliability management techniques in allocation, prediction, and growth.

Instruction: Course covers reliability measures, static and dynamic reliability models, and reliability estimation. Course taught through lecture and problem solving labs.

Student evaluation is achieved through homework (15%), exams (10%), and a final exam (25%).

Credit recommendation: In the upper division baccalaureate category, 3 semester hours in Engineering Systems Reliability (9/87).

United States Department of Agriculture, Graduate School

The Graduate School, U.S. Department of Agriculture was created in 1921 and is a nonprofit, self-supporting, continuing education institution governed by a Board appointed by the Secretary of Agriculture. The school's mission is the "improvement of government service and self-development through education and training." Although classes are attended primarily by government workers, they are open to all adults who wish to update skills, prepare for a different field of employment, or fulfill personal goals.

Instructors are practitioners in their fields, trained in educational techniques, thus assuring the highest quality in training and education. Courses are conducted in Washington, D.C. but can be conducted on-site anywhere. Correspondence programs naturally can be accomplished anywhere.

The Graduate School, USDA offers courses in more than 40 subject areas, including accounting, computer sciences, editing, paralegal, sciences and engineering, and foreign languages.

Source of official student records: Registrar's Office, Graduate School, USDA, Room 1103, South Agriculture Building, 14th and Independence Avenue, N.W., Washington, D.C. 20250.

Additional information about the courses: Program on Noncollegiate Sponsored Instruction, The Center for Adult Learning and Educational Credentials, American Council on Education, One Dupont Circle, Washington, D.C. 20036. Or, Registrar's Office, Graduate School, USDA, Room 1103, South Agriculture Building, 14th and Independence Avenue, N.W., Washington, D.C. 20250.

DAY AND EVENING PROGRAMS

ACCOUNTING

Principles of Accounting I (Evening) (EACCT101)
Location: Washington, D.C.
Length: 30 hours (3 hours per week for 10 weeks).
Dates: January 1978-Present.
Objective: To provide the student with the knowledge to record typical accounting transactions based on generally accepted accounting principles, to summarize data, and to prepare financial statements.
Learning Outcome: Upon successful completion of this course, the student will be able to understand the complete accounting cycle, including the use of special journals and subsidiary ledger accounts; prepare financial statements; journalize and post business transaction; and make adjusting and closing entries.
Instruction: Course covers accounting principles, the accounting cycle, determining cost of goods sold, gross profit, and net profit, adjusting and closing entries, deferrals and accruals, and bank reconciliation. Methodology includes lectures, proctored exercises, practice set and examinations.
Credit recommendation: In the lower division baccalaureate/associate degree category, 2 semester hours in Principles of Accounting (6/88).

Introductory Statistics I (ESTAT101)
Location: Washington, D.C.
Length: 30 hours (3 hours per week for 10 weeks).
Dates: January 1978-Present.
Objective: To provide the student with the knowledge of basic statistical concepts and measurement tools in collecting, analyzing and presenting various kinds of data in various formats.
Learning Outcome: Upon successful completion of this course, the student will be able to determine and use measures of central tendency and dispension for discrete and continuous contribution; understand and be familiar with the concepts of probability, and the use of probability distributions such as the normal, binomial and chi-square; and be able to perform low level statistical analysis and prepare interpretations.
Instruction: Course covers construction of various presentations of data, central tendency, probability and probability distributions. Methodology includes lecture, discussion, problems, and examinations.
Credit recommendation: In the upper division baccalaureate category, 2 semester hours in Business Administration, Management Science, or Statistics (6/88).

Principles of Accounting II (Evening) (EACCT102)
Location: Washington, D.C.
Length: 30 hours (3 hours per week for 10 weeks).
Dates: January 1978-Present.
Objective: To provide the student with the knowledge of how to account for plant assets, inventories, receivables and payables, division of partnership profits, and corporation equity and dividends.
Learning Outcome: Upon successful completion of this course, the student will be able to account for plant assets, inventories, receivables and payables; account for payroll, including payroll taxes; account for division of partnership profits; account for stockholders' equity, earnings, and dividends; and make entries for issuance and redemption of corporation bonds.
Instruction: Course covers concepts and principles, receivables and payables, plant assets and depreciation, pay-

roll accounting, corporation accounting, and issuance and redemption of bonds. Methodology includes lecture, problems, discussion, and examination.

Credit recommendation: In the lower division baccalaureate/associate degree category, 2 semester hours in Principles of Accounting (6/88).

Introductory Statistics II (ESTAT102)

Location: Washington, D.C.
Length: 30 hours (3 hours per week for 10 weeks).
Dates: January 1978-Present.
Objective: To provide the student with an understanding of statistical sampling, sampling distributions and to apply the same in real world applications. Comparison of means and development of inferences from statistics about populations. This course is a continuation of Introductory Statistics I (ESTAT101).
Learning Outcome: Upon successful completion of this course, the student will be able to use and apply sampling distributions to various kinds of problems and applications; compare various means, develop sample designs, test for significance and perform analysis of variance; and introduce the concepts of regression and correlation.
Instruction: Course covers sampling, sample design, various tests of significance, inference analysis of variance and design of simple experiments. Methodology includes lecture, discussion, problems, and examinations.
Credit recommendation: In the upper division baccalaureate category, 2 semester hours in Business Administration, Management Science, or Statistics (6/88).

Principles of Accounting II (Evening) (EACCT103)

Location: Washington, D.C.
Length: 30 hours (3 hours per week for 10 weeks).
Dates: January 1978-Present.
Objective: To provide the student with the essentials of manufacturing cost accounting, financial statement analysis, responsibility accounting, and breakeven analysis.
Learning Outcome: Upon successful completion of this course, the student will be able to make journal entries and prepare statements for manufacturing cost accounting; perform financial statement analysis, breakeven analysis, and differential analysis; and understand profit and cost center accounting, and accounting for nonprofit organizations.
Instruction: Course covers financial statement analysis; responsibility accounting (profit centers and cost centers); manufacturing cost accounting (process and job order); breakeven analysis; differential analysis; and individual and nonprofit organizational accounting (introductory). Methodology includes lectures, practical exercises, discussion, and examinations.
Credit recommendation: In the lower division baccalaureate/associate degree category, 2 semester hours in Principles of Accounting (6/88).

Introductory Statistics III (ESTAT103) (Correlation and Regression Analysis)

Location: Washington, D.C.
Length: 30 hours (3 hours per week for 10 weeks).
Dates: January 1978-Present.
Objective: To develop the student with the methods and techniques of correlation and regression; both linear and non-linear applications; and to understand and apply non-parametric statistical measures.
Learning Outcome: Upon successful completion of this course, the student will be able to demonstrate and develop an understanding and be able to apply linear correlation and regression analysis to data sets of various kinds; and to understand the strengths, weaknesses and uses of correlation and regression analysis in both the linear and non-linear cases.
Instruction: Course covers correlation and regression analysis, and application of non-parametric statistics. Methodology includes lecture, discussion, problems, and examinations.
Credit recommendation: In the upper division baccalaureate category, 2 semester hours in Business Administration, Management Science, or Statistics (6/88).

Cost Accounting I (Evening) (EACCT250)

Location: Washington, D.C.
Length: 30 hours (3 hours per week for 10 weeks).
Dates: January 1978-Present.
Objective: To provide the student with the practical knowledge of job order cost accounting systems and procedures. Topics covered include monitoring costs; job order cost cycle; purchase of materials; storage and issuance of materials; inventory control; timekeeping and payroll, charging labor costs into production; departmentalizing of overhead costs; setting overhead rates; applying manufacturing overhead; accounting for scrap, spoiled goods, and defective goods; and completion of the cost cycle.
Learning Outcome: Upon successful completion of this course, the student will be able to perform job order cost accounting; maintain records for purchase and storage of materials; maintain records for the control and valuation of inventory; and maintain records for the control of labor costs.
Instruction: Course covers job order cost accounting, inventory valuation, and labor costs. Methodology includes lecture, problem solving, and cost analysis.
Credit recommendation: In the upper division baccalaureate category, 1 semester hour in Accounting, Business Administration, or Cost Accounting (6/88).

Cost Accounting II (EACCT251)

Location: Washington, D.C.
Length: 30 hours (3 hours per week for 10 weeks).
Dates: January 1978-Present.
Objective: To provide the student with an understand-

ing of how to make entries and prepare statements for a process cost accounting system, and to understand the use of costs, budgeting, bids, and expenditures analysis in planning and control.

Learning Outcome: Upon successful completion of this course, the student will be able to record entries for a process control system and prepare relevant cost of production reports; prepare budgets and analyses used for planning and control of manufacturing and non-manufacturing costs.

Instruction: Course covers process cost systems, production reports, budgets used in planning and control, direct costing, standard costs, and breakeven analysis. Methodology includes lectures, class discussions, practical exercises, and examinations.

Credit recommendation: In the upper division baccalaureate category, 2 semester hours in Accounting, Business Administration, or Cost Accounting (6/88).

Auditing I (Evening) (EAUDIT310)
   Location: Washington, D.C.
   Length: 30 hours (3 hours per week for 10 weeks).
   Dates: January 1978-Present.
   Objective: To introduce generally accepted auditing procedures, professional ethics, and legal liability considerations.
   Learning Outcome: Upon successful completion of this course, the student will be able to know generally accepted auditing standards; standard audit reports, including unqualified opinion, qualified opinion, adverse opinion and disclaimer; importance of professional ethics; legal liability considerations; how to plan an audit; how to study and evaluate internal controls in an automatic data processing environment; how to gather audit evidence—how much and what kind; and statistical samplings used in auditing.
   Instruction: Course studies the role of the auditor in the American economy. Topics include professional ethics and the legal liability of auditors, planning the audit, internal control, the audit of electronic data processing systems, evidence (what kind and how much), statistical sampling, audit working papers, and examination of general records. Methodology includes lecture, analyses of practical audit problems, and chapter examinations.
   Credit recommendation: In the upper division baccalaureate category, 1 semester hour in Accounting, Auditing, or Business Administration (6/88).

Auditing II (Evening) (EAUDIT311)
   Location: Washington, D.C.
   Length: 30 hours (3 hours per week for 10 weeks).
   Dates: January 1978-Present.
   Objective: To introduce the student to the auditing techniques for working capital accounts, property, and liability accounts.
   Learning Outcome: Upon successful completion of this course, the student will be able to conduct an internal audit according to accepted auditing principles and in compliance with legal and ethical constraints; and preparation of audit reports.
   Instruction: Course covers auditing of cash, securities, and other investments; investment revenue; accounts and notes receivable; sales transactions; inventories and cost of sales; property, plant, and equipment depreciation and depletion; prepaid expenses, deferred charges, and intangible assets; accounts payable and other liabilities; interest-bearing debt and interest expense; owner's equity; and financial statements and audit reports. Methodology includes lecture, problem exercises, and chapter examinations.
   Credit recommendation: In the upper division baccalaureate category, 2 semester hours in Accounting, Auditing, or Business Administration (6/88).

Advanced Accounting I (Evening) (EACCT350)
   Location: Washington, D.C.
   Length: 30 hours (3 hours per week for 10 weeks).
   Dates: January 1978-Present.
   Objective: To provide the student with an understanding of accounting for partnerships, installment sales, mergers and acquisitions.
   Learning Outcome: Upon successful completion of this course, the student will be able to prepare a liquidation of a partnership; understand home office and brand accounting; account for installment sales; and understand accounting for mergers and acquisitions.
   Instruction: Course covers formation and liquidation of partnerships, accounting for installment sales, home office and branch operations, and mergers and acquisitions. Methodology includes lectures, class discussions, written homework, and examinations.
   Credit recommendation: In the upper division baccalaureate category, 2 semester hours in Advanced Accounting (6/88).

Advanced Accounting II (Evening) (EACCT351)
   Location: Washington, D.C.
   Length: 30 hours (3 hours per week for 10 weeks).
   Dates: January 1978-Present.
   Objective: To provide the student with an understanding of the preparation and use of corporate consolidated financial statements.
   Learning Outcome: Upon successful completion of this course, the student will be able to know the legal and financial aspects of consolidated financial statements; and understand the use of the equity and cost methods for preparing consolidated statements.
   Instruction: Course covers the legal and financial nature of consolidated statements; working papers for preparing consolidated statements; equity and cost methods; intercompany transactions in preferred stocks and bonds; interpretation of consolidated statements, including footnotes; consolidated income statements; and foreign bran-

ches and subsidiaries. Methodology includes lectures, discussions, written homework, and examinations.

Credit recommendation: In the upper division baccalaureate category, 2 semester hours in Advanced Accounting (6/88).

Advanced Accounting III (Evening) (EACCT352)
Location: Washington, D.C.
Length: 30 hours (3 hours per week for 10 weeks).
Dates: January 1978-Present.
Objective: To provide the student with an understanding of preparation of realization and liquidation statements, receivership statements, and accounting for estate and trusts.
Learning Outcome: Upon successful completion of this course, the student will be able to understand the nature of estates and trusts and how to prepare relevant financial statements; prepare a statement of realization and liquidation, and statement of affairs; and prepare financial statements for a business in receivership.
Instruction: Course covers accounting for estates and trusts; statement of realizations and liquidation; statement of affairs and its legal purpose; accounting for a business in receivership; and an introduction to accounting for estate and local governments. Methodology includes lectures, discussions, written homework, and examinations.
Credit recommendation: In the upper division baccalaureate category, 2 semester hours in Advanced Accounting (6/88).

Budget Execution and Funds Control (ECNTR416)
Location: Washington, D.C.
Length: 30 hours (3 hours per week for 10 weeks).
Dates: January 1978-Present.
Objective: To provide the student with an understanding of the concepts, procedures, and practices in the administrative control under the anti-deficiency act of the problems associated with appropriation, apportionment, obligation of the Federal Budget and its processes.
Learning Outcome: Upon successful completion of this course, the student will be able to understand the process of appropriation allotment and obligation of the Federal Budget; examine from a critical standpoint continuing legislation, special appropriations, allotments, account balances, and other special problems associated with the appropriation of the Federal Funding process.
Instruction: Course covers obligations, appropriations, apportionment, different types of appropriations—single, multiple, no year, definite year, and one-year, and continuing legislation for agencies without new budgets. Methodology includes lecture/discussion and problem solving.
Credit recommendation: In the upper division baccalaureate category, 2 semester hours in Accounting, Business Administration, or Public Administration (6/88).

COMPUTER SCIENCES

Introduction to Information Systems Technology (ECOMP110)
Location: Washington, D.C.
Length: 30 hours (10 weeks).
Dates: January 1986-Present.
Objective: To provide the student with a knowledge of the fundamentals of computers and information processing.
Learning Outcome: Upon successful completion of this course, the student will be able to recognize basic concepts, terminology and components, including hardware and software of a computer system; distinguish between the functions performed by mainframe and microcomputers; and identify the various occupational specialties in the computer field.
Instruction: Course covers overview of information systems technology; basic concepts and terminology of computers; primary computer components; understanding the differences between types of computers; running a simple computer program on a microcomputer; and discussion of computers in society. Methodology includes lectures and demonstrations with laboratory work.
Credit recommendation: In the lower division baccalaureate/associate degree category, 2 semester hours in Data Processing or Information Systems Technology (6/88).

Introduction to Computer Programming (ECOMP111)
Location: Washington, D.C.
Length: 30 hours (10 weeks).
Dates: January 1986-Present.
Objective: To provide the student with an understanding of the principles of structured computer programming and problem solution. Emphasis is placed on the algorithmic approach.
Learning Outcome: Upon successful completion of this course, the student will be able to understand the total programming process; apply the rules and guidelines of structured programming; use flowcharting concepts in problem solving; and implement a computer program in BASIC.
Instruction: Course covers problem definition, the programming process, solution implementation; structured programming and problem solving using the algorithmic approach; flowcharting, structure charts, pseudocode; data types and attributes; introduction to BASIC language; and writing, debugging, and running a BASIC program. Methodology includes lectures and demonstrations with hands-on experience.
Credit recommendation: In the lower division baccalaureate/associate degree category, 2 semester hours in Data Processing (6/88).

Introduction to Data Processing (ACOMP114)
Location: Washington, D.C.
Length: 24 hours (4 days).
Dates: September 1981-Present.
Objective: To provide the student with a knowledge of computers and their use.
Learning Outcome: Upon successful completion of this course, the student will be able to identify the components and functions of a computer system; differentiate types and uses of various hardware and software; and explain the basic concepts of data processing.
Instruction: Course covers elements of data processing including input/output; file organization; data bases and data communications; and applications of software packages. Methodology includes lecture, demonstration, and field visit.
Credit recommendation: In the lower division baccalaureate/associate degree category, 1 semester hour in Computer Science or Data Processing (6/88).

Introduction to Problem Solving (ACOMP119)
(Problem Solving for COBOL Programmers)
Location: Washington, D.C.
Length: 24 hours (4 days).
Dates: September 1983-Present.
Objective: To provide the student with the knowledge of structured techniques for elementary program design and documentation.
Learning Outcome: Upon successful completion of this course, the student will be able to select appropriate structured techniques to construct charts and diagrams for depicting and documenting systems and programs.
Instruction: Course covers structured techniques; systems analysis; top-down approach; data flow diagrams; systems flowcharts and designs; decision tables and decision trees; pseudocode; and programming features. Methodology includes lecture, workshop, and discussion.
Credit recommendation: In the lower division baccalaureate/associate degree category, 1 semester hour in Data Processing (6/88).

BASIC Programming for Beginners (ACOMP138)
Location: Washington, D.C.
Length: 30 hours (5 days).
Dates: September 1981-Present.
Objective: To provide the student with a rudimentary understanding of BASIC and executing programs using BASIC.
Learning Outcome: Upon successful completion of this course, the student will be able to design, code, debug, and execute programs written in BASIC.
Instruction: Course covers BASIC language concepts including arithmetic operations, comparing, looping, interactive programming, arrays, menus, subroutines, and sorting. Methodology includes lecture, discussion, and classroom demonstrations.
Credit recommendation: In the lower division baccalaureate/associate degree category, 1 semester hour in Data Processing (6/88).

FORTRAN Programming (ACOMP140)
Location: Washington, D.C.
Length: 60 hours (10 days).
Dates: September 1984-Present.
Objective: To provide the student with the ability to write structured FORTRAN 77 programs.
Learning Outcome: Upon successful completion of this course, the student will be able to design, program, and execute structured FORTRAN 77 programs; and use structured flowcharts and pseudocode.
Instruction: Course covers problem solution; structured programming; constants and variables; arithmetic operations; control structures; arrays; subprograms; character strings; and data types. Methodology includes lecture, discussion, and laboratory exercises.
Credit recommendation: In the lower division baccalaureate/associate degree category, 4 semester hours in Computer Science (6/88).

BASIC Programming Language (ECOMP140)
Location: Washington, D.C.
Length: 30 hours (10 weeks).
Dates: January 1984-Present.
Objective: To provide the student with a knowledge of algorithmic solutions to practical problems in computer science and other fields and the ability to program problems in BASIC.
Learning Outcome: Upon successful completion of this course, the student will be able to demonstrate programming capabilities by applying them to applications; and be able to move to more advanced programming.
Instruction: Course covers basic vocabulary language, arithmetic operations, logic operators, conditional statements, nesting, and arrays. Methodology includes lecture, discussion, demonstration, and laboratory work.
Credit recommendation: In the lower division baccalaureate/associate degree category, 2 semester hours in Computer Science or Data Processing (6/88).

PASCAL Programming (ACOMP145)
Location: Washington, D.C.
Length: 30 hours (5 days).
Dates: September 1983-Present.
Objective: To provide the student with a knowledge and application of structured PASCAL programs.
Learning Outcome: Upon successful completion of this course, the student will be able to design PASCAL programs using structured flowcharts and pseudocode; and write and execute PASCAL programs.
Instruction: Course covers basic PASCAL, data types, arithmetic operations; assignment statements, Input/Output, control structures, Begin, End, For, While, Repeat,

If, Case functions and procedures; one-dimensional arrays; set operations; and records and fields. Methodology includes lecture, demonstration, and laboratory exercises.

Credit recommendation: In the lower division baccalaureate/associate degree category, 2 semester hours in Computer Science or Data Processing (6/88).

COBOL Programming I (ECOMP145)

Location: Washington, D.C.
Length: 40 hours (10 weeks).
Dates: January 1978-Present.
Objective: To help the student to understand and write COBOL programs using the basic features of the language.
Learning Outcome: Upon successful completion of this course, the student will be able to demonstrate an understanding of the basic structure of COBOL; demonstrate an understanding of the applications of COBOL; and code, debug, and execute simple COBOL programs.
Instruction: Course covers COBOL structure, the four COBOL divisions, editing techniques, structured programming design, relational operators, table handling, and control break logic. Methodology includes lecture, discussion, and laboratory exercises.
Credit recommendation: In the lower division baccalaureate/associate degree category, 3 semester hours in Computer Science or Data Processing (6/88).

COBOL Programming II (ECOMP146)

Location: Washington, D.C.
Length: 30 hours (10 weeks).
Dates: January 1978-Present.
Objective: To provide the student with an understanding and creation of moderate to complex COBOL programs using the advanced features of the language.
Learning Outcome: Upon successful completion of this course, the student will be able to demonstrate an understanding of the advanced features of COBOL; demonstrate an understanding of the operation of a COBOL program within the total COBOL environment; and code, debug, and execute moderate to complex COBOL programs.
Instruction: Course covers sequential file processing; single and double arrays; sorting; processing ISAM files; relative file processing; and report writer. Methodology includes lecture, discussion, and laboratory exercises.
Credit recommendation: In the lower division baccalaureate/associate degree category, 2 semester hours in Computer Science or Data Processing (6/88).

Structured COBOL Programming I (ACOMP155)

Location: Washington, D.C.
Length: 72 hours (12 days).
Dates: September 1983-Present.
Objective: To provide the student with an understanding and use of structured COBOL programs in elementary business reports.
Learning Outcome: Upon successful completion of this course, the student will be able to design, code, execute, and debug elementary structured COBOL with documentation.
Instruction: Course covers COBOL Input/Output and arithmetic report editions and logic instruction use. Methodology includes lecture, demonstration, and laboratory exercises.
Credit recommendation: In the vocational certificate or lower division baccalaureate/associate degree category, 1 semester hour in Computer Science or Data Processing (6/88).

Structured COBOL Programming II (ACOMP156)

Location: Washington, D.C.
Length: 72 hours (12 days).
Dates: September 1983-Present.
Objective: To provide the student with an understanding and application of structured COBOL programs to business reports.
Learning Outcome: Upon successful completion of this course, the student will be able to use structured COBOL for compound logic statement such as nested IFS, control breaks, processing tables in memory; and design a menu program.
Instruction: Course covers nested IF statements, control break processing, multiple level control break processing, table processing, and menu programming. Methodology includes lecture, demonstration, and laboratory exercises.
Credit recommendation: In the vocational certificate or lower division baccalaureate/associate degree category, 1 semester hour in Computer Science or Data Processing (6/88).

Structured COBOL Programming III (ACOMP157)

Location: Washington, D.C.
Length: 72 hours (12 days).
Dates: September 1963-Present.
Objective: To provide the student with the knowledge to understand and create structured COBOL programs incorporating use of utilities, file organization, and debugging with storage dumps.
Learning Outcome: Upon successful completion of this course, the student will be able to use sort verbs, utilities, and JCL; create and update sequential files; create ISAM files and access randomly; use two and three dimensional tables; and use report writer and strings.
Instruction: Course covers sequential files, ISAM files, including randomly accessing and updating, sorting, and two and three dimensional tables. Methodology includes lecture, demonstration, and laboratory exercises.
Credit recommendation: In the vocational certificate or lower division baccalaureate/associate degree category, 1 semester hour in Computer Science or Data Processing

(6/88).

IBM 360/370 OS/VS Job Control Language (JCL) (ECOMP242)
Location: Washington, D.C.
Length: 35 hours (10 weeks).
Dates: January 1978-Present.
Objective: To provide the student with an understanding of the Job Control Language sufficiently to construct the majority of job streams.
Learning Outcome: Upon successful completion of this course, the student will be able to construct job streams which cover 90 percent or more of computer applications; use catalogued procedures; and debug JCL statements.
Instruction: Course covers JCL syntax rules; parameters of JOB, EXEC, and DD statements; tape processing; disk processing; catalogued procedures; in-stream procedures; and utilities. Methodology includes lecture, discussion, and laboratory exercises.
Credit recommendation: In the lower division baccalaureate/associate degree category, 2 semester hours in Data Processing (6/88).

Structured Design and Programming (ECOMP247)
Location: Washington, D.C.
Length: 30 hours (10 weeks).
Dates: September 1980-Present.
Objective: To provide the student with the ability to write, revise, and evaluate documentation of computer programs.
Learning Outcome: Upon successful completion of this course, the student will be able to write and revise documentation; and evaluate and refine documentation.
Instruction: Course covers methods of ADP documentation and writing using advanced techniques and methods; current methods of structured analysis, structured design, program coding, program development, program refinement, and program quality evaluation; surveys history of manual typing to desktop and online video documentation techniques for screen capture, text scanning, word processing, and graphics. Teams of class members are made up to write documents and make a presentation. This has the students learn to communicate ideas and form a team product in addition to learning goals. Methodology includes lecture, discussion, and laboratory exercises.
Credit recommendation: In the lower division baccalaureate/associate degree category, 2 semester hours in Data Processing or Information Systems Management (6/88).

IBM System 360/370 PL/1 (ECOMP251)
Location: Washington, D.C.
Length: 37½ hours (10 weeks).
Dates: January 1978-Present.
Objective: To provide the student with the knowledge and application of structured PL/1 programs.
Learning Outcome: Upon successful completion of this course, the student will be able to demonstrate an understanding of the concepts and terminology of structured PL/1 programming; and write and maintain structured PL/1 programs.
Instruction: Course covers program definition, procedures and statements; assignments and control statements; stream and record I/O; arrays and structures; subroutines; on-conditions and built-in functions; compiled time facilities and list processing; file structure and data definition cards. Methodology includes lecture, discussion, and laboratory exercises.
Credit recommendation: In the lower division baccalaureate/associate degree category, 3 semester hours in Data Processing (6/88).

ADP Documentation and Writing (ECOMP254)
Location: Washington, D.C.
Length: 30 hours (10 weeks).
Dates: January 1984-Present.
Objective: To provide the student with the ability to write, revise, and evaluate documentation of computer programs.
Learning Outcome: Upon successful completion of this course, the student will be able to write and revise documentation; and evaluate and refine documentation.
Instruction: Course covers methods of documentation management and planning tools, charting techniques, procedures, decision processes, programs, systems, user manuals, document types and content guidelines, document uses, word processing, desktop publishing, user interface, online documentation, and self-paced training and video documentation. A number of actual documentation of packages such as LOTUS 1-2-3, WordPerfect, dBaseIII₁, Communication Packages, and Demo Packages are evaluated. Methodology includes lecture, discussion, and laboratory exercises.
Credit recommendation: In the lower division baccalaureate/associate degree category, 2 semester hours in Data Processing or Information Systems Management (6/88).

Technical Writing (ACOMP265)
Location: Washington, D.C.
Length: 18 hours (3 days).
Dates: September 1983-Present.
Objective: To provide the student with the ability to write clear, direct procedures for accomplishing required technical tasks and to document computer programs.
Learning Outcome: Upon successful completion of this course, the student will be able to write and rewrite documents clearly; know the steps necessary to write successfully: preparation, research, organization, and revision; and know the rules of good grammar, proper punctuation, tense, word choice, etc.

Instruction: Course covers documentation overview; getting started; gathering and organizing your writing; writing styles; formats for procedures; workshops for documentation and writing; ADP terminology review and documentation; and CAI authoring system. Methodology includes lecture, discussion, and writing practice.

Credit recommendation: In the lower division baccalaureate/associate degree category, 1 semester hour in English or Technical Writing (6/88).

C Programming (ECOMP275)
Location: Washington, D.C.
Length: 30 hours (10 weeks).
Dates: September 1985-Present.
Objective: To provide the student with the knowledge and application of C language programs.
Learning Outcome: Upon successful completion of this course, the student will be able to design, write, compile, and execute C language programs.
Instruction: Course covers introduction to C, variables, types and constants, integer variables, elementary operators, and arrays; functions, local and global variables, input and output; assignment, arithmetic and unary operators; loops and control statements; pointers, pointers in functions, arrays of structures; and recursive functions. Methodology includes lecture, demonstration, and laboratory exercises.
Credit recommendation: In the lower division baccalaureate/associate degree category, 2 semester hours in Computer Science or Data Processing (6/88).

ADA Programming (ECOMP335)
Location: Washington, D.C.
Length: 30 hours (10 weeks).
Dates: January 1984-Present.
Objective: To provide the student with an understanding of the principle of ADA to permit the student to design and write ADA programs and teach ADA to others.
Learning Outcome: Upon successful completion of this course, the student will be able to make full use of ADA and software engineering features; write, compile, link, and execute ADA programs; employ information hiding and data obstruction; and develop concurrent programs using ADA's task facility.
Instruction: Course covers ADA history and basic concepts; lexical style and scalan types; control structures: IF, CASE, LOOP, and GO TO statements; composite types: array types, characters and strings, and one-dimensional array operations; subprograms, overall structure, and private types; advanced types, numeric types, and generic types; and tasking, external interfaces, string packages, and utility programs. Methodology includes lecture, demonstration, and lab work.
Credit recommendation: In the lower division baccalaureate/associate degree category, 2 semester hours in Computer Science or Data Processing (6/88).

Systems Analysis and Documentation (ACOMP345)
Location: Washington, D.C.
Length: 24 hours (4 days).
Dates: September 1983-Present.
Objective: To provide the student with a knowledge of the tools and techniques used in systems analysis.
Learning Outcome: Upon successful completion of this course, the student will be able to describe the phases of an information system analysis; and explain the structured approach used in systems analysis.
Instruction: Course covers information systems, tools of the systems analyst, phases of systems analysis, and documentation standards. Methodology includes lecture, discussion, and classroom exercises.
Credit recommendation: In the lower division baccalaureate/associate degree category, 1 semester hour in Data Processing or Information Systems Management (6/88).

Introduction to ISPF (Interactive Systems Productivity Facility) (ACOMP346)
Location: Washington, D.C.
Length: 18 hours (3 days).
Dates: September 1983-Present.
Objective: To provide the student with an understanding of the operation and application of the ISPF.
Learning Outcome: Upon successful completion of this course, the student will be able to create and edit data sets and programs in the IBM MVS environment.
Instruction: Course covers overview of ISPF; ISPF menus; managing data; editing data; partitioned data sets; data set utilities; and advanced ISPF features. Methodology includes lecture, discussion, and classroom exercises.
Credit recommendation: In the lower division baccalaureate/associate degree category, 1 semester hour in Data Processing or Systems Programming (6/88).

Systems Analysis and Design (ECOMP362)
Location: Washington, D.C.
Length: 30 hours (15 weeks).
Dates: September 1980-Present.
Objective: To provide the student with a knowledge of the tools and techniques used in systems analysis.
Learning Outcome: Upon successful completion of this course, the student will be able to identify the degree and nature of participation in the systems development process required by the analyst; identify the various activities involved in systems development; and demonstrate an awareness of the tools and techniques used in systems analysis and design.
Instruction: Course covers systems concepts, systems development life cycle, role of the systems analyst, system planning considerations, information gathering techniques, structured analysis tools, cost/benefit analysis, in-

put/output considerations, file organization and data base design, and system testing and quality assurance. Methodology includes lecture, discussion, and classroom exercises.

Credit recommendation: In the lower division baccalaureate/associate degree category, 2 semester hours in Data Processing or Information Systems Management (6/88).

Data Base Design (ECOMP364)
Location: Washington, D.C.
Length: 30 hours (10 weeks).
Dates: January 1984-Present.
Objective: To provide the student with the knowledge and use of various data base management systems and creation of an elementary data base system.
Learning Outcome: Upon successful completion of this course, the student will be able to review a data base management system and determine what kind of data structures it can handle, and the type of DBMS model it represents; and develop an elementary conceptual data base design for an application.
Instruction: Course covers purpose and use of a data base management system; various storage devices and systems used in data base work; logical relationships and several data representations; data base design and models; various data base systems such as the Relational model and CODASYL model; and data base administration. Methodology includes lecture, discussion, demonstration, and laboratory exercises.
Credit recommendation: In the lower division baccalaureate/associate degree category, 2 semester hours in Computer Science or Data Processing (6/88).

Advanced C Programming (ECOMP376)
Location: Washington, D.C.
Length: 30 hours (10 weeks).
Dates: January 1986-Present.
Objective: To provide the student with the knowledge of advanced techniques for applying the C programming language to complex computing problems.
Learning Outcome: Upon successful completion of this course, the student will be able to design, debug, and write C programs which incorporate one or more of interactive menus, graphics, text processing, file processing, and numerical algorithms.
Instruction: Course covers file management, graphics, interactive uses, construction of software tools, interaction of C with different hardware and operating systems, and construction of custom function libraries. Methodology includes lecture, demonstrations, and laboratory exercises.
Credit recommendation: In the lower division baccalaureate/associate degree category, 2 semester hours in Computer Science or Data Processing (6/88).

Structured Systems Analysis and Design (ACOMP713)
Location: Washington, D.C.
Length: 18 hours (3 days).
Dates: September 1983-Present.
Objective: To provide the student with a knowledge of the tools and techniques used in systems analysis.
Learning Outcome: Upon successful completion of this course, the student will be able to describe the phases of an information system analysis; and explain the structured approach used in systems analysis.
Instruction: Course covers information systems, tools of the systems analyst, phases of systems analysis, and documentation standards. Methodology includes lecture, discussion, and classroom exercises.
Credit recommendation: In the lower division baccalaureate/associate degree category, 1 semester hour in Data Processing or Information Systems Management (6/88).

EDITING

Principles of Editing for Publication (EEDIT140) (Principles of Editing)
Location: Washington, D.C.
Length: 40 hours (10 weeks).
Dates: January 1978-Present.
Objective: To introduce the student to the principles of editing, the tasks of an editor, and the application of these principles in production.
Learning Outcome: Upon successful completion of this course, the student will be able to convey information from a writer to a reader clearly, concisely, completely and correctly; eliminate unnecessary words, sentences from the writer's material; know how material should be organized to be effective; and know how publications are produced.
Instruction: Course covers steps in publication, design and layout, printing, form (organizational elements), tales, charts, style, and grammar. Methodology includes lecture, discussion, classroom exercises, and demonstrations.
Credit recommendation: In the lower division baccalaureate/associate degree category, 3 semester hours in Business Communications, Communications, English, or Journalism (6/88).

Proofreading (EEDIT160)
Location: Washington, D.C.
Length: 30 hours (10 weeks).
Dates: January 1984-Present.
Objective: To provide the student with the knowledge of proofreading skills.
Learning Outcome: Upon successful completion of this course, the student will be able to proofread narrative material in a manner that identifies and corrects errors in spelling, punctuation, and capitalization.

Instruction: Course covers punctuation, spelling, capitalization, and proofreading. Methodology includes exams, projects, presentations, and drills.

Credit recommendation: In the lower division baccalaureate/associate degree category, 3 semester hours in Business Communications, Communications, English, or Journalism (6/88).

Intermediate Editing (EEDIT230)
(Style and Techniques for Editors)
  Location: Washington, D.C.
  Length: 30 hours (10 weeks).
  Dates: January 1978-Present.
  Objective: To provide the student with a knowledge of intermediate editing skills and editing methods in different settings.
  Learning Outcome: Upon successful completion of this course, the student will be able to edit the substantive content of material to make it more effective; perform basic copy-editing; understand the basics of electronic editing; and edit charts, graphs and tables and reconcile them with the text.
  Instruction: Course covers proofreading and copyediting marks, editorial style (including nondiscriminatory language), statistics, graphs, charts, and careers in editing. Methodology includes classroom instruction and class exercises.
  Credit recommendation: In the lower division baccalaureate/associate degree category, 3 semester hours in Business Communications, Communications, English, or Journalism (6/88).

Printing, Layout and Design (EEDIT270)
  Location: Washington, D.C.
  Length: 30 hours (10 weeks).
  Dates: January 1978-Present.
  Objective: To provide the student with a knowledge of production concepts and the ability to solve common production problems.
  Learning Outcome: Upon successful completion of this course, the student will be able to address common production problems with increased knowledge of production concepts; develop technical vocabulary to relate in production environments; and put individual working problems in perspective, determining how they relate to others and to real life situations.
  Instruction: Course covers printing processes, typography and design, printing types, illustration, printing for the govrnment, and regulations for style, printing and binding. Methodology includes lecture, discussion, presentations, and critiques.
  Credit recommendation: In the lower division baccalaureate/associate degree category, 3 semester hours in English, Journalism, or Technical Writing (6/88).

Practice in Editing (EEDIT310)
  Location: Washington, D.C.
  Length: 30 hours (10 weeks).
  Dates: January 1985-Present.
  Objective: To provide the student with a knowledge of sensitivity to good writing, clear thinking and editing, comprehension of differences between mechanical copy preparation and substantive editing, sharpened grammar and writing skills, and knowledge and confidence as an editor.
  Learning Outcome: Upon successful completion of this course, the student will be able to copyedit letters, memos, reports, and news and feature articles; recognize grammatical errors; and recognize how well editorial material meets specific publisher or editor criteria.
  Instruction: Course covers rules of grammar and punctuation, and techniques for editing copy for publication in specialized journals. Methodology includes lecture, discussion, classroom and take home editing assignments.
  Credit recommendation: In the upper division baccalaureate category, 3 semester hours in Business Communications, Communications, English, or Journalism (6/88).

Publishing Management (EEDIT375)
  Location: Washington, D.C.
  Length: 30 hours (10 weeks).
  Dates: January 1985-Present.
  Objective: To provide the student with an understanding and application of accepted management principles to government and private publishing.
  Learning Outcome: Upon successful completion of this course, the student will be able to make the transition from editing to management; demonstrate understanding of management principles; and apply management principles to a publishing organization.
  Instruction: Course covers principles of management, government regulations on printing, copyright laws, Freedom of Information Act, Privacy Act, clearance and review procedures, reader surveys, and economics of publishing. Methodology includes lecture, discussion, handouts, and written assignments.
  Credit recommendation: In the upper division baccalaureate category, 3 semester hours in Business Communications, Communications, English, or Journalism (6/88).

Seminar in Editing (EEDIT580)
  Location: Washington, D.C.
  Length: 30 hours (10 weeks).
  Dates: February 1985-Present.
  Objective: To provide the student with an understanding of the scope and complexities of editing and the skills required of a professional, along with skills for analyzing problems encountered in editing.
  Learning Outcome: Upon successful completion of this

course, the student will be able to critique copy for ideas, quality of writing, and logical development; demonstrate basic editing skills; and analyze editorial problems arising in the planning, preparation, production, printing, and layout of publications, emphasizing the effects of technology.

Instruction: Course covers editorial issues/problems, preparation, production and management of publications, research on job-related problems, and professionalism on the job. Methodology includes lecture, discussion, case studies, and audiovisual aids.

Credit recommendation: In the upper division baccalaureate or graduate degree category, 3 semester hours in Business English, Communications, English, Journalism, or Technical Writing (6/88).

MARKETING/MANAGEMENT

Principles of Marketing (NMARKT540)
Location: Washington, D.C.
Length: 40 hours (3 weeks).
Dates: September 1974-Present.
Objective: To introduce the student to principles and concepts of marketing and the relationships between elements of marketing.
Learning Outcome: Upon successful completion of this course, the student will be able to perceive marketing problems and issues; make strategic and operational decisions responsive to problems and issues; and evaluate the proper role of the public and private sectors to control marketing practices.
Instruction: Course covers marketing concepts, marketing strategy, assessing marketing opportunities, buyer behavior, product and price management, channel management, promotion management, and marketing and public policy. Methodology includes lecture, discussion and problem solving.
Credit recommendation: In the upper division baccalaureate or graduate degree category, 3 semester hours in Business Administration, Business Management, or Marketing (6/88).

Managerial Statistics (NSTAT550)
Location: Washington, D.C.
Length: 40 hours (3 weeks).
Dates: September 1974-Present.
Objective: To allow the student to understand and apply relevant principles and concepts of basic statistics to managerial situations and positions.
Learning Outcome: Upon successful completion of this course, the student will be able to use accurate and reliable statistical measures of data; use various statistical techniques such as forecasting models, correlation and regression, sampling and risk analysis; and understand probability as a basis for using and applying statistical measures to data.
Instruction: Course covers scientific method, sources of statistics, measures of central tendency, sampling, probability, correlation and regression analysis. Methodology includes lecture, discussion, and problem solving.
Credit recommendation: In the upper division baccalaureate or graduate degree category for students not majoring in Statistics, 3 semester hours in Business Administration, Management Science, or Statistics (6/88).

Financial Management (NFINC750)
Location: Washington, D.C.
Length: 40 hours (3 weeks).
Dates: September 1974-Present.
Objective: To provide the student with an understanding of financial and managerial accounting practices and procedures in governmental and business accounting.
Learning Outcome: Upon successful completion of this course, the student will be able to demonstrate skills in financial and managerial accounting; demonstrate proficiency in governmental and business accounting practices and procedures; and use accounting as a tool to make management decisions.
Instruction: Course covers concepts of present value and inflation; capital budgeting; optimizing investment decisions; cash budgeting in financial management; current asset management; cost of capital; dividend policies; stock; portfolio analysis; and investment theory. Methodology includes lecture, discussion, and case studies.
Credit recommendation: In the upper division baccalaureate category, 3 semester hours in Accounting (but not for Accounting majors), Business Administration, Business Management, or Finance (6/88).

Management Economics for Developing Countries (NECON780)
Location: Washington, D.C.
Length: 40 hours (3 weeks).
Dates: September 1974-Present.
Objective: To allow the student to examine economic development and economic behavior of developing countries, and the dynamics of managing interdependent economies of lesser developed countries.
Learning Outcome: Upon successful completion of this course, the student will be able to demonstrate knowledge of theories of economic development in developing countries, and critically analyze goals and objectives of economic systems to include resource allocation.
Instruction: Course covers economic analysis of agriculture, forestry, extractive resources, population and demographics in developing countries. Methodology includes lecture, discussion, and projects.
Credit recommendation: In the upper division baccalaureate category, 3 semester hours in Business Administration or Economics (6/88).

International Finance (NFINC813)
Location: Washington, D.C.
Length: 40 hours (3 weeks).
Dates: September 1974-Present.
Objective: To provide the student with a knowledge of the international economic environment and its influence on corporate financial management and international business operations.
Learning Outcome: Upon successful completion of this course, the student will be able to demonstrate understanding of the international gold standard of the adjustment process of foreign exchange rates, foreign investments, capital budgeting, international financial institutions, and current issues in international finance.
Instruction: Course covers foreign adjustments of accounts, markets and exchange rates, international financial operations to include risk management capital budgeting, and international financial institutions and markets, current issues such as world debt problems, and balance of payments are explored. Methodology includes lecture, discussion, and case studies.
Credit recommendation: In the upper division baccalaureate category, 3 semester hours in Business Administration, Business Management, or Finance (6/88).

Leadership and Management Development (NMGMT846)
Location: Washington, D.C.
Length: 40 hours (3 weeks).
Dates: September 1974-Present.
Objective: To allow the student to explore the role of leadership in the management of organizations; to introduce basic management theories and their relationship to individuals and other organizations.
Learning Outcome: Upon successful completion of this course, the student will be able to understand the functions of management and organizational processes; and understand the relationship between organizations, their leaders, and human resources.
Instruction: Course covers organization, planning, control, and the basic functions of management, human resources, uses of management information, and organizational responsibilities. Methodology includes lecture and discussion.
Credit recommendation: In the upper division baccalaureate category, 3 semester hours in Business Administration or Business Management (6/88).

Project Management (NMGMT960)
Location: Washington, D.C.
Length: 40 hours (3 weeks).
Dates: September 1974-Present.
Objective: To provide the student with an understanding of principles and concepts of project management and application to projects in an international environment.
Learning Outcome: Upon successful completion of this course, the student will be able to apply project management principles and concepts in management of international projects.
Instruction: Course covers project management systems, project life cycle, time scheduling techniques, resource management, and computers as a tool for project management. Methodology includes lecture, discussion, and classroom projects.
Credit recommendation: In the upper division baccalaureate category, 3 semester hours in Administration, Business Administration, Project Management, or Public Administration (6/88).

Project Analysis (NMGMT975)
Location: Washington, D.C.
Length: 120 hours (4 weeks).
Dates: September 1974-Present.
Objective: To provide the student with knowledge and understanding of project management sufficient to manage and control projects and activities.
Learning Outcome: Upon successful completion of this course, the student will be able to understand the procedures used in analyzing projects; develop the supporting data and analyze the critical points in monitoring projects; and develop the proper tools to evaluate and estimate the benefits as well as the cost of projects.
Instruction: Course covers benefits/cost, methods of optimization, capital budgeting, statistical methods for project management, and accounting and budgeting. Methodology includes lecture, discussion, case and field studies, and extensive out-of-class preparation.
Credit recommendation: In the graduate category, 5 semester hours in Accounting, Business Administration, Management Science, or Public Administration (6/88).

LANGUAGES

CHINESE

Introductory Chinese I—Mandarin (ECHIN151)
Location: Washington, D.C.
Length: 30 hours (10 weeks).
Dates: September 1984-Present.
Objective: To develop a good pronunciation of Mandarin Chinese, a foundation in basic grammar of simple verbal sentences, and an elementary vocabulary, together with some knowledge of Chinese culture and customs.
Learning Outcome: Upon successful completion of this course, the student will be able to use proper pronunciation, including ability to read aloud pinyionized text; engage in simple dialogues in Chinese, showing mastery of simple grammatical patterns and a vocabulary of about 200 words; and recognize and reproduce about 150 characters.
Instruction: Course covers all initials and finals, including tone, stroke order in writing, and simple statements

and questions.

Credit recommendation: In the lower division baccalaureate/associate degree category, 2 semester hours in Introductory Chinese (6/88).

Introductory Chinese II (ECHIN152)

Location: Washington, D.C.
Length: 30 hours (10 weeks).
Dates: January 1985-Present.
Objective: To maintain a good pronunciation of Mandarin Chinese, become familiar with more complex grammatical patterns, and expand vocabulary.
Learning Outcome: Upon successful completion of this course, the student will be able to engage in simple conversations in Chinese, showing an active vocabulary of 400 words; and recognize and reproduce about 300 characters.
Instruction: Course covers complex expressions, tag questions, and modal particles.
Credit recommendation: In the lower division baccalaureate/associate degree category, 2 semester hours in Introductory Chinese (6/88).

Introductory Chinese III (ECHIN153)

Location: Washington, D.C.
Length: 30 hours (10 weeks).
Dates: April 1985-Present.
Objective: To maintain a good pronunciation of Mandarin Chinese, become familiar with more grammatical constructions, and expand oral and written vocabulary.
Learning Outcome: Upon successful completion of this course, the student will be able to use more advanced patterns and more practical language in conversational situations; and exhibit more competence in reading and writing.
Instruction: Course covers optative verbs and modal particle "le."
Credit recommendation: In the lower division baccalaureate/associate degree category, 2 semester hours in Introductory Chinese (6/88).

Intermediate Chinese I (ECHIN210)

Location: Washington, D.C.
Length: 30 hours (10 weeks).
Dates: September 1984-Present.
Objective: To review and continue study of crucial grammatical patterns and master socially useful conversational skills.
Learning Outcome: Upon successful completion of this course, the student will be able to demonstrate more sophisticated vocabulary in conversations, and comprehend simple speeches and written passages in Chinese.
Instruction: Course covers comparative patterns; and aspect marker and modal particle "le."
Credit recommendation: In the lower division baccalaureate/associate degree category, 2 semester hours in Intermediate Chinese (6/88).

Intermediate Chinese II (ECHIN211)

Location: Washington, D.C.
Length: 30 hours (10 weeks).
Dates: January 1985-Present.
Objective: To enable the student to work through intermediate level texts containing the important grammatical patterns and a fairly sophisticated content, and engage in everyday conversations, and to stimulate an interest in Chinese literature.
Learning Outcome: Upon successful completion of this course, the student will be able to engage in everyday conversations; and exhibit improved comprehension in reading.
Instruction: Course emphasizes more advanced reading and conversation. In addition to work on sentence structure and vocabulary, students will read longer articles and experience a gradual transition from regular textbook Chinese to "real" modern Chinese literature.
Credit recommendation: In the lower division baccalaureate/associate degree category, 2 semester hours in Intermediate Chinese (6/88).

Intermediate Chinese III (ECHIN212)

Location: Washington, D.C.
Length: 30 hours (10 weeks).
Dates: April 1985-Present.
Objective: To develop (depending on student's background), increased facility in reading and discussing texts of literary and topical interest.
Learning Outcome: Upon successful completion of this course, the student will be able to feel at ease conversing with speakers of Chinese; and give speeches and tell stories in Chinese.
Instruction: Course covers reading selections from modern Chinese literature in the form of essays, short stories, and newspaper articles. Conversation and writing exercises are based upon reading materials.
Credit recommendation: In the lower division baccalaureate/associate degree category, 2 semester hours in Intermediate Chinese (6/88).

FRENCH

Introductory French I (EFREN151)

Location: Washington, D.C.
Length: 30 hours (10 weeks).
Dates: January 1984-Present.
Objective: To understand, speak, read, and write limited basic French with relative accuracy in the context of contemporary French culture.
Learning Outcome: Upon successful completion of this course, the student will be able to understand, speak, read, and write limited basic French with relative accuracy in the context of contemporary French culture.
Instruction: Course covers vocabulary, listening, reading, writing, and grammar with emphasis on the latter

two. Methodology includes grammar presentations, oral class activities, and written assignments.

Credit recommendation: In the lower division baccalaureate/associate degree category, 2 semester hours in Introductory French I (6/88).

Introductory French II (EFREN152)
   Location: Washington, D.C.
   Length: 30 hours (10 weeks).
   Dates: January 1984-Present.
   Objective: To understand, speak, read, and write moderately complex French with relative accuracy in the context of contemporary French culture.
   Learning Outcome: Upon successful completion of this course, the student will be able to understand, speak, read, and write moderately complex French with relative accuracy in the context of contemporary French culture.
   Instruction: Course covers review and continuation of grammar study, expansion of vocabulary, development of language skills through readings and dialogues. Methodology includes grammar presentations, oral class activities, and written assignments.
   Credit recommendation: In the lower division baccalaureate/associate degree category, 2 semester hours in Introductory French II (6/88).

Introductory French III (EFREN153)
   Location: Washington, D.C.
   Length: 30 hours (10 weeks).
   Dates: January 1984-Present.
   Objective: To understand, speak, read, and write complex French with relative accuracy in the context of contemporary French culture.
   Learning Outcome: Upon successful completion of this course, the student will be able to understand, speak, read, and write complex French with relative accuracy in the context of contemporary French culture.
   Instruction: Course covers more complex structural patterns through readings and dialogues, and progressive growth in the use of the language, both in oral and written work. Methodology includes guided conversation, oral and written exercises and assignments.
   Credit recommendation: In the lower division baccalaureate/associate degree category, 2 semester hours in Introductory French III (6/88).

Intermediate French I (EFREN210)
   Location: Washington, D.C.
   Length: 30 hours (10 weeks).
   Dates: January 1984-Present.
   Objective: To expand vocabulary and consolidate grammar and develop greater proficiency in all skills including translation.
   Learning Outcome: Upon successful completion of this course, the student will be able to demonstrate greater proficiency in speaking, writing, reading, and translating and broaden understanding of French culture.
   Instruction: Course covers readings about culture and society, review of grammar, writing, and speaking. Methodology includes grammar presentation, readings, oral and written exercises and assignments.
   Credit recommendation: In the lower division baccalaureate/associate degree category, 2 semester hours in Intermediate French I (6/88).

GERMAN

Introductory German I (EGERM151)
   Location: Washington, D.C.
   Length: 30 hours (10 weeks).
   Dates: January 1984-Present.
   Objective: To provide the student with the ability to speak, read and write on an elementary level. Essential grammar skills as well as basic vocabulary are the main focus.
   Learning Outcome: Upon successful completion of this course, the student will be able to understand and use basic grammatical structures; engage in simple conversations; function in the target culture; and understand basic aspects of the target culture.
   Instruction: Course covers basic grammatical structures and vocabulary; personal information; immediate surroundings; leisure-time activities; shopping and travel; and introduction to German-speaking countries. Methodology includes lecture, discussion, classroom exercises, case studies, roleplaying, and problem solving.
   Credit recommendation: In the lower division baccalaureate/associate degree category, 2 semester hours in Introductory German I (6/88).

Introductory German II (EGERM152)
   Location: Washington, D.C.
   Length: 30 hours (10 weeks).
   Dates: January 1984-Present.
   Objective: To provide students with improved speaking, reading, and writing skills on the elementary level.
   Learning Outcome: Upon successful completion of this course, the student will be able to understand and use basic grammatical structures; engage in simple conversations; function in the target culture; understand basic aspects of the target culture; and understand and use German sentence structure.
   Instruction: Course covers basic grammatical structures and vocabulary including past and perfect tenses; daily routines; likes/dislikes; health; vacation; and more cultural information. Methodology includes lecture, discussion, classroom exercises, case studies, role playing, and problem solving.
   Credit recommendation: In the lower division baccalaureate/associate degree category, 2 semester hours in Introductory German II (6/88).

Introductory German III (EGERM153)
Location: Washington, D.C.
Length: 30 hours (10 weeks).
Dates: February 1985-Present.
Objective: Students will complete the introduction to basic grammar structures and further develop speaking, reading, and writing skills.
Learning Outcome: Upon successful completion of this course, the student will be able to use more complex structures; engage in extended conversations; and have a sounder understanding of the target culture.
Instruction: Course covers more complex structures including subjunctive; the role of women in the FRG; introduction to short stories; and further cultural input. Methodology includes lecture, discussion, classroom exercises, case studies, role playing, and problem solving.
Credit recommendation: In the lower division baccalaureate/associate degree category, 2 semester hours in Introductory German III (6/88).

Intermediate German I (EGERM210)
Location: Washington, D.C.
Length: 30 hours (10 weeks).
Dates: January 1984-Present.
Objective: To provide a grammar review and development of conversational, reading, and writing skills with an emphasis on contemporary style and vocabulary. This course is designed for participants with a working knowledge of German verb tenses, moods, and voices.
Learning Outcome: Upon successful completion of this course, the student will have reviewed present and past tenses, as well as do four cases, gained practice in speaking German, improved their writing skills, and increased their knowledge of contemporary life in the German-speaking countries.
Instruction: Course provides a grammar review and development of conversational, reading, and writing skills with an emphasis on contemporary style and vocabulary. This course is designed for participants with a working knowledge of German verb tenses, moods, and voices. Prerequisite: Introductory German III (EGERM153) or equivalent. Methodology includes classroom instruction, lecture, discussion, and drill exercises.
Credit recommendation: In the lower division baccalaureate/associate degree category, 2 semester hours in Intermediate German I (6/88).

Intermediate German II (EGERM211)
Location: Washington, D.C.
Length: 30 hours (10 weeks).
Dates: February 1985-Present.
Objective: This course emphasizes reading and writing skills as well as development of a more varied and contemporary vocabulary through study of newspapers, magazines, and recordings.
Learning Outcome: Upon successful completion of this course, the student will have reviewed prepositions, adjectives, and subjunctive mood and will have gained practice in speaking German; improved writing skills; and increased knowledge of contemporary life in the German-speaking countries.
Instruction: Course is designed for participants with a good background in the language, emphasizing reading and writing skills as well as development of a more varied and contemporary vocabulary through study of newspapers, magazines, and recordings. Methodology includes lecture, discussion, and drill exercises.
Credit recommendation: In the lower division baccalaureate/associate degree category, 2 semester hours in Intermediate German II (6/88).

Intermediate German III (EGERM212)
Location: Washington, D.C.
Length: 30 hours (10 weeks).
Dates: March 1985-Present.
Objective: A grammar review with emphasis on expanding vocabulary, idiomatic structures and conversational fluency using a variety of texts. Readings stress contemporary life in Germany.
Learning Outcome: Upon successful completion of this course, the student will have reviewed passive voice, relative clauses, and idioms, and will have gained practice in speaking German, and improved writing skills; and increased knowledge of contemporary life in the German-speaking countries.
Instruction: Course covers further development of skills in reading, writing, and vocabulary using German newspapers, magazines, and recordings.
Credit recommendation: In the lower division baccalaureate/associate degree category, 2 semester hours in Intermediate German III (6/88).

GREEK

Introductory Greek I—Modern (EGREE151)
Location: Washington, D.C.
Length: 30 hours (10 weeks).
Dates: January 1984-Present.
Objective: To introduce students to the Greek alphabet and general structure of the language with emphasis upon grammar, writing, basic vocabulary, and foundation work in speaking, comprehension and reading.
Learning Outcome: Upon successful completion of this course, the student will be able to demonstrate an understanding of the course material in a final take-home exam; construct an essay with selected words taken from the materials covered in the course; and apply knowledge learned in the course to conversation.
Instruction: Course covers the Greek alphabet; the two largest categories of regular verbs which include approximately 55 to 60 percent of verbs; common irregular verbs; masculine, feminine, and neuter nouns; information about

everyday life; and idiomatic expressions. Methodology includes classroom instruction which combine grammar skills, reading, dialogue presentation, and question and answer period.

Credit recommendation: In the lower division baccalaureate/associate degree category, 2 semester hours in Modern Greek (6/88).

Introductory Greek II (EGREE152)
Location: Washington, D.C.
Length: 30 hours (10 weeks).
Dates: February 1985-Present.
Objective: To broaden the student's knowledge of grammar, build vocabulary through reading and writing, and increase conversation skills through dialogues.
Learning Outcome: Upon successful completion of this course, the student will be able to demonstrate an understanding of the course material in a final take-home exam; construct an essay with selected words taken from the materials covered in the course; and apply knowledge learned in the course to conversation.
Instruction: Course covers conversation relative to more complex subjects; the contracted verbs; the present tense of passive voice, reflexive verbs; the imperfect (i.e., past continuous tense); factors governing time and duration of an event for the use of simple past or imperfect; the direct object; and the possessive case of nouns. Methodology includes classroom instruction which combine grammar drills, reading, dialogue presentation, and question and answer period.
Credit recommendation: In the lower division baccalaureate/associate degree category, 2 semester hours in Modern Greek (6/88).

Introductory Greek III (EGREE153)
Location: Washington, D.C.
Length: 30 hours (10 weeks).
Dates: March 1986-Present.
Objective: To improve the student's ability to understand and use grammar, increase vocabulary, and develop writing skills.
Learning Outcome: Upon successful completion of this course, the student will be able to demonstrate an understanding of the course material in a final take-home exam; write compositions with selected words taken from the materials covered in the course; and apply knowledge learned in the course to conversation.
Instruction: Course covers the future and the continuous future; comparison of adjectives and adverbs; irregular verbs and nouns; the present perfect and past perfect tenses; contractions; and techniques of composition writing. Methodology includes classroom instruction which combines grammar drills, reading, dialogue presentation, and question and answer period.
Credit recommendation: In the lower division baccalaureate/associate degree category, 2 semester hours in Modern Greek (6/88).

Intermediate Greek I (EGREE210)
Location: Washington, D.C.
Length: 30 hours (10 weeks).
Dates: January 1984-Present.
Objective: To provide the student with conversational reading and writing skills, to expand vocabulary and to provide grammar review and advanced grammar for students with a working knowledge of the basics of the language.
Learning Outcome: Upon successful completion of this course, the student will be able to demonstrate an understanding of the course material in a final take-home exam which consists of essays and questions on grammar; write compositions with selected themes; read and understand newspaper articles; and apply knowledge learned in the course to conversation.
Instruction: Course covers advanced grammar; fictional prose; Greek mythology; and current events. Methodology includes classroom sessions with emphasis on compositions and general discussion of events and situations. Grammar drills, reading and essay presentation are also parts of this course.
Credit recommendation: In the lower division baccalaureate/associate degree category, 2 semester hours in Modern Greek (6/88).

Intermediate Greek II (EGREE211)
Location: Washington, D.C.
Length: 30 hours (10 weeks).
Dates: January 1985-Present.
Objective: The course continues to develop conversational vocabulary and writing skills, expands vocabulary, and provides grammar review and advanced grammar.
Learning Outcome: Upon successful completion of this course, the student will be able to demonstrate an understanding of the course material in a final take-home exam which consists of essays, questions on grammar, and true and false statements; give an oral presentation in class; read and analyze newspaper articles; write compositions; and apply knowledge learned in the course to conversation.
Instruction: Course covers advanced grammar; fictional prose; Greek mythology; and current events. Methodology includes classroom instruction intended to improve the oral as well as the writing style of the student. Many topics are discussed which help the students to increase fluency.
Credit recommendation: In the lower division baccalaureate/associate degree category, 2 semester hours in Modern Greek (6/88).

Intermediate Greek III (EGREE212)
Location: Washington, D.C.
Length: 30 hours (10 weeks).
Dates: February 1986-Present.

Objective: To provide students with the opportunity to apply their advanced knowledge to conversational and writing activities.

Learning Outcome: Upon successful completion of this course, the student will be able to demonstrate an understanding of the course material in a final take-home exam which consists of essays, questions on Greek and American History and Geography; give an oral presentation in class; read and analyze newspaper articles; write compositions; and apply knowledge learned in the course to conversation.

Instruction: Course covers advanced grammar; fictional prose; current events; and geography and history. Methodology includes class instruction intended to improve the oral as well as the writing style of the student. Many topics are discussed which help the students to increase fluency.

Credit recommendation: In the lower division baccalaureate/associate degree category, 2 semester hours in Modern Greek (6/88).

JAPANESE

Introductory Japanese I (EJAPN151)
Location: Washington, D.C.
Length: 30 hours (10 weeks).
Dates: September 1984-Present.
Objective: To learn hiragana.
Learning Outcome: Upon successful completion of this course, the student will be able to read and write hiragana; use and understand simple copular and adjectival sentences, include negative sentences; and use roughly 40 useful expressions.
Instruction: Course covers hiragana, simple copular sentences, simple adjectival sentences, basic sentence particles, negation, and culture and general background information. Methodology includes lecture and drill.
Credit recommendation: In the lower division baccalaureate/associate degree category, 2 semester hours in Introductory Japanese (6/88).

Introductory Japanese II (EJAPN152)
Location: Washington, D.C.
Length: 30 hours (10 weeks).
Dates: January 1985-Present.
Objective: To introduce katakana and 50-75 kanji.
Learning Outcome: Upon successful completion of this course, the student will be able to read and write hiragana and katakana; recognize 50-75 kanji; write 25-50 kanji; use and understand simple verbal sentences, including commands and continuatives; know verbs of giving and receiving; and use and understand simple noun modification.
Instruction: Course covers katakana, 50-75 kanji, simple verbal sentences, and verbal gerunds.
Credit recommendation: In the lower division baccalaureate/associate degree category, 2 semester hours in Introductory Japanese (6/88).

Introductory Japanese III (EJAPN153)
Location: Washington, D.C.
Length: 30 hours (10 weeks).
Dates: April 1985-Present.
Objective: To introduce an additional 75 kanji and read a simple children's story.
Learning Outcome: Upon successful completion of this course, the student will be able to use compound sentences and noun clause modifiers; handle permission and prohibition and potential expressions; use direct-style verbal forms in discourse; read simple passages written in Japanese; and write 150 kanji.
Instruction: Course covers noun clause modification, potential expressions, "because" expressions, expressions of intention and probability, direct-style verbal forms, and 75 kanji.
Credit recommendation: In the lower division baccalaureate/associate degree category, 2 semester hours in Introductory Japanese (6/88).

Intermediate Japanese I (EJAPN210)
Location: Washington, D.C.
Length: 30 hours (10 weeks).
Dates: September 1985-Present.
Objective: To introduce the student to an additional 50 kanji; learn to use a Chinese character (kanji) dictionary; read a Japanese story; and write a Japanese letter.
Learning Outcome: Upon successful completion of this course, the student will be able to use superlatives, comparatives, conditionals, quotatives, and other verbal and adjectival constructions; be familiar with various levels and styles of speaking; and recognize and write 150-200 kanji and, within limitations, use a kanji dictionary.
Instruction: Course covers superlatives, comparatives, conditionals, quotatives, and other verbal and adjectival constructions; ways to express obligation (i.e., must, should, etc.), in the linguistic and cultural context; speech styles and levels; and use of dictionaries.
Credit recommendation: In the lower division baccalaureate/associate degree category, 2 semester hours in Intermediate Japanese (6/88).

Intermediate Japanese II (EJAPN211)
Location: Washington, D.C.
Length: 30 hours (10 weeks).
Dates: January 1986-Present.
Objective: To introduce the student to 75 more kanji.
Learning Outcome: Upon successful completion of this course, the student will be able to handle more complex Japanese patterns such as the extended predicate -rashii, -nagara, and -tearu; handle guided conversation; and recognize and write 200-275 kanji.
Instruction: Course covers extended predicate; supposition; and auxiliary verbs.

Credit recommendation: In the lower division baccalaureate/associate degree category, 2 semester hours in Intermediate Japanese (6/88).

Intermediate Japanese III (EJAPN212)
Location: Washington, D.C.
Length: 30 hours (10 weeks).
Dates: April 1986-Present.
Objective: To introduce the student to 75 more kanji.
Learning Outcome: Upon successful completion of this course, the student will be able to handle complex Japanese sentences and verbal patterns, including -tehishii, -te kureru, -te morau, -hodo, and -tameni; handle elementary non-technical conversations; and recognize and write 350 kanji.
Instruction: Course covers adjectival and copular gerund, more expressions using auxiliary verbs, degree, complex sentences, and quotatives.
Credit recommendation: In the lower division baccalaureate/associate degree category, 2 semester hours in Intermediate Japanese (6/88).

Advanced Japanese I (EJAPN250)
Location: Washington, D.C.
Length: 30 hours (10 weeks).
Dates: September 1986-Present.
Objective: To sharpen reading and translation skills, as well as speaking skills of the student.
Learning Outcome: Upon successful completion of this course, the student will be able to read and translate Japanese of moderate difficulty with the aid of a dictionary.
Instruction: Course covers reading and translation.
Credit recommendation: In the upper division baccalaureate category, 2 semester hours in Advanced Japanese (6/88).

Advanced Japanese II (EJAPN251)
Location: Washington, D.C.
Length: 30 hours (10 weeks).
Dates: January 1987-Present.
Objective: Accurate translation of Japanese materials and practice summarizing in Japanese.
Learning Outcome: Upon successful completion of this course, the student will be able to read and translate accurately Japanese of moderate difficulty; start reading newspapers; and know up to 700 kanji.
Instruction: Course covers reading and translating.
Credit recommendation: In the upper division baccalaureate category, 2 semester hours in Advanced Japanese (6/88).

Advanced Japanese III (EJAPN252)
Location: Washington, D.C.
Length: 30 hours (10 weeks).
Dates: April 1987-Present.
Objective: To further sharpen the student's reading and translating skills, and improve the ability to express themselves in spoken Japanese.
Learning Outcome: Upon successful completion of this course, the student will be able to read current materials, such as are found in newspapers and periodicals, with a dictionary and assistance from the instructor; and know 881 kanji.
Instruction: Course covers reading and translation.
Credit recommendation: In the upper division baccalaureate category, 2 semester hours in Advanced Japanese (6/88).

RUSSIAN

Introductory Russian I (ERUSS151)
Location: Washington, D.C.
Length: 30 hours (10 weeks).
Dates: January 1984-Present.
Objective: To introduce the student to the sound and writing systems of contemporary Russian. Emphasis is on the development of the basic skills—listening, speaking, reading, and writing.
Learning Outcome: Upon successful completion of this course, the student will be able to ask and respond to simple questions orally and in writing about oneself and familiar topics; understand simple phrases in a printed text.
Instruction: Course covers sound system (pronunciation and intonation); writing system (printed and cursive); and grammar—verb conjugation, case system (prepositional-singular, nominative-singular and plural, accusative-singular), motion verbs, possessive adjectives, and telling time. Methodology includes oral and written drills, lecture, and discussion.
Credit recommendation: In the lower division baccalaureate/associate degree category, 2 semester hours in Introductory Russian (6/88).

Introductory Russian II (ERUSS152)
Location: Washington, D.C.
Length: 30 hours (10 weeks).
Dates: January 1984-Present.
Objective: A continued introduction to grammatical structure and further development in listening, speaking, reading, and writing of contemporary Russian.
Learning Outcome: Upon successful completion of this course, the student will be able to carry on simple conversation on familiar topics; have conceptual understanding of verbal aspects and tenses as well as noun cases; and read simple narrative.
Instruction: Course covers grammatical case (accusative, dative, and genitive) of nouns, adjectives, and pronouns; verbs (past and future tenses, concept of aspect, imperatives); and time expressions. Methodology includes lecture, discussion, oral, and written drills.
Credit recommendation: In the lower division bac-

calaureate/associate degree category, 2 semester hours in Introductory Russian (6/88).

Introductory Russian III (ERUSS153)
   Location: Washington, D.C.
   Length: 30 hours (10 weeks).
   Dates: January 1984-Present.
   Objective: To provide the student with continued instruction in Russian grammar as well as further improvement in speaking, understanding, reading, and writing.
   Learning Outcome: Upon successful completion of this course, the student will be able to use the dative and genitive cases of nouns; understand and use the prepositional and dative case of personal pronouns and special modifiers; understand and use the prepositional case of adjective endings in the singular; understand and use the accusative case of relative adjectives; have a comfortable use of the imperfective future and imperative forms; and understand to a greater extent verb aspects and multidirectional "going" verbs.
   Instruction: Course concludes the introduction to Russian grammar as well as providing further improvement in speaking and understanding with increased emphasis on reading and writing. The course is designed for beginners who have had an extensive formal or information introduction to Russian. *Prerequisite:* Introductory Russian I (ERUSS152) or equivalent.
   Credit recommendation: In the lower division baccalaureate/associate degree category, 2 semester hours in Introductory Russian (6/88).

Intermediate Russian I (ERUSS210)
   Location: Washington, D.C.
   Length: 30 hours (10 weeks).
   Dates: January 1984-Present.
   Objective: To provide the student with vocabulary expansion through the study of word formation and usage. Development of cultural awareness through reading and commentary. Emphasis on grammatical control.
   Learning Outcome: Upon successful completion of this course, the student will be able to show greater grammatical accuracy in basic constructions; initiate and sustain a conversational exchange on familiar topics; write short compositions; and translate simple texts.
   Instruction: Course covers grammar: case usage with emphasis on genitive and instrumental (nouns, adjectives, pronouns, numerals); verbs (reflexive, motion, and conditional constructions); impersonal constructions; time expressions. Reading and translation emphasized. Methodology includes lecture, discussion, oral and written drills.
   Credit recommendation: In the lower division baccalaureate/associate degree category, 2 semester hours in Intermediate Russian (6/88).

SWEDISH

Introductory Swedish I (ESWED151)
   Location: Washington, D.C.
   Length: 30 hours (10 weeks).
   Dates: January 1985-Present.
   Objective: To introduce the student to Swedish pronunciation, grammar, and vocabulary and teach the students to express themselves on a very elementary level.
   Learning Outcome: Upon successful completion of this course, the student will be able to form simple sentences and ask simple questions in the present and past tenses; read and write on a very elementary level; and show some acquaintance with Swedish culture and customs.
   Instruction: This beginners course gives a foundation in speaking, reading, and writing Swedish and covers the basics in grammar drills and emphasized speaking.
   Credit recommendation: In the lower division baccalaureate/associate degree category, 2 semester hours in Introductory Swedish I (6/88).

Introductory Swedish II (ESWED152)
   Location: Washington, D.C.
   Length: 30 hours (10 weeks).
   Dates: January 1985-Present.
   Objective: To continue the student's development of basic language skills—comprehension, reading, speaking, and writing—begun in ESWED151.
   Learning Outcome: Upon successful completion of this course, the student will be able to form sentences in all tenses, using a broader vocabulary and with a distinct pronunciation; read simple texts and write simple narrative; and know more about Swedish culture and customs.
   Instruction: This course gives a good knowledge of the basics of the Swedish language and gives an expansion of vocabulary. Teaches pronunciation and writing and emphasizes speaking and dialogues.
   Credit recommendation: In the lower division baccalaureate/associate degree category, 2 semester hours in Introductory Swedish II (6/88).

Introductory Swedish III (ESWED153)
   Location: Washington, D.C.
   Length: 30 hours (10 weeks).
   Dates: January 1985-Present.
   Objective: To provide the student with further study of basic language skills—comprehension, reading, speaking, and writing.
   Learning Outcome: Upon successful completion of this course, the student will be able to have a conversation in Swedish with teacher or patient native speaker; read easier Swedish texts and write a letter or simple narrative with more complicated sentence structure than in ESWED152; show increased familiarity with contemporary Swedish culture and customs.
   Instruction: This course provides further improvement

in speaking, writing, and comprehension. It is designed for those with a good knowledge of basic Swedish.

Credit recommendation: In the lower division baccalaureate/associate degree category, 2 semester hours in Introductory Swedish III (6/88).

MATHEMATICS

Calculus I (EMATH210)
Location: Washington, D.C.
Length: 40 hours (10 weeks).
Dates: January 1978-Present

Objective: To provide the student with an understanding of the meaning and use of the derivative of mathematical functions.

Learning Outcome: Upon successful completion of this course, the student will be able to understand the meaning of the derivative and its relationship to the slope of the tangent line; and determine the maximum and minimum points of a curve.

Instruction: Course covers variables, functions, limits, continuity, derivatives, maxima and minima, mean value theorem, Newton's approximation of roots, and derivatives of transcendental functions. Methodology includes lectures, class exercises, and written homework.

Credit recommendation: In the lower division baccalaureate/associate degree category, 2 semester hours in Differential Calculus or Mathematics (6/88).

Calculus II (EMATH211)
Location: Washington, D.C.
Length: 40 hours (10 weeks).
Dates: January 1978-Present.

Objective: To provide the student with an understanding of the concepts and applications of the integration of mathematical functions.

Learning Outcome: Upon successful completion of this course, the student will be able to understand concepts of integration; and apply integration to the development of the area under a curve.

Instruction: Course covers simple integration, the definite integral, approximation methods of integration, trigonometric substitutions, and estimation methods. Methodology includes lectures, class exercises, and written homework.

Credit recommendation: In the lower division baccalaureate/associate degree category, 2 semester hours in Integral Calculus or Mathematics (6/88).

Calculus III (EMATH212)
Location: Washington, D.C.
Length: 40 hours (10 weeks).
Dates: January 1978-Present.

Objective: To provide the student with the knowledge to develop and solve differential equations.

Learning Outcome: Upon successful completion of this course, the student will be able to use derivatives and integrals to solve differential equations; and solve special functions, such as Fourier series and Laplace transformations.

Instruction: Course covers first order differential equations; Euler's equation; LaGrange's Method; partial derivatives; Fourier analysis; and LaPlace transforms. Methodology includes lectures, class exercises, and graded homework problems.

Credit recommendation: In the lower division baccalaureate/associate degree category, 2 semester hours in Differential Equations or Mathematics (6/88).

PARALEGAL

Courses are listed in numerical order, i.e., ELAWS 120, ELAWS 145, etc.

Business Law I (ELAWS120)
Location: Washington, D.C.
Length: 30 hours (10 weeks).
Dates: January 1984-Present.

Objective: To provide the student with an understanding of legal principles involved in contracts, sales, uniform commercial code, and torts.

Learning Outcome: Upon successful completion of this course, the student will be able to understand the basic elements of contract law; understand Article 2 of the Uniform Commercial Code (sales); identify the major difference between contract law and Article 2 of the Uniform Commercial Code; determine when one incurs contractural liability and when one does not incur this liability; and identify and describe those areas of criminal and tort law which are of particular concern to business.

Instruction: Course covers business torts and crimes, contracts, sales and warranties, and topics which relate to current legal developments. Methodology includes lecture, discussion, and case studies.

Credit recommendation: In the lower division baccalaureate/associate degree category, 2 semester hours in Business Administration or Paralegal Studies (6/88).

Environmental Law (ELAWS145)
Location: Washington, D.C.
Length: 30 hours (10 weeks).
Dates: January 1984-Present.

Objective: To provide the student with an understanding of the basic thrust of each of the environmental statues and implementation of regulations and how they relate to other areas of law.

Learning Outcome: Upon successful completion of this course, the student will be able to understand the environmental concerns and policies which led to passage of the major (and some minor) environmental statutes, with concentration on the past two decades; understand the implementation of the environmental statutes by federal agencies.

Instruction: Course covers land use planning, enviornmental planning, legislation, pollution, hazardous wastes, land use, clean air and water, and the processes under the National Environmental Protection Act. Methodology includes lecture, discussion, and case studies.

Credit recommendation: In the lower division baccalaureate/associate degree category, 2 semester hours in Environmental Science or Paralegal Studies (6/88).

Family Law (ELAWS150)
Location: Washington, D.C.
Length: 30 hours (10 weeks).
Dates: January 1984-Present.
Objective: To provide the student with knowledge of substantive and procedural aspects of domestic relations law.
Learning Outcome: Upon successful completion of this course, the student will be able to demonstrate skills in interviewing, investigation, writing, research, pleadings, relevant case law (limited), and legal analysis; identify the issues in a case, prepare a case for trial, negotiate agreements, and assist in the trial.
Instruction: Course covers legal aspects of divorce and annulment, separation, defense, adoption, legitimation, custody, habeas corpus, support, alimony, tax consulting, out-of-state divorces, validity, and jurisdiction service; analysis of separation and custody agreement as well as other documents in divorce proceedings. Methodology includes lecture, discussion, and case studies.
Credit recommendation: In the lower division baccalaureate/associate degree category, 2 semester hours in Paralegal Studies (6/88).

Wills and Probate (ELAWS166)
Location: Washington, D.C.
Length: 30 hours (10 weeks).
Dates: January 1987-Present.
Objective: To provide the student with knowledge of wills and estates from planning to administration.
Learning Outcome: Upon successful completion of this course, the student will be able to understand intestate distribution; taxes relevant to decedents and heirs; how to title property to avoid probate; how wills and trusts are drafted and the different types of each; and the process of probate and estate administration.
Instruction: Course covers how to administer the estate of a decedent and the basics of creating wills, trusts, and other instruments (deeds, joint accounts, etc.) which transfer monetary interests at death. Methodology includes lecture, discussion, and case studies.
Credit recommendation: In the lower division baccalaureate/associate degree category, 2 semester hours in Paralegal Studies (6/88).

Business Law II (ELAWS220)
Location: Washington, D.C.
Length: 30 hours (10 weeks).
Dates: January 1986-Present.
Objective: To provide the student with an understanding of legal principles involved in personal and real property, agency, corporations, and partnerships.
Learning Outcome: Upon successful completion of this course, the student will be able to understand the basic elements of personal and real property law; understand the basic elements of the law of agency, partnerships, and corporations.
Instruction: Course covers real and personal property law, agency, partnerships, and corporations. Methodology includes lecture, discussion, and case studies.
Credit recommendation: In the lower division baccalaureate/associate degree category, 2 semester hours in Business Administration or Paralegal Studies (6/88).

Tort Law (ELAWS240)
Location: Washington, D.C.
Length: 30 hours (10 weeks).
Dates: January 1987-Present.
Objective: To provide the student with an understanding of the fundamental principles of substantive tort law.
Learning Outcome: Upon successful completion of this course, the student will be able to define torts and distinguish them from contracts and form crimes; explain the basis of tort liability; describe intentional torts; define negligence; define strict liability; identify defenses to intentional torts; identify defense to an action in negligence; identify defenses to an action in strict liability; and identify recoverable damages for negligence, intentional torts, and strict liability.
Instruction: Course covers fundamental principles of torts, including consideration of liability based on negligence, intentional torts and strict liability; the relationship of tort to contract, with special attention given to recoverable damages; trespass, conversion, false imprisonment, assault, fraud, defamation, mental distress, and misuse of legal process. Methodology includes lecture, discussion, and case studies.
Credit recommendation: In the lower division baccalaureate/associate degree category, 2 semester hours in Paralegal Studies (6/88).

Administrative Law and Procedure (ELAWS310)
Location: Washington, D.C.
Length: 30 hours (10 weeks).
Dates: January 1984-Present.
Objective: To provide the student with the understanding of the legal basis of constitutional limitations, and procedural limitations on agency authority.
Learning Outcome: Upon successful completion of this course, the student will be able to appreciate the interdependence of the three branches of government and un-

derstand the role and function of administrative agencies.

Instruction: Course covers principles and practice of administrative law in the federal field, provisions of the Administrative Procedure Act dealing with formal and informal rulemaking and adjucation; notice, hearing, evidence, findings, and control by the courts; and pertinent principles of constitutional law. Methodology includes lecture, discussion, and case studies.

Credit recommendation: In the lower division baccalaureate/associate degree category, 2 semester hours in Paralegal Studies (6/88).

FOIA and the Privacy Act (ELAWS335)
Location: Washington, D.C.
Length: 30 hours (10 weeks).
Dates: January 1984-Present.
Objective: To provide the student with an understanding of the FOIA and Privacy Acts and apply the appropriate legal principles in solving relevant problems.

Learning Outcome: Upon successful completion of this course, the student will be able to understand the FOIA and Privacy Act that would enable them to file a request under either Act or respond to a request if they are employed by a federal agency; appreciate how these statues are administered by federal agencies; understand how litigation concerning these Acts is handled in federal courts; demonstrate skills in researching and analyzing federal court cases; appreciate the historical and legal foundation of these statutes in Anglo-American jurisprudence.

Instruction: Course covers the Freedom of Information Act: legislative history, publication requirements, procedures and processing request, exemptions, fees; Privacy Act: definitions, limitations of disclosure, access to records, publication and other requirements, exemptions and new system reports. Methodology includes lecture, discussion, and case studies.

Credit recommendation: In the lower division baccalaureate/associate degree category, 2 semester hours in Paralegal Studies (6/88).

Legal Research I: Legal Literature (ELAWS551)
Location: Washington, D.C.
Length: 30 hours (10 weeks).
Dates: January 1987-Present.
Objective: To provide the student with knowledge of legal materials used in researching statutory and judicial publications and emphasizes their utility, contents, and currency for the paralegal.

Learning Outcome: Upon successful completion of this course, the student will be able to identify materials in the legislative history; identify and recover published opinions; identify administrative law materials; shepardize; and identify and recover law journal articles.

Instruction: Course covers statutory materials, court cases, administrative law materials, various secondary sources, use of the computer in legal research, and updating materials. Methodology includes lecture, discussion, and case studies.

Credit recommendation: In the lower division baccalaureate/associate degree category, 2 semester hours in Paralegal Studies (6/88).

Legal Research II (ELAWS552)
Location: Washington, D.C.
Length: 30 hours (10 weeks).
Dates: December 1988-Present.
Objective: To provide the student with instruction covering the rules of legal writing, statutory interpretation, case analysis, citation checking, sheperdizing techniques, reviewing unpublished legal materials, and preparing office memoranda.

Learning Outcome: Upon successful completion of this course, the student will be able to apply rules for statutory interpretation; compile legislative histories; prepare office briefs for attorneys; check cities; shepardize cases and states; and weigh authorities.

Instruction: Course covers basic concepts for effective research and surveys the research materials required to assist attorneys in general and government practice. It also applies materials in solving problems and writing memoranda and briefs, and emphasizes writing skills and research.

Credit recommendation: In the lower division baccalaureate/associate degree category, 2 semester hours in Paralegal Studies (6/88)

CORRESPONDENCE PROGRAM

ACCOUNTING

Courses are listed in numerical order by course number, e.g. CACCT101, CACCT102, etc.

Principles of Accounting I (CACCT101)
Location: Correspondence program.
Length: 12 lessons (self-paced).
Dates: April 1982-Present.
Objective: To provide the student with the knowledge to record typical accounting transactions based on generally accepted accounting principles, summarize data, and prepare financial statements.

Learning Outcome: Upon successful completion of this course, the student will be able to understand the accounting cycle; understand the preparation and content of financial statements; understand rules for recording, accumulating, and summarizing financial transactions to include journal entries and posting to the general ledger; understand payroll accounting; understand proper accounting for transactions affecting assets, receivables, expenses, and income, deferrals, and accruals.

Instruction: Course covers accounting principles and practices, including the accounting cycle, financial statements, accounting for merchandise and cash transactions, procedures for periodic reporting, accounts receivable and accounts payable, deferrals and accruals, and payables. Methodology includes self-guided study, practical exercises, sole proprietorship practice set, and a proctored final examination.

Credit recommendation: In the lower division baccalaureate/associate degree category, 2 semester hours in Principles of Accounting (6/88).

Principles of Accounting II (CACCT102)
Location: Correspondence program.
Length: 12 lessons (self-paced).
Dates: April 1982-Present.
Objective: To provide the student with the knowledge to account for plant assets, inventories, receivables and payables, and the determination of the division of partnership profits and allocation of corporate dividends.
Learning Outcome: Upon successful completion of this course, the student will be able to account for plant assets, inventories, and receivables and payables; do partnership accounting, including division of profits; do corporation accounting including payment of dividends on preferred and common stock.
Instruction: Course covers receivables, inventories, plant assets, notes payable, partnerships, corporations, and long term debt. Methodology includes self-guided study, practical exercises, corporation practice set, and a proctored final examination.
Credit recommendation: In the lower division baccalaureate/associate degree category, 2 semester hours in Principles of Accounting (6/88).

Principles of Accounting III (CACCT103)
Location: Correspondence program.
Length: 12 lessons (self-paced).
Dates: April 1982-Present.
Objective: To provide the student with the essentials of branch and departmental accounting, manufacturing cost accounting, budgeting, financial statement analysis, and the concepts of data processing systems for accounting.
Learning Outcome: Upon successful completion of this course, the student will be able to make entries and prepare statements for departmental and branch accounting and for manufacturing cost accounting; prepare budgets for a manufacturing firm, including evaluation of capital investments; solve problems involving differential analysis; do financial statement analysis and prepare a statement of changes in financial position; become familiar with the use of a computer in accounting.
Instruction: Course covers statement of changes in financial position; financial statement analysis; accounting for decentralized operations and manufacturing operations; job order cost accounting; process cost accounting; standard cost accounting; profit reporting for management analysis; differential analysis; and accounting for individuals and nonprofit organizations. Methodology includes self-guided study, practical exercises, and a proctored final examination.
Credit recommendation: In the lower division baccalaureate/associate degree category, 2 semester hours in Principles of Accounting (6/88).

Capital Budgeting (REA Borrower Accounting-Telephone) (CACCT211)
Location: Correspondence program.
Length: 13 lessons (self-paced).
Dates: June 1981-Present.
Objective: To train potential and current office managers, accountants, and bookkeepers for closing accounting work in offices of electric utilities financed by REA.
Learning Outcome: Upon successful completion of this course, the student will be able to open, maintain, and close the accounts; understand accounting for construction costs of electrical plants; prepare financial and statistical reports; understand requesting loan funds and accounting for their repayment.
Instruction: Course covers REA books of account; accounting for construction costs; meter readings, accounting, and collecting; financial and statistical statements; and calculation of depreciation rates. Methodology includes self-paced study, written homework, and proctored final examination.
Credit recommendation: In the upper division baccalaureate category, 1 semester hour in Accounting, Business Administration, Capital Budgeting, or Public Administration (6/88).

Capital Budgeting (REA Borrower Accounting-Telephone) (CACCT212)
Location: Correspondence program.
Length: 13 lessons (self-paced).
Dates: January 1978-Present.
Objective: To provide instruction and training for those students who are now or intend in the future to be employed as accountants or bookkeepers of telephone utilities financed by REA. It may also serve as a guide to directors, managers, auditors, lawyers, or engineers who are concerned with the activities of these borrowers.
Learning Outcome: Upon successful completion of this course, the student will be able to understand accounting systems applicable to the telephone industry in general; and maintain accounting records and accounting procedures applicable to telephone utilities financed by loans approved by REA (Rural Electrical Administration) and/or the Rural Telephone Bank.
Instruction: Course covers recommended books of account and basic accounting systems applicable to the telephone industry; accounting to be performed during the periods of organization, initial construction, and operations; requesting and accounting for REA and rural telephone bank loan funds; recommended plant accounting

procedures including construction and retirement work order accounting. Methodology includes self-paced study and proctored exams.

Credit recommendation: In the upper division baccalaureate category, 1 semester hour in Accounting, Business Administration, Capital Budgeting, or Public Administration (6/88).

Cost Accounting I (CACCT250)

Location: Correspondence program.
Length: 8 lessons (self-paced).
Dates: January 1982-Present.
Objective: To provide the student with a practical knowledge of job order cost accounting systems and procedures, and the role cost accounting plays in planning and controlling operations.
Learning Outcome: Upon successful completion of this course, the student will be able to perform job order cost accounting; do accounting for purchases and storage of materials; control and value inventory; and record and control labor.
Instruction: Course covers job order cost accounting, inventory valuation procedures, and labor costs. Methodology includes self-guided study, problem solving, case analysis, and a proctored final examination.
Credit recommendation: In the upper division baccalaureate category, 1 semester hour in Accounting, Business Administration, or Cost Accounting (6/88).

Cost Accounting II (CACCT251)

Location: Correspondence program.
Length: 6 lessons (self-paced).
Dates: January 1982-Present.
Objective: To provide the student with knowledge to make entries and prepare statements for a process cost accounting system.
Learning Outcome: Upon successful completion of this course, the student will be able to record costs incurred in each step of a process manufacturing operation; prepare worksheets and costs of production reports; and make computations of equivalent units of production and unit costs.
Instruction: Course covers process cost systems, production reports, average cost of work in process, by-product costing, joint costing, and allocation of common costs. Methodology includes self-guided study, practical exercises, and a proctored final examination.
Credit recommendation: In the upper division baccalaureate category, 1 semester hour in Accounting, Business Administration, or Cost Accounting (6/88).

Cost Accounting III (CACCT252)

Location: Correspondence program.
Length: 6 lessons (self-paced).
Dates: January 1982-Present.
Objective: To provide the student with an understanding of the use of costs in planning and control, including the use of standard costs, the ability to prepare budgeted income statements, and use appropriate techniques for decision making.
Learning Outcome: Upon successful completion of this course, the student will be able to prepare various budgets used in planning and control; use a standard manufacturing cost system; prepare budgeted income statements; use breakeven analysis and differential cost analysis; and evaluate capital expenditure proposals.
Instruction: Course covers planning and control involving use of cost data, budgeting manufacturing and nonmanufacturing costs, standard costs, direct costing, breakeven analysis, capital expenditure analysis, and computerized cost accounting in a nonprofit service center. Methodology includes self-guided study, practical exercises, and a proctored final examination.
Credit recommendation: In the upper division baccalaureate category, 1 semester hour in Accounting, Business Administration, or Cost Accounting (6/88).

Federal Government Accounting (CACCT260)

Location: Correspondence program.
Length: 14 lessons (self-paced).
Dates: August 1982-Present.
Objective: To provide the student with the basic regulations, principles, and standards that govern accounting and financial reporting by U.S. Government agencies prescribed by the Comptroller General of the U.S., the General Accounting Office, and the Bureau of the Budget.
Learning Outcome: Upon successful completion of this course, the student will be able to identify terminology and concepts of federal government accounting; prepare general ledger entries.
Instruction: Course covers basic principles and practices of federal government accounting, concepts and method of fund control, practice with basic records, accounting working capital funds, allotment obligation, disbursements, and transfer appropriations.
Credit recommendation: In the upper division baccalaureate category, 2 semester hours in Government Accounting (6/88).

Federal Government Accounting II (CACCT261)

Location: Correspondence program.
Length: 12 lessons (self-paced).
Dates: August 1982-Present.
Objective: To provide the student with the ability to compile data and prepare reports based upon regulations and standards of U.S. government agencies with respect to inventory and property accounting, revolving funds, and the obligation and disbursement of funds.
Learning Outcome: Upon successful completion of this course, the student will be able to record transactions involving acquisition, depreciation, and sale of property; working capital funds and cost accounting; preparation of

business-type financial statements for federal government activities; reporting of budget execution showing status of funds apportioned, obligated, and unobligated.

Instruction: Course covers property accounting, working capital funds, financial statements for federal government activities, budget execution reports and reports on obligations, transfer of obligating authority to field offices, and statement of financial condition for Treasury Department. Methodology includes self-guided instruction, written homework problems, and proctored final examination.

Credit recommendation: In the upper division baccalaureate category, 2 semester hours in Governmental Accounting (6/88).

EDITING

Courses are listed in numerical order by course number, e.g., CEDIT140, CEDIT160, etc.

Introduction to the Editing Process (CEDIT140) (Editing)
Location: Correspondence program.
Length: 12 lessons (self-paced).
Dates: October 1988-Present.
Objective: To provide the student with a knowledge of editing techniques and publishing processes.
Learning Outcome: Upon successful completion of this course, the student will be able to perform a basic edit on a nontechnical manuscript, evidencing correct grammar, spelling, and punctuation; demonstrate various approaches to editing; demonstrate awareness of the remainder of the publishing process after an edit is completed.
Instruction: Course covers editing techniques and processes, marking up copy for typesetting and determining format, composition (typesetting), and preparing front and rear matter. Methodology includes self-paced instruction and a proctored final examination.
Credit recommendation: In the lower division baccalaureate/associate degree category, 3 semester hours in Business Communications, Communications, English, or Journalism (6/88).

Proofreading (CEDIT160)
Location: Correspondence program.
Length: 10 lessons (self-paced).
Dates: June 1988-Present.
Objective: To provide the student with an understanding and application of professional proofreading techniques.
Learning Outcome: Upon successful completion of this course, the student will be able to perform an accurate proofreading of narrative text, graphics, tabular material, mathematics text, foreign languages and illustrations; identify typography variances and critically review for technique quality; and identify and use conventional marking techniques and proofreading symbols.
Instruction: Course covers proofreading and proofmarks, measuring types and space, alternate marking systems, production process, procedures, tasks, queries and questions, and special proofreading problems. Methodology includes self-paced instruction with a proctored final examination.
Credit recommendation: In the lower division baccalaureate/associate degree category, 3 semester hours in Business English, English, Journalism, or Technical Writing (6/88).

Intermediate Editing Principles and Practices (CEDIT230)
Location: Correspondence program.
Length: 10 lessons (self-paced).
Dates: November 1982-Present.
Objective: To introduce the student to the vagaries of style emanating from ethnic geographical and environmental factors, as well as stylistic aberrations of grammar, providing the student with editing skills.
Learning Outcome: Upon successful completion of this course, the student will be able to correct copy, noting stylistic differences; make decisions on what is or what is not copyrightable; and make decisions on effectiveness of visual displays.
Instruction: Course covers copy editing, graphic design, copyright, and stylistic errors. Methodology includes self-paced instruction with a proctored final examination.
Credit recommendation: In the lower division baccalaureate/associate degree category, 3 semester hours in Communications, English, or Journalism (6/88).

Printing, Layout and Design (CEDIT270)
Location: Correspondence program.
Length: 11 lessons (self-paced).
Dates: November 1982-Present.
Objective: To provide the student with the knowledge of the process, techniques, and tools that relate to design and production of printed materials.
Learning Outcome: Upon successful completion of this course, the student will be able to identify fundamental concepts in printing, layout and design; understand the necessary theoretical background for efficient development of projects; and apply techniques and creative approaches to the job.
Instruction: Course covers planning, printing, production, print media and the printing process, composition, book binding, typography and design, photographs, layout, copyediting, and design. Methodology includes self-paced instruction with a proctored final examination.
Credit recommendation: In the lower division baccalaureate/associate degree category, 3 semester hours in English, Journalism, or Technical Writing (6/88).

Thesaurus Building (CEDIT301)
Location: Correspondence program.

Length: 11 lessons (self-paced).
Dates: August 1987-Present.
Objective: To provide the student with a knowledge of the concepts behind a thesaurus and the selection and usefulness of terms.
Learning Outcome: Upon successful completion of this course, the student will know the characteristics and value of well-constructed thesauri; develop hierarchical listings; work with existing thesauri from various sources.
Instruction: Course covers interrelationships among terms, structure (alphabetical versus hierarchical display), and sources of thesauri. Methodology includes self-paced instruction with proctored final examination.
Credit recommendation: In the vocational certificate or lower division baccalaureate/associate degree category, 1 semester hour in Information Systems Management or Library Science (6/88).

Advanced Practice in Editing (CEDIT310)
Location: Correspondence program.
Length: 11 lessons (self-paced).
Dates: March 1986-Present.
Objective: To enhance editing skills and broaden editorial perspective.
Learning Outcome: Upon successful completion of this course, the student will be able to edit a variety of manuscripts in accordance with specific style guides (e.g., GPO); fit copy to available space; write an abstract; understand basic principles of publication management.
Instruction: Course covers copy-editing, substantive editing, writing and editing for specialized audiences, and publications management. Methodology includes self-paced instruction with proctored examination.
Credit recommendation: In the upper division baccalaureate category, 3 semester hours in Business Communications, Communications, English, or Journalism (6/88).

Editing Technical Manuscripts (CEDIT350)
Location: Correspondence program.
Length: 11 lessons (self-paced).
Dates: February 1986-Present.
Objective: To provide the student with the knowledge and skill required to help experienced general editors make the transition to technical editing.
Learning Outcome: Upon successful completion of this course, the student will be able to demonstrate constructive author/editor relationships in a variety of settings; make appropriate choices of presentation concerning tables, charts, graphs, and other illustrations; and understand the special concerns of international audiences.
Instruction: Course covers technical definitions, author-editor relationships, illustrations, procedures writing, international audiences, and review of camera-ready material. Methodology includes self-paced learning with a proctored final examination.
Credit recommendation: In the upper division baccalaureate category, 3 semester hours in Business Communications, Communications, English, or Journalism (6/88).

Basic Indexing (CEDIT360)
Location: Correspondence program.
Length: 14 lessons (self-paced).
Dates: June 1987-Present.
Objective: To provide the student with the knowledge of indexing techniques.
Learning Outcome: Upon successful completion of this course, the student will be able to differentiate between material suitable for headings and subheadings, alphabetize listings accurately, and determine cross-references.
Instruction: Course covers index editing, index preparation, computers and indexing, and indexing as a business. Methodology includes self-paced learning with a proctored examination.
Credit recommendation: In the lower division baccalaureate/associate degree category, 3 semester hours in Information Systems Management or Library Science (6/88).

Applied Indexing (CEDIT361)
Location: Correspondence program.
Length: 9 lessons (self-paced).
Dates: March 1983-Present.
Objective: To provide the student with knowledge of subject indexing and techniques, including reading for content, and learning to conceptualize and synthesize information.
Learning Outcome: Upon successful completion of this course, the student will be able to distinguish between letter-by-letter and word-by-word indexing; define "merging indexes" and understand the procedure; make appropriate estimates of time and costs.
Instruction: Course covers letter-by-letter indexing; indexing, style and format differences; time and cost estimates; merging index; hierarchical indexing; comprehensive in-depth indexing. Methodology includes self-paced learning with proctored examination.
Credit recommendation: In the upper division baccalaureate category, 3 semester hours in Information Systems Management or Library Science (6/88).

Publishing Management (CEDIT375)
Location: Correspondence program.
Length: 9 lessons (self-paced).
Dates: November 1982-Present.
Objective: To provide the student with an understanding and application of accepted management principles to government and private printing.
Learning Outcome: Upon successful completion of this course, the student will be able to make the transition from editing to management; demonstrate understanding of

management principles; apply management principles to a publishing organization.

Instruction: Course covers management practice of government and private publishing entries, including selection of staff; government regulations on printing; copyright laws; Freedom of Information Act and Privacy Act; clearance and review procedures for policies, quality and content; fitting and evaluating materials for various audiences; distribution problems; reader surveys; economics of publishing; and management principles. Methodology includes self-paced instruction with a proctored final examination.

Credit recommendation: In the upper division baccalaureate category, 3 semester hours in Business Communications, Communications, English, or Journalism (6/88).

PARALEGAL

Courses are listed in numerical order by course number, e.g., CLAWS110, CLAWS120, etc.

Introduction to Law for Paralegals (CLAWS110)
Location: Correspondence program.
Length: 11 lessons (self-paced).
Dates: February 1985-Present.
Objective: To provide the student with an understanding of the role of the paralegal or lawyer's assistant through a general introduction to the American legal system.
Learning Outcome: Upon successful completion of this course, the student will be able to understand the role of a paralegal in a lawyer's office; understand fundamental principles of legal writing.
Instruction: Course covers Constitutional law, criminal law, contracts law, tort law, wills and trusts law, real estate law, consumer protection law, skills of case analysis, and components of an opinion. Methodology includes self-paced instruction with proctored examination.
Credit recommendation: In the lower division baccalaureate/associate degree category, 2 semester hours in Paralegal Studies (6/88).

Business Law I (CLAWS120)
Location: Correspondence program.
Length: 15 lessons (self-paced).
Dates: February 1985-Present.
Objective: To provide the student with knowledge of certain aspects of the substantive law applicable to many business transactions.
Learning Outcome: Upon successful completion of this course, the student will be able to apply knowledge of law to business relationships.
Instruction: Course covers aspects of law essential to conduct of modern business: contracts, bailments, sales and warranties. Methodology includes self-paced instruction with proctored examinations.
Credit recommendation: In the lower division baccalaureate/associate degree category, 2 semester hours in Business Administration or Paralegal Studies (6/88).

Business Law II (CLAWS121)
Location: Correspondence program.
Length: 11 lessons (self-paced).
Dates: February 1986-Present.
Objective: To provide the student with the knowledge of advanced aspects of substantive law applicable to business.
Learning Outcome: Upon successful completion of this course, the student will be able to apply knowledge of law to business relationships.
Instruction: Course covers aspects of law essential to conduct of modern business: agency, partnerships, corporations, corporate stock and shareholders, personal and real property, leases, and estates and trusts. Methodology includes self-paced instruction with proctored examinations.
Credit recommendation: In the lower division baccalaureate/associate degree category, 2 semester hours in Business Administration or Paralegal Studies (6/88).

Criminal Law (CLAWS135)
Location: Correspondence program.
Length: 9 lessons (self-paced).
Dates: June 1988-Present.
Objective: To provide the student with knowledge of substantive areas of criminal laws.
Learning Outcome: Upon successful completion of this course, the student will be able to understand basic principles of criminal law.
Instruction: Course covers legal aspects of criminal law: elements of specific crimes, common defenses, and the proof necessary to convict persons of crimes. Methodology includes self-paced instruction with proctored examinations.
Credit recommendation: In the lower division baccalaureate/associate degree category, 2 semester hours in Administration of Justice, Criminology, or Paralegal Studies (6/88). NOTE: Credit for this course should not be awarded as credit for a course in Criminal Procedures and Evidence.

Family Law (CLAWS150)
Location: Correspondence program.
Length: 14 lessons (self-paced).
Dates: June 1988-Present.
Objective: To introduce the student to substantive and procedural aspects of domestic relations law.
Learning Outcome: Upon successful completion of this course, the student will be able to apply knowledge of domestic relations law to client interview and case preparation.

Instruction: Course covers legal aspects of divorce, annulment, separation, adoption, legitimization, alimony, and child support, as well as related tax consequences of divorce and separation. Methodology includes self-paced instruction with proctored examinations.

Credit recommendation: In the lower division baccalaureate/associate degree category, 2 semester hours in Paralegal Studies (6/88).

Constitutional Law (CLAWS251)
   Location: Correspondence program.
   Length: 16 lessons (self-paced).
   Dates: February 1985-Present.
   Objective: To provide the student with the knowledge of the Constitution and its provisions relevant to understanding the process of constitutional decision-making.
   Learning Outcome: Upon successful completion of this course, the student will be able to apply constitutional principles to the full range of substantive and procedural areas.
   Instruction: Course covers source and scope of Judicial power; federal power to regulate interstate commerce; federal taxing and spending power; the state's exercise of police power; equal protection: racial discrimination, state action, economic, social discrimination; due process; the individual's right to privacy; freedom of speech, press, and religion; standing, mootness, and ripeness; political questions; advisory opinions. Methodology includes self-paced instruction with proctored examinations.
   Credit recommendation: In the lower division baccalaureate/associate degree category, 2 semester hours in Government and Politics/Political Science or Paralegal Studies (6/88).

Wills, Trusts and Estate Administration (CLAWS275)
   Location: Correspondence program.
   Length: 13 lessons (self-paced).
   Dates: August 1987-Present.
   Objective: To provide the student with knowledge of wills and estates from planning to administration.
   Learning Outcome: Upon successful completion of this course, the student will be able to provide effective assistance to attorneys and agencies involved in probate.
   Instruction: Course covers client interview; tax considerations, intestacy, distribution by operation of law, elements of a will, trusts, complex wills, execution and other formalities, revocations, codicils and other means of changing a will, will substitutes, and probate. Methodology includes self-paced instruction with proctored examination.
   Credit recommendation: In the lower division baccalaureate/associate degree category, 2 semester hours in Paralegal Studies (6/88).

Administrative Law and Procedure (CLAWS310)
   Location: Correspondence program.
   Length: 10 lessons (self-paced).
   Dates: February 1985-Present.
   Objective: To provide the student with an understanding of the workings of administrative agencies within the federal government.
   Learning Outcome: Upon successful completion of this course, the student will be able to appreciate the interdependent role of the three branches of the federal government; understand the role and function of federal administrative agencies.
   Instruction: Course covers principles and practice of administrative law in the federal field; provisions of Administrative Procedure Act dealing with formal and informal rulemaking and adjudication; notice, hearing, evidence, findings, and control by the courts with a discussion of pertinent and applicable principles of constitutional law. Methodology includes self-paced learning with proctored examination.
   Credit recommendation: In the lower division baccalaureate/associate degree category, 2 semester hours in Paralegal Studies (6/88).

FOIA and the Privacy Act (CLAWS335)
   Location: Correspondence program.
   Length: 9 lessons (self-paced).
   Dates: February 1986-Present.
   Objective: To provide the student with an understanding of the Freedom of Information and Privacy Acts and their case interpretation.
   Learning Outcome: Upon successful completion of this course, the student will be able to analyze substantive and procedural problems relating to Freedom of Information and Privacy Acts.
   Instruction: Course covers the Freedom of Information Act: legislative history, publication, requirements, procedures and processing requests, exemptions, fees; Privacy Act: definitions, limitations of disclosure, access to records, publication requirements, exemptions, and new systems reports. Methodology includes self-paced instruction with proctored examinations.
   Credit recommendation: In the lower division baccalaureate/associate degree category, 2 semester hours in Paralegal Studies (6/88).

Litigation (CLAWS345)
   Location: Correspondence program.
   Length: 11 lessons (self-paced).
   Dates: August 1987-Present.
   Objective: To acquaint the student with procedural aspects of the litigation process.
   Learning Outcome: Upon successful completion of this course, the student will be able to understand the litigation process; assist in preparation of documents needed for case preparation.
   Instruction: Course covers the process of civil litigation for paralegals: factual investigation of the client's case;

preparation of pleadings and pretrial motions which are necessary to commence and defend a lawsuit; discovery devices available for obtaining relevant information from opposing and third parties and what to do with that information in preparing for trial; finally, post trial proceedings and settlement documents. Methodology includes self-paced instruction with proctored examination.

Credit recommendation: In the lower division baccalaureate/associate degree category, 2 semester hours in Paralegal Studies (6/88).

Real Estate Transaction (CLAWS350)

Location: Correspondence program.
Length: 16 lessons (self-paced).
Dates: August 1987-Present.
Objective: To provide the student with the comprehension and practical knowledge of real estate laws and procedures.
Learning Outcome: Upon successful completion of this course, the student will be able to assist the lawyer in preparation of documents for various real estate transactions.
Instruction: Course covers property rights and interests; legal aspects of real estate transactions and settlement; drafting of a real estate sales contract and settlement documents. Methodology includes self-paced instruction with proctored examination.
Credit recommendation: In the lower division baccalaureate/associate degree category, 2 semester hours in Business Administration or Paralegal Studies (6/88).

Legal Research I: Legal Literature (CLAWS551)

Location: Correspondence program.
Length: 13 lessons (self-paced).
Dates: June 1988-Present.
Objective: To provide the student with knowledge of legal materials used in researching statutory and judicial publications, their utility, contents, and currency for the libraries, library technician, and paralegal.
Learning Outcome: Upon successful completion of this course, the student will be able to identify materials in the legislative history; identify and recover published opinions; identify administrative law materials; sherpardize; identify and recover law journal articles.
Instruction: Course covers statutory materials, court cases, administrative law materials, various secondary sources, use of the computer in legal research, and updating materials. Methodology includes self-paced instruction with proctored examination.
Credit recommendation: In the lower division baccalaureate/associate degree category, 2 semester hours in Paralegal Studies (6/88).

Legal Research II (CLAWS552)

Location: Correspondence program.
Length: 10 lessons (self-paced).
Dates: June 1988-Present.
Objective: To provide the student with knowledge of basic concepts for effective research and research materials required to assist attorneys in general or government practice.
Learning Outcome: Upon successful completion of this course, the student will be able to assist lawyers in research required for various legal activities; express results of research in clearly written memoranda, client letters, and other legal communications.
Instruction: Course covers statutory materials, court cases, administrative law materials, various secondary sources, use of the computer in legal research, and updating materials, writing memoranda and briefs. Methodology includes self-paced instruction with proctored examination.
Credit recommendation: In the lower division baccalaureate/associate degree category, 2 semester hours in Paralegal Studies (6/88).

Legal Writing I (CLAWS555)

Location: Correspondence program.
Length: 12 lessons (self-paced).
Dates: February 1986-Present.
Objective: To provide the student with knowledge of techniques for clear and effective legal writing.
Learning Outcome: Upon successful completion of this course, the student will be able to understand and use appropriate legal forms; communicate effectively in legal writing.
Instruction: Course covers leases, employment contracts, wills, case briefs, and interoffice memoranda. Methodology includes self-paced instruction with proctored examinations.
Credit recommendation: In the lower division baccalaureate/associate degree category, 2 semester hours in Communication Arts, Journalism, or Paralegal Studies (6/88).

Legal Writing II (CLAWS556)

Location: Correspondence program.
Length: 11 lessons (self-paced).
Dates: August 1987-Present.
Objective: To provide the student with advanced knowledge of techniques for clear and effective legal writing.
Learning Outcome: Upon successful completion of this course, the student will be able to understand and use appropriate legal forms; and communicate effectively in legal writing.
Instruction: Course covers pretrial writing in the form of a memorandum and pleadings; a trial brief; legal correspondence of various types; legislative drafting. Methodology includes self-paced instruction with proctored examination.
Credit recommendation: In the lower division bac-

calaureate/associate degree category, 2 semester hours in Communication Arts, Journalism, or Paralegal Studies (6/88).

MATHEMATICS

Calculus I (CMATH210)
Location: Correspondence program.
Length: 10 lessons (self-paced).
Dates: November 1982-Present.
Objective: To provide the student with an understanding of the meaning and use of the derivatives of mathematical functions.
Learning Outcome: Upon successful completion of this course, the student will be able to understand the meaning of the derivative, and its relationship to the slope of the tangent line; determine the maximum and minimum points of a curve.
Instruction: Course covers variables, functions, limits, continuity, derivatives, maxima and minima, mean value theorem, and approximation methods for finding roots. Methodology includes self-guided instruction, guided homework problems, and a proctored final examination.
Credit recommendation: In the lower division baccalaureate/associate degree category, 3 semester hours in Differential Calculus or Mathematics (6/88).

Calculus II (CMATH211)
Location: Correspondence program.
Length: 11 lessons (self-paced).
Dates: March 1983-Present.
Objective: To provide the student with an understanding of the concepts and applications of the integration of mathematical functions.
Learning Outcome: Upon successful completion of this course, the student will be able to understand concepts of integration; apply integration to the development of the area under a curve.
Instruction: Course covers simple integration; the definite integral; approximation methods of integration; integration of trigonometric functions. Methodology includes self-guided instruction, graded homework problems, and a proctored final examination.
Credit recommendation: In the lower division baccalaureate/associate degree category, 3 semester hours in Integral Calculus or Mathematics (6/88).

SCIENCE AND ENGINEERING

Courses are grouped below in the following sequence: Engineering, Meteorology, Physics; each grouping is arranged in numerical order by course number.

Basic Electricity (CENGN101)
Location: Correspondence program.
Length: 16 lessons (self-paced).
Dates: July 1981-Present.
Objective: To provide the student an introduction to the fundamental concepts of electricity for beginning technicians and other interested laypersons.
Learning Outcome: Upon successful completion of this course, the student will be able to understand the fundamental concepts of electricity; understand basic AC and DC circuits; understand basic electrical components such as resistors, inductors, capacitors, and motors.
Instruction: Course covers fundamental concepts and safety; DC circuits; AC circuits; inductance and capacitance; electromagnetism; electrical instruction; motors and transformers. Methodology includes self-paced instruction with proctored examination.
Credit recommendation: In the lower division baccalaureate/associate degree category, 2 semester hours in Electrical Technology (6/88).

Solid State Fundamentals (CENGN102)
Location: Correspondence program.
Length: 14 lessons (self-paced).
Dates: August 1987-Present.
Objective: This course is for electricians and electronic technicians and provides a logical, practical background in the application of solid state devices.
Learning Outcome: Upon successful completion of this course, the student will be able to repair printed circuit boards; read and understand device specifications; understand and test solid state devices and basic solid state circuits.
Instruction: Course covers PC boards, diodes, diode circuits, and testing of diodes, power supplies, other diodes (i.e., EDs and pressure sensors), transistors, transistor circuits, and transistor testing, SCRs and Triacs, integrated circuits, and introduction to fiber optics. Methodology includes self-paced instruction with proctored examination.
Credit recommendation: In the lower division baccalaureate/associate degree category, 2 semester hours in Electronics Technology (6/88).

Basic Electronics (CENGN201)
Location: Correspondence program.
Length: 16 lessons (self-paced).
Dates: July 1981-Present.
Objective: To provide the student with a basic introduction to the principles of electronics at the technical level.
Learning Outcome: Upon successful completion of this course, the student will be able to understand the basic principles of electronic components; understand basic electronic circuits; understand basic receiver and transmitter technology.
Instruction: Course covers electronic principles, diodes, transistors and electric tubes, tuned circuits, detectors, amplifiers (audio, RF, power, IF), oscillators, receivers and transmitters, and transmission lines and antennas.

Methodology includes self-paced instruction with proctored examination.

Credit recommendation: In the lower division baccalaureate/associate degree category, 3 semester hours in Electronics Technology (6/88).

Electric Transmission/Distribution (CENGN202)
  Location: Correspondence program.
  Length: 16 lessons (self-paced).
  Dates: March 1983-Present.
  Objective: To provide the student with an introduction to the concepts, principles, and devices associated with the transmission and distribution of electric energy.
  Learning Outcome: Upon successful completion of this course, the student will be able to identify the constituent parts of the total electric transmission and distribution system; perform simple computations such as power factors, regulation, efficiency, short-circuit currents, mechanical properties of lines, etc.
  Instruction: Course covers theory; transmission terminal facilities; transmission lines; mechanical design, primary and secondary distribution systems; capacitors, transformers, and system protection; planning and load characteristics; auxiliary equipment. Methodology includes self-paced instruction with proctored examination.
  Credit recommendation: In the lower division baccalaureate/associate degree category, 2 semester hours in a terminal associate degree program in Electrical Engineering Technology (6/88).

Electrical Wiring (CENGN203)
  Location: Correspondence program.
  Length: 16 lessons (self-paced).
  Dates: January 1982-Present.
  Objective: To familiarize the student with the National Electrical Code while presenting the technical and practical aspects of electrical wiring.
  Learning Outcome: Upon successful completion of this course, the student will be able to quote the National Electrical Code; read electrical blueprints; be able to wire, according to code, single- and multiple-family dwellings, commercial structures, industrial power installations, and to do this under special conditions.
  Instruction: Course covers wiring of single- and multiple-family dwellings; services for commercial and industrial establishments; and specialized and hazardous locations. Specifics include conductor sizing, grounding, panel sizing, cable types, etc. and blueprint reading. Methodology includes self-paced instruction with proctored examination.
  Credit recommendation: In the vocational certificate category, 2 semester hours in Electricians Apprentice Programs (6/88).

Hydraulics I (CENGN204)
  Location: Correspondence program.
  Length: 9 lessons (self-paced).
  Dates: March 1983-Present.
  Objective: To introduce the student to the basic principles of hydrostatics and the associated knowledge of the physical behavior of liquids and gases.
  Learning Outcome: Upon successful completion of this course, the student will be able to think analytically about technical problems associated with hyrdostatics; further understand the physical behavior of liquids and gases when subjected to various forces.
  Instruction: Course covers applicable units and their conversions: force, weight, mass, pressure, heat and area; measuring devices such as parameters, manometers, and piezometers; Pascal and Archimedes Laws; resolution of forces; moments; the hydrostatic pressure diagram; static loads on structures; the stability of dams. Methodology includes self-paced instruction with proctored examination.
  Credit recommendation: In the lower division baccalaureate/associate degree category, 2 semester hours in two-year terminal degree in Engineering Technology programs (6/88).

Strength of Materials (CENGN206)
  Location: Correspondence program.
  Length: 14 lessons (self-paced).
  Dates: August 1987-Present.
  Objective: To provide the student with the background skills, concepts, and a basic understanding of strength of materials as they relate to the design of structural members, parts and connections, by simplified approaches and the use of modern high school mathematics without the use of calculus.
  Learning Outcome: Upon successful completion of this course, the student will be able to identify basic units of measurement, terms, and solve fundamental problems involving material strengths; identify forces on structural members and solve problems involving stresses; prepare shear and moment diagrams and to solve basic problems for members subject to axial and bending stress.
  Instruction: Course covers basics of strength of materials, including stress and deformation; engineering materials, and riveted joints; thin-walled pressure vessels and welded joints; torsion; centroids and moments of inertia; shear and moment in beams; stresses, design, and deflector of beams, statically indeterminate beams; combined stresses; column; and impact loading and strain energy. Methodology includes self-paced instruction with proctored examination.
  Credit recommendation: In the lower division baccalaureate/associate degree category, 3 semester hours in Strength of Materials (6/88). NOTE: Would only apply to Engineering Technology.

Fiber Optic Communications (CENGN207)
  Location: Correspondence program.

Length: 13 lessons (self-paced).
Dates: August 1987-Present.
Objective: To provide the student with an understanding of the background theory and basic concepts of fiber optic communications and with a knowledge of fiber optic communication technology.
Learning Outcome: Upon successful completion of this course, the student will be able to understand basic physical concepts of fiber optic communications; understand the elements of a fiber optic communications system; understand the system parameters that specify fiber optic communication.
Instruction: Course covers optics and light wave fundamentals, optical fibers, integrated optics, light sources and detectors, light couplers and detectors, modulation, noise and detection, and system design. Methodology includes self-paced instruction with proctored examination.
Credit recommendation: In the lower division baccalaureate/associate degree category, 2 semester hours in Electrical Engineering (6/88).

Engineering Mechanics I (Statics) (CENGN208)
Location: Correspondence program.
Length: 9 lessons (self-paced).
Dates: August 1987-Present.
Objective: To provide the student with the background, skill, concepts, and a basic understanding of statics as it relates to engineering mechanics using simplifed approaches and modern high school mathematics without calculus. Covers applied statics and stresses practical aspects.
Learning Outcome: Upon successful completion of this course, the student will be able to identify force systems and solve problems involving force equilibrium and direction; solve problems of coplanar, parallel force and concurrent force systems; noncoplanar, parallel force and concurrent force systems; calculate and/or locate centroids, center of gravity and moments of inertia.
Instruction: Course covers basic principles, coplanar parallel and concurrent force systems, coplanar and noncoplanar nonconcurrent force systems, friction, center of gravity, centroids, and related aspects. Methodology includes self-paced instruction with proctored examination.
Credit recommendation: In the lower division baccalaureate/associate degree category, 2 semester hours in Engineering Mechanics (Statics) (6/88). NOTE: Would only apply for Engineering Technology.

Engineering Mechanics II (Dynamics) (CENGN209)
Location: Correspondence program.
Length: 9 lessons (self-paced).
Dates: August 1987-Present.
Objective: To provide students with the background, skill, concepts, and a basic understanding of dynamics as it relates to engineering mechanics using simplified approaches and modern high school mathematics without calculus. Covers applied dynamics and stresses practical aspects.
Learning Outcome: Upon successful completion of this course, the student will be able to solve problems involving rectilinear motion and kinetic forces on rigid bodies; solve problems involving rotational motion; solve problems related to impulse and momentum.
Instruction: Course covers basic problems involving rectilinear motion, kinetic forces on rigid bodies, forces on bodies traveling along any path, rotational motion, forces perpendicular to the plane of motion, and forces of impulse and momentum. Methodology includes self-paced instruction and proctored examination.
Credit recommendation: In the lower division baccalaureate/associate degree category, 2 semester hours in Engineering Mechanics (Dynamics) (6/88). NOTE: Would only apply to Engineering Technology.

Hydrology I (CENGN501)
Location: Correspondence program.
Length: 16 lessons (self-paced).
Dates: March 1983-Present.
Objective: To provide the student with the major hydrological and pertinent meteorological elements—how they are observed and the data analyzed.
Learning Outcome: Upon successful completion of this course, the student will be able to describe the hydrologic cycles; make measurements and interpretation of streamflow, precipitation, and other basic data; understand the physics of soil moisture, the infiltration and rainfall runoff relations.
Instruction: Course covers elementary meteorology and statistics; measurements and interpretation of streamflow, precipitation, and other basic data; hydrologic cycles; physics of soil moisture; infiltration theory; rainfall runoff relations. Methodology includes self-paced instruction with proctored examination.
Credit recommendation: In the upper division baccalaureate category, 3 semester hours in Hydrology in Civil Engineering (6/88).

Hydrology II (CENGN502)
Location: Correspondence program.
Length: 16 lessons (self-paced).
Dates: March 1983-Present.
Objective: To provide the student with the ability to apply the data analysis techniques applicable to the science of hydrology.
Learning Outcome: Upon successful completion of this course, the student will be able to use hydrologic data to forecast streamflow; estimate parameters needed in water control structure design.
Instruction: Course covers hydrographs and their uses; relationships between runoff, rainfall, and storm derivation; features and functions of reservoirs; calculation of sediment load in a stream. Methodology includes self-paced instruction with proctored examination.

Credit recommendation: In the upper division baccalaureate category, 3 semester hours in Hydrology in Civil Engineering (6/88).

METEOROLOGY

Dynamic Meteorology I (CMETO361)
  Location: Correspondence program.
  Length: 16 lessons (self-paced).
  Dates: April 1982-Present.
  Objective: To provide the student with the fundamentals of general meteorology.
  Learning Outcome: Upon successful completion of this course, the student will be able to understand the concepts of dynamics as applied to weather analysis; understand the concepts of dynamics as applied to weather forecasting.
  Instruction: Course covers fundamental concepts, thermodynamics, thermodynamics of water vapor, hydrostatic equilibrium and geopotential, and stability. Methodology includes self-paced instruction with proctored examination.
  Credit recommendation: In the upper division baccalaureate category, 3 semester hours in Meteorology (6/88).

Dynamic Meteorology II (CMETO362)
  Location: Correspondence program.
  Length: 10 lessons (self-paced).
  Dates: August 1982-Present.
  Objective: To provide the student with a continuation of Dynamic Meteorology I, covering the application of the general principles of mechanics and fluid motion to the study of the atmosphere and its movement.
  Learning Outcome: Upon successful completion of this course, the student will be able to apply concepts of mechanics and fluid motion to the study of the atmosphere; apply concepts of mechanics and fluid motion to weather analysis; apply concepts of mechanics and fluid motion to weather forecasting.
  Instruction: Course covers vector analysis; equations of motion; horizontal motion; variations of wind, pressure, and thermal fields in the vertical; mechanism of pressure change; weather prediction. Methodology includes self-paced instruction with proctored examination.
  Credit recommendation: In the upper division baccalaureate category, 3 semester hours in Meteorology (6/88).

PHYSICS

General Physics I (CPHYS201)
  Location: Correspondence program.
  Length: 13 lessons (self-paced).
  Dates: June 1988-Present.
  Objective: This noncalculus-based course is directed at providing the student with a working knowledge of basic physical concepts, applying the acquired principles of physics to fields of study and/or employment.
  Learning Outcome: Upon successful completion of this course, the student will be able to exhibit a working knowledge of certain basic physical concepts; relate the knowledge acquired to classes of problems in areas such as pollution, energy, water quality, etc.; describe physical phenomena in a matter universally understood by other physical scientists.
  Instruction: Course covers kinematics, dynamics, gravitation, equilibrium, energy, fluids, temperature, kinetic theory, heat, thermodynamics, waves, and sound. Methodology includes self-paced instruction with proctored examination.
  Credit recommendation: In the lower division baccalaureate/associate degree category, 3 semester hours in noncalculus-based Physics or Physical Science (6/88).

General Physics II (CPHYS202)
  Location: Correspondence program.
  Length: 11 lessons (self-paced).
  Dates: June 1988-Present.
  Objective: This noncalculus-based course is directed at providing the student with a working knowledge of physical concepts such that those principles may be applied to the field of study or employment.
  Learning Outcome: Upon successful completion of this course, the student will be able to exhibit a working knowledge of key physical concepts; relate the knowledge acquired to certain classes of problems which impact society (i.e., energy needs, radioactivity, nuclear effects, etc.).
  Instruction: This course is a continuation of General Physics I and includes the introduction of electric field, magnetism, circuits, light and electromagnetic waves, relativity, quantum theory and quantum mechanics, atoms, radioactivity, and nuclear energy. Methodology includes self-paced instruction with proctored examination.
  Credit recommendation: In the lower division baccalaureate/associate degree category, 3 semester hours in noncalculus-based Physics or Physical Science (6/88).

United States Department of Internal Revenue Service, Federal Law Enforcement Training Center

The Internal Revenue Service (IRS) administers federal tax laws and regulations. It informs the public about the requirements of the law and determines the extent of compliance and causes of noncompliance.

The IRS offers several hundred training programs covering a wide variety of clerical, secretarial, tax law, technical, and managerial subjects. Subject matter is presented through classroom training, on-the-job training, self-study courses, correspondence courses, or a combination of these methods. In addition to courses directly related to IRS operations, the Service offers basic education courses to promote employee advancement; courses to help the general public comply with the law; and courses for local, state, and foreign governments to assist them in establishing effective tax administration systems. Many of the courses are designed, developed, and maintained centrally and are conducted at the national headquarters in Washington, D.C. and at seven regional training centers: Atlanta, Chicago, Cincinnati, Dallas, New York, Philadelphia, and San Francisco.

Courses of instruction relating to the IRS's Criminal Investigation function are developed and given on site at the Federal Law Enforcement Training Center, Glynco, Georgia. The two (2) primary courses offered are Tax for Criminal Investigation (TAX-CI) and Special Agent Investigative Techniques (SAIT).

Source of official student records: Chief, Criminal Investigation Training (IRS), FLETC, Building 69, 3rd Floor, Glynco, GA 31524.

Additional information about the courses: Program on Noncollegiate Sponsored Instruction, The Center for Adult Learning and Educational Credentials, American Council on Education, One Dupont Circle, Washington, D.C. 20036.

Federal Income Tax for Criminal Investigation (Tax for Criminal Investigation TAX-CI)

Location: Federal Law Enforcement Training Center, Glynco, GA.

Length: 212 hours (5½ weeks).

Dates: July 1981-Present.

Objective: To give students a thorough and in-depth coverage of federal income tax law, its application and investigation.

Instruction: This course is a Basic Federal Income Tax Law course dealing with individuals, corporations, partnerships, and tax shelters. Provides basic tax law for all Internal Revenue Service criminal investigators.

Credit recommendation: In the lower division baccalaureate/associate degree category, 9 semester hours in United States Income Tax Law (7/87).

Special Agent Investigative Techniques (SAIT)

Location: Federal Law Enforcement Training Center, Glynco, GA.

Length: 256 hours (7½ weeks).

Dates: April 1985-Present.

Objective: Courses teaching new Internal Revenue Service Criminal Investigators the techniques necessary for the development and successful prosecution of Federal criminal tax frauds.

Instruction: This course covers pertinent testimonial and documentary evidence, the recognized methods of proving income, the determination and prosecution of income tax evasion, the organization and presentation of tax fraud evidence, and familiarization with current agency computer systems.

Credit recommendation: In the lower division baccalaureate/associate degree category, 3 semester hours in Interviewing and Interrogation, 2 semester hours in Introduction to Computers, and 3 hours in Auditing (7/87).

United States Department of Justice, Immigration and Naturalization Service, Federal Law Enforcement Training Center

The Federal Law Enforcement Training Center's U.S. Immigration and Naturalization Service provides basic training for border patrol agents through the Border Patrol Academy and for immigration inspectors, immigration examiners, criminal investigators, and deportation officers through the Immigration Officer Academy. The Academic Specialities Staff serves as a resource to both academies in educational technology and methodology. The staff also maintains liaison with area colleges and universities and with the FLETC Office of Research and Evaluation and the Instructional Services Division. The Administrative Office sets up and operates all administrative systems and procedures to serve the instructional staff and students. Varied administrative and academic activities enable the Immigration and Naturalization Service to provide a quality learning experience for trainees.

Source of official student records: Chief, Academic Specialities Staff, U.S. Immigration and Naturalization Service, Federal Law Enforcement Training Center, Glynco, GA 31520.

Additional information about the courses: Program on Noncollegiate Sponsored Instruction, The Center for Adult Learning and Educational Credentials, American Council on Education, One Dupont Circle, Washington, D.C. 20036.

Border Patrol Academy
(Border Patrol Agent Basic Training)
  Part 1: Immigration and Nationality Law
  Part 2: Criminal Investigation
  Part 3: Human Relations
  Part 4: Physical Education
  Part 5: Spanish Language

Location: U.S. Immigration and Naturalization Service, Officer Development and Training Facility, Federal Law Enforcement Training Facility, Glynco, GA.

Length: *Version 1:* 648 hours (16 weeks); residential; consisting of the following: Part 1: 148 hours; Part 2: 71 hours; Part 3, 64 hours; Part 4: 150 hours; Part 5: 198

hours (140 hours of classroom instruction plus 58 hours of supervised language laboratory). *Version 2:* 700 hours (17 weeks); residential; consisting of the following: Part 1: 148 hours; Part 2, 73 hours; Part 3: 63 hours; Part 4: 200 hours; Part 5: 216 hours (150 hours of classroom instruction plus 66 hours of supervised language laboratory).

Dates: *Version 1:* January 1970-May 1985; *Version 2:* June 1985-Present.

Objective: To provide prospective border patrol agents the skills and knowledge necessary to serve effectively in the basic law enforcement role at the entry level with the United States Immigration and Naturalization Service.

Instruction: *Part 1:* Immigration and Nationality Law. Detailed exploration of nationality, immigration, and other areas of criminal law of major importance to border patrol agents and other federal law enforcement personnel; discussion of the constitutional aspects of arrest, search and seizure, interrogation, and confessions; and identification of civil liability issues. Lectures and discussions are used.

Part 2: Criminal Investigation. Investigative methods and techniques, interviewing and interrogation, collection, preservation, reporting and disclosure of information, and recognition and handling of specific offenses.

Part 3: Human Relations. Interpersonal communications. Teaching methods include role playing.

Part 4: Physical Education. Firearms, driving, physical conditioning, defensive tactics, trauma management, survival swimming and CPR.

Part 5: Spanish Language. Basic grammar structure, up to and including the subjunctive mood, and the formation of complex sentences. Emphasis on vocabulary building and on oral and aural skills. Class periods include formal grammar presentations, translation exercises, dictation exercises, oral drill, and reading exercises supplemented by daily, supervised language laboratory use.

Credit recommendation: *Version 1:* Part 1: In the lower division baccalaureate/associate degree category or in the upper division baccalaureate category, 3 semester hours in Immigration and Nationality Law. Part 2: In the lower division baccalaureate/associate degree category or in the upper division baccalaureate category, 3 semester hours in Immigration and Nationality Law. Part 3: In the lower division baccalaureate/associate degree category, 3 semester hours in Human Relations. Part 4: In the lower division baccalaureate/associate degree category, 4 semester hours in Physical Education (11/79). Part 5: In the lower division baccalaureate/associate degree category, 8 semester hours in Spanish Language (2/81). *Version 2:* Part 1: In the lower division baccalaureate/associate degree category or in the upper division baccalaureate category, 3 semester hours in Immigration and Nationality Law. Part 2: In the lower division baccalaureate/associate degree category or in the upper division baccalaureate category, 3 semester hours in Criminal Investigation. Part 3: In the lower division baccalaureate/associate degree category, 3 semester hours in Human Relations. Part 4: In the lower division baccalaureate/associate degree category, 7 semester hours in Physical Education. Part 5: In the lower division baccalaureate/associate degree category, 12 semester hours in Spanish Language (7/87).

Immigration Officer Academy
(Immigration Officer Basic Training Course-IOBTC)
Version 1:
   Part 1. Immigration and Nationality Law
   Part 2. Criminal Investigation
   Part 3. Human Relations
   Part 4. Physical Education
   Part 5. Spanish Language
Version 2:
   Part 1. Immigration and Nationality Law
   Part 2: Specialized Training
   Part 3. Physical Education
   Part 4. Spanish Language
   Part 5. Introduction to Federal Immigration and Naturalization

Location: U.S. Immigration and Naturalization Service, Officer Development and Training Facility, Federal Law Enforcement Training Center, Glynco. GA.

Length: *Version 1:* 560 hours (14 weeks); residential; including the following: Part 1: 132 hours; Part 2: 64 hours; Part 3: 33 hours; Part 4: 128 hours; Part 5: 177 hours (134 hours of language instruction plus 43 hours of supervised language laboratory). *Version 2:* 560 hours (14 weeks); residential; including the following: Part 1: 88 hours; Part 2: 64 hours; Part 3: 128 hours; Part 4: 177 hours (136 hours of language instruction plus 41 hours of supervised language laboratory); Part 5: 103 hours.

Dates: *Version 1:* January 1980-May 1985; *Version 2:* June 1985-Present.

Objective: To provide prospective immigration officers with the skills and knowledge necessary to specialize in one of four positions: special agent, deportation officer, immigration inspector, or immigration examiner.

Instruction: *Version 1:* Part 1: Immigration and Nationality Law. Detailed exploration of nationality, immigration, and other areas of criminal law of major importance to immigration officers; discussion of the constitutional aspects of arrest, search and seizure, interrogation, and confessions; identification of civil liability issues. Lectures and discussions are used. Part 2: Criminal Investigation. Investigative methods and techniques, interviewing, and interrogation, collection, preservation, reporting and disclosure of information, and recognition and handling of specific issues. Part 3: Human Relations. Interpersonal communications. Part 4: Physical Education. Firearms, driving, physical conditioning, and defensive tactics. Part 5: Spanish Language. Basic grammatical structure, up to and including the subjunctive mood, and the formation of complex sentences. Emphasis on vocabulary building and oral and aural skills. Class periods include formal grammar presentations and translation exercises supplemented by daily, supervised language laboratory use. *Version 2:* Part 1: Immigration and Nationality Law. Detailed exploration of nationality, immigration, and other areas of criminal law of major importance to immigration officers; discussion of the constitutional aspects of arrest, search and seizure, interrogation, and confessions; identification of civil liability issues. Lectures and discussions are used. Part 2: Specialized Training. Immigration officers receive an applied, awareness oriented, training course designed to develop the ability to apply theoretical and practical aspects of their specific job requirements. Part 3: Physical Education. Firearms, driving, physical conditioning, and defensive tactics. Part 4: Spanish Language. Basic grammatical structure, up to and including the subjunctive mood, and the formation of complex sentences. Emphasis on vocabulary building and oral and aural skills. Class periods include formal grammar presentations and translation exercises supplemented by daily, supervised language laboratory use. Part 5: Introduction to Federal Immigration and Naturalization. The core curriculum covers agency organization, authority, records, and internal policies governing immigration and naturalization.

Credit recommendation: *Version 1:* Part 1: In the lower division baccalaureate/associate degree category or in the upper division baccalaureate category, 3 semester hours in Immigration and Nationality Law. Part 2: In the lower division baccalaureate/associate degree category or in the upper division baccalaureate category, 3 semester hours in Criminal Investigation. Part 3: In the lower division baccalaureate/associate degree category, 2 semester hours in Human Relations. Part 4: In the lower division baccalaureate/associate degree category, 4 semester hours in Physical Education (11/79). Part 5: In the lower division baccalaureate/associate degree category, 8 semester hours in Spanish Language. *Version 2:* Part 1: In the lower division baccalaureate/associate degree category or in the upper division baccalaureate category, 3 semester hours in Immigration and Nationality Law. Part 2: In the lower division baccalaureate/associate degree category or in the upper division baccalaureate category, 3 semester hours in Federal Law Enforcement. Part 3: In the lower division baccalaureate/associate degree category, 5 semester hours in Physical Education. Part 4: In the lower division baccalaureate/associate degree category, 8 semester hours in Spanish Language. Part 5: In the lower division baccalaureate/associate degree category, 3 semester hours in Federal Law Enforcement (2/81) (7/87). NOTE: This course has been reevaluated and continues to meet requirements for credit recommendations.

United States Department of Justice, U.S. Marshals Service, Federal Law Enforcement Training Center

The Basic Deputy U.S. Marshal Training Course provides and in-depth study of law enforcement and administrative concepts that Deputy U.S. Marshals must possess upon entry into the U.S. Marshals Service. The Basic Deputy Course consists of approximately five (5) weeks of training which is devoted to classroom instruction, practical exercises, and administrative support time. This course continues with additional training in subject areas such as warrant investigations and firearms. Instruction is also offered in operational and administrative areas, most of which are unique to the U.S. Marshals Service, and include witness security, court security, dignitary protection, process, vouchers, and personnel programs. All students are required to complete the Basic Deputy U.S. Marshals Training Course at the Federal Law Enforcement Training Center, Glynco, Georgia.

Source of official student records: Registrar/Training Coordinator, U.S. Marshals Service, Federal Law Enforcement Training Center, Building 20, Glynco, Georgia 31524.

Additional information about the courses: Program on Noncollegiate Sponsored Instruction, The Center for Adult Learning and Educational Credentials, American Council on Education, One Dupont Circle, Washington, D.C. 20036.

Deputy U.S. Marshals Basic Training School
Location: Federal Law Enforcement Training Center, Glynco, GA.
Length: 205 hours (5 weeks).
Dates: January 1980-Present.
Objective: To give students an in-depth treatment of skills and knowledge necessary for proficiency in the job of Deputy U.S. Marshal.
Instruction: This basic course covers the specialized areas of unique concern to Deputy U.S. Marshals. Prerequisite to this course is Basic Criminal Investigation.
Credit recommendation: In the lower division baccalaureate/associate degree category, 2 semester hours in Physical Education, 1 semester hour in Criminal Intelligence, 2 semester hours in Court Security Procedures or Personal Security, but not both (7/87).

United States Department of Labor, DOL Academy

The Department of Labor (DOL) Academy was established to provide leadership and direction in the development and execution of the Department's education and career development program. The Academy's objectives are to ensure that such programs are comprehensive and responsive to the needs of the employees and management of the Department. Within the Academy, courses of study, called institutes, are designed for the training needs and requirements of particular fields. This institute concept ties training and development directly with occupational career paths. The four Institutes include: Office Skills Institute—training for clerical, secretarial and support staff; Supervisory Institute—supervisory skills training, labor-management and employee relations, and Equal Employment Opportunity; Managerial Institute—a new program which bridges the gap between supervisory and executive training; and the Executive Institute—provides executives with an opportunity to gain a broader perspective on their roles, their agencies' missions and programs and the economic, social and political environment in which they operate.

The instructors for the Professional, Supervisory and Managerial Institutes are selected by the contractor, and are senior consultants with appropriate experience and degrees. They are rated in writing by each course participant and monitored by the Project Director periodically. The instructors for the Office Skills Institute are consultants recruited through advertisements and referrals, and also have the appropriate teaching credentials. These instructors are observed during their initial offering of the course, and student evaluations.

Students are required to complete a DL1-101, Training Authorization and Evaluation form for each course taken. Once the course is completed, information from the DL1-101 is entered into the Training Information System (TIS), and also filed in the participants' official personnel folder. Upon successful completion of a long-term course, a certificate of completion is granted based upon participant behavior and class participation.

Source of official student records: Registry of Credit Recommendations, The Center for Adult Learning and Educational Credentials, American Council on Education, One Dupont Circle, Washington, D.C., 20036.

Additional information about the courses:

Additional information about the courses: Program on Noncollegiate Sponsored Instruction, The Center for Adult Learning and Educational Credentials, American Council on Education, One Dupont Circle, Washington, D.C., 20036.

Communications in Management
(Communicating for Results)

Location: Washington, DC; Chicago, IL.
Length: 16 hours (2 days).
Dates: March 1988-Present.
Objective: To provide the student with a variety of communication skills that will improve working relationships with peers, subordinates, and superiors.
Learning Outcome: Upon successful completion of this course, the student will understand the complexities of the interpersonal communication process; develop strategies for minimizing typical communication problems; and develop a plan for improving their own communication skills.
Instruction: Course covers communication styles and skills. Methodology includes individual assessments, small-group work, lectures, role-plays, discussions, and practical exercises.
Credit recommendation: In the lower division baccalaureate/associate degree category, 1 semester hour in Business Management (8/88). NOTE: If both this course and Skills Training are successfully completed, then a total of 4 semester hours can be awarded.

Conflict Resolution in the Workplace
(Conflict Resolution for Support Personnel)

Location: Washington, DC and regional cities.
Length: 15 hours (2 days).
Dates: March 1989-Present.
Objective: To provide participants with techniques for minimizing and resolving conflicts.
Learning Outcome: Upon successful completion of this course, the student will be able to identify conflict situations and solutions; recognize what kinds of behavior inhibit or enhance conflict resolution; and develop strategies for resolving conflicts.
Instruction: Course covers kinds of conflict, organizational conflict, and means for resolving conflict.
Credit recommendation: In the lower division baccalaureate/associate degree category, 1 semester hour in Business Management (8/88).

Detecting and Managing Stress in the Office Environment
(Stress Management for Managers)

Location: Washington, DC; Dallas, TX; and Philadelphia, PA.
Length: 16 hours (2 days).
Dates: March 1988-Present.
Objective: To enable students to learn what causes stress in their daily lives and how to apply strategies for reducing such stress.
Learning Outcome: Upon successful completion of this course, the student will be able to explain what stress is; understand how stress develops; analyze individual responses to stress; and develop a personal plan for improving stress management.
Instruction: Course deals with stress management on a personal practical level. Methodology includes films, lectures, small-group work, and discussions.
Credit recommendation: In the lower division baccalaureate/associate degree category, 1 semester hour in Business Management (8/88). NOTE: If both this course and Skills Training are successfully completed, then a total of 4 semester hours can be awarded.

Effective Listening and Memory Development
Location: Washington, DC and regional cities.
Length: 15 hours (2 days).
Dates: May 1988-Present.
Objective: To teach participants to listen, comprehend, and recall information more effectively and efficiently.
Learning Outcome: Upon successful completion of this course, the student will be able to identify the barriers to effective listening and to suggest ways to overcome them; evaluate their own listening habits; develop more effective listening techniques; use various techniques that aid memory development; and develop a strategy for developing their own memories.
Instruction: Course covers listening as communication, remembering, and memory development.
Credit recommendation: In the lower division baccalaureate/associate degree category, 1 semester hour in Communication Skills (8/88).

Effective Writing for Federal Managers and Report Writing
1. Effective Writing Techniques
2. Report Writing

Location: DOL training sites.
Length: 1. 18 hours (4 days); 2. 16 hours (2 days).
Dates: September 1983-Present.
Objective: To recognize examples of good writing by analyzing and critiquing general communications and reports.
Learning Outcome: Upon successful completion of this course, the student will be able to write comprehensive memos; write intelligible reports; and understand the relevance of style and tone in written communications.
Instruction: Course covers principles of good writing, grammar, spelling, outlining, and paragraph organization and construction. Methodology includes lecture and discussion.
Credit recommendation: In the lower division baccalaureate/associate degree category, 2 semester hours in English (8/88). NOTE: To receive credit, students must take both courses with Effective Writing Techniques as a prerequisite to Report Writing.

Equal Employment Opportunity Programs
(EEO Workshop for Supervisors)
Location: Washington, DC and regional cities.
Length: 16 hours (2 days).
Dates: January 1980-Present.
Objective: To acquaint students with the impact of EEO and Civil Rights Laws on management policies and procedures.
Learning Outcome: Upon successful completion of this course, the student will be able to understand EEO guidelines and procedures for compliance.
Instruction: Course covers federal Civil Rights laws, decisions of the Supreme Court, and administrative procedures. Methodology includes lecture and discussion.
Credit recommendation: In the upper division baccalaureate category, 1 semester hour in Business Management (8/88).

Human Side of Management
Location: Washington, DC; Boston, MA; New York, NY; Philadelphia, PA; Atlanta, GA; Kansas City, KS; Dallas, TX; Chicago, IL; Denver, CO; San Francisco, CA; and Seattle, WA.
Length: 40 hours (5 days).
Dates: January 1980-Present.
Objective: To provide the student with an understanding of the theory and practice of organizational behavior.
Learning Outcome: Upon successful completion of this course, the student will be able to assess employee and self motivation; understand the behavior of groups and organizations; assess communication problems; and identify models of leadership.
Instruction: Course covers employee motivation, intra-organization communications, styles of leadership, and conflict and intra-group behavior. Methodology includes lecture and discussion.
Credit recommendation: In the upper division baccalaureate category, 3 semester hours in Business Management (8/88).

Keyboarding Techniques
1. Beginning Typing
2. Speedbuilding
3. Proofreading
4. Keyboarding

Location: Washington, DC and regional cities.
Length: 1. 48 hours (12 weeks); 2. 48 hours (12 weeks); 3. 24 hours (6 weeks); 4. 24 hours (6 weeks).
Dates: April 1987-Present.
Objective: To provide the student with the familiarity of all aspects of keyboarding.
Learning Outcome: Upon successful completion of this course, the student will be able to type proficiently on the alphabetic keyboard; format correspondence, reports, and tables; and proofread accurately and efficiently.
Instruction: Course covers general keyboarding, proofreading, and formatting. Methodology includes lecturettes and classroom exercises.
Credit recommendation: In the lower division baccalaureate/associate degree category, 1 semester hour in Business Education (8/88).

Negotiation Skills
(Art of Positive Negotiation)
Location: Washington, DC; Kansas City, KS; Boston, MA; San Francisco, CA; and Wilkes-Barre, PA.
Length: 24 hours (3 days).
Dates: March 1988-Present.
Objective: To provide the student with an understand-

ing of their own style of conflict management and to learn techniques for effectively handling conflicts in the workplace.

Learning Outcome: Upon successful completion of this course, the student will be able to list communication styles used in negotiation; explain common negotiating strategies, and conduct a negotiation session.

Instruction: Course covers negotiation styles and skills. Methodology includes lecture, surveys, and group discussions.

Credit recommendation: In the lower division baccalaureate/associate degree category, 1 semester hour in Business Management (8/88). NOTE: If both this course and Skills Training are successfully completed, then a total of 4 semester hours can be awarded.

Office Practices and Communications
  1. Office Practices and Procedures
  2. Telephone Techniques and Public Contact

Location: Washington, DC and regional cities.
Length: 1. 12 hours (2 days); 2. 12 hours (2 days).
Dates: June 1988-Present.
Objective: To introduce the student to effective practices in the workplace as well as the importance of clear communications.

Learning Outcome: Upon successful completion of this course, the student will be able to practice good oral and written communication; create, store, protect, control, use and file records correctly; demonstrate telephone courtesy and effective telephone techniques; proofread accurately and efficiently; and identify and use the common proofreading symbols.

Instruction: Course covers effective communication, organization skills, telephone techniques, and reading proofreaders marks. Methodology includes lecturettes and classroom exercises.

Credit recommendation: In the lower division baccalaureate/associate degree category, 1 semester hour in Business Education (8/88).

Performance Appraisal
(Performance Appraisal Workshop)

Location: Washington, DC and regional cities.
Length: 24 hours (3 days).
Dates: January 1984-Present.
Objective: To provide the student with the development of standards for conducting formal and informal performance appraisals.

Learning Outcome: Upon successful completion of this course, the student will be able to identify specific job tasks and job elements; identify appropriate indicators of levels of performance; identify adequate performance standards, and identify the need for coaching and counseling.

Instruction: Course covers the performance appraisal process; development of standards; tracking performance; techniques for coaching; land formal appraisals. Methodology includes lecture and discussion.

Credit recommendation: In the upper division baccalaureate category, 1 semester hour in Business Management (8/88).

Professional Development and Orientation
  1. Maximizing Your Potential as a DOL Professional
  2. All You Wanted to Know About Becoming a Supervisor
  3. Time Management for Professionals
  4. Professional Briefing Techniques

Location: Washington, DC and regional cities.
Length: 1. 16 hours (2 days); 2. 16 hours (2 days); 3. 16 hours (2 days); 4. 14 hours (2 days).
Dates: March 1988-Present.
Objective: To provide the student with skills and attitudes necessary to become a successful professional and understanding the system of organization in a business, agency or organization.

Learning Outcome: Upon successful completion of this course, the student will be able to set goals and prioritize tasks; manage time successfully; motivate self and others; and give effective presentations.

Instruction: Course covers decision making, self-assessment process, career ladders and development plans, and group presentations. Methodology includes lecture and discussion.

Credit recommendation: In the lower division baccalaureate/associate degree category, 2 semester hours in Professional Orientation (8/88).

Skills Training
(Skills Training for DOL Supervisors)

Location: Washington, DC and regional cities.
Length: 52 hours (7 days).
Dates: March 1988-Present.
Objective: To provide the student with the ability to understand their new role as first-line supervisors.

Learning Outcome: Upon successful completion of this course, the student will be able to improve employee performance through effective feedback; use coaching techniques to teach an employee new tasks; match the appropriate employee to a task; communicate assignments effectively; and determine when to delegate work.

Instruction: Course covers several basic techniques essential to managing the work of others and includes films, skill practice sessions, small-group work, simulation games, brief lectures, discussions, and written application plans.

Credit recommendation: In the lower division baccalaureate/associate degree category, 3 semester hours in Business Management (8/88). NOTE: If this course is successfully completed in conjunction with either Communications in Management, Detecting and Managing Stress in the Office Environment, or Negotiation Skills, then a total of 4 semester hours can be awarded.

United States Department of the Treasury, Federal Law Enforcement Training Center

The Federal Law Enforcement Training Center, established in 1970 in the Department of the Treasury, is a consolidated interagency training facility. The Center provides basic and advanced training for law enforcement personnel of more than 60 participating federal agencies. The Center conducts research in law enforcement training, methods, and curriculum content; and develops such methods and content for use in its training programs. The Center assists participating agencies in determining their needs for law enforcement training and in developing curriculum, course content, and teaching methods and techniques for the specialized courses which the agencies conduct at the Center. The Center also provides facilities, equipment, and support services necessary for the Center's numerous law enforcement training programs.

Source of official student records: Registrar's Office, Training Coordination, Federal Law Enforcement Training Center, Glynco, Georgia 31520.

Additional information about the courses: Program on Noncollegiate Sponsored Instruction, The Center for Adult Learning and Educational Credentials, American Council on Education, One Dupont Circle, Washington, D.C. 20036.

Criminal Investigator Training
Version 1:
Part 1: Criminal Law, Procedure and Evidence
Part 2: Criminal Investigation
Part 3: Physical Education
Version 2:
Part 1: Criminal Investigation
Part 2: Physical Skills Development
Location: Federal Law Enforcement Training Center, Glynco, GA.
Length: *Version 1:* 256½ hours (8 weeks); residential; Part 1: 83½ hours; Part 2: 99 hours; Part 3: 74 hours. *Version 2:* 304 hours (8 weeks); residential; Part 1: 218 hours; Part 2: 86 hours.
Dates: *Version 1:* July 1970-May 1985; *Version 2:* June 1985-Present.
Objective: To provide federal criminal investigators with the skills and knowledge to perform the investigative role effectively.
Instruction: *Version 1:* Part 1: Assault, conspiracy, and parties to criminal offenses; organized and white-collar crime; civil rights; evidence (including self-incrimination); constitutional law; entrapment; federal court procedures; arrest; search and seizure; pretrial conference and witness briefs; tactics of defendants; mock trial. Part 2: Crime scene investigation, fingerprints, photographs, questioned documents, car stop/search, informants, surveillance, undercover operations. Part 3: Firearms; defensive driving; cardiopulmonary resuscitation; defensive tactics. Lecture, discussion, workshops, and practical exercises are used. *Version 2:* Part 1: Behavioral science topics such as ethics and conduct, stress management, interviewing, investigator operations and techniques includes execution of search warrants, use of informants, surveillance, undercover operations, crime scene investigation, photography, introduction to computers, and link analysis; legal topics such as constitutional law, detention and arrest, evidence, court procedures, search and seizure, and federal statutes. Part 2: Defensive driving, firearms usage, marksmanship, CPR, defensive tactics, and arrest techniques.

Credit recommendation: *Version 1:* Part 1: In the lower division baccalaureate/associate degree category or in the upper division baccalaureate category, 3 semester hours in Criminal Law, Procedure and Evidence. Part 2: In the lower division baccalaureate/associate degree category or in the upper division baccalaureate category, 3 semester hours in Criminal Investigation. NOTE: This section duplicates the material covered in Criminal Investigation, Part 2 of Eight-Week Police Training Program; credit should not be granted for both courses. Part 3: In the lower division baccalaureate/associate degree category, 2 semester hours in Physical Education (11/78). NOTE: This section duplicates the material covered in Physical Education, Part 3 of the Eight-Week Police Training Program; credit should not be granted for both courses. *Version 2:* Part 1: In the lower division baccalaureate/associate degree category or in the upper division baccalaureate category, 7 semester hours in Criminal Justice. Part 2: In the lower division baccalaureate/associate degree category, 2 semester hours in Physical Education (7/87). NOTE: This section duplicates the material covered in Physical Skills Development, Part 2 of the Eight-Week Police Training Program; credit should not be granted for both courses. NOTE: This course has been reevaluated and continues to meet requirements for credit recommendations.

Eight-Week Police Training Program
Version 1:
Part 1: Basic Law Enforcement Procedures
Part 2: Criminal Investigation
Part 3: Physical Education
Version 2:
Part 1: Basic Law Enforcement
Part 2: Physical Skills Development
Location: Federal Law Enforcement Training Center, Glynco, GA.
Length: *Version 1:* 270 hours (8 weeks); residential; Part 1: 79 hours; Part 2: 99 hours; Part 3: 92 hours. *Version 2:* 301 hours (8 weeks); residential; Part 1: 183 hours; Part

2: 118 hours.

Dates: *Version 1:* July 1972-May 1985; *Version 2:* June 1985-Present.

Objective: To provide federal uniformed law enforcement officers with the skills and knowledge to serve effectively in the basic law enforcement role at the entry level.

Instruction: *Version 1:* Part 1: Contemporary police problems; recognition, detention, and arrest of subjects; report writing; radio communications; human relations; juvenile delinquency. Part 2: Crime scene processing, recognition and handling of specific offenses, criminalistics, application of criminal law, operation skills. Part 3: Firearms, defensive driving, cardiopulmonary resuscitation, defensive tactics, physical conditioning. Lecture, discussion, workshops, and practical exercises are used. *Version 2:* Part 1: Behavioral science topics such as communications, conflict management, interviewing techniques, and stress management; enforcement operations and techniques includes patrol procedures, report writing, VIP protection, officer safety and survival, narcotics, and criminalistics; and legal topics such as constitutional law, detention and arrest, evidence, search and seizure, and court procedures. Part 2: Defensive driving, vehicle operations, firearms usage, marksmanship, CPR, defensive tactics, and physical education.

Credit recommendation: *Version 1:* Part 1: In the lower division baccalaureate/associate degree category, 3 semester hours in Criminal Justice. Part 2: In the lower division baccalaureate/associate degree category or in the upper division baccalaureate category, 3 semester hours in Criminal Justice. NOTE 1: This section duplicates the material covered in Criminal Investigation, Part 2 of Criminal Investigator Training; credit should not be granted for both courses. Part 3: In the lower division baccalaureate/associate degree category, 3 semester hours in Physical Education (11/78). NOTE 2: This section duplicates the material covered in Physical Education, Part 3 of Criminal Investigator Training; credit should not be given for both courses. *Version 2:* Part 1: In the lower division baccalaureate/associate degree category or in the upper division baccalaureate category, 6 semester hours in Criminal Justice. Part 2: In the lower division baccalaureate/associate degree category, 3 semester hours in Physical Education (7/87). NOTE 3: This section duplicates the material covered in Physical Education, Part 2 of Criminal Investigator Training; credit should not be given for both courses. NOTE 4: This course has been reevaluated and continues to meet requirements for credit recommendations.

United States Drug Enforcement Administration

The United States Drug Enforcement Administration (DEA) of the Department of Justice has overall responsibility for enforcing the provisions of the federal drug statues. Through enforcement strategy, the gathering of drug intelligence, the use of science and technology research, close narcotics enforcement coordination with foreign countries, and the sponsorship of specialized drug training schools, the Drug Enforcement Administration exerts a unified effort designed to curb the worldwide illicit distribution of narcotics and dangerous drugs.

The National Training Institute (NTI) is the educational arm of the Drug Enforcement Administration. NTI conducts programs for special agent personnel and compliance investigators; directs an on-going executive, mid-management, and supervisory program for personnel assigned to higher-level positions; and conducts in-service programs for DEA personnel in such areas as conspiracy investigations and specialized enforcement techniques.

Source of official student records: Drug Enforcement Administration, National Training Institute, Police Programs Section, 1405 Eye Street, N.W., Washington, D.C. 20537.

Additional information about the courses: Program on Noncollegiate Sponsored Instruction, The Center for Adult Learning and Educational Credentials, American Council on Education, One Dupont Circle, Washington, D.C. 20036.

Criminal Investigation - Drug Abuse
(Two-Week Drug Law Enforcement Training School)
  Location: National Training Institute, Washington, D.C. and field locations.
  Length: 77 hours (2 weeks); residential.
  Dates: April 1968-Present.
  Objective: To introduce state and local enforcement officers to principles of criminal investigation as it relates to drug enforcement.
  Instruction: Covers four major drug-abuse areas: (1) enforcement principles and techniques, including clandestine laboratories, informants, surveillance, undercover techniques, smuggling, technical equipment, raid planning, and intelligence; (2) drug traffic patterns and drug abuse education; (3) pharmacology, stressing drug identification and field testing; (4) legal procedures, stressing evidence, search and seizure, and trial techniques. Methodology includes lecture, discussion, laboratory, demonstrations, and practical exercises.
  Credit recommendation: In the lower division baccalaureate/associate degree category, 4 semester hours in Criminal Justice or Law Enforcement (1/76).

Drug Enforcement Officers Academy
  Part 1: Criminal Investigation
  Part 2: Internship and Field Service Training
  Part 3: Drug Abuse
  Part 4: Criminal Procedures
  Part 5: Communications
  Part 6: Physical Education
  Part 7: Police Administration

Location: National Training Institute, Washington, D.C.

Length: 407 hours (10 weeks); residential; *Part 1:* 131 hours; *Part 2:* 130 hours; *Part 3:* 39 hours; *Part 4:* 37 hours; *Part 5:* 20 hours; *Part 6:* 22 hours; *Part 7:* 28 hours.

Dates: *Version 1:* October 1970-December 1985; *Version 2:* February 1988-Present.

Objective: To provide state and local enforcement officers with in-depth knowledge of the most current techniques in narcotics and dangerous drugs enforcement, and with the expertise needed to provide leadership in combating drug abuse.

Instruction: *Part 1:* Clandestine laboratories; informants; surveillance; undercover, drug-smuggling, and consipiracy investigations; technical investigative aids; photography; interview and interrogation; initiation and development of a case; raid planning and execution; concealment; field testing; determining drug-related deaths; role of intelligence information; value of news media in investigation. Lectures, discussions, classroom demonstrations, and practical and field training exercises are used. *Part 2:* Simulated transactions and practical exercises in fact finding and intelligence gathering are used to apply principles and techniques learned in the classroom. Involves planning, use of equipment, conducting raids, arrest procedures, and surveillance. Field training is reviewed through preparation of critiques and detailed reports and use of videotaped exercises. Students are supervised by staff instructors. *Part 3:* Drug identification, characteristics of various types of drugs, effects of drugs, methadone programs, national and international drug traffic patterns, social and psychological aspects of drug abuse, drug research programs. Lecture, discussion, demonstration, and field testing exercises are used. *Part 4:* The constitutional restrictions, limitations, and safeguards relative to the conduct of searches and seizures under the Fourth Amendment; forfeitures; rules of evidence; Uniform Controlled Substances Act; rules of Federal Criminal Procedure; trial techniques; mock hearings; legal aspects of electronic surveillance; identification and interrogation; conspiracy; possession with intent to distribute to others. Lectures and discussions are used. *Part 5:* Explores several theories of communications and develops requirements for effective communication; applies these principles to the presentation of formal instruction. Oral presentation of a lesson is a course requirement. Lecture, discussion, demonstration, and class participation are used. *Part 6:* Develops the physical stamina of the student through calisthenics and endurance tests. Lectures, demonstration, and class participation are used. *Part 7:* Identifies and discusses the managerial procedures needed to operate a narcotics unit within an agency's organizational structure. Covers the managerial functions of planning, supervising, and directing. Lectures and discussion are used.

Credit recommendation: *Part 1:* In the lower division baccalaureate/associate degree category, 4 semester hours in Criminal Justice or Law Enforcement (1/76). NOTE: This section duplicates the material covered in the *Two-Week Law Enforcement* course (see above). *Part 2:* In the lower division baccalaureate/associate degree category or in the upper division baccalaureate category, 3 semester hours in Criminal Justice or Law Enforcement (1/76). *Part 3:* In the lower division baccalaureate/associate degree category or in the upper division baccalaureate category, 2 semester hours in Criminal Justice or Law Enforcement (1/76). *Part 4:* In the lower division baccalaureate/associate degree category or in the upper division baccalaureate category, 3 semester hours in Criminal Justice or Law Enforcement (1/76). *Part 5:* In the lower division baccalaureate/associate degree category, 1 semester hour in Communications (1/76). *Part 6:* In the lower division baccalaureate/associate degree category, 2 semester hours in Physical Education (1/76). *Part 7:* In the lower division baccalaureate/associate degree category, 2 semester hours in Criminal Justice or Law Enforcement (1/76).

United States Food and Drug Administration

The Education and Training Staff provides technical training to the 2,800 employees of the Food and Drug Administration's Office of Regulatory Affairs. In addition, the training office coordinates and/or provides managerial and career development training for the organization.

The primary instructor is selected through the FDA contractual process. Specific criteria established by a course project staff must be met. The two FDA resource instructors are selected based on experience and knowledge of history and precedent cases. Instructors are reviewed by student course evaluations which are completed daily and at the end of the course. The course project officer observes the instructors for teaching techniques and subject matter content. End-of-course exam results also provide an indication of the primary instructor's performance.

Students who successfully complete the course are issued a letter certifying completion. The performance of students who do not pass the examination is discussed with the supervisor. Under certain circumstances, students may retake the exam after additional training. Student records are maintained in individual course files which contain a listing of students who have successfully passed the course. In addition, the Department of Health and Human Services maintains a record of completion of the training for each individual.

Source of official student records: Director, Education and Training Staff (HFC-22), Office of Regulatory Affairs, Food and Drug Administration, 5600 Fishers Lane, Rockville, Maryland 20857.

Additional information about the courses: Program on Noncollegiate Sponsored Instruction, The Center for Adult Learning and Educational Credentials, American Council on Education, One Dupont Circle, Washington, D.C. 20036.

Basic Food and Drug Law Course
  Location: Various cities throughout the United States.
  Length: 40 hours (1 week).
  Dates: January 1983-Present.
  Objective: To provide the student with an understanding of the law as it pertains to food, drugs and cosmetics, and to provide an understanding and appreciation of the litigation and policy development process.
  Learning Outcome: Upon successful completion of this course, the student will be able to explain the statutory structure, sanctions, and basis for administering the Food, Drug, and Cosmetic Act, amended, and related regulations; determine what is a food, drug and device under the statute, and distinguish the difference between a food additive, and added substance; define what a lawsuit is; know a suit is instituted and conducted in Federal District Courts, and how its various features affect FDA activities; identify the various acts prohibited by the Food, Drug, and Cosmetic Act; how precedent case decisions impact on agency actions; and to recognize and appreciate the role of voluntary compliance.
  Instruction: Course covers the litigation process, explains and defines the Food, Drug, and Cosmetic Act (Title 21), and the role of the investigation in administration of the Act. Methodology includes lecture, discussion, workshops, case studies, and examination.
  Credit recommendation: In the upper division baccalaureate category, 3 semester hours in Administrative Law, Basic Introduction to Law, Criminal Justice (Title 21), or Paralegal Studies (10/88).

United States Navy Acquisition Management Training Office

The Navy Acquisition Management Training Office (NAMTO) was established to provide world-wide acquisition training to the Navy's contracting and procurement personnel. The mission of the entity is to eliminate the inadequacies in quality, substance and availability of acquisition training. Top accomplish this objective, the program provides current, state-of-the-art instruction as prescribed in the certified acquisition and procurement courses of the Defense Management Education Training (DMET) manual and the DOD Civilian Career Program for Contracting and Acquisition Personnel (DOD Directive 1430.10-M-1.). The program also provides management advisory services and technical assistance for Navy operating officials in promoting current, cost-effective and economical contracting practices.

NAMTO was established in October 1985 under the provision of the Navy's Buy Our Spares Smart (BOSS) program and Weinburger's 10-point initiatives. The program's concept was reemphasized under the President's Blue Ribbon commission (Packard Commission) on Defense Management. NAMTO, located at NSC Norfolk, is supported by COMNAVSUPSYSCOM'S Contract Management Division with authority delegated by the Assistant Secretary of the Navy for Shipbuilding and Logistics ASN(S&L).

Source of official student records: U.S. Navy Acquisition Management Training Office, Naval Supply Center, Norfolk, VA 23512-5000.

Additional information about the courses: Program on Noncollegiate Sponsored Instruction, The Center for Adult Learning and Educational Credentials, American Council on Education, One Dupont Circle, Washington, D.C. 20036.

Advanced Contract Administration
  Location: Various locations around the country.
  Length: 67 hours (2 weeks).
  Dates: January 1986-Present.
  Objective: Development of a comprehensive management philosophy about contract management which emphasizes responsibility and accountability for government contracts.
  Learning Outcome: Upon successful completion of this course, the student will be able to identify techniques of quality assurance which can be applied to contract administration; articulate the essential nature of contract administration services with outside agencies; describe the functional components of contract administration and acquisitions; and understand the importance of overhead cost and be able to compute fair value ratios.
  Instruction: Course covers pricing and overhead, contract administration, contract financing, cost accounting standards, production management and quality assurance, claims/disputes/terminations, and subcontracting management. Methods of instruction include lecture, discussion, audiovisual aids, practice exercises, and examinations.
  Credit recommendation: In the upper division baccalaureate or graduate degree category, 3 semester hours in Business Administration, Logistics and Material Management or Procurement and Contracting (3/88).

Automation of Procurement and Accounting Data Entry (APADE)
   Part 1: Input Clerk's Course
   Part 2: Buyer's Course
   Location: Various locations around the country.
   Length: *Part 1:* 18 hours (3 days); *Part 2:* 42 hours (7 days); Part 1 is a prerequisite to Part 2.
   Dates: April 1986-Present.
   Objective: *Part 1:* Skill in use of APADE system for requisition input and inquiry; *Part 2:* Skill in use of APADE system for the entire procurement process.
   Learning Outcome: *Part 1:* Upon successful completion of this course, the student will be able to use procurement computing systems to enter requisitions, and perform an inquiry using a procurement computer system. *Part 2:* Upon successful completion of this course, the student will be able to update requisitions, process a pre-award, process a contract award, and process an award subclining, exchange data through an on-line automated data based system.
   Instruction: *Part 1:* Course covers introduction to personal computers, and requisition input and inquiry. *Part 2:* Course covers requisition update, pre-award, awards, subclining, and data exchange. Method of instruction includes lecture, discussion, practice exercises, and examinations.
   Credit recommendation: *Part 1:* In the lower division baccalaureate/associate degree category, 1 semester hour in Computer Science, Data Processing, or Procurement and Contracting. *Part 2:* In the lower division baccalaureate/associate degree category, 2 semester hours in Computer Science, Data Processing, or Procurement and Contracting (3/88).

Basic Contract Administration
   Location: Various locations around the country.
   Length: 90 hours (3 weeks).
   Dates: October 1987-Present.
   Objective: To provide the student with an understanding of the basic principles of government contracting administration, and development of a philosophy of administration of contracts.
   Learning Outcome: Upon successful completion of this course, the student will have knowledge of advantages and disadvantages of various contracts, areas of application, and limitations under various conditions; understand the lines of authority and responsibility associated with contracts under applicable federal acquisition regulations; understand quality assurance, including inspection and application warranties; and understand the role of finance, subcontracting, negotiation, and remedies associated with contract administration.
   Instruction: Course covers the acquisition process, funding, ethics in contract evaluation, types of contracts, profit, property, quality assurance, contract modification, negotiation, remedies, financing, and the role of subcontractors. Methods of instruction include lecture, discussion, case studies, and examinations.
   Credit recommendation: In the upper division baccalaureate or graduate degree category, 3 semester hours in Business Administration, Logistics and Materials Management, or Procurement and Contracting (3/88).

Becoming a More Effective Instructor (MGM-005-86)
   Location: Norfolk, San Diego, Pearl Harbor, and Charleston.
   Length: 24 hours (3 days).
   Dates: September 1986-Present.
   Objective: To provide the student with the ability to design and deliver courses for adult learners.
   Learning Outcome: Upon the successful completion of this course, the student will have an understanding of the characteristics of adult learners; skill in defining appropriate course objectives; and skill in presenting course content and in managing the learning environment.
   Instruction: Methods include lecture-discussion, out-of-class readings, role-playing, and videotaped demonstrations. Content includes designing course objectives, characteristics of adult learners and of adult learning styles, qualities of effective instructors, instructional strategies, managing the learning environment, and non-verbal communication in the classroom.
   Credit recommendation: In the upper division baccalaureate category, 1 semester hour in Methods of Adult Education (11/86).

Defense Contract Negotiation Workshop (NG-004-86)
   Location: Norfolk, San Diego, Mechanicsburg, Charleston, Jacksonville, China Lake, and Indianapolis.
   Length: 40 hours (1 week).
   Dates: January 1986-Present.
   Objective: To provide the student with knowledge of negotiation issues, strategies, and tactics. Application of this knowledge in negotiation sessions.
   Learning Outcome: Upon the successful completion of this course, the student will be able to identify the elements of effective negotiations, recognize and use negotiation strategies and tactics and prepare for negotiation sessions.
   Instruction: Methods include lecture-discussion, out-of-class readings, case studies, and group exercises. Content includes techniques for negotiating prime contracts, contract modifications, and contract terminations.
   Credit recommendation: In the vocational certificate or lower division baccalaureate/associate degree category, 1 semester hour in Acquisitions Contracting, Business Management, or Personnel Administration (11/86).

Defense Cost and Price Analysis (CP-003086)
   Location: Norfolk, San Diego, Mechanicsburg, Charleston, Jacksonville, China Lake, and Indianapolis.
   Length: 80 hours (2 weeks).

Dates: January 1986-Present.

Objective: To give the student basic understanding of cost and price relationships and of relevant policies, tools, and techniques. Application of this knowledge to contract pricing.

Learning Outcome: Upon the successful completion of this course, the student will have knowledge of cost and price theory and an ability to appropriately apply this knowledge in cost/price analysis of contractor proposals.

Instruction: Methods include lecture-discussion, out-of-class readings, and problem-solving exercises. Topics covered include pricing, cost estimates and analysis, cost projection, effects of learning rates on costs, and the role of buyers in evaluating bid proposals including profit analysis, depreciation, and legal implications.

Credit recommendation: In the lower division baccalaureate/associate degree or upper division baccalaureate category, 3 semester hours in Acquisitions Contracting or Business Management (11/86).

Government Contracting Law

Location: Various locations around the country.
Length: 64 hours (3 weeks).
Dates: October 1987-Present.

Objective: To provide the student with the knowledge and understanding of the legal aspects of contracting.

Learning Outcome: Upon successful completion of this course, the student will be able to identify legislation that is relevant to contracting law; understand basic legal principles and sources of contracting law; interpret contract language, including modifications, terminations, remedies and awards; and recognize the major elements of contracting, procurement, bid procedures, subcontracting, and funding.

Instruction: Course covers contract formation and modification, essential elements of a contract, specifications and inspection/acceptances, equitable adjustments, labor law, and termination for default and convenience. Methods of instruction include lecture, discussion, case studies, video and computer assisted instruction, and examinations.

Credit recommendation: In the upper division baccalaureate or graduate degree category, 3 semester hours in Commercial or Business Contract Law (3/88).

Management of Defense Acquisition Contracts (Basic) (MDB-001-86)

Location: Norfolk, Pearl Harbor, San Diego, Jacksonville, Philadelphia, Charleston, and Mechanicsburg.
Length: 160 hours (4 weeks).
Dates: January 1986-Present.

Objective: To give the student an introduction and expansion of basic knowledge and skills of government contracts management.

Learning Outcome: Upon the successful completion of this course, the student will have knowledge of basic contracting functions and responsibilities and skills techniques in solving operational problems of contract management.

Instruction: Through lectures and discussion, examinations, and extensive out-of-class readings, this course covers statutes, regulations and policies; elements of a contract; qualifying potential contractors; pre-solicitation considerations; patents and data; purchase by negotiation and sealed bidding; contract types and purposes; cost and pricing techniques; clauses and provisions; contract administrations; modifications; quality assurance; terminations; disputes and appeals; ethical considerations of contracting personnel; and, related contracting functions.

Credit recommendation: In the lower division baccalaureate/associate degree or upper division baccalaureate category, 3 semester hours in Acquisitions Contracting or Business Management (11/86).

Management of Defense Acquisition Contracts (Advanced) (MDA-002-86)

Location: Norfolk, San Diego, Philadelphia, Charleston, Long Beach, Pearl Harbor, and Oakland.
Length: 112 hours (14 days).
Dates: February 1986-Present.

Objective: To reinforce and extend the student's basic contract management knowledge and skills and application of theoretical concepts to acquisition planning.

Learning Outcome: Upon the successful completion of this course the student will be able to develop an acquisition strategy and to acquire or develop information needed for sound procurement decisions. The student will also have skill in evaluating offers and awards, in appropriately applying contractual mechanisms, and in identifying and solving problems associated with acquisitions contracting.

Instruction: Methods include lecture-discussion, out-of-class readings, case studies, student presentations, panels, group problem-solving, individual exercises, and open-book examinations. Content includes negotiations, value engineering, contract administration, and other pre- and post-award functions.

Credit recommendation: In the lower division baccalaureate/associate degree or upper division baccalaureate category, 3 semester hours in Acquisitions Contracting or Business Management (11/86).

Management Development Seminar

Location: Various locations around the country.
Length: 40 hours (1 week).
Dates: August 1987-Present.

Objective: To provide the student with the understanding and application of basic management concepts.

Learning Outcome: Upon successful completion of this course, the student will be able to define and apply components of the communication process; define objectives for an organizational unit; apply principles of time management; recognize types of conflict and apply resolution techniques; apply problem-solving techniques to work-related situations; and utilize team-building techniques in group situations.

Instruction: Course covers managerial communications, goal setting, time management, confrontation and conflict resolution, problem solving, and team building. Methods of instruction include lecture, discussion, case studies, use of teaching aids, examinations, and self-evaluation exercises.

Credit recommendation: In the lower division baccalaureate/associate degree category, 2 semester hours in Business Administration or Management (3/88).

Management of Managers (MGM-006-86)

Location: Norfolk, San Diego, Pearl Harbor, and Charleston.
Length: 80 hours (2 weeks).
Dates: October 1986-Present.
Objective: To provide the student with an understanding of alternate modes of behavior appropriate for the supervision of subordinate managers.
Learning Outcome: Upon the successful completion of this course, the student will have knowledge of personnel management techniques and skill in application of this knowledge, and an understanding of a manager's role in human resource development.
Instruction: Methods include lecture-discussion, out-of-class readings, demonstrations, role-playing, video presentations, and individual and group exercises. Content covered includes competencies and role of managers, communication, motivation, goal setting, coaching, delegating, time management, problem-solving, preparing presentations, stress management, situational leadership, and adapting to change.
Credit recommendation: In the upper division baccalaureate or graduate category, 3 semester hours in Business and Personnel Management or Human Resource Development (11/86).

United States Office of Personnel Management (OPM)

The Training and Investigations Group (TIG) is the federal government's central element of policy and support for federal agencies' development of executive and managerial work forces. Because of the critical role of development for and within the government-wide executive and managerial work force, TIG's Executive Programs Division is concerned exclusively with this area. Its functions include developing and administering government-wide policy and guidance to agencies; providing technical assistance to support agency implementation; and providing on an interagency basis a high quality, comprehensive, competency-based curriculum of training to support agency programs and serve as a model for other executive and management training institutions.

The Executive Programs Division is the national headquarters for development and nationwide delivery of the comprehensive, competency-based, interagency program of training for managers and prospective executives. Training delivery is carried out through three Executive Seminar Centers (Kings Point, NY; Oak Ridge, TN; and Denver, CO); the Government Executive Institute in Washington, D.C.; and OPM's five Regional Training Centers. The Regional Training Centers are located at Atlanta, Chicago, Dalls, Philadelphia, and San Francisco.

Students are nominated to OPM training programs by their employing agencies. Upon a student's successful completion of the course, the Center issues a formal notice to the employing agency for inclusion in that individual's permanent personnel file and for other agency administrative uses. Also, the Center awards certificates of successful completion to the individual.

All permanent staff are selected through the civil service merit system. The agency promotion system is used to identify internal candidates for reassignment and advancement for all positions. In addition, there is wide recruitment from other federal agencies and outside the federal government. The most productive outside recruitment resources are college and university faculties.

The permanent professional staff must be expert employee development specialists as well as highly proficient in their specialists fields. Employee development specialist expertise includes skill as a training consultant, instructor, course director, and course developer.

In addition to staffing with permanent career employees, OPM makes use of a broad range of merit-based recruitment and appointment authorities to bring to its faculties highly qualified university faculty members, experienced consultants, and others.

Source of official student records: Director, Western Executive Seminar Center, U.S. Office of Personnel Management, 1405 Curtis Street, Denver, Colorado 80202.

Additional information about the courses: Program on Noncollegiate Sponsored Instruction, The Center for Adult Learning and Educational Credentials, American Council on Education, One Dupont Circle, Washington, D.C. 20036.

Administration of Public Policy

Location: Executive Seminar Centers: Denver, CO; Kings Point, NY; and Oak Ridge, TN.
Length: 100-115 hours (2 weeks).
Dates: September 1966-Present.
Objective: To enable managers to increase awareness and understanding of elements that influence the environment of public policy processes.
Learning Outcome: Upon successful completion of this course, the student will achieve an understanding of processes affecting new and continuing policies.

Instruction: Examines the political, social, and cultural systems in which American public policy is initiated, developed, and implemented; the major policy-making centers in American government; the ways in which public policy is influenced by political and career executives in government. A major feature of this seminar is the opportunity to examine the shaping of public policy and to exchange ideas with scholars, practitioners, and other seminar participants. Lecture and discussion are used.

Credit recommendation: In the upper division baccalaureate category or in the graduate degree category, 3 semester hours in Administration of Public Policy (6/80) (7/86). NOTE: This course has been reevaluated and continues to meet requirements for credit recommendation.

Economics and Public Policy
  Location: Executive Seminar Centers: Denver, CO; Kings Point, NY; and Oak Ridge, TN.
  Length: 100-115 hours (2 weeks).
  Dates: September 1979-Present.
  Objective: To provide government managers with an examination of the nature and effect of Federal involvement in the economy and the consequences of Federal public policy and programs.
  Learning Outcome: Upon successful completion of this course, the student will achieve an understanding of processes affecting new and continuing policies.
  Instruction: Studies the U.S. economy as a market based system; origin and societal costs of Federal regulation; fiscal policy, taxation and the Federal budget as a policy instrument; the labor market and unemployment; trade policies; privatization of the delivery of public services. Lecture and discussion are utilized.
  Credit recommendation: In the upper division baccalaureate category or in the graduate degree category, 3 semester hours in Agricultural Economics, Business, Economics and Public Policy, or Social Sciences (6/80) (7/86). NOTE: This course has been reevaluated and continues to meet requirements for credit recommendations.

Executive Development Seminar
  Location: Executive Seminar Centers: Denver, CO; Kings Point, NY; and Oak Ridge, TN.
  Length: 100-110 hours (2 weeks).
  Dates: March 1980-Present.
  Objective: To assist current managers and executives in developing a broader perspective of their roles and their agencies by considering them in the context of more comprehensive social values and government policies.
  Learning Outcome: Upon successful completion of this course, the student will have completed the Senior Executive Service Candidate Program.
  Instruction: Examines the major forces acting upon an executive's decision making process. Discussion topics include: In Search of Excellence; Public Administration; Conflict and Resolutions; Role Expectations; Leadership Strategies; System Approaches to Management; Government Relations; Information Management; Federal Regulation and Managing Financial Resources. Lecture, discussion, workshops, and case studies are used.
  Credit recommendation: In the upper division baccalaureate category or in the graduate degree category, 3 semester hours in Organizational Management, Political Organization, Political Science, Public Administration or Public Affairs (6/80) (7/86). NOTE: This course has been reevaluated and continues to meet requirements for credit recommendation.

Federal Personnel Management Issues
  Location: Executive Seminar Centers: Denver, CO; Kings Point, NY; and Oak Ridge, TN.
  Length: 100-115 hours (2 weeks).
  Dates: December 1984-Present.
  Objective: To provide executives and managers with the opportunity to examine and explore in-depth issues, policy options and implementation.
  Learning Outcome: Upon successful completion of this course, the student will have achieved an understanding of the processes affecting new and continuing policies.
  Instruction: Covers current issues in Federal personnel management, government-wide implementation of effective performance management and performance-based incentives, staffing issues, merit systems protection and agency representation before related official boards, issues in Federal labor-management relations, and new approaches and demonstration projects.
  Credit recommendation: In the upper division baccalaureate category or in the graduate degree category, 3 semester hours in Public Administration, Political Science, and Business: Organizational Development (7/86).

Federal Program Management
(Formerly Seminar on Public Program Management)
  Location: Executive Seminar Centers: Denver, CO; Kings Point, NY; and Oak Ridge, TN.
  Length: *Version 1:* 65 hours (2 weeks); *Version 2:* 100-115 hours (2 weeks).
  Dates: *Version 1:* October 1966-June 1986; *Version 2:* July 1986-Present.
  Objective: Upon successful completion of this course, the student will have an understanding of the environment and operation of Federal programs, and the private managerial role in the implementation and management of programs.
  Learning Outcome: Students will learn how to implement Federal policy within operating programs.
  Instruction: Focus is on impact of Administration policy on government managers, public expectations of government responsiveness and performance, economic trends and issues, alternative delivery systems, productivity and performance management, improving financial and

general management accountability in public programs, and the legal and ethical responsibilities of the Federal program manager. Lecture and discussion are used.

Credit recommendation: *Version 1:* In the upper division baccalaureate category or in the graduate degree category, 2 semester hours in Public Administration (6/80). *Version 2:* In the upper division baccalaureate category or in the graduate degree category, 3 semester hours in Public Administration (7/86). NOTE: This course has been reevaluated and continues to meet requirements for credit recommendations.

Government Role in Technology Transfer

Location: Executive Seminar Centers: Denver, CO; Kings Point, NY; and Oak Ridge, TN.
Length: 100-115 hours (2 weeks).
Dates: March 1986-Present.
Objective: To provide participants with a conceptual framework within which they will examine some of the problems and opportunities associated with the management of technology transfer.
Learning Outcome: Upon successful completion of this course, the student will have achieved an understanding of the relationship of and potential for cooperation regarding technology transfer.
Instruction: Considers the economic environment of research and development in the U.S., identification and selection of technologies for transfer to the public and private sectors, issues associated with protecting selected technologies from unlawful transfer, applicability of U.S. patent laws and their impact on technology transfer, and implications of technology transfer for national security and the international community. Lecture and discussion are used.
Credit recommendation: In the upper division baccalaureate category or in the graduate degree category, 3 semester hours in Political Science and Public Administration (7/86).

Management Development Seminar

Location: Executive Seminar Centers: Denver, CO; Kings Point, NY; and Oak Ridge, TN.
Length: 100-115 hours (2 weeks).
Dates: October 1979-Present.
Objective: To enable participants to sharpen existing or acquire new management skills and knowledge in order to improve their managerial performance.
Learning Outcome: Upon successful completion of this course, the student will have learned managerial skills.
Instruction: Features assessment and in-depth evaluation of management styles and the organizational environment in which they function; complexity and conflict in human resource management; a survey of behavioral sciences; approaches to productivity improvement; effective time management and use of delegation; budgeting systems and sunset laws; ethical concerns of modern organizations; Civil Service reform personnel management innovations in agencies.
Credit recommendation: In the upper division baccalaureate category or in the graduate degree category, 3 semester hours in Business Administration, Educational Management, Public Administration or Personnel Management (6/80) (7/86). NOTE: This course has been reevaluated and continues to meet requirements for credit recommendations.

Management of Natural Resources
(Formerly Seminar in Environmental Quality and Natural Resources)

Location: Executive Seminar Centers: Denver, CO; Kings Point, NY; and Oak Ridge, TN.
Length: *Version 1:* 110 hours (2 weeks); *Version 2:* 100-115 hours (2 weeks).
Dates: *Version 1:* September 1979-June 1986; *Version 2:* July 1986-Present.
Objective: To provide participants with an understanding of environmental issues relating to national policy and management concerns.
Learning Outcome: Upon successful completion of this course, the student will have achieved an understanding of the processes affecting new and continuing national policies.
Instruction: Examines critical national and international issues, including the availability of natural resources. Also examines the social, political, economic, and technological forces affecting resource use in the United States; and public agencies, policies, and programs for the development, use, and protection of natural resources. Lecture, discussion, site visits, and group projects are used.
Credit recommendation: *Version 1:* In the upper division baccalaureate category or in the graduate degree category, 2 semester hours in Business, Environmental Studies, Forestry, or Social Sciences (6/80). *Version 2:* In the upper division baccalaureate category or in the graduate degree category, 3 semester hours in Business, Environmental Studies, Forestry, or Social Sciences (7/86). NOTE: This course has been reevaluated and continues to meet requirements for credit recommendations.

Managerial Competencies and Effectiveness Characteristics for Executives

Location: Executive Seminar Centers: Kings Point, NY; Denver, CO; and Oak Ridge, TN.
Length: 100-115 hours (2 weeks).
Dates: February 1986-Present.
Objective: To provide advance practice to enhance existing skills to enable advancing or transitioning managers to adapt and apply their management competencies in a broader policy context.
Learning Outcome: Upon successful completion of this course, the student will be able to transform technical or operating personnel into managers.

Instruction: Instruction emphasizes case study and intensive attention to individual influence styles and development of small group process skills. Interpersonal awareness and methods for solving conflict are discussed. Analytical skills and the ability to articulate reasoning are used in problem solving. Negotiation and mediation techniques are presented and used for conflict resolutions. Problems are structured, issues are framed, information is gathered and analyzed to develop a system for decision making.

Credit recommendation: In the upper division baccalaureate category or in the graduate degree category, 3 semester hours in Public Management, or as an elective in Behavioral Services (7/86).

Managing Money and Material Resources
Location: Executive Seminar Centers: Denver, CO; Kings Point, NY; and Oak Ridge, TN.
Length: 100-115 hours (2 weeks).
Dates: May 1986-Present.
Objective: To provide an understanding of manager's responsibilities for obtaining and allocating the money and material resources necessary to support program and policy implementation, including budget preparation, justification and administration.
Learning Outcome: Upon successful completion of this course, the student will have achieved an understanding of the processes affecting new and continuing policies.
Instruction: Covers integration of the budget with higher management priorities, budget impact on policy alternatives to higher management, preparation and justification of budgets for an agency or program, forecasting and defending an operating budget, creation of a financial management system, application of contract and procurement regulations to meet organizational objectives and management of contractor activities including contractor compliance. Lecture and discussion are used.
Credit recommendation: In the upper division baccalaureate category or in the graduate degree category, 3 semester hours in Political Science, Public Administration, or Business (7/86).

National Security Policy
Location: Executive Seminar Centers: Denver, CO; Kings Point, NY; and Oak Ridge, TN.
Length: 100-115 hours (2 weeks).
Dates: May 1985-Present.
Objective: To provide a high level overview of the complex problems involved in the administration of national security policy, and the interrelationships between political, military and technological factors affecting national security.
Learning Outcome: Upon successful completion of this course, the student will have achieved an understanding of the processes affecting new and continuing policies.
Instruction: Analyzes the rapidly changing nature of modern warfare and strategic concepts upon which national security policy is based, the structure of the defense establishment and agencies involved in policy formulation, connective defense arrangements, effect of terrorism on national and international security policy, role of intelligence in national security and anticipating national security needs.
Credit recommendation: In the upper division baccalaureate category or in the graduate degree category, 3 semester hours in Political Science or International Relations (7/86).

Seminar in Science, Technology and Public Policy
Location: Executive Seminar Centers: Denver, CO; Kings Point, NY; and Oak Ridge, TN.
Length: *Version 1:* 90 hours (2 weeks); *Version 2:* 100-115 hours (2 weeks).
Dates: *Version 1:* September 1973-June 1986; *Version 2:* July 1986-Present.
Objective: To discuss science and technology in a social and governmental context, and to examine critical issues in the management of scientific research and technological development.
Learning Outcome: Upon successful completion of this course, the student will have achieved an understanding of processes affecting new and continuing policies.
Instruction: Reviews the nature of science and technology in governmental agencies; the effects of science and technology on resource policy; organization and management of a variety of science programs. Explores the relationships between technological advances and social and economic issues. Lecture, discussion, and classroom exercises are used.
Credit recommendation: *Version 1:* In the upper division baccalaureate category or in the graduate degree category, 2 semester hours in Environmental Studies or Social Sciences (6/80). *Version 2:* In the upper division baccalaureate category or in the graduate degree category, 3 semester hours in Environmental Studies or Social Sciences (7/86). NOTE: This course has been reevaluated and continues to meet requirements for credit recommendations.

Seminar for New Managers
Location: Executive Seminar Centers: Denver, CO; Kings Point, NY; and Oak Ridge, TN.
Length: *Version 1:* 112 hours (2 weeks); *Version 2:* 100-115 hours (2 weeks).
Dates: *Version 1:* October 1977-June 1986; *Version 1:* July 1986-Present.
Objective: To provide opportunity learn and practice basic managerial skills needed to perform effectively in new administrative roles.
Learning Outcome: Upon successful completion of this course, the student will have achieved an understanding of managerial roles.

Instruction: Features assessment and evaluation of management styles, employee roles and organizational environments; application of systematic approaches to establishing goals and objectives; discussion of implications of Civil Service reform; interpretation of labor-management responsibilities of managers; interpretations and use of personal and interpersonal forces in organizations to achieve objectives; evaluation of performance to be used in a systematic approach to problem solving and decision making; allocation of resources to achieve stated objectives. Lecture, discussion, and group exercises are used.

Credit recommendation: *Version 1:* In the upper division baccalaureate category or in the graduate degree category, 3 semester hours in Business Administration, Educational Administration, Personnel Administration or Management, or Public Administration (6/80). *Version 2:* In the upper division baccalaureate category or in the graduate degree category, 3 semester hours in Business Administration, Educational Administration, Personnel Administration, Management or Public Administration (7/86). NOTE: This course has been reevaluated and continues to meet requirements for credit recommendations.

United States Postal Service - Department of Training and Development

Postal training and development programs are controlled by the Department of Training and Development, a department within the Human Resources Group located at the U.S. Postal Service Headquarters in Washington, D.C. This department ensures that all Postal training and development programs support the performance requirements and career development objectives of the 800,000 employee organization. Courses are offered at the William F. Bolger Management Academy, the Technical Training Center, and Postal Employee Development Centers at major post offices.

The Management Academy consists of the main facility in Potomac, Maryland and three field centers located in Oak Brook, Illinois; Memphis, Tennessee; and Los Angeles, California. The Technical Training Center is located on the University of Oklahoma campus in Norman, Oklahoma. The Postal Employee Development Centers are located at approximately 186 locations throughout the country.

Source of official student records: Management Academy Courses, Office of the Registrar, William F. Bolger Management Academy, 10000 Kentsdale Drive, Potomac, MD 20858-4320.

Technical Training Center Courses, Office of the Registrar, Technical Training Center, P.O. Box 1400, Norman, OK 73070-7810.

Postal Employee Development Center Courses, Office of the Registrar, William F. Bolger Management Academy, 10000 Kentsdale Drive, Potomac, MD 20858-4320.

Additional information about the courses: Program on Noncollegiate Sponsored Instruction, The Center for Adult Learning and Educational Credentials, American Council on Education, One Dupont Circle, Washington, D.C. 20036.

CORRESPONDENCE SYSTEM

The Institute delivers correspondence programs to tens of thousands of postal managers, supervisors, and other employees each year in all parts of the country. Correspondence courses provide a readily available means for employees to develop and prepare themselves for entry into more formal training in the craft, maintenance, and supervisory areas. Students applying for credit must pass a proctored final examination, successful completion of which will be indicated on the student's record.

Source of official student records: Office of the Registrar, Postal Service Management Academy, 10,000 Kentsdale Drive, Potomac, Maryland 20858-4320.

Additional information about the courses: Program on Noncollegiate Sponsored Instruction, The Center for Adult Learning and Educational Credentials, American Council on Education, One Dupont Circle, Washington, D.C. 20036.

Administration of Maintenance Programs - Module I (56170-00)
  Location: Correspondence.
  Length: Approximately 40 hours.
  Dates: January 1975-April 1984.
  Objective: To provide an understanding of the principles of managing a maintenance organization.
  Instruction: Introduction to the management elements of planning, organizing, controlling, and directing. Also covers staffing, scheduling, human interaction, motivation, safety, and communications.
  Credit recommendation: In the lower division baccalaureate/associate degree category or in the upper division baccalaureate category, 2 semester hours in General Management (2/78).

Basic Diesel Mechanics - Module I - Basic Diesel Maintenance (56160-00)
  Location: Correspondence.
  Length: Approximately 51 hours.
  Dates: March 1975-April 1984.
  Objective: To provide a foundation in the principles of diesel engines, electrical systems, and transmissions.
  Instruction: Basic diesel principles; engine structure; fuel, air intake, exhaust, lubricating, cooling electrical, and transmission systems; clutches.
  Credit recommendation: In the lower division bac-

calaureate/associate degree category, 2 semester hours or in the vocational certificate category, 3 semester hours in Diesel Mechanics (2/78).

Basic Diesel Mechanics - Module II - Mack-Diesel Maintenance (56161-00)
Location: Correspondence.
Length: Approximately 40 hours.
Dates: March 1975-April 1984.
Objective: To enable the student to describe the parts, functions, and operating principles of the Mack ENDT 673A, B, and C engines.
Instruction: Covers topics related to the Mack-diesel engine, including engine structure, fuel, air intake, exhaust, lubricating, cooling, and electrical systems; engine operation; engine testing and run-in; troubleshooting and failure analysis; shop manual organization.
Credit recommendation: In the lower division baccalaureate/associate degree category, 1 semester hour or in the vocational certificate category, 2 semester hours in Diesel Mechanics (2/78).

Basic Electricity (56150-00)
Location: Correspondence.
Length: Approximately 150 hours.
Dates: January 1972-April 1984.
Objective: To enable students to analyze and solve problems associated with AC and DC circuitry.
Instruction: Fundamental principles of electricity, including the behavior of AC and DC electrical circuits. Use of formulas and equations essential to an understanding of electricity; fundamentals of magnetism, resistance, inductance, and capacitance. No laboratory experiences included.
Credit recommendation: In the lower division baccalaureate/associate degree category, 2 semester hours in Electricity (2/78).

Basic Pneumatics and Hydraulics (56147-00)
Location: Correspondence.
Length: Approximately 80 hours.
Dates: October 1972-April 1984.
Objective: To develop a basic theoretical understanding of hydraulic and pneumatic systems.
Instruction: In logical sequence, the fundamentals of hydraulics and pneumatics and the operation of fluid power components. Topics include physics of fluids, basic systems and circuit diagrams, control and measurement of flow, component equipment functions.
Credit recommendation: In the lower division baccalaureate/associate degree category, 2 semester hours in Mechanical Technology (2/78).

Customer Service Representative (42151-00)
Location: Correspondence.
Length: Approximately 40 hours.
Dates: February 1978-April 1984.
Objective: To provide an overview of knowledge, skills, and techniques of effective salesmanship/sales management, and to enable students to design customized user service.
Instruction: Role of the customer service representative; product knowledge and customized service programs; sales processes, including precall planning and use of visual sales aids; time and territory management; customer relations and psychology of selling. Course covers same material that Customer Service Representation MAS (10068-10) covers but does not provide classroom application of principles.
Credit recommendation: In the lower division baccalaureate/associate degree category, 1 semester hour in Sales Management or Salesmanship (2/78).

Digital Electronics (56148-00)
Location: Correspondence.
Length: Approximately 30 hours.
Dates: February 1976-April 1984.
Objective: To introduce the principles of digital electronics.
Instruction: Basics of numbering systems, including methods of conversions between systems; various coding schemes; circuit introduction to Boolean algebra; elements of digital electronics.
Credit recommendation: In the lower division baccalaureate/associate degree category, 1 semester hour in Digital Electronics (2/78).

Introduction to Basic Mathematics and Electricity (56123-00)
Location: Correspondence.
Length: Approximately 50 hours.
Dates: January 1972-April 1984.
Objective: To provide an understanding of the fundamentals of mathematics necessary in the study of electricity and to introduce the principles of electricity.
Instruction: A refresher in basic arithmetic operations such as addition, subtraction, multiplication, and division. Positive and negative numbers, fractions, square roots, powers of ten. Also includes an introduction to electrical units and prefixes, elementary algebraic equations, formulas, rectangular coordinates, trigonometric relations, and vectors.
Credit recommendation: In the vocational certificate category, 3 semester hours in Basic Mathematics and Electricity (2/78).

Power Transistors (56143-00)
Location: Correspondence.
Length: Approximately 20 hours.
Dates: January 1972-April 1984.
Objective: To develop awareness of thermal, frequency, and size problems associated with power transistors.

Instruction: Considers compromises that enable both low and high frequency power transistors to operate at high temperatures and currents. Includes regulator circuits and overload protection.

Credit recommendation: In the lower division baccalaureate/associate degree category, 1 semester hour in Electronics (2/78).

Report Writing for Postal Managers (33150-00)
  Location: Correspondence.
  Length: Approximately 40 hours.
  Dates: February 1978-April 1984.
  Objective: To provide an understanding of the mechanics of report writing.
  Instruction: Review of grammar; spelling; word mechanics; usage; editing and proofreading; planning, preparation, and evaluation of written reports.
  Credit recommendation: In the lower division baccalaureate/associate degree category, 1 semester hour in Communications (2/78).

Secretary to the Postal Executive (33130-00)
  Location: Correspondence.
  Length: Approximately 40 hours.
  Dates: February 1978-April 1984.
  Objective: To provide an overview of the principles of management and business communications.
  Instruction: Principles and applications of effective communication, with emphasis on making the secretary an effective office manager.
  Credit recommendation: In the lower division baccalaureate/associate degree category, 1 semester hour in Secretarial Science (2/78).

Transistors and Transistor Applications (56142-00)
  Location: Correspondence.
  Length: Approximately 75 hours.
  Dates: January 1972-April 1984.
  Objective: To develop a theoretical understanding of transistors and their use in common electronic circuits.
  Instruction: An in-depth study of solid-state theory, transistor amplifiers, load line analysis, equivalent circuit analysis, feedback, tuned circuits, multivibrators, and modulation.
  Credit recommendation: In the lower division baccalaureate/associate degree category, 3 semester hours in Electronics (2/78).

Vehicle Accident Investigation (51159-00)
  Location: Correspondence.
  Length: Approximately 40 hours.
  Dates: February 1978-April 1984.
  Objective: To develop skills in reporting, investigating, and analyzing vehicle accidents.
  Instruction: Data collecting, interviewing, calculations, highway and human factors, road and tire evidence, vehicular evidence, forms, analysis of accidents.
  Credit recommendation: In the lower division baccalaureate/associate degree category, 1 semester hour in Industrial or Public Safety (2/78).

INSPECTION SERVICE

The courses listed below are part of the Postal Inspection Training Program of the Career Development Branch, located in Potomac, Maryland. The Program's purpose is to train law enforcement officers of the U.S. Postal Service.

Source of official student records: Office of the Registrar, Postal Service Training and Development Institute, 10000 Kentsdale Drive, Potomac, Maryland 20854.

Additional information about the courses: Program on Noncollegiate Sponsored Instruction, The Center for Adult Learning and Educational Credentials, American Council on Education, One Dupont Circle, Washington, D.C. 20036.

Introduction to Law Enforcement
(Security Force Training [12252])
  Location: Potomac, MD.
  Length: *Version 1:* 48 hours (3 weeks); residential. *Version 2:* 140 hours (4 weeks); residential.
  Dates: *Version 1:* October 1972-December 1980; *Version 2:* January 1981-December 1985.
  Objective: To develop the skills, knowledge, and attitudes required to perform as security police officers and supervisors.
  Instruction: Covers various aspects of law and legal procedures applicable to the security aspects of law enforcement. Emphasis is given to principles of security such as building control; bomb threats; building search; narcotics and dangerous drugs; arson and fire prevention; emergency medical aid; defensive tactics; and crowds, mobs, and social disorders. Program includes firearms training, a study of individual behavior and human relations, and basics of improved oral and written communications. Lectures, discussions, practical exercises, and audio visual equipment are used.
  Credit recommendation: In the lower division baccalaureate/associate degree category, 3 semester hours in Law Enforcement (2/75).

Postal Inspector Basic Training (12251)
  Part 1: Audit Procedures I
  Part 2. Audit Procedures II
  Part 3: Criminal Law I
  Part 4: Basic Criminal Investigation
  Part 5: Advanced Criminal Investigation
  Part 6: Administrative Practice
  Part 7: Personal Defense
  Location: Potomac, MD.
  Length: *Version 1:* 404 hours (16 weeks); residential.

Part 1: 50 hours; *Part 2:* 53 hours; *Part 3:* 45 hours; *Part 4:* 69 hours; *Part 5:* 71 hours; *Part 6:* 64 hours; *Part 7:* 52 hours.

Version 2: 425 hours (11 weeks); residential. *Part 1:* 72 hours; *Part 2:* 59 hours; *Part 3:* 45 hours; *Part 4:* 61 hours; *Part 5:* 80 hours; *Part 6:* 62 hours; *Part 7:* 46 hours.

Dates: *Version 1:* October 1972-January 1981; *Version 2:* February 1981-December 1985.

Objective: To train postal inspectors in all aspects of Inspection Service work and to prepare them to assume the responsibilities of their first duty assignments.

Instruction: *Part 1:* A study of types of funds and accounts, types of audits and financial investigations, and audit standards. *Part 2:* A study of audit writing and working papers; economic analysis; service, operational, and financial audits. A practical exercise is included. *Part 3:* Presents the theory, evolution, and current status of presenting evidence in criminal cases; the laws of arrest, search and seizure, and entrapment; statements and affidavits; problems of legality in presenting various kinds of physical evidence. *Part 4:* Includes principles of investigation, investigative techniques, legal practices and procedures, security operations, and preparation of case reports. *Part 5:* Builds on the instructional content of the Basic Criminal Investigation block. Stress is on use of advanced techniques and advanced technology, nonroutine methods, preventive analysis, and control operations. *Part 6:* Elements include general administrative principles; report writing; case study approaches; technical, analytical, and managerial skills; and policy development. *Part 7:* Theory and practice of selected defense skills and their application to coping successfully with situations in which the student encounters personal attack.

Credit recommendation: *Part 1:* In the upper division baccalaureate category or in the graduate degree category, 3 semester hours in Auditing, Business Administration, or Public Administration (2/75) (1/81). *Part 2:* In the upper division baccalaureate category or in the graduate degree category, 3 semester hours in Auditing, Business Administration, or Public Administration (2/75) (1/81). *Part 3:* In the graduate degree category, 3 semester hours in Criminal Law (2/75) (1/81). *Part 4:* In the lower division baccalaureate/associate degree category, 3 semester hours in Criminal Justice (2/75) (1/81). *Part 5:* In the upper division baccalaureate category, 3 semester hours in Criminal Justice (2/75) (1/81). *Part 6:* In the upper division baccalaureate category, 3 semester hours in Business Administration, Management, or Public Administration (2/75) (1/81). *Part 7:* In the lower division baccalaureate/associate degree category, 1 semester hour in Physical Education (2/75) (1/81). NOTE: *Version 1:* All participants complete Parts 1, 3, 4, 6, and 7. Trainees specializing in auditing complete Part 2 (Audit Procedures II), and those specializing in criminal investigation complete Part 5 (Advanced Criminal Investigation). *Version 2:* All participants complete Parts 1 through 7. NOTE: This course has undergone a 5-year reevaluation and continues to meet the requirements for credit recommendations.

MANAGEMENT ACADEMY

Communication Skills for Managers #11251-00 (Formerly #11451-00)

Location: Potomac, MD and Field Centers.
Length: 40 hours (5 days).
Dates: October 1982-Present.
Objective: To provide students with a knowledge of basic communication skills and concepts of reading, speaking, listening and their application.

Learning Outcome: Upon successful completion of this course, the student will be able to: identify course entry level proficiency of reading, listening, writing, and speaking skills; identify barriers and aids to effective reading, listening, writing, and speaking; demonstrate principles of effective reading, listening, talking, writing, and speaking; give and receive feedback on principles of effective listening, writing, and speaking; identify four characteristics of effective interpersonal communication; and demonstrate principles of effective briefings.

Instruction: Training consists of instructor-led lectures, exercises and the application of theories, concepts and principles used in the communication process of speaking, listening, reading, and writing. Instructional methods include video cassettes, videotaping, slides, graphics and audio cassettes.

Credit recommendation: In the lower division baccalaureate/associate degree category, 1 semester hour in Human Relations, Business Communications (3/87). NOTE: Students who receive credit for Communication Skills for Supervisors should not receive credit for this course.

Communications Skills for Supervisors #11281-00

Location: Potomac, MD and Field Centers.
Length: 40 hours (5 days).
Dates: October 1982-Present.
Objective: To provide students with oral, listening, writing and reading skills and concepts necessary to establish a foundation for effective communication in the workplace.

Learning Outcome: Upon successful completion of this course, the student will be able to: identify course entry level proficiency of reading, listening, writing, and speaking skills; identify barriers and aids to effective reading, listening, writing and speaking; demonstrate principles of effective reading, listening, talking, writing, and speaking; give and receive feedback on principles of effective listening, writing, and speaking; and identify four characteristics of effective interpersonal communication and compare pre and post course attitude toward these characteristics.

Instruction: The training consists of lectures, role play exercises, and the application of theories and concepts to the communication process. The instructional methods also include the use of video cassettes, videotaping, graphics, and audio cassettes.

Credit recommendation: In the lower division baccalaureate/associate degree or vocational certificate category, 1 semester hour in Business Communications, Human Relations (3/87). NOTE: Students who receive credit for Communication Skills for Managers should not receive credit for this course.

Constructive Conflict Resolution #11220-00
Location: Potomac, MD and Field Centers.
Length: 24 hours (3 days).
Dates: September 1985-Present.
Objective: To enable the student to identify sources of interpersonal conflict and techniques for resolving them.
Learning Outcome: Upon successful completion of this course, the student will be able to describe policies and procedures of the facility; interview and introduce a classmate; identify the other students in the class; identify how people manipulate others; and identify personal interests and career highlights.
Instruction: This course covers interpersonal problem recognition and solution by instruction in human relations and classroom exercises whose students practice interviewing, counseling, and conflict resolution.
Credit recommendation: In the lower division baccalaureate/associate degree category, 1 semester hour in Human Relations (3/87).

Customer Services Managers (MAS) #10276-00
Location: Potomac, MD.
Length: 80 hours (10 days).
Dates: October 1982-Present.
Objective: To provide the student with an understanding of the various subunits of operation in the post office and how a knowledge of these units contributes to effective management.
Learning Outcome: Upon successful completion of this course, the student will be able to manage an associate office.
Instruction: Course covers customer service management data system; unit and route reviews; growth management, staffing and scheduling, financial operations, labor relations, safety and budget responsibilities.
Credit recommendation: In the lower division baccalaureate/associate degree category, 1 semester hour in General Supervision (3/87).

Equal Employment Opportunity Administration (Woman's Program Coordinator—Special Emphasis Series)
Location: Potomac, MD.
Length: 80 hours (10 days).
Dates: January 1978-Present.
Objective: To furnish the students with basic managerial skills necessary to perform effectively as coordinator of an equal opportunity employment program.
Learning Outcome: Upon successful completion of this course, the student will understand the relationships and organizational structure; gather, analyze and interpret data; identify the needs of women that are unique; assist employees by career counseling, job applications, filing of grievances; and speak and write effectively.
Instruction: This course covers organizational relationships within the Postal Service, recruitment of women, career counseling, identification of the needs of women, development of training workshops, development and delivery of special material and the conduct of meetings.
Credit recommendation: In the lower division baccalaureate/associate degree category, 1 semester hour in Personnel Management (3/87).

Hearing Officers' Training #21275-00
Location: Potomac, MD.
Length: 24 hours (3 days).
Dates: January 1981-Present.
Objective: To provide participant with knowledge of several legal terms and the procedures for investigating the validity of various allegations.
Learning Outcome: Upon successful completion of this course, the student will be able to: perform completely and thoroughly the administrative duties of a Hearing Officer to assure appellant and management rights are not violated; conduct a pre-hearing conference consistent with regulations; conduct a formal hearing, when the appellant is not subject to the provisions of a collective bargaining agreement, in such a manner that all pertinent and valid evidence is surfaced; analyze factual materials as they relate to Step One Hearing Procedures; and write clear and concise findings of fact after conducting the hearing.
Instruction: This course is designed to prepare Hearing Officers to conduct hearings in appeals from adverse actions and disciplinary sanctions filed by employees not subject to the provisions of a collective bargaining agreement. It clarifies the functions and responsibilities of Hearing Officers by setting forth guidelines for use in preparing for the hearing. It also suggests what should be done before, during and after the hearing to assure that all of the facts are developed and recorded, proper procedures are used, and the hearing is conducted in an efficient and productive manner.
Credit recommendation: In the lower division baccalaureate/associate degree category, 1 semester hour in Paralegal Training (3/87).

1. Improving Group Performance #112200-00
2. Management Styles and Employee Motivation #11223-00
Location: Potomac, MD and Field Centers.
Length: 1. 16 hours (2 days). 2. 16 hours (2 days).
Dates: August 1986-Present.

Objective: To provide managers and supervisors with information on adversarial work relationships, individual and group motivational theories, management styles, management behavior modification techniques for self and subordinate development.

Learning Outcome: Upon successful completion of this course, students will be able to recognize the roots of the management-labor adversarial relationship, the assumptions underlying these roots, and the resulting impact on productivity; compare and contrast one's management style and the style of others in order to develop a greater understanding of individual management styles; compare and contrast major motivational theories underlying group motivation and group dynamics by applying the concepts to practical, work-related situations; and apply the newly learned and enhanced concepts of managerial behavior modification which emphasize a humanistic approach to developing our full potential and the fullest potential of our subordinates.

Instruction: The concepts and methodology of this course are designed to facilitate the learning and application of alternative approaches to management styles and employee motivation as a means of increasing organizational effectiveness. The course utilizes instrumentation to identify management styles and fine-tune people skills with exercises that have direct applicability to on-the-job activities. Principle theories and concepts are discussed in small group activities that are designed to promote feedback through a free-flow of ideas. Introductions to and closure for each module are facilitated by lecturettes and/or appropriate video. A student workbook is provided to ensure a sequential, progressive flow of the material as the subject matter moves from textbook concept to back-home application with the use of a training transfer strategy.

Credit recommendation: In the lower division baccalaureate/associate degree category, 1 semester hour in Human Relations (3/87). NOTE: To receive credit students must take both courses.

Introduction to Safety Management #21218-00
  Location: Potomac, MD.
  Length: 80 hours (10 days).
  Dates: February 1987-Present.
  Objective: To acquaint safety personnel with the technical, analytical and managerial skills necessary to perform work tasks effectively.
  Learning Outcome: Upon successful completion of this course, students will be able to perform the duties and responsibilities required of safety personnel.
  Instruction: Covers basic safety management activities and procedures including administration, planning and coordination, reviewing, monitoring, consulting, investigating, supervising, organizing and promoting within a postal safety management program.
  Credit recommendation: In the vocational certificate category, 1 semester hour in Occupational Safety (3/87).

Managing Personal Effectiveness #11221-00
  Location: Potomac, MD and Field Centers.
  Length: 24 hours (3 days).
  Dates: July 1985-Present.
  Objective: To assist managers in acquiring and principles for use at their present and higher level endeavors.
  Learning Outcome: Upon successful completion of this course, students will be able to recognize the optimal stress level that causes high performance; demonstrate the ability to identify sources and symptoms of stress; develop an understanding and awareness of holistic living; analyze the physical dimension of holistic living; develop strategies to combat stress internally; develop strategies to manage nonwork, psychological dimensions of holistic living; analyze work-related stress and develop strategies to effectively manage stress; demonstrate an understanding of crucial elements in time management that contribute to stress and ineffective use of time; develop skills that enable a manager to exercise effective control of individual and employee time; and develop a comprehensive individual strategy for maintaining personal effectiveness that integrates both time and stress management techniques.
  Instruction: Selected strategies are used to assist managers deal effectively with stress. The instructor uses exercises, questionnaires, lectures and workbooks.
  Credit recommendation: In the lower division baccalaureate/associate degree category, 1 semester hour in Human Relations (3/87).

Supervisory Leadership #17224-00
  Location: Potomac, MD, Southern, Mid-west, and Western Field Centers.
  Length: 40 hours (5 days).
  Dates: January 1986-Present.
  Objective: To provide the student with the skills to become an effective leader.
  Learning Outcome: Upon successful completion of this course, the student will have a familiarity with different leadership styles; know more about his/her own personality and that of his/her subordinates.
  Instruction: The main thrust of this course is in having the learners assess their preferred leadership style, utilizing instrumentation that was introduced in Supervisory Skills Building. The learners have evaluated their supervisory behavior during the intervening months of actual on-the-job experience. They now explore the barriers encountered on the job and discuss strategies to overcome these barriers. The main focus of the course is self-analysis; each learner evaluates his managerial behavioral style, its effectiveness in various situations with various types of subordinates, and prepares a practical change strategy. Particular emphasis is given to optimizing the learner's leadership success in the work environment. Lecture, discussion and class exercises are used.

Credit recommendation: In the lower division baccalaureate/associate degree category, 1 semester hour in Human Relations (3/87). NOTE: Students who receive credit for this course should not receive credit for Supervisory Leadership: General Management #11203-00.

Supervisory Leadership: General Management #11203-00
Location: Potomac, MD and Field Centers.
Length: 40 hours (5 days).
Dates: September 1986-Present.
Objective: To provide the student with the skills to become and effective leader.
Learning Outcome: Upon successful completion of this course, the student will have a familiarity with different leadership styles; know more about his/her own personality and that of his/her subordinates.
Instruction: The main thrust of this course is in having the learners assess their preferred leadership style, utilizing carefully selected instrumentation to disclose relative information. The learners relate their supervisory behavior to actual on-the-job experiences. They explore the barriers encountered on the job and discuss strategies for overcoming these barriers. The main focus of the course is self-analysis; each learner evaluates his/her managerial behavioral style, its effectiveness in various situations with various types of subordinates, and prepares a practical change strategy. Particular emphasis is given to optimizing probabilities for the learner's leadership success in the work environment. Lecture, discussion and class exercises are used.
Credit recommendation: In the lower division baccalaureate/associate degree category, 1 semester hour in Human Relations (3/87). NOTE: Students who receive credit for this course should not receive credit for Supervisory Leadership #17224-00.

Vehicle Maintenance Management Skills Building
Location: Potomac, MD.
Length: 80 hours (10 days).
Dates: April 1987-Present.
Objective: To train maintenance supervisors to understand and utilize principles of human relations for more productive vehicle maintenance.
Learning Outcome: Upon successful completion of this course, the student will recognize the importance of self-esteem, giving and receiving feedback, on-the-job improvement and employee motivation.
Instruction: The course covers principles of Human Relations, Human Motivation, motivation of employees and developing team work; the second half covers maintenance training that is industry specific.
Credit recommendation: In the vocational certificate category, 3 semester hours Automotive Science Supervision (3/87).

Vehicle Operations Management Skills Building
Location: Potomac, MD.
Length: 80 hours (10 days).
Dates: March 1987-Present.
Objective: To train postal supervisors in the performance of supervising functions in report writing, safety, record keeping, budgeting, labor relations.
Learning Outcome: Upon successful completion of this course, students will be able to understand the organization structure in which he/she operates and prepare standardized reports, keep records, prepare budget estimates and comply with union requirements in the vehicle operations area.
Instruction: The course covers industry specific management functions in report writing, record keeping, labor relations, safety and budgeting.
Credit recommendation: In the vocational certificate category, 3 semester hours in Management of a Vehicle Operation Service (3/87).

MANAGEMENT TRAINING SERIES (MTS)

Associate Office Management MTS (13589)
Location: PEDC Centers.
Length: Self-study.
Dates: February 1978-Present.
Objective: To enhance the supervisory and personnel management skills of incumbent associate office managers.
Instruction: Activities of an associate office with urban delivery responsibilities, including delivery and collection services, mail processing, window services, and financial procedures.
Credit recommendation: In the lower division baccalaureate/associate degree category, 1 semester hour in Personnel Administration or Supervision (3/79). NOTE: Credit should not be granted for both this course and Associate Office Management MAS (10205-00).

Associate Office Postmaster MTS (13590)
Location: PEDC Centers.
Length: Self-study.
Dates: May 1978-Present.
Objective: To strengthen the supervisory and management skills of incumbent associate office postmasters.
Instruction: Financial operations, employee and labor relations, mail processing and delivery systems, communications.
Credit recommendation: In the lower division baccalaureate/associate degree category, 1 semester hour in Personnel Administration or Supervision (3/79).

Building Equipment Maintenance Supervisor MTS (55583)
Location: PEDC Centers.
Length: Self-study.

Dates: May 1978-Present.

Objective: To enhance the supervisory knowledge and skills of first-line supervisors of building equipment maintenance personnel.

Instruction: Maintenance of building facilities, including determination of manpower requirements, scheduling of maintenance, custodial functions, energy conservation, working environment considerations, safety practices, communications, and employee relations.

Credit recommendation: In the lower division baccalaureate/associate degree category, 1 semester hour in Personnel Administration or Supervision (3/79). NOTE: Credit should not be granted for both this course and Building Equipment Maintenance Supervisors MAS (10217-00).

Building Services Maintenance Supervisor MTS (55585)

Location: PEDC Centers.
Length: Self-study.
Dates: May 1978-Present.

Objective: To enhance the supervisory knowledge and skills of incumbent first-line supervisors of building services maintenance personnel.

Instruction: Supervision of custodial personnel, determination of manpower requirements, scheduling of custodial services, energy conservation, safety practices, communications, and employee relations.

Credit recommendation: In the lower division baccalaureate/associate degree category, 1 semester hour in Personnel Administration or Supervision (3/79). NOTE: Credit should not be granted for both this course and Building Services Maintenance Supervisors MAS (10218-00).

Customer Services Representative MTS (42590)

Location: PEDC Centers.
Length: Self-study.
Dates: January 1977-Present.

Objective: To provide customer service representatives with knowledge, skills, and techniques of effective salesmanship and sales management and to enable them to design customized user services.

Instruction: Role of the customer service representative; product knowledge and customized service programs; sales processes, including precall planning and use of visual sales aids; time and territory management; customer relations and the psychology of selling.

Credit recommendation: In the lower division baccalaureate/associate degree category, 2 semester hours in Sales Management or Salesmanship (3/79). NOTE: Credit should not be granted for both this course and Customer Service Representative MAS (10268-00).

Delivery Services Supervisor MTS (44585)

Location: PEDC Centers.
Length: Self-study.
Dates: January 1978-Present.

Objective: To strengthen the supervisory skills of incumbent delivery service supervisors.

Instruction: Day-to-day supervision of delivery services and collections, mail count, and route inspections; evaluation of route inspection data; scheduling and staffing; revenue-producing programs; financial procedures; employee and labor relations activities.

Credit recommendation: In the lower division baccalaureate/associate degree category, 1 semester hour in Personnel Administration or Supervision (3/79). NOTE: Credit should not be granted for both this course and Delivery Service Supervisors MAS (10210-00).

Employee Relations Management MTS (21581)

Location: PEDC Centers.
Length: Self-study.
Dates: July 1978-Present.

Objective: To improve the managerial performance of incumbent personnel in major employee relations functions.

Instruction: The role and responsibilities of employee relations personnel with emphasis on recruitment, selection, placement, compensation and benefits, career development, records maintenance, budget and developing action plans.

Credit recommendation: In the lower division baccalaureate/associate degree category or in the upper division baccalaureate category, 2 semester hours in Industrial Relations, Personnel Administration, or Supervision (3/79). NOTE: Credit should not be granted for both this course and Employee Relations Management MAS (10270-00).

Labor Relations Management MTS (22590)

Location: PEDC Centers.
Length: Self-study.
Dates: April 1978-Present.

Objective: To help postal service managers and postal service labor relations specialists understand labor relations.

Instruction: Contract analysis, grievance procedures, employee representation, discipline and mediation/arbitration. Also includes the evolution of labor law, local implementation, and procedures for dealing with employees and union representatives.

Credit recommendation: In the lower division baccalaureate/associate degree category or in the upper division baccalaureate category, 2 semester hours in Collective Bargaining, Industrial Relations, Labor Relations, or Personnel Administration (3/79).

Mail Processing Equipment Maintenance Supervisor MTS (55596)

Location: PEDC Centers.

Length: Self-study.
Dates: May 1978-Present.
Objective: To enhance the personnel supervision knowledge and skills of incumbent first-line supervisors of mail processing equipment maintenance personnel.
Instruction: Supervision of the maintenance of mail processing equipment during mail transportation, preparation, and sorting; safety practices; communications; work environment considerations; employee relations.
Credit recommendation: In the lower division baccalaureate/associate degree category, 1 semester hour in Personnel Administration or Supervision (3/79). NOTE: Credit should not be granted for both this course and Mail Processing Equipment Maintenance Supervisors MAS (10216-00).

Mail Processing for Managers MTS (52596)
Location: PEDC Centers.
Length: Self-study.
Dates: January 1976-Present.
Objective: To provide management training for incumbent mail processing managers.
Instruction: Mail processing operations emphasizing management reporting systems use in the daily operations of Mail Processing Centers; methods improvement and plant layout to improve mail flow, enhanced employee performance with respect to performance appraisal, disciplinary actions, and grievances; proper planning and control techniques for use in mechanized and manual mail processing operations.
Credit recommendation: In the lower division baccalaureate/associate degree category, 3 semester hours in Business Administration or Management (3/79). NOTE: Credit should not be granted for both this course and Mail Processing for Supervisors MTS (52595).

Mail Processing for Supervisors MTS (52595)
Location: PEDC Centers.
Length: Self-study.
Dates: January 1976-Present.
Objective: To provide management training for incumbent mail processing supervisors.
Instruction: Mail processing operations, emphasizing management reporting systems used in the daily operations of mail processing centers; methods improvement and plant layout to improve the flow of mail; enhanced employee performance with respect to performance appraisal, disciplinary actions, and grievances; proper planning control procedures for use in manual and mechanized mail processing operations.
Credit recommendation: In the lower division baccalaureate/associate degree category, 3 semester hours in Business Administration or Management (3/79). NOTE: Credit should not be granted for both this course and Mail Processing for Managers MTS (52596).

PEDC Managers MTS (21590)
Location: PEDC Centers.
Length: Self-study.
Dates: July 1978-Present.
Objective: To improve the performance of incumbent managers in the administration of training and development activities.
Instruction: Covers the concept and operation of the Postal Employee Development Center (PEDC), the roles and responsibilities of the PEDC manager-supervisor, planning and budgeting for employee training programs, employee development programs and considerations.
Credit recommendation: In the lower division baccalaureate/associate degree category, 2 semester hours in Personnel Administration or Supervision (3/79).

Retail Sales and Services Management MTS (42591)
Location: PEDC Centers.
Length: Self-study.
Dates: April 1977-Present.
Objective: To improve the performance of incumbent managers of retail sales and services activities.
Instruction: Cost reduction and control techniques; revenue generations; interaction between managers, subordinates, and customers; principles of retail sales management.
Credit recommendation: In the lower division baccalaureate/associate degree category or in the upper division baccalaureate category, 2 semester hours in Retail Management, Sales Management, or Supervision (3/79). NOTE: Credit should not be granted for both this course and Retail Sales and Services Management MAS (10274-10).

Window Services Management MTS (41590)
Location: PEDC Centers
Length: Self-study.
Dates: March 1978-Present.
Objective: To provide management training for incumbent window services supervisors.
Instruction: Covers postal products and services; retail programs; management of window service operations; scheduling, staffing, and supervision of the sales force.
Credit recommendation: In the lower division baccalaureate/associate degree category, 1 semester hour in Personnel Administration or Supervision (3/79). NOTE: Credit should not be granted for both this course and Window Service for Managers MAS (10273-00).

THE POSTAL EMPLOYEE DEVELOPMENT CENTERS

The PEDC network, begun in 1974, consists of approximately 176 Postal Employee Development Centers (PEDC) designed to provide training to a large population of geographically dispersed postal employees. The PEDC also offers training consultant and career guidance services to all Postal Service Employees.

The courses listed below are self-instructional. Students applying for credit must pass a proctored final examination, successful completion of which will be indicated on the student's record.

Accounting I (31591-00)
Location: Self-instruction; PEDC Centers.
Length: 60 hours programmed instruction and approximately 120 hours outside problem solving.
Dates: November 1976-Present.
Objective: To provide an understanding of basic accounting theory and practice, including the preparation of financial statements.
Instruction: Fundamentals of accounting theory, including use of journals and ledgers, preparation of financial statements, and accounting for job order and process systems.
Credit recommendation: In the lower division baccalaureate/associate degree category, 3 semester hours in Accounting (2/78) (4/84). NOTE: This course has undergone reevaluation and continues to meet the requirements for credit recommendations.

Accounting II (31592-00)
Location: Self-instruction; PEDC Centers.
Length: 60 hours programmed instruction and approximately 120 hours outside problem solving.
Dates: November 1976-Present.
Objective: To provide a further understanding of accounting principles and practices, including corporate accounting.
Instruction: A continuation of Accounting I, including notes and interest, voucher system, partnership equity, budgeting, income tax, and corporate accounting.
Credit recommendation: In the lower division baccalaureate/associate degree category, 3 semester hours in Accounting (2/78) (4/84). NOTE: This course has undergone reevaluation and continues to meet the requirements for credit recommendations.

Basic Industrial Electricity (56540-00)
Location: Self-instruction; PEDC Centers.
Length: Approximately 36 hours.
Dates: December 1975-Present.
Objective: To provide introductory training in the basic theory of operation of fundamental industrial electrical circuitry.
Instruction: Basic principles of electricity and magnetism; series and parallel circuits; secondary cells, meters; transistors; motors and motor control; circuit protective devices. Self-instruction is augmented with an electrical training device.
Credit recommendation: In the lower division baccalaureate/associate degree category, 1 semester hour in Industrial Arts, or in the vocational certificate category, 1 semester hour lecture and 1 semester hour laboratory in Basic Electricity (2/78).

Bulk Conveyor Systems (55501-00)
Location: Self-instruction; PEDC Centers.
Length: Approximately 36 hours.
Dates: October 1974-Present.
Objective: To give students a basic knowledge of the fundamentals and operating principles of bulk conveyors necessary for proper maintenance.
Instruction: Bulk conveyor maintenance functions, safety considerations, use of tools, conveyor components, belt adjustments and repairs, bearing installation, maintenance of motors and drive parts, electrical principles, motor control circuits.
Credit recommendation: In the lower division baccalaureate/associate degree category, 1 semester hour in Electromechanics, or in the vocational certificate category, 2 semester hours in Electromechanics (2/78) (4/84). NOTE: This course has undergone reevaluation and continues to meet the requirements for credit recommendations.

Digital Electronics I (56548-00)
Location: Self-instruction; PEDC Centers.
Length: Approximately 36 hours.
Dates: February 1974-April 1984.
Objective: To introduce the principles of digital electronics.
Instruction: Basics of numbering systems, including methods of conversion between systems; various coding schemes; circuit introduction to Boolean algebra; elements of digital electronics.
Credit recommendation: In the lower division baccalaureate/associate degree category, 1 semester hour in Digital Electronics (2/78).

Digital Electronics II (56549-00)
Location: Self-instruction; PEDC Centers.
Length: Approximately 64 hours.
Dates: January 1974-April 1984.
Objective: To provide a study of logic circuits through the application of logic principles.
Instruction: Principles of logic functions; gates; encoding, decoding, and basic flip-flop circuits.
Credit recommendation: In the lower division baccalaureate/associate degree category, 2 semester hours in Digital Electronics (2/78).

Electronics I (56517-00)
Location: Self-instruction; PEDC Centers.
Length: Approximately 40 hours.
Dates: April 1977-April 1984.
Objective: To provide a basic understanding of electrical and electronic circuits, measuring instruments and

components, and to develop basic skills in laboratory measurement techniques.

Instruction: Elements and concepts of electricity and electronics, including types and measurement of electrical components and values. Inductance, capacitance, and resistance circuitry; components and component value determination; electrical measurement utilizing the volt-ohm meter; and the oscilloscope.

Credit recommendation: In the lower division baccalaureate/associate degree category, 1 semester hour lecture and 1 semester hour laboratory in Industrial Arts, or in the vocational certificate category, 3 semester hours in Basic Electricity/Electronics (2/78).

Electronics II (56518-00)
Location: Self-instruction; PEDC Centers.
Length: Approximately 40 hours.
Dates: January 1978-April 1984.
Objective: To provide the basic knowledge and skills required to troubleshoot simple electronic equipment and to use necessary test equipment.
Instruction: Electronic operation and troubleshooting analysis of electronic equipment at the component level, integrated circuit level, and card level.
Credit recommendation: In the lower division baccalaureate/associate degree category, 1 semester hour lecture and 2 semester hours laboratory in Electronics (2/78) (4/84).

1. Introduction to Postal Management (11561-00)
2. Introduction to Postal Supervision (11161-00)
(Formerly:
  1. Introduction to Postal Management (11561-00)
  2. Introduction to Postal Management (11561-00)
     (Formerly 11961-00)
  3. Introduction to Postal Supervision (11161-00)
Location: *Version 1:* Course 1 and 3, Self-instruction; Course 2, Postal Employe Development Centers. *Version 2:* Course 1, Postal Employe Development Centers; Course 2, Correspondence.
Length: *Version 1:* Courses 1, 2, and 3 require a total of approximately 40 hours each. *Version 2:* Courses 1 and 2 require a total of approximately 40 hours each.
Dates: *Version 1:* February 1978-April 1984. *Version 2:* May 1984-Present.
Objective: *Versions 1 and 2:* To introduce supervisory personnel to the fundamentals of supervision.
Instruction: *Versions 1 and 2:* The role of the supervisor, tools of a manager, personnel management, applied principles of management, general management functions and responsibilities.
Credit recommendation: *Version 1.* Courses 1, 2, or 3: In the lower division baccalaureate/associate degree category, 1 semester hour in Business Administration (2/78). *Version 2.* Courses 1 and 2: In the lower division baccalaureate/associate degree category, 1 semester hour in Business Administration (4/84). NOTE: This course has undergone evaluation and continues to meet the requirements for credit recommendations.

TECHNICAL TRAINING DIVISION

Accident Investigation (55646-00)
(Formerly 10011-10 and 10211-00)
Location: Technical Center, Norman, OK.
Length: 120 hours (3 weeks); residential.
Dates: June 1977-Present.
Objective: To develop the investigative and reporting skill of newly assigned claims officers.
Instruction: Covers all aspects of accident investigation for both vehicle and nonvehicle accidents, preparation of accident reports, knowledge of the Federal Tort Claims Act, technical investigation skills, preparation of exhibits and data.
Credit recommendation: In the lower division baccalaureate/associate degree category, 3 semester hours in Industrial or Public Safety (12/77) (4/84). NOTE: This course has undergone reevaluation and continues to meet the requirements for credit recommendations.

Air Brakes (FMVSS121) (55619-00)
Location: Technical Center, Norman, OK.
Length: 80 hours (2 weeks); residential; 16 hours lecture/discussion and 24 hours laboratory/workshop per week.
Dates: October 1975-Present.
Objective: To develop skills and knowledge in troubleshooting and maintenance of basic air brakes systems and antiskid systems in conformance with Federal Motor Vehicle Service (DOT) Standard #121 for fleet vehicles.
Instruction: This course combines classroom theory and practical laboratory exercises on compressors, brake valves (single and dual), governors, treadle valve, brake chambers, spring brake chambers, relay valves, safety valves, control valves, modulator assemblies, fail-safe monitors, tractor and trailer ratio relay valves, wheel speed sensors, electronic systems, and service brakes used in heavy duty vehicles.
Credit recommendation: In the lower division baccalaureate/associate degree category or in the upper division baccalaureate category, 3 semester hours in Automotive Technology, Diesel Mechanics, Industrial Education, or Transportation Technology (9/77) (4/84). NOTE: This course has undergone reevaluation and continues to meet the requirements for credit recommendations.

Allison Automatic Transmissions (55620-00)
Location: Technical Center, Norman, OK.
Length: 80 hours (2 weeks); residential; 18 hours lecture/discussion and 22 hours laboratory/workshop per week.

Dates: January 1975-Present.

Objective: To develop understanding of the operation and overhaul procedures of Allison automatic transmissions.

Instruction: Torque converters, hydraulic pumps, valve bodies, circuits, planetary gears, powerflows, internal and external inspection, disassembly and reassembly, adjustment, diagnostic procedures.

Credit recommendation: In the upper division baccalaureate category, 2 semester hours in Automotive Technology, Diesel Mechanics, Heavy Equipment Operations, or Mechanical Technology (9/77) (4/84). NOTE: This course has undergone a reevaluation and continues to meet the requirements for credit recommendations.

Automatic Business Mail Process Systems (55657-00)
Location: Technical Center, Norman, OK.
Length: 336 hours (8½ weeks); residential; 16 hours lecture/discussion and 24 hours laboratory per week.
Dates: April 1975-Present.
Objective: To develop the knowledge and skills necessary for performing preventive maintenance, system fault isolation, and repair maintenance of the Automatic Business Mail Processing System.
Instruction: In-depth study of programming and hardware associated with the PDP8E computer, including Power Fail/Auto Restart (KP-8E), Positive I/O Business Interface (KA-8E), Extended Memory Controller (KM08E), High Speed Reader/Punch (PC-04), High Speed Reader/Punch Controller (PC-8E), Data Break Interface (KD-8E), Disk File (DF32DP), Postal and Data Systems Bar/Half-Bar Code Reader (CR3000), Fairchild LSM and Power Fail/Auto Restart (KP-8E), Computer Interface, UBM/SPLSM, ABMPS software, system troubleshooting, and system maintenance.
Credit recommendation: In the upper division baccalaureate category, 3 semester hours in Computer Systems Architecture and Peripheral Devices; *and* in the lower division baccalaureate/associate degree category or in the upper division baccalaureate category, 3 semester hours in Assembly Language (for a total of 6 semester hours) (9/77) (4/84). NOTE: This course has undergone a reevaluation and continues to meet the requirements for credit recommendations.

Automatic Transmission Overhaul (55627-00)
Location: Technical Center, Norman, OK.
Length: 80 hours (2 weeks); residential; 15 hours of lecture/discussion and 25 hours of laboratory/workshop per week.
Dates: October 1970-Present.
Objective: To develop student's understanding of automatic transmission overhaul procedures; to increase effectiveness, confidence, and skills in diagnosing, disassembling, inspecting, reassembling, and adjusting automatic transmissions and components.
Instruction: Operation and service of torque converters, hydraulic pumps, valve bodies, circuits, clutches, planetary gears, power flows; internal and external inspection, adjustment, and diagnosis procedures. Includes units of instruction and workshop experiences in use of special tools and equipment. Covers the Borg Warner M-11 and M-43, Ford C-4, GM Turbohydramatic 400, and Chrysler 727 and 904 transmissions.
Credit recommendation: In the lower division baccalaureate/associate degree category, 3 semester hours in Automotive Technology, Industrial Education, or Mechanical Technology (12/74) (3/81). NOTE: This course has undergone a 5-year reevaluation and continues to meet the requirements for credit recommendations.

Automotive Diesel Mechanics
(Postal Diesel [55639-00])
Location: Technical Center, Norman, OK.
Length: 120 hours (3 weeks); residential; 15 hours of lecture/discussion and 25 hours of laboratory/workshop per week.
Dates: July 1973-Present.
Objective: To enable students to become proficient in troubleshooting, diagnosing, servicing, and repairing components in systems described below, performing diesel engine tune-ups, using test equipment, and analyzing engine performance.
Instruction: This course includes classroom presentations and shop work experiences on diesel engine systems, including fuel, air induction, exhaust, cooling, lubricating, and engine clutch; tune-up procedures; use of analyzing equipment, including the pressure prover, nozzle pop tester, and diesel timing light; proper use of shop and parts manuals, vehicle record cards, technical bulletins, measuring devices, troubleshooting charts, and preventive maintenance schedules.
Credit recommendation: In the lower division baccalaureate/associate degree category or in the upper division baccalaureate category, 5 semester hours in Automotive Technology, Diesel Mechanics, Industrial Arts, Industrial Education, or Power Technology (12/74) (3/81). NOTE: The courses Automotive Diesel Mechanics, Caterpillar Diesel (55618-00), Cummins Diesel I (55617-01), and Cummins Diesel II (55617-02) have some overlap in course material. It is therefore recommended that a maximum of 6 credits be granted for completion of two or more of these courses. This course has undergone a 5-year reevaluation and continues to meet the requirements for credit recommendations.

Automotive Electrical Systems (55625-00)
Location: Technical Center, Norman, OK.
Length: 80 hours (2 weeks); residential; 15 hours of lecture/discussion and 25 hours of laboratory/workshop per week.
Dates: July 1970-Present.

Objective: To provide students with technical knowledge in the maintenance and repair of automotive electrical systems and in the use and care of automotive testing equipment, and to increase the students' proficiency in analyzing, diagnosing, and repairing various automotive electrical systems.

Instruction: Automotive electricity and the construction, repair, and adjustment of automotive electrical systems. Includes use of automotive test equipment; battery testing;and the troubleshooting and repair of starting, charging, ignition, lighting, and instrument systems.

Credit recommendation: In the lower division baccalaureate/associate degree category, 3 semester hours in Automotive Technology or Industrial Electrical Technology (12/74) (4/84). NOTE: This course has undergone a reevaluation and continues to meet the requirements for credit recommendations.

Automotive Mechanic Fundamentals (55622-00)
  Location: Technical Center, Norman, OK.
  Length: 80 hours (2 weeks); residential; 24 hours lecture/discussion and 16 hours laboratory/workshop per week.
  Dates: January 1970-Present.
  Objective: To develop a basic understanding of the major components and systems of motor vehicles; and of the care and use of shop equipment, hand tools, diagnostic equipment, special tools, and preventive maintenance techniques. To provide a broad foundation for continued education in the automotive field.
  Instruction: Covers the basics of automotive mechanics, including shop safety, shop equipment, tire examination and maintenance, brake and suspension systems, engine operation, cooling and fuel systems, automotive electrical circuits (cranking, charging, ignition, instruments), and the testing of electrical circuits. Includes familiarization with clutches, transmissions (manual and automatic), drive lines, and rear axles.
  Credit recommendation: In the lower division baccalaureate/associate degree category, 3 semester hours in Automotive Technology, Industrial Education, or Transportation Technology (9/77) (4/84). NOTE: This course has undergone a reevaluation and continues to meet the requirements for credit recommendations.

Basic Conveyors and Controls (55666-00)
  Location: USPS Technical Training Center, Norman, OK.
  Length: 116 hours (3 weeks).
  Dates: September 1985-Present.
  Objective: To develop the ability to operate and maintain programmable controlled conveyor systems.
  Instruction: Course includes the basic understanding of the operation of programmable controllers; the interpretation of ladder logic diagrams; the installation and troubleshooting of conveyor systems, using such test instruments as: DUM's, P.C. LED indicators and CRT Programming. In addition, principles of basic fluid power, and electromechanical assemblies associated with large belt conveying systems are taught.
  Credit recommendation: In the lower baccalaureate/associate degree category, 2 semester hours in Electromechanical Systems Technology, and 1 semester hour in Programmable Controllers, or in the vocational certificate category, 4 semester hours in Electromechanical Troubleshooting (6/86).

Basic Process Control System (55670-10)
  Location: Technical Center, Norman, OK.
  Length: 480 hours (12 weeks).
  Dates: January 1981-Present.
  Objective: To prepare qualified personnel to interact with a computer and its peripherals; and to program in assembly language, use diagnostic routines, and repair peripheral equipment.
  Instruction: Introduction to computers with assembly language programming, computer architecture, and peripherals. Course covers flow charting, developing logic commands, machine language programming, and use of an editor-assembler in program development. Disk systems, magnetic tape systems, and line printers are covered. Lecture, discussion, and laboratory are used.
  Credit recommendation: In the upper division baccalaureate category, 3 semester hours in Introduction to Computers, and in the lower division baccalaureate/associate degree category, 3 semester hours in Computer Circuit Diagnostics and Repair or Electromechanical Technology (3/81).

BMC Mail Processing Mechanics (55671-00)
  Location: Technical Center, Norman, OK.
  Length: *Version 1:* 160 hours (4 weeks); residential; 24 hours lecture and 16 hours laboratory per week. *Version 2:* 200 hours (5 weeks).
  Dates: *Version 1:* January 1976-August 1982. *Version 2:* September 1982-Present.
  Objective: This course is to provide trainees with the abilities to operate, troubleshoot, adjust, and repair mechanical, electrical, electromechanical, and electronic equipment. The equipment consists of conveyors, motors, reducers, relay logic, integrated circuit logic, and pneumatic and hydraulic systems.
  Instruction: Basic and complex mechanical mechanisms; drive configurations; conveyor components; analysis and troubleshooting of electrical control systems; basic and complex mechanical, pneumatic, and electrical assemblies of sortation equipment, including drive assemblies, conveying assemblies, motors and motor controls, as well as the associated digital electronic control systems.
  Credit recommendation: In the upper division baccalaureate category, 6 semester hours in Electromechanical Technology (9/77) (4/84). NOTE: (8/82: This course

was changed to a 5-week course. The change was such as not to affect the course description or credit recommendation.) This course has undergone reevaluation and continues to meet the requirements for credit recommendations.

BMC Building Equipment Mechanic (55672-00)
   Location: Technical Center, Norman, OK.
   Length: 160 hours (4 weeks); residential; 20 hours lecture and 20 hours laboratory per week.
   Dates: March 1976-August 1980.
   Objective: To provide an understanding of air conditioning and heating systems utilized in large installations and develop skills in operating and performing preventive and repair maintenance on air conditioning and heating equipment.
   Instruction: Operation and maintenance of basic heating, ventilating and air conditioning systems, including hot water heating systems, direct expansion and chilled water systems, centrifugal compressors, automatic controls, and central automated building monitoring systems.
   Credit recommendation: In the upper division baccalaureate category, 6 semester hours in Building and Construction Management, Building Maintenance, Building Operations Management, or Electromechanical Technology (9/77).

Brakes and Suspension Systems (55623-00)
   Location: Technical Center, Norman, OK.
   Length: 80 hours (2 weeks); residential; 20 hours lecture/discussion and 20 hours laboratory/workshop per week.
   Dates: January 1974-Present.
   Objective: To develop skills and knowledge in troubleshooting and maintaining hydraulic brake systems, drum and disc, and their components; to provide an understanding of front end suspension components and geometry.
   Instruction: Shop safety, front suspension systems, wheel alignment, steering gears, wheel bearings, steering linkage, wheel balancing, springs, and attaching parts, sway control mechanisms, single and dual master cylinders, pressure differential switches, drum and caliper components, metering valves, proportional valves, brake hoses and lines, brake drums, rotors.
   Credit recommendation: In the lower division baccalaureate/associate degree category, 3 semester hours in Automotive Technology, Industrial Education, or Transportation Technology (9/77) (4/84). NOTE: This course has undergone reevaluation and continues to meet the requirements for credit recommendations.

Caterpillar Diesel (55618-00)
   Location: Technical Center, Norman, OK.
   Length: 120 hours (3 weeks); residential; 15 hours lecture and 25 hours laboratory/workshop per week.
   Dates: July 1975-Present.
   Objective: To provide an understanding of the principles of operation of the 1150 and 3208 Series Caterpillar diesel engines. To develop skill in troubleshooting, diagnosing, servicing, repairing components; performing tune-ups; and using test equipment.
   Instruction: Covers the following diesel systems: fuel, air induction, exhaust, cooling, and lubricating. Also covers tune-up procedures, use of analyzing equipment for fuel systems, troubleshooting charts, use of manuals and bulletins, and use of measuring devices.
   Credit recommendation: In the lower division baccalaureate/associate degree category or in the upper division baccalaureate category, 4 semester hours in Automotive Technology, Diesel Mechanics, Industrial Arts, Industrial Education, or Power Technology (9/77) (4/84). NOTE: The courses Automotive Diesel Mechanics, Caterpillar Diesel (55618-00), Cummins Diesel I (55617-01), and Cummins Diesel II (55617-02) have some overlap in course material. It is therefore recommended that a maximum of 6 credits be granted for completion of two or more of these courses. This course has undergone reevaluation and continues to meet the requirements for credit recommendations.

Computer Forwarding System Maintenance (55669-03)
   Location: USPS Technical Training Center, Norman, OK.
   Length: 152 hours (4 weeks).
   Dates: June 1985-Present.
   Objective: To provide the knowledge, skills, and abilities to accomplish electronic, electrical, and electromechanical repairs to a microcomputer, dual floppy disk drives, printer, and CRT display.
   Learning Outcome: Upon successful completion of this course, the student is able to diagnose and repair internal and interactive faults in and between the computer subsystems. This includes powering-up, operating the system, performing preventive maintenance, alignments and adjustments, and board/assembly replacement of faulty components.
   Instruction: Covers electromechanical and electrical adjustments, digital electronic circuitry and concepts pertinent to the Computer Forwarding System. Emphasizes use of diagnostic routines for fault isolation to the printed circuit board level and use of common test equipment to locate faults to the major component level.
   Credit recommendation: In the lower division baccalaureate/associate degree category, 3 semester hours in Digital Computer Systems Troubleshooting (6/86).

Consolidated MPLSM Training (55658-10)
   Location: USPS Technical Training Center, Norman, OK.
   Length: 92 hours (2 weeks, 1½ days).
   Dates: March 1983-January 1986.
   Objective: To teach maintenance personnel to troubleshoot and repair the various models of the Multi-Position

Letter Sorting Machine.

Learning Outcome: The course produces maintenance and repair people for the MPLSM.

Instruction: The course covers safety and the operation, documentation, preventive maintenance, and repair of several models of the MPLSM. Approximately half the time is spent in class and half on demonstration and laboratory experience.

Credit recommendation: In the vocational certificate category, 3 semester hours in Electromechanical Troubleshooting Procedures (6/86).

Cummins Diesel I (55617-01)

Location: Technical Center, Norman, OK.

Length: 80 hours (2 weeks); residential; 15 hours lecture and 25 hours laboratory/workshop per week.

Dates: June 1976-May 1980.

Objective: To provide an understanding of the principles of operation of the NTC 230 PT Model Cummins diesel engine. To develop skill in troubleshooting, diagnosing, servicing, repairing components; performing tune-ups; and using test equipment.

Instruction: Covers the following diesel systems: fuel, air induction, exhaust, cooling, and lubricating. Also covers tune-up procedures, use of analyzing equipment for fuel systems, and troubleshooting charts. (Prerequisite: Automotive Diesel Mechanics or Caterpillar Diesel [55618-00].)

Credit recommendation: In the lower division baccalaureate/associate degree category or in the upper division baccalaureate category, 3 semester hours in Automotive Technology, Diesel Mechanics, Industrial Arts, Industrial Education, or Power Technology (9/77) NOTE: The courses Automotive Diesel Mechanics, Caterpillar Diesel (55618-00), Cummins Diesel I (55617-01), and Cummins Diesel II (55617-02) have some overlap in course material. It is therefore recommended that a maximum of 6 credits be granted for completion of two or more of these courses.

Cummins Diesel III (55617-03)
(Formerly Cummins Diesel II (55617-02)

Location: Technical Center, Norman, OK.

Length: 120 hours (3 weeks); residential; 15 hours lecture and 25 hours laboratory/workshop per week.

Dates: *Version 1:* January 1977-March 1983 for Cummins Diesel II. *Version 2:* April 1983-Present for Cummins Diesel III.

Objective: To provide an understanding of the principles of operation of the NTC 230 PT Model Cummins diesel engine. To develop skill in troubleshooting, diagnosing, servicing, repairing components; performing tune-ups; and using test equipment.

Instruction: Covers the following diesel systems; fuel, air induction, exhaust cooling, and lubricating. Also covers tune-up procedures, use of analyzing equipment for fuel systems, troubleshooting charts, use of manuals and bulletins, and use of measuring devices.

Credit recommendation: In the lower division baccalaureate/associate degree category or in the upper division baccalaureate category, 4 semester hours in Automotive Technology, Diesel Mechanics, Industrial Arts, Industrial Education, or Power Technology (9/77) (4/84). NOTE: The courses Automotive Diesel Mechanics, Caterpillar Diesel (55618-00), Cummins Diesel I (55617-01), and Cummins Diesel II (55617-02) have some overlap in course material. It is therefore recommended that a maximum of 6 credits be granted for completion of two or more of these courses. This course has undergone reevaluation and continues to meet the requirements for credit recommendations. (The Cummins Diesel II course was discontinued in 1983 and replaced with the Cummins Diesel III course. The change was made because of an equipment change. This change does not affect the course description or credit recommendation.)

Customer Service and Postal Machines (55603-01)

Location: Technical Center, Norman, OK.

Length: 52 hours (1½ weeks); residential; 20 hours lecture and 32 hours laboratory/workshop.

Dates: June 1977-Present.

Objective: To develop skill in preventive maintenance, troubleshooting, analysis, and repair maintenance of postage meters.

Instruction: Troubleshooting, preventive maintenance, and repair maintenance of the Pitney Bowes Meter Machine Bases 4000 Series (R Line), and 5400 Series, Friden Meter Machine Base Model 9010, and Model 14-75 Data Recorder.

Credit recommendation: In the vocational certificate category, 1 semester hour in Mechanical Devices (9/77) (4/84). NOTE: This course has undergone reevaluation and continues to meet the requirements for credit recommendations.

Customer Vending Machines (55610-01)

Location: Technical Center, Norman, OK.

Length: 68 hours (1½ weeks); residential; 34 hours lecture and 34 hours laboratory/workshop.

Dates: July 1977-May 1982.

Objective: To develop skill in reading schematics, understanding nomenclature, and disassembly and assembly of electromechanical vending equipment.

Instruction: Use of manuals, in-line drawings, schematics, and test equipment to troubleshoot, repair, and make periodic preventive maintenance checks on vending equipment.

Credit recommendation: In the lower division baccalaureate/associate degree category, 2 semester hours in Electromechanical Technology (9/77).

Digital Computer Concepts (DCC 55699-05)
Location: USPS Technical Training Center, Norman, OK.
Length: 108 hours.
Dates: September 1985-Present.
Objective: This course enables the student to acquire basic computer concepts, including the applications of various peripheral devices.
Instruction: A lecture-lab oriented course that covers subjects such as Safety; Introduction to Computer Systems, Introduction to System Software; Introduction to System Hardware; Functional Analysis of System Operations; and Multi-User Operations, such as Commands, Media Handling and Media Installation, File Protections Schemes; Diagnostic Operating System and Computer Maintenance.
Credit recommendation: In the lower division baccalaureate/associate degree category, 2 semester hours in Computer Maintenance (6/86).

Digital Computer Systems Conversion (55699-02)
Location: USPS Technical Training Center, Norman, OK.
Length: 80 hours (10 days).
Dates: January 1986-Present.
Objective: To teach the basic skills and knowledge of computers to enable the student to attend more advanced specific computer equipment courses.
Learning Outcome: Upon successful completion of this course, the student will know basic digital computer theory and the application of equipment, firmware, and software. The concepts of maintenance and repair are stressed.
Instruction: Generic computer training that includes system operation, block diagram, programming, port location, diagnostics, preventive maintenance, and corrective maintenance. The course is half classroom work, and half laboratory.
Credit recommendation: In the vocational certificate category, 2 semester hours in Basic Computer Theory (6/86).

Digital Computer Technology (55694-00)
Location: Technical Center, Norman, OK.
Length: *Version 1:* 240 hours (6 weeks); residential; 24 hours of lecture/discussion and 16 hours of laboratory/workshop per week. *Version 2:* 320 hours (8 weeks).
Dates: *Version 1:* July 1972-July 1975; *Version 2:* July 1975-Present.
Objective: To provide programming knowledge needed to train on sophisticated digital computerized systems; to provide in-depth knowledge of the theory, operation, troubleshooting, maintenance, and repair of the PDP-8 digital computer; to familiarize the student with associate peripheral devices commonly used to communicate with high-speed computers.
Instruction: This course is designed to provide the trainee with the knowledge and skill required to proficiently and effectively repair the PDP-8 digital computer, and to familiarize the trainee with the peripheral equipment commonly associated with high-speed computers. The hardware portion of the course covers systems description, instruction set utilization, logic diagram analysis of the central processor, memory operation, programmed interrupt, data break, I-O transfer logic, and related peripheral devices. Technical maintenance includes theory of operation and practical hands-on troubleshooting exercises in the laboratory.
Credit recommendation: *Versions 1 and 2:* In the lower division baccalaureate/associate degree category, 3 semester hours in Computer Programming and 3 semester hours in Computer Technology or Electromechanical Technology (12/74) (3/81). NOTE: This course has undergone a 5-year reevaluation and continues to meet the requirements for credit recommendations.

Digital Electronics
(Advanced Digital Applications [55698-00])
Location: Technical Center, Norman, OK.
Length: 120 hours (3 weeks); residential; 20 hours lecture/discussion and 20 hours laboratory per week.
Dates: September 1975-Present.
Objective: To provide students with the basic concepts of digital circuit analysis, troubleshooting techniques, and the knowledge to prepare them to take courses associated with digital equipment maintenance at the electronic technical level.
Instruction: Applications and circuit configurations of registers, counters, multiplexers, converters (A/D, D/A), delay lines, and multivibrators. Includes instruction on the use of logic probes and oscilloscopes to troubleshoot IC circuits. The concepts of core and solid state memory circuits are an integral part of the program.
Credit recommendation: In the lower division baccalaureate/associate degree category, 3 semester hours in Digital Electronics (9/77) (4/84). NOTE: This course has undergone reevaluation and continues to meet the requirements for credit recommendations.

M36/M500B Direct Feed Facer Canceler System (55654-01)
Location: USPS Technical Training Center, Norman, OK.
Length: 114 hours (4 weeks).
Dates: January 1981-Present.
Objective: To teach maintenance mechanics to maintain, troubleshoot, and repair the Direct Feed Facer Canceler System.
Learning Outcome: Upon successful completion of this course, the student will be able to recognize system malfunctions and do adjustment/alignment replacement as necessary to restore the equipment to operating condition.

Instruction: Course covers safety, operator and maintenance documentation, theory of operation, power distribution, motor control, and jam/fault circuitry.

Credit recommendation: In the lower division baccalaureate/associate degree category, 2 semester hours in Electromechanical Troubleshooting (6/86).

Electric Vehicle (DJ5E) (55629-00)

Location: Technical Center, Norman, OK.

Length: 140 hours (3 weeks); residential; 15 hours lecture and 25 hours laboratory/workshop per week.

Dates: March 1977-May 1982.

Objective: To develop the knowledge and skills necessary to achieve proficiency in diagnostic troubleshooting, preventive maintenance, use of applicable test equipment, removal and replacement of defective components, and calibration of printed circuit boards on the Gould Electric Vehicle Propulsion System.

Instruction: Principles of operation and the technical knowledge required to perform preventive and repair maintenance of Gould Electric Powered Vehicle; electrical and electronic theory; use of test equipment, including the oscilloscope and D.V.M. schemataic interpretation and laboratory exercises on the electrical/electronic propulsion system.

Credit recommendation: In the lower division baccalaureate/associate degree category, 2 semester hours in Automotive Technology, Industrial Education, or Transportation Technology (9/77).

Electrical Power Mechanic (EPM) (55677-00)

Location: Technical Center, Norman, OK.

Length: 160 hours (4 weeks); residential; 20 hours lecture/discussion and 20 hours laboratory per week.

Dates: April 1976-December 1985.

Objective: To provide a theoretical and practical background in basic electricity.

Instruction: Basic principles of electricity; electrical power distribution; motors and motor controls; solid state devices and control circuits; electrical diagrams; instruments; troubleshooting techniques; familiarization with and utilization of basic electronic laboratory equipment.

Credit recommendation: In the lower division baccalaureate/associate category, 3 semester hours in Basic Electricity and 1 semester hour in Basic Electronic Laboratory (9/77).

Electronic Sort Processor (ESP) (55659-05) (Formerly [55659-00; 55659-01])

Location: Technical Center, Norman, OK.

Length: 280 hours (7 weeks).

Dates: April 1976-Present.

Objective: To enable maintenance personnel to perform preventive maintenance, troubleshooting analysis, and repair maintenance required to maintain the Electronic Sort Processor.

Instruction: Detailed principles of operations; circuit analysis; diagnosis, analysis, and correction of electronic faults within the Electronic Sort Processor system and associated interface module and the peripheral control board; system adjustment and alignment and associated procedures; use of operation and maintenance manuals. Requires previous formal training on electromechanical systems, logic systems, and advanced digital applications.

Credit recommendation: In the lower division baccalaureate/associate degree category, 3 semester hours as a technical elective in Electronics; or in the upper division baccalaureate category, 2 semester hours as a technical elective in Electronics (9/77) (4/84). NOTE: This course has undergone reevaluation and continues to meet the requirements for credit recommendations.

Engine Tune-up and Air Pollution Control Devices (55624-00)

Location: Technical Center, Norman, OK.

Length: 80 hours (2 weeks); residential; 15 hours of lecture/discussion and 25 hours of laboratory/workshop per week.

Dates: August 1973-Present.

Objective: To provide students with an understanding of automotive air pollution control; to train them to maintain motor vehicles equipped with air pollution control devices; to develop the students' skill in preventive maintenance and engine tune-up, use of engine analyzing and tune-up equipment, analyzing engine performance, and testing and servicing air pollution control devices.

Instruction: Vehicle air pollution terminology; compression; ignition; carburetion; tune-up procedures; use of analyzing equipment, including the oscilloscope; inspection, testing, and servicing of air pollution control devices in current use.

Credit recommendation: In the lower division baccalaureate/associate degree category, 3 semester hours in Automotive Technology, Industrial Arts, or Industrial Education (12/74) (3/81). NOTE: This course has undergone a 5-year reevaluation and continues to meet the requirements for credit recommendations.

Environmental Control I (55686-00)

Location: Technical Center, Norman, OK.

Length: 80 hours (2 weeks); residential; 20 hours lecture and 20 hours laboratory/workshop per week.

Dates: February 1970-Present.

Objective: To provide a basic understanding of air conditioning and heating systems used in commercial buildings; to develop skills in operating and performing preventive and repair maintenance on air conditioning and heating equipment.

Instruction: Operation and maintenance of forced-air systems, direct-fired heating systems, natural-draft low-pressure hot water and steam boilers, direct-expansion systems (including all reciprocating compressors), and controls for small/medium systems. Special emphasis is placed on energy conservation and safety.

Credit recommendation: In the lower division baccalaureate/associate category, 3 semester hours in Building and Construction Management, Building Maintenance, or Building Operations Management (9/77) (4/84). NOTE: This course has undergone reevaluation and continues to meet the requirements for credit recommendations.

Environmental Control II (55689-00)
  Location: Technical Center, Norman, OK.
  Length: 160 hours (4 weeks); residential; 20 hours lecture and 20 hours laboratory per week.
  Dates: July 1971-Present.
  Objective: To develop the technician's ability to operate, maintain, troubleshoot, and repair large capacity, year-round environmental control systems and to acquaint the technician with the tools and procedures used to calibrate, test, and adjust HVAC equipment and systems.
  Instruction: Operation and maintenance of large HVAC systems, including mechanical draft low and high pressure steam and hot water boilers, fuels, combustion, burners, boiler controls, pumps, hot water and steam distribution systems, air handlers, air distribution, water and air balancing, centrifugal water chillers, controls for large tonnage condensing units, and system controls. System controls include maintenance and calibration of electric, pneumatic, and electronic control equipment of the major manufacturers. Control system components are thermostats, relays, transducers, masters and submasters, single and dual input controlllers, discriminators, amplifiers, and actuators. Coverage also includes total control system functions and sequence of operation of the year-round environmental control systems with use of central control units.
  Credit recommendation: In the upper division baccalaureate category, 6 semester hours in Building and Construction Management, Building Maintenance, Building Operations Management, or Electromechanical Technology (9/77) (4/84). NOTE: This course has undergone reevaluation and continues to meet the requirements for credit recommendations.

Environmental Control III (HVAC Heating) (55689-05)
  Location: Technical Center, Norman, OK.
  Length: 36 hours (1 week).
  Dates: September 1980-Present.
  Objective: To develop students' ability to operate, provide preventive maintenance of, troubleshoot, and perform inspection procedure on heating equipment.
  Instruction: Operation, maintenance, and troubleshooting of heating systems, including steam and hot water tube boilers, cast iron boilers, natural gas or oil fired burners, float controls, combustion control, air handling units, pumps, air separators, strainers, valves, air balancing, expansion tanks, steam traps, and condensate pumps. Lecture, discussion, and laboratory are used.
  Credit recommendation: In the lower division baccalaureate/associate degree category, 1 semester hour in Environmental Control Technology (3/81).

Environmental Control IV (Advanced Air Conditioning) (55689-06)
  Location: Technical Center, Norman, OK.
  Length: 38 hours/week (3 weeks).
  Dates: October 1980-Present.
  Objective: To train students to perform preventive maintenance, troubleshooting, and minor repairs on large-capacity refrigeration equipment for air conditioning and acquaint them with the tools, procedures, and techniques for full service of large air conditioning systems.
  Instruction: Course covers troubleshooting and minor repair of large-tonnage refrigeration equipment. Repair of reciprocating compressors is emphasized. Control system maintenance and maintenance of cooling towers is also covered. Lecture and laboratory are used.
  Credit recommendation: In the lower division baccalaureate/associate degree category, 2 semester hours in Air Conditioning, Environmental Technology, or Refrigeration (3/81).

Environmental Control V (HVAC and Energy Conservation Analysis) (55689-07)
  Location: Technical Center, Norman, OK.
  Length: 36 hours (1 week).
  Dates: November 1980-Present.
  Objective: To provide training in the operation of HVAC equipment so that energy costs are kept to a minimum and the equipment is properly maintained.
  Instruction: Course covers heating and cooling load calculations; psychometric procedures for energy conservation; use of central control systems; interrelationships of the chiller, tower, pumps, air handling units, controls, boiler, and auxiliary equipment, and the interdependency of units. Total system troubleshooting. Lecture, discussion, and laboratory are used.
  Credit recommendation: In the lower division baccalaureate/associate degree category, 1 semester hour in Environmental Control Technology (3/81).

Fundamentals of Automatic Transmissions (55626-00)
  Location: Technical Center, Norman, OK.
  Length: 40 hours (1 week); residential; 24 hours lecture/discussion and 16 hours laboratory/workshop.
  Dates: March 1971-Present.
  Objective: To provide an understanding of power flows and the maintenance and adjustment of automatic transmissions.
  Instruction: Principles of operation and functions of transmission components; familiarization with parts; use

of special tools; use of technical manuals; adjustments and scheduled maintenance.

Credit recommendation: In the lower division baccalaureate/associate degree category, 1 semester hour in Automotive Technology, Industrial Education, or Mechanical Technology (9/77) (4/84). NOTE: This course has undergone reevaluation and continues to meet the requirements for credit recommendations.

Industrial Electrical Services (55687-00)
Location: Technical Center, Norman, OK.
Length: 120 hours (3 weeks); residential; 20 hours lecture/discussion and 20 hours laboratory per week.
Dates: January 1972-Present.
Objective: To provide the student with theoretical and practical knowledge of electricity and standard electrical circuits, and the basic skills of electrical wiring in a power distribution system.
Instruction: Principles of electricity, magnetism, direct current, alternating current, motors, generators, transformers, electrical power distribution, motor controls, equipment wiring, electrical lighting, and repair and preventive maintenance of a complete electrical system.
Credit recommendation: In the lower division baccalaureate/associate degree category, 1 semester hour in Industrial Electronics and 2 semester hours in Power Distribution Technology (9/77) (4/84). NOTE: This course has undergone reevaluation and continues to meet the requirements for credit recommendations.

Logic Circuits
(Digital Electronics [55693-00])
Location: Technical Center, Norman, OK.
Length: 160 hours (4 weeks); residential; 30 hours lecture/discussion and 10 hours laboratory/workshop per week.
Dates: July 1970-September 1975.
Objective: To provide students with a background in digital logic in order to prepare them for advanced training on sophisticated digital electronics equipment.
Instruction: Utilizing both theory and equipment hardware, covers the basic principles of number systems, Boolean algebra, and logic circuits such as gates, encoders, decoders, flip-flops, shift registers, and various counters found in sophisticated digital equipment.
Credit recommendation: In the lower division baccalaureate/associate degree category, 4 semester hours in Computer Systems, Electronics, or Optical Data Processing (12/74) (3/81). NOTE: This course has undergone a 5-year reevaluation and continues to meet the requirements for credit recommendations.

Mark II Facer-Canceler and Feeder Machine (55653-00)
Location: Technical Center, Norman, OK.
Length: 160 hours (4 weeks); residential; 25 hours of lecture/discussion and 15 hours of laboratory/workshop per week.
Dates: July 1969-October 1983.
Objective: To train maintenance personnel to maintain, troubleshoot, and repair facer-canceler and feeder systems.
Instruction: Component assembly identification, location, and function; repair and parts replacement; troubleshooting analysis techniques; adjustment, alignment, and preventive maintenance of an electromechanical system. Utilizes appropriate technical manuals and data, diagnostic test equipment (oscilloscopes, volt-ohm meters, etc.), and regular and special tools.
Credit recommendation: In the lower division baccalaureate/associate degree category, 3 semester hours in Electromechanical Technology or Mechanical Technology (12/74).

Microprocessor-Controlled Mark II Facer Canceler System (55653-08)
(Formerly [55653-05])
Location: USPS Technical Training Center, Norman, OK.
Length: 60 hours (8 days).
Dates: January 1983-Present.
Objective: To train maintenance mechanics to troubleshoot and repair the Microprocessor-Controlled Mark II Facer Canceler System.
Learning Outcome: Upon successful completion of this course, the maintenance mechanic is able to do routine maintenance, troubleshoot, and repair the Microprocessor-Controlled Mark II Facer Canceler System.
Instruction: Provides instruction on the facer canceler operation consisting of these major blocks: (1) familiarization, documentation and operation, (2) the equipment power distribution and motor control, (3) machine indicia recogniition gating and canceling functions. Routine preventive maintenance is stressed throughout the course.
Credit recommendation: In the vocational certificate category, 2 semester hours in Electromechanical Troubleshooting (6/86).

Model 120/121 MPLSM/ZMT On-Site Maintenance Certification (OSMC) Program (55655-02)
Location: Each postal facility maintaining Model 120/121 MPLSM/ZMT equipment.
Length: 85 hours (8½ weeks); five 2-hour sessions per week.
Dates: August 1970-Present.
Objective: To provide supplemental and supportive training for students who have completed related, prerequisite training and bring them to an adequate level of proficiency in the repair and maintenance of Multi-Position Letter-Sorter/Zip-Mail Translator Systems.
Instruction: Detailed circuit analysis of all circuits in the ZMT; detailed troubleshooting techniques and

peculiarities of equipment. Also includes some theory of operation and minor maintenance of peripheral equipment: Model 33 AST Teletype, Mohawk Data Sciences Digital Printer Series 800, EDIT, Sorensen and Lambda power supplies, and the Sequential-Chordal Trainer Console. (Prerequisite: Zip-Mail Translator [55655-01] resident training.)

Credit recommendation: In the lower division baccalaureate/associate degree category, 1 semester hour in Electromechanical Laboratory and 1 semester hour in Electronic Troubleshooting Laboratory (9/77) (4/84). NOTE: Credit should not be granted for both this course and Model 140/141 MPLSM OSMC Program, Category I (55658-05) or Model 140/141 MPLSM OSMC Program, Category II (55659-02). This course has undergone reevaluation and continues to meet the requirements for credit recommendations.

Model 140/141 Multi-Position Letter-Sorter Machine (MPLSM) (55658-01)

Location: Technical Center, Norman, OK.
Length: 80 hours (2 weeks); residential; 20 hours lecture/discussion and 20 hours laboratory per week.
Dates: January 1977-March 1983.
Objective: To train maintenance personnel to troubleshoot, repair, and perform normal preventive maintenance on the multi-position letter-sorter machine.
Instruction: Operating principles; component assembly identification, location, and function; alignment and adjustment procedures; repair and parts replacement; analysis, diagnosis, and correction of electrical and mechanical equipment malfunctions; preventive maintenance practices.
Credit recommendation: In the lower division baccalaureate/associate degree category, 3 semester hours in Electromechanical Technology (9/77). NOTE: This course is made up of a two-week session from Model 140/141 MPLSM/ZMT/ESP (55658-00) which is sometimes taken independently.

Model 140/141 MPLSM On-Site Maintenance Certification (OSMC) Program, Category I (55658-05)

Location: Each postal facility maintaining Model 140/141 MPLSM/ZMT equipment.
Length: 190 hours (19 weeks); consisting of 22 programmed modules.
Dates: November 1976-Present.
Objective: To train maintenance personnel to perform preventive maintenance, exercise diagnostic Fault Isolation Techniques, and perform corrective maintenance on the Model 140/141 Multi-Position Letter-Sorting System within minimum time frames.
Instruction: This course includes detailed training in the principles and theory of operation for the 140/141 Multi-Position Letter-Sorter, the Zip-Mail Translator, and the Electronic Sort Processor. Detailed circuit analysis, alignment procedures, and corrective maintenance techniques are included for each subassembly of the system. Electronic "Model" concepts are covered as they related to the 140/141 system. All interfacing and control functions between the Letter Sorter, the ZMT, and ESP are taught in detail. Additional training in the principles and theory of operation of keyboards, teletypes, and associate electrical circuitry.
Credit recommendation: In the lower division baccalaureate/associate degree category, 1 semester hour in Electromechanical Laboratory and 1 semester hour in Electronic Troubleshooting Laboratory (9/77) (4/84). NOTE: Credit should not be granted for Elecromechanical Laboratory for both this course and Model 140/141 MPLSM OSMC Program, Category II (55659-02). Also, credit should not be granted for both this course and Model 120/121 MPLSM/ZMT OSMC Program (55655-02). This course has undergone reevaluation and continues to meet the requirements for credit recommendations.

Model 140/141 MPLSM On-Site Maintenance Certification (OSMC) Program, Category II (55659-02)

Location: Each postal facility maintaining Model 140/141 MPLSM/ZMT equipment.
Length: 140 hours (14 weeks); consisting of 12 programmed modules.
Dates: November 1976-Present.
Objective: To train maintenance personnel to perform preventive maintenance, exercise diagnostic fault isolation techniques, and perform corrective maintenance on the Model 140/141 letter-sorting system within minimal time frames.
Instruction: This course includes detailed training in the practical application and theory of operation for the 140/141 Multi-Position Letter-Sorter, the Zip-Mail Translator, and the Electronic Sort Processor. Detailed circuit analysis, alignment procedures, and corrective maintenance techniques are included for each subassembly of the system. Electronic "Model" concepts are covered as they relate to the 140/141 system. All interfacing and control functions between the Letter Sorter, the ZMT, and the ESP are taught in detail.
Credit recommendation: In the lower division baccalaureate/associate degree category, 1 semester hour in Electromechanical Laboratory (9/77) (4/84). NOTE: Credit should not be granted for Electromechanical Laboratory for both this course and Model 140/141 MPLSM OSMC Program, Category I (55658-05) or Model 120/121 MPLSM/ZMT OSMC Program (55655-02). Credit may be granted for this course and the Electronic Troubleshooting Laboratory portion of 55655-02. This course has undergone reevaluation and continues to meet the requirements for credit recommendations.

Model 140/141 MPLSM/ZMT/ESP (55658-00)

Location: Technical Center, Norman, OK.

Length: 600 hours (15 weeks).
Dates: January 1977-Present.
Objective: To train maintenance personnel to perform preventive and corrective maintenance, and exercise diagnostic fault isolation techniques on the Model 140/141 letter-sorting system (including the Multi-Position Letter-Sorter Machine, Zip-Mail Translator, Electronic Sort Processor).
Instruction: Refer to instruction sections of Multi-Position Letter-Sorter Machine (55651-00), Zip-Mail Translator (55655-01), and Electronic Sort Processor (55659-00).
Credit recommendation: In the lower division baccalaureate/associate degree category, 3 semester hours in Computer Maintenance Technology, and 3 semester hours in Electromechanical Technology, and either 3 semester hours as a technical elective in Electronics in the lower division baccalaureate/associate degree category or 2 semester hours as a technical elective in Electronics in the upper division baccalaureate category (for a total of 9 or 8 semester hours) (9/77) (4/84). NOTE: If credit is granted for one or more of the courses cited in the Instruction section, the credit granted for this course should be reduced accordingly. If all the courses cited above are taken, no credit should be granted for this course. This course is also given as an eleven-week course for students who have completed Model 140/141 Multi-Position Letter-Sorter Machine (55658-01).

Multi-Position Letter-Sorter Machine (MPLSM) (55651-00)
Location: Technical Center, Norman, OK.
Length: 120 hours (3 weeks); residential; 20 hours of lecture/discussion and 20 hours of laboratory/workshop per week.
Dates: May 1970-Present.
Objective: To train maintenance personnel to troubleshoot, repair, and perform normal preventive maintenance on the multiposition letter-sorter machine.
Instruction: Operating principles, component assembly identification, location, and function; alignment and adjustment procedures; repair and parts replacement; analysis, diagnosis, and correction of electrical and mechanical equipment malfunctions; preventive maintenance practices.
Credit recommendation: In the lower division baccalaureate/associate degree category, 3 semester hours in Electromechanical Technology or Mechanical Technology (12/74) (3/81). NOTE: This course has undergone a 5-year reevaluation and continues to meet the requirements for credit recommendations.

Multi-Position Letter-Sorter Machines 140/141 (55658-20)
Location: USPS Technical Training Center, Norman, OK.
Length: 76 hours (2 weeks).

Dates: January 1986-Present.
Objective: To train maintenance personnel to troubleshoot, repair, and perform preventive maintenance on models 140/141 (MPLSM).
Instruction: The student is instructed in the operating principles; component assembly identification, location and function; alignment and adjustment procedures; repair and parts replacement; analysis and correction of electrical and mechanical equipment malfunctions; and preventive maintenance practices of the models 140/141 Multi-Position Letter Sorter Machines.
Credit recommendation: In the vocational certificate category, 3 semester hours in Electromechanical Troubleshooting (6/86).

Optical Character Reader I (55656-01)
Location: Technical Center, Norman, OK.
Length: 640 hours (16 weeks); residential; 30 hours lecture/discussion and 10 hours laboratory per week.
Dates: July 1971-June 1979.
Objective: To prepare electronic technicians to perform preventive and corrective maintenance on the computer-assisted Optical Character Reader I by providing the necessary theoretical background.
Instruction: Consists of a unit-by-unit analysis of the logical circuitry required for the Optical Character Reader to perform its functions. The latest modifications to the system (including Bar Code Reader) are incorporated. Covers the relationship of all the separate component units and their integration into a complete system, including the OCR, the line printer, the magnetic tape memory system, channel multiplexers, the PDP8-L computer, and interface control circuits.
Credit recommendation: In the lower division baccalaureate/associate degree category, 1 semester hour in Physics, and in the upper division baccalaureate category, 3 semester hours in Computer Technology and 5 semester hours in Computer Peripheral Devices (9/77).

Optical Character Reader I, On-Site Maintenance Certification (OSMC) Program (55656-02)
Location: Each postal facility utilizing the Optical Character Reader.
Length: 183 hours (minimum of 3 months); approximately 20 hours laboratory per week.
Dates: July 1971-Present.
Objective: To provide the electronic technician with supplemental training in the troubleshooting and repair skills necessary to maintain and repair the computer-assisted Optical Character Reader.
Instruction: Covers theoretical and hands-on training in preventive and corrective maintenance and troubleshooting techniques for use with major sections of the Optical Character Reader, including optical systems, vacuum systems, mechanical systems, electronic recognition systems, peripheral devices, and associated interfaces.

Also covers the PDP8-L computer.

Credit recommendation: In the lower division baccalaureate/associate degree category, 2 semester hours in Electromechanical Laboratory (9/77) (4/84). NOTE: This course has undergone reevaluation and continues to meet the requirements for credit recommendations.

Perimeter Office Fleet Maintenance (55638-00) (Formerly Nonpersonnel Office (NPO) Fleet Maintenance [55638-00])

Location: Technical Center, Norman, OK.

Length: 80 hours (2 weeks); residential; 28 hours lecture and 12 hours laboratory/worship per week.

Dates: February 1970-Present.

Objective: To provide knowledge of the objectives of a vehicle maintenance program with emphasis on procedure relating to reports and records, inspecting vehicles, and administering maintenance programs.

Instruction: Includes topics in vehicle maintenance handbooks, vehicle operations handbooks, position description handbooks, maintenance bulletins, modification orders, contract work orders, and contract maintenance. Also covers scheduled and repair maintenance, records and reports, and safety.

Credit recommendation: In the lower division baccalaureate/associate degree category, 2 semester hours in Automotive Service Management, Automotive Technology, or Transportation Technology (9/77) (4/84). NOTE: This course has undergone reevaluation and continues to meet the requirements for credit recommendations.

Postal Scales (55605-01)

Location: Technical Center, Norman, OK.

Length: 40 hours (1 week); residential; 15 hours lecture and 25 hours laboratory/workshop.

Dates: September 1977-Present.

Objective: To develop skill in testing, adjusting, preventive maintenance, troubleshooting, analysis, and repair maintenance of mechanical scales.

Instruction: Testing, adjusting, troubleshooting, preventive maintenance, and repair maintenance of such scales as Pitney Bowes, Pennsylvania, and Triner.

Credit recommendation: In the vocational certificate category, 1 semester hour in Mechanical Devices (9/77) (4/84). NOTE: This course has undergone reevaluation and continues to meet the requirements for credit recommendations.

Postal Source Data System (55641-01)

Location: Technical Center, Norman, OK.

Length: 520 hours (13 weeks).

Dates: July 1972-Present.

Objective: To provide students with knowledge and techniques required to maintain the PSDS system.

Instruction: Familiarization with the entire system, including input, output, and control devices; decimal, binary, and octal number systems, including the manipulation of the three systems and application of the principles to the system; electrical, mechanical, electromechanical, and electronic theory in detail sufficient for effective maintenance of the devices involved; theory of operation of input, output, and control devices; study and application of necessary test equipment; corrective maintenance procedures, based on symptom analysis and effective troubleshooting techniques; routine preventive maintenance procedures.

Credit recommendation: In the lower division baccalaureate/associate degree category, 3 semester hours in Electromechanical Technology, 6 semester hours in Computer System Analysis, and 3 semester hours in Electronic and Electromechanical Fundamentals (12/74) (3/81). NOTE: This course has undergone a 5-year reevaluation and continues to meet the requirements for credit recommendations.

Postal Source Data System On-Site Maintenance Certification (OSMC) Program (55641-02)

Location: Each postal facility utilizing the Postal Service Data Source.

Length: 240 hours; self-paced.

Dates: May 1973-Present.

Objective: To provide the electronic technician with supplemental training in the diagnostic and repair skills necessary to maintain and repair in the Postal Source Data System.

Instruction: Comprehensive theoretical and practical training in troubleshooting and repair of the following types of electronic circuits: relays, digital logic, communications, programming logic, and special purpose circuits. The technician must perform preventive maintenance, adjustment and repair of the following mechanical devices: drive belts, gears, chains, cam shafts, clutches, brakes, and associated linkages.

Credit recommendation: In the upper division baccalaureate category, 2 semester hours in Systems Troubleshooting and Maintenance Laboratory (9/77) (4/84). NOTE: This course has undergone reevaluation and continues to meet the requirements for credit recommendations.

Process Control System Line Printer (55670-31)

Location: Technical Center, Norman, OK.

Length: 120 hours (3 weeks).

Dates: April 1980-Present.

Objective: Provides electronic technicians with an in-depth understanding of functional operations, logic circuitry, diagnostic routines, and corrective maintenance procedures for the DPC Model V-306 Line Printer and interface electronics.

Instruction: Course covers electromechanical, electrical, and digital concepts pertinent to the V-306 Line Printer. Half the student's time is spent in lecture-discussion and half is spent in laboratory and directed study. (Prerequisite: Basic Process Control System [55670-10].)

Credit recommendation: In the lower division baccalaureate/associate degree category, 3 semester hours in Electromechanical Technology (3/81).

Process Control System Magnetic Tape Unit (MTU) (55670-32)

Location: Technical Center, Norman, OK.
Length: 120 hours (3 weeks).
Dates: May 1978-Present.
Objective: Provides electronic technicians with an in-depth understanding of functional operations, logic circuitry, diagnostic and maintenance techniques for the Wangco Model 1025 magnetic tape unit.
Instruction: Training involves specifics of the Wangco magnetic tape unit 1025 using lecture-discussion and laboratory. The material is presented in a format broad enough to be of general value to an electromechanical technician maintaining complex computer peripheral equipment. Lecture, discussion, laboratory, and directed study time are used. (Prerequisite: Basic Process Control System [55670-10].)
Credit recommendation: In the lower division baccalaureate/associate degree category, 1 semester hour in Computer Peripheral Maintenance or Electromechanical Equipment (3/81).

Process Control System Mail Processing Peripherals (55670-34)

Location: Technical Center, Norman, OK.
Length: 160 hours (4 weeks).
Dates: May 1981-Present.
Objective: To provide electronic technicians with an understanding of functional operations, logic circuitry, diagnostic routines, and corrective maintenance procedures for mail processing equipment, PCS interface and peripherals.
Instruction: Provides instruction on operating theory, logic circuit analysis, component function and location, troubleshooting techniques, corrective maintenance, and preventive maintenance routines. Lecture, discussion, laboratory, and directed study time are used.
Credit recommendation: In the lower division baccalaureate/associate degree category, 2 semester hours in Electromechanical Technology (3/81).

Process Control System NOVA 800 (55670-30)

Location: Technical Center, Norman, OK.
Length: 240 hours (6 weeks).
Dates: July 1978-Present.
Objective: To provide electronic technicians with an in-depth understanding of functional operations and logic circuitry associated with the NOVA 800 computer, Centronics 761 printer, and high-speed paper tape reader.
Instruction: Covers detailed hardware and logic analysis for the NOVA 800 computer. Includes the timing generator, core memory, CPU, I/O, and programmed data channels. Instruction on the Centronics 761 printer and high-speed paper tape reader covers principles of operation, logic analysis, controller software, and corrective maintenance. Lecture, discussion, laboratory, and directed study time are used. (Prerequisite: Basic Process Control System [55670-10].)
Credit recommendation: In the upper division baccalaureate category, 3 semester hours in Computer Maintenance Technology (3/81).

Security Equipment (55606-01)

Location: Technical Center, Norman, OK.
Length: 40 hours (1 week); residential; 15 hours lecture and 25 hours laboratory/workshop.
Dates: July 1977-Present.
Objective: To develop skill in maintenance and repair of combination locks and lock boxes.
Instruction: Covers troubleshooting, preventive maintenance, and repair maintenance of safe and vault combination locks and lock boxes.
Credit recommendation: In the vocational certificate category, 1 semester hour in Maintenance Mechanics or Security (9/77) (4/84). NOTE: This course has undergone reevaluation and continues to meet requirements for credit recommendations.

Self-Service Postal Center Equipment Program (55607-00)

Location: Technical Center, Norman, OK.
Length: 264 hours (6½ weeks).
Dates: July 1977-October 1979.
Objective: To develop skill in troubleshooting, servicing, and repairing of components of a number of independent mechanical and electromechanical systems.
Instruction: Burglar alarms, self-service postal scales, coin handling units and packaging machine, currency coin changer, rejectors dollar bill validators, multicommodity vending machines, multidenominational stamp vending machines, Scribe 906 multidenominational stamp vendor, and GSMC-76 multicommodity vendor.
Credit recommendation: In the lower division baccalaureate/associate degree category, 5 semester hours in Electromechanical Technology or Mechanical Technology (9/77).

Single-Position Letter-Sorter Machine (55652-00)

Location: Technical Center, Norman, OK.
Length: 120 hours (3 weeks); residential; 23 hours lecture/discussion and 17 hours laboratory per week.
Dates: January 1974-Present.
Objective: To train technicians responsible for the preventive maintenance troubleshooting, repair, and installation of digitally controlled electromechanical equipment.
Instruction: Equipment orientation; use of maintenance

manuals; system control; signal data flow; logic circuit and mechanical analysis; component assembly, identification, and replacement procedures for the single-position letter-sorter machine. (Prerequisite: The student must have passed an electromechanical examination and have a knowledge of basic electricity.)

Credit recommendation: In the lower division baccalaureate/associate degree category, 1 semester hour in Digital Systems and 1 semester hour in Electromechanical Systems (9/77) (4/84). NOTE: This course has undergone reevaluation and continues to meet the requirements for credit recommendations.

Teletype Maintenance (TTY) (55686-00)
Location: Technical Center, Norman, OK.
Length: 80 hours (2 weeks).
Dates: April 1979-Present.
Objective: To teach students preventive maintenance and corrective repair of Teletype Model 33 terminals.
Instruction: Theory followed by extensive hands-on laboratory work with the Teletype Model 33. Electrical and mechanical operation, adjustments, and maintenance of the four major units of the Model 33 - the typing unit, the keyboard, the call control unit, and the tape punch/reader. Course entails complete disassembly and reassembly of the terminal. Lecture, discussion, and laboratory are used.
Credit recommendation: In the vocational certificate category, 2 semester hours in Basic Electromechanics or Teletype Repair (3/81).

Vehicle Maintenance Analyst (55628-00)
Location: Technical Center, Norman, OK.
Length: 80 hours (2 weeks); residential; 24 hours lecture and 16 hours laboratory per week.
Dates: September 1970-Present.
Objective: To provide the participant with an understanding of the duties and responsibilities in the technical areas of vehicle inspection, maintenance analysis, corrective measures, and work interpretation; to introduce the proper methods of preparation of detailed directive work orders.
Instruction: Vehicle maintenance records; manufacturers' publications; headquarters' maintenance bulletins; modification work orders; cost and safety; preparing and analyzing work orders; use of automotive diagnostic test equipment; troubleshooting techniques; methods of analyzing vehicles; repair procedures; interim maintenance programs; the vehicle maintenance analyst's duties, responsibilities, and working relationships; the organization structure of vehicle maintenance.
Credit recommendation: In the lower division baccalaureate/associate degree category, 2 semester hours in Automotive Technology or Transportation Technology (9/77) (4/84). NOTE: This course has undergone reevaluation and continues to meet the requirements for credit recommendations.

Vehicle Maintenance Facility (VMF) Control (55634-00)
Location: Technical Center, Norman, OK.
Length: 80 hours (2 weeks); residential; 25 hours lecture/discussion and 15 hours laboratory per week.
Dates: February 1971-Present.
Objective: To provide the student with an understanding of a vehicle maintenance facility's operating policies and procedures and to develop skills in the application of these procedures to daily operations.
Instruction: Topics related to the operation of a vehicle maintenance facility, emphasizing the efficient application of management techniques to manpower control; problem identification and solving; stockroom control; fleet maintenance record and report use; shop safety; fleet-oriented programs.
Credit recommendation: In the lower division baccalaureate/associate degree category or in the upper division baccalaureate category, 3 semester hours in Automotive Service Management, Automotive Technology, or Transportation Technology (9/77) (4/84). NOTE: This course has undergone reevaluation and continues to meet the requirements for credit recommendations.

Vehicle Maintenance Facility (VMF) Utilization (55633-00)
Location: Technical Center, Norman, OK.
Length: 80 hours (2 weeks); residential; 25 hours lecture/discussion and 15 hours laboratory/workshop per week.
Dates: September 1970-Present.
Objective: To provide participants with techniques for a vehicle maintenance facility, emphasizing selection of appropriate corrective action to obtain maximum utilization of space, parts, personnel, and equipment.
Instruction: Work evaluation; repair order analysis; ratio of parts costs to labor costs; estimating; job analysis; vehicle maintenance programs; communication skills.
Credit recommendation: In the lower division baccalaureate/associate degree category or in the upper division baccalaureate category, 3 semester hours in Automotive Service Management, Automotive Technology, and Transportation Technology (9/77) (4/84). NOTE: This course has undergone reevaluation and continues to meet the requirements for credit recommendations.

Zip Mail Translator (55655-05)
(Formerly Zip-Mail Translator [55655-01])
Location: Technical Center, Norman, OK.
Length: 280 hours (7 weeks).
Dates: August 1970-Present.
Objective: To train students to troubleshoot, repair, and perform preventive maintenance on the zip-mail translator system of the letter-sorter machine.

Instruction: Component assembly identification, location, function; repair and parts replacement; troubleshooting analysis techniques; adjustment, alignment, and preventive maintenance procedures. Teaches the proper use of appropriate technical manuals and data, diagnostic test equipment, and regular and special tools.

Credit recommendation: In the lower division baccalaureate/associate degree category, 3 semester hours in Data Processing System Analysis and 3 semester hours in Computer Maintenance Technology, Data Processing Technology, or Electronics Technology (12/74) (3/81). NOTE: This course has undergone a 5-year reevaluation and continues to meet the requirements for credit recommendations.

United States Public Health Service - Indian Health Service

The Indian Health Service (IHS) is a component of the Public Health Service, Department of Health and Human Services, whose efforts are directed toward improving health services and promoting better health for all Americans. IHS serves the health needs of some 700,000 Indians and Alaska Natives who look to the federal government for assistance. The majority of the Native Americans live on federal Indian reservations in 24 states mostly west of the Mississippi, and in villages of Alaska.

The Training Center program was established in 1968 to help achieve the mission of IHS by identifying the training needs of Indian and Alaska Native people and to develop specific training programs designed to meet those needs. Training is offered in the areas of health awareness, health skills, and health management, with emphasis on development of tribal capacity to function independently.

These courses were designed for the Community Health Representatives and other tribal health workers who, as liaisons between the Native American communities, the health facilities, and the tribes, provide health services to their people.

Source of official student records: Registrar, Black Hills Training Center, 3200 Canyon Lake Drive, Rapid City, South Dakota 57001.

Additional information about the courses: Program on Noncollegiate Sponsored Instruction, The Center for Adult Learning and Educational Credentials, American Council on Education, One Dupont Circle, Washington, D.C. 20036.

Basic Maternal and Child Health (MCH100)
Location: Rapid City, SD; field locations in the U.S.
Length: 62 hours (2 weeks).
Dates: February 1977-Present.
Objective: To provide community health workers with the opportunity to increase their knowledge and skills in maternal and child health care.

Instruction: An introduction to the child-bearing cycle, family-centered maternity care, and health needs of infants and children. Content focuses on the role of allied health workers in health care management, skills training in vital signs, assessment measurements, screening of school-age children, disease prevention, and health education. The course is taught through lecture and discussion, supplemented by laboratory and field trips.

Credit recommendation: In the lower division baccalaureate/associate degree category, 3 semester hours in Allied Health, Community Health, or Public Health (9/78) (9/83). NOTE: This course has undergone a 5-year reevaluation and continues to meet the requirements for credit recommendations.

Community Health Representative (CHR100)
Location: Rapid City, SD; field locations in the U.S.
Length: 88½ hours (3 weeks).
Dates: May 1977-Present.
Objective: To introduce basic concepts of health and disease, communication skills, health planning, and community organization.

Instruction: An introduction to the tasks required of community outreach workers as related to community health problems and community resources; basic concepts of health and disease, including physical and mental health, nutrition, maternal and child health, dental health, and environmental health; the skills required in effective communication, first aid, safe driving, and community development. Lectures and discussion are used, supplemented by laboratory and field trips.

Credit recommendation: In the lower division baccalaureate/associate degree category, 4 semester hours in Allied Health, Community Health, or Public Health (9/78) (9/83). NOTE: This course has undergone a 5-year reevaluation and continues to meet the requirements for credit recommendations.

Emergency Medical Technician (EMT 200)
Location: Rapid City, SD; field locations in the U.S.
Length: 81 hours - minimum (2 weeks).
Dates: December 1979-Present.
Objective: To provide the student with the skills necessary to identify an emergency condition, assess patients with illness or injuries, and provide emergency care and safe transportation.

Instruction: Identification of common emergency medical conditions, proficiency in the use of emergency equipment and materials, recognition of symptoms of illness and injury, and proper procedures of emergency care. Lectures, films, and instructor demonstrations are used, and emphasis is placed on laboratory practice and patient-care simulation. The course is designed to prepare the student to take the National Registry Emergency Medical Technician Written Examination or its equivalent.

Credit recommendation: In the lower division baccalaureate/associate degree category, 5 semester hours in Allied Health, Emergency Medical Technology, or Nursing (2/80).

Environmental Health Concepts and Practices (EHE100)
   Location: Talihina, OK; Rapid City, SD; field locations in the U.S.
   Length: 60 hours (2 weeks).
   Dates: December 1976-September 1983.
   Objective: To create an awareness of the influence of environmental factors on health; to introduce fundamental skills essential for environmental health technicians.
   Instruction: Basic concepts of environmental health and sanitation, including water, waste disposal, zoonoses, vector-borne diseases, food-borne diseases, accident and injury prevention, housing, recreation, and public building sanitation. The course is taught primarily through lectures, supplemented with class demonstrations, laboratory, and field trips.
   Credit recommendation: In the lower division baccalaureate/associate degree category, 3 semester hours in Allied Health, Community Health, Environmental Health, or Public Health (9/78).

Health Services Research
   Location: Tucson, AZ and selected field sites.
   Length: 104 hours (3 weeks) - 60 percent lecture and discussion, 40 percent field.
   Dates: February 1974-Present.
   Objective: To design and conduct a field analysis for use in health program planning and management.
   Instruction: Principles of management, general epidemiology, types of health studies, sampling, questionnaire construction, interview techniques, and health program planning. Students design and carry out studies of health problems in field settings. Students then analyze in class the data collected during the field experience and develop comprehensive reports of the study. Lecture, discussion, and field experience are used.
   Credit recommendation: In the upper division baccalaureate category, 4 semester hours (3 hours in-class, 1 hour field experience) in Public Health (2/80).

Introduction to Human Services (HSE100)
   Location: Talihina, OK; Rapid City, SD; field locations in the U.S.
   Length: 72 hours (2 weeks).
   Dates: May 1977-September 1983.
   Objective: To increase an understanding of the roles and relationships in human services and to develop associated skills.
   Instruction: An introduction to human services, focusing on group processes, problem solving and decision making, communication skills, human behavior, and crisis counseling. The course is taught through lectures and discussion, supplemented by field experience.
   Credit recommendation: In the lower division baccalaureate/associate degree category, 3 semester hours in Guidance and Counseling, Rehabilitation Counseling, or Social Services (9/78).

Maternal and Child Nutrition
   Location: Santa Fe, NM; Rapid City, SD; Talihina, OK.
   Length: 53½ hours (2 weeks).
   Dates: March 1977-Present.
   Objective: To teach the student to identify common problems, refer to appropriate resources and provide selected basic services in the area of maternal-child nutrition.
   Instruction: Basic nutrition, maternal nutrition, growth and development, feeding infants and children, solutions to feeding and health problems, and client nutrition education. Lectures supplemented by class demonstrations, student projects, and small group sessions are used.
   Credit recommendation: In the lower division baccalaureate/associate degree category, 3 semester hours in Allied Health, Community Health, Food Science, Food Technology, Home Economics, or Public Health (2/80).

Nutrition Awareness (NCR100)
   Location: Talihina, OK; Rapid City, SD; Santa FE, NM; field locations in the U.S.
   Length: *Version 1:* 57 hours (2 weeks); *Version 2:* 60 hours (2 weeks).
   Dates: *Version 1:* May 1977-May 1979; *Version 2:* June 1979-September 1983.
   Objective: To learn about the relationship of food to health, including food selection and preparation.
   Instruction: An introduction to food and dietary habits and their impact on food selection and preparation. Content covers food needs of various age groups, meal planning, purchasing, and storage. An overview of food advertising, persuasion through advertising, and community education. The course is taught through lecture and discussion, supplemented by demonstrations, small-group work sessions, and field trips.
   Credit recommendation: In the lower division baccalaureate/associate degree category, 2 semester hours in Food Science, Food Technology, or Home Economics (9/78).

Rehabilitation and Home Health Care (RHH100)
   Location: Rapid City, SD; field locations in the U.S.
   Length: 57 hours (2 weeks).
   Dates: May 1977-September 1980.
   Objective: To equip students with the skills necessary to perform home health-care procedures.
   Instruction: Basic skills necessary for general home health care and rehabilitation, including vital signs, care

of ostomies and decubitus ulcers, bed bathing, and patient movement. Emphasis is on identifying patient problems, problem solving, and communicating health and disease information. Skills training and practice are supplemented by lectures.

Credit recommendation: In the lower division baccalaureate/associate degree category, 1 semester hour in Allied Health, Community Health, or Rehabilitation (9/78).

Skills and Techniques of Counseling (100)
  Location: Rapid City, SD.
  Length: 75 hours (2 weeks).
  Dates: February 1980-Present.
  Objective: To introduce the basic counseling techniques and skills essential in working with individuals and families.
  Instruction: An understanding of the counselor's role in the provider-client relationship; counseling skills and techniques for problem-solving and the application of "self" in the counseling process. Lecture, discussion, role playing, and hypothetical case sessions in small groups are used.
  Credit recommendation: In the lower division baccalaureate/associate degree category, 3 semester hours in Guidance and Counseling, Rehabilitation Counseling, or Social Services (2/80).

U.S. West Learning Systems

Mountain Bell Training and Education Center

The mission of Mountain Bell Training and Education Department is to develop and maintain a successful training and education resource that serves to achieve Mountain Bell's corporate and Human Resources Department objectives.

The Mountain Bell Training and Education Department is responsible for research that identifies new economic training methods and approaches made possible by advancing technology of Mountain Bell and other companies. Based on this research, provision is made for training and education required by organizational change of the company, new products and services, and employee learning needs produced by the changing society.

Source of official student records: Mountain Bell Training and Education Center, 3898 South Teller, Lakewood, Colorado 80235.

Additional information about the courses: Program on Noncollegiate Sponsored Instruction, The Center for Adult Learning and Educational Credentials, American Council on Education, One Dupont Circle, Washington, D.C. 20036.

Administration of Self-Paced Instruction: Techniques, Methods, and Psychology of Instruction
  Location: Mountain Bell Training and Education Center, Lakewood, CO.
  Length: 40-64 hours (5-8 days).
  Dates: January 1976-May 1982.
  Objective: To prepare instructors for effective teaching in a self-paced learning environment.
  Instruction: Course covers identification of behavioral objectives, criterion testing, performance management, systems approach theory. Instruction is self-paced.
  Credit recommendation: In the upper division baccalaureate category, 3 semester hours in Human Resource Development (3/81). NOTE: This course should be used for elective credit only.

Algebra I & II (1022 & 1024)
  Location: Correspondence, Mountain Bell.
  Length: 35-50 hours.
  Dates: October 1976-Present.
  Objective: To teach the student Elementary and Intermediate Algebra.
  Instruction: This course is designed to provide instruction in algebra. Topics include: first degree equations with 1 and 2 variables, inequities, absolute values, geographical methods, simultaneous solutions, exponents, quadratic equations, radicals, and logarithms.
  Credit recommendation: In the lower division baccalaureate/associate degree category, 2 semester hours in College Pre Calculus Mathematics (7/83).

Analysis and Instructional Design - AID (3107) Part I.
  Location: Mountain Bell Training and Education Center, Lakewood, CO.
  Length: 24 hours (3 days).
  Dates: October 1980-November 1982.
  Objective: To provide the student with the skills necessary for creating job aids, course design, and course materials.
  Instruction: Covers collecting data during job study relevant to determining if job aids are appropriate to any of the tasks to be treated in the training; describing performance to the level of detail necessary to make the job aid decision; comparing the job study data (such as frequency of performance, speed of performance, etc.) to each task to decide whether it will be treated by a job aid only, instruction-to-recall only, or job aid plus instruction-to-recall; selecting the formats of job aids relevant to the characteristics of task performance; designing and developing job aids such as checklists, decision tables, algorithms, cookbooks, worksheets, etc.: deriving end of course and enabling objectives for courses to be developed; relating job performance to the development of course objectives and criterion tests; and editing job aids for content, structure, and language. Self-instructional dialogues,

practice exercises, and overview presentations by the instructor.

Credit recommendation: In the upper division baccalaureate category, or graduate degree category, 6 semester hours in Analysis and Instructional Design (3/81). NOTE: Students who complete only one part of this two-part course should be awarded 3 semester hours in Analysis and Instructional Design, in the upper division baccalaureate category.

Analysis and Instructional Design - AID
Part II.
Location: Mountain Bell Training and Education Center, Lakewood, CO.
Length: 40 hours (5 days).
Dates: January 1976-December 1982.
Objective: To provide the student with the skills necessary for creating course designs and developing course materials.
Instruction: Course covers: describing job performance to a level of detail sufficient to reveal the job characteristics; analyzing the characteristics of job performance, the type of behavior, and the target student to determine potential learning problems; selecting teaching strategies based upon the characteristics of the performance and directed toward solving any potential learning problems; and designing an overall training course, planning each event of the course in detail. Also included are the preparation of instructional materials that serve the general teaching strategies of: preview, prerequisites, strengthening of concepts and procedures, isolated practice of the behaviors to be learned, appropriate step size, feedback, editing self-instructional materials and job aids, preparing performance tests, specifying general rules for selecting media and instructional activities, summarizing analysis and design decisions in course and module plans, and developmental test instructional materials and specify necessary revisions that are needed. Self-instructional dialogues, practice exercises, and overview presentations by the instructor are used.
Credit recommendation: In the upper division baccalaureate category, or graduate degree category, 6 semester hours in Analysis and Instructional Design (3/81). NOTE: Students who complete only part of this two-part course should be awarded 3 semester hours in Analysis and Instructional Design in the upper division baccalaureate category.

Advanced Management Seminar (3102)
Location: Mountain Bell Training Facilities; CO, AZ, NM, MT, UT, ID, and WY.
Length: 36 hours (4½ days).
Dates: February 1978-November 1981.
Objective: To give the students a functional understanding of performance planning and to enable them to operate effectively as second level managers.
Instruction: Covers management by objectives, manager/employee communications, performance problem analysis, group development, and conducting effective meetings. The class is taught primarily in a lecture format along with some use of discussion groups and workshops.
Credit recommendation: In the lower division baccalaureate/associate degree category, 1 semester hour in Human Relations, Leadership Management, Principles of Management, or Principles of Supervision (11/81).

Basic Data Systems Protocol (380)
Location: Mountain Bell Training and Education Center, Lakewood, CO.
Length: 24 hours (3 days).
Dates: December 1980-February 1985.
Objective: To provide experienced installation/maintenance personnel with some of the basic protocol knowledge used to establish, maintain, and repair data circuits that use line and message protocols in terminal-to-host interactive data communications.
Instruction: Covers components, functions and terms used in standard teleprocessing systems; data numbering systems (Hex, Octal, Binary, and BCD); data system codes; code protocol, error detection and correction systems; hardware and software of a host computer system, fault isolation by protocol techniques and computer-terminal interactions. Lectures and practical exercises are used.
Credit recommendation: In the lower division baccalaureate/associate degree category, 1 semester hour in Data Communication Systems Fundamentals (11/81).

Basic Electricity
Location: Mountain Bell Training and Education Center, Lakewood, CO.
Length: 40-50 hours (2 weeks).
Dates: March 1971-Present.
Objective: To introduce the student to basic concepts required for advanced study in electronics.
Instruction: Covers principles of direct current theory, alternating current theory, and the theory of magnetism. Correspondence course.
Credit recommendation: In the lower division baccalaureate/associate degree category, 3 semester hours in Electrical Technology (3/81).

Basic Electricity (911 MB)
Location: Mountain Bell Training and Education Center, Lakewood, CO.
Length: 24-40 hours (1 week).
Dates: January 1978-Present.
Objective: To acquaint the student with training in elementary electrical principles.
Instruction: Covers electrical current and voltage concepts (AC and DC); characteristics of resistance; and the relationships of current, voltage, and resistance in series

and parallel circuits. Workbooks and hands-on material are used in this self-paced training.

Credit recommendation: In the vocational certificate category, 3 semester hours in Introduction in Elementary Electrical Principles (3/81).

Basic Electronics

Location: Mountain Bell Training and Education Center, Lakewood, CO.

Length: Minimum 80 hours (2 weeks).

Dates: March 1971-Present.

Objective: To provide students with a practical knowledge of basic electronics.

Instruction: Covers the introduction to electronics and progresses through superheterodyne receivers. Correspondence course. Prerequisite: Basic Electricity.

Credit recommendation: In the lower division baccalaureate/associate degree category, 3 semester hours in Basic Electronics (3/81). NOTE: Subject to institutional examination.

Basic Engineering Economy

Location: Mountain Bell Training and Education Center, Lakewood, CO.

Length: 40 hours (1 week).

Dates: January 1981-Present.

Objective: To provide the information and expertise necessary to perform a complete engineering economy study.

Instruction: Accounting; mathematics and money; study techniques; depreciation; division of revenue; inflation; accelerated depreciation; investment tax credit. Lecture, discussion, and laboratory are used.

Credit recommendation: In the lower division baccalaureate/associate degree category or in the upper division baccalaureate category, 3 semester hours in Engineering or Engineering Technology (3/81).

Better Business Letters (1010)

Location: Correspondence, Mountain Bell.

Length: 9-10 hours.

Dates: September 1973-Present.

Objective: To provide instruction in basic business letter writing.

Instruction: The course includes instruction in letter writing techniques and basic business letter writing. Students are required to submit letters for grading and evaluation.

Credit recommendation: In the lower division baccalaureate/associate degree category, 1 semester hour in Business Communications (7/83).

BSC-BRIT-AIC Business Representative Initial Training - Account Inquiry Center (3148)

Location: Mountain Bell Training and Education Center, Lakewood, CO.

Length: 225 hours (37½ hours/week for 6 weeks).

Dates: January 1983-August 1984.

Objective: Upon completion of 3148 (formerly 3141B), the trainee will be able to: recognize information entries on telephone bills, handle referral notices, process orders, handle incoming payments, issue duplicate bills and adjustments, and understand customer provide equipment.

Instruction: Method of instruction is primarily laboratory and self-paced. It involves an extensive look at job specific techniques and exercises over a six-week period of time. Trainee evaluation is based on both written and oral examinations.

Credit recommendation: In the vocational certificate category, 3 semester hours in Customer Relations (7/83).

Business Account Inquiry Training (3141MB)

Location: Mountain Bell Training and Education Center, Lakewood, CO.

Length: 37½ hours.

Dates: October 1981-February 1985.

Objective: To train employees in the services available to the consumer of Mountain Bell products.

Instruction: Students are introduced to the various techniques in handling customer relative to bill processing, posting requirements, directory and toll information.

Credit recommendation: In the vocational certificate category, 3 semester hours in Customer Relations (9/82).

Business Demand Sales Training (3140MB)

Location: Mountain Bell Training and Education Center, Lakewood, CO.

Length: 187½ hours (8 weeks).

Dates: October 1981-March 1984.

Objective: To train employees in product knowledge and service.

Instruction: This course provides instruction in specific product services and enables the student to recommend and sell various company products and services. Handling customer requests, questions, and complaints is an integral part of the course.

Credit recommendation: In the vocational certificate category, 3 semester hours in Customer Relations (9/82).

Business Service Center Supervisor Training (3320MB)

Location: Mountain Bell Training and Education Center, Lakewood, CO.

Length: 40 hours (2 weeks).

Dates: August 1980-April 1984.

Objective: To provide training for first level managers in the fundamentals of supervision.

Instruction: Students are instructed in basic concepts of employees supervision and development. Topics in this course include leadership, organizational skills problem solving techniques and the basics of performance reviews.

Credit recommendation: In the lower division baccalaureate/associate degree category, 2 semester hours in

Principles of Supervision. NOTE: Credit should not be granted for both this course (3320MB) and 3321 (7/83).

Cable Repair Fault Locating (157)
  Location: Mountain Bell Training and Education Center, Lakewood, CO.
  Length: 40 hours (1 week).
  Dates: July 1981-Present.
  Objective: To provide employee training in the use and application of various fault locating test equipment.
  Instruction: This course is designed to provide training in the selection and use of a variety of cable fault locating equipment. Emphasized is the selection of proper fault locating test set and the analysis of obtained data in locating the fault.
  Credit recommendation: In the vocational certificate category, 1 semester hour in Electrical Technology (7/83).

Coaching Skills for Supervisors (3196)
  Location: Denver, Phoenix, Salt Lake City, Albuquerque.
  Length: 20 hours (2½ days).
  Dates: January 1984-Present.
  Objective: To introduce and develop the skills of coaching and counseling employees.
  Instruction: Lecture, discussion, and exercises are used to teach skills of coaching. Managers increase their skills and confidence in being able to confront issues and to work with employee problems.
  Credit recommendation: In the lower division baccalaureate/associate degree category, 1 semester hour in Management (4/85).

Comm-Stor II Flexible Diskette Terminal (455)
  Location: Mountain Bell Training and Education Center, Lakewood, CO.
  Length: 32 hours (4 days).
  Dates: December 1980-December 1986.
  Objective: To provide data installation/maintenance personnel with some of the basic protocol knowledge used to establish, maintain, and repair of data circuits used in a Comm-Stor II floppy-disk unit.
  Instruction: Covers floppy-disk operation, disk controller, operations parameters, refresh disk usage, disk command system, system diagnostics, and disk unit maintenance and troubleshooting. Lectures and practical exercises are used.
  Credit recommendation: In the lower division baccalaureate/associate degree category, 1 semester hour in Digital Equipment Operations (11/81).

Corporate Grammar (1065)
  Location: Correspondence Course.
  Length: 12 hours (2 days).
  Dates: November 1983-Present.
  Objective: To improve the students' grammatical usage of English in business correspondence, reports, memos, and proposals.
  Instruction: A self-instruction course which uses pre-testing analysis, a reference text, and several workbooks.
  Credit recommendation: In the lower division baccalaureate/associate division degree category, 1 semester hour in English Composition (4/85).

Dataphone II Service (414C)
  Location: Mountain Bell Training and Education Center, Lakewood, CO.
  Length: 40 hours (5 days).
  Dates: January 1981-January 1983.
  Objective: To provide the student with the required knowledge to install and maintain a Dataphone II service data set.
  Instruction: Covers a decoding of service orders and progresses through the installation, operation tests, diagnostic analysis of trouble reports (written and automatic), and the adding of optional features to the Dataphone II service data set. Lectures and hand-on experience are used.
  Credit recommendation: In the vocational certificate category, 1 semester hour in Data Communication Systems Maintenance (11/81).

DATASPEED 40 Dataphone Service (311)
  Location: Mountain Bell Training and Education Center, Lakewood, CO.
  Length: Self-paced instruction (average 40 hours).
  Dates: August 1978-January 1983.
  Objective: To afford craft persons training in the installation and field repair of the DATASPEED 40 terminal.
  Instruction: Covers the installation and operational check out of the DATASPEED 40 terminal. Similar treatment will be given to the DATASPEED 40 printer, the display monitor. A unit on troubleshooting the equipment will serve as a measure of the students growth in the course. Self-paced instruction supported with laboratory exercises.
  Credit recommendation: In the vocational certificate category, 1 semester hour in Data Communications Systems Maintenance (11/81).

Data Transmission Fundamentals
  Location: Mountain Bell Training and Education Center, Lakewood, CO.
  Length: 40 hours (1 week).
  Dates: January 1979-January 1983.
  Objective: To introduce the student to concepts of data transmission.
  Instruction: Covers basic skills necessary to establish and maintain data transmission facilities and to perform required transmission tests, analyze results to determine if requirements are met and take corrective action when necessary. Individualized, self-instructional workbooks

with audio tape and lab for hands-on experience and job relevant testing.

Credit recommendation: In the lower division baccalaureate/associate degree category, 3 semester hours in Data Transmission Fundamentals (3/81). NOTE: For elective credit only.

Design Center Engineering (942)
  Location: Mountain Bell Training and Education Center, Lakewood, CO.
  Length: 80 hours (2 weeks).
  Dates: September 1982-Present.
  Objective: To provide employee training in the design and planning of a communications distribution system.
  Instruction: Course covers: the planning, layout, and cable specifications for telephone communications subsystems.
  Credit recommendation: In the vocational certificate category, 1 semester hour in Communications Network Design (7/83).

Engineering Fundamentals
  Location: Mountain Bell Training and Education Center, Lakewood, CO.
  Length: 43-172 hours.
  Dates: January 1972-Present.
  Objective: To expose students to mathematical fundamentals necessary to pursue an engineering degree.
  Instruction: Covers basic electrical engineering concepts and the associated mathematics. Self-paced with examinations and instructor critique.
  Credit recommendation: In the lower division baccalaureate/associate degree category, 3 semester hours in Engineering Fundamentals (3/81).

Equipment Engineering Management
  Location: Mountain Bell Training and Education Center, Lakewood, CO.
  Length: 80 hours (2 weeks).
  Dates: January 1976-April 1986.
  Objective: To develop the expertise to perform equipment engineering tasks.
  Instruction: Forecasting; long-range planning; current planning; space planning; power planning; construction budgets; accounting; equipment requests; cost estimating; authorization; estimate analysis, job coordination; job inspection; closing project. Lecture, discussion, and laboratory are used.
  Credit recommendation: In the lower division baccalaureate/associate degree category, 3 semester hours in Equipment Engineering Management (3/81).

Face to Face Communication Skills
  Location: Mountain Bell Training and Education Center, Lakewood, CO.
  Length: 20 hours (2½ days).
  Dates: February 1977-August 1984.
  Objective: To enable the student to handle face-to-face communications and other types of personal interchange.
  Instruction: Covers recognition, assessment, and improvement of communication skills as they affect and influence on-the-job behavior. Course includes role playing and face-to-face confrontation. Course is instructor-led with group discussions and exercises.
  Credit recommendation: In the upper division baccalaureate degree category, 2 semester hours in Communication Skills, Interpersonal Communications, Organizational Communications, or Small Group Communications (3/81).

Facilities Economic Studies (EA SOP) (851)
  Location: Mountain Bell Training and Education Center, Lakewood, CO.
  Length: 40 hours (1 week).
  Dates: December 1978-Present.
  Objective: To provide the student with the fundamentals of engineering economics as applied to communications systems.
  Instruction: Covers the fundamentals of engineering economics with special emphasis on matters which pertain to the operation of the communications systems industry. Primarily laboratory exercises, self-paced.
  Credit recommendation: In the upper division baccalaureate category, 3 semester hours in Engineering Technology (9/82).

First Level Curriculum - Managing the Work (3121A)
  Location: Mountain Bell Training and Education Center, Lakewood, CO.
  Length: 32 hours (4 days).
  Dates: September 1982-April 1984.
  Objective: To provide newly appointed supervisors with a process for planning, organizing, and controlling the flow of work through their work groups and to give them problem solving skills that are required when something goes awry.
  Instruction: In this course, some of the principles of management are examined, including planning, organizing, and controlling. Emphasis is on the case approach. Prerequisite: 3-12 months of experience in management.
  Credit recommendation: In the lower division baccalaureate/associate degree category, 1 semester hour in Principles of Management (9/82).

First Level Curriculum - Managing Performance (3121B)
  Location: Mountain Bell Training and Education Center, Lakewood, CO.
  Length: 32 hours (4 days).
  Dates: November 1982-April 1984.
  Objective: To develop an understanding of the principles of human relations in business.

Instruction: Course offers new supervisors both knowledge and skills in analyzing performance deficiencies and identifying acceptable solutions. Specific techniques examined are: coaching, counseling, and performance appraisals. Prerequisite: 3-12 months of experience in management and supervision.

Credit recommendation: In the lower division baccalaureate/associate degree category, 1 semester hour in Human Relations in Business (9/82).

Initial Management Seminar

Location: Mountain Bell Training and Education Center, Lakewood, CO.
Length: 36 hours (1 week).
Dates: December 1974-January 1982.
Objective: To introduce the student to basic tools of effective management.
Instruction: Covers identification of job responsibilities, performance management, motivation, communication skills, work-group process, and conflict resolution. Lectures, reading, problem exercises, videotape, and discussion are used.
Credit recommendation: In the lower division baccalaureate/associate degree category, or in the upper division baccalaureate category, 3 semester hours in Human Relations, Leadership Management, Principles of Management, Supervision, or Supervisory Management (3/81). NOTE: Students who receive credit for this course should not receive credit for Initial Staff Seminar.

Initial Staff Seminar

Location: Mountain Bell Training and Education Center, Lakewood, CO.
Length: 36 hours (1 week).
Dates: October 1979-August 1982.
Objective: To develop the student skills and techniques necessary to operate efficiently and effectively in a staff role.
Instruction: Covers identification of job responsibilities, performance management, motivation, communication skills, work-group process, conflict resolution, and the role of staff and project management. Lecture, workshop, case study, discussion, and role playing are used.
Credit recommendation: In the lower division baccalaureate/associate degree category, or in the upper division baccalaureate category, 3 semester hours in Human Relations, Leadership Management, Principles of Management, Supervision, or Supervisory Management (3/81). NOTE: Students who receive credit for this course should not receive credit for Initial Management Seminar.

Initial User Training/Program Logic and Design/BASIC Programming Language (2302 or 2153))

Location: Mountain Bell Training and Education Center, Lakewood, CO.
Length: 56 hours (8 eight-hour meetings).
Dates: November 1980-Present.
Objective: To train students in coding and application of BASIC (Beginners All-Purpose Symbolic Instruction Code) programming language. Students will be able to document, build and save files, edit and construct flow chart diagrams.
Instruction: Approximately 20 increasingly complex programs are developed, projects, presentations, examinations, instructor observation and feedback will determine the course grade.
Credit recommendation: In the lower division baccalaureate/associate degree category, 3 semester hours in BASIC (7/83).

Initial User Training/Program Logic and Design/FORTRAN Programming Language (2303)

Location: Mountain Bell Training and Education Center, Lakewood, CO.
Length: 63 hours (9 eight-hour meetings).
Dates: April 1980-December 1987.
Objective: To train students in coding and application of FORTRAN programming language. Students will be able to code document, build and save files, edit and construct flow chart diagrams.
Instruction: Approximately twenty increasingly complex FORTRAN programs are developed. Students are graded through examinations, project presentations, documentations, and instructor observations and feedback.
Credit recommendation: In the lower division baccalaureate/associate degree category, 3 semester hours in FORTRAN (7/83).

Insight for Sales Managers (1112)

Location: Mountain Bell Training and Education Center, Lakewood, CO.
Length: 28 hours (3½ days).
Dates: May 1982-April 1984.
Objective: To train employees (students) in the fundamentals of supervision.
Instruction: Students are instructed in the basic principles of supervision. The purpose is to create a positive work climate and to gain insights to directing the productive energies of workers.
Credit recommendation: In the lower division baccalaureate/associate degree category, 1 semester hour in Principles of Supervision (9/82).

Instructor Training Workshop

Location: Mountain Bell Training and Education Center, Lakewood, CO.
Length: 42 hours (1 week).
Dates: January 1978-May 1982.
Objective: To develop skills for teaching the adult learner including classroom management, oral presentations, and instructional techniques incorporating media

support equipment.

Instruction: Course covers six-step instructional process and oral presentations. Trainees are given an opportunity to practice, develop, and make oral presentations. Feedback from peers, instructor, and video recordings of their presentations are provided. Lecture, discussion, and laboratory are used.

Credit recommendation: In the lower division baccalaureate/associate degree category, 3 semester hours in Education, Speech Communication, or Teaching Methods (3/81).

Introduction to Computer System Concepts (103)
 Location: Mountain Bell Training and Education Center, Lakewood, CO.
 Length: 24 hours (3 days).
 Dates: March 1982-January 1983.
 Objective: To acquaint the student with the fundamentals of computer systems.
 Instruction: Covers introduction to binary, octa-ard hexa-decimal number systems, characteristics of logic gates and functions, basic computer system components, flowcharting concepts, and data communication systems and computer interfaces. Lecture with laboratory.
 Credit recommendation: In the lower division baccalaureate/associate degree category, 1 semester hour in Computer Technology (9/82).

JCL and Operating Systems (2535)
 Location: Denver, CO and Albuquerque, NM.
 Length: 80 hours (2 weeks).
 Dates: November 1980-Present.
 Objective: To provide students with the necessary instruction for using installation standards in JCL. Includes catalogue procedures, overrides, and JE53 Control Statements.
 Instruction: Lecture, discussion, classroom exercises, and videos are used to present Installation Standards, IBM JCL and IBM VS2 System Messages.
 Credit recommendation: In the lower division baccalaureate/associate degree category, 3 semester hours in Computer Science (4/85).

**Job Design
(Job Study Workshop)**
 Location: Mountain Bell Training and Education Center, Lakewood, CO.
 Length: 40 hours (1 week).
 Dates: May 1978-December 1982.
 Objective: To provide the student with the skills necessary for doing a task analysis for the purpose of designing performance-based training material.
 Instruction: Covers complete task analysis process, including supporting documentation, summarization and verification of job content, flowcharting, and methods of data collection. Group-paced activities, including lecture, discussion, and role play are used.
 Credit recommendation: In the upper division baccalaureate category or in the graduate degree category, 3 semester hours in Human Engineering, Industrial Engineering, Personnel, Work Simplification, or Work Study Methods (3/81).

Job Design for Computer Supported Systems (3400)
 Location: Mountain Bell Training and Education Center, Lakewood, CO.
 Length: 32 hours (4 days).
 Dates: November 1983-Present.
 Objective: To learn the skills of analyzing and specifying the components of individual jobs.
 Instruction: Lecture, discussion, and exercises are used to prepare students to decompose individual jobs into components, to analyze and design new system procedures and to identify and document training needs.
 Credit recommendation: In the lower division baccalaureate/associate degree category, 1 semester hour in Management (4/85).

Loop Electronics - Design (932)
 Location: Mountain Bell Training and Education Center, Lakewood, CO.
 Length: 68 hours (8½ days).
 Dates: February 1982-Present.
 Objective: To train experienced personnel in the design of subscriber analog and digital carrier systems for new or existing plants.
 Instruction: Instruction and practical exercise utilizing special procedures which will permit the trainee to specify analog line design, analog repeaters, DB losses in cables, loss resistance, digital transmission circuits, digital repeaters, digital remote terminals, and special digital circuitry.
 Credit recommendation: In the vocational certificate category, 1 semester hour in Communication Systems (7/83).

Managing Interpersonal Relationships (3166)
 Location: Mountain Bell Training and Education Center, Lakewood, CO.
 Length: 20 hours (2½ days).
 Dates: June 1983-Present.
 Objective: To provide students with the necessary methods for building team spirit, increasing productivity, developing priorities, and resolving conflicts.
 Instruction: Lecture, discussion, and classroom exercises are used to present team building skills, decision making techniques, and conflict resolution.
 Credit recommendation: In the lower division baccalaureate/associate degree category, 2 semester hours in Career Development and Counseling (4/85). NOTE: Students must also successfully complete Psychology of Risk Taking (3243) and Managing Personal Growth (3165) to receive credit for this course.

Managing Personal Growth (3165)
Location: Mountain Bell Training and Education Center, Lakewood, CO.
Length: 16 hours (2 days).
Dates: May 1983-Present.
Objective: To provide students with the methods and techniques to recognize personal values, assess skills, strengths and weaknesses and to develop plans for improvement.
Instruction: Lecture, discussion, and classroom workshops are used to examine personal value inventories, career decision making, and performance priorities in the work environment.
Credit recommendation: In the lower division baccalaureate/associate degree category, 2 semester hours in Career Development and Counseling (4/85). NOTE: Students must also successfully complete Managing Personal Relationship (3166) and Psychology of Risk Taking (3243) to receive credit for this course.

Merchandising Management
(Phone Center Store Supervisor Training)
Location: Mountain Bell Training and Education Center, Lakewood, CO.
Length: 40 hours (1 week).
Dates: August 1978-June 1982.
Objective: To teach the student supervisory techniques related to store management.
Instruction: Covers the retail process, staffing, performance management, inventory control, retail security and safety, human resource development, and merchandising. Self-paced instruction and classroom exercises are used.
Credit recommendation: In the lower division baccalaureate/associate degree category, 2 semester hours in Merchandising or Retailing (3/81).

Methods Development Standards
Location: Mountain Bell Training and Education Center, Lakewood, CO.
Length: 133 hours (4 weeks).
Dates: September 1979-April 1984.
Objective: To provide the methods writer with the skills necessary to develop methods materials.
Instruction: Covers data collection instruments and techniques, methods design, field trials, how to plan and conduct system implementation, how to plan and conduct follow-up evaluation and maintenance of out-dated reference materials. The student is guided through each step, from gathering existing materials to conducting a field trial of the developed materials. Lecture, laboratories, and discussion are used.
Credit recommendation: In the vocational certificate category or in the lower division baccalaureate/associate degree category, 6 semester hours in Performance Technology or Technical Writing (3/81).

Methods Development Standards Workshop (3133)
Location: Mountain Bell Training and Education Center, Lakewood, CO.
Length: 24 hours (3 days).
Dates: November 1981-October 1986.
Objective: To provide students with an understanding of the systematic process required for the development and evaluation of work methods projects.
Instruction: Covers phases of methods development, evaluation of job activities, flowcharting, and the collection and analysis of field trial data. The course is taught in a format which includes lectures, discussion, and classroom exercises.
Credit recommendation: In the lower division baccalaureate/associate degree category, 1 semester hour in Introduction to Production Management, Principles of Management, or Supervision of Methods and Procedures (11/81).

Mountain Bell 139 Sequence
1. 139A: 21A Communication System Installation
2. 139C: 7A Communication System Installation
3. 139D: 4A Communication System Installation
4. 139E: 600 Series Modular Panels

Location: Mountain Bell Training and Education Center, Lakewood, CO.
Length: Self-paced instruction (average 80 hours).
Dates: March 1977-January 1983.
Objective: To teach key system installers how to install the major equipment components and to identify features of the 21A, 7A, and 4A Communication Systems, and of the 600 Series Modular Panels.
Instruction: Provides specialized training in ComKey 2152, ComKey 718, and ComKey 416 system installations; and 620A, 641A, and 642A Modular Panel installations. Self-paced courses with laboratory support.
Credit recommendation: In the vocational certificate category, 2 semester hours in Communication Systems Installation (11/81).

Mountain Bell 139 and 141 Sequence
1. 139: Key Telephone Installation - Phase I
2. 141: Key Telephone System Repair

Location: Mountain Bell Training and Education Center, Lakewood, CO.
Length: Self-paced instruction (average 88 hours).
Dates: August 1972-January 1983.
Objective: To train experienced personnel to perform all of the necessary installation tasks, testing procedures, diagnostic procedures, and repair procedures needed to verify and ensure the proper operation of all components of a key telephone system.
Instruction: Covers all aspects of the key telephone system, including component placement, wiring procedures, basic electrical components, grounding procedures, fault diagnosis using wiring diagrams, and component level re-

pair and troubleshooting. Self-paced and practical exercises are used.

Credit recommendation: In the vocational certificate category, 2 semester hours in Communication Systems Installation (11/81).

Mountain Bell 160-163 Sequence
1. **160: Introduction to Data Systems**
2. **162A: Using the Oscilloscope**
3. **163B/163.2: Data Test Equipment 914C**

Location: Mountain Bell Training and Education Center, Lakewood, CO.
Length: Self-paced instruction (average 64 hours).
Dates: July 1973-January 1983.
Objective: To provide the student with a fundamental understanding of data systems features and terminology, and with the skills required to perform data tests on Bell System voice bank data sets.
Instruction: Covers data terminology, and data numbering system and codes; data set types and characteristics; the system concepts in data communications; data test center features and functions; and descriptions of test and equipment available to assist in data systems repair. In addition, the general features of the 465 Oscilloscope and specific characteristics and uses of the 914C Data Test Set will be taught. A combination of self-paced instruction and laboratory verification methods are used.
Credit recommendation: In the lower division baccalaureate/associate degree category, 1 semester hour in Data Communication Systems Fundamentals (11/81).

Mountain Bell 167-179 Sequence
1. **167: 200 Series Data Sets**
2. **179: 921A Data Test Set**

Location: Mountain Bell Training and Education Center, Lakewood, CO.
Length: Self-paced instruction (average 72 hours).
Dates: November 1976-January 1983.
Objective: To train experienced personnel to install and maintain the family of 200 Series Data Sets (Modems) and to equip them with the skills to operate the 921A Data Test Set.
Instruction: Covers the operation and use of a specialized test set used to test synchronous and nonsynchronous modems; and the installations, use, testing, and maintenance of a series of medium-speed (300 to 2400 baud) and high-speed (2400 baud and up) modem units, including wiring methods (RS323, EIA), carrier operations, transmission losses, wiring procedures, fault analysis, and unit testing and maintenance. Self-paced instruction and practical exercises are used.
Credit recommendation: In the lower division baccalaureate/associate degree category, 2 semester hours in Data Communication Systems Fundamentals (11/81).

Mountain Bell 298-343 Sequence
1. **298: CSS-201S Installation and First-Tier Maintenance**
2. **343: Dimension PBX-CES-201L Installation and Maintenance**

Location: Mountain Bell Training and Education Center, Lakewood, CO.
Length: Self-paced instruction (144 hours).
Dates: April 1977-January 1983.
Objective: To train experienced installation personnel to install and maintain (at the module level) a digital signal communications system (100, 400, and 200 Private Business Exchange).
Instruction: Covers operation, use, installation, and first-level (module-level) maintenance of digitally controlled signal processing system, including central processor operation and maintenance, software descriptions, installation testing, and software diagnostic programs for system troubleshooting. Instruction and practical exercises are used.
Credit recommendation: In the lower division baccalaureate/associate degree category, 3 semester hours in Digital Signal Processing Systems (11/81).

Mountain Bell 345 & 370 Sequence
1. **345: Dimension Custom Telephone Service**
2. **370: Horizon 32A**

Location: Mountain Bell Training and Education Center, Lakewood, CO.
Length: Self-paced instruction (average 48 hours).
Dates: January 1978-January 1983.
Objective: To provide trained maintenance personnel with the knowledge of the operation, installation, testing, and maintenance of a custom telephone service system (Horizon 32A and Dimension 400 PBX).
Instruction: Covers operation, use, installation, and maintenance of a custom telephone system primarily related to the Horizon 32A and Dimension 400 PBX. Self-paced instruction and practical exercises are used.
Credit recommendation: In the vocational certificate category, 1 semester hour in Communication Systems Practices (11/81).

Mountain Bell 507AA/508AA Sequence
1. **507AA: Introduction to Electronic Switching Systems/Second Generation**
2. **508AA: Common Peripheral Units/Second Generation**

Location: Mountain Bell Training and Education Center, Lakewood, CO.
Length: Self-paced instruction (average 245 hours).
Dates: November 1981-Present.
Objective: To provide the student with entry-level skills and knowledge for first- and second-generation electronic switching technology.
Instruction: Covers Electronic Switching Systems over-

view, numbering systems, diodes and transistors, logic circuits, hardware, oscilloscope usage, basic ESS communication buses, principal components, skills required for locating trouble. Self-paced, practical exercises under direct supervision of an administrator.

Credit recommendation: In the lower division baccalaureate/associate degree category, 3 semester hours in Introduction to Electronic Switching Systems (11/81).

Mountain Bell 507B-508B/OJT Sequence
1. **507B: Introduction to No. 1 Electronic Switching Systems (ESS)**
2. **508B-OJT: No. 1 ESS Peripheral Units - On-the-Job Training**

Location: Mountain Bell Training and Education Center, Lakewood, CO.
Length: Self-paced instruction (average 55 hours).
Dates: November 1981-Present.
Objective: To provide the student with the skills needed to progress to more advanced No. 1-level ESS and to provide the student with practice and skills associated with No. 1 ESS peripheral equipment maintenance.
Instruction: Covers operations, use, fault diagnosis, and repair of No.1 level ESS and their related peripheral units, including component identification from schematics, block diagram analysis, program diagnostics and listing, testing procedures for service lines and equipment, logic circuit testing, and central processor hardware operations. Self-paced instruction and practical on-the-job exercises are used.
Credit recommendation: In the vocational certificate category, 1 semester hour in Switching Systems Maintenance (11/81).

Mountain Bell 508K Sequence
1. **508KA: No. 1/1A Remreed Peripheral Maintenance**
2. **508KB: No. 1/1A ESS CIT/MUT Peripheral Unit Maintenance**
3. **508KD: No. 1/1A ESS DCT - Operation and Maintenance**
4. **508KF: No. 1 ESS Ferreed Operation and Maintenance**

Location: Mountain Bell Training and Education Center, Lakewood, CO.
Length: Self-paced instruction (average 211 hours).
Dates: November 1981-June 1982.
Objective: To provide the student with the general knowledge and maintenance procedures required to work on first- and second-generation Electronic Switching Systems (ESS) peripherals.
Instruction: Covers operation, design, maintenance, and fault diagnosis of first and second generation electronic switching system Remreed switching network and its related equipment, including switching path networks, trunk switching frames, junction switching, network maintenance, pulse distribution diagnostics, trunk circuit analysis, and digital switching diagnostics. Self-paced instruction and practical exercises are used.
Credit recommendation: In the vocational certificate category, 5 semester hours in Switching Systems Maintenance (11/81).

Mountain Bell 509B: No. 1 ESS Central Processor and Program Fundamentals
Location: Mountain Bell Training and Education Center, Lakewood, CO.
Length: Self-paced instruction (average 113 hours).
Dates: November 1981-Present.
Objective: To provide the student with the skills necessary to characterize data failures in No. 1 Electronic Switching Systems Program Store or Call Store memory systems and to isolate the failure to specific hardware location.
Instruction: Covers operation, maintenance, and repair of an advanced-level Electronic Switching System control unit, including logic circuit analysis, block diagram and timing analysis, address operations, computer system operations, memory addressing (32K and 8K), program instruction codes, core memory operations, program diagnostics, troubleshooting procedures, and repair methods. Self-paced instruction and practical exercises are used.
Credit recommendation: In the lower division baccalaureate/associate degree category, 3 semester hours in Computer Systems or Logic Circuit Fundamentals (11/81).

Mountain Bell 534 Sequence
1. **534A: No. 1 ESS Central Office Language, Hardware, and Maintenance**
2. **534B: Program Store Hardware and Maintenance**
3. **534C: Call Store Maintenance**
4. **534D: No. 1 ESS Central Processor Hardware and Programming**
5. **534E: Master Control Centers and Associated Frames Diagnostics**

Location: Mountain Bell Training and Education Center, Lakewood, CO.
Length: Self-paced instruction (average 268 hours).
Dates: November 1981-May 1984.
Objective: To provide the student with the skills, knowledge, and techniques required to maintain the central processor free of hardware faults.
Instruction: Course covers central control, program store, call store, signal processor, and master control center. Five modules containing a total of 15 individual units. Tests after each unit. Must obtain 100% on each test prior to continuing. Self-paced, practical exercises under direct supervision of an administrator.
Credit recommendation: In the vocational certificate category, 6 semester hours in Digital Hardware Maintenance (11/81).

Mountain Bell 539 Sequence
1. **539A: No. 1 ESS Stored Program Organization**
2. **539B: No. 1 ESS Parameters**
3. **539C: No. 1 ESS Translations**
4. **539D: No. 1 ESS Call Processing**
5. **539E: No. 1 ESS Maintenance and Alarm Printouts**
6. **539F: No. 1 ESS Maintenance Procedures**

Location: Mountain Bell Training and Education Center, Lakewood, CO.

Length: Self-paced instruction (average 240 hours).

Dates: November 1981-May 1984.

Objective: To develop the skills that will enable an individual to perform tasks in the area of software maintenance for No. 1 Electronic Switching Systems.

Instruction: Covers use of generic program documentation, locating and clearing parameter and translation problems, applied knowledge of No. 1 ESS Call Processing, resolving audit error printouts, and off-line testing. Self-paced instruction with graded exams serving as the measure of goal accomplishment.

Credit recommendation: In the vocational certificate category, 6 semester hours in Switching System Software Diagnostics (11/81).

Mountain Bell Sequence (849-850)
1. **Preparation OSP Engineering Work Plans**
2. **Advanced OSP Engineering Work Plans**

Location: Mountain Bell Training and Education Center, Lakewood, CO.

Length: 120 hours (3 weeks).

Dates: July 1979-April 1984.

Objective: To provide students with the knowledge to be able to analyze a designer's rough sketch for discrepancies, obtain answers to those discrepancies, select materials, and draw the work plans to standard.

Instruction: Covers the information needed to produce standard work plans including cable sizes and lengths, cable locations, cable types (i.e., aerial, buried, underground, etc.), and advanced work plan concepts leading to field assignments and identifications, for the purpose of equipping new facilities and/or modifying existing facilities. Group discussion, laboratory exercises, self-paced.

Credit recommendation: In the lower division baccalaureate/associate degree category, 4 semester hours in Communication Systems (9/82).

Mountain Bell Sequence (849 & 941)
1. **Preparation OSP Engineering Work Plans**
2. **Engineering Tools and Field Survey**

Location: Mountain Bell Training and Education Center, Lakewood, CO.

Length: 85-95 hours (10 days).

Dates: August 1982-April 1984.

Objective: To teach the student how to draw, analyze, and amend engineering work plans associated with outside communication systems.

Instruction: Covers details of reading, drawing, and interpreting communication line construction work plans. Group discussion, laboratory exercises, self-paced.

Credit recommendation: In the lower division baccalaureate/associate degree category, 3 semester hours in Communication Systems Practices (9/82).

Mountain Bell Sequence (933, 935-937, 939)
1. **Electrical Protection OSP (933)**
2. **Principles of Electricity (939)**
3. **Principles of Transmission (937)**
4. **Resistance Design (936)**
5. **Unified Loop Design (935)**

Location: Mountain Bell Training and Education Center, Lakewood, CO.

Length: Self-paced instruction (average 60 hours).

Dates: October 1981-Present.

Objective: To provide students with the skills needed to insure protection of and to effect the design of the outside plant components of a communication system.

Instruction: Covers basic electrical and communication terminology including topics on electrical protection procedures, unified loop design, and transmission losses and impairments. Primarily self-paced.

Credit recommendation: In the vocational certificate category, 2 semester hours in Engineering Technology (9/82).

Mountain Bell 1021/26/35 Sequence
1. **1021: Communication Analysis**
2. **1026: System Implementation**
3. **1035: Customer Administration Panel - Dimension 2000**

Location: Mountain Bell Training and Education Center, Lakewood, CO.

Length: Self-paced instruction (average 200 hours).

Dates: March 1978-May 1981.

Objective: To provide the student with the tools necessary to analyze the customer's needs, suggest and install the proper product, supervise training and start-up procedures, and follow-up to insure greatest benefit and acceptance.

Instruction: *Course 1:* Stresses the techniques available in order to ascertain precisely the communication needs of the customer. *Course 2:* Provides opportunity to use this information to suggest the proper product. *Course 3:* Provides sufficient in-depth training in the use and capabilities of an advanced PBX and its peripheral equipment to enable the seller to knowledgeably demonstrate and discuss the machine with the prospective buyer. Even though the applications are specific, the principles used are fundamental and therefore applicable to a variety of situations in all areas of technical marketing. Self-paced instruction with laboratory support is used.

Credit recommendation: In the lower division baccalaureate/associate degree category, 3 semester hours in

Applications of Technical Marketing (11/81).

Mountain Bell Sequence 3305 MBA-MBE
Competitive Selling - Demand Sales Center (3305 MBA)
Face to Face Selling (3305 MBB)
WATS Orders - Demand Sales Center (3305 MBC)
Horizon Subsequent Activity A & B (3305 MBD)
Variable Term Payment Plan/Variable Term Telephone Lease Agreement (3305 MBE)
   Location: Mountain Bell Training and Education Center, Lakewood, CO.
   Length: 83 hours (59 days).
   Dates: October 1981-April 1984.
   Objective: To train students in specific selling skills on products and service relative to Mountain Bell.
   Instruction: This five-course sequence provides instruction to students in basic selling techniques involving competitive research, consumer approaches, customer benefits, handling objections, and closing the sale.
   Credit recommendation: In the lower division baccalaureate/associate degree category, 2 semester hours in Principles of Salesmanship (9/82).

New Age Thinking for Achieving Your Potential (3127)
   Location: Mountain Bell Training and Education Center, Lakewood, CO.
   Length: 24 hours (3 days).
   Dates: March 1980-May 1984.
   Objective: To guide the participant toward an understanding and acceptance of his or her own talents and resources, instill belief in personal ability to succeed, and expand vision of available opportunities.
   Instruction: This course is designed to make the individual aware of the potential for self-development. Participants explore goal-setting, communications, problem solving, self-esteem, motivation, and acceptance of and planning for change. Method of instruction includes filmed lectures, classroom discussion, and laboratory work.
   Credit recommendation: In the lower division baccalaureate/associate degree category, 1 semester hour in Human Potential Seminar (9/82).

Performance Data Collection and Analysis (3143)
   Location: Mountain Bell Training and Education Center, Lakewood, CO.
   Length: 32 hours (1 week).
   Dates: January 1982-Present.
   Objective: A comprehensive presentation of data collection methods and analysis of in job performance. Students will learn to determine causes of performance deficiencies and recommend solutions.
   Instruction: The course is designed to provide instruction in specific data collection techniques, such as sample sizes and data sources. The design of data collection instruments are presented. Worksheets and flow charts are utilized. A Deficiency Analysis Summary is used to conclude reports.
   Credit recommendation: In the upper division baccalaureate or graduate degree category, 2 semester hours in Human Engineering, Industrial Engineering, Management Information Systems, or Work Study Methods (4/85).

Performance Driven Selling (3065)
   Location: Mountain Bell Training and Education Center, Lakewood, CO.
   Length: 32 hours (1 week).
   Dates: July 1981-Present.
   Objective: To train students in specific selling techniques.
   Instruction: This course provides some of the basics of selling. The course instruction includes cases and role-playing exercises which require students to solve marketing problems using skills acquired in the course.
   Credit recommendation: In the lower division baccalaureate/associate degree category, 1 semester hour of elective credit in a Marketing or Marketing/Sales Program (7/83).

PL/I Series (2030)
   Location: Mountain Bell Training and Education Center, Lakewood, CO.
   Length: 96 hours (12 days).
   Dates: June 1982-Present.
   Objective: To provide students with instruction for coding, compiling, and executing PL/I procedures.
   Instruction: The course is offered in a self-paced laboratory setting. Students receive direct programming experience in all phases of the PL/I language.
   Credit recommendation: In the lower division baccalaureate/associate degree category, 3 semester hours in Computer Science (4/85).

Power Writing (3195)
   Location: Mountain Bell Training and Education Center, Lakewood, CO.
   Length: 24 hours (1 week).
   Dates: November 1982-Present.
   Objective: To improve the students' ability to write business letters, reports, memos, and proposals.
   Instruction: Lecture, discussion, and practical workshop assignments are utilized to teach topic organization, conciseness, and clarity of style, proper grammar and sentence structure.
   Credit recommendation: In the lower division baccalaureate/associate degree category, 1 semester hour in English Composition (4/85).

Programmer Basic Training
   Location: Mountain Bell Training and Education Cen-

ter, Lakewood, CO.

Length: 473 hours (13 weeks).

Dates: January 1978-Present.

Objective: To introduce students to the physical structure and major concepts of a computer; to develop skills in designing and implementing structured COBOL programs and required documentation; to prepare students to create and modify JCL to execute programs and procedures.

Instruction: Data processing concepts; data representation; structured programming, design, implementation and case problems; COBOL; JCL, including cataloged procedures; TSO; and, utilities. The COBOL unit of the course emphasizes understanding diagnostic messages, making appropriate corrections to COBOL code, debugging, modularity, the SORT verb, and modular debugging. Students are required to take written tests and execute case studies. Lecture, discussion, workshop, and independent study are used.

Credit recommendation: In the lower division baccalaureate/associate degree category or in the upper division baccalaureate category, 6 semester hours in Computer Sciences, Information Sciences, or Technology. In the upper division baccalaureate category, 3 semester hours in Engineering (3/81). NOTE: These credit recommendations are not additive.

Psychology of Risk Taking (3243)

Location: Mountain Bell Training and Education Center, Lakewood, CO.

Length: 20 hours (2½ days).

Dates: April 1984-January 1988.

Objective: To provide understanding of risk taking and its impact on behavior and performance.

Instruction: Lecture, discussion, and exercises are used to provide coverage of risk taking behavior. The seminar defines risk taking looks at the impact of this type of behavior on performance and helps to identify opportunities for risk taking in the work setting.

Credit recommendation: In the lower division baccalaureate/associate degree category, 2 semester hours in Career Development and Counseling (4/85). NOTE: Students must also have successfully completed Managing Personal Growth (3165) and Managing Interpersonal Relationships (3166) to receive credit for this course.

Put It In Writing (3161MB)

Location: Mountain Bell Training Centers.

Length: 24 hours (1 week).

Dates: November 1982-May 1987.

Objective: To teach students the principles of clear writing, and how to compose accurate, concise, and efficient business letters, write comprehensive memos and reports, and to critique the writing of others.

Instruction: Lecture, discussion, and workshop assignments are supported by audio/slide presentation.

Credit recommendation: In the lower division baccalaureate/associate degree category, 1 semester hour in English, Technical, or Business Writing (4/85).

Residence Account Service Center Learning (RASCL) (3201MB)

Location: Mountain Bell Training and Education Center, Lakewood, CO.

Length: Self-Paced, 112 hours - minimum (3 weeks); 150 hours - maximum (4 weeks).

Dates: December 1981-June 1984.

Objective: To provide training to non-management personnel in performing service representative functions in the Residence Account Service Center.

Instruction: This course trains the service representative to handle customer questions and complaints in a professional manner, take effective action to collect overdue bills, explain and adjust customers' bills, answer questions about long distance calls, and use a variety of reference documents. Methodology includes self-paced learning under an instructor's guidance and practice sessions in a customer contact simulation center.

Credit recommendation: In the vocational certificate category, 3 semester hours in Customer Relations (9/82).

Residence Telephone Order Center Curriculum (RTOCC) (3200MB)

Location: Mountain Bell Training and Education Center, Lakewood, CO.

Length: Self-Paced, 187½ hours - minimum (5 weeks); 225 hours - maximum (6 weeks).

Dates: May 1981-December 1983.

Objective: To provide training to non-management personnel in performing service representative functions in the Residence Telephone Order Center.

Instruction: In this course service representatives are trained to handle customer questions and complaints in a professional manner, quote the amount on customer bills, sell company products and services, and use a variety of reference documents. Methodology includes self-paced learning under an instructor's guidance and practice sessions in a customer contact simulation center.

Credit recommendation: In the vocational certificate category, 3 semester hours in Customer Relations (9/82).

Second Level Management Performance Based Curriculum

Location: Mountain Bell Training and Education Center, Lakewood, CO.

Length: 96 hours (12 days).

Dates: November 1981-April 1984.

Objective: To provide students with skills training aimed at modeling the performance of successful second level managers in the Bell System.

Instruction: Covers the identification and solution of job related problems using a problem solving model; use of "thought pattern development" to improve written communication; development of a job definition; managing time more effectively; establishing goals; communicating more effectively in interviewing, negotiation, feedback, and coaching situations; planning, organizing, and monitoring work flow; subordinate growth utilizing the "subordinate development system." Classroom lectures, discussions, and workshops are utilized in six separate learning modules.

Credit recommendation: In the lower division baccalaureate/associate degree category, 2 semester hours in Principles of Supervision or Principles of Job Administration (11/81).

Sights on Selling (1111)
Location: Mountain Bell Training and Education Center, Lakewood, CO.
Length: 40 hours (1 week).
Dates: February 1982-April 1984.
Objective: To develop an understanding of the basic selling process to be used in the phone center store.
Instruction: Students are instructed in the basic selling process involving relating, customer needs, information gathering, product recommendation, and follow-up.
Credit recommendation: In the lower division baccalaureate/associate degree category, 1 semester hour in Principles of Salesmanship (9/82).

Situational Leadership Workshop (3169)
Location: Mountain Bell Training and Education Center, Lakewood, CO.
Length: 20 hours (2½ days).
Dates: December 1983-Present.
Objective: To provide an understanding of styles of leadership and to learn to match one's leadership style to the needs of subordinates and job situations.
Instruction: Lecture, discussion, and exercises are used to teach how a manager's leadership style influences subordinate performance; how to apply situational leadership in the work environment. Mazlor, Herzberg, and McClelland are introduced to support the situational leadership approach.
Credit recommendation: In the lower division baccalaureate/associate degree category, 1 semester hour in Management (4/85).

Subscribers Carrier Planning (931)
Location: Mountain Bell Training and Education Center, Lakewood, CO.
Length: 36 hours (4½ days).
Dates: December 1982-June 1986.
Objective: To train experienced personnel in the application of LROPP (Long Range Outside Plant Planning) and the FA (Feeder Administration) process steps required to complete the fundamental Subscriber Carrier Plan (FSCP).
Instruction: Instruction and practical exercises are given in the use and interpretation of several specialized computer programs including LROPP, FA, FSCP, PGP (Pair Gain Planning) and the RDES editor. Includes terminal usage, file creation and editing files.
Credit recommendation: In the vocational certificate category, 1 semester hour in Communications Technology (7/83).

Supervisor Training for Business Service Order Entry Center and Service Order Entry Center Special Services (3321)
Location: Mountain Bell Training and Education Center, Lakewood, CO.
Length: 56 hours (over 2½ week period).
Dates: September 1979-April 1984.
Objective: To provide training for first level managers in the fundamentals of supervision.
Instruction: Students are instructed in basic concepts of employee supervision and development. Topics in this course include leadership, organizational skills, problem-solving techniques and the basics of performance reviews.
Credit recommendation: In the lower division baccalaureate/associate degree category, 1 semester hour in Principles of Supervision. NOTE: Credit should not be granted for both this course (3321) and 3320MB (7/83).

Synchronous DATASPEED 40 (388)
Location: Mountain Bell Training and Education Center, Lakewood, CO.
Length: Self-paced instruction (average 40 hours).
Dates: November 1978-December 1985.
Objective: To train personnel to install, test, and troubleshoot various DATASPEED 40 arrangements which provide users with a flexible, interactive, and efficient station for application on computer controlled systems.
Instruction: Covers installation, testing, and troubleshooting various computer input-output equipment cluster controllers including equipment arrangement, coding information (ASCII, EBCDIC, and HEX), code interpretations, and troubleshooting procedures for CRT display, keyboard, connecting cables, and controllers to the module level. Self-paced instruction and practical exercises are used.
Credit recommendation: In the lower division baccalaureate/associate degree category, 1 semester hour in Digital Equipment Operations (11/81).

Testing Human Performance (3402)
Location: Mountain Bell Training and Education Center, Lakewood, CO.
Length: 24 hours (3 days).
Dates: December 1983-Present.
Objective: To provide an introduction to and basic skills of testing and evaluation of human performance.
Instruction: Lecture, discussion, and exercises are used

to teach the basics of testing and evaluating human performance. Different approaches to testing are considered and elementary forms of statistical analysis are introduced.

Credit recommendation: In the lower division baccalaureate/associate degree category, 1 semester hour in Management (4/85).

TTC No. 366 Circuit Reading

Location: Mountain Bell Training and Education Center, Lakewood, CO.

Length: 36-48 hours (1 week).

Dates: January 1979-Present.

Objective: To enable students to read standard schematic diagrams and drawings.

Instruction: Course consists of six individualized and self-paced modules. Printed reference materials, standard drawings, and schematics, Bell System practices and a glossary are provided, as required, for each module. A trainee workbook with pre and final tests and an administrator's guide is provided for each module. Student-paced, individualized with instructor evaluated exam.

Credit recommendation: In the vocational certificate category, 3 semester hours in Basic Circuit Reading (3/81).

VSAM (2922)

Location: Denver, CO and Albuquerque, NM.

Length: 40 hours (5 days).

Dates: January 1982-April 1987.

Objective: To provide students with instructional tools to use VSAM data sets, interpret VSAM output messages, and to state how alternate indexes are used.

Instruction: Lecture, discussion, laboratory exercises, and videos are used to teach VSAM commands and performance optimization features of VSAM.

Credit recommendation: In the lower division baccalaureate/associate degree category, 2 semester hours in Computer Science as an elective (4/85).

Wang Initial Word Processing/Wang Glossary Training (3175/3182)

Location: Mountain Bell Training and Education Center, Lakewood, CO.

Length: 32 hours (4 eight-hour days).

Dates: April 1980-Present.

Objective: To provide students with training on CRT (Cathode Ray Video Screen Typing) Word Processing equipment by creating, editing, printing, and storing information on diskettes or other technological devices. Students completing this course should be able to transfer their knowledge to a variety of CRT Word Processing equipment.

Instruction: Students participate in instructor led discussions, classroom exercises, and individual assignments involving the capabilities of current word processing equipment.

Credit recommendation: In the lower division baccalaureate/associate degree category, 2 semester hours in Word Processing Application (7/83).

Writing Procedures and Users Guides (3401)

Location: Mountain Bell Training and Education Center, Lakewood, CO.

Length: 32 hours (4 days).

Dates: November 1983-Present.

Objective: To train managers to use state-of-the-art documentation principles to the design and make presentations of user documents.

Instruction: Lecture, discussion, and exercises are used in this workshop which emphasizes principles of design for instructing performance aid and procedural documents. It is designed for documenting work flows or procedures for computer-based systems.

Credit recommendation: In the lower division baccalaureate/associate degree category, 1 semester hour in Technical Writing (4/85).

Northwestern Bell Telephone Company, Training and Education Department

Northwestern Bell Telephone Company is part of U.S. West Learning Systems and provides telecommunications services in Iowa, Minnesota, Nebraska, North and South Dakota.

The primary responsibility for training is resident in the Training and Education Department which comprises six major groups serving all segments of the business. Course offerings are extensive ranging from job specific technical skills to those in the disciplines of management, organization effectiveness, accounting, data processing, telecommunications, engineering, communication skills, interpersonal skills, instructional technology, and trainer training.

The department is also responsible for continuing education programs including tuition aid which are available to all Northwestern Bell employees out-of-hours for self-improvement and career advancement.

Source of official student records: Training and Education Department, Northwestern Bell Telephone Company, Staff Manager-Administration, 2800 Wayzata Boulevard, Minneapolis, MN 55405.

Additional information about the courses: Program on Noncollegiate Sponsored Instruction, The Center for Adult Learning and Educational Credentials, American Council on Education, One Dupont Circle, Washington, D.C. 20036.

AC/DC Basic Electronics (NM54009)

Location: Des Moines, IA; Minneapolis, MN; and Omaha, NE.

Length: 160 hours (80 AC, 80 DC) (4 weeks).

Dates: December 1981-Present.

Objective: To provide supervisors and craft personnel with a basic background in AC and DC electronics.

Instruction: Covers a noncalculus treatment of fundamental electrical quantities, Ohm's Law, electromagnetism, schematics, instrumentation, basic mathematics, component operation, circuit design, transformers and impedance. Self-paced with a classroom facilitator.

Credit recommendation: In the lower division baccalaureate/associate degree category, 3 semester hours in Electronic Technology (10/83).

Air Dryer Maintenance Course (5) (DM02000, DM02000A, B, C, and D)

Location: Des Moines, IA.
Length: 36 hours (4½ days).
Dates: March 1982-Present.

Objective: To provide experienced personnel with the skills and knowledge to maintain and repair a variety of devices to remove moisture from communications lines.

Instruction: Instruction and practical exercises in the operation of several air drying compressor systems including oilless piston types, water seal/liquid ring types, heat reactivated/water seal types, and oil lubricated types, the identification of system components, standard operation procedures, general maintenance procedures, and troubleshooting and repair practices.

Credit recommendation: In the lower division baccalaureate/associate degree category, 1 semester hour in Pneumatics (10/83).

Assistant Manager Initial Training (AMIT) Phase I and II (2212, 2213)

Location: Minneapolis, MN.
Length: 86 hours.
Dates: April 1982-Present.

Objective: This course teaches the student the administrative procedures and job designed functions of the Assistant Manager. It addresses the duties associated with the development function of the Assistant Managers job design.

Instruction: Instruction is given in work force planning and analysis. Students learn review procedures for service representatives, as well as summarization of customer calls. Workload and performance evaluations are detailed and discussed.

Credit recommendation: In the lower division baccalaureate/associate degree category, 2 semester hours in Principles of Supervision (10/83).

Basic Carrier (NM54304)

Location: Minneapolis, MN.
Length: 40 hours (1 week).
Dates: June 1982-Present.

Objective: To provide students and supervisors with a fundamental background in basic transmission theory and operation as applied to the telephone environment.

Instruction: Lectures and limited practical exercises covering transmission principles including characteristic impedance, losses and noise; carrier system principles including descriptions of AM modulation, balanced bridge modulation, lattice modulation, and filter operation; high frequency carrier line characteristics; fundamentals of digital transmission including differences, between analog and digital signals, time division multiplexing and digital terminals; as each of these items pertain to the telephone system.

Credit recommendation: In the lower division baccalaureate/associate degree category, 1 semester hour in Communication Systems Practices (10/83).

Basic Carrier for Outside Forces (DM53045)

Location: Des Moines, IA.
Length: 40 hours (1 week).
Dates: May 1982-Present.

Objective: To provide students and supervisors with the fundamentals of both analog and digital type carrier systems.

Instruction: Instruction and practical exercises in the fundamentals of analog carriers including frequency combining and separating, multi-channel operation, signal loss, loss measurements and troubleshooting and digital carriers including carrier components encoding and decoding, loss measurements, and specialized digital apparatus.

Credit recommendation: In the lower division baccalaureate/associate degree category, 1 semester hour in Communication Systems Practices (10/83).

Basic Telephone Accounting (AC79400)

Location: Des Moines, IA; Minneapolis, MN; and Omaha, NE.
Length: 32 hours (4 days).
Dates: March 1981-Present.

Objective: To enable the student to understand the nature and purpose of accounting.

Instruction: Instruction covers the basic accounting cycle, and financial statements. Students apply general accounting principles and processes to telephone accounting in preparing specific financial reports. Course uses lectures, visual aids, workbook exercises and case problems.

Credit recommendation: In the lower division baccalaureate/associate degree category, 2 semester hours in Principles of Accounting (10/83).

Basic Trainer Skills Workshops (BTSW) (HR3200)

Location: Des Moines, IA; Minneapolis, MN; and Omaha, NE.
Length: 40 hours.
Dates: September 1979-Present.

Objective: To develop both understanding and skills in training new instructors, people who give presentations, and Quality of Work Life facilitators.

Instruction: The course focuses on adult learning styles, ethical considerations, modes of instruction, training skills, and self assessment techniques. Lectures with videotaping of practice sessions are utilized.

Credit recommendation: In the lower division baccalaureate/associate degree category, 1 semester hour in Teaching Methods or Speech Communications (10/83).

BM 0167 200 Series Data Sets
  Location: Des Moines, IA.
  Length: 42 hours (self-paced).
  Dates: November 1976-Present.
  Objective: To train personnel to install and maintain the family of 200 Series Data Sets (Modems).
  Instruction: Covers the operation of a specialized test set to test synchronous and asynchronous modems; the installation, use, testing, and maintenance of a series of medium speed, high speed modem units, including the RS-323-E1A, carrier operations, transmission losses, wiring procedures, fault analysis, unit testing and maintenance.
  Credit recommendation: In the lower division baccalaureate/associate degree category, 1 semester hour in Electronic Communications Technology (4/85).

Business Office Supervisor Training (RC72210)
  Location: Des Moines, IA and Minneapolis, MN.
  Length: 120 hours (3 weeks).
  Dates: January 1972-Present.
  Objective: To present the skills necessary to perform the business office supervisor's job along with the activities and procedures necessary to carry them out.
  Instruction: Instruction is provided in the areas of job enrichment problem-solving, documentation, interviewing, evaluation, and follow-up. Role playing and student presentations are used as the instructional mode.
  Credit recommendation: In the lower division baccalaureate/associate degree category, 3 semester hours in Principles of Supervision (10/83).

Business Representative Initial Training/Account System Inquiry (80)
  Location: Minneapolis, MN.
  Length: 195 hours (self-paced and laboratory).
  Dates: September 1982-Present.
  Objective: To train students to respond to customer inquiries and account processing.
  Instruction: Covers telephone billings, referral notices, payments, duplicate bills, and adjustments. Methodology includes self-paced learning activities and practical exercises.
  Credit recommendation: In the vocational certificate category, 3 semester hours in Customer Relations (10/83).

Cable Repair-Air Leak Locating (DM0446)
  Location: Des Moines, IA.
  Length: 32 hours.
  Dates: July 1980-Present.
  Objective: To provide the student with skills and knowledge helpful in the locating of leaks in cable air systems.
  Instruction: This training provides the student with knowledge on how to locate leaks in a non-pipe or pipe system, using the cable pressurization computer (slide rule) and the gradient system. It is a self-paced instruction consisting of workbooks, cassette tapes and cable simulators.
  Credit recommendation: In the lower division baccalaureate/associate degree category, 1 semester hour in Pneumatics (10/83).

Circuit Reading (Business) (BM016)
  Location: Des Moines, IA and Minneapolis, MN.
  Length: 30 hours (4 days).
  Dates: September 1982-Present.
  Objective: To teach the student how to identify electronic components and their applications in interpreting communication circuits and systems.
  Instruction: Covers the reading of circuits, basic terminology, symbols and abbreviations and the relationship these terms and symbols have to circuit design.
  Credit recommendation: In the lower division baccalaureate/associate degree category, 1 semester hour in Communication Systems Practices (10/83).

Clerical Supervisor's Training (RC72220)
  Location: Des Moines, IA and Minneapolis, MN.
  Length: 80 hours (2 weeks).
  Dates: June 1975-Present.
  Objective: To provide the basic skills necessary to perform the clerical supervisor's job, along with the activities and procedures necessary to carry them out.
  Instruction: Instruction is given in the area of job enrichment, problem-solving, interviewing, performance evaluation, and documentation. Teaching methods include role playing and student presentations.
  Credit recommendation: In the lower division baccalaureate/associate degree category, 2 semester hours in Principles of Supervision (10/83).

COMM STOR II Flexible Diskette Terminal (BMO 455)
  Location: Des Moines, IA.
  Length: 40 hours (1 week).
  Dates: December 1980-Present.
  Objective: To provide the student with knowledge and skills necessary to perform installations and maintenance of the COMM-STOR II Floppy Disk Unit.
  Instruction: An instructor-led presentation in a classroom environment covering such topics as: floppy disk

operation, disk controller, operations parameters, refresh disk usage, disk command system, system diagnostics, disk units maintenance and troubleshooting; to include practice exercises.

Credit recommendation: In the lower division baccalaureate/associate degree category, 2 semester hours in Electronic Communications Technology (4/85).

Consumer Relations Practicum (BC 52310)
Location: Minneapolis and Des Moines Training Centers.
Length: 120 hours (3 weeks).
Dates: March 1984-Present.
Objective: To provide the students with basic customer contact skills and the associated clerical activities required of a service representative.
Instruction: Lecture, classroom exercise, simulation and problem solving are used to teach customer contact skills in handling incoming calls, service orders, adjustments, and payment procedures.
Credit recommendation: In the lower division baccalaureate/associate degree category, 1 semester hour in Economics or Marketing (4/85).

Criterion Referenced Instruction Workshop (HR39152)
Location: Des Moines, IA; Minneapolis, MN; and Omaha, NE.
Length: 80 hours (minimum 2 weeks); 120 hours (maximum 3 weeks); self-paced and classroom instruction.
Dates: November 1980-Present.
Objective: To develop an understanding of the process in preparing, operating, and instructing a criterion referenced training program.
Instruction: Students follow a manual through the role of course developer and the supervisors of the learning process. Goal analysis, performance analysis, task analysis, and preparing criterion materials are discussed. Both workshop and self-paced instruction is used.
Credit recommendation: In the upper division baccalaureate category, 1 semester hour in Instructional Design (10/83).

Data Speed 40 (BM0311)
Location: Des Moines, IA.
Length: 80 hours (Self-paced).
Dates: August 1978-Present.
Objective: To provide personnel with the skills and knowledge necessary to perform installation, test, and maintenance activities on the Data Speed 40 terminal, printer, and display monitor.
Instruction: Consists of a series of color video cassette recordings and a workbook. The package is self-paced with employees "hands-on" performance. Course content includes component access/installation, operational checkout, printer and monitor adjustment, and troubleshooting.

Credit recommendation: In the vocational certificate category, 2 semester hours in Data Communication System Installation and Maintenance (4/85).

Data Transmission Fundamentals (BM0160 & BM0161)
Location: Des Moines, IA.
Length: 49 hours (2 weeks).
Dates: January 1979-Present.
Objective: To provide the student with a fundamental understanding of data systems features, terminology, and concepts of data transmission.
Instruction: To handle the basic skills necessary to establish and maintain data transmission facilities, to perform required transmission tests, analyze results to determine if requirements are met, and take corrective action when necessary.
Credit recommendation: In the lower division baccalaureate/associate category, 3 semester hours in Electronic Communications Technology (4/85).

Dataphone II (BM0414C)
Location: Des Moines, IA.
Length: 64 hours (2 weeks).
Dates: January 1981-Present.
Objective: To provide personnel with the knowledge and skills necessary to perform installation and repair procedures on Dataphone II equipment.
Instruction: Lecture and laboratory exercises in the installation and maintenance of data sets, installation and testing the diagnostic console and network controller of Dataphone II equipment.
Credit recommendation: In the vocational certificate category, 3 semester hours in Data Communication Systems Maintenance (4/85).

Digital Techniques (NM54015)
Location: Des Moines, IA; Minneapolis, MN; and Omaha, NE.
Length: 150 hours (4 days).
Dates: August 1980-Present.
Objective: To provide students and supervisors with the knowledge of digital electronic fundamentals.
Instruction: Self-paced instruction and practical exercises in digital techniques, semiconductor devices for digital circuits, digital logic circuits, digital integrated circuits including TTL, ECL, MOS and CMOS, Boolean algebra, flip-flops, registers, sequential logic, combinational logic including decoders, multiplexers, de-multiplaners and ROMS, and the application of these to digital design.
Credit recommendation: In the lower division baccalaureate/associate degree category, 3 semester hours in Digital Systems (10/83).

Dimension 400 PBX Installation and Maintenance (BM0298)
  Location: Des Moines, IA.
  Length: 72 hours (2 weeks).
  Dates: November 1980-Present.
  Objective: To provide personnel with the necessary training to install and maintain a Dimension 400 PBX (Private Business Exchange) at the block diagram level.
  Instruction: This is an instructor-led hands-on course covering operation, use, installation, and maintenance of a digital signal processing system. Includes central processor operation and maintenance, software descriptions, installation testing, and software diagnostic programs for system troubleshooting.
  Credit recommendation: In the lower division baccalaureate/associate degree category, 3 semester hours in Electronic Communications Technology (4/85).

Electronic Circuits (NM54013)
  Location: Des Moines, IA; Minneapolis, MN; and Omaha, NE.
  Length: 100 hours (2½ weeks).
  Dates: August 1980-Present.
  Objective: To provide supervisors and craft personnel with a basic background in electronic circuit structure and operations.
  Instruction: Covers basic amplifiers, operational amplifiers, power supplies, oscillators, pulse circuits, modulation circuits and detector circuits. Self-paced material with a classroom facilitator.
  Credit recommendation: In the lower division baccalaureate/associate degree category, 2 semester hours in Electronics Technology (10/83).

Electronic Switching Systems - No. 1 ESS Peripheral Units (OJT) 507B, 508B (OJI)
  Location: Northwestern Bell Centers.
  Length: 52 hours (Self-paced).
  Dates: January 1978-Present.
  Objective: To provide hands-on practice and the necessary knowledge to progress to more advanced No. 1 level ESS and ESS peripheral units operation and maintenance.
  Instruction: Lecture and laboratory exercises in fault diagnosis and repair of No. 1 level electronics switching systems and their related peripheral units. Analysis is at the block diagram level and includes program diagnosis, testing procedures for service lines and equipment, logic circuit testing, and central processor hardware options.
  Credit recommendation: In the vocational certificate category, 1 semester hour in Electronic Switching Systems Maintenance (4/85).

1/1A Electronic Switching System - Method of Operation 1, NE34535
  Location: Des Moines, IA.
  Length: 3-6 hours (1 day).
  Dates: January 1977-Present.
  Objective: To provide the student with knowledge of terminology of memory organization and equipment component functions, and the ability to trace outgoing, incoming, intraoffice, and tandem calls, and identify hardware and software components and functions.
  Instruction: Covers the operation, features, and documentation of the No. 1 Electronic Switching System. An introduction to the No. 1 Electronic Switching System.
  Credit recommendation: In the vocational certificate category, 1 semester hour in Electronic Switching Systems (4/85).

1/1A Electronic Switching System (508KA, KB, KD, KF)
  Location: Minneapolis Training Center.
  Length: Self-paced instruction (average 152 hours).
  Dates: April 1985-Present.
  Objective: To provide the student with the general knowledge and maintenance procedures required to work on first, second, and third generation Electronic Switching System (ESS) Peripherals.
  Instruction: Covers operation, maintenance, and fault diagnosis of first, second, and third generation ESS Remreed Switching network and its related equipment, including switching path networks, trunk switching frames, junction switching, network maintenance, pulse distribution diagnostics, trunk circuit analysis, and digital switching diagnostics. Self-paced instruction and practice exercises are used.
  Credit recommendation: In the vocational certificate category, 6 semester hours in Electronic Communications Technology or in the lower division baccalaureate/associate degree category, 4 semester hours in Electronic Communications Technology (4/85).

Experienced Trainer's Laboratory (HR38028)
  Location: Des Moines, IA; Minneapolis, MN; and Omaha, NE.
  Length: 36 hours (4½ days).
  Dates: January 1983-Present.
  Objective: To develop understanding and skills in updating experienced trainer's skills.
  Instruction: Emphasis is on updating the knowledge and skills gained on the job and through previous training workshops. Students will apply improved teaching techniques in role playing sessions which will be followed by written, oral, and video taped feedback.
  Credit recommendation: In the lower division baccalaureate/associate degree category, 1 semester hour in Introduction to Teaching Methods or Speech Communication (10/83).

Hardwired Administration Workshop (HAW-B) (NE39261)
  Location: Des Moines, IA (or suitcased to contract lo-

cation).
Length: 36 hours (1 week).
Dates: January 1983-Present.
Objective: To teach the daily and monthly activities involved in an inventory and investment record keeping system.
Instruction: An instructor led course providing instruction in material identification, interpretation, and listing in appropriate format for entry in a computerized inventory management system. Specific topics include central office property record keeping, batch billing, company engineered orders, job status updates, miscellaneous property records, retirement and online formats, and reconciliation formats.
Credit recommendation: In the lower division baccalaureate/associate degree category, 2 semester hours in Technical Management (4/85).

Horizon 32A (BM0370)
Location: Des Moines, IA.
Length: 36 hours (1 week).
Dates: June 1980-Present.
Objective: To train personnel to operate, install, test, and maintain a custom telephone service system (Horizon 32A).
Instruction: Provides lecture and laboratory instruction for personnel to install and maintain the Horizon Communication System. Topics include identification and operating of MET and CAP button, testing all available features of the system and the performance of maintenance tests, including warm start, alarm test, skip memory test, pooled line test. Features of Type B common equipment are identified along with new circuit pack, and changes in existing circuit packs in the Horizon Communication System.
Credit recommendation: In the vocational certificate category, 1 semester hour in Communication Systems Practices (4/85).

If It's to Be, It's Up to Me - A Value Added Seminar (RD02268)
Location: Minneapolis, MN; Omaha, NE; Des Moines, IA.
Length: 24 hours (3 days).
Dates: July 1983-Present.
Objective: To instruct students in the process of company and individual evaluations and to provide techniques for implementing change.
Instruction: Lecture, discussion, simulations, and problem solving are used to evaluate the interaction between corporate goals and values and those of employees. The impact of organizational and individual change is analyzed.
Credit recommendation: In the lower division baccalaureate/associate degree category, 1 semester hour in Management (4/85).

Insights for Sales Managers (RD32216)
Location: Minneapolis, MN.
Length: 28 hours (3½ days).
Dates: April 1982-Present.
Objective: To train students in the fundamentals of supervision.
Instruction: Students are instructed in the basic principles of supervision. The purpose is to create a positive work climate and to gain insights to directing the productive energies of workers. Methodology includes lectures, video tapes and related exercises, role playing, and self-assessment exercises.
Credit recommendation: In the lower division baccalaureate/associate degree category, 1 semester hour in Principles of Supervision or Sales Management (10/83).

Instructional Module Development (HR39273)
Location: Des Moines, IA; Minneapolis, MN; and Omaha, NE.
Length: 40 hours (minimum 1 week); 80 hours (maximum 2 weeks).
Dates: November 1980-Present.
Objective: To prepare students to develop instructional modules and delivery systems.
Instruction: Course covers complete development of an instructional module including the description of a module, the objectives to be met by an instructional module, the selection of delivery systems, preparation and writing, testing, and revision. Methodology is mostly self-paced and modular.
Credit recommendation: In the upper division baccalaureate category, 1 semester hour in Instructional Design (10/83).

Introduction to Electronic Systems Concepts (BM0100)
Location: Des Moines, IA and Minneapolis, MN.
Length: 24 hours (3 days).
Dates: March 1982-Present.
Objective: To familiarize the student with the fundamentals of computer systems as applied to present day communications.
Instruction: An instructor-led, multimedia course designed to acquaint the trainee with the following electronic systems concepts: numbering systems, logic circuits, computer concepts, programming fundamentals, and data communications.
Credit recommendation: In the lower division baccalaureate/associate degree category, 1 semester hour in Computer Technology/Electronics Technology (10/83).

Introduction to ESS (2nd Generation)
1. Introduction to ESS - Common - 507AA
1A Technology Common Peripheral Units - 508AA
Location: Minneapolis Training Center, Minneapolis, MN.
Length: Self-paced instruction (average 209 hours).

Dates: November 1981-Present.

Objective: To provide the student with entry-level skills and knowledge for first and second generation electronic switching technology.

Instruction: Covers Electronic Switching Systems overview, numbering systems, diodes and transistors, logic circuits, hardware, oscilloscope usage, basic ESS communication buses, principal components, skills required for locating trouble.

Credit recommendation: In the lower division baccalaureate/associate degree category, 3 semester hours in Electronic Communications Technology (4/85).

1. Introduction to Hewlett Packard (DM53020)
2. Introduction to DBMS (DM53021)

Location: Des Moines, IA.
Length: 40 hours (5 days).
Dates: January 1983-Present.

Objective: To teach the use of the HP/125, with specific attention to Data Base Management System.

Instruction: Lecture and exercises are used to allow students to gain proficiency in using HP/125 microcomputer and to use data base management program.

Credit recommendation: In the vocational certificate category, 1 semester hour in Computer Science (4/85).

Introduction to Hewlett Packard (DM53020)
Introduction to Super CALC 2 (DM53055)

Location: Des Moines, IA.
Length: 40 hours (5 days).
Dates: January 1983-Present.

Objective: To teach the use of the HP/125, with specific attention to the Super CALC 2, spreadsheet program.

Instruction: Lecture and exercises are used to allow students to gain proficiency in using HP/125 microcomputer and to use Super CALC 2, spreadsheet program.

Credit recommendation: In the vocational certificate category, 1 semester hour in Computer Science (4/85).

Introduction to Telephone Dialing Systems
1. NE34555: Step-by-Step Method of Operation

Location: Des Moines, IA.
Length: 36 hours (1 week).
Dates: October 1975-Present.

Objective: To provide the student with the ability to describe the SXS switching components and the functions of the components, and to identify the switching paths of calls through the SXS system.

Instruction: Covers the basic step-by-step (SXS switch, terminal banks, types of selectors and measurement items), and the function and operation of the originating, terminating, and distributing stages. Also covered are selector multiple grading, selector arrangements, and trunking. A familiarization of DDD and Touch-Tone is included.

Credit recommendation: In the lower division baccalaureate/associate degree category, 1 semester hour in Electronic Communications Technology (4/85).

Key Systems (BM0139)
Location: Des Moines, IA; Minneapolis, MN.
Length: Self-paced (approximately 100 hours).
Dates: August 1975-Present.

Objective: To train newly assigned key system technicians to install or repair a basic key telephone system. The trainee will perform all the necessary installation tasks and testing procedures needed to verify the proper operation of the component parts of the system.

Instruction: Lecture and laboratory instruction in location of Bell Systems practices information, grounding and bonding power units, connection and tracing wiring in key telephone sets, and installation of manual and touch-tone dial intercoms, CO/PBX lines, power failure services, and common audible signaling. Also includes reading and interpretation of the USOC Manual, and basic service order (business).

Credit recommendation: In the vocational certificate category, 2 semester hours in Communication Systems Installation Techniques (4/85).

Labor Relations Seminar (HR78005)
Location: Des Moines, IA; Minneapolis, MN; Omaha, NE.
Length: 18 hours (2 days).
Dates: September 1975-Present.

Objective: To provide training in labor relations techniques aimed at managing employee grievances and to recognize behaviors that affect Union/Management relationships.

Instruction: Lecture, discussion, guest speakers, and case problems are utilized to understand the general labor relations agreement. Emphasis is placed on informal grievance meeting procedures.

Credit recommendation: In the lower division baccalaureate/associate degree category, 1 semester hour in Management (4/85).

Loop Electronics-Construction and Maintenance Supervision (DM73049)
Location: Des Moines, IA.
Length: 40 hours (1 week).
Dates: June 1982-Present.

Objective: To provide supervisors responsible for the installation, testing and maintenance of digital subscriber Loop carrier systems with the appropriate installation, testing, and maintenance procedures for those systems.

Instruction: Lectures and practical exercises in the operation, testing and troubleshooting of a specialized digital subscribe Loop carrier system including discussions of modulations procedures, equipment submodules, and to maintenance and repair of the items found in this digital communication system.

Credit recommendation: In the lower division baccalaureate/associate degree category, 1 semester hour in Communication Systems Practices (10/83).

Time Management (HR38014)
Managing the Job (HR38015)
Managing the Flow of Work (HR38016)
Developing Subordinates (HR38017)

Location: Des Moines, IA; Minneapolis, MN; and Omaha, NE.

Length: 40 hours (5 days).

Dates: January 1981-Present.

Objective: To provide newly appointed second level managers (i.e., supervisor of supervisors) an understanding of some of the basic principles of management.

Instruction: Course offers new second-level managers a basic understanding of some of the principles of management. Topics covered include time management; goal setting; problem-solving; interviewing and negotiating; planning and monitoring the work flow; and developing subordinates. Methodology includes lectures, case studies, discussions, self-paced instruction, and role playing.

Credit recommendation: In the lower division baccalaureate/associate degree category, 2 semester hours in Principles of Management (2/84).

Managing the Work (HR38009) and Managing Performance (HR38010)

Location: Des Moines, IA; Minneapolis, MN; and Omaha, NE.

Length: 56 hours.

Dates: February 1982-Present.

Objective: To provide newly appointed first level supervisors an understanding of the principles of supervision.

Instruction: Course offers new supervisors an introduction to the knowledge and skills required in managing the performance and work of subordinates. Specific techniques examined are planning and monitoring, problem-solving, coaching, counseling, and providing performance feedback.

Credit recommendation: In the lower division baccalaureate/associate degree category, 2 semester hours in Principles of Supervision (2/84).

Managing to Write (HR38012) and Defining the Job (HR38013); Managing Problem Solving (HR38011)

Location: Des Moines, IA; Minneapolis, MN; and Omaha, NE.

Length: 48 hours (6 days).

Dates: November 1980-Present.

Objective: To provide newly appointed second level managers with an understanding of the basic principles of business communications.

Instruction: Course offers newly appointed second level managers with the knowledge and skills needed to write memos, letters, documents, and job definitions. Topics covered include setting specific correspondence objectives, establishing tone, building writing strategies, and writing job definitions. Methodology includes lectures, discussions, and self-paced workbooks.

Credit recommendation: In the lower division baccalaureate/associate degree category, 2 semester hours in Business Communications (2/84).

Microprocessor Programming and Applications (NM54017)

Location: Des Moines, IA; Minneapolis, MN; and Omaha, NE.

Length: 200 hours (5 weeks).

Dates: August 1980-Present.

Objective: To provide supervisors and craft personnel with a fundamental knowledge of microprocessor programming and applications.

Instruction: Covers number systems and codes, microcomputers, computer arithmetic, programming, microprocessor usage, interfacing, programming experiments and interfacing experiments. Self-paced with classroom facilitators and laboratory exercises.

Credit recommendation: In the lower division baccalaureate/associate degree category, 4 semester hours in Computer Technology (10/83).

Methods Developers' Workshop (HR38021)

Location: Des Moines, IA; Minneapolis, MN; and Omaha, NE.

Length: 80 hours (2 weeks).

Dates: January 1980-Present.

Objective: To enable the performer to develop methods in a systematic way that can enhance teaching effectiveness.

Instruction: Objective identification, flowcharting, instructional aids, methods development and follow-up are all stressed in a systematic manner. Methodology emphasizes case studies; lecture, discussion, laboratory and demonstration.

Credit recommendation: In the upper division baccalaureate category, 1 semester hour in Vocational Education (10/83).

New Age Thinking for Achieving Your Potential (RD02267)

Location: Des Moines, IA; Minneapolis, MN; and Omaha, NE.

Length: 28 hours (3½ days).

Dates: January 1982-Present.

Objective: To guide the participant toward an understanding and acceptance of his or her own talents and resources, instill belief in personal ability to succeed, and expand vision of available opportunities.

Instruction: This course is designed to make the individual aware of the potential for self-development. Participants explore goal-setting, communications, problem-solving, self-esteem, motivation, and acceptance of and planning for change. Method of instruction includes filmed lectures, classroom discussion, and laboratory work.

Credit recommendation: In the lower division baccalaureate/associate degree category, 1 semester hour in Human Potential Seminar (10/83).

No. 1 ESS Processor Hardware and Maintenance
1. **Central Control Language Hardware and Maintenance - 534A**
2. **Program Store Maintenance - 534B**
3. **32K Call Store Maintenance - 534C**
4. **Signal Processor Language Hardware and Maintenance - 534D**
5. **Master Control Center and Associated Frames Diagnostics - 534E**
   Location: Minneapolis, MN.
   Length: Self-paced instruction (average 299 hours).
   Dates: November 1981-Present.
   Objective: To provide the student with the skills, knowledge, and techniques required to maintain the central processor free of hardware faults.
   Instruction: Course covers central control, program store, call store, signal processor, and master control center. Five modules. Tests after each unit. Must obtain 100 percent on each test prior to continuing. Self-paced, practical exercises under supervision of an administrator.
   Credit recommendation: In the vocational certificate category, 6 semester hours in Electronic Communications Technology (4/85).

No. 1 ESS Software Maintenance
1. **Generic Program - 539A**
2. **Parameters - 539B**
3. **Translations - 539C**
4. **Call Processing - 539D**
5. **Maintenance and Alarm Printouts - 539E**
6. **Maintenance Procedures - 539F**
   Location: Minneapolis, MN.
   Length: Self-paced instruction (average 233 hours).
   Dates: November 1981-Present.
   Objective: To develop the skills that will enable an individual to perform tasks in the area of software maintenance for No. 1 Electronic Switching Systems (ESS).
   Instruction: Covers use of generic program documentation locating and clearing parameter and translation problems, applied knowledge of No. 1 ESS call processing, resolving audit error printouts, and off-line testing. Self-paced instruction with graded exams.
   Credit recommendation: In the vocational certificate category, 6 semester hours in Switching System Software Diagnostics (4/85).

No. 5 Crossbar - Method of Operation
1. **No. 5 Method of Operation - 34565**
   Location: Des Moines, IA.
   Length: 36 hours (1 week).
   Dates: January 1976-Present.
   Objective: To give students a general understanding of the No. 5 Crossbar Switching System, plus a detailed knowledge of the various equipment components and their functions on different types of calls.
   Instruction: Covers the crossbar switch, all components of No. 5 Crossbar equipment, trunking arrangements, linkage, special features such as tandem and coin junctor operation, paired and tripled trunk lines, paired line links, etc. Included is an explanation of load and service registers.
   Credit recommendation: In the vocational certificate category, 2 semester hours in Data Communications Fundamentals (4/85).

Performance Data Collection and Analysis (HR38024)
   Location: Des Moines, IA; Minneapolis, MN; and Omaha, NE.
   Length: 40 hours.
   Dates: December 1982-Present.
   Objective: To identify performance deficiencies.
   Instruction: Topics include identification of performance deficiencies; deficiency analysis; identification of job-related tasks, skills, knowledges and abilities; data collection and appropriate instruments. Modes of instruction include role playing, lectures and individual group exercises.
   Credit recommendation: In the lower division baccalaureate/associate degree category, 1 semester hour in Principles of Supervision (10/83).

Plug-In Administration Workshop (NE39404)
   Location: Des Moines, IA.
   Length: 36 hours (1 week).
   Dates: January 1983-Present.
   Objective: To provide the student with knowledge of inventory and record data, monthly billing reconciliations, annual batch run reports, inventory management activities, controlling expenditures, and management decision strategies used in each phase of inventory cycle.
   Instruction: Covers analysis of output products in order to manage inventory efficiency. The management of inventory and control systems is covered with many practical examples.
   Credit recommendation: In the lower division baccalaureate/associate degree category, 2 semester hours in Technical Management (4/85).

Plug-In Operations Workshop (PIOW) NE39403
   Location: Des Moines, IA.
   Length: 36 hours (1 week).
   Dates: January 1983-Present.

Objective: To provide the trainee with information pertaining to equipment inventory control; to include the identification of basic situations that can be used to develop practices peculiar to a local setting.

Instruction: A group-paced and instructor-led course designed to teach the processing of data entries and the analysis of the output products of the Plug-In Inventory Control System/Detailed Continuing Property Record; a detailed description of operations and procedures is covered in a day-to-day activity to enable an ongoing analysis of the student's comprehension.

Credit recommendation: In the lower division baccalaureate/associate degree category, 2 semester hours in Technical Management (4/85).

Professional Telephone Sales (RC51014)
Location: Minneapolis, MN.
Length: 166 hours (4 weeks).
Dates: May 1984-Present.
Objective: To instruct students in professional telephone sales techniques. Basic sales procedures are used to match customer needs with company products.
Instruction: Self-instructional exercises and simulations are used to develop product knowledge, sales skills, and closing techniques.
Credit recommendation: In the lower division baccalaureate/associate degree category, 1 semester hour in Marketing (4/85).

Q CALC (1209)
Location: Des Moines, IA.
Length: 24 hours (3 days).
Dates: September 1984-Present.
Objective: To provide instruction in Q CALC Electronic Spreadsheet.
Instruction: Lecture, discussion and classroom exercises are used to present the initial features of the Q CALC Spreadsheet. Self-paced instruction is used for the remainder of the course.
Credit recommendation: In the vocational certificate category, 1 semester hour in Computer Science (4/85).

Representative Course Administrative Training (RCAT) (RC71016)
Location: Minneapolis Training Center.
Length: 35 hours (1 week).
Dates: December 1983-Present.
Objective: To provide the student with the skills needed to instruct the adult learner, administer self-instruction training, conduct evaluations and recommend remedial action.
Instruction: Lecture, classroom exercises, and simulations are used to cover problem recognition, problem solving, positive reinforcement, questioning and answering techniques, and listening skills associated with self-instruction modes of learning.
Credit recommendation: In the lower divison baccalaureate/associate degree category, 1 semester hour in Education (4/85).

Residence Telephone Order Center RITC-RTOC (RC51014)
Location: Minneapolis, MN.
Length: 149 hours (3.9 weeks).
Dates: April 1982-August 1984.
Objective: To prepare service representatives for customer contact interaction and to recommend various company products.
Instruction: Instruction is given in microfiche reading, selling skills, customer relations, repair calls, and contact memoranda. Students learn consumer interaction techniques through the use of the Customer Contact Simulation Unit.
Credit recommendation: In the lower division baccalaureate/associate degree category, 3 semester hours in Customer Relations (10/83).

Residence Account Service Center (RITL-RASC) (1013)
Location: Minneapolis, MN.
Length: 113 hours (3 weeks).
Dates: January 1982-Present.
Objective: To provide training to non-management personnel in performing service representative functions.
Instruction: This course trains the service representative to handle customer questions and complaints in a professional manner, take effective action to collect overdue bills, explain and adjust customer's bills, answer questions about long distance calls, and use a variety of reference documents. Methodology includes self-paced learning under an instructor's guidance and practice sessions in a Customer Contract Simulation Unit.
Credit recommendation: In the vocational certificate category, 3 semester hours in Customer Relations (10/83).

Semiconductor Devices (NM54011)
Location: Des Moines, IA; Minneapolis, MN; and Omaha, NE.
Length: 100 hours (2½ weeks).
Dates: August 1980-Present.
Objective: To provide supervisors and craft personnel with a fundamental knowledge of semiconductor structure and operation.
Instruction: Covers semiconductor structure, diodes, zence diodes, special applications bipolar transistors, field effect transistors, thynistors, integrated circuits and optoelectronic devices. Self-paced with classroom facilitator.
Credit recommendation: In the lower division baccalaureate/associate degree category, 2 semester hours in Electronics Technology (10/83).

Sights on Selling (RD02266)
  Location: Des Moines, IA and Minneapolis, MN.
  Length: 40 hours (1 week).
  Dates: April 1982-Present.
  Objective: To develop an understanding of the basic selling process to be used in telephone center stores.
  Instruction: Students are instructed in the basic selling process involving customer needs, information gathering, product recommendation and follow-up. Methodology includes video tapes, role playing, lecture and discussion.
  Credit recommendation: In the lower division baccalaureate/associate degree category, 1 semester hour in Principles of Salesmanship (10/83).

Sights on Selling-Instructor Certification (RD32265)
  Location: Des Moines, IA and Minneapolis, MN.
  Length: 64 hours (8 days).
  Dates: December 1981-Present.
  Objective: To develop an understanding of the basic selling process to be used in telephone center stores and acquire the skills necessary for training "new trainers."
  Instruction: Students are instructed in the basic selling process involving customer needs, information gathering, product recommendation and follow-up. In addition, co-training, sub-group activities and practice skill of giving and receiving feedback is covered. Methodology includes role playing, video tapes, lecture, and discussion.
  Credit recommendation: In the lower division baccalaureate/associate degree category, 1 semester hour in Principles of Salesmanship and 1 semester hour in Introduction to Teaching Methods (10/83).

Supervisory Relationships Training (HR78006)
  Location: Des Moines, IA; Minneapolis, MN; Omaha, NE.
  Length: 16 hours (2 days).
  Dates: January 1976-Present.
  Objective: To instruct participants in an objective, non-defensive approach to handling problems with employees.
  Instruction: Lecture, discussion, classroom exercises, and role playing used to analyze and plan discussions about productivity, quality, absenteeism, and other problem areas. Emphasis is placed on open communication.
  Credit recommendation: In the lower division baccalaureate/associate degree category, 1 semester hour in Management (4/85).

Test Development Workshop (HR38019)
Performance Analysis Workshop (HR39327)
Job Aid Workshop (HR39600)
  Location: Des Moines, IA; Minneapolis, MN; and Omaha, NE.
  Length: 72 hours (9 days).
  Dates: January 1980-Present.
  Objective: To train students in the development of instructional design and measurement techniques.
  Instruction: Students are instructed in the development and use of performance testing, analysis and job aid development, performance analysis, and learning strategies. Different evaluation procedures are analyzed, discussed, and validated. The course administrator provides feedback.
  Credit recommendation: In the upper division baccalaureate category, 2 semester hours in Instructional Development (10/83).

Word Processing (DM53020)
  Location: Des Moines, IA.
  Length: 20 hours (1 week).
  Dates: January 1983-Present.
  Objective: To provide the student with entry level theory in operating the Hewlett Packard 125 Microcomputer.
  Instruction: Lecture and laboratory exercises are used to instruct in disc formatting, editing, filing, and retrieval.
  Credit recommendation: In the vocational certificate category, 2 semester hours in Information Processing or Word Processing (4/85). NOTE: To receive credit for this course, students must successfully complete Introduction to HP 125 Word Processing (DM53057).

Word Processing (DM53057)
  Location: Des Moines, IA.
  Length: 28 hours (3½ days).
  Dates: January 1983-Present.
  Objective: To provide students with advanced theory in operating the HP 125 Microcomputer.
  Instruction: Lecture and laboratory exercises are used to train students in advance editing techniques and special function applications.
  Credit recommendation: In the vocational certificate category, 2 semester hours in Information Processing or Word Processing (4/85). NOTE: Students who receive credit for this course must have successfully completed Introduction to HP 125 Word Processing (DM53020)

Western Regional CUNA School for Credit Union Personnel

Western Regional CUNA (Credit Union National Association) School for Credit Union Personnel serves credit union employees in thirteen western states. Overall authority for school policies belongs to a policy committee comprised of industrial officials from these states. The policy committee has delegated the authority and responsibility for operating the school to a local administrative committee, which is comprised of credit union managers and staff members.

Because the school is located at Pomona College, it draws upon the college's resources including faculty and classrooms. The California Credit Union League provides administrative support and supplies all requested audiovisual and other equipment.

Source of official student records: Manager of Training Services, Western Regional CUNA School, California Credit Union League, 2322 So. Garey Avenue, Pomona, CA 91766.

Additional information about the courses: Program on Noncollegiate Sponsored Instruction, The Center for Adult Learning and Educational Credentials, American Council on Education, One Dupont Circle, Washington, D.C. 20036.

Western Regional CUNA School for Credit Union Personnel
   Location: Claremont, CA.
   Length: 3 two-week periods over 3 years.
   Dates: *Version 1:* August 1979-August 1981; *Version 2:* August 1982-Present.
   Objective: To provide credit union employees and officials with technical and managerial knowledge and skills.
   Instruction: *Area 1:* Business Management: principles, methods, and procedures essential to successful management with a focus on the major functions of management. (1) Planning: the decision making process, goal setting, organizational policies; (2) Organizing: structure, hierarchy and roles; (3) Leading/Directing: leadership styles, motivating, time management; (4) Controlling: the controlling process, evaluating budgeting. *Area 2:* Personnel Administration: staffing process, record keeping, evaluation and appraisal, compensation, discipline and conflict resolution, training and development, and work analysis. *Area 3:* Marketing and Advertising: marketing functions, practice, and research: advertising policy and problems germane to the credit union industry; economic principles and sociological factors underlying these areas. *Area 4:* Financial Management: cash management, budgeting, money and banking, payment systems, forecasting, portfolio management, risk management, business law, legal and regulatory problems. *Area 5:* Communications: effective oral and written communication. The following skills are emphasized: listening, providing feedback, understanding others, public speaking, and business writing. *Area 6:* Human Relations: the development of productive and satisfying work relationships. The following skills are emphasized: nonverbal communication, building a relationship, decision making, problem solving, stress diagnosis and management, and time management. Methodology includes lectures, cases, small group discussion, survey/questionnaire grids, and interactive group experiences.
   Credit recommendation: *Version 1:* In the lower division baccalaureate/associate degree category, 9 semester hours as follows: Same as Version 2 (below) except that there are no semester hours for Area 2. *Version 2:* In the lower division baccalaureate/associate degree category, 10 semester hours as follows: *Area 1:* 3 semester hours in Business Administration, Management, or Supervision; *Area 2:* 1 semester hour in Business Administration or Personnel Management; *Area 3:* 1 semester hour in Business Administration or Marketing; *Area 4:* 3 semester hours in Finance or Business Administration; *Area 5:* 1 semester hour in Business Administration, Communications, or Psychology; *Area 6:* 1 semester hour in Business Administration, Behavioral Sciences, or Psychology (1/82).

Westinghouse Electric Corporation, Defense and Electronics Center

Westinghouse Defense and Electronics Center (D&EC) is engaged in the design, production, and support of defense systems. Areas of concentration and expertise include avionics, command and control, electrical systems, electronic countermeasures, integrated logistics support, instrumentation, marine products, ocean systems, and space and information systems. Situated in Baltimore, Maryland, Westinghouse D&EC is the cities largest employer with over 18,000 employees.

The Personnel Development Department offers both day and evening courses for all management, professional, and clerical personnel. The day courses focus on general management, business, and behavioral science topics. The evening courses from the Westinghouse School of Applied Engineering Science offer engineering, computer science, management, and special studies curricula.

Training is generally conducted at the Baltimore site; however, some courses can be presented at different plant locations.

Source of official student records: Personnel Development Department, Westinghouse Electric Corporation, P.O. Box 1693, MS-4450, Baltimore, MD 21203.

Additional information about the courses: Program on Noncollegiate Sponsored Instruction, The Center for Adult Learning and Educational Credentials, American Council on Education, One Dupont Circle, Washington, D.C. 20036.

Advanced Microprocessing (577)
   Location: Various Baltimore-Washington International Westinghouse plant locations.
   Length: 30 hours (12 weeks).
   Dates: May 1983-December 1988.
   Objective: To learn microprocessor I/O architecture along with programming the microprocessor I/O devices. Learning to use an assembler on the 6800 and 8085 and perform a team project, presenting the results.
   Instruction: Four programs written using an assembler on the 6800 and 8085 microcomputers. Problems include I/O programming using interrupts and timing constraints. The student uses the ISIS Operating System. Homework problems are done each week from the text-

book. Midterm and final exam are used.

Credit recommendation: In the upper division baccalaureate category, 2 semester hours in Electrical Engineering or Computer Science (5/83).

Advanced Microwave Circuit Design (321.2)

Location: Various Baltimore-Washington International Westinghouse plant locations.

Length: 105 hours.

Dates: May 1983-December 1988.

Objective: To provide trained or experienced microwave engineer with the advanced circuit design techniques primarily as applied to microwave integrated circuits.

Instruction: Instruction and outside exercises dealing with transmission lines, Smith charts and matching concepts, S parameters, microwave integrated circuit systems, detectors, mixers, GaAs monolithic circuits, energy bands, doping, FET switches, phase shifters, PIN attenvators, matching networks, LN amplifiers, amplifier stability, microwave oscillators, and feedback techniques.

Credit recommendation: In the upper division baccalaureate or graduate degree category, 3 semester hours in Advanced Electromagnetic Field Theory or Microwave Theory (5/83).

Applied Engineering Software (584)

Location: Various Baltimore-Washington International Westinghouse plant locations.

Length: 30 hours (12 weeks).

Dates: February 1981-Present.

Objective: To teach FORTRAN 77 with simple applications, to learn to run programs on UNIVAC & UAX systems. Use of editors and subroutine packages. Students write, debug, and run programs on the above computers.

Instruction: Text FORTRAN 77 by Weissner and Orgawich. Lectures and recitation. Homework problems to write, debug and run 10 program. Midterm exams on use of editors and control language to run programs. Also questions on use of FORTRAN 77.

Credit recommendation: In the lower division baccalaureate/associate degree or upper division baccalaureate category, 3 semester hours in Engineering or Computer Science (5/83).

Basic Microprocessing (576)

Location: Various Baltimore-Washington International Westinghouse plant locations.

Length: 30 hours (12 weeks).

Dates: September 1976-December 1988.

Objective: To teach the fundamentals of microprocessor architecture and program simple machine language problems.

Instruction: Three single programs are run by the students on a microprocessor trainer. No sixteen bit microprocessors are discussed or used. No hardware or interfacing. Basically this is a programming course on M6800 and Intel 8085 in machine language. Homework is done from problems in the text. Midterm and final exam done in class with students writing programs.

Credit recommendation: In the lower division baccalaureate/associate degree or upper division baccalaureate category, 2 semester hours in Electrical Engineering or Computer Science (5/83).

Basic Microwave (321.1)

Location: Various Baltimore-Washington International Westinghouse plant locations.

Length: 102 hours.

Dates: May 1983-December 1988.

Objective: To provide trained or experienced individuals with the necessary background for understanding and designing microwave circuits and devices.

Instruction: Instruction and outside exercises dealing with electrostatics, laplace equations, potential distributions, numerical methods, gradients and divergence, magnetostatics, boundary conditions, Maxwell equations, wave equations, polarization, reflections, transmission line theory and analogy, guided waves, wave guides and propagation in stripline, coax, microstrip and slotguide.

Credit recommendation: In the upper division baccalaureate or graduate degree category, 3 semester hours in Electromagnetic Field Theory (5/83).

Introduction to Electronic Filtering I (390.1)

Location: Various Baltimore-Washington International Westinghouse plant locations.

Length: 30 hours.

Dates: May 1973-Present.

Objective: To acquaint the student with the mathematical concepts associated with electronic filtering. The student will be better able to identify design specification for various classes of filters.

Instruction: Includes the mathematical aspects of impulse and step responses, super position and convolution integrates, transfer function, attenuation and phase functions, group delay function, noise bandwidth, poles and zeros; and their relationships to the design of filtering systems. Analysis is carried out on both theoretical and realizable filter characteristics in both the time and frequency domain.

Credit recommendation: In the upper division baccalaureate or graduate degree category, 3 semester hours in Linear System Theory (5/83).

Introduction to Electronic Filtering II (390.2)

Location: Various Baltimore-Washington International Westinghouse plant locations.

Length: 30 hours.

Dates: February 1983-Present.

Objective: To acquaint the student with the intricate details and techniques of the design of electronic filters.

Instruction: Includes optimum linear filters, matched filters, digital filters, surface-wave filters, allepass filters for phase and group delay equalization, characteristics of insertion loss, impedance transformations, time-domain synthesis, and filter components and approximations.

Credit recommendation: In the graduate degree category, 3 semester hours in Electronic Filter Design (5/83).

LISP: The Artificial Intelligence Language (589.2)

Location: Various Baltimore-Washington International Westinghouse plant locations.
Length: 42-66 hours.
Dates: May 1983-Present.
Objective: To provide experienced personnel with a working knowledge of MACLISP, a dialect of the list processing language LISP.
Instruction: Lectures and outside exercises dealing with the use of MACLISP which can be used for Artificial Intelligence programming, especially those used in expert systems. Emphasis is placed on computer usage only in a final student project. Homework assignments do not require usage of a computer. Specific topics covered include: list operations, recursive program structures, interactive structures, MACRO and MAP. Functions, input/output functions, state space search, goal driven programming, knowledge representation and natural language interfaces.
Credit recommendation: In the upper division baccalaureate category, 2 semester hours in LISP Program Language in Computer Science (5/83).

Probability and Random Processes I (590.1)

Location: Various Baltimore-Washington International Westinghouse plant locations.
Length: 30 hours.
Dates: September 1982-December 1988.
Objective: To provide the student with an introduction to the foundations of probability theory and random processes.
Instruction: Included are the formulation of mathematical models of non-deterministic systems, elementary theory, probabilistic models, joint and conditional probabilities, and statistical independence, discrete and continuous random variables, impulsive densities, elementary decision theory and functions of random and vector random variables.
Credit recommendation: In the upper division baccalaureate category, 2 semester hours in Engineering and/or Computer Science (5/83).

Probability and Random Processes II (590.2)

Location: Various Baltimore-Washington International Westinghouse plant locations.
Length: 30 hours.
Dates: January 1983-December 1988.
Objective: To expand the elementary treatment of probability theory to concepts of statistical inference and basic estimation theory.
Instruction: Covers topics such as moments of random variables, characteristic functions, chebyshev inequality, prediction theory, central limit theorem, statistical inference; and estimation theory. The concept of stationary noise is explained and the role of the covariance function in minimum mean square predictions is introduced.
Credit recommendation: In the upper division baccalarueate category, 2 semester hours in Engineering and/or Computer Science (5/83).

MANAGEMENT COURSES

Effective Technical Presentations

Location: Various Baltimore-Washington International Westinghouse plant locations; Sunnyvale, CA.
Length: 23 hours (3 days).
Dates: June 1974-Present.
Objective: To provide theory and practice of effective technical presentation.
Instruction: The course covers techniques and tips of oral presentation, including visual aids (slides, charts, models). Student presentations are videotaped and critiqued by student participants and in-house management personnel.
Credit recommendation: In the vocational certificate category, 1 semester hour in Technical Communications (5/83).

Human Interaction and Communication
1. Transactional Analysis B120
2. Communications Workshop B100

Location: Various Baltimore-Washington International Westinghouse plant locations; Sunnyvale, CA.
Length: 39 hours.
Dates: September 1974-Present.
Objective: To give the student an understanding of dynamics of human interaction which includes developing techniques for interacting with others; analysis of communication barriers; and development of effective communications skills.
Instruction: Lecture, discussion, role playing, and individual/group exercises that focus on personal awareness and development, establishing and improving relationships with others, and elements of effective communication (listening, inferring, interpreting written and oral messages, group membership, interviewing, and gaining trust).
Credit recommendation: In the lower division baccalaureate/associate degree category, 1 semester hour in Communications, Human Relations, or Speech (5/83).

Leadership Development Workshop (B310)

Location: Local hotels in Baltimore, MD; Sunnyvale, CA.
Length: 24 hours (3 days).

Dates: January 1975-December 1988.

Objective: To survey the various models of leadership and motivational theories and their relationship to the workplace; to improve perceptions of ones leadership style and its effect on others in the work situation; to practice a systematic problem-solving method for use with a subordinate and with small groups; and to explore effective ways of planning and organizing your time.

Instruction: Presents a basic overview of leadership styles, motivational theories, time management, and problem-solving methods for beginning level management personnel. Lecture, discussion, and laboratory exercises are used.

Credit recommendation: In the lower division baccalaureate/associate degree category, 1 semester hour in Behavioral Science, Human Relations, Human Services or Management Science (5/83).

Management Functions and Policies

Location: Airport Square II, Elkridge Landing Road, Baltimore, MD.

Length: 24 hours (3 days).

Dates: June 1981-December 1988.

Objective: To develop management skills and performance, through the application of current behavioral theories, and to familiarize participants with Westinghouse corporate policies.

Instruction: The course, designed for second level management, uses lectures, discussion, role-playing, and other group exercises to examine such concepts as power, motivation, persuasion, and organizational climate, and to improve participants' problem-solving and decision-making skills.

Credit recommendation: In the upper division baccalaureate category, 1 semester hour in Management (5/83).

Management Techniques Seminar (B110)

Location: Airport Square II, Elkridge Landing Road, Baltimore, MD.

Length: 30 hours (4 days).

Dates: January 1979-December 1988.

Objective: To provide a pre-supervisory learning experience to assist professionals in determining their interest in a management career; to provide realistic management case studies and situations for problem-solving analysis; to provide an overview of communication techniques and transactional analysis; and to provide participants an opportunity to explore their behavioral patterns and cooperation style through inventory assessments.

Instruction: Presents an introduction to management techniques for professionals, technical personnel, and non-management personnel. The course covers leadership theory, employee performance behavior, motivation, communication, and decision theory. Lecture, discussion, outside preparation, and laboratory exercises are used.

Credit recommendation: In the lower division baccalaureate/associate degree category, 1 semester hour in Behavioral Science, Human Relations, Human Services or Management Science (5/83).

Models for Management Seminar

Location: Airport Square II, Elkridge Landing Road, Baltimore, MD.

Length: 30 hours.

Dates: June 1973-Present.

Objective: To provide a broad overview and synthesis of behavioral science concepts which apply to managerial practices, and to assist individual participants to assess their own management practices.

Instruction: This course is designed for management personnel. Through readings, lectures, and discussion, participants survey the behavioral concepts of Lewin, Maslow, Herzberg, and others, and apply them to case studies of management problems. Students complete self-appraisals, solicit appraisals from associates, and do individual and group exercises.

Credit recommendation: In the upper division baccalaureate or graduate degree category, 2 semester hours in Management (5/83).

WESTINGHOUSE CONTRACT MANAGEMENT PRO-SEMINAR

The Contracts Department for the Defense Business Unit is located at the Westinghouse Defense and Electronic Center in Baltimore, Maryland. The Contracts Department provides on-site or off-site classroom setting for the weekly course sessions, as well as any textbooks and reading materials required during the course. The department also maintains several resource centers containing 1,200 volumes of law, contracts, and accounting information, as well as complete sets of government regulations. Students have access to these resources. The Training and Development Department acts as a liaison with academic providers of education and training programs, authorizes tuition reimbursement benefits for employees pursuing continuing advanced education, collaborates with local educational institutions on special programs, and provides training services and consultation for employees. Course development is centrally coordinated by an instructional design team consisting of the Education, Training and Development Department and selected experienced and qualified Contracts staff.

Source of official student records: Director of the Westinghouse School of Applied Engineering Science, Westinghouse Defense and Electronics Center, Post Office Box 746, Mail Stop 4450, Baltimore, Maryland 21203.

Additional information about the courses: Program on Noncollegiate Sponsored Instruction, The Center for Adult Learning and Educational Credentials, American

Council on Education, One Dupont Circle, Washington, D.C. 20036.

Principles of Government Contract Management (Contracts Management Pro-Seminar)
Location: Baltimore area Defense and Electronic Center at on-site classrooms or a suitable conference facility.
Length: 39 hours (13 weeks); one 3-hour meeting per week.
Dates: May 1987-Present.
Objective: To enable the student to acquire a basic knowledge and understanding of the government procurement process from acquisition planning through contract closeout. Study will include government acquisition planning and budgeting, types of contracts, role and responsibilities of the contracting officer.
Learning Outcome: Upon successful completion of this course, students will have a sensitivity and understanding of the totality of the acquisition process. The course is designed to respond to government initiatives on professionalization, and students will enhance their expertise in the field of contract management.
Instruction: Course covers history of government regulation and cost accounting standards; government acquisition process review of *current* regulatory environment; government funding processes; solicitation procedures and activities (government and contractor); contract types; negotiations and mock negotiation; financial concepts, such as progress payments, advance payments, contract financing, cash flow strategies, and prompt payment requirements; allowable costs, defective pricing and audits, government vs. internal audits, risk management; laws and regulations; change management and administration; claims and claims avoidance; claims identification and processing, methods of computing price adjustments and modifying contract terms; warranty; terminations, disputes, contract closeout; international contracting considerations; the role and authority of an on-site government procurement office. Lecture, discussion, and self-assessment programs are used.
Credit recommendation: In the graduate category, 3 semester hours in Acquisition Management or Logistics and Materials Management (6/87).

Westinghouse Electric Corporation, Education Center Department

Westinghouse Electric Corporation is engaged primarily in the manufacture of products for the generation, transmission, and use of electricity. The Westinghouse Education Center Training Department offers formal course work to all management and professional employees throughout the corporation. Courses cover general management and business topics as well as more specialized subjects in the fundamental areas of manufacturing, engineering, finance, sales, marketing, etc.

Training for all employees is most frequently conducted in the Pittsburgh area. However, many courses can be presented at different plant or division sites.

Source of official student records: Director, Westinghouse Education Center, Ardmore Blvd. and Brinton Rd., Pittsburgh, PA 15221.

Additional information about the courses: Program on Noncollegiate Sponsored Instruction, The Center for Adult Learning and Educational Credentials, American Council on Education, One Dupont Circle, Washington, D.C. 20036.

Business Management Course (871)
Location: Pittsburgh, PA.
Length: 48 hours (6 days).
Dates: January 1972-Present.
Objective: To conduct self-assessment and relate that assessment to team effort; to apply accounting and financial tools and concepts in achieving managerial control; and to develop skills in applying behavioral concepts and processes in integrating individual needs with organizational goals.
Instruction: Covers the development of organizational and personal potential; managerial and financial concepts such as measurement of performance, financial statements, capital expenditures, and factors underlying depreciation policies; inventory policies; capital budgeting; analysis of production costs; standard cost systems, including direct costing vs. absorption costing; profitability improvement program; dynamics of individual/organizational growth. Utilizes lectures, instructions, workshops, demonstrations, group problem solving, and case studies.
Credit recommendation: In the upper division baccalaureate category, 2 semester hours in Accounting, Finance, or Management (11/77) (7/82). NOTE: This course has undergone a 5-year reevaluation and continues to meet requirements for credit recommendations.

Computer Concepts (885)
Location: Pittsburgh, PA.
Length: 30 hours (3 days).
Dates: April 1975-Present.
Objective: To provide an understanding of data processing needs within the framework of information systems logic and to provide an understanding of the problems of computer control.
Instruction: Includes introduction to data processing fundamentals; corporate applications; interaction with the computer via terminals.
Credit recommendation: In the lower division baccalaureate/associate degree category, 2 semester hours in Computer Science or Data Processing (11/77) (7/82). NOTE: This course has undergone a 5-year reevaluation and continues to meet requirements for credit recommen-

dations.

Dynamics of Applied Marketing Management (771)
  Location: Pittsburgh, PA.
  Length: 40 hours (5 days).
  Dates: August 1977-Present.
  Objective: To provide an opportunity for the utilization of selected marketing concepts in the decision making process and to help the participants become more effective decision makers on more complex and long-range marketing planning issues.
  Instruction: An in-depth coverage of a variety of decision making tools and techniques is applied to an ongoing case study prepared to simulate the point of view of a corporate divisional marketing manager. Participants are expected to apply increasingly more difficult concepts including, but not restricted to, product pricing matrices, short- and long-run forecasting techniques, promotional strategy analysis, product life cycles, and investment decisions. The course requires extensive analysis leading to development of a detailed five-year, long-range strategic plan for the case firm.
  Credit recommendation: In the upper division baccalaureate category or in the graduate degree category, 3 semester hours in Marketing (11/77) (7/82). NOTE: This course has undergone a 5-year reevaluation and continues to meet requirements for credit recommendations.

Introduction to Economic Analysis (637)
(Alternative Title: Economics of Competition Seminar)
  Location: Pittsburgh, PA.
  Length: 24 hours (3 days).
  Dates: *Version 1:* November 1967-June 1982; *Version 2:* July 1982-Present.
  Objective: To introduce the interrelationships of operating a business in today's economic system and the impact of national and international forces on making business decisions and to aid the student in visualizing problem solving solutions within an environment of current and anticipated economic and social changes.
  Instruction: An overview of economics; the foundation of economic freedom and competitive markets; Adam Smith to John M. Keynes; the American enterprise system, other economic systems and future directions; economic roles of government and business; competition, monopoly, and government policy; labor organizations, labor markets, and public policy; consumerism, population; the environment, waste disposal, and ecology; energy and shortages; population and poverty; the economic role of women; economics of national security; productivity and labor costs; economic challenges of the future; economic growth; the United States, the mature economics, and the emerging nations; the national economy-prices, inflation, indexes and indexation, controls, and forecasting; achieving economic stability; monetary and fiscal policies; the U.S. in the world economy.
  Credit recommendation: *Version 1:* In the lower division baccalaureate/associate degree category, 2 semester hours in Macro-Economics (11/77). *Version 2:* In the lower division baccalaureate/associate degree or in the upper division baccalaureate category, 2 semester hours in Macro-Economics (7/82). NOTE: This course has undergone a 5-year reevaluation and continues to meet requirements for credit recommendations.

Management Functions and Policies (869/870)
  Location: Pittsburgh, PA.
  Length: 40 hours (5 days).
  Dates: November 1967-Present.
  Objective: To develop effective management skills; to understand corporate activities and policies; to integrate theory and concepts into practical application of principles, techniques, and skills of effective management; and to facilitate behavior change leading to individual performance improvement and growth in capabilities and responsibilities.
  Instruction: Covers functions of the manager; managerial financial control; Westinghouse business simulation; group dynamics; team building; corporate policy review; continuing growth and development. Includes lectures, workshops, simulation, films, case studies.
  Credit recommendation: In the upper division baccalaureate category, 3 semester hours in Management (11/77) (7/82). NOTE: This course has undergone a 5-year reevaluation and continues to meet requirements for credit recommendations.

Management Techniques (867/868)
  Location: Pittsburgh, PA.
  Length: 40 hours (5 days).
  Dates: November 1967-Present.
  Objective: To introduce basic and common functions and principles of management.
  Instruction: The management cycle - a system approach; the planning function of management; organizing function of management; implementing function of management; review function of management; feedback function of management; action plan for results. Course includes lectures, case studies, simulation, in-basket techniques, role playing, and films.
  Credit recommendation: In the lower division baccalaureate/associate degree category or in the upper division baccalaureate category, 3 semester hours in Management (11/77) (7/82). NOTE: This course has undergone a 5-year reevaluation and continues to meet requirements for credit recommendations.

Marketing Communications Concepts and Planning Seminar (767)
  Location: Charlottesville, VA.
  Length: 40 hours (5 days).
  Dates: August 1972-Present.

Objective: To provide the participant with a framework for understanding the interrelated role of the communications task with those of the entire marketing function.

Instruction: Development of marketing strategy with emphasis on analysis of communications media channels for implementing that strategy. Case studies, lectures, and group studies are utilized.

Credit recommendation: In the upper division baccalaureate category, 3 semester hours in Marketing or Advertising Management (11/77) (7/82). NOTE: This course has undergone a 5-year reevaluation and continues to meet requirements for credit recommendations.

Marketing Management (761)
(Alternative Title: Sales Management Course)

Location: Charlottesville, VA.
Length: 40 hours (5 days).
Dates: July 1973-Present.

Objective: To develop a framework for understanding the various managerial elements that ultimately affect certain sales/marketing tasks which are required for effectively implementing the marketing strategy.

Instruction: Course concentrates on marketing strategy using various case studies. One segment of the course concentrates on management of the marketing effort. Another segment concentrates on development of marketing strategy. Topics include administration, coaching, counseling evaluation, organization, development, personnel selection, training, and compensation.

Credit recommendation: In the upper division baccalaureate category, 3 semester hours in Marketing (11/77) (7/82). NOTE: This course has undergone a 5-year reevaluation and continues to meet requirements for credit recommendations.

Marketing Research (762)
(Alternative Title: Marketing Analysis and Forecasting Seminar)

Location: Pittsburgh, PA.
Length: 24 hours (3 days).
Dates: April 1974-Present.

Objective: To develop the participant's knowledge and decision making skills in marketing forecasting and planning through application of tools and techniques of information gathering and data analysis.

Instruction: Gathering and analyzing marketing information and the application of forecasting techniques in marketing planning utilizes workshops, lectures, and case studies.

Credit recommendation: In the upper division baccalaureate category, 2 semester hours in Marketing (11/77) (7/82). NOTE: This course has undergone a 5-year reevaluation and continues to meet requirements for credit recommendations.

Marketing Strategy and Business Planning Seminar (790)

Location: Pittsburgh, PA.
Length: 24 hours (3 days).
Dates: April 1976-Present.

Objective: To develop an understanding of strategy formation as it relates to the marketing process.

Instruction: Course stresses quantitative and financial application. Topics covered are product line portfolio management; price and cost experience curve relationships; planning marketing strategy; allocation of resources; product life cycle and the international strategic marketing plan. Course emphasizes application, testing, and effects of various ratios and other quantitative techniques to long-range planning problems. Case study, discussion, team consultation, and simulation are used.

Credit recommendation: In the upper division baccalaureate category or in the graduate degree category, 2 semester hours in Marketing (11/77) (7/82). NOTE: This course has undergone a 5-year reevaluation and continues to meet the requirements for credit recommendations.

Multinational Marketing Seminar (770)
(Alternative Title: Multinational Seminar)

Location: Pittsburgh, PA.
Length: 40 hours (5 days).
Dates: August 1971-Present.

Objective: To increase a student's knowledge and sensitivity of the many considerations involved in marketing products and services throughout the world.

Instruction: Focuses on global environmental analysis; development of multinational marketing strategy; planning business strategy for a multinational division, business unit, group, and corporation. Utilities case studies, articles, group workshops, lectures, and discussions.

Credit recommendation: In the upper division baccalaureate category or in the graduate degree category, 3 semester hours in Marketing (11/77) (7/82). NOTE: This course has undergone a 5-year reevaluation and continues to meet requirements for credit recommendations.

Organizational Behavior (900/890/830)
(Alternative Title: Models for Management)

Location: Pittsburgh, PA.
Length: 24 hours (3 days).
Dates: January 1973-Present.

Objective: To introduce participants to the behavioral science concepts as they apply to managerial practices.

Instruction: Course surveys the behavioral concepts associated with McGregor, Brunswick, Lewin, Luft and Ingham, Maslow, Herzberg, and Blake and Mouton. Lectures, discussions, workshops, self-assessment exercises, and team activity are used.

Credit recommendation: In the lower division baccalaureate/associate degree category or in the upper division baccalaureate category, 2 semester hours in

Management, particularly organizational development or leadership styles (11/77) (7/82). NOTE: This course has undergone a 5-year reevaluation and continues to meet requirements for credit recommendations.

1. Principles of Marketing (752)
(Alternative Title: Marketing Management Course)
2. Professional Marketing Course (456)
   Location: Pittsburgh, PA; Lansing, MI.
   Length: 1. 40 hours (5 days); 2. 40 hours (5 days).
   Dates: January 1970-Present.
   Objective: To increase the manager's understanding of an array of elements of marketing and how they relate to each other.
   Instruction: Covers marketing in business; sales force strategy; marketing communications; pricing decision; developing marketing strategy; market planning; product life cycle; trade-offs in marketing decisions; new product development; multinational marketing; financial evaluation of marketing decisions; marketing strategy and the sales force; managing the product mix. Utilizes lectures, case studies, and workshops.
   Credit recommendation: Course 1 or Course 2: In the lower division baccalaureate/associate degree category or in the upper division baccalaureate category, 3 semester hours in Marketing (11/77) (7/82). NOTE: A total of 3 credits should be granted for either the Marketing Management course or the Professional Marketing course, but not both. These courses have undergone a 5-year reevaluation and continue to meet requirements for credit recommendations.

Problem Solving and Decision Making for First Level Supervisors of Salaried Personnel (832/833)
   Location: Pittsburgh, PA.
   Length: 28 hours (3½ days).
   Dates: January 1975-Present.
   Objective: To introduce and supply basic concepts for analyzing problems and opportunities, identifying and evaluating alternatives, and choosing a course of action.
   Instruction: Topics presented are situation analysis, priority setting, problem solving, results planning, and various decision making techniques which include creative analysis and unit comparison. Lecture, discussion, and classroom exercises are used.
   Credit recommendation: In the lower division baccalaureate/associate degree category, 2 semester hours in Management (7/82).

Problem Solving and Decision Making for Middle Managers (866)
   Location: Pittsburgh, PA.
   Length: 40 hours (5 days).
   Dates: January 1975-Present.
   Objective: To introduce and apply a number of concepts for analyzing problems and opportunities, identifying and evaluating alternatives, and choosing a course of action.
   Instruction: Topics presented are situation analysis, priority setting, problem solving, results planning and various decision making techniques which include creative, sequential (decision tree), and feasibility analysis, as well as unit comparison. Lecture, discussion, and classroom exercises are used.
   Credit recommendation: In the upper division baccalaureate or graduate degree category, 3 semester hours in Management (7/82).

Techniques of Finance and Accounting (864)
   Location: Pittsburgh, PA.
   Length: 40 hours (5 days).
   Dates: February 1975-Present.
   Objective: To develop an understanding and appreciation of financial and accounting concepts and to apply the products of accounting to managerial decision making.
   Instruction: Classification and recording of transactions; understanding of the derivation of financial statements; application of selected accounting and financial concepts to managerial decision making. Includes lectures and workshops dealing with accounting problems. This course does not include principles of accounting.
   Credit recommendation: In the lower division baccalaureate/associate degree category or in the upper division baccalaureate category, 3 semester hours in Accounting or Finance (11/77) (7/82). NOTE: This course has undergone a 5-year reevaluation and continues to meet the requirements for credit recommendations.

Wholesaling (768)
(Alternative Title: Concepts of Distribution Management)
   Location: Pittsburgh, PA.
   Length: 32 hours (4 days).
   Dates: December 1974-Present.
   Objective: To develop an understanding of the manufacturer-distributor/wholesaler relationship.
   Instruction: Covers financial analysis; management of inventory; management of accounts receivable; cash flow analysis; market and product profitability analysis, developing the distributors market segments with users, OEM's, government and utilities and REA's; joint planning and objectives setting with the manufacturer and distributor.
   Credit recommendation: In the upper division baccalaureate category, 1 semester hour in Marketing (11/77) (7/82). NOTE: This course has undergone a 5-year reevaluation and continues to meet requirements for credit recommendations.

Westinghouse Electric Corporation, Integrated Logistic Support Division

There are several educational/training components in the Integrated Logistic Support Division (ILSD). The ILSD Education and Training section of the division's Human Resources Department administers training programs of the division providing counseling, course planning and acquisition, and actual training instructors. The ILSD Controllers Department provides financial reporting, controls, and training for the entire division's organization where 99 percent of the customers are U.S. Government agencies and armed forces (U.S. Air Force, U.S. Navy, and U.S. Army).

The ILSD Division of the Westinghouse Electric Corporation is headquartered in the Hunt Valley Business Community off Interstate 83 and Shawan Roads, 7 miles north of the Baltimore Beltway (I-695). The ILSD Controllers Department rents modern classrooms from the Loyola College of Baltimore, Hunt Valley Campus.

The Manager of ILSD Controllers Administration and Planning is the Dean of the Professional Training School. His secretary is the registrar. Instructors grade the exams and homework problems and submit them to the Dean and Registrar.

Instructors are selected by the Division's Controller and the Manager of Administration and Planning (who acts as the Dean). Members of the teaching staff must be recognized experts in their specialty areas, a members of the Controllers Department Management, and recognized as competent teachers.

Source of official student records: Manager, Integrated Logistic Support Division Administration and Planning, Westinghouse Electric Corporation, Mail Stop 7043, 1111 Schilling Road, Hunt Valley, Maryland 21030.

Additional information about the courses: Program on Noncollegiate Sponsored Instruction, The Center for Adult Learning and Educational Credentials, American Council on Education, One Dupont Circle, Washington, D.C. 20036.

Government Contracts Accounting and Control (Controllers Professional Training School)
Location: Hunt Valley, MD.
Length: 84 hours (21 weeks).
Dates: October 1984-Present.
Objective: To train the professional in the government accounting and control systems used by contractors.
Instruction: This course consists of a variety of interrelated topics covering six major modules in the areas of corporate organization, corporate and governmental accounting and government contracts, estimating, pricing and rate setting, and management information systems. The methodology utilizes lectures, workshops, homework projects and problems, case studies, discussions, quizzes, graded homework and exams. (Prerequisites: Bachelor's degree with a strong background in Accounting, Finance, Business Administration, or Computer Sciences.)
Credit recommendation: In the upper division baccalaureate or graduate category, 3 semester hours in Governmental Procurement and Contract Administration, Logistics and Materials Management, or Government Accounting (8/85).

Westinghouse Electric Corporation, Nuclear Services Division (Formerly Water Reactor Divisions)

The Nuclear Services Division of Westinghouse Electric Corporation provides operational support and servicing for commercial nuclear power plants for the electric utility industry. The Nuclear Services Division offers formal training programs to utility nuclear plant operators, technicians, engineers, and other personnel. This division also conducts training programs for Westinghouse field service personnel, engineers, and instructor personnel. The Division operates two computerized nuclear power plant full-scope simulators and mobile instrumentation training unit trailers. Personnel in this division also develop course materials utilized by electric utility training center staffs.

Courses include reactor theory and principles, operational systems, thermodynamics, instrumentation and control technology, control room simulator training, instructional skill development, and other highly specialized courses related to nuclear technology and engineering.

Educational programs and specialty courses are offered at the Pittsburgh, Pennsylvania and Zion, Illinois facilities, as well as nuclear utility plant sites.

Source of official student records: Academic Administrator, Training and Operational Services - East, P.O. Box 598, Pittsburgh, Pennsylvania 15230 or Academic Dean, Training and Operational Services - West, 505 Shiloh Boulevard, Zion, Illinois 60099.

Additional information about the courses: Program on Noncollegiate Sponsored Instruction, The Center for Adult Learning and Educational Credentials, American Council on Education, One Dupont Circle, Washington, D.C. 20036.

Basic Nuclear Systems (NIC 210)
Location: Pittsburgh, PA; Zion, IL; or on-site utility locations.
Length: *Version 1:* 35 hours (1 week); *Version 2:* 30 hours (1 week).
Dates: *Version 1:* January 1981-July 1988; *Version 2:* August 1988-Present.
Objective: To provide the student with information regarding basic nuclear systems.

Instruction: Course provides an introduction to 4 components of nuclear power plant operations: (1) primary plant mechanical systems, (2) secondary plant and support systems, (3) electrical systems, and (4) instrumentation and control systems.

Credit recommendation: In the lower division baccalaureate/associate degree category, 1 semester hour in Engineering Technology or Nuclear Technology (12/81) (8/88). NOTE: This course has been reevaluated and continues to meet requirements for credit recommendations.

Comprehensive Analysis of Technical, Thermal, and Radiological Limits (NPO 317)

Location: Pittsburgh, PA; Zion, IL; or on-site utility locations.

Length: 30 hours (1 week).

Dates: *Version 1:* September 1982-February 1985; *Version 2:* March 1985-July 1988; *Version 3:* August 1988-Present.

Objective: To provide the student with an understanding of the content, bases, and application of technical specifications, emergency plan requirements, significant licensee events, and core thermal limits.

Instruction: *Versions 1 and 2:* Topics include analysis of technical specification content, bases, and application, emergency plan implementation, significant licensee events, and core thermal performance including hot channel factors, and natural circulation considerations. Material is presented in seminar format with frequent student discourse. *Version 3:* Topics include analysis of technical specifications, content, bases, and application of technical specifications, emergency plan requirements, significant licensee events, radiation problems and current PWR safety problems. Instruction is also provided in diagnostic theory, principles, applications, team work, and communications. Material is presented in seminar format with frequent student participation.

Credit recommendation: *Version 1:* In the lower division baccalaureate/associate degree category, 1 semester hour in Engineering Technology or Nuclear Technology (9/82). *Versions 2 and 3:* In the upper division baccalaureate category, 1 semester hour in Engineering Technology or Nuclear Technology (3/85) (8/88). NOTE: This course involves analysis of nuclear power plant conditions through: (1) interpretation of readings from plant instrumentation, and (2) integration of this information with a detailed knowledge of plant systems (obtained from prerequisite courses). These types of "operations-oriented problem-solving skills" are those of a technologist—one who has completed a baccalaureate-level technology degree. NOTE: This course has been reevaluated and continues to meet requirements for credit recommendations.

Control and Protection Instrumentation Systems (NPS 227)

Location: Zion, IL.

Length: 35 hours (1 week).

Dates: *Version 1:* March 1972-February 1985; *Version 2:* March 1985-June 1986.

Objective: To provide the student with an understanding of the various components and functions of control and protection instrumentation systems utilized in the nuclear power plant.

Instruction: Course covers the following systems: in-core and excore nuclear instrumentation, rod control, rod position indication, reactor protection, and radiation monitoring. Methods include lecture, discussion, and plant tours.

Credit recommendation: *Version 1:* In the lower division baccalaureate/associate degree category, 1 semester hour in Nuclear Technology (9/82). *Version 2:* In the upper division baccalaureate category, 1 semester hour in Nuclear Technology (3/85). NOTE: Course content involves the application of instrumentation to the control and protection of reactors.

Digital Metal Impact Monitoring System (NIC 272)

Location: Pittsburgh, PA.

Length: *Version 1:* 31 hours (1 week); *Version 2:* 30 hours (1 week).

Dates: *Version 1:* April 1983-July 1988; *Version 2:* August 1988-Present.

Objective: To provide the student with the knowledge and skills necessary to operate and maintain the metal impact monitor system.

Instruction: The course includes topics which address the need for the digital metal impact monitor system (DMIMS), how the system detects loose parts, discriminates against other signals and may locate loose parts, accelerometer and microprocessor operation, memory console, test generator operation, alarms, and system testing and troubleshooting.

Credit recommendation: In the vocational certificate degree or lower division baccalaureate/associate degree category, 1 semester hour in Nuclear Technology Laboratory (8/83) (8/88). NOTE: This course has been reevaluated and continues to meet requirements for credit recommendations.

Digital Rod Position Indicating System (NIC-360)

Location: Pittsburgh, PA; Zion, IL; or on-site utility locations.

Length: 49 hours (7 days).

Dates: January 1981-Present.

Objective: To provide the student with an understanding of digital position indication systems with application to nuclear reactor control rod systems.

Instruction: Course covers description of the digital circuits employed in position sensing and control with specific applications to a pressurized water reactor control rod system. Methodology includes lecture, laboratory, and discussion.

Credit recommendation: In the lower division baccalaureate/associate degree category, 1 semester hour in Engineering Technology or Nuclear Technology (12/81) (8/88). NOTE: This course has been reevaluated and continues to meet requirements for credit recommendations.

Eddy Current - Level I (NST 210)
Location: Pittsburgh, PA and Spartanburg, SC.
Length: 42 hours plus 173 hours of Field Proficiency.
Dates: January 1982-Present.
Objective: To provide nuclear service trainees with theory and operational skills in Eddy Current - Level I testing and data collection procedures.
Instruction: Course covers concepts of magnetic circuits, including permeability, reactance, impedance, induced currents, eddy currents, bridge circuits, magnetic field sensor and signal processing, alternating current signals, use of multiple frequency test or, oscilloscope operation; steam generator tube inspection system operation.
Credit recommendation: In the lower division baccalaureate/associate degree category, 3 semester hours in Electrical Systems for Nuclear Service Technology; or 2 semester hours in Electricity and 1 semester hour in Electrical Systems Laboratory, or General Technical Electronics (11/82) (8/88). NOTE: This course has been reevaluated and continues to meet requirements for credit recommendations.

Electrical Sciences (NEP 241)
Location: Zion, IL and on-site utility locations.
Length: 73 hours (2 weeks).
Dates: *Version 1:* September 1981-July 1988; *Version 2:* August 1988-Present.
Objective: *Version 1:* To provide the student with an understanding of electrical and electronic theory applied to the operation of selected nuclear power station equipment, including process instrumentation and control systems. *Version 2:* To provide the student with an understanding of the basic aspects of electrical science with emphasis on applying these fundamentals to power plant equipment.
Instruction: *Version 1:* Topics covered include basic electrical theory; AC and DC circuits; AC circuit analysis; theory and operation of motors, generators, and transformers; semiconductor theory and application and process instrumentation. Lecture and discussion are used. *Version 2:* Course covers basic electrical theory, AC and DC circuits; AC circuit analysis; theory and operation of motors, generators, and transformers. Information on the design and operation of electrical power systems, including power factors, protective relaying, voltage regulation and system control and regulation is also included. Methodology includes lecture and discussion.
Credit recommendation: *Version 1:* In the lower division baccalaureate/associate degree category, 2 semester hours in Industrial Technology or Nuclear Technology (9/82). *Version 2:* In the upper division baccalaureate category, 2 semester hours in Electrical Science (8/88). NOTE: This course has been reevaluated and continues to meet requirements for credit recommendations.

Electrical Systems (NPS 213)
Location: Zion, IL.
Length: 35 hours (1 week).
Dates: March 1972-June 1986.
Objective: To familiarize the student with various electrical generating and distribution systems of a nuclear power plant.
Instruction: Topics include main generation, 345 KV power distribution, auxiliary, power emergency diesel generation, AC instrument and DC control power, and electric systems operation during normal and off-normal conditions. Lecture, laboratory, plant tours are used.
Credit recommendation: In the lower division baccalaureate/associate degree category, 1 semester hour in Industrial Technology or Nuclear Technology (9/82).

Engineered Safeguard Systems (NPS 221)
Location: Zion, IL.
Length: 35 hours (1 week).
Dates: *Version 1:* March 1972-February 1985; *Version 2:* March 1985-June 1986.
Objective: To provide the student with an understanding of the components and functions of the engineered safeguard systems utilized in a nuclear power plant.
Instruction: Federal safety and protection requirements, design and construction of containment building, fire protection systems, ventilation, spray systems, and injection systems. Lecture, discussion, laboratory, and plant tours.
Credit recommendation: *Version 1:* In the lower division baccalaureate/associate degree category, 1 semester hour in Engineering Technology, Industrial Safety, or Nuclear Technology (9/82). *Version 2:* In the upper division baccalaureate category, 1 semester hour in Mechanical Engineering Technology, Industrial Safety, or Nuclear Technology (3/85). NOTE: Course contains material on ventilation systems and moderately complex cooling systems similar to content of upper division ET courses, particularly in Mechanical Technology.

General Employee Training (SPC 219)
(Formerly Radiological Education Maintenance [SPC 219])
Location: Pittsburgh, PA or Zion, IL.
Length: *Version 1:* 35 hours (5 days); *Version 2:* 24 hours (4 days).
Dates: *Version 1:* October 1980-July 1988; *Version 2:* August 1988-Present.
Objective: To provide the student with basic theory and practice related to radiation safety and general industrial safety.

Instruction: Course covers instruction in industrial safety, basic radiation physics, radiation monitoring, biological effects of radiation exposure, protection standards and limits, and principles of exposure and contamination control. Methods utilized include lecture, demonstration, and hands-on experiences.

Credit recommendation: In the lower division baccalaureate/associate degree or in the upper division baccalaureate category, 1 semester hour in Industrial Safety or Nuclear Technology (7/82) (8/88). NOTE: This course has been reevaluated and continues to meet requirements for credit recommendations.

Heat Transfer, Fluid Flow and Thermodynamics (SPC 321)

Location: Zion, IL.
Length: 67 hours (2 weeks).
Dates: April 1982-December 1983.
Objective: To provide the student with an understanding of fluid mechanics, thermal sciences, and the thermodynamics associated with operation of the pressurized water reactor system.
Instruction: Topics include the basic properties of fluids and water, heat exchanger designs, heat transfer rates, thermodynamics cycles, fluid mechanics, pumps and piping, safety factors, and system limitations. Emphasis is placed on site specific information. Lecture, laboratory, and discussion methods are utilized.
Credit recommendation: In the lower division baccalaureate/associate degree category, 2 semester hours in Engineering Technology or Nuclear Technology (9/82).

Inadequate Core Cooling Monitoring System (NIC 270)
(Formerly Reactor Vessel Level Instrumentation System [NIC 270])

Location: Pittsburgh, PA and on-site at request of utility power plant.
Length: *Version 1:* 34 hours (1 week); *Version 2:* 58 hours (2 weeks).
Dates: *Version 1:* March 1983-July 1988; *Version 2:* August 1988-Present.
Objective: *Version 1:* To provide an overall view of the operation, calibration, and maintenance of a microprocessor-based reactor vessel level instrument system. *Version 2:* To provide an overall view of the operation, calibration, and maintenance of a microprocessor-based core cooling monitoring system.
Instruction: *Version 1:* Course covers pressure and temperature transducers, reactor vessel monitoring techniques, differential measurements, related console operations, set point adjustments, and system troubleshooting. *Version 2:* Topics include pressure and temperature transducers, reactor vessel monitoring techniques, differential measurements, related console operations, set point adjustments, incore thermocouples-thermodynamics, saturated steam conditions, and system troubleshooting.
Credit recommendation: *Version 1:* In the lower division baccalaureate/associate degree category, 1 semester hour in Nuclear Service Technology Instrument Laboratory (8/83). *Version 2:* In the lower division baccalaureate/associate degree category, 2 semester hours in Nuclear Technology (1 lecture credit and 1 laboratory credit) (8/88). NOTE: This course has been reevaluated and continues to meet requirements for credit recommendations.

Instructional Skills Workshop (ISM 463)

Location: Pittsburgh, PA; Zion, IL; or on-site utility locations.
Length: 80 hours (2 weeks).
Dates: November 1980-Present.
Objective: To familiarize instructors or instructor candidates with theories, methods, and materials that can enhance teaching effectiveness.
Instruction: Course covers stressing transfer of cognitions and performance competencies on topics such as characteristics of adult learners, audiovisual methods, tests and measurements, instructional methods, and curriculum development. Methodology includes lecture, discussion, and demonstration methods.
Credit recommendation: In the upper division baccalaureate category, 2 semester hours in Education or Industrial Training (12/81) (8/88). NOTE: This course has been reevaluated and continues to meet requirements for credit recommendations.

Integrated Plant Operations (NPO 323)

Location: Pittsburgh, PA; Zion, IL; or on-site utility locations.
Length: *Version 1:* 80 hours (2 weeks); *Version 2:* 160 hours (4 weeks).
Dates: *Version 1:* September 1982-July 1988; *Version 2:* August 1988-Present.
Objective: To enable the student to apply the concepts of nuclear theory, heat transfer, fluid mechanics, and thermodynamics to analysis of plant operating status for both steady state and transient operations.
Instruction: *Version 1:* Course covers recognition, mitigation, and potential radiological consequences of core damage, evaluation of plant conditions based on visual display in control room and synthesis of theoretical, thermal, design, operational and administrative knowledge. Methodology includes lecture, discussion, and simulator exercises. *Version 2:* Classroom topics include core cooling and resulting damage situations; transient and accident analysis; introduction to probabilistic risk assessment; application of fluid dynamic, thermodynamic and reactor physics and control concepts, safety and emergency system design concepts; and application of operating procedures and administrative limits and controls. Simulator sessions include malfunctions during power op-

erations and periodic tests, mitigating core damage scenarios, malfunctions during power and solid plant operations and practice simulator examinations.

Credit recommendation: *Version 1:* In the upper division baccalaureate degree category, 2 semester hours in Nuclear Technology (9/82). *Version 2:* In the upper division baccalaureate category, 2 semester hours in Nuclear Technology and 1 semester hour in Nuclear Technology Laboratory (8/88). NOTE: This course has been reevaluated and continues to meet requirements for credit recommendations.

Introduction to Nuclear Power Plants (NPS 211)
Location: Zion, IL.
Length: 35 hours (1 week).
Dates: March 1972-January 1983.
Objective: To provide the student with an understanding of the overall pressurized water reactor system to include potential radiation hazards, location of major pieces of equipment, and plant emergency procedures.
Instruction: Using drawings of the power plant, the student develops an understanding of blueprint symbology and general power plant layout. Using this information potential radiation hazards are identified and the radiation protection guidelines applicable to the situation are developed. Use is made of the federal radiation regulations and power plant legal documents in developing the radiation guidelines.
Credit recommendation: In the lower division baccalaureate/associate degree category, 1 semester hour in Nuclear Technology (9/82). NOTE: Credit should not be granted for both this course and Radioactivity, Radiation Detection, and Radiation Safety (NEP 213).

Introduction to Power Plant Operations (SPC 106)
Location: Pittsburgh, PA; Zion, IL; or on-site utility locations.
Length: 45 hours (6 days).
Dates: July 1982-Present.
Objective: To provide the student with an overview of pressurized water reactor plant basic design, basic system components, elementary operation, and various transient conditions.
Instruction: Course covers description of control room, reactor instrumentation, reactor protection systems, engineered safeguards systems, and plant operations. Operational exercises on simulator include plant heatup, reactor startup, steam plant startup, power range operations, and plant transients.
Credit recommendation: In the lower division baccalaureate/associate degree category, 1 semester hour in Nuclear Technology (7/82) (8/88). NOTE: This course has been reevaluated and continues to meet requirements for credit recommendations.

Large Pressurized Water Reactor Core Control (NEP 219)
Location: Zion, IL or on-site utility locations.
Length: 67 hours (2 weeks).
Dates: *Version 1:* January 1975-February 1985; *Version 2:* March 1985-Present.
Objective: To provide the student with a basic understanding of reactor operation and control by induced and inherent reactivity effects during normal steady state and normal power operations.
Instruction: Reactor vessel and core construction, basic pressurized water reactor operation and control, core structure, reactivity coefficients and fission product poisoning, chemical shim and control rod reactivity effects, estimated critical condition and shutdown margin calculations, heatup and startup considerations, and plant chemistry. Material presented by lecture and student exercise problems.
Credit recommendation: *Version 1:* In the lower division baccalaureate/associate degree category, 2 semester hours in Engineering Technology or Nuclear Technology (9/82). *Version 2:* In the upper division baccalaureate category, 2 semester hours in Engineering Technology or Nuclear Technology (3/85) (8/88). NOTE: Course covers material that is normally covered in upper level nuclear technology programs in 4-year colleges including nuclear reactor kinetics and operations. The course prerequisites include a course which also is at the level of an upper division nuclear engineering textbook. NOTE: This course has been reevaluated and continues to meet requirements for credit recommendations.

Materials Considerations of Pressurized Water Reactors (NEP 513)
Location: Pittsburgh, PA; Zion, IL; or on-site utility company locations.
Length: 35 hours (1 week).
Dates: March 1985-Present.
Objective: To provide the student with an understanding of the important role of materials in nuclear power systems, the fundamentals of materials science and the methods employed to select and test these materials.
Instruction: Course covers the type and selection of nuclear materials, metallurgy, strength of materials, fracture, mechanisms, corrosion, radiation damage, failure mechanisms, non-destructive testing and inspection, codes and standards. Lecture and discussion are utilized.
Credit recommendation: In the upper division baccalaureate category, 1 semester hour in Nuclear Materials (3/85) (8/88). NOTE: This course has been reevaluated and continues to meet requirements for credit recommendations.

Mechanical Plugging of Steam Generator (NST 201)
Location: Pittsburgh, PA; Spartanburg, SC; and Westinghouse R&D Center, Churchill, PA.

Length: 62 hours plus 20 hours Field Proficiency.
Dates: January 1982-Present.
Objective: To provide the student with the skills necessary to perform Mechanical Plugging procedures on a Steam Generator.
Instruction: Course covers the proper use of the SM-3 Mechanical Plugging Tool for Steam Generators; proper repair and maintenance of the SM-3; procedures used to train the Heat Exchange Plug Installer (Jumper); and duties and responsibilities of the manway operator.
Credit recommendation: In the lower division baccalaureate/associate degree category, 2 semester hours in Nuclear Technology (11/82) (8/88). NOTE: This course has been reevaluated and continues to meet requirements for credit recommendations.

Microprocessor Basics (NIC 120)
(Formerly 8080 Microprocessor and Nuclear Applications [NIC 120])
Location: Pittsburgh, PA.
Length: 70 hours (2 weeks).
Dates: *Version 1:* January 1983-July 1988; *Version 2:* August 1988-Present.
Objective: *Version 1:* To provide the student with a hands-on introduction and survey of the 8080 microprocessor and associated minicomputer circuitry; machine language use, and interfacing techniques. *Version 2:* To provide the student with a hands-on introduction and survey of the 8080 and the 8086 microprocessor hardware components, operation, and software machine operation.
Instruction: *Version 1:* Instructional material includes: study of an 8080 based microcomputer system; decoding and encoding machine language programs; conducting interfacing experiments; and troubleshooting faults in the system using microprocessor trainers. *Version 2:* Instructional materials include study of both the 8080 and the 8086 microprocessor systems, software development using machine language, timing and control signal operation, and troubleshooting techniques to locate system faults in microprocessor systems.
Credit recommendation: *Version 1:* In the lower division baccalaureate/associate degree category, 2 semester hours in Introduction to Microprocessor Systems (8/83). *Version 2:* In the upper division baccalaureate category, 2 semester hours in Microprocessor Systems (8/88). NOTE: This course has been reevaluated and continues to meet requirements for credit recommendations.

Mitigating Core Damage (SPC 359)
Location: Pittsburgh, PA; Zion, IL; or on-site utility locations.
Length: 40 hours (5 days).
Dates: *Version 1:* June 1980-July 1988; *Version 2:* August 1988-Present.
Objective: To provide the student with instruction on the effects of certain accidents on reactor core cooling and anomalous responses of plant instrumentation to the post accident environment.
Instruction: *Version 1:* Topics include major assumptions used in plant accident evaluations, review of plant thermal limits, in-core instrumentation and its response during accident situations, post-accident primary chemistry, radiation monitoring, vital process and disposal of gases during an accident, potential core damaging situations, and core cooling methods. *Version 2:* Topics include post-accident core cooling, small break loss of coolant accident with no high head safety injection, pressurized thermal shock, loss of feedwater, loss of all AC power, instrument qualification and accident response, accident response of incore and excore instrumentation, post-accident core damage assessment, radiological aspects of core damage and improbable (Class 9) events.
Credit recommendation: *Version 1:* In the upper division baccalaureate degree category, 1 semester hour in Nuclear Technology (7/82). *Version 2:* In the upper division baccalaureate category, 2 semester hours in Nuclear Technology (8/88). NOTE: This course has been reevaluated and continues to meet requirements for credit recommendations.

Nuclear Instrumentation (System) (NIC 335)
Location: Pittsburgh, PA; Zion, IL; or on-site utility locations.
Length: *Version 1:* 42 hours (6 days); *Version 2:* 58 hours (8 days).
Dates: *Version 1:* January 1981-July 1988; *Version 2:* August 1988-Present.
Objective: *Version 1:* To provide the student with an understanding of leakage neutron conversion process to signals usable by the operator, and of nuclear instrumentation, systems functions, and the symbols. *Version 2:* To provide the student with a brief understanding of radiation detector theory as it applies to neutron leakage detection in nuclear power reactors. Provides component level theory of operation of signal conversion electronics to produce reactor control and protection signals.
Learning Outcome: Upon successful completion of this course, the student will be able to apply detector and electronics theory to perform system troubleshooting, calibration, and maintenance to meet required performance tolerances.
Instruction: *Version 1:* In this course, nuclear instrumentation equipment, the system functions, symbology, and details of the individual drawers, power supplies, circuitry, and equipment maintenance are introduced. Methods include lecture, simulation exercises, and written examination. *Version 2:* Topics include system functions, symbology, power supplies, circuitry, detector theory of operation and construction, time domain reflectometer and installation and maintenance.
Credit recommendation: In the upper division baccalaureate category, 1 semester hour in Engineering Tech-

nology or Nuclear Technology (12/81) (8/88). NOTE: This course has been reevaluated and continues to meet requirements for credit recommendations.

Nuclear Reactor Theory (NEP 211)
Location: Pittsburgh, PA; Zion, IL; or on-site utility locations.
Length: 53 hours (1½ weeks).
Dates: *Version 1:* January 1975-February 1985; *Version 2:* March 1985-Present.
Objective: To provide the student with an understanding of first principles of the physical basis of nuclear reactor neutron physics, including neutron diffusion and slowing down theory and reactor kinetics.
Instruction: Topics covered include fundamental characteristics of matter at the atomic level, radioactive decay, photon and neutron shielding, reactor criticality, reactor kinetics, and reactor control. Theoretical development proceeds through the six-factor formula and the in-hour equations. Lecture and discussion are used.
Credit recommendation: *Version 1:* In the lower division baccalaureate/associate degree category, 2 semester hours in Nuclear Engineering or Nuclear Technology (9/82). *Version 2:* In the upper division baccalaureate category, 2 semester hours in Nuclear Engineering or Nuclear Technology (3/83) (8/88). NOTE: Course requires previous knowledge of Physics and Mathematics through differential equations. Topics covered in the area of Nuclear Reactions, Neutron Physics, and Reactor Physics. NOTE: This course has been reevaluated and continues to meet requirements for credit recommendations.

Nuclear Refueling (NST 160)
Location: Pittsburgh, PA and Spartanburg, SC.
Length: *Version 1:* 56 hours (7 days); *Version 2:* 40 hours (1 week).
Dates: *Version 1:* January 1980-July 1988; *Version 2:* August 1988-Present.
Objective: *Version 1:* To provide the student with an in-depth knowledge of reactor theory and systems, fuel construction, fuel handling and reactor construction. *Version 2:* To provide the student with a basic knowledge of reactor theory, plant systems, fuel construction, reactor disassembly and reassembly, refueling tool operation, and fuel handling.
Instruction: Instruction is accomplished through lectures, discussions, video tapes, slide presentations, practical exercises (labs) and exams.
Credit recommendation: *Version 1:* In the lower division baccalaureate/associate degree category, 3 semester hours in Nuclear Technology or Engineering Technology (11/82). *Version 2:* In the lower division baccalaureate/associate degree category, 2 semester hours in Nuclear Technology (8/88). NOTE: This course has been reevaluated and continues to meet requirements for credit recommendations.

Plant Operations (NPS 229)
Location: Zion, IL.
Length: 36 hours (1 week).
Dates: March 1972-June 1986.
Objective: To provide the student with an understanding of individual systems and to enable him or her to use that knowledge for analysis of normal and off-normal plant operating conditions.
Instruction: Topics include accident analysis, plant transients, normal and off-normal operations, hot channel factors, local operating stations, and station emergency plans. Methodology includes lecture, discussion, and plant tours.
Credit recommendation: In the upper division baccalaureate degree category, 1 semester hour in Nuclear Technology (9/82).

1. **Plant Transient Response Casualty Training (NPO 315)**
2. **Plant Casualty Training (Minor) (NPO 319)**
3. **Plant Casualty Training (Major) (NPO 321)**
   Location: Pittsburgh, PA; Zion, IL; or on-site utility locations.
   Length: *Version 1:* 21 days (4 weeks); *Version 2:* 25 days (5 weeks).
   Dates: *Version 1:* January 1980-July 1988; *Version 2:* August 1988-Present.
   Objective: To provide the student with the comprehensive knowledge required to analyze normal and abnormal plant operation and to take appropriate procedural steps to attain and maintain a safe, stable condition.
   Learning Outcome: Upon successful completion of this course, the student will be able to analyze and diagnose instrument response and to take appropriate corrective actions for anticipated operational transients, minor, and major casualties.
   Instruction: *Version 1:* Course provides nuclear reactor operator students with the knowledge and practice necessary to analyze and diagnose instrument response and to take appropriate corrective actions for anticipated operational transients, minor, and major casualties. Methodology includes lectures, student presentations, workshops, and simulator operations. *Version 2:* The two weeks of classroom instruction review plant systems and procedures emphasizing potential failures as well as providing detailed discussions of about ten significant plant accident scenarios. The three weeks of simulator instruction include accident scenarios and transients associated plant startup and shutdown as well as all major operational casualties analyzed by the safety analysis.
   Credit recommendation: *Version 1:* In the upper division baccalaureate category, 3 semester hours in Nuclear Technology (12/81). *Version 2:* In the upper division baccalaureate category, 2 semester hours in Nuclear Technology and 2 semester hours in Nuclear Technology Laboratory (8/88). NOTE: This course has been reeva-

luated and continues to meet requirements for credit recommendations.

Pressurized Water Reactor (PWR) Information Course (SPC 250)

Location: Pittsburgh, PA; Zion, IL; or on-site utility locations.

Length: 60 hours (2 weeks).

Dates: September 1979-Present.

Objective: To introduce the student to the fundamental principles and practices regarding pressurized water reactor systems.

Instruction: Lecture and discussion in nuclear reactor fundamentals, thermal hydraulics, and generation systems.

Credit recommendation: In the lower division baccalaureate/associate degree category, 2 semester hours in Engineering Technology or Nuclear Technology (12/81) (8/88). NOTE: This course has been reevaluated and continues to meet requirements for credit recommendations.

1. Pressurized Water Reactor (PWR) Operations Familiarization (NPO 311)
2. Pressurized Water Reactor (PWR) Normal Plant Operations (NPO 313)

Location: Pittsburgh, PA; Zion, IL; or on-site utility locations.

Length: *Versions 1 and 2:* 98 hours (3 weeks); *Version 3:* 70 hours (2 weeks).

Dates: *Version 1:* January 1980-February 1985; *Version 2:* March 1985-July 1988; *Version 3:* August 1988-Present.

Objective: To provide the student with knowledge and reactor simulator operational experience necessary for the operator to execute the appropriate procedures to operate a pressurized water reactor.

Instruction: *Versions 1 and 2:* Course combines lectures on fundamental theory, radiation protection, plant systems operation, proper application of administrative controls, including technical specifications, with simulator (laboratory) exercises which demonstrate integrated plant operation. *Version 3:* Course applies and integrates the knowledge from lectures on fundamental theory, radiation protection, plant systems operation, proper application of administrative controls, including technical specifications, with simulator (laboratory) exercises which demonstrate plant startup, normal, shutdown, and refueling operations.

Credit recommendation: *Version 1:* In the lower division baccalaureate/associate degree category, 3 semester hours in Nuclear Technology (12/81). *Version 2:* In the upper division baccalaureate category, 3 semester hours in Nuclear Technology (3/85). NOTE: This course involves analysis of nuclear power plant conditions through: (1) interpretation of readings from plant instrumentation, and (2) integration of this information with a detailed knowledge of plant systems (obtained from prerequisite courses). These types of "operations-oriented problem-solving skills" are those of a technologist—one who has completed a baccalaureate-level technology degree. *Version 3:* In the upper division baccalaureate category, 2 semester hours in Nuclear Technolgoy (1 lecture credit and 1 laboratory credit) (8/88). NOTE: This course has been reevaluated and continues to meet requirements for credit recommendations.

Process Instrumentation (NIC 320)
(Formerly 7300 Process Transducer Instrumentation [NIC 320])

Location: Pittsburgh, PA; Zion, IL; or on-site utility locations.

Length: 105 hours (3 weeks).

Dates: January 1981-Present.

Objective: To provide the student with an understanding of process system cards, controllers, and circuits so that he or she can achieve timely and accurate maintenance and improve instrument troubleshooting techniques.

Instruction: Course provides signal information pertaining to circuits for measuring the physical process parameters that are essential for the safe and efficient operation of the nuclear power plant, including symbology. Signal information includes the measure of temperature, pressure, level, and flow in the NSSS.

Credit recommendation: In the lower division baccalaureate/associate degree category, 2 semester hours in Engineering Technology or Nuclear Technology (12/81) (8/88). NOTE: This course has been reevaluated and continues to meet requirements for credit recommendations.

PWR Plant Radiochemistry (CHM 560)
(Formerly CH-560)

Location: POTC Monroeville, PA; Westinghouse Forest Hills Facility/Waltz Mill Analytical Labs, Madison, PA; and various utilities.

Length: *Version 1:* 240 hours (5 weeks/8 hours a day); *Version 2:* 120 hours (3 weeks).

Dates: *Version 1:* August 1982-July 1988; *Version 2:* August 1988-Present.

Objective: This course is designed to build the proficiency of the student in recognizing and solving various plant analytical chemistry problems.

Instruction: *Version 1:* Course is a mixture of lecture and laboratory periods with about 40 percent occurring in lecture. Laboratory practice is on an individual or small group basis. Course covers pressurized water reactor systems, a review of chemistry-related mathematics and physics, instruction in plant chemistry fundamentals, and interpretation of primary and secondary sampling results. *Version 2:* Course is about 40 percent lecture and the remainder of the time is the laboratory using state-of-the-art radioanalysis equipment. Topics include counting statistics, gas-filled detectors, scintillation detectors, semiconductor detectors, pulse height analysis, coincidence and anti-coincidence counters, isotopic exchange and separations, limits of detection, decay and growth radioactivity, sources of radioactivity, regulatory review and practical laboratory exercises to analyze unknown samples.

Credit recommendation: *Version 1:* In the upper division baccalaureate category, 4 semester hours in Chemistry or Nuclear Technology (8/83). *Version 2:* In the upper division baccalaureate category, 2 semester hours in Chemistry or Nuclear Technology (8/88). NOTE: This course has been reevaluated and continues to meet requirements for credit recommendations.

Quality Assurance/Quality Control (NST 240)
Location: Pittsburgh, PA; Spartanburg, SC; and through self-study.
Length: Estimated 160 hours.
Dates: October 1982-Present.
Objective: To introduce requirements for the procedures and applications of nuclear steam generation quality assurance/quality control principles and techniques.
Instruction: Students will develop an awareness of QA/QC concepts and actions, working under the supervision of a mentor with this self-study course, within which one unit requires laboratory exercises in non-destructive examination of materials. Formal written examination is required.
Credit recommendation: In the lower division baccalaureate/associate degree or upper division baccalaureate category, 3 semester hours in Nuclear Technology (11/82) (8/88). NOTE: This course has been reevaluated and continues to meet requirements for credit recommendations.

Radioactivity, Radiation Detection, and Radiation Safety (NEP 213)
Location: Zion, IL and on-site utility locations.
Length: 46 hours (1½ weeks).
Dates: *Version 1:* January 1975-July 1988; *Version 2:* August 1988-Present.
Objective: To enable the student to apply the mathematical principles of radiation exposure control and applicable federal regulations in order to protect himself or herself, co-workers, and the public from unnecessary radiation exposure.
Instruction: *Version 1:* Course covers fundamentals of radioactive decay; shielding of charged particle, neutron or photon sources; biological effects of radiation; radiation detection; reactor control instrumentation; and radiation hazards due to corrosion products. Lecture and discussion are used. *Version 2:* Course covers fundamentals of radioactive decay, shielding of charged particles, neutron and photon sources, biological effects of radiation, radiation detection, radiation hazards due to corrosion products, chemistry and corrosion fundamentals, and primary and secondary chemistry control. Lecture and discussion formats are used.
Credit recommendation: *Version 1:* In the lower division baccalaureate/associate degree category, 1 semester hour in Nuclear Technology, Industrial Safety Technology, Health Physics (9/82). NOTE: Credit should not be granted for both this course and Introduction to Nuclear Power Plants (NPS-211). *Version 2:* In the upper division baccalaureate category, 1 semester hour in Nuclear Technology (8/88). NOTE: This course has been reevaluated and continues to meet requirements for credit recommendations.

Reactor Support Systems - Part I (NPS 217)
Location: Zion, IL.
Length: 35 hours (1 week).
Dates: March 1979-June 1986.
Objective: To give the student an understanding of the components and instrumentation associated with selected reactor auxiliary systems.
Instruction: Topics include the chemical and volume control system, reactor makeup control system, boron thermal regeneration system, residual heat removal system, component cooling water system, and integrated primary system operation. Lecture and discussion are used.
Credit recommendation: In the lower division baccalaureate/associate degree category, 1 semester hour in Nuclear Technology (9/82).

Reactor Support Systems - Part II (NPS219)
Location: Zion, IL.
Length: 35 hours (1 week).
Dates: March 1972-June 1986.
Objective: To enable the student to develop an understanding of the components, flow path, function, and operation of selected reactor auxiliary systems.
Instruction: Topics covered include the boron recycle system, the primary chemistry and sampling system, the waste disposal systems, the fuel handling system, and the spent fuel pool cooling system. Lecture and discussion are used.
Credit recommendation: In the lower division baccalaureate/associate degree category, 1 semester hour in Nuclear Technology (9/82).

Reactor Systems and Components (NPS 215)
Location: Zion, IL.
Length: 35 hours (1 week).
Dates: March 1972-June 1986.
Objective: To develop in the student an ability to relate the design criteria, function, and operation of the individual components of the reactor coolant system.
Instruction: Topics include the reactor coolant system, the reactor vessel and internals, core components, pressurizer pressure and level control, reactor coolant system temperature instrumentation, reactor coolant pumps, and

reactor systems operation. Lecture and discussion are used.

Credit recommendation: In the lower division baccalaureate/associate degree category, 1 semester hour in Nuclear Technology (9/82).

ROD Control System (NIC 355)

Location: Pittsburgh, PA; Zion, IL; or on-site utility locations.

Length: 70 hours (10 days).

Dates: *Version 1:* January 1981-July 1988; *Version 2:* August 1988-Present.

Objective: *Version 1:* To provide specific information on the operation, maintenance, and troubleshooting of the control system of a pressurized water nuclear reactor. *Version 2:* To provide specific information on the operation, maintenance, and troubleshooting of the rod control system of a pressurized water nuclear reactor.

Instruction: Course furnishes a description of the rod control system function and then concentrates on the details of the operation and circuit testing procedures. Material presented in lecture format with several laboratory periods.

Credit recommendation: In the lower division baccalaureate/associate degree category, 2 semester hours in Engineering Technology or Nuclear Technology (12/81) (8/88). NOTE: This course has been reevaluated and continues to meet requirements for credit recommendations.

7100 Process Instrumentation Scaling (NIC 432)

Location: Pittsburgh, PA; Zion, IL; or on-site utility locations.

Length: 35 hours (1 week).

Dates: January 1981-December 1986.

Objective: To provide students with information pertinent to signal scaling principles and methods.

Instruction: Lecture and problem solving on signal scaling topics, such as terminology, principles, and application of signal scaling principles to system.

Credit recommendation: In the upper division baccalaureate category, 1 semester hour in Engineering Technology or Nuclear Technology (12/81).

7300 Process Instrumentation Scaling (NIC 380)

Location: Pittsburgh, PA; Zion, IL; or on-site utility locations.

Length: 35 hours (1 week).

Dates: January 1981-Present.

Objective: To provide the student with information pertinent to signal scaling principles and methods.

Instruction: Lecture and problem solving on signal scaling topics such as terminology, methods, setpoints, and application of signal scaling principles to systems.

Credit recommendation: In the upper division baccalaureate category, 1 semester hour in Engineering Technology or Nuclear Technology (12/81) (8/88). NOTE: This course has been reevaluated and continues to meet requirements for credit recommendations.

Simulator Instructor Skills and Methods (ISM 464)

Location: Pittsburgh, PA; Zion, IL; or on-site utility company locations.

Length: 40 hours (1 week).

Dates: *Version 1:* March 1985-July 1988; *Version 2:* August 1988-Present.

Objective: To introduce the student to the skills, techniques, and insights necessary to effectively use a nuclear power plant simulator as an audiovisual training aid.

Instruction: *Version 1:* Topics include training philosophy, motivation techniques for the adult learner, establishment of an educational environment, and use of the simulator to enhance learning. *Version 2:* Topics include training philosophy, adult learning techniques and motivation as applied to the simulator environment. Simulator topics include shift and instructor turnover techniques, scenario development and implementation, differences between teaching and auditing, evaluation and administrative records, and student feedback methods. Course includes significant instructor demonstration on the simulator.

Credit recommendation: In the upper division baccalaureate category, 1 semester hour in Education or Industrial Training (3/85) (8/88). NOTE: This course has been reevaluated and continues to meet requirements for credit recommendations.

Sold State Protection System (SSPS) (NIC 350)

Location: Pittsburgh, PA; Zion, IL; or on-site utility locations.

Length: 56 hours (8 days).

Dates: January 1981-Present.

Objective: To provide the student with an understanding of the solid state protection system, its functions, operation of circuits, operating conditions, testing, and interface with other systems.

Instruction: The course covers solid state protective systems functions, circuitry, operations, testing procedures, and their interrelationships with other instrumentation components and systems. Introduction is provided in SSPS equipment, the system functions, symbology, circuit operation, and equipment maintenance. Lecture and laboratory exercises are used.

Credit recommendation: In the lower division baccalaureate/associate degree category, 2 semester hours in Engineering Technology or Nuclear Technology (12/81) (8/88). NOTE: This course has been reevaluated and continues to meet requirements for credit recommendations.

Station Nuclear Engineering - PWR Theory and Systems (SNE 520)

Location: Pittsburgh, PA.

Length: 120 hours (4 weeks).

Dates: February 1981-February 1985.
Objective: To provide the student with sufficient pressurized water reactor (PWR) theory and systems knowledge to effectively interact with other nuclear power plant personnel in the performance of station nuclear engineering duties.
Instruction: The course begins with an in-depth review of PWR theory, nuclear physics, neutron diffusion theory, reactor kinetics and inherent feedback mechanisms. Instruction on PWR plant systems follows the review. The purpose of each system, how it functions and interconnects with other systems and the reasons for certain design aspects of the system are studied.
Credit recommendation: In the upper division baccalaureate category, 3 semester hours in Nuclear Technology (8/83).

Station Nuclear Engineering (SNE 560)
Location: Pittsburgh, PA.
Length: 120 hours (4 weeks).
Dates: February 1981-Present.
Objective: To give the student an overview of pressurized water reactor response during normal operations and specifically during transient and accident conditions.
Instruction: 24 hours lecture/week for 3 weeks and 1 week of simulator (laboratory) training. Provides an introduction to signal conditioning, normal and abnormal transient response, instrument failure response and plant response during accident conditions. Student is also introduced to selected topics in mitigating core damage during postulated accident conditions. The classroom phase completes with an in-depth study of core control with emphasis on methods of handling xenon oscillations and flux distributions. Students spend final week operating the SNUPPS II reactor plant simulator.
Credit recommendation: In the upper division baccalaureate category, 3 semester hours in Nuclear Technology (8/83) (8/88). NOTE: This course has been reevaluated and continues to meet requirements for credit recommendations.

Steam Cycle Support Systems (NPS 225)
Location: Zion, IL.
Length: 35 hours (1 week).
Dates: *Version 1:* March 1972-February 1985; *Version 2:* March 1985-June 1986.
Objective: To provide the student with an understanding of the components and functions of the steam cycle support systems of a nuclear power plant.
Instruction: Topics include circulating water systems, service water systems, the generator and turbine auxiliary systems, and the turbine control and protection systems. Lecture, laboratory, and plant tours are used.
Credit recommendation: *Version 1:* In the lower division baccalaureate/associate degree category, 1 semester hour in Nuclear Technology (9/82). *Version 2:* In the upper division baccalaureate category, 1 semester hour in Nuclear Technology or Mechanical Engineering Technology (3/85) NOTE: This is a continuation of course sequence in which prerequisite course NPS 223 is defined to be upper division.

Steam Cycle Systems (NPS 223)
Location: Zion, IL.
Length: 35 hours (1 week).
Dates: *Version 1:* March 1972-February 1985; *Version 2:* March 1985-June 1986.
Objective: To familiarize the student with the various steam cycle systems of a nuclear plant.
Instruction: Topics include the steam systems, the condensate and feedwater systems, the steam dump system, the auxiliary feedwater system, the steam generator water level control system, and secondary chemistry and sampling system. Lecture and discussion are used.
Credit recommendation: *Version 1:* In the lower division baccalaureate/associate degree category, 1 semester hour in Nuclear Technology (9/82). *Version 2:* In the upper division baccalaureate category, 1 semester hour in Nuclear Technology or Mechanical Engineering Technology (3/85). NOTE: Course content requires working knowledge of thermal science and fluid dynamics as prerequisites.

Thermal Sciences (NEP 221)
Location: Zion, IL or on-site utility locations.
Length: 67 hours (2 weeks).
Dates: *Version 1:* September 1979-February 1985; *Version 2:* March 1985-Present.
Objective: To provide the student with an understanding of fluid mechanics, thermal sciences, and the thermodynamics associated with operation of the pressurized water reactor system.
Instruction: Topics include the basic properties of fluids and matter, heat exchanger designs, heat transfer rates, thermodynamics cycles, fluid mechanics, pumps and piping, safety factors, and system limitations. Lecture and laboratory discussion methods are utilized.
Credit recommendation: *Version 1:* In the lower division baccalaureate/associate degree category, 2 semester hours in Engineering Technology or Nuclear Technology (9/82). *Version 2:* In the upper division baccalaureate category, 2 semester hours in Mechanical Engineering Technology or Nuclear Technology (3/85) (8/88). NOTE: Course topics include heat transfer, thermodynamics, and fluid mechanics and is taught assuming a complete background in physics and calculus. NOTE: This course has been reevaluated and continues to meet requirements for credit recommendations.

Transient and Accident Analysis (SPC 361)
Location: Pittsburgh, PA; Zion, IL; or on-site utility locations.

Length: 60 hours (10 days).
Dates: *Version 1:* June 1980-July 1988; *Version 2:* August 1988-Present.
Objective: To provide the student with instruction on the effects on the nuclear power plant systems of normal transients, abnormal transients, and accident occurrences.
Instruction: Course covers the analysis of the effects of normal and abnormal transients on nuclear power plant systems response and is developed from an analytical basis. This is followed by an evaluation of accident accident occurrences on the power systems. Lecture and classroom participation by the student is the mode of instruction.
Credit recommendation: *Version 1:* In the upper division baccalaureate degree category, 1 semester hour in Nuclear Technology (7/82). *Version 2:* In the upper division baccalaureate category, 2 semester hours in Nuclear Technology (8/88). NOTE: This course has been reevaluated and continues to meet requirements for credit recommendations.

Westinghouse Electric Corporation, Water Reactor Divisions

See WESTINGHOUSE ELECTRIC CORPORATION, NUCLEAR SERVICES DIVISION

Whirlpool Corporation

The Whirlpool Corporation is engaged primarily in engineering, procuring, manufacturing and marketing of home appliances and other durable goods and services to meet the needs of global customers. Headquartered in Benton Harbor, Michigan, Whirlpool employs some twenty-four thousand employees world-wide.

The Whirlpool Corporate Educational Center is located adjacent to the corporate headquarters and was dedicated in December of 1982.

The mission of the Whirlpool Corporate Educational Center is to increase the management effectiveness of employees and customers by providing solutions to human performance problems. The training that the center provides helps accelerate professional and managerial development.

Courses are identified for development as a part of the Corporate Strategic Planning Process. All courses are systematically designed and based on a description of the audience, their skill requirements, and the training they require to perform assigned duties. Classrooms, audio-visual support, and other student/instructor facilities have been designed to ensure effective learning environments.

Source of official student records: Director of Educational Development, Whirlpool Corporate Educational Center, 2000 US 33 North, Benton Harbor, Michigan 49022.

Additional information about the courses: Program on Noncollegiate Sponsored Instruction, The Center for Adult Learning and Educational Credentials, American Council on Education, One Dupont Circle, Washington, D.C. 20036.

Advertising Analysis and Action Planning
Location: Corporate Educational Center, Benton Harbor, MI.
Length: 36 hours (4 days).
Dates: December 1985-Present.
Objective: To provide the student with the skills and understanding of the fundamentals of advertising, to include the analysis of factors influencing development of promotional plans.
Instruction: Minimum lecture, discussion, role playing, classroom exercise, and problem solving under intensive instructor supervision. Preparation and outside reading required of highly structured and specific textual material.
Credit recommendation: In the lower division baccalaureate/associate degree category, 2 semester hours in Advertising (12/85).

Appliance Service Training
(Service Professional Seminar)
Location: Corporate Educational Center, Benton Harbor, MI.
Length: 120 hours (3 weeks).
Dates: October 1986-Present.
Learning Outcome: Upon successful completion of this course, the student will be able to operate, diagnose and repair appliances, and to use appropriate customer interaction techniques to assist in the appliance diagnosis and repair.
Instruction: Practice in the following areas: basic electricity; appliance operation, assembly/disassembly; component location, removal, testing and replacement; identification of installation errors and external problems; general troubleshooting and communication techniques for customer interaction. Students: written practices, videotaped skill practices, and performance tests; instructor: demonstrations.
Credit recommendation: In the lower division baccalaureate/associate degree or vocational certificate category, 6 semester hours in Household Appliance Maintenance (11/86).

Builder Selling Skills
Location: Corporate Educational Center, Benton Harbor, MI.
Length: 36 hours (4½ days).
Dates: November 1984-Present.
Objective: To provide the student with the skills and an understanding of sales techniques as specifically applied to the homebuilding industry.

Instruction: Lecture/discussions, extensive role playing, classroom exercises and problem solving under intensive supervision of the instructor. Preparation and substantial outside reading required of highly structured and specific textual materials.

Credit recommendation: In the lower division baccalaureate/associate degree category, 2 semester hours in Sales (12/85).

Dealer Coaching and Selling Skills

Location: Corporate Educational Center, Benton Harbor, MI.
Length: 36 hours (4½ days).
Dates: December 1985-Present.
Objective: To provide the student with skills and sales techniques in assessing needs and circumstances of the potential customer; and to develop sales coaching skills directed towards needs satisfaction selling.
Instruction: Lecture, discussion, role playing, classroom exercises, and problem solving under intensive supervision of the instructor. Preparation and substantial outside reading required of highly structured and specific textual material.
Credit recommendation: In the lower division baccalaureate/associate degree category, 2 semester hours in Sales Management (12/85).

Dealer Development
(Bringing Out the Best in Your Dealers)

Location: Corporate Educational Center, Benton Harbor, MI.
Length: 42 hours (5 days).
Dates: October 1985-Present.
Learning Outcome: Upon successful completion of this course, the student will be able to assist dealers in analyzing their territories, inventories, account development, pricing, outlet image and sales activity.
Instruction: Practice in assisting dealer to determine optimum inventory; developing and presenting plan to improve dealer's store image; developing pricing to support dealer's sales strategy and produce the desired gross margin; systematically analyzing potential new accounts and making constructive recommendations; refining planning skills; coaching accounts' salespeople in effective product selling techniques. Students: written practices, videotaped skill practices, and performance tests; instructor: lecture.
Credit recommendation: In the lower division baccalaureate/associate degree category, 2 semester hours in Marketing (11/86).

Generating a Personal Target Plan of Action

Location: Corporate Educational Center, Benton Harbor, MI.
Length: 36 hours (4½ days).
Dates: December 1985-Present.

Objective: To provide the student with the skills and an understanding of sales, market trends, and the ability to develop marketing plans and targets towards sales objectives.
Instruction: Lecture, discussion, role playing, classroom exercises, and problem solving under intensive supervision of the instructor. Preparation and substantial outside reading required of highly structured and specific textual material.
Credit recommendation: In the lower division baccalaureate/associate degree category, 2 semester hours in Salesmanship (12/85).

Indirect Sales Development Techniques
(Building Excellent Indirect Accounts)

Location: Corporate Educational Center, Benton Harbor, MI.
Length: 42 hours (5 days).
Dates: May 1986-Present.
Learning Outcome: Upon successful completion of this course, the student will be able to effectively identify and consult with new indirect accounts.
Instruction: Practice in prospecting new accounts; inventorying indirect accounts; improving indirect account's display space; developing indirect account's pricing; identifying staff selling skills' deficiencies; planning, developing, and implementing selling skills training; and evaluating performance on new selling techniques. Students: written practices, videotaped skill practices, and performance tests; instructor: lecture.
Credit recommendation: In the lower division baccalaureate/associate degree category, 2 semester hours in Marketing (11/86).

Manufactured Housing Selling Skills

Location: Corporate Educational Center, Benton Harbor, MI.
Length: 20 hours (2½ days).
Dates: June 1984-Present.
Objective: To provide the student with the skills and an understanding of sales to dealers of manufactured housing and the ability to exercise techniques associated with successful sales.
Instruction: Lecture, discussion, role playing, classroom exercises, and problem solving under intensive supervision of the instructor. Preparation and substantial outside reading required of highly structured and specific textual material.
Credit recommendation: In the lower division baccalaureate/associate degree category, 1 semester hour in Sales (12/85).

Prospecting for New Accounting; Developing Existing Accounts

Location: Corporate Educational Center, Benton Harbor, MI.

Length: 36 hours (4 days).
Dates: December 1985-Present.
Objective: To provide the student with the skills and knowledge of sales techniques associated with the development of new customers and the servicing and expansion of sales to existing customers.
Instruction: Lecture, discussion, role playing, classroom exercises, and problem solving under intensive supervision of the instructor. Preparation and substantial outside reading required of highly structured and specific textual material.
Credit recommendation: In the lower division baccalaureate/associate degree category, 2 semester hours in Sales Management (12/85).

Sales Analysis and Planning
(Effective Territory Analyses and Action Planning)
Location: Corporate Educational Center, Benton Harbor, MI.
Length: 42 hours (5 days).
Dates: April 1986-Present.
Learning Outcome: Upon successful completion of this course, the student will be able to identify inadequately penetrated markets, develop sales objectives, identify shortcomings in existing accounts, forecast sales, and coach selling techniques.
Instruction: Practice in analyzing market penetration; setting sales objectives; identifying account's shortcomings and appropriate replacement, if necessary; forecasting sales for market segments; preparing account presentation; selecting time investments; completing weekly report; identifying poor selling performance; demonstrating good selling skills; and providing feedback. Students: written practices, videotaped skill practices, and performance tests; instructor: lecture.
Credit recommendation: In the lower division baccalaureate/associate degree category, 2 semester hours in Marketing (11/86).

Sales Management I
(Sales Manager Excellence in Pricing, Programming, and Promotion Strategies)
Location: Corporate Educational Center, Benton Harbor, MI.
Length: 42 hours (5 days).
Dates: November 1985-Present.
Learning Outcome: Upon successful completion of this course, the student will be able to develop sales pricing and programming, develop merchandising booklets, and plan promotions.
Instruction: Practice in developing an optimally balanced program and merchandising booklets; and planning promotions. Students: written practices, videotaped skill practices, and performance tests; instructor: lecture.
Credit recommendation: In the lower division baccalaureate/associate degree category, 2 semester hours in Marketing (11/86).

Sales Management II
(Coaching and Training Territory Managers)
Location: Corporate Educational Center, Benton Harbor, MI.
Length: 42 hours (5 days).
Dates: April 1986-Present.
Learning Outcome: Upon successful completion of this course, the student will be able to coach and identify the differences in selling techniques, and develop sales training activities.
Instruction: Practice in describing coach selling groundrules; identifying poor performance; demonstrating appropriate selling skills; providing feedback; conducting sales training; identifying skill deficiencies; planning, developing, and implementing selling skills training, and providing feedback. Students: written practices, videotaped skill practices, and performance tests; instructor: lecture.
Credit recommendation: In the lower division baccalaureate/associate degree category, 2 semester hours in Marketing (11/86).

Sales Management for Builders
(Action Planning, Pricing, and Programming)
Location: Corporate Educational Center, Benton Harbor, MI.
Length: 42 hours (5 days).
Dates: April 1986-Present.
Learning Outcome: Upon successful completion of this course, the student will be able to identify inadequately penetrated markets, set market objectives, analyze pricing structures and set prices.
Instruction: Practice in analyzing market segment penetration; setting sales objectives; identifying staff's shortcomings; setting staff's sales objectives; scheduling time investments; reviewing accounts analysis forms; developing pricing programs; completing quotations; and completing upgrade appliance worksheet. Students: written practices, videotaped skill practices, and performance tests; instructor: lecture.
Credit recommendation: In the lower division baccalaureate/associate degree category, 2 semester hours in Marketing (11/86).

Sales Management Seminar
(Increasing the Effectiveness of Your Retail Territory Managers)
Location: Corporate Educational Center, Benton Harbor, MI.
Length: 42 hours (5 days).
Dates: August 1985-Present.
Learning Outcome: Upon successful completion of this course, the student will be able to set sales objectives, evaluate territory development, interpret reports related

to overall marketing activity, and train and evaluate staff's selling techniques.

Instruction: Practice in setting sales objectives; identifying staff's shortcomings; identifying inadequate market penetration; setting sales goals; estimating time investments; reviewing activity reports; demonstrating selling techniques; and coaching others to use selling techniques. Students: written practices, videotaped skill practices, and performance tests; instructor: lecture.

Credit recommendation: In the lower division baccalaureate/associate degree category, 2 semester hours in Marketing (11/86).

Sales, Promotions and Advertising Strategies
(Effective Selling Skills, Winning Promotions and Advertising Strategies)
Location: Corporate Educational Center, Benton Harbor, MI.
Length: 42 hours (5 days).
Dates: September 1985–Present.
Learning Outcome: Upon successful completion of this course, the student will be able to: given the appropriate sales materials on an account, make a full sales presentation to a dealer; and, to develop a dealer's advertising strategy and evaluation plan of that strategy.

Instruction: Practice in determining purpose/benefit statement for call; using questions to identify dealer's needs; selecting features/benefits to satisfy dealer's needs; handling dealer's objections; closing deal; defining account image; describing customer population, identifying primary and secondary markets; determining appropriate monthly advertising and promotion budgets; selecting promotional themes; calculating costs/selecting media; developing a promotion evaluation plan; drafting advertising content/copy; and preparing advertisement. Students: written practices, videotaped skill practices, and performance tests; instructor: lecture.

Credit recommendation: In the lower division baccalaureate/associate degree category, 2 semester hours in Marketing (11/86).

Sales Training Techniques
(Conduct Sales Training)
Location: Corporate Educational Center, Benton Harbor, MI.
Length: 16 hours (2 days).
Dates: March 1986–Present.
Learning Outcome: Upon successful completion of this course, the student will be able to identify sales skills deficiencies, plan, develop and conduct sales training through demonstration of sales skills and performance, and evaluate performance.

Instruction: Practice in determining deficiencies in staff's selling skills; planning, developing, and implementing sales training; and providing feedback to staff on new selling techniques. Students: written practices, videotaped skill practices, and performance tests; instructor: lecture.

Credit recommendation: In the lower division baccalaureate/associate degree category, 1 semester hour in Marketing (11/86).

Wisconsin Public Service Corporation

Wisconsin Public Service Corporations's (WPSC) Nuclear Training Group is charged with the responsibility of providing such scientific, engineering, technical, managerial and operational educational and training to the Nuclear Department's personnel as is required for the safe and economic operation of the Kewaunee Nuclear Power Plant (KNPP).

A major portion of such education and training is directed to personnel who will serve as Equipment, Auxiliary, Reactor and Senior Reactor Operators at KNPP. The subject matter taught these individuals is notably technical and scientific.

To accomplish its education and training of personnel, WPSC's Nuclear Training Group is comprised of individuals with terminal degrees in scientific and engineering disciplines, persons with many years of experience in nuclear power generation who hold United States Nuclear Regulatory Commission Senior Reactor Operator Licenses on the facility and a cadre of support personnel with varying discipline knowledge and appropriate experience.

A library of scientific, engineering, technical and operations supporting materials exists for the trainee's use. A full scale multi-million dollar KNPP specific training simulator exists which is capable of generating hundreds of scenarios for operators to practice and master plant operations.

Extensive means exist for external assistance in course development and revision. In the case of courses on topics such as nuclear theory, fluid mechanics, thermodynamics, etc., basic sciences such as physics, chemistry, and mathematics, university faculty from several institutions routinely aid in program and course development. Additionally, professors of nuclear science, nuclear engineering, physics and chemistry have assisted the Nuclear Training Group in delivering education/training to WPSC personnel. Other consultants from nationally known nuclear power plant vendors also assist the training staff in development and delivery of courseware.

Source of official student records: Superintendent, Nuclear Training, Wisconsin Public Service Corporation, P.O. Box 19002, Green Bay, Wisconsin 54307-9002.

Additional information about the courses: Program on Noncollegiate Sponsored Instruction, The Center for Adult Learning and Educational Credentials, American Council on Education, One Dupont Circle, Washington, D.C. 20036.

Nuclear Systems Overview
  Location: Kewaunee, WI.
  Length: 73½ hours (2 weeks).
  Dates: January 1984-Present.
  Objective: To provide students with an understanding of the operation of nuclear power plant systems.
  Learning Outcome: Upon successful completion of this course, the student will have a knowledge of nomenclature, understanding of concepts, and ability to define and describe operating systems of nuclear power plants.
  Instruction: Method of instruction is lecture-discussion with supplemental readings. Content includes reactor coolant, chemical volume control, rod control, main stream, main turbine, main feedwater, main generator, electrical, radioactive waste, and radiation monitoring systems, plus instrumentation and accident analysis.
  Credit recommendation: In the lower division baccalaureate/associate degree category, 2 semester hours in Nuclear Engineering Technology (12/86). NOTE: Credit should not be awarded for this course if participants have completed the Reactor Operator fundamentals course.

Radiation Monitoring Systems
  Location: Kewaunee Nuclear Training Center, WI.
  Length: 62 hours (5 weeks).
  Dates: January 1985-Present.
  Objective: To provide the student with a knowledge of radiation monitoring systems.
  Learning Outcome: Upon successful completion of this course, the student will understand the function and characteristics of radiation monitoring systems and the chemistry relevant to the primary sampling system.
  Instruction: Course covers purposes, operations; and equipment of radiation monitoring system and of the primary sampling system. The chemistry relevant to the primary sampling system such as deposits and corrosion is discussed.
  Credit recommendation: In the vocational certificate category, 1 semester hour in Nuclear Technology (8/86).

Reactor Operation Fundamentals Chemistry
  Location: Kewaunee Nuclear Training Center, WI.
  Length: 40 hours (1 week).
  Dates: January 1981-Present.
  Objective: To give the student instruction in fundamentals of chemistry.
  Learning Outcome: Upon successful completion of this course, the student will understand the fundamentals of chemistry and be able to perform stoichiometric calculations.
  Instruction: Course covers fundamentals and principles of chemistry including atomic theory, law of mass action, bonding, solution concentrations, pH, and electrochemistry (non laboratory).
  Credit recommendation: In the lower division baccalaureate/associate degree category, 1 semester hour in General Chemistry (8/86). NOTE: Credit should not be awarded for both Introduction to Fundamentals of Power Plant Chemistry and this course.

Reactor Operator Fundamentals: Core Physics
  Location: Kewaunee Nuclear Training Center, WI.
  Length: 150 hours (4 weeks).
  Dates: January 1981-Present.
  Objective: To provide a survey of (a) plant specific reactor core components and coolant flow; (b) the effects of various coefficients on core reactivity; and (c) core power distribution and reactivity control during reactor operation.
  Learning Outcome: Upon successful completion of this course, the student will be able to describe, define, and/or calculate reactor components, the multiplication factor, reactivity and reactivity changes, the effects of various coefficients (doppler, temperature, void, etc.), fission product poisoning, lumped and distributed poisons, power distribution and reactivity control often contrasting parameters at BOL with EOL.
  Instruction: By means of lecture, discussion, problem solution, and supervised self study the following topics are surveyed: reactor core construction; reactivity and fuel effects; moderator temperature effects and power defect; fission product poisoning; chemical shim control; control rod reactivity effect; estimated critical condition and shutdown; reactivity considerations; nuclear power distribution in a PWR core; and reactivity control during power operation.
  Credit recommendation: In the lower division baccalaureate/associate degree category, 3 semester hours in Nuclear Engineering/Nuclear Engineering Technology (8/86).

Reactor Operator Fundamentals: Heat Transfer and Fluid Flow
  Location: Kewaunee Nuclear Training Center, WI.
  Length: 160 hours (4 weeks).
  Dates: January 1981-Present.
  Objective: To provide the student with an understanding of basic concepts of heat transfer and fluid mechanics as applied to pressurized water reactors.
  Learning Outcome: Upon successful completion of this course, the student will have an understanding of the basic laws of heat transfer, thermodynamics, and fluid mechanics and be able to apply these concepts to the operation of a pressurized water reactor.
  Instruction: Instructional units that include lectures, discussions, guided problem-solving, and self study in the following subject areas: properties of water, reactor heat transfer, reactor thermodynamics, heat exchangers, steam generator thermodynamics, turbine thermodynamics and the rankine cycle, fluid mechanics in the turbine, condensor/tertiary thermodynamics, piping and pump fluid mechanics instrumentation, steady state and normal

transients, and core thermal parameters and limits.

Credit recommendation: In the lower division baccalaureate/associate degree category, 2 semester hours in Heat Transfer and Fluid Mechanics (8/86).

Reactor Operator Fundamentals: Mathematics

Location: Kewaunee Nuclear Training Center, WI.
Length: 37 hours (1 week).
Dates: January 1981-Present.
Objective: To develop skills in solving linear and quadratic equations, use of mensuration formulae, exponents, logarithms, graphs, and to introduce basic concepts of calculus.
Learning Outcome: Upon successful completion of this course, the student will be able to solve linear, quadratic, and exponential equations; construct graphs, find slopes and intercepts; and calculate basic trigonometric functions using calculator.
Instruction: A lecture/discussion course in the fundamentals of algebra, exponentials, and logarithms, graphs, and an introduction to calculus concepts of integrals and derivatives.
Credit recommendation: In the lower division baccalaureate/associate degree category, 1 semester hour in Mathematics (Algebra and Trigonometry) (8/86).

Reactor Operator Fundamentals: Radiation

Location: Kewaunee Nuclear Training Center, WI.
Length: 80 hours (2 weeks).
Dates: January 1981-Present.
Objective: To provide students with fundamental knowledge of the properties and effects of nuclear radiation.
Learning Outcome: Upon successful completion of this course, the student will have an understanding of physical and biological effects of nuclear radiation, radiation detection and protection and be able to perform determinations of half-lives and activities.
Instruction: Lecture course covers radioactive decay, interaction of radiation with matter, biological effects of radiation, radiation detectors, and radiation protection and regulations.
Credit recommendation: In the upper division baccalaureate category, 3 semester hours in Nuclear Science (Radiology/Health Physics) (8/86). NOTE: Credit should not be granted for both Auxiliary Operator: Theory and Administration and this course.

Reactor Operator Fundamentals: Reactor Theory

Location: Kewaunee Nuclear Training Center, WI.
Length: 112 hours (3 weeks).
Dates: January 1981-Present.
Objective: To provide a survey of information on the structure of the atom, properties of the neutron, nuclear interactions, radioactive decay, static and kinetic reactor behavior.
Learning Outcome: Upon successful completion of this course, the student will be able to describe, define, and/or calculate basic properties of the atom, the neutron, and radioisotopes as they relate to the steady state or dynamic behavior of a reactor core.
Instruction: By means of lecture, discussion, problem solution, and supervised self study the following topics are surveyed: properties of energy and matter; atomic physics; nuclear reactions; neutron physics; reactor statics; reactor kinetics, and subcritical reactor behavior.
Credit recommendation: In the lower division baccalaureate/associate degree category, 2 semester hours in Nuclear Engineering/Nuclear Engineering Technology (8/86).

Reactor Operator Simulator Training (Normal Operations; Abnormal Operations; Abnormal/Emergency; and Emergency Function Restoration)

Location: Kewaunee, WI.
Length: 297 hours (8.6 weeks) in four separate course modules.
Dates: January 1984-Present.
Objective: To provide students with knowledge of normal, abnormal, and emergency nuclear power plant operation.
Learning Outcome: Upon successful completion of this course, the student will have the knowledge and skill to startup, normal operation, and shutdown of nuclear power plants; and ability to diagnose and mitigate malfunctions and to institute appropriate emergency operating procedures in nuclear power plants.
Instruction: Methods of instruction are lecture-discussion and extensive laboratory training utilizing a simulator. Content includes normal startup, shutdown, and full power operation of a nuclear power plant; occasional expected malfunctions; rare abnormal/emergency malfunctions; and emergency operating procedures for taking appropriate corrective action when malfunctions occur in nuclear power plants.
Credit recommendation: In the upper division baccalaureate category, 3 semester hours in Nuclear Engineering Technology (12/86).

Reactor Operator Systems: Administration and Emergency Planning

Location: Kewaunee Nuclear Training Center, WI.
Length: 173½ hours (4½ weeks).
Dates: January 1981-Present.
Objective: To provide the student with instruction in nuclear plant management as it relates to compliance with technical specifications, selected portions of Title 10 of the Code of Federal Regulations, Emergency Planning and Fire Protection.
Learning Outcome: Upon successful completion of this course, the student will be able to (a) describe and explain

the implications, definitions, limitations, compliance, and basis for the various sections of technical specifications, (b) describe and interpret the interrelationships of emergency planning with off-site organizations, and (c) describe and explain principles of fire protection and the associated alarm responses, and technical specification implications.

Instruction: Subjects related to Administration and Emergency Planning as described in: technical specifications; administrative control directives; Title 10 Code of Federal Regulations; emergency planning; emergency plant implementation, and fire protection.

Credit recommendation: In the upper division baccalaureate category, 2 semester hours in Nuclear Plant Management (8/86).

Reactor Operator Systems: Electrical Generation and Distribution Systems
   Location: Kewaunee Nuclear Training Center, WI.
   Length: 105 hours (9 days).
   Dates: January 1981-Present.
   Objective: To provide the student with instruction on power plant electrical generation and distribution systems — design, components, instrumentation and functions — as they apply to a reactor operator.
   Learning Outcome: Upon successful completion of this course, the student will have an understanding of the electrical generation and distribution system of a power plant.
   Instruction: Instructional units that include lectures, discussions, on-the-job training, and self study on the following topics: main generator and generator auxiliaries, protection relating, substation and electrical distribution, 4160 Volt electrical system, 480 Volt electrical system and emergency systems.
   Credit recommendation: In the lower division baccalaureate/associate degree category, 1 semester hour in Electrical or Nuclear Engineering Technology (8/86).

Reactor Operator Systems: Emergency Diesel Generator Mechanical/Electrical Systems
   Location: Kewaunee Nuclear Training Center, WI.
   Length: 51 hours (7 days).
   Dates: January 1981-Present.
   Objective: To provide the student with instruction on the diesel generator mechanical/electrical systems of a nuclear power plant as they apply to a reactor operator.
   Learning Outcome: Upon successful completion of this course, the student will have an understanding of the diesel generator mechanical/electrical systems of a nuclear power plant.
   Instruction: Instructional units that include lecture, discussion, on-the-job training and self study on the following topics: diesel generator — mechanical, diesel generator — electrical, and load shedding and sequencing.
   Credit recommendation: In the lower division baccalaureate/associate degree category, 1 semester hour in Nuclear Engineering Technology (8/86).

Reactor Operator Systems: Integrated Reactor Protection and Safety Features
   Location: Kewaunee Nuclear Training Center, WI.
   Length: 58 hours (1½ weeks).
   Dates: January 1981-Present.
   Objective: To provide the student with descriptions, purposes, operating limits, interlocks, alarms and associated procedures for reactor protection systems and engineered safeguards systems.
   Learning Outcome: Upon successful completion of this course, the student will be able to describe and become familiar with the operation, functions, locations, operating limits, instrumentation, procedures and technical specification implications of all the system components.
   Instruction: Subjects related to integrated reactor protection and safety features including the integrated safety features and the reactor protection and safeguards logic.
   Credit recommendation: In the lower division baccalaureate/associate degree category, 1 semester hour in Nuclear Engineering Technology (8/86).

Reactor Operator Systems: Plant Secondary Coolant and Auxiliary Systems
   Location: Kewaunee Nuclear Training Center, WI.
   Length: 189 hours (24 days).
   Dates: January 1981-Present.
   Objective: To provide the student with instruction on the plant secondary coolant and auxiliary systems of a nuclear power plant as they apply to a reactor operator.
   Learning Outcome: Upon successful completion of this course, the student will have an understanding of the plant/secondary coolant and auxiliary systems.
   Instruction: Instructional units that include lecture, discussion, on-the-job training and self study on the following topics: Related to plant, secondary coolant and auxiliary systems. Station and instrument air, main steam and steam pumps, steam pump control, bleed steam, feedwater heaters, heater drains, circulating water, main turbine and auxiliaries, turbine control system, air removal, condensate system, main feed water, makeup water, secondary sampling system, secondary chemistry control.
   Credit recommendation: In the lower division baccalaureate/associate degree category, 3 semester hours in Nuclear Engineering Technology (8/86).

Reactor Operator Systems: Plant Ventilation Systems
   Location: Kewaunee Nuclear Training Center, WI.
   Length: 84 hours (2 weeks and 1 day).
   Dates: January 1981-Present.
   Objective: To provide the student with instruction on the plant ventilation systems of a nuclear power plant as they apply to a reactor operator.
   Learning Outcome: Upon successful completion of this

course, the student will have an understanding of the various ventilation systems of a nuclear power plant.

Instruction: Instructional units that include lecture discussion, on-the-job training and self study on the following plant ventilation systems: turbine building and screenhouse, auxiliary building, shield building, reactor building, containment building, and post LOCA hydrogen control, and control room air conditioning.

Credit recommendation: In the lower division baccalaureate/associate degree category, 1 semester hour in Nuclear Engineering Technology (8/86).

Reactor Operator Systems: Reactor Core Design, Components, Instrumentation, and Functions
  Location: Kewaunee Nuclear Training Center, WI.
  Length: 54 hours (1½ weeks).
  Dates: January 1981-Present.
  Objective: To provide a description and familiarization of reactor vessel internal components, incore and excore nuclear instrumentation.
  Learning Outcome: Upon successful completion of this course, the student will be able: (a) to locate and describe the function of reactor vessel internals, explain safety limits associated with these components; (b) to understand some basic instrumentation theory, explain functions of the instrumentation and the associated readouts and interlocks; (c) to understand the relationship with other plant components, technical specification limits.
  Instruction: Subjects related to design, components instrumentation and functions of the reactor core including the reactor vessel and internals, excore and incore instrumentation.
  Credit recommendation: In the lower division baccalaureate/associate degree category, 1 semester hour in Nuclear Engineering Technology (8/86).

Reactor Operator Systems: Reactor Emergency and Auxiliary Coolant Systems
  Location: Kewaunee Nuclear Training Center, WI.
  Length: 138 hours (4 weeks).
  Dates: January 1981-Present.
  Objective: To provide the student with descriptions, purposes, associated interlocks and alarms, and procedures for all system components.
  Learning Outcome: Upon successful completion of this course, the student will be able to describe and become familiar with the operation, functions, locations, interconnections, interactions, limits, precautions, and procedures where applicable of all the system components.
  Instruction: Covers subjects related to the reactor emergency and auxiliary coolant systems including: chemical and volume control; component cooling; residual heat removal; internal containment spray, and safety injection.
  Credit recommendation: In the lower division baccalaureate/associate degree category, 2 semester hours in Nuclear Engineering Technology (8/86).

Reactor Operator Systems: Reactor Primary Coolant System
  Location: Kewaunee Nuclear Training Center, WI.
  Length: 123½ hours (3½ weeks).
  Dates: January 1981-Present.
  Objective: To provide the student with descriptions, purposes flow paths, arrangements, indications, normal and abnormal procedure for all system components.
  Learning Outcome: Upon successful completion of this course, the student will be able to describe and become familiar with the operation, functions, locations, interconnections, interactions, tests, instrumentation, limits, and procedures (normal and abnormal) for all the components of the primary coolant system.
  Instruction: Covers subjects related to reactor primary coolant system including: reactor coolant system; pressurizer and pressure relief tank; pressurizer pressure instrumentation and pressure control; pressurizer level control; reactor coolant pumps, and steam generators and level control.
  Credit recommendation: In the lower division baccalaureate/associate degree category, 3 semester hours in Nuclear Engineering Technololgy (8/86).

Reactor Operator Systems: Rod Control
  Location: Kewaunee Nuclear Training Center, WI.
  Length: 59 hours (1½ weeks).
  Dates: January 1981-Present.
  Objective: To provide a description and familiarization with the rod control system, rod position indications and the rod insertion limit and temperature instrumentation.
  Learning Outcome: Upon successful completion of this course, the student will be able to: (a) locate and describe the functions of rod control system, position indicators, and temperature instrumentation and (b) relate the system to technical specifications.
  Instruction: Subjects related to the rod control system including the full length control rods, rod position indication and RCS temperature monitoring and rod insertion limits.
  Credit recommendation: In the lower division baccalaureate/associate degree category, 1 semester hour in Nuclear Engineering Technology (8/86).

Reactor Operator Systems: Special Auxiliary Systems
  Location: Kewaunee Nuclear Training Center, WI.
  Length: 82 hours (4 weeks).
  Dates: January 1981-Present.
  Objective: To provide the student with instruction on the special auxiliary systems of a nuclear power plant as they apply to a reactor operator.
  Learning Outcome: Upon successful completion of this course, the student will have an understanding of the special auxiliary systems of a nuclear power plant.
  Instruction: Instructional units that include lecture, discussions, on-the-job training, and self study on the follow-

ing special auxiliary systems: auxiliary feedwater system, source water system, refueling and spent fuel pool system.

Credit recommendation: In the lower division baccalaureate/associate degree category, 1 semester hour in Nuclear Engineering Technology (8/86).

Senior Reactor Operator: Operational Administration
Location: Kewaunee Nuclear Training Center, WI.
Length: 96 hours (3 weeks).
Dates: January 1981-Present.
Objective: To provide the student with in-depth knowledge of nuclear plant operational administration.
Learning Outcome: Upon successful completion of this course, the student will be able to: describe organizational responsibilities, supervisor responsibilities and duties of plant personnel from plant manager to radiation protection personnel as outlined in the course description.
Instruction: Subjects related to operational administration including: Supervisor training; plant organization; operations; reactor engineering and corporate engineering organization; maintenance and supply; chemistry; radiation radiological protection; plant safety organization; plant emergencies; plant security; project and program control techniques; operational quality assurance program; regulatory requirements, and plant shutdown and special activities.
Credit recommendation: In the upper division baccalaureate category, 3 semester hours in Nuclear Engineering (8/86).

Senior Reactor Operator: Plant Systems Review and Upgrade
Location: Kewaunee Nuclear Training Center, WI.
Length: 200 hours (5 weeks).
Dates: January 1981-Present.
Objective: To provide the student with an in-depth and integrated knowledge of all plant systems.
Learning Outcome: Upon successful completion of this course, the student will be able to: describe, explain, and analyze the bases, design requirements, precautions, limitations, procedures, and technical specification implications of all plant systems.
Instruction: Subjects related to plant systems including: reactor core; rod control system; reactor primary coolant system; reactor emergency and auxiliary coolant systems; plant ventilation systems; special auxiliary systems; emergency diesel generator mechanical/electrical systems; integrated reactor protection and safety features; radiological and non-radiological waste disposal systems; radiation monitoring systems; plant secondary coolant and auxiliary systems; electrical generation and distribution systems, and fire emergencies.
Credit recommendation: In the upper division baccalaureate category, 4 semester hours in Nuclear Engineering (8/86).

Senior Reactor Operator Simulator Training (Abnormal Operations; and Abnormal Emergency Operations)
Location: Kewaunee, WI.
Length: 177 hours (3.6 weeks) in two separate course modules.
Dates: January 1984-Present.
Objective: To give students conceptual understanding of nuclear power plant design and operation, and of abnormal/emergency operating conditions. Understanding of interaction among various nuclear power plant operating systems.
Learning Outcome: Upon successful completion of this course, the students will have technical, operational, and conceptual understanding of nuclear power plant operations; and ability to diagnose and solve problems encountered in abnormal/emergency nuclear power plant operation.
Instruction: Method of instruction is hands-on laboratory training utilizing a simulator. Content includes performance of routine water power plant operation, response to selected abnormal events, and diagnosis and mitigation of nuclear power plant malfunctions.
Credit recommendation: In the upper division baccalaureate category, 2 semester hours in Nuclear Engineering Technology (12/86).

Wolf Creek Nuclear Operating Corporation (Formerly Kansas Gas & Electric)

Wolf Creek Nuclear Operating Corporation is the licensee and operator of the Wolf Creek Generating Station (WCGS), an 1150Mw nuclear power plant. WCGS provides electric service to the southeast quadrant of Kansas. The training effort is tasked to provide academic and technical training to plant operators, technicians, and professional and support personnel to ensure the facility's safe and reliable operation.

The structure of the training organization has four functions: Operations Training provides classroom, simulator and in-plant experiential segments to plant-licensed and non-licensed operators. The simulator, a replica of the plant master control board, is used to present real-time scenarios of normal and transient operations. The Technical Training Section provides technical crafts training; the General Section conducts company-wide and professional training; the Academic Section supervises the academic standards, and the procedural integrity of the training effort to ensure compliance with regulatory and advisory agencies.

The plant operations personnel training program is organized in two parts: Non-Licensed Operator (NLO) systems courses are organized around a set of generic objectives to prepare the employee to work in all watch stations within the plant. The sequence is offered over a three-year period with formal classroom training interspersed with on-the-job training and individual plant systems qualification. The Licensed Operator (LO) sequence is 48 weeks of theory, systems instrumentation and control, and control and mitigation of transients designed to train reactor control room operators to meet the criteria for licensing by the Nuclear Regulatory Commission. Both NLO and LO programs have continuing and requalification programs designed to maintain and enhance the skill and knowledge levels of the plant operators.

The Technical Training programs are organized around the primary technician tasks: mechanical maintenance technician, electrical maintenance technician, instrumentation and control technician, health physics technician, and chemistry technician. The programs provide initial and fundamental courses, skills courses, and continuing and requalification courses designed to maintain and enhance the skill and knowledge levels of the plant technicians.

The General Training programs provide company-wide training for all employees and specialty training for professional and management personnel.

Source of official student records: Manager, Training, Wolf Creek Nuclear Operating Corporation, P.O. Box 411, Burlington, Kansas 66839.

Additional information about the courses: Program on Noncollegiate Sponsored Instruction, The Center for Adult Learning and Educational Credentials, American Council on Education, One Dupont Circle, Washington, D.C. 20036.

CHEMISTRY TECHNICIAN

Instrument Analysis (CF0116200)

Location: Wolf Creek Generating Station, Burlington, KS.

Length: 69 hours (1.7 weeks); 21 hours lecture/discussion, 48 hours on-the-job training.

Dates: January 1987-Present.

Objective: To provide the student with sufficient instruction on the measurement of nuclear power plant chemistry parameters.

Learning Outcome: Upon successful completion of this course, the student will be able to operate chemical instruments; understand the principles of chemistry measurements; interpret experimental results, and determine if the instruments are operating properly.

Instruction: Course includes theoretical and practical aspects of instrumental analysis based upon the measurement of potentiometric, conductometric, spectrophotometric, atomic absorption, gas chromatography, ion chromatography, and other chemicals.

Credit recommendation: In the lower division baccalaureate/associate degree category, 1 semester hour in Nuclear Reactor Technology (4/88).

Radiation Detection and Measurement (CN0100060)

Location: Wolf Creek Generating Station, Burlington, KS.

Length: 148 hours (3 weeks); 96 hours classroom and 52 hours on-the-job training.

Dates: November 1986-Present.

Objective: To provide the student with an instruction on how to perform radioactive analysis at WCGS and interpret the results.

Learning Outcome: Upon successful completion of this course, the student will be able to perform gamma isotopic, beta and alpha analysis; quantify the activity of various samples; and evaluate the results to determine if they are statistically correct.

Instruction: Course covers atomic structure, radionuclide identification, radiation interactions with matter, modes of decay, radiation detection, radiochemical analysis, fission product release mechanisms, activity calculations, counting statistics and practical experience in calibration, operation, and data evaluation of counting systems.

Credit recommendation: In the lower division baccalaureate/associate degree category, 3 semester hours in Nuclear Reactor Technology (4/88).

ELECTRICAL MAINTENANCE

Basic Electricity/Electronics (ME0035302)

Location: Wolf Creek Generating Station, Burlington, KS.

Length: 116 hours (3 weeks); 102 hours lecture, 12 hours lab, 6 hours videotape.

Dates: November 1987-Present.

Objective: To provide the student with an understanding of the theory of AC and DC electricity and basic electronics.

Learning Outcome: Upon successful completion of this course, the student will be able to discuss and understand the simple theory of electricity and electronics and apply this information to future courses and equipment.

Instruction: Course covers resistance, capacitance and induction; series and parallel circuits; magnetism; Ohms Law; sample transistor theory and operation; and applications of the above to maintenance of electronic equipment. Methodology includes lecture, lab, videotapes, and computer-assistance.

Credit recommendation: In the lower division baccalaureate/associate degree category, 3 semester hours in Engineering/Engineering Technology (4/88). NOTE: This course must be combined with Measurement and Test Equipment (ME0035303) for credit recommendation.

Circuit Protection (ME0035307)

Location: Wolf Creek Generating Station, Burlington, KS.

Length: 88 hours (2 weeks, 1 day); 82 hours lecture, 2 hours videotape, 4 hours lab.

Dates: November 1987-Present.

Objective: To provide theory of circuit protection, a working knowledge of equipment used for circuit protection, and how to maintain this equipment.

Learning Outcome: Upon successful completion of this course, the student will be able to become familiar with the theory of circuit protection and operation of devices used for circuit protection to the working environment.

Instruction: Course covers the theory, operation, and maintenance of circuit breakers; motor control; protection devices; and bus and switchgear. Methodology includes lecture and videotapes.

Credit recommendation: In the vocational certificate category, 2 semester hours in Circuit Protection Techniques (4/88).

Conduit, Cable and Wire (ME0035309)

Location: Wolf Creek Generating Station, Burlington, KS.

Length: 56 hours (1 week, 2 days).

Dates: November 1987-Present.

Objective: To familiarize the student with the various types of cable and wire, their uses, methods of testing power cable to locating faults.

Learning Outcome: Upon successful completion of this course, the student will be able to describe the different types of cables, and describe the steps in testing and cable fault location.

Instruction: Course covers cable and wire; cable fault location, radar cable fault location, and power cable testing. Methodology includes lecture.

Credit recommendation: In the vocational certificate category, 1 semester hour in Wiring and Cableing (4/88).

Electrical Maintenance Fundamentals (ME0035301)

Location: Wolf Creek Generating Station, Burlington, KS.

Length: 84 hours (2 weeks); 4 hours videotapes, 76 hours lecture.

Dates: June 1987-Present.

Objective: To familiarize the student with basic fundamentals of print reading, maintenance procedures, scaffolding, rigging and personal safety required to perform successfully in electrical craft.

Learning Outcome: Upon successful completion of this course, the student will be able to read prints, describe maintenance practices, perform a job safely, and have a working knowledge of scaffolding, rigging and cranes.

Instruction: Course covers basic communication, safety and maintenance, print reading and scaffolding. Methodology includes lecture and videotapes.

Credit recommendation: In the vocational certificate category, 2 semester hours in Electrical Maintenance (4/88).

Heating, Ventilation and Air Conditioning (ME0035305)

Location: Wolf Creek Generating Station, Burlington, KS.

Length: 80 hours (2 weeks); 70 hours lecture, 2 hours videotapes, 8 hours lab.

Dates: November 1987-Present.

Objective: To provide the student with background in the basics of air conditioning, air handling, and in the maintenance and troubleshooting of such equipment.

Learning Outcome: Upon successful completion of this course, the student will be able to describe the operation and maintenance of heating, ventilating and air conditioning equipment.

Instruction: Course covers electrical circuit theory applied to motors and controls, charging refrigeration and heat pump equipment, and maintenance procedures. Methodology includes lecture, videotapes, and lab.

Credit recommendation: In the vocational certificate category, 1 semester hour in Basic Electricity (4/88).

Measurement and Test Equipment (ME0035303)

Location: Wolf Creek Generating Station, Burlington, KS.

Length: 59 hours (1½ weeks).

Dates: November 1987-Present.

Objective: To provide the student with a knowledge of the test equipment used at WCGS and its proper use in the field.

Learning Outcome: Upon successful completion of this course, the student will be able to identify the proper piece of test equipment for the situation and use it correctly.

Instruction: Course covers operation and use of electronic test equipment. Methodology includes lecture.

Credit recommendation: In the lower division baccalaureate/associate degree category, 3 semester hours in Engineering/Engineering Technology (4/88). NOTE: This course must be combined with Basic Electricity/Electronics (ME0035302) for credit recommendation.

Motors and Generators (ME0035306)

Location: Wolf Creek Generating Station, Burlington, KS.

Length: 96 hours (2 weeks, 2 days); 80 hours lecture, 4 hours videotapes, 6 hours lab.

Dates: November 1987-Present.

Objective: To provide the student with the theory of motors and generators, the Altorex Exciter, and motor operated valves.

Learning Outcome: Upon successful completion of this course, the student will be able to describe theory and operation of motors and generators.

Instruction: Course covers AC motors and generators, generator excitor, and motor operated valves. Methodology includes lecture, videotapes, and lab.

Credit recommendation: In the lower division baccalaureate/associate degree category, 3 semester hours in Engineering/Engineering Technology (4/88). NOTE: This course must be combined with Transformers (ME0035304) for credit recommendation.

Transformers (ME0035304)

Location: Wolf Creek Generating Station, Burlington, KS.

Length: 80 hours (2 weeks); 77 hours lecture, 3 hours lab.

Dates: November 1987-Present.

Objective: To provide the student with knowledge of the theory, operation, testing, and maintenance of transformers.

Learning Outcome: Upon successful completion of this course, the student will be able to describe the theory of transformers and their maintenance.

Instruction: Course covers transformer theory, transformer connections, and transformer testing and maintenance. Methodology includes lecture.

Credit recommendation: In the lower division baccalaureate/associate degree category, 3 semester hours in Engineering/Engineering Technology (4/88). NOTE: This course must be combined with Motors and Generators (ME0035306) for credit recommendation.

Troubleshooting/DC Sources (ME0035308)

Location: Wolf Creek Generating Station, Burlington, KS.

Length: 72 hours (1 week, 4 days).

Dates: November 1987-Present.

Objective: To provide the student with the necessary knowledge to troubleshoot electrical circuits and maintain DC power sources.

Learning Outcome: Upon successful completion of this course, the student will be able to troubleshoot electrical circuits and discuss the theory and operation of DC power sources.

Instruction: Course covers troubleshooting electrical circuits, battery testing/maintenance, and battery chargers/inverters/cathodic protection. Methodology includes lecture and lab exercises.

Credit recommendation: In the vocational certificate category, 2 semester hours in Basic DC Circuit Maintenance (4/88).

HEALTH PHYSICS TECHNICIAN

Health Physics Fundamentals (HF1100000)

Location: Wolf Creek Generating Station, Burlington, KS.

Length: 200 hours (5 weeks); 125 hours lecture/discussion, 75 hours problem-solving.

Dates: January 1987-Present.

Objective: To provide the health physics technician instructor in basic math, chemistry, and physics.

Learning Outcome: Upon successful completion of this course, the student will be able to explain and to apply basic math, chemistry, and physics concepts.

Instruction: Course covers introductory concepts in math (40%), chemistry (20%), and physics (40%). Methodology includes lecture and problem solving.

Credit recommendation: In the lower division baccalaureate/associate degree category, 2 semester hours in General Science (4/88).

Health Physics Technician Initial Training (HP1100000)

Location: Wolf Creek Generating Station, Burlington, KS.

Length: 492 hours (12.3 weeks); 192 hours classroom and 300 hours in-the-plant laboratory training.

Dates: June 1987-Present.

Objective: To qualify to perform the job functions of a Health Physics Technician.

Learning Outcome: Upon successful completion of this course, the student will be able to perform contamination surveys, radiation surveys, airborne surveys, decontamination, and to prepare Radiation Work Permits (RWPs).

Instruction: Course covers radiation surveillance, radioactive waste, respiratory protection, radiation dosimetry, instrumentation and computers. Methodology includes lecture, discussion, and on-the-job training.

Credit recommendation: In the lower division baccalaureate/associate degree category, 3 semester hours in Nuclear Science (Health Physics) (4/88). NOTE: This recommendation may be viewed as 2 semester hours for the classroom activity and 1 semester hour for the on-the-job training.

Health Physics Theory (HT1100000)

Location: Wolf Creek Generating Station, Burlington, KS.

Length: 120 hours (3 weeks); 75 hours lecture/discussion, 45 hours supervised self-study.

Dates: January 1987-Present.

Objective: To provide the student with sufficient instruction on the theory of health physics as it applies to day-to-day job assignments.

Learning Outcome: Upon successful completion of this course, the student will be able to answer plant personnel questions dealing with radiation protection principles, and to explain radioactivity, radioactive decay, internal and external exposure, and methods of measurement.

Instruction: Course covers nuclear physics and reactor technology, radioactivity, radiation interactions with matter, radiation units and biological effects, radiation detection and measurement, personnel dosimetry, external radiation protection, internal exposure, gamma spectroscopy, and counting statistics. Methodology includes lecture/discussion.

Credit recommendation: In the lower division baccalaureate/associate degree category, 2 semester hours in Nuclear Engineering Technology (4/88).

Health Physics WCGS Plant Systems (HP1400000)

Location: Wolf Creek Generating Station, Burlington, KS.

Length: 120 hours (3 weeks); 99 hours lecture/discussion, 21 hours supervised self-study.

Dates: March 1987-Present.

Objective: To provide the student with knowledge of the WCGS plant systems and an understanding of the health physics concerns for each system.

Learning Outcome: Upon successful completion of this course, the student will be able to work around plant systems more efficiently and effectively, and to explain the general operation, as related to the health physics concerns, of the various plant systems and the components of each system.

Instruction: Course covers plant systems related to the purpose, components and operation, health physics concerns, and their interrelationships with other plant systems. Methodology includes lecture, discussion, and supervised self-study.

Credit recommendation: In the lower division baccalaureate/associate degree category, 2 semester hours in Nuclear Science (Health Physics) (4/88).

INSTRUMENTS AND CONTROL TECHNICIAN

Instrument and Control Maintenance Fundamentals (IC0035301)

Location: Wolf Creek Generating Station, Burlington, KS.

Length: 576 hours (14½ weeks).

Dates: November 1987-Present.

Objective: To provide the background in math, physics, and chemistry necessary to understand control functions in a nuclear plant and develop certain manual skills needed to function as an instrument mechanic.

Learning Outcome: Upon successful completion of this course, the student will be able to understand the functioning of controls in nuclear plants and to perform certain maintenance functions.

Instruction: Course covers basic algebra, including logs and exponents, basic physics (mechanics), chemistry, electronics, physical and chemical measurements, and techniques of joining. Methodology includes lecture.

Credit recommendation: In the lower division baccalaureate/associate degree category, 2 semester hours in Introduction to Physical Science (4/88).

Instrument and Control Maintenance Initial Training (IC0035302)

Location: Wolf Creek Generating Station, Burlington, KS.

Length: 234 hours (6 weeks); 125 hours lecture, 109 hours lab.

Dates: January 1988-Present.

Objective: To provide the student the fundamental background in digital electronics, process control, and transients in core operation.

Learning Outcome: Upon successful completion of this course, the student will be able to completely describe the operation of control devices used in controlling nuclear reactions.

Instruction: Course covers digital electronics, process control fundamentals, and core transients. Methodology includes lecture and lab exercises.

Credit recommendation: In the lower division baccalaureate/associate degree category, 3 semester hours in Digital Electronics (4/88).

LICENSED OPERATOR

Students completing this sequence should not be granted credit for Professional Training courses: Introduction to Pressure Water Reactors (PT1300000), Pressurized Water Reactor Information course (PT400000), or Introduction to Power Plant Operations (PT4535400).

Abnormal Operations Course (LO0035306)

Location: Wolf Creek Generating Station, Burlington, KS.

Length: 160 hours (4 weeks); 80 hours classroom, 80 hours lab/simulator.

Dates: January 1988-Present.

Objective: To provide the student with an understanding of system interrelationships associated with abnormal plant operations that result from instrument or system failures.

Learning Outcome: Upon successful completion of this course, the student will be able to perform reactor operations during abnormal plant conditions.

Instruction: Course covers management, operation, and analysis of plant system during abnormal operations. Methodology includes lecture and on-the-job training.

Credit recommendation: In the upper division baccalaureate category, 2 semester hours in Nuclear Engineering Technology (4/88).

Diagnostics and Mitigating Core Damage (LO0035307)

Location: Wolf Creek Generating Station, Burlington, KS.

Length: 40 hours (1 week).

Dates: January 1988-Present.

Objective: To provide the student with an understanding of indications of core damage and of methods for

mitigating core damage.
Learning Outcome: Upon successful completion of this course, the student will be able to demonstrate, through examinations and subsequent simulator exercises, an understanding of mitigating core damage.
Instruction: Course covers management, response, evaluation, and analysis of typical failures that could result in core damage. Methodology includes lecture and on-the-job training.
Credit recommendation: In the upper division baccalaureate category, 1 semester hour in Nuclear Engineering Technology (4/88).

Licensed Operator Fundamentals (LO0035301)
Location: Wolf Creek Generating Station, Burlington, KS.
Length: 320 hours (8 weeks).
Dates: January 1988-Present.
Objective: To provide the student with an understanding of the fundamentals of reactor physics, reactor kinetics, heat transfer, fluid flow, and radiation protection relative to reactor operation.
Learning Outcome: Upon successful completion of this course, the student will be able to demonstrate a clear conceptual understanding of basic sciences associated with reactor operation.
Instruction: Course covers reactor physics, reactor kinetics, heat transfer, fluid flow, and radiation protection. Methodology includes lecture and on-the-job training.
Credit recommendation: In the upper division baccalaureate category, 5 semester hours in Nuclear Engineering Technology (4/88).

Licensed Operator Systems (LO0035302)
Location: Wolf Creek Generating Station, Burlington, KS.
Length: 320 hours (8 weeks).
Dates: January 1988-Present.
Objective: To provide the student with an understanding of the operation, instrumentation, control and system interrelationships among safety, primary and secondary, fuel handling, waste processing and auxiliary systems.
Instruction: Course covers instrumentation and control, system interrelationships, primary and secondary systems, fuel handling system, waste processing systems, and auxiliary systems. Methodology includes lecture and on-the-job training.
Credit recommendation: In the lower division baccalaureate/associate degree category, 4 semester hours in Nuclear Engineering Technology (4/88).

Normal Operations Course (LO0035305)
Location: Wolf Creek Generating Station, Burlington, KS.
Length: 160 hours (4 weeks); 80 hours classroom, 80 hours lab/simulator.
Dates: January 1988-Present.
Objective: To provide the student with an understanding of system interrelationships associated with plant heatups, cooldowns, startup, and shutdowns.
Learning Outcome: Upon successful completion of this course, the student will be able to perform normal plant operations associated with plant heatups, cooldowns, startups, and shutdowns.
Instruction: Course covers management, operation, and analysis of plant systems during normal operating conditions. Methodology includes lecture and on-the-job training.
Credit recommendation: In the upper division baccalaureate category, 2 semester hours in Nuclear Engineering Technology (4/88).

Shift Technical Advisor (LO0035308)
Location: Wolf Creek Generating Station, Burlington, KS.
Length: 80 hours (2 weeks); 20 hours lecture, 60 hours simulator.
Dates: June 1987-Present.
Objective: To provide the student with the skills necessary to perform and to supervise reactor operations relative to normal and abnormal operations and to fuel and radioactivate material management.
Learning Outcome: Upon successful completion of this course, the student will be able to demonstrate competence beyond the senior reactor operator level (through simulator exercises and examination) relative to normal and abnormal operation and to fuel and radioactive materials management. Methodology includes lecture and simulator exercises.
Instruction: Course covers reactor plant management and operations under normal and abnormal conditions. Methodology includes lecture and simulator exercises.
Credit recommendation: In the upper division baccalaureate category, 1 semester hour in Nuclear Engineering Technology (4/88).

SRO Supervisory and Teamwork (LO0035304)
Location: Wolf Creek Generating Station, Burlington, KS.
Length: 40 hours (1 week).
Dates: January 1988-Present.
Objective: To provide the training necessary to instill a supervisory attitude in SRO License candidates.
Learning Outcome: Upon successful completion of this course, the student will be able to demonstrate satisfactory supervisory ability during simulator training.
Instruction: Course covers communication, leadership, motivation, and decision making. Methodology includes lecture and on-the-job training.
Credit recommendation: In the upper division baccalaureate category, 1 semester hour in Nuclear Engineering Technology (4/88).

SRO Technical Training (LO0035303)
Location: Wolf Creek Generating Station, Burlington, KS.
Length: 80 hours (2 weeks).
Dates: January 1988-Present.
Objective: To provide the student with expertise in the areas of plant design, safety, and thermodynamics that exceed the SRO level, and thereby be qualified for a supervisory position.
Learning Outcome: Upon successful completion of this course, the student will be able to perform selected simulator exercises that demonstrate technical confidence in providing advice during plant recovery.
Instruction: Course covers management of hazardous and radioactive material and administrative and operating procedures relative to normal and abnormal plant operation. Methodology includes lecture and on-the-job training.
Credit recommendation: In the upper division baccalaureate category, 2 semester hours in Nuclear Engineering Technology (4/88).

MECHANICAL MAINTENANCE

Advanced Mechanical Maintenance, Part II (MM0035303)
Location: Wolf Creek Generating Station, Burlington, KS.
Length: 138 hours (3½ weeks).
Dates: February 1988-Present.
Objective: To provide the student with the basic theories of pneumatic and hydraulic circuits and the skills to read engineering prints of such circuits.
Learning Outcome: Upon successful completion of this course, the student will demonstrate the ability to read prints of hydraulic and pneumatic circuits, describe hydraulic and pneumatic circuits, and describe the function and maintenance of various types of rotating machinery.
Instruction: Course covers the physics of hydraulic and pneumatic circuits and rotating machinery, and the reading of blueprints for such equipment. Methodology includes lecture and labs.
Credit recommendation: In the lower division baccalaureate/associate degree category, 3 semester hours in Basic Mechanical Engineering Fundamentals (4/88).

General Advanced Mechanical Maintenance, Part I (MM0035302)
Location: Wolf Creek Generating Station, Burlington, KS.
Length: 168 hours (4.2 weeks).
Dates: February 1988-Present.
Objective: To familiarize the student with materials used in nuclear plants.
Learning Outcome: Upon successful completion of this course, the student will be able to understand and explain the types of corrosion in nuclear plants and to outline preventative measures; understand the heat transfer aspects of nuclear plants; and have a basic understanding of joining techniques, i.e., welding and bolting.
Instruction: Course covers corrosion chemistry, properties of materials, heat transfer, welding, practices specific to various equipment items.
Credit recommendation: In the lower division baccalaureate/associate degree category, 3 semester hours in Basic Engineering/Engineering Technology (4/88).

General Physics and Math for Maintenance Personnel (MB0035301)
Location: Wolf Creek Generating Station, Burlington, KS.
Length: 80 hours (2 weeks).
Dates: November 1987-Present.
Objective: To provide the student with background physics and mathematics so as to enhance the understanding of maintenance jobs.
Learning Outcome: Upon successful completion of this course, the student will be able to use the various physics formulas necessary to work.
Instruction: Course covers fractions, signed numbers, units conversions, scientific notation, algebra, exponents, logs, vectors, linear motion, and rotational motion. Methodology includes lecture.
Credit recommendation: In the vocational certificate category, 2 semester hours in Introductory Physics/Math (4/88).

NON-LICENSED OPERATOR

Students completing this sequence should not be granted credit for professional training courses: Introduction to Pressure Water Reactors (PT1300000), Pressurized Water Reactor Information course (PT1400000), or Introduction to Power Plant Operation (PT4535400).

Auxiliary Building Segment (NO1400000)
(Formerly Auxiliary and Radiation Systems, Part I [NL0209])
Location: Wolf Creek Generating Station, Burlington, KS.
Length: *Version 1:* 160 hours (4 weeks). *Version 2:* 344 hours (9 weeks).
Dates: *Version 1:* July 1983-January 1987. *Version 2:* February 1987-Present.
Objective: To develop in the student an understanding of radioactive, potentially contaminated plant systems, basic metallurgy, basic reactor technology and safety systems.
Instruction: The training consists of lecture-discussion enhanced with plant inspections, demonstrations, videotapes, problem-solving sessions. Topics include basic reactor technology and basic metallurgy, reactor coolant

system, reactor coolant support systems, boron thermal regeneration system, safety injection system, and safeguard electrical systems. Student progress is measured by examination.

Credit recommendation: *Version 1:* In the lower division baccalaureate/associate degree category, 2 semester hours in Nuclear Technology (12/83). *Version 2:* In the lower division baccalaureate/associate degree category, 3 semester hours in Nuclear Engineering Technology (4/88). NOTE: This course has been reevaluated and continues to meet requirements for recommendations.

Non-Licensed Operator Fundamentals (NO1100000)
(Formerly Introduction to Plant Operations [NL0101])

Location: Wolf Creek Generating Station, Burlington, KS.

Length: *Version 1:* 160 hours (4 weeks); *Version 2:* 240 hours (6 weeks).

Dates: *Version 1:* July 1981-January 1987; *Version 2:* February 1987-Present.

Objective: To develop a basic understanding of mechanical and electrical systems and how these systems are combined to accomplish overall system objectives. This overview will enable students to understand and to explain the function and basic operating principles of common plant components with emphasis on the physical processes occuring within the component. The student will have a basic understanding of heat transfer, fluid flow, corrosion, water chemistry, and electric generation.

Instruction: The training consists of lecture-discussion enhanced by plant inspections, videotapes, demonstrations, and problem-solving sessions. Topics covered include heat transfer, fluid flow, erosion, water chemistry, plant component theory, bearing basics, print reading, and electrical generation. Student progress is measured by examination.

Credit recommendation: *Version 1:* In the lower division baccalaureate/associate degree category, 3 semester hours in Nuclear Engineering Technology (12/83). *Version 2:* In the lower division baccalaureate/associate degree category, 4 semester hours in Nuclear Engineering Technology (4/88). NOTE: This course has been reevaluated and continues to meet requirements for credit recommendations.

Radwaste Operator Segment (NO1500000)
(Formerly Auxiliary and Radiation, Part II [NL0211])

Location: Wolf Creek Generating Station, Burlington, KS.

Length: 160 hours (4 weeks).

Dates: July 1983-Present.

Objective: Upon completion of this course the student will be able to describe the process of transferring spent fuel, including the spent fuel pool cooling and cleanup systems. The student will be able to trace the flowpath and explain the processes/procedures for the treatment of contaminated waste. The student will be able to properly use detection instruments, shielding, and stay-times to limit radioactive exposure.

Instruction: The training consists of lecture-discussion, enhanced by plant inspections, demonstrations, videotapes, and problem-solving exercises. Topics covered include spent fuel pool, spent fuel pool cooling and cleanup systems, boron recycle system, liquid, gaseous, and solid radwaste systems, and radiation monitoring systems. The instruction also includes radiation protection fundamentals, reactor protection and safety, fuel handling, and reactor plant chemistry. Student progress is measured by examination.

Credit recommendation: In the lower division baccalaureate/associate degree category, 3 semester hours in Nuclear Engineering Technology (12/83) (4/88). NOTE: This course has been reevaluated and continues to meet requirements for credit recommendations.

Site Operations Segment (NO1200000)
(Formerly Site and Support Operations [NL0103])

Location: Wolf Creek Generating Station, Burlington, KS.

Length: *Version 1:* 160 hours (4 weeks). *Version 2:* 232 hours (6 weeks).

Dates: *Version 1:* July 1981-January 1987. *Version 2:* February 1987-Present.

Objective: To provide the student with a basic understanding of site auxiliary or support systems. The student demonstrates an understanding of thermodynamics as it applies to heat exchangers.

Instruction: The training consists of lecture-discussion enhanced by plant inspections, demonstrations, videotapes, and problem-solving sessions. Topics covered include thermodynamics, electrical distribution, plant circulating water systems, auxiliary boiler fuel oil system, service gas systems, and fire protection systems. Student progress is measured by examination.

Credit recommendation: *Version 1:* In the lower division baccalaureate/associate degree category, 2 semester hours in Nuclear Technology (12/83). *Version 2:* In the lower division baccalaureate/associate degree category, 3 semester hours in Nuclear Engineering Technology (4/88). NOTE: This course has been reevaluated and continues to meet requirements for credit recommendations.

Turbine Building Segment (NO1300000)
(Formerly Nuclear Power Generation [NL0205])

Location: Wolf Creek Generating Station, Burlington, KS.

Length: *Version 1:* 240 hours (8 weeks). *Version 2:* 312 hours (8 weeks).

Dates: *Version 1:* July 1983-January 1987. *Version 2:* February 1987-Present.

Objective: To provide the student with an understanding of steam cycle components and systems, of the conversion of heat energy to electrical energy, of electrical motor/generator theory, and of the practical applications of alternating current electrical circuitry. This understanding is then related to the systems making up the Wolf Creek Generating Station.

Instruction: The training consists of lecture-discussion enhanced by plant inspections, demonstrations, videotapes, and problem-solving sessions. Topics covered include the steam system, feed and condensate system, the turbine system, motor/generators, service and instrument air system, and miscellaneous waste systems. Progress is measured by examination.

Credit recommendation: *Version 1:* In the lower division baccalaureate/associate degree category, 3 semester hours in Nuclear Technology (12/83). *Version 2:* In the lower division baccalaureate/associate degree category, 4 semester hours in Nuclear Engineering Technology (4/88). NOTE: This course has been reevaluated and continues to meet requirements for credit recommendations.

PROFESSIONAL TRAINING

Classroom Instructor Workshop (TI1231800)
Location: Wolf Creek Generating Station, Burlington, KS.
Length: 40 hours (1 week).
Dates: August 1987-Present.
Objective: To provide the training personnel with the knowledge and skills to design, develop, and evaluate effective performance-based instruction.
Learning Outcome: Upon successful completion of this course, the student will be able to develop learning objectives, select instructional methods, write lesson plans and conduct instruction, and develop and administer evaluation instruments.
Instruction: This course covers practice in planning and developing learning hierarchies, practice in training system design, practice in job and task analysis, practice in preparing lesson plans, familiarization with characteristics of different instructional media, practice in preparing and administering performance measuring instruments, and practice in "microteaching." Methodology includes lecture and student discussion (microteaching).
Credit recommendation: In the upper division baccalaureate category, 2 semester hours in Technical Education (Instructional Design) (4/88).

Fire Brigade, Basic (FB1231400)
Location: Wolf Creek Generating Station, Burlington, KS.
Length: 48 hours (1.2 weeks); 28 hours lecture, 20 hours lab.
Dates: June 1987-Present.
Objective: To train the student in the procedures required to safely function as a member of a fire brigade and to choose the proper techniques for fighting fires unique to a nuclear facility.
Learning Outcome: Upon successful completion of this course, the student will be able to use various fire fighting equipment and to direct its use; choose and use proper protective clothing and equipment for fire fighting; and properly identify potential fire hazards before a fire, and actual hazards during one.
Instruction: Course covers basic fire chemistry, protective clothing and breathing apparatus, fire fighting tactics, fire fighting tools and their use, fire protection systems, and use of hoses, nozzles, and extinguishers. Methodology includes lecture, demonstration, labs, and videotapes.
Credit recommendation: In the lower division baccalaureate/associate degree category, 1 semester hour in Fire Protection (4/88).

Introduction to Power Plant Operations (PT4535400)
Location: Wolf Creek Generating Station, Burlington, KS.
Length: 40 hours (1 week); 20 hours lecture, 20 hours control room simulator.
Dates: June 1986-Present.
Objective: To brief professionals and supervisors on the basics of integrated nuclear power operations.
Learning Outcome: Upon successful completion of this course, the student will be able to relate their own job responsibilities to the operational response of the entire power plant.
Instruction: Course covers, through control room simulation, the following plant operations and responses: startup, steady state operations, shutdowns, and selected accidents. Methodology includes lecture and work on control room simulator.
Credit recommendation: In the lower division baccalaureate/associate degree category, 2 semester hours in Nuclear Reactor Technology (4/88).

Introduction to Pressurized Water Reactors (PT1300000)
Location: Wolf Creek Generating Station, Burlington, KS.
Length: 24 hours (8 hours per day for 3 days).
Dates: July 1987-Present.
Objective: To provide a basic understanding of how a nuclear power plant generates electricity, and know the function of major plant systems and safety features.
Learning Outcome: Upon successful completion of this course, the student will be able to discuss the basic operation of a pressurized water reactor.
Instruction: Course covers overview of Wolf Creek Generating Plant, fundamentals of pressurized water reactors, primary systems, secondary systems, auxiliary systems, safety systems, and review of plant operation and accident analysis. Methodology includes lecture.
Credit recommendation: In the vocational certificate category, 2 semester hours in Nuclear Power Plant Tech-

nology (4/88).

Pressurized Water Reactor Information Course (PT1400000)
   Location: Wolf Creek Generating Station, Burlington, KS.
   Length: 120 hours (1 day a week for 15 weeks).
   Dates: January 1987-Present.
   Objective: To provide the student with an understanding of the basic operation, major systems, safety features, and fundamental theory of operation of Wolf Creek Generating Station.
   Learning Outcome: Upon successful completion of this course, the student will be able to discuss basic pressurized water reactor operation and theory, and to discuss Wolf Creek Generating Station's plant systems, integrated plant operation, and safety features.
   Instruction: Course covers theory of pressurized water reactor operation, pressurized water reactor systems, integrated plant operation, and safety features. Methodology includes lecture, plant tour, control room simulator, and demonstration.
   Credit recommendation: In the lower division baccalaureate/associate degree category, 3 semester hours in Nuclear Reactor Theory (4/88).

Supervision I (PS0131200)
   Location: Wolf Creek Generating Station, Burlington, KS.
   Length: 40 hours (1 week).
   Dates: March 1987-Present.
   Objective: To introduce practicing, newly appointed or potential supervisors to the basics of supervision, equal opportunity employment laws, and employee behavior reliability.
   Learning Outcome: Upon successful completion of this course, the student will be able to perform the role as supervisor effectively, to practice equal opportunity employment, and to recognize and deal with aberrant behavior, drug- or alcohol-related problems according to company policy.
   Instruction: Course covers basics of supervision-leadership, basics of supervision-employee communications, basics of supervision-command responsibility and limits, basics of supervision-employee motivation, basics of supervision-problem solving and decision making, fundamental principles of team building, equal employment opportunity, and employee behavior reliability. Methodology includes lecture.
   Credit recommendation: In the lower division baccalaureate/associate degree category, 2 semester hours in Human Relations, Leadership, Management, Supervision, or Supervisory Management (4/88).

SECURITY

General Security Qualification Information (SC0035301)
   Location: Wolf Creek Generating Station, Burlington, KS.
   Length: 40 hours (1 week).
   Dates: July 1983-Present.
   Objective: To provide introduction to security devices, duties of security general, legal issues, and law enforcement.
   Learning Outcome: Upon successful completion of this course, the student will be able to competently perform duties as a security guard.
   Instruction: Course covers physical security, barrier devices, detection devices, sabotage devices, legal issues, law enforcement, leadership, and NRC requirements. Methodology includes lecture.
   Credit recommendation: In the lower division baccalaureate/associate degree category, 2 semester hours in Criminal Justice (4/88). NOTE: This course must be combined with Communications Qualification Training (SC0035032) for credit recommendation.

Communications Qualification Training (SC0035302)
   Location: Wolf Creek Generating Station, Burlington, KS.
   Length: 40 hours (1 week).
   Dates: July 1983-Present.
   Objective: To provide training in communication techniques, both verbal and nonverbal and to be cognizant of the requirements for proper reporting.
   Learning Outcome: Upon successful completion of this course, the student will be able to use and to interpret information from various communication systems in use at the site, and to be able to fill out proper security reports.
   Instruction: Course covers observation and perception, listening, radio codes, hand signals, and traffic control. Methodology includes lecture.
   Credit recommendation: In the lower division baccalaureate/associate degree category, 2 semester hours in Criminal Justice (4/88). NOTE: This course must be combined with General Security Qualification Information (SC0035301) for credit recommendation.

Weapons Qualification Training (SC0035303)
   Location: Wolf Creek Generating Station, Burlington, KS.
   Length: 80 hours (2 weeks).
   Dates: November 1983-Present.
   Objective: To train security officers in the use of firearms.
   Learning Outcome: Upon successful completion of this course, the student will be able to qualify in use of revolvers and shotguns.
   Instruction: Course covers use of revolvers and shot-

guns, weapons safety and care. Methodology includes lecture and range lab.

Credit recommendation: In the lower division baccalaureate/associate degree category, 1 semester hour in Criminal Justice (4/88).

Xerox Corporation

Xerox Corporation is an information-processing organization with interests in copiers/duplicators, education, aerospace, and medical diagnostics. Xerox activities extend to 113 countries.

A variety of residential training courses is offered to Xerox employees from the United States and Canada at the International Center for Training and Management Development. Each division within the corporation conducts training programs for its employees.

CORPORATE MANAGEMENT TRAINING PROGRAM

The Corporate Management Training Program has the responsibility for designing, administering, and/or delivering management and professional training programs for Xerox employees in the United States and other countries. Based at the Xerox International Center for Training and Management Development in Leesburg, Virginia, Corporate Management Training conducts middle-management and professional development programs as part of its international "building blocks" system for human resource development. Executive-level programs are administered by corporate management training and delivered by faculty members of The Harvard Graduate School of Business Administration.

Source of official student records: Xerox Corporation, Corporate Human Resource Development, Stamford, Connecticut 06904.

Additional information about the courses: Program on Noncollegiate Sponsored Instruction, The Center for Adult Learning and Educational Credentials, American Council on Education, One Dupont Circle, Washington, D.C. 20036.

Executive Seminar I

Location: Exeter, NH; Leesburg, VA; Pala Mesa, CA.

Length: 50 hours (10 days, with 10 hours required reading before the course and a minimum of 50 hours of outside reading during the course).

Dates: March 1981-December 1988.

Objective: To enable the participant to develop a broader, more general management perspective by strengthening the skills necessary to formulate and implement short- and long-range policy and strategy; by developing a greater understanding of financial policy and economic forces affecting corporate decisions; and by understanding the management of organizational structure, human resources, and interpersonal relationships.

Instruction: Covers three major sections: (1) Business policy - choice of market opportunities; design of departmental, divisional, group, and corporate strategies; and planning action to get expected results. (2) Human and organizational problems - the corporation as a human organization and satisfying individual needs to maximize performance. (3) Practical problems as well as corporate finance in the domestic and international areas. Lecture, discussion, and case studies are used.

Credit recommendation: In the upper division baccalaureate category or in the graduate degree category, 6 semester hours in Business Administration or Management (11/81).

Finance for the Nonfinancial Manager/Financial Decision Making

Location: Xerox International Center for Training and Management Development, Leesburgh, VA; Xerox Management Center, Rochester, NY.

Length: 40 hours (5 days).

Dates: July 1979-December 1988.

Objective: To improve the business decision making of managers. To guide participants in making competent expenditure analyses using real-world examples. To facilitate learning by allowing participants to apply financial decision-making techniques and concepts.

Instruction: Covers reducing the element of risk in business decisions through the systematic analysis of expenditures. Major topics include time value of money, net cash flow, capital expenditure analysis, buy versus lease, return on investment, and present-worth analysis. Course uses a participative and experiential mode with examples from the participants' own environments. A full-day's simulation to allow application of course learnings is also included.

Credit recommendation: In the lower division baccalaureate/associate degree category or in the upper division baccalaureate category, 3 semester hours in Business Administration or Management (11/81).

Managing the Personnel Function

Location: Xerox International Center for Training and Management Development, Leesburg, VA.

Length: 62 hours (5 days, 3 open-ended evening sessions, and 10 hours required reading before the course).

Dates: March 1979-December 1988.

Objective: To enable the participant to develop greater awareness of the interaction and interdependence of all functions within the Personnel Department; to develop the skills of identifying critical personnel issues and of recommending and implementing detailed courses of action in response to such issues.

Instruction: Focuses on particpants' preparation of a

human resource plan for a fictitious company. All aspects of the fictitious company's organizational structure, compensation/benefit programs and practices, climate, employee mix, attitudes, and so forth are studied and analyzed. Course provides maximum participant involvement and interaction, and optimum experiential learning using the case study method.

Credit recommendation: In the lower division baccalaureate/associate degree category or in the upper division baccalaureate category or in the graduate degree category, 3 semester hours in Personnel Management (11/81). NOTE: Credit category for this course depends heavily on the background and/or educational experience of the participant.

Managing Tasks Through People
Location: Xerox International Center for Training and Management Development, Leesburg, VA.
Length: 80 hours (2 weeks), residential; plus 6 hours precourse work and 10 hours of outside preparation per week.
Dates: *Version 1:* March 1976-January 1981; *Version 2:* February 1981-December 1988.
Objective: *Version 1:* To improve the effectiveness of middle managers by providing them with managerial information, skills, and techniques. *Version 2:* To improve the effectiveness of middle managers by providing them with managerial information, skills, and techniques for working with and through people in both planning and implementing work.
Instruction: *Version 1:* Topics in administrative and behavioral management, including planning, decision making, management practices, performance objectives and analysis, and interactive skills. Methodology includes lecture and discussion, group exercises, short cases, and videotape presentations. *Version 2:* Covers management practices, methods for clarifying job objectives, decision making, interpersonal skills, planning, nonverbal communication, managing change, influencing and negotiating, setting performance objectives, analyzing performance problems, counseling, feedback and reinforcement, and group dynamics. Lecture, discussion, and group exercises with an emphasis on case analysis and presentation are used. Course is a tool for thorough evaluation and follow-up at all managerial levels.
Credit recommendation: *Version 1:* In the upper division baccalaureate category, 2 semester hours in Administrative and Behavioral Management (11/81). *Version 2:* In the upper division baccalaureate category, 4 semester hours in Business Administration or Management; or in the graduate degree category, 3 semester hours in Introduction to Behavioral Management (11/81).

THE CORPORATE SALES AND SYSTEMS TRAINING PROGRAMS

The Corporate Sales and Systems Training group has the responsibility for designing, administering, and delivering professional training programs for Xerox marketing systems, and customer support staffs in the United States and Canada.

Based at the Xerox International Center for Training and Management Development in Leesburg, Virginia, the sales and systems instruction staff conducts professional training programs for newly appointed and incumbent Xerox marketing, sales, and systems representatives in a building block structure.

Source of official student records: Sales Training, Xerox International Center for Training and Management Development, Leesburg, Virginia 22075.

Additional information about the courses: Program on Noncollegiate Sponsored Instruction, The Center for Adult Learning and Educational Credentials, American Council on Education, One Dupont Circle, Washington, D.C. 20036.

Account Management I
Location: Xerox International Center for Training and Management Development, Leesburg, VA.
Length: 40 hours (1 week).
Dates: December 1977-December 1988.
Objective: To provide students with the skills necessary to prepare and give major-account presentations.
Instruction: Includes knowledge of IBM, Kodak, offset environment, the sold process (stressing lease purchase analysis), terminology and application of financial decision making, and survey methods. Lecture, workshops, laboratory, student presentations, and problem solving are used.
Credit recommendation: In the upper division baccalaureate category, 1 semester hour in Salesmanship (12/81).

1. **Account Management II**
2. **Account Management III**
Location: Xerox International Center for Training and Management Development, Leesburg, VA.
Length: 1. 40 hours (1 week); 2. 40 hours (1 week).
Dates: December 1977-December 1988.
Objective: To develop the knowledge and skill required for successful major-account management by allowing the student to develop and present an internal account review, prepare and give a major-account presentation, and effectively implement the major-account strategy in the field.
Instruction: Covers the long selling cycle, developing and writing an account action plan, preparing and presenting an internal account review, repairing and giving a major-account presentation. Xerox high volume products and capabilities and the impact of productivity within

major accounts are also covered. Lecture, workshops, classroom exercises, presentations, and problem solving are used.

Credit recommendation: In the upper division baccalaureate category, 1 semester hour in Salesmanship (12/81). NOTE: This credit recommendation applies for either Account Management II or Account Management III but not for both.

Account Representative School

Location: Xerox International Center for Training and Management Development, Leesburg, VA.

Length: 36 hours (5 days) and 30 hours of self-paced preschool study.

Dates: June 1978-December 1988.

Objective: To improve student knowledge and capabilities in salesmanship, using a variety of marketing strategies including principles of financial analysis.

Instruction: Sales strategies applicable to sophisticated business decision making are explained through an analysis of capital budgeting, financial analysis, cash flow analysis, and other tools used in the formulation of investment proposals. Methodology includes extensive use of case studies and exercises in addition to the creation and presentation of proposals. Students are tested on their understanding of tools, techniques, and concepts, and are provided with follow-up remedial assistance at the branch-office level.

Credit recommendation: In the upper division baccalaureate category, 1 semester hour in Financial Analysis (5/79). NOTE: Credit recommendations in Financial Analysis are not cumulative.

Advanced Salesmanship
(Xerox Office Products Division Basic Marketing School - Sales)

Location: Xerox International Center for Training and Management Development, Leesburg, VA.

Length: 120 hours (3 weeks).

Dates: January 1980-December 1988.

Objective: To provide the student with the skills of selling and knowledge of the marketplace for office information processing systems.

Instruction: Stresses skills needed to sell information processing products through the establishment of sales cycles, systems architecture, communications, competition strategy, and pricing and financing. Lecture, discussion, and role plays are used. (Prerequisite: Course admission presupposes formal sales experience and/or major account representation.)

Credit recommendation: In the upper division baccalaureate category, 3 semester hours in Advanced Salesmanship (12/81).

1. Basic Sales School
2. Advanced Sales School

Location: Xerox International Center for Training and Management Development, Leesburg, VA.

Length: 1. 360 hours (9 weeks); 240 hours of self-paced preschool study and 120 hours (3 weeks) of classroom instruction in residence. 2. 140 hours; 100 hours of self-paced preschool study and 40 hours (1 week) of classroom instruction in residence.

Dates: July 1976-December 1988.

Objective: To provide students with the conceptual and technical backgrounds necessary to enable them to perform successfully in selling and marketing positions.

Instruction: Analysis of the market-system environment, basic business functions, business communications, financial analysis, principles of organization and management, product capabilities, analysis of the sales cycle, selling techniques, psychology of persuasion, client-need analysis, marketing strategies, account and territory management, analysis of the competition. Use of lectures, cases, role playing, self-paced instruction, discussions, videotapes, and, in the preschool component of the advanced sales course, field sales apprenticeship.

Credit recommendation: In the lower division baccalaureate/associate degree category, 3 semester hours in Introduction to Business Management, and in the upper division baccalaureate category, 6 semester hours in Sales and Marketing (2/77).

Basic Sales Training/Business Products Division

Location: Xerox International Center for Training and Management Development, Leesburg, VA.

Length: 80 hours (2 weeks).

Dates: December 1978-December 1988.

Objective: To provide the fundamental skills of selling and knowledge of the marketplace in order to prepare students to perform effectively as marketing representatives.

Instruction: Imparts the basic skills needed to sell copier/duplicator products. Covers the value of the consulting role in uncovering problem areas, recommending solutions, overcoming obstacles, methodology and outline for territory and account management through the sales cycle. Students learn the role of the marketing representative through role plays, audiotapes, discussion, testing, and workshops.

Credit recommendation: In the lower division baccalaureate/associate degree category, 3 semester hours in Basic Salesmanship (12/81). NOTE: Students who receive credit for this course should not receive credit for Basic Sales Training/Information Systems Division.

Basic Sales Training/Information Systems Division
(Formerly Basic Sales Training)

Location: Xerox International Center for Training and Management Development, Leesburg, VA.

Length: *Version 1:* 160 hours of self-paced preschool study and 80 hours (2 weeks) of classroom instruction in residence. *Version 2:* 80 hours (2 weeks).

Dates: *Version 1:* July 1976-February 1982; *Version 2:* July 1981-December 1988.

Objective: To provide the fundamental skills of selling and knowledge of the marketplace in order to prepare students to perform effectively as marketing representatives.

Instruction: *Version 1:* Consists of two parts. Part one is a programmed learning unit pursued on a self-study basis. This unit covers the market system of resource allocation, the functional areas of business, business communications, organizational principles, financial analysis, etc. Part two is an in-residence unit consisting of lectures, cases, role playing, discussion, videotapes, and team projects. This unit covers selling techniques and selling philosophy as well as client-need analysis, account and territory management, assessment of competition, and basic product knowledge. *Version 2:* Imparts the basic skills needed to sell copier/duplicator products. Covers the value of the consulting role in uncovering problem areas, recommending solutions, and overcoming obstacles. Also covers methodology and outline for territory and account management through the sales cycle. Students learn the role of the marketing representative through role plays, audiotapes, discussion, testing, and workshops.

Credit recommendation: *Version 1:* In the upper division baccalaureate category, 3 semester hours in Salesmanship (5/79). *Version 2:* In the lower division baccalaureate/associate degree category, 3 semester hours in Basic Salesmanship (12/81). NOTE: Students who receive credit for this course should not receive credit for Basic Sales Training/Business Products Division.

Executive Sales Seminar

Location: Xerox International Center for Training and Management Development, Leesburg, VA.

Length: 36 hours (5 days).

Dates: May 1979-December 1988.

Objective: To teach the student sales theory and the elements of good technical sales performance.

Instruction: The structure of presentation, executive persuasion, presentation skills, and style of selling. Additionally, students elect several topics from areas such as productivity analysis, lease-purchase analysis, nonverbal communication, the dimensions of decision making, and product familiarization.

Credit recommendation: In the upper division baccalaureate category, 2 semester hours of Advanced Salesmanship or 2 hours of Business Communications (5/79).

Geo-Combo School

Location: Xerox International Center for Training and Management Development, Leesburg, VA.

Length: 36 hours (5 days).

Dates: September 1978-December 1988.

Objective: To provide the breadth of product knowledge needed in markets where salespersons are not specialized by product line.

Instruction: A study of the various products offered by Xerox Corporation is integrated with development of systems analysis of office requirements and basic sales techniques. Methodology includes the use of written exercises in problem solving, lecture, discussion, sales presentations, evaluation, and feedback.

Credit recommendation: In the upper division baccalaureate category, 1 semester hour in Financial Analysis (5/79). NOTE: Credit recommendations in Financial Analysis are not cumulative.

High Volume Sales Executive School

Location: Xerox International Center for Training and Management Development, Leesburg, VA.

Length: 36 hours (1 week) in residence.

Dates: May 1979-December 1988.

Objective: To provide sales executives with the skills and knowledge necessary to market the most sophisticated Xerox photocopy equipment.

Instruction: Xerox high-volume machine familiarization, the sales sequence, sales financing, capital budgeting, competitive purchase plans, analysis of competitive products, concepts of productivity and turnaround time, and productive work relationships. Lectures, discussion, workshop, case studies, and simulations are used.

Credit recommendation: In the upper division baccalaureate category, 1 semester hour in Financial Analysis (5/79). NOTE: Credit recommendations in Financial Analysis are not cumulative.

Marketing Management
(Systems Analyst School - Support)

Location: Xerox International Center for Training and Management Development, Leesburg, VA.

Length: 80 hours (2 weeks).

Dates: April 1981-December 1988.

Objective: To provide students with the knowledge and skills to assist in systems analysis, systems design, installation coordination, and follow-up assistance; to provide an understanding of the characteristics of the marketplace, business organizations, functions, and problems.

Instruction: Covers characteristics of the marketplace, functions of a systems analyst, consultative techniques, cost justification, and management of information data analysis system (MIDAS). Lectures, discussions, workshops, and case studies are used.

Credit recommendation: In the upper division baccalaureate category, 3 semester hours in Marketing Management (12/81).

OS Basic Sales School
1. OS Product School
2. OS Sales School

Location: Xerox International Center for Training and Management Development, Leesburg, VA.

Length: 200 hours (5 weeks) in residence and 160 hours of self-paced instruction.

Dates: September 1978-December 1988.

Objective: To provide the knowledge-base necessary for performing such personal selling activities as offices systems analysis, product mix analysis, and customer problem solving.

Instruction: Course objectives achieved through an introduction to Xerox and competing products, a study of offices systems, and an in-depth analysis of sales strategies and techniques. Methodology includes independent study verified by examination, lectures, discussion, role playing, and case analysis.

Credit recommendation: In the upper division baccalaureate category, 4 semester hours in Salesmanship; and in the lower division baccalaureate/associate degree category, 2 semester hours in Public Speaking (5/79).

Records Processing
(Marker Support Specialist/860 Product School Support)

Location: Xerox International Center for Training and Management Development, Leesburg, VA.

Length: 36 hours (1 week).

Dates: May 1980-December 1988.

Objective: To provide the student with the knowledge and skills necessary to understand and operate a records processing package.

Instruction: Covers review of word processing, disc logic, software control, and problem reports. Records processing demonstrations and case studies are used.

Credit recommendation: In the upper division baccalaureate category, 2 semester hours in Office Administration (12/81).

Sales Accounts Management
(Account Management Training Program)

Location: Xerox International Center for Training and Management Development, Leesburg, VA.

Length: 73 hours; 36 hours of self-paced preschool instruction and 37 hours (1 week) classroom instruction in residence.

Dates: January 1977-December 1988.

Objective: To prepare the student to analyze and meet the needs of major customer accounts for information processing systems.

Instruction: Effective executive sales calls and account presentation skills, executive decision making, major account-reporting systems, industry marketing resources, account reviews, comparative analysis and financial justification of large information-processing systems. Lectures, discussions, role play, and one major presentation are used.

Credit recommendation: In the upper division baccalaureate category, 2 semester hours in Marketing and Sales Management (2/77).

Word Processing
(Xerox Office Products Division 860 Product School - Sales)

Location: Xerox International Center for Training and Management Development, Leesburg, VA.

Length: 36 hours (1 week).

Dates: August 1980-December 1988.

Objective: To provide the student with the knowledge and skills necessary to operate a word processing system; to provide the student with hardware training for a variety of applications.

Instruction: Includes an overview of customer/office applications, communications, vocabulary, and applications and procedures of word processing. Hands-on training and demonstrations are used.

Credit recommendation: In the lower division baccalaureate/associate degree category, 2 semester hours in Business Education or Office Practices (12/81).

XEROX SERVICE TRAINING

Xerox Service Training provides training to its technical representatives from the United States, Canada, and Latin America operations at the Xerox International Center for Training and Development. The training, centered around the design of criterion-referenced instruction, provides the technical representative with skills and knowledge in the areas of customer satisfaction, electrical/electronic diagnosis and repair, mechanical operations, adjustment and repair, digital circuitry and logic, computers, and microprocessor technology. Service Training delivers over 50 different training programs ranging from one week to seven weeks in duration.

Source of official student records: Xerox International Center for Training and Management Development, P.O. Box 2000, Leesburg, Virginia 22075.

Additional information about the courses: Program on Noncollegiate Sponsored Instruction, The Center for Adult Learning and Educational Credentials, American Council on Education, One Dupont Circle, Washington, D.C. 20036.

1824/1860 (A42)

Location: Xerox International Center for Training and Management Development, Leesburg, VA.

Length: 80 hours (2 weeks); residential.

Dates: January 1976-December 1988.

Objective: To provide an introduction to photographic processes and the technical knowledge and skills required to adjust, troubleshoot, service, and repair a copier that prints from microfilm.

Instruction: Troubleshooting using schematic analysis is emphasized. Knowledge of image reproduction, principles of operation, component assembly identification, adjustment procedures, repair and service of electrical and mechanical components. Also covers customer relations skills. Practical laboratory exercises are used to strengthen repair skills.

Credit recommendation: In the lower division baccalaureate/associate degree category, 2 semester hours in Electromechanical Technology (6/78). NOTE: Credit recommendations in Electromechanical Technology are not cumulative.

2080 (A39)

Location: Xerox International Center for Training and Management Development, Leesburg, VA.

Length: 120 hours (3 weeks) of criterion-referenced instruction.

Dates: September 1979-December 1988.

Objective: To teach technicians advanced troubleshooting to enable them to maintain an electronic-intensive, electromechanical copying device which reduces, enlarges, and makes size-for-size copies in an engineering/printshop environment - specifically, the 2080 photocopier.

Instruction: Topics include component location and function, system operation, logic circuitry, use of electronic instruments, mechanisms, xerography, optics, fault analysis, diagnostic techniques necessary to troubleshoot, adjustment, and alignment of a complex electromechanical system.

Credit recommendation: In the lower division baccalaureate/associate degree category, 2 semester hours in Electromechanical Technology and 1 semester hour in Digital Systems or Instrumentation and Measurement (11/81). NOTE: Credit recommendations in Electromechanical Technology are not cumulative.

6500 Color Copier (A24)

Location: Xerox International Center for Training and Management Development, Leesburg, VA.

Length: 80 hours (2 weeks); 2½ hours of lecture, 10 hours of discussion, and 17½ hours of self-paced study and laboratory per week.

Dates: January 1975-December 1988.

Objective: To train maintenance personnel to troubleshoot, align, adjust, and repair color copiers equipped with time-sharing devices.

Instruction: In-depth study of theory and applications of color and light phenomena; advanced logic functions and time sharing; familiarization with color copier modules; identification, location, and function of electrical, mechanical, optical, and xerographic components and modules; ;use of precision measuring and adjusting tools; fault analysis, diagnostics, and adjustment/alignment techniques.

Credit recommendation: In the lower division baccalaureate/associate degree category, 2 semester hours in Electromechanical Technology and Maintenance, 1 semester hour in Digital Systems, and 1 semester hour in Principles of Color Photography (3/75) (11/81). NOTE: This course has undergone a 5-year reevaluation and continues to meet the requirements for credit recommendations. Credit recommendations in Electromechanical Technology are not cumulative.

3400/3450 Combination XT

Location: Xerox International Center for Training and Management Development, Leesburg, VA.

Length: Approximately 80 hours (2 weeks); 2 hours of lecture, 30 hours of discussion, and 40 hours of laboratory.

Dates: February 1980-December 1988.

Objective: To provide trainees with the knowledge and skill required to maintain, fault diagnose, and repair the Xerox 3450 copier.

Instruction: The topics covered, under supervised, self-paced instruction, include equipment operation, troubleshooting, main driver and power distribution, paper supply/feed, document transportation, optics, xerographics, copy transformation and fusing, sorter and 3450 copier logic circuits.

Credit recommendation: In the lower division baccalaureate/associate degree category, 1 semester hour in Electromechanical Technology (11/81). NOTE: Credit recommendations in Electromechanical Technology are not cumulative.

Computer Forms Printer (Duplicator)

Location: Xerox International Center for Training and Management Development, Leesburg, VA.

Length: 120 hours (3 weeks); 14 hours of lecture, 3 hours of discussion, and 23 hours of laboratory per week.

Dates: January 1975-January 1977.

Objective: To provide knowledge necessary for advanced troubleshooting to maintain an electronic-intensive, electromechanical, data-processing-type office machine designed for computer printout input with collator output features.

Instruction: Component location and function, system operation, logic circuitry; use of electronic instruments (CRO, etc.); mechanisms; xerography; fault analysis diagnosis techniques necessary to troubleshoot, adjust, and align a complex electromechanical system.

Credit recommendation: In the lower division baccalaureate/associate degree category, 2 semester hours in Electromechanical Technology and 1 semester hour in Digital Systems (3/75) (11/81). NOTE: This course has undergone a 5-year reevaluation and continues to meet the requirements for credit recommendations. Credit recommendations in Electromechanical Technology are not cumulative.

660 Copier (A20)
(Formerly New Hire Copier [A20])
Location: Xerox International Center for Training and Management Development, Leesburg, VA.

Length: *Version 1:* 160 hours (4 weeks); 4 hours of lecture, 16 hours of discussion, and 20 hours of laboratory per week. *Version 2:* 80 hours (2 weeks); 1 hour of lecture, 1 hour of discussion, and 38 hours of laboratory per week.

Dates: *Version 1:* January 1975-September 1977; *Version 2:* October 1977-December 1988.

Objective: To teach the occupational skills of diagnosis and correction of mechanical and electrical equipment malfunction in the 660 copier.

Instruction: Topics are xerographic equipment, specific component location, symbolic representation of functions and operation, the system operation of the 660 copier.

Credit recommendation: In the lower division baccalaureate/associate degree category, 2 semester hours in Electromechanical Technology (3/75) (11/81). NOTE: This course has undergone a 5-year reevaluation and continues to meet requirements for credit recommendations. Credit recommendations in Electromechanical Technology are not cumulative.

3450 Copier (Stand Alone) H15
Location: Xerox International Center for Training and Management Development, Leesburg, VA.

Length: 120 hours (3 weeks); 2 hours of lecture, 2 hours of discussion, and 36 hours of laboratory per week.

Dates: July 1981-December 1988.

Objective: To provide technicians with the knowledge and skill required to maintain, fault diagnose, and repair the Xerox 3450 copier.

Instruction: The topics studied, under a supervised self-paced format, are theory of AC and DC circuits, microelectronics, logic circuits, troubleshooting, and machine self-diagnostics.

Credit recommendation: In the lower division baccalaureate/associate degree category, 2 semester hours in Electromechanical Technology and 1 semester hour in Optics and Logic Circuits (11/81). NOTE: Credit recommendations in Electromechanical Technology are not cumulative.

4000 Cross-Training (A22)
Location: Xerox International Center for Training and Management Development, Leesburg, VA.

Length: 120 hours (3½ weeks); 4 hours of lecture, 8 hours of discussion, and 28 hours of laboratory/workshop per week.

Dates: June 1974-December 1988.

Objective: To train maintenance personnel to perform the normal preventive maintenance, troubleshooting analysis, and repair maintenance that the copier machine requires.

Instruction: Functions of logic circuitry; operating principles; component assembly identification, location, and function; alignment and adjustment procedures; repair and parts replacement; fault analysis, diagnosis, and correction of electrical and mechanical equipment and malfunctions.

Credit recommendation: In the lower division baccalaureate/associate degree category, 2 semester hours in Electromechanical Technology and 1 semester hour in Digital Systems (3/75) (11/81). NOTE: This course has undergone a 5-year reevaluation and continues to meet the requirements for credit recommendations. Credit recommendations in Electromechanical Technology are not cumulative.

9400 Duplicator (Stand Alone)
Location: Xerox International Center for Training and Management Development, Leesburg, VA.

Length: 160 hours (4 weeks); 2 hours or less of lecture, 1 to 2 hours of discussion, and 36 hours of laboratory per week.

Dates: July 1979-December 1988.

Objective: To provide experienced technicians with the knowledge and skills to perform all phases of repair and maintenance of the 9400 copier.

Instruction: Supervised self-paced instruction in solid state and logic devices, machine control and diagnostics, service documentation, fault analysis, power and control, optics, xerographics, and complex electromechanical devices.

Credit recommendation: In the lower division baccalaureate/associate degree category, 3 semester hours in Electromechanical Technology, 1 semester hour in Computer Technology, and 1 semester hour in General Systems (11/81). NOTE: Credit recommendations in Electromechanical Technology are not cumulative.

9200 Duplicator
(A03) New Hires
(A33) Cross-Trainees
Location: Xerox International Center for Training and Management Development, Leesburg, VA.

Length: Self-paced instruction (average 172-240 hours).

Dates: January 1975-December 1988.

Objective: To provide participants with the knowledge and skills necessary to install, perform preventive maintenance on, troubleshoot, and repair a complex electromechanical duplicating system.

Instruction: Systems fault analysis; xerography; functional operation of optics; systems accounting; theory of AC and DC circuits; fundamental principles of solid state devices, logic elements, flip-flops, and their use in control and timing circuits; operation of complex mechanical mechanisms, and their adjustment and timing sequences in relation to electronic control systems.

Credit recommendation: In the lower division baccalaureate/associate degree category, 3 semester hours in

Electromechanical Technology and 1 semester hour in Digital Systems (3/75) (11/81). NOTE: This course has undergone a 5-year reevaluation and continues to meet the requirements for credit recommendations. Credit recommendations in Electromechanical Technology are not cumulative.

9400 Duplicator (A27)
Location: Xerox International Center for Training and Management Development, Leesburg, VA.
Length: 80 hours (2 weeks); self-paced, residential.
Dates: July 1977-December 1988.
Objective: To provide experienced technical personnel with the advanced diagnostic skills and theory required to service and repair a microprocessor-controlled duplicator system.
Instruction: For experienced technical personnel, an updating in the difference between the 9400 and 9200 copiers. Includes servicing, troubleshooting, and repair procedures using automatic microprocessor-controlled programs and check charts. Practical laboratory exercises are also used. (Prerequisite: 9200 Duplicator.)
Credit recommendation: In the lower division baccalaureate/associate degree category, 2 semester hours in Electromechanical Technology (6/78). NOTE: Credit recommendations in Electromechanical Technology are not cumulative.

840 Engineering Printing System (A41)
Location: Xerox International Center for Training and Management Development, Leesburg, VA.
Length: 80 hours (2 weeks); 4 hours of lecture, 16 hours of discussion, and 20 hours of laboratory per week.
Dates: January 1975-December 1988.
Objective: To provide knowledge necessary to maintain electromechanical office copying equipment, and to provide in-depth knowledge of the theory, operation, diagnostics, and maintenance techniques required to develop a proficient and effective method of maintaining the equipment.
Instruction: Component assembly identification, location, function, repair, and parts replacement; troubleshooting analysis techniques; adjustment, alignment, and preventive maintenance philosophy of an electromechanical system. Utilizes appropriate technical manuals and data, diagnostic test equipment (volt-ohm meter, ammeter), regular and special tools.
Credit recommendation: In the lower division baccalaureate/associate degree category, 2 semester hours in Electromechanical Technology (3/75) (11/81). NOTE: This course has undergone a 5-year reevaluation and continues to meet the requirements for credit recommendations. Credit recommendations in Electromechanical Technology are not cumulative.

9700 EPS
Location: Xerox International Center for Training and Management Development, Leesburg, VA.
Length: 280 hours (7 weeks); 1 hour of lecture, 4 hours of discussion, and 35 hours of laboratory per week.
Dates: January 1981-December 1988.
Objective: To provide the trainee with the knowledge and skill to install, operate, troubleshoot, perform preventive maintenance on, and repair a complex electronic printing system (specifically the Xerox 9700 unit) which is controlled by a minicomputer.
Instruction: Supervised, self-paced instruction on topics which include xerographics, laser, illuminated scanner, oscilloscope, minciomputer, magnetic-tape unit, disk, image generator, stacker, operator training, and various aspects of print (initiation of print, feed, registration, transportation, and fusing of the copy paper).
Credit recommendation: In the lower division baccalaureate/associate degree category, 3 semester hours in Electromechanical Technology, 2 semester hours in Computer Technology, and 2 semester hours in Laser, Optics, and Magnetic Tape Technology (11/81). NOTE: Credit recommendations in Electromechanical Technology are not cumulative.

800 ETS/CETS (A71)
Location: Xerox International Center for Training and Management Development, Leesburg, VA.
Length: 90 hours (2 weeks and 2 days); residential.
Dates: February 1978-December 1988.
Objective: To provide the technical knowledge and skills necessary to operate, troubleshoot, repair, and maintain an electric typing system.
Instruction: An in-depth study of the logic circuits and the interrelationship of electromechanical components, including printers, magnetic tape units, mechanical and magnetic card units, and computer memory devices. emphasis is on operating diagnostic aids, routine maintenance and repair, and replacement of faulty electrical or mechanical components.
Credit recommendation: In the lower division baccalaureate/associate degree category, 2 semester hours in Electromechanical Technology (6/78). NOTE: Credit recommendations in Electromechanical Technology are not cumulative.

3100 Family (A26)
(Formerly 3100 Copier Cross-Train [A23])
Location: Xerox International Center for Training and Management Development, Leesburg, VA.
Length: *Version 1:* 70 hours (1½ weeks); 62 hours residential, 8 hours of postschool, 6 hours of lecture, and 34 hours of laboratory per week. *Version 2:* 88 hours (2 weeks); 6 hours of lecture, and 34 hours of laboratory per week.
Dates: *Version 1:* February 1975-November 1980; *Ver-*

sion 2: December 1980-December 1988.

Objective: To prepare individuals to perform fault analysis, operational diagnosis, and alignment/adjustment of an electronic intensive copier machine.

Instruction: CRI format. Solid state electronic circuit functions, mechanisms and their adjustment; use of precision devices, xerographic principles, optical modules, and Mod III electrometer. Laboratory project is oriented to module understanding and fault analysis.

Credit recommendation: In the lower division baccalaureate/associate degree category, 3 semester hours in Electromechanical Technology (3/75) (11/81). NOTE: This course has undergone a 5-year reevaluation and continues to meet the requirements for credit recommendations. Credit recommendations in Electromechanical Technology are not cumulative.

Instructional Methods "Product Technical Specialist" (P11)

Location: Xerox International Center for Training and Management Development, Leesburg, VA.

Length: Approximately 80 hours (2 weeks); 22 hours of workshop and 12 hours of laboratory per week.

Dates: November 1980-December 1988.

Objective: To teach instructors instructional methods, skills, principles of human behavior, techniques for student questioning and feedback, counseling, coaching, and methods for performance analysis.

Instruction: Identification of optional/mandatory requirements for optimal training paybacks. Student responsibilities of recall and implementation are covered to ensure student/instructor compatibility during training. Laboratory experience is provided to state/observe/practice the major principles covered in the course and to evaluate student behavior in response to the principles being applied.

Credit recommendation: In the lower division baccalaureate/associate degree category, 3 semester hours in Human Relations or Leadership Training (11/81).

850 DTS (A73)

Location: Xerox International Center for Training and Management Development, Leesburg, VA.

Length: 45-52 hours (1 week, 2 days); self-paced, residential.

Dates: January 1978-December 1988.

Objective: To provide functional knowledge of a complete microprocessor-controlled typing system and of the technical skills required to operate, troubleshoot, service, and repair the total system.

Instruction: Operation, adjustment, and maintenance of a microprocessor-controlled typewriter system using automated diagnostic aids. Systems covered include magnetic disk units, display units, typing console, and printers. Troubleshooting practices are covered using flow chart analysis to pinpoint problem areas. Laboratory exercises are also used.

Credit recommendation: In the lower division baccalaureate/associate category, 1 semester hour in Electromechanical Technology (6/78).

860 IPS
(Formerly 850 DTS [A73])

Location: Xerox International Center for Training and Management Development, Leesburg, VA.

Length: *Version 1:* 45-52 hours (1 week, 2 days); self-paced, residential. *Version 2:* 56 hours (7 days); self-paced, residential.

Dates: *Version 1:* January 1978-November 1980; *Version 2:* December 1980-December 1988.

Objective: To provide functional knowledge of a complete microprocessor-controller information processing system and of the technical skills required to operate, troubleshoot, service, and repair the total system.

Instruction: Supervised, self-paced instruction, operation, adjustment, and maintenance of a microprocessor-controlled information processing system. Automated diagnostic aids are used. Systems covered include magnetic disk units, typing console, and printers. Troubleshooting practices are covered using flow chart analysis to pinpoint problem areas. Laboratory exercises are also used.

Credit recommendation: In the lower division baccalaureate/associate degree category, 1 semester hour in Electromechanical Technology (11/18). NOTE: Students who have completed the 800 ETS/CETS (A71) course should not receive credit for this course. Credit recommendations in Electromechanical Technology are not cumulative.

600 Microfilm Enlarger Printer (A40)

Location: Xerox International Center for Training and Management Development, Leesburg, VA.

Length: 80 hours (2 weeks); 4 hours of lecture, 12 hours of discussion, and 24 hours of laboratory per week.

Dates: January 1975-December 1988.

Objective: To prepare individuals to perform fault analysis, diagnosis, and alignment/adjustment of the electrical circuitry and the mechanical components of a microfilm enlarger printer.

Instruction: Electrical components and their assembly into an operational system; electrical schematic diagrams and their use in fault analysis/troubleshooting and correction. Basic mechanical adjustment/alignment techniques and procedures.

Credit recommendation: In the vocational certificate category, 2 semester hours in Electromechanical Technology (3/75) (11/81). NOTE: This course has undergone a 5-year reevaluation and continues to meet the requirements for credit recommendations. Credit recommendations in Electromechanical Technology are not cumulative.

4000 New Hire (A02)

Location: Xerox International Center for Training and Management Development, Leesburg, VA.

Length: 136 hours (3½ weeks); 8 hours of lecture, 8 hours of discussion, and 24 hours of laboratory/workshop per week.

Dates: June 1974-December 1988.

Objective: To train maintenance personnel to perform the normal preventive maintenance, troubleshooting analysis, and repair maintenance that the copier machine requires.

Instruction: Electrostatics, optics, photo conduction, and the principles of xerography; functions of logic circuitry; operating principles; component assembly identification, location, and function, alignment and adjustment procedures; repair and parts replacement; fault analysis, diagnosis, and correction of electrical and mechanical equipment malfunctions; preventive maintenance practices.

Credit recommendation: In the lower division baccalaureate/associate degree category, 2 semester hours in Electromechanical Technology and 1 semester hour in Digital Systems (3/75) (11/81). NOTE: This course has undergone a 5-year reevaluation and continues to meet the requirements for credit recommendations. Credit recommendations in Electromechanical Technology are not cumulative.

New Hire Copier (A00)

Location: Xerox International Center for Training and Management Development, Leesburg, VA.

Length: 160 hours (4 weeks); 4 hours of lecture, 16 hours of discussion, and 20 hours of laboratory per week.

Dates: January 1975-December 1988.

Objective: To provide the occupational skill to diagnose and correct mechanical and electrical equipment malfunction in copiers.

Instruction: Familiarization with xerographic equipment, specific component location, symbolic representation of functions and operation, the system operation of basic copiers.

Credit recommendation: In the vocational certificate category, 3 semester hours in Electromechanical Technology (3/75) (11/81). NOTE: This course has undergone a 5-year reevaluation and continues to meet the requirements for credit recommendations. Credit recommendations in Electromechanical Technology are not cumulative.

New Hire 7000 Duplicator (A06)
7000 Duplicator XT (A35)
(Formerly New Hire Duplicator 3600 [A06])
(Formerly A01)

Location: Xerox International Center for Training and Management Development, Leesburg, VA.

Length: *Version 1:* 152 hours (19 days); residential; 12 hours of lecture and 28 hours of laboratory per week. *Version 2:* 180 hours (25 days). *Version 3:* 136 hours (3½ weeks); 6 hours lecture and 34 hours of laboratory per week.

Dates: *Version 1:* January 1975-January 1977; *Version 2:* February 1977-January 1979; *Version 3:* February 1979-December 1988.

Objective: To teach the occupational skills of diagnosis and correction of mechanical and electrical equipment malfunction in copiers.

Instruction: Topics are xerographic equipment, specific component location, symbolic representation of functions and operation, the system operation of the 660 copier, systems fault analysis (troubleshooting) techniques necessary to adjust and replace faulty components.

Credit recommendation: In the vocational certificate category, 3 semester hours in Electromechanical Technology (3/75) (11/81). NOTE: This course has undergone a 5-year reevaluation and continues to meet the requirements for credit recommendations. Credit recommendations in Electromechanical Technology are not cumulative.

Selling Products/Services by Telephone (Customer Support Techniques)

Location: Xerox International Center for Training and Management Development, Leesburg, VA.

Length: 200 hours; 160 hours of self-paced preschool study and 40 hours (1 week) of classroom instruction in residence.

Dates: April 1976-December 1988.

Objective: To enable the student to serve customer needs and/or problems via the telephone.

Instruction: Aspects of customer relations, including preparation for the call and determining customer attitude, promoting products and services to the satisfied customer, solving problems for the dissatisfied customer, and follow-up activities. Lectures, discussion, role plays, and workshops are used.

Credit recommendation: In the lower division baccalaureate/associate degree category, 2 semester hours in Office Techniques (2/77).

Telecopier 200 (A56)

Location: Xerox International Center for Training and Management Development, Leesburg, VA.

Length: 56 hours (7½ days); residential.

Dates: January 1977-December 1988.

Objective: To train students to adjust and repair the Xerox Telecopier 200.

Instruction: Use of operation and service manuals; isolation and repair of malfunctions using a check-sheet troubleshooting procedure. Lectures are used to teach operation and repair practices; and laboratory exercises provide practical experience on actual systems, including instructor- and student-inserted system problems which students locate by following check-sheet procedures.

Credit recommendation: In the vocational certificate category, 1 semester hour in Troubleshooting (6/78).

Telecopier 400/410 (A57)

Location: Xerox International Center for Training and Management Development, Leesburg, VA.

Length: 30-35 hours (1 week); self-paced, residential.

Dates: April 1978-December 1988.

Objective: To train students to adjust and repair the Xerox Telecopier 400/410.

Instruction: Use of operation and service manuals; isolation and repair of malfunctions using a check-sheet troubleshooting procedure. Self-paced instruction is used for learning operation and repair practices; and laboratory exercises provide practical experience on actual systems, including instructor- and student-inserted system problems which students locate by following check-sheet procedures.

Credit recommendation: In the vocational certificate category, 1 semester hour in Troubleshooting (6/78).

8200/9500 Update

Location: Xerox International Center for Training and Management Development, Leesburg, VA.

Length: Approximately 65 hours (1 week and 2 days); 1½ days of lecture, ½ day of discussion, and 38 hours of laboratory per week.

Dates: February 1980-December 1988.

Objective: To provide students with the advanced knowledge necessary to install, operate, and maintain complex electromechanical duplicating systems that are controlled by a microprocessor. To train representatives in advancements in systems and to introduce new technology.

Instruction: Criterion-referenced instruction (laboratory-based), which requires the student to reach individually based performance levels before advancing to additional modules. Lecture/discussion, problem solving, and fault analysis are used.

Credit recommendation: In the lower division baccalaureate/associate degree category, 1 semester hour in Computer Science or Electromechanical Technology (11/81). NOTE: Credit recommendations in Electromechanical Technology are not cumulative.

5400/5600 Update Combination

Location: Xerox International Center for Training and Management Development, Leesburg, VA.

Length: 56-80 hours (7-10 days).

Dates: December 1980-December 1988.

Objective: To develop sufficient updated expertise in the technology associated with the 5400/5600 system. To enable students to understand and use appropriate documentation to service the equipment.

Instruction: The course is a self-paced, laboratory-based experience built around teaching modules. The student is required to reach a specified level of performance before advancing to additional modules.

Credit recommendation: In the lower division baccalaureate/associate degree category, 1 semester hour in Electromechanical Technology (11/81). NOTE: Credit recommendations in Electromechanical Technology are not cumulative.

3400 Update Training (H31)

Location: Xerox International Center for Training and Management Development, Leesburg, VA.

Length: 43-65 hours; self-paced, residential.

Dates: January 1978-December 1988.

Objective: To train experienced technical personnel to service, troubleshoot, and repair a 3400 series duplicator.

Instruction: For experienced technical personnel, an updating in the differences between the 3100 and 3400 copiers. Includes servicing, troubleshooting, and repair procedures, using automatic diagnostic programs and check charts. Practical laboratory exercises are also used. (Prerequisite: 3100 Family [A26].)

Credit recommendation: In the lower division baccalaureate/associate degree category, 1 semester hour in Electromechanical Technology (6/78). NOTE: Credit recommendations in Electromechanical Technology are not cumulative.

5400 Update Training (A28)

Location: Xerox International Center for Training and Management Development, Leesburg, VA.

Length: 80 hours (2 weeks); self-paced, residential.

Dates: October 1977-December 1988.

Objective: To prepare experienced technical personnel to diagnose, repair, and adjust faulty components or subsystems within the copier-duplicator.

Instruction: Instructs experienced technical representatives to train persons in the operation of the 5400 copier; troubleshooting procedures using check charts and some automated diagnostic processes. Laboratory exercises are also used. (Prerequisite: 4000 New Hire [A02], or 4000 Cross Training [A22].)

Credit recommendation: In the lower division baccalaureate/associate degree category, 1 semester hour in Electromechanical Technology (6/78). NOTE: Credit recommendations in Electromechanical Technology are not cumulative.

Yankee Atomic Electric Company

Yankee Atomic Electric Company is a nuclear-powered electricity generating facility located in Rowe, Massachusetts, with corporate headquarters in Boston, Massachusetts. Through its Rowe Training Department, the company provides job performance-based training to its employees. Yankee's commitment to the principle of Training Systems Development, a systematic approach to training, is evidenced by its status as a fully accredited member of the National Academy for Nuclear Training, a division of the Institute of Nuclear Power Operators.

The Y.A.E.C. Reactor Operator Qualification Course prepares entry-level candidates for the position of Control Room Operator. The 34-week program consists of 880 hours of classroom instruction and 480 hours of on-shift training. The course is based on learning objectives from Yankee's specific Job and Task Analysis. Its intent is to develop participants' skills and knowledge and prepare them for professional licensing examinations.

The credit recommended applies to individuals who successfully complete the entire Reactor Operators Training Course during the period from January 1, 1983 to November 1, 1991. The program is offered at the Yankee Atomic Electric Training Center in Rowe, Massachusetts.

Source of official student records: Director of Training, Yankee Atomic Electric Company, HC 87, P.O. Box 160, Rowe, Massachusetts 01367.

Additional information about the courses: Vermont State Colleges, Office of External Programs, P.O. Box 34, Waterbury, Vermont 05676.

Reactor Operator Training Program
Location: Rowe, MA.
Length: 34 weeks.
Dates: January 1, 1983-November 1, 1991.
Objective: To develop participants' skills and knowledge in operating a pressurized water reactor.
Instruction: See individual courses below.
Credit recommendation: 22 semester hours recommended only after completing the entire program (10/88). NOTE: See description of separate components below.

Reactor Physics
Instruction: A non-calculus-based reactor neutronics course with an emphasis on applications. Course topics include: atomic physics (including radioactive decay and radiation), cross sections, the fission process, neutron moderation and diffusion, neutron balance and the four and six factor formulas, the multiplication factor, delayed and prompt neutrons, subcritical multiplication, elementary kinetics, reactor control, reactivity coefficients, fission product poisons, core fluxes, and decay heat.
Credit recommendation: In the lower division baccalaureate/associate degree category, 3 semester hours in Reactor Physics (10/88).

Essentials of Electricity
Instruction: An algebra-based survey of essential properties of DC and AC circuits, motors, generators, and distribution systems. Relationships between current and voltage in series and parallel resistive circuits are studied. Phase relationships between voltage and current in capacitive and inductive circuit elements are discussed. Electronic amplifier concepts are introduced. Aspects of electrical safety are covered.
Credit recommendation: In the lower division baccalaureate/associate degree category, 3 semester hours in Essentials of Electricity (10/88).

Applied Technical Mathematics
Instruction: This course covers applications of concepts including ratios, graphing, basic algebraic operations, linear equations, logarithms, trigonometry, unit conversions, geometry, and graphical integration and differentiation.
Credit recommendation: In the lower division baccalaureate/associate degree category, 3 semester hours in Applied Technical Mathematics (10/88).

Power Plant Technology
Instruction: A non-calculus treatment of the Rankine cycle and components. Properties of substances, work, heat, first and second law, Carnot and Rankine cycles are covered. Fluid properties, fluid mechanics, Bernoulli's equation, laminar and turbulent flow, friction, and pump work are also covered. Principles of conduction, convection, and radiation are presented, including boiling heat transfer and natural circulation.
Credit recommendation: In the lower division baccalaureate/associate degree category, 3 semester hours in Power Plant Technology (10/88).

Introductory Chemistry
Instruction: An introduction to basic chemistry with applications to corrosion control.
Credit recommendation: In the lower division baccalaureate/associate degree category, 1 semester hour in Introductory Chemistry (10/88).

Pressurized Water Reactor (PWR) Plant Systems
Instruction: An overview of main and auxiliary systems involved in power generation, with particular attention to pressurized water reactors.
Credit recommendation: In the upper division baccalaureate category, 3 semester hours in PWR Plant Systems (10/88).

Pressurized Water Reactor (PWR) Plant Systems Laboratory
Instruction: Laboratory experience supporting PWR Plant Systems course materials.
Credit recommendation: In the upper division baccalaureate category, 3 semester hours in PWR Plant Systems Laboratory (10/88).

Pressurized Water Reactor (PWR) Simulator Laboratory I
Instruction: This course provides the knowledge and

PWR simulator experience necessary to execute the appropriate procedures to operate a pressurized water reactor.

Credit recommendation: In the upper division baccalaureate category, 3 semester hours in PWR Simulator Laboratory (10/88).

Young Women's Christian Association of the U.S.A.

The Young Women's Christian Association of the U.S.A. is an autonomous women's membership movement, with programs and services in more than five thousand locations in the United States. It is a multiservice agency whose programs are designed to meet the needs of the community, with special emphasis on the program needs of teen and adult women. More than two and half million persons participate in its programs.

The National Training Program, developed by the National Board of the YWCA for Associations across the country, provides leadership training for professional staff and corporate volunteers. Its goal is to strengthen the skills of women within the YWCA so that they can utilize their human, financial, and physical resources more effectively. The program includes basic and advanced management courses, advanced program development, and training for new staff. Courses are conducted in selected facilities around the country, using classroom instruction, workshops, and individual assignments.

Source of official student records: Director of Membership-Leadership Development, National Board, YWCA, 135 West 50th Street, New York, New York 10022.

Additional information about the courses: Program on Noncollegiate Sponsored Instruction, The Center for Adult Learning and Educational Credentials, American Council on Education, One Dupont Circle, Washington, D.C. 20036.

Advanced Management Workshop: Financial Administration and Development
(Formerly Advanced Management Workshop in Finance)

Location: Atlanta, GA; Cincinnati, OH; San Diego, CA; Milwaukee, WI; Washington, DC; Bloomington, IN.

Length: *Version 1:* 28¼ hours (5 days); residential. *Version 2:* 55 hours (7 days).

Dates: *Version 1:* March 1977-June 1982; *Version 2:* July 1983-Present.

Objective: To provide students with the principles and methods applicable to securing and managing financial resources.

Instruction: Use of case budgeting as a management tool; the auditor's role; financial reporting; asset and purchasing control; fund raising opportunities and strategies; planning; foundation and government funding. Methodology includes lecture, discussion, and case studies.

Credit recommendation: *Version 1:* In the graduate degree category, 2 semester hours in Administration or Education (3/77). *Version 2:* In the graduate degree category, 3 semester hours in Administration, Organization, Management, or Business Education (6/83). NOTE: This course has undergone a five-year reevaluation and continues to meet requirements for ACE credit recommendations.

Advanced Management Workshop in Personnel Administration

Location: Various locations nationally.

Length: 33 hours (5 days); residential.

Dates: March 1977-June 1983.

Objective: To provide professionals and volunteers with training in principles and methods of establishing sound personnel policies and practices.

Instruction: Effective personnel administration; policy and procedure formulation; Board of staff roles in personnel administration; affirmative action compliance; performance appraisal; wage and salary administration; and ERISA compliance. Methodology includes simulations, lectures, small-group discussion, and case studies assignments.

Credit recommendation: In the graduate degree category, 2 semester hours in Business and Public Administration, Guidance and Counseling, or Industrial Psychology (3/77).

Encore: The YWCA Post Mastectomy Group Rehabilitation Program Opportunity - Energies Revived)
(Encore Training Workshop: Encouragement - Normally - Counseling - Opportunity - Energies Revived))

Location: Pittsburgh, PA; Providence, RI; Milwaukee, WI; Atlanta, GA; San Diego, CA; Cincinnati, OH.

Length: 44.75 hours (8 days).

Dates: July 1979-Present.

Objective: To provide professionals and volunteers with training and knowledge of anatomical, physical, medical, and psychosocial aspects of breast cancer and mastectomy.

Instruction: The course is a workshop to acquire updated knowledge and skills in meeting the special physical and psychosocial needs of the post-mastectomy woman. Assessment is made of personal attitudes, abilities, strengths and limitations as an Encore leader including evaluation of community to gain administrative aspects of programming and to ensure higher quality of national standards with Encore. Methodology includes lectures, small group discussion, and techniques for instructing floor and water exercises.

Credit recommendation: In the upper division bac-

Management Training for Staff with Executive Potential

Location: Various locations nationally.
Length: *Version 1:* 59½ hours (8 days); residential. *Version 2:* 57¼ hours (7 days); residential.
Dates: March 1977-Present.
Objective: To provide professional staff with managerial skills required for executive performance in voluntary organizations.
Instruction: Management concepts; allocation of human and other resources; management and organization processes; team development; personal assessment and career planning. Methodology includes lecture, discussion case studies, and role play.
Credit recommendation: In the upper division baccalaureate category or in the graduate degree category, 3 semester hours in Adult Education, Business Administration, Community Affairs, Public Administration, Sociology, or Social Work (3/77) (6/83). NOTE: This course covers much of the same material as Management Workshop for Executive Staff. Credit should not be awarded for both. This course has undergone a 5-year reevaluation and continues to meet requirements for ACE credit recommendations.

Management Workshop for Executive Staff

Location: Various locations nationally.
Length: 52 hours (8 days); residential.
Dates: March 1977-Present.
Objective: To provide executive staff with managerial skills applicable to the voluntary organization environment.
Instruction: Management and organization processes; planning; problem solving and decision making; control and evaluation; supervision; conflict management; personnel and financial administration; communications. Methodology includes lecture, discussion, case histories, role playing, and small-group learning teams.
Credit recommendation: In the upper division baccalaureate category or in the graduate degree category, 3 semester hours in Adult Education, Business Administration, Community Affairs, Public Administration, Sociology, or Social Work (3/77) (6/83). NOTE: This course covers much of the same material as Management Training for Staff with Executive Potential. Credit should not be awarded for both. This course has undergone a 5-year reevaluation and continues to meet the requirements for credit recommendations.

Management Workshop for Student Leadership
(Formerly Management Workshop for Student YWCA Staff)

Location: El Paso, TX; Athens, GA; San Diego, CA.
Length: *Version 1:* 49 hours (8 days); residential. *Version 2:* 33 3/4 hours (4½ days); residential.
Dates: *Version 1:* March 1977-June 1983; *Version 2:* July 1983-Present.
Objective: To provide the staff of YWCA's that primarily serve postsecondary students with the managerial skills to effectively utilize human, financial, and physical resources.
Instruction: Management training and the planning function; program development; current social forces and trends in higher education; building student involvement and pluralistic leadership; development of YWCA Boards; sound financial planning. Methodology includes lecture, simulations, audiovisual aids and workshops.
Credit recommendation: *Version 1:* In the graduate degree category, 3 semester hours in Business Administration, Community Affairs, Guidance and Counseling, Public Administration, or Sociology (3/77). *Version 2:* In the graduate degree category, 2 semester hours in Adult Education, Business Administration, Community Affairs, Guidance and Counseling, Public Administration, Social Work, or Sociology (6/83). NOTE: Students who receive credit for this course should not receive credit for An Overview of the Role of Voluntary Leaders in the YWCA (Presidential Leadership and Association Committee Chairpersons' Workshop). This course has undergone a 5-year reevaluation and continues to meet requirements for credit recommendations.

Presidential Leadership and Association Committee Chairpersons' Workshop
(An Overview of the Role of Voluntary Leaders in the YWCA)

Location: Various locations nationally.
Length: *Version 1:* 27¼ hours (4 days); residential. *Version 2:* 37¼ hours (5 days); residential.
Dates: *Version 1:* March 1977-June 1983; *Version 2:* July 1983-Present.
Objective: To provide an overview of volunteer leadership responsibilities.
Instruction: Provides a conceptual basis for planning, budgeting, communicating, decision making, and problem solving. Clarifies leadership roles and management responsibilities of executive directors, presidents, and chairpersons. Methodology includes lecture, discussion, and small-group interaction.
Credit recommendation: *Version 1:* In the lower division baccalaureate/associate degree category or in the upper division baccalaureate category, 2 semester hours in Business Administration, Sociology, or Urban or Community Affairs (3/77). *Version 2:* In the upper division baccalaureate or graduate degree category, 2 semester hours in Business Administration, Social Work, Sociology, or Urban or Community Affairs (6/83). NOTE: Students who receive credit for this course should not receive credit for Management Workshop for Student Leadership

(Management Workshop for Student YWCA Staff). This course has undergone a 5-year reevaluation and continues to meet requirements for credit recommendations.

Program Development Workshop
  Location: Various locations nationally.
  Length: *Version 1:* 39¼ hours (8 days); residential. *Version 2:* 52 hours (7 days); residential.
  Dates: March 1977-Present.
  Objective: To provide professional staff with knowledge and practical experience in program design, development, and delivery.
  Instruction: The course is a practicum in program-planning process. Methodology includes lecture and discussion; emphasis is on practical application, to include designing, implementing, and evaluating a program.
  Credit recommendation: In the upper division baccalaureate category or in the graduate degree category, 3 semester hours in Curriculum Development, Guidance and Counseling, Social Work, or Sociology (3/77) (6/83). NOTE: This course has undergone a 5-year reevaluation and continues to meet requirements for ACE credit recommendations.

Staff Development II
  Location: Various locations nationally.
  Length: 54 hours (8 days); residential.
  Dates: March 1977-June 1983.
  Objective: To provide relatively new staff with insight into the human responsibilities and skills required of voluntary association professionals.
  Instruction: Working with volunteers; the planning process; finance; program development; analyzing community needs and resources; conflict management; team building; group work techniques; proposal writing; financial resources. Methodology includes lecture, group discussion and interaction, role play, and group and community interaction.
  Credit recommendation: In the lower division baccalaureate/associate degree category or in the upper division baccalaureate category, 3 semester hours in Business Administration, Community Affairs, Guidance and Counseling, Social Work or Sociology (3/77).

Appendix and Index

Appendix: List of Evaluators

Carolyn Adams
Assistant, Dean, College of Liberal Arts
Temple University
Philadelphia, PA

Dewey A. Adams
Chairperson, Comprehensive Vocational Education
Ohio State University
Columbus, OH

Don Adams
Professor of Technology
Oklahoma State University
Stillwater, OK

Joseph D. Adams
Assistant Division Chairman for English
Northern Virginia Community College
Annadale, VA

Richard August Ahrens
Professor of Nutrition
College of Human Ecology
University of Maryland
College Park, MD

Frank Alberico
Professor
Joliet Junior College
Joliet, IL

Louis Albert
Director of Special Projects
American Association for Higher Education
Washington, DC

Leonard Alberts
Professor, Drafting and Design Department
Pennsylvania Institute of Technology
Upper Darby, PA

Don Albright
Professor of Mathematics and Chemistry
Northwestern College
St. Paul, MN

Dave Alexander
Education Specialist
George Meany Center for Labor Studies
Silver Spring, MD

Richard Allen
Assistant Dean for Career Education and Community Service
Northern Oklahoma College
Tonkawa, OK

Clayton Allein
Industrial Educational Department
University of Texas
Tyler, TX

Gemmy Allen
Marketing and Management Instructor
Mountain View College
Dallas, TX

Richard A. Almonte
Consultant, Vocational Education
Department of Education
Bureau of Vocational-Technical Education
Providence, RI

Roy Alvarez
Cornell University
Ithaca, NY

James M. Anderson
Professor of Civil Engineering
Department of Civil Engineering
University of California
Berkeley, CA

Edwin L. Andrews
Chairman, Division of Arts and Sciences
SUNY Agricultural and Tech College
Cobleskill, NY

Frank Angell
Professor of Insurance and Finance
New York University
School of Business
New York, NY

Roanne Angiello
Dean, Business Technologies Division
Bergen Community College
Paramus, NJ

Richard Anthony
Professor, Engineering Technology Department
Cuyahoga Community College
Cleveland, OH

Charles Ardolino
Faculty Member and Administrator
Coastline Community College
Fountain Valley, CA

Kathleen F. Arns
Assistant Vice President for Vocational Curricula
Oakton Community College
Des Plaines, IL

Gerard Arsenault
Professor
Cumberland County College
Vineland, NJ

Appendix: List of Evaluators

William F. Atchison
Professor, Department of Computer Science
University of Maryland
College Park, MD

Roger Atherton
Director, Division of Management
College of Business Administration
Oklahoma University
Norman, OK

Clarence Avery
Professor, School of Accounting
University of Central Florida
Orlando, FL

Alexander W. Avtgis
Department Head, Electrical/Electronic Engineering
 Technology
Wentworth Institute of Technology
Boston, MA

Robert Azar
Chairman, Department of Mechanical Engineering
Western New England College
Springfield, MA

Sandra Bailey
Program Head, Medical Records Technology Program
Northern Virginia Community College
Annandale, VA

W. E. Bailey
Automotive Center Coordinator
Oklahoma State University
School of Technical Training
Okmulgee, OK

Carl D. Baird
Professor
University of Florida
Gainesville, FL

James R. Baker
Professor of Imaging Systems
Virginia Polytechnical Institute
Blacksburg, VA

Dennis M. Bakewicz
Professor
Essex County College
Newark, NJ

Joseph Balabon
Director MIS
Mercer County Community College
Trenton, NJ

Lowell N. Ballew
Head, Computer Science Department
East Texas State University
Commerce, TX

Gary Ballman
Professor, Medical Laboratory Technology
Northern Virginia Community College
Annandale, VA

Guy R. Banville
Associate Dean, School of Business
St. Louis University
St. Louis, MO

Thomas C. Barker
Dean, School of Allied Health Professions
Medical College of Virginia Campus
Virginia Commonwealth University
Richmond, VA

Joan Barnacle
Instructor of Medical Assisting
Indian Valley College
Novato, CA

Eugene W. Bartel
Senior Research Associate
Carnegie-Melon University
Pittsburgh, PA

Richard A. Bassler
Director of Computer Systems Applications Program
The American University
Washington, DC

D. L. Bates
Associate Professor of Management
California State University
Long Beach, CA

Harish Batra
Chairman, Department of Finance and Business Law
University of Wisconsin
Whitewater, WI

Colin Battle
Chairperson, Division of Business Administration
Broward Community College
Pompano Beach, FL

William Bauer
Vice President of Academic Affairs
Community College of Beaver County
Monaca, PA

Jon Bauman
Professor of Music
Department of Music
Frostburg State University
Frostburg, MD

John R. Beaton
Dean, College of Human Ecology
University of Maryland
College Park, MD

William A. Beck
President, Guthrie Foundation for Medical Research
Sayre, PA

Leon Bedard
Chariman, Science and Technology
Mt. Wachusett Community College
Gardener, MA

Susanne Bensel
Professor, Modern Language Department
Johns Hopkins University
Washington, DC

Kenneth Benson
Chairman of Health, Urban and Outdoor Recreation
Kean College
Union, NJ

Billie D. Berger
Consultant
Yale, OK

Leslie H. Berk
Chairman, Division of Administrative Services
Director of Continuing and Management Education
Franklin University
Columbus, OH

Adele Berlin
Professor, Department of Far Eastern and Near Eastern Languages
University of Maryland
College Park, MD

Thomas Berry
Professor, Department of Slavic Languages
University of Maryland
College Park, MD

Don Biederman
Director of Telecommunications Technical Program
Skyline College
San Bruno, CA

Patrick Biesty
Dean of Business and Social Sciences
County College of Morris
Sparta, NJ

Leland Biggs
Professor, Business Administration and Economics
Montgomery College
Rockville, MD

Phyllis Bigpond
Executive Director
Phoenix Indian Center
Phoenix, AZ

George Biles
Professor of Personnel Administration
School of Business Administration
The American University
Washington, DC

Beatrice Black
University of the District of Columbia
Washington, DC

Patsy Blackshear
Director, Division of Budget
D.C. Government
Washington, DC

Bishop B. Blackwell
Professor of Aeronautical Science
Embry-Riddle Aeronautical University
Bunnell, FL

Jose A. Blakeley
Assistant Professor, Computer Science Department
Indiana University
Bloomington, IN

Santos Blan
Business and Governmental Studies
Community College of Denver
Denver, CO

Lewis Blazy
Former Assistant Professor of Computer Science and Psychology
Fairfax, VA

Roland L. Bliss
Assistant Professor of Business
Department of Business
Los Angeles Technical College
Los Angeles, CA

Carl Bogt
Dean, Business School
Bowling Green State University
Bowling Green, OH

Arthur H. Boisselle
Coordinator, Business Management
Pikes Peak Community College
Colorado Springs, CO

J. Lyle Bootman
College of Pharmacy
University of Arizona
Tucson, AZ

William Boras
Associate Professor
Computer Information System
School of Business
Ferris State College
Big Rapids, MI

Vera Borkovec
Associate Professor, Department of Language & Foreign Studies
American University
Washington, DC

George W. Boulware
Professor of Business Administration
David Lipscomb College
Nashville, TN

Edward K. Bowdon
Professor and Head, Department of Engineering Technology
Texas A & M University
Tyler, TX

Robert L. Bowers
Chairman, Division of Business and Public Services
J. Sargeant Reynolds Community College
Richmond, VA

Doreen Boyce
Chairman, Department of Economics and Management
Hood College
Frederick, MD

Paul Boyd
Chairman, Electronics Department
University of the District of Columbia
Van Ness Campus
Washington, DC

Barbara Koerber Boyington
Wanamassa, NJ

Anthony D. Branch
Dean, Graduate College
Golden Gate University
San Francisco, CA

William Brant
Director of Education and Research
Administrative Management Society
The American College
Bryn Mawr, PA

Robert Braswell
Technical Director, Armament Development and Test Center
Eglin AFB, FL

Martha Braunig
President
MJB Associates
Denver, CO

Eugene Brill
Coordinator of Marketing and Management Programs
Grossmont College
El Cajon, CA

Audrey Bronson
Professor of Psychology
Cheyney State College
Cheyney, PA

Jacqueline Brophy
Director of Labor Liberal Arts Program
Cornell University
New York State School of Industrial and Labor Relations
New York, NY

Gilbert Brown
Professor of Nuclear Engineering
University of Lowell
Lowell, MA

Kenneth W. Brown
Coordinator of Teacher Certifying Program for the College of Technology
Houston, TX

Melanie Brown
Assistant Professor, Business Education
The University of the District of Columbia
Washington, DC

Robert Brucker
Field Consultant
Erie, PA

Alfred Buchanan
Plantsville, CT

John Bullard
Assistant Dean for Graduate and Continuing Education
Uniformed Services
University of Health Sciences
Bethesda, MD

Edward Burns
Warner-Lambert
Adjunct
Morris County College
Randolph, NJ

Herbert Burns
Department Head, Accounting and Finance
Central Piedmont Community College
Charlotte, NC

Jack Burson
Professor, Technology Department
McNeese State University
Lake Charles, LA

Anderson Byrd
Director
University Police
Rutgers University
Camden, NJ

Roy Byrd
Chairman, Department of Technology
Cameron University
Lawton, OK

Kenneth L. Cammie
Adjunct Faculty Member
Computer Engineering Technology
Prince Georges Community College
Largo, MD

Dave Camp
Chairman, Department of Criminal Justice
Georgia State University
Atlanta, GA

Gerald R. Camp
Associate Professor and Coordinator of Data Processing
University of Akron
Akron, OH

John Campbell
Supervision/Management Education Coordinator, Department of Business Education
San Jose City College
San Jose, CA

Layard Campbell
Automatic Fire Sprinkler System
Norwalk, CT

Filemon Campo-Flores
Associate Professor, Department of Management
California State University
Long Beach, CA

Robert Carbone
Professor of Higher and Adult Education
Department of Educational Policy, Planning and
  Administration
University of Maryland
College Park, MD

Patrick W. Carlton
Associate Professor of Educational Administration
Division of Administrative and Educational Services
College of Education
Dulles Graduate Studies Center
Washington, DC

William A. Carr, Jr.
Chief of Vocational Training (retired)
U.S. Government Printing Office
Arlington, VA

Paula Carroll
Associate Director, Administrative Computer Center
University of Maryland
College Park, MD

Frank H. Cassell
Northwestern University
Graduate School of Management
Evanston, IL

Don B. Chaffin
Professor, Department of Industrial and Operating
  Engineering
University of Michigan
Ann Arbor, MI

Neal Chalofsky
Visiting Assistant Professor of Human Resource
  Development
School of Education & Human Development
George Washington University
Washington, DC

Aime J. Chapdelaine, Jr.
Assistant Professor, Electronics Program
Northern Virginia Community College
Annandale, VA

Miriam Chaplin
Associate Professor of Education
Rutgers University
Camden, NJ

Julius Chapman
Associate Dean of Academic Affairs
Dean of Minority Affairs
Towson State University
Baltimore, MD

James J. Chastain
Professor of Insurance and Director for the Center of
  Insurance Education
School of Business
Howard University
Washington, DC

Harlan Cheney
Professor of Business Economics and Finance
College of Business
The University of the District of Columbia
Washington, DC

Robert Chenoweth
Department Chairman of Data Processing (retired)
Morris County College
Randolph, NJ

Umbok Cheong
Foreign Service Institute
Department of State
Washington, DC

James W. Chester
Instructor, Department of Business
Cameron University
Lawton, OK

Michael Chier
Professor
Milwaukee School of Engineering
Milwaukee, WI

Robert J. Chinnis
Associate Professor of Biology
Biology Department
The American University
Washington, DC

Marc Christophe
Lecturer, Romance Languages Department
Howard University
Washington, DC

Robert Christopher
Chairman, Mechanical Engineering
University of Colorado
Boulder, CO

Vincent P. Cieri
Chief, Training Development
Project MGR-ARTADS
Fort Monmouth, NJ

Joseph J. Cioch
Professor and Head
Department of Restaurant, Hotel and Institutional
  Management
Purdue University
West Lafayette, IN

Joseph Cirrincione
Associate Professor, Department of Geography
University of Maryland
College Park, MD

Appendix: List of Evaluators

Donald Clark, Jr.
Lecturer/Supervisor, Language Laboratory and German Department
Johns Hopkins University
Baltimore, MD

Edward Clark
Coordinator of Electronics Technology
Atlantic Community College
Mays Landing, NJ

William Clark
Associate Professor, Department of Industrial Management
Tidewater Community College
Portsmouth, VA

Alvin Clay
Dean, Commerce and Finance
Villanova University
Villanova, PA

Preston Clement
Professor
Mercer Community College
Trenton, NJ

Alexander Cloner
Dean, School of Public Administration
University of Southern California
Sacramento Campus
Sacramento, CA

Mary Ann Coffland
Professor and Chair, Department of Italian
George Washington University
Washington, DC

Jean A. Coffman
Assistant Professor
Hawaii Pacific College
Honolulu, HI

Jerry S. Cohen
Associate Professor, Business Administration
Somerset County College
Somerville, NJ

Daniel Cokewood
Chair, Department of Technology
Kean College
Union, NJ

James Nathan Cole
Florida Junior College
Jacksonville, FL

Gary Collins
Instructor, Public Services Department (Fire Sciences)
San Joaquin Delta College
Stockton, CA
Captain, Stockton Fire Department

James Comer
Associate Professor
University of Cincinnati
Cincinnati, OH

Larry Connatser
Director, Office of Continuing Professional Studies
Virginia Commonwealth University
Richmond, VA

Frank W. Connolly
Director of Academic Computing Services
The American University
Washington, DC

Thomas J. Connolly
Chairman and Professor of Aeronautical Science
Embry-Riddle Aeronautical University
Bunnell, FL

Thomas G. Cook
Dean, Lifelong Learning
Ferris State University
Big Rapids, MI

Ralph (Spade) Cooley
Engineering Manager, Nuclear Training
Nutech
Bethesda, MD

Robert Cotner
Chairman, English and Philosophy Department
Montgomery College
Rockville, MD

James E. Couch
School of Technology
Florida International University
Miami, FL

Amy Coury
Professor of Nursing
Los Angeles Harbor College
Los Angeles, CA

Richard Coutant
Representative
Scott, Foresman and Co.
Syracuse, NY

John R. Cox
Professor of Finance
California State University, Los Angeles
Los Angeles, CA

Michael Crone
DeVry Institute of Technology
Atlanta, GA

Constance Crowley
Assistant Clinical Professor
Family Health Care Nursing
University of California
San Francisco, CA

Joseph Crowley
Professor, Department of Marketing and Management
Community College of Philadelphia
Philadelphia, PA

David Cummins
Assistant Professor of Insurance Department
Wharton School
University of Pennsylvania
Philadelphia, PA

Nancy Curry
Chairperson, Department of Child Development and Child Care
University of Pittsburgh
Pittsburgh, PA

Alan Czarapata
Professor of Engineering Technology
Montgomery College
Rockville, MD

Nell Dale
Department of Computer Science
University of Texas
Austin, TX

Gordon Darkenwald
Professor of Education
Department of Educational Administration
Rutgers University
New Brunswick, NJ

Jerome Darnell
Professor of Business
College of Business Administration
University of Colorado
Boulder, CO

James Daschbach
Professor, Department of Aerospace and Mechanical Engineering
Notre Dame University
Notre Dame, IN

Boyd Daugherty
Professor of Electrical Engineering
Washington Technical School
Washington, DC

Hope S. Daugherty
Program Leader, 4-H Extension Service
U.S. Department of Agriculture
Washington, DC

Dan A. Davis
Associate Dean, College of Liberal Studies
The University of Oklahoma
Norman, OK

Herbert J. Davis
Associate Professor of Business Administration
Program Director, Business Management
School of Government and Business Administration
The George Washington University
Washington, DC

Lance Davis
Administrator, Corporate Education
Thomas A. Edison State College
Trenton, NJ

Larry Davis
Professor
Manager
East Texas State University
Texarkana, TX

Leonard Davis
Professor of Communications
West Virginia University
Morgantown, WV

Monte Davis
Professor, Nuclear Research Center
Georgia Institute of Technology
Atlanta, GA

Robert L. Davis
Dean of Engineering
University of Missouri
Rolla, MO

Mary Day
Director of Continuing Education
School of Social Work
Howard University
Washington, DC

Lloyd M. DeBoer
Chairman, Business Administration Department
George Mason University
Fairfax, VA

Lynne Delay
Professor of the Graduate Program for Administrators
Consultant for the Port Authority of New York and New Jersey
Rider College
Lawrenceville, NJ

Robert de Iongh
Business Department
San Francisco City College
San Francisco, CA

Eugene Deloatch
School of Engineering
Howard University
Washington, DC

Thomas Delutis
President, Information Systems Architects
Fairfax, VA

Donal A. Dermody
Professor, School of Hotel Administration
Cornell University
Ithaca, NY

Richard Devalin
Professor, Restaurant Management
Los Angeles Trade Technical School
Los Angeles, CA

Kenneth Dickie
Professor, Department of Educational Leadership
Western Michigan University
Kalamazoo, MI

Simonne Dickinson, CTC
Director, Division of World-Wide Travel
AAA, Automobile Club of Washington
Seattle, WA

Richard Diklich
Instructor, Automotive Technology
Longview Community College
Lee's Summit, MO

Mervin Dissinger
Washington's Crossing, PA

John diStasio
Business and Office Occupations Division
Pikes Peak Community College
Colorado Springs, CO

Robert Dompka
Montgomery College
Rockville, MD

R. D. Draper
Psychology Department
Montclair State College
Upper Montclair, NJ

Li-Chuang Duke
Professor of Chinese
School of Advanced International Studies
Johns Hopkins University
Washington, DC

Howard Dunn
Professor of Data Processing
Mercer County Community College
Trenton, NJ

Margaret Dunn
Associate Professor of English
Kean College of New Jersey
Dunellen, NJ

William J. Dunne
Associate Dean, College of Business Administration
University of Illinois
Chicago, IL

Kenneth J. Dwyer
Hudson County Community College
Belleville, NJ

Charles Edelson
Assistant Dean of the College of Business and Management
University of Maryland
College Park, MD

Robert Edmister
Professor of Finance
College of Business and Management
University of Maryland
College Park, MD

Warren Eidness
Chairman, Department of Chemistry
Normandale Community College
Bloomington, MN

Joel Eigen
Professor, Sociology Department
Franklin and Marshall College
Lancaster, PA

Adel I. El-Ansary
Professor of Marketing and Business Administration
School of Government and Business Administration
The George Washington University
Washington, DC

Norb Elbert
Associate Professor of Management
Denver Technical University
Denver, CO

Kenneth Elsner
Director of Student Teaching
Central State University
Edmond, OK

William Enslin
Department Chairman of Management
Glassboro State College
Glassboro, NJ

Donald C. Eteson
Professor of Electrical Engineering
Worcester Polytechnic Institute
Worcester, MA

John B. Eubanks
Professor of History of Religions
Howard University
School of Religion
Washington, DC

Michael Evans
Director of Tourism, Food and Lodging Administration
University of Tennessee
Knoxville, TN

W. Buell Evans
Computing Center
Emory University
Atlanta, GA

Ormond C. Ewers
Head, Department of Business Administration
Suffolk Community College
Long Island, NY

Marvin Eyler
Dean, College of Physical Education, Recreation and Health
University of Maryland
College Park, MD

Robert F. Fair
Professor and Assistant Dean of Executive Programs
The Colgate Darden Graduate School of Business
    Administration
University of Virginia
Charlottesville, VA

Gary W. Falkenberg
Professor of Management
Oakland Community College
Auburn Hills Campus
Auburn Heights, MI

James L. Faltinek
Vice President and Director
Association Services Division
Bank Marketing Association
Chicago, IL

Scott Feinerman
Coordinator, Travel Services Education
Los Angeles Airport College Center and Los Angeles
 Trade-Technical College
Los Angeles, CA

Otto Feinstein
Director, University Studies and Weekend College
College of Lifelong Learning
Wayne State University
Detroit, MI

Ali Fekrat
Professor, College of Business Administration
Georgetown University
Washington, DC

Carol Felder
Assistasnt Professor of English
Somerset County College
Somerville, NJ

Lewis R. Fibel
Vice President and Dean of Faculty
Sullivan County Community College
Loch Sheldrake, NY

Carl Fields
Chairman, Nuclear Engineering Technology Program
Penn State University
Monaca, PA

Arnold Finchum
Chairman, Engineering, Technology Department
California Polytechnic State University, San Luis Obispo
San Luis Obispo, CA

Arthur Finkle
Rider College
Trenton, NJ

Diana Fischer
Computer Technology
Prince Georges Community College
Largo, MD

James Fisk
Department of Chemistry
Sanford University
Birmingham, AL

Patrick S. Fitzsimons
Assistant Chief
Office of Management Analysis
New York City Police Department
New York, NY

William Fleisher
U.S. Customs Service
Philadelphia, PA

Stevenson W. Fletcher
Head, Hotel, Restaurant and Travel Administration
University of Massachusetts
Amherst, MA

William Ford
Chief, Juvenile Probation Officer
Bucks County Courthouse
Doylestown, PA

Ernest Foreman
Professor of Management and Information Science
George Washington University
Washington, DC

Roger Formissano
Graduate School of Business
University of Wisconsin
Madison, WI

Edward L. Foss
Director, Marine Division
Cape Fear Technical Institute
Wilmington, NC

Joe Fox
President, Mid-State Bank & Trust Co.
Altoona, PA

Donald D. Fraser
Professor
Essex County College
Newark, NJ

Robert O. Freedman
Dean of Graduate Studies
Baltimore Hebrew College
Baltimore, MD

David A. Frisby
Director, Antioch College
Philadelphia, PA

James J. Fyfe
Associate Professor
The American University
School of Justice
Washington, DC

Joel D. Galloway
Dean, School of Technology
Ferris State University
Big Rapids, MI

Connolly Gamble
Executive Secretary, Society for Advancement of Continuing Education for Ministry (SACEM)
Collegeville, PA

John Gannon
Assistant Professor, Aeronautical Science
Embry-Riddle Aeronautical University
Bunnell, FL

Roberto Garcia
Assistant Professor, Electrical Engineering Department
University of Texas
Arlington, TX

Cara Gargano
Professor of Dance
Long Island University
C.W. Post Campus
Greenvale, NY

Leonard Garrett
Professor, Computer Information Systems
Temple University
Philadelphia, PA

Patrick Garrett
Chairman, Electrical Engineering Technology
Ohio College of Applied Science
University of Cincinnati
Cincinnati, OH

H. Donald Garrison
Associate Professor
Technology Department
University of Texas
Tyler, TX

William George
Associate Professor of Marketing
College of Commerce and Finance
Villanova University
Villanova, PA

James L. George
Assistant Dean of Business Administration
School of Business Administration
University of Southern California
Los Angeles, CA

Katherine L. George
Senior Editor and Communications Section Manager
American Society of Association Executives
Washington, DC

Robert E. Georges
Associate Dean and Director (retired)
College of Administrative Sciences
The Ohio State University
Columbus, OH

Ronald Gepner
Associate Professor
Mercer County Community College
Trenton, NJ

Victor Gerdes
Academic Vice President
College of Insurance
New York, NY

Michael Gerli
Associate Professor, School of Languages and Linguistics
Georgetown University
Washington, DC

Mattie Giles
Professor, Social Welfare
University of the District of Columbia
Washington, DC

David Giltinan
Professor, Physics Department
Edinboro State College
Edinboro, PA

Dolores C. Gioffre
Assistant Professor
Montclair State College
Upper Montclair, NJ

Alan Gitlin
Assistant Administrator
Westbrook Hospital
Richmond, VA

Helmut Golatz
Head of Department of Labor Studies
Pennsylvania State University
University Park, PA

Murray Goldman
Chairman, Physics Department
Community College of Philadelphia
Philadelphia, PA

William T. Gordon
Instructor, Automotives Department
Daytona Beach Community College
Daytona Beach, FL

S. K. Gosh
Associate Professor, Department of Civil Engineering, Mechanics, and Metallurgy
University of Illinois
Chicago, IL

Anita Gottlieb
National Representative, National Treasury Employees Union
Washington, DC

John W. Gould
Associate Professor of Business Communication
Director of Center for Business Communication
Graduate School of Business
University of Southern California
Los Angeles, CA

Steele Gow
Dean, School of General Studies
University of Pittsburgh
Pittsburgh, PA

Richard Grahn
Manager, Well Control School
Ventura Community College
Ventura, CA

George Graves
Professor, Aerospace Engineering
California State Polytechnic University, Pomona
Pomona, CA

David E. Gray
Vice President for Administration and Staff Coordination
California State University, Long Beach
Long Beach, CA

John Grede
Chicago, IL

William Green
Assistant Professor, Department of Welding Engineering
Ohio State University
Columbus, OH

Robert Gregg
Dean of Technology
Southeastern Illinois College
Harrisburg, IL

Alton L. Greenfield
Specialist, Reading Education
Minnesota Department of Education
St. Paul, MN

Ellihu D. Grossman
Professor, Department of Chemical Engineering
Drexel University
Philadelphia, PA

Albert B. Grubbs, Jr.
Associate Professor, Department of Engineering Technology
Texas A & M University
College Station, TX

Ben Guild
Instructor, Department of Computer Science
Wright State University
Dayton, OH

John D. Guilfoil
Associate Dean, College of Business and Public Administration
New York University
New York, NY

Manak C. Gupta
Professor of Finance
School of Business Administration
Temple University
Philadelphia, PA

Sandra Gustavson
Chair, Department of Insurance, Legal Studies and Real Estate
University of Georgia
Athens, GA

Effie Hacklander
Associate Dean, College of Human Ecology
University of Maryland
College Park, MD

William Haeberle
Professor of Management
Graduate School of Business
Indiana University
Bloomington, IN

Charles Hague
Technical Consultant, Reynolds Metals Company
Richmond, VA

William Halal
Associate Professor of Management
School of Business
The American University
Washington, DC

Nancy Lynch Hale
Chairperson, Business Education Office
Administrative Department
Pace University
New York, NY

Charles P. Hall, Jr.
Professor of Insurance and Risk and of Health Administration
Temple University
Philadelphia, PA

John W. Hall
Professoer and Chairman, Risk Management and Insurance Department
College of Business Administration
Georgia State University
Atlanta, GA

Arthur J. Halligan
Director, Conferences and Institutes Division
University of Maryland, University College
College Park, MD

G. Victor Hallman
Dean, Examinations
American Institute for Property and Liability/Insurance Institute of America
Malvern, PA

Howard B. Hamilton
Professor, Electrical Engineering
University of Pittsburgh
Pittsburgh, PA

Richard J. Hammel
Assistant Professor of Pharmacy Administration
Associacte in Family and Community Medicine
University of Arizona
Tucson, AZ

David W. Hampton
Professor of Management
School of Business Administration
San Diego State University
San Diego, CA

Thomas M. Handler
Business Division
Middlesex County College
Edison, NJ

Lyman L. Handy
Chair, Department of Petroleum Engineering
School of Engineering
University of Southern California
Los Angeles, CA

Eloise Hansen
Executive Head, Medical Assisting Department
De Anza College
Cupertino, CA

Richard Hanson
Professor of Business
Somerset County College
Somerville, NJ

Stanley Hanson
Executive, Mathematics Career Panel
National Security Agency
Fort Meade, MD

Muhammad I. Haque
Associate Professor, Department of
  Civil/Mechanical/Environmental Engineering
The George Washington University
Washington, DC

R. L. Hardy
Civil Engineering Department
Iowa State University
Ames, IA

Robert Haring
Professor, College of Business Administration
University of Arkansas
Fayetteville, AR

John Harrington
Professor of Finance
Seton Hall University
South Orange, NJ

Charles Harper
Assistant Professor of Finance
University of Houston
Houston, TX

Gary Harris
Assistant Professor of Electrical Engineering
Department of Electrical Engineering
Howard University
Washington, DC

Ronald Hart
Director of MIS
Essex County College
Newark, NJ

Richard M. Harter
Assistant Professor of Electronics
Champlain College
Burlington, VT

Adele W. Hartig
Instructor
Bergen Community College
Franklin Lakes, NJ

Barron Harvey
Associate Professor of Business Administration
Howard University
Washington, DC

Mike Harvey
Chairman, Department of Marketing
Edwin L. Cox School of Business
Southern Methodist University
Dallas, TX

Howard Hauck
Adjunct Professor of Data Processing
Passaic County College
Patterson, NJ

Stanley L. Havens
Coordinator, Admissions and Records
Wytheville Community College
Wytheville, VA

Rev. Jack Healy, O. Carm.
Rochester, NY

Sean D. Healy
Professor
Kean College of New Jersey
Union, NJ

Peter D. Hechler
Associate Professor of Management
School of Business and Economics
California State University, Los Angeles
Los Angeles, CA

Russell Heiserman
Professor
School of Technology
Oklahoma State University
Stillwater, OK

Andrew Heitzman
Associate Professor of Special Education
State University College of Arts and SCiences
Geneseo, NY

Gail Henderson
Ohio Department of Education
Division of Vocational Education
Columbus, OH

William G. Heuson
Professor of Finance
School of Business Administration
University of Miami
Coral Gables, FL

Donald Hill
Executive Vice Chancellor Emeritus
City College of Chicago
Carlsbad, CA

John P. Hill
Chairman, Public Services Technologies Division
Thomas Nelson Community College
Hampton, VA

Leo Hilton
Coordinator, Urban Education Graduate Program
William Patterson College
Wayne, NJ

Bob Hinders
Instructor of Electronics
Western Iowa Tech Community College
Sioux City, IA

Rodney J. Hinkle
Academic Dean
Fisher Junior College
Boston, MA

Clete Hinton
Director, Weekend College
William Rainey Harper College
Palatine, IL

Ben A. Hirst, Jr.
Executive Director, Vocational Technical Education Consortium of States (V-TECS)
Commission on Occupational Education Institutions
Atlanta, GA

John F. Hitchcock
Bridgewater, NJ

Mary J. Hitchcock
Professor, Food Science, Nutrition and Food Systems Administration Department
College of Home Economics
University of Tennessee
Knoxville, TN

William J. Hoben
Dean of the School of Business Administration
University of Dayton
Dayton, OH

Alfred E. Hofflander
Professor of Finance and Insurance
Graduate School of Management
University of California at Los Angeles
Los Angeles, CA

Michael Hogue
Assistant Professor of Insurance
Wharton School
University of Pennsylvania
Philadelphia, PA

JoAnn Hoiles
Professor, Business Studies
Somerset County College
Somerville, NJ

Robert Holland
Professor, School of Business Administration
The George Washington University
Washington, DC

Jerry Holman
President, Qualifications Evaluation Systems Corporation
Gaithersburg, MD

Milton C. Holmen
Professor of Managament and Public Administration
School of Business Administration
University of Southern California, Los Angeles
Los Angeles, CA

Robert K. Holz
Chairman, Department of Geography
University of Texas at Austin
Austin, TX

Cecilia Hopkins
Director, Division of Business
College of San Mateo
San Mateo, CA

Henry F. Houser
Assistant Professor and Director, Center for Business and Economic Development
Auburn University
Montgomery, AL

Chester Howarth
Director of Distributive Education and Mid-Management
Florida Junior College at Jacksonville
Jacksonville, FL

Gregg Hricenak
Assistant Academic Dean of Technology
Westmoreland County Community College
Youngwood, PA

George L. Huebner
Professor, Department of Meteorology
Texas A & M University
College Station, TX

Sister Mary Huey
Associate Professor of Education
Fontbonne College
St. Louis, MO

Carlyle Hughes
Chairman, Department of Management
University of the District of Columbia
Washington, DC

M. Gweneth Humphreys
Chairman, Mathematics Department
Randolph Macon Woman's College
Lynchburg, VA

Bobby R. Hunt
Professor of Computer Science
University of Arizona
Tucson, AZ

Emanuel Hurwitz
Assistant Dean, College of Education
University of Illinois—Chicago
Chicago, IL

James F. Huston
Professor, Department of Education
Edinboro State College
Edinboro, PA

Shu-fen C. Hwang
Lecturer, Chinese/Japanese Department
School of Languages & Linguistics
Georgetown University
Washington, DC

John P. Hyde
Curriculum Director
Ottawa Area Vocational Center
Holland, MI

Elmer Hyden
Assistant Dean
Business and Industrial Technology
Tyler Junior College
Tyler, TX

John Hyland
Chairman, Social Sciences Department
LaGuardia Community College
Long Island City, NY

Elizabeth Iannizzi
Professor, Department of Secretarial Science
New York City Community College
Brooklyn, NY

Emilio F. Iodice
Director, Office of Consumer Goods and Services
The Bureau of Industrial Economics
U.S. Department of Commerce
Washington, DC

Betty Ipock
Director, Associate Degree Nursing Program
Missouri Southern State College
Joplin, MO

Eleanor Irwin
Pittsburgh Child Guidance Center
Pittsburgh, PA

J. R. Isaac
Professor, Department of Computer Science and Engineering
Indian Institute of Technology
Powai, Bombay INDIA

Sterling H. Ivison
Assistant Professor of Finance
The American University
Washington, DC

Glen Jackson
Fort Washington, DC

Keith Jackson
Department of Electrical Engineering
Howard University
Washington, DC

David C. Jacobs
Assistant Professor, Department of Management
American University
Washington, DC

Rhoda L. Jacobs
Associate Professor of Business Administration
County College of Morris
Hackettstown, NJ

Robert W. Jefferson
Professor and Chairperson
Department of Marketing and Finance
Western Illinois University
Macomb, IL

Betty L. Jehn
Instructor, Computer Science Department
University of Dayton
Dayton, OH

Lawrence Jehn
Professor, Computer Science Department
University of Dayton
Dayton, OH

James John
Dean of Engineering
University of Massachusetts
Amherst, MA

James Johnson
Assistant Professor, Department of Civil Engineering
Howard University
Washington, DC

Merritt Johnson
Longview, TX

Thomas A. Johnson
Dean of Banking, Finance, and Credit Program
William Rainey Harper College
Palatine, IL

Willie Johnson
Coordinator and Professor, Masters of Public Administration Program
Department of Social and Behavioral Sciences
Savannah State College
Savannah, GA

Webb Jones
Director of Vocational and Technical Education
East Texas State University
Commerce, TX

Ethel K. Jorgensen
Professor of Business Administration and Finance
Department of Business Administration
Los Angeles Valley College
Van Nuys, CA

Rodney Jurist
Department Chairman of Business Education
Rider College
Lawrenceville, NJ

Thomas Jurkanin
Assistant Manager, Illinois Local Government Law Enforcement Officers Training Board
Springfield, IL

Eugene Kadow
Dean, Extended Day and Summer Session
San Bernardino Valley College
San Bernardino, CA

Arthur Kane
Director, Education Department
Department Federation of Government Employees
Washington, DC

Joseph Kanyan
Director and Associate Professor, Department of Music
George Mason University
Fairfax, VA

Charles Kardon
Certified Life University
Dayton, OH

Ralph Katerberg
Associate Professor of Organizational Behavior
University of Cincinnati
Cincinnati, OH

Saul W. Katz
Associate Dean of Continuing Education
Kingsborough Community College
Brooklyn, NY

William Keane
National Director, Continuing Education
Price, Waterhouse, & Co.
New York, NY

Larry G. Keating
Associate Professor and Acting Chairman, Department of Electrical Engineering Technology
Metropolitan State College
Denver, CO

James R. Keiser
Associate Professor of Hotel and Institutional Administration
Assistant Head of Food Service and Housing Administration
Pennsylvania State University
University Park, PA

J. Roland Kelley
Chairman, Business Administration
Tarrant County Junior College System
Northeast Campus
Hurst, TX

Clyde Kesler
Professor of Civil Engineering and of Theoretical and Applied Mechanics
University of Illinois
Urbana, IL

Judy Kieffer
Associate Professor of Nursing
University of Louisville
Louisville, KY

Geoffrey King
Chair, Department of Management
California State University, Fullerton
Fullerton, CA

Jerry King
Dean of Vocational Education
Trinity Valley Community College
Athens, TX

Paul Kinney
Dean, Business School
California State University
Chico, CA

Russell Kline
Professor of Technology
Oklahoma State University
Oklahoma City, OK

Alyce O. Klussman
Financial Service Associates, Inc.
Washington, DC

Ron Knipfer
Dean, Department of Engineering Technology
Sinclair Community College
Dayton, OH

Glenn Knudsvig
Director, English Composition Board and Coordinator of Instructional Development
University of Michigan
Ann Arbor, MI

Bert Kobayashi
Department Chairman, Health and Physical Education
University of California, San Diego
La Jolla, CA

George Kocher
Director, Mining Resource Center
Mt. Carmel, IL

James Koerlin
Dean, School of Telecommunication Management
Golden Gate University
San Francisco, CA

Mary Kohls
Department Chairman of Data Processing
Austin Community College
Austin, TX

Michael Kolesnick
Coordinator of Instruction and Advisement
Community College of Vermont
Rutland, VT

Michael Kolivosky
Dean of Continuing Education
Hillsdale College
Hillsdale, MI

David Korn
Chairman, German-Russian Department
Howard University
Washington, DC

Stanley H. Kossen
Instructor, Business and Economics
Merritt College
Oakland, CA

Joe Kossik
Professor, Business and Governmental Studies
Community College of Denver
Denver, CO

Sanford Kravitz
Professor of Public Affairs
School of Public Affairs and Services
Florida International University
North Miami, FL

Eugene J. Kray
Dean of Community Education
Delaware County Community College
Media, PA

Charles O. Kroncke
Associate Professor of Business
Graduate School of Business
University of Wisconsin—Madison
Madison, WI

Steven Kubriki
Professor
Stockton College
Stockton, NJ

Bernard Kuhn
Assistant Professor of Criminal Justice
University of Baltimore
Baltimore, MD

John Kurutz
U.S. Postal Service Headquarters
Office of Career Development and Training
Washington, DC

Robert Lager
Chairman, Department of Russian
School of Language and Linguistics
Georgetown University
Washington, DC

Marilyn Lair
Associate Professor of Business
Cameron University
Lawton, OK

Betty G. Lall
Director, Union University Urban Affairs Program
Cornell University
New York, NY

David R. Lambert
Associate Professor of Marketing
School of Management
Suffolk University
Boston, MA

Gerald E. Lampe
Professor and Director, Language Studies
SAIS of Johns Hopkins University
Washington, DC

Jon Larkin, Esq.
Adjunct Professor
University of Maryland
College Park, MD

Eric Larson
Elgin Community College
Elgin, IL

Kenneth R. Lauer
Professor of Civil Engineering
University of Notre Dame
Notre Dame, IN

William C. Lauer
Visiting Professor, Business Education Department
Rider College
Lawrenceville, NJ

Arthur C. Laufer
Professor of Management
California State University, Long Beach
Long Beach, CA

Joseph Launie
Department of Finance, Insurance and Real Estate
School of Business
California State University
Northridge, CA

Richard V. Lechowich
Professor and Head, Department of Food Science and Technology
Virginia Polytechnic Institute and State University
Blacksburg, VA

C. W. Lee
Professor, Department of Accounting/Data Processing/Law
School of Management
California State University, Dominguez Hills
Carson, CA

Fred E. Lee
Associate Director, Professional Development Institute
College of Business
North Texas State University
Richardson, TX

Hugh M. Lee
Lecturer, Classics Department
Howard University
Washington, DC

Arch Leean
Chairman, Art Department
St. Olaf College
Northfield, MN

Claudette Lefebre
Associate Professor, Department of Leisure Studies
New York University
New York, NY

William J. Lenicka
Associate Vice President for Academic Affairs
Georgia Institute of Technology
Atlanta, GA

Richard Leininger
Associate Professor, School of Business and Management
Saginaw Valley State College
University Center, MI

Mary M. Leonard
Assistant Professor and Psychologist
University of Maryland
College Park, MD

Thomas Leonard
Chairman, Aeronautics Department
San Jose State University
San Jose, CA

Edward Leven
Acting Dean, Graduate School of Management
Golden Gate University
San Francisco, CA

James S. Levine
Associate Professor of Russian Language and Linguistics
Department of Foreign Languages and Literature
George Mason University
Fairfax, VA

Viola Levitt
Associate Dean, Health Technology Department
Prince Georges Community College
Largo, MD

Tamara Lewis
Professor
Davenport College—South Bend
Granger, IN

Charles Libera
Coordinator, Business and Public Administration
Metropolitan State University
St. Paul, MN

Diana L. Linton
The George Meany Center for Labor Studies
Silver Spring, MD

M. A. Littlejohn
Electrical Engineering Department
North Carolina State University
Raleigh, NC

Anne Lloyd
Professor of Urban Education
Department of Urban Education
Temple University
Philadelphia, PA

Gary Lloyd
Director, Council on Social Work Education
New York, NY

Joseph P. Longo, Jr.
Dean, School of Intelligence Information Systems
Defense Intelligence College
Washington, DC

David Lucht
Vice President, Firepro, Inc.
Wellesley Hills, MA

Norbert Ludkey
Program Coordinator, Computer and Information Science
City College of San Francisco
San Francisco, CA

John A. Ludrick
Assistant to the Dean, School of Education
Southwestern Oklahoma State University
Weatherford, OK

Robert Luke
Visiting Assistant Professor of Adult Education and Human Resources
The George Washington University
Washington, DC

Donald Lundberg
Chairman, Hotel and Restaurant Management
California State Polytechnic University
Pomona, CA

Jack Luskin
Radiological Laboratory
Lowell University
Lowell, MA

Barnaby McAusian
Assistant Professor
Burlington County College
Pemberton, NJ

Neal McBryde
Dean, Bee County College
Beeville, TX

Herbert E. McCartney
Automotive Program Head
Northern Virginia Community College
Alexandria, VA

Michael McCaskey
School of Languages and Linguistics
Georgetown University
Washington, DC

Thomas J. McCoy
Business Division
Middlesex County College
Edison, NJ

Phyllis McCracken
Coordinator of Continuing Education
Erie Institute for Nursing
Villa Maria College
Erie, PA

Kenneth McCreedy
Assistant Professor, School of Community Services
Department of Administration of Justice and Public Safety
Virginia Commonwealth University
Richmond, VA

Keith MacDonald
Associate Professor
Ferris State College
Big Rapids, MI

William E. McDonald
Arts Advisor, ESAA
U.S. Office of Education
Washington, DC

Garnett McDonough
Chair, Law, Legal Assisting and Real Estate Department
Sinclair Community College
Dayton, OH

James A. McDonough
Professor of Civil Engineering
Virginia Military Institute
Lexington, VA

Paul E. McDuffee
Director, Airline Flight Operators Certificate Program
Embry-Riddle Aeronautical University
Bunnell, FL

Phil McGee
Director, Center for Leadership Education and Development
Greenville Technical College
Greenville, SC

Robert McLeod
National Training Manager
National Fire Sprinkler Association
Sarasota, FL

Donald Ian MacInnes
Director, Teacher Education Laboratory
Presbyterian School of Christian Education
Richmond, VA

Robert McIntosh
Professor of Tourism
School of Hotel, Restaurant and Institutional Management
College of Business
Michigan State University
East Lansing, MI

Ron McKeen
Professor, Department of Mathematics
Virginia Technical University
Dulles International Airport
Falls Church, VA

John R. MacKenzie
Associate Professor and Director of Labor Studies Center
University of the District of Columbia
Washington, DC

Archibald J. McKillop
Instructor of Business Management Science
Mount San Antonio College
Walnut, CA

George W. McKinney, Jr.
Virginia Bankers' Professor of Bank Management
McIntire School of Commerce
University of Virginia
Charlottesville, VA

Miles MacMahon
Professor of Physics and Mathematics
Essex County College
Newark, NJ

Dale McNabb
Associate Director for Small Businesses
Air Force Systems Command
Andrews Air Force Base
Washington, DC

Dorothy McNutt
Chairman, Business Division
College of the Mainland
Texas City, TX

Robert McQuitty
Lecturer
Management Department
Webster College
St. Louis, MO

Robert McVicker
Director, Cooperative Education
University of Lowell
Lowell, MA

John F. Magnotti, Jr.
Director, Procurement Management Program
American University
Washington, DC

William J. Mahon
Editor & Publisher
The Hearing Journal
Maynard, MA

Patricia Malone
Assistant Professor, Business Department
Rider College
Lawrenceville, NJ

Anthony Maltese
Chairman, Department of Communications
William Patterson College
Wayne, NJ

Anthony Mann
Chairman and Professor, Computer Information Systems
Sinclair Community College
Dayton, OH

William March
Dean, College of Graduate Studies
Embry-Riddle Aeronautical University
Bunnell, FL

Julius Mariasis
Associate Professor, Business Administration Division
Massachusetts Bay Community College
Wellesley Hills, MA

Leonard Marks
Instructor, Fire Science Department
Santa Ana College
Santa Ana, CA

Joseph H. Martin
President, Martin & Benner Appraisal Co.
Lawrenceville, NJ

William R. Martin
Professor of Education
Department of Education
George Mason University
Fairfax, VA

Santo Marzullo
Chairman, Department of Technical Teacher Training
Washington Technical Institute
Washington, DC

Rocci S. Mastroberti
Chairman, Business Division
Anne Arundel Community College
Arnold, MD

William J. Mathias
Dean, College of Criminal Justice
University of South Carolina
Columbia, SC

Charles Maxey
Assistant Professor, Department of Organizational Behavior
School of Business Administration
University of Southern California
Los Angeles, CA

Lee Maxwell
Professor, Electrical Engineering
Colorado State University
Fort Collins, CO

Paul D. Maxwell
Assistant Dean and Director of Business Administration
Northeastern University
Boston, MA

Brigitte May
Professor, Department of Modern Language and Linguistics
University of Maryland—Baltimore County
Catonsville, MD

John Mayer
Associate Professor of Nuclear Engineering
Worcester Polytechnic Institute
Worcester, MA

Patricia Mayer
Associate Professor, Dance Department
Rutgers University
Douglas Campus
New Brunswick, NJ

Vadim Medish
Professor, Department of Language and Foreign Studies
The American University
Washington, DC

Charles Medler
Chair, Department of Electrical Engineering
California State University, Fullerton
Fullerton, CA

Robert Mehman
Newton, PA

William Melnicoe
Chair, Department of Criminal Justice
California State University, Sacramento
Sacramento, CA

Arnold Meltzer
Professor of Electrical Engineering
George Washington University
Washington, DC

Steven J. Meltzer
Chief, Management Training Branch
Internal Revenue Service
Washington, DC

Sidney Messer
Professor, Engineering Department
City College of San Francisco
San Francisco, CA

Paul Mercado
Chairman, Drafting and Design Department
Pennsylvania Institute of Technology
Upper Darby, PA

John Mercier
Professor, Department of Communications
Glassboro State College
Glassboro, NJ

Richard L. Meyer
Associate Professor of Finance
College of Business Administration
University of South Florida
Tampa, FL

David Michaels
Professor of Management and Law
Northern Virginia Community College
Annandale, VA

Joseph Migliaccio
Statistician, U.S. Department of Treasury
Washington, DC
Visiting Lecturer in Mathematics
Northern Virginia Community College
Alexandria, VA

Wilbert L. Miles
Managerial Consultant & Psychotherapist
University of Colorado
Denver, CO

Lawrence F. Miller
Associate Professor of Nuclear Engineering
Department of Nuclear Engineering
University of Tennessee
Knoxville, TN

Vergil V. Miller
Dean, College of Business Administration
Oklahoma State University
Stillwater, OK

Jake Milliones
Assistant Professor, Department of Psychology
University of Pittsburgh
Pittsburgh, PA

Sam Mills
Assistant Director of Continuing Education
J. Sargeant Reynolds Community College
Richmond, VA

Stuart Milner
Assistant Professor of Educational Technology
School of Education
Catholic University of America
Washington, DC

Robert Minter
Chairman, Division of Administrative Services
University of Denver
Denver, CO

Herbert Mitchell
Dean, College of Business
Virginia Polytechnic Institute and State University
Blacksburg, VA

Nancy Mitry
Assistant Professor, Department of Management
School of Business
San Diego State University
San Diego, CA

Jan L. Mize
Director, Computer Science Department
Georgia State University
Atlanta, GA

Nancy Moeller
Associate Dean
Hiram Weekend College
Hiram, OH

Francis H. Moffitt
Professor of Photogrammetry
Civil Engineering Department
University of California
Berkeley, CA

Richard A. Molenaar
Assistant Professor
University of North Dakota
Grand Forks, ND

Jack Monks
Associate Professor, Technology Department
McNeese State University
Lake Charles, LA

Jose G. Montero
Associate Professor
Northern Virginia Community College
Annandale, VA

A. Thompson Montgomery
Associate Professor of Accounting
School of Business
San Francisco State University
San Francisco, CA

James M. Moore
Professor, Department of Industrial Engineering and
   Operations Research
Virginia Polytechnic Institute and State University
Blacksburg, VA

R. Kenneth Moore
Lecturer, Business Administration
School of Business and Public Administration
California State University
Sacramento, CA

Harry More
Professor, Adminstration of Justice
San Jose State University
San Jose, CA

Russell Morey
Chairperson, Management Department
Western Illinois University
Macomb, IL

Jim Lee Morgan
Professor of Management
West Los Angeles College
Culver City, CA

W. J. Morgan, Jr.
Professor, School of Hotel, Food and Travel
Florida International University
Miami, FL

Joseph M. Moricz
Dean of Business Programs
Robert Morris College
Coraopolis, PA

Richard Mortimer
Chairman, Department of Mechanical Engineering
Drexel University
Philadelphia, PA

Joanne Moncrief
Chief Copy Editor
National Journal Magazine
Washington, DC

George Mostoller
Director of Engineering Technology
University of Pittsburgh—Johnstown
Johnstown, PA

Homer J. Mottice
Professor, Department of Accounting
Florida State University
Tallahassee, FL

Eiko Muira
Professor, HEALL Department
University of Maryland
College Park, MD

Marie Mullaney
Livingston, NJ

Donald J. Mullineaux
Chairholder, DuPont Endowed Chair in Banking and
 Financial Services
College of Business and Economics
University of Kentucky
Lexington, KY

James Murphy
Riverdale, MD

Richard J. Murphy
Professor of Mechanical Engineering
Northeastern University
Boston, MA

Richard A. Myren
Dean and Professor, School of Justice
The American University
Washington, DC

Sumiko Nagasawa
Visiting Instructor, Chinese/Japanese Department
Georgetown University
Washington, DC

John Nagohosian
Director, Division of Industrial Technology
Henry Ford Community College
Dearborn, MI

Anthony Natale
Trenton State College
Trenton, NJ

Prabhaker Nayak
William Paterson College
Wayne, NJ

Richard G. Nehrbass
Assitant Professor, Management and Marketing
School of Management
California State University, Dominguez Hills
Carson, CA

Edward A. Nelson
Professor, Department of Finance and Business Law
School of Business and Economics
California State University
Los Angeles, CA

Richard S. Nelson
Professor of Business
San Francisco State University
San Francisco, CA

Charles P. Nemeth
Professor
Wilmington, DE

Howard Newhouse
Vice President for Public Relations
The Berkeley Schools
New York, NY

Joe M. Newton
Coordinator, Management Studies
Bakersfield College
Bakersfield, CA

Jens C. Nielsen
Coordinator, School Hospitality Industry Administration
Triton College
River Grove, IL

Thomas Niles
Director of Monmouth Adult Education Commission
Monmouth College
West Long Branch, NJ

Gerard Nistal
Professor and Chair, Division of Business and Economics
Holy Cross College
New Orleans, LA

David Novicki
Division Director
Research Applications and Educational Services
Michigan State University
East Lansing, MI

James Null
Dean, College of Arts and Sciences and Professor of Public
 Administration
Graduate School of Public Affairs
University of Colorado at Colorado Springs
Colorado Springs, CO

Michael O'Brien
Chairman, Marine Science
Thomas Nelson Community College
Hampton, VA

Rev. Richard O'Brien
Jesuit Community
Georgetown University
Washington, DC

Charles E. O'Rear
Professor and Chairman, Department of Forensics
The George Washington University
Graduate School of Arts and Sciences
Washington, DC

Frank O'Rourke
Sicklerville, NJ

Robert Oberg
Department of Computer Sciences
Framingham State College
Framingham, MA

Herbert Oestreich
School of Business
San Jose State University
San Jose, CA

Martin Oettinger
Associate Professor, Department of Economics
University of California, Davis
Davis, CA

Van Norwood Oliphant
Professor of Management
Memphis State University
Memphis, TN

Harold Oliver
Educational Advisor
U.S. Army Ordnance Center and School
Aberdeen Proving Ground, MD

Alan Oppenheim
Professor and Director of M.B.A. Program
Montclair State College
Upper Montclair, NJ

Rosa Oppenheim
Associate Professor, Quantitative Methods
Graduate School of Management
Rutgers University
New Brunswick, NJ

Howard P. Osborn
Director, Training and Development
Maryland Casualty Company
Baltimore, MD

Rose-Marie G. Oster
Professor, Germanic and Slavic Languages and Literature
University of Maryland
College Park, MD

Leo B. Osterhaus
Dean, Center of Business Administration
St. Edwards University
Austin, TX

Dula Pacquiao
Edison, NJ

Jim Painter
Durham Technical Institute
Durham, NC

Ray Palmer
Vice Chairman, Electrical Engineering and Computer Science
Milwaukee School of Engineering
Milwaukee, WI

Yvonne Panaro
Professor, Department of Italian
Georgetown University
Washington, DC

Frank Paone
President, Detroit College of Business
Dearborn, MI

Salvatore Paratore
Associate Professor, Department of Education
The George Washington University
Washington, DC

Kenneth M. Parzych
Professor and Chairman, Department of Economics and Management Science
Eastern Connecticut State College
Willimantic, CT

Phillip Pastras
Professor of English
Middlesex County College
Edison, NJ

James Patterson
Consultant, Marketing and Communication
Tucson, AZ

Walter Pauk
Director, Reading-Study Center, and Professor of Education
Cornell University
Ithaca, NY

John Paulson
Arizona Division of Emergency Services
Phoenix, AZ

James Pellegrino
Associate Professor of Vocational Education
School of Education
University of Pittsburgh
Pittsburgh, PA

John L. Penkala
State College, PA

Lawrence Hobdy Perkins
Director, Vocational Research and Services
University of Western Florida
Pensacola, FL

David A. Perreault
Coordinator of Computer Engineering
School of Engineering
Boston University
Boston, MA

Louis Peterka
Santa Rosa, CA

Frances Peterson
Chair, Business Department
Rio Hondo College
Whittier, CA

James Phelps
Professor of Nuclear Engineering
University of Lowell
Lowell, MA

A. J. Phillips
NJATC
Lanham, MD

Kenneth Phillips
Chair, Department of Industrial Studies
California State University—Los Angeles
Los Angeles, CA

Lawrence C. Phillips
Professor of Accounting
Case Western Reserve University
School of Management
Cleveland, OH

John E. Phipps
Associate Chairman, Flight Technology Department
Embry-Riddle Aeronautical University
Daytona Beach, FL

Bruce Piringer
Director, Fire and Rescue Training
University of Missouri
Columbia, MO

Rosemary Pittman
Director, Nurse Practioner Program
School of Nursing
University of Washington
Seattle, WA

Chester C. Platt
Associate Dean for Area 8
Coastine Community College
Mountain Valley, CA

Robert Pleasure
Executive Director, The George Meany Center for Labor Studies
Silver Spring, MD

Mark Plovick
Associate Dean of the Graduate School of Management
Clark University
Worcester, MA

Richard Podlesnik
School of Business Administration
Fort Lewis College
Durango, CO

Alan Pollock
Instructor of Insurance
Business Division
Long Beach City College
Long Beach, CA

Richard Pontinen
Chairman and Professor of Physics
Hamline University
St. Paul, MN

Thomas Poppendieck
Director of Academic Computing
Hamline University
St. Paul, MN

Samuel I. Porrath
Chairman of the Institute of Transportation, Travel and Tourism
Niagara University
Niagara, NY

Harry Powell
Instructor, Department of Criminal Justice
Sierra College
Rocklin, CA

Walter M. Presz, Jr.
Professor (M.E.)
Western New England College
Springfield, MA

Stanley D. Price
Dean, Graduate School of Banking and Finance
Golden Gate University
San Francisco, CA

Paul W. Prins
Associate Dean, School of Theology
Ferris State University
Big Rapids, MI

Preston Probasco
Acting Director, Cybernetic Systems
School of Social Science
San Jose State University
San Jose, CA

Jose Quevedo
Miami, FL

Roseann M. Quinn
Professor
Chestnut Hill College
Philadelphia, PA

Samuel Rabinowitz
Rutgers University
Camden, NJ

Ronald Racster
Professor, College of Administrative Science
Ohio State University
Columbus, OH

Denis T. Raihall
Professor of Administration
Drexel University
Philadelphia, PA

William L. Raley
Director, Adult Vocational Education
College of the Mainland
Texas City, TX

Felicenne Ramey
Assistant Professor of Business Law
School Business and Public Administration
California State University
Sacramento, CA

Wayne Ramp
Professor, Department of Vocational Education Studies
Southern Illinois University
Carbondale, IL

S. Robert Ramsey
Associate Professor, Hebrew & East Asian Languages & Literatures
University of Maryland
College Park, MD

Richard L. Rath
Senior Editor, Yachting Magazine
Cos Cob, CT

Gayle Rayburn
Professor of Accounting
College of Business Administration
Memphis State University
Memphis, TN

Irving S. Reed
Professor of Electrical Engineering
University of Southern California
Los Angeles, CA

Lary Reed
Executive Vice President
Navarro College
Corsicana, TX

Robert Reed
Director, Emergency Administration and Planning Institute
University of North Texas
Denton, TX

Howard Reichbart
Associate Professor, Hotel, Restaurant, and Institutional Management
Northern Virginia Community College
Annandale, VA

Wallace Reiff
Associate Dean and Professor of Finance
College of Business Administration
Florida Technical College
Orlando, FL

Mary E. Reilly
Chair, Secretarial Science Department
Middlesex County College
Edison, NJ

Benjamin Resnik
Academic Advisement Coordinator
Communications Department
Glassboro State College
Glassboro, NJ

Charles R. Rhyner
Professor of Physics
University of Wisconsin
Green Bay, WI

Harriett Rice
Associate Professor, Business Administration Department
Los Angeles City College
Los Angeles, CA

George Rich
Professor of Physical Education
Department of Physical Education
California State University—Northridge
Northridge, CA

Marc Riedel
Research Associate, Center for Studies in Criminology and Criminal Law
University of Pennsylvania
Philadelphia, PA

Albert D. Robinson
Coordinator, Electrical/Electronic Department
Washtenaw Community College
Ann Arbor, MI

Gerald D. Robinson
Professor of Management and Supervision
Macomb Community College
Warren, MI

Gordon Robinson
Professor, Nuclear Engineering Department
Pennsylvania State University
University Park, PA

Yvonne Rodgers
C.A. Fredd State Technical College
Tuscaloosa, AL

Stewart Rodnon
Professor of English
Rider College
Lawrenceville, NJ

Lloyd Rogers
Assistant Dean of Business
Sacramento City College
Sacramento, CA

Johnson Roney III
Director, Registrations and Student Records
Mercer County Community College
Trenton, NJ

James F. Rooney
Professor, School of Social Service
Catholic University
Washington, DC

Gene Roth
Professor, College of Education
Idaho State University
Pocatello, ID

Charlene Rothkopf
Marriott Corporation
Washington, DC

John Rouselle
Purdue University
West Lafayette, IN

Patrick C. Runde
Associate Dean, School of Allied Health
University of Wisconsin
Madison, WI

John E. Ryan
Associate Dean, Academic Affairs
McGeorge School of Law
Sacramento, CA

Steve Saffron
Director of American Indian Program
Scottsdale Community College
Scottsdale, AZ

Charles Sahrbeck
Director of Management Training (retired)
General Motors Corporation
Flint, MI

Ann Barbara Sakurai
Chair and Professor, Math and Computer Science
  Department
Webster University
St. Louis, MO

Octavio Salati
Professor of Electrical Engineering and Science
College of Engineering and Applied Science
Moore School of Electrical Engineering
University of Pennsylvania
Philadelphia, PA

Tom S. Sale
Chairman, Department of Finance and Economics
Louisiana Tech University
Ruston, LA

Charles Sanders
Professor of Management
School of Business and Public Management
The University of the District of Columbia
Washington, DC

Richard Sandhusen
Assistant Professor, Marketing Department
Rider College
Lawrenceville, NJ

Mel Sandler
Associate Professor, Whittemore School of Business and
  Economics
University of New Hampshire
Durham, NH

Rebecca J. Sartin
Health Technologies
Pima Community College
Tucson, AZ

Annabelle Sartore
Chair, Department of Management
School of Business
California State University, Long Beach
Long Beach, CA

Henry Sauer
Program Manager, Biomedical and Environmental Special
  Programs
Chemical Manufacturers Association
Washington, DC

Lyman Savory
Instructor, Wellsville School of Vocational Studies
Alfred Agricultural Technical College (SUNY)
Wellsville, NY

Charles R. Sayre
Assistant Director, Law Enforcement Training
Eastern Kentucky University
Richmond, KY

Ralph M. Scarrow
Professor, California State Polytechnic Institute—Pomona
Pomona, CA

Susan Schaefer
Associate Professor, Management Science Department
California State University
Hayward, CA

Daniel J. Schleef
Professor of Mechanical Engineering
Department of Mechanical and Industrial Engineering
University of Cincinnati
Cincinnati, OH

Donald Schmidt
Professor
Hudson Valley Community College
Troy, NY

William Schmitt
Temple University
Philadelphia, PA

Penelope Scambly Schott
Assistant Professor of English
Somerset County College
Somerville, NJ

Stephen Schneider
Assistant Dean of Instruction
Suffolk County Community College
Brentwood, NY

Charles Schuler
Professor, Industrial Arts Department
California State College
California, PA

Helene Schwarberg
Assistant Department Head
University of Cincinnati
Cincinnati, OH

Robert Scully
Professor of Business
Burlington County College
Pemberton, NJ

John H. Seabrook
Westfield, NJ

Jennie Seaton
Virginia Commonwealth University
Richmond, VA

Gabriella Sechi
Assistant Professor, Department of Engineering Technology
Trenton State College
Trenton, NJ

Ronald L. Seeber
Associate Dean, New York State School of Industrial and Labor Relations
Cornell University
Ithaca, NY

Morley Segal
Professor, School of Government and Public Administration
The American University
Washington, DC

Barry Seldes
Trenton, NJ

Genevieve Semple
Belmar, NJ

Walter Senska
Apprenticeship Coordinator
Department of Applied Technology
Macomb Community College
Warren, MI

Mohammed Sesay
Professor, Department of Mathematics
University of the District of Columbia
Washington, DC

Robert Settlage
Director of Maternity and Infant Care Project
Central Health Services Region
County of Los Angeles
University of Southern California
Los Angeles, CA

John Shaffer
Director of Aviation
University of Albuquerque
Albuquerque, NM

Hugh M. Shane
Chairperson, Department of Management
Western Illinois University
Macomb, IL

Bill Shannon, Esq.
Professor of Paralegal Studies
Northern Virginia Community College
Alexandria, VA

Harry Sheather
Professor
Union County College
Cranford, NJ

Larry Short
Director of Graduate Program
Management Department
Drake University
Des Moines, IA

Phillip Shrotman
District Coordinator for Cooperative Work Experience Education
Office of Cooperative Education
Long Beach City College
Long Beach, CA

Milton Shuch
Associate Professor and Chairman
Department of Management and Director of Price Retailing Program
Simmons College
Boston, MA

S. Cabell Shull
Chairman, Department of Economics and Finance
University of Mississippi
University, MS

Louis Shuster
Professor of Management
School of Business and Public Administration
California State College
Bakersfield, CA

Jerrold Siegel
Professor, Department of Math and Computer Science
University of Missouri—St. Louis
St. Louis, MO

Ned J. Sifferlen
Vice President for Instruction
Sinclair Community College
Dayton, OH

Kemp Sigmon
Dean, Industrial Division
Spartanburg Technical College
Spartanburg, SC

Eugene Simko
School of Business Administration
Monmouth College
West Long Branch, NJ

Gale Simons
Professor, Department of Nuclear Engineering
Kansas State University
Manhattan, KS

Don Simonson
Oklahoma Bankers' Professor of Finance
University of Oklahoma
Norman, OK

Richard W. Simpson
Director, Bureau of Regulations, Rates and Policies
Pennsylvania Insurance Department
Harrisburg, PA

John H. Sims
Chairman, Management Science Department
California State University
Hayward, CA

Delavan Sipes
Associate Professor of Electronics
Biomedical Engineering Technology Coordinator
Schoolcraft College
Livonia, MI

Gunnil Sjoberg
Senior Lecturer
University of Pennsylvania—Philadelphia
Philadelphia, PA

Robert Small
Fairleigh Dickinson University
Rutherford, NJ

James B. Smathers
Professor, Department of Radiation and Oncology
University of California
Los Angeles, CA

Wayne Smeltz
Trenton, NJ

Charles R. Smith
Associate Professor of Finance
School of Business
San Diego State University
San Diego, CA

Paul L. Smith, Jr.
Research Professor of Meteorology and Electrical Engineering
Institute of Atmospheric Sciences
South Dakota School of Mines and Technology
Rapid City, SD

Robert J. Smith
Professor, Management Department
School of Business Administration
California State University, Long Beach
Long Beach, CA

Walter S. Smith
Department Head, Automotive Center
Oklahoma State Technical Institute
Okmulgee, OK

Ed Solinski
Computer Technological Department
Indiana University—Purdue
Indianapolis, IN

Wilbur H. Somerton
Department of Mechanical Engineering
College of Engineering
University of California
Berkeley, CA

Judy Sparks
Department of Management and Organization
School of Business Administration
University of Southern California
Los Angeles, CA

Patrick Michael Sparks
Assistant Professor, Business Administration
School of Business and Public Administration
California State University
Sacramento, CA

Michael G. Spencer
Associate Professor, Department of Electrical Engineering
Howard University
Washington, DC

Robert G. Sperring
Director, Company Training
Eastman Kodak Company
Rochester, NY

Terry Spradley
Professor of Technology
Technical Education Division
Cameron University
Lawton, OK

Langley A. Spurlock
Director of Biomedical and Environmental Special Programs
Chemical Manufacturers Association
Washington, DC

Robert Stafford
Professor, Computer Information Systems Department
Temple University
Philadelphia, PA

Lawrence R. Stapel
Instructor, Fullerton College
Fullerton, CA
Employment Manager
Beckman Instruments

James Starky
Chairman of Economics Department
University of Rhode Island
Kingston, RI

Henry H. Stick
Associate Dean & Director of the School of Business
  Administration
University of Dayton
Dayton, OH

James Stinchcomb
Chairman, Department of Administration of Justice and
  Public Safety
Virginia Commonwealth University
Richmond, VA

John W. Stockman
Professor, Department of Organizational Behavior and
  Environment
California State University
Sacramento, CA

James B. Stone
Chairman, Division of Specialized Allied Studies
Mining Occupational and Transportation Safety Department
Marshall University
Huntington, WV

Stanton Stone
Rockford Police Department
Rockford, IL

Sue Strasinger
Health and Public Service Department
Northern Virginia Community College
Alexandria, VA

John C. Strayer
Director, Pennsylvania Institute of Technology
Upper Darby, PA

George B. Strother
School of Business
University of Wisconsin—Madison
Madison, WI

Carolyn Stumpf
Director, Cooperative Education in Business
Georgian Court College
Lakewood, NJ

Allen Stubberud
Associate Dean, School of Engineering
University of California, Irvine
Irvine, CA

Bill Studyvin
Assistant Professor, Department of Technology
Pittsburg State University
Pittsburg, KS

Jerry Suhodolsky
Field Engineer
Tektronix, Inc.
Cleveland, OH

Thomas F. Sullivan
Professor, Business Department
Fisher College
Boston, MA

Paul Sultan
Professor of Economics and Management
Southern Illinois University
Edwardsville, IL

Vaidy Sunderam
Professor, Department of Mathematics & Computer Science
Emory University
Atlanta, GA

Tom Sutherland
Professor of Technology
Cameron University
Lawson, OK

Carl F. Swanson
Instructor/Master Mariner
Marine Science Department
Southern Maine Vocational Technical Institute
South Portland, ME

William Swyter
Dean of the Faculty
Montgomery College
Rockville, MD

Jesse Symms
Chairman, Electronics Department
College of the Mainland
Texas City, TX

Richard Szukalski
Chairperson, Business Department
City College of San Francisco
San Francisco, CA

Tom Tahnk
Instructor
Metropolitan State University
St. Paul, MN

Connie Talbert
Dean, College of Business
Arkansas State University
State University, AR

Edward Tangman
Chairman, Engineering Technologies Division
Northern Virginia Community College
Annandale, VA

Charlotte M. Tatro
Director, Institute for Women's Research and Studies
Florida International University
Miami, FL

Estelle Taylor
Chairperson, English Department
Howard University
Washington, DC

Harvey Taylor
Attorney
Washington, DC

James C. Taylor
Dean, School of Hotel and Restaurant Management
University of Houston
Houston, TX

Gerald Thebeau
Union Central Life Insurance and Adjunct Professor
Webster College
St. Louis, MO

Barbara N. Thomas
Director, Washington School for Secretaries
Washington, DC

Bonnie Thomas-Moore
Assistant Professor and Coordinator
Food Service Management Program
University of Akron
Akron, OH

B. J. Thompson
Professor, Industrial Studies
(Fire Protection Administration)
San Diego State University
San Diego, CA
California State University
Los Angeles, CA
Fire Chief, City of Santa Ana

Duly H. Thompson
Associate Professor and Director of Law Enforcement
Anne Arundel Community College
Arnold, MD

A. L. Thurman
Associate Chairman, Department of American Thought and Language
University College
Michigan State University
East Lansing, MI

Miller Tiger
Training Specialist
Oklahoma State Department of Vocational-Technical Education
Stillwater, OK

Terry J. Tinney
Associate Professor of Marketing
St. Louis University
Glen Carbon, IL

Edward S. Todd
Office of the Secretary of Defense
Internal Security Affairs
Washington, DC

Ralph Todd
Chairman, Management Education Department
American River College
Sacramento, CA

Leon J. Tolle, Jr.
Professor, School of Business
Our Lady of the Lake University
San Antonio, TX

W. Sanford Topham
Associate Professor and Clinical Engineering Administrator
Department of Biomedical Engineering
Case Western Reserve University
Cleveland, OH

Joseph L. Tramutola, Jr.
Mendham, NJ

Konstantinos Triantis
Assistant Professor, Department of Industrial Engineering and Operations Research
Northern Virginia Graduate Center
Virginia Tech
Falls Church, VA

Stuart J. Travis
Associate Professor and Head, Computer Information Systems Department
School of Business
Ferris State College
Big Rapids, MI

Edward Troicke
Associate Professor of Electrical Engineering
Broome County Community College
McDonough, NY

Donald Trucksess
Adjunct Instructor
Somerset County College
Somerville, NJ

Franklin D. Trumpy
Group Leader, Math/Science/Engineering
Des Moines Area Community College
Ankeny, IA

Norma Jean Tucker
Dean of Instruction
Merritt College
Oakland, CA

Woodie L. Tucker
Professor of Business Education and Office Administration
Virginia Commonwealth University
Richmond, VA

Robert E. Tumelty
Professor and Director, Health Care Administration Program
California State University
Long Beach, CA

Frederick Turner
Professor of Communications
Rider College
Lawrenceville, NJ

Hester Turner
Attorney
New York, NY

Robert Turrill
Assistant Dean, Graduate Programs
School of Business
University of Southern California
Los Angeles, CA

Charles E. Tychsen
Professor, Business Division
Northern Virginia Community College
Annandale, VA

David Tyrell
Middlesex Community College
Edison, NJ

Don Uhlenberg
Professor
University of North Dakota
Grand Forks, ND

Joseph G. Uy
Lecturer, Department of Engineering and Engineering Technology
Montgomery College
Rockville, MD

Charles Vanderbosh
Director of Education and Training
Baltimore City Police Department
Baltimore, MD

Jack Vernon
Professor of Otalaryngology
Oregon Health Sciences University
Portland, OR

Paul D. VonHoltz
Assistant Professor of Industrial Education and Technology
Glassboro State College
Glassboro, NJ

L. W. VonTersch
Dean, College of Engineering
Michigan State University
East Lansing, MI

Joseph A. Wagner
Associate Professor, North Central Technical College
Ohio State University
Mansville, OH

Samuel Wagner
Associate Dean, School of Business Administration
Temple University
Philadelphia, PA

Arthur Wainer
Professor of Chemistry and Nutrition
Department of Chemistry
Edinboro State College
Edinboro, PA

Henry Walbasser
Professor of Education and Director of Graduate Studies
University of Maryland
Baltimore County Campus
Baltimore, MD

Harold R. Walt
Dean of College of Business and Professor of Management
University of San Francisco
San Francisco, CA

Richard Walls
Professor of Educational Psychology and Rehabilitation
West Virginia University
Morgantown, WV

David Ward
Associate Professor of Finance
College of Business Administration
University of Wisconsin
Oshkosh, WI

Dean Warner
Associate Professor, Business Education
Rider College
Lawrenceville, NJ

Craig Washington
Chairman, Associate Professor
Automotive Engineering and Public Service Division
Northern Virginia Community College
Alexandria, VA

Richard Waters
Coordinator, Hotel, Restaurant Management and Food Serives
Long Beach City College
Long Beach, CA

Jack Waxman
Chairman, Business Education Division
Diablo Valley College
Pleasant Hill, CA

K. Mark Weaver
Associate Professor of Management
The University of Alabama
University, AL

Ian Webb
Instructor in Electronics
West Valley College
Saratoga, CA

Robert S. Weinbeck
Assistant Professor of Meteorology
Department of Earth Sciences
State University of New York—Brockport
Brockport, NY

Howard Weiner
Assistant Professor, Data Processing, Business Division
Northern Virginia Community College
Annandale, VA

Steven Weisbart
Assistant Professor, Department of Insurance
Georgia State University
Atlanta, GA

Marvin Weiss
Dean of Business
New York Institute of Technology
New York, NY

Inge B. Wekerle
Department of Foreign Language & Literature
George Mason University
Fairfax, VA

Anne Weldon
School of Language Studies
Foreign Service Institute
State Department
Washington, DC

David Y. Wen
Professor and Chairman, Computer Science Department
Diablo Valley College
Pleasant Hill, CA

Terrence W. West
Professor, County College of Morris
Hackettstown, NJ

Glenn Whan
Professor of Chemical and Nuclear Engineering
University of New Mexico
Albuquerque, NM

Robert A. Wheeler
Director, Associate Degree Program
Dickinson State College
Dickinson, ND

C. Eugene White
Associate Professor, School of Pharmacy
VCU/MCV Station
Richmond, VA

Richmond White
Chairman, Division of Engineering, Physics, Mathematics, and Technology
Texarkana Community College
Texarkana, TX

Gerald H. Whitlock
Professor of Management and Psychology
University of Tennessee
Knoxville, TN

William E. Whitsell
Professor, Department of Economics
Franklin and Marshall University
Lancaster, PA

Gary Wilcox
Dean of Arts and Sciences
Des Moines Area Community College
Ankeny, IA

Elsie Wilkens
Assistant Director of Education
St. John's Mercy Medical Center
St. Louis, MO

Gene Williams
Assistant Vice Chancellor for Administration and Finance
University of Kentucky
Lexington, KY

James F. Williams
Associate Professor, Computer Science Department
Montgomery Community College
Rockville, MD

Ronald J. Williams
Professor, Del Mar College
Corpus Christie, TX

Hugh H. Wilson
Professor, Department of Ceramic Engineering
Clemson University
Clemson, SC

Kennedy Wilson
Former Professor of Commerce
University of Virginia
Falls Church, VA

Robert R. Wilson
Assistant Director of Extension Service and Director of the Department of Independent Study
University of Michigan
Ann Arbor, MI

Wayne Wilson
Professor of Management
South Oklahoma City Junior College
Oklahoma City, OK

Richard Winchell
Center for Public Affairs
Arizona State University
Tempe, AZ

Leonard Winner
Instructor, Elgin Community College
Elgin, IL

Marvin Wittrock
Department Head, Central Piedmont Community College
Charlotte, NC

F. Stanton Woerth
Director, Industrial Relations
College of Engineering Technology
Temple University
Philadelphia, PA

John Wolfe
Assistant Dean of Continuing Education
University of Kansas—Lawrence
Lawrence, KS

Ronald Wolfe
School of Languages and Linguistics
Georgetown University
Washington, DC

Glenn L. Wood
Professor of Finance
School of Business and Public Administration
California State College
Bakersfield, CA

Wendell Wood
Manager, Management Development and Training Department
Agriculture Equipment Group
International Harvester Company
Chicago, IL

Richard Woodring
Dean, College of Engineering
Drexel University
Philadelphia, PA

Nell Woodward
Associate Professor, Food Services
Division of Consumer and Health Services
Orange Coast College
Costa Mesa, CA

Ronald Woolf
Professor of Management
College of Business Administration
University of Oklahoma
Norman, OK

George B. Wright
Assistant Professor, Department of Engineering Technology
Texas A & M University
College Station, TX

John D. Wright
Associate Professor, Engineering Technology
Frederick Community College
Frederick, MD

Ray Wright
Chairman, Computer Science Department
Roosevelt University
Chicago, IL

Sally Jo Wright
Chair, Graduate Business Administration Program
Sangamon State University
Springfield, IL

Albert Wrisley
Hotel, Restaurant and Travel Administration
University of Massachusetts
Amherst, MA

Emily Wughalter
Professor, Physical Education and Sport
New York University
New York, NY

Paul E. Wynant
Dean, Business Techhnology
Sinclair Community College
Dayton, OH

La Monte Wyche
Associate Professor of School Psychology
Howard University
Washington, DC

Barbara Ann Wyles
Associate Dean for Curriculum Services
Northern Virginia Community College
Annandale, VA

Raymond Yarbrough
Associate Professor of Electrical Engineering and Computer Science
University of Santa Clara
Santa Clara, CA

Dewey Yeager
Division Head of Engineering
Oklahoma State University Technical Branch
Oklahoma City, OK

Stanley Yeldell
Professor, Law/Justice Department
Glassboro State College
Glassboro, NJ

Charles Young
Project Manager, Swimmer Systems
Naval Surface Weapons Center
Silver Spring, MD

Darroch Young
Chair, Business Division
Santa Monica City College
Santa Monica, CA

Mary E. Young
Chairperson, Business Education Department
Suffolk Community College
Selden, NY

Ralph Young
Private Economic Consultant
Washington, DC

Conrad C. Youngren
Associate Professor of Engineering
SUNY Maritime College
Bronx, NY

Steve Zabetakis
Associate Professor
Hagerstown Junior College
Hagerstown, MD

Kathleen Zaepfel
Morganville, NJ

Thomas H. Zepf
Chairman and Professor, Department of Physics
Creighton University
Omaha, NE

Alvin J. T. Zumbrun
Criminal Justice Program Coordinator
Catonsville Community College
Catonsville, MD

Index

AC Circuits

Mercer County Vocational-Technical Schools - Division of Adult Education

    AC Circuits

AC Electronics

Chrysler Institute Associate Degree Program

    Fundamental Electronics II

AC Machinery

Joint Apprenticeship Training Committee, International Brotherhood of Electrical Workers Local Union 269, and the National Electrical Contractors Association of Southern New Jersey

    Electrician Apprentice

AC Motors

International Correspondence Schools

    A-C and D-C Motors and Controls

Accident Control

Sun Refining and Marketing Company

    Refinery Operator Program

Accident Prevention

National Mine Health and Safety Academy

    Accident Analysis and Problem Identification; Accident Prevention in the Mining Industry; Accident Prevention Techniques

Accounting

Abu Dhabi National Oil Company Career Development Center/GDC, Inc.

    Principles of Accounting

American Bankers Association

    Accounting Principles I; Accounting Principles II; Analyzing Financial Statements

American Institute for Property and Liability Underwriters/Insurance Institute of America

    Accounting and Finance; (AIAF 111) Statutory Accounting for Property and Liability Insurers; (APA 91) Principles of Premium Auditing; (APA 92) Premium Auditing Applications; Management, Accounting, and Finance

American Institute of Banking - Washington, D.C. Chapter

    Accounting I; Accounting II; Analyzing Financial Statements; Banking Law; Banking Law/Lending; Banking Law/Operations; Business Law; Business Law: Selected Topics

AT&T - Marketing Education - Somerset Seminars

    A Cost Model for Communications; Cash Flow Analysis I; Fundamentals of Finance and Accounting; Private Line Cost Models and Studies - PLIAC

Bell Atlantic Corporation

    Accounting for Equipment Engineers; Basic Accounting; Basic Telephone Accounting; Cost and Accounting Systems; Fundamentals of Revenue Accounting; Introduction to Property and Cost Accounting; Payroll Accounting

Bell Communications Research Training and Education Center

    Capital Recovery: Theory; Finance and Accounting Issues and Concepts in the Modern Corporation; Quantitative Forecasting Methods

Certified Employee Benefit Specialist Program

    Accounting and Information Systems; CEBS Course VI

Chrysler Institute Associate Degree Program

    Plant Finance Overview

Control Data

    Analytic Accounting

Credit Union National Association - Certified Credit Union Executive Program

    Accounting I #400

David C.D. Rogers Associates

    Finance and Accounting for Managers

Florida Bankers' Association

    Accounting

Garden State AIB

    Accounting I; Accounting II

General Electric Company

    Advanced Financial Accounting; Auditing; Financial Accounting; Management Accounting; Management Cost Accounting

Institute of Management and Production

    Basic Accounting; Basics of Accounting and Financial Control

International Correspondence Schools

    Accounting I; Accounting II; Cost Accounting; Federal Taxation; Intermediate Accounting I; Intermediate Accounting II; Managerial Accounting

Katharine Gibbs School

    Accounting Essentials #401; Accounting I #403; Accounting I #409; Accounting II #403.2

Opportunities Academy of Management Training, Inc.

    Introduction of Accounting and Internal Control; Managerial Accounting

Pacific Bell

    Introduction to Basic Accounting

Professional Secretaries International

    Part IV: Accounting

United States Department of Agriculture, Graduate School

    Advanced Accounting I; Advanced Accounting II; Advanced Accounting III; Auditing I; Auditing II; Budget Execution and Funds Control; Capital Budgeting; Cost Accounting I; Cost Accounting II; Cost

Accounting III; Federal Government Accounting; Federal Government Accounting II; Financial Management; Principles of Accounting I; Principles of Accounting II; Principles of Accounting III; Project Analysis

United States Postal Service - Department of Training and Development

Accounting I; Accounting II

U.S. West Learning Systems

Basic Telephone Accounting

Westinghouse Electric Corporation, Education Center Department

Business Management Course; Techniques of Finance and Accounting

Accounts Receivable Collection Techniques

Control Data

Accounts Receivable Collection Techniques

Acquisition Management

Westinghouse Electric Corporation, Defense and Electronics Center

Contracts Management Pro-Seminar; Principles of Government Contract Management

Acquisitions Contracting

United States Navy Acquisition Management Training Office

Defense Contract Negotiation Workshop; Defense Cost and Price Analysis; Management of Defense Acquisition Contracts

Administration

Federal Aviation Administration

Advanced Secretarial Course (14016); Basic Clerical/Secretarial Techniques (14015)

General Electric Company

Management Processes

Independent School Management

Women as School Administrators in Private-Independent Schools

Opportunities Academy of Management Training, Inc.

Advanced Affective Educational Techniques; Advanced Management Skill Training; Affective Education; Corporate Training for Nonprofit Organizations; Employment and Training, Planning Proposal Writing and Fund Development; Improving Management Skills; Management and Ownership Training; Management Control in Nonprofit Organizations; Personnel Management; Program Assessment and Evaluation; Program Planning Design and Implementation; Proposal Writing and Fund Development; Team Building; Tool for Better Management

United States Department of Agriculture, Graduate School

Project Management

Young Women's Christian Association of the U.S.A.

Advanced Management Workshop: Financial Administration and Development

Administration of Justice

National Sheriffs' Association

Fundamentals of Adult Detention

United States Department of Agriculture, Graduate School

Criminal Law

Administrative Assistant

Katharine Gibbs School

Administrative Assistant II

Administrative Law

Disabled American Veterans

Disabled American Veterans Continuing Training Program for National Service Officers

National Emergency Training Center

Code Management: A Systems Approach

New Jersey Department of Personnel, Division of Management Training and Employee Services

Managerial Tools for Today's Executive

United States Food and Drug Administration

Basic Food and Drug Law Course

Administrative Management

Credit Union National Association - Certified Credit Union Executive Program

Personnel Administration #300

NCR Corporation

Administrative Management

Xerox Corporation

Managing Tasks Through People

Adult Basic Education

Laubach Literacy Action

Teaching of Basic Reading and Writing Skills to Adult Nonreaders

Adult Education

Opportunities Academy of Management Training, Inc.

Advanced Motivation; Employment and Training, Planning Proposal Writing and Fund Development; Proposal Writing and Fund Development

Young Women's Christian Association of the U.S.A.

Management Training for Staff with Executive Potential; Management Workshop for Executive Staff; Management Workshop for Student Leadership

Adult Education Methods

United States Navy Acquisition Management Training Office

Becoming a More Effective Instructor

Advertising

AT&T - Corporate Education Center, Management Education Training Division

Concepts of Promotional Strategy

AT&T - Marketing Education - Somerset Seminars

Advanced Consumer Promotion Management I and II;

Direct Marketing; Theory and Practice of Promotion Management

Whirlpool Corporation
Advertising Analysis and Action Planning

Advertising Management

Westinghouse Electric Corporation, Education Center Department
Marketing Communications Concepts and Planning Seminar

Aeronautical Engineering

Federal Aviation Administration
Certification and Surveillance of NDT Repair Stations and Facilities (22520); Introduction to Aircraft Flutter (22504); Introduction to Aircraft Vibration (22505); Loads Analysis for Small Airplanes (22521); Non-Destructive Testing (22502)

Aeronautical Science

Federal Aviation Administration
Flow Management Weather Coordinator (50112/55138)

Aeronautical Studies

Federal Aviation Administration
Non-Radar Air Traffic Control (50123)

Aerospace

General Electric Company
Aerodynamics; Gas Turbine Fundamentals

Aerospace Engineering

Defense Mapping Agency - Inter American Geodetic Survey Cartographic School
Satellite Doppler Positioning

Affirmative Action

Pacific Bell
Affirmative Action

Affirmative Action Programs

Control Data
Affirmative Action Management Sequence

Agricultural Economics

United States Office of Personnel Management (OPM)
Economics and Public Policy

Agricultural Land Brokerage

National Association of REALTORS®
Agricultural Land Brokerage (FLI-220)

Agricultural Land Valuation

National Association of REALTORS®
Agricultural Land Valuation (FLI-161)

Agriculture

Defense Mapping Agency - Inter American Geodetic Survey Cartographic School
Introduction to Remote Sensing/Image Analysis

Air Conditioning

Federal Aviation Administration
Air Conditioning (44106)

United States Postal Service - Department of Training and Development
Environmental Control IV

Air Conditioning Technology

Seafarers Harry Lundeberg School of Seamanship
Refrigeration Systems Maintenance and Operation

Air Traffic Control

Federal Aviation Administration
Basic Aviation and Air Traffic (50312); Phase VII Clearance Delivery (55027)

Aircraft Control

Federal Aviation Administration
Radar Air Traffic Control Phase 10-A (50026)

Aircraft Maintenance Technology

Federal Aviation Administration
Emergency Evacuation and Survival Equipment (Airworthiness) (21843)

Airport Control Tower Operations

Federal Aviation Administration
Radar Air Traffic Control Phase 10-A (50026); Radar Position Certification (55031); Terminal Phase III - Control Tower Operation (50023); Terminal Phase IV, Non-Radar Air Traffic Control (50024)

Airport Engineering

Federal Aviation Administration
Project Engineering (06018)

Airport Management

Federal Aviation Administration
Airport Management for Internationals (06032); Airport Master Planning (06022); Airport Planning for Non-Federal Aviation Administration Personnel (06013); Environmental Assessment (12000); Flight Data (55026); Ground Control (55028); Local Control (55029); Non-Radar Terminal Control (55030); Radar Air Traffic Control Phase 10-A (50026)

Alcohol Abuse

National Mine Health and Safety Academy
Substance Abuse or

Algebra

Abu Dhabi National Oil Company Career Development Center/GDC, Inc.
Industrial Mathematics III

Chrysler Institute Associate Degree Program
Industrial Mathematics-Algebra

Control Data
Algebra

General Electric Company
> College Algebra; Technical Mathematics

International Correspondence Schools
> Technical Mathematics I

Omaha Public Power District
> Basic Mathematics or

Allied Health

Certified Medical Representatives Institute, Inc.
> Cardiovascular System; Clinical Drug Interactions; Digestive System; Endocrine System; Healthcare Community; Integumentary System; Musculoskeletal System; Nervous System; Reproductive Systems; Respiratory System; Sensory Organs; Trends and Issues in Healthcare; Urinary System

United States Public Health Service - Indian Health Service
> Basic Maternal and Child Health; Community Health Representative; Emergency Medical Technician; Environmental Health Concepts and Practices; Maternal and Child Nutrition; Rehabilitation and Home Health Care

Young Women's Christian Association of the U.S.A.
> Encore: The YWCA Post Mastectomy Group Rehabilitation Program; Encore Training Workshop: Encouragement - Normally - Counseling - Opportunity - Energies Revived

Allied Health Careers

American Medical Record Association
> Orientation to the Health Care Field

Alternating Current

The Cittone Institute
> Alternating Current Module

Computer Processing Institute
> Alternating Current Theory; Alternating Current Theory Laboratory

American Jurisprudence

American Institute for Paralegal Studies, Inc.
> American Jurisprudence

American Literature

International Correspondence Schools
> American Literature

Analog Instrumentation

Abu Dhabi National Oil Company Career Development Center/GDC, Inc.
> Digital and Analog Instruments

Analytic Geometry

International Correspondence Schools
> Analytic Geometry and Calculus

Anatomy

Certified Medical Representatives Institute, Inc.
> Cardiovascular System; Digestive System; Endocrine System; Integumentary System; Musculoskeletal System; Nervous System; Reproductive Systems; Respiratory System; Sensory Organs; Urinary System

Applied Health Physics

National Registry of Radiation Protection Technologists
> National Registry of Radiation Protection Technologists

Applied Sciences

Omaha Public Power District
> Applied Thermodynamics

Arabic

National Cryptologic School
> Arabic Syria Course; Basic Modern Standard Arabic; Intermediate Arabic Structure; Levantine Arabic Course

Archaeology

Seminary Extension, Southern Baptist Seminaries
> Biblical Backgrounds

Architectural Drawing

Portsmouth Naval Shipyard: Apprenticeship Training
> Architectural Drawing

Architectural Engineering

New England Telephone Company
> Asbestos Recognition and Abatement

Architectural Science

General Motors Corporation
> Plant Layout and Materials Handling

Architecture

National Emergency Training Center
> Fallout Shelter Analysis

Armenian Civilization and Culture

Armenian National Education Committee (Formerly Woodside Armenian Center)
> Introduction to Armenian Civilization and Culture

Armenian History

Armenian National Education Committee (Formerly Woodside Armenian Center)
> Armenian Ancient and Medieval History; Modern Armenian History

Arson Investigation

National Emergency Training Center
> Fire Arson Investigation

Art Education

Art Instruction Schools
> Advanced Drawing and Painting; Advanced Illustration; Art in Advertising; Basic Drawing and Design I; Basic Drawing and Design II; Cartooning; Design, Composition, and Reproduction; Figure Drawing and Studio Techniques; Fundamentals of Art; Painting Techniques; Specialized Art

Artificial Intelligence

General Motors Corporation - Technical Staffs Group and Lansing Automotive Division (Formerly Advanced Engineering Staff [AES])

    Artificial Intelligence

National Cryptologic School

    Combinatorial Mathematics

Assembler Language

Applied Learning (Formerly ASI/DELTAK)

    Assembler Language Programming; 4080 MVS/SP JES 2; 5600 Assembler Language Programming: Basic Techniques; 5610 Assembler Language Programming: Binary Instruction Set

Brick Computer Science Institute

    Assembler Programming

The Chubb Institute

    Applications Laboratory; Basic Program Design; Programming Fundamentals

Computer Learning Center

    Assembler Language Coding

Assembly Language

The Cittone Institute

    Microprocessor Technology

NCR Corporation

    NCR 605/608 Hardware and Programming

United States Postal Service - Department of Training and Development

    Automatic Business Mail Process Systems

Asset Management

Certified Employee Benefit Specialist Program

    Asset Management; CEBS Course VII

Astronomy

National Cryptologic School

    Introduction to Astrodynamics

Audiology

American Conference of Audioprosthology

    Program in Audioprosthology

Auditing

United States Department of Agriculture, Graduate School

    Auditing I; Auditing II

United States Department of Internal Revenue Service, Federal Law Enforcement Training Center

    Special Agent Investigative Techniques

United States Postal Service - Department of Training and Development

    Postal Inspector Basic Training

Automated Office Administration

Professional Secretaries International

    Part VI: Office Administration and Technology; Part VI: Office Technology

Automated Office Management

Blake Business School

    Electronic Office Procedures

Automated Systems

Ford National Development and Training Center (Formerly UAW—Ford National Development and Training Center)

    Brand Oriented Robot Workshop; Introduction to Automated Systems; Robotics Overview; Robotics/Automation Evaluation and Application Methodology

Automation Design

Ford National Development and Training Center (Formerly UAW—Ford National Development and Training Center)

    Automation Friendly Design; Introduction to Design for Automation; Robotics Overview

Automotive Electronics Service

General Motors Corporation - Technical Staffs Group and Lansing Automotive Division (Formerly Advanced Engineering Staff [AES])

    Automotive Electronics

Automotive Engineering

United States Army Materiel Command - AMC (Formerly DARCOM - United States Army Materiel Development and Readiness Command)

    Automotive Principles

Automotive Fundamentals

General Motors Corporation - Technical Staffs Group and Lansing Automotive Division (Formerly Advanced Engineering Staff [AES])

    Automotive Fundamentals

Automotive Performance

General Motors Corporation - Technical Staffs Group and Lansing Automotive Division (Formerly Advanced Engineering Staff [AES])

    Chassis Design and Vehicle Dynamics; Vehicle Performance and Transmission Design

Automotive Science Supervision

United States Postal Service - Department of Training and Development

    Vehicle Maintenance Management Skills Building

Automotive Service Management

United States Postal Service - Department of Training and Development

    Perimeter Office Fleet Maintenance; Vehicle Maintenance Facility Control; Vehicle Maintenance Facility Utilization

Automotive Technology

Chrysler Motors Advanced Technical Training

    Electronic Fuel Injection Systems; Vehicle Electrical/Electronic Systems

Federal Aviation Administration

>Engine Control Panels (40127)

Sandy Corporation - Marketing Educational Services

>Financial Management for Parts Managers; Financial Management for Sales Managers; Financial Management for Service Managers; Fundamentals of Management for Parts Managers; Fundamentals of Management for Sales Managers; Fundamentals of Management for Service Managers; General Motors Field Management Development Program; Operations Management for Parts Managers; Operations Management for Sales Managers; Operations Management for Service Managers; Personnel Management for Parts Managers; Personnel Management for Sales Managers; Personnel Management for Service Managers

United States Postal Service - Department of Training and Development

>Air Brakes; Allison Automatic Transmissions; Automatic Transmission Overhaul; Automotive Diesel Mechanics; Automotive Electrical Systems; Automotive Mechanic Fundamentals; Brakes and Suspension Systems; Caterpillar Diesel; Cummins Diesel I; Cummins Diesel III; Electric Vehicle; Engine Tune-up and Air Pollution Control Devices; Fundamentals of Automatic Transmissions; Perimeter Office Fleet Maintenance; Postal Diesel; Vehicle Maintenance Analyst; Vehicle Maintenance Facility Control; Vehicle Maintenance Facility Utilization

Aviation Maintenance Technology

Federal Aviation Administration

>Aircraft Maintenance Reliability Programs (21813); Allison Convair 580 Maintenance and Inspection (21831); B-727 Aircraft and JT8D Engine Maintenance and Inspection (21838); DC-9 Airframe and Powerplant Maintenance and Inspection (21840); General Aviation Jet Powerplants (21814); Introduction to Executive Jet-Powered Aircraft (21816); Lear Jet and Sabreliner Aircraft Systems (21817)

Aviation Management

Federal Aviation Administration

>Advanced Air Traffic Control for International Participants (50003); Airspace Management (50010); Evaluation of Aviation Management Systems (22600); Fundamentals of Air Traffic Control (50022); Fundamentals of Air Traffic Control (50122); Non-Radar Air Traffic Control (50123); Radar Position Certification (55031)

Aviation Technology

Federal Aviation Administration

>Air Carrier Operations Indoctrination (20700); Air Carrier Operations Indoctrination (21607); Assistant Controller Position Qualification and Certification (55126); B-727 Aircraft Systems (21808); B-737 Aircraft Systems (21806); DC-9 Aircraft Systems (21807); Enroute Radar Initial Qualification Training, Phase 10A (50125 [formerly 50124]); Final Radar Control Position - Phase XIII (55133); Final Radar-Associated/Non-Radar Control Position Qualification and Certification (55130); General Aviation Aircraft Alteration (21811); General Purpose Helicopter (21812); Initial Radar Control Position Qualification and Certification - Phase XII (55132); Initial Radar Position Qualification Certification Phase (55129); Non-Radar Air Traffic Control (50123); On-the-Job Training, Final Functional Area Checkout (55104); On-the-Job Training in NAS (55103); Predevelopmental, Phase III Field Environmental Training (55313); Predevelopmental, Phase IV - Option Determination (55314); Preliminary Radar-Associated/Non-Radar Control Training and Assistant Controller Duties (55127); Radar Associated/Non-Radar Controller Training (55128); Terminal Phase III - Control Tower Operation (50023)

Avionics

Federal Aviation Administration

>Flight Control System (22462); Flight Control Systems (22462); Omega/Area Navigation Systems (21845)

Baking

Seafarers Harry Lundeberg School of Seamanship

>Cook and Baker

Bank Accounting

American Bankers Association

>Bank Accounting

Bank Auditing

American Bankers Association

>Bank Control and Audit

Bank Lending

Graduate School of Banking at Colorado

>Bank Lending

Bank Management

American Bankers Association

>Investment Basics and Beyond; Trust Investments

Florida Bankers' Association

>Commercial Bank Management

Garden State AIB

>Bank Management; Bank Management Seminar

Graduate School of Banking at Colorado

>Management of Financial Institutions

Graduate School of Banking at the University of Wisconsin-Madison (Central States Conference of Bankers Associates)

>Management of Financial Institutions

New England School of Banking

>Commercial Banking Major; Trust Banking Major

Bank Marketing

American Bankers Association

>Marketing for Bankers

Garden State AIB

>Financial Marketing

Bank Operations

American Bankers Association

>Concepts of Data Processing; Deposit Operations; Principles of Banking; Securities Processing

Banking

American Bankers Association

> Bank Investments; Bank Management; Banking and the Plastic Card; Commercial Lending: 200-Level Curriculum; Commercial Lending; Commercial Loan Officer Development; Consumer Credit 200-Level Curriculum; Consumer Lending; Current Issues in Bank Management; Financial Planning for Bankers; International Banking; PDP 200-Level General Banking Curriculum; Personal Financial Planning; The Trust Business

American Institute of Banking - Washington, D.C. Chapter

> Bank Investments; Bank Management; Cash Management I and II; Commercial Banking; Installment Credit; Management of Commercial Bank Funds; Principles of Banking; Principles of Commercial Banking

Garden State AIB

> Principles of Banking

Institute of Financial Education

> Commercial Banking; Commercial Lending for Savings Institutions; Consumer Lending; Income Property Lending; Individual Retirement Accounts/Keogh Plans; Marketing for Financial Institutions; Mortgage Loan Servicing; NOW Accounts; Real Estate Law I; Real Estate Law II; Residential Mortgage Lending

School of Banking of the South

> Commercial Lending and Credit Analysis; Management of Financial Institutions

Banking Law

American Bankers Association

> Law and Banking: Applications; Law and Banking

BASIC

Blake Business School

> Computer Programming

Brick Computer Science Institute

> Basic Programming

The Cittone Institute

> BASIC Programming with Flowcharting

Control Data

> Introduction to Programming in BASIC

General Electric Company

> Computer Science

General Motors Corporation - Technical Staffs Group and Lansing Automotive Division (Formerly Advanced Engineering Staff [AES])

> Computer Programming in BASIC

International Correspondence Schools

> Computer Literacy and Programming in BASIC; Computer Science I; Computer Science II

NCR Corporation

> Advanced 2950 Programming; BASIC for the 2157; BASIC Programming

U.S. West Learning Systems

> Initial User Training/Program Logic and Design/BASIC Programming Language

Basic Skills

Institute of Financial Education

> Basic Business English

Behavioral Management

Xerox Corporation

> Managing Tasks Through People

Behavioral Science

Federal Aviation Administration

> Academy Instructor Training (Basic) (10520); Facility Instructor Training (10501)

Ford National Development and Training Center (Formerly UAW—Ford National Development and Training Center)

> Group Problem Solving

National Cryptologic School

> Transactional Analysis

National Emergency Training Center

> Personal Effectiveness; Team Effectiveness

Western Regional CUNA School for Credit Union Personnel

> Western Regional CUNA School for Credit Union Personnel

Westinghouse Electric Corporation, Defense and Electronics Center

> Leadership Development Workshop; Management Techniques Seminar

Behavioral Services

United States Office of Personnel Management (OPM)

> Managerial Competencies and Effectiveness Characteristics for Executives

Biochemistry

Certified Medical Representatives Institute, Inc.

> Biochemistry

Biology

Certified Medical Representatives Institute, Inc.

> Cardiovascular System; Digestive System; Endocrine System; Human Body, Pathology and Treatment; Integumentary System; Musculoskeletal System; Nervous System; Reproductive Systems; Respiratory System; Urinary System

Biomedical Engineering

American Sterilizer Company (AMSCO)

> Hospital Engineering Seminar

General Electric Company

> Basics of Ultrasound

Biomedical Equipment Maintenance

American Sterilizer Company (AMSCO)

> Basic Biomedical Equipment Maintenance

926 *Index*

Blueprint Reading

Abu Dhabi National Oil Company Career Development Center/GDC, Inc.

    Mechanical Blueprint Reading

Chrysler Institute Associate Degree Program

    Print Reading

Blueprint Reading and Sketching

Electrical Workers, Local Union 102 of the International Brotherhood of Electrical Workers

    Electrician Apprentice

Electrical Workers, Local Union 164 of the International Brotherhood of Electrical Workers, AFL-CIO, Bergen and Hudson Counties, New Jersey, and the Bergen-Hudson County Chapter of the National Electrical Contractors Association Joint Apprenticeship Training Program

    Electrician Apprentice

Electrical Workers, Local Union 26 of the International Brotherhood of Electrical Workers and the Washington, D.C. Chapter of the National Electrical Contractors Association, Joint School

    Electrician Apprentice

Joint Apprenticeship Training Committee, International Brotherhood of Electrical Workers Local Union 269, and the National Electrical Contractors Association of Southern New Jersey

    Electrician Apprentice

Omaha Joint Electrical Apprenticeship and Training Committee

    Electrical Apprenticeship Training

Portsmouth Naval Shipyard: Apprenticeship Training

    Blueprint Reading and Shop Sketching

Body Conditioning

Bergen County Police Academy

    Basic Police Training Course

Boiler and Water Treatment

Abu Dhabi National Oil Company Career Development Center/GDC, Inc.

    Boilers and Water Treatment I and II

Boiler Control Process

Abu Dhabi National Oil Company Career Development Center/GDC, Inc.

    Boiler Control

Boiler Repair and Maintenance

Abu Dhabi National Oil Company Career Development Center/GDC, Inc.

    Boiler Repair and Maintenance

Bookkeeping

Abu Dhabi National Oil Company Career Development Center/GDC, Inc.

    Accounting I, II, and III; Bookkeeping I; Bookkeeping II

Brokerage Accounting and Operation

National Association of Securities Dealers, Inc.

    Investments and/or Brokerage Accounting; Securities, Regulation, Law, and Self-Regulation

Building and Construction Management

United States Postal Service - Department of Training and Development

    BMC Building Equipment Mechanic; Environmental Control I; Environmental Control II

Building Maintenance

United States Postal Service - Department of Training and Development

    BMC Building Equipment Mechanic; Environmental Control I; Environmental Control II

Building Operations Management

United States Postal Service - Department of Training and Development

    BMC Building Equipment Mechanic; Environmental Control I; Environmental Control II

Business

Abu Dhabi National Oil Company Career Development Center/GDC, Inc.

    Orientation to Business Careers

American Bankers Association

    Financial Planning for Bankers; Personal Financial Planning

American Institute for Property and Liability Underwriters/Insurance Institute of America

    (AAI 81) Principles of Insurance Production; (AAI 82) Multiple-Lines Insurance Production; (AAI 83) Agency Operations and Sales Management; (AIC 31) Principles of Insurance and Property Loss Adjusting; (AIC 32) Principles of Insurance and Liability Claims Adjusting; (AIC 35) Property Insurance Adjusting; (AIC 36) Liability Insurance Adjusting; (INS 21) Property and Liability Insurance Principles; (INS 22) Personal Insurance; Management

American International Group, Inc.

    Counselor Selling; Supervisory Management

ARA Services, Inc.

    Advanced Management Skills Workshop; Management by Objectives; Management Expectancy; Service Management Seminar; Supervisory Skills Workshop

AT&T - Center for Systems Education (Formerly AT&T Company Data Systems Education Group)

    Programmer Basic Training

AT&T - Marketing Education - Somerset Seminars

    Strategy Analysis for Finance and Marketing

Bell Atlantic Corporation

    Fundamentals of Data Transmission: Testing and Service; Peripheral Installation and Maintenance; Programmer Basic Training; Trainer Skills Workshop

Bell Communications Research, Inc.

    Basic Programming Sequence UNIX System Files and Commands OS402, Advanced Use of the UNIX Text; Introduction to "C" Language Programming for

Index 927

Experienced Programmers

Bell Communications Research Training and Education Center

Cost Analysis: Service Industry; Data Communications - PC Communications; Innovative Marketing Strategies; Product Life Cycle Management; Strategy Analysis for Finance and Marketing

Blake Business School

Business Management

Crawford Risk Management Services

Advanced Casualty Claims Adjusting; Advanced Property Loss Adjusting; Casualty Claim Adjusting; Property Loss Adjusting; Specialized Rehabilitation Counseling; Workers' Compensation Claims Adjusting

David C.D. Rogers Associates

Competition in Telecommunications; Concepts of Corporate Planning

Federal Aviation Administration

Fundamentals of Procurement (07001); Program Analysis and Review (14026); Relocation Assistance (06027)

Garden State AIB

Financial Marketing; Fundamentals of Supervision; Trust Operations

General Electric Company

Management Processes

Graduate School of Banking at Colorado

Bank Lending; Management of Financial Institutions; Marketing Management

Institute of Financial Education

Commercial Law I; Commercial Law II; Introduction to the Savings Institution Business; Savings Institution Operations

Institute of Management and Production

Business Administration

Insurance Educational Association

Liability Insurance Adjusting; Principles of Insurance and Liability Claim Adjusting; Principles of Insurance and Property Loss Adjusting; Property Insurance Adjusting - Advanced

Jamaican Institute of Management

Introduction to Business and Principles of Management

Katharine Gibbs School

Introduction to Business

Massachusetts Bankers Association, Inc.

MSFS-Business Policy; MSFS-Human Resource Management; MSFS-Investments; MSFS-Lending Fundamentals; MSFS-Marketing of Financial Services; MSFS-Principles of Management

National Emergency Training Center

Code Management: A Systems Approach; Fire Service Information Management

Opportunities Academy of Management Training, Inc.

Management and Ownership Training

Pacific Bell

Arbitration Advocacy; Contemporary Collective Bargaining; Labor Laws and Labor History; Right of Way Appraisal; Right of Way

United States Office of Personnel Management (OPM)

Economics and Public Policy; Management of Natural Resources; Managing Money and Material Resources

Business Administration

American Bankers Association

Concepts of Data Processing; Management Fundamentals

American Institute for Property and Liability Underwriters/Insurance Institute of America

(AIM 41) The Process of Management; (AIM 42) Management and Human Resources; (AIM 43) Managerial Decision Making; (AIM 44) Management in a Changing World; (ARM 54) Structure of Risk Management Process; (ARM 55) Risk Control; (ARM 56) Risk Financing; (ARP 101) Business Research Methods; (ARP 102) Strategic Planning for Insurers; (AU 61) Principles of Property Liability and Underwriting; (AU 62) Personal Lines Underwriting; (AU 63) Commercial Liability Underwriting; (AU 64) Commercial Property and Multiple-Lines Underwriting; Economics, Government, and Business

American Institute of Banking - Washington, D.C. Chapter

Accounting I; Bank Investments; Bank Marketing: Theory and Applications; Banking Law; Banking Law/Lending; Banking Law/Operations; Business Law; Business Law: Selected Topics; Cash Management I and II; Consumer Credit; Fundamentals of Bank Data Processing; Installment Credit; International Banking; Law and Banking I; Management of Commercial Bank Funds; Principles of Banking; Real Estate Finance; Trust Banking

AT&T - Center for Systems Education (Formerly AT&T Company Data Systems Education Group)

Concepts of the Integrated Systems Provisioning Process; Data Gathering for System Development; Human Performance Engineering; Information Systems Analysis Workshop; Introduction to Project Management; Introductory Project Management; Performance Analysis Workshop; Project Leadership Workshop; Project Management and Leadership; Project Management Workshops; Project Manager Workshop

AT&T - Marketing Education - Somerset Seminars

Advanced Market Planning; Advanced Service Management Seminar; Competitive Pricing Strategy and Tactics; Computer Assisted Market Planning; Concepts of Capital Costs; Cost Analysis for Marketing Studies; Demand Analysis Techniques; Demand Analysis Techniques Seminar; Economics for Pricing Network Services; Evaluation of AT&T Interexchange Culture: A Management Technique; Financial Planning Control and Decision Making; Introduction to Regulated Utilities; Local Network Services Seminar; Measured Service Issues Seminar; Network Services Issues Seminar; Principles of Marketing Management; Public Switched Network Seminar; Rate Seminar; Restructure of Private Line Issues; Service Planning Seminar; Special Network Services Seminar; Stakeholder Analysis; Strategic Marketing and Process; Telephone Bypass Opportunities and Local Access; Terminal Products Issues Seminar

Bell Atlantic Corporation

Advanced Lotus 1-2-3; Computer Literacy/Do I need a PC?; Developing Additional Managerial Skills; Developing Managers; Human Relations in Business;

Introduction to dBase III; Introduction to IBM PC-XT and DOS; Introduction to Lotus 1-2-3

Bell Communications Research Training and Education Center

Competitive Pricing: Strategy and Tactics; Cost Studies for New Technology; Financial Planning, Control and Decision Making

College for Financial PlanningR

Estate Planning; Financial Paraplanner Program; Introduction to Financial Planning; Investments; Retirement Planning and Employee Benefits; Risk Management; Tax Planning and Management

Contel Service Corporation

FORTRAN

Continental Telecom, Inc.

Basic Supervisory Management Program - CORE; Better Business Writing; Management Studies Workshop; Orientation to Management

David C.D. Rogers Associates

Finance and Accounting for Managers

Defense Mapping Agency - Inter American Geodetic Survey Cartographic School

Cartographic Management; Field Surveys Supervisor; Geodetic Management; Photogrammetric Production Supervisor

Federal Aviation Administration

Advanced Procurement and Contracting (07007); Briefing and Presentation Techniques (14010); Conference Techniques in Every-Day Management (14000); Discrimination Complaints Investigation Course (01525); Facilitator's Training Course (01523); Managing Change (01306); Procurement for Technical Personnel (07004); Work Group Facilitator's Course (01528)

General Electric Company

Advanced Methods and Models; An Introduction to Finance; Basic Mathematics; Economic Analysis of Alternatives; Effective Creativity; GESIMTEL; Introduction to Probability Theory and Descriptive Statistics; Mathematical Methods and Models; Modeling; Operations Research and Applications Training; Probabilistic Models; Regression Analysis; Statistical Inference; Survey of Accounting and Financial Techniques; Time-Sharing System and Applications

Health Insurance Association of America

Group Life/Health Insurance: Part C; Group Life/Health Insurance: Parts A and B; Individual Health Insurance: Parts A and B

Illinois Fire Service Institute

Fire Department Management I; Fire Department Management II; Fire Department Management III; Fire Department Management IV

Indian Health Service - Tribal Management Support Center

Health Service Personnel Administration; Principles of Management and Leadership

Institute of Financial Education

Principles of Management

Institute of Management and Production

Basic Language for Microcomputer Users; Business Administration; COBOL Programming; Data Processing Program; Introduction to Data Processing; Systems Analysis and Design

Insurance Educational Association

Management and Human Resources; Management in a Changing World; Managerial Decision Making; Process of Management

International Correspondence Schools

Introduction to Business

Jewish Hospital of St. Louis

Management I; Management II

Kepner-Tregoe, Inc.

Apex; Fulcrum; Genco; Managing Involvement; Problem Solving and Decision Making; Project Management; Vertex

Knight-Ridder, Inc.

Improving Personnel Selection; Newspaper Production Techniques

McDonald's Corporation

Managing the McDonald's Team

National Cryptologic School

Behavioral Sciences Concepts and Applications in Management; Cryptologic Management for Interns; Cryptologic Management for Managers; Cryptologic Management for Supervisors; Economics/Business Administration Statistics; Introduction to Management; Introduction to Supervision; Managerial Grid Seminar; Probability and Statistics; Procurement; Procurement Management for Technical Personnel; Social Sciences Statistics

National Emergency Training Center

Fire Executive Development III; Fire Service Financial Management; Fire Service Leadership/Communications; Fire Service Organizational Theory; Interpersonal Dynamics in Fire Service Organizations; Strategic Analysis of Fire Department Operations

NCR Corporation

Executive Development Program - International Economy; Executive Development Program - Law; Introduction to Quality Improvement

New England Telephone Company

Concepts of Total System Development; Introduction to Project Management; Programmer Basic Training

O/E Learning, Inc.

Personal Finances

Opportunities Academy of Management Training, Inc.

Functions of a Manager

Pacific Bell

Advanced DOS; Beginning WordPerfect; Intermediate Word Perfect; Advanced WordPerfect; Communications with Microcomputers; Data Processing/Data Communications; DOS Concepts and Beginning RBASE 5000 for Hard Disk PC Systems; DOS Concepts, Wordstar, and Lotus 1-2-3 for the Hard Disk PC System; DOS for the Hard Disk; EDP Concepts for Business; Introduction to DBASE II/III; Introduction to Personal Computing; Methods Development Workshop; Multimate Mod. I; Multimate Mod. II; Paradox Users Series: Introduction to Paradox; Using Paradox (1425A); Applying Paradox (1425B); PC and

Symphony Users Series: Hard Disk and DOS; Beginning Symphony; Advanced Symphony; PC and Wordstar Users Series: Beginning WI Hard Disk and DOS; Beginning Wordstar; Advanced Wordstar; Spreadsheets, Graphics, Word Processing and Database Using Symphony; Strategic Management Writing; Word Processing Concepts and the Use of Displaywrite; Word Processing Concepts and the Use of Multimate

The Palmer School

Accounting; Business Law I; Business Law II; Introduction to Business

School of Banking of the South

Legal Environment of Business

United States Army Materiel Command - AMC (Formerly DARCOM - United States Army Materiel Development and Readiness Command)

Procurement Policies and Procedures for Engineers; Project Management; Systems Engineering

United States Department of Agriculture, Graduate School

Auditing I; Auditing II; Budget Execution and Funds Control; Business Law I; Business Law II; Capital Budgeting; Correlation and Regression Analysis; Cost Accounting I; Cost Accounting II; Cost Accounting III; Financial Management; International Finance; Introductory Statistics I; Introductory Statistics II; Introductory Statistics III; Leadership and Management Development; Management Economics for Developing Countries; Managerial Statistics; Principles of Marketing; Project Analysis; Project Management; Real Estate Transaction

United States Navy Acquisition Management Training Office

Advanced Contract Administration; Basic Contract Administration; Management Development Seminar

United States Office of Personnel Management (OPM)

Management Development Seminar; Seminar for New Managers

United States Postal Service - Department of Training and Development

Introduction to Postal Management; Introduction to Postal Supervision; Mail Processing for Managers MTS; Mail Processing for Supervisors MTS; Postal Inspector Basic Training

Western Regional CUNA School for Credit Union Personnel

Western Regional CUNA School for Credit Union Personnel

Xerox Corporation

Executive Seminar I; Finance for the Nonfinancial Manager/Financial Decision Making; Managing Tasks Through People

Young Women's Christian Association of the U.S.A.

Management Training for Staff with Executive Potential; Management Workshop for Executive Staff; Management Workshop for Student Leadership; Presidential Leadership and Association Committee Chairpersons' Workshop; Staff Development II

Business Analysis

AT&T - Marketing Education - Somerset Seminars

Advanced Quantitative Methods in Marketing; Analysis of Marketing Data for Management Decision Making; Application of Multivariate Techniques; Marketing Statistics; Statistical Analysis in Marketing

Business and Public Administration

Young Women's Christian Association of the U.S.A.

Advanced Management Workshop in Personnel Administration

Business and Society

The Center for Leadership Development

Business and Society

Business Communications

Abu Dhabi National Oil Company Career Development Center/GDC, Inc.

Business Communications

AT&T - Center for Systems Education (Formerly AT&T Company Data Systems Education Group)

Information-Mapping, Structured Writing

AT&T - Marketing Education - Somerset Seminars

Marketing Communications Workshop; Witness Preparation; Witness Support

Bell Communications Research Training and Education Center

Management Communications Workshop; Witness and Marketing Support; Witness Preparation

Blake Business School

Business Communications III

Continental Telecom, Inc.

Better Business Writing

Control Data

Better Business Letters

Dana Corporation

Business Practices

English Language Institute of America, Inc.

Practical English and the Command of Words

Georgia Computer Campus (Formerly Georgia Computer Programming Project for Severely Handicapped Persons)

Business Communication Skills

Institute of Management and Production

Communication

International Correspondence Schools

Business Communication; Communications/Modern Language Expression

Katharine Gibbs School

Business Writing

National Management Association

Supervisory and Management Skills Program

National Mine Health and Safety Academy

Effective Writing

NCR Corporation

Technical and Report Writing

New England Telephone Company

Business Meeting Skills; Communications Workshop; Writer's Workshop

Pacific Bell

    Strategic Management Writing; System Design Consultant Communication Skills

United States Department of Agriculture, Graduate School

    Advanced Practice in Editing; Editing; Editing Technical Manuscripts; Intermediate Editing; Introduction to the Editing Process; Practice in Editing; Principles of Editing; Principles of Editing for Publication; Proofreading; Publishing Management; Style and Techniques for Editors

United States Postal Service - Department of Training and Development

    Communication Skills for Managers #11251-00; Communications Skills for Supervisors #11281-00

U.S. West Learning Systems

    Better Business Letters; Managing to Write and Defining the Job; Managing Problem Solving

Xerox Corporation

    Executive Sales Seminar

Business Contract Law

United States Navy Acquisition Management Training Office

    Government Contracting Law

Business Correspondence

Abu Dhabi National Oil Company Career Development Center/GDC, Inc.

    Business Correspondence

Business Data Processing

Blake Business School

    Introduction to Data Processing

Business Education

United States Department of Labor, DOL Academy

    Keyboarding Techniques; Office Practices and Communications

Xerox Corporation

    Word Processing; Xerox Office Products Division 860 Product School - Sales

Young Women's Christian Association of the U.S.A.

    Advanced Management Workshop: Financial Administration and Development

Business English

Katharine Gibbs School

    Business English

United States Department of Agriculture, Graduate School

    Proofreading; Seminar in Editing

Business Entities

PJA School

    Business Entities

Business Finance

AT&T - Marketing Education - Somerset Seminars

    Financial Awareness Plus Seminar; Financial Awareness Seminar; Introduction to Finance

Business Insurance

Credit Union National Association - Certified Credit Union Executive Program

    Risk Management and Insurance #500

Business Law

American Educational Institute, Inc.

    Legal Principles

American Institute for Paralegal Studies, Inc.

    Business Law; Business Law I

American Institute for Property and Liability Underwriters/Insurance Institute of America

    (AIC 31) Principles of Insurance and Property Loss Adjusting; (AIC 32) Principles of Insurance and Liability Claims Adjusting; (AIC 35) Property Insurance Adjusting; (AIC 36) Liability Insurance Adjusting; Insurance and Business Law; The Legal Environment of Insurance

American Institute of Banking - Washington, D.C. Chapter

    Banking Law; Banking Law/Lending; Banking Law/Operations; Business Law; Business Law: Selected Topics

AT&T - Marketing Education - Somerset Seminars

    Witness Preparation; Witness Support

Bell Communications Research Training and Education Center

    Witness Preparation

Blake Business School

    Business Law

Certified Employee Benefit Specialist Program

    CEBS Course V; Contemporary Legal Environment of Employee Benefit Plans

Chrysler Institute Associate Degree Program

    Business Law

Crawford Risk Management Services

    Advanced Casualty Claims Adjusting

Credit Union National Association - Certified Credit Union Executive Program

    Business Law #1000

Insurance Educational Association

    Law of Torts; Legal Environment of Insurance; Liability Insurance Adjusting; Principles of Insurance and Liability Claim Adjusting; Principles of Insurance and Property Loss Adjusting; Property Insurance Adjusting - Advanced

International Correspondence Schools

    Business Law I; Business Law II

Katharine Gibbs School

    Business Law #603

National Academy for Paralegal Studies, Inc.

    Business Law 1

National Emergency Training Center

    Managing the Code Process

Professional Secretaries International
> Part II: Business Law

Business Management

AT&T - Center for Systems Education (Formerly AT&T Company Data Systems Education Group)
> Consulting Skills Workshop; Interpersonal Management Skills for Information Systems; Managing the Data Systems Manager; Managing the D.P. Professional

Federal Aviation Administration
> Construction Contracting (07013); Evaluation of Aviation Management Systems (22600); Operations and Supply Support (07014)

International Correspondence Schools
> Introduction to Computer Concepts

International PADI, Inc.
> Retail Store Sales and Operations

Jewish Hospital of St. Louis
> Motivational Dynamics I; Motivational Dynamics II

Maynard Management Institute
> Industrial Engineering Basics; Industrial Engineering for the Supervisor

National Emergency Training Center
> Personal Effectiveness; Strategic Analysis of Executive Leadership; Team Effectiveness

United States Army Materiel Command - AMC (Formerly DARCOM - United States Army Materiel Development and Readiness Command)
> Acquisition and Contracting; Quality Assurance

United States Department of Agriculture, Graduate School
> Financial Management; International Finance; Leadership and Management Development; Principles of Marketing

United States Department of Labor, DOL Academy
> Communications in Management; Conflict Resolution in the Workplace; Detecting and Managing Stress in the Office Environment; Equal Employment Opportunity Programs; Human Side of Management; Negotiation Skills; Performance Appraisal; Skills Training

United States Navy Acquisition Management Training Office
> Defense Contract Negotiation Workshop; Defense Cost and Price Analysis; Management of Defense Acquisition Contracts; Management of Managers

Xerox Corporation
> Advanced Sales School; Basic Sales School

Business Mathematics

Abu Dhabi National Oil Company Career Development Center/GDC, Inc.
> Business Mathematics I and II; Business Mathematics I, II and III

Blake Business School
> Business Math I; Business Math II

Institute for Business and Technology
> Business Mathematics

Institute of Financial Education
> Business Math Review

International Correspondence Schools
> Business Statistics; Math for Business and Finance

Katharine Gibbs School
> Mathematics for Business

Business Organizations

American Center for Technical Arts and Sciences (Formerly Mainline Paralegal Institute)
> Business and Corporate Law I

Business Policy

Bell Communications Research Training and Education Center
> Concepts of Corporate Planning

Massachusetts Bankers Association, Inc.
> MSFS-Business Policy

NCR Corporation
> Advanced Management Skills

New England School of Banking
> Commercial Banking Major

Business Statistics

United States Army Materiel Command - AMC (Formerly DARCOM - United States Army Materiel Development and Readiness Command)
> Statistical Analysis

Business Systems

Brick Computer Science Institute
> EDP Applications and Systems

Business Systems Analysis

Control Data
> Business Systems Analyst Sequence

Business Writing

U.S. West Learning Systems
> Put It In Writing

Business/Consumer Direct Marketing

AT&T - Corporate Education Center, Management Education Training Division
> Business/Consumer Direct Marketing Application

C Language Programming

AT&T - Center for Systems Education (Formerly AT&T Company Data Systems Education Group)
> C Initial Designer Training

Bell Communications Research Training and Education Center
> C Language Programming

NCR Corporation
> "C" Programming Advanced; "C" Programming for Entry Level Programmers; "C" Programming

Cable

Wolf Creek Nuclear Operating Corporation (Formerly Kansas Gas & Electric)
> Conduit, Cable and Wire

CAI

Control Data
> CREATE Curriculum

Calculus

Abu Dhabi National Oil Company Career Development Center/GDC, Inc.
> Industrial Mathematics IV

Control Data
> Calculus 1; Calculus 2

International Correspondence Schools
> Analytic Geometry and Calculus

United States Department of Agriculture, Graduate School
> Calculus I; Calculus II

Capacity Requirements Planning

Digital Equipment Corporation
> Capacity Requirements Planning

Capital Budgeting

United States Department of Agriculture, Graduate School
> Capital Budgeting

Capital Markets

New England School of Banking
> Commercial Banking Major

Capitalization Theory and Techniques

National Association of REALTORS®
> Capitalization Theory and Techniques - Part A (EX 1B-1); Capitalization Theory and Techniques - Part B (EX 1B-2); Capitalization Theory and Techniques - Part C (EX 1B-3)

Cardiopulmonary Resuscitation

National Mine Health and Safety Academy
> First Responder

Seafarers Harry Lundeberg School of Seamanship
> Chief Steward; Chief/Assistant Engineer - Uninspected Motor Vessels; Original Third Assistant Engineer, Steam and/or Motor - Inspected

Cardiovascular Anatomy

General Electric Company
> Nuclear Cardiology

Cardiovascular Physiology

General Electric Company
> Nuclear Cardiology

Career Counseling

Opportunities Academy of Management Training, Inc.
> Advanced Job Development

Career Development

Pacific Bell
> Goal Setting Skills; Managing Performance

Career Development and Counseling

U.S. West Learning Systems
> Managing Interpersonal Relationships; Managing Personal Growth; Psychology of Risk Taking

Career Planning

Knight-Ridder, Inc.
> Career Planning and Counseling

Cargo Handling

Seafarers Harry Lundeberg School of Seamanship
> Third Mate - Inspected Vessels

Cartographic Technology

Defense Mapping Agency - Inter American Geodetic Survey Cartographic School
> Automated Cartography-Digitizing System Operator; Color Separation Technician

Cartography

Defense Mapping Agency - Inter American Geodetic Survey Cartographic School
> Aeronautical Cartography; Automated Cartography; Basic Photographic Sciences; Cartographic Techniques for Space Imagery; Cartographic Techniques for Thematic Mapping; Cartography; Control Surveys; Digital Methods of Terrain Modeling; Introduction to Automated Cartography; Introduction to Computer Programming Using FORTRAN, Independent Study; Introduction to Digital Image Analysis; Introduction to Minicomputers, Independent Study; Map Maintenance; Modern Cartography; Nautical Cartography; Orthophotography; Photogrammetry; Preparation of Landsat Mosaics

Casualty Insurance

American Institute for Property and Liability Underwriters/Insurance Institute of America
> (INS 23) Commercial Insurance

Celestial Navigation

Seafarers Harry Lundeberg School of Seamanship
> Celestial Navigation; Third Mate - Inspected Vessels

Cell Chemistry

Technical Training Project, Inc.
> Laboratory Technician Program

Central Processor Maintenance

Bell Communications Research Training and Education Center
> 1A Maintenance Program - Control Processor Maintenance

Central Service Department Seminar

American Sterilizer Company (AMSCO)
> Advanced Management Central Service Seminar

Index 933

Chemical Engineering

General Motors Corporation - Technical Staffs Group and Lansing Automotive Division (Formerly Advanced Engineering Staff [AES])
> Corrosion; Polymer Engineering

Chemical Process Technology

Abu Dhabi National Oil Company Career Development Center/GDC, Inc.
> Applied Chemistry I and II

Chemical Technology

Technical Training Project, Inc.
> Laboratory Technician Program

Chemical Unit Operations

Sun Refining and Marketing Company
> Basic Operator Training

Chemical Unit Operations Technology

Sun Refining and Marketing Company
> Refinery Operator Program

Chemistry

Abu Dhabi National Oil Company Career Development Center/GDC, Inc.
> Applied Chemistry I and II; Chemistry for Technologists I and II and Chemical Calculations

Carolina Power & Light Company
> COC: Chemistry and Material Science; Reactor Operator Theory: Chemistry

Control Data
> Chemistry 1; Chemistry 2

Duquesne Light Company
> Chemistry Fundamentals

General Electric Company
> Boiling Water Reactor Chemistry for Technicians; Boiling Water Reactor Chemistry; Introduction to Chemistry I; Introduction to Chemistry II

National Emergency Training Center
> Instructors Program Level I—Chemistry of Hazardous Materials

Omaha Public Power District
> Basic Concepts of Water Chemistry; Chemistry Lecture; Radiochemistry I; Radiochemistry II

Technical Training Project, Inc.
> Laboratory Technician Program

Westinghouse Electric Corporation, Nuclear Services Division (Formerly Water Reactor Divisions)
> PWR Plant Radiochemistry

Yankee Atomic Electric Company
> Introductory Chemistry

Chemistry for the Oil and Gas Industry

Baroid Corporation Career Development Center (Formerly NL Industries, Inc.)
> Production Treating Chemicals

Child Welfare

Police Training Institute
> Child Sex Exploitation

Chinese

United States Department of Agriculture, Graduate School
> Intermediate Chinese I; Intermediate Chinese II; Intermediate Chinese III; Introductory Chinese II; Introductory Chinese III; Introductory Chinese I—Mandarin

Chinese (Mandarin)

National Cryptologic School
> Chinese Refresher II; Intermediate Readings in Chinese; Newspaper/Broadcast Chinese I

CICS/VS

Brick Computer Science Institute
> CICS/VS

Circuit Protection Techniques

Wolf Creek Nuclear Operating Corporation (Formerly Kansas Gas & Electric)
> Circuit Protection

Circuit Reading

U.S. West Learning Systems
> TTC No. 366 Circuit Reading

Circuits Testing

International Correspondence Schools
> Circuits and Components Testing

City Planning

Federal Aviation Administration
> Relocation Assistance (06027)

Civil Engineering

Defense Mapping Agency - Inter American Geodetic Survey Cartographic School
> Automated Cartography; Automated Geodetic Computations and Adjustments; Control Surveys; Geodetic Computations and Adjustments; Geodetic Computations; Gravity Surveys; Land Gravity Surveys; Satellite Doppler Positioning

Federal Aviation Administration
> Airport Engineering (06012); Airport NAVAIDS and Lighting (06019); Airport Paving (06005); Project Engineering (06018); Recurrent Engineering (06021)

National Emergency Training Center
> Fallout Shelter Analysis; Wildland/Urban Interface Fire Protection: A National Problem with Local Solutions

Civil Engineering Technology

Defense Mapping Agency - Inter American Geodetic Survey Cartographic School
> Automated Geodetic Computations and Adjustments; Control Surveys; Geodetic Computations and Adjustments; Geodetic Computations; Gravity Surveys; Hydrographic Surveying; Land Gravity Surveys; Satellite Doppler Positioning

Pacific Bell
: Right of Way Appraisal; Right of Way

Civil Law

American Institute for Paralegal Studies, Inc.
: Basic Civil Law

National Academy for Paralegal Studies, Inc.
: Basic Civil Law

Civil Litigation

American Center for Technical Arts and Sciences (Formerly Mainline Paralegal Institute)
: Civil Litigation

Omega Institute
: Civil Litigation Practice

Clinic Administration

General Electric Company
: Management Processes

Clinical Engineering

American Sterilizer Company (AMSCO)
: Hospital Engineering Seminar

Clinical Medicine

General Electric Company
: Principles of Cardiovascular Monitoring

Clinical Practice

American Medical Record Association
: Health Record Management in Nursing Homes

CMI

Control Data
: CREATE Curriculum

Coal Mine Ventilation

National Mine Health and Safety Academy
: Ventilation

Coal Preparation

National Mine Health and Safety Academy
: Coal Preparation

Coastwise Navigation

Seafarers Harry Lundeberg School of Seamanship
: Third Mate - Inspected Vessels

Coastwise Navigation and Piloting

Seafarers Harry Lundeberg School of Seamanship
: Able Seaman

COBOL

Applied Learning (Formerly ASI/DELTAK)
: Advanced COBOL Programming; ANS COBOL Language; Structured ANS COBOL - Entry Level; Structured COBOL Programming; 1627 Advanced COBOL: Processing Non-Sequential Files; 1628 Advanced COBOL: Coding with VSAM Files; 1629 Advanced COBOL: Sorting and Advanced Programming Structures; 1633 Advanced Structured COBOL

AT&T - Center for Systems Education (Formerly AT&T Company Data Systems Education Group)
: Initial Designer Training 2

Brick Computer Science Institute
: Advanced ANSI COBOL; Introduction to ANSI COBOL

The Chubb Institute
: Applications Laboratory; COBOL Language

The Cittone Institute
: COBOL

Computer Learning Center
: Structured Programming in COBOL

Control Data
: Structured COBOL Programming

National Institute of Information Technology
: Certificate in COBOL Programming; COBOL Programming and Application

NCR Corporation
: Advanced NCR VRX COBOL; COBOL Programming; COBOL 74 - Self-Instruction; COBOL 74 VRX/E; COBOL 74; Introduction to Interactive COBOL Programming; Structured COBOL

Collective Bargaining

United States Postal Service - Department of Training and Development
: Labor Relations Management MTS

Color Photography

Xerox Corporation
: 6500 Color Copier

Color Printing

Defense Mapping Agency - Inter American Geodetic Survey Cartographic School
: Cartographic Techniques for Thematic Mapping

Commercial Contract Law

United States Navy Acquisition Management Training Office
: Government Contracting Law

Commercial Investment

National Association of REALTORS®
: Case Studies in Commercial Investment Real Estate Brokerage (CI-105)

Commercial Law

American Bankers Association
: Law and Banking: Applications; Law and Banking

American Educational Institute, Inc.
: Legal Principles; Liability; Property

Certified Employee Benefit Specialist Program
: CEBS Course V; Contemporary Legal Environment of

Employee Benefit Plans

Institute of Financial Education
Commercial Law I; Commercial Law II

Commercial Lending

Institute of Financial Education
Commercial Lending for Savings Institutions

Communication

Indian Health Service - Tribal Management Support Center
Training the Trainer

Communication Skills

Bell Atlantic Corporation
Designing and Conducting Role Play

United States Department of Labor, DOL Academy
Effective Listening and Memory Development

U.S. West Learning Systems
Face to Face Communication Skills

Communication Systems Installation

U.S. West Learning Systems
Mountain Bell 139 and 141 Sequence; Mountain Bell 139 Sequence; 139: Key Telephone Installation - Phase I; 139A: 21A Communication System Installation; 139C: 7A Communication System Installation; 139D: 4A Communication System Installation; 139E: 600 Series Modular Panels; 141: Key Telephone System Repair

Communication Systems Installation Techniques

U.S. West Learning Systems
Key Systems

Communication Systems Maintenance

U.S. West Learning Systems
Dataphone II Service; DATASPEED 40 Dataphone Service

Communications

AT&T - Center for Systems Education (Formerly AT&T Company Data Systems Education Group)
Interpersonal Management Skills for Information Systems

AT&T - Marketing Education - Somerset Seminars
Public Switched Network Seminar

Bell Atlantic Corporation
Effective Communicating; Oral Communication; Outside Plant Trunk Facilities Design; Programming Languages, Architecture and Operating Systems, and Communications

Control Data
Communications and Consulting Skills Sequence

General Electric Company
Effective Listening

Institute for Citizen Involvement in Education
Public Policy and Public Schools

Institute of Financial Education
Communication Skills for Business: Talking and Listening; Effective Speaking

International Correspondence Schools
Communications

Knight-Ridder, Inc.
Interpersonal and Organizational Communications; Making Effective Presentations

Laubach Literacy Action
Writing for New Readers

National Emergency Training Center
Public Fire Education Specialist

National Management Association
Supervisory and Management Skills Program

National Mine Health and Safety Academy
Communication Skills I or Communication, Interpersonal, Small Group

National Weather Service Training Center
Weather Service Operations

New England Telephone Company
Communications Workshop; Investment in Excellence

Opportunities Academy of Management Training, Inc.
Adult Basic Education

Pacific Bell
Effective Communicating Seminar

Seminary Extension, Southern Baptist Seminaries
Advanced Exposition

United States Army Materiel Command - AMC (Formerly DARCOM - United States Army Materiel Development and Readiness Command)
Written Communications

United States Department of Agriculture, Graduate School
Advanced Practice in Editing; Editing; Editing Technical Manuscripts; Intermediate Editing; Intermediate Editing Principles and Practices; Introduction to the Editing Process; Legal Writing I; Legal Writing II; Practice in Editing; Principles of Editing; Principles of Editing for Publication; Proofreading; Publishing Management; Seminar in Editing; Style and Techniques for Editors

United States Drug Enforcement Administration
Drug Enforcement Officers Academy

United States Postal Service - Department of Training and Development
Report Writing for Postal Managers

U.S. West Learning Systems
Face to Face Communication Skills

Western Regional CUNA School for Credit Union Personnel
Western Regional CUNA School for Credit Union Personnel

Westinghouse Electric Corporation, Defense and Electronics Center
Communications Workshop B100; Human Interaction and Communication; Transactional Analysis B120

Communications Circuit Design

GTE Service Corporation - GTE Telephone Operations Network Training
> Special Circuits Design Engineering

Communications Electronics

Federal Aviation Administration
> ILS Wilcox Mark 1-A (40235)

Communications Engineering

GTE Service Corporation - GTE Telephone Operations Network Training
> Fiber Optic Communications Engineering

Communications Engineering Technology

GTE Service Corporation - GTE Telephone Operations Network Training
> Basic Transmission Engineering

Communications Network Design

U.S. West Learning Systems
> Design Center Engineering

Communications Network Subsystem

GTE Service Corporation - GTE Telephone Operations Network Training
> Digital Network Concepts

Communications Systems

GTE Service Corporation - GTE Telephone Operations Network Training
> Customer Loop Design

Henkels & McCoy, Inc.
> Cable Television Technician Course; Key System Installer

U.S. West Learning Systems
> Advanced OSP Engineering Work Plans; Loop Electronics - Design; Mountain Bell Sequence; Preparation OSP Engineering Work Plans

Communications Systems Practices

Bell Atlantic Corporation
> Custom Telephone Service System; Custom Telephone Service System Repair 208, Dimension 400 Repair-Tier 2 209, Horizon Computer; Dimension 400 Repair - Tier 2, Course 209; Dimension 400 Tier 1 Installation and Repair, Course 208; Horizon Communications Systems, Course 237

U.S. West Learning Systems
> Basic Carrier for Outside Forces; Basic Carrier; Circuit Reading; Engineering Tools and Field Survey; Horizon 32A; Loop Electronics-Construction and Maintenance Supervision; Mountain Bell Sequence; Mountain Bell 345 & 370 Sequence; Preparation OSP Engineering Work Plans; 345: Dimension Custom Telephone Service; 370: Horizon 32A

Communications Technology

Bell Communications Research Training and Education Center
> Planning, Design, and Operation of Telecommunication Systems

Professional Secretaries International
> Part VI: Office Administration and Technology; Part VI: Office Technology

U.S. West Learning Systems
> Subscribers Carrier Planning

Communications Theory

General Electric Company
> B-Course

Community Affairs

Young Women's Christian Association of the U.S.A.
> Management Training for Staff with Executive Potential; Management Workshop for Executive Staff; Management Workshop for Student Leadership; Presidential Leadership and Association Committee Chairpersons' Workshop; Staff Development II

Community Development

National Emergency Training Center
> Strategic Analysis of Fire Prevention Programs

Community Health

American Medical Record Association
> Orientation to the Health Care Field

United States Public Health Service - Indian Health Service
> Basic Maternal and Child Health; Community Health Representative; Environmental Health Concepts and Practices; Maternal and Child Nutrition; Rehabilitation and Home Health Care

Community Services

Indian Health Service - Tribal Management Support Center
> Training the Trainer

Competitive Marketing Analysis

Bell Communications Research Training and Education Center
> Competitive Analysis

David C.D. Rogers Associates
> Finance and Accounting in the Competitive Environment

Composition

Bell Atlantic Corporation
> Effective Writing

Chrysler Institute Associate Degree Program
> Writing Skills

Computational Research Methods

National Cryptologic School
> APL Programming

Computer Aided Analysis of Electronic Circuits

General Motors Corporation - Technical Staffs Group and Lansing Automotive Division (Formerly Advanced Engineering Staff [AES])
> Computer-Aided Electrical Engineering

Computer Aided Design

INACOMP Computer Centers, Inc.
> Computer Aided Design

Computer Aided Design and Manufacturing

General Motors Corporation - Technical Staffs Group and Lansing Automotive Division (Formerly Advanced Engineering Staff [AES])
> Computer Integrated Design and Manufacturing

Computer and Digital Equipment Diagnostics and Repair

National Weather Service Training Center
> Automation of Field Operations and Services M-05-07, M-08-04; Upper Air Minicomputer M-03-06

Computer Applications

Data Processing Training, Inc.
> Computer Literacy; Introduction to Spreadsheet Applications

Computer Architecture

Bell Communications Research Training and Education Center
> Data Communications - System Network Architecture; 3B Processor - Operations and Data Base Management; 3B20 Duplex Computer Systems Maintenance

General Motors Corporation - Technical Staffs Group and Lansing Automotive Division (Formerly Advanced Engineering Staff [AES])
> Computer Architecture

Computer Circuit Diagnostics and Repair

United States Postal Service - Department of Training and Development
> Basic Process Control System

Computer Circuits

The Cittone Institute
> Microprocessor Technology

Computer Disk Drives

Dow Jones & Company, Inc.
> CDC 9710/9715 Disk Drives; CDC 9766 Disk Drive

Computer Electronics

Federal Aviation Administration
> Computer Display Channel for Technicians (43426)

Computer Engineering

Control Data
> Introduction to Microprocessors

NCR Corporation
> Data Communications: Concepts; Data Communications: Fault Analysis; Telecommunications; Video Display: Fault Analysis; Video Displays: Concepts

United States Army Materiel Command - AMC (Formerly DARCOM - United States Army Materiel Development and Readiness Command)
> Computer Simulation and Communication Techniques; Computer Techniques for Engineers; Current Topics in Software Engineering; Economic Analysis and Software Life-Cycle Costs; Microprocessor Controls; Software Engineering Concepts II; Software Engineering Using ADA II; Software Engineering Workshop; Systems Engineering

Computer Equipment Repair

Federal Aviation Administration
> IBM 029 Card Punch and IBM 129 Card Punch - Print-Verifier (43456)

Computer Fundamentals

Applied Learning (Formerly ASI/DELTAK)
> Introduction to Computer Fundamentals; 5140 ADP Concepts; 5141 ADP Fundamentals

Computer Graphics

Defense Mapping Agency - Inter American Geodetic Survey Cartographic School
> Modern Cartography

General Motors Corporation - Technical Staffs Group and Lansing Automotive Division (Formerly Advanced Engineering Staff [AES])
> Computer Graphics

Computer Hardware

Control Data
> Computer Hardware

Northern Telecom, Inc., Digital Switching Systems - Technical Training Center
> DMS-10 System Maintenance; DMS-100/200 System Maintenance

Computer Information Systems

AT&T - Center for Systems Education (Formerly AT&T Company Data Systems Education Group)
> Analysis and Design Strategies; Concepts of the Integrated Systems Provisioning Process; Data Analysis and Logical Data Structuring; Data Gathering for System Development; Human Factors in Computer Systems; Logical Data Structuring; Personnel Subsystem Testing and Evaluation; Structured Test Plans; Task Analysis

Institute of Management and Production
> Computer Concepts in Business

International Correspondence Schools
> Introduction to Computer Concepts

Pacific Bell
> Advanced PC Users Series: Operating Systems, Project Management (1426), Local Networks (1423); Basic Network Design; Computer Systems Concepts; dBASE III Users Series: Introduction to dBASE III; Using dBASE III (1405B); Applying dBASE III (1405C); Electronic Spreadsheets: Enhancing Lotus 1-2-3 with Freelance, HAL, and Manuscript; Electronic Spreadsheets: EXCEL on MacIntosh; Integrated Application Software: Beginning DOS and Total Engineering Support System; Integrated Application

938 Index

Software: Total Engineering Support System (TESS) and PC-DOS (1436); Structured COBOL; Systems Analysis and Design; Word Processing Concepts: MS-Word on MacIntosh

Southwestern Bell Telephone Company

Introduction to C Programming; Introduction to UNIXR Operating Systems and Shell Programming; Report Writing Using the Fourth Generation Language FOCUS; UNIXR Systems Programming; Use of Fourth Generation Language FOCUS

Computer Literacy

Abu Dhabi National Oil Company Career Development Center/GDC, Inc.

Introduction to Data Processing and Computer Applications

AT&T - Center for Systems Education (Formerly AT&T Company Data Systems Education Group)

Data Processing Concepts for Users; Information System Seminar for the Executive

International Correspondence Schools

Computer Literacy and Programming in BASIC; Computer Science I; Computer Science II

Computer Mainframe Operations and Maintenance

Unisys Corporation

Introduction to Computer Mainframe Operation and Maintenance

Computer Maintenance

Unisys Corporation

Introduction to Large Computer Mainframes Operation and Maintenance (337800); Introduction to Software Concepts

United States Postal Service - Department of Training and Development

Digital Computer Concepts

Computer Maintenance Technology

United States Postal Service - Department of Training and Development

Model 140/141 MPLSM/ZMT/ESP; Process Control System NOVA 800; Zip Mail Translator

Computer Networking

Bell Atlantic Corporation

Computer Network Architecture; Information Networks

Computer Operations

Applied Learning (Formerly ASI/DELTAK)

Computer Operations; 4160 Multiple Virtual System XA

Contel Service Corporation

Distributed Customer Record Information System

Federal Aviation Administration

Adaptation and Operations (53122); NAS Data Processing Functions (53129); On-the-Job Training, Final Functional Area Checkout (55104)

NCR Corporation

Introduction to VRX Operating System; NCS Operations; VRX Operations

Unisys Corporation

Introduction to Computer Systems Operation

Computer Organization

The Chubb Institute

Assembler Language

Computer Peripheral Maintenance

United States Postal Service - Department of Training and Development

Process Control System Magnetic Tape Unit

Computer Peripheral Operations

Federal Aviation Administration

ARTS III Operating and Programming the Disc System (53012)

Computer Peripherals

The Cittone Institute

Computer System, Peripherals and Robotics

Unisys Corporation

Introduction to Tape Subsystems

United States Postal Service - Department of Training and Development

Optical Character Reader I

Computer Programming

AT&T - Center for Systems Education (Formerly AT&T Company Data Systems Education Group)

Programmer Productivity Techniques

Federal Aviation Administration

Air Traffic Control Automated Radar Terminal System; ARTS III: A Programmer (53010); Hardware Familiarization and Programming EARTS Software (53133)

General Electric Company

Computer Programming and Data Analysis; Data Analysis and Probability Evaluation; Introduction to Computers; Manufacturing Information Systems

General Motors Corporation - Technical Staffs Group and Lansing Automotive Division (Formerly Advanced Engineering Staff [AES])

Computer Programming in BASIC

National Institute of Information Technology

Computer-Based Business Systems; Diploma in Systems Management

United States Postal Service - Department of Training and Development

Digital Computer Technology

Computer Science

Applied Learning (Formerly ASI/DELTAK)

Understanding Data Processing

AT&T - Center for Systems Education (Formerly AT&T Company Data Systems Education Group)

Analysis and Design Strategies; Assembler Language Coding; Basic FORTRAN; Bisync Protocol Analysis; Computer Communications System Architecture;

Computer Communications System Operations; Data Analysis and Logical Data Structuring; Data Gathering for System Development; Data Security and Controls; Human Factors in Computer Systems; IMS/VS Batch Programming; IMS/VS Data Base Implementation; IMS/VS Logical Data Base Implementation; IMS/VS Physical Data Base Design; Introduction and Techniques (IE3320 and IE3324); IMS/VS Physical Data Base Implementation; IMS/VS Programming - Teleprocessing; IMS/VS Programming; Introduction to Assembler Language Coding; Introduction to FORTRAN; Logical Data Base Design; Logical Data Structuring; Modems and Facilities; MVS Workshop; Physical Data Base Design; PL/1 Workshop; Programmer Basic Training; Structured Test Plans; Teleprocessing in the Host; Terminals and Line Protocol; X.25 Network Architecture

Bell Atlantic Corporation

Information Transmission and Networking; Network Management and Applications; Programmer Basic Training; Programmer Basic Training - COBOL; #5 Electronic Switching Systems Method of Operation

Bell Communications Research, Inc.

Basic Programming Sequence UNIX System Files and Commands OS402, Advanced Use of the UNIX Text; Basic Word Processing Sequence Equation Processing Using the UNIX System WP122, Table Processing Using; Introduction to "C" Language Programming for Experienced Programmers

Bell Communications Research Training and Education Center

Advanced "C" Language Programming; Data Communications - PC Communications; Introduction to UNIXR Operating System; Software Fault Analysis

Chrysler Institute Associate Degree Program

Computer Usage in Manufacturing Operations

Computer Learning Center of Philadelphia

Assembler Language; OS Job Control Language; Structured Programming in COBOL

Computer Learning Center of Washington

Assembler Language Programming; COBOL Programming; FORTRAN Programming; Introduction to Data Processing; Introduction to Data Processing for Programmers; Systems Analysis and Design

Contel Service Corporation

ADE Training; Advanced DATATRIEVE with FMS; Advanced dBASE III Plus; Advanced Lotus 1-2-3; Azrex Training; BASIC Micro Programming; BASIC Programming; COBOL-74 Specifics; Computer Fundamentals for Engineering Applications; DATATRIEVE Training; DPS MOD600 Utilization; FORTRAN; Honeywell Job Control Language; Intermediate Timeshare; Introduction to Data Processing and Data Communications; Introduction to dBASE III Plus; Introduction to Systems Analysis and Design; Introduction to Time Sharing; Lotus 1-2-3; VAX/VMS Commands and Utilities I; VAX/VMS Commands and Utilities II; VAX/VMS Minicomputer Concepts; 20/20

Control Data

Ada Programming Fundamentals; Advanced Ada and Software Engineering; Computer Literacy; Data Communications; Introduction to Microprocessors; Job Control Language; PASCAL

Defense Mapping Agency - Inter American Geodetic Survey Cartographic School

Automated Cartography; Automated Cartography-Digitizing System Operator; Digital Methods of Terrain Modeling; Introduction to Computer Programming Using FORTRAN, Independent Study; Introduction to Digital Image Analysis; Introduction to Minicomputers, Independent Study; Modern Cartography; Photogrammetric Applications Program

Federal Aviation Administration

Adaptation and Operations (53122); ARTS II For Data Systems Specialist (53020); ARTS III for Data Systems Specialist (53003); ARTS III Operating and Programming the Disc System (53012); Basic Assembler Language (53135); Common Digitizer Height Only (43477); Computer Based Support for Managerial Decision Making (01307); Computer Display Channel Processor (43423); Data Processing Subsystem (42027); Direct Access Radar Channel System for Engineers (43479); Direct Access Radar Channel System Software (43520); Flight Data Processing and Monitor for Jovial Programming System (43469); IBM System 360 Operating System (43468); IBM 360 Operating System (12003); IBM 9020-A Processing (43461); IBM 9020-A System Hardware for Engineers (43489); IBM 9020-A/D System Common Hardware for Engineers (43491); IBM 9020-D System Hardware for Engineers (43490); Interface Buffer Adapter and Generator (42024); Jovial Programming (12002); NAS Enroute Operational Program for Engineers (43470); NAS System Interfaces for Systems Performance Specialists (43471); On-the-Job Training in NAS (55103); Radar Data Processing for Systems Performance Specialist (43483); Ultra Programming (42008)

General Electric Company

Advanced Computer Techniques; Advanced Programming Techniques; C Programming; C-Course; Computer Science; GESIMTEL; Information Systems; Time-Sharing System and Applications

General Motors Corporation - Technical Staffs Group and Lansing Automotive Division (Formerly Advanced Engineering Staff [AES])

Advanced Artificial Intelligence; Compiler Design; Database Systems; Information Structures; Pattern Recognition

Institute of Financial Education

Introduction to Electronic Data Processing

Institute of Management and Production

Basic Language for Microcomputer Users; COBOL Programming; Data Processing Program; Introduction to Data Processing; Report Program Generator II; Systems Analysis and Design

Knight-Ridder, Inc.

Application of Modern Computer Technology to Newspaper Operations

National Cryptologic School

ALGOL Programming; FORTRAN Programming; General Programming Techniques; Introduction to Computer Science; Introduction to Computer Software; Introduction to Computing; Modern Computer Architecture; Systems Software

National Institute of Information Technology

Certificate in COBOL Programming; COBOL Programming and Application

NCR Corporation

    Data Communications: Concepts; Data Communications: Fault Analysis; RM/COS Operating System; Telecommunications; UNIX® Operating System; UNIX® System Administration; Video Display: Fault Analysis; Video Displays: Concepts

New England Telephone Company

    Programmer Basic Training

Ohio Bell Telephone Company

    Data Processing Concepts

Pacific Bell

    Computer Systems Concepts; Data Processing/Data Communications; Introduction to "C" Programming; Introduction to Data Base Management Systems; Introduction to JCL; Structured COBOL; UNISYS Database Concepts and UNISYS 1100 Series System Concepts (52698 and 52691); Utilities

Southwestern Bell Telephone Company

    Data Communications Technology; Fiber Optics; IMS/VS: DL/I Programming; Introduction to C Programming; Introduction to UNIXR Operating Systems and Shell Programming; Report Writing Using the Fourth Generation Language FOCUS; UNIX® Systems Programming; Use of Fourth Generation Language FOCUS

Texas Utilities Electric Corporation (Formerly Texas Utilities Generating Company - TUGCo)

    Microprocessor I; Microprocessor II; Microprocessor III

Unisys Corporation

    B7900 Hardware and Maintenance; CP3680/CP3685 Maintenance; Introduction to Large Computer Mainframes Operation and Maintenance (337800); Introduction to Software Concepts; Maintenance and Operation; Operations and Software; S3000 Document Processor

United States Army Materiel Command - AMC (Formerly DARCOM - United States Army Materiel Development and Readiness Command)

    Computer Science; Computer Simulation and Communication Techniques; Computer Simulation for System Design; Computer Techniques for Engineers; Current Topics in Software Engineering; Embedded Computer Algorithms; Engineering Applications for Computers; Software Configuration Management; Software Engineering Concepts I; Software Engineering Concepts II; Software Engineering Using ADA I; Software Engineering Using ADA II; Software Engineering Workshop; Systems Engineering

United States Department of Agriculture, Graduate School

    ADA Programming; Advanced C Programming; BASIC Programming Language; C Programming; COBOL Programming I; COBOL Programming II; Data Base Design; FORTRAN Programming; Introduction to Data Processing; PASCAL Programming; Structured COBOL Programming I; Structured COBOL Programming II; Structured COBOL Programming III

United States Navy Acquisition Management Training Office

    Automation of Procurement and Accounting Data Entry

U.S. West Learning Systems

    Introduction to DBMS; Introduction to Hewlett Packard; Introduction to Super CALC 2; JCL and Operating Systems; PL/I Series; Programmer Basic Training; Q CALC; VSAM

Westinghouse Electric Corporation, Defense and Electronics Center

    Advanced Microprocessing; Applied Engineering Software; Basic Microprocessing; LISP: The Artificial Intelligence Language; Probability and Random Processes I; Probability and Random Processes II

Westinghouse Electric Corporation, Education Center Department

    Computer Concepts

Xerox Corporation

    8200/9500 Update

Computer Science Technology

Federal Aviation Administration

    Computer Display Channel for Software (43451)

Computer Software

Southwestern Bell Telephone Company

    Specialized Telephone Software Applications

United States Army Materiel Command - AMC (Formerly DARCOM - United States Army Materiel Development and Readiness Command)

    Economic Analysis and Software Life-Cycle Costs

Computer Supported Marketing Techniques

National Association of REALTORS®

    Real Estate Business Decision-Making Computer Simulated Management Game (CRB-305)

Computer System Analysis

United States Postal Service - Department of Training and Development

    Postal Source Data System

Computer System Architecture

Unisys Corporation

    Microcomputer System Maintenance

United States Postal Service - Department of Training and Development

    Automatic Business Mail Process Systems

Computer System Maintenance and Repair

National Weather Service Training Center

    Automation of Field Operations and Services M-04-04

Computer Systems

Bell Atlantic Corporation

    New Jersey Bell 509B: No. 1 ESS Central Processor and Program Fundamentals; Programmer Basic Training; Programming Languages, Architecture and Operating Systems, and Communications

The Chubb Institute

    Assembler Language

The Cittone Institute

    Computer System, Peripherals and Robotics

Pacific Bell

    1 ESS Central Processor and Programming

Fundamentals

United States Postal Service - Department of Training and Development

Digital Electronics; Logic Circuits

U.S. West Learning Systems

Mountain Bell 509B: No. 1 ESS Central Processor and Program Fundamentals

Computer Systems Networking

NCR Corporation

Problem Determination for SNA

Computer Systems Technology

Federal Aviation Administration

Computer Update Equipment (43416)

Computer Technology

Bell Atlantic Corporation

Computer-Based PBX Systems 208, Dimension 400 Repair-Tier 2 209, CSS 201-2000 Dimension Installation; Electronic Switching Systems; Fundamentals of Data Transmission; Fundamentals of Data Transmission: Testing and Service; Microcomputer Based PBX Systems: Installation and Maintenance; Peripheral Installation and Maintenance

Control Data

Data Representation

Dow Jones & Company, Inc.

CDC 9710/9715 Disk Drives; CDC 9766 Disk Drive; DataBak; Pagination

Federal Aviation Administration

ARTS III for Data Systems Specialist (53003); Central Control and Monitoring System (CCMS) Maintenance (43472); Test Equipment Console Test (43419)

General Electric Company

Computer Science

Unisys Corporation

Introduction to COBOL Processor Operation and Maintenance

United States Postal Service - Department of Training and Development

Digital Computer Technology; Optical Character Reader I

U.S. West Learning Systems

Introduction to Computer System Concepts; Introduction to Electronic Systems Concepts; Microprocessor Programming and Applications

Xerox Corporation

9400 Duplicator; 9700 EPS

Computer Theory

United States Postal Service - Department of Training and Development

Digital Computer Systems Conversion

Computers

Chrysler Institute Associate Degree Program

Computer Usage in Manufacturing Operations

The Cittone Institute

Introduction to Computers

GTE Service Corporation - GTE Telephone Operations Network Training

Data Communications Concepts

National Weather Service Training Center

Computer Technology Y-03-01

United States Department of Internal Revenue Service, Federal Law Enforcement Training Center

Special Agent Investigative Techniques

United States Postal Service - Department of Training and Development

Basic Process Control System

Computers in Business

Abu Dhabi National Oil Company Career Development Center/GDC, Inc.

Computers in Business

Concrete

International Correspondence Schools

Concrete; Reinforced Concrete Design

Conduit Layout

Bell Atlantic Corporation

Basic Drafting; Conduit Drafting

Constitutional Law and Governmental Agencies

Omega Institute

Constitutional Law and Governmental Agencies

Construction

Institute of Financial Education

Housing Construction

Construction Technology

GTE Service Corporation - GTE Telephone Operations Network Training

Basic Engineering—Outside Plant

National Emergency Training Center

Building Construction: Non-Combustible and Fire Resistive; Building Construction: Principles—Wood and Ordinary Construction

Pacific Bell

Building Industry Consultant

Consumer Credit

American Bankers Association

Banking and the Plastic Card; Consumer Lending

Consumer Credit Management

American Bankers Association

Consumer Credit 200-Level Curriculum

American Institute of Banking - Washington, D.C. Chapter

Consumer Credit

Consumer Finance

Control Data
> Consumer Finance

Consumer Lending

Institute of Financial Education
> Consumer Lending

Consumer Marketing Management

AT&T - Corporate Education Center, Management Education Training Division
> Consumer Marketing Strategies

Contemporary Business Issues

National Management Association
> Supervisory and Management Skills Program

Contract Administration

Westinghouse Electric Corporation, Integrated Logistic Support Division
> Controllers Professional Training School; Government Contracts Accounting and Control

Contract Law

Omega Institute
> Contract Law

Conveyor Operation and Maintenance

Seafarers Harry Lundeberg School of Seamanship
> Conveyorman

Corporate Finance

AT&T - Marketing Education - Somerset Seminars
> Financial Awareness Plus Seminar; Financial Awareness Seminar; Introduction to Finance

First Fidelity Bank, N.A., N.J., Management Training Program
> Corporate Finance

NCR Corporation
> Financial Management

Corporate Financial Management

Control Data
> Foundations of Corporate Financial Management

Corporate Law

Omega Institute
> Corporate Law

Corporate Planning

David C.D. Rogers Associates
> Concepts of Corporate Planning

Corporate Strategy

Bell Communications Research Training and Education Center
> Concepts of Corporate Planning

Corrections

Police Training Institute
> Basic Correctional Officers

Cost Accounting

Bell Atlantic Corporation
> Introduction to Property and Cost Accounting

Bell Communications Research Training and Education Center
> Capital Cost Methodology

United States Department of Agriculture, Graduate School
> Cost Accounting I; Cost Accounting II; Cost Accounting III

Cost Analysis

General Electric Company
> Economic Analysis of Alternatives; Introduction to Accounting Principles; Managerial Accounting and Cost Analysis; Operating Costs, Budgets, and Measurements

Counseling

Jewish Hospital of St. Louis
> Assertiveness Training; Stress Management

New Jersey Department of Human Services
> Prediction and Prevention of Aggressive Behavior in the System

Opportunities Academy of Management Training, Inc.
> Advanced Motivation

Police Training Institute
> Advanced Law for Youth Officers; Youth Officers

Counseling Psychology

Opportunities Academy of Management Training, Inc.
> Advanced Motivation

Counselor Education

Independent School Management
> Extending Student Counselor's Role in Private-Independent Schools

Counterpoint

Tritone Music
> 18th-Century Counterpoint

Course Development

Unisys Corporation
> Principles and Practice of Course Development

Court Room Procedures

National Mine Health and Safety Academy
> Courtroom Procedures

Court Security Procedures

United States Department of Justice, U.S. Marshals Service, Federal Law Enforcement Training Center
> Deputy U.S. Marshals Basic Training School

Credit and Collections

Credit Union National Association - Certified Credit Union Executive Program
>Credit and Collections #900

Credit Management

American Bankers Association
>Commercial Lending; Consumer Lending; Income Property Construction Lending; Residential Mortgage Lending

Credit Unions

Credit Union National Association - Certified Credit Union Executive Program
>Introduction to Credit Unions #100

Crime Prevention

Police Training Institute
>Crime Prevention Officers

Criminal Intelligence

United States Department of Justice, U.S. Marshals Service, Federal Law Enforcement Training Center
>Deputy U.S. Marshals Basic Training School

Criminal Investigation

Bergen County Police Academy
>Basic Police Training Course

Police Training Institute
>Criminal Investigation; Fundamentals of Burglary Investigation; Homicide/Sex Investigation

United States Department of Justice, Immigration and Naturalization Service, Federal Law Enforcement Training Center
>Border Patrol Academy; Immigration Officer Academy

United States Department of the Treasury, Federal Law Enforcement Training Center
>Criminal Investigator Training

Criminal Justice

American Institute for Paralegal Studies, Inc.
>Introduction to Criminal Justice

Illinois Fire Service Institute
>Arson Investigation I; Arson Investigation II

National Academy for Paralegal Studies, Inc.
>Introduction to Criminal Justice

National Emergency Training Center
>Arson Detection; Fire Arson Investigation

National Sheriffs' Association
>Fundamentals of Adult Detention

Opportunities Academy of Management Training, Inc.
>Employment and Training Services to Ex-Offenders

Police Training Institute
>Advanced Law for Youth Officers; Basic Correctional Officers; Child Sex Exploitation; Police Community Relations; Youth Officers

United States Department of the Treasury, Federal Law Enforcement Training Center
>Criminal Investigator Training; Eight-Week Police Training Program

United States Drug Enforcement Administration
>Criminal Investigation - Drug Abuse; Drug Enforcement Officers Academy

United States Food and Drug Administration
>Basic Food and Drug Law Course

United States Postal Service - Department of Training and Development
>Postal Inspector Basic Training

Wolf Creek Nuclear Operating Corporation (Formerly Kansas Gas & Electric)
>Communications Qualification Training; General Security Qualification Information; Weapons Qualification Training

Criminal Law

American Center for Technical Arts and Sciences (Formerly Mainline Paralegal Institute)
>Criminal Law

American Institute for Paralegal Studies, Inc.
>Criminal Law and Procedure

Bergen County Police Academy
>Basic Police Training Course

Police Training Institute
>Basic Law Enforcement III; Basic Law Enforcement IV; Law for Police II

United States Department of the Treasury, Federal Law Enforcement Training Center
>Criminal Investigator Training

United States Postal Service - Department of Training and Development
>Postal Inspector Basic Training

Criminal Procedures

American Institute for Paralegal Studies, Inc.
>Criminal Law and Procedure

PJA School
>Criminal Law

Criminology

Police Training Institute
>Advanced Law for Youth Officers; Youth Officers

United States Department of Agriculture, Graduate School
>Criminal Law

Curriculum

Federal Aviation Administration
>Designing Programmed Instruction (10525)

Curriculum Design

Pacific Bell
>Development of Instructional Materials; Job Aid Analysis and Design

Curriculum Development

Federal Aviation Administration

> Air Traffic Control Specialist and/or Facility Instructor Training (10510); Curriculum Development (10512)

NCR Corporation

> Computer Assisted Instruction Development Techniques

Young Women's Christian Association of the U.S.A.

> Program Development Workshop

Customer Relations

New England Telephone Company

> Telemarketing

Pacific Bell

> Account Inquiry Initial Training; Marketing Residence Service Representative Basic-RASC; Marketing Residence Service Representative Basic-RTOC

Southwestern Bell Telephone Company

> Account Inquiry Center

U.S. West Learning Systems

> BSC-BRIT-AIC Business Representative Initial Training - Account Inquiry Center; Business Account Inquiry Training; Business Demand Sales Training; Business Representative Initial Training/Account System Inquiry; Residence Account Service Center Learning; Residence Account Service Center; Residence Telephone Order Center Curriculum; Residence Telephone Order Center RITC-RTOC

Data Analysis

General Electric Company

> Computer Programming and Data Analysis; Data Analysis and Probability Evaluation; Introduction to Computers; Manufacturing Information Systems

Data Analysis and Regression

AT&T - Marketing Education - Somerset Seminars

> Data Analysis and Regression

Data Base Concepts

Applied Learning (Formerly ASI/DELTAK)

> Data Base Concepts; 3801-3807 Data Base: An Introduction; 3808 AITC: How A Data Base Management System Works; 3809 AITC: Data Dictionary; 3810 Data Base Concepts and Fundamentals

NCR Corporation

> NCR TOTAL

Data Base Design

Applied Learning (Formerly ASI/DELTAK)

> Data Base Design; 1527 IMS Data Base Design; 4505 IMS Concepts

Data Base III

The Cittone Institute

> Data Base III

Data Base Management

Bell Atlantic Corporation

> Information Management System

Control Data

> Introduction to Data Processing and Data Base Management

NCR Corporation

> Data Base Design; PROGRESS Programming Fundamentals

Data Communication System Installation and Maintenance

U.S. West Learning Systems

> Data Speed 40

Data Communication Systems

U.S. West Learning Systems

> Basic Data Systems Protocol; Mountain Bell 160-163 Sequence; Mountain Bell 167-179 Sequence; 160: Introduction to Data Systems; 162A: Using the Oscilloscope; 163B/163.2: Data Test Equipment 914C; 167: 200 Series Data Sets; 179: 921A Data Test Set

Data Communication Systems Maintenance

U.S. West Learning Systems

> Dataphone II

Data Communications

Applied Learning (Formerly ASI/DELTAK)

> Data Communications; 3501 Fundamentals of Data Communications; 3505 Data Communications Transmission; 4530 IMS/VS Data Communications Programming Overview; 4574 IMS/VS MFS: Concepts and Terminology; 4575 IMS/VS MFS: Control Statement Coding

AT&T - Center for Systems Education (Formerly AT&T Company Data Systems Education Group)

> Bisync Protocol Analysis; Computer Communications System Architecture; Computer Communications System Operations; Modems and Facilities; Teleprocessing in the Host; Terminals and Line Protocol; X.25 Network Architecture

Bell Atlantic Corporation

> #5 Electronic Switching Systems Method of Operation

Bell Communications Research Training and Education Center

> Data Services - Digital Data System; Protocol Concepts-1; Protocol Concepts-2

GTE Service Corporation - GTE Telephone Operations Network Training

> Advanced Data Communications Analysis; Data Communications Concepts

Pacific Bell

> Protocol-Asynchronous and Bisynchronous

Southwestern Bell Telephone Company

> Phone Trunk Testing

Unisys Corporation

> Fundamentals of Data Communications

U.S. West Learning Systems

> No. 5 Crossbar - Method of Operation; No. 5 Method of Operation - 34565

Data Communications Concepts

Ohio Bell Telephone Company

    Data Communications Concepts

Data Communications Technology

Bell Communications Research Training and Education Center

    DC-Basic Protocols; DC-Introduction to Data Communications

Data Entry

Federal Aviation Administration

    Adaptation and Operations (53122); NAS Data Processing Functions (53129)

Data Networks

Bell Communications Research Training and Education Center

    Data Services - Data in the Network; Protocol Concepts-2

Data Processing

Applied Learning (Formerly ASI/DELTAK)

    Understanding Data Processing

AT&T - Center for Systems Education (Formerly AT&T Company Data Systems Education Group)

    Assembler Language Coding; Basic FORTRAN; Bisync Protocol Analysis; COBOL Workshop; Computer Communications System Architecture; Computer Communications System Operations; Data Security and Controls; IMS/VS Batch Programming; IMS/VS Data Base Implementation; IMS/VS Logical Data Base Implementation; IMS/VS Physical Data Base Design; Introduction and Techniques (IE3320 and IE3324); IMS/VS Physical Data Base Implementation; IMS/VS Programming - Teleprocessing; IMS/VS Programming; Introduction to Assembler Language Coding; Introduction to FORTRAN; Logical Data Base Design; Modems and Facilities; MVS Workshop; Physical Data Base Design; PL/1 Workshop; Teleprocessing in the Host; Terminals and Line Protocol; X.25 Network Architecture

Bell Atlantic Corporation

    An Introduction to Time Share and Basic Language Programming; C Programming; Data Processing/Data Communications; Introduction to Honeywell Time Share; Programmer Basic Training; Time Share Basic

Bell Communications Research Training and Education Center

    Advanced "C" Language Programming

Blake Business School

    Computer Theory

Brick Computer Science Institute

    Introduction to Data Processing

The Chubb Institute

    Introduction to Computer Systems; Programming Fundamentals

Computer Learning Center

    Introduction to Data Processing

Computer Learning Center of Philadelphia

    Assembler Language; DOS Operations; Introduction to Data Processing; OS Job Control Language; OS Operations; Structured Programming in COBOL

Computer Learning Center of Washington

    Assembler Language Programming; COBOL Programming; FORTRAN Programming; Introduction to Data Processing; Introduction to Data Processing for Programmers; Systems Analysis and Design

Contel Service Corporation

    ADE Training; Advanced DATATRIEVE with FMS; Advanced dBASE III Plus; Advanced Lotus 1-2-3; Azrex Training; BASIC Micro Programming; BASIC Programming; COBOL-74 Specifics; Computer Fundamentals for Engineering Applications; DATATRIEVE Training; DPS MOD600 Utilization; FORTRAN; Honeywell Job Control Language; Intermediate Timeshare; Introduction to Data Processing and Data Communications; Introduction to dBASE III Plus; Introduction to Designing Oracle/SQLForms; Introduction to Oracle/SQLCalc; Introduction to Oracle/SQLPlus; Introduction to Systems Analysis and Design; Introduction to Time Sharing; Lotus 1-2-3; Personal Computer; VAX/VMS Commands and Utilities I; VAX/VMS Commands and Utilities II; VAX/VMS Minicomputer Concepts; 20/20

Control Data

    Introduction to Data Processing and Data Base Management

Data Processing Training, Inc.

    Introduction to Spreadsheet Applications

Federal Aviation Administration

    Air Traffic Control Automated Radar Terminal System; ARTS II For Data Systems Specialist (53020); ARTS III: A Programmer (53010); ARTS III for Data Systems Specialist (53003); ARTS III Operating and Programming the Disc System (53012); Basic Assembler Language (53135); Computer Based Support for Managerial Decision Making (01307); IBM 360 Operating System (12003); Jovial Programming (12002); On-the-Job Training in NAS (55103)

General Electric Company

    C Programming

Georgia Computer Campus (Formerly Georgia Computer Programming Project for Severely Handicapped Persons)

    Advanced Programming: PASCAL and COBOL; COBOL II; Introduction to Data Processing - COBOL I

Health Insurance Association of America

    Group Life/Health Insurance: Part C; Group Life/Health Insurance: Parts A and B

Institute of Financial Education

    Introduction to Electronic Data Processing

Institute of Management and Production

    Basic Language for Microcomputer Users; COBOL Programming; Computer Concepts in Business; Data Processing Program; Introduction to Data Processing; Management of Data Processing Installations; Report Program Generator II; Systems Analysis and Design

International Correspondence Schools

    Introduction to Computer Concepts

International Monetary Fund

 CMC 100 Overview of Personal Computers; CMC 101 Microcomputer Fixed Disk Management; CMC 200 Lotus 1-2-3; CMC 201 Advanced Lotus 1-2-3

Katharine Gibbs School

 Introduction to Data Processing

National Cryptologic School

 Burroughs B6700/7000 Advanced Technical Skills; Burroughs B6700/7000 Systems Software; CDC 6600 Series Advanced Technical Skills; CDC 6600 Series System Software; COBOL Programming; IBM Assembly Language Programming; IBM 360 Job Control Language; IBM 360 System Software; IBM 370 Job Control Language; Introduction to Computer Software; Introduction to Computer Systems Operations; Introduction to the 370 MVS Operating System; Model 204 Information Retrieval Language; PDP-11 Programming; Phase V CDC 7600 System Software Concepts; Phase VI CDC 7600 System Advanced Technical Skills; PL/1 Programming; Programming for Operators; Systems Software; Univac 1100 Advanced Training Skills; Univac 1100 Systems Software; Univac 494 Advanced Technical Skills; Univac 494 HOLDER System Software; Univac 494RYE System Software; 370 MVS Advanced Technical Skills

NCR Corporation

 Automatic Teller Machine/Automated System Generator H05835; Data Processing: Concepts and Systems; EDP Concepts; Elementary Systems and Software - NEAT/3; Fundamentals of Computers and Programming Logic; Interactive Manufacturing Control Systems II; ITEM; Modular Lodging System Installation; Variable Item Processing System; 2140 Programming and System Installation; 2160 Food Service System Installation - UO2445

New England Telephone Company

 Programmer Basic Training

Northern Telecom, Inc., Digital Switching Systems - Technical Training Center

 DMS-10 System Maintenance; DMS-10 System Translations; DMS-100/200 System Maintenance; DMS-100/200 System Translations

O/E Learning, Inc.

 Lotus

Pacific Bell

 Advanced DOS; Advanced Lotus 1-2-3; Advanced PC Users Series: Operating Systems, Project Management (1426), Local Networks (1423); Basic Network Design; Beginning Lotus 1-2-3; Beginning WordPerfect; Intermediate Word Perfect; Advanced WordPerfect; Communications with Microcomputers; Data Processing/Data Communications; dBASE III Users Series: Introduction to dBASE III; Using dBASE III (1405B); Applying dBASE III (1405C); DOS Concepts and Beginning RBASE 5000 for Hard Disk PC Systems; DOS Concepts, Wordstar, and Lotus 1-2-3 for the Hard Disk PC System; DOS for the Hard Disk; EDP Concepts for Business; Electronic Spreadsheets: Enhancing Lotus 1-2-3 with Freelance, HAL, and Manuscript; Electronic Spreadsheets: EXCEL on MacIntosh; Fiber Optics: Sales or Technical; Fundamentals of Computer Operations; Integrated Application Software: Beginning DOS and Total Engineering Support System; Integrated Application Software: Total Engineering Support System (TESS) and PC-DOS (1436); Intermediate Lotus 1-2-3; Introduction to "C" Programming; Introduction to Data Base Management Systems; Introduction to DBASE II/III; Introduction to JCL; Introduction to Personal Computing; Multimate Mod. I; Multimate Mod. II; MVS Concepts; Paradox Users Series: Introduction to Paradox; Using Paradox (1425A); Applying Paradox (1425B); PC and Symphony Users Series: Hard Disk and DOS; Beginning Symphony; Advanced Symphony; PC and Wordstar Users Series: Beginning WI Hard Disk and DOS; Beginning Wordstar; Advanced Wordstar; Spreadsheets, Graphics, Word Processing and Database Using Symphony; Structured COBOL; UNISYS Database Concepts and UNISYS 1100 Series System Concepts (52698 and 52691); UNISYS Peripheral Subsystems; Utilities; Word Processing Concepts and the Use of Displaywrite; Word Processing Concepts and the Use of Multimate; Word Processing Concepts: MS-Word on MacIntosh

Southwestern Bell Telephone Company

 IMS Basic Data Communications Programming and Message Format Service; IMS/VS: DL/I Programming; Introduction to C Programming; Introduction to UNIXR Operating Systems and Shell Programming; Report Writing Using the Fourth Generation Language FOCUS; UNIXR Systems Programming; Use of Fourth Generation Language FOCUS

Unisys Corporation

 Introduction to Computer Systems Operation

United States Army Materiel Command - AMC (Formerly DARCOM - United States Army Materiel Development and Readiness Command)

 Management Information Systems

United States Department of Agriculture, Graduate School

 ADA Programming; ADP Documentation and Writing; Advanced C Programming; BASIC Programming for Beginners; BASIC Programming Language; C Programming; COBOL Programming I; COBOL Programming II; Data Base Design; IBM System 360/370 PL/1; IBM 360/370 OS/VS Job Control Language; Introduction to Computer Programming; Introduction to Data Processing; Introduction to Information Systems Technology; Introduction to ISPF (ACOMP346); Introduction to Problem Solving; PASCAL Programming; Problem Solving for COBOL Programmers; Structured COBOL Programming I; Structured COBOL Programming II; Structured COBOL Programming III; Structured Design and Programming; Structured Systems Analysis and Design; Systems Analysis and Design; Systems Analysis and Documentation

United States Navy Acquisition Management Training Office

 Automation of Procurement and Accounting Data Entry

Westinghouse Electric Corporation, Education Center Department

 Computer Concepts

Data Processing Systems Analysis

United States Postal Service - Department of Training and Development

 Zip Mail Translator

Data Processing Technology

United States Postal Service - Department of Training and Development

 Zip Mail Translator

Data Protocol

Bell Atlantic Corporation
>Basic Data Protocol

Data Transmission

Ohio Bell Telephone Company
>Transmission Principles

Pacific Bell
>Transmission Fundamentals

U.S. West Learning Systems
>Data Transmission Fundamentals

DC Circuit Maintenance

Wolf Creek Nuclear Operating Corporation (Formerly Kansas Gas & Electric)
>Troubleshooting/DC Sources

DC Circuits

Mercer County Vocational-Technical Schools - Division of Adult Education
>DC Circuits

DC Electronics

Chrysler Institute Associate Degree Program
>Fundamental Electronics I

DC Motors

International Correspondence Schools
>A-C and D-C Motors and Controls

Debtor/Creditor Relations

American Center for Technical Arts and Sciences (Formerly Mainline Paralegal Institute)
>Debtor/Creditor Relations

Decedent's Estates

American Center for Technical Arts and Sciences (Formerly Mainline Paralegal Institute)
>Estates, Trusts, and Wills

Decision and Risk Analysis

AT&T - Marketing Education - Somerset Seminars
>Decision and Risk Analysis

Decision Making

Control Data
>Problem Analysis and Decision Making

National Emergency Training Center
>Code Management: A Systems Approach

Dental Assisting

General Electric Company
>Radiological Techniques in Dentistry

Dental Hygiene

General Electric Company
>Radiological Techniques in Dentistry

Development Education

New England Telephone Company
>Writer's Workshop

Developmental Studies

Applied Learning (Formerly ASI/DELTAK)
>Fundamental Study Skills: Technical Math and Reading

Diesel Engine Technology

Seafarers Harry Lundeberg School of Seamanship
>Chief/Assistant Engineer - Uninspected Motor Vessels; Diesel Engines

Diesel Engines

Seafarers Harry Lundeberg School of Seamanship
>Diesel Engines

Diesel Mechanics

Federal Aviation Administration
>Diesel Engine Generators (44102)

United States Postal Service - Department of Training and Development
>Air Brakes; Allison Automatic Transmissions; Automotive Diesel Mechanics; Basic Diesel Mechanics - Module I - Basic Diesel Maintenance; Basic Diesel Mechanics - Module II - Mack-Diesel Maintenance; Caterpillar Diesel; Cummins Diesel I; Cummins Diesel III; Postal Diesel

Diesel Power

Seafarers Harry Lundeberg School of Seamanship
>Original Third Assistant Engineer, Steam and/or Motor - Inspected

Diesel Technology

Federal Aviation Administration
>Engine Control Panels (40127)

Seafarers Harry Lundeberg School of Seamanship
>Fireman, Oiler, and Watertender; Refrigerated Containers/Advanced Maintenance

Differential Equations

United States Department of Agriculture, Graduate School
>Calculus III

Digital and Computer Circuitry

National Weather Service Training Center
>Automation of Field Operations and Services M-05-07, M-08-04

Digital Circuits

Bell Atlantic Corporation
>Advanced Electronics Course; Fundamentals of Digital Circuits

Brick Computer Science Institute
>Micro Electronics with Lab

Digital Communications

Dow Jones & Company, Inc.
> AVANTI; DataBak

Digital Communications Technology

Bell Communications Research Training and Education Center
> Principles of Digital Transmission

Digital Computer Systems Troubleshooting

United States Postal Service - Department of Training and Development
> Computer Forwarding System Maintenance

Digital Controls

Federal Aviation Administration
> Computer Display Channel for Technicians (43426)

Digital Data Communications

Bell Communications Research Training and Education Center
> Data Services - Digital Data System Maintenance

Digital Data Transmission

Bell Communications Research Training and Education Center
> Data Services - Network Terminal Equipment; Digital Cross Connect System Fundamentals

Digital Electronics

The Cittone Institute
> Digital Electronics

Computer Processing Institute
> Digital Techniques and Circuits; Digital Techniques and Circuits Laboratory

Federal Aviation Administration
> Computer Display Channel for Technicians (43426)

United States Postal Service - Department of Training and Development
> Advanced Digital Applications; Digital Electronics; Digital Electronics I; Digital Electronics II; Digital Electronics

Wolf Creek Nuclear Operating Corporation (Formerly Kansas Gas & Electric)
> Instrument and Control Maintenance Initial Training

Digital Equipment Diagnostics and Repair

National Weather Service Training Center
> AMOS III-70/73 S-02-02; Device for Automatic Remote Data Collection B-07-02

Digital Equipment Operations

U.S. West Learning Systems
> Comm-Stor II Flexible Diskette Terminal; Synchronous DATASPEED 40

Digital Hardware Maintenance

Bell Atlantic Corporation
> New Jersey Bell 534 Sequence; New Jersey Bell 534K Sequence

Pacific Bell
> 1 AESS Attached Processor System Maintenance; 1 AESS Common Peripheral Units; 1 AESS Processor Hardware Language; 1 ESS Central Processor Hardware Maintenance; 1 ESS Common Peripheral Units

U.S. West Learning Systems
> Mountain Bell 534 Sequence; 534A: No. 1 ESS Central Office Language, Hardware, and Maintenance; 534B: Program Store Hardware and Maintenance; 534C: Call Store Maintenance; 534D: No. 1 ESS Central Processor Hardware and Programming; 534E: Master Control Centers and Associated Frames Diagnostics

Digital Instrumentation

Abu Dhabi National Oil Company Career Development Center/GDC, Inc.
> Digital and Analog Instruments

Digital Signal Processing Systems

U.S. West Learning Systems
> Mountain Bell 298-343 Sequence; 298: CSS-201S Installation and First-Tier Maintenance; 343: Dimension PBX-CES-201L Installation and Maintenance

Digital Systems

National Weather Service Training Center
> Digital Video Integrator Processor R-13-02; WSR - 57/DVIP Radar System R-08-06; WSR 74C Radar System R-12-04

United States Postal Service - Department of Training and Development
> Single-Position Letter-Sorter Machine

U.S. West Learning Systems
> Digital Techniques

Xerox Corporation
> Computer Forms Printer; 2080; 4000 Cross-Training; 4000 New Hire; 6500 Color Copier; 9200 Duplicator

Direct Access Storage Device

Applied Learning (Formerly ASI/DELTAK)
> VSAM and Access Methods Services; 4040 MVS/SP; 4214 VSAM and Basic AMS

Direct Current

The Cittone Institute
> Direct Current

Disc File Techniques

Applied Learning (Formerly ASI/DELTAK)
> VSAM and Access Methods Services; 4040 MVS/SP; 4214 VSAM and Basic AMS

Disk Operation and Maintenance

Unisys Corporation
> Introduction to Fixed Disk Drive Operation and Maintenance of Medium and Small Systems; Introduction to Fixed Disk Drive Operation and Maintenance of Small Systems

Disk Pack Drive Maintenance and Operations

Unisys Corporation

> Introduction to Disk Pack Drive Operation and Maintenance

Distributive Education

Opportunities Academy of Management Training, Inc.

> Advanced Job Development

DL/1 Programming

Applied Learning (Formerly ASI/DELTAK)

> DL/1 Programming; 4511 DL/1 Programming: Transversing the Hierarchy; 4515 DL/1 Programming: An overview; 4520 DL/1 Programming: Basic Techniques

Domestic Relations

Omega Institute

> Domestic Relations

DOS/Operations

Computer Learning Center

> DOS/Operations

Drafting

Abu Dhabi National Oil Company Career Development Center/GDC, Inc.

> Electrical and Electronic Drawing; Industrial Drawing and Sketching; Process Flow Sheets

Control Data

> Advanced ICEM Design/Drafting; Basic ICEM Design/Drafting; ICEM Solid Modeling

United States Army Materiel Command - AMC (Formerly DARCOM - United States Army Materiel Development and Readiness Command)

> Blueprint Reading

Drama

Katharine Gibbs School

> Introduction to Theatre

Drilling Fluids Technology

Baroid Corporation Career Development Center (Formerly NL Industries, Inc.)

> Completion/Workover Fluids Technology; Drilling Fluids Technology - Basic; Drilling Fluids Technology - Comprehensive; Drilling Fluids Technology - Intermediate; Drilling Fluids Technology - Refresher

Drug Abuse

National Mine Health and Safety Academy

> Substance Abuse or

Drug Interactions

Certified Medical Representatives Institute, Inc.

> Clinical Drug Interactions

Dual-Process Minicomputer Operation and Maintenance

Unisys Corporation

> Introduction to Dual-Processor Mini-Computer Operation and Maintenance (321965) (321966)

Early Childhood Curriculum

Educational Information and Resource Center (EIRC)

> Early Childhood Curriculum

Early Childhood Education

The Christopher Academy

> (a) St. Nicholas Montessori Training Course I

Earth Science

Defense Mapping Agency - Inter American Geodetic Survey Cartographic School

> Digital Methods of Terrain Modeling; Introduction to Computer Programming Using FORTRAN, Independent Study; Introduction to Digital Image Analysis; Introduction to Minicomputers, Independent Study; Orthophotography; Photogrammetry

Earthwork

International Correspondence Schools

> Earthwork

Econometrics

AT&T - Marketing Education - Somerset Seminars

> Demand Analysis Techniques

Economic Analysis

United States Army Materiel Command - AMC (Formerly DARCOM - United States Army Materiel Development and Readiness Command)

> Economic Analysis; Techniques in Cost Estimation

Economic Geography

Opportunities Academy of Management Training, Inc.

> Fundamentals of the Local Economic Development Process

Economics

Abu Dhabi National Oil Company Career Development Center/GDC, Inc.

> Introduction to Economics

American Bankers Association

> Money and Banking

American Institute for Property and Liability Underwriters/Insurance Institute of America

> (AIAF 113) Insurance Company Finance; Economics; Economics, Government, and Business

American Institute of Banking - Washington, D.C. Chapter

> Economics; Money and Banking

AT&T - Marketing Education - Somerset Seminars

> Advanced Economic Principles of Network Services Pricing; Cost Analysis for Marketing Studies; Demand Analysis Techniques; Demand Analysis Techniques Seminar; Economics for Pricing Network Services; Microeconomics Seminar; Network Cost System and

Workshop; Public Switched Network Seminar

Bell Communications Research Training and Education Center
    Cost Analysis: Service Industry

Blake Business School
    Economics

The Center for Leadership Development
    Economics

Certified Employee Benefit Specialist Program
    CEBS Course IX; Employee Benefit Plans and the Economy

Chrysler Institute Associate Degree Program
    Basic Economics

Control Data
    Economics

Credit Union National Association - Certified Credit Union Executive Program
    Economics #600

David C.D. Rogers Associates
    Competition in Telecommunications

Florida Bankers' Association
    Macroeconomics and Introduction to Money and Banking

Garden State AIB
    Economics

General Electric Company
    Advanced Methods and Models; Basic Mathematics; Introduction to Probability Theory and Descriptive Statistics; Mathematical Methods and Models; Modeling; Probabilistic Models; Regression Analysis; Statistical Inference

Institute of Financial Education
    Economics I; Economics II; Economics

Insurance Educational Association
    Economics

International Correspondence Schools
    Economics I; Economics II

Massachusetts Bankers Association, Inc.
    MSFS-Business Policy; MSFS-Investments; MSFS-Lending Fundamentals

National Cryptologic School
    Economics/Business Administration Statistics; Mathematical Statistics; Probability and Statistics; Probability Theory; Social Sciences Statistics

Opportunities Academy of Management Training, Inc.
    Community Economic Development Policy and Analysis; Fundamentals of the Local Economic Development Process

Pacific Bell
    Arbitration Advocacy; Contemporary Collective Bargaining; Labor Laws and Labor History

Professional Secretaries International
    Part III: Economics and Management

School of Banking of the South
    Economics

United States Army Materiel Command - AMC (Formerly DARCOM - United States Army Materiel Development and Readiness Command)
    Economic Analysis and Software Life-Cycle Costs

United States Department of Agriculture, Graduate School
    Management Economics for Developing Countries

United States Office of Personnel Management (OPM)
    Economics and Public Policy

U.S. West Learning Systems
    Consumer Relations Practicum

Education

AT&T - Center for Systems Education (Formerly AT&T Company Data Systems Education Group)
    Advanced Techniques of Instruction; Basic Training Development Skills Workshop; Techniques of Instruction; Test Design for Course Developers; User Documentation/Performance Aids Workshop

Bell Atlantic Corporation
    Methodology; Trainer Skills Workshop

Bell Communications Research Training and Education Center
    Field Test Results and Analysis; Fundamentals of Instructional Media; Fundamentals of Media Selection Workshop; Test Development; Training Needs Analysis and Data Collection

Federal Aviation Administration
    On-the-Job Training Techniques (14018); Principles of Instruction (14022)

Illinois Fire Service Institute
    Curriculum and Course Design II; Curriculum and Course Design III

International PADI, Inc.
    Instructor Development; Underwater Photography Instructor

Jerrico Corporation
    Train the Trainer

Laubach Literacy Action
    Teaching English to Speakers of Other Languages; Writing for New Readers

National Emergency Training Center
    Fire Science Course Development; Fire Service Instructional Methodology; Methods and Techniques of Adult Learning

National Weather Service Training Center
    Instructor Training

NCR Corporation
    Course Development Workshop; Effective Teaching

Opportunities Academy of Management Training, Inc.
    Adult Basic Education; Advanced Adult Basic Education; Advanced Affective Educational Techniques; Advanced Counseling; Affective Education; Counseling for the Disadvantaged; Employment Analysis: Development and Placement for the Disadvantaged;

Employment and Training Services to Ex-Offenders; Employment and Training Services to Limited English-Speaking Populations; Job Development for the Disadvantaged; Manpower Services to Disadvantaged Youth; Methods in Prevocational Training; Motivating the Disadvantaged; Open-Entry/Open-Exit Skill Training; Prevocational Training; Vocational Education Instruction

Pacific Bell

    CBT Design and Development; Ease Authoring

Seminary Extension, Southern Baptist Seminaries

    Dynamics of Teaching

Texas Utilities Electric Corporation (Formerly Texas Utilities Generating Company - TUGCo)

    Supervisor-Employee Relations

U.S. West Learning Systems

    Instructor Training Workshop; Representative Course Administrative Training

Westinghouse Electric Corporation, Nuclear Services Division (Formerly Water Reactor Divisions)

    Instructional Skills Workshop; Simulator Instructor Skills and Methods

Young Women's Christian Association of the U.S.A.

    Advanced Management Workshop: Financial Administration and Development

Educational Administration

Bell Atlantic Corporation

    Developing Additional Managerial Skills; Developing Managers

Independent School Management

    Catholic School Governance: Managing Change; Fund Raising for Private-Independent Schools; In-Service Workshop for Private-Independent School Headmasters; Presiding Over the Private-Independent School Board of Trustees

National Emergency Training Center

    Advanced Fire Safety

United States Office of Personnel Management (OPM)

    Seminar for New Managers

Educational Management

United States Office of Personnel Management (OPM)

    Management Development Seminar

Educational Methodology

Bell Atlantic Corporation

    Trainer Workshop

Knight-Ridder, Inc.

    Knight-Ridder Supervisory Training

McDonald's Corporation

    Training Consultants; Training Consultant's Development

National Emergency Training Center

    Instructors Program Level I—Chemistry of Hazardous Materials

Pacific Bell

    Introduction to CBT: Design and Development

Educational Methods

Federal Aviation Administration

    Academy Instructor Training (Basic) (10520); Facility Instructor Training (10501)

National Emergency Training Center

    Methods and Techniques of Adult Learning

Educational Program Management

Federal Aviation Administration

    Air Traffic Control Specialist and/or Facility Instructor Training (10510)

Educational Psychology

Institute for Citizen Involvement in Education

    Public Policy and Public Schools

Opportunities Academy of Management Training, Inc.

    Program Assessment and Evaluation

Effective Listening

Ford National Development and Training Center (Formerly UAW—Ford National Development and Training Center)

    Time Management and Effective Listening

Electomechanical Troubleshooting

United States Postal Service - Department of Training and Development

    M36/M500B Direct Feed Facer Canceler System

Electrical Circuits

Duquesne Light Company

    Electrical Circuits and Applications

GTE Service Corporation - GTE Telephone Operations Network Training

    Metallic Trunk Carrier Transmission Engineering

Omaha Public Power District

    Electrical Circuits Lab

Southwestern Bell Telephone Company

    Fundamental Electrical Circuits/Telehone Transmission; Wiring Specialized Telephone Circuits

Electrical Communications

Bell Communications Research Training and Education Center

    Transmission Theory and Applications

Electrical Construction

Electrical Workers, Local Union 102 of the International Brotherhood of Electrical Workers

    Electrician Apprentice

Electrical Workers, Local Union 164 of the International Brotherhood of Electrical Workers, AFL-CIO, Bergen and Hudson Counties, New Jersey, and the Bergen-Hudson County Chapter of the National Electrical Contractors Association Joint Apprenticeship Training Program

    Electrician Apprentice

Electrical Workers, Local Union 26 of the International Brotherhood of Electrical Workers and the Washington, D.C. Chapter of the National Electrical Contractors Association, Joint School

    Electrician Apprentice

Omaha Joint Electrical Apprenticeship and Training Committee

    Electrical Apprenticeship Training

Electrical Construction Materials and Methods

Electrical Workers, Local Union 164 of the International Brotherhood of Electrical Workers, AFL-CIO, Bergen and Hudson Counties, New Jersey, and the Bergen-Hudson County Chapter of the National Electrical Contractors Association Joint Apprenticeship Training Program

    Electrician Apprentice

Electrical Workers, Local Union 26 of the International Brotherhood of Electrical Workers and the Washington, D.C. Chapter of the National Electrical Contractors Association, Joint School

    Electrician Apprentice

Electrical Control Systems

Chrysler Motors Advanced Technical Training

    Industrial Electrical Controls

Electrical Engineering

AT&T - Marketing Education - Somerset Seminars

    Special Network Services Seminar

Bell Atlantic Corporation

    Data Management for Switching Networks; Data Management No. 5 Crossbar

Bell Communications Research Training and Education Center

    Transmission Theory and Applications

General Electric Company

    C-Course; Computer-aided Circuit Design and Analysis; Feedback Control Theory and Design of Digital Control Systems (E-316)

General Motors Corporation - Technical Staffs Group and Lansing Automotive Division (Formerly Advanced Engineering Staff [AES])

    Advanced Artificial Intelligence; Advanced Computer Graphics and Computer Aided Design; Analytical Methods in Robotics; Basic Circuits and Electronics; Compiler Design; Database Systems; Design and Analysis of Experiments; Digital Signal Processing; Geometrical and Physical Optics; Modern Control Theory; Pattern Recognition; Random Variables and Signals

Omaha Public Power District

    Basic Electronics; Electrical Circuits Lab; Electrical Circuits, Machinery and Instruments; Electronics Lab; Fundamentals of Digital Electronics

Unisys Corporation

    CP3680/CP3685 Maintenance; Maintenance and Operation; S3000 Document Processor

United States Army Materiel Command - AMC (Formerly DARCOM - United States Army Materiel Development and Readiness Command)

    Advanced Microprocessors; Electrical Fields and Circuits

United States Department of Agriculture, Graduate School

    Fiber Optic Communications

Westinghouse Electric Corporation, Defense and Electronics Center

    Advanced Microprocessing; Basic Microprocessing

Electrical Engineering Applications of Fourier Analysis

National Cryptologic School

    Fourier Analysis for Cryptanalysis

Electrical Engineering Technology

Bell Communications Research Training and Education Center

    Principles of Digital Transmission

Carolina Power & Light Company

    COC: Electrical Science, Instrumentation and Control; Reactor Operator Theory: Electrical Sciences; Senior Reactor Operator Theory: Electrical Science

United States Department of Agriculture, Graduate School

    Electric Transmission/Distribution

Electrical Instrumentation

Texas Utilities Electric Corporation (Formerly Texas Utilities Generating Company - TUGCo)

    Electrical Wiring and National Electric Code

Electrical Machinery

Electrical Workers, Local Union 102 of the International Brotherhood of Electrical Workers

    Electrician Apprentice

Joint Apprenticeship Training Committee, International Brotherhood of Electrical Workers Local Union 269, and the National Electrical Contractors Association of Southern New Jersey

    Electrician Apprentice

Mercer County Vocational-Technical Schools - Division of Adult Education

    Electrical Machinery

Electrical Machines

International Correspondence Schools

    Electrical Machines

Electrical Maintenance

Seafarers Harry Lundeberg School of Seamanship

    Refrigerated Containers/Advanced Maintenance

Wolf Creek Nuclear Operating Corporation (Formerly Kansas Gas & Electric)

    Electrical Maintenance Fundamentals

Electrical Measurements

General Electric Company

    Applied Electrical Principles

International Correspondence Schools

    Electrical/Electronic Measurements and Instruments

Index 953

Electrical Networks

Bell Communications Research Training and Education Center
    Central Office Grounding

Electrical Permissibility

National Mine Health and Safety Academy
    Electrical Permissibility; Electricity and Permissibility for the Non-Electrical Inspector

Electrical Power

Federal Aviation Administration
    Cable Fault Analysis Engine Control Panels (40121)

Electrical Power Circuits

Abu Dhabi National Oil Company Career Development Center/GDC, Inc.
    Electrical Theory and Laboratory Level IV

Electrical Power Technology

Chrysler Motors Advanced Technical Training
    Industrial Electrical Controls

Omaha Public Power District
    Motors, Generators and Transformers

Electrical Systems for Nuclear Service Technology

Westinghouse Electric Corporation, Nuclear Services Division (Formerly Water Reactor Divisions)
    Eddy Current - Level I

Electrical Technology

Bell Atlantic Corporation
    Computer-Based PBX Systems 208, Dimension 400 Repair-Tier 2 209, CSS 201-2000 Dimension Installation; Digital Technology; Electronic Switching Systems; FA; Fundamentals of Data Transmission; Fundamentals of Data Transmission: Testing and Service; General Transmission Concepts; Interoffice Facilities Current Planning; Light Wave Design; Loop Electronics Design; Loop Electronics Planning; LROPP; Microcomputer Based PBX Systems: Installation and Maintenance; Peripheral Installation and Maintenance

Bell Communications Research Training and Education Center
    Principles of Telecommunications Environmental Hazards and Protection

Federal Aviation Administration
    Electrical Principles (47600); Engine Control Panels (40127); Exide Uninterruptible Power Supply (40145)

International Correspondence Schools
    A-C and D-C Motors and Controls; Circuits and Components Testing; Electrical Installation Practices; Electrical/Electronic Measurements and Instruments; Electronic Circuits; Electronic Instrumentation and Control; Industrial Systems; Introduction to Microprocessors; Linear and Digital Integrated Circuits; Microprocessor Application

Omaha Public Power District
    Basic Electronics; Electrical Circuits, Machinery and Instruments

Southwestern Bell Telephone Company
    Fundamentals of Electricity in Telephony; Noise Reduction

Texas Utilities Electric Corporation (Formerly Texas Utilities Generating Company - TUGCo)
    Batteries and DC Circuits; Control Circuits; Control Wiring Diagrams and Electrical Troubleshooting; Electrical Protective Devices; Solid State Devices; Three-Phase Motors; Wiring and the National Electrical Code

United States Department of Agriculture, Graduate School
    Basic Electricity

U.S. West Learning Systems
    Basic Electricity; Cable Repair Fault Locating

Westinghouse Electric Corporation, Nuclear Services Division (Formerly Water Reactor Divisions)
    Electrical Sciences

Electrical Troubleshooting

Texas Utilities Electric Corporation (Formerly Texas Utilities Generating Company - TUGCo)
    Transformers

Electricity

Abu Dhabi National Oil Company Career Development Center/GDC, Inc.
    Basic Electricity; Electrical Circuits; Electrical Math I and II; Electrical Theory I; Electrical Theory II

Bell Atlantic Corporation
    Basic Electricity and Electronics Course

Electrical Workers, Local Union 102 of the International Brotherhood of Electrical Workers
    Electrician Apprentice

Electrical Workers, Local Union 164 of the International Brotherhood of Electrical Workers, AFL-CIO, Bergen and Hudson Counties, New Jersey, and the Bergen-Hudson County Chapter of the National Electrical Contractors Association Joint Apprenticeship Training Program
    Electrician Apprentice

Electrical Workers, Local Union 26 of the International Brotherhood of Electrical Workers and the Washington, D.C. Chapter of the National Electrical Contractors Association, Joint School
    Electrician Apprentice

General Electric Company
    Electricity I & II

International Correspondence Schools
    Fundamentals of Electricity

Joint Apprenticeship Training Committee, International Brotherhood of Electrical Workers Local Union 269, and the National Electrical Contractors Association of Southern New Jersey
    Electrician Apprentice

Omaha Joint Electrical Apprenticeship and Training Committee
    Electrical Apprenticeship Training

Pacific Bell
> Basic Electricity

Seafarers Harry Lundeberg School of Seamanship
> Chief/Assistant Engineer - Uninspected Motor Vessels; Marine Electrical Maintenance; Original Third Assistant Engineer, Steam and/or Motor - Inspected; Qualified Members of the Engine Department, Eight-Week Version; Qualified Members of the Engine Department, Four-Week Version; Qualified Members of the Engine Department, Six-Week Version; Qualified Members of the Engine Department, Twelve-Week Version

Texas Utilities Electric Corporation (Formerly Texas Utilities Generating Company - TUGCo)
> AC Circuits

United States Department of Agriculture, Graduate School
> Electrical Wiring

United States Postal Service - Department of Training and Development
> Basic Electricity; Basic Industrial Electricity; Electrical Power Mechanic; Electronics I; Introduction to Basic Mathematics and Electricity

Westinghouse Electric Corporation, Nuclear Services Division (Formerly Water Reactor Divisions)
> Eddy Current - Level I

Wolf Creek Nuclear Operating Corporation (Formerly Kansas Gas & Electric)
> Heating, Ventilation and Air Conditioning

Yankee Atomic Electric Company
> Essentials of Electricity

Electricity and DC Circuits

Computer Processing Institute
> Basic Electricity and DC Circuits

Electro-Hydraulic Control Systems

Seafarers Harry Lundeberg School of Seamanship
> Electro-Hydraulic System Maintenance

Electromagnetic Field Theory

Westinghouse Electric Corporation, Defense and Electronics Center
> Advanced Microwave Circuit Design; Basic Microwave

Electromechanical Equipment

United States Postal Service - Department of Training and Development
> Process Control System Magnetic Tape Unit

Electromechanical Maintenance

Xerox Corporation
> 6500 Color Copier

Electromechanical Systems

United States Postal Service - Department of Training and Development
> Single-Position Letter-Sorter Machine

Electromechanical Technology

Abu Dhabi National Oil Company Career Development Center/GDC, Inc.
> Electrical Theory

Federal Aviation Administration
> Basic Multi Channel Recorder Theory (44006)

General Electric Company
> Basics of Ultrasound

Unisys Corporation
> Introduction to Non-Impact Printers; Maintenance and Operation of Character Recognition System; Microfilm Module Installation and Maintenance

United States Postal Service - Department of Training and Development
> Basic Conveyors and Controls; Basic Process Control System; BMC Building Equipment Mechanic; BMC Mail Processing Mechanics; Customer Vending Machines; Digital Computer Technology; Environmental Control II; Mark II Facer-Canceler and Feeder Machine; Model 120/121 MPLSM/ZMT On-Site Maintenance Certification Program (55655-02); Model 140/141 MPLSM On-Site Maintenance Certification Program, Category I Category II; Model 140/141 MPLSM/ZMT/ESP; Model 140/141 Multi-Position Letter-Sorter Machine; Multi-Position Letter-Sorter Machine; Optical Character Reader I, On-Site Maintenance Certification Program; Postal Source Data System; Process Control System Line Printer; Process Control System Mail Processing Peripherals; Self-Service Postal Center Equipment Program

Xerox Corporation
> Computer Forms Printer; New Hire Copier; New Hire 7000 Duplicator; 1824/1860; 2080; 3100 Family; 3400 Update Training; 3400/3450 Combination XT; 3450 Copier H15; 4000 Cross-Training; 4000 New Hire; 5400 Update Training; 5400/5600 Update Combination; 600 Microfilm Enlarger Printer; 6500 Color Copier; 660 Copier; 7000 Duplicator XT; 800 ETS/CETS; 8200/9500 Update; 840 Engineering Printing System; 850 DTS; 860 IPS; 9200 Duplicator; 9400 Duplicator; 9700 EPS

Electromechanical Troubleshooting

Southwestern Bell Telephone Company
> I/IA ESS Overview and Software

United States Postal Service - Department of Training and Development
> Basic Conveyors and Controls; Consolidated MPLSM Training; Microprocessor-Controlled Mark II Facer Canceler System; Multi-Position Letter-Sorter Machines 140/141

Electromechanics

United States Postal Service - Department of Training and Development
> Bulk Conveyor Systems; Teletype Maintenance

Electron Video Technology

Federal Aviation Administration
> Bright Radar Indicator Tower Equipment (40345)

Electronic Aids to Navigation

Seafarers Harry Lundeberg School of Seamanship
> First Class Pilot; Master/Mate Freight and Towing

Electronic Circuits

Computer Processing Institute
> Electronics Circuits I & II

International Correspondence Schools
> Electronic Circuits

Electronic Communication Systems

Pacific Bell
> Loop Lightwave Engineering

Electronic Communications

Bell Atlantic Corporation
> Radio License - Second Class

Federal Aviation Administration
> AN/GRN-27 (40232); Data Receiver Group/IFDS (43417); ILS (Wilcox Mark I-D/E/F) (47702); ILS Concepts (40233)

Electronic Communications Technology

Bell Communications Research Training and Education Center
> Applied Communications Fundamentals

Federal Aviation Administration
> Bright 2/4 Radar Indicator (40327)

U.S. West Learning Systems
> BM 0167 200 Series Data Sets; Central Control Language Hardware and Maintenance - 534A; COMM STOR II Flexible Diskette Terminal; Data Transmission Fundamentals; Dimension 400 PBX Installation and Maintenance; Introduction to ESS - Common - 507AA; Introduction to ESS; Introduction to Telephone Dialing Systems; Master Control Center and Associated Frames Diagnostics - 534E; NE34555: Step-by-Step Method of Operation; No. 1 ESS Processor Hardware and Maintenance; Program Store Maintenance - 534B; Signal Processor Language Hardware and Maintenance - 534D; 1A Technology Common Peripheral Units - 508AA; 1/1A Electronic Switching System; 32K Call Store Maintenance - 534C

Electronic Engineering Technology

General Motors Corporation - Technical Staffs Group and Lansing Automotive Division (Formerly Advanced Engineering Staff [AES])
> Basic Electrical Circuits and Instrumentation

GTE Service Corporation - GTE Telephone Operations Network Training
> Protection and Noise

Electronic Filter Design

Westinghouse Electric Corporation, Defense and Electronics Center
> Introduction to Electronic Filtering II

Electronic Installation Practices

International Correspondence Schools
> Electrical Installation Practices

Electronic Instrumentation

International Correspondence Schools
> Electronic Instrumentation and Control

Electronic Maintenance

Bell Atlantic Corporation
> Repair Transmission

Electronic Measurements

International Correspondence Schools
> Electrical/Electronic Measurements and Instruments

Electronic Switching Systems

Bell Atlantic Corporation
> New Jersey Bell 507AA/AA Sequence

U.S. West Learning Systems
> Mountain Bell 507AA/508AA Sequence; 1/1A Electronic Switching System - Method of Operation 1, NE34535; 507AA: Introduction to Electronic Switching Systems/Second Generation; 508AA: Common Peripheral Units/Second Generation

Electronic Switching Systems Maintenance

U.S. West Learning Systems
> Electronic Switching Systems - No. 1 ESS Peripheral Units 507B, 508B

Electronic Systems

National Weather Service Training Center
> ART Rawin System J-12-03; GMD RAWIN System J-10-03

Electronic Technology

General Motors Corporation - Technical Staffs Group and Lansing Automotive Division (Formerly Advanced Engineering Staff [AES])
> Introduction to Microcomputers

Unisys Corporation
> Introduction to Large Computer Mainframes Operation and Maintenance (337800)

U.S. West Learning Systems
> AC/DC Basic Electronics

Electronic Troubleshooting

United States Postal Service - Department of Training and Development
> Model 120/121 MPLSM/ZMT On-Site Maintenance Certification Program (55655-02); Model 140/141 MPLSM On-Site Maintenance Certification Program, Category I

Electronics

Abu Dhabi National Oil Company Career Development Center/GDC, Inc.
> Electronic Devices and Circuits; Electronic Instrumentation; Industrial Electronics

Bell Atlantic Corporation
  Basic Electricity and Electronics Course

Brick Computer Science Institute
  Basic Electronics I; Basic Electronics II

Electrical Workers, Local Union 102 of the International Brotherhood of Electrical Workers
  Electrician Apprentice

Electrical Workers, Local Union 164 of the International Brotherhood of Electrical Workers, AFL-CIO, Bergen and Hudson Counties, New Jersey, and the Bergen-Hudson County Chapter of the National Electrical Contractors Association Joint Apprenticeship Training Program
  Electrician Apprentice

Electrical Workers, Local Union 26 of the International Brotherhood of Electrical Workers and the Washington, D.C. Chapter of the National Electrical Contractors Association, Joint School
  Electrician Apprentice

Federal Aviation Administration
  Central Control and Monitoring System (CCMS) Remote Operator (43474); Omega/Area Navigation Systems (21845)

Ford National Development and Training Center (Formerly UAW—Ford National Development and Training Center)
  Allen-Bradley Programmable Controller Maintenance Program; Basic Electronic Measuring Equipment; Basic Electronics; Modicon Programmable Controller Maintenance Training Program; Programmable Logic Controller Maintenance; Programmable Logic Controller Maintenance Training Program; Solid State Electronics; Use of the Volt-Ohm-Millian Meter; Using the Oscilloscope

General Electric Company
  Basic Electronics; Electricity I & II

Joint Apprenticeship Training Committee, International Brotherhood of Electrical Workers Local Union 269, and the National Electrical Contractors Association of Southern New Jersey
  Electrician Apprentice

Mercer County Vocational-Technical Schools - Division of Adult Education
  Survey of Basic Electronics

Omaha Joint Electrical Apprenticeship and Training Committee
  Electrical Apprenticeship Training

Omaha Public Power District
  Basic Electronics; Electronics Lab; Fundamentals of Digital Electronics

Southwestern Bell Telephone Company
  Attached Processor Maintenance; Computer CPU and Peripheral Maintenance; Computer CPU Maintenance; Specialized Computer Peripheral Maintenance

Texas Utilities Electric Corporation (Formerly Texas Utilities Generating Company - TUGCo)
  Electronics I; Electronics II; Electronics III; Electronics IV; Electronics V; Electronics VI

Unisys Corporation
  Introduction to Software Concepts; Maintenance and Operation of Character Recognition System

United States Postal Service - Department of Training and Development
  Digital Electronics; Electrical Power Mechanic; Electronic Sort Processor; Electronics I; Electronics II; Logic Circuits; Model 140/141 MPLSM/ZMT/ESP; Power Transistors; Transistors and Transistor Applications

U.S. West Learning Systems
  Basic Electronics

Westinghouse Electric Corporation, Nuclear Services Division (Formerly Water Reactor Divisions)
  Eddy Current - Level I

Electronics Systems

National Weather Service Training Center
  WBRT RAWIN System J-11-03; Weather Bureau Radar Remote Recorder R-06-02; Weather Bureau Radar Remote 1 and 2 R-05-03

Electronics Technology

Applied Learning (Formerly ASI/DELTAK)
  Basic Electricity and Electronics; Digital Circuits and Devices; Introduction to Microprocessors; Microelectronics: Devices and Applications; Semiconductors: Circuits and Devices

Bell Atlantic Corporation
  Advanced Peripheral Processor Maintenance; Digital Technology; FA; Interoffice Facilities Current Planning; Light Wave Design; Loop Electronics Design; Loop Electronics Planning; LROPP

Bell Communications Research Training and Education Center
  Principles of Telecommunications Environmental Hazards and Protection

Federal Aviation Administration
  Air Route Surveillance Radar-3 (40331); Air Traffic Control Beacon Integrator 5 (ATCBI) (40383); Air Traffic Control Beacon Integrator 5 (40383); Air Traffic Control Beacon Interrogator (40335); Airport Surveillance Radar (ASR) (40342); Automated Radar Terminal System (ARTS II) for Supervisors (42029); Automated Radar Terminal System (ARTS III-A) Update (42014); Automated Radar Terminal System Common Course (42009); Automated Radar Terminal System II (42031); Automated Radar Tracking System III-A (42011); Back-Up Emergency Communications (BUEC) System (40008 - 40009); Back-up Emergency Communications (BUEC) System (40027 - 40028); Common Digitizer Height Only (43477); Communications Equipment (40029); Computer Display Channel Processor (43423); Continuous Data Recording System (42025); Data Terminal Equipment, Display and Keyboard (40019); Direct Access Radar Channel System for Engineers (43479); Direct Access Radar Channel System for Technicians (43473); Direct Access Radar Channel System Software (43520); Distance Measuring Equipment Cardion DME-9639 (40258); Electrical Principles (47600); Electronics Technician Qualification Course Phase I (40509); Enroute Automated Radar Tracking System Data Acquisition Subsystem (42028); Enroute Automated Radar Tracking System Display (EARTS) (43467); Enroute Automated Radar Tracking System (42021); Exide Uninterruptible Power Supply (40145); High Capacity Voice Recorder Runway Visual

Range Equipment Type (40016); IBM 9020-A Processing (43461); IBM 9020-A System Hardware for Engineers (43489); IBM 9020-A/D System Common Hardware for Engineers (43491); IBM 9020-D System Hardware for Engineers (43490); ILS Capture Effect Glide Slope (40240); Input/Output Processor (IOP) (42017); Interface Buffer Adapter and Generator (42024); Mark 1F-Instrument Handling System (47703); Power Conditioning System for Radar Microwave Link (40122); Radar Beacon Interrogator ATCBI-5 (40339); Radar Beacon Performance Remote System Monitor (40378); Radar Microwave Link System (40344/76); Radar Microwave Link/Repeater (RML) (40320); Runway Visual Range Equipment Tasker 500 Series (40252); Solid State Direction Finder Equipment (40257); Solid State Video Mappers (40328); Solid State VOR Transmitter Assembly (40230); Surveillance Radar Unit (40307); VHF/UHF Direction Finder Equipment (40225)

International Correspondence Schools

A-C and D-C Motors and Controls; Applications of Industrial Electronics; Circuits and Components Testing; Electrical Installation Practices; Electrical Machines; Electrical/Electronic Measurements and Instruments; Electronic Circuits; Electronic Instrumentation and Control; Fundamentals of Electronics; Industrial Systems; Introduction to Microprocessors; Linear and Digital Integrated Circuits; Microprocessor Application; Pulse and Logic Circuits

Pacific Bell

Cable Fault Locating; Cable Repair - Fault Locating; ESS Introduction; SCC Trunk Tester

Southwestern Bell Telephone Company

Data Communications Technology; Digital Circuit Technology; Fiber Optics; Introduction to ESS and Minicomputer Fundamentals

Unisys Corporation

Introduction to COBOL Processor Operation and Maintenance

United States Army Materiel Command - AMC (Formerly DARCOM - United States Army Materiel Development and Readiness Command)

Electronics

United States Department of Agriculture, Graduate School

Basic Electronics; Solid State Fundamentals

United States Postal Service - Department of Training and Development

Postal Source Data System; Zip Mail Translator

U.S. West Learning Systems

Electronic Circuits; Introduction to Electronic Systems Concepts; Semiconductor Devices

Elementary Education Administration

Independent School Management

Managing the Private-Independent Elementary School

Emergency Management

National Emergency Training Center

Basic Skills For Emergency Program Managers; Civil Defense Systems, Programs and Policies; Command and Control of Fire Department Operations at Catastrophic Disasters; Emergency Medical Service and Administration: An Overview; Emergency Planning Course; Exercise Design; Exercise Design—Train-the-Trainer; Hazardous Materials Contingency Planning; Introduction to Emergency Management; Microcomputer Applications in Emergency Management; Module IV: Creative Financing; Natural Hazards Mitigations; Natural Hazards Recovery; Shelter Systems Officer; Shelter Systems Officer Train-the Trainer; Tactical Operations for Company Officers II

Emergency Medical Care

Bergen County Police Academy

Basic Police Training Course

Emergency Medical Services

Illinois Fire Service Institute

Hazardous Materials: Chemistry

Emergency Medical Technology

United States Public Health Service - Indian Health Service

Emergency Medical Technician

Emergency Medicine

General Electric Company

Principles of Cardiovascular Monitoring

Emergency Planning

National Emergency Training Center

Fallout Shelter Analysis

Employee Benefits

Certified Employee Benefit Specialist Program

CEBS Course I; CEBS X; Contemporary Benefit Issues and Administration; Life, Health, and Other Group Benefit Programs

Employee Development

Pacific Bell

Managing Performance; Planning Controlling the Work; Taking Charge of Time

Employee Retirement Income Security Act

American Center for Technical Arts and Sciences (Formerly Mainline Paralegal Institute)

Employee Retirement Income Security Act

Employment Discrimination Law

American Center for Technical Arts and Sciences (Formerly Mainline Paralegal Institute)

Employment Discrimination Law

Engineering

AT&T - Center for Systems Education (Formerly AT&T Company Data Systems Education Group)

Programmer Basic Training

AT&T - Marketing Education - Somerset Seminars

Local Network Services Seminar

Bell Atlantic Corporation

Basic Engineering Economy; Capital Utilization Criteria; Concepts in Engineering for Nontechnical Majors; Engineering Economy; General Engineering;

Programmer Basic Training; Programmer Basic Training - COBOL

Contel Service Corporation

FORTRAN

Control Data

Mechanisms

Federal Aviation Administration

Airport Engineering (06012); Airport NAVAIDS and Lighting (06019); Airport Paving (06005); Recurrent Engineering (06021)

General Electric Company

Abnormal Event Analysis; A-Course; Boiling Water Reactor Chemistry for Technicians; Boiling Water Reactor Chemistry; BWR Observation Training; BWR Operator Training; BWR Technology; BWR/6 Operator Training; Core Management Engineering; Corrosion in Boiling Water Reactors; Degraded Core Training, Part I; Designing with Microprocessors; Engineering Fundamentals; Feedwater Control; Fundamentals of Nuclear Engineering; GE MAC 5000 Instrumentation; Health Physics and Radiological Emergencies; Health Physics Technology; High Temperature Metallurgy; Materials Engineering I; Nuclear Engineering for Operators; Nuclear Instrumentation; Nuclear Materials; Process Instrumentation and Control; Radiological Engineering; Recirculation Flow Control; Rod Control and Information System; Rod Drive Control System; Station Nuclear Engineering Refresher; Station Nuclear Engineering

General Motors Corporation

Design of Computerized Real-Time Data Acquisitions, and Process Control Systems; Engineering Economy Analysis of Plant Projects; Human Performance; Introduction to Data Sampling and Analysis; Introduction to Human Performance; Introduction to Industrial Statistics; Introduction to Minicomputer Programming; Methods Analysis and Basic Time Study; Noise Control; Plant Layout and Materials Handling; Project Management Using Network Planning Techniques; Quality Control and Industrial Statistics I; Quality Control and Industrial Statistics II; Reliability Engineering

Insurance Educational Association

Hazard Identification and Analysis

National Emergency Training Center

Chemistry of Hazardous Materials; Hazardous Materials Tactical Considerations; Hazardous Substance Specialist; Planning for a Hazardous Materials Incident

New England Telephone Company

Programmer Basic Training

United States Army Materiel Command - AMC (Formerly DARCOM - United States Army Materiel Development and Readiness Command)

Chemical Safety in the Industrial Environment; Microprocessor Controls

U.S. West Learning Systems

Basic Engineering Economy; Engineering Fundamentals; Programmer Basic Training

Westinghouse Electric Corporation, Defense and Electronics Center

Applied Engineering Software; Probability and Random Processes I; Probability and Random Processes II

Wolf Creek Nuclear Operating Corporation (Formerly Kansas Gas & Electric)

Basic Electricity/Electronics; General Advanced Mechanical Maintenance, Part I; Measurement and Test Equipment; Motors and Generators; Transformers

Engineering Administration

Central Intelligence Agency

Issues in Program Management in Government Procurement

National Emergency Training Center

Fire Service Information Management; Management of Emergency Medical Services

New England Telephone Company

Concepts of Total System Development; Introduction to Project Management

Engineering Analysis

General Electric Company

A-Course

Engineering Communications

AT&T - Marketing Education - Somerset Seminars

Special Network Services Seminar

Engineering Data Base Library

Control Data

ICEM Engineering Data Library

Engineering Drawing

General Motors Corporation - Technical Staffs Group and Lansing Automotive Division (Formerly Advanced Engineering Staff [AES])

Technical Drawing

Portsmouth Naval Shipyard: Apprenticeship Training

Engineering Drawings - The Application of Mechanical Design

Engineering Drawing Interpretation

General Electric Company

Mechanical Drawing I & II

Engineering Economics

AT&T - Marketing Education - Somerset Seminars

Concepts of Capital Costs; Public Switched Network Seminar

Bell Atlantic Corporation

Time Share Cable Sizing Program

Bell Communications Research Training and Education Center

Cost Analysis: Service Industry; Economic Evaluation; Planning, Design, and Operation of Telecommunication Systems

Board of Engineers for Rivers and Harbors - U.S. Army Corps of Engineers

Water Resources Planning Associates Program

GTE Service Corporation - GTE Telephone Operations Network Training

Engineering Economics

Pacific Bell

    Basic Engineering Economy; Engineering Economy - Advanced; Principles of Engineering Economy and Economic Alternative Selection for Outside Plant

Southwestern Bell Telephone Company

    Economic Study Module

Engineering Economy

International Correspondence Schools

    Engineering Economy

Engineering Graphics

General Motors Corporation - Technical Staffs Group and Lansing Automotive Division (Formerly Advanced Engineering Staff [AES])

    Geometric Tolerancing

Portsmouth Naval Shipyard: Apprenticeship Training

    Engineering Graphics; Mechanical Drawing

Engineering Management

Federal Aviation Administration

    Facility Management and Administration for International Participants (50004 and 14002)

General Electric Company

    Economic Analysis of Alternatives; GESIMTEL; Introduction to Probability Theory and Descriptive Statistics; Modeling; Operations Research and Applications Training; Statistical Inference; Time-Sharing System and Applications

Engineering Materials

International Correspondence Schools

    Engineering Materials; Technical Materials

Engineering Mechanics

General Motors Corporation - Technical Staffs Group and Lansing Automotive Division (Formerly Advanced Engineering Staff [AES])

    Fracture and Fatigue Considerations in Design

Engineering Science

Defense Mapping Agency - Inter American Geodetic Survey Cartographic School

    Introduction to Remote Sensing/Image Analysis

Engineering Service and Technology for Computer-Controlled Sterilizers

American Sterilizer Company (AMSCO)

    Engineering Service and Technology for Computer-Controlled Sterilizers

Engineering Systems Reliability

United States Army Materiel Command - AMC (Formerly DARCOM - United States Army Materiel Development and Readiness Command)

    Systems Reliability

Engineering Technology

Abu Dhabi National Oil Company Career Development Center/GDC, Inc.

    Electrical Circuits

American Sterilizer Company (AMSCO)

    AMSCAR Service Training or AMSCAR Distribution Systems; Customer Service V/Eagle 2000 Series Sterilizers; Electromechanical Theories and Practices of Health Care Equipment; Engineering Technology Laboratory I; Engineering Technology Laboratory II; Engineering Technology Laboratory III; Training Seminar for Hospital Corporation of America

AT&T - Center for Systems Education (Formerly AT&T Company Data Systems Education Group)

    Programmer Basic Training

Bell Atlantic Corporation

    Basic Engineering Economy; Capital Utilization Criteria; Engineering Economy

Defense Mapping Agency - Inter American Geodetic Survey Cartographic School

    Automated Cartography-Digitizing System Operator; Color Separation Technician

General Electric Company

    Abnormal Event Analysis; APT Programming; Boiling Water Reactor Chemistry for Shift Technical Advisors; Boiling Water Reactor Chemistry for Technicians; Boiling Water Reactor Chemistry; BWR Hot License Qualification; BWR Observation Training; BWR Operator Training; BWR Technology; BWR/6 Operator Training; Computer-Aided Manufacturing; Core Management Engineering; Degraded Core Training, Part I; Engineering Fundamentals; Feedwater Control; Fundamentals of Nuclear Engineering; GE MAC 5000 Instrumentation; Health Physics and Radiological Emergencies; Health Physics Technology; Interactive Graphics; Manufacturing Methods and Processes; Nuclear Engineering for Operators; Nuclear Instrumentation; Nuclear Materials; Process Instrumentation and Control; Radiological Engineering; Recirculation Flow Control; Rod Control and Information System; Rod Drive Control System; Station Nuclear Engineering Refresher; Station Nuclear Engineering

General Motors Corporation

    Design of Computerized Real-Time Data Acquisitions, and Process Control Systems; Engineering Economy Analysis of Plant Projects; Introduction to Data Sampling and Analysis; Introduction to Industrial Statistics; Introduction to Minicomputer Programming; Methods Analysis and Basic Time Study; Nondestructive Evaluation; Project Management Using Network Planning Techniques; Quality Control and Industrial Statistics I; Quality Control and Industrial Statistics II; Reliability Engineering; Resistance Welding

General Motors Corporation - Technical Staffs Group and Lansing Automotive Division (Formerly Advanced Engineering Staff [AES])

    Hydraulics and Pneumatics

International Correspondence Schools

    Engineering Materials; Engineering Mechanics; Fluid Mechanics; Kinematics; Manufacturing Processes; Mechanical Design I; Mechanical Design II; Mechanics of Materials; Planning and Control; Plant Facilities; Reinforced Concrete Design; Technical Materials; Tool Design I; Tool Design II

NCR Corporation

    Introduction to Quality Improvement

Northern Telecom, Inc., Digital Switching Systems - Technical Training Center

> Digital Multiplex System-1 System Maintenance; Digital Multiplex System-10 Method of Operation/Traffic Provisioning; Digital Multiplex System-100/200 System Method of Operation/Traffic Provisioning

Unisys Corporation

> Introduction to Multi-Processor System Maintenance

United States Army Materiel Command - AMC (Formerly DARCOM - United States Army Materiel Development and Readiness Command)

> Army Manufacturing and Testing Technology

United States Department of Agriculture, Graduate School

> Engineering Mechanics I; Engineering Mechanics II; Hydraulics I

U.S. West Learning Systems

> Basic Engineering Economy; Electrical Protection OSP; Facilities Economic Studies; Mountain Bell Sequence; Principles of Electricity; Principles of Transmission; Resistance Design; Unified Loop Design

Westinghouse Electric Corporation, Nuclear Services Division (Formerly Water Reactor Divisions)

> Basic Nuclear Systems; Comprehensive Analysis of Technical, Thermal, and Radiological Limits (NPO 317); Digital Rod Position Indicating System; Engineered Safeguard Systems; Heat Transfer, Fluid Flow and Thermodynamics; Large Pressurized Water Reactor Core Control; Nuclear Instrumentation; Nuclear Refueling; Pressurized Water Reactor Information Course; Process Instrumentation; ROD Control System; Sold State Protection System; Thermal Sciences; 7100 Process Instrumentation Scaling; 7300 Process Instrumentation Scaling

Wolf Creek Nuclear Operating Corporation (Formerly Kansas Gas & Electric)

> Basic Electricity/Electronics; General Advanced Mechanical Maintenance, Part I; Measurement and Test Equipment; Motors and Generators; Transformers

Engines

General Motors Corporation - Technical Staffs Group and Lansing Automotive Division (Formerly Advanced Engineering Staff [AES])

> Engine Design

English

Bell Atlantic Corporation

> Written Communication Skills

Chrysler Institute Associate Degree Program

> Introduction to Writing

English Language Institute of America, Inc.

> Practical English and the Command of Words

Institute of Financial Education

> Basic Business English

Katharine Gibbs School

> Business Writing

Laubach Literacy Action

> Writing for New Readers

United States Department of Agriculture, Graduate School

> Advanced Practice in Editing; Editing; Editing Technical Manuscripts; Intermediate Editing; Intermediate Editing Principles and Practices; Introduction to the Editing Process; Practice in Editing; Principles of Editing; Principles of Editing for Publication; Printing, Layout and Design; Proofreading; Publishing Management; Seminar in Editing; Style and Techniques for Editors; Technical Writing

United States Department of Labor, DOL Academy

> Effective Writing for Federal Managers and Report Writing

U.S. West Learning Systems

> Put It In Writing

English as a Second Language

Abu Dhabi National Oil Company Career Development Center/GDC, Inc.

> (Basic English I, II, III, IV; Business English; Technical English); English as a Second Language

Opportunities Academy of Management Training, Inc.

> Employment and Training Services to Limited English-Speaking Populations

English Composition

Bell Atlantic Corporation

> English Grammar and Usage

Blake Business School

> Business Communications II

International Correspondence Schools

> Composition and Rhetoric

Katharine Gibbs School

> Effective Writing; English I; English II; English III; Fundamentals of Writing

U.S. West Learning Systems

> Corporate Grammar; Power Writing

Environmental Control

New England Telephone Company

> Asbestos Recognition and Abatement

Environmental Control Technology

United States Postal Service - Department of Training and Development

> Environmental Control III; Environmental Control V (55689-07)

Environmental Engineering

International Union of Operating Engineers

> Hazardous Waste Materials Training

Environmental Health

United States Public Health Service - Indian Health Service

> Environmental Health Concepts and Practices

Environmental Management

National Emergency Training Center

> Wildland/Urban Interface Fire Protection: A National

Problem with Local Solutions

Environmental Science

Board of Engineers for Rivers and Harbors - U.S. Army Corps of Engineers
>Water Resources Planning Associates Program

Control Data
>WILDWAYS: Understanding Wildlife Conservation

Federal Aviation Administration
>Environmental Assessment (12000); Environmental System Control (40133); Heating, Ventilating, Air Conditioner (40132)

National Emergency Training Center
>Command and Control of Fire Department Operations at Catastrophic Disasters

United States Department of Agriculture, Graduate School
>Environmental Law

Environmental Studies

United States Office of Personnel Management (OPM)
>Management of Natural Resources; Seminar in Science, Technology and Public Policy

Environmental Technology

United States Postal Service - Department of Training and Development
>Environmental Control IV

Equipment Engineering Management

U.S. West Learning Systems
>Equipment Engineering Management

Estate Planning

National Association of REALTORS®
>Estate Planning (FLI-160)

Estate Taxation

New England School of Banking
>Trust Banking Major

Estates and Trusts

American Institute for Paralegal Studies, Inc.
>Estates and Trusts; Estates and Trusts II

National Academy for Paralegal Studies, Inc.
>Estates and Trusts; Estates and Trusts II

Omega Institute
>Estates and Trusts

Ethics

Seminary Extension, Southern Baptist Seminaries
>Introduction to Christian Ethics

Evaluation and Measurement

Federal Aviation Administration
>Instructional Testing (10513)

Extension Education

National Emergency Training Center
>Methods and Techniques of Adult Learning

Family Law

American Center for Technical Arts and Sciences (Formerly Mainline Paralegal Institute)
>Family Law

American Institute for Paralegal Studies, Inc.
>Family Law

Farm Appraisal

National Association of Independent Fee Appraisers
>Farm, Ranch, and Rural Appraisal

Federal Law Enforcement

United States Department of Justice, Immigration and Naturalization Service, Federal Law Enforcement Training Center
>Immigration Officer Academy

Federal Taxation and Real Estate

National Association of REALTORS®
>Introduction to Federal Taxes and Real Estate (FLI-166)

Feedback Control

General Motors Corporation - Technical Staffs Group and Lansing Automotive Division (Formerly Advanced Engineering Staff [AES])
>Feedback Control Systems

Filing Systems

American Medical Record Association
>Numbering and Filing Systems; Indexes; Registers

Finance

American Bankers Association
>Analyzing Financial Statements; Bank Investments; Bank Management; Commercial Lending: 200-Level Curriculum; Commercial Loan Officer Development; Current Issues in Bank Management; Investment Basics and Beyond; PDP 200-Level General Banking Curriculum; Statement Analysis; The Trust Business; Trust Investments

American Institute for Property and Liability Underwriters/Insurance Institute of America
>Accounting and Finance; (AIAF 113) Insurance Company Finance; Management, Accounting, and Finance

American Institute of Banking - Washington, D.C. Chapter
>Analyzing Financial Statements; Bank Investments; Bank Marketing: Theory and Applications; Banking Law; Banking Law/Lending; Banking Law/Operations; Business Law; Business Law: Selected Topics; Cash Management I and II; Commercial Loan Case Simulation; Consumer Credit; Installment Credit; International Banking; Management of Commercial Bank Funds; Principles of Banking; Principles of Commercial Banking; Real Estate Finance; Trust Banking

AT&T - Marketing Education - Somerset Seminars

> A Cost Model for Communications; Capital Cost Methodology; Cash Flow Analysis I; Concepts of Capital Costs; Cost Analysis for Marketing Studies; Financial Awareness Plus Seminar; Financial Awareness Seminar; Fundamentals of Finance and Accounting; Introduction to Finance; Private Line Cost Models and Studies - PLIAC; Public Switched Network Seminar; Witness Preparation

Bell Atlantic Corporation

> Accounting Witness Support Training; Rate Regulations

Bell Communications Research Training and Education Center

> Capital Recovery: Theory; Finance and Accounting Issues and Concepts in the Modern Corporation; Quantitative Forecasting Methods; Witness Preparation

College for Financial Planning®

> Investments

Control Data

> Fundamentals of Finance and Accounting for Non-Financial Managers

David C.D. Rogers Associates

> Finance and Accounting for Managers

Graduate School of Banking at Colorado

> Bank Lending; Management of Financial Institutions

Graduate School of Banking at the University of Wisconsin-Madison (Central States Conference of Bankers Associates)

> Commercial Lending; Investments; Management of Financial Institutions

Institute of Financial Education

> Commercial Banking; Financial Statement Analysis

Institute of Management and Production

> Business Administration

Insurance Educational Association

> Accounting and Finance

International Correspondence Schools

> Principles of Finance; Securities and Investments

Massachusetts Bankers Association, Inc.

> MSFS-Investments; MSFS-Lending Fundamentals

Raymond James & Associates, Inc. and Employee Benefits Education and Planning Service, Inc.

> Personal Financial Planning; Personal Investment Planning

School of Banking of the South

> Commercial Lending and Credit Analysis; Management of Financial Institutions

Southwestern Bell Telephone Company

> Financial Selling Skills

United States Department of Agriculture, Graduate School

> Financial Management; International Finance

Western Regional CUNA School for Credit Union Personnel

> Western Regional CUNA School for Credit Union Personnel

Westinghouse Electric Corporation, Education Center Department

> Business Management Course; Techniques of Finance and Accounting

Finance Banking

American Bankers Association

> Agriculture Lending: 200-Level Curriculum

Financial Analysis

AT&T - Marketing Education - Somerset Seminars

> Financial Planning Control and Decision Making

Bell Communications Research Training and Education Center

> Financial Planning, Control and Decision Making

Xerox Corporation

> Account Representative School; Geo-Combo School; High Volume Sales Executive School

Financial Decision Making

AT&T - Marketing Education - Somerset Seminars

> Financial Planning Control and Decision Making

Bell Communications Research Training and Education Center

> Financial Planning, Control and Decision Making

Financial Institutions

Institute of Financial Education

> Accounting Practices for Savings Institutions; Accounting Principles for Savings Institutions; Financial Institutions I; Financial Institutions II; Money and Banking

Financial Institutions Marketing

Institute of Financial Education

> Marketing for Financial Institutions

Financial Management

American Institute for Property and Liability Underwriters/Insurance Institute of America

> Management, Accounting, and Finance

AT&T - Marketing Education - Somerset Seminars

> Advanced Service Management Seminar; Analysis for Service Decisions; Financial Management in Telecommunications; Service Plan Financial Analysis

Bell Communications Research Training and Education Center

> Capital Cost Methodology

Jamaican Institute of Management

> Financial Management and Advanced Financial Management

Knight-Ridder, Inc.

> Financial Management for Non-Financial Executives

NCR Corporation

> Financial Management

Ohio Bell Telephone Company

> Financial Operations

United States Army Materiel Command - AMC (Formerly DARCOM - United States Army Materiel Development and Readiness Command)
> Financial Management

Financial Planning

College for Financial Planning®
> Introduction to Financial Planning; Retirement Planning and Employee Benefits

Financial Resource Development

Independent School Management
> Operating the Private-Independent School Development Program - 3dd

Financial Statement Analysis

AT&T - Marketing Education - Somerset Seminars
> Financial Management in Telecommunications; Financial Statement Analysis

Bell Communications Research Training and Education Center
> Financial Management in Telecommunications

Financial Statements

Garden State AIB
> Analyzing Financial Statements

Finite Element Analysis

General Motors Corporation - Technical Staffs Group and Lansing Automotive Division (Formerly Advanced Engineering Staff [AES])
> Finite Element Methods

Fire Administration

National Emergency Training Center
> Advanced Fire Safety; Fire Risk Analysis; Firefighter Safety and Survival: Company Officer's Responsibility; Incident Command System; Plans Review for Inspectors; Use Of Microcomputers For Fire Service Management

Fire Engineering

National Emergency Training Center
> Plans Review for Inspectors

Fire Management

National Emergency Training Center
> Firefighter Safety and Survival: Company Officer's Responsibility; Plans Review for Inspectors; Use Of Microcomputers For Fire Service Management

Fire Prevention Chemistry

National Emergency Training Center
> Instructors Program Level I—Chemistry of Hazardous Materials

Fire Prevention Engineering

National Emergency Training Center
> Strategic Analysis of Fire Prevention Programs

Fire Protection

Insurance Educational Association
> Fire Protection Engineering

Wolf Creek Nuclear Operating Corporation (Formerly Kansas Gas & Electric)
> Fire Brigade, Basic

Fire Science

Illinois Fire Service Institute
> Arson Investigation I; Arson Investigation II; Curriculum and Course Design I; Curriculum and Course Design II; Curriculum and Course Design III; Fire Department Management I; Fire Department Management II; Fire Department Management III; Fire Department Management IV; Fire Prevention Officer I; Hazardous Materials: Chemistry; Tactics and Strategy II

National Emergency Training Center
> Advanced Incident Command; Arson Detection; Building Construction: Non-Combustible and Fire Resistive; Building Construction: Principles—Wood and Ordinary Construction; Command and Control of Fire Department Operations at Catastrophic Disasters; Command and Control of Fire Department Operations; Community Fire Defenses: Challenges and Solutions; Community Fire Protection: Planning; Emergency Medical Service and Administration: An Overview; Fire Arson Investigation; Fire Command Operations; Fire Prevention Specialist I; Fire Prevention Specialist II; Fire Risk Analysis; Fire Science Course Development; Fire Service Financial Management; Fire Service Information Management; Fire Service Instructional Methodology; Fire Service Leadership/Communications; Fire Service Organizational Theory; Firefighter Health and Safety: Program Implementation and Management; Firefighter Safety and Survival: Company Officer's Responsibility; Incident Command System; Interpersonal Dynamics in Fire Service Organizations; Introduction to Fire Safety Education; Leadership and Incident Command/Communications Course; Management of a Fire Preventive Program; Management of Emergency Medical Services; Managing the Code Process; Plans Review for Inspectors; Public Fire Education Specialist; Strategic Analysis of Fire Department Operations; Tactical Operations for Company Officers I; Tactical Operations for Company Officers II; Team Effectiveness; Use Of Microcomputers For Fire Service Management

Fire Science Chemistry

National Emergency Training Center
> Chemistry of Hazardous Materials; Hazardous Materials Tactical Considerations; Hazardous Substance Specialist; Planning for a Hazardous Materials Incident

Fire Science Management

National Emergency Training Center
> Fire Executive Development III

Fire Sprinkler System Technology

Automatic Sprinkler Apprenticeship Program, Joint Apprenticeship and Training Committee, Local 669
> Architectural Working Drawings for Sprinkler Fitters; The Automatic Fire Sprinkler; Basic Drawing for the Sprinkler System; Blueprint Reading for the Sprinkler Fitter; Economics of the Sprinkler Industry; Human Relations; Hydraulics for the Sprinkler Apprentice; Installation of Sprinkler Systems; Introduction to

Automatic Sprinklers; Reading Automatic Sprinkler Piping Drawings; Safety, Rigging, and Scaffolding; Special Application Sprinkler Systems; Sprinkler System Alarms; Sprinkler Systems Calculations; Sprinkler Systems Water Supply; Technical Reports; Types of Fire Protection Systems; Use and Care of Tools

Fire Technology

Illinois Fire Service Institute

Arson Investigation II; Curriculum and Course Design I; Curriculum and Course Design II; Curriculum and Course Design III; Fire Prevention Officer I; Hazardous Materials: Chemistry; Tactics and Strategy II

National Emergency Training Center

Plans Review for Inspectors

Firefighting

Sun Refining and Marketing Company

Refinery Operator Program

First Aid

Abu Dhabi National Oil Company Career Development Center/GDC, Inc.

First Aid

Electrical Workers, Local Union 164 of the International Brotherhood of Electrical Workers, AFL-CIO, Bergen and Hudson Counties, New Jersey, and the Bergen-Hudson County Chapter of the National Electrical Contractors Association Joint Apprenticeship Training Program

Electrician Apprentice

Electrical Workers, Local Union 26 of the International Brotherhood of Electrical Workers and the Washington, D.C. Chapter of the National Electrical Contractors Association, Joint School

Electrician Apprentice

General Electric Company

Principles of Cardiovascular Monitoring

Joint Apprenticeship Training Committee, International Brotherhood of Electrical Workers Local Union 269, and the National Electrical Contractors Association of Southern New Jersey

Electrician Apprentice

Omaha Joint Electrical Apprenticeship and Training Committee

Electrical Apprenticeship Training

Seafarers Harry Lundeberg School of Seamanship

Able Seaman; Celestial Navigation; Chief Steward; Chief/Assistant Engineer - Uninspected Motor Vessels; Original Third Assistant Engineer, Steam and/or Motor - Inspected; Qualified Members of the Engine Department, Twelve-Week Version

First Aid and Life Saving

Seafarers Harry Lundeberg School of Seamanship

First Class Pilot; Master/Mate Freight and Towing

Flight Technology

Federal Aviation Administration

Boeing 727 Inspector Pilot and Flight Engineer Initial Qualification Course (20007); Federal Aviation Administration Douglas DC-9 Air Carrier Training Unit (20006)

Fluid Mechanics

International Correspondence Schools

Fluid Mechanics

Omaha Public Power District

Introduction to Thermodynamics

Sun Refining and Marketing Company

Refinery Operator Program

Wisconsin Public Service Corporation

Reactor Operator Fundamentals: Heat Transfer and Fluid Flow

Fluid Mechanics Technology

Sun Refining and Marketing Company

Refinery Operator Program

Fluid Power

Abu Dhabi National Oil Company Career Development Center/GDC, Inc.

Fundamentals of Fluids

Fluid Power Systems

Control Data

Fluid Power Systems

Fluid Power Technology

Chrysler Motors Advanced Technical Training

Hydraulic Systems Analysis

Focus Group Techniques

AT&T - Corporate Education Center, Management Education Training Division

Industrial Interviewing and Focus Group Techniques

Food Management

Seafarers Harry Lundeberg School of Seamanship

Chief Steward

Food Operations

Ponderosa Inc.

Steakhouse Training and Education Program

Food Preparation

Seafarers Harry Lundeberg School of Seamanship

Assistant Cook Utility; Chief Cook; Towboat Cook

Food Production

Jerrico Corporation

Basic Management Training Program

Ponderosa Inc.

Steakhouse Training and Education Program

Seafarers Harry Lundeberg School of Seamanship

Assistant Cook Utility; Chief Cook; Chief Steward; Cook and Baker

Food Science

United States Public Health Service - Indian Health Service
  Maternal and Child Nutrition; Nutrition Awareness

Food Service Equipment

McDonald's Corporation
  Advanced Operations

Food Service Equipment Engineering

McDonald's Corporation
  Applied Equipment

Food Service Management

Del Taco Corporation
  Manager Training Program, Phases I, II, and III

Del Taco, Inc.
  Manager Candidate Course; Manager Training Program, Phases I, II, and III

McDonald's Corporation
  Basic Operations; Field Consultants; Intermediate Operations; Management Development Program I, II, III, & IV; Operations Department Head's Class; Supervisory Management Skills

Food Service Operations

Seafarers Harry Lundeberg School of Seamanship
  Basic Steward

Food Service Organization and Supervision

Seafarers Harry Lundeberg School of Seamanship
  Chief Steward

Food Technology

United States Public Health Service - Indian Health Service
  Maternal and Child Nutrition; Nutrition Awareness

Foreign Service

Federal Aviation Administration
  Introduction to Foreign Service (14007)

Forensic Science

Police Training Institute
  Crime Scene Technician

Forestry

Defense Mapping Agency - Inter American Geodetic Survey Cartographic School
  Introduction to Remote Sensing/Image Analysis

United States Office of Personnel Management (OPM)
  Management of Natural Resources

FORTRAN

Control Data
  Structured FORTRAN Programming

International Correspondence Schools
  Computer Science III—Computer and FORTRAN Fundamentals

U.S. West Learning Systems
  Initial User Training/Program Logic and Design/FORTRAN Programming Language

French

National Cryptologic School
  Intermediate French Translation

United States Department of Agriculture, Graduate School
  Intermediate French I; Introductory French I; Introductory French II; Introductory French III

Front-line Supervision

Federal Aviation Administration
  A Positive Approach to Discipline (14001); Effective Organization of Work (14006); Fundamentals of Supervision (14002); Human Relations in Supervision (14003)

Gas Turbine Technology

General Electric Company
  Gas Turbine Technology

Geodetic Science

Defense Mapping Agency - Inter American Geodetic Survey Cartographic School
  Automated Geodetic Computations and Adjustments; Control Surveys; Geodesy; Geodetic Computations and Adjustments; Geodetic Computations; Gravity Surveys; Hydrographic Surveying; Land Gravity Surveys; Photogrammetry; Satellite Doppler Positioning

Geography

Defense Mapping Agency - Inter American Geodetic Survey Cartographic School
  Automated Cartography; Introduction to Remote Sensing/Image Analysis

Geological Science

Defense Mapping Agency - Inter American Geodetic Survey Cartographic School
  Introduction to Remote Sensing/Image Analysis

Geology

Baroid Corporation Career Development Center (Formerly NL Industries, Inc.)
  Directional Drilling Technology; Directional Drilling; Drilling Engineering; Programmed Drilling Technology

Geophysics

Defense Mapping Agency - Inter American Geodetic Survey Cartographic School
  Gravity Surveys; Land Gravity Surveys

National Cryptologic School
  Introduction to Astrodynamics

German

National Cryptologic School
  German for Reading Knowledge; Intermediate German Review; Introduction to German

United States Department of Agriculture, Graduate School
> Intermediate German I; Intermediate German II; Intermediate German III; Introductory German I; Introductory German II; Introductory German III

Gerontological Studies

New Jersey Department of Human Services
> Gerontology Training Series

Government

Pacific Bell
> Arbitration Advocacy; Contemporary Collective Bargaining; Labor Laws and Labor History

Government and Politics

United States Department of Agriculture, Graduate School
> Constitutional Law

Governmental Procurement

Westinghouse Electric Corporation, Integrated Logistic Support Division
> Controllers Professional Training School; Government Contracts Accounting and Control

Governmental Regulations (Pharmaceutical)

Certified Medical Representatives Institute, Inc.
> Governmental Regulations

Grammar

Bell Atlantic Corporation
> English Grammar and Usage

Graphics

Abu Dhabi National Oil Company Career Development Center/GDC, Inc.
> Industrial Drawing and Sketching

Knight-Ridder, Inc.
> Newspaper Production Techniques

Graphics Design

Knight-Ridder, Inc.
> Effective Newspaper Design and Graphics Editing

Greek

United States Department of Agriculture, Graduate School
> Intermediate Greek I; Intermediate Greek II; Intermediate Greek III; Introductory Greek II; Introductory Greek III; Introductory Greek I—Modern

Group Life and Health Insurance

Certified Employee Benefit Specialist Program
> CEBS Course I; Life, Health, and Other Group Benefit Programs

Guidance and Counseling

United States Public Health Service - Indian Health Service
> Introduction to Human Services; Skills and Techniques of Counseling

Young Women's Christian Association of the U.S.A.
> Advanced Management Workshop in Personnel Administration; Management Workshop for Student Leadership; Program Development Workshop; Staff Development II

Hardware Maintenance

Bell Atlantic Corporation
> Teletype Fundamentals

Unisys Corporation
> B7900 Hardware and Maintenance

Harmony

Tritone Music
> Chromatic Harmony; Diatonic Harmony

Hazardous Materials

National Mine Health and Safety Academy
> Hazardous Materials

New England Telephone Company
> Asbestos Recognition and Abatement

Health Administration

General Electric Company
> Management Processes

Health and Safety

Insurance Educational Association
> Hazard Identification and Analysis

Health Care Administration

American Medical Record Association
> Health Record Management in Nursing Homes

Certified Medical Representatives Institute, Inc.
> Healthcare Community; Trends and Issues in Healthcare

Health Insurance Association of America
> Group Life/Health Insurance: Part C; Group Life/Health Insurance: Parts A and B

Insurance Educational Association
> Workers' Compensation Rehabilitation

National Emergency Training Center
> Management of Emergency Medical Services

Health Care Delivery Systems

American Medical Record Association
> Orientation to the Health Care Field; Trends in Health Care Delivery

Health Care Systems Management

American Medical Record Association
> Supervisory Principles and Practice

Health Education

General Electric Company
> Principles of Cardiovascular Monitoring

National Mine Health and Safety Academy
> First Responder

Index 967

Health Facilities Management

Jewish Hospital of St. Louis
> Nursing Management

Health Hazards in Mining

National Mine Health and Safety Academy
> Health Hazards in Mining

Health Information Services

American Medical Record Association
> Planning for Health Information Services

Health Information Statistics

American Medical Record Association
> Health Statistics

Health Legislation

National Mine Health and Safety Academy
> Mine Safety and Health Legislation

Health Physics

Carolina Power & Light Company
> COC: Health Physics; Radiation Control and Measurement Laboratory

Duquesne Light Company
> Radiation, Radiation Protection, and Radiation Survey

General Electric Company
> Health Physics and Radiological Emergencies; Health Physics Technology; Nuclear Materials; Radiological Engineering

Westinghouse Electric Corporation, Nuclear Services Division (Formerly Water Reactor Divisions)
> Radioactivity, Radiation Detection, and Radiation Safety

Wolf Creek Nuclear Operating Corporation (Formerly Kansas Gas & Electric)
> Health Physics Technician Initial Training; Health Physics WCGS Plant Systems

Health Promotion

National Emergency Training Center
> Firefighter Health and Safety: Program Implementation and Management

Young Women's Christian Association of the U.S.A.
> Encore: The YWCA Post Mastectomy Group Rehabilitation Program; Encore Training Workshop: Encouragement - Normally - Counseling - Opportunity - Energies Revived

Health Safety

National Emergency Training Center
> Emergency Medical Service and Administration: An Overview; Firefighter Health and Safety: Program Implementation and Management

Health Science

American Sterilizer Company (AMSCO)
> Advanced Management Central Service Seminar; Central Service Department Seminar; Combined Central Service, Operating Room, and Infection Control Seminar; Hospital Engineering Seminar; Materials Management in Hospitals

Certified Medical Representatives Institute, Inc.
> Cardiovascular System; Digestive System; Endocrine System; Integumentary System; Musculoskeletal System; Nervous System; Reproductive Systems; Respiratory System; Sensory Organs; Urinary System

Crawford Risk Management Services
> Specialized Rehabilitation Counseling

Heat Transfer

Abu Dhabi National Oil Company Career Development Center/GDC, Inc.
> Heat Transfer Technology

Wisconsin Public Service Corporation
> Reactor Operator Fundamentals: Heat Transfer and Fluid Flow

Heavy Equipment Operations

United States Postal Service - Department of Training and Development
> Allison Automatic Transmissions

Hebrew

National Cryptologic School
> Basic Hebrew Refresher; Basic Modern Standard Hebrew; Intermediate Hebrew Reading Comprehension; Intermediate Hebrew Structure

Helping Skills

National Mine Health and Safety Academy
> Communication Skills I or Communication, Interpersonal, Small Group

Highway Construction and Design

International Correspondence Schools
> Highway Construction and Design I; Highway Construction and Design II

History

Katharine Gibbs School
> History of Modern World I; History of Modern World II; Introduction to Modern Civilization #701 or #813.; Modern World: A World in Flux #701.2 or #814

Seminary Extension, Southern Baptist Seminaries
> Biblical Backgrounds; How to Understand the Bible

Home Economics

United States Public Health Service - Indian Health Service
> Maternal and Child Nutrition; Nutrition Awareness

Homes and Condominiums as Investment Vehicles

National Association of REALTORS®
> Making Money Selling and Investing in Single Family Residences (RS-204)

Homiletics

Seminary Extension, Southern Baptist Seminaries
> Advanced Exposition

968 *Index*

Hospital Administration

American Medical Record Association
> Federal Health Programs; Health Record Content and Format; Medical Staff; Trends in Health Care Delivery

General Electric Company
> Management Processes

Hospital Statistics

American Medical Record Association
> Health Statistics

Household Appliance Maintenance

Whirlpool Corporation
> Appliance Service Training

Human Anatomy

Disabled American Veterans
> Disabled American Veterans Continuing Training Program for National Service Officers

Human Behavior

National Management Association
> Supervisory and Management Skills Program

Human Biology

Certified Medical Representatives Institute, Inc.
> Sensory Organs

Human Disease

Certified Medical Representatives Institute, Inc.
> Introduction to Disease States

Human Engineering

U.S. West Learning Systems
> Job Design; Job Study Workshop; Performance Data Collection and Analysis

Human Factors Engineering

National Mine Health and Safety Academy
> Human Factors Engineering

Human Pathology

Certified Medical Representatives Institute, Inc.
> Introduction to Disease States

Human Physiology

Certified Medical Representatives Institute, Inc.
> Physiology

Human Potential

U.S. West Learning Systems
> New Age Thinking for Achieving Your Potential

Human Relations

Bell Atlantic Corporation
> First Level Curriculum-Managing Performance; Human Relations in Business; Negotiation Skills Workshop

Control Data
> Affirmative Action Management Sequence

Federal Aviation Administration
> Advanced Instructor Training (10511)

New England Telephone Company
> Investment in Excellence

Pacific Bell
> Interpersonal Skills; Problem Solving; Winning

United States Department of Justice, Immigration and Naturalization Service, Federal Law Enforcement Training Center
> Border Patrol Academy; Immigration Officer Academy

United States Postal Service - Department of Training and Development
> Communication Skills for Managers #11251-00; Communications Skills for Supervisors #11281-00; Constructive Conflict Resolution #11220-00; Improving Group Performance #112200-00; Management Styles and Employee Motivation #11223-00; Managing Personal Effectiveness #11221-00; Supervisory Leadership: General Management #11203-00; Supervisory Leadership #17224-00

U.S. West Learning Systems
> Advanced Management Seminar; First Level Curriculum - Managing Performance; Initial Management Seminar; Initial Staff Seminar

Westinghouse Electric Corporation, Defense and Electronics Center
> Communications Workshop B100; Human Interaction and Communication; Leadership Development Workshop; Management Techniques Seminar; Transactional Analysis B120

Wolf Creek Nuclear Operating Corporation (Formerly Kansas Gas & Electric)
> Supervision I

Xerox Corporation
> Instructional Methods "Product Technical Specialist"

Human Resource Development

General Electric Company
> Career Planning Workshop

International Monetary Fund
> MGT 3 Management Development Course

Jewish Hospital of St. Louis
> Motivational Dynamics I; Motivational Dynamics II

National Weather Service Training Center
> Instructor Training

United States Navy Acquisition Management Training Office
> Management of Managers

U.S. West Learning Systems
> Administration of Self-Paced Instruction: Techniques, Methods, and Psychology of Instruction

Human Resource Management

Bell Communications Research Training and Education Center
> Facilitating Groups and Meetings; Innovation -

Achieving the Future; Managing Change in a Changing Environment; Managing Costly Group Problems; Managing the Boss

Blake Business School
> Human Relations

International Correspondence Schools
> Personnel Management

Massachusetts Bankers Association, Inc.
> MSFS-Human Resource Management

McDonald's Corporation
> Personnel Manager Program; Personnel Orientation Program

National Emergency Training Center
> Fire Command Operations; Strategic Analysis of Executive Leadership

Human Resource Policies and Practices

McDonald's Corporation
> Personnel Assistant Program

Human Resource Selection Management

McDonald's Corporation
> Personnel Recruiter Program

Human Resource Supervision

McDonald's Corporation
> Personnel Supervisor Program

Human Resources

Bell Atlantic Corporation
> Handling Grievances; Social Awareness #196; Supervisory Relationships Training; Time Management #190

Crawford Risk Management Services
> Specialized Rehabilitation Counseling

Opportunities Academy of Management Training, Inc.
> Comprehensive Employment and Training Act

Human Resources Management

AT&T - Center for Systems Education (Formerly AT&T Company Data Systems Education Group)
> Basic Training Development Skills Workshop; Techniques of Instruction; User Documentation/Performance Aids Workshop

Certified Employee Benefit Specialist Program
> CEBS Course VIII; Personnel and Labor Relations

NCR Corporation
> Behavior Modeling

New Jersey Department of Personnel, Division of Management Training and Employee Services
> Leading and Directing; Organizing; Planning

Professional Secretaries International
> Part I: Behavioral Science in Business

Human Services

Ford National Development and Training Center (Formerly UAW—Ford National Development and Training Center)
> Employe Involvement Process; Group Problem Solving; Successful Retirement Planning: Instructor Training

New Jersey Department of Human Services
> Gerontology Training Series; Prediction and Prevention of Aggressive Behavior in the System; Psychiatric Rehabilitation Practitioner Training; Training for Trainers - Crisis Recognition, Prevention, and Intervention

Opportunities Academy of Management Training, Inc.
> Manpower Services to Disadvantaged Youth

Westinghouse Electric Corporation, Defense and Electronics Center
> Leadership Development Workshop; Management Techniques Seminar

Humanities

Bell Atlantic Corporation
> Fundamentals of Data Transmission; Fundamentals of Data Transmission: Testing and Service; Peripheral Installation and Maintenance

Katharine Gibbs School
> Humanities I; Humanities II; Humanities: The American Experience; Introduction to the Humanities

Seminary Extension, Southern Baptist Seminaries
> How to Understand the Bible; New Testament Survey, Part III

Hydraulics

Abu Dhabi National Oil Company Career Development Center/GDC, Inc.
> Hydraulics and Pneumatics I and II

Chrysler Institute Associate Degree Program
> Industrial Hydraulics

Chrysler Motors Advanced Technical Training
> Industrial Hydraulic Technology

Ford National Development and Training Center (Formerly UAW—Ford National Development and Training Center)
> Basic Hydraulics

Seafarers Harry Lundeberg School of Seamanship
> Hydraulics

Hydrographic Science

Defense Mapping Agency - Inter American Geodetic Survey Cartographic School
> Hydrographic Surveying

Hydrology

National Weather Service Training Center
> Flash Flood Forecasting

United States Department of Agriculture, Graduate School
> Hydrology I; Hydrology II

IBM Series/1

Brick Computer Science Institute

    IBM Series/1 Disk and Magnetic Tape System with Telecommunications

Image Processing

General Motors Corporation - Technical Staffs Group and Lansing Automotive Division (Formerly Advanced Engineering Staff [AES])

    Image Processing

Imagery Analysis

National Photographic Interpretation Center

    National Imagery Analysis Course

Imagery Interpretation

National Photographic Interpretation Center

    National Imagery Analysis Course

Immigration and Nationality Law

United States Department of Justice, Immigration and Naturalization Service, Federal Law Enforcement Training Center

    Border Patrol Academy; Immigration Officer Academy

Immunology

Certified Medical Representatives Institute, Inc.

    Immune System

IMS Concepts

Applied Learning (Formerly ASI/DELTAK)

    Data Base Design; 1527 IMS Data Base Design; 4505 IMS Concepts

Income Property Appraisal

National Association of Independent Fee Appraisers

    Income Property Appraising

Income Tax Law (U.S.)

United States Department of Internal Revenue Service, Federal Law Enforcement Training Center

    Federal Income Tax for Criminal Investigation

Industrial Arts

Knight-Ridder, Inc.

    Newspaper Production Techniques

United States Army Materiel Command - AMC (Formerly DARCOM - United States Army Materiel Development and Readiness Command)

    Electronics

United States Postal Service - Department of Training and Development

    Automotive Diesel Mechanics; Basic Industrial Electricity; Caterpillar Diesel; Cummins Diesel I; Cummins Diesel III; Electronics I; Engine Tune-up and Air Pollution Control Devices; Postal Diesel

Industrial Controls

Chrysler Motors Advanced Technical Training

    Microprocessors 6800/6502

Industrial Education

Ohio Bell Telephone Company

    Trainer Workshop

United States Postal Service - Department of Training and Development

    Air Brakes; Automatic Transmission Overhaul; Automotive Diesel Mechanics; Automotive Mechanic Fundamentals; Brakes and Suspension Systems; Caterpillar Diesel; Cummins Diesel I; Cummins Diesel III; Electric Vehicle; Engine Tune-up and Air Pollution Control Devices; Fundamentals of Automatic Transmissions; Postal Diesel

Industrial Electrical Controls

Chrysler Motors Advanced Technical Training

    Programmable Controllers PLC-2 Family Advanced Program; Programmable Controllers PLC-2 Family; Programmable Controllers PLC-3 and PLC 3/10 Advanced Program; Programmable Controllers PLC-3 and PLC-3/10; Programmable Controllers PLC-5 Family; Programmable Controllers—Modicon 484; Programmable Controllers—Modicon 584

Industrial Electrical Technology

Texas Utilities Electric Corporation (Formerly Texas Utilities Generating Company - TUGCo)

    DC Motors and Generators; Electrical Troubleshooting; Transformers and Circuit Breakers

United States Postal Service - Department of Training and Development

    Automotive Electrical Systems

Industrial Electricity

Abu Dhabi National Oil Company Career Development Center/GDC, Inc.

    Electrical Theory

Electrical Workers, Local Union 26 of the International Brotherhood of Electrical Workers and the Washington, D.C. Chapter of the National Electrical Contractors Association, Joint School

    Electrician Apprentice

Mercer County Vocational-Technical Schools - Division of Adult Education

    Industrial Electricity

Omaha Joint Electrical Apprenticeship and Training Committee

    Electrical Apprenticeship Training

Industrial Electromechanical Programs

Ford National Development and Training Center (Formerly UAW—Ford National Development and Training Center)

    Advanced Relay Logic Program; Electro-Mechanical Logic Controls for Industrial Machines; Relay Logic Program

Industrial Electronics

Abu Dhabi National Oil Company Career Development Center/GDC, Inc.

    Industrial Electronics

Chrysler Motors Advanced Technical Training

    Industrial Electronics; Microprocessors 6800/6502

International Correspondence Schools
> Applications of Industrial Electronics

United States Postal Service - Department of Training and Development
> Industrial Electrical Services

Industrial Electronics Laboratory

Seafarers Harry Lundeberg School of Seamanship
> Variable Speed DC Drives

Industrial Engineering

AT&T - Center for Systems Education (Formerly AT&T Company Data Systems Education Group)
> Human Factors in Computer Systems; Human Performance Engineering; Performance Analysis Workshop

AT&T - Marketing Education - Somerset Seminars
> Demand Analysis Techniques; Demand Analysis Techniques Seminar; Public Switched Network Seminar; Special Network Services Seminar

General Electric Company
> Industrial Engineering; Manufacturing Materials and Processes; Product Engineering; Regression Analysis

General Motors Corporation - Technical Staffs Group and Lansing Automotive Division (Formerly Advanced Engineering Staff [AES])
> Advanced Robotic Systems; Analytical Methods in Robotics; Noise Control

Maynard Management Institute
> Clerical MOST; Fundamental Principles of Supervision; Fundamentals of Cost Reduction; Fundamentals of Methods Engineering and Time Study; Fundamentals of Time Study; Industrial Engineering Basics; Industrial Engineering for the Supervisor; Maintenance Planner and Scheduler; Maxi MOST Computer Supplementary Module; Maxi MOST; Methods Engineering; Mini MOST Computer Supplementary Module; MOST Computer; MOST Computer Systems; Predetermined Time System—Basic MOST; Predetermined Time Systems—Mini MOST; Predetermined Time Systems—MTM-1; Predetermined Time Systems—MTM-2; Predetermined Time Systems—MTM2B; Predetermined Time Systems—MTM3; Standard Data Development; Supervisor's Cost Reduction; Time Study Engineering; Universal Maintenance Standards

National Emergency Training Center
> Firefighter Health and Safety: Program Implementation and Management

NCR Corporation
> Project Planning and Management; Project Planning and Management for Software Development

United States Army Materiel Command - AMC (Formerly DARCOM - United States Army Materiel Development and Readiness Command)
> Advanced Topics in Reliability and Maintainability Engineering; Computer Simulation Techniques; Computers in Manufacturing; Design by Reliability; Design of Engineering Experiments; Experimental Design; Human Factors Engineering in Systems Design; Human Operations in Complex Systems; Logistics Support Analysis; Maintainability Analysis; Problems in Maintainability Engineering I; Problems in Maintainability Engineering II; Production Modeling Techniques; Production Systems Design; Reliability Analysis and Design; Reliability, Availability, and Maintainability; Reliability Engineering; Statistical Methods and Systems Reliability; Statistical Methods in Reliability and Maintainability; Statistical Methods in Reliability; Statistical Quality Control; Techniques in Operations Research; Test and Evaluation Management

U.S. West Learning Systems
> Job Design; Job Study Workshop; Performance Data Collection and Analysis

Industrial Engineering Technology

Bell Atlantic Corporation
> Outside Plant Engineering Education Program,, (NE09CIC)

Industrial Equipment Repair

Abu Dhabi National Oil Company Career Development Center/GDC, Inc.
> Repair and Maintenance of Rotating Equipment I and II

Industrial Hydraulics

General Electric Company
> Industrial Hydraulics

Industrial Hygiene

National Mine Health and Safety Academy
> Resident IV Industrial Hygiene II

Industrial Instrument Installation

Abu Dhabi National Oil Company Career Development Center/GDC, Inc.
> Instrument Technology

Industrial Instrumentation

Abu Dhabi National Oil Company Career Development Center/GDC, Inc.
> Instrumentation

Industrial Maintenance

Abu Dhabi National Oil Company Career Development Center/GDC, Inc.
> Boiler Repair and Maintenance; Plant Materials and Equipment

Industrial Management

General Electric Company
> Computer-Aided Manufacturing; Conventional Metal Removal; Fabricated Parts Seminar; Joining; Manufacturing Methods and Processes; Miscellaneous Processes; Non-Conventional Metal Removal; Numerical Control; Quality Control; Rotating Parts Seminar; Sheet Metal

NCR Corporation
> Data Pathing Systems Engineering Management; Industrial Data Systems; Systems Engineering Management

972 *Index*

United States Army Materiel Command - AMC (Formerly DARCOM - United States Army Materiel Development and Readiness Command)

    Issues; Maintainability Analysis and Design; Operational Analysis for Production Systems; Physical Inventory; Preservation and Packaging; Product Assurance Management and Engineering II; Product Reliability and Safety; Production Planning and Control; Program Planning and Control; Receiving; Safety Engineering Tools and Techniques; Software Quality; Warehousing and Materiels Handling

Industrial Marketing

AT&T - Corporate Education Center, Management Education Training Division

    Concepts in Industrial Marketing

AT&T - Marketing Education - Somerset Seminars

    Advanced Market Planning; Computer Assisted Market Planning

Industrial Marketing Research

AT&T - Corporate Education Center, Management Education Training Division

    Applications in Industrial Marketing Research

Industrial Mathematics

Abu Dhabi National Oil Company Career Development Center/GDC, Inc.

    Industrial Mathematics I and II

Industrial Processes

Omaha Public Power District

    Process Measurement Fundamentals

Industrial Psychology

Bell Communications Research Training and Education Center

    Facilitating Groups and Meetings; Innovation - Achieving the Future; Managing Change in a Changing Environment; Managing Costly Group Problems; Managing the Boss

Chrysler Institute Associate Degree Program

    Principles of Industrial Psychology

Katharine Gibbs School

    Industrial and Organizational Psychology

Young Women's Christian Association of the U.S.A.

    Advanced Management Workshop in Personnel Administration

Industrial Real Estate

National Association of REALTORS®

    Industrial Real Estate (SIR-I); Industrial Real Estate (SIR-II)

Industrial Relations

Bell Atlantic Corporation

    Management/Union Relations Workshop

Certified Employee Benefit Specialist Program

    CEBS Course VIII; Personnel and Labor Relations

Chrysler Institute Associate Degree Program

    Labor Relations

Jamaican Institute of Management

    Personnel Management and Industrial Relations

United States Postal Service - Department of Training and Development

    Employee Relations Management MTS; Labor Relations Management MTS

Industrial Safety

Abu Dhabi National Oil Company Career Development Center/GDC, Inc.

    Electrical Safety

American Institute for Property and Liability Underwriters/Insurance Institute of America

    (ALCM 71) Hazard Identification and Analysis; (ALCM 72) Loss Control Applications and Management

Bell Communications Research Training and Education Center

    Central Office Grounding; Electrical Protection Fundamentals

Seafarers Harry Lundeberg School of Seamanship

    Chief/Assistant Engineer - Uninspected Motor Vessels; Original Third Assistant Engineer, Steam and/or Motor - Inspected

United States Army Materiel Command - AMC (Formerly DARCOM - United States Army Materiel Development and Readiness Command)

    Chemical Safety in the Industrial Environment

United States Postal Service - Department of Training and Development

    Accident Investigation; Vehicle Accident Investigation

Westinghouse Electric Corporation, Nuclear Services Division (Formerly Water Reactor Divisions)

    Engineered Safeguard Systems; General Employee Training

Industrial Safety Technology

Westinghouse Electric Corporation, Nuclear Services Division (Formerly Water Reactor Divisions)

    Radioactivity, Radiation Detection, and Radiation Safety

Industrial Security

Department of Defense, Defense Security Institute

    Defense Industrial Security Programs I and II; Industrial Security Specialist Course—Basic and Advanced; Principles of Industrial Security

Industrial Systems

International Correspondence Schools

    Industrial Systems

Industrial Technology

Abu Dhabi National Oil Company Career Development Center/GDC, Inc.

    Boiler Control; Boilers and Water Treatment I and II; Instrumentation; Mechanical Elements; Plant Materials and Equipment; Process Static Equipment II; Repair and Maintenance of Rotating Equipment I and II; Repair and Maintenance of Static Equipment I and II; Utility Systems

Applied Learning (Formerly ASI/DELTAK)

Basic and Advanced Troubleshooting in Electronic Systems; Course 1 - Introduction to Industrial Control; Course 2 - Introduction to Programmable Control

Bell Atlantic Corporation

Computer-Based PBX Systems 208, Dimension 400 Repair-Tier 2 209, CSS 201-2000 Dimension Installation; Electronic Switching Systems; Fundamentals of Data Transmission; Fundamentals of Data Transmission: Testing and Service; Microcomputer Based PBX Systems: Installation and Maintenance; Peripheral Installation and Maintenance

General Electric Company

Descriptive Geometry I; Descriptive Geometry II

Westinghouse Electric Corporation, Nuclear Services Division (Formerly Water Reactor Divisions)

Electrical Sciences; Electrical Systems

Industrial Training

Westinghouse Electric Corporation, Nuclear Services Division (Formerly Water Reactor Divisions)

Instructional Skills Workshop; Simulator Instructor Skills and Methods

Industrial Valuation

National Association of REALTORS®

Industrial Valuation (EX 7)

Infection Control Seminar

American Sterilizer Company (AMSCO)

Advanced Management Central Service Seminar

Information Mapping

Pacific Bell

Information Mapping

Information Processing

U.S. West Learning Systems

Word Processing

Information Science

AT&T - Center for Systems Education (Formerly AT&T Company Data Systems Education Group)

Concepts of the Integrated Systems Provisioning Process; Programmer Basic Training

Bell Atlantic Corporation

Programmer Basic Training; Programmer Basic Training - COBOL

Chrysler Institute Associate Degree Program

Computer Usage in Manufacturing Operations

General Electric Company

Information Systems

New England Telephone Company

Programmer Basic Training

Ohio Bell Telephone Company

Data Processing Concepts

Pacific Bell

Principles of Digital Technology

U.S. West Learning Systems

Programmer Basic Training

Information Security

Department of Defense, Defense Security Institute

Information Security Management; Principles of Information Security

Information Systems

AT&T - Center for Systems Education (Formerly AT&T Company Data Systems Education Group)

Information Systems Analysis Workshop

Bell Atlantic Corporation

Network Management and Applications; Programmer Workshop I

NCR Corporation

IMOS TRAN-PRO Concepts; IMOS TRAN-PRO Installation and Support

Pacific Bell

Advanced DOS; Communications with Microcomputers; Introduction to DBASE II/III; Network Traffic Concepts

Information Systems Design

AT&T - Center for Systems Education (Formerly AT&T Company Data Systems Education Group)

System Design

Information Systems Management

American Institute for Property and Liability Underwriters/Insurance Institute of America

(AIAF 112) Insurance Information Systems

Insurance Data Management Association

Data Administration

United States Department of Agriculture, Graduate School

ADP Documentation and Writing; Applied Indexing; Basic Indexing; Structured Design and Programming; Structured Systems Analysis and Design; Systems Analysis and Design; Systems Analysis and Documentation; Thesaurus Building

Information Systems Technology

United States Department of Agriculture, Graduate School

Introduction to Information Systems Technology

Information Technology

Bell Atlantic Corporation

Introduction to Information Technology—Basic Concepts and Market Structure

Input/Output Device Maintenance

Bell Communications Research Training and Education Center

1A Maintenance Program - Auxiliary Unit Maintenance

Instructional Design and Development

AT&T - Professional Development Division
  Instructional Design and Development Workshop

New England Telephone Company
  Trainer Skills Workshop

Pacific Bell
  Instructor Competencies

U.S. West Learning Systems
  Analysis and Instructional Design - AID; Criterion Referenced Instruction Workshop; Instructional Module Development; Job Aid Workshop; Performance Analysis Workshop; Test Development Workshop

Wolf Creek Nuclear Operating Corporation (Formerly Kansas Gas & Electric)
  Classroom Instructor Workshop

Instructional Methods

Southwestern Bell Telephone Company
  Trainer Skills Workshop

Unisys Corporation
  Introduction to Teaching Methods

Instructional Skills

Ford National Development and Training Center (Formerly UAW—Ford National Development and Training Center)
  Instructional Skills Workshop

Instructional Technology

AT&T - Center for Systems Education (Formerly AT&T Company Data Systems Education Group)
  Advanced Techniques of Instruction

Instructional Writing

AT&T - Professional Development Division
  Instructional Writing Workshop

Instructor Skills

AT&T - Professional Development Division
  Basic Instructors Skills

Instrument Diagrams

Abu Dhabi National Oil Company Career Development Center/GDC, Inc.
  Piping and Instrument Diagrams

Instrument Repair and Calibration

Abu Dhabi National Oil Company Career Development Center/GDC, Inc.
  Instrument Repair and Calibration I and II

Instrument Technology

Abu Dhabi National Oil Company Career Development Center/GDC, Inc.
  Hydraulics and Pneumatics I and II; Instrument Repair and Calibration I and II; Instrument Technology; Introduction to Instrumentation; Piping and Instrument Diagrams; Pneumatic Instrumentation; Process Control I and II; Process Control III

Instrumental Methods

Technical Training Project, Inc.
  Laboratory Technician Program

Instrumentation

Abu Dhabi National Oil Company Career Development Center/GDC, Inc.
  Introduction to Instrumentation

Electrical Workers, Local Union 26 of the International Brotherhood of Electrical Workers and the Washington, D.C. Chapter of the National Electrical Contractors Association, Joint School
  Electrician Apprentice

Omaha Joint Electrical Apprenticeship and Training Committee
  Electrical Apprenticeship Training

Instrumentation and Measurement

Xerox Corporation
  2080

Instrumentation Technology

Abu Dhabi National Oil Company Career Development Center/GDC, Inc.
  Analytical Equipment; Process Simulators I and II

Insurance

American Institute for Property and Liability Underwriters/Insurance Institute of America
  (AAI 81) Principles of Insurance Production; (AAI 82) Multiple-Lines Insurance Production; Accounting and Finance; (AIAF 111) Statutory Accounting for Property and Liability Insurers; (AIAF 112) Insurance Information Systems; (AIAF 113) Insurance Company Finance; (AIC 31) Principles of Insurance and Property Loss Adjusting; (AIC 32) Principles of Insurance and Liability Claims Adjusting; (AIC 35) Property Insurance Adjusting; (AIC 36) Liability Insurance Adjusting; (ALCM 71) Hazard Identification and Analysis; (ALCM 72) Loss Control Applications and Management; Analysis of Insurance Functions; (APA 91) Principles of Premium Auditing; (APA 92) Premium Auditing Applications; (ARM 54) Structure of Risk Management Process; (ARM 55) Risk Control; (ARM 56) Risk Financing; (ARP 101) Business Research Methods; (ARP 102) Strategic Planning for Insurers; (AU 61) Principles of Property Liability and Underwriting; (AU 62) Personal Lines Underwriting; (AU 63) Commercial Liability Underwriting; (AU 64) Commercial Property and Multiple-Lines Underwriting; Commercial Liability Risk Management and Insurance; Commercial Property Risk Management and Insurance; (INS 21) Property and Liability Insurance Principles; (INS 22) Personal Insurance; (INS 23) Commercial Insurance; Insurance and Business Law; Insurance Company Operations; Insurance Issues and Professional Ethics; Insurance Principles and Practices; The Legal Environment of Insurance; Personal Risk Management and Insurance; Principles of Risk Management and Insurance

American International Group, Inc.
  New Career Employee Training Program; Principles of Insurance

College for Financial Planning®
: Estate Planning; Risk Management

Crawford Risk Management Services
: Advanced Casualty Claims Adjusting; Advanced Property Loss Adjusting; Casualty Claim Adjusting; Property Loss Adjusting; Specialized Rehabilitation Counseling; Workers' Compensation Claims Adjusting

Health Insurance Association of America
: Group Life/Health Insurance: Part C; Group Life/Health Insurance: Parts A and B; Individual Health Insurance: Parts A and B

Illinois Fire Service Institute
: Arson Investigation I; Arson Investigation II

Insurance Educational Association
: Accounting and Finance; Automobile Insurance; Casualty Insurance; Commercial Automobile Insurance Coverages; Commercial Inland Marine; Commercial Liability Insurance Coverages; Commercial Liability Risk Management and Insurance; Commercial Liability Underwriting; Commercial Multi-Peril Package Policies; Commercial Property and Multiple-Line Underwriting; Commercial Property Insurance Coverages; Commercial Property Risk Management and Insurance; Fire Protection Engineering; Hazard Identification and Analysis; Insurance Company Operations; Insurance Issues and Professional Ethics; Law of Torts; Legal Environment of Insurance; Liability Insurance Adjusting; Personal Lines Insurance; Personal Lines Underwriting; Personal Risk Management and Insurance; Principles of Insurance and Liability Claim Adjusting; Principles of Insurance and Property Loss Adjusting; Principles of Insurance; Principles of Property and Liability Underwriting; Principles of Risk Management and Insurance; Property Insurance Adjusting - Advanced; Property Insurance; Risk Control; Risk Financing; Structure of the Risk-Management Process; Surety Bonding; Workers' Compensation; Workers' Compensation Claims - Medical Terms and Applications; Workers' Compensation Claims; Workers' Compensation: Permanent Disability Rating; Workers' Compensation Rehabilitation

National Emergency Training Center
: Arson Detection; Fire Arson Investigation

Professional Insurance Agents
: PIA Insurance School at Drake University

International Banking

American Bankers Association
: International Banking

International Business

American Institute of Banking - Washington, D.C. Chapter
: International Banking

International Finance

American Bankers Association
: Letters of Credit

International Relations

United States Office of Personnel Management (OPM)
: National Security Policy

Interpersonal Communications

Chrysler Institute Associate Degree Program
: Interpersonal Communications

NCR Corporation
: Introduction to Time Management, Public Speaking, and Stress Management

Ohio Bell Telephone Company
: Listening Skills

Portsmouth Naval Shipyard: Apprenticeship Training
: Human Behavior and Leadership

Interpersonal Dynamics

National Management Association
: Supervisory and Management Skills Program

Interpersonal Relations

American Medical Record Association
: Supervisory Principles and Practice

National Mine Health and Safety Academy
: Communication Skills I or Communication, Interpersonal, Small Group

Interpersonal Skills

Pacific Bell
: The Versatile Organization

Southwestern Bell Telephone Company
: Negotiating Successfully

Interrogation

United States Department of Internal Revenue Service, Federal Law Enforcement Training Center
: Special Agent Investigative Techniques

Interrogation Procedures

National Mine Health and Safety Academy
: Applied Communication Techniques

Interviewing

AT&T - Corporate Education Center, Management Education Training Division
: Industrial Interviewing and Focus Group Techniques

National Mine Health and Safety Academy
: Applied Communication Techniques

United States Department of Internal Revenue Service, Federal Law Enforcement Training Center
: Special Agent Investigative Techniques

Inventory Management

Bell Communications Research Training and Education Center
: Inventory Management

Digital Equipment Corporation
: Inventory Management

Investigation

National Emergency Training Center
    Arson Detection

Investment Analysis

Certified Employee Benefit Specialist Program
    Asset Management; CEBS Course VII

Investment Management

Certified Employee Benefit Specialist Program
    Asset Management; CEBS Course VII

Investments

Graduate School of Banking at the University of Wisconsin-Madison (Central States Conference of Bankers Associates)
    Investments

Institute of Financial Education
    Personal Investments

National Association of Securities Dealers, Inc.
    Investments and/or Brokerage Accounting; Securities, Regulation, Law, and Self-Regulation

Iraqi

National Cryptologic School
    Basic Colloquial Iraqi

Italian

National Cryptologic School
    Basic Italian; Intermediate Italian Translation; Rapid Survey of Italian Structure

Japanese

National Cryptologic School
    Basic Japanese Level I; Basic Japanese Level II; Basic Japanese Level III; Basic Japanese Level IV

United States Department of Agriculture, Graduate School
    Advanced Japanese I; Advanced Japanese II; Advanced Japanese III; Intermediate Japanese I; Intermediate Japanese II; Intermediate Japanese III; Introductory Japanese I; Introductory Japanese II; Introductory Japanese III

Job Administration

U.S. West Learning Systems
    Second Level Management Performance Based Curriculum

Job Control Language

Computer Learning Center
    Introduction to Data Processing; OS/Operations

Job Definition

Bell Atlantic Corporation
    Developing Subordinates; Managing the Flow of Work; Managing the Job

Journalism

Knight-Ridder, Inc.
    Newspaper Production Techniques

United States Department of Agriculture, Graduate School
    Advanced Practice in Editing; Editing; Editing Technical Manuscripts; Intermediate Editing; Intermediate Editing Principles and Practices; Introduction to the Editing Process; Legal Writing I; Legal Writing II; Practice in Editing; Principles of Editing; Principles of Editing for Publication; Printing, Layout and Design; Proofreading; Publishing Management; Seminar in Editing; Style and Techniques for Editors

Junior High School Administration

Independent School Management
    Managing the Private-Independent Middle School

Juvenile Delinquency

Police Training Institute
    Advanced Law for Youth Officers; Youth Officers

Juvenile Justice

Opportunities Academy of Management Training, Inc.
    Manpower Services to Disadvantaged Youth

Police Training Institute
    Advanced Law for Youth Officers; Youth Officers

Key Telephone Equipment Installation Repair

Bell Atlantic Corporation
    Installation and Service of Key Telephone Customer Equipment 2152 Installation 128, Residence Key Telephone System 139, Key Systems

Keyboarding

Institute for Business and Technology
    Keyboarding

Kinematics

International Correspondence Schools
    Kinematics

Kitchen Supervision

Seafarers Harry Lundeberg School of Seamanship
    Assistant Cook Utility; Chief Cook

Korean

National Cryptologic School
    Basic Korean Refresher Course; Basic Korean Structure I; Basic Korean Structure II; Basic Korean Structure III; Basic Korean Structure IV

Labor Education

Seafarers Harry Lundeberg School of Seamanship
    Union Education

Labor Planning

National Emergency Training Center
    Strategic Analysis of Fire Prevention Programs

Labor Policy

Opportunities Academy of Management Training, Inc.
    Comprehensive Employment and Training Act

Labor Relations

Certified Employee Benefit Specialist Program
    CEBS Course VIII; Personnel and Labor Relations

Federal Aviation Administration
    Labor Relations for Management (01202)

Institute of Management and Production
    Collective Bargaining; Industrial Relations, Issues, and Review; Labor Laws in Jamaica; Labor Relations in Jamaica

New England Telephone Company
    Labor Relations

Pacific Bell
    Arbitration Advocacy; Contemporary Collective Bargaining; Labor Laws and Labor History

Seafarers Harry Lundeberg School of Seamanship
    Union Leadership

United States Postal Service - Department of Training and Development
    Labor Relations Management MTS

Labor Studies

Ford National Development and Training Center (Formerly UAW—Ford National Development and Training Center)
    Employe Involvement Process; Successful Retirement Planning: Instructor Training

New England Telephone Company
    Labor Relations

Pacific Bell
    Arbitration Advocacy; Contemporary Collective Bargaining; Labor Laws and Labor History

Seafarers Harry Lundeberg School of Seamanship
    Union Leadership

Labor-Management Relations

Dana Corporation
    Fundamentals of Supervision III

Land Return Analysis

National Association of REALTORS®
    Land Return Analysis (FLI-164)

Land Surveying

International Correspondence Schools
    Geodetic Surveying; Land Surveying

Laser, Optics, and Magnetic Tape Technology

Xerox Corporation
    9700 EPS

Law

AT&T - Marketing Education - Somerset Seminars
    Measured Service Issues Seminar; Network Services Issues Seminar; Restructure of Private Line Issues; Terminal Products Issues Seminar

Institute of Management and Production
    Business Administration

United States Food and Drug Administration
    Basic Food and Drug Law Course

Law and Banking

Garden State AIB
    Business and Banking Law 1

Law Enforcement

Bell Communications Research Training and Education Center
    Security Personnel Basic Training School

Illinois Fire Service Institute
    Arson Investigation I; Arson Investigation II; Hazardous Materials: Chemistry

Police Training Institute
    Basic Law Enforcement I; Basic Law Enforcement II

United States Drug Enforcement Administration
    Criminal Investigation - Drug Abuse; Drug Enforcement Officers Academy

United States Postal Service - Department of Training and Development
    Introduction to Law Enforcement; Security Force Training

Law for Police

Police Training Institute
    Law for Police II

Law Office Administration

American Center for Technical Arts and Sciences (Formerly Mainline Paralegal Institute)
    Law Office Administration

Leadership

Bell Atlantic Corporation
    Human Relations in Business

Independent School Management
    Overview of Business and Financial Management in Private-Independent Schools; Presiding Over the Private-Independent School Board of Trustees; Women as School Administrators in Private-Independent Schools

Southwestern Bell Telephone Company
    Leadership Skills Workshop

Wolf Creek Nuclear Operating Corporation (Formerly Kansas Gas & Electric)
    Supervision I

Leadership Management

U.S. West Learning Systems
    Advanced Management Seminar; Initial Management Seminar; Initial Staff Seminar

Leadership Training

Xerox Corporation
    Instructional Methods "Product Technical Specialist"

Legal Aspects of Health Information

American Medical Record Association
    Legal Aspects of Health Information

Legal Environment of Business

American Educational Institute, Inc.
    Legal Principles

Certified Employee Benefit Specialist Program
    CEBS Course V; Contemporary Legal Environment of Employee Benefit Plans

Legal Office Practice

Katharine Gibbs School
    Legal Office Practice

Legal Research

American Center for Technical Arts and Sciences (Formerly Mainline Paralegal Institute)
    Techniques of Legal Research

American Institute for Paralegal Studies, Inc.
    Introduction to Legal Research and Writing; Legal Research and Writing II

National Academy for Paralegal Studies, Inc.
    Introduction to Legal Research and Writing; Legal Analysis and Writing; Legal Research and Writing II

Legal Research and Writing

Omega Institute
    Legal Research and Writing

Legal Studies

PJA School
    Civil Litigation; Domestic Relations; Legal Research; Wills and Estates

Legal Writing

American Center for Technical Arts and Sciences (Formerly Mainline Paralegal Institute)
    Techniques of Legal Research

American Institute for Paralegal Studies, Inc.
    Introduction to Legal Research and Writing; Legal Research and Writing II

National Academy for Paralegal Studies, Inc.
    Introduction to Legal Research and Writing; Legal Analysis and Writing; Legal Research and Writing II

Liability Insurance

American Educational Institute, Inc.
    Liability

Library Science

United States Department of Agriculture, Graduate School
    Applied Indexing; Basic Indexing; Thesaurus Building

Life Insurance

Certified Employee Benefit Specialist Program
    CEBS Course II; Pension Plans

Lightwave Cable Application

Bell Atlantic Corporation
    Lightwave Design; Subscriber Carrier

Linear and Digital Electronics

International Correspondence Schools
    Linear and Digital Integrated Circuits

National Weather Service Training Center
    Integrated Circuits and Application Concepts Y-02-03

Linear System Theory

Westinghouse Electric Corporation, Defense and Electronics Center
    Introduction to Electronic Filtering I

Linguistics

Laubach Literacy Action
    Teaching English to Speakers of Other Languages

National Cryptologic School
    Introduction to Linguistic Theory

Liquid Cargo Operations

Seafarers Harry Lundeberg School of Seamanship
    Liquid Cargo Operations

LISP Program Language

Westinghouse Electric Corporation, Defense and Electronics Center
    LISP: The Artificial Intelligence Language

Literature

Katharine Gibbs School
    Modern American Literature 704, 706, or 722.

Litigation

American Institute for Paralegal Studies, Inc.
    Litigation, Pleadings and Arbitration

Litigation Values

National Association of REALTORS®
    Litigation Valuation (EX 4)

Loan and Discount

Garden State AIB
    Loan and Discount

Local Area Networks

Bell Communications Research Training and Education Center
    Data Communications - Local Area Network

Logic

Chrysler Institute Associate Degree Program
    Creative Thinking in the Industrial Environment

Logic Circuit Fundamentals

Bell Atlantic Corporation
> New Jersey Bell 509B: No. 1 ESS Central Processor and Program Fundamentals

Pacific Bell
> 1 ESS Central Processor and Programming Fundamentals

U.S. West Learning Systems
> Mountain Bell 509B: No. 1 ESS Central Processor and Program Fundamentals

Logic Circuits

International Correspondence Schools
> Pulse and Logic Circuits

Logistics

Federal Aviation Administration
> Material Management (07015); Operations and Supply Support (07014); Procurement for Technical Personnel (07004)

Logistics and Materials Management

Bell Atlantic Corporation
> Procurement Management Fundamentals

United States Navy Acquisition Management Training Office
> Advanced Contract Administration; Basic Contract Administration

Westinghouse Electric Corporation, Defense and Electronics Center
> Contracts Management Pro-Seminar; Principles of Government Contract Management

Westinghouse Electric Corporation, Integrated Logistic Support Division
> Controllers Professional Training School; Government Contracts Accounting and Control

Machine Language Programming

Dow Jones & Company, Inc.
> Pagination

Machine Organization

The Chubb Institute
> Introduction to Computer Systems; Programming Fundamentals

Machine Shop Practices

Seafarers Harry Lundeberg School of Seamanship
> Liquid Cargo Operations

Machine Technology

General Motors Corporation
> Introduction to Minicomputer Programming

Macroeconomics

Certified Employee Benefit Specialist Program
> CEBS Course IX; Employee Benefit Plans and the Economy

Katharine Gibbs School
> Economics I - #506 or #806

Westinghouse Electric Corporation, Education Center Department
> Introduction to Economic Analysis

Mainframe Processor Operations and Maintenance

Unisys Corporation
> Large Mainframe Central Processing Operation and Maintenance

Maintenance Mechanics

United States Postal Service - Department of Training and Development
> Security Equipment

Management

Abu Dhabi National Oil Company Career Development Center/GDC, Inc.
> Principles of Management

American Bankers Association
> Management Fundamentals

American Institute for Property and Liability Underwriters/Insurance Institute of America
> (AIM 41) The Process of Management; (AIM 42) Management and Human Resources; (AIM 43) Managerial Decision Making; (AIM 44) Management in a Changing World; (ARM 55) Risk Control; (ARM 56) Risk Financing; (ARP 101) Business Research Methods; (ARP 102) Strategic Planning for Insurers; Management

American Sterilizer Company (AMSCO)
> Advanced Management Central Service Seminar; Central Service Department Seminar; Combined Central Service, Operating Room, and Infection Control Seminar; Materials Management in Hospitals

AT&T - Center for Systems Education (Formerly AT&T Company Data Systems Education Group)
> Introduction to Project Management; Introductory Project Management; Personnel Subsystem Testing and Evaluation; Project Leadership Workshop; Project Management and Leadership; Project Management Workshops; Project Manager Workshop; Task Analysis

AT&T - Marketing Education - Somerset Seminars
> Advanced Service Management Seminar; Cost Analysis for Marketing Studies; Evaluation of AT&T Interexchange Culture: A Management Technique; Financial Planning Control and Decision Making; Marketing Communications Workshop; Rate Seminar; Stakeholder Analysis; Witness Preparation; Witness Support

Bell Atlantic Corporation
> Developing Subordinates; Dynamics of Management; First Level Curriculum-Managing Performance; Human Relations in Business; Initial Management Training; Initial Supervisory Training; Introduction to Management; Management Relationships Training; Managing the Flow of Work; Managing the Job; Orientation for New Managers; Orientation for New Managers/Supervisors; Orientation for New Supervisors; Transactional Analysis

Bell Communications Research Training and Education Center

    Innovative Marketing Strategies; Management Communications Workshop; Witness Preparation

The Center for Leadership Development

    Applied Management; Principles of Management

Certified Employee Benefit Specialist Program

    CEBS Course IV; Management Principles

Chrysler Institute Associate Degree Program

    The Environment of Business; Principles and Structuring of Organizations Management; Principles of Management; Problem Solving and Productivity

Continental Telecom, Inc.

    Basic Supervisory Management Program - CORE; Management Studies Workshop; Orientation to Management

Control Data

    Basic Management; Managerial Planning, Organizing, and Controlling Curriculum; Managerial Success Curriculum

Crawford Risk Management Services

    Advanced Branch Office Management; Branch Office Management

Credit Union National Association - Certified Credit Union Executive Program

    Management #200

Dale Carnegie & Associates, Inc.

    Dale Carnegie Management Seminar

Dana Corporation

    Asset Management; Fundamentals of Supervision III; Intermediate Management; Managerial Styles Seminar; Manufacturing Costs and Controls; Principles of Organizational Behavior; Problem Solving and Decision Making; Supervisory Management

Defense Mapping Agency - Inter American Geodetic Survey Cartographic School

    Cartographic Data Base Concepts; Cartographic Management; Field Surveys Supervisor; Geodetic Management; Photogrammetric Production Supervisor

Federal Aviation Administration

    Advanced Secretarial Course (14016); Basic Clerical/Secretarial Techniques (14015); Basic Obstruction Evaluation and Airport/Airspace Analysis (12051); Briefing and Presentation Techniques (14010); Budgeting and Resource Management (14024); Computer Based Support for Managerial Decision Making (01307); Conference Techniques in Every-Day Management (14000); Constructive Discipline (01203); Developing Human Relations Skills; Discrimination Complaints Investigation Course (01525); Facilitator's Training Course (01523); Federal Procurement Law (07010); Labor Relations (14028); Management by Objectives (14004); Management for Program Managers (01509); Managerial Effectiveness (01302); Managerial Initial Course (01300); Managing Change (01306); Material Management (07015); Obstruction Evaluation and Airport/Airspace Analysis (12050); Performance Improvement and Employee Appraisal (01201); Procurement for Technical Personnel (07004); Program Analysis and Review (14026); Staff Specialist; Staff Specialist (14019 Books I & II); Supervisory Guide (14021); Work Group Facilitator's Course (01528)

Ford National Development and Training Center (Formerly UAW—Ford National Development and Training Center)

    Employe Involvement Process

General Electric Company

    Computer-Aided Manufacturing; Effective Management Planning; Fabricated Parts Seminar; Management Processes; Manufacturing Methods and Processes; Non-Conventional Metal Removal; Rotating Parts Seminar

General Motors Corporation

    Basic Management for First-Line Supervisors - Engineering/Technical (0004); Basic Management for First-Line Supervisors in Manufacturing; Basic Management for First-Line Supervisors of Salaried Employees; Human Performance; Intermediate Management for General Supervisors in Manufacturing; Intermediate Management for General Supervisors of Salaried Employees (0011); Introduction to Human Performance; Project Management Using Network Planning Techniques

Graduate School of Banking at the University of Wisconsin-Madison (Central States Conference of Bankers Associates)

    Principles of Management

Illinois Fire Service Institute

    Fire Department Management I; Fire Department Management II; Fire Department Management III; Fire Department Management IV

Indian Health Service - Tribal Management Support Center

    Using the Computer as a Management Tool

Institute of Certified Professional Managers

    Administrative Skills for the Manager; Interpersonal Skills for the Manager; Personal Skills for the Manager

Institute of Financial Education

    Human Resources Management; Principles of Management; Supervisory Personnel Management I; Supervisory Personnel Management II

Institute of Management and Production

    Business Administration; Management of Data Processing Installations

Insurance Educational Association

    Management and Human Resources; Management; Management in a Changing World; Managerial Decision Making; Process of Management

International Correspondence Schools

    Industrial Psychology; Introduction to Business; Principles of Management

International Monetary Fund

    MGT 3 Management Development Course

Jamaican Institute of Management

    Introduction to Business and Principles of Management; Principles of Management

Jerrico Corporation

    Basic Management Training Program; Basic Management Training Program Course; Executive Career Development Workshop; Supervisory Development Course; Train the Trainer

Jewish Hospital of St. Louis

    Management I; Management II

Kepner-Tregoe, Inc.

Apex; Fulcrum; Genco; Government Management Seminar; Managing Involvement; Problem Solving and Decision Making; Project Management; Vertex

Knight-Ridder, Inc.

Effective Management Skills; Improving Personnel Selection; Interpersonal and Organizational Communications; Organization and Team Development; Problem Solving and Decision Making; Training, Developing, and Evaluating Your Employees

Massachusetts Bankers Association, Inc.

MSFS-Principles of Management

Maynard Management Institute

Maintenance Planner and Scheduler

McDonald's Corporation

Advanced Restaurant Management; Management Skills; Managing the McDonald's Team

National Association of REALTORS®

Management Practices and Techniques (702); Public Housing Management

National Cryptologic School

Behavioral Sciences Concepts and Applications in Management; Cryptologic Management for Interns; Cryptologic Management for Managers; Cryptologic Management for Supervisors; Introduction to Management; Introduction to Supervision; Managerial Grid Seminar; Organizational Problem Solving for Executives; Organizational Problem Solving for Managers

National Emergency Training Center

Advanced Fire Safety; Code Management: A Systems Approach; Community Fire Protection: Planning; Executive Development for Emergency Program Managers; Fire Risk Analysis; Fire Service Information Management; Fire Service Leadership/Communications; Fire Service Organizational Theory; Incident Command System; Interpersonal Dynamics in Fire Service Organizations; Management of a Fire Preventive Program; Personal Effectiveness; Strategic Analysis of Fire Department Operations

National Management Association

Supervisory and Management Skills Program

NCR Corporation

Coaching and Counseling; Executive Development Program - International Economy; Executive Development Program - Law; Influence Management; Introduction to Management; Principles of Management; Targeted Performance Management

New England Telephone Company

Concepts of Total System Development; Introduction to Project Management; Principles of Supervision: Managerial Task Cycle; Programmer Basic Training; Situational Leadership II; Stress Management: A Positive Strategy

New Jersey Department of Personnel, Division of Management Training and Employee Services

Organizing; Planning

Ohio Bell Telephone Company

Communications Skills Workshop; Innovative Problem Solving; Risk Management Workshop

Opportunities Academy of Management Training, Inc.

Advanced Management Skill Training; Corporate Training for Nonprofit Organizations; Employment and Training, Planning Proposal Writing and Fund Development; Functions of a Manager; Improving Management Skills; Management and Ownership Training; Management Control in Nonprofit Organizations; Management Skills for Economic Development; Personnel Management; Program Assessment and Evaluation; Program Planning Design and Implementation; Proposal Writing and Fund Development; Seminar on the Job Training Partnership Act; Team Building; Tool for Better Management

Pacific Bell

Computer Systems Concepts; Introduction to Management and Supervision; Introduction to Management Skills; Management Skill Development Series; Strategic Management Writing

Police Training Institute

Management Techniques

Professional Secretaries International

Part III: Economics and Management

San Diego Employers Association, Inc.

Advanced Workshop for Supervisors; Graduate Seminar for Supervisors; Workshop for Supervisors

Sandy Corporation - Marketing Educational Services

Dealership Management Development; Financial Management for Parts Managers; Financial Management for Sales Managers; Financial Management for Service Managers; Fundamentals of Management for Parts Managers; Fundamentals of Management for Sales Managers; Fundamentals of Management for Service Managers; General Motors Field Management Development Program; Operations Management for Parts Managers; Operations Management for Sales Managers; Operations Management for Service Managers; Personnel Management for Parts Managers; Personnel Management for Sales Managers; Personnel Management for Service Managers

School of Banking of the South

Business Policy

Texas Utilities Electric Corporation (Formerly Texas Utilities Generating Company - TUGCo)

Supervisor-Employee Relations; Supervisory Development

United States Army Materiel Command - AMC (Formerly DARCOM - United States Army Materiel Development and Readiness Command)

Administrative Systems; Administrative Systems and Design; Cataloging; Commodity Command Standard System; Defense Inventory Management Simulation; Defense Inventory Simulation; Department of Army Publication; Direct Support/General Support Supply Procedures; End of Course Projects; Engineering Management; Integrated Logistics Support; Introduction to CCSS; Logistic Support Exercise; Maintenance Management; Maintenance Management Program: Research Project; Management Analysis; Management of Major Items; Management of Secondary Items; Management Techniques—Parts I and II; Principles of Management; Procurement Policies and Procedures for Engineers; Product/Production Planning and Control; Project Management; Research Project; Security Assistance Management; Standard Army Intermediate Level Supply Subsystem; Stratification; Supply

Simulation; Techniques of Management; Transportation Management

United States Navy Acquisition Management Training Office
    Management Development Seminar

United States Office of Personnel Management (OPM)
    Seminar for New Managers

United States Postal Service - Department of Training and Development
    Administration of Maintenance Programs - Module I; Mail Processing for Managers MTS; Mail Processing for Supervisors MTS; Postal Inspector Basic Training

U.S. West Learning Systems
    Advanced Management Seminar; Coaching Skills for Supervisors; Developing Subordinates; First Level Curriculum - Managing the Work; If It's to Be, It's Up to Me - A Value Added Seminar; Initial Management Seminar; Initial Staff Seminar; Job Design for Computer Supported Systems; Labor Relations Seminar; Managing the Flow of Work; Managing the Job; Methods Development Standards Workshop; Situational Leadership Workshop; Supervisory Relationships Training; Testing Human Performance; Time Management

Western Regional CUNA School for Credit Union Personnel
    Western Regional CUNA School for Credit Union Personnel

Westinghouse Electric Corporation, Defense and Electronics Center
    Management Functions and Policies; Models for Management Seminar

Westinghouse Electric Corporation, Education Center Department
    Business Management Course; Management Functions and Policies; Management Techniques; Organizational Behavior; Problem Solving and Decision Making for First Level Supervisors of Salaried Personnel; Problem Solving and Decision Making for Middle Managers

Wolf Creek Nuclear Operating Corporation (Formerly Kansas Gas & Electric)
    Supervision I

Xerox Corporation
    Executive Seminar I; Finance for the Nonfinancial Manager/Financial Decision Making; Managing Tasks Through People

Young Women's Christian Association of the U.S.A.
    Advanced Management Workshop: Financial Administration and Development

Management Communication

Pacific Bell
    Effective Presentations; Leading Discussion Meetings

Management Development

Bell Atlantic Corporation
    Developing Managers

New Jersey Department of Human Services
    Executive Development Seminar; Special Management Topics

Management Information Systems

Abu Dhabi National Oil Company Career Development Center/GDC, Inc.
    Management Information Systems

AT&T - Center for Systems Education (Formerly AT&T Company Data Systems Education Group)
    COBOL Workshop

Bell Atlantic Corporation
    #5 Electronic Switching Systems Method of Operation

New Jersey Department of Personnel, Division of Management Training and Employee Services
    Managerial Tools for Today's Executive

Pacific Bell
    Advanced Lotus 1-2-3; Advanced PC Users Series: Operating Systems, Project Management (1426), Local Networks (1423); Beginning Lotus 1-2-3; Beginning WordPerfect; Intermediate Word Perfect; Advanced WordPerfect; DOS Concepts and Beginning RBASE 5000 for Hard Disk PC Systems; DOS Concepts, Wordstar, and Lotus 1-2-3 for the Hard Disk PC System; DOS for the Hard Disk; Intermediate Lotus 1-2-3; Introduction to Data Base Management Systems; Introduction to JCL; Multimate Mod. I; Multimate Mod. II; Paradox Users Series: Introduction to Paradox; Using Paradox (1425A); Applying Paradox (1425B); PC and Symphony Users Series: Hard Disk and DOS; Beginning Symphony; Advanced Symphony; PC and Wordstar Users Series: Beginning WI Hard Disk and DOS; Beginning Wordstar; Advanced Wordstar; Performance Data Collection and Analysis; Spreadsheets, Graphics, Word Processing and Database Using Symphony; UNISYS Database Concepts and UNISYS 1100 Series System Concepts (52698 and 52691); Utilities; Word Processing Concepts and the Use of Displaywrite; Word Processing Concepts and the Use of Multimate

U.S. West Learning Systems
    Performance Data Collection and Analysis

Management Practices

NCR Corporation
    Corporate Management

Management Psychology

Bell Atlantic Corporation
    New Age Thinking; The Total Manager; Whole Brain Applications

Management Report Writing

Pacific Bell
    Writing Management Reports

Management Science

Ford National Development and Training Center (Formerly UAW—Ford National Development and Training Center)
    Group Problem Solving

United States Department of Agriculture, Graduate School
    Correlation and Regression Analysis; Introductory Statistics I; Introductory Statistics II; Introductory Statistics III; Managerial Statistics; Project Analysis

Westinghouse Electric Corporation, Defense and Electronics Center

    Leadership Development Workshop; Management Techniques Seminar

Management Skills

Board of Engineers for Rivers and Harbors - U.S. Army Corps of Engineers

    Water Resources Planning Associates Program

Management Supervision

American Bankers Association

    Supervisory Training

Managerial Accounting

Bell Atlantic Corporation

    Introduction to Property and Cost Accounting

Bell Communications Research Training and Education Center

    Managerial Accounting

Control Data

    Managerial Accounting

Credit Union National Association - Certified Credit Union Executive Program

    Accounting II #410

First Fidelity Bank, N.A., N.J., Management Training Program

    Managerial Accounting

General Electric Company

    Economic Analysis of Alternatives; Introduction to Accounting Principles; Managerial Accounting and Cost Analysis; Operating Costs, Budgets, and Measurements

NCR Corporation

    Financial Management for D&PG Managers; Financial Management

Managerial Communications

AT&T - Center for Systems Education (Formerly AT&T Company Data Systems Education Group)

    Information-Mapping, Structured Writing; Preparing Technical Presentations

Manufacturing

General Motors Corporation - Technical Staffs Group and Lansing Automotive Division (Formerly Advanced Engineering Staff [AES])

    Automated Manufacturing; Design for Manufacturability

Manufacturing Engineering

Chrysler Institute Associate Degree Program

    Manufacturing Engineering Survey

Chrysler Motors Advanced Technical Training

    Industrial Robotics

General Motors Corporation

    Nondestructive Evaluation; Resistance Welding

General Motors Corporation - Technical Staffs Group and Lansing Automotive Division (Formerly Advanced Engineering Staff [AES])

    Advanced Artificial Intelligence; Advanced Computer Graphics and Computer Aided Design; Advanced Robotic Systems; Analytical Methods in Robotics; Corrosion; Heat and Mass Transfer; Information Structures; Manufacturing Processes; Polymer Engineering; Polymer Processes; Random Variables and Signals

Manufacturing Engineering Technology

General Electric Company

    Applied Engineering Mechanics; Computer-Aided Manufacturing; Conventional Metal Removal; Engineering Graphics I; Engineering Graphics II; Fabricated Parts Seminar; Fundamentals of Numerical Control; Joining; Machine Shop Theory; Manufacturing Engineering; Manufacturing Methods and Processes; Measurements; Mechanics of Materials; Metallurgy/Materials; Miscellaneous Processes; Non-Conventional Metal Removal; Numerical Control; Quality Control; Rotating Parts Seminar; Sheet Metal; Tool Design

General Motors Corporation - Technical Staffs Group and Lansing Automotive Division (Formerly Advanced Engineering Staff [AES])

    Resistance Welding Processes

Texas Utilities Electric Corporation (Formerly Texas Utilities Generating Company - TUGCo)

    Measurements

Manufacturing Management

General Electric Company

    Cases in Manufacturing Management; Manufacturing Engineering; Manufacturing Management; Materials Management; Quality Control

Manufacturing Processes

General Electric Company

    Shop Theory/Materials and Processes

International Correspondence Schools

    Manufacturing Processes

Manufacturing Technology

Chrysler Institute Associate Degree Program

    Production Processes Survey

Map Drafting

Defense Mapping Agency - Inter American Geodetic Survey Cartographic School

    Aeronautical Cartography

Map Reading and Interpretation

Defense Mapping Agency - Inter American Geodetic Survey Cartographic School

    Aeronautical Cartography; Cartographic Data Base Concepts; Cartographic Techniques for Space Imagery; Cartographic Techniques for Thematic Mapping; Cartography; Map Maintenance; Preparation of Landsat Mosaics

Marine Engineering

Seafarers Harry Lundeberg School of Seamanship
> Basic Engine; Fireman, Oiler, and Watertender

Marine Investigation/Regulations

Seafarers Harry Lundeberg School of Seamanship
> First Class Pilot

Marine Meteorology

Seafarers Harry Lundeberg School of Seamanship
> First Class Pilot; Master/Mate Freight and Towing; Third Mate - Inspected Vessels

Market Service Representation

Pacific Bell
> Marketing Service Representative Basic Training

Marketing

American Institute for Property and Liability Underwriters/Insurance Institute of America
> (AAI 83) Agency Operations and Sales Management

American Institute of Banking - Washington, D.C. Chapter
> Bank Marketing: Theory and Applications; Consumer Credit

AT&T - Corporate Education Center, Management Education Training Division
> Fundamentals of Marketing Research

AT&T - Marketing Education - Somerset Seminars
> Analysis of Marketing Data for Management Decision Making; Competitive Marketing Strategies; Competitive Pricing Strategy and Tactics; Computer Assisted Market Planning; Concepts of Service and Segment Management; Consumer Marketing; Fundamentals of Modern Marketing; Integrated Marketing and Financial Strategy; Introduction to Regulated Utilities; Market Segmentation/Buyer Behavior; Marketing Research; Marketing Statistics; Marketing Strategy; Principles of Marketing Management; Rate Seminar; Regulated Pricing and Marketing; Service Planning Seminar; Statistical Analysis in Marketing; Strategic Marketing and Process; Telephone Bypass Opportunities and Local Access

Bell Atlantic Corporation
> Account Executive Selling Skills; Advanced Systems Selling for Accounting Executives; Market Administrator - Voice, Intercity, PBX; Selling Skills

Bell Communications Research Training and Education Center
> Advanced Strategic Marketing Management; Competitive Analysis; Competitive Marketing Strategies; Competitive Pricing: Strategy and Tactics; Finance and Accounting in the Competitive Environment; Innovative Marketing Strategies; Marketing Analysis; Marketing Strategy; Product and Market Plans-Design and Implementation; Product Life Cycle Management

Credit Union National Association - Certified Credit Union Executive Program
> Marketing #700

David C.D. Rogers Associates
> Advanced Competitive Strategic Analysis; Advanced Marketing Strategies; Finance and Accounting in the Competitive Environment; Marketing Tools and Strategies

Graduate School of Banking at Colorado
> Marketing Management

Health Insurance Association of America
> Individual Health Insurance: Parts A and B

Institute of Management and Production
> Business Administration; Marketing

International Correspondence Schools
> Advertising Principles; Principles of Marketing; Retailing

Jamaican Institute of Management
> Principles of Marketing and Marketing Management

Katharine Gibbs School
> Principles of Marketing #543

Knight-Ridder, Inc.
> Marketing

Massachusetts Bankers Association, Inc.
> MSFS-Marketing of Financial Services

National Cryptologic School
> Procurement; Procurement Management for Technical Personnel

Pacific Bell
> Account Executive Selling Skills; Public Packet Switching Service; Telemarketing Concepts and Sales Process; Telemarketing Design and Implementation Workshop

Pitney-Bowes Incorporated
> Introduction to Selling

Southwestern Bell Telephone Company
> Financial Selling Skills

United States Department of Agriculture, Graduate School
> Principles of Marketing

U.S. West Learning Systems
> Consumer Relations Practicum; Mountain Bell 1021/26/35 Sequence; Performance Driven Selling; Professional Telephone Sales; 1021: Communication Analysis; 1026: System Implementation; 1035: Customer Administration Panel - Dimension 2000

Western Regional CUNA School for Credit Union Personnel
> Western Regional CUNA School for Credit Union Personnel

Westinghouse Electric Corporation, Education Center Department
> Dynamics of Applied Marketing Management; Marketing Communications Concepts and Planning Seminar; Marketing Management; Marketing Research; Marketing Strategy and Business Planning Seminar; Multinational Marketing Seminar; Principles of Marketing; Professional Marketing Course; Wholesaling

Whirlpool Corporation
> Dealer Development; Indirect Sales Development Techniques; Sales Analysis and Planning; Sales Management for Builders; Sales Management I; Sales Management II; Sales Management Seminar; Sales,

Promotions and Advertising Strategies; Sales Training Techniques

Marketing Decision Making

AT&T - Corporate Education Center, Management Education Training Division

Marketing Decision Making

Marketing Management

AT&T - Marketing Education - Somerset Seminars

Advanced Market Planning; Competitive Pricing Strategy and Tactics; Computer Assisted Market Planning; Principles of Marketing Management

Bell Communications Research Training and Education Center

Competitive Pricing: Strategy and Tactics

Jamaican Institute of Management

Principles of Marketing and Marketing Management

Knight-Ridder, Inc.

Advertising Sales Management; Circulation Management

NCR Corporation

Data Center Sales Management; District Sales Management

Xerox Corporation

Account Management Training Program; Marketing Management; Sales Accounts Management; Systems Analyst School - Support

Marketing Research

AT&T - Marketing Education - Somerset Seminars

Advanced Quantitative Methods in Marketing; Analysis of Marketing Data for Management Decision Making; Application of Multivariate Techniques; Marketing Research

International Correspondence Schools

Marketing Research

Marketing Segmentation

AT&T - Marketing Education - Somerset Seminars

Concepts of Service and Segment Management

Marketing Strategies

David C.D. Rogers Associates

Advanced Marketing Strategies

Master Planning

Digital Equipment Corporation

Master Planning

Material Damage Appraisal

Crawford Risk Management Services

Heavy Equipment Material Damage Appraisal; Material Damage Appraisal

Material Requirements Planning

Digital Equipment Corporation

Material Requirements Planning

Material Science

Carolina Power & Light Company

Reactor Operator Theory: Material Science; Reactor Operator Theory: Material Sciences

Materials

General Motors Corporation - Technical Staffs Group and Lansing Automotive Division (Formerly Advanced Engineering Staff [AES])

Modern Engineering Materials

Materials Management

Federal Aviation Administration

Advanced Procurement and Contracting (07007)

Mathematical Modeling

National Cryptologic School

Introduction to Astrodynamics

Mathematical Statistics

United States Army Materiel Command - AMC (Formerly DARCOM - United States Army Materiel Development and Readiness Command)

Mathematical Statistics

Mathematics

Abu Dhabi National Oil Company Career Development Center/GDC, Inc.

Electrical Math I and II; Industrial Mathematics I and II

Bell Atlantic Corporation

Basic Mathematics

Bell Communications Research Training and Education Center

Data Analysis and Regression—Advanced; Data Analysis and Regression—Basic

Brick Computer Science Institute

Basic Mathematics for Electronics

Carolina Power & Light Company

Reactor Operator Theory: Mathematics

Chrysler Institute Associate Degree Program

Industrial Mathematics

Defense Mapping Agency - Inter American Geodetic Survey Cartographic School

Photogrammetric Aerotriangulation; Photogrammetric Applications Program; Semianalytical and Analytical Triangulation

Electrical Workers, Local Union 102 of the International Brotherhood of Electrical Workers

Electrician Apprentice

Electrical Workers, Local Union 164 of the International Brotherhood of Electrical Workers, AFL-CIO, Bergen and Hudson Counties, New Jersey, and the Bergen-Hudson County Chapter of the National Electrical Contractors Association Joint Apprenticeship Training Program

Electrician Apprentice

Electrical Workers, Local Union 26 of the International Brotherhood of Electrical Workers and the Washington, D.C. Chapter of the National Electrical Contractors Association, Joint School

    Electrician Apprentice

General Electric Company

    A-Course; Calculus I; Calculus II; College Math I; College Math II; Probability Theory; Probability Theory for Engineering Applications; Statistical Inference; Technical Mathematics

International Correspondence Schools

    Applied Math; Technical Mathematics I; Technical Mathematics II

Joint Apprenticeship Training Committee, International Brotherhood of Electrical Workers Local Union 269, and the National Electrical Contractors Association of Southern New Jersey

    Electrician Apprentice

National Cryptologic School

    Combinatorial Mathematics; Fourier Analysis for Cryptanalysis; Introduction to Computer Science Math

National Mine Health and Safety Academy

    General Math or Introduction to Algebra

National Union of Hospital and Health Care Employees, District 1199C

    Algebra and Calculus; Calculus I

Omaha Joint Electrical Apprenticeship and Training Committee

    Electrical Apprenticeship Training

Omaha Public Power District

    Algebra; Applied Calculus; Trigonometry

Portsmouth Naval Shipyard: Apprenticeship Training

    Basic Mathematics and Algebra; Geometry, Trigonometry, and Statistics

Technical Training Project, Inc.

    Laboratory Technician Program

Texas Utilities Electric Corporation (Formerly Texas Utilities Generating Company - TUGCo)

    Basic Shop Mathematics

United States Department of Agriculture, Graduate School

    Calculus I; Calculus II; Calculus III

United States Postal Service - Department of Training and Development

    Introduction to Basic Mathematics and Electricity

U.S. West Learning Systems

    Algebra I & II

Wisconsin Public Service Corporation

    Reactor Operator Fundamentals: Mathematics

Wolf Creek Nuclear Operating Corporation (Formerly Kansas Gas & Electric)

    General Physics and Math for Maintenance Personnel

Yankee Atomic Electric Company

    Applied Technical Mathematics

Mathematics of Life Insurance

Control Data

    Mathematics of Life Insurance

Mechanical Design

International Correspondence Schools

    Mechanical Design I; Mechanical Design II

Portsmouth Naval Shipyard: Apprenticeship Training

    Machine Design; Mechanical Design

Mechanical Devices

United States Postal Service - Department of Training and Development

    Customer Service and Postal Machines; Postal Scales

Mechanical Drawing

International Correspondence Schools

    Mechanical Drawing

Mechanical Engineering

General Electric Company

    Aerodynamics; Applied Mechanical Principles; Feedback Control Theory and Design of Digital Control Systems (E-316); Gas Turbine Fundamentals; Mechanical Design and Mechanical Vibration Theory

General Motors Corporation - Technical Staffs Group and Lansing Automotive Division (Formerly Advanced Engineering Staff [AES])

    Advanced Artificial Intelligence; Advanced Computer Graphics and Computer Aided Design; Advanced Finite Element Methods; Advanced Robotic Systems; Analytical Methods in Robotics; Combustion Engine Emissions and Control; Corrosion; Design and Analysis of Experiments; Design Sensitivities and Optimization; Fracture and Fatigue Considerations in Design; Geometrical and Physical Optics; Heat and Mass Transfer; Machine Elements; Machine Tool Design; Mechanical Power Transmissions; Modern Control Theory; Polymer Engineering; Random Variables and Signals; Strength of Materials; Turbomachinery

Omaha Public Power District

    Applied Thermodynamics

United States Army Materiel Command - AMC (Formerly DARCOM - United States Army Materiel Development and Readiness Command)

    Automotive Principles; Engineering Materiels; Product/Production Engineering I; Product/Production Engineering II; Product/Production Engineering III; Statics and Dynamics; Strength of Materiels; Thermodynamics

Mechanical Engineering Fundamentals

Wolf Creek Nuclear Operating Corporation (Formerly Kansas Gas & Electric)

    Advanced Mechanical Maintenance, Part II

Mechanical Engineering Technology

Westinghouse Electric Corporation, Nuclear Services Division (Formerly Water Reactor Divisions)

    Engineered Safeguard Systems; Steam Cycle Support Systems; Steam Cycle Systems; Thermal Sciences

Mechanical Technology

Abu Dhabi National Oil Company Career Development Center/GDC, Inc.

> Mechanical Elements; Process Rotating Equipment I; Process Rotating Equipment II; Process Static Equipment; Utility Systems

United States Postal Service - Department of Training and Development

> Allison Automatic Transmissions; Automatic Transmission Overhaul; Basic Pneumatics and Hydraulics; Fundamentals of Automatic Transmissions; Mark II Facer-Canceler and Feeder Machine; Multi-Position Letter-Sorter Machine; Self-Service Postal Center Equipment Program

Mechanics

International Correspondence Schools
> Mechanics of Materials

Mechanisms

General Electric Company
> Mechanisms

Medical and Health-Related Career Programs

Syntex Laboratories, Inc.

> Advanced Medical Education: Arthritis I, II, III; Advanced Medical Education Course: Dermatology I, II, III; Advanced Medical Education: Obstetrics and Gynecology I, II, III

Medical Ethics

Certified Medical Representatives Institute, Inc.
> Ethics

Medical Instrumentation Technology

Bell Atlantic Corporation

> Fundamentals of Data Transmission; Fundamentals of Data Transmission: Testing and Service; Peripheral Installation and Maintenance

Medical Office Assisting

American Medical Record Association
> Health Record Content and Format

Medical Office Practice

Katharine Gibbs School
> Medical Office Practice

Medical Office Transcription

American Medical Record Association
> Medical Transcription

Medical Record Classification Systems

American Medical Record Association
> Nomenclature and Classification Systems

Medical Record Science

American Medical Record Association

> Health Record Content and Format; Legal Aspects of Health Information; Medical Staff; Nomenclature and Classification Systems

Medical Record Services

American Medical Record Association
> Planning for Health Information Services

Medical Record Technology

American Medical Record Association

> Directed Clinical Practice; Health Record Management in Nursing Homes; Independent Study Program in Medical Record Technology; Orientation to the Health Care Field

Medical Report Transcription

American Medical Record Association
> Medical Transcription

Medical Science

American Medical Record Association
> Basic Pathology of Disease Process

Medical Secretarial Transcription

American Medical Record Association
> Medical Transcription

Medical Technology

Insurance Educational Association
> Workers' Compensation Claims - Medical Terms and Applications

Medical Terminology

American Medical Record Association
> Medical Terminology

Certified Medical Representatives Institute, Inc.
> Medical Terminology

Medical/Surgical Nursing

Jewish Hospital of St. Louis
> Basic Critical Care Nursing Course

Medicine Mathematics

General Electric Company
> Nuclear Medicine Registration and Certification

Merchandising

U.S. West Learning Systems
> Merchandising Management; Phone Center Store Supervisor Training

Metallurgical Engineering

General Motors Corporation - Technical Staffs Group and Lansing Automotive Division (Formerly Advanced Engineering Staff [AES])
> Nondestructive Testing and Evaluation

Metallurgy

General Electric Company
> High Temperature Metallurgy; Metallurgy

Portsmouth Naval Shipyard: Apprenticeship Training
> Metallurgy

Meteorological Instrumentation

National Weather Service Training Center
> Surface Instruments Maintenance Training X-02-04

Meteorological Instrumentation Laboratory

National Weather Service Training Center
> Upper Air Observations

Meteorology

Federal Aviation Administration
> Flow Management Weather Coordinator (50112/55138)

National Weather Service Training Center
> Air Pollution Meteorology; Basic Meteorological Technician; Flash Flood Forecasting; Fundamentals of Meteorology; Introduction to Meteorology; Radar Meteorology - A Short Course; Radar Meteorology - WSR-57; Radar Meteorology - WSR-74; Radar Meteorology; Weather Service Operations

United States Department of Agriculture, Graduate School
> Dynamic Meteorology I; Dynamic Meteorology II

Methods Development

Bell Atlantic Corporation
> Methods Development Standards

Microbiology

Certified Medical Representatives Institute, Inc.
> Microbiology

Microcomputer Applications

Data Processing Training, Inc.
> Computer Literacy; Introduction to Microcomputer Applications; Introduction to Spreadsheet Applications

INACOMP Computer Centers, Inc.
> Advanced Computer Literacy; Basic Computer Literacy

O/E Learning, Inc.
> Computer Awareness Training Phase II

Microcomputer Concepts

Pacific Bell
> Microcomputer Fundamentals

Microcomputer Hardware

Brick Computer Science Institute
> Micro Computer Hardware and Software with Lab

Microcomputer Operations

Blake Business School
> Data Entry Applications

Microcomputer Software

Brick Computer Science Institute
> Micro Computer Hardware and Software with Lab

Microcomputer Technology

Federal Aviation Administration
> Fundamentals of Digital Logic (54004)

Microcomputers

Computer Processing Institute
> Microprocessor Electronics; Microprocessor Electronics Laboratory

National Weather Service Training Center
> Microprocessor: Fundamental Concepts and Applications Y-04-02

New Jersey Department of Personnel, Division of Management Training and Employee Services
> Managerial Tools for Today's Executive

O/E Learning, Inc.
> Computer Awareness Training Phase I

Microeconomics

Katharine Gibbs School
> Economics II - #809, #542, or #506.2

Microprocessor Applications

International Correspondence Schools
> Microprocessor Application

Microprocessor Based Systems

Bell Atlantic Corporation
> New Jersey Bell 1 A ESS Overview and Maintenance; New Jersey Bell 1 ESS System Overview and Maintenance

Microprocessor Electronics

Computer Processing Institute
> Microprocessor Electronics; Microprocessor Electronics Laboratory

Microprocessor Fundamentals

Northern Telecom, Inc., Digital Switching Systems - Technical Training Center
> DMS-10 System Maintenance; DMS-100/200 System Maintenance

Microprocessor Programming

GTE Service Corporation - GTE Telephone Operations Network Training
> Microprocessor Fundamentals

Microprocessor Systems

Westinghouse Electric Corporation, Nuclear Services Division (Formerly Water Reactor Divisions)
> Microprocessor Basics

Microprocessor Technology

Federal Aviation Administration
> Fundamentals of Digital Logic (54004); Fundamentals of Microprocessors (22470)

Microprocessors

International Correspondence Schools
> Introduction to Microprocessors

Microwave Engineering Design

GTE Service Corporation - GTE Telephone Operations Network Training

>Microwave Radio Engineering

Microwave Theory

Westinghouse Electric Corporation, Defense and Electronics Center

>Advanced Microwave Circuit Design

Military Science

United States Army Intelligence and Threat Analysis Center

>Introduction to Strategic Intelligence Production

United States Army Materiel Command - AMC (Formerly DARCOM - United States Army Materiel Development and Readiness Command)

>Aircraft; Army Manufacturing Technology; Army Systems Management and Engineering; Cost Estimating for Engineering; Introduction to the Army in the Field; Maintainability Case Studies; Materiel Acquisition Management; Military Standard Data Systems; Missiles and Rockets; Product Assurance Management and Engineering I; Software Technical Data Package Development; Supply, Storage, and Transportation Procedures; Systems Safety Management; Technical Data Package Development; Technical Data Package Development/Preparation; Unit and Organization Supply Procedures

Mine Atmosphere and Detection Instruments

National Mine Health and Safety Academy

>Coal Mine Dust Control

Mine Disaster Procedures

National Mine Health and Safety Academy

>Mine Disaster Procedures

Mine Electricity

National Mine Health and Safety Academy

>Electricity and Permissibility for the Non-Electrical Inspector; Mine Electricity

Mine Haulage and Transportation

National Mine Health and Safety Academy

>Mine Haulage and Transportation

Mine Health

National Mine Health and Safety Academy

>Philosophical Concepts of Mine Safety and Health

Mine Hoist Operations

National Mine Health and Safety Academy

>Hoisting

Mine Safety

National Mine Health and Safety Academy

>Coal Mine Explosion Prevention; Mine Safety and Health Legislation; Philosophical Concepts of Mine Safety and Health

Mineral Engineering

Baroid Corporation Career Development Center (Formerly NL Industries, Inc.)

>Directional Drilling Technology; Directional Drilling; Drilling Engineering; Programmed Drilling Technology

Mini Processor Maintenance

Bell Communications Research Training and Education Center

>1A Maintenance Program - Attached Processor Systems

Mining

Baroid Corporation Career Development Center (Formerly NL Industries, Inc.)

>Directional Drilling; Programmed Drilling Technology

National Mine Health and Safety Academy

>Introduction to Mining; Man, Machine and the Environment

Mining Engineering

Baroid Corporation Career Development Center (Formerly NL Industries, Inc.)

>Directional Drilling Technology; Drilling Engineering

Money and Banking

First Fidelity Bank, N.A., N.J., Management Training Program

>Money and Banking

Garden State AIB

>Money and Banking

Motion and Time Study

Chrysler Institute Associate Degree Program

>Introduction to Industrial Engineering

Motor Control Circuits

Abu Dhabi National Oil Company Career Development Center/GDC, Inc.

>Electrical Lab IV; Electrical Theory III

Motor Control Ladder Diagram Analysis

Abu Dhabi National Oil Company Career Development Center/GDC, Inc.

>Electrical Diagrams

Motor Controls

Electrical Workers, Local Union 102 of the International Brotherhood of Electrical Workers

>Electrician Apprentice

Electrical Workers, Local Union 164 of the International Brotherhood of Electrical Workers, AFL-CIO, Bergen and Hudson Counties, New Jersey, and the Bergen-Hudson County Chapter of the National Electrical Contractors Association Joint Apprenticeship Training Program

>Electrician Apprentice

Electrical Workers, Local Union 26 of the International Brotherhood of Electrical Workers and the Washington, D.C. Chapter of the National Electrical Contractors Association, Joint School

>Electrician Apprentice

Joint Apprenticeship Training Committee, International Brotherhood of Electrical Workers Local Union 269, and the National Electrical Contractors Association of Southern New Jersey

    Electrician Apprentice

Omaha Joint Electrical Apprenticeship and Training Committee

    Electrical Apprenticeship Training

Multivariate Analysis

Bell Communications Research Training and Education Center

    Multivariate Analysis

Music Appreciation

Tritone Music

    Music Appreciation: Music from the Middle Ages Through the Classical Period; Music Appreciation: Music of the 19th Century; Music Appreciation: Music of the 20th Century and Music of Canada

MVS Concepts and Facilities

Applied Learning (Formerly ASI/DELTAK)

    Introduction to MVS/XA Concepts and Facilities

National Electrical Code

Electrical Workers, Local Union 102 of the International Brotherhood of Electrical Workers

    Electrician Apprentice

Electrical Workers, Local Union 164 of the International Brotherhood of Electrical Workers, AFL-CIO, Bergen and Hudson Counties, New Jersey, and the Bergen-Hudson County Chapter of the National Electrical Contractors Association Joint Apprenticeship Training Program

    Electrician Apprentice

Electrical Workers, Local Union 26 of the International Brotherhood of Electrical Workers and the Washington, D.C. Chapter of the National Electrical Contractors Association, Joint School

    Electrician Apprentice

Joint Apprenticeship Training Committee, International Brotherhood of Electrical Workers Local Union 269, and the National Electrical Contractors Association of Southern New Jersey

    Electrician Apprentice

Mercer County Vocational-Technical Schools - Division of Adult Education

    National Electrical Code

Omaha Joint Electrical Apprenticeship and Training Committee

    Electrical Apprenticeship Training

National Security Affairs

United States Army Intelligence and Threat Analysis Center

    Introduction to Strategic Intelligence Production

Navigation

Defense Mapping Agency - Inter American Geodetic Survey Cartographic School

    Nautical Cartography

Seafarers Harry Lundeberg School of Seamanship

    Coastwise Navigation and Piloting; Towboat Operator

NEAT/3

NCR Corporation

    Elementary Systems and Software - NEAT/3; NEAT/3 Programming

Negotiation

The Negotiation Institute

    The Art of Negotiation

Network Systems Analysis

GTE Service Corporation - GTE Telephone Operations Network Training

    Traffic Concepts

Network Theory

GTE Service Corporation - GTE Telephone Operations Network Training

    Introduction to Packet Switching Networks

New Age Thinking

Bell Atlantic Corporation

    New Age Thinking

New Venture Management

AT&T - Corporate Education Center, Management Education Training Division

    Marketing Entre/Intrapreneurship

Newspaper Design

Knight-Ridder, Inc.

    Effective Newspaper Design and Graphics Editing

Newsroom Management

Knight-Ridder, Inc.

    Newsroom Management

Noise Rejection Techniques

Bell Communications Research Training and Education Center

    Principles of Noise Measurements and Mitigation

Nuclear Cardiology

General Electric Company

    Nuclear Cardiology

Nuclear Engineering

Duquesne Light Company

    Basic Nuclear Physics; Mitigating Core Damage/Accident Transient Analysis; Simulator Training

General Motors Corporation - Technical Staffs Group and Lansing Automotive Division (Formerly Advanced Engineering Staff [AES])

    Nondestructive Testing and Evaluation

Omaha Public Power District

    Reactor Theory and Core Physics

Westinghouse Electric Corporation, Nuclear Services Division (Formerly Water Reactor Divisions)
    Nuclear Reactor Theory

Wisconsin Public Service Corporation
    Senior Reactor Operator: Operational Administration; Senior Reactor Operator: Plant Systems Review and Upgrade

Nuclear Engineering Technology

Carolina Power & Light Company
    COC: Heat Transfer, Fluid Flow, and Thermodynamics; COC: Reactor Theory; Nuclear Engineering Fundamentals Laboratory; Nuclear Reactor Operations Laboratory; Reactor Operator: Emergency Operating Procedures; Reactor Operator: Simulator; Reactor Operator Systems: Nuclear Steam Supply Systems and Design Considerations; Reactor Operator Systems: Plant Systems Review and Upgrade Review; Reactor Operator Systems: Power Plant Engineering Systems; Reactor Operator Theory: Heat Transfer, Fluid Flow, and Thermodynamics; Reactor Operator Theory: Mitigating Core Damage; Reactor Operator Theory: Operation and Administration; Reactor Operator Theory: Radiation Protections and Chemistry; Reactor Operator Theory: Radiological Control; Reactor Operator Theory: Reactor Core Analysis and Mitigating Core Damage; Reactor Operator Theory: Reactor Theory; Senior Reactor Operator: Advanced Transient and Accident Analysis; Senior Reactor Operator: Emergency Operating Procedures; Senior Reactor Operator: Plant Systems Review and Upgrade; Senior Reactor Operator: Reactor Core Analysis and Mitigating Core Damage; Senior Reactor Operator: Simulator; Senior Reactor Operator Theory: Mitigating Core Damage; Senior Reactor Operator Theory: Transient and Accident Analysis

Duquesne Light Company
    Basic Nuclear Physics; Radiation, Radiation Protection, and Radiation Survey; Reactor Plant Systems; Reactor Theory; Turbine Plant Systems

Omaha Public Power District
    Radiation Protection and Detection; Radiological Protection

Wisconsin Public Service Corporation
    Mechanical/Electrical Systems; Reactor Operator Fundamentals: Core Physics; Reactor Operator Fundamentals: Reactor Theory; Reactor Operator Simulator Training; Reactor Operator Systems: Electrical Generation and Distribution Systems; Reactor Operator Systems: Emergency Diesel Generator; Reactor Operator Systems: Integrated Reactor Protection and Safety Features; Reactor Operator Systems: Plant Secondary Coolant and Auxiliary Systems; Reactor Operator Systems: Plant Ventilation Systems; Reactor Operator Systems: Reactor Core Design, Components, Instrumentation, and Functions; Reactor Operator Systems: Reactor Emergency and Auxiliary Coolant Systems; Reactor Operator Systems: Reactor Primary Coolant System; Reactor Operator Systems: Rod Control; Reactor Operator Systems: Special Auxiliary Systems; Senior Reactor Operator Simulator Training

Wolf Creek Nuclear Operating Corporation (Formerly Kansas Gas & Electric)
    Abnormal Operations Course; Auxiliary Building Segment; Diagnostics and Mitigating Core Damage; Health Physics Theory; Licensed Operator Fundamentals; Licensed Operator Systems; Non-Licensed Operator Fundamentals; Normal Operations Course; Radwaste Operator Segment; Shift Technical Advisor; Site Operations Segment; SRO Supervisory and Teamwork; SRO Technical Training; Turbine Building Segment

Nuclear Materials

Westinghouse Electric Corporation, Nuclear Services Division (Formerly Water Reactor Divisions)
    Materials Considerations of Pressurized Water Reactors

Nuclear Medicine

General Electric Company
    Advanced Concepts in Nuclear Medicine; Basics of Nuclear Medicine; Comprehensive Nuclear Medicine; Dynamics in Nuclear Medicine; Nuclear Cardiology; Nuclear Medicine Registration and Certification; Quality Control and Compliance in Nuclear Medicine

Nuclear Plant Management

Carolina Power & Light Company
    Senior Reactor Operator: Administration, Procedures, and Bases; Senior Reactor Operator: Operational Administration; Senior Reactor Operator Theory: Operation and Administration

Wisconsin Public Service Corporation
    Reactor Operator Systems: Administration and Emergency Planning

Nuclear Plant Materials

Duquesne Light Company
    Materials for Power Plants

Nuclear Power Plant Technology

Wolf Creek Nuclear Operating Corporation (Formerly Kansas Gas & Electric)
    Introduction to Pressurized Water Reactors

Nuclear Reactor Technology

Wolf Creek Nuclear Operating Corporation (Formerly Kansas Gas & Electric)
    Instrument Analysis; Introduction to Power Plant Operations; Radiation Detection and Measurement

Nuclear Reactor Theory

Wolf Creek Nuclear Operating Corporation (Formerly Kansas Gas & Electric)
    Pressurized Water Reactor Information Course

Nuclear Science

Carolina Power & Light Company
    COC: Health Physics; Radiation Control and Measurement Laboratory

Wisconsin Public Service Corporation
    Reactor Operator Fundamentals: Radiation

Wolf Creek Nuclear Operating Corporation (Formerly Kansas Gas & Electric)
    Health Physics Technician Initial Training; Health Physics WCGS Plant Systems

Nuclear Technology

Duquesne Light Company
    Thermodynamics for Licensed Operators

992 *Index*

Omaha Public Power District
> Reactor Theory and Core Physics

Westinghouse Electric Corporation, Nuclear Services Division (Formerly Water Reactor Divisions)
> Basic Nuclear Systems; Comprehensive Analysis of Technical, Thermal, and Radiological Limits (NPO 317); Control and Protection Instrumentation Systems; Digital Metal Impact Monitoring System; Digital Rod Position Indicating System; Electrical Sciences; Electrical Systems; Engineered Safeguard Systems; General Employee Training; Heat Transfer, Fluid Flow and Thermodynamics; Inadequate Core Cooling Monitoring System; Integrated Plant Operations; Introduction to Nuclear Power Plants; Introduction to Power Plant Operations; Large Pressurized Water Reactor Core Control; Mechanical Plugging of Steam Generator; Mitigating Core Damage; Nuclear Instrumentation; Nuclear Reactor Theory; Nuclear Refueling; Plant Casualty Training; Plant Operations; Plant Transient Response Casualty Training; Pressurized Water Reactor Information Course; Pressurized Water Reactor Normal Plant Operations; Pressurized Water Reactor Operations Familiarization; Process Instrumentation; PWR Plant Radiochemistry; Quality Assurance/Quality Control; Radioactivity, Radiation Detection, and Radiation Safety; Reactor Support Systems - Part I; Reactor Support Systems - Part II; Reactor Systems and Components; ROD Control System; Sold State Protection System; Station Nuclear Engineering - PWR Theory and Systems; Station Nuclear Engineering; Steam Cycle Support Systems; Steam Cycle Systems; Thermal Sciences; Transient and Accident Analysis; 7100 Process Instrumentation Scaling; 7300 Process Instrumentation Scaling

Wisconsin Public Service Corporation
> Radiation Monitoring Systems

Wolf Creek Nuclear Operating Corporation (Formerly Kansas Gas & Electric)
> Site Operations Segment; Turbine Building Segment

Nuclear Theory

Duquesne Light Company
> Radiation Technician Training Program

Numerical Control

Control Data
> ICEM Numerical Control

Numerical Control Programming and Applications

General Electric Company
> Fundamentals of Numerical Control and Numerical Control Programming

Nursing

Certified Medical Representatives Institute, Inc.
> Anatomy; Cardiovascular System; Clinical Drug Interactions; Digestive System; Endocrine System; Integumentary System; Introduction to Disease States; Musculoskeletal System; Nervous System; Reproductive Systems; Respiratory System; Sensory Organs; Urinary System

Crawford Risk Management Services
> Specialized Rehabilitation Counseling

United States Public Health Service - Indian Health Service
> Emergency Medical Technician

Young Women's Christian Association of the U.S.A.
> Encore: The YWCA Post Mastectomy Group Rehabilitation Program; Encore Training Workshop: Encouragement - Normally - Counseling - Opportunity - Energies Revived

Nursing Home Administration

American Medical Record Association
> Federal Health Programs

Nursing Management

Jewish Hospital of St. Louis
> Nursing Management

Nursing Pharmacology

Certified Medical Representatives Institute, Inc.
> Pharmacology I; Pharmacology II

Occupational Counseling

Opportunities Academy of Management Training, Inc.
> Advanced Job Development

Occupational Education

National Mine Health and Safety Academy
> Research Applications in Occupational Education

Occupational Health and Safety

National Emergency Training Center
> Fire Command Operations; Firefighter Health and Safety: Program Implementation and Management; Strategic Analysis of Fire Prevention Programs

Occupational Therapy

Certified Medical Representatives Institute, Inc.
> Anatomy

Oceanography

Defense Mapping Agency - Inter American Geodetic Survey Cartographic School
> Nautical Cartography

Office Administration

Independent School Management
> The Compleat Private-Independent School Secretary

Katharine Gibbs School
> Administrative Assistant I

Professional Secretaries International
> Part VI: Office Administration and Technology; Part VI: Office Technology

Xerox Corporation
> Marker Support Specialist/860 Product School Support; Records Processing

Office Automation

Bell Communications Research Training and Education Center
> UNIX® Software For Managers

Office Leasing Administration

National Association of REALTORS®
> Office Leasing Administration (SIR-III)

Office Management

Credit Union National Association - Certified Credit Union Executive Program
> Personnel Administration #300

Federal Aviation Administration
> Advanced Secretarial Course (14016); Basic Clerical/Secretarial Techniques (14015)

Indian Health Service - Tribal Management Support Center
> Office Management and Administration; Wang Word Processing

National Association of REALTORS®
> How to Plan for Profit and Growth (CRB-301)

Police Training Institute
> First Line Supervision or Police Supervision

Professional Secretaries International
> Part VI: Office Administration and Technology; Part VI: Office Technology

Office Practices

American International Group, Inc.
> Administrative Secretary Skills Seminar

Xerox Corporation
> Word Processing; Xerox Office Products Division 860 Product School - Sales

Office Procedures

Abu Dhabi National Oil Company Career Development Center/GDC, Inc.
> Office Procedures

Katharine Gibbs School
> Office Procedures

Professional Secretaries International
> Part V: Communication Applications; Part V: Office Administration and Communication; Part VI: Office Administration and Technology; Part VI: Office Technology

Office Procedures for Legal Secretary

Katharine Gibbs School
> Legal Secretary

Office Systems Technology

Contel Service Corporation
> ALL-IN-1 Version 2; Freelance Plus Graphics; Lotus 1-2-3 Macros; Personal Computer; WordPerfect 5.0: Module 1; WordPerfect 5.0: Module 2

Office Techniques

Xerox Corporation
> Selling Products/Services by Telephone

Office Technology

Institute for Business and Technology
> Office Technology

Online Systems Design

NCR Corporation
> Online Systems Design

Operating Room Service Seminar

American Sterilizer Company (AMSCO)
> Advanced Management Central Service Seminar

Operating Systems

Bell Communications Research Training and Education Center
> UNIX® Shell Programming; UNIX® System Administration

The Chubb Institute
> Operating Systems

NCR Corporation
> IMOS V Operating System; IRX Operating System; ITX Operating System Advanced; ITX Operating System; NCR Century to VRX Migration; VRX Problem-Solving Techniques

Operations

Bell Atlantic Corporation
> Methods Developers' Workshop

Operations Management

Bell Communications Research Training and Education Center
> Quality Assurance for Product Selection, Acquisition and Maintenance (QAPSAM)

General Electric Company
> Principles of Production and Inventory Management; Value Analysis; Value Engineering

NCR Corporation
> Field Engineering Management; Introduction to Quality Circles; Project Planning and Management; Project Planning and Management for Software Development

Operations Research

AT&T - Marketing Education - Somerset Seminars
> Demand Analysis Techniques; Demand Analysis Techniques Seminar

Bell Communications Research Training and Education Center
> Data Analysis and Regression—Advanced; Data Analysis and Regression—Basic

National Cryptologic School
> Combinatorial Mathematics; Introduction to Astrodynamics

United States Army Materiel Command - AMC (Formerly DARCOM - United States Army Materiel Development and Readiness Command)
> Problem Solving Techniques; Techniques in Operations Research

Optical Data Processing

United States Postal Service - Department of Training and Development

    Digital Electronics; Logic Circuits

Optics

General Motors Corporation - Technical Staffs Group and Lansing Automotive Division (Formerly Advanced Engineering Staff [AES])

    Integrated Optics

Optics and Logic Circuits

Xerox Corporation

    3450 Copier H15

Opto-Electronics

Bell Communications Research Training and Education Center

    Fiber Optic Systems - Maintenance; Fiber Optic Systems - Technical Overview

Oral Communication

American International Group, Inc.

    Effective Oral Presentation

Dale Carnegie & Associates, Inc.

    Dale Carnegie Course

General Electric Company

    Effective Presentation and Career Management Skills; Effective Presentation

McDonald's Corporation

    Presentation Skills I & II

Portsmouth Naval Shipyard: Apprenticeship Training

    Oral Communications

Oral Presentations

Southwestern Bell Telephone Company

    Communispond Effective Presentation Skills

Organization

Young Women's Christian Association of the U.S.A.

    Advanced Management Workshop: Financial Administration and Development

Organizational Behavior

AT&T - Marketing Education - Somerset Seminars

    Evaluation of AT&T Interexchange Culture: A Management Technique; Marketing Communications Workshop; Stakeholder Analysis; Witness Preparation; Witness Support

Bell Communications Research Training and Education Center

    Facilitating Groups and Meetings; Innovation - Achieving the Future; Management Communications Workshop; Managing Change in a Changing Environment; Managing Costly Group Problems; Managing the Boss; Witness Preparation

The Center for Leadership Development

    Organizational Behavior

Certified Employee Benefit Specialist Program

    CEBS Course IV; Management Principles

General Electric Company

    Supervisory Development and Organization Renewal Workshop

General Motors Corporation

    Intermediate Management for General Supervisors in Manufacturing; Intermediate Management for General Supervisors of Salaried Employees (0011)

Knight-Ridder, Inc.

    Organization and Team Development

National Emergency Training Center

    Strategic Analysis of Executive Leadership

New Jersey Department of Human Services

    Executive Development Seminar

New Jersey Department of Personnel, Division of Management Training and Employee Services

    Leading and Directing; Planning

Ohio Bell Telephone Company

    Leadership Strategies Workshop

Pacific Bell

    Influence Management; Interpersonal Skills

Professional Secretaries International

    Part I: Behavioral Science in Business

Organizational Development

Bell Communications Research Training and Education Center

    Facilitating Groups and Meetings; Managing Change in a Changing Environment; Managing Costly Group Problems; Managing the Boss

New Jersey Department of Human Services

    Executive Development Seminar

New Jersey Department of Personnel, Division of Management Training and Employee Services

    Organizational and Human Resources Development

Opportunities Academy of Management Training, Inc.

    Employment and Training, Planning Proposal Writing and Fund Development; Proposal Writing and Fund Development

United States Office of Personnel Management (OPM)

    Federal Personnel Management Issues

Organizational Management

General Electric Company

    Supervisory Development and Organization Renewal Workshop

United States Office of Personnel Management (OPM)

    Executive Development Seminar

Organizational Psychology

Bell Communications Research Training and Education Center

    Facilitating Groups and Meetings; Innovation - Achieving the Future; Managing Change in a Changing

Environment; Managing Costly Group Problems; Managing the Boss

Katharine Gibbs School
Industrial and Organizational Psychology

Oscilloscopes

Bell Atlantic Corporation
Oscilloscopes

OS/JCL

Brick Computer Science Institute
OS/JCL with VSAM Concepts

Pagination Systems

Dow Jones & Company, Inc.
Pagination

Paralegal Studies

American Institute for Paralegal Studies, Inc.
Introduction to Criminal Justice

National Academy for Paralegal Studies, Inc.
Introduction to Criminal Justice

PJA School
Civil Litigation

United States Department of Agriculture, Graduate School
Administrative Law and Procedure; Business Law I; Business Law II; Constitutional Law; Criminal Law; Environmental Law; Family Law; FOIA and the Privacy Act; Introduction to Law for Paralegals; Legal Research I: Legal Literature; Legal Research II; Legal Writing I; Legal Writing II; Litigation; Real Estate Transaction; Tort Law; Wills and Probate; Wills, Trusts and Estate Administration

United States Food and Drug Administration
Basic Food and Drug Law Course

Paralegal Training

United States Postal Service - Department of Training and Development
Hearing Officers' Training #21275-00

PASCAL

NCR Corporation
PASCAL Programming

Pastoral Counseling

Seminary Extension, Southern Baptist Seminaries
The Pastor as Counselor

Pastoral Ministries

Seminary Extension, Southern Baptist Seminaries
The Pastor as a Person; Pastoral Ministries

Pathophysiology

American Medical Record Association
Basic Pathology of Disease Process

Disabled American Veterans
Disabled American Veterans Continuing Training Program for National Service Officers

Patrol Techniques

Police Training Institute
Basic Law Enforcement III; Basic Law Enforcement IV

Pension Plans

Certified Employee Benefit Specialist Program
CEBS Course II; Pension Plans

Performance Analysis

Bell Atlantic Corporation
Performance Analysis Workshop #204

Performance Appraisal

Bell Atlantic Corporation
Performance Appraisal

Pacific Bell
Improving Performance; Managing Professional Growth

Performance Management

Bell Atlantic Corporation
Performance Appraisal

Performance Technology

U.S. West Learning Systems
Methods Development Standards

Peripheral Device Theory and Operation

Unisys Corporation
Microcomputer System Maintenance

Personal Computers

Bell Communications Research Training and Education Center
Data Communications - Personal Computer Fundamentals

NCR Corporation
Personal Computers: Concepts; Personal Computers: DOS

Personal Finance

American Institute of Banking - Washington, D.C. Chapter
Introduction to Financial Planning

Credit Union National Association - Certified Credit Union Executive Program
Financial Counseling #800

Institute of Financial Education
Personal Money Management

International Correspondence Schools
Personal Financial Management

Personal Growth and Development

Pacific Bell
New Age Thinking for Achieving Your Potential

Personal Law

Institute for Business and Technology
> Business Law

Personal Security

United States Department of Justice, U.S. Marshals Service, Federal Law Enforcement Training Center
> Deputy U.S. Marshals Basic Training School

Personal Selling

Southwestern Bell Telephone Company
> Fundamentals of Selling

Personnel

Bell Atlantic Corporation
> Job Study Workshop; Management Appraisal Plan Training; Supervisory Relationships - Trainer Workshop; Supervisory Relationships Training

Chrysler Institute Associate Degree Program
> Industrial Supervisory Practices

Jerrico Corporation
> Train the Trainer

U.S. West Learning Systems
> Job Design; Job Study Workshop

Personnel Administration

Certified Employee Benefit Specialist Program
> CEBS Course VIII; CEBS X; Contemporary Benefit Issues and Administration; Personnel and Labor Relations

Defense Mapping Agency - Inter American Geodetic Survey Cartographic School
> Field Surveys Supervisor; Geodetic Management; Photogrammetric Production Supervisor

General Electric Company
> Employee Relations in Manufacturing; Individual and Group Relations on the Job; Management Processes; Manufacturing Organization and Supervision; Personnel Administration

Indian Health Service - Tribal Management Support Center
> Health Service Personnel Administration

Jewish Hospital of St. Louis
> Management I; Management II

Knight-Ridder, Inc.
> Career Planning and Counseling; Improving Personnel Selection; Knight-Ridder Supervisory Training

National Association of REALTORS®
> How to Manage the Finances: Risks of a Real Estate Brokerage (CRB-302); How to Recruit, Train, and Retain Real Estate Sales Associates and Increase Productivity (CRB-304)

National Weather Service Training Center
> Station Management and Supervision

Police Training Institute
> First Line Supervision or Police Supervision

United States Navy Acquisition Management Training Office
> Defense Contract Negotiation Workshop

United States Office of Personnel Management (OPM)
> Seminar for New Managers

United States Postal Service - Department of Training and Development
> Associate Office Management MTS; Associate Office Postmaster MTS; Building Equipment Maintenance Supervisor MTS; Building Services Maintenance Supervisor MTS; Delivery Services Supervisor MTS; Employee Relations Management MTS; Labor Relations Management MTS; Mail Processing Equipment Maintenance Supervisor MTS; PEDC Managers MTS; Window Services Management MTS

Personnel Development

General Electric Company
> Career Planning Workshop

Ohio Bell Telephone Company
> New Age Thinking for Achieving Your Potential

Personnel Management

Bell Atlantic Corporation
> Management/Union Relations Workshop

Chrysler Institute Associate Degree Program
> Personnel Practices Survey

Del Taco Corporation
> Manager Training Program, Phases I, II, and III

Del Taco, Inc.
> Manager Training Program, Phases I, II, and III

Illinois Fire Service Institute
> Fire Department Management IV

Institute of Financial Education
> Human Resources Management

Institute of Management and Production
> Human Resource Development; Introduction to Personnel management; Personnel Management; Personnel Management: Skills and Techniques

International Correspondence Schools
> Personnel Management

Jamaican Institute of Management
> Personnel Management and Industrial Relations

McDonald's Corporation
> Advanced Operations; Management Skills Development; Supervisory Management Skills

National Management Association
> Supervisory and Management Skills Program

NCR Corporation
> Behavior Modeling; Development and Production Management

Omaha Public Power District
> Introduction to Management Skills; Introduction to Personnel Management

United States Navy Acquisition Management Training Office
> Management of Managers

United States Office of Personnel Management (OPM)
> Management Development Seminar

United States Postal Service - Department of Training and Development
> Equal Employment Opportunity Administration

Western Regional CUNA School for Credit Union Personnel
> Western Regional CUNA School for Credit Union Personnel

Xerox Corporation
> Managing the Personnel Function

Personnel Relations

Bell Atlantic Corporation
> Negotiation Skills Workshop

Personnel Security

Department of Defense, Defense Security Institute
> Personnel Security Investigations Course

Personnel Security Adjudications

Department of Defense, Defense Security Institute
> DoD Basic Personnel Security Adjudications Correspondence Course; DoD Basic Personnel Security Adjudications Course; Personnel Security Adjudications

Personnel Security Investigations

Department of Defense, Defense Security Institute
> Personnel Security Investigations Course

Personnel Supervision

Defense Mapping Agency - Inter American Geodetic Survey Cartographic School
> Cartographic Management

Ponderosa Inc.
> Steakhouse Training and Education Program

Persuasive Communications

Public Service Electric & Gas
> Systematic Analysis of Ideas

Petrochemical Process Systems

Abu Dhabi National Oil Company Career Development Center/GDC, Inc.
> Process Systems I and II

Petroleum Engineering

Baroid Corporation Career Development Center (Formerly NL Industries, Inc.)
> Directional Drilling Technology; Directional Drilling; Drilling Engineering; Drilling Technology; Programmed Drilling Technology

Petroleum Technology

Abu Dhabi National Oil Company Career Development Center/GDC, Inc.
> Fuels and Lubricants; Introduction to Technology I and II; Refrigeration, Cryogenics and Corrosion

Baroid Corporation Career Development Center (Formerly NL Industries, Inc.)
> Basic Well Control; Drilling Fluids Technology; Drilling Technology; Oilwell Pipe Recovery; Systems Approach to Production Logging

Pharmaceutical History

Certified Medical Representatives Institute, Inc.
> History of the Pharmaceutical Industry; Pharmaceutical Industry

Pharmaceutical Marketing

Certified Medical Representatives Institute, Inc.
> Pharmaceutical Marketing

Pharmacology

Certified Medical Representatives Institute, Inc.
> Cardiovascular System; Digestive System; Endocrine System; Integumentary System; Introduction to Pharmacology; Musculoskeletal System; Nervous System; Pharmacology I; Pharmacology II; Reproductive Systems; Respiratory System; Sensory Organs; Urinary System

Philosophy

The Catholic Home Study Institute
> The Philosophy of Communism

Seminary Extension, Southern Baptist Seminaries
> Introduction to Christian Ethics

Photogrammetry

Defense Mapping Agency - Inter American Geodetic Survey Cartographic School
> Advanced Photogrammetry; Automated Cartography; Basic Photographic Sciences; Control Surveys; Digital Methods of Terrain Modeling; Introduction to Computer Programming Using FORTRAN, Independent Study; Introduction to Digital Image Analysis; Introduction to Minicomputers, Independent Study; Map Maintenance; Orthophotography; Photogrammetric Aerotriangulation; Photogrammetric Applications Program; Photogrammetry; Satellite Doppler Positioning; Semianalytical and Analytical Triangulation

Photographic Laboratory Color Processing

Defense Mapping Agency - Inter American Geodetic Survey Cartographic School
> Cartographic Techniques for Space Imagery; Preparation of Landsat Mosaics

Photographic Science

Defense Mapping Agency - Inter American Geodetic Survey Cartographic School
> Basic Photographic Sciences; Cartographic Techniques for Thematic Mapping

Photography

Defense Mapping Agency - Inter American Geodetic Survey Cartographic School
> Cartographic Techniques for Space Imagery; Preparation of Landsat Mosaics

998 *Index*

Unisys Corporation
    Microfilm Module Installation and Maintenance

Physical Distribution Management

AT&T - Corporate Education Center, Management Education Training Division
    Strategic Physical Distribution Management

Physical Education

Bergen County Police Academy
    Basic Police Training Course

International PADI, Inc.
    Advanced Open Water Diver; Divemaster; Instructor Development; Open Water Diver; Professional Scuba Equipment Repair; Rescue Diver; Retail Store Sales and Operations; Underwater Photography Instructor

United States Department of Justice, Immigration and Naturalization Service, Federal Law Enforcement Training Center
    Border Patrol Academy; Immigration Officer Academy

United States Department of Justice, U.S. Marshals Service, Federal Law Enforcement Training Center
    Deputy U.S. Marshals Basic Training School

United States Department of the Treasury, Federal Law Enforcement Training Center
    Criminal Investigator Training; Eight-Week Police Training Program

United States Drug Enforcement Administration
    Drug Enforcement Officers Academy

United States Postal Service - Department of Training and Development
    Postal Inspector Basic Training

Physical Science

International Correspondence Schools
    Physical Science

National Emergency Training Center
    Chemistry of Hazardous Materials; Hazardous Materials Tactical Considerations; Hazardous Substance Specialist; Instructors Program Level I—Chemistry of Hazardous Materials; Planning for a Hazardous Materials Incident

United States Department of Agriculture, Graduate School
    General Physics I; General Physics II

Wolf Creek Nuclear Operating Corporation (Formerly Kansas Gas & Electric)
    Instrument and Control Maintenance Fundamentals

Physical Therapy

Certified Medical Representatives Institute, Inc.
    Anatomy

Physicians' Assistants

American Medical Record Association
    Federal Health Programs

Physics

Abu Dhabi National Oil Company Career Development Center/GDC, Inc.
    Applied Physics I and II

Control Data
    Physics I

General Electric Company
    Basics of Ultrasound; Industrial Physics; Radioisotope Handlers

International Correspondence Schools
    Physics

National Cryptologic School
    Fourier Analysis for Cryptanalysis

Omaha Public Power District
    Basic Concepts of Mechanics, Heat, Electricity and Atomic Physics (ACEOPS 88-14)

Portsmouth Naval Shipyard: Apprenticeship Training
    Physics

Southwestern Bell Telephone Company
    Fundamentals of Electricity in Telephony; Noise Reduction

United States Department of Agriculture, Graduate School
    General Physics I; General Physics II

United States Postal Service - Department of Training and Development
    Optical Character Reader I

Wolf Creek Nuclear Operating Corporation (Formerly Kansas Gas & Electric)
    General Physics and Math for Maintenance Personnel

Physiology

Certified Medical Representatives Institute, Inc.
    Cardiovascular System; Digestive System; Endocrine System; Integumentary System; Musculoskeletal System; Nervous System; Reproductive Systems; Respiratory System; Sensory Organs; Urinary System

Piloting and Coastwise Navigation

Seafarers Harry Lundeberg School of Seamanship
    First Class Pilot; Master/Mate Freight and Towing

Piping Diagrams

Abu Dhabi National Oil Company Career Development Center/GDC, Inc.
    Piping and Instrument Diagrams

Planning

National Emergency Training Center
    Civil Defense Systems, Programs and Policies

Planning and Operations

Bell Atlantic Corporation
    Outside Plant Engineering Education Program,, (NE09CIC)

Plant Material and Practices

Abu Dhabi National Oil Company Career Development Center/GDC, Inc.
> Plant Materials and Equipment

Plant Utility Systems

Abu Dhabi National Oil Company Career Development Center/GDC, Inc.
> Utility Systems

Pleadings and Arbitration

American Institute for Paralegal Studies, Inc.
> Litigation, Pleadings and Arbitration

PL/I Programming

Applied Learning (Formerly ASI/DELTAK)
> Introduction to PL/I Programming

Pneumatic Instrumentation

Abu Dhabi National Oil Company Career Development Center/GDC, Inc.
> Pneumatic Instrumentation

Pneumatic Logic Controls

Chrysler Motors Advanced Technical Training
> Air Logic

Pneumatics

Abu Dhabi National Oil Company Career Development Center/GDC, Inc.
> Hydraulics and Pneumatics I and II

Chrysler Motors Advanced Technical Training
> Industrial Pneumatic Technology

Pacific Bell
> Air Dryer Maintenance; Cable Pressurization Engineering

U.S. West Learning Systems
> Air Dryer Maintenance Course; Cable Repair-Air Leak Locating

Police Administration

Police Training Institute
> Management Techniques

Police Function and Human Behavior

Police Training Institute
> Basic Law Enforcement IV

Police Science

Police Training Institute
> Crime Scene Technician; First Line Supervision or Police Supervision; Police Community Relations

Policy Development

National Emergency Training Center
> Code Management: A Systems Approach

Political Organization

United States Office of Personnel Management (OPM)
> Executive Development Seminar

Political Science

The Catholic Home Study Institute
> The Philosophy of Communism

Institute for Citizen Involvement in Education
> Public Policy and Public Schools

United States Army Intelligence and Threat Analysis Center
> Introduction to Strategic Intelligence Production

United States Department of Agriculture, Graduate School
> Constitutional Law

United States Office of Personnel Management (OPM)
> Federal Personnel Management Issues; Government Role in Technology Transfer; Managing Money and Material Resources; National Security Policy

Portuguese

National Cryptologic School
> Basic Portuguese; Basic Portuguese Transcription; Portuguese for Spanish Linguistics; Rapid Survey of Portuguese

Power Distribution Technology

United States Postal Service - Department of Training and Development
> Industrial Electrical Services

Power Plant Chemistry

Wisconsin Public Service Corporation
> Reactor Operation Fundamentals Chemistry

Power Plant Technology

Seafarers Harry Lundeberg School of Seamanship
> Original Third Assistant Engineer, Steam and/or Motor - Inspected; Qualified Members of the Engine Department, Twelve-Week Version

Yankee Atomic Electric Company
> Power Plant Technology

Power Technology

United States Postal Service - Department of Training and Development
> Automotive Diesel Mechanics; Caterpillar Diesel; Cummins Diesel I; Cummins Diesel III; Postal Diesel

Power Tools

Abu Dhabi National Oil Company Career Development Center/GDC, Inc.
> Hand and Power Tools I

Practical Arts

Federal Aviation Administration
> Air Conditioning (44106); Final Radar Control Position - Phase XIII (55133); Final Radar-Associated/Non-Radar Control Position Qualification and Certification (55130); Initial Radar Control Position Qualification and Certification - Phase

XII (55132); Predevelopmental, Phase III Field Environmental Training (55313); Predevelopmental, Phase IV - Option Determination (55314)

Precalculus

Control Data
> Precalculus

Preschool Environment

Educational Information and Resource Center (EIRC)
> Relationship Within the Preschool Setting

Pressurized Water Reactor Plant Systems

Yankee Atomic Electric Company
> Pressurized Water Reactor Plant Systems; Pressurized Water Reactor Plant Systems Laboratory

Pressurized Water Reactor Simulator

Yankee Atomic Electric Company
> Pressurized Water Reactor Simulator Laboratory I

Pricing

AT&T - Corporate Education Center, Management Education Training Division
> Strategic Pricing for Profitability

Pricing Strategies

AT&T - Marketing Education - Somerset Seminars
> Economics for Pricing Network Services

Problem Analysis

Control Data
> Problem Analysis and Decision Making

Problem Solving

Bell Atlantic Corporation
> Defining the Job; Managing the Problem-Solving Process; Managing to Write

Process Control

Abu Dhabi National Oil Company Career Development Center/GDC, Inc.
> Process Simulators I and II

Process Control Instrumentation

Duquesne Light Company
> Instrumentation and Control Fundamentals

Seafarers Harry Lundeberg School of Seamanship
> Process Control Instrumentation

Process Measurements

Omaha Public Power District
> Process Measurement Fundamentals

Process Static Equipment

Abu Dhabi National Oil Company Career Development Center/GDC, Inc.
> Process Static Equipment II

Procurement and Contracting

Bell Atlantic Corporation
> Procurement Management Fundamentals

United States Navy Acquisition Management Training Office
> Advanced Contract Administration; Automation of Procurement and Accounting Data Entry; Basic Contract Administration

Production Activity Control

Digital Equipment Corporation
> Production Activity Control

Production Control

Chrysler Institute Associate Degree Program
> Procurement and Production Control

Production Engineering

United States Army Materiel Command - AMC (Formerly DARCOM - United States Army Materiel Development and Readiness Command)
> Problems in Product/Production Engineering I & II

Production Facilities Planning

International Correspondence Schools
> Plant Facilities

Production Management

Bell Communications Research Training and Education Center
> Quality Assurance for Product Selection, Acquisition and Maintenance (QAPSAM)

International Correspondence Schools
> Production Management

NCR Corporation
> Introduction to Quality Circles; Project Planning and Management; Project Planning and Management for Software Development

U.S. West Learning Systems
> Methods Development Standards Workshop

Production Operation Management

Bell Communications Research Training and Education Center
> Inventory Management

Production Planning and Control

International Correspondence Schools
> Planning and Control

Professional Appraisal Standards

National Association of REALTORS®
> Professional Appraisal Standards (EX 2-3/8-3)

Professional Orientation

United States Department of Labor, DOL Academy
> Professional Development and Orientation

Index 1001

Program Management

Central Intelligence Agency
  Issues in Program Management in Government Procurement

Programmed Instruction

Federal Aviation Administration
  Designing Programmed Instruction (10525)

Programming

Bell Atlantic Corporation
  Programmer Basic Training

Control Data
  Structured Programming with FORTRAN 77

General Electric Company
  Computer Science

NCR Corporation
  IMOS TRAN-PRO Programming; NCR 7750 DDPS and RPS Systems and Programming

New England Telephone Company
  Programmer Basic Training

Programming Language Systems and Software

Bell Communications Research Training and Education Center
  3B20 Duplex Computer-System Software

Programming Languages

Bell Atlantic Corporation
  Programming Languages, Architecture and Operating Systems, and Communications

Project Management

Kepner-Tregoe, Inc.
  Project Management

Pacific Bell
  Project Management: Sales Version or Staff Version

United States Department of Agriculture, Graduate School
  Project Management

Promotion

AT&T - Corporate Education Center, Management Education Training Division
  Concepts of Promotional Strategy

Property and Liability Contract Analysis

Professional Insurance Agents
  PIA Insurance School at Drake University

Property Brokering

National Association of REALTORS®
  Brokering Transitional Properties (FLI-230)

Property Insurance

American Educational Institute, Inc.
  Property

Property Management

National Association of REALTORS®
  Property Management I; Property Management II; Property Management III; Property Management IV; Property Management (RM-304); Property Management V; Real Estate Investment Management

Psychiatric Rehabilitation Training Development

New Jersey Department of Human Services
  Psychiatric Rehabilitation Practitioner Training

Psychology

AT&T - Center for Systems Education (Formerly AT&T Company Data Systems Education Group)
  Interpersonal Management Skills for Information Systems

The Catholic Home Study Institute
  Catechesis of the High School Student

Certified Medical Representatives Institute, Inc.
  Behavioral Pathology and Treatment; Psychology

Chrysler Institute Associate Degree Program
  Applied Behavioral Science; Introduction to Psychology

Federal Aviation Administration
  Advanced Instructor Training (10511)

Institute of Financial Education
  Human Relations in Business

International Correspondence Schools
  General Psychology; Industrial Psychology

Jewish Hospital of St. Louis
  Assertiveness Training; Motivational Dynamics I; Motivational Dynamics II; Stress Management

Katharine Gibbs School
  Introduction to Psychology #805

New England Telephone Company
  Investment in Excellence; Stress Management: A Positive Strategy

Opportunities Academy of Management Training, Inc.
  Advanced Affective Educational Techniques; Affective Education; Motivating the Disadvantaged

Police Training Institute
  Child Sex Exploitation

Western Regional CUNA School for Credit Union Personnel
  Western Regional CUNA School for Credit Union Personnel

Public Administration

AT&T - Marketing Education - Somerset Seminars
  Concepts of Capital Costs; Demand Analysis Techniques; Evaluation of AT&T Interexchange Culture: A Management Technique; Introduction to Regulated Utilities; Local Network Services Seminar; Marketing Communications Workshop; Measured Service Issues Seminar; Network Services Issues Seminar; Public Switched Network Seminar; Rate Seminar; Restructure of Private Line Issues; Special Network Services Seminar; Stakeholder Analysis;

Terminal Products Issues Seminar

Bell Communications Research Training and Education Center

Management Communications Workshop

Continental Telecom, Inc.

Basic Supervisory Management Program - CORE; Orientation to Management

Defense Mapping Agency - Inter American Geodetic Survey Cartographic School

Cartographic Management; Field Surveys Supervisor; Geodetic Management; Photogrammetric Production Supervisor

Federal Aviation Administration

Constructive Discipline (01203); Equal Employment Opportunity Counselor Effectiveness Training (01505); Management for Program Managers (01509); Managerial Effectiveness (01302); Managerial Initial Course (01300); Performance Improvement and Employee Appraisal (01201); Relocation Assistance (06027); Resource Management (01303); Staff Specialist

Indian Health Service - Tribal Management Support Center

Health Service Personnel Administration; Principles of Management and Leadership; Using the Computer as a Management Tool

Kepner-Tregoe, Inc.

Apex; Government Management Seminar

National Emergency Training Center

Basic Skills For Emergency Program Managers; Civil Defense Systems, Programs and Policies; Community Fire Protection: Planning; Emergency Medical Service and Administration: An Overview; Emergency Planning Course; Exercise Design; Exercise Design—Train-the-Trainer; Fallout Shelter Analysis; Fire Executive Development III; Fire Service Financial Management; Fire Service Leadership/Communications; Fire Service Organizational Theory; Hazardous Materials Contingency Planning; Interpersonal Dynamics in Fire Service Organizations; Introduction to Emergency Management; Management of a Fire Preventive Program; Microcomputer Applications in Emergency Management; Module IV: Creative Financing; Radiological Emergency Preparedness Planning; Shelter Systems Officer; Shelter Systems Officer Train-the Trainer; State Radiological Officer Management; Strategic Analysis of Fire Department Operations

National Weather Service Training Center

Station Management and Supervision

New England Telephone Company

Asbestos Recognition and Abatement

New Jersey Department of Personnel, Division of Management Training and Employee Services

Management Functions in State Government

Opportunities Academy of Management Training, Inc.

Comprehensive Employment and Training Act; Seminar on the Job Training Partnership Act

United States Department of Agriculture, Graduate School

Budget Execution and Funds Control; Capital Budgeting; Project Analysis; Project Management

United States Office of Personnel Management (OPM)

Executive Development Seminar; Federal Personnel Management Issues; Federal Program Management; Government Role in Technology Transfer; Management Development Seminar; Managing Money and Material Resources; Seminar for New Managers

United States Postal Service - Department of Training and Development

Postal Inspector Basic Training

Young Women's Christian Association of the U.S.A.

Management Training for Staff with Executive Potential; Management Workshop for Executive Staff; Management Workshop for Student Leadership

Public Affairs

International Correspondence Schools

Public Relations

United States Office of Personnel Management (OPM)

Executive Development Seminar

Public and Urban Policy

Opportunities Academy of Management Training, Inc.

Manpower Services to Disadvantaged Youth; Program Assessment and Evaluation

Public Communication

International Correspondence Schools

Public Relations

Public Finances

New Jersey Department of Personnel, Division of Management Training and Employee Services

Managerial Tools for Today's Executive

Public Health

United States Public Health Service - Indian Health Service

Basic Maternal and Child Health; Community Health Representative; Environmental Health Concepts and Practices; Health Services Research; Maternal and Child Nutrition

Public Health Administration

American Medical Record Association

Federal Health Programs

Public Information

International Correspondence Schools

Public Relations

National Emergency Training Center

Public Fire Education Specialist

Public Management

Illinois Fire Service Institute

Fire Department Management I; Fire Department Management II; Fire Department Management III

National Emergency Training Center

Fire Command Operations; Strategic Analysis of Executive Leadership

National Weather Service Training Center
   Station Management and Supervision

United States Office of Personnel Management (OPM)
   Managerial Competencies and Effectiveness Characteristics for Executives

Public Policy

Institute for Citizen Involvement in Education
   Public Policy and Public Schools

United States Army Intelligence and Threat Analysis Center
   Introduction to Strategic Intelligence Production

United States Office of Personnel Management (OPM)
   Economics and Public Policy

Public Policy Administration

United States Office of Personnel Management (OPM)
   Administration of Public Policy

Public Relations

Institute of Management and Production
   Principles of Public Relations

International Correspondence Schools
   Public Relations

Public Safety

United States Postal Service - Department of Training and Development
   Accident Investigation; Vehicle Accident Investigation

Public Speaking

AT&T - Center for Systems Education (Formerly AT&T Company Data Systems Education Group)
   Preparing Technical Presentations

Dale Carnegie & Associates, Inc.
   Dale Carnegie Course

McDonald's Corporation
   Presentation Skills I & II

National Mine Health and Safety Academy
   Public Speaking and Briefing Techniques

Xerox Corporation
   OS Basic Sales School

Public Works

National Emergency Training Center
   Civil Defense Systems, Programs and Policies

Pumps

Sun Refining and Marketing Company
   Refinery Operator Program

Purchasing

Abu Dhabi National Oil Company Career Development Center/GDC, Inc.
   Principles of Purchasing

Digital Equipment Corporation
   Purchasing

Purchasing Management

NCR Corporation
   Purchasing Education - Phase I; Purchasing Education - Phase II

Quality and Reliability Engineering

United States Army Materiel Command - AMC (Formerly DARCOM - United States Army Materiel Development and Readiness Command)
   Problems in Quality and Reliability Engineering II

Quality Assurance

General Motors Corporation - Technical Staffs Group and Lansing Automotive Division (Formerly Advanced Engineering Staff [AES])
   Manufacturing Quality Assurance

Quality Control

Chrysler Institute Associate Degree Program
   Quality Control Survey

United States Army Materiel Command - AMC (Formerly DARCOM - United States Army Materiel Development and Readiness Command)
   Production Quality Control; Statistical Quality Control

Quantitative Methods

AT&T - Marketing Education - Somerset Seminars
   Advanced Quantitative Methods in Marketing; Analysis of Marketing Data for Management Decision Making; Application of Multivariate Techniques; Network Cost System and Workshop

National Association of REALTORS®
   Quantitative Methods (EX 11)

Quantitative Research Methods

National Cryptologic School
   APL Programming

Quantity Food Production

Seafarers Harry Lundeberg School of Seamanship
   Chief Cook; Chief Steward; Cook and Baker

Radar Meteorology

National Weather Service Training Center
   Meteorology; Radar Users' Course

Radar Systems

Federal Aviation Administration
   Radar Data Processing for Systems Performance Specialist (43483)

National Weather Service Training Center
   WSR - 57/DVIP Radar System R-08-06; WSR 74C Radar System R-12-04

Radar Technology

Federal Aviation Administration
   Airport Surveillance Radar System ASR-8 (40333)

Radiation Biology

General Electric Company
> Radioisotope Handlers

Radiation Chemistry

General Electric Company
> Radioisotope Handlers

Radiation Detection and Measurement

National Registry of Radiation Protection Technologists
> National Registry of Radiation Protection Technologists

Radiation Emergency Management

National Emergency Training Center
> Fundamentals for Radiological Officers

Radiation Physics

General Electric Company
> Radioisotope Handlers

Radiation Protection and Control

National Registry of Radiation Protection Technologists
> National Registry of Radiation Protection Technologists

Radiation Protection Technology

Omaha Public Power District
> Airborne Radioactivity Monitoring and Control; Dosimetry and Contamination Control; Environmental Radioactivity and Accident Evaluation; Health Physics Fundamentals; Introduction to Nuclear Physics and Power Reactors; Radiation Biology and Exposure Control; Radiation Measurements, Calculations and Material Handling

Radiation Safety

Duquesne Light Company
> Radiation, Radiation Protection, and Radiation Survey

General Electric Company
> Quality Control and Compliance in Nuclear Medicine; Radioisotope Handlers

Radio Systems

National Weather Service Training Center
> NOAA Weather Radio B-16-03

Radio Systems Engineering

Bell Atlantic Corporation
> MRSE

Radiographic Equipment

General Electric Company
> Computed Tomography Series

Radiography

General Electric Company
> Computed Tomography Series

Radiological Science

National Emergency Training Center
> Fundamentals: For Radiological Monitor and Radiological Response Teams; Fundamentals for Radiological Officers; Radiological Accident Assessment; Radiological Emergency Response

National Registry of Radiation Protection Technologists
> National Registry of Radiation Protection Technologists

Radiological Science Education

National Emergency Training Center
> Radiological Monitors Instructor; Train the Trainer for Radiological Instructors III

Radiology Sciences

General Electric Company
> Introduction to Radiologic Techniques; Quality Assurance in Radiology; Radiological Series; Radiology Registration and Certification; Standardization of Radiologic Techniques; Understanding X-Ray Generation

Ranch Appraisal

National Association of Independent Fee Appraisers
> Farm, Ranch, and Rural Appraisal

Range Management

National Emergency Training Center
> Wildland/Urban Interface Fire Protection: A National Problem with Local Solutions

Reactor Operator

Wisconsin Public Service Corporation
> Nuclear Systems Overview

Reactor Physics

Yankee Atomic Electric Company
> Reactor Physics

Reading Comprehension

Bell Atlantic Corporation
> Skillful Reading

Reading Education

Laubach Literacy Action
> Teaching of Basic Reading and Writing Skills to Adult Nonreaders

Real and Personal Property

Omega Institute
> Real and Personal Property

Real Estate

American Institute for Paralegal Studies, Inc.
> Real Estate; Real Estate Transfer and Ownership

American Institute of Banking - Washington, D.C. Chapter
> Real Estate Finance

Federal Aviation Administration
> Land Appraisal and Title Opinion (06028); Real Estate

for Federal Aviation Administration Contracting Officers (07005)

Fox & Lazo, Inc.
>Professional Real Estate Orientation CII

Institute of Financial Education
>Housing Construction; Income Property Lending; Real Estate Law I; Real Estate Law II; Real Estate Principles I; Real Estate Principles II; Residential Appraising; Residential Mortgage Lending

National Academy for Paralegal Studies, Inc.
>Real Estate; Real Estate Transfer and Ownership

National Association of REALTORS®
>Fundamentals of Real Estate Investment and Taxation (CI-101); Graduate Realtors Institute (GRI) Courses I, II, III.; Real Estate Investment Analysis (CI-102)

New Jersey Association of Realtors
>Graduate Realtors Institute Course I; Graduate Realtors Institute Course II; Graduate Realtors Institute Course III; Graduate Realtors Institute Course IV

Pacific Bell
>Right of Way Appraisal; Right of Way

PJA School
>Real Property

Real Estate Analysis

National Association of REALTORS®
>Introduction to Real Estate Investment Analysis (EX 6)

Real Estate Appraisal

American Bankers Association
>Real Estate Appraisal I; Real Estate Appraisal II

Control Data
>Principles of Real Estate Appraisal

National Association of Independent Fee Appraisers
>Principles of Residential Real Estate Appraising

National Association of REALTORS®
>Principles of Real Estate Appraisal (EX 1A-1/8-1)

Real Estate Asset Management

National Association of REALTORS®
>Asset Management (703)

Real Estate Finance

American Bankers Association
>Income Property Underwriting; Real Estate Finance

Garden State AIB
>Real Estate and Mortgage Principles

Real Estate Investment

National Association of REALTORS®
>Behavioral Aspects of Investment (CI-104)

Real Estate Investment and Taxation

National Association of REALTORS®
>Advanced Real Estate Taxation and Investments (CI-103)

Real Estate Law

American Center for Technical Arts and Sciences (Formerly Mainline Paralegal Institute)
>Real Estate Law

American Institute for Paralegal Studies, Inc.
>Real Estate Transfer and Ownership

Real Estate Management

National Association of REALTORS®
>Case Studies in Commercial Investment Real Estate Brokerage (CI-105)

Real Estate Management Information Systems

National Association of REALTORS®
>Real Estate Office Management

Real Estate Marketing

National Association of REALTORS®
>Alternative Real Estate Marketing Techniques (FLI-163); Sales Strategies for the Residential Specialist (RS202)

Real Estate Marketing Analysis

National Association of REALTORS®
>Real Estate Market Analysis (EX 10)

Real Estate Marketing Management

National Association of REALTORS®
>How to Improve Image and Increase Market Share (CRB-303)

Real Estate Planning

National Association of REALTORS®
>Real Estate Planning (501) (Residential); Real Estate Planning (502) (Office Buildings); Real Estate Planning (503) (Commercial Stores and Shopping Centers)

Real Estate Sales

National Association of REALTORS®
>Listing Strategies for the Residential Specialist (RS-201)

Real Estate Securities Licensing

National Association of REALTORS®
>Real Estate Securities Licensing Course (22L)

Real Estate Valuation

National Association of REALTORS®
>Basic Real Estate Valuation (EX 1A-2); Case Studies in Real Estate Valuation (EX 2-1)

Real Time Processing and Control

General Motors Corporation - Technical Staffs Group and Lansing Automotive Division (Formerly Advanced Engineering Staff [AES])
>Computer Information Processing and Control

Recordkeeping

Abu Dhabi National Oil Company Career Development Center/GDC, Inc.
> Recordkeeping

Records Management

Blake Business School
> Records Management

Recreation

International PADI, Inc.
> Advanced Open Water Diver; Divemaster; Instructor Development; Open Water Diver; Professional Scuba Equipment Repair; Rescue Diver; Underwater Photography Instructor

Refinery Process Instrumentation and Control

Sun Refining and Marketing Company
> Refinery Operator Program

Refrigeration

Seafarers Harry Lundeberg School of Seamanship
> Qualified Members of the Engine Department, Eight-Week Version; Qualified Members of the Engine Department, Four-Week Version; Qualified Members of the Engine Department, Six-Week Version; Qualified Members of the Engine Department, Twelve-Week Version; Refrigeration Systems Maintenance and Operation

United States Postal Service - Department of Training and Development
> Environmental Control IV

Refrigeration Technology

Seafarers Harry Lundeberg School of Seamanship
> Fireman, Oiler, and Watertender; Refrigerated Containers/Advanced Maintenance

Rehabilitation

New Jersey Department of Human Services
> Prediction and Prevention of Aggressive Behavior in the System; Training for Trainers - Crisis Recognition, Prevention, and Intervention

United States Public Health Service - Indian Health Service
> Rehabilitation and Home Health Care

Rehabilitation Counseling

Crawford Risk Management Services
> Specialized Rehabilitation Counseling

United States Public Health Service - Indian Health Service
> Introduction to Human Services; Skills and Techniques of Counseling

Religion

Seminary Extension, Southern Baptist Seminaries
> Biblical Backgrounds; History of Christian Thought; History of Christianity; How to Understand the Bible; Introduction to Christian Ethics; New Testament Survey, Part III; New Testament Theology; Public Worship; Systematic Theology

Religious Education

The Catholic Home Study Institute
> Catechesis of the High School Student

Religious Studies

The Catholic Home Study Institute
> Christian Spirituality in the Catholic Tradition; The Church and Human Destiny; God, Man, and the Universe; Introduction to Sacred Scripture; Jesus Christ, Mary, and the Grace of God; Nature of Christian Spirituality; The Philosophy of Communism; The Ten Commandments Today, Part A; The Ten Commandments Today, Part B; Theology of the Sacraments, Part One; Theology of the Sacraments, Part Two

Remote Sensing

Defense Mapping Agency - Inter American Geodetic Survey Cartographic School
> Cartographic Techniques for Space Imagery; Fundamentals of Remote Sensing; Introduction to Remote Sensing; Introduction to Remote Sensing/Image Analysis

Remote Sensing Interpretation

National Photographic Interpretation Center
> Active Remote Sensor Image Analysis Training Program

Remote Sensing Techniques

National Photographic Interpretation Center
> National Imagery Analysis Course

Research Methods

Certified Medical Representatives Institute, Inc.
> Pharmaceutical and Medical Research; Research Methods

Residential Valuation

National Association of REALTORS®
> Residential Valuation (EX 8-2)

Restaurant Finance

McDonald's Corporation
> Advanced Restaurant Management

Restaurant Management

McDonald's Corporation
> Advanced Operations; Advanced Restaurant Management; Area Supervisor's Development Program; Field Consultant Development Program

Retail Management

United States Postal Service - Department of Training and Development
> Retail Sales and Services Management MTS

Retail Merchandising

Sandy Corporation - Marketing Educational Services
> General Motors Field Management Development Program

Retailing

NCR Corporation
> Retail Environments: Concepts

U.S. West Learning Systems
> Merchandising Management; Phone Center Store Supervisor Training

Retirement Arrangements

Certified Employee Benefit Specialist Program
> CEBS Course III; Social Security, Savings Plans, and Other Retirement Arrangements

Rhetoric

International Correspondence Schools
> Composition and Rhetoric

Risk Management

American Institute for Property and Liability Underwriters/Insurance Institute of America
> (ALCM 71) Hazard Identification and Analysis; (ALCM 72) Loss Control Applications and Management; (ARM 54) Structure of Risk Management Process; (ARM 55) Risk Control; (ARM 56) Risk Financing; Commercial Liability Risk Management and Insurance; Commercial Property Risk Management and Insurance; Insurance Company Operations; Insurance Issues and Professional Ethics; The Legal Environment of Insurance; Personal Risk Management and Insurance; Principles of Risk Management and Insurance

Crawford Risk Management Services
> Advanced Casualty Claims Adjusting; Advanced Property Loss Adjusting; Casualty Claim Adjusting; Property Loss Adjusting; Specialized Rehabilitation Counseling; Workers' Compensation Claims Adjusting

Credit Union National Association - Certified Credit Union Executive Program
> Risk Management and Insurance #500

River Piloting

Seafarers Harry Lundeberg School of Seamanship
> Towboat Operator

Robotic Dynamics and Control

General Motors Corporation - Technical Staffs Group and Lansing Automotive Division (Formerly Advanced Engineering Staff [AES])
> Robotic Systems

Robotics

Chrysler Motors Advanced Technical Training
> Advanced Cincinnati Milacron T3786; ASEA IRB/90; Industrial Robotics; KUKA IR662/100; PRAB F600 Control; PRAB F700 Control

The Cittone Institute
> Computer System, Peripherals and Robotics

Ford National Development and Training Center (Formerly UAW—Ford National Development and Training Center)
> Introduction to Robotics; Robotics Overview; Specific Application Instruction; Specific Manufacture Robot Training

O/E Learning, Inc.
> Robotics Awareness Training Phase III

Roof and Rib Control

National Mine Health and Safety Academy
> Roof Control for the Specialist

RPG II

Brick Computer Science Institute
> Advanced RPG II; RPG II Programming

The Cittone Institute
> RPG II and RPG III

Computer Learning Center
> RPG II Programming

Control Data
> Introduction to RPG II Programming

Rules of the Road

Seafarers Harry Lundeberg School of Seamanship
> Celestial Navigation; First Class Pilot; Master/Mate Freight and Towing; Third Mate - Inspected Vessels

Rural Appraisal

National Association of Independent Fee Appraisers
> Farm, Ranch, and Rural Appraisal

Rural Valuation

National Association of REALTORS®
> Rural Valuation (EX 3)

Russian

National Cryptologic School
> Accelerated Intermediate Intensive Russian; Advanced Russian Conversation and Composition I; Advanced Russian Conversation and Composition II; Advanced Russian Reading; Advanced Russian Translation; Basic Conversation and Composition; Comprehensive Russian; Intensive Basic and Intermediate Russian; Intermediate Intensive Russian; Intermediate Russian; Intermediate Russian Reading; Intermediate Russian Structure I; Intermediate Spoken Russian I; Russian Refresher; Russian Structure I; Russian Structure II; Russian Textual Analysis I; Russian Textual Analysis II; Russian Translation Techniques; Workshop in Russian Stylistics

United States Department of Agriculture, Graduate School
> Intermediate Russian I; Introductory Russian I; Introductory Russian II; Introductory Russian III

Russian Linguistics

National Cryptologic School
> Russian Linguistics

Safety

Electrical Workers, Local Union 164 of the International Brotherhood of Electrical Workers, AFL-CIO, Bergen and Hudson Counties, New Jersey, and the Bergen-Hudson County Chapter of the National Electrical Contractors Association Joint Apprenticeship Training Program
> Electrician Apprentice

Electrical Workers, Local Union 26 of the International Brotherhood of Electrical Workers and the Washington, D.C. Chapter of the National Electrical Contractors Association, Joint School

    Electrician Apprentice

Joint Apprenticeship Training Committee, International Brotherhood of Electrical Workers Local Union 269, and the National Electrical Contractors Association of Southern New Jersey

    Electrician Apprentice

National Mine Health and Safety Academy

    Accident Analysis and Problem Identification; Accident Prevention in the Mining Industry; Accident Prevention Techniques

Omaha Joint Electrical Apprenticeship and Training Committee

    Electrical Apprenticeship Training

Seafarers Harry Lundeberg School of Seamanship

    Able Seaman; Celestial Navigation; Qualified Members of the Engine Department, Twelve-Week Version

Sun Refining and Marketing Company

    Refinery Operator Program

Safety and Fire Prevention

Abu Dhabi National Oil Company Career Development Center/GDC, Inc.

    Safety and Fire Prevention

Safety Engineering

United States Army Materiel Command - AMC (Formerly DARCOM - United States Army Materiel Development and Readiness Command)

    Principles of Radiological Safety Engineering; Principles of Safety; Problems in Safety Engineering; Radiological Safety and Hazards Evaluation; Safety Aspects of Facilities Design; Safety in the Occupational Environment I; Safety in the Occupational Environment II; Systems Safety Engineering

Safety Management

United States Postal Service - Department of Training and Development

    Introduction to Safety Management #21218-00

Sailing

Offshore Sailing School, Ltd.

    Advanced Sailing; Bareboat Cruising Preparation; Learn to Sail; Sailboat Racing

Sales

International Correspondence Schools

    Principles of Marketing

Southwestern Bell Telephone Company

    Communispond Effective Presentation Skills; Negotiating Successfully; Sales Presentation Skills; Versatile Sales Person

Whirlpool Corporation

    Builder Selling Skills; Manufactured Housing Selling Skills

Sales and Marketing

Xerox Corporation

    Advanced Sales School; Basic Sales School

Sales Forecasting

AT&T - Marketing Education - Somerset Seminars

    Forecasting for Marketing Managers

Sales Management

Dana Corporation

    Sales Development

International Correspondence Schools

    Sales Management

NCR Corporation

    Systemedia District Management

Southwestern Bell Telephone Company

    Effective Sales Management; Sales Strategies and Tactics—Account Executive

United States Postal Service - Department of Training and Development

    Customer Service Representative; Customer Services Representative MTS; Retail Sales and Services Management MTS

U.S. West Learning Systems

    Insights for Sales Managers

Whirlpool Corporation

    Dealer Coaching and Selling Skills; Prospecting for New Accounting; Developing Existing Accounts

Xerox Corporation

    Account Management Training Program; Sales Accounts Management

Sales Supervision

Southwestern Bell Telephone Company

    Introduction to Sales Training Supervision

Salesmanship

American International Group, Inc.

    Counselor Selling

Bell Atlantic Corporation

    Account Executive Phase I; Account Executive Phase II; Personal Selling I; Personal Selling II

Control Data

    Selling: The Psychological Sequence; Selling: The Strategic Approach Sequence

Dale Carnegie & Associates, Inc.

    Dale Carnegie Sales Course

Fox & Lazo, Inc.

    Professional Real Estate Orientation CII

Institute of Financial Education

    Techniques for Customer Counseling

Pacific Bell

    Basic Selling Skills; Inside Selling Skills; Sales Skills

Southwestern Bell Telephone Company
> Fundamentals of Selling; Versatile Sales Person

United States Postal Service - Department of Training and Development
> Customer Service Representative; Customer Services Representative MTS

U.S. West Learning Systems
> Competitive Selling - Demand Sales Center; Face to Face Selling; Horizon Subsequent Activity A & B; Mountain Bell Sequence 3305 MBA-MBE; Sights on Selling; Sights on Selling-Instructor Certification; Variable Term Payment Plan/Variable Term Telephone Lease Agreement (3305 MBE); WATS Orders - Demand Sales Center

Whirlpool Corporation
> Generating a Personal Target Plan of Action

Xerox Corporation
> Account Management I; Account Management II; Account Management III; Advanced Salesmanship; Basic Sales Training/Business Products Division; Basic Sales Training/Information Systems Division; Executive Sales Seminar; OS Basic Sales School; Xerox Office Products Division Basic Marketing School - Sales

Savings Association Operations

Institute of Financial Education
> Deposit Accounts and Services; Managing Deposit Accounts and Services

Savings Plans

Certified Employee Benefit Specialist Program
> CEBS Course III; Social Security, Savings Plans, and Other Retirement Arrangements

School Administration

Independent School Management
> Administering the Small Private-Independent School; Marketing the Private-Independent School: Student Recruitment and Retention; Operating a Private-Independent School Business Office; Overview of Business and Financial Management in Private-Independent Schools; Private-Independent School Scheduling: Designs, Process, Techniques

School Business Management

Independent School Management
> Advanced Business Management for Private-Independent Schools

School Curriculum

Independent School Management
> Private-Independent School Curriculum Analysis and Coordination

Science

Carolina Power & Light Company
> COC: Mathematics and Physics

International Correspondence Schools
> Technical Science

National Emergency Training Center
> Chemistry of Hazardous Materials

Wolf Creek Nuclear Operating Corporation (Formerly Kansas Gas & Electric)
> Health Physics Fundamentals

Seamanship

Seafarers Harry Lundeberg School of Seamanship
> Able Seaman; Advanced Deck - Inland and Oceans; Basic Deck; First Class Pilot; Lifeboat; Master/Mate Freight and Towing; Third Mate - Inspected Vessels

Secretarial Accounting

Blake Business School
> Accounting Essentials

Secretarial Procedures

American International Group, Inc.
> Administrative Secretary Skills Seminar

Katharine Gibbs School
> Administrative Procedures; Administrative Secretary I and II; Advanced Secretarial Procedures I and II; Secretarial Procedures

Secretarial Science

American International Group, Inc.
> Basic Typewriting; Introduction to Gregg Shorthand Theory; Shorthand and Transcription

Blake Business School
> Electronic Office Procedures; Office Procedures; Shorthand I; Shorthand II; Shorthand III; Shorthand IV

Control Data
> Office Communication and Behavior

Indian Health Service - Tribal Management Support Center
> Office Management and Administration; Wang Word Processing

Katharine Gibbs School
> Machine Transcription

National Cryptologic School
> Clerical Orientation

United States Postal Service - Department of Training and Development
> Secretary to the Postal Executive

Secretarial Studies

Independent School Management
> The Compleat Private-Independent School Secretary

Securities, Regulation, and Law

National Association of Securities Dealers, Inc.
> Investments and/or Brokerage Accounting; Securities, Regulation, Law, and Self-Regulation

Security

United States Postal Service - Department of Training and Development
> Security Equipment

Security Administration

Department of Defense, Defense Security Institute
> DoD Security Specialist Course; Introduction to Security Administration

Security Management

Bell Communications Research Training and Education Center
> Security Personnel Basic Training School

Semiconductor Devices

Computer Processing Institute
> Electronics Circuits I & II

Federal Aviation Administration
> Semi-Conductor Devices (44417)

Semiconductor Principles

The Cittone Institute
> Semiconductor Principles Module

Sheet Metal Fabrication and Design

Portsmouth Naval Shipyard: Apprenticeship Training
> Pattern Drafting; Sheet Metal Fabrication and Design

Ship Systems and Auxiliary Equipment

Seafarers Harry Lundeberg School of Seamanship
> Original Third Assistant Engineer, Steam and/or Motor - Inspected

Shop Practices

Electrical Workers, Local Union 26 of the International Brotherhood of Electrical Workers and the Washington, D.C. Chapter of the National Electrical Contractors Association, Joint School
> Electrician Apprentice

Omaha Joint Electrical Apprenticeship and Training Committee
> Electrical Apprenticeship Training

Shop Practices and Procedures

Abu Dhabi National Oil Company Career Development Center/GDC, Inc.
> Hand and Power Tools I; Hand and Power Tools II and III; Repair and Maintenance of Static Equipment I and II; Welding

Shorthand

Katharine Gibbs School
> Intermediate Gregg Shorthand and Transcription; Introduction to Gregg Shorthand; Shorthand I and II; Shorthand I; Shorthand II; Shorthand III and IV; Shorthand III

Professional Secretaries International
> Part V: Communication Applications; Part V: Office Administration and Communication

Skills Development

Bell Atlantic Corporation
> Skillful Reading

Small Business Management

American Conference of Audioprosthology
> Program in Audioprosthology

Control Data
> Building Your Own Business and Obtaining Financing

Small Group Communications

U.S. West Learning Systems
> Face to Face Communication Skills

Social Insurance

American Educational Institute, Inc.
> Worker's Compensation

Certified Employee Benefit Specialist Program
> CEBS Course III; Social Security, Savings Plans, and Other Retirement Arrangements

Social Psychology

Certified Medical Representatives Institute, Inc.
> Psychology

Social Science

Abu Dhabi National Oil Company Career Development Center/GDC, Inc.
> Ecomomic Geography I

Bell Atlantic Corporation
> Developing Additional Managerial Skills; Developing Managers

Federal Aviation Administration
> Developing Human Relations Skills

Katharine Gibbs School
> Economic History #703

National Sheriffs' Association
> Fundamentals of Adult Detention

United States Office of Personnel Management (OPM)
> Economics and Public Policy; Management of Natural Resources; Seminar in Science, Technology and Public Policy

Social Security

Certified Employee Benefit Specialist Program
> CEBS Course III; Social Security, Savings Plans, and Other Retirement Arrangements

Social Services

United States Public Health Service - Indian Health Service
> Introduction to Human Services; Skills and Techniques of Counseling

Social Welfare

Opportunities Academy of Management Training, Inc.
> Advanced Counseling; Advanced Job Development; Counseling for the Disadvantaged; Employment Analysis: Development and Placement for the Disadvantaged; Employment and Training Services to Ex-Offenders; Employment and Training Services to Former Drug Abusers; Employment and Training

Services to Older Workers; Job Development for the Disadvantaged

Social Work

Ford National Development and Training Center (Formerly UAW—Ford National Development and Training Center)
> Group Problem Solving

Opportunities Academy of Management Training, Inc.
> Advanced Counseling; Advanced Motivation; Community Involvement; Community Participation in Local Economic Development; Employment and Training Services to Ex-Offenders; Employment and Training Services to Limited English-Speaking Populations; Manpower Services to Disadvantaged Youth

Police Training Institute
> Child Sex Exploitation

Young Women's Christian Association of the U.S.A.
> Management Training for Staff with Executive Potential; Management Workshop for Executive Staff; Management Workshop for Student Leadership; Presidential Leadership and Association Committee Chairpersons' Workshop; Program Development Workshop; Staff Development II

Sociology

Bell Communications Research Training and Education Center
> Security Personnel Basic Training School

Chrysler Institute Associate Degree Program
> Sociology

Ford National Development and Training Center (Formerly UAW—Ford National Development and Training Center)
> Group Problem Solving

International Correspondence Schools
> Introduction to Sociology

Jewish Hospital of St. Louis
> Assertiveness Training

Katharine Gibbs School
> Introduction to Sociology #815, 806, or 819

Opportunities Academy of Management Training, Inc.
> Community Economic Development Policy and Analysis; Employment and Training Services to Older Workers

Police Training Institute
> Advanced Law for Youth Officers; Child Sex Exploitation; Police Community Relations; Youth Officers

Seminary Extension, Southern Baptist Seminaries
> Introduction to Christian Ethics

Young Women's Christian Association of the U.S.A.
> Management Training for Staff with Executive Potential; Management Workshop for Executive Staff; Management Workshop for Student Leadership; Presidential Leadership and Association Committee Chairpersons' Workshop; Program Development Workshop; Staff Development II

Software Engineering

United States Army Materiel Command - AMC (Formerly DARCOM - United States Army Materiel Development and Readiness Command)
> Advanced Microprocessors; Current Topics in Software Engineering; Economic Analysis and Software Life-Cycle Costs; Embedded Computer Algorithms; Software Configuration Management; Software Engineering Concepts I; Software Engineering Concepts II; Software Engineering Using ADA II; Software Engineering Workshop; Systems Engineering

Software Systems

Bell Communications Research Training and Education Center
> 1A Maintenance Program - Advanced System Testing

Solid State Devices

Brick Computer Science Institute
> Active Circuits and Lab

Solid State Electronics

National Weather Service Training Center
> RAMOS S-03-02

Spanish

National Cryptologic School
> Basic Spanish Structure; Intermediate Spanish Translation; Spanish Refresher Course - Reading; Spanish Refresher Course - Transcription; Spanish Refresher Course - Translation; Spanish Refresher Course

United States Department of Justice, Immigration and Naturalization Service, Federal Law Enforcement Training Center
> Border Patrol Academy; Immigration Officer Academy

Special Education

New Jersey Department of Human Services
> Prediction and Prevention of Aggressive Behavior in the System; Training for Trainers - Crisis Recognition, Prevention, and Intervention

Speech

American International Group, Inc.
> Effective Oral Presentation

Bell Atlantic Corporation
> Oral Communication; Oral Communication Skills

Chrysler Institute Associate Degree Program
> Speech Skills

Dana Corporation
> Effective Speaking

General Electric Company
> Effective Listening

Institute for Citizen Involvement in Education
> Public Policy and Public Schools

Katharine Gibbs School
> Oral Communication

Knight-Ridder, Inc.
: Making Effective Presentations

National Mine Health and Safety Academy
: Public Speaking and Briefing Techniques

Public Service Electric & Gas
: Oral Presentation Skills

Southwestern Bell Telephone Company
: Communispond Effective Presentation Skills

United States Army Materiel Command - AMC (Formerly DARCOM - United States Army Materiel Development and Readiness Command)
: Oral Communications

Westinghouse Electric Corporation, Defense and Electronics Center
: Communications Workshop B100; Human Interaction and Communication; Transactional Analysis B120

Speech Communications

NCR Corporation
: Presentation Skills

U.S. West Learning Systems
: Basic Trainer Skills Workshops; Experienced Trainer's Laboratory; Instructor Training Workshop

Stamping Technology

Chrysler Institute Associate Degree Program
: Stamping Technology

Statics

General Electric Company
: Statics

Statics and Dynamics

International Correspondence Schools
: Engineering Mechanics

United States Department of Agriculture, Graduate School
: Engineering Mechanics I; Engineering Mechanics II

Statistics

AT&T - Marketing Education - Somerset Seminars
: Advanced Quantitative Methods in Marketing; Application of Multivariate Techniques; Marketing Statistics; Statistical Analysis in Marketing

Bell Atlantic Corporation
: Traffic Theory/Basic Network Design

Bell Communications Research Training and Education Center
: Data Analysis and Regression—Advanced; Data Analysis and Regression—Basic; Scientific Sampling I; Scientific Sampling II

Chrysler Institute Associate Degree Program
: Introduction to Statistics

General Motors Corporation - Technical Staffs Group and Lansing Automotive Division (Formerly Advanced Engineering Staff [AES])
: Statistics for Technicians

National Cryptologic School
: Mathematical Statistics; Probability Theory

National Union of Hospital and Health Care Employees, District 1199C
: Elementary Statistics

Pacific Bell
: Voice Network Design

Portsmouth Naval Shipyard: Apprenticeship Training
: Basic Mathematics and Algebra; Geometry, Trigonometry, and Statistics

United States Army Materiel Command - AMC (Formerly DARCOM - United States Army Materiel Development and Readiness Command)
: Engineering Statistics; Mathematical Statistics for Product Assurance; Mathematical Statistics I; Mathematical Statistics II; System Assessment Techniques; Test Engineering and Analysis

United States Department of Agriculture, Graduate School
: Correlation and Regression Analysis; Introductory Statistics I; Introductory Statistics II; Introductory Statistics III; Managerial Statistics

Steam Generation Systems

Seafarers Harry Lundeberg School of Seamanship
: Qualified Members of the Engine Department, Eight-Week Version; Qualified Members of the Engine Department, Six-Week Version; Qualified Members of the Engine Department, Twelve-Week Version

Steam Turbine Technology

General Electric Company
: Steam Turbine Technology

Stenoscript

Katharine Gibbs School
: Stenoscript

Strategic Management

Bell Communications Research Training and Education Center
: Innovative Marketing Strategies; Product and Market Plans-Design and Implementation; Product Life Cycle Management

National Emergency Training Center
: Tactical Operations for Company Officers II

NCR Corporation
: Advanced Management Skills

Strategic Marketing

Bell Communications Research Training and Education Center
: Marketing Strategy

Strategic Marketing Analysis

Bell Communications Research Training and Education Center
: Marketing Analysis

David C.D. Rogers Associates
: Marketing Tools and Strategies

Strategic Marketing Management

AT&T - Corporate Education Center, Management Education Training Division
> Product Management Concepts

Strategic Planning

National Emergency Training Center
> Tactical Operations for Company Officers I

Strength of Materials

General Electric Company
> Statics; Strength of Materials

Portsmouth Naval Shipyard: Apprenticeship Training
> Strength of Materials

United States Department of Agriculture, Graduate School
> Strength of Materials

Stress

National Mine Health and Safety Academy
> Stress - Its Implications in Health and Safety

Stress Management

Bell Atlantic Corporation
> Stress Management

Structural Engineering

General Electric Company
> Modern Structural Analysis I; Survey of Topics in Structural Analysis

Structural Steel Design

International Correspondence Schools
> Structural Steel Design

Structured Design

NCR Corporation
> Structured Design

Structured Systems Analysis

Applied Learning (Formerly ASI/DELTAK)
> Introduction to Systems Analysis; 4701 Developing a Changeable System: Structured Systems Development (consists of 4702-4705); 4711 Structured Systems Analysis & Design: Using Data Flow Diagrams (consists of 4712-4714); 4715 Structured Analysis & Design: Structured Analysis

Student Personnel Administration

Independent School Management
> The Private-Independent School Admissions Office

Student Teaching

Federal Aviation Administration
> Air Traffic Control Specialist and/or Facility Instructor Training (10510)

Studio Art

Art Instruction Schools
> Advanced Drawing and Painting; Advanced Illustration; Art in Advertising; Basic Drawing and Design I; Basic Drawing and Design II; Cartooning; Design, Composition, and Reproduction; Figure Drawing and Studio Techniques; Fundamentals of Art; Painting Techniques; Specialized Art

Study Skills

Chrysler Institute Associate Degree Program
> Reading and Study Skills

Substance Abuse

National Mine Health and Safety Academy
> Substance Abuse or

Supervision

Abu Dhabi National Oil Company Career Development Center/GDC, Inc.
> Introduction to Supervision

American International Group, Inc.
> Supervisory Management

Control Data
> Managerial Success Curriculum

Federal Aviation Administration
> Basic Employment Practices (14029); Position Management and Classification (14030); Use and Conservation of Personnel, Money, and Materials (14005)

Garden State AIB
> Fundamentals of Supervision

Institute of Management and Production
> Fundamentals of Supervisory Practice; Principles of Supervision; Supervisory Management—Part I; Supervisory Management—Part II

International Correspondence Schools
> Principles of Management

Jamaican Institute of Management
> Principles of Supervision

Knight-Ridder, Inc.
> Effective Human Relations

National Emergency Training Center
> Personal Effectiveness; Strategic Analysis of Executive Leadership; Team Effectiveness

National Management Association
> Supervisory and Management Skills Program

New England Telephone Company
> Principles of Supervision: Managerial Task Cycle; Situational Leadership II; Stress Management: A Positive Strategy

New Jersey Department of Human Services
> Management II Basic; Management III Basic

Pacific Bell
> Assistant Manager Initial Training Business; Interpersonal Skills; Introduction to Management and Supervision; Problem Solving; Strategic Management Writing; Winning

1014 *Index*

Police Training Institute

    First Line Supervision or Police Supervision

Public Service Electric & Gas

    Supervisory Training Program

Southwestern Bell Telephone Company

    Assistant Manager Job Design; Leadership Skills Workshop; Supervisory Skills Workshop

United States Postal Service - Department of Training and Development

    Associate Office Management MTS; Associate Office Postmaster MTS; Building Equipment Maintenance Supervisor MTS; Building Services Maintenance Supervisor MTS; Customer Services Managers #10276-00; Delivery Services Supervisor MTS; Employee Relations Management MTS; Mail Processing Equipment Maintenance Supervisor MTS; PEDC Managers MTS; Retail Sales and Services Management MTS; Window Services Management MTS

U.S. West Learning Systems

    Advanced Management Seminar; Assistant Manager Initial Training; Business Office Supervisor Training; Business Service Center Supervisor Training; Clerical Supervisor's Training; Initial Management Seminar; Initial Staff Seminar; Insight for Sales Managers; Insights for Sales Managers; Managing the Work and Managing Performance; Methods Development Standards Workshop; Performance Data Collection and Analysis; Second Level Management Performance Based Curriculum; Supervisor Training for Business Service Order Entry Center and Service Order Entry Center Special Services

Western Regional CUNA School for Credit Union Personnel

    Western Regional CUNA School for Credit Union Personnel

Wolf Creek Nuclear Operating Corporation (Formerly Kansas Gas & Electric)

    Supervision I

Supervisory Management

Federal Aviation Administration

    Interpersonal Behavior In Problem Solving; Supervisor's Course - Phase I (01260); Supervisor's Course - Phase II (01226)

Maynard Management Institute

    Fundamental Principles of Supervision

McDonald's Corporation

    Supervisory Management Skills

U.S. West Learning Systems

    Initial Management Seminar; Initial Staff Seminar

Wolf Creek Nuclear Operating Corporation (Formerly Kansas Gas & Electric)

    Supervision I

Surveying

Defense Mapping Agency - Inter American Geodetic Survey Cartographic School

    Advanced Photogrammetry; Automated Geodetic Computations and Adjustments; Control Surveys; Digital Methods of Terrain Modeling; Geodesy; Geodetic Computations and Adjustments; Geodetic Computations; Gravity Surveys; Hydrographic Surveying; Introduction to Computer Programming Using FORTRAN, Independent Study; Introduction to Minicomputers, Independent Study; Land Gravity Surveys; Nautical Cartography; Photogrammetry; Satellite Doppler Positioning

International Correspondence Schools

    Basic Surveying I; Basic Surveying II

Surveying Science

Defense Mapping Agency - Inter American Geodetic Survey Cartographic School

    Geodesy

Surveying Technology

Defense Mapping Agency - Inter American Geodetic Survey Cartographic School

    Automated Cartography-Digitizing System Operator; Automated Geodetic Computations and Adjustments; Color Separation Technician; Geodetic Computations and Adjustments; Geodetic Computations; Gravity Surveys; Hydrographic Surveying; Land Gravity Surveys

Swedish

United States Department of Agriculture, Graduate School

    Introductory Swedish I; Introductory Swedish II; Introductory Swedish III

Switching System Maintenance

Bell Atlantic Corporation

    New Jersey Bell 507B; New Jersey Bell 507K: Introduction to the 1A Processor; New Jersey Bell 508K Sequence

Pacific Bell

    1 AESS Peripheral Units; 1 AESS Processor Introduction; 1 ESS Method of Operation; 1 ESS Translations Basic; 2 ESS Method of Operation

U.S. West Learning Systems

    Mountain Bell 507B-508B/OJT Sequence; Mountain Bell 508K Sequence; 507B: Introduction to No. 1 Electronic Switching Systems; 508B-OJT: No. 1 ESS Peripheral Units - On-the-Job Training; 508KA: No. 1/1A Remreed Peripheral Maintenance; 508KB: No. 1/1A ESS CIT/MUT Peripheral Unit Maintenance; 508KD: No. 1/1A ESS DCT - Operation and Maintenance; 508KF: No. 1 ESS Ferreed Operation and Maintenance

Switching System Software Diagnostics

Bell Atlantic Corporation

    New Jersey Bell 539 Sequence; New Jersey Bell 539K Sequence

Pacific Bell

    1 AESS System Operation; 1 ESS System Operations

U.S. West Learning Systems

    Call Processing - 539D; Generic Program - 539A; Maintenance and Alarm Printouts - 539E; Maintenance Procedures - 539F; Mountain Bell 539 Sequence; No. 1 ESS Software Maintenance; Parameters - 539B; Translations - 539C; 539A: No. 1 ESS Stored Program Organization; 539B: No. 1 ESS Parameters; 539C: No. 1 ESS Translations; 539D: No. 1 ESS Call Processing; 539E: No. 1 ESS Maintenance and Alarm Printouts;

539F: No. 1 ESS Maintenance Procedures

System Management

New England Telephone Company
> Programmer Basic Training

System Safety Engineering

National Mine Health and Safety Academy
> System Safety Engineering

Systems Analysis

AT&T - Marketing Education - Somerset Seminars
> Data Gathering, System Analysis, and Design; Demand Analysis Techniques; Demand Analysis Techniques Seminar; Network Cost System and Workshop

Defense Mapping Agency - Inter American Geodetic Survey Cartographic School
> Cartographic Data Base Concepts

NCR Corporation
> Basic Systems Analysis Skills

Systems Application

Bell Atlantic Corporation
> Programmer Workshop I

Systems Design

AT&T - Center for Systems Education (Formerly AT&T Company Data Systems Education Group)
> C Initial Designer Training; Initial Designer Training 2

Systems Implementation

NCR Corporation
> STORES System Generation and Installation U07445; STORES Systems and Operations

Systems Maintenance

United States Postal Service - Department of Training and Development
> Postal Source Data System On-Site Maintenance Certification Program

Systems Programmming

United States Department of Agriculture, Graduate School
> Introduction to ISPF (ACOMP346)

Systems Troubleshooting

United States Postal Service - Department of Training and Development
> Postal Source Data System On-Site Maintenance Certification Program

System/370 Concepts and Facilities

Applied Learning (Formerly ASI/DELTAK)
> 1414 308X Architecture for the Application Programmer

Tax Accounting

College for Financial Planning®
> Tax Planning and Management

Tax Advantaged Investments

National Association of REALTORS®
> Tax Advantaged Investments - Self Study Program

Taxation

National Association of REALTORS®
> Advanced Real Estate Taxation and Investments (CI-103); Fundamentals of Real Estate Investment and Taxation (CI-101)

Teacher Education Adult Learning

Bell Communications Research Training and Education Center
> Adult Instructional Methodology: I; Adult Instructional Methodology II

Teaching Methods

Illinois Fire Service Institute
> Curriculum and Course Design I; Curriculum and Course Design II; Curriculum and Course Design III

National Mine Health and Safety Academy
> Instructor Training

Sun Refining and Marketing Company
> Introduction to Teaching Techniques

U.S. West Learning Systems
> Basic Trainer Skills Workshops; Experienced Trainer's Laboratory; Instructor Training Workshop; Sights on Selling-Instructor Certification

Teaching Technical Courses

Duquesne Light Company
> Instructor Development

Teaching Techniques

Police Training Institute
> Field Training Officer; Introduction to Teaching Techniques; Police In-Service Trainers; Police Instructors

Team Building

New Jersey Department of Human Services
> Executive Development Seminar

Technical Communications

Westinghouse Electric Corporation, Defense and Electronics Center
> Effective Technical Presentations

Technical Drawing Interpretation

General Electric Company
> Mechanical Drawing I & II

Technical Education

Wolf Creek Nuclear Operating Corporation (Formerly Kansas Gas & Electric)
> Classroom Instructor Workshop

1016 *Index*

Technical Management

U.S. West Learning Systems

    Hardwired Administration Workshop; Plug-In Administration Workshop; Plug-In Operations Workshop NE39403

Technical Programs

Texas Utilities Electric Corporation (Formerly Texas Utilities Generating Company - TUGCo)

    Blueprint Reading; Schematics and Symbols

Technical Report Writing

Federal Aviation Administration

    Report Analysis and Consolidation (14027); Writing Improvement (14014)

NCR Corporation

    Effective Technical Writing

Technical Writing

Bell Atlantic Corporation

    Methods Developers' Workshop

General Electric Company

    Technical Communications

United States Army Materiel Command - AMC (Formerly DARCOM - United States Army Materiel Development and Readiness Command)

    Written Communications

United States Department of Agriculture, Graduate School

    Printing, Layout and Design; Proofreading; Seminar in Editing; Technical Writing

U.S. West Learning Systems

    Methods Development Standards; Put It In Writing; Writing Procedures and Users Guides

Technology

Bell Atlantic Corporation

    Programmer Basic Training; Programmer Basic Training - COBOL

United States Army Materiel Command - AMC (Formerly DARCOM - United States Army Materiel Development and Readiness Command)

    Safety Considerations in Electrical/Electronic Systems Design

U.S. West Learning Systems

    Programmer Basic Training

Telecommunications

Bell Communications Research Training and Education Center

    Digital Switch Hardware Maintenance; Digital Switch Programming; General Transmission Concepts; Introduction to Telecommunications Concepts; Introduction to UNIXR Operating System; Principles of Digital Technology; Protocol Concepts-1

David C.D. Rogers Associates

    Competition in Telecommunications

Dow Jones & Company, Inc.

    AVANTI; DataBak

NCR Corporation

    VRX Telecommunications

Pacific Bell

    Basic Network Design; Cable Fault Locating; Fiber Optics: Sales or Technical; Network Traffic Concepts; Principles of Digital Technology; Protocol-Asynchronous and Bisynchronous

Southwestern Bell Telephone Company

    Cable Repair - Fault Locating; Data Communications Technology; Design Center Engineering; Digital Circuit Technology; Economic Study Module; Fiber Optics; Light Guide Design; Loop Electronics Design; Loop Engineering Assignment Data; Loop Technology Planning Fundamentals; Subscriber Loop Carrier 96

Telecommunications Equipment Maintenance

Bell Communications Research Training and Education Center

    DMS 100 Family - Hardware Maintenance for Peripherals; Telephone Switch Peripheral Equipment Maintenance I; Telephone Switch Peripheral Equipment Maintenance II; TOPS Facilities Management

Telecommunications Management

Bell Communications Research Training and Education Center

    Planning, Design, and Operation of Telecommunication Systems

Pacific Bell

    Network Fundamentals

Telecommunications Management Technology

Bell Communications Research Training and Education Center

    Applied Communications Fundamentals

Telecommunications Programming

Bell Communications Research Training and Education Center

    Telecommunications Switch Programming

Telecommunications Software Support

Bell Communications Research Training and Education Center

    ISDN Switching Fundamentals

Telecommunications Technology

Bell Communications Research Training and Education Center

    Data Communications - Facility at CPE Testing; Data Communications - Integrated Services Digital Network; DC-Basic Protocols; DC-Introduction to Data Communications; Digital Carrier Maintenance; DMS-100 Family Capacities; Switch Capacities

Pacific Bell

    Information Transport Technologies; Network Fundamentals

Telemarketing

New England Telephone Company

    Telemarketing

Telephone Switching
Bell Atlantic Corporation
> Trunk Tester

Teleprocessing
Southwestern Bell Telephone Company
> Phone Trunk Testing

Teletype Repair
United States Postal Service - Department of Training and Development
> Teletype Maintenance

Television Theory
Pacific Bell
> Television Fundamentals and Signal Analysis

Tests and Measurements
Institute for Citizen Involvement in Education
> Public Policy and Public Schools

Theatre
Katharine Gibbs School
> Introduction to Theatre

Theology
The Catholic Home Study Institute
> Christian Spirituality in the Catholic Tradition; The Church and Human Destiny; God, Man, and the Universe; Introduction to Sacred Scripture; Jesus Christ, Mary, and the Grace of God; Nature of Christian Spirituality; The Ten Commandments Today, Part A; The Ten Commandments Today, Part B; Theology of the Sacraments, Part One; Theology of the Sacraments, Part Two

Seminary Extension, Southern Baptist Seminaries
> History of Christian Thought; New Testament Theology; Systematic Theology

Thermodynamics
Omaha Public Power District
> Introduction to Thermodynamics

Time and Stress Management
National Association of REALTORS®
> Personal and Career Management for the Residential Specialist (RS-203)

Time Management
Ford National Development and Training Center (Formerly UAW—Ford National Development and Training Center)
> Time Management and Effective Listening

Tool Design
International Correspondence Schools
> Tool Design I; Tool Design II

Tool Making
General Electric Company
> Tool Design

Topographic Drawing
International Correspondence Schools
> Topographic Drawing and Surveying

Topographic Surveying
International Correspondence Schools
> Topographic Drawing and Surveying

Torts
American Institute for Paralegal Studies, Inc.
> Personal and Injury Litigation - Torts II; Torts and Personal Injury

National Academy for Paralegal Studies, Inc.
> Personal and Injury Litigation - Torts II

Omega Institute
> Torts

Towboat Operations
Seafarers Harry Lundeberg School of Seamanship
> Towboat Operator

Traffic
Police Training Institute
> Basic Law Enforcement III

Training and Development
AT&T - Center for Systems Education (Formerly AT&T Company Data Systems Education Group)
> Basic Training Development Skills Workshop; Techniques of Instruction; User Documentation/Performance Aids Workshop

Bell Atlantic Corporation
> Trainer Skills Workshop

New England Telephone Company
> Trainer Skills Workshop

Training Methods
National Emergency Training Center
> Methods and Techniques of Adult Learning

Training Procedures
New Jersey Department of Human Services
> Psychiatric Rehabilitation Trainer Development

Training Techniques
Bell Atlantic Corporation
> Trainer Workshop

Transcription
Professional Secretaries International
> Part V: Communication Applications; Part V: Office Administration and Communication

Transmission Engineering
GTE Service Corporation - GTE Telephone Operations Network Training
> Basic Data Transmission Engineering

Transportation Technology

United States Postal Service - Department of Training and Development

> Air Brakes; Automotive Mechanic Fundamentals; Brakes and Suspension Systems; Electric Vehicle; Perimeter Office Fleet Maintenance; Vehicle Maintenance Analyst; Vehicle Maintenance Facility Control; Vehicle Maintenance Facility Utilization

Trial Practices

National Mine Health and Safety Academy
> Courtroom Procedures

Trigonometry

General Electric Company
> Technical Mathematics; Trigonometry

International Correspondence Schools
> Technical Mathematics II

Omaha Public Power District
> Basic Mathematics or

Troubleshooting

Ford National Development and Training Center (Formerly UAW—Ford National Development and Training Center)
> Troubleshooting Strategy

Xerox Corporation
> Telecopier 200; Telecopier 400/410

Trust Banking

American Institute of Banking - Washington, D.C. Chapter
> Trust Banking

Trust Functions and Services

Garden State AIB
> Trust Business

Trust Operations

Garden State AIB
> Trust Operations

Turkish

National Cryptologic School
> Basic Modern Turkish

Typewriting

Abu Dhabi National Oil Company Career Development Center/GDC, Inc.
> Typewriting

Blake Business School
> Typing I; Typing II; Typing III; Typing IV

Institute for Business and Technology
> Typing

Katharine Gibbs School
> Advanced Typewriting; Beginning Typewriting; Intermediate Typewriting; Typewriting; Typing I or III; Typing II or IV

Professional Secretaries International
> Part V: Communication Applications; Part V: Office Administration and Communication

Ultrasound Equipment

General Electric Company
> Basics of Ultrasound; Quality Control and Compliance in Ultrasound

Underground Conduit Design and Administration

Bell Atlantic Corporation
> Underground Conduit Design and Administration

Unibody Repair

Applied Power, Inc. - Blackhawk Automotive Division
> New Science of Unibody Repair

UNIX Operating System

Bell Communications Research Training and Education Center
> UNIX® System Tools 1; UNIX® System Tools 2

NCR Corporation
> UNIX® System Tuning

UNIX Shell Programming

NCR Corporation
> UNIX® Shell Programming

Urban Affairs

Police Training Institute
> Police Community Relations

Young Women's Christian Association of the U.S.A.
> Presidential Leadership and Association Committee Chairpersons' Workshop

Urban Education

Opportunities Academy of Management Training, Inc.
> Advanced Job Development; Comprehensive Employment and Training Act; Program Assessment and Evaluation

Urban Planning

Federal Aviation Administration
> Relocation Assistance (06027)

National Emergency Training Center
> Wildland/Urban Interface Fire Protection: A National Problem with Local Solutions

Urban Policy

National Emergency Training Center
> Wildland/Urban Interface Fire Protection: A National Problem with Local Solutions

Urban Services Delivery

National Emergency Training Center
> Civil Defense Systems, Programs and Policies

Urban Studies

Opportunities Academy of Management Training, Inc.
> Community Corporate Planning Process; Community Economic Development Policy and Analysis; Community Involvement; Community Participation in Local Economic Development; Employment and Training, Planning Proposal Writing and Fund Development; Employment and Training Services to Limited English-Speaking Populations; Employment and Training Services to Older Workers; Fundamentals of the Local Economic Development Process; Management Skills for Economic Development; Proposal Writing and Fund Development; Seminar on the Job Training Partnership Act

Valuation Analysis and Report Writing

National Association of REALTORS®
> Valuation Analysis and Report Writing (EX 2-2)

Value Engineering

General Electric Company
> Value Engineering

Vehicle Operation Service

United States Postal Service - Department of Training and Development
> Vehicle Operations Management Skills Building

Visual Arts

International PADI, Inc.
> Underwater Photography Instructor

VLSI Design

General Motors Corporation - Technical Staffs Group and Lansing Automotive Division (Formerly Advanced Engineering Staff [AES])
> VLSI Design

Vocational Education

U.S. West Learning Systems
> Methods Developers' Workshop

Vocational/Technical Education

Texas Utilities Electric Corporation (Formerly Texas Utilities Generating Company - TUGCo)
> ARC Welding; Basic Hydraulics and Troubleshooting; Basic Metallurgy; Basic Pneumatics and Troubleshooting; Basic Vibration Training and Simple Balancing; Better Plant Operation Through Chemistry; Boiler Fundamentals and Operation; Coupling and Shaft Alignment Level I; Coupling and Shaft Alignment Level II; Drive Components; Electrical Distribution; Elements of Mechanics; Fluid Power Systems; Generator Fundamentals and Operation; Heat Rate Improvement; Lubrication and Bearings; Materials; Oxyacetylene Welding; Piping Systems and Pumps; Plant Protective Devices; Power Plant Auxiliary Equipment; Power Plant Fundamentals; Power Plant Simulator Training; Principles and Applications of Lubrication; Principles of Bearings Operation; Pumps and Piping; Pumps; Rigging, Hydraulic Crane, Forklift; Safety and Relief Valves; Turbine Fundamentals and Operation; Valves

VSAM Access Methods

Applied Learning (Formerly ASI/DELTAK)
> VSAM and Access Methods Services; 4040 MVS/SP; 4214 VSAM and Basic AMS

Waste Management

International Union of Operating Engineers
> Hazardous Waste Materials Training

Water Chemistry

Abu Dhabi National Oil Company Career Development Center/GDC, Inc.
> Water Chemistry; Water Facilities Chemistry

Water Resources Planning

Board of Engineers for Rivers and Harbors - U.S. Army Corps of Engineers
> Water Resources Planning Associates Program

Welding

Abu Dhabi National Oil Company Career Development Center/GDC, Inc.
> Welding

Chrysler Motors Advanced Technical Training
> Resistance Welding Technology; Weld Controllers

Seafarers Harry Lundeberg School of Seamanship
> Conveyorman; Welding

Well Logging

Baroid Corporation Career Development Center (Formerly NL Industries, Inc.)
> Basic Concepts of Open-Hole Logging; Cased-Hole Log Interpretation; Cased-Hole Wireline Logging

Whole Brain Applications

Bell Atlantic Corporation
> Whole Brain Applications

Wills, Trusts, and Estates

New England School of Banking
> Trust Banking Major

Wiring

Wolf Creek Nuclear Operating Corporation (Formerly Kansas Gas & Electric)
> Conduit, Cable and Wire

Wiring Procedures

Abu Dhabi National Oil Company Career Development Center/GDC, Inc.
> Electrical Lab I; Electrical Lab II

Word Processing

Bell Communications Research, Inc.
> Basic Word Processing Sequence Equation Processing Using the UNIX System WP122, Table Processing Using

Blake Business School
> Microcomputer Operation: Word Processing

Applications; Word Processing Applications: Wang; Word Processing Applications: Wordstar, Display Write 4, WordPerfect, Multimate; Word Processing I; Word Processing II Basic Function; Word Processing III Application; Word Processing IV

Contel Service Corporation
    DECMATE Word Processing

Institute for Business and Technology
    Introduction to Word Processing

Katharine Gibbs School
    Word Processing Concepts

Pacific Bell
    Wang Word Processing Training

U.S. West Learning Systems
    Wang Initial Word Processing/Wang Glossary Training; Word Processing

Work Simplification

U.S. West Learning Systems
    Job Design; Job Study Workshop

Work Study Methods

U.S. West Learning Systems
    Job Design; Job Study Workshop; Performance Data Collection and Analysis

Workers' Compensation

American Educational Institute, Inc.
    Worker's Compensation

Workshop Leadership Methods

Bell Atlantic Corporation
    Instructor Training Workshop

World Resources

AT&T - Marketing Education - Somerset Seminars
    International Marketing

Writing, Fundamentals of

Blake Business School
    Business Communications I

Writing Skills

Bell Atlantic Corporation
    Effective Writing

Written Communications

Bell Atlantic Corporation
    Effective Writing; English Grammar and Usage

General Electric Company
    Effective Presentation

Institute of Financial Education
    Effective Business Writing

Ref.
LB
3051
A599
1989

North Dakota State University
Fargo, North Dakota
58105